W9-BSW-585

TABLE OF CONTENTS

ACKNOWLEDGEMENTS

Larry Bigman (Frazetta-Williamson data); Glenn Bray (Kurtzman data); Dan Malan & Charles Heffelfinger (Classic Comics data); Gary Carter (DC data); J. B. Clifford Jr. (E. C. data); Gary Coddington (Superman data); Wilt Conine (Fawcett data); Dr. S. M. Davidson (Cupples & Leon data); Al Dellinges (Kubert data); Kevin Hancer (Tarzan data); Charles Heffelfinger and Jim Ivey (March of Comics listing); R. C. Holland and Ron Pussell (Seduction and Parade of Pleasure data); Grant Irwin (Quality data); Richard Kravitz (Kelly data); Phil Levine (giveaway data); Fred Nardelli (Frazetta data); Michelle Nolan (love comics); Mike Nolan (MLJ, Timely, Nedor data); George Olshevsky (Timely data); Richard Olson (LOA data); Scott Pell ('50s data); Greg Robertson (National data); Frank Scigliano (Little Lulu data); Gene Seger (Buck Rogers data); Rick Sloane (Archie data); David R. Smith, Archivist, Walt Disney Productions (Disney data); Don and Maggie Thompson (Four Color listing); Mike Tiefenbacher, Jerry Sinkovec, and Richard Yudkin (Atlas and National data); Raymond True (Classic Comics data); Jim Vadeboncoeur Jr. (Williamson and Atlas data); Kim Weston (Disney and Barks data); Cat Yronwode (Spirit data); Andrew Zerbe and Gary Behymer (M. E. data).

My appreciation must also be extended to Don Maris, John Snyder, Steve Geppi, Bruce Hamilton, and Jon Warren, who loaned material for photographing, and especially to Hugh and Louise O'Kennon for their support and help. Special acknowledgement is also given to Ron Pussell, Ken Mitchell, Scott Pell, Michelle Nolan, Terry Stroud, and especially to Larry Boyd for submitting an unusual amount of corrective data; to Dr. Richard Olson for rewriting grading definitions; to Larry Breed for his suggestions on re-organizing the introductory section; to Dan Malan for revamping the Classics section; to Terry Stroud, Hugh O'Kennon, Jon Warren, Dave Smith, Rod Dyke, Jay Maybruck, Jack Mallette, Joe Vereneault, James Payette, John Snyder, Gary Carter, Bill Cole, Rick Sloane, Stephen Fishler, Jerry Weist, Walter Wang, Steve Geppi, Joe Mannarino, Richard Dell, Gary Colabuono, Mark Brown and Ron Pussell, (pricing); to Tom Inge for his "Chronology of the American Comic Book;" to Tom Andrae for his interview with Jerry Siegel and Joe Shuster; to L. B. Cole and Jerry Ordway for their outstanding cover art; to Landon Chesney and Dave Noah for their work on the key comic book list; to L. B. Cole, Steve Saffel, and Jerry DeFuccio for their counsel and help; to Bill Spicer and Zetta DeVoe (Western Publishing Co.) for their contribution of data; and especially to Bill for his kind permission to reprint portions of his and Jerry Bails' **America's Four Color Pastime**; and to Walter Presswood, Dave Noah, and Jeff Overstreet for their help in editing this volume.

I will always be indebted to Jerry Bails, Landon Chesney, Bruce Hamilton and Larry Bigman whose advice and concern have helped in making **The Comic Book Price Guide** a reality; to my wife Martha for her encouragement and help in putting this reference work together; and to everyone who placed ads in this edition.

Acknowledgement is also due to the following people who have so generously contributed much needed data for this edition:

Aaron Andrade
Jeffrey Backenger
Stephen Baer
Jim Bahler
Sheila Barnard
Tim Barnes
Steven Barrington
Jon S. Berk
John Binder, M.D.
Jeff Birkel
Jacques Boivin
Larry Boyd
Chris Brayshaw
Sergio Candido
Steven A. Carey
Douglas Chambers
Dixon Chandler
Guy Chiapparino
Nick Christonikos
David Clark
L.B. Cole
Mark D. Combs
James W. Cook, Jr.
Dan Crawford
Kate & Amata Crawford
Tim Crawford
Jim Crocker
David H. Curtis
Stephen Fishler
Michael Francis
Danny Fuchs
Alberto Gonzalez
Brett S. Greene
Joseph Grissell
Michael J. Gronsky
John Hauser
Steve Haynie
W.G. 'Wally' Helaney
Anton Hermus

Jef Hinds
Brian Hoag
Thomas R. Horvitz
Jno. B. Hosier
Stanley Hosmer
Ken Huebschman, Jr.
Jon Huston
Bill Hutchison
Mark Johnson
Norral Johnson
Terry Julian
Ken Kaake
Stephen Kanzee
Chris Khalaf
Jeff Kramer
Timothy A. Krubsack
Tony Lee
Phil Levine
Frank Lopiccolo, Jr.
Don Mangus
Don Maris
Chris Mason
Robert Mathis
Greg Matson
Duncan McAlpine
James P. McLoughlin
Raymund Messner
Harry W. Miller
Ken Mitchell
Robert E. Myers
Frank T. Nama
Art Nestor
Ralph Pay
Scott Pell
C.M. Peterson
Jim Pitts
George Poulios
Brian Powell
Scott Reno
Mike Rivera
Jim Rossow
Michael Joseph Rouse
Michael Sanchez
Joe Sarno
Chuck Schadrack
Jerry A. Schulz
Robert Scott
Ian Scudamore
Steve Sibra
David R. Smith
Ed Sobolak
David Sorochty
Dan Stevenson
Ray Storch
Evan Stuart
Bill Teichert
Brad Tenan
Harry Thomas
Peter R. Thorpe
Mike Tickal
John Verzyl
Henry Vogel
Jeff Walker
Lawrence Watt-Evans
David Welch
William J. Wieder
Donald F. Wilcher
Don Wilmoth
Garth Wood
Dan Wright, Ph.D.
Joseph Young
Catherine Yronwode

PREFACE

Comic book values listed in this reference work were recorded from convention sales, dealers' lists, adzines, and by special contact with dealers and collectors from coast to coast. Prices paid for rare comics vary considerably from one locale to another. We have attempted to list a realistic average between the lowest and highest range observed. The reader should keep in mind that the prices listed only reflect the market just prior to publication. Any new trends that have developed since the preparation of this book would not be shown.

The values listed are reports, not estimates. Each new edition of the guide is actually an average report of sales that occurred during the year; not an estimate of what we feel the books will be bringing next year. Even though many prices listed will remain current throughout the year, the wise user of this book would keep abreast of current market trends to get the fullest potential out of his invested dollar.

By the same token, many of the scarcer books are seldom offered for sale in top condition. This makes it difficult to arrive at a realistic market value. Some of the issues in this category are: Action No. 1, All-American No. 16, Batman No. 1, Black and White No. 20, Captain America No. 1, Captain Marvel No. 1, Detective No. 27, Double Action No. 2, the No-Number Feature Books, Green Giant No. 1, March of Comics No. 4, Marvel No. 1, More Fun No. 52, Motion Picture Funnies Weekly No. 1, Silver Streak No. 6, Superman No. 1, Tough Kid Squad No. 1, Whiz No. 2 (No. 1), Wonder No. 1, Amazing Man No. 5, and Wow No. 1.

Some rare comics were published in a complete black and white format; i.e., All-New No. 15, Blood Is the Harvest, Boy Explorers No. 2, Eerie No. 1, Flash Gordon No. 5, If the Devil Would Talk, Is This Tomorrow, and Stuntman No. 3. As we have learned in the case of Eerie No. 1, the collector or investor in these books would be well advised to give due consideration to the possibility of counterfeits before investing large sums of money.

This book is the most comprehensive listing of comic books ever attempted. Comic book titles, dates of first and last issues, publishing companies, origin and special issues are listed when known.

The Guide will be listing only American comic books due to space limitation. Some variations of the regular comic book format will be listed. These basically include those pre-1933 comic strip reprint books with varying size—usually with cardboard covers, but sometimes with hardback. As forerunners of the modern comic book format, they deserve to be listed despite their obvious differences in presentation. Other books that will be listed are giveaway comics—but only those that contain known characters, work by known artists, or those of special interest.

All titles are listed as if they were one word, ignoring spaces, hyphens and apostrophes. Page counts listed will always include covers.

IMPORTANT. Prices listed in this book are in U. S. currency and are for your reference only. This book is not a dealer's price list, although some dealers may base their prices on the values listed. The true value of any comic book is what you are willing to pay. Prices listed herein are an indication of what collectors (not dealers) would probably pay. For one reason or another, these collectors might want certain books badly, or else need specific issues to complete their runs and so are willing to pay more. Dealers are not in a position to pay the full prices listed, but work on a percentage depending largely on the amount of investment required and the quality of material offered. Usually they will pay from 20 to 70 percent of the list price depending on how long it will take them to sell the collection after making the investment; the higher the demand and better the condition, the more the percentage. Most dealers are faced with expenses such as advertising, travel, telephone and mailing, plus convention costs. These costs all go in before the books are sold. The high demand books usually sell right away but there are many other titles that are difficult to sell due to low demand. Sometimes a dealer will have cost tied up in this type of material for several years before finally moving it. Remember, his position is that of handling, demand and overhead. Most dealers are victims of these economics.

Everyone connected with the publication of this book advocates the collecting of comic books for fun and pleasure, as well as for nostalgia, art, and cultural values. Second to this is investment, which, if wisely placed in the best quality books (condition and contents considered), will yield dividends over the long term. The publisher of this reference work is a collector and has no comic books for sale.

TERMINOLOGY

Many of the following terms and abbreviations are used in the comic book market and are explained here:

a—Story art; **a(i)**—Story art inks; **a(p)**—Story art pencils; **a(r)**—Story art reprint.

B&W—Black and white art.

Bondage cover—Usually denotes a female in bondage.

c—Cover art; **c(i)**—Cover inks; **c(p)**—Cover pencils; **c(r)**—Cover reprint.

Cameo—When a character appears briefly in one or two panels.

Edgar Church—Refers to a large NM-Mint collection of comics originating from Denver, Colorado (Previously called Mile High collection).

Colorist—Artist that applies color to the pen and ink art.

Con—A Convention or public gathering of fans.

Cosmic Aeroplane—Refers to a large collection discovered by Cosmic Aeroplane Books.

Debut—The first time that a character appears anywhere.

Drug propaganda story—Where comic makes an editorial stand about drug abuse.

Drug use story—Shows the actual use of drugs: shooting, taking a trip, harmful effects, etc.

Fanzine—An amateur fan publication.

File Copy—A high grade comic originating from the publisher's file.

First app.—Same as debut.

Flashback—When a previous story is being recalled.

G. A.—Golden Age (1930s—1950s).

Headlight—Protruding breasts.

i—Art inks.

Infinity cover—Shows a scene that repeats itself to infinity.

Inker—Artist that does the inking.

Intro—Same as debut.

JLA—Justice League of America.

JSA—Justice Society of America.

Lamont Larson—Refers to a large high grade collection of comics. Many of the books have Lamont or Larson written on the cover.

Logo—The title of a strip or comic book as it appears on the cover or title page.

Mile High(See Edgar Church)

nd—No date.

nn—No number.

N. Y. Legis. Comm.—New York Legislative Committee to Study the Publication of Comics (1951).

Origin—When the story of the character's creation is given.

p—Art pencils.

Penciler—Artist that does the pencils.

POP—Parade of Pleasure, book about the censorship of comics.

Poughkeepsie—Refers to a large collection of Dell Comics' "file copies"

believed to have originated from Poughkeepsie, N. Y.
R or r—Reprint.
Rare—10 to 20 copies estimated to exist.
Reprint comics—Comic books that contain newspaper strip reprints.
S. A.—Silver Age (1956—Present).
Scarce—20 to 100 copies estimated to exist.
Silver proof—A black & white actual size print on thick glossy paper given to the colorist to indicate colors to the engraver.
S&K—Simon and Kirby (artists).
SOTI—**Seduction of the Innocent**, book about the censorship of comics.
Splash panel—A large panel that usually appears at the front of a comic story.
Very rare—1 to 10 copies estimated to exist.
X-over—When one character crosses over into another's strip.
Zine—See Fanzine.

Marvel comic books are cover coded for the direct sales (comic shop), newsstand, and foreign markets. They are all first printings, with the special coding being the only difference. The comics sold to the comic shops have to be coded differently, as they are sold on a no-return basis while newsstand comics are not. The Price Guide has not detected any price difference between these versions.

Direct Sales (Comic Shops)

Newsstand

Newsstand Overseas

Marvel Reprints: In recent years Marvel has reprinted some of their comics. There has been confusion in identifying the reprints from the originals. However, in 99 percent of the cases, the reprints will list "reprint," or "2nd printing," etc. in the indicia, along with a later copyright date in some cases. The only known exceptions are a few of the movie books such as *Star Wars*, the *Marvel Treasury Editions*, and tie-in books such as *G. I. Joe*. These books were reprinted and not identified as reprints. The *Star Wars* reprints have a large diamond with no date and a blank UPC symbol on the cover. The other reprints will have some cover variation such as a date missing, different colors, etc.

Gold Key comics were sold with two different labels: Whitman and Gold Key. There are collectors who prefer the Gold Key labels to Whitman, although the Price Guide does not differentiate in the price. Beginning in 1980, all comics produced by Western carried the Whitman label.

Many of the better artists are pointed out. When more than one artist worked on a story, their names are separated by a (/). The first name did the pencil drawings and the second did the inks. When two or more artists work on a story, only the most prominent will be noted in some cases. There has been some confusion in past editions as to which artists to list and which to leave out. We wish all good artists could be listed, but due to space limitation, only the most popular can. The following list of artists are considered to be either the most collected in the comic field or are historically significant and should be pointed out. Artists designated below with an (*) indicate that only their most noted work will be listed. The rest will eventually have all their work shown as the information becomes available. This list could change from year to year as new artists come into prominence.

Adams, Neal
*Aparo, Jim
*Austin, Terry
Baker, Matt
Barks, Carl
Beck, C. C.
Brunner, Frank
*Buscema, John
Byrne, John
*Check, Sid
Cole, Jack
Cole, L. B.
Craig, Johnny
Crandall, Reed
Davis, Jack
Disbrow, Jayson
*Ditko, Steve
Eisner, Will
*Elder, Bill
Evans, George
Everett, Bill
Feldstein, Al
Fine, Lou
Foster, Harold
Fox, Matt
Frazetta, Frank
Giffen, Keith
Golden, Michael
Gottfredson, Floyd
*Guardineer, Fred
Gustavson, Paul
*Heath, Russ
Howard, Wayne
Ingels, Graham
Jones, Jeff
Kamen, Jack
Kane, Bob
*Kane, Gil
Kelly, Walt
Kinstler, E. R.
Kirby, Jack
Krenkel, Roy
Krigstein, Bernie
*Kubert, Joe
Kurtzman, Harvey
Manning, Russ
*Meskin, Mort
Miller, Frank
Moreira, Ruben
*Morisi, Pete
*Nasser, Mike
*Newton, Don
Nostrand, Howard
Orlando, Joe
Pakula, Mac (Toth inspired)
*Palais, Rudy
*Perez, George
Powell, Bob
Raboy, Mac
Raymond, Alex
Ravielli, Louis
*Redondo, Nestor
Rogers, Marshall
Schomburg, Alex
Siegel & Shuster
Simon & Kirby (S&K)
*Simonson, Walt
Smith, Barry
Smith, Paul
Stanley, John
Starlin, Jim
Steranko, Jim
Torres, Angelo
Toth, Alex
Tuska, George
Ward, Bill
Williamson, Al
Woggon, Bill
Wolverton, Basil
Wood, Wallace
Wrightson, Bernie

The following abbreviations are used with the cover reproductions throughout the book for copyright credit purposes. The companies they represent are listed here:

ACE—Ace Periodicals
ACG—American Comics Group
AJAX—Ajax-Farrell
AP—Archie Publications
ATLAS—Atlas Comics (see below)
AVON—Avon Periodicals
BP—Better Publications
C & L—Cupples & Leon
CC—Charlton Comics
CEN—Centaur Publications
CCG—Columbia Comics Group
CG—Catechetical Guild
CHES—Harry 'A' Chesler
CLDS—Classic Det. Stories
CM—Comics Magazine
DC—DC Comics, Inc.
DELL—Dell Publishing Co.
DMP—David McKay Publishing
DS—D. S. Publishing Co.
EAS—Eastern Color Printing Co.
EC—E. C. Comics
ENWIL—Enwil Associates
EP—Elliott Publications
ERB—Edgar Rice Burroughs
FAW—Fawcett Publications
FF—Famous Funnies
FH—Fiction House Magazines
FOX—Fox Features Syndicate
GIL—Gilberton
GK—Gold Key
GP—Great Publications
HARV—Harvey Publications
HILL—Hillman Periodicals
HOKE—Holyoke Publishing Co.
KING—King Features Syndicate
LEV—Lev Gleason Publications
ME—Magazine Enterprises
MEG—Marvel Ent. Group
MLJ—MLJ Magazines
NOVP—Novelty Press
PG—Premier Group
PINE—Pines
PMI—Parents' Magazine Institute
PRIZE—Prize Publications
QUA—Quality Comics Group
REAL—Realistic Comics
RH—Rural Home
S & S—Street and Smith Publishers
SKY—Skywald Publications
STAR—Star Publications
STD—Standard Comics
STJ—St. John Publishing Co.
SUPR—Superior Comics
TC—Tower Comics
TM—Trojan Magazines
TOBY—Toby Press
UFS—United Features Syndicate
VITL—Vital Publications
WDC—The Walt Disney Company
WEST—Western Publishing Co.
WHIT—Whitman Publishing Co.
WHW—William H. Wise
WMG—William M. Gaines (E. C.)
WP—Warren Publishing Co.
YM—Youthful Magazines
Z-D—Ziff-Davis Publishing Co.

TIMELY/MARVEL/ATLAS COMICS. "A Marvel Magazine" and "Marvel Group" was the symbol used between December 1946 and May 1947 (not used on all titles/issues during period). The Timely Comics symbol was used between July 1942 and September 1942 (not on all titles/issues during period). The round "Marvel Comic" symbol was used between February 1949 and June 1950. Early comics code symbol (star and bar) was used between April 1952 and February 1955. The Atlas globe symbol was used between December 1951 and September 1957. The M over C symbol (beginning of Marvel Comics) was used between July 1961 until the price increased to 12 cents on February 1962.

TIMELY/MARVEL/ATLAS Publishers' Abbreviation Codes:

ACI—Animirth Comics, Inc.
AMI—Atlas Magazines, Inc.
ANC—Atlas News Co., Inc.
BPC—Bard Publishing Corp.
BFP—Broadcast Features Pubs.
CBS—Crime Bureau Stories

CIDS—Classic Detective Stories
CCC—Comic Combine Corp.
CDS—Current Detective Stories
CFI—Crime Files, Inc.
CmPI—Comedy Publications, Inc.
CmPS—Complete Photo Story
CnPC—Cornell Publishing Corp.
CPC—Chipiden Publishing Corp.
CPI—Crime Publications, Inc.
CPS—Canam Publ. Sales Corp.
CSI—Classics Syndicate, Inc.
DCI—Daring Comics, Inc.
EPC—Euclid Publishing Co.
EPI—Emgee Publications, Inc.
FCI—Fantasy Comics, Inc.
FPI—Foto Parade, Inc.
GPI—Gem Publishing, Inc.
HPC—Hercules Publishing Corp.
IPS—Interstate Publishing Corp.
JPI—Jaygee Publications, Inc.
LBI—Lion Books, Inc.
LCC—Leading Comic Corp.
LMC—Leading Magazine Corp.
MALE—Male Publishing Corp.
MAP—Miss America Publ. Corp.
MCI—Marvel Comics, Inc.
MgPC—Margood Publishing Corp.
MjMC—Marjean Magazine Corp.
MMC—Mutual Magazine Corp.
MPC—Medalion Publishing Corp.
MPI—Manvis Publications, Inc.
NPI—Newsstand Publications, Inc.
NPP—Non-Pareil Publishing Corp.
OCI—Official Comics, Inc.
OMC—Official Magazine Corp.
OPI—Olympia Publications, Inc.
PPI—Postal Publications, Inc.
PrPI—Prime Publications, Inc.
RCM—Red Circle Magazines, Inc.
SAI—Sports Actions, Inc.
SePI—Select Publications, Inc.
SnPC—Snap Publishing Co.
SPC—Select Publishing Co.
SPI—Sphere Publications, Inc.
TCI—Timely Comics, Inc.
TP—Timely Publications
20 CC—20th Cent. Comics Corp.
USA—U.S.A. Publications, Inc.
VPI—Vista Publications, Inc.
WFP—Western Fiction Publishing
WPI—Warwick Publications, Inc.
YAI—Young Allies, Inc.
ZPC—Zenith Publishing Co., Inc.

YOUR INFORMATION IS NEEDED: In order to make future Guides more accurate and complete, we are interested in any relevant information or facts that you might have. **Relevant and significant data includes:**

Works by the artists named elsewhere. **Caution:** Most artists did not sign their work and many were imitated by others. When submitting this data, advise whether the work was signed or not. In many cases, it takes an expert to identify certain artists—so extreme caution should be observed in submitting this data.

Issues mentioned by Wertham and others in **Seduction**, **Parade...**
Origin issues.
First and last appearances of strips or characters.
Title continuity information.
Beginning and ending numbers of runs.
Atomic bomb, Christmas, Flag and infinity covers.
Swipes.
Photo covers.

To record something in the Guide, **documented** facts are needed. Please send a photo copy of indicia or page in question if possible.

Non-relevent data—Most giveaway comics will not be listed. Literally thousands of titles came out, many of which have educational themes. We will only list significant collectible giveaways such as March of Comics, Disney items, communist books (but not civil defense educational comics), and books that contain illustrated stories by top artists or top collected characters.

We are also interested in receiving **page counts** for all comic books. When submitting data, please use the following procedure: **1.** All info is to be **Typed** on 3x5 index cards. **2.** Each card should contain **Complete** info on either: **(a)** Complete run if less than 100 issues (i.e. Aces High #1-5). **(b)** 100 issue groups if the run is greater than 100 issues (i.e. Action comics #1-100, 101-200, 201-300, 301-400, 401-500). **(c)** Block of issues after the last complete run of 100 issues (i.e. Action Comics #501-596). **3.** Count **Each** side of **Each** sheet as a page (count covers as well). Most comic books will have page counts of either 36, 52, 68, 84, or 100. **4.** Make special notes if the number of pages before the center staple is **Not One-Half** the number of pages in the entire issue.

5. Your index card should look like this:

ACTION COMICS

1 - 60	68 pages
61 - 74	60 pages (34 pages before center staple)
75 - 100	52 pages

6. Provider may, if he wishes, list his name, address, phone number on back of card.

7. Send to: Page Count Project, **Overstreet Publ., Inc.,** 780 Hunt Cliff Dr. NW, Cleveland, Tenn. 37311.

Advertise in the Guide

This book reaches more serious comic collectors than any other publication and has proven ad results due to its world-wide circulation and use. Your ad will pull all year long until the new edition comes out.

Display Ad space is sold in full, half, fourth, and eighth page sizes. Shop listings are sold for the **State Directory**. Ad rates are set in the early fall prior to each edition's release. Write at that time for rates (Between Oct.—Dec.).

PRINTED SIZES

Full Page—8" long x 5" wide. **Half Page**—4" long x 5" wide.
Fourth Page—4" long x 2½" wide. **Eighth Page**—2" long x 2½" wide.

Classified Ads will be retyped and reduced about one-half. No artwork permitted. Rate is based on your 4" typed line. **Display Classified Ads:** The use of borders, bold face type, cuts or other decorations change your classified ad to display—rates same as regular display.

NOTE: Submit your ad on white paper in a proportionate version of the actual printed size. All Full to Quarter page advertisers will receive a complimentary copy of the Guide. The **New Guide** will be professionally done throughout. . .so to reflect a consistently high quality from cover to cover, we must ask that all ads be neatly and professionally done. **Full Payment** must be sent with all ads. All but classified ads will be run as is.

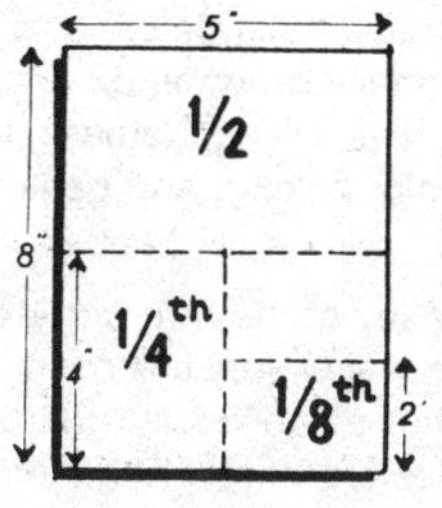

AD DEADLINE - COLOR—Dec. 15th
AD DEADLINE - Black & White—Jan. 15th

Overstreet Publications, Inc.
780 Hunt Cliff Dr. N.W.
Cleveland, Tennessee 37311

The **Price Guide** has become the **Standard Reference Work** in the field and is distributed to tens of thousands of comic collectors throughout the world. Don't miss this opportunity to advertise in the Guide.

NOTICE: All advertisements are accepted and placed in the Price Guide in good faith. However, we cannot be held responsible for any losses incurred in your dealings with the advertisers. If, after receiving legitimate complaints, and there is sufficient evidence to warrant such action, these advertisers will be dropped from future editions.

SPECIAL NOTICE

If copyrighted characters are planned for your ad, the following must be done: Send a copy of your ad layout (including characters) to the company(s) or copyright owner(s) involved requesting permission for their use. A copy of this permission must be sent to us with your ad. DC Comics and Marvel Comics have indicated that you will have no problem getting permission, so if you must use their characters. . .write for the permission. For DC, write: Public Relations, DC Comics, Inc. 666 Fifth Ave., New York, NY, 10103. For Marvel, write: Marvel Comics, 387 Park Ave. South, New York, NY 10016. Other companies such as Disney could be more of a problem. At any rate, we cannot accept any ads with copyrighted chracters without a copy of the permission.

GRADING COMIC BOOKS

Before a comic book's true value can be assessed, its condition or state of preservation must be determined. In most comic books, especially in the rarer issues, the better the condition, the more desirable the book. The scarcer first and/or origin issues in PRISTINE MINT condition will bring several times the price of the same book in POOR condition. The grading of a comic book is done by simply looking at the book and describing its condition, which may range from absolutely perfect newsstand condition (PRISTINE MINT) to extremely worn, dirty, and torn (POOR). Numerous variables influence the evaluation of a comic's condition and **all** must be considered in the final evaluation. More important characteristics include tears, missing pieces, wrinkles, stains, yellowing, brittleness, tape repairs, water marks, spine roll, writing, and cover lustre. The significance of each of these will be described more fully in the grading scale definitions. As grading is the most subjective aspect of determining a comic's value, it is very important that the grader must be careful and not allow wishful thinking to influence what the eyes see. It is also very important to realize that older comics in above MINT condition are extremely scarce and are rarely advertised for sale; most of the nicer comics advertised range from VERY FINE to NEAR MINT. To the novice, grading will appear difficult at first, but as experience is gained, accuracy will improve. Whenever in doubt, consult with a reputable dealer or experienced collector in your area. The following grading guide is given to aid the panelologist.

GRADING DEFINITIONS

The hardest part of evaluating a comic is being honest and objective with yourself, and knowing what characteristics to look for in making your decision. The following characteristics should be checked in evaluating books, especially those in higher grades: degree of cover lustre, degree of color fading, staples, staple areas, spine condition, top and bottom of spine, edges of cover, centering, brittleness, browning/yellowing, flatness, tightness, interior damage, tape, tears, folds, water marks, color flaking, and general cleanliness.

WARNING ABOUT RESTORATION:

Many of the rare and expensive key books are being upgraded from lower grades to fine or very fine condition through restoration. It has been brought to our attention that some dealers have been selling these books to unsuspecting collectors/investors—not telling them of the restoration. In some cases these restored books are being priced the same as unrestored books. **Very Important:** Examine books very closely for repairing or restoration before purchase. The more expensive the book, the greater the likelihood of restoration. Major things to look for are: bleaching, whitening, trimming, interior spine and tear reinforcement, gluing, restapling, missing pieces replaced, wrinkles pressed out of covers, recoloring and reglossing covers. Dealers should state that a book has been restored and not expect to get as much as a book unrestored in that condition would bring. **Note:** Cleaning, stain removal, rolled spine removal, staple replacement, etc., if professionally done, would not be considered restoration as long as the printed condition of the comic has not been changed.

VERY IMPORTANT: A book must be graded in its entirety; not by just the cover alone. A book in any of the grades listed must be in its **ORIGINAL UNRESTORED** condition. **Restored books** must be graded as such; i.e., a restored book grading fine might only be worth the same as a Very Good or even a Good copy in its unrestored state. The value of an extensively restored book may improve a half-grade from its original unrestored state. After examining these characteristics a comic may be assigned to one of the following grades:

PRISTINE MINT (PM): Absolutely perfect in every way, regardless of age. The cover has full lustre, is crisp, and shows no imperfections of any sort. The cover and all pages are extra white and fresh; the spine is tight, flat, and clean; not even the slightest blemish can be detected around staples, along spine, at corners or edges. Arrival dates pencilled on the cover are acceptable. As comics must be truly perfect to be graded PM, they are obviously extremely scarce even on the newsstand. Books prior to 1960 in this grade bring 20 to 250 per cent more.

MINT (M): Like new or newsstand condition, as above, but with very slight loss of lustre, or a slight off-centered cover, or a minor printing error. Could have pencilled arrival dates, slight color fading, and white to extra white cover and pages. Any defects noticeable would be very minor and attributable to the cutting, folding and stapling process.

NEAR MINT (NM): Almost perfect; tight spine, flat and clean; just enough minor defects of wear noticeable with close inspection to keep it out of the MINT category; i.e., a small flake of color missing at a staple, corner or edge, or slight discoloration on inside cover or pages; near perfect cover gloss retained.

VERY FINE (VF): Slight wear beginning to show; possibly a small wrinkle or crease at staples or where cover has been opened a few times; still clean and flat with most of cover gloss retained. Slight yellowing acceptable.

FINE (FN): Tight cover with some wear, but still relatively flat, clean and shiny with no subscription crease, writing on cover, yellowed margins or tape repairs. Stress lines around staples and along spine beginning to show; minor color flaking possible at spine, staples, edges or corners. Slight yellowing acceptable.

VERY GOOD (vg): Obviously a read copy with original printing lustre and gloss almost gone; some discoloration, but not soiled; some signs of wear and minor markings, but none that deface the cover; usually needs slight repair around staples and along spine which could be rolled; cover could have a minor tear or crease where a corner was folded under or a loose centerfold; no chunks missing. Slight yellowing acceptable.

GOOD (g): An average used copy complete with both covers and no panels missing; slightly soiled or marked with possible creases, minor tears or splits, rolled spine and small color flaking, but perfectly sound and legible. A well-read copy, but perfectly acceptable with no chunks missing. **Minor** tape repairs usually occur and slight browning (no brittleness) acceptable, although tape repairs should be considered a defect and priced accordingly.

FAIR (f): Very heavily read and soiled, but complete with possibly a small chunk out of cover; tears needing repairs and multiple folds and wrinkles likely; damaged by the elements, but completely sound and legible, bringing 50-70% of good price.

POOR (p): Damaged; heavily weathered; soiled; or otherwise unsuited for collection purposes.

COVERLESS (c): Coverless comics turn up frequently, are usually hard to sell and in many cases are almost worthless. It takes ingenuity and luck to get a good price; e.g., color Xerox covers will increase the salability. A cover of an expensive book is scarcer and worth more. However, certain "high demand" issues could bring up to 30 percent of the good price.

IMPORTANT: Comics in all grades with fresh extra white pages usually bring more. Books with defects such as pages or panels missing, coupons cut, torn or taped covers and pages, brown or brittle pages, restapled, taped spines, pages or covers, watermarked, printing defects, rusted staples, stained, holed, or other imperfections that detract from the original beauty, are worth less than if free of these defects.

Many of the early strip reprint comics were printed in hardback with dust jackets.

Books with dust jackets are worth more. The value can increase from 20 to 50 percent depending on the rarity of book. Usually, the earlier the book, the greater the percentage. Unless noted, prices listed are without dust jackets. The condition of the dust jacket should be graded independently of the book itself.

STORAGE OF COMIC BOOKS

Acids left in comic book paper during manufacture are the primary cause of aging and yellowing. Improper storage can accelerate the aging process.

The importance of storage is proven when looking at the condition of books from large collections that have surfaced over the past few years. In some cases, an entire collection has brown or yellowed pages approaching brittleness. Collections of this type were probably stored in too much heat or moisture, or exposed to atmospheric pollution (sulfur dioxide) or light. On the other hand, other collections of considerable age (30 to 50 years) have emerged with snow white pages and little sign of aging. Thus we learn that proper storage is imperative to insure the long life of our comic book collections.

Store books in a dark, cool place with an ideal relative humidity of 50 percent and a temperature of 40 to 50 degrees or less. Air conditioning is recommended. Do not use regular cardboard boxes, since most contain harmful acids. Use acid-free boxes instead. Seal books in Mylar[1] or other suitable wrappings or bags and store them in the proper containers or cabinets, to protect them from heat, excessive dampness, ultraviolet light (use tungsten filament lights), polluted air, and dust.

Many collectors seal their books in plastic bags and store them in a cool dark room in cabinets or on shelving. Plastic bags should be changed every two to three years, since most contain harmful acids. Cedar chest storage is recommended, but the ideal method of storage is to stack your comics (preferably in Mylar[1] bags) vertically in acid-free boxes. The boxes can be arranged on shelving for easy access. Storage boxes, plastic bags, backing boards, Mylar[1] bags, archival supplies, etc. are available from dealers. (See ads in this edition.)

Some research has been done on deacidifying comic book paper, but no easy or inexpensive, clear-cut method is available to the average collector. The best and longest-lasting procedure involves soaking the paper in solutions or spraying each page with specially prepared solutions. These procedures should be left to experts. Covers of comics pose a special problem in deacidifying due to their varied composition of papers used.

Here is a list of persons who offer services in restoration or archival supplies:

—Bill Cole, P.O. Box 60, Wollaston, MA 02170. Archival supplies, storage protection, deacidification solutions.

—The Art Conservatory, Mark Wilson, P. O. Box 705, Union City, CA 94587. Restoration

—Comic Conservation Lab, Jef Hines, P.O. Box 5L, Bakersfield, CA 93385. PH: (805) 872-8428. Restoration & preservation supplies.

—The Restoration Lab, P.O. Box 632, New Town Branch, Boston, MA 02258. PH: (617) 924-4297. Restoration.

—Lee Tennant Ent., Inc. 6963 W. 111th St., P.O. Box 296, Worth, IL 60482. (312) 448-2938 or 1-800-356-6401 for out of state

[1]***Mylar is a registered trademark of the DuPont Company.***

1987 MARKET REPORT

by Bob Overstreet[1]

Prices in the comic marketplace continued to post strong gains throughout the past year. Economic stability in the first three quarters of 1987 provided the necessary background for further price increases during the summer months. Turbulence in the financial markets last Fall had cast a cloud of uncertainty over many minds, but prices remained stable in the fourth quarter as sales proceeded at a brisk pace. Since prior price increases have been of a more stable nature, one would expect little impact on the comic marketplace should the national economy turn downward. Should the economy remain stable throughout the coming election year, one would again expect similar price increases.

Batman and related comics (*Detective*), the hottest title of 1986, was again the hottest title of 1987 along with all pre-hero DC titles: *New Comics, New Fun, New Adventure, Detective* and *More Fun*.

The past year saw a definite scarcity of high grade Golden-Age number ones and keys for sale. The market is becoming more aware of the importance of books with a "pedigree." Dealers were asking and getting 1.5 to 2 times mint guide for high grade copies from the following known collections: Denver, San Francisco, Larson, Pennsylvania, et al.

The big news for 1987 was the sale of a *Superman* #1 in NM for $14,000 cash and a Barks painting valued at $45,000. The (Church) copy of *Marvel* #1 traded for $82,000 and an *Action* #1 in VF-NM sold for $34,500 cash (the same copy that sold for $28,000 in 1986).

1987 was a year of readjustment for the comics from the Edgar Church (Mile High) collection. A somewhat different pricing structure was evident, more reminiscent of Edgar Church activity during the 1982-1984 period. A large number of Church books again became concentrated in the possession of three to four individual collector/brokers; large numbers of Church books traded at one time thus affecting the overall market value of many issues. As we reported in Overstreet #16 and #17, the key books from this particular collection sold for multiples of 3.5 mint guide list and over to several individuals. These books, primarily key DC comics, Timely comics, Centaurs, early MLJ and key Fiction House runs did not, for the most part, become available for sale over the past year. Most books which were offered for sale came from the vast assortment of the remaining titles contained in this historic collection. Copies of other than flawed or damaged Church books (books which were contained in this collection and were perfect - perhaps 10 per cent of the collection as a whole), continued to sell at a significant premium over mint guide list. Due to two primary factors, the large bulk transactions mentioned above and the fact that many comics demonstrated a substantial increase, in their list price over the last two years, the market showed resistance in paying previous years' multiples of guide list for these books. The premium paid over mint guide list fluctuated between 1.5 and 2 times for most titles. The more desirable key issues still maintained a value in excess of 3 times mint guide.

Once again, it is important to note that while the value of Church books has a relation to the overall market, sales of these books need be viewed as distinct; they reflect the special appeal and demand for these particular books from this particular collection. For a more detailed history of the Edgar Church collection (previously called

[1]*With helpful assistance from Steve Geppi, Hugh O'Kennon, Ron Pussell, Jay Maybruck, Joe Vereneault, Dan Malan, Rick Sloane, John Snyder, Terry Stroud, Gary Colabuono, Walter Wang, James Payette, Jon Warren, Stephen Fishler, Bruce Hamilton, Gary Carter, Mark Wilson and Joe Mannarino.*

the Mile High collection) refer to the market report in Overstreet #16.

The past year was a year of change at Overstreet Publications. The Official Overstreet #17 passed 100,000 in circulation due to our new alignment with Ballantine Books. In the Fall, Ballantine published *The Official Comic Book Price Guide Companion*, a mass market paperback that included up-to-date listings and prices for the more volatile recent comics and a new price guide section for Big Little Books! This new book will be an annual published in the Fall of each year. Look for it!

A more detailed recap of the market follows, broken down by periods, publishers and/or genres:

1930s Titles: Supplies of these early books were not able to meet demand, forcing prices to higher and higher levels—especially on certain key titles. The highest demand titles from this period were again the prehero DCs: *New Fun, New Comics, More Fun, Adventure, Detective,* etc. The Church copies of *Detective* #8 & 10 sold for $1,000 each, and #18 for $1,200. Other *Detective* sales are: #16VF - $1,200; #3Fn+ - $1,950 & #8Fn+ - $1,500. *More Fun* sales: #15,16,41-50 (Church) at 2.8 X Mint guide; #14Fn+ - $600; #14 Fair - $175; #20G - $150. *New Comics* sales: #1VG (restored) - $800; #6VF - $450; #1VG,4VG,6F,8VG,9VG,11G - 1.75 X mint guide. *New Adventure* sales: #14VG-Fn - 1.75 x guide; #14VF - $400; #31Fn - $150; #30VG - $95. A *New Book Of Comics* #1 in Fn+ brought $1,275. A *Famous Funnies Series 1* in VF sold for $2,000. Other *Famous Funnies* sales are: #1Fair - $350; #1Fn - $975; #2Fn+ - $500; #3VG - $250; #4VG - $150; 93-99 (Church) 2.5 x guide. Early issues of *Jumbo* were in high demand. A few recorded sales were: #1VF+(restored) - $2,950; #1Fn - $1,050; #3G+ - $200; #4Fn - $775, VG - $450; #8G+ - $400, GVG - $345.

A *Skippy's Own Book Of Comics* #1 in Fn sold for $750 & in VF for $1,050. *Funnies On Parade* #1VF (minor repair) brought $1,250. Other sales of 1930s comics are: *Amazing Mystery Funnies* #1Fn+ - $600; *Detective Picture Stories* #1FVF - $800; *All-American* #1Fn - $500; *Funny Picture Stories* #1VF - $400; *Popular Comics* #1G - $400; *Star Comics* #1VG - $310; V2#2Fn - $70; #1,3 (Church) 3X guide; *Star Ranger* #1,3,4,6 (Church) 3X guide; #1Fr-G - $100; #3FVF - $200; *Sun Fun* #1VG+ - $60; *Tip Top* #7NM - $175, 25FVF - $70; *The Comics* #1Fn - $475; *Favorite Comics* #2,3VGF - $100 each; *Wow* #4('36)VG - $750, 4Fn - $950 (auction). Most 1930s titles remained scarce and continue to show excellent growth as demand for these books is on the increase.

1940s Titles: The first three quarters of last year showed a strong demand for the superhero titles, as well as the westerns and all Fiction House titles. The last quarter, however, was not as active with a slight drop-off in demand. The DC superhero were the most sought after, followed by Centaur, Fox, Timely and MLJ. Overall, most titles from this period enjoyed good sales throughout the year, especially when graded accurately and priced fairly.

DC—One of the top collected companies, most all DC titles showed strong price increases again this year. *Action Comics* #1 again became the most valuable comic book last year passing *Marvel Comics* #1 in listed value. A high grade collection of mostly early 40s DCs was purchased by a Midwest dealer last year who brought them to San Diego to sell at the convention. During the first hour of the con he sold $11,000 worth comprised mostly of *Batmans, Detectives* and a few *Supermans*. They were all priced at over guide list with many of them selling to anxious buyers. *Batman* #1, *Detective* #27, *Action* #1, *Superman* #1, *All-American* #16, *All Star* #3, *Green Lantern* #1 and *Flash* #1 were all hot books in 1987. A VG restored *Action* #1 sold for $9,500; another copy in VF brought $34,500; and a Fn restored fetched $12,000. A very sharp NM copy of *Superman* #1 sold for $14,000 cash plus a Barks painting valued at $45,000; a Fn #1 sold for $12,000; a VF restored sold for $17,000 & a VG copy for $9,000. Other DC sales are as follows: *Action* #17VF+ - $850; #18VF+ - $650; #64 (Church) over 3x guide; *All-American* #1VF-NM - $700; #16VG+ - $2,500; #19VF - $750; #25NM - $750; #61 (Church) - $1,900; #73NM - $120; #100NM - $250;

All Star #1 (Larson) - $3,000; #2NM + (Church) 3.75 x guide; #3VF (restored) - $4,400; #3Fn + - $2,200; #29M - $500; *All Flash* #1VF - $775; #2NM - $400; #3,7,16,17, 19,21,22,24-29,32 (Church) over 3x guide; *Batman* #5VF - $700; 6NM - $700; #9NM - $700; #11M - $800; #14VF - $575; #21NM - $300; *Big All-American* VG + - $800; *Detective* #27Fn + (restored) - $9,300; #27Fn (restored) - $7,500; #33Fn - $2,000; #33VF - $4,000; #41VF - $625; #43VF - $400; #45NM - $400; #50VF - $400; #59M - $450; #61NM - $350; #72M - $300; #80VF - $250; #93NM - $225; *Flash Comics* #1 (Church) - $15,400; #1M - $4,900; #2NM - $1,650; #8VF - $375; #104VF - $800; NM - $350 cash, $1,004 trade; *Green Lantern* #1VG + - $800; *More Fun* #52VG (restored) - $2,350; *Star Spangled* #13-15,17 (S.F.) 2.1x guide; *Superman* #2VF (restored) - $1,200; #4VF + - $1,250; #5FVF - $725; #7VF + - $800; #14VF + - $500. #14NM - $800; #19NM - $500; #22NM - $400.

Most all DC superhero and other titles were very strong in 1987 and continue to be the company to watch in the years ahead.

Timely—Mixed reports on this perennial favorite. *Captain America* seemed to be the strongest title with *Marvel Mystery, Human Torch and Sub-Mariner* holding their own. *Namora, Sun Girl* and *Blonde Phantom* remained hard to find. The Church copy of *Marvel Comics* #1 traded again for $82,000 early in the year. The Church *Captain America* #1 sold for $14,500 and the Denver copy brought $8,500! Another copy in NM + sold for $8,000 and a FN + (restored) brought $2,000; a #3 in VG + sold for $650; the 132pg. B&W sold for $850 in VG and another copy sold for $1,200 in G. An *All Winners* #1NM sold for $1,450; A #1VG (2nd Series) sold for $160; A *Human Torch* #1VF brought $2,500; A *Marvel Comics* #1Fn + sold for $20,700; a #6 in VG + brought $455; *Sub-Mariner* #32M - $400; *Mystic* #1 (Denver) - $3,000; another #1VF-NM - $2,200; another #1VF - $1,400; *Mystic* #5VF + - $700; *Red Raven* #1NM - $4,000; *Terrytoons* #1NM - $225; *Tough Kid Squad* #1VF + - $1,450. Currently prices on most Timelys seem to be leveling off where supplies are meeting current demand.

Fox—Early issues of *Mystery Men, Wonderworld, Blue Beetle, Fantastic* and *Weird* were in high demand; especially those issues with Lou Fine covers. The late 1940s titles—*Blue Beetle, Phantom Lady, Rulah, Zoot, Jo-Jo,* etc. were in high demand. *Wonder* #1NM (Windy City) - $2,000; #1VF - $1,050; *Mystery Men* #3-9 (Denver) - 1.5x guide; *Zoot* #14VG + - $50; *Rex Dexter* #1Fn - $250; *V-Comics* #1VF - $275; *Wonderworld* #3Fn - $200; #9 (Denver) 1.5x guide.

Centaur—All Centaurs remained scarce and in high demand showing solid increases for the year. A collector brought an incomplete run of *Amazing-Man* to the San Diego con last year to sell, and soon had several buyers wanting the set. Needless to say they sold quickly to one of the buyers. This company's books are still very volatile and continue to be an excellent area for investment. A few documented sales are: *Amazing Mystery Funnies* V1#3Fn - $165; V2#2VF - $200; V2#7VF + - $1,225; V2#8VG - $170; V2#9Fn - $165; *The Arrow* #1VF - $350; *Green Giant* #1VG (restored) - $770; *C-M-O Comics* #1NM - $200; *Funny Pages* V3#1VF - $200; V2#10G - $175; V3#9Fn - $175; #42VF - $195; *Keen Detective Funnies* V2#8GVG - $70; V2#9VG-Fn - $80; *Stars & Stripes* #3 (Larson) 1.5x guide.

Fawcett—*Captain Marvel, Marvel Family, Captain Midnight* & *Spy Smasher* were in the highest demand. Most titles of this company again enjoyed slow to moderate sales. Early issues of *Master* were not available. *Nickel, Bulletman, Captain Jr.,* etc. showed moderate sales with *Whiz* and later issues of *Master* selling slower. A Fawcett *Flash* #1 in Fn + sold for $5,000, while a *Thrill* #1 in VG sold for $9,000 cash. A *Whiz* #1 in VG (restored) sold for $3,900; a *Wow Comics* #2 in VF brought $400; a *Slam Bang* #1 in NM fetched $375; another copy in VG sold for $125. A *Master* #1Fn - $800; *Nickel* #1Fn - $300; *Minuteman* #1Fn - $200; *Golden Arrow* #1VF - $100. No high grade copies of *Whiz* #1 or *Captain Marvel* #1 turned up in 1987. *Captain Video* and *Vic Torry & His Flying Saucer* were hot.

Gleason—Renewed interest in *Daredevil* and *Silver Streak* with moderate sales in *Boy* and *Crime Does Not Pay*. A *Daredevil* #1 in Fn+ sold for $650. A *Silver Streak* #6 in VF sold for $1,200; a #7 in NM brought $925. A *Captain Battle Jr.* #1NM sold for $250.

Disney—Interest in all Disney titles picked up during the year due (in part) to Gladstone's high quality and popular new titles. However, most Disney comics were selling at and around current guide prices with a few exceptions. A *Donald Duck Surprise Party* in Fn sold for $600; a *Four Color* #16 in FVF sold for $1,500; another copy in FVF (restored) brought $700; a *March Of Comics* #41 in NM brought $1,300; a #20 in Fn sold for $500; a *Mickey Mouse Magazine* set in Vg-Fn (minus V2#3, V5#12) sold for $5,500; a *Walt Disney C&S* #1 in NM brought $2,600; a *Four Color* #4 in VG sold for $475. The demand for *Four Color* #4, 9 & 16 in NM-M picked up as well as for early *Comics and Stories* in high grade. Copies of *Adventures Of Mickey Mouse, Book 1* (not listed) were selling for $200 - $400. This book has the first mention & appearance of *Donald Duck*. A few high grade early Disney's surfaced last year from the publisher's files and sold quickly to anxious buyers.

Quality—*Blackhawk, Military* and *Plastic Man* were strong with *Hit Comics, National, Smash, Police, Feature,* etc. showing slow to moderate demand. A *Police* #11 in NM sold for $750.

Fiction House—A very strong selling company throughout the year. *Jumbo* #1-8 remained very scarce and in high demand. *Planet* continues to be the most in demand title but *Jumbo, Jungle, Rangers, Wings, Ghost, Sheena,* etc. all enjoyed good sales. A *Sheena* #1 (Denver) sold for 1.5x guide; a *Jungle Girl* #1 in VF brought $225. A high grade collection of most Fiction House titles surfaced from NW Georgia early in the year. This collection covered the mid to late issue number range and sold briskly to local collectors. The paper quality was unusually fresh, supple and white.

MLJ—*Pep* continued to be the most popular title. Most MLJ titles had slow to moderate sales. *Pep Comics* #17,21 (Church) sold for over 3x guide; a #22 in M sold for $2,000; a #1 in VF brought $800; *Blackhood* #10,12,16,18,19 (Church) sold for over 3x guide; *Zip Comics* (Church) #39-47 sold for over 3x guide; *Archie* was slow to moderate with *Archie Comics* #1-15 remaining hard to find. An *Archie* #1VF sold for $1,050. *Katy Keene* was still very strong.

Harvey—*Green Hornet* was a very hot title with *Champ, Champion, Black Cat, All New, Speed*, etc. having moderate demand. The later Harvey's, *Richie Rich*, etc. remained slow. A *Green Hornet* #1 in VF+ sold for $500. A *Speed* #1VF sold for $500. Demand for *Dick Tracy* is meeting current supplies.

Classic Comics—This year saw continued strong growth in the *Classics* field. Many dealers have felt that *Classics* were a sleeper for the last few years. There were many new discoveries of rare non-series items (giveaways, gift boxes, etc.) and foreign *Classics*. Early originals saw very strong growth, plus international trading drove up demand for any cheap copy of U.S. #'s 8,14,20,21,33,40,43,44,53,66,73,74,84,95,110 & 169. All giveaways and other non-series items have been pulled from the main listings and placed in a new section called "Classics Non-Series Items." The *Classics* section has again been revamped due mostly to continuing research by Dan Malan. Thanks Dan. A *Classic* #1 in VF+ sold for $1,250; a #2 in VF+ brought $600; a #8 in NM sold for $550, to list a few examples.

Miscellaneous—The '40s produced many other collectible titles. *Airboy, Air Fighters, Tip Top* and *Sparkler* with *Tarzan* covers, *Superworld, Miracle, Doc Savage, Shadow* all sold very well. Some odd titles like *Thirty Seconds Over Tokyo* and *Remember Pearl Harbor* were in high demand. A *Superworld* #1 (Denver) sold for $1,500. Another copy in VF brought $600. Here are a few other sales: *Atoman* #1VF - $100; *Dynamic* #1VF - $250; *Lightning* #4VF - $200; *Fighting Yank* #1Fn - $225; *Hyper Mystery* #1VF - $250; *Sure Fire* #1VF - $300; *Whirlwind* #1NM - $300; *Crash* #1VF - $400; *Target* #1VG - $250.

1950s Titles—Most titles from this period showed high demand throughout the year. The superhero, T.V., western, and horror titles all had strong sales. Late in the year a high grade 50s collection came out of New Jersey and sold briskly to anxious buyers at over-guide prices. In highest demand were the Atlas horror, E.C. horror, DC funny animal, humor and superhero titles.

TV Comics—Interest in most TV related titles stayed strong last year. Some of the more collected titles were *Leave It To Beaver, Avengers* with Emma Peel, *Bewitched, I Love Lucy, Monkees, Space Ghost, Three Stooges, Jonny Quest, Wild, Wild West, Rocky & Bullwinkle, Lippy The Lion, Mister Magoo, Howdy Doody,* and *Rawhide* just to name a few. This genre is on the move and deserves a close look in anyone's investment portfolio. A *Howdy Doody* #1 in Fn sold for $100.

E.C.—Most E.C. titles were a little stronger than in previous years, especially for *Mad, Frontline Combat* and the horror titles. However most E.C.s are selling at current price levels. A set of E.C. annuals and a set of the horror titles in high grade brought 35% over mint guide late in the year. A *Crime SuspenStories* #1NM sold for $325. A *Tales From The Crypt* #20VF brought $250. A VF *Lucky Fights It Through* brought $1,625 at auction.

DC—Many of the more obscure titles showed high demand. *Alan Ladd, Jackie Gleason* and *Sergeant Bilko* were very hot. *Danger Trail, New Advs. of Charlie Chan, Feature Films, Frontier Fighters* and *Jimmy Wakely* also sold at a fast clip. *Tommy Tomorrow* issues remained scarce. The humor DCs showed moderate sales. *Scribbly, Sugar and Spike, Fox & The Crow* showed steady sales. Demand is picking up for the war DCs—*Our Army At War, Our Fighting Forces* and *G.I. Combat*. Of course the most volatile area are the superhero titles with all prices up. *Action, Adventure, Batman, World's Finest, Detective,* etc. supplies could not meet demand. *Challengers* #1-8 were moderate-hot. *Mystery In Space* #53-80 and *Phantom Stranger* sold well. *Showcase* #1-35 are up, especially the *Challengers, Flash, Green Lantern* and *Adam Strange* issues. All late '50s 10-cent DCs remained very hard to get with a huge demand.

Atlas—The horror and science fiction titles were strong, especially *Marvel Tales* and *Journey Into Unknown Worlds*. The crime titles showed moderate demand with the war titles holding their own and romance titles slow.

Westerns—This genre continues to have strong sales. The Dell titles—*Roy Rogers, Gene Autry, Lone Ranger, Red Rider*, etc. had steady sales. The later issues of *Lone Ranger* were in higher demand. All TV Dell westerns remained strong. NM copies of *Rawhide* sold for $100 last year. *The Rifleman, Gunsmoke, Maverick, Have Gun Will Travel, The Rebel,* etc. also enjoyed good sales. The Fawcett westerns were very hot with low supplies and high demand; especially *Lash LaRue, Tex Ritter, Ken Maynard, Tom Mix, Bob Colt, Bob Steele, Rod Cameron, Bill Boyd, Hopalong Cassidy* and *Rocky Lane*. The *Fawcett Movie* and *Motion Picture Comics* enjoyed moderate sales. The M.E. westerns were up. *Tim Holt, Red Mask* (esp. the 3-D issues), *Ghost Rider, Straight Arrow* and *Durango Kid* had strong demand. The Atlas westerns showed increased demand. *Black Rider, Rawhide Kid* and *Kid Colt* were selling very well. *Whip Wilson, Rex Hart* and *Reno Browne* were very hot and not available, while *Tex Morgan* and *Tex Taylor* held their own. *Prize Western* with *American Eagle* by Severin and *Crack Western* had good sales. However, the following titles were highly sought after with very limited supplies: *Cisco Kid* (1944), *Cowboy Western* with *Sunset Carson, Hoot Gibson, Tim McCoy* and *Sunset Carson. John Wayne* remained very popular in all movie comics issues as well as the St. John run. A *Ken Maynard* #1M sold for $150.

Dell/Gold Key Giants—These books stayed in high demand with a near complete set in mint condition selling for 1.5x mint guide. The small supply of mint copies that came out two or three years ago have now been mostly absorbed into collections. A *Peter Pan Treasure Chest* in NM sold for $250; a *Dell Giant* #30 (Disneyland USA) and #43(Mighty Mouse) brought $75 each.

Art Comics—Steve Ditko comics are very strong; especially *The Thing* and *Captain Atom* in *Space Adventures.* Matt Baker is holding his own while Frank Frazetta continued to sell very well. Matt Fox showed increased demand for his few comic appearances in Atlas comics and *Chilling Tales* issues. Alex Toth sales were up and Sid Check and Bill Everett showed solid demand. Disbrow and L.B. Cole had slower sales while Kirby was up. Eisner *Spirit* prices are still at a plateau. Barks and John Stanley still remained very popular.

Baseball & Sport Comics—Probably due to the hugh increase in demand for sports cards in recent years, comic books of this theme are really coming into their own. Especially in high demand are the Fawcett titles like *Phil Rizzuto, Ralph Kiner, The Pride Of The Yankees, Jackie Robinson, Thrilling True Stories Of. . .*, etc.

Good Girl Art Comics—Overall, this remained a popular area of collecting. The Fox titles like *Phantom Lady, Rulah, Jo-Jo, Crimes By Women, Women Outlaws* and later *Blue Beetle*, etc. showed high demand. *Undercover Girl, Brenda Starr* and *Seven Seas* were hot.

3-D Comics—These books remained very popular with the more obscure, harder to find titles having greater demand.

Horror Comics—E.C. horror was stronger than in previous years. ACG titles like *Adventures Into The Unknown* #1-20 and *Forbidden Worlds* #1-10 sold well. Harvey titles were available in the market. Atlas horror enjoyed high demand as well as the more obscure companys' titles like *Baffling Mysteries, Dark Mysteries, Mysterious Adventures, The Beyond, Voodoo*, etc. A *Skeleton Hand* #1VF sold for $50. A *Phantom Witch Doctor* #1NM sold for $125. An *Out of The Night* #1VF sold for $75. A *Mask* #1VG fetched $125.

Humor Comics—Average sales overall. The hottest titles were *Casper* (St. John), *Laurel & Hardy* (St. John), and *Three Stooges* (all issues). Demand for *Pogo* and *Powerhouse Pepper* was up. The Dell *Looney Tunes* and *New Funnies* had increased popularity as well as all D.C. and ACG humor titles.

Seduction Of The Innocent Comics—Demand for these books picked up during the year. Comics with extreme violence, spanking, transvestism, etc. and especially the SOTI issues were very strong.

Miscellaneous Items—"Atomic" type books held their own; *Juke Box Comics* are still in high demand. Negro theme comics like *Negro Heroes, Negro Romances*, etc. are very popular. *Space Patrol* was hot. Love comics overall were slow with a pickup of interest in the photo cover issues. Here are a few sales: *Strange Worlds* (Avon) #1NM - $250; *Flying Saucers* #1VF - $200; *Forbidden Worlds* #1VF - $175; *Thunda* #1Fn - $550.

1960s-1970s Titles—1987 saw a strong increase in demand for most 1960s titles, while most 1970s titles remained stable. DC sales were up; especially Legion issues. All the key DC Silver Age titles like early *Showcase*, early *Brave and The Bold*, early *Justice League, Flash* and *Green Lantern* remained scarce in high grade. There was also increased demand for *Aquaman, Rip Hunter, Sea Devils, The Atom* and especially in fine-mint condition. *Strange Adventures* with Atomic Knights, as well as Doom Patrol in *My Greatest Adventure* were hot. Marvels showed a high demand for early 60s very fine - mint issues of *Spiderman, Hulk, Fantastic Four, Tales Of Suspense, Avengers, Tales To Astonish*, etc. with a stronger demand for *X-Men. Amazing Adult Fantasy* issues were hot. An *Amazing Fantasy* #15NM sold for $2,200; a *Fantastic Four* #1M brought $1,900; a *Spiderman* #1M sold for $1,000; another copy in NM sold for $855; an *X-Men* #1 sold for $700; a *Showcase* #4NM for $1,400; a *Strange Adventures* #9FVF for $250; a *Tales Of Suspense* #39FVF for $160; a *Flash* #123VG for $25; a #109NM for $82; a #105VF for $400 and a *Star Wars* (35 cents) #1NM brought $175.

1980s Titles—1987 marked the return of DC Comics to the top of the heap in the direct sales market. After making huge strides towards closing the gap between themselves and Marvel Comics in 1985 and 1986 with projects such as *Dark Knight* and *Man of Steel*, DC regained the number one position in dollar sales during the Summer of 1987. Their rise to the top was certainly in large measure the result of editorial improvements in their mainline titles such as *Justice League, Flash, Wonder Woman, Superman* and *Batman*, all of which had significant changes in artists, writers or editors in 1986-87. continued quality efforts in the marketing and promotion areas got the word out to the distributors, retailers and fans, and a continued commitment to create innovative titles, formats and schedules made following the DC Universe interesting and exciting. *Watchmen* continued the success it had developed with its early issues and by the time the series ended fans were clamoring for more *Watchmen* material. Buttons, T-Shirts, portfolios, watches, trade paperbacks and the like followed to the delight of fandom. The *Green Arrow Long Bow Hunters* mini-series was a success that emulated the success of *Dark Knight* the year earlier. The same perfect bound "prestige format," also known as "bookshelf format" was utilized for the *Blackhawk* mini-series which was also highly successful.

Millenium was an eight issue weekly series that tied into most of the DC Universe. Its success laid the groundwork for additional weeklies announced by both DC and Marvel for the Spring of 1988. *The Shadow* and *Doc Savage* were popular projects which successfully took Golden Age pulp heroes and brought them to the readers of today.

Marvel was in somewhat of a state of flux during the early part of 1987 as they lost their editor in chief for many years, Jim Shooter. Shooter resigned in March of 1988 and was replaced by Tom Defalco. While all deadlines were met and the transition was certainly smooth, it did take a while for Marvel to regain the energy and drive necessary to produce new and innovative products for the direct market. *The Fall of the Mutants* project was a bigger than expected success as readers clamored for all the cross-over titles. The Marvel mainline titles continued to dominate the industry in unit sales and there were a few pleasant surprises. *X-Men* continues to be the leading title in unit sales and all the *Mutant* spin offs are doing extremely well. *The Punisher* and *Silver Surfer* titles were huge successes from their premiere issues and continue to do very well. *The Nam* was a surprise hit as was *Solo Avengers*. 1987 was declared a rebuilding year for both the Epic and New Universe lines. New, improved offerings are promised for both in 1988.

The direct sales market came to national prominence with the premiere on November 7, 1987 of the ABC network primetime show, Sable, based on the Mike Grell character published by First Comics. It marked the first time a character born and raised entirely in the direct sales market received this kind of national exposure. The early ratings were very strong and hopefully, the show will be renewed for the Fall season. This is an historic First and marks the emergence of this marketplace into the mainstream entertainment industry.

1987 witnessed the Japanese invasion as First Comics, Eclipse Comics and many other smaller publishers brought over original Japanese comics to translate and reproduce for the American market. Although sales did not approach the sales figures in Japan where comics sell in the millions of copies per issue, they did very well and their success will undoubtedly foster more Japanese translations in 1988. *Lone Wolf* and *Cub* from First led the invasion from the Far East. The success of these titles have generated considerable interest in the back issues which are commanding premium prices.

1987 saw the demise of several direct sales distributors as well as publishers. Glenwood, Alternate Realities and Sunrise Comics all closed their doors during 1987. Their bankruptcies underline the fragility of the direct sales market at the distributor level. The repercussions felt by the publishers at the inability of the distributors to pay their bills as well as a dramatic reduction in the interest and sales of many small press products caused many small publishers to go out of the comic book business as well. Aaargh!, Amazing, Elite, Imperial, Lodestone, Showcase, Solson, Timeline, and Wonder, to name a few. Those that have survived, have in some cases reduced their frequencies and/or number of offerings as the marketplace makes the final adjustments to last years black and white glut. This instability at the new issue level has greatly affected the back issue market for these publications. The cancellation of many titles, the re-scheduling of others and the general cautious attitude of the collectors of the small press titles have caused back issue sales and prices to continue on their downward spiral. There are of course notable exceptions including *Teenage Mutant Ninja Turtles, Boris the Bear* and *Flaming Carrot.*

In summary, 1987 continued the market effects begun in late 1986 as the small independent publications continued their downward trends while ongoing titles of the larger more reliable publishers remained stable and high quality limited series showed large price increases as speculative interests snapped up available copies.

You will note that many of the more recent black and white comics have been deleted from the listings in this edition. We have been observing the proliferation of these type of publications in recent years, not knowing exactly how to react as far as guide listings were concerned. We have noticed that many of these black & whites were vanity press type publications; while still others could be classified as undergrounds. After much deliberation we have decided for the time being not to list most of these type comics. However, we will continue to list the more important titles (those with collector value) in the Bulletins and Update.

INVESTOR'S DATA

The following table denotes the rate of appreciation of the top 50 most valuable Golden Age titles over the past year and the past five years (1983-1988). The retail value for a complete mint run of each title in 1988 is compared to its value in 1987 and 1983. The 1971 values are also included as an interesting point of reference. The rate of return for 1988 over 1987, and the yearly average rate of return for each year since 1983, is given.

For example, a complete mint run of *Detective Comics* retails at $118,121 in 1988, $107,328 in 1987, and $47,228 in 1983. The rate of increase of 1988 over 1987 can be easily calculated at 10.1%, while the average yearly increase or rate of return over the past five years is 30.0%. This means that the mint value of this title has increased an average of 30.0% each year over the past five years. However, the rate of increase would be less for fine condition and much less for good condition over the same period.

The place in rank is given for each title by year, with its corresponding mint value. This table can be very useful in forecasting trends in the market place. For instance, the investor might want to know which title is yielding the best dividend from one year to the next, or one might just be interested in seeing how the popularity of titles changes from year to year. For instance, *Famous Funnies* was in 8th place in 1971 and has dropped to 25th place in 1988. But this title could be on the move to reclaim its original position, as it has changed from 38th place to 25th in the past five years and currently continues to show a strong price increase (1988 over 1987).

Batman overtook *Whiz* for the number 9 spot, and *Classic Comics* overtook *Marge's Little Lulu* for the number 36 spot this year. *Daredevil* entered the top 50 jumping from 54th to 50th spot. *Green Lantern* increased by 17.7% from 1987, but shows a yearly average increase of 23.6%. *Jumbo Comics* was up 23.9% and *More Fun* up 21.5%.

The following tables are meant as a guide to the investor and it is hoped that they might aid him in choosing titles in which to invest. However, it should be pointed out that trends may change at anytime and that some titles can meet market resistance with a slowdown in price increases, while others can develop into real comers from a presently dormant state. In the long run, if the investor sticks to the titles that are appreciating steadily each year, he shouldn't go very far wrong.

The Silver Age titles continued to show movement, especially early issues of Marvel's and DC's in high grade. Golden Age titles are continuing to appreciate faster than economic inflationary values during the same period.

TOP 50 TITLES

TOP 50 TITLES & RATE OF INCREASE OVER 1987 AND 1983 GUIDE VALUES

Title	1988 Guide Rank	1988 Guide Value	%Change From '87 Value	Avg.Yrly. Return '83-'88	1987 Guide Rank	1987 Guide Value	1983 Guide Rank	1983 Guide Value	1971 Guide Rank	1971 Guide Value
Detective Comics	1	$118,121	+10.1	+30.0	1	$107,328	3	$47,228	4	$2,747
Action Comics	2	100,221	+ 9.9	+17.8	2	91,230	1	52,986	7	2,354
Marvel Mystery Comics	3	76,530	+ 3.9	+10.6	3	73,654	2	49,970	5	2,584
More Fun Comics	4	75,410	+21.5	+25.4	4	62,048	5	33,252	3	2,816
Four Color	5	65,053	+11.2	+14.4	5	58,480	4	37,792	1	4,229
Adventure Comics	6	62,226	+14.2	+22.0	6	54,475	7	29,627	2	3,066
Superman	7	59,577	+11.8	+16.5	7	53,276	6	32,684	13	1,460
Captain America	8	41,875	+13.9	+14.5	8	36,759	9	24,260	17	1,303
Batman	9	39,943	+16.6	+22.1	10	34,260	13	18,964	19	1,246
All Star Comics	10	39,080	+14.5	+22.5	11	34,128	14	18,380	10	1,657
Whiz Comics	11	$36,953	+ 3.7	+ 9.6	9	$35,623	8	$24,975	14	$1,357
Flash Comics	12	34,350	+14.9	+22.6	12	29,902	15	16,125	15	1,344
All American Comics	13	32,965	+14.3	+22.5	13	28,853	16	15,520	24	1,189
Donald Duck	14	28,454	+ 6.1	+ 5.9	14	26,825	10	22,014	53	604
Walt Disney's C & S	15	26,111	+ 7.7	+ 4.1	15	24,233	11	21,627	12	1,487
Planet Comics	16	23,233	+ 8.4	+14.1	16	21,429	18	13,643	50	613
Police Comics	17	21,793	+ 6.5	+10.8	18	20,467	17	14,163	30	903
Jumbo Comics	18	20,914	+23.9	+26.0	22	16,886	27	9,101	16	1,320
Spirit	19	20,839	− 1.8	+ 1.1	17	21,224	12	19,783	44	645
World's Best & Finest	20	20,725	+11.3	+13.2	19	18,624	20	12,502	33	841
Mickey Mouse Magazine	21	$18,717	+12.4	+11.2	23	$16,654	21	$12,010	18	$1,252
Captain Marvel Advs.	22	17,989	+ 6.0	+ 8.5	21	16,977	19	12,613	29	1,009
Master Comics	23	17,866	+11.0	+13.4	24	16,094	23	10,693	28	1,021
Star Spangled Comics	24	17,454	+13.9	+19.0	26	15,326	28	8,959	35	830
Famous Funnies	25	16,957	+17.9	+33.6	29	14,377	38	6,326	8	2,343
Human Torch	26	16,620	+ 4.2	+ 9.4	25	15,956	22	11,290	46	632
Pep Comics	27	16,511	+ 8.6	+15.8	27	15,204	26	9,230	31	880
Dick Tracy	28	16,457	+ 2.4	+12.1	20	16,066	24	10,264	25	1,116
Sensation Comics	29	15,731	+ 9.6	+15.7	30	14,358	29	8,809	41	681
Submariner	30	15,107	+ 4.9	+ 9.6	28	14,408	25	10,210	54	601
Green Lantern	31	$15,025	+17.7	+23.6	32	$12,770	34	$6,885	87	390
Feature Book	32	14,317	+ 4.2	+13.1	31	13,744	30	8,647	26	$1,069
King Comics	33	13,903	+17.5	+27.1	34	11,831	51	5,899	6	2,490
Wonder Woman	34	13,775	+ 9.2	+13.5	33	12,617	32	8,234	64	537
Jungle Comics	35	12,983	+10.2	+21.8	35	11,786	41	6,214	32	861
Classic Comics	36	12,920	+19.9	+23.5	38	10,780	49	5,942	189	65
Tip Top Comics	37	12,793	+17.6	+23.8	37	10,879	52	5,848	9	2,088
Marge's Little Lulu	38	12,306	+ 8.9	+21.5	36	11,305	50	5,925	135	219
Amazing-Man Comics	39	11,935	+11.6	+31.4	40	10,695	60	4,645	108	314
Silver Streak Comics	40	11,729	+10.6	+14.1	41	10,608	35	6,873	86	394
Feature & Feature Funnies	41	$11,448	+10.6	+26.9	42	$10,353	56	$4,883	22	$1,214
Hit Comics	42	11,413	+ 6.4	+11.8	39	10,726	33	7,188	67	523
Military Comics	43	11,343	+12.4	+17.0	43	10,094	42	6,130	68	520
Popular Comics	44	11,079	+15.2	+28.1	49	9,616	61	4,610	11	1,598
Target Comics	45	10,730	+ 7.3	+14.4	45	10,003	39	6,236	38	746
National Comics	46	10,461	+ 6.6	+12.4	47	9,810	37	6,451	42	676
Large Feature Comic	47	10,360	+ 4.6	+ 4.8	46	9,901	31	8,361	27	1,058
Superboy	48	10,298	+ 2.5	+13.1	44	10,044	40	6,218	94	360
Ace Comics	49	10,079	+10.8	+25.8	50	9,097	62	4,404	23	1,212
Daredevil	50	10,064	+14.4	+14.7	54	8,798	53	5,794	45	639

The following tables show the rate of return of the 50 most valuable Golden Age books, the 20 most valuable Silver Age titles and the 20 most valuable Silver Age books over the past year. It also shows the average yearly rate of return over the past five years (1988-1983). Comparisons can be made in the same way as in the previous table of the Top 50 titles. Ranking in many cases is relative since so many books have the same value. These books are listed alphabetically within the same value.

50 MOST VALUABLE GOLDEN AGE BOOKS AND RATE OF RETURN

Issue	1988 Guide Rank	1988 Guide Value	%Change From '87 Value	Avg.Yrly. Return '83-'88	1987 Guide Rank	1987 Guide Value	1983 Guide Rank	1983 Guide Value
Action Comics #1	1	$28,650	+14.6	+20.9	2	$25,000	2	$14,000
Marvel Comics #1	2	27,000	+ 3.8	+10.9	1	26,000	1	17,500
Superman #1	3	20,800	+15.6	+21.6	3	18,000	3	10,000
Detective Comics #27	4	20,000	+14.3	+31.3	4	17,500	5	7,800
Whiz Comics #1	5	16,250	+ 8.3	+20.6	5	15,000	4	8,000
Detective Comics #1	6	9,100	+21.3	+71.0	7	7,500	25	2,000
More Fun Comics #52	7	8,500	+21.4	+17.8	8	7,000	10	4,500
Batman #1	8	8,400	+10.5	+10.5	6	7,600	6	5,500
Double Action Comics #2	9	6,500	+12.1	+ 7.1	9	5,800	9	4,800
Captain America #1	10	6,300	+10.5	+ 5.2	10	5,700	7	5,000
Captain Marvel Advs. #1	11	$6,000	+ 5.3	+ 6.7	10	$5,700	10	$4,500
All American Comics #16	12	5,900	+16.3	+20.7	12	5,075	16	2,900
All Star Comics #3	13	5,740	+20.6	+40.4	15	4,760	30	1,900
More Fun Comics #53	14	5,500	+14.6	+16.7	14	4,800	15	3,000
Motion Pic. Funnies Wkly. #1	15	5,000	+ 0.0	+ 0.0	13	5,000	7	5,000
Wow Comics #1	15	5,000	+ 6.4	+ 6.3	16	4,700	12	3,800
Action Comics #2	17	4,725	+ 3.8	+ 9.5	17	4,550	13	3,200
Detective Comics #28	18	4,400	+ 4.8	+20.0	18	4,200	22	2,200
Flash Comics #1	18	4,400	+14.3	+27.6	20	3,850	33	1,850
Marvel Mystery Comics #2	18	4,400	+ 4.8	+ 7.5	18	4,200	13	3,200
Detective Comics #33	21	$4,200	+12.1	+25.4	21	$3,745	33	$1,850
Detective Comics #38	21	4,200	+12.1	+32.5	21	3,745	38	1,600
New Fun Comics #1	21	4,200	+20.0	+56.4	22	3,500	70	1,100
Action Comics #3	24	3,640	+ 7.1	+10.3	24	3,400	19	2,400
Amazing-Man Comics #5	25	3,500	+14.8	+50.0	26	3,050	77	1,000
All Star Comics #1	26	3,300	+17.9	+24.0	30	2,800	45	1,500
New Fun Comics #2	27	3,250	+16.1	+88.3	30	2,800	-	600
Human Torch #1	28	3,200	+ 6.7	+ 6.7	27	3,000	19	2,400
Walt Disney C&S #1	28	3,200	+10.3	+ 4.6	29	2,900	17	2,600
Marvel Mystery Comics #5	30	3,185	+ 1.1	+ 4.5	25	3,150	17	2,600
Superman #2	31	$3,150	+ 7.1	+ 8.6	28	$2,940	22	$2,200
Action Comics #5	32	3,000	+ 7.1	+10.0	30	2,800	25	2,000
Daring Mystery Comics #1	32	3,000	+ 8.5	+14.3	34	2,765	37	1,750
Donald Duck March of Comics #4	32	3,000	+15.4	+ 5.0	37	2,600	19	2,400
Red Raven Comics #1	35	2,900	+ 7.4	+ 9.0	35	2,700	25	2,000
Action Comics #7	36	2,800	+14.3	+15.0	39	2,450	38	1,600
Action Comics #10	36	2,800	+14.3	+15.0	39	2,450	38	1,600
Dick Tracy Feature Book nn	36	2,800	+ 0.0	+15.0	30	2,800	38	1,600
Detective Comics #2	39	2,765	+15.2	+41.4	43	2,400	95	900
Captain America #2	40	2,700	+ 8.0	+ 8.4	38	2,500	30	1,900
Detective Comics #29	40	$2,700	+12.5	+21.5	43	$2,400	58	$1,300
Popeye Feature Book nn	40	2,700	+ 0.0	+16.0	35	2,700	45	1,500
Big Book Of Fun Comics #1	43	2,625	+25.0	+85.0	51	2,100	-	500
Marvel Mystery Comics #3	44	2,520	+ 2.9	+ 8.0	39	2,450	36	1,800
Mystic Comics #1	44	2,520	+ 4.3	+13.6	42	2,415	45	1,500
Action Comics #4	46	2,500	+ 5.0	+11.3	46	2,380	38	1,600
Batman #2	46	2,500	+13.6	+18.5	47	2,200	58	1,300
Detective Comics #31	46	2,500	+15.2	+25.5	49	2,170	70	1,100
Green Lantern #1	46	2,500	+19.0	+27.6	51	2,100	75	1,050
Sub-Mariner Comics #1	46	2,500	+ 4.2	+ 7.0	43	2,400	33	1,850

20 MOST VALUABLE SILVER AGE TITLES AND RATE OF INCREASE

Issue	1988 Guide Rank	1988 Guide Value	%Change From '87 Value	Avg.Yrly. Return '83-'88	1987 Guide Rank	1987 Guide Value	1983 Guide Rank	1983 Guide Value
Showcase	1	$7,311	+14.4	+ 8.1	1	$6,391	1	$5,196
Fantastic Four	2	6,132	+13.2	+ 5.8	2	5,417	2	4,749
Amazing Spider-Man	3	5,825	+15.0	+ 7.8	3	5,064	3	4,189
The Flash	4	5,048	+23.8	+11.7	4	4,076	5	3,188
Brave and The Bold	5	4,412	+15.3	+ 7.3	5	3,826	4	3,228
X-Men	6	4,127	+26.6	+23.6	7	3,259	11	1,894
Sugar and Spike	7	3,884	+12.9	+21.8	6	3,439	13	1,858
Justice League	8	3,541	+32.6	+16.7	10	2,670	8	1,932
Tales To Astonish/Inc. Hulk	9	3,265	+12.6	+ 3.5	8	2,900	6	2,779
Green Lantern	10	3,014	+19.5	+11.7	11	2,523	10	1,902
Richie Rich	11	$2,728	+ 0.6	+ 0.4	9	$2,713	7	$2,668

Issue	1988 Guide Rank & Value		%Change From '87 Value	Avg.Yrly. Return '83-'88	1987 Guide Rank & Value		1983 Guide Rank & Value	
Avengers	12	2,620	+22.5	+ 7.8	14	2,139	12	1,888
Challengers Of The Unknown	13	2,587	+15.1	+10.2	12	2,248	14	1,716
Superman's Pal J. Olsen	14	2,463	+11.0	+ 5.6	13	2,219	9	1,925
Cerebus	15	2,187	+50.7	+437.3	20	1,451	-	-
Superman's Girl Friend L. Lane	16	1,910	+ 9.5	+ 5.2	16	1,745	16	1,516
Mystery In Space #53 up	17	1,790	+ 9.9	+ 9.9	18	1,629	19	1,199
Journey Into Mystery/Thor	18	1,748	+ 5.1	+ 1.3	17	1,663	15	1,644
Harvey Hits	19	1,612	+ 4.8	+ 1.4	19	1,538	17	1,508
Daredevil	20	1,567	+22.0	+10.4	22	1,284	21	1,030

20 MOST VALUABLE SILVER AGE BOOKS AND RATE OF RETURN

Issue	1988 Guide Rank & Value		%Change From '87 Value	Avg.Yrly. Return '83-88	1987 Guide Rank & Value		1983 Guide Rank & Value	
Amazing Fantasy #15	1	$1,500	+25.0	+ 5.0	4	$1,200	1	$1,200
Showcase #4	2	1,450	+16.0	+ 6.4	2	1,250	3	1,100
Fantastic Four #1	3	1,380	+10.4	+ 3.0	2	1,250	1	1,200
Adventure #247	4	1,350	+ 2.3	+29.1	1	1,320	6	550
Amazing Spider-Man #1	5	1,000	+11.1	+ 8.6	5	900	4	700
Incredible Hulk #1	6	660	+ 4.8	+ 1.1	6	630	5	625
Detective Comics #225	7	640	+21.9	+14.1	7	525	14	375
X-Men #1	8	600	+25.0	+22.9	11	480	24	280
Justice League #1	9	575	+17.3	+26.0	10	490	30	250
Brave & The Bold #28	10	550	+25.0	+16.1	15	440	22	305
Fantastic Four #2	10	550	+10.0	+ 5.0	8	500	8	440
Flash #105	10	550	+31.0	+14.4	19	420	20	320
Tales To Astonish #27	10	550	+19.6	+ 7.5	13	460	12	400
Brave & The Bold #1	14	540	+ 8.0	+ 5.4	8	500	10	425
Avengers #1	15	520	+18.2	+ 9.7	15	440	15	350
Showcase #8	16	510	+20.0	+10.0	18	425	18	340
Superman's Pal J. Olsen #1	17	500	+ 5.0	+ 3.8	12	476	11	420
Showcase #22	18	495	+19.3	+13.0	21	415	23	300
Journey Into Mystery #83	19	475	+ 5.6	− 0.2	14	450	7	480
Showcase #1	20	450	+ 7.1	+5.7	19	420	15	350

The following table lists the really hot current titles over the past year. From one year to another, this list can change drastically.

HOT TITLES & RATE OF INCREASE 1988 GUIDE OVER 1987 GUIDE

Title	Increase	Title	Increase	Title	Increase
Nam, The	227.8%	G.I. Joe Spec. Missions	88.9%	Iron Man	39.4%
Justice League ('87)	224.1%	G.I. Joe Order of Battle	85.2%	Aquaman	38.2%
Groo, The Wanderer ('82)	181.4%	X-Men vs. Avengers	83.3%	New Mutants	36.9%
Punisher ('87)	180.0%	Gumby's Summer Fun Spec.	80.0%	West Coast Avengers ('84)	34.5%
Elfquest ('79)	167.8%	Strikeforce: Morituri	76.4%	Green Arrow ('83)	32.4%
Marshall Law	150.0%	Sgt. Fury	71.9%	Saga of Swamp Thing	32.2%
Green Arrow: Long Bow	136.2%	West Coast Avengers ('85)	68.0%	Superman ('87)	31.5%
Elfquest ('87)	128.6%	Star Trek ('84)	66.9%	Sea Devils	30.6%
Longshot	128.4%	Groo, The Wanderer ('85)	65.7%	Our Fighting Forces	30.2%
Flash ('87)	127.3%	Elektra: Assassin	64.2%	Rip Hunter	28.0%
Doom Patrol	120.8%	Spiderman vs. Wolverine	60.0%	Marvel Tales	27.2%
X-Factor	105.9%	G. I. Joe	54.9%	Silver Surfer	25.7%
Watchmen	100.0%	Mage	54.4%	Nick Fury, Agent of Shield	25.0%
Grendel ('86)	96.0%	Cerebus	50.7%	Classic X-Men	24.8%
Young All-Stars	96.0%	Elfquest ('85)	50.5%	Scout	23.5%
Wonder Woman ('87)	94.7%	Shadow ('87)	50.0%	Speed Racer	23.1%
Legends	92.7%	Atom, The	47.9%	Metal Men	23.0%
Web of Spiderman	92.7%	Albedo	45.3%	Ronin	21.3%
Punisher ('86)	90.7%	Teen Titans	43.3%	Iron Fist	21.0%
Wolverine	90.3%	Flaming Carrot	43.1%	Strange Tales	20.5%

THE FIRST WAVE OF COMIC BOOKS 1933-1943 (Key books listed and ranked)

The first modern format comic book came out in 1933 and represents the beginning of comic books as we know them today. The impact of these early characters and ideas are today deeply engrained in American folklore and continue to feed and inspire this ever changing industry.

Over the years historians, collectors and bibliofiles have tried to make some sense out of this era. The question 'what are considered to be the most important books?' has been a topic of discussion and debate for many years. With certain criteria considered, how would the top key issues be ranked in order of importance? How would they relate to each other? In an attempt to answer some of these questions, the following list has been prepared. The books are grouped chronologically in the order they were published. The most important books are ranked into seven tiers, with the top six designated with stars. The more important the book is, the more stars it receives. The following criteria were used to determine the importance and placement of each book in each tier:

A. Durability of character(s)
b. Durability of title
c. Popularity of character(s)
d. First appearance anywhere of a major character
e. First issue of a title
f. Originality of character (first of a type)
g. First or most significant work of a major artist
h. Starts a trend
i. First of a genre
j. Historical significance
k. First of a publisher
l. First appearance in comic books of a character from another medium

This list was compiled by several people* and represents a collective opinion of all. The list is not perfect, not by any means. Adjustments will be made over time as more input is received. The final ranking of a book depends greatly on the overall importance and impact of that book on the comic book market. Obviously, the further you get away from the top key books, the more difficult it becomes for proper ranking. For this reason, books ranked in the lower numbered tiers could change drastically. The final rating given a book is not based entirely on the quantity of points it receives, but rather the overall weight of the points it does receive. For example, the first appearance of *The Fighting Yank* is not as important as the first appearance of *Superman* who was a trend setting character and long lasting.

In the comics market there are several comics that have become high demand, valuable books due primarily to rarity. A list of the top key books ranked due to value, demand and rarity would look entirely different than what we have here. As we have learned in coins, stamps and other hobbies, rarity is an important factor that affects value and it is not our intention to demean the collectibility of any particular book that is rare. Quite the contrary. There are many rare books that would enhance anyone's collection. Consideration of rarity, for the ranking of books in this list has been kept at a minimum.

The following list covers the period 1933 through 1943 and includes **every** key book of this period of which we are currently aware. Any omissions will be added in future lists. It should be noted that many other issues, although highly collectible, were not considered important for the purpose of this list: i.e., origin issues, early issues in a run, special cover and story themes, etc.

Special thanks is due **Landon Chesney who contributed considerable energy and thought to the individual write-ups; to **David Noah** who polished and edited, and to the following people who contributed their time and ideas to the compilation of this list: Hugh O'Kennon, Steve Geppi, Richard Halegua, John Snyder, Joe Tricarichi, Walter Wang, Jon Warren, Bruce Hamilton, Ray Belden and Chuck Wooley*

NOTE: All **first issues** are included as well as books that introduce an important new character, or has key significance in some other way.

CHRONOLOGICAL LIST OF KEY COMIC BOOKS FOR PERIOD 1933 - 1943

(All first issus listed)

GENRE CODES (Main theme)

An - Anthology (mixed)	**H** - Costumed/Superhero	**Mg** - Magic	**Sp** - Sport
Av - Aviation	**Hr** - Horror	**M** - Movie	**TA** - Teen-Age
Cr - Crime	**Hm** - Humor	**R** - Strip Reprints	**Tr** - True Fact
D - Detective	**J** - Jungle	**Re** - Religious	**W** - War
F - Funny Animal	**Lit** - Literature	**SF** - Science Fiction	**Ws** - Western

NOTE: The stars signify the ranking of books into seven different tiers of importance. The top (most important) books receive six stars (1st tier), dropping to no star (7th tier) as their significance diminishes. The following information is provided for each comic: 1. Ranking, 2. Title, 3. Issue number, 4. Date, 5. Publisher, 6. Genre code, 7. Description. 8. Criteria codes.

ANTEDILUVIAN PERIOD

1933 ■

★★★★ **FUNNIES ON PARADE** nn (1933, Eastern Color, R)-The very first comic book in the modern format reprinting popular strip characters. Given away to test the feasibility of demand for repackaged Sunday newspaper funnies. (An 8-page tabloid folded down to 32 pages).
(a,c,d,e,h,i,j,k,l)

★★★★ **FAMOUS FUNNIES, A CARNIVAL OF COMICS** nn (1933, Eastern Color, R)-The second comic book. Given away to test reader demand. Its success set up another test to come in the following year to see if the public would actually pay 10¢ for this type of product (an 8-page tabloid folded down to 32 pages). The first of three first issues for this title.
(a,b,c,e,f,h,j)

★ **CENTURY OF COMICS** nn (1933, Eastern Color, R)-The third comic book. A 100-pager given away with three times the contents of the previous two books.
(e,j)

1934 ■

★ **SKIPPY'S OWN BOOK OF COMICS** nn (1934, Eastern Color, R)-The fourth comic book. The first to feature a single character-this wasn't tried again until ***Superman*** No. 1.
(e,j)

★★★★ **FAMOUS FUNNIES, SERIES I** (1934, Eastern Color, R)-The first comic book sold to the general public (through chain stores). The acid test, its unprecedented success set up the beginning of the first continuous series (anthology reprint) title in comics, and started the chain reaction.
(a,b,c,e,f,h,j)

★★★★★ **FAMOUS FUNNIES** No. 1 (7/34, Eastern Color, R)-Satisfied with the public response, this issue began the series and was the first comic book sold to the general public through newsstand distribution.
(a,b,c,e,f,h,j)

★ **FAMOUS FUNNIES** No. 3 (9/34, Eastern Color, R)-This issue ushered in the famous and very popular *Buck Rogers* strip reprints. Not trend setting, but important for the survival of the run which lasted 22 years.
(a,b,c,f,i,j,l)

1935 ■

★★★★ **NEW FUN COMICS** No. 1 (2/35, DC, An)-The first prototype of the modern comic in that it featured an anthology format of continuing characters and original rather than reprinted material. First of the DC line and the first tabloid-size book (albeit short-lived), surviving 13 years as ***More Fun Comics***.
(b,e,h,i,j,k)

★ **MICKEY MOUSE MAGAZINE** No. 1 (Sum/35, K.K., F)-Magazine-size protocomic introducing the already legendary transfer characters to the fledgling comic book market. This title first appeared in 1933 as a black & white giveaway comic, and after going through format changes, eventually led to the ultimate "funny animal" comic, ***Walt Disney's Comics & Stories***, to come five years later.
(a,b,c,e,g,j,k)

★ **NEW COMICS** No. 1 (12/35, DC, An)-DC felt enough confidence in the market to issue a second anthology title featuring original, continuing characters. It was second only to ***New Fun*** of its kind. Evolved into ***Adventure Comics***, warhorse of the DC line. DC parlayed the second most perfect comic book title (the first is ***Action***) into a forty plus year run.
(b,e,h,j)

1936 ■

MORE FUN COMICS No. 7 (1/36, DC, An)-DC cancelled the title ***New Fun*** due to the appearance of ***New Comics***, continuing the series under this changed title.
(b,e,j)

★★★ **POPULAR COMICS** No. 1 (2/36, Dell, R)-The second anthology format title of continuing reprint strips. First of the Dell line, the third publisher to enter the field. Featuring the first comic book appearance of *Dick Tracy, Little Orphan Annie, Terry & the Pirates* and others, lasting 13 years.
(a,b,c,e,j,k,l)

BIG BOOK OF FUN COMICS (Spr/36, DC, An)-The first annual in comics (56 pages, large size; reprints from ***New Fun*** No. 1-5).
(e,h,i,j)

★★★ **KING COMICS** No. 1 (4/36, McKay, R)-Ties as the third continuous series reprint title. The first of a publisher (4th to enter the field). Showcase title of all the King Feature characters-the most popular and widely circulated in the world, featuring Segar's *Popeye* and Raymond's *Flash Gordon* series as the mainstay, lasting 16 years.
(a,b,c,e,j,k,l)

★★★ **TIP TOP COMICS** No. 1 (4/36, UFS, R)-Ties as the third continuous series reprint anthology title. The first of a publisher (5th to enter the field). Featuring the *Tarzan* and *Li'l Abner* series and surviving 25 years.
(a,b,c,e,j,k,l)

★ **COMICS MAGAZINE, THE** (Funny Pages) No. 1 (5/36, Comics Mag., An)-The third anthology format title of original material. The first of a publisher (6th to enter the field). This book is unique in that its cover and entire contents were purchased from DC. This material created gaps in the story line continuity of DC's titles ***More Fun*** and ***New Adventure*** from which it came.
(e,j,k)

WOW COMICS No. 1 (7/36, McKay, An)-The fourth anthology title of original material. McKay's second series (first with original contents), lasting only 4 issues to 11/36. The Unpublished inventory formed the basis of the Eisner/Iger shop.
(e)

NEW BOOK OF COMICS No. 1 (6-8/36, DC, An)-The

The second annual in comics; 100 pages, reprinting popular strips from ***More Fun*** and ***New Comics***. Second and last issue appeared in Spring of 1938.
(e)

FUNNIES, THE No. 1 (10/36, Dell, R)-Having published this title six years earlier as a tabloid, Dell brought it back as a regular comic book. Featuring more popular strip characters, this became Dell's second comic book title and ran for 6 years.
(b,e)

FUNNY PAGES No. 6 (11/36, Comics Mag., An)-Continued from ***The Comics Magazine****; introduced The Clock*(?), the first masked hero (detective type, transition hero) in a comic book.
(a,b,c,d,e,f,h,i,j)

FUNNY PICTURE STORIES No. 1 (11/36, Comics Mag., An)-Actually this company's second title, featuring their popular original character, *The Clock*, who appeared on the cover. Title continues for 3 years.
(e)

DETECTIVE PICTURE STORIES No. 1 (12/36, Comic Mag., D)-The first anthology comic title series devoted to a single theme and the first to focus on this subject. Popular in pulps, magazines and films of the time, lasted 7 issues.
(e,h,i,j)

1937 ■

NEW ADVENTURE COMICS No. 12 (1/37, DC, An)-Title change from ***New Comics***, continues series.
(e)

STAR COMICS No. 1 (2/37, Chesler, An)-Ties as first of a publisher. Anthology format of continuing original material, but short lived (2½ years). Large-size format.
(e,k)

STAR RANGER No. 1 (2/37, Chesler, Ws)-Ties as first of a publisher, and as the first continuous series western anthology title (see ***Western Picture Stories***). Large-size format of original material, lasting only 1 year.
(e,i,j,k)

WESTERN PICTURE STORIES No. 1 (2/37, Comics Mag, Ws)-Ties with ***Star Ranger*** as the first anthology comic title of original material to focus on this subject, the second of a single theme, not lasting out the year.
(e,i,j)

COMICS, THE No. 1 (3/37, Dell, R)-Dell's third anthology reprint title. The first comic book appearance of *Tom Mix*, lasting only one year.
(e,d)

★★★ **DETECTIVE COMICS** No. 1 (3/37, DC, D)-Inaugurated the longest run in comics. Initially a pulpy anthology of mystery men and private eyes, it emerged as the first important title on a single theme with the debut of the implacable *Batman* in '39 (Siegel and Shuster's *Slam Bradley* series is a flavorful example of title's '37-'38 period).
(a,b,c,e,f,h,i,j)

ACE COMICS No. 1 (4/37, McKay, R)-Due to the enormous success of McKay's first series, ***King Comics***, this companion title was published featuring, among others, Raymond's *Jungle Jim*, lasting 12 years.
(a,b,c,e,j,l)

WESTERN ACTION THRILLERS No. 1 (4/37, Dell, Ws)-The third title devoted to westerns. A one-shot of 100 pages.
(e)

FEATURE BOOK nn (Popeye)(1937, McKay, R)-A new concept. The first series of comic books representing a divergence from the normal anthology format. Each issue in the run is actually a one-shot devoted to a single character. More than one issue in the run can be devoted to the same character. These books began in a B&W, magazine-size format. Improvements on this concept came a year later with UFS's ***Single Series*** (in color, comic book size), and still a year later with Dell's ***Four Color*** series, the only one to last.
(a,b,c,e,h,i,j)

FEATURE FUNNIES No. 1 (10/37, Chesler, R)-Another reprint title to add to the list, surviving 13 years as ***Feature Comics***; carrying *Joe Palooka, Mickey Finn* and others.
(e)

100 PAGES OF COMICS No. 101 (1937, Dell, R)-Another 100-page reprint anthology book (Dell's 2nd) with a western cover. Only one issue.
(e)

1938 ■

ACE COMICS No. 11 (2/38, McKay, R)-First comic book appearance of *The Phantom*. Premiere mystery man and first costumed hero. The Ghost Who Walks never made the impact in comics that he enjoyed as a syndicated star.
(a,b,c,f,i,j,l)

FUNNY PAGES V2/6 (3/38, Centaur, An)-Ties with ***Funny Picture Stories***, ***Star Comics*** and ***Star Ranger*** as first of a publisher. Series picked up from Chesler, ending two years later.
(k)

FUNNY PICTURE STORIES V2/6 (3/38, Centaur, An)-Ties with ***Funny Pages***, ***Star Comics***, and ***Star Ranger*** as first of a publisher. Series picked up from Comics Magazine, ending one year later.
(k)

STAR COMICS No. 10 (3/38, Centaur, An)-Ties with ***Funny Pages***, ***Funny Picture Stories***, and ***Star Ranger*** as first of a publisher. Series picked up from Chesler, ending one year later.
(k)

STAR RANGER V2/10 (3/38, Centaur, Ws)-Ties with ***Funny Picture Stories***, ***Star Ranger***, and ***Funny Pages*** as first of a publisher. Series picked up from Chesler, lasting 2 more issues.
(k)

COMICS ON PARADE No. 1 (4/38, UFS, R)-The second title of this publisher, featuring much the same reprint strips as ***Tip Top***, their first. This series survived 17 years.
(a,b,c,e,j)

MAMMOTH COMICS No. 1 (1938, Whitman, R)-First of a publisher, in the same format as the McKay ***Feature Books***. Only one issue.
(e,k)

SUPER COMICS No. 1 (5/38, Dell, R)-A dynamic new title, Dell's fourth. Debuted with some of the heavy weights transferred from the already successful ***Popular Comics***. This new line-up of *Dick Tracy, Terry & The Pirates,* etc. proved to be a sound marketing strategy, lasting 11 years. (a,b,c,e,j)

GOLDEN AGE PERIOD

★★★★★★ **ACTION COMICS** No. 1 (6/38, DC, H)-The ultimate refinement of the anthology, continuing character title. The first appearance of *Superman*, the quintessential hero with extraordinary powers. Arguably the most imitated character in all of fiction. Standard bearer of the DC line. The most important comic book ever published, and in tandem with ***Superman***, one of the most influential, prevailed beyond four decades.
(a,b,c,d,e,f,h,i,j)

CIRCUS COMICS No. 1 (6/38, Globe, An)-A unique short-lived title featuring a top artist line-up. Introduced Wolverton's *Spacehawks*, later to appear in ***Target Comics*** as *Spacehawk*. First of a publisher.
(d,e,f,j,k)

CRACKAJACK FUNNIES No. 1 (6/38, Dell, R)-A new Dell title, replacing the defunct ***The Comics*** with a similar but different mix of reprint strips. Lasted 4 years.
(e)

COWBOY COMICS No. 13 (7/38, Centaur, Ws)-Continued from ***Star Ranger*** and lasted only two issues. The fourth western anthology title.
(e)

KEEN DETECTIVE FUNNIES No. 8 (7/38, Centaur, An)-Continued from ***Detective Picture Stories***, this title became one of Centaur's mainstays introducing the *Masked Marvel* one year later, lasting 2 years.
(e)

LITTLE GIANT COMICS No. 1 (7/38, Centaur, An)-Small-size diversion from the regular format and short-lived (4 issues).
(e)

AMAZING MYSTERY FUNNIES No. 1 (8/38, Centaur, An)-Standard bearer of the Centaur line. Top artist line-up due to its production by the Everett shop. Ran for two years.
(e,g)

LITTLE GIANT MOVIE FUNNIES No. 1 (8/38, Centaur, An)-A miniature-sized format comic lasting two issues. A small cartoon panel appears on the right edge of each page giving the illusion of motion when riffled (a flip book) (the cover is set up to represent a movie theater).
(e,i)

★ **FUNNY PAGES** V2/10 (9/38, Centaur, H)-First appearance of *The Arrow* who is the very first costumed hero originating in the comic book (3 months after *Superman*). A primitive percursor of the more refined archers to come, *The Arrow* executed his adversaries with the medieval bluntness his uniform suggested.
(a,b,d,f,h,i,j)

★★★ **JUMBO COMICS** No. 1 (9/38, FH, J)-Publisher of the most perused, but least read, of Golden Age comics, Fiction House did not so much initiate a trend as continue the trusty formula that sustained their line of pulps, cheesecake cast against a variety of single theme adventurous backgrounds (aviation, s/f, jungle & war). ***Jumbo*** was the pilot model of the FH line and the first of the exploitation comics. The debut of *Sheena, Queen of the Jungle* heralded hordes of jungle goddesses to follow. The line overall is perhaps best remembered as a showcase for Matt Baker's patented 'calendar girl' art which, after Caniff and Raymond, was the most pervasive of Golden Age styles, enduring 15 years.
(a,b,c,e,f,h,i,j,k,l)

DETECTIVE COMICS No. 20 (10/38, DC, H)-First appearance of *The Crimson Avenger*, a *Shadow* look-a-like, who was the second comic book costumed hero (4 months after *Superman*).
(b,c,d,f,h,i,j)

LITTLE GIANT DETECTIVE FUNNIES No. 1 (10/38, Centaur, An)-Small-size format only lasting a few issues.
(e)

STAR RANGER FUNNIES No. 15 (10/38, Centaur, An)-Links to ***Star Ranger*** and ***Cowboy Comics***, only lasting a few months. (Packaged by the Iger Shop.)
(e)

★★★ **DONALD DUCK** nn (1938, Whitman, F)-The first *Donald Duck*, as well as the first Walt Disney comic book; in the format of McKay's ***Feature Book*** (B&W with color cover), reprinting 1936 & 1937 Sunday comics. The first funny animal comic devoted to a single character. Precursor to great things to come for this character.
(a,b,c,e,f,i,j,l)

★★ **SINGLE SERIES** nn (Captain & The Kids) (1938, UFS, R)-UFS refined McKay's one-shot ***Feature Book*** format by adding color and adopting the standard comic book size, resulting in a more marketable package. Dell adopted this format for their ***Four Color*** series, which started a year later. This is UFS' third continuous series title.
(e,f,h,i,j)

COCOMALT BIG BOOK OF COMICS No. 1 (1938, Chesler, An)-A one-shot mixed anthology Charles Biro creation, packaged by the Chesler shop (top-notch art).
(e)

NICKEL COMICS No. 1 (1938, Dell, An)-A small-size divergent format one-shot, lasting only one issue.
(e)

1939 ■

ALL-AMERICAN COMICS No. 1 (4/39, DC, R)-DC finally bends to the reprint anthology format, but includes some original material for flavor. *Scribbly* by Mayer begins; a ten-year run.
(a,b,c,d,e,j)

NEW YORK WORLD'S FAIR (3-5/39, DC, H)-The first newsstand comic with a commercial tie-in, capitalizing on the enormous publicity of a real life public event, featuring DC's top characters. The thick format, as well as the title segued into ***World's Finest Comics*** two years later.
(a,c,e,i,j)

★ **MOVIE COMICS** No. 1 (4/39, DC, M)-A unique but short-lived idea. The notion of adapting films to comics in fumetti form (the panels were half-tones of stills from the films) was a good one, but didn't work any better in '39 than it does today. (The first movie adaption comic in standard comic book form and probably the first attempt at a fumetti continuity.)
(e,f,j,i)

★★★★★ **DETECTIVE COMICS** No. 27 (5/39, DC, H)-Reliable but predictable 'funny paper' cops 'n robbers anthology came into focus with the debut of *The Batman*. DC's second powerhouse set another standard for the industry to follow. The 'dynamic' hero—costumed athlete sans extraordinary powers—proved a viable alternative for the burgeoning competition to mimic, but Bob Kane broke the mold. The character's unique personna defied any but the most oblique imitation. ***Detective*** shared standard bearer honors with ***Action*** and provided the initials by which the company was known. One of the top four comics.
(a,b,c,d,f,h,j)

KEEN KOMICS V2/1 (5/39, Centaur, An)-A large size mixed anthology comic changing to regular size with number two. Packaged by the Everett shop and lasting only three issues.
(e)

★★ **WONDER COMICS** No. 1 (5/39, Fox, H)-Salutory effort of Fox (packaged by Eisner/Iger). First, and shortest-lived, of *Superman* imitations. Historically significant because the debut of Fox's *Wonder Man* prompted DC's first attempt to successfully defend their copyright on *Superman*. (A precedent that would prove decisive when the Man of Steel confronted a more formidable courtroom adversary a decade hence). Only one more issue followed.
(d,e,j,k)

★★★ **MOTION PICTURE FUNNIES WEEKLY** No.1 (5/39? Funnies, Inc., H)-Produced as a theatre giveaway, this title featured the first appearance of *Sub-Mariner*. His official newsstand debut occurred later in the year in ***Marvel Comics*** No. 1. Only seven known copies exist.
(a,c,d,e,f,g,h,i,j,k)

FEATURE COMICS No. 21 (6/39, Quality, An)-Continues from ***Feature Funnies*** of two years earlier. A discreet title change, indicating that original adventure comics were becoming a significant alternative to the formerly dominant reprints.
(b,e,k)

★★ **ADVENTURE COMICS** No. 40 (7/39, DC, H)-The *Sandman*, a transition crime fighter who stuck tenaciously to the trusty regalia of the pulp heroes. Finally, the pressure to adopt modern togs was brought to bear. The original mystery man vanished into oblivion, replaced by a swashbuckling Kirby hero.
(a,b,c,d,j)

AMAZING MYSTERY FUNNIES V2/7 (7/39, Centaur, H)-Debut of *The Fantom of the Fair*, mystery man, whose headquarters were under the World's Fair (An unexpected attraction for Fair goers). Destined for extinction with the 1940 wind-up of the Fair. Top artist line-up and exciting cover concepts.
(c,d,j)

COMIC PAGES V3/4 (7/39, Centaur, An)-A mixed anthology series continuing from ***Funny Picture Stories*** of three years earlier, lasting 3 issues.
(e)

KEEN DETECTIVE FUNNIES V2/7 (7/39, Centaur, H)-*The Masked Marvel*, super sleuth, and his three confederates began a terror campaign against lawless gangs. His big amphibian plane, secret laboratory and projected red shadow were devices used in the strip, lasting one year.
(d,j)

★★★ **MUTT AND JEFF** nn (Sum/39, DC, R)-This one shot represented a significant departure for DC. Formerly they had avoided the reprint title, preferring to develop their own original characters. This title was obviously a test to see if the market would support an entire book devoted to a single character (or in this case characters). This book has the honor of being the very first *newsstand* comic devoted to a single reprint strip. After a very slow start (four issues in four years), ***Mutt And Jeff*** was made a quarterly and soon became a popular run lasting 26 astounding years. It was the only successful reprint series of a single character to enjoy a respectible run. The syndicated *Mutt and Jeff* strip was, after *The Katzenjammer Kids*, the oldest continuously published newspaper strip.
(a,b,c,e,j)

★★★★★ **SUPERMAN** No. 1 (Sum/39, DC, H)-This landmark issue signaled a major turning point for the industry. Arguably, the second most important comic ever published (***Action*** being the first), and possibly the most influential. *Superman* was the first original character promoted from headling an anthology title to starring in a book of his own. More importantly, this tandem exposure demonstrated to the industry that it could survive on its own original material, independent of the proven syndicated stars. As other publishers were attracted to the field in the months to come, they emulated not only *Superman*, but the tandem anthology/headline format that had contributed to his unprecedented success. A double trend setter. Contains reprint material from ***Action*** No. 1-4. Title has continued beyond four decades.
(a,b,c,e,h,i,j)

WONDERWORLD COMICS No. 3 (7/39, Fox, H)-After the *Wonder Man* debacle, Fox bounces back with a revised title and a new lead character (courtesy of the Iger shop). *The Flame* got off to a brilliant start, but was snuffed out when Iger and Fox parted company, lasting 3 years.
(a,c,d,e,j)

MAGIC COMICS No. 1 (8/39, McKay, R)-King Features' third reprint anthology (after ***King*** and ***Ace Comics***) featured such popular syndicated stars as *Mandrake, Henry,* and *Blondie*. By 1940 *Blondie* had become the most widely syndicated newspaper strip in the world, and became the prime cover feature for the balance of the run, title enduring 10½ years.
(a,b,c,e,j)

★ **MYSTERYMEN COMICS** No. 1 (8/39, Fox, H)-Fox was on firm ground with a trio of potential contenders: ***Wonderworld's*** *The Flame* and, debuting in this title, *The Blue Beetle* and *The Green Mask*. These early products of the Eisner/Iger shop are worth a second look. Potential glows from every page. Soon, due to the E/I and Fox break up, the characters sunk into hack oblivion.
(a,c,d,e,j)

SMASH COMICS No. 1 (8/39, Quality, An)-This is the first title that Quality developed entirely on their own, (previous titles having been purchased from other publishers). The series lacked originality until the debut of Lou Fine's *Ray* which began in issue No. 14.
(b,e,j)

AMAZING MAN COMICS No. 5 (9/39, Centaur, H)-Everett's *A-Man* was launched here, the first Centaur character to headline his own title. The first costumed hero to shrink (*Minimidget*) begins. (This concept was better used later in Quality's *Doll Man*.) Top artist line-up in this series which

ended in early 1942. The standard bearer of the Centaur line.
(e,j)

SPEED COMICS No. 1 (10/39, Harvey, H)-First of a publisher. *Shock Gibson* is the main hero. The characters in this series lacked the charisma of the competition's best; had a few bright moments when top artists entered the line-up, surviving as an average run for 7 years.
(a,b,e,k)

BEST COMICS No. 1 (11/39, BP, H) First of a publisher. Debut of the Red Mask. An experimental large format book that read sideways; it failed to find an audience after four issues and folded.
(e,j,k)

BLUE RIBBON COMICS No. 1 (11/39, MLJ, An)-First of a publisher. Contents unremarkable (*Rang-A-Tang, The Wonder Dog*, for example). An MLJ anthology that failed to survive beyond 1942 despite the influx of super heroes.
(e,j,k)

★★★★★ **MARVEL COMICS** No. 1 (11/39, Timely, H)-Timely, the first publisher to hit with a smash twin bill in their inaugural title (courtesy of the Everett shop). From the onset, the formula of iconoclast as hero would prove to be Timely's most successful newsstand strategy. *The Human Torch* and *Sub-Mariner* won immediate reader approval, paving the way for more marvels to come from the pre-eminent Thrill Factory of comicdom. Possibly The most sought after of all Golden Age comics. Title lasted 10 years.
(a,b,c,d,e,f,g,h,i,j,k)

CHAMPION COMICS No. 2 (12/39, Harvey, An)-Early transitional anthology title with a sports theme, changing over to costumed heroes early on. None of the characters caught on enough to sustain the run for more than four years.
(e)

FANTASTIC COMICS No. 1 (12/39, Fox, H)-Biblical character *Samson* debuts. This series is more noted for the Lou Fine covers (Iger Shop). *Stardust* begins, one of the most bizarre super heroes in comics (Almost child-like, almost surrealistic art and plotting). He assassinated wrong doers regularly.
(e)

★★ **FEATURE COMICS** No. 27 (12/39, Quality, H)-Debut of the *Dollman* (Quality's first super hero), who was the second, but most significant, with the power to shrink (See ***Amazing Man***). The stories were generally undistinguished but Quality's high standards of illustration (Eisner in this case) lent the strip a credibility that would have been lacking in lesser hands. This title lasted 11 years.
(a,b,c,d,j)

★ **SILVER STREAK COMICS** No. 1 (12/39, Lev, An)-First of a publisher. Debut of *The Claw*, one of the most bizarre villains in the annals of comics. Standing 100 feet tall with claws and fangs was the ultimate refinement of the 'yellow peril' theme from the pulps. Such a formidable figure had to have an adversary to match (See ***Silver Streak*** No. 7). The first comic book to display a metallic silver logo to insure prominence on the stands.
(a,c,d,e,f,k)

TOP-NOTCH COMICS No. 1 (12/39, MLJ, H)-*The Wizard*, one of MLJ's top characters debuted. Their second anthology title, lasting 4½ years.
(a,b,c,d,e,j)

LARGE FEATURE COMIC nn (1939, Dell, R)-Black and white, magazine size, one-shot series with color covers (identical to McKay ***Feature Books*** of two years earlier), lasting four years.
(a,c,e)

CAPTAIN EASY nn (1939, Hawley, R)-First of a publisher. A one-shot reprint comic devoted to a single character, already proven successful by other publishers.
(a,c,e,k)

★★ **FOUR COLOR** No. 1 (Dick Tracy)(1939, Dell, R)-Exact format of UFS's ***Single Series*** of one year earlier. The most successful of the one-shot continuity titles, lasting 23 years. This series also provided a testing arena for new characters and concepts.
(a,b,c,e,j)

LONE RANGER COMICS, THE nn (1939, giveaway, Ws)-Fifth western title, first of a major character. This one-shot may have had newsstand distribution as price (10 cents) was stamped on cover.
(a,c,e)

1940 ■

★★ **BLUE BEETLE, THE** No. 1 (Wint/39-40, Fox, H)-The star of the second continuous series title devoted to a single character exemplified the pioneer 'crime fighter' of the early comics. His uniform was as simple and direct as the four-color medium itself– unadorned, form-fitting chain mail. Disdaining cloak, cape and the cover of night, *Blue Beetle* trounced crime where he found it, usually in the street and in broad daylight. Striking figure made an indelible impression on readers and, had Fox been more committed to long term development, would have doubtless gone the distance. The series eventually succumbed to tepid scripts and lack-lustre art, but the character was of sufficient personal appeal to survive, in memory, not only the demise of his title but legions of better produced, longer tenured heroes.

★★★★★ **FLASH COMICS** No. 1 (1/40, DC, H)-DC reinforced its arsenal with two more dynamos: *The Flash* (first, and most significant hero with lightning speed), and *The Hawkman* (first and most significant winged hero). Both trend setters, with series lasting beyond 40 years.
(a,b,c,d,e,f,h,i,j)

★★ **FLASH COMICS** No. 1 (1/40, Faw, H)-An in-house b&w proof produced to secure pre-publication copyright. Important changes made before the book was officially released were, a title change from ***Flash*** to ***Whiz*** (DC had already gone to press with their ***Flash Comics***), and the name of the lead character was changed from *Captain Thunder* to *Captain Marvel*. (8 known copies exist.)
(e,f,g,j,k)

THRILL COMICS No. 1 (1/40, Faw, H)-Identical to ***Flash Comics*** listed above, only a different title. Only three known copies exist.
(e,f,g,j,k)

JUNGLE COMICS No. 1 (1/40, FH, J)-The second single theme anthology series of this subject (cloned from ***Jumbo***). The title more perfectly suggested the 'jungle' theme with format selling rather than strong characters. Third series of a publisher, lasting as long as its parent (14½ years), with no competition until six years later.
(a,b,c,d,e,j)

★★ **PEP COMICS** No. 1 (1/40, MLJ, H)-Debut of *The*

Shield, the first patriotic hero, later eclipsed by Simon & Kirby's *Captain America*, the bombshell of 1941. MLJ's third and longest lasting (over 40 years) anthology title. Archie eventually takes over the series.
(a,b,c,d,e,f,h,i,j)

★★★★ **PLANET COMICS** No. 1 (1/40, FH, SF)-The publisher's fourth anthology title of continuing characters. The first and by far the most successful science fiction run in comics. As with ***Jumbo*** and ***Jungle***, this title had no competition for many years. Fiction Houses's style of action-packed covers and art made up for the routine plotting, lasting 14 years.
(a,b,c,e,f,h,i,j)

MIRACLE COMICS No. 1 (2/40, Hillman, H)-A mixed anthology series similar to ***Rocket Comics*** published a month later. First of a publisher. Covers have good eye-appeal, ending with the fourth issue.
(e,k)

★★★ **MORE FUN COMICS** No. 52,53 (2,3/40, DC, H)-DC modernizes its first anthology title, introducing the ominous *Spectre* in this two-part origin series. This frightening ethereal hero was too much a match for his adversaries, but gave DC an exciting alternative to their swelling ranks of wondermen. A trend setter, lasting 4 years in this title.
(a,b,c,d,f,h,i,j)

SCIENCE COMICS No. 1 (2/40, Fox, SF)-With qualifications, the second science fiction anthology title (very few of the stories dealt with outer space). Aside from the Lou Fine covers (No. 1 & 2), the artwork was not attractive and the series died after eight issues. First *Eagle* (the second winged hero).
(e)

TARGET COMICS No. 1 (2/40, Novelty, H)-First of a publisher. An early Everett shop super hero production. First *White Streak* by Burgos (the second android super hero). Top artist line-up featuring above average covers and stories, lasting 10 years.
(b,e,k)

THRILLING COMICS No. 1 (2/40, Better, H)-The first successful anthology title by this publisher (their second series). Debut of *Dr. Strange*. Logo carried over from the pulp. The Schomburg covers are the highlight of the run. The title lasted 11 years, switching to a jungle theme near the end.
(a,b,c,e,j)

★★★★★ **WHIZ COMICS** No. 2 (2/40, Faw, H)-After ***Action***, the most significant of all hero/adventure anthologies was this late entry from Fawcett. Origin, first appearance of *Captain Marvel*, humor hero par excellence. The most accessible of miracle men came from behind to eclipse the competition's best. He also founded the industry's first character dynasty (Marvel's *Junior, Mary* and even *Bunny*), a tactic that would prove as fundamental to comics' merchandising as DC's hero team concept. Landmark first issue also introduced such secondary stalwarts as *Sivana, Old Shazam, Spy Smasher* (the definitive aviator/mysteryman), and *Ibis the Invincible*, most memorable of comic book sorcerers. Flagship of the Fawcett line and a perennial favorite for 13 years.
(a,b,c,d,e,f,g,j,k)

ZIP COMICS No. 1 (2/40, MLJ, H)-MLJ's fourth anthology title (featuring *Steel Sterling*). Interesting stylized covers and art. Series lasted four years. With the exception of *Wilbur* (an Archie clone), none of the characters reached their own titles.
(a,b,c,d,j)

★★ **ADVENTURE COMICS** No. 48 (3/40, DC, H)-Debut of *The Hourman*. A substantial secondary feature that sold a few books for DC, but never received adequate creative support. Interesting premise came to dominate all the stories resulting in monotonous repetition.
(a,b,c,d,e,j)

COLOSSUS COMICS No. 1 (3/40, Sun, H)-An early esoteric book which ties to the esoteric ***Green Giant*** comic.
(e)

★★★ **DONALD DUCK FOUR COLOR** No. 4 (3/40?, Dell, F)-The first comic book devoted to this important transfer character. Still confined to one page gag strips. Full potential not yet reached.
(a,b,c,j)

MASTER COMICS No. 1 (3/40, Faw, H)-An experimental format at first (magazine size, priced at 15¢ and 52 pages). Debut of *Master Man*, an imitation of *Superman*, killed by DC after six issues; just in time for *Bulletman* to become the lead figure with issue no. 7, transferred from the defunct ***Nickel Comics***.
(b,e,j,k)

MYSTIC COMICS No. 1 (3/40, Timely, H)-Unusual anthology title (their third) in that each issue featured a practically new line-up of costumed heroes. High impact covers and art, lasting only 10 issues.
(e)

PRIZE COMICS No. 1 (3/40, Prize, H)-High quality anthology series with the debut of *Power Nelson*. First of a publisher. Dick Briefer's unique *Frankenstein* was introduced in No. 7 as well as Simon & Kirby's *Black Owl*. The covers have tremendous eye-appeal.
(a,b,e,j,k)

ROCKET COMICS No. 1 (3/40, Hillman, H)-The title is misleading. This is actually a mixed anthology title with science fiction covers; short-lived with only three issues. Companion mag to ***Miracle Comics***. The second Hillman title.
(e)

★ **SHADOW COMICS** No. 1 (3/40, S&S, H)-The venerable pulp publisher tested the comic waters with a heavyweight who had dominated both the pulp and radio markets but never quite found his metier in a medium that relied on action over ethereal atmosphere. *Doc Savage*, another renowned pulp character, debuted in this issue. A respectable but undistinguished run (9 years) probably sustained by popularity of radio program.
(a,b,c,e,f,i,j,k,l)

SLAM BANG COMICS No. 1 (3/40, Faw, An)-Fawcett's third title was an ill conceived adventure anthology starring civilian heroes. This formula had gone out two years before with the appearance of *Superman*. The title was retired after 8 issues.
(e)

SUN FUN KOMIKS No. 1 (3/40, Sun, Hm)-An esoteric one-shot printed in black and red. A satire on comic books. The first of its kind not to be fully developed until ***Mad*** of 12 years hence.
(e,i,j)

★★★★ **DETECTIVE COMICS** No. 38 (4/40, DC, H)-DC in-

itiates yet another breakthrough concept—the apprentice costumed hero. Origin, first appearance of *Robin*, the first and most enduring juvenile aide. For the first time in popular literature, the youthful apprentice was accepted as an equal by his partner. Bob Kane set another standard for the industry to mimic. The foreboding and enigmatic *Batman* was never the same after this issue.
(a,b,c,d,f,h,i,j)

EXCITING COMICS No. 1 (4/40, Better, H)-A sister anthology title to ***Thrilling***, becoming Better's second successful series. This title launched *The Black Terror* in No. 9, with Schomburg doing the covers early on (a poor man's Timely). Title lasted 9 years with jungle theme covers at the end.
(b,e,j)

★★ **NEW YORK WORLD'S FAIR** (3-5/40, DC, H)-The second comic book produced for a public event, ending the series. The first book to feature *Superman* and *Batman* together on a cover, as well as the first to showcase all of a company's stars, all in one book.
(a,c,j)

SUPERWORLD COMICS No. 1 (4/40, Gernsback, SF)-Following the success of ***Planet***, this title takes the honors as the third continuous series science fiction anthology. But Gernsback soon learned that 'raw' science fiction without a unique art style or gimmick (cheesecake) wouldn't sell. Disappeared after only three issues.
(e,k)

WEIRD COMICS No. 1 (4/40, Fox, H)-Another mixed anthology title with costumed heroes. The first to capitalize on this title, which became more common a decade later. Early issues by the Iger shop. First *Birdman* (the third winged hero). First *Thor*, from Greek mythology. Title lasted 2 years.
(e)

BIG SHOT COMICS No. 1 (5/40, CCG, Av)-First *Skyman*, the second aviation hero (noted for his flying wing)(See ***Whiz***). The first of a publisher. Mixed anthology series with original and reprint strips (*Joe Palooka*), lasting 9 years.
(a,b,c,d,e,j,k)

CRACK COMICS No. 1 (5/40, Quality, H)-Debut of Fine's *Black Condor* (the fourth winged hero). *Madame Fatal* begins, a bizarre hero who dresses as a woman to fight crime. A top quality series, lasting 9 years.
(a,b,c,d,e)

CRASH COMICS No. 1 (5/40, Tem/Holyoke, H)-The first Simon & Kirby art team-up, whose loose style of action reached maturity a year later with *Captain America*. Kirby was on his way to becoming one of the most influencial artists in comics. First of a publisher. A short lived mixed anthology series with costumed heroes, lasting 5 issues.
(e,g,k)

DOC SAVAGE COMICS No. 1 (5/40, S&S, H)-The legendary Man of Bronze headlined Street & Smith's second comic title. But it soon became evident that the original 'super man' was out of his depth. His prose adventures, which crackled with vitality in the pulps, seemed bland and derivative in the four-color medium. Outclassed by the characters he inspired, Doc and his title were retired after 3 years of so-so performance.
(c,e)

HYPER MYSTERY COMICS No. 1 (5/40, Hyper, H)-First of a publisher. A costumed hero anthology title which could not compete with the many heroes on the market at this time, lasting 2 issues.
(e,k)

★ **MORE FUN COMICS** No. 55 (5/40, DC, H)-First *Dr. Fate*, DC's second supernatural hero was given immediate cover exposure. Above average art and stories; colorful costume, lasting 3½ years and not achieving his own title.
(a,b,c,d,j)

★★★ **NICKEL COMICS** No. 1 (5/40, Faw, H)-Introduced *Bulletman*, Fawcett's third costumed hero. This book was experimental, selling for 5¢, came out biweekly, and lasting only 8 issues. (After *Bulletman* was moved to ***Master Comics***, he won his own title in 1941.)
(a,c,d,e,j)

WAR COMICS No. 1 (5/40, Dell, W)-The first single theme anthology series devoted to war. The combat genre did not find a significant market until the outbreak of the Korean conflict a decade later.
(e,i,j)

AMAZING ADVENTURE FUNNIES No. 1 (6/40, Centaur, H)-Outstanding collection of Centaur's best characters reprinted from earlier titles. Centaur was increasingly thrown back to all reprint books. Conjecture is that Timely's sudden success pre-empted all of the Everett shop's time.
(c,e)

★★★★ **BATMAN** No. 1 (Spr/40, DC, H)-Has arrival date of 4/25/40. DC's second strongest character achieved stardom and was given his own title. Assembled from ***Detective Comics***' inventory, containing the last solo appearance of *The Batman. The Joker* and *The Cat* debut. Title has run uninterrupted over four decades.
(a,b,c,e,j)

BLUE BOLT No. 1 (6/40, Novelty, H)-Second of a publisher. Costumed hero anthology title. Important early Simon & Kirby development began in No. 3. The heroes in this series could not be sustained, with *Dick Cole* eventually taking over, lasting 9 years.
(a,b,c,d,e,j)

CYCLONE COMICS No. 1 (6/40, Bilbara, An)-An anthology title with emphasis on subjects other than costumed hero. First of a publisher, expiring after 5 issues.
(e,j,k)

FUTURE COMICS No. 1 (6/40, McKay, R)-McKay's first new title in about a year. A reprint anthology with a science fiction theme (the fourth ever). This issue is noted for *The Phantom's* origin and science fiction cover. Went down for the count after 4 issues.
(e)

★★★**SPIRIT, THE** No. 1 (6/2/40, Eisner, D)-A weekly comic book (the only in comics) featuring the blockbuster strip distributed through newspapers. Notably, one of the best written and illustrated strips ever. A trend setter. Ingenious themes; capital atmospheric art with movie-like continuity and humorous plotting. Focus on special effects, lighting and unusual angles, lasting 12 years and endlessly revived.
(a,b,c,d,e,f,h,i,j)

STARTLING COMICS No. 1 (6/40, Better, H)-Better's third companion anthology series; *Wonder Man* and *Captain Future* begin. *The Fighting Yank* debuted in No. 10. Schomburg covers began early giving the books more impact. Cover theme changed to science fiction at the end.

(a,b,c,e,j)

SURE-FIRE COMICS No. 1 (6/40, Ace, H)-First of a publisher. A super hero anthology title of average quality lasting 4 issues before a title change.
(e,k)

WHIRLWIND COMICS No. 1 (6/40, Nita, H)-First of a publisher. A Three-issue run of mediocre quality with no sustaining characters.
(e,k)

★★★★ **ALL-AMERICAN COMICS** No. 16 (7/40, DC, H)-DC scored with another winning variation on the mystery man/adventure theme. Origin and first appearance of most enduring of DC's magic oriented heroes. The ancient fable of the magic lamp was transformed into a modern and more accessible, more mysterious form. *The Green Lantern's* chant became a staple of school boy mythology and another great career was launched. Series ended in 1949, although the name continued beyond 4 decades.
(a,b,c,d,j)

★★★ **ALL-STAR COMICS** No. 1 (Sum/40, DC, H)-The first continuous series showcase comic (see ***New York World's Fair***, 1940) for giving more exposure to top characters, who all headlined anthology series but as yet were not strong enough to have titles of their own. (This abundance of popular characters was unique to DC, forcing them to come up with this new format.)
(a,b,c,e)

FLAME, THE No. 1 (Sum/40, Fox, H)-One of Fox's top characters given prominence, reprinted from ***Wonderworld***. Lou Fine art in this issue, but the quality dropped early on, with the title lasting only 1½ years.
(c,e)

GREEN MASK, THE No. 1 (Sum/40, Fox, H)-Fox's emerald mystery man achieved stardom, but was squelched early on due to sub-standard art. An intriguing concept that was resurrected several times over the next 15 years, none of which were successful.
(c,e)

★ **MARVEL MYSTERY COMICS** No. 9 (7/40, Timely, H)-Epic battle issue. The first time in comics that two super heroes appeared together in one story. *Sub-Mariner* and *The Human Torch* each give up their usual space and battle for 22 pages. A coming together of the ancient basic elements, Water and Fire. Ignited newsstands everywhere.
(a,b,c,h,j)

HIT COMICS No. 1 (7/40, Quality, H)-Quality's fourth anthology title. Distinguished primarily by Iger shop graphics (Lou Fine). Non-memorable characters until *Kid Eternity* took over as main feature two years later. Series lasted 10 years.
(a,b,e,j)

NATIONAL COMICS No. 1 (7/40, Quality, H)-Of equal quality to ***Hit***, Lou Fine at his very best (covers and story art). Debut of *Uncle Sam*, Quality's top patriot. Legendary artist line-up with series lasting 9 years.
(a,b,c,d,e,f,j)

OKAY COMICS No. 1 (7/40, UFS, R)-Not having published a new title since 1938 (***Single Series***), United decides to make a comeback. Three new titles are released simultaneously with a fourth the following month. This one-shot issue features *The Captain and the Kids* and *Hawkshaw the Detective*.
(e)

OK COMICS No. 1 (7/40, UFS, H)-United tries their first super hero anthology title, but the characters were not strong enough to endure the stiff competition, lasting only two issues. Their second new title for the month.
(e)

SHIELD-WIZARD COMICS No. 1 (Sum/40, MLJ, H)-MLJ gave their top two characters joint stardom. A unique concept, titling a book after more than one character to insure its survival—a first in comics. The series lasted 4 years (the dual title wasn't enough).
(c,e)

SPARKLER COMICS No. 1 (7/40, UFS, R)-A two-issue reprint anthology series featuring *Jim Hardy* in No. 1 and *Frankie Doodle* in No. 2. United's third new title for the month.
(c,e)

SUPER-MYSTERY COMICS No. 1 (7/40, Ace, H)-Ace's second title, featuring more prominent characters and art, becoming their mainstay run. The series lasted 9 years, sustained by colorful covers and top artists.
(a,b,c,e)

FANTOMAN No. 2 (8/40, Centaur, H)-Centaur's second title reprinting their top characters and lasting three issues. Their second series of repackaged material.
(e)

HEROIC COMICS No. 1 (8/40, Eastern Color, H)-Seven years after introducing ***Famous Funnies***, Eastern came out with their second anthology title (their third ever). Original rather than reprinted material. *Hydroman*, a spin-off of the *Sub-Mariner* debuted. Eventually the format was changed to true stories of heroism, lasting 15 years. Top artists included throughout the run.
(e)

RED RAVEN COMICS No. 1 (8/40, Timely, H)-A one-shot esoteric super hero book featuring Kirby art. Highly sought after due to its lineage and rarity. Timely's fourth title.
(e)

★★★★ **SPECIAL EDITION COMICS** No. 1 (8/40, Fawcett, H)-Due to the enormous popularity of ***Whiz's*** explosive character, a single theme (Fawcett's first) anthology one-shot of *Captain Marvel* was published. A few months later, he began his own series. Beck cover and story art—high quality throughout.
(a,c,e,j)

UNITED COMICS No. 1 (8/40, UFS, R)-The popular *Fritzi Ritz* strip was featured and sustained the run for 12½ years. United's fourth and only successful title in their recent comeback attempt beginning a month earlier. The first comic book series to focus on the career girl theme (proto-type of *Katy Keene*).
(a,b,c,e)

CRASH COMICS No. 4(9/40, Holyoke, H)-*Catman* debuted for two issues then stayed dormant for six months before appearing in his own title.
(a,c,d,j)

MASKED MARVEL No. 1 (9/40, Centaur, H)-After exposure in ***Keen Detective Funnies***, the crimson sleuth was given his own title, lasting only 3 issues.
(e)

★ **MICKEY MOUSE MAGAZINE** V5/12, (9/40, K.K. F)-This historically significant publication was one step remov-

ed from becoming the first official funny animal series. As a magazine, it had evolved through various sizes and formats to finally become a full-fledged comic book. The following month, a title change to ***Walt Disney's Comics & Stories*** completed the transition.
(a,c,h,j)

PRIZE COMICS No. 7 (9/40, Prize, H)-Debut of Dick Briefer's *Frankenstein* series, and *The Black Owl* by Simon & Kirby. Above average strips with eye-catching covers.
(a,b,c,d,j)

★ **RED RYDER COMICS** No. 1 (9/40, Hawley/Dell, Ws)-A one-shot devoted to the popular strip character by Fred Harman, not becoming a continuous series until Dell picked up the title a year later. Ties with ***Tom Mix*** as the second book devoted to a single western character, but the first to receive widespread newsstand distribution. Lasted 17 years due to popular movie series. The second title of a publisher.
(a,b,c,e,f,h,i,j,l)

★ ★ ★ **SILVER STREAK COMICS** No. 6 (9/40, Lev, H)-High impact cover of *The Claw* by Jack Cole. Debut of *Daredevil with his unprecedented costume of dichromatic symmetry. (See **Silver Streak** no. 7.)*
(a,b,c,d,f,j)

SKY BLAZERS No. 1 (9/40, Hawley, Av)-Ties with ***Red Ryder*** as 2nd of a publisher. Inspired by the radio show, not lasting beyond 2 issues.
(e)

★ ★ **TOM MIX** No. 1 (9/40, Ralston, Ws)-The first continuous series single theme western comic, but a giveaway by Ralston—not sold on the stands.
(a,b,c,e,j,k)

★ **WINGS COMICS** No. 1 (9/40, FH, Av)-The publisher's fifth single theme anthology title. The first to focus entirely on aviation (a subject of high appeal to boys of the era). With no competition, the series lasted 14 years.
(a,b,c,e,h,i,j)

ALL-AMERICAN COMICS No. 19 (10/40, DC, H)-Debut of *The Atom* (a hero for short people). Good filler material as a back-up to the main feature, who lasted 4½ years.
(a,b,c,d,f,h,j)

ARROW, THE No. 1 (10/40, Centaur, H)-The very first costume hero (pre-*Batman*) was given prominence after a two-year run in ***Funny Pages***. Folded after 3 issues (Centaur phasing out).
(e)

BIG 3 No. 1 (Fall/40, Fox, H)-Fox's first showcase anthology title featuring their top characters together in one magazine. A good idea, but not surviving more than 7 issues.
(e)

BILL BARNES COMICS No. 1 (10/40, S&S, Av)-The celebrated pulp ace got his own comic title, but after three years failed to find an audience. Street & Smith's third title.
(c,e,l)

CHAMP COMICS No. 11 (10/40, Harvey, H)-Continued from ***Champion***, now featuring super heroes in full swing. Later on the popular and saleable Simon & Kirby art style was copied as an attempt to sustain the run. The title ended in 1944.
(e)

★ ★ ★ **HUMAN TORCH, THE** No. 2 (Fall/40, Timely, H)-From the pages of ***Marvel Mystery***, the android flys into his own title. Inspired concept. High impact, eye-catching character, making appearances over the next 40 years.
(a,b,c,e,j)

REX DEXTER OF MARS No. 1 (Fall/40, Fox, SF)-A modest success in ***Mysterymen***, but not important enough to carry a title of his own. Expired after one issue.
(e)

SAMSON No. 1 (Fall/40, Fox, H)-One of Fox's top characters from ***Fantastic*** achieves stardom. Lack-luster art leads to the early death of the run the following year.
(e)

SPORT COMICS No. 1 (10/40, S&S, Sp)-A good idea 'real life' comic series featuring notable sport figures and lasting (through a title change) for 9 years. The first comic series devoted entirely to this theme (see ***Champion** and **Fight***).
(b,c,e,h,i,j)

SUPER SPY No. 1 (10/40, Centaur, H)-Late Centaur super hero anthology title, introducing *The Sparkler*. Interesting early vintage comic with only two issues published.
(e)

TOP-NOTCH COMICS No. 9 (10/40, MLJ, H)-Debut of *The Black Hood*, key MLJ hero. One of the few at MLJ to later star in his own title. The costume had eye-appeal which sustained the character, lasting 3 years.
(c,d,j)

★ ★ ★ ★ ★ **WALT DISNEY'S COMICS AND STORIES** No. 1 (10/40, Dell, F)-The first funny animal continuous series comic book title. Miscellaneous collection of proven Disney characters began to come into focus around consistently high quality strips by Taliaferro and Gottfredson, who consistently delivered the goods. The definitive funny animal anthology comic after which all others were modeled. A trend setter. Suspected to have achieved the highest circulation of any comic, lasting beyond 40 years.
(a,b,c,e,h,i,j)

WESTERN DESPERADO COMICS No. 8 (10/40, Fawcett, Ws)-Fawcett's first western theme anthology title, only one issue.
(e)

DETECTIVE EYE No. 1 (11/40, Centaur, H)-More exposure for characters from ***Keen Detective Funnies***, lasting 2 issues.
(e)

HI-SPOT COMICS No. 2 (11/40, Hawley, An)-A one-shot book featuring an Edgar Rice Burroughs strip, *David Innes of Pellucidar*.
(e)

WHAM COMICS No. 1 (11/40, Centaur, H)-Another short-lived anthology title, similar to ***Super Spy*** (reprinting earlier material).
(e)

★ ★ **GREEN HORNET COMICS** No. 1 (12/40, Harvey, H)-The respected radio and movie hero tried his wings in comics. Intriguing concept, with a few high points of good artists in the run. He never excelled in the medium, but did present a respectable run of 9 years—probably sustained by the popularity of the radio program.
(a,b,c,e,l)

LIGHTNING COMICS No. 4 (12/40, Ace, H)-Continued from ***Sure-Fire***, becoming Ace's third title. Colorful covers (some exceptional) could not sustain the run beyond 18 months.

(e)

DOUBLE COMICS (1940, Elliot, H)-The first attempt at repackaging (and remarketing) remaindered comics. First of a publisher. Elliot produced these unique books for four years, taking advantage of the insatiable public demand for comics.
(e,h,j,k)

GREEN GIANT COMICS No. 1 (1940, Funnies, Inc., H)-A very rare one-shot test comic. Conjecture is that its circulation was limited to the New York City area only.
(e,j)

1941 ■

★★★★★ **ALL-STAR COMICS** No. 3 (Wint/40-41, DC, H)-A breakthrough concept, second in importance only to the creation of the super hero. For the first time in comics, top characters come together in one book to form a crime fighting organization *The Justice Society*. A trend setter. Unprecedented in all of literature (the gods of Mt. Olympus weren't on speaking terms; the Knights of the Round Table didn't foregather to confront a common foe). Forerunner of *The Justice League*, and inspiration for many hero groups that followed.
(a,b,c,f,h,i,j)

BUCK ROGERS No. 1 (Wint/40-41, FF, R)-Due to the enormous popularity of the strip in ***Famous Funnies***, he earned his own title, which is the first continuous title devoted to a reprint character. Unfortunately, like many other transfer characters, the series didn't last, running only 6 issues.
(a,c,e)

SILVER STREAK COMICS No. 7 (1/41, Lev, H)-Epic clash between *Daredevil* and *The Claw* began in this issue. (Rivaled only by the *Torch-Sub-Mariner* brouhaha). Early enthusiastic work by Jack Cole. *DD's* costume colors change to red and blue, giving him a sinister, demonic appearance (unforgettable). Smash hit series launched *DD* to stardom with own title.
(a,c,f,j)

WOW COMICS No. 1 (Wint/40-41, Faw, H)-Featuring the costumed hero *Mr. Scarlet* (imitation of *Batman*), drawn by Kirby. Included other features with small impact to the comic scene. The major feature of this title was *Mary Marvel*, a *Captain Marvel* clone, who dominated from No. 9 on. This particular issue is highly prized due to its rarity and early Kirby art.
(b,e)

★★★★ **CAPTAIN MARVEL ADVENTURES** nn (1-2/41?, Faw, H)-Following the wake of ***Special Edition***, the celebrated character started his own series (this issue illustrated by Kirby), reaching a two-week publication frequency at one point, lasting 13 years.
(a,b,c,e,j)

BLUE RIBBON COMICS No. 9 (2/41, MLJ, H)-Inspired by DC's *The Spectre*, *Mr. Justice* began this issue and survived to the end of the run (1942).
(d)

★★★★★ **CAPTAIN AMERICA COMICS** No. 1 (3/41, Timely, H)-Simon & Kirby's most classic creation; a patriotic paragon (the second but foremost of patriotic heroes) that set the comics market reeling. A trend setter. One of the top ten most sought after books. With a few interruptions, the character has survived beyond 40 years.
(a,b,c,d,e,g,j)

JACKPOT COMICS No. 1 (Spr/41, MLJ, H)-MLJ's first showcase title to give more exposure to their top characters. The mediocre scripts and art could only keep the run alive for 2 years.
(c,e)

★★★ **SUB-MARINER COMICS** No. 1 (Spr/41, Timely, H)-The aquatic anti-hero is given prominence. The potential of the character was never fully realized. High impact covers, sustaining the run for 8 years.
(a,b,c,e,j)

★★★ **WORLD'S BEST COMICS** No. 1 (Spr/41, DC, H)-Using the successful format of ***The World's Fair*** books, DC created this title to feature their top two attractions, *Batman* and *Superman*. This was the first thick format continuous series comic (as ***World's Finest***). Series lasted beyond 40 years without interruption.
(a,b,c,e,h,j)

★★★ **MICKEY MOUSE FOUR COLOR** No. 16 (4/41?, Dell, F)-The first comic devoted to this world renowned character. The subject of this landmark issue was Gottfredson's classic, *The Phantom Blot*.
(a,b,c,j)

★★ **ADVENTURE COMICS** No. 61 (4/41, DC, H)-*Starman* was introduced as DC continued to create new characters. Visually, an intriguing alternative with enough appeal to last 3½ years in this run, but not quite strong enough to appear in his own title.
(a,b,c,d,j)

TRUE COMICS No. 1 (4/41, PM, TR)-The second anthology series based on true stories (see ***Sport Comics***). The first of a publisher, lasting 9 years.
(b,e,h,i,j,k)

AMERICA'S GREATEST COMICS No. 1 (5/41?, Faw, H)-Fawcett's first showcase anthology title (in thick format) featuring their top characters, lasting 8 issues.
(a,c,e)

ARMY AND NAVY No. 1 (5/41, S&S, W)-S&S's fifth anthology title, the second ever with a war theme, lasting 5 issues.
(e)

CATMAN COMICS No. 1 (5/41, Holyoke, H)-Continued from ***Crash***, *Catman* got his own series. Second of a publisher. Adequate, but unexceptional covers and stories. Expired after 5 years.
(a,b,c,e)

EXCITING COMICS No. 9 (5/41, BP, H)-Debut of *The Black Terror*, nemesis of crime. Editors never adequatelly capitalized on the tremendous eye-appeal of the character. Indifferent scripts, lack-luster art disappointed more often than not. The indomitable character endured despite lack of staff support. Logical yet striking appearance of costume sustained character.
(a,b,c,d,j)

STARS AND STRIPES COMICS No. 2 (5/41, Centaur, H)-After the failure of Centaur's last flurry of reprint books a year earlier, they tried to make a comeback. Following Timely's newsstand hit, Centaur picked up on the patriotic theme with the first of three books of this type, lasting only 5 issues.
(e)

SUPER MAGIC No. 1 (5/41, S&S, Mg)-A one-shot book

featuring *Blackstone the Magician* and *Rex King*. The first title to focus on magicians. The title was modified to ***Super Magician*** and the series lasted 6 years.
(b,e,i,j)

LIBERTY SCOUTS No. 2 (6/41, Centaur, H)-Centaur's second patriotic theme series lasted only two issues.
(e)

★★★ **ALL FLASH COMICS** No. 1 (Sum/41, DC, H)-The hero of speed achieved stardom and was given his own title. Momentarily retired after 6 years.
(a,b,c,e)

★ **ALL WINNERS COMICS** No. 1 (Sum/41, Timely, H)-First Timely showcase title to give more exposure to their top characters. High impact covers and characters sustained run for 5 years.
(a,c,e)

★★ **BULLETMAN** No. 1 (7/41, Faw, H)-The hit of ***Master Comics***, receives his own title, lasting 5 years. The Raboy cover and silver logo gets the series off to a good start.
(a,c,e)

CAPTAIN BATTLE COMICS No. 1 (Sum/41, Lev, H)-The third patriotic hero (see ***Pep Comics*** and ***Captain America***) from ***Silver Streak*** is given his own title. Lacked necessary distinctiveness to compete, folding with the second issue.
(e)

★★ **DAREDEVIL COMICS** No. 1 (7/41, Lev, H)-High impact cover, inspired costume design and massive support from Biro's strong, complex plotting sustained momentum of "The Greatest Name in Comics" splash debut. Immediately stood out from the hordes of rival strongmen glutting the stands. Series prevailed for 15 years.
(a,b,c,e,j)

EAGLE, THE No. 1 (7/41, Fox, H)-Another publisher on the patriotic band wagon. *The Eagle* only flew for four issues.
(e)

FUNNIES, THE No. 57 (7/41, Dell, H)-Debut of *Captain Midnight*, a patriotic aviation hero who was an established attraction on radio. He was also featured in Dell's ***Popular Comics*** before being picked up by Fawcett as a regular series.
(a,c,d,j)

MINUTEMAN No. 1 (7/4l, Faw, H)-Fawcett's answer to a patriotic hero who began in ***Master Comics***. This less than distinguished hero only lasted three issues in his own title.
(e)

PEP COMICS No. 17 (7/41, MLJ, H)-Landmark issue. The first time in comics that a major character (*The Comet*) actually died, and a new character (*The Hangman*) was created in the same story.
(a,b,c,d,h)

SPARKLER COMICS No. 1 (7/41, UFS, R)-After three years of costumed heroes glutting the stands, UFS tries its second costumed hero series. Debut of *Sparkman*, a colorful character who eventually gave way to *Tarzan* and other reprint characters, title proved competitive through 14 years.
(a,b,c,e,j)

★ **YOUNG ALLIES** No. 1 (Sum/41, Timely, H)-The first sidekick group in comics. The *Red Skull* guest-starred to give the title a good send-off. Proto-type of the more successful *Teen Titans* of 25 years hence, it managed a respectable run of 5 years.
(e,f,h,i,j)

CAPTAIN FEARLESS No. 1 (8/41, Helnit, H)-Third of a publisher. An interesting mix of super patriots not lasting beyond the second issue.
(e)

★★★★ **MILITARY COMICS** No. 1 (8/41, Qua, Av)-Otherwise predictable war-theme anthology (the third of its kind) sparked by debut of aviation feature of geniune classic proportions. The crack *Blackhawk* team took command of the series and continued at the helm 9 years after a title change (to ***Modern Comics***) indicated the public had grown jaded with war-themes generally. Ace concept (air-borne privateers meet the axis on its own terms) backed by sterling Iger graphics (the shop's piece de resistance) and top-drawer scripting propelled feature into its own title and a phenomenal 40 year run (with interruptions). The introduction of *Blackhawk*, and *Plastic Man* later the same month, lifted Quality into the first rank of comics publishers. A masterpiece of collaborative art.
(a,b,c,d,e,f,h,i,j)

OUR FLAG COMICS No. 1 (8/41, Ace, H)-Ace joined the other publishers with a host of patriotic strongmen debuting in this book. High impact patriotic cover. Series lasted 5 issues.
(e,j)

POCKET COMICS No. 1 (8/41, Harv, H)-An experimental pocket size comic book series featuring Harvey's top characters. Most divergent forms didn't last long and this was no exception, expiring after 4 issues.
(e)

★★★★ **POLICE COMICS** No. 1 (8/41, Quality, H)-Debut of one of the most ingenious super heroes in comics, *Plastic Man*. An original concept, fully exploited by Jack Cole in the ensuing years. Sheer entertainment with the incomparable *Cole* at the top of his form. Shares standard bearer honors with ***Military***, lasting 12 years.
(a,b,c,d,e,f,i,j)

★ **RED RYDER COMICS** No. 3 (8/41, Hawley, Ws)-The first continuous series single theme western comic for newsstand sales. Ties back to a one-shot issue of a year earlier. Title lasted 16 years due to popular movie series.
(a,b,c,e,f,h,i,j)

SPITFIRE COMICS No. 1 (8/41, Harvey, Av)-An experimental aviation pocket size comic book, lasting 2 issues.
(e)

★ **UNCLE SAM QUARTERLY** No. 1 (8/41, Qua, H)-Eisner's version of a patriotic hero, the star of ***National Comics***, is given his own book, lasting 8 issues. Usual Iger shop excellence.
(e)

USA COMICS No. 1 (8/41, Timely, H)-Timely, extending the patriotic theme, created another showcase title for introducing new characters. After five issues, their trend setting *Captain America* was brought in to save the run and it endured 4 years.
(a,c,e)

VICTORY COMICS No. 1 (8/41, Hill, H)-Classic Everett Nazi war cover. Hillman tried their third title, this time with a patriotic costumed hero theme, again unsuccessfully. It lasted only 4 issues.
(e)

BANNER COMICS No. 3 (9/41, Ace, H)-Debut of *Captain Courageous*, a derivative patriotic hero—not prominent enough to survive more than 3 issues.
(e)

CALLING ALL GIRLS No. 1 (9/41, PMI, TR)-Second of a publisher. The true fact anthology, with biographies of famous persons and sketches of historic events (occassionally mixed with magazine-type photo features), was a comics format pioneered by Parent's Magazine Institute. Here the target audience was adolescent girls. Similar titles were cloned later on. Enjoyed a run of 7 years.
(b,e,f,h,i,j)

FOUR FAVORITES No. 1 (9/41, Ace, H)-Ace's first showcase title featuring their top characters together in one book, lasting 6 years.
(e)

REAL HEROES COMICS No. 1 (9/41, PMI, TR)-With the success of ***True Comics***, the publisher attempted another title based on true stories. Their third series, lasting 5 years. ***Heroic Comics*** was later converted to this theme.
(e)

REAL LIFE COMICS No. 1 (9/41, BP, TR)-Inspired by the newsstand success of PMI's ***True Comics***, this publisher came out with their version, lasting 11 years.
(b,e)

STARTLING COMICS No. 10 (9/41, BP, H)-Debut of *The Fighting Yank*, America's super patriot. Interesting variation on the patriotic theme in that he could call up heroes from the American revolution to assist in the modern fight against crime. Tremendous eye-appeal of character never fully realized due to low standard story art. High impact Schomburg covers sustained the run.
(a,b,c,d,j)

SUPER MAGICIAN COMICS No. 2 (9/41, S&S, Mg)-The first continuous series anthology title on the subject of magic, continuing from ***Super Magic*** and lasting 6 years.
(e,j)

YANKEE COMICS No. 1 (9/41, Chesler, H)-Chesler re-entered the comic market with this patirotic title. Debut of *Yankee Doodle Jones*. Sensational patriotic cover. Despite its visual appeal, it endured only 4 issues.
(e)

★★★★ **CLASSIC COMICS** No. 1 (10/41, Gil, Lit)-First and most enduring of 'educational' theme comics, Gilberton drew on works of great literature for their highly visible newsstand product. One of the few lines that could be endorsed without reservation by parents and educators, its marketing success was not tied to single-theme titles or continuing characters. Variable art quality somewhat diminished the overall impact of the line. The only comic publisher to place each issue into endless reprints while continuing to publish new titles on a monthly basis, lasting 30 years.
(a,b,c,e,f,h,i,j,k)

DOLL MAN No. 1 (Fall/41, Qua, H)-After a successful two-year run in ***Feature***, the mighty mite leaped into his own title, lasting 12 years. The proto-type of the Silver Age Atom.
(a,b,c,e,j)

DYNAMIC COMICS No. 1 (10/41, Chesler, H)-Chesler's second patriotic super hero series. Debut of *Major Victory*. Suspended after three issues and brought back with a format change in 1944, lasting four more years.
(e)

★★★ **GREEN LANTERN** No. 1 (Fall/41, DC, H)-Having headlined ***All-American*** for one year, one of DC's foremost heroes achieved the distinction of his own title. It ran for 8 years and went on to become one of the key revival characters of the Silver Age.
(a,b,c,e)

★★★★ **LOONEY TUNES & MERRY MELODIES** No. 1 (Fall/41, Dell, F)-The companion title to the enormously successful ***WDC&S***. Dell's second funny animal anthology featured *Bugs Bunny, Porky Pig* and *Elmer Fudd*. This was the first comic book appearance of Warner Brothers film characters. The series ran for 21 years.
(a,b,c,e,h,j,l)

RANGERS COMICS No. 1(10/41, FH, W)-The publisher's sixth single theme anthology title (war theme). Standard FH style of cheesecake art and covers, lasting 11 years.
(a,b,c,e)

SKYMAN No. 1 (Fall/41, CCG, Av)-After a year's successful run in ***Big Shot***, he was given his own title. Second of a publisher, lasting only 4 issues. (He remained the main feature in ***Big Shot*** for 9 years.)
(a,c,e)

★★ **SPYSMASHER** No. 1 (Fall/41, Faw, Av)-Popular war hero graduating from ***Whiz*** into his own title, lasting 2 years. Maiden issue featured unusual logo printed in metallic silver.
(a,c,e)

STAR SPANGLED COMICS No. 1(10/41, DC, H)-DC's first patriotic theme title featuring the *Star Spangled Kid*. Due to the weak contents, the title had a dramatic format change with No. 7 when *The Guardian* and *The Newsboy Legion* were introduced.
(b,e)

WORLD FAMOUS HEROES MAGAZINE No. 1 (10/41, Comic Corp, TR)-Similar theme to PMI's ***Real Heroes***, and Eastern's ***Heroic***, with stories of famous people, lasting 4 issues.
(e)

AIR FIGHTERS COMICS No. 1 (11/41, Hill, Av)-An early attempt at an aviation theme comic (like ***Wings***), lasting only one issue. A year later the title was revived more successfully with a new 'dynamic' character in *Airboy*.
(e)

GREAT COMICS No. 1 (11/41, Great, H)-First of a publisher, featuring super heroes. The third and last issue is a classic: *Futuro* takes *Hitler* to hell.
(e,j,k)

MAN OF WAR No. 1 (11/41, Centaur, H)-Centaur's third and last patriotic theme title, lasting 2 issues. Conjecture is that Centaur itself expired with this book.
(e)

SCOOP COMICS No. 1 (11/41, Chesler, H)-Chesler's third attempt at a comeback with this anthology of super heroes. Debut of *Rocketman* and *Rocketgirl*, lasting 8 issues.
(e)

U.S. JONES No. 1 (11/41, Fox, H)-Fox's second patriotic theme title, lasting 2 issues.
(e)

★★★★ **ALL-STAR COMICS** No. 8 (11-12/41, DC, H)-*Wonder Woman*, the first super-heroine, created by Charles Moulton and drawn by H.G. Peters, debuted in this issue as an 8 page add-on. Her origin continued in ***Sensation***

No. 1, where she becomes the lead feature. A trend setter. (a,b,c,d,f,h,i,j)

BANG-UP COMICS No. 1 (12/41, Progressive, H)-A new publisher entered the field. This series was mediocre in its content only surviving 3 issues.
(e,k)

CAPTAIN AERO COMICS No. 7 (12/41, Hoke, Av)-Cashing in on the popularity of *Spy Smasher* and *Captain Midnight*, this publisher began with another aviation hero. With strong, colorful covers, the series lasted 5 years.
(e)

CHOICE COMICS No. 1 (12/41, Great, H)-The publisher's second title. A mixed anthology, lasting 3 issues.
(e)

MASTER COMICS No. 21 (12/41, Faw, H)-*Captain Marvel* and *Bulletman* team-up to fight *Captain Nazi*. A classic battle sequence, rare in comics at this time. High impact (classic) Raboy cover and story art.
(a,b,c)

PIONEER PICTURE STORIES No. 1 (12/41, S&S, TR)-An anthology of true stories about heroes (ala ***Heroic Comics***), lasting 9 issues.
(e)

★★★★ **PEP COMICS** No. 22 (12/41, MLJ, TA)-The eternal sophomore and his friends began the first of over forty consecutive terms at Riverdale High. Never rose above pat formula, but survived vagaries of shifting market that did in a host of illustrious predecessors and glut of imitators (many of which originated at MLJ itself). Auxillary characters achieved stardom with their own titles. Trend setter, lasting beyond 40 years.
(a,b,c,d,f,h,i,j)

PUNCH COMICS No. 1 (12/41, Chesler, H)-Chesler's fourth attempt to get back into the market. A mixed anthology series with a successful format, lasting 6 years.
(e)

★★★ **WHIZ COMICS** No. 25 (12/12/41, Faw, H)-*Captain Marvel* was cloned for the second time (see *Lt. Marvels*) into a junior size as *Captain Marvel Jr.* Classic art by Mac Raboy gave the character a slick streamlined 'Raymond' look. He was given immediate headlining in ***Master Comics***. This was the first significant character cloned.
(a,b,c,d,j)

X-MAS COMICS No. 1 (12/41, Faw, H)-A new concept. Earlier in the year, Fawcett began over-running certain selected comics with indicias, page numbers, etc. removed. These comics were then bound up into a thick book (324 pgs.) to be sold as a special comic for Christmas. This successful format evolved into several other titles and lasted for 11 years.
(a,b,c,e,f,h,j)

CAPTAIN MARVEL THRILL BOOK nn (1941, Faw, H)-A large-size black & white comic reprinting popular *Captain Marvel* stories, lasting one issue. (Half text, half illustration.)
(e)

DICKIE DARE No. 1 (1941, Eastern, R)-Another single theme anthology title of the popular strip, lasting 4 issues.
(e)

DOUBLE UP nn (1941, Elliott, H)-The same idea as ***Double***, except this was a one-shot remarketing of remaindered digest-sized issues of ***Speed, Spitfire*** and ***Pocket***. Probably a special deal to Elliott due to heavy returns?
(e)

FACE, THE No. 1 (1941, CCG, H)-The popular strip from ***Big Shot*** achieved brief stardom, lasting only two issues.
(e)

KEY RING COMICS (1941, Dell, An)-A special formated comic series of 16 pages each to put in a two-ring binder (sold as a set of five).
(e)

TRAIL BLAZERS No. 1 (1941, S&S, TR)-True fact anthology of heroic deeds, lasting 4 issues.
(e)

USA IS READY No. 1 (1941, Dell, W)-Dell's second war title lasting one issue.
(e)

★★★ **ANIMAL COMICS** No. 1 (12-1/41-42, Dell, F)-Debut of Walt Kelly's classic character, *Pogo*, which became syndicated in 1948. Dell's third funny animal single theme anthology title following the success of ***WDC&S*** and ***Looney Tunes***. The first funny animal comic with original characters at Dell.
(a,c,d,e,j)

1942 ■

BIG CHIEF WAHOO No. 1 (Wint/41-42, Eastern, R)-Popular transfer strip debuts in his own comic series, lasting 23 issues.
(c,e)

FOUR MOST No. 1 (Wint/41-42, Novelty, H)-A showcase title featuring Novelty's best characters from ***Target*** and ***Blue Bolt***. Series taken over by *Dick Cole* with No. 3 on. Their third title.
(a,b,c,e)

★ **LEADING COMICS** No. 1 (Wint/41-42, DC, H)-Like ***All-Star***, this title provided a showcase for DC's secondary heroes (a poor man's ***All-Star***). Series ran 14 issues then changed to a funny animal format for the rest of its 7 year existance.
(e)

★★★★★ **SENSATION COMICS** No. 1 (1/42, DC, H)-*Wonder Woman's* origin continued from ***All-Star*** No. 8 (her first appearance). A very strong character from the onset, achieving stardom instantly as a headline feature of this series. She won her own title within a few months which has run uninterrupted for over 40 years. (One of the few characters to achieve this kind of exposure.)
(a,b,c,e,f,h,j)

SPECIAL COMICS No. 1 (Wint/41-42, MLJ, H)-A one-shot special featuring *The Hangman* from ***Pep Comics***. A hit on the stands, the character was launched into his own series with No. 2.
(c,e)

V...- COMICS No. 1 (1/42, Fox,H)-Another short-lived title from Fox. His third patriotic theme comic. Introduced *V-Man*, lasted only two issues.
(e)

AMERICA'S BEST COMICS No. 1 (2/42, BP, H)-A showcase title to give more exposure to their top characters. The high impact covers (many by Schomburg) sustained the run, lasting 7 years.
(a,b,c,e)

CAMP COMICS No. 1 (2/42, Dell, Hm)-A mixed (humorous) anthology title with pretty girl photo covers. An unusual format slanted to the soldier boys at camp.
(e)

★★ **GENE AUTRY COMICS** No. 1 (2/42, Faw, Ws)-The second newsstand continuous series western title devoted to a single character. *Gene* ties with *Roy Rogers* as the most popular cowboy star of the sound era. Title survived 18 years.
(a,b,c,e,h,j,l)

JINGLE JANGLE COMICS No. 1 (2/42, Eastern Color, Hm)-A young children's comic, containing illustrations and script by George Carlson, a children's book heavyweight (*Uncle Wiggily*). Eastern's second anthology title of original material (see ***Heroic***), lasting 7 years.
(a,b,e,j)

TRUE SPORT PICTURE STORIES No. 5 (2/42, S&S, Sp)-Continued from ***Sport Comics***, lasting 7 years.
(e)

CAPTAIN COURAGEOUS COMICS No. 6 (3/42, Ace, H)-Introduced in ***Banner***, the character was given his own title but lasted only one issue.
(e)

TOUGH KID SQUAD No. 1 (3/42, Timely, H)-Timely's second series devoted to sidekicks (see ***Young Allies***). Highly prized due to its rarity.
(e)

★★ **BOY COMICS** No. 3 (4/42, Lev, H)-Gleason's second successful title, introducing *Crimebuster*. This series survived 14 years due to Biro's strong, complex plotting.
(a,b,c,d,e,j)

COMEDY COMICS No. 9 (4/42, Timely, H)-The title is misleading. A super hero anthology title changing to a humorous and funny animal format early on.
(e)

HANGMAN COMICS No. 2 (Spr/42, MLJ, H)-The smash hit of ***Pep Comics*** received his own series, but lasted only 7 issues.
(e)

★ **JOKER COMICS** No. 1 (4/42, Timely, Hm)-First *Powerhouse Pepper* by Wolverton. Wolverton, an original if there ever was one, stood totally aloof from the mainstream of comic art. His effect on later comics ranging from the original ***Mad*** to the sixties undergrounds, is incalculable. (He tried to fit in, but the effect of playing it straight made his work even more bizzarre.)
(a,b,c,d,e,f,g,j)

SHEENA, QUEEN OF THE JUNGLE No. 1 (Spr/42, FH, J)-After three years exposure in ***Jumbo Comics***, *Sheena* finally graduated to her own title, lasting 18 issues spread over 11 years.
(a,b,c,e)

★★ **STAR SPANGLED COMICS** No. 7 (4/42, DC, H)-Debut of *The Guardian* and *The Newsboy Legion* by Simon and Kirby (vintage). Title lasted 11 years.
(a,b,c,d,j)

WAMBI, JUNGLE BOY No. 1 (Spr/42, FH, J)-From ***Jungle Comics***. Not strong enough to carry his own title which had erratic publishing (18 issues in 11 years).
(e)

★★★★ **CRIME DOES NOT PAY** No. 22 (6/42, Lev, C)-Aside from being the first crime comic, this title was the first of any to be deliberately targeted at the adult reader. Inspired by the widely read ***True Detective*** - style magazines of the time. Implicit and unsavory subject matter, in the context of what was popularly understood as publications for children, assured the attention and disapproval of Wertham and others. Established conventions of graphically depicted violence that would be exploited to the extreme in the horror comics of a decade later. Arguably the third most influential comic ever published (after ***Action*** and ***Superman***), ***CDNP*** was a belated trend setter. Gleason had the field all to himself for six years. Then, in 1948 the industry suffered a severe slump in sales. In desperation, publishers turned en masse to the formerly untapped 'crime' market. This move was abetted in part by Gleason himself. In mid-1947 he had begun publishing circulation figures on the covers of ***CDNP***, reporting sales of 5 million - 6 million copies (per issue?), an astounding record for a comics periodical and, an open invitation to imitation.
(a,b,c,e,f,h,i,j)

★ **DETECTIVE COMICS** No. 64 (6/42, DC, H)-Simon and Kirby introduce the *Boy Commandos*. A more timely version of the *Newsboy Legion*, this popular series found the Axis plagued with a platoon of wise-cracking juveniles. An immediate hit, the lads were rewarded with a quarterly of their own within a matter of months.
(a,c,d,j)

FAIRY TALE PARADE No. 1 (6-7/42, Dell, F)-Dell's second continuous series funny animal title with original characters. Its popularity was carried entirely by the imaginative illustrative genius of Walt Kelly.
(c,e)

DIXIE DUGAN No. 1 (7/42, CCG, R)-Popular strip character given own title, lasting 7 years (13 issues).
(e)

KRAZY KOMICS No. 1 (7/42, Timely, F)-With four funny animal anthology titles on the stands (all by Dell), Timely entered this new developing field. This series had a humorous format with no strong characters, lasting 4 years. The second publisher in this genre.
(e)

NEW FUNNIES No. 65 (7/42, Dell, F)-The funny animal fever was catching on as Dell gave stardom to their newly acquired characters, *Andy Panda* and *Woody Woodpecker*. Lantz created these characters who became an instant success for Dell's ***The Funnies***. This was Dell's fifth funny animal series (with only six on the stands).
(a,b,c,e,j)

OAKY DOAKS No. 1 (7/42, Eastern Color, R)-A one-shot strip reprint book which couldn't compete on the stands.
(e)

WAR VICTORY ADVENTURES No. 1 (Sum/42, Harv, W)-A unique super hero title produced to promote purchase of war savings bonds, lasting 3 issues.
(e)

★★★★ **WONDER WOMAN** No. 1 (Sum/42, DC, H)-One of the few characters in comics to make her own title just months from her debut in ***All-Star*** No. 8. The only mythological character to flourish in the comics format, her only concession to the present was adopting a modern costume. The amazing Amazon was a trend setter whose popularity has lasted beyond 40 years.

(a,b,c,e,j)

WAR HEROES No. 1 (7-9/42, Dell, W)-Dell's third war title, lasting 11 issues.
(e)

★ **CAPTAIN MIDNIGHT** No. 1 (9/42, Faw, Av)-This book heralds one of the most changed transfer characters adapted successfully to the comic book format. Fawcett's version of the character is the most memorable (see ***The Funnies*** No. 57), lasting 6 years. Kept alive by the long lasting radio series and a movie serial. A spin-off of *Spy Smasher*.
(a,b,c,e)

FIGHTING YANK No. 1 (9/42, BP, H)-After a year's exposure in ***Startling***, the colonial hero was given his own series. The outstanding Schomburg covers sustained the run, lasting 7 years.
(a,b,c,e,j)

OUR GANG COMICS No. 1 (9-10/42, Dell, F)-A strong early licensed group from MGM films who didn't quite come across as well in the comic medium due to necessary changes in the stereotyping of *Buckwheat* and others. The comic version is mainly collected due to the outstanding art by Walt Kelly and the back-up strips by Carl Barks.
(a,b,c,e,f,j,l)

★ **COO COO COMICS** No. 1 (10/42, BP, F)-Seeing the stands beginning to swell with Dell's funny animal titles (5), Better got on the band wagon. *Super Mouse* debuted, the first funny animal super hero (cloned from *Superman*). (7 funny animal titles now on the stands.)
(a,b,c,d,e,f,h,i,j)

★★★★★ **DONALD DUCK FOUR COLOR** No. 9 (10/42, Dell, F)-Debut of anonymous artist, who breathed life into the character and turned the strip into full-length adventure stories. Carl Barks' successful adaptation won him the position as *Donald Duck's* biographer for almost three decades beginning with ***Walt Disney's Comics and Stories*** No. 31.
(a,b,c,g,h,j)

★ **JUNGLE GIRL** No. 1 (Fall/42, Faw, J)-Inspired by the popular film serial, *Perils of Nyoka*, this one-shot introduced the jungle heroine to comics. The series was picked up again in 1945 (retitled ***Nyoka***, lasting 8 years.
(a,b,c,e,f,j,l)

PICTURE STORIES FROM THE BIBLE No. 1 (Fall/42, DC, TR)-The pilot model of M. C. Gaines' projected 'educational comics' line was laudable in concept but squelched at the stands by abysmal art, pedantic scripting and the normal resistance of kids to anything even remotely preachy. Sustained primarily by lot sales to educators and church groups. Ironically, the first comic ever to bear the EC seal.
(a,c,e,i,j,l)

SUPERSNIPE COMICS No. 6 (10/42, S&S, H)-Probably the best, and certainly the most original comic book character of this pulp publisher. A super hero parody lasting 7 years.
(a,b,c,e,f,j)

★ **TERRY-TOONS COMICS** No. 1 (10/42, Timely, F)-20th Century Fox's characters enter the comic field with this book. Timely's second funny animal anthology series (8 titles are now on the stands). 20th Century Fox's *Mighty Mouse* appeared in films the following year and entered this run with No. 38.
(a,b,c,e,j,l)

★ **AIR FIGHTERS** No. 2 (11/42, Hill, Av)-First appearance of one ot the top aviation features also marked Hillman's first successful title. Engaging origin featured air-minded monk who designed and built the premier imaginary aircraft in all of comics. At the controls of the unusual bat-winged orinthopter, dubbed *Birdie*, was the youth who would become known as *Airboy*. He managed to make the standard garb of the pilot—goggles, scarf, flight jacket, et al—look as if they were designed expressly for him. Thoughtful scripting and complimentary art (ala Caniff) propelled this feature through the war years and beyond. Duration 11 years. (*The Heap*, one of the most original characters in comics, began in the next issue.)
(a,b,c,d,j)

★★ **CAPTAIN MARVEL JR** No. 1 (11/42, Faw, H)-Fawcett's second most popular hero (from ***Master***) was given his own series. Raboy classic covers/story art sustained the run, lasting 11 years.
(a,b,c,e)

MICKEY FINN No. 1 (11/42, Eastern Color, R)-The popular transfer character tried his wings in a title of his own. Like *Sparky Watts*, only 17 issues came out in a 10 year period.
(a,c,e)

NAPOLEON AND UNCLE ELBY No. 1 (11/42, Eastern Color, R)-A one-shot single theme anthology title of the popular transfer strip.
(e)

SPARKY WATTS No. 1 (11/42, CCG, R)-Humorous, off-beat character (proven in ***Big Shot***) is given own title, struggling through 10 issues in 7 years.
(a,c,e)

STRICTLY PRIVATE No. 1 (11/42, Eastern Color, R)-A two-issue run of the famous strip, not surviving as a comic book.
(e)

TOPIX No. 1 (11/42, CG, Re)-The first continuous series comic with a religious theme, lasting 10 years. First of a publisher.
(b,e,i,j,k)

★ **CAPTAIN MARVEL ADVENTURES** No. 18 (12/11/42, Faw, H)-*Captain Marvel* is cloned again. Debut of *Mary Marvel* and *The Marvel Family*. *Mary Marvel* was given instant stardom in ***Wow***.
(a,b,c,d,j)

FAWCETT'S FUNNY ANIMAL COMICS No. 1 (12/42, Faw, F)-The first appearance of *Hoppy The Marvel Bunny*, (cloned from *Captain Marvel*), lasting 13 years. The second funny animal super hero (see ***Coo Coo***). Fawcett joined Dell, Timely and Better entering the funny animal market (10 titles now on the stands). (*Captain Marvel* himself introduced *Hoppy* on the cover.)
(a,b,c,d,e,h,j)

FUNNY BOOK No. 1 (12/42, PMI, F)-Another publisher entered the funny animal market with this book. Weak concepts overall, the title lasting 9 issues over 4 years (10 titles now on the stands).
(e)

GIFT COMICS No. 1 (12/42, Faw, H)-Fawcett's second thick-format title containing original comics to be released at Christmas with ***Holiday*** and ***Xmas*** for 50¢.
(a,c,e)

HIT COMICS No. 25 (12/42, Qua, H)-*Kid Eternity* debuts. Recurring war-era theme of life after life was given novel twist in this long running series. Youthful hero, dying ahead of his appointed time, was not only miraculously restored to life but granted the ability to call on all the great heroes of the past for assistance in solving crimes (see *The Fighting Yank*). Intriguing concept was given usual stellar Iger shop treatment.
(a,b,c,d,j)

HOLIDAY COMICS No. 1 (12/42, Faw, H)-Fawcett's third thick-format title of original comics to be released at Christmas with ***Gift*** and ***Xmas*** for 25¢.
(a,c,e)

SANTA CLAUS FUNNIES No. 1 (12/42, Dell, F)-A special Christmas book illustrated by Kelly. A successful concept that was repeated annually for 20 years.
(a,b,c,e)

AMERICA IN ACTION nn (1942, Dell, W)-A one-shot war anthology book.
(e)

FAMOUS STORIES No. 1 (1942, Dell, Lit)-An educational theme comic, similar to ***Classic Comics***, not lasting beyond the 2nd issue.
(e)

JOE PALOOKA No. 1 (1942, CCG, R)-With proven success in ***Big Shot*** (not to mention syndication), the character became a star in his own title. Early issues boast "over 1,000,000 copies sold." The series lasted 19 years.
(a,b,c,e)

WAR STORIES No. 1 (1942, Dell, W)-Dell's fourth war theme anthology title, lasting 8 issues. *Night Devils*, a mysterious costumed war team debuted in No. 3.
(e)

1943 ■

ALL NEW COMICS No. 1 (1/43, Harv, H)-A super hero anthology title of mediocre quality, lasting 15 issues.
(e)

★★★ **ARCHIE COMICS** No. 1 (Wint/42-43, AP, TA)-Early stardom for a non-super hero theme. A successful formula with many spin-off characters, lasting beyond 40 years.
(a,b,c,d,e,h,i,j)

BLACK TERROR No. 1 (Wint/42-43, BP, H)-Fighting his way from ***Exciting***, the character begins his own series. Sterling costume. High impact Schomburg covers mislead the buyer as to the quality of the contents. Lasted 7 years.
(a,b,c,e,j)

BOY COMMANDOS No. 1 (Wint/42-43, DC, W)-After *Captain America*, this was the second title that Simon and Kirby had all to themselves. Pat variation of favorite S&K theme: Kid group with adult mentor. Seldom rose above the expected, but S&K were at their loosest and the strip conveys the sense of fun they probably had doing it. Earlier covers, sans redundant blurbs and intrusive dialogue balloons, are superb poster art.
(a,b,c,e,j)

CAPTAIN BATTLE No. 3 (Wint/42-43, Mag. Press, H)-After a year's delay, the character from ***Silver Streak*** was given another chance, only lasting 3 issues.
(e)

CLUE COMICS No. 1 (1/43, Hill, H)-Hillman's second most successful title. Unusual heroes and bizarre villains sustained run for four years.
(e)

COMIC CAVALCADE No. 1 (Wint/42-43, DC, H)-Following the success of ***World's Finest***, DC launched this companion book in thick format featuring their next tier of top characters, *Wonder Woman, The Flash* and *Green Lantern*.
(a,b,c,e)

COMICS DIGEST No. 1 (Wint/42-43, PMI, TR)-A one-shot war theme reprint anthology (pocket size) from ***True Comics***.
(e)

FLYING CADET No. 1 (1/43, Flying Cadet, Av)-A true theme World War II aviation anthology (with real photos), lasting 4 years.
(e)

GOLDEN ARROW No. 1 (Wint/42-43, Faw, Ws)-Fawcett's original western character from ***Whiz*** finally given own title, lasting 6 issues.
(a,e)

HELLO PAL COMICS No. 1 (1/43, Harv, An)-Unusual format featuring photographic covers of movie stars. *Rocketman* and *Rocketgirl* appear (see ***Scoop***), lasting 3 issues.
(e)

MISS FURY COMICS No. 1 (Wint/42-43, Timely, H)-A strong transfer character by Tarpe Mills. Noteworthy and unique in that she rarely appeared in costume.
(a,c,e,f,j)

MAJOR HOOPLE COMICS No. 1 (1/43, BP, R)-A one-shot comic of the famous strip character, as Better tried to enter the reprint market.
(e)

REAL FUNNIES No. 1 (1/43, Nedor, F)-The publisher's second funny animal title (11 titles now on stands), only lasting 3 issues. First appearance of *The Black Terrier* (cloned from *The Black Terror*), the third funny animal super hero.
(e)

RED DRAGON COMICS No. 5 (1/43, S&S, An)-Pulpy anthology series not strong enough to last over 5 issues.
(e)

DON WINSLOW OF THE NAVY No. 1 (2/43, Faw, W)-His comic book career was launched here with an introduction by *Captain Marvel* himself. Successful adaptation of this popular transfer character, lasting 12 years.
(a,b,c,e,j,l)

HEADLINE COMICS No. 1 (2/43, Prize, TR)-Taking up the "True" theme of PMI's ***True*** and ***Real Heroes*** and Better's ***Real Life***, Prize entered the field with this, their second title, which lasted 13 years.
(b,e)

HOPALONG CASSIDY No. 1 (2/43, Faw, Ws)-A one-shot issue continuing as a series three years later. The third continuous series newsstand western title, lasting 16 years. A transfer character kept alive by William Boyd's strong following in the movies and on TV.
(a,b,c,e)

IBIS, THE INVINCIBLE No. 1 (2/43, Faw, Mg)-As a solid back-up feature in ***Whiz***, he was invincible, but not invincible enough to support a title of his own. The title expired after 6 issues.
(e)

KID KOMICS No. 1 (2/43, Timely, H)-Timely's third series devoted to sidekicks. The Schomburg covers and guest appearances of secondary characters sustained the run through 10 issues.
(e)

ALL HERO COMICS No. 1 (3/43, Faw, H)-Fawcett's second title that showcased their top characters (see ***America's Greatest***). A thick format one-shot.
(a,c,e)

CAPTAIN MARVEL ADVENTURES No. 22 (3/43, Faw, H)-Begins the 25-issue *Mr. Mind* serial which captured nationwide attention at the time. Tremendous and brilliant marketing strategy by Fawcett. An epic by any standard, unmatched before or since.
(c,d,f,h,i,j)

COMEDY COMICS No. 14 (3/43, Timely, F)-The first *Super Rabbit* (the fourth funny animal super hero) (the 12th title on the stands). Given his own title the following year. (An imitation of *Hoppy The Marvel Bunny*.)
(a,c,d,e,j)

FUNNY FUNNIES No. 1 (4/43, BP, F)-A one-shot funny animal title (their third) (13 titles now on the stands). No enduring characters.
(e)

★★★★ **WALT DISNEY'S COMICS AND STORIES** No. 31 (4/43, Dell, F)-Anonymous staffer who defined what funny animal continuity is all about began this issue (2nd Barks *DD* story; see ***DD Four Color*** No. 9). Cinched long-term success of Disney anthology. One of a half-dozen absolute masters of the form, Carl Barks' achievement on individual stories is exceeded only by remarkable consistency of the series over the length of its run (over 40 years).
(a,b,c,j)

GOOFY COMICS No. 1 (6/43, Nedor, F)-Nedor's fourth funny animal title and one of the most enduring, lasting 10 years. No memorable characters. (13 funny animal titles on the stands.)
(b,e)

JOLLY JINGLES No. 10 (Sum/43, MLJ, F)-A new publisher tried their hand at funny animals, introducing *Super Duck* (the fifth funny animal super hero). (A hybrid of *Superman* and *Donald Duck*.) (14 titles on the stands.)
(a,c,d,e,j)

★★ **PLASTIC MAN** No. 1 (Sum/43, Qua, H)-After a slow start, this title outlasts ***Police Comics***, surviving 13 years. One of the top hero concepts carried by the exciting plotting/art of Jack Cole.
(a,b,c,e)

HAPPY COMICS No. 1 (8/43, Standard, F)-Their fifth funny animal title. No memorable characters, lasting 7 years (14 titles on the stands.)
(b,e)

ALL-SELECT COMICS No. 1 (Fall/43, Timely, H)-Timely's second showcase title featuring their top three characters (see ***All Winners***). Series carried by Schomburg covers (a proven sales feature), lasting 3 years.
(a,c,e)

ALL SURPRISE No. 1 (Fall/43, Timely, F)-Timely's fourth funny animal title, giving more exposure to their leading character, *Super Rabbit*, lasting 4 years. (15 titles on the stands.)
(e)

SUPER RABBIT No. 1 (Fall/43, Timely, F)-After his debut in ***Comedy Comics***, *Super Rabbit* is given his own title, lasting 5 years. (15 titles on the stands.)
(e)

CAPTAIN BATTLE JR No. 1 (Fall/43, Comic House, H)-Clone of *Captain Battle*. The *Claw* vs. *The Ghost*, lasting 2 issues.
(e)

GIGGLE COMICS No. 1 (10/43, ACG, F)-Ties as first title of a new publisher, reinforcing the trend to funny animals. The quality and style of ACG's whole line was heavily influenced by the mastery of the teacher-artist of Ken Hultgren, the series' artist (beginning in 1944). This title lasted 12 years. (17 titles on the stands.)
(a,b,c,e,j,k)

HA HA COMICS No. 1 (10/43, ACG, F)-Ties as first title of a new publisher, reinforcing the trend to funny animals. A double impact-with sister title on the stands. Ingenious plotting and art by Ken Hultgren begins the following year. This series lasted 12 years. (17 titles on the stands.)
(a,b,c,e,j,k)

SUSPENSE COMICS No. 1 (12/43, Continental, D)-Debut of *The Grey Mask* (imitation of *The Spirit*). Atmospheric radio drama in a comic book form, lasting 3 years.
(e)

AVIATION CADETS nn (1943, S&S, Av)-A World War II aviation anthology one-shot. Navy pre-flight training involving sports.
(e)

COLUMBIA COMICS No. 1 (1943, Wise, R)-More exposure for Columbia's reprint characters, *Joe Palooka, Dixie Duggan*, etc., lasting 3 issues.
(e)

POWERHOUSE PEPPER No. 1 (1943, Timely, Hm)-The protagonist of ***Joker Comics*** of a year earlier, Wolverton's humorous plotting made this character a memorable one. Popular enough to receive his own title.
(a,c,e,j)

TINY TOTS COMICS No. 1 (1943, Dell, F)-A one-shot anthology book of funny animals with Walt Kelly art.
(e)

TREASURE COMICS nn (1943, Prize, H)-Rebinding of coverless copies of ***Prize*** No. 7-11 from 1942. A very rare book with only one copy known to exist.
(e)

UNITED STATES MARINES nn (1943, Wise, W)-A documentary style war anthology series mixed with magazine-type photo features from the front, surviving one year. The title was resurrected for a brief period after the Korean conflict.
(e)

ALL FUNNY COMICS No. 1 (Wint/43-44, DC, Hm)-DC's first all funny anthology title. A popular series with the humorous plotting of *Genius Jones*, lasting 4½ years.
(e,j)

BLACK HOOD COMICS No. 9 (Wint/43-44, MLJ, H)-The Man of Mystery graduates from ***Top-Notch*** into his own title, lasting 11 issues.
(e)

CHRONOLOGICAL LIST OF COMIC BOOK TITLES BY PUBLISHER FOR PERIOD 1933 - 1943

(The indented titles are key books other than No. 1's)

ACE MAGAZINES

Sure-Fire No. 1, 6/40
Super Mystery No. 1, 7/40
Lightning No. 4, 12/40
Our Flag No. 1, 8/41
Banner No. 3, 9/41
Four Favorites No. 1, 9/41
Captain Courageous No. 6, 3/42

AMERICAN COMICS GROUP

Giggle No. 1, 10/43
Ha Ha No. 1, 10/43

BETTER PUBL. (Standard)

Best No. 1, 11/39
Thrilling No. 1, 2/40
Exciting No. 1, 4/40
  Exciting No. 9, 5/41
Startling No. 1, 6/40
Real Life No. 1, 9/41
  Startling No. 10, 9/41
America's Best No. 1, 2/42
Fighting Yank No. 1, 9/42
Coo Coo No. 1, 10/42
Black Terror No. 1, Wint/42-43
Major Hoople No. 1, 1/43
Real Funnies No. 1, 1/43
Funny Funnies No. 1, 4/43
Goofy No. 1, 6/43
Happy No. 1, 8/43

BILBARA PUBLISHING CO.

Cyclone No. 1, 6/40

CENTAUR PUBLICATIONS

Funny Pages V2/6, 3/38
Funny Pic. Stories V2/6, 3/38
Star Comics No. 10, 3/38
Star Ranger No. 10, 3/38
Cowboy No. 13, 7/38
Keen Detective No. 8, 7/38
Little Giant No. 1, 7/38
Amazing Mystery Funnies No. 1, 8/38
Little Giant Movie No. 1, 8/38
  Funny Pages V2/10, 9/38
Star Ranger Funnies No. 15, 10/38
Little Giant Det. No. 1, 10/38
Keen Komics V2/1, 5/39
  Amazing Mystery Funnies V2/7, 7/39
Comic Pages V3/4, 7/39
  Keen Detective V2/7, 7/39
Amazing Man No. 5, 9/39
Amazing Adventure Funnies No. 1, 6/40
Fantoman No. 2, 8/40
Masked Marvel No. 1, 9/40
Arrow, The No. 1, 10/40
Super Spy No. 1, 10/40
Detective Eye No. 1, 11/40
Wham No. 1, 11/40
Stars and Stripes No. 2, 5/41
Liberty Scouts No. 2, 6/41
World Famous Heroes No. 1, 10/41
Man Of War No. 1, 11/41

CATECHETICAL GUILD

Topix No. 1, 11/42

HARRY 'A' CHESLER

Star No. 1, 2/37
Star Ranger No. 1, 2/37
Feature Funnies No. 1, 10/37
Cocomalt Big Book No. 1, 1938
Yankee No. 1, 9/41
Dynamic No. 1, 10/41
Scoop No. 1, 11/41
Punch No. 1, 12/41

COLUMBIA COMICS GROUP

Big Shot No. 1, 5/40
Skyman No. 1, Fall/41
Face, The No. 1, 1941
Dixie Duggan No. 1, 7/42
Joe Palooka No. 1, 1942
Sparky Watts No. 1, 11/42

COMICS MAGAZINE

Comics Magazine No. 1, 5/36
Funny Pages No. 6, 11/36
Funny Picture Stories No. 1, 11/36
Detective Picture Stories No. 1, 12/36
Western Picture Stories No. 1, 2/37

DC COMICS

New Fun No. 1, 2/35
New Comics No. 1, 12/35
More Fun No. 7, 1/36
Big Book of Fun No. 1, Spr/36
New Book of Comics No. 1, 6-8/36
New Adventure No. 12, 1/37
Detective No. 1, 3/37
Action No. 1, 6/38
  Detective No. 20, 10/38
Adventure No. 32, 11/38
All-American No. 1, 4/39
New York World's Fair 3-5/39
Movie No. 1, 4/39
  Detective No. 27, 5/39
  Adventure No. 40, 7/39
Mutt and Jeff No. 1, Sum/39
Superman No. 1, Sum/39
Double Action No. 2, 1/40
Flash No. 1, 1/40
  More Fun No. 52,53, 2,3/40
  Adventure No. 48, 3/40
Batman No. 1, Spr/40
New York World's Fair 3-5/40
  More Fun No. 55, 5/40
  All-American No. 16, 7/40
All-Star No. 1, Sum/40
  All-American No. 19, 10/40
  All-Star No. 3, Wint/40-41
  Adventure No. 61, 4/41
World's Best No. 1, Spr/41
All Flash No. 1, Sum/41
World's Finest No. 2, Sum/41
Green Lantern No. 1, Fall/41
Star Spangled No. 1, 10/41
  All-Star No. 8, 11-12/41
Leading No. 1, Wint/41-42
Sensation No. 1, 1/42
  Star Spangled No. 7, 4/42
  Detective No. 64, 6/42
Wonder Woman No. 1, Sum/42
Pic. Stories/Bible No. 1, Fall/42
Boy Commandos No. 1, Wint/42-43
Comic Cavalcade No. 1, Wint/42-43
All Funny No. 1, Wint/43-44

DELL PUBLISHING CO.

Popular No. 1, 2/36
Funnies No. 1, 10/36
Comics No. 1, 3/37
West. Action Thrillers No. 1, 4/37
100 Pages of Comics No. 1, 1937
Super No. 1, 5/38
Crackajack No. 1, 6/38
Nickel No. 1, 1938
Large Feature Comic No. 1, 1939
Four-Color No. 1, 1939
Donald Duck 4-Color No. 4, 3/40?
War No. 1, 5/40
W.D.'s Comics & Stories No. 1, 10/40
Mickey Mouse 4-Color No. 16, 4/41
  Funnies No. 57, 7/41
Red Ryder No. 3, 8/41
Looney Tunes No. 1, Fall/41
Key Ring No. 1, 1941
Large Feature No. 1, 1941
USA Is Ready No. 1, 1941
Animal No. 1, 12-1/41-42
Camp No. 1, 2/42
Fairy Tale Parade No. 1, 6-7/42
New Funnies No. 65, 7/42
War Heroes No. 1, 7-9/42
Our Gang No. 1, 9-10/42
Santa Claus Funnies No. 1, 12/42
America In Action No. 1, 1942
Donald Duck 4-Color No. 9, 1942
Famous Stories No. 1, 1942
War Stories No. 1, 1942
  W.D. Comics & Stories No. 31, 4/43
Tiny Tots No. 1, 1943

EASTERN COLOR

Funnies On Parade nn, 1933
F. F., A Carnival-- nn, 1933
Century Of Comics nn, 1933
Skippy's Own Book nn, 1934
Famous Funnies Series 1, 1934
Famous Funnies No. 1, 7/34
Heroic No. 1, 8/40
Buck Rogers No. 1, Wint/40-41
Dickie Dare No. 1, 1941
Big Chief Wahoo No. 1, Wint/41-42
Jingle Jangle No. 1, 2/42
Oaky Doaks No. 1, 7/42
Mickey Finn No. 1, 11/42
Napoleon & Uncle Elby No. 1, 11/42
Strictly Private No. 1, 11/42
Tiny Tots No. 1, 1943

WILL EISNER

Spirit No. 1, 6/2/40

ELLIOT PUBLICATIONS

Double 1940
Double Up 1941

FAWCETT PUBLICATIONS

Flash No. 1, 1/40
Whiz No. 2, 2/40
Master No. 1, 3/40
Slam Bang No. 1, 3/40
Nickel No. 1, 5/40
Special Edition No. 1, 8/40
Western Desperado No. 8, 10/40
Wow No. 1, Wint/40-41
Captain Marvel No. 1, 1-2/41
America's Greatest No. 1, 5/41
Bulletman No. 1, 7/41
Minuteman No. 1, 7/41
Capt. Marvel Thrill Book 1941
Gene Autry No. 1, Fall/41
Spysmasher No. 1, Fall/41
  Master No. 21, 12/41
  Whiz No. 25, 12/12/41
Xmas No. 1, 12/41
Captain Midnight No. 1, 9/42
Jungle Girl No. 1, Fall/42
Captain Marvel Jr. No. 1, 11/42
  Captain Marvel No. 18, 12/11/42
Fawcett's Funny Animals No. 1, 12/42
Gift No. 1, 12/42
Holiday No. 1, 12/42
Golden Arrow No. 1, Wint/42-43
Don Winslow No. 1, 2/43

Hopalong Cassidy No. 1, 2/43
Ibis No. 1, 2/43
All Hero No. 1, 3/43
  Captain Marvel No. 22, 3/43

FICTION HOUSE

Jumbo No. 1, 9/38
Fight No. 1, 1/40
Jungle No. 1, 1/40
Planet No. 1, 1/40
Wings No. 1, 9/40
Rangers No. 1, 10/41
Sheena No. 1, Spr/42
Wambi No. 1, Spr/42

FLYING CADET

Flying Cadet No. 1, 1/43

FOX FEATURES SYNDICATE

Wonder No. 1, 5/39
Wonderworld No. 3, 7/39
Mysterymen No. 1, 8/39
Fantastic No. 1, 12/39
Blue Beetle No. 1, Wint/39-40
Science No. 1, 2/40
Weird No. 1, 4/40
Flame, The No. 1, Sum/40
Green Mask No. 1, Sum/40
Big 3 No. 1, Fall/40
Rex Dexter No. 1, Fall/40
Samson No. 1, Fall/40
Eagle, The No. 1, 7/41
U.S. Jones No. 1, 11/41
V-Comics No. 1, 1/42

FUNNIES, INC.

Motion Pic. Funn. Weekly No. 1, 5/39?
Green Giant No. 1, 1940

LEV GLEASON

Silver Streak No. 1, 12/39
  Silver Streak No. 6, 9/40
  Silver Streak No. 7, 1/41
Captain Battle No. 1, Sum/41
Daredevil No. 1, 7/41
Boy No. 3, 4/42
Crime Does Not Pay No. 22, 6/42
Captain Battle No. 3, Wint/42-43
Captain Battle Jr. No. 1, Fall/43

HUGO GERNSBACK

Superworld No. 1, 4/40

GILBERTON PUBLICATIONS

Classic No. 1, 10/41

GLOBE SYNDICATE

Circus No. 1, 6/38

GREAT PUBLICATIONS

Great No. 1, 11/41
Choice No. 1, 12/41

HARVEY PUBLICATIONS (Helnit)

Speed No. 1, 10/39
Champion No. 2, 12/39
Champ No. 11, 10/40
Green Hornet No. 1, 12/40
Pocket No. 1, 8/41
War Victory No. 1, Sum/42
All New No. 1, 1/43
Hello Pal No. 1, 1/43

HAWLEY PUBLICATIONS

Captain Easy nn, 1939
Red Ryder No. 1, 9/40

Sky Blazers No. 1, 9/40
Hi-Spot No. 2, 11/40

HILLMAN PERIODICALS

Miracle No. 1, 2/40
Rocket No. 1, 3/40
Victory No. 1, 8/41
Air Fighters No. 1, 11/41
  Air Fighters No. 2, 11/42
Clue No. 1, 1/43

HOLYOKE (Continental)

Crash No. 1, 5/40
  Crash No. 4, 9/40
Catman No. 1, 5/41
Captain Fearless No. 1, 8/41
Captain Aero No. 7, 12/41
Suspense No. 1, 12/43

HYPER PUBLICATIONS

Hyper Mystery No. 1, 5/40

K.K. PUBLICATIONS

Mickey Mouse Mag. No. 1, Sum/35
Mickey Mouse Mag. V5/12, 9/40

DAVID MCKAY PUBL.

King No. 1, 4/36
Wow No. 1, 5/36
Ace No. 1, 4/37
Feature Book nn, 1-4/37
Magic No. 1, 8/39
Future No. 1, 6/40

MLJ MAGAZINES

Blue Ribbon No. 1, 11/39
Top-Notch No. 1, 12/39
Pep No. 1, 1/40
Zip No. 1, 2/40
Shield-Wizard No. 1, Sum/40
  Top-Notch No. 9, 10/40
  Blue Ribbon No. 9, 2/41
Jackpot No. 1, Spr/41
  Pep No. 17, 7/41
  Pep No. 22, 12/41
Special No. 1, Wint/41-42
Hangman No. 2, Spr/42
Archie No. 1, Wint/42-43
Jolly Jingles No. 10, Sum/43
Black Hood No. 9, Wint/43-44

NITA PUBLICATIONS

Whirlwind No. 1, 6/40

NOVELTY PUBLICATIONS

Target No. 1, 2/40
Blue Bolt No. 1, 6/40
Four Most No. 1, Wint/41-42

PARENT'S MAGAZINE INST.

True No. 1, 4/41
Calling All Girls No. 1, 9/41
Real Heroes No. 1, 9/41
Funny Book No. 1, 12/42
Comics Digest No. 1, Wint/42-43

PRIZE PUBLICATIONS

Prize No. 1, 3/40
  Prize No. 7, 9/40
Headline No. 1, 2/43
Treasure nn, 1943

PROGRESSIVE PUBLISHERS

Bang-Up No. 1, 12/41

QUALITY COMICS GROUP

Feature No. 21, 6/39
Smash No. 1, 8/39
  Feature No. 27, 12/39
Crack No. 1, 5/40
Hit No. 1, 7/40
National No. 1, 7/40
Military No. 1, 8/41
Police No. 1, 8/41
Uncle Sam No. 1, 8/41
Doll Man No. 1, Fall/41
  Hit No. 25, 12/42
Plastic Man No. 1, Sum/43

RALSTON-PURINA CO.

Tom Mix No. 1, 9/40

STREET AND SMITH PUBL.

Shadow No. 1, 3/40
Doc Savage No. 1, 5/40
Bill Barnes No. 1, 10/40
Sport No. 1, 10/40
Army and Navy No. 1, 5/41
Super Magic No. 1, 5/41
Super Magician No. 2, 9/41
Pioneer Pic. Stories No. 1, 12/41
Trail Blazers No. 1, 1941
True Sport Pic. Stories No. 5, 2/42
Supersnipe No. 6, 10/42
Devil Dogs No. 1, 1942
Remember Pearl Harbor nn, 1942
Red Dragon No. 5, 1/43
Aviation Cadets No. 1, 1943

SUN PUBLICATIONS

Colossus No. 1, 3/40
Sun Fun No. 1, 3/40

TIMELY COMICS (Marvel)

Marvel No. 1, 11/39
Marvel Mystery No. 2, 12/39
Daring Mystery No. 1, 1/40
Mystic No. 1, 3/40
  Marvel Mystery No. 9, 7/40
Red Raven No. 1, 8/40
Human Torch No. 2, Fall/40
Captain America No. 1, 3/41
Sub-Mariner No. 1, Spr/41
All-Winners No. 1, Sum/41
Young Allies No. 1, Sum/41
USA No. 1, 8/41
Tough Kid Squad No. 1, 3/42
Comedy No. 9, 4/42
Joker No. 1, 4/42
Krazy No. 1, 7/42
Terry-Toons No. 1, 10/42
Miss Fury No. 1, Wint/42-43
Kid Komics No. 1, 2/43
  Comedy No. 14, 3/43
All-Select No. 1, Fall/43
All-Surprise No. 1, Fall/43
Super Rabbit No. 1, Fall/43
Powerhouse Pepper No. 1, 1943

UNITED FEATURES SYND.

Tip Top No. 1, 4/36
Comics On Parade No. 1, 4/38
Single Series No. 1, 1938
Okay No. 1, 7/40
O.K. No. 1, 7/40
Sparkler No. 1, 7/40
United No. 1, 8/40
Sparkler No. 1, 7/41

WHITMAN PUBLISHING CO.

Mammoth No. 1, 1937
Donald Duck nn, 1938

WILLIAM H. WISE

Columbia Comics No. 1, 1943
United States Marines No. 1, 1943

COMICS WITH LITTLE IF ANY VALUE

There exists in the comic book market, as in all other collector's markets, items, usually of recent origin, that have relatively little if any value. Why even mention it? We wouldn't, except for one thing—this is where you could probably take your worst beating, investment-wise. Since these books are listed by dealers in such profusion, at prices which will vary up to 500 percent from one dealer's price list to another, determining a realistic "market" value is almost impossible. And since the same books are listed repeatedly, list after list, month after month, it is difficult to determine whether or not these books are selling. In some cases, it is doubtful that they are even being collected. Most dealers must get a minimum price for their books; otherwise, it would not be profitable to handle. This will sometimes force a value on an otherwise valueless item. Since new comics are now priced at 75 cents or more each, most dealers who handle them get a minimum price of at least 90 cents. This is the **available** price to obtain a **reading** copy. However, this is not what dealers will pay to restock. Since many of these books are not yet collector's items, their salvage value would be very low. You may not get more than 5 cents to 10 cents per copy selling them back to a dealer. This type of material, from an investment point of view, would be of maximum risk since the salvage value is so low. For this reason, recent comics should be bought for enjoyment as reading copies and if they go up in value, consider it a bonus. On the other hand, you might buy a vastly over-priced golden-age comic and still expect to recover your loss after a reasonable passage of time. This, unfortunately, is not true of so many titles that we are put in a rather awkward position of listing.

THE PRICE GUIDE'S POSITION: We don't want to leave a title out just because it is presently valueless. And at the same time, we don't want to presume to "establish" what is collectible and what isn't. The passage of time and a change in collectors' interests can make almost any comic potentially valuable. Some books, by virtue of their age, will someday obtain a value as a cultural or historical curiosity. Therefore, we feel that all books, regardless of the demand for them, should be listed.

Since speculation in the comic book market began around 1964, most all titles since that time have been saved and are in plentiful supply. These books have been included for your information and can be found listed throughout The Guide with values assigned (under $1.00). The collector would be well advised to compare prices between several dealers' lists before ordering this type of material.

COLLECTING FOREIGN COMICS AND AMERICAN REPRINTS

One extremely interesting source of comics or early vintage—one which does not necessarily have to be expensive—is the foreign market. Many American strips, from both newspapers and magazines, are reprinted abroad (both in English and in other languages) months and even years after they appear in the states. By working out trade agreements with foreign collectors, one can obtain, for practically the cover price, substantial runs of a number of newspaper strips and reprints of American comic books dating back five, ten, or occasionally even twenty or more years. These reprints are often in black and white, and sometimes the reproduction is poor, but this is not always the case. In any event, this is a source of material that every serious collector should look into.

Once the collector discovers comics published in foreign lands, he often becomes fascinated with the original strips produced in these countries. Many are excellent, and have a broader range of appeal than those of American comic books.

CANADIAN REPRINTS (E.C.s: by J. B. Clifford)

Several E.C. titles were published in Canada by Superior Comics from 1949 to at least 1953. Canadian editions of the following E.C. titles are known: (Pre-Trend) *Saddle Romances, Moon Girl, A Moon A Girl. . . Romance, Modern Love, Saddle*

Justice; (New-Trend) *Crypt of Terror—Tales From the Crypt, Haunt of Fear, Vault of Horror, Weird Science, Weird Fantasy, Two-Fisted Tales, Frontline Combat,* and *Mad. Crime SuspenStories* was also published in Canada under the title *Weird SuspenStories* (Nos. 1-3 known). No reprints of *Shock SuspenStories* by Superior are known, nor have any "New Direction" reprints ever been reported. No reprints later than January 1954 are known. Canadian reprints sometimes exchanged cover and contents with adjacent numbers (e.g., a *Frontline Combat* 12 with a *Frontline Combat* No. 11 cover). They are distinguished both in cover and contents. As the interior pages are always reprinted poorly, these comics are of less value (about ½) than the U.S. editions; they were printed from asbestos plates made from the original plates. On some reprints, the Superior seal replaces the E.C. seal. Superior publishers took over Dynamic in 1947.

CANADIAN REPRINTS (Dells: by Ronald J. Ard)

Canadian editions of Dell comics, and presumably other lines, began in March-April, 1948 and lasted until February-March, 1951. They were a response to the great Canadian dollar crisis of 1947. Intensive development of the post-war Canadian economy was financed almost entirely by American capital. This massive import or money reached such a level that Canada was in danger of having grossly disproportionate balance of payments which could drive it into technical bankruptcy in the midst of the biggest boom in its history. The Canadian government responded by banning a long list of imports. Almost 500 separate items were involved. Alas, the consumers of approximately 499 of them were politically more formidable than the consumers of comic books.

Dell responded by publishing its titles in Canada, through an arrangement with Wilson Publishing Company of Toronto. This company had not existed for a number of years and it is reasonable to assume that its sole business was the production and distribution of Dell titles in Canada. There is no doubt that they had a captive market. If you check the publication data on the U. S. editions of the period you will see the sentence "Not for sale in Canada." Canada was thus the only area of the Free World in those days technically beyond the reach of the American comic book industry.

We do not know whether French editions existed of the Dell titles put out by Wilson. The English editions were available nationwide. They were priced at 10 cents and were all 36 pages in length, at a time when their American parents were 52 pages. The covers were made of coarser paper, similar to that used in the Dell Four Color series in 1946 and 1947 and were abandoned as the more glossy cover paper became more economical. There was also a time lag of from six to eight weeks between, say, the date an American comic appeared and the date that the Canadian edition appeared.

Many Dell covers had seasonal themes and by the time the Canadian edition came out (two months later) the season was over. Wilson solved this problem by switching covers around so that the appropriate season would be reflected when the books hit the stands. Most Dell titles were published in Canada during this period including the popular Atom Bomb giveaway, *Walt Disney Comics and Stories* and the *Donald Duck* and *Mickey Mouse* Four Color one-shots. The quality of the Duck one-shots is equal to that of their American counterparts and generally bring about 30 percent less.

By 1951 the Korean War had so stimulated Canadian exports that the restrictions on comic book importation, which in any case were an offense against free trade principle, could be lifted without danger of economic collapse. Since this time Dell, as well as other companies, have been shipping direct into Canada.

CANADIAN REPRINTS (DCs: by Doug A. England)

Many DC comics were reprinted in Canada by National Comics Publications Limited and Simcoe Publishing and Distributing Co., both of Toronto, for years 1948-1950 at least. Like the Dells, these issues were 36 pages rather than the 52 pages offered in the U.S. editions, and the inscription "Published in Canada" would appear in place of "A 52 Page Magazine" or "52 Big Pages" appearing on U.S. editions. These issues contained no advertisements and some had no issue numbers.

HOW TO START COLLECTING

Most collectors of comic books begin by buying new issues in mint condition directly off the newsstand or from their local comic store. (Subscription copies are available from several mail-order services.) Each week new comics appear on the stands that are destined to become true collectors items. The trick is to locate a store that carries a complete line of comics. In several localities this may be difficult. Most panelologists frequent several magazine stands in order not to miss something they want. Even then, it pays to keep in close contact with collectors in other areas. Sooner or later, nearly every collector has to rely upon a friend in Fandom to obtain for him an item that is unavailable locally.

Before you buy any comic to add to your collection, you should carefully inspect its condition. Unlike stamps and coins, defective comics are generally not highly prized. The cover should be properly cut and printed. Remember that every blemish or sign of wear depreciates the beauty and value of your comics.

The serious panelologist usually purchases extra copies of popular titles. He may trade these multiples for items unavailable locally (for example, foreign comics), or he may store the multiples for resale at some future date. Such speculation is, of course, a gamble, but unless collecting trends change radically in the future, the value of certain comics in mint condition should appreciate greatly, as new generations of readers become interested in collecting.

COLLECTING BACK ISSUES

In addition to current issues, most panelologists want to locate back issues. Some energetic collectors have had great success in running down large hoards of rare comics in their home towns. Occasionally, rare items can be located through agencies that collect old papers and magazines, such as the Salvation Army. The lucky collector can often buy these items for much less than their current market value. Placing advertisements in trade journals, newspapers, etc., can also produce good results. However, don't be discouraged if you are neither energetic nor lucky. Most panelologists build their collections slowly but systematically by placing mail orders with dealers and other collectors.

Comics of early vintage are extremely expensive if they are purchased through a regular dealer or collector, and unless you have unlimited funds to invest in your hobby, you will find it necessary to restrict your collecting in certain ways. However you define your collection, you should be careful to set your goals well within your means.

PROPER HANDLING OF COMIC BOOKS

Before picking up an old rare comic book, caution should be exercised to handle it properly. Old comic books are very fragile and can be easily damaged. Because of this, many dealers hesitate to let customers personally handle their rare comics. They would prefer to remove the comic from its bag and show it to the customer themselves. In this way, if the book is damaged, it would be the dealer's responsibility—not the customer's. Remember, the slightest crease or chip could render an otherwise Mint book to Near Mint or even Very Fine. The following steps are pro-

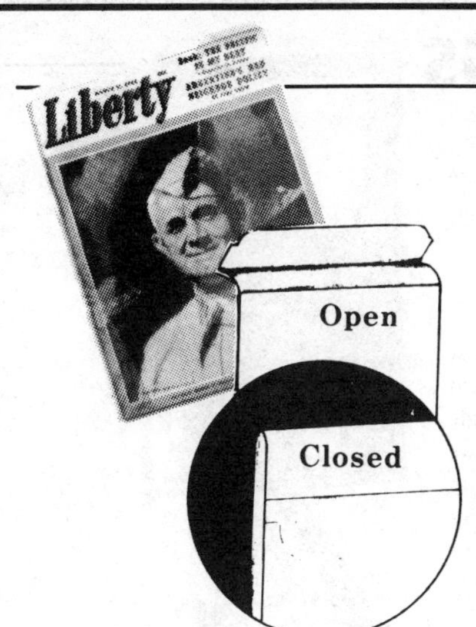

TIME-LOKS®

Lock out the harmful effects of time! Our exclusive self-locking flap is the key to Time-Loks® dependability. And it makes preserving your collection easy. Your collectibles can't slide out and harmful pollutants can't get in.

As with all our Mylar® sleeves, Time-Loks® are sealed using our exclusive heat sealing process.

SATISFACTION GUARANTEED

Cat.#	Description	Size (inches)	Price per 50	Wt. (lbs.)	Price per 100	Wt. (lbs.)	Price per 500	Wt. (lbs.)	Price per 1000	Wt. (lbs.)
714TLF	Standard Size late 60's to present	7¼x10⅝	44.00	(2)	79.50	(5)	360.00	(19)	655.00	(40)
734TLF	Silver/Gold Silver from 1940's to 1960's	7¾x10⅝	45.00	(2)	82.00	(5)	372.00	(20)	676.50	(42)
814TLF	Super Gold Size larger comics of early 40's	8¼x11	46.50	(3)	84.50	(5)	384.00	(20)	698.00	(42)
878TLF	Magazine Size	8⅝x11	50.50	(3)	91.50	(6)	415.50	(23)	755.00	(44)

Bill Cole Enterprises, Inc.
P.O.Box 60 • Dept.48 • Randolph, MA 02368-0060
617-986-2653

What to look for in MYLAR®

CALL IN TOLL-FREE TO ORDER WITH YOUR MASTERCARD, VISA OR BCE CARD
1-800-225-8249

Bill Cole Enterprises' Mylar® sleeves are made using an exclusive heat sealing process. This process produces welds nearly twice as strong as those created through electronic sealing. Make sure to look for Mylar® sealed with this exclusive process to insure durability!

All references to Mylar® refer to uncoated archival quality polyester film such as Mylar® Type D by DuPont Co. or equivalent material such as Melinex® 516 by ICI Corp.

Time-Loks® is a registered trademark of Bill Cole Enterprises, Inc.

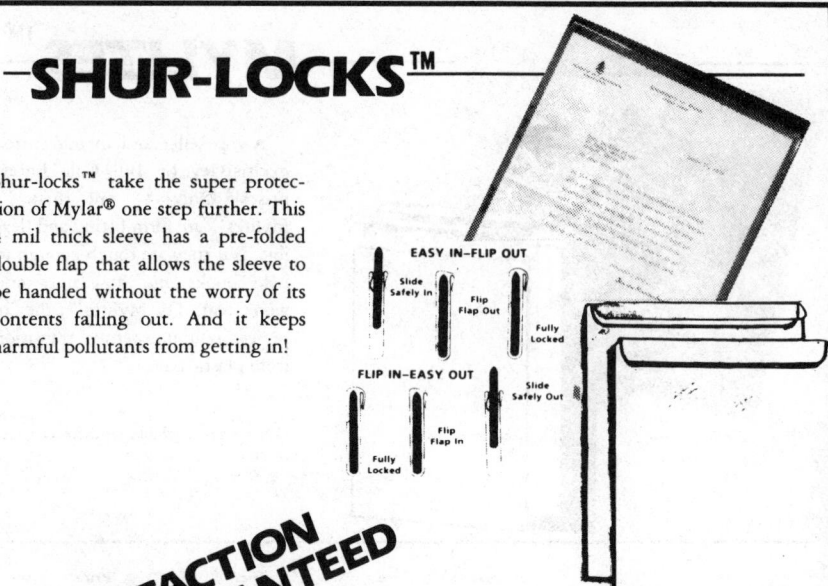

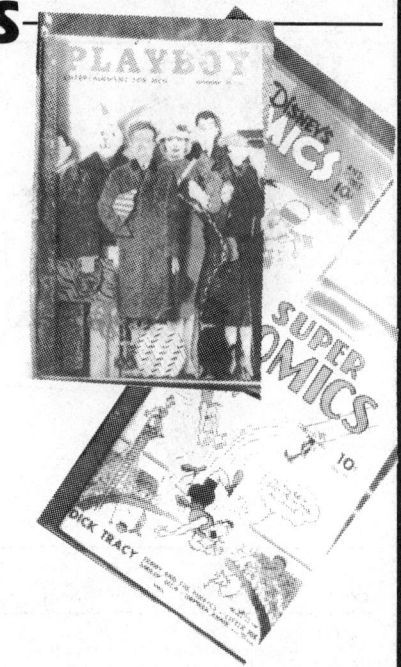

ARCHIVAL SUPPLIES

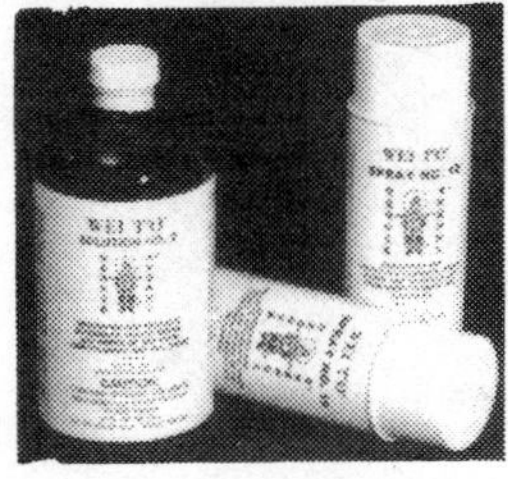

Wei t'o®

Wei t'o® non-aqueous sprays and solutions can safely be used to prevent deterioration of your comics and other paper collectables. One application offers indefinite preservation. And, when used in conjunction with Mylar® and acid-free cardboard, it is the ultimate paper preservation system available.

Cat. #	Description	Size	Price Ea.	Wt. (lbs.)
80/12	Aerosol Spray, for thicker paper and boards	1 pt.	18.40	(3)
81/10	Aerosol Spray, for general use	1 pt.	18.40	(3)
82/2	Solution	1 qt.	28.75	(6)

Wei t'o® is a registered trademark of Wei t'o Associates, Inc.

84

Cat.#	Description	Size	Price Ea.	Wt. (lbs.)
84	Document Repair Tape	1"x98'	15.35	(½)
92	Archival Double-Faced Tape	¼"x18'	6.35	(½)
91	Document Cleaning Pad	—	2.60	(½)
77	PH indicator test strips (measures ph of paper)	100/pkg	10.00	(½)

91

All references to Mylar® refer to uncoated archival quality polyester film such as Mylar® Type D by DuPont Co. or, equivalent material such as Melinex® 516 by ICI Corp.

also from
Bill Cole Enterprises, Inc.

Specialists in rock'n'roll, pop, jazz, blues, country/western, biographies, autobiographies, price guides, discographies, reference books and much, much more. The Music Book Enz™ is the mail order source for strange pop culture books, imports, independents. Books you want — and books you didn't know existed!

Send your name and address for a free copy of our catalog to:

MUSIC BOOK ENZ
c/o Bill Cole Enterprises, Inc.
PO Box 60 Dept.48, Randolph, MA 02368-0060

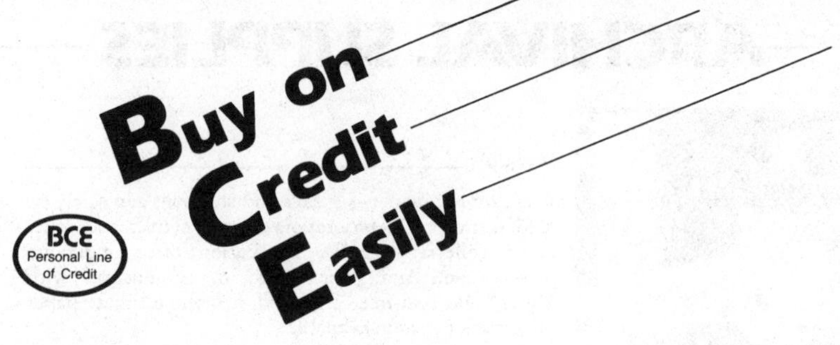

We are pleased to announce our new "**Buy on Credit Easily**" a personal line of Credit to simplify your buying power. This Credit service is unique in that there is no annual fee no credit cards to lose, no need to mail checks with orders, and we can now accept credit orders from anywhere in the world. Not only that, but with your personal line of credit you won't be running up your other credit balances.

Ordering will be simple and easy once your account is approved and established. Just give us your account number, expiration date and your personal identification code. We will automatically process your order.

You will receive a monthly statement and there will be no finance charge assessed if your current purchases are paid within 30 days. If you choose to pay only a portion of your statement, then interest will be charged on the unpaid balance only.

We invite you to apply for your personal line of Credit.

Just send us a long self-addressed stamped envelope and your application will be sent to you by return mail Please allow 4 weeks for processing. Applicants must be 18 years of age or older.

Send requests to:

"Credit Approval"
Bill Cole Enterprises, Inc.
PO Box 60 Dept. 48
Randolph, MA 02368-0060

ONLY

from

Bill Cole Enterprises, Inc.

RARE COMIC ART IS MY BAG
. . .and I love to trade bags of money, or other art for items of special interest to me. I'll pay top dollar for original artwork by Carl Barks, E.C. Segar, and other classic cartoonists, as well as paintings, cartoon movie posters from the '30s and '40s, and other rare comic oriented esoterica.
If you have rare material for sale **contact me first**. If you don't, you may be selling your collection short.
Bruce Hamilton
P. O. Box 1432
Prescott, AZ 86302
(602) 776-1300

ACTION COMICS
SUPERMAN
64 PAGES OF ACTION!
ALL IN FULL COLOR
THE COMPLETE STORY OF THE DARING EXPLOITS OF THE ONE AND ONLY SUPERMAN
1940's
ACTION COMICS
SUPERMAN
No. 12
WORLD'S GREATEST ADVENTURE-STRIP CHARACTER!
10¢
1950's
SUPERMAN
Featuring The Super-Family From Out of Space!
SUPERMAN
1960's
LOIS LANE
1970's
ADVENTURES OF SUPERMAN
1
15¢
ACTION COMICS
20¢
SUPERMAN!
1980's
ADVENTURES OF SUPERMAN
SUPERMAN
HISTORIC LAST ISSUE:
A Very Special Story by ALAN MOORE, CURT SWAN & GEORGE PEREZ
FIRST ALL-NEW ISSUE!
SUPERMAN & THE TEEN TITANS
ACTION COMICS
THE MAN OF STEEL IS OUT FOR BLOOD
DAILY PLANET

OVER 1 BILLION COMICS SOLD
HARVEY COMICS FOR FUN READING AND PROFITABLE COLLECTING!
HARVEY COM
STARS SHINE BRIGH
RICHIE RICH
CASPER
BABY
LITTLE DOT
SAD SACK
HOT STUFF
WENDY
GHOSTLY TRIO
...AND BRIGHTER!
...YEAR AFTER YEAR!
HARVEY COMICS
SPOOKY
YOUR PARENTS READ THEM!
THEIR PARENTS READ THEM!
CONGRATULATIONS!
NOW YOU'RE A
HARVEY COMICS KID!
LITTLE LOTTA
© 1987 HARVEY PUBLICATIONS INC. ©1987 SAD SACK INC.
HARVEY
HARVEY
HARVEY
HARVEY
AND PROFITABLE COLLECTING!
OVER 1 BILLION COMICS SOLD SINCE 1940!

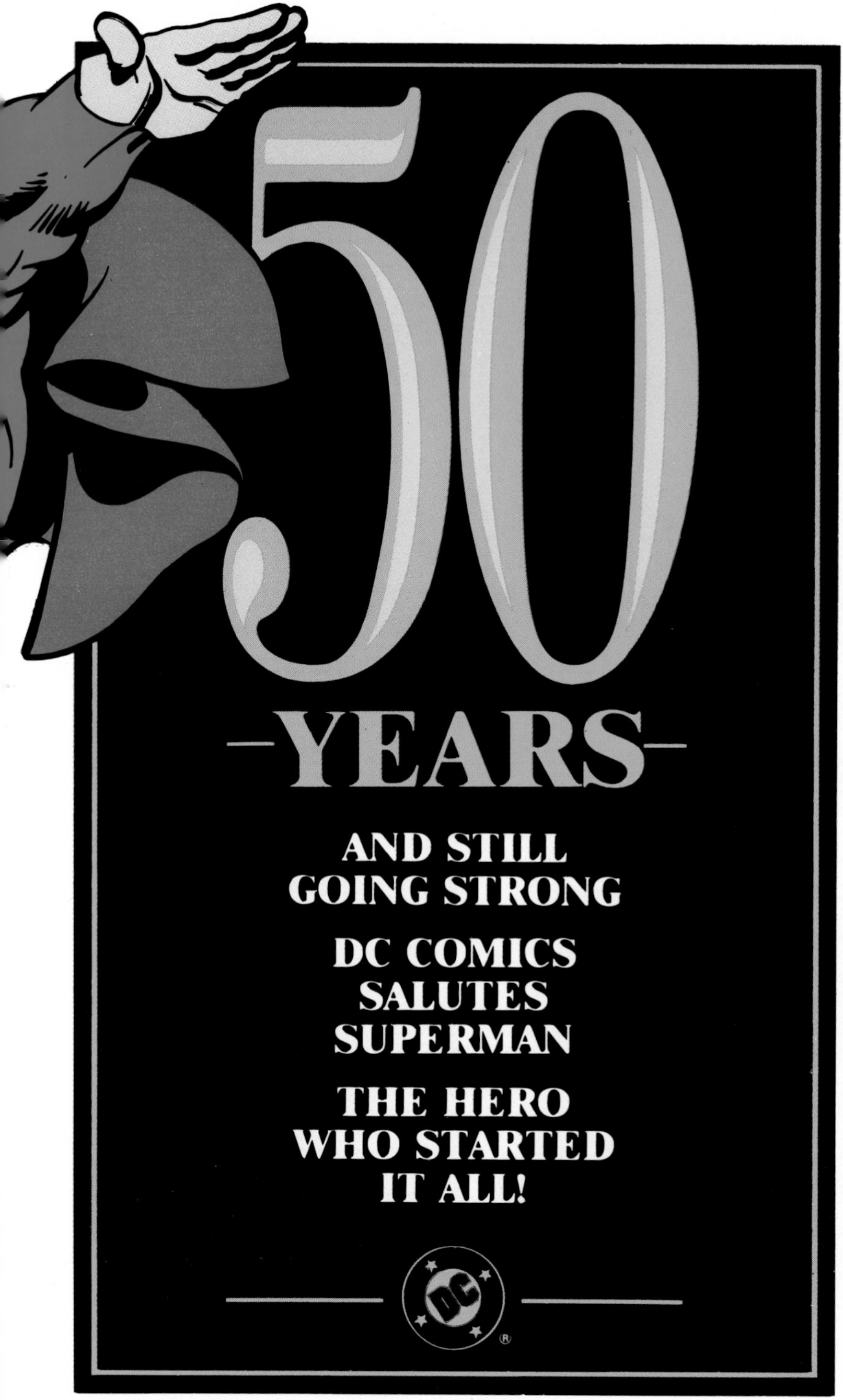

1. **Superman**® wood jointed doll, c. 1939, Ideal toys. Considered to be the first **Superman**® toy ever made.

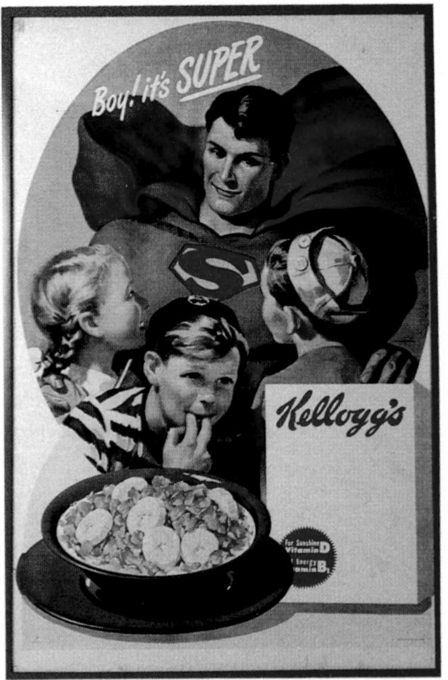

2. **Superman**® Pep cereal poster, c. 1947, Kelloggs, 27"x41" supermarket poster for Pep cereal who sponsored his radio show.

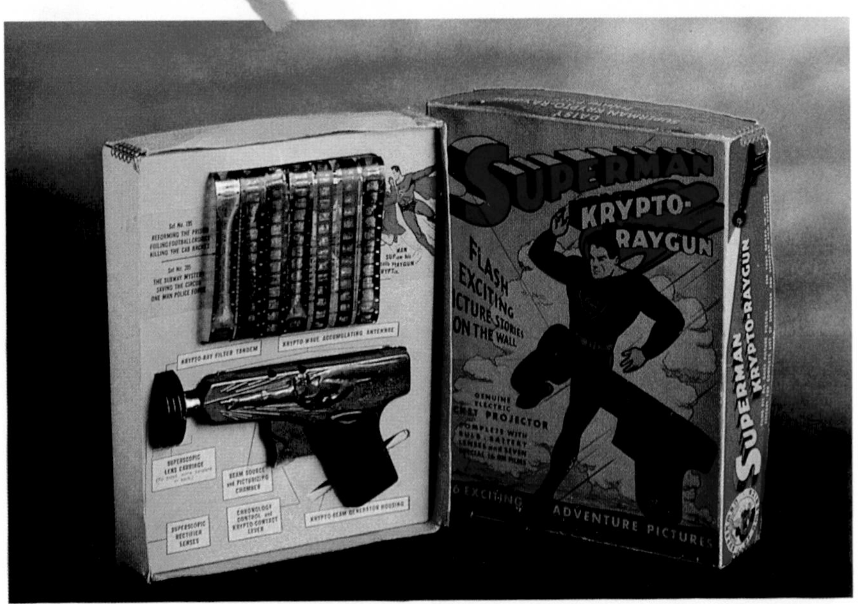

3. **Superman**® Krypto-Raygun, c. 1939, Daisy Manufacturing Co. Difficult to find Mint in the box with all seven film strips.

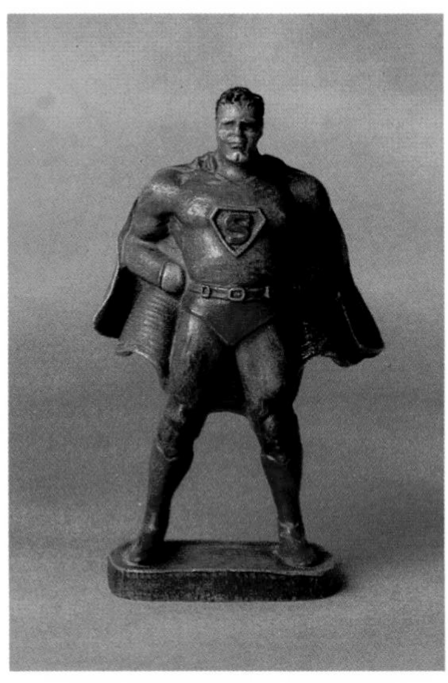

4. **Superman**® Sirocco Figure, c. 1942, 6" pressed-wood figure of **Superman.**® Probably un-licensed.

5. **Superman**® Silent Flame Table Lighter, c. 1942, Dunhill, battery operated cigarette lighter featuring a 3" chrome figure of **Superman.**®

6. **Superman**® Tank, c. 1958, Line Mar Toys, battery operated tank, well designed toy that performs several actions.

7. **Superman**® Pocket Watch, c. 1959, Bradley Time Co. Beautiful watch that also has a stop-watch mechanism.

8. **Superman**® Racing The Airplane, c. 1940, Marx. This toy features the only three-dimensional painted metal figure of **Superman**® produced in the 1940s.

All photos courtesy of Danny Fuchs, "America's Foremost Superman Collector."

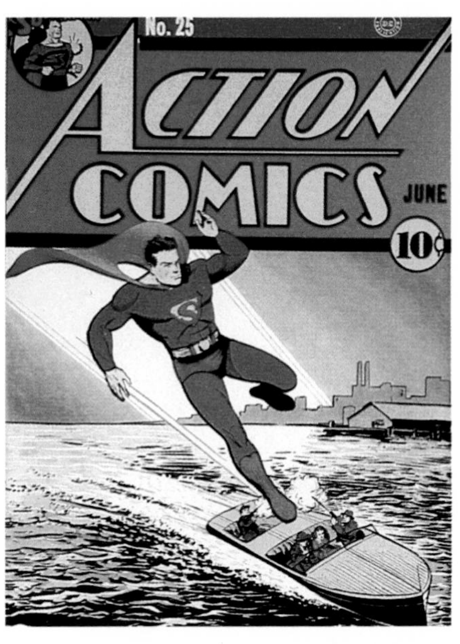

Action Comics #25, 1940. © DC

Adventure Comics #73, 1942. Origin & 1st app. Manhunter by Simon & Kirby. © DC

Air Fighters Comics V2#2, 1943. 1st app. Valkyrie. © HILL

All-American Comics #19, 1940. Origin & 1st app. The Atom. © DC

All Star Comics #7, 1941. © DC

Amazing-Man Comics #7, 1939. Bill Everett cover art. © CEN

America's Best Comics #24, 1947. Schomburg cover art. © Nedor

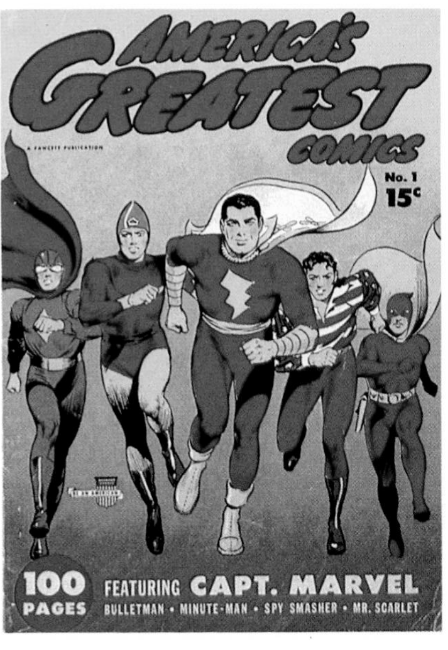

America's Greatest Comics #1, 1941. © FAW

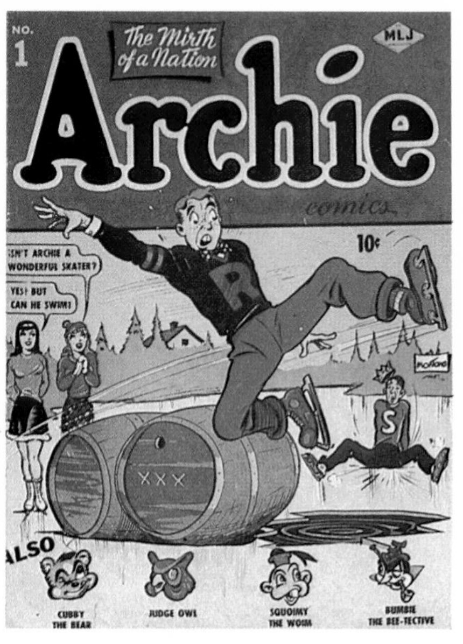

Archie Comics #1, 1942. © AP

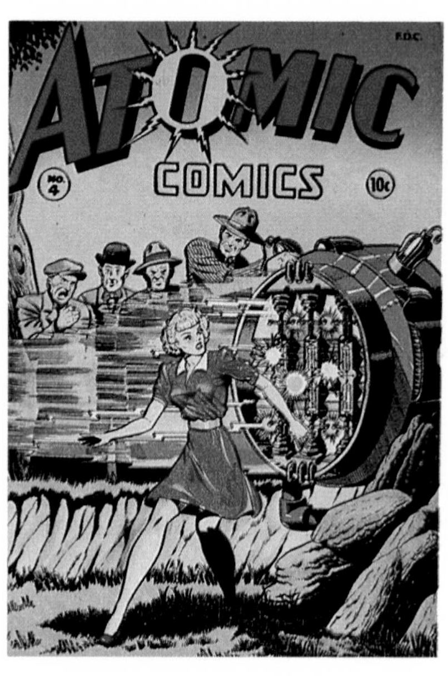

Atomic Comics #4, 1946. Matt Baker cover art. © Green Publ. Co.

The Blue Beetle #2, 1940. © FOX

Bob Colt #1, 1950. © FAW

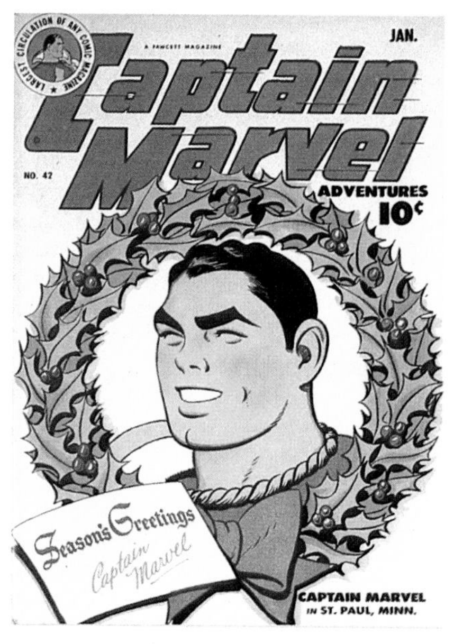

Captain Marvel Adventures #42, 1945. © FAW

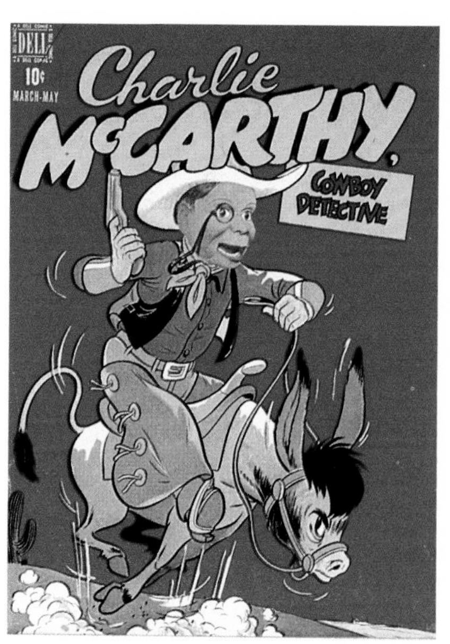

Charlie McCarthy #1, 1949. © Edger Bergen

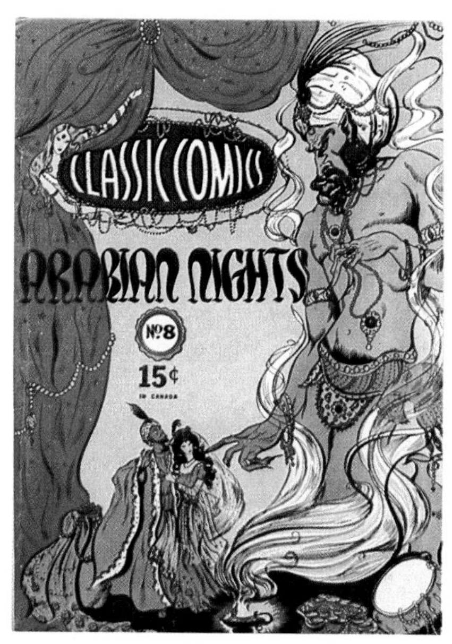

Classic Comics #8(HRN 20), 1944. © GIL

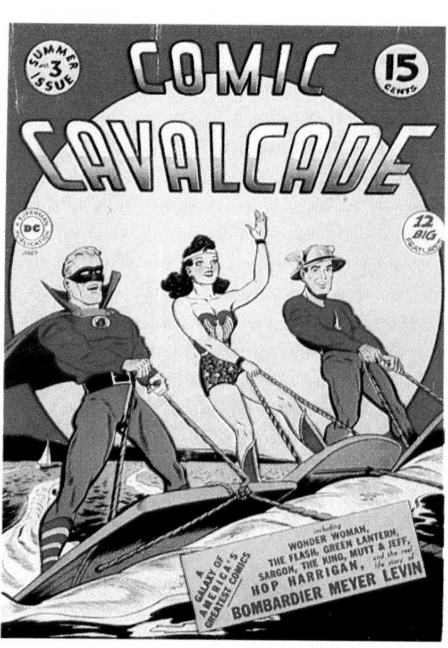

Comic Cavalcade #3, 1943. © DC

Detective Comics #24, 1939. © DC

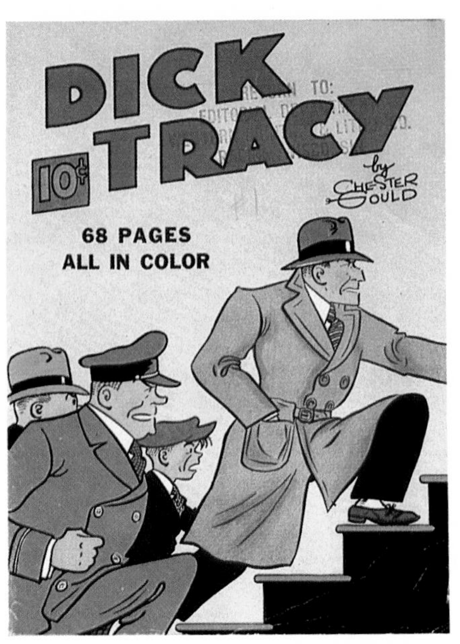

Dick Tracy #1 (Four Color), 1939. © Chicago Tribune

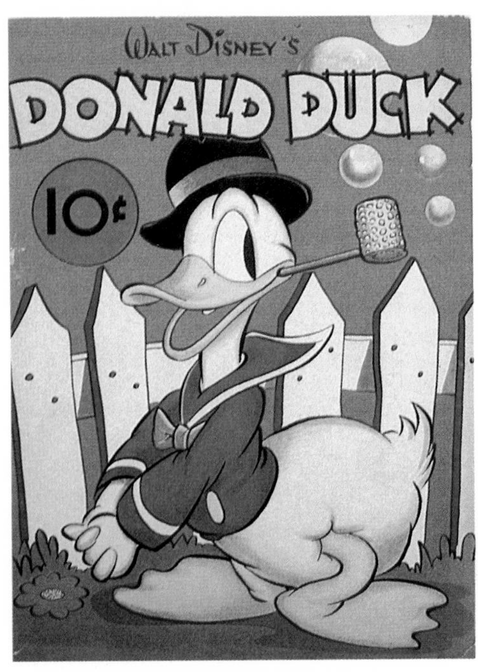

Donald Duck nn, 1938. The 1st Donald Duck & Walt Disney comic book. © WDC

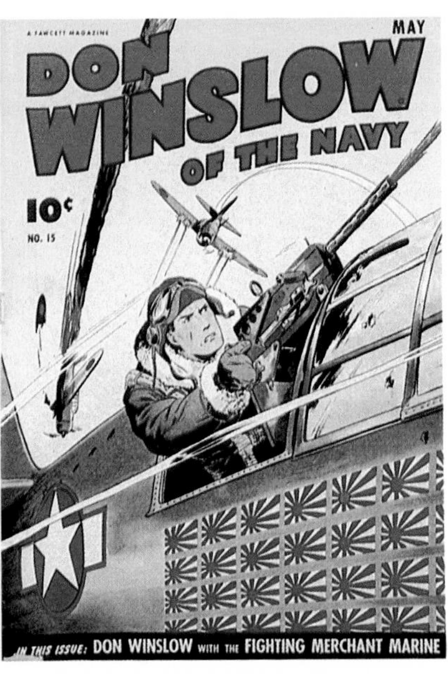

Don Winslow #15, 1944. © FAW

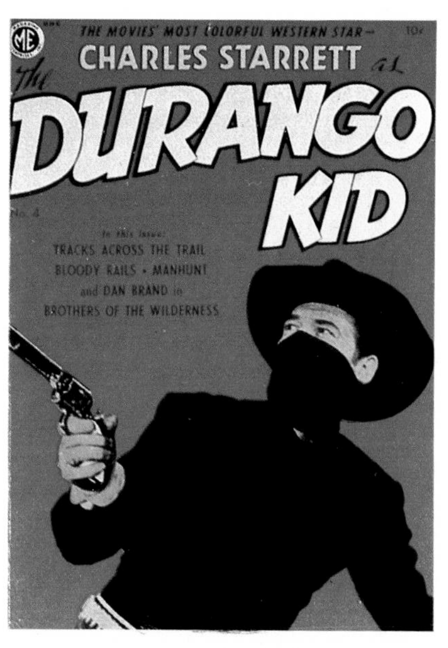

The Durango Kid #4, 1950. © ME

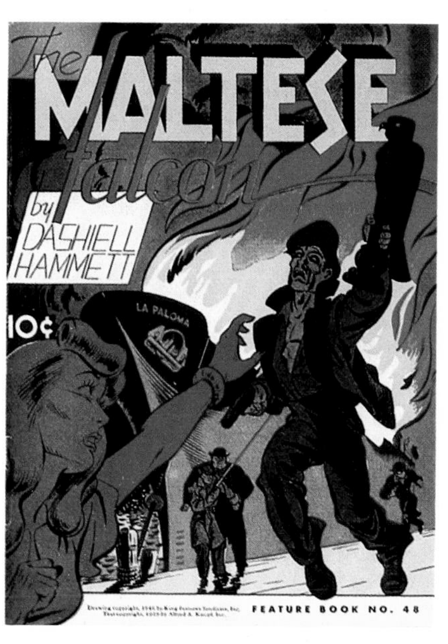

Feature Book #48, 1946. © King

Feature Comics #85, 1945. © QUA

Flash Comics #9, 1940. © DC

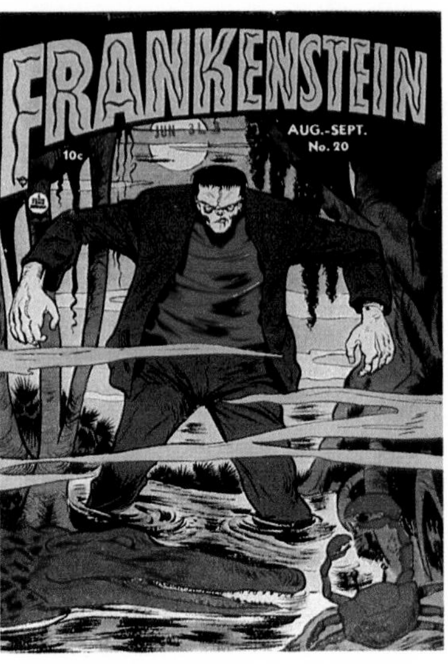

Above: Frankenstein #20, 1952. © PRIZE

Left: 40 Big Pages of Mickey Mouse #945, 1936, © WDC

Funny Pages #36, 1940. Mad Ming cover. © CEN

The Ghost Rider #6, 1951. © ME

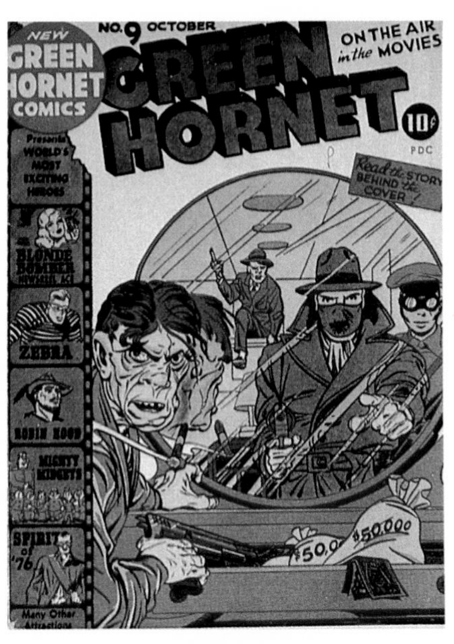

Green Hornet #9, 1942. © Green Hornet

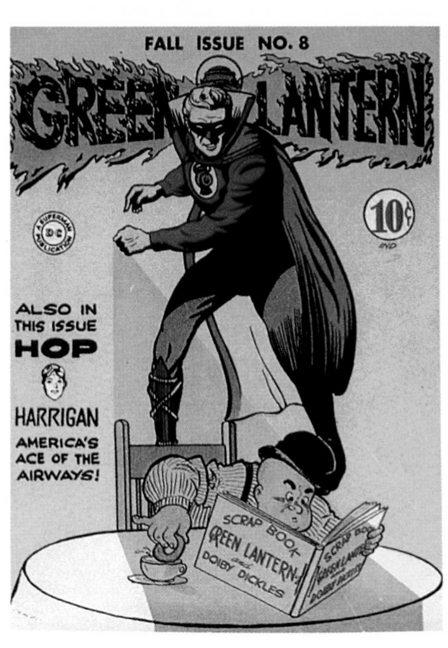

Green Lantern #8, 1943. © DC

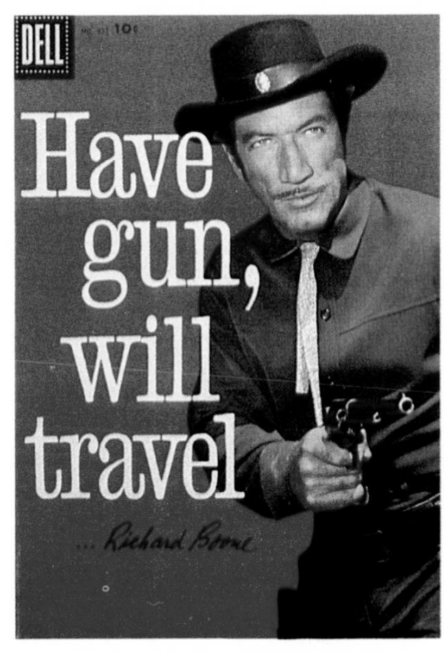

Have Gun, Will Travel Four Color #931, 1958. © CBS

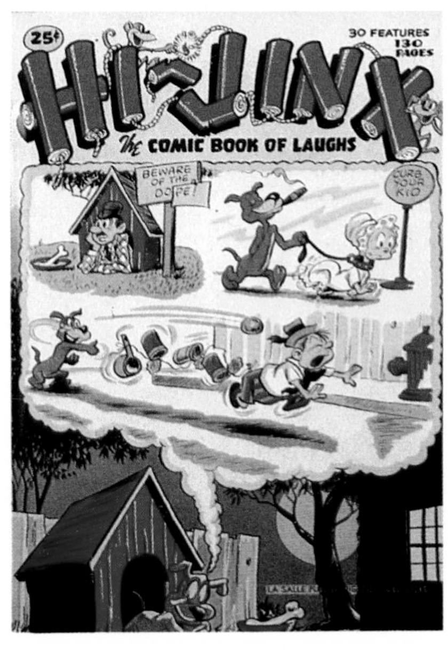

Hi-Jinx Annual, 1940s. © ACG

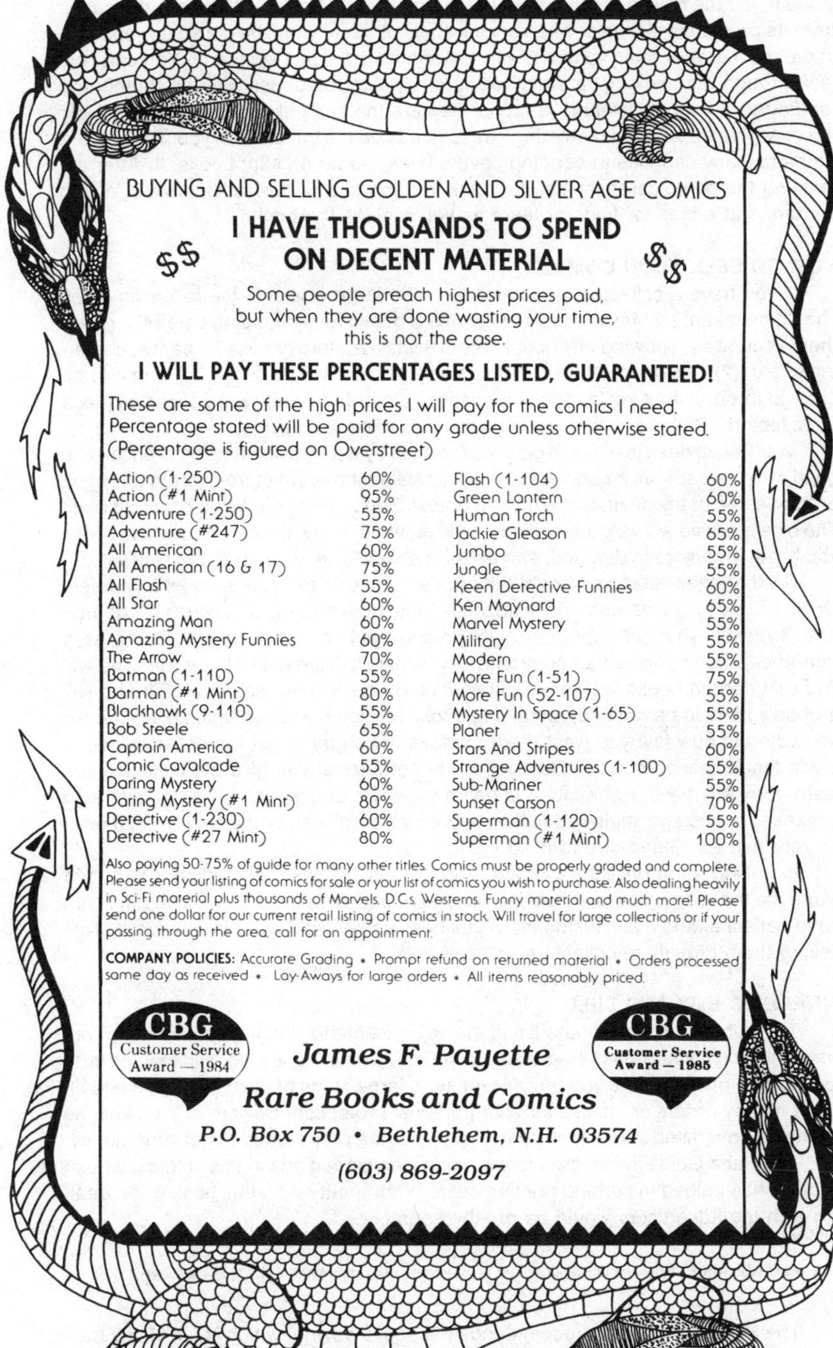

BUYING AND SELLING GOLDEN AND SILVER AGE COMICS
I HAVE THOUSANDS TO SPEND ON DECENT MATERIAL
$$
$$
Some people preach highest prices paid, but when they are done wasting your time, this is not the case.
I WILL PAY THESE PERCENTAGES LISTED, GUARANTEED!
These are some of the high prices I will pay for the comics I need. Percentage stated will be paid for any grade unless otherwise stated. (Percentage is figured on Overstreet)
Action (1-250) 60%
Action (#1 Mint) 95%
Adventure (1-250) 55%
Adventure (#247) 75%
All American 60%
All American (16 & 17) 75%
All Flash 55%
All Star 60%
Amazing Man 60%
Amazing Mystery Funnies 60%
The Arrow 70%
Batman (1-110) 55%
Batman (#1 Mint) 80%
Blackhawk (9-110) 55%
Bob Steele 65%
Captain America 60%
Comic Cavalcade 55%
Daring Mystery 60%
Daring Mystery (#1 Mint) 80%
Detective (1-230) 60%
Detective (#27 Mint) 80%
Flash (1-104) 60%
Green Lantern 60%
Human Torch 55%
Jackie Gleason 65%
Jumbo 55%
Jungle 55%
Keen Detective Funnies 60%
Ken Maynard 65%
Marvel Mystery 55%
Military 55%
Modern 55%
More Fun (1-51) 75%
More Fun (52-107) 55%
Mystery In Space (1-65) 55%
Planet 55%
Stars And Stripes 60%
Strange Adventures (1-100) 55%
Sub-Mariner 55%
Sunset Carson 70%
Superman (1-120) 55%
Superman (#1 Mint) 100%
Also paying 50-75% of guide for many other titles. Comics must be properly graded and complete. Please send your listing of comics for sale or your list of comics you wish to purchase. Also dealing heavily in Sci-Fi material plus thousands of Marvels. D.C.s. Westerns. Funny material and much more! Please send one dollar for our current retail listing of comics in stock. Will travel for large collections or if your passing through the area. call for an appointment.
COMPANY POLICIES: Accurate Grading * Prompt refund on returned material * Orders processed same day as received * Lay-Aways for large orders * All items reasonably priced.
CBG Customer Service Award — 1984
CBG Customer Service Award — 1985
James F. Payette
Rare Books and Comics
P.O. Box 750 • Bethlehem, N.H. 03574
(603) 869-2097

vided to aid the novice in the proper handling of comic books: 1. Remove the comic from its protective sleeve or bag very carefully. 2. Gently lay the comic (un-opened) in the palm of your hand so that it will stay relatively flat and secure. 3. You can now leaf through the book by carefully rolling or flipping the pages with the thumb and forefinger of your other hand. Caution: Be sure the book always remains relatively flat or slightly rolled. Avoid creating stress points on the covers with your fingers and be particularly cautious in bending covers back too far on Mint books. 4. After examining the book, carefully insert it back into the bag or protective sleeve. Watch corners and edges for folds or tears as you replace the book.

HOW TO SELL YOUR COMICS

If you have a collection of comics for sale, large or small, the following steps should be taken. (1) Make a detailed list of the books for sale, being careful to grade them accurately, showing any noticeable defects; i.e., torn or missing pages, centerfolds, etc. (2) Decide whether to sell or trade wholesale to a dealer all in one lump or to go through the long laborious process of advertising and selling piece by piece to collectors. Both have their advantages and disadvantages.

In selling to dealers, you will get the best price by letting everything go at once—the good with the bad—all for one price. Simply select names either from ads in this book or from some of the adzines mentioned below. Send them your list and ask for bids. The bids received will vary depending on the demand, rarity and condition of the books you have. The more in demand, and better the condition, the higher the bids will be.

On the other hand, you could become a "dealer" and sell the books yourself. Order a copy of one or more of the adzines. Take note how most dealers lay out their ads. Type up your ad copy, carefully pricing each book (using the Guide as a reference). Send finished ad copy with payment to adzine editor to be run. You will find that certain books will sell at once while others will not sell at all. The ad will probably have to be retyped, remaining books repriced, and run again. Price books according to how fast you want them to move. If you try to get top dollar, expect a much longer period of time. Otherwise, the better deal you give the collector, the faster they will move. Remember, in being your own dealer, you will have overhead expenses in postage, mailing supplies and advertising cost. Some books might even be returned for refund due to misgrading, etc.

In selling all at once to a dealer, you get instant cash, immediate profit, and eliminate the long process of running several ads to dispose of the books; but if you have patience, and a small amount of business sense, you could realize more profit selling them directly to collectors yourself.

WHERE TO BUY AND SELL

Throughout this book you will find the advertisements of many reputable dealers who sell back-issue comics magazines. If you are an inexperienced collector, be sure to compare prices before you buy. Never send large sums of cash through the mail. Send money orders or checks for your personal protection. Beware of bargains, as the items advertised sometimes do not exist, but are only a fraud to get your money.

The Price Guide is indebted to everyone who placed ads in this volume, whose support has helped in curbing printing costs. Your mentioning this book when dealing with the advertisers would be greatly appreciated.

THE BUYERS GUIDE, Krause Publications, 700 E. State St., Iola, WI 54997. PH: (715) 445-2214

The Price Guide highly recommends the above adzine, which is full of ads buying and selling comics, pulps, radio tapes, premiums, toys and other related items. You can also place ads to buy or sell your comics in the above publication.

COMIC BOOK MAIL ORDER SERVICES

The following offer a mail order service on new comic books. Write for rates and details:

COLLECTOR'S CHOICE, 3405 Keith St., Cleveland, TN 37311

THE COMIC SOURCE, Bruce B. Brittain, P.O. Box 863605, Plano, TX 75086-3605

DOUG SULIPA'S COMIC WORLD, 315 Ellice Ave., Winnipeg, Man., Canada R3B 1X7

FANTACO ENTERPRISES, INC., 21 Central Ave., Albany, NY 12210-1391. PH: (518) 463-1400.

FRIENDLY FRANK'S Distribution, Inc., 3990 Broadway, Gary IN 46408-2705 (219)884-5052 or 884-5053
1025 North Vigo, Gary, IN 46403

GEPPI'S SUBSCRIPTION SERVICE, 1720 Belmont Ave., Bay-C, Baltimore, MD 21207

HEROES AREN'T HARD TO FIND, 1214 Thomas Ave., Charlotte, NC 28205

PRESIDENTIAL COMIC BOOK SERVICE, P. O. Box 41, Scarsdale, NY 10583

STYX COMIC SERVICE, P. O. Box 3791, Station B, Winnipeg, Manitoba, Can. R2W 3R6

LEE TENNANT Ent.—6963 W. 111th St., P.O. Box 296, Worth, IL 60482 (312)448-2938

WESTFIELD COMICS, 8608 University Green, P.O. Box 470, Middleton, WI 53562 (608)836-1945

COMIC BOOK CONVENTIONS

As is the case with most other aspects of comic collecting, comic book conventions, or cons as they are referred to, were originally conceived as the comic-book counterpart to science-fiction fandom conventions. There were many attempts to form successful national cons prior to the time of the first one that materialized, but they were all stillborn. It is interesting that after only three relatively organized years of existence, the first comic con was held. Of course, its magnitude was nowhere near as large as most established cons held today.

What is a comic con? As might be expected, there are comic books to be found at these gatherings. Dealers, collectors, fans, whatever they call themselves can be found trading, selling, and buying the adventures of their favorite characters for hours on end. Additionally if at all possible, cons have guests of honor, usually professionals in the field of comic art, either writers, artists, or editors. The committees put together panels for the con attendees where the assembled pros talk about certain areas of comics, most of the time fielding questions from the assembled audience. At cons one can usually find displays of various and sundry things, usually original art. There might be radio listening rooms; there is most certainly a daily showing of different movies, usually science-fiction or horror type. Of course there is always the chance to get together with friends at cons and just talk about comics; one also has a good opportunity to make new friends who have similar interests and with whom one can correspond after the con.

It is difficult to describe accurately what goes on at a con. The best way to find out is to go to one or more if you can.

The addresses below are those currently available for conventions to be held in the upcoming year. Unfortunately, addresses for certain major conventions are unavailable as this list is being compiled. Once again, the best way to keep abreast of conventions is through the various adzines. Please remember when writing for convention information to include a self-addressed, stamped envelope for reply. Most conventions are non-profit, so they appreciate the help. Here is the list:

COMIC BOOK CONVENTIONS FOR 1988

(Note: All convention listings must be submitted to us by December 1 of each year)

ARIZONA COMIC DEALER NETWORK—P.O. Box 28283, Tempe, AZ 85283. PH: (602) 838-3629. News of conventions in the state.

ATLANTA FANTASY FAIR XIV, June 24-26, 1988, Atlanta Hilton and Towers, Atlanta, GA. Info: Atlanta Fantasy Fair, 482 Gardner Rd., Stockbridge, GA 30281. PH: (404) 961-2347.

ATLANTA SPRING COMICS FAIR II, (Mar., 5-6, 1988), Radisson Inn, I-75 & Howell Mill Rd., Atlanta, GA. Info: The Atlanta Spring Comics Fair, c/o The Atlanta Fantasy Fair, 482 Gardner Rd., Stockbridge, GA 30281. PH: (404) 961-2347.

CAROLINA CON VII—Sponsored by The Carolina Pictorial Fiction Assn., Greenville, SC. Send SASE to S. Haynie, Rt. 6, Box 307, Easley, SC 29640

CHATTANOOGA COMIC CON, Collector's Choice, 3405 Keith St., Cleveland, TN 37311. Held in Spring and Fall each year.

CHICAGO COMICON—Larry Charet, 1219-A West Devon Ave., Chicago, IL 60660. Phone (312) 274-1832.

CHICAGO-MONTHLY MINI CON—Write Larry Charet, 1219-A West Devon Ave., Chicago, IL 60660.

CHILDHOOD TREASURES SHOW AND CONVENTION, July 22-24, 1988, Dallas, TX. Write: Don Maris, Box 111266, Arlington, TX 76007. Phone (817)261-8745 before 10pm Central Time.

CREATION CON—145 Jericho Turnpike, Mineola, NY 11501. Phone (516) 746-9626. Holds major conventions in the following cities: Atlanta, Boston, Cincinnati, Cleveland, Detroit, London, Los Angeles, Philadelphia, Rochester, San Francisco, and Washington, D.C. Write or call for details.

DALLAS FANTASY FAIR, March 11-13, 1988, Marriott Park Central, 7750 I-635 at Coit Rd., July 1-3, 1988, Sheraton Park Central, I-635 at Coit Rd., Nov. 25-27, 1988, Marriott Park Central, 7750 I-635 at Coit Rd. (These are 1988 Bulldog Prod. Conventions). For info: Larry Lankford (214) 349-3367.

DETROIT AREA COMIC BOOK/BASEBALL CARD SHOWS. Held every 2-3 weeks in Royal Oak and Livonia Mich., write: Michael Goldman, Suite 231, 19827 W. 12 Mile Rd., Southfield, MI 48076. PH: (313) 350-2633.

EL PASO FANTASY FESTIVAL—c/o Rita's Fantasy Shop, No. 34 Sunrise Center, El Paso, TX 79904. PH: (915) 757-1143. Late July-Early August.

FANTACON MEGA-SHOW, Sept. 10,11, 1988, The Governor Nelson A. Rockefeller Empire State Plaza Convention Center in Albany, N.Y. for info: Tom Skulan, Convention Chairman, FantaCon, 21 Central Ave., Albany, NY 12210-1391. Please send SASE with inquiry or call (518) 463-1400.

ISLAND NOSTALGIA COMIC BOOK/BASEBALL CARD SHOWS, Hauppauge, N.Y.-Holiday Inn off L.I.E. exit 55, 1740 Express Drive South, Hauppauge, N.Y., 6-7 p.m. daily. For more info call Dennis (516) 724-7422.

KANSAS CITY MINI-CON—c/o Kansas City Comic Book Club, 136 East Longfellow, Kansas City, MO 64119. Three times a year.

LONG ISLAND COMIC BOOK & COLLECTOR'S MARKET CONVENTION—(Held monthly). Rockville Centre Holiday Inn, 173 Sunrise Hwy., Long Island, NY. For info: Cosmic Comics & Books of Rockville Centre, 139 N. Park Ave., Rockville Centre, NY 11570. (516) 763-1133.

LOS ANGELES COMIC BOOK & SCIENCE FICTION CONVENTION, Bruce Schwartz, 1802 West Olive Ave., Burbank, CA 91506. Has monthly shows. PH: (818) 954-8432.

MICHIANA COMICON, April 4 & Oct. 10, 1987. Write Jim Rossow, 53100 Poppy Road, South Bend, IN 46628.

MOBI-CON, Howard Johnson's Motor Lodge, 3132 Government Blvd. (US 90 at I-65) June, 10-12, 1988. For information: P.O. Box 161257, Mobile, AL 36616. (205) 661-4060.

MO-KAN COMIC FESTIVAL—c/o Kansas City Comic Book Club, 136 East Longfellow, Kansas City, MO 64119. Once a year.

NEWCON '88—Don Phelps, P. O. Box 85, Cohasset, MA 02025.

SAN DIEGO COMIC-CON—Box 17066, San Diego, CA 92117. July-Aug., 1988.

THE SAN FERNANDO VALLEY COMIC BOOK CONVENTION, held up to 9 times yearly at the Los Angeles Science Fantasy Society, 11513 Burbank Blvd., North Hollywood, CA. Write: Rob Gustavson, 11684 Ventura Bl., No. 335, Studio City, CA 91604. Phone (1-818-792-5667 or 1-213-426-0393).

SEATTLE CENTER CON, Apr, July, 1988, Box 2043, Kirkland, Wash, 98033. Phone (206) 822-5709 or 827-5129.

SEATTLE QUEST NORTHWEST, Seattle, Wash. Write: Ron Church or Steve Sibra, P.O. Box 82676, Kenmore, WA 98028.

THE SUNDAY FUNNIES, Will Murray, 334 E. Squantum St., Quincy, MA 02I71. Phone (617)328-5224.

COMIC BOOK CLUBS

ALABAMA—The Mobile Panelology Assoc. meets 1st Monday of each month at 2301 Airport Blvd. (Back Bldg. Mobile Recreation Dept.), Mobile, Ala.; 7:00 p.m. to 9:00 p.m. Club business address: 161 West Grant St., Chickasaw, AL 36611. (205) 456-4514. Founded 1973.

ARIZONA—Arizona Comic Dealer Network, P. O. Box 28283, Tempe, AZ 85283. Phone (602) 838-3629. Clearinghouse for dealer and fan activities.

CALIFORNIA—The California Comic Book Collectors Club, c/o Matt Ornbaun, 23601 Hwy. 128, Yorkville, CA 95494. Send 50 cents and SASE for information and enrollment.

Alpha Omega—c/o Donald Ensign, 6011 Agnes Ave., Temple City, CA 91780. Puts out bi-monthly pub.

USC Comics Club, University of Southern California Intramural Recreation Dept., Heritage Hall 103, University Park, Los Angeles, CA 90089-0601. PH 213-743-5127.

GEORGIA—The Defenders of Dreams, Inc., c/o Will Rose, 3121 Shady Grove Rd., Carrollton, GA 30117. (Publishes its own clubzine *Excalibur* bi-monthly and a pulpzine *Real Pulp Adventures*.) Send business size SASE for details.

IDAHO—Mr. O's Comic Book Collectors Club, S. 1200 Agate Rd., Coeur D'Alene, Idaho 83814.

MASSACHUSETTS—The Gloo Club, c/o Ron Holmes, 140 Summit St., New Bedford, Mass. 02740. Write for details and send SASE. (This club is both national and international.)

MISSOURI—The Kansas City Comic Book Club meets the last Sunday of each month at 75th & Quivera (Sun Savings Building), Shawnee, Kansas; 1:30-3:30 p.m. Club business address: 136 East Longfellow, Kansas City, MO 64119. Puts on three conventions a year, publishes monthly newsletter, and gives away free comics to first 20 members that attend meetings. Annual dues $5.00.

OKLAHOMA—Fandom International. For information, write to: Dan DePalma, 5823 E. 22 St., Tulsa, OK 74114. Phone 834-8035.

TEXAS—The Gulf Coast Comic Collectors' Society (GCCCS). Write to GCCCS Headquarters, c/o Mike Mills, 4318 Iroquois St., Houston, TX 77504.

THE HISTORY OF COMICS FANDOM

At this time it is possible to discern two distinct and largely unrelated movements in the history of Comics Fandom. The first of these movements began about 1953 as a response to the then-popular, trend-setting EC lines of comics. The first true comics fanzines of this movement were short-lived. Bhob Stewart's EC FAN BULLETIN was a hectographed newsletter that ran two issues about six months apart; and Jimmy Taurasi's FANTASY COMICS, a newsletter devoted to all science-fiction comics of the period, was a monthly that ran for about six months. These were followed by other newsletters, such as Mike May's EC FAN JOURNAL, and George Jennings' EC WORLD PRESS. EC fanzines of a wider and more critical scope appeared somewhat later. Two of the finest were POTRZEBIE, the product of a number of fans, and Ron Parker's HOOHAH. Gauging from the response that POTRZEBIE received from a plug in an EC letter column, Ted White estimated the average age of EC fans to lie in the range of 9 to 13, while many EC fans were in their mid-teens. This fact was taken as discouraging to many of the faneds, who had hoped to reach an older audience. Consequently, many of them gave up their efforts in behalf of Comics Fandom, especially with the demise of the EC groups, and turned their attention to science-fiction fandom with its longer tradition and older membership. While the flourish of fan activity in response to the EC comics was certainly noteworthy, it is fair to say that it never developed into a full-fledged, independent, and self-sustaining movement.

The second comics fan movement began in 1960. It was largely a response to (though it later became a stimulus for) the Second Heroic Age of Comics. Most fan historians date the Second Heroic Age from the appearance of the new FLASH comics magazine (numbered 105 and dated February 1959). The letter departments of Julius Schwartz (editor at National Periodicals), and later those of Stan Lee (Marvel Group) and Bill Harris (Gold Key) were most influential in bringing comics readers into Fandom. Beyond question, it was the reappearance of the costumed hero that sparked the comics fan movement of the sixties. Sparks were lit among some science-fiction fans first, when experienced fan writers, who were part of an established tradition, produced the first in a series of articles on the comics of the forties—ALL IN COLOR FOR A DIME. The series was introduced in XERO No. 1 (September 1960), a general fanzine for science-fiction fandom edited and published by Dick Lupoff.

Meanwhile, outside science-fiction fandom, Jerry Bails and Roy Thomas, two strictly comics fans of long-standing, conceived the first true comics fanzine in response to the Second Heroic Age. The fanzine, ALTER EGO, appeared in March 1961. The first several issues were widely circulated among comics fans, and were to influence profoundly the comics fan movement to follow. Unlike the earlier EC fan movement, this new movement attracted many fans in their twenties and thirties. A number of these older fans had been active collectors for years but had been largely unknown to each other. Joined by scores of new, younger fans, this group formed the nucleus of a new movement that is still growing and shows every indication of being self-sustaining. Although it has borrowed a few of the more appropriate terms coined by science-fiction fans, Comics Fandom of the Sixties was an independent if fledging movement, without, in most cases, the advantages and disadvantages of a longer tradition. What Comics Fandom did derive from science-fiction fandom it did so thanks largely to the fanzines produced by so-called double fans. The most notable of this type is COMIC ART, edited and published by Don and Maggie Thompson.

HOW TO SELECT FANZINES

In the early 1960s, only a few comic fanzines were being published. A fan could easily afford to subscribe to them all. Today, the situation has radically changed, and it has become something of a problem to decide which fanzines to order.

Fanzines are not all of equal quality or general interest. Even different issues of the same fanzine may vary significantly. To locate issues that will be of interest to you, learn to look for the names of outstanding amateur artists, writers, and editors, and consult fanzine review columns. Although you may not always agree with the judgements of the reviewers, you will find these reviews to be a valuable source of information about the content and quality of the current fanzines.

When ordering a fanzine, remember that print runs are small and the issue you may want may be out of print (OP). Ordinarily in this case, you will receive the next issue. Because of irregular publishing schedules that nearly all fanzines must, of necessity, observe, allow up to 90 days or more for your copy to reach you. It is common courtesy when addressing an inquiry to an ama-publisher to enclose a self-addressed, stamped envelope.

FAN PUBLICATIONS OF INTEREST

NOTE: We must be notified each year by December 1 for listing to be included, due to changes of address, etc. Please send sample copy.

AFTERMATH-Gulf Coast Comics, P.O. Box 310, Winnie, TX 77665. For science fiction fans. $2.50 postpaid. Back issues & reprints available.

ALPHA OMEGA, for Christian artists and fans, bi-mo. $3.75 for 3 issues. For info: Donald Ensign, 6011 Agnes Ave., Temple City, CA 91780.

AMAZING HEROES—4359 Cornell Rd., Agoura, CA 91301. Sample copy $2.50.

ANNIE PEOPLE, Jon Merrill, P.O. Box 431, Cedar Knolls, NJ 07927. Bi-monthly Little Orphan Annie newsletter.

THE CLASSICS JOURNAL—Mike Strauss, 26 Madera, San Carlos, CA 94070.

COMICANA, 3, Boolimba Cres., Narrabundah, A.C.T., 2604 Australia. Covers all aspects of comic books; includes a special Australian section.

COMIC ART AND FANTASY—Stephen Barrington, 161 West Grant Street, Chickasaw, AL 36611. Published quarterly for comics, gaming & sf fans. $1.00 for two issues.

THE COMIC CORNER—Gulf Coast Comic Collectors' Society (GCCCS). For sample copy and subscription info, write: The Comic Corner, c/o Mike Mills, 4318 Iroquois St., Pasadena, TX 77504.

THE COMICS FORUM—Kansas City Comic Book Club, 136, East Longfellow, Kansas City, MO 64119. (News, reviews, interviews, and classifieds.)

COMICS INTERVIEW—c/o Fictioneer Books Ltd., #1 Screamer Mtn., Clayton, GA 30525.

THE COMICS JOURNAL—4359 Cornell Rd., Agoura, CA 91301. Sample copy $3.50.

COMIX EMPORIUM NEWSLETTER—P.O. Box 3742, Silver Spring, MD 20901. Pub. 8 times a year, w/Marvel, DC & major independents news. Sample free.

THE COMPLETE EC LIBRARY—Russ Cochran, P. O. Box 437, West Plains, MO 65775. (A must for all EC collectors. Reprinting of the complete EC line is planned. Write for details.)

THE DUCKBURG TIMES—Irregular Barks/Disney fanzine. Sample copy $1.50. Dana Gabbard, 3010 Wilshire Blvd., #362, Los Angeles, CA 90010.

FANDOM JOURNAL—Kevin Collier, 18129 136th Ave. Apt. B, Nunica, MI 49448. (Monthly newspaper on small press comics and zines. 25 cent postpaid for sample.)

FANTACO'S CHRONICLES SERIES, Roger Green, Editor, FantaCo Enterprises Inc., 21 Central Ave., Albany, NY 12210-1391. Sample copy $3.00.

FANTASY ADVERTISER—Martin Skidmore, 25 Cornleaze, Withywood, Bristol, BS13 7SG, England.

FAWCETT COLLECTORS OF AMERICA & ME, TOO!—Bill & Teresa Harper, 301 E. Buena Vista Ave., North Augusta, SC 29841.

THE GLOO CLUB NEWS—Ron Holmes, 140 Summit St., New Bedford, Mass. 02740. Pub. 6 times/year. Write for details.

HELLFIRE—c/o David & Paul Roach, 36 Lakeside Dr., Lakeside Cardiff, S-Glam Wales, U.K., CF2 6DF. Has articles on American, British, European comics.

KATY KEENE NEWSLETTER—QUARTERLY—Craig Leavitt, 1125 11th St., Modesto, CA 95354. ($6 yr. subscription)

NEMO: THE CLASSIC COMICS LIBRARY—4359 Cornell Rd., Agoura, CA 91301. Reprints classic strips with articles.

THE STANLEY STEAMER, Jon Merrill, P.O. Box 431, Cedar Knolls, NJ 07927. Bi-monthly Little Lulu fanzine.

COLLECTING STRIPS

Collecting newspaper comic strips is somewhat different than collecting magazines, although it can be equally satisfying.

Obviously, most strip collectors begin by clipping strips from their local paper, but many soon branch out to strips carried in out-of-town papers. Naturally this can become more expensive and it is often frustrating, because it is easy to miss editions of out-of-town papers. Consequently, most strip collectors work out trade agreements with collectors in other cities in order to get an uninterrupted supply of the strips they want. This usually necessitates saving local strips to be used for trade purposes only.

Back issues of strips dating back several decades are also available from time to time from dealers. The prices per panel vary greatly depending on the age, condition, and demand for the strip. When the original strips are unavailable, it is sometimes possible to get photostatic copies from collectors, libraries, or newspaper morgues.

COLLECTING ORIGINAL ART

In addition to magazines and strips, some enthusiasts also collect the original art for the comics. These black and white, inked drawings are usually done on illustration paper at about 30 per cent up (i.e., 30 per cent larger than the original printed panels). Because original art is a one-of-a-kind article, it is highly prized and often difficult to obtain.

Interest in original comic art has increased tremendously in the past several years. Many companies now return the originals to the artists who have in turn offered them for sale, usually at cons but sometimes through agents and dealers. As with any other area of collecting, rarity and demand governs value. Although the masters' works bring fine art prices, most art is available at moderate prices. Comic strips are the most popular facet with collectors, followed by comic book art. Once scarce, current and older comic book art has surfaced within the last few years. In 1974 several original painted covers of vintage comic books and coloring books turned up from Dell, Gold Key, Whitman, and Classic Comics.

The following are sources for original art:

Tony Dispoto
Comic Art Showcase
P. O. Box 425
Lodi, NJ 07644

Russ Cochran
P. O. Box 437
West Plains, MO 65775

The Cartoon Museum
Jim Ivey
4310 S. Semoran
Orlando, FL 32807

Cartoon Carnival
2 Rabbit Run
Wallingford, PA 19086
PH: 215-566-1292

Graphic Collectibles
Mitch Itkowitz
174 Jewett Ave.
Staten Island, NY 10302

Museum Graphics
Jerome K. Muller
Box 743
Costa Mesa, CA 92627

Artman
Bruce Bergstrom
1620 Valley St.
Fort Lee, NJ 07024

TRH Gallery (Tom Hervitz)
1090 N. Palm Canyon Dr. #B
Palm Springs, CA 92262
PH: 1-619-320-9599

Steve Herrington
30 W. 70th St.
New York, NY 10023

The Comic Character Shop
Old Firehouse Antiques
110 Alaskan Way South
Seattle, WA 98104
PH: (206) 283-0532

Collector's Paradise Gallery
Harry Kleiman
P. O. Box 1540
Studio City, CA 91604

San Mateo Original Art
306 Baldwin Ave.
San Mateo, CA 94401
PH: (415) 344-1536

Carsten Lagua
Havensteinstr. 54
1000 Berlin 46
West Germany

Original Artwork
Martin Hilland
AM Josefshaus 6
4040 Neuss 21
West Germany

Richard Halegua
Comic Art & Graffix
Gallery
2033 Madison Rd.
Cincinnati, OH 45208
(513) 321-4208

A Chronology of the Development of THE AMERICAN COMIC BOOK

By M. Thomas Inge

Precursors: The facsimile newspaper strip reprint collections constitute the earliest "comic books." The first of these was a collection of Richard Outcault's **Yellow Kid** from the Hearst **New York American** in March 1897. Commercial and promotional reprint collections, usually in cardboard covers, appeared through the 1920s and featured such newspaper strips as **Mutt and Jeff, Foxy Grandpa, Buster Brown,** and **Barney Google**. During 1922 a reprint magazine, **Comic Monthly**, appeared with each issue devoted to a separate strip, and in 1929 George Delacorte published 13 issues of **The Funnies** in tabloid format with original comic pages in color, becoming the first four-color comic newsstand publication.

1933: The Ledger syndicate published a small broadside of their Sunday comics on 7" by 9" plates. Employees of Eastern Color Printing Company in New York, sales manager Harry I. Wildenberg and salesman Max C. Gaines, saw it and figured that two such plates would fit a tabloid page, which would produce a book about 7½" x 10" when folded. Thus 10,000 copies of **Funnies on Parade**, containing 32 pages of Sunday newspaper reprints, was published for Proctor and Gamble to be given away as premiums. Some of the strips included were: **Joe Palooka, Mutt and Jeff, Hairbreadth Harry,** and **Reg'lar Fellas**. M. C. Gaines was very impressed with this book and convinced Eastern Color that he could sell a lot of them to such big advertisers as Milk-O-Malt, Wheatena, Kinney Shoe Stores, and others to be used as premiums and radio give-aways. So, Eastern Color printed **Famous Funnies: A Carnival of Comics**, and then **Century of Comics**, both as before, containing Sunday newspaper reprints. Mr. Gaines sold these books in quantities of 100,000 to 250,000.

1934: The give-away comics were so successful that Mr. Gaines believed that youngsters would buy comic books for ten cents like the "Big Little Books" coming out at that time. So, early in 1934, Eastern Color ran off 35,000 copies of **Famous Funnies, Series 1**, 64 pages of reprints for Dell Publishing Company to be sold for ten cents in chain stores. Selling out promptly on the stands, Eastern Color, in May 1934, issued **Famous Funnies** No. 1 (dated July 1934) which became, with issue No. 2 in July, the first monthly comic magazine. The title continued for over 20 years through 218 issues, reaching a circulation peak of nearly one million copies. At the same time, Mr. Gaines went to the sponsors of Percy Crosby's **Skippy**, who was on the radio, and convinced them to put out a Skippy book, advertise it on the air, and give away a free copy to anyone who bought a tube of Phillip's toothpaste. Thus 500,000 copies of **Skippy's Own Book of Comics** was run off and distributed through drug stores everywhere. This was the first four-color comic book of reprints devoted to a single character.

1935: Major Malcolm Wheeler-Nicholson's National Periodical Publications issued in February a tabloid-sized comic publication called **New Fun**, which became **More Fun** after the sixth issue and converted to the normal comic-book size after issue eight. **More Fun** was the first comic book of a standard size to publish original material and continued publication until 1949. **Mickey Mouse Magazine** began in the summer, to become **Walt Disney's Comics and Stories** in 1940, and combined original material with reprinted newspaper strips in most issues.

1936: In the wake of the success of **Famous Funnies**, other publishers, in conjunction with the major newspaper strip syndicates, inaugurated more reprint comic books: **Popular Comics** (News-Tribune, February), **Tip Top Comics** (United Features, April), **King Comics** (King Features, April), and **The Funnies** (new series, NEA, October). Four issues of **Wow Comics**, from David McKay and Henle Publications, appeared, edited by S. M. Iger and including early art by Will Eisner, Bob Kane, and Alex Raymond. The first non-reprint comic book devoted to a single theme was **Detective Picture Stories** issued in December by The Comics Magazine Company.

1937: The second single-theme title, **Western Picture Stories**, came in February from The Comics Magazine Company, and the third was **Detective Comics**, an offshoot of **More Fun**, which began in March to be published to the present. The book's initials, "D.C.," have long served to refer to National Periodical Publications, which was purchased from Major Nicholson by Harry Donenfeld late this year.

1938: "DC" copped a lion's share of the comic book market with the publication of **Action Comics** No. 1 in June which contained the first appearance of Superman by writer Jerry Siegel and artist Joe Shuster, a discovery of Max C. Gaines. The "man of steel" inaugurated the "Golden Era" in comic book history. Fiction House, a pulp publisher, entered the comic book field in September with **Jumbo Comics**, featuring Sheena, Queen of the Jungle, and appearing in over-sized format for the first eight issues.

1939: The continued success of "DC" was assured in May with the publication of **Detective Comics** No. 27 containing the first episode of Batman by artist Bob Kane and writer Bill Finger. **Superman Comics** appeared in the summer. Also, during the summer, a black and white premium comic titled **Motion Picture Funnies Weekly** was published to be given away at motion picture theatres. The plan was to issue it weekly and to have continued stories so that the kids would come back week after week not to miss an episode. Four issues were planned but only one came out. This book contains the first appearance and origin of the Sub-Mariner by Bill Everett (8 pages) which was later reprinted in **Marvel Comics**. In November, the first issue of **Marvel Comics** came out, featuring the Human Torch by Carl Burgos and the Sub-Mariner reprint with color added.

1940: The April issue of **Detective Comics** No. 38 introduced Robin the Boy Wonder as a sidekick to Batman, thus establishing the "Dynamic Duo" and a major precedent for later costume heroes who would also have boy companions. **Batman Comics** began in the spring. Over 60 different comic book titles were being issued, including **Whiz Comics** begun in February by Fawcett Publications. A creation of writer Bill Parker and artist C. C. Beck, **Whiz's** Captain Marvel was the only superhero ever to surpass Superman in comic book sales. Drawing on their own popular pulp magazine heroes, Street and Smith Publications introduced **Shadow Comics** in March and **Doc Savage Comics** in May. A second trend was established with the summer appearance of the first issue of **All-Star Comics**, which brought several superheroes together in one story and in its third issue that winter would announce the establishment of the Justice Society of America.

1941: Wonder Woman was introduced in the winter issue of **All-Star Comics** No. 8, the creation of psychologist William Moulton Marston and artist Harry Peters. **Captain Marvel Adventures** began this year. By the end of 1941, over 160 titles were being published, including **Captain America** by Jack Kirby and Joe Simon, **Police Comics** with Jack Cole's Plastic Man and later Will Eisner's Spirit, **Military Comics** with Blackhawk by Eisner and Charles Cuidera, **Daredevil Comics** with the original character by Charles Biro, **Air Fighters** with Airboy also by Biro, and **Looney Tunes & Merrie Melodies** with Porky Pig, Bugs Bunny, and Elmer Fudd, reportedly created by Bob Clampett for the Leon Schlesinger Productions animated films and drawn for the comics by Chase Craig. Also, Albert Kanter's Gilberton Company initiated the **Classics Illustrated** series with **The Three Musketeers**.

1942: Crime Does Not Pay by editor Charles Biro and publisher Lev Gleason, devoted to factual accounts of criminals' lives, began a different trend in realistic crime stories. **Wonder Woman** appeared in the summer. John Goldwater's character Archie, drawn by Bob Montana, first published in **Pep Comics**, was given his own magazine **Archie Comics**, which has remained popular over 40 years. The first issue of **Animal Comics** contained Walt Kelly's "Albert Takes the Cake," featuring the new character of Pogo. In mid-1942, the undated Dell Four Color title, No. 9, **Donald Duck Finds Pirate Gold**, appeared with art by Carl Barks and Jack Hannah. Barks, also featured in **Walt Disney's Comics and Stories**, remained the most popular delineator of Donald Duck and later introduced his greatest creation, Uncle Scrooge, in **Christmas on Bear Mountain** (Dell Four Color No. 178). The fantasy work of George Carlson appeared in the first issue of **Jingle Jangle Comics**, one of the most imaginative titles for children ever to be published.

1945: The first issue of **Real Screen Comics** introduced the Fox and the Crow by James F. Davis, and John Stanley began drawing the **Little Lulu** comic book based on a popular feature in the **Saturday Evening Post** by Marjorie Henderson Buell from 1935 to 1944. Bill Woggon's Katy Keene appears in issue No. 5 of **Wilbur Comics** to be followed by appearances in **Laugh, Pep, Suzie** and her own comic book in 1950. The popularity of Dick Briefer's satiric version of the Frankenstein monster, originally drawn for **Prize Comics** in 1941, led to the publication of **Frankenstein Comics** by Prize Publications.

1950: The son of Max C. Gaines, William M. Gaines, who earlier had inherited his father's firm Educational Comics (later Entertaining Comics), began publication of a series of well-written and masterfully drawn titles which would establish a "New Trend" in comics magazines: **Crypt of Terror** (later **Tales from the Crypt**, April), **The Vault of Horror** (April), **The Haunt of Fear** (May), **Weird Science** (May), **Weird Fantasy** (May), **Crime SuspenStories** (October), and **Two-Fisted Tales** (November), the latter stunningly edited by Harvey Kurtzman.

1952: In October "E.C." published the first number of **Mad** under Kurtzman's creative editorship.

1953: All Fawcett titles featuring Captain Marvel were ceased after many years of litigation in the courts during which National Periodical Publications claimed that the super-hero was an infringement on the copyrighted Superman.

1954: The appearance of Fredric Wertham's book **Seduction of the Innocent** in the spring was the culmination of a continuing war against comic books fought by those who believed they corrupted youth and debased culture. The U. S. Senate Subcommittee on Juvenile Delinquency investigated comic books and in response the major publishers banded together in October to create the Comics Code Authority and adopted, in their own words, "the most stringent code in existence for any communications media."

1955: In an effort to avoid the Code, "E.C." launched a "New Direction" series of titles, such as **Impact, Valor, Aces High, Extra, M.D.**, and **Psychoanalysis**, none of which lasted beyond the year. **Mad** was changed into a larger magazine format with issue No. 24 in July to escape the Comics Code entirely.

1956: Beginning with the Flash in **Showcase** No. 4, Julius Schwartz began a popular revival of "DC" superheroes which would lead to the "Silver Age" in comic book history.

1960: After several efforts at new satire magazines (**Trump** and **Humbug**), Harvey Kurtzman, no longer with Gaines, issued in August the first number of another abortive effort, **Help!**, where the early work of underground cartoonists Jay Lynch, Skip Williamson, Gilbert Shelton, and Robert Crumb appeared.

1961: Stan Lee edited in November the first **Fantastic Four**, featuring Mr. Fantastic, the Human Torch, the Thing, and the Invisible Girl, and inaugurated an enormously popular line of titles from Marvel Comics featuring a more contemporary style of superhero.

1962: Lee introduced **The Amazing Spider-Man** in August, with art by Steve Ditko, **The Hulk** in May and **Thor** in August, the last two produced by Dick Ayers and Jack Kirby.

1963: Marvel's **The X-Men**, with art by Jack Kirby, began a successful run in November, but the title would experience a revival and have an even more popular reception in the 1980s.

1965: James Warren issued **Creepy**, a larger black and white comic book, outside Comics Code's control, which emulated the "E.C." horror comic line. Warren's **Eerie** began in September and **Vampirella** in September 1969.

1967: Robert Crumb's **Zap** No. 1 appeared, the first popular underground comic book.

1970: Editor Roy Thomas at Marvel begins **Conan the Barbarian** based on fiction by Robert E. Howard with art by Barry Smith.

1972: The Swamp Thing by Berni Wrightson begins in November from "DC."

1973: In February, "DC" revived the original Captain Marvel with new art by C. C. Beck and reprints in the first issue of **Shazam** and in October **The Shadow** with scripts by Denny O'Neil and art by Mike Kaluta.

1974: "DC" began publication in the spring of a series of over-sized facsimile reprints of the most valued comic books of the past under the general title of "Famous First Editions," beginning with a reprint of **Action** No. 1 and including afterwards **Detective Comics** No. 27, **Sensation Comics** No. 1, **Whiz Comics** No. 2, **Batman** No. 1, **Wonder Woman** No. 1, **All-Star Comics** No. 3, and **Flash Comics** No. 1.

1975: In the first collaborative effort between the two major comic book publishers of the previous decade, Marvel and "DC" produced together an over-sized comic-book version of **MGM's Marvelous Wizard of Oz** in the fall, and then the following year in an unprecedented cross-over produced **Superman vs. the Amazing Spider-Man**, written by Gerry Conway, drawn by Ross Andru, and inked by Dick Giordano.

1976: Frank Brunner's Howard the Duck, who had appeared earlier in Marvel's **Fear** and **Man-Thing**, was given his own book in January, which because of distribution problems became an over-night collector's item. After decades of litigation, Jerry Siegel and Joe Shuster were given financial recompense and recognition by National Periodical Publications for their creation of Superman, after several friends of the team made a public issue of the case.

1977: Stan Lee's **Spider-Man** was given a second birth, fifteen years after his first, through a highly successful newspaper comic strip, which began syndication on January 3 with art by John Romita. This invasion of the comic strip by comic book characters continued with the appearance on June 6 of Marvel's **Howard the Duck**, with story by Steve Gerber and visuals by Gene Colan. In an unusually successful collaborative effort, Marvel began publication of the comic book adaption of the George Lucas film **Star Wars**, with script by Roy Thomas and art by Howard Chaykin, at least three months before the film was released nationally on May 25. The demand was so great that all six issues of **Star Wars** were reprinted at least seven times, and the installments were reprinted in two volumes of an over-sized Marvel Special Edition and a single paperback volume for the book trade.

1978: In an effort to halt declining sales, Warner Communications drastically cut back on the number of "DC" titles and overhauled its distribution process in June. The interest of the visual media in comic book characters reached a new high with the Hulk, Spider-Man, and Doctor Strange, the subjects of television shows; with various projects begun to produce film versions of Flash Gordon, Dick Tracy, Popeye, Conan, The Phantom, and Buck Rogers; and with the movement reaching an outlandish peak of publicity with the release of **Superman** in December. Two significant applications of the comic book format to traditional fiction appeared this year: **A Contract with God and Other Tenement Stories** by Will Eisner and **The Silver Surfer** by Stan Lee and Jack Kirby. Eclipse Enterprises published Paul Gulacy's **Sabre**, the first graphic album produced for the direct sales market, and initiated a policy of paying royalties and granting copyrights to comic book creators.

1979: The Micronauts with art by Michael Golden debuted from Marvel in January.

1980: Publication of the November premier issue of **The New Teen Titans**, with art by George Perez and story by Marv Wolfman, brought back to widespread popularity a title originally published by "DC" in 1966.

1981: The distributor Pacific Comics began publishing titles for direct sales through comic shops with the inaugural issue of Jack Kirby's **Captain Victory and the Galactic Rangers** and offered royalties to artists and writers on the basis of sales. "DC" would do the same for regular newsstand comics in November (with payments retroactive to July 1981), and Marvel followed suit by the end of the year.

1982: The first slick format comic book in regular size appeared, **Marvel Fanfare** No. 1, with a March date. The premier March issue of **Captain Carrot and His Amazing Zoo Crew**, with story by Roy Thomas and art by Scott Shaw, revived the concept of funny animal superheroes of the 1940s.

1983: This year saw more comic book publishers, aside from Marvel and DC, issuing more titles than has existed in the past 40 years, most small independent publishers relying on direct sales, such as Americomics, Capital, Eagle, Eclipse, First, Pacific, and Red Circle, and with Archie, Charlton, and Whitman publishing on a limited scale. Frank Miller's mini-series **Ronin** demonstrated a striking use of sword-play and martial arts typical of Japanese comic book art, and Howard Chaykin's stylish but controversial **American Flagg** appeared with an October date on its first issue.

1985: Ohio State University's Library of Communication and Graphic Arts hosted the first major exhibition devoted to the comic book May 19 through August 2. In what was billed as an irreversible decision, the silver age superheroine Supergirl was killed in the seventh (October) issue of **Crisis on Infinite Earths**, a limited series intended to reorganize and simplify the DC universe on the occasion of the publisher's 50th anniversary.

1986: In recognition of its twenty-fifth anniversary, Marvel began publication of several new ongoing titles comprising Marvel's "New Universe," a self-contained fictional world. DC attracted extensive publicity and media coverage with its revisions of the character of **Superman** by John Byrne and of **Batman** in the **Dark Knight** series by Frank Miller. **Watchmen**, a limited-series graphic novel by Alan Moore and artist Dave Gibbons, began publication with a September issue from DC and Marvel's **The 'Nam**, written by Vietnam verteran Doug Murray and penciled by Michael Golden, began with its December issue. DC issued guidelines in December for labelling their titles as either for mature readers or for readers of all ages; in response, many artists and writers publicly objected or threatened to resign.

1987: Art Spiegelman's **Maus: A Survivor's Tale** was nominated for the National Book Critics Circle Award in biography, the first comic book to be so honored. A celebration of Superman's fiftieth Birthday began with the opening of an exhibition on his history at the Smithsonian's Museum of American History in Washington, D.C., in June.

THE MAN BEHIND THE COVER
L.B. Cole

by Christopher Irons

A rare glimpse of L.B. Cole in his studio.

When I was called upon to do a *short* biographical piece about L.B. Cole, I found that in order to do justice to the man, I would of necessity have to enumerate only the highlights of his truly remarkable career. Here then is the mere essence of this consummate artist's achievements.

He received the coveted Inkpot Award for his contribution to the comics industry at the San Diego Comics Convention in 1981. He was awarded the Prestigious Landseer Society Award for wildlife illustration.

Working in close conjunction with the Professors of Ichthyology at the American Museum Of Natural History, he illustrated the color sections of fish in *The New Book Of Knowledge* and *The Encyclopedia International* by Grolier. He was called upon to paint the cover of *Robins* for the Director of Wildlife Management of the Massachusetts Audubon Society published by Follett. He was the publisher of *World Rod And Gun Magazine* and illustrated all the covers plus a picture-for-framing in each issue.

His work in the comics industry included running the Dell Comics Division when the company pulled out of Western. He was the art director for *Classics Illustrated* when Gilberton updated many of their titles and introduced *The World Around Us series.* He was editor and art director at Continental where he produced *Catman, Captain Aero, Suspense, Contact, Terrific,* etc. plus illustrating all the covers and many inside stories. Leonard was the Art Director for *Alfred Hitchcock Magazine.* He was the Editor, Art Director and eventually Publisher at Star Publications, producing their highly successful line of comics, paperbacks, coloring books, crossword puzzles, how-to books and mens books. All this, plus work throughout the industry resulted in some 1500 covers for varied publications.

He is the holder of two Doctorates and is currently involved in illustrating a definitive laboratory textbook in Anatomy and Physiology.

For relaxation and to satisfy an inner desire he is painting a series on the early American West in a style reminiscent of Remington but in a technique uniquely his own. The paintings I've seen are magnificent and are truly of museum quality. There has been sudden, hectic activity among collectors, both foreign and domestic to garner his original art and printed copies of his originals for investment purposes and as collectibles. He has in his possession, safely stored, some 30 to 40 choice pieces of original art and printed proofs. I can truly state, "I wish I owned them."

This then is merely the tip of the iceberg. For an in-depth look at L.B. Cole, I suggest reading Overstreet's *Comic Book Price Guide* number 11, page A-55, by E.B. Boatner.

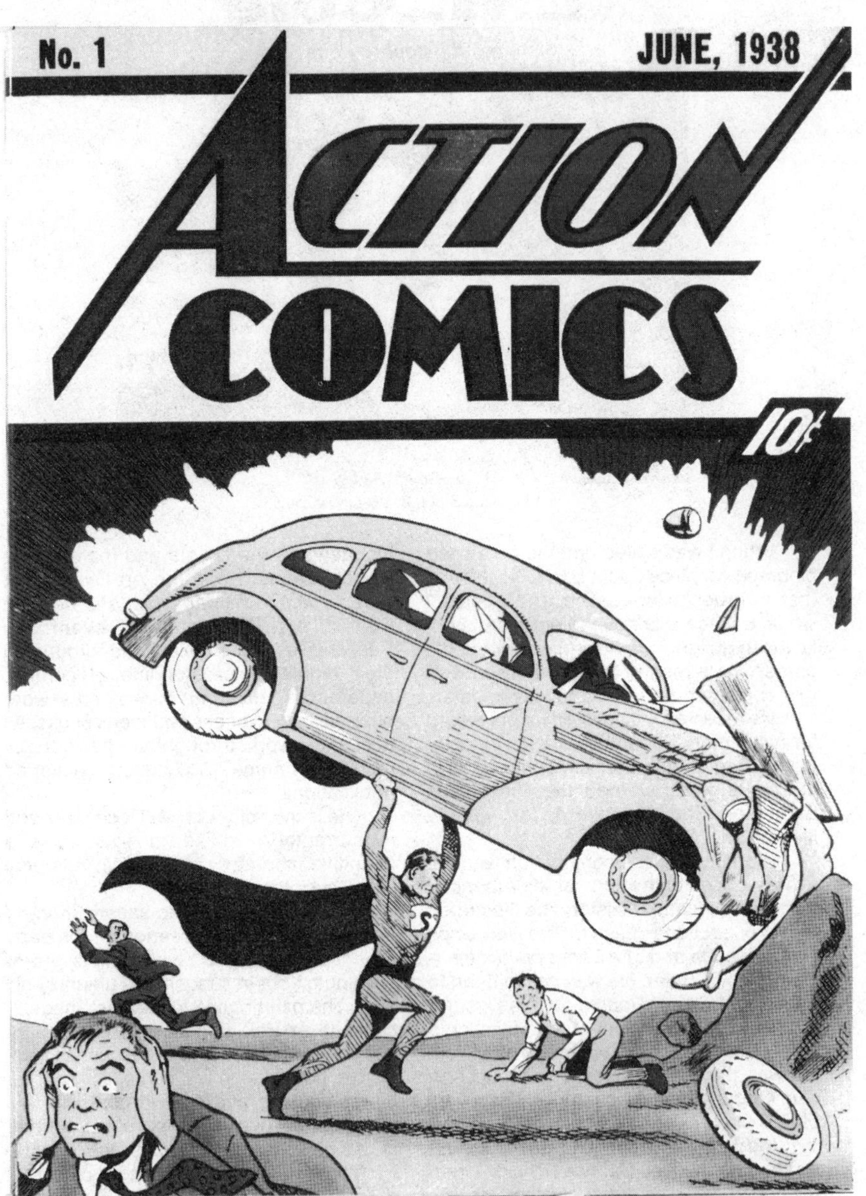

Action Comics #1, June, 1938. The first appearance of *Superman*. This book is the most important and influential comic book ever published. Consequently, it is one of the most sought after and one of the top three most valuable comic books. Superman is TM & © DC Comics, Inc.

Of Supermen and Kids with Dreams:

An Interview with Jerry Siegel and Joe Shuster

Superman is one of the most popular fictional creations of all time. His image and costume have become omnipresent icons used to merchandise every conceivable product, so cliched they are the subject of countless parodies. Yet initially the concept was so original it revolutionized the comic book medium, creating a boom in a new type of protagonist, the superhero, and transforming what was virtually a cottage industry into a multimillion dollar business. But of all the costume strongmen this revolution spawned, only Superman has been consistently popular for so long a time, boasting a career which now spans half a century. Nor has this popularity been confined to one medium. Superman has starred in radio and TV shows, movie serials, newspaper comic strips, animated cartoons, even the Broadway stage, and since the late seventies, in a series of blockbuster feature films. Like his great abilities, Superman's popularity would seem to know no bounds.

However, Superman's potential was far from obvious in the beginning. Our familiarity with the superhero makes us forget what a daringly original concept it was. Sheldon Mayer, famous creator of Scribbly, and an early champion of Superman, recalls the anxieties that publishing the man of steel's exploits first evoked. "When DC publisher Harry Donenfeld first saw that cover of Superman holding that car in the air, he really got worried. He felt that nobody would believe it, that it was ridiculous. . .crazy." Donenfeld's nervousness was well justified, for this cover of **Action Comics** No. 1 (June, 1938) showed things the public had never seen before and the inside story was even more fantastic, revealing a man hurtling skyscrapers, outracing an express train and possessing a skin so tough bullets bounced off his chest. Other publishers had not been so bold or farsighted. Superman's creators hawked their brainchild to every major newspaper syndicate and comic book publisher only to be rejected or offered unsatisfactory deals. Amazingly, the hottest property in comics lay gathering dust on the shelf for almost five years.

Superman was created by two 18 year old high school kids: Jerry Siegel who invented the character and wrote the strip and Joe Shuster who drew it. Close friends and neighbors, Siegel and Shuster grew up in Cleveland, Ohio during the nadir of the Depression. Shuster was so poor he had to draw on wall paper and the backs of calendars and Siegel was not much better off. Both dreamed of lifting themselves out of poverty and obscurity by becoming rich and famous cartoonists, and it was this dream which carried them through rejection after heart-wrenching rejection. Through it all they maintained a faith in their creations and a will to succeed. When Siegel, an aspiring science fiction writer, could not get published, he started his own primitive fanzine called **Science Fiction: the Advance Guard of Future Civilization** to get his rejected stories into print. Cranked out on the high school mimeograph machine, it was one of the first publications of its kind and boasted art by Shuster. The third issue of this fanzine, dated January, 1933, contained Siegel's first Superman story entitled "The Reign of the Super-

THOMAS ANDRAE

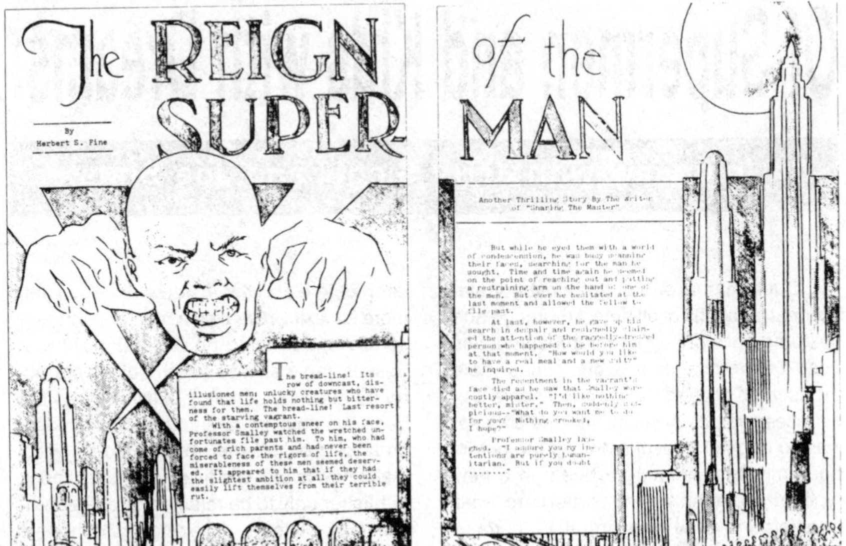

The REIGN of the SUPER-MAN

By
Herbert S. Fine

Another Thrilling Story By The Writer of "Snaring The Master"

The bread-line! Its row of downcast, disillusioned men; unlucky creatures who have found that life holds nothing but bitterness for them. The bread-line! Last resort of the starving vagrant.

With a contemptous sneer on his face, Professor Smalley watched the wretched unfortunates file past him. To him, who had come of rich parents and had never been forced to face the rigors of life, the miserableness of these men seemed deserved. It appeared to him that if they had the slightest ambition at all they could easily lift themselves from their terrible rut.

But while he eyed them with a world of condescension, he was busy scanning their faces, searching for the man he sought. Time and time again he seemed on the point of reaching out and putting a restraining arm on the hand of one of the men. But ever he hesitated at the last moment and allowed the fellow to file past.

At last, however, he gave up his search in despair and resignedly claimed the attention of the raggedly-dressed person who happened to be before him at that moment. "How would you like to have a real meal and a new suit?" he inquired.

The resentment in the vagrant's face died as he saw that Smalley wore costly apparel. "I'd like nothing better, mister." Then, suddenly suspicious--"What do you want me to do for you? Nothing crooked, I hope?"

Professor Smalley laughed. "I assure you my intentions are purely humanitarian. But if you doubt ...."

The Superman as an evil genius hovering over the breadline from the opening pages of **The Reign of the Superman** by Herbert S. Fine (a.k.a. Jerry Siegel); from **Science Fiction: the Vanguard of Future Civilization** #3, January, 1933. Collection of Richard Lupoff.

man." Surprisingly, the protagonist of this tale was not a hero but a super-villain, an evil genius bent on world domination who bears a striking resemblance to Luthor, later Superman's arch-nemesis.

Siegel's casting of his first superman as a villain was no fluke, but followed the established conventions in the science fiction of the period. While there had been heroic supermen in science fiction before Siegel's creation of Superman, they were used only rarely. The first physical superman of a heroic mold was Edgar Rice Burroughs' John Carter of Mars who, like Burroughs' more famous creation Tarzan, first appeared just before World War I. Carter was an Earthman who had been magically transported to Mars; because that planet had a lesser gravity than Earth, he was able to leap great distances and became superstrong. John Carter's abilities may have been similar to those of heroes in myths and legends, but their sources were radically different. His powers were neither gifts from the gods nor made possible through the miraculous suspension of natural law, but due solely to natural processes and given a psuedo-scientific rationale.

However, there was another image of the superman which came to predominate in science fiction. The concept of a wholly naturalistic superman did not originate with Burroughs' Mars stories; perhaps the earliest tale of a being possessed of supernatural strength through psuedo-scientific means was Mary Shelley's **Frankenstein** (1818). Unlike John Carter, Shelley's creature was neither a heroic individual nor even a normal human being, but a murderous monster synthetically created in the laboratory. Following the lead of **Frankenstein**, most science fiction portrayed the superman as a sometimes sympathetic but always monstrous, threatening and socially deviant being.

Despite its early appearance, the superman theme did not really catch on until the early thirties when a flood of stories about mental and physical supermen appeared either as separate novels or short stories in the science fiction pulps which had captured the popular imagination at that time. Most important of these was Philip Wylie's novel about a physical superman, **Gladiator**, said to have inspired Siegel's creation of Superman. But **Gladiator** and virtually all other early tales of supermen differ from Siegel and Shuster's Superman in one crucial respect. With the exception of the John Carter stories which took place outside Earthly society and in which the super-strength of the hero was not a major emphasis, all the tales of mentally and physically super-human beings end tragically and futilely. Whether he becomes an outcast whose superior powers, abnormal appearance, or strange personality alienates him from humanity or a tyranical monster so dangerous he threatens to enslave the world, convention dictates that the superman cannot continue to exist. By the end of the story he must either die or be robbed of his power.

Siegel's decision to make Superman into a hero marks an innovative break with science fiction tradition. Superman differs from his predecessors in being neither alienated from society nor a misanthropic, power-mad menace but a truly messianic figure, a "savior of the helpless and oppressed. . . sworn to devote his life to those in need." Unlike previous supermen, he chooses a place for himself in society and aids his fellows and in turn is accepted, even glorified by them. He is a "man of tomorrow" who represents mankind's highest potentialities and ideals, but whose powers, remarkably, pose no threat. Superman would undergo an ontogeny of changes before emerging as the figure we are familiar with today, acquiring a blue union suit and red cape, a dual identity, and a girl reporter as a love interest, modeled after Siegel's future wife Joanne. But let his creators tell their own story, a tale of two kids who dared to dream the impossible dream, whose wildest fantasies all came true.

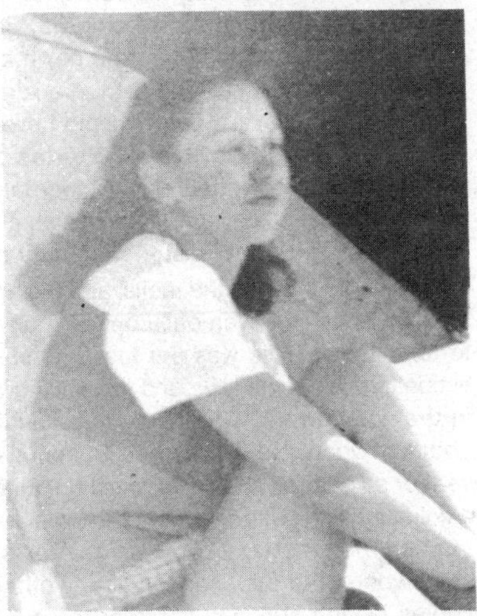

Photo of Joanne Carter Siegel on the beach at Santa Monica, California, ca. 1938, a few years after posing as Lois Lane for Joe Shuster. Photo by Joseph Kulik.

NOTE: For a comprehensive discussion of the early superman and the historical context surrounding Siegel and Shuster's creation of Superman c.f. Thomas Andrae, "From Menace to Messiah: the Prehistory of the Superman in Science Fiction Literature," ***Discourse: Journal for Theoretical Studies in Media and Culture****, #2 (Summer, 1980).*

THE SIEGEL AND SHUSTER INTERVIEW:

How did the two of you meet?

Joe: I came from Canada when I was about 10 years old, and our family settled in Cleveland, Ohio. It was in Glenville High School that I met Jerry Siegel; we were both on the staff of the Glenville High paper.

Jerry: Before that you went to a junior high school . . .

Joe: Yes, it was Alexander Hamilton Junior High School, where I was staff artist on their school paper, ***The Federalist***. And I did a comic strip called, of all things, ***Jerry the Journalist***. It wasn't influenced by anything in particular. The script was given to me.

Jerry: Strangely enough, it was written by a cousin of mine—he was the editor of the paper. I don't know the details, but when Joe moved from that neighborhood down into the neighborhood where I was living, it was shortly before that I was talking to my cousin—I told him I was interested in comics, and I was starting to collaborate through the mail with some cartoonist—and he told me about Joe. He said that Joe was very good and was moving into my neighborhood and the two of us ought to get together. That's what led to the two of us meeting.

Joe: We were just a few blocks away from each other, matter of fact. We were about 16 at the time.

Jerry: Something like that. We were high school kids.

Was the material in your high school paper your first published artwork?

Joe: Yes, the first that had ever been published. It was a humorous strip, a

High school graduation pictures of (left to right) Jerry Siegel, Joe Shuster and Lois Amster, the inspiration for Lois Lane (1934). By this time Siegel and Shuster had already created their legendary character.

cartoon.

Jerry: It was a gag, complete in itself, each separate one.

What was the high school like?

Jerry: It was Glenville High School, and while we were students there, there were also some students who in later years achieved considerable celebrity—among them Jerome Lawrence, who later was co-writer of **Inherit the Wind** and **Auntie Mame.** And then Seymour Heller, who was also a student there, later became the manager of Liberace. There were some other fellers who did quite well in the later years. Some of them worked on the newspaper.

What were your interests at that time besides the high school paper?

Joe: I tried to build up my body. I was so skinny, I went in for weight-lifting and athletics. I used to get all the body-building magazines—from the second-hand stores—and read them...

Jerry: I used to go to the school gym and see Joe in action; he was pretty good.

Joe: ...I put a lot of effort into it for about four or five years.

Jerry: Joe, do you mind if I tell a little funny story at your expense?

Joe: Not about the time in Miami!

Jerry: No, I'm talking about the barbells. Joe was interviewed years ago, and he was really good with the barbells. But newsmen being the way they are, they waited until after Joe had raised and lowered the thing many times. When he put it down and collapsed, that's the picture they wanted: a funny shot instead of all the terrific lifting he had done.

Joe: Incidentally, Jerry and I did the first science-fiction fanzine, called **Science Fiction**—

Jerry: And here's something of interest which the fan field doesn't know, because the information didn't come fully back to me until just a short time ago. Recently I bought a copy of **The Encyclopaedia of Science Fiction**—the title was something like that; it's published in England. At the front of the book they list certain 'firsts'; and they had me down as the publisher of a science-fiction fanzine which I put out several years before I even met Joe. It was called **Cosmic Stories**. It was strictly a typewritten and hectographed publication, I believe; I believe that I wrote most of it or at least a great deal of it. It was sold through the mails, and the article says that not even one copy is known to exist today. This was the first science-fiction fanzine in the U.S., and for all I know, in the whole world. This was when I was about 14 years old, back in 1929, about a year or so before I met Joe. It must be quite a collector's item if any copies exist. It's not impossible that a copy might exist somewhere, but the chances of any other copies having survived is rather remote.

Do you recall any of the stories you wrote for that?

Jerry: Yes. As a matter of fact, I even recall that I called the thing The Fantastic Fiction Publishing Company or something like that; and I actually mimeographed and sold through the mails pamphlets that I wrote under the pseudonym Hugh Langley—or whatever. I don't have copies of those, but I do remember that when I showed the material to my English teacher, she gave me a little lecture that it was a pity I was wasting my time writing such trash when there were so many wonderful types of literature I could be writing instead. And I said, "Well, I like this kind of stuff, and that's why I write it."

Joe: We were both great science-fiction fans, reading **Amazing Stories** and **Wonder Stories** in those days.

Jerry: When Joe and I met, it was like the right chemicals coming together. I loved his artwork, the stuff that he showed me—and he showed me stuff that he had drawn even years earlier, when he was a teenager, science-fiction stuff. I thought he had the flair—though he was a beginner—I thought he had the flair of a Frank R. Paul, who was one of the best science-fiction illustrators in the field.

Joe: And I was an avid reader of H. G. Wells—

Jerry: Right. And to our astonishment, we found that both of us were great science-fiction fans, Joe as well as I; and we were both reading the same type of material.

Joanne Siegel: In Fact, the three of us were destined to meet, because we were kids all playing at being grown up, trying desperately to be grown up. And since that first day of our friendship, we're still together.

Joe: Not only that, but when I first met Joe, to my intense delight, he showed me that he was a collector. He was collecting some of the early *Tarzan* pages by Hal Foster, and, later, early *Flash Gordons*; and I found that we were both absolutely interested in the same type of thing. And I was crazy about the artists that he was crazy about, and yet he had this wonderful flair. I didn't know then that someday he would be as famous as those other cartoonists; but I thought, "Gee whiz, I would just love to work with him."

Joe, what was the first artwork of yours that Jerry saw?

Joe: That was when I was about 14 years old. I drew a picture on the back of a calendar in pencil. In those days, they used to give out free calendars. I had no art paper, so I took whatever else I could. A lot of my work was done on brown wrapping paper and on the back of wallpaper. The drawing Jerry first saw was on the back of a calendar sheet about 14 inches wide by 17 inches long. It showed the world of tomorrow: a beautiful scene of spaceships, rocketships, and futuristic skyscrapers in the city of the future. At the bottom I put my name and the date and "The City of the Future: 1980." That was in 1926 or 1927. It was one of the few things I've ever saved.

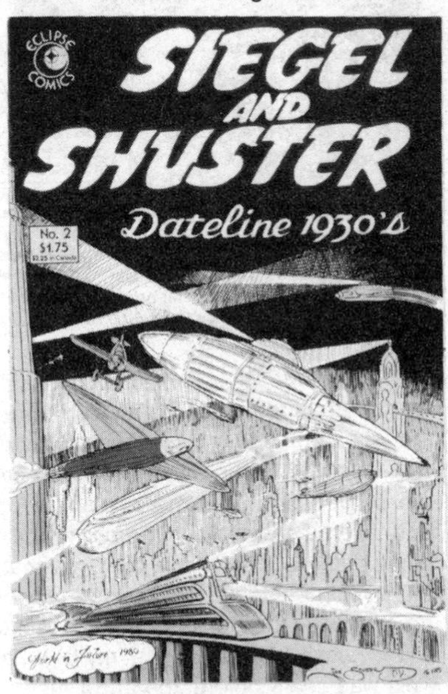

"The City of the Future: 1980" (May 2, 1931). This was the first of Shuster's artwork that Siegel ever saw. Drawn when the artist was 16 years old, it bears a close resemblance to scenes from Fritz Lang's science fiction classic *Metropolis* (1928), the film which inspired the name of Superman's home city. Cover to **Siegel and Shuster: Dateline 1930s** #2 published by Eclipse Comics; © Joe Shuster.

Jerry: 1980 seemed like the distant future then.

Joe: My favorite comic strip in those days was *Little Nemo* by Winsor McCay. It was very imaginative, and that was the sort of fantasy I grew up with and loved.

The two page Dr. Occult episode from the *"Koth and the Seven"* story in **More Fun** #16, December, 1936. Although they were initially unable to get Superman into print, Siegel and Shuster could not resist putting some of their ideas for this strip into their published work. In the above serial which ran in **More Fun** #14-17, Dr. Occult became a red and blue suited superhero who could fly. And the villain, Koth, was an alien from another planet who, like Superman, came to Earth after escaping his planet's destruction. Dr. Occult's costume and flying abilities reflect the influence of Edgar Rice Burroughs' *John Carter of Mars*, one of Siegel's favorite characters. © DC Comics, Inc.

Jerry: Me, too. I used to love *Little Nemo*. And I remember that when I was a kid, someone had told me how you could rub a printed drawing with a candlewax candle, put it down on a piece of blank paper, and take a heavy object and rub the back of the paper, and the whole thing, color and all, would be transferred. I used to love to do that with the comics, including *Little Nemo*, which was also one of my favorites. This was years before Joe and I met.

Joe: Also, Jerry and I did a comic book together—

Jerry: That was later; it was after we did our fanzine **Science Fiction**. I've already mentioned how in 1929 I put out this fanzine. I definitely wanted to be a science-fiction writer. Since I was running into a little trouble in getting other people to go along with my desires and publish my stuff, I began publishing it myself. Then, after I met Joe, we immediately began working on a wide variety of different types of comic strips—funny strips and adventure strips. We did a strip about a cave man and showed it around to the syndicates. That was one of our first collaborations, but not the very first. It wasn't too long after that that *Alley Oop* came out, and we did a double-take. And then another strip that I had done before getting together with Joe—I worked with another artist through the mails—was called *The Time Crusaders*. It was about some fellows who travelled around in a time machine and had adventures in the past and future. I presented it, and not too long after that, *Brick Bradford* came out.

Joe: One of the first comic strips we ever did together was called *Interplanetary Police*.

Jerry: Right, it was one of our first strips—perhaps the very first. I really can't give you too much detail, except that, as the title suggests, it was about the adventures of the police in the distant future, with the adventures taking place on various worlds.

Something funny in connection with it—I submitted it to United Features Syndicate. Joe and I waited breathlessly. Then one day we got a letter in the mail, and it said United Features Syndicate on it, and my heart started pounding, and I opened it. There was a real short letter, and the first line was, "Congratulations!" And I thought, "Boy, we've made it." Then what was the rest of the letter? "This is an interesting strip, but we can't use it."—something like that, which was quite a letdown.

We did various other strips. We also did a strip about two pals who own some sort of mechanism which enables them to peer anywhere in the world, through walls or anything, and listen in on what gangsters are saying, and then get busy scotching the villainy. In a way, that was a forerunner of Superman's super-vision and X-ray vision, only done with a mechanism. I don't remember the title—*Ralph* something.

Another early strip that Joe and I did was called *Snoopy and Smiley*. It was a comedy strip a la Laurel and Hardy or Charlie Chaplin or Lord knows what. It didn't sell. Around this time I contacted J. Allen St. John, who had done all the illustrations for the *Tarzan* books; and I worked up with him in my script something called *Rex Carson of the Ether Patrol*. His drawings were very nice. It was submitted around, nothing happened to it, and eventually it just got lost over the years. But then right around this time, Joe and I started our fanzine **Science Fiction**, where I did the first *Superman* story I ever wrote, and Joe did the first *Superman* illustration that he ever did.

Joe: It (the magazine) was subtitled "The Advance Guard of Future Civilization."

Jerry: In the third issue of our fanzine I wrote a story called "The Reign of the Superman." I wrote it under the pseudonym of Herb S. Fine which was a combination of the names of one of my cousins and my

Doctor Occult, the Ghost Detective by Leger and Reuths (Siegel & Shuster) from **New Fun** #6 (1st Doctor Occult), October, 1935. © DC Comics, Inc.

Henri Duval, Soldier of Fortune by Siegel and Shuster from **New Fun** #6, October, 1935. © DC Comics, Inc. This and the preceding strips represent some of the first published work by Siegel and Shuster.

Opening sequence of a two page *Dr. Mystic* story from **The Comics Magazine** #1, May, 1936, which begins the *"The Koth and the Seven"* story that continues in **More Fun** #14, Oct., 1936. © The Comics Magazine Publ.

mother's maiden name. Joe did the illustrations for it.

Joe: I did all the illustrations for the magazine, and also for all the other stories.

Jerry: I recall that we did a one-panel cartoon feature in the magazine; it was a sort of "Believe It or Not" of the future called *Queeriosities*.

Joe: In the magazine we had letters to the editor; we had invited readers to write in—

Jerry: And one of (those readers) was Julius Schwartz, who is currently the editor of *Superman*. And he wrote in, saying some nice things, including the fact that he liked Joe's work. Forrest Ackerman was a contributor—

Joanne: Of stories?

Jerry: I believe so—I haven't seen the stuff in years. Also, Mort Weisinger and Julius Schwartz collaborated on a sort of science-fiction gossip column which ran in the fanzine; they may have done it under a pseudonym.

How did you come up with the idea for "The Reign of the Superman?"

Jerry: Well, as a science-fiction fan, I knew of the various themes in the field. The superman theme has been one of the themes ever since Samson and Hercules; and I just sat down and wrote a story of that type—only in this story, the superman was a villain.

Had you read any stories featuring supermen as villains?

Jerry: If they existed, I didn't know about them. After all, there were tons of things published.

The bald-domed, menacing Superman in "The Reign" looks a lot like Lex Luther, the villain in later Superman stories. Did you consciously base Luthor on the early character?

Joe: The evil Superman was just my idea of a villain—I suppose he looks a lot like Telly Savalas.

Did you intend a switch on the traditional Superman theme by making him a villain?

Jerry: No, it wasn't a switch at all. That's just the way I thought that I'd play it. I was just a young kid, and my thoughts didn't go in those directions; that was just the story that occurred to me. That was published in the January 1933 issue of **Science Fiction**. A couple of months after I published this story, it occurred to me that a superman as a hero rather than a villain might make a great comic strip character in the vein of Tarzan, only more super and sensational than that great character. Joe and I drew it up as a comic book—this was in early 1933. We interested a publisher in putting it out, but then he changed his mind, and that was the end of that particular version of Superman—called *The Superman*. Practically all of it was torn up, by the way. Joe got very upset and tore up and threw away most of it.

Does any of it still exist?

Joe: We saved the cover. The rest of the drawings were a crude version of Superman. It wasn't really Superman—that was before he evolved into a costumed figure. He was simply wearing a T-shirt and pants; he was more like Slam Bradley (another

Siegel & Shuster collaboration) than anything else, just a man of action. But we called him *The Superman*. That was the second time we used the name, but the first time it was used for a character of goodwill. I'm a perfectionist, and I think the fact that the drawings had been turned down made me want to tear them up. I simply destroyed them. I said, "If we ever do it again, I'm going to redo it properly." It was a very low period for us.

Jerry: In later years—maybe 10 or 15 years ago—I asked Joe what he remembered of this story, and he remembered a scene of a character crouched on the edge of a building, with a cape almost a la Batman. We don't specifically recall if the character had a costume or not. The publisher who turned it down published *Detective Dan*. The sketch that was publish-

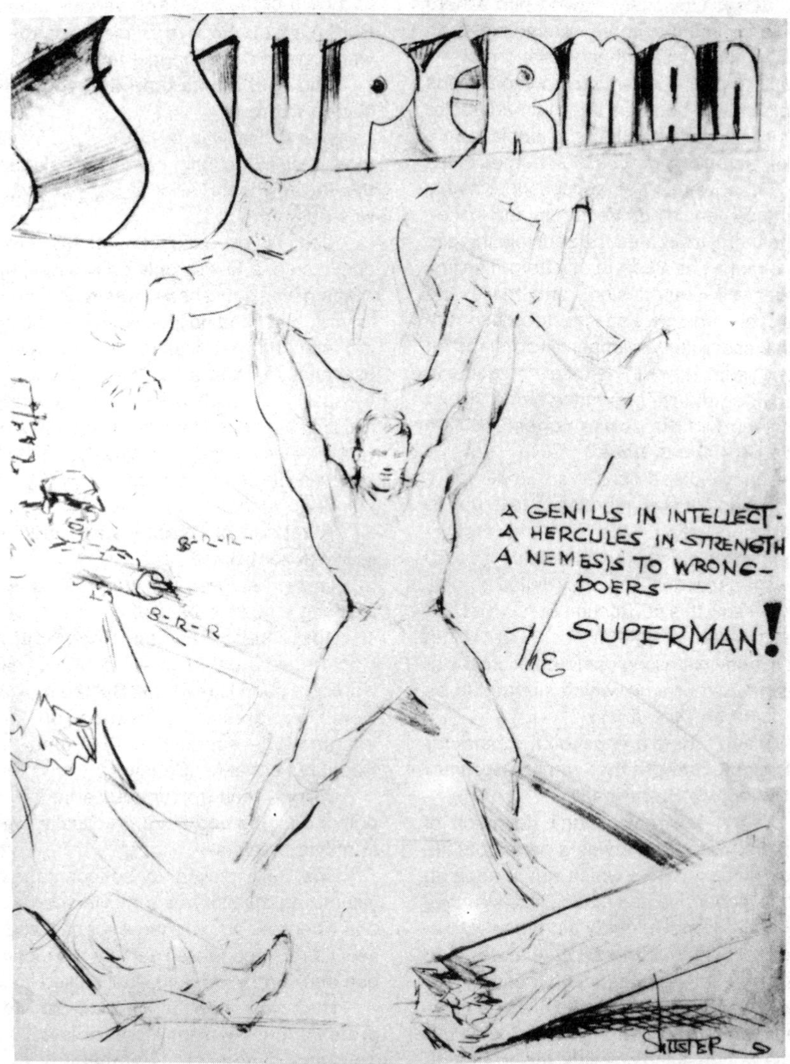

A pencilled concept-sketch for the first version of Superman (1933), called *"The Superman"* and drawn in comic book format. The interior art for this story was destroyed by Shuster during a time of depression. Note that Superman sports a strongman's outfit rather than his familiar cape and tights. Superman is TM & © DC Comics, Inc.

ed in Steranko's book was one of the sketches that Joe made at that time for this story—to show the publisher. In that particular sketch, the character is not in costume; but Joe and I—especially Joe—seem to recall that there were some scenes in there in which the character had a bat-like cape.

What was your reason for changing Superman from a villain to a hero?

Jerry: Obviously, having him a hero would be infinitely more commercial than having him a villain. I understand that the comic strip *Dr. Fu Manchu* ran into all sorts of difficulties because the main character was a villain. And with the example before us of Tarzan and other action heroes of fiction who were very successful, mainly because people admired them and looked up to them, it seemed the sensible thing to do to make *The Superman* a hero. The first piece was a short story, and that's one thing; but creating a successful comic strip with a character you hope will continue for many years, it would definitely be going in the wrong direction to make him a villain.

Was *The Superman* conceived as a strip or a comic book?

Jerry: It was conceived strictly as a comic book. It was intended to take up the entire publication. When Joe and I first got together, we did attempt to prepare and sell newspaper strips; but they failed to sell. When I saw this publication *Detective Dan*, it occurred to me that we could get up an even more interesting comic book character than that other strip, which seemed to be a takeoff on *Dick Tracy*.

Wasn't there a Popeye-like character with great strength that you created very early, before Superman?

Jerry: We really didn't do much of anything with that. It was a series of little short stories I wrote which ran in my high school paper. Joe and I made little sketches for it, but we never really did much with it. That was *Goober, the Mighty*; it was a la Popeye, but it was satirical. Of course, we liked Popeye—especially the animated cartoons, which had a strong influence on me in the writing—and possibly Joe, too, for all I know...

Joe: Yes.

Jerry: ...because the super-strength and action in the animated cartoons, rather than in the comic strip, were absolutely sensational. I thought, "This is really great, but it's done strictly as comedy. What if it featured a straight adventure character? You could end up with a very dynamic adventure strip." So that was one of the influences on Superman. There were many. There was Tarzan, who was the greatest action hero of the time, and various others. But I think the Popeye animated cartoons were one of the strongest influences.

You said at one time that you did a Tarzan satire.

Jerry: That was it—*Goober, the Mighty* took place in the jungle and kind of kidded the Tarzan theme. A lot of our early work was humorous.

Joe: We even did a Laurel and Hardy comic strip, a few sample daily strips, but it was never published. I was really a cartoonist, and I had no idea what we'd be going into. I loved illustration, but I was essentially—I had a flair for comedy.

Jerry: We both loved the comic strips; it just so happened that the adventure stuff was what we managed to market, and that's what we did from there on.

Joe: Yeah.

What sort of comedy strips did you enjoy at that time?

Jerry: I enjoyed *Li'l Abner*. That was a strong influence on me.

Joe: Alex Raymond and Burne Hogarth were my idols—also Milt Caniff, Hal Foster, and Roy Crane. But the movies were the greatest influence on our imagination—especially the films of Douglas Fairbanks, Senior.

Jerry: I read tremendous amounts of pulps; and Joe and I, we practically lived in movie theaters—

Joe: Jerry picked up the technique of visualizing the story as a movie scenario; and whenever he gave me a script, I would see it as a screenplay. That was the technique that Jerry used, and I just picked it up.

Had you had a chance to see professionally-written screenplays?

Jerry: Not at all. As a matter of fact, when we broke into the field, we both indulged in what we thought was very experimental stuff. In the writing, I tried to incorporate what was so popular in the pulp field into the comics field. I used a great number of captions along with dialogue balloons, visualizing the way a pulp comic should be. I feel now that we were pioneering, and that much of the stuff that followed was influenced by the way we handled our very early work, like *Slam Bradley* especially.

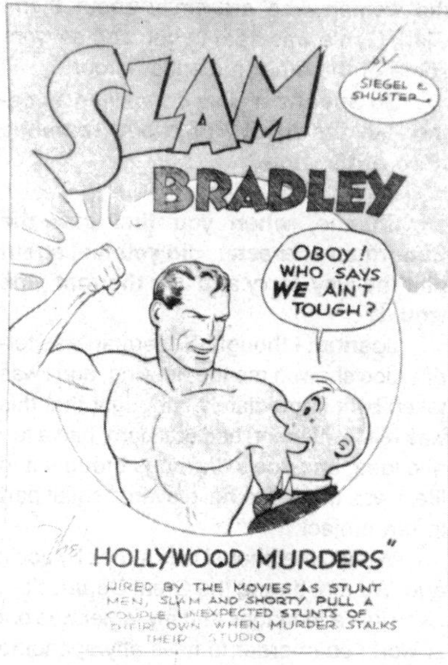

Slam Bradley by Siegel and Shuster, a dry run for Superman. From **Detective Comics** #4, 1937. © DC Comics, Inc..

Slam Bradley was a dry run for Superman. Superman had already been created, and we didn't want to give away the Superman idea; but we just couldn't resist putting into *Slam Bradley* some of the slambang stuff which we knew would be in *Superman* if and when we got *Superman* launched.

Where did Slam Bradley come from?

Joe: Oh, that's a very important part of our lives, a very important part of our background. Jerry often says that Slam Bradley was really the forerunner of Superman, because we turned it out with no restrictions, complete freedom to do what we wanted; the only problem was that we had a deadline. We had to work very fast, so Jerry suggested that we save time by putting less than six panels to a page—four panels or three panels, and sometimes two panels. I think one day we just had one panel to a page. The kids loved it because it was spectacular—I could do so much more. Later on, the editors stopped us from doing that; they said the kids were not getting their money's worth.

The actual character of Slam Bradley was Jerry's idea. They wanted an action strip, and Jerry came up with the idea of a man of action with a sense of humor. The character had a devil-may-care attitude very much like that of Fairbanks, Senior's Zorro. Still, he couldn't fly, and he didn't have a costume.

When you first conceived Superman, did you have the dual-identity theme in mind?

Jerry: That occurred to me in late 1934, when I decided that I'd like to do *Superman* as a newspaper strip. I approached Joe about it, and he was enthusiastic about the possibility. I was up late one night, and more and more ideas kept coming to me, and I kept writing out several weeks of syndicate scripts for the proposed newspaper strip. When morning came, I had written several weeks of material, and I dashed over to Joe's place and showed it to him. (This was the story that appeared in *Action Comics* No. 1, June, 1938, the first published appearance of *Superman*.)

Joe: That was one very important day in our lives. We just sat down, and I worked straight through. I think I had brought in some sandwiches to eat, and we worked all day long.

Jerry: Of course, Joe had worked on that earlier version of Superman, and when I came to him with this new version of it, he was immediately sold. And when I saw the drawings that were emerging from his pencil, I almost flipped. I knew he had matured a great deal since he had done *The Superman*, and I thought he was doing a great job on the new art.

Joe: I was caught up in Jerry's enthusiasm, and I started drawing as fast as I could use my pencil. My imagination just picked the concept right up from Jerry.

Jerry: You see, Clark Kent grew not only out of my private life, but also out of Joe's. As a high school student, I thought that someday I might become a reporter, and I had crushes on several attractive girls who either didn't know I existed or didn't care I existed. As a matter of fact, some of them looked like they *hoped* I didn't exist. It occurred to me,"What if I was real terrific? What if I had something special going for me, like jumping over buildings or throwing cars around or something like that? Then maybe they would notice me." That night when all the thoughts were coming to me, the concept came to me that Superman could have a dual identity, and that in one of his identities he could be meek and mild, as I was, and wear glasses, the way I do. The heroine, who I figured would be a girl reporter, would think he was some sort of a worm; yet she would be crazy about this Superman character who could do all sorts of fabulous things. In fact, she was real wild about him, and a big inside joke was that the fellow she was crazy about was also the fellow whom she loathed. By coincidence, Joe was a carbon copy (of me).

Joe: I was mild-mannered, wore glasses, was very shy with women.

Jerry: So in the artwork, he was able to translate it; and he wasn't just drawing it, he was feeling it.

Did heroes like Zorro have any influence on the dual-identity motif?

Jerry: Definitely. I loved **The Mark of Zorro**, and I'm sure that had some influence on me. I did also see **The Scarlet Pimpernel** but didn't care much for it. But the shy reporter with glasses came out of our own personal lives. Of course we loved Douglas Fairbanks as Robin Hood, and that influenced both of us—me in the writing, and Joe in the art. I'm sure that subliminally we remembered Rudolph Valentino in **The Sheik**, and the tremendous romantic appeal to women of a guy in costume.

Yet the early Superman avoided women.

Jerry: Yes. I figured that the character would be so advanced that he would be invulnerable in other ways than physically. Secretly, I kind of enjoyed the thought that women, who just didn't care at all about somebody like Clark Kent, would go ape over somebody like Superman. I enjoyed the fact that he wasn't that affected by all their admiration. When you come down to it, some of the greatest lovers of all time simply aren't that crazy about women—it's the women who are crazy about them. Clark Gable was hard to get, and so were some of the other romantic heroes.

So Superman was conceived as being like the ideal Hollywood romantic hero of the time?

Jerry: That's right.

Joanne, when you first saw the Superman character, did you feel about him the way Jerry and Joe thought girls would?

Joanne: I thought Superman was terrific. Joe showed me the drawing, and I was taken by it immediately. I thought that this was really different; and that Jerry had a terrific idea, and Joe's drawings brought it to life. I was thrilled to have even a small part in the project.

When I met them I was struck by Joe's age. We met during the Great Depression. I was just a teenager, and my father was out of work; so in order to have any spending money, I had to earn my own money. I found that no one would hire me because I had no skills or training, and even grown people were having trouble getting jobs. I had read an article about modeling, and I thought maybe I could get away with that. So I practiced various poses in front of a mirror, and I put an ad in the *Cleveland Plain Dealer* in the Situation Wanted column, advertising myself as a model, and Joe happened to see it. We corresponded, and he signed all his letters "Mr. Joseph Shuster," so I thought he was an older man. We set up an appointment at his apartment, where he lived with his parents, brother, and sister. I went there on a Saturday afternoon because I was going to school during the week. I was so nervous, because I thought he was going to say I was too young.

It was a freezing cold day, and I was absolutely frozen by the time I got there, because I lived on the other side of town. I pounded on the door, and it opened a little bit; and I saw a young boy on the other side, and I said, "I'm the model that Mr. Shuster is expecting." He said, "Come on in," and we got to talking. I asked if I could leave my coat on, because I was still cold. Right away we got excited—we were talking about not only the weather, but movies and everything. Finally I said, "Does Mr. Shuster know that I'm here?" And he said, "I'm Mr. Shuster." That was the way we met.

We went in the back, and I posed for him that day—I posed for him every Saturday after that. When I came out to the living room, Jerry was waiting over there to meet me, because he knew I was going to be coming. I was absolutely astounded with his energy—talk about super-energy! He was sitting on a chair, his feet were going, he was flipping through magazines, anxiously waiting to meet me. (To Jerry:) You made a shambles of that house...We hit it off just great. Then we found that we had all been on our school papers, so we felt that we had a real common bond there. I was at a different school, but I had been on my school paper, and I had wanted to be a girl reporter; so I was very thrilled that I was posing as a girl reporter. We've been together ever since.

And you dated Jerry?

Joe: I started dating her first.

Joanne: Right. We dated first...

Jerry: I was just a bystander.

Joanne: ...and many years later, Jerry and I and Joe had a reunion at the Hotel Plaza in New York at a great cartoonists' ball.

Jerry: It was a costume ball. Tell them who you came as.

Joanne: I came as Dixie Dugan, because I had my hair exactly like hers at that time. Joe took me down to the Brooks costume company and rented an enormous ballgown for me, so I looked exactly like Dixie Dugan. Jerry and Joe were having problems at that time—there was litigation—and I just didn't feel like going as Lois Lane under those circumstances. But Lois Lane also wore her hair that way, remember? After this reunion at the ball, Jerry and I started dating, and a few months later, we were married. That was in 1948.

How did Lois Lane come about?

Joanne: Joe was redrawing the strip, and it was going to be more realistic, rather than cartoony. I used to model for him every Saturday until he had enough drawings. He made so many stock drawings that it got to the point where he didn't need any more.

Joe: To me she *was* Lois Lane.

Joanne: We became such good friends by that time, we decided we would always stay friends. I did a lot of traveling but kept in touch with Joe—we corresponded. I did a lot of modeling in Boston after that, but the job with Joe was my first modeling job. I posed for a lot of painters and illustrators in Boston and Provincetown and New York—and some photographers in New York. I never did fashion modeling; I never was tall enough. I wanted to grow more, but this was as high as I got.

Did you have a chance to make suggestions about Lois Lane in the early Stages?

An early, rather romanticized portrait of Lois Lane, c. 1942-43.

Joanne: No, I had no part in that at all. Jerry thought of Lois Lane long before I came on the scene.

Joe: She was a great inspiration for me, though. She encouraged me, she was very enthusiastic about the strip; it meant a lot to me.

Joanne: Many times he used to write to me and say that he was about to give up on it; and I'd say, "Keep at it and you'll make it." I had such a feeling about the strip and about them. I told him, "You're going to be very famous some day." But Jerry was the brains behind Lois. People get the word *model* confused. There's the model that's an inspiration, and the model that poses. I was the model that posed; he thought of Lois Lane before I came on the scene.

Joe, did you have any male models for Superman or Clark as you did for Lois?

Joe: No, he was just inspired by many of the heroes in fiction and the classics. And of course, I was inspired by the movies. In the silent films, my hero was Douglas Fairbanks Senior, who was very agile and athletic. So I think he might have been an inspiration to us, even in his attitude. He had a stance which I often used in drawing Superman. You'll see in many of his roles—including Robin Hood—that he always stood with his hands on his hips and his feet spread apart, laughing—taking nothing seriously. Clark Kent, I suppose, had a little bit of Harold Lloyd in him.

The stance of laughing at evil is more characteristic of the early Superman, who toys with crooks and suspends them from telephone wires.

Joe: That's the one I drew. Jerry and I always felt that the character was enjoying himself. He was having fun—he wasn't taking himself seriously. It was always a lark for him, as you can see in my early drawings.

Where did Superman's costume come from?

Joe: It was inspired by the costume pictures that Fairbanks did. They greatly influenced us. He did **The Mark of Zorro**, and **Robin Hood**, and a marvelous one called **The Black Pirate**—those are three that I recall that we loved. Fairbanks would swing on ropes very much like Superman flying—or like Tarzan on a vine.

Before I ever put anything on paper, Jerry and I would talk back and forth. Jerry would say, "Well, how about this, or how about that, or how about doing him like this?" And I agreed the feeling of action as he was flying or jumping or leaping—a flowing cape would give it movement. It really helped, and it was very easy to draw.

I also had classical heroes and strongmen in mind, and this shows in the footwear. In the third version, Superman wore sandals laced halfway up the calf. You can still see this on the cover of *Action 1*, though they were covered over in red to look like boots when the comic was printed.

Who came up with the "S" insignia, and how many versions did it go through?

Joe: Jerry and I discussed it in detail. We said, "Let's put something on the front." I think initially we wanted to use the first letter of the character's name. We thought S was perfect. After we came up with it, we kiddingly said, "Well, it's the first letter of Siegel and Shuster." Progressively, as the strip evolved, the emblem became larger and larger. You'll notice at the beginning it was quite small.

It was almost a more simple triangle at the beginning, wasn't it?

Joe: Actually, it was made like a shield. I can't describe it, but I was thinking of what they call a crest. Yes, I had a heraldic crest in the back of my mind when I made it. It was a little fancy triangle with curves at the top.

Did you forsee the merchandising possibilities inherent in Superman?

Jerry: One day, I read an article in some leading maga zine of the time about how Tarzan was merchandised by Stephen Slesinger so successfully. And I thought, "Wow! Superman is even more super than Tarzan; the same thing could happen with Superman." And I mentioned it to Joe—he got real enthused—and I walked in a day or two later, and he had made a big drawing of Superman showing how the character could be merchandised on boxtops, T-shirts, and everything. We put this merchandising business into one of the very early Superman stories. The publisher looked at it and thought it was a good idea, and

Superman has been a terrific earner from character merchandising ever since.

Joe: In this drawing, we just let our imagination run wild. We visualized Superman toys, games, and a radio show—that was before TV—and Superman movies. We even visualized Superman billboards. And it's all come true.

How did you name the Superman characters?

Joe: Jerry created all the names. We were great movie fans, and were inspired a lot by the actors and actresses we saw. As for Clark Kent, he combined the names of Clark Gable and Kent Taylor. And Metropolis, the city in which Superman operated, came from the Fritz Lang movie, which we both loved.

What led you to make Superman a visitor from another planet?

Joe: Jerry reversed the usual formula of the superhero who goes to another planet. He put the superhero in ordinary, familiar surroundings, instead of the other way around, as was done in most science fiction. That was the first time I can recall that it had ever been done.

Were you influenced by the Edgar Rice Burroughs John Carter of Mars stories?

Jerry: I don't think they had much of an influence on me when I wrote "The Reign of the Superman". However, when I did the version in 1934, (which years later, in 1938, was published in revised form, in *Action Comics No. 1*) the John Carter stories did influence me. Carter was able to leap great distances because the planet Mars was smaller than the planet Earth; and he had great strength. I visualized the planet Krypton as a huge planet, much larger than Earth; so whoever came to Earth from that planet would be able to leap great distances and lift great weights.

Initially, Superman only leapt great distances. How did his flying evolve?

Joe: He was mostly leaping tall buildings in the beginning. There were cases where he would leap off a tall building or swoop down, and at that point he would look like he was flying, I suppose. It was just natural to draw him like that.

Some critics claim that Superman first flew in the animated cartoons, and that this influenced you to make the comic book character fly.

Joe: Not that I recall.

How did you do the artwork for the Superman story published in *Action 1*?

Joe: I think we did the roughs in pencil, then transferred them to other paper.

Jerry: He was a very meticulous

Photos taken in 1941 of Jerry Siegel (left) and Joe Shuster (right). Courtesy of Joe Shuster and Gary Coddington.

worker. This was in the days when he didn't have to turn out tons of work, so he had the time to put his best efforts into it. In later years, he was absolutely swamped with work and had trouble with his eyes.

Joe: Somebody once pointed out to me that it was so meticulous. It had to be, because I couldn't see. I had to get down to about an inch above the paper in order to see the fine lines.

Jerry: That's true. His head was very close to the paper. And on top of that, his family had financial problems, and his apartment in Cleveland didn't have heat. Joe would be working often wearing gloves, and several sweaters, and a jacket or two—he was working under that handicap, on top of his vision problems.

Joe: *Action No. 1* was taken directly from the newspaper strip—it was pasted up. They were in a rush to meet the deadline on the first issue. Everything happened very fast. They made the decision to publish it and said to us, "Just go out and turn out 13 pages based on your strip." It was a rush job, and one of the things I like least to do is to rush my artwork. I'm too much of a perfectionist to do anything which is mediocre. The only solution Jerry and I could come up with was to cut up the strips into panels and paste the panels on a sheet the size of the page. If some panels were too long, we would shorten them, cut them off; if they were too short, we would extend them. You see, some of the panels were extended to fit the size of the page; it was quite an art job.

How did this art compare with the drawings for "The Superman" which you tore up?

Joe: Those early sketches looked too cartoony. I really wanted to do detailed

Superman newspaper strip #1, c. 1934. Siegel and Shuster's first unpublished version of Superman's origin. Shuster redrew these three panels for the first page of **Action Comics** #1, Superman's first published appearance (drawings of Superman after he had come to Earth as a babe and his discovery by a passing motorist are missing from the panels shown here, but were originally part of the daily strip. Presumably they are similar to the ones published in the comic book version). Note that, with the exception of the fancy cuffs and more prominent lacing

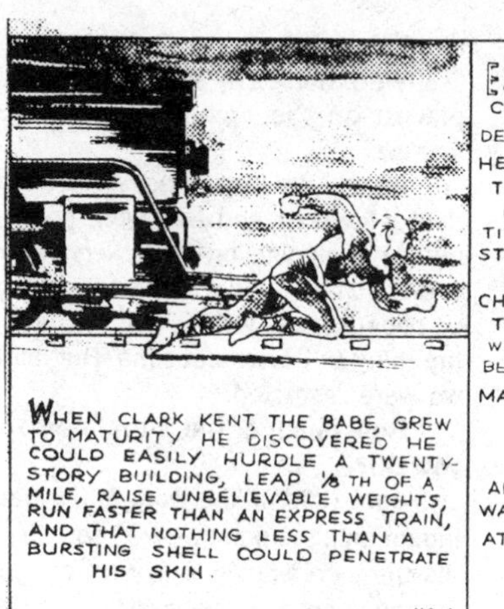

Superman is TM & © DC Comics, Inc.

on his boots, Superman's costume is the same as that in **Action** #1. Because he could not afford craft tint paper, Shuster simulated the effect by using a toothbrush to flick ink dots on the figures of Superman and the buildings of Krypton. Superman is TM & © DC Comics, Inc.

SUPERMAN!
CHAMPION OF THE OPPRESSED, THE PHYSICAL MARVEL WHO HAD SWORN TO DEVOTE HIS EXISTENCE TO HELPING THOSE IN NEED!

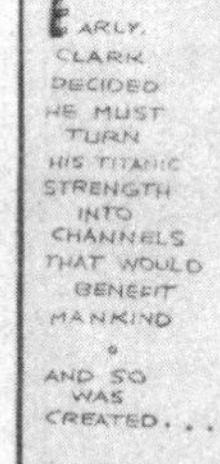

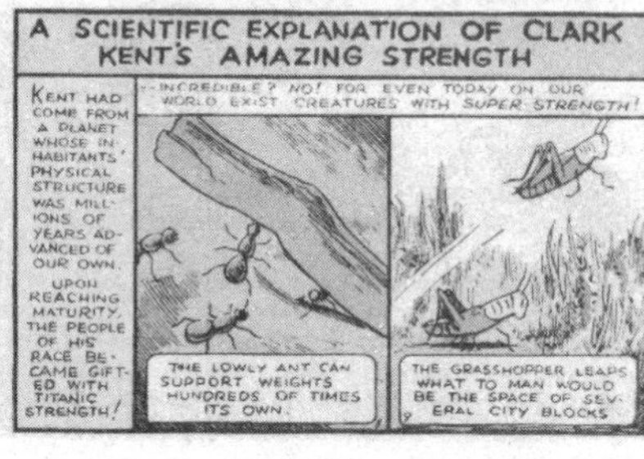

The first page of **Action Comics** #1 (June, 1938), Superman's first published appearance. Siegel instructed Shuster to draw the four panels of Superman demonstrating his powers in this page to replace the single figure of Superman outracing an express train in daily strip #1. Shuster redrew Superman in civilian garb so that his first appearance in costume would be more spectacular. In comparing this page with the newspaper strip, notice that Shuster had to delete some of the buildings in his redrawing of the first panel to make room for the Superman logo and the Siegel and Shuster byline. Perhaps because of time pressure, Shuster also greatly simplified this panel in redrawing it. Note his omission of the doomed Kryptonians and a third rocket ship as well as the less detailed buildings. Superman is TM & © DC Comics, Inc.

drawings—I was taking anatomy classes—but unfortunately I wasn't able to do it because of the time element. We had to turn the stuff out like a factory. Sometimes I wanted to sit down and spend an hour or two on one drawing, but it wasn't possible. I had to produce a complete page—or two or three—in one day. I took a lot of pride in my work, and I hated to do a mediocre job. Evidently, some of the writers enjoyed my work best of all for that very reason. I think Jules Feiffer called it crude. At the same time, he said it came to life. It was not polished. Some of the early drawings were very well drawn, and in great detail, because I had plenty of time to work on each panel. Later I was able to capture the action scenes very well, but I just didn't have time to put in all details—the polishing.

Jules Feiffer also mentioned something which no one has ever mentioned before. He said that one reason the kids loved my Superman artwork so much was the fact that it was almost like something they would draw. They could idenify with that kind of drawing. I won't say that it was childlike, but I took Feiffer's remark as a compliment. He didn't denigrate my work.

Were there any editorial restrictions placed on the early Superman comic strips?

Joe: In the beginning, we had a great deal of freedom, and Jerry wrote completely out of his imagination—very, very freely. We even had no editorial supervision to speak of, because they were in such a rush to get the thing in before deadline. But later on, we were restricted.

How much of the Superman art did you do?

Joe: I did all the work at the beginning up until the point where I couldn't handle the increasingly heavy art production burden alone. I needed and got assistance.

Who was the first artist you hired?

Joe: So much time has passed that it would be difficult for us to accurately answer that question. At that time, the strip was sold to the McClure Syndicate. As time went on, I had quite a production staff, but I was always involved in the drawing. Not all of the aspects of it, but I was involved in the initial layouts, the pencilling; and I did all the faces of Superman, every one of

Like his predecessors in science fiction, Superman was initially an outlaw and in early issues was wanted by the police. He was also a social activist whom Siegel conceived as a "thorn in the side of the establishment." Here he destroys an entire slum area to force the government to erect low cost housing in order to wipe out the conditions which fostered juvenile delinquency while the national guard attacks him with aerial bombardments. From **Action Comics** #8 (Jan., 1939). Superman is TM & © DC Comics, Inc.

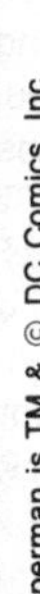

them—which was very tedious, because Jerry insisted (and I agreed with him) that there was nobody else that could really catch the spirit, the feeling, of Superman. I did all the figures, too, as a matter of fact. My staff did mainly the backgrounds and the inking, the polishing up of the pencilling—because a lot of my pencils were quite rough. But they were very spontaneous. What I did was get the initial action of the figure, and they would go on from there. The one thing they did not ink was Superman's face. For about an eight or ten-year period, I did every face of Superman.

What was your and Jerry's method of working before Superman required a production staff?

Joe: We worked very closely. At the beginning, he would sit down next to me at the drawing board. We would sit side by side. It was a real collaboration. He would have his script, and he would describe the scene to me. First he would read the scene to me, and I would absorb it and visualize it. And he'd say, "That's just what I had in mind," or "Let's make a few changes here." He would even describe the positions of Superman he wanted and how the character would act. It was almost like a movie scenario. He did almost everything except draw it. He really visualized everything for me, and I picked it up.

Jerry was one of the first I can remember—at least in the comic books—who really used the style of a screen writer. He would describe each scene, and the shot used—long shot, medium, close-up, overhead shot. It was marvelous. I guess he evolved the technique for himself, because we were both movie buffs. He would study the techniques of the movie serials, but he never saw a written screenplay.

What influence did you have on the

portrayal of Superman in other media—the Max Fleischer cartoons, for instance?

Joe: It was purely accidental. I was just down in Miami for a visit, and somebody who knew me said, "How would you like to come down and visit the Studios?" I said, "Yeah, I'd love to see them doing **Superman**. They were just starting on it. I went down there, and I was fascinated with it. And I suggested, "I wouldn't mind drawing some shots for you showing how Superman looks in side view, front view, three-quarter view; how Clark Kent would look, and Lois Lane would look." They said, "Fine, they'd love to have me do it." So I just sat down and spent a couple of days there drawing model sheets. I loved doing it, and I loved being involved in it. And we were lucky enough to receive a credit line on the cartoons afterwards.

Were you involved in the radio show much?

Joe: No, not really. Jerry may have been consulted about some of the initial scripts. But I remember meeting Bud Collyer, who played Superman. I think the show was very well done.

Did you ever watch any filming of the TV show?

Joe: No, but I met some of the cast later on. Several years ago we had a reunion and were interviewed on one of the stations in Los Angeles—Channel 13. We did an hour show, and I met the girl who played Lois Lane—Noel Neill—and Jack Larson (Jimmy Olsen).

Did you and Jerry have any part in casting the Superman movie?

Joe: That would have been great, but we were never approached as to who would play what part. But I had certain people in mind. One of the people I had in mind for newspaper editor Perry White was the fellow who played Lou Grant—Ed Asner. He was marvelous as a newspaper editor.

But you've met the stars of the film.

Jerry: Yes, at the Los Angeles premiere. I thought that Christopher Reeve was great as Superman. He really captured the sense of humor that Joe and I intended the early character to have.

What do you think has made Superman so popular for over 40 years?

Jerry: If you're interested in what made *Superman* what it is, here's one of the keys to what made it universally acceptable. Joe and I had certain inhibitions...which led to wish fulfillment which we expressed through our interest in science-fiction and our comic strip. That's where the dual-identity concept came from, and Clark Kent's problems with Lois. I imagine there are a lot of people in this world who are similarly frustrated. Joe and I both felt that way in high school, and he was able to put the feeling into sketches.

Joanne: Most teenage boys have disappointments with girls—

Jerry: True! That's why I say it's a universal theme, and that's why so many people could relate to it.

Joanne: That's why love songs are so popular. They're all full of passion for someone who doesn't care about the singer.

Jerry: There's one other comment that I would like to add before we close. It has been very frustrating for Joe and me to have been off the character that we originated and loved for so many years. We are grateful that, in our senior years—we're both almost 69—that the corporation which owns Superman is treating us well.

Joanne: We have a good relationship with DC and Warner's.

Thanks to Gary Coddington, "World's Foremost Superman Authority," for his help with this interview.

The Siegel and Shuster interview originally appeared in ***Nemo*** *no. 2 by Fantagraphics Books.*

DIRECTORY OF COMIC AND NOSTALGIA SHOPS

This is a current up-to-date list, but is not all-inclusive. We cannot assume any responsibility in your dealings with these shops. This list is provided for your information only. When planning your trips, it would be advisable to make appointments in advance. To get your shop included in the next edition, write for rates. Items stocked by these shops are listed just after the telephone numbers and are coded as follows:

(a) Golden Age comics
(b) Silver Age comics
(c) New comics, magazines
(d) Pulps
(e) Paperbacks
(f) Big Little Books
(g) Magazines (old)
(h) Books (old)
(i) Movie posters, lobby cards
(j) Original art
(k) Toys (old)
(l) Records (old)
(m) Gum trading cards
(n) Underground comics
(o) Old radio show tapes
(p) Premiums
(q) Comic related posters
(r) Comic supplies
(s) Role playing games
(t) Star Trek items
(u) Dr. Who items
(v) Japanese animation items

ALABAMA:

Discount Comic Book Shop
1301 Noble Street
Anniston, AL 36201
PH:205-238-8373 (a-e,l,m)

Court St. Books & Collectibles
416 N. Court St.
Florence, AL 35630
No phone (a-c,e,g-i,l-n,r,t)

ARIZONA:

AAA Best Comics, Etc.
9204 N. Seventh St., #12
Phoenix, AZ 85020
PH:602-997-4012 (a-c,g,q,r,v)

All About Books & Comics
529 E. Camelback
Phoenix, AZ 85012
PH:602-277-0757 (a-e,g,h,l-n,q-u)

All About Books & Comics West
4208 W. Dunlap
Phoenix, AZ 85051
PH:602-435-0410 (a-e,g,h,l-n,q-u)

High Desert Books & Comics
116 El Camino Real
Sierra Vista, AZ 85635
PH:602-458-1606 (a-c,e,g,h,n,q-v)

Marty Hay—Comics
329 E. Main St.
Springerville, AZ 85938
PH:602-333-2222 (a,b,d-f,h-j,r)

The Comic Corner
5031 E. Fifth St.
Tucson, AZ 85711
PH:602-326-2677 (b,c,e)

Fantasy Comics
6001 E. 22nd St.
Tucson, AZ 85711
PH:602-748-7483 (b,c,n,q,r)

Fantasy Comics
2745 N. Campbell
Tucson, AZ 85719
PH:602-325-9790 (b,c,n,q,r)

ARKANSAS:

Paperbacks Plus
2207 Rogers Avenue
Fort Smith, AR 72901
PH:501-452-5446 (b,c,e,g-i,n,q,r)

Alternate Worlds Books & Comics
117 Third St.
Hot Springs, AR 71913
PH:501-624-2040 (a-c,e,j,q-s)

Pie-Eyes
5211 W. 65th St.
Little Rock, AR 72209
PH:501-568-1414 (a-i,k-n,p-u)

Collector's Edition Comics
5310 MacArthur Drive
North Little Rock, AR 72118
PH:501-753-2586 (a-c,e,h,q-s)

TNT Collectors Hut
503 W. Hale Ave.
Osceola, AR 72370
PH:501-563-5760 (b,c,e,l,m,r)

CALIFORNIA:

Comic Heaven
24 W. Main Street
Alhambra, CA 91801
PH:818-289-3945 (a-c,g,j,q-t)

California Comics & Books
Benton Park Center
2517 South H Street
Bakersfield, CA 93304
PH:805-833-3810 (a-c,g,j,m,q-t,v)

Comics & Comix
2461 Telegraph Ave.
Berkeley, CA 94704
PH:415-483-1744
(a-c,e,g,h,m,n,q,r)

Fantasy Kingdom
1802 W. Olive Ave.
Burbank, CA 91506
PH:818-954-8432 (a-c,g,i,k,m,r,t-v)

Comics & Comix
6135 Sunrise
Citrus Heights, CA 95610
PH:916-969-0717
(a-c,e,g,h,m,n,q,r)

Superior Comics
1630 Superior
Costa Mesa, CA 92627
PH:714-631-3933
(a-c,e-k,m,n,p-t,v)

Graphitti Comics & Games
4325 Overland Ave.
Culver City, CA 90230
PH:213-559-2058 (b,c,g,i,l,q-s)

Comic Quest
24346 Muirlands
El Toro, CA 92630
PH:714-951-9668 (b,c,j,q-s)

The Comic Gallery
675 N. Broadway
Escondido, CA 92025
PH:619-745-5660 (a-c,j,m,n,q-t,v)

The Comic Castle
320 - 2nd St., Suite 2H
Eureka, CA 95501
PH:707-444-BOOK (b,c,g,n,q,r)

Comics & Comix
Solano Mall
Fairfield, CA 94533
PH:707-427-1202
(a-c,e,g,h,m,n,q,r)

Wonderland Comics
1407 N. Van Ness
Fresno, CA 93728
PH:209-968-3950 (a-i,k,n,q-s)

Adventureland Comics
106 N. Harbor Blvd.
Fullerton, CA 92632
PH:714-738-3698 (a-c,q,r,v)

Book Bazaar
520 N. Harbor Blvd.
Fullerton, CA 92632
PH:714-525-4967 (b,e-h,n)

Comic Castle
107 W. Amerige
Fullerton, CA 92632
PH:714-879-6160 (a-v)

Geoffrey's Comics
15530 Crenshaw Blvd.
Gardena, CA 90249
PH:213-538-3198
(a-c,g,j,m-o,q,r,t,v)

Fantasy Illustrated
12531 Harbor Blvd.
Garden Grove, CA 92640
PH:714-537-0087 (a-f,h,m)

Shooting Star Comics
700 E. Colorado Blvd.
Glendale, CA 91205
PH:818-502-1535 (a-c,j,m,n,q-s,v)

The American Comic Book Co.
2670 E. Florence
Huntington Park, CA 90255
PH:213-589-4500 (a-k,m,n,p)

Comic Time
770 E. La Habra Blvd.
La Habra, CA 90631
PH:213-691-2921 (a-c,m,n,q-s)

The Compleat Paperbacker
15711 E. Amar Rd.
La Puente, CA 91744
PH:818-330-0400 (a,b,d,e,g,n)

The American Comic Co.
3972 Atlantic Ave.
Long Beach, CA 90807
PH:213-426-0393 (a-k,m,n,p)

Pacific Fantasy Bookstore
5622 East Second Street
Long Beach, CA 90803
PH:213-434-5136 (c,e,g,j,n)

R-B Sport Collectors Dugout and The Comic Strip
4125 Norse Way
Long Beach, CA 90808
PH:213-492-2116 (b,c,g,m,q,r)

"The Original" Another World
1615 Colorado Blvd.
Los Angeles, CA 90041
PH:213-257-7757 (b-e,q-v)

Golden Apple Comics
7711 Melrose Ave.
Los Angeles, CA 90046
PH:213-658-6047 (a-c,f,g,j,m,n)

Golden Apple Comics #3
8934 West Pico Blvd.
Los Angeles, CA 90035
PH:213-274-2008 (a-c,f,g,j,m,n)

Graphitti Westwood—UCLA
960 Gayley Ave.
Los Angeles, CA 90024
PH:213-824-3656 (a-c,g,i,l-n,q-s)

Bonanza Books & Comics
Roseburg Square
813 W. Roseburg Avenue
Modesto, CA 95350-5058
PH:209-529-0415 (a-f,m,o-v)

Modesto Coin Center
145 Woodrow Ave., Suite D
Modesto, CA 95350
PH:209-521-6500 (c,e,m,n,p-u)

Ninth Nebula: The Comic Book Shop
11517 Burbank Blvd. (in back)
North Hollywood, CA 91601
PH:818-509-2901 (a-c,f-j,l-n,q-v)

Golden Apple Comics #2
8962 Reseda Blvd.
Northridge, CA 91324
PH:818-993-7804 (a-c,f,g,j,m,n)

Freedonia Funnyworks
350 S. Tustin Ave.
Orange, CA 92666
PH:714-639-5830 (a-c,e-k,m,n,p-r)

Desert Comics
174 N. Palm Canyon Dr.
Palm Springs, CA 92262
PH:619-325-5805

Comics & Comix
405 California
Palo Alto, CA 94306
PH:415-328-8100
(a-c,e,g,h,m,n,q,r)

Lee's Comics
3429 Alma St.
(In Alma Plaza)
Palo Alto, CA 94306
PH:415-493-3957
(a-c,e-g,j,m-o,q,r,t-v)

Funtime Comics & Fantasy
147 Pomona Mall East
Pomona, CA 91766
PH:714-629-8860 (a-v)

Galaxy Comics & Cards
1503 Aviation Blvd.
Redondo Beach, CA 90278
PH:213-374-7440 (a-m,q-s)

Markstu Discount Comics
3642 - 7th St.
Riverside, CA 92501
PH:714-684-8544
(a-c,e-i,k-m,o,q,s)

Comics & Comix
921 K Street Mall
Sacramento, CA 95814
PH:916-442-5142
(a-c,e,g,h,m,n,q,r)

The Comic Gallery
4224 Balboa Ave.
San Diego, CA 92117
PH:619-483-4853 (a-c,j,m,n,q-t,v)

Golden State Comics
4688 Boundary St.
San Diego, CA 92116
PH:619-283-3666 (a-c,g,r)

Comics & Comix
700 Lombard
San Francisco, CA 94133
PH:415-982-3511
(a-c,e,g,h,m,n,q,r)

Comics & Comix
650 Irving
San Francisco, CA 94122
PH:415-665-5888
(a-c,e,g,h,m,n,q,r)

Comics and Da-Kind
1643 Noriega St.
San Francisco, CA 94122
PH:415-753-9678 (a-c,e,m,q,r)

San Francisco Card Exchange
1316 - 18th Ave.
San Francisco, CA 94122
PH:415-665-TEAM (a,b,g,i,m,r,t)

Gary's Corner Bookstore
1051 So. San Gabriel Blvd.
San Gabriel, CA 91776
PH:818-285-7575 (b,c,e,m,q-s)

Comic Collector Shop
73 E. San Fernando
San Jose, CA 95113
PH:408-287-2254 (a-g,l,n,q,r)

The Comic Shop
16390 E. 14th St.
San Leandro, CA 94578
PH:415-278-9545 (a-c,g,m,q,r)

The Sub
879 Higuera St.
San Luis Obispo, CA 93401
PH:805-541-3735 (c,e,g,h,n,q-v)

San Mateo Comic Books, Baseball Cards & Original Art
306 Baldwin Ave.
San Mateo, CA 94401
PH:415-344-1536 (a-c,g,j,l-n,q,r)

Brian's Books
3225 Cabrillo Ave.
Santa Clara, CA 95051
PH:408-985-7481 (a-c,g,m,q-s)

R & K Comics
3153 El Camino Real
Santa Clara, CA 95051
PH:408-554-6512
(a-c,f,m,n,q,r,t,v)

Atlantis Fantasyworld
707 Pacific Avenue
Santa Cruz, CA 95060
PH:408-426-0158 (a-c,g-i,n,o,q-u)

Markgraf's Comic Books
121 S. Broadway
Santa Maria, CA 93454
PH:805-925-7470 (a,c,g,i,m,q-t)

Hi De Ho Comics & Fantasy
525 Santa Monica Blvd.
Santa Monica, CA 90401
PH:213-394-2820
(a-d,f,g,i,j,m,n,q,r)

Superior Comics
220 Pier Ave.
Santa Monica, CA 90405
PH:213-396-7005
(a-c,e-k,m,n,p-t,v)

Super Hero Universe #8
Sycamore Plaza
3064 Cochran St.
Simi Valley, CA 93065
PH:805-583-3027 (b,c,e,g,n,p-s)

Cheap Comics
12123 Garfield Ave.
South Gate, CA 90280
PH:213-408-0900
(c-e,h,i,k,m-o,r-u)

Joe & Elisa Escove Collectables
725 N. El Dorado
Stockton, CA 95202
PH:209-941-2646 (c,e,m,p-u)

The American Comic Book Co.
12206 Ventura Blvd.
Studio City, CA 91604
PH:818-980-4976 (a-k,m,n,p)

Wild & Free Comic Book Corp.
(Mail Order)
11684 Ventura Blvd. #335
Studio City, CA 91604
PH:818-509-2901 (a-c,f-j,l-n,q-s)

Roleplayers
5933 Adobe Rd.
29 Palms, CA 92277
PH:619-367-6282

Ralph's Comic Corner
2408 E. Main St.
Ventura, CA 93003
PH:805-653-2732 (a-d,m,n,q-s)

The Second Time Around Bookshop
391 E. Main St.
Ventura, CA 93001
PH:805-643-3154 (a,b,d-h,l,n,s,t)

Comic Castle
14464 - 7th St. Unit C
Victorville, CA 92392
PH:619-245-8006 (a-v)

Graphitti Comics & Records
Amfac Hotel (Rear) LAX
8639 Lincoln Blvd. #102
Westchester, L.A., CA 90045
PH:213-641-8661 (b,c,g,i,l,q-s)

Franco's Comic & Game Center
14153 E. Whittier Blvd., #109
Whittier, CA 90605
PH:213-698-9669 (a-c,m,n,q-s)

COLORADO:

The Colorado Comics/Heroes & Dragons
220 N. Tejon St.
Colorado Springs, CO 80903
PH:719-635-2516 (a-c,e,n,q-u)

Heroes & Dragons
The Citadel
Colorado Springs, CO 80909
PH:719-550-9570 (b,c,e,o,q-v)

CONNECTICUT:

Space Travelers
77 Minerva St.
Derby, CT 06418
PH:203-734-6400 (a-c,e,g,n,q-v)

The Nostalgia Shop
2980 Whitney Ave.
Hamden, CT 06518
PH:203-281-0577 (a-k,m,p-v)

Comic World Superstore
168 Bridgeport Ave. (U.S. 1)
Milford, CT 06460
PH:203-877-1562 (a-c,m,q-s,u)

Wholesale City
166 Bridgeport Ave. (U.S. 1)
Milford, CT 06460
PH:203-877-1562 (c,m,q,r)

F & S Comics & Fantasy Shop
54 Bank St.
New Milford, CT 06776
PH:203-355-3426 (a-k,m-u)

Jim's Comic Book Shop
1629 East Main St.
Waterbury, CT 06705
PH:203-753-2450 (a-c,m,q-s,u)

DELAWARE:

Comics & Robots II, Inc.
46½ E. Main St., 2nd Floor
Newark, DE 19711
PH:302-454-7115 (a-c,k,n,q,r,v)

Comics & Robots
509 Philadelphia Pike
Wilmington, DE 19809
PH:302-764-6792 (a-c,k,n,q,r,v)

DISTRICT OF COLUMBIA:

Another World
1504 Wisconsin Ave.
Georgetown,
Washington, DC 20007
PH:202-333-8650 (a-c,k,q-s)

FLORIDA:

The Funny Farm
422 26th St. W.
Bradenton, FL 34205
PH:813-747-7714 (a,b,f,k,m,p,r)

The Time Machine II
Southwood Mall
5748 - 14 St. W.
Bradenton, FL 34207
PH:813-758-3684 (a-c,e,n,q-v)

Comics Etc.
1271-125 Semoran Blvd.
Lake Howell Square
Casselberry, FL 32707
PH:407-679-5665 (b,c,e,m,q-t)

Phil's Comic Shoppe
3275 University Dr.
(in the Coral Springs Mall)
Coral Springs, FL 33065
PH:305-752-0580 (c,m,q,r)

Cliff's Books
209 N. Woodland Blvd. (17-92)
De Land, FL 32720
PH:904-734-6963 (a-h,j-u)

Family Book Shop
1301 N. Woodland Blvd.
(near Daytona Beach & Orlando)
De Land, FL 32720
PH:904-736-6501
(b,c,e,g,h,m,n,r,s)

Intergalactic Comics and Collectibles
109 E. Semoran Blvd.
(17-92 & 436, at Zayre Plaza)
Fern Park, FL 32730
PH:305-260-0017 (a-i,k-m,p-v)

Novel Ideas
804 W. University Ave.
Gainesville, FL 32601
PH:904-374-8593 (b,c,e,n,q-v)

Past—Present—Future Comics
6186 S. Congress Ave., Suite A4
Lantana, FL 33462
PH:305-433-3068 (b,c,q-s)

Geppi's Comic World
2200 East Bay Drive #203
Largo, FL 34601
PH:813-585-0325 (a-c,f)

Dr. Fun Comics
530 Savage Ct.
Longwood, FL 32750
PH:305-332-7722 (a-i,m,n,r,t)

Acevedo's Collectables
195 S. State Road 7
Margate, FL 33063
PH:305-977-7352 (b,c,g,i,k,m,r)

Star-Gate
277 N. Babcock Street
Melbourne, FL 32935
PH:305-259-2374 (a-c,e,g-j,m,p-v)

Comics & Fantasy
105 Bank St.
New Port Richey, FL 33552
PH:813-846-1261
(a-c,e,g,i-k,m,n,q-s)

Phil's Comic Shoppe
263 Rock Island Rd.
N. Lauderdale, FL 33068
PH:305-726-1622 (b,c,m,n,q,r)

Tropic Comics South
742 N.E. 167 St.
N. Miami Beach, FL 33162
PH:305-940-8700 (a-c,i,n,q,r)

The Cartoon Museum
4300 S. Semoran, Suite 109
Orlando, FL 32822-2453
PH:305-273-0141 (a-k,m,n,p-r)

Coliseum of Comics
4103 S. Orange Blossom Tr.
Orlando, FL 32809
PH:407-422-5757 (b,c,g,m,n,q-s)

Enterprise 1701
2814 Corrine Drive
Orlando, FL 32803
PH:407-896-1701 (c,e,o,q-v)

Sincere Comics
Town & Country Plaza
3300 N. Pace Blvd.
Pensacola, FL 32505
PH:904-432-1352 (b-e,j,n,q-s)

Champions
1739 N. University Dr.
Plantation, FL 33322
PH:305-475-2633 (b,c,m,r)

Tropic Comics
313 S. State Rd. 7
Plantation, FL 33317
PH:305-587-8878 (a-c,i,n,q,r)

Comic Exchange, Inc.
8432 W. Oakland Park Blvd.
Sunrise, FL 33351
PH:305-742-0777 (b-e,g,q-v)

GEORGIA:

Art Moods Cards & Comics
1058 Mistletoe Rd.
Decatur, GA 30033
PH:404-321-1899 (a-c,f,g,m,q-s)

Stone Mountain Supplies
645 S. Main St.
Stone Mountain, GA 30083
PH:404-498-6676 (r)

HAWAII:

Jelly's Comics & Books
404 Piikoi Street
Honolulu, HI 96814
PH:808-538-6667, 538-7771
(a-c,e,g,h,j,l-n,p-t,v)

Compleat Comics Company
1728 Kaahumanu Avenue
Wailuku, Maui, HI 96793
PH:808-242-5875 (a-c,m,n,q-s)

IDAHO:

King's Komix Kastle
1706 N. 18th St. (appointments)
Boise, ID 83702
PH:208-343-7142 (a-i,m,n,q,r)

King's Komix Kastle II
2560 Leadville (drop in)
Mail: 1706 N. 18th
Boise, ID 83706
PH:208-343-7055 (a-i,m,n,q,r)

New Mythology Comics & Science Fiction
1725 Broadway
Boise, ID 83706
PH:208-344-6744 (a-e,n,q-s)

ILLINOIS:

Friendly Frank's Distribution
(Wholesale Whse.—retailers only)
727 Factory Rd.
Addison, IL 60101

Friendly Frank's Comics
11941 S. Cicero
Alsip, IL 60658
PH:312-371-6760 (a-d,f,g,i,j,n,q,r)

Moondog's Comicland
Plaza Verde Center
1231 W. Dundee Rd.
Buffalo Grove, IL 60090
PH:312-259-6060 (a-c,m,r,s,u,v)

The Book Nook
501 N. Neil St.
Champaign, IL 61820
PH:217-356-4773 (a-c,e-j,n,o,q-v)

Comics for Heroes
1702 W. Foster
Chicago, IL 60640
PH:312-769-4745 (a-c,m,n,q-v)

Comics for Heroes
3937 W. Lawrence
Chicago, IL 60625
PH:312-478-8585 (a-c,m,n,q-v)

Larry Laws (Mail Order)
Phone for Appointment
831 Cornelia
Chicago, IL 60657
PH:312-477-9247 (g,h)

Joe Sarno's Comic Kingdom
5941 W. Irving Park Rd.
Chicago, IL 60634
PH:312-545-2231 (a-c,j,m,q-s)

Yesterday
1143 W. Addison St.
Chicago, IL 60613
PH:312-248-8087 (a,b,d-g,i-n,r,t)

Moondog's Comicland
114 S. Waukegan Rd.
Deerbrook Mall
Deerfield, IL 60015
PH:312-272-6080 (a-c,m,r,s,u,v)

The Paper Escape
318 W. 1st Street
Dixon, IL 61021
PH:815-284-7567 (b,c,e,g,m,q-t)

Graham Crackers Comics
5228 South Main Street
Downers Grove, IL 60515
PH:312-852-1810 (a-d,f,n,q-s)

GEM Comics
156 N. York Rd.
Elmhurst, IL 60126
PH:312-833-8787 (a-c,q-s)

Galaxy of Books
Rt. 137 & Sheridan Rd.
Great Lakes Depot
Great Lakes, IL 60064
PH:312-473-1099 (a-c,e,q,r,t,u)

Friendly Frank's Comics
3427 Ridge Road
Lansing, IL 60438
PH:312-418-1220 (a-d,f,g,i,j,n,q,r)

Moondog's Comicland
139 W. Prospect Ave.
Mt. Prospect, IL 60056
PH:312-398-6060 (a-c,m,r,s,u,v)

Graham Crackers Comics
5 East Chicago Ave.
Naperville, IL 60540
PH:312-355-4310 (a-d,f,n,q-s)

Tomorrow Is Yesterday
5600 N. Second St.
Rockford, IL 61111
PH:815-633-0330 (a-g,i,j,m,q-v)

Moondog's COMICLAND
1403 W. Schaumburg Rd.
Schaumburg Plaza
Schaumburg, IL 60194
PH:312-529-6060 (a-c,m,r,s,u,v)

B.J.'s Comic/Country Corner
260 N. Ardmore Ave.
Villa Park, IL 60181
PH:312-834-0383 (a-r)

Unicorn Comics & Cards
216 S. Villa Avenue
Villa Park, IL 60181
PH:312-279-5777
(a-c,e,g,h,j,l-n,q-s)

Heroland Comics
6963 W. 111th St.
Worth, IL 60482
PH:312-448-2937 (a-c,j,m-s)

Galaxy of Books
1908 Sheridan Road
Zion, IL 60099
PH:312-872-3313
(a-c,e,f,h,l,q,r,t,u)

INDIANA:

25th Century Five & Dime
106 E. Kirkwood, P.O. Box 7
Bloomington, IN 47402
PH:812-332-0011
(b,c,e,g-i,m,n,q-u)

The Bookstack
112 W. Lexington Ave.
Elkhart, IN 46516
PH:219-293-3815 (b,c,e,h)

Books, Comics and Things
2212 Maplecrest Rd.
Fort Wayne, IN 46815
PH:219-749-4045 (a-c,e-h,m,q-u)

Books, Comics and Things
6105 West Jefferson Blvd.
Westland Mall
Fort Wayne, IN 46804
PH:219-436-0159 (a-c,e-h,m,q-u)

Broadway Comic Book & Baseball Card Shop
2423 Broadway
Fort Wayne, IN 46807
PH:219-744-1456 (a-i,m,p-t)

Friendly Frank's Distr., Inc.
(Wholesale only)
3990 Broadway
Gary, IN 46408
PH:219-884-5052 (c,g,n,r,s)

Friendly Frank's Comics
220 Main Street
Hobart, IN 46342
PH:219-942-6020 (a-d,f,g,i,j,n,q,r)

Comic Carnival & Nostalgia Emporium
6265 N. Carrollton Ave.
Indianapolis, IN 46220
PH:317-253-8882 (a-j,m-p)

Comic Carnival & Nostalgia Emporium
5002 S. Madison Ave.
Indianapolis, IN 46227
PH:317-787-3773 (a-j,m-p)

Comic Carnival & Nostalgia Emporium
982 N. Mitthoeffer Rd.
Indianapolis, IN 46229
PH:317-898-5010 (a-j,m-p)

John's Comic Closet
4610 East 10th St.
Indianapolis, IN 46201
PH:317-357-6611
(b,c,e,g-j,m,n,q-u)

IOWA:

Oak Leaf Comics
23 - 5th S.W.
Mason City, IA 50401
PH:515-424-0333 (a-c,e,f,h-v)

The Comiclogue
520 Elm St., P.O. Box 65304
West Des Moines, IA 50265
PH:515-279-9006 (a-c,j,k,m-r,t,u)

KANSAS:

The Comic Corner
2220 Iowa
Lawrence, KS 66046
PH:913-841-4294 (a-v)

Air Capital Comics
954 S. Oliver
Wichita, KS 67218
PH:316-681-0219 (a-v)

KENTUCKY:

Comic Book World
7130 Turfway Road
Florence, KY 41042
PH:606-371-9562 (a-c,e,m,q-v)

Comic Connection
929 South Limestone
Lexington, KY 40503
PH:606-255-4707 (a-i,m,n,q-s)

LOUISIANA:

Comic Book Emporium
5201 Nicholson Dr., Suite H
Beau Chene Shopping Village
Baton Rouge, LA 70820
PH:504-767-1227 (b,c,e,h,i,n,q-u)

B.T. & W.D. Giles
P. O. Box 271
Keithville, LA 71047
PH:318-925-6654 (a,b,d-f,h)

B S I Comics
5039 Fairfield St.
Metairie, LA 70006
PH:504-889-2665 (a-c,g,q,r,t,v)

The Bookworm of N.O.E.
7011 Read Blvd.
New Orleans, LA 70127
PH:504-242-7608 (c,e,q-u)

Comix Plus
637 Carollo Dr.
Slidell, LA 70458
PH:504-649-HERO (b,c,q,r)

MAINE:

Lippincott Books
624 Hammond St.
Bangor, ME 04401
PH:207-942-4398 (a,b,d-h,n,p,r,t)

Moonshadow Comics
10 Exchange St.
Portland, ME 04101
PH:207-772-3870
(a-c,e,g,i,j,n,q-s)

MARYLAND:

Universal Comics
5300 East Drive
Arbutus, MD 21227
PH:301-242-4578 (a-c,e,g,k,q,r,t)

Comic Book Kingdom
4307 Harford Road
Baltimore, MD 21214
PH:301-426-4529 (a-h,m,r)

Geppi's Comic World
7019 Security Blvd.
Hechinger's Square
at Security Mall
Baltimore, MD 21207
PH:301-298-1758 (a-c,f)

Geppi's Comic World
Harbor Place
Upper Level, Light St. Pavilion
301 Light St.
Baltimore, MD 21202
PH:301-547-0910 (a-c,f)

Big Planet Comics
4865 Cordell Ave. (2nd Floor)
Bethesda, MD 20814
PH:301-654-6856 (c,j,n,q,r)

Bookcom — Book & Comic Outlet
15528 Annapolis Rd.
Freestate Mall
Bowie, MD 20715
PH:301-464-3570 (a-c,e,q,r)

Alternate Worlds
9924 York Road
Cockeysville, MD 21030
PH:301-667-0440 (b,c,n,q-v)

The Closet of Comics
7319 Baltimore Ave.
College Park, MD 20740
PH:301-699-0498 (a-c,e,g,n,q,r)

Bookcom — E.T. Home Video
Marlboro Pike
Forestville Plaza
Forestville, MD 20747
PH:301-568-6661 (b,c,e,l,r)

Collectors Choice
368 Armstrong Ave.
Laurel, MD 20707
PH:301-725-0887 (a-n,p-r,t,u)

Comic Classics
365 Main Street
Laurel, MD 20707
PH:301-792-4744, 490-9811
(a-c,e,m,n,q,r,t-v)

Bookcom
8265 Rt. 3 & Old Mill Rd.,
Suite 12
Millersville, MD 21108
PH:301-987-1602 (a-c,e,q,r)

Bookcom — Book & Comic Outlet
7736 Riverdale Rd.
Carrollton Mall
New Carrollton, MD 20784
PH:301-731-5851 (a-c,e,m,n,q,r)

Geppi's Comic World
8317 Fenton St.
Silver Spring, MD 20910
PH:301-588-2546 (a-c,e,f)

The Barbarian Book Shop
11254 Triangle Lane
Wheaton, MD 20902
PH:301-946-4184 (a-c,e,h,n,q-v)

MASSACHUSETTS:

New England Comics
140A Harvard Ave.
Allston (Boston), MA 02134
PH:617-783-1848 (a-g,n,q-s)

New England Comics
139A Brighton Ave.
Allston (Boston), MA 02134
PH:617-783-3955 (a-g,n,q-s)

Comically Speaking
1310B Mass. Ave.
Arlington, MA 02174
PH:617-643-XMEN
(a-e,g,i,m,n,q-s)

Bargain Books and Collectibles
247 So. Main St.
Attleboro, MA 02703
PH:617-226-1668 (b,c,q-t,v)

Super Hero Universe #3
41 West St.
Boston, MA 02111
PH:617-423-6676 (a-c,e,g,m,p-s)

New England Comics
748 Crescent Street
East Crossing Plaza
Brockton, MA 02402
PH:617-559-5068 (a-g,n,q-s)

The Million Year Picnic
99 Mt. Auburn St.
Cambridge, MA 02138
PH:617-492-6763 (a-s)

Super Hero Universe #1
1105 Massachusetts Ave.
Cambridge, MA 02138
PH:617-354-5344 & 800-338-0637
(b,c,e,g,n,p-r)

Bop City Comics
66 Hollis St. (Rt. 126)
Framingham, MA 01701
PH:617-872-2317

New England Comics
12A Pleasant St.
Malden, MA 02148
PH:617-322-2404 (a-g,n,q-s)

Imagine That Bookstore
59 Main St.
North Adams, MA 01247
PH:413-663-5195 (b-i,l,m,o,q-u)

New England Comics
714A Washington Street
Norwood, MA 02062
PH:617-769-4552 (a-g,n,q-s)

Imagine That Bookstore
58 Dalton St.
Pittsfield, MA 01201
PH:413-445-5934 (b-i,l,m,o,q-u)

New England Comics
1350 Hancock Street
Quincy, MA 02169
PH:617-770-1848 (a-g,n,q-s)

Pages of Reading
25 Harnden Street
Reading, MA 01867
PH:617-944-9613 (b,c,e,h,l,q-u)

Bill Cole (appointment only)
121 Liberty St.
South Quincy, MA 02169
PH:617-963-5510 (a,b)

The Outer Limits
457 Moody St.
Waltham, MA 02154
PH:617-891-0444
(a-c,e-i,k,m,n,q-v)

Golden Age Buyers
457-A Moody St.
Waltham, MA 02154
PH:617-891-0444 (a-c)

Bookstore Restaurant, Inc.
Kendrick Ave., Mayo Beach
Wellfleet, MA 02667
PH:617-349-3154 (a-e,g-i)

Bop City Comics
22 Front St.
Midtown Mall
Worcester, MA 01608
PH:617-797-4646

That's Entertainment
151 Chandler Street
Worcester, MA 01609
PH:617-755-4207 (a-i,k-m,q-v)

MICHIGAN:

Dave's II, Comics & Collectibles
623 E. William (3rd Floor)
Ann Arbor, MI 48104
PH:313-665-6969 (a-n,p-r,t-v)

Tom & Terry Comics
508 Lafayette Ave.
Bay City, MI 48708
PH:517-895-5525 (b,c,m,q,r)

The Reading Place
107 W. Lawrence Ave.
Charlotte, MI 48813
PH:517-543-7922 (b,c,e,m,r)

Taurus Comics
202 E. State St.
Cheboygan, MI 49721
PH:616-627-2820 (a-c,g-i,k,q-s)

Curious Book Shop
307 E. Grand River Ave.
East Lansing, MI 48823
PH:517-332-0112 (a-k,m-p)

Argos Book Shop
1405 Robinson Rd. S.E.
Grand Rapids, MI 49506
PH:616-454-0111 (a-h,m,n)

Tardy's Collector's Corner, Inc.
2009 Eastern Ave. S.E.
Grand Rapids, MI 49507
PH:616-247-7828
(a-c,f,g,j,m,n,q,r)

Capital City Comics & Books
2004 E. Michigan Ave.
Lansing, MI 48912
PH:517-485-0416 (a-j,n,p-v)

Taurus Comics
116 Spring St.
Marquette, MI 49855
PH:906-225-1499 (a-c,g-i,k,q-s)

Taurus Comics
609 Huron Ave.
Port Huron, MI 48060
PH:313-984-5556 (a-c,g-i,k,q-s)

Dave's Comics & Collectibles
816 W. 11 Mile Road
Royal Oak, MI 48067
PH:313-548-1230 (a-n,p-r,t-v)

Book Stop
1160 Chicago Drive
Wyoming, MI 49509-1004
PH:616-245-0090
(a-c,e,g,m,n,q,r,t)

MINNESOTA:

Collector's Connection
101 East Superior Street
Duluth, MN 55802
PH:218-722-9551 (b,c,e,m,q-s)

Midway Book & Comic
1579 University Ave.
St. Paul, MN 55104
PH:612-644-7605 (a-h,n,q-u)

MISSISSIPPI:

Star Store
4212 North State St.
Jackson, MS 39206
PH:601-362-8001 (a-v)

Spanish Trail Books
1006 Thorn Ave.
Ocean Springs, MS 39564
PH:601-875-1144 (a-h,t,u)

MISSOURI:

The Paperback Rack
126 E. 69 Highway
Kansas City, MO 64119
PH:816-452-7478 (b-e,n,r)

B & R Comix Center
4747 Morganford
St. Louis, MO 63116
PH:314-353-4013 (b,c,g,j,n,q,r,u)

Mo's Comics & Stories
4530 Gravois
St. Louis, MO 63116
PH:314-353-9500
(a-d,f,k,m,p-r,t,u)

The Book Rack
300 W. Olive
Springfield, MO 65806
PH:417-865-4945 (b-f,h,i,q,r)

MONTANA:

Marvel-Us Comics
510 Central Avenue
Inside of Antique Town
Great Falls, MT 59401
PH:406-761-7161

The Book Exchange
Holiday Village Shopping Center
Missoula, MT 59801
PH:406-728-6342 (a-c,e,g,h,n,q-s)

NEBRASKA:

Star Realm
7305 South 85th St.
Omaha, NE 68128
PH:402-331-4844 (b,c,e,i-m,q-u)

NEVADA:

Fandom's COMICWORLD OF RENO
2001 East Second St.
Reno, NV 89502
PH:702-786-6663 (a-c,g,q,r)

Stella Enterprises
126 'B' Street
P.O. Box 251
Sparks, NV 89432
PH:702-359-7812 (a-c,f,g,j,m,q,r)

NEW HAMPSHIRE:

James F. Payette
P. O. Box 750
Bethlehem, NH 03574
PH:603-869-2097 (a,b,d-h)

Collectibles Unlimited
30A Warren St.
Concord, NH 03301
PH:603-228-3712 (a-c,m,n,q-u)

Comic Store
66 Lake Ave.
Manchester, NH 03101
PH:603-668-6705 (b,c,j,n,o,q-v)

Comic Store
300 Main St.
Simoneau Plaza
Nashua, NH 03060
PH:603-881-HULK (b,c,j,m-o,q-v)

NEW JERSEY:

Thunder Road Comics & Cards
424 High Street
Burlington, NJ 08016
(a-c,m,n,q,r,v)

Fat Moose Comics & Games
235 Ridgedale Avenue
Cedar Knolls, NJ 07927
PH:201-898-4734 (b,c,q-s)

Rainbow Collectables
Laurel Hill Plaza, Store #6
Clementon, NJ 08021
PH:609-627-1711 (a-c,g,m,r)

Comic Relief
24 Mill Run Plaza
Route 130
Delran, NJ 08075
PH:609-461-1770 (a-c,j,n,q,r,t-v)

Collector's Center
729 Edgar Road
Elizabeth, NJ 07202
PH:201-355-7942 (a,b,m,r)

Shore Video Comics & Baseball Cards
615 Lacey Road
Forked River, NJ 08731
PH:609-693-3831 (b,c,m,q,r)

Comic Relief
106 Clifton Avenue
Lakewood, NJ 08701
PH:201-363-3899 (a-c,j,n,q,r,t-v)

Comic Relief
156-A Mercer Mall
Route 1
Lawrenceville, NJ 08648
PH:609-452-7548 (a-c,j,n,q,r,t-v)

The Hobby Shop
Route 34
Strathmore Shopping Center
Matawan, NJ 07747
PH:201-583-0505 (a-c,f,m,q-s)

Comic Museum
58 High St.
Mount Holly, NJ 08060
PH:609-261-0996 (a-c,h,n,q,r,u,v)

A & S Comics
7113 Bergenline Ave.
North Bergen, NJ 07047
PH:201-869-0280 (b,c,m,q-s)

Comicrypt II
521 White Horse Pike
Oaklyn, NJ 08107
PH:609-858-3877
(a-e,g,i,j,m,n,q-s)

Passaic Book Center
594 Main Ave.
Passaic, NJ 07055
PH:201-778-6646 (a-h,l,n,q,r,t,u)

Mr. Collector
311 Union Ave.
Paterson, NJ 07502
PH:201-595-0781 (a-c,g,h,m,r)

Sparkle City
(by appointment)
Sewell, NJ
PH:609-589-3606 (a,b,d,f)

Philip M. Levine Associates, Rare & Esoteric Books
P. O. Box 246 (appointment only)
Three Bridges, NJ 08887
PH:201-788-1088, 984-2772
(a,b,d,f-h,k,m,n,p,r)

Mr. Collector
327 Union Blvd.
Totowa Boro, NJ 07512
PH:201-595-0900 (a-c,g,h,m,r)

Thunder Road Comics & Cards
Parkway Shopping Center
831 Parkway Ave.
Trenton, NJ 08618
PH:609-771-1055 (a-c,m,n,q,r,v)

Comic Book Emporium
643 Chestnut St.
Union, NJ 07083
PH:201-964-9673 (a-c,n,q-v)

Comic Relief
116-B Main Street
Off Route 35
Woodbridge, NJ 07095
PH:201-855-2922 (a-c,j,n,q,r,t-v)

NEW MEXICO:

The Comic Warehouse
9308 Menaul N.E.
Albuquerque, NM 87112
PH:505-293-3065

Captain Comics Specialty Shop
109 W. 4th St.
Clovis, NM 88101
PH:505-769-1543 (a-c,g,n,q,r)

NEW YORK:

FantaCo Comic Shop
21 Central Avenue
Albany, NY 12210
PH:518-463-1400
(c,e,g,h,m-o,q-v)

FantaCo Enterprises, Inc.
21 Central Avenue
Albany, NY 12210-1391
PH:518-463-3667 (e,g,h,i,m-o)

FantaCo Publications
21 Central Avenue
Albany, NY 12210-1391
PH:518-463-1400 (c,e)

FantaCon
21 Central Avenue
Albany, NY 12210
PH:518-463-1400 (a-o,q-v)

Long Island Comics
1670-D Sunrise Hwy.
Bay Shore, NY 11706
PH:516-665-4342 (a-c,g,j,q-t)

Captain Comics
3104 E. Tremont Ave.
Bronx, NY 10461
PH:212-823-9532 (a-c,g,m,q-s)

Wow Comics
642 Pelham Parkway S.
Bronx, NY 10462
PH:212-829-0461 (a-c,m,n,q-s)

Fantasy Headquarters
2203 Bath Ave.
Brooklyn, NY 11214
PH:718-372-3695 (a-c,g,m,n,q-t)

Metropolis Comics
(by appointment)
P. O. Box 165
Brooklyn, NY 11214
PH:718-837-2538
(a,b,d,g,h,j,k,m,p)

Pinocchio Discounts
1814 McDonald Ave. near Ave. P
Brooklyn, NY 11223
PH:718-645-2573 (a,c,g,m)

The World of Fantasy
737 Long Island Ave.
Deer Park, NY 11729
PH:516-586-7314 (a-d,f,m-o,q,r)

The Book Stop
384 East Meadow Ave.
East Meadow, NY 11554
PH:516-794-9129 (a-c,e,g,n,r)

Continental Comics & Cards
71-05 Austin St.
Forest Hills, NY 11375
PH:718-544-4487 (a-r)

Little Nemo Shop
108 - 30 Ascan Avenue
Forest Hills, NY 11375
PH:718-263-5296 (a-j,l,r,t)

Video Ventures
777 Hempstead Turnpike
Franklin Square, NY 11010
PH:516-488-4105 (a-d,g,i,j,n-r)

Fantazia Record & Book Exchange
2 So. Central Ave.
Hartsdale, NY 10530
PH:914-946-3306 (a-j,l-n,q,r)

Park Avenue Books (formerly Brighton-Nostrand Books)
17 E. Park Ave.
Long Beach, NY 11561
(a-h,n,r-u)

Dolgoff's Comic Kingdom
156 Mamaroneck Ave.
Mamaroneck, NY 10543
PH:914-698-9473 (a-d,j,m,n,r)

Creation Science Fiction & Comic World
145 Jericho Turnpike
Mineola, NY 11501
PH:516-747-4050 (c,k,q,r,t-v)

Action Comics
318 E. 84th St.
(Between 1st & 2nd Ave.)
New York, NY 10028
PH:212-249-7344 (a-c,j,k,m,n,q-s)

Big Apple Comics
2489 Broadway (92 - 93 St.)
New York, NY 10025
PH:212-724-0085 (a-d,j,m,n,r)

Funny Business
656 Amsterdam Ave.
(corner 92nd St.)
New York, NY 10025
PH:212-799-9477 (a-c,g,n,o,q,r)

Jerry Ohlinger's Movie Material Store, Inc.
242 West 14th St.
New York, NY 10011
PH:212-989-0869 (g,i,l)

St. Mark's Comics
11 St. Mark's Pl.
New York, NY 10003
PH:212-598-9439 (a-c,e,g,j,m-v)

Supersnipe Comic Book Euphorium
Box 1102, Gracie Station
New York, NY 10028
PH:212-879-9628 (a-d,g,j,r,t)

West Side Comics & Video
107 W. 86
New York, NY 10024
PH:212-724-0432 (a-c,n,o,q,r)

M & M Comics
100 Main St.
Nyack, NY 10960
PH:914-358-3335 (a-g,i,j,m,n,q-s)

Corner-Stone Comic Shop
110 Margaret St.
Plattsburgh, NY 12901
PH:518-561-0520 (a-c,h,q,r)

Flash Point — The Science Fiction and Fantasy Shop
105 West Broadway
Port Jefferson, NY 11777
PH:516-331-9401 (b,c,e,g,k,q-v)

Iron Vic Comics
1 Raymond Ave.
Poughkeepsie, NY 12603
PH:914-473-8365 (a-d,g,j,m,n,r)

Empire Comics
1176 Mt. Hope Ave.
Rochester, NY 14620
PH:716-442-0371 (a-c,f,h,k,q-s)

Empire Comics
572 Stone Rd.
Rochester, NY 14616
PH:716-663-6877 (a-c,h,k,q-s)

Amazing Comics
12 Gillette Ave.
Sayville, NY 11782
PH:516-567-8069 (a-c,j,q-s)

Comix 4-U, Inc.
1121 State St., 2nd Floor
Schenectady, NY 12304
PH:518-372-6612 (a-c,e,g,n,q,r)

Electric City Comics
1704 Van Vranken Ave.
Schenectady, NY 12308
PH:518-377-1500 (a-c,g,j,n,q,r)

Jim Hanley's Universe
3842 Richmond Avenue
(at the Eltingville train station)
Staten Island, NY 10312
PH:718-948-6377 or 718-WIT-NESS (a-g,k,m,n,p-v)

Comic Book Heaven
(formerly of Q.P. Market)
48-14 Skillman Avenue
Sunnyside, Queens, NY 11104
PH:718-899-4175 (b,c,m,q-s)

The Twilight Book & Game Emporium
1411 North Salina Street
Syracuse, NY 13208
PH:315-471-3139 (a-e,m,o,q-v)

Ravenswood
1411 Oriskany St. W.
Utica, NY 13502
PH:315-735-3699
(a-c,g,i,k-n,p-r,t-v)

NORTH CAROLINA:

Super Giant Books
344 Merrimon Ave.
Asheville, NC 28801
PH:704-254-2103 (a-c,e,h,j)

Heroes Aren't Hard to Find
1214 Thomas Ave.
Charlotte, NC 28205
PH:704-375-7462 (a-c,g,i,j,q-s)
Heroes Hotline: 704-375-HERO

Books Do Furnish a Room
1809 W. Markham Ave.
Durham, NC 27705-4806
PH:919-286-1076
(b-d,f,h,l,n,q,r,v)

Heroes Are Here
117 S. Center St.
Goldsboro, NC 27530
PH:919-734-3131 (a-c,e,m,q,r)

Tales Resold
207 S. Berkeley Blvd.
Goldsboro, NC 27530
PH:919-778-6520 (a-c,e-h,j,l,q-u)

Acme Comics
348 S. Elm Street
Greensboro, NC 27401
PH:919-272-5994 (a-c,n,q,r)

Crazy Dave's Comic Book Detective Agency
108 E. 5th St., P.O. Box 603
Greenville, NC 27835
(a-r) 11-7 daily & by appt.

The Nostalgia News Stand
919 Dickinson Ave.
Greenville, NC 27834
PH:919-758-6909 (b,c,e,n,q,r)

Book & Comic Connection
#30 East Plaza Prof. Center
Havelock, NC 28532
PH:919-447-4815 (a-c,h,i,n,r,s,u)

Heroes Aren't Hard to Find
100 Main Avenue N.W.
Hickory, NC 28601
PH:704-322-3444 (a-c,q,r)

Heroes Are Here
1005 Vernon Ave.
Kinston, NC 28501
PH:919-523-6613 (a-c,m,q,r)

Heroes Aren't Hard to Find
Carmel Commons Shopping Ctr.
6648 Carmel Rd.
Pineville, NC 28134
PH:704-542-8842

Tales Resold
213 E. Franklin St.
Raleigh, NC 27604
PH:919-833-4383 (a-c,e-h,j,l,q-u)

The Booktrader
121 Country Club Road
Rocky Mount, NC 27801
PH:919-443-3993 (b,c,e,r)

Heroes Aren't Hard to Find
1000 Brookstown Ave.
Winston-Salem, NC 27101
PH:919-724-6987 (a-c,n,q-s)

NORTH DAKOTA:

Book Nook
308 So. 3rd St.
Grand Forks, ND 58201
PH:701-772-3649 (b,c,e,g,h,q,r)

Collector's Corner
306 N. 4th St., P.O. Box 101
Grand Forks, ND 58201
PH:701-772-2518 (a-g,m,n,q-u)

Book Trader
Dakota Square Mall
Minot, ND 58701
PH:701-838-1694 (c,e,h,q,r,t)

Tom's Coin, Stamp, Gem, Comic & Baseball Shop
2 First St. S.W.
Minot, ND 58701
PH:701-852-4522 (a-g,i-k,m,n,p-r)

OHIO:

Book Exchange
112 W. Columbus, P.O.Box 55
Bellefontaine, OH 43311
PH:513-593-0381 (a-c,e,g-i)

Comics, Cards & Collectables
533 Market Ave. North
Canton, OH 44702
PH:216-456-8907 (a-c,k,m,r-t)

Comic Book World
5526 Colerain Ave.
Cincinnati, OH 45273
PH:513-541-8002 (a-c,e,m,q-v)

Comic Book World
3805 North Bend Rd.
Cincinnati, OH 45211
PH:513-662-0440 (a-c,m,q-s)

Collectors Warehouse Inc.
5437 Pearl Road
Cleveland, OH 44129
PH:216-842-2896 (a-n,q-v)

The Book Nook
Carriage House Plaza
1016 Tiffin Ave.
Findlay, OH 45840
PH:419-423-9738 (b,c,e,q,r)

Troll & Unicorn Comics
#1, 5050 Nebraska Avenue
Huber Heights, OH 45424
PH:513-233-6535 (a-d,n,p-r,t,u)

Comic Book City
2601 Hubbard Road
Madison, OH 44057
PH:216-428-4786 (a-c,m,n,q-u)

Rich's Comic Shoppe
Middletown, OH
PH:513-424-1095 (a-c,i,m,q,r,t)

StarQuest Books
985 W. Main St.
Four Seasons Mall
Tipp City, OH 45371
PH:513-667-2574 (b,c,e,m,q-v)

Monarch Cards & Comics
2620 Airport Hwy.
Toledo, OH 43609
PH:419-382-1451 (b,c,m,q,r)

Funnie Farm Bookstore
328 N. Dixie Drive
Airline Shopping Center
Vandalia, OH 45377
PH:513-898-2794 (a-c,e,m,q-s)

Dark Star Books
231 Xenia Ave.
Yellow Springs, OH 45387
PH:513-767-9400
(a-c,e-h,m,n,q-v)

OKLAHOMA:

New World Bookstore
6219 N. Meridian
Oklahoma City, OK 73112
PH:405-721-7634 (a-e,g,m,n,q-v)

New World Bookstore
8017 S. Western
Oklahoma City, OK 73159
PH:405-631-0088 (a-e,g,m,n,q-v)

The Comic Empire of Tulsa
3122 S. Mingo Rd.
Tulsa, OK 74146
PH:918-664-5808 (a-c,f,n,q,r,t,u)

Starbase 21
2130 S. Sheridan
Tulsa, OK 74114
PH:918-838-3388 (a-g,i,j,m,r)

Want List Comics
Box 701932 (appointment only)
Tulsa, OK 74170-1932
PH:918-491-9191 (a-c,f,g,i-m,o-q)

OREGON:

Pegasus Books
4390 S.W. Lloyd
Beaverton, OR 97005
PH:503-643-4222
(a-c,e,f,i,j,m,o,q-v)

Comics Plus
964 Charnelton St.
Eugene, OR 97401
PH:503-344-2206
(a-c,e,m,n,q,r,t-v)

Emerald City Comics
770 East 13th
Eugene, OR 97401
PH:503-345-2568 (a-g,i,j,m-o,q-v)

House of Fantasy
2005 E. Burnside
P. O. Box 472
Gresham, OR 97030
PH:503-661-1815 (a-c,m,q-u)

Nelscott Books
3412 S.E. Hwy. 101
Lincoln City, OR 97367
PH:503-994-3513 (a,b,d-f,h,r)

Harti Comics & Cards
Danielson Hilltop Mall
358 Warner-Milne Rd., #G-104
Oregon City, OR 97045
PH:503-655-5986 (b,c,m,r)

The Comic Shop
(Mail Order Service)
P. O. Box 18178
Portland, OR 97218
(a-c,e,m,q-v)

Pegasus Books
5015 N.E. Sandy Blvd.
Portland, OR 97213
PH:503-284-4693 (a-c,e,i,m,q-v)

Pegasus Books
1401 S.E. Division
Portland, OR 97214
PH:503-233-0768 (a-c,e,i,m,o,q-v)

Lady Jayne's
19060 S.W. Boones Ferry Rd.
Tualatin, OR 97062
PH:503-692-0753 (c,e,q-s)

PENNSYLVANIA:

Cap's Comic Cavalcade
1980 Catasauqua Rd.
Allentown, PA 18103
PH:215-264-5540 (a-g,j,m-v)

Dreamscape Comics
404 West Broad St.
Bethlehem, PA 18018
PH:215-867-1178 (b,c,j,n,q-v)

Dreamscape Comics
9 East Third St.
Bethlehem, PA 18015
PH:215-867-1178 (b,c,j,n,q-v)

Mr. Monster's Comic Crypt & House of Horrors
347 Ferry Street
Easton, PA 18042
PH:215-250-0659 (a-c,o,q,r,t)

Golden Unicorn Comics
860 Alter St.
Hazleton, PA 18201
PH:717-455-4645 (a-c,q,r)

Ott's Trading Post
201 Allegheny Street
Hollidaysburg, PA 16648
PH:814-696-3494 (a-c,f,l,n)

Charlie's Collectors Corner
100D West Second Street
Hummelstown, PA 17036
PH:717-566-7216 (b,c,m,r)

The Comic Store
The Golden Triangle
1264 Lititz Pike
Lancaster, PA 17601
PH:717-39-SUPER
(a-c,e,g,h,n,q-s)

Comic Relief
4153 Woerner Ave.
Off 5 Points
Levittown, PA 19057
PH:215-945-7954 (a-c,j,n,q,r,t-v)

Paperback Trader
Whitpain Shopping Center
1502 De Kalb Pike
Norristown, PA 19401
PH:215-279-8855 (c,e,g,q,r,t,u)

Comicrypt IV
7598 Haverford Ave.
North Philadelphia, PA 19151
PH:215-473-6333 (b,c,g,q,r)

Comicrypt V
5736 North 5th St.
North Philadelphia, PA 19120
PH:215-924-8210 (b,c,g,q,r)

Fat Jack's Comicrypt
2006 Sansom Street
Philadelphia, PA 19103
PH:215-963-0788 (a-c,e,g,n,q,r)

Sparkle City Comics
Philadelphia, PA
(Philly area by appointment)
PH:609-589-3606 (a,b,d,f)

Book Swap
110 South Fraser St.
State College, PA 16801
PH:814-234-6005 (a-c,e,g,h,n,q-v)

Comicrypt III
2966 Kensington Ave.
West Philadelphia, PA 19134
PH:215-423-3876 (b,c,g,q,r)

RHODE ISLAND:

Starship Excalibur
60 Washington St.
Providence, RI 02903-1731
PH:401-273-8390
(a-c,e,i,j,m-o,q-v)

Starship Excalibur
834 Hope St.
Providence, RI 02906-3744
PH:401-861-1177
(a-c,e,i,j,m-o,q-v)

Super Hero Universe #2
#56 Arcade Mall
65 Weybossett St.
Providence, RI 02903
PH:401-331-5637 (b,c,e,g,p-r)

Starship Excalibur
832 Post Rd., Warwick Plaza
Warwick, RI 02888
PH:401-941-8890
(a-c,e,i,j,m-o,q-v)

SOUTH CAROLINA:

Super Giant Comics & Records
Market Place/Cinema Center
3466 Clemson Blvd.
Anderson, SC 29621
PH:803-225-9024 (a-c,e,j,l,q,r)

Silver City — Comics - Science Fiction - Gaming
904 Knox Abbott Drive
Cayce, SC 29033
PH:803-791-4021 (a-e,g,q-u)

Heroes Aren't Hard to Find
1415-A Laurens Rd.
Greenville, SC 29607
PH:803-235-3488 (a-c,i,j,q-s)

Haven for Heroes
1123 South Sea Village
Hwy. 544
Myrtle Beach, SC 29587
PH:803-238-9975 (a-c,e,m,q,r)

Super Giant Comics
Suite 30 - West Oak Square
2811 Reidville Rd.
Spartanburg, SC 29301
PH:803-576-4990 (a-c,j,q,r)

TENNESSEE:

Enterprise Comics
4154 N. Bonny Oaks Drive
Chattanooga, TN 37406
PH:615-629-6217 (a-e,g,i,l,m,q,r)

White Book Shop
Super Flea Market
4307 Rossville Blvd.
Chattanooga, TN 37407
PH:404-820-1449 (a-e,r)

Collector's Choice
3405 Keith St., Shoney's Plaza
Cleveland, TN 37311
PH:615-472-6649 (b,c,g,i,m,q-v)

Mountain Empire Comics and Collectibles III
1210 N. Roan St.
Johnson City, TN 37602
PH:615-929-8245 (b,c,e,i,q-s)

Mountain Empire Comics and Collectibles II
1451 E. Center St.
Kingsport, TN 37664
PH:615-245-0364 (b,c,e,g,h,q-s)

Collector's Choice
2104 Cumberland Ave.
Knoxville, TN 37916
PH:615-546-2665 (b,c,g,i,m,q-v)

Memphis Comics & Records
3669 Hickory Hill
Memphis, TN 38115
PH:901-360-8220 (a-v)

Memphis Comics & Records
665 S. Highland
Memphis, TN 38111
PH:901-452-1304 (a-v)

Memphis Comics & Records
964 June Rd.
Memphis, TN 38119
PH:901-763-1733 (a-v)

Nostalgia World Inc.
2492 Summer Ave.
Memphis, TN 38112
PH:901-327-6522 (a-c,g,l,m,r)

Book Rack
Hillwood Plaza
6648 Charlotte Pike
Nashville, TN 37209
PH:615-352-3563 (b,c,e,r)

Book Rack
Rivergate Plaza
752 Two Mile Pike
Nashville, TN 37072
PH:615-859-9814 (b,c,e,r)

Walt's Paperback Books
2604 Franklin Rd.
Nashville, TN 37204
PH:615-298-2506 (b,c,e,o,r)

Collector's Dream World
Rt. 4 Box 155 — Parkway
(just inside Pigeon Forge)
Sevierville, TN 37862
PH:615-428-4261 (a-d,f,i,k,m,p,q)

TEXAS:

Lone Star Comics & Science Fiction
511 East Abram Street
Arlington, TX 76010
PH:817-Metro 265-0491
(a-c,e,g,h,m,q-s)

Lone Star Comics & Science Fiction
5721 W. I-20 at Green Oaks Blvd.
Arlington, TX 76016
PH:817-478-5405
(b,c,e,g,h,m,q-s)

Lone Star Comics & Science Fiction
7738 Forest Lane
Dallas, TX 75230
PH:214-373-0934
(a-c,e,h,m,n,q-s)

Remember When
2431 Valwood Parkway
Dallas, TX 75234
PH:214-243-3439
(a-c,e,g,i,j,m,o,q-s)

B & D Trophy Shop
4404 N. Shepherd
Houston, TX 77018
PH:713-694-8436 (a-c,i,r)

Third Planet #1
2339 Bissonnet
Houston, TX 77005
PH:713-528-1067 (a-s)

Third Planet #2
10001 Long Point, Suite K
Houston, TX 77055
PH:713-984-9922 (a-s)

Third Planet #3
3806 So. Shaver
Houston, TX 77034
PH:713-941-1490 (a-s)

Lone Star Comics & Science Fiction
2550 N. Beltline Road
Irving, TX 75062
PH:214-659-0317
(a-c,e,g,h,m,q-s)

Alan's Comics, Cards, & Games
100 N. Green
P. O. Box 1301
Longview, TX 75606
PH:214-753-0493 (a-c,m,q-v)

Lone Star Comics & Science Fiction
3600 Gus Thomasson, Suite 107
Mesquite, TX 75150
PH:214-681-2040 (b,c,e,m,q-s)

Lone Star Comics & Science Fiction
4032 Kemp Street
Wichita Falls, TX 76308
PH:817-691-3034
(a-c,e,g,h,m,q-s,u)

UTAH:

The Bookshelf
2456 Washington Blvd.
Ogden, UT 84401
PH:801-621-4752 (b,c,e,h,l,m,q-v)

The Baseball Card Shop & Comics Too! I
3169 Highland Dr.
Salt Lake City, UT 84106
PH:801-466-3981 (b,c,m,r)

The Baseball Card Shop & Comics Too! II
8560 South 1300 East
Sandy, UT 84092
PH:801-566-6777 (b,c,m,r)

VERMONT:

Comics Outpost
27 Granite St.
Barre, VT 05641
PH:802-476-4553 (a-c,q-s,u)

Earth Prime Comics
127 Bank St.
Burlington, VT 05401
PH:802-863-3666 (a-c,n,q,r)

Comics City, Inc.
28 Main St.
Winooski, VT 05404
PH:802-655-7422 (b,c,e,m,n,q-v)

VIRGINIA:

Capital Comics Center Storyland, U.S.A.
2008 Mt. Vernon Ave.
Alexandria, VA 22301 (D.C. area)
PH:703-548-3466 (a-c,e,f,m,n,q-u)

Geppi's Comic World Inc.
8330A Richmond Highway
Alexandria, VA 22309
PH:703-360-0120 (a-c,f)

Geppi's Crystal City Comics
1755 Jefferson Davis Hwy.
Crystal City Underground
Arlington, VA 22202
PH:703-521-4618 (a-c,f)

Mountain Empire Comics and Collectibles I
4 Piedmont Street
Bristol, VA 24201
PH:703-466-6337 (a-e,i,k-m,q-s)

Burke Centre Books
5741 Burke Centre Pkwy.
Burke, VA 22015
PH:703-250-5114 (a-h,m,q-s)

Fantasia Comics and Records
1419½ University Ave.
Charlottesville, VA 22903
PH:804-971-1029 (b,c,l,n,q-s,v)

Trilogy Shop #3
3580-F Forest Haven Ln.
Chesapeake, VA 23321
PH:804-483-4173 (b,c,e,m,q-s)

Zeno's Books
1112 Sparrow Road
Chesapeake, VA 23325
PH:804-420-2344 (a-j,m-o,q,r)

Hole in the Wall Books
905 West Broad St.
Falls Church, VA 22046
PH:703-536-2511 (b-e,g,h,l,q-s)

Marie's Books and Things
1701 Princess Anne St.
Fredericksburg, VA 22401
PH:703-373-5196 (a-m)

American Comics
6581 Commerce Court
Gainesville, VA 22065
PH:703-347-7081 (c,q-s)

Bender's
17 East Mellen St.
Hampton, VA 23663
PH:804-723-3741 (a-k,m,n,p-s)

Franklin Farm Books
13320-I Franklin Farm Rd.
Herndon, VA 22071
PH:703-437-9530 (a-h,m,q-s)

Sam's Comics & Collectibles
13262 Warwick Blvd.
Newport News, VA 23602
PH:804-874-5581 (a-c,m,n,q,r,t)

World's Best Comics & Collectibles
9825 Jefferson Ave.
Newport News, VA 23605
PH:804-595-9005 (a-c,e-i,q-s)

Trilogy Shop #2
340 E. Bayview Blvd.
Norfolk, VA 23503
PH:804-587-2540 (b,c,e,m,q-s)

Ward's Comics
3405 Clifford St.
Portsmouth, VA 23707
PH:804-397-7106 (b,c,q-s)

Dave's Comics
7019-E Three Chopt Rd.
Richmond, VA 23226
PH:804-282-1211 (b,c,e,g,m,q-v)

Nostalgia Plus
5610 Patterson Ave.
Richmond, VA 23226
PH:804-282-5532 (a-c,g,n,r)

B & D Comic Shop
3514 Williamson Rd. N.W.
Roanoke, VA 24012
PH:703-563-4161 (b,c,e,g,n,q-v)

Trilogy Shop #1
5773 Princess Anne Rd.
Virginia Beach, VA 23462
PH:804-490-2205 (b,c,e,m,q-s)

Trilogy Shop #4
867 S. Lynnhaven Rd.
Virginia Beach, VA 23452
PH:804-468-0412 (b,c,e,m,q-s)

Zeno's Books
338 Constitution Dr.
Virginia Beach, VA 23462
PH:804-490-1517 (a-j,m-o,q,r)

WASHINGTON:

Tales of Kirkland
(formerly Wally's)
128 Park Lane
Kirkland, WA 98033
PH:206-822-7333
(a-c,e,g,h,j,n,q,r)

The Coin House
777 Stevens Dr.
Richland, WA 99352
PH:509-943-6547 (a-c,m,q,r)

The Comic Character Shop
Old Firehouse Antique Mall
110 Alaskan Way South
Seattle, WA 98104
PH:206-283-0532 (a,b,h-k,q)

Gemini Book Exchange
9614 - 16th Ave. S.W.
Seattle, WA 98106
PH:206-762-5543 (b,c,e,g,q-s)

Golden Age Collectables
1501 Pike Place Market
401 Lower Level
Seattle, WA 98101
PH:(206)622-9799 (a-d,f,i,j,n,o)

Psycho 5 Comics & Cards Shop
12513 Lake City Way
Seattle, WA 98125
PH:206-367-1620 (a-c,m,q,r,v)

Rocket Comics
119 N. 85th
Seattle, WA 98103
PH:206-784-7300 (a-d,i,j,n,q,r)

Zanadu Comics
"A Sense of Wonder" Bookstore
1923 3rd Ave.
Seattle, WA 98101
PH:206-443-1316
(b,c,e-h,j,n,o,q-v)

The Book Exchange
K-Mart Center
N. 6504 Division
Spokane, WA 99208
PH:509-489-2053 (a-c,e,g,h,n,q-s)

The Book Exchange
U-City E.
E. 10812 Sprague
Spokane, WA 99206
PH:509-928-4073 (a-c,e,g,h,n,q-s)

Collectors Nook
213 North "I" St.
Tacoma, WA 98403
PH:206-272-9828 (a,b,d,e,g,h,m)

Pegasus Books
813 Grand Blvd.
Vancouver, WA 98661
PH:206-693-1240 (a-c,e,i,m,q-v)

Galaxy Comics
1720 - 5th St., Suite D
Wenatchee, WA 98801
PH:509-663-4330 (b,c,g,q-s)

WEST VIRGINIA:

Comic World
613 West Lee St.
Charleston, WV 25302
(a-c,g,q,r)

Comic World
1204 - 4th Avenue
Huntington, WV 25701
PH:304-522-3923 (a-c,g,q,r)

Books and Things
2506 Pike Street
Parkersburg, WV 26101
PH:304-422-0666 (b,c,e,h,q-u)

WISCONSIN:

River City Cards & Comics
115 South 6th Street
La Crosse, WI 54601
PH:608-782-5540 (b,c,f,i,m,q,r)

Capital City Comics
1910 Monroe St.
Madison, WI 53711
PH:608-251-8445 (a-c,f,n,q,r)

20th Century Books
108 King Street
Madison, WI 53703
PH:608-251-6226 (b-e,g,h,n,q-v)

Comics & Books
125 S. Central
Marshfield, WI 54449
PH:715-384-4941 (a-c,e,m,r,s)

Time Traveler Bookstore
7143 West Burleigh
Milwaukee, WI 53210
PH:414-442-0203 (a-h)

CANADA:

ALBERTA:

Comic Centre
8120 Deddington Blvd.
Calgary, Alberta, Can. T3K 2A8
(a-c,g,j,n,q,r)

Comic Centre
120 - 8th Avenue S.W.
Calgary, Alberta, Can. T2P 1B3
PH:403-263-8330 (a-c,g,j,m,n,q-s)

BRITISH COLUMBIA:

Funny Pages
382 Tranquille Rd.
Kamloops, B.C., Can. V2B 3G4
PH:604-376-3120 (a-c,j,n,q,r)

Page After Page
1763 Harvey Ave.
Kelowna, B.C., Can. V1Y 6G4
PH:604-860-6554 (a,c,e,h,q,r)

Ted's Paperback & Comics
269 Leon Ave.
Kelowna, B.C., Can. V1Y 6J1
PH:604-763-1258 (a-c,e,h,l)

The Comic Shop
2089 West 4th Avenue
Vancouver, B.C., Can. V6J 1N3
PH:604-738-8122 (a-c,e,n,q-s)

Golden Age Collectables
830 Granville St.
Vancouver, B.C., Can. V3Z 1K3
PH:604-683-2819 (a-d,f,i,j,n,o)

Island Fantasy Comic Service Ltd.
#29 Market Square
560 Johnson St.
Victoria, B.C., Can. V8W 3C6
PH:604-381-1134 (a-c,f,j,n,q-v)

MANITOBA:

Calvin Slobodian
859 - 4th Avenue
Rivers, Man., Can. R0K 1X0
PH:204-328-7846 (a-d,f,g,j,r)

NEW BRUNSWICK:

1,000,000 Comix
345 Mountain Rd.
Moncton, N.B., Can. E1C 2M4
PH:506-855-0056
(a-d,f-h,j,m,n,p-v)

ONTARIO:

1,000,000 Comix
2400 Guelph Line
Burlington, Ont., Can. L7P 4M7
PH:416-332-5600
(a-d,f-h,j,m,n,p-v)

Starlite Comics and Books
132 Westminster Drive South
Cambridge (Preston),
Ont., Can. N3H 1S8
PH:519-653-6571 (a-h,q,r)

Bid Time Return
225 Queens Ave.
London, Ont., Can. N6A 1J8
PH:519-679-0295 (a-k,m,n,q-s)

The Comic Book Collector
616 Dundas St.
London, Ont., Can. N5W 2Y8
PH:519-433-6004 (a-d,n,q)

1,000,000 Comix
Burnhamthorpe Rd.
South Common Mall
Mississauga, Ont., Can. L5L 3A2
PH:416-828-8208
(a-d,f-h,j,m,n,p-v)

Comics Unlimited
875 Eglinton Ave. W. #11
Toronto, Ont., Can. M6C 3Z9
PH:416-781-5579 (b,c,m,p-r)

Queen's Comics & Memorabilia
1009 Kingston Rd.
(at Victoria Pk.)
Toronto, Ont., Can. M4E 1T3
PH:416-698-8757 (b,c,m,q,r)

QUEBEC:

1,000,000 Comix
5010 Samson Blvd.
Chomedy, Laval, Que., Can.
PH:514-688-5626
(a-d,f-h,j,m,n,p-v)

1,000,000 Comix
7019 Cote St. Luc Rd.
Cote St. Luc, Que., Can.
H4U 1J2 PH:514-486-1175
(a-d,f-h,j,m,n,p-v)

Capitaine Quebec
4305 Blvd. St. Jean
Shakespeare Plaza
Dollard des Ormeaux, Que., Can.
H9H 2A4 PH:514-620-1866
(a-c,e,g,m,n,q-v)

Capitaine Quebec
5108 Decarie at Queen Mary Rd.
Montreal, Que., Can. H3X 2H9
PH:514-487-0970
(a-c,e,g,m,n,q-v)

Cosmix
11819 Laurentien Blvd.
Montreal, Que., Can. H4J 2M1
PH:514-337-6183 (a-c,e,g,i,q-t,v)

Multinational Comic Distribution
5595 Place D'aiguillon
Montreal, Que., Can. H4J 1L8
PH:514-336-2440 (a-c,g,m,q,r)

Multinational Comics/Cards
8918 A Lajeunesse
Montreal, Que., Can. H2M 1R9
PH:514-336-2440 (a-c,e,g,m,q,r,t)

Premiere Issue
54 St. Cyrille W.
Quebec City, Que., Can.
G1R 2A4
PH:418-648-8204 (a-c,e,g,i,q-t)

Comics Plus (a 1,000,000 Comix affiliate)
1475 MacDonald St.
St. Laurent, Montreal, Que., Can.
PH:514-334-0732
(a-d,f-h,j,m,n,p-v)

AUSTRALIA:

Comic Collectors Paradise
Leaf St.
Shailer Park 4128
Queensland, Australia
PH:07-801-2010

DENMARK:

Komics
Mejlgade 48
8000 Aarhus C., Denmark
PH:06-19-47-49 (c,q,s)

ENGLAND:

Forbidden Planet
7 Deer Walk, Specialist Arcade
Central Milton Keynes, England
MK9 3AB
PH:0908-677556 (a-c,e,j,q,s-u)

Comic Showcase
76 Neal Street
Covent Garden,
London WC2, England
PH:01-240-3664 (a-c,j,n,q,r)

Forbidden Planet
23 Denmark St.
London WC2H 8NN, England
PH:01-836-4179 (a-f,j,n,q-s)

Forbidden Planet 2
58 St. Giles High Street
London, WC2H 8LH, England
PH:01-379-6042 (e,g,i,o,t-v)

Forbidden Planet Mail Order
P. O. Box 378
London E3 4RD, England
PH:01-980-9711 (a-f,i,o,q,s-v)

Forbidden Planet
29 Sydney Street, Brighton,
Sussex, BN1 4EP, England
PH:0273-687620 (a-c,e,f,i,j,n,q-v)

DIRECTORY OF ADVERTISERS (Cl = Classified, c = color)

DIRECTORY OF ADVERTISERS (continued)

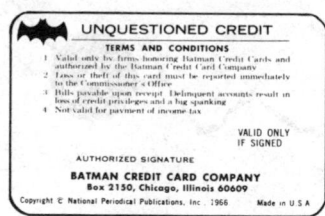

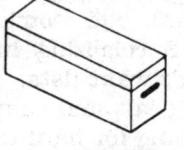

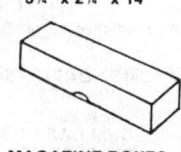

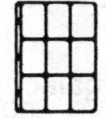

© Comics Magazine Co.

BUYING

OLD COMIC BOOKS!

IMMEDIATE CASH $

© DC Comics, Inc.

© DC Comics, Inc.

IF YOU HAVE THESE OR **ANY** OTHER COMIC BOOKS TO SELL **CONTACT US!**

© Marvel Comics

TOP PRICES PAID!

- NOBODY PAYS MORE **OR** AS FAST! SEND US A LIST OF WHAT YOU HAVE FOR A **QUICK** RESPONSE, OR GIVE US A ☎ AT (206) 423-8673.

© DC Comics, Inc.

© DC Comics, Inc.

- NO COLLECTION IS TOO LARGE OR TOO SMALL!
- WE WILL TRAVEL ANYWHERE TO VIEW LARGE COLLECTIONS.

© DC Comics, Inc.

- WE ARE EXPERT AT **GRADING** AND **PRICING**, AND HAVE THE CAPITAL TO BACK UP ANY OFFER WITH CASH.

☞ QUICK, SIMPLE, REPUTABLE ☜

© DC Comics, Inc.

© Eastern Color

WORLD'S FINEST COMICS

P.O. Box 1609 Longview, WA. 98632

☎ (206) 423-8673 Ask for Mark Wilson

© Centaur Publ.

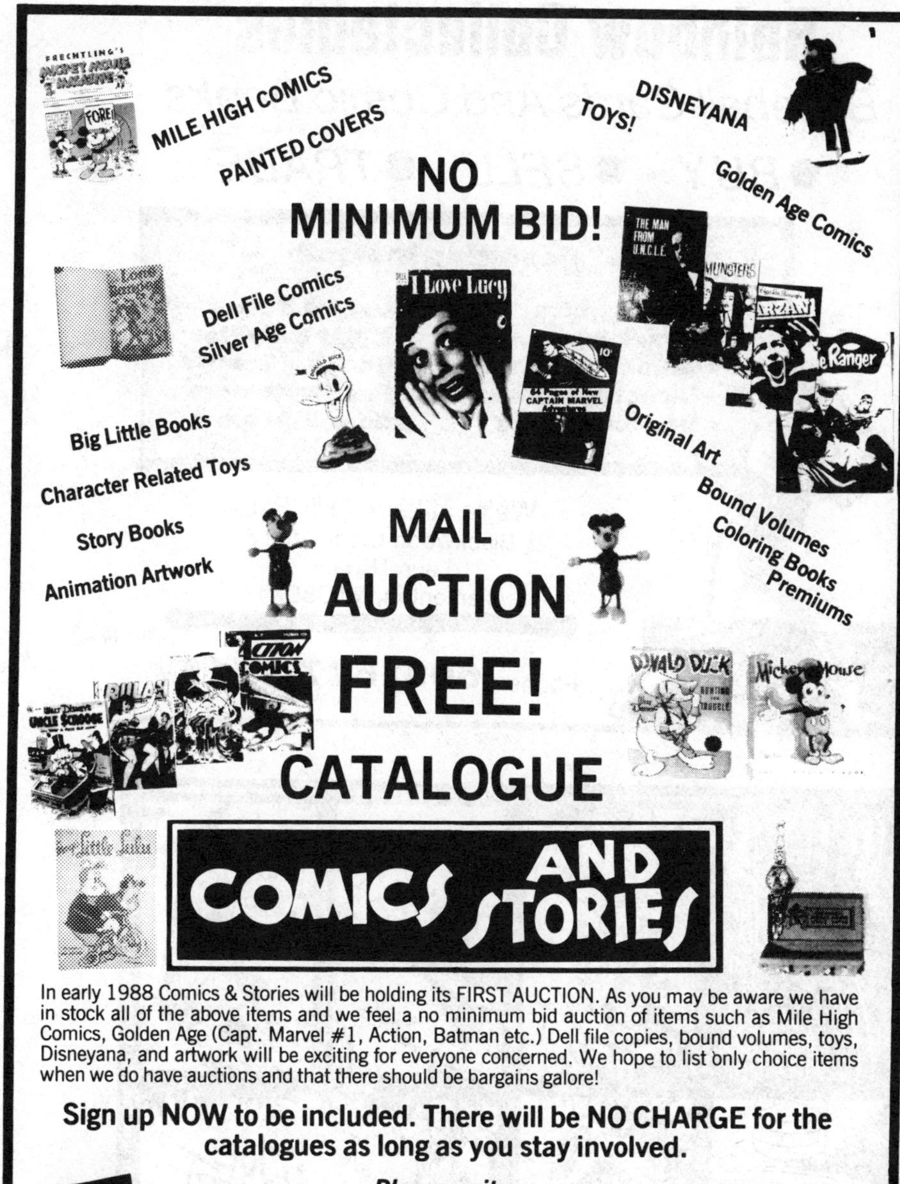

MILE HIGH COMICS

PAINTED COVERS

DISNEYANA

TOYS!

NO MINIMUM BID!

Golden Age Comics

Dell File Comics

Silver Age Comics

Original Art

Big Little Books

Character Related Toys

Story Books

Animation Artwork

Bound Volumes

Coloring Books

Premiums

MAIL AUCTION

FREE!

CATALOGUE

COMICS AND STORIES

In early 1988 Comics & Stories will be holding its FIRST AUCTION. As you may be aware we have in stock all of the above items and we feel a no minimum bid auction of items such as Mile High Comics, Golden Age (Capt. Marvel #1, Action, Batman etc.) Dell file copies, bound volumes, toys, Disneyana, and artwork will be exciting for everyone concerned. We hope to list only choice items when we do have auctions and that there should be bargains galore!

Sign up NOW to be included. There will be NO CHARGE for the catalogues as long as you stay involved.

Please write:

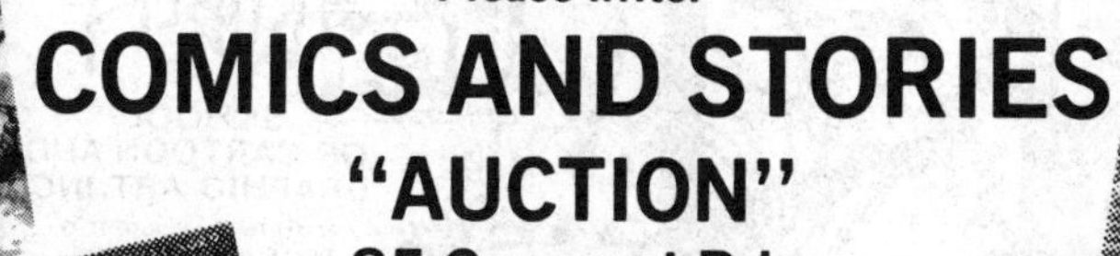

COMICS AND STORIES

"AUCTION"

85 Crescent Rd.
Wanaque, NJ 07465
(201) 839-2192

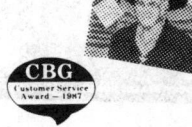

Rainbow Collectables

Baseball Cards And Comic Books

● BUY ● SELL ● TRADE

Featuring In Depth

- ★ New Comics
- ★ Silver Age
- ★ Golden Age
- ★ Direct Sale Items
- ★ Baseball Cards
- ★ Bags & Boxes
- ★ Mylar & Mylites
- ★ Backing Boards
- ★ Plastic Holders
- ★ Card Binders

We're at Laurel Hill Plaza
Blackwood-Clementon &
Laurel Roads
Clementon, NJ 08021

Phone: **(609) 627-1711**

ED KALB

P.O. Box 4111, Mesa, AZ 85211-4111, 1-602-832-5176 (anytime 9-9 MST)

"SERVING COLLECTORS WORLDWIDE SINCE 1967"

QUALITY MATERIAL AND FAST DEPENDABLE SERVICE ARE GUARANTEED. All items are returnable for refund or exchange, no explanation necessary.

CONDITION—Fine to Mint. 90% Near Mint to Mint. We send the best quality on hand - **We're looking for satisfied customers!**

ALTERNATE CHOICES—are greatly appreciated, but not a must. Your alternate selections are used **only** when your first choice is out of stock. Refunds are sent when an item is out of stock. Please note if you prefer credit vouchers.

POSTAGE—Please add $2.00 to all orders to help with postage. All orders are insured. Foreign customers are appreciated. Foreign lands please add extra postage and specify air or surface delivery. All unused postage (foreign) shall be reimbursed.

HOW TO ORDER—Simply list on any sheet of paper what you would like. Add $2.00 for postage. Print your name and address clearly. Payment with order please. All orders are securely packaged and sent out **promptly**.

All prices are per item.

All items are original first printings

10% DISCOUNT—To qualify for your 10% discount simply include a list of alternate choices that equal or exceed the value of your original order. All items qualify for discount except those with value of $15 or more. Deduct your 10% discount before adding postage (see postage).

This price list is good through March 1989.

The following is a sample listing of our inventory. For our complete catalog please send 50 cents. Catalog will be mailed free with any order.

ACTION COMICS
315-329 .... 3.50
330-349 .... 2.50
350-380 .... 2.00
381-392 .... 3.00
393-413 .... 1.50
414-550 .... 1.00
551-599, up .... .75

ADVENTURE COMICS
370-393 .... 2.50
394-441 .... 1.50
442-490 .... 1.00
491-503 Digests .. 2.00

ADVENTURES INTO THE UNKNOWN-ACG
113-174 .... 2.00

AIRBOY (Eclipse)
5-30, up 2.00

ALIEN LEGION (1984)
1 .... 4.00
2-25, up 2.00

ALL STAR
58-74 .... 1.50

ALL STAR SQUADRON
1 .... 4.00
2-25 .... 1.50
26-70, up .... .75

ALPHA FLIGHT
1 .... 4.00
2-12 .... 2.00
13-25 .... 1.50
26-60, up .... .75

AMAZING ADVENTURES (1970)
1-18 .... 2.00
19-39 .... 1.00

AMERICAN FLAGG!
5-50, up 2.00

AQUAMAN (1986)
1-4 .... 3.00

ASTONISHING TALES (1970)
1-25 .... 2.00
26-36 .... 1.00

AVENGERS
20-30 .... 4.50
31-52,54-56,59-92 .... 3.00
53,57,58 .... 10.00
93,100 .... 15.00
94-96 .... 7.50
97-99 .... 5.00
101-112 .... 2.50
113-138 .... 2.00
139-163 .... 1.50
164-166,181-191 .. 2.50
167-180,192-250 .. 1.00
251-295, up .... .75
Annual 1 .... 7.50
2-5,7 .... 4.00
6,8-16, up 2.00
Giant Size 1-5 .... 3.00

BATMAN
180-189 .... 3.00
190-231 .... 2.00
Giants on above .. 4.00
263-369 .... 1.00
370-399 .... .75
400-425, up 1.00

BEAUTY AND THE BEAST
1-4 .... 1.50

BLACK DRAGON
1-6 .... 3.50

BLACKHAWK
201-243 .... 2.00

BLUE DEVIL
1 .... 4.00
2-30 .... 1.00

BRAVE & THE BOLD
103-120 .... 1.50
121-150 .... 1.00
151-199 .... .75

CAMELOT 3000
1 .... 4.00
2-12 .... 2.00

CAPTAIN ACTION
1-5 .... 3.00

CAPTAIN AMERICA
100 .... 15.00
101-108 .... 3.50
109-111,113,117 .. 6.00
112,114-116,118 .. 2.50
119-159 .... 2.00
160-171,176-199, 201-246 .... 1.00
200,247-255 .... 2.00
256-330 .... .75
331-345, up 1.00

CAPTAIN MARVEL
1 .... 7.50
2,11,25,26 .... 4.00
3-10,12-24,27-34 .. 2.00
35-62 .... 1.00

CAT (1972)
1-4 .... 2.00

CEREBUS
84-98 .... 2.00

CHAMPIONS
1,17 .... 4.00
2-16 .... 1.50

CONAN THE BARBARIAN
1 .... 60.00
2,3 .... 25.00
4,5 .... 15.00
6-11,14,15 .... 12.00
12,13,16,23 .... 10.00
17-22,24 .... 7.50
25-36,38-49 .... 2.00
50-69 .... 1.50
70-100 .... 1.00
101-200, up .... .75
Annual 2-10 .... 2.00
Giant Size 1-5 .... 2.50

CONAN THE KING/ KING CONAN
1 .... 4.00
2-50, up 1.50

COYOTE
1 .... 4.00
2-20, up 2.00

CREEPY (Magazine)
2-19 .... 4.00
20-69 .... 2.50
70-145 .... 2.00

CRISIS ON INFINITE EARTHS
1-12 .... 2.00

DAREDEVIL
19-29 .... 4.00
30-40,50-53 .... 2.50
41-49,54-79 .... 2.00
80-99,101-130,132-137, 139-157 .... 1.50
100,131,138 .... 4.00
159-161,163,164 .. 7.50
165-167,169,170 .. 6.00
171-175,182-184 .. 4.00
185-200 .... 1.50
201-225 .... 1.00
226,228-233 .... 2.00
234-260, up 1.00

DAZZLER
1,2,38 .... 2.50
3-37,39-42 .... 1.00

DC COMICS PRESENTS
1 .... 4.00
2-25 .... 1.50
27-50 .... 1.00
51-97 .... .75

DC CHALLENGE
1-12 .... 1.50

DEFENDERS
1 .... 15.00
2-10 .... 4.00
11-20 .... 2.00
21-54,100 .... 1.50
55-99 .... 1.00
101-124,126-149 .... .75
125,150-152 .... 2.00
Giant Size 1-5 .... 3.00

DETECTIVE COMICS
350-368,370-394 .. 2.00
411-437 .... 1.50
446-465 .... 1.00
466-481 .... 2.50
482-500 .... 1.50
501-585, up 1.00

DNAGENTS (Eclipse)
1-23 .... 2.00

DOC SAVAGE (Robeson, paperbacks)
1-96 .... 2.00

DOC SAVAGE (1972)
1-8, Giant 1 .... 2.00

DOCTOR SOLAR
6-31 .... 2.00

DOCTOR STRANGE
169 .... 6.00
170-183 .... 2.00

DOCTOR STRANGE (1974)
1 .... 6.00
2-5 .... 2.00
6-26 .... 1.50
27-50 .... 1.00
51-95, up .... .75

DOCTOR WHO (1984)
1 .... 4.00
2-23 .... 2.00

DOOM PATROL (1987)
1 .... 2.00
2-up 1.50

DREDSTAR
1-26 .... 2.00

EERIE (Magazine)
2-12 .... 4.00
14-16,19-69 .... 2.50
70-139 .... 2.00

ELECTRIC WARRIOR
2-20, up 2.00

ELEKTRA ASSASSIN
1-8 .... 2.00

ELEMENTALS
3-15, up 2.00

FAMOUS MONSTERS OF FILMLAND (Mag.)
34-100 .... 4.00
101-129 .... 2.50
130-191 .... 2.00

FANTASTIC FOUR
34-40 .... 10.00
41-47 .... 7.50
51-60,66,67 .... 5.00
61-65,72,74-77 .... 4.00
68-71,78-99 .... 2.50
100 .... 8.00
101-111,113-120,124-129 .... 2.00
121-123 .... 4.00
130-157 .... 1.50
158-262 .... 1.25
263-320, up .... .75
Annual 4-10 .... 4.00
11-19, up 2.00

FLASH
175-216,220-232 .. 2.00
233-250 .... 1.00
251-299 .... .75
300,306-313,350 .. 1.50
314-349 .... .75

FLASH (1987)
2-up 1.50

FLASH GORDON
King 1-9 .... 4.50
Charlton 12-18 .... 2.50
Gold Key 19-37 .... 1.50

FLY/FLYMAN
25-39 .... 2.50

FURY OF FIRESTORM
1 .... 3.00
2-19 .... 1.00
20-65, up .... .75

GARGOYLE
1-4 .... 1.50

GHOST RIDER (1967)
1-7 .... 2.00

GHOST RIDER
1 .... 7.50
2-20 .... 2.00
21-81 .... 1.00

G.I. JOE
28-39 .... 4.00
40-50 .... 2.00
51-75, up 1.00
Special Missions
1 .... 2.50
2-15, up 1.00

GODZILLA
2-24 .... 1.00

GREEN LANTERN
77-80,85,86 .... 10.00
81-84,87,89 .... 7.50
88,90-100 .... 1.50
101-119 .... 1.00
120-140,145-159, 162-199,201-220 .... .75

HISTORY OF THE DC UNIVERSE
1,2 .... 3.00

HOWARD THE DUCK
2-31,Annual 1 .... 1.50

INCREDIBLE HULK
102 .... 12.00
103-110 .... 4.00
111-119 .... 2.50
120-140 .... 2.00
142-161,163-179 .. 1.50
183-199,201-249 .. 1.00
251-271,273-299,301-313,315-349, up .... .75

INFINITY INC.
1 .... 4.00
2-50, up 1.50

INHUMANS
1 .... 3.00
2-12 .... 1.50

INVADERS
1 .... 5.00
2-9 .... 2.00
10-41 .... 1.00

IRON FIST
1 .... 6.00
3-13 .... 2.00

IRON MAN
3-19 .... 4.00
20-29 .... 3.00
30-46,48-50 .... 2.00
51,52,54,57-69 .... 1.50
70-117,119-150 .... 1.25
100,118,169,170 .. 3.00
151-168,171-179 .. 1.00
180-230, up .... .75
Annuals 2-8, up .. 2.00

JIMMY OLSEN
70-89 .... 2.50
90-163 .... 1.50

JONAH HEX
2-19 .... 1.50
20-49 .... 1.00
50-92 .... .75

JON SABLE
6-50, up 2.00

JUDGE DREDD
2-32 .... 2.00

JUSTICE
1 .... 2.00
2-20, up 1.00

JUSTICE LEAGUE OF AMERICA
101-117 .... 2.50
118-160 .... 1.50
161-219 .... 1.00
220-261 .... .75

JUSTICE LEAGUE INTERNATIONAL
2-15, up 1.50

KAMANDI
2-59 .... 1.00

KID COLT OUTLAW
120-139 .... 1.50

KITTY & WOLVERINE
1-6 .... 2.00

KORAK (Gold Key)
2-11 .... 4.00
12-45 .... 2.00

LAND OF THE GIANTS
1-5 .... 5.00

LEGENDS
1-6 .... 1.50

LEGION OF SUPER—HEROES
259,285-287 .... 4.50
260-284,288-310 .. 1.50
311-350, up .... .75

Ed Kalb, page 2

LEGION OF SUPER—HEROES (1984)
2-50, up ... 1.50

LOIS LANE
37-59 ... 3.00
60-137 ... 1.50

MAD (Magazine)
80-119 ... 4.00
120-150 ... 2.00

MAGIK
1-4 ... 1.50

MAN OF STEEL
1-6 ... 1.50

MARVEL CLASSICS
1-35 ... 1.50

MARVEL FANFARE
1,2 ... 7.00
3-5 ... 3.00
6-45, up ... 1.50

MARVEL SAGA
1-25, up ... 1.50

MARVEL TALES
3-10 ... 4.00
11-19 ... 2.50
20-33 ... 2.00
34-100 ... 1.00

MARVEL TEAM UP
1 ... 15.00
2-4 ... 6.00
5-10 ... 4.00
11-29 ... 2.00
30-52,54-70,75,79 ... 1.50
53 ... 6.00
71-74,76-78,80-88,90-99,101-116,118 ... 1.00
89,100,117 ... 4.00
119-149 ... .75
Annual 1 ... 9.00
2-7 ... 2.00

MARVEL TWO IN ONE
1 ... 8.50
2-10 ... 2.50
11-42 ... 1.50
44-49,56-82 ... 1.00
43,50-55,83,84 ... 2.00
85-100 ... .75

MARVEL UNIVERSE (1985)
1-18, up ... 2.00

MASTER OF KUNG FU
16-50 ... 1.50
51-79 ... 1.00
80-125 ... .75

METAL MEN
30-44 ... 2.00
45-56 ... 1.00

MICRONAUTS
1 ... 4.00
2-5 ... 2.00
6-59 ... 1.00

MIGHTY SAMSON
6-31 ... 2.00

MOON KNIGHT
1 ... 4.00
2-15 ... 1.50
16-38 ... 1.00

MS. MARVEL
1 ... 3.00
2-23 ... 1.00

NAM
5-10 ... 3.00
11-20, up ... 1.50

NEW DNAGENTS (1985)
1-17 ... 2.00

NEW MUTANTS
1 ... 4.00
2-19 ... 1.50
20-65, up ... 1.00

NEW TEEN TITANS (1980)
1 ... 17.50
2-4 ... 7.50
5-8 ... 4.00
9-19 ... 2.00
20-95, up ... 1.00

NEW TEEN TITANS (1984)
1 ... 5.00
2-4 ... 3.00
5-45, up ... 1.50

NEXUS (First)
1-45, up ... 2.00

NICK FURY (1968)
1 ... 8.50
2-7 ... 3.00
8-18 ... 2.00

NIGHTMASK
1 ... 2.00
2-20, up ... 1.00

NOVA
1 ... 3.00
2-25 ... 1.00

OMEGA MEN
1 ... 3.00
2-38 ... 1.50

PETER PARKER/ SPECTACULAR SPIDER—MAN
1 ... 6.00
2-10 ... 2.00
11-26,29,30 ... 1.50
27,28 ... 6.50
31-63,65-68,71-80,84-100 ... 1.00
64 ... 8.00
69,70,81-83 ... 4.00
101-145, up ... .75
Annual 1-5 ... 2.00

POWERMAN/IRON FIST (1972-1986)
1 ... 6.00
2-39 ... 1.50
40-47,51-56,58-69 ... 1.00
70-125 ... .75

POWER PACK
2-12 ... 1.50
13-45, up ... 1.00

PUNISHER (1987)
1 ... 2.00
2-15, up ... 1.00

QUESTION, THE
1 ... 3.00
2-15, up ... 1.50

RAWHIDE KID
45-76 ... 1.50

RIP HUNTER
13-29 ... 2.50

ROM
1,17,18 ... 4.00
2-16 ... 1.50
19-75 ... .75

SAVAGE SWORD OF CONAN (Magazine)
2-19 ... 4.00
20-150, up ... 2.00

SCOUT, THE
1-25, up ... 2.00

SEA DEVILS
16-35 ... 2.00

SECRET ORIGINS (1986)
1-25, up ... 1.50

SECRET WARS I
1 ... 4.00
2,3 ... 3.00
4-12 ... 2.00

SECRET WARS II
1-10 ... 1.50

SGT. FURY
14-19 ... 3.00
20-29 ... 2.00
30-69 ... 1.50

SHADOW (1973)
1 ... 4.00
2-12 ... 2.00

SHAZAM (1973)
1,8,12-17 ... 2.50
2-7,9-11,18-35 ... 1.00

SILVER SURFER ('68)
1 ... 50.00
3,5-7 ... 12.00
8-18 ... 5.00

SILVER SURFER ('87)
1 ... 2.00
2-15, up ... 1.00

SPACE FAMILY ROBINSON
2-19 ... 4.00
20-36 ... 2.50
37-59 ... 1.50

SPECTRE (1987)
1 ... 2.00
2-10, up ... 1.50

SPIDER—MAN (Amaz)
30-38 ... 7.50
41-49 ... 4.50
51-95 ... 2.50
96-98,101,102 ... 7.50
103-120,123-128,130-133,136-139 ... 2.00
134,135,161,162,174,175 ... 4.00
140-160,163-173,176-199 ... 1.50
200-203 ... 4.00
204-237,239-251,253-255 ... 1.50
238,252 ... 7.50
256-305, up ... 1.00
Annual 4-10,14,15 ... 4.00
11-13,16-21, up ... 2.00
Giant Size 1-3,5,6 ... 2.50

SPIDER-WOMAN
1,37,38,50 ... 2.50
2-36,39-49 ... 1.00

SPIRIT (1983)
1-45, up ... 2.00

STAR SPANGLED WAR STORIES
111-133 ... 2.00

STAR WARS
1 ... 5.00
2-44 ... 1.50
45-107 ... .75

STRANGE ADVENTURES
185-204 ... 1.50
206-216 ... 4.50
217-244 ... 1.50

STRANGE TALES
131-139 ... 4.00
140-168 ... 2.50
178-181 Warlock ... 2.00

STRANGE TALES '87
1 ... 2.00
2-15, up ... 1.00

SUB-MARINER
1 ... 12.00
2 ... 4.00
3-10 ... 3.00
11-39 ... 2.00
40-72 ... 1.00

SUPERBOY
102-120 ... 3.00
121-140 ... 2.00
141-219 ... 1.50
Giants on above ... 4.00
220-258 ... 1.00

SUPERMAN
190-245 ... 2.00
Giants on above ... 4.00
255-339 ... 1.00
340-435, up ... .75

SUPERMAN (1987)
1-15, up ... 1.50

SUPERMAN FAMILY
164-222 ... 1.50

SWAMP THING ('72)
2-10 ... 2.50
11-24 ... 1.50

SWAMP THING ('82)
1-19,36-70, up ... 1.00

TALES OF SUSPENSE
61-69 ... 4.00
70-99 ... 2.50

TALES TO ASTONISH
63-70 ... 4.00
71-92,94-101 ... 2.00

TARZAN (Gold Key)
147-155 ... 4.00
156-169 ... 2.50
170-206 ... 2.00

TARZAN (DC)
207-235 ... 1.50
236-258 ... 1.00

TEEN TITANS (old)
23-43 ... 2.00
44-53 ... 1.50

THOR (Journey Into Mystery)
120-125 ... 4.50
127-139 ... 2.50
140-179 ... 2.00
182-192,194-229 ... 1.50
230-300 ... 1.00
301-336 ... .75
338-350 ... 1.00
351-395, up ... .75
Annuals 3-13, up ... 2.00

T.H.U.N.D.E.R. AGENTS (Tower)
2-20 ... 5.00

TOMAHAWK
87-140 ... 1.50

TOMB OF DRACULA
1 ... 7.50
2-10 ... 2.50
11-70 ... 1.00

TRANSFORMERS
1,2 ... 5.00
3,4 ... 3.00
5-10 ... 1.50
11-45, up ... 1.00

TUROK
51-69 ... 2.00
70-130 ... 1.50

TWISTED TALES
1-10 ... 2.00

VAMPIRELLA (Mag.)
15-39 ... 4.00
40-110 ... 2.00

VIGILANTE
1 ... 4.00
2-50, up ... 1.50

VOYAGE TO BOTTOM OF THE SEA
2-16 ... 4.50

WALT DISNEY'S COMICS & STORIES
321-429 ... 2.00
430-521 ... 1.50

WARLORD
2-10 ... 4.00
11-29 ... 2.00
30-50 ... 1.50
51-120, up ... .75

WATCHMEN
1 ... 4.00
2-12 ... 2.00

WEB OF SPIDER—MAN
1 ... 5.00
2-9 ... 1.50
10-45, up ... 1.00

WEIRD TALES (pulps) -please write

WEST COAST AVENGERS
1 ... 4.00
2-9 ... 1.50
10-35, up ... 1.00

WHAT IF?
1 ... 6.00
2-12 ... 2.50
13,27,28,31 ... 4.00
14-26,29,30,32-47 ... 2.00

WHO'S WHO (DC Universe)
1-24 ... 1.50

WONDER WOMAN
181-200 ... 2.00
201-249 ... 1.00
250-329 ... .75

WONDER WOMAN '87
1 ... 2.50
2-15, up ... 1.50

WORLDS FINEST
143-150 ... 4.00
151-179 ... 2.00
180-282 ... 1.50
283-323 ... 1.00

X-FACTOR
1 ... 4.00
2-15 ... 1.50
16-30, up ... 1.00

X-MEN
94 ... 80.00
95 ... 30.00
96-101,108,109 ... 22.00
102-107,110-113 ... 12.00
114-119,122-130 ... 8.50
120,121 ... 22.00
131-142 ... 7.50
143-149 ... 4.00
150-175 ... 2.50
176-189,193,200 ... 2.00
190-192,194-209 ... 1.50
210-235, up ... 1.00
Annual 5-11, up ... 2.00

YOUNG ALL STARS
1 ... 2.50
2-15, up ... 1.50

—WE ARE BUYING—

We are paying 80 to 100% of guide for many comics. Our new buying catalog consists of over 250 comic titles with prices we pay per issue. Publishers include (1935-1988): Marvel, DC, Gold Key, Dell, Fawcett, Fiction House, Timely, Atlas, Standard, EC and others.

We buy many "off" brand titles and can appreciate your lower grade material. If you're a dealer with overstock or a collector looking for cash - **write for our Buying Catalog** #11. Self addressed stamped envelope, please.

(Buying Catalog #11 also features prices we pay for Big Little Books, Pulps, Paperbacks, Gum Cards, Monster, Mad magazines and G.I. Joe dolls).

ED KALB

P.O. Box 4111, Mesa, AZ 85211-4111

BUYING

GOLDEN AGE COMICS
CLASSICS
DISNEY — PULPS
HOUDINI (pre 1927)

SELLING

Send $1.00 for each of the following Catalogues:

- **Giant 1988 COMIC CATALOGUE**-covers Marvel, DC, Dell, Independents, Archie, Harvey, Gold & Silver Age, Disneyana
- **1988 PULP CATALOGUE** -our BIGGEST yet!
- **VINTAGE Paperbacks**-issued in two parts

Fantasy Illustrated
12531 Harbor Blvd.
Garden Grove, CA 92640
☎ (714) 537-0087
Just 1½ miles So. of Disneyland

BRIGHTON-NOSTRAND BOOKS
Now
PARK AVENUE BOOKS
Moved to
The Waldbaums Shopping Center
17 E. Park Ave.
Long Beach, NY 11561
COMICS-HUGE SELECTION-COMICS
OLD COMIC CATALOG $1.00 postage
Send S.A.S.E. for wholesale list
Park Avenue Books
17 E. Park Ave.
Long Beach, NY 11561

CLASSIC COMICS AND CLASSICS ILLUSTRATED

Classic Comics/Illustrated and all related items. Send for **FREE CATALOG**. Phil Gaudino, 84-19 106 St., Richmond Hill, NY 11418.

BUYING OR SELLING—Call (718) 847-6850 nightly 7 to 10 p.m.

CURIOUS BOOK SHOP
307 E. Grand River
East Lansing, MI 48823
(517) 332-0112

Mid-Michigan's Largest Selection of:
SCIENCE FICTION • PULPS • BOOKS
COMICS • B-L-B's • PAPERBACKS
MAGAZINES • ORIGINAL ART

ALWAYS BUYING QUALITY ITEMS!

VISIT OUR 2ND SHOP:
ARGOS BOOK SHOP
1405 Robinson Rd.
Grand Rapids, MI 49506
(616) 454-0111

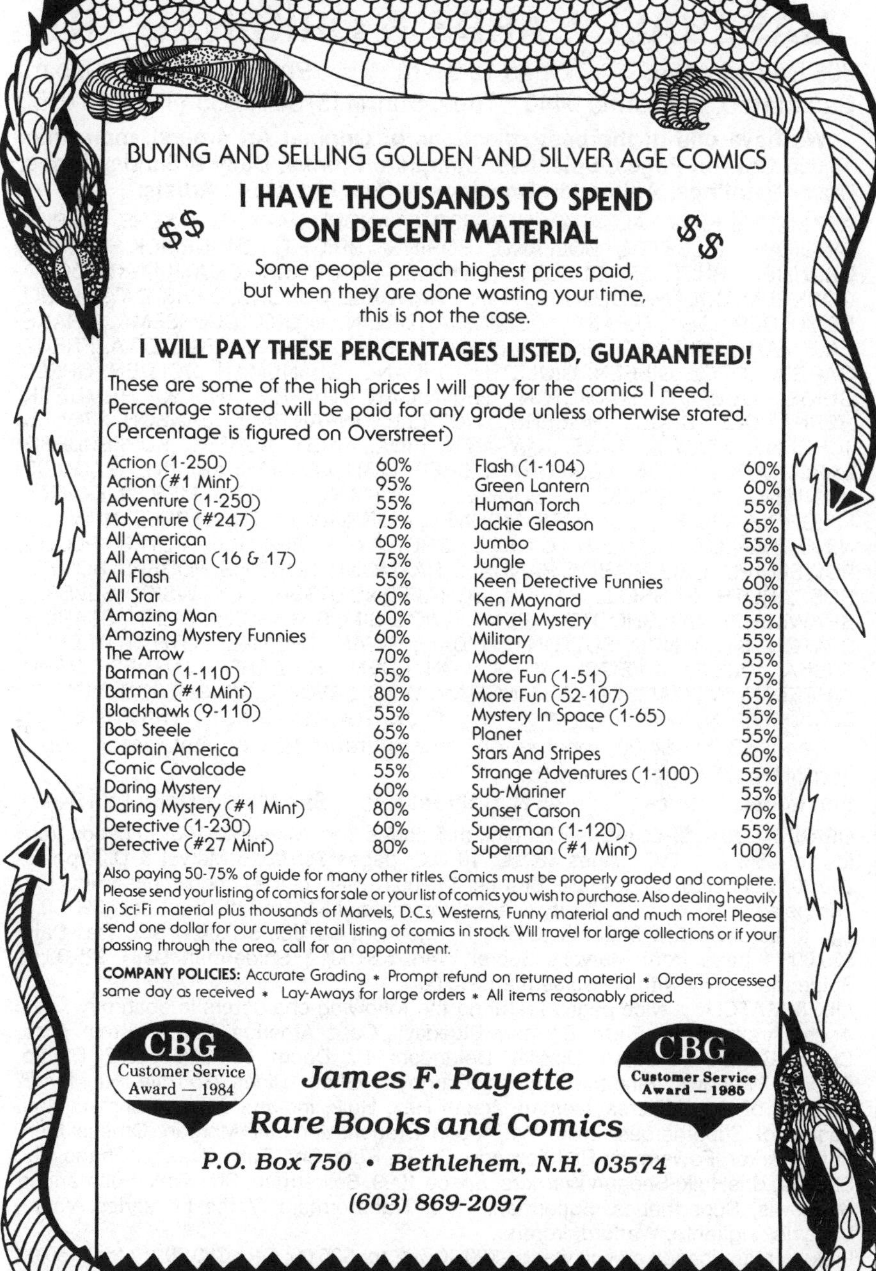

BUYING AND SELLING GOLDEN AND SILVER AGE COMICS
I HAVE THOUSANDS TO SPEND ON DECENT MATERIAL
$$
$$
Some people preach highest prices paid, but when they are done wasting your time, this is not the case.
I WILL PAY THESE PERCENTAGES LISTED, GUARANTEED!
These are some of the high prices I will pay for the comics I need. Percentage stated will be paid for any grade unless otherwise stated. (Percentage is figured on Overstreet)
Action (1-250) 60%
Action (#1 Mint) 95%
Adventure (1-250) 55%
Adventure (#247) 75%
All American 60%
All American (16 & 17) 75%
All Flash 55%
All Star 60%
Amazing Man 60%
Amazing Mystery Funnies 60%
The Arrow 70%
Batman (1-110) 55%
Batman (#1 Mint) 80%
Blackhawk (9-110) 55%
Bob Steele 65%
Captain America 60%
Comic Cavalcade 55%
Daring Mystery 60%
Daring Mystery (#1 Mint) 80%
Detective (1-230) 60%
Detective (#27 Mint) 80%
Flash (1-104) 60%
Green Lantern 60%
Human Torch 55%
Jackie Gleason 65%
Jumbo 55%
Jungle 55%
Keen Detective Funnies 60%
Ken Maynard 65%
Marvel Mystery 55%
Military 55%
Modern 55%
More Fun (1-51) 75%
More Fun (52-107) 55%
Mystery In Space (1-65) 55%
Planet 55%
Stars And Stripes 60%
Strange Adventures (1-100) 55%
Sub-Mariner 55%
Sunset Carson 70%
Superman (1-120) 55%
Superman (#1 Mint) 100%
Also paying 50-75% of guide for many other titles. Comics must be properly graded and complete. Please send your listing of comics for sale or your list of comics you wish to purchase. Also dealing heavily in Sci-Fi material plus thousands of Marvels, D.C.s, Westerns, Funny material and much more! Please send one dollar for our current retail listing of comics in stock. Will travel for large collections or if your passing through the area, call for an appointment.
COMPANY POLICIES: Accurate Grading * Prompt refund on returned material * Orders processed same day as received * Lay-Aways for large orders * All items reasonably priced.
CBG Customer Service Award — 1984
CBG Customer Service Award — 1985
James F. Payette
Rare Books and Comics
P.O. Box 750 • Bethlehem, N.H. 03574
(603) 869-2097

comic book store
NINTH NEBULA
11517 Burbank Bl., REAR
North Hollywood
CALIFORNIA
USA 91601
NEW COMIC BOOKS ARRIVE VIA AIR MAIL AT 7:00 P.M. THURS. EVENING
MARVEL CATALOG: $1.00
1-818-509-2901
THE FINEST COMIC BOOK STORE IN SOUTHERN CALIFORNIA
D.C. SUPERMAN
LIST: FREE! *

Panther Comics

#1

ACTION COMICS No. 1
AMAZING FANTASY No. 15
(1st SPIDERMAN)
AVENGERS No. 1
BATMAN No. 1
CLASSIC COMICS No. 1
FANTASTIC FOUR No. 1
SPIDERMAN No. 1
SUPERMAN No. 1
WALT DISNEY COMICS & STORIES No. 1

Sleuthing done dirt cheap!

Can't find that number one (or origin issue)? Then why not try me?

Yes, I have **all** of the **No.1** issues shown above & other **hard-to-find** comics especially those much sought after **early Marvels** (there are always available in stock a near complete set of all Marvel titles).

And besides this I also have the following:

(A) WALT DISNEY COMICS - all titles: Mickey Mouse, Donald Duck, Uncle Scrooge. Firestone & other Giveways & Disney Collectibles; pop-ups, figures, games, Disney posters etc., etc.

(B) DC COMICS (Golden Age, Silver Age up to the present-old Flash, Green Lantern, Superman, Batman, as well as super-heroes of the 70's).

(C) (GOLDEN AGE & SILVER AGE) comics- these include Quality, Timely, Fox, Avon, Fiction House, Fawcett, Motion Picture Comics, Dell, Westerns, Funny Animal Comics, Classics, etc.

(D) MAD comics - Panic, Humbug, Trump, Help & Horror, Crime & **EC** comics.

(E) Hundreds of **BIG LITTLE BOOKS**- all titles at **Less** than catalog prices. Also available-the **original** Cupples & Leon comic "books".

(F) Rare **PULPS**-science fiction & pulp hero titles; **ARKHAM HOUSE** books

(G) ORIGINAL ART-including **Carl Barks** (Uncle Scrooge artist); Windsor McCay (**Little Nemo** artist); George Herriman (**Krazy Kat** artist) & other fine classic as well as modern artists.

(H) SUNDAY COMIC PAGES -Just about every major & minor comic strip character from the early **1900's to the 1950's.** Strips include; **Little Nemo, Krazy Kat, Mickey Mouse, Donald Duck, Popeye, Tarzan, Flash Gordon, Prince Valiant, Terry & The Pirates, Dick Tracy, Superman, Pogo &** many, many more too numerous to list here.

I also **BUY & TRADE,** so let me know what you have. For my latest **GIANT** 1988 catalog "Number One Plus", write to the address below enclosing $1.00 in cash (or stamps). Hurry now or you could miss out on getting that issue you've been looking for!

SPECIAL – SPECIAL: MOVIE SALE

A ONCE IN A LIFE-TIME OFFER! Huge Catalog listing hundreds and hundreds of rare (and **ORIGINAL**) movie posters, lobby cards, autographed photos from the 1930's to the 1970's. You'll find your favorite movie stars as: Bogart, Gable, Garbo, Garland, Laurel & Hardy, Presley, Disney Titles & many, many more. Wide selection from B-Westerns, Horror, Science-Fiction, Comedy, Musicals, Etc. Act **NOW** to receive my "1988 **MOVIE CATALOG**"

(NOTE: Those wishing to receive **ONLY** the Movie Catalog **MUST** enclose .50 cents & a self-addressed stamped envelope. Want lists also welcomed. If you wish to receive **BOTH** the Comic & the Movie catalog, send **$1.50**)

write: **HAL VERB**
P.O. BOX 1815
SAN FRANCISCO, CA. 94101

OVER 18,000 DIFFERENT COMICS IN STOCK
BUY—SELL—TRADE
with Marty Hay
or else!!
Enclose 1 stamp each for Buying or Selling List!
© 1988 Marvel Comics. All rights reserved.

SECOND GENESIS

3 WEST COAST WAREHOUSES FOR RETAILER SERVICE

Complete line of comic book publishers: Marvel,DC, Gladstone, First, Eclipse, Comico, Dark Horse and all the independent publishers.

Specialty products: Trade Paperbacks, T-Shirts, Games, Calendars, Graphic Novels, and more.

Supplies: Long and short comic boxes, magazine boxes, dividers, 9 different sizes of polypropylene bags, baseball sheets, backing boards and mylar products.

Call one of our warehouses for our thick monthly catalog.
Providing wholesale services to retailers since 1976.

NEW PUBLISHERS: Solicitation material or new product information should go to our Portland Warehouse.

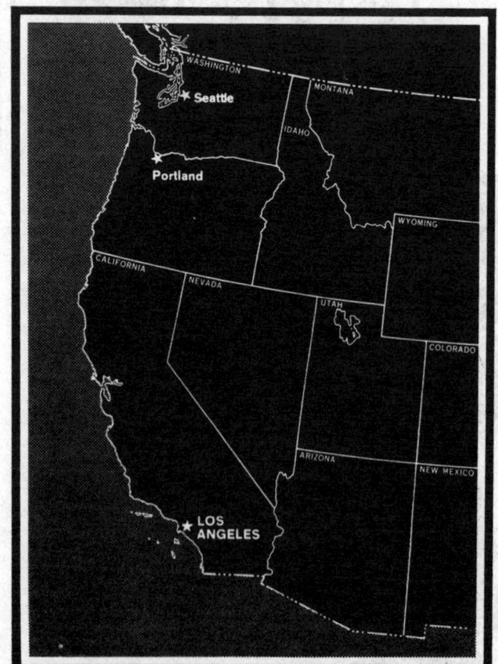

SEATTLE WAREHOUSE
Manager: Al Clover
815 Thomas Street
Seattle, WA 98109
(206) 624-6210

PORTLAND WAREHOUSE
Manager: Kathy Moullet
5860 NE Going Street
Portland, OR 97218
Please call directory assistance for new number.

LOS ANGELES WAREHOUSE
Manager: Erica Barnes
6223 Randolph Street
Commerce, CA 90040
(213) 888-0466

PHILIP M. LEVINE AND SONS
RARE AND ESOTERIC BOOKS
P.O. BOX 246, THREE BRIDGES, N.J. 08887
PH: (201) 788-1088, 984-2772
SEND US ALL OF YOUR OLD COMIC BOOKS TODAY.
We will make you an immediate cash offer. If we don't buy your books we will pay the postage both ways. We are always buying and selling comics, giveaway comics, big little books, paperbacks, true crime paperbacks, Seduction of the Innocent and related censorship material, radio premiums, early crime magazines, "Cardboard Age" comics, pulps, Catechetical Guild comics and related material, Golden Age comics, Silver Age comics, old toys, and old Japanese toys. We do not publish a selling list. Send us your want lists.
YOU CAN COME AND SEE US AT ALL NEW YORK AREA "CREATION" COMIC SHOWS.
Don't forget to send us your books. We have been buying and selling comic books for 31 years.
HEY DAVID, DID YOU SEE THAT?!
YEAH! WE BETTER GO HOME AND TELL MOM! COME ON JEFFREY!

© DC

© DC

© DC

© MCG

© FH

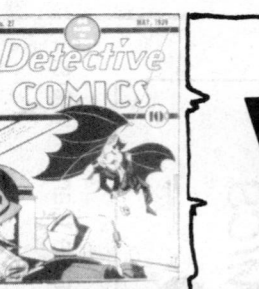

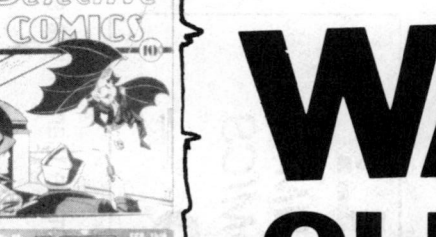

WE PAY MORE

Always have, always will

☎ (317) 293-2551

OVER
$1,000,000
WORTH
OF COLLECTIBLES
IN STOCK

SELL/BUY
ART
COMICS
COINS
TOYS
PREMIUMS
BIG LITTLE BOOKS

NATIONAL COMIC & COIN COLLECTIBLES

President: John K. Snyder, Jr.

Vice President: Steve A. Geppi

Box 34404

Indianapolis, Indiana 46234

☎ (317) 293-2551

COLLECTOR'S CHOICE

—SUBSCRIPTION SERVICE—

812 SCENIC DR.
CLEVELAND TENN. 37311

NEVER PAY SHIPPING AGAIN !!

20 % OFF EVERYTHING!!

LOOKING FOR A NEW COMIC MAIL ORDER SERVICE?

In the past few years we have seen a lot of mail order services come and go. Most offering wild discounts, but in the end taking most or all of your discount back in service charges, handling charges and so forth. What makes us so different you ask? First, we have been in the mail-order business since 1983. Each of those years we have grown steadily. We have encountered every problem known to man, so you can be assured we have all the bugs out of our service. Second, we offer a fair discount which adds up to big savings when you take into account that we pay ALL shipping charges. We make enough to keep us in business so you can have a cheap source month after month. Third, we feel we have built our business on something few of our competitors remember...SERVICE! SOUND TOO GOOD TO BE TRUE ? Give us a try. We have hundreds of happy customers who ARE GLAD THEY DID!

- We pay ALL shipping charges for orders shipped once a month
- WE give you a FREE comic bag with each comic ordered!
- MONTHLY STATEMENTS- each month you will receive an exact statement clearly showing all transactions for your records.
- Each month you will receive a newsletter to assist you in making your comic selections.
- Fast,Accurate,Dependable,and Friendly SERVICE!
- SELECTION ! Our's can't be beat
- SATISFACTION GUARANTEED ! WE will gladly refund the unused portion of your order if you are EVER unsatisfied with your order!
- PACKING SECOND TO NONE !!

IT'S SO EASY

Call us at 615-479-2788 or 615-472-6649 for a copy of our simple instructions and listing of all titles that we carry. Then just sit back...

WE'LL DO THE REST!

Multi-Book & Periodical Inc

4128 South Service Rd.,
Burlington, Ontario L7L 4X5

TELEPHONE 416-632-5573

CANADA

THE DIRECT COMIC BOOK DISTRIBUTOR.

WE ARE STRICTLY WHOLESALE AND CURRENTLY DEALING WITH ALL COM BOOK PUBLISHERS AND RELATED PUBLISHERS.

SO YOU THINK YOUR TOO SMALL TO DEAL WITH A DIRECT DISTRIBUTOR? TA TO US, WE HAVE SPECIAL START—UP PACKAGES TO HELP YOU TO BECO THAT MAJOR DEALER IN THE NEAR FUTURE. WE HAVE THANKFUL ACCOUN THAT STARTED OUT THIS WAY.

FAST, DEPENDABLE SERVICE.
MULTI-BOOK CARRIES A HUGE SUPPLY OF EXTRA COMIC EACH WEEK FOR YOUR RE-ORDERING CONVENIENCE. YOU ARE CAUGHT SHORT, GIVE US A CALL.

WHEN YOU BECOME A WEEKLY SHIP OUT DEALER. YOU WILL ENJOY O WEEKLY BACK ISSUE LIST ALONG WITH HIGHLY DISCOUNTED SPECIALS TH WE OFFER. OUR MONTHLY NEW COMIC BOOK CATALOGUE IS AVAILABLE REQUEST. GO FOR IT!

WE ALSO CARRY A LARGE SELECTION OF FANTASY GAMES AND RELAT PRODUCT. AS WELL AS COMIC BAGS, COMIC BOXES, DIVIDERS, MAGAZI BOXES, BACKING BOARDS AND MORE!

ALL DEALER ENQUIRIES ARE HELD IN THE STRICTEST CONFIDENCE.

Comics and Stories features one of the finest selections of all Golden Age comics—DC's, Timelys, Fawcetts, Marvels and of course Dells.

All the Key #1's are our specialty.

Our latest "find" includes a selection of all Dells.

These are the first legal "file" (never distributed) copies available to the public. We are proud to announce that we encompass all the classic Dell & Disney Titles as well as the photo cover T.V. and movie titles.

Remember: I love Lucy, Maverick, Lawman, The Munsters, Star Trek, The Three Stooges, Lancer, Land of the Giants, My Favorite Martian, Mr. Ed, Sergeant Preston, Lost in Space, The Twilight Zone, Rocky & Bullwinkle, Sea Hunt, Man from U.N.C.L.E., Girl from U.N.C.L.E., The Phanthom, Bonanza, Roy Rogers, Gene Autry, Rex Allen, Wild Wild West, Wyatt Earp, Have Gun Will Travel, Peanuts, Bozo, Cisco Kid, Tarzan, Mickey Mouse, Donald Duck & all the Disney Titles, Gunsmoke, Howdy Doody, The Jetsons, Lassie, Nancy, Rin Tin Tin, Four Color Comics, Little Lulu, Heroic, Famous Funnies, Raggedy Ann, Jingle Jangle, and all the Hot Hanna-Barbera titles.

WE'VE DONE IT!

Due to an unprecedented amount of requests for the hot Dell file copies, and our recent purchases of MILE HIGHS, bound volumes, and Key Golden Age Books, we have decided to meet these demands with our first full catalogue.

The principal catalogue will include over 15,000 Legal Dell file copies as featured in the 17th Overstreet Comic Book Price Guide, 99% of which are NM-Mint condition.

The supplementary catalogue includes a selection of Mile Highs, as well as other "Pedigree" Key Golden Age.

To be included on our mailing list and receive BOTH our catalogues send $2.00 To:

COMICS & STORIES
85 Crescent Rd., Wanaque, N.J. 07465
(201) 839-2192

(Viewing By Appointment Only)

Please indicate your specific interests.

P.O. BOX 1102, Gracie Station, N.Y., N.Y. 10028. PH: (212) 879-962

SUPERSNIPE COMIC BOOK AND ART CATALOG

Free on request to Dept. 018

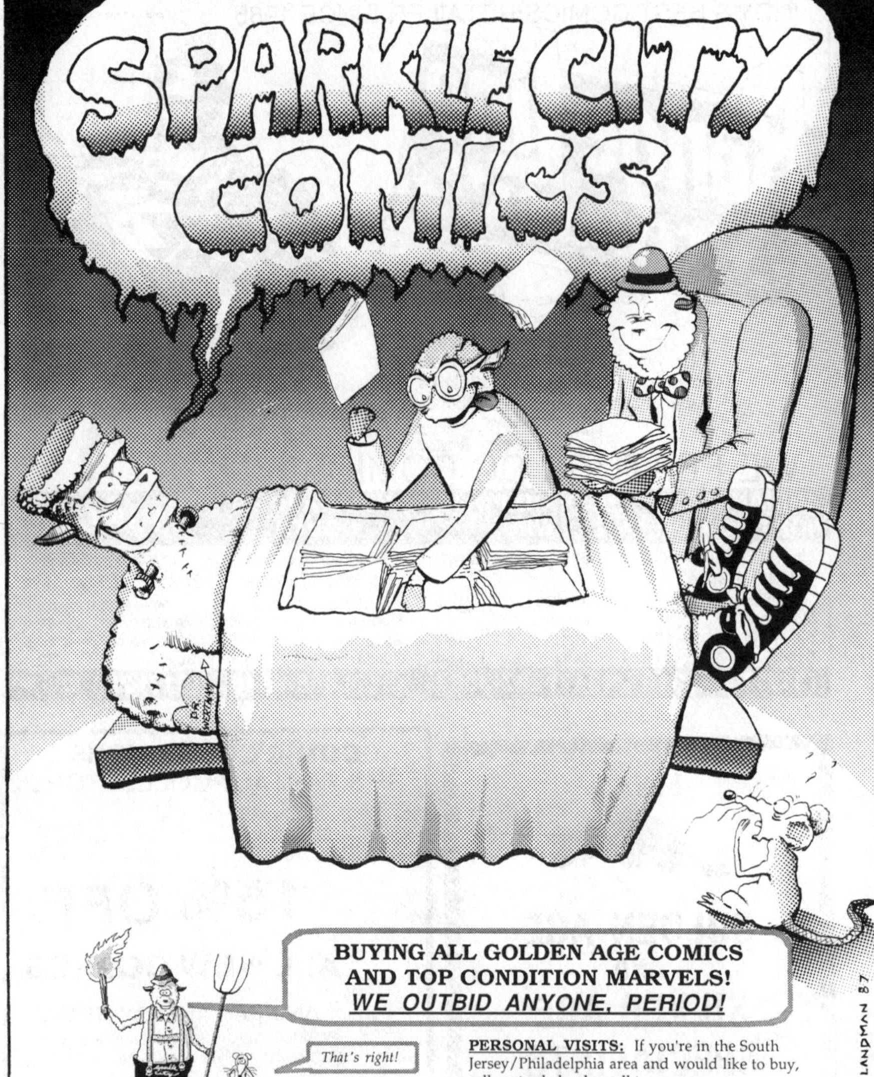

WANT LISTS: Our nationally renowned want list service has constantly located comics quickly for thousands of collectors! Our expanded staff can now efficiently handle want lists on both expensive, high demand issues and on lower priced popular titles! Best of all, our want list prices make all other national mail order prices laughable! When you send us your want list, we don't have to spend thousands of dollars placing extensive detailed ads in the price guide or in monthly comics and we *PASS ON THE SAVINGS DIRECTLY TO YOU!*

THIS IS THE AGE OF SPARKLE CITY!

We want you as a customer and Hans and the Herd are ready to prove that SPARKLE CITY offers the best service and lowest prices this side of Sagebrush, Denmark!!!

PERSONAL VISITS: If you're in the South Jersey/Philadelphia area and would like to buy, sell, or trade books, call to arrange an appointment!

CONSIGNMENT SALES SERVICE: Our staff will be glad to sell your comics on commission! Call or write for details! Receive up to 90% of guide on quality books!

BUYING AT TOP DOLLAR: If you decide to sell your books outright, we pay top dollar on individual books and collections! Call or write for immediate quotes! We will come to you to buy your books! And we will come right away!

call or write:

SPARKLE CITY COMICS

P.O. BOX 67, SEWELL N.J. 08080

(609) 589-3606

Plus: *Dark Horse Presents*, *The Wizard of 4th Street*, *Mecha*, *The Mark*, *Boris the Bear Color Classics*, *Wolverton's Gateway to Horror*, and more! Dark Horse *is* your best bet!

ANDROMEDA
PUBLICATIONS LTD.
C. VESS 87.
ONE OF
CANADA'S
LARGEST
COMIC
DISTRIBUTORS
We Specialize in:
• Dependable Service
• Faster Reorder Turnaround
• A Large and Diverse
Line of Product
SEND FOR OUR FREE
MONTHLY CATALOG
SWAMPTHING © 1988 DC COMICS INC.
ANDROMEDA PUBLICATIONS LTD.
2113 Dundas St. W. Toronto, Ontario CANADA
M6R 1X1 416-535-9100

New & Rare Comics
Movie Posters • Magazines
Records • Games •
Art • Books • T-Shirts • Stuff
VISIT...
Graphitti
L.A.'s #1 DISCOUNT COMIC STORES
ATLANTIC OCEAN
AFRICA
NEW YORK
WASHINGTON D.C.
CHICAGO
ROCKY MTS
GRAND CANYON
HOLLYWOOD
L.A.
GRAPHITTI-WESTCHESTER
8639 LINCOLN
#102
(213) 641-8661
(REAR OF AMFAC HOTEL)
3
GRAPHITTI
1
GRAPHITTI - WESTWOOD
960 GAYLEY AVE.
LOS ANGELES CA. 90024
(213) 824-3656
SEND $1.00 FOR CATALOG
CENTURY CITY
COMICS
GAYLEY AVE
WESTWOOD
AMFAC HOTEL
GRAPHITTI
GRAPHITTI
LINCOLN
OVERLAND
COMICS
MANCHESTER
SANTA MONICA
2
GRAPHITTI-CULVER CITY
4325 OVERLAND
(213) 559-2058
PACIFIC OCEAN

E. Gerber Products
We Specialize in
"Mile High" comics*
and other
High Grade
Comics 1933-'65
3/4 mile
Write or Call for FREE
Catalog or Buy Quote!
1/2 mile
E. Gerber Products, Inc.
P.O. Box 906 (m)
Minden, Nev. 89423
702-883 4100 (9-1, M-S)
1/4 mile
Nevada
Sea Level
*The Edgar Church Collection

RESERVE your copy/s by July 15th

We are Printing Only Enough Books to Fill Reserve Orders. After July Please Inquire for Future Print Runs.

Scheduled Publication: 9/'88

Distributed by:

E. Gerber, Inc.
PO Box 906
Minden, Nev.
89423

702-883 4100

Write or Call for
Wholesale
Prices

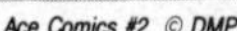
Ace Comics #2, © DMP

Action Adventure #3, © Gillmor

Action Comics #1, © DC

The correct title listing for each comic book can be determined by consulting the indicia (publication data) on the beginning interior pages of the comic. The official title is determined by those words of the title in capital letters only, and not by what is on the cover.

Titles are listed in this book as if they were one word, ignoring spaces, hyphens, and apostrophes, to make finding titles easier.

A-1 (See A-One)

ABBIE AN' SLATS (. . .With Becky No. 1-4) (See Fight for Love, Giant Comics Edition 2, Sparkler Comics, Tip Topper,Treasury of Comics, & United Comics)
1940; March, 1948 - No. 4, Aug, 1948 (Reprints)
United Features Syndicate

	Good	Fine	Mint
Single Series 25 ('40)	15.00	45.00	105.00
Single Series 28	12.00	36.00	84.00
1 (1948)	7.00	21.00	50.00
2-4: 3 r-/Sparkler No. 68-72	3.70	11.00	26.00

ABBOTT AND COSTELLO (. . .Comics)(See Treasury of Comics)
Feb, 1948 - No. 40, Sept?, 1956 (Mort Drucker art in most issues)
St. John Publishing Co.

	Good	Fine	Mint
1	17.00	51.00	120.00
2	8.50	25.50	60.00
3-9 (#8, 8/49; #9, 2/50)	5.00	15.00	35.00
10-Son of Sinbad story by Kubert (new)	11.50	34.50	80.00
11,13-20 (#11, 10/50; #13, 8/51; #15, 12/52)	3.00	9.00	21.00
12-Movie issue	4.00	12.00	28.00
21-30: 28 r-No. 8. 30-Painted-c	2.35	7.00	16.00
31-40	2.00	6.00	14.00
3-D No. 1 (11/53)-Infinity-c	16.00	48.00	112.00

ABBOTT AND COSTELLO (TV)
Feb, 1968 - No. 22, Aug, 1971 (Hanna-Barbera)
Charlton Comics

	Good	Fine	Mint
1	1.35	4.00	9.00
2-10	.70	2.00	4.50
11-22	.50	1.50	3.00

ABC (See America's Best TV Comics)

ABRAHAM LINCOLN LIFE STORY (See Dell Giants)

ABSENT-MINDED PROFESSOR, THE (See 4-Color Comics No. 1199)

ACE COMICS
April, 1937 - No. 151, Oct-Nov, 1949
David McKay Publications

	Good	Fine	Mint
1-Jungle Jim by Alex Raymond, Krazy Kat begin	115.00	375.00	805.00
2	43.00	130.00	300.00
3-5	30.00	90.00	210.00
6-10	22.00	65.00	154.00
11-The Phantom begins(In brown costume, 2/38)	30.00	90.00	210.00
12-20	16.50	50.00	115.00
21-25,27-30	13.50	40.00	95.00
26-Origin Prince Valiant	43.00	130.00	300.00
31-40: 37-Krazy Kat ends	10.00	30.00	70.00
41-60	8.00	24.00	56.00
61-64,66-76-(7/43; last 68pgs.)	7.00	21.00	50.00
65-(8/42; Flag-c)	8.00	24.00	56.00
77-84 (3/44; all 60pgs.)	6.50	19.00	46.00
85-99 (52 pgs.)	5.50	17.00	38.00
100 (7/45; last 52 pgs.)	6.50	19.00	46.00
101-134: 128-11/47; Brick Bradford begins. 134-Last Prince Valiant (All 36 pgs.)	4.70	14.00	33.00
135-151: 135-6/48; Lone Ranger begins	3.70	11.00	26.00

ACE KELLY (See Tops Comics & Tops In Humor)

ACE KING (See Advs. of the Detective)

ACES HIGH
Mar-Apr, 1955 - No. 5, Nov-Dec, 1955
E.C. Comics

	Good	Fine	Mint
1-Not approved by code	7.00	21.00	50.00
2	6.00	18.00	42.00
3-5	5.00	15.00	35.00

NOTE: *All have stories by* ***Davis, Evans, Krigstein,*** *and* ***Wood; Evans*** *c-1-5.*

ACTION ADVENTURE (War) (Formerly Real Adventure)
June, 1955 - No. 4, Oct, 1955
Gillmor Magazines

	Good	Fine	Mint
V1#2-4	1.15	3.50	8.00

ACTION COMICS (See Special Edition)
June, 1938 - No. 583, Sept, 1986; No. 584, Jan, 1987 - Present
National Periodical Publ./Detective Comics/DC

1-Origin & 1st app. Superman by Siegel & Shuster, Marco Polo, Tex Thompson, Pep Morgan, Chuck Dawson & Scoop Scanlon; intro. Zatara; Superman story missing 4 pgs. which were included when reprinted in Superman No. 1. Mentioned in **POP**, pg. 86

Good	Fine	Vf-NM
4400.00	13,200.00	28,650.00

(Only one known copy exists in Mint condition which has not sold)

1-Reprint, Oversize 13½"x10." **WARNING:** This comic is an exact reprint of the original except for its size. DC published it in 1974 with a second cover titling it as a **Famous First Edition**. There have been many reported cases of the outer cover being removed and the interior sold as the original edition. The reprint with the new outer cover removed is practically worthless.

	Good	Fine	Mint
1(1976,1983)-Giveaway; paper cover, 16pgs. in color; reprints complete Superman story from No. 1 ('38)	.70	2.00	4.00
2	675.00	2025.00	4725.00
3 (Scarce)	520.00	1560.00	3640.00
4	355.00	1065.00	2500.00
5 (Rare)	430.00	1290.00	3000.00
6-1st Jimmy Olsen (called office boy)	340.00	1020.00	2400.00
7,10-Superman covers	400.00	1200.00	2800.00
8,9	300.00	900.00	2100.00
11,12,14: 14-Clip Carson begins, ends #41	150.00	450.00	1050.00
13-Superman cover; last Scoop Scanlon	180.00	540.00	1260.00
15-Superman cover	190.00	570.00	1330.00
16	120.00	360.00	840.00
17-Superman cover; last Marco Polo	150.00	450.00	1050.00
18-Origin 3 Aces	105.00	335.00	735.00
19-Superman covers begin	135.00	405.00	945.00
20-'S' left off Superman's chest-No. 20. 20-Clark Kent works at 'Daily Star'	130.00	390.00	910.00
21,22,24,25: 24-Kent at Daily Planet. 25-Last app. Gargantua T. Potts, Tex Thompson's sidekick	80.00	240.00	560.00
23-1st app. Luthor & Black Pirate; Black Pirate by Moldoff	105.00	315.00	735.00
26-30	57.00	170.00	400.00
31,32	45.00	135.00	315.00
33-Origin Mr. America	52.00	155.00	365.00
34-40: 37-Origin Congo Bill. 40-Intro Star Spangled Kid & Stripsey	45.00	135.00	315.00
41	42.00	125.00	295.00
42-Origin Vigilante; Bob Daley becomes Fat Man; origin Mr. America's magic flying carpet; The Queen Bee & Luthor app; Black Pirate ends; not in #41	58.00	175.00	405.00
43-50: 44-Fat Man's i.d. revealed to Mr. America. 45-Intro. Stuff	42.00	125.00	295.00
51-1st app. The Prankster	35.00	105.00	245.00
52-Fat Man & Mr. America become the Ameri-commandos; origin Vigilante retold	42.00	125.00	295.00

53-60: 56-Last Fat Man. 59-Kubert Vigilante begins?, ends #70.

ACTION COMICS (Continued)	Good	Fine	Mint
60-First app. Lois Lane as Superwoman	30.00	90.00	210.00
61-63,65-70: 63-Last 3 Aces	27.00	81.00	190.00
64-Intro Toyman	30.00	90.00	210.00
71-79: 74-Last Mr. America	24.00	72.00	170.00
80-2nd app. & 1st Mr. Mxyztplk-c (1/45)	35.00	105.00	250.00
81,82,84-90	24.00	72.00	170.00
83-Intro Hocus & Pocus	24.00	72.00	120.00
91-99: 93-X-Mas-c. 99-1st small logo(7/46)	21.00	63.00	148.00
100	38.00	115.00	265.00
101-Nuclear explosion-c	25.00	75.00	175.00
102-120: 105,117-X-Mas-c	21.00	63.00	148.00
121-126,128-140: 135,136,138-Zatara by Kubert	19.00	57.00	133.00
127-Vigilante by Kubert; Tommy Tomorrow begins	30.00	90.00	210.00
141-157,159-161: 156-Lois Lane as Super Woman. 160-Last 52 pgs.	19.00	57.00	133.00
158-Origin Superman	20.00	60.00	140.00
162-180: 168,176-Used in **POP**, pg. 90	13.00	40.00	90.00
181-201: 191-Intro. Janu in Congo Bill. 198-Last Vigilante. 201-Last pre-code ish	13.00	40.00	90.00
202-220	10.00	30.00	70.00
221-240: 224-1st Golden Gorilla story	7.00	21.00	50.00
241,243-251: 248-Congo Bill becomes Congorilla. 251-Last Tommy Tomorrow	5.00	15.00	35.00
242-Origin & 1st app. Brainiac (7/58); 1st mention of Shrunken City of Kandor	16.50	50.00	115.00
252-Origin & 1st app. Supergirl and Metallo (5/59)	33.00	100.00	230.00
253-2nd app. Supergirl	5.25	16.00	37.00
254-1st meeting of Bizarro & Superman	4.70	14.00	33.00
255-1st Bizarro Lois & both Bizarros leave Earth to make Bizarro World	4.00	12.00	28.00
256-260: 259-Red Kryptonite used	3.00	8.00	21.00
261-1st X-Kryptonite which gave Streaky his powers; last Congorilla in Action; origin & 1st app. Streaky The Super Cat	3.00	9.00	21.00
262-266,268-270: 263-Origin Bizarro World	2.65	8.00	18.50
267(8/60)-3rd Legion app; 1st app. Chameleon Boy, Colossal Boy, & Invisible Kid	21.00	62.00	145.00
271-275,277-281: 280-Congorilla app.	2.30	7.00	16.00
276(5/61)-6th Legion app; 1st app. Brainiac 5, Phantom Girl, Triplicate Girl, Bouncing Boy, Sun Boy, & Shrinking Violet; Supergirl joins Legion	7.00	21.00	50.00
282-Brainiac 5 cameo (last 10 cent issue)	2.30	7.00	16.00
283(12/61)-Legion of Super-Villains app.	2.50	7.50	17.50
284(1/62)-Mon-el app.	2.50	7.50	17.50
285(2/62)-12th Legion app; Brainiac 5 cameo; Supergirl's existance revealed to world	3.00	9.00	21.00
286(3/62)-Legion of Super Villains app.	1.85	5.50	13.00
287(4/62)-14th Legion app.(cameo)	1.85	5.50	13.00
288-Mon-el app.; r-origin Supergirl	1.85	5.50	13.00
289(6/62)-16th Legion app.(Adult); Lightning Man & Saturn Woman's marriage 1st revealed	1.85	5.50	13.00
290(7/62)-17th Legion app; Phantom Girl app.	1.85	5.50	13.00
291,292,294-299: 292-2nd app. Superhorse (see Adv. 293). 297-Mon-el app; 298-Legion app.	1.10	3.25	6.50
293-Origin Comet(Superhorse)	1.65	4.90	11.50
300	1.50	4.50	10.00
301-303,305-308,310-320: 306-Brainiac 5, Mon-el app. 307-Saturn Girl app. 314-r-origin Supergirl; J.L.A. x-over. 317-Death of Nor-Kan of Kandor. 319-Shrinking Violet app.	.90	2.75	5.50
304-Origin & 1st app. Black Flame	.90	2.75	5.50
309-Legion app.	1.10	3.25	6.50
321-333,335-340: 336-Origin Akvar(Flamebird). 340-Origin, 1st app. Parasite	.70	2.00	4.00
334-Giant G-20; origin Supergirl; Legion-r	1.25	3.75	7.50
341-346,348-359	.55	1.60	3.20
347,360-Gnt. Supergirl G-33,G-45; 360-Legion-r; r-origin Supergirl	.90	2.75	5.50
361-372,374-380: 365-Legion app. 370-New facts about Superman's origin. 376-Last Supergirl in Action. 377-Legion begins	.35	1.00	2.00
373-Giant Supergirl G-57; Legion-r	.65	1.90	3.80
381-392: 392-Last Legion in Action. Saturn Girl gets new costume.		.50	1.00
393-402-All Superman issues		.50	1.00
403-413: All 52pg. ish; 411-Origin Eclipso-(r). 413-Metamorpho begins; ends #418.		.50	1.00
414-424: 419-Intro. Human Target. 421-Intro Capt. Strong; Green Arrow begins. 422/423-Origin Human Target		.50	1.00
425-Adams-a; Atom begins	.35	1.00	2.00
426-436,438-439,442,444-450		.50	1.00
440-1st Grell-a on Green Arrow	.50	1.50	3.00
441-Grell-a on Green Arrow	.25	.75	1.50
437,443-100pg. Giants	.30	.90	1.80
451-499: 454-Last Atom. 458-Last Green Arrow. 487-488, 44pgs. 487-1st app. Microwave Man; origin Atom retold		.50	1.00
500-Infinity-c; Superman life story; $1.00 size; 68 pgs.; shows Legion statues in museum		.60	1.20
501-520: 511-514-New Airwave. 513-The Atom begins. 517-Aquaman begins; ends #541		.40	.80
521-534,537-543,545: 521-Intro. & 1st app. The Vixen. 532-New Teen Titans cameo		.40	.80
535,536-Omega Men app.; 536-New Teen Titans cameo.		.40	.80
544: (Mando paper); 68pgs.; Origins New Luthor & Brainiac; Omega Men cameo		.40	.80
546-J.L.A. & New Teen Titans guest		.40	.80
547-559,561,562,564		.40	.80
560,563,565: Ambush Bug app.	.25	.75	1.50
566-582		.50	1.00
583-Allan Moore scripts	.50	1.50	3.00
584-Byrne-a begins; New Teen Titans app.		.60	1.20
585-600		.50	1.00
Annual 1 (10/87)	.25	.75	1.50
Wheaties Giveaway (1947, 32 pgs., 6½x8¼", nn)-Vigilante story based on movie serial. NOTE: *All copies were taped to Wheaties boxes and never found in mint condition. The mint grade applies to slight tape residue on book.*	23.00	70.00	160.00

NOTE.: ***Supergirl's*** *origin in 262, 280, 285, 291, 305, 309.* ***Adams*** *c-356, 358, 359, 361-64, 366, 367, 370-74, 377-79i, 398-400, 402, 404-06, 419p, 466, 468, 473i, 485.* ***Bailey*** *a-24, 25.* ***Giffen*** *a-560, 563p, 565; c-539p, 560p, 563p.* ***Grell*** *a-440-442, 444-446, 450-452, 456-458; c-456.* ***Guardineer*** *a-24, 25; c-8, 11, 12, 14-16, 18. 25.* ***Bob Kane's*** *Clip Carson-14-41.* ***Gil Kane*** *a-493r, 539-541, 544-546, 551-554; c-535p, 540, 541, 544p, 545-49, 551-554.* ***Meskin*** *a-42-121(most).* ***Moldoff*** *a-23-25.* ***Perez*** *c-529p.* ***Starlin*** *a-509.* ***Staton*** *a-525p, 526p, 531p, 535p, 536p.* ***Toth*** *a-406, 407, 413, 418, 419, 425, 431.* ***Tuska*** *a-486p, 550.* ***Williamson*** *a-568i.*

ACTION FORCE

Mar, 1987 - Present (Magazine size, $1.00, color, weekly)
Marvel Comics Ltd. (British)

	Good	Fine	Mint
1-British G.I. Joe series	.85	2.55	5.00
2	.50	1.50	3.00
3-8	.35	1.00	2.00
9-14	.70	2.00	4.00

ACTUAL CONFESSIONS (Formerly Love Adventures)

No. 13, October, 1952 - No. 14, December, 1952
Atlas Comics (MPI)

	Good	Fine	Mint
13,14	1.15	3.50	8.00

ACTUAL ROMANCES

October, 1949 - No. 2, Jan, 1950 (52 pgs.)
Marvel Comics (IPS)

Action Comics #66, © DC

Action Comics #145, © DC

Action Comics #308, © DC

Adam-12 #2, © DC

Adventure Comics #83, © DC

Adventure Comics #247, © DC

ACTUAL ROMANCES (continued) — Good / Fine / Mint

1 — 2.50 7.50 17.50
2 — 1.25 3.75 8.75

ADAM AND EVE
1975, 1978 (35-49 cents)
Spire Christian Comics (Fleming H. Revell Co.)

By Al Hartley — .25 .50

ADAM-12 (TV)
Dec, 1973 - No. 10, Feb, 1976 (photo covers)
Gold Key

1 — .85 2.50 5.00
2-10 — .50 1.50 3.00

ADDAMS FAMILY (TV)
Oct, 1974 - No. 3, Apr, 1975 (Hanna-Barbera)
Gold Key

1 — 1.15 3.50 7.00
2,3 — .70 2.00 4.00

ADLAI STEVENSON
December, 1966
Dell Publishing Co.

12-007-612-Life story; photo-c — 2.35 7.00 16.00

ADULT TALES OF TERROR ILL. (See Terror Ill.)

ADVENTURE BOUND (See 4-Color Comics No. 239)

ADVENTURE COMICS (Formerly New Adventure)
No. 32, 11/38 - No. 490, 2/82; No. 491, 9/82 - No. 503, 9/83
(The longest continously published comic book title)
National Periodical Publications/DC Comics

32-Anchors Aweigh (ends #52), Barry O'Neil (ends #60, not in #33), Captain Desmo (ends #47), Dale Daring (ends #47), Federal Men (ends #70), The Golden Dragon (ends #36), Rusty & His Pals (ends #52) by Bob Kane, Todd Hunter (ends #38) and Tom Brent (ends #39) begin — 54.00 162.00 380.00
33-38: 37-c-used on Double Action 2 — 32.00 96.00 225.00
39(1/39)-Jack Wood begins, ends #42: 1st mention of Marijuana in comics — 35.00 105.00 245.00
40-Intro. & 1st app. The Sandman. Socko Strong begins, ends #54 — 240.00 720.00 1680.00
41 — 70.00 210.00 490.00
42-47: 47-Steve Conrad Adventurer begins, ends #76 — 48.00 145.00 335.00
48-Intro. & 1st app. The Hourman by Bernard Baily — 230.00 690.00 1610.00
49,50: 50-Cotton Carver by Jack Lehti begins, ends #59? — 52.00 156.00 365.00
51-60: 53-Intro Jimmy "Minuteman" Martin & the Minutemen of America in Hourman; ends #78. 58-Paul Kirk Manhunter begins, ends #72 — 48.00 145.00 335.00
61-Intro/1st app. Starman by Jack Burnley — 185.00 555.00 1300.00
62-65,67,68: 67-Origin The Mist — 44.00 132.00 310.00
66-Origin Shining Knight — 60.00 180.00 425.00
69-Intro. Sandy the Golden Boy (Sandman's sidekick) by Bob Kane; Sandman dons new costume — 55.00 165.00 385.00
70-Last Federal Men — 44.00 132.00 310.00
71-Jimmy Martin becomes costume aide to the Hourman; intro Hourman's Miracle Ray machine — 42.00 125.00 290.00
72-1st Simon & Kirby Sandman — 155.00 465.00 1085.00
73-Origin Manhunter by Simon & Kirby; begin new series — 200.00 600.00 1400.00
74-76: 74-Thorndyke replaces Jimmy, Hourman's assistant — 65.00 195.00 455.00
77-Origin Genius Jones; Mist story — 65.00 195.00 455.00
78-80-Last Simon & Kirby Manhunter & Burnley Starman — 65.00 195.00 455.00

Good / Fine / Mint

81-90: 83-Last Hourman. 84-Mike Gibbs begins, ends #102 — 40.00 120.00 280.00
91-Last Simon & Kirby Sandman — 37.00 110.00 260.00
92-99,101,102-Last Starman, Sandman, & Genius Jones. Most-S&K-c. 92-Last Manhunter — 27.00 81.00 190.00
100 — 40.00 120.00 280.00
103-Aquaman, Green Arrow, Johnny Quick, Superboy begin; 1st small logo (4/46) — 74.00 222.00 520.00
104 — 33.00 100.00 230.00
105-110 — 29.00 87.00 200.00
111-120: 113-X-Mas-c — 25.00 75.00 175.00
121-126,128-130: 128-1st meeting Superboy-Lois Lane — 20.00 60.00 140.00
127-Brief origin Shining Knight retold — 22.00 65.00 154.00
131-140: 132-Shining Knight 1st return to King Arthur time; origin aide Sir Butch — 17.00 50.00 120.00
141,143-149 — 17.00 50.00 120.00
142-Origin Shining Knight & Johnny Quick retold — 18.00 54.00 125.00
150,151,153,155,157,159,161,163-All have 6-pg. Shining Knight stories by Frank Frazetta. 159-Origin Johnny Quick — 32.00 95.00 225.00
152,154,156,158,160,162,164-169: 166-Last Shining Knight. 168-Last 52 pgs. — 15.70 47.00 110.00
170-180 — 14.00 43.00 100.00
181-199: 189-B&W and color illo in **POP** — 13.00 40.00 90.00
200 — 15.70 47.00 110.00
201-209: 207-Last Johnny Quick (not in 205). 209-Last Pre-code ish; origin Speedy — 13.00 40.00 90.00
210-1st app. Krypto — 55.00 165.00 385.00
211-220 — 10.00 30.00 70.00
221-246: 237-1st Intergalactic Vigilante Squadron (Legion tryout) — 9.00 27.00 63.00
247(4/58)-1st Legion of Super Heroes app.; 1st app. Cosmic Boy, Lightning Lad, & Saturn Girl (origin) — 193.00 580.00 1350.00
248-255: All Kirby Green Arrow. 253-1st meeting Superboy-Robin. 255-Intro. Red Kryptonite in Superboy (used in #252 but with no effect) — 5.50 16.50 38.00
256-Origin Green Arrow by Kirby — 11.50 34.00 80.00
257-259 — 5.50 16.50 38.00
260-Origin Aquaman retold — 8.30 25.00 58.00
261-266,268,270: 262-Origin Speedy in Green Arrow. 270-Congorilla begins, ends #281,283 — 4.30 13.00 30.00
267(12/59)-2nd Legion of Super Heroes — 38.00 114.00 265.00
269-Intro. Aqualad; last Green Arrow (not in #206) — 5.70 17.00 40.00
271-Origin Luthor — 4.30 13.00 30.00
272-280: 275-Origin Superman-Batman team retold (see World's Finest #94). 276-Intro Sunboy. 279-Intro White Kryptonite in Superboy. 280-1st meeting Superboy-Lori Lemaris — 3.15 9.50 22.00
281,284,287-289: 281-Last Congorilla. 284-Last Aquaman in Adv. 287,288-Intro. Dev-Em, the Knave from Krypton. 287-1st Bizarro Perry White & J. Olsen. 289-Legion cameo (statues) — 2.65 8.00 18.00
282(3/61)-5th Legion app; intro & origin Star Boy — 8.00 24.00 55.00
283-Intro. The Phantom Zone — 4.30 13.00 30.00
285-1st Bizarro World story (ends #299) in Adv. (See Action #255) — 4.30 13.00 30.00
286-1st Bizarro Mxyzptlk — 3.50 10.50 24.00
290(11/61)-8th Legion app; origin Sunboy in Legion (last 10 cent ish.) — 6.50 19.50 46.00
291,292,295-299: 292-1st Bizarro Lana Lang & Lucy Lane. 295-1st Bizarro Titano. 299-1st Gold Kryptonite (8/62) — 2.30 7.00 16.00

ADVENTURE COMICS (continued) — Good / Fine / Mint

293(2/62)-13th Legion app; Mon-el & Legion Super Pets (intro & origin) app. (1st Superhorse). 1st Bizarro Luthor & Kandor — 4.85 14.50 34.00

294-1st Bizarro M. Monroe, Pres. Kennedy — 2.65 8.00 18.00

300-Legion series begins; Mon-el leaves Phantom Zone (temporarily), joins Legion — 22.00 65.00 152.00

301-Origin Bouncing Boy — 7.00 21.00 50.00

302-305: 303-1st app. Matter Eater Lad. 304-Death of Lightning Lad in Legion — 4.00 12.00 28.00

306-310: 306-Intro. Legion of Substitute Heroes. 307-Intro. Element Lad in Legion. 308-1st app. Lightning Lass in Legion — 3.00 9.00 21.00

311-320: 312-Lightning Lad back in Legion. 315-Last new Superboy story; Colossal Boy app. 316-Origins & powers of Legion given. 317-Intro. Dream Girl in Legion; Lightning Lass becomes Light Lass; Hall of Fame series begins. 320-Dev-Em 2nd app. — 2.35 7.00 16.00

321-Intro Time Trapper — 1.75 5.25 12.00

322-326,328-330: 329-Intro Legion of Super Bizarros — 1.60 4.80 11.00

327-Intro Timber Wolf in Legion — 1.60 4.80 11.00

331-340: 337-Chlorophyll Kid & Night Girl app. 340-Intro Computo in Legion — 1.50 4.50 10.00

341-Triplicate Girl becomes Duo Damsel — 1.25 3.75 7.50

342-345,347,350: 345-Last Hall of Fame; returns in 356,371 — 1.10 3.25 6.50

346-1st app. Karate Kid, Princess Projectra, Ferro Lad, & Nemesis Kid — 1.25 3.75 7.50

348-Origin Sunboy & intro Dr. Regulus in Legion — 1.25 3.75 7.50

349-Intro Universo & Rond Vidar — 1.25 3.75 7.50

351-1st app. White Witch — 1.10 3.25 6.50

352,354-360: 355-Insect Queen joins Legion (4/67) — .90 2.75 5.50

353-Death of Ferro Lad in Legion — 1.50 4.50 10.00

361-364,366,368-370: 369-Intro Mordru in Legion — .70 2.10 4.20

365-Intro Shadow Lass; lists origins & powers of L.S.H. — .85 2.60 5.20

367-New Legion headquarters — .85 2.60 5.20

371-Intro. Chemical King — .85 2.60 5.20

372-Timber Wolf & Chemical King join — .85 2.60 5.20

373,374,376-380: Last Legion in Adv. — .70 2.10 4.20

375-Intro Quantum Queen — .85 2.60 5.20

381-389,391-400: 381-Supergirl begins. 399-Unpubbed G.A. Black Canary. 400-New costume for Supergirl — .60 1.20

390-Giant Supergirl G-69 — .65 2.00 4.00

401,402,404-410: 409-52pg. issues begin; ends #420 — .60 1.20

403-68pg. Giant G-81 — .65 2.00 4.00

411-415: 412-Animal Man origin reprint/Str. Adv. #180. 413-Hawkman by Kubert; G.A. Robotman-r/Det. 178; Zatanna begins, ends #421 — .40 .80

416-Giant DC-10. GA-r — .60 1.20

417-Morrow Vigilante; Frazetta Shining Knight r-/Adv. #161; origin The Enchantress — .60 1.20

418-424: Last Supergirl in Adv. — .40 .80

425-New look, content change to adventure; Toth-a, origin Capt. Fear — .25 .75 1.50

426-458: 427-Last Vigilante. 428-430-Black Orchid app. 431-440-Spectre app. 435-Mike Grell's 1st comic work ('74). 440 New Spectre origin. 441-452-Aquaman app. 445-447-The Creeper app. 449-451-Martian Manhunter app. 453-458-Superboy app; intro Mighty Girl No. 453. 457,458-Eclipso app. — .40 .80

459-466($1.00 size, 68pgs.): 459-Flash (ends 466), Deadman (ends 466), Wonder Woman (ends 464), Gr. Lantern (ends 460), New Gods begin (ends 460). 460-Aquaman begins; ends 478. 461-Justice Society begins; ends 466; death Earth II Batman (also #462) — .45 .90

467-490: 467-Starman, Plasticman begin, end 478. 469,470-Origin Starman. 479-Dial 'H' For Hero begins, ends 490. — .40 .80

491-499: 491-100pg. Digest size begins; r-Legion of Super Heroes/Adv. 247 & 267; Spectre, Aquaman, Superboy, S&K Sandman, Bl. Canary-r & new Shazam by Newton begin. 493-Challengers of the Unknown begins by Tuska w/brief origin. 492,495,496,499-S&K Sandman-r/Adventure in all; 494-499-Spectre-r/Spectre 1-3, 5-7. 493-495,497-499-G.A. Captain Marvel-r. 498-Plastic Man-r begin; origin Bouncing Boy-r/#30 — .60 1.20

500-All Legion-r (Digest size, 148 pgs.) — .25 .80 1.60

501-503-G.A.-r — .60 1.20

NOTE: *Bizarro covers-285, 286, 288, 294, 295. Vigilante app.-420, 426, 427.* **Adams** *a(r)-495i-498i; c-365-369, 371-373, 375-379, 381-383.* **Austin** *a-449i-451i.* **Ditko** *a-467p-478p; c-467p.* **Giffen** *c-491p-494p, 500p.* **Grell** *a-435-437, 440.* **Guardineer** *c-45.* **Kaluta** *c-425.* **G. Kane** *a-414r, 425; c-496-499, 537.* **Kirby** *a-250-256.* **Kubert** *a-413.* **Meskin** *a-81, 127.* **Moldoff** *a-494i; c-49.* **Morrow** *a-413-415, 417, 422, 502r, 503r.* **Newton** *a-459-461, 464-466, 491p, 492p.* **Orlando** *a-457p, 458p.* **Perez** *c-484-486, 490p.* **Simon/Kirby** *c-73-97, 101, 102.* **Starlin** *c-471.* **Staton** *a-445-447i, 456-458p, 459, 460, 461p-465p, 466, 467p-478p, 502p(r); c-458, 461(back).* **Toth** *a-418, 419, 425, 431, 495p-497p.* **Tuska** *a-494p.*

ADVENTURE COMICS
No date (early 1940s) Paper cover, 32 pgs.
IGA

Two different issues; Super-Mystery reprints from 1941 — 13.00 40.00 90.00

ADVENTURE IN DISNEYLAND (Giveaway)
May, 1955 (16 pgs., soft-c) (Dist. by Richfield Oil)
Walt Disney Productions

nn — 3.00 9.00 21.00

ADVENTURE INTO FEAR
1951
Superior Publ. Ltd.

1 — 5.70 17.00 40.00

ADVENTURE INTO MYSTERY
May, 1956 - No. 8, July, 1957
Atlas Comics (BFP No. 1/OPI No. 2-8)

	Good	Fine	Mint
1-Everett-c	5.70	17.00	40.00
2-Flying Saucer story	3.00	9.00	21.00
3,6,8: 3,6-Everett-c	2.50	7.50	17.50
4-Williamson-a, 4 pgs; Powell-a	5.70	17.00	40.00
5-Everett-c/a, Orlando-a	2.70	8.00	19.00
7-Torres-a; Everett-c	3.50	10.50	24.00

ADVENTURE IS MY CAREER
1945 (44 pgs.)
U.S. Coast Guard Academy/Street & Smith

nn-Simon, Milt Gross-a — 5.00 15.00 35.00

ADVENTURES (No. 2 Spectacular. . . on cover)
11/49 - No. 2, 2/50 (No. 1 . . . in Romance on cover)
St. John Publishing Co. (Slightly large size)

1(Scarce); Bolle, Starr-a(2) — 9.00 27.00 63.00

2(Scarce)-Slave Girl; China Bombshell app.; Bolle, L. Starr-a — 16.00 48.00 110.00

ADVENTURES FOR BOYS
December, 1954
Bailey Enterprises

Comics, text, & photos — 1.60 4.80 11.00

ADVENTURES IN PARADISE (See 4-Color No. 1301)

ADVENTURES IN ROMANCE (See Adventures)

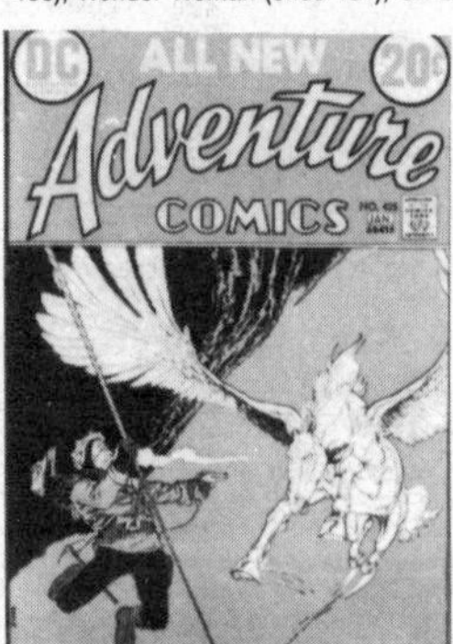

Adventure Comics #425, © DC

Adventure Into Mystery #1, © MCG

Adventures #2, © BP

Adventures Into Darkness #8, © BP

Adventures Into Terror #12, © MCG

Advs. of Bob Hope #107, © DC

ADVENTURES IN SCIENCE (See Classics Special)

ADVENTURES IN 3-D
Nov, 1953 - No. 2, Jan, 1954
Harvey Publications

	Good	Fine	Mint
1-Nostrand, Powell-a, 2-Powell-a	8.00	24.00	56.00

ADVENTURES INTO DARKNESS (See Seduction of/Innocent 3-D)
No. 5, Aug, 1952 - No. 14, 1954
Better-Standard Publications/Visual Editions

	Good	Fine	Mint
5-Katz c/a; Toth-a(p)	5.00	15.00	35.00
6-Tuska, Katz-a	4.00	12.00	28.00
7-Katz c/a	4.00	12.00	28.00
8,9-Toth-a(p)	5.00	15.00	35.00
10,11-Jack Katz-a	3.15	9.50	22.00
12-Toth-a?; lingerie panels	4.00	12.00	28.00
13-Toth-a(p); Cannibalism story cited by T. E. Murphy articles	4.50	13.50	31.50
14	3.15	9.50	22.00

NOTE: ***Fawcette** a-13. **Moriera** a-5. **Sekowsky** a-10, 11, 13(2).*

ADVENTURES INTO TERROR (Formerly Joker Comics)
No. 43, Nov, 1950 - No. 31, May, 1954
Marvel/Atlas Comics (CDS)

	Good	Fine	Mint
43	7.00	21.00	50.00
44(2/51)	5.00	15.00	35.00
3(4/51), 4	3.50	10.50	24.00
5-Wolverton-c panel/Mystic #6. Atom Bomb story	4.50	13.50	31.50
6,8: 8-Wolverton text illo r-/Marvel Tales 104	3.00	9.00	21.00
7-Wolverton-a "Where Monsters Dwell", 6 pgs.; Tuska-c	17.00	50.00	120.00
9,10,12-Krigstein-a. 9-Decapitation panels	3.85	11.50	27.00
11,13-20	2.50	7.50	17.50
21-24,26-31	2.15	6.50	15.00
25-Matt Fox-a	3.50	10.50	24.00

NOTE: ***Colan** a-3, 5, 14, 24, 25, 29; c-27. **Everett** c-13, 21, 25. **Heath** a-43, 44, 4-6, 22, 24, 26; c-43, 9, 11. **Lazarus** a-7. **Maneely** a-7, 10, 11. **Don Rico** a-4, 5. **Sekowsky** a-43, 3, 4. **Sinnott** a-8, 9, 11. **Tuska** a-14.*

ADVENTURES INTO THE UNKNOWN
Fall, 1948 - No. 174, Aug, 1967 (No. 1-33, 52 pgs.)
American Comics Group

(1st continuous series horror comic)

	Good	Fine	Mint
1-Guardineer-a; adapt. of 'Castle of Otranto' by Horace Walpole	33.00	100.00	230.00
2	15.00	45.00	105.00
3-Feldstein-a, 9 pgs.	18.00	54.00	125.00
4,5	10.50	32.00	74.00
6-10	7.50	23.00	52.00
11-16,18-20	5.00	15.00	35.00
17-Story similar to movie 'The Thing'	7.50	23.00	52.00
21-26,28-30	4.50	13.50	31.00
27-Williamson/Krenkel-a, 8 pgs.	14.00	42.00	100.00
31-50	3.00	9.00	21.00
51(1/54) - 59 (3-D effect). 52-E.C. swipe/Haunt Of Fear 14	7.00	21.00	50.00
60-Woodesque-a by Landau	2.15	6.50	15.00
61-Last pre-code ish (1-2/55)	1.85	5.50	13.00
62-70	1.30	4.00	9.00
71-90	.85	2.50	6.00
91,95,96(#95 on inside),107,116-All contain Williamson-a	2.65	8.00	18.00
92-94,97-99,101-106,108-115,117-127: 109-113,118-Whitney painted-c	.65	1.90	4.00
100	.80	2.40	4.80
128-Williamson-a(r)/Forbidden Worlds 63	.80	2.40	4.80
129-150	.35	1.00	2.00
151-153: 153-Magic Agent app.		.50	1.00
154-Nemesis begins (origin), ends #170	.40	1.20	2.40
155-167,169-174: 157-Magic Agent app.	.30	.80	1.60
168-Ditko-a(p)	.40	1.20	2.40

NOTE: *"Spirit of Frankenstein" series in 5, 6, 8-10, 12, 16. **Buscema** a-100, 106, 108-110, 158r, 165r. **Craig** a-152, 160. **Goode** a-45, 47, 60. **Landau** a-51, 59-63. **Lazarus** a-51, 79; c-51. **Torres** a-116.*

ADVENTURES INTO WEIRD WORLDS
Jan, 1952 - No. 30, June, 1954
Marvel/Atlas Comics (ACI)

	Good	Fine	Mint
1-Atom bomb panels	8.00	24.00	56.00
2	4.50	13.50	31.00
3-6,8,9	3.50	10.50	24.00
7-Tongue ripped out	4.50	13.50	31.00
10-Krigstein, Everett-a	3.85	11.50	27.00
11-20	2.50	7.50	17.50
21-Hitler in hell story	2.30	7.00	16.00
22,23,25,26	2.00	6.00	14.00
24-Man holding hypo and splitting in two	5.35	16.00	37.00
27-Matt Fox end of world story-a; severed head cover	5.70	17.00	40.00
28-Atom bomb story; decapitation panels	2.15	6.50	15.00
29,30	1.70	5.00	12.00

NOTE: ***Everett** a-4, 5; c-6, 8, 10-13, 18, 19, 22, 24; a-4, 25. **Fass** a-7. **Forte** a-21, 24. **Heath** a-1, 4, 17, 22; c-7. **Rico** a-13. **Maneely** a-3, 11, 20, 22, 25; c-3, 25-27, 29. **Reinman** a-28. **Robinson** a-13. **Sinnott** a-25, 30. **Tuska** a-1, 12, 15. **Wildey** a-28. Bondage c-22.*

ADVENTURES IN WONDERLAND
April, 1955 - No. 5, Feb, 1956 (Jr. Readers Guild)
Lev Gleason Publications

	Good	Fine	Mint
1-Maurer-a	2.50	7.50	17.50
2-4	1.45	4.35	10.00
5-Christmas issue	1.60	4.80	11.00

ADVENTURES OF ALAN LADD, THE
Oct-Nov, 1949 - No. 9, Feb-Mar, 1951
National Periodical Publications

	Good	Fine	Mint
1-Photo-c	24.00	72.00	170.00
2-Photo-c	14.00	42.00	100.00
3-6: Last photo-c	12.00	36.00	84.00
7-9	10.00	30.00	70.00

NOTE: ***Moreira** a-3-7.*

ADVENTURES OF ALICE
1945 (Also see Alice in Wonderland & . . .at Monkey Island)
Civil Service Publ./Pentagon Publishing Co.

	Good	Fine	Mint
1	4.50	13.50	32.00
2-Through the Magic Looking Glass	3.50	10.50	24.00

ADVENTURES OF BOB HOPE, THE (Also see True Comics 59)
Feb-Mar, 1950 - No. 109, Feb-Mar, 1968 (#1-10, 52pgs.)
National Periodical Publications

	Good	Fine	Mint
1-Photo-c	34.00	102.00	240.00
2-Photo-c	17.00	50.00	120.00
3,4-Photo-c	11.50	34.00	80.00
5-10	8.50	26.00	60.00
11-20	5.00	15.00	35.00
21-30	3.50	10.50	24.00
31-40	2.65	8.00	18.00
41-50	1.70	5.00	12.00
51-70	1.00	3.00	7.00
71-93,95-105	.70	2.00	4.00
94-Aquaman cameo	.85	2.50	5.00
106-109-Adams c/a	2.50	7.50	15.00

NOTE: *Kitty Karr of Hollywood in No. 17-20,28. Liz in No. 26. Miss Beverly Hills of Hollywood in No. 7, 10, 13, 14. Miss Melody Lane of Broadway in No. 15. Rusty in No.*

ADVENTURES OF BOB HOPE (continued)
23, 25. Tommy in No. 24. No 2nd feature in No. 2-4, 6, 8, 11, 12, 28-on.

ADVENTURES OF DEAN MARTIN AND JERRY LEWIS, THE
(The Adventures of Jerry Lewis No. 41 on)
July-Aug, 1952 - No. 40, Oct, 1957
National Periodical Publications

	Good	Fine	Mint
1	26.00	78.00	180.00
2	12.00	36.00	85.00
3-10	7.00	21.00	49.00
11-20	4.00	12.00	28.00
21-30	3.00	9.00	21.00
31-40	2.15	6.50	15.00

ADVENTURES OF G. I. JOE
1969 (3¼"x7") (20 & 16 pgs.)
Giveaways

First Series: 1-Danger of the Depths. 2-Perilous Rescue. 3-Secret Mission to Spy Island. 4-Mysterious Explosion. 5-Fantastic Free Fall. 6-Eight Ropes of Danger. 7-Mouth of Doom. 8-Hidden Missile Discovery. 9-Space Walk Mystery. 10-Fight for Survival. 11-The Shark's Surprise. **Second Series:** 2-Flying Space Adventure. 4-White Tiger Hunt. 7-Capture of the Pygmy Gorilla. 12-Secret of the Mummy's Tomb. **Third Series:** Reprinted surviving titles of First Series. **Fourth Series:** 13-Adventure Team Headquarters. 14-Search For the Stolen Idol. each.... .30 .60

ADVENTURES OF HAWKSHAW (See Hawkshaw The Detective)
1917 (9-3/4 x 13½", 48 pgs., Color & two-tone)
The Saalfield Publishing Co.

By Gus Mager (only 24 pgs. of strips, reverse of each page is blank) 15.00 45.00 105.00

ADVENTURES OF HOMER COBB, THE
September, 1947 (Oversized)
Say/Bart Prod. (Canadian)

	Good	Fine	Mint
1-(Scarce)-Feldstein-a	17.00	50.00	120.00

ADVENTURES OF HOMER GHOST
June, 1957 - No. 2, August, 1957
Atlas Comics

	Good	Fine	Mint
V1No.1, V1No. 2	1.15	3.50	8.00

ADVENTURES OF JERRY LEWIS, THE (Advs. of Dean Martin & Jerry Lewis No. 1-40)(See Super DC Giant)
No. 41, Nov, 1957 - No. 124, May-June, 1971
National Periodical Publications

	Good	Fine	Mint
41-60	1.85	5.50	13.00
61-80: 68,74-Photo-c	1.15	3.50	8.00
81-91,93-96,98-100	.80	2.40	4.80
92-Superman cameo	.90	2.70	5.40
97-Batman/Robin x-over	.90	2.70	5.40
101-104-Adams c/a; 102-Beatles app.	2.50	7.50	15.00
105-Superman x-over	.80	2.40	4.80
106-111,113-116	.35	1.00	2.00
112-Flash x-over	.50	1.50	3.00
117-Wonder Woman x-over	.50	1.50	3.00
118-124		.60	1.20

ADVENTURES OF MARGARET O'BRIEN, THE
1947 (20 pgs. in color; slick cover; regular size) (Premium)
Bambury Fashions (Clothes)

	Good	Fine	Mint
In "The Big City"-movie adaptation (Scarce)	13.00	40.00	90.00

ADVENTURES OF MIGHTY MOUSE (Mighty Mouse Advs. No. 1)
No. 2, Jan, 1952 - No. 18, May, 1955
St. John Publishing Co.

	Good	Fine	Mint
2	6.00	18.00	42.00
3-5	4.00	12.00	28.00
6-18	2.50	7.50	17.50

ADVENTURES OF MIGHTY MOUSE (2nd Series)
(Two No. 144's; formerly Paul Terry's Comics; No. 129-137 have nn's)(Becomes Mighty Mouse No. 161 on)
No. 126, Aug, 1955 - No. 160, Oct, 1963
St. John/Pines/Dell/Gold Key

	Good	Fine	Mint
126(8/55), 127(10/55), 128(11/55)-St. John	1.85	5.50	13.00
nn(129, 4/56)-144(8/59)-Pines	1.50	4.50	10.00
144(10-12/59)-155(7-9/62) Dell	1.15	3.50	8.00
156(10/62)-160(10/63) Gold Key	1.15	3.50	8.00

NOTE: *Early issues titled "Paul Terry's Adventures of ...."*

ADVENTURES OF MIGHTY MOUSE (Formerly Mighty Mouse)
No. 166, Mar, 1979 - No. 172, Jan, 1980
Gold Key

	Good	Fine	Mint
166-172	.50	1.50	3.00

ADVS. OF MR. FROG & MISS MOUSE (See Dell Jr. Treasury No. 4)

ADVENTURES OF OZZIE AND HARRIET, THE (Radio)
Oct-Nov, 1949 - No. 5, June-July, 1950
National Periodical Publications

	Good	Fine	Mint
1-Photo-c	22.00	65.00	155.00
2	16.00	48.00	110.00
3-5	13.00	39.00	90.00

ADVENTURES OF PATORUZU
Aug, 1946 - Winter, 1946
Green Publishing Co.

	Good	Fine	Mint
nn's-Contains Animal Crackers reprints	1.30	4.00	9.00

ADVENTURES OF PINKY LEE, THE (TV)
July, 1955 - No. 5, Dec, 1955
Atlas Comics

	Good	Fine	Mint
1	7.50	22.50	52.00
2-5	4.50	13.50	32.00

ADVENTURES OF PIPSQUEAK, THE (Formerly Pat the Brat)
No. 34, Sept., 1959 - No. 39, July, 1960
Archie Publications (Radio Comics)

	Good	Fine	Mint
34	2.00	6.00	14.00
35-39	1.15	3.50	8.00

ADVENTURES OF QUAKE & QUISP, THE (See Quaker Oats "Plenty of Glutton")

ADVENTURES OF REX THE WONDER DOG, THE (Rex. . No. 1)
Jan-Feb, 1952 - No. 45, May-Jun, 1959; No. 46, Nov-Dec, 1959
National Periodical Publications

	Good	Fine	Mint
1-(Scarce)-Toth-a	42.00	126.00	295.00
2-(Scarce)-Toth-a	21.00	62.00	145.00
3-(Scarce)-Toth-a	17.00	51.00	120.00
4,5	12.00	36.00	84.00
6-10	8.00	24.00	56.00
11-Atom bomb c/story	5.50	16.50	38.00
12-19: Last precode, 1-2/55	4.50	13.50	31.50
20-46	2.85	8.50	20.00

NOTE: ***Infantino, Gil Kane*** *art in most issues.*

ADVENTURES OF ROBIN HOOD, THE (Formerly Robin Hood)
No. 7, 9/57 - No. 8, 11/57 (Based on Richard Greene TV Show)
Magazine Enterprises (Sussex Publ. Co.)

	Good	Fine	Mint
7,8-Richard Greene photo-c. 7-Powell-a	2.50	7.50	17.50

ADVENTURES OF ROBIN HOOD, THE
March, 1974 - No. 7, Jan, 1975 (Disney Cartoon) (36 pgs.)
Gold Key

	Good	Fine	Mint
1(90291-403)-Part-r of $1.50 editions	.60	1.80	3.60
2-7: 1-7, part-r	.45	1.25	2.50

ADVENTURES OF SLIM AND SPUD, THE
1924 (3¾"x9¾")(104 pg. B&W strip reprints)
Prairie Farmer Publ. Co.

	Good	Fine	Mint
	7.00	21.00	50.00

Advs. of Dean Martin and Jerry Lewis #35, © DC

Advs. of Mighty Mouse #3, © STJ

Advs. of Rex The Wonder Dog #22, © DC

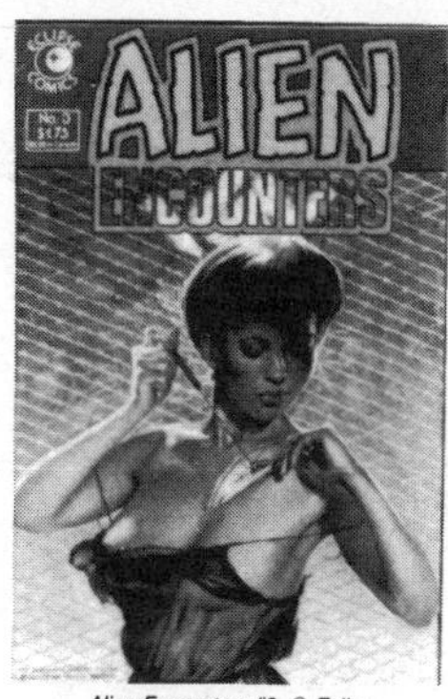

Alien Encounters #3, © Eclipse

All-American Comics #2, © DC

All-American Comics #29, © DC

	Good	Fine	Mint
AL CAPP'S SHMOO (continued)	13.00	40.00	90.00

AL CAPP'S WOLF GAL
1951 - No. 2, 1952
Toby Press

1,2-Edited-r from Li'l Abner No. 63,64	16.00	48.00	110.00

ALEXANDER THE GREAT (See 4-Color No. 688)

ALF (TV)
Mar, 1988 - Present ($1.00, color)
Marvel Comics

1,2-Post-a		.50	1.00

ALGIE
Dec, 1953 - No. 3, 1954
Timor Publ. Co.

1	1.50	4.50	10.00
2,3	.85	2.50	6.00
Accepted Reprint #2(nd)	.55	1.65	4.00
Super Reprint 15	.40	1.20	2.80

ALICE (New Advs. in Wonderland)
1952
Ziff-Davis Publ. Co.

10-Spanking-c; Berg-a	8.00	24.00	56.00
11-Dave Berg-a	4.00	12.00	28.00
2-Dave Berg-a	3.00	9.00	21.00

ALICE AT MONKEY ISLAND (See The Advs. of Alice)
No. 3, 1946
Pentagon Publ. Co. (Civil Service)

3	3.15	9.50	22.00

ALICE IN BLUNDERLAND
1952 (Paper cover, 16 pages in color)
Industrial Services

nn-Facts about big government waste and inefficiency	12.00	36.00	84.00

ALICE IN WONDERLAND (See Advs. of Alice, 4-Color No. 331,341, Dell Jr. Treasury No. 1, Movie Comics, Single Series No. 24, Walt Disney Showcase No. 22, and World's Greatest Stories)

ALICE IN WONDERLAND
1965; 1982
Western Printing Company/Whitman Publ. Co.

...Meets Santa Claus(1950s), nd, 16pgs	2.75	8.00	16.00
Rexall Giveaway(1965, 16 pgs., 5x7¼") Western Printing (TV-Hanna-Barbera)	2.00	6.00	12.00
Wonder Bakery Giveaway(16 pgs, color, nn, nd) (Continental Baking Co. (1969)	2.00	6.00	12.00
1-(Whitman; 1982)-r/4-Color 331		.40	.80

ALICE IN WONDERLAND MEETS SANTA
nd (16 pgs., 6-5/8x9-11/16", paper cover)
No publisher (Giveaway)

	10.00	30.00	60.00

ALIEN ENCOUNTERS (Replaces Alien Worlds)
June, 1985 - No. 14, Aug, 1987 ($1.75; Baxter) (Mature readers)
Eclipse Comics

1-14: Nudity, strong language	.35	1.00	2.00

ALIEN LEGION
April, 1984 - No. 20, Sept, 1987
Epic Comics (Marvel)

1-$2.00 cover, high quality paper	.60	1.75	3.50
2-5	.35	1.00	2.00
6-10	.30	.85	1.70
11-20		.75	1.50

NOTE: *Austin a-1i, 4i; c-3i-5i.*

ALIEN LEGION (2nd series)
Aug, 1987 - Present ($1.25, color)
Epic Comics (Marvel)

	Good	Fine	Mint
V2#1,2	.25	.75	1.50

ALIENS, THE (Captain Johner and...)(Also see Magnus Robot...
Sept-Dec, 1967; No. 2, May, 1982
Gold Key

1-Reprints from Magnus #1,3,4,6-10, all by Russ Manning	1.00	3.00	6.00
2-Magnus-r/#1 by Manning		.50	1.00

ALIEN TERROR (See 3-D Alien Terror)

ALIEN WORLDS
12/82; No. 2, 6/83 - No. 7, 4/84; No. 8, 11/84 - No. 9, 1/85
(Baxter paper, $1.50)
Pacific Comics No. 1-7/Eclipse No. 8, 9

1-Williamson, Redondo-a; nudity	.60	1.75	3.50
2-7: 4-Nudity scenes	.50	1.50	3.00
8-Williamson-a	.30	.85	1.70
9-($1.75 cover)	.35	1.00	2.00

NOTE: ***Bolton** c-5, 9. **Brunner** a-6p, 9; c-6. **Conrad** a-1. **Corben** a-7. **J. Jones** a-4p. **Krenkel** a-6. **Morrow** a-7. **Perez** a-7. **Stevens** a-2, 4i; c-2, 4. **Williamson/Frazetta** a-4r/Witzend No. 1.*

ALIEN WORLDS 3-D (See 3-Dimensional Alien Worlds)

ALL-AMERICAN COMICS (...Western #103-126, ...Men of War #127 on)
April, 1939 - No. 102, Oct, 1948
National Periodical Publications/All-American

1-Hop Harrigan, Scribbly, Toonerville Folks, Ben Webster, Spot Savage, Mutt & Jeff, Red White & Blue, Adv. in the Unknown, Tippie, Reg'lar Fellers, Skippy, Bobby Thatcher, Mystery Men of Mars, Daiseybelle, & Wiley of West Point begin	132.00	396.00	925.00
2-Ripley's Believe It or Not begins, ends #24	58.00	175.00	405.00
3-5: 5-The American Way begins, ends #10	40.00	120.00	280.00
6,7: 6-Last Spot Savage; Popsicle Pete begins, ends #26, 28. 7-Last Bobby Thatcher	30.00	90.00	210.00
8-The Ultra Man begins	50.00	150.00	350.00
9,10: 10-X-Mas-c	35.00	105.00	245.00
11-15: 12-Last Toonerville Folks. 15-Last Tippie & Reg'lar Fellars	28.00	85.00	200.00
16-Origin & 1st app. Green Lantern (Rare), created by Martin Nodell. Inspired by Aladdin's Lamp; the suggested alter ego name Alan Ladd, was never capitalized on. It was changed to Alan Scott before appearance of movie star Alan Ladd	900.00	2700.00	5900.00
(Prices vary widely on this book)			
17-(Scarce)	240.00	720.00	1680.00
18	120.00	360.00	840.00
19-Origin & 1st app. The Atom; Last Ultra Man	175.00	525.00	1225.00
20-Atom dons costume; Hunkle becomes Red Tornado; Rescue on Mars begins, ends #25; 1 pg. origin Green Lantern	105.00	315.00	735.00
21-23: 21-Last Wiley of West Point & Skippy. 23-Last Daiseybelle; 3 Idiots begin, end #82	72.00	215.00	505.00
24-Sisty & Dinky become the Cyclone Kids; Ben Webster ends. Origin Dr. Mid-Nite & Sargon, The Sorcerer in text with app.	77.00	230.00	540.00

25-Origin & 1st story app. Dr. Mid-Nite by Stan Asch; Hop Harrigan becomes Guardian Angel; last Adventure in the Unknown

ALL-AMERICAN COMICS (continued) Good Fine Mint

125.00 375.00 875.00

26-Origin & 1st story app. Sargon, the Sorcerer

85.00 255.00 600.00

27: No. 27-32 are misnumbered in indicia with correct No. appearing on cover. Intro. Doiby Dickles, Green Lantern's sidekick

85.00 255.00 600.00

28-Hop Harrigan gives up costumed i.d. 48.00 145.00 335.00

29,30 48.00 145.00 335.00

31-40: 35-Doiby learns Green Lantern's i. d. 35.00 105.00 245.00

41-50: 50-Sargon ends 30.00 90.00 210.00

51-60: 59-Scribbly & the Red Tornado ends 25.00 75.00 175.00

61-Origin Solomon Grundy 62.00 185.00 435.00

62-70: 70-Kubert Sargon; intro Sargon's helper, Maximillian O'Leary

25.00 75.00 175.00

71-Last Red White & Blue 20.00 60.00 140.00

72-Black Pirate begins (not in #74-82); last Atom

20.00 60.00 140.00

73-80: 73-Winky, Blinky & Noddy begins, ends #82

20.00 60.00 140.00

81-88,90: 90-Origin Icicle 20.00 60.00 140.00

89-Origin Harlequin 25.00 75.00 175.00

91-99-Last Hop Harrigan 20.00 60.00 140.00

100-1st app. Johnny Thunder by Alex Toth 38.00 115.00 265.00

101-Last Mutt & Jeff 25.00 75.00 175.00

102-Last Green Lantern, Black Pirate & Dr. Mid-Nite

25.00 75.00 175.00

NOTE: *No Atom in 47,62-69.* ***Kinstler*** *Black Pirate-89.* ***Stan Aschmeier*** *a-25, 40, 55, 70; c-7.* ***Moldoff*** *c-16-23.* ***Paul Reinman*** *a-55, 70; c-55, 70.* ***Toth*** *a-88, 92, 96, 98-102; c-92, 96-102.*

ALL-AMERICAN MEN OF WAR (Previously All-American Western)
No. 127, Aug-Sept, 1952 - No. 117, Sept-Oct, 1966
National Periodical Publications

127 (1952) 17.00 50.00 120.00

128 (1952) 11.00 33.00 75.00

2(12-1/'52-53)-5 8.50 25.50 60.00

6-10 5.50 16.50 38.00

11-20 3.85 11.50 27.00

21-28 3.00 9.00 21.00

29,30,32-Wood-a 3.50 10.50 24.00

31,33-50 1.50 4.50 10.00

51-66 1.00 3.00 7.00

67-1st Gunner & Sarge by Andru 1.00 3.00 7.00

68-80 .70 2.00 4.00

81-100: 82-Johnny Cloud begins, ends #111,114,115

.35 1.00 2.00

101-117: 112-Balloon Buster series begins, ends #114,116; 115-Johnny Cloud app. .60 1.20

NOTE: ***Colan*** *a-112.* ***Drucker*** *a-47,65,74,77.* ***Heath*** *a-27, 32, 47, 95, 112; c-95, 100, 112.* ***Krigstein*** *a-128('52), 2, 3, 5.* ***Kirby*** *a-29.* ***Kubert*** *a-29, 36, 38, 41, 43, 47, 49, 50, 52, 53, 55, 56, 60, 63, 65, 69, 71-73, 103, 114; c-41, 77, 114. Tank Killer in 69, 71, 76 by* ***Kubert.***

ALL-AMERICAN SPORTS
October, 1967
Charlton Comics

1 .30 .60

ALL-AMERICAN WESTERN (Formerly All-American Comics; Becomes All-American Men of War)
No. 103, Nov, 1948 - No. 126, June-July, 1952 (52pgs, 103-121)
National Periodical Publications

103-Johnny Thunder & his horse Black Lightning continues by Toth, ends No. 126; Foley of The Fighting 5th, Minstrel Maverick, & Overland Coach begin; Captain Tootsie by Beck; mentioned in **Love and Death** 14.00 42.00 100.00

104-Kubert-a 10.00 30.00 70.00

105,107-Kubert-a 9.00 27.00 63.00

Good Fine Mint

106,108-110,112: 112-Kurtzman "Pot-Shot Pete," 1pg.

7.00 21.00 50.00

111,114-116-Kubert-a 8.00 24.00 56.00

113-Intro. Swift Deer, J. Thunder's new sidekick; classic Toth-c; Kubert-a 9.00 27.00 63.00

117-120,122-125 6.00 18.00 42.00

121-Kubert-a 6.00 18.00 42.00

126-Last issue 6.00 18.00 42.00

NOTE: ***Kubert*** *a-103-105, 107, 111, 112(1 pg.), 113-116, 121.* ***Toth*** *c/a 103-126.*

ALL COMICS
1945
Chicago Nite Life News

1 4.50 13.50 32.00

ALLEY OOP (See 4-Color No. 3 and Super Book No. 9)

ALLEY OOP
No. 10, 1947 - No. 18, Oct, 1949
Standard Comics

10 12.00 36.00 84.00

11-18: 17,18-Schomburg-c 9.00 27.00 63.00

ALLEY OOP
Nov, 1955 - No. 3, March, 1956 (Newspaper reprints)
Argo Publ.

1 9.00 27.00 63.00

2,3 6.00 18.00 42.00

ALLEY OOP
12-2/62-63 - No. 2, 9-11/63
Dell Publishing Co.

1,2 5.00 15.00 35.00

ALL-FAMOUS CRIME
1949 - No. 10, Nov, 1951
Star Publications

1 4.50 13.50 32.00

2 2.65 8.00 18.00

3-5 2.35 7.00 16.00

6-8,10 2.00 6.00 14.00

9-Used in **SOTI**, illo-"The wish to hurt or kill couples in lovers' lanes is not uncommon perversion;" L.B. Cole-c/a(r)/Law-Crime No. 3 8.00 24.00 56.00

NOTE: *All have* ***L.B. Cole*** *covers.*

ALL FAMOUS CRIME STORIES (See Fox Giants)

ALL-FAMOUS POLICE CASES
Oct, 1951 - No. 16, Sept, 1954
Star Publications

1 4.50 13.50 32.00

2 2.65 8.00 18.00

3-6,9-16 2.35 7.00 16.00

7-Kubert-a 3.00 9.00 21.00

8-Marijuana story 3.00 9.00 21.00

NOTE: ***L. B. Cole*** *c-all; a-15, 1pg.* ***Hollingsworth*** *a-15.*

ALL-FLASH (. . .Quarterly No. 1-5)
Summer, 1941 - No. 32, Dec-Jan, 1947-48
National Periodical Publications/All-American

1-Origin The Flash retold by E. Hibbard 200.00 600.00 1400.00

2-Origin recap 78.00 234.00 545.00

3,4 53.00 160.00 370.00

5-Winky, Blinky & Noddy begins, ends #32 42.00 125.00 295.00

6-10 36.00 108.00 250.00

11-13: 12-Origin The Thinker. 13-The King app.

28.00 84.00 195.00

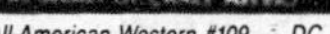
All-American Western #109, © DC

All-Famous Police Cases #16, © STAR

All-Flash #13, © DC

ALL-FLASH (continued) Good Fine Mint
14-Green Lantern cameo 32.00 95.00 225.00
15-20: 18-Mutt & Jeff begins, ends #22 25.00 75.00 175.00
21-31 23.00 70.00 160.00
32-Origin The Fiddler; 1st Star Sapphire 27.00 81.00 190.00
NOTE: *Book length stories in 2-13,16. Bondage c-31, 32.*

ALL FOR LOVE (Young Love V3/5-on)
Apr-May, 1957 - V3No.4, Dec-Jan, 1959-60
Prize Publications
V1No.1 2.30 7.00 16.00
2-6: 5-Orlando-c 1.30 4.00 9.00
V2No.1-6 .85 2.50 6.00
V3No.1-4: 2-Powell-a .70 2.00 4.00

ALL FUNNY COMICS
Winter, 1943-44 - No. 23, May-June, 1948
Tilsam Publ./National Periodical Publications (Detective)
1-Genius Jones, Buzzy (ends #4), Dover & Clover begin; Bailey-a 17.00 51.00 120.00
2 8.00 24.00 56.00
3-10 5.50 16.50 38.00
11-13,15,18,19-Genius Jones app. 4.50 13.50 31.50
14,17,20-23 3.30 10.00 23.00
16-DC Super Heroes app. 8.50 25.50 60.00

ALL GOOD COMICS (See Fox Giants)
Spring, 1946 (36 pgs.)
Fox Features Syndicate
1-Joy Family, Dick Transom, Rick Evans, One Round Hogan 6.00 18.00 42.00

ALL GOOD
Oct, 1949 (260 pages) (50 cents)
St. John Publishing Co.
(8 St. John comics bound together) 38.00 115.00 265.00
NOTE: *Also see Li'l Audrey Yearbook & Treasury of Comics.*

ALL GREAT (See Fox Giants)
1946 (36 pgs.)
Fox Features Syndicate
1-Crazy House, Bertie Benson Boy Detective, Gussie the Gob 4.85 14.50 34.00

ALL GREAT
nd (1945?) (132 pgs.)
William H. Wise & Co.
nn-Capt. Jack Terry, Joan Mason, Girl Reporter, Baron Doomsday; Torture scenes 13.50 40.00 95.00

ALL GREAT (Dagar, Desert Hawk No. 14 on)
No. 14, Oct, 1947 - No. 13, Dec, 1947
Fox Features Syndicate
14-Brenda Starr-r (Scarce) 13.50 40.00 95.00
13-Origin Dagar, Desert Hawk; Brenda Starr (all-r); Kamen-c 13.00 40.00 90.00

ALL-GREAT CONFESSIONS (See Fox Giants)

ALL GREAT CRIME STORIES (See Fox Giants)

ALL GREAT JUNGLE ADVENTURES (See Fox Giants)

ALL HERO COMICS
March, 1943 (100 pgs.) (Cardboard cover)
Fawcett Publications
1-Captain Marvel Jr., Capt. Midnight, Golden Arrow, Ibis the Invincible, Spy Smasher, & Lance O'Casey 60.00 180.00 420.00

ALL HUMOR COMICS
Spring, 1946 - No. 17, December, 1949
Quality Comics Group
1 5.00 15.00 35.00
2-Atomic Tot sty; Gustavson-a 2.50 7.50 18.00
3-9: 5-1st app. Hickory? 8-Gustavson-a 1.85 5.50 13.00
10-17 1.30 4.00 9.00

ALL LOVE (. . . Romances No. 26)(Formerly Ernie)
No. 26, May, 1949 - No. 32, May, 1950
Ace Periodicals (Current Books)
26(No. 1)-Ernie, Lily Belle app. 2.30 7.00 16.00
27-L. B. Cole-a 2.65 8.00 18.50
28-32 1.50 4.50 10.00

ALL-NEGRO COMICS
June, 1947 (15 cents)
All-Negro Comics
1 (Rare) 65.00 195.00 455.00
NOTE: *Seldom found in fine or mint condition; many copies have brown pages.*

ALL-NEW COLLECTORS' EDITION (Formerly Ltd. Collectors' Ed.)
Jan, 1978 - No. C-62, 1979 (No. 54-58: 76 pgs.)
DC Comics, Inc.
C-53-Rudolph the Red-Nosed Reindeer .50 1.00
C-54-Superman Vs. Wonder Woman .25 .75 1.50

Good Fine Mint
C-55-Superboy & the Legion of Super-Heroes .70 2.00 4.00
C-56-Superman Vs. Muhammad Ali: story & wraparound Adams-c .35 1.00 2.00
C-58-Superman Vs. Shazam .60 1.20
C-60-Rudolph's Summer Fun(8/78) .60 1.20
C-62-Superman the Movie (68 pgs.; 1979) .60 1.20

ALL-NEW COMICS (. . . Short Story Comics No. 1-3)
Jan, 1943 - No. 14, Nov, 1946; No. 15, Mar-Apr, 1947
Family Comics (Harvey Publications)
1-Steve Case, Crime Rover, Johnny Rebel, Kayo Kane, The Echo, Night Hawk, Ray O'Light, Detective Shane begin; Red Blazer on cover only; Sultan-a 46.00 138.00 320.00
2-Origin Scarlet Phantom by Kubert 23.00 70.00 160.00
3 17.00 51.00 120.00
4,5 15.00 45.00 105.00
6-The Boy Heroes & Red Blazer (text story) begin, end #12; Black Cat app.; intro. Sparky in Red Blazer 17.00 51.00 120.00
7-Kubert, Powell-a; Black Cat & Zebra app. 17.00 51.00 120.00
8-Shock Gibson app.; Kubert, Powell-a; Schomburg bondage-c 17.00 51.00 120.00
9-Black Cat app.; Kubert-a 17.00 51.00 120.00
10-The Zebra app.; Kubert-a(3) 15.00 45.00 105.00
11-Girl Commandos, Man In Black app. 15.00 45.00 105.00
12-Kubert-a 15.00 45.00 105.00
13-Stuntman by Simon & Kirby; Green Hornet, Joe Palooka, Flying Fool app. 17.00 51.00 120.00
14-The Green Hornet & The Man in Black Called Fate by Powell, Joe Palooka app. 15.00 45.00 105.00
15-(Rare)-Small size (5½x8½"; B&W; 32 pgs.). Distributed to mail subscribers only. Black Cat and Joe Palooka app. Estimated value....$200-250
NOTE: *Also see Boy Explorers No. 2, Flash Gordon No. 5, and Stuntman No. 3.* ***Powell*** *a-11.* ***Schomburg*** *c-7,8,10,11.*

ALL PICTURE ADVENTURE MAGAZINE
Oct, 1952 - No. 2, Nov, 1952 (100 pg. Giants)
St. John Publishing Co.
1-War comics 11.00 33.00 77.00
2-Horror-crime comics 15.00 45.00 105.00
NOTE: *Above books contain three St. John comics rebound; variations possible.* ***Baker*** *art known in both.*

ALL PICTURE ALL TRUE LOVE STORY
October, 1952 (100 pages)
St. John Publishing Co.
1-Canteen Kate by Matt Baker 22.00 65.00 155.00

ALL-PICTURE COMEDY CARNIVAL
October, 1952 (100 pages)
St. John Publishing Co.
1-(4 rebound comics)-Contents can vary; Baker-a 20.00 60.00 140.00

ALL REAL CONFESSION MAGAZINE (See Fox Giants)

ALL ROMANCES (Mr. Risk No. 7 on)
Aug, 1949 - No. 6, June, 1950
A. A. Wyn (Ace Periodicals)
1 3.00 9.00 21.00
2 1.50 4.50 10.00
3-6 1.15 3.50 8.00

ALL-SELECT COMICS (Blonde Phantom No. 12 on)
Fall, 1943 - No. 11, Fall, 1946
Timely Comics (Daring Comics)
1-Capt. America, Human Torch, Sub-Mariner begin; Black Widow app. 150.00 450.00 1050.00
2-Red Skull app. 66.00 200.00 460.00
3-The Whizzer begins 46.00 138.00 320.00
4,5-Last Sub-Mariner 38.00 114.00 265.00
6-The Destroyer app. 30.00 90.00 210.00
7-9: 8-No Whizzer 30.00 90.00 210.00
10-The Destroyer & Sub-Mariner app.; last Capt. America & Human Torch issue 30.00 90.00 210.00
11-1st app. Blonde Phantom; Miss America app.; all Blonde Phantom-c 50.00 150.00 350.00
NOTE: ***Schomburg*** *c-2,4,9,10. No. 7 & 8 show 1944 in indicia, but should be 1945.*

ALL SPORTS COMICS (Formerly Real Sports Comics; becomes All Time Sports Comics No. 4 on)
No. 2, Dec-Jan, 1948-49, No. 3, Feb-Mar, 1949
Hillman Periodicals
2-Krigstein-a(p), Powell, Starr-a 6.00 18.00 42.00
3-Mort Lawrence-a 4.50 13.50 32.00

ALL STAR COMICS (. . . Western No. 58 on)
Summer, 1940 - No. 57, Feb-Mar, 1951; No. 58, Jan-Feb, 1976 - No. 74, Sept-Oct, 1978
National Periodical Publ./All-American/DC Comics
1-The Flash(No.1 by Harry Lampert), Hawkman(by Shelly), Hourman, The Sandman, The Spectre, Biff Bronson, Red White &

ALL STAR COMICS (continued)

	Good	Fine	Mint
Blue begin; Ultra Man's only app.	472.00	1415.00	3300.00
2-Green Lantern, Johnny Thunder begin	220.00	660.00	1540.00
3-Origin Justice Society of America; Dr. Fate & The Atom begin, Red Tornado cameo; last Red White & Blue; reprinted in Famous First Edition	820.00	2460.00	5740.00
4	210.00	630.00	1470.00
5-Intro. & 1st app. Shiera Sanders as Hawkgirl	180.00	540.00	1260.00
6-Johnny Thunder joins JSA	180.00	540.00	1260.00
7-Batman, Superman, Flash cameo; last Hourman; Doiby Dickles app.	125.00	375.00	875.00
8-Origin & 1st app. Wonder Woman(added as 8pgs. making book 76pgs.;origin cont'd in Sensation No. 1); Dr. Fate dons new helmet; Dr.Mid-Nite, Hop Harrigan text stories & Starman begin; Shiera app.; Hop Harrigan JSA guest	300.00	900.00	2100.00
9-Shiera app.	125.00	375.00	875.00
10-Flash, Green Lantern cameo, Sandman new costume	125.00	375.00	875.00
11-Wonder Woman begins; Spectre cameo; Shiera app.	115.00	345.00	805.00
12-Wonder Woman becomes JSA Secretary	115.00	345.00	805.00
13-15: Sandman w/Sandy in No. 14 & 15; 15-Origin Brain Wave; Shiera app.	105.00	315.00	735.00
16-19: 19-Sandman w/Sandy	82.00	245.00	575.00
20-Dr. Fate & Sandman cameo	82.00	245.00	575.00
21-Spectre & Atom cameo; Dr. Fate by Kubert; Dr. Fate, Sandman end	70.00	210.00	490.00
22,23: 22-Last Hop Harrigan; Flag-c. 23-Origin Psycho Pirate; last Spectre & Starman	70.00	210.00	490.00
24-Flash & Green Lantern cameo; Mr. Terrific only app.; Wildcat, JSA guest; Kubert Hawkman begins	70.00	210.00	490.00
25-27: 25-The Flash & Green Lantern start again. 27-Wildcat, JSA guest	65.00	195.00	455.00
28-32	55.00	165.00	385.00
33-Solomon Grundy, Hawkman, Doiby Dickles app.	105.00	315.00	735.00
34,35-Johnny Thunder cameo in both	52.00	155.00	365.00
36-Batman & Superman JSA guests	102.00	305.00	715.00
37-Johnny Thunder cameo; origin Injustice Society; last Kubert Hawkman	55.00	165.00	385.00
38-Black Canary begins; JSA Death issue	62.00	185.00	435.00
39,40: 39-Last Johnny Thunder	42.00	125.00	295.00
41-Black Canary joins JSA; Injustice Society app.	40.00	120.00	280.00
42-Atom & the Hawkman don new costume	40.00	120.00	280.00
43-49	40.00	120.00	280.00
50-Frazetta art, 3 pgs.	50.00	150.00	350.00
51-56	40.00	120.00	280.00
57-Kubert-a, 6 pgs. (Scarce)	52.00	155.00	365.00
58('76)-Flash, Hawkman, Dr. Mid-Nite, Wildcat, Dr. Fate, Green Lantern, Star Spangled Kid, & Robin app.; intro Power Girl		.25	.50
59-74: 69-1st app. Huntress		.25	.50

NOTE: *No Atom-27, 36; no Dr. Fate-13; no Flash-8, 9, 11-23; no Green Lantern-8, 9, 11-23; no Johnny Thunder-5, 36; no Wonder Woman-9, 10, 23.* ***Baily*** *a-1-10, 12, 13, 14i, 15-20.* ***Buckler*** *c-63, 66p.* ***Burnley*** *Starman-8-13; c-12, 13.* ***Grell*** *c-58.* ***Kubert*** *Hawkman-24-30, 33-37.* ***Moldoff*** *Hawkman-3-23; c-11.* ***Simon & Kirby*** *Sandman -14-17, 19.* ***Giffen*** *a-60p-63p.* ***Staton*** *a-66-74p; c-71-74.* ***Toth*** *a-37(2), 38(2), 40, 41; c-38, 41.* ***Wood*** *a-58i-63i, 64, 65; c-63-65.*

ALL-STAR SQUADRON
Sept, 1981 - No. 67, March, 1987
DC Comics

	Good	Fine	Mint
1-Original Atom, Hawkman, Dr. Mid-Nite, Robotman (origin), Plastic Man, Johnny Quick, Liberty Belle, Shining Knight begin	.25	.75	1.50
2		.50	1.00
3-24: 5-Danette Reilly becomes new Firebrand. 12-Origin G.A. Hawkman retold. 23-Intro/origin The Amazing Man		.40	.80
25-1st Infinity, Inc.	.70	2.10	4.20
26-Origin Infinity, Inc.	.60	1.75	3.50
27-49: 31-Origin Freedom Fighters of Earth-X. 41-Origin Starman. 47-Origin Dr. Fate		.40	.80
50-Double size; Crisis x-over	.25	.75	1.50
51-53-Crisis x-over		.50	1.00
54-67: 61-Origin Liberty Belle. 62-Origin The Shining Knight. 63-Origin Robotman. 65-Origin Johnny Quick. 66-Origin Tarantula		.40	.80
Annual 1(11/82)-Retells origin of G.A. Atom, Guardian & Wildcat		.50	1.00
Annual 2(11/83)-Infinity, Inc. app.		.50	1.00
Annual 3(9/84)		.65	1.30

NOTE: ***Kubert*** *c-2, 7-18.*

ALL-STAR STORY OF THE DODGERS, THE
April, 1979 (Full Color) ($1.00)
Stadium Communications

	Good	Fine	Mint
1		.50	1.00

ALL STAR WESTERN (All Star No. 1-57)
Apr-May, 1951 - No. 119, June-July, 1961
National Periodical Publications

	Good	Fine	Mint
58-Trigger Twins (end #116), Strong Bow, The Roving Ranger & Don Caballero begin	15.00	45.00	105.00
59,60: Last 52 pgs.	7.00	21.00	50.00
61-66: 61,64-Toth-a	6.00	18.00	42.00
67-Johnny Thunder begins; Gil Kane-a	7.00	21.00	50.00
68-81: Last precode, 2-3/55	3.35	10.00	23.50
82-98	2.50	7.50	17.50
99-Frazetta-a r-/Jimmy Wakely #4	5.00	15.00	35.00
100	3.35	10.00	23.50
101-107,109-116,118,119	2.00	6.00	14.00
108-Origin Johnny Thunder	4.00	12.00	28.00
117-Origin Super Chief	3.50	10.50	24.50

NOTE: ***Infantino*** *art in most issues. Madame app.-No. 117-119.*

ALL-STAR WESTERN (Weird Western Tales No. 12 on)
Aug-Sept, 1970 - No. 11, Apr-May, 1972
National Periodical Publications

	Good	Fine	Mint
1-Pow-Wow Smith-r; Infantino-a	.50	1.50	3.00
2-Outlaw begins; El Diablo by Morrow begins	.35	1.00	2.00
3-8: 3-Origin El Diablo. 5-Last Outlaw ish. 6-Billy the Kid begins, ends #8	.35	1.00	2.00
9-Frazetta-a, 3pgs.(r)	.70	2.00	4.00
10-Jonah Hex begins	2.35	7.00	14.00
11	.70	2.00	4.00

NOTE: ***Adams*** *c-1-5;* ***Aparo*** *a-5.* ***G. Kane*** *a-3, 4, 6, 8.* ***Morrow*** *a-2-4, 10, 11. No. 7-11 have 52 pages.*

ALL SURPRISE
Fall, 1943 - No. 12, Winter, 1946-47
Timely/Marvel (CPC)

	Good	Fine	Mint
1-Super Rabbit & Gandy & Sourpuss	8.50	25.50	60.00
2	4.00	12.00	28.00
3-10,12	3.00	9.00	21.00
11-Kurtzman "Pigtales" art	4.70	14.00	33.00

ALL TEEN (Formerly All Winners; Teen Comics No. 21 on)
No. 20, January, 1947
Marvel Comics (WFP)

	Good	Fine	Mint
20	2.50	7.50	18.00

ALL THE FUNNY FOLKS
1926 (hardcover, 112 pgs., 11½x3½") (Full color)

All-Select Comics #7, © MCG

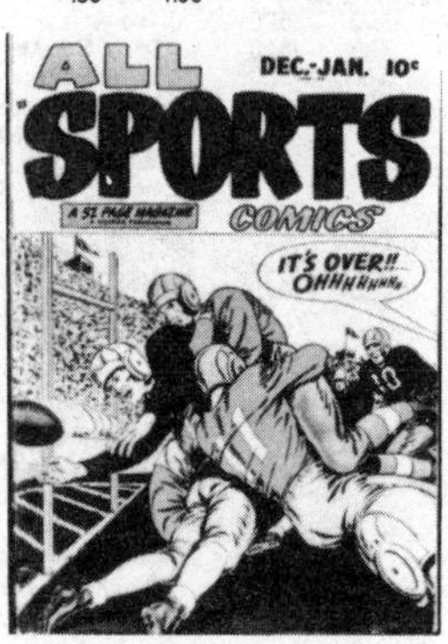

All Sports Comics #2, © HILL

All Star Comics #22, © DC

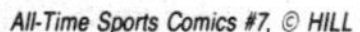
All-Time Sports Comics #7, © HILL

All-True Crime #40, © MCG

All Winners Comics V2#1, © MCG

ALL THE FUNNY FOLKS (continued)
World Press Today, Inc. — Good Fine Mint
nn-Barney Google, Spark Plug, Jiggs & Maggie, Tillie The Toiler, Happy Hooligan, Hans & Fritz, Toots & Casper, etc. 15.00 45.00 105.00

ALL-TIME SPORTS COMICS (Formerly All Sports Comics)
No. 4, Apr-May, 1949 - No. 7, Oct-Nov, 1949
Hillman Periodicals
4 4.00 12.00 28.00
5-7: 5-Powell-a. 7-Krigstein-a(p) 3.00 9.00 21.00

ALL TOP
1944 (132 pages)
William H. Wise Co.
Capt. V, Merciless the Sorceress, Red Robbins, One Round Hogan, Mike the M.P., Snooky, Pussy Katnip app. 11.50 34.50 80.00

ALL TOP COMICS (My Experience No. 19 on)
1945; No. 2, Sum, 1946 - No. 18, Mar, 1949; 1957 - 1959
Fox Features Synd./Green Publ./Norlen Mag.
1-Cosmo Cat & Flash Rabbit begin 8.00 24.00 56.00
2 4.50 13.50 32.00
3-7 3.50 10.50 25.00
8-Blue Beetle, Phantom Lady, & Rulah, Jungle Goddess begin (11/47); Kamen-c 52.00 155.00 365.00
9-Kamen-c 30.00 90.00 210.00
10-Kamen bondage-c 30.00 90.00 210.00
11-13,15-17: 15-No Blue Beetle 22.00 65.00 154.00
14-No Blue Beetle; used in **SOTI**, illo-"Corpses of colored people strung up by their wrists." 30.00 90.00 210.00
18-Dagar, Jo-Jo app; no Phantom Lady or Blue Beetle 18.00 54.00 125.00
6(1957-Green Publ.)-Patoruzu the Indian; Cosmo Cat on cover only 1.50 4.50 10.00
6(1958-Literary Ent.)-Muggy Doo; Cosmo Cat on cover only 1.50 4.50 10.00
6(1959-Norlen)-Atomic Mouse; Cosmo Cat on cover only 1.50 4.50 10.00
6(1959)-Little Eva 1.50 4.50 10.00
6(Cornell)-Supermouse on-c 1.50 4.50 10.00
NOTE: *Jo-Jo by* ***Kamen****-12,18.*

ALL TRUE ALL PICTURE POLICE CASES
Oct, 1952 - No. 2, Nov, 1952 (100 pages)
St. John Publishing Co.
1-Three rebound St. John crime comics 20.00 60.00 140.00
2-Three comics rebound 17.00 51.00 120.00
NOTE: *Contents may vary.*

ALL-TRUE CRIME (. . .Cases No. 26-35; formerly Official True Crime Cases)
No. 26, Feb, 1948 - No. 52, Sept, 1952
Marvel/Atlas Comics(OFI No. 26,27/CFI No. 28,29/LCC No. 30-46/LMC No. 47-52)
26(No. 1) 4.00 12.00 28.00
27(4/48)-Electric chair-c 3.50 10.50 24.00
28-41,43-48,50-52 1.50 4.50 10.00
42-Krigstein-a 2.85 8.50 20.00
49-Used in **POP**, Pg. 79; Krigstein-a 3.50 10.50 24.00
NOTE: ***Robinson*** *a-47.* ***Tuska*** *a-48(3).*

ALL-TRUE DETECTIVE CASES (Kit Carson No. 5 on)
Feb-Mar, 1954 - No. 4, Aug-Sept, 1954
Avon Periodicals
1 9.00 27.00 63.00
2-Wood-a 8.50 25.50 60.00
3-Kinstler-c 3.75 11.25 26.00

Good Fine Mint
4-Wood(?), Kamen-a 7.00 21.00 50.00
nn(100 pgs.)-7 pg. Kubert-a, Kinstler back-c 20.00 60.00 140.00

ALL TRUE ROMANCE (. . . Illustrated No. 3)
3/51 - No. 34, 3/58; No. 3, 9/57 - No. 4, 11/57
Artful Publ. #1-3/Harwell(Comic Media) #4-20?/Ajax-Farrell(Excellent Publ.)/Four Star Comic Corp.
1 (3/51) 5.50 16.50 38.50
2 3.50 10.50 24.00
3(12/51)-No. 5(5/52) 3.00 9.00 21.00
6-Wood-a, 9 pgs. (exceptional) 8.00 24.00 56.00
7-10 2.15 6.50 15.00
11-13,16-19 (2/54) 1.60 4.80 11.00
14-Marijuana story 2.50 7.50 17.00
20-22: Last precode (Ajax, 3/55) 1.50 4.50 10.00
23-27,29-34 (29-34 exist?) 1.20 3.60 8.40
28 (9/56)-L. B. Cole, Disbrow-a 2.50 7.50 17.00
3,4(Farrell, 1957) .60 1.80 4.00

ALL WESTERN WINNERS (Formerly All Winners; becomes Western Winners with No. 5; see Two-Gun Kid No. 5)
No. 2, Winter, 1948-49 - No. 4, April, 1949
Marvel Comics(CDS)
2-Black Rider (Origin & 1st app.) & his horse Satan, Kid Colt & his horse Steel, & Two-Gun Kid & his horse Cyclone begin 14.00 42.00 100.00
3-Anti-Wertham editorial 10.00 30.00 70.00
4-Black Rider i.d. revealed 10.00 30.00 70.00

ALL WINNERS COMICS (All Teen #20; #1 adv. as All Aces)
Summer, 1941 - No. 19, Fall, 1946; No. 21, Winter, 1946-47
(no No. 20) (No. 21 continued from Young Allies No. 20)
USA No. 1-7/WFP No. 10-19/YAI No. 21
1-The Angel & Black Marvel only app.; Capt. America by Simon & Kirby, Human Torch & Sub-Mariner begin 250.00 750.00 1750.00
2-The Destroyer & The Whizzer begin; Simon & Kirby Captain America 120.00 360.00 840.00
3,4 92.00 275.00 645.00
5,6: 6-The Black Avenger only app.; no Whizzer story 63.00 190.00 440.00
7-10 52.00 155.00 365.00
11-18: 12-Last Destroyer; no Whizzer story; no Human Torch No. 14-16 33.00 100.00 230.00
19-(Scarce)-1st app. & origin All Winners Squad 80.00 240.00 560.00
21-(Scarce)-All Winners Squad, Miss America app; bondage-c 75.00 235.00 525.00
NOTE: ***Everett*** *Sub-Mariner-1, 3, 4;* ***Burgos*** *Torch-1, 3, 4.* ***Schomburg*** *c-12, 14, 15.*

(2nd Series - August, 1948, Marvel Comics (CDS))
(Becomes All Western Winners with No. 2)
1-The Blonde Phantom, Capt. America, Human Torch, & Sub-Mariner app. 64.00 192.00 450.00

ALL YOUR COMICS (See Fox Giants)
Spring, 1946 (36 pages)
Fox Feature Syndicate (R. W. Voight)
1-Red Robbins, Merciless the Sorceress app. 6.00 18.00 42.00

ALMANAC OF CRIME (See Fox Giants)

AL OF FBI (See Little Al of the FBI)

ALONG THE FIRING LINE WITH ROGER BEAN
1916 (Hardcover, B&W) (6x17") (66 pages)
Chas. B. Jackson
3-by Chic Jackson (1915 daily strips) 7.00 21.00 50.00

ALPHA AND OMEGA
1978 (49 cents)
Spire Christian Comics (Fleming H. Revell)

	Good	Fine	Mint
		.30	.60

ALPHA FLIGHT (See X-Men #120,121)
Aug, 1983 - Present (#52-on are direct sale only)
Marvel Comics Group

	Good	Fine	Mint
1-Byrne-a begins (52pgs.)-Wolverine & Nightcrawler cameo	.80	2.40	4.80
2-Vindicator becomes Guardian; origin Marrina & Alpha Flight	.55	1.60	3.20
3-5: 3-Concludes origin Alpha Flight	.45	1.30	2.60
6-11: 6-Origin Shaman. 7-Origin Snowbird. 10,11-Origin Sasquatch	.35	1.00	2.10
12-Double size; death of Guardian	.40	1.25	2.50
13-16: 13,16-Wolverine app.	.25	.75	1.50
17-X-Men x-over; Wolverine cameo	.55	1.60	3.20
18-28: 20-New headquarters. 25-Return of Guardian. 28-Last Bryne issue		.75	1.50
29-39		.60	1.20
40-49,51-53		.50	1.00
50-Double size		.65	1.30
54,55		.40	.80
Annual 1 (9/86, $1.25)	.30	.90	1.80
Annual 2(12/87), $1.25)		.65	1.30

NOTE: ***Austin** c-1i, 2i, 53i.*

ALPHA TRACK
Feb, 1986 - Present (?) ($1.75 cover)
Fantasy General Comics

	Good	Fine	Mint
1,2	.25	.75	1.50

ALPHA WAVE
March, 1987 - Present ($1.75, color)
Darkline Comics

	Good	Fine	Mint
1	.25	.75	1.50

ALPHONSE & GASTON & LEON
1903 (15x10'' Sunday strip reprints in color)
Hearst's New York American & Journal

	Good	Fine	Mint
by Fred Opper	25.00	75.00	175.00

ALTER EGO
May, 1986 - No. 4, Nov, 1986 (mini-series)
First Comics

	Good	Fine	Mint
1	.30	.90	1.80
2-4		.70	1.40

ALVIN (TV) (See 4-Color Comics No. 1042)
Oct-Dec, 1962 - No. 28, Oct, 1973
Dell Publishing Co.

	Good	Fine	Mint
12-021-212	2.15	6.50	15.00
2	1.50	4.50	10.00
3-10	1.15	3.50	8.00
11-28	1.00	3.00	6.00
Alvin For President (10/64)	.85	2.50	5.00
...& His Pals in Merry Christmas with Clyde Crashcup & Leonardo 1(02-120-402)-12-2/64, reprinted in 1966 (12-023-604)	1.15	3.50	8.00

AMAZING ADULT FANTASY (Amazing Adventures #1-6; Amazing Fantasy #15)
No. 7, Dec, 1961 - No. 14, July, 1962
Marvel Comics Group (AMI)

	Good	Fine	Mint
7: Ditko-a No. 7-14; c-7-13	10.00	30.00	70.00
8-Last 10 cent issue	8.00	24.00	56.00
9-14: 12-1st app. Mailbag. 13-Anti-communist story	7.00	21.00	50.00

AMAZING ADVENTURE FUNNIES (Fantoman No. 2 on)
June, 1940 - No. 2, Sept. 1940
Centaur Publications

	Good	Fine	Mint
1-The Fantom of the Fair by Gustavson (r-/Amaz. Mystery Funnies V2/7, V2/8), The Arrow, Skyrocket Steele From the Year X by Everett (r-/AMF 2); Burgos-a	82.00	245.00	575.00
2-Reprints. Pub. after Fantoman #2	60.00	180.00	420.00

NOTE: ***Burgos** a-1(2). **Everett** a-1(3). **Gustavson** a-1(5), 2(3). **Pinajian** a-2.*

AMAZING ADVENTURES (Also see Science Comics)
1950 - No. 6, Fall, 1952 (Painted covers)
Ziff-Davis Publ. Co.

1950 (no month given) (8½x11'') (8 pgs.) Has the front & back cover plus Schomburg story used in Amazing Advs. #1 (Sent to subscribers of Z-D s/f magazines & ordered through mail for 10 cents. Used to test market) Estimated value....180.00

	Good	Fine	Mint
1-Wood, Schomburg, Anderson, Whitney-a	28.00	84.00	185.00
2-5-Anderson-a. 3-Starr-a	10.00	30.00	70.00
6-Krigstein-a	14.00	43.00	100.00

AMAZING ADVENTURES (Amazing Adult Fantasy No. 7)
June, 1961 - No. 6, Nov, 1961
Atlas Comics (AMI)/Marvel Comics No. 3 on

	Good	Fine	Mint
1-Origin Dr. Droom (1st Marvel-Age Superhero) by Kirby; Ditko & Kirby-a in all; Kirby c-1-6	17.00	51.00	120.00
2	8.50	25.50	60.00
3-6: Last Dr. Droom	6.50	19.50	45.00

AMAZING ADVENTURES
Aug, 1970 - No. 39, Nov, 1976
Marvel Comics Group

	Good	Fine	Mint
1-Inhumans by Kirby(p) & Black Widow begin; Adams-a(p)	.40	1.20	2.40
2-4: Last Kirby Inhumans	.25	.80	1.60
5-8-Adams-a; 8-Last Black Widow	.50	1.50	3.00
9,10: 10-Last Inhumans (origin-r by Kirby)		.60	1.20
11-New Beast begins(Origin), ends #17; X-Men cameo	.60	1.75	3.50
12-17	.30	.90	1.80
18-War of the Worlds begins; 1st app. Killraven; Adams-a(p)	.40	1.25	2.50
19-39: 35-Giffen's first art (3/76)		.30	.60

NOTE: ***Adams** c-6-8. **Buscema** a-1p, 2p. **Colan** a-3-5p, 26p. **Ditko** a-24r. **Everett** inks-3-5, 7, 9. **Giffen** a-35i, 38p. **G. Kane** c-11, 25p, 29p. **Ploog** a-12i. **Russell** c-33i, 39. **Starlin** c-15p, 27. **Sutton** a-11-15p.*

AMAZING ADVENTURES
December, 1979 - No. 14, January, 1981
Marvel Comics Group

	Good	Fine	Mint
V2#1: r-/X-Men No. 1,38	.30	.80	1.60
2-14: 2,4,6-X-Men-r. 7,8-Origin Iceman	.25	.75	1.50

NOTE: ***Byrne** c-6p, 9p. **Kirby** a-1-14r; c-7, 9. **Steranko** a-12r. **Tuska** a-7-9.*

AMAZING ADVENTURES OF CAPTAIN CARVEL AND HIS CARVEL CRUSADERS, THE (See Carvel Comics)

AMAZING CHAN & THE CHAN CLAN, THE (TV)
May, 1973 - No. 4, Feb, 1974 (Hanna-Barbera)
Gold Key

	Good	Fine	Mint
1	.50	1.50	3.00
2-4	.35	1.00	2.00

AMAZING COMICS (Complete No. 2)
Fall, 1944
Timely Comics (EPC)

1-The Destroyer, The Whizzer, The Young Allies, Sergeant Dix

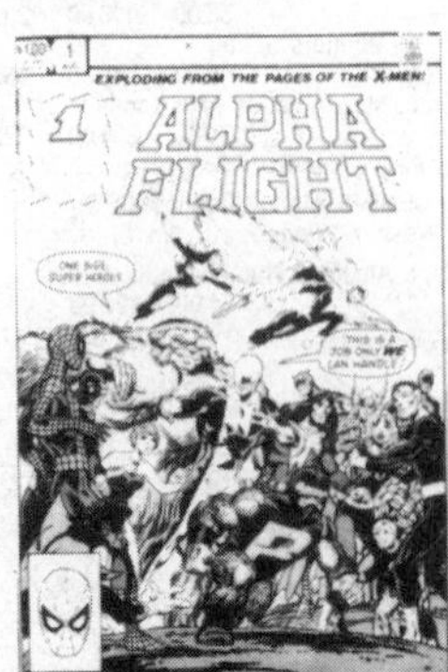

Alpha Flight #1, © MCG

Amazing Adventure Funnies #1, © CEN

Amazing Adventures #2('61), © MCG

Amazing-Man Comics #13, © CEN

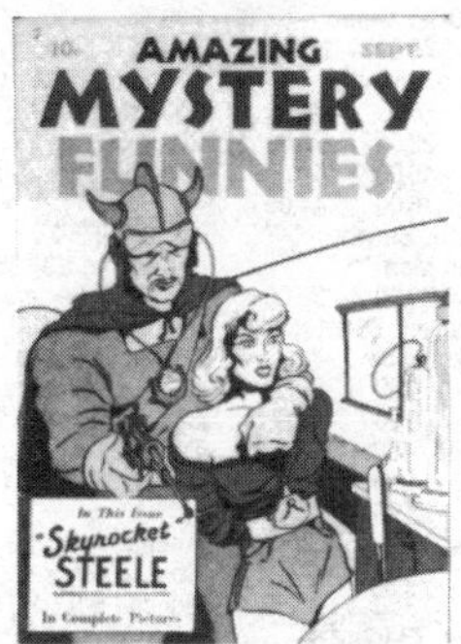

Amazing Mystery Funnies V1#2, © CEN

Amazing Spider-Man #1, © MCG

AMAZING COMICS (continued) — Good / Fine / Mint

	Good	Fine	Mint
	65.00	195.00	455.00

AMAZING DETECTIVE CASES (Formerly Suspense No. 2?)
No. 3, Nov, 1950 - No. 14, Sept, 1952
Marvel/Atlas Comics (CCC)

	Good	Fine	Mint
3	4.00	12.00	28.00
4-6	2.00	6.00	14.00
7-10	1.70	5.00	12.00
11,14: 11-(3/52)-change to horror	2.00	6.00	14.00
12-Krigstein-a	2.65	8.00	18.00
13-Everett-a; electrocution-c/story	3.00	9.00	21.00

NOTE: ***Maneely** c-13. **Sekowsky** a-12. **Sinnott** a-13. **Tuska** a-10.*

AMAZING FANTASY (. . . Adult Fantasy No. 7-14)
No. 15, Aug, 1962 (Sept, 1962 shown in indicia)
Marvel Comics Group (AMI)

	Good	Fine	Mint
15-Origin & 1st app. of Spider-Man by Ditko; Kirby/Ditko-c	150.00	600.00	1500.00

AMAZING GHOST STORIES (Formerly Nightmare)
No. 14, Oct, 1954 - No. 16, Feb, 1955
St. John Publishing Co.

	Good	Fine	Mint
14-Pit & the Pendulum story by Kinstler; Baker-c	9.00	27.00	63.00
15-Reprints Weird Thrillers #5; Baker-c, Powell-a	6.00	18.00	42.00
16-Kubert reprints of Weird Thrillers #4; Baker-c; Roussos, Tuska, Kinstler-a	6.50	19.50	45.00

AMAZING HIGH ADVENTURE
8/84; No. 2, 10/85; No. 3, 10/86 - Present (Baxter No. 3,4)
Marvel Comics

	Good	Fine	Mint
1-5	.35	1.00	2.00

NOTE: ***Bissette** a-5. **Bolton** c/a-5. **Severin** a-1, 3, 5. **P. Smith** a-2. **Williamson** a-2i.*

AMAZING-MAN COMICS (Formerly Motion Pic. Funnies Wkly?)
No. 5, Sept, 1939 - No. 27, Feb, 1942
Centaur Publications

	Good	Fine	Mint
5(No.1)(Rare)-Origin A-Man the Amazing Man by Bill Everett; The Cat-Man by Tarpe Mills (also No. 8), Mighty Man by Filchock, Minimidget & sidekick Ritty, & The Iron Skull by Burgos begins	500.00	1500.00	3500.00
6-Origin The Amazing Man retold; The Shark begins; Ivy Menace by Tarpe Mills app.	160.00	480.00	1120.00
7-Magician From Mars begins; ends #11	96.00	290.00	675.00
8-Cat-Man dresses as woman	70.00	210.00	490.00
9-Magician From Mars battles the 'Elemental Monster,' swiped into The Spectre in More Fun 54 & 55	68.00	205.00	475.00
10,11: 11-Zardi, the Eternal Man begins; ends #16; Amazing Man dons costume; last Everett issue	60.00	180.00	420.00
12,13	68.00	205.00	475.00
14-Reef Kinkaid, Rocke Wayburn (ends #20), & Dr. Hypno (ends #21) begin; no Zardi or Chuck Hardy	45.00	135.00	315.00
15,17-20: 15-Zardi returns; no Rocke Wayburn. 17-Dr. Hypno returns; no Zardi	33.00	100.00	230.00
16-Mighty Man's powers of super strength & ability to shrink & grow explained; Rocke Wayburn returns; no Dr. Hypno; Al Avison (a character) begins, ends #18 (a tribute to the famed artist)	35.00	105.00	245.00
21-Origin Dash Dartwell (drug-use story); origin & only app. T.N.T.	33.00	100.00	230.00
22-Dash Dartwell, the Human Meteor & The Voice app; last Iron Skull & The Shark; Silver Streak app..	33.00	100.00	230.00
23-Two Amazing Man stories; intro/origin Tommy the Amazing Kid; The Marksman only app.	35.00	105.00	245.00
24,27: 24-King of Darkness, Nightshade, & Blue Lady begin; end #26	33.00	100.00	230.00
25,26 (Scarce)-Meteor Martin by Wolverton in both; 26-Electric Ray app.	72.00	215.00	505.00

NOTE: ***Everett** a-5-11; c-5-11. **Gilman** a-14-20. **Giunta/Mirando** a-7-10. **Sam Glanzman** a-14-16, 18-21, 23. **Louis Glanzman** a-6, 9-11, 14-21; c-14-19, 21. **Robert Golden** a-9. **Gustavson** a-6; c-22, 23. **Lubbers** a-14-21. **Simon** a-10. **Frank Thomas** a-6, 9-11, 14, 15, 17-21.*

AMAZING MYSTERIES (Formerly Sub-Mariner No. 31)
No. 32, May, 1949 - No. 35, Jan, 1950
Marvel Comics (CCC)

	Good	Fine	Mint
32-The Witness app; 1st Marvel horror comic	17.00	51.00	120.00
33-Horror format	5.00	15.00	35.00
34,35-Change to Crime	3.50	10.50	25.00

AMAZING MYSTERY FUNNIES
Aug, 1938 - No. 24, Sept, 1940 (All 52 pgs.)
Centaur Publications

	Good	Fine	Mint
V1#1-Everett-c(1st); Dick Kent Adv. story; Skyrocket Steele in the Year X on cover only	142.00	425.00	995.00
2-Everett 1st-a (Skyrocket Steele)	70.00	210.00	490.00
3	42.00	125.00	295.00
3(#4, 12/38)-nn on cover, #3 on inside; bondage-c	35.00	105.00	245.00
V2#1-4,6: 2-Drug use story. 3-Air-Sub DX begins by Burgos. 4-Dan Hastings, Sand Hog begins (ends #5). 6-Last Skyrocket Steele	30.00	90.00	210.00
5-Classic Everett-c	35.00	105.00	245.00
7 (Scarce)-Intro. The Fantom of the Fair; Everett, Gustavson, Burgos-a	150.00	450.00	1050.00
8-Origin & 1st app. Speed Centaur	60.00	180.00	420.00
9-11: 11-Self portrait and biog. of Everett; Jon Linton begins	35.00	105.00	245.00
12 (Scarce)-Wolverton Space Patrol-a (12/39)	85.00	255.00	595.00
V3#1(#17, 1/40)-Intro. Bullet; Tippy Taylor serial begins, ends #24 (cont. in The Arrow 2)	35.00	105.00	245.00
18,20	30.00	90.00	210.00
19,21-24-All have Space Patrol by Wolverton	60.00	180.00	420.00

NOTE: ***Burgos** a-V2#3-9. **Eisner** a-V1#2, 3(2). **Everett** a-V1#2-4, V2#1, 3-6; c-V1#1-4, V2#3, 5, 18. **Filchock** a-V2#9. **Guardineer** a-V1#4, V2#4-6; **Gustavson** a-V2#4, 5, 9-12, V3#1, 19, 20; c-V2#7, 9, 12, V3#1, 21, 22; **McWilliams** a-V2#9, 10. **Tarpe Mills** a-V2#2, 4-6, 9-12, V3#1. **Leo Morey**(Pulp artist) c-V2#10; text illo-V2#11. **Frank Thomas** c-V2/11. **Webster** a-V2#4.*

AMAZING SAINTS
1974 (39 cents)
Logos International

	Good	Fine	Mint
True story of Phil Saint		.20	.40

AMAZING SPIDER-MAN, THE (See All Detergent Comics, Amazing Fantasy, Aurora, Marvel Fanfare, Marvel Graphic Novel, Marvel Spec. Ed., Marvel Tales, Marvel Team-Up, Marvel Treasury Ed., Official Marvel Index To . . ., Spectacular . . ., Spider-Man Digest, Spider-Man Vs. Wolverine, Spidey Super Stories, Superman Vs. . . ., & Web of Spiderman)

AMAZING SPIDER-MAN, THE
March, 1963 - Present
Marvel Comics Group

	Good	Fine	Mint
1-Retells origin by Steve Ditko; F.F. x-over; intro. John Jameson & The Chameleon; Kirby-c	110.00	360.00	1000.00
1-Reprint from the Golden Record Comic set	2.00	6.00	14.00
with record	5.15	15.50	36.00
2-Intro the Vulture & the Terrible Tinkerer	54.00	136.00	380.00
3-Human Torch cameo; intro. & 1st app. Doc Octopus	31.00	79.00	220.00
4-Origin & 1st app. The Sandman; Intro. Betty Brant & Liz Allen	27.00	70.00	192.00
5,6: 5-Dr. Doom app. 6-1st app. Lizard	21.00	53.00	148.00

AMAZING SPIDER-MAN, THE (continued)

	Good	Fine	Mint
7-10: 8-Fantastic 4 app. 9-1st app. Electro (origin). 10-1st app. Big Man & Enforcers	16.00	39.00	110.00
11-13,15: 11-1st app. Bennett Brant. 13-1st app. Mysterio. 15-Intro. Kraven the Hunter	10.00	25.00	72.00
14-Intro. Green Goblin; Hulk x-over	11.00	28.00	78.00
16-19: 18-Fant.-4 app; 19-Intro. Ned Leeds	6.00	16.00	44.00
20-Intro & origin The Scorpion	6.00	16.00	44.00
21-30: 22-1st app. Princess Python. 25-1st app. Spencer Smythe. 26-1st app. Crime Master. 28-Origin/1st app. Molten Man	4.30	10.50	30.00
31-38: 31-Intro. Harry Osborn, Gwen Stacy & Prof. Warren. 36-1st app. Looter. 37-Intro. Norman Osborn. 38-Last Ditko issue	2.40	6.00	17.00
39,40-Green Goblin in both; origin #40	2.40	6.00	17.00
41-49: 41-1st app. Rhino. 42-1st app. Mary Jane Watson. 46-Intro. Shocker	1.50	4.50	10.00
50-Intro. Kingpin	2.15	6.50	13.00
51-60: 52-Intro. Joe Robertson. 56-Intro. Capt. George Stacy. 57,58-Ka-Zar app. 59-Intro. Brainwasher (alias Kingpin)	1.10	3.30	6.60
61-80: 67-Intro. Randy Robertson. 73-Intro. Silvermane. 78-Intro. Prowler	.85	2.50	5.00
81-89: 83-Intro. Schemer & Vanessa (Kingpin's wife).	.75	2.20	4.40
90-Death of Capt. Stacey	1.15	3.50	7.00
91-93,95,99: 93-Intro. Arthur Stacy	.75	2.20	4.40
94-Origin retold	.85	2.50	6.60
96-98-Drug books not approved by CCA	1.85	5.50	11.00
100-Anniversary issue	2.50	7.50	15.00
101-Intro. Morbius	1.30	4.00	8.00
102-Origin Morbius (52 pgs.)	1.30	4.00	8.00
103-112: 108-Intro. Sha-Shan. 110-Intro. Gibbon	.60	1.75	3.50
113,114-Starlin a(i); 113-Intro. Hammerhead	.70	2.00	4.00
115-118	.60	1.75	3.50
119,120	.70	2.90	4.00
121-Death of Gwen Stacy (r-/in Marvel Tales #98)	2.85	8.50	20.00
122-Death of Green Goblin	2.85	8.50	20.00
123-128: 124-Intro. Man Wolf, origin-#125.	.40	1.35	2.70
129-1st app. The Punisher	3.15	9.40	22.00
130-133,136-140: 139-Intro. Grizzly. 140-Intro. Glory Grant	.35	1.10	2.20
134-Punisher cameo; intro Tarantula	.95	2.80	5.60
135-Punisher app.	1.35	4.00	8.00
141-160: 143-Intro. Cyclone	.30	.90	1.80
161-Nightcrawler app. from X-Men; Punisher cameo	1.20	3.50	7.00
162-Punisher, Nightcrawler app.	1.35	4.00	8.00
163-173,176-81: 167-1st app. Will O' The Wisp. 171-Nova app. 177-180-Green Goblin app. 181-Origin retold; gives life history of Spider-Man	.25	.75	1.50
174,175-Punisher app.	.70	2.00	5.00
182-188		.55	1.10
189,190-Byrne-a(p)	.35	1.00	2.10
191-199,204,205,207-219: 194-1st Black Cat. 196-Faked death of Aunt May. 210-Intro. & 1st app. Madame Web. 212-Intro. Hydro Man		.50	1.00
200-Giant origin issue	.40	1.25	2.50
201,202-Punisher app.	.75	2.25	4.50
203-2nd Dazzler app.	.35	1.00	2.00
206-Byrne-a(p)	.25	.75	1.50
220-237: 226,227-Black Cat returns. 236-Tarantula dies. 235-Origin Will-'O-The-Wisp		.50	1.00
238-1st app. Hobgoblin	.65	1.90	3.80

	Good	Fine	Mint
239	.35	1.00	2.00
240-251: 241-Origin The Vulture		.55	1.10
252-Spider-Man dons new costume (5/84)	.85	2.50	5.00
253-1st app. The Rose	.50	1.50	3.00
254	.25	.75	1.50
255-260: 259-Sp-M back to old costume. 261-Hobgoblin app.		.60	1.20
261-274,276-284		.50	1.00
275-Origin-r($1.25)	.30	.90	1.80
285-Punisher app.	.55	1.70	3.40
286-288,290-292		.45	.90
289-Double size, origin Hobgoblin	.35	1.10	2.20
293-Six part, Kraven	.35	1.00	2.00
294		.50	1.00
295-298		.40	.80
Annual 1 (1964)-Origin S-M; Intro. Sinister Six	7.40	22.00	52.00
Annual 2	2.30	7.00	16.00
Special 3,4	1.35	4.00	8.00
Special 5-8 (12/71)	.70	2.00	4.00
King Size 9 ('73)-Green Goblin app.	.35	1.00	2.00
Giant-Size 1(7/74)-Kirby/Ditko-r	.50	1.50	3.00
Giant-Size 2(10/74)	.25	.75	1.50
Giant-Size 3(1/75), 5(7/75), 6(9/75)	.25	.75	1.50
Giant-Size 4(4/75)-Punisher app.	1.15	3.50	7.00
Annual 10(6/76)-Old Human Fly app.	.35	1.00	2.00
Annual 11(9/77), 12(8/78)	.35	1.00	2.00
Annual 13(11/79)-Byrne-a	.50	1.50	3.00
Annual 14(12/80)-Miller c/a(p), 40pgs.	.70	2.00	4.00
Annual 15(1981)-Miller c/a(p); Punisher app.	.85	2.60	5.20
Annual 16(12/82)-Origin/1st app. new Capt. Marvel (female heroine)		.60	1.20
Annual 17(12/83), 18 (1984)		.60	1.20
Annual 19(11/85)		.65	1.30
Annual 20(11/86)-Origin Iron Man of 2020		.65	1.30
Annual 21-Special wedding issue	.45	1.35	3.20
Annual 21-Wedding issue, 2nd cover	.40	1.25	2.90
Aim Toothpaste giveaway(36pgs., reg. size)-Green Goblin app.	.35	1.00	2.00
Aim Toothpaste giveaway (16pgs., reg. size)-Dr. Octopus app.		.50	1.00
All Detergent Giveaway ('79, 36 pgs.), nn-Origin-r	.70	2.00	4.00
Giveaway-Acme & Dingo Children's Boots(1980)-Spider-Woman app.		.50	1.00
...& Power Pack ('84, nn)(Nat'l Committee for Prevention of Child Abuse. (two versions, mail offer & store giveaway)-Mooney-a; Byrne-c		.30	.60
...& The Hulk (Special Edition)(6/8/80; 20 pgs.; Chicago Tribune giveaway)	.70	2.00	4.00
...& The Incredible Hulk (1981, 1982; 36 pgs.), Sanger Harris, Dallas Times, Kansas City Star, The Jones Store-giveaway; 16 pgs. (1983)	.50	1.50	3.00
..., Captain America, The Incredible Hulk, & Spider-Woman ('81) (7-11 Stores giveaway; 36 pgs.)		.30	.60
Giveaway-Esquire & Eye Magazines(2/69)-Miniature-Still attached	3.00	9.00	18.00
..., Storm & Powerman ('82; 20 pgs.)(American Cancer Society)-giveaway		.30	.60
...Vs. The Hulk (Special Edition; 1979)(Supplement to Columbus Dispatch)-Giveaway	.50	1.50	3.00
...vs. the Prodigy Giveaway, 16 pgs. in color ('76)-5x6½"-Sex education; (1 million printed;35-50 cents)		.25	.50

NOTE: ***Austin** a-248i, Annual 13i; c-188i, 241i, 242i, 248i. **J. Buscema** a(p)-72, 73, 76-81, 84, 85. **Byrne** a-189p, 190p, 206p, Annual 3r, 6r, 7r, 13p, Gnt-Size 1r, 3-5r; c-189p, 268, 296, Annual 12. **Ditko** a-1-38, Annual 1, 2, Gnt-Size 4r; c-1-38. **Gil Kane***

Amazing Spider-Man #21, © MCG

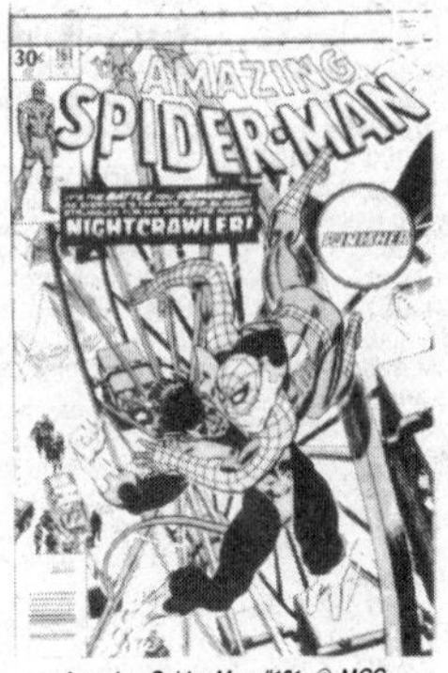

Amazing Spider-Man #161, © MCG

Amazing Spider-Man #250, © MCG

The American Air Forces #3, © ME

American Flagg! #12, © First Comics

America's Best #13, © STD

AMAZING SPIDER-MAN (continued) — Good — Fine — Mint

a(p)-89-105, 120-124, 150, Annual 10, 12i; c-90p, 96, 98, 99, 101-105p, 129p, 131p, 132p, 137-140p, 143p, 148p, 149p, 151p, 153p, 160p, 161p, Annual 10p. ***Kirby*** *a-8.* ***Miller*** *c-218, 219.* ***Mooney*** *a-65i, 67-82i, 84-88i, 173i, 178i, 189i, 190i, 192i, 193i, 196-202i, 211-219i, 221i, 226i, 227i, 229-233i, Annual 11i, 17i.* ***Nasser*** *c-228p.* ***Pollard*** *a-193-195p, 197p; c-187, 190.* ***Simonson*** *c-222.* ***Starlin*** *a-187p.*

AMAZING WILLIE MAYS, THE
No date (Sept, 1954)
Famous Funnies Publ.

nn 23.00 70.00 160.00

AMAZING WORLD OF SUPERMAN (See Superman)

AMBUSH (See 4-Color Comics No. 314)

AMBUSH BUG (Also see Son of...)
June, 1985 - No. 4, Sept, 1985 (mini-series)
DC Comics

1-Giffen c/a begins .50 1.00
2-4 .40 .80
...Stocking Stuffer (2/86)-Giffen c/a .65 1.30

AMERICA IN ACTION
1942; Winter, 1945 (36 pages)
Dell(Imp. Publ. Co.)/Mayflower House Publ.

1942-Dell-(68 pages) 7.00 21.00 50.00
1(1945)-Has 3 adaptations from American history; Kiefer, Schrotter & Webb-a 4.50 13.50 32.00

AMERICA MENACED!
1950 (Paper cover)
Vital Publications

Anti-communism. estimated value.... 150.00

AMERICAN AIR FORCES, THE (See A-1 Comics)
Sept-Oct, 1944 - 1945; 1951 - 1954
William H. Wise(Flying Cadet Publ. Co./Hasan(No.1)/Life's Romances/Magazine Ent. No. 5 on)

1-Article by Zack Mosley, creator of Smilin' Jack 5.00 15.00 35.00
2-4 3.50 10.50 25.00

NOTE: *All part comic, part magazine. Art by* ***Whitney, Chas. Quinlan, H. C. Kiefer,*** *and* ***Tony Dipreta.***

5(A-1 45)(Formerly Jet Powers), 6(A-1 54),7(A-1 58),8(A-1 65) 9(A-1 67),10(A-1 74),11(A-1 79),12(A-1 91) 2.00 6.00 14.00

NOTE: ***Powell*** *c/a-5-12.*

AMERICAN COMICS
1940's
Theatre Giveaways (Liberty Theatre, Grand Rapids, Mich. known)

Many possible combinations. "Golden Age" superhero comics with new cover added and given away at theaters. Following known: Superman #59, Capt. Marvel #20, Capt. Marvel Jr. #5, Action #33, Classics Comics #8, Whiz #39. Value would vary with book and should be 70-80 percent of the original.

AMERICAN FLAGG! (Also see First Comics Graphic Novel 3, and Howard Chaykin's...)
Oct, 1983 - No. 50, Mar, 1988
First Comics

1-Chaykin c/a begins .85 2.50 5.00
2-5 .45 1.40 3.00
6-12 .40 1.20 2.20
13-20 .30 .90 1.80
21-40: 21-27: Alan Moore scripts. 31-Origin Bob Violence .25 .75 1.50
41-50 .25 .75 1.50
Special 1 (11/86) .35 1.00 2.00

AMERICAN GRAPHICS
No. 1, 1954; No. 2, 1957 (25 cents)
Henry Stewart

Good — Fine — Mint

1-The Maid of the Mist, The Last of the Eries (Indian Legends of Niagara) (Sold at Niagara Falls) 3.00 9.00 21.00
2-Victory at Niagara & Laura Secord (Heroine of the War of 1812) 2.00 6.00 14.00

AMERICAN INDIAN, THE (See Picture Progress)

AMERICAN LIBRARY
1944 (68 pages) (15 cents, B&W, text & pictures)
David McKay Publications

3-6: 3-Look to the Mountain. 4-Case of the Crooked Candle (Perry Mason). 5-Duel in the Sun. 6-Wingate's Raiders 5.50 16.50 38.00

NOTE: *Also see Guadalcanal Diary & Thirty Seconds Over Tokyo (part of series?).*

AMERICA'S BEST COMICS
Feb, 1942 - No. 31, July, 1949
Nedor/Better/Standard Publications

1-The Woman in Red, Black Terror, Captain Future, Doc Strange, The Liberator, & Don Davis, Secret Ace begin 50.00 150.00 350.00
2-Origin The American Eagle; The Woman in Red ends 25.00 75.00 175.00
3-Pyroman begins 18.00 54.00 125.00
4 16.00 48.00 110.00
5-Last Captain Future-not in #4; Lone Eagle app. 14.00 42.00 100.00
6,7: 6-American Crusader app. 12.00 36.00 84.00
8-Last Liberator 10.00 30.00 70.00
9-The Fighting Yank begins; The Ghost app. 10.00 30.00 70.00
10-14: 10-Flag-c. 14-American Eagle ends 9.00 27.00 63.00
15-20 8.00 24.00 56.00
21-Infinity-c 7.00 21.00 50.00
22-Capt. Future app. 7.00 21.00 50.00
23-Miss Masque begins; last Doc Strange 9.00 27.00 63.00
24-Miss Masque bondage-c 8.00 24.00 56.00
25-Last Fighting Yank; Sea Eagle app. 7.00 21.00 50.00
26-The Phantom Detective & The Silver Knight app.; Frazetta text illo & some panels in Miss Masque 9.00 27.00 63.00
27-31: 27,28-Commando Cubs. 27-Doc Strange. 28-Tuska Bl. Terror. 29-Last Pyroman 7.00 21.00 50.00

NOTE: *American Eagle not in 3, 8, 9, 13. Fighting Yank not in 10, 12. Liberator not in 2, 6, 7. Pyroman not in 9, 11, 14-16, 23, 25-27.* ***Schomburg (Xela)*** *c-5, 7-31. Bondage c-18.*

AMERICA'S BEST TV COMICS (TV)
1967 (Produced by Marvel Comics)
American Broadcasting Company

1-Spider-Man, Fantastic Four, Casper, King Kong, George of the Jungle, Journey to the Center of the Earth app. (Promotes new TV cartoon show) 1.15 3.50 8.00

AMERICA'S BIGGEST COMICS BOOK
1944 (196 pages) (One Shot)
William H. Wise

1-The Grim Reaper, The Silver Knight, Zudo, the Jungle Boy, Commando Cubs, Thunderhoof app. 18.00 54.00 125.00

AMERICA'S FUNNIEST COMICS
1944 (80 pages) (15 cents)
William H. Wise

nn(#1), 2 8.50 25.50 60.00

AMERICA'S GREATEST COMICS
5?/1941 - No. 8, Summer, 1943 (100 pgs.) (Soft cardboard covers)
Fawcett Publications

1-Bulletman, Spy Smasher, Capt. Marvel, Minute Man & Mr. Scarlet begin; Mac Raboy-c 110.00 330.00 770.00

AMERICA'S GREATEST (continued)

	Good	Fine	Mint
2	52.00	156.00	365.00
3	35.00	105.00	245.00
4-Commando Yank begins; Golden Arrow, Ibis the Invincible & Spy Smasher cameo in Captain Marvel	30.00	90.00	210.00
5	30.00	90.00	210.00
6	22.00	65.00	155.00
7-Balbo the Boy Magician app.; Captain Marvel, Bulletman cameo un Mr. Scarlet	22.00	65.00	155.00
8-Capt. Marvel Jr. & Golden Arrow app.; Spy Smasher x-over in Capt. Midnight; no Minute Man or Commando Yank	22.00	65.00	155.00

AMERICA'S SWEETHEART SUNNY (See Sunny)

AMERICA VS. THE JUSTICE SOCIETY
Jan, 1985 - No. 4, Apr, 1985 (mini-series)
DC Comics

	Good	Fine	Mint
1-Double size; Alcala-a in all	.30	.90	1.80
2-4		.60	1.20

AMERICOMICS
April, 1983 - No. 6, Mar, 1984 (Baxter paper)
Americomics

	Good	Fine	Mint
1-Intro/origin The Shade; The Slayer, Captain Freedom and The Liberty Corps intro.	.30	.90	1.80
2-6: 2-Messenger, & Tara on Jungle Island app. 3-New & old Blue Beetle battle. 4-Origin Dragonfly & Shade. 6-Origin the Scarlet Scorpion.	.30	.90	1.80
Special 1(8/83, $2.00)-Sentinels of Justice (Blue Beetle, Captain Atom, Nightshade, & The Question)	.30	.90	1.80

NOTE: *Perez* c-1.

AMETHYST
Jan, 1985 - No. 16, Aug, 1986
DC Comics

	Good	Fine	Mint
1		.50	1.00
2-16: 8-Fire Jade's i.d. revealed		.45	.90
Special 1 (10/86)		.65	1.30

AMETHYST
Nov, 1987 - No. 4, Feb, 1988 ($1.25, color, mini-series)
DC comics

	Good	Fine	Mint
1	.25	.75	1.50
2-4		.60	1.25

AMETHYST, PRINCESS OF GEMWORLD
May, 1983 - No. 12, May, 1984 (12 issue maxi-series)
DC Comics

	Good	Fine	Mint
1-60 cents cover price	.25	.75	1.50
1-35 cents; tested in Austin & Kansas City	1.35	4.00	8.00
2-35 cents; tested in Austin & Kansas City	1.00	3.00	8.00
2-12: Perez-c(p) No. 6-11		.50	1.00
Annual 1(9/84)		.65	1.30

ANARCHO DICTATOR OF DEATH (See Comics Novel)

ANCHORS ANDREWS (The Saltwater Daffy)
Jan, 1953 - No. 4, July, 1953 (Anchors the Saltwater... No. 4)
St. John Publishing Co.

	Good	Fine	Mint
1-Canteen Kate by Matt Baker, 9 pgs.	7.00	21.00	50.00
2-4	2.00	6.00	14.00

ANDY & WOODY (See March of Comics No. 40,55,76)

ANDY BURNETT (See 4-Color Comics No. 865)

ANDY COMICS (Formerly Scream Comics; becomes Ernie Comics)
No. 20, June, 1948 - No. 21, Aug?, 1948
Current Publications (Ace Magazines)

	Good	Fine	Mint
20,21-Archie-type comic	1.70	5.00	12.00

ANDY DEVINE WESTERN
Dec, 1950 - No. 10, 1952
Fawcett Publications

	Good	Fine	Mint
1	17.00	51.00	120.00
2	8.00	24.00	56.00
3-10 (Exist?)	6.00	18.00	42.00

ANDY GRIFFITH SHOW, THE (See 4-Color No. 1252,1341)

ANDY HARDY COMICS (See Movie Comics No. 3, Fiction House)
April, 1952 - No. 6, Sept-Nov, 1954
Dell Publishing Co.

	Good	Fine	Mint
4-Color 389	1.70	5.00	12.00
4-Color 447,480,515,5,6	1.15	3.50	8.00
...& the New Automatic Gas Clothes Dryer ('52, 16 pgs., 5x7¼") Bendix Giveaway (soft-c)	2.00	6.00	14.00

ANDY PANDA (Also see Walter Lantz ...., New Funnies & The Funnies)
1943 - Nov-Jan, 1961-62 (Walter Lantz)
Dell Publishing Co.

	Good	Fine	Mint
4-Color 25('43)	22.00	65.00	154.00
4-Color 54('44)	12.00	36.00	84.00
4-Color 85('45)	8.00	24.00	56.00
4-Color 130('46),154,198	4.00	12.00	28.00
4-Color 216,240,258,280,297	2.30	7.00	16.00
4-Color 326,345,358	1.30	4.00	9.00
4-Color 383,409	1.00	3.00	7.00
16(11-1/52-53) - 30	.70	2.10	5.00
31-56	.55	1.80	4.00

(See March of Comics No. 5,22,79, & Super Book No. 4,15,27.)

ANGEL
Aug, 1954 - No. 16, Nov-Jan, 1958-59
Dell Publishing Co.

	Good	Fine	Mint
4-Color 576(8/54)	1.00	3.00	7.00
2(5-7/55) - 16	.55	1.80	4.00

ANGEL AND THE APE (Meet Angel No. 7) (See Limited Collector's Edition C-34 & Showcase No. 77)
Nov-Dec, 1968 - No. 6, Sept-Oct, 1969
National Periodical Publications

	Good	Fine	Mint
1-Not Wood-a	.25	.75	1.50
2-6-Wood inks in all	.25	.75	1.50

ANGELIC ANGELINA
1909 (11½x17"; 30 pgs.; 2 colors)
Cupples & Leon Company

	Good	Fine	Mint
By Munson Paddock	10.00	30.00	70.00

ANGEL LOVE
Aug, 1986 - No. 8, Mar, 1987 (mini-series)
DC Comics

	Good	Fine	Mint
1-8		.40	.80
Special 1		.60	1.20

ANGEL OF LIGHT, THE (See The Crusaders)

ANIMAL ADVENTURES
Dec, 1953 - No. 3, Apr?, 1954
Timor Publications/Accepted Publications (reprints)

	Good	Fine	Mint
1	1.50	4.50	10.00
2,3	.85	2.50	6.00
1-3 (reprints, nd)	.70	2.10	5.00

ANIMAL ANTICS (Movie Town... No. 24 on)
Mar-Apr, 1946 - No. 23, Nov-Dec, 1949
National Periodical Publications

	Good	Fine	Mint
1-Raccoon Kids begins by Otto Feur; some-c by Grossman	17.00	51.00	120.00

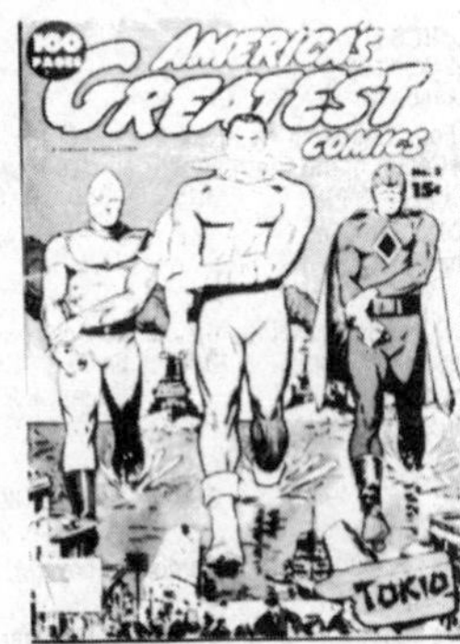

America's Greatest Comics #3, © FAW

Amethyst, Princess of Gemworld #1, © DC

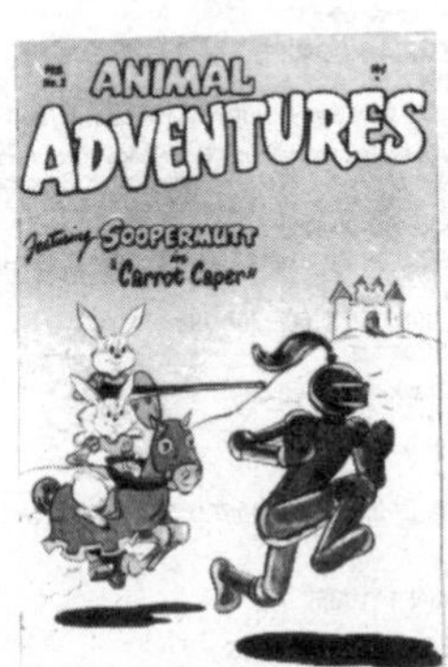

Animal Adventures #2, © Timor

Animal Comics #10, © DELL

Annie Oakley and Tagg #1(7/65), © GK

Anthro #3, © DC

ANIMAL ANTICS (continued) — Good / Fine / Mint
2 — 8.00 24.00 56.00
3-10 — 5.50 16.50 38.00
11-23 — 3.50 10.50 24.00
NOTE: ***Post*** *a-10,14,15,19; c-10.*

ANIMAL COMICS
Dec-Jan, 1941-42 - No. 30, Dec-Jan, 1947-48
Dell Publishing Co.
1-1st Pogo app. by Walt Kelly (Dan Noonan art in most issues) — 83.00 250.00 580.00
2-Uncle Wiggily begins — 34.00 100.00 235.00
3,5 — 23.00 70.00 160.00
4,6,7-No Pogo — 13.00 40.00 90.00
8-10 — 16.00 48.00 110.00
11-15 — 10.00 30.00 70.00
16-20 — 6.50 20.00 45.00
21-30: 25-30-"Jigger" by John Stanley — 4.60 14.00 32.00
NOTE: ***Dan Noonan*** *a-18-30.* ***Gollub*** *art in most later issues.*

ANIMAL CRACKERS (Also see Advs. of Patoruzu)
1946; No. 31, July, 1950; 1959
Green Publ. Co./Norlen/Fox Feat.(Hero Books)
1-Super Cat begins — 4.00 12.00 28.00
2 — 2.00 6.00 14.00
3-10 (Exist?) — 1.15 3.50 8.00
31(Fox)-Formerly My Love Secret — 2.30 7.00 16.00
9(1959-Norlen) — .70 2.00 5.00
nn, nd ('50s), no publ.; infinity-c — .70 2.00 5.00

ANIMAL FABLES
July-Aug, 1946 - No. 7, Nov-Dec, 1947
E. C. Comics(Fables Publ. Co.)
1-Freddy Firefly (clone of Human Torch), Korky Kangaroo, Petey Pig, Danny Demon begin — 22.00 65.00 154.00
2-Aesop Fables begin — 13.00 40.00 90.00
3-6 — 11.00 33.00 77.00
7-Origin Moon Girl — 38.00 115.00 265.00

ANIMAL FAIR (Fawcett's. . .)
March, 1946 - No. 11, Feb, 1947
Fawcett Publications
1 — 7.00 21.00 50.00
2 — 3.50 10.50 25.00
3-6 — 2.65 8.00 18.00
7-11 — 2.00 6.00 14.00

ANIMAL FUN
1953
Premier Magazines
1-(3-D) — 18.00 54.00 125.00

ANIMAL WORLD, THE (See 4-Color Comics No. 713)

ANIMATED COMICS
No date given (Summer, 1947?)
E. C. Comics
1 (Rare) — 55.00 165.00 385.00

ANIMATED FUNNY COMIC TUNES (See Funny Tunes)

ANIMATED MOVIE-TUNES (Movie Tunes No. 3)
Fall, 1945 - No. 2, Sum, 1946
Margood Publishing Corp. (Timely)
1,2-Super Rabbit, Ziggy Pig & Silly Seal — 6.50 19.50 45.00

ANIMAX
Dec, 1986 - No. 4, June, 1987
Star Comics (Marvel)
1-4: Based on toys — .40 .80

ANNETTE (See 4-Color Comics No. 905)

ANNETTE'S LIFE STORY (See 4-Color No. 1100)

ANNIE
Oct, 1982 - No. 2, Nov, 1982
Marvel Comics Group — Good / Fine / Mint
1,2-Movie adaptation — .25 .50
Treasury Edition (Tabloid size) — .35 1.00 2.00

ANNIE OAKLEY (Also see Two-Gun Kid, Wild Western, & Tessie The Typist No. 19)
Spring, 1948 - No. 4, 11/48; No. 5, 6/55 - No. 11, 6/56
Marvel/Atlas Comics(MPI No. 1-4/CDS No. 5 on)
1 (1st Series, '48)-Hedy Devine app. — 12.00 36.00 84.00
2 (7/48, 52 pgs.)-Kurtzman-a, "Hey Look," 1pg; Intro. Lana; Hedy Devine app; Captain Tootsie by Beck — 9.00 27.00 63.00
3,4 — 7.00 21.00 50.00
5 (2nd Series)(1955) — 4.50 13.50 32.00
6-8: 8-Woodbridge-a — 3.50 10.50 24.00
9-Williamson-a, 4 pgs. — 4.00 12.00 28.00
10,11: 11-Severin-c — 3.00 9.00 21.00

ANNIE OAKLEY AND TAGG (TV)
1953 - No. 18, Jan-Mar, 1959; July, 1965 (all photo-c)
Dell Publishing Co./Gold Key
4-Color 438 — 5.00 15.00 35.00
4-Color 481,575 — 3.50 10.50 25.00
4(7-9/55)-10 — 3.00 9.00 21.00
11-18(1-3/59) — 2.35 7.00 16.00
1(7/65-Gold Key)-Photo-c — 2.00 6.00 14.00
NOTE: ***Manning*** *a-13. Photo back c-4, 9, 11.*

ANOTHER WORLD (See Strange Stories From. . .)

ANTHRO (See Showcase)
July-Aug, 1968 - No. 6, July-Aug, 1969
National Periodical Publications
1-Howie Post-a in all — .70 2.00 4.00
2-6: 6-Wood c/a inks — .40 1.25 2.50

ANTONY AND CLEOPATRA (See Ideal, a Classical Comic)

ANYTHING GOES
Oct, 1986 - No. 6, 1987 (mini-series)(Adults, $2.00)
Fantagraphics Books
1-Flaming Carrot app. (1st in color?) — .60 1.75 3.50
2-6: 2-Alan Moore scripts. 3-Capt. Jack, Cerebus app. 5-TMNT app. — .35 1.00 2.00

A-1 COMICS (A-1 appears on covers No. 1-17 only)(See individual title listings. 1st two issues not numbered.)
1944 - No. 139, Sept-Oct, 1955
Life's Romances Publ.-No. 1/Compix/Magazine Ent.
nn-Kerry Drake, Johnny Devildog, Rocky, Streamer Kelly (Slightly large size) — 11.50 34.00 80.00
1-Dotty Dripple(1 pg.), Mr. Ex, Bush Berry, Rocky, Lew Loyal (20 pgs.) — 4.35 13.00 30.00
2-8,10-Texas Slim & Dirty Dalton, The Corsair, Teddy Rich, Dotty Dripple, Inca Dinca, Tommy Tinker, Little Mexico & Tugboat Tim, The Masquerader & others — 1.70 5.00 12.00
9-Texas Slim (all) — 1.70 5.00 12.00
11-Teena — 2.30 7.00 16.00
12,15-Teena — 1.70 5.00 12.00
13-Guns of Fact & Fiction (1948). Used in **SOTI**, pg. 19; narcotics, junkie mentioned; Ingels & J. Craig-a — 11.50 34.00 80.00
14-Tim Holt Western Adventures #1 (1948) — 28.00 84.00 195.00
16-Vacation Comics — 1.30 4.00 9.00
17-Tim Holt #2. Last issue to carry A-1 on cover (9-10/48) — 17.00 50.00 120.00

A-ONE COMICS (continued)	Good	Fine	Mint
18-Jimmy Durante-Photo-c	9.00	27.00	62.00
19-Tim Holt #3	12.00	36.00	84.00
20-Jimmy Durante-Photo-c	9.00	27.00	62.00
21-Joan of Arc(1949)-Movie adapt.; Ingrid Bergman photo-cvrs & interior photos; Whitney-a	10.00	30.00	70.00
22-Dick Powell(1949)	6.50	19.50	45.00
23-Cowboys 'N' Indians #6	2.00	6.00	14.00
24-Trail Colt #1-Frazetta, r-in Manhunt #13; Ingels-c; L. B. Cole-a	24.00	72.00	168.00
25-Fibber McGee & Molly(1949) (Radio)	3.00	9.00	21.00
26-Trail Colt #2-Ingels-c	17.00	51.00	120.00
27-Ghost Rider #1(1950)-Origin G.R.	30.00	90.00	210.00
28-Christmas-(Koko & Kola #6)(5/47)	1.15	3.50	8.00
29-Ghost Rider #2-Frazetta-c (1950)	31.50	95.00	220.00
30-Jet Powers #1-Powell-a	13.00	40.00	90.00
31-Ghost Rider #3-Frazetta-c & origin ('51)	31.50	95.00	220.00
32-Jet Powers #2	9.50	28.00	65.00
33-Muggsy Mouse #1('51)	2.00	6.00	14.00
34-Ghost Rider #4-Frazetta-c (1951)	31.50	95.00	220.00
35-Jet Powers #3-Williamson/Evans-a	18.00	54.00	125.00
36-Muggsy Mouse #2; Racist-c	3.50	10.50	24.00
37-Ghost Rider #5-Frazetta-c (1951)	31.50	95.00	220.00
38-Jet Powers #4-Williamson & Wood-a	18.00	54.00	125.00
39-Muggsy Mouse #3	1.00	3.00	7.00
40-Dogface Dooley #1('51)	2.00	6.00	14.00
41-Cowboys 'N' Indians #7	1.60	4.70	11.00
42-Best of the West #1-Powell-a	17.00	51.00	120.00
43-Dogface Dooley #2	1.30	4.00	9.00
44-Ghost Rider #6	10.00	30.00	70.00
45-American Air Forces #5-Powell-c/a	2.00	6.00	14.00
46-Best of the West #2	8.50	25.50	60.00
47-Thun'da, King of the Congo #1-Frazetta-c/a('52)	100.00	300.00	700.00
48-Cowboys 'N' Indians #8	1.60	4.70	11.00
49-Dogface Dooley #3	1.30	4.00	9.00
50-Danger Is Their Business #11 (1952)-Powell-a	3.70	11.00	26.00
51-Ghost Rider #7 ('52)	10.00	30.00	70.00
52-Best of the West #3	7.00	21.00	50.00
53-Dogface Dooley #4	1.30	4.00	9.00
54-American Air Forces #6(8/52)-Powell-a	2.00	6.00	14.00
55-U.S. Marines #5-Powell-a	2.35	7.00	16.00
56-Thun'da #2-Powell-c/a	12.00	36.00	84.00
57-Ghost Rider #8	8.50	25.50	60.00
58-American Air Forces #7-Powell-a	2.00	6.00	14.00
59-Best of the West #4	7.00	21.00	50.00
60-The U.S. Marines #6-Powell-a	2.35	7.00	16.00
61-Space Ace #5(1953)-Guardineer-a	13.00	40.00	90.00
62-Starr Flagg, Undercover Girl #5	15.00	45.00	105.00
63-Manhunt #13-Frazetta reprinted from A-1 #24	15.00	45.00	105.00
64-Dogface Dooley #5	1.30	4.00	9.00
65-American Air Forces #8-Powell-a	2.00	6.00	14.00
66-Best of the West #5	7.00	21.00	50.00
67-American Air Forces #9-Powell-a	2.00	6.00	14.00
68-U.S. Marines #7-Powell-a	2.35	7.00	16.00
69-Ghost Rider #9(10/52)	8.50	25.50	60.00
70-Best of the West #6	5.00	15.00	35.00
71-Ghost Rider #10(12/52)	8.50	25.50	60.00
72-U.S. Marines #8-Powell-a(3)	2.35	7.00	16.00
73-Thun'da #3-Powell-c/a	9.00	27.00	62.00
74-American Air Forces #10-Powell-a	2.00	6.00	14.00
75-Ghost Rider #11(3/52)	6.50	19.50	45.00
76-Best of the West #7	5.00	15.00	35.00
77-Manhunt #14 (classic cover)	9.50	28.00	65.00
78-Thun'da #4-Powell-c/a	9.00	27.00	62.00

	Good	Fine	Mint
79-American Air Forces #11-Powell-a	2.00	6.00	14.00
80-Ghost Rider #12(6/52)	6.50	19.50	45.00
81-Best of the West #8	5.00	15.00	35.00
82-Cave Girl #11(1953)-Powell-c/a; origin	20.00	60.00	140.00
83-Thun'da #5-Powell-c/a	8.00	24.00	56.00
84-Ghost Rider #13(8/53)	6.50	19.50	45.00
85-Best of the West #9	5.00	15.00	35.00
86-Thun'da #6-Powell-c/a	8.00	24.00	56.00
87-Best of the West #10	5.00	15.00	35.00
88-Bobby Benson's B-Bar-B Riders #20	3.00	9.00	21.00
89-Home Run #3-Powell-a; Stan Musial photo-c	4.35	13.00	30.00
90-Red Hawk #11(1953)-Powell-c/a	3.50	10.50	24.00
91-American Air Forces #12-Powell-a	2.00	6.00	14.00
92-Dream Book of Romance #5-photo-c; Guardineer-a	2.30	7.00	16.00
93-Great Western #8('54)-Origin The Ghost Rider; Powell-a	7.00	21.00	50.00
94-White Indian #11-Frazetta-a(r)	18.00	54.00	126.00
95-Muggsy Mouse #4	1.00	3.00	7.00
96-Cave Girl #12, with Thun'da; Powell-c/a	14.00	42.00	100.00
97-Best of the West #11	5.00	15.00	35.00
98-Undercover Girl #6-Powell-c	13.00	40.00	90.00
99-Muggsy Mouse #5	1.00	3.00	7.00
100-Badmen of the West #1-Meskin-a(?)	8.50	25.50	60.00
101-White Indian #12-Frazetta-a(r)	18.00	54.00	126.00
101-Dream Book of Romance #6 (4-6/54); Marlon Brando photo-c; Powell, Bolle, Guardineer-a	5.70	17.00	40.00
103-Best of the West #12-Powell-a	5.00	15.00	35.00
104-White Indian #13-Frazetta-a(r)('54)	18.00	54.00	126.00
105-Great Western #9-Ghost Rider app.; Powell-a, 6 pgs.; Bolle-c	3.50	10.50	24.00
106-Dream Book of Love #1 (6-7/54)-Powell, Bolle-a; Montgomery Clift, Donna Reed photo-c	3.50	10.50	24.00
107-Hot Dog #1	2.30	7.00	16.00
108-Red Fox #15 (1954)-L.B. Cole c/a; Powell-a	7.00	21.00	50.00
109-Dream Book of Romance #7 (7-8/54). Powell-a; photo-c	2.30	7.00	16.00
110-Dream Book of Romance #8 (10/54)	2.30	7.00	16.00
111-I'm a Cop #1 ('54); drug mention story; Powell-a	4.60	14.00	32.00
112-Ghost Rider #14 ('54)	6.50	17.50	45.00
113-Great Western #10; Powell-a	3.50	10.50	24.00
114-Dream Book of Love #2-Guardineer, Bolle-a; Peter Lorre, Victor Mature photo-c	2.30	7.00	16.00
115-Hot Dog #3	1.30	4.00	9.00
116-Cave Girl #13-Powell-c/a	14.00	42.00	100.00
117-White Indian #14	6.50	19.50	45.00
118-Undercover Girl #7-Powell-c	13.00	40.00	90.00
119-Straight Arrow's Fury #1 (origin)	4.35	13.00	30.00
120-Badmen of the West #2	5.00	15.00	35.00
121-Mysteries of Scotland Yard #1; r-from Manhunt	4.60	14.00	32.00
122-Black Phantom #1(11/54)	13.00	40.00	90.00
123-Dream Book of Love #3(10-11/54)	2.30	7.00	16.00
124-Dream Book of Romance #8(10-11/54)	2.30	7.00	16.00
125-Cave Girl #14-Powell-c/a	14.00	42.00	100.00
126-I'm a Cop #2-Powell-a	2.30	7.00	16.00
127-Great Western #11('54)-Powell-a	3.50	10.50	24.00
128-I'm a Cop #3-Powell-a	2.30	7.00	16.00
129-The Avenger #1('55)-Powell-c	12.00	36.00	84.00
130-Strongman #1-Powell-a	8.00	24.00	56.00
131-The Avenger #2('55)-Powell-c/a	6.00	18.00	42.00
132-Strongman #2	5.70	17.00	40.00
133-The Avenger #3-Powell-c/a	6.00	18.00	42.00

A-1 Comics #18, © ME

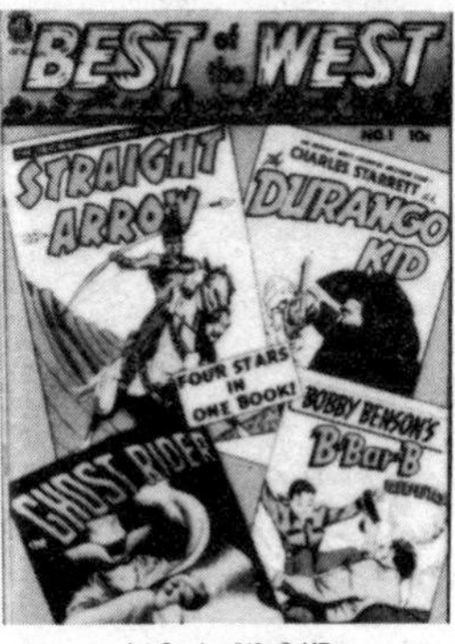

A-1 Comics #42, © ME

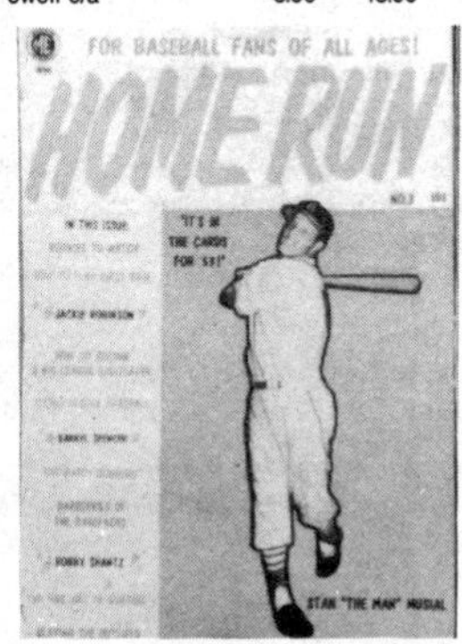

A-1 Comics #89, © ME

Apache Kid #14, © MCG

Approved Comics #12, © STJ

Aquaman #1(1962), © DC

A-1 COMICS (continued)	**Good**	**Fine**	**Mint**
134-Strongman #3	5.70	17.00	40.00
135-White Indian #15	6.50	19.50	45.00
136-Hot Dog #4	1.30	4.00	9.00
137-Africa #1-Powell-c/a(4)	10.50	30.00	70.00
138-The Avenger #4-Powell-c/a	6.00	18.00	42.00
139-Strongman #4-Powell-a	5.70	17.00	40.00

NOTE: ***Bolle** a-110. Photo-c-110.*

APACHE
1951
Fiction House Magazines

1-Baker-c	7.00	21.00	50.00
I.W. Reprint No. 1	.70	2.00	4.00

APACHE HUNTER
1954 (18 pgs. in color) (promo copy) (saddle stitched)
Creative Pictorials

Severin, Heath stories	13.00	39.00	90.00

APACHE KID (Formerly Reno Browne; Western Gunfighters #20 on)
(Also see Two-Gun Western & Wild Western)
No. 53, 12/50 - No. 10, 1/52; No. 11, 12/54 - No. 19, 4/56
Marvel/Atlas Comics(MPC No. 53-10/CPS No. 11 on)

53(No.1)-A. Kid & his horse Nightwind (origin) begin	6.00	18.00	42.00
2(2/51)	3.00	9.00	21.00
3-5	2.00	6.00	14.00
6-10 (1951-52)	1.70	5.00	12.00
11-19 (1954-56)	1.30	4.00	9.00

NOTE: ***Heath** c-11, 13. **Maneely** c-12,14-16. **Severin** c-17.*

APACHE MASSACRE (See Chief Victorio's. . .)

APACHE TRAIL
Sept, 1957 - No. 4, June, 1958
Steinway/America's Best

1	2.50	7.50	17.50
2-4: 2-Tuska-a	1.30	4.00	9.00

APPROVED COMICS
March, 1954 - No. 12, Aug, 1954 (All painted-c)(no c-price)
St. John Publishing Co.

1-The Hawk No. 5-r	3.00	9.00	21.00
2-Invisible Boy-r(3/54)-Origin; Saunders-c	6.00	18.00	42.00
3-Wild Boy of the Congo #11-r(4/54)	3.00	9.00	21.00
4-Kid Cowboy-r	3.00	9.00	21.00
5-Fly Boy-r	3.00	9.00	21.00
6-Daring Adv.-r(5/54); Krigstein-a(2); Baker-c	4.50	13.50	32.00
7-The Hawk #6-r	3.00	9.00	21.00
8-Crime on the Run; Powell-a; Saunders-c	3.00	9.00	21.00
9-Western Bandit Trails #3-r, with new-c; Baker c/a	4.00	12.00	28.00
11-Fightin' Marines #3-r; Kanteen Kate app; Baker-c/a	4.50	13.50	32.00
12-North West Mounties #4-r(8/54); new Baker-c	4.50	13.50	32.00

AQUAMAN (See Showcase, Brave & the Bold, Super DC Giant, Adventure, DC Super-Stars No. 7, Detective, DC Comics Presents No. 5, DC Special Series No. 1, DC Special No. 28, and World's Finest)

AQUAMAN
Jan-Feb, 1962 - No. 56, Mar-Apr, 1971; No. 57, Aug-Sept, 1977 - No. 63, Aug-Sept, 1978
National Periodical Publications/DC Comics

	Good	**Fine**	**Mint**
1-Intro. Quisp	8.50	25.50	60.00
2	3.70	11.00	26.00
3-5	3.00	9.00	21.00
6-10	2.15	6.50	15.00
11-20: 11-Intro. Mera. 18-Aquaman weds Mera; JLA cameo	1.15	3.50	7.00
21-30: 23-Birth of Aquababy. 26-Huntress app.(3-4/66). 29-Intro. Ocean Master, Aquaman's step-brother	.75	2.20	4.40
31,32,34-40	.70	2.00	4.00
33-Intro. Aqua-Girl	.85	2.50	5.00
41-47,49	.50	1.50	3.00
48-Origin reprinted	.50	1.50	3.00
50-52-Adams Deadman	1.40	4.20	8.40
53-56('71): 56-Intro Crusader	.25	.75	1.50
57('77)-63: 58-Origin retold		.45	.90

NOTE: ***Aparo** a-40-59; c-57-60, 63. **Newton** a-60-63.*

AQUAMAN
Feb, 1986 - No. 4, May, 1986 (mini-series)
DC Comics

1-New costume	.85	2.50	5.00
2-4	.35	1.40	2.80

AQUANAUTS (See 4-Color No. 1197)

ARABIAN NIGHTS (See Cinema Comics Herald)

ARAK/SON OF THUNDER (See Warlord #48)
Sept, 1981 - No. 50, Nov, 1985
DC Comics

1-Origin; 1st app. Angelica, Princess of White Cathay		.60	1.20
2-4: 3-Intro Valda, The Iron Maiden		.45	.90
5-10: 8-Viking Prince begins, ends No. 11		.35	.70
11-20: 12-Origin Valda. 20-Origin Angelica		.35	.70
21-23,25-27		.35	.70
24-$1.00 size		.45	.90
28-49 (75 cent cover)		.35	.70
50-Double size		.60	1.20
Annual 1(10/84)		.45	.90

NOTE: ***Alcala** a-10i-12i, 13, 14, 15i-26i; c-13-15, 16i-18i, 19, 20i-25i.*

ARCHIE AND BIG ETHEL
1982 (69 cents)
Spire Christian Comics (Fleming H. Revell Co.)

		.30	.60

ARCHIE AND ME (See Archie Gnt. Series Mag. 578)
Oct, 1964 - No. 162, 1987
Archie Publications

1	6.50	19.50	45.00
2	3.00	9.00	21.00
3-5	1.70	5.00	12.00
6-10	.85	2.50	5.00
11-20	.35	1.00	2.00
21-42		.50	1.00
43-63-(All Giants)		.50	1.00
64-162-(Regular size)		.30	.60

ARCHIE AND MR. WEATHERBEE
1980 (59¢)
Spire Christian Comics (Fleming H. Revell Co.)

nn		.30	.60

ARCHIE. . .ARCHIE ANDREWS, WHERE ARE YOU? (. . .Comics Digest No. 9, 10; . . .Comics Digest Mag. No. 11 on)
Feb, 1977 - Present (Digest size, 160-128 pages)
Archie Publications

1	.30	.80	1.60
2,3,5,7-9-Adams-a; 8-r-/origin The Fly by S&K. 9-Steel Sterling-r	.35	1.00	2.00
4,6,10-54 ($1.00-$1.25): 17-Katy Keene sty		.50	1.00

ARCHIE AS PUREHEART THE POWERFUL

ARCHIE AS PUREHEART THE POWERFUL (continued)
Sept, 1966 - No. 6, Nov, 1967
Archie Publications (Radio Comics)

	Good	Fine	Mint
1	3.00	9.00	21.00
2	1.70	5.00	12.00
3-6	1.00	3.00	7.00

NOTE: *Evilheart cameos in all. Title: . . .As Capt. Pureheart the Powerful-No. 4,6; . . .As Capt. Pureheart-No. 5.*

ARCHIE AT RIVERDALE HIGH (See Archie Gnt. Ser. Mag. 573)
Aug, 1972 - No. 114, 1987
Archie Publications

	Good	Fine	Mint
1	2.00	6.00	12.00
2	1.00	3.00	6.00
3-5	.50	1.50	3.00
6-10	.25	.75	1.50
11-30		.50	1.00
31-114: 96-Anti-smoking issue		.30	.60

ARCHIE COMICS (Archie No. 158 on)(See Everything's. . ., Jackpot, Oxydol-Dreft, and Pep)(First Teen-age comic)(Radio)
Winter, 1942-43 - No. 19, 3-4/46; No. 20, 5-6/46 - Present
MLJ Magazines No. 1-19/Archie Publ.No. 20 on

	Good	Fine	Mint
1 (Scarce)-Jughead, Veronica app.	250.00	750.00	1750.00
2	93.00	280.00	650.00
3 (60 pgs.)	68.00	205.00	475.00
4,5	46.00	140.00	325.00
6-10	32.00	95.00	225.00
11-20: 15,17,18-Dotty & Ditto by Woggon	20.00	60.00	140.00
21-30: 23-Betty & Veronica by Woggon	13.00	40.00	90.00
31-40	9.00	27.00	62.00
41-50	5.70	17.00	40.00
51-70 (1954): 65-70-Katy Keene app.	3.50	10.50	25.00
71-99: 72-74-Katy Keene app.	2.00	6.00	14.00
100	3.00	9.00	18.00
101-130 (1962)	1.15	3.50	8.00
131-160	.70	2.00	4.00
161-200	.35	1.00	2.00
201-240		.50	1.00
241-282		.30	.60
283-Cover/story plugs "International Children's Appeal" which was a fraudulent charity, according to TV's 20/20 news program broadcast July 20, 1979.		.60	1.25
284-355: 300-Anniversary issue		.25	.50
Annual 1('50)-116 pgs. (Scarce)	65.00	195.00	455.00
Annual 2('51)	35.00	105.00	245.00
Annual 3('52)	17.00	51.00	120.00
Annual 4,5(1953-54)	13.00	40.00	90.00
Annual 6-10(1955-59)	7.00	21.00	50.00
Annual 11-15(1960-65)	3.00	9.00	21.00
Annual 16-20(1966-70)	1.00	3.00	6.00
Annual 21-26(1971-75)	.45	1.25	2.50
Annual Digest 27('75)-49('83-'86)(. . .Magazine No. 35 on)		.40	.80
. . .All-Star Specials(Winter '75)-$1.25; 6 remaindered Archie comics rebound in each; titles: "The World of Giant Comics," "Giant Grab Bag of Comics," "Triple Giant Comics," and "Giant Spec. Comics"	.50	1.50	3.00
Mini-Comics (1970-Fairmont Potato Chips Giveaway-Miniature)(8 issues-nn's., 8 pgs. each)	1.00	3.00	6.00
Official Boy Scout Outfitter(1946)-9½x6½", 16 pgs., B. R. Baker Co. (Scarce)	18.00	54.00	125.00
Shoe Store giveaway (1948, Feb?)	5.00	15.00	35.00

ARCHIE COMICS DIGEST (. . .Magazine No. 37 on)
Aug, 1973 - Present (Small size, 160-128 pages)
Archie Publications

	Good	Fine	Mint
1	2.00	6.00	12.00
2	1.00	3.00	6.00
3-5	.50	1.50	3.00
6-10	.25	.75	1.50
11-33: 32,33-The Fly-r by S&K		.50	1.00
34-88: 36-Katy Keene story		.30	.60

NOTE: ***Adams*** *a-1,2,4,5,19-21,24,25,27,29,31,33.*

ARCHIE GETS A JOB
1977
Spire Christian Comics (Fleming H. Revell Co.)

	Good	Fine	Mint
		.30	.60

ARCHIE GIANT SERIES MAGAZINE
1954 - Present (No No. 36-135, no No. 252-451)
Archie Publications

	Good	Fine	Mint
1-Archie's Christmas Stocking	38.00	115.00	265.00
2-Archie's Christmas Stocking('55)	19.00	57.00	132.00
3-5-Archie's Christmas Stocking('56-'58)	12.00	36.00	84.00
6-Archie's Christmas Stocking('59)	12.00	36.00	84.00
7-Katy Keene Holiday Fun(9/60)	9.00	27.00	63.00
8-Betty & Veronica Summer Fun (10/60)			
9-The World of Jughead (12/60)			
10-Archie's Christmas Stocking (1/61)			
each. . . .	8.00	24.00	56.00
11-Betty & Veronica Spectacular (6/61)	5.00	15.00	35.00
12-Katy Keene Holiday Fun (9/61)	6.00	18.00	42.00
13-Betty & Veronica Summer Fun (10/61)			
14-The World of Jughead (12/61)			
15-Archie's Christmas Stocking (1/62)			
16-Betty & Veronica Spectacular (6/62)			
17-Archie's Jokes (9/62); Katy Keene app.			
18-Betty & Veronica Summer Fun (10/62)			
19-The World of Jughead (12/62)			
20-Archie's Christmas Stocking (1/63)			
each. . . .	5.00	15.00	35.00
21-Betty & Veronica Spectacular (6/63)			
22-Archie's Jokes (9/63)			
23-Betty & Veronica Summer Fun (10/63)			
24-The World of Jughead (12/63)			
25-Archie's Christmas Stocking (1/64)			
26-Betty & Veronica Spectacular (6/64)			
27-Archie's Jokes (8/64)			
28-Betty & Veronica Summer Fun (9/64)			
29-Around the World with Archie (10/64)			
30-The World of Jughead (12/64)			
each. . . .	3.00	9.00	18.00
31-Archie's Christmas Stocking (1/65)			
32-Betty & Veronica Spectacular (6/65)			
33-Archie's Jokes (8/65)			
34-Betty & Veronica Summer Fun (9/65)			
35-Around the World with Archie (10/65)			
136-The World of Jughead (12/65)			
137-Archie's Christmas Stocking (1/66)			
138-Betty & Veronica Spectacular (6/66)			
139-Archie's Jokes (6/66)			
140-Betty & Veronica Summer Fun (8/66)			
141-Around the World with Archie (9/66)			
each. . . .	2.35	7.00	14.00
142-Archie's Super-Hero Special (10/66)-Origin Capt. Pureheart, Capt. Hero, and Evilheart	2.00	6.00	12.00
143-The World of Jughead (12/66)			
144-Archie's Christmas Stocking (1/67)			
145-Betty & Veronica Spectacular (6/67)			
146-Archie's Jokes (6/67)			
147-Betty & Veronica Summer Fun (8/67)			
148-World of Archie (9/67)			

Archie Comics #3, © AP

Archie Comics #34, © AP

Archie Comics #117, © AP

ARCHIE GIANT SERIES MAG. (continued)
149-World of Jughead (10/67)
150-Archie's Christmas Stocking (1/68)
151-World of Archie (2/68)
152-World of Jughead (2/68)
153-Betty & Veronica Spectacular (6/68)
154-Archie Jokes (6/68)
155-Betty & Veronica Summer Fun (8/68)
156-World of Archie (10/68)
157-World of Jughead (12/68)
158-Archie's Christmas Stocking (1/69)
159-Betty & Veronica Christmas Spect. (1/69)
160-World of Archie (2/69)

	Good	Fine	Mint
each....	1.20	3.50	7.00

161-World of Jughead (2/69)
162-Betty & Veronica Spectacular (6/69)
163-Archie's Jokes (8/69)
164-Betty & Veronica Summer Fun (9/69)
165-World of Archie (9/69)
166-World of Jughead (9/69)
167-Archie's Christmas Stocking (1/70)
168-Betty & Veronica Christmas Spect. (1/70)
169-Archie's Christmas Love-In (1/70)
170-Jughead's Eat-Out Comic Book Mag. (12/69)
171-World of Archie (2/70)
172-World of Jughead (2/70)
173-Betty & Veronica Spectacular (6/70)
174-Archie's Jokes (8/70)
175-Betty & Veronica Summer Fun (9/70)
176-Li'l Jinx Giant Laugh-Out (8/70)
177-World of Archie (9/70)
178-World of Jughead (9/70)
179-Archie's Christmas Stocking (1/71)
180-Betty & Veronica Christmas Spect. (1/71)
181-Archie's Christmas Love-In (1/71)
182-World of Archie (2/71)
183-World of Jughead (2/71)
184-Betty & Veronica Spectacular (6/71)
185-Li'l Jinx Giant Laugh-Out (6/71)
186-Archie's Jokes (8/71)
187-Betty & Veronica Summer Fun (9/71)
188-World of Archie (9/71)
189-World of Jughead (9/71)
190-Archie's Christmas Stocking (12/71)
191-Betty & Veronica Christmas Spect. (2/72)
192-Archie's Christmas Love-In (1/72)
193-World of Archie (3/72)
194-World of Jughead (4/72)
195-Li'l Jinx Christmas Bag (1/72)
196-Sabrina's Christmas Magic (1/72)
197-Betty & Veronica Spectacular (6/72)
198-Archie's Jokes (8/72)
199-Betty & Veronica Summer Fun (9/72)
200-World of Archie (10/72)

each....	.45	1.25	2.50

201-Betty & Veronica Spectacular (10/72)
202-World of Jughead (11/72)
203-Archie's Christmas Stocking (12/72)
204-Betty & Veronica Christmas Spect. (2/73)
205-Archie's Christmas Love-In (1/73)
206-Li'l Jinx Christmas Bag (12/72)
207-Sabrina's Christmas Magic (12/72)
208-World of Archie (3/73)
209-World of Jughead (4/73)
210-Betty & Veronica Spectacular (6/73)
211-Archie's Jokes (8/73)
212-Betty & Veronica Summer Fun (9/73)
213-World of Archie (10/73)
214-Betty & Veronica Spectacular (10/73)
215-World of Jughead (11/73)
216-Archie's Christmas Stocking (12/73)
217-Betty & Veronica Christmas Spect. (2/74)
218-Archie's Christmas Love-In (1/74)
219-Li'l Jinx Christmas Bag (12/73)
220-Sabrina's Christmas Magic (12/73)
221-Betty & Veronica Spectacular (Advertised as World of Archie) (6/74)
222-Archie's Jokes (Advertised as World of Jughead)(8/74)
223-Li'l Jinx (8/74)
224-Betty & Veronica Summer Fun (9/74)
225-World of Archie (9/74)
226-Betty & Veronica Spectacular (10/74)
227-World of Jughead (10/74)
228-Archie's Christmas Stocking (12/74)
229-Betty & Veronica Christmas Spect. (12/74)
230-Archie's Christmas Love-In (1/75)
231-Sabrina's Christmas Magic (1/75)
232-World of Archie (3/75)
233-World of Jughead (4/75)
234-Betty & Veronica Spectacular (6/75)
235-Archie's Jokes (8/75)
236-Betty & Veronica Summer Fun (9/75)
237-World of Archie (9/75)
238-Betty & Veronica Spectacular (10/75)
239-World of Jughead (10/75)
240-Archie's Christmas Stocking (12/75)
241-Betty & Veronica Christmas Spectacular (12/75)
242-Archie's Christmas Love-In (1/76)
243-Sabrina's Christmas Magic (1/76)
244-World of Archie (3/76)
245-World of Jughead (4/76)
246-Betty & Veronica Spectacular (6/76)
247-Archie's Jokes (8/76)
248-Betty & Veronica Summer Fun (9/76)
249-World of Archie (9/76)
250-Betty & Veronica Spectacular (10/76)
251-World of Jughead (10/76)

	Good	Fine	Mint
each....		.50	1.00

452-Archie's Christmas Stocking (12/76)
453-Betty & Veronica Christmas Spect. (12/76)
454-Archie's Christmas Love-In (1/77)
455-Sabrina's Christmas Magic (1/77)
456-World of Archie (3/77)
457-World of Jughead (4/77)
458-Betty & Veronica Spectacular (6/77)
459-Archie's Jokes (8/77)-Shows 8/76 in error
460-Betty & Veronica Summer Fun (9/77)
461-World of Archie (9/77)
462-Betty & Veronica Spectacular (10/77)
463-World of Jughead (10/77)
464-Archie's Christmas Stocking (12/77)
465-Betty & Veronica Christmas Spectacular (12/77)
466-Archie's Christmas Love-In (1/78)
467-Sabrina's Christmas Magic (1/78)
468-World of Archie (2/78)
469-World of Jughead (2/78)
470-Betty & Veronica Spectacular (6/78)
471-Archie's Jokes (8/78)
472-Betty & Veronica Summer Fun (9/78)
473-World of Archie (9/78)
474-Betty & Veronica Spectacular (10/78)
475-World of Jughead (10/78)
476-Archie's Christmas Stocking (12/78)
477-Betty & Veronica Christmas Spectacular (12/78)
478-Archie's Christmas Love-In (1/79)
479-Sabrina Christmas Magic (1/79)
480-The World of Archie (3/79)
481-World of Jughead (4/79)
482-Betty & Veronica Spectacular (6/79)
483-Archie's Jokes (8/79)
484-Betty & Veronica Summer Fun (9/79)
485-The World of Archie (9/79)
486-Betty & Veronica Spectacular (10/79)
487-The World of Jughead (10/79)
488-Archie's Christmas Stocking (12/79)
489-Betty & Veronica Christmas Spect. (1/80)
490-Archie's Christmas Love-in (1/80)
491-Sabrina's Christmas Magic (1/80)
492-The World of Archie (2/80)
493-The World of Jughead (4/80)
494-Betty & Veronica Spectacular (6/80)
495-Archie's Jokes (8/80)
496-Betty & Veronica Summer Fun (9/80)
497-The World of Archie (9/80)
498-Betty & Veronica Spectacular (10/80)
499-The World of Jughead (10/80)
500-Archie's Christmas Stocking (12/80)
501-Betty & Veronica Christmas Spect. (12/80)
502-Archie's Christmas Love-in (1/81)
503-Sabrina Christmas Magic (1/81)
504-The World of Archie (3/81)
505-The World of Jughead (4/81)
506-Betty & Veronica Spectacular (6/81)
507-Archie's Jokes (8/81)
508-Betty & Veronica Summer Fun (9/81)
509-The World of Archie (9/81)
510-Betty & Vernonica Spectacular (9/81)
511-The World of Jughead (10/81)
512-Archie's Christmas Stocking (12/81)
513-Betty & Veronica Christmas Spectacular (12/81)
514-Archie's Christmas Love-in (1/82)
515-Sabrina's Christmas Magic (1/82)
516-The World of Archie (3/82)
517-The World of Jughead (4/82)
518-Betty & Veronica Spectacular (6/82)
519-Archie's Jokes (8/82)
520-Betty & Veronica Summer Fun (9/82)
521-The World of Archie (9/82)
522-Betty & Veronica Spectacular (10/82)
523-The World of Jughead (10/82)

ARCHIE'S GIANT SERIES MAG. (continued)
524-Archie's Christmas Stocking (1/83)
525-Betty and Veronica Christmas Spectacular (1/83)
526-Betty and Veronica Spectacular (5/83)
527-Little Archie (8/83)
528-Josie and the Pussycats (8/83)
529-Betty and Veronica Summer Fun (8/83)
530-Betty and Veronica Spectacular (9/83)
531-The World of Jughead (9/83)
532-The World of Archie (10/83)
533-Space Pirates by Frank Bolling (10/83)
534-Little Archie (1/84)
535-Archie's Christmas Stocking (1/84)
536-Betty and Veronica Christmas Spectacular (1/84)
537-Betty and Veronica Spectacular (6/84)
538-Little Archie (8/84)
539-Betty and Veronica Summer Fun 8/84)
540-Josie and the Pussycats (8/84)
541-Betty and Veronica Spectacular (9/84)
542-The World of Jughead (9/84)
543-The World of Archie (10/84)
544-Sabrina the Teen-Age Witch (10/84)
545-Little Archie (12/84)
546-Archie's Christmas Stocking (12/84)
547-Betty and Veronica Christmas Spectacular (12/84)
548-
549-Little Archie
550-Betty and Veronica Summer Fun
551-Josie and the Pussycats
552-Betty and Veronica Spectacular
553-The World of Jughead
554-The World of Archie
555-Betty's Diary
556-Little Archie (1/86)
557-Archie's Christmas Stocking (1/86)
558-Betty & Veronica Christmas Spectacular (1/86)
559-Betty & Veronica Spectacular
560-
561-Betty & Veronica Summer Fun
562-Josie and the Pussycats
563-Betty & Veronica Spectacular
564-World of Jughead
565-World of Archie
566-Little Archie
567-Archie's Christmas Stocking
568-Betty & Veronica Christmas Spectacular
569-Betty & Veronica Spring Spectacular
570-Little Archie
571-Josie & the Pussycats
572-Betty & Veronica Summer Fun
573-Archie At Riverdale High
574-World of Archie
575-Betty & Veronica Spectacular
576-Pep
577-World of Jughead
578-Archie And Me
579-Archie's Christmas Stocking
580-Betty and Veronica Christmas Spectacular
581-Little Archie Christmas Special

	Good	Fine	Mint
each....		.40	.80

ARCHIE'S ACTIVITY COMICS DIGEST MAGAZINE
1985 (Annual, 128 pgs.; digest size)
Archie Enterprises

	Good	Fine	Mint
1-4		.50	1.00

ARCHIE'S CAR
1979 (49 cents)
Spire Christian Comics (Fleming H. Revell Co.)

	Good	Fine	Mint
nn		.30	.60

ARCHIE'S CHRISTMAS LOVE-IN (See Archie Giant Series Mag. No. 169, 181, 192, 205, 218, 230, 242, 454, 466, 478, 490, 502, 514)

ARCHIE'S CHRISTMAS STOCKING (See Archie Giant Series Mag. No. 1-6, 10, 15, 20, 25, 31, 137, 144, 150, 158, 167, 179, 190, 203, 216, 228, 240, 452, 464, 476, 488, 500, 512, 524, 535, 546, 557, 567)

ARCHIE'S CLEAN SLATE
1973 (35-49 cents)
Spire Christian Comics (Fleming H. Revell Co.)

	Good	Fine	Mint
1(Some issues have nn)	.35	1.00	2.00

ARCHIE'S DATE BOOK
1981
Spire Christian Comics (Fleming H. Revell Co.)

	Good	Fine	Mint
		.30	.60

ARCHIE'S DOUBLE DIGEST QUARTERLY MAGAZINE
1981 - Present ($1.95, 256pgs.) (A.D.D. Magazine No. 10 on)
Archie Comics

	Good	Fine	Mint
1-33: 6-Katy Keene sty	.25	.75	1.50

ARCHIE'S FAMILY ALBUM
1978 (36 pages) (39 cents)
Spire Christian Comics (Fleming H. Revell Co.)

	Good	Fine	Mint
		.30	.60

ARCHIE'S FESTIVAL
1980 (49 cents)
Spire Christian Comics (Fleming H. Revell Co.)

	Good	Fine	Mint
		.30	.60

ARCHIE'S GIRLS, BETTY AND VERONICA (Becomes Betty & Veronica)
1950 - No. 347, 1987
Archie Publications (Close-Up)

	Good	Fine	Mint
1	58.00	175.00	405.00
2	30.00	90.00	210.00
3-5	17.00	51.00	120.00
6-10: 10-2pg. Katy Keene app.	13.00	40.00	90.00
11-20: 11,13,14,17-19-Katy Keene app. 20-Debbie's Diary, 2pgs.	8.00	24.00	56.00
21-30: 27-Katy Keene app.	6.50	19.50	45.00
31-50	4.30	13.00	30.00
51-74	2.65	8.00	18.00
75-Betty & Veronica sell soul to devil	5.50	16.50	38.00
76-99	1.30	4.00	9.00
100	2.00	6.00	14.00
101-140: 118-Origin Superteen. 119-Last Superteen story	.75	2.25	4.50
141-180	.35	1.00	2.00
181-220		.40	.80
221-347: 300-Anniversary issue		.25	.50
Annual 1 (1953)	30.00	90.00	210.00
Annual 2(1954)	14.00	42.00	100.00
Annual 3-5 ('55-'57)	10.00	30.00	70.00
Annual 6-8 ('58-'60)	7.00	21.00	50.00

ARCHIE SHOE-STORE GIVEAWAY
1944-49 (12-15 pgs. of games, puzzles, stories like Superman-Tim books, No nos. - came out monthly)
Archie Publications

	Good	Fine	Mint
(1944-47)-issues	8.35	25.00	55.00
2/48-Peggy Lee photo-c	5.00	15.00	35.00
3/48-Marylee Robb photo-c	5.00	15.00	35.00
4/48-Gloria DeHaven photo-c	5.00	15.00	35.00
5/48,6/48,7/48	5.00	15.00	35.00

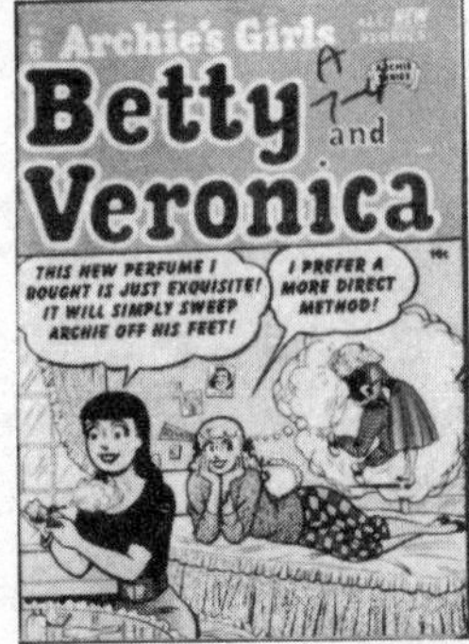

Archie's Girls, Betty and Veronica #6, © AP

Archie's Girls, Betty and Veronica #52, © AP

Archie's Girls...Annual #8, © AP

Archie's Joke Book Magazine #78, © AP

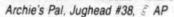

Archie's Pal, Jughead #38, © AP

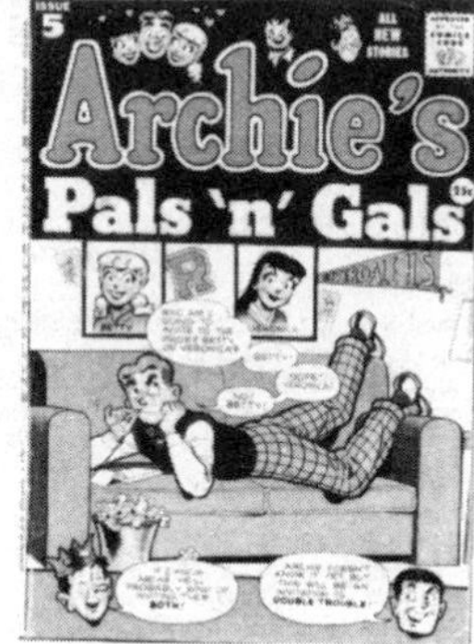

Archie's Pals 'n' Gals #5, © AP

ARCHIE SHOE-STORE GIVEAWAY (cont.)

	Good	Fine	Mint
8/48-Story on Shirley Temple	5.00	15.00	35.00
10/48-Archie as Wolf on cover	5.00	15.00	35.00
5/49-Kathleen Hughes photo-c	4.00	12.00	28.00
7/49	4.00	12.00	28.00
8/49-Archie photo-c from radio show	5.00	15.00	35.00
10/49-Gloria Mann photo-c from radio show	5.00	15.00	35.00
11/49,12/49	4.00	12.00	28.00

ARCHIE'S JOKEBOOK COMICS DIGEST ANNUAL (See Jokebook . .)

ARCHIE'S JOKE BOOK MAGAZINE (See Joke Book . . .)
1953 - No. 3, Sum, 1954; No. 15, Fall, 1954 - No. 288, 11/82
Archie Publications

	Good	Fine	Mint
1953-One Shot(No.1)	38.00	115.00	265.00
2	20.00	60.00	140.00
3 (nn.4-14)	13.00	40.00	90.00
15-20: 14-17-Katy Keene app.	9.00	27.00	63.00
21-30	6.00	18.00	42.00
31-40,42,43	3.00	9.00	21.00
40-1st professional comic work by Neal Adams ('59), 1 pg.	11.50	34.00	80.00
44-47-Adams-a in all, 1-2 pgs.	6.00	18.00	42.00
48-Four pgs. Adams-a	6.00	18.00	42.00
49-60 (1962)	2.00	6.00	12.00
61-80	1.15	3.50	7.00
81-100	.60	1.75	3.50
101-140	.25	.75	1.50
141-200		.40	.80
201-288		.25	.50
Drug Store Giveaway (No. 39 w/new-c)	2.00	6.00	12.00

ARCHIE'S JOKES (See Archie Giant Series Mag. No. 17, 22, 27, 33, 139, 146, 154, 163, 174, 186, 198, 211, 222, 235, 247, 459, 471, 483, 495, 519)

ARCHIE'S LOVE SCENE
1973 (35-49 cents)
Spire Christian Comics (Fleming H. Revell Co.)

	Good	Fine	Mint
1(Some issues have nn)	.35	1.00	2.00

ARCHIE'S MADHOUSE (Madhouse Ma-ad No. 67 on)
Sept, 1959 - No. 66, Feb, 1969
Archie Publications

	Good	Fine	Mint
1-Archie begins	13.00	40.00	90.00
2	6.50	20.00	45.00
3-5	5.00	15.00	35.00
6-10	3.75	11.25	26.00
11-16 (Last w/regular characters)	2.65	8.00	18.00
17-21,23-30 (New format)	1.00	3.00	6.00
22-1st app. Sabrina, the Teen-age Witch (10/62)	3.00	9.00	18.00
31-40	.25	.75	1.50
41-66: 43-Mighty Crusaders cameo		.25	.50
Annual 1 (1962-63)	2.65	8.00	18.00
Annual 2 (1964)	1.20	3.50	7.00
Annual 3 (1965)-Origin Sabrina The Teen-Age Witch	.70	2.00	4.00
Annual 4-6('66-69)(Becomes Madhouse Ma-ad Annual No. 7 on)	.35	1.00	2.00

NOTE: *Cover title to 61-65 is "Madhouse" and to 66 is "Madhouse Ma-ad Jokes."*

ARCHIE'S MECHANICS
Sept, 1954 - 1955
Archie Publications

	Good	Fine	Mint
1-(15 cents; 52 pgs.)	50.00	150.00	350.00
2-(10 cents)	30.00	90.00	210.00
3-(10 cents)	25.00	75.00	175.00

ARCHIE'S ONE WAY
1972 (35 cents, 39 cents, 49 cents) (36 pages)
Spire Christian Comics (Fleming H. Revell Co.)

	Good	Fine	Mint
nn	.35	1.00	2.00

ARCHIE'S PAL, JUGHEAD (Jughead No. 127 on)
1949 - No. 126, Nov, 1965
Archie Publications

	Good	Fine	Mint
1	55.00	165.00	385.00
2	26.00	78.00	180.00
3-5	16.00	48.00	110.00
6-10: 7-Suzie app.	10.00	30.00	70.00
11-20	7.50	22.50	52.00
21-30: 23-25,28-30-Katy Keene app. 28-Debbie's Diary app.	5.00	15.00	35.00
31-50	3.00	9.00	21.00
51-70	2.35	7.00	16.00
71-100	1.35	4.00	8.00
101-126	.85	2.50	5.00
Annual 1 (1953)	23.00	70.00	160.00
Annual 2 (1954)	13.00	40.00	90.00
Annual 3-5 (1955-57)	8.50	25.50	60.00
Annual 6-8 (1958-60)	6.00	18.00	42.00

ARCHIE'S PALS 'N' GALS
1952-53 - No. 6, 1957-58; No. 7, 1958 - Present
Archie Publications

	Good	Fine	Mint
1-(116 pages)	30.00	90.00	210.00
2(Annual)('53-'54)	16.00	48.00	110.00
3-5(Annual, '54-57)	10.00	30.00	70.00
6-10('58-'60)	5.00	15.00	35.00
11-20	2.65	8.00	18.00
21-40: 29-Beatle satire	1.35	4.00	9.50
41-60	.70	2.00	4.00
61-80	.25	.75	1.50
81-110		.50	1.00
111-195		.30	.60

ARCHIE'S PARABLES
1973, 1975 (36 pages, 39-49 cents)
Spire Christian Comics (Fleming H. Revell Co.)

	Good	Fine	Mint
By Al Hartley		.40	.80

ARCHIE'S RIVAL REGGIE (Reggie No. 15 on)
1950 - No. 14, Aug, 1954
Archie Publications

	Good	Fine	Mint
1	40.00	120.00	280.00
2	20.00	60.00	140.00
3-5	13.00	40.00	90.00
6-10	8.00	24.00	56.00
11-14: Katy Keene in No. 10-14, 1-2pgs.	6.00	18.00	42.00

ARCHIE'S ROLLER COASTER
1981 (69 cents)
Spire Christian Comics (Fleming H. Revell Co.)

	Good	Fine	Mint
nn		.40	.80

ARCHIE'S SOMETHING ELSE
1975 (36 pages, 39-49 cents)
Spire Christian Comics (Fleming H. Revell Co.)

	Good	Fine	Mint
nn		.40	.80

ARCHIE'S SONSHINE
1973, 1974 (36 pages, 39-49 cents)
Spire Christian Comics (Fleming H. Revell Co.)

	Good	Fine	Mint
nn	.35	1.00	2.00

ARCHIE'S SPORTS SCENE
1983
Spire Christian Comics (Fleming H. Revell Co.)

	Good	Fine	Mint
nn		.40	.80

ARCHIE'S STORY & GAME COMICS DIGEST MAGAZINE
Nov, 1986 - Present (Digest size, $1.25, $1.35, 128 pgs.)
Archie Enterprises

	Good	Fine	Mint
1-6		.60	1.25

ARCHIE'S SUPER HERO SPECIAL (See Archie Giant Series Magazine No. 142)

ARCHIE'S SUPER HERO SPECIAL (. . .Comics Digest Mag. 2)
Jan, 1979 - No. 2, Aug, 1979 (148 pages, 95 cents)
Archie Publications (Red Circle)

	Good	Fine	Mint
1-Simon & Kirby r-/Double Life of Pvt. Strong No. 1,2; Black Hood, The Fly, Jaguar, The Web app.		.40	.80
2-Contains contents to the never published Black Hood No. 1; origin Black Hood; Adams, Wood, McWilliams, Morrow, S&K(r)-a; Adams-c. The Shield, The Fly, Jaguar, Hangman, Steel Sterling, The Web, The Fox-r		.40	.80

ARCHIE'S TV LAUGH-OUT
Dec, 1969 - No. 106, 1986
Archie Publications

	Good	Fine	Mint
1	3.35	10.00	20.00
2	1.35	4.00	8.00
3-5	.70	2.00	4.00
6-10	.25	.75	1.50
11-20		.40	.80
21-106		.25	.50

ARCHIE'S WORLD
1973, 1976 (39-49 cents)
Spire Christian Comics (Fleming H. Revell Co.)

	Good	Fine	Mint
		.40	.80

ARION, LORD OF ATLANTIS
Nov, 1982 - No. 36, Oct, 1985
DC Comics

	Good	Fine	Mint
1-Story cont'd from Warlord 62		.60	1.20
2-36: 4-Origin		.35	.70
Special #1 (11/85)		.55	1.10

ARISTOCATS (See Movie Comics & Walt Disney Showcase No. 16)

ARISTOKITTENS, THE (. . . Meet Jiminy Cricket No. 1)(Disney)
Oct, 1971 - No. 9, Oct, 1975 (No. 6: 52 pages)
Gold Key

	Good	Fine	Mint
1	.50	1.50	3.00
2-9	.25	.75	1.50

ARIZONA KID, THE (Also see Wild Western)
March, 1951 - No. 6, Jan, 1952
Marvel/Atlas Comics(CSI)

	Good	Fine	Mint
1	5.00	15.00	35.00
2-4: 2-Heath-a(3)	3.00	9.00	21.00
5,6	2.65	8.00	18.00

ARK, THE (See The Crusaders)

ARMAGEDDON FACTOR, THE
1987 - Present ($1.95, color)
AC Comics

	Good	Fine	Mint
1-3: Sentinels of Justice, Dragonfly	.35	1.00	2.00

ARMY AND NAVY (Supersnipe No. 6 on)
May, 1941 - No. 5, Sept, 1942
Street & Smith Publications

	Good	Fine	Mint
1-Cap Fury & Nick Carter	18.00	54.00	125.00
2-Cap Fury & Nick Carter	8.00	24.00	56.00
3,4	6.00	18.00	42.00
5-Supersnipe app.; see Shadow V2#3 for 1st app.	17.00	51.00	120.00

ARMY ATTACK
July, 1964 - No. 47, Feb, 1967
Charlton Comics

	Good	Fine	Mint
V1#1	.30	.80	1.60
2-4(2/65)		.40	.80
V2#38(7/65)-47 (formerly U.S. Air Force #1-37)		.30	.60

NOTE: ***Glanzman** a-1-3. **Montes/Bache** a-44.*

ARMY AT WAR (Also see Our Army at War, Cancelled Comic Cavalcade)
Oct-Nov, 1978
DC Comics

	Good	Fine	Mint
1-Kubert-c		.30	.60

ARMY WAR HEROES (Also see Iron Corporal)
Dec, 1963 - No. 38, June, 1970
Charlton Comics

	Good	Fine	Mint
1	.50	1.50	3.00
2-20		.50	1.00
21-38: 23-Origin & 1st app. Iron Corporal series by Glanzman. 24-Intro. Archer & Corp. Jack series		.40	.80
Modern Comics Reprint 36 ('78)		.30	.60

NOTE: ***Montes/Bache** a-1,16,17,21,23-25,27-30.*

AROUND THE BLOCK WITH DUNC & LOO (See Dunc and Loo)

AROUND THE WORLD IN 80 DAYS (See 4-Color Comics No. 784 and A Golden Picture Classic)

AROUND THE WORLD UNDER THE SEA (See Movie Classics)

AROUND THE WORLD WITH ARCHIE (See Archie Giant Series Mag. No. 29, 35, 141)

AROUND THE WORLD WITH HUCKLEBERRY & HIS FRIENDS (See Dell Giant No. 44)

ARRGH! (Satire)
Dec, 1974 - No. 5, Sept, 1975
Marvel Comics Group

	Good	Fine	Mint
1		.40	.80
2-5		.25	.50

NOTE: ***Alcala** a-2; c-3. **Everett** a-1r, 2r. **Maneely** a-4r. **Sekowsky** a-1p. **Sutton** a-1.*

ARROW, THE (See Funny Pages)
Oct, 1940 - No. 2, Nov, 1940; No. 3, Oct, 1941
Centaur Publications

	Good	Fine	Mint
1-The Arrow begins(r/Funny Pages)	75.00	225.00	525.00
2-Tippy Taylor serial cont's/Amaz. Myst. Funnies 24	45.00	135.00	315.00
3-Origin Dash Dartwell, the Human Meteor; origin The Rainbow-r; bondage-c	45.00	135.00	315.00

NOTE: ***Gustavson** a-1,2; c-3.*

ARROWHEAD (See Black Rider, Wild Western)
April, 1954 - No. 4, Nov, 1954
Atlas Comics (CPS)

	Good	Fine	Mint
1-Arrowhead & his horse Eagle begin	3.50	10.50	25.00
2-4	2.30	7.00	16.00

NOTE: ***Maneely** c-2. **Sinnott** a-1-4.*

ASSASSINS, INC.
1987 - Present ($1.95, color)
Silverline comics

	Good	Fine	Mint
1	.35	1.00	1.90

ASTONISHING (Marvel Boy No. 1,2)
No. 3, April, 1951 - No. 63, Aug, 1957
Marvel/Atlas Comics(20CC)

	Good	Fine	Mint
3-Marvel Boy cont'd.	23.00	70.00	160.00
4-6-Last Marvel Boy; 4-Stan Lee app.	18.00	54.00	125.00
7-10	4.35	13.00	30.00
11,12,15,17,18,20	3.50	10.50	24.00

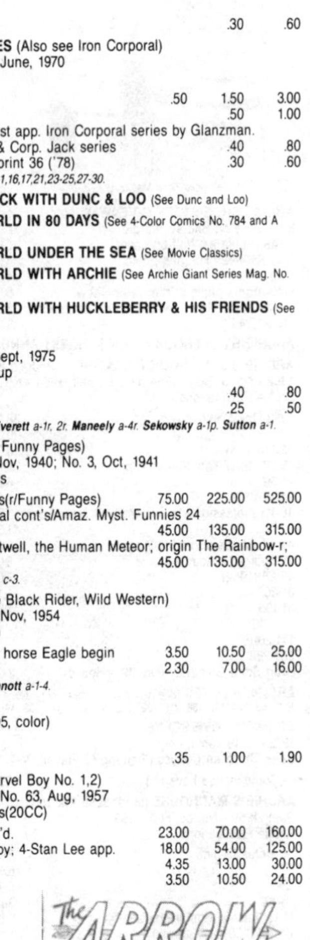

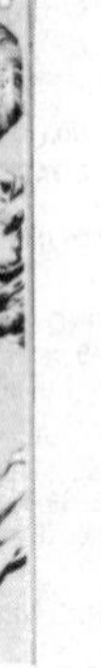

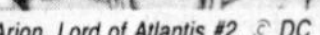
Arion, Lord of Atlantis #2, © DC

Army War Heroes #1, © CC

The Arrow #3, © CEN

Astonishing #14, © MCG

The Atom #8, © DC

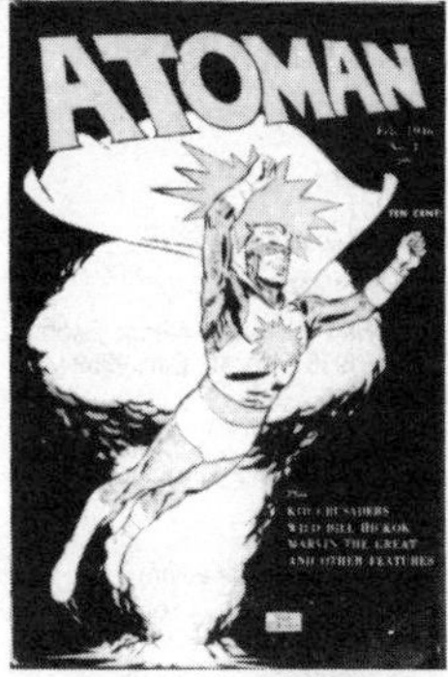

Atoman #1, © Spark Publications

ASTONISHING (continued) — **Good** **Fine** **Mint**
13,14,16,19-Krigstein-a 3.70 11.00 26.00
21,22,24 2.65 8.00 18.00
23-E.C. swipe-'The Hole In The Wall' from VOH 16
3.50 10.50 24.00
25-Crandall-a 3.50 10.50 24.00
26-29 2.85 8.50 20.00
30-Tentacled eyeball story 4.00 12.00 28.00
31-37-Last pre-code issue 2.30 7.00 16.00
38-43,46,48-52,56,58,59,61 1.50 4.50 10.00
44-Crandall swipe/Weird Fantasy 22 2.70 8.00 19.00
45,47-Krigstein-a 2.70 8.00 19.00
53-Crandall, Ditko-a 2.00 6.00 14.00
54-Torres-a 2.00 6.00 14.00
55-Crandall, Torres-a 2.65 8.00 18.00
57-Williamson/Krenkel-a, 4 pgs. 4.00 12.00 28.00
60-Williamson/Mayo-a, 4 pgs. 4.00 12.00 28.00
62-Torres, Woodbridge, Powell -a 1.70 5.00 12.00
63-Last issue; Woodbridge-a 1.70 5.00 12.00

NOTE: ***Berg** a-36, 53, 56. **Cameron** a-50. **Gene Colan** a-12, 20, 29, 56. **Ditko** a-50, 53. **Drucker** a-41. **Everett** a-3-5(3), 6, 10, 12, 37, 47, 48, 58, 61; c-3-5, 13, 15, 16, 18, 29, 47, 49, 51, 53-55, 57, 59-63. **Fass** a-34. **Fuje** a-11. **Heath** c/a-8; c-9, 26. **Kirby** a-56. **Lawrence** a-28, 37, 38, 42. **Maneely** c-31, 33, 34, 56. **Moldoff** a-33. **Morrow** a-52, 61. **Orlando** a-47, 58, 61. **Powell** a-43, 44, 48. **Ravielli** a-28. **Reinman** a-34. **Robinson** a-20. **J. Romita** a-7, 24, 43, 57, 61. **Roussos** a-55. **Sekowsky** a-13. **Severin** c-46. **Sinnotta**-30. **Ed Win** a-20. Canadian reprints exist.*

ASTONISHING TALES (See Ka-Zar)
Aug, 1970 - No. 36, July, 1976
Marvel Comics Group

1-Ka-Zar by Kirby(p) & Dr. Doom by Wood begin
.25 .75 1.50
2-Kirby, Wood-a .50 1.00
3-6: Smith-a(p); Wood-a-#3,4. 5-Red Skull app.
.40 1.25 2.50
7-9: 8-Last Dr. Doom. (52 pgs.) .35 .70
10-Smith-a(p) .40 1.25 2.50
11-Origin Ka-Zar & Zabu .50 1.00
12-Man-Thing by Adams .40 1.25 2.50
13-20: 20-Last Ka-Zar .35 .70
21-24: 21-It! the Living Colossus begins, ends #24 .25 .50
25-Deathlok the Demolisher begins; Perez 1st work, 2pgs. (8/74)
.35 1.20 2.40
26-30: 29-Guardians of the Galaxy app. .50 1.00
31-36: 31-Wrightson-c(i) .30 .60

NOTE: ***Buckler** a-13i, 16p, 25, 26p, 27p, 28, 29p-36p; c-13, 25p, 26-30, 32-35p, 36. **John Buscema** a-9, 12p-14p, 16p; c-4-6p, 12p. **Colan** a-7p, 8p. **Ditko** a-21r. **Everett** a-6i. **G. Kane** a-11p, 15p; c-10p, 11p, 14, 15p, 21p. **McWilliams** a-30i. **Starlin** a-19p; c-16p. **Sutton & Trimpe** a-8. **Tuska** a-5p, 6p, 8p. **Wood** a-1-4.*

ASTRO BOY (TV) (Also see March of Comics No. 285)
August, 1965
Gold Key

1(10151-508) 6.50 20.00 45.00

ASTRO BOY, THE ORIGINAL
Sept, 1987 - Present ($1.50, color)
Now Comics

1 .60 1.80 3.60
2,3 .35 1.00 2.00
4,5 .25 .80 1.60

ASTRO COMICS
1969 - 1979 (Giveaway)
American Airlines (Harvey)

nn-Harvey's Casper, Spooky, Hot Stuff, Stumbo the Giant, Little Audrey, Little Lotta, & Richie Rich reprints .70 2.00 4.00

ATARI FORCE
Jan, 1984 - No. 20, Aug, 1985 (Mando paper)
DC Comics — **Good** **Fine** **Mint**
1-1st app. Tempest, Packrat, Babe, Morphea, & Dart
.25 .75 1.50
2-20 .45 .90
Special 1 (4/86) .25 .80 1.60

NOTE: ***Byrne** c-Special 1i. **Giffen** a-12p, 13i. **Rogers** a-18p, Special 1p.*

A-TEAM, THE (TV)
March, 1984 - No. 3, May, 1984
Marvel Comics Group

1-3 .30 .60

ATLANTIS, THE LOST CONTINENT (See 4-Color No. 1188)

ATLAS (See First Issue Special)

ATOM, THE (See Action, All-American, Brave & the Bold, D.C. Special Series #1, Detective, Showcase, Sword Of The Atom & World's Finest)

ATOM, THE (. . .& the Hawkman No. 39 on)
June-July, 1962 - No. 38, Aug-Sept, 1968
National Periodical Publications

1-Intro Plant-Master 9.30 28.00 65.00
2 4.00 12.00 28.00
3-1st Time Pool story; 1st app. Chronos (origin)
3.50 10.50 24.00
4,5: 4-Snapper Carr x-over 3.00 9.00 21.00
6-10: 7-Hawkman x-over. 8-Justice League, Dr. Light app.
2.15 6.50 15.00
11-15 1.30 4.00 9.00
16-20: 19-Zatanna x-over 1.00 3.00 6.00
21-30: 29-Golden Age Atom x-over .70 2.00 4.00
31-38: 31-Hawkman x-over. 36-G.A. Atom x-over. 37-Intro. Major Mynah; Hawkman cameo .50 1.50 3.00

NOTE: ***Anderson** a-1-11i, 13i; c-inks-1-25, 31-35, 37. **Sid Greene** a-8i-38i. **Gil Kane** a-1p-38p; c-1p-28p, 29, 33p, 34. Pool stories also in 6, 9,12, 17, 21, 27, 35.*

ATOM AGE (See Classics Special)

ATOM-AGE COMBAT
June, 1952 - No. 5, April, 1953; Feb, 1958
St. John Publishing Co.

1 15.00 45.00 105.00
2 10.00 30.00 70.00
3,5: 3-Mayo-a, 6 pgs. 7.00 21.00 50.00
4 (Scarce) 9.00 27.00 63.00
1(2/58-St. John) 6.00 18.00 42.00

ATOM-AGE COMBAT
Nov, 1958 - No. 3, March, 1959
Fago Magazines

1 8.00 24.00 56.00
2,3 5.50 16.50 38.00

ATOMAN
Feb, 1946 - No. 2, April, 1946
Spark Publications

1-Origin Atoman; Robinson/Meskin-a; Kidcrusaders, Wild Bill Hickok, Marvin the Great app. 18.00 54.00 125.00
2: Robinson/Meskin-a 11.50 34.50 80.00

ATOM & HAWKMAN, THE (Formerly The Atom)
No. 39, Oct-Nov, 1968 - No. 45, Oct-Nov, 1969
National Periodical Publications

39-45: 43-1st app. Gentlemen Ghost, origin-44
.40 1.25 2.50

NOTE: ***Sid Greene** a-40i-45i. **Kubert** a-40p, 41p; c-39-45.*

ATOM ANT (TV)
January, 1966 (Hanna-Barbera)
Gold Key

1(10170-601) 3.00 9.00 18.00

ATOMIC ATTACK (Formerly Attack, first series)
No. 5, Jan, 1953 - No. 8, Oct, 1953
Youthful Magazines

	Good	Fine	Mint
5-Atomic bomb-c	11.50	34.50	80.00
6-8	5.70	17.00	40.00

ATOMIC BOMB
1945 (36 pgs.)
Jay Burtis Publications

	Good	Fine	Mint
1-Airmale & Stampy	6.00	18.00	42.00

ATOMIC BUNNY (Formerly Atomic Rabbit)
No. 12, Aug, 1958 - No. 19, Dec, 1959
Charlton Comics

	Good	Fine	Mint
12	3.50	10.50	25.00
13-19	1.70	5.00	12.00

ATOMIC COMICS
1946 (Reprints)
Daniels Publications (Canadian)

	Good	Fine	Mint
1-Rocketman, Yankee Boy, Master Key; bondage-c	7.00	21.00	50.00
2-4	4.30	13.00	30.00

ATOMIC COMICS
Jan, 1946 - No. 4, July-Aug, 1946
Green Publishing Co.

	Good	Fine	Mint
1-Radio Squad by Siegel & Shuster; Barry O'Neal app.; Fang Gow cover-r/Det. Comics	18.00	54.00	125.00
2-Inspector Dayton; Kid Kane by Matt Baker; Lucky Wings, Congo King, Prop Powers (only app.) begin	15.00	45.00	105.00
3,4: 3-Zero Ghost Detective app.; Baker-a(2) each; 4-Kamen-c	8.00	24.00	56.00

ATOMIC MOUSE (See Blue Bird, Giant & Wotalife Comics)
3/53 - No. 54, 6/63; No. 1, 12/84; V2/10, 9/85 - No. 13, ?/86
Capitol Stories/Charlton Comics

	Good	Fine	Mint
1-Origin	7.00	21.00	50.00
2	3.50	10.50	25.00
3-10: 5-Timmy The Timid Ghost app.; see Zoo Funnies	2.65	8.00	18.00
11-13,16-25	1.50	4.50	10.00
14,15-Hoppy The Marvel Bunny app.	1.70	5.00	12.00
26-(68 pages)	2.65	8.00	18.00
27-40: 36,37-Atom The Cat app.	1.15	3.50	8.00
41-54	.45	1.35	3.00
1 (1984)		.40	.80
V2/10 (10/85) -13-Fago-r. No.12(1/86)		.40	.75

ATOMIC RABBIT (Atomic Bunny No. 12 on; see Wotalife Comics)
August, 1955 - No. 11, March, 1958
Charlton Comics

	Good	Fine	Mint
1-Origin; Al Fago-a	6.00	18.00	42.00
2	3.00	9.00	21.00
3-10-Fago-a in most	2.30	7.00	16.00
11-(68 pages)	2.65	8.00	18.00

ATOMIC SPY CASES
Mar-Apr, 1950
Avon Periodicals

	Good	Fine	Mint
1-Painted-c; No Wood-a	11.50	34.50	80.00

ATOMIC THUNDERBOLT, THE
Feb, 1946 - No. 2, April, 1946
Regor Company

	Good	Fine	Mint
1,2: 1-Intro. Atomic Thunderbolt & Mr. Murdo	6.50	20.00	46.00

ATOMIC WAR!
Nov, 1952 - No. 4, April, 1953
Ace Periodicals (Junior Books)

	Good	Fine	Mint
1-Atomic bomb-c	34.00	100.00	235.00
2,3: 3-Atomic bomb-c	23.00	70.00	160.00
4-Used in **POP**, pg. 96 & illo.	24.00	72.00	168.00

ATOM THE CAT (Formerly Tom Cat)
No. 9, Oct, 1957 - No. 17, Aug, 1959
Charlton Comics

	Good	Fine	Mint
9	2.35	7.00	16.00
10,13-17	1.15	3.50	8.00
11-(64pgs)-Atomic Mouse app., 12(100pgs)	2.00	6.00	14.00

ATTACK
May, 1952 - No. 4, Nov, 1952; No. 5, Jan, 1953 - No. 5, Sept, 1953
Youthful Mag./Trojan No. 5 on

	Good	Fine	Mint
1-(1st series)-Extreme violence	5.00	15.00	35.00
2,3	2.35	7.00	16.00
4-Krenkel-a, 7 pgs, Harrison-a. (Becomes Atomic Attack No. 5 on)	2.65	8.00	18.00
5-(No. 1, Trojan, 2nd series)	2.35	7.00	16.00
6-8 (No. 2-4), 5	1.75	5.25	12.00

ATTACK
No. 54, 1958 - No. 60, Nov, 1959
Charlton Comics

	Good	Fine	Mint
54(100 pages)	2.00	6.00	14.00
55-60	.45	1.35	3.00

ATTACK!
1962 - No. 15, 3/75; No. 16, 8/79 - No. 48, 10/84
Charlton Comics

	Good	Fine	Mint
nn(No. 1)-('62) Special Edition	.35	1.00	2.00
2('63), 3(Fall, '64)		.50	1.00
V4No.3(10/66), 4(10/67)-(Formerly Special War Series No. 2; becomes Attack At Sea V4No.5)		.30	.60
1(9/71)		.50	1.00
2-15(3/75): 4-American Eagle app.		.40	.80
16(8/79) - 47		.30	.60
48(10/84)-Wood-r; S&K-c		.40	.80
Modern Comics 13('78)-r		.20	.40

ATTACK!
1975 (39, 49 cents) (36 pages)
Spire Christian Comics (Fleming H. Revell Co.)

	Good	Fine	Mint
nn		.40	.80

ATTACK AT SEA (Formerly Attack!, 1967)
October, 1968
Charlton Comics

	Good	Fine	Mint
V4#5		.30	.60

ATTACK ON PLANET MARS
1951
Avon Periodicals

	Good	Fine	Mint
nn-Infantino, Fawcette, Kubert & Wood-a; adaptation of Tarrano the Conqueror by Ray Cummings	43.00	130.00	300.00

AUDREY & MELVIN (Formerly Little. . .)
No. 62, September, 1974
Harvey Publications

	Good	Fine	Mint
62		.30	.60

AUGIE DOGGIE (TV) (See Whitman Comic Books)
October, 1963 (Hanna-Barbera)
Gold Key

	Good	Fine	Mint
1	2.50	7.50	15.00

Atomic Comics #4, © Green Publishing

Atomic Mouse #27, © CC

Attack #4, © YM

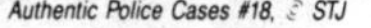
Authentic Police Cases #18, © STJ

The Avengers #48, © MCG

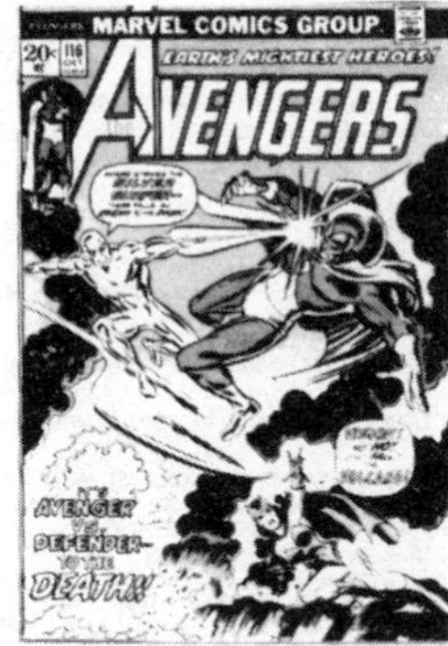

The Avengers #116, © MCG

AURORA COMIC SCENES INSTRUCTION BOOKLET
1974 (Slick paper, 8 pgs.)(6¼x9¾")(in full color)
(Included with superhero model kits)
Aurora Plastics Co.

	Good	Fine	Mint
181-140-Tarzan; Adams-a	.35	1.00	2.00
182-140-Spider-Man; 183-140-Tonto(Gil Kane art); 184-140-Hulk; 185-140-Superman; 186-140-Superboy; 187-140-Batman; 188-140-The Lone Ranger(1974-by Gil Kane); 192-140-Captain America (1975); 193-140-Robin each....		.50	1.00

AUTHENTIC POLICE CASES
Feb, 1948 - No. 38, Mar, 1955
St. John Publishing Co.

	Good	Fine	Mint
1-Hale the Magician by Tuska begins	10.00	30.00	70.00
2-Lady Satan, Johnny Rebel app.	6.00	18.00	42.00
3-Veiled Avenger app.; blood drainage story plus 2 Lucky Coyne stories; used in **SOTI**, illo. from Red Seal #16	21.50	64.00	150.00
4,5: 4-Masked Black Jack app. 5-Late 1930s Jack Cole-a(r); transvestism story	5.70	17.00	40.00
6-Matt Baker-c; used in **SOTI**, illo-"An invitation to learning", r-in Fugitives From Justice #3; Jack Cole-a; also used by the N.Y. Legis. Comm.	21.50	64.00	150.00
7,8,10-14: 7-Jack Cole-a; Matt Baker art begins #8; Vic Flint in #10-14	6.00	18.00	42.00
9-No Vic Flint	5.00	15.00	35.00
15-Drug c/story; Vic Flint app.; Baker-c	6.85	20.50	48.00
16,18,20,21,23	3.50	10.50	24.00
17,19,22-Baker-c	3.70	11.00	26.00
24-28 (All 100 pages): 26-Transvestism	10.00	30.00	70.00
29,30	2.15	6.50	15.00
31,32,37-Baker-c	2.50	7.50	17.50
33-Transvestism; Baker-c	3.00	9.00	21.00
34-Drug-c by Baker	3.50	10.50	24.00
35-Baker c/a(2)	3.35	10.00	23.00
36-Vic Flint strip-r; Baker-c	2.50	7.50	17.50
38-Baker c/a	3.35	10.00	23.00

NOTE: ***Matt Baker** c-7-16, 22, 36-38; a-13, 16. Bondage c-1, 3.*

AVENGER, THE (See A-1 Comics)
1955 - No. 4, Aug-Sept, 1955
Magazine Enterprises

	Good	Fine	Mint
1(A-1 129)-Origin	12.00	36.00	84.00
2(A-1 131), 3(A-1 133), 4(A-1 138)	6.00	18.00	42.00
IW Reprint #9('64)-Reprints #1 (new cover)	1.20	3.50	7.00

NOTE: ***Powell** a-2-4; c-1-4.*

AVENGERS, THE (See Kree/Skrull War Starring..., Marvel Super Action, Marvel Super Heroes('66), Marvel Treas. Ed., Marvel Triple Action, & Tales Of Suspense)
Sept, 1963 - Present
Marvel Comics Group

	Good	Fine	Mint
1-Origin The Avengers (Thor, Iron Man, Hulk, Ant-Man, Wasp)	74.00	185.00	520.00
2	25.00	62.00	175.00
3	16.00	39.00	110.00
4-Revival of Captain America who joins the Avengers	30.00	75.00	210.00
4-Reprint from the Golden Record Comic set	1.50	4.50	10.00
With Record....	4.00	12.50	28.00
5-Hulk leaves	9.40	23.50	66.00
6-10: 6-Intro The Masters of Evil. 8-Intro Kang. 9-Intro Wonder Man who dies in same story	7.00	17.50	50.00
11-15: 15-Death of Zemo	4.50	11.50	32.00
16-19: 16-New Avengers line-up (Hawkeye, Quicksilver, Scarlet Witch join; Thor, Iron Man, Giant-Man & Wasp leave.) 19-Intro. Swordsman; origin Hawkeye	3.40	8.50	24.00
20-22: Wood inks	2.50	6.40	18.00
23-30: 28-Giant-Man becomes Goliath	1.70	5.00	10.00
31-40	1.10	3.30	6.60
41-50: 48-Intro/Origin new Black Knight	.85	2.50	5.00
51,52,54-56: 52-Black Panther joins; Intro The Grim Reaper. 54-Intro new Masters of Evil	.85	2.50	5.00
53-X-Men app.	1.30	4.00	8.00
57-Intro. The Vision	2.35	7.00	14.00
58-Origin The Vision	2.00	6.00	12.00
59-65,68-70: 59-Intro. Yellowjacket. 60-Wasp & Yellowjacket wed. 63-Goliath becomes Yellowjacket; Hawkeye becomes the new Goliath	1.00	3.00	6.00
66,67: Smith-a	1.45	4.40	8.80
71-1st Invaders; Black Knight joins	.90	2.70	5.40
72-80: 80-Intro. Red Wolf	.75	2.20	4.40
81,82,84-91: 87-Origin The Black Panther. 88-Written by Harlan Ellison	.75	2.20	4.40
83-Intro. The Liberators (Wasp, Valkyrie, Scarlet Witch, Medusa & the Black Widow)	.90	2.70	5.40
92-Adams-c	.90	2.70	5.40
93-(52 pgs.)-Adams c/a	4.30	13.00	26.00
94-96-Adams c/a	2.65	8.00	16.00
97-G.A. Capt. America, Sub-Mariner, Human Torch, Patriot, Vision, Blazing Skull, Fin, Angel, & New Capt. Marvel x-over;	1.10	3.20	6.60
98-Goliath becomes Hawkeye; Smith c/a(i)	1.85	5.50	11.00
99-Smith/Sutton-a	1.75	5.25	10.50
100-Smith c/a; featuring everyone who was an Avenger	3.00	9.00	18.00
101-106,108,109: 101-Harlan Ellison scripts	.70	2.10	4.20
107-Starlin-a(p)	.75	2.30	4.60
110,111-X-Men app.	1.05	3.20	6.40
112-1st app. Mantis	.70	2.10	4.20
113-120: 116-118-Defenders/Silver Surfer app.	.55	1.65	3.70
121-130: 123-Origin Mantis	.55	1.60	3.20
131-133,136-140	.45	1.30	2.60
134,135-True origin The Vision	.55	1.60	3.20
141-149: 144-Origin & 1st app. Hellcat	.35	1.15	2.30
150-Kirby-a(r); new line-up begins: Capt. America, Scarlet Witch, Iron Man, Wasp, Yellowjacket, Vision & The Beast	.40	1.25	2.50
151-163: 151-Wonderman returns with new costume	.40	1.15	2.30
164-166-Byrne-a	.70	2.10	4.20
167-170	.35	1.10	2.20
171-180	.30	.85	1.70
181-191-Byrne-a. 181-New line-up: Capt. America, Scarlet Witch, Iron Man, Wasp, Vision, The Beast & The Falcon. 183-Ms Marvel joins. 186-Origin Quicksilver & Scarlet Witch	.45	1.30	2.60
192-199,201,202: Perez-a. 195-1st Taskmaster	.30	.85	1.70
200-Dbl size; Ms. Marvel leaves	.30	.85	1.70
203-220: 211-New line-up: Capt. America, Iron Man, Tigra, Thor, Wasp & Yellowjacket. 213-Yellowjacket leaves. 216-Tigra leaves		.60	1.20
221-230: 221-Hawkeye & She-Hulk join. 227-Capt. Marvel (Female) joins; origins of Ant-Man, Wasp, Giant-Man, Goliath, Yellowjacket, & Avengers		.60	1.20
231-250: 231-Ironman leaves. 232-Starfox (Eros) joins. 234-Origin Quicksilver, Scarlet Witch. 236-New logo. 238-Origin Blackout. 240-Spider-Woman revived		.60	1.20
251-262,264-271,273-290		.60	1.20
263-X-Factor tie-in	.30	.90	1.80
272-Alpha Flight guest	.30	.85	1.70
Annual 7(11/77)-Starlin c/a; Warlock dies	1.05	3.15	6.30

THE AVENGERS (continued)

	Good	Fine	Mint
Annual 8(10/78)	.35	1.10	2.20
Annual 9(10/79)-Newton-a	.30	.85	1.70
Annual 10(10/81)-Golden-p; X-Men cameo	.30	.85	1.70
Annual 11(12/82), 12(1/84), 13(11/84),		.55	1.10
Annual 14(11/85), 15(10/86), 16(10/87)		.70	1.40
Special 1(9/67)	2.65	8.00	16.00
Special 2(9/68)	1.05	3.20	6.40
Special 3(9/69)	1.05	3.20	6.40
Special 4(1/71), 5(1/72)	.75	2.30	4.60
Special 6(11/76)	.55	1.60	3.20
Giant Size 1(8/74)	.70	2.10	4.20
Giant Size 2(11/74)(death of the Swordsman), 3(2/75)	.55	1.60	3.20
Giant Size 4(6/75)(Vision marries Scarlet Witch), 5(12/75)	.35	1.10	2.20

NOTE: ***Austin*** *c(i)-157, 167, 168, 170-77, 181, 183-88, 198-201, Annual 8.* ***Buckler*** *a-101p, 102p, 106p, Gnt.-Size 1p; c-101p, 102p, 106-108p.* ***John Buscema*** *a-41-44p, 46p, 47p, 49, 50, 51-62p, 68-71, 74-77, 79-85, 87-91, 97, 105p, 121p, 124p, 125p, 152, 153p, 255p-279p, 281p-286p; c-41-66, 68-71, 73-91, 97-99, 178, 256p-259p, 261p-279p, 281p-286p.* ***Byrne*** *a-164-66p, 181-191p, 233p, Annual 13, 14p; c-186-190p, 233p, 260.* ***Colan*** *c/a(p)-63-65, 111, 206-208, 210.* ***Guice*** *a-Annual 12p.* ***Kane*** *c-37p, 159p.* ***Kane/Everett*** *c-97.* ***Kirby*** *a-1-8p, Special 3, 4p; c-1-30, 148, 151-158; layouts-14-16.* ***Marcos*** *a(i)-154-177, Annual 8; c-163i.* ***Miller*** *c-193p.* ***Mooney*** *a-86i, 179p, 180p.* ***Nebres*** *a-178i; c-179i.* ***Newton*** *a-204p, Annual 9p.* ***Perez*** *a(p)-141, 144, 148, 154p, 155p, 160p, 161, 162, 167, 168, 170, 171, 194, 195, 196p, 198-202, Annual 6(p), 8; c-160-162p, 164-166p, 170-74p, 181p, 183-85p, 191p, 192p, 194-201p, Annual 8.* ***Starlin*** *c-121.* ***Staton*** *a-127-134i.* ***Tuska*** *a-47i, 48i, 51i, 53i, 54i, 106p, 107p, 135p, 137-140p, 163p.*

AVENGERS, THE (TV)
Nov, 1968 ("John Steed & Emma Peel" cover title) (15 cents)
Gold Key

	Good	Fine	Mint
1-Photo-c	8.00	24.00	56.00

A-V IN 3-D
Dec, 1984 (28 pgs., w/glasses)
Aardvark-Vanaheim

	Good	Fine	Mint
1-Cerebus, Flaming Carrot, Normalman	.75	2.25	4.50

AVIATION ADVENTURES AND MODEL BUILDING
Dec, 1946 - No. 17, Feb, 1947 (True Aviation Adv. . . No. 15)
Parents' Magazine Institute

	Good	Fine	Mint
16,17-Half comics and half pictures	2.65	8.00	18.00

AVIATION CADETS
1943
Street & Smith Publications

	Good	Fine	Mint
	4.85	14.50	34.00

AWFUL OSCAR (Formerly & becomes Oscar with No. 13)
No. 11, June, 1949 - No. 12, Aug, 1949
Marvel Comics

	Good	Fine	Mint
11,12	2.30	7.00	16.00

AXA
Apr, 1987 - Present ($1.75, color)
Eclipse Comics

	Good	Fine	Mint
1,2	.25	.80	1.60

AXEL PRESSBUTTON (Pressbutton No. 5; see Laser Eraser & Pressbutton)
11/84 - No. 6, 7/85 ($1.50-$1.75)
Eclipse Comics

	Good	Fine	Mint
1-r/Warrior (British mag.); Bolland-c; origin Laser Eraser & Pressbutton; Baxter paper	.25	.75	1.50
2-6	.30	.90	1.80

AZTEC ACE
3/84 - No. 15, 9/85 (Baxter paper, 36 pgs. No. 2 on)
Eclipse Comics

	Good	Fine	Mint
1-$2.25 cover (52 pgs.)	.50	1.50	3.00
2,3-$1.50 cover	.35	1.00	2.00
4-15-$1.75-$1.50 cover	.35	1.00	2.00

NOTE: ***N. Redondo*** *a-1i-8i, 10i; c-6-8i.*

BABE (. . . Darling of the Hills, later issues)(Also see Big Shot, Sparky Watts)
June-July, 1948 - No. 11, Apr-May, 1950
Prize/Headline/Feature

	Good	Fine	Mint
1-Boody Rogers-a	7.00	21.00	50.00
2-Boody Rogers-a	5.00	15.00	35.00
3-11-All by Boody Rogers	3.70	11.00	26.00

BABE AMAZON OF OZARKS
No. 5, 1948
Standard Comics

	Good	Fine	Mint
5	3.50	10.50	24.00

BABE RUTH SPORTS COMICS
April, 1949 - No. 11, Feb, 1951
Harvey Publications

	Good	Fine	Mint
1-Powell-a	8.50	26.00	60.00
2-Powell-a	7.00	21.00	50.00
3-11: Powell-a in most	5.00	15.00	35.00

BABES IN TOYLAND (See 4-Color No. 1282 & Golden Pix Story Book ST-3)

BABY HUEY AND PAPA (See Paramount Animated. . .)
May, 1962 - No. 33, Jan, 1968 (Also see Casper The Friendly. .)
Harvey Publications

	Good	Fine	Mint
1	6.75	20.00	40.00
2	3.35	10.00	20.00
3-5	2.00	6.00	12.00
6-10	1.35	4.00	8.00
11-20	.70	2.00	4.00
21-33	.35	1.00	2.00

BABY HUEY DUCKLAND
Nov, 1962 - No. 15, Nov, 1966 (25 cent Giant)
Harvey Publications

	Good	Fine	Mint
1	4.00	12.00	24.00
2-5	1.70	5.00	10.00
6-15	.85	2.50	5.00

BABY HUEY, THE BABY GIANT (Also see Casper, Harvey Hits #22, Harvey Comics Hits #60, & Paramount Animated Comics)
9/56 - No. 97, 10/71; No. 98, 10/72; No. 99, 10/80
Harvey Publications

	Good	Fine	Mint
1-Infinity-c	18.00	56.00	125.00
2	10.00	30.00	70.00
3-Baby Huey takes anti-pep pills	6.00	18.00	42.00
4,5	4.35	13.00	30.00
6-10	2.15	6.50	15.00
11-20	1.35	4.00	9.00
21-40	1.00	3.00	7.00
41-60	.70	2.00	4.00
61-79(12/67)	.35	1.00	2.00
80(12/68) - 98-All Giants	.50	1.50	3.00
99		.50	1.00

BABY SNOOTS (Also see March of Comics No. 359,371,396,401, 419,431,443,450,462,474,485)
Aug, 1970 - No. 22, Nov, 1975
Gold Key

	Good	Fine	Mint
1	.50	1.50	3.00
2-22: 22-Titled Snoots, the Forgetful Elefink		.60	1.20

BACHELOR FATHER (TV)
No. 1332, 4-6/62 - No. 2, 1962
Dell Publishing Co.

Aztec Ace #1, © Eclipse Comics

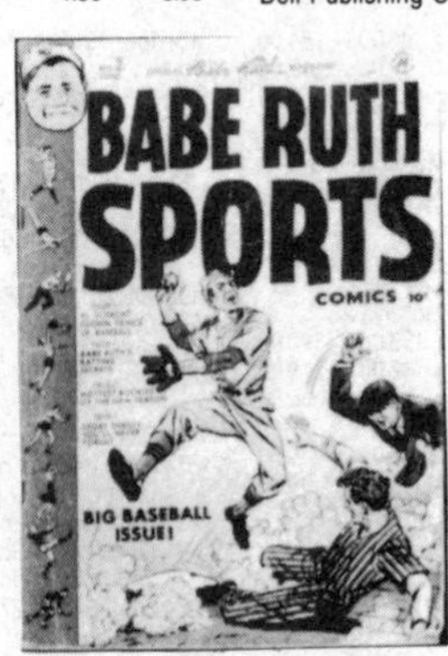

Babe Ruth Sports Comics #2, © HARV

Baby Huey, The Baby Giant #1, © HARV

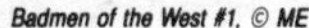
Badmen of the West #1, © ME

Baffling Mysteries #7, © ACE

Bang-Up Comics #1, © Progressive Publ.

BACHELOR FATHER (continued) — Good / Fine / Mint
4-Color 1332 (#1) 3.50 10.50 24.00
2-Written by Stanley 3.50 10.50 24.00

BACHELOR'S DIARY
1949
Avon Periodicals
1(Scarce)-King Features panel cartoons & text-r; pin-up, girl wrestling photos 17.00 51.00 120.00

BADGE OF JUSTICE
No. 22, 1/55 - No. 23, 3/55; 4/55 - No. 4, 10/55
Charlton Comics
22(1/55) 2.30 7.00 16.00
23(3/55), 1 1.50 4.50 10.00
2-4 1.15 3.50 8.00

BADGER, THE
Oct, 1983 - Present (Baxter paper)
Capital Comics/First Comics No. 5 on
1-Badger, Ham the Weather Wizard begin 1.00 3.00 6.00
2-4 .75 2.25 4.50
5(5/85) .70 2.00 4.00
6 .60 1.75 3.50
7-10 .55 1.60 3.20
11-34 .35 1.00 2.00

BADMEN OF THE WEST
1951 (Giant - 132 pages)
Avon Periodicals
1-Contains rebound copies of Jesse James, King of the Bad Men of Deadwood, Badmen of Tombstone; other combinations possible. Issues with Kubert-a.... 15.00 45.00 105.00

BADMEN OF THE WEST! (See A-1 Comics)
1953 - No. 3, 1954
Magazine Enterprises
1(A-1 100)-Meskin-a? 8.50 25.50 60.00
2(A-1 120), 3: 2-Larsen-a 5.00 15.00 35.00

BADMEN OF TOMBSTONE
1950
Avon Periodicals
nn 6.00 18.00 42.00

BAFFLING MYSTERIES (Formerly Indian Braves No. 1-4; Heroes of the Wild Frontier No. 26-on)
No. 5, Nov, 1951 - No. 26, Oct, 1955
Periodical House (Ace Magazines)
5 7.00 21.00 50.00
6,7,9,10: 10-E.C. Crypt Keeper swipe on-c 4.00 12.00 28.00
8-Woodish-a by Cameron 5.00 15.00 35.00
11-24: 24-Last pre-code ish 4.00 12.00 28.00
25-Reprints; surrealistic-c 4.35 13.00 30.00
26-Reprints 2.70 8.25 19.00

NOTE: ***Cameron** a-8,16-18,20-22. **Colan** a-5, 11, 25r/5. **Sekowsky** a-5, 6, 22. Bondage c-20. Reprints in 18(1), 19(1), 24(3).*

BALBO (See Mighty Midget Comics)

BALDER THE BRAVE
Nov, 1985 - No. 4, 1986 (mini-series)
Marvel Comics Group
1-4: Simonson c/a .50 1.00

BALLAD OF HALO JONES, THE
Sept, 1987 - Present
Quality Comics
1-3: Alan Moore scripts begin .60 1.25

BALOO & LITTLE BRITCHES
April, 1968 (Walt Disney)
Gold Key — Good / Fine / Mint
1-From the Jungle Book 1.70 5.00 10.00

BALTIMORE COLTS
1950 (Giveaway)
American Visuals Corp.
Eisner-c 22.00 65.00 154.00

BAMBI (See 4-Color No. 12,30,186, Movie Classics, Movie Comics, and Walt Disney Showcase No. 31)

BAMBI (Disney)
1941, 1942, 1984
K. K. Publications (Giveaways)/Whitman Publ. Co.
1941-Horlick's Malted Milk & various toy stores - text & pictures; most copies mailed out with store stickers on cover 13.00 40.00 90.00
1942-Same as 4-Color 12, but no price (Same as '41 issue?) (Scarce) 18.00 54.00 125.00
1-(Whitman, 1984; 60 cents)-r/4-Color 186 .30 .60

BAMM BAMM & PEBBLES FLINTSTONE (TV)
Oct, 1964 (Hanna-Barbera)
Gold Key
1 1.70 5.00 10.00

BANANA OIL
1924 (52 pages)(Black & White)
MS Publ. Co.
Milt Gross-a; not reprints 9.00 27.00 63.00

BANANA SPLITS, THE (TV) (See March of Comics No. 364)
June, 1969 - No. 8, Oct, 1971 (Hanna-Barbera)
Gold Key
1 .85 2.50 5.00
2-8 .40 1.20 2.40

BAND WAGON (See Hanna-Barbera . . .)

BANG-UP COMICS
Dec, 1941 - No. 3, June, 1942
Progressive Publishers
1-Cosmo Mann & Lady Fairplay begin; Buzz Balmer by Rick Yager in all (origin #1) 32.00 95.00 225.00
2,3 19.00 57.00 132.00

BANNER COMICS (Captain Courageous No. 6)
No. 3, Sept., 1941 - No. 5, Jan, 1942
Ace Magazines
3-Captain Courageous & Lone Warrior & Sidekick Dicky begin 40.00 120.00 280.00
4,5: 4-Flag-c 26.00 78.00 182.00

BARBARIANS, THE
June, 1975
Atlas Comics/Seaboard Periodicals
1-Origin, only app. Andrax; Iron Jaw app. .50 1.00

BARBIE & KEN
May-July, 1962 - No. 5, Nov-Jan, 1963-64
Dell Publishing Co.
01-053-207(#1) 5.00 15.00 35.00
2-5 3.50 10.50 24.00

BARKER, THE
Autumn, 1946 - No. 15, Dec, 1949
Quality Comics Group/Comic Magazine
1 5.00 15.00 35.00
2 2.50 7.50 17.50
3-10 1.70 5.00 12.00

BARKER, THE (continued)

	Good	Fine	Mint
11-14	1.15	3.50	8.00
15-Jack Cole-a(p)	1.70	5.00	12.00

NOTE: ***Jack Cole** art in some issues.*

BARNEY AND BETTY RUBBLE (TV) (Flintstones' Neighbors)
Jan, 1973 - No. 23, Dec, 1976 (Hanna-Barbera)
Charlton Comics

	Good	Fine	Mint
1	1.00	3.00	6.00
2-10	.60	1.80	3.60
11-23	.40	1.20	2.40

BARNEY BAXTER
1938 - 1956
David McKay/Dell Publishing Co./Argo

	Good	Fine	Mint
Feature Books 15(McKay-1938)	15.00	45.00	105.00
4-Color 20(1942)	13.00	40.00	90.00
4,5	6.50	19.50	45.00
1,2(1956-Argo)	2.65	8.00	18.00

BARNEY BEAR HOME PLATE
1979 (49 cents)
Spire Christian Comics (Fleming H. Revell Co.)

	Good	Fine	Mint
		.30	.60

BARNEY BEAR LOST AND FOUND
1979 (49 cents)
Spire Christian Comics (Fleming H. Revell Co.)

	Good	Fine	Mint
nn		.30	.60

BARNEY BEAR OUT OF THE WOODS
1980 (49 cents)
Spire Christian Comics (Fleming H. Revell Co.)

	Good	Fine	Mint
nn		.30	.60

BARNEY BEAR SUNDAY SCHOOL PICNIC
1981 (69 cents)
Spire Christian Comics (Fleming H. Revell Co.)

	Good	Fine	Mint
nn		.30	.60

BARNEY BEAR THE SWAMP GANG!
1980 (59 cents)
Spire Christian Comics (Fleming H. Revell Co.)

	Good	Fine	Mint
nn		.30	.60

BARNEY BEAR WAKES UP
1977 (39 cents)
Spire Christian Comics (Fleming H. Revell Co.)

	Good	Fine	Mint
nn		.30	.60

BARNEY GOOGLE AND SPARK PLUG (See Comic Monthly & Giant Comic Album)
1923 - 1928 (Daily strip reprints; B&W) (52 pages)
Cupples & Leon Co.

	Good	Fine	Mint
1-By Billy DeBeck	14.00	42.00	100.00
2-6	9.00	27.00	63.00

NOTE: *Started in 1918 as newspaper strip; Spark Plug began 1922, 1923.*

BARNEY GOOGLE & SNUFFY SMITH
1942 - April, 1964
Dell Publishing Co./Gold Key

	Good	Fine	Mint
4-Color 19('42)	20.00	60.00	140.00
4-Color 40('44)	11.00	32.00	75.00
Large Feature Comic 11(1943)	11.00	32.00	75.00
1(10113-404)-Gold Key (4/64)	1.50	4.50	9.00

BARNEY GOOGLE & SNUFFY SMITH
June, 1951 - No. 4, Feb, 1952 (Reprints)
Toby Press

	Good	Fine	Mint
1	4.50	13.50	31.50
2,3	2.65	8.00	18.00
4-Kurtzman-a "Pot Shot Pete," 5 pgs.; reprints/John Wayne #5	3.50	10.50	24.00

BARNEY GOOGLE AND SNUFFY SMITH
March, 1970 - No. 6, Jan, 1971
Charlton Comics

	Good	Fine	Mint
1	1.00	3.00	6.00
2-6	.70	2.00	4.00

BARNYARD COMICS (Dizzy Duck No. 32 on)
June, 1944 - No. 31, Sept, 1950; 1957
Nedor/Polo Mag./Standard(Animated Cartoons)

	Good	Fine	Mint
1(nn, 52 pgs.)	7.00	21.00	50.00
2 (52 pgs.)	3.50	10.50	25.00
3-5	2.00	6.00	14.00
6-12,16	1.65	5.00	11.50
13-15,17,21,23,26,27,29-All contain Frazetta text illos	3.00	9.00	21.00
18-20,22,24,25-All contain Frazetta-a & text illos	8.00	24.00	56.00
28,30,31	1.00	3.00	7.00
10(1957)(Exist?)	.50	1.50	4.00

BARRY M. GOLDWATER
March, 1965 (Complete life story)
Dell Publishing Co.

	Good	Fine	Mint
12-055-503: Photo-c	2.35	7.00	14.00

BASEBALL COMICS
Spring, 1949 (Reprinted later as a Spirit section)
Will Eisner Productions

	Good	Fine	Mint
1-Will Eisner c/a	28.00	84.00	195.00

BASEBALL HEROES
1952 (One Shot)
Fawcett Publications

	Good	Fine	Mint
nn (Scarce)	25.00	75.00	175.00

BASEBALL THRILLS
No. 10, Sum, 1951 - No. 3, Sum, 1952 (Saunders painted-c No.1,2)
Ziff-Davis Publ. Co.

	Good	Fine	Mint
10(No. 1)	12.00	36.00	84.00
2-Powell-a(2)(Late Sum, '51)	7.00	21.00	50.00
3-Kinstler c/a	7.00	21.00	50.00

BASICALLY STRANGE (Magazine)
December, 1982 (B&W, $1.95)
JC Comics (Archie Comics Group)

	Good	Fine	Mint
1-(21,000 printed; all but 1,000 destroyed—pages out of sequence).	.30	1.00	2.00
1-Wood, Toth-a; Corben-c. Reprints & new art	.30	1.00	2.00

BASIC HISTORY OF AMERICA ILLUSTRATED
1976 (B&W)
Pendulum Press

07-1999 America Becomes a World Power 1890-1920
07-2251 The Industrial Era 1865-1915
07-226x Before the Civil War 1830-1860
07-2278 Americans Move Westward 1800-1850
07-2286 The Civil War 1850-1876 - Redondo-a
07-2294 The Fight for Freedom 1750-1783
07-2308 The New World 1500-1750
07-2316 Problems of the New Nation 1800-1830
07-2324 Roaring Twenties and the Great Depression 1920-1940
07-2332 The United States Emerges 1783-1800
07-2340 America Today 1945-1976
07-2359 World War II 1940-1945

	Good	Fine	Mint
Softcover			1.50
Hardcover			4.50

Barney Google and Snuffy Smith #1, © TOBY

Barry M. Goldwater #12-055-503, © DELL

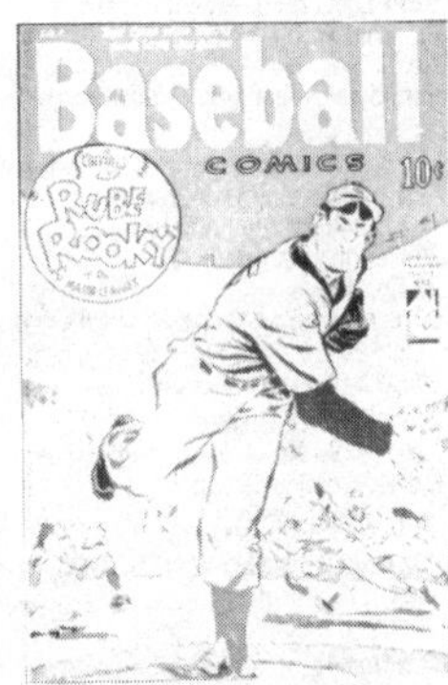

Baseball Comics #1, © Will Eisner

Batman #3, © DC

Batman #45, © DC

Batman #150, © DC

BASIL (. . .the Royal Cat)
Jan, 1953 - No. 4, Sept, 1953
St. John Publishing Co.

	Good	Fine	Mint
1	1.70	5.00	12.00
2-4	.85	2.50	6.00
I.W. Reprint 1		.50	1.00

BAT LASH (See DC Spec. Series #16, Showcase #76 & Weird Western Tales)
Oct-Nov, 1968 - No. 7, Oct-Nov, 1969
National Periodical Publications

	Good	Fine	Mint
1	.25	.80	1.60
2-7		.50	1.00

BATMAN (See Aurora, The Best of DC #2, The Brave & the Bold, Detective, Dynamic Classics, 80-Page Giants, Limited Coll. Ed., DC 100-Page Super Spec., Shadow of the.., 3-D Batman, Untold Legends of.. & World's Finest)

BATMAN
Spring, 1940 - Present
National Periodical Publ./Detective Comics/DC Comics

	Good	Fine	Mint
1-Origin The Batman retold by Bob Kane; see Detective #33 for 1st origin; 1st app. Joker & The Cat (Catwoman); has Batman story without Robin originally planned for Detective #38. This book was created entirely from the inventory of Det. Comics	1200.00	3600.00	8400.00
(Prices vary widely on this book)			
1-Reprint, oversize 13½"x10." **WARNING:** This comic is an exact duplicate reprint of the original except for its size. DC published it in 1974 with a second cover titling it as a **Famous First Edition**. There have been many reported cases of the outer cover being removed and the interior sold as the original edition. The reprint with the new outer cover removed is practically worthless.			
2	357.00	1070.00	2500.00
3-1st Catwoman in costume; 1st Puppetmaster app.	228.00	685.00	1600.00
4	185.00	555.00	1300.00
5-1st app. of the Batmobile with its bat-head front	140.00	420.00	980.00
6-10: 8-Infinity-c	100.00	300.00	700.00
11-Classic Joker-c	85.00	255.00	600.00
12-15: 13-Jerry Siegel, creator of Superman appears in a Batman story	80.00	240.00	560.00
16-Intro Alfred	95.00	265.00	665.00
17-20	50.00	150.00	350.00
21-26,28-30: 22-1st Alfred solo. 25-Only Joker/Penguin team-up	45.00	135.00	315.00
27-Christmas-c	48.00	145.00	335.00
31,32,34-40: 32-Origin Robin retold	30.00	90.00	210.00
33-Christmas-c	35.00	105.00	245.00
41-46: 45-Christmas-c	25.00	75.00	175.00
47-1st detailed origin The Batman	72.00	215.00	505.00
48-1000 Secrets of Bat Cave	28.00	84.00	195.00
49,50: 49-1st Vicki Vale & Mad Hatter. 50-Two-Face impostor app.	25.00	75.00	175.00
51-60: 57-Centerfold is a 1950 calendar	23.00	70.00	160.00
61-Origin Batman Plane II	23.00	70.00	160.00
62-Origin Catwoman	30.00	90.00	210.00
63-73: 68-Two-Face app. 72-Last 52 pgs.	19.00	57.00	132.00
74-Used in **POP**, pg. 90	20.00	60.00	140.00
75-77,79,80	19.00	57.00	132.00
78-(9/53)-Ron Kar, The Man Hunter from Mars story-the 1st lawman of Mars to come to Earth (green skinned)	22.00	65.00	154.00
81-89: 84-Two-Face app. 86-Intro Batmarine (Batman's submarine). 89-Last Pre-Code ish.	18.00	54.00	125.00
90-99: 92-1st app. Bat-Hound	11.50	34.50	80.00
100	36.00	107.00	250.00
101-110: 105-1st Batwoman in Batman	8.50	25.50	60.00
111-120: 113-1st app. Fatman	6.50	19.50	45.00
121-130: 127-Superman cameo. 129-Origin Robin retold; Bondage-c	5.50	16.50	38.00
131-143: Last 10 cent issue. 131-Intro 2nd Batman & Robin series. 133-1st Bat-Mite in Batman. 134-Origin The Dummy. 139-Intro old Bat-Girl	3.70	11.00	26.00
144-150	2.70	8.15	19.00
151-170: 164-New Batmobile; New look & Mystery Analysts series begins	2.00	6.00	12.00
171-Riddler app.(5/65), 1st since 12/48	2.65	8.00	18.00
172-175,177-180	1.15	3.50	7.00
176-80-Pg. Giant G-17	1.35	4.00	8.00
181,183,184,186,188-190: 181-Batman & Robin poster insert; Intro Poison Ivy	.85	2.50	5.00
182,185,187-80 Pg. Gnt. G-24,G-27,G-30	1.00	3.00	6.00
191,192,194-197,199: 197-New Bat-Girl app.	.60	1.80	3.60
193-80-Pg. Giant G-37; Batcave blueprints	.70	2.00	4.00
198-80-Pg. Giant G-43; Origin-r	.70	2.00	4.00
200-Retells origin of Batman & Robin	1.35	4.00	8.00
201,202,204-207,209,210	.40	1.20	2.40
203-80 Pg. Giant G-49	.55	1.70	3.40
208-80 Pg. Giant G-55; New origin Batman by Gil Kane	.55	1.70	3.40
211,212,214-217: 216-Alfred given a new last name-"Pennyworth." (see Det. 96)	.40	1.20	2.40
213-80-Pg. Giant G-61; origin Alfred; new origin Robin	.55	1.70	3.40
218-80-Pg. Giant G-67	.55	1.70	3.40
219-Adams-a	1.05	3.15	6.30
220,221,224-227,229-231	.40	1.20	2.40
222-Beatles take-off	.70	2.00	4.00
223,228,233-80-Pg. Giant G-73,G-79,G-85	.55	1.60	3.20
232-Adams-a; Intro Ras Al Ghul	1.05	3.15	6.30
234,237: Adams-a. 234-52pg. ish begin, end No. 242. 237-GA Batman-r	1.05	3.15	6.30
235,236,239-242: 241-r-Batman #5	.30	.90	1.80
238-DC-8 100 pg. Super Spec.; unpubbed G.A. Atom, Sargon, Plastic Man stories; Doom patrol origin-r; Batman, Legion, Aquaman-r; Adams-c	.40	1.25	2.50
243-245-Adams-a	.70	2.10	4.20
246-250,252,253	.30	.90	1.80
251-Adams-a; Joker app.	.70	2.00	4.00
254-100pg. editions begin	.35	1.10	2.20
255-Adams-a; tells of Bruce Wayne's father who wore bat costume & fought crime	.70	2.00	4.00
256-261-Last 100pg. ish; part-r	.35	1.10	2.20
262-365,367,369,370: 262-68pgs. 266-Catwoman back to old costume. 311-Batgirl reteams w/Batman. 332-Catwoman's 1st solo. 345-New Dr. Death app.	.25	.75	1.50
366-Jason Todd 1st in Robin costume	.50	1.50	3.00
368-1st new Robin in costume (Jason Todd)	.70	2.00	4.00
371-399		.60	1.20
400 ($1.50, 64pgs.)-Dark Knight special; intro by Steven King; Art Adams/Austin-a	.75	2.20	4.40
401-403,407-418: 408-410-New origin Jason Todd (Robin)		.60	1.20
404-Miller scripts begin (end 407); Year 1	.60	1.80	3.60
405,406: Year 1 cont.	.40	1.20	2.40
Annual 1(8-10/61)-Swan-c	11.00	28.00	75.00
Annual 2	4.30	11.00	30.00
Annual 3(Summer, '62)	3.00	7.50	21.00
Annual 4,5	2.15	5.40	15.00
Annual 6,7(7/64)	1.70	4.30	12.00
Annual 8(10/82)		.70	1.40
Annual 9(7/85), 10(8/86), 11('87)	.25	.80	1.60
Pizza Hut giveaway(12/77)-exact r-/of #122, 123		.25	.50
Prell Shampoo giveaway('66)-16 pgs. "The Joker's Practical Jokes" (6-7/8"x3-3/8")	1.00	3.00	6.00

BATMAN (continued)

	Good	Fine	Mint
Special 1(4/84)-Golden c/a(p)	.25	.80	1.60

NOTE: ***Art Adams** a-400p. **Neal Adams** c-200, 203, 210, 217, 219, 220-22, 224-27, 229, 230, 232, 234, 236-41, 243-46, 251, 255. **Burnley** a-10, 12-18, 20, 25, 27; c-28. **Byrne** c-401, Annual 11i. **Colan** a-340p, 343p-45p, 348p-51p, 373p, 383p; c-343p, 345p, 350p. **J. Cole** a-238r. **Giffen** c-354p. **Golden** a-295, 303p. **Grell** a-287, 288p, 289p, 290; c-287-90. **Kaluta** c-242, 248, 253. **Bob Kane** a-1, 2; c-1-5, 7. **G. Kane** a-(R)-254, 255, 259, 261, 353i. **Kubert** a-238r, 400; c-310,319p, 327, 328, 344. **Lopez** a-336p, 337p, 353p; c-272, 311, 313, 314, 318, 321, 353. **Mooney** a-255r. **Newton** a-305, 306, 328p, 331p, 332p, 337p, 338p, 346p, 352-57p, 360p-72p, 374p-378p; c-374p, 378p. **Perez** a-400. **Robinson/Roussos** a-12-17, 20, 22, 24, 25, 27, 28, 31, 33, 37. **Robinson** a-12, 14, 18, 22-32, 34, 36, 37, 255r, 260r, 261r; c-6, 8-10, 12-15, 18, 21, 24, 26, 27, 30, 37, 39. **Simonson** a-300p, 312p, 321p; c-300p, 312p, 366, 413i. **P. Smith** a-Annual 9. **Starlin** c/a-402. **Staton** a-334. **Wrightson** a-265i, 400; c-320r.*

BATMAN (Kellogg's Poptarts comics)
1966 (set of 6) (16 pages)
National Periodical Publications

	Good	Fine	Mint
"The Man in the Iron Mask," "The Penguin's Fowl Play," "The Joker's Happy Victims," "The Catwoman's Catnapping Caper," "The Mad Hatter's Hat Crimes," "The Case of the Batman II" each....	.70	2.00	4.00

NOTE: *All above were folded and placed in Poptarts boxes. **Infantino** art on Catwoman and Joker issues.*

BATMAN AND THE OUTSIDERS (The Advs. of the Outsiders #33 on)(Also see The Outsiders & Brave & The Bold #200)
Aug, 1983 - No. 32, Apr, 1986 (Mando paper No. 5 on)
DC Comics

	Good	Fine	Mint
1-Batman, Halo, Geo-Force, Katana, Metamorpho & Black Lightning begin	.40	1.25	2.50
2-4	.25	.75	1.50
5-(75 cent ish. begin)-New Teen Titans app.	.30	.90	1.80
6-10: 9-Halo begins		.60	1.20
11-20: 11,12-Origin Katana. 18-More facts about Metamorpho's origin		.50	1.00
21-32: 28-31-Lookers origin		.45	.90
Annual 1 (9/84)-Miller/Aparo-c; Aparo-i	.25	.75	1.50
Annual 2 (9/85)-Metamorpho & Sapphire Stagg wed; Aparo-c		.65	1.30

NOTE: ***Aparo** a-1-9, 11, 12p, 16-20; c-1-4, 5i, 6-21. **B. Kane** a-3r. **Layton** a-19i, 20i. **Lopez** a-3p. **Perez** c-5p. **B. Willingham** a-14p.*

BATMAN FAMILY, THE
Sept-Oct, 1975 - No. 20, Oct-Nov, 1978 (No.1-4, 17-on: 68 pages)
(Combined with Detective Comics with No. 481)
National Periodical Publications/DC Comics

	Good	Fine	Mint
1-Origin Batgirl-Robin team-up (The Dynamite Duo); reprints plus one new story begins; Adams-a(r).	.25	.80	1.60
2-5: 3-Batgirl & Robin learn each's i.d.		.40	.80
6-10,14-16: 10-1st revival Batwoman		.30	.60
11-13: Rogers-p. 11-New stories begin; Man-Bat begins	.35	1.00	2.00
17-($1.00 size)-Batman, Huntress begin; Starlin-a		.60	1.20
18-20: Huntress by Staton in all. 20-Origin Ragman retold		.40	.80

NOTE: ***Aparo** a-17; c-11-16. **Austin** a-12i. **Chaykin** a-14p. **Michael Golden** a-15-17, 18-20p. **Grell** a-1; c-1. **Gil Kane** a-2r. **Kaluta** c-17, 19. **Newton** a-13. **Robinson** a-1r ,3i(r), 9r. **Russell** a-18i, 19i. **Starlin** c-18, 20.*

BATMAN MINIATURE (See Batman Kellogg's)

BATMAN RECORD COMIC
1966 (One Shot)
National Periodical Publications

	Good	Fine	Mint
1-With record	4.50	13.50	31.50
Comic only	1.35	4.00	8.00

BATMAN SPECTACULAR (See DC Special Series No. 15)

BATMAN: THE DARK KNIGHT RETURNS
March, 1986 - No. 4, 1986
DC Comics

	Good	Fine	Mint
1-Miller story & a(p); set in the future	4.15	12.50	25.00
1-2nd printing	1.30	4.00	8.00
1-3rd printing	.60	1.75	3.50
2-Carrie Kelly becomes Robin (female)	2.15	6.50	13.00
2-2nd printing	.85	2.50	5.00
2-3rd printing	.50	1.50	3.00
3-Death of Joker	.75	2.25	4.50
3-2nd printing	.60	1.80	3.60
4-Death of Alfred	.70	2.00	4.00
Hardcover, signed & numbered edition ($40.00)(4000 copies)	43.00	130.00	260.00
Hardcover, trade edition	8.35	25.00	50.00
Softcover, trade edition	2.65	8.00	16.00

BATMAN: THE SON OF THE DEMON
Sept, 1987 (80 pgs, hardcover, $14.95)
DC Comics

	Good	Fine	Mint
1	2.85	8.60	20.00
Softcover reprint; new-c ($8.95)	1.70	5.00	10.00

BATMAN VS. THE INCREDIBLE HULK (See DC Special Series No. 27)

BAT MASTERSON (TV)
Aug-Oct, 1959; Feb-Apr, 1960 - No. 9, Nov-Jan, 1961-62
Dell Publishing Co.

	Good	Fine	Mint
4-Color 1013 (8-10/59)	3.50	10.50	24.00
2-9: Gene Barry photo-c on all	2.65	8.00	18.00

BATS (See Tales Calculated to Drive You...)

BATTLE
March, 1951 - No. 70, June, 1960
Marvel/Atlas Comics(FPI No. 1-62/Male No. 63 on)

	Good	Fine	Mint
1	4.50	13.50	31.50
2	2.00	6.00	14.00
3-9: 4-1st Buck Pvt. O'Toole	1.50	4.50	10.00
10-Pakula-a	1.70	5.00	12.00
11-20: 11-Check-a	1.00	3.00	7.00
21,23-Krigstein-a	1.70	5.00	12.00
22,24-36: 36-Everett-a	.85	2.50	6.00
37-Kubert-a (Last precode, 2/55)	1.35	4.00	9.00
38-40,42-48	.70	2.10	4.00
41-Kubert/Moskowitz-a	1.35	4.00	9.00
49-Davis-a	1.70	5.00	12.00
50-54,56-58	.60	2.00	4.00
55-Williamson-a, 5 pgs.	2.35	7.00	16.00
59-Torres-a	1.20	3.50	8.00
60-62: Combat Kelly app.-No. 60,62; Combat Casey app.-No. 61	.50	1.50	3.00
63-65: 63-Ditko-a. 64,65-Kirby-a	1.20	3.50	8.00
66-Kirby, Davis-a	1.35	4.00	9.00
67-Williamson/Crandall-a, 4 pgs; Kirby, Davis-a	2.35	7.00	16.00
68-Kirby/Williamson-a, 4 pgs; Kirby/Ditko-a	2.35	7.00	16.00
69-Kirby-a	1.00	3.00	7.00
70-Kirby/Ditko-a	1.00	3.00	7.00

NOTE: ***Andru** a-37. **Berg** a-8, 14, 60-62. **Colan** a-33. **Everett** a-36, 50, 70; c-56, 57. **Heath** a-6, 9, 13, 31, 69; c-6, 9, 26, 37. **Kirby** c-64-69. **Maneely** a-4, 31; c-4, 61. **Orlando** a-47. **Powell** a-53, 55. **Reinman** a-26, 32. **Robinson** a-9, 39. **Romita** a-26. **Severin** a-28, 32-34, 66-68; c-36. **Sinnott** a-33, 37. **Tuska** a-32. **Woodbridge** a-52, 55.*

BATTLE ACTION
Feb, 1952 - No. 12, 5/53; No. 13, 11/54 - No. 30, 8/57
Atlas Comics (NPI)

	Good	Fine	Mint
1-Pakula-a	4.00	12.00	28.00
2	1.70	5.00	12.00
3,4,6,7,9,10: 6-Robinson c/a	1.15	3.50	8.00
5-Used in **POP**, pg. 93,94	1.35	4.00	9.00

Batman: The Dark Knight #2, © DC

Bat Masterson #2, © ZIV TV Programs

Battle 26, © MCG

Battle Cry #9, © Stanmor Publ.

Battlefront #22, © MCG

Battle Squadron #1, © Stanmor Publ.

BATTLE ACTION (continued)

	Good	Fine	Mint
8-Krigstein-a	1.70	5.00	12.00
11-15 (Last precode, 2/55)	1.00	3.00	7.00
16-26,28,29	.85	2.50	6.00
27,30-Torres-a	1.35	4.00	9.00

NOTE: *Battle Brady app. 5,6,10-12.* ***Check*** *a-11.* ***Everett*** *c-13, 25.* ***Heath*** *a-8; c-21.* ***Maneely*** *a-1.* ***Reinman*** *a-1.* ***Woodbridge*** *a-28,30.*

BATTLE ATTACK
Oct, 1952 - No. 8, Dec, 1955
Stanmor Publications

	Good	Fine	Mint
1	2.50	7.50	18.00
2	1.30	3.85	9.00
3-8: 3-Hollingsworth-a	1.00	3.00	7.00

BATTLE BRADY (Men in Action No. 1-9)
No. 10, Jan, 1953 - No. 14, June, 1953
Atlas Comics (IPC)

	Good	Fine	Mint
10	2.30	7.00	16.00
11-Used in **POP**, pg. 95 plus B&W & color illos.	2.00	6.00	14.00
12-14	1.15	3.50	8.00

BATTLE CLASSICS (See Cancelled Comic Cavalcade)
Sept-Oct, 1978 (44 pages)
DC Comics

	Good	Fine	Mint
1-Kubert-r, new Kubert-c		.40	.80

BATTLE CRY
1952(May) - No. 20, Sept, 1955
Stanmor Publications

	Good	Fine	Mint
1	2.85	8.50	20.00
2	1.50	4.50	10.00
3,5-10: 8-Pvt. Ike begins, ends No. 12,17	1.00	3.00	7.00
4-Classic E.C. swipe	1.50	4.50	10.00
11-Opium-c	1.70	5.00	12.00
12-20	.70	2.00	5.00

NOTE: ***Hollingsworth*** *a-9; c-20.*

BATTLEFIELD (War Adventures on the. . .)
April, 1952 - No. 11, May, 1953
Atlas Comics (ACI)

	Good	Fine	Mint
1-Pakula, Reinman-a	3.50	10.50	24.00
2-5	1.50	4.50	10.00
6-11	.85	2.50	6.00

NOTE: ***Colan*** *a-11.* ***Everett*** *c-8.* ***Heath*** *a-1, 5p; c-2, 9, 11.* ***Ravielli*** *a-11.*

BATTLEFIELD ACTION (Formerly Foreign Intrigues)
No. 16, Nov, 1957 - No. 62, 2-3/66; No. 63, 7/80 - No. 89, 11/84
Charlton Comics

	Good	Fine	Mint
16	.85	2.50	6.00
17,18,20-30	.35	1.00	2.40
19-Check-a	.60	1.80	4.00
31-62(1966)		.30	.60
63-89(1983-'84)		.30	.60

NOTE: ***Montes/Bache*** *a-43,55,62.* ***Glanzman*** *a-87r.*

BATTLE FIRE
April, 1955 -No. 7, 1955
Aragon Magazine/Stanmor Publications

	Good	Fine	Mint
1	1.50	4.50	10.00
2	.70	2.00	5.00
3-7	.60	1.80	4.00

BATTLE FOR A THREE DIMENSIONAL WORLD
May, 1983 (20 pgs., slick paper w/stiff covers, $3.00)
3D Cosmic Publications

	Good	Fine	Mint
nn-Kirby c/a in 3-D; shows history of 3-D	.50	1.50	3.00

BATTLEFRONT
June, 1952 - No. 48, Aug, 1957
Atlas Comics (PPI)

	Good	Fine	Mint
1-Heath-c	4.00	12.00	28.00
2	2.00	6.00	14.00
3-5-Robinson-a(4) in each	1.70	5.00	12.00
6-10: Combat Kelly in No. 6-10	1.50	4.50	10.00
11-22,24-28: Last precode (2/55). Battle Brady in #14,16	.85	2.50	6.00
23-Check-a	1.20	3.50	8.00
29-39	.75	2.25	4.50
40,42-Williamson-a	2.35	7.00	16.00
41,44-47	.85	1.75	3.50
43-Check-a	1.00	3.00	7.00
48-Crandall-a	1.20	3.50	8.00

NOTE: ***Ayers*** *a-19.* ***Berg*** *a-44.* ***Colan*** *a-21, 22, 33.* ***Drucker*** *a-28, 29.* ***Everett*** *a-44.* ***Heath*** *c-23, 27, 29.* ***Maneely*** *c/a-22.* ***Morisi*** *a-42.* ***Morrow*** *a-41.* ***Orlando*** *a-47.* ***Powell*** *a-19, 21, 25, 29, 47.* ***Robinson*** *a-1, 2, 4, 5; c-4, 5.* ***Robert Sale*** *a-19.* ***Severin*** *c-40.* ***Woodbridge*** *a-45, 46.*

BATTLEFRONT
No. 5, June, 1952
Standard Comics

	Good	Fine	Mint
5-Toth-a	3.50	10.50	24.00

BATTLE GROUND
Sept, 1954 - No. 20, Aug, 1957
Atlas Comics (OMC)

	Good	Fine	Mint
1	3.50	10.50	24.00
2-Jack Katz-a	1.70	5.00	12.00
3,4-Last precode (3/55)	1.15	3.50	8.00
5-8,10	.85	2.50	6.00
9-Krigstein-a	1.70	5.00	12.00
11,13,18-Williamson-a in each	2.35	7.00	16.00
12,15-17,19,20	.75	2.25	4.50
14-Kirby-a	1.00	3.00	7.00

NOTE: ***Colan*** *a-11.* ***Drucker*** *a-7, 12, 13.* ***Heath*** *c-5.* ***Orlando*** *a-17.* ***Pakula*** *a-11.* ***Severin*** *a-5, 12, 19.* ***Tuska*** *a-11.*

BATTLE HEROES
Sept, 1966 - No. 2, Nov, 1966 (25 cents)
Stanley Publications

	Good	Fine	Mint
1,2	.30	.80	1.60

BATTLE OF THE BULGE (See Movie Classics)

BATTLE OF THE PLANETS (TV)
6/79 - No. 10, 12/80 (Based on syndicated cartoon by Sandy Frank)
Gold Key/Whitman No. 6 on

	Good	Fine	Mint
1		.40	.80
2-10: Mortimer a-1-4,7-10		.30	.60

BATTLE REPORT
Aug, 1952 - No. 6, June, 1953
Ajax/Farrell Publications

	Good	Fine	Mint
1	1.70	5.00	12.00
2-6	.85	2.50	6.00

BATTLE SQUADRON
April, 1955 - No. 5, Dec, 1955
Stanmor Publications

	Good	Fine	Mint
1	1.50	4.50	10.00
2-5	.70	2.00	5.00

BATTLESTAR GALACTICA (TV)(Also see Marvel Super Spec. #8)
March, 1979 - No. 23, January, 1981
Marvel Comics Group

	Good	Fine	Mint
1		.35	.70
2-23: 1-3-Partial-r		.25	.50

NOTE: ***Austin*** *c-9i, 10i.* ***Golden*** *c-18.* ***Simonson*** *a(p)-4, 5, 11-20, 22, 23; c-4p, 5p, 11p-15p.*

BATTLE STORIES (See X-Mas Comics)
Jan, 1952 - No. 11, Sept, 1953
Fawcett Publications

	Good	Fine	Mint
1-Evans-a	4.00	12.00	28.00
2	1.70	5.00	12.00
3-11	1.35	4.00	9.00

BATTLE STORIES
1963 - 1964
Super Comics

	Good	Fine	Mint
Reprints #10-12,15-18; 15-r-/Amer. Air Forces by Powell	.35	1.00	2.00

BEACH BLANKET BINGO (See Movie Classics)

BEAGLE BOYS, THE (Walt Disney)
11/64; No. 2, 11/65; No. 3, 8/66 - No. 47, 2/79 (See WDC&S #134)
Gold Key

	Good	Fine	Mint
1	2.35	7.00	14.00
2-5	1.35	4.00	8.00
6-10	.85	2.50	5.00
11-20: 11,14,19-r	.50	1.50	3.00
21-47: 27-r	.25	.75	1.50

BEAGLE BOYS VERSUS UNCLE SCROOGE
March, 1979 - No. 12, Feb, 1980
Gold Key

	Good	Fine	Mint
1	.25	.80	1.60
2-12: 9-r		.40	.80

BEANBAGS
Winter, 1951 - No. 2, Spring, 1952
Ziff-Davis Publ. Co. (Approved Comics)

	Good	Fine	Mint
1,2	3.00	9.00	21.00

BEANIE THE MEANIE
1958 - No. 3, May, 1959
Fago Publications

	Good	Fine	Mint
1-3	1.00	3.00	7.00

BEANY AND CECIL (TV) (Bob Clampett's. . .)
Jan, 1952 - 1955; July-Sept, 1962 - No. 5, July-Sept, 1963
Dell Publishing Co.

	Good	Fine	Mint
4-Color 368	8.00	24.00	56.00
4-Color 414,448,477,530,570,635(1/55)	6.00	18.00	42.00
01-057-209	6.00	18.00	42.00
2-5	4.00	12.00	28.00

BEAR COUNTRY (Disney)(See 4-Color No. 758)

BEATLES, THE (Jimmy Olsen 79, Marvel Comics Super Special 4, My Little Margie 54, Not Brand Echh, Strange Tales 130, Summer Love, Teen Confessions 37, Tippy's Friends & Tippy Teen)

BEATLES, LIFE STORY, THE
Sept-Nov, 1964 (35 cents)
Dell Publishing Co.

	Good	Fine	Mint
1-(Scarce)-Stories with color photo pin-ups	25.00	75.00	175.00

BEATLES YELLOW SUBMARINE (See Movie Comics under Yellow. . .)

BEAUTY AND THE BEAST, THE
Jan, 1985 - No. 4, Apr, 1985 (Mini-series)
Marvel Comics Group

	Good	Fine	Mint
1-Dazzler & the Beast		.40	.80
2-4		.40	.80

BEAVER VALLEY (See 4-Color No. 625)

BEDKNOBS AND BROOMSTICKS (See Walt Disney Showcase No. 6 & 50)

BEDLAM!
9/85 - No. 2, 9/85 (B&W-r in color)
Eclipse Comics

	Good	Fine	Mint
1,2-Bissette-a	.30	.90	1.75

BEDTIME STORY (See Cinema Comics Herald)

BEEP BEEP, THE ROAD RUNNER (TV)(Also see Daffy)
7/58 - No. 14, 8-10/62; 10/66 - No. 105, 1983
Dell Publishing Co./Gold Key No. 1-88/Whitman No. 89 on

	Good	Fine	Mint
4-Color 918	2.30	7.00	16.00
4-Color 1008,1046	1.50	4.50	10.00
4(2-4/60)-14(Dell)	1.00	3.00	7.00
1	1.15	3.50	8.00
2-5	.55	1.65	4.00
6-14	.40	1.20	2.80
15-18,20-40	.35	1.00	2.00
19-w/pull-out poster	1.35	4.00	8.00
41-60		.60	1.20
61-105		.40	.80
Kite Fun Book-Giveaway ('67,'71), 16pgs., soft-c, 5x7¼"	.70	2.00	4.00

(See March of Comics No. 351,353,375,387,397,416,430,442,455)

NOTE: 5,8-10,35,53,59-62,68-r; 96-102, 104 ⅓-r.

BEETLE BAILEY (Also see Comics Reading Library & Sarge Snorkel)
No. 459, 5/53 - No. 38, 5-7/62; No. 39, 11/62 - No. 53, 5/66; No. 54, 8/66 - No. 65, 12/67; No. 67, 2/69 - No. 119, 11/76; No. 120, 4/78 - No. 132, 4/80
Dell Publishing Co./Gold Key No. 39-53/King No. 54-66/Charlton No. 67-119/Gold Key No. 120-131/Whitman No. 132

	Good	Fine	Mint
4-Color 469 (No. 1)-By Mort Walker	3.00	9.00	21.00
4-Color 521,552,622	2.00	6.00	14.00
5(2-4/56)-10(5-7/57)	1.50	4.50	10.00
11-20(4-5/59)	1.00	3.00	7.00
21-38(5-7/62)	.70	2.10	5.00
39-53(5/66)	.45	1.35	3.00
54-119 (No. 66 publ. overseas only?)	.50	1.00	1.50
120-132		.50	1.00
Bold Detergent Giveaway('69)-same as regular ish (No. 67) minus price		.40	.80
Cerebral Palsy Assn. Giveaway V2No.71('69)-V2No.73)(No. 1), 1/70, Charlton		.40	.80
Giant Comic Album(1972, 59 cents, 11x14") Color cover, B&W interior, Modern Promotions (r)		.40	.80
Red Cross Giveaway, 16pp, 5x7", 1969, paper-c		.40	.80

BEE 29, THE BOMBARDIER
Feb, 1945
Neal Publications

	Good	Fine	Mint
1-(Funny animal)	4.00	12.00	28.00

BEHIND PRISON BARS
1952
Realistic Comics (Avon)

	Good	Fine	Mint
1-Kinstler-c	12.00	36.00	84.00

BEHOLD THE HANDMAID
1954 (Religious) (25 cents with a 20 cent sticker price)
George Pflaum

	Good	Fine	Mint
	4.00	12.00	28.00

BELIEVE IT OR NOT (See Ripley's. . .)

BEN AND ME (See 4-Color No. 539)

BEN BOWIE AND HIS MOUNTAIN MEN
1952 - No. 17, Nov-Jan, 1958-59
Dell Publishing Co.

	Good	Fine	Mint
4-Color 443 (No. 1)	2.65	8.00	18.00
4-Color 513,557,599,626,657	1.70	5.00	12.00
7(5-7/56)-11: 11-Intro/origin Yellow Hair	1.30	4.00	9.00

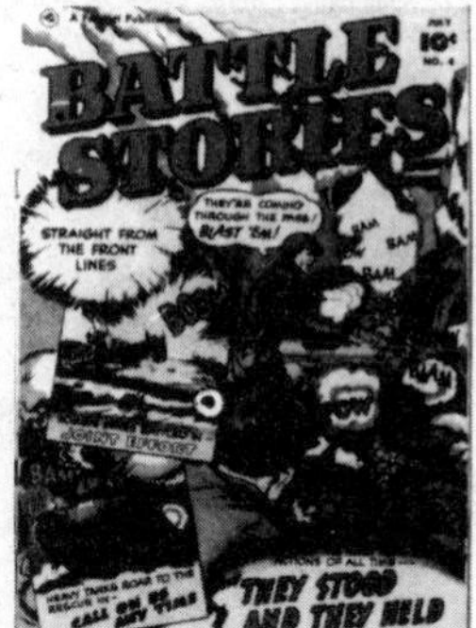

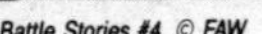
Battle Stories #4, © FAW

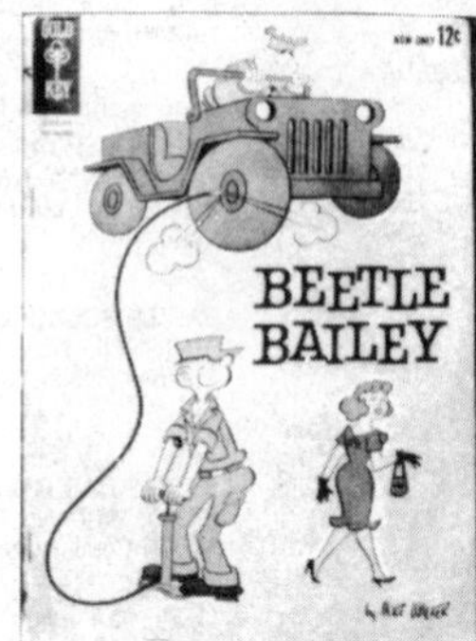

Beetle Bailey #39, © KING

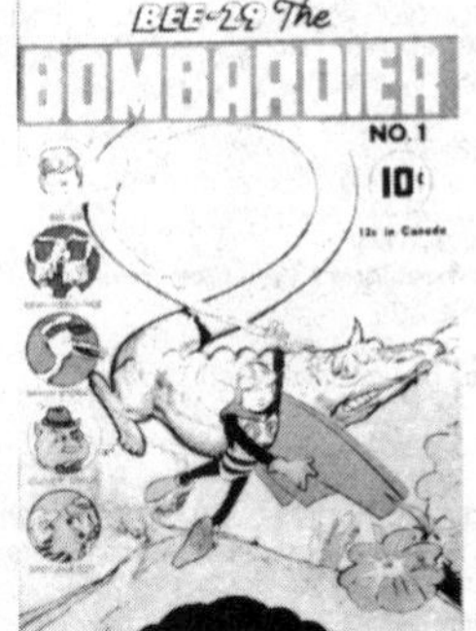

Bee 29, the Bombardier #1, © Neal Publ.

Ben Casey #5, © Bing Crosby Prod.

The Berrys #1, © Argo Publ.

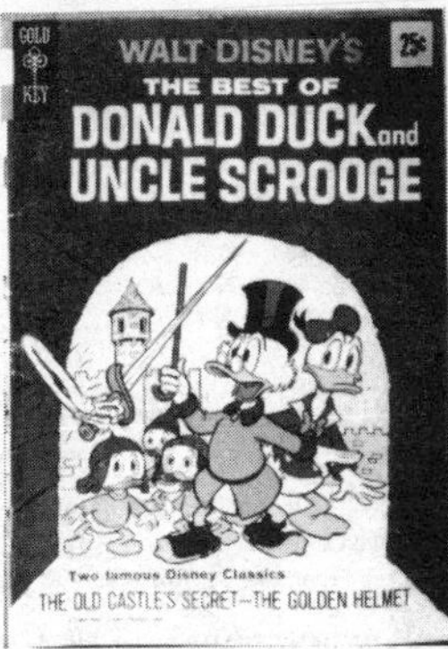

The Best of Donald Duck & U. S. #1, © WDC

BEN BOWIE (continued)

	Good	Fine	Mint
12-17	1.00	3.00	7.00

BEN CASEY (TV)
June-July, 1962 - No. 10, June-Aug, 1965 (Photo-c)
Dell Publishing Co.

12-063-207	2.00	6.00	14.00
2(10/62)-10	1.30	4.00	9.00

BEN CASEY FILM STORY (TV)
November, 1962 (25 cents) (Photo-c)
Gold Key

30009-211-All photos	4.00	12.00	28.00

BENEATH THE PLANET OF THE APES (See Movie Comics)

BEN FRANKLIN KITE FUN BOOK
1975, 1977 (16 pages; 5-1/8"x6-5/8")
Southern Calif. Edison Co./PG&E('77)

	.35	1.00	2.00

BEN HUR (See 4-Color No. 1052)

BEN ISRAEL
1974 (39 cents)
Logos International

		.50	1.00

BEOWULF (See First Comics Graphic Novel)
April-May, 1975 - No. 6, Feb-Mar, 1976
National Periodical Publications

1		.45	.90
2-6		.25	.50

BERNI WRIGHTSON, MASTER OF THE MACABRE
July, 1983 - No. 5, Nov, 1984 ($1.50; Baxter paper)
Pacific Comics/Eclipse Comics No. 5

1-Wrightson c/a-r begins	.30	1.00	2.00
2-5	.25	.75	1.50

BERRYS, THE
May, 1956
Argo Publ.

1-Reprints daily & Sunday strips & daily Animal Antics by Ed Nofziger	1.85	5.50	13.00

BEST COMICS
Nov, 1939 - 1940 (large size, reads sideways)
Better Publications

1-(Scarce)-Red Mask begins	25.00	75.00	175.00
2-4: 4-Cannibalism sty	15.00	45.00	105.00

BEST FROM BOY'S LIFE, THE
Oct, 1957 - No. 5, Oct, 1958 (35 cents)
Gilberton Company

1-Space Conquerors & Kam of the Ancient Ones app.; also No. 3	3.00	9.00	18.00
2,3,5	1.30	4.00	9.00
4-L.B. Cole-a	1.70	5.00	12.00

BEST LOVE (Formerly Sub-Mariner No. 32)
No. 33, Aug, 1949 - No. 36, April, 1950 (Photo-c 33-35)
Marvel Comics (MPI)

33-Kubert-a	3.50	10.50	24.00
34	1.70	5.00	12.00
35,36-Everett-a	2.65	8.00	18.00

BEST OF BUGS BUNNY, THE
Oct, 1966 - No. 2, Oct, 1968
Gold Key

1-Giant	1.50	4.50	12.00
2	1.00	3.00	6.00

BEST OF DC, THE (Blue Ribbon Digest) (See Limited Coll. Ed. C-52)
9-10/79 - No. 71, 4/86 (100-148 pgs; all reprints)
DC Comics

	Good	Fine	Mint
1-17,19-34,36-71		.40	.80
18-The New Teen Titans	.25	.80	1.60
35-The Year's Best Comics Stories(148pgs.)		.60	1.20

NOTE: **Adams** a-26, 51. **Aparo** a-9, 14, 26, 30; c-9, 14, 26. **Austin** a-51i. **Buckler** a-40p; c-22. **Giffen** a-50, 52; c-33p. **Grell** a-33p. **Grossman** a-37. **Heath** a-26. **Kaluta** a-40. **G. Kane** c-40, 44. **Kubert** a-21, 26. **Layton** a-21. **S. Mayer** c-29, 37, 41, 43, 47; a-28, 29, 37, 41, 43, 47, 58, 65, 68. **Moldoff** c-64p. **Morrow** a-40; c-40. **W. Mortimer** a-39p. **Newton** a-5, 51. **Perez** a-24, 50p; c-18, 21, 23. **Rogers** a-14, 51p. **Spiegle** a-52. **Starlin** a-51. **Staton** a-5, 21. **Tuska** a-24. **Wolverton** a-60. **Wood** a-60, 63; c-60, 63. **Wrightson** a-60. New art in No. 14, 18, 24.

BEST OF DENNIS THE MENACE, THE
Summer, 1959 - No. 5, Spring, 1961 (100 pages)
Hallden/Fawcett Publications

1 (all reprints; Wiseman-a)	2.00	6.00	14.00
2-5	1.30	4.00	9.00

BEST OF DONALD DUCK, THE
Nov, 1965 (36 pages)
Gold Key

1-Reprints 4-Color 223 by Barks	5.00	15.00	30.00

BEST OF DONALD DUCK & UNCLE SCROOGE, THE
Nov, 1964 - No. 2, Sept, 1967 (25 cent giant)
Gold Key

1(30022-411)('64)-Reprints 4-Color 189 & 408 by Carl Barks No. 189-c redrawn by Barks	6.00	18.00	36.00
2(30022-709)('67)-Reprints 4-Color 256 & "Seven Cities of Cibola" & U.S. 8 by Barks	5.00	15.00	30.00

BEST OF HORROR AND SCIENCE FICTION COMICS
1987 ($2.00, color)
Bruce Webster

1-Wolverton, Frazetta, Powell-r	.35	1.00	2.00

BEST OF MARMADUKE, THE
1960 (a dog)
Charlton Comics

1-Brad Anderson's strip reprints	.60	1.80	4.20

BEST OF MS. TREE, THE
1987 - No. 4, 1988 ($2.00, mini-series)
Pyramid Comics

1-3	.35	1.00	2.00

BEST OF THE WEST (See A-1 Comics)
1951 - No. 12, April-June, 1954
Magazine Enterprises

1(A-1 42)-Ghost Rider, Durango Kid, Straight Arrow, Bobby Benson begin	17.00	51.00	120.00
2(A-1 46)	8.50	25.50	60.00
3(A-1 52), 4(A-1 59), 5(A-1 66)	7.00	21.00	50.00
6(A-1 70), 7(A-1 76), 8(A-1 81), 9(A-1 85), 10(A-1 87), 11(A-1 97), 12(A-1 103)	5.00	15.00	35.00

NOTE: **Borth** a-12. **Guardineer** a-5, 12. **Powell** a-1,12.

BEST OF UNCLE SCROOGE & DONALD DUCK, THE
November, 1966 (25 cents)
Gold Key

1(30030-611)-Reprints part 4-Color 159 & 456 & Uncle Scrooge 6,7 by Carl Barks	5.00	15.00	30.00

BEST OF WALT DISNEY COMICS, THE
1974 (In color; $1.50; 52 pages) (Walt Disney)
8½x11" cardboard covers; 32,000 printed of each
Western Publishing Co.

96170-Reprints 1st two stories less 1 pg. each from 4-Color 62	1.00	3.00	7.00

BEST OF WALT DISNEY (continued) **Good Fine Mint**

96171-Reprints Mickey Mouse and the Bat Bandit of Inferno Gulch from 1934 (strips) by Gottfredson 1.00 3.00 7.00

96172-Reprints Uncle Scrooge 386 & two other stories 1.00 3.00 7.00

96173-Reprints "Ghost of the Grotto" (from 4-Color 159) & "Christmas on Bear Mtn." (from 4-Color 178) 1.00 3.00 7.00

BEST ROMANCE
No. 5, Feb-Mar, 1952 - No. 7, Aug, 1952
Standard Comics (Visual Editions)

5-Toth-a 4.00 12.00 28.00
6,7-Photo-c 1.50 4.50 10.00

BEST SELLER COMICS (See Tailspin Tommy)

BEST WESTERN (Formerly Terry Toons?) (Western Outlaws & Sheriffs No. 60 on)
No. 58, June, 1949 - No. 59, Aug, 1949
Marvel Comics (IPC)

58,59-Black Rider, Kid Colt, Two-Gun Kid app. 4.00 12.00 28.00

BETTY AND HER STEADY (Going Steady with Betty No. 1)
No. 2, Mar-Apr, 1950
Avon Periodicals

2 4.50 13.50 31.50

BETTY AND ME
Aug, 1965 - Present
Archie Publications

1 6.00 18.00 36.00
2 3.00 9.00 18.00
3-5: 3-Origin Superteen. Superteen in new costume No. 4-7; dons new helmet No. 5, ends No. 8 2.00 6.00 12.00
6-10 .85 2.50 5.00
11-30 .35 1.00 2.00
31-55 (52 pages No. 36-55) .50 1.00
56-164 .30 .60

BETTY AND VERONICA (Also see Archie's Girls. . .)
June, 1987 - Present
Archie Enterprises

1-8 .40 .75

BETTY & VERONICA ANNUAL DIGEST (. . .Digest Mag. #2-4; . . .Comics Digest Mag. #5 on)
November, 1980 - Present ($1.00 - 1.25)
Archie Publications

1, 2(11/81-Katy Keene sty), 3(8/82), 4-6(11/83), 7-29('87) .40 .80

BETTY & VERONICA CHRISTMAS SPECTACULAR (See Archie Giant Series Mag. #159, 168, 180, 191, 204, 217, 229, 241, 453, 465, 477, 489, 501, 513, 525, 536, 547, 558, 568)

BETTY & VERONICA DOUBLE DIGEST MAGAZINE
1987 - Present (Digest size, 256 pgs., $2.25)
Archie Enterprises

1-5 .35 1.10 2.25

BETTY & VERONICA SPECTACULAR (See Archie Giant Series Mag. #11, 16, 21, 26, 32, 138, 145, 153, 162, 173, 184, 197, 201, 210, 214, 221, 226, 234, 238, 246, 250, 458, 462, 470, 482, 486, 494, 498, 506, 510, 518, 522, 526, 530, 537, 552, 559, 563, 569, 575)

BETTY & VERONICA SUMMER FUN (See Archie Giant Series Mag. #8, 13, 18, 23, 28, 34, 140, 147, 155, 164, 175, 187, 199, 212, 224, 236, 248, 460, 484, 496, 508, 520, 529, 539, 550, 561)

BETTY BOOP IN 3-D
Sept, 1986
Blackthorne Publ.

Good Fine Mint
1 .40 1.25 2.50

BETTY'S DIARY (See Archie Giant Series Mag. No. 555)
April, 1986 - Present
Archie Enterprises

1-15 .40 .75

BEVERLY HILLBILLIES (TV)
4-6/63 - No. 18, 8/67; No. 19; No. 20, 10/70; No. 21, Oct, 1971
Dell Publishing Co.

1 4.35 13.00 30.00
2 2.15 6.50 15.00
3-10 1.70 5.00 12.00
11-21 1.35 4.00 8.00

NOTE: *No. 1,2,3,5,8-14,17,18,20,21 are photo covers.*

BEWARE (Formerly Fantastic; Chilling Tales No. 13 on)
No. 10, June, 1952 - No. 12, Oct, 1952
Youthful Magazines

10-Pit & the Pendulum adaptation; Wildey, Harrison-a; atom bomb-c 8.50 25.50 60.00
11-Harrison-a; Ambrose Bierce adapt. 6.00 18.00 42.00
12-Used in **SOTI**, pg. 388; Harrison-a 7.00 21.00 50.00

BEWARE
No. 13, 1/53 - No. 13, 1/55; No. 14, 3/55, No. 15, 5/55
Trojan Magazines No. 13-16,5-13/Merit Publ. No. 14,15

13(#1)-Harrison-a 8.50 25.50 60.00
14(#2) 6.00 18.00 42.00
15,16(#3,4)-Harrison-a 5.00 15.00 35.00
5,9,12,13 5.00 15.00 35.00
6-Ill. in **SOTI**-"Children are first shocked and then desensitized by all this brutality." Corpse on cover swipe/V.O.H. #26; girl on cover swipe/Advs. Into Darkness #10 12.00 36.00 84.00
7,8-Check-a 6.00 18.00 42.00
10-Frazetta/Check-c; Disbrow, Check-a 25.00 75.00 175.00
11-Disbrow-a; heart torn out, blood drainage 6.00 18.00 42.00
14-Krenkel/Harrison-c; dismemberment, severed head panels 5.50 16.50 38.00
15-Harrison-a 5.00 15.00 35.00

NOTE: ***Fass** a-6; c-6, 11. **Hollingsworth** a-16(4),9; c-16(4),8,9. **Kiefer** a-6,10.*

BEWARE! (Tomb of Darkness No. 9 on)
March, 1973 - No. 8, May, 1974
Marvel Comics Group

1-Everett-c .30 .60
2-8: 6-Tuska-a. 7-Torres r-/Mystical Tales #7 .20 .40

BEWARE TERROR TALES
May, 1952 - No. 8, July, 1953
Fawcett Publications

1-E.C. art swipe/Haunt of Fear 5 & Vault of Horror 26 7.00 21.00 50.00
2 4.35 13.00 30.00
3-8: 8-Tothish-a 3.50 10.50 24.00

NOTE: ***Andru** a-2. **Bernard Bailey** a-1; c-1-5. **Powell** a-1, 2, 8. **Sekowsky** a-2.*

BEWARE THE CREEPER (See Adventure, Brave & the Bold, First Issue Special, Showcase, and World's Finest)
May-June, 1968 - No. 6, March-April, 1969
National Periodical Publications

1 .85 2.50 5.00
2-6 .70 2.00 4.00

NOTE: ***Ditko** a-1-4, 5p; c-1-5. **G. Kane** c-6. **Sparling** a-6p.*

BEWITCHED (TV)
4-6/65 - No. 11, 10/67; No. 12 - No. 14, Oct, 1969
Dell Publishing Co.

Beverly Hillbillies #21, © Filmways TV Prod.

Beware #11, © YM

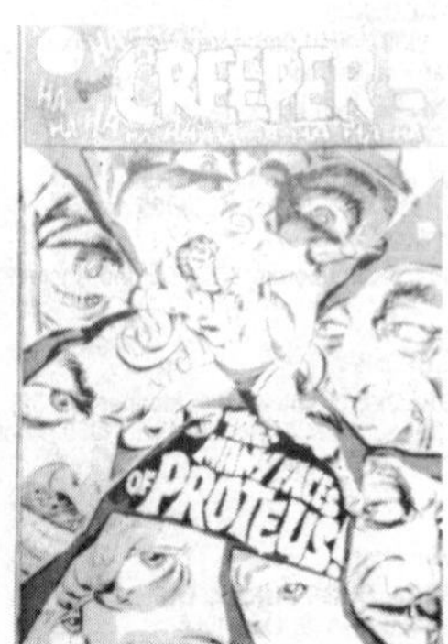

Beware the Creeper #2, © DC

Bewitched #11, © Screen Gems

The Beyond #1, © ACE

Big Shot Comics #14, © CCG

BEWITCHED (continued)

	Good	Fine	Mint
1	4.35	13.00	30.00
2	2.65	8.00	18.00
3-14: Photo-c #3-13	1.70	5.00	12.00

BEYOND, THE
Nov, 1950 - No. 30, Jan, 1955
Ace Magazines

	Good	Fine	Mint
1-Bakerish-a(p)	11.00	32.00	75.00
2-Bakerish-a(p)	6.00	18.00	42.00
3-10: 10-Woodish-a by Cameron	4.35	13.00	30.00
11-17,19,20	3.00	9.00	21.00
18-Used in **POP**, pgs. 81,82	3.50	10.50	24.00
21-26,28-30	2.65	8.00	18.00
27-Used in **SOTI**, pg. 111	3.00	9.00	21.00

NOTE: ***Cameron*** *a-10, 11p, 12p, 15, 20-27, 30; c-20.* ***Colan*** *a-6, 13, 17.* ***Sekowsky*** *a-2, 3, 5, 7, 11, 14, 27r. No. 1 was to appear as Challenge of the Unknown No. 7.*

BEYOND THE GRAVE
7/75 - No. 6, 6/76; No. 7, 1/83 - No. 17, 10/84
Charlton Comics

	Good	Fine	Mint
1-Ditko-a	.30	.80	1.60
2,4-6-Ditko-a		.60	1.20
3-No Ditko-a		.30	.60
7-17: ('83-'84) Reprints		.30	.60
Modern Comics Reprint 2('78)		.20	.40

NOTE: ***Ditko*** *c-2,3,6.* ***Sutton*** *c-15.*

BIBLE TALES FOR YOUNG FOLK (. . .Young People No. 3-5)
Aug, 1953 - No. 5, Mar, 1954
Atlas Comics (OMC)

	Good	Fine	Mint
1	5.50	16.50	38.00
2-Everett, Krigstein-a	4.50	13.50	31.50
3-5	3.00	9.00	21.00

BIG ALL-AMERICAN COMIC BOOK, THE
1944 (One Shot) (132 pages)
All-American/National Periodical Publ.

	Good	Fine	Mint
1-Wonder Woman, Green Lantern, Flash, The Atom, Wildcat, Scribbly, The Whip, Ghost Patrol, Hawkman by Kubert (1st on Hawkman), Hop Harrigan, Johnny Thunder, Little Boy Blue, Mr. Terrific, Mutt & Jeff app.; Sargon on cover only	172.00	515.00	1200.00

BIG BOOK OF FUN COMICS (1st DC Annual)
Spring, 1936 (52 pages, large size) (1st comic book annual)
National Periodical Publications

	Good	Fine	Mint
1 (Very rare)-r-/New Fun No. 1-5	375.00	1125.00	2625.00

BIG BOOK ROMANCES
February, 1950(no date given) (148 pages)
Fawcett Publications

	Good	Fine	Mint
1-Contains remaindered Fawcett romance comics - several combinations possible	12.00	36.00	84.00

BIG BOY (See Adventures of the. . .)

BIG CHIEF WAHOO
Wint?, 1941-42 No. 23, 1945?
Eastern Color Printing/George Dougherty

	Good	Fine	Mint
1-Newspaper reprints	16.00	48.00	110.00
2-Steve Roper app.	8.00	24.00	56.00
3-5	5.00	15.00	35.00
6-10	4.00	12.00	28.00
11-23	3.00	9.00	21.00

NOTE: *Kerry Drake in some issues.*

BIG CIRCUS, THE (See 4-Color No. 1036)

BIG COUNTRY, THE (See 4-Color No. 946)

BIG DADDY ROTH
Oct-Nov, 1964 - No. 4, Apr-May, 1965 (Magazine; 35 cents)
Millar Publications

	Good	Fine	Mint
1-Toth-a	6.00	18.00	42.00
2-4-Toth-a	4.50	13.50	31.50

BIG HERO ADVENTURES (See Jigsaw)

BIG JIM'S P.A.C.K.
No date (16 pages)
Mattel, Inc. (Marvel Comics)

	Good	Fine	Mint
Giveaway with Big Jim doll		.15	.30

BIG JOHN AND SPARKIE (Formerly Sparkie, Radio Pixie)
1952
Ziff-Davis Publ. Co.

	Good	Fine	Mint
4	5.00	15.00	35.00

BIG LAND, THE (See 4-Color No. 812)

BIG RED (See Movie Comics)

BIG SHOT COMICS
May, 1940 - No. 104, Aug, 1949
Columbia Comics Group

	Good	Fine	Mint
1-Intro. Skyman; The Face (Tony Trent), The Cloak (Spy Master), Marvelo, Monarch of Magicians, Joe Palooka, Charlie Chan, Tom Kerry, Dixie Dugan, Rocky Ryan begin	54.00	160.00	375.00
2	24.00	72.00	170.00
3-The Cloak called Spy Chief; Skyman-c	20.00	60.00	140.00
4,5	18.00	54.00	125.00
6-10	14.50	43.50	100.00
11-14: 14-Origin Sparky Watts	12.00	36.00	84.00
15-Origin The Cloak	13.00	40.00	90.00
16-20	8.00	24.00	56.00
21-30: 29-Intro. Capt. Yank; Bo (a dog) newspaper strip reprints by Frank Beck begins, ends #104	6.00	18.00	42.00
31-40: 32-Vic Jordan newspaper strip reprints begin, ends #52	5.00	15.00	35.00
41-50: 42-No Skyman. 50-Origin The Face retold	4.00	12.00	28.00
51-60	3.50	10.50	24.00
61-70: 63 on-Tony Trent, the Face	3.00	9.00	21.00
71-80: 73-The Face cameo. 74,80: The Face app. in Tony Trent. 78-Last Charlie Chan strip reprints	2.65	8.00	18.00
81-90: 85-Tony Trent marries Babs Walsh	2.00	6.00	14.00
91-99,101-104: 69-94-Skyman in Outer Space	1.70	5.00	12.00
100	2.15	6.50	15.00

NOTE: ***Mart Bailey*** *art on "The Face"-No. 1-104.* ***Guardineer*** *a-5. Sparky Watts by* ***Boody Rogers****-No. 14-42, 77-104, (by others No. 43-76). Others than Tony Trent wear "The Face" mask in No. 46-63, 93. Skyman by* ***Ogden Whitney****-No. 1, 2, 4, 12-37, 49, 70-101. Skyman covers-No. 1, 6, 10, 11, 14, 16, 20, 27, 89, 95, 100.*

BIG TEX
June, 1953
Toby Press

	Good	Fine	Mint
1-Contains (3) John Wayne stories-r with name changed to Big Tex	3.00	9.00	21.00

BIG-3
Fall, 1940 - No. 7, Jan, 1942
Fox Features Syndicate

	Good	Fine	Mint
1-Blue Beetle, The Flame, & Samson begin	62.00	185.00	435.00
2	27.00	81.00	190.00
3-5	22.00	65.00	154.00
6-Last Samson; bondage-c	19.00	57.00	132.00
7-V-Man app.	19.00	57.00	132.00

BIG TOP COMICS, THE
1951 (no month)
Toby Press

	Good	Fine	Mint
1,2	2.00	6.00	14.00

BIG TOWN (Radio/TV)
Jan, 1951 - No. 50, Mar-Apr, 1958 (No. 1-9, 52pgs.)
National Periodical Publications

	Good	Fine	Mint
1-Dan Barry-a begins	17.00	51.00	120.00
2	8.00	24.00	56.00
3-10	5.00	15.00	35.00
11-20	3.00	9.00	21.00
21-31: Last pre-code (1-2/55)	2.00	6.00	14.00
32-50	1.50	4.50	10.00

BIG VALLEY, THE (TV)
6/66 - No. 5, 10/67; No. 6, 10/69
Dell Publishing Co.

	Good	Fine	Mint
1: Photo-c #1-5	2.65	8.00	18.00
2-6: 6 r-/#1	1.30	4.00	9.00

BILL BARNES COMICS (. . . America's Air Ace Comics No. 2 on)
(Air Ace V2No.1 on; also see Shadow Comics)
Oct, 1940(No. month given) - No. 12, Oct, 1943
Street & Smith Publications

	Good	Fine	Mint
1-23 pgs.-comics; Rocket Rooney begins	28.00	84.00	195.00
2-Barnes as The Phantom Flyer app.; Tuska-a	17.00	51.00	120.00
3-5	14.50	43.50	100.00
6-12	10.00	30.00	70.00

BILL BATTLE, THE ONE MAN ARMY (Also see Master No. 133)
Oct, 1952 - No. 4, Apr, 1953 (All photo-c)
Fawcett Publications

	Good	Fine	Mint
1	2.35	7.00	16.00
2	1.15	3.50	8.00
3,4	1.00	3.00	7.00

BILL BOYD WESTERN (Movie star; see Hopalong Cassidy & Western Hero)
Feb, 1950 - No. 23, June, 1952 (36pgs., 1-3,7,11,14-on)
Fawcett Publications

	Good	Fine	Mint
1-Bill Boyd & his horse Midnite begin; photo front/back-c	16.00	48.00	110.00
2-Painted-c	11.50	34.50	80.00
3-Photo-c begin, end #23; last photo back-c	10.00	30.00	70.00
4-6(52pgs.)	8.00	24.00	56.00
7,11(36pgs.)	6.50	19.50	45.00
8-10,12,13(52pgs.)	7.00	21.00	50.00
14-22	5.50	16.50	38.50
23-Last issue	6.00	18.00	42.00

BILL BUMLIN (See Treasury of Comics No. 3)

BILL ELLIOTT (See Wild Bill Elliott)

BILL STERN'S SPORTS BOOK
Spring-Summer, 1951 - V2No.2, Winter, 1952
Ziff-Davis Publ. Co.(Approved Comics)

	Good	Fine	Mint
V1#10(1951)	5.00	15.00	35.00
2(Sum'52-reg. size)	3.50	10.50	24.00
V2#2(1952,96 pgs.)-Krigstein, Kinstler-a	7.00	21.00	50.00

BILLY AND BUGGY BEAR
1958; 1964
I.W. Enterprises/Super

	Good	Fine	Mint
I.W. Reprint #1(early Timely funny animal), #7(1958)	.35	1.00	2.00
Super Reprint #10(1964)	.35	1.00	2.00

BILLY BUCKSKIN WESTERN (2-Gun Western No. 4)
Nov, 1955 - No. 3, March, 1956
Atlas Comics (IMC No. 1/MgPC No. 2,3)

	Good	Fine	Mint
1-Mort Drucker-a; Maneely-c/a	4.00	12.00	28.00
2-Mort Drucker-a	2.00	6.00	14.00
3-Williamson, Drucker-a	4.00	12.00	28.00

BILLY BUNNY (Black Cobra No. 6 on)
Feb-Mar, 1954 - No. 5, Oct-Nov, 1954
Excellent Publications

	Good	Fine	Mint
1	2.00	6.00	14.00
2	1.00	3.00	7.00
3-5	.75	2.25	5.00

BILLY BUNNY'S CHRISTMAS FROLICS
1952 (100 pages)
Farrell Publications

	Good	Fine	Mint
1	4.35	13.50	31.50

BILLY MAKE BELIEVE (See Single Series No. 14)

BILLY THE KID (Formerly Masked Raider)
No. 9, Nov, 1957 - No. 121, Dec, 1976; No. 122, Sept, 1977 - No. 123, Oct, 1977; No. 124, Feb, 1978 - No. 153, Mar, 1983
Charlton Publ. Co.

	Good	Fine	Mint
9	2.65	8.00	18.00
10,12,14,17-19	1.70	5.00	12.00
11-(68 pgs., origin, 1st app. The Ghost Train)	2.00	6.00	14.00
13-Williamson/Torres-a	2.65	8.00	18.00
15-Origin; 2pgs. Williamson-a	2.65	8.00	18.00
16-Two pgs. Williamson	2.65	8.00	18.00
20-22,25-Severin-a(3-4)	2.65	8.00	18.00
23,24,26-30	.85	2.50	6.00
31-40	.60	1.80	4.20
41-60	.50	1.50	3.00
61-80: 66-Bounty Hunter series begins. Not in No. 79,82,84-86		.40	.80
81-123: 87-Last Bounty Hunter. 111-Origin The Ghost Train; Sutton-a. 117-Gunsmith & Co., The Cheyenne Kid app.		.30	.60
124(2/78)-129		.30	.60
130-153		.30	.60
Modern Comics 109 (1977 reprint)		.15	.30

NOTE: *Severin a(r)-121-129,134.*

BILLY THE KID ADVENTURE MAGAZINE
Oct, 1950 - No. 30, 1955
Toby Press

	Good	Fine	Mint
1-Williamson/Frazetta, 4 pgs; photo-c	11.50	34.00	80.00
2-Photo-c	3.00	9.00	21.00
3-Williamson/Frazetta "The Claws of Death," 4 pgs. plus Williamson-a	16.00	48.00	110.00
4,5,7,8,10: 7-Photo-c	2.00	6.00	14.00
6-Frazetta story assist on 'Nightmare;" photo-c	5.00	15.00	35.00
9-Kurtzman Pot-Shot Pete; photo-c	4.50	13.50	31.50
11,12,15-20	1.85	5.50	13.00
13-Kurtzman r-/John Wayne 12 (Genius)	2.30	7.00	16.00
14-Williamson/Frazetta; r-of #1, 2 pgs.	5.00	15.00	35.00
21,23-30	1.30	4.00	9.00
22-Williamson/Frazetta r(1pg.)-/#1; photo-c	1.70	5.00	12.00

BILLY THE KID AND OSCAR
Winter, 1945 - No. 3, Summer, 1946 (funny animal)
Fawcett Publications

	Good	Fine	Mint
1	4.00	12.00	28.00
2,3	2.00	6.00	14.00

BILLY WEST (Bill West No. 9,10)
1949 - No. 9, Feb, 1951; No. 10, Feb, 1952
Standard Comics (Visual Editions)

	Good	Fine	Mint
1	4.00	12.00	28.00
2	2.00	6.00	14.00

Big Town #3, © DC

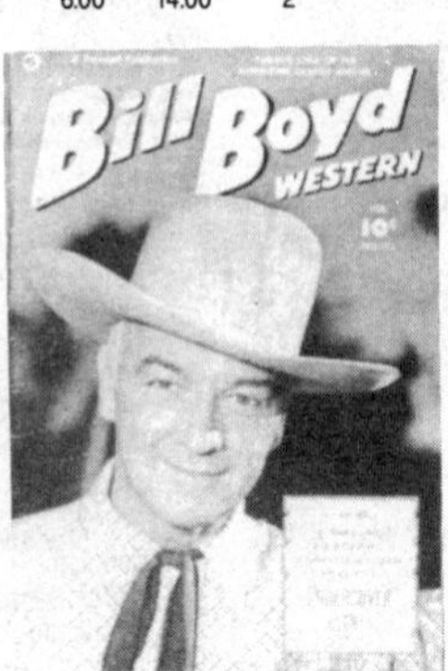

Bill Boyd Western #11, © FAW

Billy the Kid Adventure Mag. #6, © TOBY

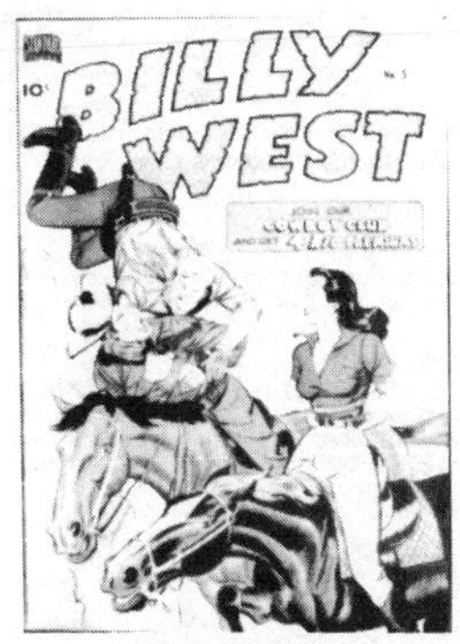

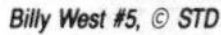

Billy West #5, © STD

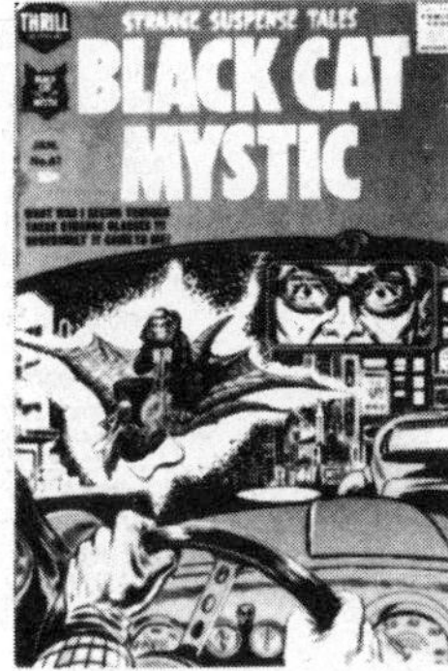

Black Cat Mystic #61, © HARV

Black Diamond Western #52, © LEV

BILLY WEST (continued)

	Good	Fine	Mint
3-10: 7,8-Schomburg-c	1.50	4.50	10.00

NOTE: ***Celardo*** *a-1-6,9; c-1-3.* ***Moreira*** *a-3.* ***Roussos*** *a-2.*

BING CROSBY (See Feature Films)

BINGO (. . .Comics) (H. C. Blackerby)
1945 (Reprints National material)
Howard Publ.

	Good	Fine	Mint
1-L. B. Cole opium-c	8.00	24.00	56.00

BINGO, THE MONKEY DOODLE BOY
Aug, 1951; Oct, 1953
St. John Publishing Co.

	Good	Fine	Mint
1(8/51)-by Eric Peters	2.30	7.00	16.00
1(10/53)	1.50	4.50	10.00

BINKY (Formerly Leave It to. . .)
No. 72, 4-5/70 - No. 81, 10-11/71; No. 82, Summer/77
National Periodical Publ./DC Comics

	Good	Fine	Mint
72-81		.50	1.00
82('77)-(One Shot)		.30	.60

BINKY'S BUDDIES
Jan-Feb, 1969 - No. 12, Nov-Dec, 1970
National Periodical Publications

	Good	Fine	Mint
1	.35	1.00	2.00
2-12		.50	1.00

BIONIC WOMAN, THE (TV)
October, 1977 - No. 5, June, 1978
Charlton Publications

	Good	Fine	Mint
1-5		.50	1.00

BIZARRE ADVENTURES (Formerly Marvel Preview)
No. 25, 3/81 - No. 34, 2/83 (Magazine-$1.50, 25-33)
Marvel Comics Group

	Good	Fine	Mint
25-Lethal Ladies. 26-King Kull		.60	1.20
27-Phoenix, Iceman & Nightcrawler app. 28-The Unlikely Heroes; Elektra by Miller; Adams-a	.25	.75	1.50
29-Horror. 30-Tomorrow. 31-After The Violence Stops; new Hangman story; Miller-a. 32-Gods. 33-Horror		.60	1.20
34 ($2.00, Baxter paper, comic size)-Son of Santa; Christmas spec.; Howard the Duck by P. Smith	.25	.75	1.50

NOTE: ***Alcala*** *a-27i.* ***Austin*** *a-25i, 28i.* ***J. Buscema*** *a-27p, 29, 30p; c-26.* ***Byrne*** *a-31(2pgs.).* ***Golden*** *a-25p, 28p.* ***Gulacy*** *a-25; c-25, 27.* ***Perez*** *a-27p.* ***Reese*** *a-31i.* ***Rogers*** *a-25p.* ***Simonson*** *a-29; c-29.* ***Paul Smith*** *a-34.*

BIZARRE 3-D ZONE (Blackthorne 3-D Series No. 5)
July, 1986 (One shot)($2.25)
Blackthorne Publishing

	Good	Fine	Mint
1-D. Stevens-a	.40	1.25	2.50

BLACK AND WHITE (See Large Feature Comic, Series I)

BLACKBEARD'S GHOST (See Movie Comics)

BLACK BEAUTY (See 4-Color No. 440)

BLACK CAT COMICS (. .West. No. 16-19; . .Mystery No. 30 on)
June-July, 1946 - No. 29, June, 1951 (See All-New #7,9)
Harvey Publications (Home Comics)

	Good	Fine	Mint
1-Kubert-a	24.00	72.00	170.00
2-Kubert-a	14.00	42.00	100.00
3	10.00	32.00	70.00
4-The Red Demons begin (The Demon #4 & 5)	10.00	32.00	70.00
5,6-The Scarlet Arrow app. in ea. by Powell; S&K-a in both. 6-origin Red Demon	11.50	34.00	80.00
7-Vagabond Prince by S&K plus 1 more story	11.50	34.00	80.00
8-S&K-a; Kerry Drake begins, ends #13	10.00	32.00	70.00
9-Origin Stuntman (r-/Stuntman #1)	14.00	43.00	100.00
10-20: 14,15,17-Mary Worth app. plus Invisible Scarlet O'Neil-#15,20,24	7.00	21.00	50.00
21-26	6.00	18.00	42.00
27-Used in **SOTI**, pg. 193; X-Mas-c	7.00	21.00	50.00
28-Intro. Kit, Black Cat's new sidekick	7.00	21.00	50.00
29-Black Cat bondage-c; Black Cat stories	6.00	18.00	42.00

BLACK CAT MYSTERY (Formerly Black Cat; . . .Western Mystery #54; . . .Western #55,56; . . .Mystery #57; . . .Mystic #58-62; Black Cat #63-65)
No. 30, Aug, 1951 - No. 65, April, 1963
Harvey Publications

	Good	Fine	Mint
30-Black Cat on cover only	5.00	15.00	35.00
31,32,34,37,38,40	4.00	12.00	28.00
33-Used in **POP**, pg. 89; electrocution-c	4.00	12.00	28.00
35-Atomic disaster cover/story	5.00	15.00	35.00
36,39-Used in **SOTI**: #36-Pgs. 270,271; #39-Pgs. 386-388	8.50	25.50	60.00
41-43	3.50	10.50	24.00
44-Eyes, ears, tongue cut out; Nostrand-a	4.00	12.00	28.00
45-Classic "Colorama" by Powell; Nostrand-a	6.50	19.50	45.00
46-49,51-Nostrand-a in all	4.00	12.00	28.00
50-Check-a; Warren Kremer?-c showing a man's face burning away	6.50	19.50	45.00
52,53 (r-#34 & 35)	3.50	10.50	24.00
54-Two Black Cat stories	4.00	12.00	28.00
55,56-Black Cat app.	3.00	9.00	21.00
57(7/56)-Simon?-c	2.65	8.00	18.00
58-60-Kirby-a(4)	4.00	12.00	28.00
61-Nostrand-a; "Colorama" r-/45	3.50	10.50	24.00
62(3/58)-E.C. story swipe	2.65	8.00	18.00
63-Giant(10/62); Reprints; Black Cat app.; origin Black Kitten	4.00	12.00	28.00
64-Giant(1/63); Reprints; Black Cat app.	4.00	12.00	28.00
65-Giant(4/63); Reprints; Black Cat app.	4.00	12.00	28.00

NOTE: ***Kremer*** *a-37, 39, 43; c-36, 37, 47.* ***Meskin*** *a-51.* ***Palais*** *a-30, 31(2), 32(2), 33-35, 37-40.* ***Powell*** *a-32-35, 36(2), 40, 41, 43-53, 57.* ***Simon*** *c-63-65.* ***Sparling*** *a-44. Bondage-c No. 32, 34, 43.*

BLACK COBRA
No. 1, 10-11/54; No. 6(No. 2), 12-1/54-55; No. 3, 2-3/55
Ajax/Farrell Publications

	Good	Fine	Mint
1	8.00	24.00	56.00
6(No. 2)-Formerly Billy Bunny	5.00	15.00	35.00
3-(pre-code)-Torpedoman app.	5.00	15.00	35.00

BLACK DIAMOND
May, 1983 - No. 5, 1984 (no month) ($2.00-$1.75)(Baxter paper)
Americomics

	Good	Fine	Mint
1-Movie adaptation; Colt back up begins	.40	1.25	2.50
2,3-Movie adaptation	.40	1.25	2.50
4,5	.25	.75	1.50

NOTE: ***Bill Black*** *a-1i; c-1.* ***Gulacy*** *c-2-5.*

BLACK DIAMOND WESTERN (Desperado No. 1-8)
No. 9, Mar, 1949 - No. 60, Feb, 1956 (No. 9-28, 52 pgs.)
Lev Gleason Publications

	Good	Fine	Mint
9-Origin	6.00	18.00	42.00
10	3.50	10.50	24.00
11-15	3.00	9.00	21.00
16-28-Wolverton's Bing Bang Buster	3.50	10.50	24.00
29,30,32-40	1.70	5.00	12.00
31-One pg. Frazetta-a	2.15	6.50	15.00
41-50,53-59	1.50	4.50	10.00
51-3-D effect c/story	3.50	10.50	24.00
52-3-D effect story	3.00	9.00	21.00

BLACK DIAMOND WEST. (continued) — Good / Fine / Mint
60-Last issue 1.70 5.00 12.00
NOTE: ***Guardineer** a-18. **Morisi** a-55. **Tuska** a-48.*

BLACK DRAGON, THE
5/85 - No. 6, 10/85 (Baxter paper; mini-series; adults only)
Epic Comics (Marvel)
1: Bolton c/a No. 1-6 .70 2.00 4.00
2 .40 1.25 2.50
3-6 .35 1.00 2.00

BLACK FURY (Wild West No. 58) (See Blue Bird)
May, 1955 - No. 57, Mar-Apr, 1966 (Horse stories)
Charlton Comics Group
1 2.00 6.00 14.00
2 1.00 3.00 7.00
3-15 .75 2.25 5.00
16-18-Ditko-a 2.00 6.00 14.00
19-30 .45 1.35 3.00
31-57 .50 1.00

BLACK GOLD
1945? (8 pgs. in color)
Esso Service Station (Giveaway)
Reprints from True Comics 3.00 9.00 21.00

BLACK GOLIATH
Feb, 1976 - No. 5, Nov, 1976
Marvel Comics Group
1 .40 .80
2-5: 1-3-Tuska-a(p) .30 .60

BLACKHAWK (Formerly Uncle Sam No. 1-8)
No. 9, Winter, 1944 - No. 243, 10-11/68; No. 244, 1-2/76 - No. 250, 1-2/77; No. 251, 10/82 - No. 273, 11/84
Comic Magazines(Quality)No. 9-107(12/56); National Periodical Publ. No. 108(1/57)-250; DC Comics No. 251 on
9 (1944) 80.00 240.00 560.00
10 (1946) 38.00 115.00 265.00
11-15: 14-Ward-a; 13,14-Fear app. 27.00 81.00 190.00
16-20: 20-Ward Blackhawk 21.00 63.00 146.00
21-30 16.00 48.00 110.00
31-40: 31-Chop Chop by Jack Cole 12.00 36.00 84.00
41-49,51-60 8.50 25.50 60.00
50-1st Killer Shark; origin in text 10.00 30.00 70.00
61-Used in **POP**, pg. 91 8.50 25.50 60.00
62-Used in **POP**, pg. 92 & color illo 8.50 25.50 60.00
63-65,67-70,72-80: 70-Return of Killer Shark. 75-Intro. Blackie the Hawk 7.00 21.00 50.00
66-B&W and color illos in **POP** 8.00 24.00 56.00
71-Origin retold; flying saucer-c; A-Bomb panels 7.00 21.00 50.00
81-86: Last precode, 3/55 6.00 18.00 42.00
87-92,94-99,101-107 4.50 13.50 31.50
93-Origin in text 5.50 16.50 38.00
100 5.50 16.50 38.00
108-Re-intro. Blackie, the Hawk, their mascot; not in #115 10.00 30.00 70.00
109-117 3.00 9.00 21.00
118-Frazetta r-/Jimmy Wakely 4, 3 pgs. 5.70 17.00 40.00
119-130 1.70 5.00 12.00
131-142,144-163,165,166: 133-Intro. Lady Blackhawk. 166-Last 10 cent issue 1.30 4.00 9.00
143-Kurtzman r-/Jimmy Wakely 4 1.50 4.50 10.00
164-Origin retold 1.50 4.50 10.00
167-180 .70 2.00 4.00
181-190 .50 1.50 3.00
191-197,199-202,204-210: Combat Diary series begins. 197-New look for Blackhawks .40 1.20 2.40
198-Origin retold .50 1.50 3.00
203-Origin Chop Chop .50 1.50 3.00
211-243(1968): 228-Batman, Green Lantern, Superman, The Flash cameos. 230-Blackhawks become superheroes. 242-Return to old costumes .35 1.00 2.00
244 ('76) -250: 250-Chuck dies .60 1.20
251-Origin retold; Black Knights return .40 .80
252-264: 252-Intro Domino. 253-Part origin Hendrickson. 258-Blackhawk's Island destroyed. 259-Part origin Chop-Chop .40 .80
265-273 (75 cent cover price) .40 .80
NOTE: ***Chaykin** a-260; c-257-60, 262. **Crandall** a-10, 11, 13, 16, 18-20, 22-26, 30-33, 36(2), 37, 39-44, 46-50, 52-58, 60, 63, 64, 66, 67; c-18-20, 22-on(most). **Evans** a-244, 245, 246i, 248-250i. **G. Kane** c-263, 264. **Kubert** c-244, 245. **Newton** a-266p. **Severin** a-257. **Spiegle** a-261-67, 269-73; c-265-72. **Toth** a-260p. **Ward** a-16-27(Chop Chop, 8pgs. ea.); pencilled stories-No. 17-63(approx.). **Wildey** a-268.*

BLACKHAWK
Mar, 1988 - No. 3, May, 1988 ($2.95 mini-series)
DC Comics
1-3 .50 1.50 3.00

BLACKHAWK INDIAN TOMAHAWK WAR, THE
1951
Avon Periodicals
nn-Kinstler-c; Kit West story 6.00 18.00 42.00

BLACK HOLE (See Walt Disney Showcase #54)
March, 1980 - No. 4, September, 1980 (Disney movie)
Whitman Publ. Co.
11295-Photo-c; Spiegle-a .50 1.00
2,3-Spiegle-a; 3-McWilliams-a; photo-c .50 1.00
4-Spiegle-a .40 .80

BLACK HOOD, THE
Jan, 1983 - No. 3, Oct, 1983 (Printed on Mandell paper)
Red Circle Comics (Archie)
1-Morrow, McWilliams, Wildey-a; Toth-c .60 1.20
2,3: MLJ's The Fox by Toth, c/a .50 1.00
(Also see Archie's Super-Hero Special Digest #2)

BLACK HOOD COMICS (Formerly Hangman #2-8; Laugh Comics #20 on; also see Top-Notch #9)
No. 9, Winter, 1943-44 - No. 19, Summer, 1946
MLJ Magazines
9-The Hangman & The Boy Buddies cont'd 25.00 75.00 175.00
10-The Hangman & Dusty, the Boy Detective app.; Fuje-a 12.00 36.00 84.00
11-Dusty app.; no Hangman 10.00 30.00 70.00
12-18: 17-Bondage-c 10.00 30.00 70.00
19-I.D. exposed 11.00 35.00 77.00

BLACK JACK (Rocky Lane's. . ., formerly Jim Bowie)
No. 20, Nov, 1957 - No. 30, Nov, 1959
Charlton Comics
20 2.00 6.00 14.00
21,27,29,30 1.15 3.50 8.00
22-(68 pages) 1.70 5.00 12.00
23-Williamson/Torres-a 3.50 10.50 24.00
24-26,28-Ditko-a 2.15 6.50 15.00

BLACK KNIGHT, THE
May, 1953; 1963
Toby Press
1-Bondage-c 5.50 16.50 38.00
Super Reprint No. 11 (1963) .85 2.50 5.00

BLACK KNIGHT, THE (Also see Marvel Super Heroes & Tales To

Blackhawk #76, © DC

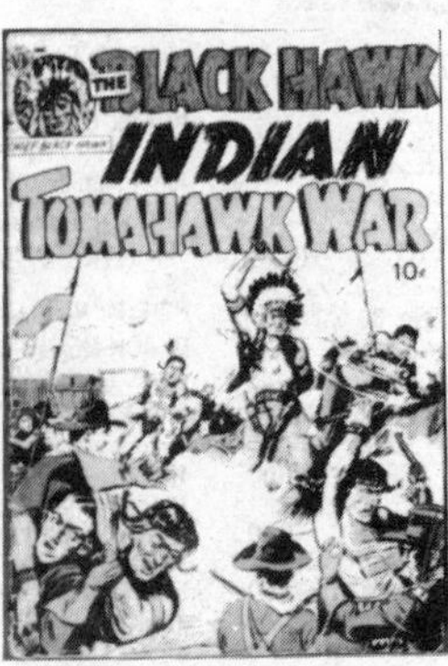

Blackhawk Indian Tomahawk War #1, © AVON

Black Hood Comics #16, © MLJ

Black Magic V7#4, © Headline

Black Rider #21, © MCG

The Black Terror #19, © STD

BLACK KNIGHT, THE (continued)
Astonish)
May, 1955 - No. 5, April, 1956
Atlas Comics (MgPC)

	Good	Fine	Mint
1-Origin Crusader; Maneely c/a	30.00	90.00	210.00
2	22.00	65.00	154.00
3-5: 4-Maneely c/a	17.00	51.00	120.00

BLACK LIGHTNING (See Brave & The Bold, Cancelled Comic Cavalcade, DC Comics Presents No. 16, Detective and World's Finest)
April, 1977 - No. 11, Sept-Oct, 1978
National Periodical Publications/DC Comics

	Good	Fine	Mint
1		.40	.80
2-11: 4-Intro Cyclotronic Man		.25	.50

NOTE: ***Buckler** c-1-3p, 6-11p.*

BLACK MAGIC (. . . Magazine) (Becomes Cool Cat)
10-11/50 - V4/1, 6-7/53: V4/2, 9-10/53 - V5/3, 11-12/54; V6/1, 9-10/57 - V7/2, 11-12/58: V7/3, 7-8/60 - V8/5, 11-12/61 (V1/1-5, 52pgs.; V1/6-V3/3, 44pgs.)
Crestwood Publ. V1No.1-4,V6No.1-V7No.2/Headline V1No.5-V5No.3,V7No.3-V8No.5

	Good	Fine	Mint
V1/1-S&K-a, 10 pgs.; Meskin-a(2)	12.00	36.00	84.00
2-S&K-a, 17 pgs.; Meskin-a	5.70	17.00	40.00
3-6(8-9/51)-S&K, Roussos, Meskin-a	4.35	13.00	30.00
V2/1(10-11/51),4,5,7(#13),9(#15),11(#17),12(#18)-S&K-a	3.50	10.50	24.00
2,3,6,8,10(#16)	2.35	7.00	16.00
V3/1(#19, 12/52) - 6(#24, 5/53)-S&K-a	2.65	8.00	18.00
V4/1(#25, 6-7/53), 2(#26, 9-10/53)-S&K-a(3-4)	3.00	9.00	21.00
3(#27, 11-12/53)-S&K-a; Ditko-a(1st in comics)	8.00	24.00	56.00
4(#28)-Eyes ripped out/story-S&K, Ditko-a	7.00	21.00	50.00
5(#29, 3-4/54)-S&K, Ditko-a	6.00	18.00	42.00
6(#30, 5-6/54)-S&K, Powell?-a	2.65	8.00	18.00
V5/1(#31, 7-8/54 - 3(#33, 11-12/54)-S&K-a	2.65	8.00	18.00
V6/1(#34, 9-10/57), 2(#35, 11-12/57)	1.50	4.50	10.00
3(1-2/58) - 6(7-8/58)	1.50	4.50	10.00
V7/1(9-10/58) - 3(7-8/60)	1.15	3.50	8.00
4(9-10/60), 5(11-12/60)-Torres-a	1.60	4.70	11.00
6(1-2/61)-Powell-a(2)	1.15	3.50	8.00
V8/1(3-4/61)-Powell-c/a	1.15	3.50	8.00
2(5-6/61)-E.C. story swipe/W.F. #22; Ditko, Powell-a	1.60	4.70	11.00
3(7-8/61)-E.C. story swipe/W.F. #22; Powell-a(2)	1.50	4.50	10.00
4(9-10/61)-Powell-a(5)	1.15	3.50	8.00
5-E.C. story swipe/W.S.F. #28; Powell-a(3)	1.50	4.50	10.00

NOTE: ***Bernard Baily** a-V4/6?, V5/3(2). **Grandenetti** a-V2/3, 11. **Kirby** c-V1/1-6, V2/1-12, V3/1-6, V4/1, 2, 4-6, V5/1-3. **McWilliams** a-V3/2i. **Meskin** a-V1/1(2), 2, 3, 4(2), 5(2), 6, V2/1, 2, 3(2), 4(3), 5, 6(2), 7-9, 11, 12i, V3/1(2), 5, 6, V5/1(2), 2. **Orlando** a-V6/1, 4, V7/2; c-V6/1-6. **Powell** a-V5/1?. **Roussos** a-V1/3-5, 6(2), V2/3(2), 4, 5(2), 6, 8, 9, 10(2), 11, 12p, V3/1(2), 2i, 5, V5/2. **Simon** a-V2/12, V3/2, V7/5? c-V4/3?, V7/3?, 4, 5?, 6?, V8/1-5. **Simon & Kirby** a-V1/1, 2(2), 3-6, V2/1, 4, 5, 7, 9, 11?, 12, V3/1-6, V4/1(3), 2(4), 3(2), 4(2), 5, 6, V5/1-3; c-V2/1. **Leonard Starr** a-V1/1. **Tuska** a-V6/3, 4. **Woodbridge** a-V7/4.*

BLACK MAGIC
Oct-Nov, 1973 - No. 9, Apr-May, 1975
National Periodical Publications

	Good	Fine	Mint
1-S&K reprints		.30	.60
2-9-S&K reprints		.20	.40

BLACKMAIL TERROR (See Harvey Comics Library)

BLACKMAN
No Date (1981)
Leader Comics Group

	Good	Fine	Mint
V1No.1		.30	.60

BLACKOUTS (See Broadway Hollywood. . .)

BLACK PANTHER, THE (Also see Jungle Action)
1/77 - No. 15, 5/79
Marvel Comics Group

	Good	Fine	Mint
1		.40	.80
2-15		.25	.50

NOTE: ***J. Buscema** c-15p. **Kirby** c/a 1-12. **Layton** c-13i.*

BLACK PHANTOM (See Tim Holt & Wisco)
Nov, 1954 - No. 2, Feb?, 1955 (Female outlaw)
Magazine Enterprises

	Good	Fine	Mint
1 (A-1 122)-The Ghost Rider app.; Headlight c/a	14.00	42.00	100.00
2 (Rare)	18.00	54.00	125.00

BLACK RIDER (Formerly Western Winners; Western Tales of Black Rider #28-31; Gunsmoke Western #32 on)(Also see All Western Winners, Best Western, Kid Colt, Outlaw Kid, Rex Hart, Two-Gun Kid, Two-Gun Western, Western Gunfighters, Western Winners, Wild Western)
No. 8, 3/50 - No. 18, 1/52; No. 19, 11/53 - No. 27, 3/55
Marvel/Atlas Comics(CDS No. 8-17/CPS No. 19 on)

	Good	Fine	Mint
8 (No. 1)-Black Rider & his horse Satan begin; 52pgs begin, end No. 14; photo-c	12.00	36.00	84.00
9	6.00	18.00	42.00
10-Origin Black Rider	8.00	24.00	56.00
11-14(Last 52pgs.)	4.35	13.00	30.00
15-19: 19-Two-Gun Kid app.	4.00	12.00	28.00
20-Classic-c; Two-Gun Kid app.	4.35	13.00	30.00
21-26: 21-23-Two-Gun Kid app. 24,25-Arrowhead app. 26-Kid Colt app.	3.00	9.00	21.00
27-Last issue; Kid Colt app.	3.50	10.50	24.00

NOTE: ***Jack Keller** a-15, 27. **Maneely** a-14; c-16, 17, 25, 27. **Syd Shores** a-23(3), 24(3), 25; c-19, 23. **Sinnott** a-24, 25. **Tuska** a-12, 20, 21.*

BLACK RIDER RIDES AGAIN!, THE
September, 1957
Atlas Comics (CPS)

	Good	Fine	Mint
1-Kirby-a(3); Powell-a; Severin-c	5.00	15.00	35.00

BLACKSTONE (See Wisco Giveaways & Super Magician Comics)

BLACKSTONE, MASTER MAGICIAN COMICS
Mar-Apr, 1946 - No. 3, July-Aug, 1946
Vital Publications/Street & Smith Publ.

	Good	Fine	Mint
1	9.00	27.00	63.00
2,3	6.00	18.00	42.00

BLACKSTONE, THE MAGICIAN
No. 2, May, 1948 - No. 4, Sept, 1948 (no No.1)
Marvel Comics (CnPC)

	Good	Fine	Mint
2-The Blonde Phantom begins	18.00	54.00	125.00
3,4-(. . . Detective on cover only). 3,4-Bondage-c	15.00	45.00	105.00

BLACKSTONE, THE MAGICIAN DETECTIVE FIGHTS CRIME
Fall, 1947
E. C. Comics

	Good	Fine	Mint
1-1st app. Happy Houlihans	24.00	72.00	168.00

BLACK SWAN COMICS
1945
MLJ Magazines (Pershing Square Publ. Co.)

	Good	Fine	Mint
1-The Black Hood reprints from Black Hood No. 14; Bill Woggon-a; Suzie app.	7.00	21.00	50.00

BLACK TARANTULA (See Feature Presentations No. 5)

BLACK TERROR (See Exciting & America's Best)
Wint, 1942-43 - No. 27, June, 1949
Better Publications/Standard

	Good	Fine	Mint
1-Black Terror, Crime Crusader begin	50.00	150.00	350.00
2	25.00	75.00	175.00
3	18.00	54.00	125.00
4,5	14.00	42.00	100.00
6-10: 7-The Ghost app.	10.00	30.00	70.00
11-19	9.00	27.00	62.00
20-The Scarab app.	9.00	27.00	62.00
21-Miss Masque app.	10.00	30.00	70.00
22-Part Frazetta-a on one Black Terror story	11.00	33.00	77.00
23	9.00	27.00	62.00
24-¼ pg. Frazetta-a	10.00	30.00	70.00
25-27	9.00	27.00	62.00

NOTE: ***Schomburg (Xela)** c-2-27; bondage c-2, 17, 24. **Meskin** a-27. **Moreira** a-27. **Robinson/Meskin** a-23, 24(3), 25, 26. **Roussos/Mayo** a-24. **Tuska** a-26, 27.*

BLACK ZEPPELIN (See Gene Day's. . .)

BLADERUNNER
Oct, 1982 - No. 2, Nov, 1982
Marvel Comics Group

	Good	Fine	Mint
1-Movie adaptation; Williamson c/a		.30	.60
2-Movie adapt. concludes; Williamson a		.30	.60

BLAKE HARPER (See City Surgeon. . .)

BLAST (Satire Magazine)
Feb, 1971 - No. 2, May, 1971
G & D Publications

	Good	Fine	Mint
1-Wrightson & Kaluta-a	1.70	5.00	10.00
2-Kaluta-a	1.20	3.50	7.00

BLAST-OFF (Three Rocketeers)
October, 1965
Harvey Publications (Fun Day Funnies)

	Good	Fine	Mint
1-Kirby/Williamson-a(2); Williamson/Crandall-a; Williamson/Torres/Krenkel-a; Kirby/Simon-c	2.00	6.00	12.00

BLAZE CARSON (Rex Hart No. 6 on)
(See Kid Colt, Tex Taylor, Wild Western, Wisco)
Sept, 1948 - No. 5, June, 1949
Marvel Comics (USA)

	Good	Fine	Mint
1	6.00	18.00	42.00
2	4.00	12.00	28.00
3-Used by N.Y. State Legis. Comm.(Injury to eye splash); Tex Morgan app.	5.50	16.50	38.00
4,5: 4-Two-Gun Kid app. 5-Tex Taylor app.	3.50	10.50	24.00

BLAZE THE WONDER COLLIE
No. 2, Oct, 1949 - No. 3, Feb, 1950
Marvel Comics(SePI)

	Good	Fine	Mint
2(#1), 3-photo-c (Scarce)	8.00	24.00	56.00

BLAZING BATTLE TALES
July, 1975
Seaboard Periodicals (Atlas)

	Good	Fine	Mint
1-Intro. Sgt. Hawk & the Sky Demon by Severin; McWilliams, Sparling-a; Thorne-c		.30	.60

BLAZING COMBAT (Magazine) (35 cents)
Oct, 1965 - No. 4, July, 1966 (Black & White)
Warren Publishing Co.

	Good	Fine	Mint
1-Frazetta-c	6.75	20.00	40.00
2-Frazetta-c	2.50	7.50	15.00
3,4-Frazetta-c; 4-Frazetta ½ pg. ad	1.70	5.00	10.00
. . . Anthology (reprints from No. 1-4)	.70	2.00	4.00

NOTE: *Above has art by **Colan, Crandall, Evans, Morrow, Orlando, Severin, Torres, Toth, Williamson,** and **Wood.***

BLAZING COMICS
June, 1944 - #3, 9/44; #4, 2/45; #5(V2#2), 3/55 - #6(V2#3), 1955?
Enwil Associates/Rural Home

	Good	Fine	Mint
1-The Green Turtle, Red Hawk, Black Buccaneer begin; origin Jun-Gal	16.00	48.00	110.00
2-4: 3-Briefer-a	10.00	30.00	70.00
5(3/55, V2#2-inside)-Black Buccaneer-c, 6(V2#3-inside, 1955)-Indian/Jap-c	2.00	6.00	14.00

NOTE: *No. 5 & 6 contain remaindered comics rebound and the contents can vary. Cloak & Daggar, Will Rogers, Superman 64, Star Spangled 130, Kaanga known. Value would be half of contents.*

BLAZING SIXGUNS
December, 1952
Avon Periodicals

	Good	Fine	Mint
1-Kinstler c/a; Larsen/Alascia-a(2), Tuska?-a; Jesse James, Kit Carson, Wild Bill Hickok app.	7.00	21.00	50.00

BLAZING SIXGUNS
1964
I.W./Super Comics

	Good	Fine	Mint
I.W. Reprint No. 1,8,9: 8-Kinstler-c; 9-Ditko-a	.40	1.20	2.40
Super Reprint No. 10,11,15,16(Buffalo Bill, Swift Deer),17(1964)	.35	1.00	2.00
12-Reprints Bullseye No. 3; S&K-a	2.00	6.00	12.00
18-Powell's Straight Arrow	.85	2.50	5.00

BLAZING SIX-GUNS
Feb, 1971 - No. 2, April, 1971 (52 pages)
Skywald Comics

	Good	Fine	Mint
1-The Red Mask, Sundance Kid begin, Avon's Geronimo reprint by Kinstler		.50	1.00
2-Wild Bill Hickok, Jesse James, Kit Carson-r		.40	.80

BLAZING WEST
Fall, 1948 - No. 22, Mar-Apr, 1952
American Comics Group(B&I Publ./Michel Publ.)

	Good	Fine	Mint
1-Origin & 1st app. Injun Jones, Tenderfoot & Buffalo Belle; Texas Tim & Ranger begins, ends No. 13	6.00	18.00	42.00
2,3	3.00	9.00	21.00
4-Origin & 1st app. Little Lobo; Starr-a	2.30	7.00	16.00
5-10: 5-Starr-a	1.85	5.50	13.00
11-13	1.50	4.50	10.00
14-Origin & 1st app. The Hooded Horseman; Whitney-c	3.50	10.50	24.00
15-22: 15,16,19-Starr-a	1.70	5.00	12.00

BLAZING WESTERN
Jan, 1954 - No. 5, Sept, 1954
Timor Publications

	Good	Fine	Mint
1-Ditko-a; Text story by Bruce Hamilton	4.00	12.00	28.00
2-4	1.70	5.00	12.00
5-Disbrow-a	2.00	6.00	14.00

BLESSED PIUS X
No date (32 pages; ½ text, ½ comics) (Paper cover)
Catechetical Guild (Giveaway)

	Good	Fine	Mint
	3.00	9.00	21.00

BLITZKRIEG!
Jan-Feb, 1976 - No. 5, Sept-Oct, 1976
National Periodical Publications

	Good	Fine	Mint
1-Kubert-c on all		.25	.50
2-5		.20	.40

BLONDE PHANTOM (Formerly All-Select #1-11; Lovers #23 on)
(Also see Blackstone, Millie The Model #2 and Marvel Mystery)
No. 12, Winter, 1946-47 - No. 22, March, 1949
Marvel Comics (MPC)

The Black Terror #27, © STD

Blaze Carson #1, © MCG

Blazing West #15, © ACG

Blonde Phantom #17, © MCG

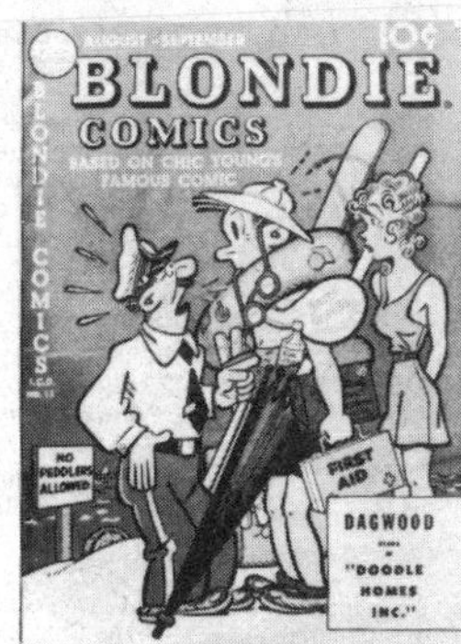

Blondie Comics #13, © KING

Blue Beetle #56 (Fox), © DC

BLONDIE PHANTOM (continued)

	Good	Fine	Mint
12-Miss America begins, ends #14	40.00	120.00	280.00
13-Sub-Mariner begins	27.00	81.00	190.00
14,15; 14-Male Bondage-c. 15-Kurtzman's 'Hey Look'	23.00	70.00	160.00
16-Captain America with Bucky app.; Kurtzman's "Hey Look"	23.00	70.00	160.00
17-22: 22-Anti Wertham editorial	21.50	65.00	150.00

BLONDIE (See Dagwood, Daisy & Her Pups, Eat Right to Work . . ., & Comics Reading Libraries)
1942 - 1946
David McKay Publications

	Good	Fine	Mint
Feature Books 12 (Rare)	35.00	105.00	245.00
Feature Books 27-29,31,34(1940)	7.00	21.00	50.00
Feature Books 36,38,40,42,43,45,47	6.00	18.00	42.00
. . . 1944, hard-c, 1938-'44 daily strip-r, B&W, 128 pgs.	8.50	25.50	60.00

BLONDIE & DAGWOOD FAMILY
Oct, 1963 - No. 4, Dec, 1965 (68 pages)
Harvey Publications (King Features Synd.)

	Good	Fine	Mint
1	1.15	3.50	8.00
2-4	.85	2.50	5.00

BLONDIE COMICS (. . . Monthly No. 16-141)
Spring, 1947 - No. 163, Nov, 1965; No. 164, Aug, 1966 - No. 175, Dec, 1967; No. 177, Feb, 1969 - No. 222, Nov, 1976
David McKay No. 1-15/Harvey No. 16-163/King No. 164-175/ Charlton No. 177 on

	Good	Fine	Mint
1	8.00	24.00	56.00
2	4.00	12.00	28.00
3-5	3.50	10.50	24.00
6-10	2.50	7.50	17.50
11-15	1.85	5.50	13.00
16-(3/50; Harvey)	2.00	6.00	14.00
17-20	1.50	4.50	10.00
21-30	1.15	3.50	8.00
31-50	1.00	3.00	6.00
51-80	.85	2.50	5.00
81-100	.75	2.25	4.50
101-130: 125-80 pg. ish.	.70	2.00	4.00
131-136,138,139	.50	1.50	3.00
137,140-(80 pages)	.85	2.50	5.00
141-166(#148,155,157-159,161-163 are 68 pgs.)	.85	2.50	5.00
167-One pg. Williamson ad		.50	1.00
168-175,177-222(No #176)		.30	.60
Blondie, Dagwood & Daisy 1(100 pgs., 1953)	7.00	21.00	50.00
1950 Giveaway	1.50	4.50	10.00
1962,1964 Giveaway	.40	1.20	2.40
N. Y. State Dept. of Mental Hygiene Giveaway-('50,'56,'61) Regular size (Diff. issues) 16 pages; no #	1.00	3.00	6.00

BLOOD: A TALE
Feb, 1988 - No. 4, 1988 ($3.25, adults)
Epic comics (Marvel)

	Good	Fine	Mint
1	.75	2.25	4.50
2-4	.60	1.80	3.60

BLOOD IS THE HARVEST
1950 (32 pages) (paper cover)
Catechetical Guild

	Good	Fine	Mint
(Scarce)-Anti-communism(13 known copies)	64.00	190.00	450.00
Black & white version (5 known copies), saddle stitched	30.00	90.00	200.00

Untrimmed version (only one known copy); estimated value-$800

NOTE: *In 1979 nine copies of the color version surfaced from the old Guild's files plus the five black & white copies.*

BLOOD OF THE BEAST
Sum, 1986 - No. 4 (mini-series; $2.00, color)
Fantagraphics Books

	Good	Fine	Mint
1-4	.35	1.00	2.00

BLOOD OF THE INNOCENT (See Warp Graphics Annual)
1/7/86 - No. 4, 1/28/86 (Weekly mini-series; adults only)
WaRP Graphics

	Good	Fine	Mint
1-4	.50	1.50	3.00
Bound Volume	1.30	4.00	7.95

BLOOD RITES (See Americomics Graphic Novel)

BLUE BEETLE, THE (Also see Mystery Men & Weekly Comic Mag.)
Winter, 1939-40 - No. 60, Aug, 1950
Fox Publ. No. 1-11, 31-60; Holyoke No. 12-30

	Good	Fine	Mint
1-Reprints from Mystery Men 1-5; Blue Beetle origin; Yarko the Great-r/from Wonder/Wonderworld 2-5 all by Eisner; Master Magician app.; (Blue Beetle in 4 different costumes)	100.00	300.00	700.00
2-K-51-r by Powell/Wonderworld 8,9	45.00	135.00	315.00
3-Simon-c	32.00	95.00	225.00
4-Marijuana drug mention story	24.00	72.00	170.00
5-Zanzibar The Magician by Tuska	20.00	60.00	140.00
6-Dynamite Thor begins; origin Blue Beetle	18.00	54.00	125.00
7,8-Dynamo app. in both. 8-Last Thor	16.00	48.00	110.00
9,10-The Blackbird & The Gorilla app. in both. 10-Bondage/hypo-c	14.00	42.00	100.00
11(2/42)-The Gladiator app.	14.00	42.00	100.00
12(6/42)-The Black Fury app.	14.00	42.00	100.00
13-V-Man begins, ends #18; Kubert-a	17.00	51.00	120.00
14,15-Kubert-a in both. 14-Intro. side-kick (c/text only), Sparky (called Spunky #17-19)	16.00	48.00	110.00
16-18	11.50	34.00	80.00
19-Kubert-a	14.00	42.00	100.00
20-Origin/1st app. Tiger Squadron; Arabian Nights begin	14.00	42.00	100.00
21-26: 24-Intro. & only app. The Halo. 26-General Patton sty & photo	10.00	30.00	70.00
27-Tamaa, Jungle Prince app.	8.50	25.50	60.00
28-30(2/44)	7.00	21.00	50.00
31(6/44)-40: "The Threat from Saturn" serial in #34-38	5.70	17.00	40.00
41-45	4.50	13.50	31.50
46-The Puppeteer app.	5.00	15.00	35.00
47-Kamen & Baker-a begin	27.00	81.00	190.00
48-50	22.00	66.00	154.00
51,53	20.00	60.00	140.00
52-Kamen bondage-c	27.00	81.00	190.00
54-Used in **SOTI**. Illo-"Children call these 'headlights' comics"	55.00	165.00	385.00
55,57(7/48)-Last Kamen issue	19.00	57.00	132.00
56-Used in **SOTI**, pg. 145	24.00	72.00	170.00
58(4/50)-60-No Kamen-a	3.70	11.00	26.00

NOTE: ***Kamen** a-47-51, 53, 55-57; c-47, 49-52. **Powell** a-4(2). Bondage-c 9, 10, 12, 46, 52.*

BLUE BEETLE (Formerly The Thing; becomes Mr. Muscles No. 22 on) (See Space Adventures)
No. 18, Feb, 1955 - No. 21, Aug, 1955
Charlton Comics

	Good	Fine	Mint
18,19-(Pre-1944-r). 19-Bouncer, Rocket Kelly-r	3.50	10.50	24.00
20-Joan Mason by Kamen	5.00	15.00	35.00
21-New material	3.50	10.50	24.00

BLUE BEETLE (Unusual Tales #1-49; Ghostly Tales #55 on)
V2No.1, 6/64 - V2No.5, 3-4/65; V3No.50, 7/65 - V3No.54, 2-3/66; No. 1, 6/67 - No. 5, 11/68
Charlton Comics

BLUE BEETLE (continued) — Good / Fine / Mint

V2#1-Origin Dan Garrett-Blue Beetle 1.70 5.00 12.00
2-5, V3#50-54 1.30 4.00 9.00
1(1967)-Question series begins by Ditko 2.00 6.00 14.00
2-Origin Ted Kord-Blue Beetle; Dan Garrett x-over 1.30 4.00 9.00
3-5 (#1-5-Ditko-c/a) .85 2.50 6.00
1,3(Modern Comics-1977)-Reprints .15 .30

NOTE: *#6 only appeared in the fanzine 'The Charlton Portfolio.'*

BLUE BEETLE
June, 1986 - Present
DC Comics

1-Origin retold; intro. Firefist .35 1.00 2.00
2-10: 2-Origin Firefist. 5-7-The Question app. .45 .90
11-17: 14-New Teen Titans x-over .40 .80
18-23 ($1.00) .50 1.00

BLUE BIRD COMICS
Late 1940's - 1964 (Giveaway)
Various Shoe Stores/Charlton Comics

nn(1947-50)(36 pgs.)-Several issues; Human Torch, Sub-Mariner app. in some 3.35 10.00 20.00
1959-Li'l Genius, Timmy the Timid Ghost, Wild Bill Hickok (All #1) .70 2.00 4.00
1959-(6 titles; all #2) Black Fury #1,4,5, Freddy #4, Li'l Genius, Timmy the Timid Ghost #4, Masked Raider #4, Wild Bill Hickok (Charlton) .70 2.00 4.00
1959-(#5) Masked Raider #21 .70 2.00 4.00
1960-(6 titles)(All #4) Black Fury #8,9, Masked Raider, Freddy #8,9, Timmy the Timid Ghost #9, Li'l Genius #9 (Charlton) .30 .80 1.60
1961,1962-(All #10's) Atomic Mouse #12,13,16, Black Fury #11,12, Freddy, Li'l Genius, Masked Raider, Six Gun Heroes, Texas Rangers in Action, Timmy the Ghost, Wild Bill Hickok, Wyatt Earp #3,11-13,16-18 (Charlton) .50 1.00
1963-Texas Rangers #17 (Charlton) .40 .80
1964-Mysteries of Unexplored Worlds #18, Teenage Hotrodders #18, War Heroes #18 (Charlton) .30 .60
1965-War Heroes #18 .25 .50

NOTE: *More than one issue of each character could have been published each year. Numbering is sporatic.*

BLUE BIRD CHILDREN'S MAGAZINE, THE
1957 (16 pages; soft cover; regular size)
Graphic Information Service

V1#2-6: Pat, Pete & Blue Bird app. .40 1.20 2.40

BLUE BOLT
June, 1940 - No. 101 (V10No.2), Sept-Oct, 1949
Funnies, Inc. No. 1/Novelty Press/Premium Group of Comics

V1#1-Origin Blue Bolt by Joe Simon, Sub-Zero, White Rider & Super Horse, Dick Cole, Wonder Boy & Sgt. Spook 92.00 275.00 645.00
2-Simon-a 55.00 165.00 385.00
3-1 pg. Space Hawk by Wolverton; S&K-a 44.00 132.00 305.00
4,5-S&K-a in each; 5-Everett-a begins on Sub-Zero 35.00 105.00 245.00
6,8-10-S&K-a 32.00 95.00 225.00
7-S&K c/a 33.00 100.00 230.00
11,12 14.00 43.00 100.00
V2#1-Origin Dick Cole & The Twister; Twister x-over in Dick Cole, Sub-Zero, & Blue Bolt. Origin Simba Karno who battles Dick Cole through V2/5 & becomes main supporting character V2/6 on; battle-c 10.00 30.00 70.00
2-Origin The Twister retold in text 6.00 18.00 42.00
3-5: 5-Intro. Freezum 4.35 13.00 30.00
6-Origin Sgt. Spook retold 3.50 10.50 24.00
7-12: 7-Lois Blake becomes Blue Bolt's costume aide; last Twister 3.00 9.00 21.00
V3#1-3 2.15 6.50 15.00
4-12: 4-Blue Bolt abandons costume 2.00 6.00 14.00
V4#1-Hitler, Tojo, Mussolini-c 2.00 6.00 14.00
V4#2-12: 3-Shows V4#3 on-c, V4#4 inside (9-10/43). 8-Last Sub-Zero 1.65 4.75 11.00
V5#1-8, V6#1-3,5-10, V7#1-12 1.30 4.00 9.00
V6#4-Racist cover 1.50 4.50 10.00
V8#1-6,8-12, V9#1-5,7,8 1.15 3.50 8.00
V8#7,V9#6,9-L. B. Cole-c 1.75 5.25 12.00
V10#1(#100) 1.50 4.50 10.00
V10#2(#101)-Last Dick Cole, Blue Bolt 1.35 4.00 9.00

NOTE: ***Everett** c-V1#4,11, V2#1,2. **Gustavson** a-V1#1-12, V2#1-7. **Rico** a-V6#10, V7#4. Blue Bolt not in V9#8.*

BLUE BOLT (Becomes Ghostly Weird Stories #120 on; continuation of Novelty Blue Bolt) (. .Weird Tales #112-119)
No. 102, Nov-Dec, 1949 - No. 119, May-June, 1953
Star Publications

102-The Chameleon, & Target app. 8.00 24.00 56.00
103,104-The Chameleon app.; last Target-#104 7.00 21.00 50.00
105-Origin Blue Bolt (from #1) retold by Simon; Chameleon & Target app.; opium den story 19.00 57.00 132.00
106-Blue Bolt by S&K begins; Spacehawk reprints from Target by Wolverton begins, ends #110; Sub-Zero begins; ends #109 15.00 45.00 105.00
107-110: 108-Last S&K Blue Bolt reprint. 109-Wolverton-c(r)/inside Spacehawk splash. 110-Target app. 15.00 45.00 105.00
111-Red Rocket & The Mask-r; last Blue Bolt; 1pg. L. B. Cole-a 17.00 51.00 120.00
112-Last Torpedo Man app. 15.00 45.00 105.00
113-Wolverton's Spacehawk r-/Target V3#7 15.00 45.00 105.00
114,116: 116-Jungle Jo-r 15.00 45.00 105.00
115-Sgt. Spook app. 17.00 51.00 120.00
117-Jo-Jo & Blue Bolt-r 15.00 45.00 105.00
118-"White Spirit" by Wood 17.00 51.00 120.00
119-Disbrow/Cole-c; Jungle Jo-r 15.00 45.00 105.00
Accepted Reprint #103(1957?, nd) 3.00 9.00 21.00

NOTE: ***L. B. Cole** c-102-108, 110 on. **Disbrow** a-112(2), 113(3), 114(2), 115(2), 116-118. **Hollingsworth** a-117. **Palais** a-112r.*

BLUE CIRCLE COMICS
June, 1944 - No. 6, April, 1945
Enwil Associates/Rural Home

1-The Blue Circle begins; origin Steel Fist 8.00 24.00 56.00
2 4.00 12.00 28.00
3-5: Last Steel Fist 3.00 9.00 21.00
6-Colossal Features-r 3.00 9.00 21.00

BLUE DEVIL
June, 1984 - No. 31, Dec, 1986
DC Comics

1 .35 1.00 2.00
2-5: 4-Origin Nebiros .60 1.20
6-10: 7-Gil Kane-a .50 1.00
11-16 .45 .90
17-19: Crisis x-over .50 1.00
20-30: 27-Godfrey Goose app. .45 .90
31-Double size .65 1.30
Annual 1 (11/85)-Team-ups with Black Orchid, The Creeper, Demon, Madame Xanadu, Man-Bat & Phantom Stranger .25 .70 1.40

BLUE PHANTOM, THE
June-Aug, 1962
Dell Publishing Co.

Blue Beetle #1 (1967), © DC

Blue Bolt V3#1, © NOVP

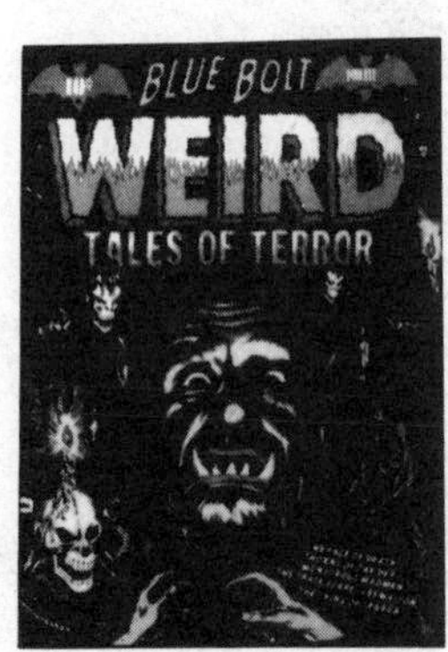

Blue Bolt #111, © STAR

Blue Ribbon Comics #1, © MLJ

Bobby Benson's B-Bar-B Riders #5, © ME

Bob Colt #4, © FAW

	Good	Fine	Mint
BLUE PHANTOM, THE (continued)			
1(01-066-208)-by Fred Fredericks	1.70	5.00	12.00

BLUE RIBBON COMICS (. . . Mystery Comics No. 9-18)
Nov, 1939 - No. 22, March, 1942 (1st MLJ series)
MLJ Magazines

	Good	Fine	Mint
1-Dan Hastings, Ricky the Amazing Boy, Rang-A-Tang the Wonder Dog begin; Little Nemo app. (not by W. McCay); Jack Cole-a(3)	100.00	300.00	700.00
2-Bob Phantom, Silver Fox (both in #3), Rang-A-Tang Club & Cpl. Collins begin; Jack Cole-a	40.00	120.00	280.00
3-J. Cole-a	27.00	81.00	190.00
4-Doc Strong, The Green Falcon, & Hercules begin; origin & 1st app. The Fox & Ty-Gor, Son of the Tiger	30.00	90.00	210.00
5-8: 8-Last Hercules	18.00	54.00	125.00
9-(Scarce)-Origin & 1st app. Mr. Justice	93.00	280.00	650.00
10-12: 12-Last Doc Strong	36.00	108.00	252.00
13-Inferno, the Flame Breather begins, ends #19. Devil-c	36.00	108.00	252.00
14,15,17,18: 15-Last Green Falcon	33.00	100.00	230.00
16-Origin & 1st app. Captain Flag	62.00	185.00	435.00
19-22: 20-Last Ty-Gor. 22-Origin Mr. Justice retold	28.00	85.00	200.00

BLUE RIBBON COMICS (Teen-Age Diary Secrets No. 6)
Feb, 1949 - No. 6, Aug, 1949 (See Heckle & Jeckle)
Blue Ribbon (St. John)

	Good	Fine	Mint
1,3-Heckle & Jeckle	3.00	9.00	21.00
2(4/49)-Diary Secrets; Baker-c	5.00	15.00	35.00
4(6/49)-Teen-Age Diary Secrets; Baker c/a(2)	6.00	18.00	42.00
5(8/49)-Teen-Age Diary Secrets; Oversize; photo-c; Baker-a(2)- Continues as Teen-Age Diary Secrets	6.00	18.00	42.00
6-Dinky Duck(8/49)	1.30	4.00	9.00

BLUE-RIBBON COMICS
Oct, 1983 - No. 14, Dec, 1984
Red Circle Prod./Archie Ent. No. 5 on

	Good	Fine	Mint
1-The Fly No. 1-r		.50	1.00
2-4: 3-Origin Steel Sterling		.50	1.00
5-14: 5-S&K Shield-r. 6,7-The Fox app. 8,11-Black Hood. 12-Thunder Agents. 13-Thunder Bunny. 14-Web & Jaguar		.50	1.00

NOTE: ***Adams** a(r)-8. **Buckler** a-4i. **Nino** a-2i. **McWilliams** a-8. **Morrow** a-8.*

BLUE STREAK (See Holyoke One-Shot No. 8)

BLYTHE (See 4-Color No. 1072)

B-MAN (See Double-Dare Adventures)

BO (Also see Big Shot No. 29; Tom Cat No. 4 on)
June, 1955 - No. 3, Oct, 1955 (a dog)
Charlton Comics Group

	Good	Fine	Mint
1-3-Newspaper reprints by Frank Beck	3.00	9.00	21.00

BOATNIKS, THE (See Walt Disney Showcase No. 1)

BOB & BETTY & SANTA'S WISHING WELL
1941 (12 pages) (Christmas giveaway)
Sears Roebuck & Co.

	Good	Fine	Mint
	6.00	18.00	42.00

BOBBY BENSON'S B-BAR-B RIDERS (See Best of The West, & Model Fun)
May-June, 1950 - No. 20, May-June, 1953
Magazine Enterprises

	Good	Fine	Mint
1-Powell-a	11.00	33.00	75.00
2	5.70	17.00	40.00
3-5: 4-Lemonade Kid-c	4.60	14.00	32.00
6-8,10	3.50	10.50	24.00
9,11,13-Frazetta-c; Ghost Rider in #13-15 (Ayers-a).	16.00	48.00	110.00
12,17-20(A-1 88)	3.00	9.00	21.00
14-Bondage-c	4.00	12.00	28.00
15-Ghost Rider-c	4.00	12.00	28.00
16-Photo-c	4.00	12.00	28.00
. . . in the Tunnel of Gold-(1936, 5¼x8"; 100 pgs.) Radio giveaway by Hecker-H.O. Company(H.O. Oats); contains 22 color pages of comics, rest in novel form	4.60	14.00	32.00
. . . And The Lost Herd-same as above	4.60	14.00	32.00

NOTE: ***Ayers** a-13-15, 20. **Powell** a-1-12(4 ea.), 13(3), 14-16(Red Hawk only); c-1-8,10,12. Lemonade Kid in most 1-13.*

BOBBY COMICS
May, 1946
Universal Phoenix Features

	Good	Fine	Mint
1-by S. M. Iger	3.50	10.50	24.00

BOBBY SHELBY COMICS
1949
Shelby Cycle Co./Harvey Publications

	Good	Fine	Mint
	1.85	5.50	13.00

BOBBY SHERMAN (TV)
Feb, 1972 - No. 7, Oct, 1972
Charlton Comics

	Good	Fine	Mint
1-7-Based on TV show "Getting Together"	1.20	3.50	7.00

BOBBY THATCHER & TREASURE CAVE
1932 (86 pages; B&W; hardcover; 7x9")
Altemus Co.

	Good	Fine	Mint
Reprints; Storm-a	5.00	15.00	35.00

BOBBY THATCHER'S ROMANCE
1931
The Bell Syndicate/Henry Altemus Co.

	Good	Fine	Mint
nn-By Storm	5.00	15.00	35.00

BOB COLT (Movie star)(See X-Mas Comics)
Nov, 1950 - No. 10, May, 1952
Fawcett Publications

	Good	Fine	Mint
1-Bob Colt, his horse Buckskin & sidekick Pablo begin; photo front/back-c begin	14.00	42.00	100.00
2	11.50	34.50	80.00
3-5	10.00	30.00	70.00
6-Flying Saucer story	8.50	25.50	60.00
7-10: 9-Last photo back-c	7.00	21.00	50.00

BOB HOPE (See Adventures of. . .)

BOB SCULLY, TWO-FISTED HICK DETECTIVE
No date (1930's) (36 pages; 9½x12"; B&W; paper cover)
Humor Publ. Co.

	Good	Fine	Mint
By Howard Dell; not reprints	4.35	13.00	30.00

BOB SON OF BATTLE (See 4-Color No. 729)

BOB STEELE WESTERN (Movie star)
Dec, 1950 - No. 10, June, 1952
Fawcett Publications

	Good	Fine	Mint
1-Bob Steele & his horse Bullet begin; photo front/back-c begin	14.00	42.00	100.00
2	11.50	34.50	80.00
3-5: 4-Last photo back-c	10.00	30.00	70.00
6-10: 10-Last photo-c	7.00	21.00	50.00

BOB SWIFT (Boy Sportsman)
May, 1951 - No. 5, Jan, 1952
Fawcett Publications

	Good	Fine	Mint
1	2.15	6.50	15.00
2-5: Saunders painted-c #1-5	1.30	4.00	9.00

BOLD ADVENTURES
Oct, 1983 - No. 3, June, 1984
Pacific Comics

	Good	Fine	Mint
1-Time Force, Spitfire, & The Weirdling begin	.30	.90	1.80
2,3	.25	.75	1.50

NOTE: ***Kaluta*** *c-3.* ***Nebres*** *a-3.* ***Nino*** *a-2, 3.* ***Severin*** *a-3.*

BOLD STORIES (Also see Candid Tales, It Rhymes With Lust)
Mar, 1950 - July, 1950 (Digest size; 144 pgs.; full color)
Kirby Publishing Co.

	Good	Fine	Mint
March issue (Very Rare) - Contains "The Ogre of Paris" by Wood	34.00	102.00	240.00
May issue (Very Rare) - Contains "The Cobra's Kiss" by Graham Ingels (21 pgs.)	25.00	75.00	175.00
July issue (Very Rare) - Contains "The Ogre of Paris" by Wood	27.00	81.00	190.00

BOMBARDIER (See Bee 29, the Bombardier & Cinema Comics Herald)

BOMBA, THE JUNGLE BOY
Sept-Oct, 1967 - No. 7, Sept-Oct, 1968
National Periodical Publications

	Good	Fine	Mint
1-Infantino/Anderson-c		.60	1.20
2-7		.40	.80

BOMBER COMICS
March, 1944 - No. 4, Winter, 1944-45
Elliot Publ. Co./Melverne Herald/Farrell/Sunrise Times

	Good	Fine	Mint
1-Wonder Boy, & Kismet, Man of Fate begin	14.00	42.00	100.00
2-4: 2-4-Have Classics Comics ad to HRN 20	10.00	30.00	70.00

BONANZA (TV)
June-Aug, 1960 - No. 37, Aug, 1970 (All Photo-c)
Dell/Gold Key

	Good	Fine	Mint
4-Color 1110	4.60	14.00	32.00
4-Color 1221,1283, also No. 01070-207, 01070-210	4.00	12.00	28.00
1(12/62-Gold Key)	4.00	12.00	28.00
2	2.65	8.00	18.00
3-10	2.00	6.00	14.00
11-20	1.50	4.50	10.00
21-37: 29-r	1.00	3.00	7.00

BONGO (See Story Hour Series)

BONGO & LUMPJAW (See 4-Color #706,886, & Walt Disney Showcase #3)

BON VOYAGE (See Movie Classics)

BOOK OF ALL COMICS
1945 (196 pages)
William H. Wise

	Good	Fine	Mint
Green Mask, Puppeteer	17.00	51.00	120.00

BOOK OF COMICS, THE
No date (1944) (132 pages) (25 cents)
William H. Wise

	Good	Fine	Mint
nn-Captain V app.	17.00	51.00	120.00

BOOK OF LOVE (See Fox Giants)

BOOSTER GOLD
Feb, 1986 - Present
DC comics

	Good	Fine	Mint
1	.50	1.50	3.00
2-5	.30	.90	1.80
6-10: 6-Origin		.60	1.20
11-25: 23-Byrne-c(i)		.50	1.00

BOOTS AND HER BUDDIES
No. 5, 9/48 - No. 9, 9/49; 12/55 - No. 3, 1956
Standard Comics/Visual Editions/Argo (NEA Service)

	Good	Fine	Mint
5-Strip-r	5.70	17.00	40.00
6,8	3.50	10.50	24.00
7-(Scarce)-Spanking panels(3)	13.00	40.00	90.00
9-(Scarce)-Frazetta-a, 2 pgs.	16.00	48.00	110.00
1-3(Argo-1955-56)-Reprints	1.60	4.70	11.00

BOOTS & SADDLES (See 4-Color No. 919,1029,1116)

BORDER PATROL
May-June, 1951 - No. 3, Sept-Oct, 1951
P. L. Publishing Co.

	Good	Fine	Mint
1	3.00	9.00	21.00
2,3	1.70	5.00	12.00

BORIS KARLOFF TALES OF MYSTERY (. . .Thriller No. 1,2)
No. 3, April, 1963 - No. 97, Feb, 1980 (TV)
Gold Key

	Good	Fine	Mint
3-8,10-(Two #5's, 10/63,11/63)	1.15	3.50	7.00
9-Wood-a	1.50	4.50	9.00
11-Williamson-a, Orlando-a, 8 pgs.	1.50	4.50	9.00
12-Torres, McWilliams-a; Orlando-a(2)	1.00	3.00	6.00
13,14,16-20	.70	2.00	4.00
15-Crandall,Evans-a	.85	2.50	5.00
21-Jones-a	.85	2.50	5.00
22-50: 23-Reprint; photo-c	.35	1.00	2.00
51-74: 74-Origin & 1st app. Taurus		.60	1.20
75-79,87-97: 78,81-86,88,90,92,95,97-Reprints		.40	.80
80-86-(52 pages)		.40	.80
Story Digest 1(7/70-Gold Key)-All text	.50	1.50	3.00

(See Mystery Comics Digest No. 2,5,8,11,14,17,20,23,26)

NOTE: ***Bolle*** *a-51-54, 56, 58, 59.* ***McWilliams*** *a-12, 14, 18, 19, 80, 81, 93.* ***Orlando*** *a-11-15, 21.*

BORIS KARLOFF THRILLER (TV) (Becomes Boris Karloff Tales of Mystery No. 3)
Oct, 1962 - No. 2, Jan, 1963 (80 pages)
Gold Key

	Good	Fine	Mint
1-Photo-c	2.00	6.00	16.00
2	1.75	5.25	14.00

BORIS THE BEAR INSTANT COLOR CLASSICS
July, 1987 - Present ($1.75, $1.95, color)
Dark Horse Comics

	Good	Fine	Mint
1	.30	.90	1.75
2-5	.35	1.00	1.95

BORN AGAIN
1978 (39 cents)
Spire Christian Comics (Fleming H. Revell Co.)

	Good	Fine	Mint
Watergate, Nixon, etc.		.50	1.00

BOUNCER, THE (Formerly Green Mask?)
1944 - No. 14, Jan, 1945
Fox Features Syndicate

	Good	Fine	Mint
nn(1944)-Same as #14	6.00	18.00	42.00
11(#1)(9/44)-Origin	6.00	18.00	42.00
12-14	4.60	14.00	32.00

BOUNTY GUNS (See 4-Color No. 739)

BOY AND HIS BOT, A
Jan, 1987 ($1.95, color)
Now Comics

	Good	Fine	Mint
1	.35	1.00	2.00

BOY AND THE PIRATES, THE (See 4-Color No. 1117)

BOY COMICS Captain Battle No. 1&2; Boy Illustories No. 43-108)
(Stories by Charles Biro)
No. 3, April, 1942 - No. 119, March, 1956

Bonanza #16, © NBC

Border Patrol #1, © P.L. Publ.

The Bouncer #11, © FOX

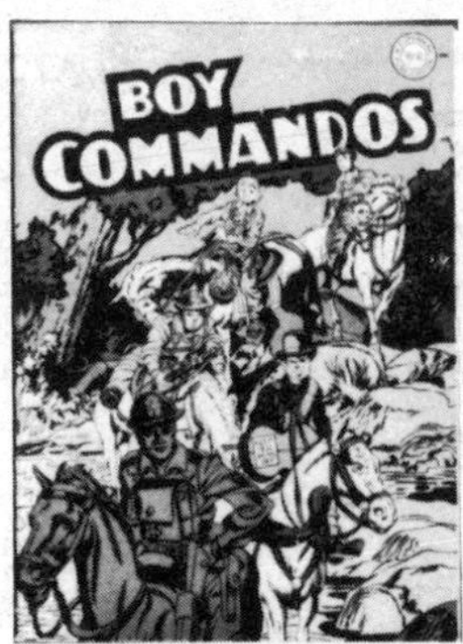

Boy Commandos #6, © DC

Boy Meets Girl #19, © LEV

Bozo the Clown #6, © Capitol Records

BOY COMICS (continued)
Lev Gleason Publications

	Good	Fine	Mint
3(No.1)-Origin Crimebuster, Bombshell & Young Robin Hood; Yankee Longago,Case 1001-1008, Swoop Storm, & Boy Movies begin; intro. Iron Jaw	80.00	240.00	560.00
4-Hitler, Tojo, Mussolini-c	35.00	105.00	245.00
5	30.00	90.00	210.00
6-Origin Iron Jaw; origin & death of Iron Jaw's son; Little Dynamite begins, ends #39	60.00	180.00	420.00
7,9: 7-Flag-c	25.00	75.00	175.00
8-Death of Iron Jaw	28.00	84.00	195.00
10-Return of Iron Jaw; classic Biro-c	35.00	105.00	245.00
11-14	17.00	51.00	120.00
15-Death of Iron Jaw	21.00	62.00	146.00
16,18-20	11.00	32.00	76.00
17-Flag-c	12.00	36.00	84.00
21-26	7.00	21.00	50.00
27-29-(68 pages). 28-Yankee Longago ends	8.50	25.50	60.00
30-Origin Crimebuster retold	9.00	27.00	63.00
31-40: 32(68pgs.)-Swoop Storm, Young Robin Hood ends. 34-Suicide c/story	3.50	10.50	24.00
41-50	2.30	7.00	16.00
51-59: 57-Dilly Duncan begins, ends #71	1.70	5.00	12.00
60-Iron Jaw returns	2.15	6.50	15.00
61-Origin Crimebuster & Iron Jaw retold	2.65	8.00	18.00
62-Death of Iron Jaw explained	3.00	9.00	21.00
63-72	1.60	4.70	11.00
73-Frazetta 1-pg. ad	1.70	5.00	12.00
74-80: 80-1st app. Rocky X of the Rocketeers; becomes "Rocky X" #101; Iron Jaw, Sniffer & the Deadly Dozen begins, ends #118	1.50	4.50	10.00
81-88	1.50	4.50	10.00
89-92-The Claw serial app. in all	1.70	5.00	12.00
93-Claw cameo; Check-a(Rocky X)	2.30	7.00	16.00
94-97,99	1.50	4.50	10.00
98-Rocky X by Sid Check	2.65	8.00	18.00
100	2.00	6.00	14.00
101-107,109,111,119: 111-Crimebuster becomes Chuck Chandler. 119-Last Crimebuster	1.50	4.50	10.00
108,110,112-118-Kubert-a	2.00	6.00	14.00

(See Giant Boy Book of Comics)

NOTE: *Boy Movies in 3-5,40,41. Iron Jaw app.-3, 4, 6, 8, 10, 11, 13-15; returns-60-62, 68, 69, 72-79, 81-118.* ***Briefer*** *a-18, 19.* ***Fuje*** *a-55, 18 pgs.* ***Palais*** *a-19.*

BOY COMMANDOS (See Detective Comics)
Winter, 1942-43 - No. 36, Nov-Dec, 1949
National Periodical Publications

	Good	Fine	Mint
1-Origin Liberty Belle; The Sandman & The Newsboy Legion x-over in Boy Commandos; S&K-a, 48 pgs.	110.00	330.00	770.00
2-Last Liberty Belle; S&K-a, 46 pgs.	55.00	165.00	385.00
3-S&K-a, 45 pgs.	38.00	115.00	265.00
4,5	22.00	65.00	154.00
6-8,10: 6-S&K-a	15.00	45.00	105.00
9-No S&K-a	10.00	30.00	70.00
11-Infinity-c	11.00	33.00	76.00
12-20	8.00	24.00	56.00
21,22,24-30	5.00	15.00	35.00
23-S&K c/a(all)	6.00	18.00	42.00
31-35: 32-Dale Evans app. on-c. 34-Intro. Wolf, their mascot	3.50	10.50	24.00
36	4.35	13.00	30.00

NOTE: *Most issues signed by* ***Simon & Kirby*** *are not by them.* ***S&K*** *c-1-9.*

BOY COMMANDOS
Sept-Oct, 1973 - No. 2, Nov-Dec, 1973
National Periodical Publications

	Good	Fine	Mint
1,2-G.A. S&K reprints		.30	.60

BOY DETECTIVE
May-June, 1951 - No. 4, May, 1952
Avon Periodicals

	Good	Fine	Mint
1	7.00	21.00	50.00
2,3: 3-Kinstler-c	4.60	14.00	32.00
4-Kinstler c/a	8.00	24.00	56.00

BOY EXPLORERS COMICS (Terry and The Pirates No. 3 on)
May-June, 1946 - No. 2, Sept-Oct, 1946
Family Comics (Harvey Publications)

	Good	Fine	Mint
1-Intro The Explorers, Duke of Broadway, Calamity Jane & Danny Dixon...Cadet; S&K-c/a, 24 pgs	35.00	105.00	245.00
2-(Rare)-Small size (5½x8½"; B&W; 32 pgs.) Distributed to mail subscribers only; S&K-a. Estimated value			$250-$400

(Also see All New No. 15, Flash Gordon No. 5, and Stuntman No. 3)

BOY ILLUSTORIES (See Boy Comics)

BOY LOVES GIRL (Boy Meets Girl No. 1-24)
No. 25, July, 1952 - No. 57, June, 1956
Lev Gleason Publications

	Good	Fine	Mint
25(#1)	2.30	7.00	16.00
26,27,29-42: 30-33-Serial, 'Loves of My Life.' 39-Lingerie panels	1.50	4.50	10.00
28-Drug propaganda story	2.35	7.00	16.00
43-Toth-a	3.00	9.00	21.00
44-50: 50-Last pre-code (2/55)	1.15	3.50	8.00
51-57: 57-Ann Brewster-a	.70	2.00	6.00

BOY MEETS GIRL (Boy Loves Girl No. 25 on)
Feb, 1950 - No. 24, June, 1952 (No. 1-17, 52 pgs.)
Lev Gleason Publications

	Good	Fine	Mint
1-Guardineer-a	3.50	10.50	24.00
2	1.70	5.00	12.00
3-10	1.35	4.00	9.00
11-24	1.15	3.50	8.00

NOTE: ***Briefer*** *a-24.* ***Fuje*** *c-3,7. Painted-c 1-17. Photo-c 19-21,23.*

BOYS' AND GIRLS' MARCH OF COMICS (See March of Comics)

BOYS' RANCH (Also see Western Tales & Witches' Western Tales)
Oct, 1950 - No. 6, Aug, 1951 (No.1-3, 52 pgs.; No. 4-6, 36 pgs.)
Harvey Publications

	Good	Fine	Mint
1-S&K-a(3)	28.00	84.00	200.00
2-S&K-a(3)	22.00	65.00	154.00
3-S&K-a(2); Meskin-a	19.00	57.00	132.00
4-S&K-c/a, 5pgs.	14.00	42.00	100.00
5,6-S&K splashes & centerspread only; Meskin-a	7.00	21.00	50.00
Shoe Store Giveaway #5,6 (Identical to regular issues except S&K centerfold replaced with ad)	5.70	17.00	40.00

NOTE: ***Simon & Kirby*** *c-1-6.*

BOZO THE CLOWN (TV) (Bozo No. 7 on)
July, 1950 - No. 4, Oct-Dec, 1963
Dell Publishing Co.

	Good	Fine	Mint
4-Color 285	5.00	15.00	35.00
2(7-9/51)-7(10-12/52)	3.00	9.00	21.00
4-Color 464,508,551,594(10/54)	3.00	9.00	21.00
1(nn, 5-7/62) - 4(1963)	1.50	4.50	10.00
Giveaway-1961, 16 pgs., 3½x7¼", Apsco Products	1.00	3.00	6.00

BOZO THE CLOWN 3-D
1987 ($2.50)
Blackthorne Publishing

	Good	Fine	Mint
1	.40	1.25	2.50

BOZZ CHRONICLES, THE
Dec, 1985 - No. 6, 1986 (Adults only)

BOZZ CHRONICLES (continued)
Epic Comics (Marvel)

	Good	Fine	Mint
1	.35	1.00	2.00
2-6	.25	.80	1.60

BRADY BUNCH, THE (TV)
Feb, 1970 - No. 2, May, 1970
Dell Publishing Co.

	Good	Fine	Mint
1,2	1.35	4.00	8.00
Kite Fun Book (PG&E, 1976)	.70	2.00	4.00

BRAIN, THE
Sept, 1956 - 1958
Sussex Publ. Co./Magazine Enterprises

	Good	Fine	Mint
1	1.85	5.50	13.00
2,3	1.00	3.00	7.00
4-7	.75	2.25	5.00
I.W. Reprints #1,3,4,8,9,10('63),14	.30	.80	1.60
I.W. Reprint #2-Reprints Sussex #2 with new cover added	.30	.80	1.60
Super Reprint #17,18(nd)	.30	.80	1.60

BRAIN BOY
April-June, 1962 - No. 6, Sept-Nov, 1963
Dell Publishing Co.

	Good	Fine	Mint
4-Color 1330-Gil Kane-a; origin	3.50	10.50	24.00
2(7-9/62),3-6: 4-origin retold	2.00	6.00	14.00

BRAND ECHH (See Not Brand Echh)

BRAND OF EMPIRE (See 4-Color No. 771)

BRAVADOS, THE (See Wild Western Action)
August, 1971 (52 pages) (One-Shot)
Skywald Publ. Corp.

	Good	Fine	Mint
1-Red Mask, The Durango Kid, Billy Nevada-r		.30	.60

BRAVE AND THE BOLD, THE (See Super DC Giant)
Aug-Sept, 1955 - No. 200, July, 1983
National Periodical Publications/DC Comics

	Good	Fine	Mint
1-Kubert Viking Prince, Silent Knight, Golden Gladiator begin	77.00	230.00	540.00
2	32.00	95.00	226.00
3,4	18.00	54.00	125.00
5-Robin Hood begins	12.50	38.00	88.00
6-10: 6-Kubert Robin Hood; G. Gladiator last app.; Silent Knight; no V. Prince	13.00	40.00	92.00
11-22: 22-Last Silent Knight	10.00	30.00	70.00
23-Kubert Viking Prince origin	12.30	37.00	86.00
24-Last Kubert Viking Prince	12.30	37.00	86.00
25-27-Suicide Squad	3.50	10.50	24.00
28-Justice League intro.; origin Snapper Carr	78.00	235.00	550.00
29,30-Justice League	31.00	92.00	220.00
31-33-Cave Carson	3.00	9.00	21.00
34-Origin Hawkman & Byth by Kubert	9.30	28.00	65.00
35,36-Kubert Hawkman; origin Shadow Thief #36	4.85	14.50	34.00
37-39-Suicide Squad. 38-Last 10 cent ish.	2.15	6.60	15.00
40,41-Cave Carson Inside Earth; #40 has Kubert art	3.00	9.00	21.00
42,44-Kubert Hawkman	3.50	10.50	24.00
43-Origin Hawkman by Kubert	3.70	11.00	26.00
45-49-Infantino Strange Sports Stories	.70	2.00	4.00
50-The Green Arrow & Manhunter From Mars	1.00	3.00	6.00
51-Aquaman & Hawkman	.75	2.20	4.40
52-Kubert Sgt. Rock, Haunted Tank, Johnny Cloud, & Mlle. Marie	1.20	3.50	7.00
53-Toth Atom & The Flash	1.20	3.50	7.00
54-Kid Flash, Robin & Aqualad; 1st app./origin Teen Titans (6-7/64)	6.85	21.00	48.00
55-Metal Men & The Atom	.55	1.60	3.20
56-The Flash & Manhunter From Mars	.55	1.60	3.20
57-Intro & Origin Metamorpho	.55	1.60	3.20
58-Metamorpho by Fradon	.55	1.60	3.20
59-Batman & Green Lantern	.55	1.60	3.20
60-Teen Titans	2.65	8.00	16.00
61,62-Origin Starman & Black Canary by Anderson. 62-Huntress app.	.85	2.50	5.00
63-Supergirl & Wonder Woman	.50	1.50	3.00
64-Batman Versus Eclipso	.50	1.50	3.00
65-Flash & Doom Patrol	.50	1.50	3.00
66-Metamorpho & Metal Men	.50	1.50	3.00
67-Infantino Batman & The Flash	.50	1.50	3.00
68-72	.50	1.50	3.00
73-78	.40	1.20	2.40
79-Batman-Deadman by Adams	1.70	5.00	10.00
80-Batman-Creeper; Adams-a	1.35	4.00	8.00
81-Batman-Flash; Adams-a	1.35	4.00	8.00
82-Batman-Aquaman; Adams-a; origin Ocean Master retold	1.35	4.00	8.00
83-Batman-Teen Titans; Adams-a	2.50	7.50	15.00
84-Batman(GA)-Sgt. Rock; Adams-a	1.35	4.00	8.00
85-Batman-Green Arrow; new costume for Green Arrow by Adams	1.35	4.00	8.00
86-Batman-Deadman; Adams-a	1.35	4.00	8.00
87-92	.35	1.00	2.00
93-Batman-House of Mystery; Adams-a	1.35	4.00	8.00
94-Batman-Teen Titans	.50	1.50	3.00
95-99: 97-Origin Deadman-r	.35	1.00	2.00
100-Batman-Gr. Lantern-Gr. Arrow-Black Canary-Robin; Deadman by Adams	1.00	3.00	6.00
101-Batman-Metamorpho; Kubert Viking Prince	.25	.75	1.50
102-Batman-Teen Titans; Adams-a(p)	.50	1.50	3.00
103-116		.50	1.00
117-148,150		.40	.80
149-Batman-Teen Titans		.60	1.20
151-199: 196-Origin Ragman retold		.30	.60
200-Double-sized (64 pgs.); printed on Mando paper; Earth One & Earth Two Batman team-up; Intro/1st app. Batman & The Outsiders	.40	1.25	2.50

NOTE: ***Adams** a-79-86, 93, 100r, 102; c-75, 76, 79-86, 88-90, 93, 95, 99, 100r. **Anderson** a-115r; c-72i, 96i. **Aparo** a-98, 100-02, 104-25, 126i, 127-36, 138-45, 147, 148i, 149-52, 154, 155, 157-62, 168-70, 173-78, 180-82, 184, 186i-89i, 191i-93i, 195, 196, 200; c-105-09, 111-36, 137i, 138-75, 177, 180-84, 186-200. **Austin** a-166i. **Buckler** a-185, 186p; c-137, 178p, 185p, 186p. **Giordano** a-143, 144. **Infantino** a-67p, 72p, 97r, 98r, 172p, 183p, 190p, 194p; c-45-49, 67p, 69p, 70p, 72p, 96p, 98r. **Kaluta** c-176. **Kane** a-115r. **Kubert &/or Heath** a-1-24; reprints-101, 113, 115, 117. **Kubert** c-22-24, 34-36, 40, 42-44, 52. **Mooney** a-114r. **Newton** a-153p, 156p, 165p. **Roussos** a-114r. **Staton** 148p. 52 pgs.-97, 100; 64 pgs.-120; 100 pgs.-112-117.*

BRAVE AND THE BOLD SPECIAL, THE (See DC Special Series No. 8)

BRAVE EAGLE (See 4-Color No. 705,770,816,879,929)

BRAVE ONE, THE (See 4-Color No. 773)

BRAVE STARR IN 3-D
1987 - Present ($2.50, with glasses)
Blackthorne Publishing

	Good	Fine	Mint
1-Based on TV show	.40	1.25	2.50

BREEZE LAWSON, SKY SHERIFF (See Sky Sheriff)

BRENDA LEE STORY, THE
September, 1962
Dell Publishing Co.

	Good	Fine	Mint
01-078-209	4.00	12.00	28.00

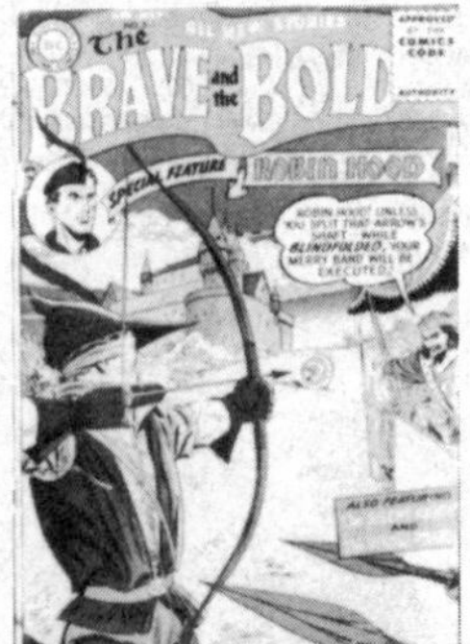

The Brave and the Bold #5, © DC

The Brave and the Bold #30, © DC

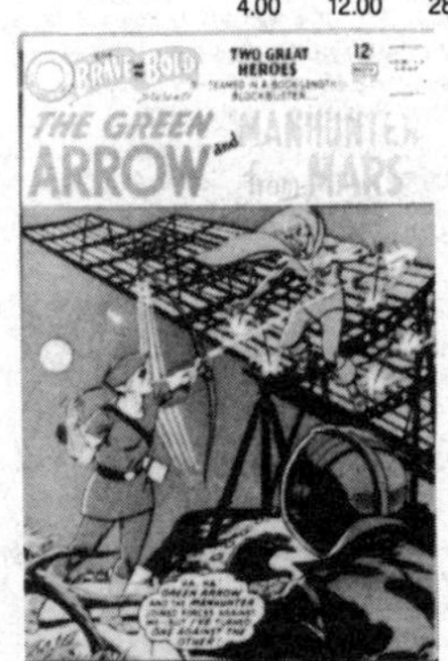

The Brave and the Bold # 50, © DC

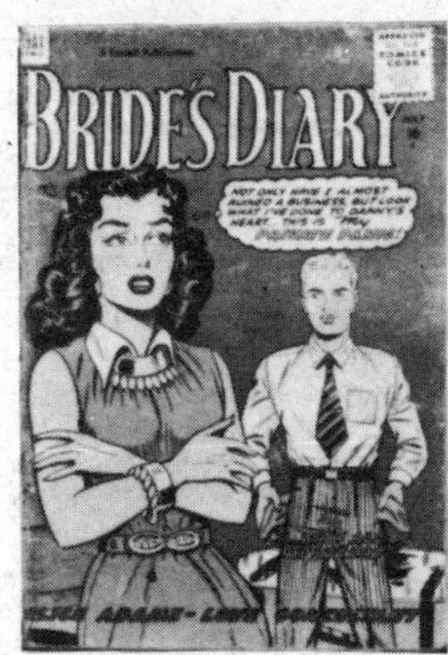

Bride's Diary #5, © AJAX

Broadway Hollywood Blackouts #1, © Stanhall

Brother Power, The Geek #1, © DC

BRENDA STARR (Also see All Great)
No. 13, 9/47; No. 14, 3/48; V2No.3, 6/48 - V2No.12, 12/49
Four Star Comics Corp./Superior Comics Ltd.

	Good	Fine	Mint
V1#13-By Dale Messick	24.00	72.00	170.00
14-Kamen bondage-c	24.00	72.00	170.00
V2#3-Baker-a?	20.00	60.00	140.00
4-Used in **SOTI**, pg. 21; Kamen bondage-c	22.00	65.00	154.00
5-10	17.00	51.00	120.00
11,12 (Scarce)	20.00	60.00	140.00

NOTE: *Newspaper reprints plus original material through #6. All original #7 on.*

BRENDA STARR (. . . Reporter)(Young Lovers No. 16 on?)
No. 13, June, 1955 - No. 15, Oct, 1955
Charlton Comics

13-15-Newspaper-r	11.00	33.00	76.00

BRENDA STARR REPORTER
October, 1963
Dell Publishing Co.

1	7.00	21.00	50.00

BRER RABBIT (See 4-Color No. 129,208,693, Walt Disney Showcase No. 28, and Wheaties)

BRER RABBIT IN "A KITE TAIL"
1955 (16 pages, 5x7¼", soft-c) (Walt Disney) (Premium)
Pacific Gas & Electric Co./Southern Calif. Edison

(Rare)-Kite fun book	14.00	42.00	100.00

BRER RABBIT IN "ICE CREAM FOR THE PARTY"
1955 (16 pages, 5x7¼", soft-c) (Walt Disney) (Premium)
American Dairy Association

(Rare)	8.00	24.00	56.00

BRICK BRADFORD
1948 - 1949 (Ritt & Grey reprints)
King Features Syndicate/Standard

5	7.00	21.00	50.00
6-8: 7-Schomburg-c	6.00	18.00	42.00

BRIDE'S DIARY
No. 4, May, 1955 - No. 10, Aug, 1956
Ajax/Farrell Publ.

4 (#1)	2.30	7.00	16.00
5-8	1.60	4.70	11.00
9,10-Disbrow-a	2.00	6.00	14.00

BRIDES IN LOVE (Hollywood Romances & Summer Love No. 46 on)
Aug, 1956 - No. 45, Feb, 1965
Charlton Comics

1	2.30	7.00	16.00
2	1.30	4.00	9.00
3-10	.85	2.50	6.00
11-20	.50	1.50	3.00
21-45	.30	.90	1.80

BRIDES ROMANCES
Nov, 1953 - No. 23, Dec, 1956
Quality Comics Group

1	4.00	12.00	28.00
2	2.00	6.00	14.00
3-10	1.60	4.70	11.00
11-14,16,17,19-22	1.15	3.50	8.00
15-Baker-a(p); Colan-a	1.30	4.00	9.00
18-Baker-a	1.65	5.00	11.50
23-Baker c/a	2.50	7.50	17.00

BRIDE'S SECRETS
Apr-May, 1954 - No. 19, May, 1958
Ajax/Farrell(Excellent Publ.)/Four-Star Comic

	Good	Fine	Mint
1	4.00	12.00	28.00
2	2.00	6.00	14.00
3-6: Last precode (3/55)	1.50	4.50	10.00
7-19: 12-Disbrow-a. 18-Hollingsworth-a	1.15	3.50	8.00

BRIDE-TO-BE ROMANCES (See True . . .)

BRIGAND, THE (See Fawcett Movie Comics No. 18)

BRINGING UP FATHER (See Large Feature Comic No. 9 & 4-Color No. 37)

BRINGING UP FATHER
1917 (16½x5½"; cardboard cover; 100 pages; B&W)
Star Co. (King Features)

(Rare) Daily strip reprints by George McManus (no price on cover)	25.00	75.00	175.00

BRINGING UP FATHER
1919 - 1934 (by George McManus)
(10x10"; stiff cardboard covers; B&W; daily strip reprints; 52 pgs.)
(No. 22 is 9¼x9½")
Cupples & Leon Co.

1	20.00	60.00	140.00
2-10	10.00	30.00	70.00
11-26 (Scarcer)	15.00	45.00	105.00
The Big Book 1(1926)-Thick book (hardcover); 10¼x10¼", 142pgs.	25.00	75.00	175.00
The Big Book 2(1929)	20.00	60.00	140.00

NOTE: *The Big Books contain 3 regular issues rebound and probably with dust jackets.*

BRINGING UP FATHER, THE TROUBLE OF
1921 (9x15") (Sunday reprints in color)
Embee Publ. Co.

(Rare)	25.00	75.00	175.00

BROADWAY HOLLYWOOD BLACKOUTS
Mar-Apr, 1954 - No. 3, July-Aug, 1954
Stanhall

1	4.00	12.00	28.00
2,3	2.65	8.00	18.00

BROADWAY ROMANCES
January, 1950 - No. 5, Sept, 1950
Quality Comics Group

1-Ward c/a, 9pgs.; Gustavson-a	14.00	42.00	100.00
2-Ward-a, 9pgs., photo-c	8.50	25.50	60.00
3-5: 4,5-Photo-c	3.70	11.00	26.00

BROKEN ARROW (See 4-Color No. 855,947)

BROKEN CROSS, THE (See The Crusaders)

BRONCHO BILL (See Sparkler comics)
1939 - 1940; No. 5, 1?/48 - No. 16, 8?/50
United Features Syndicate/Standard(Visual Editions) No. 5-on

Single Series 2 ('39)	20.00	60.00	140.00
Single Series 19 ('40)(#2 on cvr)	16.00	48.00	110.00
5	4.00	12.00	28.00
6(4/48)-10(4/49)	2.30	7.00	16.00
11(6/49)-16	1.85	5.50	13.00

NOTE: *Schomburg c-6,7,9-13,16.*

BROTHER POWER, THE GEEK
Sept-Oct, 1968 - No. 2, Nov-Dec, 1968
National Periodical Publications

1-Origin; Simon-c(i?)	1.00	3.00	6.00
2	.50	1.50	3.00

BROTHERS, HANG IN THERE, THE
1979 (49 cents)
Spire Christian Comics (Fleming H. Revell Co.)

	Good	Fine	Mint
		.30	.60

BROTHERS OF THE SPEAR (Also see Tarzan)
6/72 - No. 17, 2/76; No. 18, 5/82
Gold Key/Whitman No. 18 on

	Good	Fine	Mint
1	1.00	3.00	6.00
2	.70	2.00	4.00
3-10	.45	1.25	2.50
11-17		.50	1.00
18-Manning-r/No. 2; Leopard Girl-r		.40	.80

NOTE: *Painted-c No. 2-17.* ***Spiegle*** *a-13-17.*

BROTHERS, THE CULT ESCAPE, THE
1980 (49 Cents)
Spire Christian Comics (Fleming H. Revell Co.)

	Good	Fine	Mint
		.30	.60

BROWNIES (See 4-Color No. 192, 244, 293, 337, 365, 398, 436, 482, 522, 605 & New Funnies)

BRUCE GENTRY
Jan, 1948 - No. 2, Nov, 1948; No. 3, Jan, 1949 - No. 8, July, 1949
Better/Standard/Four Star Publ./Superior No. 3

	Good	Fine	Mint
1-Ray Bailey strip reprints begin, end No. 3; E. C. emblem appears as a monogram on stationery in story; negligee panels	17.00	51.00	120.00
2,3	12.00	36.00	84.00
4-8	9.00	27.00	63.00

NOTE: ***Kamenish*** *a-2-4,6,7; c-1-4,6-8.*

BRUTE, THE
Feb, 1975 - No. 3, July, 1975
Seaboard Publ. (Atlas)

	Good	Fine	Mint
1-Origin & 1st app; Sekowsky-a		.40	.80
2,3: 2-Sekowsky-a		.25	.50

BUCCANEER
No date (1963)
I. W. Enterprises

	Good	Fine	Mint
I.W. Reprint #1(r-/Quality #20), #8(r-/#23)	1.00	3.00	6.00
Super Reprint #12('64, r-/#21)-Crandall-a	1.00	3.00	6.00

BUCCANEERS (Formerly Kid Eternity)
No. 19, Jan, 1950 - No. 27, May, 1951 (No.24-27: 52 pages)
Quality Comics Group

	Good	Fine	Mint
19-Captain Daring, Black Roger, Eric Falcon & Spanish Main begin; Crandall-a	17.00	51.00	120.00
20,23-Crandall-a	13.00	40.00	90.00
21-Crandall c/a	16.00	48.00	110.00
22-Bondage-c	8.50	25.50	60.00
24,26: 24-Adam Peril, U.S.N. begins; last Spanish Main	8.00	24.00	56.00
25-Origin & 1st app. Corsair Queen	8.00	24.00	56.00
27-Crandall c/a	14.00	42.00	100.00

BUCCANEERS, THE (See 4-Color No. 800)

BUCKAROO BANZAI
Dec, 1984 - No. 2, Feb, 1985
Marvel Comics Group

	Good	Fine	Mint
1,2-r/Marvel Super Special		.40	.80

BUCK DUCK
June, 1953 - No. 4, Dec, 1953
Atlas Comics (ANC)

	Good	Fine	Mint
1-(funny animal)	2.30	7.00	16.00
2-4-(funny animal)	1.50	4.50	10.00

BUCK JONES
No. 299, Oct, 1950 - No. 850, Oct, 1957 (All Painted-c)
Dell Publishing Co.

	Good	Fine	Mint
4-Color 299(#1)-Buck Jones & his horse Silver-B begin; painted back-c begins, ends #5	7.00	21.00	50.00
2(4-6/51)	4.00	12.00	28.00
3-8(10-12/52)	3.00	9.00	21.00
4-Color 460,500,546,589	3.00	9.00	21.00
4-Color 652,733,850	2.00	6.00	14.00

BUCK ROGERS (In the 25th Century)
1933 (36 pages in color) (6x8")
Kelloggs Corn Flakes Giveaway

	Good	Fine	Mint
370A(Rare) by Phil Nowlan & Dick Calkins; 1st Buck Rogers radio premium (tells origin)	25.00	75.00	175.00

BUCK ROGERS (Also see Famous Funnies, Pure Oil Comics, Salerno Carnival of Comics, 24 Pages of Comics, & Vicks Comics)
Winter, 1940-41 - No. 6, Sept, 1943
Famous Funnies

	Good	Fine	Mint
1-Sunday strip reprints by Rick Yager; begins with strip No. 190	100.00	300.00	700.00
2	60.00	180.00	420.00
3,4	48.00	145.00	335.00
5-Story continues with Famous Funnies No. 80; ½ Buck Rogers, ½ Sky Roads	43.00	130.00	300.00
6-Reprints of 1939 dailies; contains B.R. story "Crater of Doom" (2 pgs.) by Calkins not reprinted from Famous Funnies	43.00	130.00	300.00

BUCK ROGERS
No. 100, Jan, 1951 - No. 9, May-June, 1951
Toby Press

	Good	Fine	Mint
100(7)	11.50	34.50	80.00
101(8), 9-All Anderson-a('47-'49-r/dailies)	10.00	30.00	70.00

BUCK ROGERS (. . . in the 25th Century No. 5 on) (TV)
10/64; No. 2, 7/79 - No. 16, 5/82 (no No. 10)
Gold Key/Whitman No. 7 on

	Good	Fine	Mint
1(10128-410)	2.65	8.00	16.00
2(8/79)-Movie adaptation	.35	1.00	2.00
3-9,11-16: 3,4-Movie adaptation; 5-new stories		.50	1.00
Giant Movie Edition 11296(64pp, Whitman, $1.50), reprints GK No. 2-4 minus cover	.35	1.00	2.00
Giant Movie Edition 02489(Western/Marvel, $1.50), reprints GK No. 2-4 minus cover	.35	1.00	2.00

NOTE: ***Bolle*** *a-2p-4p.* *McWilliams a-2i-4i, 5-11. Painted-c No. 1-13.*

BUCKSKIN (See 4-Color No. 1011,1107 (Movie))

BUDDIES IN THE U.S. ARMY
Nov, 1952 - No. 2, 1953
Avon Periodicals

	Good	Fine	Mint
1	6.00	18.00	42.00
2-Mort Lawrence c/a	4.60	14.00	32.00

BUDDY TUCKER & HIS FRIENDS
1906 (11x17") (In color)
Cupples & Leon Co.

	Good	Fine	Mint
1905 Sunday strip reprints by R. F. Outcault	16.00	48.00	110.00

BUFFALO BEE (See 4-Color No. 957,1002,1061)

BUFFALO BILL (Also see Super West. Comics & West. Act. Thrillers)
No. 2, Oct., 1950 - No. 9, Dec, 1951
Youthful Magazines

	Good	Fine	Mint
2	2.65	8.00	18.00
3-9	1.50	4.50	10.00

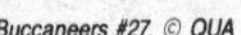
Buccaneers #27, © QUA

Buck Jones #4, © DELL

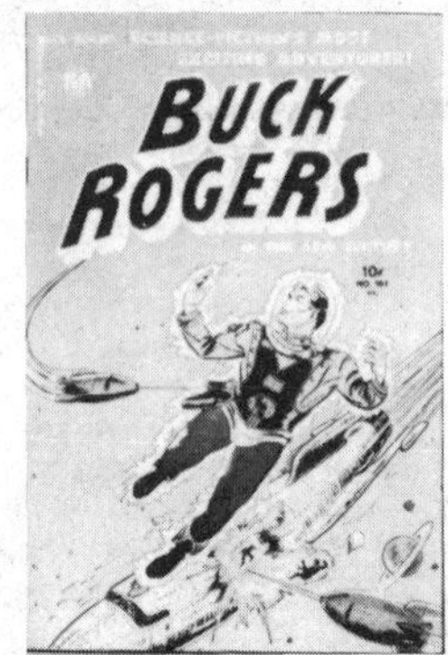

Buck Rogers #101 (Toby), © KING

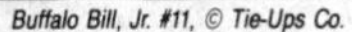
Buffalo Bill, Jr. #11, © Tie-Ups Co.

Bugs Bunny and Porky Pig #1, © L. Schlesinger-Warner Bros.

Bulletman #10, © FAW

BUFFALO BILL CODY (See Cody of the Pony Express)

BUFFALO BILL, JR. (TV) (Also see Western Roundup)
Jan, 1956 - No. 13, Aug-Oct, 1959; 1965 (All photo-c)
Dell Publishing Co./Gold Key

	Good	Fine	Mint
4-Color 673 (#1)	3.00	9.00	21.00
4-Color 742,766,798,828,856(11/57)	2.15	6.50	15.00
7(2-4/58)-13	1.75	5.25	12.00
1(6/65-Gold Key)	1.35	4.00	8.00

BUFFALO BILL PICTURE STORIES
June-July, 1949 - No. 2, Aug-Sept, 1949
Street & Smith Publications

1,2-Wildey, Powell-a in each	4.00	12.00	28.00

BUFFALO BILL'S PICTURE STORIES
1909 (Soft cardboard cover)
Street & Smith Publications

	8.00	24.00	56.00

BUGALOOS (TV)
Sept, 1971 - No. 4, Feb, 1972
Charlton Comics

1-4	.35	1.00	2.00

NOTE: *No. 3(1/72) went on sale late in 1972 (after No. 4) with the 1/73 issues.*

BUGHOUSE (Satire)
Mar-Apr, 1954 - No. 4, Sept-Oct, 1954
Ajax/Farrell (Excellent Publ.)

V1#1	5.00	15.00	35.00
2-4	3.00	9.00	21.00

BUGHOUSE FABLES
1921 (48 pgs.) (4x4½") (10 cents)
Embee Distributing Co. (King Features)

1-Barney Google	6.00	18.00	42.00

BUG MOVIES
1931 (52 pages) (B&W)
Dell Publishing Co.

Not reprints; Stookie Allen-a	5.00	15.00	35.00

BUGS BUNNY (See Dell Giants for annuals)
1942 - No. 245, 1983
Dell Publishing Co./Gold Key No. 86-218/Whitman No. 219 on

Large Feature Comic 8(1942)-(Rarely found in fine-mint condition)	47.00	141.00	330.00
4-Color 33 ('43)	23.00	70.00	160.00
4-Color 51	16.00	48.00	110.00
4-Color 88	9.00	27.00	63.00
4-Color 123('46),142,164	5.00	15.00	35.00
4-Color 187,200,217,233	4.00	12.00	28.00
4-Color 250-Used in **SOTI**, pg. 309	4.00	12.00	28.00
4-Color 266,274,281,289,298('50)	3.00	9.00	21.00
4-Color 307,317(#1),327(#2),338,347,355,366,376,393	2.00	6.00	14.00
4-Color 407,420,432	1.50	4.50	10.00
28(12-1/52-53)-30	1.00	3.00	7.00
31-50	.65	2.00	4.50
51-85(7-9/62)	.50	1.50	3.50
86(10/62)-88-Bugs Bunny's Showtime-(80 pgs.)(25 cents)	1.50	4.50	12.00
89-100	.50	1.50	3.00
101-120	.40	1.25	2.50
121-140	.35	1.00	2.00
141-170		.60	1.20
171-228,230-245		.30	.60
229-Swipe of Barks story/WDC&S 223		.35	.70

NOTE: *Reprints-100, 102, 104, 123, 143, 144, 147, 167, 173, 175-77, 179-85, 187, 190.*

	Good	Fine	Mint
...Comic-Go-Round 11196-(224 pgs.)($1.95)(Golden Press, 1979)	.40	1.20	2.40
Kite Fun Book ('60,'68)-Giveaway, 16 pgs., 5x7¼"	.50	1.50	3.00
Winter Fun 1(12/67-Gold Key)-Giant	1.25	3.75	10.00

BUGS BUNNY (See The Best of...; Camp Comics; Comic Album #2, 6, 10, 14; Dell Giant #28, 32, 46; Golden Comics Digest #1, 3, 5, 6, 8, 10, 14, 15, 17, 21, 26, 30, 34, 39, 42, 47; March of Comics #44, 59, 75, 83, 97, 115, 132, 149, 160, 179, 188, 201, 220, 231, 245, 259, 273, 287, 301, 315, 329, 343, 363, 367, 380, 392, 403, 415, 428, 440, 452, 464, 476, 487; Puffed Wheat, Story Hour Series #802, Super Book #14, 26; and Whitman Comic Books)

BUGS BUNNY (Puffed Rice Giveaway)
1949 (32 pages each, 3-1/8x6-7/8")
Quaker Cereals

A1-Traps the Counterfeiters, A2-Aboard Mystery Submarine, A3- Rocket to the Moon, A4-Lion Tamer, A5-Rescues the Beautiful Princess, B1-Buried Treasure, B2-Outwits the Smugglers, B3-Joins the Marines, B4-Meets the Dwarf Ghost, B5-Finds Aladdin's Lamp, C1-Lost in the Frozen North, C2-Secret Agent, C3-Captured by Cannibals, C4-Fights the Man from Mars, C5-And the Haunted Cave

each....	1.70	5.00	10.00

BUGS BUNNY (3-D)
1953 (Pocket size) (15 titles)
Cheerios Giveaway

each....	4.30	13.00	30.00

BUGS BUNNY & PORKY PIG
Sept, 1965 (100 pages; paper cover; giant)
Gold Key

1(30025-509)	2.00	6.00	14.00

BUGS BUNNY'S ALBUM (See 4-Color No. 498,585,647,724)

BUGS BUNNY LIFE STORY ALBUM (See 4-Color No. 838)

BUGS BUNNY MERRY CHRISTMAS (See 4-Color No. 1064)

BULLETMAN (See Fawcett Miniatures, Master Comics, Mighty Midget Comics, Nickel Comics & X-Mas Comics)
Sum, 1941 - No. 12, 2/12/43; No. 14, Spr, 1946 - No. 16, Fall, 1946 (nn 13)
Fawcett Publications

1	100.00	300.00	700.00
2	65.00	195.00	455.00
3	43.00	130.00	300.00
4,5	35.00	105.00	245.00
6-10: 7-Ghost Stories as told by the night watchman of the cemetery begins; Eisnerish-a	30.00	90.00	210.00
11,12,14-16 (nn 13)	26.00	78.00	182.00
...Well Known Comics (1942)-Paper-c, glued binding; printed in red (Bestmaid/Samuel Lowe giveaway)	12.00	36.00	72.00

NOTE: ***Mac Raboy*** *c-1-3,5,10.*

BULLS-EYE (Cody of The Pony Express No. 8 on)
7-8/54 - No. 5, 3-4/55; No. 6, 6/55; No. 7, 8/55
Mainline No. 1-5/Charlton No. 6,7

1-S&K-c, 2 pages	20.00	60.00	140.00
2-S&K c/a	20.00	60.00	140.00
3-5-S&K c/a(2)	12.00	36.00	84.00
6-S&K c/a	10.00	30.00	70.00
7-S&K c/a(3)	12.00	36.00	84.00
Great Scott Shoe Store giveaway-Reprints #2 with new cover	8.00	24.00	56.00

BULLS-EYE COMICS
No. 11, 1944
Harry 'A' Chesler

11-Origin K-9, Green Knight's sidekick, Lance; The Green Knight, Lady Satan, Yankee Doodle Jones app.	11.50	34.50	80.00

BULLWHIP GRIFFIN (See Movie Comics)

BULLWINKLE (TV) (. . .and Rocky No. 20 on; See March of Comics No. 233, and Rocky & Bullwinkle)
3-5/62 - No. 11, 4/74; No. 12, 6/76 - No. 19, 3/78; No. 20, 4/79 - No. 25, 2/80 (Jay Ward)
Dell/Gold Key

	Good	Fine	Mint
4-Color 1270 (3-5/62)	4.00	12.00	28.00
01-090-209 (Dell, 7-9/62)	4.00	12.00	28.00
1(11/62, Gold Key)	3.00	9.00	21.00
2(2/63)	2.30	7.00	16.00
3(4/72)-11(4/74-Gold Key)	1.00	3.00	6.00
12(6/76)-reprints	.50	1.50	3.00
13(9/76), 14-new stories	.50	1.50	3.00
15-25	.50	1.50	3.00
Mother Moose Nursery Pomes 01-530-207 (5-7/62-Dell)	3.50	10.50	24.00

NOTE: *Reprints-6,7,20-24.*

BULLWINKLE (. . .& Rocky No. 2 on)(TV)
July, 1970 - No. 7, July, 1971
Charlton Comics

	Good	Fine	Mint
1	1.00	3.00	6.00
2-7	.70	2.00	4.00

BULLWINKLE AND ROCKY
Nov, 1987 - Present
Star Comics (Marvel)

	Good	Fine	Mint
1-3		.50	1.00

BULLWINKLE AND ROCKY 3-D
Mar, 1987 (Blackthorne 3-D Series #18, $2.50)
Blackthorne Publ.

	Good	Fine	Mint
1	.45	1.25	2.50

BUNNY
Dec, 1966 - No. 20, Dec, 1971; No. 21, Nov, 1976
Harvey Publications

	Good	Fine	Mint
1	1.00	3.00	6.00
2,4-6,8,10,21	.50	1.50	3.00
3,7,9,11-20-All Giants	1.00	3.00	6.00

BURKE'S LAW (TV)
1-3/64; No. 2, 5-7/64; No. 3, 3-5/65 (Gene Barry photo-c)
Dell Publishing Co.

	Good	Fine	Mint
1-Photo-c	2.00	6.00	12.00
2,3	1.35	4.00	8.00

BURNING ROMANCES (See Fox Giants)

BUSTER BEAR
Dec, 1953 - No. 10, June, 1955
Quality Comics Group (Arnold Publ.)

	Good	Fine	Mint
1	2.00	6.00	14.00
2	1.00	3.00	7.00
3-10	.85	2.50	6.00
I.W. Reprint #9,10 (Super on inside)	.30	.80	1.60

BUSTER BROWN
1903 - 1909 (11x17" strip reprints in color)
Frederick A. Stokes Co.

	Good	Fine	VF
. . .& His Resolutions (1903) by R. F. Outcault	32.00	105.00	245.00
. . .Abroad (1904)-86 pgs.; hardback; 8x10¼"; B&W; by R. F. Outcault(76pgs.)	28.00	84.00	195.00
. . .His Dog Tige & Their Troubles (1904)	28.00	84.00	195.00
. . .Pranks (1905)	28.00	84.00	195.00
. . .Antics (1906)-11x17", 30 pages color strip reprints	28.00	84.00	195.00
. . .Mary Jane & Tige (1906)	28.00	84.00	195.00
. . .My Resolutions (1906)-68 pgs.; B&W; hardcover; Sunday panel reprints	28.00	84.00	195.00
Collection of Buster Brown Comics (1908)	28.00	84.00	195.00
Buster Brown Up to Date (1909)	28.00	84.00	195.00
. . .The Little Rogue (1916)(10x15¾," 62pp, in color)	20.00	60.00	140.00

NOTE: *Rarely found in fine or mint condition.*

BUSTER BROWN
1906 - 1917 (11x17" strip reprints in color)
Cupples & Leon Co./N. Y. Herald Co.
(By R. F. Outcault)

	Good	Fine	VF
. . .His Dog Tige & Their Jolly Times (1906)	25.00	75.00	175.00
. . .Latest Frolics (1906), 58 pgs.	23.00	70.00	160.00
. . .Amusing Capers (1908)	23.00	70.00	160.00
. . .And His Pets (1909)	23.00	70.00	160.00
. . .On His Travels (1910)	23.00	70.00	160.00
. . .Happy Days (1911)	23.00	70.00	160.00
. . .In Foreign Lands (1912)	21.00	64.00	150.00
. . .And the Cat (1917)	20.00	60.00	140.00

NOTE: *Rarely found in fine or mint condition.*

BUSTER BROWN COMICS (Also see My Dog Tige)
1945 - 1959 (No. 5: paper cover)
Brown Shoe Co.

	Good	Fine	Mint
nn, nd (#1)	8.00	24.00	56.00
2	4.00	12.00	28.00
3-10	2.00	6.00	14.00
11-20	1.60	4.70	11.00
21-24,26-28	1.30	4.00	9.00
25,31,33-37,40-43-Crandall-a in all	3.65	11.00	25.00
29,30,32-"Interplanetary Police Vs. the Space Siren" by Crandall	3.65	11.00	25.00
38,39	1.00	3.00	7.00
. . .Goes to Mars (2/58-Western Printing), slick-c, 20 pgs., reg. size	2.00	6.00	12.00
. . .In "Buster Makes the Team!" (1959-Custom Comics)	1.00	3.00	7.00
. . .In The Jet Age ('50s), slick-c, 20 pgs., 5x7¼"	1.30	4.00	9.00
. . .Of the Safety Patrol ('60-Custom Comics)	1.00	3.00	7.00
. . .Out of This World ('59-Custom Comics)	1.00	3.00	7.00
. . .Safety Coloring Book (1958)-Slick paper, 16 pages	1.00	3.00	7.00

BUSTER BUNNY
Nov, 1949 - No. 16, Oct, 1953
Standard Comics(Animated Cartoons)/Pines

	Good	Fine	Mint
1-Frazetta 1 pg. text illo.	2.65	8.00	18.00
2	1.30	4.00	9.00
3-16	1.00	3.00	7.00

BUSTER CRABBE
Nov, 1951 - No. 12, 1953
Famous Funnies

	Good	Fine	Mint
1-Frazetta drug pusher back-c	14.00	42.00	100.00
2-Williamson/Evans-c	17.00	51.00	120.00
3-Williamson/Evans c/a	19.00	57.00	132.00
4-Frazetta c/a, 1pg.; bondage-c	23.00	70.00	160.00
5-Frazetta-c; Williamson/Krenkel/Orlando-a, 11pgs. (per Mr. Williamson)	110.00	330.00	770.00
6,8,10-12	3.50	10.50	24.00
7,9-One pg. of Frazetta in each	4.00	12.00	28.00

BUSTER CRABBE (The Amazing Adventures of. .)
Dec, 1953 - No. 4, June, 1954
Lev Gleason Publications

	Good	Fine	Mint
1	5.70	17.00	40.00

Bullwinkle Mother Moose Nursery Pomes #1, © Jay Ward Prod.

Burke's Law #3, © Four Star

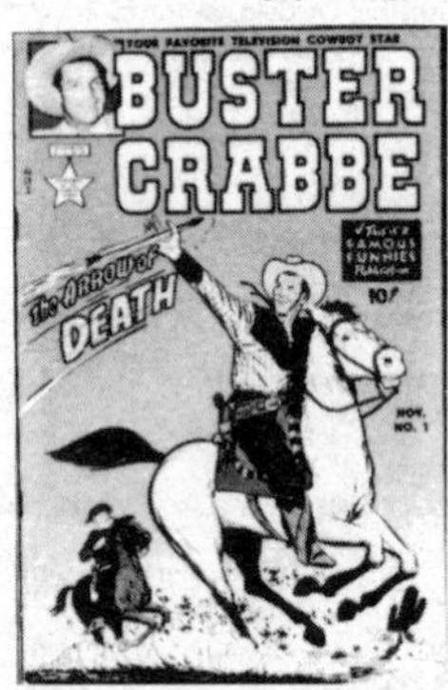

Buster Crabbe #1, © FF

Buzzy #9, © DC

Calling All Girls #11, © PMI

Camera Comics #8, © U.S. Camera

BUSTER CRABBE (continued)

	Good	Fine	Mint
2,3-Toth-a	8.00	24.00	56.00
4-Flash Gordon-c	5.70	17.00	40.00

BUTCH CASSIDY
June, 1971 - No. 3, Oct, 1971 (52 pages)
Skywald Comics

	Good	Fine	Mint
1-Red Mask reprint, retitled Maverick; Bolle-a		.40	.80
2-Whip Wilson reprint		.30	.60
3-Dead Canyon Days reprint/Crack Western No. 63; Sundance Kid app.; Crandall-a		.30	.60

BUTCH CASSIDY (. . . & the Wild Bunch)
1951
Avon Periodicals

	Good	Fine	Mint
1-Kinstler c/a	8.50	25.50	60.00

NOTE: ***Reinman*** *story; Issue No. on inside spine.*

BUTCH CASSIDY (See Fun-In No. 11 & Western Adventure Comics)

BUZ SAWYER
June, 1948 - 1949
Standard Comics

	Good	Fine	Mint
1-Roy Crane-a	7.00	21.00	50.00
2-Intro his pal Sweeney	4.50	13.50	31.50
3-5	3.70	11.00	26.00

BUZ SAWYER'S PAL, ROSCOE SWEENEY (See Sweeney)

BUZZY (See All Funny Comics)
Winter, 1944-45 - No. 75, 1-2/57; No. 76, 10/57; No. 77, 10/58
National Periodical Publications/Detective Comics

	Good	Fine	Mint
1 (52 pgs. begin)	12.00	36.00	84.00
2	6.00	18.00	42.00
3-5	4.35	13.00	30.00
6-10	2.80	8.60	20.00
11-20	2.15	6.50	15.00
21-30	1.70	5.00	12.00
31,35-38	1.30	4.00	9.00
32-34,39-Last 52 pgs. Scribbly by Mayer in all (These four stories were done for Scribbly #14 which was delayed for a year)	1.50	4.50	10.00
40-77	1.00	3.00	7.00

BUZZY THE CROW (See Harvey Hits #18 & Paramount Animated Comics #1)

CADET GRAY OF WEST POINT (See Dell Giants)

CAIN'S HUNDRED (TV)
May-July, 1962 - No. 2, Sept-Nov, 1962
Dell Publishing Co.

	Good	Fine	Mint
nn(01-094-207)	1.30	4.00	9.00
2	.85	2.50	6.00

CALL FROM CHRIST
1952 (36 pages)
Catechetical Educational Society (Giveaway)

	Good	Fine	Mint
	2.30	7.00	16.00

CALLING ALL BOYS (Tex Granger No. 18 on)
Jan, 1946 - No. 17, May, 1948
Parents' Magazine Institute

	Good	Fine	Mint
1	3.00	9.00	21.00
2	1.60	4.70	11.00
3-9,11-17	1.30	4.00	9.00
10-Gary Cooper photo-c	2.35	7.00	16.00

CALLING ALL GIRLS
Sept, 1941 - No. 72, April, 1948 (Part magazine, part comic)
Parents' Magazine Institute

	Good	Fine	Mint
1	4.35	13.00	30.00
2	2.30	7.00	16.00
3-Shirley Temple photo-c	3.00	9.00	21.00
4-10: 9-Flag-c	1.60	4.70	11.00
11-20	1.15	3.50	8.00
21-39,41-43(10-11/45)-Last issue with comics	.75	2.25	5.00
40-Liz Taylor photo-c	.85	2.50	6.00
44-51(7/46)-Last comic book size issue	.50	1.50	3.00
52-72	.35	1.00	2.00

NOTE: ***Jack Sparling*** *art in many issues.*

CALLING ALL KIDS
Dec-Jan, 1945-46 - No. 26, Aug, 1949
Parents' Magazine Institute

	Good	Fine	Mint
1	2.65	8.00	18.00
2	1.30	4.00	9.00
3-10	.85	2.50	6.00
11-26	.55	1.65	4.00

CALVIN (See Li'l Kids)

CALVIN & THE COLONEL (TV)
No. 1354, 4-6/62 - No. 2, July-Sept, 1962
Dell Publishing Co.

	Good	Fine	Mint
4-Color 1354	3.00	9.00	21.00
2	2.00	6.00	14.00

CAMELOT 3000
12/82 - No. 11, 7/84; No. 12, 4/85 (Direct Sale; Mando paper)
DC Comics (Maxi-series)

	Good	Fine	Mint
1	.35	1.00	2.00
2,3	.25	.70	1.40
4-6: 5-Intro Knights of New Camelot		.60	1.20
7-12		.50	1.00

NOTE: ***Austin*** *a-7i-12i.*

CAMERA COMICS
July, 1944 - No. 9, Summer, 1946
U.S. Camera Publishing Corp./ME

	Good	Fine	Mint
nn (7/44)	8.00	24.00	56.00
nn (9/44)	6.00	18.00	42.00
1(10/44)-The Grey Comet	6.00	18.00	42.00
2	3.70	11.00	26.00
3-Nazi WW II-c; ½ photos	3.50	10.50	24.00
4-9: All ½ photos	2.65	8.00	18.00

CAMP COMICS
Feb, 1942 - No. 3, April, 1942 (All have photo-c)
Dell Publishing Co.

	Good	Fine	Mint
1-"Seaman Sy Wheeler" by Kelly, 7 pgs.; Bugs Bunny app.	30.00	90.00	210.00
2-Kelly-a, 12 pgs.; Bugs Bunny app.	23.00	70.00	160.00
3-(Scarce)-Kelly-a	30.00	90.00	210.00

CAMP RUNAMUCK (TV)
April, 1966
Dell Publishing Co.

	Good	Fine	Mint
1	1.35	4.00	8.00

CAMPUS LOVES
Dec, 1949 - No. 5, Aug, 1950
Quality Comics Group (Comic Magazines)

	Good	Fine	Mint
1-Ward c/a, 9 pgs.	13.00	40.00	90.00
2-Ward c/a	10.00	30.00	70.00
3,4	4.60	14.00	32.00
5-Spanking panels (2)	6.00	18.00	42.00

NOTE: ***Gustavson*** *a-1-5. Photo-c-3-5.*

CAMPUS ROMANCE (. . . Romances on cover)
Sept-Oct, 1949 - No. 3, Feb-Mar, 1950
Avon Periodicals/Realistic

CAMPUS ROMANCE (continued)

	Good	Fine	Mint
1-Walter Johnson-a; c-/Avon paperback 348	10.00	30.00	70.00
2-Grandenetti-a; c-/Avon paperback 151	8.50	25.50	60.00
3-c-/Avon paperback 201	8.50	25.50	60.00
Realistic reprint	3.50	10.50	24.00

CANADA DRY PREMIUMS (See Swamp Fox, The & Terry & The Pirates)

CANCELLED COMIC CAVALCADE
Summer, 1978 - No. 2, Fall, 1978 (8½x11"; B&W)
(Xeroxed pages on one side only w/blue cover and taped spine)
DC Comics, Inc.

1-(412 pages) Contains xeroxed copies of art for: Black Lightning No. 12, cover to No. 13; Claw No. 13,14; The Deserter No. 1; Doorway to Nightmare No. 6; Firestorm No. 6; The Green Team No. 2,3.

2-(532 pages) Contains xeroxed copies of art for: Kamandi #60 (including Omac), #61; Prez #5; Shade #9 (including The Odd Man); Showcase #105 (Deadman), 106 (The Creeper); The Vixen #1; and covers to Army at War #2, Battle Classics #3, Demand Classics #1 & 2, Dynamic Classics #3, Mr. Miracle #26, Ragman #6, Weird Mystery #25 & 26, & Western Classics #1 & 2. (Rare)

(One set sold in 1986 for $550.00)

NOTE: In June, 1978, DC cancelled several of their titles. For copyright purposes, the unpublished original art for these titles was xeroxed, bound in the above books, published and distributed. Only 35 copies were made.

CANDID TALES (Also see Bold Stories & It Rhymes With Lust)
April, 1950, June, 1950 (Digest size) (144 pages) (Full color)
Kirby Publishing Co.

	Good	Fine	Mint
(Scarce) Contains Wood female pirate story, 15 pgs., and 14 pgs. in June issue; Powell-a	35.00	105.00	245.00

NOTE: *Another version exists with Dr. Kilmore by Wood; no female pirate story.*

CANDY
Fall, 1944 - No. 3, Spring, 1945
William H. Wise & Co.

	Good	Fine	Mint
1-Two Scoop Scuttle stories by Wolverton	11.50	34.50	80.00
2,3-Scoop Scuttle by Wolverton, 2-4 pgs.	8.50	25.50	60.00

CANDY
Fall, 1947 - No. 64, July, 1956
Quality Comics Group

	Good	Fine	Mint
1-Gustavson-a	5.70	17.00	40.00
2-Gustavson-a	3.00	9.00	21.00
3-10	2.00	6.00	14.00
11-30	1.50	4.50	10.00
31-63	1.15	3.50	8.00
64-Ward-c(p)?	1.65	5.00	11.50
Super Reprint No. 2,10,12,16,17,18('63-'64)	.50	1.50	3.00

NOTE: ***Jack Cole*** *1-2 pg. art in many issues.*

CANNONBALL COMICS
Feb, 1945 - No. 2, Mar, 1945
Rural Home Publishing Co.

	Good	Fine	Mint
1-The Crash Kid, Thunderbrand, The Captive Prince & Crime Crusader begin	17.00	51.00	120.00
2	10.00	30.00	70.00

CANTEEN KATE (Also see All Picture All True Love Story & Fightin' Marines)
June, 1952 - No. 3, Nov, 1952
St. John Publishing Co.

	Good	Fine	Mint
1-Matt Baker c/a	23.00	70.00	160.00
2-Matt Baker c/a	20.00	60.00	140.00
3-(Rare)-Used in **POP**, pg. 75; Baker c/a; transvestism story	24.00	72.00	170.00

CAP'N CRUNCH COMICS (See Quaker Oats)
1963; 1965 (16 pgs.; miniature giveaways; 2½x6½")
Quaker Oats Co.

	Good	Fine	Mint
(1963 titles)-"The Picture Pirates," "The Fountain of Youth," "I'm Dreaming of a Wide Isthmus." (1965 titles)-"Bewitched, Betwitched, & Betweaked," Seadog Meets the Witch Doctor"	.75	2.25	5.00

CAP'N QUICK & A FOOZLE
July, 1985 - No. 3, Nov, 1985 ($1.50; Baxter paper)
Eclipse Comics

	Good	Fine	Mint
1-3-Rogers c/a	.25	.75	1.50

CAPTAIN ACTION
Oct-Nov, 1968 - No. 5, June-July, 1969
National Periodical Publications

	Good	Fine	Mint
1-Origin; Wood-a	.35	1.00	2.00
2-5: 2,3,5-Kane/Wood-a	.25	.75	1.50
. . . & Action Boy('67)-Ideal Toy Co. giveaway	.25	.75	1.50

CAPTAIN AERO COMICS (Samson No. 1-6; also see Veri Best Sure Fire & Veri Best Sure Shot Comics)
V1No.7(No.1), Dec, 1941 - V2No.4(No.10), Jan, 1943; V3No.9(No. 11), Sept, 1943 - V4No.3(No.17), Oct, 1944; No. 21, Dec, 1944 - No. 26, Aug, 1946 (no No. 18-20)
Holyoke Publishing Co.

	Good	Fine	Mint
V1#7(#1)-Flag-Man & Solar, Master of Magic, Captain Aero, Cap Stone, Adventurer begin	38.00	115.00	265.00
8(#2)-Pals of Freedom app.	22.00	65.00	154.00
9(#3)-Alias X begins; Pals of Freedom app.	22.00	65.00	154.00
10(#4)-Origin The Gargoyle; Kubert-a	22.00	65.00	154.00
11,12(#5,6)-Kubert-a; Miss Victory app. in #6	19.00	57.00	132.00
V2#1(#7)	11.00	32.00	76.00
2(#8)-Origin The Red Cross	11.00	32.00	76.00
3(#9)-Miss Victory app.	8.00	24.00	56.00
4(#10)-Miss Victory app.	6.00	18.00	42.00
V3#9 - V3#13(#11-15): 11,15-Miss Victory app.	4.35	13.00	30.00
V4#2, V4#3(#16,17)	3.50	10.50	24.00
21-24,26-L. B. Cole-c	6.35	19.00	44.00
25-L. B. Cole S/F-c	8.00	24.00	56.00

NOTE: ***Hollingsworth*** *a-23.* ***Infantino*** *a-23.*

CAPTAIN AMERICA (See All-Select, All Winners, Aurora, The Invaders, Marvel Double Feature, Marvel Fanfare, Marvel Mystery, Marvel Super-Action, Marvel Super Heroes, Marvel Team-Up, Marvel Treasury Special, USA Comics, Young Allies, and Young Men)

CAPTAIN AMERICA (Tales of Suspense #1-99; . . . and the Falcon #134-223)
No. 100, April, 1968 - Present
Marvel Comics Group

	Good	Fine	Mint
100-Flashback on Cap's revival with Avengers & Sub-Mariner	2.00	6.00	12.00
101	1.00	3.00	6.00
102-108	.85	2.50	5.00
109-Origin Capt. America	1.00	3.00	6.00
110,111,113-Steranko c/a. 110-Rick becomes Cap's partner. 111-Death of Steve Rogers. 113-Cap's funeral	1.70	5.00	10.00
112,114-116,118-120	.35	1.00	2.00
117-1st app. The Falcon	.40	1.25	2.50
121-130: 121-Retells origin	.30	.90	1.80
131-139: 133-The Falcon becomes Cap's partner; origin Modok. 137,138-Spider-Man x-over	.35	1.00	2.00
140-Origin Grey Gargoyle retold	.35	1.00	2.00
141-150: 143-(52 pgs.)		.60	1.20
151-171,176-179: 155-Origin; redrawn with Falcon added. 164-1st app. Nightshade. 176-End of Capt. America		.50	1.00
172-175-X-Men x-over	.70	2.10	4.20
180-Intro & origin of Nomad		.50	1.00
181-Intro & origin of new Capt. America		.50	1.00
182,184,185,187-192		.40	.80

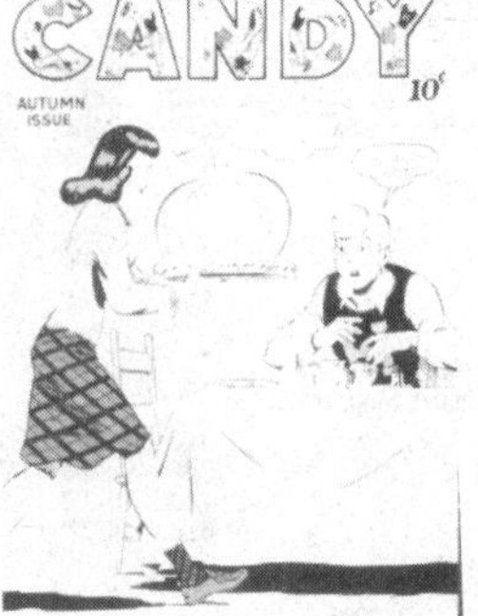

Candy #1 (2nd series), © QUA

Captain Aero #13, © HOKE

Captain America #110, © MCG

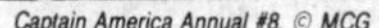
Captain America Annual #8, © MCG

Captain America Comics #1, © MCG

Captain America Comics #69, © MCG

CAPTAIN AMERICA (continued)	**Good**	**Fine**	**Mint**
183-Death of New Cap; Nomad becomes Cap		.50	1.00
186-True origin The Falcon		.60	1.20
193-199,201-240,242-246		.40	.80
200	.25	.75	1.50
241-Punisher app.		.50	1.00
247-255-Byrne-a. 255-Origin	.25	.75	1.50
256-280: 269-1st Team America		.40	.80
281-331: 281-1950s Bucky returns. 282-Bucky becomes Nomad. 284-Patriot (Jack Mace) app. 285-Death of Patriot. 298-Origin Red Skull		.40	.80
332-Old Cap resigns	.85	2.50	5.00
333-Intro new Captain	.70	2.00	4.00
334	.40	1.25	2.50
335,336	.25	.75	1.50
337-340		.50	1.00
...& The Campbell Kids (1980, 36pg. giveaway, Campbell's soup/U.S. Dept. of Energy)	.35	1.00	2.00
Giant Size 1(12/75)	.30	.90	1.80
Special 1(1/71)	.40	1.25	2.50
Special 2(1/72)	.40	1.25	2.50
Annual 3(4/76), 4(8/77)-Kirby c/a, 5(1981), 6(11/82), 7('83),		.60	1.20
Annual 8(9/86)-Wolverine feat.	.40	1.25	2.50

NOTE: ***Austin*** *c-225i, 239i, 246i.* ***Buscema*** *a-115p, 217p; c-136p, 217.* ***Byrne*** *part c-223, 238, 239, 247p-54p, 290, 291; a-247-254p, 255.* ***Colan*** *a(p)-116-137, 256, Annual 5; c(p)-116-123, 126, 129.* ***Everett*** *a-136i, 137i; c-126i.* ***Gil Kane*** *a-145p; c-147p, 149p, 150p, 170p, 172-174, 180, 181p, 183-190p, 215, 216, 220, 221.* ***Kirby*** *a(p)-100-109, 112, 193-214, 216, Giant Size 1, Special 1, 2(layouts), Annual 3,4; c-100-109, 112, 126p, 193-214.* ***Miller*** *c-241p, 244p, 245p, 255p, Annual No. 5.* ***Mooney*** *a-149i.* ***Morrow*** *a-144.* ***Perez*** *c-243p, 246p.* ***Roussos*** *a-140i, 168i.* ***Starlin/Sinnott*** *c-162.* ***Sutton*** *a-244i.* ***Tuska*** *a-112i, 215p, Special 2.* ***Wood*** *a-127i.*

CAPTAIN AMERICA COMICS
Mar, 1941 - No. 75, Jan, 1950; No. 76, 5/54 - No. 78, 9/54
(No. 74 & 75 titled Capt. America's Weird Tales)
Timely/Marvel Comics (TCI 1-20/CmPS 21-68/MjMC 69-75/Atlas Comics (PrPI 76-78)

	Good	Fine	Mint
1-Origin & 1st app. Captain America & Bucky by S&K; Hurricane, Tuk the Caveboy begin by S&K; Red Skull app.	900.00	2700.00	6300.00
(Prices vary widely on this book)			
2-S&K Hurricane; Tuk by Avison (Kirby splash)	385.00	1155.00	2700.00
3-Red Skull app; Stan Lee's 1st text.	271.00	810.00	1900.00
4	180.00	540.00	1260.00
5	165.00	495.00	1155.00
6-Origin Father Time; Tuk the Caveboy ends	140.00	420.00	980.00
7-Red Skull app	140.00	420.00	980.00
8-10-Last S&K issue, (S&K centerfold #6-10)	118.00	355.00	825.00
11-Last Hurricane, Headline Hunter; Al Avison Captain America begins, ends #20	85.00	255.00	595.00
12-The Imp begins, ends No. 16; Last Father Time	85.00	255.00	595.00
13-Origin The Secret Stamp; classic-c	90.00	270.00	630.00
14,15	85.00	255.00	595.00
16-Red Skull unmasks Cap	90.00	270.00	630.00
17-The Fighting Fool only app.	70.00	210.00	490.00
18,19-Human Torch begins #19	65.00	195.00	455.00
20-Sub-Mariner app.; no H. Torch	65.00	195.00	455.00
21-25: 25-Cap drinks liquid opium	57.00	170.00	400.00
26-30: 27-Last Secret Stamp. 30-Last 68 pg. issue	52.00	155.00	365.00
31-36,38-40: 31-60 pg. issues begin	45.00	135.00	315.00
37-Red Skull app.	47.00	140.00	330.00
41-45,47: 41-Last Jap War-c. 47-Last German War-c	40.00	120.00	280.00
46-German Holocaust-c	40.00	120.00	280.00
48-58,60	37.00	110.00	260.00
59-Origin retold	50.00	150.00	350.00
61-Red Skull c/story	45.00	135.00	315.00
62,64,65: 65-"Hey Look" by Kurtzman	37.00	110.00	260.00
63-Intro/origin Asbestos Lady	40.00	120.00	280.00
66-Bucky is shot; Golden Girl teams up with Captain America & learns his i.d; origin Golden Girl	45.00	135.00	315.00
67-Captain America/Golden Girl team-up; Mxyztplk swipe; last Toro in Human Torch	37.00	110.00	260.00
68,70-Sub-Mariner/Namora, and Captain America/Golden Girl team-up in each. 70-Science fiction c/story	37.00	110.00	260.00
69-Human Torch/Sun Girl team-up	37.00	110.00	260.00
71-Anti Wertham editorial; The Witness, Bucky app.	30.00	90.00	210.00
72,73	30.00	90.00	210.00
74-(Scarce)(1949)-Titled "C.A.'s Weird Tales;" Red Skull app.	65.00	195.00	455.00
75(2/50)-Titled "C.A.'s Weird Tales;" no C.A. app.; horror cover/stories	45.00	135.00	315.00
76-78(1954); Human Torch/Toro story	27.00	81.00	190.00
132-Pg. Issue (B&W-1942)(Canadian)	200.00	600.00	1400.00
Shoestore Giveaway No. 77	16.00	48.00	110.00

NOTE: *Bondage c-3, 7, 15, 16, 34.* ***Crandall*** *a-2i, 3i.* ***Schomburg*** *c-26-29, 31, 33, 37-39, 41-43, 45-54, 58.* ***Shores*** *c-20-25, 30, 32, 34-36, 40, 59, 61-63.* ***S&K*** *c-1, 2, 5-7, 9, 10.*

CAPTAIN AMERICA SPECIAL EDITION
Feb, 1984 - No. 2, Mar, 1984 ($2.00; Baxter paper)
Marvel Comics Group

	Good	Fine	Mint
1,2-Steranko-r, c/a	.40	1.25	2.50

CAPTAIN AND THE KIDS, THE (See Famous Comics Cartoon Books)

CAPTAIN AND THE KIDS, THE (See Comics on Parade, Okay Comics & Sparkler Comics)
1938 - 4-Color No. 881, Feb, 1958
United Features Syndicate/Dell Publ. Co.

	Good	Fine	Mint
Single Series 1('38)	30.00	90.00	210.00
Single Series 1(Reprint)(12/39-"Reprint" on cover)	17.00	51.00	120.00
1(Summer, 1947-UFS)	5.00	15.00	35.00
2	2.65	8.00	18.00
3-10	1.85	5.50	13.00
11-20	1.50	4.50	10.00
21-32(1955)	1.15	3.50	8.00
50th Anniversary issue('48)-Contains a 2 page history of the strip, including an account of the famous Supreme Court decision allowing both Pulitzer & Hearst to run the same strip under different names.	2.65	8.00	18.00
Special Summer issue, Fall issue (1948)	2.00	6.00	14.00
4-Color 881 (Dell)	1.50	4.50	10.00

CAPTAIN ATOM
1950 - 1951 (5x7¼") (5 cents, 52 pgs.)
Nationwide Publishers

	Good	Fine	Mint
1-Sci/fic	2.30	7.00	16.00
2-7	1.70	5.00	12.00

CAPTAIN ATOM (Formerly Strange Suspense Stories No. 77)
No. 78, Dec, 1965 - No. 89, Dec, 1967 (Also see Space Advs.)
Charlton Comics

	Good	Fine	Mint
78-Origin retold	1.70	5.00	12.00
79-81	1.50	4.50	10.00
82-Intro. Nightshade	1.50	4.50	10.00
83-86: Ted Kord Blue Beetle in all	1.15	3.50	8.00
87-89-Nightshade by Aparo in all	1.15	3.50	8.00

CAPTAIN ATOM (continued) — Good | Fine | Mint
83-85(Modern Comics-1977)-reprints — .15 | .30
NOTE: *Aparo a-87-89. Ditko c/a(p) 78-87; c-88, 89. #90 only published in fanzine 'The Charlton Bullseye' #1, 2.*

CAPTAIN ATOM
March, 1987 - Present
DC Comics
1-44 pgs. ($1.00)-Origin/1st app. with new costume — .35 | 1.00 | 2.00
2-Reg. size — .50 | 1.00
3-13: 5-Firestorm x-over. 6-Intro. new Dr. Spectro — .40 | .80

CAPTAIN BATTLE (Boy No. 3 on) (See Silver Streak)
Summer, 1941 - No. 2, Fall, 1941
New Friday Publ./Comic House
1-Origin Blackout by Rico; Captain Battle begins — 40.00 | 120.00 | 280.00
2 — 25.00 | 75.00 | 175.00

CAPTAIN BATTLE (2nd Series)
Wint, 1942-43 - No. 5, Sum, 1943 (No.3: 52pgs., nd)(No.5: 68pgs.)
Magazine Press/Picture Scoop No. 5
3-Origin Silver Streak-r/SS#3; Origin Lance Hale-r/Silver Streak; Simon-a(r) — 20.00 | 60.00 | 140.00
4 — 14.00 | 42.00 | 100.00
5-Origin Blackout retold — 14.00 | 42.00 | 100.00

CAPTAIN BATTLE, JR.
Fall, 1943 - No. 2, Winter, 1943-44
Comic House (Lev Gleason)
1-The Claw vs. The Ghost — 32.00 | 95.00 | 225.00
2-Wolverton's Scoop Scuttle; Don Rico-c/a; The Green Claw story — 28.00 | 84.00 | 195.00

CAPTAIN BRITAIN (Also see Marvel Team-Up No. 65,66)
Oct. 13, 1976 - No. 39, July 6, 1977 (Weekly)
Marvel Comics International
1-Origin; with Capt. Britain's face mask inside — .85 | 2.50 | 5.00
2-Origin, conclusion; Britain's Boomerang inside — .60 | 1.80 | 3.60
3-Vs. Bank Robbers — .35 | 1.00 | 2.00
4-7-Vs. Hurricane — .35 | 1.00 | 2.00
8-Vs. Bank Robbers — .35 | 1.00 | 2.00
9-13-Vs. Dr. Synne — .30 | .90 | 1.80
14,15-Vs. Mastermind — .30 | .90 | 1.80
16-20-With Capt. America; 17 misprinted & color section reprinted in No. 18 — .30 | .90 | 1.80
21-23,25,26-With Capt. America — .30 | .90 | 1.80
24-With C.B.'s Jet Plane inside — .60 | 1.80 | 3.60
27-Origin retold — .30 | .90 | 1.80
28-32-Vs. Lord Hawk — .25 | .75 | 1.50
33-35-More on origin — .30 | .90 | 1.80
36-Star Sceptre — .25 | .75 | 1.50
37-39-Vs. Highwayman & Munipulator — .25 | .75 | 1.50
Annual(1978,Hardback,64pgs.)-Reprints No. 1-7 with pin-ups of Marvel characters — 1.35 | 4.00 | 8.00
Summer Special (1980, 52pp)-Reprints — .35 | 1.00 | 2.00
NOTE: *No. 1,2, & 24 are rarer in mint due to inserts. Distributed in Great Britain only. Nick Fury-r by Steranko in 1-20, 24-31, 35-37. Fantastic Four-r by J. Buscema in all. New Buscema-a in 24-30. Story from No. 39 continues in Super Spider-Man (British weekly) No. 231-247. Following cancellation of his series, new Captain Britain stories appeared in "Super Spider-Man" (British weekly) No. 231-247. Captain Britain stories which appear in Super-Spider-Man No. 248-253 are reprints of Marvel Team-Up No. 65&66. Capt. Britain strips also appeared in Hulk Comic (weekly) 1, 3-30, 42-55, 57-60, in Marvel Superheroes (monthly) 377-388, in Daredevils (monthly) 1-11, Mighty World of Marvel (monthly) 7-16 & Captain Britain (monthly) 1-present.*

CAPTAIN CANUCK
7/75 - No. 4, 7/77; No. 4, 7-8/79 - No. 14, 3-4/81
Comely Comix (Canada) (All distr. in U. S.)
Good | Fine | Mint
1-1st app. Bluefox — .40 | 1.25 | 2.50
2-1st app. Dr. Walker, Redcoat & Kebec — .30 | .90 | 1.80
3(5-7/76)-1st app. Heather — .30 | .90 | 1.80
4(1st printing-2/77)-10x14½"; (5.00); B&W; 300 copies serially numbered and signed with one certificate of authenticity. — 5.00 | 15.00 | 30.00
4(2nd printing-7/77)-11x17", B&W; only 15 copies printed; signed by creator Richard Comely, serially #'d and two certificates of authenticity inserted; orange cardboard covers (Very Rare) — 8.00 | 25.00 | 50.00
4(7-8/79)-1st app. Tom Evans & Mr. Gold; origin The Catman — .40 | .80
5-Origin Capt. Canuck's powers; 1st app. Earth Patrol & Chaos Corps — .40 | .80
6-14: 8-Jonn 'The Final Chapter'. 9-1st World Beyond. 11-1st 'Chariots of Fire' story. — .40 | .80
Summer Special 1(7-9/80, 95-, 64pgs.) — .50 | 1.00
NOTE: *30,000 copies of No. 2 were destroyed in Winnipeg.*

CAPTAIN CARROT AND HIS AMAZING ZOO CREW
March, 1982 - No. 20, Nov, 1983 (Also see New Teen Titans)
DC Comics
1-Superman app. — .50 | 1.00
2-20: 3-Re-intro Dodo & The Frog. 9-Re-intro Three Mouseketeers, the Terrific Whatzit. 10,11- Pig Iron reverts back to Peter Porkchops. 20-The Changeling app. — .35 | .70

CAPTAIN CARVEL AND HIS CARVEL CRUSADERS (See Carvel Comics)

CAPTAIN COURAGEOUS COMICS (Banner No. 3-5)
March, 1942
Periodical House (Ace Magazines)
6-Origin & 1st app. The Sword; Lone Warrior, Capt. Courageous app. — 30.00 | 90.00 | 210.00

CAPT'N CRUNCH COMICS (See Cap'n. . .)

CAPTAIN DAVY JONES (See 4-Color No. 598)

CAPTAIN EASY
1939 - No. 17, Sept, 1949; April, 1956
Hawley/Dell Publ./Standard(Visual Editions)/Argo
Hawley(1939)-Contains reprints from The Funnies & 1938 Sunday strips by Roy Crane — 25.00 | 75.00 | 175.00
4-Color 24 (1943) — 17.00 | 51.00 | 120.00
4-Color 111(6/46) — 7.00 | 21.00 | 50.00
10(Standard-10/47) — 3.50 | 10.50 | 24.00
11-17: All contain 1930's & '40's strip-r — 2.65 | 8.00 | 18.00
Argo 1(4/56)-(r) — 2.00 | 6.00 | 14.00
NOTE: *Schomburg c-13,16.*

CAPTAIN EASY & WASH TUBBS (See Famous Comics Cartoon Books)

CAPTAIN ELECTRON
Aug, 1986 - Present ($2.25, color)
Brick Computer Science Institute
1,2-Disbrow-a — .35 | 1.00 | 2.00

CAPTAIN EO 3-D (Disney)
July, 1987 (Eclipse 3-D Special #18, $3.50, baxter)
Eclipse Comics
1-Adapts 3-D movie — .60 | 1.75 | 3.50
1-Large size (11x15")-Sold only at Disney Theme parks ($6.95) — 1.20 | 3.50 | 6.95

CAPTAIN FEARLESS COMICS (Also see Holyoke One-Shot #6 & Old Glory Comics)
August, 1941 - No. 2, Sept, 1941

Captain Battle, Jr. #1, © LEV

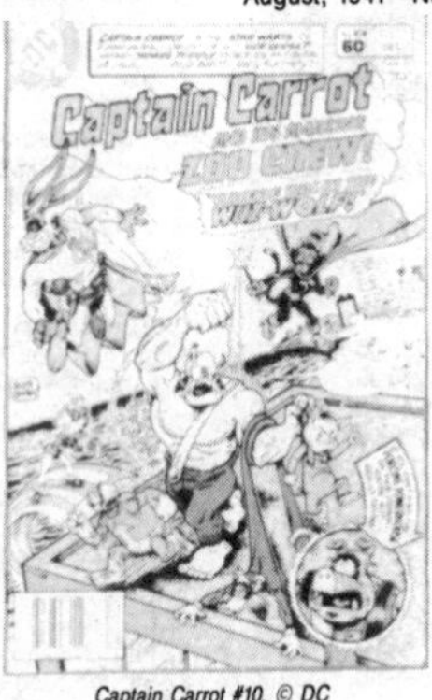

Captain Carrot #10, © DC

Captain Courageous 6, © ACE

Captain Flash #3, © Sterling Comics

Captain Marvel #6, © MCG

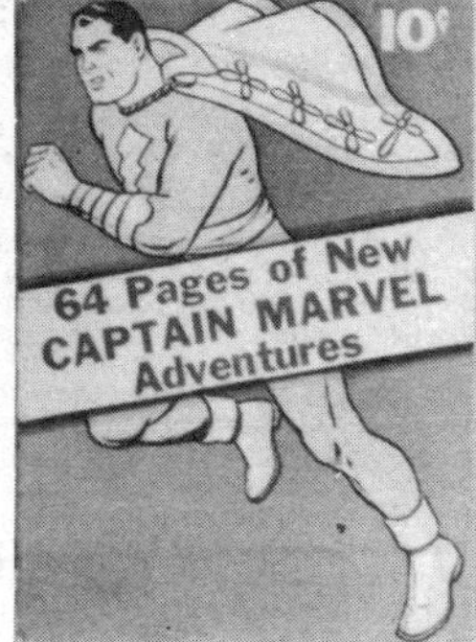

Captain Marvel Adventures #1, © FAW

CAPTAIN FEARLESS (continued)
Helnit Publishing Co. (Holyoke Publishing Co.)

	Good	Fine	Mint
1-Origin Mr. Miracle, Alias X, Captain Fearless, Citizen Smith Son of the Unknown Soldier; Miss Victory begins	25.00	75.00	175.00
2-Grit Grady, Captain Stone app.	14.00	42.00	100.00

CAPTAIN FLASH
Nov, 1954 - No. 4, July, 1955
Sterling Comics

1-Origin; Sekowsky-a; Tomboy (female super hero) begins Last pre-code ish	9.00	27.00	62.00
2-4	5.50	16.50	38.00

CAPTAIN FLEET
Fall, 1952
Ziff-Davis Publishing Co.

1	5.00	15.00	35.00

CAPTAIN FLIGHT COMICS
Mar, 1944 - No. 11, Feb-Mar, 1947
Four Star Publications

nn	8.00	24.00	56.00
2	4.50	13.50	31.50
3,4: 4-Rock Raymond begins, ends #7	3.70	11.00	26.00
5-Bondage, torture-c; Red Rocket begins; the Grenade app.	5.50	16.50	38.00
6,7	4.35	13.00	30.00
8-Yankee Girl, Black Cobra begin; intro. Cobra Kid	7.50	22.50	52.00
9-Torpedoman app.; last Yankee Girl; Kinstler-a	7.50	22.00	52.00
10-Deep Sea Dawson, Zoom of the Jungle, Rock Raymond, Red Rocket, & Black Cobra app; L. B. Cole bondage-c	7.50	22.00	52.00
11-Torpedoman, Blue Flame app.; last Black Cobra, Red Rocket; L. B. Cole-c	7.50	22.00	52.00

NOTE: *L. B. Cole c-7-11.*

CAPTAIN FORTUNE PRESENTS
1955 - 1959 (16 pages; 3¼x6-7/8") (Giveaway)
Vital Publications

"Davy Crockett in Episodes of the Creek War," "Davy Crockett at the Alamo," "In Sherwood Forest Tells Strange Tales of Robin Hood" ('57), "Meets Bolivar the Liberator"('59), "Tells How Buffalo Bill Fights the Dog Soldiers"('57), "Young Davy Crockett"	.85	2.50	5.00

CAPTAIN GALLANT (. . . of the Foreign Legion) (TV)
(Texas Rangers in Action No. 5 on?)
1955 - No. 4, Sept, 1956
Charlton Comics

1-Buster Crabbe	5.00	15.00	35.00
2-4	2.30	7.00	16.00
Heinz Foods Premium(1955; regular size)-U.S. Pictorial; contains Buster Crabbe photos; Don Heck-a	1.70	5.00	12.00
Non-Heinz version (same as above except pictures of show replaces ads)	1.70	5.00	12.00

CAPTAIN HERO (See Jughead as. . .)

CAPTAIN HERO COMICS DIGEST MAGAZINE
Sept, 1981
Archie Publications

1-Reprints of Jughead as Super-Guy		.30	.60

CAPTAIN HOBBY COMICS
Feb, 1948 (Canadian)
Export Publication Ent. Ltd. (Dist. in U.S. by Kable News Co.)

1	2.00	6.00	14.00

CAPTAIN HOOK & PETER PAN (See 4-Color No. 446 and Peter Pan)

CAPTAIN JET (Fantastic Fears No. 7 on)
May, 1952 - No. 5, Jan, 1953
Four Star Publ./Farrell/Comic Media

	Good	Fine	Mint
1-Bakerish-a	5.00	15.00	35.00
2	3.50	10.50	24.00
3-5,6(?)	2.65	8.00	18.00

CAPTAIN JUSTICE
March, 1988 - No. 2, April, 1988
Marvel Comics

1,2-Based on TV series, True Colors	.25	.75	1.50

CAPTAIN KANGAROO (See 4-Color No. 721,780,872)

CAPTAIN KIDD (Formerly Dagar; My Secret Story #26 on)(Also see Fantastic Comics)
No. 24, June, 1949 - No. 25, Aug, 1949
Fox Feature Syndicate

24,25	5.40	16.00	38.00

CAPTAIN MARVEL (See All Hero, All-New Coll. Ed., America's Greatest, Fawcett Min., Gift, Limited Coll. Ed., Marvel Family, Master No. 21, Mighty Midget Comics, Shazam, Special Edition Comics, Whiz, Wisco, and X-Mas)

CAPTAIN MARVEL (. . . Presents the Terrible 5 No. 5)
April, 1966 - No. 4, Nov, 1966 (25 cents)
M. F. Enterprises

nn-(#1 on page 5)-Origin	.35	1.00	2.00
2,4		.60	1.20
3-(#3 on page 4)-Fights the Bat		.60	1.20

CAPTAIN MARVEL (See Marvel Spotlight, Marvel Graphic Novel & Marvel Super-Heroes 12)
May, 1968 - No. 19, Dec, 1969; No. 20, June, 1970 - No. 21, Aug, 1970; No. 22, Sept, 1972 - No. 62, May, 1979
Marvel Comics Group

1	1.50	4.50	10.00
2-5	.50	1.50	3.00
6-10	.35	1.00	2.00
11-Smith/Trimpe-c; Death of Una	.50	1.50	3.00
12-24: 17-New costume		.60	1.20
25-Starlin c/a	1.35	4.00	8.00
26-Starlin c/a	1.00	3.00	6.00
27-34-Starlin c/a. 29-C.M. gains more powers	.75	2.25	4.50
35,37-40: 39-Origin Watcher		.50	1.00
36-Starlin-a, 3pgs.	.25	.70	1.40
41,43-Wrightson part inks; cover No. 43(inks)		.50	1.00
42,44-48,50		.40	.80
49-Starlin in part		.50	1.00
51-62: 53-Inhumans app.		.30	.60
Giant-Size 1 (12/75)	.40	1.20	2.40

NOTE: ***Alcala** a-35. **Austin** a-46i, 49-53i; c-52i. **Buscema** a-18p-21p. **Colan** a(p)-1-4; c(p)-1-4, 8, 9. **Heck** a-5p-10p, 16p. **Gil Kane** a-17p-21p, Gnt-Size 1p; c-17p-24p, 37p, 53. **McWilliams** a-40.*

CAPTAIN MARVEL ADVENTURES (See Special Edition Comics for pre-No. 1)
1941 - No. 150, Nov, 1953
Fawcett Publications

	Good	Fine	VF-NM
nn(#1)-Captain Marvel & Sivana by Jack Kirby. The cover was printed on unstable paper stock and is rarely found in Fine or Mint condition; blank inside-c	857.00	2570.00	6000.00

(Prices vary widely on this book)

	Good	Fine	Mint
2-(Advertised as #3, which was counting Special Edition Comics as the real #1); Tuska-a	143.00	430.00	1000.00
3-Metallic silver-c	71.00	212.00	500.00
4-Three Lt. Marvels app.	50.00	150.00	350.00
5	43.00	130.00	300.00

CAPTAIN MARVEL ADVS. (continued) — **Good** / **Fine** / **Mint**

6-10 — 33.00 100.00 230.00
11-15: 13-Two-pg. Capt. Marvel pin-up. 15-Comic cards on back-c begin, end #26 — 26.00 77.00 180.00
16,17: 17-Painted-c — 23.00 70.00 160.00
18-Origin & 1st app. Mary Marvel & Marvel Family; painted-c (12/11/42) — 35.00 105.00 245.00
19-Mary Marvel x-over; Christmas-c — 21.00 63.00 150.00
20,21-Attached to the cover, each has a miniature comic just like the Mighty Midget Comics #11, except that each has a full color promo ad on the back cover. Most copies were circulated without the miniature comic. These issues with miniatures attached are very rare, and should not be mistaken for copies with the similar Mighty Midget glued in its place. The Mighty Midgets had blank back covers except for a small victory stamp seal. Only the Capt. Marvel and Captain Marvel Jr. No. 11 miniatures have been positively documented as having been affixed to these covers. Each miniature was only partially glued by its back cover to the Captain Marvel comic making it easy to see if it's the genuine miniature rather than a Mighty Midget.
with comic attached.... — 50.00 150.00 350.00
20,21-Without miniature — 18.50 55.00 130.00
22-Mr. Mind serial begins — 32.00 95.00 225.00
23-25 — 17.00 50.00 115.00
26-30: 26-Flag-c — 14.50 43.50 100.00
31-35: 35-Origin Radar — 13.00 40.00 90.00
36-40: 37-Mary Marvel x-over — 11.50 34.50 80.00
41-46: 42-Christmas-c. 43-Captain Marvel 1st meets Uncle Marvel; Mary Batson cameo. 46-Mr. Mind serial ends — 10.00 30.00 70.00
47-50 — 8.65 26.00 60.00
51-53,55-60: 52-Origin & 1st app. Sivana Jr.; Capt. Marvel Jr. x-over — 6.00 18.00 42.00
54-Special oversize 68-pg. issue — 8.00 24.00 56.00
61-The Cult of the Curse serial begins — 9.00 27.00 63.00
62-66-Serial ends; Mary Marvel x-over in #65. 66-Atomic War-c — 6.00 18.00 42.00
67-77,79: 69-Billy Batson's Christmas; Uncle Marvel, Mary Marvel, Capt. Marvel Jr. x-over. 71-Three Lt. Marvels app. No. 79-Origin Mr. Tawny — 5.35 16.00 38.00
78-Origin Mr. Atom — 6.00 18.00 42.00
80-Origin Capt. Marvel retold — 9.50 28.50 65.00
81-84,86-90: 81,90-Mr. Atom app. 82-Infinity-c. 86-Mr. Tawny app. — 6.00 18.00 42.00
85-Freedom Train issue — 7.25 21.50 50.00
91-99: 96-Mr. Tawny app. — 4.35 13.00 30.00
100-Origin retold — 10.00 30.00 70.00
101-120: 116-Flying Saucer ish (1/51) — 4.35 13.00 30.00
121-Origin retold — 5.70 17.00 40.00
122-141,143-149: 138-Flying Saucer issue (11/52). 141-Pre-code horror story "The Hideous Head-Hunter" — 4.00 12.00 28.00
142-Used in **POP**, pgs. 92,96 — 4.35 13.00 30.00
150-(Low distribution) — 10.00 30.00 70.00
Bond Bread Giveaways-(24 pgs.; pocket size-7¼x3½"; paper cover): "...& the Stolen City ('48)," "The Boy Who Never Heard of C.M.,""Meets the Weatherman"-(1950)(reprint)
each.... — 13.00 40.00 80.00
...Well Known Comics (1944; 12 pgs.; 8½x10½")-printed in red & in blue; soft-c; glued binding)-Bestmaid/Samuel Lowe Co. giveaway — 16.00 48.00 96.00

CAPTAIN MARVEL ADVENTURES (Also see Whiz)
1945 (6x8") (Full color, paper cover)
Fawcett Publications (Wheaties Giveaway)

"Captain Marvel & the Threads of Life" plus 2 other stories (32pgs.) — 16.00 48.00 110.00

NOTE: *All copies were taped at each corner to a box of Wheaties and are never found in Fine or Mint condition.*

CAPTAIN MARVEL AND THE GOOD HUMOR MAN
1950
Fawcett Publications — **Good** / **Fine** / **Mint**

nn — 16.00 48.00 110.00

CAPTAIN MARVEL AND THE LTS. OF SAFETY
1950 - 1951 (3 issues - no No.'s)
Ebasco Services/Fawcett Publications

"Danger Flies a Kite"('50)," "Danger Takes to Climbing"('50), "Danger Smashes Street Lights"('51) — 10.00 30.00 70.00

CAPTAIN MARVEL COMIC STORY PAINT BOOK (See Comic Story....)

CAPTAIN MARVEL, JR. (See Fawcett Miniatures, Marvel Family, Master Comics, Mighty Midget Comics, and Shazam)

CAPTAIN MARVEL, JR.
Nov, 1942 - No. 119, June, 1953 (nn 34)
Fawcett Publications

1-Origin Capt. Marvel Jr. retold (Whiz No. 25); Capt. Nazi app. — 100.00 300.00 700.00
2-Vs. Capt. Nazi; origin Capt. Nippon — 50.00 150.00 350.00
3,4 — 36.00 108.00 250.00
5-Vs. Capt. Nazi — 29.00 87.00 200.00
6-10: 8-Vs. Capt. Nazi. 9-Flag-c — 22.00 65.00 154.00
11,12,15-Capt. Nazi app. — 18.50 56.00 130.00
13,14,16-20: 16-Capt. Marvel & Sivana x-over. 19-Capt. Nazi & Capt. Nippon app. — 12.00 36.00 84.00
21-30: 25-Flag-c — 8.00 24.00 56.00
31-33,36-40: 37-Infinity-c — 5.00 15.00 35.00
35-#34 on inside; cover shows origin of Sivana Jr. which is not on inside. Evidently the cover to #35 was printed out of sequence and bound with contents to #34 — 5.00 15.00 35.00
41-50 — 3.50 10.50 24.00
51-70 — 3.50 10.50 24.00
71-99,101-103 — 3.00 9.00 21.00
100 — 3.50 10.50 24.00
104-Used in **POP**, pg. 89 — 3.50 10.50 24.00
105-114,116-119: 119-Electric chair-c — 2.85 8.50 20.00
115-Injury to eye-c; Eyeball story w/ injury-to-eye panels — 4.00 12.00 28.00
...Well Known Comics (1944; 12 pgs.; 8½x10½")(Printed in blue; paper-c, glued binding)-Bestmaid/Samuel Lowe Co. giveaway — 12.00 36.00 72.00

NOTE: ***Mac Raboy** c-1-10,12-14,16,19,22,25,27,28,30-33,57 among others.*

CAPTAIN MARVEL PRESENTS THE TERRIBLE FIVE
Aug, 1966; V2No.5, Sept, 1967 (no No.2-4) (25 cents)
M. F. Enterprises

1 — .35 1.00 1.50
V2#5-(Formerly Capt. Marvel) — .30 .80 1.20

CAPTAIN MARVEL'S FUN BOOK
1944 (½" thick) (cardboard covers)
Samuel Lowe Co.

Puzzles, games, magic, etc.; infinity-c — 7.00 21.00 50.00

CAPTAIN MARVEL SPECIAL EDITION (See Special Edition)

CAPTAIN MARVEL STORY BOOK
Summer, 1946 - No. 4, Summer?, 1948
Fawcett Publications

1-½ text — 23.00 70.00 160.00
2-4 — 16.00 48.00 110.00

CAPTAIN MARVEL THRILL BOOK (Large-Size)
1941 (Black & White; color cover)
Fawcett Publications

1-Reprints from Whiz #8,10, & Special Edition #1 (Rare)

Captain Marvel Adventures #44, © FAW

Captain Marvel, Jr. #12, © FAW

Captain Marvel Story Book #4, © FAW

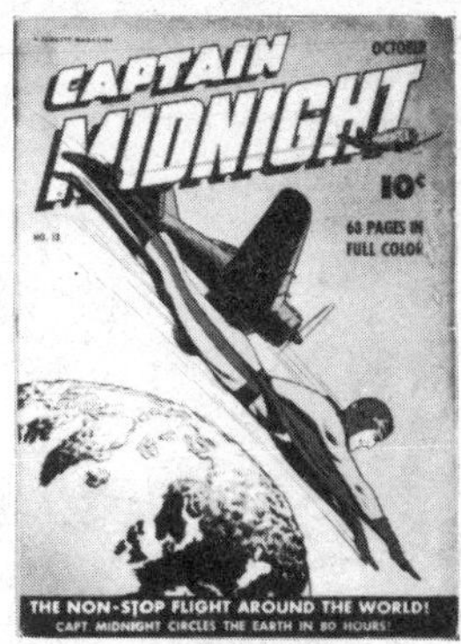

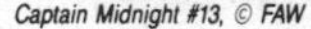
Captain Midnight #13, © FAW

Captain Science #5, © YM

Captain Video #3, © FAW

CAPTAIN MARVEL THRILL BK. (continued) Good Fine VF-NM
142.00 425.00 1000.00
NOTE: *Rarely found in Fine or Mint condition.*

CAPTAIN MIDNIGHT (Radio, films, TV) (See The Funnies & Popular Comics) (Becomes Sweethearts No. 68 on)
Sept, 1942 - No. 67, Fall, 1948
Fawcett Publications

	Good	Fine	Mint
1-Origin Captain Midnight; Captain Marvel cameo on cover	75.00	225.00	525.00
2	38.00	115.00	265.00
3-5	26.00	78.00	180.00
6-10: 9-Raboy-c. 10-Raboy Flag-c	18.00	54.00	125.00
11-20: 11,17-Raboy-c	11.50	34.50	80.00
21-30	8.50	25.50	60.00
31-40	6.50	19.50	45.00
41-59,61-67	4.60	14.00	32.00
60-Flying Saucer ish (2/48)-3rd of this theme; see Shadow Comics V7#10	8.00	24.00	56.00

CAPTAIN NICE (TV)
Nov, 1967 (One Shot)
Gold Key
1(10211-711)-Photo-c 2.00 6.00 12.00

CAPTAIN PARAGON (Also see Bill Black's Fun Comics)
Dec, 1983 - No. 4, 1985? (#3 is in color)
Americomics
1-4: 1-Ms. Victory begins .35 1.00 2.00

CAPTAIN PARAGON AND THE SENTINELS OF JUSTICE
April, 1985 - Present? ($1.75; color)
AC Comics
1-Capt. Paragon, Commando D., Nightveil, Scarlet Scorpion, Stardust & Atoman begin .35 1.00 2.00
2-5 .30 .90 1.80

CAPTAIN PUREHEART (See Archie as . . .)

CAPTAIN ROCKET
November, 1951
P. L. Publ. (Canada)
1 13.00 40.00 90.00

CAPTAIN SAVAGE AND HIS LEATHERNECK RAIDERS
Jan, 1968 - No. 19, Mar, 1970 (See Sgt. Fury No. 10)
Marvel Comics Group
1-Sgt. Fury & Howlers cameo .40 .80
2-19: 2-Origin Hydra .25 .50

CAPTAIN SCIENCE (Fantastic No. 8 on)
Nov, 1950 - No. 7, Dec, 1951
Youthful Magazines
1-Wood-a; origin 38.00 115.00 265.00
2 16.00 48.00 110.00
3,6,7; 3-Bondage c-swipe/Wings 94. 6,7-Bondage-c 13.00 40.00 90.00
4,5-Wood/Orlando-c/a(2) each 34.00 100.00 240.00

CAPTAIN SILVER'S LOG OF SEA HOUND (See Sea Hound)

CAPTAIN SINDBAD (Movie Adaptation) (See Movie Comics)

CAPTAIN STEVE SAVAGE (. . .& His Jet Fighters, No. 2-13)
1950 - 1952? No. 5, 9-10/54 - No. 13, 5-6/56
Avon Periodicals
nn(1st series)-Wood art, 22 pgs. (titled ". . .Over Korea") 17.00 51.00 120.00
1(4/51)-Reprints nn ish (Canadian) 8.50 25.50 60.00
2-Kamen-a 4.35 13.00 30.00
3-11 2.65 8.00 18.00

	Good	Fine	Mint
12-Wood-a, 6pp	5.15	15.50	36.00
13-Check, Lawrence-a	3.50	10.50	24.00

NOTE: ***Kinstler*** *c-2-5, 7-9, 11.* ***Lawrence*** *a-8.* ***Ravielli*** *a-5, 9.*

5(9-10/54-2nd series)(Formerly Sensational Police Cases) 3.00 9.00 21.00
6-Reprints nn ish; Wood-a 5.00 15.00 35.00
7-13 1.50 4.50 10.00

CAPTAIN STONE (See Holyoke One-Shot No. 10)

CAPT. STORM
May-June, 1964 - No. 18, Mar-Apr, 1967
National Periodical Publications
1-Origin .35 1.00 2.00
2-18: 3,6-Kubert-a. 12-Kubert-c .50 1.00

CAPTAIN 3-D
December, 1953
Harvey Publications
1-Kirby/Ditko-a 4.00 12.00 24.00
NOTE: *Many copies surfaced in 1979, causing a set-back in price.*

CAPTAIN THUNDER AND BLUE BOLT
Sept, 1987 - Present ($1.95, color)
Hero Comics
1-Origin Blue Bolt .35 1.00 1.95
2-5: 3-Origin Capt. Thunder .35 1.00 1.95

CAPTAIN TOOTSIE & THE SECRET LEGION (Advs. of. .)
Oct, 1950 - No. 2, Dec, 1950
Toby Press
1-Not Beck-a 9.00 27.00 62.00
2-Not Beck-a 5.70 17.00 40.00

CAPTAIN VENTURE & THE LAND BENEATH THE SEA
Oct, 1968 - No. 2, Oct, 1969
Gold Key (See Space Family Robinson)
1,2: 1-r/Space Family Robinson serial; Spiegle-a in both 2.00 6.00 12.00

CAPTAIN VICTORY AND THE GALACTIC RANGERS
Nov, 1981 - No. 13, Jan, 1984 ($1.00) (36-48 pgs.)
Pacific Comics (Sold only through comic shops)
1-1st app. Mr. Mind .25 .75 1.50
2-13: 3-Adams-a .50 1.00
Special Issue #1(10/83)-Kirby c/a(p) .50 1.00
NOTE: ***Conrad*** *a-10.* ***Ditko*** *a-6.* ***Kirby*** *a-1-13p; c-1-13.*

CAPTAIN VIDEO (TV) (See X-Mas Comics)
Feb, 1951 - No. 6, Dec, 1951 (No. 1,5,6-36pgs.; 2-4, 52pgs.)
Fawcett Publications
1-George Evans-a(2) 27.00 81.00 190.00
2-Used in **SOTI**, pg. 382 20.00 60.00 140.00
3-6-All Evans-a 18.00 54.00 125.00
NOTE: *Minor* ***Williamson*** *assist on most issues. Photo c-1, 5, 6; painted c-2-4.*

CAPTAIN WILLIE SCHULTZ (Also see Fightin' Army)
No. 76, Oct, 1985 - No. 77, Jan, 1986
Charlton Comics
76,77 .40 .75

CAPTAIN WIZARD COMICS (Also see Meteor)
1946
Rural Home
1-Capt. Wizard dons new costume; Impossible Man, Race Wilkins app. 6.00 18.00 42.00

CARDINAL MINDSZENTY (The Truth Behind the Trial of. . .)
1949 (24 pages; paper cover, in color)
Catechetical Guild Education Society

CARDINAL MINDSZENTY (continued)

	Good	Fine	Mint
nn-Anti-communism	8.35	25.00	50.00
Press Proof-(Very Rare)-(Full color, 7½x11¾", untrimmed) Only two known copies			150.00
Preview Copy (B&W, stapled), 18 pgs.; contains first 13 pgs. of Cardinal Mindszenty and was sent out as an advance promotion. Only one known copy			$150.00 - $250.00

NOTE: *Regular edition also printed in French.*

CARE BEARS (TV, Movie)
Nov, 1985 - Present
Star Comics

	Good	Fine	Mint
1-10: Post-a		.35	.70
11-15 ($1.00 cover)		.45	.90

CAREER GIRL ROMANCES (Formerly Three Nurses)
June, 1964 - No. 78, Dec, 1973
Charlton Comics

	Good	Fine	Mint
V4#24-31,33-78		.40	.80
32-Presley, Hermans Hermits, Johnny Rivers line drawn-c	1.15	3.50	8.00

CAR 54, WHERE ARE YOU? (TV)
Mar-May, 1962 - No. 7, Sept-Nov, 1963; 1964 - 1965 (All photo-c)
Dell Publishing Co.

	Good	Fine	Mint
4-Color 1257(3-5/62)	2.00	6.00	14.00
2(6-8/62)-7	1.15	3.50	8.00
2,3(10-12/64), 4(1-3/65)-Reprints No. 2,3,&4 of 1st series	.85	2.50	6.00

CARNATION MALTED MILK GIVEAWAYS (See Wisco)

CARNIVAL COMICS
1945
Harry 'A' Chesler/Pershing Square Publ. Co.

	Good	Fine	Mint
1	3.50	10.50	24.00

CARNIVAL OF COMICS
1954 (Giveaway)
Fleet-Air Shoes

	Good	Fine	Mint
nn-Contains a comic bound with new cover; several combinations possible; Charlton's Eh! known	1.00	3.00	7.00

CAROLINE KENNEDY
1961 (One Shot)
Charlton Comics

	Good	Fine	Mint
	3.70	11.00	26.00

CAROUSEL COMICS
V1No.8, April, 1948
F. E. Howard, Toronto

	Good	Fine	Mint
V1#8	1.50	4.50	10.00

CARTOON KIDS
1957 (no month)
Atlas Comics (CPS)

	Good	Fine	Mint
1-Maneely c/a	1.30	4.00	9.00

CARVEL COMICS (Amazing Advs. of Capt. Carvel)
1975 (25 cents; No.3-5: 35 cents) (No.4,5: 3¼x5")
Carvel Corp. (Ice Cream)

	Good	Fine	Mint
1-3		.15	.30
4,5(1976)-Baseball theme	.85	2.50	5.00

CASE OF THE SHOPLIFTER'S SHOE (Perry Mason) (See Feature Book No. 50 McKay)

CASE OF THE WASTED WATER, THE
1972? (Giveaway)
Rheem Water Heating

	Good	Fine	Mint
Neal Adams-a	2.00	6.00	14.00

CASE OF THE WINKING BUDDHA, THE
1950 (132 pgs.; 25 cents; B&W; 5½x7-5½x8")
St. John Publ. Co.

	Good	Fine	Mint
Charles Raab-a; reprinted in Authentic Police Cases No. 25	11.00	32.00	75.00

CASEY-CRIME PHOTOGRAPHER (Two-Gun Western No. 5 on)
Aug, 1949 - No. 4, Feb, 1950 (Radio)
Marvel Comics (BFP)

	Good	Fine	Mint
1: Photo-c	5.00	15.00	35.00
2-4: Photo-c	3.50	10.50	24.00

CASEY JONES (See 4-Color No. 915)

CASPER AND. . .
1987 - Present
Harvey Comics

	Good	Fine	Mint
1-The Ghostly Trio		.40	.75
2-4 ($1.00)		.50	1.00

CASPER AND NIGHTMARE (See Harvey Hits No. 37, 45, 52, 56, 59, 62, 65, 68, 71, 75)

CASPER AND NIGHTMARE (Nightmare & Casper No. 1-5) (25 cents)
No. 6, 11/64 - No. 44, 10/73; No. 45, 6/74 - No. 46, 8/74
Harvey Publications

	Good	Fine	Mint
6	2.00	6.00	12.00
7-10	1.00	3.00	6.00
11-20	.50	1.50	3.00
21-46	.35	1.00	2.00

CASPER AND SPOOKY (See Harvey Hits No. 20)
Oct, 1972 - No. 7, Oct, 1973
Harvey Publications

	Good	Fine	Mint
1	.85	2.50	5.00
2-7	.35	1.00	2.00

CASPER AND THE GHOSTLY TRIO
Nov, 1972 - No. 7, Nov, 1973
Harvey Publications

	Good	Fine	Mint
1	.85	2.50	5.00
2-7	.35	1.00	2.00

CASPER AND WENDY
Sept, 1972 - No. 8, Nov, 1973
Harvey Publications

	Good	Fine	Mint
1	.85	2.50	5.00
2-8	.35	1.00	2.00

CASPER CAT
1958; 1963
I. W. Enterprises/Super

	Good	Fine	Mint
1,7-Reprint, Super No. 14('63)	.35	1.00	2.00

CASPER DIGEST
Oct, 1986 - Present ($1.25, digest-size)
Harvey Publications

	Good	Fine	Mint
1-4		.50	1.00

CASPER DIGEST STORIES
2/80 - No. 4, 11/80 (95 cents; 132 pgs.; digest size)
Harvey Publications

	Good	Fine	Mint
1	.50	1.50	3.00
2-4	.35	1.00	2.00

CASPER DIGEST WINNERS
April, 1980 - No. 3, Sept, 1980 (95 cents; 132 pgs.; digest size)
Harvey Publications

	Good	Fine	Mint
1	.35	1.00	2.00
2,3	.25	.75	1.50

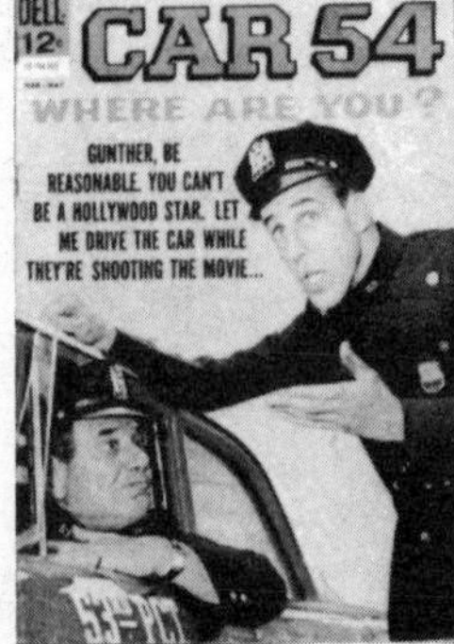

Car 54, Where Are You? #5 ('62), © Eupolis Prod.

Caroline Kennedy no #, © CC

Casper Cat #1, © I.W.

Casper, The Friendly Ghost #22, © Paramount

The Cat #4, © MCG

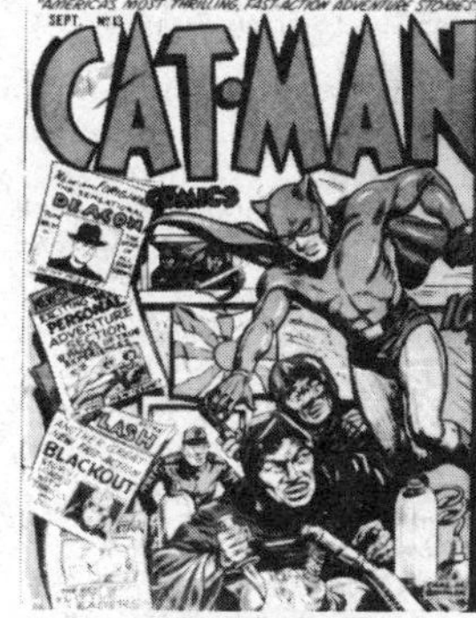

Catman Comics #13, © HOKE

CASPER HALLOWEEN TRICK OR TREAT
January, 1976
Harvey Publications

	Good	Fine	Mint
1	.35	1.00	2.00

CASPER IN SPACE (Formerly Casper Spaceship)
No. 6, June, 1973 - No. 8, Oct, 1973
Harvey Publications

6-8	.35	1.00	2.00

CASPER'S GHOSTLAND
Winter, 1958-59 - No. 97, 12/77; No. 98, 12/79 (25 cents)
Harvey Publications

1	6.00	18.00	40.00
2	3.35	10.00	23.00
3-10	2.75	8.00	18.00
11-20: 13-X-Mas-c	1.70	5.00	11.50
21-40	1.00	3.00	7.00
41-60	.75	2.25	5.00
61-80	.50	1.50	3.00
81-97: 94-X-Mas-c	.35	1.00	2.00
98		.50	1.00

CASPER SPACESHIP (Casper in Space No. 6 on)
Aug, 1972 - No. 5, April, 1973
Harvey Publications

1	.85	2.50	5.00
2-5	.35	1.00	2.00

CASPER STRANGE GHOST STORIES
October, 1974 - No. 14, Jan, 1977
Harvey Publications

1	.70	2.00	4.00
2-14	.35	1.00	2.00

CASPER, THE FRIENDLY GHOST (See Famous TV Funday Funnies, The Friendly Ghost..., Nightmare &..., Richie Rich, Tastee-Freez & Treasury of Comics)

CASPER, THE FRIENDLY GHOST (Becomes Harvey Comics Hits No. 61 (No. 6), and then continued with Harvey issue No. 7)
9/49 - No. 3, 8/50; 9/50 - No. 5, 5/51
St. John Publishing Co.

1(1949)-Origin & 1st app. Baby Huey	40.00	120.00	280.00
2,3	25.00	75.00	175.00
1(9/50)	30.00	90.00	210.00
2-5	20.00	60.00	140.00

CASPER, THE FRIENDLY GHOST (Paramount Picture Star...)
No. 7, Dec, 1952 - No 70, July, 1958
Harvey Publications (Family Comics)

Note: No. 6 is Harvey Comics Hits No. 61 (10/52)

7-Baby Huey begins, ends No. 17?	14.00	42.00	100.00
8-10: 8-Spooky begins, ends No. 70?	7.00	21.00	50.00
11-19: 19-1st app. Nightmare (4/54)	5.00	15.00	35.00
20-Wendy the Witch begins (1st app, 5/54)	6.00	18.00	42.00
21-30: 24-Infinity-c	4.30	13.00	30.00
31-40	3.75	11.25	26.00
41-50	3.00	9.00	21.00
51-70	2.30	7.00	16.00
American Dental Association (Giveaways):			
...'s Dental Health Activity Book-1977	.30	.80	1.60
...Presents Space Age Dentistry-1972	.40	1.20	2.40
..., His Den, & Their Dentist Fight the Tooth Demons-1974	.40	1.20	2.40

CASPER T.V. SHOWTIME
Jan, 1980 - No. 5, Oct, 1980
Harvey Comics

1	.35	1.00	2.00
2-5		.50	1.00

CASTILIAN (See Movie Classics)

CAT, T.H.E. (TV) (See T.H.E. Cat)

CAT, THE (See Movie Classics)

CAT, THE
Nov, 1972 - No. 4, June, 1973
Marvel Comics Group

	Good	Fine	Mint
1-Origin The Cat; Wood, Mooney-a(i)	.40	1.25	2.50
2-Mooney-a(i), 3-Everett inks	.25	.80	1.60
4-Starlin/Weiss-a(p)	.30	.90	1.80

CAT FROM OUTER SPACE (See Walt Disney Showcase #46)

CATHOLIC COMICS (See Heroes All Catholic...)
June, 1946 - V3No.10, July, 1949
Catholic Publications

1	7.00	21.00	50.00
2	3.50	10.50	24.00
3-13(7/47)	2.35	7.00	16.00
V2No.1-10	1.50	4.50	10.00
V3No.1-10	1.15	3.50	8.00

CATHOLIC PICTORIAL
1947
Catholic Guild

1-Toth-a(2) (Rare)	14.00	40.00	80.00

CATMAN COMICS (Crash No. 1-5)
5/41 - No. 17, 1/43; No. 18, 7/43 - No. 22, 12/43; No. 23, 3/44 - No. 26, 11/44; No. 27, 4/45 - No. 30, 12/45; No. 31, 6/46 - No. 32, 8/46
Holyoke Publishing Co./Continental Magazines V2No.12, 7/44 on

1(V1No.6)-Origin The Deacon & Sidekick Mickey, Dr. Diamond & Rag-Man; The Black Widow app.; The Catman by Chas. Quinlan & Blaze Baylor begin	50.00	150.00	350.00
2(V1#7)	25.00	75.00	175.00
3(V1#8), 4(V1#9): 3-The Pied Piper begins	20.00	60.00	140.00
5(V2#10)-Origin Kitten; The Hood begins (c-redated), 6,7(V2#11,12)	15.00	45.00	105.00
8(V2#13,3/42)-Origin Little Leaders; Volton by Kubert begins (his 1st comic book work)	22.00	65.00	154.00
9(V2#14)	12.00	36.00	84.00
10(V2#15)-Origin Blackout; Phantom Falcon begins	12.00	36.00	84.00
11(V3#1)-Kubert-a	11.50	34.00	80.00
12(V3#2) - 18(V3#8, 7/43)	10.00	30.00	70.00
19(V2#6) - 23(V2#10, 3/44): 19-Hitler-c	10.00	30.00	70.00
nn(V3#13, 5/44)-Rico-a; Schomburg bondage-c	8.00	24.00	56.00
nn(V2#12, 7/44)	8.00	24.00	56.00
nn(V3#1, 9/44)-Origin The Golden Archer; Leatherface app.;	7.00	21.00	50.00
nn(V3#2, 11/44)-L. B. Cole-c	14.00	42.00	100.00
27-Origin Kitten retold; L. B. Cole Flag-c	16.00	48.00	110.00
28-Catman learns Kitten's I.D.; Dr. Macabre, Deacon app.; L. B. Cole-c/a	17.00	51.00	120.00
29-32-L. B. Cole-c; bondage-#30	14.00	42.00	100.00

CAUGHT
Aug, 1956 - No. 5, April, 1957
Atlas Comics (VPI)

1	3.00	9.00	21.00
2,4: 4-Severin-c; Maneely-a	1.30	4.00	9.00
3-Torres-a	2.30	7.00	16.00
5-Crandall, Krigstein-a; Severin-c	3.00	9.00	21.00

CAVALIER COMICS
1945; 1952 (Early DC reprints)
A. W. Nugent Publ. Co.

CAVALIER COMICS (continued)	Good	Fine	Mint
2(1945)-Speed Saunders, Fang Gow	6.00	18.00	42.00
2(1952)	2.65	8.00	18.00

CAVE GIRL
1953 - 1954
Magazine Enterprises

	Good	Fine	Mint
11(A-1 82)-Origin	20.00	60.00	140.00
12(A-1 96), 13(A-1 116), 14(A-1 125)-Thunda by Powell	14.00	42.00	100.00

NOTE: ***Powell** c/a in all.*

CAVE KIDS (TV)
Feb, 1963 - No. 16, Mar, 1967 (Hanna-Barbera)
Gold Key

	Good	Fine	Mint
1	1.00	3.00	7.00
2-5	.70	2.00	4.00
6-16	.50	1.50	3.00

CENTURION OF ANCIENT ROME, THE
1958 (no month listed) (36 pages) (B&W)
Zondervan Publishing House

	Good	Fine	Mint
(Rare) All by Jay Disbrow Estimated Value....			180.00

CENTURIONS
June, 1987 - No. 4, Sept,1987 (mini-series)
DC Comics

	Good	Fine	Mint
1-4		.45	.90

CENTURY OF COMICS
1933 (100 pages) (Probably the 3rd comic book)
Eastern Color Printing Co.

Bought by Wheatena, Milk-O-Malt, John Wanamaker, Kinney Shoe Stores, & others to be used as premiums and radio giveaways. No publisher listed.

	Good	Fine	Mint
nn-Mutt & Jeff, Joe Palooka, etc. reprints	200.00	600.00	1400.00

CEREBUS JAM
Apr, 1985
Aardvark-Vanaheim

	Good	Fine	Mint
1-Eisner, Austin-a	.85	2.50	5.00

CEREBUS THE AARDVARK
Dec, 1977 - Present
Aardvark-Vanaheim

	Good	Fine	Mint
1-2000 print run; most copies poorly printed	73.00	220.00	440.00

Note: There is a counterfeit version known to exist. It can be distinguished from the original in the following ways: inside cover is glossy instead of flat, black background on the front cover is blotted or spotty. These counterfeits sell for between $50.00 and $75.00.

	Good	Fine	Mint
2	35.00	105.00	210.00
3-Origin Red Sophia	26.00	78.00	155.00
4-Origin Elrod the Albino	17.50	52.50	105.00
5,6	14.00	42.50	85.00
7-10	10.00	30.00	60.00
11,12: 11-Origin Moon Roach	10.00	30.00	60.00
13-15: 14-Origin Lord Julius	6.00	18.00	36.00
16-20	4.15	12.50	25.00
21-Scarce	15.00	45.00	90.00
22	3.65	11.00	22.00
23-28	1.85	5.50	11.00
29-31	2.15	6.50	13.00
32-40	1.00	3.00	6.00
41-50,52	.85	2.50	5.00
51-Not reprinted	3.00	9.00	18.00
53-Intro. Wolveroach	1.15	3.50	7.00
54-Wolveroach 1st full story	2.00	6.00	12.00
55,56-Wolveroach	1.00	3.00	7.00
57-60	.60	1.75	3.50
61,62: Flaming Carrot app.	.85	2.50	5.00
63-68	.70	2.00	4.00
69-75	.55	1.60	3.20
76-79	.50	1.50	3.00
80-85	.45	1.25	2.50
86-105	.30	1.00	2.00

CHALLENGE OF THE UNKNOWN (Formerly Love Experiences)
No. 6, Sept, 1950 (See Web Of Mystery No. 19)
Ace Magazines

	Good	Fine	Mint
6-'Villa of the Vampire' used in N.Y. Joint Legislative Comm. Publ; Sekowsky-a	6.00	18.00	42.00

CHALLENGER, THE
1945 - No. 4, Oct-Dec, 1946
Interfaith Publications

	Good	Fine	Mint
nn; nd; 32 pgs.; Origin the Challenger Club; Anti-Fascist with funny animal filler	6.50	19.50	45.00
2-4-Kubert-a; 4-Fuje-a	10.00	30.00	70.00

CHALLENGERS OF THE UNKNOWN (See Showcase, Super DC Giant, and Super Team Family)
4-5/58 - No.77, 12-1/70-71; No.78, 2/73 - No.80, 6-7/73; No.81, 6-7/77 - No.87, 6-7/78
National Periodical Publications/DC Comics

	Good	Fine	Mint
1-Kirby/Stein-a(2)	45.00	135.00	315.00
2-Kirby/Stein-a(2)	22.00	65.00	154.00
3-Kirby/Stein-a(2)	18.00	54.00	125.00
4-8-Kirby/Wood-a plus c-#8	14.00	42.00	100.00
9,10	5.70	17.00	40.00
11-15: 14-Origin Multi-Man	4.35	13.00	30.00
16-22: 18-Intro. Cosmo, the Challs Spacepet. 22-Last 10 cent issue	3.00	9.00	21.00
23-30	1.50	4.50	10.00
31-40: 31-Retells origin of the Challengers	1.00	3.00	7.00
41-60: 43-New look begins. 48-Doom Patrol app. 49-Intro. Challenger Corps. 51-Sea Devils app. 55-Death of Red Ryan. 60-Red Ryan returns	.50	1.50	3.00
61-63,66-73: 69-Intro. Corinna	.35	1.00	2.00
64,65-Kirby origin-r, parts 1 & 2	.35	1.00	2.00
74-Deadman by Tuska/Adams	1.00	3.00	6.00
75-87: 82-Swamp Thing begins		.40	.80

NOTE: ***Adams** c-67, 68, 70, 72, 74i, 81i. **Buckler** c-83-86p. **Giffen** a-83-87p. **Kirby** a-75-80r; c-75, 77, 78. **Kubert** c-64, 66, 69, 76, 79. **Nasser** c/a-81p, 82p. **Tuska** a-73. **Wood** r-76.*

CHALLENGE TO THE WORLD
1951 (36 pages) (10 cents)
Catechetical Guild

	Good	Fine	Mint
nn	5.00	14.00	28.00

CHAMBER OF CHILLS (...of Clues No. 27 on)
No. 21, June, 1951 - No. 26, Dec, 1954
Harvey Publications/Witches Tales

	Good	Fine	Mint
21	9.00	27.00	62.00
22,24	6.00	18.00	42.00
23-Excessive violence; eyes torn out	6.00	18.00	42.00
5(2/52)-Decapitation, acid in face scene	6.00	18.00	42.00
6-Woman melted alive	4.50	13.50	31.50
7-Used in **SOTI**, pg. 389; decapitation/severed head panels	4.50	13.50	31.50
8-10: 8-Decapitation panels	3.70	11.00	26.00
11,12,14	3.50	10.50	24.00
13,15-24-Nostrand-a in all; c-#20. 13,21-Decapitation panels. 18-Atom bomb panels	5.70	17.00	40.00
25,26	3.00	9.00	21.00

Centurions #1, © DC

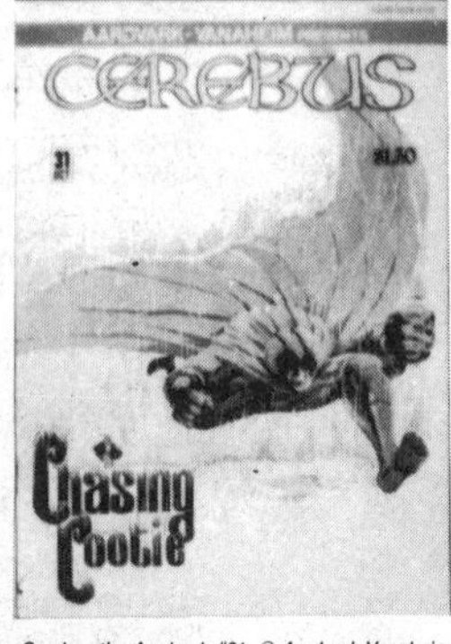

Cerebus the Aardvark #31, © Aardvark-Vanaheim

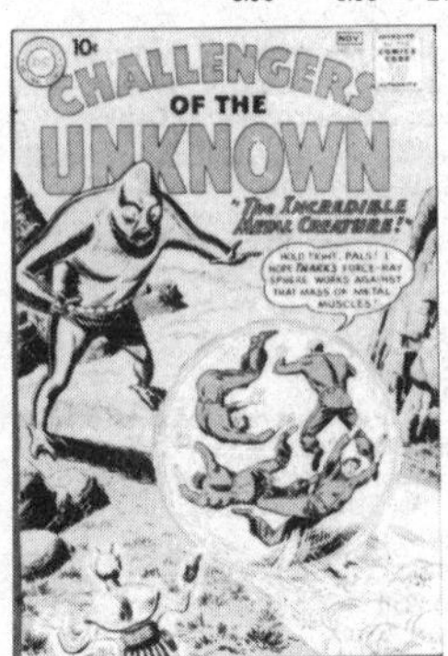

Challengers of the Unknown #16, © DC

Champion Comics #10, © HARV

The Champions #11, © MCG

Charlie McCarthy #3, © Edgar Bergen

CHAMBER OF CHILLS (continued)

NOTE: *About half the issues contain bondage, torture, sadism, perversion, gore, cannabalism, eyes ripped out, acid in face, etc.* ***Kremer*** *a-12, 17.* ***Palais*** *a-21(1), 23.* ***Nostrand/Powell*** *a-13, 15, 16.* ***Powell*** *a-21, 23, 24('51), 5-8, 11, 13, 18-21, 23-25. Bondage-c-21, 24('51), 7. 25 r-No. 5; 26 r-No. 9.*

CHAMBER OF CHILLS
Nov, 1972 - No. 25, Nov, 1976
Marvel Comics Group

	Good	Fine	Mint
1-Harlan Ellison adapt.		.40	.80
2-25		.20	.40

NOTE: ***Adkins*** *a-1i, 2i.* ***Brunner*** *a-2-4; c-4.* ***Ditko*** *r-14, 16, 19, 23, 24.* ***Everett*** *a-3i, 11r, 21r.* ***Heath*** *a-1r.* ***Gil Kane*** *c-2p.* ***Powell*** *a-13r.* ***Russell*** *a-1p, 2p.* ***Williamson/Mayo*** *a-13r.* ***Robert E. Howard*** *horror story adaptation-2, 3.*

CHAMBER OF CLUES (Formerly Chamber of Chills)
Feb, 1955 - No. 28, April, 1955
Harvey Publications

	Good	Fine	Mint
27-Kerry Drake r-/No. 19; Powell-a	4.30	13.00	30.00
28-Kerry Drake	2.30	7.00	16.00

CHAMBER OF DARKNESS (Monsters on the Prowl #9 on)
Oct, 1969 - No. 8, Dec, 1970
Marvel Comics Group

	Good	Fine	Mint
1-Buscema-a(p)		.40	.80
2-Adams script		.40	.80
3-Smith, Buscema-a		.60	1.20
4-A Conanesque tryout by Smith; reprinted in Conan No. 16	1.25	3.75	7.50
5-8: 5-H.P. Lovecraft adapt.		.30	.60
7-Wrightson c/a, 7pgs. (his 1st work at Marvel); Wrightson draws himself in 1st & last panels	.35	1.00	2.00
1(1/72-25 cent Special)		.40	.80

NOTE: ***Adkins/Everett*** *a-8.* ***Craig*** *a-5.* ***Ditko*** *a-6-8r.* ***Kirby*** *a(p)-4, 5, 7.* ***Kirby/Everett*** *c-5.* ***Severin/Everett*** *c-6.* ***Wrightson*** *c-7, 8.*

CHAMP COMICS (Champion No. 1-10)
No. 11, Oct, 1940 - No. 29, March, 1944
Worth Publ. Co./Champ Publ./Family Comics(Harvey Publ.)

	Good	Fine	Mint
11-Human Meteor cont'd.	27.00	81.00	190.00
12-18: 14,15-Crandall-c	20.00	60.00	140.00
19-The Wasp app.	20.00	60.00	140.00
20-The Green Ghost app.	20.00	60.00	140.00
21-29: 22-The White Mask app. 23-Flag-c	17.00	51.00	120.00

CHAMPION (See Gene Autry's...)

CHAMPION COMICS (Champ No. 11 on)
No. 2, Dec, 1939 - No. 10, Aug, 1940 (no No.1)
Worth Publ. Co.(Harvey Publications)

	Good	Fine	Mint
2-The Champ, The Blazing Scarab, Neptina, Liberty Lads, Jungleman, Bill Handy, Swingtime Sweetie begin	35.00	105.00	245.00
3-7: 7-The Human Meteor begins?	20.00	60.00	140.00
8-10-Kirbyish-c; bondage #10	22.00	65.00	154.00

CHAMPIONS, THE
October, 1975 - No. 17, Jan, 1978
Marvel Comics Group

	Good	Fine	Mint
1-The Angel, Black Widow, Ghost Rider, Hercules, Ice Man (The Champions) begin; Kane/Adkins-c; Venus x-over	.50	1.50	3.00
2-10: 2,3-Venus x-over		.50	1.00
11-15,17-Byrne-a	.50	1.50	3.00
16		.30	.60

NOTE: ***Buckler/Adkins*** *c-3.* ***Kane/Layton*** *c-11.* ***Layton*** *a-11i-13i.* ***Tuska*** *a-3p, 4p.*

CHAMPIONS
June, 1986 - No. 6, Feb, 1987 (limited series)
Eclipse Comics

	Good	Fine	Mint
1-6: Based on role playing game		.65	1.30

CHAMPIONS
Sept, 1987 - Present ($1.95, color)
Hero Comics

	Good	Fine	Mint
1-5	.35	1.00	2.00

CHAMPION SPORTS
Oct-Nov, 1973 - No. 3, Feb-Mar, 1974
National Periodical Publications

	Good	Fine	Mint
1-3		.30	.60

CHAOS (See The Crusaders)

CHARLIE CHAN (See The New Advs. of...)

CHARLIE CHAN (The Adventures of) (Zaza The Mystic No. 10 on)
6-7/48 - No.5, 2-3/49; No.6, 6/55 - No.9, 3/56
Crestwood(Prize) No.1-5; Charlton No.6(6/55) on

	Good	Fine	Mint
1-S&K-c, 2 pages; Infantino-a	17.00	51.00	120.00
2-S&K-c	10.00	30.00	70.00
3-5-All S&K-c	9.00	27.00	62.00
6(6/55-Charlton)-S&K-c	6.00	18.00	42.00
7-9	3.50	10.50	24.00

CHARLIE CHAN
Oct-Dec, 1965 - No. 2, Mar, 1966
Dell Publishing Co.

	Good	Fine	Mint
1-Springer-a	1.70	5.00	10.00
2	1.00	3.00	6.00

CHARLIE CHAPLIN
1917 (9x16"; large size; softcover; B&W)
Essanay/M. A. Donohue & Co.

	Good	Fine	Mint
Series 1, No. 315-Comic Capers (9¾x15¾")-18pp by Segar, Series 1, No. 316-In the Movies	35.00	105.00	245.00
Series 1, No. 317-Up in the Air. No. 318-In the Army	35.00	105.00	245.00
...Funny Stunts-(12½x16-3/8") in color	24.00	72.00	170.00

NOTE: *All contain* ***Segar*** *-a; pre-Thimble Theatre.*

CHARLIE McCARTHY (See Edgar Bergen Presents...)
No. 171, Nov, 1947 - No. 571, July, 1954 (See True Comics #14)
Dell Publishing Co.

	Good	Fine	Mint
4-Color 171	5.00	15.00	35.00
4-Color 196-Part photo-c; photo back-c	6.00	18.00	42.00
1(3-5/49)-Part photo-c; photo back-c	6.00	18.00	42.00
2-9(7/52; No. 5,6-52 pgs.)	2.30	7.00	16.00
4-Color 445,478,527,571	1.70	5.00	12.00

CHARLTON BULLSEYE
June, 1981 - No. 10, Dec, 1982; Nov, 1986
Charlton Publications

	Good	Fine	Mint
1-Blue Beetle, The Question		.40	.80
2-10: 2-1st app. Neil The Horse. 6-Origin & 1st app. Thunderbunny		.30	.60

CHARLTON CLASSICS
April, 1980 - No. 9, Aug, 1981
Charlton Comics

	Good	Fine	Mint
1		.30	.60
2-9		.25	.50

CHARLTON CLASSICS LIBRARY (1776)
V10No.1, March, 1973 (One Shot)
Charlton Comics

	Good	Fine	Mint
1776 (title) - Adaptation of the film musical "1776"; given away at movie theatres	.35	1.00	2.00

CHARLTON PREMIERE (Formerly Marine War Heroes)
V1No.19, July, 1967; V2No.1, Sept, 1967 - No. 4, May, 1968
Charlton Comics

V1No.19-Marine War Heroes, V2No.1-Trio; intro. Shape, Tyro Team, &

CHARLTON PREMIERE (continued) Good Fine Mint
Spookman, 2-Children of Doom, 3-Sinistro Boy Fiend; Blue Beetle Peacemaker x-over, 4-Unlikely Tales; Ditko-a .40 .80

CHARLTON SPORT LIBRARY - PROFESSIONAL FOOTBALL
Winter, 1969-70 (Jan. on cover) (68 pages)
Charlton Comics
1 .50 1.50 3.00

CHASING THE BLUES
1912 (52 pages) (7½x10"; B&W; hardcover)
Doubleday Page
by Rube Goldberg 20.00 60.00 140.00

CHECKMATE (TV)
Oct, 1962 - No. 2, Dec, 1962
Gold Key
1,2-Photo-c 2.00 6.00 14.00

CHECKMATE
April, 1988 - Present
DC Comics
1 .65 1.30

CHEERIOS PREMIUMS (Disney)
1947 (32 pages) (Pocket size; 16 titles)
Walt Disney Productions

	Good	Fine	Mint
Set "W"-Donald Duck & the Pirates	3.35	10.00	20.00
Pluto Joins the F.B.I.	2.00	6.00	12.00
Bucky Bug & the Cannibal King	2.00	6.00	12.00
Mickey Mouse & the Haunted House	3.00	9.00	18.00
Set "X"-Donald Duck, Counter Spy	2.75	8.00	16.00
Goofy Lost in the Desert	2.00	6.00	12.00
Br'er Rabbit Outwits Br'er Fox	2.00	6.00	12.00
Mickey Mouse at the Rodeo	3.00	9.00	18.00
Set "Y"-Donald Duck's Atom Bomb by Carl Barks	57.00	170.00	380.00
Br'er Rabbit's Secret	2.00	6.00	12.00
Dumbo & the Circus Mystery	2.75	8.00	16.00
Mickey Mouse Meets the Wizard	3.00	9.00	18.00
Set "Z"-Donald Duck Pilots a Jet Plane (not by Barks)	2.75	8.00	16.00
Pluto Turns Sleuth Hound	2.00	6.00	12.00
The Seven Dwarfs & the Enchanted Mtn.	2.75	8.00	16.00
Mickey Mouse's Secret Room	3.00	9.00	18.00

CHEERIOS 3-D GIVEAWAYS (Disney)
1954 (Pocket size) (24 titles)
Walt Disney Productions
(Glasses were cut-outs on boxes)
Glasses only.... 4.00 12.00 28.00

(Set 1)
1-Donald Duck & Uncle Scrooge, the Firefighters
2-Mickey Mouse & Goofy, Pirate Plunder
3-Donald Duck's Nephews, the Fabulous Inventors
4-Mickey Mouse, Secret of the Ming Vase
5-Donald Duck with Huey, Dewey, & Louie; ...the Seafarers (title on 2nd page)
6-Mickey Mouse, Moaning Mountain
7-Donald Duck, Apache Gold
8-Mickey Mouse, Flight to Nowhere
(per book).... 5.00 15.00 35.00

(Set 2)
1-Donald Duck, Treasure of Timbuktu
2-Mickey Mouse & Pluto, Operation China
3-Donald Duck in the Magic Cows
4-Mickey Mouse & Goofy, Kid Kokonut
5-Donald Duck, Mystery Ship
6-Mickey Mouse, Phantom Sheriff
7-Donald Duck, Circus Adventures
8-Mickey Mouse, Arctic Explorers
(per book).... Good 5.00 Fine 15.00 Mint 35.00

(Set 3)
1-Donald Duck & Witch Hazel
2-Mickey Mouse in Darkest Africa
3-Donald Duck & Uncle Scrooge, Timber Trouble
4-Mickey Mouse, Rajah's Rescue
5-Donald Duck in Robot Reporter
6-Mickey Mouse, Slumbering Sleuth
7-Donald Duck in the Foreign Legion
8-Mickey Mouse, Airwalking Wonder
(per book).... 5.00 15.00 35.00

CHESTY AND COPTIE
1946 (4 pages) (Giveaway) (Disney)
Los Angeles Community Chest
(Very Rare) by Floyd Gottfredson 14.00 42.00 100.00

CHESTY AND HIS HELPERS
1943 (12 pgs., Disney giveaway, 5½x7¼")
Los Angeles War Chest
nn-Chesty & Coptie 17.00 51.00 120.00

CHEYENNE (TV)
No. 734, Oct, 1956 - No. 25, Dec-Jan, 1961-62
Dell Publishing Co.

	Good	Fine	Mint
4-Color 734(#1)-Ty Hardin photo-c begin	5.00	15.00	35.00
4-Color 772,803	4.00	12.00	28.00
4(8-10/57) - 12-Last Ty Hardin photo-c	3.50	10.50	24.00
13-25 (All Clint Walker photo-c)	3.00	9.00	21.00

CHEYENNE AUTUMN (See Movie Classics)

CHEYENNE KID (Wild Frontier No. 1-7)
No. 8, July, 1957 - No. 99, Nov, 1973
Charlton Comics

	Good	Fine	Mint
8 (No. 1)	2.00	6.00	14.00
9,15-17,19	1.00	3.00	7.00
10-Williamson/Torres-a(3); Ditko-c	5.50	16.50	38.00
11,12-Williamson/Torres-a(2) ea.; 11-(68 pgs.)	5.50	16.50	38.00
13-Williamson/Torres-a, 5 pgs.	3.50	10.50	24.00
14,18-Williamson-a, 5 pgs.?	3.50	10.50	24.00
20-22,25-Severin c/a(3) each	1.70	5.00	12.00
23,24,27-29	.75	2.25	5.00
26,30-Severin-a	.85	2.50	6.00
31-59	.35	1.00	2.00
60-99: 66-Wander by Aparo begins, ends #87. Apache Red begins #88, origin #89		.30	.60
Modern Comics Reprint 87,89('78)		.20	.40

CHICAGO MAIL ORDER (See C-M-O Comics)

CHIEF, THE (Indian Chief No. 3 on)
No. 290, Aug, 1950 - No. 2, Apr-June, 1951
Dell Publishing Co.
4-Color 290, 2 3.00 9.00 21.00

CHIEF CRAZY HORSE (See Wild Bill Hockok #21)
1950
Avon Periodicals
nn: Fawcette-c 10.00 30.00 70.00

CHIEF VICTORIO'S APACHE MASSACRE
1951
Avon Periodicals
nn-Williamson/Frazetta-a, 7 pgs.; Larsen-a; Kinstler-c 30.00 90.00 210.00

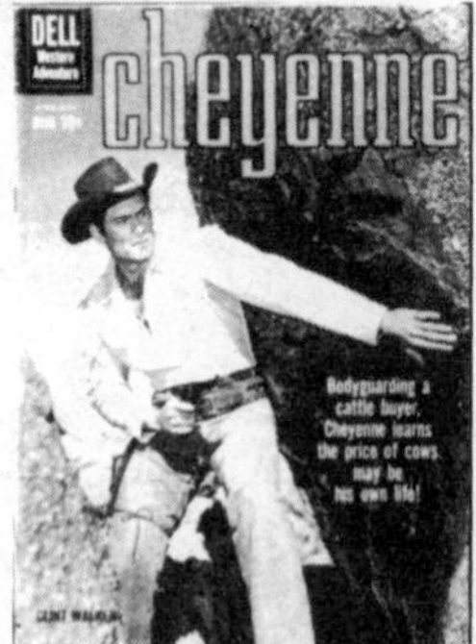

Cheyenne #15, © Warner Bros.

Cheyenne Kid #47, © CC

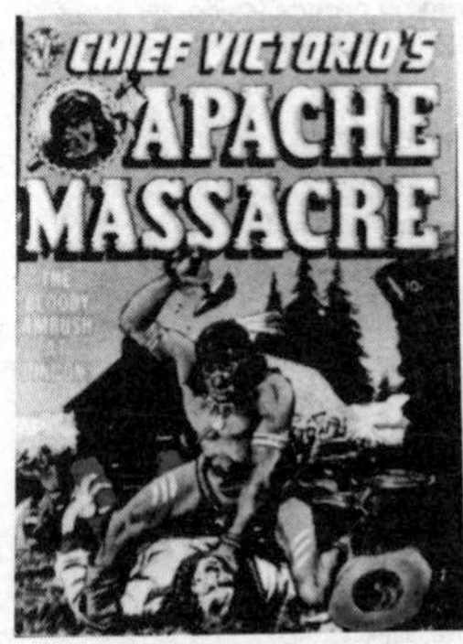

Chief Victorio's Apache Massacre #1, © AVON

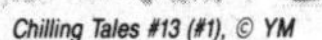
Chilling Tales #13 (#1), © YM

Choice Comics #2, © GP

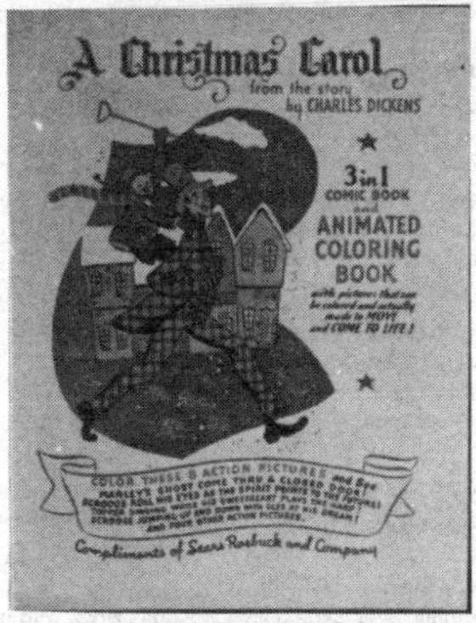

A Christmas Carol, 1940s, © Sears

CHILDREN OF FIRE
Nov, 1987 - No. 3, 1988 (Color)
Fantagor Press

	Good	Fine	Mint
1-3	.35	1.00	2.00

CHILDREN'S BIG BOOK
1945 (68 pages; stiff covers) (25 cents)
Dorene Publ. Co.

	Good	Fine	Mint
Comics & fairy tales; David Icove-a	5.00	15.00	35.00

CHILI (Millie's Rival)
5/69 - No. 17, 9/70; No. 18, 8/72 - No. 26, 12/73
Marvel Comics Group

	Good	Fine	Mint
1	.70	2.00	4.00
2-5	.35	1.00	2.00
6-17		.50	1.00
18-26		.40	.80
Special 1(12/71)		.40	.80

CHILLING ADVENTURES IN SORCERY (. . .as Told by Sabrina No.1, 2) (Red Circle Sorcery No. 6 on)
9/72 - No. 2, 10/72; No. 3, 10/73 - No. 5, 2/74
Archie Publications (Red Circle Prod.)

	Good	Fine	Mint
1,2-Sabrina cameo in both	.50	1.50	3.00
3-Morrow c/a, all	.35	1.00	2.00
4,5-Morrow c/a, 5,6 pgs.	.35	1.00	2.00

CHILLING TALES (Formerly Beware)
No. 13, Dec, 1952 - No. 17, Oct, 1953
Youthful Magazines

	Good	Fine	Mint
13(No.1)-Harrison-a; Matt Fox c/a	10.00	30.00	70.00
14-Harrison-a	6.00	18.00	42.00
15-Has No. 14 on-c; Matt Fox-c; Harrison-a	8.00	24.00	56.00
16-Poe adapt.-'Metzengerstein'; Rudyard Kipling adapt.-'Mark of the Beast,' by Kiefer; bondage-c	6.00	18.00	42.00
17-Matt Fox-c; Sir Walter Scott & Poe adapt.	8.00	24.00	56.00

CHILLING TALES OF HORROR (Magazine)
V1No.1, 6/69 - V1No.7, 12/70; V2No.2, 2/71 - V2No.5, 10/71
(52 pages; black & white) (50 cents)
Stanley Publications

	Good	Fine	Mint
V1No.1	.40	1.25	2.50
2-7: 7-Cameron-a	.30	.90	1.80
V2No.2-Spirit of Frankenstein r-/Adv. into Unknown No. 16; V2No.3,5	.30	.90	1.80
V2No.4-r-9 pg. Feldstein-a from Adv. into Unknown No. 3	.40	1.25	2.50

NOTE: *Two issues of V2No.2 exist, Feb, 1971 and April, 1971.*

CHILLY WILLY (See 4-Color No. 740,852,967,1017,1074,1122,1177,1212,1281)

CHINA BOY (See Wisco)

CHIP 'N' DALE (Walt Disney)(See WDC&S #204)
11/53 - No. 30, 6-8/62; 9/67 - No. 83, 1982
Dell Publishing Co./Gold Key/Whitman No. 65 on

	Good	Fine	Mint
4-Color 517	1.70	5.00	12.00
4-Color 581,636	1.30	4.00	9.00
4(12/55-2/56)-10	.75	2.25	5.00
11-30	.55	1.65	4.00
1(Gold Key reprints, 1967)	.50	1.50	3.00
2-10	.25	.75	1.50
11-20		.50	1.00
21-83		.30	.60

NOTE: *All Gold Key/Whitman issues have reprints except No. 32-35, 38-41, 45-47. No. 23-28, 30-42, 45-47, 49 have new covers.*

CHITTY CHITTY BANG BANG (See Movie Comics)

CHOICE COMICS
Dec, 1941 - No. 3, Feb, 1942
Great Publications

	Good	Fine	Mint
1-Origin Secret Circle; Atlas the Mighty app.; Zomba, Jungle Fight, Kangaroo Man, & Fire Eater begin	37.00	110.00	260.00
2	24.00	72.00	170.00
3-Features movie 'The Lost City" classic cover; continues in Great Comics #3	35.00	105.00	245.00

CHOO CHOO CHARLIE
Dec, 1969
Gold Key

	Good	Fine	Mint
1-John Stanley-a	3.00	9.00	21.00

CHRISTIAN HEROES OF TODAY
1964 (36 pages)
David C. Cook

	Good	Fine	Mint
	.70	2.00	4.00

CHRISTMAS (See A-1 No. 28)

CHRISTMAS ADVENTURE, A (See Classics Comics Giveaway)

CHRISTMAS ADVENTURE, THE
1963 (16 pages)
S. Rose (H. L. Green Giveaway)

	Good	Fine	Mint
	.85	2.50	5.00

CHRISTMAS ALBUM (See March of Comics No. 312)

CHRISTMAS & ARCHIE ($1.00)
Jan, 1975 (68 pages) (10¼x13¼")
Archie Comics

	Good	Fine	Mint
1	1.70	5.00	10.00

CHRISTMAS AT THE ROTUNDA (Titled Ford Rotunda Christmas Bk. 1957 on) (Regular size)
Given away every Christmas at one location
1954 - 1961
Ford Motor Co. (Western Printing)

	Good	Fine	Mint
1954-56 issues (nn's)	1.75	5.25	12.00
1957-61 issues (nn's)	1.15	3.50	8.00

CHRISTMAS BELLS (See March of Comics No. 297)

CHRISTMAS CARNIVAL
1952 (100 pages) (One Shot)
Ziff-Davis Publ. Co./St. John Publ. Co. No. 2

	Good	Fine	Mint
nn	6.00	18.00	42.00
2-Reprints Ziff-Davis issue plus-c	4.35	13.00	30.00

CHRISTMAS CAROL, A (See March of Comics No. 33)

CHRISTMAS CAROL, A
No date (1942-43) (32 pgs.; 8¼x10¾"; paper cover)
Sears Roebuck & Co. (Giveaway)

	Good	Fine	Mint
nn-Comics & coloring book	5.00	15.00	30.00

CHRISTMAS CAROL, A
1940s ? (20 pgs.)
Sears Roebuck & Co. (Christmas giveaway)

	Good	Fine	Mint
Comic book & animated coloring book	4.00	12.00	24.00

CHRISTMAS CAROLS
1959 ? (16 pgs.)
Hot Shoppes Giveaway

	Good	Fine	Mint
	1.20	3.50	7.00

CHRISTMAS COLORING FUN
1964 (20 pgs.; slick cover; B&W inside)
H. Burnside

	Good	Fine	Mint
	.70	2.00	4.00

CHRISTMAS DREAM, A
1950 (16 pages) (Kinney Shoe Store Giveaway)
Promotional Publishing Co.

CHRISTMAS DREAM, A (continued) Good Fine Mint
nn 1.35 4.00 8.00

CHRISTMAS DREAM, A
1952? (16 pgs.; paper cover)
J. J. Newberry Co. (Giveaway)
1.35 4.00 8.00

CHRISTMAS DREAM, A
1952 (16 pgs.; paper cover)
Promotional Publ. Co. (Giveaway)
1.35 4.00 8.00

CHRISTMAS EVE, A (See March of Comics No. 212)

CHRISTMAS FUN AROUND THE WORLD
No date (early 50's) (16 pages; paper cover)
No publisher
2.00 6.00 12.00

CHRISTMAS IN DISNEYLAND (See Dell Giants)

CHRISTMAS JOURNEY THROUGH SPACE
1960
Promotional Publishing Co.
Reprints 1954 issue Jolly Christmas Book with new slick cover
1.50 4.50 10.00

CHRISTMAS ON THE MOON
1958 (20 pgs.; slick cover)
W. T. Grant Co. (Giveaway)
1.75 5.25 12.00

CHRISTMAS PARADE (See Dell Giant No. 26, Dell Giants, March of Comics No. 284, & Walt Disney's . . .)

CHRISTMAS PARADE (Walt Disney's)
1/63 (no month) - No. 9, 1/72 (No.1,5: 80pgs.; No.2-4,7-9: 36pgs.)
Gold Key

	Good	Fine	Mint
1 (30018-301)-Giant	3.50	10.50	24.00
2-Reprints 4-Color 367 by Barks	3.75	11.00	26.00
3-Reprints 4-Color 178 by Barks	3.75	11.00	26.00
4-Reprints 4-Color 203 by Barks	3.75	11.00	26.00
5-Reprints Christmas Parade 1(Dell) by Barks; giant	3.75	11.00	26.00
6-Reprints Christmas Parade 2(Dell) by Barks(64pp)-Giant	3.75	11.00	30.00
7,9: 7-Pull-out poster	1.75	5.25	12.00
8-Reprints 4-Color 367 by Barks; pull-out poster	3.75	11.00	26.00

CHRISTMAS PARTY (See March of Comics No. 256)

CHRISTMAS PLAY BOOK
1946 (16 pgs.; paper cover)
Gould-Stoner Co. (Giveaway)
2.75 8.00 16.00

CHRISTMAS ROUNDUP
1960
Promotional Publishing Co.
Marv Levy c/a 1.00 3.00 7.00

CHRISTMAS STORIES (See 4-Color No. 959,1062)

CHRISTMAS STORY (See March of Comics No. 326)

CHRISTMAS STORY BOOK (See Woolworth's Christmas Book)

CHRISTMAS STORY CUT-OUT BOOK, THE
1951 (36 pages) (15 cents)
Catechetical Guild
393-½ text, ½ comics 2.75 8.00 16.00

CHRISTMAS TREASURY, A (See Dell Giants & March of Comics No. 227)

CHRISTMAS USA (Through 300 Years) (Also see Uncle Sam's. . .)
1956
Promotional Publ. Co. (Giveaway) Good Fine Mint
Marv Levy c/a 1.00 3.00 6.00

CHRISTMAS WITH ARCHIE
1973, 1974 (52 pages) (49 cents)
Spire Christian Comics (Fleming H. Revell Co.)
nn .60 1.20

CHRISTMAS WITH MOTHER GOOSE (See 4-Color No. 90,126,172,201,253)

CHRISTMAS WITH SANTA (See March of Comics No. 92)

CHRISTMAS WITH SNOW WHITE AND THE SEVEN DWARFS
1953 (16 pages, paper cover)
Kobackers Giftstore of Buffalo, N.Y.
3.00 9.00 18.00

CHRISTOPHERS, THE
1951 (36 pages) (Some copies have 15 cent sticker)
Catechetical Guild (Giveaway)
nn-Hammer & sickle dripping blood-c; Stalin as Satan in Hell
25.00 75.00 175.00

CHROME
1986 - No. 6? ($1.50, color)
Hot Comics

	Good	Fine	Mint
1	.45	1.25	2.50
2-6	.25	.75	1.50

CHRONICLES OF CORUM, THE
Jan, 1987 - Present ($1.75, deluxe series)
First Comics
1-8: Adapt. M. Moorcock's novel .30 .90 1.80

CHUCKLE, THE GIGGLY BOOK OF COMIC ANIMALS
1945 (132 pages) (One Shot)
R. B. Leffingwell Co.
1-Funny animal 7.00 21.00 50.00

CHUCK NORRIS AND THE KARATE KOMMANDOS (TV)
Jan, 1987 - No. 5, Sept, 1987
Star Comics (Marvel)

	Good	Fine	Mint
1-Ditko-a		.50	1.00
2-5		.40	.80

CHUCK WAGON (See Sheriff Bob Dixon's. . .)

CICERO'S CAT
July-Aug, 1959 - No. 2, Sept-Oct, 1959
Dell Publishing Co.
1,2 1.70 5.00 12.00

CIMARRON STRIP (TV)
January, 1968
Dell Publishing Co.
1 2.00 6.00 14.00

CINDER AND ASHE
Mar, 1988 - No. 4, June, 1988 ($1.75, mini-series)
DC Comics
1,2 .30 .90 1.75

CINDERELLA (See 4-Color No. 272,786, & Movie Comics)

CINDERELLA
April, 1982
Whitman Publishing Co.
nn-r-/4-Color 272 .30 .60

CINDERELLA IN "FAIREST OF THE FAIR"
1955 (16 pages, 5x7¼", soft-c) (Walt Disney)

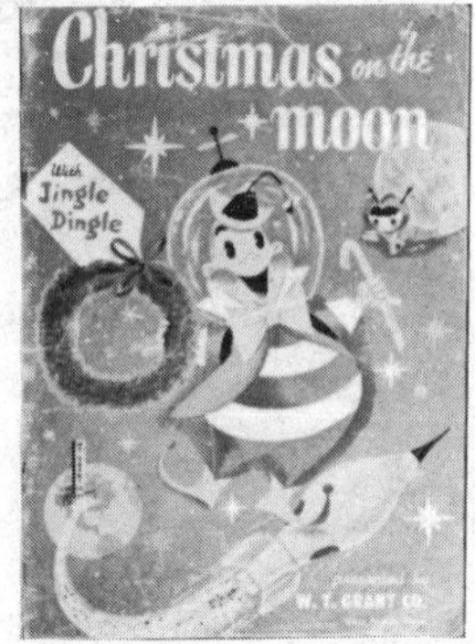

Christmas On the Moon, no #, © W.T. Grant

Christmas Parade #3, © WDC

Chuckle, The Giggly Book... #1, © Leffingwell

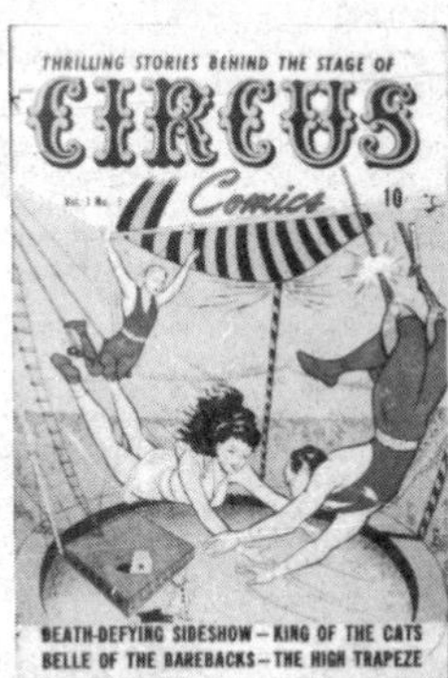

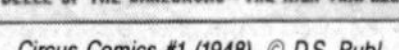

Circus Comics #1 (1948), © D.S. Publ.

Cisco Kid Comics #1 (1944), © B. Bailey

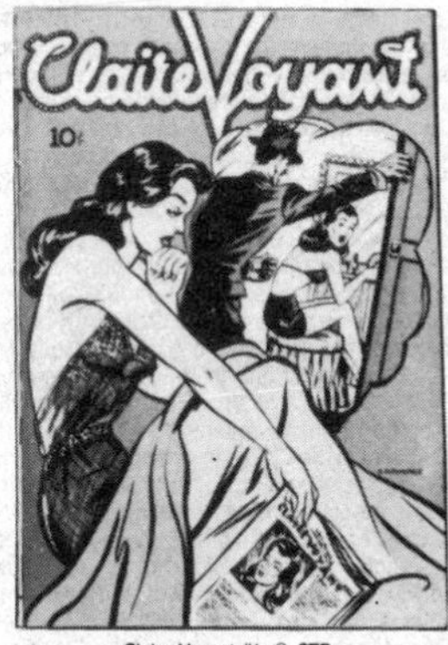

Claire Voyant #1, © STD

CINDERELLA (continued)
American Dairy Association (Premium)

	Good	Fine	Mint
nn	5.00	15.00	30.00

CINDERELLA LOVE
No. 10, 1950; No. 11, 4/51 - No. 12, 9/51; No. 4, 10-11/51 - No. 11, Fall, 1952; No. 12, 10/53 - No. 15, 8/54; No.25, 12/54 -No.29, 10/55 (no No.16-24)
Ziff-Davis/St. John Publ. Co. No. 12 on

	Good	Fine	Mint
10 (1st Series, 1950)	3.70	11.00	26.00
11(4/51), 12(9/51)	1.70	5.00	12.00
4-8: 7-Photo-c	1.50	4.50	10.00
9-Kinstler-a	2.35	7.00	16.00
10-Whitney painted-c	2.00	6.00	14.00
11(Fall/'52)-Crandall-a; Saunders painted-c	3.00	9.00	21.00
12(St. John-10/53)-No.14	1.35	4.00	9.00
15 (8/54)-Matt Baker-c	2.65	8.00	18.00
25(2nd Series)(Formerly Romantic Marriage)	1.35	4.00	9.00
26-Baker-c; last precode (2/55)	3.00	9.00	21.00
27,28	1.00	3.00	7.00
29-Matt Baker-c	2.65	8.00	18.00

CINDY COMICS (. . .Smith No. 39,40; Crime Can't Win No. 41 on)(Formerly Krazy Komics)
No. 27, Fall, 1947 - No. 40, July, 1950
Timely Comics

	Good	Fine	Mint
27-Kurtzman-a, 3 pgs: Margie, Oscar begin	5.50	16.50	38.00
28-31-Kurtzman-a	3.00	9.00	21.00
32-40	2.00	6.00	14.00

NOTE: ***Kurtzman's*** *"Hey Look"-#27(3), 29(2), 30(2), 31; "Giggles 'N' Grins"- #28.*

CINEMA COMICS HERALD
1941 - 1943 (4-pg. movie "trailers," paper-c, 7½x10½")
Paramount Pictures/Universal/RKO/20th Century Fox/Republic (Giveaway)

	Good	Fine	Mint
"Mr. Bug Goes to Town"-(1941)	3.35	10.00	20.00
"Bedtime Story"	3.35	10.00	20.00
"Lady For A Night," John Wayne, Joan Blondell (1942)	3.35	10.00	20.00
"Reap The Wild Wind"-(1942)	3.35	10.00	20.00
"Thunder Birds"-(1942)	3.35	10.00	20.00
"They All Kissed the Bride"	3.35	10.00	20.00
"Arabian Nights," nd	3.35	10.00	20.00
"Bombardier"-(1943)	3.35	10.00	20.00
"Crash Dive"-(1943)-Tyrone Power	3.35	10.00	20.00

NOTE: *The 1941-42 issues contain line art with color photos. The 1943 issues are line art.*

CIRCUS (. . .the Comic Riot)
June, 1938 - No. 3, Aug, 1938
Globe Syndicate

	Good	Fine	Mint
1-(Scarce)-Spacehawks (2 pgs.), & Disk Eyes by Wolverton (2 pgs.), Pewee Throttle by Cole (2nd comic book work; see Star Comics V1/11), Beau Gus, Ken Craig & The Lords of Crillon, Jack Hinton by Eisner, Van Bragger by Kane	150.00	450.00	1050.00
2,3-(Scarce)-Eisner, Cole, Wolverton, Bob Kane-a in each	75.00	225.00	525.00

CIRCUS BOY (See 4-Color No. 759,785,813)

CIRCUS COMICS
1945 - No. 2, June, 1945; Winter, 1948-49
Farm Women's Publishing Co./D. S. Publ.

	Good	Fine	Mint
1	3.50	10.50	24.00
2	2.00	6.00	14.00
1(1948)-D.S. Publ.; 2 pgs. Frazetta	13.00	40.00	90.00

CIRCUS OF FUN COMICS
1945 - 1947 (a book of games & puzzles)
A. W. Nugent Publishing Co.

	Good	Fine	Mint
1	3.50	10.50	24.00
2,3	2.00	6.00	14.00

CIRCUS WORLD (See Movie Classics)

CISCO KID, THE (TV)
July, 1950 - No. 41, Oct-Dec, 1958
Dell Publishing Co.

	Good	Fine	Mint
4-Color 292(No.1)-Cisco Kid, his horse Diablo, & sidekick Pancho & his horse Loco begin; painted-c begin	7.00	21.00	50.00
2(1/51)-5	3.75	11.25	26.00
6-10	3.35	10.00	23.00
11-20	2.65	8.00	18.00
21-36-Last painted-c	2.35	7.00	16.00
37-41: All photo-c	3.50	10.50	24.00

NOTE: ***Buscema*** *a-40.* ***Ernest Nordli*** *painted-c-5-16,20,35.*

CISCO KID COMICS
Winter, 1944 - No. 3, 1945
Bernard Bailey/Swappers Quarterly

	Good	Fine	Mint
1-Illustrated Stories of the Operas: Faust; Funnyman by Giunta; Cisco Kid begins	20.00	60.00	140.00
2,3	14.00	42.00	100.00

CITIZEN SMITH (See Holyoke One-Shot No. 9)

CITY OF THE LIVING DEAD (See Fantastic Tales No. 1)
1952
Avon Periodicals

	Good	Fine	Mint
nn-Hollingsworth c/a	17.00	51.00	120.00

CITY SURGEON (Blake Harper. . .)
August, 1963
Gold Key

	Good	Fine	Mint
1(10075-308)	1.15	3.50	8.00

CIVIL WAR MUSKET, THE (Kadets of America Handbook)
1960 (36 pages) (Half-size; 25 cents)
Custom Comics, Inc.

	Good	Fine	Mint
nn	1.50	4.50	10.00

CLAIRE VOYANT (Also see Keen Teens)
1946 - 1947 (Sparling strip reprints)
Leader Publ./Standard/Pentagon Publ.

	Good	Fine	Mint
nn	26.00	78.00	180.00
2-Kamen-c	20.00	60.00	140.00
3-Kamen bridal-c; contents mentioned in **Love and Death**, a book by Gershom Legman('49) referenced by Dr. Wertham	32.00	95.00	225.00
4-Kamen bondage-c	20.00	60.00	140.00

CLANCY THE COP
1930 - 1931 (52 pages; B&W) (not reprints) (10"x10")
Dell Publishing Co. (Soft cover)

	Good	Fine	Mint
1,2-Vep-a	5.00	15.00	35.00

UNDERSTANDING CLASSICS ILLUSTRATED

by Dan Malan

Since 1982, this book has been listing every **Classics** edition. That became possible because of Charles Heffelfinger's 1978 book, **The Classics Handbook**, detailing and illustrating every **Classics** edition. But there are still some areas of confusion, and this revised and expanded introduction will attempt to alleviate those problem areas.

THE HISTORY OF CLASSICS

The **Classics** series was the brainchild of Al Kanter, who sought for a way to introduce children to quality literature. In October 1941 his Gilberton Co. began the series **Classic Comics** with **The Three Musketeers**, with 64 pages of storyline. The early years saw irregular schedules and numerous printers, not to mention some second-class artwork and liberal story adaptations. With No. 13 the page total was dropped to 56 (except for No. 33, originally scheduled to be No. 9), and with No. 15 the next-issue ad on the outside back cover moved indoors. In 1945 the Iger shop began producing Classics, beginning with No. 23. In 1947 the search for a "classier" logo title produced **Classics Illustrated**, beginning with No. 35, **The Last Days Of Pompeii**. With No. 45 the story length dropped again to 48 pages, which was to become the standard.

What was probably the most important development for the success of the **Classics** series began in 1951 with the introduction of painted covers, instead of the old line drawn covers, beginning with No. 81, **The Odyssey**. That served as a good excuse to raise the cover price from 10 to 15 cents and did not hinder the growth of the series. From 1947 to 1953 **Classics** artwork was dominated by H.C. Kiefer and Alex Blum, together accounting for nearly 50 titles. Their distinctive styles gave real personality to the **Classics** series. **Classics** flourished during the fifties, and they diversified with **Juniors**, **Specials**, and **World Around Us** series.

But in the early sixties financial troubles set in. In 1962 the issuing of new titles ended with No. 167, **Faust**. In 1967 the company was sold to the Catholic publisher, Twin Circle. They issued two new titles in 1969 as part of an attempted revival, but succumbed to major distribution problems.

One of the major trademarks of the **Classics** series was the proliferation of reprint variations. Some titles had as many as 25 reprint editions. Reprinting began in 1943. Some of the **Classic Comic** (CC) reprints (r) had the logo format revised to the banner logo, and had the motto added under the banner. Then, reprints of all the CC titles were changed over to the new logo title, **Classics Illustrated** (CI), but still had line drawn covers (LDC). Nos. 13, 18, 29 and 41 received second covers (LDC2), replacing covers considered too violent. During 1948 and 1949, reprints of title Nos. 13 to 44 had pages reduced to 48 (except for No. 26, which had 48 pages to begin with).

Starting in the mid-fifties, 70 of the 80 LDC titles were reissued with new painted covers (PC). Thirty of them also received new interior artwork (A2). The new artwork was generally higher quality with larger art panels and more faithful but abbreviated storylines. There were also 29 second painted covers (PC2) issued, mostly by Twin Circle. The last reprints were issued in 1971. Altogether there were 199 interior artwork variations (169 (0)s plus 30 A2 editions) and 272 different covers (169 (0)s, four LDC2s, 70 new PCs of LDC (0) titles, and 29 PC2s). It is mildly astounding to realize that there were over 1,350 editions in the U.S. **Classics** series.

FOREIGN CLASSICS ILLUSTRATED

If U.S. **Classics** variations are mildly astounding, the veritable plethora of foreign **Classics** variations will boggle your imagination. While research on some countries is ongoing, we have definite information about series in 15 languages, 20 countries of origin (some with two or three series), and 30 distribution countries. There were nearly 200 new **Classics** titles in foreign series and over 300 new foreign covers of U.S. **Classics** titles. Altogether, there were over 4,000 foreign **Classics** editions.

Except for four **Classic Comic** reprints in Canada in 1946, foreign **Classics** began in 1948. But the early series were scattered/isolated and often brief. In the mid-fifties, when the U.S. began developing its PC/A2 editions, that U.S. development was coordinated with multi-European country series utilizing the same editions in nine languages at once. This was the main thrust of foreign **Classics**. And when the U.S. stopped issuing new titles in the early sixties, the European series continued with 80 new European titles, which continued until 1976. There were also 84 new Greek History & Mythology titles. Countries with large numbers of new covers of U.S. titles were Brazil, Mexico, Greece, and the early Australian series.

Here is a chronological list of countries with **Classics** series:

Canada	Japan	Sweden
Australia	Germany	New Zealand
Brazil	Mexico	Finland
Netherlands	Italy	France
Greece	Norway	Singapore
Great Britain	Iceland	Belgium
Argentina	Denmark	

Other listed distribution countries included Austria, Switzerland, Luxemburg, Spain, Morocco, and South Africa.

REFERENCE WORKS ON CLASSICS

The Classics Handbook (3rd edition - 1986) by Charles Heffelfinger. This work identifies and illustrates all U.S. **Classics** editions. It also has illustrations of all **Juniors**, **Specials** & **World Around Us**, plus information on giveaways, artists, etc.

The Classics Index (1986) by Tom Fisher. This comprehensive subject index covers all **Classics** title stories and filler articles, plus all **Juniors**, **Specials** & **World Around Us**.

The Foreign Classics Handbook (preliminary draft - 1986) by Dan Malan. This draft details over 30 series in 20 countries. It also includes a cross-reference index for all U.S. titles/artwork/covers, and a cross-reference comparison chart for all European country series.

All of these works are available through Bob Levy, 2456 East 18 Street, Brooklyn, NY 11235. Write to him for further details.

IDENTIFYING CLASSICS EDITIONS

HRN: This is the highest number on the reorder list. It is crucial to understanding the various **Classics** editions. It is shown in parentheses.

ORIGINALS (0): This is the all-important First Edition. There is one basic rule and two secondary rules (with exceptions) that apply here.

Rule No. 1: All (0)s and only (0)s have an ad for the next title (issue). **Exceptions:** No. 14(15) (reprint) has an ad on the last inside page of the text. No. 14(O) has an ad on the outside back cover and also says 10 cents on the front cover. Nos. 55(75) and 57(75) (reprints) have ads for the next issue. (Rules 2 and 3 apply here.) Nos. 168(O) and 169(O) do not have ads for the next issue. (No. 168 was never reprinted; No. 169(O) has HRN (166), No. 169(169) is the only reprint.)

Rule No. 2: All (0)s and only (0)s (Nos. 1-80) list 10 cents on the front cover. **Exceptions:** Nos. 39(71) and 46(62) (reprints) say 10 cents on the front cover. (Rules 1 and 3 apply here.)

Rule No. 3: All (0)s have HRN very close to the issue No. of that title. **Exceptions:** Many reprints also have HRN very close to the title number. Some CC(r)s, 58(62), 60(62), 149(149), 152(149), 153(149), (r)s of titles in 160's. (Rules 1 and 2 apply here.)

For information on variations of (O)s, see the next section (**TIPS. .**).

DATES: Many **Classics** editions do not list a date, and others actually list an incorrect date. The dates listed in the price guide are calculated by the HRN. It is safer to go by the HRN to identify an edition. Dates listed in **Classics** are important on editions with HRNs of (167), (166), and (169). By then new titles were no longer being issued, and the date listed in the **Classic** itself does identify the edition (except for '62/63 which were issued in late 1962 to early 1963, but still listed original date).

COVERS: A change from CC to LDC does not indicate a new cover, only a new logo title, while a change from LDC to PC does indicate a new cover. Keep in mind that there are only four new LDC covers—13, 18, 29 and 41. New PCs can be identified by the HRN, and PC2s should be identified by the HRN and the listed date. Remember that many little details can change on a cover and it will still be listed as the same cover.

NOTES: If a front cover states "15 cents in Canada," that does not necessarily mean that it is a Canadian edition. Check the return address to be certain. An HRN listed in the price guide with a "/" in it means that there are two different reorder lists in the front and back covers. Twin Circle editions have a back cover different from regular **Classics**.

TIPS ON LISTING CLASSICS FOR SALE

It may be easy to just list "Edition 17," but **Classics** collectors think of issues in terms of what the HRN is, and whether it is an (0) or an (r), and whether it is a CC, LDC, PC, A2, PC2, stiff cover, etc.

ORIGINALS: The best way to list Originals is to just say (0), unless there are variations of Originals, such as HRN (Nos. 95, 108, 160), printer (Nos. 18-22), color (Nos. 51, 61), etc.

REPRINTS: Just list HRN if it is 165 or below; above that, HRN and date. Also, please list type of logo/cover/art for the convenience of buyers. They will appreciate it.

CLASSIC COMICS (See America in Action, Stories by Famous Authors, Story of the Commandos, & The World Around Us)

CLASSIC COMICS (. . .'s Illustrated No. 35 on)
10/41 - No. 34, 2/47; No. 35, 3/47 - No. 169, Winter/71
(Painted Covers No. 81 on)
Gilberton Publications

Abbreviations:
A-Art; C or c—Cover; CC—Classic Comics; CI—Classics Ill.; Ed—Edition; LDC—Line Drawn Cover; PC—Painted Cover; r—Reprint

1. The Three Musketeers

Ed	HRN	Date	Details	A	C	**Good**	**Fine**	**Mint**
1	—	F/41	Original	1	1	150.00	450.00	1050.00
2	10	5/43	10 cents price removed; CC-r	1	1	12.00	36.00	84.00
3	15	11/43	Long Isl. Ind. Ed.; CC-r	1	1	8.50	25.50	60.00
4	18/20	6/44	Sunrise Times Ed.; CC-r	1	1	8.00	24.00	56.00
5	21	7/44	Richmond Courier Ed.; CC-r	1	1	6.50	19.50	45.00
6	28	6/46	CC-r	1	1	5.00	15.00	35.00
7	36	4/47	LDC-r	1	1	2.30	7.00	16.00
8	60	6/49	LDC-r	1	1	1.50	4.50	10.00
9	64	10/49	LDC-r	1	1	1.30	4.00	9.00
10	78	12/50	15 cents-c; LDC-r	1	1	1.30	4.00	9.00
11	93	3/52	LDC-r	1	1	1.00	3.00	7.00
12	114	11/53	Last LDC-r	1	1	1.00	3.00	7.00
13	134	9/56	New-c; old-a; 64 pg. PC-r	1	2	1.50	4.50	10.00
14	143	3/58	Old-a; PC-r; 64 pg.	1	2	1.15	3.50	8.00
15	150	5/59	New-a; PC-r; Evans/Crandall-a	2	2	1.15	3.50	8.00
16	149	3/61	PC-r	2	2	.70	2.00	4.00
17	167	'62/63	PC-r	2	2	.70	2.00	4.00

Classic Comics #3, © GIL

Classic Comics #4, © GIL

Classic Comics #5 (HRN 36), © GIL

CLASSIC COMICS (continued)

Ed	HRN	Date	Details	A	C	Good	Fine	Mint
18	167	4/64	PC-r	2	2	.70	2.00	4.00
19	167	1/65	PC-r	2	2	.70	2.00	4.00
20	167	3/66	PC-r	2	2	.70	2.00	4.00
21	166	11/67	PC-r	2	2	.70	2.00	4.00
22	166	Spr/69	New 25¢ price; stiff-c; PC-r	2	2	.70	2.00	4.00
23	169	Spr/71	PC-r; stiff-c	2	2	.70	2.00	4.00

2. Ivanhoe

Ed	HRN	Date	Details	A	C	Good	Fine	Mint
1	—	1941	Original	1	1	71.00	210.00	500.00
2	1	5/43	'Presents' removd. from cover; CC-r	1	1	10.00	30.00	70.00
3	15	11/43	Long Isl. Ind. ed.; CC-r	1	1	7.00	21.00	50.00
4	18/20	6/44	Sunrise Times ed.; CC-r	1	1	6.50	19.50	45.00
5	21	7/44	Richmond Courier ed.; CC-r	1	1	5.70	17.00	40.00
6	28	6/46	Last 'Comics'-r	1	1	5.00	15.00	35.00
7	36	4/47	1st LDC-r	1	1	2.30	7.00	16.00
8	60	6/49	LDC-r	1	1	1.50	4.50	10.00
9	64	10/49	LDC-r	1	1	1.15	3.50	8.00
10	78	12/50	C-price 15¢; LDC-r	1	1	1.15	3.50	8.00
11	89	11/51	LDC-r	1	1	.85	2.50	6.00
12	106	4/53	LDC-r	1	1	.85	2.50	6.00
13	121	7/54	Last LDC-r	1	1	.85	2.50	6.00
14	136	1/57	New-c&a; PC-r	2	2	1.70	5.00	12.00
15	142	1/58	PC-r	2	2	.70	2.00	4.00
16	153	11/59	PC-r	2	2	.70	2.00	4.00
17	149	3/61	PC-r	2	2	.70	2.00	4.00
18	167	'62/63	PC-r	2	2	.70	2.00	4.00
19	167	5/64	PC-r	2	2	.70	2.00	4.00
20	167	1/65	PC-r	2	2	.70	2.00	4.00
21	167	3/66	PC-r	2	2	.70	2.00	4.00
22	166	9/67	PC-r	2	2	.70	2.00	4.00
23	166	R/1968	PC-r	2	2	.70	2.00	4.00
24	169	Win/69	Stiff-c	2	2	.70	2.00	4.00
25	169	Win/71	PC-r; stiff-c	2	2	.70	2.00	4.00

3. The Count of Monte Cristo

Ed	HRN	Date	Details	A	C	Good	Fine	Mint
1	—	3/42	Original	1	1	60.00	180.00	420.00
2	10	5/43	CC-r	1	1	10.00	30.00	70.00
3	15	11/43	Long Isl. Ind. ed.; CC-r	1	1	7.00	21.00	50.00
4	18/20	6/44	Sunrise Times ed.; CC-r	1	1	6.50	19.50	45.00
5	20	6/44	Sunrise Times ed.; CC-r	1	1	6.00	18.00	42.00
6	21	7/44	Richmond Courier ed.; CC-r	1	1	5.50	16.50	38.00
7	28	6/46	CC-r	1	1	5.00	15.00	35.00
8	36	4/47	1st LDC-r	1	1	2.30	7.00	16.00
9	60	6/49	LDC-r	1	1	1.50	4.50	10.00
10	62	8/49	LDC-r	1	1	1.50	4.50	10.00
11	71	5/50	LDC-r	1	1	1.15	3.50	8.00
12	87	9/51	Price 15¢; LDC-r	1	1	.85	2.50	6.00
13	113	11/53	LDC-r	1	1	.85	2.50	6.00
14	135	11/56	New-c&a; PC-r	2	2	1.50	4.50	10.00
15	143	3/58	PC-r	2	2	.70	2.00	4.00
16	153	11/59	PC-r	2	2	.70	2.00	4.00
17	161	3/61	PC-r	2	2	.70	2.00	4.00
18	167	'62/63	PC-r	2	2	.70	2.00	4.00
19	167	7/64	PC-r	2	2	.70	2.00	4.00
20	167	7/65	PC-r	2	2	.70	2.00	4.00
21	167	7/66	PC-r	2	2	.70	2.00	4.00
22	166	R/1968	Price 25¢; PC-r	2	2	.70	2.00	4.00
23	169	Win/69	Stiff-c; PC-r	2	2	.70	2.00	4.00

4. The Last of the Mohicans

Ed	HRN	Date	Details	A	C	Good	Fine	Mint
1	—	8/42	Original	1	1	43.00	130.00	300.00
2	12	6/43	Price balloon deleted; CC-r	1	1	8.50	25.50	60.00
3	15	11/43	Long Isl. Ind. ed.; CC-r	1	1	8.00	24.00	56.00
4	20	6/44	Long Isl. Ind. ed.; CC-r	1	1	7.00	21.00	50.00
5	21	7/44	Queens Home News ed.; CC-r	1	1	5.50	16.50	38.00
6	28	6/46	Last CC-r	1	1	5.00	15.00	35.00
7	36	4/47	1st LDC-r	1	1	2.30	7.00	16.00
8	60	6/49	LDC-r	1	1	1.50	4.50	10.00
9	64	10/49	LDC-r	1	1	1.30	4.00	9.00
10	78	12/50	New price 15¢; LDC-r	1	1	.85	2.50	6.00
11	89	11/51	LDC-r	1	1	.85	2.50	6.00
12	117	3/54	Last LDC-r	1	1	.85	2.50	6.00
13	135	11/56	New-c; PC-r	1	2	1.50	4.50	10.00
14	141	11/57	PC-r	1	2	1.30	4.00	9.00
15	150	5/59	New-a; PC-r; Severin, L.B. Cole-a	2	2	1.50	4.50	10.00
16	161	3/61	PC-r	2	2	.85	2.50	5.00
17	167	'62/63	PC-r	2	2	.70	2.00	4.00
18	167	6/64	PC-r	2	2	.70	2.00	4.00
19	167	8/65	PC-r	2	2	.70	2.00	4.00
20	167	8/66	PC-r	2	2	.70	2.00	4.00
21	166	R/1967	New price 25¢; PC-r	2	2	.70	2.00	4.00
22	169	Spr/69	Stiff-c; PC-r	2	2	.70	2.00	4.00

5. Moby Dick

Ed	HRN	Date	Details	A	C	Good	Fine	Mint
1	—	9/42	Original	1	1	43.00	130.00	300.00
2	10	5/43	C-price removed; CC-r; Conray Products ed.	1	1	9.00	27.00	63.00
3	15	11/43	Long Isl. Ind. ed.; CC-r	1	1	8.00	24.00	56.00
4	18/20	6/44	Sunrise Times ed.; CC-r	1	1	6.00	18.00	42.00
5	20	7/44	Sunrise Times ed.; CC-r	1	1	5.50	16.50	38.00
6	21	7/44	Sunrise Times ed.; CC-r	1	1	5.50	16.50	38.00
7	28	6/46	CC-r	1	1	5.00	15.00	35.00
8	36	4/47	1st LDC-r	1	1	2.30	7.00	16.00
9	60	6/49	LDC-r	1	1	1.50	4.50	10.00
10	62	8/49	LDC-r	1	1	1.50	4.50	10.00
11	71	5/50	LDC-r	1	1	1.15	3.50	8.00
12	87	9/51	New price 15¢; LDC-r	1	1	.85	2.50	6.00
13	118	4/54	LDC-r	1	1	.85	2.50	6.00
14	131	3/56	New c&a; PC-r	2	2	1.50	4.50	10.00
15	138	5/57	PC-r	2	2	.70	2.00	4.00
16	148	1/59	PC-r	2	2	.70	2.00	4.00
17	158	9/60	PC-r	2	2	.70	2.00	4.00
18	167	'62/63	PC-r	2	2	.70	2.00	4.00
19	167	6/64	PC-r	2	2	.70	2.00	4.00
20	167	7/65	PC-r	2	2	.70	2.00	4.00
21	167	3/66	PC-r	2	2	.70	2.00	4.00

CLASSIC COMICS (continued)

Ed	HRN	Date	Details	A	C	Good	Fine	Mint
22	166	9/67	PC-r	2	2	.70	2.00	4.00
23	166	Win/69	New-c&price 25¢; Stiff-c; PC-r	2	3	1.50	4.50	10.00
24	169	Win/71	PC-r	2	3	1.50	4.50	10.00

6. A Tale of Two Cities

Ed	HRN	Date	Details	A	C	Good	Fine	Mint
1	—	11/42	Original-Zeckerberg-c/a	1	1	43.00	130.00	300.00
2	14	9/43	C-price deleted; CC-r	1	1	9.00	27.00	63.00
3	18	3/44	Long Isl. Ind. ed.; CC-r	1	1	8.00	24.00	56.00
4	20	6/44	Sunrise Times ed.; CC-r	1	1	7.00	21.00	50.00
5	28	6/46	Last CC-r	1	1	5.00	15.00	35.00
6	51	9/48	1st LDC-r	1	1	2.00	6.00	14.00
7	64	10/49	LDC-r	1	1	1.50	4.50	10.00
8	78	12/50	C-price now 15¢; LDC-r	1	1	.85	2.50	6.00
9	89	11/51	LDC-r	1	1	.85	2.50	6.00
10	117	3/54	LDC-r	1	1	.85	2.50	6.00
11	132	5/56	New-c&a; PC-r; Joe Orlando-a	2	2	1.70	5.00	12.00
12	140	9/57	PC-r	2	2	.60	1.80	3.60
13	147	11/57	PC-r	2	2	.60	1.80	3.60
14	152	9/59	PC-r	2	2	.60	1.80	3.60
15	153	11/59	PC-r	2	2	.60	1.80	3.60
16	149	3/61	PC-r	2	2	.60	1.80	3.60
17	167	'62/63	PC-r	2	2	.60	1.80	3.60
18	167	6/64	PC-r	2	2	.60	1.80	3.60
19	167	8/65	PC-r	2	2	.60	1.80	3.60
20	166	5/67	PC-r	2	2	.60	1.80	3.60
21	166	Fall/68	PC-r(Exist?)	2	2	.60	1.80	3.60
22	166	Fall/68	New-c&price 25¢; PC-r	2	3	1.50	4.50	10.00
23	169	Sum-70	Stiff-c; PC-r	2	3	1.50	4.50	10.00

7. Robin Hood

Ed	HRN	Date	Details	A	C	Good	Fine	Mint
1	—	12/42	Original	1	1	38.00	115.00	265.00
2	12	6/43	P.D.C. on cvr. deleted; CC-r	1	1	9.00	27.00	63.00
3	18	3/44	Long Isl. Ind. ed.; CC-r	1	1	7.00	21.00	50.00
4	20	6/44	Nassau Bulletin ed.; CC-r	1	1	6.50	19.50	45.00
5	22	10/44	Queens Cty. Times ed.; CC-r	1	1	5.70	17.00	40.00
6	28	6/46	CC-r	1		5.00	15.00	35.00
7	51	9/48	LDC-r	1	1	2.00	6.00	14.00
8	60	6/49	LDC-r (exist?)	1	1	3.00	9.00	21.00
9	64	10/49	LDC-r	1	1	1.50	4.50	10.00
10	78	12/50	LDC-r	1	1	1.00	3.00	7.00
11	97	7/52	LDC-r	1	1	.85	2.60	6.00
12	106	3/53	LDC-r	1	1	.85	2.60	6.00
13	121	7/54	LDC-r	1	1	.85	2.60	6.00
14	129	11/55	New-c; PC-r	1	2	1.50	4.50	10.00
15	136	1/57	New-a; PC-r	2	2	1.50	4.50	10.00
16	143	3/58	PC-r	2	2	.70	2.00	4.00
17	153	11/59	PC-r	2	2	.70	2.00	4.00
18	164	10/61	PC-r	2	2	.70	2.00	4.00
19	167	'62/63	PC-r	2	2	.70	2.00	4.00
20	167	6/64	PC-r	2	2	.70	2.00	4.00
21	167	5/65	PC-r	2	2	.70	2.00	4.00
22	167	7/66	PC-r	2	2	.70	2.00	4.00
23	166	12/67	PC-r	2	2	.70	2.00	4.00
24	169	Sum-69	Stiff-c; PC-r	2	2	.70	2.00	4.00

8. Arabian Nights

Ed	HRN	Date	Details	A	C	Good	Fine	Mint
1	—	2/43	Original-Lilian Chestney c/a	1	1	80.00	240.00	560.00
2	14	9/43	CC-r (exist?)	1	1	50.00	150.00	350.00
3	17	1/44	Long Isl. ed.; CC-r	1	1	30.00	90.00	210.00
4	20	6/44	Nassau Bulletin ed.; 'Three Men Named Smith;' 64 pgs.; CC-r	1	1	25.00	75.00	175.00
5	28	6/46	CC-r	1	1	15.00	45.00	105.00
6	51	9/48	LDC-r	1	1	10.00	30.00	70.00
7	64	10/49	LDC-r	1	1	8.50	25.50	60.00
8	78	12/50	LDC-r	1	1	8.00	24.00	56.00
9	164	10/61	New-c&a; PC-r	2	2	6.50	17.50	45.00

9. Les Miserables

Ed	HRN	Date	Details	A	C	Good	Fine	Mint
1	—	3/43	Original	1	1	30.00	90.00	210.00
2	14	9/43	CC-r	1	1	10.00	30.00	70.00
3	18	3/44	Nassau Bulletin ed.; CC-r	1	1	8.00	24.00	56.00
4	20	6/44	Richmond Courier ed.; CC-r	1	1	7.00	21.00	50.00
5	28	6/46	CC-r	1	1	5.00	15.00	35.00
6	51	9/48	LDC-r	1	1	2.30	7.00	16.00
7	71	5/50	LDC-r	1	1	2.00	6.00	14.00
8	87	9/51	New price 15 cents; LDC-r	1	1	1.70	5.00	12.00
9	161	3/61	New-c&a; PC-r	2	2	1.50	4.50	10.00
10	167	9/63	PC-r	2	2	1.15	3.50	8.00
11	167	12/65	PC-r	2	2	1.15	3.50	8.00
12	166	R/1968	New-c & price 25 cents; PC-r	2	3	1.70	5.00	12.00

10. Robinson Crusoe (Used in **SOTI**, pg. 142)

Ed	HRN	Date	Details	A	C	Good	Fine	Mint
1	—	4/43	Original-Stanley Zeckerberg c/a	1	1	35.00	105.00	245.00
2	14	9/43	CC-r	1	1	9.00	27.00	63.00
3	18	3/44	Nassau Bulletin ed.; pg.64 has Bill of Rights; CC-r	1	1	7.00	21.00	50.00
4	20	6/44	Queens Home News ed.; CC-r	1	1	6.00	18.00	42.00
5	23	?/45	CC-r	1	1	5.00	15.00	35.00
6	28	6/46	CC-r	1	1	5.00	15.00	35.00
7	51	9/48	LDC-r	1	1	2.00	6.00	14.00
8	64	10/49	LDC-r	1	1	1.50	4.50	10.00
9	78	12/50	New price 15 cents; LDC-r	1	1	1.15	3.50	8.00
10	97	7/52	LDC-r	1	1	1.00	3.00	7.00
11	114	12/53	LDC-r	1	1	1.00	3.00	7.00
12	130	1/56	New-c; PC-r	1	2	1.50	4.50	10.00
13	140	9/57	New-a; PC-r	2	2	1.50	4.50	10.00
14	153	11/59	PC-r	2	2	.55	1.70	3.40
15	164	10/61	PC-r	2	2	.55	1.70	3.40
16	167	'62/63	PC-r	2	2	.55	1.70	3.40
17	167	7/64	PC-r	2	2	.55	1.70	3.40
18	167	5/65	PC-r	2	2	.55	1.70	3.40
19	167	6/66	PC-r	2	2	.55	1.70	3.40
20	166	Fall/68	New price 25 cents; PC-r	2	2	.55	1.70	3.40
21	166	R/68	(No Twin Circle ad)	2	2	.55	1.70	3.40

Classic Comics #6 (HRN 20), © GIL

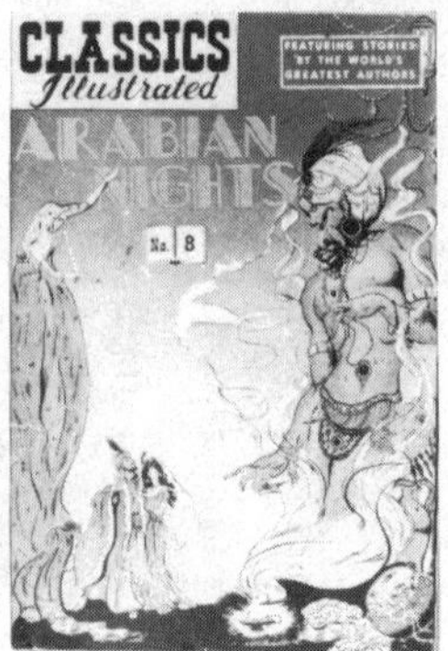

Classics Illustrated #8 (HRN 51), © GIL

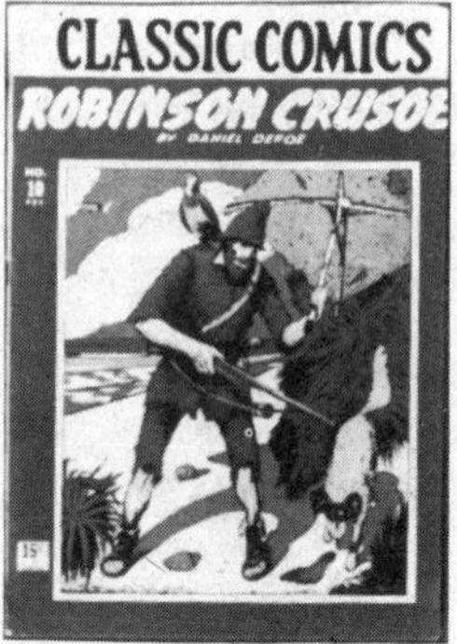

Classic Comics #10 (HRN 14), © GIL

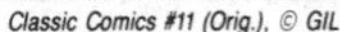
Classic Comics #11 (Orig.), © GIL

Classic Comics #13, © GIL

Classic Comics #14 (HRN 21), © GIL

CLASSIC COMICS (continued)

Ed	HRN	Date	Details	A	C	Good	Fine	Mint
22	169	Sm/70	Stiff-c; PC-r	2	2	.85	2.50	5.00

11. Don Quixote

Ed	HRN	Date	Details	A	C	Good	Fine	Mint
1	—	5/43	Original	1	1	35.00	105.00	245.00
2	18	3/44	Nassau Bulletin ed.; CC-r	1	1	8.00	24.00	56.00
3	21	7/44	Queens Home News ed.; CC-r	1	1	7.00	21.00	50.00
4	28	6/46	CC-r	1	1	5.00	15.00	35.00
5	110	8/53	New-PC; PC-r	1	2	2.35	7.50	16.00
6	156	5/60	Pgs. reduced 64 to 48; PC-r	1	2	1.15	3.50	8.00
7	165	1962	PC-r	1	2	.70	2.00	4.00
8	167	1/64	PC-r	1	2	.70	2.00	4.00
9	167	11/65	PC-r	1	2	.70	2.00	4.00
10	166	R/1968	New-c&price 25 cents; PC-r	1	3	1.70	5.00	12.00

12. Rip Van Winkle and the Headless Horseman

Ed	HRN	Date	Details	A	C	Good	Fine	Mint
1	—	6/43	Original	1	1	40.00	120.00	280.00
2	15	11/43	Long Isl. Ind. ed.; CC-r	1	1	10.00	30.00	70.00
3	20	6/44	Long Isl. Ind. ed.;	1	1	8.00	24.00	56.00
4	22	10/44	Queens Cty. Times ed.; CC-r	1	1	7.00	21.00	50.00
5	28	6/46	CC-r	1	1	5.00	15.00	35.00
6	60	6/49	1st LDC-r	1	1	1.70	5.00	12.00
7	62	8/49	LDC-r	1	1	1.50	4.50	10.00
8	71	5/50	LDC-r	1	1	1.00	3.00	7.00
9	89	11/51	New price 15 cents; LDC-r	1	1	.85	2.50	6.00
10	118	4/54	LDC-r	1	1	.85	2.50	6.00
11	132	5/56	New-c; PC-r	1	2	1.50	4.50	10.00
12	150	5/59	New-a; PC-r	2	2	1.50	4.50	10.00
13	158	9/60	PC-r	2	2	.70	2.00	4.00
14	167	'62/63	PC-r	2	2	.70	2.00	4.00
15	167	12/63	PC-r	2	2	.70	2.00	4.00
16	167	4/65	PC-r	2	2	.70	2.00	4.00
17	167	4/66	PC-r	2	2	.70	2.00	4.00
18	166	R/1968	New-c&price 25 cents; PC-r; stiff-c	2	3	1.50	4.50	10.00
19	169	Sm/70	PC-r; stiff-c	2	3	1.50	4.50	10.00

13. Dr. Jekyll and Mr. Hyde (Used in **SOTI**, pg. 143)

Ed	HRN	Date	Details	A	C	Good	Fine	Mint
1	—	8/43	Original	1	1	40.00	120.00	280.00
2	15	11/43	Long Isl. Ind. ed.; CC-r	1	1	10.00	30.00	70.00
3	20	6/44	Long Isl. Ind. ed.; CC-r	1	1	8.00	24.00	56.00
4	28	6/46	No c-price; CC-r	1	1	6.00	18.00	42.00
5	60	6/49	New-c; Pgs. reduced from 56 to 48; H.C. Kiefer-c; LDC-r	1	2	1.70	5.00	12.00
6	62	8/49	LDC-r	1	2	1.00	3.00	7.00
7	71	5/50	LDC-r	1	2	1.00	3.00	7.00
8	87	9/51	Date returns (erroneous); LDC-r	1	2	1.00	3.00	7.00
9	112	10/53	New-c&a; PC-r	2	3	1.70	5.00	12.00
10	153	11/59	PC-r	2	3	.70	2.00	4.00
11	161	3/61	PC-r	2	3	.70	2.00	4.00
12	167	'62/63	PC-r	2	3	.70	2.00	4.00
13	167	8/64	PC-r	2	3	.70	2.00	4.00
14	167	11/65	PC-r	2	3	.70	2.00	4.00
15	166	R/1968	New price 25 cents; PC-r	2	3	.70	2.00	4.00
16	169	Wn/69	PC-r; stiff-c	2	3	.70	2.00	4.00

14. Westward Ho!

Ed	HRN	Date	Details	A	C	Good	Fine	Mint
1	—	9/43	Original	1	1	80.00	240.00	560.00
2	15	11/43	Long Isl. Ind. ed.; CC-r	1	1	40.00	120.00	280.00
3	21	7/44	Pg.56 new; CC-r	1	1	27.00	81.00	190.00
4	28	6/46	No c-price; Pg.56 new; CC-r	1	1	23.00	70.00	160.00
5	53	11/48	Pgs. reduced from 56 to 48; LDC-r	1	1	16.00	48.00	110.00

15. Uncle Tom's Cabin (Used in **SOTI**, pgs. 102, 103)

Ed	HRN	Date	Details	A	C	Good	Fine	Mint
1	—	11/43	Original	1	1	30.00	90.00	210.00
2	15	11/43	Price circle blank; Long Isl. Ind. ed; CC-r	1	1	11.50	34.50	80.00
3	21	7/44	Nassau Bulletin ed.; CC-r	1	1	10.00	30.00	70.00
4	28	6/46	No c-price; CC-r	1	1	5.70	17.00	40.00
5	53	11/48	1st pgs. reduced 56 to 48; LDC-r	1	1	3.50	10.50	24.00
6	71	5/50	LDC-r	1	1	2.00	6.00	14.00
7	89	11/51	New price 15¢; LDC-r	1	1	1.75	5.25	12.00
8	117	3/54	New-c/lettering changes; PC-r	1	2	1.50	4.50	10.00
9	128	9/55	'Picture Progress' promo; PC-r	1	2	1.20	3.50	8.00
10	137	3/57	PC-r	1	2	.70	2.00	4.00
11	146	9/58	PC-r	1	2	.70	2.00	4.00
12	154	1/60	PC-r	1	2	.70	2.00	4.00
13	161	3/61	PC-r	1	2	.70	2.00	4.00
14	167	'62/63	PC-r	1	2	.70	2.00	4.00
15	167	6/64	PC-r	1	2	.70	2.00	4.00
16	167	5/65	PC-r	1	2	.70	2.00	4.00
17	166	5/67	PC-r	1	2	.70	2.00	4.00
18	166	Wn/69	New-stiff-c; PC-r	1	3	1.50	4.50	10.00
19	169	Sm/70	PC-r; stiff-c	1	3	1.50	4.50	10.00

16. Gullivers Travels

Ed	HRN	Date	Details	A	C	Good	Fine	Mint
1	—	12/43	Original-Lilian Chestney c/a	1	1	25.00	75.00	175.00
2	18/20	6/44	Price deleted; Queens Home News ed; CC-r	1	1	8.00	24.00	56.00
3	22	10/44	Queens Cty. Times ed.; CC-r	1	1	7.00	21.00	50.00
4	28	6/46	CC-r	1	1	5.00	15.00	35.00
5	60	6/49	Pgs. reduced to 48; LDC-r	1	1	1.50	4.50	10.00
6	62	8/49	LDC-r	1	1	1.50	4.50	10.00
7	64	10/49	LDC-r (exist?)	1	1	1.00	3.00	7.00
8	78	12/50	New c-price 15 cents; LDC-r	1	1	1.00	3.00	7.00
9	89	11/51	LDC-r	1	1	1.00	3.00	7.00
10	155	3/60	New-c; PC-r	1	2	1.50	4.50	10.00
11	165	1962	PC-r	1	2	.70	2.00	4.00
12	167	5/64	PC-r	1	2	.70	2.00	4.00
13	167	11/65	PC-r	1	2	.70	2.00	4.00
14	166	R/1968	New price 25 cents; PC-r	1	2	.70	2.00	4.00

CLASSIC COMICS (continued)

Ed	HRN	Date	Details	A	C	Good	Fine	Mint
15	169	Wn/69	PC-r; stiff-c	1	2	.70	2.00	4.00

17. The Deerslayer

Ed	HRN	Date	Details	A	C	Good	Fine	Mint
1	—	1/44	Original	1	1	25.00	75.00	175.00
2	18	3/44	Price removd; CC-r	1	1	7.00	21.00	50.00
3	22	10/44	Queens Cty. Times ed.; CC-r	1	1	6.00	18.00	42.00
4	28	6/46	CC-r	1	1	5.00	15.00	35.00
5	60	6/49	Pgs.reduced to 48; LDC-r	1	1	1.50	4.50	10.00
6	64	10/49	LDC-r	1	1	1.00	3.00	7.00
7	85	7/51	C-price 15¢; LDC-r	1	1	.85	2.50	6.00
8	118	4/54	LDC-r	1	1	.85	2.50	6.00
9	132	5/56	LDC-r	1	1	.70	2.00	4.00
10	167	11/66	Last LDC-r	1	1	.70	2.00	4.00
11	166	R/1968	New-c & price 25 cents; PC-r	1	2	1.50	4.50	10.00
12	169	Spr/71	Stiff-c; letters from parents & educators; PC-r	1	2	1.50	4.50	10.00

18. The Hunchback of Notre Dame

Ed	HRN	Date	Details	A	C	Good	Fine	Mint
1	—	3/44	Orig.; Gilberton ed.	1	1	32.00	95.00	225.00
2	—	3/44	Orig.; Island Pub. Co. ed.	1	1	28.00	84.00	195.00
3	18/20	6/44	Queens Home News ed.; CC-r	1	1	7.00	21.00	50.00
4	22	10/44	Queens Cty. Times ed.; CC-r	1	1	5.50	16.50	38.00
5	28	6/46	CC-r	1	1	4.60	14.00	32.00
6	60	6/49	New-c; 8pgs. deleted; Kiefer-c; LDC-r	1	2	1.30	4.00	9.00
7	62	8/49	LDC-r	1	2	1.00	3.00	7.00
8	78	12/50	C-price 15 cents; LDC-r	1	2	.85	2.50	6.00
9	89	11/51	LDC-r	1	2	.85	2.50	6.00
10	118	4/54	LDC-r	1	2	.85	2.50	6.00
11	140	9/57	New-c; PC-r	1	3	2.30	7.00	16.00
12	146	9/58	PC-r	1	3	1.70	5.00	12.00
13	158	9/60	New-c&a; PC-r; Evans/Crandall-a	2	4	2.00	6.00	14.00
14	165	1962	PC-r	2	4	.50	1.50	3.00
15	167	9/63	PC-r	2	4	.50	1.50	3.00
16	167	10/64	PC-r	2	4	.50	1.50	3.00
17	167	4/66	PC-r	2	4	.50	1.50	3.00
18	166	R/1968	New price 25¢; PC-r	2	4	.50	1.50	3.00
19	169	Sm/70	Stiff-c; PC-r	2	4	.50	1.50	3.00

19. Huckleberry Finn

Ed	HRN	Date	Details	A	C	Good	Fine	Mint
1	—	4/44	Orig.; Gilberton ed.	1	1	20.00	60.00	140.00
2	—	4/44	Orig.; Island Pub. Co. ed.	1	1	18.00	54.00	125.00
3	18	3/44	Nassau Bulletin ed.; CC-r	1	1	7.00	21.00	50.00
4	22	10/44	Queens Cty. Times ed.; CC-r	1	1	5.00	15.00	35.00
5	28	6/46	CC-r	1	1	4.60	14.00	32.00
6	60	6/49	Pgs. reduced to 48; LDC-r	1	1	1.50	4.50	10.00
7	62	8/49	LDC-r	1	1	1.00	3.00	7.00
8	78	12/50	LDC-r	1	1	.85	2.50	6.00
9	89	11/51	LDC-r	1	1	.85	2.50	6.00
10	117	3/54	LDC-r	1	1	.85	2.50	6.00
11	131	3/56	New-c&a; PC-r	2	2	1.50	4.50	10.00
12	140	9/57	PC-r	2	2	.70	2.00	4.00
13	150	5/59	PC-r	2	2	.70	2.00	4.00
14	158	9/60	PC-r	2	2	.70	2.00	4.00
15	165	1962	PC-r	2	2	.70	2.00	4.00
16	167	'62/63	PC-r	2	2	.70	2.00	4.00
17	167	6/64	PC-r	2	2	.70	2.00	4.00
18	167	6/65	PC-r	2	2	.70	2.00	4.00
19	167	10/65	PC-r	2	2	.70	2.00	4.00
20	166	9/67	PC-r	2	2	.70	2.00	4.00
21	166	Win/69	New price 25 cents; PC-r; stiff-c	2	2	.70	2.00	4.00
22	169	Sm/70	PC-r; stiff-c	2	2	.70	2.00	4.00

20. The Corsican Brothers

Ed	HRN	Date	Details	A	C	Good	Fine	Mint
1	—	6/44	Orig.; Gilberton ed.	1	1	22.00	65.00	154.00
2	—	6/44	Orig.; Courier ed.	1	1	20.00	60.00	140.00
3	—	6/44	Orig.; Long Island Ind. ed.; CC-r	1	1	20.00	60.00	140.00
4	22	10/44	Queens Cty. Times ed.; CC-r	1	1	9.00	27.00	63.00
5	28	6/46	CC-r	1	1	8.00	24.00	56.00
6	60	6/49	CI logo; no price; 48 pgs.; LDC-r	1	1	7.00	21.00	50.00
7	62	8/49	LDC-r	1	1	6.00	18.00	42.00
8	78	12/50	C-price 15 cents; LDC-r	1	1	5.00	15.00	35.00
9	97	7/52	LDC-r	1	1	5.00	15.00	35.00

21. 3 Famous Mysteries ("The Sign of the 4," "The Murders in the Rue Morgue," "The Flayed Hand")

Ed	HRN	Date	Details	A	C	Good	Fine	Mint
1	—	7/44	Orig.; Gilberton ed.	1	1	40.00	120.00	280.00
2	—	7/44	Orig. Island Pub. Co.; nd or indicia	1	1	35.00	105.00	245.00
3	—	7/44	Original; Richmond Courier Ed.	1	1	37.00	110.00	260.00
4	22	10/44	Nassau Bulletin ed.; CC-r	1	1	16.00	48.00	110.00
5	30	9/46	CC-r	1	1	14.00	42.00	100.00
6	62	8/49	LDC-r	1	1	9.00	27.00	63.00
7	70	4/50	LDC-r	1	1	11.00	33.00	60.00
8	85	7/51	Price 15 cents; LDC-r	1	1	8.00	24.00	56.00
9	114	12/53	New-c; PC-r	1	2	11.00	33.00	60.00

22. The Pathfinder

Ed	HRN	Date	Details	A	C	Good	Fine	Mint
1	—	10/44	Orig.; Gilberton ed.	1	1	18.00	54.00	125.00
2	—	10/44	Original; Island Pub. Co. ed.	1	1	16.00	48.00	110.00
3	—	10/44	Original; Queens County Times ed.	1	1	16.00	48.00	110.00
4	30	9/46	C-price removed; CC-r	1	1	8.00	24.00	56.00
5	60	6/49	Pgs. reduced to 48; LDC-r	1	1	1.50	4.50	10.00
6	62	8/49	LDC-r (exist?)	1	1	.80	2.30	5.60
7	70	4/50	LDC-r	1	1	.80	2.30	5.60
8	85	7/51	15¢ c-price; LDC-r	1	1	.55	1.60	3.80
9	118	4/54	LDC-r	1	1	.55	1.60	3.80
10	132	5/56	LDC-r	1	1	.55	1.60	3.80
11	146	9/58	LDC-r	1	1	.55	1.60	3.80
12	167	11/63	New-c; PC-r	1	2	2.65	8.00	18.00
13	167	12/65	PC-r	1	2	1.70	5.00	12.00

Classics Illustrated #17 (HRN 60), © GIL

Classic Comics #20, © GIL

Classics Illustrated #22 (HRN 85), © GIL

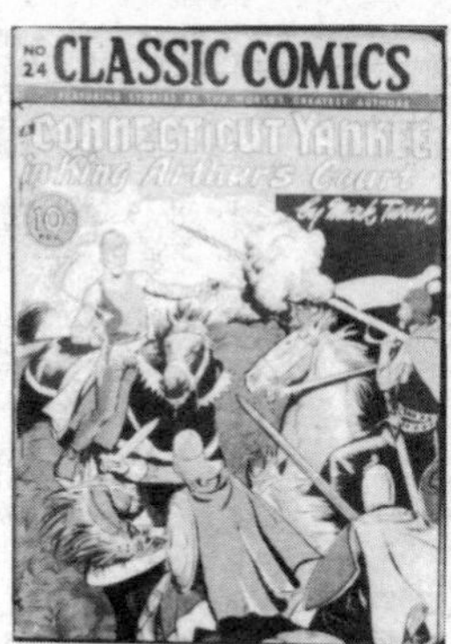

Classic Comics #24 (Orig.), © GIL

Classics Illustrated #26, © GIL

Classic Comics #29 (Orig.), © GIL

CLASSIC COMICS (continued)

Ed	HRN	Date	Details	A	C	Good	Fine	Mint
14	166	8/67	PC-r	1	2	1.70	5.00	12.00

23. Oliver Twist (1st Classic produced by the Iger Shop)

Ed	HRN	Date	Details	A	C	Good	Fine	Mint
1	—	7/45	Original	1	1	16.00	48.00	110.00
2	30	9/46	Price circle blank; CC-r	1	1	5.00	15.00	35.00
3	60	6/49	Pgs. reduced to 48; LDC-r	1	1	1.50	4.50	10.00
4	62	8/49	LDC-r	1	1	1.15	3.50	8.00
5	71	5/50	LDC-r	1	1	.70	2.00	5.00
6	85	7/51	15¢ c-price; LDC-r	1	1	.70	2.00	5.00
7	94	4/52	LDC-r	1	1	.70	2.00	5.00
8	118	4/54	LDC-r	1	1	.70	2.00	5.00
9	136	1/57	New-PC, old-a; PC-r	1	2	1.50	4.50	10.00
10	150	5/59	Old-a; PC-r	1	2	1.15	3.50	8.00
11	164	1961	Old-a; PC-r	1	2	1.15	3.50	8.00
12	164	1961	New-a; PC-r; Evans/Crandall-a	2	2	1.70	5.00	12.00
13	167	'62/63	PC-r	2	2	.50	1.50	3.00
14	167	8/64	PC-r	2	2	.50	1.50	3.00
15	167	12/65	PC-r	2	2	.50	1.50	3.00
16	166	R/1968	New price 25¢; PC-r	2	2	.50	1.50	3.00
17	169	Win/69	Stiff-c; PC-r	2	2	.70	2.00	4.00

24. A Connecticut Yankee in King Arthur's Court

Ed	HRN	Date	Details	A	C	Good	Fine	Mint
1	—	9/45	Original	1	1	15.00	45.00	105.00
2	30	9/46	Price circle blank; CC-r	1	1	5.00	15.00	35.00
3	60	6/49	8 pgs. deleted; LDC-r	1	1	1.50	4.50	10.00
4	62	8/49	LDC-r	1	1	1.50	4.50	10.00
5	71	5/50	LDC-r	1	1	.70	2.00	5.00
6	87	9/51	15¢ c-price; LDC-r	1	1	.70	2.00	5.00
7	121	7/54	LDC-r	1	1	.70	2.00	5.00
8	140	9/57	New-c&a; PC-r	2	2	1.30	4.00	9.00
9	153	11/59	PC-r	2	2	.50	1.50	3.00
10	164	1961	PC-r	2	2	.50	1.50	3.00
11	167	'62/63	PC-r	2	2	.50	1.50	3.00
12	167	7/64	PC-r	2	2	.50	1.50	3.00
13	167	6/66	PC-r	2	2	.50	1.50	3.00
14	166	R/1968	New price 25¢; PC-r	2	2	.50	1.50	3.00
15	169	Spr/71	PC-r; stiff-c	2	2	.50	1.50	3.00

25. Two Years Before the Mast

Ed	HRN	Date	Details	A	C	Good	Fine	Mint
1	—	10/45	Original; Webb/Heames-a&c	1	1	16.00	48.00	110.00
2	30	9/46	Price circle blank; CC-r	1	1	5.00	15.00	35.00
3	60	6/49	8 pgs. deleted; LDC-r	1	1	1.50	4.50	10.00
4	62	8/49	LDC-r	1	1	.85	2.50	6.00
5	71	5/50	LDC-r	1	1	.70	2.00	5.00
6	85	7/51	15¢c-price; LDC-r	1	1	.70	2.00	5.00
7	114	12/53	LDC-r	1	1	.70	2.00	5.00
8	156	5/60	3 pgs. replaced by fillers; new-c; PC-r	1	2	1.00	3.00	7.00
9	167	12/63	PC-r	1	2	.50	1.50	3.00
10	167	12/65	PC-r	1	2	.50	1.50	3.00
11	166	9/67	PC-r	1	2	.50	1.50	3.00
12	169	Win/69	New price 25¢; stiff-c; PC-r	1	2	.50	1.50	3.00

26. Frankenstein

Ed	HRN	Date	Details	A	C	Good	Fine	Mint
1	—	12/45	Original; Webb/Brewster a&c	1	1	38.00	115.00	265.00
2	30	9/46	Price circle blank; CC-r	1	1	14.00	42.00	100.00
3	60	6/49	LDC-r	1	1	4.00	12.00	28.00
4	62	8/49	LDC-r	1	1	3.00	9.00	21.00
5	71	5/50	LDC-r	1	1	2.65	8.00	18.00
6	82	4/51	15¢ c-price; LDC-r	1	1	2.30	7.00	16.00
7	117	3/54	LDC-r	1	1	1.75	5.25	12.00
8	146	9/58	New Saunders-c PC-r	1	2	1.75	5.25	12.00
9	153	11/59	PC-r	1	2	.50	1.50	3.00
10	160	1/61	PC-r	1	2	.50	1.50	3.00
11	165	1962	PC-r	1	2	.50	1.50	3.00
12	167	'62/63	PC-r	1	2	.50	1.50	3.00
13	167	6/64	PC-r	1	2	.50	1.50	3.00
14	167	6/65	PC-r	1	2	.50	1.50	3.00
15	167	10/65	PC-r	1	2	.50	1.50	3.00
16	166	9/67	PC-r	1	2	.50	1.50	3.00
17	169	Fall/69	New price 25¢; PC-r; stiff-c	1	2	.50	1.50	3.00
18	169	Spr/71	PC-r; stiff-c	1	2	.50	1.50	3.00

27. The Adventures of Marco Polo

Ed	HRN	Date	Details	A	C	Good	Fine	Mint
1	—	4/46	Original	1	1	16.00	48.00	110.00
2	30	9/46	Last 'Comics' reprint; CC-r	1	1	5.00	15.00	35.00
3	70	4/50	8 pgs. deleted; no c-price; LDC-r	1	1	1.00	3.00	7.00
4	87	9/51	15¢c-price; LDC-r	1	1	.70	2.00	5.00
5	117	3/54	LDC-r	1	1	.70	2.00	5.00
6	154	1/60	New-c; PC-r	1	2	1.15	3.50	8.00
7	165	1962	PC-r	1	2	.50	1.50	3.00
8	167	4/64	PC-r	1	2	.50	1.50	3.00
9	167	6/66	PC-r	1	2	.50	1.50	3.00
10	169	Spr/69	New price 25¢; stiff-c; PC-r	1	2	.50	1.50	3.00

28. Michael Strogoff

Ed	HRN	Date	Details	A	C	Good	Fine	Mint
1	—	6/46	Original	1	1	16.00	48.00	110.00
2	51	9/48	8 pgs. cut; LDC-r	1	1	5.00	15.00	35.00
3	115	1/54	New-c; PC-r	1	2	1.70	5.00	12.00
4	155	3/60	PC-r	1	2	.70	2.00	5.00
5	167	11/63	PC-r	1	2	.70	2.00	5.00
6	167	7/66	PC-r	1	2	.70	2.00	5.00
7	169	Sm/69	New price 25¢ stiff-c; PC-r	1	3	1.50	4.50	10.00

29. The Prince and the Pauper

Ed	HRN	Date	Details	A	C	Good	Fine	Mint
1	—	7/46	Orig.; "Horror"-c	1	1	30.00	90.00	210.00
2	60	6/49	8 pgs. cut; new-c by Kiefer; LDC-r	1	2	1.50	4.50	10.00
3	62	8/49	LDC-r	1	2	1.15	3.50	8.00
4	71	5/50	LDC-r	1	2	.85	2.50	6.00
5	93	3/52	LDC-r	1	2	.70	2.00	5.00
6	114	12/53	LDC-r	1	2	.70	2.00	5.00
7	128	9/55	New-c; PC-r	1	3	1.15	3.50	8.00
8	138	5/57	PC-r	1	3	.50	1.50	3.00
9	150	5/59	PC-r	1	3	.50	1.50	3.00
10	164	1961	PC-r	1	3	.50	1.50	3.00
11	167	'62/63	PC-r	1	3	.50	1.50	3.00
12	167	7/64	PC-r	1	3	.50	1.50	3.00

CLASSIC Comics (continued)

Ed	HRN	Date	Details	A	C	Good	Fine	Mint
13	167	11/65	PC-r	1	3	.50	1.50	3.00
14	166	R/1968	New price 25¢; PC-r	1	3	.50	1.50	3.00
15	169	Sm/70	PC-r; stiff-c	1	3	.50	1.50	3.00

30. The Moonstone

Ed	HRN	Date	Details	A	C	Good	Fine	Mint
1	—	9/46	Original; Rico c/a	1	1	16.00	48.00	110.00
2	60	6/49	LDC-r; 8pgs. cut	1	1	3.00	9.00	21.00
3	70	4/50	LDC-r	1	1	2.00	6.00	14.00
4	155	3/60	New L.B. Cole-c; PC-r	1	2	5.00	15.00	35.00
5	165	1962	PC-r; L.B. Cole-c	1	2	2.00	6.00	14.00
6	167	1/64	PC-r; L.B. Cole-c	1	2	1.35	4.00	8.00
7	167	9/65	PC-r; L.B. Cole-c	1	2	1.00	3.00	6.00
8	166	R/1968	New price 25¢; PC-r	1	2	.70	2.00	4.00

31. The Black Arrow

Ed	HRN	Date	Details	A	C	Good	Fine	Mint
1	—	10/46	Original	1	1	13.00	40.00	90.00
2	51	9/48	CI logo; LDC-r 8pgs. deleted	1	1	1.50	4.50	10.00
3	64	10/49	LDC-r	1	1	1.00	3.00	7.00
4	87	9/51	15¢ c-price; LDC-r	1	1	.70	2.00	5.00
5	108	6/53	LDC-r	1	1	.70	2.00	5.00
6	125	3/55	LDC-r	1	1	.70	2.00	5.00
7	131	3/56	New-c; PC-r	1	2	.85	2.50	6.00
8	140	9/57	PC-r	1	2	.50	1.50	3.00
9	148	1/59	PC-r	1	2	.50	1.50	3.00
10	161	3/61	PC-r	1	2	.50	1.50	3.00
11	167	'62/63	PC-r	1	2	.50	1.50	3.00
12	167	7/64	PC-r	1	2	.50	1.50	3.00
13	167	11/65	PC-r	1	2	.50	1.50	3.00
14	166	R/1968	25¢ new price; PC-r	1	2	.50	1.50	3.00

32. Lorna Doone

Ed	HRN	Date	Details	A	C	Good	Fine	Mint
1	—	12/46	Original; Matt Baker c&a	1	1	13.00	40.00	90.00
2	53/64	10/49	8 pgs. deleted; LDC-r	1	1	3.65	11.00	25.00
3	85	7/51	15¢ price, LDC-r; Baker c&a	1	1	3.00	9.00	21.00
4	118	4/54	LDC-r	1	1	2.00	6.00	14.00
5	138	5/57	New-c; old-c becomes new title pg.; PC-r	1	2	1.35	4.00	9.00
6	150	5/59	PC-r	1	2	.70	2.00	4.00
7	165	1962	PC-r	1	2	.70	2.00	4.00
8	167	'62/63	PC-r	1	2	.70	2.00	4.00
9	167	1/64	PC-r	1	2	.70	2.00	4.00
10	167	11/65	PC-r	1	2	.70	2.00	4.00
11	166	R/1968	New-c; PC-r	1	3	1.50	4.50	10.00

33. The Adventures of Sherlock Holmes

Ed	HRN	Date	Details	A	C	Good	Fine	Mint
1	—	1/47	Original; Kiefer-c	1	1	48.00	145.00	335.00
2	53	11/48	'A Study in Scarlet' (17 pgs.) deleted; LDC-r	1	1	23.00	70.00	160.00
3	71	5/50	LDC-r	1	1	16.00	48.00	110.00
4	89	11/51	15¢ price; LDC-r	1	1	14.00	42.00	100.00

34. Mysterious Island

Ed	HRN	Date	Details	A	C	Good	Fine	Mint
1	—	2/47	Original; Last 'Classic Comic.' Webb/Heames c/a	1	1	15.00	45.00	105.00
2	60	6/49	8 pgs. deleted; LDC-r	1	1	1.50	4.50	10.00
3	62	8/49	LDC-r	1	1	1.00	3.00	7.00
4	71	5/50	LDC-r	1	1	1.00	3.00	7.00
5	78	12/50	15¢ price circle; LDC-r	1	1	.85	2.50	6.00
6	92	2/52	LDC-r	1	1	.85	2.50	6.00
7	117	3/54	LDC-r	1	1	.85	2.50	6.00
8	140	9/57	New-c; PC-r	1	2	.85	2.50	6.00
9	156	5/60	PC-r	1	2	.70	2.00	4.00
10	167	10/63	PC-r	1	2	.70	2.00	4.00
11	167	5/64	PC-r	1	2	.70	2.00	4.00
12	167	6/66	PC-r	1	2	.70	2.00	4.00
13	166	R/1968	New price 25¢; PC-r	1	2	.70	2.00	4.00

35. Last Days of Pompeii

Ed	HRN	Date	Details	A	C	Good	Fine	Mint
1	—	3/47	Original; 1st 'Classics Illus.;'' LDC; Kiefer c/a	1	1	15.00	45.00	105.00
2	161	3/61	New c&a; 15¢; PC-r; Jack Kirby-a	2	2	2.30	7.00	16.00
3	167	1/64	PC-r	2	2	1.00	3.00	6.00
4	167	7/66	PC-r	2	2	1.00	3.00	6.00
5	169	Spr/70	New price 25¢; stiff-c; PC-r	2	2	1.15	3.50	8.00

36. Typee

Ed	HRN	Date	Details	A	C	Good	Fine	Mint
1	—	4/47	Original	1	1	7.00	21.00	50.00
2	64	10/49	No c-price; 8 pg. ed.; LDC-r	1	1	2.65	8.00	18.00
3	155	3/60	New-c; PC-r	1	2	1.30	4.00	9.00
4	167	9/63	PC-r	1	2	1.20	3.50	7.00
5	167	7/65	PC-r	1	2	1.20	3.50	7.00
6	169	Sm/69	New price 25¢; stiff-c; PC-r	1	2	.85	2.50	6.00

37. The Pioneers

Ed	HRN	Date	Details	A	C	Good	Fine	Mint
1	37	5/47	Original; Palais-c/a	1	1	7.00	21.00	50.00
2	62	8/49	8 pgs. cut; LDC-r	1	1	2.65	8.00	18.00
3	70	4/50	LDC-r	1	1	.70	2.00	5.00
4	92	2/52	15¢ c-price; LDC-r	1	1	.50	1.50	3.50
5	118	4/54	LDC-r	1	1	.50	1.50	3.50
6	131	3/56	LDC-r	1	1	.50	1.50	3.50
7	132	5/56	LDC-r	1	1	.50	1.50	3.50
8	153	11/59	LDC-r	1	1	.50	1.50	3.50
9	167	5/64	LDC-r	1	1	.50	1.50	3.00
10	167	6/66	LDC-r	1	1	.50	1.50	3.00
11	166	R/1968	New-c&price 25¢; PC-r	1	2	1.50	4.50	10.00

38. Adventures of Cellini

Ed	HRN	Date	Details	A	C	Good	Fine	Mint
1	—	6/47	Original; Froehlich c/a	1	1	14.00	42.00	100.00
2	164	1961	New-c&a; PC-r	2	2	1.50	4.50	10.00
3	167	12/63	PC-r	2	2	1.00	3.00	6.00
4	167	7/66	PC-r	2	2	1.00	3.00	6.00
5	169	Spr/70	Stiff-c; new price 25¢; PC-r	2	2	1.35	4.00	8.00

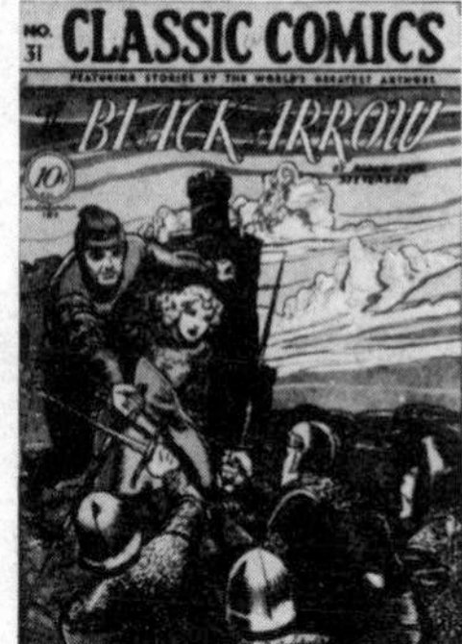

Classic Comics #31 (Orig.), © GIL

Classics Illustrated #34 (HRN 167), © GIL

Classics Illustrated #37, © GIL

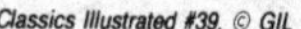
Classics Illustrated #39, © GIL

Classics Illustrated #41 (Orig.), © GIL

Classics Illustrated #43 (Orig.), © GIL

CLASSICS ILLUSTRATED (continued)

39. Jane Eyre

Ed	HRN	Date	Details	A	C	Good	Fine	Mint
1	—	7/47	Original	1	1	11.00	33.00	76.00
2	60	6/49	No c-price; 8 pgs. cut; LDC-r	1	1	3.00	9.00	21.00
3	62	8/49	LDC-r	1	1	2.00	6.00	14.00
4	71	5/50	LDC-r	1	1	2.00	6.00	14.00
5	92	2/52	15¢ c-price; LDC-r	1	1	1.30	4.00	9.00
6	118	4/54	LDC-r	1	1	1.30	4.00	9.00
7	142	1/58	New-c; old-a; PC-r	1	2	1.70	5.00	12.00
8	154	1/60	Old-a; PC-r	1	2	1.35	4.00	9.00
9	165	1962	New-a; PC-r	2	2	1.70	5.00	12.00
10	167	12/63	PC-r	2	2	1.00	3.00	6.00
11	167	4/65	PC-r	2	2	1.00	3.00	6.00
12	167	8/66	PC-r	2	2	1.00	3.00	6.00
13	166	R/1968	New-c; PC-r	2	3	3.00	9.00	21.00

40. Mysteries ("The Pit and the Pendulum," "The Advs. of Hans Pfall," "The Fall of the House of Usher")

Ed	HRN	Date	Details	A	C	Good	Fine	Mint
1	—	8/47	Original; Kiefer-c/a, Froehlich, Griffiths-a	1	1	38.00	115.00	265.00
2	62	8/49	LDC-r; 8pgs cut	1	1	11.50	34.00	80.00
3	75	9/50	LDC-r	1	1	8.50	25.50	60.00
4	92	2/52	15¢ c-price; LDC-r	1	1	7.00	21.00	50.00

41. Twenty Years After

Ed	HRN	Date	Details	A	C	Good	Fine	Mint
1	—	9/47	Original; 'horror'-c	1	1	23.00	70.00	160.00
2	62	8/49	New-c; no c-price 8 pgs. cut; LDC-r; Kiefer-c	1	2	2.00	6.00	14.00
3	78	12/50	C-price 15¢; LDC-r	1	2	1.15	3.50	8.00
4	156	5/60	New-c; PC-r	1	3	1.00	3.00	7.00
5	167	12/63	PC-r	1	3	.70	2.00	4.00
6	167	11/66	PC-r	1	3	.70	2.00	4.00
7	169	Spr/70	New price 25¢; stiff-c; PC-r	1	3	.70	2.00	4.00

42. Swiss Family Robinson

Ed	HRN	Date	Details	A	C	Good	Fine	Mint
1	42	10/47	Orig.; Kiefer a&c	1	1	6.50	19.50	45.00
2	62	8/49	No c-price; 8 pgs. cut; LDC-r; not all have 'gift box' ad	1	1	1.30	4.00	9.00
3	75	9/50	LDC-r	1	1	.85	2.50	6.00
4	93	3/52	LDC-r	1	1	.85	2.50	6.00
5	117	3/54	LDC-r	1	1	.85	2.50	6.00
6	131	3/56	New-c; old-a; PC-r	1	2	1.50	4.50	10.00
7	137	3/57	Old-a; PC-r	1	2	1.35	4.00	9.00
8	141	11/57	Old-a; PC-r	1	2	1.35	4.00	9.00
9	152	9/59	New-a; PC-r	2	2	.85	2.50	6.00
10	158	9/60	PC-r	2	2	.70	2.00	4.00
11	167	10/47	PC-r	2	2	.70	2.00	4.00
12	165	12/63	PC-r	2	2	.70	2.00	4.00
13	167	12/63	PC-r	2	2	.70	2.00	4.00
14	167	4/65	PC-r	2	2	.70	2.00	4.00
15	167	5/66	PC-r	2	2	.70	2.00	4.00
16	166	11/67	PC-r	2	2	.45	1.30	2.60
17	169	Spr/69	PC-r	2	2	.45	1.30	2.60
18	169	Spr/70	New price 25¢; stiff-c; PC-r	2	2	.45	1.30	2.60
19	169	Sm/70	Stiff-c; PC-r	2	2	.50	1.50	3.00

43. Great Expectations (Used in **SOTI**, pg. 311)

Ed	HRN	Date	Details	A	C	Good	Fine	Mint
1	—	11/47	Original; Kiefer-a/c	1	1	40.00	120.00	280.00
2	62	8/49	No c-price; 8 pgs. cut; LDC-r	1	1	30.00	90.00	210.00

44. Mysteries of Paris (Used in **SOTI**, pg. 323)

Ed	HRN	Date	Details	A	C	Good	Fine	Mint
1	44	12/47	Original; 56 pgs.; Kiefer-a/c	1	1	30.00	90.00	210.00
2	62	8/47	No c-price; 8 pgs. cut; LDC-r; not all have 'gift box' ad	1	1	14.00	42.00	100.00
3	78	12/50	C-price 15¢; LDC-r	1	1	10.00	30.00	70.00

45. Tom Brown's School Days

Ed	HRN	Date	Details	A	C	Good	Fine	Mint
1	44	1/48	Original; 1st 48pg. issue	1	1	5.00	15.00	35.00
2	64	10/49	No c-price; LDC-r	1	1	2.35	7.00	16.00
3	161	3/61	New-c&a; PC-r	2	2	1.30	4.00	9.00
4	167	2/64	PC-r	2	2	1.00	3.00	7.00
5	167	8/66	PC-r	2	2	1.00	3.00	7.00
6	166	R/1968	New price 25¢; PC-r	2	2	1.00	3.00	7.00

46. Kidnapped

Ed	HRN	Date	Details	A	C	Good	Fine	Mint
1	47	4/48	Original; Webb-c/a	1	1	5.70	17.00	40.00
2	62	8/49	Red price circle blank or w/10¢ price; LDC-r	1	1	1.50	4.50	10.00
3	78	12/50	15¢ price; LDC-r	1	1	.70	2.00	5.00
4	87	9/51	LDC-r	1	1	.70	2.00	5.00
5	118	4/54	LDC-r	1	1	.60	1.80	4.20
6	131	3/56	New-c; PC-r	1	2	1.00	3.00	7.00
7	140	9/57	PC-r	1	2	.60	1.80	4.20
8	150	5/59	PC-r	1	2	.60	1.80	4.20
9	156	5/60	PC-r	1	2	.60	1.80	4.20
10	164	1961	Reduced pg.width; PC-r	1	2	.45	1.40	2.80
11	167	'62/63	PC-r	1	2	.45	1.40	2.80
12	167	3/64	PC-r	1	2	.45	1.40	2.80
13	167	6/65	PC-r	1	2	.45	1.40	2.80
14	167	12/65	PC-r	1	2	.45	1.40	2.80
15	167	9/67	PC-r	1	2	.45	1.40	2.80
16	166	Win/69	New price 25¢; PC-r; stiff-c	1	2	.45	1.40	2.80
17	169	Sm/70	PC-r; stiff-c	1	2	.50	1.50	3.00

47. Twenty Thousand Leagues Under the Sea

Ed	HRN	Date	Details	A	C	Good	Fine	Mint
1	47	5/48	Orig.; Kiefer-a&c	1	1	8.00	24.00	56.00
2	64	10/49	No c-price; LDC-r	1	1	1.20	3.50	8.00
3	78	12/50	15¢ price; LDC-r	1	1	1.00	3.00	7.00
4	94	4/52	LDC-r	1	1	1.00	3.00	7.00
5	118	4/54	LDC-r	1	1	1.00	3.00	7.00
6	128	9/55	New-c; PC-r	1	2	.85	2.50	5.00
7	133	7/56	PC-r	1	2	.85	2.50	5.00
8	140	9/57	PC-r	1	2	.85	2.50	5.00
9	148	1/59	PC-r	1	2	.85	2.50	5.00
10	156	5/60	PC-r	1	2	.85	2.50	5.00
11	165	'62/63	PC-r	1	2	.85	2.50	5.00
12	167	5/48	PC-r	1	2	.85	2.50	5.00
13	167	3/64	PC-r	1	2	.85	2.50	5.00
14	167	8/65	PC-r	1	2	.70	2.10	4.20
15	167	10/66	PC-r	1	2	.85	2.50	5.00
16	166	R/1968	New price 25¢; new-c; PC-r	1	3	1.50	4.50	10.00

CLASSICS ILLUSTRATED (continued)

Ed	HRN	Date	Details	A C	Good	Fine	Mint
17	169	Spr/70	Stiff-c; PC-r	1 3	1.50	4.50	10.00

48. David Copperfield

Ed	HRN	Date	Details	A C	Good	Fine	Mint
1	47	6/48	Original; Kiefer a/c	1 1	6.00	18.00	42.00
2	64	10/49	Price circle replaced by motif of boy reading; LDC-r	1 1	1.50	4.50	10.00
3	87	9/51	15¢ c-price; LDC-r	1 1	.80	2.30	5.60
4	121	7/54	New-c; PC-r	1 2	.80	2.30	5.60
5	130	1/56	PC-r	1 2	.80	2.30	5.60
6	140	9/57	PC-r	1 2	.80	2.30	5.60
7	148	1/59	PC-r	1 2	.80	2.30	5.60
8	156	5/60	PC-r	1 2	.80	2.30	5.60
9	167	'62/63	PC-r	1 2	.60	1.80	3.60
10	167	4/64	PC-r	1 2	.60	1.80	3.60
11	167	6/65	PC-r	1 2	.60	1.80	3.60
12	166	5/67	PC-r	1 2	.60	1.80	3.60
13	166	R/67	PC-r	1 2	.60	1.80	3.60
14	166	Spr/69	New price 25¢; PC-r; stiff-c	1 2	.50	1.50	3.00
15	169	Win/69	Stiff-c; PC-r	1 2	.50	1.50	3.00

49. Alice in Wonderland

Ed	HRN	Date	Details	A C	Good	Fine	Mint
1	47	7/48	Original; 1st Blum a & c	1 1	10.00	30.00	70.00
2	64	10/49	No c-price; LDC-r	1 1	2.00	6.00	14.00
3	85	7/51	15¢ c-price; LDC-r	1 1	1.50	4.50	10.00
4	155	3/60	New PC, similar to orig.; PC-r	1 2	1.50	4.50	10.00
5	165	1962	PC-r	1 2	1.00	3.00	7.00
6	167	3/64	PC-r	1 2	1.00	3.00	7.00
7	167	6/66	PC-r	1 2	1.00	3.00	7.00
8	166	Fall/68	New-c; soft-c; 25¢ price; PC-r	1 3	2.00	6.00	14.00
9	166	Fall/68	Soft & Stiff-c; PC-r	1 3	3.50	10.50	24.00

50. Adventures of Tom Sawyer (Used in **SOTI**, pg. 37)

Ed	HRN	Date	Details	A C	Good	Fine	Mint
1	51	8/48	Original; Aldo Rubano a&c	1 1	5.00	15.00	35.00
2	51	9/48	Original	1 1	4.00	12.00	28.00
3	64	10/49	No c-price; LDC-r	1 1	1.50	4.50	10.00
4	78	12/50	15¢ price; LDC-r	1 1	.85	2.50	6.00
5	94	4/52	LDC-r	1 1	.85	2.50	6.00
6	114	12/53	LDC-r (exist?)	1 1	.85	2.50	6.00
7	117	3/54	LDC-r	1 1	.85	2.50	6.00
8	132	5/56	LDC-r	1 1	.85	2.50	6.00
9	140	9/57	New-c; PC-r	1 2	1.30	4.00	9.00
10	150	5/59	PC-r	1 2	1.15	3.50	8.00
11	164	1961	New-a; PC-r	2 2	.85	2.50	6.00
12	167	'62/63	PC-r	2 2	.70	2.00	4.00
13	167	1/65	PC-r	2 2	.70	2.00	4.00
14	167	5/66	PC-r	2 2	.70	2.00	4.00
15	166	12/67	PC-r	2 2	.70	2.00	4.00
16	169	Fall/69	New price 25¢; PC-r; stiff-c	2 2	.50	1.50	3.00
17	169	Win/71	PC-r	2 2	.50	1.50	3.00

51. The Spy

Ed	HRN	Date	Details	A C	Good	Fine	Mint
1	51	9/48	Original; maroon-c	1 1	5.00	15.00	35.00
2	51	9/48	Original; violet-c	1 1	5.00	15.00	35.00
3	89	11/51	New price 15¢; LDC-r	1 1	.85	2.50	6.00
4	121	7/54	LDC-r	1 1	.85	2.50	6.00
5	139	7/57	New-c; PC-r	1 2	.85	2.50	6.00
6	156	5/60	PC-r	1 2	.70	2.00	4.00
7	167	11/63	PC-r	1 2	.70	2.00	4.00
8	167	7/66	PC-r	1 2	.70	2.00	4.00
9	166	Win/69	New price 25¢; Soft & stiff-c; PC-r	1 2	.70	2.00	4.00

52. The House of the Seven Gables

Ed	HRN	Date	Details	A C	Good	Fine	Mint
1	53	10/48	Orig.; Griffiths a&c	1 1	5.00	15.00	35.00
2	89	11/51	New price 15¢; LDC-r	1 1	.85	2.50	6.00
3	121	7/54	LDC-r	1 1	.85	2.50	6.00
4	142	1/58	New-c&a; PC-r Woodbridge-a	2 2	1.00	3.00	7.00
5	156	5/60	PC-r	2 2	.70	2.00	4.00
6	165	1962	PC-r	2 2	.70	2.00	4.00
7	167	5/64	PC-r	2 2	.70	2.00	4.00
8	167	3/66	PC-r	2 2	.70	2.00	4.00
9	166	R/1968	New price 25¢; PC-r	2 2	.50	1.50	3.00
10	169	Spr/70	Stiff-c; PC-r	2 2	.50	1.50	3.00

53. A Christmas Carol

Ed	HRN	Date	Details	A C	Good	Fine	Mint
1	53	11/48	Original & only ed; Kiefer-a,c	1 1	8.00	24.00	56.00

54. Man in the Iron Mask

Ed	HRN	Date	Details	A C	Good	Fine	Mint
1	55	12/48	Original; Froehlich-a, Kiefer-c	1 1	5.00	15.00	35.00
2	93	3/52	New price 15¢; LDC-r	1 1	.85	2.50	6.00
3	111	9/53	LDC-r	1 1	.60	1.80	4.20
4	142	1/58	New-c&a; PC-r	2 2	.85	2.50	6.00
5	154	1/60	PC-r	2 2	.50	1.50	3.00
6	165	1962	PC-r	2 2	.50	1.50	3.00
7	167	5/64	PC-r	2 2	.50	1.50	3.00
8	167	4/66	PC-r	2 2	.50	1.50	3.00
9	166	Win/69	New price 25¢; stiff-c; PC-r	2 2	.50	1.50	3.00

55. Silas Marner (Used in **SOTI**, pgs. 311, 312)

Ed	HRN	Date	Details	A C	Good	Fine	Mint
1	55	1/49	Original	1 1	6.00	18.00	42.00
2	75	9/50	Price circle blank; 'Coming Next' ad; LDC-r	1 1	2.00	6.00	14.00
3	97	7/52	LDC-r	1 1	.85	2.50	6.00
4	121	7/54	New-c; PC-r	1 2	.85	2.50	6.00
5	130	1/56	PC-r	1 2	.50	1.50	3.00
6	140	9/57	PC-r	1 2	.50	1.50	3.00
7	154	1/60	PC-r	1 2	.50	1.50	3.00
8	165	1962	PC-r	1 2	.50	1.50	3.00
9	167	2/64	PC-r	1 2	.50	1.50	3.00
10	167	5/64	PC-r	1 2	.50	1.50	3.00
11	167	6/65	PC-r	1 2	.50	1.50	3.00
12	166	5/67	PC-r	1 2	.50	1.50	3.00
13	166	Win/69	New price 25¢; PC-r; stiff-c	1 2	.50	1.50	3.00

56. The Toilers of the Sea

Ed	HRN	Date	Details	A C	Good	Fine	Mint
1	55	2/49	Original; A.M. Froehlich a,c	1 1	8.50	25.50	60.00
2	165	1962	New-c&a; PC-r;	2 2	2.65	8.00	18.00

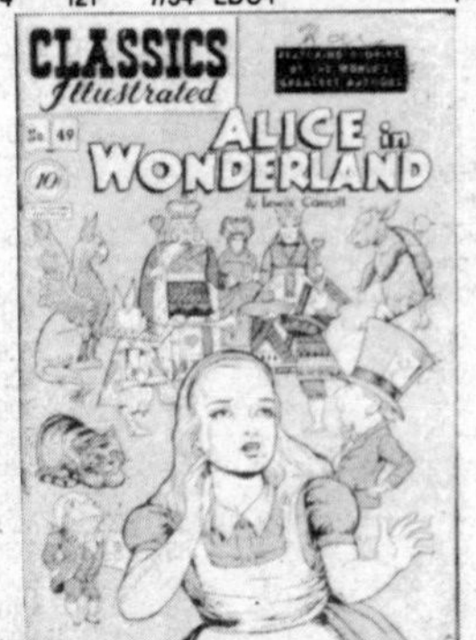

Classics Illustrated #49 (Orig.), © GIL

Classics Illustrated #52 (Orig.), © GIL

Classics Illustrated #55 (Orig.), © GIL

Classics Illustrated #57 (Orig.), © GIL

Classics Illustrated #61, © GIL

Classics Illustrated #64 (Orig.), © GIL

CLASSICS ILLUSTRATED (continuted)

Ed	HRN	Date	Details	A	C	Good	Fine	Mint
			Angelo Torres-a					
3	167	3/64	PC-r	2	2	2.00	6.00	14.00
4	167	10/66	PC-r	2	2	2.00	6.00	14.00

57. The Song of Hiawatha

Ed	HRN	Date	Details	A	C	Good	Fine	Mint
1	55	3/49	Original; Alex Blum a&c	1	1	4.00	14.00	32.00
2	75	9/50	No c-price; 'Coming Next'ad; LDC-r	1	1	2.00	6.00	14.00
3	94	4/52	15¢ c-price; LDC-r	1	1	.85	2.50	6.00
4	118	4/54	LDC-r	1	1	.60	1.80	4.20
5	134	9/56	New-c; PC-r	1	2	.70	2.00	5.00
6	139	7/57	PC-r	1	2	.50	1.50	3.00
7	154	1/60	PC-r	1	2	.50	1.50	3.00
8	167	'62/63	Has orig.date; PC-r	1	2	.50	1.50	3.00
9	167	9/64	PC-r	1	2	.50	1.50	3.00
10	167	10/65	PC-r	1	2	.50	1.50	3.00
11	166	R/Fall 1968	New price 25¢; PC-r	1	2	.50	1.50	3.00

58. The Prairie

Ed	HRN	Date	Details	A	C	Good	Fine	Mint
1	60	4/49	Original; Palais c/a	1	1	4.60	14.00	32.00
2	62	8/49	LDC-r	1	1	2.65	8.00	18.00
3	78	12/50	15¢ price in double circle; LDC-r	1	1	1.70	5.00	12.00
4	114	12/53	LDC-r	1	1	.75	2.20	5.25
5	131	3/56	LDC-r	1	1	.70	2.00	5.00
6	132	5/56	LDC-r	1	1	.70	2.00	5.00
7	146	9/58	New-c; PC-r	1	2	.85	2.50	6.00
8	155	3/60	PC-r	1	2	.50	1.50	3.00
9	167	5/64	PC-r	1	2	.50	1.50	3.00
10	167	4/66	PC-r	1	2	.50	1.50	3.00
11	169	Sm/69	New price 25¢; stiff-c; PC-r	1	2	.50	1.50	3.00

59. Wuthering Heights

Ed	HRN	Date	Details	A	C	Good	Fine	Mint
1	60	5/49	Original; Kiefer a/c	1	1	7.00	21.00	50.00
2	85	7/51	15¢ price; LDC-r	1	1	2.00	6.00	14.00
3	156	5/60	New-c; PC-r	1	2	1.30	4.00	9.00
4	167	1/64	PC-r	1	2	.50	1.50	3.00
5	167	10/66	PC-r	1	2	.50	1.50	3.00
6	169	Sm/69	New price 25¢; stiff-c; PC-r	1	2	.50	1.50	3.00

60. Black Beauty

Ed	HRN	Date	Details	A	C	Good	Fine	Mint
1	62	6/49	Original; Froehlich c/a	1	1	5.00	15.00	35.00
2	62	8/49	LDC-r	1	1	3.50	10.50	24.00
3	85	7/51	New price 15¢ LDC-r	1	1	2.20	6.50	15.00
4	158	9/60	New L.B. Cole -c&a; PC-r	2	2	2.65	8.00	18.00
5	167	2/64	PC-r	2	2	1.50	4.50	9.00
6	167	3/66	PC-r	2	2	1.20	3.50	7.00
7	167	3/66	'Open book'blank; (See Classics Ill. Golden Records)					
8	166	R/1968	New-c&price, 25¢; PC-r	2	3	3.50	10.50	24.00

61. The Woman in White

Ed	HRN	Date	Details	A	C	Good	Fine	Mint
1	62	7/49	Original; Blum-c/a Maroon & Violet-c	1	1	5.00	15.00	35.00
2	156	5/60	New-c; PC-r	1	2	1.50	4.50	10.00
3	167	1/64	PC-r	1	2	1.35	4.00	8.00
4	166	R/1968	New price 25¢; PC-r	1	2	1.00	3.00	6.00

62. Western Stories ("The Luck of Roaring Camp" and "The Outcasts of Poker Flat")

Ed	HRN	Date	Details	A	C	Good	Fine	Mint
1	62	8/49	Original; Kiefer-a,c	1	1	5.00	15.00	35.00
2	89	11/51	New price 15¢; LDC-r	1	1	1.00	3.00	7.00
3	121	7/54	LDC-r	1	1	.85	2.50	6.00
4	137	3/57	New-c; PC-r	1	2	1.00	3.00	7.00
5	152	9/59	PC-r	1	2	.85	2.50	6.00
6	167	10/63	PC-r	1	2	.85	2.50	6.00
7	167	6/64	PC-r	1	2	.70	2.00	4.00
8	167	11/66	PC-r	1	2	.70	2.00	4.00
9	166	R/1968	New-c&price 25¢; PC-r	1	3	1.70	5.00	12.00

63. The Man Without a Country

Ed	HRN	Date	Details	A	C	Good	Fine	Mint
1	62	9/49	Original; Kiefer-a,c	1	1	5.00	15.00	35.00
2	78	12/50	C-price 15¢ in double circle; LDC-r	1	1	2.00	6.00	14.00
3	156	5/60	New-c, old-a; PC-r	1	2	2.35	7.00	16.00
4	165	1962	New-a & text pgs.; PC-r; A. Torres-a	2	2	1.00	3.00	7.00
5	167	3/64	PC-r	2	2	.70	2.00	4.00
6	167	8/66	PC-r	2	2	.70	2.00	4.00
7	169	Sm/69	New price 25¢; stiff-c; PC-r	2	2	.70	2.00	4.00

64. Treasure Island

Ed	HRN	Date	Details	A	C	Good	Fine	Mint
1	62	10/49	Original; Blum-a,c	1	1	5.00	15.00	35.00
2	82	4/51	New price 15¢; LDC-r	1	1	1.00	3.00	7.00
3	117	3/54	LDC-r	1	1	.70	2.00	5.00
4	131	3/56	New-c; PC-r	1	2	.70	2.00	5.00
5	138	5/57	PC-r	1	2	.50	1.50	3.00
6	146	9/58	PC-r	1	2	.50	1.50	3.00
7	158	9/60	PC-r	1	2	.50	1.50	3.00
8	165	1962	PC-r	1	2	.50	1.50	3.00
9	167	'62/63	PC-r	1	2	.50	1.50	3.00
10	167	6/64	PC-r	1	2	.50	1.50	3.00
11	167	12/65	PC-r	1	2	.50	1.50	3.00
12	166	10/67	PC-r	1	2	.50	1.50	3.00
13	166	10/67	w/Grit ad stapled in book	1	2	1.70	5.00	10.00
14	169	Spr/69	New price 25¢; stiff-c; PC-r	1	2	.50	1.50	3.00

65. Benjamin Franklin

Ed	HRN	Date	Details	A	C	Good	Fine	Mint
1	64	11/49	Original; Kiefer-c Iger Shop-a	1	1	5.00	15.00	35.00
2	131	3/56	New-c; PC-r	1	2	1.00	3.00	7.00
3	154	1/60	PC-r	1	2	.50	1.50	3.00
4	167	2/64	PC-r	1	2	.50	1.50	3.00
5	167	4/66	PC-r	1	2	.50	1.50	3.00
6	169	Fall/69	New price 25¢; stiff-c; PC-r	1	2	.50	1.50	3.00

CLASSICS ILLUSTRATED (continued)

66. The Cloister and the Hearth

Ed	HRN	Date	Details	A	C	Good	Fine	Mint
1	67	12/49	Original & only ed; Kiefer-a & c	1	1	11.00	33.00	76.00

67. The Scottish Chiefs

Ed	HRN	Date	Details	A	C	Good	Fine	Mint
1	67	1/50	Original; Blum-a&c	1	1	4.35	13.00	30.00
2	85	7/51	New price 15¢; LDC-r	1	1	1.00	3.00	7.00
3	118	4/54	LDC-r	1	1	.70	2.00	5.00
4	136	1/57	New-c; PC-r	1	2	.70	2.00	5.00
5	154	1/60	PC-r	1	2	.50	1.50	3.00
6	167	11/63	PC-r	1	2	.50	1.50	3.00
7	167	8/65	PC-r	1	2	.50	1.50	3.00

68. Julius Caesar (Used in SOTI, pgs. 36, 37)

Ed	HRN	Date	Details	A	C	Good	Fine	Mint
1	70	2/50	Original; Kiefer-a,c	1	1	5.00	15.00	35.00
2	85	7/51	New price 15¢; LDC-r	1	1	1.00	3.00	7.00
3	108	6/53	LDC-r	1	1	.70	2.00	5.00
4	156	5/60	New L.B. Cole-c; PC-r	1	2	2.00	6.00	14.00
5	165	1962	New-a by Evans, Crandall; PC-r	2	2	2.00	6.00	14.00
6	167	2/64	PC-r	2	2	.70	2.00	4.00
7	167	10/65	Tarzan books inside cover; PC-r	2	2	.50	1.50	3.00
8	166	R/1967	PC-r	2	2	.50	1.50	3.00
9	169	Win/69	PC-r; stiff-c	2	2	.50	1.50	3.00

69. Around the World in 80 Days

Ed	HRN	Date	Details	A	C	Good	Fine	Mint
1	70	3/50	Original; Kiefer-a/c	1	1	5.00	15.00	35.00
2	87	9/51	New price 15¢; LDC-r	1	1	1.00	3.00	7.00
			(Coward Shoe ad)			1.15	3.50	8.00
3	125	3/55	LDC-r	1	1	.80	2.30	5.60
4	136	1/57	New-c; PC-r	1	2	.85	2.50	6.00
5	146	9/58	PC-r	1	2	.70	2.00	4.00
6	152	9/59	PC-r	1	2	.70	2.00	4.00
7	164	1961	PC-r	1	2	.70	2.00	4.00
8	167	'62/63	PC-r	1	2	.70	2.00	4.00
9	167	7/64	PC-r	1	2	.70	2.00	4.00
10	167	11/65	PC-r	1	2	.70	2.00	4.00
11	166	7/67	PC-r	1	2	.50	1.50	3.00
12	169	Spr/69	New price 25¢; stiff-c; PC-r	1	2	.50	1.50	3.00

70. The Pilot

Ed	HRN	Date	Details	A	C	Good	Fine	Mint
1	71	4/50	Original; Blum-a,c	1	1	3.50	10.50	24.00
2	75	10/50	New price 15¢ LDC-r	1	1	1.00	3.00	7.00
3	92	2/52	LDC-r	1	1	.85	2.50	6.00
4	125	3/55	LDC-r	1	1	.75	2.20	5.25
5	156	5/60	New-c; PC-r	1	2	1.00	3.00	7.00
6	167	2/64	PC-r	1	2	.70	2.00	4.00
7	167	5/66	PC-r	1	2	.70	2.00	4.00

71. The Man Who Laughs

Ed	HRN	Date	Details	A	C	Good	Fine	Mint
1	71	5/50	Original; Blum-a,c	1	1	6.50	17.50	45.00
2	165	1962	New-c&a; PC-r	2	2	4.35	13.00	30.00
3	167	4/64	PC-r	2	2	3.50	10.50	24.00

72. The Oregon Trail

Ed	HRN	Date	Details	A	C	Good	Fine	Mint
1	73	6/50	Original; Kiefer-a,c	1	1	3.50	10.50	24.00
2	89	11/51	New price 15¢; LDC-r	1	1	.75	2.20	5.25
3	121	7/54	LDC-r	1	1	.70	2.00	5.00
4	131	3/56	New-c; PC-r	1	2	.85	2.50	6.00
5	140	9/57	PC-r	1	2	.75	2.20	5.25
6	150	5/59	PC-r	1	2	.70	2.00	4.00
7	164	1961	PC-r	1	2	.70	2.00	4.00
8	167	'62/63	PC-r	1	2	.70	2.00	4.00
9	167	8/64	PC-r	1	2	.70	2.00	4.00
10	167	10/65	PC-r	1	2	.70	2.00	4.00
11	166	R/1968	New price 25¢; PC-r	1	2	.50	1.50	3.00

73. The Black Tulip

Ed	HRN	Date	Details	A	C	Good	Fine	Mint
1	75	7/50	1st & only ed.; Alex Blum-a & c	1	1	12.00	36.00	84.00

74. Mr. Midshipman Easy

Ed	HRN	Date	Details	A	C	Good	Fine	Mint
1	75	8/50	1st & only edition	1	1	12.00	36.00	84.00

75. The Lady of the Lake

Ed	HRN	Date	Details	A	C	Good	Fine	Mint
1	75	9/50	Original; Kiefer-a/c	1	1	3.50	10.50	24.00
2	85	7/51	New price 15¢; LDC-r	1	1	1.15	3.50	8.00
3	118	4/54	LDC-r	1	1	.70	2.00	5.00
4	139	7/57	New-c; PC-r	1	2	.70	2.00	5.00
5	154	1/60	PC-r	1	2	.50	1.50	3.00
6	165	1962	PC-r	1	2	.50	1.50	3.00
7	167	4/64	PC-r	1	2	.50	1.50	3.00
8	167	5/66	PC-r	1	2	.50	1.50	3.00
9	169	Spr/69	New price 25¢; stiff-c; PC-r	1	2	.50	1.50	3.00

76. The Prisoner of Zenda

Ed	HRN	Date	Details	A	C	Good	Fine	Mint
1	75	10/50	Original; Kiefer-a,c	1	1	3.00	9.00	21.00
2	85	7/51	New price 15¢; LDC-r	1	1	1.20	3.50	8.00
3	111	9/53	LDC-r	1	1	.85	2.50	6.00
4	128	9/55	New-c; PC-r	1	2	1.00	3.00	7.00
5	152	9/59	PC-r	1	2	.50	1.50	3.00
6	165	1962	PC-r	1	2	.50	1.50	3.00
7	167	4/64	PC-r	1	2	.50	1.50	3.00
8	167	9/66	PC-r	1	2	.50	1.50	3.00
9	169	Fall/69	New price 25¢; stiff-c; PC-r	1	2	.60	1.80	3.60

77. The Iliad

Ed	HRN	Date	Details	A	C	Good	Fine	Mint
1	78	11/50	Original; Blum-a,c	1	1	3.00	9.00	21.00
2	87	9/51	New price 15¢; LDC-r	1	1	1.15	3.50	8.00
3	121	7/54	LDC-r	1	1	.75	2.20	5.25
4	139	7/57	New-c; PC-r	1	2	.85	2.50	6.00
5	150	5/59	PC-r	1	2	.50	1.50	3.00
6	165	1962	PC-r	1	2	.50	1.50	3.00
7	167	10/63	PC-r	1	2	.50	1.50	3.00
8	167	7/64	PC-r	1	2	.50	1.50	3.00
9	167	5/66	PC-r	1	2	.50	1.50	3.00
10	166	R/1968	New price 25¢; PC-r	1	2	.50	1.50	3.00

Classics Illustrated #66 (Orig.), © GIL

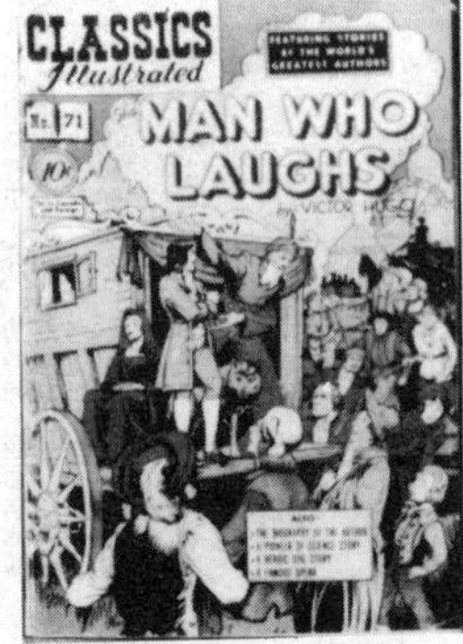

Classics Illustrated #71, © GIL

Classics Illustrated #73, © GIL

Classics Illustrated #78 (HRN 128), © GIL

Classics Illustrated #84 (HRN 167), © GIL

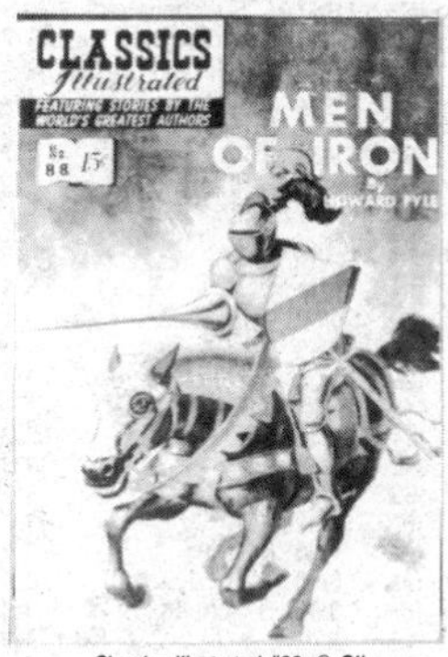

Classics Illustrated #88, © GIL

CLASSICS ILLUSTRATED (continued)

78. Joan of Arc

Ed	HRN	Date	Details	A C	Good	Fine	Mint
1	78	12/50	Original; Kiefer-a,c	1 1	3.00	9.00	21.00
2	87	9/51	New price 15¢; LDC-r	1 1	1.15	3.50	8.00
3	113	11/53	LDC-r	1 1	.70	2.00	5.00
4	128	9/55	New-c; PC-r	1 2	1.00	3.00	7.00
5	140	9/57	PC-r	1 2	.50	1.50	3.00
6	150	5/59	PC-r	1 2	.50	1.50	3.00
7	159	11/60	PC-r	1 2	.50	1.50	3.00
8	167	'62/63	PC-r	1 2	.50	1.50	3.00
9	167	12/63	PC-r	1 2	.50	1.50	3.00
10	167	6/65	PC-r	1 2	.50	1.50	3.00
11	166	6/67	PC-r	1 2	.50	1.50	3.00
12	166	Win/69	New-c&price, 25¢; PC-r; stiff-c	1 3	1.70	5.00	12.00

79. Cyrano de Bergerac

Ed	HRN	Date	Details	A C	Good	Fine	Mint
1	78	1/51	Orig.; movie promo inside front-c; Blum-a & c	1 1	3.00	9.00	21.00
2	85	7/51	New price 15¢; LDC-r	1 1	1.15	3.50	8.00
3	118	4/54	LDC-r	1 1	.85	2.50	6.00
4	133	7/56	New-c; PC-r	1 2	1.50	4.50	10.00
5	156	5/60	PC-r	1 2	1.15	3.50	8.00
6	167	8/64	PC-r	1 2	1.15	3.50	8.00

80. White Fang (Last line drawn cover)

Ed	HRN	Date	Details	A C	Good	Fine	Mint
1	79	2/51	Orig.; Blum-a&c	1 1	3.00	9.00	21.00
2	87	9/51	LDC-r	1 1	.85	2.50	6.00
3	125	3/55	LDC-r	1 1	.70	2.00	5.00
4	132	5/56	New-c; PC-r	1 2	.70	2.00	5.00
5	140	9/57	PC-r	1 2	.45	1.30	2.60
6	153	11/59	PC-r	1 2	.45	1.30	2.60
7	167	'62/63	PC-r	1 2	.45	1.30	2.60
8	167	9/64	PC-r	1 2	.45	1.30	2.60
9	167	7/65	PC-r	1 2	.45	1.30	2.60
10	166	6/67	PC-r	1 2	.45	1.30	2.60
11	169	Fall/69	New price 25¢; PC-r; stiff-c	1 2	.50	1.50	3.00

81. The Odyssey (1st painted cover)

Ed	HRN	Date	Details	A C	Good	Fine	Mint
1	82	3/51	Original; Blum-c	1 1	2.00	6.00	14.00
2	167	8/64	PC-r	1 1	.85	2.50	6.00
3	167	10/66	PC-r	1 1	.85	2.50	6.00
4	169	Spr/69	New, stiff-c; PC-r	1 2	1.50	4.50	10.00

82. The Master of Ballantrae

Ed	HRN	Date	Details	A C	Good	Fine	Mint
1	82	4/51	Original; Blum-c	1 1	2.00	6.00	14.00
2	167	8/64	PC-r	1 1	.85	2.50	6.00
3	166	Fall/68	New, stiff-c; PC-r	1 2	1.50	4.50	10.00

83. The Jungle Book

Ed	HRN	Date	Details	A C	Good	Fine	Mint
1	85	5/51	Original; Blum-c Bossert/Blum-a	1 1	2.00	6.00	14.00
2	110	8/53	PC-r	1 1	.70	2.00	4.00
3	125	3/55	PC-r	1 1	.35	1.10	2.20
4	134	5/56	PC-r	1 1	.35	1.10	2.20
5	142	1/58	PC-r	1 1	.35	1.10	2.20
6	150	5/59	PC-r	1 1	.35	1.10	2.20
7	159	11/60	PC-r	1 1	.35	1.10	2.20
8	167	'62/63	PC-r	1 1	.35	1.10	2.20
9	167	3/65	PC-r	1 1	.35	1.10	2.20
10	167	11/65	PC-r	1 1	.35	1.10	2.20
11	167	5/66	PC-r	1 1	.35	1.10	2.20
12	166	R/1968	New c&a; stiff-c; PC-r	2 2	1.50	4.50	10.00

84. The Gold Bug and Other Stories ("The Gold Bug," "The Tell-Tale Heart," "The Cask of Amontillado")

Ed	HRN	Date	Details	A C	Good	Fine	Mint
1	85	6/51	Original; Blum-c/a Palais, Laverly-a	1 1	6.50	19.50	45.00
2	167	7/64	PC-r	1 1	4.00	12.00	28.00

85. The Sea Wolf

Ed	HRN	Date	Details	A C	Good	Fine	Mint
1	85	8/51	Original; Blum-a&c	1 1	2.00	6.00	14.00
2	121	7/54	PC-r	1 1	.50	1.50	3.00
3	132	5/56	PC-r	1 1	.50	1.50	3.00
4	141	11/57	PC-r	1 1	.50	1.50	3.00
5	161	3/61	PC-r	1 1	.50	1.50	3.00
6	167	2/64	PC-r	1 1	.50	1.50	3.00
7	167	11/65	PC-r	1 1	.50	1.50	3.00
8	169	Fall/69	New price 25¢; stiff-c; PC-r	1 1	.50	1.50	3.00

86. Under Two Flags

Ed	HRN	Date	Details	A C	Good	Fine	Mint
1	87	8/51	Original; first delBourgo-a	1 1	2.00	6.00	14.00
2	117	3/54	PC-r	1 1	.40	1.20	2.40
3	139	7/57	PC-r	1 1	.40	1.20	2.40
4	158	9/60	PC-r	1 1	.40	1.20	2.40
5	167	2/64	PC-r	1 1	.40	1.20	2.40
6	167	8/66	PC-r	1 1	.40	1.20	2.40
7	169	Sm/69	New price 25¢; stiff-c; PC-r	1 1	.50	1.50	3.00

87. A Midsummer Nights Dream

Ed	HRN	Date	Details	A C	Good	Fine	Mint
1	87	9/51	Original; Blum c/a	1 1	2.30	7.00	16.00
2	161	3/61	PC-r	1 1	.85	2.50	5.00
3	167	4/64	PC-r	1 1	.70	2.00	4.00
4	167	5/66	PC-r	1 1	.70	2.00	4.00
5	169	Sm/69	New price 25¢; stiff-c; PC-r	1 1	.50	1.50	3.00

88. Men of Iron

Ed	HRN	Date	Details	A C	Good	Fine	Mint
1	89	10/51	Original	1 1	2.00	6.00	14.00
2	154	1/60	PC-r	1 1	.70	2.00	4.00
3	167	1/64	PC-r	1 1	.70	2.00	4.00
4	166	R/1968	New price 25¢; PC-r	1 1	.70	2.00	4.00

89. Crime and Punishment (Cover illo. in **POP**)

Ed	HRN	Date	Details	A C	Good	Fine	Mint
1	89	11/51	Original; Palais-a	1 1	2.30	7.00	16.00
2	152	9/59	PC-r	1 1	.50	1.50	3.00
3	167	4/64	PC-r	1 1	.50	1.50	3.00
4	167	5/66	PC-r	1 1	.50	1.50	3.00
5	169	Fall/69	New price 25¢ stiff-c; PC-r	1 1	.50	1.50	3.00

90. Green Mansions

Ed	HRN	Date	Details	A C	Good	Fine	Mint
1	89	12/51	Original; Blum-a&c	1 1	2.65	8.00	18.00

CLASSICS ILLUSTRATED (continued)

Ed	HRN	Date	Details	A	C	Good	Fine	Mint
2	148	1/59	New L.B. Cole -c; PC-r	1	2	1.35	4.00	8.00
3	165	1962	PC-r	1	2	.50	1.50	3.00
4	167	4/64	PC-r	1	2	.50	1.50	3.00
5	167	9/66	PC-r	1	2	.50	1.50	3.00
6	169	Sm/69	New price 25¢; stiff-c; PC-r	1	2	.50	1.50	3.00

91. The Call of the Wild

Ed	HRN	Date	Details	A	C	Good	Fine	Mint
1	92	1/52	Orig.; delBourgo-a	1	1	2.00	6.00	14.00
2	112	10/53	PC-r	1	1	.50	1.50	3.00
3	125	3/55	'Picture Progress' on back-c; PC-r	1	1	.70	2.00	4.00
4	134	9/56	PC-r	1	1	.50	1.50	3.00
5	143	3/58	PC-r	1	1	.50	1.50	3.00
6	165	1962	PC-r	1	1	.40	1.20	2.40
7	167	1962	PC-r	1	1	.40	1.20	2.40
8	167	4/65	PC-r	1	1	.40	1.20	2.40
9	167	3/66	PC-r	1	1	.40	1.20	2.40
10	167	3/66	Record ed.; PC-r (See Classics Ill. Golden Records)	1	1			
11	166	11/67	PC-r	1	1	.40	1.20	2.40
12	169	Spr/70	New price 25¢; stiff-c; PC-r	1	1	.40	1.20	2.40

92. The Courtship of Miles Standish

Ed	HRN	Date	Details	A	C	Good	Fine	Mint
1	92	2/52	Original; Blum-a&c	1	1	2.00	6.00	14.00
2	165	1962	PC-r	1	1	.50	1.50	3.00
3	167	3/64	PC-r	1	1	.50	1.50	3.00
4	166	5/67	PC-r	1	1	.50	1.50	3.00
5	169	Win/69	New price 25¢ stiff-c; PC-r	1	1	.50	1.50	3.00

93. Pudd'nhead Wilson

Ed	HRN	Date	Details	A	C	Good	Fine	Mint
1	94	3/52	Orig.; Kiefer-a&c;	1	1	2.00	6.00	14.00
2	165	1962	New-c; PC-r	1	2	.85	2.50	6.00
3	167	3/64	PC-r	1	2	.85	2.50	6.00
4	166	R/1968	New price 25¢; soft-c; PC-r	1	2	.85	2.50	6.00

94. David Balfour

Ed	HRN	Date	Details	A	C	Good	Fine	Mint
1	94	4/52	Original; Palais-a	1	1	2.00	6.00	14.00
2	167	5/64	PC-r	1	1	1.15	3.50	8.00
3	166	R/1968	New price 25¢; PC-r	1	1	1.15	3.50	8.00

95. All Quiet on the Western Front

Ed	HRN	Date	Details	A	C	Good	Fine	Mint
1	96	5/52	Orig.; delBourgo-a	1	1	5.00	15.00	35.00
2	99	5/52	Orig.	1	1	4.00	12.00	28.00
3	167	10/64	PC-r	1	1	2.00	6.00	14.00
4	167	11/66	PC-r	1	1	2.00	6.00	14.00

96. Daniel Boone

Ed	HRN	Date	Details	A	C	Good	Fine	Mint
1	97	6/52	Original; Blum-a	1	1	2.00	6.00	14.00
2	117	3/54	PC-r	1	1	.50	1.50	3.00
3	128	9/55	PC-r	1	1	.50	1.50	3.00
4	132	5/56	PC-r	1	1	.50	1.50	3.00
5	134	——	'Story of Jesus' on back-c; PC-r	1	1	.50	1.50	3.00
6	158	9/60	PC-r	1	1	.50	1.50	3.00
7	167	1/64	PC-r	1	1	.50	1.50	3.00
8	167	5/65	PC-r	1	1	.50	1.50	3.00
9	167	11/66	PC-r	1	1	.50	1.50	3.00
10	166	Win/69	New-c; price 25¢; PC-r; stiff-c	1	2	1.50	4.50	10.00

97. King Solomon's Mines

Ed	HRN	Date	Details	A	C	Good	Fine	Mint
1	96	7/52	Orig.; Kiefer-a	1	1	2.35	7.00	16.00
2	118	4/54	PC-r	1	1	1.00	3.00	7.00
3	131	3/56	PC-r	1	1	.70	2.00	4.00
4	141	9/51	PC-r	1	1	.70	2.00	4.00
5	158	9/60	PC-r	1	1	.70	2.00	4.00
6	167	2/64	PC-r	1	1	.70	2.00	4.00
7	167	9/65	PC-r	1	1	.70	2.00	4.00
8	169	Sm/69	New price 25¢; stiff-c; PC-r	1	1	.85	2.50	5.00

98. The Red Badge of Courage

Ed	HRN	Date	Details	A	C	Good	Fine	Mint
1	98	8/52	Original	1	1	2.00	6.00	14.00
2	118	4/54	PC-r	1	1	.45	1.30	2.60
3	132	5/56	PC-r	1	1	.45	1.30	2.60
4	142	1/58	PC-r	1	1	.45	1.30	2.60
5	152	9/59	PC-r	1	1	.45	1.30	2.60
6	161	3/61	PC-r	1	1	.45	1.30	2.60
7	167	'62/63	Has orig.date; PC-r	1	1	.45	1.30	2.60
8	167	9/64	PC-r	1	1	.45	1.30	2.60
9	167	10/65	PC-r	1	1	.45	1.30	2.60
10	166	R/1968	New-c&price 25¢; PC-r; stiff-c	1	2	1.75	5.25	12.00

99. Hamlet (Used in **POP**, pg. 102)

Ed	HRN	Date	Details	A	C	Good	Fine	Mint
1	98	9/52	Original; Blum-a	1	1	2.35	7.00	16.00
2	121	7/54	PC-r	1	1	.70	2.00	4.00
3	141	11/57	PC-r	1	1	.70	2.00	4.00
4	158	9/60	PC-r	1	1	.70	2.00	4.00
5	167	'62/63	Has orig.date; PC-r	1	1	.70	2.00	4.00
6	167	7/65	PC-r	1	1	.70	2.00	4.00
7	166	4/67	PC-r	1	1	.70	2.00	4.00
8	169	Spr/69	New-c&price 25¢; PC-r; stiff-c	1	2	1.50	4.50	10.00

100. Mutiny on the Bounty

Ed	HRN	Date	Details	A	C	Good	Fine	Mint
1	100	10/52	Original	1	1	2.00	6.00	12.00
2	117	3/54	PC-r	1	1	.50	1.50	3.00
3	132	5/56	PC-r	1	1	.50	1.50	3.00
4	142	1/58	PC-r	1	1	.50	1.50	3.00
5	155	3/60	PC-r	1	1	.50	1.50	3.00
6	167	'62/63	Has orig.date; PC-r	1	1	.50	1.50	3.00
7	167	5/64	PC-r	1	1	.50	1.50	3.00
8	167	3/66	PC-r	1	1	.50	1.50	3.00
9	167	3/66	No # or price; (See Classics Ill. Golden Records)					
10	169	Spr/70	PC-r; stiff-c	1	1	.50	1.50	3.00

101. William Tell

Ed	HRN	Date	Details	A	C	Good	Fine	Mint
1	101	11/52	Original; Kiefer-c delBourgo-a	1	1	2.00	6.00	12.00
2	118	4/54	PC-r	1	1	.45	1.30	3.00
3	141	11/57	PC-r	1	1	.50	1.50	3.00
4	158	9/60	PC-r	1	1	.50	1.50	3.00
5	167	'62/63	Has orig.date; PC-r	1	1	.50	1.50	3.00
6	167	11/64	PC-r	1	1	.50	1.50	3.00
7	166	4/67	PC-r	1	1	.50	1.50	3.00
8	169	Win/69	New price 25¢; stiff-c; PC-r	1	1	.50	1.50	3.00

Classics Illustrated #91 (HRN 112), © GIL

Classics Illustrated #97 (HRN 131), © GIL

Classics Illustrated #99, © GIL

Classics Illustrated #103, © GIL

Classics Illustrated #107 (HRN 167) © GIL

Classics Illustrated #111 (HRN 167), © GIL

CLASSICS ILLUSTRATED (continued)

102. The White Company

Ed	HRN	Date	Details	A	C	Good	Fine	Mint
1	101	12/52	Original; Blum-a	1	1	2.65	8.00	18.00
2	165	1962	PC-r	1	1	1.50	4.50	10.00
3	167	4/64	PC-r	1	1	1.50	4.50	10.00

103. Men Against the Sea (Palais-a)

Ed	HRN	Date	Details	A	C	Good	Fine	Mint
1	104	1/53	Original; Kiefer-c, Palais-a	1	1	2.00	6.00	14.00
2	114	12/53	PC-r	1	1	1.30	4.00	9.00
3	131	3/56	New-c; PC-r	1	2	1.30	4.00	9.00
4	149	3/59	PC-r	1	2	.70	2.00	4.00
5	158	9/60	PC-r	1	2	.70	2.00	4.00
6	167	3/64	PC-r	1	2	.70	2.00	4.00

104. Bring 'Em Back Alive

Ed	HRN	Date	Details	A	C	Good	Fine	Mint
1	105	2/53	Original; Kiefer c/a	1	1	2.00	6.00	14.00
2	118	4/54	PC-r	1	1	.50	1.50	3.00
3	133	7/56	PC-r	1	1	.50	1.50	3.00
4	150	5/59	PC-r	1	1	.50	1.50	3.00
5	158	9/60	PC-r	1	1	.50	1.50	3.00
6	167	10/63	PC-r	1	1	.50	1.50	3.00
7	167	9/65	PC-r	1	1	.50	1.50	3.00
8	169	Win/69	New price 25¢; stiff-c; PC-r	1	1	.50	1.50	3.00

105. From the Earth to the Moon

Ed	HRN	Date	Details	A	C	Good	Fine	Mint
1	106	3/53	Original; Blum-a	1	1	1.50	4.50	10.00
2	118	4/54	PC-r	1	1	.40	1.20	2.40
3	132	3/56	PC-r	1	1	.40	1.20	2.40
4	141	11/57	PC-r	1	1	.40	1.20	2.40
5	146	9/58	PC-r	1	1	.40	1.20	2.40
6	156	5/60	PC-r	1	1	.40	1.20	2.40
7	167	'62/63	Has orig.date; PC-r	1	1	.40	1.20	2.40
8	167	5/64	PC-r	1	1	.40	1.20	2.40
9	167	5/65	PC-r	1	1	.40	1.20	2.40
10	166	10/67	PC-r	1	1	.40	1.20	2.40
11	169	Sm/69	New price 25¢; stiff-c; PC-r	1	1	.35	1.00	2.00
12	169	Spr/71	PC-r	1	1	.35	1.00	2.00

106. Buffalo Bill

Ed	HRN	Date	Details	A	C	Good	Fine	Mint
1	107	4/53	Orig.; delBourgo-a	1	1	1.50	4.50	10.00
2	118	4/54	PC-r	1	1	.40	1.20	2.40
3	132	3/56	PC-r	1	1	.40	1.20	2.40
4	142	1/58	PC-r	1	1	.40	1.20	2.40
5	161	3/61	PC-r	1	1	.40	1.20	2.40
6	167	3/64	PC-r	1	1	.40	1.20	2.40
7	166	7/67	PC-r	1	1	.40	1.20	2.40
8	169	Fall/69	PC-r; stiff-c	1	1	.40	1.20	2.40

107. King of the Khyber Rifles

Ed	HRN	Date	Details	A	C	Good	Fine	Mint
1	108	5/53	Original	1	1	1.70	5.00	12.00
2	118	4/54	PC-r	1	1	.70	2.00	4.00
3	146	9/58	PC-r	1	1	.70	2.00	4.00
4	158	9/60	PC-r	1	1	.70	2.00	4.00
5	167	'62/63	Has orig.date; PC-r	1	1	.70	2.00	4.00
6	167	'62/63	PC-r	1	1	.70	2.00	4.00
7	167	10/66	PC-r	1	1	.70	2.00	4.00

108. Knights of the Round Table

Ed	HRN	Date	Details	A	C	Good	Fine	Mint
1	108	6/53	Original; Blum-a	1	1	2.00	6.00	14.00
2	109	6/53	Original; Blum-a	1	1	2.00	6.00	14.00
3	117	3/54	PC-r	1	1	.50	1.50	3.00
4	153	11/59	PC-r	1	1	.50	1.50	3.00
5	165	1962	PC-r	1	1	.50	1.50	3.00
6	167	4/64	PC-r	1	1	.50	1.50	3.00
7	166	4/67	PC-r	1	1	.50	1.50	3.00
8	169	Sm/69	New price 25¢; stiff-c; PC-r	1	1	.50	1.50	3.00

109. Pitcairn's Island

Ed	HRN	Date	Details	A	C	Good	Fine	Mint
1	110	7/53	Original; Palais-a	1	1	2.65	8.00	18.00
2	165	1962	PC-r	1	1	.70	2.00	5.00
3	167	3/64	PC-r	1	1	.70	2.00	5.00
4	166	6/67	PC-r	1	1	.70	2.00	5.00

110. A Study in Scarlet

Ed	HRN	Date	Details	A	C	Good	Fine	Mint
1	111	8/53	Original	1	1	6.00	18.00	42.00
2	165	1962	PC-r	1	1	4.00	12.00	28.00

111. The Talisman

Ed	HRN	Date	Details	A	C	Good	Fine	Mint
1	112	9/53	Original; last H.C. Kiefer-a	1	1	3.65	11.00	25.00
2	165	1962	PC-r	1	1	.50	1.50	3.00
3	167	5/64	PC-r	1	1	.50	1.50	3.00
4	166	Fall/68	New price 25¢; PC-r	1	1	.50	1.40	2.80

112. Adventures of Kit Carson

Ed	HRN	Date	Details	A	C	Good	Fine	Mint
1	113	10/53	Original; Palais-a	1	1	3.00	9.00	21.00
2	129	11/55	PC-r	1	1	.50	1.40	2.80
3	141	11/57	PC-r	1	1	.50	1.40	2.80
4	152	9/59	PC-r	1	1	.50	1.40	2.80
5	161	3/61	PC-r	1	1	.50	1.40	2.80
6	167	'62/63	PC-r	1	1	.50	1.40	2.80
7	167	2/65	PC-r	1	1	.50	1.40	2.80
8	167	5/66	PC-r	1	1	.50	1.40	2.80
9	166	Win/69	New-c&price 25¢; PC-r; stiff-c	1	2	1.15	3.50	8.00

113. The Forty-Five Guardsmen

Ed	HRN	Date	Details	A	C	Good	Fine	Mint
1	114	11/53	Orig.; delBourgo-a	1	1	3.50	10.50	24.00
2	166	7/67	PC-r	1	1	1.70	5.00	12.00

114. The Red Rover

Ed	HRN	Date	Details	A	C	Good	Fine	Mint
1	115	12/53	Original	1	1	3.50	10.50	24.00
2	166	7/67	PC-r	1	1	1.70	5.00	12.00

115. How I Found Livingstone

Ed	HRN	Date	Details	A	C	Good	Fine	Mint
1	116	1/54	Original	1	1	3.50	10.50	24.00
2	167	1/67	PC-r	1	1	1.70	5.00	12.00

116. The Bottle Imp

Ed	HRN	Date	Details	A	C	Good	Fine	Mint
1	117	2/54	Orig.; Cameron-a	1	1	4.00	12.00	28.00
2	167	1/67	PC-r	1	1	1.70	5.00	12.00

117. Captains Courageous

Ed	HRN	Date	Details	A	C	Good	Fine	Mint
1	118	3/54	Orig.; Costanza-a	1	1	2.65	8.00	18.00
2	167	2/67	PC-r	1	1	.85	2.50	5.00

CLASSICS ILLUSTRATED (continued)

Ed	HRN	Date	Details	A	C	Good	Fine	Mint
3	169	Fall/69	New price 25¢; stiff-c; PC-r	1	1	.70	2.00	4.00

118. Rob Roy

Ed	HRN	Date	Details	A	C	Good	Fine	Mint
1	119	4/54	Original; Rudy & Walter Palais-a	1	1	3.50	10.50	24.00
2	167	2/67	PC-r	1	1	1.70	5.00	12.00

119. Soldiers of Fortune

Ed	HRN	Date	Details	A	C	Good	Fine	Mint
1	120	5/54	Original Shaffenberger-a	1	1	3.00	9.00	21.00
2	166	3/67	PC-r	1	1	1.00	3.00	6.00
3	169	Spr/70	New price 25¢; stiff-c; PC-r	1	1	.70	2.00	4.00

120. The Hurricane

Ed	HRN	Date	Details	A	C	Good	Fine	Mint
1	121	1954	Orig.; Cameron-a	1	1	3.00	9.00	21.00
2	166	3/67	PC-r	1	1	1.70	5.00	12.00

121. Wild Bill Hickok

Ed	HRN	Date	Details	A	C	Good	Fine	Mint
1	122	7/54	Original	1	1	2.00	6.00	14.00
2	132	5/56	PC-r	1	1	.40	1.20	2.40
3	141	11/57	PC-r	1	1	.40	1.20	2.40
4	154	1/60	PC-r	1	1	.40	1.20	2.40
5	167	'62/63	PC-r	1	1	.40	1.20	2.40
6	167	8/64	PC-r	1	1	.40	1.20	2.40
7	166	4/67	PC-r	1	1	.40	1.20	2.40
8	169	Win/69	PC-r; stiff-c	1	1	.50	1.50	3.00

122. The Mutineers

Ed	HRN	Date	Details	A	C	Good	Fine	Mint
1	123	9/54	Original	1	1	1.50	4.50	10.00
2	136	1/57	PC-r	1	1	.40	1.20	2.40
3	146	9/58	PC-r	1	1	.40	1.20	2.40
4	158	9/60	PC-r	1	1	.40	1.20	2.40
5	167	11/63	PC-r	1	1	.35	1.00	2.00
6	167	3/65	PC-r	1	1	.35	1.00	2.00
7	166	8/67	PC-r	1	1	.35	1.00	2.00

123. Fang and Claw

Ed	HRN	Date	Details	A	C	Good	Fine	Mint
1	124	11/54	Original	1	1	2.00	6.00	14.00
2	133	7/56	PC-r	1	1	.45	1.30	2.60
3	143	3/58	PC-r	1	1	.45	1.30	2.60
4	154	1/60	PC-r	1	1	.45	1.30	2.60
5	167	'62/63	Has orig.date; PC-r	1	1	.45	1.30	2.60
6	167	9/65	PC-r	1	1	.45	1.30	2.60

124. The War of the Worlds

Ed	HRN	Date	Details	A	C	Good	Fine	Mint
1	125	1/55	Orig.; Cameron c/a	1	1	1.50	4.50	10.00
2	131	3/56	PC-r	1	1	.45	1.30	2.60
3	141	11/57	PC-r	1	1	.45	1.30	2.60
4	148	1/59	PC-r	1	1	.45	1.30	2.60
5	156	5/60	PC-r	1	1	.45	1.30	2.60
6	165	1962	PC-r	1	1	.45	1.30	2.60
7	167	'62/63	PC-r	1	1	.45	1.30	2.60
8	167	11/64	PC-r	1	1	.45	1.30	2.60
9	167	11/65	PC-r	1	1	.45	1.30	2.60
10	166	R/1968	New price 25¢; PC-r	1	1	.45	1.30	2.60
11	169	Sm/70	PC-r; stiff-c	1	1	.50	1.50	3.00

125. The Ox Bow Incident

Ed	HRN	Date	Details	A	C	Good	Fine	Mint
1	—	3/55	Original	1	1	1.50	4.50	10.00
2	143	3/58	PC-r	1	1	.40	1.20	2.40
3	152	9/59	PC-r	1	1	.40	1.20	2.40
4	149	3/61	PC-r	1	1	.40	1.20	2.40
5	167	'62/63	PC-r	1	1	.40	1.20	2.40
6	167	11/64	PC-r	1	1	.40	1.20	2.40
7	166	4/67	PC-r	1	1	.40	1.20	2.40
8	169	Win/69	New price 25¢; stiff-c; PC-r	1	1	.40	1.20	2.40

126. The Downfall

Ed	HRN	Date	Details	A	C	Good	Fine	Mint
1	—	5/55	Orig.; 'Picture Progress' replaces reorder list; Cameron c/a	1	1	1.50	4.50	10.00
2	167	8/64	PC-r	1	1	.70	2.00	4.00
3	166	R/1968	New price 25 ¢ PC-r	1	1	.70	2.00	4.00

127. The King of the Mountains

Ed	HRN	Date	Details	A	C	Good	Fine	Mint
1	128	7/55	Original	1	1	1.50	4.50	10.00
2	167	6/64	PC-r	1	1	.70	2.00	5.00
3	166	F/1968	New price 25¢; PC-r	1	1	.70	2.00	5.00

128. Macbeth (Used in **POP**, pg. 102)

Ed	HRN	Date	Details	A	C	Good	Fine	Mint
1	128	9/55	Orig.; last Blum-a	1	1	2.65	8.00	18.00
2	143	3/58	PC-r	1	1	.45	1.30	2.60
3	158	9/60	PC-r	1	1	.45	1.30	2.60
4	167	'62/63	PC-r	1	1	.45	1.30	2.60
5	167	6/64	PC-r	1	1	.45	1.30	2.60
6	166	4/67	PC-r	1	1	.45	1.30	2.60
7	166	R/1968	New Price 25¢; PC-r	1	1	.35	1.00	2.00
8	169	Spr/70	Stiff-c; PC-r	1	1	.35	1.00	2.00

129. Davy Crockett

Ed	HRN	Date	Details	A	C	Good	Fine	Mint
1	129	11/55	Orig.; Cameron-a	1	1	3.50	10.50	24.00
2	167	9/66	PC-r	1	1	2.00	6.00	14.00

130. Caesar's Conquests

Ed	HRN	Date	Details	A	C	Good	Fine	Mint
1	130	1/56	Original; Orlando-a	1	1	1.50	4.50	10.00
2	142	1/58	PC-r	1	1	.40	1.20	2.40
3	152	9/59	PC-r	1	1	.40	1.20	2.40
4	149	3/61	PC-r	1	1	.40	1.20	2.40
5	167	'62/63	PC-r	1	1	.40	1.20	2.40
6	167	10/64	PC-r	1	1	.40	1.20	2.40
7	167	4/66	PC-r	1	1	.40	1.20	2.40

131. The Covered Wagon

Ed	HRN	Date	Details	A	C	Good	Fine	Mint
1	131	3/56	Original	1	1	1.50	4.50	10.00
2	143	3/58	PC-r	1	1	.40	1.20	2.40
3	152	9/59	PC-r	1	1	.40	1.20	2.40
4	158	9/60	PC-r	1	1	.40	1.20	2.40
5	167	'62/63	PC-r	1	1	.40	1.20	2.40
6	167	11/64	PC-r	1	1	.40	1.20	2.40
7	167	4/66	PC-r	1	1	.40	1.20	2.40
8	169	Win/69	New price 25 cents; stiff-c; PC-r	1	1	.40	1.20	2.40

Classics Illustrated #124 (Orig.), © GIL

Classics Illustrated #127 (Orig.), © GIL

Classics Illustrated #130 (Orig.), © GIL

Classics Illustrated #133 (HRN 167), © GIL

Classics Illustrated #138, © GIL

Classics Illustrated #140 (HRN 160), © GIL

CLASSICS ILLUSTRATED (continued)

131. The Covered Wagon

Ed	HRN	Date	Details	A	C	Good	Fine	Mint
1	131	3/56	Original	1	1	1.50	4.50	10.00
2	143	3/58	PC-r	1	1	.40	1.20	2.40
3	152	9/59	PC-r	1	1	.40	1.20	2.40
4	158	9/60	PC-r	1	1	.40	1.20	2.40
5	167	'62/63	PC-r	1	1	.40	1.20	2.40
6	167	11/64	PC-r	1	1	.40	1.20	2.40
7	167	4/66	PC-r	1	1	.40	1.20	2.40
8	169	Win/69	New price 25 cents; stiff-c; PC-r	1	1	.40	1.20	2.40

132. The Dark Frigate

Ed	HRN	Date	Details	A	C	Good	Fine	Mint
1	132	5/56	Original	1	1	1.50	4.50	10.00
2	150	5/59	PC-r	1	1	.40	1.20	2.40
3	167	1/64	PC-r	1	1	.40	1.20	2.40
4	166	5/67	PC-r	1	1	.40	1.20	2.40

133. The Time Machine

Ed	HRN	Date	Details	A	C	Good	Fine	Mint
1	132	7/56	Orig.; Cameron-a	1	1	2.30	7.00	16.00
2	142	1/58	PC-r	1	1	.60	1.80	4.20
3	152	9/59	PC-r	1	1	.60	1.80	4.20
4	158	9/60	PC-r	1	1	.60	1.80	4.20
5	167	'62/63	PC-r	1	1	.60	1.80	4.20
6	167	6/64	PC-r	1	1	.60	1.80	4.20
7	167	3/66	PC-r	1	1	.60	1.80	4.20
8	167	3/66	No # or price; (See Classics Ill. Golden Record)					
9	166	12/67	PC-r	1	1	.60	1.80	4.20
10	169	Win/71	New price 25 cents; stiff-c; PC-r	1	1	.85	2.50	6.00

134. Romeo and Juliet

Ed	HRN	Date	Details	A	C	Good	Fine	Mint
1	134	9/56	Original; Evans-a	1	1	1.50	4.50	10.00
2	161	3/61	PC-r	1	1	.50	1.50	3.00
3	167	9/63	PC-r	1	1	.50	1.50	3.00
4	167	5/65	PC-r	1	1	.50	1.50	3.00
5	166	6/67	PC-r	1	1	.50	1.50	3.00
6	166	Win/69	New c&price 25¢; stiff-c; PC-r	1	2	2.30	7.00	16.00

135. Waterloo

Ed	HRN	Date	Details	A	C	Good	Fine	Mint
1	135	11/56	Orig.; G. Ingels-a	1	1	1.50	4.50	10.00
2	153	11/59	PC-r	1	1	.50	1.50	3.00
3	167	'62/63	PC-r	1	1	.50	1.50	3.00
4	167	9/64	PC-r	1	1	.50	1.50	3.00
5	166	R/1968	New price 25 cents; PC-r	1	1	.50	1.50	3.00

136. Lord Jim

Ed	HRN	Date	Details	A	C	Good	Fine	Mint
1	136	1/57	Original; Evans-a	1	1	1.50	4.50	10.00
2	165	'62/63	PC-r	1	1	.50	1.50	3.00
3	167	3/64	PC-r	1	1	.50	1.50	3.00
4	167	9/66	PC-r	1	1	.50	1.50	3.00
5	169	Sm/69	New price 25 cents; stiff-c; PC-r	1	1	.50	1.50	3.00

137. The Little Savage

Ed	HRN	Date	Details	A	C	Good	Fine	Mint
1	136	3/57	Original; Evans-a	1	1	1.50	4.50	10.00
2	148	1/59	PC-r	1	1	.50	1.50	3.00
3	156	5/60	PC-r	1	1	.50	1.50	3.00
4	167	'62/63	PC-r	1	1	.50	1.50	3.00
5	167	10/64	PC-r	1	1	.50	1.50	3.00
6	166	8/67	PC-r	1	1	.50	1.50	3.00
7	169	Spr/70	New price 25 cents; stiff-c; PC-r	1	1	.50	1.50	3.00

138. A Journey to the Center of the Earth

Ed	HRN	Date	Details	A	C	Good	Fine	Mint
1	136	5/57	Original	1	1	1.50	4.50	10.00
2	146	9/58	PC-r	1	1	.50	1.50	3.00
3	156	5/60	PC-r	1	1	.50	1.50	3.00
4	158	9/60	PC-r	1	1	.50	1.50	3.00
5	167	'62/63	PC-r	1	1	.50	1.50	3.00
6	167	6/64	PC-r	1	1	.50	1.50	3.00
7	167	4/66	PC-r	1	1	.50	1.50	3.00
8	166	R/1968	New price 25 cents; PC-r	1	1	.50	1.50	3.00

139. In the Reign of Terror

Ed	HRN	Date	Details	A	C	Good	Fine	Mint
1	139	7/57	Original; Evans-a	1	1	1.50	4.50	10.00
2	154	1/60	PC-r	1	1	.50	1.50	3.00
3	167	'62/63	Has orig.date; PC-r	1	1	.50	1.50	3.00
4	167	7/64	PC-r	1	1	.50	1.50	3.00
5	166	R/1968	New price 25 cents; PC-r	1	1	.50	1.50	3.00

140. On Jungle Trails

Ed	HRN	Date	Details	A	C	Good	Fine	Mint
1	140	9/57	Original	1	1	1.50	4.50	10.00
2	150	5/59	PC-r	1	1	.50	1.50	3.00
3	160	1/61	PC-r	1	1	.50	1.50	3.00
4	167	9/63	PC-r	1	1	.50	1.50	3.00
5	167	9/65	PC-r	1	1	.50	1.50	3.00

141. Castle Dangerous

Ed	HRN	Date	Details	A	C	Good	Fine	Mint
1	141	11/57	Original	1	1	1.50	4.50	10.00
2	152	9/59	PC-r	1	1	.50	1.50	3.00
3	167	'62/63	PC-r	1	1	.40	1.20	2.40
4	166	7/67	PC-r	1	1	.40	1.20	2.40

142. Abraham Lincoln

Ed	HRN	Date	Details	A	C	Good	Fine	Mint
1	142	1/58	Original	1	1	1.50	4.50	10.00
2	154	1/60	PC-r	1	1	.40	1.20	2.40
3	158	9/60	PC-r	1	1	.40	1.20	2.40
4	167	10/63	PC-r	1	1	.40	1.20	2.40
5	167	7/65	PC-r	1	1	.40	1.20	2.40
6	166	11/67	PC-r	1	1	.40	1.20	2.40
7	169	Fall/69	New price 25 cents; stiff-c; PC-r	1	1	.50	1.50	3.00

143. Kim

Ed	HRN	Date	Details	A	C	Good	Fine	Mint
1	143	3/58	Original; Orlando-a	1	1	1.50	4.50	10.00
2	165	'62/63	PC-r	1	1	.40	1.20	2.40
3	167	11/63	PC-r	1	1	.40	1.20	2.40
4	167	8/65	PC-r	1	1	.40	1.20	2.40
5	169	Win/69	New price 25 cents; stiff-c; PC-r	1	1	.50	1.50	3.00

144. The First Men in the Moon

Ed	HRN	Date	Details	A	C	Good	Fine	Mint
1	143	5/58	Original; Wood-bridge/Williamson/Torres-a	1	1	2.00	6.00	14.00
2	153	11/59	PC-r	1	1	.50	1.50	3.00
3	161	3/61	PC-r	1	1	.50	1.50	3.00

CLASSICS ILLUSTRATED (continued)

Ed	HRN	Date	Details	A C	Good	Fine	Mint
4	167	'62/63	PC-r	1 1	.50	1.50	3.00
5	167	12/65	PC-r	1 1	.50	1.50	3.00
6	166	Fall/68	New-c&price 25¢; PC-r; stiff-c	1 2	.85	2.50	6.00
7	169	Win/69	Stiff-c; PC-r	1 2	.85	2.50	6.00

145. The Crisis

Ed	HRN	Date	Details	A C	Good	Fine	Mint
1	143	7/58	Original; Evans-a	1 1	1.50	4.50	10.00
2	156	5/60	PC-r	1 1	.45	1.40	2.80
3	167	10/63	PC-r	1 1	.45	1.40	2.80
4	167	3/65	PC-r	1 1	.45	1.40	2.80
5	166	R/1968	New price 25¢; PC-r	1 1	.45	1.40	2.80

146. With Fire and Sword

Ed	HRN	Date	Details	A C	Good	Fine	Mint
1	143	9/58	Original; Woodbridge-a	1 1	1.50	4.50	10.00
2	156	5/60	PC-r	1 1	.70	2.00	4.00
3	167	11/63	PC-r	1 1	.70	2.00	4.00
4	167	3/65	PC-r	1 1	.70	2.00	4.00

147. Ben-Hur

Ed	HRN	Date	Details	A C	Good	Fine	Mint
1	147	11/58	Original; Orlando-a	1 1	1.70	5.00	12.00
2	153	11/59	PC-r	1 1	.50	1.50	3.00
3	158	9/60	PC-r	1 1	.50	1.50	3.00
4	167	'62/63	Orig.date; but PC-r	1 1	.50	1.50	3.00
5	167	———	PC-r	1 1	.50	1.50	3.00
6	167	2/65	PC-r	1 1	.50	1.50	3.00
7	167	9/66	PC-r	1 1	.50	1.50	3.00
8	166	Fall/68	New-c&price 25¢; PC-r; hard cover. . .	1 2	1.50	4.50	10.00
			soft cover.		2.65	8.00	18.00

148. The Buccaneer

Ed	HRN	Date	Details	A C	Good	Fine	Mint
1	148	1/59	Orig.; Evans/Jenny-a; Saunders-c	1 1	1.50	4.50	10.00
2	568	———	Juniors list only PC-r	1 1	.85	2.50	6.00
3	167	'62/63	PC-r	1 1	.50	1.50	3.00
4	167	9/65	PC-r	1 1	.50	1.50	3.00
5	169	Sm/69	New price 25¢; PC-r; stiff-c	1 1	.50	1.50	3.00

149. Off on a Comet

Ed	HRN	Date	Details	A C	Good	Fine	Mint
1	149	3/59	Orig.; G.McCann-a	1 1	1.70	5.00	12.00
2	155	3/60	PC-r	1 1	.50	1.50	3.00
3	149	3/61	PC-r	1 1	.50	1.50	3.00
4	167	12/63	PC-r	1 1	.40	1.20	2.40
5	167	2/65	PC-r	1 1	.40	1.20	2.40
6	167	10/66	PC-r	1 1	.40	1.20	2.40
7	166	Fall/68	New-c&price 25¢; PC-r	1 2	1.50	4.50	10.00

150. The Virginian

Ed	HRN	Date	Details	A C	Good	Fine	Mint
1	150	5/59	Original	1 1	2.00	6.00	14.00
2	164	1961	PC-r	1 1	.85	2.50	6.00
3	167	'62/63	PC-r	1 1	.85	2.50	6.00
4	167	12/65	PC-r	1 1	.85	2.50	6.00

151. Won By the Sword

Ed	HRN	Date	Details	A C	Good	Fine	Mint
1	150	7/59	Original	1 1	2.00	6.00	14.00
2	164	1961	PC-r	1 1	.70	2.00	4.00
3	167	10/63	PC-r	1 1	.70	2.00	4.00
4	167	1963	PC-r	1 1	.70	2.00	4.00
5	166	7/67	PC-r	1 1	.70	2.00	4.00

152. Wild Animals I Have Known

Ed	HRN	Date	Details	A C	Good	Fine	Mint
1	152	9/59	Orig.; L.B. Cole c/a	1 1	2.00	6.00	14.00
2	149	3/61	PC-r	1 1	.70	2.00	4.00
3	167	9/63	PC-r	1 1	.50	1.50	3.00
4	167	8/65	PC-r	1 1	.50	1.50	3.00
5	169	Fall/69	New price 25¢; stiff-c; PC-r	1 1	.50	1.50	3.00

153. The Invisible Man

Ed	HRN	Date	Details	A C	Good	Fine	Mint
1	153	11/59	Original	1 1	1.50	4.50	10.00
2	149	3/61	PC-r	1 1	.50	1.50	3.00
3	167	'62/63	PC-r	1 1	.50	1.50	3.00
4	167	2/65	PC-r	1 1	.50	1.50	3.00
5	167	9/66	PC-r	1 1	.50	1.50	3.00
6	166	Win/69	New price 25¢; PC-r; stiff-c	1 1	.50	1.50	3.00
7	169	Spr/71	Stiff-c; letters spelling 'Invisible Man' are 'solid' not'invisible;' PC-r	1 1	.50	1.50	3.00

154. The Conspiracy of Pontiac

Ed	HRN	Date	Details	A C	Good	Fine	Mint
1	154	1/60	Original	1 1	2.00	6.00	14.00
2	167	11/63	PC-r	1 1	1.00	3.00	7.00
3	167	7/64	PC-r	1 1	1.00	3.00	7.00
4	166	12/67	PC-r	1 1	1.00	3.00	7.00

155. The Lion of the North

Ed	HRN	Date	Details	A C	Good	Fine	Mint
1	154	3/60	Original	1 1	1.15	3.50	8.00
2	167	1/64	PC-r	1 1	1.00	3.00	7.00
3	166	R/1967	New price 25¢; PC-r	1 1	1.00	3.00	7.00

156. The Conquest of Mexico

Ed	HRN	Date	Details	A C	Good	Fine	Mint
1	156	5/60	Orig.; Bruno Premiani-a&c	1 1	1.50	4.50	10.00
2	167	1/64	PC-r	1 1	.70	2.00	5.00
3	166	8/67	PC-r	1 1	.70	2.00	5.00
4	169	Spr/70	New price 25¢; stiff-c; PC-r	1 1	.70	2.00	5.00

157. Lives of the Hunted

Ed	HRN	Date	Details	A C	Good	Fine	Mint
1	156	7/60	Orig.; L.B. Cole-c	1 1	1.70	5.00	12.00
2	167	2/64	PC-r	1 1	1.30	4.00	9.00
3	166	10/67	PC-r	1 1	1.30	4.00	9.00

158. The Conspirators

Ed	HRN	Date	Details	A C	Good	Fine	Mint
1	156	9/60	Original	1 1	1.75	5.25	12.00
2	167	7/64	PC-r	1 1	1.30	4.00	9.00
3	166	10/67	PC-r	1 1	1.30	4.00	9.00

159. The Octopus

Ed	HRN	Date	Details	A C	Good	Fine	Mint
1	159	11/60	Orig.; Gray Morrow & Evans-a;	1 1	1.50	4.50	10.00

Classics Illustrated #148, © GIL

Classics Illustrated #149, © GIL

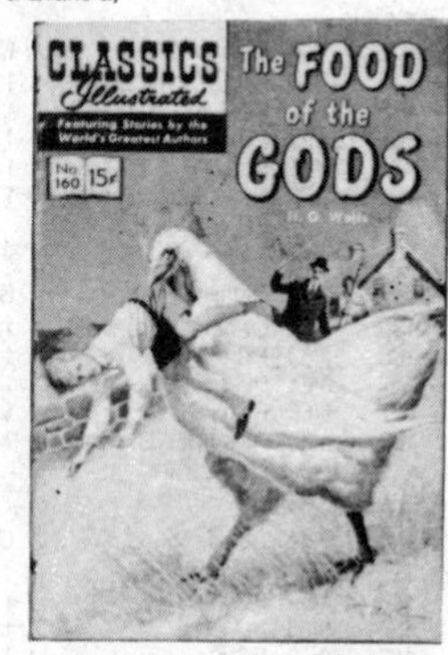

CLASSICS
Illustrated
The FOOD
of the
GODS
No. 160
15¢

Classics Illustrated #160 (Orig.), © GIL

Classics Illustrated #163 (Orig.), © GIL

Classics Illustrated #166 (HRN 167), © GIL

Classics Illustrated #169 (Orig.), © GIL

CLASSICS ILLUSTRATED (continued)

Ed	HRN	Date	Details	A C	Good	Fine	Mint
			L.B. Cole-c				
2	167	2/64	PC-r	1 1	.70	2.00	5.00
3	166	R/1967	New price 25; PC-r	1 1	.70	2.00	5.00

160. The Food of the Gods

Ed	HRN	Date	Details	A C	Good	Fine	Mint
1	159	1/61	Original	1 1	2.00	6.00	14.00
2	160	1/61	Original; same, except for HRN	1 1	2.00	6.00	14.00
3	167	1/64	PC-r	1 1	1.00	3.00	7.00
4	166	6/67	PC-r	1 1	1.00	3.00	7.00

161. Cleopatra

Ed	HRN	Date	Details	A C	Good	Fine	Mint
1	161	3/61	Original	1 1	2.65	8.00	18.00
2	167	1/64	PC-r	1 1	1.50	4.50	10.00
3	166	8/67	PC-r	1 1	1.50	4.50	10.00

162. Robur the Conqueror

Ed	HRN	Date	Details	A C	Good	Fine	Mint
1	162	5/61	Original	1 1	2.00	6.00	14.00
2	167	7/64	PC-r	1 1	1.15	3.50	8.00
3	166	8/67	PC-r	1 1	1.15	3.50	8.00

163. Master of the World

Ed	HRN	Date	Details	A C	Good	Fine	Mint
1	163	7/61	Original; Gray Morrow-a	1 1	2.00	6.00	14.00
2	167	1/65	PC-r	1 1	.70	2.00	5.00
3	166	R/1968	New price 25¢; PC-r	1 1	.70	2.00	5.00

164. The Cossack Chief

Ed	HRN	Date	Details	A C	Good	Fine	Mint
1	164	(1961)	Original; undated	1 1	2.30	7.00	16.00
2	167	4/65	PC-r	1 1	1.15	3.50	8.00
3	166	Fall/68	New price 25¢ PC-r	1 1	1.15	3.50	8.00

165. The Queen's Necklace

Ed	HRN	Date	Details	A C	Good	Fine	Mint
1	164	1/62	Original; Morrow-a	1 1	2.30	7.00	16.00
2	167	4/65	PC-r	1 1	1.15	3.50	8.00
3	166	Fall/68	New price 25¢; PC-r	1 1	1.15	3.50	8.00

166. Tigers and Traitors

Ed	HRN	Date	Details	A C	Good	Fine	Mint
1	165	5/62	Original	1 1	2.65	8.00	18.00
2	167	2/64	PC-r	1 1	1.50	4.50	10.00
3	167	11/66	PC-r	1 1	1.50	4.50	10.00

167. Faust

Ed	HRN	Date	Details	A C	Good	Fine	Mint
1	165	8/62	Original	1 1	5.50	16.50	38.00
2	167	2/64	PC-r	1 1	2.65	8.00	18.00
3	166	6/67	PC-r	1 1	2.65	8.00	18.00

168. In Freedom's Cause

Ed	HRN	Date	Details	A C	Good	Fine	Mint
1	169	Win/69	Original; Evans/ Crandall-a; stiff-c	1 1	4.00	12.00	28.00

169. Negro Americans—The Early Years

Ed	HRN	Date	Details	A C	Good	Fine	Mint
1	166	Spr/69	Orig. & last issue; Stiff-c	1 1	5.00	15.00	35.00
2	169	Spr/69	Stiff-c	1 1	4.00	12.00	28.00

CLASSICS NON-SERIES ITEMS
by Dan Malan

In this section we are attempting to organize the wide variety of Classics items which were not really part of the regular series. These include **Giveaways, Newspaper Editions, Gift Boxes, Giants,** and **Records**. All of these either are or contain comic books. There are many other non-comic book Classics collectibles not listed here, including posters, racks, binders, original letters from Gilberton/Twin Circle personnel, and publications containing ads for Classics, such as the teachers' magazine *The Instructor*.

The rarity of almost all of these items must be emphasized. Except for the Twin Circle editions and the 1969 Christmas giveaway, all items listed here vary from scarce to very rare. Some of these items have not been offered for sale in the last five years or so, and there are some items of which only one copy is known to exist. It is therefore very difficult to arrive at an accurate market value. Through the Worldwide Classics Newsletter we have attempted to determine what collectors would pay for these items if they were offered for sale. Three items have been reproduced (Shelter/Westinghouse/Daynor) with color photocopy outsides and black and white photocopy interiors. They state "W.C.N. Reprint" on the front cover. All dealers are encouraged to seek out these rare items.

NEWSPAPER CLASSICS—These are similar to the Spirit Sections, and were issued for one year, from 3/30/47 to 3/21/48. They were printed in the Sunday Funnies sections of various newspapers. At this point the known newspapers are the *New York Post, Queens Home News, Newark Star-Ledger, Chicago Sun, Milwaukee Journal, Indianapolis Star,* and *St. Louis Post-Dispatch*. Each section contains 16 reduced comic book pages. They are very significant because they predate the original comic book editions by as much as three years, and contain 64 pages of text of Classics titles that were issued with 48 pages. The last five newspaper titles were converted from a comic book page format to a comic strip format. Some newspapers did not complete the 14-title series. All of these editions are very rare, and only one copy is known to exist of the newspaper edition of No. 92, Miles Standish. *Indianapolis Star* editions are in black and white, and would be worth slightly less, and *St. Louis Post-Dispatch* editions are in strip format throughout, and would be worth slightly more.

The above newspaper editions must be distinguished from the Twin Circle newspaper editions issued from 1967-1976 of over 100 Classics titles, included with the Catholic newspaper. Those later newspaper editions are listed in Charles Heffelfinger's Handbook.

Cl#	Section	Date	Good	Fine	Mint
#46. Kidnapped					
	1 of 4	3/30/47	5.00	15.00	35.00
	2 of 4	4/06/47	5.00	15.00	35.00
	3 of 4	4/13/47	5.00	15.00	35.00
	4 of 4	4/20/47	5.00	15.00	35.00
#47. 20,000 Leagues Below the Sea					
	1 of 4	4/27/47	5.00	15.00	35.00
	2 of 4	5/04/47	5.00	15.00	35.00
	3 of 4	5/11/47	5.00	15.00	35.00
	4 of 4	5/18/47	3.00	9.00	21.00
#48. David Copperfield					
	1 of 4	5/25/47	5.00	15.00	35.00
	2 of 4	6/01/47	5.00	15.00	35.00
	3 of 4	6/08/47	5.00	15.00	35.00
	4 of 4	6/15/47	5.00	15.00	35.00
#49. Alice in Wonderland					
	1 of 4	6/22/47	5.00	15.00	35.00
	2 of 4	6/29/47	5.00	15.00	35.00
	3 of 4	7/06/47	5.00	15.00	35.00
	4 of 4	7/13/47	5.00	15.00	35.00
#51. The Spy					
	1 of 4	7/20/47	5.00	15.00	35.00
	2 of 4	7/27/47	5.00	15.00	35.00
	3 of 4	8/03/47	5.00	15.00	35.00
	4 of 4	8/10/47	5.00	15.00	35.00

NEWSPAPER CLASSICS (continued)

Cl#	Section	Date	Good	Fine	Mint
#50. Tom Sawyer					
	1 of 4	8/17/47	5.00	15.00	35.00
	2 of 4	8/24/47	5.00	15.00	35.00
	3 of 4	8/31/47	5.00	15.00	35.00
	4 of 4	9/07/47	5.00	15.00	35.00
#52. House of the Seven Gables					
	1 of 4	9/14/47	5.00	15.00	35.00
	2 of 4	9/21/47	5.00	15.00	35.00
	3 of 4	9/28/47	5.00	15.00	35.00
	4 of 4	10/05/47	5.00	15.00	35.00
#68. Julius Caesar					
	1 of 4	10/12/47	6.00	18.00	42.00
	2 of 4	10/19/47	6.00	18.00	42.00
	3 of 4	10/26/47	6.00	18.00	42.00
	4 of 4	11/02/47	6.00	18.00	42.00
#55. Silas Marner					
	1 of 4	11/09/47	6.00	18.00	42.00
	2 of 4	11/16/47	6.00	18.00	42.00
	3 of 4	11/23/47	6.00	18.00	42.00
	4 of 4	11/30/47	6.00	18.00	42.00
#53. A Christmas Carol					
	1 of 3	12/07/47	7.00	21.00	50.00
	2 of 3	12/14/47	7.00	21.00	50.00
	3 of 3	12/21/47	7.00	21.00	50.00
#75. Lady of the Lake					
	1 of 4	12/28/47	6.00	18.00	42.00
	2 of 4	1/04/48	6.00	18.00	42.00
	3 of 4	1/11/48	6.00	18.00	42.00
	4 of 4	1/18/48	6.00	18.00	42.00
#54. Man in the Iron Mask					
	1 of 4	1/25/48	6.00	18.00	42.00
	2 of 4	2/01/48	6.00	18.00	42.00
	3 of 4	2/08/48	6.00	18.00	42.00
	4 of 4	2/15/48	6.00	18.00	42.00
#56. Toilers of the Sea					
	1 of 4	2/22/48	7.00	21.00	50.00
	2 of 4	2/29/48	7.00	21.00	50.00
	3 of 4	3/07/48	7.00	21.00	50.00
	4 of 4	3/14/48	7.00	21.00	50.00
#92. The Courtship of Miles Standish					
	1 of 1	3/21/48	20.00	60.00	140.00

Note: St. Louis Post-Dispatch sections worth 50% more than above.
* Listing researched and contributed by Dan Malan.

CLASSICS GIFT BOXES (Very Rare)

Classic Comics Library Gift Boxes (& Classics Illustrated...)
Note: *Prices listed are for the box ONLY! The value of any contents should be determined independently. There are variations of these boxes: two-piece/one-piece with end flaps; different colors or illustrations on the box-face; and Classic Comics/Classics Illustrated logo change. Each variation is by itself very rare.*

Box A containing #1-5 first appeared 12/42 as advertised on #7 (0). When first offered, it would have contained originals, but later would have contained reprints. The initial box-face illustration showed stories 1-6, but actually only contained 1-5.
Box B containing #6-10 first appeared 11/43 as advertised on #15 (0). When first offered, it would have contained either originals or the first reprint edition, but later would contain current reprints.
Box C containing #11-15 also first appeared 11/43 as per #15 (0), with same edition content variations as Box B.
Box D containing #16-20 first appeared 6/44 as advertised on #20 (0). When first offered, it would have contained partly originals and first reprint editions, but later would contain current reprints.

Box A/B/C/D (any variations)...... 47.00 140.00 330.00

Christmas Gift Boxes (Very Rare)

Series 4V (1950?) contained early LDC reprints of 17, 24, 47, 50.
Series 4W contained 64, 76 (first LDC reprints), & 82, 98 (originals).
Series 4X contained 52, 69, 80 (first LDC reprints) & 97 (original).
Series 4Y contained 19, 67, 79 (early LDC reprints) & 91 (original).
Series 4Z contained 63 (first LDC reprint) & 86, 90, 95 (originals).

NOTE: *Series 4W, 4X, 4Y, 4Z probably all came out Christmas 1952.*

Series 4V/4W/4X/4Y/4Z each...... 40.00 120.00 280.00

CLASSICS GIVEAWAYS (Arranged in chronological order)

1942—Double Comics containing CC#1 (orig.) (diff. cover) (not actually a giveaway) (very rare) (see also Double Comics) 100.00 300.00 700.00
12/42—Saks 34th St. Giveaway containing CC#7 (orig.) (diff. cover) (very rare) 70.00 210.00 500.00
2/43—American Comics containing CC#8 (orig.) (Liberty Theatre Giveaway) (diff. cover) (only one known copy) (see American Comics) 60.00 180.00 420.00
12/44—Robin Hood Flour Co. Giveaway - #7-CC(R) (diff. cover) (rare) (edition probably 7 [22]) 57.00 170.00 400.00

NOTE: *How are above editions determined without CC covers? 1942 is dated 1942, and CC#1-first reprint did not come out until 5/43. 12/42 and 2/43 are determined by blue note at bottom of first text page only in original edition. 12/44 is estimate from page width—each reprint edition had progressively slightly smaller page width.*

1951—Shelter Thru the Ages (C.I. Educational Series) (actually Giveaway by the Ruberoid Co.) (16 pgs.) (contains original artwork by H. C. Kiefer) (there are back cover ad variations) (scarce) 35.00 105.00 245.00
1952—George Daynor Biography Giveaway (CC logo) (partly comic book/pictures/newspaper articles) (story of man who built Palace Depression out of junkyard swamp in NJ) (64 pgs.) (very rare) 70.00 210.00 500.00
1953—Westinghouse/Dreams of a Man (C.I. Educational Series) (Westinghouse bio./Westinghouse Co. giveaway) (contains original artwork by H. C. Kiefer) (16 pgs.) (also French/Spanish/Italian versions) (scarce) 35.00 105.00 245.00

NOTE: *Reproductions of 1951, 1952, and 1953 exist — color photocopy covers and black & white photocopy interior ("W.C.N. Reprint")* 1.00 3.00 7.00

51-53—Coward Shoe Giveaways (all editions very rare) (two variations of back cover Coward Shoe ads) 5 (87), 12 (89), 49 (85), 69 (87), 96 (0), 98 (0), 100 (0), 101 (0), 103 (0), 104 (0), 105 (0), 108 (0), 112 (0). (some above editions recently discovered—some only one copy currently known to exist) 12.00 36.00 84.00
1956—Ben Franklin 5-10 Store Giveaway (#65-PC with back cover ad) (scarce) 13.00 40.00 90.00
1956—Ben Franklin Insurance Co. Giveaway (#65-PC with diff. back cover ad) (very rare) 20.00 60.00 140.00
11/56—Sealtest Co. Edition - #4 (135) (identical to regular edition except for Sealtest logo printed, not stamped, on front cover) (only one copy known to exist) 15.00 45.00 105.00
1958—Get-Well Giveaway containing #15-CI (new cartoon-type cover) (Pressman Pharmacy) (only one copy known to exist) 15.00 45.00 105.00
67-68—Twin Circle Giveaway Editions - all HRN 166, with back cover ad for National Catholic Press.

	Good	Fine	Mint
2(R68), 4(R67), 10(R68), 13(R68), 48(R67), 68(R67)......	1.50	4.50	10.00
16 (R68)......	4.00	12.00	28.00
128 (R68)......	2.35	7.00	16.00
535 (576-R68)......	5.00	15.00	35.00

12/69—Christmas Giveaway ("A Christmas Adventure") (reprints Picture Parade #4-1953, new cover) (4 ad variations)

	Good	Fine	Mint
Stacy's Dept. Store......	1.65	5.00	12.00
Anne & Hard Store......	5.00	15.00	35.00
"Merry Christmas" & blank ad space..	2.00	6.00	14.00

CLASSICS ILLUSTRATED RECORDS

1958—Science Fiction Record: C.I. #105, 124, 133, 144 (narration of Classics Illustrated stories) (very rare) 15.00 45.00 105.00
1958—C. I. Juniors Record: C.I. Juniors #502, 504, 505, 507, 509, 512, 513, 514, 520, 525, 531, 535 (Robert Q. Lewis narration of Juniors stories) (advertised on some Juniors editions) (very rare) 14.00 42.00 98.00
1966—Golden Records Great Literature Series (SLP-189: Black Beauty, SLP-190: Mutiny on the Bounty, SLP-191: The Time Machine, SLP-192: The Call of the Wild) ($2.49 retail for comic and record) (scarce)

	Good	Fine	Mint
Comic only......	1.50	4.50	10.00
Comic & Record......	11.00	33.00	76.00

CLASSICS ILLUSTRATED GIANTS
February, 1948 (One-Shots - "OS")
Gilberton Publications

These Giant Editions were on sale for two years, beginning in 1948. They were 50 cents on the newsstand and 60 cents by mail. They are actually four classics in one volume. All the stories are reprints of the Classics Illustrated Series. NOTE: *There were also British hardback Adventure & Indian Giants in 1952, with the same covers but different contents: Adventure - 2, 7, 10; Indian - 17, 22, 37, 58. They are also rare.*

"An Illustrated Library of Great Adventure Stories" - reprints of No. 6,7,8,10 (Rare); Kiefer-c 60.00 180.00 420.00
"An Illustrated Library of Exciting Mystery Stories" - reprints of No. 30,21,40,13 (Rare) 62.00 185.00 435.00
"An Illustrated Library of Great Indian Stories" - reprints of No. 4,17, 22,37 (Rare) 55.00 165.00 385.00

CLASSICS ILLUSTRATED JUNIOR
Oct, 1953 - Spring, 1971
Famous Authors Ltd. (Gilberton Publications)

Original editions have ad for the next issue. Reprints are worth 50 per cent less than originals. Prices listed are for originals.

	Good	Fine	Mint
501-Snow White & the Seven Dwarfs; Alex Blum-a	10.00	30.00	70.00
502-The Ugly Duckling	5.00	15.00	35.00
503-Cinderella	2.00	6.00	14.00
504-The Pied Piper	1.50	4.50	10.00
505-The Sleeping Beauty	1.15	3.50	8.00

Classics Illustrated Junior #518, © GIL

Classics Illustrated Special Issue #167A, © GIL

Classic X-Men #1, © MCG

CLASSICS ILL. JR. (continued)	**Good**	**Fine**	**Mint**
506-The Three Little Pigs	1.15	3.50	8.00
507-Jack & the Beanstalk	1.50	4.50	10.00
508-Goldilocks & the Three Bears	1.15	3.50	8.00
509-Beauty and the Beast	1.50	4.50	10.00
510-Little Red Riding Hood	1.50	4.50	10.00
511-Puss-N-Boots	1.15	3.50	8.00
512-Rumpel Stiltskin	1.50	4.50	10.00
513-Pinocchio	4.00	12.00	28.00
514-The Steadfast Tin Soldier	4.60	14.00	32.00
515-Johnny Appleseed	1.70	5.00	12.00
516-Aladdin and His Lamp	4.60	14.00	32.00
517-The Emperor's New Clothes	1.70	5.00	12.00
518-The Golden Goose	1.70	5.00	12.00
519-Paul Bunyan	1.50	4.50	10.00
520-Thumbelina	2.65	8.00	18.00
521-King of the Golden River	1.70	5.00	12.00
522-The Nightingale	1.50	4.50	10.00
523-The Gallant Tailor	1.15	3.50	8.00
524-The Wild Swans	1.15	3.50	8.00
525-The Little Mermaid	1.15	3.50	8.00
526-The Frog Prince	1.70	5.00	12.00
527-The Golden-Haired Giant	1.15	3.50	8.00
528-The Penny Prince	1.50	4.50	10.00
529-The Magic Servants	1.15	3.50	8.00
530-The Golden Bird	1.15	3.50	8.00
531-Rapunzel	1.70	5.00	12.00
532-The Dancing Princesses	1.50	4.50	10.00
533-The Magic Fountain	1.50	4.50	10.00
534-The Golden Touch	1.50	4.50	10.00
535-The Wizard of Oz	4.00	12.00	28.00
536-The Chimney Sweep	1.15	3.50	8.00
537-The Three Fairies	1.15	3.50	8.00
538-Silly Hans	1.15	3.50	8.00
539-The Enchanted Fish	4.00	12.00	28.00
540-The Tinder-Box	6.00	18.00	42.00
541-Snow White & Rose Red	2.00	6.00	14.00
542-The Donkey's Tale	3.00	9.00	21.00
543-The House in the Woods	1.50	4.50	10.00
544-The Golden Fleece	4.00	12.00	28.00
545-The Glass Mountain	1.70	5.00	12.00
546-The Elves & the Shoemaker	2.65	8.00	18.00
547-The Wishing Table	1.30	4.00	9.00
548-The Magic Pitcher	1.00	3.00	7.00
549-Simple Kate	1.00	3.00	7.00
550-The Singing Donkey	1.00	3.00	7.00
551-The Queen Bee	1.30	4.00	9.00
552-The Three Little Dwarfs	2.65	8.00	18.00
553-King Thrushbeard	1.00	3.00	7.00
554-The Enchanted Deer	1.30	4.00	9.00
555-The Three Golden Apples	1.00	3.00	7.00
556-The Elf Mound	1.00	3.00	7.00
557-Silly Willy	.75	2.25	5.00
558-The Magic Dish; L.B. Cole-c	1.30	4.00	9.00
559-The Japanese Lantern; 1 pg. Ingels-a; L.B. Cole-c	3.50	10.50	24.00
560-The Doll Princess; L.B. Cole-c	1.30	4.00	9.00
561-Hans Humdrum; L.B. Cole-c	1.30	4.00	9.00
562-The Enchanted Pony; L.B. Cole-c	2.65	8.00	18.00
563-The Wishing Well; L.B. Cole-c	1.70	5.00	12.00
564-The Salt Mountain; L.B. Cole-c	1.30	4.00	9.00
565-The Silly Princess; L.B. Cole-c	1.70	5.00	12.00
566-Clumsy Hans; L.B. Cole-c	1.00	3.00	7.00
567-The Bearskin Soldier; L.B. Cole-c	1.00	3.00	7.00
568-The Happy Hedgehog; L.B. Cole-c	1.70	5.00	12.00
569-The Three Giants	1.00	3.00	7.00
570-The Pearl Princess	.85	2.50	6.00
571-How Fire Came to the Indians	1.15	3.50	8.00
572-The Drummer Boy	.85	2.50	6.00
573-The Crystal Ball	1.75	3.50	8.00
574-Brightboots	1.00	3.00	7.00
575-The Fearless Prince	1.30	4.00	9.00
576-The Princess Who Saw Everything	1.70	5.00	12.00
577-The Runaway Dumpling	5.50	16.50	38.00

NOTE: *Last reprint - Spring, 1971.* ***Costanza*** *&* ***Shaffenberger*** *art in many issues.*

CLASSICS ILLUSTRATED LIBRARY GIFT BOX (See Classic Comics Non-Series. . .)

CLASSICS ILLUSTRATED SPECIAL ISSUE
Dec, 1955 - July, 1962 (100 pages) (35 cents)
Gilberton Co. (Came out semi-annually)

	Good	Fine	Mint
129-The Story of Jesus (titled ...Special Edition) "Jesus on Mountain" cover	2.35	7.00	16.00
"Three Camels" cover(12/58)	5.00	15.00	35.00
"Mountain" cover (1968 re-issue; has black 50 cent circle)	.75	2.25	5.00
132A-The Story of America (6/56)	2.00	6.00	14.00
135A-The Ten Commandments(12/56)	3.35	10.00	23.00
138A-Adventures in Science(6/57)	2.75	8.00	18.00
141A-The Rough Rider (Teddy Roosevelt)(12/57)	1.15	3.50	8.00
144A-Blazing the Trails West(6/58)- 73 pages of Crandall/Evans plus Severin-a	1.15	3.50	8.00
147A-Crossing the Rockies(12/58)-Crandall/Evans-a	4.00	12.00	28.00
150A-Royal Canadian Police(6/59)-Ingels, Sid Check-a	4.00	12.00	28.00
153A-Men, Guns & Cattle(12/59)-Evans-a, 26 pgs.	3.00	9.00	21.00
156A-The Atomic Age(6/60)-Crandall/Evans, Torres-a	2.00	6.00	14.00
159A-Rockets, Jets and Missiles(12/60)-Evans, Morrow-a	2.35	7.00	16.00
162A-War Between the States(6/61)-Kirby & Crandall/Evans-a	3.50	10.50	24.00
165A-To the Stars(12/61)-Torres, Crandall/Evans, Kirby-a	2.65	8.00	18.00
166A-World War II('62)-Torres, Crandall/Evans, Kirby-a	2.35	7.00	16.00
167A-Prehistoric World(7/62)-Torres & Crandall/Evans-a	3.65	11.00	25.00
nn Special Issue-The United Nations (50 cents); (Scarce)-Not Williamson-a (1960)	15.00	45.00	105.00

NOTE: *158A appeared as DC's Showcase No. 43, "Dr. No" and was only published in Great Britain as 158A with different cover.*

CLASSICS LIBRARY (See King Classics)

CLASSIC X-MEN
Sept, 1986 - Present
Marvel Comics Group

	Good	Fine	Mint
1-Begins-r of New X-Men	.55	1.60	3.20
2-4	.35	1.10	2.20
5-10	.30	.95	1.90
11-15	.25	.80	1.60
16-20		.65	1.30

CLAW THE UNCONQUERED (See Cancelled Comic Cavalcade)
5-6/75 - No. 9, 9-10/76; No. 10, 4-5/78 - No. 12, 8-9/78
National Periodical Publications/DC Comics

	Good	Fine	Mint
1		.50	1.00
2,3: 3-Nudity panel		.40	.80
4-12: 9-Origin		.25	.50

NOTE: ***Giffen*** *a-8-12p.* ***Kubert*** *c-10-12.* ***Layton*** *a-9i, 12i.*

CLAY CODY, GUNSLINGER
Fall, 1957
Pines Comics

	Good	Fine	Mint
1	1.30	4.00	9.00

CLEAN FUN, STARRING "SHOOGAFOOTS JONES"
1944 (24 pgs.; B&W; oversized covers) (10 cents)
Specialty Book Co.

Humorous situations involving Negroes in the Deep South			
White cover issue....	2.75	8.00	16.00
Dark grey cover issue....	3.00	9.00	18.00

CLEMENTINA THE FLYING PIG (See Dell Jr. Treasury)

CLEOPATRA (See Ideal, a Classical Comic No. 1)

CLIFF MERRITT SETS THE RECORD STRAIGHT
Giveaway (2 different issues)
Brotherhood of Railroad Trainsmen

...and the Very Candid Candidate by Al Williamson	.40	1.20	2.40
...Sets the Record Straight by Al Williamson (2 diff.-c: one by Williamson, the other by McWilliams)	.40	1.20	2.40

CLIFFORD MCBRIDE'S IMMORTAL NAPOLEON & UNCLE ELBY
1932 (12x17"; softcover cartoon book)
The Castle Press

Intro. by Don Herod	6.00	18.00	42.00

CLIMAX!
July, 1955 - No. 2, Sept, 1955
Gillmor Magazines

1,2 (Mystery)	4.00	12.00	28.00

CLINT & MAC (See 4-Color No. 889)

CLOAK AND DAGGER
Fall, 1952
Ziff-Davis Publishing Co.

1-Saunders painted-c	10.00	30.00	70.00

CLOAK AND DAGGER (Also see Marvel Fanfare)
Oct, 1983 - No. 4, Jan, 1984 (Mini-series)
Marvel Comics Group

1-Austin c/a(i) in all	.25	.75	1.50
2-4: 4-Origin		.50	1.00

CLOAK AND DAGGER (Also see Strange Tales, 2nd series)
July, 1985 - No. 11, Jan, 1987
Marvel Comics Group

1	.25	.75	1.50
2-10: 9-Art Adams-a		.50	1.00
11 ($1.25)		.60	1.25

CLOSE SHAVES OF PAULINE PERIL, THE (TV?)
June, 1970 - No. 4, March, 1971 (Jay Ward?)
Gold Key

1	1.00	3.00	6.00
2-4	.70	2.00	4.00

CLOWN COMICS (No. 1 titled Clown Comic Book)
1945 - No. 3, Wint, 1946
Clown Comics/Home Comics/Harvey Publ.

nn	3.50	10.50	24.00
2,3	2.00	6.00	14.00

CLUBHOUSE RASCALS (#1 titled ...Presents?)
June, 1956 - No. 2, Oct, 1956 (Also see Three Rascals)
Sussex Publ. Co. (Magazine Enterprises)

1,2: 2-The Brain app.	1.50	4.50	10.00

CLUB "16"
June, 1948 - No. 4, Dec, 1948
Famous Funnies

	Good	Fine	Mint
1	4.00	12.00	28.00
2-4	2.00	6.00	14.00

CLUE COMICS (Real Clue Crime V2No.4 on)
Jan, 1943 - No. 15(V2No.3), May, 1947
Hillman Periodicals

1-Origin The Boy King, Nightmare, Micro-Face, Twilight, & Zippo	35.00	105.00	245.00
2	19.00	57.00	132.00
3	14.00	42.00	100.00
4	11.50	35.00	80.00
5	10.00	30.00	70.00
6,8,9	7.00	21.00	50.00
7-Classic torture-c	10.00	30.00	70.00
10-Origin The Gun Master	7.00	21.00	50.00
11	5.00	15.00	35.00
12-Origin Rackman	7.00	21.00	50.00
V2#1-Nightro new origin; Iron Lady app.; Simon & Kirby-a	9.00	27.00	62.00
V2#2-S&K-a(2)-Bondage/torture-c; man attacks & kills people with electric iron. Infantino-a	10.00	30.00	70.00
V2#3-S&K-a(3)	10.00	30.00	70.00

CLUTCHING HAND, THE
July-Aug, 1954
American Comics Group

1	7.00	21.00	50.00

CLYDE BEATTY COMICS
October, 1953 (84 pages)
Commodore Productions & Artists, Inc.

1-Photo front/back-c; includes movie scenes and comics	10.00	30.00	70.00
...African Jungle Book('56)-Richfield Oil Co. 16 pg. giveaway, soft-c	4.60	14.00	32.00

CLYDE CRASHCUP (TV)
Aug-Oct, 1963 - No. 5, Sept-Nov, 1964
Dell Publishing Co.

1-All written by John Stanley	3.00	9.00	21.00
2-5	2.00	6.00	14.00

C-M-O COMICS
1942 (68 pages, full color)
Chicago Mail Order Co.(Centaur)

1-Invisible Terror, Super Ann, & Plymo the Rubber Man app. (All Centaur costume heroes)	28.00	84.00	195.00
2-Invisible Terror, Super Ann app.	20.00	60.00	140.00

COCOMALT BIG BOOK OF COMICS
1938 (Regular size; full color; 52 pgs.)
Harry 'A' Chesler (Cocomalt Premium)

1-(Scarce)-Biro-c/a; Little Nemo by Winsor McCay Jr., Dan Hastings; Guardineer, Jack Cole, Gustavson, Bob Wood-a	45.00	135.00	315.00

CODE NAME: ASSASSIN (See First Issue Special)

CODENAME: DANGER
Aug, 1985 - No. 2? ($1.50 cover)
Lodestone Publ.

1,2	.25	.75	1.50

CODENAME SPITFIRE (Formerly Spitfire And The Troubleshooters)
No. 10, July, 1987 - No. 12, Oct, 1987
Marvel Comics Group

10-12		.40	.80

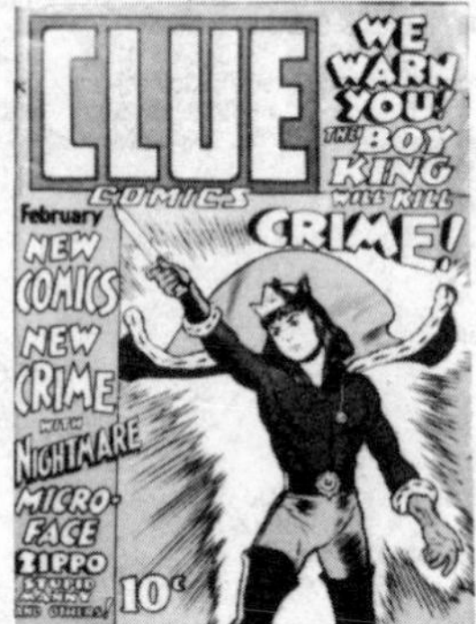

Clue Comics #2, © HILL

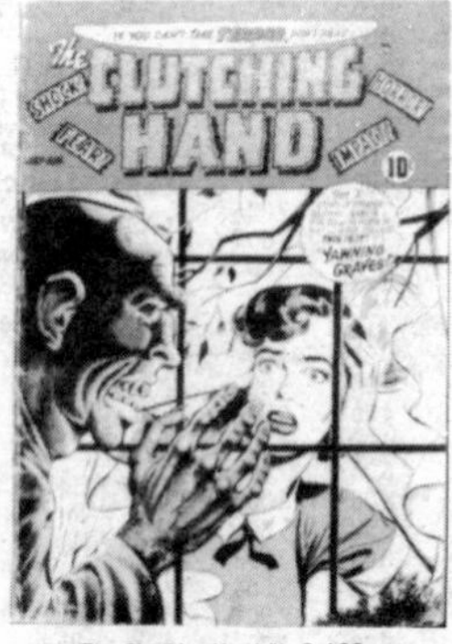

The Clutching Hand #1, © ACG

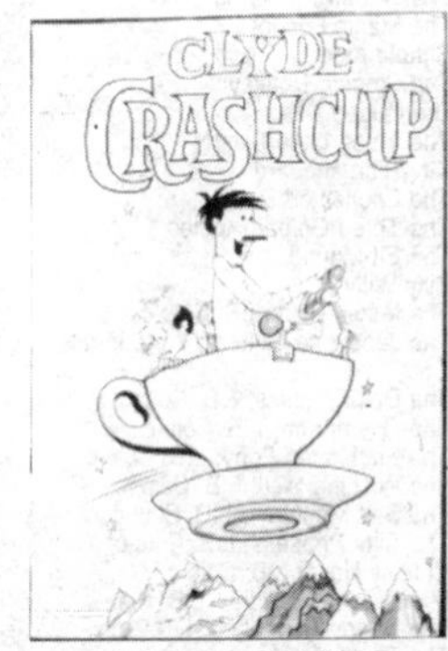

Clyde Crashcup #5, © DELL

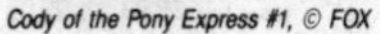
Cody of the Pony Express #1, © FOX

Colt .45 #9, © Warner Bros.

Combat Casey #17, © MCG

CODY OF THE PONY EXPRESS (See Colossal Features Magazine)
Sept, 1950 - No. 3, Jan, 1951 (See Women Outlaws)
Fox Features Syndicate

	Good	Fine	Mint
1-3 (actually #3-5)	4.00	12.00	28.00

CODY OF THE PONY EXPRESS (Buffalo Bill . . .) (Outlaws of the West #11 on; Formerly Bullseye) (See Colossal Features Magazine)
No. 8, Oct, 1955; No. 9, Jan, 1956; No. 10, June, 1956
Charlton Comics

8-Bullseye on splash pg; not S&K-a	2.30	7.00	16.00
9,10	1.50	4.50	10.00

CO-ED ROMANCES
November, 1951
P. L. Publishing Co.

1	2.30	7.00	16.00

COLLECTORS ITEM CLASSICS (See Marvel Collectors Item Classics)

COLOSSAL FEATURES MAGAZINE (Formerly I Loved) (See Cody of the Pony Express)
No. 33, May, 1950 - No. 34, July, 1950; No. 3, Sept, 1950
Fox Features Syndicate

33,34-Cody of the Pony Express begins (based on serial). 34-Photo-c	4.60	14.00	32.00
3-Authentic criminal cases	4.00	12.00	28.00

COLOSSAL SHOW, THE (TV)
October, 1969
Gold Key

1	1.70	5.00	12.00

COLOSSUS COMICS (See Green Giant & Motion Pic. Fun. Wkly)
March, 1940
Sun Publications (Funnies, Inc.?)

1-(Scarce)-Tulpa of Tsang (hero); Colossus app.	75.00	225.00	525.00

NOTE: *Cover by artist that drew Colossus in Green Giant Comics.*

COLT .45 (TV)
No. 924, 8/58 - No. 1058, 11-1/59-60; No. 4, 2-4/60 - No. 9, 5-7/61
Dell Publishing Co.

4-Color 924-Wayde Preston photo-c on all	4.00	12.00	28.00
4-Color 1004,1058; #4,5,7-9	3.00	9.00	21.00
6-Toth-a	4.00	12.00	28.00

COLUMBIA COMICS
1943
William H. Wise Co.

1-Joe Palooka, Charlie Chan, Capt. Yank, Sparky Watts, Dixie Dugan begin	11.00	32.00	76.00
2-4	6.50	19.50	45.00

COMANCHE (See 4-Color No. 1350)

COMANCHEROS, THE (See 4-Color No. 1300)

COMBAT
June, 1952 - No. 11, April, 1953
Atlas Comics (ANC)

1	3.00	9.00	21.00
2	1.30	4.00	9.00
3,5-9,11	1.00	3.00	7.00
4-Krigstein-a	2.00	6.00	14.00
10-B&W and color illos. in **POP**	2.00	6.00	14.00

NOTE: *Combat Casey in 7,8,10,11.* ***Heath*** *c-1.* ***Maneely*** *a-1.* ***Pakula*** *a-1.* ***Reinman*** *a-1.*

COMBAT
Oct-Nov, 1961 - No. 40, Oct, 1973 (no No.9)
Dell Publishing Co.

	Good	Fine	Mint
1	1.35	4.00	8.00
2-5	.70	2.00	4.00
6,7,8(4-6/63), 8(7-9/63)	.45	1.25	2.50
10-27		.50	1.00
28-40(reprints #1-14)		.30	.60

NOTE: ***Glanzman*** *c/a-1-27.*

COMBAT CASEY (Formerly War Combat)
No. 6, Jan, 1953 - No. 34, July, 1957
Atlas Comics (SAI)

6 (Indicia shows 1/52 in error)	2.35	7.00	16.00
7-Spanking panel	3.00	9.00	21.00
8-Used in **POP**, pg. 94	1.70	5.00	12.00
9	1.00	3.00	7.00
10,13-19-Violent art by R. Q. Sale; Battle Brady x-over #10	1.70	5.00	12.00
11,12,20-Last Precode (2/55)	.70	2.00	5.00
21-34	.70	2.00	5.00

NOTE: ***Everett*** *a-6.* ***Heath*** *c-10, 17, 30.* ***Powell*** *a-29(5), 30(5), 34.* ***Severin*** *c-26, 33.*

COMBAT KELLY
Nov, 1951 - No. 44, Aug, 1957
Atlas Comics (SPI)

1-Heath-a	5.00	15.00	35.00
2	2.30	7.00	16.00
3-10	1.35	4.00	9.00
11-Used in **POP**, pages 94,95 plus color illo.	2.30	7.00	16.00
12-Color illo. in **POP**	2.30	7.00	16.00
13-16	.70	2.00	5.00
17-Violent art by R. Q. Sale; Combat Casey app.	2.30	7.00	16.00
18-20,22-44: 18-Battle Brady app. 28-Last precode (1/55). 38-Green Berets story(8/56)	.85	2.50	6.00
21-Transvestism-c	1.70	5.00	12.00

NOTE: ***Berg*** *a-8, 12-14, 16, 17, 19-23, 25, 26, 28, 31-36, 42-44.* ***Colan*** *a-42.* ***Maneely*** *a-6, 8; c-8.* ***Severin*** *c-41, 42.* ***Whitney*** *a-5.*

COMBAT KELLY (and the Deadly Dozen)
June, 1972 - No. 9, Oct, 1973
Marvel Comics Group

1-Intro. Combat Kelly; Mooney-a		.40	.80
2-9		.30	.60

COMBINED OPERATIONS (See The Story of the Commandos)

COMEDY CARNIVAL
no date (1950's) (100 pages)
St. John Publishing Co.

nn-Contains rebound St. John comics	10.00	30.00	70.00

COMEDY COMICS (1st Series) (Daring Mystery No. 1-8) (Margie No. 35 on)
No. 9, April, 1942 - No. 34, Fall, 1946
Timely Comics (TCI 9,10)

9-(Scarce)-The Fin by Everett, Capt. Dash, Citizen V, & The Silver Scorpion app.; Wolverton-a; 1st app. Comedy Kid; satire on Hitler & Stalin	75.00	225.00	525.00
10-(Scarce)-Origin The Fourth Musketeer, Victory Boys; Monstro, the Mighty app.	55.00	165.00	385.00
11-Vagabond, Stuporman app.	18.00	54.00	125.00
12,13	4.35	13.00	30.00
14-Origin & 1st app. Super Rabbit	19.00	57.00	132.00
15-20	4.35	13.00	30.00
21-32	3.15	9.50	22.00
33-Kurtzman-a, 5 pgs.	4.35	13.00	30.00
34-Wolverton-a, 5 pgs.	6.00	18.00	42.00

COMEDY COMICS (2nd Series)
May, 1948 - No. 10, Jan, 1950
Marvel Comics (ACI)

1-Hedy, Tessie, Millie begin; Kurtzman's "Hey Look" (he draws

COMEDY COMICS (continued)

	Good	Fine	Mint
himself)	10.00	30.00	70.00
2	4.00	12.00	28.00
3,4-Kurtzman's "Hey Look"(?&3)	6.00	18.00	42.00
5-10	2.00	6.00	14.00

COMET, THE
Oct, 1983 - No. 2, Dec, 1983
Red Circle Comics

	Good	Fine	Mint
1-Origin The Comet; The American Shield begins		.50	1.00
2-Origin continues		.50	1.00

COMET MAN, THE
Feb, 1987 - No. 6, July, 1987 (mini-series)
Marvel Comics Group

	Good	Fine	Mint
1-6		.50	1.00

COMIC ALBUM
Mar-May, 1958 - No. 18, June-Aug, 1962
Dell Publishing Co.

	Good	Fine	Mint
1-Donald Duck	3.00	9.00	21.00
2-Bugs Bunny	1.15	3.50	8.00
3-Donald Duck	2.65	8.00	18.00
4-Tom & Jerry	1.15	3.50	8.00
5-Woody Woodpecker	1.15	3.50	8.00
6-Bugs Bunny	1.15	3.50	8.00
7-Popeye (9-11/59)	2.00	6.00	14.00
8-Tom & Jerry	1.15	3.50	8.00
9-Woody Woodpecker	1.15	3.50	8.00
10-Bugs Bunny	1.15	3.50	8.00
11-Popeye (9-11/60)	2.00	6.00	14.00
12-Tom & Jerry	1.15	3.50	8.00
13-Woody Woodpecker	1.15	3.50	8.00
14-Bugs Bunny	1.15	3.50	8.00
15-Popeye	2.00	6.00	14.00
16-Flintstones (12-2/61-62)-3rd app.	2.00	6.00	14.00
17-Space Mouse-3rd app.	1.15	3.50	8.00
18-Three Stooges; photo-c	3.50	10.50	24.00

COMIC BOOK (Also see Comics From Weatherbird)
1954 (Giveaway)
American Juniors Shoe

Contains a comic rebound with new cover. Several combinations possible. Contents determines price.

COMIC BOOK MAGAZINE
1940 - 1943 (Similar to Spirit Sections)
(7¾x10¾"; full color; 16-24 pages each)
Chicago Tribune & other newspapers

	Good	Fine	Mint
1940 issues	5.00	15.00	35.00
1941, 1942 issues	4.00	12.00	28.00
1943 issues	3.35	10.00	23.00

NOTE: *Published weekly. Texas Slim, Kit Carson, Spooky, Josie, Nuts & Jolts, Lew Loyal, Brenda Starr, Daniel Boone, Captain Storm, Rocky, Smokey Stover, Tiny Tim, Little Joe, Fu Manchu appear among others. Early issues had photo stories with pictures from the movies; later issues had comic art.*

COMIC BOOKS (Series 1)
1950 (16 pgs.; 5¼x8½"; full color; bound at top; paper cover)
Metropolitan Printing Co. (Giveaway)

	Good	Fine	Mint
1-Boots and Saddles; intro. The Masked Marshal	3.35	10.00	23.00
1-The Green Jet; Green Lama by Raboy	17.00	52.00	120.00
1-My Pal Dizzy (Teen-age)	1.70	5.00	12.00
1-New World; origin Atomaster (costumed hero)	4.65	14.00	32.00
1-Talullah (Teen-age)	1.70	5.00	12.00

COMIC CAPERS
Fall, 1944 - No. 6, Summer, 1946
Red Circle Mag./Marvel Comics

	Good	Fine	Mint
1-Super Rabbit, The Creeper, Silly Seal, Ziggy Pig, Sharpy Fox begin	7.00	21.00	50.00
2	4.00	12.00	28.00
3-6	2.65	8.00	18.00

COMIC CAVALCADE
Winter, 1942-43 - No. 63, June-July, 1954
(Contents change with No. 30, Dec-Jan, 1948-49 on)
All-American/National Periodical Publications

	Good	Fine	Mint
1-The Flash, Green Lantern, Wonder Woman, Wildcat, The Black Pirate by Moldoff (also #2), Ghost Patrol, and Red White & Blue begin; Scribbly app., Minute Movies	140.00	420.00	980.00
2-Mutt & Jeff begin; last Ghost Patrol & Black Pirate; Minute Movies	70.00	210.00	490.00
3-Hop Harrigan & Sargon, the Sorcerer begin; The King app.	52.00	155.00	365.00
4-The Gay Ghost, The King, Scribbly, & Red Tornado app.	43.00	130.00	300.00
5-Christmas-c	36.00	108.00	250.00
6-10: 7-Red Tornado & Black Pirate app.; last Scribbly. 9-X-mas-c	32.00	95.00	225.00
11,12,14-20: 12-Last Red White & Blue. 15-Johnny Peril begins, ends #29. 19-Christmas-c	28.00	84.00	195.00
13-Solomon Grundy app.	48.00	145.00	335.00
21-23	28.00	84.00	195.00
24-Solomon Grundy x-over in Gr. Lantern	32.00	95.00	225.00
25-29: 25-Black Canary app.; X-mas-c. 26-28-Johnny Peril app. 28-Last Mutt & Jeff. 29-Last Flash, Wonder Woman, Green Lantern & Johnny Peril	21.00	64.00	150.00
30-The Fox & the Crow, Dodo & the Frog & Nutsy Squirrel begin	15.00	45.00	105.00
31-35	7.00	21.00	50.00
36-49	5.00	15.00	35.00
50-62(Scarce)	7.00	21.00	50.00
63(Rare)	12.00	36.00	84.00
Giveaway (1945, 16 pages, paper-c, in color)-Movie "Tomorrow The World" (Nazi theme)	25.00	75.00	175.00
Giveaway (c. 1944-45; 8 pgs, paper-c, in color)-The Twain Shall Meet-r/C. Cavlacade	15.00	45.00	105.00

NOTE: ***Grossman** a-30-63. **Sheldon Mayer** a(2-3)-40-63. **Post** a-31, 36. **Reinman** a-15, 20. **Toth** a-26-28(Green Lantern); c-23, 27. Atom app.-22, 23.*

COMIC COMICS
April, 1946 - No. 10, Feb, 1947
Fawcett Publications

	Good	Fine	Mint
1-Captain Kidd	4.60	14.00	32.00
2-10-Wolverton-a, 4 pgs. each. 5-Captain Kidd app.	5.00	15.00	35.00

COMIC CUTS (Also see The Funnies)
5/19/34 - 7/28/34 (5 cents; 24 pages) (Tabloid size in full color)
(Not reprints; published weekly; created for newsstand sale)
H. L. Baker Co., Inc.

	Good	Fine	Mint
V1#1 - V1#7(6/30/34), V1#8(7/14/34), V1#9(7/28/34)-Idle Jack strips	6.50	19.50	45.00

COMIC LAND
March, 1946
Fact and Fiction

	Good	Fine	Mint
1-Sandusky & the Senator, Sam Stuper, Marvin the Great, Sir Passer, Phineas Gruff app.; Irv Tirman & Perry Williams art	3.00	9.00	21.00

COMIC MONTHLY
Jan, 1922 - No. 12, Dec, 1922 (32 pgs.)(8½x9")(10 cents)
(1st monthly newsstand comic publication) (Reprints 1921 B&W

Comic Album #4, © M.G.M.

Comic Cavalcade #10, © DC

Comic Land #1, © Fact and Fiction

Comic Pages V3#5, © CEN

The Comics #4, © DELL

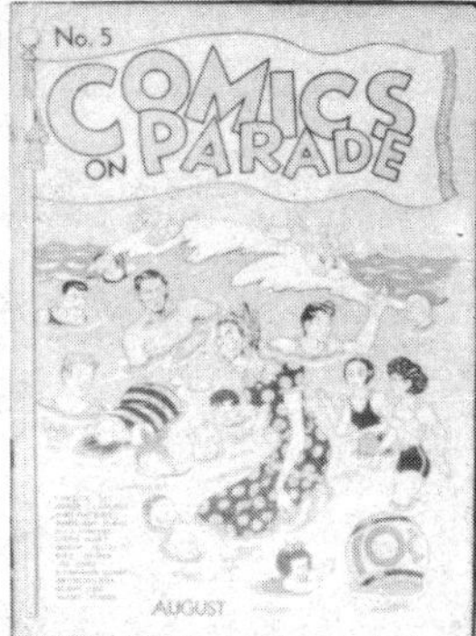

Comics On Parade #5, © UFS

COMIC MONTHLY (continued)
dailies)
Embee Dist. Co.

	Good	Fine	Mint
1-Polly & Her Pals	30.00	90.00	210.00
2-Mike & Ike	5.70	17.00	40.00
3-S'Matter, Pop?	5.70	17.00	40.00
4-Barney Google	11.50	34.00	80.00
5-Tillie the Toiler	8.50	25.50	60.00
6-Indoor Sports	4.60	14.00	32.00
7-Little Jimmy	4.60	14.00	32.00
8-Toots and Casper	4.60	14.00	32.00
9,10-Foolish Questions	4.60	14.00	32.00
11-Barney Google & Spark Plug in the Abadaba Handicap	4.60	14.00	32.00
12-Polly & Her Pals	4.60	14.00	32.00

COMICO PRIMER (See Primer)

COMIC PAGES (Formerly Funny Picture Stories)
V3No.4, July, 1939 - V3No.6, Dec, 1939
Centaur Publications

	Good	Fine	Mint
V3#4-Bob Wood-a	20.00	60.00	140.00
5,6	14.00	42.00	100.00

COMIC PAINTING AND CRAYONING BOOK
1917 (32 pages)(10x13½")(No price on cover)
Saalfield Publ. Co.

	Good	Fine	Mint
Tidy Teddy by F. M. Follett, Clarence the Cop, Mr. & Mrs. Butt-In. Regular comic stories to read or color	6.50	19.50	45.00

COMICS (See All Good)

COMICS, THE
March, 1937 - No. 11, 1938 (Newspaper strip reprints)
Dell Publishing Co.

	Good	Fine	Mint
1-1st Tom Mix in comics; Wash Tubbs, Tom Beatty, Myra North Arizona Kid, Erik Noble & International Spy w/Doctor Doom begin	43.00	130.00	300.00
2	23.00	70.00	160.00
3-11: 3-Alley Oop begins	17.00	51.00	120.00

COMICS AND STORIES (See Walt Disney's . . .)

COMICS CALENDAR, THE (The 1946 . . .)
1946 (116 pgs.; 25 cents)(Stapled at top)
True Comics Press (ordered through the mail)

	Good	Fine	Mint
(Rare) Has a "strip" story for every day of the year in color	16.00	48.00	110.00

COMICS DIGEST (Pocket size)
Winter, 1942-43 (100 pages) (Black & White)
Parents' Magazine Institute

	Good	Fine	Mint
1-Reprints from True Comics (non-fiction World War II stories)	4.60	14.00	32.00

COMIC SELECTIONS (Shoe store giveaway)
1944-46 (Reprints from Calling All Girls, True Comics, True Aviation, & Real Heroes)
Parents' Magazine Press

	Good	Fine	Mint
1	1.50	4.50	10.00
2-5	1.15	3.50	8.00

COMICS FOR KIDS
1945 (no month); No. 2, Sum, 1945 (Funny animal)
London Publishing Co./Timely

	Good	Fine	Mint
1,2-Puffy Pig, Sharpy Fox	4.60	14.00	32.00

COMICS FROM WEATHER BIRD (Also see Comic Book, Free Comics to You, Weather Bird & Edward's Shoes)
1954 - 1957 (Giveaway)
Weather Bird Shoes

Contains a comic bound with new cover. Many combinations possible. Contents would determine price. Some issues do not contain complete comics, but only parts of comics. Value equals 40 to 60 percent of contents.

COMICS HITS (See Harvey Comics Hits)

COMICS MAGAZINE, THE (. . . Funny Pages #3)(Funny Pages #6 on)
May, 1936 - No. 5, Sept, 1936 (Paper covers)
Comics Magazine Co.

	Good	Fine	Mint
1: Dr. Mystic, The Occult Detective by Siegel & Shuster (1st episode continues in More Fun #14); 1pg. Kelly-a; Sheldon Mayer-a	95.00	288.00	670.00
2: Federal Agent by Siegel & Shuster; 1pg. Kelly-a	55.00	165.00	385.00
3-5	42.00	125.00	295.00

COMICS NOVEL (Anarcho, Dictator of Death)
1947
Fawcett Publications

	Good	Fine	Mint
1-All Radar	16.00	48.00	110.00

COMICS ON PARADE (No. 30 on, continuation of Single Series)
April, 1938 - No. 104, Feb, 1955
United Features Syndicate

	Good	Fine	Mint
1-Tarzan by Foster; Captain & the Kids, Little Mary Mixup, Abbie & Slats, Ella Cinders, Broncho Bill, Li'l Abner begin	90.00	270.00	630.00
2	42.00	125.00	295.00
3	32.00	95.00	225.00
4,5	22.00	65.00	154.00
6-10	18.00	54.00	125.00
11-20	15.00	45.00	105.00
21-29: 22-Son of Tarzan begins. 29-Last Tarzan issue	13.00	40.00	90.00
30-Li'l Abner	10.00	30.00	70.00
31-The Captain & the Kids	7.00	21.00	50.00
32-Nancy & Fritzi Ritz	5.70	17.00	40.00
33-Li'l Abner	8.50	25.50	60.00
34-The Captain & the Kids (10/41)	6.00	18.00	42.00
35-Nancy & Fritzi Ritz	5.70	17.00	40.00
36-Li'l Abner	8.50	25.50	60.00
37-The Captain & the Kids (6/42)	6.00	18.00	42.00
38-Nancy & Fritzi Ritz; infinity-c	5.70	17.00	40.00
39-Li'l Abner	8.50	25.50	60.00
40-The Captain & the Kids (3/43)	6.00	18.00	42.00
41-Nancy & Fritzi Ritz	4.35	13.00	30.00
42-Li'l Abner	8.00	24.00	56.00
43-The Captain & the Kids	6.00	18.00	42.00
44-Nancy & Fritzi Ritz (3/44)	4.35	13.00	30.00
45-Li'l Abner	6.50	19.50	45.00
46-The Captain & the Kids	5.70	17.00	40.00
47-Nancy & Fritzi Ritz	4.35	13.00	30.00
48-Li'l Abner (3/45)	6.50	19.50	45.00
49-The Captain & the Kids	5.50	16.50	38.00
50-Nancy & Fritzi Ritz	4.35	13.00	30.00
51-Li'l Abner	5.50	16.50	38.00
52-The Captain & the Kids (3/46)	3.70	11.00	26.00
53-Nancy & Fritzi Ritz	3.70	11.00	26.00
54-Li'l Abner	5.50	16.50	38.00
55-Nancy & Fritzi Ritz	3.70	11.00	26.00
56-The Captain & the Kids (r-/Sparkler)	3.70	11.00	26.00
57-Nancy & Fritzi Ritz	3.70	11.00	26.00
58-Li'l Abner	5.50	16.50	38.00
59-The Captain & the Kids	3.50	10.50	24.00
60-70-Nancy & Fritzi Ritz	3.50	10.50	24.00
71-76-Nancy only	2.30	7.00	16.00
77-99,101-104-Nancy & Sluggo	2.30	7.00	16.00
100-Nancy & Sluggo	3.00	9.00	21.00

Special Issue, 7/46; Summer, 1948 - The Capt. & the Kids app.

COMICS ON PARADE (continued)	Good	Fine	Mint
	2.30	7.00	16.00
Bound Volume (Very Rare) includes No. 1-12; bound by publisher in pictorial comic boards & distributed at the 1939 World's Fair and through mail order from ads in comic books (Also see Tip Top)	142.00	425.00	1000.00

NOTE: *Li'l Abner reprinted from Tip Top.*

COMICS READING LIBRARIES (Educational Series)
1973, 1977, 1979 (36 pages in color) (Giveaways)
King Features (Charlton Publ.)

	Good	Fine	Mint
R-01-Tiger, Quincy		.15	.30
R-02-Beetle Bailey, Blondie & Popeye		.15	.30
R-03-Blondie, Beetle Bailey		.30	.60
R-04-Tim Tyler's Luck, Felix the Cat	.70	2.00	4.00
R-05-Quincy, Henry		.15	.30
R-06-The Phantom, Mandrake	1.35	4.00	8.00
1977 reprint(R-04)	.70	2.00	4.00
R-07-Popeye, Little King	.70	2.00	4.00
R-08-Prince Valiant(Foster), Flash Gordon	4.00	12.00	24.00
1977 reprint	1.35	4.00	8.00
R-09-Hagar the Horrible, Boner's Ark		.15	.30
R-10-Redeye, Tiger		.15	.30
R-11-Blondie, Hi & Lois		.25	.50
R-12-Popeye-Swee'pea, Brutus	.70	2.00	4.00
R-13-Beetle Bailey, Little King		.15	.30
R-14-Quincy-Hamlet		.15	.30
R-15-The Phantom, The Genius	1.70	5.00	10.00
R-16-Flash Gordon, Mandrake	4.00	12.00	24.00
1977 reprint	1.35	4.00	8.00
Other 1977 editions....		.15	.30
1979 editions(68pgs.)		.20	.40

NOTE: *Above giveaways available with purchase of $45.00 in merchandise. Used as a reading skills aid for small children.*

COMICS REVUE
June, 1947 - No. 5, Jan, 1948
St. John Publ. Co. (United Features Synd.)

	Good	Fine	Mint
1-Ella Cinders & Blackie	4.00	12.00	28.00
2-Hap Hopper (7/47)	2.65	8.00	18.00
3-Iron Vic (8/47)	2.30	7.00	16.00
4-Ella Cinders (9/47)	2.65	8.00	18.00
5-Gordo No. 1 (1/48)	2.30	7.00	16.00

COMIC STORY PAINT BOOK
1943 (68 pages) (Large size)
Samuel Lowe Co.

	Good	Fine	Mint
1055-Captain Marvel & a Captain Marvel Jr. story to read & color; 3 panels in color per page (reprints)	28.00	84.00	200.00

COMIX BOOK (B&W Magazine - $1.00)
Oct, 1974 - No. 5, 1976
Marvel Comics Group/Krupp Comics Works No. 4

	Good	Fine	Mint
1-Underground comic artists; 2 pg. Wolverton-a	.70	2.00	4.00
2-Wolverton-a (1 pg.)	.40	1.20	2.40
3-Low distribution (3/75)	.50	1.50	3.00
4(2/76), 4(5/76), 5	.40	1.20	2.40

NOTE: *Print run No. 1-3: 200-250M; No. 4&5: 10M each.*

COMIX INTERNATIONAL
July, 1974 - No. 5, Spring, 1977 (Full color)
Warren Magazines

	Good	Fine	Mint
1-Low distribution; all Corben remainders from Warren	4.00	12.00	24.00
2-Wood, Wrightson-r	1.20	3.50	7.00
3-5: 4-Crandall-a	.70	2.00	4.00

NOTE: *No. 4 had two printings with extra* ***Corben*** *story in one.*

COMMANDER BATTLE AND THE ATOMIC SUB
July-Aug, 1954 - No. 7, July-Aug, 1955
American Comics Group (Titan Publ. Co.)

	Good	Fine	Mint
1 (3-D effect)	14.00	48.00	100.00
2	5.40	16.00	38.00
3-H-Bomb-c; Atomic Sub becomes Atomic Spaceship	7.00	21.00	50.00
4-7: 6,7-Landau-a	5.50	16.50	38.00

COMMANDMENTS OF GOD
1954, 1958
Catechetical Guild

	Good	Fine	Mint
300-Same contents in both editions; different-c	2.75	8.00	16.00

COMMANDO ADVENTURES
June, 1957 - No. 2, Aug, 1957
Atlas Comics (MMC)

	Good	Fine	Mint
1,2-Severin-c; 2-Drucker-a	1.50	4.50	10.00

COMMANDO YANK (See Mighty Midget Comics)

COMPLETE BOOK OF COMICS AND FUNNIES
1944 (196 pages) (One Shot) (25 cents)
William H. Wise & Co.

	Good	Fine	Mint
1-Origin Brad Spencer, Wonderman; The Magnet, The Silver Knight by Kinstler, & Zudo the Jungle Boy app.	17.00	51.00	120.00

COMPLETE BOOK OF TRUE CRIME COMICS
No date (Mid 1940's) (132 pages) (25 cents)
William H. Wise & Co.

	Good	Fine	Mint
nn-Contains Crime Does Not Pay rebound (includes #22)	42.00	125.00	295.00

COMPLETE COMICS (Formerly Amazing No. 1)
Winter, 1944-45
Timely Comics (EPC)

	Good	Fine	Mint
2-The Destroyer, The Whizzer, The Young Allies & Sergeant Dix	43.00	128.00	300.00

COMPLETE LOVE MAGAZINE (Formerly a pulp with same title)
V26/2, May-June, 1951 - V32/4(No.191), Sept, 1956
Ace Periodicals (Periodical House)

	Good	Fine	Mint
V26/2-Painted-c (52 pgs.)	2.30	7.00	16.00
V26/3-6(2/52), V27/1(4/52)-6(1/53)	1.50	4.50	10.00
V28/1(3/53), V28/2(5/53), V29/3(7/53)-6(12/53)	1.30	4.00	8.00
V30/1(2/54), V30/1(No. 176, 4/54)-6(No.181, 1/55)	1.15	3.50	8.00
V31/1(No.182, 3/55)-Last precode	1.00	3.00	7.00
V31/2(5/55)-6(No.187, 1/56)	.85	2.50	6.00
V32/1(No.188, 3/56)-4(No.191, 9/56)	.80	2.40	5.50

NOTE: *(34 total issues). Photo-c V27/5-on. Painted-c V26/3.*

COMPLETE MYSTERY (True Complete Mystery No. 5 on)
Aug, 1948 - No. 4, Feb, 1949 (Full length stories)
Marvel Comics (PrPl)

	Good	Fine	Mint
1-Seven Dead Men	11.00	33.00	76.00
2-Jigsaw of Doom!	7.00	21.00	50.00
3-Fear in the Night; Burgos-a	7.00	21.00	50.00
4-A Squealer Dies Fast	7.00	21.00	50.00

COMPLETE ROMANCE
1949
Avon Periodicals

	Good	Fine	Mint
1-(Scarce)-Reprinted as Women to Love	22.00	65.00	154.00

COMPLIMENTARY COMICS
No date (1950's)
Sales Promotion Publ. (Giveaway)

	Good	Fine	Mint
1-Strongman by Powell, 3 stories	3.35	10.00	20.00

Comics Revue #3, © UFS

Complete Comics #2, © MCG

Complete Mystery #3, © MCG

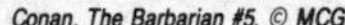
Conan, The Barbarian #5, © MCG

Confessions of Romance #8, © STAR

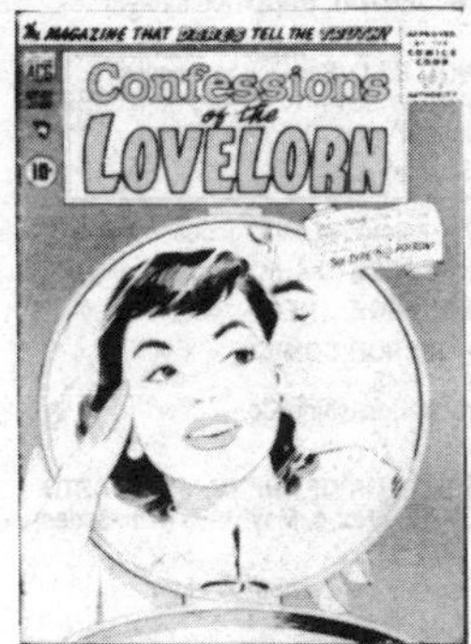

Confessions of the Lovelorn #82, © ACG

CONAN (See Chamber of Darkness #4, Handbook of . . ., King Conan, Marvel Treasury Ed., Robert E. Howard's. . ., Savage Sword of Conan, and Savage Tales)

CONAN SAGA, THE
June, 1987 - Present (B&W magazine, $2.00)
Marvel Comics

	Good	Fine	Mint
1-Barry Smith-r begin	.35	1.00	2.00
2-10	.35	1.00	2.00

CONAN, THE BARBARIAN
Oct, 1970 - Present
Marvel Comics Group

	Good	Fine	Mint
1-Origin Conan by Barry Smith; Kull app.	12.50	37.50	75.00
2	5.00	15.00	30.00
3-(low distribution in some areas)	8.50	25.00	50.00
4,5	4.25	12.50	25.00
6-10: 8-Hidden panel message, pg. 14. 10-52 pgs.; Black Knight-r; Kull story by Severin	3.00	9.00	18.00
11-13: 11-52 pgs. 12-Wrightson c(i)	2.35	7.00	14.00
14,15-Elric app.	3.00	9.00	18.00
16,19,20: 16-Conan-r/Savage Tales #1	1.70	5.00	10.00
17,18-No Smith-a	1.00	3.00	6.00
21,22: 22-has r-from #1	1.35	4.00	8.00
23-1st app. Red Sonja	1.70	5.00	10.00
24-1st full story Red Sonja; last Smith-a	1.70	5.00	10.00
25-Buscema-a begins	1.00	3.00	6.00
26-30	.60	1.75	3.50
31-36,38-40	.40	1.20	2.40
37-Adams c/a	.85	2.50	5.00
41-43,46-49	.25	.75	1.50
44,45-Adams inks, c-45;	.35	1.00	2.00
50-57,60	.25	.80	1.60
58-2nd Belit app.(see Gnt-Size 1)	.50	1.50	3.00
59-Origin Belit	.25	.75	1.50
61-99		.50	1.00
100-(52 pg. Giant)-Death of Belit	.40	1.25	2.50
101-114,116-193		.35	.70
115-double size		.60	1.20
194-199: $1.00 cover		.50	1.00
200-double size	.25	.75	1.50

NOTE: ***Adams** a-116r(i); c-49i. **Austin** a-125, 126; c-125i, 126i. **Brunner** c-17i. c-40. **Buscema** a-25-36p, 38, 39, 41-56p, 58-63p, 65-67p, 68, 70-78p, 84-86p, 88-91p, 93-126p, 136p, 140, 141-44p, 146-58p, 159, 161, 162, 163p, 165p-185p, 187p-190p, Annual 2-5p, 7p; c(p)-26, 36, 44, 46, 52, 56, 58, 59, 64, 65, 72, 78-80, 83-91, 93-103, 105-26, 136-51, 155-159, 161, 162, 168, 169, 171, 172, 174, 175, 178-185, 188, 189. **Golden** c-152. **Kaluta** c-167. **Gil Kane** a-12p, 17p, 18p, 127-30, 131-134p, Gnt-Size 1p-4p; c-12p, 17p, 18p, 23, 25, 27-32, 34, 35, 38, 39, 41-43, 45-51, 53-55, 57, 60-63, 65-71, 73p, 76p, 127-34, Gnt-Size 1, 3, 4. **Russell** a-21. **Simonson** c-135. **Smith** a-1p-11p, 12, 13p-15p, 16, 19-21, 23, 24; c-1-11, 13-16, 19-24p. **Sutton** inks-Gnt-Size 1-3. **Wood** a-47r. Issues No. 3-5, 7-9, 11, 16-18, 21, 23, 25, 27-30, 35, 37, 38, 42, 45, 52, 57, 58, 65, 69-71, 73, 79-83, 99, 100, 104, 114, Annual 2 have original Robert E. Howard stories adapted. Issues #32-34 adapted from Norvell Page's novel **Flame Winds.***

	Good	Fine	Mint
Giant Size 1(9/74)-Smith r-/#3; start adaptation of Howard's "Hour of the Dragon." 1st app. Belit	.70	2.00	4.00
Giant Size 2(12/74)-Smith r-/#5; Sutton-a; Buscema-c	.70	2.00	4.00
Giant Size 3(4/75-Smith r-/#6; Sutton-a), Giant Size 4(6/75; Smith r-/#7), Giant Size 5('75; Smith r-/#14,15; Kirby-c)	.30	.90	1.80
King Size 1(9/73-35 cents)-Smith r-/#2,4; Smith-c	1.00	3.00	6.00
Annual 2(6/76)-50 cents; new stories	.40	1.20	2.40
Annual 3(2/78)-reprints	.30	.80	1.60
Annual 4(10/78), 5(12/79)-Buscema-a/part-c	.25	.70	1.40
Annual 6(10/81)-Kane c/a	.25	.70	1.40
Annual 7(11/82), 8(2/84)		.60	1.20
Annual 9(12/84), 10(2/87), 11('87)		.60	1.20
Special Edition 1(Red Nails)	.50	1.50	3.00

CONAN THE BARBARIAN MOVIE SPECIAL
Oct, 1982 - No. 2, Nov, 1982
Marvel Comics Group

	Good	Fine	Mint
1,2-Movie adapt.; Buscema-a		.25	.50

CONAN THE DESTROYER
Jan, 1985 - No. 2, Mar, 1985 (Movie adaptation)
Marvel Comics Group

	Good	Fine	Mint
1,2-r/Marvel Super Special		.40	.80

CONAN THE KING (Formerly King Conan)
No. 20, Jan, 1984 - Present
Marvel Comics Group

	Good	Fine	Mint
20-45		.60	1.20

NOTE: ***Kaluta** c-20-23, 24i, 26, 27.*

CONDORMAN
Oct, 1981 - No. 3, Jan, 1982
Whitman Publ.

	Good	Fine	Mint
1-3: 1,2-Movie adaptation		.30	.60

CONFESSIONS ILLUSTRATED (Magazine)
Jan-Feb, 1956 - No. 2, Spring, 1956
E. C. Comics

	Good	Fine	Mint
1-Craig, Kamen, Wood, Orlando-a	5.50	16.50	38.00
2-Craig, Crandall, Kamen, Orlando-a	6.50	19.50	45.00

CONFESSIONS OF LOVE
4/50 - No. 2, 7/50 (25 cents; 132 pgs. in color)(7¼x5¼")
Artful Publ.

	Good	Fine	Mint
1-Bakerish-a	17.00	51.00	120.00
2-Art & text; Bakerish-a	8.50	25.50	60.00

CONFESSIONS OF LOVE (Confessions of Romance No. 7)
No. 11, July, 1952 - No. 6, Aug, 1953
Star Publications

	Good	Fine	Mint
11	3.50	10.50	24.00
12,13-Disbrow-a	3.50	10.50	24.00
14, 6	2.00	6.00	14.00
4-Disbrow-a	2.75	8.00	18.00
5-Wood/?-a	4.00	12.00	28.00

NOTE: *All have **L. B. Cole** covers.*

CONFESSIONS OF ROMANCE (Formerly Confessions of Love)
No. 7, Nov, 1953 - No. 11, Nov, 1954
Star Publications

	Good	Fine	Mint
7	3.50	10.50	24.00
8	2.35	7.00	16.00
9-Wood-a	6.00	18.00	42.00
10,11-Disbrow-a	3.00	9.00	21.00

NOTE: ***L. B. Cole** covers on all.*

CONFESSIONS OF THE LOVELORN (Formerly Lovelorn)
No. 52, Aug, 1954 - No. 114, June-July, 1960
American Comics Group (Regis Publ./Best Synd. Features)

	Good	Fine	Mint
52 (3-D effect)	8.50	25.50	60.00
53,55	1.50	4.50	10.00
54 (3-D effect)	7.00	21.00	50.00
56-Communist propaganda sty, 10pgs; last pre-code (2/55)	2.00	6.00	14.00
57-90	1.00	3.00	7.00
91-Williamson-a	4.00	12.00	28.00
92-99,101-114	.85	2.50	6.00
100	1.00	3.00	7.00

NOTE: ***Whitney** a-most issues. 106,107-painted-c.*

CONFIDENTIAL DIARY (Formerly High School Confidential Diary; Three Nurses No. 18 on)
No. 12, May, 1962 - No. 17, March, 1963
Charlton Comics

CONFIDENTIAL DIARY (continued) — Good / Fine / Mint
12-17 .35 1.00 2.00

CONGO BILL (See Action Comics)
Aug-Sept, 1954 - No. 7, Aug-Sept, 1955
National Periodical Publications — Good / Fine / VF-NM
1-(Scarce) 23.00 70.00 160.00
2-(Scarce) 20.00 60.00 140.00
3-7 (Scarce), 4-Last precode 17.00 51.00 120.00

CONNECTICUT YANKEE, A (See King Classics)

CONQUEROR, THE (See 4-Color No. 690)

CONQUEROR COMICS
Winter, 1945
Albrecht Publishing Co. — Good / Fine / Mint
nn 5.00 15.00 35.00

CONQUEROR OF THE BARREN EARTH
Feb, 1985 - No. 4, May, 1985 (Mini-series)
DC Comics
1-Back-up series from Warlord .60 1.20
2-4 .50 1.00

CONQUEST
1953 (6 cents)
Store Comics
1-Richard the Lion Hearted, Beowulf, Swamp Fox 1.50 4.50 10.00

CONQUEST
Spring, 1955
Famous Funnies
1-Crandall-a, 1 pg.; contains contents of 1953 issue 2.00 6.00 14.00

CONTACT COMICS
July, 1944 - No. 12, May, 1946
Aviation Press
nn-Black Venus, Flamingo, Golden Eagle, Tommy Tomahawk begin 11.50 34.00 80.00
2-5: 3-Last Flamingo. 3,4-Black Venus by L. B. Cole. 5-The Phantom Flyer app. 8.50 25.50 60.00
6,11-Kurtzman's Black Venus; 11-Last Golden Eagle, last Tommy Tomahawk; Feldstein-a 11.50 34.00 80.00
7-10,12: 12-Sky Rangers, Air Kids, Ace Diamond app. 7.00 21.00 50.00
NOTE: ***L. B. Cole** a-9; c-1-12. **Giunta** a-3. **Hollingsworth** a-5, 10. **Palais** a-11,12.*

CONTEMPORARY MOTIVATORS
1977 - 1978 (5-3/8x8")(31 pgs., B&W, $1.45)
Pendelum Press
14-3002 The Caine Mutiny; 14-3010 Banner in the Sky; 14-3029 God Is My Co-Pilot; 14-3037 Guadalcanal Diary; 14-3045 Hiroshima; 14-3053 Hot Rod; 14-3061 Just Dial a Number; 14-307x Star Wars; 14-3088 The Diary of Anne Frank; 14-3096 Lost Horizon 1.50
NOTE: *Also see Now Age III. Above may have been dist. the same.*

CONTEST OF CHAMPIONS (See Marvel Superhero. . .)

COO COO COMICS (. . . the Bird Brain No. 57 on)
Oct, 1942 - No. 62, April, 1952
Nedor Publ. Co./Standard (Animated Cartoons)
1-1st app./origin Super Mouse (cloned from Superman)-The first funny animal super hero 7.00 21.00 50.00
2 3.50 10.50 24.00
3-10 (3/44) 2.15 6.50 15.00
11-33: 33-1pg. Ingels-a 1.50 4.50 10.00
34-40,43-46,48-50-Text illos by Frazetta in all 2.65 8.00 18.00
41-Frazetta-a(2) 8.00 24.00 56.00
42,47-Frazetta-a & text illos. 5.50 16.50 38.00

Good / Fine / Mint
51-62 1.15 3.50 8.00

"COOKIE"
April, 1946 - No. 55, Aug-Sept, 1955
Michel Publ./American Comics Group(Regis Publ.)
1 6.00 18.00 42.00
2 3.00 9.00 21.00
3-10 2.00 6.00 14.00
11-20 1.50 4.50 10.00
21-30 1.15 3.50 8.00
31-34,36-55 .85 2.50 6.00
35-Starlett O'Hara story 1.15 3.50 8.00

COOL CAT (Formerly Black Magic)
V8/6, Mar-Apr, 1962 - V9/2, July-Aug, 1962
Prize Publications
V8#, nn(V9#), V9# 1.00 3.00 7.00

COPPER CANYON (See Fawcett Movie Comics)

CORBEN SPECIAL, A
May, 1984 (One-shot)
Pacific Comics
1-Corben c/a; E.A. Poe Adaptation .35 1.00 2.00

CORKY & WHITE SHADOW (See 4-Color No. 707)

CORLISS ARCHER (See Meet. . .)

CORPORAL RUSTY DUGAN (See Rusty Dugan)

CORPSES OF DR. SACOTTI, THE (See Ideal a Classical Comic)

CORSAIR, THE (See A-1 Comics No. 5,7,10)

COSMIC BOOK, THE
Dec, 1986 - Present ($1.95, color)
Ace Comics
1 .35 1.00 2.00
2-B&W begins .25 .80 1.60

COSMIC BOY
Dec, 1986 - No. 4, Mar, 1987 (mini-series)
DC Comics
1-Legends tie-in, all issues .25 .75 1.50
2-4 .50 1.00

COSMO CAT (Also see Wotalife Comics)
July-Aug, 1946 - No. 10, Oct, 1947; 1957; 1959
Fox Publications/Green Publ. Co./Norlen Mag.
1 6.00 18.00 42.00
2 3.00 9.00 21.00
3-Origin 3.00 9.00 21.00
4-10 2.00 6.00 14.00
2-4(1957-Green Publ. Co.) .85 2.50 6.00
2-4(1959-Norlen Mag.) .75 2.25 5.00
I.W. Reprint No. 1 .35 1.00 2.00

COSMO THE MERRY MARTIAN
Sept, 1958 - No. 6, Oct, 1959
Archie Publications (Radio Comics)
1-Bob White-a in all 5.00 15.00 35.00
2-6 3.50 10.50 24.00

COTTON WOODS (See 4-Color No. 837)

COUGAR, THE (Cougar No. 2)
April, 1975 - No. 2, July, 1975
Seaboard Periodicals (Atlas)
1-Adkins-a(p) .40 .80
2-Origin .25 .50

COUNTDOWN (See Movie Classics)

Congo Bill #5, © DC

Contact Comics #10, © Aviation Press

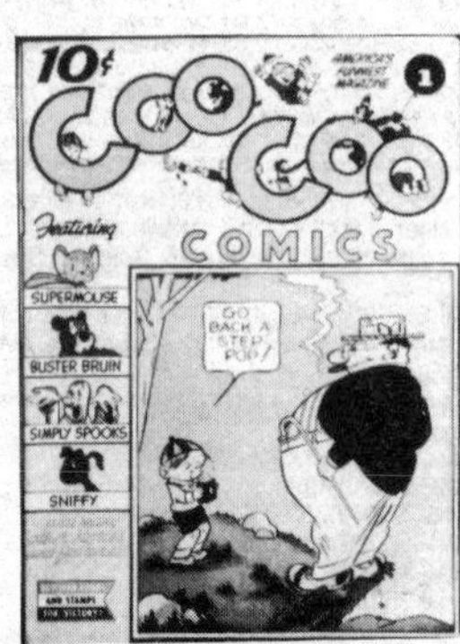

Coo Coo Comics #1, © STD

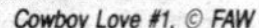
Cowboy Love #1, © FAW

Cowboy Western #67, © CC

Cowgirl Romances #28, © MCG

COUNT OF MONTE CRISTO, THE (See 4-Color No. 794)

COURAGE COMICS
1945
J. Edward Slavin

	Good	Fine	Mint
1,2,77	3.00	9.00	21.00

COURTSHIP OF EDDIE'S FATHER (TV)
Jan, 1970 - No. 2, May, 1970
Dell Publishing Co.

	Good	Fine	Mint
1,2-Bill Bixby photo-c	1.50	4.50	10.00

COVERED WAGONS, HO (See 4-Color No. 814)

COWBOY ACTION (Western Thrillers No. 1-4; Quick Trigger Western No. 12 on)
No. 5, March, 1955 - No. 11, March, 1956
Atlas Comics (ACI)

	Good	Fine	Mint
5	3.00	9.00	21.00
6-10	1.70	5.00	12.00
11-Williamson-a, 4 pgs., Baker-a	4.00	12.00	28.00

NOTE: ***Maneely** c/a-5. **Severin** c-10.*

COWBOY COMICS (. . .Stories No. 14, formerly Star Ranger) (Star Ranger Funnies No. 15 on)
No. 13, July, 1938 - No. 14, Aug, 1938
Centaur Publishing Co.

	Good	Fine	Mint
13-(Rare)-Ace and Deuce, Lyin Lou, Air Patrol, Aces High, Lee Trent, Trouble Hunters begin	38.00	115.00	265.00
14	27.00	81.00	190.00

NOTE: ***Guardineer** a-13, 14. **Gustavson** a-13, 14.*

COWBOY IN AFRICA (TV)
March, 1968
Gold Key

	Good	Fine	Mint
1(10219-803)-Chuck Connors photo-c	1.70	5.00	12.00

COWBOY LOVE (Becomes Range Busters?)
7/49 - V2/10, 6/50; No. 11, 1951; No. 28, 2/55 - No. 31, 8/55
Fawcett Publications/Charlton Comics No. 28 on

	Good	Fine	Mint
V1#1-Rocky Lane photo back-c	4.35	13.00	30.00
2	1.70	5.00	12.00
V1#3,4,6 (12/49)	1.50	4.50	10.00
5-Bill Boyd photo back-c (11/49)	2.65	8.00	18.00
V2#7-Williamson/Evans-a	4.00	12.00	28.00
V2#8-11	1.15	3.50	8.00
V1#28-31(1955-Charlton)(Formerly Romantic Story?; becomes Sweetheart Love Story?)	.85	2.50	6.00

NOTE: ***Powell** a-10. Photo c-1-11 No. 1-3,5-7,9,10, 52 pgs.*

COWBOY ROMANCES (Young Men No. 4 on)
Oct, 1949 - No. 3, Mar, 1950
Marvel Comics (IPC)

	Good	Fine	Mint
1-Photo-c	6.50	19.50	45.00
2-William Holden, Mona Freeman 'Streets of Laredo' photo-c	4.60	14.00	32.00
3	3.70	11.00	26.00

COWBOYS 'N' INJUNS (. . .'N' Indians No. 6 on)
1946 - No. 5, 1947; No. 6, 1949 - No. 8, 1952
Compix No. 1-5/Magazine Enterprises No. 6 on

	Good	Fine	Mint
1	2.65	8.00	18.00
2-5-All funny animal western	1.60	4.70	11.00
6(A-1 23)-half violent, half funny	2.00	6.00	14.00
7(A-1 41, 1950), 8(A-1 48)-All funny	1.60	4.70	11.00
I.W. Reprint No. 1,7 (reprinted in Canada by Superior, No. 7)	.35	1.00	2.00
Super Reprint No. 10 (1963)	.35	1.00	2.00

COWBOY WESTERN COMICS (Formerly Jack In The Box; Becomes Space Western No. 40-45 & Wild Bill Hickok & Jingles No. 68 on; title: . . .Heroes No. 47 & 48; Cowboy Western No. 49 on (TV))
No. 17, 7/48 - No. 39, 8/52; No. 46, 10/53; No. 47, 12/53; No. 48 Spr, '54; No. 49, 5-6/54 - No. 67, 3/58 (nn 40-45)
Charlton(Capitol Stories)

	Good	Fine	Mint
17	4.35	13.00	30.00
18,19-Orlando c/a	3.00	9.00	21.00
20-25	1.85	5.50	13.00
26-Photo-c	3.00	9.00	21.00
27,30-Sunset Carson photo-c	14.00	42.00	100.00
28,29-Sunset Carson app.	6.00	18.00	42.00
31-39,47-50 (no No.40-45)	1.30	4.00	9.00
46-(Formerly Space Western)-space western story	4.35	13.00	30.00
51-66	1.15	3.50	8.00
67-Williamson/Torres-a, 5 pgs.	5.00	15.00	35.00

NOTE: *Many issues trimmed 1" shorter.*

COWGIRL ROMANCES (Formerly Jeanie)
No. 28, Jan, 1950
Marvel Comics (CCC)

	Good	Fine	Mint
28(No.1)-Photo-c	7.00	21.00	50.00

COWGIRL ROMANCES
1950 - No. 12, Winter, 1952-53 (No. 1-3, 52 pgs.)
Fiction House Magazines

	Good	Fine	Mint
1-Kamen-a	12.00	36.00	84.00
2	6.00	18.00	42.00
3-5	5.00	15.00	35.00
6-9,11,12	4.00	12.00	28.00
10-Frazetta?/Williamson-a; Kamen/Baker-a	16.00	48.00	110.00

COW PUNCHER (. . .Comics)
Jan, 1947; No. 2, Sept, 1947 - No. 7, 1949
Avon Periodicals

	Good	Fine	Mint
1-Clint Cortland, Texas Ranger, Kit West, Pioneer Queen begin; Kubert-a; Alabam stories begin	17.00	51.00	120.00
2-Kubert, Kamen/Feldstein-a; Kamen bondage-c	14.00	42.00	100.00
3-5,7: 3-Kiefer story	9.00	27.00	63.00
6-Opium drug mention story; bondage, headlight-c; Reinman-a	11.00	33.00	76.00

COWPUNCHER
1953 (nn) (Reprints Avon's No. 2)
Realistic Publications

	Good	Fine	Mint
Kubert-a	5.00	15.00	35.00

COWSILLS, THE (See Harvey Pop Comics)

COYOTE
June, 1983 - No. 16, Mar, 1986 (Adults only) ($1.50)
Epic Comics (Marvel)

	Good	Fine	Mint
1-Origin	.25	.75	1.50
2-5: 2-Origin concludes	.25	.75	1.50
6-16: 7,9-Ditko-p. 14-Badger x-over from First Comics	.25	.75	1.50

CRACKAJACK FUNNIES (Giveaway)
1937 (32 pgs.; full size; soft cover; full color)(Before No. 1?)
Malto-Meal

	Good	Fine	Mint
Features Dan Dunn, G-Man, Speed Bolton, Freckles, Buck Jones, Clyde Beatty, The Nebbs, Major Hoople, Wash Tubbs	38.00	115.00	265.00

CRACKAJACK FUNNIES
June, 1938 - No. 43, Jan, 1942
Dell Publishing Co.

1-Dan Dunn, Freckles, Myra North, Wash Tubbs, Apple Mary, The Nebbs, Don Winslow, Tom Mix, Buck Jones, Major Hoople, Clyde

CRACKAJACK FUNNIES (continued)	Good	Fine	Mint
Beatty, Boots begin	62.00	185.00	435.00
2	30.00	90.00	210.00
3	23.00	70.00	160.00
4,5	18.00	54.00	125.00
6-8,10	14.00	42.00	100.00
9-Red Ryder strip-r begin by Harman; 1st app. in comics & 1st cover	20.00	60.00	140.00
11-14	12.00	36.00	84.00
15-Tarzan text feature begins by Burroughs; not in No. 26,35	13.00	40.00	90.00
16-24	10.00	30.00	70.00
25-The Owl begins; in new costume No. 26 by Frank Thomas	23.00	70.00	160.00
26-30: 28-Owl-c	17.00	51.00	120.00
31-Owl covers begin	15.00	45.00	105.00
32-Origin Owl Girl	17.00	51.00	120.00
33-38: 36-Last Tarzan ish	11.00	33.00	77.00
39-Andy Panda begins (intro/1st app.)	12.00	36.00	84.00
40-43: 42-Last Owl cover	11.00	33.00	77.00

NOTE: ***McWilliams** art in most issues.*

CRACK COMICS (. . .Western No. 63 on)
May, 1940 - No. 62, Sept, 1949
Quality Comics Group

	Good	Fine	Mint
1-Origin The Black Condor by Lou Fine, Madame Fatal, Red Torpedo, Rock Bradden & The Space Legion; The Clock, Alias the Spider, Wizard Wells, & Ned Bryant begin; Powell-a; Note: Madame Fatal is a man dressed up as a woman	155.00	465.00	1085.00
2	75.00	225.00	585.00
3	60.00	180.00	420.00
4	52.00	156.00	364.00
5-10: 10-Tor, the Magic Master begins	40.00	120.00	280.00
11-20	35.00	105.00	245.00
21-24-Last Fine Black Condor	27.00	81.00	190.00
25,26	18.00	54.00	125.00
27-Intro & origin Captain Triumph by Alfred Andriola (Kerry Drake artist)	35.00	105.00	245.00
28-30	15.00	45.00	105.00
31-39: 31-Last Black Condor	9.00	27.00	62.00
40-46	6.00	18.00	42.00
47-57,59,60-Capt. Triumph by Crandall	7.00	21.00	50.00
58,61,62-Last Captain Triumph	5.00	15.00	35.00

NOTE: *Black Condor by **Fine**: No. 1, 2, 4-6, 8, 10-24; by **Sultan**: No. 3, 7; by **Fugitani**: No. 9. **Crandall** c-55, 59, 60. **Guardineer** a-17. **Gustavson** a-17. **McWilliams** art-No. 15-21, 23-27.*

CRACKED (Magazine) (Satire)
Feb-Mar, 1958 - Present
Major Magazines

	Good	Fine	Mint
1-One pg. Williamson	5.00	15.00	35.00
2-1st Shut-Ups & Bonus Cut-Outs	2.50	7.50	17.50
3-6	1.15	3.50	8.00
7-10: 7-R/1st 6 covers on-c	.85	2.50	6.00
11-12, 13(nn,3/60), 14-17, 18(nn,2/61), 19,20	.75	2.25	4.50
21-27(11/62), 27(No.28, 2/63; misnumbered), 29(5/63)	.45	1.25	2.50
31-60		.60	1.20
61-100: 99-Alfred E. Neuman on-c		.50	1.00
101-235: 234-Don Martin-a		.40	.80
Biggest. . .(Winter, 1977)		.60	1.20
Biggest, Greatest. . .nn('65)	.85	2.50	5.00
Biggest, Greatest. . .2('66) - #12('76)	.25	.75	1.50
. . .Digest 1(Fall, '86, 148p) - #5	.35	1.00	2.00
. . .Collectors' Edition ('73; formerly . . .Special) 4	.50	1.50	3.00
5-70		.60	1.25
. . .Shut-Ups (2/72-'72; Cracked Special #3) 1,2	.50	1.50	3.00
. . .Special 3('73; formerly Cracked Shut-Ups; . . .Collectors' Edition #4 on)	.50	1.50	3.00
Extra Special. . .1('76), 2('76)		.60	1.20
Giant. . .nn('65)	.85	2.50	5.00
Giant. . .2('66)-12('76), nn(9/77)-48('87)		.60	1.20
King Sized. . .1('67)	.85	2.50	5.00
King Sized. . .2('68)-11('77)	.50	1.50	3.00
King Sized. . .12-22 (Sum/'86)		.60	1.20
Super. . .1('68)	.85	2.50	5.00
Super. . .2('69)-34('87): 2-Spoof on Beatles movie by Severin	.50	1.50	3.00
Super. . .1('87, 100p))Severin & Elder-a	.45	1.40	2.75

NOTE: ***Burgos** a-1-10. **Davis** a-5, 11-17, 24, 80; c-12-14, 16. **Elder** a-5, 6, 10-13; c-10. **Everett** a-1-10, 23-25, 61; c-1. **Heath** a-1-3, 6, 13, 14, 17, 110; c-6. **Jaffee** a-5, 6. **Morrow** a-8-10. **Reinman** a-1-4. **Severin** a-in most all issues. **Shores** a-3-7. **Torres** a-7-10. **Ward** a-22-24, 143, 144, 149, 150, 152, 153, 156. **Williamson** a-1 (1 pg.). **Wolverton** a-10 (2 pgs.), Giant nn('65).*

CRACK WESTERN (Formerly Crack; Jonesy No. 85 on)
No. 63, Nov, 1949 - No. 84, May, 1953 (36pgs., 63-68,74-on)
Quality Comics Group

	Good	Fine	Mint
63(#1)-Two-Gun Lil (origin & 1st app.)(ends #84), Arizona Ames, his horse Thunder (sidekick Spurs & his horse Calico), Frontier Marshal (ends #70), & Dead Canyon Days (ends #69) begin; Crandall-a	7.00	21.00	50.00
64,65-Crandall-a	5.00	15.00	35.00
66,68-Photo-c. 66-Arizona Ames becomes A. Raines (ends #84)	5.00	15.00	35.00
67-Randolph Scott photo-c; Crandall-a	6.00	18.00	42.00
69(52pgs.)-Crandall-a	5.00	15.00	35.00
70(52pgs.)-The Whip (origin & 1st app.) & his horse Diablo begin (ends #84); Crandall-a	5.00	15.00	35.00
71(52pgs.)-Frontier Marshal becomes Bob Allen F. Marshal (ends #84); Crandall-c/a	6.00	18.00	42.00
72(52pgs.)-Tim Holt photo-c	5.00	15.00	35.00
73(52pgs.)-Photo-c	3.50	10.50	24.00
74,77,79,80,82	2.65	8.00	18.00
75,76,78,81,83-Crandall-c	3.50	10.50	24.00
84-Crandall c/a	5.00	15.00	35.00

CRASH COMICS (Catman No. 6 on)
May, 1940 - No. 5, Nov, 1940
Tem Publishing Co.

	Good	Fine	Mint
1-The Blue Streak, Strongman (origin), The Perfect Human, Shangra begin; Simon & Kirby-a(1st team-up)	70.00	210.00	490.00
2-Simon & Kirby-a	35.00	105.00	245.00
3-Simon & Kirby-a	28.00	84.00	200.00
4-Origin & 1st app. The Catman; S&K-a	45.00	135.00	315.00
5-S&K-a	28.00	84.00	200.00

NOTE: *Solar Legion by **Kirby** No. 1-5 (5 pgs. each).*

CRASH DIVE (See Cinema Comics Herald)

CRASH RYAN
Oct, 1984 - No. 4, Jan, 1985 (Baxter paper, limited series)
Epic Comics (Marvel)

	Good	Fine	Mint
1	.35	1.00	2.00
2-4	.25	.75	1.50

CRAZY
Dec, 1953 - No. 7, July, 1954
Atlas Comics (CSI)

	Good	Fine	Mint
1-Everett c/a	5.70	17.00	40.00
2	4.35	13.00	30.00
3-7	3.50	10.50	24.00

NOTE: ***Berg** a-1, 2. **Burgos** c-5. **Drucker** a-6. **Everett** a-1-4. **Heath** a-3, 7; c-7. **Maneely** a-1-7; c-3. **Post** a-3, 5, 6.*

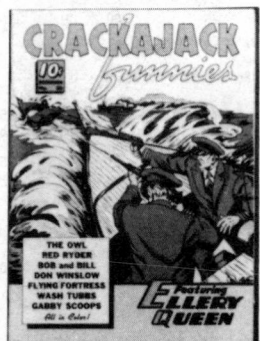

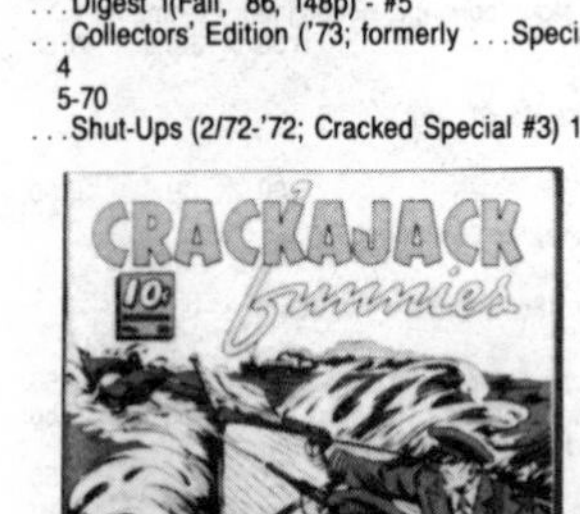

Crackajack Funnies #30, © DELL

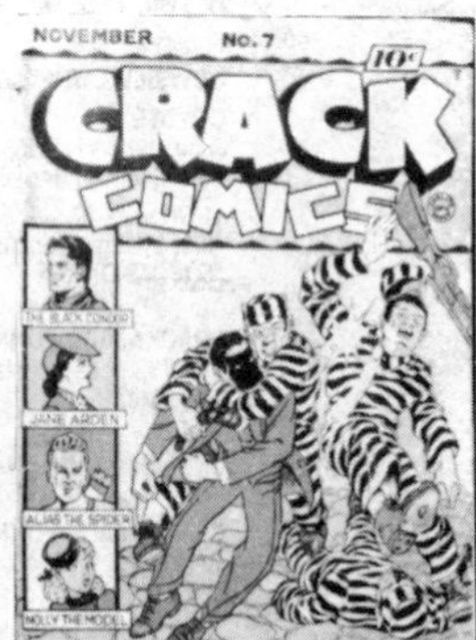

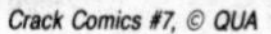
Crack Comics #7, © QUA

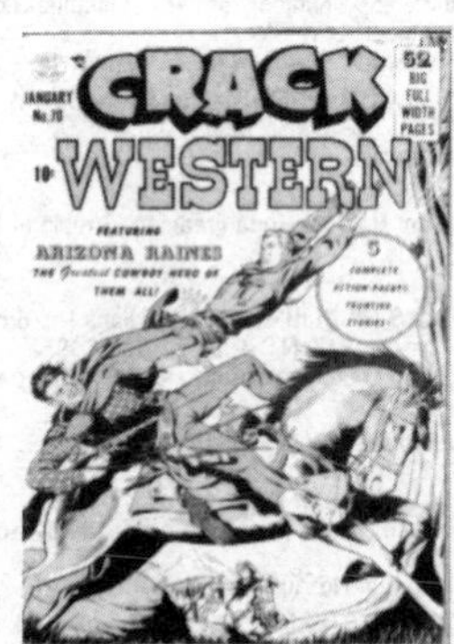

Crack Western #70, © QUA

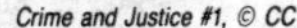
Crime and Justice #1, © CC

Crime and Punishment #5, © LEV

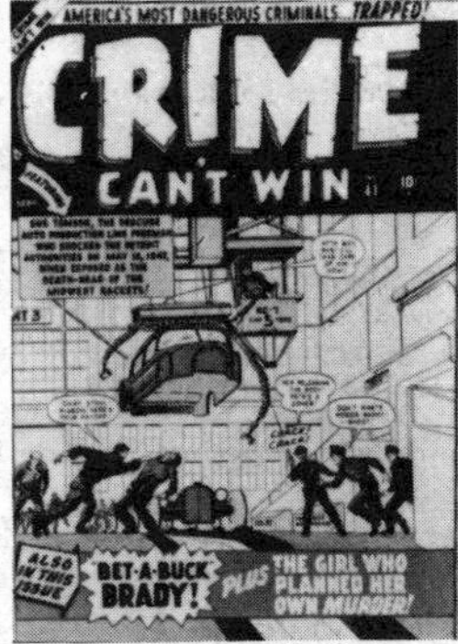

Crime Can't Win #41 (#1), © MCG

CRAZY (People Who Buy This Magazine Is. . .) (Formerly This Magazine Is. . .)
V3No.3, Nov, 1957 - V4No.8, Feb, 1959 (Magazine) (Satire)
Charlton Publications

	Good	Fine	Mint
V3#3 - V4#7	.50	1.50	3.00
V4#8-Davis-a, 8 pgs.	1.00	3.00	6.00

CRAZY (Satire)
Feb, 1973 - No. 3, June, 1973
Marvel Comics Group

	Good	Fine	Mint
1-3-Not Brand Echh-r		.30	.60

CRAZY (Magazine) (Satire)
Oct, 1973 - No. 94, Mar, 1983 (40 cents) (Black & White)
Marvel Comics Group

	Good	Fine	Mint
1-Wolverton(1 pg.), Ploog, Bode-a; 3 pg. photo story of Adams & Giordano	.35	1.00	2.00
2-Adams-a; Kurtzman's "Hey Look" reprint, 2 pgs.; Buscema-a		.60	1.20
3,5,6,8: 3-Drucker-a		.40	.80
4,7-Ploog-a		.40	.80
9-16-Eisner-a		.40	.80
17-81,83-94: 43-E.C. swipe from Mad 131. 76-Best of. . Super Special		.30	.60
82-Super Special ish; X-Men on-c	.30	.60	1.20
Super Special 1(Summer,'75, 100pgs.)-Ploog, Adams-r	.30	.80	1.60

NOTE: ***Austin** a-82i. **Buscema** a-82. **Byrne** c-82p. **Cardy** c-7,8. **Freas** c-1,2,4,6; a-7. **Rogers** a-82.*

CRAZY, MAN, CRAZY (Magazine) (Satire)
June, 1956
Humor Magazines

	Good	Fine	Mint
V2#2-Wolverton-a, 3pgs.	3.50	10.50	24.00

CREATURE, THE (See Movie Classics)

CREATURES ON THE LOOSE (Tower of Shadows No. 1-9)
No. 10, March, 1971 - No. 37, Sept, 1975
Marvel Comics Group

	Good	Fine	Mint
10-First King Kull story; Wrightson-a	1.35	4.00	8.00
11-15: 13-Crandall-a		.40	.80
16-Origin Warrior of Mars		.50	1.00
17-20		.30	.60
21,22: Steranko-c; Thongor begins #22, ends #29		.25	.50
23-37: 30-Manwolf begins		.25	.50

NOTE: ***Ditko** r-15, 17, 18, 20, 22, 24, 27, 28. **Everett** a-16i(r). **Gil Kane** a-16p(r); c-16, 20, 25, 29, 33p, 35p, 36p. **Morrow** a-20, 21. **Perez** a-33-37; c-34p. **Tuska** a-32p.*

CREEPER, THE (See Beware. . . & First Issue Special)

CREEPY (Magazine)(See Warren Presents)
1964 - No. 145, Feb, 1983; No. 146, 1985 (B&W)
Warren Publishing Co./Harris Publ. #146

	Good	Fine	Mint
1-Frazetta-a	.85	2.50	5.00
2	.50	1.50	3.00
3-13: 7,10-Frazetta-c	.35	1.00	2.00
14-Adams 1st Warren work	.60	1.75	3.50
15-25	.35	1.00	2.00
26-40: 32-Harlan Ellison story	.25	.75	1.50
41-47,49-54,56-61: 61-Wertham parody		.60	1.20
48,55-(1973, 1974 Annuals)	.35	1.00	2.00
62-64,66-145		.50	1.00
65-(1975 Annual)	.25	.75	1.50
146 ($2.95)	.50	1.50	3.00
Year Book 1968, 1969	.50	1.50	3.00
Year Book 1970-Adams, Ditko-a(r)	.50	1.50	3.00
Annual 1971,1972	.35	1.00	2.00

NOTE: *Above books contain many good artists works: **Adams, Brunner, Corben, Craig (Taycee), Crandall, Ditko, Evans, Frazetta, Heath, Jeff Jones, Krenkel, McWilliams, Morrow, Nino, Orlando, Ploog, Severin, Torres, Toth, Williamson, Wood, & Wrightson**; covers by **Crandall, Davis, Frazetta, Morrow, SanJulian, Todd/Bode**; Otto Binder's "Adam Link" stories in No. 2, 4, 6, 8, 9, 12, 13, 15 with **Orlando** art.*

CREEPY THINGS
July, 1975 - No. 6, June, 1976
Charlton Comics

	Good	Fine	Mint
1		.50	1.00
2-6		.40	.80
Modern Comics Reprint 2-6('77)		.25	.50

NOTE: ***Ditko** a-3,5. **Sutton** c-3,4.*

CRIME AND JUSTICE (Rookie Cop? No. 27 on)
March, 1951 - No. 26, Sept, 1955
Capitol Stories/Charlton Comics

	Good	Fine	Mint
1-Spanking panel	9.00	27.00	62.00
2	2.30	7.00	16.00
3-8,10,13: 6-Negligee panels	2.00	6.00	14.00
9-Classic story "Comics Vs. Crime"	5.00	15.00	35.00
11-Narcotics story	4.00	12.00	28.00
12-Bondage-c	3.50	10.50	24.00
14-Color illos in **POP**; gory story of man who beheads women	5.70	17.00	40.00
15-17,19-26	1.50	4.50	10.00
18-Ditko-a	9.00	27.00	62.00

NOTE: ***Ayers** a-17. **Shuster** a-19-21; c-19. Bondage c-11.*

CRIME AND PUNISHMENT (Title inspired by 1935 film)
April, 1948 - No. 74, Aug, 1955
Lev Gleason Publications

	Good	Fine	Mint
1	7.00	21.00	50.00
2	3.50	10.50	24.00
3-Used in **SOTI**, pg. 112; injury-to-eye panel; Fuje-a	5.70	17.00	40.00
4,5	2.65	8.00	18.00
6-10	2.00	6.00	14.00
11-20	1.70	5.00	12.00
21-30	1.50	4.50	10.00
31-38,40-44	1.30	4.00	9.00
39-Drug mention story "The 5 Dopes"	3.50	10.50	24.00
45-"Hophead Killer" drug story	3.25	9.75	22.00
46-One page Frazetta	1.85	5.50	13.00
47-57,60-65,70-74	1.15	3.50	8.00
58-Used in **POP**, pg. 79	2.85	8.50	20.00
59-Used in **SOTI**, illo-"What comic-book America stands for"	10.00	30.00	70.00
66-Toth c/a(4); 3-D effect ish(3/54)	12.00	36.00	84.00
67-"Monkey on His Back"-heroin story; 3-D effect ish.	9.00	27.00	62.00
68-3-D effect ish; Toth-c (7/54).	8.00	24.00	56.00
69-"The Hot Rod Gang"-dope crazy kids	4.35	13.00	30.00

NOTE: ***Everett** a-31. **Fuje** a-3, 12, 13, 17, 18, 26, 27. **Guardineer** a-2, 3, 10, 14, 17, 18, 26-28, 40-44. **Kinstler** c-69. **McWilliams** a-41, 48, 49. **Tuska** a-28, 30.*

CRIME CAN'T WIN (Formerly Cindy Smith)
No. 41, 9/50 - No. 43, 2/51; No. 4, 4/51 - No. 12, 9/53
Marvel/Atlas Comics (TCI 41/CCC 42,43,4-12)

	Good	Fine	Mint
41	4.35	13.00	30.00
42	2.65	8.00	18.00
43-Horror story	2.65	8.00	18.00
4(4/51), 5-9,11,12	2.00	6.00	14.00
10-Possible use in **SOTI**, pg. 161	2.65	8.00	18.00

NOTE: ***Robinson** a-9-11. **Tuska** a-43.*

CRIME CASES COMICS (Formerly Willie Comics)
No. 24, 8/50 - No. 27, 3/51; No. 5, 5/51 - No. 12, 7/52
Marvel/Atlas Comics(CnPC No.24-8/MJMC No.9-12)

	Good	Fine	Mint
24 (52 pgs.)	3.00	9.00	21.00

CRIME CASES COMICS (continued)

	Good	Fine	Mint
25,26	2.00	6.00	14.00
27-Morisi-a	2.00	6.00	14.00
5-12: 11-Robinson-a, 12-Tuska-a	1.70	5.00	12.00

CRIME CLINIC
No. 10, July-Aug, 1951 - No. 5, Summer, 1952
Ziff-Davis Publishing Co.

	Good	Fine	Mint
10-Painted-c	7.00	21.00	50.00
11,4,5-Painted-c	4.60	14.00	32.00
3-Used in **SOTI**, pg. 18	6.00	18.00	42.00

NOTE: *Painted covers by* ***Saunders.***

CRIME DETECTIVE COMICS
Mar-Apr, 1948 - V3/8, May-June, 1953
Hillman Periodicals

	Good	Fine	Mint
V1#1-The Invisible 6, costumed villains app; Fuje-c	5.00	15.00	35.00
2	2.30	7.00	16.00
3,4,7,10-12	1.70	5.00	12.00
5-Krigstein-a	2.85	8.50	20.00
6-McWilliams-a	1.70	5.00	12.00
8-Kirbyish-a by McCann	2.30	7.00	16.00
9-Used in **SOTI**, pg. 16 & "Caricature of the author in a position comic book publishers wish he were in permanently" illo.	17.00	51.00	120.00
V2#1,4,7-Krigstein-a	2.30	7.00	16.00
2,3,5,6,8-12 (1-2/52)	1.30	4.00	9.00
V3#1-Drug use-c	1.70	5.00	12.00
2-8	1.15	3.50	8.00

NOTE: ***Briefer*** *a-V3#1.* ***Kinstlerish*** *-a by McCann-V2#7, V3#2.* ***Powell*** *a-11.*

CRIME DETECTOR
Jan, 1954 - No. 5, Sept, 1954
Timor Publications

	Good	Fine	Mint
1	4.00	12.00	28.00
2	2.00	6.00	14.00
3,4	1.70	5.00	12.00
5-Disbrow-a (classic)	5.70	17.00	40.00

CRIME DOES NOT PAY (Formerly Silver Streak No. 1-21)
No. 22, June, 1942 - No. 147, July, 1955 (1st crime comic)
Comic House/Lev Gleason/Golfing (Title inspired by film)

	Good	Fine	Mint
22(23 on cover, 22 on indicia)-Origin The War Eagle & only app.; Chip Gardner begins; No. 22 rebound in True Crime, Complete Book of (Scarce)	68.00	205.00	475.00
23 (Scarce)	38.00	115.00	265.00
24-Intro. & 1st app. Mr. Crime (Scarce)	33.00	100.00	230.00
25-30	17.00	51.00	120.00
31-40	10.00	30.00	70.00
41-Origin & 1st app. Officer Common Sense	6.50	19.50	45.00
42-Electrocution-c	7.00	21.00	50.00
43-46,48-50	5.00	15.00	35.00
47-Electric chair-c	7.00	21.00	50.00
51-62,65-70	2.65	8.00	18.00
63,64-Possible use in **SOTI**, pg. 306. #63-Contains Biro-Gleason's self censorship code of 12 listed restrictions (5/48)	2.65	8.00	18.00
71-99: 87-Chip Gardner begins, ends #99.	1.70	5.00	12.00
100	2.00	6.00	14.00
101-104,107-110: 102-Chip Gardner app.	1.30	4.00	9.00
105-Used in **POP**, pg. 84	2.65	8.00	18.00
106,114-Frazetta, 1 pg.	2.00	6.00	14.00
111-Used in **POP**, pgs. 80,81 & injury-to-eye story illo	2.65	8.00	18.00
112,113,115-130	1.15	3.50	8.00
131-140	1.00	3.00	7.00
141,142-Last pre-code ish; Kubert-a(1)	2.30	7.00	16.00
143,147-Kubert-a, one each	2.30	7.00	16.00
144-146	1.00	3.00	7.00
1(Golfing-1945)	1.30	4.00	9.00
The Best of...(1944)-128 pgs.; Series contains 4 rebound issues	25.00	75.00	175.00
...1945 issue	20.00	60.00	140.00
...1946-48 issues	17.00	51.00	120.00
...1949-50 issues	12.00	36.00	84.00
...1951-53 issues	10.00	30.00	70.00

NOTE: *Many issues contain violent covers and stories. Whodunnit by* ***Guardineer****-39-105, 108-110; Chip Gardner by* ***Bob Fujitani (Fuje)****-88-103; c-103.* ***Alderman*** *a-41-43.* ***Kubert*** *c-143.* ***Landau****-a-118.* ***Maurer*** *a-41, 42.* ***McWilliams*** *a-91, 93, 95, 100-103.* ***Palais*** *a-41-43.* ***Powell*** *a-146, 147.* ***Tuska*** *a-51, 52, 56, 61, 63, 64, 66, 67. Bondage c-62, 98.*

CRIME EXPOSED
June, 1948; Dec, 1950 - No. 14, June, 1952
Marvel Comics (PPI)/Marvel Atlas Comics (PrPI)

	Good	Fine	Mint
1(6/48)	5.70	17.00	40.00
1(12/50)	3.50	10.50	24.00
2	2.00	6.00	14.00
3-9,11,14	1.70	5.00	12.00
10-Used in **POP**, pg. 81	2.00	6.00	14.00
12-Krigstein & Robinson-a	2.00	6.00	14.00
13-Used in **POP**, pg. 81; Krigstein-a	2.65	8.00	18.00

NOTE: ***Maneely*** *c-8.* ***Robinson*** *a-11,12.* ***Tuska*** *a-3, 4.*

CRIMEFIGHTERS
April, 1948 - No. 10, Nov, 1949
Marvel Comics (CmPS 1-3/CCC 4-10)

	Good	Fine	Mint
1-Some copies are undated & could be reprints	5.00	15.00	35.00
2	2.30	7.00	16.00
3-Morphine addict story	3.00	9.00	21.00
4-10: 6-Anti-Wertham editorial. 9,10-Photo-c	1.70	5.00	12.00

CRIME FIGHTERS (...Always Win)
No. 11, Sept, 1954 - No. 13, Jan, 1955
Atlas Comics (CnPC)

	Good	Fine	Mint
11,12: 11-Maneely-a	1.70	5.00	12.00
13-Pakula, Reinman, Severin-a	2.00	6.00	14.00

CRIME FIGHTING DETECTIVE (Shock Detective Cases No. 20 on; formerly Criminals on the Run?)
No. 11, Apr-May, 1950 - No. 19, June, 1952
Star Publications

	Good	Fine	Mint
11-L. B. Cole c/a, 2pgs.	3.00	9.00	21.00
12,13,15-19: 17-Young King Cole & Dr. Doom app.; L. B. Cole-c on all	2.35	7.00	16.00
14-L. B. Cole-c/a, r-/Law-Crime No. 2	3.00	9.00	21.00

CRIME FILES
No. 5, Sept, 1952 - No. 6, Nov, 1952
Standard Comics

	Good	Fine	Mint
5-Alex Toth-a; used in **SOTI**, pg. 4 (text)	8.00	24.00	56.00
6-Sekowsky-a	3.00	9.00	21.00

CRIME ILLUSTRATED (Magazine)
Nov-Dec, 1955 - No. 2, Spring, 1956
E. C. Comics

	Good	Fine	Mint
1-Ingels & Crandall-a	7.00	21.00	50.00
2-Ingels & Crandall-a	5.70	17.00	40.00

NOTE: ***Craig*** *a-2.* ***Crandall*** *a-1, 2; c-2.* ***Evans*** *a-1.* ***Davis*** *a-2.* ***Ingels*** *a-1, 2.* ***Krigstein/Crandall*** *a-1.* ***Orlando*** *a-1, 2; c-1.*

CRIME INCORPORATED (Formerly Crimes Incorporated)
No. 2, Aug, 1950; No. 3, Aug, 1951
Fox Features Syndicate

	Good	Fine	Mint
2	5.50	16.50	38.00

Crime Does Not Pay #25, © LEV

Crimefighters #1, © MCG

Crime Files #6, © STD

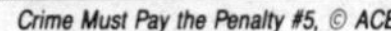
Crime Must Pay the Penalty #5, © ACE

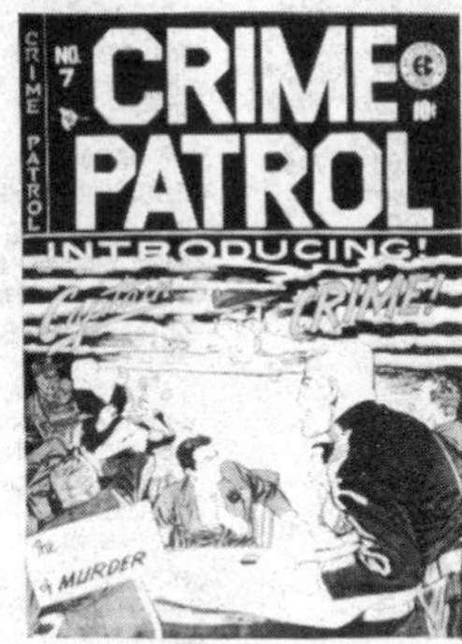

Crime Patrol #7, © EC

Crimes By Women #3, © FOX

	Good	Fine	Mint

CRIME INCORPORATED (continued)
3(1951)-Hollingsworth-a 3.70 11.00 26.00

CRIME MACHINE (Magazine)
Feb, 1971 - No. 2, May, 1971 (B&W)
Skywald Publications
1-Kubert-a(2)(r)(Avon) 1.00 3.00 7.00
2-Torres, Wildey-a; violent c/a .70 2.00 5.00

CRIME MUST LOSE! (Formerly Sports Action?)
No. 4, Oct, 1950 - No. 12, April, 1952
Sports Action (Atlas Comics)
4-Ann Brewster-a in all; c-used in N.Y. Legis. Comm. documents 3.50 10.50 24.00
5-10,12 1.70 5.00 12.00
11-Used in **POP**, pg. 89 2.30 7.00 16.00
NOTE: ***Robinson*** *a-9.*

CRIME MUST PAY THE PENALTY (Formerly Four Favorites; Penalty No. 47,48)
No. 33, 2/48; No. 2, 6/48 - No. 48, 1/56
Ace Magazines (Current Books)
33(2/48)-Becomes Four Teeners No. 34? 6.50 19.50 45.00
2(6/48)-Extreme violence; Palais-a? 4.35 13.00 30.00
3-'Frisco Mary' story used in Senate Investigation report, pg. 7 2.00 6.00 14.00
4,8-Transvestism story 4.00 12.00 28.00
5-7,9,10 1.70 5.00 12.00
11-20: 18-2pg. text on cocaine 1.30 4.00 9.00
21-32,34-40,42-48 1.15 3.50 8.00
33(7/53)-"Dell Fabry-Junk King"-drug story; mentioned in **Love and Death** 3.00 9.00 21.00
41-Drug story-"Dealers in White Death" 3.00 9.00 21.00
NOTE: ***Cameron*** *a-30-32,34,39-41.* ***Colan*** *a-20, 31.* ***Kremer*** *a-3, 37r.* ***Palais*** *a-2?, 5?.*

CRIME MUST STOP
October, 1952
Hillman Periodicals
V1#1(Scarce)-Similar to Monster Crime; Mort Lawrence-a 24.00 72.00 165.00

CRIME MYSTERIES (Secret Mysteries No. 16 on; combined with Crime Smashers No. 11? on)
May, 1952 - No. 15, Sept, 1954
Ribage Publishing Corp. (Trojan Magazines)
1-Transvestism story 16.00 48.00 110.00
2-Marijuana story (7/52) 12.00 36.00 84.00
3-One pg. Frazetta 7.00 21.00 50.00
4-Cover shows girl in bondage having her blood drained; 1 pg. Frazetta 16.00 48.00 110.00
5-10 6.00 18.00 42.00
11-14 5.00 15.00 35.00
15-Acid in face-c 10.00 30.00 70.00
NOTE: ***Hollingsworth*** *a-10-12, 15; c-12, 15.* ***Woodbridge*** *a-13. Bondage-c-1, 8, 12.*

CRIME ON THE RUN (See Approved Comics)
1949
St. John Publishing Co.
8 (Exist?) 2.65 8.00 18.00

CRIME ON THE WATERFRONT (Formerly Famous Gangsters)
No. 4, May, 1952 (Painted cover)
Realistic Publications
4 11.00 33.00 76.00

CRIME PATROL (International #1-5; International Crime Patrol #6, becomes Crypt of Terror #17 on)
No. 7, Summer, 1948 - No. 16, Feb-Mar, 1950
E. C. Comics

	Good	Fine	Mint

7-Intro. Captain Crime 28.00 84.00 195.00
8-14: 12-Ingels-a 25.00 75.00 175.00
15-Intro. of Crypt Keeper & Crypt of Terror; used by N.Y. Legis. Comm.-last pg. Feldstein-a 57.00 170.00 400.00
16-2nd Crypt Keeper app. 47.00 140.00 330.00
NOTE: ***Craig*** *c/a in most.*

CRIME PHOTOGRAPHER (See Casey. . .)

CRIME REPORTER
Aug, 1948 - No. 3, Dec, 1948 (Shows Oct.)
St. John Publ. Co.
1-Drug club story 15.00 45.00 105.00
2-Used in **SOTI**: illo-"Children told me what the man was going to do with the red-hot poker;" r-/Dynamic #17 with editing; Baker-c; Tuska-a 30.00 90.00 210.00
3-Baker-c; Tuska-a 11.00 32.00 76.00

CRIMES BY WOMEN
June, 1948 - No. 15, Aug, 1951; 1954
Fox Features Syndicate
1 33.00 100.00 230.00
2 17.00 51.00 120.00
3-Used in **SOTI**, pg. 234 20.00 60.00 140.00
4,5,7,9,11-15 16.00 48.00 110.00
6-Classic girl fight-c; acid-in-face panel 18.00 54.00 125.00
8-Used in **POP** 17.00 51.00 120.00
10-Used in **SOTI**, pg. 72 17.00 51.00 120.00
54(M.S. Publ.-'54)-Reprint; (formerly My Love Secret) 8.00 24.00 56.00

CRIMES INCORPORATED (Formerly My Past)
No. 12, June, 1950 (Crime Incorporated No. 2 on)
Fox Features Syndicate
12 3.70 11.00 26.00

CRIMES INCORPORATED (See Fox Giants)

CRIME SMASHER
Summer, 1948 (One Shot)
Fawcett Publications
1 (Spy Smasher) 12.00 36.00 84.00

CRIME SMASHERS (Secret Mysteries No. 16 on)
Oct, 1950 - No. 15, Mar, 1953
Ribage Publishing Corp.(Trojan Magazines)
1-Used in **SOTI**, pg. 19,20, & illo-"A girl raped and murdered;" Sally the Sleuth begins 24.00 72.00 170.00
2-Kubert-c 11.50 34.00 80.00
3,4 8.50 25.00 60.00
5-Wood-a 14.00 42.00 100.00
6,8-11 6.50 19.50 45.00
7-Female heroin junkie sty 7.00 21.00 50.00
12-Injury to eye panel; 1pg. Frazetta 8.50 25.50 60.00
13-Used in **POP**, pgs. 79,80; 1pg. Frazetta 8.00 24.00 56.00
14,15 6.50 19.50 45.00
NOTE: ***Hollingsworth*** *a-14.* ***Kiefer*** *a-15. Bondage c-7,9.*

CRIME SUSPENSTORIES (Formerly Vault of Horror No. 12-14)
No. 15, Oct-Nov, 1950 - No. 27, Feb-Mar, 1955
E. C. Comics
15-Identical to #1 in content; #1 printed on outside front cover. #15 (formerly "The Vault of Horror") printed and blackened out on inside front cover with Vol. 1, No. 1 printed over it. Evidently, several of No. 15 were printed before a decision was made not to drop the Vault of Horror and Haunt of Fear series. The print run was stopped on No. 15 and continued on No. 1. All of No. 15 were changed as described above. 60.00 180.00 420.00
1 50.00 150.00 350.00
2 30.00 90.00 210.00
3-5 21.00 63.00 145.00

CRIME SUSPENSTORIES (continued)	Good	Fine	Mint
6-10	16.00	48.00	110.00
11,12,14,15	11.00	33.00	75.00
13,16-Williamson-a	15.00	45.00	105.00
17-Williamson/Frazetta-a, 6 pgs.	17.00	52.00	120.00
18	8.00	24.00	55.00
19-Used in **SOTI**, pg. 235	10.00	30.00	70.00
20-Cover used in **SOTI**, illo-"Cover of a children's comic book"	13.00	40.00	90.00
21,25-27	6.50	19.50	45.00
22,23-Used in Senate investigation on juvenile delinquency. 22-Ax decapitation-c	11.00	33.00	76.00
24-'Food For Thought' similar to 'Cave In' in Amaz. Det. #13 ('52)	6.50	19.50	45.00

NOTE: ***Craig** a-1-21; c-1-18,20-22. **Crandall** a-18-26. **Davis** a-4, 5, 7, 9-12, 20. **Elder** a-17, 18. **Evans** a-15, 19, 21, 23, 25, 27; c-23, 24. **Feldstein** c-19. **Ingels** a-1-12, 14, 15, 27. **Kamen** a-2, 4-18, 20-27; c-25-27. **Krigstein** a-22, 24, 25, 27. **Kurtzman** a-1, 3. **Orlando** a-16, 22, 24, 26. **Wood** a-1, 3. Issues No. 11-15 have E. C. "quickie" stories. No. 25 contains the famous "Are You a Red Dupe?" editorial.*

CRIMINALS ON THE RUN (Formerly Young King Cole)
(Crime Fighting Detective No. 11 on?)
Aug-Sept, 1948 - No. 10, Dec-Jan, 1949-50
Premium Group (Novelty Press)

	Good	Fine	Mint
V4#1-Young King Cole begins	6.00	18.00	42.00
2-6: 6-Dr. Doom app.	4.60	14.00	32.00
7-Classic "Fish in the Face" cover by L. B. Cole	11.00	33.00	76.00
V5#1,2	4.60	14.00	32.00
10-L. B. Cole-c	4.60	14.00	32.00

NOTE: *Most issues have **L. B. Cole** covers. **McWilliams** a-V4#6,7, V5#2; c-V4#5.*

CRISIS ON INFINITE EARTHS (See Official . . . Index)
Apr, 1985 - No. 12, Mar, 1986 (12 issue maxi-series)
DC Comics

	Good	Fine	Mint
1-1st DC app. Blue Beetle & Detective Karp from Charlton; Perez-c on all	.70	2.00	4.00
2	.50	1.50	3.00
3	.40	1.25	2.50
4-6: 6-Intro Charlton's Capt. Atom, Nightshade, Question, Judomaster, Peacemaker & Thunderbolt	.35	1.00	2.00
7-Double size; death of Supergirl	.40	1.25	2.50
8-Death of Flash	.40	1.25	2.50
9-11: 9-Intro. Charlton's Ghost. 10-Intro. Charlton's Banshee, Dr. Spectro, Image, Punch & Jewellee	.35	1.00	2.00
12-Double size; deaths of Dove, Kole, Lori Lemaris, Sunburst, G.A. Robin & Huntress; Kid Flash becomes new Flash	.50	1.50	3.00

CROSLEY'S HOUSE OF FUN (Also see Tee and Vee Crosley. . .)
1950 (32 pgs.; full color; paper cover)
Crosley Div. AVCO Mfg. Corp. (Giveaway)

	Good	Fine	Mint
Strips revolve around Crosley appliances	1.70	5.00	10.00

CROSS AND THE SWITCHBLADE, THE
1972 (35-49 cents)
Spire Christian Comics/Fleming H. Revell Co.

	Good	Fine	Mint
1(Some issues have nn)		.40	.80

CROSSFIRE
1973 (39,49cents)
Spire Christian Comics (Fleming H. Revell Co.)

	Good	Fine	Mint
nn		.40	.80

CROSSFIRE
5/84 - No. 17, 3/86; No. 18, 1/87 - No. 26 (Baxter paper)
Eclipse Comics

	Good	Fine	Mint
1-DNAgents x-over; Spiegle c/a begins	.30	.90	1.80
2-17: 12,13-Death of Marilyn Monroe	.25	.75	1.50
18-26 (B&W)	.30	.90	1.80

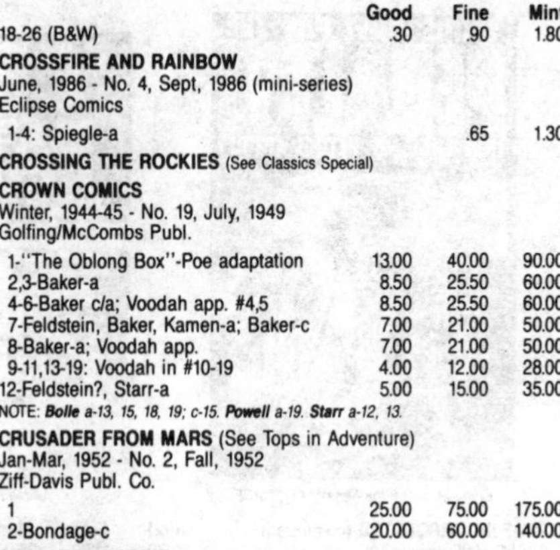

CROSSFIRE AND RAINBOW
June, 1986 - No. 4, Sept, 1986 (mini-series)
Eclipse Comics

	Good	Fine	Mint
1-4: Spiegle-a		.65	1.30

CROSSING THE ROCKIES (See Classics Special)

CROWN COMICS
Winter, 1944-45 - No. 19, July, 1949
Golfing/McCombs Publ.

	Good	Fine	Mint
1-"The Oblong Box"-Poe adaptation	13.00	40.00	90.00
2,3-Baker-a	8.50	25.50	60.00
4-6-Baker c/a; Voodah app. #4,5	8.50	25.50	60.00
7-Feldstein, Baker, Kamen-a; Baker-c	7.00	21.00	50.00
8-Baker-a; Voodah app.	7.00	21.00	50.00
9-11,13-19: Voodah in #10-19	4.00	12.00	28.00
12-Feldstein?, Starr-a	5.00	15.00	35.00

NOTE: ***Bolle** a-13, 15, 18, 19; c-15. **Powell** a-19. **Starr** a-12, 13.*

CRUSADER FROM MARS (See Tops in Adventure)
Jan-Mar, 1952 - No. 2, Fall, 1952
Ziff-Davis Publ. Co.

	Good	Fine	Mint
1	25.00	75.00	175.00
2-Bondage-c	20.00	60.00	140.00

CRUSADER RABBIT (See 4-Color No. 735,805)

CRUSADERS, THE
1974 - Vol. 16, 1985 (36 pg.) (39-69 cents) (Religious)
Chick Publications

	Good	Fine	Mint
Vol. 1-Operation Bucharest('74). Vol. 2-The Broken Cross('74). Vol. 3-Scarface('74). Vol. 4-Exorcists('75). Vol. 5-Chaos('75). each. . . .		.40	.80
Vol. 6-Primal Man?('76)-(Disputes evolution theory). Vol. 7-The Ark-(Claims proof of existence, destroyed by Bolsheviks). Vol. 8-The Gift-(Life story of Christ). Vol. 9-Angel of Light-(Story of the Devil). Vol. 10-Spellbound?-(Tells how rock music is Satanical & produced by witches). 11-Sabotage?. 12-Alberto. 13-Double-Cross 14-The Godfathers. (No. 6-14 low in distribution; Loaded in religious propaganda.). 15-The Force. 16-The Four Horsemen		.40	.80

CRYIN' LION, THE
Fall, 1944 - No. 3, Spring, 1945
William H. Wise Co.

	Good	Fine	Mint
1	4.35	13.00	30.00
2,3	2.65	8.00	18.00

CRYPT OF SHADOWS
Jan, 1973 - No. 21, Nov, 1975
Marvel Comics Group

	Good	Fine	Mint
1-Wolverton-a r-/Advs. Into Terror No. 7		.30	.60
2-21		.25	.50

NOTE: ***Briefer** a-2r. **Ditko** a-13r, 18-20r. **Everett** a-6, 14r; c-2i. **Heath** a-1r. **Mort Lawrence** a-1r. **Maneely** a-2r. **Moldoff** a-8. **Powell** a-12r, 14r.*

CRYPT OF TERROR (Tales From the Crypt No. 20 on; formerly Crime Patrol)
No. 17, Apr-May, 1950 - No. 19, Aug-Sept, 1950
E. C. Comics

	Good	Fine	Mint
17	70.00	210.00	490.00
18,19	52.00	156.00	365.00

NOTE: ***Craig** c/a-17-19. **Feldstein** a-17-19. **Ingels** a-19. **Kurtzman** a-18. **Wood** a-18. Canadian reprints known; see Table of Contents.*

CUPID
Jan, 1950 - No. 2, Mar, 1950
Marvel Comics (U.S.A.)

CRIME
SUSPENSTORIES
10¢
AN ILLUSTRATED
TERROR-TALE
HAUNT OF FEAR!

Crime Suspenstories #5, © EC

Crisis On Infinite Earths #2, © DC

Crown Comics #19, © Golfing

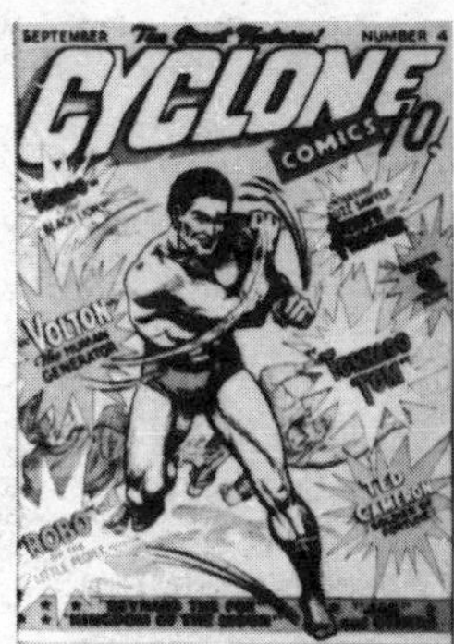

Cyclone Comics #4, © Bilbara Publ.

Dagar, Desert Hawk #15, © FOX

Daisy and Donald 1, © WDC

CUPID (continued) — **Good** **Fine** **Mint**
1,2: 1-Photo-c 3.50 10.50 24.00

CURIO
1930's(?) (Tabloid size, 16-20 pages)
Harry 'A' Chesler
5.00 15.00 35.00

CURLY KAYOE COMICS
1946 - 1948; 1948 - 1950; Jan, 1958
United Features Syndicate/Dell Publ. Co.
1 (1946) 5.00 15.00 35.00
2 2.65 8.00 18.00
3-8 1.85 5.50 13.00
United Presents . . . (Fall, 1948) 1.85 5.50 13.00
4-Color 871 (Dell, 1/58) 1.70 5.00 12.00

CUSTER'S LAST FIGHT
1950
Avon Periodicals
nn-Partial reprint of Cowpuncher #1 8.50 25.50 60.00

CUTIE PIE
May, 1955 - No. 5, Aug, 1956
Junior Reader's Guild/Lev Gleason
1 1.70 5.00 12.00
2-5 1.00 3.00 7.00

CYCLONE COMICS
June, 1940 - No. 5, Nov, 1940
Bilbara Publishing Co.
1-Origin Tornado Tom; Volton begins, Mister Q app.
35.00 105.00 245.00
2 17.00 51.00 120.00
3-5 14.00 42.00 100.00

CYNTHIA DOYLE, NURSE IN LOVE (Formerly and becomes Sweetheart Diary No. 75 on)
No. 66, Oct, 1962 - No. 74, Feb, 1964
Charlton Publications
66-74 (#74, exist?) .30 .80 1.60

DAFFY (. . . Duck No. 18 on)
No. 457, 3/53 - No. 30, 7-9/62; No. 31, 10-12/62 - No. 145, 1983 (no No. 132,133)
Dell Publishing Co./Gold Key No. 31-127/Whitman No. 128 on
4-Color 457-Elmer Fudd x-overs begin 1.50 4.50 10.00
4-Color 536,615('55) 1.15 3.50 8.00
4(1-3/56)-11('57) .85 2.50 6.00
12-19(1958-59) .75 2.25 5.00
20-40(1960-64) .60 1.75 3.50
41-60(1964-68) .35 1.00 2.00
61-90(1969-73)-Road Runner in most .60 1.20
91-131,134-145(1974-83) .40 .80
Mini-Comic 1 (1976; 3¼x6½") .25 .50

NOTE: *Reprint issues-No.41-46, 48, 50, 53-55, 58, 59, 67, 69, 73, 81, 96, 103-08; 136-142, 144, 145(⅓-⅔-r). (See March of Comics No. 277, 288, 313, 331, 347, 357, 375, 387, 397, 402, 413, 425, 437, 460).*

DAFFYDILS
1911 (52 pgs.; 6x8"; B&W; hardcover)
Cupples & Leon Co.
by Tad 7.00 21.00 50.00

DAFFY TUNES COMICS
June, 1947 - No. 2, Aug, 1947
Four Star Publications
nn 2.30 7.00 16.00
2-Al Fago c/a 2.65 8.00 18.00

DAGAR, DESERT HAWK (Capt. Kidd No. 24-on; formerly All Great)
No. 14, Feb, 1948 - No. 23, Apr, 1949 (No No.17,18)
Fox Features Syndicate — **Good** **Fine** **Mint**
14-Tangi & Safari Cary begin; Edmond Good bondage-c/a
22.00 65.00 154.00
15,16-E. Good-a; 15-Bondage-c 14.00 42.00 100.00
19,20,22 11.00 33.00 76.00
21-'Bombs & Bums Away' panel in 'Flood of Death' story used in **SOTI** 14.00 42.00 100.00
23-Bondage-c 14.00 42.00 100.00

NOTE: *Tangi by* ***Kamen****-14-16,19; c-21.*

DAGAR THE INVINCIBLE (Tales of Sword & Sorcery . . .)
10/72 - No. 18, 12/76; No. 19, 4/82 (See Dan Curtis)
Gold Key
1-Origin; intro. Villains Olstellon & Scorpio 1.00 3.00 6.00
2-5: 3-Intro. Graylin, Dagar's woman; Jarn x-over
.50 1.50 3.00
6-1st Dark Gods story .35 1.00 2.00
7-10: 9-Intro. Torgus. 10-1st Three Witches story
.35 1.00 2.00
11-18: 13-Durak & Torgus x-over; story continues in Dr. Spektor No. 15. 14-Dagar's origin retold. 18-Origin retold .60 1.20
19-Origin-r/No. 18 .40 .80

NOTE: *Durak app.-7,12,13. Tragg app.-5,11.*

DAGWOOD (Chic Young's) (Also see Blondie)
Sept, 1950 - No. 140, Nov, 1965
Harvey Publications
1 6.00 18.00 42.00
2 3.00 9.00 21.00
3-10 2.50 7.50 17.50
11-30 1.50 4.50 10.00
31-70 1.00 3.00 6.00
71-100 .70 2.00 4.00
101-128,130,135 .50 1.50 3.00
129,131-134,136-140-All are 68-pg. issues .85 2.50 5.00

NOTE: *Popeye and other one page strips appeared in early issues.*

DAGWOOD SPLITS THE ATOM (Also see Topix V8No.4)
1949 (Science comic with King Features characters) (Giveaway)
King Features Syndicate
nn-½ comic, ½ text; Popeye, Olive Oyl, Henry, Mandrake, Little King, Katzenjammer Kids app. 2.65 8.00 18.00

DAISY AND DONALD (See Walt Disney Showcase No. 8)
May, 1973 - No. 59, 1984 (no No. 48)
Gold Key/Whitman No. 42 on
1-Barks r-/WDC&S 280,308 .50 1.50 3.00
2-5: 4-Barks r-/WDC&S 224 .35 1.00 2.00
6-10 .25 .75 1.50
11-20 .50 1.00
21-47,49,50: 32-r-/WDC&S 308. 50-r-/No. 3 .40 .80
51-Barks r-/4-Color 1150 .50 1.00
52-59: 52-r-/No. 2. 55-r-/No. 5 .35 .70

DAISY & HER PUPS (Blondie's Dogs)
No. 21, 7/51 - No. 27, 7/52; No. 8, 9/52 - No. 25, 7/55
Harvey Publications
21-27: 26,27 have No. 6 & 7 on cover but No. 26 & 27 on inside
1.00 3.00 6.00
8-25: 19-25-Exist? .85 2.50 5.00

DAISY COMICS
Dec, 1936 (Small size: 5¼x7½")
Eastern Color Printing Co.
Joe Palooka, Buck Rogers (2 pgs. from Famous Funnies No. 18), Napoleon Flying to Fame, Butty & Fally 14.00 42.00 100.00

DAISY DUCK & UNCLE SCROOGE PICNIC TIME (See Dell Giant No.33)

DAISY DUCK & UNCLE SCROOGE SHOW BOAT (See Dell Giant No.55)

DAISY DUCK'S DIARY (See 4-Color No. 600,659,743,858,948,1055,1150,1247 & WDC&S #298)

DAISY HANDBOOK
1946 - 1948 (132 pgs.)(10 cents)(Pocket-size)
Daisy Manufacturing Co.

	Good	Fine	Mint
1-Buck Rogers, Red Ryder	13.00	40.00	90.00
2-Captain Marvel & Ibis the Invincible, Red Ryder, Boy Commandos & Robotman; 2 pgs. Wolverton-a; contains 8pg. color catalog	13.00	40.00	90.00

DAISY LOW OF THE GIRL SCOUTS
1954, 1965 (16 pgs.; paper cover)
Girl Scouts of America

1954-Story of Juliette Gordon Low	2.00	6.00	14.00
1965	.50	1.50	3.00

DAISY MAE (See Oxydol-Dreft)

DAISY'S RED RYDER GUN BOOK
1955 (132 pages)(25 cents)(Pocket-size)
Daisy Manufacturing Co.

Boy Commandos, Red Ryder, 1 pg. Wolverton-a	9.00	27.00	62.00

DAKOTA LIL (See Fawcett Movie Comics)

DAKOTA NORTH
1986 - No. 5, Feb, 1987
Marvel Comics Group

1-5		.40	.80

DAKTARI (Ivan Tors) (TV)
7/67 - No. 3, 10/68; No. 4, 9/69 (Photo-c)
Dell Publishing Co.

1	1.15	3.50	8.00
2-4	.85	2.50	6.00

DALE EVANS COMICS (Also see Queen of the West . . .)
Sept-Oct, 1948 - No. 24, July-Aug, 1952 (No. 1-19, 52 pgs.)
National Periodical Publications

1-Dale Evans & her horse Buttermilk begin; Sierra Smith begins by Alex Toth	17.00	51.00	120.00
2-Alex Toth-a	12.00	36.00	84.00
3-11-Alex Toth-a	10.00	30.00	70.00
12-24	5.00	15.00	35.00

NOTE: *Photo-c-1, 2, 4-14.*

DALGODA
Aug, 1984 - No. 8, Feb, 1986
Fantagraphics Books

1-Full color, high quality paper ($2.25 cover price). Fujitake a/c	.40	1.25	2.50
2-8-($1.50 cover price). 2,3-Debut Grimwood's Daughter	.30	.90	1.80

DALTON BOYS, THE
1951
Avon Periodicals

1-(No. on spine)-Kinstler-c	8.50	25.50	60.00

DAN CURTIS GIVEAWAYS
1974 (24 pages) (3x6") (in color, all reprints)
Western Publishing Co.

1-Dark Shadows, 2-Star Trek, 3-The Twilight Zone, 4-Ripley's Believe It or Not!, 5-Turok, Son of Stone, 6-Star Trek, 7-The Occult Files of Dr. Spektor, 8-Dagar the Invincible, 9-Grimm's Ghost Stories Set . . .	.50	1.50	3.00

DANDEE
1947
Four Star Publications

	Good	Fine	Mint
	2.30	7.00	16.00

DAN DUNN (See Detective Dan & Super Book nn)

DANDY COMICS (Also see Happy Jack Howard)
Spring, 1947 - No. 7, Spring, 1948
E. C. Comics

1-Vince Fago-a in all	15.00	45.00	105.00
2	11.00	33.00	76.00
3-7	9.00	27.00	62.00

DANGER
January, 1953 - No. 11, Aug, 1954
Comic Media/Allen Hardy Assoc.

1-Heck-a	4.00	12.00	28.00
2,3,5-7,9-11	1.70	5.00	12.00
4-Marijuana cover/story	5.00	15.00	35.00
8-Bondage/torture/headlights panels	5.00	15.00	35.00

NOTE: ***Morisi** a-2,5,6(3); c-2. Contains some-r from Danger & Dynamite.*

DANGER (Jim Bowie No. 15 on; formerly Comic Media title)
No. 12, June, 1955 - No. 14, Oct, 1955
Charlton Comics Group

12(#1)	3.00	9.00	21.00
13,14: 14 r-/#12	1.70	5.00	12.00

DANGER
1964
Super Comics

Super Reprint No. 10-12 (Black Dwarf; No. 11-r-/from Johnny Danger), No. 15,16 (Yankee Girl & Johnny Rebel), No. 17 (Capt. Courage & Enchanted Dagger), No. 18(nd) (Gun-Master, Annie Oakley, The Chameleon; L.B. Cole-a)	.70	2.00	4.00

DANGER AND ADVENTURE (Formerly This Magazine Is Haunted; Robin Hood and His Merry Men No. 28 on)
No. 22, Feb, 1955 - No. 27, Feb, 1956
Charlton Comics

22-Ibis the Invincible, Nyoka app.	3.00	9.00	21.00
23-Nyoka, Lance O'Casey app.	3.00	9.00	21.00
24-27: 24-Mike Danger & Johnny Adventure begin	2.00	6.00	14.00

DANGER IS OUR BUSINESS!
1953(Dec.) - No. 10, June, 1955
Toby Press

1-Captain Comet by Williamson/Frazetta-a, 6 pgs. (Science Fiction)	25.00	75.00	175.00
2	3.15	9.50	22.00
3-10	2.65	8.00	18.00
I.W. Reprint No. 9('64)-Williamson/Frazetta-a r-/No. 1; Kinstler-c	7.00	21.00	40.00

DANGER IS THEIR BUSINESS (See A-1 Comics No. 50)

DANGER MAN (See 4-Color No. 1231)

DANGER TRAIL
July-Aug, 1950 - No. 5, Mar-Apr, 1951
National Periodical Publications

1-King Farrady begins, ends No. 4; Toth-a	28.00	84.00	200.00
2-Toth-a	23.00	70.00	160.00
3-5-Toth-a in all; Johnny Peril app. #5	20.00	60.00	140.00

DANIEL BOONE (See The Exploits of . . ., 4-Color No. 1163, The Legends of . . ., Frontier Scout . . ., Fighting . . ., & March of Comics No. 306)

DAN'L BOONE
Sept, 1955 - No. 8, Sept, 1957
Magazine Enterprises/Sussex Publ. Co. No. 2 on

1	3.00	9.00	21.00

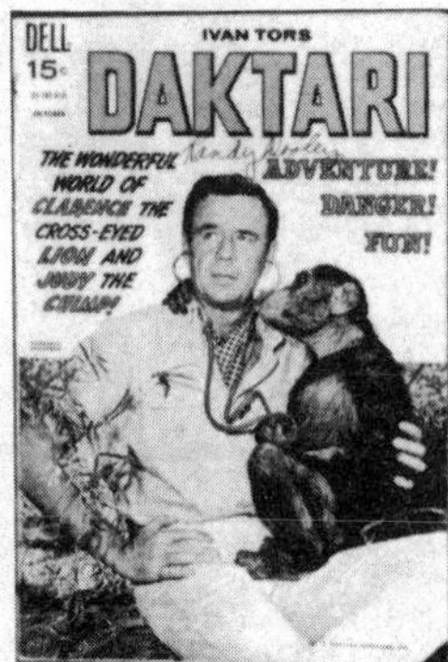

Daktari #4, © Ivan Tors Films

Dale Evans Comics #6, © DC

Danger #2, © Comics Media

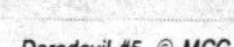
Daredevil #5, © MCG

Daredevil #184, © MCG

Daredevil Comics #22, © LEV

DAN'L BOONE (continued)

	Good	Fine	Mint
2	1.70	5.00	12.00
3-8	1.30	4.00	9.00

DANIEL BOONE (TV) (See March of Comics No. 306)
Jan, 1965 - No. 15, Apr, 1969
Gold Key

	Good	Fine	Mint
1	1.50	4.50	10.00
2-5	.85	2.50	5.00
6-15: 6-Photo-c	.70	2.00	4.00

DANNY BLAZE (Nature Boy No. 3 on)
Aug, 1955 - No. 2, Oct, 1955
Charlton Comics

	Good	Fine	Mint
1,2	2.30	7.00	16.00

DANNY DINGLE (See Single Series No. 17 & Sparkler Comics)

DANNY KAYE'S BAND FUN BOOK
1959
H & A Selmer (Giveaway)

	Good	Fine	Mint
	2.00	6.00	14.00

DANNY THOMAS SHOW, THE (See 4-Color No. 1180,1249)

DARBY O'GILL & THE LITTLE PEOPLE (See 4-Color No. 1024 & Movie Comics)

DAREDEVIL (. . .& the Black Widow #92-107; see Marvel Advs. & Marvel Super Heroes, '66)
April, 1964 - Present
Marvel Comics Group

	Good	Fine	Mint
1-Origin Daredevil	43.00	107.00	300.00
2-Fantastic Four cameo	19.00	48.00	135.00
3-Origin, 1st app. The Owl	11.00	27.00	75.00
4,5: 5-Wood-a begins	6.40	16.00	45.00
6,7,9,10: 7-dons new costume	4.30	11.00	30.00
8-Origin & 1st app. Stilt-Man	4.30	11.00	30.00
11-15: 12-Romita's 1st work at Marvel. 13-Facts about Ka-Zar's origin; Kirby-a	2.65	8.00	18.00
16-20: 16,17-Spider-Man x-over. 18-Origin & 1st app. Gladiator	1.70	5.00	12.00
21-40	1.15	3.50	7.00
41-49: 41-Death Mike Murdock. 43-vs. Capt. America	.70	2.00	4.00
50-52-Smith-a	1.15	3.50	7.00
53-Origin retold	.75	2.25	4.50
54-56,58-60	.40	1.25	2.50
57-Reveals i.d. to Karen Page	.60	1.80	3.60
61-99: 62-1st app. Nighthawk. 81-Oversize issue; Black Widow begins	.35	1.10	2.20
100-Origin retold	1.00	3.00	6.00
101-106,108-113,115-120	.25	.70	1.40
107-Starlin-c	.30	.90	1.80
114-1st app. Deathstalker	.30	.90	1.80
121-130,132-137: 124-1st app. Copperhead; Black Widow leaves. 126-1st New Torpedo.		.60	1.20
131-Origin & 1st app. Bullseye	.75	2.25	4.50
138-Byrne-a	.45	1.40	2.80
139-150: 142-Nova cameo. 148-30 & 35 cent issues exist. 150-1st app. Paladin		.60	1.20
151-Reveals i.d. to Heather Glenn		.60	1.20
152-157		.50	1.00
158-Frank Miller art begins (5/79); origin & death of Deathstalker	3.75	15.00	30.00
159	1.85	5.50	11.00
160,161	1.50	4.50	9.00
162	.35	1.00	2.00
163,164: 163-Hulk cameo. 164-Origin	1.25	3.75	7.50
165-167,170	1.00	3.00	6.00
168-Intro/origin Elektra	2.50	7.50	15.00
169-Elektra app.	1.25	3.75	7.50
171-175: 174,175-Elektra app.	.70	2.00	4.00
176-180-Elektra app. 179-Anti-smoking issue mentioned in the Congressional Record	.40	1.25	2.50
181-Double size; death of Elektra	.45	1.40	2.80
182-184-Punisher app. by Miller	.85	2.50	5.00
185-189: 187-New Black Widow. 189-Death of Stick		.70	1.40
190-Double size; return of Elektra, part origin		.70	1.40
191-Last Miller Daredevil		.70	1.40
192-195,197-210: 208-Harlan Ellison scripts		.60	1.20
196-Wolverine app.	.60	1.80	3.60
211-225		.50	1.00
226-Frank Miller plots begin		.60	1.20
227-Miller scripts begin	.70	2.00	4.00
228-233-Last Miller script	.35	1.00	2.00
234-248,250-255		.50	1.00
249-Wolverine app.	.35	1.00	2.00
Giant Size 1 ('75)	.35	1.10	2.20
Special 1(9/67)-new art	.60	1.75	3.50
Special 2(2/71)(Wood-r), 3(1/72)-r	.35	1.10	2.20
Annual 4(10/76)	.35	1.10	2.20

NOTE: ***Art Adams*** *c-238p, 239.* ***Austin*** *a-191i; c-151i, 200i.* ***John Buscema*** *a-136, 137p, 234p, 235p; c-86p, 136i, 137p, 142, 219.* ***Byrne*** *c-200p, 201, 203, 223.* ***Colan*** *a(p)-20-49, 53-82, 84-98, 100, 110, 112, 124, 153, 154, 156, 157, Spec. 1p; c(p)-20-42, 44-49, 53-60, 71, 92, 98, 138, 153, 154, 156, 157, Annual 1.* ***Craig*** *a-50i, 52i.* ***Ditko*** *a-162, 234p, 235p; c-162.* ***Everett*** *a/c-1; inks-21, 83.* ***Gil Kane*** *a-141p, 146-48p, 151p; c(p)-85, 90, 91, 93, 94, 115, 116, 119, 120, 125-28, 133, 139, 147, 152.* ***Kirby*** *c-2-4, 5p, 12p, 13p, 136p.* ***Layton*** *c-202.* ***Miller*** *script-168-182, 183(part), 184-191; a-158-161p, 163-184p, 191p; c-158-161p, 163-184p, 185-189, 190p, 191.* ***Orlando*** *a-2-4p.* ***Powell*** *a-9p, 11p, Special 1r, 2r.* ***B. Smith*** *a-83p, 236p.* ***Smith*** *c-51p, 52p.* ***Simonson*** *c-199.* ***Starlin*** *a-105p.* ***Steranko*** *c-44i.* ***Tuska*** *a-39i, 145p.* ***Williamson*** *a-237i, 239i, 248-250i; c-248-250i.* ***Wood*** *a-5-9i, 10, 11i, Spec. 2i; c-5i, 6-11, 164i.*

DAREDEVIL COMICS (See Silver Streak)
July, 1941 - No. 134, Sept, 1956 (Charles Biro stories)
Lev Gleason Publications (Funnies, Inc. No. 1)

(No. 1 titled "Daredevil Battles Hitler")

	Good	Fine	Mint
1-The Silver Streak, Lance Hale, Cloud Curtis, Dickey Dean, Pirate Prince team up with Daredevil and battle Hitler; Daredevil battles the Claw; Origin of Hitler feature story	210.00	630.00	1470.00
2-London, Pat Patriot, Nightro, Real American No. 1, Dickie Dean, Pirate Prince, & Times Square begin; intro. & only app. The Pioneer, Champion of America	120.00	360.00	840.00
3-Origin of 13	67.00	200.00	470.00
4	55.00	165.00	385.00
5-Intro. Sniffer & Jinx; Ghost vs. Claw begins by Bob Wood, ends No. 20	50.00	150.00	350.00
6-(#7 on indicia)	40.00	120.00	280.00
7-10: 8-Nightro ends	36.00	108.00	250.00
11-London, Pat Patriot end; bondage/torture-c	32.00	95.00	225.00
12-Origin of The Claw; Scoop Scuttle by Wolverton begins (2-4 pgs.), ends #22, not in #21	45.00	135.00	315.00
13-Intro. of Little Wise Guys	45.00	135.00	315.00
14	24.00	72.00	170.00
15-Death of Meatball	35.00	105.00	245.00
16,17	22.00	65.00	154.00
18-New origin of Daredevil-Not same as Silver Streak No. 6	45.00	135.00	315.00
19,20	20.00	60.00	140.00
21-Reprints cover of Silver Streak No. 6(on inside) plus intro. of The Claw from Silver Streak No. 1	28.00	84.00	195.00
22-30	11.50	34.00	80.00
31-Death of The Claw	18.00	54.00	125.00
32-37: 34-Two Daredevil stories begin, end #68			

DAREDEVIL COMICS (continued) Good Fine Mint

8.00 24.00 56.00

38-Origin Daredevil retold from No. 18 16.00 48.00 110.00

39,40 8.00 24.00 56.00

41-50: 42-Intro. Kilroy in Daredevil 5.00 15.00 35.00

51-69-Last Daredevil ish. 3.50 10.50 24.00

70-Little Wise Guys take over book; McWilliams-a; Hot Rock Flanagan begins, ends No. 80 2.30 7.00 16.00

71-79,81: 79-Daredevil returns 1.70 5.00 12.00

80-Daredevil x-over 1.70 5.00 12.00

82,90-One page Frazetta ad in both 2.00 6.00 14.00

83-89,91-99,101-134 1.50 4.50 10.00

100 2.30 7.00 16.00

NOTE: ***Wolverton's*** *Scoop Scuttle-12-20, 22.* ***Bolle*** *a-125.* ***Maurer*** *a-75.* ***McWilliams*** *a-73, 75, 79, 80.*

DARING ADVENTURES (Also see Approved Comics)
Nov, 1953 (3-D)
St. John Publishing Co.

1 (3-D)-Reprints lead story/Son of Sinbad No. 1 by Kubert 18.00 54.00 125.00

DARING ADVENTURES
1963 - 1964
I.W. Enterprises/Super Comics

I.W. Reprint No. 9-Disbrow-a(3) 2.00 6.00 12.00

Super Reprint No. 10,11('63)-r/Dynamic No. 24,16; 11-Marijuana story; Yankee Boy app. 1.00 3.00 6.00

Super Reprint No. 12('64)-Phantom Lady from Fox(r/No. 14,15) 6.00 18.00 40.00

Super Reprint No. 15('64)-Hooded Menace 5.00 15.00 35.00

Super Reprint No. 16('64)-r/Dynamic No. 12 1.00 3.00 6.00

Super Reprint No. 17('64)-Green Lama by Raboy from Green Lama No. 3 2.00 6.00 12.00

Super Reprint No. 18-Origin Atlas 1.00 3.00 6.00

DARING COMICS (Formerly Daring Mystery) (Jeanie No. 13 on)
No. 9, Fall, 1944 - No. 12, Fall, 1945
Timely Comics (HPC)

9-Human Torch & Sub-Mariner begin 32.00 95.00 225.00

10-The Angel only app. 29.00 85.00 200.00

11,12-The Destroyer app. 29.00 85.00 200.00

DARING CONFESSIONS (Formerly Youthful Hearts)
No. 4, 11/52 - No. 7, 5/53; No. 8, 10/53
Youthful Magazines

4-Doug Wildey-a 3.70 11.00 26.00

5-8: 6,8-Wildey-a 2.65 8.00 18.00

DARING LOVE (Radiant Love No. 2 on)
Sept-Oct, 1953
Gillmor Magazines

1 3.00 9.00 21.00

DARING LOVE (Formerly Youthful Romances)
No. 15, 12/52; No. 16, 2/53-c, 4/53-Indicia; No. 17-4/53-c & indicia
Ribage/Pix

15 3.00 9.00 21.00

16,17: 17-Photo-c 2.30 7.00 16.00

NOTE: ***Colletta*** *a-15.* ***Wildey*** *a-17.*

DARING LOVE STORIES (See Fox Giants)

DARING MYSTERY COMICS (Comedy No. 9 on; title changed to Daring with No. 9)
Jan, 1940 - No. 8, Jan, 1942
Timely Comics (TPI 1-6/TCI 7,8)

1-Origin The Fiery Mask by Joe Simon; Monako, Prince of Magic, John Steele, Soldier of Fortune, Doc Doyle begin; Flash Foster & Barney Mullen, Sea Rover only app; bondage-c 428.00 1285.00 3000.00

2-(Rare)-Origin The Phantom Bullet & only app.; The Laughing Mask & Mr. E only app.; Trojak the Tiger Man begins, ends #6; Zephyr Jones & K-4 & His Sky Devils app., also #4 205.00 615.00 1435.00

3-The Phantom Reporter, Dale of FBI, Breeze Barton, Captain Strong & Marvex the Super-Robot only app.; The Purple Mask begins 147.00 440.00 1030.00

4-Last Purple Mask; Whirlwind Carter begins; Dan Gorman, G-Man app. 105.00 315.00 735.00

5-The Falcon begins; The Fiery Mask, Little Hercules app. by Sagendorf in the Segar style; bondage-c 100.00 300.00 700.00

6-Origin & only app. Marvel Boy by S&K; Flying Flame, Dynaman, & Stuporman only app.; The Fiery Mask by S&K; S&K bondage-c 125.00 375.00 875.00

7-Origin The Blue Diamond, Captain Daring by S&K, The Fin by Everett, The Challenger, The Silver Scorpion & The Thunderer by Burgos; Mr. Millions app. 125.00 375.00 875.00

8-Origin Citizen V; Last Fin, Silver Scorpion, Capt. Daring by Borth, Blue Diamond & The Thunderer; S&K-c; Rudy the Robot only app. 95.00 285.00 665.00

NOTE: ***Schomburg*** *c-1-4.* ***Simon*** *a-2,3,5.*

DARING NEW ADVENTURES OF SUPERGIRL, THE
Nov, 1982 - No. 13, Nov, 1983 (Supergirl No. 14-on)
DC Comics

1-Origin retold .40 .80

2-13: 13-New costume; flag-c .25 .50

NOTE: ***Buckler*** *c-1p, 2p.* ***Giffen*** *c-3p, 4p.* ***Gil Kane*** *c-6, 8, 9, 11-13.*

DARK CRYSTAL, THE
April, 1983 - No. 2, May, 1983
Marvel Comics Group

1,2-Movie adaptation, part 1&2 .25 .50

DARK KNIGHT (See Batman: The Dark Knight Returns)

DARKLON THE MYSTIC
Oct, 1983 (One shot)
Pacific Comics

1-Starlin c/a(r) .25 .75 1.50

DARK MANSION OF FORBIDDEN LOVE, THE (Becomes Forbidden Tales of Dark Mansion No. 5 on)
Sept-Oct, 1971 - No. 4, Mar-Apr, 1972
National Periodical Publications

1-4: 2-Adams-c. 3-Jeff Jones-c .40 .80

DARK MYSTERIES
June-July, 1951 - No. 25, 1955
"Master"-"Merit" Publications

1-Wood c/a, 8 pgs. 22.00 65.00 154.00

2-Wood/Harrison c/a, 8 pgs. 18.00 54.00 125.00

3-9: 7-Dismemberment, hypo blood drainage stories 5.50 16.50 38.00

10-Cannibalism story 6.50 19.50 45.00

11-13,15-18: 11-Severed head panels. 13-Dismemberment-c/story 4.60 14.00 32.00

14-Several E.C. Craig swipes 5.00 15.00 35.00

19-Injury to eye panel 6.50 19.50 45.00

20-Female bondage, blood drainage story 5.00 15.00 35.00

21,22-Last pre-code ish, mis-dated 3/54 instead of 3/55 4.00 12.00 28.00

23-25 3.00 9.00 21.00

NOTE: ***Cameron*** *a-1, 2.* ***Myron Fass*** *c/a-21.* ***Harrison*** *a-3, 7; c-3.* ***Hollingsworth*** *a-7-17, 20, 21, 23.* ***Wildey*** *a-5.* ***Woodish*** *art by Fleishman-9; c-10. Bondage-c, 10, 18, 19.*

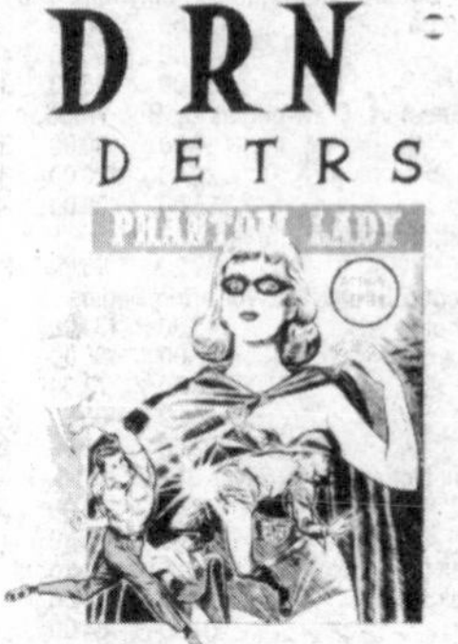

Daring Adventures #12, © Super Comics

Daring Comics #9, © MCG

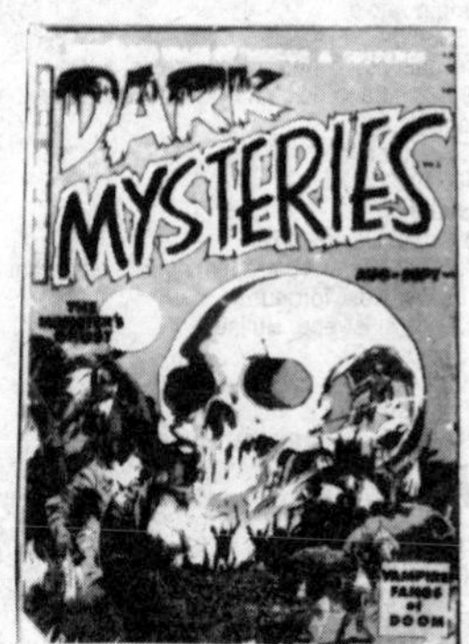

Dark Mysteries #2, © Master

A Date With Judy #7, © DC

Davy Crockett #1, © CC

The Dazzler #24, © MCG

DARK SHADOWS
October, 1957 - 1958
Steinway Comic Publications (Ajax)

	Good	Fine	Mint
1	3.50	10.50	24.00
2,3	2.00	6.00	14.00

DARK SHADOWS (TV) (See Dan Curtis)
March, 1969 - No. 35, Feb, 1976 (Photo-c, 1-7)
Gold Key

	Good	Fine	Mint
1(30039-903)-with pull-out poster	4.60	14.00	32.00
2	2.30	7.00	16.00
3-with pull-out poster	3.00	9.00	21.00
4-7: Last photo-c	2.00	6.00	14.00
8-10	1.50	4.50	10.00
11-20	1.15	3.50	8.00
21-35: 30-last painted-c	.85	2.50	5.00
Story Digest 1 (6/70)	.85	2.50	5.00

DARLING LOVE
Oct-Nov, 1949 - No. 11, 1952 (no month)
Close Up/Archie Publ. (A Darling Magazine)

	Good	Fine	Mint
1	4.60	14.00	32.00
2	2.35	7.00	16.00
3-8,10,11: 5,6-photo-c	2.00	6.00	14.00
9-Krigstein-a	3.35	10.00	23.00

DARLING ROMANCE
Sept-Oct, 1949 - No. 7, 1951
Close Up (MLJ Publications)

	Good	Fine	Mint
1	4.60	14.00	32.00
2	2.35	7.00	16.00
3-7	2.00	6.00	14.00

DASTARDLY & MUTTLEY IN THEIR FLYING MACHINES (See Fun-In No. 1-4,6)

DASTARDLY & MUTTLEY KITE FUN BOOK (Giveaway)
1969 (16 pages) (5x7", soft-c) (Hanna-Barbera's)
Florida Power & Light Co./Sou. Calif. Edison/Pacific Gas & Electric

	Good	Fine	Mint
	.75	2.25	5.00

DATE WITH DANGER
No. 5, Dec, 1952 - No. 6, Feb, 1953
Standard Comics

	Good	Fine	Mint
5,6	2.65	8.00	18.00

DATE WITH DEBBI
1-2/69 - No. 17, 9-10/71; No. 18, 10-11/72
National Periodical Publications

	Good	Fine	Mint
1	.85	2.50	5.00
2-18	.50	1.50	3.00

DATE WITH JUDY, A (Radio/TV)
Oct-Nov, 1947 - No. 79, Oct-Nov, 1960 (No. 1-25, 52 pgs.)
National Periodical Publications

	Good	Fine	Mint
1	10.00	30.00	70.00
2	5.00	15.00	35.00
3-10	3.70	11.00	26.00
11-20	2.35	7.00	16.00
21-40	1.70	5.00	12.00
41-45: 45-Last pre-code (2-3/55)	1.30	4.00	9.00
46-79: 79-Drucker c/a	1.00	3.00	7.00

DATE WITH MILLIE, A (Life With Millie No. 8 on)
Oct, 1956 - No. 7, Aug, 1957; Oct, 1959 - No. 7, Oct, 1960
Atlas/Marvel Comics (MPC)

	Good	Fine	Mint
1(10/56)-(1st Series)	5.00	15.00	35.00
2	2.30	7.00	16.00
3-7	2.00	6.00	14.00
1(10/59)-(2nd Series)	3.00	9.00	21.00
2-7	1.60	4.70	11.00

DATE WITH PATSY, A
September, 1957
Atlas Comics

	Good	Fine	Mint
1	2.65	8.00	18.00

DAVID AND GOLIATH (See 4-Color No. 1205)

DAVID CASSIDY (TV?)(See Swing With Scooter #33)
Feb, 1972 - No. 14, Sept, 1973
Charlton Comics

	Good	Fine	Mint
1	1.00	3.00	6.00
2-14: 7,9-Photo-c	.70	2.00	4.00

DAVID LADD'S LIFE STORY (See Movie Classics)

DAVY CROCKETT (See Dell Giants, Fightin . . ., Frontier Fighters, It's Game Time, Western Tales & Wild Frontier)

DAVY CROCKETT
1951
Avon Periodicals

	Good	Fine	Mint
nn-Tuska?, Reinman-a; Fawcette-c	8.00	24.00	56.00

DAVY CROCKETT (. . . King of the Wild Frontier No. 1,2)(TV)
5/55 - No. 671, 12/55; No. 1, 12/63; No. 2, 11/69 (Walt Disney)
Dell Publishing Co./Gold Key

	Good	Fine	Mint
4-Color 631-Fess Parker photo-c	2.65	8.00	18.00
4-Color 639-Photo-c	2.30	7.00	16.00
4-Color 664,671(Marsh-a)-Photo-c	3.00	9.00	21.00
1(12/63-Gold Key)-r	1.50	4.50	10.00
2(11/69)-r; Fess Parker photo-c	1.00	3.00	6.00
..Christmas Book (no date, 16pgs, paper-c) Sears giveaway	1.70	5.00	12.00
..In the Raid at Piney Creek (1955, 16pgs, 5x7¼")American Motors giveaway; slick, photo-c	3.50	10.50	24.00
..Safety Trails (1955, 16pgs, 3¼x7") Cities Service giveaway	3.00	9.00	21.00

DAVY CROCKETT (. . . Frontier Fighter #1,2; Kid Montana #9 on)
Aug, 1955 - No. 8, Jan, 1957
Charlton Comics

	Good	Fine	Mint
1	2.65	8.00	18.00
2	1.30	4.00	9.00
3-8	1.00	3.00	7.00
Hunting With . . . ('55, 16 pgs.)-Ben Franklin Store giveaway (Publ.-S. Rose)	1.15	3.50	8.00

DAYS OF THE MOB (See In the Days of the Mob)

DAZEY'S DIARY
June-Aug, 1962
Dell Publishing Co.

	Good	Fine	Mint
01-174-208: Bill Woggon-a?	2.00	6.00	14.00

DAZZLER, THE (Also see Marvel Graphic Novel & X-Men #130)
March, 1981 - No. 42, Mar, 1986
Marvel Comics Group

	Good	Fine	Mint
1-X-Men app; Alcala art	.25	.75	1.50
2-X-Men app.		.50	1.00
3-20: 23,24-Power Man & Iron Fist app. 32-The Inhumans app.		.40	.80
21-Double size; photo-c; many cameos		.50	1.00
22-37		.35	.70
38-X-Men app.	.35	1.00	2.00
39-42		.40	.80

NOTE: *No. 1 distributed only through comic shops.* ***Alcala*** *a-1i, 2i.* ***Guice*** *a-42.*

DC CHALLENGE
11/85 - No. 12, 10/86 ($1.25-$2.00; 12 issue maxi-series)
DC Comics

DC CHALLENGE (continued) Good Fine Mint
1 .25 .75 1.50
2-11 .65 1.30
12($2.00)-Perez/Austin-c .35 1.00 2.00

DC COMICS PRESENTS
July-Aug, 1978 - No. 97, Sept, 1986
DC Comics

(Superman team-ups with No. 1-on)

1 .40 1.25 2.50
2-10 .25 .75 1.50
11,12,14-20 .60 1.20
13-Legion of Super Heroes .45 1.25 2.50
21-25 .50 1.00
26-(10/80)-Green Lantern; intro Cyborg, Starfire, Raven, New Teen Titans; Starlin-c/a; Sargon the Sorcerer back-up; 16 pgs. preview of the New Teen Titans 2.35 7.00 14.00
27-85: 41-16 pg. W. Woman insert; 1st app. in new costume. 43-Legion app. 52-1st app. Ambush Bug. 59,81-Ambush Bug app. .40 .80
86,88-Crisis x-over .50 1.00
87-Double size; Crisis x-over .65 1.30
89-96: 90-Origin Capt. Atom retold .45 .90
97-Double size .65 1.30
Annual 1(9/82)-G.A. Superman .60 1.20
Annual 2(7/83)-Intro/origin Superwoman .60 1.20
Annual 3(9/84)-Shazam; intro Capt. Thunder .60 1.20
Annual 4(10/85)-Superwoman .65 1.30

NOTE: ***Adkins** a-2, 54; c-2. **Alcala** a-48. **Buckler** a-12p, 33p, 34p, 45p, 49p, Annual 1p; c-30p, 33p, 34p, 49p, 50p, Annual 1p. **Giffen** a/c-52p, 59p, 81p. **Gil Kane** a-28, 35, Annual 3; c-48p, 56, 58, 60, 62, 64, 68, Annual 2, 3. **Kubert** c/a-66. **Morrow** c/a-65. **Newton** a/c-54p. **Orlando** c-53i. **Perez** a-26p, 61p; c-38, 61, 94. **Starlin** a-26-29p, 36p, 37p; c-26-29, 36, 37, 93. **Staton** a(p)-9-11, 15, 16, 19, 21, 23, 39, 96p; c-15p. **Williamson** i-79, 85, 87.*

DC GRAPHIC NOVEL (Also see DC Science Fiction . . .)
Nov, 1983 - Present ($5.95, 68 pgs.)
DC Comics

1-Star Raiders 1.00 3.00 6.00
2-Warlords; not from the regular Warlord series 1.00 3.00 6.00
3-The Medusa Chain; Ernie Colon story/a 1.00 3.00 6.00
4-The Hunger Dogs; Kirby-c/a 1.00 3.00 6.00
5-Me And Joe Priest 1.00 3.00 6.00
6-Metalzoic 1.20 3.50 7.00
7-Space Clusters 1.00 3.00 6.00

DC 100 PAGE SUPER SPECTACULAR (50 cents)
(Title is 100 Page. . .No. 14 on)(Square bound)
1971 - No. 13, 6/72; No. 14, 2/73 - No. 22, 11/73 (No No.1-3)
National Periodical Publications

4-Weird Mystery Tales-Johnny Peril & Phantom Stranger; cover & splashes by Wrightson; origin Jungle Boy of Jupiter .60 1.20
5-Love stories; Wood Inks, 7pgs. .60 1.20
6-"World's Greatest Super-Heroes"-JLA, JSA, Spectre, Johnny Quick, Vigilante, Wildcat & Hawkman; Adams wrap-around-c .25 .75 1.50
7-(See Superman No. 245),8-(See Batman No. 238)
9-(See Our Army at War No. 242),10-(See Adventure No. 416)
11-(See Flash No. 214),12-(See Superboy No. 185)
13-(See Superman No. 252)
14-22: 21-r/Showcase 54. 22-r/All Flash 13 .40 .80

NOTE: ***Anderson** a-11, 14, 18i, 22. **B. Baily** a-18r, 20r. **Burnley** a-20r. **Crandall** a-14p(r), 20r. **Drucker** a-4r. **Infantino** a-17, 20, 22. **G. Kane** a-18. **Kubert** a-6, 7, 16, 17; c-16,19. **Meskin** a-4, 22. **Mooney** a-15r, 21r. **Toth** a-17, 20.*

DC SCIENCE FICTION GRAPHIC NOVEL
1985 - Present? ($5.95)
DC Comics Good Fine Mint
SF1-Hell on Earth by Robert Bloch, SF2-Nightwings by Robert Silverberg, SF3-Frost & Fire by Bradbury 1.00 3.00 5.95
SF4-Merchants of Venus 1.00 3.00 5.95
SF5-Demon With A Glass Hand by Ellison; M. Rogers-a. SF6-The Magic Goes Away by Niven, SF7-Sandkings by George R.R. Martin 1.00 3.00 5.95

DC SPECIAL (Also see Super DC. . .)
10-12/68 - No. 15, 11-12/71; No. 16, Spr/75 - No. 29, 8-9/77
National Periodical Publications

1-All Infantino ish; Flash, Batman, Adam Strange-r (68 pgs.) begin .60 1.20
2-4,6-11,13,14 .40 .80
5-All Kubert ish. Viking Prince, Sgt. Rock-r .40 .80
12-Viking Prince; Kubert-c .40 .80
15-G.A. Plastic Man origin r/Police No. 1; origin Woozy by Cole Last 68 pg. ish .40 .80
16-27: 16-Super Heroes Battle Super Gorillas .40 .80
28-Earth Shattering Disaster Stories; Legion of Super-Heroes story .40 .80
29-Secret Origin of the Justice Society .40 .80

NOTE: ***Adams** c-3, 4, 6, 11, 29. **Buckler** a-27p; c-27p. **Grell** a-20; c-17. **Heath** a-12r. **G. Kane** a-6p, 17r, 19-21r. **Kubert** a-6r, 12r, 22. **Staton** a-29p. **Toth** a-13.*

DC SPECIAL BLUE-RIBBON DIGEST
Mar-Apr, 1980 - No. 24, Aug, 1982
DC Comics

1-24 .50 1.00

NOTE: ***Adams** a-16(6)r, 17r, 23r; c-16. **Aparo** a-6r, 24r; c-23. **Grell** a-8, 10; c-10. **Heath** a-14. **Kaluta** a-17r. **Gil Kane** a-22r. **Kirby** a-23r. **Kubert** a-3, 18r, 21r; c-7, 12, 14, 17, 18, 21, 24. **Morrow** a-24r. **Orlando** a-17r, 22r; c-1, 20. **Perez** c-19p. **Toth** a-21r, 24r. **Wood** a-3, 17r, 24r. **Wrightson** a-16r, 17r, 24r.*

DC SPECIAL SERIES
9/77 - No. 16, Fall, 1978; No. 17, 8/79 - No. 27, Fall, 1981
(No. 23 & 24 - digest size; No. 25-27 - over-sized)
National Periodical Publications/DC Comics

1-Five-Star Super-Hero Spectacular; Atom, Flash, Green Lantern, Aquaman, Batman, Kobra app.; Adams-c; Staton, Nasser-a .50 1.00
2(No.1)-Original Swamp Thing Saga, The(9-10/77)-reprints Swamp Thing No. 1&2 by Wrightson; Wrightson wrap-around-c .50 1.00
3-20,22-24: 10-Origin Dr. Fate, Lightray & Black Canary .25 .50
21-Miller-a (1st on Batman) .50 1.50 3.00
25-Superman II The Adventure Continues (Sum '81); photos from movie($2.95) (Same as All-New Coll. Ed. C-64?) .35 1.00 2.00
26-Superman and His Incredible Fortress of Solitude (Sum '81) ($2.50) (Same as All-New Co.. Ed. C-63?) .35 1.00 2.00
27-Batman vs. The Incredible Hulk($2.50) .35 1.00 2.00

DC SPOTLIGHT
1985 (50th anniversary special)
DC Comics (giveaway)

1 .40 .80

DC SUPER-STARS
March, 1976 - No. 18, Winter, 1978 (No.3-18: 52 pgs.)
National Periodical Publications/DC Comics

1-Teen Titans (68 pgs.) .60 1.20
2-16,18 .30 .60
17-Secret Origins of Super-Heroes(1st app./origin of The Huntress); Origin Green Arrow by Grell; Legion app. .60 1.20

NOTE: ***Aparo** c-7, 14, 17, 18. **Austin** a-11i. **Buckler** a-14p; c-10. **Grell** a-17. **G. Kane** a-1r, 10r. **Kubert** c-15. **Layton** c/a-16i, 17i. **Mooney** a-4r, 6r. **Morrow** c/a-11r. **Nasser** a-11. **Newton** c/a-16p. **Staton** a-17; c-17. No. 10, 12-18 contain all new material; the rest*

DC Challenge #2, © DC

DC Comics Presents #50, © DC

DC Special Series #21, © DC

Dead-Eye Western #3, © HILL

Deadman #2 ('85), © DC

Death Valley #1, Comic Media

DC SUPER-STARS (continued)
are reprints.

D-DAY (Also see Special War Series)
Sum/63; No. 2, Fall/64; No. 4, 9/66; No. 5, 10/67; No. 6, 11/68
Charlton Comics (no No. 3)

	Good	Fine	Mint
1(1963)-Montes/Bache-c	.50	1.50	3.00
2(Fall,'64)-Wood-a(3)	1.00	3.00	7.00
4-6('66-'68)-Montes/Bache-a #5	.35	1.00	2.00

DEAD END CRIME STORIES
April, 1949 (52 pages)
Kirby Publishing Co.

nn-(Scarce)-Powell, Roussos-a	19.00	57.00	132.00

DEAD-EYE WESTERN COMICS
Nov-Dec, 1948 - V3No.1, Apr-May, 1953
Hillman Periodicals

V1#1(52 pgs.)-Krigstein, Roussos-a	5.00	15.00	35.00
V1#2,3(52 pgs.)	2.65	8.00	18.00
V1#4-12	1.50	4.50	10.00
V2#1,2,5-8,10-12	1.15	3.50	8.00
3,4-Krigstein-a	2.30	7.00	16.00
9-One pg. Frazetta ad	1.60	4.70	11.00
V3#1	1.00	3.00	7.00

NOTE: ***Briefer** a-V1No.8. Kinstleresque stories by **McCann**-12, V2No.1,2, V3No.1.*

DEADLIEST HEROES OF KUNG FU
Summer, 1975 (Magazine)
Marvel Comics Group

1	.30	.90	1.80

DEADLY HANDS OF KUNG FU, THE
April, 1974 - No. 33, Feb, 1977 (75 cents) (B&W - Magazine)
Marvel Comics Group

1(V1#4 listed in error)-Origin Sons of the Tiger; Shang-Chi, Master of Kung Fu begins; Bruce Lee photo pin-up	.40	1.25	2.50
2,3,5	.30	.90	1.80
4-Bruce Lee painted-c by Adams; 8 pg. biog of B. Lee	.40	1.25	2.50
6-14	.30	.90	1.80
15-(Annual 1, Summer '75)	.30	.90	1.80
16-19,21-27,29-33: 19-1st White Tiger		.60	1.20
20-Origin The White Tiger; Perez-a	.30	.90	1.80
28-Origin Jack of Hearts; Bruce Lee life story	.40	1.25	2.50
Special Album Edition 1(Summer, '74)-Adams-i	.30	.90	1.80

NOTE: ***Adams** c-1, 2-4, 11, 12, 14, 17. **Giffen** a-22p, 24p. **G. Kane** a-23p. **Kirby** a-5r. **Perez** a(p)-6-14, 16, 17, 19, 21. **Rogers** a-32, 33. **Starlin** a-1, 2r, 15r. **Staton** a-28p, 31, 32. Sons of the Tiger in 1, 3, 4, 6-14, 16-19.*

DEADMAN
May, 1985 - No. 7, Nov, 1985
DC Comics

1-Deadman-r by Infantino, Adams	.35	1.00	2.00
2-7	.30	.90	1.80

DEADMAN
Mar, 1986 - No. 4, June, 1986 (mini-series)
DC Comics

1-4-Lopez-c/a		.45	.90

DEAD OF NIGHT
Dec, 1973 - No. 11, Aug, 1975
Marvel Comics Group

1-Reprints		.30	.60
2-11: 11-Kane/Wrightson-c		.25	.50

NOTE: ***Ditko** a-7r, 10r.*

DEAD WHO WALK, THE (Also see Strange Myst., Super-r #15,16)
1952 (One Shot)
Realistic Comics

	Good	Fine	Mint
nn	20.00	60.00	140.00

DEADWOOD GULCH
1931 (52 pages) (B&W)
Dell Publishing Co.

By Gordon Rogers	5.00	15.00	35.00

DEAN MARTIN & JERRY LEWIS (See Adventures of . . .)

DEAR BEATRICE FAIRFAX
No. 5, Nov, 1950 - No. 9, Sept, 1951 (Vern Greene art)
Best/Standard Comics(King Features)

5	3.00	9.00	21.00
6-9	1.70	5.00	12.00

NOTE: ***Schomburg** air brush-c-5-9.*

DEAR HEART (Formerly Lonely Heart)
No. 15, July, 1956 - No. 16, Sept, 1956
Ajax

15,16	1.70	5.00	12.00

DEAR LONELY HEART (. . . Illustrated No. 1-6)
Mar, 1951; No. 3, Dec, 1951 - No. 8, Oct, 1952
Artful Publications

1	8.00	24.00	56.00
2	3.70	11.00	26.00
3-Matt Baker Jungle Girl story	8.00	24.00	56.00
4-8	3.35	10.00	23.00

DEAR LONELY HEARTS (Lonely Heart #9 on)
Aug, 1953 - No. 8, Oct, 1954
Harwell Publ./Mystery Publ. Co.

1	3.00	9.00	21.00
2-8	1.65	5.00	11.00

DEARLY BELOVED
Fall, 1952
Ziff-Davis Publishing Co.

1-Photo-c	6.00	18.00	42.00

DEAR NANCY PARKER
June, 1963 - No. 2, Sept, 1963
Gold Key

1,2	1.50	4.50	10.00

DEATH OF CAPTAIN MARVEL (See Marvel Graphic Novel #1)

DEATH RATTLE (Formerly an Underground)
V2/1, 10/85 - Present ($1.95, Baxter paper)(Mature readers)
Kitchen Sink Press

V2/1-Corben-c	.35	1.00	2.00
2-5: 2-Unpubbed Spirit sty by Eisner. 5-Robot Woman by Wolverton-r	.35	1.00	2.00
6,7: 6-B&W issues begin	.35	1.00	2.00

DEATH VALLEY
Oct, 1953 - No. 6, Aug, 1954?
Comic Media

1-Old Scout	3.50	10.50	24.00
2	2.00	6.00	14.00
3-6	1.30	4.00	9.00

DEATH VALLEY (Becomes Frontier Scout, Daniel Boone No.10-13)
No. 7, 6/55 - No. 9, 10/55 (Cont. from Comic Media series)
Charlton Comics

7-9	1.30	4.00	9.00

DEBBIE DEAN, CAREER GIRL
April, 1945 - No. 2, 1945
Civil Service Publ.

Good Fine Mint

DEBBIE DEAN (continued)
1,2-Newspaper reprints by Bert Whitman 6.00 18.00 42.00

DEBBI'S DATES
Apr-May, 1969 - No. 11, Dec-Jan, 1970-71
National Periodical Publications
1-11: 4-Adams text illo. .25 .75 1.50

DEEP, THE (Movie)
November, 1977
Marvel Comics Group
1-Infantino c/a .40 .80

DEFENDERS, THE (TV)
Sept-Nov, 1962 - No. 2, Feb-Apr, 1963
Dell Publishing Co.
12-176-211(#1), 304(#2) 1.15 3.50 8.00

DEFENDERS, THE (Also see Marvel Feature & Marvel Treas. Ed.; The New. . .#140-on)
Aug, 1972 - No. 152, Feb, 1986
Marvel Comics Group
1-The Hulk, Doc Strange, & Sub-Mariner begin 1.70 5.00 10.00
2 .85 2.50 5.00
3-5: 4-Valkyrie joins .70 2.00 4.00
6-10: 9,10-Avengers app. 10-Thor-Hulk battle .40 1.25 2.50
11-20: 12-Xemnu, The Titan app. 13,14-Squadron Sinister app.; Sub-Mariner leaves, Nighthawk joins. 15,16-Magneto app. 17-19-Powerman, Wrecking Crew app. .25 .75 1.50
21-30: 25-Powerman app. 26-29-Guardians of the Galaxy app. 27-1st app. Starhawk (cameo). 28-Starhawk app. .50 1.00
31-46: 31,32-Origin Nighthawk. 35-Intro. New Red Guardian. 44-Hellcat joins. 45-Dr. Strange leaves .50 1.00
47-51-Giffen-a; Moon Knight x-over; 47-Wonderman app. .25 .75 1.50
52-Giffen-a(p) .50 1.00
53,54-Giffen & Golden-a .50 1.00
55-99: 55-Origin Red Guardian. 57-Ms. Marvel app. 62-64-Nova & others cameo. 77-Origin Omega. 99-Silver Surfer app. .40 .80
100-Double size; Silver Surfer app. .50 1.00
101-124: 101,107,123-Silver Surfer app. 106-Death of Nighthawk .40 .80
125-($1.25)Double size; 1st app. Mad Dog; Hellcat & Son of Satan wed; intro. new Defenders .60 1.20
126-149,151: 140-Moondragon new costume .30 .60
150-Double size; origin Cloud .65 1.30
152-Double size; ties in with X-Factor & Secret Wars II .75 1.50

NOTE: ***Art Adams** c-142p. **Austin** a-53i; c-65i, 119i, 145i. **Frank Bolle** a-7i, 10i, 11i. **Buckler** c(p)-34, 38, 76, 77, 79-86, 90, 91. **J. Buscema** c-66. **Ditko** a-Gnt-Size 1-4r. **Everett** r-Gnt-Size 1-4. **Giffen** a-42-49p, 50, 51p, 52p, 53p, 54p. **Golden** a-53p, 54p; c-94, 96. **Guice** c-129. **G. Kane** c(p)-13, 16, 18, 19, 21-26, 31-33, 35-37, 40, 41, 52, 55, Gnt-Size 2, 4. **Kirby** c-42-45. **Mooney** a-3i, 31-34i, 62i, 63i, 85i. **Nasser** c-88p. **Perez** c(p)-51, 53, 54. **Rogers** c-98. **Starlin** c-110. **Tuska** a-57p. Silver Surfer in No. 2, 3, 6, 8-11, 92, 98-101, 107, 112-115, 122-125.*

Annual 1(11/76) .35 1.00 2.00
Giant Size 1(7/74)-Silver Surfer app.; Starlin-a; Everett, Ditko, & Kirby-r .50 1.50 3.00
Giant Size 2(10/74)-G. Kane-a; Everett, Ditko-r .50 1.00
Giant Size 3(1/75)-Starlin, Newton, Everett-a .50 1.00
Giant Size 4(4/75), 5(7/75)-Guardians app. .50 1.00

DEFENDERS OF THE EARTH (TV)
Jan, 1987 - No. 5, Sept, 1987
Star Comics (Marvel)
1-3: The Phantom, Mandrake The Magician, Flash Gordon begin .35 .70

Good Fine Mint

4,5 ($1.00) .45 .90

THE DEFINITIVE DIRECTORY OF THE DC UNIVERSE (See Who's Who. . .)

DELECTA OF THE PLANETS (See Fawcett Miniatures & Don Fortune)

DELLA VISION (Patty Powers #4 on)
April, 1955 - No. 3, Aug, 1955
Atlas Comics
1 5.00 15.00 35.00
2,3 3.70 11.00 26.00

DELL GIANT COMICS
No. 21, Sept, 1959 - No. 55, Sept, 1961 (Most 84 pages, 25 cents)
Dell Publishing Co.
21-M.G.M.'s Tom & Jerry Picnic Time (84pp, stapled binding) 3.00 9.00 24.00
22-Huey, Dewey & Louie Back to School(10/59, 84pp, square binding begins) 3.00 12.00 30.00
23-Marge's Little Lulu & Tubby Halloween Fun (10/59)-Stanley-a 6.00 24.00 60.00
24-Woody Woodpeckers Family Fun (11/59) 2.00 8.00 20.00
25-Tarzan's Jungle World(11/59)-Marsh-a 3.50 14.00 35.00
26-Christmas Parade-Barks-a, 16pgs.(Disney; 12/59)-Barks draws himself on wanted poster pg. 13 8.00 32.00 80.00
27-Man in Space r-/4-Color 716,866, & 954 (100 pages, 35 cents) (Disney)(TV) 3.00 12.00 30.00
28-Bugs Bunny's Winter Fun (2/60) 2.00 8.00 20.00
29-Marge's Little Lulu & Tubby in Hawaii (4/60)-Stanley-a 6.00 24.00 60.00
30-Disneyland USA(6/60)-Reprinted in Vacation in Disneyland 4.00 16.00 40.00
31-Huckleberry Hound Summer Fun (7/60)(TV) 2.50 10.00 25.00
32-Bugs Bunny Beach Party 2.00 8.00 20.00
33-Daisy Duck & Uncle Scrooge Picnic Time (9/60) 3.50 14.00 35.00
34-Nancy & Sluggo Summer Camp (8/60) 2.50 10.00 25.00
35-Huey, Dewey & Louie Back to School (10/60) 3.00 12.00 30.00
36-Marge's Little Lulu & Witch Hazel Halloween Fun(10/60)-Stanley-a 6.00 24.00 60.00
37-Tarzan, King of the Jungle(11/60)-Marsh-a 3.00 12.00 30.00
38-Uncle Donald & His Nephews Family Fun (11/60) 3.00 12.00 30.00
39-Walt Disney's Merry Christmas(12/60) 3.00 12.00 30.00
40-Woody Woodpecker Christmas Parade(12/60) 2.60 8.00 20.00
41-Yogi Bear's Winter Sports (12/60)(TV) 2.50 10.00 25.00
42-Marge's Little Lulu & Tubby in Australia (4/61) 6.00 24.00 60.00
43-Mighty Mouse in Outer Space (5/61) 7.00 28.00 70.00
44-Around the World with Huckleberry & His Friends (7/61)(TV) 2.50 10.00 25.00
45-Nancy & Sluggo Summer Camp (8/61) 2.50 10.00 25.00
46-Bugs Bunny Beach Party (8/61) 2.00 8.00 20.00
47-Mickey & Donald in Vacationland (8/61) 3.00 12.00 30.00
48-The Flintstones (No. 1)(Bedrock Bedlam)(7/61)(TV) 3.50 14.00 35.00
49-Huey, Dewey & Louie Back to School (9/61) 3.00 12.00 30.00
50-Marge's Little Lulu & Witch Hazel Trick 'N' Treat (10/61) 6.00 24.00 60.00
51-Tarzan, King of the Jungle by Jesse Marsh (11/61) 3.00 12.00 30.00
52-Uncle Donald & His Nephews Dude Ranch (11/61) 3.00 12.00 30.00

The Defenders #11, © MCG

Dell Giant Comics #23, © WEST

Dell Giant Comics #48, © Hanna-Barbera

Bugs Bunny's Christmas Funnies #2, © L. Schlesinger

Donald Duck Beach Party #2, © WDC

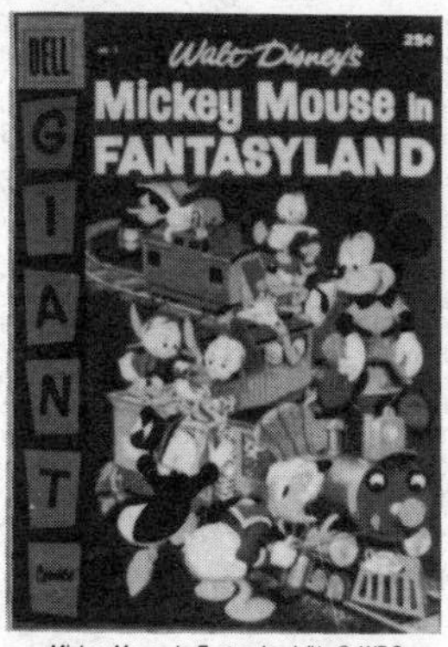

Mickey Mouse in Fantasyland #1, © WDC

DELL GIANT COMICS (continued) **Good Fine Mint**

53-Donald Duck Merry Christmas(12/61)-Not by Barks
3.00 12.00 30.00

54-Woody Woodpecker Christmas Party(12/61)-issued after No. 55
2.25 9.00 22.50

55-Daisy Duck & Uncle Scrooge Showboat (9/61)-1st app. Daisy Duck's nieces, April, May & June 4.00 16.00 40.00

NOTE: *All issues printed with & without ad on back cover.*

(OTHER DELL GIANT EDITIONS)

Abraham Lincoln Life Story 1(3/58, 100p) 2.50 10.00 25.00

Bugs Bunny Christmas Funnies 1(11/50, 116p)
6.00 24.00 60.00

...**Christmas Funnies** 2(11/51, 116p) 4.00 16.00 40.00

...**Christmas Funnies** 3-5(11/52-11/54, 100p)-Becomes Christmas Party No. 6 2.75 11.00 27.50

...**Christmas Funnies** 7-9(12/56-12/58, 100p)
2.25 9.00 22.50

...**Christmas Party** 6(11/55, 100p)-Formerly B.B. Christmas Funnies #5 2.75 11.00 27.50

...**County Fair** 1(9/57, 100p) 3.00 12.00 30.00

...**Halloween Parade** 1(10/53, 100p) 5.00 20.00 50.00

...**Halloween Parade** 2(10/54, 100p)-Trick 'N' Treat Halloween Fun No. 3-on 3.50 14.00 35.00

...**Trick 'N' Treat Halloween Fun** 3,4(10/55-10/56, 100p)-Formerly Halloween Parade 2 3.00 12.00 30.00

...**Vacation Funnies** 1(7/51, 112p) 6.00 24.00 60.00

...**Vacation Funnies** 2('52, 100p) 4.00 16.00 40.00

...**Vacation Funnies** 3-5('53-'55, 100p) 3.00 12.00 30.00

...**Vacation Funnies** 6-9('54-6/59, 100p) 2.50 10.00 25.00

Cadet Gray of West Point 1(4/58, 100p)-Williamson-a, 10pgs. Buscema-a, photo-c 3.50 14.00 35.00

Christmas In Disneyland 1(12/57, 100p)-Barks-a, 18pgs.
7.00 28.00 70.00

Christmas Parade 1(11/49)-Barks-a, 25pgs; r-in G.K. Christmas Parade 5 30.00 120.00 300.00

Christmas Parade 2('50)-Barks-a, 25pgs; r-in G.K. Christmas Parade 6 17.50 70.00 175.00

Christmas Parade 3-7('51-'55, 116-100p) 3.50 14.00 35.00

Christmas Parade 8(12/56, 100p)-Barks-a, 8pgs.
7.00 28.00 70.00

Christmas Parade 9(12/58, 100p)-Barks-a, 20pgs.
9.00 36.00 90.00

Christmas Treasury, A 1(11/54, 100p) 4.50 18.00 45.00

Davy Crockett, King Of The Wild Frontier 1(9/55, 100p)-Photo-c; Marsh-a 7.50 30.00 75.00

Disneyland Birthday Party 1(10/58, 100p)-Barks-a, 16pgs.
6.00 24.00 60.00

Donald and Mickey In Disneyland 1(5/58, 100p)
3.00 12.00 30.00

Donald Duck Beach Party 1(7/54, 100p) 5.00 20.00 50.00

...**Beach Party** 2('55, 100p) 3.50 14.00 35.00

...**Beach Party** 3-5('56-'58, 100p) 2.75 11.00 27.50

...**Beach Party** 6(8/59, 84p)-Stapled 2.25 9.00 22.50

Donald Duck Fun Book 1,2('53-10/54, 100p)-Games, puzzles, comics & cut-outs (Rare) 8.00 32.00 80.00

Donald Duck In Disneyland 1(9/55, 100p) 3.00 12.00 30.00

Golden West Rodeo Treasury 1(10/57, 100p) 3.50 14.00 35.00

Huey, Dewey and Louie Back To School 1(9/58, 100p)
3.50 14.00 35.00

Lady and The Tramp 1(6/55, 100p) 3.50 14.00 35.00

Life Stories of American Presidents 1(11/57, 100p)-Buscema-a
2.25 9.00 22.50

Lone Ranger Golden West 3(8/55, 100p)-Formerly West. Treasury
4.50 18.00 45.00

...**Movie Story** nn(3/56, 100p)-Origin Lone Ranger in text; Clayton Moore photo-c 12.00 48.00 120.00

Good Fine Mint

...**Western Treasury** 1(9/53, 100p)-Origin L. Ranger, Silver, & Tonto 10.00 40.00 100.00

...**Western Treasury** 2(8/54, 100p)-Becomes Golden West No. 3
5.00 20.00 50.00

Marge's Little Lulu & Alvin Story Telling Time 1(3/59)-r/No.2,5,3, 11,30,10,21,17,8,14,16; Stanley-a 7.00 28.00 70.00

...**& Her Friends** 4(3/56, 100p)-Stanley-a 6.00 24.00 60.00

...**& Her Special Friends** 3(3/55, 100p)-Stanley-a
6.00 24.00 60.00

...**& Tubby At Summer Camp** 5(10/57, 100p)-Stanley-a
6.00 24.00 60.00

...**& Tubby At Summer Camp** 2(10/58, 100p)-Stanley-a
6.00 24.00 60.00

...**& Tubby Halloween Fun** 6(10/57, 100p)-Stanley-a
6.00 24.00 60.00

...**& Tubby Halloween Fun** 2(10/58, 100p)-Stanley-a
6.00 24.00 60.00

...**& Tubby In Alaska** 1(7/59, 100p)-Stanley-a
6.00 24.00 60.00

...**On Vacation** 1(7/54, 100p)-r/4C-110,14,4C-146,5,4C-97,4, 4C-158,3,1; Stanley-a 9.00 36.00 90.00

...**& Tubby Annual** 1(3/53, 100p)-r/4C-165,4C-74,4C-146,4C-97, 4C-158,4C-139,4C-131; Stanley-a 14.00 56.00 140.00

...**& Tubby Annual** 2('54, 100p)-r/4C-139,6,4C-115,4C-74,5, 4C-97,3,4C-146,18; Stanley-a 13.00 52.00 130.00

Marge's Tubby & His Clubhouse Pals 1(10/56, 100p)-1st app. Gran'pa Feeb, written by Stanley; Tripp-a
8.00 32.00 80.00

Mickey Mouse Almanac 1(12/57, 100p)-Barks-a, 8pgs.
8.00 32.00 80.00

...**Birthday Party** 1(9/53, 100p)-r-/entire 48pgs. of Gottfredson's "M.M. in Love Trouble" from WDC&S 36-39. Quality equal to original. Also reprints one story each from 4-Color 27, 29, & 181 plus 6 panels of highlights in the career of Mickey Mouse
13.00 52.00 130.00

...**Club Parade** 1(12/55, 100p)-R-/4-Color 16 with some art redrawn by Paul Murry & recolored with night scenes turned into day; quality much poorer than original 10.00 40.00 100.00

...**In Fantasy Land** 1(5/57, 100p) 4.50 18.00 45.00

...**In Frontier Land** 1(5/56, 100p)-M.M. Club issue
4.50 18.00 45.00

...**Summer Fun** 1(8/58, 100p)-Mobile cut-outs on back-c; becomes Summer Fun No. 2 4.50 18.00 45.00

Moses & The Ten Commandments 1(8/57, 100p)-Not based on movie; Dell's adapt; Sekowsky-a 2.75 11.00 27.50

Nancy & Sluggo Travel Time 1(9/58, 100p) 3.00 12.00 30.00

Peter Pan Treasure Chest 1(1/53, 212p)-Disney; contains movie adapt. plus other stories 20.00 80.00 200.00

Picnic Party 6,7(7/55-6/56, 100p)(Formerly Vacation Parade)-Uncle Scrooge, Mickey & Donald 3.00 12.00 30.00

Picnic Party 8(7/57, 100p)-Barks-a, 6pgs. 5.00 20.00 50.00

Pogo Parade 1(9/53, 100p)-Kelly-a(r-/Pogo from Animal Comics in this order: No. 11,13,21,14,27,16,23,9,18,15,17)
16.00 64.00 160.00

Raggedy Ann & Andy 1(2/55, 100p) 5.00 20.00 50.00

Santa Claus Funnies 1(11/52, 100p)-Dan Noonan -**A Christmas Carol** adaptation 4.00 16.00 40.00

Silly Symphonies 1(9/52, 100p)-r/Chicken Little, M. Mouse "The Brave Little Tailor," Mother Pluto, Three Little Pigs, Lady, Bucky Bug, Wise Little Hen, Little Hiawatha, Pedro, The Grasshopper & The Ants 8.00 32.00 80.00

Silly Symphonies 2(9/53, 100p)-r/M. Mouse-"The Sorcerer's Apprentice," Little Hiawatha, Peculiar Penguins, Lambert The Sheepish Lion, Pluto, Spotty Pig, The Golden Touch, Elmer Elephant, The Pelican & The Snipe 6.00 24.00 60.00

Silly Symphonies 3(2/54, 100p)-r/Mickey & The Beanstalk

DELL GIANTS (continued) Good Fine Mint

(4-Color 157), Little Minnehaha, Pablo, The Flying Gauchito, Pluto, & Bongo 6.00 24.00 60.00

Silly Symphonies 4(8/54, 100p)-r/Dumbo (4-Color 234), Morris The Midget Moose, The Country Cousin, Bongo, & Clara Cluck 4.50 18.00 45.00

Silly Symphonies 5(2/55, 100p)-r/Cinderella (4-Color 272), Bucky Bug, Pluto, Little Hiawatha, The 7 Dwarfs & Dumbo, Pinocchio 4.50 18.00 45.00

Silly Symphonies 6(8/55, 100p)-r/Pinocchio(WDC&S 63), The 7 Dwarfs & Thumper (WDC&S 45), M. Mouse-"Adventures With Robin Hood," Johnny Appleseed, Pluto & Peter Pan, & Bucky Bug; Cut-out on back-c 4.50 18.00 45.00

Silly Symphonies 7(2/57, 100p)-r/Reluctant Dragon (4-Color 13), Ugly Duckling, M. Mouse & Peter Pan, Jiminy Cricket, Peter & The Wolf, Brer Rabbit, Bucky Bug; Cut-out on back-c 5.50 22.00 55.00

Silly Symphonies 8(2/58, 100p)-r/Thumper Meets The 7 Dwarfs (4-Color 19), Jiminy Cricket, Niok, Brer Rabbit; Cut-out on back-c 4.50 18.00 45.00

Silly Symphonies 9(2/59, 100p)-r/Paul Bunyan, Humphrey Bear, Jiminy Cricket, The Social Lion, Goliath II; Cut-out on back-c 4.50 18.00 45.00

Sleeping Beauty 1(4/59, 100p) 7.00 28.00 70.00

Summer Fun 2(8/59, 100p)(Formerly M. Mouse...)-Barks-a(2), 24 pgs. 5.50 22.00 55.00

Tales From The Tomb (See Tales From The Tomb)

Tarzan's Jungle Annual 1(8/52, 100p) 4.50 18.00 45.00

...Annual 2(8/53, 100p) 3.50 14.00 35.00

...Annual 3-7('54-9/58, 100p)(two No. 5s)-Manning-a-No. 3,5-7; Marsh-a in No. 1-7 2.50 10.00 25.00

Tom And Jerry Back To School 1(9/56, 100p) 3.00 12.00 30.00

...Picnic Time 1(7/58, 100p) 2.50 10.00 25.00

...Summer Fun 1(7/54, 100p)-Droopy written by Barks 5.00 20.00 50.00

...Summer Fun 2-4(7/55-7/57, 100p) 2.50 10.00 25.00

...Toy Fair 1(6/58, 100p) 3.00 12.00 30.00

...Winter Carnival 1(12/52, 100p)-Droopy written by Barks 7.00 28.00 70.00

...Winter Carnival 2(12/53, 100p)-Droopy written by Barks 4.00 16.00 40.00

...Winter Fun 3(12/54, 100p) 3.00 12.00 30.00

...Winter Fun 4-7(12/55-11/58, 100p) 2.50 10.00 25.00

Treasury of Dogs, A 1(10/56, 100p) 2.25 9.00 22.50

Treasury of Horses, A 1(9/55, 100p) 2.25 9.00 22.50

Uncle Scrooge Goes To Disneyland 1(8/57, 100p)-Barks-a, 20pgs. 7.00 28.00 70.00

Universal Presents-Dracula-The Mummy & Other Stories
02-530-311 (9-11/63, 84p)-R-/Dracula 12-231-212, The Mummy 12-437-211 & part of Ghost Stories No. 1 2.50 10.00 25.00

Vacation In Disneyland 1(8/58, 100p) 3.50 14.00 35.00

Vacation Parade 1(7/50, 130p)-Donald Duck & M. Mouse; Barks-a, 55 pgs. 50.00 200.00 500.00

Vacation Parade 2(7/51, 100p) 7.00 28.00 70.00

Vacation Parade 3-5(7/52-7/54, 100p)-Picnic Party No. 6 on 3.50 14.00 35.00

Western Roundup 1(6/52, 100p)-Photo-c; Gene Autry, Roy Rogers, Johnny Mack Brown, Rex Allen, & Bill Elliott begin; photo back-c begin, end No. 14,16,18 7.00 28.00 70.00

Western Roundup 2(2/53, 100p)-Photo-c 4.50 18.00 45.00

Western Roundup 3-5(7-9/53 - 1-3/54)-Photo-c 4.00 16.00 40.00

Western Roundup 6-10(4-6/54 - 4-6/55)-Photo-c 3.50 14.00 35.00

Western Roundup 11-13,16,17(100p)-Photo-c; Manning-a. 11-Flying A's Range Rider, Dale Evans begin 3.25 13.00 32.50

Western Roundup 14,15,25(1-3/59; 100p)-Photo-c 3.00 12.00 30.00

Western Roundup 18(100p)-Toth-a; last photo-c; Gene Autry ends 4.00 16.00 40.00

Western Roundup 19-24(100p)-Manning-a; 19-Buffalo Bill Jr. begins. 21-Rex Allen, Johnny Mack Brown end. 22-Jace Pearson's.. Texas Rangers, Rin Tin Tin, Tales of Wells Fargo & Wagon Train begin 2.75 11.00 27.50

Woody Woodpecker Back To School 1(10/52, 100p) 2.75 11.00 27.50

...Back To School 2-4,6('53-10/57, 100p)-County Fair No. 5 2.25 9.00 22.50

...County Fair 5(9/56, 100p)-Formerly Back To School 2.25 9.00 22.50

...County Fair 2(11/58, 100p) 2.25 9.00 22.50

DELL JUNIOR TREASURY (15¢)
June, 1955 - No. 10, Oct, 1957
Dell Publishing Co.

	Good	Fine	Mint
1-Alice in Wonderland-Reprints 4-Color 331 (52 pgs.)	5.00	15.00	35.00
2-Aladdin & the Wonderful Lamp	4.35	13.00	30.00
3-Gulliver's Travels(1/56)	3.00	9.00	21.00
4-Advs. of Mr. Frog & Miss Mouse	4.00	12.00	28.00
5-The Wizard of Oz(7/56)	4.35	13.00	30.00
6-Heidi (10/56)	3.00	9.00	21.00
7-Santa and the Angel	3.00	9.00	21.00
8-Raggedy Ann and the Camel with the Wrinkled Knees	3.00	9.00	21.00
9-Clementina the Flying Pig	3.50	10.50	24.00
10-Adventures of Tom Sawyer	4.00	12.00	28.00

DEMON, THE (See Detective No. 482-485)
8-9/72 - No. 16, 1/74; 1/87 - No. 4, 4/87 (mini series)
National Periodical Publications

	Good	Fine	Mint
1-Origin; Kirby-c/a in 1-16		.50	1.00
2-16		.30	.60
1-4('87)		.40	.80

DEMON DREAMS
Feb, 1984 - No. 2, May, 1984
Pacific Comics

	Good	Fine	Mint
1,2-Mostly r-/Heavy Metal	.25	.75	1.50

DEMON-HUNTER
September, 1975
Seaboard Periodicals (Atlas)

	Good	Fine	Mint
1-Origin; Buckler c/a		.30	.60

DENNIS THE MENACE (See The Best of... & The Very Best of...)
8/53 - No. 14, 1/56; No. 15, 3/56 - No. 31, 11/58; No. 32, 1/59 - No. 166, 11/79
Standard Comics/Pines No.15-31/Hallden (Fawcett) No.32 on

	Good	Fine	Mint
1-1st app. Mr. & Mrs. Wilson, Ruff & Dennis' mom & dad; Wiseman-a, written by Fred Toole-most issues	18.00	54.00	125.00
2	9.00	27.00	62.00
3-10	4.60	14.00	32.00
11-20	2.65	8.00	18.00
21-40: 22-1st app. Margaret w/blonde hair. 31-1st Joey app.	1.30	4.00	9.00
41-60	.75	2.25	5.00
61-90	.50	1.50	3.00
91-166	.30	.80	1.60
...& Dirt('59,'68)-Soil Conservation giveaway; r-No. 36; Wiseman c/a	.25	.70	1.40
...Away We Go('70)-Caladayl giveaway	.25	.70	1.40
...Coping with Family Stress-giveaway		.30	.60
...Takes a Poke at Poison('61)-Food & Drug Assn. giveaway;			

Tom and Jerry's Back To School #1, © M.G.M.

Vacation Parade #5, © WDC

Western Roundup #4, © DELL

Dennis the Menace #4, © FAW

Dennis the Menace Giant #26, © FAW

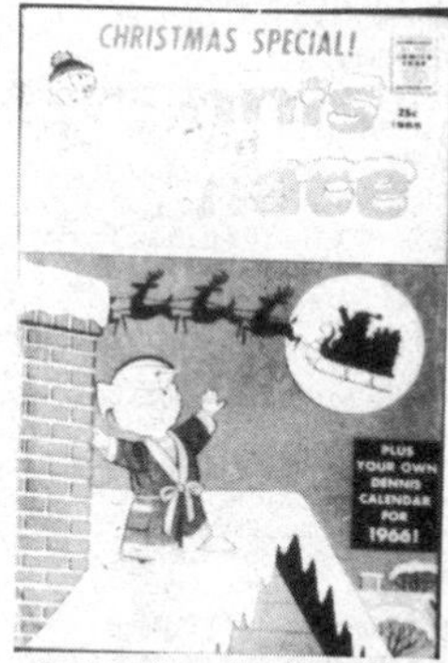

Dennis the Menace Giant #35, © FAW

DENNIS THE MENACE (continued)

	Good	Fine	Mint
Wiseman c/a	.35	1.00	2.00
...Takes a Poke at Poison-Revised 1/66, 11/70, 1972, 1974, 1977, 1981		.30	.60

NOTE: *Wiseman c/a-1-46,53,68,69.*

DENNIS THE MENACE (Giants) (No. 1 titled Giant Vacation Special; becomes D.T.M. Bonus Magazine No. 76 on)
(No. 1-8,18,23,25,30,38: 100 pgs.; rest to No. 41: 84 pgs.; No. 42-75: 68 pgs.)
Summer, 1955 - No. 75, Dec, 1969
Standard/Pines/Hallden(Fawcett)

	Good	Fine	Mint
nn-Giant Vacation Special(Summer '55-Standard)	4.50	13.50	36.00
nn-Christmas issue (Winter '55)	3.50	10.50	28.00
2-Giant Vacation Special (Summer '56-Pines)			
3-Giant Christmas issue (Winter '56-Pines)			
4-Giant Vacation Special (Summer '57-Pines)			
5-Giant Christmas issue (Winter '57-Pines)			
6-In Hawaii (Giant Vacation Special)(Summer '58-Pines)-Reprinted Summer '59 plus 3 more times			
6-Giant Christmas issue (Winter '58) each....	2.50	7.50	20.00
7-In Hollywood (Winter '59-Hallden)			
8-In Mexico (Winter '60, 100 pgs.-Hallden/Fawcett)			
8-In Mexico (Summer '62, 2nd printing)			
9-Goes to Camp (Summer '61, 84 pgs., 2nd printing-Summer '62)-1st CCA approved ish.			
10-X-Mas issue (Winter '61)			
11-Giant Christmas issue (Winter '62)			
12-Triple Feature (Winter '62) each....	2.00	6.00	16.00
13-Best of Dennis the Menace (Spring '63)-Reprints			
14-And His Dog Ruff (Summer '63)			
15-In Washington, D.C. (Summer '63)			
16-Goes to Camp (Summer '63)-Reprints No. 9			
17-& His Pal Joey (Winter '63)			
18-In Hawaii (Reprints No. 6)			
19-Giant Christmas issue (Winter '63)			
20-Spring Special (Spring '64) each....	1.25	3.75	10.00
21-40	1.00	3.00	6.00
41-75	.50	1.50	3.00

NOTE: *Wiseman c/a-1-8,12,14,15,17,20,22,27,28,31,35,36,41,49.*

DENNIS THE MENACE
Nov, 1981 - No. 13, Nov, 1982
Marvel Comics Group

	Good	Fine	Mint
1,2-New art		.25	.50
3-13: 3-Part-r. 4,5-r		.25	.50

NOTE: *Hank Ketcham c-most; a-3,12. Wiseman a-4,5.*

DENNIS THE MENACE AND HIS DOG RUFF
Summer, 1961
Hallden/Fawcett

	Good	Fine	Mint
1-Wiseman c/a	2.25	6.75	18.00

DENNIS THE MENACE AND HIS FRIENDS
1969; No. 5, Jan, 1970 - No. 46, April, 1980 (All reprints)
Fawcett Publications

	Good	Fine	Mint
Dennis T.M. & Joey No. 2 (7/69)	1.35	4.00	8.00
Dennis T.M. & Ruff No. 2 (9/69)	1.00	3.00	6.00
Dennis T.M. & Mr. Wilson No. 1 (10/69)	1.00	3.00	6.00
Dennis & Margaret No. 1 (Winter '69)	.50	1.50	3.00
5-10: No. 5-Dennis T.M. & Margaret. No. 6-& Joey. No. 7-& Ruff. No. 8-& Mr. Wilson	.25	.70	1.40
11-20	.25	.70	1.40
21-37		.60	1.20
38(begin digest size, 148 pgs., 4/78, 95 cents) - 46		.60	1.20

NOTE: *Titles rotate every four issues, beginning with No. 5.*

DENNIS THE MENACE AND HIS PAL JOEY
Summer, 1961 (10 cents) (See Dennis the Menace Giants No. 45)
Fawcett Publications

	Good	Fine	Mint
1-Wiseman c/a	2.30	7.00	16.00

DENNIS THE MENACE AND THE BIBLE KIDS
1977 (36 pages)
Word Books

	Good	Fine	Mint
1-Jesus. 2-Joseph. 3-David. 4-The Bible Girls. 5-Moses. 6-More About Jesus. 7-The Lord's Prayer. 8-Stories Jesus told. 9-Paul, God's Traveller. 10-In the Beginning each....		.25	.50

NOTE: *Ketcham c/a in all.*

DENNIS THE MENACE BONUS MAGAZINE (Formerly Dennis the Menace Giants Nos. 1-75)
No. 76, 1/70 - No. 194, 10/79; (No. 76-124: 68 pgs.; No. 125-163: 52 pgs.; No. 164 on: 36 pgs.)
Fawcett Publications

	Good	Fine	Mint
76-90	.30	.90	1.80
91-110		.60	1.20
111-140		.40	.80
141-194		.30	.60

DENNIS THE MENACE BIG BONUS SERIES
No. 10, 1980 - No. 11, 1980
Fawcett Publications

	Good	Fine	Mint
10,11		.50	1.00

DENNIS THE MENACE COMICS DIGEST
April, 1982 - No. 3, Aug, 1982 (Digest Size, $1.25)
Marvel Comics Group

	Good	Fine	Mint
1-3-Reprints	.20	.60	1.25

NOTE: *Hank Ketcham c-all. Wiseman a-all. A few thousand No. 1's were published with a DC emblem on cover.*

DENNIS THE MENACE FUN BOOK
1960 (100 pages)
Fawcett Publications/Standard Comics

	Good	Fine	Mint
1-Part Wiseman-a	2.25	6.75	18.00

DENNIS THE MENACE POCKET FULL OF FUN!
Spring, 1969 - No. 50, March, 1980 (196 pages) (Digest size)
Fawcett Publications (Hallden)

	Good	Fine	Mint
1-Reprints in all issues	.70	2.00	4.00
2-10	.35	1.00	2.00
11-28		.50	1.00
29-50: 35,40,46-Sunday strip-r		.40	.80

NOTE: *No. 1-28 are 196 pgs.; No. 29-36: 164 pgs.; No. 37: 148 pgs.; No. 38 on: 132 pgs. No. 8, 11, 15, 21, 25, 29 all contain strip reprints.*

DENNIS THE MENACE TELEVISION SPECIAL
Summer, 1961 - No. 2, Spring, 1962 (Giant)
Fawcett Publications (Hallden Div.)

	Good	Fine	Mint
1	2.00	6.00	16.00
2	1.25	3.75	10.00

DENNIS THE MENACE TRIPLE FEATURE
Winter, 1961 (Giant)
Fawcett Publications

	Good	Fine	Mint
1-Wiseman c/a	1.75	5.25	14.00

DEPUTY, THE (See 4-Color No. 1077,1130,1225)

DEPUTY DAWG (TV) (Also see New Terrytoons)
Oct-Dec, 1961 - No. 1, Aug, 1965
Dell Publishing Co./Gold Key

DEPUTY DAWG (continued)

	Good	Fine	Mint
4-Color 1238,1299	3.50	10.50	24.00
1(10164-508)	3.00	9.00	21.00

DEPUTY DAWG PRESENTS DINKY DUCK AND HASHIMOTO-SAN
August, 1965 (TV)
Gold Key

1(10159-508)	3.00	9.00	21.00

DESIGN FOR SURVIVAL (Gen. Thomas S. Power's. . .)
1968 (36 pages in color) (25 cents)
American Security Council Press

nn-Propaganda against the Threat of Communism-Aircraft cover	3.00	9.00	18.00
Twin Circle edition-cover shows panels from inside	1.70	5.00	10.00

DESPERADO (Black Diamond Western No. 9 on)
June, 1948 - No. 8, Feb, 1949
Lev Gleason Publications

1-Biro-c	4.60	14.00	32.00
2	2.30	7.00	16.00
3-8: 3-Story with over 20 killings	1.70	5.00	12.00

NOTE: *Barry a-2. Kida a-3-7. Fuje a-4, 8. Guardineer a-6, 7. Ed Moore a-4, 6.*

DESTINATION MOON (See Fawcett Movie Comics, Space Adventures #20, 23, & Strange Adventures #1)

DESTROYER DUCK
1982 (no month) - No. 7, 5/84 (2-7: Baxter paper) ($1.50)
Eclipse Comics

1-Origin D. Duck & Groo	1.30	4.00	8.00
2-7: 2-Starling back-up begins	.25	.75	1.50

NOTE: *Adams c-1i. Kirby a-1-5p; c-1-5p. Miller c-7.*

DESTRUCTOR, THE
February, 1975 - No. 4, Aug, 1975
Atlas/Seaboard

1-Origin; Ditko/Wood-a; Wood-c(i)		.60	1.20
2-4: 2-Ditko/Wood-a. 3,4-Ditko-a(p)		.40	.80

DETECTIVE COMICS (See Special Edition)
March, 1937 - Present
National Periodical Publications/DC Comics

	Good	Fine	Vf-NM
1-(Scarce)-Slam Bradley & Spy by Siegel & Shuster, Speed Saunders by Guardineer, Flat Foot Flannigan by Gustavson, Cosmo, the Phantom of Disguise, Buck Marshall, Bruce Nelson begin; Chin Lung-c from 'Claws of the Red Dragon' serial; Flessel-c (1st?)	1400.00	4200.00	9100.00
(No copy is known to exist beyond VF condition)			
2 (Rare)	425.00	1275.00	2765.00
3 (Rare)	350.00	1050.00	2280.00

	Good	Fine	Mint
4,5: 5-Larry Steele begins	180.00	540.00	1260.00
6,7,9,10	120.00	360.00	840.00
8-Mister Chang-c	150.00	450.00	1050.00
11-17,19: 17-1st app. Fu Manchu in Det.	100.00	300.00	700.00
18-Fu Manchu-c	135.00	405.00	945.00
20-The Crimson Avenger begins (intro. & 1st app.)	140.00	420.00	980.00
21,23-25	70.00	210.00	490.00
22-1st Crimson Avenger-c (12/38)	90.00	270.00	630.00
26	74.00	220.00	520.00

	Good	Fine	Vf-NM
27-1st app. The Batman & Commissioner Gordon by Bob Kane	3100.00	9300.00	20,000

(No copy known to exist beyond VF-NM condition)
Prices vary widely on this book)

27-Reprint, Oversize 13½"x10." **WARNING:** This comic is an exact duplicate reprint of the original except for its size. DC published it in 1974 with a second cover titling it as Famous First Edition. There have been many reported cases of the outer cover being removed and the interior sold as the original edition. The reprint with the new outer cover removed is practically worthless.

	Good	Fine	Mint
27(1984)-Oreo Cookies giveaway (32 pgs., paper-c, r-/Det. 27, 38 & Batman No. 1 (1st Joker)	1.00	3.00	6.00
28	630.00	1890.00	4400.00
29-Batman-c; Doctor Death app.	385.00	1155.00	2700.00
30,32: 30-Dr. Death app. 32-Batman uses gun	214.00	642.00	1500.00
31-Classic Batman-c; 1st Julie Madison, Bat Plane (Bat-Gyro) & Batarang	357.00	1070.00	2500.00
33-Origin The Batman; Batman gunholster-c	600.00	1800.00	4200.00
34-Steve Malone begins; 2nd Crimson Avenger-c	171.00	513.00	1200.00
35-37: Batman-c. 35-Hypo-c. 36-Origin Hugo Strange. 37-Cliff Crosby begins	185.00	555.00	1300.00
38-Origin/1st app. Robin the Boy Wonder	600.00	1800.00	4200.00
39	164.00	490.00	1150.00
40-Origin & 1st app. Clay Face; 1st Joker cover app.	128.00	385.00	900.00
41-Robin's 1st solo	107.00	320.00	750.00
42-45: 44-Crimson Avenger dons new costume. 45-1st Joker story in Det. (3rd app.)	72.00	215.00	525.00
46-50: 48-1st time car called Batmobile; Gotham City 1st mention. 49-Last Clay Face	68.00	205.00	480.00
51-57,59: 59-Last Steve Malone; 2nd Penguin; Wing becomes Crimson Avenger's aide	54.00	162.00	380.00
58-1st Penguin app.; last Speed Saunders	85.00	255.00	595.00
60-Intro. Air Wave	55.00	165.00	385.00
61-63: 63-Last Cliff Crosby; 1st app. Mr. Baffle	53.00	160.00	370.00
64-Origin & 1st app. Boy Commandos by Simon & Kirby	135.00	405.00	945.00
65-Boy Commandos-c	70.00	210.00	490.00
66-Origin & 1st app. Two-Face	75.00	225.00	525.00
67,69,70	45.00	135.00	315.00
68-Two-Face app.	50.00	150.00	350.00
71-75: 74-1st Tweedledum & Tweedledee; S&K-a	38.00	115.00	265.00
76-Newsboy Legion & The Sandman x-over in Boy Commandos; S&K-a	48.00	145.00	335.00
77-79: All S&K-a	38.00	115.00	265.00
80-Two-Face app.; S&K-a	40.00	120.00	280.00
81,82,84-90: 81-1st Cavalier app. 85-Last Spy. 89-Last Crimson Avenger	35.00	105.00	245.00
83-1st "Skinny" Alfred; last S&K Boy Commandos? Note: most issues No. 84 on signed S&K are not by them	38.00	115.00	265.00
91-99: 96-Alfred's last name 'Beagle' revealed, later changed to 'Pennyworth'-Batman 214	32.00	95.00	225.00
100	48.00	145.00	335.00
101-120: 114-1st small logo(7/46)	30.00	90.00	210.00
121-130: 126-Electrocution-c	28.00	84.00	195.00
131-137,139: 137-Last Air Wave	25.00	75.00	175.00
138-Origin Robotman (See Star Spangled No. 7, 1st app.); series ends No. 202	43.00	130.00	300.00
140-1st app. The Riddler	57.00	170.00	400.00
141,143-150: 150-Last Boy Commandos	25.00	75.00	175.00
142-2nd Riddler app.	29.00	87.00	200.00
151-Origin & 1st app. Pow Wow Smith	26.00	78.00	185.00
152,154,155,157-160: 152-Last Slam Bradley	25.00	75.00	175.00
153-1st Roy Raymond app.; origin The Human Fly	25.50	76.00	180.00
156(2/50)-The new classic Batmobile	25.50	76.00	180.00

Detective Comics #2, © DC

Detective Comics #31, © DC

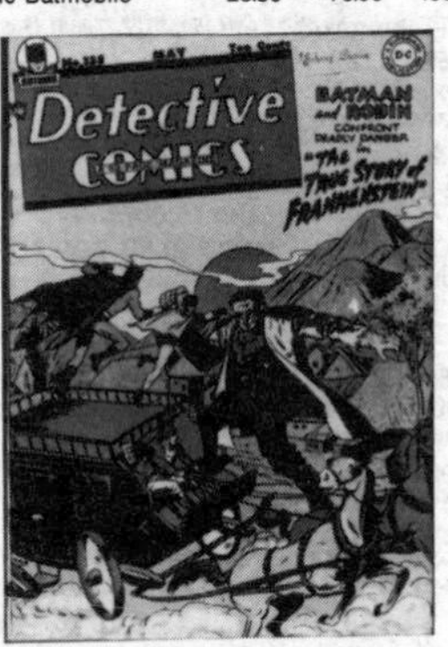

Detective Comics #135, © DC

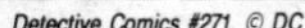
Detective Comics #271, © DC

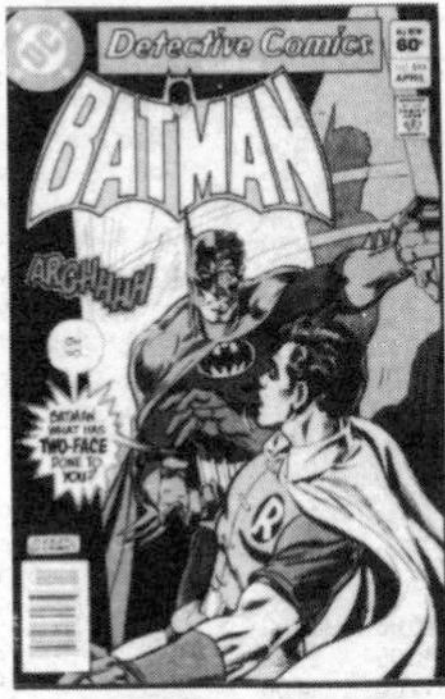

Detective Comics #513, © DC

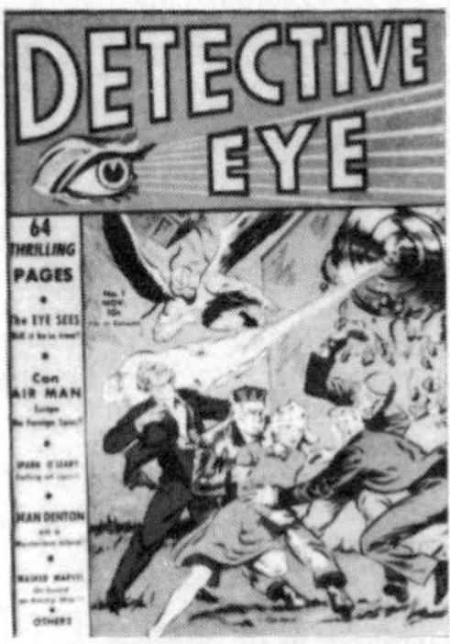

Detective Eye #1, © CEN

DETECTIVE COMICS (continued) — Good / Fine / Mint

161-167,169-176: Last 52 pgs. 25.50 76.00 180.00
168-Origin the Joker 57.00 170.00 400.00
177-189,191-199,201-204,206-212,214-216: 187-Two-Face app. 202-Last Robotman & Pow Wow Smith. 216-Last precode (2/55) 18.00 54.00 125.00
190-Origin Batman retold 22.00 65.00 155.00
200 25.50 76.00 180.00
205-Origin Batcave 24.00 72.00 165.00
213-Origin Mirror Man 24.00 72.00 165.00
217-224 16.50 50.00 115.00
225-(11/55)-Intro. & 1st app. Martian Manhunter-John Jones, later changed to J'onn J'onzz (1st National Silver Age hero); also see Batman 78 91.00 273.00 640.00
226 25.00 75.00 175.00
227-229 15.00 45.00 105.00
230-Mad Hatter app. 18.00 54.00 125.00
231-Origin Martian Manhunter retold 11.50 34.00 80.00
232,234-240 10.00 30.00 70.00
233-Origin & 1st app. Batwoman 16.00 48.00 110.00
241-260: 246-Intro. Diane Meade, J. Jones' girl. 257-Intro. & 1st app. Whirly Bats 8.00 24.00 55.00
261-264,266,268-270: 261-1st app. Dr. Double X. 262-Origin Jackal 5.00 15.00 35.00
265-Batman's origin retold 6.50 19.50 45.00
267-Origin & 1st app. Bat-Mite 5.70 17.00 40.00
271-280: 276-2nd Bat-Mite 4.00 12.00 28.00
281-297: 287-Origin J'onn J'onzz retold. 292-Last Roy Raymond. 293-Aquaman begins, ends No. 300. 297-Last 10 cent issue (11/61) 2.65 8.00 18.00
298-1st modern Clayface 3.60 10.80 25.00
299-327,329,330: 311-Intro. Zook in John Jones; 1st app. Catman. 322-Batgirl's 1st app. in Det 326-Last J'onn J'onzz; intro. Idol-Head of Diabolu. 327-Elongated Man begins; new Batman costume 1.30 4.00 9.00
328-Death of Alfred 1.30 4.00 9.00
331-368,370: 345-Intro The Block Buster. 351-Elongated Man new costume. 355-Zatanna x-over in Elongated Man. 356-Alfred brought back in Batman. 359-Intro/origin new Batgirl 1.00 3.00 6.00
369-Adams-a 1.70 5.00 12.00
371-390: 383-Elongated Man series ends. 387-r/1st Batman story from No. 27 .40 2.25 4.50
391-394,396,398,399,401,403,405,406,409: 392-1st app. Jason Bard. 400,401-1st Batgirl/Robin team-up .60 1.75 3.50
395,397,400,402,404,407,408,410-Adams-a. 400-Origin & 1st app. Man-Bat 1.20 3.50 8.00
411-420: 414-52 pgs. begin, end #424. 418-Creeper x-over .60 1.75 3.50
421-436: 424-Last Batgirl; 1st She-Bat. 426-Elongated Man begins, ends #436. 428,434-Hawkman begins, ends #467 .40 1.20 2.40
437-New Manhunter begins by Simonson, ends #443 .50 1.50 3.00
438-439(100 pgs.): 439-Origin Manhunter .65 1.90 3.60
440(100 pgs.)-G.A. Manhunter, Hawkman, Dollman, Gr. Lantern; Toth-a .50 1.50 3.00
441(100 pgs.)-G.A. Plastic Man, Batman, Ibis-r .50 1.50 3.00
442(100 pgs.)-G.A. Newsboy Legion, Bl. Canary, Elongated Man, Dr. Fate-r .50 1.50 3.00
443(100 pgs.)-Origin The Creeper-r; death of Manhunter; G.A. Gr. Lantern, Spectre-r .50 1.50 3.00
444,445(100 pgs.): 444-G.A. Kid Eternity-r. 445-G.A. Dr. Midnite-r .30 .90 1.80
446-460: 457-Origin retold & updated .30 .90 1.80
461-465,469,470,480 .30 .90 1.80
466-468,471-476,478,479-Rogers-a .90 2.70 5.50

Good / Fine / Mint

477-Adams-a(r); Rogers-a, 3pgs. .70 2.10 4.20
481-(Combined with Batman Family, 12/78-1/79)(Begin $1.00 issues) .70 2.10 4.20
482-Starlin/Russell, Golden-a; origin Demon-r .40 1.20 2.40
483-40th Anniversary ish.; origin retold; Newton Batman begins .30 .85 1.70
484-495: 485-Death of Batwoman. 487-The Odd Man by Ditko. 490-Black Lightning begins.491(492 on inside) .30 .85 1.70
496-499,501-520: 519-Last Batgirl .30 .85 1.70
500-($1.50)-Batman/Deadman team-up .60 1.70 3.50
521-525: 521-Green Arrow series begins .30 .85 1.70
526-Batman's 500th app. in Det. Comics (68 pgs., $1.50) .60 1.75 3.50
527-571: 535-Intro. new Robin (Jason Todd). 554-1st new Bl. Canary. 567-H. Ellison scripts .25 .70 1.40
572 (60 pgs., $1.25)-50th Anniversary .35 1.10 2.20
573,574,576-584: 574-Origin Batman & Jason Todd retold. 579-New logo .50 1.00
575-Year 2 begins .60 1.70 3.50

NOTE: **Adams** *c-369, 370, 372, 383, 385, 389, 391, 392, 394-422, 439.* **Aparo** *a-437, 438, 444-46, 500; c-430, 437, 440-46, 448, 468-70, 480, 484(back), 492-9, 500-02, 508, 509, 515, 518-22.* **Austin** *a-450i, 451i, 463i-68i, 471i-76i; c-474-76i, 478i.* **Baily** *a-443r.* **Buckler** *a-434, 446p, 479p; c-467p, 482p, 505p, 506p, 511p, 513-16p, 518p.* **Colan** *a(p)-510, 512, 517, 523, 528-38, 540-46, 555-64, 567; c(p)-510, 512, 528, 530-35, 537, 538, 540, 541, 543-45, 556-58, 560-64.* **J. Craig** *a-488.* **Ditko** *a-443r, 483-85, 487.* **Golden** *a-482p.* **Grell** *a-445, 455, 463p, 464p; c-455.* **Gustavson** *a-441r.* **Kaluta** *c-423, 424, 426-28, 431, 434, 438, 484, 486, 572.* **Bob Kane** *a-Most early ish. No. 27 on, 297r, 438-40r, 442r, 443r.* **Gil Kane** *a(p)-368, 370-74, 384, 385, 388-407, 438r, 439r, 520.* **Kubert** *a-438r, 439r, 500; c-348-500.* **Meskin** *a-420r.* **Mooney** *a-444r.* **Moreira** *a-153-300, 419r, 444r, 445r.* **Newton** *a(p)-480, 481, 483-99, 501-09, 511, 513-16, 518-20, 524, 526, 539; c-526p.* **Robinson** *a-part: 66, 68, 71-73; all: 74-76, 79, 80; c-62, 64, 66, 68-74, 76, 79, 82, 86, 88, 442r, 443r.* **Rogers** *a-467, 478p, 479p, 481p; c-471p, 472p, 473, 474-479p.* **Roussos** *Airwave-76-105(most).* **Russell** *a-481i, 482i.* **Simon/Kirby** *a-440r, 442r.* **Simonson** *a-437-43, 450, 469, 470, 500.* **Starlin** *a-481p, 482p; c-503, 504, 567p.* **Starr** *a-444r.* **Toth** *a-414r, 416r, 418r, 424r, 440-44r, 527.* **Tuska** *a-486p, 490p.* **Wrightson** *c-425.*

DETECTIVE DAN,SECRET OP. 48
1933 (36 pgs.; 9½x12") (B&W; Softcover)
Humor Publ. Co.

By Norman Marsh; forerunner of Dan Dunn 6.00 18.00 42.00

DETECTIVE EYE (See Keen Detective Funnies)
Nov, 1940 - No. 2, Dec, 1940
Centaur Publications

1-Air Man & The Eye Sees begins; The Masked Marvel app. 70.00 210.00 490.00
2-Origin Don Rance and the Mysticape; Binder-a 52.00 156.00 365.00

DETECTIVE PICTURE STORIES (Keen Det. Funnies No. 8 on?)
Dec, 1936 - No. 7, 1937 (1st comic of a single theme)
Comics Magazine Company

1 80.00 240.00 560.00
2-The Clock app. 40.00 120.00 280.00
3,4: 4-Eisner-a 32.00 95.00 225.00
5-7: 5-Kane-a 28.00 84.00 195.00

DETECTIVES, THE (See 4-Color No. 1168,1219,1240)

DETECTIVES, INC. (See Eclipse Graphic Album Series)
April, 1985 - No. 2, April, 1985 (Both have April dates)
Eclipse Comics

1,2: 2-Nudity .35 1.00 2.00

DEVIL DINOSAUR
April, 1978 - No. 9, Dec, 1978
Marvel Comics Group

1-9 .25 .50

NOTE: **Byrne** *a(i)-4-8. All* **Kirby** *c/a.* **Kirby/Byrne** *c-9.*

DEVIL-DOG DUGAN (Tales of the Marines No. 4 on)
July, 1956 - No. 3, Nov, 1956
Atlas Comics (OPI)

	Good	Fine	Mint
1-Severin-c	2.65	8.00	18.00
2-Iron Mike McGraw x-over; Severin-c	1.35	4.00	9.00
3	1.35	4.00	9.00

DEVIL DOGS
1942
Street & Smith Publishers

	Good	Fine	Mint
1-Boy Rangers	7.00	21.00	50.00

DEVILINA
Feb, 1975 - No. 2, May, 1975 (Magazine) (B&W)
Atlas/Seaboard

	Good	Fine	Mint
1,2: 1-Reese-a	.50	1.50	3.00

DEVIL KIDS STARRING HOT STUFF
July, 1962 - No. 107, Oct, 1981 (Giant-Size No. 45? on)
Harvey Publications (Illustrated Humor)

	Good	Fine	Mint
1	6.75	20.00	45.00
2	3.35	10.00	21.00
3-10 (1/64)	2.35	7.00	14.00
11-20	1.35	4.00	8.00
21-30	1.00	3.00	6.00
31-50 ('71)	.70	2.00	4.00
51-70	.40	1.20	2.40
71-90	.30	.80	1.60
91-107		.30	.60

DEXTER COMICS
Summer, 1948 - No. 5, July, 1949
Dearfield Publ.

	Good	Fine	Mint
1	2.65	8.00	18.00
2	1.60	4.70	11.00
3-5	1.15	3.50	8.00

DEXTER THE DEMON (Formerly Melvin The Monster)
No. 7, Sept, 1957
Atlas Comics (HPC)

	Good	Fine	Mint
7	1.00	3.00	7.00

DIARY CONFESSIONS (Formerly Ideal Romance)
No. 9, May, 1955 - No. 10, July, 1955
Stanmor/Key Publ.

	Good	Fine	Mint
9	2.30	7.00	16.00
10	1.50	4.50	10.00

DIARY LOVES (Formerly Love Diary #1; G. I. Sweethearts #32 on)
No. 2, Nov, 1949 - No. 31, April, 1953
Quality Comics Group

	Good	Fine	Mint
2-Ward c/a, 9 pgs.	8.50	25.00	60.00
3 (1/50)	3.00	9.00	21.00
4-Crandall-a	4.85	14.50	34.00
5-7,10	2.15	6.50	15.00
8,9-Ward-a 6,8 pgs. plus Gustavson-#8	5.70	17.00	40.00
11,13,14,17-20	1.70	5.00	12.00
12,15,16-Ward-a 9,7,8 pgs.	4.85	14.50	34.00
21-Ward-a, 7 pgs.	4.00	12.00	28.00
22-31: 31-Whitney-a	1.30	4.00	9.00

NOTE: *Photo c-13-27.*

DIARY OF HORROR
December, 1952
Avon Periodicals

	Good	Fine	Mint
1-Hollingsworth c/a; bondage-c	14.00	42.00	100.00

DIARY SECRETS (Formerly Teen-Age Diary Secrets)
No. 10, Feb, 1952 - No. 30, Sept, 1955
St. John Publishing Co.

	Good	Fine	Mint
10	6.50	19.50	45.00
11-Spanking panel	8.50	25.50	60.00
12-16,18,19	4.85	14.50	34.00
17,20-Kubert-a	5.70	17.00	40.00
21-30: 28-Last precode (3/55)	3.00	9.00	21.00

(See Giant Comics Ed. for Annual)
NOTE: ***Baker** c/a most issues.*

DICK COLE (Sport Thrills No. 11 on)
Dec-Jan, 1948-49 - No. 10, June-July, 1950
Curtis Publ./Star Publications

	Good	Fine	Mint
1-Sgt. Spook; L. B. Cole-c; McWilliams-a; Curt Swan's 1st work	6.00	18.00	42.00
2	4.00	12.00	28.00
3-10	3.50	10.50	24.00
Accepted Reprint #7(V1#6 on-c)(1950's)-Reprints #7 L.B. Cole-c	2.00	6.00	14.00
Accepted Reprint #9(nd)-(Reprints #9 & #8-c)	2.00	6.00	14.00

NOTE: ***L. B. Cole** a-all; c 1,3,4,6-10. Dick Cole in 1-9.*

DICKIE DARE
1941 - No. 4, 1942
Eastern Color Printing Co.

	Good	Fine	Mint
1-Caniff-a, Everett-c	15.00	45.00	105.00
2	9.00	27.00	62.00
3,4-Half Scorchy Smith by Noel Sickles who was very influential in Milton Caniff's development	10.00	30.00	70.00

DICK POWELL (See A-1 Comics No. 22)

DICK QUICK, ACE REPORTER (See Picture News)

DICK'S ADVENTURES IN DREAMLAND (See 4-Color No. 245)

DICK TRACY (See Merry Christmas, Popular Comics, Super Comics, Tastee-Freez, Limited Coll. Ed., Harvey Comics Library, & Super Book No. 1, 7, 13, 25, nn)

DICK TRACY
May, 1937 - Jan, 1938
David McKay Publications

	Good	Fine	Mint
Feature Books nn - 100 pgs., part reprinted as 4-Color No. 1 (appeared before Large Feat. Comics, 1st Dick Tracy comic book) (Very Rare-three known copies) Estimated Value....	400.00	1200.00	2800.00
Feature Books 4 - Reprints nn issue but with new cover added	72.00	215.00	500.00
Feature Books 6,9	57.00	170.00	400.00

DICK TRACY
1939 - No. 24, Dec, 1949
Dell Publishing Co.

	Good	Fine	Mint
Large Feat. Comic 1(1939)	75.00	225.00	525.00
Large Feat. Comic 4	43.00	130.00	300.00
Large Feat. Comic 8,11,13,15	37.00	110.00	260.00
4-Color 1(1939)('35-r)	100.00	300.00	700.00
4-Color 6(1940)('37-r)-(Scarce)	65.00	195.00	455.00
4-Color 8(1940)('38-'39-r)	40.00	120.00	280.00
Large Feature Comics 3(1941)	35.00	105.00	245.00
4-Color 21('41)('38-r)	38.00	115.00	265.00
4-Color 34('43)('39-'40-r)	28.00	85.00	195.00
4-Color 56('44)('40-r)	20.00	60.00	140.00
4-Color 96('46)('40-r)	16.00	48.00	110.00
4-Color 133('47)('40-'41-r)	13.00	40.00	90.00
4-Color 163('47)('41-r)	10.00	30.00	70.00
4-Color 215('48)-Titled "Sparkle Plenty," Tracy-r	7.00	21.00	50.00
Buster Brown Shoes giveaway-36 pgs. in color (1938,'39-r)-by Gould	24.00	72.00	168.00

Gillmore Giveaway-(See Super Book)
...Hatful of Fun(no date, 1950-52)-32 pgs.; 8½x10"-Dick Tracy

Devil Kids #8, © HARV

Diary Secrets #27, © STJ

Dickie Dare #3, © EAS

Dick Tracy, 1958 Esso Giveaway, © N.Y. News Synd.

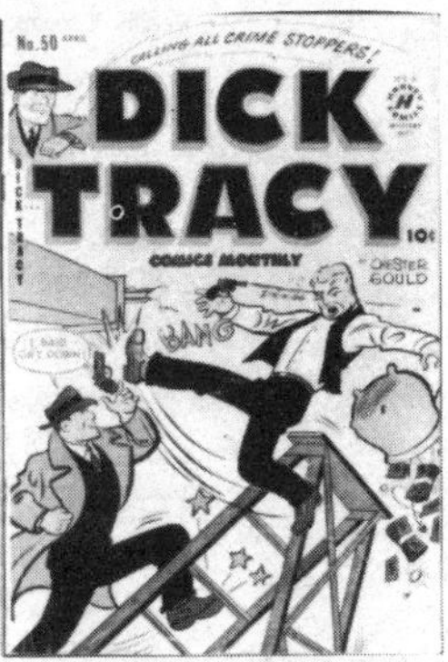

Dick Tracy #50, © N.Y. News Synd.

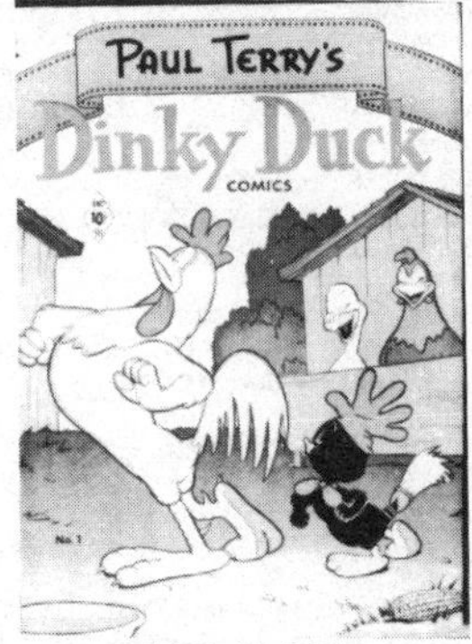

Dinky Duck #1, © STJ

DICK TRACY (continued)	**Good**	**Fine**	**Mint**
hat promotion; D. Tracy games, magic tricks. Miller Bros. premium	6.00	18.00	42.00
Motorola Giveaway('53)-Reprints Harvey Comics Library No. 2	3.00	9.00	21.00
Popped Wheat Giveaway('47)-'40-r; 16 pgs. in color; Sig Feuchtwanger publ.; Gould-a	.85	2.50	5.00
. . . Presents the Family Fun Book-Tip Top Bread Giveaway, no date, number (1940); 16 pgs. in color; Spy Smasher, Ibis, Lance O'Casey app. Fawcett Publ.	25.00	75.00	175.00
Same as above but without app. of heroes & Dick Tracy on cover only	7.50	22.50	45.00
Service Station giveaway(1958)-16 pgs. in color, regular size; Harvey Info. Press(slick cover)	1.70	5.00	12.00
Shoe Store Giveaway (1939, 16p)-Gould-a	10.00	30.00	70.00
1(1/48)('34-r)	30.00	90.00	210.00
2,3	15.00	45.00	105.00
4-10	13.00	40.00	90.00
11-18: 13-Bondage-c	9.00	27.00	62.00
19-1st app. Sparkle Plenty, B.O. Plenty & Gravel Gertie in a 3-pg. strip not by Gould	6.00	18.00	42.00
20-1st app. Sam Catchem c/a not by Gould	5.00	15.00	35.00
21-24-Only 2 pg. Gould-a in each	5.00	15.00	35.00

NOTE: No. 19-24 have a 2 pg. biography of a famous villain illustrated by Gould: 19-Little Face; 20-Flattop; 21-Breathless Mahoney; 22-Measles; 23-Itchy; 24-The Brow.

DICK TRACY (Cont'd. from Dell series)
No. 25, Mar, 1950 - No. 145, April, 1961
Harvey Publications

	Good	Fine	Mint
25	13.00	40.00	90.00
26-28,30: 28-Bondage-c	11.00	33.00	76.00
29-1st app. Gravel Gertie in a Gould-r	13.00	40.00	90.00
31,32,34,35,37-40	9.00	27.00	62.00
33-"Measles the Teen-Age Dope Pusher"	11.00	33.00	76.00
36-1st app. B.O. Plenty in a Gould-r	11.00	33.00	76.00
41-50	8.00	24.00	56.00
51-56,58-80: 51-2pgs Powell-a	7.00	21.00	50.00
57-1st app. Sam Catchem, Gould-r	9.00	27.00	62.00
81-99,101-140	5.50	16.50	38.00
100	5.75	17.25	40.00
141-145 (25 cents)	5.00	15.00	35.00

*NOTE: **Powell** a(1-2pgs.)-43,44,104,145. No. 110-120, 141-145 are all reprints from earlier issues.*

DICK TRACY & DICK TRACY JR. CAUGHT THE RACKETEERS, HOW
1933 (88 pages) (7x8½") (Hardcover)
Cupples & Leon Co.

	Good	Fine	Mint
2-(numbered on pg. 84)-Continuation of Stooge Viller book (daily strip reprints from 8/3/33 thru 11/8/33) (Rarer than No. 1)	35.00	105.00	245.00
with dust jacket	55.00	165.00	385.00
Book 2 (32 pgs.; soft-c; has strips 9/18/33-11/8/33)	17.00	51.00	120.00

DICK TRACY & DICK TRACY JR. AND HOW THEY CAPTURED "STOOGE" VILLER (See Treasure Box of Famous Comics)
1933 (7x8½") (Hard cover; One Shot; 100 pgs.)
Reprints 1932 & 1933 Dick Tracy daily strips
Cupples & Leon Co.

	Good	Fine	Mint
nn(No.1)-1st app. of "Stooge" Viller	25.00	75.00	175.00
with dust jacket	40.00	120.00	280.00

DICK TRACY, EXPLOITS OF
1946 (Strip reprints) (Hardcover) ($1.00)
Rosdon Books, Inc.

	Good	Fine	Mint
1-Reprints the complete case of "The Brow" from early 1940's	18.00	54.00	125.00
with dust jacket	30.00	90.00	210.00

DICK TRACY MONTHLY
May, 1986 - Present ($2.00, B&W)
Blackthorne Publ.

	Good	Fine	Mint
1-7: Gould-r	.35	1.00	2.00
3-D Special 1('86)('58-r)	.60	1.75	3.50

DICK TRACY SHEDS LIGHT ON THE MOLE
1949 (16 pgs.) (Ray-O-Vac Flashlights giveaway)
Western Printing Co.

	Good	Fine	Mint
Not by Gould	4.35	13.00	30.00

DICK TURPIN (See Legend of Young . . .)

DICK WINGATE OF THE U.S. NAVY
1951; 1953 (no month)
Superior Publ./Toby Press

	Good	Fine	Mint
nn-U.S. Navy giveaway	1.15	3.50	8.00
1(1953, Toby)	1.70	5.00	12.00

DIE, MONSTER, DIE (See Movie Classics)

DIG 'EM
1973 (16 pgs.) (2-3/8x6")
Kellogg's Sugar Smacks Giveaway

	Good	Fine	Mint
4 different		.50	1.00

DILLY (From Daredevil Comics)
May, 1953 - No. 3, Sept, 1953
Lev Gleason Publications

	Good	Fine	Mint
1-Biro-c	1.85	5.50	13.00
2,3-Biro-c	1.00	3.00	7.00

DIME COMICS
1945; 1951
Newsbook Publ. Corp.

	Good	Fine	Mint
1-Silver Streak app.; L. B. Cole-c	13.00	40.00	90.00
1(1951), 5	1.65	5.00	11.00

DINGBATS (See First Issue Special)

DING DONG
1946
Compix/Magazine Enterprises

	Good	Fine	Mint
1	2.65	8.00	18.00
2	1.30	4.00	9.00
3-5	.85	2.50	6.00

DINKY DUCK (Paul Terry's . . .) (See Blue Ribbon Comics)
11/51 - No. 16, 9/55; No. 16, Fall/'56; No. 17, 5/57 - No. 19, Summer/'58
St. John Publishing Co./Pines No. 16 on

	Good	Fine	Mint
1	2.65	8.00	18.00
2	1.30	4.00	9.00
3-10	.85	2.50	6.00
11-16(9/55)	.75	2.25	5.00
16(Fall,'56) - 19	.55	1.65	4.00

DINKY DUCK & HASHIMOTO-SAN (See Deputy Dawg Presents . . .)

DINO (TV)(The Flintstones)
Aug, 1973 - No. 20, Jan, 1977
Charlton Publications

	Good	Fine	Mint
1	.50	1.50	3.00
2-20		.50	1.00

DINOSAUR REX
Sum, 1986 - No. 3, 1986 (mini-series; $2.00)
Upshot Graphics (Fantagraphics Books)

	Good	Fine	Mint
1-3	.35	1.00	2.00

DINOSAURUS (See 4-Color No. 1120)

DIPPY DUCK
October, 1957
Atlas Comics (OPI)

	Good	Fine	Mint
1-Maneely-a	1.30	4.00	9.00

DIRTY DOZEN (See Movie Classics)

DISNEYLAND BIRTHDAY PARTY (Also see Dell Giants)
Aug, 1985 ($2.50)
Gladstone Publishing Co.

1-R-/Dell Giant with new-photo-c	.40	1.25	2.50
...Comics Digest #1-(Digest)		.60	1.25

DISNEYLAND, USA (See Dell Giant No. 30)

DIVER DAN (TV)
Feb-Apr, 1962 - No. 2, June-Aug, 1962
Dell Publishing Co.

4-Color 1254, 2	2.00	6.00	14.00

DIXIE DUGAN
July, 1942 - No. 13, 1949
McNaught Syndicate/Columbia/Publication Ent.

1-Joe Palooka x-over by Ham Fisher	10.00	30.00	70.00
2	6.00	18.00	42.00
3	4.60	14.00	32.00
4,5(1945-46)	2.65	8.00	18.00
6-13(1948-49)	2.00	6.00	14.00

DIXIE DUGAN
Nov, 1951 - V4/4, Feb, 1954
Prize Publications (Headline)

V3No.1	2.65	8.00	18.00
2-4	1.70	5.00	12.00
V4No.1-4(No.5-8)	1.30	4.00	9.00

DIZZY DAMES
Sept-Oct, 1952 - No. 6, July-Aug, 1953
American Comics Group (B&M Distr. Co.)

1	3.50	10.50	24.00
2	2.15	6.50	15.00
3-6	1.30	4.00	9.00

DIZZY DON COMICS
1942 - No. 22, Oct, 1946 (B&W)
F. E. Howard Publications/Dizzy Don Ent. Ltd (Canada)

1	2.00	6.00	14.00
2	1.15	3.50	8.00
3-21	1.00	3.00	7.00
22-Full color, 52pgs.	1.70	5.00	12.00

DIZZY DUCK (Formerly Barnyard Comics)
No. 32, Nov, 1950 - No. 39, Mar, 1952
Standard Comics

32	2.65	8.00	18.00
33-39	1.30	4.00	9.00

DNAGENTS (The New DNAgents V2/1 on)(Also see Surge)
March, 1983 - No. 24, July, 1985 ($1.50, Baxter paper)
Eclipse Comics

1-Origin	.55	1.65	3.30
2-10: 4-Amber app.	.45	1.40	2.80
11-24: 18-Infinity-c	.35	1.00	2.00

NOTE: ***Spiegle** a-9. **Dave Stevens** c-24.*

DOBERMAN (See Sgt. Bilko's Private...)

DOBIE GILLIS (See The Many Loves of...)

DOC CARTER VD COMICS
1949 (16 pages in color) (Paper cover)
Health Publications Institute, Raleigh, N. C. (Giveaway)

Good	Fine	Mint
17.00	51.00	120.00

DOC SAVAGE
November, 1966
Gold Key

1-Adaptation of the Thousand-Headed Man; James Bama-c r-/'64 Doc Savage paperback	2.00	6.00	14.00

DOC SAVAGE
Oct, 1972 - No. 8, Jan, 1974
Marvel Comics Group

1		.40	.80
2-8: 2,3-Steranko-c		.25	.50
Giant-Size 1(1975)-Reprints No. 1 & 2		.30	.60

NOTE: ***Mooney** a-1i, Gnt-Size 1r. No. 1,2 adapts pulp story "The Man of Bronze," No. 3,4 adapts "Death in Silver," No. 5,6 adapts "The Monsters," No. 7,8 adapts "The Brand of The Werewolf."*

DOC SAVAGE (Magazine)
Aug, 1975 - No. 8, Spr, 1977 (Black & White)
Marvel Comics Group

1-Cover from movie poster	.25	.75	1.50
2-8		.50	1.00

NOTE: ***John Buscema** a-1,3.*

DOC SAVAGE
Nov, 1987 - No. 4, Feb, 1988 ($1.75, mini-series)
DC Comics

1-Adam & Andy Kubert c/a	.40	1.25	2.50
2-4	.35	1.00	2.00

DOC SAVAGE COMICS (Also see Shadow Comics)
May, 1940 - No. 20, Oct, 1943
Street & Smith Publications

1-Doc Savage, Cap Fury, Danny Garrett, Mark Mallory, The Whisperer, Captain Death, Billy the Kid, Sheriff Pete & Treasure Island begin; Norgil, the Magician app.	90.00	270.00	630.00
2-Origin & 1st app. Ajax, the Sun Man; Danny Garrett, The Whisperer end	45.00	135.00	315.00
3	34.00	102.00	240.00
4-Treasure Island ends; Tuska-a	25.00	75.00	175.00
5-Origin & 1st app. Astron, the Crocodile Queen, not in No. 9 & 11; Norgil the Magician app.	22.00	65.00	150.00
6-9: 6-Cap Fury ends; origin & only app. Red Falcon in Astron story. 8-Mark Mallory ends. 9-Supersnipe app.	18.00	54.00	125.00
10-Origin & only app. The Thunderbolt	18.00	54.00	125.00
11,12	14.00	42.00	100.00
V2#1-8(#13-20): 16-The Pulp Hero, The Avenger app. 17-Sun Man ends; Nick Carter begins	14.00	42.00	100.00

DR. ANTHONY KING, HOLLYWOOD LOVE DOCTOR
1952(Jan.) - No. 3, May, 1953; No. 4, May, 1954
Minoan Publishing Corp./Harvey Publications No. 4

1	4.00	12.00	28.00
2-4: 4-Powell-a	2.65	8.00	18.00

DR. ANTHONY'S LOVE CLINIC (See Mr. Anthony's...)

DR. BOBBS (See 4-Color No. 212)

DR. FATE (See First Issue Special, The Immortal..., Justice League, More Fun, & Showcase)

DOCTOR FATE
July, 1987 - No. 4, Oct, 1987 (mini-series, $1.50, Baxter)
DC Comics

1-Giffen c/a begins	.35	1.10	2.00
2-4	.30	.90	1.80

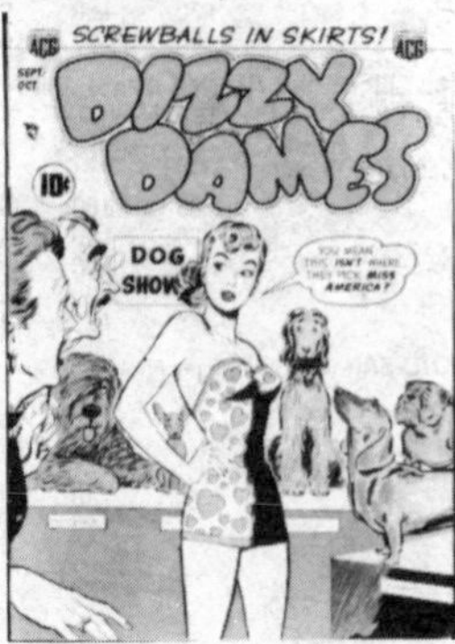

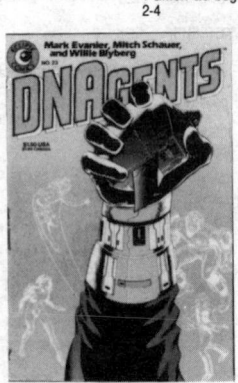

Dizzy Dames #1, © ACG

DNAgents #23, © Evanier & Meugniot

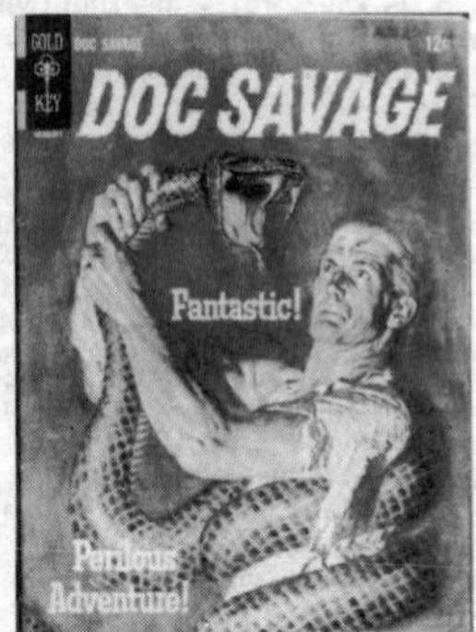

Doc Savage #1, © GK

Doctor Solar #10, © GK

Doctor Strange #170, © MCG

Doll Man #6, © QUA

DR. FU MANCHU (See The Mask of. . .)
1964
I.W. Enterprises

	Good	Fine	Mint
1-Reprints Avon's "Mask of Dr. Fu Manchu;" Wood-a	6.75	20.00	45.00

DOCTOR GRAVES (Formerly The Many Ghosts of. . .)
No. 73, Sept, 1985 - No. 75, Jan, 1986
Charlton Comics

	Good	Fine	Mint
73-75		.40	.75

DR. JEKYLL AND MR. HYDE (See A Star Presentation)

DR. KILDARE (TV)
No. 1337, 4-6/62 - No. 9, 4-6/65 (All photo-c)
Dell Publishing Co.

	Good	Fine	Mint
4-Color 1337('62)	2.65	8.00	18.00
2-9	1.70	5.00	12.00

DR. MASTERS (See The Adventures of Young. . .)

DOCTOR SOLAR, MAN OF THE ATOM
10/62 - No. 27, 4/69; No. 28, 4/81 - No. 31, 3/82
Gold Key/Whitman No. 28 on (Painted-c No. 1-27)

	Good	Fine	Mint
1-Origin Dr. Solar (1st Gold Key comic-No. 10000-210)	3.50	10.50	24.00
2-Prof. Harbinger begins	1.70	5.00	12.00
3-5: 5-Intro. Man of the Atom in costume	1.30	4.00	9.00
6-10	1.00	3.00	7.00
11-14,16-20	.70	2.00	5.00
15-Origin retold	.85	2.50	6.00
21-27	.60	1.80	4.00
28-31: 29-Magnus Robot Fighter begins. 31-The Sentinel app.		.40	.80

NOTE: ***Frank Bolle** a-6-19, 29-31; c-29i, 30i. **Bob Fugitani** a-1-5. **Spiegle** a-29-31. **Al McWilliams** a-20-23.*

DOCTOR SPEKTOR (See The Occult Files of. . .)

DOCTOR STRANGE (Strange Tales No. 1-168) (Also see Marvel Fanfare, Marvel Graphic Novel, Marvel Premiere, Marvel Treas. Ed. and Strange Tales, 2nd Series)
No. 169, 6/68 - No. 183, 11/69; 6/74 - No. 81, 2/87
Marvel Comics Group

	Good	Fine	Mint
169(#1)-Origin; panel swipe/M.D. #1-c	.85	2.50	5.00
170-183: 177-New costume	.35	1.00	2.00
1(6/74)-Brunner c/a	1.00	3.00	7.00
2-5	.50	1.50	3.00
6-26: 21-Origin/Str. Tales 169	.30	.90	1.80
27-40		.65	1.30
41-80: 56-Origin retold		.50	1.00
81	.25	.75	1.50

NOTE: ***Adkins** a-169, 170, 171i; c-169-71, 172i, 173. **Adams** a-4i. **Austin** a-48-60i, 66i, 68i, 70i; c-38i, 47-53i, 55i, 58-60i, 70i. **Brunner** a-1-5p; c-1-6, 22, 28-30, 33. **Colan** a(p)-172-78, 180-83, 6-18, 36-45, 47; c(p)-172, 174-83, 11-21, 23, 27, 35, 36, 47. **Ditko** a-179r, 3r. **Everett** c-183i. **Golden** a-55p; c-42-44, 46, 55p. **G. Kane** c(p)-8-10. **Miller** c-46p. **Nebres** a-20, 22, 23, 24i, 26i, 32i; c-32i, 34. **Rogers** a-48-53p; c-47p-53p. **Russell** a-34i, 46i, Annual 1. **B. Smith** c-179. **Paul Smith** a-54p, 56p, 65, 66p, 68p, 69, 71, 72; c-56, 65, 66, 68, 71. **Starlin** a-23p, 26; c-25, 26. **Sutton** a-27-29p, 34p.*

	Good	Fine	Mint
Annual 1(1976)-Russell-a	.35	1.00	2.00
Giant Size 1(11/75)-Str. Tales-r	.35	1.00	2.00
. . ./Silver Dagger (Special Edition)(2/83)($2.50, Baxter paper)-r-/ Dr. Strange 1,2,4,5 & Strange Tales 127; Wrightson-c	.35	1.00	2.00

DOCTOR STRANGE CLASSICS
Mar, 1984 - No. 4, June, 1984 ($1.50 cover price; Baxter paper)
Marvel Comics Group

	Good	Fine	Mint
1-4: Ditko reprints	.25	.75	1.50

DR. TOM BRENT, YOUNG INTERN
Feb, 1963 - No. 5, Oct, 1963
Charlton Publications

	Good	Fine	Mint
1	.30	.80	1.60
2-5		.50	1.00

DR. VOLTZ (See Mighty Midget Comics)

DOCTOR WHO (Also see Marvel Premiere #57-60)
Oct, 1984 - No. 23, Aug, 1986 (Direct sales, Baxter paper, $1.50)
Marvel Comics Group

	Good	Fine	Mint
1-($1.50 cover)-British-r	.40	1.25	2.50
2-23	.30	.90	1.80

DR. WHO & THE DALEKS (See Movie Classics)

DO-DO
1950 - 1951 (5x7¼" Miniature) (5 cents)
Nation Wide Publishers

	Good	Fine	Mint
1 (52 pgs.); funny animal	1.00	3.00	7.00
2-7	.70	2.00	5.00

DODO & THE FROG, THE (Formerly Funny Stuff)
9-10/54 - No. 88, 1-2/56; No. 89, 8-9/56; No. 90, 10-11/56; No. 91, 9/57; No. 92, 11/57 (See Comic Cavalcade)
National Periodical Publications

	Good	Fine	Mint
80-Doodles Duck by Sheldon Mayer	3.50	10.50	24.00
81-91: Doodles Duck by Sheldon Mayer in No. 81,83-90	2.00	6.00	14.00
92-(Scarce)-Doodles Duck by S. Mayer	3.50	10.50	24.00

DOGFACE DOOLEY
1951 - 1953
Magazine Enterprises

	Good	Fine	Mint
1(A-1 40)	2.00	6.00	14.00
2(A-1 43), 3(A-1 49), 4(A-1 53), 5(A-1 64)	1.30	4.00	9.00
I.W. Reprint No.1('64), Super Reprint No.17	.60	1.80	3.60

DOG OF FLANDERS, A (See 4-Color No. 1088)

DOGPATCH (See Al Capp's. . . & Mammy Yokum)

DOINGS OF THE DOO DADS, THE
1922 (34 pgs.; 7¾x7¾"; B&W) (50 cents)
(Red & White cover; square binding)
Detroit News (Universal Feat. & Specialty Co.)

	Good	Fine	Mint
Reprints 1921 newspaper strip "Text & Pictures" given away as prize in the Detroit News Doo Dads contest; by Arch Dale	6.00	18.00	42.00

DOLLFACE & HER GANG (See 4-Color No. 309)

DOLL MAN
Fall, 1941 - No. 7, Fall, '43; No. 8, Spring, '46 - No. 47, Oct, 1953
Quality Comics Group

	Good	Fine	Mint
1-Dollman (by Cassone) & Justin Wright begin	86.00	260.00	600.00
2-The Dragon begins; Crandall-a(5)	48.00	145.00	335.00
3	32.00	95.00	225.00
4	24.00	72.00	168.00
5-Crandall-a	21.00	62.00	146.00
6,7(1943)	16.00	48.00	110.00
8(1946)-1st app. Torchy by Bill Ward	19.00	57.00	132.00
9	14.00	42.00	100.00
10-20	11.00	33.00	75.00
21-30	10.00	30.00	70.00
31-36,38,40: Jeb Rivers app. #32-34	8.00	24.00	56.00
37-Origin Dollgirl; Dollgirl bondage-c	10.00	30.00	70.00
39-"Narcotics. . .the Death Drug"-c-/story	8.00	24.00	56.00
41-47	6.00	18.00	42.00
Super Reprint #11('64, r-#20),15(r-#23),17(r-#28): Torchy app.-#15,17	1.35	4.00	8.00

NOTE: ***Ward** Torchy in 8, 9, 11, 12, 14-24, 27; by **Fox**-No. 30, 35-47. **Crandall** a-2,5,10,13 & Super No. 11,17,18. Bondage-c #27,37,38,39.*

DOLLY
1951 (Funny animal)
Ziff-Davis Publ. Co.

	Good	Fine	Mint
10	1.30	4.00	9.00

DOLLY DILL
1945
Marvel Comics/Newsstand Publ.

1	5.50	16.50	38.00

DOLLY DIMPLES & BOBBY BOONCE'
1933
Cupples & Leon Co.

	5.00	15.00	35.00

DOMINO CHANCE
May, 1984 - No. 9, May, 1985
Chance Ent.

1	2.50	7.50	15.00
1-Reprint, May 1985	.50	1.50	3.00
2-6,9		.50	1.00
7-1st app. Gizmo, 2 pgs.	1.35	4.00	8.00
8-1st full Gizmo story	2.00	6.00	12.00

DONALD AND MICKEY IN DISNEYLAND (See Dell Giants)

DONALD AND MICKEY MERRY CHRISTMAS (Formerly Famous Gang)
1943 - 1949 (20 pgs.)(Giveaway) Put out each Christmas; 1943 issue titled "Firestone Presents Comics" (Disney)
K. K. Publ./Firestone Tire & Rubber Co.

1943-Donald Duck reprint from WDC&S No. 32 by Carl Barks	53.00	160.00	370.00
1944-Donald Duck reprint from WDC&S No. 35 by Barks	50.00	150.00	350.00
1945-"Donald Duck's Best Christmas," 8 pgs. Carl Barks; intro. & 1st app. Grandma Duck in comic books	64.00	190.00	450.00
1946-Donald Duck in "Santa's Stormy Visit," 8 pgs. Carl Barks	47.00	140.00	330.00
1947-Donald Duck in "Three Good Little Ducks," 8 pgs. Carl Barks	40.00	120.00	280.00
1948-Donald Duck in "Toyland," 8 pgs. Carl Barks	37.00	110.00	260.00
1949-Donald Duck in "New Toys," 8 pgs. Carl Barks	46.00	138.00	320.00

DONALD AND THE WHEEL (See 4-Color No. 1190)

DONALD DUCK (See Cheerios, Mickey Mouse Mag., Story Hour Series, Uncle Scrooge, Walt Disney's C&S, Wheaties & Whitman Comic Books)

DONALD DUCK (Also see The Wise Little Hen)
1935, 1936 (Linen-like text & color pictures; 1st Donald Duck book ever) (9½x13")
Whitman Publishing Co./Grosset & Dunlap/K.K.

978(1935)-16 pgs.; story book	45.00	135.00	315.00
nn(1936)-36 pgs.; reprints '35 edition with expanded ill. & text	36.00	108.00	250.00
with dust jacket....	50.00	150.00	350.00

DONALD DUCK (Walt Disney's) (10 cents)
1938 (B&W) (8½x11½") (Cardboard covers)
Whitman/K.K. Publications

(Has Donald Duck with bubble pipe on front cover)

	Good	Fine	VF-NM
nn-The first Donald Duck & Walt Disney comic book; 1936 & 1937 Sunday strip-r(in B&W); same format as the Feature Books; 1st strips with Huey, Dewey & Louie	90.00	270.00	630.00

(Prices vary widely on this book)

DONALD DUCK (See 4-Color listings for titles & 4-Color No. 1109 for origin story) (See Gladstone Comic Album)
1940 - No. 84, 9-11/62; No. 85, 12/62 - No. 245, 1984; No. 246, 10/86 - Present
Dell Publishing Co./Gold Key No. 85-216/Whitman No. 217-245/ Gladstone No. 246 on

	Good	Fine	Mint
4-Color 4(1940)-Daily 1939 strip-r by Al Taliaferro	270.00	810.00	1900.00
Large Feat. Comic 16(1/41?)-1940 Sunday strips-r in B&W	145.00	435.00	1015.00
Large Feat. Comic 20('41)-Comic Paint Book, r-single panels from Large Feat. 16 at top of each page to color; daily strip-r across bottom of each page	205.00	615.00	1435.00
4-Color 9('42)-"Finds Pirate Gold;"-64 pgs. by Carl Barks & Jack Hannah (pgs. 1,2,5,12-40 are by Barks, his 1st comic book work; © 8/17/42)	315.00	945.00	2200.00
4-Color 29(9/43)-"Mummy's Ring" by Carl Barks; reprinted in Uncle Scrooge & Donald Duck No. 1('65) & W.D. Comics Digest No. 44('73)	215.00	645.00	1505.00

(Prices vary widely on all above books)

4-Color 62(1/45)-"Frozen Gold;" 52 pgs. by Carl Barks, reprinted in The Best of W.D. Comics	118.00	354.00	825.00
4-Color 108(1946)-"Terror of the River;" 52 pgs. by Carl Barks	85.00	255.00	595.00
4-Color 147(5/47)-in "Volcano Valley" by Carl Barks	60.00	180.00	420.00
4-Color 159(8/47)-in "The Ghost of the Grotto;" 52 pgs. by Carl Barks-reprinted in Best of Uncle Scrooge & Donald Duck No. 1 ('66) & The Best of W.D. Comics; two Barks stories	52.00	156.00	364.00
4-Color 178(12/47)-1st Uncle Scrooge by Carl Barks; reprinted in Gold Key Christmas Parade No. 3 & The Best of W.D. Comics	58.00	175.00	405.00
4-Color 189(6/48)-by Carl Barks; reprinted in Best of Donald Duck & Uncle Scrooge No. 1('64)	52.00	156.00	364.00
4-Color 199(10/48)-by Carl Barks; mentioned in **Love and Death**	52.00	156.00	364.00
4-Color 203(12/48)-by Barks; reprinted as Gold Key Christmas Parade No. 4	36.00	108.00	250.00
4-Color 223(4/49)-by Barks; reprinted as Best of Donald Duck No. 1('65)	50.00	150.00	350.00
4-Color 238(8/49), 256(12/49)-by Barks; No. 256-reprinted in Best of Donald Duck & Uncle Scrooge No. 2('67) & W.D. Comics Digest No. 44('73)	27.00	81.00	190.00
4-Color 263(2/50)-Two Barks stories	27.00	81.00	190.00
4-Color 275(5/50), 282(7/50), 291(9/50), 300(11/50)-All by Carl Barks; No. 275,282 reprinted in W.D. Comics Digest No. 44('73)	25.00	75.00	175.00
4-Color 308(1/51), 318(3/51)-by Barks; No. 318-reprinted in W.D. Comics Digest No. 34	21.00	63.00	147.00
4-Color 328(5/51)-by Carl Barks (drug issue)	23.00	70.00	160.00
4-Color 339(7-8/51), 379-not by Barks	4.35	13.00	30.00
4-Color 348(9-10/51), 356,394-Barks-c only	6.00	18.00	42.00
4-Color 367(1-2/52)-by Barks; reprinted as Gold Key Christmas Parade No. 2 & again as No. 8	19.00	57.00	132.00
4-Color 408(7-8/52), 422(9-10/52)-All by Carl Barks. No. 408-reprinted in Best of Donald Duck & Uncle Scrooge No. 1('64)	19.00	57.00	132.00
26(11-12/52)-In "Trick or Treat"(Barks-a, 36pgs.) 1st story r-/Walt Disney Digest #16	20.00	60.00	140.00
27-30-Barks-c only	4.00	12.00	28.00
31-40	2.30	7.00	16.00
41-44,47-50	1.70	5.00	12.00
45-Barks-a, 6 pgs.	6.50	19.50	45.00
46-"Secret of Hondorica" by Barks, 24 pgs.; reprinted in Donald Duck #98 & 154	7.50	22.00	52.00
51-Barks, ½ pg.	1.60	4.70	11.00

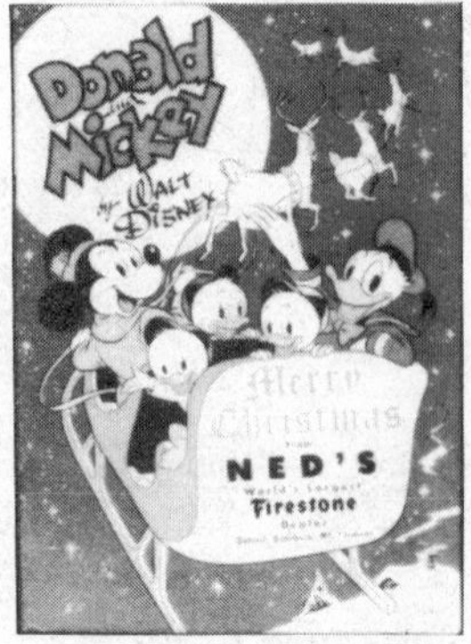

Donald & Mickey Merry Christmas 1948, © WDC

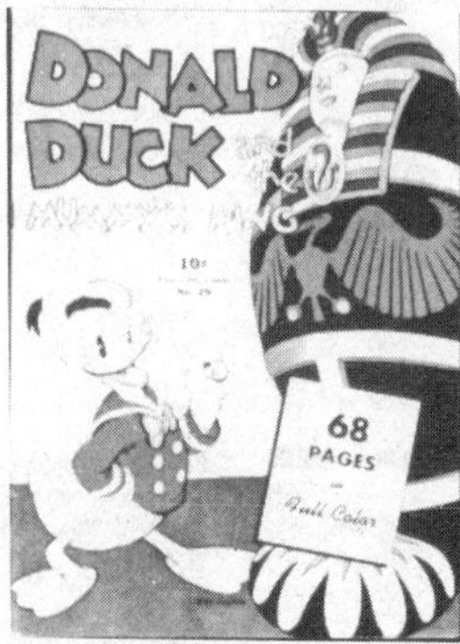

Donald Duck 4-Color 29, © WDC

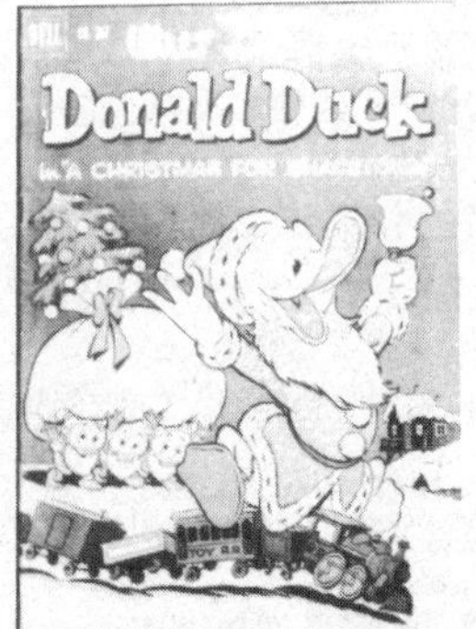

Donald Duck 4-Color 367, © WDC

A 64 PAGE CLASSIC!
Walt Disney's
Donald Duck
finds Pirate Gold!

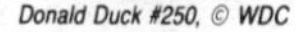
Donald Duck #250, © WDC

Donald Duck Album #1 (G.K.), © WDC

Donald Duck Tells About Kites, PG&E, © WDC

DONALD DUCK (continued)	**Good**	**Fine**	**Mint**
52-"Lost Peg-Leg Mine" by Barks, 10 pgs.	6.50	19.50	45.00
53,55-59	1.50	4.50	10.00
54-"Forbidden Valley" by Barks, 26 pgs.	7.50	22.00	52.00
60-"D.D. & the Titanic Ants" by Barks, 20 pgs. plus 6 more pgs.	6.50	19.50	45.00
61-67,69,70	1.15	3.50	8.00
68-Barks-a, 5 pgs.	3.75	11.25	26.00
71-Barks-r, ½ pg.	1.30	4.00	9.00
72-78,80,82-97,99,100: 96-Donald Duck Album	1.00	3.00	7.00
79,81-Barks-a, 1pg.	1.30	4.00	9.00
98-Reprints #46 (Barks)	2.15	6.50	15.00
101-133: 112-1st Moby Duck	.85	2.50	6.00
134-Barks-r/#52 & WDC&S 194	1.00	3.00	7.00
135-Barks-r/WDC&S 198, 19 pgs.	.70	2.00	5.00
136-153,155,156,158	.50	1.50	3.00
154-Barks-r(#46)	.70	2.00	5.00
157-Barks-r(#45)	.40	1.25	2.50
159-Reprints/WDC&S #192	.40	1.25	2.50
160-Barks-r(#26)	.40	1.25	2.50
161-163,165-170	.25	.75	1.50
164-Barks-r(#79)	.40	1.25	2.50
171-173,175-187,189-191		.60	1.20
174-Reprints 4-Color 394	.35	1.00	2.00
188-Barks-r/#68	.35	1.00	2.00
192-Barks-r(40 pgs.) from Donald Duck #60 & WDC&S #226,234 (52 pgs.)	.40	1.25	2.50
193-200,202-207,209-211,213-218: 217 has 216 on-c		.50	1.00
201-Barks-r/Christ. Parade 26, 16pgs.	.35	1.00	2.00
208-Barks-r/#60	.35	1.00	2.00
212-Barks-r/WDC&S 130	.35	1.00	2.00
219-Barks-r/WDC&S 106,107, 2 pgs. ea.		.60	1.20
220-227,231-245		.35	.70
228-Barks-r/F.C. 275	.25	.75	1.50
229-Barks-r/F.C. 282	.25	.75	1.50
230-Barks-r/#52 & WDC&S 194	.25	.75	1.50
246-249,251-253: 246-Barks-r/FC 422. 248-Barks-r/DD 54. 249-Barks-r/DD 26. 251-Barks-r/'45 Firestone		.40	.75
250-Barks-r/4-Color 9, 64 pgs.	.35	1.00	2.00
254-256,258-262: 254-Barks-r/FC 328. 256-Barks-r/FC 147.		.50	.95
257-Barks-r/Vac. Parade #1 (52 pgs.)	.25	.75	1.50
Mini-Comic No. 1(1976)-(3¼x6½"); Reprints/Donald Duck #150			.10

NOTE: *Carl* ***Barks*** *wrote all issues he illustrated, but No. 117, 126, 138 contain his script only. Issues 4-Color No.189, 199, 203, 223, 238, 256, 263, 275, 282, 308, 348, 356, 367, 394, 408, 422, 26-30, 35, 44, 46, 52, 55, 57, 60, 65, 70-73, 77-80, 83, 101, 103, 105, 106, 111, 126 all have* ***Barks*** *covers. No. 96 titled "Comic Album," No. 99-"Christmas Album." New art issues-106-46, 148-63, 167, 169, 170, 172, 173, 175, 178, 179, 196, 209, 223, 225, 236.*

DONALD DUCK
1944 (16 pg. Christmas giveaway)(paper cover)(2 versions)
K. K. Publications

	Good	Fine	Mint
Kelly cover reprint	37.00	110.00	260.00

DONALD DUCK ADVENTURES
Nov, 1987 - Present
Gladstone Publishing

	Good	Fine	Mint
1-3		.50	.95

DONALD DUCK ALBUM (See Duck Album & Comic Album No. 1,3)
May-July, 1959 - Oct, 1963
Dell Publishing Co./Gold Key

	Good	Fine	Mint
4-Color 995,1182, 01204-207 (1962-Dell)	2.00	6.00	14.00
4-Color 1099,1140,1239-Barks-c	2.30	7.00	16.00
1(8/63-Gold Key)-Barks-c	2.00	6.00	14.00
2(10/63)	1.00	3.00	7.00

DONALD DUCK AND THE BOYS (Also see Story Hour Series)
1948 (Hardcover book; 5¼x5½") 100pgs., ½art, ½text
Whitman Publishing Co.

	Good	Fine	Mint
845-Partial r-/WDC&S No. 74 by Barks	17.00	51.00	120.00

(Prices vary widely on this book)

DONALD DUCK AND THE RED FEATHER
1948 (4 pages) (8½x11") (Black & White)
Red Feather Giveaway

	Good	Fine	Mint
	4.60	14.00	32.00

DONALD DUCK BEACH PARTY (See Dell Giants)
Sept, 1965 (25 cents)
Gold Key

	Good	Fine	Mint
1(#10158-509)-Barks-r/WDC&S #45	3.00	9.00	21.00

DONALD DUCK BOOK (See Story Hour Series)

DONALD DUCK COMIC PAINT BOOK (See Large Feat. Comic No. 20)

DONALD DUCK COMICS DIGEST
1986 - No. 5, 1987? ($1.25-$1.50, 96 pgs.)
Gladstone Publishing

	Good	Fine	Mint
1-3: 1-Barks c/a-r		.60	1.25
4,5	.25	.75	1.50

DONALD DUCK FUN BOOK (See Dell Giants)

DONALD DUCK IN DISNEYLAND (See Dell Giants)

DONALD DUCK IN "THE LITTERBUG"
1963 (16 pgs., 5x7¼", soft-c) (Disney giveaway)
Keep America Beautiful

	Good	Fine	Mint
	1.70	5.00	12.00

DONALD DUCK MARCH OF COMICS
1947 - 1951 (Giveaway) (Disney)
K. K. Publications

	Good	Fine	Mint
nn(No.4)-"Maharajah Donald;" 30 pgs. by Carl Barks-(1947)	428.00	1285.00	3000.00
20-"Darkest Africa" by Carl Barks-(1948); 22 pgs.	257.00	770.00	1800.00
41-"Race to South Seas" by Carl Barks-(1949); 22 pgs.(On Disney's band list)	200.00	600.00	1400.00
56-(1950)-Barks-a on back-c	22.00	65.00	140.00
69-(1951)-Not Barks	19.00	57.00	125.00
263	6.00	18.00	36.00

DONALD DUCK MERRY XMAS (See Dell Giant No. 53)

DONALD DUCK PICNIC PARTY (See Picnic Party under Dell Giant)

DONALD DUCK "PLOTTING PICNICKERS"
1962 (16 pgs., 3¼x7", soft-c) (Disney)(Also see Ludwig Von Drake & Mickey Mouse)
Fritos Giveaway

	Good	Fine	Mint
	1.35	7.00	14.00

DONALD DUCK'S SURPRISE PARTY
1948 (16 pgs.) (Giveaway for Icy Frost Twins Ice Cream Bars)
Walt Disney Productions

	Good	Fine	Mint
(Rare)Kelly c/a	100.00	300.00	700.00

DONALD DUCK TELLS ABOUT KITES
11/54 (Giveaway) (8 pgs. - no cover) (Disney)
Southern California Edison Co./Pacific Gas & Electric Co./Florida Power & Light Co.

	Good	Fine	Mint
Fla. Power, S.C.E. & version with blank label issues-Barks pencils-8 pgs.; inks-7 pgs. (Rare)	285.00	850.00	1800.00

P.G.&E. issue-7th page redrawn changing middle 3 panels to show P.G.&E. in story line; (All Barks; last page Barks pencils only)

DONALD DUCK KITE (continued)

	Good	Fine	Mint
(Scarce)	250.00	750.00	1600.00

(Prices vary widely on above books)

NOTE: *These books appeared one month apart in the fall and were distributed on the West and East Coasts.*

DONALD DUCK, THIS IS YOUR LIFE (See 4-Color No. 1109)

DONALD DUCK XMAS ALBUM (See regular Donald Duck No. 99)

DONALD IN MATHMAGIC LAND (See 4-Color No. 1051, 1198)

DONATELLO, TEENAGE MUTANT NINJA TURTLE
Aug, 1986 (One-shot, $1.50, B&W, 44 pgs.)
Mirage Studios

	Good	Fine	Mint
1	.85	2.50	5.00

DONDI (See 4-Color No. 1176,1276)

DON FORTUNE MAGAZINE
Aug, 1946 - No. 6, Feb, 1947
Don Fortune Publishing Co.

	Good	Fine	Mint
1-Delecta of the Planets by C. C. Beck in all	6.50	19.50	45.00
2	4.00	12.00	28.00
3-6: 3-Bondage-c	3.00	9.00	21.00

DON NEWCOMBE
1950 (Baseball)
Fawcett Publications

	Good	Fine	Mint
nn	12.00	36.00	84.00

DON'T GIVE UP THE SHIP (See 4-Color No. 1049)

DON WINSLOW OF THE NAVY (See 4-Color #2,22, & Super Book #5,6)

DON WINSLOW OF THE NAVY (See TV Teens; Movie, Radio, TV)
Feb, 1943 - No. 73, Sept, 1955 (Fightin' Navy No. 74 on)
Fawcett Publications/Charlton No. 70 on

	Good	Fine	Mint
1-Captain Marvel on cover	35.00	105.00	245.00
2	17.00	51.00	120.00
3	12.00	36.00	84.00
4,5	9.00	27.00	62.00
6-Flag-c	7.00	21.00	50.00
7-10	5.70	17.00	40.00
11-20	3.70	11.00	26.00
21-40	2.85	8.50	20.00
41-63	2.30	7.00	16.00
64(12/48)-Matt Baker-a	2.85	8.50	20.00
65(1/51)-69(9/51): All photo-c. 65-Flying Saucer attack	3.50	10.50	24.00
70(3/55)-73: 70-73 r-/No. 26,58 & 59	1.85	5.50	13.00

DOOM PATROL, THE (My Greatest Adv. No. 1-85; see DC Spec. Bl. Ribbon Digest 19, Official . . . Index & Showcase No. 94-96)
3/64 - No. 121, 9-10/68; 2/73 - No. 124, 6-7/73
National Periodical Publications

	Good	Fine	Mint
86-1pg. origin	4.00	12.00	28.00
87-99: 88-Origin The Chief. 91-Intro. Mento. 99-Intro. Beast Boy who later became the Changeling in the New Teen Titans	2.85	8.50	20.00
100-Origin Beast Boy; Robot-Maniac series begins	3.60	10.70	25.00
101-110: 102-Challengers/Unknown app. 105-Robot-Maniac series ends. 106-Negative Man begins (origin)	1.70	5.00	12.00
111-120	1.50	4.50	10.00
121-Death of Doom Patrol; Orlando-c	4.00	12.00	28.00
122-124(reprints)	.35	1.00	2.00

DOOM PATROL
Oct, 1987 - Present
DC Comics

	Good	Fine	Mint
1	.35	1.00	2.00
2,3		.50	1.00
. . . Suicide Squad Special 1(3/88)	.25	.75	1.50

DOOMSDAY + 1
7/75 - No. 6, 5/76; No. 7, 6/68 - No. 12, 5/79
Charlton Comics

	Good	Fine	Mint
1	1.00	3.00	6.00
2	.75	2.25	4.50
3-6: 4-Intro Lor	.70	2.00	4.00
V3#7-12 (reprints #1-6)	.30	.80	1.60
5 (Modern Comics reprint, 1977)		.20	.40

NOTE: ***Byrne** c/a-1-12; Painted covers-2-7.*

DOOMSDAY SQUAD, THE
Aug, 1986 - No. 7, Feb, 1987 ($2.00)
Fantagraphics Books

	Good	Fine	Mint
1,2: 1-Byrne-a	.35	1.00	2.00
3-Usagi Yojimbo app. (1st in color)	.85	2.50	5.00
4-7	.35	1.00	2.00

DOORWAY TO NIGHTMARE (See Cancelled Comic Cavalcade)
Jan-Feb, 1978 - No. 5, Sept-Oct, 1978
DC Comics

	Good	Fine	Mint
1-5-Madame Xanadu in all. 4-Craig-a		.30	.60

NOTE: ***Kaluta** covers on all. Merged into The Unexpected with No. 190.*

DOPEY DUCK COMICS (Wacky Duck No. 3) (See Super Funnies)
Fall, 1945 - No. 2, April, 1946
Timely Comics (NPP)

	Good	Fine	Mint
1,2-Casper Cat, Krazy Krow	7.00	21.00	50.00

DOROTHY LAMOUR (Formerly Jungle Lil)
No. 2, June, 1950 - No. 3, Aug, 1950
Fox Features Syndicate

	Good	Fine	Mint
2,3-Wood-a(3) each, photo-c	8.00	24.00	56.00

DOT AND DASH AND THE LUCKY JINGLE PIGGIE
1942 (12 pages)
Sears Roebuck Christmas giveaway

	Good	Fine	Mint
Contains a war stamp album and a punch out Jingle Piggie bank	3.50	10.50	24.00

DOT DOTLAND (Formerly Little Dot . . .)
No. 62, Sept, 1974 - No. 63, November, 1974
Harvey Publications

	Good	Fine	Mint
62,63		.60	1.20

DOTTY (. . . & Her Boy Friends) (Formerly Four Teeners; Glamorous Romances No. 41 on)
No. 35, July, 1948 - No. 40, May, 1949
Ace Magazines (A. A. Wyn)

	Good	Fine	Mint
35	3.50	10.50	24.00
36,38-40	1.85	5.50	13.00
37-Transvestism story	2.00	6.00	14.00

DOTTY DRIPPLE (Horace & Dotty Dripple No. 25 on)
1946 - No. 24, June, 1952 (See A-1 No. 1-8, 10)
Magazine Ent.(Life's Romances)/Harvey No. 3 on

	Good	Fine	Mint
nn (nd) (10 cent)	2.65	8.00	18.00
2	1.30	4.00	9.00
3-10: 3,4-Powell-a	.85	2.50	6.00
11-24	.75	2.25	5.00

DOTTY DRIPPLE AND TAFFY
No. 646, Sept, 1955 - No. 903, May, 1958
Dell Publishing Co.

	Good	Fine	Mint
4-Color 646	1.70	5.00	12.00
4-Color 691,718,746,801,903	1.30	4.00	9.00

DOUBLE ACTION COMICS
No. 2, Jan, 1940 (Regular size; 68 pgs.; B&W, color cover)

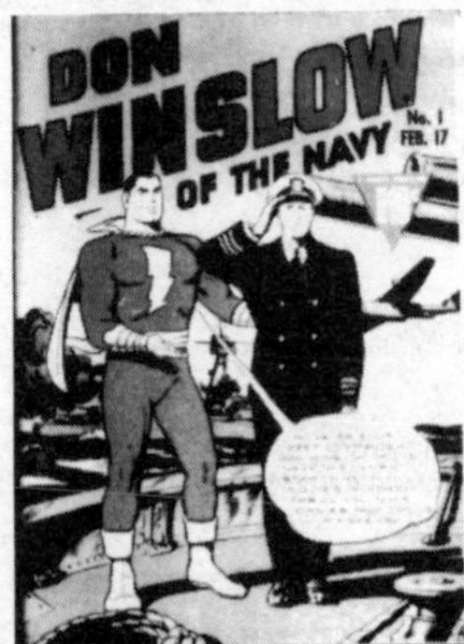

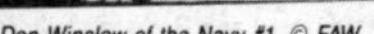
Don Winslow of the Navy #1, © FAW

The Doom Patrol #90, © DC

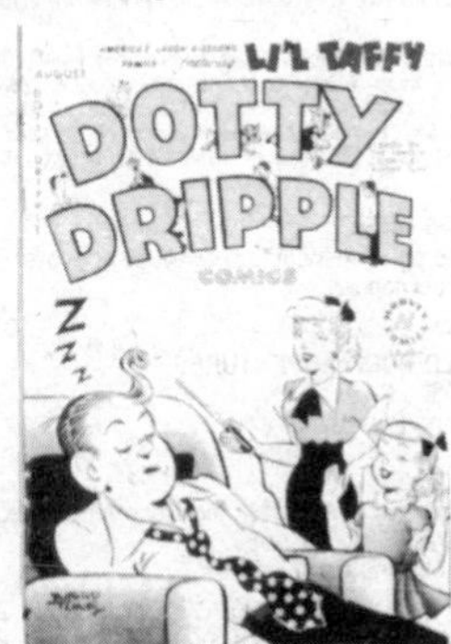

Dotty Dripple #13, © HARV

Double Comics 1940, © Elliot Publ.

Down With Crime #7, © FAW

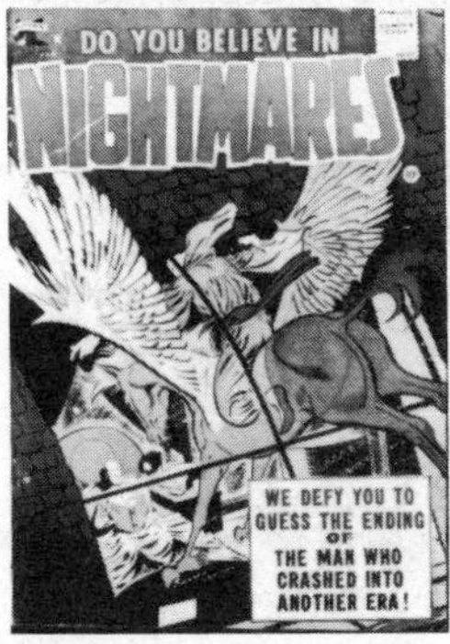

Do You Believe in Nightmares? #1, © STJ

DOUBLE ACTION COMICS (continued)
National Periodical Publications

	Good	Fine	Mint
2-Contains original stories(?); pre-hero DC contents; same cover as Adventure No. 37. (Five known copies) (not an ashcan) Estimated value....			6500.00

NOTE: *The cover to this book was probably reprinted from Adventure No. 37. No. 1 exists as an ash can copy with B&W cover; contains a coverless comic on inside with 1st & last page missing.*

DOUBLE COMICS
1940 - 1944 (132 pages)
Elliot Publications

	Good	Fine	Mint
1940 issues	80.00	240.00	560.00
1941 issues	55.00	165.00	385.00
1942 issues	40.00	120.00	280.00
1943,44 issues	30.00	90.00	210.00

NOTE: Double Comics consisted of an almost endless combination of pairs of remaindered, unsold issues of comics representing most publishers and usually mixed publishers in the same book; e.g., a Captain America with a Silver Streak, or a Feature with a Detective, etc., could appear inside the same cover. The actual contents would have to determine its price. Prices listed are for average contents. Any containing rare origin or first issues are worth much more. Covers also vary in same year. Value would be approximately 50 percent of contents.

DOUBLE-CROSS (See The Crusaders)

DOUBLE-DARE ADVENTURES
Dec, 1966 - No. 2, March, 1967 (35-25 cents, 68 pgs.)
Harvey Publications

	Good	Fine	Mint
1-Origin Bee-Man, Glowing Gladiator, & Magic-Master; Simon/Kirby-a	.70	2.00	5.00
2-Williamson/Crandall-a; r-/Alarming Adv. #3('63)	1.00	3.00	7.00

NOTE: ***Powell** a-1. **Simon/Sparling** c-1,2.*

DOUBLE LIFE OF PRIVATE STRONG, THE
June, 1959 - No. 2, Aug, 1959
Archie Publications/Radio Comics

	Good	Fine	Mint
1-Origin The Shield; Simon & Kirby c/a; The Fly app.	14.00	42.00	100.00
2-S&K c/a; Tuska-a; The Fly app.	9.00	27.00	62.00

DOUBLE TALK (Also see Two-Faces)
No date (1962?) (32 pgs.; full color; slick cover)
Christian Anti-Communism Crusade (Giveaway)
Feature Publications

	Good	Fine	Mint
	15.00	45.00	90.00

DOUBLE TROUBLE
Nov, 1957 - No. 2, Jan, 1958?
St. John Publishing Co.

	Good	Fine	Mint
1,2	1.30	4.00	9.00

DOUBLE TROUBLE WITH GOOBER
No. 417, Aug, 1952 - No. 556, May, 1954
Dell Publishing Co.

	Good	Fine	Mint
4-Color 417	1.50	4.50	10.00
4-Color 471,516,556	1.00	3.00	7.00

DOUBLE UP
1941 (200 pages) (Pocket size)
Elliott Publications

	Good	Fine	Mint
1-Contains rebound copies of digest sized issues of Pocket Comics, Speed Comics, & Spitfire Comics	35.00	105.00	245.00

DOVER BOYS (See Adventures of the...)

DOVER THE BIRD
Spring, 1955
Famous Funnies Publishing Co.

	Good	Fine	Mint
1	1.30	4.00	9.00

DOWN WITH CRIME
Nov, 1952 - No. 7, Nov, 1953
Fawcett Publications

	Good	Fine	Mint
1	7.00	21.00	50.00
2,4-Powell-a each	4.00	12.00	28.00
3-Used in **POP**, pg. 106; heroin drug cover/story	6.00	18.00	42.00
5-Bondage-c	4.00	12.00	28.00
6-Used in **POP**, pg. 80	3.50	10.50	24.00
7	3.00	9.00	21.00

DO YOU BELIEVE IN NIGHTMARES?
Nov, 1957 - No. 2, Jan, 1958
St. John Publishing Co.

	Good	Fine	Mint
1-Ditko c/a(most)	9.00	27.00	62.00
2-Ayers-a	4.00	12.00	28.00

D.P. 7
Nov, 1986 - Present
Marvel Comics Group

	Good	Fine	Mint
1	.40	1.25	2.50
2,3	.25	.75	1.50
4-18		.50	1.00
Annual #1 (11/87)-Intro. The Witness		.65	1.30

DRACULA (See Tomb of..., Marvel Graphic Novel & Movie Classics under Universal Presents as well as Dracula)

DRACULA (See Movie Classics for No. 1)
11/66 - No. 4, 3/67; No. 6, 7/72 - No. 8, 7/73 (No No.5)
Dell Publishing Co.

	Good	Fine	Mint
2-Origin Dracula (11/66)	.35	1.00	2.00
3,4-Intro. Fleeta #4('67)	.25	.75	1.50
6-('72)-r-/#2 w/origin		.50	1.00
7,8: 7 r-/#3, 8-r/#4		.40	.80

DRACULA (Magazine)
1979 (120 pages) (full color)
Warren Publishing Co.

	Good	Fine	Mint
Book 1-Maroto art; Spanish material translated into English	1.00	3.00	6.00

DRACULA LIVES! (Magazine)
1973(no month) - No. 13, July, 1975 (B&W) (75 cents)
Marvel Comics Group

	Good	Fine	Mint
1-Boris-c	.50	1.50	3.00
2-Origin; Adams c/a; Starlin-a	.50	1.50	3.00
3-Adams-a(i)	.50	1.50	3.00
4-Ploog-a	.45	1.25	2.50
5(V2#1)-13: 5-Dracula series begins	.35	1.00	2.00
Annual 1('75)-Adams-a(r)	.35	1.00	2.00

NOTE: ***Alcala** a-9. **Buscema** a-3p, 6p. **Buckler** a-1p. **Colan** a(p)-1, 5, 6, 8. **Evans** a-7. **Heath** a-1r, 13. **Pakula** a-6r.*

DRAG 'N' WHEELS (Formerly Top Eliminator)
No. 30, Sept, 1968 - No. 59, May, 1973
Charlton Comics

	Good	Fine	Mint
30-59-Scot Jackson feat.		.40	.80
Modern Comics Reprint 58('78)		.20	.40

DRAGONFLY
Sum, 1985 - Present ($1.75)(No. 1&3, color)
Americomics

	Good	Fine	Mint
1-5	.30	.90	1.75

DRAGONSLAYER
October, 1981 - No. 2, Nov, 1981
Marvel Comics Group

	Good	Fine	Mint
1,2-Paramount Disney movie adaptation		.25	.50

DRAGOON WELLS MASSACRE (See 4-Color No. 815)

DRAGSTRIP HOTRODDERS (World of Wheels No. 17 on)
Sum, 1963; No. 2, Jan, 1965 - No. 16, Aug, 1967
Charlton Comics

	Good	Fine	Mint
1	.50	1.50	3.00
2-16		.50	1.00

DRAMA OF AMERICA, THE
1973 (224 pages) ($1.95)
Action Text

1-"Students' Supplement to History"	.50	1.50	3.00

DREADSTAR ($1.50) (Also see Marvel Graphic Novel)
Nov, 1982 - Present (Direct sale, Baxter paper)
Epic Comics (Marvel)/First Comics No. 27 on

1	.85	2.50	5.00
2	.60	1.70	3.50
3-5	.50	1.50	3.00
6-10	.40	1.25	2.50
11-26: 12-New costume. 16-New powers	.35	1.10	2.20
27-First Comics; new look	.35	1.10	2.20
28-35: New look	.35	1.00	2.00
Annual 1 (12/83)-Reprints The Price	.40	1.25	2.50

NOTE: ***Starlin** c/a-1-19, Annual 1. **Wrightson** a-6, 7.*

DREADSTAR AND COMPANY
July, 1985 - No. 6, Dec, 1985
Epic Comics (Marvel)

1-Reprints of Dreadstar series		.55	1.10
2-6		.40	.80

DREAM BOOK OF LOVE (See A-1 Comics No. 106,114,123)

DREAM BOOK OF ROMANCE (See A-1 No. 92,101,109,110,124)

DREAM OF LOVE
1958 (Reprints)
I. W. Enterprises

1,2,8,9: 1-Powell-a. 8,9-Kinstler-c	.50	1.50	3.00

DREAMS OF THE RAREBIT FIEND
1905
Doffield & Co.?

By Winsor McCay (Very Rare) (Three copies known to exist)
Estimated value.... $500.00—$900.00

DRIFT MARLO
May-July, 1962 - No. 2, Oct-Dec, 1962
Dell Publishing Co.

01-232-207, 2(12-232-212)	1.00	3.00	7.00

DRISCOLL'S BOOK OF PIRATES
1934 (124 pgs.) (B&W; hardcover; 7x9")
David McKay Publ. (Not reprints)

By Montford Amory	6.00	18.00	42.00

DROIDS
April, 1986 - No. 8, June, 1987 (Based on Sat. morning cartoon)
Star Comics (Marvel)

1-R2D2, C-3PO from Star Wars		.40	.80
2-8: 3-Romita/Williamson-a		.40	.80

DRUM BEAT (See 4-Color No. 610)

DUCK ALBUM (See Donald Duck Album)
Oct, 1951 - Sept, 1957
Dell Publishing Co.

4-Color 353-Barks-c	2.65	8.00	18.00
4-Color 450-Barks-c	2.30	7.00	16.00
4-Color 492,531,560,586,611,649,686	1.70	5.00	12.00
4-Color 726,782,840	1.50	4.50	10.00

DUDLEY (Teen-age)
Nov-Dec, 1949 - No. 3, Mar-Apr, 1950
Feature/Prize Publications

	Good	Fine	Mint
1-By Boody Rogers	5.00	15.00	35.00
2,3	2.65	8.00	18.00

DUDLEY DO-RIGHT (TV)
Aug, 1970 - No. 7, Aug, 1971 (Jay Ward)
Charlton Comics

1	1.70	5.00	12.00
2-7	1.15	3.50	8.00

DUKE OF THE K-9 PATROL
April, 1963
Gold Key

1 (10052-304)	1.75	5.25	12.00

DUMBO (See 4-Color #17,234,668, Movie Comics, & Walt Disney Showcase #12)

DUMBO (Walt Disney's...)
1941 (K.K. Publ. Giveaway)
Weatherbird Shoes/Ernest Kern Co.(Detroit)

16 pgs., 9x10" (Rare)	22.00	65.00	154.00
52 pgs., 5½x8½", slick cover in color; B&W interior; half text, half reprints/4-Color No. 17	13.00	40.00	90.00

DUMBO COMIC PAINT BOOK (See Large Feat. Comic No. 19)

DUMBO WEEKLY
1942 (Premium supplied by Diamond D-X Gas Stations)
Walt Disney Productions

1	10.00	30.00	60.00
2-16	5.00	15.00	30.00

NOTE: *A cover and binder came separate at gas stations. Came with membership card.*

DUNC AND LOO (1-3 titled "Around the Block with Dunc and Loo")
Oct-Dec, 1961 - No. 8, Oct-Dec, 1963
Dell Publishing Co.

1	4.35	13.00	30.00
2	3.00	9.00	21.00
3-8	2.00	6.00	14.00

NOTE: *Written by **John Stanley**; **Bill Williams** art.*

DUNE
April, 1985 - No. 3, June, 1985
Marvel Comics

1-3-r/Marvel Super Special; movie adaptation		.40	.80

DURANGO KID, THE (Also see Best of the West, White Indian, & Great Western) (Charles Starrett starred in Columbia's Durango Kid movies)
Oct-Nov, 1949 - No. 41, Oct-Nov, 1955 (All 36pgs.)
Magazine Enterprises

1-Charles Starrett photo-c; Durango Kid & his horse Raider begin; Dan Brand & Tipi (origin) begin by Frazetta & continue through #16	33.00	100.00	230.00
2(Starrett photo-c)	21.00	63.00	150.00
3-5(All-Starrett photo-c)	19.00	57.00	132.00
6-10	13.50	40.50	94.00
11-16-Last Frazetta ish.	12.00	36.00	84.00
17-Origin Durango Kid	9.00	27.00	62.00
18-Fred Meagher-a on Dan Brand begins	4.35	13.00	30.00
19-30: 19-Guardineer c/a(3) begin, end #41. 23-Intro. The Red Scorpion	4.60	14.00	32.00
31-Red Scorpion returns	4.00	12.00	28.00
32-41-Bolle/Frazetta-a (Dan Brand)	5.00	15.00	35.00

NOTE: *#6,8,14,15 contain **Frazetta** art not reprinted in White Indian. **Guardineer** a(3)-19-41; c-19-41. **Fred Meagher** a-18-29 at least.*

DWIGHT D. EISENHOWER
December, 1969

Dreadstar Annual #1, © First Comics

Dumbo Weekly #8, © WDC

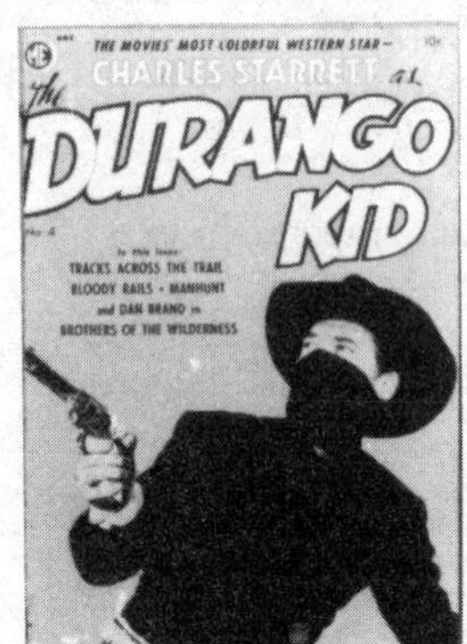

The Durango Kid #4, © ME

Dynamic Comics #14, © CHES

Dynamo #3, © TC

The Eagle #3, © FOX

DWIGHT D. EISENHOWER (continued)
Dell Publishing Co.

	Good	Fine	Mint
01-237-912 - Life story	2.00	6.00	12.00

DYNABRITE COMICS
1978 - 1979 (69 cents; 48 pgs.)(10x7-1/8"; cardboard covers)
(Blank inside covers)
Whitman Publishing Co.

11350 - Walt Disney's Mickey Mouse & the Beanstalk (4-C 157)
11350-1 - Mickey Mouse Album (4-C 1057,1151,1246)
11351 - Mickey Mouse & His Sky Adventure (4-C 214,343)
11352 - Donald Duck (4-C 408, Donald Duck 45,52)-Barks
11352-1 - Donald Duck (4-C 318, 10 pg. Barks/WDC&S 125,128)-Barks-c(r)
11353 - Daisy Ducks Diary (4-C 1055,1150) - Barks-a
11354 - Goofy: A Gaggle of Giggles
11354-1 - Super Goof Meets Super Thief
11355 - Uncle Scrooge (Barks-a/U.S. 12,33)
11355-1 - Uncle Scrooge (Barks-a/U.S. 13,16) - Barks-c(r)
11356 - Bugs Bunny(?)
11357 - Star Trek (r-Star Trek 33 & 41)
11358 - Star Trek (r-Star Trek 34,36)
11359 - Bugs Bunny-r
11360 - Winnie the Pooh Fun and Fantasy (Disney-r)
11361 - Gyro Gearloose & the Disney Ducks (4-C 1047,1184)-Barks-c(r)

	Good	Fine	Mint
each....		.40	.80

DYNAMIC ADVENTURES
No. 8,9, 1964
I. W. Enterprises

	Good	Fine	Mint
8-Kayo Kirby by Baker?	1.20	3.50	7.00
9-Reprints Avon's "Escape From Devil's Island"-Kinstler-c	1.35	4.00	8.00
nn(no date)-Reprints Risks Unlimited with Rip Carson, Senorita Rio	1.20	3.50	7.00

DYNAMIC CLASSICS (See Cancelled Comic Cavalcade)
Sept-Oct, 1978 (44 pgs.)
DC Comics

	Good	Fine	Mint
1-Adams Batman, Simonson Manhunter-r		.30	.60

DYNAMIC COMICS (No No.4-7)
Oct, 1941 - No. 3, Feb, 1942; No. 8, 1944 - No. 25, May, 1948
Harry 'A' Chesler

	Good	Fine	Mint
1-Origin Major Victory by Charles Sultan (reprinted in Major Victory #1), Dynamic Man & Hale the Magician; The Black Cobra only app.	50.00	150.00	350.00
2-Origin Dynamic Boy & Lady Satan; intro. The Green Knight & sidekick Lance Cooper	24.00	72.00	170.00
3	20.00	60.00	140.00
8-Dan Hastings, The Echo, The Master Key, Yankee Boy begin; Yankee Doodle Jones app.; hypo story	20.00	60.00	140.00
9-Mr. E begins; Mac Raboy-c	21.00	62.00	145.00
10	17.00	51.00	120.00
11-15: 15-The Sky Chief app.	12.00	36.00	84.00
16-Marijuana story	13.50	40.50	95.00
17(1/46)-Illustrated in **SOTI**, "The children told me what the man was going to do with the hot poker," but Wertham saw this in Crime Reporter #2	18.00	54.00	125.00
18,19,21,22,24,25	8.00	24.00	56.00
20-Bare-breasted woman-c	10.00	30.00	70.00
23-Yankee Girl app.	8.00	24.00	56.00
I.W. Reprint #1,8('64): 1-r/#23	.70	2.00	4.00

NOTE: ***Kinstler** c-IW #1. **Tuska** art in many issues, #3, 9, 11, 12, 16, 19. Bondage c-16.*

DYNAMITE (Johnny Dynamite No. 10 on)
May, 1953 - No. 9, Sept, 1954
Comic Media/Allen Hardy Publ.

	Good	Fine	Mint
1-Pete Morisi-a; r-as Danger No. 6	5.70	17.00	40.00
2	3.00	9.00	21.00
3-Marijuana story; Johnny Dynamite begins by Pete Morisi	4.00	12.00	28.00
4-Injury-to-eye, prostitution; Morisi-a	5.00	15.00	35.00
5-9-Morisi-a in all	2.65	8.00	18.00

DYNAMO
Aug, 1966 - No. 4, June, 1967 (25 cents)
Tower Comics

	Good	Fine	Mint
1-Crandall/Wood, Ditko/Wood-a; Weed series begins; NoMan & Lightning cameos; Wood c/a	1.70	5.00	12.00
2-4: Wood c/a in all	1.30	4.00	9.00

NOTE: ***Adkins/Wood** a-2. **Ditko** a-4. **Tuska** a-2,3.*

DYNAMO JOE (Also see Mars & First Advs.)
May, 1986 - Present
First Comics

	Good	Fine	Mint
1	.50	1.50	3.00
2-11: 4-Cargonauts begin	.25	.75	1.50
12-16 ($1.75)	.30	.90	1.75
Special 1(1/87)-Mostly-r/Mars	.25	.75	1.50

DYNOMUTT (TV)(See Scooby-Doo, 3rd series)
Nov, 1977 - No. 6, Sept, 1978
Marvel Comics Group

	Good	Fine	Mint
1-6		.50	1.00

EAGLE, THE (1st Series)
July, 1941 - No. 4, Jan, 1942
Fox Features Syndicate

	Good	Fine	Mint
1-The Eagle begins; Rex Dexter of Mars app. by Briefer	50.00	150.00	350.00
2-The Spider Queen begins (origin)	25.00	75.00	175.00
3,4: 3-Joe Spook begins (origin)	20.00	60.00	140.00

EAGLE (2nd Series)
Feb-Mar, 1945 - No. 2, Apr-May, 1945
Rural Home Publ.

	Good	Fine	Mint
1-Aviation stories	6.50	19.50	45.00
2-Lucky Aces	5.50	16.50	38.00

NOTE: ***L. B. Cole** c/a.*

EARTH MAN ON VENUS (An...) (Also see Strange Planets)
1951
Avon Periodicals

	Good	Fine	Mint
nn-Wood-a, 26 pgs.	76.00	228.00	535.00

EASTER BONNET SHOP (See March of Comics No. 29)

EASTER WITH MOTHER GOOSE (See 4-Color No. 103,140,185,220)

EAT RIGHT TO WORK AND WIN
1942 (16 pages) (Giveaway)
Swift & Company

	Good	Fine	Mint
Blondie, Henry, Flash Gordon by Alex Raymond, Toots & Casper, Thimble Threatre (Popeye), Tillie the Toiler, The Phantom, The Little King, & Bringing Up Father - original strips just for this book - (in daily strip form which shows what foods we should eat and why)	18.00	54.00	125.00

E. C. CLASSIC REPRINTS
May, 1973 - No. 12, 1976 (E. C. Comics reprinted in full color minus ads)
East Coast Comix Co.

	Good	Fine	Mint
1-The Crypt of Terror #1 (Tales From the Crypt #46)	.70	2.00	4.00
2-Weird Science #15('52)	.50	1.50	3.00
3-Shock SuspenStories #12	.35	1.00	2.00
4-12: 4-Haunt of Fear #12. 5-Weird Fantasy #13('52). 6-Crime SuspenStories #25. 7-Vault of Horror #26. 8-Shock SuspenStories #6 9-Two-Fisted Tales #34. 10-Haunt of Fear #23. 11-Weird Science #12(#1). 12-Shock SuspenStories #2	.35	1.00	2.00

EC CLASSICS
1985 - Present (High quality paper; r-/8 stories in color)
Russ Cochran

	Good	Fine	Mint
(All No. 1)-Shock Suspenstories, Two-Fisted Tales, Vault of Horror, Weird Fantasy	.85	2.50	4.95

ECHO OF FUTUREPAST
May, 1984 - Present? (52 pgs., $2.95)
Pacific Comics/Continuity Comics

	Good	Fine	Mint
1-Adams c/a begins	.60	1.80	3.50
2-11	.50	1.50	3.00

NOTE: ***Adams** a-1-6; c-1-3, 5p, 8. **Golden** a-1-6; c-6. **Toth** a-6, 7.*

ECLIPSE GRAPHIC ALBUM SERIES
Oct, 1978 - Present (8½x11")
Eclipse Comics

	Good	Fine	Mint
1-Sabre (10/78)	1.35	4.00	7.95
1-Sabre (2nd print, 1/79)	1.35	4.00	7.95
2-Night Music (11/79)	1.35	4.00	7.95
3-Detectives, Inc. (5/80)	1.35	4.00	7.95
4-Stewart The Rat ('80)	1.35	4.00	7.95
5-The Price (10/81)-Starlin-a	1.35	4.00	7.95
6-I Am Coyote (11/84)-Rogers c/a	1.35	4.00	7.95
7-The Rocketeer (9/85)-Stevens-a	1.35	4.00	7.95
8-Zorro In Old California ('86)	1.15	3.50	6.95
8-Hard cover	2.00	6.00	11.95
9-The Sacred And The Profane ('86, soft-c)	2.50	7.50	14.95
9-Hard cover	4.00	12.50	24.95
10-Somerset Holmes ('86)-Adults, soft-c	2.50	7.50	14.95
10-Hard cover	4.00	12.50	24.95

ECLIPSE MONTHLY
8/83 - No. 10, 7/84 (Baxter paper; 1-3: 52 pgs., $2.00)
Eclipse Comics

	Good	Fine	Mint
1-3: ($2.00)-Cap'n Quick and a Foozle by Rogers, Static by Ditko, Dope by Trina Robbins, Rio by Doug Wildey, The Masked Man by Boyer begin. 3-Ragamuffins begins	.35	1.00	2.00
4-8 ($1.50 cover)	.25	.75	1.50
9,10-($1.75 cover)	.30	.90	1.80

NOTE: ***Boyer** c-6. **Ditko** a-3. **Rogers** a-3-5; c-2, 4. **Wildey** a-1, 2, 5, 6, 9; c-5, 10.*

E. C. 3-D CLASSICS (See Three Dimensional . . .)

EDDIE STANKY (Baseball Hero)
1951 (New York Giants)
Fawcett Publications

	Good	Fine	Mint
nn	6.00	18.00	42.00

EDGAR BERGEN PRESENTS CHARLIE McCARTHY
1938 (36 pgs.; 15x10½"; in color)
Whitman Publishing Co. (Charlie McCarthy Co.)

	Good	Fine	Mint
764 (Scarce)	35.00	105.00	245.00

EDGE OF CHAOS
July, 1983 - No. 3, Jan, 1984
Pacific Comics

	Good	Fine	Mint
1-3-Morrow c/a; all contain nudity	.25	.75	1.50

EDWARD'S SHOES GIVEAWAY
1954 (Has clown on cover)
Edward's Shoe Store

Contains comic with new cover. Many combinations possible. Contents determines price, 50-60 percent of original. (Similar to Comics From Weatherbird & Free Comics to You)

ED WHEELAN'S JOKE BOOK STARRING FAT & SLAT (See Fat & Slat)

EERIE (Strange Worlds No. 18 on)
No. 1, Jan, 1947; No. 1, May-June, 1951 - No. 17, Aug-Sept, 1954
Avon Periodicals

	Good	Fine	Mint
1(1947)-1st horror comic; Kubert, Fugitani-a; bondage-c	32.00	95.00	225.00
1(1951)-Reprints story/'47 No. 1	19.00	57.00	130.00
2-Wood c/a; bondage-c	21.00	64.00	150.00
3-Wood-c, Kubert, Wood/Orlando-a	21.00	64.00	150.00
4,5-Wood-c	19.00	57.00	130.00
6,13,14	6.50	19.50	45.00
7-Wood/Orlando-c; Kubert-a	12.00	36.00	84.00
8-Kinstler-a; bondage-c; Phantom Witch Doctor story	7.00	21.00	50.00
9-Kubert-a; Check-c	8.50	25.50	60.00
10,11-Kinstler-a	7.00	21.00	50.00
12-25-pg. Dracula story from novel	10.00	30.00	70.00
15-Reprints No. 1('51)minus-c(bondage)	4.60	14.00	32.00
16-Wood-a r-/No. 2	6.00	18.00	42.00
17-Wood/Orlando & Kubert-a; reprints No. 3 minus inside & outside Wood-c	8.50	25.50	60.00

NOTE: ***Hollingsworth** a-9-11; c-10,11.*

EERIE
1964
I. W. Enterprises

	Good	Fine	Mint
I.W. Reprint No. 1(1964)-Wood-c(r)	1.20	3.50	7.00
I.W. Reprint No. 2,6,8: 8-Dr. Drew by Grandenetti from Ghost No. 9	.85	2.50	5.00
I.W. Reprint No. 9-From Eerie No. 2(Avon); Wood-c	1.35	4.00	8.00

EERIE (Magazine)(See Warren Presents)
No. 1, Sept, 1965; No. 2, Mar, 1966 - No. 139, Feb, 1983
Warren Publishing Co.

1-24 pgs., black & white, small size (5¼x7¼"), low distribution; cover from inside back cover of Creepy No. 2; stories reprinted from Creepy No. 7, 8. At least three different versions exist.

First Printing - B&W, 5¼" wide x 7¼" high, evenly trimmed. On page 18, panel 5, in the upper left-hand corner, the large rear view of a bald headed man blends into solid black and is unrecognizable. Overall printing quality is poor.

	Good	Fine	Mint
	13.00	40.00	90.00

Second Printing - B&W, 5¼x7¼", with uneven, untrimmed edges (if one of these were trimmed evenly, the size would be less than as indicated). The figure of the bald headed man on page 18, panel 5 is clear and discernible. The staples have a ¼" blue stripe.

	Good	Fine	Mint
	7.00	20.00	40.00

Other unauthorized reproductions for comparison's sake would be practically worthless. One known version was probably shot off a first printing copy with some loss of detail; the finer lines tend to disappear in this version which can be determined by looking at the lower right-hand corner of page one, first story. The roof of the house is shaded with straight lines. These lines are sharp and distinct on original, but broken on this version.

	Good	Fine	Mint
	1.35	4.00	8.00

NOTE: ***The Comic Book Price Guide** recommends that, before buying, you consult an expert.*

	Good	Fine	Mint
2-Frazetta-c	1.00	3.00	6.00
3-Frazetta-c, 1 pg.	.70	2.00	4.00
4-10: 4-Frazetta ½ page	.50	1.50	3.00
11-25	.45	1.25	2.50
26-41,43-45	.35	1.00	2.00
42-(1973 Annual)	.50	1.50	3.00
46-50,52,53,56-78: 78-The Mummy-r		.75	1.50
51-(1974 Annual)	.50	1.50	3.00
54,55-Color Spirit story by Eisner, 12/21/47 & 6/16/46	.35	1.00	2.00
79,80-Origin Darklon the Mystic by Starlin		.75	1.50
81-139		.60	1.20
Year Book 1970-Reprints	.85	2.50	5.00
Year Book 1971-Reprints	.85	2.50	5.00
Year Book 1972-Reprints	.70	2.00	4.00

NOTE: *The above books contain art by many good artists: **Adams, Brunner, Corben, Craig (Taycee), Crandall, Ditko, Eisner, Evans, Jeff Jones, Kinstler, Krenkel, McWilliams, Morrow, Orlando, Ploog, Severin, Starlin, Torres, Toth, Williamson, Wood,** and **Wrightson;** covers by **Bode', Corben, Davis, Frazetta, Morrow,** and*

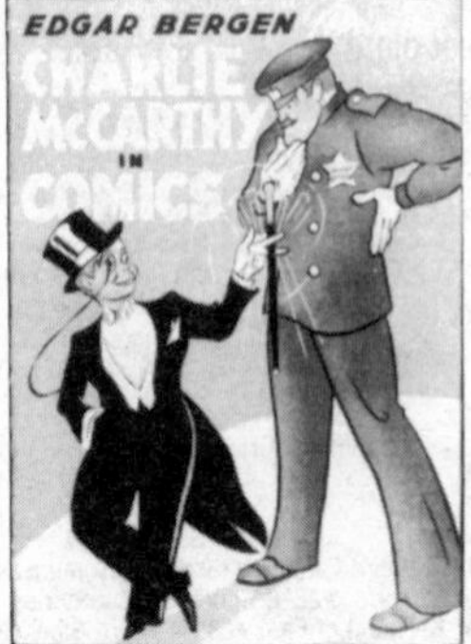

Edgar Bergen Presents ... #764, © E. Bergen

Eerie #1 ('51), © AVON

Eerie #1, © WP

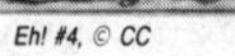
Eh! #4, © CC

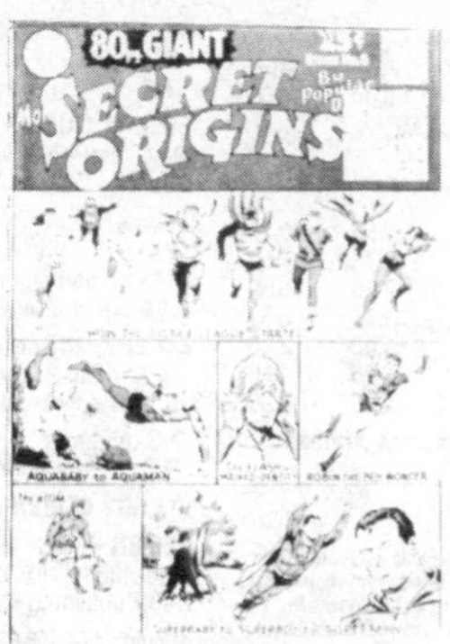

80 Page Giant #8, © DC

80 Page Giant #12, © DC

EERIE (continued)
Orlando. Annuals from 1973-on are included in regular numbering. 1970-74 Annuals are complete reprints. Annuals from 1975-on are in the format of the regular issues.

EERIE ADVENTURES (Also see Weird Adventures)
Winter, 1951
Ziff-Davis Publ. Co.

	Good	Fine	Mint
1-Powell-a(2), Kinstler-a; used in **SOTI**; bondage-c; Krigstein back-c	7.00	21.00	50.00

NOTE: Title dropped due to similarity to Avon's Eerie & legal action.

EERIE TALES (Magazine)
1959 (Black & White)
Hastings Associates

1-Williamson, Torres, Tuska-a, Powell(2), & Morrow(2)-a	3.50	10.50	24.00

EERIE TALES
1964
Super Comics

Super Reprint No. 10,11,12,18: Purple Claw in No. 11,12; No. 12 r-Avon Eerie No. 1('51)	.70	2.00	4.00
15-Wolverton-a, Spacehawk-r/Blue Bolt Weird Tales No. 113; Disbrow-a	2.00	6.00	12.00

EGBERT
Spring, 1946 - No. 20, 1950
Arnold Publications/Quality Comics Group

1-Funny animal; intro Egbert & The Count	7.00	21.00	50.00
2	3.50	10.50	24.00
3-10	2.00	6.00	15.00
11-20	1.30	4.00	9.00

EH! (. . . Dig This Crazy Comic) (From Here to Insanity No. 8 on)
Dec, 1953 - No. 7, Nov-Dec, 1954 (Satire)
Charlton Comics

1-Davisish-a by Ayers, Woodish-a by Giordano; Atomic Mouse app.	7.00	21.00	50.00
2	4.60	14.00	32.00
3-7: 4,6-Sexual innuendo-c	4.35	13.00	30.00

80 PAGE GIANT (. . . Magazine No. 1-15) (25 cents)
8/64 - No. 15, 10/65; No. 16, 11/65 - No. 89, 7/71 (All-r)
National Periodical Publications (No.57-89: 68 pages)

1-Superman	4.50	13.50	36.00
2-Jimmy Olsen	1.75	5.25	14.00
3-Lois Lane	1.00	3.00	8.00
4-Flash-G.A.-r; Infantino-a	1.00	3.00	8.00
5-Batman; has Sunday newspaper strip	1.00	3.00	8.00
6-Superman	1.00	3.00	8.00
7-Sgt. Rock's Prize Battle Tales; Kubert c/a	1.00	3.00	8.00
8-More Secret Origins-origins of JLA, Aquaman, Robin, Atom, & Superman; Infantino-a	3.35	10.00	27.00
9-Flash(reprints Flash No. 123)-Infantino-a	1.00	3.00	8.00
10-Superboy	1.00	3.00	8.00
11-Superman-All Luthor issue	.65	2.00	5.20
12-Batman; has Sunday newspaper strip	.65	2.00	5.20
13-Jimmy Olsen	.65	2.00	5.20
14-Lois Lane	.65	2.00	5.20
15-Superman and Batman	.65	2.00	5.20

Continued as part of regular series under each title in which that particular book came out, a Giant being published instead of the regular size. Issues No. 16 to No. 89 are listed for your information. See individual titles for prices.

16-JLA #39 (11/65)
17-Batman #176
18-Superman #183
19-Our Army at War #164
20-Action #334
21-Flash #160
22-Superboy #129
23-Superman #187
24-Batman #182
25-Jimmy Olsen #95
26-Lois Lane #68
27-Batman No. 185
28-World's Finest #161
29-JLA #48
30-Batman #187
31-Superman #193
32-Our Army at War #177
33-Action #347
34-Flash #169
35-Superboy #138
36-Superman #197
37-Batman #193
38-Jimmy Olsen #104
39-Lois Lane #77
40-World's Finest #170
41-JLA #58
42-Superman #202
43-Batman #198
44-Our Army at War #190
45-Action #360
46-Flash #178
47-Superboy #147
48-Superman #207
49-Batman #203
50-Jimmy Olsen #113
51-Lois Lane #86
52-World's Finest #179
53-JLA #67
54-Superman #212
55-Batman #208
56-Our Army at War #203
57-Action #373
58-Flash #187
59-Superboy #156
60-Superman #217
61-Batman #213
62-Jimmy Olsen #122
63-Lois Lane #95
64-World's Finest #188
65-JLA #76
66-Superman #222
67-Batman #218
68-Our Army at War #216
69-Adventure #390
70-Flash #196
71-Superboy #165
72-Superman #227
73-Batman #223
74-Jimmy Olsen #131
75-Lois Lane #104
76-World's Finest #197
77-JLA #85
78-Superman #232
79-Batman #228
80-Our Army at War #229
81-Adventure #403
82-Flash #205
83-Superboy #174
84-Superman #239
85-Batman #233
86-Jimmy Olsen #140
87-Lois Lane #113
88-World's Finest #206
89-JLA #93

87TH PRECINCT (TV)
Apr-June, 1962 - No. 2, July-Sept, 1962
Dell Publishing Co.

	Good	Fine	Mint
4-Color 1309; Krigstein-a	5.00	15.00	35.00
2	4.00	12.00	28.00

EINHERIAR: THE CHOSEN
1987 (color, $1.50)
Vanguard Graphics (Canadian)

1	.25	.75	1.50

EL BOMBO COMICS
1946
Standard Comics/Frances M. McQueeny

nn(1946)	4.00	12.00	28.00
1(no date)	4.00	12.00	28.00

EL CID (See 4-Color No. 1259)

EL DORADO (See Movie Classics)

ELECTRIC WARRIOR
May, 1986 - No. 18, Oct, 1987 (Baxter paper)
DC Comics

1	.50	1.50	3.00
2-5	.35	1.00	2.00
6-18	.30	.85	1.70

ELEKTRA: ASSASSIN
Aug, 1986 - No. 8, Mar, 1987 (limited series)(Adults)
Epic Comics (Marvel)

1-Miller scripts in all	.40	2.25	4.50
2	.60	1.80	3.60
3-8	.40	1.20	2.40

ELEKTRA SAGA, THE
Feb, 1984 - No. 4, June, 1984 ($2.00 cover; Baxter paper)

ELEKTRA SAGA (continued)
Marvel Comics Group

	Good	Fine	Mint
1-4-r/Daredevil 168-190; Miller a/c	1.00	3.00	6.00

ELEMENTALS, THE (Also see The Justice Machine)
June, 1984 - Present ($1.50; Baxter paper)
Comico The Comic Co.

1-Willingham c/a, 1-8	2.50	7.50	15.00
2	1.25	3.75	7.50
3	.85	2.50	5.00
4-7	.60	1.75	3.50
8-10: 9-Bissette-a(p)	.35	1.00	2.00
11-20	.25	.75	1.50
Special 1 (3/86)-Willingham-a(p)	.35	1.00	2.00

ELFQUEST (Also see Fantasy Quarterly & Warp Graphics Annual)
No. 2, Aug, 1978 - No. 21, Feb, 1985
No. 1, April, 1979
WaRP Graphics, Inc.

NOTE: *Elfquest* was originally published as one of the stories in Fantasy Quarterly No. 1. When the publisher went out of business, the creative team, Wendy and Richard Pini, formed WaRP Graphics and continued the series, beginning with Elfquest No. 2. Elfquest No. 1, which reprinted the story from Fantasy Quarterly, was published about the same time Elfquest No. 4 was released. Thereafter, most issues were reprinted as demand warranted, until Marvel announced it would reprint the entire series under its Epic imprint (Aug., 1985).

1(4/79)-Reprints Elfquest story from Fantasy Quarterly No. 1			
1st printing ($1.00 cover)	1.80	5.50	11.00
2nd printing ($1.25 cover)	.35	1.00	2.00
3rd printing ($1.50 cover)	.35	1.00	2.00
2(8/78)-5: 1st printing ($1.00 cover)	1.15	3.50	7.00
2nd printing ($1.25 cover)	.35	1.00	2.00
3rd printing ($1.50 cover)	.35	1.00	2.00
6-9: 1st printing ($1.25 cover)	.90	2.75	5.50
2nd printing ($1.50 cover)	.35	1.00	2.00
10-21: ($1.50 cover); 16-8pg. preview of A Distant Soil	.65	1.90	3.80

ELFQUEST
Aug, 1985 - Present
Epic Comics (Marvel)

1-Reprints in color the Elfquest epic by WaRP Graphics	.70	2.00	4.00
2-5	.35	1.00	2.00
6-10	.25	.75	1.50
11-21		.50	1.00
22-32 ($1.00)		.60	1.20

ELFQUEST: SIEGE AT BLUE MOUNTAIN
Dec, 1986 - No. 8, 1988 (mini-series)($1.75, B&W)
WaRp Graphics/Apple Comics

1	.70	2.00	4.00
2-5	.35	1.00	2.00
2-2nd printing	.30	.90	1.80
6-8	.30	.90	1.80

ELLA CINDERS (See Comics Revue #1,4, Famous Comics Cartoon Book, Sparkler Comics & Treasury of Comics)

ELLA CINDERS
1938 - 1940
United Features Syndicate

Single Series 3(1938)	18.00	54.00	125.00
Single Series 21(#2 on-c, #21 on inside), 28('40)	14.00	42.00	100.00

ELLA CINDERS
March, 1948 - No. 5, 1949
United Features Syndicate

	Good	Fine	Mint
1	6.00	18.00	42.00
2	3.00	9.00	21.00
3-5	2.30	7.00	16.00

ELLERY QUEEN
May, 1949 - No. 4, Nov, 1949
Superior Comics Ltd.

1-Kamen c; L.B. Cole-a	16.00	48.00	110.00
2,4	10.00	30.00	70.00
3-Drug use stories(2)	11.00	33.00	75.00

NOTE: *Iger shop art-all issues.*

ELLERY QUEEN (TV)
1-3/52 - No. 2, Summer/52 (Saunders painted covers)
Ziff-Davis Publishing Co.

1-Saunders-c	14.00	42.00	100.00
2-Saunders bondage, torture-c	14.00	42.00	100.00

ELLERY QUEEN (See 4-Color No. 1165,1243,1289)

ELMER FUDD (Also see Camp Comics & Daffy)
May, 1953 - No. 1293, Mar-May, 1962
Dell Publishing Co.

4-Color 470,558,628,689('56)	1.15	3.50	8.00
4-Color 725,783,841,888,938,977,1032,1081,1131,1171,1222, 1293('61)	.85	2.50	6.00

(See Super Book #10,22)

ELMO COMICS
January, 1948 (Daily strip-r)
St. John Publishing Co.

1-By Cecil Jensen	4.00	12.00	28.00

ELRIC OF MELNIBONE (See First Comics Graphic Novel)
Apr, 1983 - No. 6, Apr, 1984 ($1.50, Baxter paper)
Pacific Comics

1-Russell c/a(i) in all	.35	1.10	2.20
2-6	.35	1.00	2.00

ELRIC: SAILOR ON THE SEAS OF FATE
Aug, 1985 - No. 7, June, 1986 (Limited series; $1.75 cover)
First Comics

1-Adapts M. Moorcock's novel	.40	1.25	2.50
2-7	.30	.90	1.80

ELRIC: THE VANISHING TOWER
Aug, 1987 - No. 6, 1988 ($1.75, color)
First Comics

1-6	.30	.90	1.80

ELRIC: WEIRD OF THE WHITE WOLF
Oct, 1986 - No. 5, June, 1987 (limited series)
First Comics

1-5: Adapts M. Moorcock's novel	.30	.90	1.80

ELSIE THE COW
Oct-Nov, 1949 - No. 3, July-Aug, 1950
D. S. Publishing Co.

1-(36 pages)	9.50	28.50	66.00
2,3	6.50	19.50	45.00
Borden Milk Giveaway-(16 pgs., nn) (3 issues, 1957)	3.00	9.00	21.00
Elsie's Fun Book(1950; Borden Milk)	4.50	13.50	31.00
Everyday Birthday Fun With . . . (1957; 20 pgs.)(100th Anniversary); Kubert-a	3.50	10.50	24.00

ELVIRA'S HAUNTED HOLIDAYS
Mar, 1987
DC Comics

1-Colan-a		.60	1.25

The Elementals #5, © Comico

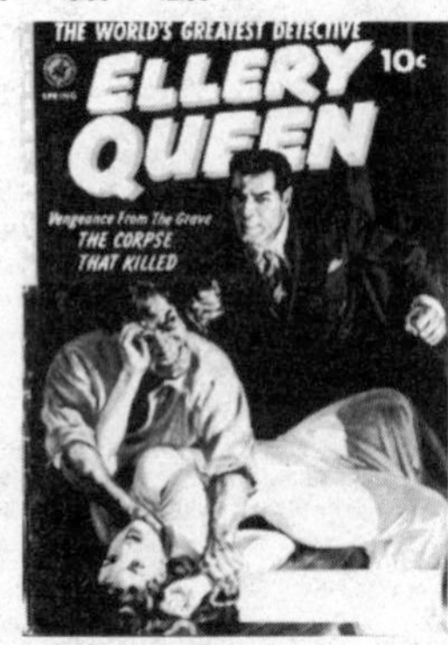

Ellery Queen #1, © Ziff-Davis

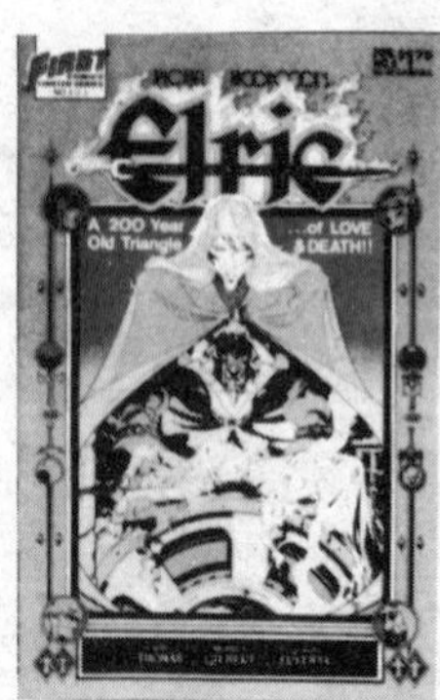

Elric: Sailor on the Seas of Fate #5, © First

E-Man #3, © First Comics

Enchanting Love #2, © Kirby Publ.

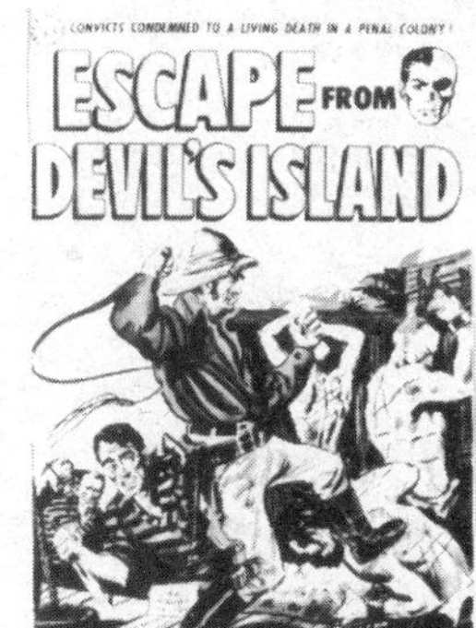

Escape From Devil's Island #1, © AVON

ELVIRA'S HOUSE OF MYSTERY
Jan, 1986 - No. 11, Jan, 1987
DC Comics

	Good	Fine	Mint
1 ($1.50, 68pgs.)-Photo back-c	.40	1.25	2.50
2-10: 6-Reads sideways. 7-Sci/fic ish. 9-Photo-c		.50	1.00
11-Double-size Halloween ish		.50	1.00
Special #1 (3/87, $1.25)		.60	1.25

NOTE: ***Ayers/DeZuniga** a-5. **Bolland** c-1. **Spiegel** a-1. **Sevens** c-11.*

ELVIS PRESLEY (See Career Girl Rom. 32, I Love You 60 & Young Lovers 18)

E-MAN
Oct, 1973 - No. 10, Sept, 1975 (Painted-c No. 7-10)
Charlton Comics

	Good	Fine	Mint
1-Origin E-Man; Staton c/a in all	1.20	3.50	7.00
2-Ditko-a	.70	2.00	4.00
3,4: 3-Howard-a. 4-Ditko-a	.70	2.00	4.00
5-Miss Liberty Belle app. by Ditko	.50	1.50	3.00
6,7,9,10-Byrne-a in all	.70	2.00	4.00
8-Full-length story; Nova begins as E-Man's partner	.85	2.50	5.00
1-4,9,10(Modern Comics reprints, '77)		.15	.30

NOTE: *Killjoy app.-No. 2,4. Liberty Belle app.-No. 5. Rog 2000 app.-No. 6, 7, 9, 10. Travis app.-No. 3. **Tom Sutton** a-1.*

E-MAN (Also see The Original . . . & Michael Mauser)
Apr, 1983 - No. 25, Aug, 1985 (Direct Sale only, $1.00-$1.25)
First Comics

	Good	Fine	Mint
1		.50	1.00
2-10: 2-X-Men satire. 3-X-Men/Phoenix satire. 6-Origin retold. 10-Origin Nova Kane		.50	1.00
11-25: 13-Chaos x-over from Warp		.50	1.00

NOTE: ***Staton** a-1-5, 6-25p; c-1-25.*

EMERGENCY (Magazine)
June, 1976 - No. 4, Jan, 1977 (B&W)
Charlton Comics

	Good	Fine	Mint
1-Adams c/a, Heath, Austin-a	.50	1.50	3.00
2-Adams-c	.30	.80	1.60
3-Adams-a	.35	1.00	2.00
4-Alcala-a	.30	.80	1.60

EMERGENCY (TV)
June, 1976 - No. 4, Dec, 1976
Charlton Comics

	Good	Fine	Mint
1-Staton-c, Byrne-a	.50	1.50	3.00
2-4: 2-Staton-c	.25	.75	1.50

EMERGENCY DOCTOR
Summer, 1963 (One Shot)
Charlton Comics

	Good	Fine	Mint
1	.30	.80	1.60

EMIL & THE DETECTIVES (See Movie Comics)

EMMA PEEL & JOHN STEED (See The Avengers)

EMPIRE STRIKES BACK, THE (See Marvel Comics Super Special 16)

ENCHANTED APPLES OF OZ, THE (See First Comics Graphic Novel)

ENCHANTING LOVE
Oct, 1949 - No. 6, July, 1950
Kirby Publishing Co.

	Good	Fine	Mint
1-Photo-c	4.35	13.00	30.00
2-Photo-c; Powell-a	2.35	7.00	16.00
3,4,6	2.00	6.00	14.00
5-Ingels-a, 9 pgs.; photo-c	8.00	24.00	56.00

ENCHANTMENT VISUALETTES (Magazine)
Dec, 1949 - No. 5, April, 1950
World Editions

	Good	Fine	Mint
1-Contains two romance comic strips each; painted-c	7.00	21.00	50.00
2	6.00	18.00	42.00
3-5	5.00	15.00	35.00

ENEMY ACE (See Star-Spangled War Stories)

ENSIGN O'TOOLE (TV)
Aug-Oct, 1963 - No. 2, 1964
Dell Publishing Co.

	Good	Fine	Mint
1,2	1.15	3.50	8.00

ENSIGN PULVER (See Movie Classics)

EPIC ILLUSTRATED (Magazine)
Spring, 1980 - No. 34, Mar, 1986 (B&W/Color) ($2.00-$2.50)
Marvel Comics Group

	Good	Fine	Mint
1	.35	1.00	2.00
2-10	.25	.75	1.50
11,13-15: 14-Revenge of the Jedi preview. 15-Vallejo-c & interview; ties into Dreadstar No. 1	.25	.75	1.50
12-Wolverton Spacehawk-r edited & recolored with article on him	.25	.75	1.50
16-B. Smith c/a(2)	.25	.75	1.50
17-26: 26-Galactus series begins, ends No. 34; Cerebus the Aardvark story by Dave Sim	.25	.75	1.50
27-34: ($2.50): 28-Cerebus app.	.40	1.25	2.50

NOTE: ***Adams** a-7; c-6. **Austin** a-15-20i. **Bode** a-19, 23, 27r. **Bolton** a-7, 10-12, 15, 18, 22-25; c-10, 18, 22, 23. **Boris** c/a-15. **Brunner** c-12. **Buscema** a-1p, 9p, 11p-13p. **Byrne/Austin** a-26-34. **Chaykin** a-2; c-8. **Conrad** a-2-5, 7-9, 25-34. **Corben** a-15; c-2. **Frazetta** c-1. **Golden** a-3. **Gulacy** c/a-3. **Jeff Jones** c-25. **Kaluta** a-17r, 21, 24r, 26; c-4, 28. **Nebres** a-1. **Reese** a-12. **Russell** a-2-4, 9, 14, 33. **Smith** a-7, 16; c-7, 16. **Starlin** a-1-9, 14, 15, 34. **Steranko** c-19. **Williamson** a-27, 34. **Wrightson** a-13p, 22, 25, 27, 34; c-30.*

EPSILON WAVE
Oct, 1985 - Present
Independent Comics/Elite Comics No. 5 on

	Good	Fine	Mint
1-Seadragon app.	.50	1.50	3.00
2-4: 2,3-Seadragon app.	.25	.75	1.50
5-10: 6-Seadragon app.	.25	.75	1.50
V2/1,2 (B&W)	.30	.80	1.60

ERNIE COMICS (Formerly Andy Comics No. 21; All Love Romances No. 26 on)
Sept, 1948 - No. 25, Mar, 1949
Current Books/Ace Periodicals

	Good	Fine	Mint
nn(9/48,11/48; No. 22,23)	2.65	8.00	18.00
24,25	1.50	4.50	10.00

ESCAPADE IN FLORENCE (See Movie Comics)

ESCAPE FROM DEVIL'S ISLAND
1952
Avon Periodicals

	Good	Fine	Mint
1-Kinstler-c; r/as Dynamic Adv. No. 9	14.00	42.00	100.00

ESCAPE FROM FEAR
1956, 1962, 1969 (8 pages full color) (On birth control)
Planned Parenthood of America (Giveaway)

	Good	Fine	Mint
1956 edition	13.00	40.00	80.00
1962 edition	10.00	30.00	60.00
1969 edition	5.00	15.00	30.00

ESCAPE TO WITCH MOUNTAIN (See Walt Disney Showcase No. 29)

ESPERS
July, 1986 - Present (Mando paper)
Eclipse Comics

	Good	Fine	Mint
1-7	.35	1.00	2.00

ESPIONAGE (TV)
May-July, 1964 - No. 2, Aug-Oct, 1964
Dell Publishing Co.

	Good	Fine	Mint
1,2	1.15	3.50	8.00

ETERNAL BIBLE, THE
1946 (Large size) (16 pages in color)
Authentic Publications

	Good	Fine	Mint
1	4.50	13.50	31.00

ETERNALS, THE
July, 1976 - No. 19, Jan, 1978
Marvel Comics Group

	Good	Fine	Mint
1-Origin		.40	.80
2-19: 2-1st app. Ajak & The Celestials		.25	.50
Annual 1(10/77)		.25	.50

NOTE: ***Kirby** c/a(p) in all. Price changed from 25 cents to 30 cents during run of #1.*

ETERNALS, THE
10/85 - No. 12, 9/86 (12 issue maxi-series, mando paper)
Marvel Comics Group

	Good	Fine	Mint
1 ($1.25 cover)	.25	.75	1.50
2-11 (75 cents cover)		.45	.90
12-Double size ($1.25)-Simonson-a		.65	1.30

ETERNITY SMITH
Sept, 1986 - No. 5, 1987
Renegade Press

	Good	Fine	Mint
1		.65	1.30
2-5	.25	.70	1.40

ETERNITY SMITH
Sept, 1987 - Present ($1.95, color)
Hero Comics

	Good	Fine	Mint
V2#1-5	.30	.95	1.90

ETTA KETT
No. 11, Dec, 1948 - No. 14, Sept, 1949
King Features Syndicate/Standard

	Good	Fine	Mint
11	4.00	12.00	28.00
12-14	2.30	7.00	16.00

EVANGELINE (Also see Primer)
1/84 - No. 2, 6/84; V2#1, 5/87 - Present (Color; Baxter)
Comico/First Comics V2/1 on

	Good	Fine	Mint
1	1.00	3.00	6.00
2	.50	1.50	3.00
V2#1 (5/87)	.30	.90	1.80
2-7	.30	.90	1.80
Special #1 ('86, $2.00, color)	.35	1.00	2.00

EVA THE IMP
1957 - No. 2, Nov, 1957
Red Top Comic/Decker

	Good	Fine	Mint
1,2	1.00	3.00	7.00

EVEL KNIEVEL
1974 (20 pages) (Giveaway)
Marvel Comics Group (Ideal Toy Corp.)

	Good	Fine	Mint
nn		.40	.80

EVERYBODY'S COMICS (See Fox Giants)

EVERYTHING HAPPENS TO HARVEY
Sept-Oct, 1953 - No. 7, Sept-Oct, 1954
National Periodical Publications

	Good	Fine	Mint
1	8.00	24.00	56.00
2	5.00	15.00	35.00
3-7	4.00	12.00	28.00

EVERYTHING'S ARCHIE
May, 1969 - Present (Giant issues No. 1-20)
Archie Publications

	Good	Fine	Mint
1	4.00	12.00	28.00
2	2.00	6.00	14.00
3-5	1.20	3.50	8.00
6-10	.70	2.00	4.50
11-20	.35	1.00	2.00
21-40		.50	1.00
41-134		.30	.60

EVERYTHING'S DUCKY (See 4-Color No. 1251)

EWOKS (TV)
June, 1985 - Present
Star Comics (Marvel)

	Good	Fine	Mint
1-13: 10-Williamson-a		.35	.70
14 ($1.00)		.45	.90

EXCALIBER
Apr, 1988 - Present
Marvel Comics

	Good	Fine	Mint
1 ($3.25)	.55	1.60	3.25

EXCITING COMICS
April, 1940 - No. 69, Sept, 1949
Nedor/Better Publications/Standard Comics

	Good	Fine	Mint
1-Origin The Mask, Jim Hatfield, Sgt. Bill King, Dan Williams begin	56.00	168.00	390.00
2-The Sphinx begins; The Masked Rider app.	24.00	72.00	168.00
3	20.00	60.00	140.00
4	16.00	48.00	110.00
5	12.00	36.00	84.00
6-8	10.00	30.00	70.00
9-Origin/1st app. of The Black Terror & sidekick Tim	56.00	168.00	390.00
10-13	23.00	70.00	160.00
14-Last Sphinx, Dan Williams	14.00	42.00	100.00
15-Origin The Liberator	18.00	54.00	125.00
16-20: 20-The Mask ends	10.00	30.00	70.00
21,23-30: 28-Crime Crusader begins, ends #58	10.00	30.00	70.00
22-Origin The Eaglet; The American Eagle begins	10.00	30.00	70.00
31-38: 35-Liberator ends, not in 31-33	9.50	28.00	65.00
39-Origin Kara, Jungle Princess	12.00	36.00	84.00
40-50: 42-The Scarab begins. 49-Last Kara, Jungle Princess. 50-Last American Eagle	11.00	33.00	76.00
51-Miss Masque begins	14.00	42.00	100.00
52-54: Miss Masque ends	11.00	33.00	76.00
55-Judy of the Jungle begins(origin), ends #69; 1 pg. Ingels-a	14.50	43.50	100.00
56-58: All airbrush-c	12.00	36.00	84.00
59-Frazetta art in Caniff style; signed Frank Frazeta (one t), 9 pgs.	18.00	56.00	125.00
60-65: 60-Rick Howard, the Mystery Rider begins	12.00	36.00	84.00
66-Robinson/Meskin-a	12.00	36.00	84.00
67-69	7.00	21.00	50.00

NOTE: ***Schomburg (Xela)** c-28-68; airbrush c-57-66. Black Terror by **R. Moreira**-No. 65. **Roussos** a-62. Bondage-c 9, 13, 20, 23, 25, 30, 59.*

EXCITING ROMANCES
1949 - No. 4, 1951(no month); No. 5, 9/51 - No. 12, 1/53
Fawcett Publications

	Good	Fine	Mint
1(1949)-Photo-c	3.50	10.50	24.00
2-4-(? - 1951): 4-Photo-c	2.50	7.50	18.00
5-12	1.50	4.50	10.00

Evangeline V2#1, © First Comics

Exciting Comics #66, © STD

Exciting Romances #12, © FAW

Explorer Joe #1, © Z-D

Extra! #1, © EC

The Face #1, © CCG

EXCITING ROMANCES (continued)
NOTE: ***Powell** a-8-10. Photo-c, 1,4-7,11 at least.*

EXCITING ROMANCE STORIES (See Fox Giants)

EXCITING WAR
No. 5, Sept, 1952 - No. 8, May, 1953; No. 9, Nov, 1953
Standard Comics (Better Publ.)

	Good	Fine	Mint
5	2.35	7.00	16.00
6,7,9	1.35	4.00	9.00
8-Toth-a	3.00	9.00	21.00

EXORCISTS (See The Crusaders)

EXOTIC ROMANCES (Formerly True War Romances)
No. 22, Oct, 1955 - No. 31, Nov, 1956
Quality Comics Group (Comic Magazines)

	Good	Fine	Mint
22	3.50	10.50	24.00
23-26,29	1.70	5.00	12.00
27,31-Baker c/a	3.85	11.50	27.00
28,30-Baker-a	3.50	10.50	24.00

EXPLOITS OF DANIEL BOONE
Nov, 1955 - No. 6, Sept, 1956
Quality Comics Group

	Good	Fine	Mint
1	5.15	15.50	36.00
2	2.85	8.50	20.00
3-6	2.35	7.00	16.00

EXPLOITS OF DICK TRACY (See Dick Tracy)

EXPLORER JOE
Winter, 1951 - No. 2, Oct-Nov, 1952
Ziff-Davis Comic Group (Approved Comics)

	Good	Fine	Mint
1-Saunders painted-c	4.60	14.00	32.00
2-Krigstein-a	5.70	17.00	40.00

EXPOSED (. . .True Crime Cases)
Mar-Apr, 1948 - No. 9, July-Aug, 1949
D. S. Publishing Co.

	Good	Fine	Mint
1	5.70	17.00	40.00
2-Giggling killer story with excessive blood; two eye injury panels	6.50	19.50	45.00
3,8,9	3.00	9.00	21.00
4-Orlando-a	3.50	10.50	24.00
5-Breeze Lawson, Sky Sheriff by E. Good	2.65	8.00	18.00
6-Ingels-a; used in **SOTI**, illo.-"How to prepare an alibi."	14.00	42.00	100.00
7-Illo. in **SOTI**, "Diagram for housebreakers"; used by N.Y. Legis. Comm.	13.00	40.00	90.00

EXTRA
1948
Magazine Enterprises

	Good	Fine	Mint
1-Giant; consisting of rebound ME comics. Two versions known: (1)-Funny Man by Siegel & Shuster, Space Ace, Undercover Girl, & (2)-All Funnyman	20.00	60.00	140.00

EXTRA!
Mar-Apr, 1955 - No. 5, Nov-Dec, 1955
E. C. Comics

	Good	Fine	Mint
1	6.00	18.00	42.00
2-5	4.00	12.00	28.00

NOTE: ***Craig, Crandall, Severin** art in all.*

FACE, THE (Tony Trent, the Face No. 3 on)
1941 (See Big Shot Comics)
Columbia Comics Group

	Good	Fine	Mint
1-The Face	25.00	75.00	175.00
2	17.00	51.00	120.00

FAIRY TALE PARADE (See Famous Fairy Tales)
June-July, 1942 - No. 121, Oct, 1946 (Most all by Walt Kelly)
Dell Publishing Co.

	Good	Fine	Mint
1-Kelly-a begins	78.00	234.00	545.00
2(8-9/42)	44.00	132.00	305.00
3-5 (10-11/42 - 2-4/43)	28.00	84.00	195.00
6-9 (5-7/43 - 11-1/43-44)	22.00	65.00	155.00
4-Color 50('44)	21.00	63.00	145.00
4-Color 69('45)	18.00	54.00	125.00
4-Color 87('45)	16.00	48.00	110.00
4-Color 104,114('46)-Last Kelly ish.	12.00	36.00	84.00
4-Color 121('46)-Not Kelly	8.00	24.00	56.00

NOTE: *#1-9, 4-Color #50,69 have **Kelly** c/a; 4-Color #87, 104, 114-**Kelly** art only. #9 has a redrawn version of The Reluctant Dragon. This series contains all the classic fairy tales from Jack In The Beanstalk to Cinderella.*

FAIRY TALES
No. 10, 1951 - No. 11, June-July, 1951
Ziff-Davis Publ. Co. (Approved Comics)

	Good	Fine	Mint
10,11	4.60	14.00	32.00

FAITHFUL
November, 1949 - No. 2, Feb, 1950
Marvel Comics/Lovers' Magazine

	Good	Fine	Mint
1,2-Photo-c	2.65	8.00	18.00

FALCON
Nov, 1983 - No. 4, Feb, 1984 (mini-series)
Marvel Comics Group

	Good	Fine	Mint
1-Paul Smith c/a(p)		.50	1.00
2-4: 2-Smith-c		.50	1.00

FALLEN ANGELS
April, 1987 - No. 8, Nov, 1987 (mini-series)
Marvel Comics Group

	Good	Fine	Mint
1	.50	1.50	3.00
2,3	.35	1.00	2.00
4,5	.25	.75	1.50
6-8		.50	1.00

FALLING IN LOVE
Sept-Oct, 1955 - No. 143, Oct-Nov, 1973
Arleigh Publ. Co./National Periodical Publications

	Good	Fine	Mint
1	10.00	30.00	70.00
2	4.35	13.00	30.00
3-10	3.00	9.00	21.00
11-20	1.70	5.00	12.00
21-40	1.30	4.00	9.00
41-50	.85	2.50	6.00
51-100	.50	1.50	3.00
101-107,109-143		.60	1.20
108-Wood-a, 4pgs. (7/69)	.35	1.00	2.00

FALL OF THE HOUSE OF USHER, THE (See Corben Special, A)

FALL OF THE ROMAN EMPIRE (See Movie Comics)

FAMILY AFFAIR (TV)
Feb, 1970 - No. 4, Oct, 1970 (25 cents)
Gold Key

	Good	Fine	Mint
1-Pull-out poster; photo-c	2.00	6.00	14.00
2-4: 3,4-Photo-c	1.15	3.50	8.00

FAMILY FUNNIES
No. 9, Aug-Sept, 1946
Parents' Magazine Institute

	Good	Fine	Mint
9	2.00	6.00	14.00

FAMILY FUNNIES (Tiny Tot Funnies No. 9 on)
Sept, 1950 - No. 8, April?, 1951
Harvey Publications

	Good	Fine	Mint
1-Mandrake	3.00	9.00	21.00

FAMILY FUNNIES (continued) — Good / Fine / Mint

2-Flash Gordon, 1 pg. 2.35 7.00 16.00
3-8: 4,5,7-Flash Gordon, 1 pg. 2.00 6.00 14.00
1(black & white) 1.20 3.50 8.00

FAMOUS AUTHORS ILL. (See Stories by. . .)

FAMOUS COMICS (Also see Favorite Comics)
No date; Mid 1930's (24 pages) (paper cover)
Zain-Eppy/United Features Syndicate

Reprinted from 1934 newspaper strips in color; Joe Palooka, Hairbreadth Harry, Napoleon, The Nebbs, etc. 17.00 51.00 120.00

FAMOUS COMICS
1934 (100 pgs., daily newspaper reprints)
(3½x8½"; paper cover) (came in a box)
King Features Syndicate (Whitman Publ. Co.)

684(#1)-Little Jimmy, Katzenjammer Kids, & Barney Google 13.00 40.00 90.00
684(#2)-Polly, Little Jimmy, Katzenjammer Kids 13.00 40.00 90.00
684(#3)-Little Annie Rooney, Polly, Katzenjammer Kids 13.00 40.00 90.00
. . . . Box price. . . . 4.70 17.00 40.00

FAMOUS COMICS CARTOON BOOKS
1934 (72 pgs.; 8x7¼"; daily strip reprints)
Whitman Publishing Co. (B&W; hardbacks)

1200-The Captain & the Kids; Dirks reprints credited to Bernard Dibble 9.50 28.00 66.00
1202-Captain Easy & Wash Tubbs by Roy Crane 13.50 40.50 95.00
1203-Ella Cinders 9.00 27.00 62.00
1204-Freckles & His Friends 7.50 22.00 52.00
NOTE: *Called Famous Funnies Cartoon Books inside.*

FAMOUS CRIMES
June, 1948 - No. 19, Sept, 1950; No. 20, Aug, 1951
Fox Features Syndicate/M.S. Dist. No. 51,52

1-Blue Beetle app. & crime story r-/Phantom Lady No. 16 12.00 36.00 84.00
2-Shows woman dissolved in acid; lingerie-c/panels 8.50 25.50 60.00
3-Injury-to-eye story used in **SOTI**, pg. 112; has two electrocution stories 12.00 36.00 84.00
4-6 5.00 15.00 35.00
7-"Tarzan, the Wyoming Killer" used in **SOTI**, pg. 44; drug trial/possession story 10.00 30.00 70.00
8-20: 17-Morisi-a 3.70 11.00 26.00
51(nd, 1953) 4.35 13.00 30.00
52 2.65 8.00 18.00

FAMOUS FAIRY TALES
1943 (32 pgs.); 1944 (16 pgs.) (Soft covers)
K. K. Publ. Co. (Giveaway)

1943-Reprints from Fairy Tale Parade No. 2,3; Kelly inside art 40.00 120.00 260.00
1944-Kelly inside art 28.00 85.00 180.00

FAMOUS FEATURE STORIES
1938 (68 pgs., 7½x11")
Dell Publishing Co.

1-Tarzan, Terry & the Pirates, King of the Royal Mtd., Buck Jones, Dick Tracy, Smilin' Jack, Dan Dunn, Don Winslow, G-Man, Tailspin Tommy, Mutt & Jeff, & Little Orphan Annie reprints - all illustrated text 33.00 100.00 230.00

FAMOUS FIRST EDITION (See Limited Collectors Edition)
($1.00; 10x13½"-Giant Size)(72pgs.; No.6-8, 68 pgs.)
1974 - No. 8, Aug-Sept, 1975; C-61, Sept, 1978
National Periodical Publications/DC Comics — Good / Fine / Mint

C-26-Action No. 1 1.00 3.00 7.00
C-28-Detective No. 27 1.00 3.00 7.00
C-30-Sensation No. 1(1974) 1.00 3.00 7.00
F-4-Whiz No. 2(No.1)(10-11/74)-Cover not identical to original 1.00 3.00 7.00
F-5-Batman No. 1(F-6 on inside) 1.00 3.00 7.00
F-6-Wonder Woman No. 1 .85 2.50 6.00
F-7-All-Star Comics No. 3 1.00 3.00 7.00
F-8-Flash No. 1(8-9/75) .85 2.50 6.00
C-61-Superman No. 1(9/78) 1.00 3.00 7.00
Hardbound editions w/dust jackets ($5.00) (Lyle Stuart, Inc.)
C-26,C-28,C-30,F-4,F-6 known 1.75 5.25 12.00

Warning: The above books are almost **exact** reprints of the originals that they represent except for the Giant-Size format. None of the originals are Giant-Size. The first five issues and C-61 were printed with two covers. Reprint information can be found on the outside cover, but not on the inside cover which was reprinted exactly like the original (inside and out).

FAMOUS FUNNIES
1933 - No. 218, July, 1955
Eastern Color

A Carnival of Comics (probably the second comic book), 36 pgs., no date given, no publisher, no number; contains strip reprints of The Bungle Family, Dixie Dugan, Hairbreadth Harry, Joe Palooka, Keeping Up With the Jones, Mutt & Jeff, Reg'lar Fellers, S'Matter Pop, Strange As It Seems, and others. This book was sold by M. C. Gaines to Wheatena, Milk-O-Malt, John Wanamaker, Kinney Shoe Stores, & others to be given away as premiums and radio giveaways (1933). 180.00 540.00 1260.00

Series 1-(Very rare)(nd-early 1934)(68 pgs.) No publisher given (Eastern Color Printing Co.); sold in chain stores for 10 cents. 35,000 print run. Contains Sunday strip reprints of Mutt & Jeff, Reg'lar Fellers, Nipper, Hairbreadth Harry, Strange As It Seems, Joe Palooka, Dixie Dugan, The Nebbs, Keeping Up With the Jones, and others. Inside front and back covers and pages 1-16 of Famous Funnies Series 1, #s 49-64 reprinted from **Famous Funnies, A Carnival of Comics,** and most of pages 17-48 reprinted from **Funnies on Parade.** This was the first comic book sold. 260.00 780.00 1820.00

No. 1 (Rare)(7/34-on stands 5/34) - Eastern Color Printing Co. First monthly newsstand comic book. Contains Sunday strip reprints of Toonerville Folks, Mutt & Jeff, Hairbreadth Harry, S'Matter Pop, Nipper, Dixie Dugan, The Bungle Family, Connie, Ben Webster, Tailspin Tommy, The Nebbs, Joe Palooka, & others. 220.00 660.00 1540.00

2 (Rare) 75.00 225.00 525.00
3-Buck Rogers Sunday strip reprints by Rick Yager begins, ends # 218; not in No. 191-208; the number of the 1st strip reprinted is pg. 190, Series No. 1 100.00 300.00 700.00
4 50.00 150.00 350.00
5 37.00 110.00 260.00
6-10 32.00 95.00 225.00
11,12,18-Four pgs. of Buck Rogers in each issue, completes stories in Buck Rogers No. 1 which lacks these pages; No. 18-Two pgs. of Buck Rogers reprinted in Daisy Comics No. 1 27.00 81.00 190.00
13-17,19,20: 14-Has two Buck Rogers panels missing. 17-1st Christmas-c on a newsstand comic 21.00 62.00 145.00
21,23-30: 27-War on Crime begins 14.00 42.00 100.00
22-Four pgs. of Buck Rogers needed to complete stories in Buck Rogers No. 1 16.00 48.00 110.00
31,32,34,36,37,39,40 11.50 34.50 80.00
33-Careers of Baby Face Nelson & John Dillinger traced 11.50 34.50 80.00
35-Two pgs. Buck Rogers omitted in Buck Rogers No. 2 14.00 42.00 100.00
38-Full color portrait of Buck Rogers 12.00 36.00 84.00
41-60: 55-Last bottom panel, pg. 4 in Buck Rogers redrawn in Buck Rogers No. 3 9.00 27.00 62.00
61-64,66,67,69,70 8.00 24.00 56.00
65,68-Two pgs. Kirby-a-"Lightnin & the Lone Rider" 8.50 25.50 60.00
71,73,77-80: 80-Buck Rogers story continues from B. R. No. 5 6.00 18.00 42.00

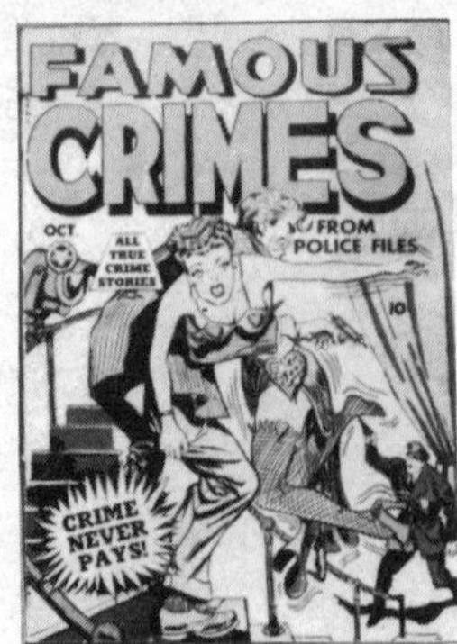

Famous Crimes #3, © FOX

Famous Feature Stories #1, © DELL

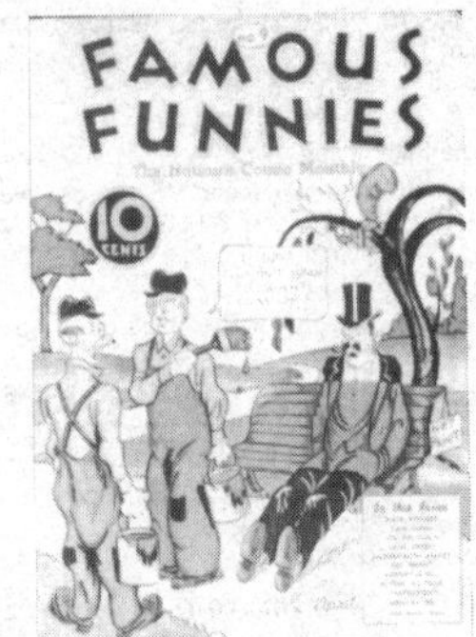

Famous Funnies #9, © EAS

Famous Funnies #211, © EAS

Famous Stars #5, © Z-D

Fantastic Adventures #17, © Super Comics

FAMOUS FUNNIES (continued) — Good / Fine / Mint

72-Speed Spaulding begins by Marvin Bradley (artist), ends No. 88. This series was written by Edwin Balmer & Philip Wylie and later appeared as film & book "When Worlds Collide." 8.00 24.00 56.00
74-76-Two pgs. Kirby-a in all 6.00 18.00 42.00
81-Origin Invisible Scarlet O'Neil; strip begins No. 82, ends No. 167 5.00 15.00 35.00
82-Buck Rogers-c 6.00 18.00 42.00
83-87,90: 87 has last Buck Rogers full page-r. 90-Bondage-c 5.00 15.00 35.00
88-Buck Rogers in "Moon's End" by Calkins, 2 pgs.(not reprints). Beginning with No. 88, all Buck Rogers pages have rearranged panels 5.50 16.50 38.00
89-Origin Fearless Flint, the Flint Man 5.50 16.50 38.00
91-93,95,96,98-99,101-110: 105-Series 2 begins (Strip Page No. 1) 4.35 13.00 30.00
94-Buck Rogers in "Solar Holocaust" by Calkins, 3 pgs.(not reprints) 5.00 15.00 35.00
97-War Bond promotion, Buck Rogers by Calkins, 2 pgs.(not reprints) 5.00 15.00 35.00
100 5.00 15.00 35.00
111-130 3.50 10.50 24.00
131-150: 137-Strip page No. 110½ omitted 2.30 7.00 16.00
151-162,164-168 2.00 6.00 14.00
163-St. Valentine's Day-c 2.65 8.00 18.00
169,170-Two text illos. by Williamson, his 1st comic book work 5.00 15.00 35.00
171-180: 171-Strip pgs. 227,229,230, Series 2 omitted. 172-Strip Pg. 232 omitted 2.00 6.00 14.00
181-190: Buck Rogers ends with start of strip pg. 302, Series 2 1.70 5.00 12.00
191-197,199,201,203,206-208: No Buck Rogers 1.50 4.50 10.00
198,202,205-One pg. Frazetta ads; no Buck Rogers 1.85 5.50 13.00
200-Frazetta 1 pg. ad 2.00 6.00 14.00
204-Used in **POP**, pgs. 79,99 2.15 6.50 15.00
209-Buck Rogers begins with strip pg. 480, Series 2; Frazetta-c 23.00 70.00 160.00
210-216: Frazetta-c. 211-Buck Rogers ads by Anderson begins, ends #217. #215-Contains B. Rogers strip pg. 515-518, series 2 followed by pgs. 179-181, Series 3 23.00 70.00 160.00
217,218-Buck Rogers ends with pg. 199, Series 3 1.70 5.00 12.00

NOTE: ***Rick Yager*** *did the Buck Rogers Sunday strips reprinted in Famous Funnies. The Sundays were formerly done by Russ Keaton and Lt. Dick Calkins did the dailies, but would sometimes assist Yager on a panel or two from time to time. Strip No. 169 is Yager's first full Buck Rogers page. Yager did the strip until 1958 when* ***Murphy Anderson*** *took over.* ***Tuska*** *art from 4/26/59 - 1965. Virtually every panel was rewritten for Famous Funnies. Not identical to the original Sunday page. The Buck Rogers reprints run continuously through Famous Funnies issue No. 190 (Strip No. 302) with no break in story line. The story line has no continuity after No. 190. The Buck Rogers newspaper strips came out in four series: Series 1, 3/30/30 - 9/21/41 (No. 1 - 600); Series 2, 9/28/41 -10/21/51 (No. 1 -525)(Strip No. 110½ (½ pg.) published in only a few newspapers); Series 3, 10/28/51 -2/9/58 (No. 100-428)(No No. 1-99); Series 4, 2/16/58 - 6/13/65 (No numbers, dates only).* ***Everett*** *c-86.* ***Moulton*** *a-100.*

FAMOUS FUNNIES
1964
Super Comics

Reprint No. 15-18 .40 1.20 2.40

FAMOUS GANG BOOK OF COMICS (Donald & Mickey Merry Christmas 1943 on)
Dec, 1942 (32 pgs.; paper cover) (Christmas giveaway)
Firestone Tire & Rubber Co.

(Rare)-Porky Pig, Bugs Bunny, Sniffles; r-/Looney Tunes 67.00 200.00 500.00

FAMOUS GANGSTERS (Crime on the Waterfront No. 4)
April, 1951 - No. 3, Feb, 1952
Avon Periodicals/Realistic — Good / Fine / Mint

1-Narcotics mentioned; Capone, Dillinger; c-/Avon paperback No. 329 13.00 40.00 90.00
2-Wood-c/a (1 pg.); r-/Saint No. 7 & retitled "Mike Strong" 14.00 42.00 100.00
3-Lucky Luciano & Murder, Inc; c-/Avon paperback 66 14.00 42.00 100.00

FAMOUS INDIAN TRIBES
July-Sept, 1962; July, 1972
Dell Publishing Co.

12-264-209 (The Sioux) .85 2.50 6.00
2(7/72)-Reprints above .25 .75 1.50

FAMOUS STARS
Nov-Dec, 1950 - No. 6, Spring, 1952 (All photo covers)
Ziff-Davis Publ. Co.

1-Shelley Winters, Susan Peters, Ava Gardner, Shirley Temple 11.50 34.50 80.00
2-Betty Hutton, Bing Crosby, Colleen Townsend, Gloria Swanson; Everett-a(2) 8.50 25.50 60.00
3-Farley Granger, Judy Garland's ordeal, Alan Ladd 8.00 24.00 56.00
4-Al Jolson, Bob Mitchum, Ella Raines, Richard Conte, Vic Damone; Crandall-a, 6pgs. 7.00 21.00 50.00
5-Liz Taylor, Betty Grable, Esther Williams, George Brent; Krigstein-a 10.00 30.00 70.00
6-Gene Kelly, Hedy Lamarr, June Allyson, William Boyd, Janet Leigh, Gary Cooper 7.00 21.00 50.00

NOTE: ***Whitney*** *a-1,3.*

FAMOUS STORIES (. . .Book No. 2)
1942
Dell Publishing Co.

1-Treasure Island 10.00 30.00 70.00
2-Tom Sawyer 10.00 30.00 70.00

FAMOUS TV FUNDAY FUNNIES
Sept, 1961
Harvey Publications

1-Casper the Ghost 3.00 9.00 21.00

FAMOUS WESTERN BADMEN (Formerly Redskin)
No. 13, Dec, 1952 - No. 15, 1953
Youthful Magazines

13 3.50 10.50 24.00
14,15 2.15 6.50 15.00

FANTASTIC (Formerly Capt. Science; Beware No. 10 on)
No. 8, Feb, 1952 - No. 9, April, 1952
Youthful Magazines

8-Capt. Science by Harrison 10.00 30.00 70.00
9-Harrison-a 6.00 18.00 42.00

FANTASTIC (Fantastic Fears No. 1-9)
No. 10, Nov-Dec, 1954 - No. 11, Jan-Feb, 1955
Ajax/Farrell Publ.

10,11 3.50 10.50 24.00

FANTASTIC ADVENTURES
1963 - 1964 (Reprints)
Super Comics

9,10,12,15,16,18: 16-Briefer-a. 18-r/Superior Stories No. 1 1.00 3.00 6.00
11-Wood-a; r/Blue Bolt No. 118 1.70 5.00 10.00
17-Baker-a(2) r-/Seven Seas 6 1.35 4.00 8.00

FANTASTIC COMICS
Dec, 1939 - No. 23, Nov, 1941

FANTASTIC COMICS (continued)
Fox Features Syndicate

	Good	Fine	Mint
1-Intro/Origin Samson; Stardust, The Super Wizard, Space Smith, Sub Saunders, Capt. Kidd begin	100.00	300.00	700.00
2-Powell text illos	50.00	150.00	350.00
3-5: 3-Powell text illos	40.00	120.00	280.00
6-9: 6,7-Simon-c	33.00	100.00	230.00
10-Intro/origin David, Samson's aide	25.00	75.00	175.00
11-17: 16-Stardust ends	19.00	57.00	132.00
18-Intro. Black Fury & sidekick Chuck; ends #23	22.00	65.00	154.00
19,20	19.00	57.00	132.00
21-The Banshee begins(origin); ends #23	22.00	65.00	154.00
22	19.00	57.00	132.00
23-Origin The Gladiator	22.00	65.00	154.00

NOTE: ***Lou Fine*** *c-1-5.* ***Tuska*** *a-3-5, 8. Bondage c-6, 8, 9.*

FANTASTIC FEARS (Formerly Captain Jet) (Fantastic No. 10 on)
No. 7, May, 1953 - No. 9, Sept-Oct, 1954
Ajax/Farrell Publ.

	Good	Fine	Mint
7(5/53)	7.00	21.00	50.00
8(7/53)	4.60	14.00	32.00
3,4	3.50	10.50	24.00
5-1st Ditko story is written by Bruce Hamilton reprinted in Weird V2#8	20.00	60.00	140.00
6-Decapitation of girl's head with paper cutter (classic)	10.00	30.00	70.00
7(5-6/54), 9(9-10/54)	3.50	10.50	24.00
8(7-8/54)-Contains story intended for Jo-Jo; name changed to Kaza; decapitation story	5.00	15.00	35.00

FANTASTIC FOUR (See Marvel Coll. Item Classics, Marvel Treas. Ed, Marvel Triple Action & Official Marvel Index to. . .)
Nov, 1961 - Present
Marvel Comics Group

	Good	Fine	Mint
1-Origin & 1st app. The Fantastic Four (Reed Richards: Mr. Fantastic, Johnny Storm: The Human Torch, Sue Storm: The Invisible Girl, & Ben Grimm: The Thing); origin The Mole Man	145.00	580.00	1380.00
1-Golden Record Comic Set-r	2.00	6.00	12.00
with record. . . .	5.15	15.50	36.00
2-Vs. The Skrulls (last 10 cent issue)	78.00	185.00	550.00
3-Fantastic Four don costumes & establish Headquarters	63.00	157.00	440.00
4-1st Silver Age Sub-Mariner app.	48.00	120.00	340.00
5-Origin & 1st app. Doctor Doom	38.00	116.00	270.00
6-10: 6-Sub-Mariner, Dr. Doom team up. 7-1st app. Kurrgo. 8-1st app. Puppet-Master & Alicia Masters	24.00	60.00	170.00
11-Origin The Impossible Man	18.00	45.00	126.00
12-Fantastic Four Vs. The Hulk	16.00	41.00	115.00
13-15: 13-Intro. The Watcher; 1st app. The Red Ghost	12.00	30.00	84.00
16-20: 18-Origin The Super Skrull. 19-Intro. Rama-Tut. 20-Origin The Molecule Man	8.50	21.00	60.00
21-30: 21-Intro. The Hate Monger. 25,26-The Thing Vs. the Hulk. 28-X-Men app. 30-Intro. Diablo	4.70	12.00	33.00
31-40: 31-Avengers x-over. 33-1st app. Attuma. 35-Intro/1st app. Dragon Man. 36-Intro/1st app. Madam Medusa & the Frightful Four (Sandman, Wizard, Paste Pot Pete). 39-Wood inks on Daredevil	2.45	6.00	17.00
41-47: 41-43-Frightful Four app. 44-Intro. Gorgan. 45-Intro. The Inhumans	1.75	5.25	10.50
48-Intro/1st app. The Silver Surfer, & Galactus (3/66)	5.15	15.50	31.00
49,50-Silver Surfer x-over	2.65	8.00	15.80
51-60: 52-Intro. The Black Panther; origin-#53. Silver Surfer x-over in #55-60,61(cameo). 54,59,60-Inhumans cameo	1.40	4.20	8.40
61-65,68-70	1.05	3.15	6.30
66,67-1st app. & origin Him (Warlock)	1.40	4.20	8.40
71,73,78-80	.70	2.10	4.20
72,74-77: Silver Surfer app.	1.40	4.20	8.40
81-90: 81-Crystal joins & dons costume. 82,83-Inhumans app. 84-87-Dr. Doom app.	.70	2.00	4.00
91-99,101,102: 94-Intro. Agatha Harkness. Last Kirby issue #102,108	.70	2.00	4.00
100	2.10	6.30	12.60
103-111	.45	1.40	2.80
112-Hulk Vs. Thing	.70	2.10	4.20
113-120: 116-(52 pgs.)	.45	1.30	2.60
121-123-Silver Surfer x-over	.70	2.10	4.20
124-127,129-140: 126-Origin F.F. retold. 129-Intro. Thundra. 130-Sue leaves F.F. 132-Medusa joins. 133-Thundra Vs. Thing	.35	1.05	2.10
128-Four pg. insert of F.F. Friends & Fiends	.55	1.60	3.20
141-149,151-154,158-160: 142-Kirbyish art by Buckler begins. 151-Origin Thundra. 159-Medusa leaves, Sue rejoins	.35	1.05	2.10
150-Crystal & Quicksilver's wedding	.45	1.30	2.60
155-157: Silver Surfer in all	.35	1.05	2.10
161-180: 164-The Crusader (old Marvel Boy) revived; origin #165. 176-Re-intro Impossible Man; Marvel artists app.	.25	.80	1.60
181-199: 190-191-F.F. breaks up		.60	1.20
200-Giant size-FF re-united	.55	1.60	3.20
201-208,219		.50	1.00
209-216,218,220,221-Byrne-a. 209-1st Herbie the Robot. 220-Brief origin	.25	.80	1.60
217-Dazzler app. by Byrne	.45	1.30	2.60
222-231		.50	1.00
232-Byrne-a begins	.40	1.25	2.50
233-235,237-249: Byrne-a. 238-Origin Frankie Ray	.35	1.05	2.10
236-20th Anniversary issue(11/81, 64pgs., $1.00)-Brief origin F.F.	.45	1.30	2.60
250-Double size; Byrne-a; Skrulls impersonate New X-Men	.45	1.30	2.60
251-259: Byrne c/a. 252-Reads sideways; Annihilus app.	.30	.95	1.90
260-Alpha Flight app.	.35	1.30	2.60
261-285: 261-Silver Surfer. 262-Origin Galactus	.25	.80	1.60
286-Ties in w/X-Factor	.55	1.60	3.20
287-295		.50	1.00
296-Barry Smith c/a; Thing rejoins	.30	.90	1.80
297-300		.50	1.00
301-305,307-315		.40	.80
306-New team begins		.60	1.20
Giant-Size 2(8/74) - 4: Formerly G-S Super-Stars	.55	1.60	3.20
Giant-Size 5(5/75), 6(8/75)	.30	.85	1.70
Annual 1('63)-Origin F.F.; Ditko-i	10.00	25.00	70.00
Annual 2('64)-Dr. Doom origin & x-over	4.50	11.00	32.00
Annual 3('65)-Reed & Sue wed	2.00	5.00	14.00
Special 4(11/66)-G.A. Torch x-over & origin retold	1.00	3.00	6.00
Special 5(11/67)-New art; Intro. Psycho-Man; Silver Surfer, Black Panther, Inhumans app.	.75	2.25	4.50
Special 6(11/68)-Intro. Annihilus; no reprints; birth of Franklin Richards	.70	2.00	4.00
Special 7(11/69), 8(12/70), 9(12/71), 10('73)	.45	1.40	2.80
Annual 11(6/76), 12(2/78)	.25	.80	1.60
Annual 13(10/78), 14(1/80)	.25	.80	1.60

Fantastic Comics #1, © FOX

Fantastic Four #1, © MCG

Fantastic Four #48, © MCG

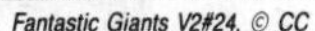
Fantastic Giants V2#24, © CC

Fantasy Masterpieces #6, © MCG

Fast Fiction #1, © Seaboard Publ.

FANTASTIC FOUR (continued)

	Good	Fine	Mint
Annual 15(10/80), 16(10/81), 17(9/83)	.25	.80	1.60
Annual 18(11/84), 19(11/85), 20(9/87)	.25	.80	1.60
Special Edition 1 (5/84)-r/Annual #1; Byrne c/a	.25	.80	1.60
Giveaway (nn, 1981, 32pgs., Young Model Builders Club)	.25	.80	1.60

NOTE: ***Austin*** *c(i)-232-236, 238, 240-42, 250i, 286i.* ***Buckler*** *a-142-163p, 168, 169; c-140-49p, 151-59p, 161-63pp, 165, 166p, 169, 170p, 216.* ***John Buscema*** *a(p)-107, 108(****w/Kirby & Romita****),109-130, 132, 134-141, 160, 173-175, 202, 296p-309p, Annual 11, 13, Gnt-Size 1-4; c(p)-107-122, 124-129, 133-139, 202, Annual 12p, Special 10.* ***Byrne*** *a-209-218p, 220p, 221p, 232-65, 266i, 267-73, 274-93p; c-211-14p, 220p, 232-236p, 237, 238p, 239, 240-42p, 243-49, 250p, 251-67, 269-77, 278p-81p, 283p, 284, 285, 286p, 288-293.* ***Ditko*** *a-13i, Gnt Size 2r, Annual 16.* ***G. Kane*** *c-150p, 160p.* ***Kirby*** *a-1-102p, 108, 180r, 189r, 236p(r), Special 1-10, Giant-Size 5, 6r; c-1-101, 164, 167, 171-177, 180, 181, 190, 200, Annual 11, Giant-Size 5, Special 1-7, 9.* ***Marcos*** *a-Annual 14i.* ***Mooney*** *a-118i, 152i.* ***Perez*** *a-164-167, 170-172, 176-178, 184-188, 191p, 192p. Annual 14p, 15p; c(p)-183-88, 191, 192, 194-197.* ***Simonson*** *c-212.* ***Steranko*** *c-130-132p.*

FANTASTIC FOUR INDEX (See Official . . .)

FANTASTIC FOUR ROAST
May, 1982 (One Shot, Direct Sale)
Marvel Comics Group

	Good	Fine	Mint
1-Celebrates 20th anniversary of Fantastic Four No. 1; Golden, Miller, Buscema, Rogers, Byrne, Anderson, Austin-a, c(i)	.40	1.25	2.50

FANTASTIC FOUR VERSUS THE X-MEN
Feb, 1987 - No. 4, May, 1987 (mini-series)
Marvel Comics Group

	Good	Fine	Mint
1	.60	1.80	3.60
2-4	.30	.90	1.80

FANTASTIC GIANTS (Konga No. 1-23)
September, 1966 (25 cents, 68 pgs.)
Charlton Comics

	Good	Fine	Mint
V2#24-Origin Konga & Gorgo reprinted; two new Ditko stories	2.00	6.00	12.00

FANTASTIC TALES
1958 (no date) (Reprint)
I. W. Enterprises

	Good	Fine	Mint
1-Reprints Avon's "City of the Living Dead"	1.35	4.00	8.00

FANTASTIC VOYAGE (See Movie Comics)
Aug, 1969 - No. 2, Dec, 1969
Gold Key

	Good	Fine	Mint
1,2 (TV)	1.70	5.00	12.00

FANTASTIC VOYAGES OF SINDBAD, THE
Oct, 1965 - No. 2, June, 1967
Gold Key

	Good	Fine	Mint
1,2	2.15	6.50	15.00

FANTASTIC WORLDS
No. 5, Sept, 1952 - No. 7, Jan, 1953
Standard Comics

	Good	Fine	Mint
5-Toth, Anderson-a	10.00	30.00	70.00
6-Toth story	8.50	25.50	60.00
7	5.00	15.00	35.00

FANTASY FEATURES
1987 - Present ($1.75, color)
Americomics

	Good	Fine	Mint
1	.30	.90	1.80

FANTASY MASTERPIECES (Marvel Super Heroes No. 12 on)
Feb, 1966 - No. 11, Oct, 1967; Dec, 1979 - No. 14, Jan, 1981
Marvel Comics Group

	Good	Fine	Mint
1-Photo of Stan Lee	1.00	3.00	6.00
2	.35	1.00	2.00
3-G.A. Captain America-r begin; 1st Giant	.35	1.00	2.00
4-6-Capt. America-r	.35	1.00	2.00
7-Begin G.A. Sub-Mariner, Torch-r	.35	1.00	2.00
8-Torch battles the Sub-Mariner r-/Marvel Mystery #9	.35	1.00	2.00
9-Origin Human Torch r-/Marvel Comics #1	.35	1.00	2.00
10-All Winners-r	.35	1.00	2.00
11-Reprint of origin Toro & Black Knight	.35	1.00	2.00
V2#1(12/79)-52 pgs.; 75 cents; r-/origin Silver Surfer from S. Surfer #1 with editing; J. Buscema-a	.35	1.00	2.00
2-4-Silver Surfer-r	.35	1.00	2.00
5-14-Silver Surfer-r		.50	1.00

NOTE: ***Buscema*** *c-V2No.7-9(in part).* ***Ditko*** *a-1-3r, 7r, 9r.* ***Everett*** *a-9r.* ***Matt Fox*** *a-9i(r).* ***Kirby*** *a-2-4r, 8r, 11r.* ***Starlin*** *a-8-13r. Some direct sale V2No14's had a 50 cent cover price.*

FANTASY QUARTERLY (Also see Elfquest)
Spring, 1978
Independent Publishers Syndicate

	Good	Fine	Mint
1-1st app. Elfquest (2nd printing exist?)	9.15	27.50	55.00

FANTOMAN (Formerly Amazing Adv. Funnies)
No. 2, Aug, 1940 - No. 4, Dec, 1940
Centaur Publications

	Good	Fine	Mint
2-The Fantom of the Fair, The Arrow, Little Dynamite-r begin; origin The Ermine by Filchock; Burgos, J. Cole, Ernst, Gustavson-a	55.00	165.00	385.00
3,4: Gustavson-a(r). 4-Bondage-c	37.00	110.00	260.00

FARGO KID (Formerly Justice Traps the Guilty)
V11No.3(No.1), June-July, 1958 - V11No.5, Oct-Nov, 1958
Prize Publications

	Good	Fine	Mint
V11#3(#1)-Origin Fargo Kid, Severin-c/a; Williamson-a(2)	6.50	19.50	45.00
V11#4,5-Severin c/a	3.70	11.00	26.00

FARMER'S DAUGHTER, THE
2-3/54 - No. 3, 6-7/54; No. 4, 10/54
Stanhall Publ./Trojan Magazines

	Good	Fine	Mint
1-Lingerie, nudity panel	6.50	19.50	45.00
2-4(Stanhall)	3.50	10.50	24.00

FASHION IN ACTION
Aug, 1986 - Present ($1.75, Baxter)
Eclipse Comics

	Good	Fine	Mint
Summer Special 1	.30	.85	1.70
Winter Special 1(2/87, $2.00)	.30	.90	1.80

FASTEST GUN ALIVE, THE (See 4-Color No. 741)

FAST FICTION (. . . Action) (Stories by Famous Authors Illustrated No. 6 on)
Oct, 1949 - No. 5, Mar, 1950 (All have Kiefer-c)
Seaboard Publ./Famous Authors Ill.

	Good	Fine	Mint
1-Scarlet Pimpernel; Jim Lavery-a	16.00	48.00	110.00
2-Captain Blood; H. C. Kiefer-a	14.00	42.00	100.00
3-She, by Rider Haggard; Vincent Napoli-a	22.00	65.00	154.00
4-(52pgs, 1/50)-The 39 Steps; Lavery-a	10.00	30.00	70.00
5-Beau Geste; Kiefer-a	10.00	30.00	70.00

NOTE: ***Kiefer*** *a-2, 5; c-2, 3, 5.* ***Lavery*** *a-1, 4; c-1, 4.* ***Napoli*** *a-3.*

FAST WILLIE JACKSON
October, 1976 - No. 7, 1977
Fitzgerald Periodicals, Inc.

	Good	Fine	Mint
1		.50	1.00
2-7		.40	.80

FAT ALBERT (. . . & the Cosby Kids) (TV)
March, 1974 - No. 29, Feb, 1979
Gold Key

FAT ALBERT (continued)	Good	Fine	Mint
1	.35	1.00	2.00
2-29		.40	.80

FAT AND SLAT (Ed Wheelan) (Gunfighter No. 5 on)
Summer, 1947 - No. 4, Spring, 1948
E. C. Comics

	Good	Fine	Mint
1	14.00	42.00	100.00
2	11.00	33.00	76.00
3,4	9.50	28.50	66.00

FAT AND SLAT JOKE BOOK
Summer, 1944 (One Shot, 52 pages)
All-American Comics (William H. Wise)

	Good	Fine	Mint
by Ed Wheelan	10.00	30.00	70.00

FATE (See Hand of Fate, & Thrill-O-Rama)

FATHER OF CHARITY
No date (32 pgs.; paper cover)
Catechetical Guild Giveaway

	Good	Fine	Mint
	2.00	6.00	12.00

FATHOM
May, 1987 - No. 3, July, 1987 ($1.50, mini-series, color)
Comico

	Good	Fine	Mint
1-3	.25	.75	1.50

FATIMA...CHALLENGE TO THE WORLD
1951, 36 pgs. (15 cent cover)
Catechetical Guild

	Good	Fine	Mint
nn (not same as 'Challenge to the World')	3.00	9.00	18.00

FATMAN, THE HUMAN FLYING SAUCER
April, 1967 - No. 3, Aug-Sept, 1967 (68 pgs.)
Lightning Comics(Milson Publ. Co.) (Written by Otto Binder)

	Good	Fine	Mint
1-Origin Fatman & Tinman by C. C. Beck	2.00	6.00	14.00
2-Beck-a	1.75	5.25	12.00
3-(Scarce)-Beck-a	3.50	10.50	24.00

FAUNTLEROY COMICS (Superduck Presents. . .)
1950 - No. 3, 1952
Close-Up/Archie Publications

	Good	Fine	Mint
1	3.50	10.50	24.00
2,3	1.75	5.25	12.00

FAVORITE COMICS (Also see Famous Comics)
1934 (36 pgs.)
Grocery Store Giveaway (Dif Corp.) (detergent)

	Good	Fine	Mint
Book No. 1-The Nebbs, Strange As It Seems, Napoleon, Dixie Dugan, Joe Palooka, S'Matter Pop, Hairbreadth Harry, etc. reprints	16.00	48.00	110.00
Book No. 2,3	13.00	40.00	90.00

FAWCETT MINIATURES (See Mighty Midget)
1946 (12-24 pgs.; 3¾x5") (Wheaties giveaways)
Fawcett Publications

	Good	Fine	Mint
Captain Marvel-"And the Horn of Plenty;" Bulletman story	2.35	7.00	16.00
Captain Marvel-"& the Raiders From Space;" Golden Arrow story	2.35	7.00	16.00
Captain Marvel Jr.-"The Case of the Poison Press!" Bulletman story	2.35	7.00	16.00
Delecta of the Planets-C. C. Beck art; B&W inside; 12 pgs.; 3 printing variations (coloring) exist. Only 6 known copies exist	8.00	24.00	56.00

FAWCETT MOTION PICTURE COMICS (See Motion Picture Comics)

FAWCETT MOVIE COMIC
1949 - No. 20, Dec, 1952 (All photo-c)
Fawcett Publications

	Good	Fine	Mint
nn-"Dakota Lil"-George Montgomery & Rod Cameron('49)	20.00	60.00	140.00
nn-"Copper Canyon"-Ray Milland & Hedy Lamarr('50)	14.00	42.00	100.00
nn-"Destination Moon"-(1950)	45.00	135.00	315.00
nn-"Montana"-Errol Flynn & Alexis Smith('50)	14.00	42.00	100.00
nn-"Pioneer Marshal"-Monte Hale(1950)	14.00	42.00	100.00
nn-"Powder River Rustlers"-Rocky Lane(1950)	16.00	48.00	110.00
nn-"Singing Guns"-Vaughn Monroe & Ella Raines(1950)	14.00	42.00	100.00
7-"Gunmen of Abilene"-Rocky Lane; Bob Powell-a(1950)	16.00	48.00	110.00
8-"King of the Bullwhip"-Lash LaRue; Bob Powell-a(1950)	20.00	60.00	140.00
9-"The Old Frontier"-Monte Hale; Bob Powell-a(2/51; mis-dated 2/50)	14.00	42.00	100.00
10-"The Missourians"-Monte Hale(4/51)	14.00	42.00	100.00
11-"The Thundering Trail"-Lash LaRue(6/51)	20.00	60.00	140.00
12-"Rustlers on Horseback"-Rocky Lane(8/51)	16.00	48.00	110.00
13-"Warpath"-Edmond O'Brien & Forrest Tucker(10/51)	13.00	40.00	90.00
14-"Last Outpost"-Ronald Reagan(12/51)	32.00	95.00	225.00
15-(Scarce)-"The Man From Planet X"-Robert Clark; Shaffenberger-a (2/52)	150.00	450.00	1050.00
16-"10 Tall Men"-Burt Lancaster	10.00	30.00	70.00
17-"Rose of Cimarron"-Jack Buetel & Mala Powers	6.50	19.50	45.00
18-"The Brigand"-Anthony Dexter; Shaffenberger-a	7.00	21.00	50.00
19-"Carbine Williams"-James Stewart; Costanza-a	9.00	27.00	62.00
20-"Ivanhoe"-Liz Taylor	12.00	36.00	84.00

FAWCETT'S FUNNY ANIMALS (No. 1-26, 80-on titled "Funny Animals;" Li'l Tomboy No. 92 on?)
12/42 - No. 79, 4/53; No. 80, 6/53 - No. 83, 12?/53; No. 84, 4/54 - No. 91, Feb, 1956
Fawcett Publications/Charlton Comics No. 84 on

	Good	Fine	Mint
1-Capt. Marvel on cover; intro. Hoppy The Marvel Bunny, cloned from Capt. Marvel	21.00	62.00	150.00
2	10.00	30.00	70.00
3-5	7.00	21.00	50.00
6,7,9,10	5.00	15.00	35.00
8-Flag-c	5.70	17.00	40.00
11-20	3.00	9.00	21.00
21-40: 26-St. Valentines Day-c	1.85	5.50	13.00
41-88,90,91	1.30	4.00	9.00
89-Merry Mailman ish	1.65	5.00	11.50

NOTE: *Marvel Bunny in all issues to at least No. 68 (not in 49-54).*

FAZE ONE FAZERS
1986 - No. 4, Sept, 1986 (mini-series)
Americomics (AC Comics)

	Good	Fine	Mint
1-4	.50	1.50	3.00

F.B.I., THE
April-June, 1965
Dell Publishing Co.

	Good	Fine	Mint
1-Sinnott-a	1.00	3.00	7.00

F.B.I. STORY, THE (See 4-Color No. 1069)

FEAR (Adventure into. . .)
Nov, 1970 - No. 31, Dec, 1975 (No.1-6 - Giant Size)
Marvel Comics Group

Fat and Slat #3, © WMG

Fawcett Movie Comic #11, © FAW

Fawcett's Funny Animals #33, © FAW

Feature Books #11, © DMP

Feature Comics #34, © QUA

Feature Films #2, © DC

FEAR (continued)

	Good	Fine	Mint
1-Reprints Fantasy & Sci-Fi stories		.60	1.20
2-9: 9-Everett-a		.30	.60
10-Man-Thing begins; Morrow c/a(p)	.70	2.00	4.00
11-Adams-c	.25	.75	1.50
12-Starlin/Buckler-a	.25	.75	1.50
13-18		.30	.60
19-Intro. Howard the Duck; Val Mayerick-a	1.70	5.00	10.00
20-Morbius, the Living Vampire begins, ends No. 31; Gulacy-a(p)		.30	.60
21-31: 30-Evans-a		.30	.60

NOTE: ***Bolle** a-13i. **Brunner** c-15-17. **Buckler** a-11p, 22p; c-13p, 22p. **Chaykin** a-10i. **Colan** a-23r. **Craig** a-10p. **Ditko** a-6-8r. **Everett** a-10i, 21r. **Gil Kane** a-21p; c(p)-20, 21, 23-28, 31. **Kirby** a-8r, 9r. **Maneely** a-24r. **Mooney** a-11i, 26r. **Paul Reinman** a-14r. **Russell** a-23p, 24p. **Severin** c-8. **Starlin** c-12p.*

FEARBOOK
April, 1986 (One shot) ($1.75, adults)
Eclipse Comics

	Good	Fine	Mint
1-Scholastic Mag.-r; Bissette-a	.30	.90	1.80

FEAR IN THE NIGHT (See Complete Mystery No. 3)

FEARLESS FAGAN (See 4-Color No. 441)

FEATURE BOOK (Dell) (See Large Feature Comic)

FEATURE BOOKS (Newspaper-r, early issues)
May, 1937 - No. 57, 1948
David McKay Publications

	Good	Fine	Mint
nn-Popeye & the Jeep (#1, 100 pgs.); reprinted as Feature Books #3 (Very Rare; only 3 known copies, 1-vf, 2-in low grade) Estimated value....	385.00	1155.00	2700.00
nn-Dick Tracy (#1)-Reprinted as Feature Book #4 (100 pgs.) & in part as 4-Color #1 (Rare, less than 10 known copies) Estimated value....	400.00	1200.00	2800.00

NOTE: *Above books were advertised together with different covers from Feature Books No. 3 & 4.*

	Good	Fine	Mint
1-King of the Royal Mtd. (#1)	35.00	105.00	245.00
2-Popeye(6/37) by Segar	47.00	140.00	330.00
3-Popeye(7/37) by Segar; same as nn issue but a new cover added	40.00	120.00	280.00
4-Dick Tracy(8/37)-Same as nn issue but a new cover added	72.00	215.00	500.00
5-Popeye(9/37) by Segar	32.00	95.00	225.00
6-Dick Tracy(10/37)	57.00	170.00	400.00
7-Little Orphan Annie (#1) (Rare)	70.00	210.00	490.00
8-Secret Agent X-9-Not by Raymond	20.00	60.00	140.00
9-Dick Tracy(1/38)	57.00	170.00	400.00
10-Popeye(2/38)	32.00	95.00	225.00
11-Little Annie Rooney (#1)	16.00	48.00	110.00
12-Blondie (#1) (4/38) (Rare)	35.00	105.00	245.00
13-Inspector Wade	10.00	30.00	70.00
14-Popeye(6/38) by Segar (Scarce)	46.00	138.00	320.00
15-Barney Baxter (#1) (7/38)	15.00	45.00	105.00
16-Red Eagle	8.50	25.50	60.00
17-Gangbusters (#1)	20.00	60.00	140.00
18,19-Mandrake	20.00	60.00	140.00
20-Phantom (#1)	37.00	110.00	260.00
21-Lone Ranger	37.00	110.00	260.00
22-Phantom	32.00	95.00	225.00
23-Mandrake	20.00	60.00	140.00
24-Lone Ranger(1941)	37.00	110.00	260.00
25-Flash Gordon (#1)-Reprints not by Raymond	50.00	150.00	350.00
26-Prince Valiant(1941)-Harold Foster-a; newspaper strips reprinted, pgs. 1-28,30-63	68.00	205.00	475.00
27-29,31,34-Blondie	7.00	21.00	50.00
30-Katzenjammer Kids (#1)	8.00	24.00	56.00
32,35,41,44-Katzenjammer Kids	6.00	18.00	42.00
33(nn)-Romance of Flying-World War II photos	5.70	17.00	40.00
36,38,40,42,43,45,47-Blondie	6.00	18.00	42.00
37-Katzenjammer Kids; has photo & biog of Harold H. Knerr(1883-1949) who took over strip from Rudolph Dirks in 1914	7.00	21.00	50.00
39-Phantom	22.00	65.00	154.00
46-Mandrake in the Fire World-(58 pgs.)	16.00	48.00	110.00
48-Maltese Falcon('46)	34.00	102.00	240.00
49,50-Perry Mason	10.00	30.00	70.00
51,54-Rip Kirby by Raymond; origin-#51	16.00	48.00	110.00
52,55-Mandrake	14.00	42.00	100.00
53,56,57-Phantom	17.00	51.00	120.00

NOTE: *All Feature Books through #25 are over-sized 8½x11-3/8" comics with color covers and black and white interiors. The covers are rough, heavy stock. The page counts, including covers, are as follows: nn, #3,4-100 pgs.; #1,2-52 pgs.; #5-25 are all 76 pgs. #33 was found in bound set from publisher.*

FEATURE COMICS (Formerly Feature Funnies)
No. 21, June, 1939 - No. 144, May, 1950
Quality Comics Group

	Good	Fine	Mint
21	17.00	51.00	120.00
22-26: 23-Charlie Chan begins	13.00	40.00	90.00
26-(nn, nd)-c-in one color, (10 cents, 36pgs.; issue No. blanked out. 2 variations exist, each contain half of the regular No. 26)	4.60	14.00	32.00
27-Origin & 1st app. of Dollman by Eisner	135.00	405.00	945.00
28-1st Fine Dollman	60.00	180.00	420.00
29,30	36.00	108.00	250.00
31-Last Clock & Charlie Chan issue	30.00	90.00	210.00
32-37: 32-Rusty Ryan & Samar begin. 37-Last Fine Dollman	23.00	70.00	160.00
38-41: 38-Origin the Ace of Space. 39-Origin The Destroying Demon, ends #40. 40-Bruce Blackburn in costume	16.50	50.00	115.00
42-USA, the Spirit of Old Glory begins	10.00	30.00	70.00
43,45-50: 46-Intro. Boyville Brigadiers in Rusty Ryan. 48-USA ends	10.00	30.00	70.00
44-Dollman by Crandall begins, ends #63; Crandall-a(2)	15.00	45.00	105.00
51-55	8.50	25.50	60.00
56-Marijuana story in "Swing Session"	9.00	27.00	62.00
57-Spider Widow begins	8.50	25.50	60.00
58-60: 60-Raven begins, ends #71	8.50	25.50	60.00
61-68 (5/43)	8.00	24.00	56.00
69,70-Phantom Lady x-over in Spider Widow	8.50	25.50	60.00
71-80: 71-Phantom Lady x-over. 72-Spider Widow ends	5.70	17.00	40.00
81-99	4.60	14.00	32.00
100	5.70	17.00	40.00
101-144: 139-Last Dollman. 140-Intro. Stuntman Stetson	4.35	13.00	30.00

NOTE: ***Celardo** a-37-43. **Crandall** a-44-60, 62, 63-on(most). **Gustavson** a-(Rusty Ryan)-32-47. **Powell** a-34, 64-73.*

FEATURE FILMS
Mar-Apr, 1950 - No. 4, Sept-Oct, 1950 (Photo-c 2,3)
National Periodical Publications

	Good	Fine	Mint
1-"Captain China" with John Payne & Gail Russell	24.00	72.00	170.00
2-"Riding High" with Bing Crosby	20.00	60.00	140.00
3-"The Eagle & the Hawk" with John Payne, Rhonda Fleming & D. O'Keefe	20.00	60.00	140.00
4-"Fancy Pants"-Bob Hope & Lucille Ball	22.00	65.00	154.00

FEATURE FUNNIES (Feature Comics No. 21 on)
Oct, 1937 - No. 20, May, 1939
Harry 'A' Chesler

FEATURE FUNNIES (continued) — Good / Fine / Mint

1(V9/1-indicia)-Joe Palooka, Mickey Finn, The Bungles, Jane Arden, Dixie Dugan, Big Top, Ned Bryant, Strange As It Seems, & Off the Record strip reprints begin 87.00 260.00 600.00
2-The Hawk app. (11/37) 40.00 120.00 280.00
3-Hawks of Seas begins by Eisner, ends #12; The Clock begins; Christmas-c 30.00 90.00 210.00
4,5 22.00 65.00 154.00
6-12: 11-Archie O'Toole by Bud Thomas begins, ends #22 18.00 54.00 125.00
13-Espionage, Starring Black X begins by Eisner, ends #20 20.00 60.00 140.00
14-20 15.00 45.00 105.00

FEATURE PRESENTATION, A (Feature Presentations Mag. #6) (Formerly Women in Love) (Also see Startling Terror Tales #11)
No. 5, April, 1950
Fox Features Syndicate

5-Black Tarantula 14.00 42.00 100.00

FEATURE PRESENTATIONS MAGAZINE (Formerly A Feature Presentation #5; becomes Feature Stories Mag. #3 on)
No. 6, July, 1950
Fox Features Syndicate

6-Moby Dick; Wood-c 11.00 33.00 76.00

FEATURE STORIES MAGAZINE (Formerly Feat. Present. Mag. #6)
No. 3, Aug, 1950 - No. 4, Oct, 1950
Fox Features Syndicate

3-Jungle Lil, Zegra stories; bondage-c 10.00 30.00 70.00
4 7.00 21.00 50.00

FEDERAL MEN COMICS (See The Comics Magazine, New Adv. Comics, New Book of Comics & New Comics)
1945 (DC reprints from 1930's)
Gerard Publ. Co.

2-Siegel & Shuster-a; cover redrawn from Detective #9; spanking panel 8.50 25.50 60.00

FELIX'S NEPHEWS INKY & DINKY
Sept, 1957 - No. 7, Oct, 1958
Harvey Publications

1-Cover shows Inky's left eye with 2 pupils 4.00 12.00 28.00
2-7 1.75 5.25 12.00

NOTE: *Contains no* ***Messmer*** *art.*

FELIX THE CAT
1927 - 1931 (24 pgs.; 8x10¼")(1926,'27 color strip reprints)
McLoughlin Bros.

260-(Rare)-by Otto Messmer 57.00 170.00 400.00

FELIX THE CAT (See The Funnies, March of Comics & Popular)
1943 - No. 118, 11/61; 9-11/62 - No. 12, 7-9/65
Dell Publ. No.1-19/Toby No.20-61/Harvey No.62-118/Dell

4-Color 15 35.00 105.00 245.00
4-Color 46('44) 24.00 72.00 170.00
4-Color 77('45) 20.00 60.00 140.00
4-Color 119('46) 14.00 42.00 100.00
4-Color 135('46) 11.50 34.00 80.00
4-Color 162(9/47) 9.00 27.00 63.00
1(2-3/48)(Dell) 11.50 34.00 80.00
2 5.70 17.00 40.00
3-5 4.60 14.00 32.00
6-19(2-3/51-Dell) 3.50 10.50 24.00
20-30(Toby): 28-2/52 some copies have No. 29 on cover, No. 28 on inside 3.00 9.00 21.00
31,34,35-No Messmer-a 1.50 4.50 10.00
32,33,36-61(6/55-Toby)-Last Messmer ish. 2.00 6.00 14.00
62(8/55)-100 (Harvey) .85 2.50 6.00
101-118(11/61) .75 2.25 5.00
12-269-211(9-11/62)(Dell) 1.50 4.50 10.00
2-12(7-9/65)(Dell, TV) .75 2.25 5.00
...& His Friends 1(12/53-Toby) 3.00 9.00 21.00
...& His Friends 2-4 2.00 6.00 14.00
3-D Comic Book 1(1953-One Shot) 17.00 51.00 120.00
Summer Annual 2('52)-Early 1930s Sunday strip-r (Exist?) 17.00 51.00 120.00
Summer Annual nn('53, 100 pgs., Toby)-1930s daily & Sunday-r 12.00 36.00 84.00
Winter Annual 2('54, 100 pgs., Toby)-1930s daily & Sunday-r 9.00 27.00 62.00
Summer Annual 3('55) (Exist?) 7.00 21.00 50.00

(See March of Comics No. 24,36,51)

NOTE: *4-Color No. 15, 46, 77 and the Toby Annuals are all daily or Sunday newspaper reprints from the 1930's drawn by Otto Messmer, who created Felix in 1915 for the Sullivan animation studio. He drew Felix from the beginning under contract to Pat Sullivan. In 1946 he went to work for Dell and wrote and pencilled most of the stories and inked some of them through the Toby Press issues. No. 107 reprints No. 71 interior; No. 110 reprints No. 56 interior.*

FEMFORCE
Apr, 1985 - Present ($1.75 cover; in color)
Americomics

1: Black-a .50 1.50 3.00
2-9 .30 .90 1.80
Special 1 (Fall, '84)(B&W, 52pgs.) .25 .75 1.50

FERDINAND THE BULL (See Mickey Mouse Mag. V4/3)
1938 (10 cents)(Large size; some color, rest B&W)
Dell Publishing Co.

nn 6.50 19.50 45.00

FIBBER McGEE & MOLLY (See A-1 Comics No. 25)

55 DAYS AT PEKING (See Movie Comics)

FIGHT AGAINST CRIME (Fight Against the Guilty #22,23)
May, 1951 - No. 21, Sept, 1954
Story Comics

1 6.50 19.50 45.00
2 3.00 9.00 21.00
3 2.65 8.00 18.00
4-Drug story-"Hopped Up Killers" 5.70 17.00 40.00
5-Frazetta, 1 pg. 2.65 8.00 18.00
6-Used in **POP**, pgs. 83,84 3.50 10.50 24.00
7 3.50 10.50 24.00
8-Last crime format issue 2.65 8.00 18.00

NOTE: *No. 9-21 contain violent, gruesome stories with blood, dismemberment, decapitation, E.C. style plot twists and several E.C. swipes.*

9-11,13 6.00 18.00 42.00
12-Morphine drug story-"The Big Dope" 8.00 24.00 56.00
14-Tothish art by Ross Andru 6.00 18.00 42.00
15-B&W & color illos in **POP** 7.00 21.00 50.00
16-E.C. story swipe/Haunt of Fear No. 19; Tothish-a by Ross Andru; bondage-c 7.00 21.00 50.00
17-Wildey E.C. swipe/Shock SuspenStories No. 9; knife through neck-c (1/54) 7.00 21.00 50.00
18,19 5.70 17.00 40.00
20-Decapitation cover; contains hanging, ax murder, blood & violence 16.00 48.00 110.00
21-E.C. swipe 7.00 21.00 50.00

NOTE: ***Cameron*** *a-5.* ***Hollingsworth*** *a-3, 9, 10, 13.* ***Wildey*** *a-15, 16.*

FIGHT AGAINST THE GUILTY (Formerly Fight Against Crime)
No. 22, Dec, 1954 - No. 23, Mar, 1955
Story Comics

22-Tothish-a by Ross Andru; Ditko-a; E.C. story swipe 6.00 18.00 42.00

Feature Presentations Magazine #6, © FOX

Felix the Cat #20, © KING

Fight Against Crime #8, © Story Comics

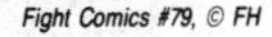
Fight Comics #79, © FH

Fighting American #4, © PRIZE

Fighting Indians of the Wild West! #1, © AVON

FIGHT AGAINST THE GUILTY (cont'd)	**Good**	**Fine**	**Mint**
23-Hollingsworth-a	3.70	11.00	26.00

FIGHT COMICS
Jan, 1940 - No. 86, Summer, 1953
Fiction House Magazines

	Good	Fine	Mint
1-Origin Spy Fighter, Starring Saber; Fine/Eisner-c; Eisner-a	70.00	210.00	490.00
2	33.00	100.00	230.00
3-Rip Regan, the Power Man begins	28.00	84.00	195.00
4,5: 4-Fine-c	22.00	65.00	154.00
6-10	18.00	54.00	125.00
11-14: Rip Regan ends	16.00	48.00	110.00
15-1st Super American	22.00	65.00	154.00
16-Captain Fight begins; Spy Fighter ends	22.00	65.00	154.00
17,18: Super American ends	19.00	57.00	132.00
19-Captain Fight ends; origin & 1st app. Senorita Rio; Rip Carson, Chute Trooper begins	19.00	57.00	132.00
20	15.00	45.00	105.00
21-30	10.00	30.00	70.00
31,33-35: 31-Decapitation-c	9.50	28.50	66.00
32-Tiger Girl begins	10.00	30.00	70.00
36-47,49,50: 44-Capt. Fight returns	9.00	27.00	62.00
48-Used in **Love and Death** by Legman	10.00	30.00	70.00
51-Origin Tiger Girl	13.00	40.00	90.00
52-60	7.00	21.00	50.00
61-Origin Tiger Girl retold	8.00	24.00	56.00
62-65-Last Baker issue	7.00	21.00	50.00
66-77	6.00	18.00	42.00
78-Used in **POP**, pg. 99	6.00	18.00	42.00
79-The Space Rangers app.	6.00	18.00	42.00
80-85	5.00	15.00	35.00
86-Two Tigerman stories by Evans; Moreira-a	6.00	18.00	42.00

NOTE: *Bondage c-No. 20, 21, 30, 32, 40, 41, 43, 44, 52. Lingerie, headlights panels are common. Tiger Girl by* ***Baker****-No. 36-60,62-65; Kayo Kirby by* ***Baker****-No. 52-64, 67.* ***Eisner*** *c-1-3, 5, 10, 11.* ***Kamen*** *a-54?, 57?.* ***Tuska*** *a-1, 5, 8, 10.*

FIGHT FOR FREEDOM
1949, 1951 (16 pgs.) (Giveaway)
National Association of Mfgrs./General Comics

	Good	Fine	Mint
Dan Barry-a; used in **POP**, pg. 102	5.00	15.00	30.00

FIGHT FOR LOVE
1952 (no month)
United Features Syndicate

	Good	Fine	Mint
nn-Abbie & Slats newspaper-r	6.50	19.50	45.00

FIGHTING AIR FORCE (See United States Fighting Air Force)

FIGHTIN' AIR FORCE (Formerly Sherlock Holmes?; War and Attack No. 54 on)
No. 3, Feb, 1956 - No. 53, Feb-Mar, 1966
Charlton Comics

	Good	Fine	Mint
V1#3	1.15	3.50	8.00
4-10	.60	1.80	4.20
11(68 pgs.)(3/58)	.85	2.50	6.00
12 (100 pgs.)	1.15	3.50	8.00
13-30	.30	.90	2.00
31-50: 50-American Eagle begins		.40	.80
51-53		.30	.60

NOTE: ***Glanzman*** *a-13,24; c-24.*

FIGHTING AMERICAN
Apr-May, 1954 - No. 7, Apr-May, 1955
Headline Publications/Prize

	Good	Fine	Mint
1-Origin Fighting American & Speedboy; S&K c/a(3)	65.00	195.00	455.00
2-S&K-a(3)	33.00	100.00	230.00
3,4-S&K-a(3)	28.00	84.00	195.00
5-S&K-a(2), Kirby/?-a	28.00	84.00	195.00
6-Four pg. reprint of origin, plus 2 pgs. by S&K	25.00	75.00	175.00
7-Kirby-a	24.00	72.00	168.00

NOTE: ***Simon & Kirby*** *covers on all.*

FIGHTING AMERICAN
October, 1966 (25 cents)
Harvey Publications

	Good	Fine	Mint
1-Origin Fighting American & Speedboy by S&K-r; S&K-c/a(3); 1 pg. Adams ad	1.50	4.50	10.00

FIGHTIN' ARMY (Formerly Soldier and Marine Comics; see Capt. Willy Schultz)
No. 16, 1/56 - No. 127, 12/76; No. 128, 9/77 - No. 172, 11/84
Charlton Comics

	Good	Fine	Mint
16	.75	2.25	5.00
17-19,21-30	.35	1.00	2.50
20-Ditko-a	.85	2.50	6.00
31-45	.25	.75	1.50
46-60		.40	.80
61-80: 75-The Lonely War of Willy Schultz begins, ends #92		.30	.60
81-172: 89,90,92-Ditko-a; Devil Brigade in #79,82,83		.30	.60
108(Modern Comics-1977)-Reprint		.15	.30

NOTE: ***Aparo*** *c-154.* ***Montes/Bache*** *a-48,49,51,69,75,76, 170r.*

FIGHTING DANIEL BOONE
1953
Avon Periodicals

	Good	Fine	Mint
nn-Kinstler c/a, 22 pgs.	8.00	24.00	56.00
I.W. Reprint #1-Kinstler c/a; Lawrence/Alascia-a	1.00	3.00	6.00

FIGHTING DAVY CROCKETT (Formerly Kit Carson)
No. 9, Oct-Nov, 1955
Avon Periodicals

	Good	Fine	Mint
9-Kinstler-c	3.50	10.50	24.00

FIGHTIN' 5, THE (Formerly Space War; also see The Peacemaker)
7/64 - No. 41, 1/67; No. 42, 10/81 - No. 49, 12/82
Charlton Comics

	Good	Fine	Mint
V2No.28-Origin Fightin' Five	.35	1.00	2.00
29-39,41		.50	1.00
40-Peacemaker begins	.35	1.00	2.00
42-49: Reprints		.30	.60

FIGHTING FRONTS!
Aug, 1952 - No. 5, Jan, 1953
Harvey Publications

	Good	Fine	Mint
1	1.70	5.00	12.00
2-Extreme violence; Nostrand/Powell-a	2.30	7.00	16.00
3-5: 3-Powell-a	1.20	3.50	8.00

FIGHTING INDIAN STORIES (See Midget Comics)

FIGHTING INDIANS OF THE WILD WEST!
Mar, 1952 - No. 2, Nov, 1952
Avon Periodicals

	Good	Fine	Mint
1-Kinstler, Larsen-a	7.00	21.00	50.00
2-Kinstler-a	4.60	14.00	32.00
100 Pg. Annual(1952, 25 cents)-Contains three comics rebound	15.00	45.00	105.00

FIGHTING LEATHERNECKS
Feb, 1952 - No. 6, Dec, 1952
Toby Press

1-"Duke's Diary"-full pg. pin-ups by Sparling

FIGHTING LEATHERNECKS (continued)	Good	Fine	Mint
	4.60	14.00	32.00
2-"Duke's Diary"	3.00	9.00	21.00
3-5-"Gil's Gals"-full pg. pin-ups	3.00	9.00	21.00
6-(Same as No. 3-5?)	2.00	6.00	14.00

FIGHTING MAN, THE (War)
May, 1952 - No. 8, July, 1953
Ajax/Farrell Publications(Excellent Publ.)

	Good	Fine	Mint
1	2.00	6.00	14.00
2	1.00	3.00	7.00
3-8	.85	2.50	6.00
Annual 1 (100 pgs, 1952)	11.50	34.00	80.00

FIGHTIN' MARINES (Formerly The Texan; see Approved Comics)
No. 15, 8/51 - No. 10, 12/52; No. 14, 5/55 - No. 132, 11/76;
No. 133, 10/77 - No. 176, 9/84 (no No. 11-13)
St. John(Approved Comics)/Charlton Comics No. 14 on

	Good	Fine	Mint
15(No.1)-Matt Baker c/a "Leatherneck Jack;" slightly large size; Fightin' Texan No. 16 & 17?	8.50	25.50	60.00
2-1st Canteen Kate by Baker; slightly large size	11.50	34.00	80.00
3-9-Canteen Kate by Matt Baker; Baker c-No. 2,3,5-9	6.00	18.00	42.00
10 (12/52; last St. John issue; see Approved Comics)-Baker-c	1.50	4.50	10.00
14 (5/55; 1st Charlton issue; formerly?)-Canteen Kate by Baker	4.60	14.00	32.00
15-Baker-c	1.50	4.50	10.00
16,18-20-Not Baker-c	.85	2.50	6.00
17-Canteen Kate by Baker	4.60	14.00	32.00
21-24	.50	1.50	3.50
25-(68 pgs.)(3/58)-Check-a(5)	1.15	3.50	8.00
26-(100 pgs.)(8/58)	2.00	6.00	14.00
27-50		.60	1.20
51-81,83-100: 78-Shotgun Harker & the Chicken series begin		.40	.80
82-(100 pgs.)	.50	1.50	3.00
101-121		.30	.60
122-Pilot issue for "War" title (Fightin' Marines Presents War)		.30	.60
123-176		.30	.60
120(Modern Comics reprint, 1977)		.20	.40

NOTE: *No. 14 & 16 (CC) reprints St. John issue; No. 16 reprints St. John insignia on cover.* ***Colan*** *a-3, 7.* ***Glanzman*** *c/a-92, 94.* ***Montes/Bache*** *a-48, 53, 55, 64, 65, 72-74, 77-83, 176r.*

FIGHTING MARSHAL OF THE WILD WEST (See The Hawk)

FIGHTIN' NAVY (Formerly Don Winslow)
No. 74, 1/56 - No. 125, 4-5/66; No. 126, 8/83 - No. 133, 10/84
Charlton Comics

	Good	Fine	Mint
74	.70	2.00	5.00
75-81	.35	1.10	2.50
82-Sam Glanzman-a	.35	1.10	2.50
83-99,101-105	.25	.75	1.50
100	.35	1.00	2.00
106-125 ('66), 126-133('84)		.30	.60

NOTE: ***Montes/Bache*** *a-109.* ***Glanzman*** *a-131r.*

FIGHTING PRINCE OF DONEGAL, THE (See Movie Comics)

FIGHTIN' TEXAN (Formerly The Texan & Fightin' Marines No. 15?)
No. 16, Oct, 1952 - No. 17, Dec, 1952
St. John Publishing Co.

	Good	Fine	Mint
16,17-Tuska-a each. 17-Cameron-c/a	2.30	7.00	16.00

FIGHTING UNDERSEA COMMANDOS
1952 - No. 5, April, 1953
Avon Periodicals

	Good	Fine	Mint
1	4.00	12.00	28.00
2	2.65	8.00	18.00
3-5: 3-Ravielli-c. 4-Kinstler-c	2.35	7.00	16.00

FIGHTING WAR STORIES
Aug, 1952 - 1953
Men's Publications/Story Comics

	Good	Fine	Mint
1	1.75	5.25	12.00
2	.90	2.75	6.00
3-5	.60	1.80	4.00

FIGHTING YANK (See Startling & America's Best)
Sept, 1942 - No. 29, Aug, 1949
Nedor/Better Publ./Standard

	Good	Fine	Mint
1-The Fighting Yank begins; Mystico, the Wonder Man app; bondage-c	50.00	150.00	350.00
2	24.00	72.00	170.00
3	16.00	48.00	110.00
4	11.50	34.50	80.00
5-10: 7-The Grim Reaper app.	10.00	30.00	70.00
11-The Oracle app.	8.50	25.50	60.00
12-17: 12-Hirohito bondage-c.	8.50	25.50	60.00
18-The American Eagle app.	6.50	19.50	45.00
19,20	6.50	19.50	45.00
21,23,24: 21-Kara, Jungle Princess app. 24-Miss Masque app.	10.00	30.00	70.00
22-Miss Masque-c/story	11.50	34.00	80.00
25-Robinson/Meskin-a; strangulation, lingerie panel; The Cavalier app.	11.50	34.00	80.00
26-29: All-Robinson/Meskin-a. 28-One pg. Williamson-a	11.00	33.00	76.00

NOTE: ***Schomburg (Xela)*** *c-4-29; airbrush-c 28, 29. Bondage c-4, 8, 11, 15, 17.*

FIGHT THE ENEMY
Aug, 1966 - No. 3, Mar, 1967 (25 cents)
Tower Comics

	Good	Fine	Mint
1-Lucky 7 & Mike Manly begin	.40	1.20	2.40
2-Boris Vallejo, McWilliams-a	1.00	3.00	6.00
3-Wood-a ½pg; McWilliams, Bolle-a	.30	.80	1.60

FILM FUNNIES
Nov, 1949 - No. 2, Feb, 1950
Marvel Comics (CPC)

	Good	Fine	Mint
1	5.50	16.50	38.00
2	3.70	11.00	26.00

FILM STARS ROMANCES
Jan-Feb, 1950 - No. 3, May-June, 1950
Star Publications

	Good	Fine	Mint
1-Rudy Valentino story; L. B. Cole-c; lingerie panels	13.00	40.00	90.00
2-Liz Taylor/Robert Taylor photo-c	14.00	42.00	100.00
3-Photo-c	11.00	33.00	76.00

FINAL CYCLE, THE
July, 1987 - No. 4, 1988 (mini-series, color)
Dragon's Teeth Productions

	Good	Fine	Mint
1	.60	1.75	3.50

FIRE AND BLAST
1952 (16 pgs.; paper cover) (Giveaway)
National Fire Protection Assoc.

	Good	Fine	Mint
Mart Baily A-Bomb cover; about fire prevention	12.00	35.00	70.00

FIRE BALL XL5 (See Steve Zodiac)

FIRE CHIEF AND THE SAFE OL' FIREFLY, THE
1952 (16 pgs.) (Safety brochure given away at schools)

Fightin' Marines #5, © STJ

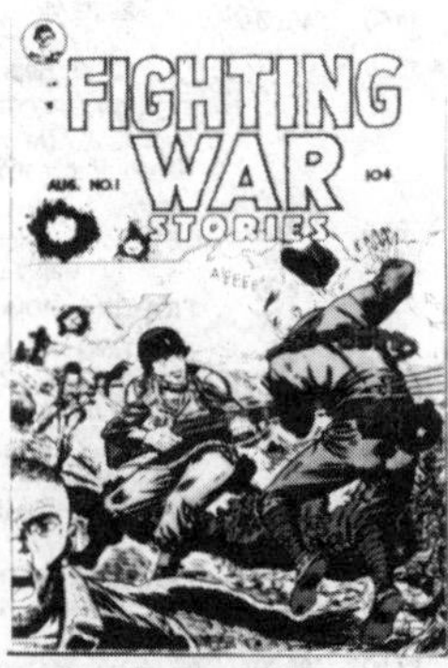

Fighting War Stories #1, © Men's Publ.

Fighting Yank #22, © STD

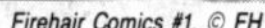
Firehair Comics #1, © FH

First Issue Special #7, © DC

First Romance Magazine #16, © HARV

FIRE CHIEF. . . (continued)
National Board of Fire Underwriters (produced by American Visuals Corp.) (Eisner)

	Good	Fine	Mint
(Rare) Eisner c/a	25.00	75.00	175.00

FIREHAIR COMICS (Pioneer West Romances #3-6; also see Rangers Comics)
Winter/48-49 - No. 2, Spr/49; No. 7, Spr/51 - No. 11, Spr/52
Fiction House Magazines (Flying Stories)

1	16.00	48.00	110.00
2	7.00	21.00	50.00
7-11	6.00	18.00	42.00
I.W. Reprint 8-Kinstler-c; reprints Rangers #57; Dr. Drew story by Grandenetti (nd)	.85	2.50	5.00

FIRESTAR
March, 1986 - No. 4, June, 1986 (From TV Spider-Man series)
Marvel Comics Group

1-X-Men & New Mutants app.	.35	1.00	2.00
2-4: 3-Art Adams c(p)	.25	.75	1.50

FIRESTONE (See Donald & Mickey)

FIRESTORM (See Cancelled Comic Cavalcade, DC Comics Presents & Flash #289)
March, 1978 - No. 5, Oct-Nov, 1978 (See The Fury of. . .)
DC Comics

1-Origin & 1st app.	.50	1.50	3.00
2-5: 2-Origin Multiplex. 3-Origin Killer Frost. 4-1st app. Hyena	.35	1.00	2.00

FIRESTORM, THE NUCLEAR MAN (Formerly Fury of Firestorm)
No. 65, Nov, 1987 - Present
DC Comics

65-70		.40	.80
Annual 5 (10/87)		.65	1.30

FIRST ADVENTURES
Dec, 1985 - No. 5, Apr, 1986
First Comics

1-5: 1-Blaze Barlow, Whisper & Dynamo Joe begin		.65	1.30

FIRST AMERICANS, THE (See 4-Color No. 843)

FIRST CHRISTMAS, THE (3-D)
1953 (25 cents) (Oversized - 8¼x10¼")
Fiction House Magazines (Real Adv. Publ. Co.)

nn-(Scarce)-Kelly Freas-c	24.00	72.00	170.00

FIRST COMICS GRAPHIC NOVEL
Jan, 1984 - Present (52-176 pgs, high quality paper)
First Comics

	Good	Fine	Mint
1-Beowulf ($5.95)	1.00	3.00	6.00
1-2nd printing	1.15	3.50	7.00
2-Time Beavers ($5.95)	1.00	3.00	6.00
3($11.95, 100 pgs.)-Hard Times; American Flagg-r	2.00	6.00	11.95
4-Nexus ($6.95)-r/B&W 1-3	1.30	4.00	8.00
5-The Enchanted Apples of Oz ($7.95, 52pp)-Intro by Harlan Ellison (1986)	1.35	4.00	7.95
6-Elric of Melnibone ($14.95, 176pp)-r with new color	2.50	7.50	14.95
7-The Secret Island Of Oz ($7.95)	1.35	4.00	7.95
8-Teenage Mutant Ninja Turtles (132 pgs., r-/TMNT No. 1-3 in color w/12 pgs. new-a ($9.95)	1.70	5.00	9.95
9-Time 2: The Epiphany by Chaykin, 52 pgs. ($7.95)	1.35	4.00	7.95
10-Teenage Mutant Ninja Turtles	1.70	5.00	9.95
11-Sailor On The Sea of Fate	2.50	7.50	14.95
12-American Flagg!	2.00	6.00	11.95
13-The Ice King Of Oz	1.35	4.00	7.95
14-Teenage Mutant Ninja Turtles Book III	1.70	5.00	9.95

FIRST ISSUE SPECIAL
April, 1975 - No. 13, April, 1976
National Periodical Publications

1-Intro. Atlas; Kirby c/a	.25	.75	1.50
2-7: 2-Green Team (See Cancelled Comic Cavalcade). 3-Metamorpho. 4-Lady Cop. 5-Manhunter; Kirby c/a. 6-Dingbats; Kirby c/a, 7-The Creeper		.50	1.00
8-The Warlord (origin); Grell c/a	2.50	7.50	15.00
9-Dr. Fate; Kubert-c; Simonson-a		.30	.60
10-13: 10-The Outsiders. 11-Code Name: Assassin; Redondo-a. 12-Origin/1st app. new Starman. 13-Return of the New Gods		.30	.60

FIRST KISS
Dec, 1957 - No. 40, Jan, 1965
Charlton Comics

V1#1	1.00	3.00	7.00
V1#2-10	.50	1.50	3.00
11-40		.50	1.00

FIRST LOVE ILLUSTRATED
2/49 - No. 9, 6/50; No. 10, 1/51 - No. 86, 3/58; No. 87, 9/58 - No. 88, 11/58; No. 89, 11/62, No. 90, 2/63
Harvey Publications(Home Comics)(True Love)

1-Powell-a(2)	3.50	10.50	24.00
2-Powell-a	2.00	6.00	14.00
3-"Was I Too Fat To Be Loved" story	2.50	7.50	17.00
4-10	1.70	5.00	12.00
11-30: 30-Lingerie panel	1.00	3.00	7.00
31-34,37,39-49: 49-Last pre-code (2/55)	.85	2.50	6.00
35-Used in **SOTI**, illo-"The title of this comic book is First Love;"	8.00	24.00	56.00
36-Communism story, "Love Slaves"	1.15	3.50	8.00
38-Nostrand-a	2.00	6.00	14.00
50-90	.50	1.50	3.50

NOTE: ***Disbrow** a-13. **Orlando** c-87. **Powell** a-1, 3-5, 7, 10, 11, 13-17, 19-24, 26-29, 33, 35-41, 43, 45, 46, 50, 54, 55, 57, 58, 61-63, 65, 71-73, 76, 79r, 82, 84, 88.*

FIRST MEN IN THE MOON (See Movie Comics)

FIRST ROMANCE MAGAZINE
8/49 - #6, 6/50; #7, 6/51 - #50, 2/58; #51, 9/58 - #52, 11/58
Home Comics(Harvey Publ.)/True Love

1	3.50	10.50	24.00
2	2.00	6.00	14.00
3-5	1.70	5.00	12.00
6-10	1.35	4.00	9.00
11-20	1.00	3.00	7.00
21-27,29-32: 32-Last pre-code (2/55)	.70	2.00	5.00
28-Nostrand-a(Powell swipe)	1.70	5.00	12.00
33-52	.50	1.50	3.50

NOTE: ***Powell** a-1-5,8-10,14,18,20-22,24,25,28,36,46,48,51.*

FIRST TRIP TO THE MOON (See Space Advs. No. 20)

5-STAR SUPER-HERO SPEC. (See DC Special Series No. 1)

FLAME, THE
Summer, 1940 - No. 8, Jan, 1942
Fox Features Syndicate

1-Flame stories from Wonderworld No. 5-9; origin The Flame; Lou Fine-a, 36 pgs., r-/Wonderworld 3,10	100.00	300.00	700.00
2-Fine-a(2). Wing Turner by Tuska	50.00	150.00	350.00
3-8: 3-Powell-a	25.00	75.00	175.00

FLAME, THE (Formerly Lone Eagle)
No. 5, Dec-Jan, 1954-55 - No. 4, June-July, 1955
Ajax/Farrell Publications (Excellent Publ.)

	Good	Fine	Mint
5(No.1)	8.50	25.50	60.00
2-4	5.70	17.00	40.00

FLAMING CARROT
Summer-Fall, 1981 (One Shot) (Large size, 8½x11")
Kilian Barracks Press

	Good	Fine	Mint
1-By Bob Burden	14.00	42.50	85.00

FLAMING CARROT (Also see Anything Goes)
5/84 - No. 5, 1/85; No. 6, 3/85 - Present (B&W)
Aardvark-Vanaheim/Renegade Press No. 6 on

	Good	Fine	Mint
1-Bob Burden story/a	7.00	21.00	40.00
2	4.00	12.00	24.00
3	3.00	9.00	18.00
4,5	2.00	6.00	12.00
6-9	1.25	3.75	7.50
10-17	.40	1.25	2.50

FLAMING LOVE
Dec, 1949 - No. 6, Oct, 1950 (Photo covers No. 2-6)
Quality Comics Group (Comic Magazines)

	Good	Fine	Mint
1-Ward-c, 9 pgs.	14.00	42.00	100.00
2	6.00	18.00	42.00
3-Ward-a, 9 pgs.; Crandall-a	10.00	30.00	70.00
4-6: 4-Gustavson-a	5.00	15.00	35.00

FLAMING WESTERN ROMANCES
Nov-Dec, 1949 - No. 3, Mar-Apr, 1950
Star Publications

	Good	Fine	Mint
1-L. B. Cole-c	11.00	33.00	75.00
2-L. B. Cole-c	7.00	21.00	50.00
3-Robert Taylor, Arlene Dahl photo-c with biographies inside; L. B. Cole-c; spanking panel	17.00	51.00	120.00

FLASH, THE (Formerly Flash Comics)(See Adventure, The Brave & the Bold, DC Comics Presents, DC Special Series, DC Super-Stars, Green Lantern, Showcase, Super Team Family, & World's Finest)
No. 105, Feb-Mar, 1959 - No. 350, Oct, 1985
National Periodical Publications/DC Comics

	Good	Fine	Mint
105-Origin Flash(retold), & Mirror Master	78.00	195.00	550.00
106-Origin Grodd & Pied Piper	31.00	78.00	220.00
107-109	13.00	33.00	88.00
110-Intro/origin Kid Flash & The Weather Wizard	16.00	40.00	110.00
111,115	6.30	16.00	44.00
112-Intro & origin Elongated Man	7.00	18.00	50.00
113-Origin Trickster	5.70	14.00	40.00
114-Origin Captain Cold	5.70	14.00	40.00
116-120: 117-Origin Capt. Boomerang. 119-Elongated Man marries Sue Dearborn	4.60	12.00	32.00
121,122: 122-Origin & 1st app. The Top	3.50	9.00	24.00
123-Re-intro. Golden Age Flash; origins of both Flashes; 1st mention of an Earth II where DC Golden Age heroes live	24.00	60.00	165.00
124-Last 10 cent issue	2.85	7.00	20.00
125-128,130: 128-Origin Abra Kadabra	1.50	4.50	9.00
129-G.A. Flash x-over; J.S.A. cameo (1st since 2-3/51)	7.00	16.00	44.00
131-136,138-140: 136-1st Dexter Miles. 139-Origin Prof. Zoom. 140-Origin & 1st app. Heat Wave	1.50	4.50	9.00
137-G.A. Flash x-over; J.S.A. cameo; 1st Silver Age app. Vandall Savage	2.00	6.00	12.00
141-150	.90	2.75	5.50
151-159: 151-G.A. Flash x-over	.70	2.00	4.00
160-80-Pg. Giant G-21-G.A.-r Flash & Johnny Quick	.90	2.75	5.50
161-168,170: 165-Silver Age Flash weds Iris West. 167-New facts about Flash's origin. 170-Dr. Mid-Nite, Dr. Fate, G.A. Flash x-over	.35	1.10	2.20
169-80-Pg. Giant G-34	.75	2.20	4.40
171-177,179,180: 171-JLA, Green Lantern, Atom flashbacks. 173-G.A. Flash x-over. 174-Barry Allen reveals I.D. to wife. 175-2nd Superman/Flash race; JLA cameo	.35	1.10	2.20
178-80-Pg. Giant G-46	.55	1.70	3.40
181-186,188-190: 186-Re-intro. Sargon	.30	.85	1.70
187-68-Pg. Giant G-58	.35	1.10	2.20
191-195,197-200	.30	.85	1.70
196-68-Pg. Giant G-70	.35	1.05	2.10
201-204,206-210: 201-New G.A. Flash story. 208-52 pg. begin, end No. 213,215,216. 206-Elongated Man begins		.65	1.30
205-68-Pg. Giant G-82	.35	1.05	2.10
211-213,216,220: 211-G.A. Flash origin (#104). 213-All-r.		.65	1.30
214-Giant DC-11; origin Metal Men-r; 1st pubbed G.A. Flash story	.35	1.05	2.10
215 (52 pgs.)-Flash-r/Showcase 4; G.A. Flash x-over, r-in #216		.65	1.30
217-219: Adams-a in all. 217-Green Lantern/Green Arrow series begins. 219-Last Green Arrow	.85	2.60	5.20
221-225,227,228,230,231		.50	1.00
226-Adams-a	.55	1.60	3.20
229,232,233-(100 pgs. each)	.35	1.05	2.10
234-270: 243-Death of The Top. 246-Last Green Lantern. 256-Death of The Top retold. 267-Origin of Flash's uniform. 270-Intro The Clown		.50	1.00
271-274,277-288,290: 286-Intro/origin Rainbow Raider		.50	1.00
275,276-Iris West Allen dies	.30	.85	1.70
289-Perez 1st DC art; new Firestorm series begins, ends #304		.50	1.00
291-299,301-305: 291-Intro/origin Colonel Computron. 298-Intro/origin Shade. 301-Atomic Bomb-c. 303-The Top returns. 305-G.A. Flash x-over		.50	1.00
300-52pgs.; origin Flash retold	.30	.85	1.70
306-Dr. Fate by Giffen begins, ends 313	.35	1.05	2.10
307-313-Giffen-a. 309-Origin Flash retold	.25	.75	1.50
314-330: 324-Death of Reverse Flash (Prof. Zoom). 328-Iris West Allen's death retold		.50	1.00
331-349: 344-Origin Kid Flash		.50	1.00
350-Double size ($1.25)	.55	1.60	3.20
Annual 1(10-12/63, 84pgs.)-Origin Elongated Man & Kid Flash-r; origin Grodd, G.A. Flash-r	5.50	14.00	38.00

NOTE: ***Adams*** *c-194, 195, 203, 204, 206-208, 211, 213, 215, 246.* ***Aparo*** *c-311.* ***Austin*** *a-233i, 234i.* ***Buckler*** *a-271p, 272p; c(p)-247-50, 252, 253p, 255, 256p, 258, 262, 265-67, 269-71.* ***Giffen*** *a-306p-313p; c-310p, 315.* ***Sid Greene*** *a-167-74i, 229i(r).* ***Grell*** *a-237p, 238p, 240-43p; c-236.* ***G. Kane*** *a-195p, 197-99p, 229r, 232r; c-197-99, 312p.* ***Kubert*** *a-108p, 215i(r); c-189-191.* ***Lopez*** *c-272.* ***Meskin*** *a-229r, 232r.* ***Perez*** *a-289-293p; c-293.* ***Starlin*** *a-294-296p.* ***Staton*** *c-263p, 264p. Green Lantern x-over-131, 143, 168, 171, 191.*

FLASH
June, 1987 - Present
DC Comics

	Good	Fine	Mint
1-Guice c/a in all; New Teen Titans app.	1.00	3.00	6.00
2,3: 3-Intro. Kilgore	.45	1.40	2.80
4-6: 5-Intro. Speed McGee	.25	.70	1.40
7-12		.50	1.00
Annual #1 (9/87)	.25	.75	1.50

FLASH COMICS (Whiz Comics No. 2 on)
Jan, 1940 (12 pgs., B&W, regular size)
(Not distributed to newsstands; printed for in-house use)

The Flame #2, © AJAX

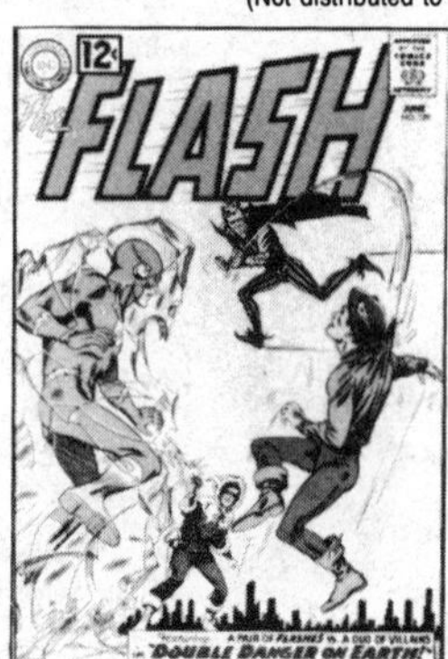

The Flash #129, © DC

Flash #1 ('87), © DC

Flash Comics #21, © DC

Flash Comics #101, © DC

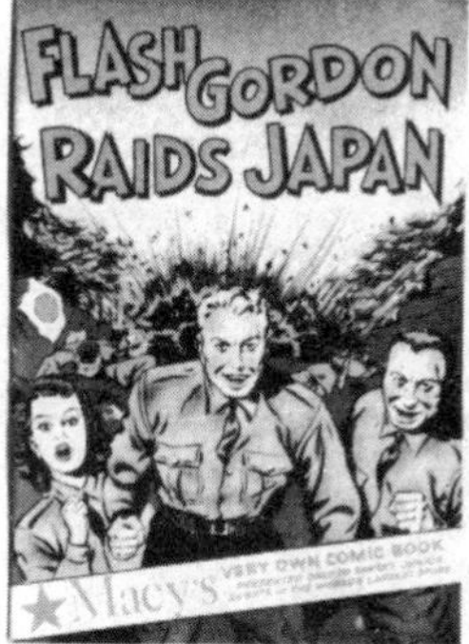

Flash Gordon, Macy's Giveaway, © KING

FLASH COMICS (continued)
Fawcett Publications

NOTE: **Whiz Comics** No. 2 was preceded by two books, **Flash Comics** and **Thrill Comics**, both dated Jan, 1940, (12 pgs, B&W, regular size) and were not distributed. These two books are identical except for the title. It is believed that the complete 68 page issue of Fawcett's **Flash** and **Thrill Comics** No. 1 was finished and ready for publication with the January date. Since D.C. Comics was also about to publish a book with the same date and title, Fawcett hurriedly printed up the black and white version of **Flash Comics** to secure copyright before D.C. The inside covers are blank, with the covers and inside pages printed on a high quality uncoated paper stock. The eight page origin story of Captain Thunder is composed of pages 1-7 and 13 of the Captain Marvel story essentially as they appeared in the first issue of **Whiz Comics**. The balloon dialogue on page thirteen was relettered to tie the story into the end of page seven in **Flash** and **Thrill Comics** to produce a shorter version of the origin story for copyright purposes. Obviously, D.C. acquired the copyright and Fawcett dropped **Flash** as well as **Thrill** and came out with **Whiz Comics** a month later. Fawcett never used the cover to **Flash** and **Thrill** No. 1, designing a new cover for **Whiz Comics**. Fawcett also must have discovered that Captain Thunder had already been used by another publisher. All references to Captain Thunder were relettered to Captain Marvel before appearing in **Whiz**.

1 (nn on-c, No. 1 on inside)-Origin & 1st app. Captain Thunder.
Eight copies of **Flash** and three copies of **Thrill** exist. All 3 copies of Thrill sold in 1986 for between $4,000-$10,000 each. A vg copy of Flash sold in 1987 for $9000 cash; another copy sold in 1987 for $2000 cash, $10,000 trade.

FLASH COMICS (The Flash No. 105 on) (Also see All-Flash)
Jan, 1940 - No. 104, Feb, 1949
National Periodical Publications/All-American

	Good	Fine	Mint
1-Origin The Flash by Harry Lampert, Hawkman by Gardner Fox, The Whip, & Johnny Thunder by Stan Asch; Cliff Cornwall by Moldoff, Minute Movies begin; Moldoff (Shelly) cover; 1st app. Shiera Sanders who later becomes Hawkgirl, #24; reprinted in Famous First Edition	630.00	1890.00	4400.00
2-Rod Rian begins, ends #11	200.00	600.00	1400.00
3-The King begins, ends #41	150.00	450.00	1050.00
4-Moldoff (Shelly) Hawkman begins	130.00	390.00	910.00
5	115.00	345.00	805.00
6,7	90.00	270.00	630.00
8-10: 8-Male bondage-c	73.00	220.00	510.00
11-20: 12-Les Watts begins; "Sparks" #16 on. 17-Last Cliff Cornwall	53.00	160.00	370.00
21-23	43.00	130.00	300.00
24-Shiera becomes Hawkgirl	53.00	160.00	370.00
25-30: 28-Last Les Sparks. 29-Ghost Patrol begins(origin, 1st app.), ends #104	37.00	110.00	260.00
31-40: 35-Origin Shade	30.00	90.00	210.00
41-50	26.00	78.00	180.00
51-61: 59-Last Minute Movies. 61-Last Moldoff Hawkman	21.00	64.00	150.00
62-Hawkman by Kubert begins	30.00	90.00	210.00
63-70: 66-68-Hop Harrigan in all	24.00	72.00	170.00
71-80: 80-Atom begins, ends #104	24.00	72.00	170.00
81-85	24.00	72.00	170.00
86-Intro. The Black Canary in Johnny Thunder; rare in Mint due to black ink smearing on white cover	65.00	195.00	455.00
87-90: 88-Origin Ghost	30.00	90.00	210.00
91,93-99: 98-Atom dons new costume	40.00	120.00	280.00
92-1st solo Black Canary	65.00	195.00	455.00
100,103(Scarce)	73.00	220.00	510.00
101,102(Scarce)	59.00	177.00	410.00
104-Origin The Flash retold (Scarce)	143.00	430.00	1000.00
Wheaties Giveaway (1946, 32 pgs., 6½x8¼")-Johnny Thunder, Ghost Patrol, The Flash & Kubert Hawkman app. NOTE: All known copies were taped to Wheaties boxes and are never found in mint condition. Copies with light tape residue bring the listed prices in all grades	25.00	75.00	175.00

NOTE: ***Infantino** a-86p, 90, 93-95, 99-104. **Kinstler** a-87, 89(Hawkman). **Chet Kozlak** c-77, 79, 81. **Krigstein** a-94. **Kubert** a-62-76, 83, 85, 86, 88-104; c-63, 65, 67, 70, 71, 73, 75, 83, 85, 86, 88, 89, 91, 94, 96, 98, 100, 104. **Moldoff** c/a-3.*

FLASH DIGEST, THE (See DC Spec. Series 24)

FLASH GORDON (See Eat Right to Work..., Feature Book #25 (McKay), King Classics, King Comics, March of Comics #118, 133, 142, Street Comix & Wow comics, 1st series)

FLASH GORDON
No. 10, 1943 - No. 512, Nov, 1953
Dell Publishing Co.

	Good	Fine	Mint
4-Color 10(1943)-by Alex Raymond; reprints/"The Ice Kingdom"	50.00	150.00	350.00
4-Color 84(1945)-by Alex Raymond; reprints/"The Fiery Desert"	30.00	90.00	210.00
4-Color 173,190: 190-Bondage-c	10.00	30.00	70.00
4-Color 204,247	8.00	24.00	56.00
4-Color 424	6.00	18.00	42.00
2(5-7/53-Dell)-Evans-a	3.50	10.50	24.00
4-Color 512	3.50	10.50	24.00
Macy's Giveaway(1943)-(Rare)-20 pgs.; not by Raymond	60.00	160.00	320.00

FLASH GORDON (See Tiny Tot Funnies)
Oct, 1950 - No. 4, April, 1951
Harvey Publications

	Good	Fine	Mint
1-Alex Raymond-a; bondage-c	17.00	51.00	120.00
2-Alex Raymond-a	13.00	40.00	90.00
3,4-Alex Raymond-a	12.00	36.00	80.00

5-(Rare)-Small size-5½x8½"; B&W; 32 pgs.; Distributed to some mail subscribers only Estimated value.... $200.00—$300.00
(Also see All-New No. 15, Boy Explorers No. 2, and Stuntman No. 3)

FLASH GORDON
1951 (Paper cover; 16 pgs. in color; regular size)
Harvey Comics (Gordon Bread giveaway)

	Good	Fine	Mint
1 (1938), 2(1941?)-Reprints by Raymond each....	10.00	30.00	60.00

NOTE: *Most copies have brittle edges.*

FLASH GORDON
June, 1965
Gold Key

	Good	Fine	Mint
1 (1947 reprint)	1.75	5.25	12.00

FLASH GORDON (Also see Comics Reading Libraries)
9/66 - No. 18, 1/70; No. 19, 10-11/78 - No. 37, 3/82
(Painted covers No. 19-30,34)
King, No.1-11(12/67)/Charlton, No.12(2/69)-18/Gold Key, No.19-27/Whitman No. 28 on

	Good	Fine	Mint
1-Army giveaway(1968)("Complimentary" on cover)(Same as regular No. 1 minus Mandrake story & back-c)	1.20	3.50	8.00
1-Williamson c/a(2); E.C. swipe/Incred. S.F. 32. Mandrake sty	1.50	4.50	10.00
2-Bolle, Gil Kane-c/a; Mandrake sty	1.15	3.50	8.00
3-Williamson-c	1.30	4.00	9.00
4-Secret Agent X-9 begins, Williamson-c/a(3)	1.30	4.00	9.00
5-Williamson c/a(2)	1.30	4.00	9.00
6,8-Crandall-a. 8-Secret Agent X-9-r	1.50	4.50	12.00
7-Raboy-a	1.00	3.00	7.00
9,10-Raymond-r	1.30	4.00	9.00
11-Crandall-a	.85	2.50	6.00
12-Crandall c/a	1.00	3.00	7.00
13-Jeff Jones-a	1.00	3.00	7.00
14-17: 17-Brick Bradford sty	.50	1.50	3.00
18-Kaluta-a	.70	2.00	4.00
19(9/78, G.K.), 20-30(10/80)	.35	1.00	2.00
30 (7/81; re-issue)		.30	.60
31-33: Movie adapt; Williamson-a		.50	1.00
34-37: Movie adapt		.40	.80

NOTE: ***Aparo** a-8. **Bolle** a-21, 22. **Buckler** a-9, 10. **Crandall** c-6. **Estrada** a-3. **Gene Fawcette** a-29, 30, 34, 37. **McWilliams** a-31-33, 36.*

FLASH GORDON GIANT COMIC ALBUM
1972 (11x14"; cardboard covers; 48 pgs.; B&W; 59 cents)
Modern Promotions, N. Y.

	Good	Fine	Mint
Reprints 1968, 1969 dailies by Dan Barry	.25	.70	1.40

FLASH SPECTACULAR, THE (See DC Special Series No. 11)

FLAT TOP
11/53 - No. 3, 5/54; No. 4, 3/55 - No. 6, 7/55
Mazie Comics/Harvey Publ.(Magazine Publ.) No. 4 on

	Good	Fine	Mint
1	1.15	3.50	8.00
2,3	.70	2.00	4.00
4-6	.50	1.50	3.00

FLESH AND BONES
June, 1986 - No. 4, Dec, 1986 (mini-series)
Upshot Graphics (Fantagraphics Books)

	Good	Fine	Mint
1: Dalgoda by Fujitake-r	.40	1.25	2.50
2-4	.35	1.00	2.00

FLINTSTONE KIDS, THE (TV)
Aug, 1987 - Present
Star Comics (Marvel)

	Good	Fine	Mint
1-4		.50	1.00

FLINTSTONES, THE (TV)(See Dell Giant No.48 for No. 1)
No. 2, Nov-Dec, 1961 - No. 60, Sept, 1970 (Hanna-Barbera)
Dell Publ. Co./Gold Key No. 7 (10/62) on

	Good	Fine	Mint
2	2.30	7.00	16.00
3-6(7-8/62)	1.50	4.50	10.00
7 (10/62; 1st GK)	1.50	4.50	10.00
8-10: Mr. & Mrs. J. Evil Scientist begin?	1.30	4.00	9.00
11-1st app. Pebbles (6/63)	1.70	5.00	12.00
12-15,17-20	1.15	3.50	8.00
16-1st app. Bamm-Bamm (1/64)	1.50	4.50	10.00
21-30: 26,27-The Grusomes app.	.85	2.50	6.00
31-33,35-40: 31-Xmas-c. 33-Meet Frankenstein & Dracula. 39-Reprints	.70	2.00	5.00
34-1st app. The Great Gazoo	.85	2.50	6.00
41-60	.60	1.80	4.00
At N. Y. World's Fair('64)-J.W. Books(25 cents)-1st printing; no date on-c	1.75	5.25	12.00
At N. Y. World's Fair (1965 on-c; re-issue). NOTE: Warehouse find in 1984	.35	1.00	2.00
Bigger & Boulder 1(30013-211)G.K. Giant(25 cents); 84 pgs.	2.00	6.00	16.00
Bigger & Boulder 2-(25 cents)(1966)-reprints B&B No. 1	1.75	5.25	14.00
...With Pebbles & Bamm Bamm(100 pgs., G.K.)-30028-511 (paper-c, 25 cents)(11/65)	2.00	6.00	14.00

NOTE: *(See Comic Album No. 16, Bamm-Bamm & Pebbles Flintstone, Dell Giant 48, March of Comics No. 229, 243, 271, 289, 299, 317, 327, 341, Pebbles Flintstone, and Whitman Comic Books.)*

FLINTSTONES, THE (TV)(...& Pebbles)
Nov, 1970 - No. 50, Feb, 1977 (Hanna-Barbera)
Charlton Comics

	Good	Fine	Mint
1	1.15	3.50	8.00
2	.70	2.00	4.00
3-7,9,10	.50	1.50	3.00
8-"Flintstones Summer Vacation," 52 pgs. (Summer, 1971)	.70	2.00	4.00
11-20	.35	1.00	2.00
21-50: 42-Byrne-a, 2pgs.	.25	.75	1.50

(Also see Barney & Betty Rubble, Dino, The Great Gazoo, and Pebbles & Bamm-Bamm)

FLINTSTONES, THE (TV)(See Yogi Bear, 3rd series)
October, 1977 - No. 9, Feb, 1979 (Hanna-Barbera)
Marvel Comics Group

	Good	Fine	Mint
1-9: 1-Yogi Bear begins		.25	.50

FLINTSTONES CHRISTMAS PARTY, THE (See The Funtastic World of Hanna-Barbera No. 1)

FLINTSTONES 3-D
Apr, 1987 - Present ($2.25)
Blackthorne Publ.

	Good	Fine	Mint
1,2	.40	1.25	2.50

FLIP
April, 1954 - No. 2, June, 1954 (Satire)
Harvey Publications

	Good	Fine	Mint
1,2-Nostrand-a each. 2-Powell-a	6.00	18.00	42.00

FLIPPER (TV)
April, 1966 - No. 3, Nov, 1967 (Photo-c)
Gold Key

	Good	Fine	Mint
1	1.75	5.25	12.00
2,3	1.15	3.50	8.00

FLIPPITY & FLOP
12-1/51-52 - No. 46, 8-10/59; No. 47, 9-11/60
National Periodical Publ. (Signal Publ. Co.)

	Good	Fine	Mint
1	9.00	27.00	62.00
2	4.35	13.00	30.00
3-5	3.70	11.00	26.00
6-10	3.00	9.00	21.00
11-20	2.15	6.50	15.00
21-47	1.50	4.50	10.00

FLY, THE
May, 1983 - No. 9, Oct, 1984 (See The Advs. of...)
Archie Enterprises, Inc.

	Good	Fine	Mint
1-Mr. Justice app; origin Shield.		.50	1.00
2-9: 2-Flygirl app.		.40	.80

NOTE: ***Buckler** a-1, 2. **Ditko** a-2-9; c-4p-8p. **Nebres** c-4, 5i, 6, 7i. **Steranko** c-1-3.*

FLY BOY (Also see Approved Comics)
Spring, 1952 - No. 4, 1953
Ziff-Davis Publ. Co. (Approved)

	Good	Fine	Mint
1-Saunders painted-c	4.60	14.00	32.00
2-Saunders painted-c	3.00	9.00	21.00
3,4-Saunders painted-c	2.35	7.00	16.00

FLYING ACES
July, 1955 - No. 5, March, 1956
Key Publications

	Good	Fine	Mint
1	1.50	4.50	10.00
2-5: 2-Trapani-a	.85	2.50	6.00

FLYING A'S RANGE RIDER, THE (TV) (See 4-Color #404 for No. 1) (See Western Roundup)
No. 2, June-Aug, 1953 - No. 24, Aug, 1959 (All photo-c)
Dell Publishing Co.

	Good	Fine	Mint
2	3.50	10.50	24.00
3-10	3.00	9.00	21.00
11-16,18-24	2.65	8.00	18.00
17-Toth-a	3.50	10.50	24.00

FLYING CADET (WW II Plane Photos)
Jan, 1943 - 1947 (½ photos, ½ comics)
Flying Cadet Publishing Co.

	Good	Fine	Mint
V1#1	4.60	14.00	32.00
2	2.30	7.00	16.00
3-9 (Two #6's, Sept. & Oct.)	1.70	5.00	12.00
V2#1-7(#10-16)	1.30	4.00	9.00
8(#17)-Bare-breasted woman-c	4.35	13.00	30.00

The Flintstones With Pebbles... #1, © Hanna-Barbera

Flip #1, © HARV

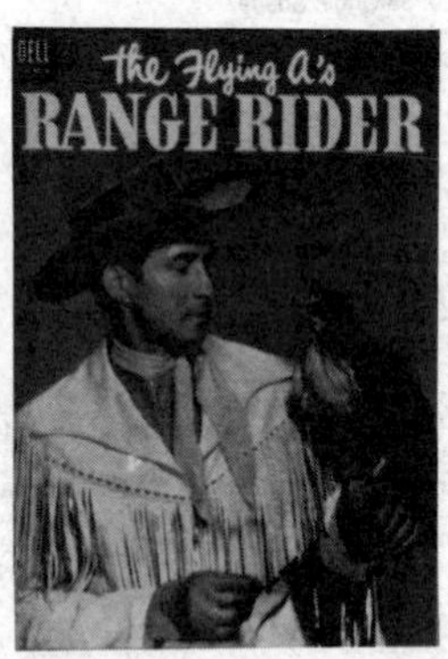

The Flying A's Range Rider #6, © Tie-Ups

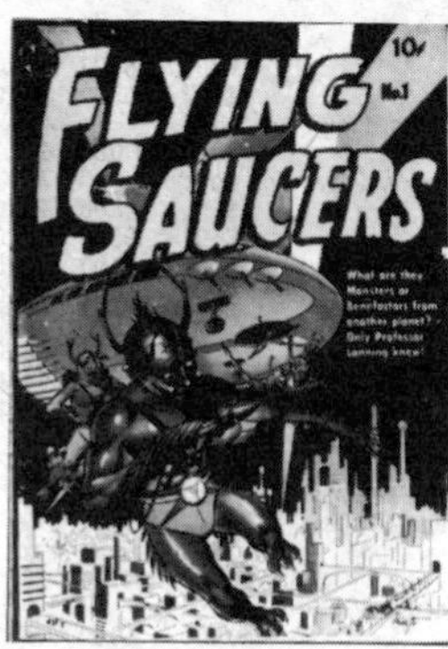

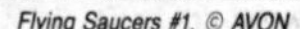
Flying Saucers #1, © AVON

For a Night of Love #1, © AVON

Forbidden Worlds #14, © ACG

FLYIN' JENNY
1946 - 1947 (1945 strip reprints)
Pentagon Publ. Co.

	Good	Fine	Mint
nn	4.60	14.00	32.00
2-Baker-c	6.00	18.00	42.00

FLYING MODELS
May, 1954 (16 pgs.) (5 cents)
H-K Publ. (Health-Knowledge Publs.)

V61#3 (Rare)	3.00	9.00	21.00

FLYING NUN (TV)
Feb, 1968 - No. 4, Nov, 1968
Dell Publishing Co.

1	1.35	4.00	8.00
2-4	.85	2.50	5.00

FLYING NURSES (See Sue & Sally Smith. . .)

FLYING SAUCERS
1950 - 1953
Avon Periodicals/Realistic

1(1950)-Wood-a, 21 pgs.	33.00	100.00	230.00
nn(1952)-Cover altered plus 2 pgs. of Wood-a not in original	30.00	90.00	210.00
nn(1953)-Reprints above	17.00	50.00	120.00

FLYING SAUCERS (Comics)
April, 1967 - No. 4, Nov, 1967; No. 5, Oct, 1969
Dell Publishing Co.

1	.85	2.50	5.00
2-5	.50	1.50	3.00

FLY MAN (Formerly Adv. of The Fly; Mighty Comics. . .No. 40 on)
No. 32, July, 1965 - No. 39, Sept, 1966
Mighty Comics Group (Radio Comics) (Archie)

32,33-Comet, Shield, Black Hood, The Fly & Flygirl x-over; re-intro. Wizard, Hangman No. 33	.85	2.50	5.00
34-Shield begins	.85	2.50	5.00
35-Origin Black Hood	.85	2.50	5.00
36-Hangman x-over in Shield; re-intro. & origin of Web	.85	2.50	5.00
37-Hangman, Wizard x-over in Flyman; last Shield issue	.85	2.50	5.00
38-Web story	.85	2.50	5.00
39-Steel Sterling story	.85	2.50	5.00

FOLLOW THE SUN (TV)
May-July, 1962 - No. 2, Sept-Nov, 1962 (Photo-c)
Dell Publishing Co.

01-280-207(No.1), 12-280-211(No.2)	1.75	5.25	12.00

FOODINI (TV)(The Great. .; see Pinhead &. . ., & Jingle Dingle)
March, 1950 - No. 5, 1950
Continental Publications (Holyoke)

1 (52 pgs.)	4.60	14.00	32.00
2	2.30	7.00	16.00
3-5	1.60	4.70	11.00

FOOEY (Magazine) (Satire)
Feb, 1961 - No. 4, May, 1961
Scoff Publishing Co.

1	1.20	3.50	7.00
2-4	.70	2.00	4.00

FOOFUR
Aug, 1987 - Present
Star Comics (Marvel)

1-5		.50	1.00

FOOTBALL THRILLS
Fall-Winter, 1951-52 - No. 2, 1952
Ziff-Davis Publ. Co.

	Good	Fine	Mint
1-Powell a(2); Saunders painted-c	7.00	21.00	50.00
2-Saunders painted-c	5.00	15.00	35.00

FOR A NIGHT OF LOVE
1951
Avon Periodicals

nn-Two stories adapted from the works of Emile Zola; Astarita, Ravielli-a; Kinstler-c	16.00	48.00	110.00

FORBIDDEN LOVE
Mar, 1950 - No. 4, Sept, 1950
Quality Comics Group

1-(Scarce)Classic photo-c; Crandall-a	50.00	150.00	350.00
2,3(Scarce)-Photo-c	22.00	65.00	150.00
4-(Scarce)Ward/Cuidera-a; photo-c	24.00	72.00	170.00

FORBIDDEN LOVE (See Dark Mansion of. . .)

FORBIDDEN TALES OF DARK MANSION (Dark Mansion of Forbidden Love #1-4)
No. 5, May-June, 1972 - No. 15, Feb-Mar, 1974
National Periodical Publications

5-15: 13-Kane/Howard-a		.25	.50

NOTE: *Alcala a-9-11, 13. Chaykin a-7,15. Evans a-14. Kaluta c-7-11, 13. G. Kane a-13. Kirby a-6. Nino a-8, 12, 15. Redondo a-14.*

FORBIDDEN WORLDS
7-8/51 - No. 34, 10-11/54; No. 35, 8/55 - No. 145, 8/67
(No.1-5: 52 pgs.; No.6-8: 44 pgs.)
American Comics Group

1-Williamson/Frazetta-a, 10pgs.	45.00	135.00	315.00
2	17.00	51.00	120.00
3-Williamson/Wood/Orlando-a, 7pgs.	21.00	62.00	145.00
4	9.00	27.00	62.00
5-Williamson/Krenkel-a, 8pgs.	17.00	51.00	120.00
6-Harrison/Williamson-a, 8pgs.	15.00	45.00	105.00
7,8,10	5.70	17.00	40.00
9-A-Bomb explosion story	6.50	19.50	45.00
11-20	4.00	12.00	28.00
21-33: 24-E.C. swipe by Landau	3.00	9.00	21.00
34(10-11/54)(Becomes Young Heroes #35 on)-Last pre-code ish; A-Bomb explosion story	3.00	9.00	21.00
35(8/55)-62	1.50	4.50	10.00
63,69,76,78-Williamson-a in all; w/Krenkel #69	3.00	9.00	21.00
64,66-68,70-72,74,75,77,79-90	.85	2.50	6.00
65-"There's a New Moon Tonight" listed in #114 as holding 1st record fan mail response	1.00	3.00	7.00
73-Intro., 1st app. Herbie by Whitney	12.50	37.50	75.00
91-93,95,97-100	.70	2.00	4.00
94-Herbie app.	4.00	12.00	24.00
96-Williamson-a	2.35	7.00	14.00
101-109,111-113,115,117-120	.50	1.50	3.00
110,114,116-Herbie app. 114 contains list of editor's top 20 ACG stories	2.00	6.00	12.00
121-124: 124-Magic Agent app.	.40	1.20	2.40
125-Magic Agent app.; intro. & origin Magicman series, ends #141	.50	1.50	3.00
126-130	.40	1.10	2.20
131,132,134-141: 136-Nemesis x-over in Magicman. 140-Mark Midnight app. by Ditko	.30	.90	1.80
133-Origin & 1st app. Dragonia in Magicman (1-2/66); returns #138	.30	.90	1.80
142-145	.25	.70	1.40

NOTE: *Buscema a-75, 79, 81, 82, 140r. Disbrow a-10. Ditko a-137p, 138, 140. Landau a-24, 28, 31-34, 48, 86r, 96, 143-45. Lazarus a-23. Moldoff a-31, 139r. Whitney a-115, 116, 137; c-40, 46, 57, 60, 68, 79, 90, 93, 94, 100, 102, 103, 106-108, 114, 129.*

FORCE, THE (See The Crusaders)

FORD ROTUNDA CHRISTMAS BOOK (See Christmas at the Rotunda)

FOREIGN INTRIGUES (Formerly Johnny Dynamite; Battlefield Action No. 16 on)
No. 13, 1956 - No. 15, Aug, 1956
Charlton Comics

	Good	Fine	Mint
13-15-Johnny Dynamite continues	1.70	5.00	12.00

FOREMOST BOYS (See Four Most)

FOREST FIRE (Also see Smokey The Bear)
1949 (dated-1950) (16 pgs., paper-c)
American Forestry Assn.(Commerical Comics)

	Good	Fine	Mint
nn-Intro/1st app. Smokey The Forest Fire Preventing Bear; created by Rudy Wendelein; Wendelein/Sparling-a; 'Carter Oil Co.' on back-c of original	10.00	30.00	70.00

FOREVER, DARLING (See 4-Color No. 681)

FOREVER PEOPLE
Feb-Mar, 1971 - No. 11, Oct-Nov, 1972
National Periodical Publications

	Good	Fine	Mint
1-Superman x-over; Kirby-c/a begins	.70	2.00	4.00
2-11: 4-G.A.-r begin, end No. 9	.35	1.00	2.00

NOTE: *Kirby c/a(p)-1-11; No. 4-9 contain Sandman reprints from Adventure No. 85, 84, 75, 80, 77, 74 in that order. No. 1-3, 10-11 are 36pgs; No. 4-9 are 52pgs.*

FOREVER PEOPLE
Feb, 1988 - No. 6, 1988 ($1.25, mini-series)
DC Comics

	Good	Fine	Mint
1,2		.60	1.25

FOR GIRLS ONLY
Nov, 1953 (Digest size, 100 pgs.)
Bernard Bailey Enterprises

	Good	Fine	Mint
1-½ comic book, ½ magazine	6.00	18.00	42.00

FORGOTTEN STORY BEHIND NORTH BEACH, THE
No date (8 pgs.; paper cover)
Catechetical Guild

	Good	Fine	Mint
	3.00	9.00	18.00

FOR LOVERS ONLY (Formerly Hollywood Romances)
No. 60, Aug, 1971 - No. 87, Nov, 1976
Charlton Comics

	Good	Fine	Mint
60-87		.25	.50

40 BIG PAGES OF MICKEY MOUSE
1936 (44 pgs.; 10¼x12½''; cardboard cover)
Whitman Publishing Co.

	Good	Fine	Mint
945-Reprints Mickey Mouse Magazine #1, but with a different cover. Ads were eliminated and some illustrated stories had expanded text. The book is ¾'' shorter than Mickey Mouse Mag. #1, but the reprints are the same size. (Rare)	40.00	120.00	280.00

48 FAMOUS AMERICANS
1947 (Giveaway) (Half-size in color)
J. C. Penney Co. (Cpr. Edwin H. Stroh)

	Good	Fine	Mint
Simon & Kirby-a	6.75	20.00	40.00

FOR YOUR EYES ONLY (See James Bond)

FOUR COLOR
Sept?, 1939 - No. 1354, Apr-June, 1962
Dell Publishing Co.

NOTE: *Four Color only appears on issues #19-25, 1-99,101. Dell Publishing Co. filed these as Series I, #1-25, and Series II, #1-1354. Issues beginning with #710? were printed with and without ads on back cover. Issues without ads are worth more.*

SERIES I:

	Good	Fine	Mint
1(nn)-Dick Tracy	100.00	300.00	700.00
2(nn)-Don Winslow of the Navy (#1) (Rare) (11/39?)	60.00	180.00	420.00
3(nn)-Myra North (1/40?)	22.00	65.00	154.00
4-Donald Duck by Al Taliaferro('40)(Disney) (3/40?)	270.00	810.00	1900.00
(Prices vary widely on this book)			
5-Smilin' Jack (#1) (5/40?)	35.00	105.00	245.00
6-Dick Tracy (Scarce)	65.00	195.00	455.00
7-Gang Busters	17.00	51.00	120.00
8-Dick Tracy	40.00	120.00	280.00
9-Terry and the Pirates-r/Super 9-29	37.00	110.00	260.00
10-Smilin' Jack	32.00	95.00	225.00
11-Smitty (#1)	19.00	57.00	132.00
12-Little Orphan Annie	28.00	84.00	195.00
13-Walt Disney's Reluctant Dragon('41)-Contains 2 pages of photos from film; 2 pg. foreword to Fantasia by Leopold Stokowski; Donald Duck, Goofy, Baby Weems & Mickey Mouse (as the Sorcerer's Apprentice) app. (Disney)	64.00	192.00	450.00
14-Moon Mullins (#1)	17.00	51.00	120.00
15-Tillie the Toiler (#1)	17.00	51.00	120.00
16-Mickey Mouse (#1) (Disney) by Gottfredson	250.00	750.00	1750.00
(Prices vary widely on this book)			
17-Walt Disney's Dumbo, the Flying Elephant (#1)(1941)-Mickey Mouse, Donald Duck, & Pluto app. (Disney)	65.00	195.00	455.00
18-Jiggs and Maggie (#1)(1936-'38-r)	17.00	51.00	120.00
19-Barney Google and Snuffy Smith (#1)-(1st issue with Four Color on the cover)	20.00	60.00	140.00
20-Tiny Tim	17.00	51.00	120.00
21-Dick Tracy	38.00	115.00	265.00
22-Don Winslow	13.00	40.00	90.00
23-Gang Busters	12.00	36.00	84.00
24-Captain Easy	17.00	51.00	120.00
25-Popeye	35.00	105.00	245.00

SERIES II:

	Good	Fine	Mint
1-Little Joe	22.00	65.00	154.00
2-Harold Teen	13.00	40.00	90.00
3-Alley Oop (#1)	29.00	85.00	200.00
4-Smilin' Jack	26.00	78.00	180.00
5-Raggedy Ann and Andy (#1)	27.00	81.00	190.00
6-Smitty	11.00	33.00	76.00
7-Smokey Stover (#1)	18.00	54.00	125.00
8-Tillie the Toiler	10.00	30.00	70.00
9-Donald Duck Finds Pirate Gold, by Carl Barks & Jack Hannah (Disney) (c. 8/17/42)	315.00	945.00	2200.00
(Prices vary widely on this book)			
10-Flash Gordon by Alex Raymond; r-/from ''The Ice Kingdom''	50.00	150.00	350.00
11-Wash Tubbs	16.00	48.00	110.00
12-Walt Disney's Bambi (#1)	29.00	85.00	200.00
13-Mr. District Attorney (#1)	12.00	36.00	84.00
14-Smilin' Jack	21.00	62.00	148.00
15-Felix the Cat (#1)	35.00	105.00	245.00
16-Porky Pig (#1)(1942)-''Secret of the Haunted House''	32.00	95.00	225.00
17-Popeye	28.00	84.00	195.00
18-Little Orphan Annie's Junior Commandos; Flag-c	21.00	64.00	150.00
19-Walt Disney's Thumper Meets the Seven Dwarfs (Disney); r-in Silly Symphonies	31.00	92.00	220.00
20-Barney Baxter	13.00	40.00	90.00
21-Oswald the Rabbit (#1)(1943)	18.00	54.00	125.00
22-Tillie the Toiler	8.00	24.00	56.00
23-Raggedy Ann and Andy	20.00	60.00	140.00
24-Gang Busters	12.00	36.00	84.00

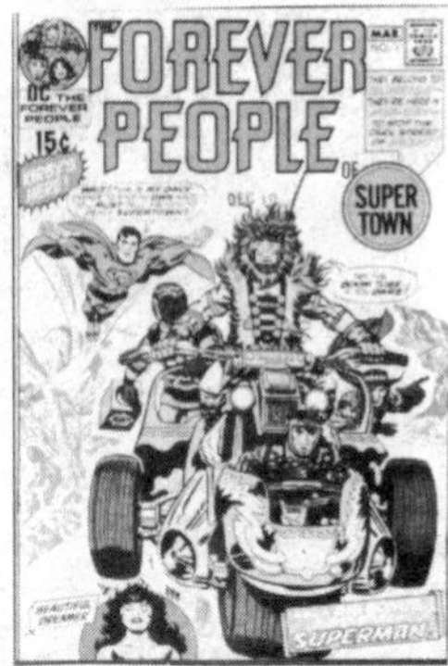

Forever People #1 (1st series), © DC

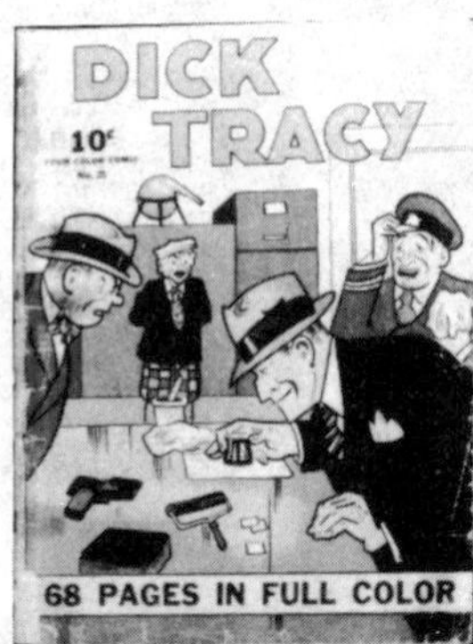

Four Color #21 (1st series), © N.Y. News Synd.

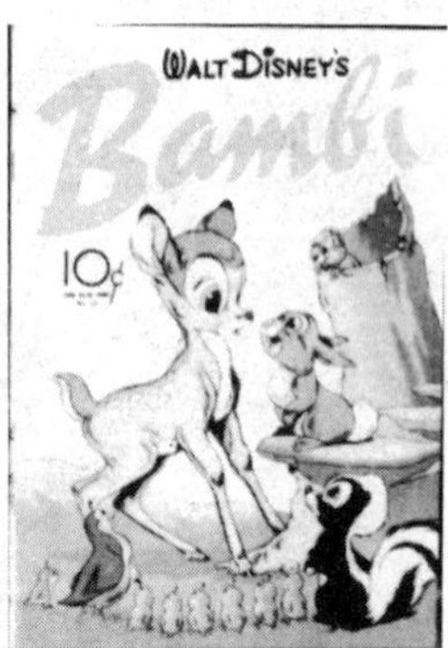

Four Color #12 (2nd series), © WDC

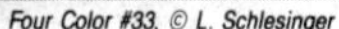
Four Color #33, © L. Schlesinger

Four Color #82, © Lone Ranger

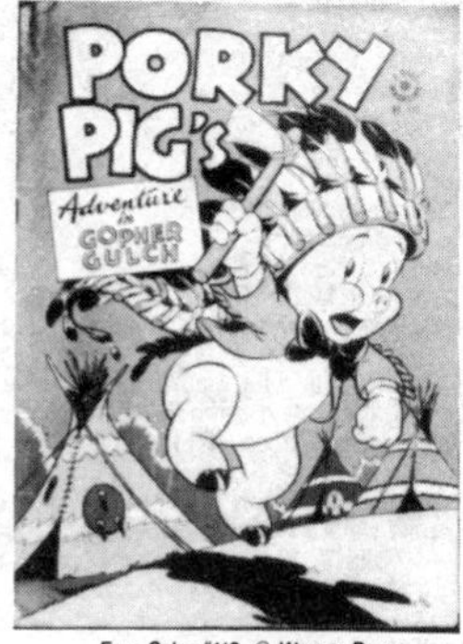

Four Color #112, © Warner Bros.

FOUR COLOR (continued)	**Good**	**Fine**	**Mint**
25-Andy Panda (#1) (Walter Lantz)	22.00	65.00	154.00
26-Popeye	26.00	78.00	180.00
27-Walt Disney's Mickey Mouse and the Seven Colored Terror	45.00	135.00	315.00
28-Wash Tubbs	12.00	36.00	84.00
29-Donald Duck and the Mummy's Ring, by Carl Barks (Disney) (9/43)	215.00	645.00	1505.00
(Prices vary widely on this book)			
30-Bambi's Children(1943)-Disney	27.00	81.00	190.00
31-Moon Mullins	10.00	30.00	70.00
32-Smitty	9.00	27.00	62.00
33-Bugs Bunny "Public Nuisance #1"	23.00	70.00	160.00
34-Dick Tracy	28.00	85.00	195.00
35-Smokey Stover	10.00	30.00	70.00
36-Smilin' Jack	12.00	36.00	84.00
37-Bringing Up Father	10.00	30.00	70.00
38-Roy Rogers (#1, c. 4/44)-1st western comic with photo-c	42.00	125.00	295.00
39-Oswald the Rabbit('44)	13.00	40.00	90.00
40-Barney Google and Snuffy Smith	11.00	32.00	75.00
41-Mother Goose and Nursery Rhyme Comics (#1)-All by Kelly	17.00	51.00	120.00
42-Tiny Tim (1934-r)	9.50	28.50	65.00
43-Popeye (1938-'42-r)	17.00	51.00	120.00
44-Terry and the Pirates	22.00	65.00	154.00
45-Raggedy Ann	15.00	45.00	105.00
46-Felix the Cat and the Haunted Castle	24.00	72.00	170.00
47-Gene Autry (© 6/16/44)	30.00	90.00	210.00
48-Porky Pig of the Mounties by Carl Barks (7/44)	62.00	185.00	435.00
49-Snow White and the Seven Dwarfs (Disney)	24.00	72.00	170.00
50-Fairy Tale Parade-Walt Kelly art (1944)	21.00	63.00	145.00
51-Bugs Bunny Finds the Lost Treasure	16.00	48.00	110.00
52-Little Orphan Annie	15.00	45.00	105.00
53-Wash Tubbs	8.50	25.50	60.00
54-Andy Panda	12.00	36.00	84.00
55-Tillie the Toiler	6.00	18.00	42.00
56-Dick Tracy	20.00	60.00	140.00
57-Gene Autry	24.00	72.00	170.00
58-Smilin' Jack	12.00	36.00	84.00
59-Mother Goose and Nursery Rhyme Comics-Kelly c/a	15.00	45.00	105.00
60-Tiny Folks Funnies	9.00	27.00	62.00
61-Santa Claus Funnies(11/44)-Kelly art	19.00	57.00	132.00
62-Donald Duck in Frozen Gold, by Carl Barks (Disney) (1/45)	118.00	354.00	825.00
63-Roy Rogers-Photo-c	28.00	84.00	195.00
64-Smokey Stover	7.00	21.00	50.00
65-Smitty	7.00	21.00	50.00
66-Gene Autry	24.00	72.00	170.00
67-Oswald the Rabbit	8.50	25.50	60.00
68-Mother Goose and Nursery Rhyme Comics, by Walt Kelly	15.00	45.00	105.00
69-Fairy Tale Parade, by Walt Kelly	18.00	54.00	125.00
70-Popeye and Wimpy	14.00	42.00	100.00
71-Walt Disney's Three Caballeros, by Walt Kelly(c. 4/45)-(Disney)	57.00	170.00	400.00
72-Raggedy Ann	13.00	40.00	90.00
73-The Gumps (No.1)	6.00	18.00	42.00
74-Marge's Little Lulu (No.1)	84.00	250.00	590.00
75-Gene Autry and the Wildcat	20.00	60.00	140.00
76-Little Orphan Annie	11.50	34.00	80.00
77-Felix the Cat	20.00	60.00	140.00
78-Porky Pig and the Bandit Twins	11.50	34.00	80.00
79-Walt Disney's Mickey Mouse in The Riddle of the Red Hat by Carl Barks(8/45)	57.00	171.00	400.00
80-Smilin' Jack	10.00	30.00	70.00
81-Moon Mullins	5.50	16.50	38.00
82-Lone Ranger	24.00	72.00	170.00
83-Gene Autry in Outlaw Trail	20.00	60.00	140.00
84-Flash Gordon by Alex Raymond-Reprints from "The Fiery Desert"	30.00	90.00	210.00
85-Andy Panda and the Mad Dog Mystery	8.00	24.00	56.00
86-Roy Rogers-Photo-c	21.00	62.00	148.00
87-Fairy Tale Parade by Walt Kelly; Dan Noonan cover	16.00	48.00	110.00
88-Bugs Bunny's Great Adventure	9.00	27.00	63.00
89-Tillie the Toiler	5.50	16.50	38.00
90-Christmas with Mother Goose by Walt Kelly (11/45)	15.00	45.00	105.00
91-Santa Claus Funnies by Walt Kelly (11/45)	14.00	42.00	100.00
92-Walt Disney's The Wonderful Adventures Of Pinocchio(1945); Donald Duck by Kelly, 16 pgs. (Disney)	24.00	72.00	168.00
93-Gene Autry in The Bandit of Black Rock	16.00	48.00	110.00
94-Winnie Winkle (1945)	7.00	21.00	50.00
95-Roy Rogers Comics-Photo-c	21.00	62.00	148.00
96-Dick Tracy	16.00	48.00	110.00
97-Marge's Little Lulu (1946)	45.00	135.00	315.00
98-Lone Ranger, The	21.00	64.00	150.00
99-Smitty	6.00	18.00	42.00
100-Gene Autry Comics-Photo-c	16.00	48.00	110.00
101-Terry and the Pirates	14.00	42.00	100.00

NOTE: *No. 101 is last issue to carry "Four Color" logo on cover; all issues beginning with No. 100 are marked ". . .O. S." (One Shot) which can be found in the bottom left-hand panel on the first page; the numbers following "O. S." relate to the year/month issued.*

	Good	**Fine**	**Mint**
102-Oswald the Rabbit-Walt Kelly art, 1 pg.	8.50	25.50	60.00
103-Easter with Mother Goose by Walt Kelly	14.00	42.00	100.00
104-Fairy Tale Parade by Walt Kelly	14.00	42.00	100.00
105-Albert the Alligator and Pogo Possum (No.1) by Kelly (4/46)	54.00	160.00	380.00
106-Tillie the Toiler	4.60	14.00	32.00
107-Little Orphan Annie	11.00	32.00	76.00
108-Donald Duck in The Terror of the River, by Carl Barks (Disney) (c. 4/16/46)	85.00	255.00	595.00
109-Roy Rogers Comics	17.00	51.00	120.00
110-Marge's Little Lulu	32.00	95.00	220.00
111-Captain Easy	7.00	21.00	50.00
112-Porky Pig's Adventure in Gopher Gulch	7.00	21.00	50.00
113-Popeye	8.00	24.00	56.00
114-Fairy Tale Parade by Walt Kelly	14.00	42.00	100.00
115-Marge's Little Lulu	32.00	95.00	220.00
116-Mickey Mouse and the House of Many Mysteries (Disney)	14.00	42.00	100.00
117-Roy Rogers Comics-Photo-c	12.00	36.00	84.00
118-Lone Ranger, The	21.00	64.00	150.00
119-Felix the Cat	14.00	42.00	100.00
120-Marge's Little Lulu	28.00	84.00	195.00
121-Fairy Tale Parade-(not Kelly)	8.00	24.00	56.00
122-Henry (No.1)(10/46)	5.00	15.00	35.00
123-Bugs Bunny's Dangerous Venture	5.00	15.00	35.00
124-Roy Rogers Comics-Photo-c	12.00	36.00	84.00
125-Lone Ranger, The	15.00	45.00	105.00
126-Christmas with Mother Goose by Walt Kelly (1946)	12.00	36.00	84.00
127-Popeye	8.00	24.00	56.00
128-Santa Claus Funnies-"Santa & the Angel" by Gollub; "A Mouse in the House" by Kelly	12.00	36.00	84.00
129-Walt Disney's Uncle Remus and His Tales of Brer Rabbit (No.1) (1946)	11.50	34.00	80.00
130-Andy Panda (Walter Lantz)	4.00	12.00	28.00

FOUR COLOR (continued)	Good	Fine	Mint
131-Marge's Little Lulu	28.00	84.00	195.00
132-Tillie the Toiler('47)	4.60	14.00	32.00
133-Dick Tracy	13.00	40.00	90.00
134-Tarzan and the Devil Ogre	32.00	95.00	225.00
135-Felix the Cat	11.50	34.00	80.00
136-Lone Ranger, The	15.00	45.00	105.00
137-Roy Rogers Comics-Photo-c	12.00	36.00	84.00
138-Smitty	5.00	15.00	35.00
139-Marge's Little Lulu (1947)	26.00	78.00	185.00
140-Easter with Mother Goose by Walt Kelly	12.00	36.00	84.00
141-Mickey Mouse and the Submarine Pirates (Disney)	13.00	40.00	90.00
142-Bugs Bunny and the Haunted Mountain	5.00	15.00	35.00
143-Oswald the Rabbit & the Prehistoric Egg	3.50	10.50	24.00
144-Roy Rogers Comics ('47)-Photo-c	12.00	36.00	84.00
145-Popeye	8.00	24.00	56.00
146-Marge's Little Lulu	26.00	78.00	185.00
147-Donald Duck in Volcano Valley, by Carl Barks (Disney)(5/47)	60.00	180.00	420.00
148-Albert the Alligator and Pogo Possum by Walt Kelly (5/47)	45.00	135.00	315.00
149-Smilin' Jack	7.00	21.00	50.00
150-Tillie the Toiler (6/47)	3.50	10.50	24.00
151-Lone Ranger, The	12.00	36.00	84.00
152-Little Orphan Annie	8.00	24.00	56.00
153-Roy Rogers Comics-Photo-c	9.00	27.00	62.00
154-Walter Lantz Andy Panda	4.00	12.00	28.00
155-Henry (7/47)	4.00	12.00	28.00
156-Porky Pig and the Phantom	5.00	15.00	35.00
157-Mickey Mouse & the Beanstalk (Disney)	13.00	40.00	90.00
158-Marge's Little Lulu	26.00	78.00	185.00
159-Donald Duck in the Ghost of the Grotto, by Carl Barks (Disney) (8/47)	52.00	156.00	364.00
160-Roy Rogers Comics-Photo-c	9.00	27.00	62.00
161-Tarzan and the Fires Of Tohr	28.00	84.00	195.00
162-Felix the Cat (9/47)	9.00	27.00	63.00
163-Dick Tracy	10.00	30.00	70.00
164-Bugs Bunny Finds the Frozen Kingdom	5.00	15.00	35.00
165-Marge's Little Lulu	26.00	78.00	185.00
166-Roy Rogers Comics-52 pgs.,Photo-c	9.00	27.00	62.00
167-Lone Ranger, The	12.00	36.00	84.00
168-Popeye (10/47)	8.00	24.00	56.00
169-Woody Woodpecker (No.1)-"Manhunter in the North"; drug use story	5.70	17.00	40.00
170-Mickey Mouse on Spook's Island (11/47)(Disney)-reprinted in M. M. No. 103	11.50	34.00	80.00
171-Charlie McCarthy (No.1) and the Twenty Thieves	5.00	15.00	35.00
172-Christmas with Mother Goose by Walt Kelly (11/47)	12.00	36.00	84.00
173-Flash Gordon	10.00	30.00	70.00
174-Winnie Winkle	4.00	12.00	28.00
175-Santa Claus Funnies by Walt Kelly ('47)	12.00	36.00	84.00
176-Tillie the Toiler (12/47)	3.50	10.50	24.00
177-Roy Rogers Comics-36 pgs, Photo-c	9.00	27.00	62.00
178-Donald Duck "Christmas on Bear Mountain" by Carl Barks; 1st app. Uncle Scrooge (Disney)(12/47)	58.00	175.00	405.00
179-Uncle Wiggily (No.1)-Walt Kelly-c	8.00	24.00	56.00
180-Ozark Ike (No.1)	6.00	18.00	42.00
181-Walt Disney's Mickey Mouse in Jungle Magic	11.50	34.00	80.00
182-Porky Pig in Never-Never Land (2/48)	5.00	15.00	35.00
183-Oswald the Rabbit (Lantz)	3.50	10.50	24.00
184-Tillie the Toiler	3.50	10.50	24.00
185-Easter with Mother Goose by Walt Kelly (1948)	11.50	34.00	80.00

	Good	Fine	Mint
186-Walt Disney's Bambi (4/48)-Reprinted as Bambi No. 3('56)	7.00	21.00	50.00
187-Bugs Bunny and the Dreadful Dragon	4.00	12.00	28.00
188-Woody Woodpecker (Lantz, 5/48)	4.35	13.00	30.00
189-Donald Duck in The Old Castle's Secret, by Carl Barks (Disney) (6/48)	52.00	156.00	364.00
190-Flash Gordon ('48)	10.00	30.00	70.00
191-Porky Pig to the Rescue	5.00	15.00	35.00
192-The Brownies (No.1)-by Walt Kelly (7/48)	11.50	34.00	80.00
193-M.G.M. Presents Tom and Jerry (No.1)(1948)	6.50	19.50	45.00
194-Mickey Mouse in The World Under the Sea (Disney)-Reprinted in M.M. No. 101	11.50	34.00	80.00
195-Tillie the Toiler	3.00	9.00	21.00
196-Charlie McCarthy in The Haunted Hide-Out	6.00	18.00	42.00
197-Spirit of the Border (No.1) (Zane Grey) (1948)	5.00	15.00	35.00
198-Andy Panda	4.00	12.00	28.00
199-Donald Duck in Sheriff of Bullet Valley, by Carl Barks; Barks draws himself on wanted poster, last page; used in **Love & Death** (Disney) (10/48)	52.00	156.00	364.00
200-Bugs Bunny, Super Sleuth (10/48)	4.00	12.00	28.00
201-Christmas with Mother Goose by Walt Kelly	11.00	32.00	76.00
202-Woody Woodpecker	2.65	8.00	18.00
203-Donald Duck in the Golden Christmas Tree, by Carl Barks (Disney) (12/48)	36.00	108.00	250.00
204-Flash Gordon (12/48)	8.00	24.00	56.00
205-Santa Claus Funnies by Walt Kelly	11.00	32.00	76.00
206-Little Orphan Annie	5.50	16.50	38.00
207-King of the Royal Mounted	11.50	34.00	80.00
208-Brer Rabbit Does It Again (Disney)(1/49)	7.00	21.00	50.00
209-Harold Teen	2.30	7.00	16.00
210-Tippie and Cap Stubbs	2.30	7.00	16.00
211-Little Beaver (No.1)	3.00	9.00	21.00
212-Dr. Bobbs	2.30	7.00	16.00
213-Tillie the Toiler	3.00	9.00	21.00
214-Mickey Mouse and His Sky Adventure (2/49)(Disney)-Reprinted in M.M. No. 105	8.50	25.50	60.00
215-Sparkle Plenty (Dick Tracy reprints by Gould)	7.00	21.00	50.00
216-Andy Panda and the Police Pup (Lantz)	2.30	7.00	16.00
217-Bugs Bunny in Court Jester	4.00	12.00	28.00
218-3 Little Pigs and the Wonderful Magic Lamp (Disney)(3/49)	6.50	19.50	45.00
219-Swee'pea	6.50	19.50	45.00
220-Easter with Mother Goose by Walt Kelly	11.00	32.00	76.00
221-Uncle Wiggily-Walt Kelly cover in part	6.50	19.50	45.00
222-West of the Pecos (Zane Grey)	4.00	12.00	28.00
223-Donald Duck "Lost in the Andes" by Carl Barks (Disney-4/49) (square egg story)	50.00	150.00	350.00
224-Little Iodine (No.1), by Hatlo (4/49)	3.75	11.25	26.00
225-Oswald the Rabbit (Lantz)	2.30	7.00	16.00
226-Porky Pig and Spoofy, the Spook	3.50	10.50	24.00
227-Seven Dwarfs (Disney)	6.50	19.50	45.00
228-Mark of Zorro, The (No.1) ('49)	14.00	42.00	100.00
229-Smokey Stover	2.65	8.00	18.00
230-Sunset Pass (Zane Grey)	4.00	12.00	28.00
231-Mickey Mouse and the Rajah's Treasure (Disney)	8.50	25.50	60.00
232-Woody Woodpecker (Lantz, 6/49)	2.65	8.00	18.00
233-Bugs Bunny, Sleepwalking Sleuth	4.00	12.00	28.00
234-Dumbo in Sky Voyage (Disney)	5.70	17.00	40.00
235-Tiny Tim	3.00	9.00	21.00
236-Heritage of the Desert (Zane Grey)('49)	4.00	12.00	28.00

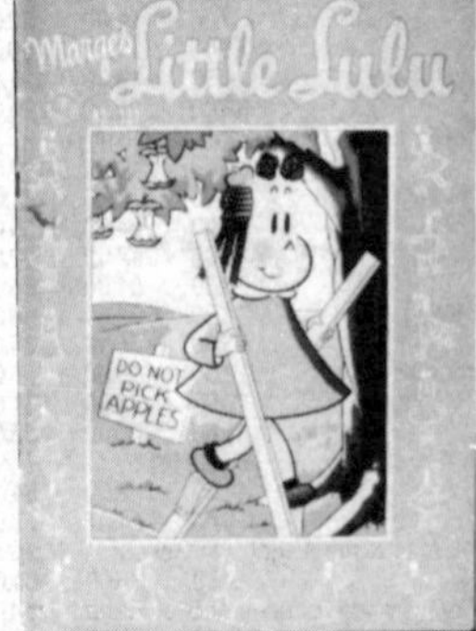

Four Color #131, © WEST

Four Color #172, © DELL

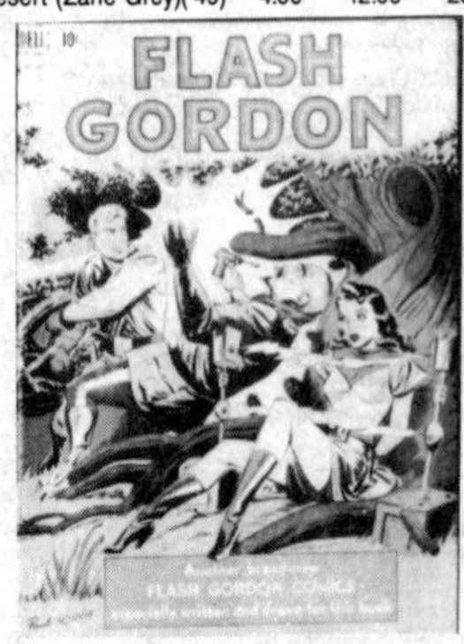

Four Color #190, © KING

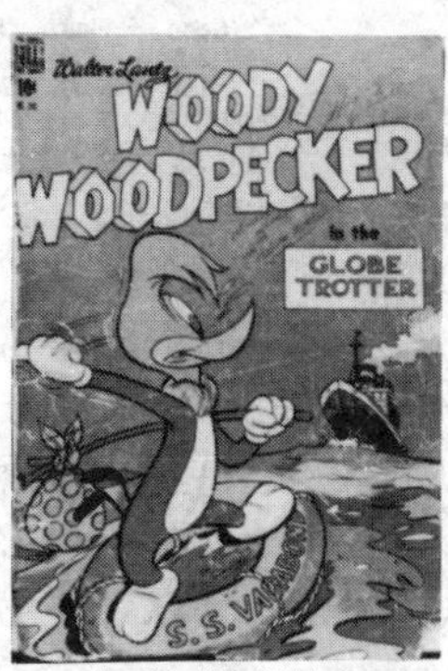

Four Color #249, © W. Lantz

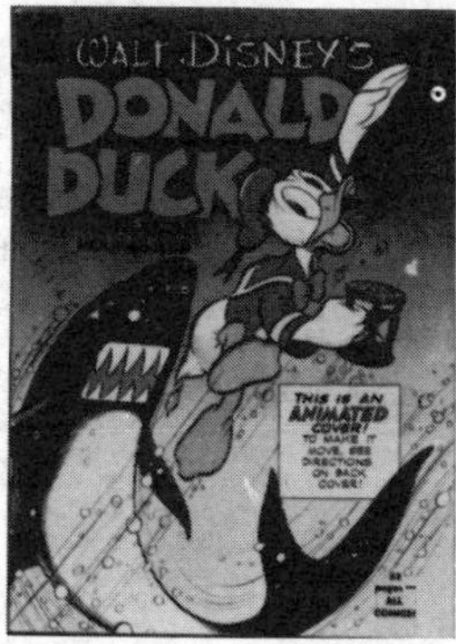

Four Color #291, © WDC

Four Color #323, © DELL

FOUR COLOR (continued)	Good	Fine	Mint
237-Tillie the Toiler	3.00	9.00	21.00
238-Donald Duck in Voodoo Hoodoo, by Carl Barks (Disney) (8/49)	27.00	81.00	190.00
239-Adventure Bound (8/49)	2.30	7.00	16.00
240-Andy Panda (Lantz)	2.30	7.00	16.00
241-Porky Pig, Mighty Hunter	3.50	10.50	24.00
242-Tippie and Cap Stubbs	1.70	5.00	12.00
243-Thumper Follows His Nose (Disney)	5.70	17.00	40.00
244-The Brownies by Walt Kelly	10.00	30.00	70.00
245-Dick's Adventures in Dreamland (9/49)	3.00	9.00	21.00
246-Thunder Mountain (Zane Grey)	3.00	9.00	21.00
247-Flash Gordon	8.00	24.00	56.00
248-Mickey Mouse and the Black Sorcerer (Disney)	8.50	25.50	60.00
249-Woody Woodpecker in the Globetrotter" (10/49)	2.65	8.00	18.00
250-Bugs Bunny in Diamond Daze-Used in **SOTI**, pg. 309	4.00	12.00	28.00
251-Hubert at Camp Moonbeam	2.30	7.00	16.00
252-Pinocchio(Disney)-not Kelly; origin	6.50	19.50	45.00
253-Christmas with Mother Goose by Walt Kelly	9.50	28.50	65.00
254-Santa Claus Funnies by Walt Kelly; Pogo & Albert story by Kelly (11/49)	11.00	32.00	76.00
255-The Ranger (Zane Grey) (1949)	3.00	9.00	21.00
256-Donald Duck in "Luck of the North" by Carl Barks (Disney) (12/49)-Shows No. 257 on inside	27.00	81.00	190.00
257-Little Iodine	2.85	8.50	20.00
258-Andy Panda and the Balloon Race (Lantz)	2.30	7.00	16.00
259-Santa and the Angel (Gollub art-condensed from No. 128) & Santa at the Zoo (12/49)-two books in one	3.50	10.50	24.00
260-Porky Pig, Hero of the Wild West(12/49)	3.50	10.50	24.00
261-Mickey Mouse and the Missing Key (Disney)	8.50	25.50	60.00
262-Raggedy Ann and Andy	3.50	10.50	24.00
263-Donald Duck in "Land of the Totem Poles" by Carl Barks (Disney)(2/50)-has two Barks stories	27.00	81.00	190.00
264-Woody Woodpecker in the Magic Lantern (Lantz)	2.65	8.00	18.00
265-King of the Royal Mounted (Zane Grey)	7.00	21.00	50.00
266-Bugs Bunny on the Isle of Hercules"(2/50)-Reprinted in Best of B.B. No. 1	3.00	9.00	21.00
267-Little Beaver-Harmon c/a	2.00	6.00	14.00
268-Mickey Mouse's Surprise Visitor (1950) (Disney)	8.50	25.50	60.00
269-Johnny Mack Brown (No.1)-Photo-c	8.00	24.00	56.00
270-Drift Fence (Zane Grey) (3/50)	3.00	9.00	21.00
271-Porky Pig in Phantom of the Plains	3.50	10.50	24.00
272-Cinderella (Disney)(4/50)	4.65	14.00	32.00
273-Oswald the Rabbit (Lantz)	2.30	7.00	16.00
274-Bugs Bunny, Hare-brained Reporter	3.00	9.00	21.00
275-Donald Duck in "Ancient Persia" by Carl Barks (Disney) (5/50)	25.00	75.00	175.00
276-Uncle Wiggily	3.70	11.00	26.00
277-Porky Pig in Desert Adventure (5/50)	3.50	10.50	24.00
278-Bill Elliott Comics (No.1)-Photo-c	7.00	21.00	50.00
279-Mickey Mouse and Pluto Battle the Giant Ants (Disney); r-/in M.M. No. 102	7.00	21.00	50.00
280-Andy Panda in The Isle Of Mechanical Men (Lantz)	2.30	7.00	16.00
281-Bugs Bunny in The Great Circus Mystery	3.00	9.00	21.00
282-Donald Duck and the Pixilated Parrot by Carl Barks (Disney) (c. 5/23/50)	25.00	75.00	175.00
283-King of the Royal Mounted (7/50)	7.00	21.00	50.00
284-Porky Pig in The Kingdom of Nowhere	3.50	10.50	24.00
285-Bozo the Clown and His Minikin Circus (No.1)(TV)	5.00	15.00	35.00
286-Mickey Mouse in The Uninvited Guest (Disney)	7.00	21.00	50.00
287-Gene Autry's Champion in The Ghost Of Black Mountain (No.1)-Photo-c	4.00	12.00	28.00
288-Woody Woodpecker in Klondike Gold (Lantz)	2.65	8.00	18.00
289-Bugs Bunny in "Indian Trouble"	3.00	9.00	21.00
290-The Chief	3.00	9.00	21.00
291-Donald Duck in "The Magic Hourglass" by Carl Barks (Disney) (9/50)	25.00	75.00	175.00
292-The Cisco Kid Comics (No.1)	7.00	21.00	50.00
293-The Brownies-Kelly c/a	9.50	28.50	65.00
294-Little Beaver	2.00	6.00	14.00
295-Porky Pig in President Porky (9/50)	3.50	10.50	24.00
296-Mickey Mouse in Private Eye for Hire (Disney)	7.00	21.00	50.00
297-Andy Panda in The Haunted Inn (Lantz, 10/50)	2.30	7.00	16.00
298-Bugs Bunny in Sheik for a Day	3.00	9.00	21.00
299-Buck Jones & the Iron Horse Trail (No.1)	7.00	21.00	50.00
300-Donald Duck in "Big-Top Bedlam" by Carl Barks (Disney) (11/50)	25.00	75.00	175.00
301-The Mysterious Rider (Zane Grey)	3.00	9.00	21.00
302-Santa Claus Funnies (11/50)	2.30	7.00	16.00
303-Porky Pig in The Land of the Monstrous Flies	2.30	7.00	16.00
304-Mickey Mouse in Tom-Tom Island (Disney) (12/50)	5.00	15.00	35.00
305-Woody Woodpecker (Lantz)	1.70	5.00	12.00
306-Raggedy Ann	3.00	9.00	21.00
307-Bugs Bunny in Lumber Jack Rabbit	2.00	6.00	14.00
308-Donald Duck in "Dangerous Disguise" by Carl Barks (Disney) (1/51)	21.00	63.00	147.00
309-Betty Betz' Dollface and Her Gang ('51)	2.30	7.00	16.00
310-King of the Royal Mounted (1/51)	4.60	14.00	32.00
311-Porky Pig in Midget Horses of Hidden Valley	2.30	7.00	16.00
312-Tonto (No.1)	7.00	21.00	50.00
313-Mickey Mouse in The Mystery of the Double-Cross Ranch (No. 1)(Disney)	5.00	15.00	35.00
314-Ambush (Zane Grey)	3.00	9.00	21.00
315-Oswald the Rabbit (Lantz)	1.50	4.50	10.00
316-Rex Allen (No.1)-Photo-c; Marsh-a	8.50	25.50	60.00
317-Bugs Bunny in Hair Today Gone Tomorrow (No.1)	2.00	6.00	14.00
318-Donald Duck in "No Such Varmint" by Carl Barks (No. 1) Indicia shows #317 (Disney, c. 1/23/51)	21.00	63.00	147.00
319-Gene Autry's Champion	3.00	9.00	21.00
320-Uncle Wiggily (No. 1)	3.00	9.00	21.00
321-Little Scouts (No.1)	1.70	4.00	9.00
322-Porky Pig in Roaring Rockets (No.1)	2.30	7.00	16.00
323-Susie Q. Smith (3/51)	1.50	4.50	10.00
324-I Met a Handsome Cowboy (3/51)	4.35	13.00	30.00
325-Mickey Mouse in The Haunted Castle (No. 2)(Disney)(4/51)	5.00	15.00	35.00
326-Andy Panda (No. 1, Lantz)	1.30	4.00	9.00
327-Bugs Bunny and the Rajah's Treasure (No. 2)	2.00	6.00	14.00
328-Donald Duck in Old California (No.2) by Carl Barks-Peyote drug use issue (Disney) (5/51)	23.00	70.00	160.00
329-Roy Roger's Trigger (No.1)(5/51)-Photo-c	5.00	15.00	35.00
330-Porky Pig Meets the Bristled Bruiser (No.2)	2.30	7.00	16.00
331-Alice in Wonderland (Disney) (1951)	5.70	17.00	40.00
332-Little Beaver	2.00	6.00	14.00

FOUR COLOR (continued)	Good	Fine	Mint
333-Wilderness Trek (Zane Grey) (5/51)	3.00	9.00	21.00
334-Mickey Mouse and Yukon Gold (Disney) (6/51)	5.00	15.00	35.00
335-Francis the Famous Talking Mule (No.1)	1.70	5.00	12.00
336-Woody Woodpecker (Lantz)	1.70	5.00	12.00
337-The Brownies-not by Walt Kelly	2.65	8.00	18.00
338-Bugs Bunny and the Rocking Horse Thieves	2.00	6.00	14.00
339-Donald Duck and the Magic Fountain-not by Carl Barks (Disney) (7-8/51)	4.35	13.00	30.00
340-King of the Royal Mounted (7/51)	4.60	14.00	32.00
341-Unbirthday Party with Alice in Wonderland (Disney) (7/51)	5.70	17.00	40.00
342-Porky Pig the Lucky Peppermint Mine	1.70	5.00	12.00
343-Mickey Mouse in The Ruby Eye of Homar-Guy-Am (Disney)-Reprinted in M.M. No. 104	4.00	12.00	28.00
344-Sergeant Preston from Challenge of The Yukon (No.1)(TV)	4.00	12.00	28.00
345-Andy Panda in Scotland Yard (8-10/51)(Lantz)	1.30	4.00	9.00
346-Hideout (Zane Grey)	3.00	9.00	21.00
347-Bugs Bunny the Frigid Hare (8-9/51)	2.00	6.00	14.00
348-Donald Duck "The Crocodile Collector"-Barks-c only (Disney) (9-10/51)	5.00	15.00	35.00
349-Uncle Wiggily	3.00	9.00	21.00
350-Woody Woodpecker (Lantz)	1.70	5.00	12.00
351-Porky Pig and the Grand Canyon Giant (9-10/51)	1.70	5.00	12.00
352-Mickey Mouse in The Mystery of Painted Valley (Disney)	4.00	12.00	28.00
353-Duck Album (No.1)-Barks-c (Disney)	2.65	8.00	18.00
354-Raggedy Ann & Andy	3.00	9.00	21.00
355-Bugs Bunny Hot-Rod Hare	2.00	6.00	14.00
356-Donald Duck in "Rags to Riches"-Barks-c only (Disney)	5.00	15.00	35.00
357-Comeback (Zane Grey)	2.30	7.00	16.00
358-Andy Panda (Lantz)(11-1/52)	1.30	4.00	9.00
359-Frosty the Snowman (No.1)	2.30	7.00	16.00
360-Porky Pig in Tree of Fortune (11-12/51)	1.70	5.00	12.00
361-Santa Claus Funnies	2.30	7.00	16.00
362-Mickey Mouse and the Smuggled Diamonds (Disney)	4.00	12.00	28.00
363-King of the Royal Mounted	4.00	12.00	28.00
364-Woody Woodpecker (Lantz)	1.50	4.50	10.00
365-The Brownies-not by Kelly	2.65	8.00	18.00
366-Bugs Bunny Uncle Buckskin Comes to Town (12-1/52)	2.00	6.00	14.00
367-Donald Duck in "A Christmas for Shacktown" by Carl Barks (Disney) (1-2/52)	19.00	57.00	132.00
368-Bob Clampett's Beany and Cecil (No.1)	8.00	24.00	56.00
369-The Lone Ranger's Famous Horse Hi-Yo Silver (No.1); Silver's origin	4.35	13.00	30.00
370-Porky Pig in Trouble in the Big Trees	1.70	5.00	12.00
371-Mickey Mouse in The Inca Idol Case ('52) (Disney)	4.00	12.00	28.00
372-Riders of the Purple Sage (Zane Grey)	2.30	7.00	16.00
373-Sergeant Preston (TV)	3.00	9.00	21.00
374-Woody Woodpecker (Lantz)	1.50	4.50	10.00
375-John Carter of Mars (E. R. Burroughs)-Jesse Marsh-a; origin	9.50	28.50	65.00
376-Bugs Bunny, "The Magic Sneeze"	2.00	6.00	14.00
377-Susie Q. Smith	1.50	4.50	10.00
378-Tom Corbett, Space Cadet (No.1)(TV)-McWilliams-a	5.00	15.00	35.00
379-Donald Duck in "Southern Hospitality"-not by Barks (Disney)	4.35	13.00	30.00

	Good	Fine	Mint
380-Raggedy Ann & Andy	3.00	9.00	21.00
381-Marge's Tubby (No.1)	11.00	33.00	76.00
382-Snow White and the Seven Dwarfs (Disney)-origin; partial reprint of 4-Color No. 49 (Movie)	5.00	15.00	35.00
383-Andy Panda (Lantz)	1.00	3.00	7.00
384-King of the Royal Mounted (3/52)(Zane Grey)	4.00	12.00	28.00
385-Porky Pig in The Isle of Missing Ships (3-4/52)	1.70	5.00	12.00
386-Uncle Scrooge No. 1 by Carl Barks (Disney) in "Only a Poor Old Man" (3/52)	56.00	168.00	390.00
387-Mickey Mouse in High Tibet (Disney) (4-5/52)	4.00	12.00	28.00
388-Oswald the Rabbit (Lantz)	1.50	4.50	10.00
389-Andy Hardy Comics (No.1)	1.70	5.00	12.00
390-Woody Woodpecker (Lantz)	1.50	4.50	10.00
391-Uncle Wiggily	2.65	8.00	18.00
392-Hi-Yo Silver	2.65	8.00	18.00
393-Bugs Bunny	2.00	6.00	14.00
394-Donald Duck in Malayalaya-Barks-c only (Disney)	5.00	15.00	35.00
395-Forlorn River (Zane Grey) (1952)-First Nevada (5/52)	2.30	7.00	16.00
396-Tales of the Texas Rangers (No.1)(TV)-Photo-c	4.35	13.00	30.00
397-Sergeant Preston of the Yukon (TV)(5/52)	3.00	9.00	21.00
398-The Brownies-not by Kelly	2.65	8.00	18.00
399-Porky Pig in The Lost Gold Mine	1.70	5.00	12.00
400-Tom Corbett, Space Cadet (TV)-McWilliams c/a	4.00	12.00	28.00
401-Mickey Mouse and Goofy's Mechanical Wizard (Disney) (6-7/52)	3.50	10.50	24.00
402-Mary Jane and Sniffles	5.50	16.50	38.00
403-Li'l Bad Wolf (Disney) (6/52)	2.00	6.00	14.00
404-The Range Rider (No.1)(TV)-Photo-c	4.60	14.00	32.00
405-Woody Woodpecker (Lantz)	1.50	4.50	10.00
406-Tweety and Sylvester (No.1)	1.30	4.00	9.00
407-Bugs Bunny, Foreign-Legion Hare	1.50	4.50	10.00
408-Donald Duck and the Golden Helmet by Carl Barks (Disney) (7-8/52)	19.00	57.00	132.00
409-Andy Panda (7-9/52)	1.00	3.00	7.00
410-Porky Pig in The Water Wizard	1.70	5.00	12.00
411-Mickey Mouse and the Old Sea Dog (Disney) (8-9/52)	3.50	10.50	24.00
412-Nevada (Zane Grey)	2.30	7.00	16.00
413-Robin Hood (Disney-Movie) (8/52)-Photo-c	2.30	7.00	16.00
414-Bob Clampett's Beany and Cecil (TV)	6.00	18.00	42.00
415-Rootie Kazootie (No.1)(TV)	3.00	9.00	21.00
416-Woody Woodpecker (Lantz)	1.50	4.50	10.00
417-Double Trouble with Goober (No.1)	1.50	4.50	10.00
418-Rusty Riley, a Boy, a Horse, and a Dog (No.1)-Frank Godwin-a (strip reprints) (8/52)	2.00	6.00	14.00
419-Sergeant Preston (TV)	3.00	9.00	21.00
420-Bugs Bunny in The Mysterious Buckaroo (8-9/52)	1.50	4.50	10.00
421-Tom Corbett, Space Cadet (TV)-McWilliams-a	4.00	12.00	28.00
422-Donald Duck and the Gilded Man, by Carl Barks (Disney) (9-10/52) (No.423 on inside)	19.00	57.00	132.00
423-Rhubarb, Owner of the Brooklyn Ball Club (The Millionaire Cat) (No.1)	1.15	3.50	8.00
424-Flash Gordon-Test Flight in Space (9/52)	6.00	18.00	42.00
425-Zorro, the Return of	6.50	19.50	45.00
426-Porky Pig in The Scalawag Leprechaun	1.70	5.00	12.00
427-Mickey Mouse and the Wonderful Whizzix (Disney) (10-11/52)-			

Four Color #334, © WDC

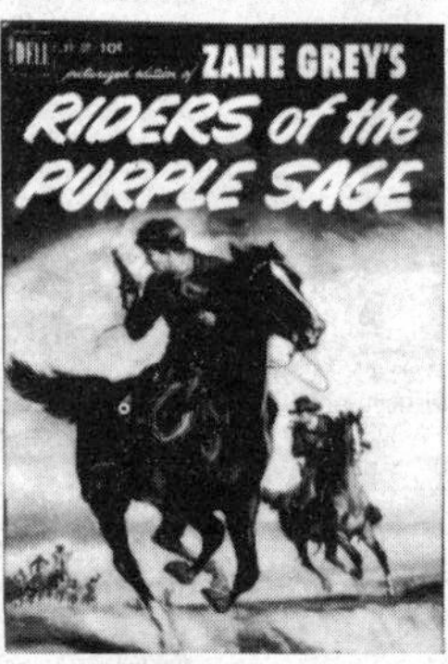

Four Color #372, © Zane Grey

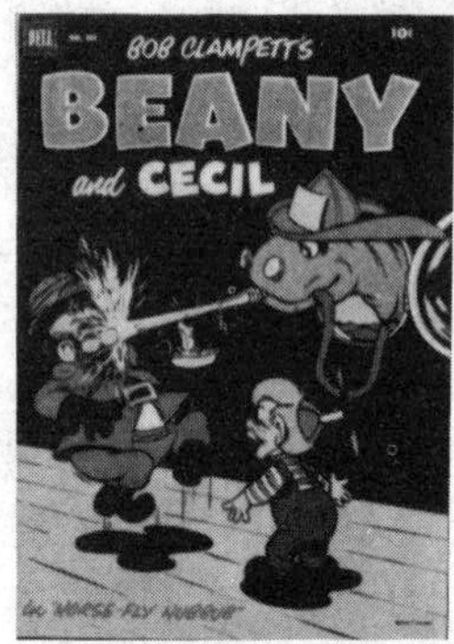

Four Color #414, © Bob Clampett

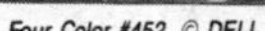
Four Color #452, © DELL

Four Color #475, © M.G.M.

Four Color #505, © WDC

FOUR COLOR (continued)	Good	Fine	Mint
reprinted in M.M. No. 100	3.50	10.50	24.00
428-Uncle Wiggily	2.30	7.00	16.00
429-Pluto in "Why Dogs Leave Home" (Disney)(10/52)			
	2.00	6.00	14.00
430-Marge's Tubby, the Shadow of a Man-Eater			
	6.00	18.00	42.00
431-Woody Woodpecker (10/52)(Lantz)	1.50	4.50	10.00
432-Bugs Bunny and the Rabbit Olympics	1.50	4.50	10.00
433-Wildfire (Zane Grey)	2.30	7.00	16.00
434-Rin Tin Tin-"In Dark Danger" (No.1)(TV)(11/52)-Photo-c			
	4.00	12.00	28.00
435-Frosty the Snowman	1.70	5.00	12.00
436-The Brownies-not by Kelly (11/52)	2.30	7.00	16.00
437-John Carter of Mars (E. R. Burroughs)-Marsh-a			
	8.00	24.00	56.00
438-Annie Oakley (No.1) (TV)	5.00	15.00	35.00
439-Little Hiawatha (Disney) (12/52)	2.00	6.00	14.00
440-Black Beauty (12/52)	1.70	5.00	12.00
441-Fearless Fagan	1.15	3.50	8.00
442-Peter Pan (Disney) (Movie)	5.00	15.00	35.00
443-Ben Bowie and His Mountain Men (No.1)	2.65	8.00	18.00
444-Marge's Tubby	6.00	18.00	42.00
445-Charlie McCarthy	1.70	5.00	12.00
446-Captain Hook and Peter Pan (Disney) (Movie) (1/53)			
	5.00	15.00	35.00
447-Andy Hardy Comics	1.15	3.50	8.00
448-Bob Clampett's Beany and Cecil (TV)	6.00	18.00	42.00
449-Tappan's Burro (Zane Grey) (2-4/53)	2.30	7.00	16.00
450-Duck Album-Barks-c (Disney)	2.30	7.00	16.00
451-Rusty Riley-Frank Godwin-a (strip reprints) (2/53)			
	1.70	5.00	12.00
452-Raggedy Ann & Andy ('53)	3.00	9.00	21.00
453-Susie Q. Smith (2/53)	1.30	4.00	9.00
454-Krazy Kat Comics-not by Herriman	2.00	6.00	14.00
455-Johnny Mack Brown Comics(3/53)-Photo-c			
	3.00	9.00	21.00
456-Uncle Scrooge Back to the Klondike (No.2) by Barks (3/53)			
(Disney)	26.00	78.00	180.00
457-Daffy (No.1)	1.50	4.50	10.00
458-Oswald the Rabbit (Lantz)	1.00	3.00	7.00
459-Rootie Kazootie (TV)	2.65	8.00	18.00
460-Buck Jones (4/53)	3.00	9.00	21.00
461-Marge's Tubby	6.00	18.00	42.00
462-Little Scouts	.85	2.50	6.00
463-Petunia (4/53)	1.30	4.00	9.00
464-Bozo (4/53)	3.00	9.00	21.00
465-Francis the Famous Talking Mule	1.00	3.00	7.00
466-Rhubarb, the Millionaire Cat	.85	2.50	6.00
467-Desert Gold (Zane Grey) (5-7/53)	2.30	7.00	16.00
468-Goofy (No.1) (Disney)	3.00	9.00	21.00
469-Beetle Bailey (No.1)(5/53)	3.00	9.00	21.00
470-Elmer Fudd	1.15	3.50	8.00
471-Double Trouble with Goober	1.00	3.00	7.00
472-Wild Bill Elliott (6/53)-Photo-c	3.50	10.50	24.00
473-Li'l Bad Wolf (Disney)	1.50	4.50	10.00
474-Mary Jane and Sniffles	4.60	14.00	32.00
475-M.G.M.'s The Two Mouseketeers (No.1)	1.50	4.50	10.00
476-Rin Tin Tin (TV)-Photo-c	3.00	9.00	21.00
477-Bob Clampett's Beany and Cecil (TV)	6.00	18.00	42.00
478-Charlie McCarthy	1.70	5.00	12.00
479-Queen of the West Dale Evans (No.1)	5.50	16.50	38.00
480-Andy Hardy Comics	1.15	3.50	8.00
481-Annie Oakley And Tagg (TV)	3.50	10.50	25.00
482-Brownies-not by Kelly	2.30	7.00	16.00
483-Little Beaver (7/53)	1.70	5.00	12.00
484-River Feud (Zane Grey) (8-10/53)	2.30	7.00	16.00

	Good	Fine	Mint
485-The Little People-Walt Scott (No.1)	2.00	6.00	14.00
486-Rusty Riley-Frank Godwin strip-r	1.70	5.00	12.00
487-Mowgli, the Jungle Book (Rudyard Kipling's)			
	2.00	6.00	14.00
488-John Carter of Mars (Burroughs)-Marsh-a	7.00	21.00	50.00
489-Tweety and Sylvester	1.00	3.00	7.00
490-Jungle Jim (No.1)	2.65	8.00	18.00
491-Silvertip (No.1) (Max Brand)-Kinstler-a			
(8/53)	4.00	12.00	24.00
492-Duck Album (Disney)	1.70	5.00	12.00
493-Johnny Mack Brown-Photo-c	3.00	9.00	21.00
494-The Little King (No.1)	2.65	8.00	18.00
495-Uncle Scrooge (No.3)(Disney)-by Carl Barks (9/53)			
	23.00	70.00	160.00
496-The Green Hornet	7.00	21.00	50.00
497-Zorro (Sword of. . .)	6.50	19.50	45.00
498-Bugs Bunny's Album (9/53)	1.30	4.00	9.00
499-M.G.M.'s Spike and Tyke (No.1)(9/53)	1.30	4.00	9.00
500-Buck Jones	3.00	9.00	21.00
501-Francis the Famous Talking Mule	1.00	3.00	7.00
502-Rootie Kazootie (TV)	2.65	8.00	18.00
503-Uncle Wiggily (10/53)	2.30	7.00	16.00
504-Krazy Kat-not by Herriman	2.00	6.00	14.00
505-The Sword and the Rose (Disney) (10/53) (TV)-Photo-c			
	3.00	9.00	21.00
506-The Little Scouts	.85	2.50	6.00
507-Oswald the Rabbit (Lantz)	1.00	3.00	7.00
508-Bozo (10/53)	3.00	9.00	21.00
509-Pluto (Disney) (10/53)	2.00	6.00	14.00
510-Son of Black Beauty	1.70	5.00	12.00
511-Outlaw Trail (Zane Grey)-Kinstler-a	2.65	8.00	18.00
512-Flash Gordon (11/53)	3.50	10.50	24.00
513-Ben Bowie and His Mountain Men	1.70	5.00	12.00
514-Frosty the Snowman	1.50	4.50	10.00
515-Andy Hardy	1.15	3.50	8.00
516-Double Trouble With Goober	1.00	3.00	7.00
517-Chip 'N' Dale (No.1)(Disney)	1.70	5.00	12.00
518-Rivets (11/53)	1.15	3.50	8.00
519-Steve Canyon (No.1)-not by Milton Caniff	4.00	12.00	28.00
520-Wild Bill Elliott-Photo-c	3.50	10.50	24.00
521-Beetle Bailey (12/53)	2.00	6.00	14.00
522-The Brownies	2.30	7.00	16.00
523-Rin Tin Tin (TV)-Photo-c	3.00	9.00	21.00
524-Tweety and Sylvester	1.00	3.00	7.00
525-Santa Claus Funnies	1.70	5.00	12.00
526-Napoleon	1.15	3.50	8.00
527-Charlie McCarthy	1.70	5.00	12.00
528-Queen of the West Dale Evans-Photo-c	4.00	12.00	28.00
529-Little Beaver	1.70	5.00	12.00
530-Bob Clampett's Beany and Cecil (TV) (1/54)			
	6.00	18.00	42.00
531-Duck Album (Disney)	1.70	5.00	12.00
532-The Rustlers (Zane Grey) (2-4/54)	2.30	7.00	16.00
533-Raggedy Ann and Andy	3.00	9.00	21.00
534-Western Marshal (Ernest Haycox's)-Kinstler-a			
	3.00	9.00	21.00
535-I Love Lucy (No. 1)(TV) (2/54)-photo-c	8.00	24.00	56.00
536-Daffy (3/54)	1.15	3.50	8.00
537-Stormy, the Thoroughbred. . . (Disney-Movie) on top ⅔ of each page; Pluto story on bottom ⅓ of each page (2/54)			
	2.00	6.00	14.00
538-The Mask of Zorro-Kinstler-a	7.00	21.00	50.00
539-Ben and Me (Disney) (3/54)	1.50	4.50	10.00
540-Knights of the Round Table (3/54) (Movie)-Photo-c			
	3.50	10.50	24.00
541-Johnny Mack Brown-Photo-c	3.00	9.00	21.00

FOUR COLOR (continued)	Good	Fine	Mint
542-Super Circus Featuring Mary Hartline (TV) (3/54)	2.30	7.00	16.00
543-Uncle Wiggily (3/54)	2.30	7.00	16.00
544-Rob Roy (Disney-Movie)-Manning-a; photo-c	3.50	10.50	24.00
545-The Wonderful Adventures of Pinocchio-Partial reprint of 4-Color 92 (Disney-Movie)	2.65	8.00	18.00
546-Buck Jones	3.00	9.00	21.00
547-Francis the Famous Talking Mule	1.00	3.00	7.00
548-Krazy Kat-not by Herriman (4/54)	1.70	5.00	12.00
549-Oswald the Rabbit (Lantz)	1.00	3.00	7.00
550-The Little Scouts	.85	2.50	6.00
551-Bozo (4/54)	3.00	9.00	21.00
552-Beetle Bailey	2.00	6.00	14.00
553-Susie Q. Smith	1.30	4.00	9.00
554-Rusty Riley (Frank Godwin strip-r)	1.75	5.25	12.00
555-Range War (Zane Grey)	2.30	7.00	16.00
556-Double Trouble With Goober (5/54)	1.00	3.00	7.00
557-Ben Bowie and His Mountain Men	1.70	5.00	12.00
558-Elmer Fudd (5/54)	1.15	3.50	8.00
559-I Love Lucy (No. 2)(TV)-Photo-c	5.70	17.00	40.00
560-Duck Album (Disney)	1.70	5.00	12.00
561-Mr. Magoo (5/54)	4.00	12.00	28.00
562-Goofy (Disney)	2.30	7.00	16.00
563-Rhubarb, the Millionaire Cat (6/54)	.85	2.50	6.00
564-Li'l Bad Wolf (Disney)	1.50	4.50	10.00
565-Jungle Jim	2.00	6.00	14.00
566-Son of Black Beauty	1.75	5.25	12.00
567-Prince Valiant (No.1)-by Bob Fuje (Movie)-Photo-c	5.70	17.00	40.00
568-Gypsy Colt (Movie)	2.30	7.00	16.00
569-Priscilla's Pop	1.30	4.00	9.00
570-Bob Clampett's Beany and Cecil (TV)	6.00	18.00	42.00
571-Charlie McCarthy	1.70	5.00	12.00
572-Silvertip (Max Brand)(7/54); Kinstler-a	3.00	9.00	21.00
573-The Little People by Walt Scott	1.50	4.50	10.00
574-The Hand of Zorro	6.50	19.50	45.00
575-Annie Oakley and Tagg(TV)-Photo-c	3.50	10.50	25.00
576-Angel (No.1) (8/54)	1.00	3.00	7.00
577-M.G.M.'s Spike and Tyke	1.00	3.00	7.00
578-Steve Canyon (8/54)	3.50	10.50	24.00
579-Francis the Famous Talking Mule	1.00	3.00	7.00
580-Six Gun Ranch (Luke Short-8/54)	2.00	6.00	14.00
581-Chip 'N' Dale (Disney)	1.30	4.00	9.00
582-Mowgli Jungle Book (Kipling)	1.70	5.00	12.00
583-The Lost Wagon Train (Zane Grey)	2.30	7.00	16.00
584-Johnny Mack Brown-Photo-c	3.00	9.00	21.00
585-Bugs Bunny's Album	1.30	4.00	9.00
586-Duck Album (Disney)	1.70	5.00	12.00
587-The Little Scouts	.85	2.50	6.00
588-King Richard and the Crusaders (Movie) (10/54) Matt Baker-a; photo-c	7.00	21.00	50.00
589-Buck Jones	3.00	9.00	21.00
590-Hansel and Gretel	3.00	9.00	21.00
591-Western Marshal (Ernest Haycox's)-Kinstler-a	3.00	9.00	21.00
592-Super Circus (TV)	2.30	7.00	16.00
593-Oswald the Rabbit (Lantz)	1.00	3.00	7.00
594-Bozo (10/54)	3.00	9.00	21.00
595-Pluto (Disney)	1.70	5.00	12.00
596-Turok, Son of Stone (No.1)	19.00	57.00	132.00
597-The Little King	1.70	5.00	12.00
598-Captain Davy Jones	1.50	4.50	10.00
599-Ben Bowie and His Mountain Men	1.70	5.00	12.00
600-Daisy Duck's Diary (No.1)(Disney)(11/54)	2.00	6.00	14.00
601-Frosty the Snowman	1.50	4.50	10.00
602-Mr. Magoo and Gerald McBoing-Boing	4.00	12.00	28.00
603-M.G.M.'s The Two Mouseketeers	1.00	3.00	7.00
604-Shadow on the Trail (Zane Grey)	2.30	7.00	16.00
605-The Brownies-not by Kelly (12/54)	2.30	7.00	16.00
606-Sir Lancelot (not TV)	5.00	15.00	35.00
607-Santa Claus Funnies	1.70	5.00	12.00
608-Silvertip-"Valley of Vanishing Men" (Max Brand)-Kinstler-a	3.00	9.00	21.00
609-The Littlest Outlaw (Disney-Movie) (1/55)-Photo-c	2.65	8.00	18.00
610-Drum Beat (Movie); Alan Ladd photo-c	4.60	14.00	32.00
611-Duck Album (Disney)	1.70	5.00	12.00
612-Little Beaver (1/55)	1.30	4.00	9.00
613-Western Marshal (Ernest Haycox's) (2/55)-Kinstler-a	3.00	9.00	21.00
614-20,000 Leagues Under the Sea (Disney) (Movie) (2/55)	2.65	8.00	18.00
615-Daffy	1.15	3.50	8.00
616-To the Last Man (Zane Grey)	2.30	7.00	16.00
617-The Quest of Zorro	6.50	19.50	45.00
618-Johnny Mack Brown-Photo-c	3.00	9.00	21.00
619-Krazy Kat-not by Herriman	1.70	5.00	12.00
620-Mowgli Jungle Book (Kipling)	1.70	5.00	12.00
621-Francis the Famous Talking Mule	1.00	3.00	7.00
622-Beetle Bailey	2.00	6.00	14.00
623-Oswald the Rabbit (Lantz)	.85	2.50	6.00
624-Treasure Island (Disney-Movie) (4/55)-Photo-c	2.30	7.00	16.00
625-Beaver Valley (Disney-Movie)	1.50	4.50	10.00
626-Ben Bowie and His Mountain Men	1.70	5.00	12.00
627-Goofy (Disney) (5/55)	2.30	7.00	16.00
628-Elmer Fudd	1.15	3.50	8.00
629-Lady and the Tramp with Jock (Disney)	2.00	6.00	14.00
630-Priscilla's Pop	1.15	3.50	8.00
631-Davy Crockett, Indian Fighter (No.1)(Disney)(5/55)(TV)-Fess Parker photo-c	2.65	8.00	18.00
632-Fighting Caravans (Zane Grey)	2.30	7.00	16.00
633-The Little People by Walt Scott	1.50	4.50	10.00
634-Lady and the Tramp Album (Disney) (6/55)	1.70	5.00	12.00
635-Bob Clampett's Beany and Cecil (TV)	6.00	18.00	42.00
636-Chip 'N' Dale (Disney)	1.30	4.00	9.00
637-Silvertip (Max Brand)-Kinstler-a	3.00	9.00	21.00
638-M.G.M.'s Spike and Tyke (8/55)	1.00	3.00	7.00
639-Davy Crockett at the Alamo (Disney) (7/55)(TV)-Fess Parker photo-c	2.30	7.00	16.00
640-Western Marshal (Ernest Haycox's)-Kinstler-a	3.00	9.00	21.00
641-Steve Canyon ('55)-by Caniff	3.50	10.50	24.00
642-M.G.M.'s The Two Mouseketeers	1.00	3.00	7.00
643-Wild Bill Elliott-Photo-c	3.00	9.00	21.00
644-Sir Walter Raleigh (5/55)-Based on movie "The Virgin Queen"-Photo-c	3.00	9.00	21.00
645-Johnny Mack Brown-Photo-c	3.00	9.00	21.00
646-Dotty Dripple and Taffy (No.1)	1.70	5.00	12.00
647-Bugs Bunny's Album (9/55)	1.30	4.00	9.00
648-Jace Pearson of the Texas Rangers (TV)-Photo-c	3.00	9.00	21.00
649-Duck Album (Disney)	1.70	5.00	12.00
650-Prince Valiant - by Bob Fuje	3.50	10.50	24.00
651-King Colt (Luke Short)(9/55)-Kinstler-a	2.65	8.00	18.00
652-Buck Jones	2.00	6.00	14.00
653-Smokey the Bear (No.1) (10/55)	2.00	6.00	14.00
654-Pluto (Disney)	1.70	5.00	12.00
655-Francis the Famous Talking Mule	1.00	3.00	7.00
656-Turok, Son of Stone (No.2) (10/55)	13.00	40.00	90.00

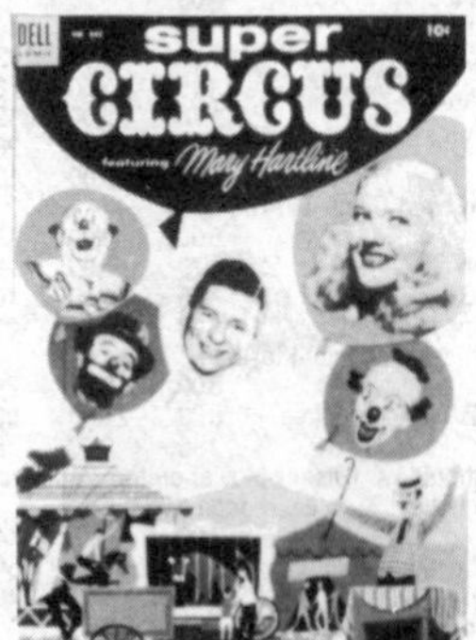

Four Color #542, © DELL

Four Color #595, © WDC

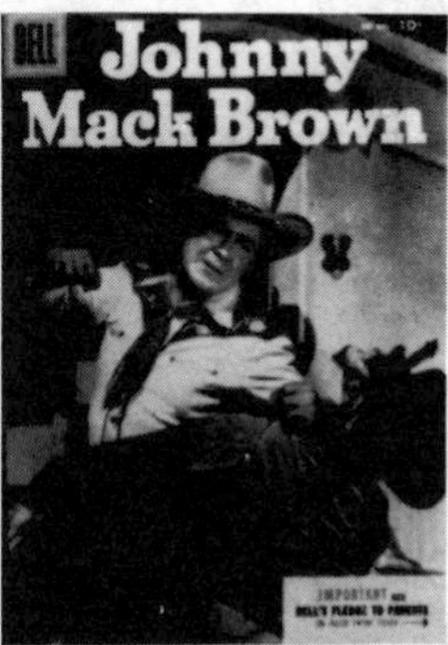

Four Color #645, © DELL

Four Color #669, © WDC

Four Color #703, © WDC

Four Color #735, © DELL

FOUR COLOR (continued)	Good	Fine	Mint
657-Ben Bowie and His Mountain Men	1.70	5.00	12.00
658-Goofy (Disney)	2.30	7.00	16.00
659-Daisy Duck's Diary (Disney)	1.70	5.00	12.00
660-Little Beaver	1.30	4.00	9.00
661-Frosty the Snowman	1.50	4.50	10.00
662-Zoo Parade (TV)-Marlin Perkins (11/55)-Photo-c	2.00	6.00	14.00
663-Winky Dink (TV)	3.00	9.00	21.00
664-Davy Crockett in the Great Keelboat Race (TV) (Disney)(11/55)-Fess Parker photo-c	3.00	9.00	21.00
665-The African Lion (Disney-Movie) (11/55)	2.00	6.00	14.00
666-Santa Claus Funnies	1.70	5.00	12.00
667-Silvertip and the Stolen Stallion (Max Brand) (12/55)-Kinstler-a	3.00	9.00	21.00
668-Dumbo (Disney) (12/55)	3.50	10.50	24.00
668-Dumbo (Disney) (1/58) different cover, same contents	3.50	10.50	24.00
669-Robin Hood (Disney-Movie) (12/55)-reprint of No. 413-Photo-c	2.00	6.00	14.00
670-M.G.M's Mouse Musketeers (No.1)(1/56)-Formerly the Two Mouseketeers	1.00	3.00	7.00
671-Davy Crockett and the River Pirates (TV) (Disney) (12/55)-Jesse Marsh-a; Fess Parker photo-c	3.00	9.00	21.00
672-Quentin Durward (1/56)(Movie)-Photo-	3.00	9.00	21.00
673-Buffalo Bill, Jr. (No.1)(TV)-Photo-c	3.00	9.00	21.00
674-The Little Rascals (No.1) (TV)	2.00	6.00	14.00
675-Steve Donovan, Western Marshal (No.1)(TV)-Kinstler-a; photo-c	3.50	10.50	24.00
676-Will-Yum!	1.15	3.50	8.00
677-Little King	1.70	5.00	12.00
678-The Last Hunt (Movie)-Photo-c	3.00	9.00	21.00
679-Gunsmoke (No.1) (TV)	5.00	15.00	35.00
680-Out Our Way with the Worry Wart (2/56)	1.30	4.00	9.00
681-Forever, Darling (Movie) with Lucille Ball & Desi Arnaz (2/56)-Photo-c	4.35	13.00	30.00
682-When Knighthood Was in Flower (Disney-Movie)-Reprint of No. 505-Photo-c	2.65	8.00	18.00
683-Hi and Lois (3/56)	1.00	3.00	7.00
684-Helen of Troy (Movie)-Buscema-a; photo-c	5.70	17.00	40.00
685-Johnny Mack Brown-Photo-c	3.00	9.00	21.00
686-Duck Album (Disney)	1.70	5.00	12.00
687-The Indian Fighter (Movie)-Kirk Douglas Photo-c	2.65	8.00	18.00
688-Alexander the Great (Movie) (5/56) Buscema-a; photo-c	3.50	10.50	24.00
689-Elmer Fudd (3/56)	1.15	3.50	8.00
690-The Conqueror (Movie) - John Wayne-Photo-c	7.00	21.00	50.00
691-Dotty Dripple and Taffy	1.30	4.00	9.00
692-The Little People-Walt Scott	1.50	4.50	10.00
693-Song of the South (Disney)(1956)-Partial reprint of No. 129	2.00	6.00	14.00
694-Super Circus (TV)-Photo-c	2.30	7.00	16.00
695-Little Beaver	1.30	4.00	9.00
696-Krazy Kat-not by Herriman (4/56)	1.70	5.00	12.00
697-Oswald the Rabbit (Lantz)	.85	2.50	6.00
698-Francis the Famous Talking Mule	1.00	3.00	7.00
699-Prince Valiant-by Bob Fuje	3.50	10.50	24.00
700-Water Birds and the Olympic Elk (Disney-Movie)(4/56)	2.35	7.00	16.00
701-Jiminy Cricket (No.1)(Disney)(5/56)	2.35	7.00	16.00
702-The Goofy Success Story (Disney)	2.00	6.00	14.00
703-Scamp (No.1) (Disney)	1.70	5.00	12.00
704-Priscilla's Pop (5/56)	1.15	3.50	8.00
705-Brave Eagle (No.1) (TV)-Photo-c	2.00	6.00	14.00

	Good	Fine	Mint
706-Bongo and Lumpjaw (Disney)(6/56)	1.50	4.50	10.00
707-Corky and White Shadow (Disney)(5/56)-Mickey Mouse Club (TV)-Photo-c	2.30	7.00	16.00
708-Smokey the Bear	1.50	4.50	10.00
709-The Searchers (Movie) - John Wayne photo-c	11.00	32.00	76.00
710-Francis the Famous Talking Mule	1.00	3.00	7.00
711-M.G.M's Mouse Musketeers	.85	2.50	6.00
712-The Great Locomotive Chase (Disney-Movie) (9/56)-Photo-c	2.65	8.00	18.00
713-The Animal World (Movie) (8/56)	2.30	7.00	16.00
714-Spin and Marty (No.1)(TV)(Disney)-Mickey Mouse Club (6/56)-Photo-c	3.50	10.50	24.00
715-Timmy (8/56)	1.50	4.50	10.00
716-Man in Space (Disney-Movie)	2.00	6.00	14.00
717-Moby Dick (Movie)-Photo-c	4.60	14.00	32.00
718-Dotty Dripple and Taffy	1.30	4.00	9.00
719-Prince Valiant - by Bob Fuje	3.50	10.50	24.00
720-Gunsmoke (TV)-Photo-c	3.50	10.50	24.00
721-Captain Kangaroo (TV)-Photo-c	5.00	15.00	35.00
722-Johnny Mack Brown-Photo-c	3.00	9.00	21.00
723-Santiago (Movie)-Kinstler-a(9/56); Alan Ladd photo-c	4.60	14.00	32.00
724-Bugs Bunny's Album	1.30	4.00	9.00
725-Elmer Fudd (9/56)	.85	2.50	6.00
726-Duck Album (Disney)	1.50	4.50	10.00
727-The Nature of Things (TV) (Disney)-Jesse Marsh-a	2.00	6.00	14.00
728-M.G.M's Mouse Musketeers	.85	2.50	6.00
729-Bob Son of Battle (11/56)	1.70	5.00	12.00
730-Smokey Stover	1.70	5.00	12.00
731-Silvertip and The Fighting Four (Max Brand)-Kinstler-a	3.00	9.00	21.00
732-Zorro, the Challenge of (10/56)	6.50	19.50	45.00
733-Buck Jones	2.00	6.00	14.00
734-Cheyenne (No.1)(TV)(10/56)-Photo-c	5.00	15.00	35.00
735-Crusader Rabbit (No. 1) (TV)	4.35	13.00	30.00
736-Pluto (Disney)	1.30	4.00	9.00
737-Steve Canyon-Caniff-a	3.50	10.50	24.00
738-Westward Ho, the Wagons (Disney-Movie)-Photo-c	2.00	6.00	14.00
739-Bounty Guns (Luke Short)-Drucker-a	2.00	6.00	14.00
740-Chilly Willy (No.1)(Walter Lantz)	1.15	3.50	8.00
741-The Fastest Gun Alive (Movie) (9/56)-Photo-c	2.65	8.00	18.00
742-Buffalo Bill, Jr. (TV)-Photo-c	2.15	6.50	15.00
743-Daisy Duck's Diary (Disney) (11/56)	1.70	5.00	12.00
744-Little Beaver	1.30	4.00	9.00
745-Francis the Famous Talking Mule	1.00	3.00	7.00
746-Dotty Dripple and Taffy	1.30	4.00	9.00
747-Goofy (Disney)	2.30	7.00	16.00
748-Frosty the Snowman (11/56)	1.30	4.00	9.00
749-Secrets of Life (Disney-Movie)-Photo-c	2.00	6.00	14.00
750-The Great Cat Family (Disney-Movie)	2.30	7.00	16.00
751-Our Miss Brooks (TV)-Photo-c	3.00	9.00	21.00
752-Mandrake, the Magician	3.70	11.00	26.00
753-Walt Scott's Little People (11/56)	1.50	4.50	10.00
754-Smokey the Bear	1.50	4.50	10.00
755-The Littlest Snowman (12/56)	2.00	6.00	14.00
756-Santa Claus Funnies	1.70	5.00	12.00
757-The True Story of Jesse James (Movie)-Photo-c	4.00	12.00	28.00
758-Bear Country (Disney-Movie)	2.00	6.00	14.00
759-Circus Boy (TV)-The Monkees' Mickey Dolenz photo-c	5.00	15.00	35.00
760-The Hardy Boys (No. 1) (TV) (Disney)-Mickey Mouse Club-			

FOUR COLOR (continued)

	Good	Fine	Mint
Photo-c	3.50	10.50	24.00
761-Howdy Doody (TV) (1/57)	3.50	10.50	24.00
762-The Sharkfighters (Movie)(1/57)(Scarce); Buscema-a; photo-c	6.50	17.50	45.00
763-Grandma Duck's Farm Friends (No. 1) (Disney)	2.30	7.00	16.00
764-M.G.M's Mouse Musketeers	.85	2.50	6.00
765-Will-Yum!	1.00	3.00	7.00
766-Buffalo Bill, Jr. (TV)-Photo-c	2.15	6.50	15.00
767-Spin and Marty (TV)(Disney)-Mickey Mouse Club (2/57)	3.00	9.00	21.00
768-Steve Donovan, Western Marshal (TV)-Kinstler-a; photo-c	3.00	9.00	21.00
769-Gunsmoke (TV)	3.50	10.50	24.00
770-Brave Eagle (TV)-Photo-c	1.50	4.50	10.00
771-Brand of Empire (Luke Short)(3/57)-Drucker-a	2.00	6.00	14.00
772-Cheyenne (TV)-Photo-c	4.00	12.00	28.00
773-The Brave One (Movie)-Photo-c	2.00	6.00	14.00
774-Hi and Lois (3/57)	1.00	3.00	7.00
775-Sir Lancelot and Brian (TV)-Buscema-a; photo-c	4.60	14.00	32.00
776-Johnny Mack Brown-Photo-c	3.00	9.00	21.00
777-Scamp (Disney)	1.15	3.50	8.00
778-The Little Rascals (TV)	1.70	5.00	12.00
779-Lee Hunter, Indian Fighter (3/57)	2.00	6.00	14.00
780-Captain Kangaroo (TV)-Photo-c	5.00	15.00	35.00
781-Fury (No.1)(TV)(3/57)-Photo-c	4.00	12.00	28.00
782-Duck Album (Disney)	1.50	4.50	10.00
783-Elmer Fudd	.85	2.50	6.00
784-Around the World in 80 Days (Movie) (2/57)-Photo-c	3.00	9.00	21.00
785-Circus Boy (TV) (4/57)-The Monkees' Mickey Dolenz photo-c	5.00	15.00	35.00
786-Cinderella (Disney) (3/57)-Partial reprint of No. 272	2.00	6.00	14.00
787-Little Hiawatha (Disney) (4/57)	1.50	4.50	10.00
788-Prince Valiant - by Bob Fuje	3.50	10.50	24.00
789-Silvertip-Valley Thieves (Max Brand) (4/57)-Kinstler-a	3.00	9.00	21.00
790-The Wings of Eagles (Movie) (John Wayne)-Toth-a; photo-c	8.00	24.00	56.00
791-The 77th Bengal Lancers (TV)-Photo-c	3.50	10.50	24.00
792-Oswald the Rabbit (Lantz)	.85	2.50	6.00
793-Morty Meekle	1.50	4.50	10.00
794-The Count of Monte Cristo (5/57) (Movie)-Buscema-a	5.00	15.00	35.00
795-Jiminy Cricket (Disney)	1.70	5.00	12.00
796-Ludwig Bemelman's Madeleine and Genevieve	2.00	6.00	14.00
797-Gunsmoke (TV)-Photo-c	3.50	10.50	24.00
798-Buffalo Bill, Jr. (TV)-Photo-c	2.15	6.50	15.00
799-Priscilla's Pop	1.15	3.50	8.00
800-The Buccaneers (TV)-Photo-c	4.00	12.00	28.00
801-Dotty Dripple and Taffy	1.30	4.00	9.00
802-Goofy (Disney) (5/57)	2.30	7.00	16.00
803-Cheyenne (TV)-Photo-c	4.00	12.00	28.00
804-Steve Canyon-Caniff-a (1957)	3.50	10.50	24.00
805-Crusader Rabbit (TV)	4.00	12.00	28.00
806-Scamp (Disney) (6/57)	1.15	3.50	8.00
807-Savage Range (Luke Short)-Drucker-a	2.00	6.00	14.00
808-Spin and Marty (TV)(Disney)-Mickey Mouse Club-Photo-c	3.00	9.00	21.00
809-The Little People-Walt Scott	1.50	4.50	10.00
810-Francis the Famous Talking Mule	1.00	3.00	7.00
811-Howdy Doody (TV) (7/57)	3.50	10.50	24.00

	Good	Fine	Mint
812-The Big Land(Movie); Alan Ladd photo-c	4.60	14.00	32.00
813-Circus Boy (TV)-The Monkees' Mickey Dolenz photo-c	5.00	15.00	35.00
814-Covered Wagons, Ho! (Disney)-Donald Duck (TV)(6/57)	2.00	6.00	14.00
815-Dragoon Wells Massacre (Movie)-photo-c	4.00	12.00	28.00
816-Brave Eagle (TV)-photo-c	1.50	4.50	10.00
817-Little Beaver	1.30	4.00	9.00
818-Smokey the Bear (6/57)	1.50	4.50	10.00
819-Mickey Mouse in Magicland (Disney) (7/57)	2.00	6.00	14.00
820-The Oklahoman (Movie)-Photo-c	4.00	12.00	28.00
821-Wringle Wrangle (Disney)-Based on movie "Westward Ho, the Wagons"-Marsh-a; Fess Parker photo-c	3.00	9.00	21.00
822-Paul Revere's Ride with Johnny Tremain (TV)(Disney)-Toth-a	5.70	17.00	40.00
823-Timmy	1.15	3.50	8.00
824-The Pride and the Passion (Movie)(8/57)-Frank Sinatra photo-c	3.50	10.50	24.00
825-The Little Rascals (TV)	1.70	5.00	12.00
826-Spin and Marty and Annette (TV)(Disney)-Mickey Mouse Club-Annette photo-c	6.00	18.00	42.00
827-Smokey Stover (8/57)	1.70	5.00	12.00
828-Buffalo Bill, Jr. (TV)-Photo-c	2.15	6.50	15.00
829-Tales of the Pony Express (TV) (8/57)-Painted-c	2.00	6.00	14.00
830-The Hardy Boys (TV)(Disney)-Mickey Mouse Club (8/57)-Photo-c	3.00	9.00	21.00
831-No Sleep 'Til Dawn (Movie)-Photo-c	3.00	9.00	21.00
832-Lolly and Pepper (No.1)	1.70	5.00	12.00
833-Scamp (Disney) (9/57)	1.15	3.50	8.00
834-Johnny Mack Brown-Photo-c	3.00	9.00	21.00
835-Silvertip-The Fake Rider (Max Brand)	2.30	7.00	16.00
836-Man in Flight (Disney) (TV)(9/57)	2.00	6.00	14.00
837-All-American Athlete Cotton Woods	2.00	6.00	14.00
838-Bugs Bunny's Life Story Album (9/57)	1.70	5.00	12.00
839-The Vigilantes (Movie)	3.50	10.50	24.00
840-Duck Album (Disney)	1.50	4.50	10.00
841-Elmer Fudd	.85	2.50	6.00
842-The Nature of Things (Disney-Movie)('57)-Jesse Marsh-a (TV series)	2.30	7.00	16.00
843-The First Americans (Disney)(TV)-Marsh-a	2.30	7.00	16.00
844-Gunsmoke (TV)-Photo-c	3.50	10.50	24.00
845-The Land Unknown (Movie)-Alex Toth-a	8.00	24.00	56.00
846-Gun Glory (Movie)-by Alex Toth-photo-c	7.00	21.00	50.00
847-Perri (squirrels) (Disney-Movie)-Two different covers published	1.50	4.50	10.00
848-Marauder's Moon	2.65	8.00	18.00
849-Prince Valiant-by Bob Fuje	3.50	10.50	24.00
850-Buck Jones	2.00	6.00	14.00
851-The Story of Mankind (Movie) (1/58)-Photo-c	3.00	9.00	21.00
852-Chilly Willy (2/58)(Lantz)	.85	2.50	6.00
853-Pluto (Disney) (10/57)	1.30	4.00	9.00
854-The Hunchback of Notre Dame (Movie)-Photo-c	6.00	18.00	42.00
855-Broken Arrow (TV)-Photo-c	2.65	8.00	18.00
856-Buffalo Bill, Jr. (TV)-Photo-c	2.15	6.50	15.00
857-The Goofy Adventure Story (Disney) (11/57)	2.00	6.00	14.00
858-Daisy Duck's Diary (Disney) (11/57)	1.70	5.00	12.00
859-Topper and Neil (TV)(11/57)	1.30	4.00	9.00
860-Wyatt Earp (No.1)(TV)-Manning-a; photo-c	5.00	15.00	35.00
861-Frosty the Snowman	1.30	4.00	9.00

Four Color #762, © United Artists

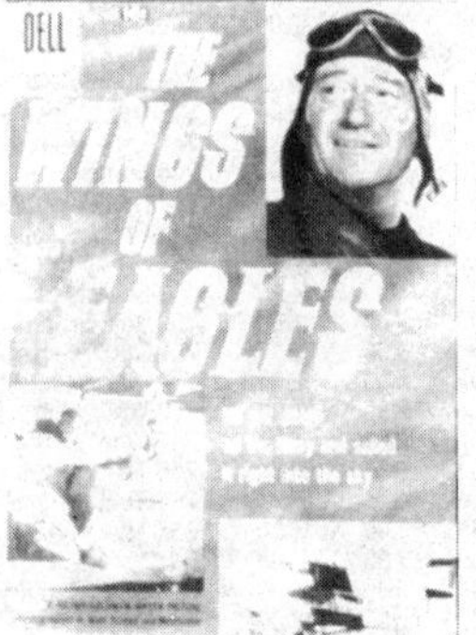

Four Color #790, © M.G.M.

Four Color #836, © WDC

Four Color #880, © DELL

Four Color #904, © DELL

Four Color #937, © Hanna-Barbera

FOUR COLOR (continued)	**Good**	**Fine**	**Mint**
862-The Truth About Mother Goose (Disney-Movie) (11/57)	3.50	10.50	24.00
863-Francis the Famous Talking Mule	1.00	3.00	7.00
864-The Littlest Snowman	2.00	6.00	12.00
865-Andy Burnett (TV) (Disney) (12/57)-Photo-c	3.00	9.00	21.00
866-Mars and Beyond (Disney-Movie)	2.00	6.00	14.00
867-Santa Claus Funnies	1.70	5.00	12.00
868-The Little People (12/57)	1.50	4.50	10.00
869-Old Yeller (Disney-Movie)-Photo-c	2.65	8.00	18.00
870-Little Beaver (1/58)	1.30	4.00	9.00
871-Curly Kayoe	1.70	5.00	12.00
872-Captain Kangaroo (TV)-Photo-c	5.00	15.00	35.00
873-Grandma Duck's Farm Friends (Disney)	2.00	6.00	14.00
874-Old Ironsides (Disney-Movie with Johnny Tremain) (1/58)	2.30	7.00	16.00
875-Trumpets West (Luke Short) (2/58)	2.00	6.00	14.00
876-Tales of Wells Fargo (No.1) (TV) (2/58)-Photo-c	3.50	10.50	24.00
877-Frontier Doctor with Rex Allen (TV)-Alex Toth-a; photo-c	6.00	18.00	42.00
878-Peanuts (No.1)-Schulz-c only (2/58)	4.35	13.00	30.00
879-Brave Eagle (TV)(2/58)-Photo-c	1.50	4.50	10.00
880-Steve Donovan, Western Marshal-Drucker-a (TV)-Photo-c	2.00	6.00	14.00
881-The Captain and the Kids	1.50	4.50	10.00
882-Zorro (Disney)-1st Disney issue by Alex Toth (TV) (2/58)-Photo-c	5.00	15.00	35.00
883-The Little Rascals (TV)	1.70	5.00	12.00
884-Hawkeye and the Last of the Mohicans (TV)-Photo-c	2.30	7.00	16.00
885-Fury (TV) (3/58)-Photo-c	3.00	9.00	21.00
886-Bongo and Lumpjaw (Disney, 3/58)	1.30	4.00	9.00
887-The Hardy Boys (Disney)(TV)-Mickey Mouse Club (1/58)-Photo-c	3.00	9.00	21.00
888-Elmer Fudd (3/58)	.85	2.50	6.00
889-Clint and Mac (Disney)(TV)-Alex Toth-a (3/58)-Photo-c	5.70	17.00	40.00
890-Wyatt Earp (TV)-by Russ Manning; photo-c	3.50	10.50	24.00
891-Light in the Forest (Disney-Movie) (3/58)-Photo-c	2.30	7.00	16.00
892-Maverick (No.1) (TV) (4/58)	4.60	14.00	32.00
893-Jim Bowie (TV)-Photo-c	2.30	7.00	16.00
894-Oswald the Rabbit (Lantz)	.85	2.50	6.00
895-Wagon Train (No.1)(TV)(3/58)-Photo-c	4.00	12.00	28.00
896-The Adventures of Tinker Bell (Disney)	3.00	9.00	21.00
897-Jiminy Cricket (Disney)	1.70	5.00	12.00
898-Silvertip (Max Brand)-Kinstler-a (5/58)	3.00	9.00	21.00
899-Goofy (Disney)	2.00	6.00	14.00
900-Prince Valiant-by Bob Fuje	3.50	10.50	24.00
901-Little Hiawatha (Disney)	1.50	4.50	10.00
902-Will-Yum!	1.00	3.00	7.00
903-Dotty Dripple and Taffy	1.30	4.00	9.00
904-Lee Hunter, Indian Fighter	1.70	5.00	12.00
905-Annette (Disney,TV, 5/58)-Mickey Mouse Club-Photo-c	9.50	28.50	65.00
906-Francis the Famous Talking Mule	1.00	3.00	7.00
907-Sugarfoot (No.1)(TV)Toth-a; photo-c	7.00	21.00	50.00
908-The Little People and the Giant-Walt Scott (5/58)	1.50	4.50	10.00
909-Smitty	1.30	4.00	9.00
910-The Vikings (Movie)-Buscema-a; photo-c	4.35	13.00	30.00
911-The Gray Ghost (TV)(Movie)-Photo-c	3.50	10.50	24.00
912-Leave It to Beaver (No.1)(TV)-Photo-c	8.50	25.50	60.00
913-The Left-Handed Gun (Movie) (7/58); Paul Newman photo-c	5.00	15.00	35.00

	Good	**Fine**	**Mint**
914-No Time for Sergeants (Movie)-Photo-c; Toth-a	6.00	18.00	42.00
915-Casey Jones (TV)-Photo-c	2.30	7.00	16.00
916-Red Ryder Ranch Comics	1.60	4.70	11.00
917-The Life of Riley (TV)-Photo-c	5.00	15.00	35.00
918-Beep Beep, the Roadrunner (No.1)(7/58)-Two different back covers published	2.30	7.00	16.00
919-Boots and Saddles (No.1)(TV)-Photo-c	3.50	10.50	24.00
920-Zorro (Disney-TV)(6/58)Toth-a; photo-c	5.00	15.00	35.00
921-Wyatt Earp (TV)-Manning-a; photo-c	3.50	10.50	24.00
922-Johnny Mack Brown by Russ Manning-Photo-c	3.50	10.50	24.00
923-Timmy	1.15	3.50	8.00
924-Colt .45 (No.1)(TV)(8/58)-Photo-c	4.00	12.00	28.00
925-Last of the Fast Guns (Movie) (8/58)-Photo-c	3.00	9.00	21.00
926-Peter Pan (Disney)-Reprint of No. 442	2.00	6.00	14.00
927-Top Gun (Luke Short) Buscema-a	2.00	6.00	14.00
928-Sea Hunt (No.1) (TV)-Lloyd Bridges photo-c	4.35	13.00	30.00
929-Brave Eagle (TV)-Photo-c	1.50	4.50	10.00
930-Maverick (TV) (7/58)-James Garner photo-c	4.00	12.00	28.00
931-Have Gun, Will Travel (No.1) (TV)-Photo-c	4.35	13.00	30.00
932-Smokey the Bear (His Life Story)	1.50	4.50	10.00
933-Zorro (Disney)-by Alex Toth (TV)(9/58)	5.00	15.00	35.00
934-Restless Gun (No.1)(TV)-Photo-c	4.60	14.00	32.00
935-King of the Royal Mounted	3.00	9.00	21.00
936-The Little Rascals (TV)	1.70	5.00	12.00
937-Ruff and Reddy (No.1)(TV)(Hanna-Barbera)	2.30	7.00	16.00
938-Elmer Fudd (9/58)	.85	2.50	6.00
939-Steve Canyon - not by Caniff	3.00	9.00	21.00
940-Lolly and Pepper	1.30	4.00	9.00
941-Pluto (Disney) (10/58)	1.30	4.00	9.00
942-Pony Express (TV)	2.00	6.00	14.00
943-White Wilderness (Disney-Movie) (10/58	2.30	7.00	16.00
944-The 7th Voyage of Sindbad (Movie) (9/58)-Buscema-a	8.00	24.00	56.00
945-Maverick (TV)-James Garner photo-c	4.00	12.00	28.00
946-The Big Country (Movie)-Photo-c	3.00	9.00	21.00
947-Broken Arrow (TV)-Photo-c	2.65	8.00	18.00
948-Daisy Duck's Diary (Disney) (11/58)	1.70	5.00	12.00
949-High Adventure (Lowell Thomas')(TV)-Photo-c	2.00	6.00	14.00
950-Frosty the Snowman	1.30	4.00	9.00
951-The Lennon Sisters Life Story (TV)-Toth-a, 32pgs.-Photo-c	7.00	21.00	50.00
952-Goofy (Disney) (11/58)	2.00	6.00	14.00
953-Francis the Famous Talking Mule	1.00	3.00	7.00
954-Man in Space-Satellites (Disney-Movie)	2.00	6.00	14.00
955-Hi and Lois (11/58)	1.00	3.00	7.00
956-Ricky Nelson (No.1)(TV)-Photo-c	8.50	25.50	60.00
957-Buffalo Bee (No.1)(TV)	2.30	7.00	16.00
958-Santa Claus Funnies	1.50	4.50	10.00
959-Christmas Stories-(Walt Scott's Little People)(1951-56 strip reprints)	1.50	4.50	10.00
960-Zorro (Disney)(TV)(12/58)-Toth art	5.00	15.00	35.00
961-Jace Pearson's Tales of the Texas Rangers (TV)-Spiegle-a; photo-c	3.00	9.00	21.00
962-Maverick (TV) (1/59)-James Garner photo-c	4.00	12.00	28.00
963-Johnny Mack Brown-Photo-c	3.00	9.00	21.00
964-The Hardy Boys (TV)(Disney)-Mickey Mouse Club (1/59)-Photo-c	3.00	9.00	21.00

FOUR COLOR (continued)	Good	Fine	Mint
965-Grandma Duck's Farm Friends (Disney) (1/59)	2.00	6.00	14.00
966-Tonka (starring Sal Mineo; Disney-Movie)-Photo-c	3.00	9.00	21.00
967-Chilly Willy (2/59)(Lantz)	.85	2.50	6.00
968-Tales of Wells Fargo (TV)-Photo-c	3.00	9.00	21.00
969-Peanuts (2/59)	3.50	10.50	24.00
970-Lawman (No.1)(TV)-Photo-c	4.60	14.00	32.00
971-Wagon Train (TV)-Photo-c	3.00	9.00	21.00
972-Tom Thumb (Movie)-George Pal	5.00	15.00	35.00
973-Sleeping Beauty and the Prince (Disney) (5/59)	4.00	12.00	28.00
974-The Little Rascals (TV)(3/59)	1.70	5.00	12.00
975-Fury (TV)-Photo-c	3.00	9.00	21.00
976-Zorro (Disney)(TV)-Toth-a; photo-c	5.00	15.00	35.00
977-Elmer Fudd	.85	2.50	6.00
978-Lolly and Pepper	1.30	4.00	9.00
979-Oswald the Rabbit (Lantz)	.85	2.50	6.00
980-Maverick (TV) (4-6/59)-James Garner & Jack Kelly photo-c	4.00	12.00	28.00
981-Ruff and Reddy (TV)(Hanna-Barbera)	1.70	5.00	12.00
982-The New Adventures of Tinker Bell (TV-Disney)	3.00	9.00	21.00
983-Have Gun, Will Travel (TV) (4-6/59)-Photo-c	3.50	10.50	24.00
984-Sleeping Beauty's Fairy Godmothers (Disney)	4.00	12.00	28.00
985-Shaggy Dog (Disney-Movie)-Photo-c	2.30	7.00	16.00
986-Restless Gun (TV)-Photo-c	3.50	10.50	24.00
987-Goofy (Disney) (7/59)	2.00	6.00	14.00
988-Little Hiawatha (Disney)	1.50	4.50	10.00
989-Jiminy Cricket (Disney) (5-7/59)	1.70	5.00	12.00
990-Huckleberry Hound (No.1)(TV)(Hanna-Barbera)	2.30	7.00	16.00
991-Francis the Famous Talking Mule	1.00	3.00	7.00
992-Sugarfoot (TV)-Toth-a; photo-c	7.00	21.00	50.00
993-Jim Bowie (TV)-Photo-c	2.30	7.00	16.00
994-Sea Hunt (TV)-Lloyd Bridges photo-c	3.50	10.50	24.00
995-Donald Duck Album (Disney) (5-7/59)	2.00	6.00	14.00
996-Nevada (Zane Grey)	2.00	6.00	14.00
997-Walt Disney Presents-Tales of Texas John Slaughter (TV-Disney)-Photo-c	2.65	8.00	18.00
998-Ricky Nelson (TV)-Photo-c	8.50	25.50	60.00
999-Leave It to Beaver (TV)-Photo-c	7.00	21.00	50.00
1000-The Gray Ghost (Movie) (6-8/59)-Photo-c	3.50	10.50	24.00
1001-Lowell Thomas' High Adventure (TV) (8-10/59)-Photo-c	2.00	6.00	14.00
1002-Buffalo Bee (TV)	2.00	6.00	14.00
1003-Zorro (TV) (Disney)-Photo-c	4.00	12.00	28.00
1004-Colt .45 (TV) (6-8/59)-Photo-c	3.00	9.00	21.00
1005-Maverick (TV)-James Garner photo-c	4.00	12.00	28.00
1006-Hercules (Movie)-Buscema-a	6.00	18.00	42.00
1007-John Paul Jones (Movie)-Photo-c	2.30	7.00	16.00
1008-Beep Beep, the Road Runner (7-9/59)	1.50	4.50	10.00
1009-The Rifleman (No.1) (TV)-Photo-c	6.00	18.00	42.00
1010-Grandma Duck's Farm Friends (Disney)-by Carl Barks	6.00	18.00	42.00
1011-Buckskin (No.1)(TV)-Photo-c	3.50	10.50	24.00
1012-Last Train from Gun Hill (Movie) (7/59)-Photo-c	3.50	10.50	24.00
1013-Bat Masterson (No.1) (TV) (8/59)-Gene Barry photo-c	3.50	10.50	24.00
1014-The Lennon Sisters (TV)-Toth-a; photo-c	6.50	19.50	45.00
1015-Peanuts-Schulz-c	3.50	10.50	24.00
1016-Smokey the Bear Nature Stories	1.15	3.50	8.00

	Good	Fine	Mint
1017-Chilly Willy (Lantz)	.85	2.50	6.00
1018-Rio Bravo (Movie)(6/59)-John Wayne; Toth-a; John Wayne, Dean Martin & Ricky Nelson photo-c	10.00	30.00	70.00
1019-Wagon Train (TV)-Photo-c	3.00	9.00	21.00
1020-Jungle Jim-McWilliams-a	1.70	5.00	12.00
1021-Jace Pearson's Tales of the Texas Rangers (TV)-Photo-c	2.65	8.00	18.00
1022-Timmy	1.15	3.50	8.00
1023-Tales of Wells Fargo (TV)-Photo-c	3.00	9.00	21.00
1024-Darby O'Gill and the Little People (Disney-Movie)-Toth-a; Photo-c	5.70	17.00	40.00
1025-Vacation in Disneyland (8-10/59)-Carl Barks-a (Disney)	6.00	18.00	42.00
1026-Spin and Marty (TV)(Disney)-Mickey Mouse Club (9-11/59)-Photo-c	2.65	8.00	18.00
1027-The Texan (TV)-Photo-c	3.00	9.00	21.00
1028-Rawhide (No.1)(TV)-Clint Eastwood photo-c	8.50	25.50	60.00
1029-Boots and Saddles (9/59, TV)-Photo-c	2.65	8.00	18.00
1030-Spanky and Alfalfa, the Little Rascals (TV)	1.50	4.50	10.00
1031-Fury (TV)-Photo-c	3.00	9.00	21.00
1032-Elmer Fudd	.85	2.50	6.00
1033-Steve Canyon-not by Caniff; photo-c	3.00	9.00	21.00
1034-Nancy and Sluggo Summer Camp (9-11/59)	1.70	5.00	12.00
1035-Lawman (TV)-Photo-c	3.50	10.50	24.00
1036-The Big Circus (Movie)-Photo-c	2.00	6.00	14.00
1037-Zorro (Disney)(TV)-Tufts-a; Annette Funicello photo-c	6.50	19.50	45.00
1038-Ruff and Reddy (TV)(Hanna-Barbera)('59)	1.70	5.00	12.00
1039-Pluto (Disney) (11-1/60)	1.30	4.00	9.00
1040-Quick Draw McGraw (No.1)(TV)(Hanna-Barbera)(12-2/60)	2.30	7.00	16.00
1041-Sea Hunt (TV)-Toth-a; Lloyd Bridges photo-c	5.00	15.00	35.00
1042-The Three Chipmunks (Alvin, Simon & Theodore) (No.1)(TV) (10-12/59)	.85	2.50	6.00
1043-The Three Stooges (No.1)-Photo-c	5.00	15.00	35.00
1044-Have Gun, Will Travel (TV)-Photo-c	3.50	10.50	24.00
1045-Restless Gun (TV)-Photo-c	3.50	10.50	24.00
1046-Beep Beep, the Road Runner (11-1/60)	1.50	4.50	10.00
1047-Gyro Gearloose (No.1)(Disney)-Barks c/a	6.00	18.00	42.00
1048-The Horse Soldiers (Movie) (John Wayne)-Sekowsky-a	9.00	27.00	62.00
1049-Don't Give Up the Ship (Movie) (8/59)-Jerry Lewis photo-c	3.50	10.50	24.00
1050-Huckleberry Hound (TV)(Hanna-Barbera)(10-12/59)	1.70	5.00	12.00
1051-Donald in Mathmagic Land (Disney-Movie)	3.00	9.00	21.00
1052-Ben-Hur (Movie) (11/59)-Manning-a	5.00	15.00	35.00
1053-Goofy (Disney) (11-1/60)	2.00	6.00	14.00
1054-Huckleberry Hound Winter Fun (TV)(Hanna-Barbera)(12/59)	1.70	5.00	12.00
1055-Daisy Duck's Diary (Disney)-by Carl Barks (11-1/60)	5.00	15.00	35.00
1056-Yellowstone Kelly (Movie)-Photo-c	2.30	7.00	16.00
1057-Mickey Mouse Album (Disney)	1.70	5.00	12.00
1058-Colt .45 (TV)-Photo-c	3.00	9.00	21.00
1059-Sugarfoot (TV)-Photo-c	4.35	13.00	30.00
1060-Journey to the Center of the Earth (Movie)-Photo-c	6.00	18.00	42.00
1061-Buffalo Bee (TV)	2.00	6.00	14.00
1062-Christmas Stories-(Walt Scott's Little People strip-r)			

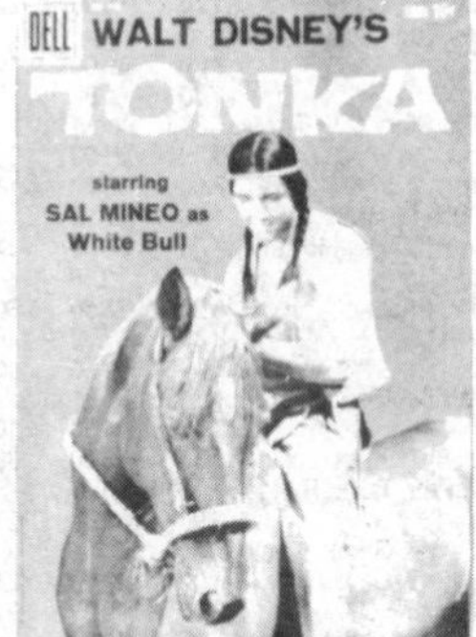

Four Color #966, © WDC

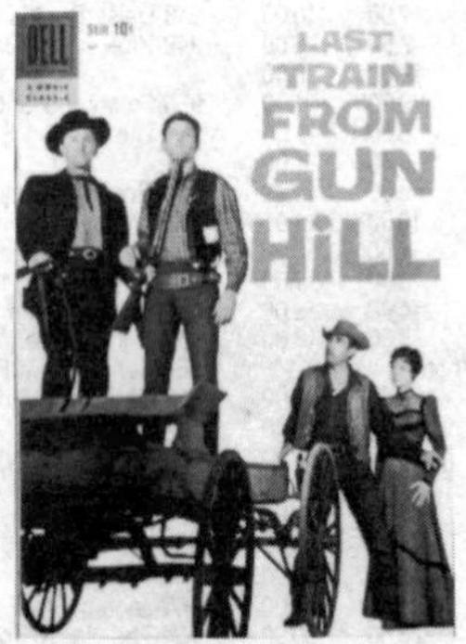

Four Color #1012, © DELL

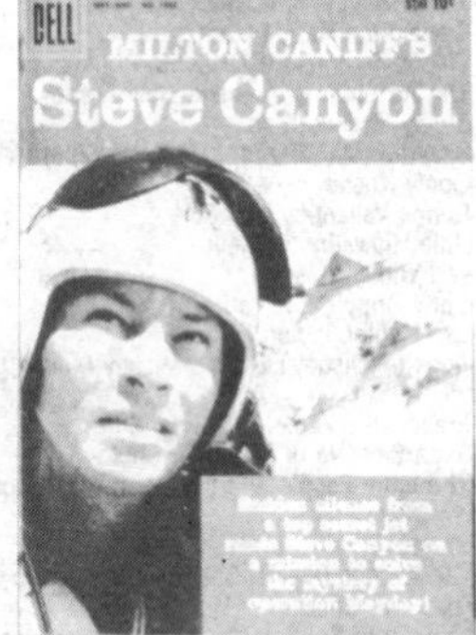

Four Color #1033, © Milton Caniff

Four Color #1067, © Hanna Barbera

Four Color #1106, © Warner Bros.

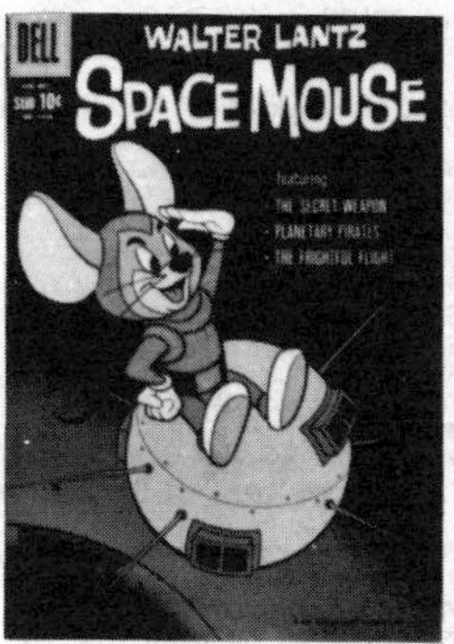

Four Color #1132, © W. Lantz

FOUR COLOR (continued)	Good	Fine	Mint
	1.50	4.50	10.00
1063-Santa Claus Funnies	1.50	4.50	10.00
1064-Bugs Bunny's Merry Christmas (12/59)	1.30	4.00	9.00
1065-Frosty the Snowman	1.30	4.00	9.00
1066-77 Sunset Strip (No.1)(TV)-Toth-a (1-3/60)-Photo-c	5.00	15.00	35.00
1067-Yogi Bear (No.1)(TV)(Hanna-Barbera)	2.65	8.00	18.00
1068-Francis the Famous Talking Mule	1.00	3.00	7.00
1069-The FBI Story (Movie)-Toth-a; photo-c	6.00	18.00	42.00
1070-Solomon and Sheba (Movie)-Sekowsky-a; photo-c	4.60	14.00	32.00
1071-The Real McCoys (No.1)(TV)-Toth-a; photo-c	5.00	15.00	35.00
1072-Blythe (Marge's)	2.00	6.00	14.00
1073-Grandma Duck's Farm Friends-Barks c/a (Disney)	6.00	18.00	42.00
1074-Chilly Willy (Lantz)	.85	2.50	6.00
1075-Tales of Wells Fargo (TV)-Photo-c	3.00	9.00	21.00
1076-The Rebel (No.1)(TV)-Sekowsky-a; photo-c	5.00	15.00	35.00
1077-The Deputy (No.1)(TV)-Buscema-a; Henry Fonda photo-c	5.00	15.00	35.00
1078-The Three Stooges (2-4/60)-Photo-c	3.50	10.50	24.00
1079-The Little Rascals (TV)(Spanky & Alfalfa)	1.50	4.50	10.00
1080-Fury (TV) (2-4/60)-Photo-c	3.00	9.00	21.00
1081-Elmer Fudd	.85	2.50	6.00
1082-Spin and Marty (Disney)(TV)-Photo-c	2.65	8.00	18.00
1083-Men into Space (TV)-Anderson-a; photo-c	2.65	8.00	18.00
1084-Speedy Gonzales	1.30	4.00	9.00
1085-The Time Machine (H.G. Wells) (Movie) (3/60)-Alex Toth-a	6.50	19.50	45.00
1086-Lolly and Pepper	1.30	4.00	9.00
1087-Peter Gunn (TV)-Photo-c	3.50	10.50	24.00
1088-A Dog of Flanders (Movie)-Photo-c	2.00	6.00	14.00
1089-Restless Gun (TV)-Photo-c	3.50	10.50	24.00
1090-Francis the Famous Talking Mule	1.00	3.00	7.00
1091-Jacky's Diary (4-6/60)	2.30	7.00	16.00
1092-Toby Tyler (Disney-Movie)-Photo-c	2.00	6.00	14.00
1093-MacKenzie's Raiders (Movie)-Photo-c	3.50	10.50	24.00
1094-Goofy (Disney)	2.00	6.00	14.00
1095-Gyro Gearloose (Disney)-Barks-c/a	5.00	15.00	35.00
1096-The Texan (TV)-Photo-c	3.00	9.00	21.00
1097-Rawhide (TV)-Manning-a; Clint Eastwood photo-c	6.00	18.00	42.00
1098-Sugarfoot (TV)-Photo-c	4.35	13.00	30.00
1099-Donald Duck Album (Disney) (5-7/60) - Barks-c	2.30	7.00	16.00
1100-Annette's Life Story (Disney-Movie)(5/60)-Photo-c	10.00	30.00	70.00
1101-Robert Louis Stevenson's Kidnapped (Disney-Movie) (5/60); photo-c	3.00	9.00	21.00
1102-Wanted: Dead or Alive (No.1)(TV) (5-7/60); Steve McQueen photo-c	5.00	15.00	35.00
1103-Leave It to Beaver (TV)-Photo-c	7.00	21.00	50.00
1104-Yogi Bear Goes to College (TV)(Hanna-Barbera)(6-8/60)	1.70	5.00	12.00
1105-Gale Storm (Oh! Susanna) (TV)-Toth-a; photo-c	6.50	19.50	45.00
1106-77 Sunset Strip (TV)(6-8/60)-Toth-a; photo-c	4.35	13.00	30.00
1107-Buckskin (TV)-Photo-c	3.00	9.00	21.00
1108-The Troubleshooters (TV)-Photo-c	2.65	8.00	18.00
1109-This Is Your Life, Donald Duck (Disney)(TV)(8-10/60)-Gyro flash-back to WDC&S 141. Origin Donald Duck (1st told)	5.70	17.00	40.00
1110-Bonanza (No.1) (TV) (6-8/60)-Photo-c	4.60	14.00	32.00
1111-Shotgun Slade (TV)	3.00	9.00	21.00
1112-Pixie and Dixie and Mr. Jinks (No.1)(TV)(Hanna-Barbera) (7-9/60)	2.00	6.00	14.00
1113-Tales of Wells Fargo (TV)-Photo-c	3.00	9.00	21.00
1114-Huckleberry Finn (Movie) (7/60)-Photo-c	2.30	7.00	16.00
1115-Ricky Nelson (TV)-Manning-a; photo-c	8.50	25.50	60.00
1116-Boots and Saddles (TV)(8/60)-Photo-c	2.65	8.00	18.00
1117-Boy and the Pirates (Movie)-Photo-c	3.00	9.00	21.00
1118-The Sword and the Dragon (Movie) (6/60)-Photo-c	3.50	10.50	24.00
1119-Smokey the Bear Nature Stories	1.15	3.50	8.00
1120-Dinosaurus (Movie)-Painted-c	2.65	8.00	18.00
1121-Hercules Unchained (Movie)(8/60)-Crandall/Evans-a	4.60	14.00	32.00
1122-Chilly Willy (Lantz)	.85	2.50	6.00
1123-Tombstone Territory (TV)-Photo-c	3.50	10.50	24.00
1124-Whirlybirds (No.1) (TV)-Photo-c	3.50	10.50	24.00
1125-Laramie (No.1)(TV)-Photo-c	4.35	13.00	30.00
1126-Sundance (TV) (8-10/60)-Photo-c	4.35	13.00	30.00
1127-The Three Stooges-Photo-c	3.50	10.50	24.00
1128-Rocky and His Friends (No.1)(TV) (Jay Ward) (8-10/60)	5.70	17.00	40.00
1129-Pollyanna (Disney-Movie)-Photo-c	5.00	15.00	35.00
1130-The Deputy (TV)-Buscema-a; photo-c	4.35	13.00	30.00
1131-Elmer Fudd (9-11/60)	.85	2.50	6.00
1132-Space Mouse (Lantz)(8-10/60)	1.15	3.50	8.00
1133-Fury (TV)-Photo-c	3.00	9.00	21.00
1134-Real McCoys (TV)-Toth-a; photo-c	5.00	15.00	35.00
1135-M.G.M.'s Mouse Musketeers	.85	2.50	6.00
1136-Jungle Cat (Disney-Movie) (9-11/60)-Photo-c	3.00	9.00	21.00
1137-The Little Rascals (TV)	1.50	4.50	10.00
1138-The Rebel (TV)-Photo-c	4.35	13.00	30.00
1139-Spartacus (Movie) (11/60)-Buscema-a; photo-c	5.00	15.00	35.00
1140-Donald Duck Album (Disney)	2.30	7.00	16.00
1141-Huckleberry Hound for President (TV)(Hanna-Barbera)(10/60)	1.70	5.00	12.00
1142-Johnny Ringo (TV)-Photo-c	3.50	10.50	24.00
1143-Pluto (Disney) (11-1/61)	1.30	4.00	9.00
1144-The Story of Ruth (Movie)-Photo-c	5.00	15.00	35.00
1145-The Lost World (Movie)-Gil Kane-a; photo-c	5.00	15.00	35.00
1146-Restless Gun (TV)-Photo-c	3.50	10.50	24.00
1147-Sugarfoot (TV)-Photo-c	4.35	13.00	30.00
1148-I Aim at the Stars-the Wernher Von Braun Story (Movie) (11-1/61)-Photo-c	2.30	7.00	16.00
1149-Goofy (Disney) (11-1/61)	2.00	6.00	14.00
1150-Daisy Duck's Diary (Disney) (12-1/61) by Carl Barks	5.00	15.00	35.00
1151-Mickey Mouse Album (Disney) (11-1/61)	1.70	5.00	12.00
1152-Rocky and His Friends (Jay Ward) (TV) (12-2/61)	5.15	15.50	36.00
1153-Frosty the Snowman	1.15	3.50	8.00
1154-Santa Claus Funnies	1.50	4.50	10.00
1155-North to Alaska (Movie) - J. Wayne-Photo-c	8.00	24.00	56.00
1156-Walt Disney Swiss Family Robinson (Movie) (12/60)-Photo-c	3.00	9.00	21.00
1157-Master of the World (Movie) (7/61)	3.00	9.00	21.00
1158-Three Worlds of Gulliver (2 issues with different covers) (Movie)-Photo-c	3.00	9.00	21.00
1159-77 Sunset Strip (TV)-Toth-a; photo-c	4.35	13.00	30.00
1160-Rawhide (TV)-Clint Eastwood photo-c	6.00	18.00	42.00

FOUR COLOR (continued)	Good	Fine	Mint
1161-Grandma Duck's Farm Friends (Disney) by Carl Barks (2-4/61)	6.00	18.00	42.00
1162-Yogi Bear Joins the Marines (TV)(Hanna-Barbera)(5-7/61)	1.70	5.00	12.00
1163-Daniel Boone (3-5/61); Marsh-a	2.65	8.00	18.00
1164-Wanted: Dead or Alive (TV); Steve McQueen photo-c	4.35	13.00	30.00
1165-Ellery Queen (No.1)(3-5/61)	4.35	13.00	30.00
1166-Rocky and His Friends (Jay Ward) (TV)	5.15	15.50	36.00
1167-Tales of Wells Fargo (TV)-Photo-c	3.00	9.00	21.00
1168-The Detectives (TV)-Photo-c	3.50	10.50	24.00
1169-New Adventures of Sherlock Holmes	9.00	27.00	62.00
1170-The Three Stooges-Photo-c	3.50	10.50	24.00
1171-Elmer Fudd	.85	2.50	6.00
1172-Fury (TV)-Photo-c	3.00	9.00	21.00
1173-The Twilight Zone (No.1)-Crandall/Evans-c/a (TV) (5/61)	4.60	14.00	32.00
1174-The Little Rascals (TV)	1.50	4.50	10.00
1175-M.G.M.'s Mouse Musketeers (3-5/61)	.85	2.50	6.00
1176-Dondi (Movie)-Origin; photo-c	1.70	5.00	12.00
1177-Chilly Willy (Lantz)(4-6/61)	.85	2.50	6.00
1178-Ten Who Dared (Disney-Movie) (12/60)	2.30	7.00	16.00
1179-The Swamp Fox (TV)(Disney)-Photo-c	3.00	9.00	21.00
1180-The Danny Thomas Show (TV)-Toth-a; photo-c	6.50	19.50	45.00
1181-Texas John Slaughter (TV)(Disney)(4-6/61)-Photo-c	2.00	6.00	14.00
1182-Donald Duck Album (Disney) (5-7/61)	2.00	6.00	14.00
1183-101 Dalmatians (Disney-Movie) (3/61)	2.65	8.00	18.00
1184-Gyro Gearloose; Barks c/a (Disney) (5-7/61) Two variations exist	5.00	15.00	35.00
1185-Sweetie Pie	1.50	4.50	10.00
1186-Yak Yak (No.1) by Jack Davis (2 versions - one minus 3-pg. Davis-c/a)	4.00	12.00	28.00
1187-The Three Stooges (6-8/61)-Photo-c	3.50	10.50	24.00
1188-Atlantis, the Lost Continent (Movie) (5/61)-Photo-c	5.00	15.00	35.00
1189-Greyfriars Bobby (Disney-Movie, 11/61)-Photo-c	2.65	8.00	18.00
1190-Donald and the Wheel (Disney-Movie) (11/61); Barks-c	3.00	9.00	21.00
1191-Leave It to Beaver (TV)-Photo-c	7.00	21.00	50.00
1192-Ricky Nelson (TV)-Manning-a; photo-c	8.50	25.50	60.00
1193-The Real McCoys (TV)(6-8/61)-Photo-c	4.35	13.00	30.00
1194-Pepe (Movie) (4/61)-Photo-c	1.70	5.00	12.00
1195-National Velvet (No.1)(TV)-Photo-c	2.30	7.00	16.00
1196-Pixie and Dixie and Mr. Jinks (TV)(Hanna-Barbera)(7-9/61)	1.70	5.00	12.00
1197-The Aquanauts (TV)(5-7/61)-Photo-c	3.00	9.00	21.00
1198-Donald in Mathmagic Land - reprint of No. 1051 (Disney-Movie)	2.65	8.00	18.00
1199-The Absent-Minded Professor (Disney-Movie) (4/61)-Photo-c	3.00	9.00	21.00
1200-Hennessey (TV) (8-10/61)-Gil Kane-a; photo-c	3.50	10.50	24.00
1201-Goofy (Disney) (8-10/61)	2.00	6.00	14.00
1202-Rawhide (TV)-Clint Eastwood photo-c	6.00	18.00	42.00
1203-Pinocchio (Disney) (3/62)	2.00	6.00	14.00
1204-Scamp (Disney)	.85	2.50	6.00
1205-David and Goliath (Movie) (7/61)-Photo-c	3.00	9.00	21.00
1206-Lolly and Pepper (9-11/61)	1.30	4.00	9.00
1207-The Rebel (TV)-Sekowsky-a; photo-c	4.35	13.00	30.00
1208-Rocky and His Friends (Jay Ward) (TV)	4.60	14.00	32.00
1209-Sugarfoot (TV)-Photo-c	4.35	13.00	30.00
1210-The Parent Trap (Disney-Movie)(8/61)(Haley Mills photo-c)	6.00	18.00	42.00

	Good	Fine	Mint
1211-77 Sunset Strip (TV)-Manning-a; photo-c	3.50	10.50	24.00
1212-Chilly Willy (Lantz)(7-9/61)	.85	2.50	6.00
1213-Mysterious Island (Movie)-Photo-c	4.00	12.00	28.00
1214-Smokey the Bear	1.15	3.50	8.00
1215-Tales of Wells Fargo (TV) (10-12/61)-Photo-c	3.00	9.00	21.00
1216-Whirlybirds (TV)-Photo-c	3.50	10.50	24.00
1218-Fury (TV)-Photo-c	3.00	9.00	21.00
1219-The Detectives (TV)-Photo-c	2.65	8.00	18.00
1220-Gunslinger (TV)-Photo-c	3.00	9.00	21.00
1221-Bonanza (TV) (9-11/61)-Photo-c	4.00	12.00	28.00
1222-Elmer Fudd (9-11/61)	.85	2.50	6.00
1223-Laramie (TV)-Gil Kane-a; photo-c	3.50	10.50	24.00
1224-The Little Rascals (TV)(10-12/61)	1.50	4.50	10.00
1225-The Deputy (TV)-Photo-c	4.35	13.00	30.00
1226-Nikki, Wild Dog of the North (Disney-Movie) (9/61)-Photo-c	2.00	6.00	14.00
1227-Morgan the Pirate (Movie)-Photo-c	4.60	14.00	32.00
1229-Thief of Baghdad (Movie)-Evans-a; photo-c	6.50	19.50	45.00
1230-Voyage to the Bottom of the Sea (No.1)(Movie)-Photo-c	3.00	9.00	21.00
1231-Danger Man (TV)(9-11/61); Patrick McGoohan photo-c	3.50	10.50	24.00
1232-On the Double (Movie)	2.00	6.00	14.00
1233-Tammy Tell Me True (Movie) (1961)	3.50	10.50	24.00
1234-The Phantom Planet (Movie) (1961)	3.00	9.00	21.00
1235-Mister Magoo (12-2/62)	3.50	10.50	24.00
1235-Mister Magoo (3-5/65) 2nd printing - reprints of '61 issue	2.00	6.00	14.00
1236-King of Kings (Movie)-Photo-c	4.00	12.00	28.00
1237-The Untouchables (No.1)(TV)-not by Toth; photo-c	3.50	10.50	24.00
1238-Deputy Dawg (TV)	3.50	10.50	24.00
1239-Donald Duck Album (Disney) (10-12/61)-Barks-c	2.30	7.00	16.00
1240-The Detectives (TV)-Tufts-a; photo-c	2.65	8.00	18.00
1241-Sweetie Pie	1.50	4.50	10.00
1242-King Leonardo and His Short Subjects (No.1)(TV)(11-1/62)	3.50	10.50	24.00
1243-Ellery Queen	3.50	10.50	24.00
1244-Space Mouse (Lantz)(11-1/62)	1.15	3.50	8.00
1245-New Adventures of Sherlock Holmes	9.00	27.00	62.00
1246-Mickey Mouse Album (Disney)	1.70	5.00	12.00
1247-Daisy Duck's Diary (Disney) (12-2/62)	1.70	5.00	12.00
1248-Pluto (Disney)	1.30	4.00	9.00
1249-The Danny Thomas Show (TV)-Manning-a; photo-c	5.70	17.00	40.00
1250-The Four Horsemen of the Apocalypse (Movie)-Photo-c	3.50	10.50	24.00
1251-Everything's Ducky (Movie) (1961)	2.30	7.00	16.00
1252-The Andy Griffith Show (TV)-Photo-c; 1st show aired 10/3/60	5.70	17.00	40.00
1253-Space Man (No.1) (1-3/62)	2.65	8.00	18.00
1254-"Diver Dan" (TV) (2-4/62)-Photo-c	2.00	6.00	14.00
1255-The Wonders of Aladdin (Movie) (1961)	3.00	9.00	21.00
1256-Kona, Monarch of Monster Isle (No.1)(2-4/62)-Glanzman-a	2.65	8.00	18.00
1257-Car 54, Where Are You? (No.1) (TV) (3-5/62)-Photo-c	1.75	5.25	12.00
1258-The Frogmen (No.1)-Evans-a	2.65	8.00	18.00
1259-El Cid (Movie) (1961)-Photo-c	3.00	9.00	21.00
1260-The Horsemasters (TV, Movie - Disney) (12-2/62)-Annette Funicello photo-c	3.50	10.50	24.00
1261-Rawhide (TV)-Clint Eastwood photo-c	6.00	18.00	42.00
1262-The Rebel (TV)-Photo-c	4.35	13.00	30.00

Four Color #1180, © DELL

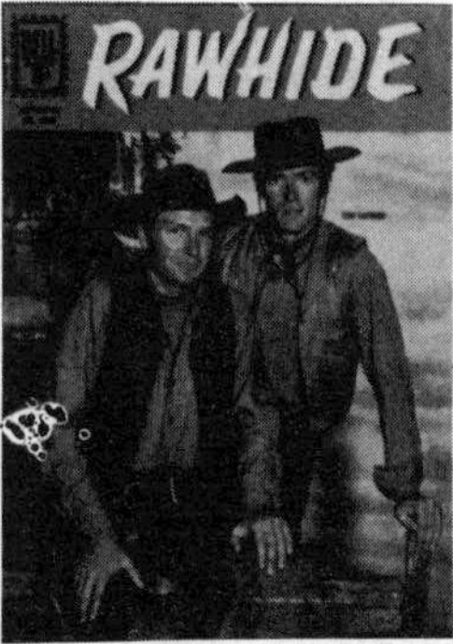

Four Color #1202, © CBS

Four Color #1237, © DELL

Four Color #1265, © Brennan-Westgate

Four Favorites #29, © ACE

Four Most V2#3, © NOVP

FOUR COLOR (continued)

	Good	Fine	Mint
1263-77 Sunset Strip (TV) (12-2/62)-Manning-a; photo-c	3.50	10.50	24.00
1264-Pixie and Dixie and Mr. Jinks (TV)(Hanna-Barbera)	1.70	5.00	12.00
1265-The Real McCoys (TV)-Photo-c	4.35	13.00	30.00
1266-M.G.M.'s Spike and Tyke (12-2/62)	.85	2.50	6.00
1267-Gyro Gearloose; Barks c/a, 4 pgs. (Disney) (12-2/62)	3.70	11.00	26.00
1268-Oswald the Rabbit (Lantz)	.85	2.50	6.00
1269-Rawhide (TV)-Clint Eastwood photo-c	6.00	18.00	42.00
1270-Bullwinkle and Rocky (No.1)(Jay Ward)(TV)(3-5/62)	4.00	12.00	28.00
1271-Yogi Bear Birthday Party (TV)(Hanna-Barbera)(11/61)	1.50	4.50	10.00
1272-Frosty the Snowman	1.15	3.50	8.00
1273-Hans Brinker (Disney-Movie)-Photo-c	2.65	8.00	18.00
1274-Santa Claus Funnies	1.50	4.50	10.00
1275-Rocky and His Friends (Jay Ward) (TV)	4.60	14.00	32.00
1276-Dondi	1.50	4.50	10.00
1278-King Leonardo and His Short Subjects (TV)	3.50	10.50	24.00
1279-Grandma Duck's Farm Friends (Disney)	2.00	6.00	14.00
1280-Hennessey (TV)-Photo-c	2.65	8.00	18.00
1281-Chilly Willy (Lantz)(4-6/62)	.85	2.50	6.00
1282-Babes in Toyland (Disney-Movie) (1/62); Annette Funicello photo-c	4.60	14.00	32.00
1283-Bonanza (TV) (2-4/62)-Photo-c	4.00	12.00	28.00
1284-Laramie (TV)-Heath-a; photo-c	3.50	10.50	24.00
1285-Leave It to Beaver (TV)-Photo-c	7.00	21.00	50.00
1286-The Untouchables (TV)-Photo-c	3.50	10.50	24.00
1287-Man from Wells Fargo (TV)-Photo-c	3.00	9.00	21.00
1288-The Twilight Zone (TV) (4/62)-Crandall/Evans c/a	3.70	11.00	26.00
1289-Ellery Queen	3.50	10.50	24.00
1290-M.G.M.'s Mouse Musketeers	.85	2.50	6.00
1291-77 Sunset Strip (TV)-Manning-a; photo-c	3.50	10.50	24.00
1293-Elmer Fudd (3-5/62)	.85	2.50	6.00
1294-Ripcord (TV)	2.65	8.00	18.00
1295-Mister Ed, the Talking Horse (No.1)(TV)(3-5/62)-Photo-c	2.30	7.00	16.00
1296-Fury (TV) (3-5/62)-Photo-c	3.00	9.00	21.00
1297-Spanky, Alfalfa and the Little Rascals (TV)	1.50	4.50	10.00
1298-The Hathaways (TV)-Photo-c	2.00	6.00	14.00
1299-Deputy Dawg (TV)	3.50	10.50	24.00
1300-The Comancheros (Movie) (1961)-John Wayne	9.00	27.00	62.00
1301-Adventures in Paradise (TV) (2-4/62)	2.00	6.00	14.00
1302-Johnny Jason, Teen Reporter (2-4/62)	1.15	3.50	8.00
1303-Lad: A Dog (Movie)-Photo-c	2.30	7.00	16.00
1304-Nellie the Nurse (3-5/62)-Stanley-a	4.65	14.00	32.00
1305-Mister Magoo (3-5/62)	3.50	10.50	24.00
1306-Target: the Corrupters (TV) (3-5/62)	2.30	7.00	16.00
1307-Margie (TV) (3-5/62)	2.00	6.00	14.00
1308-Tales of the Wizard of Oz (TV) (3-5/62)	5.00	15.00	35.00
1309-87th Precinct (TV) (4-6/62)-Krigstein-a; photo-c	5.00	15.00	35.00
1310-Huck and Yogi Winter Sports (TV)(Hanna-Barbera)(3/62)	1.50	4.50	10.00
1311-Rocky and His Friends (Jay Ward) (TV)	4.60	14.00	32.00
1312-National Velvet (TV)-Photo-c	2.00	6.00	14.00
1313-Moon Pilot (Disney-Movie)-Photo-c	2.30	7.00	16.00
1328-The Underwater City (Movie)-Evans-a (1961)-Photo-c	3.50	10.50	24.00
1330-Brain Boy (No.1)-Gil Kane-a	3.50	10.50	24.00
1332-Bachelor Father (TV)	3.50	10.50	24.00
1333-Short Ribs (4-6/62)	2.30	7.00	16.00
1335-Aggie Mack (4-6/62)	1.70	5.00	12.00
1336-On Stage - not by Leonard Starr	2.30	7.00	16.00
1337-Dr. Kildare (No.1) (TV)-Photo-c	2.65	8.00	18.00
1341-The Andy Griffith Show (TV) (4-6/62)-Photo-c	5.00	15.00	35.00
1348-Yak Yak (No.2)-Jack Davis c/a	3.50	10.50	24.00
1349-Yogi Bear Visits the U.N. (TV)(Hanna-Barbera)(1/62)	3.00	9.00	21.00
1350-Comanche (Disney-Movie)(1962)-Reprints 4-Color 966 (title change from "Tonka" to "Comanche")(4-6/62)-Sal Mineo photo-c	2.00	6.00	14.00
1354-Calvin & the Colonel (TV)(4-6/62)	3.00	9.00	21.00

NOTE: *Missing numbers probably do not exist.*

FOUR FAVORITES (Crime Must Pay the Penalty No. 33 on)
Sept, 1941 - No. 32, Dec, 1947
Ace Magazines

	Good	Fine	Mint
1-Vulcan, Lash Lightning, Magno the Magnetic Man & The Raven begin; Flag-c	35.00	105.00	245.00
2-The Black Ace only app.	17.00	51.00	120.00
3-Last Vulcan	15.00	45.00	105.00
4,5: 4-The Raven & Vulcan end; Unknown Soldier begins, ends No. 28. 5-Captain Courageous begins, ends No. 28; not in No. 6	14.00	42.00	100.00
6-8: 6-The Flag app.; Mr. Risk begins	11.00	32.00	76.00
9,11-Kurtzman-a; 11-L.B. Cole-a	15.00	45.00	105.00
10-Classic Kurtzman c/a	17.00	51.00	120.00
12-L.B. Cole-a	9.00	27.00	63.00
13-20: 18-Palais c/a	7.00	21.00	50.00
21-No Unknown Soldier; The Unknown app.	5.50	16.50	38.00
22-Captain Courageous drops costume	5.50	16.50	38.00
23-26: 23-Unknown Soldier drops costume. 26-Last Magno	5.50	16.50	38.00
27-32	4.35	13.00	30.00

FOUR HORSEMEN, THE (See The Crusaders)

FOUR HORSEMEN OF THE APOCALYPSE, THE (See 4-Color No. 1250)

FOUR MOST (. . .Boys No. 32-41)
Winter, 1941-42 - V8No.5(No. 36), 9-10/49; No. 37, 11-12/49 - No. 41, 6-7/50
Novelty Publications/Star Publications No. 37-on

	Good	Fine	Mint
V1#1-The Target by Sid Greene, The Cadet & Dick Cole begin w/origins retold; produced by Funnies Inc.	35.00	105.00	245.00
2-Last Target	17.00	51.00	120.00
3-Flag-c	15.00	45.00	105.00
4-1pg. Dr. Seuss(signed)	12.00	36.00	84.00
V2#1-4, V3#1-4	2.65	8.00	18.00
V4#1-4	2.00	6.00	14.00
V5#1-The Target & Targeteers app.	1.70	5.00	12.00
2-5	1.70	5.00	12.00
V6#1-White Rider & Super Horse begins	1.70	5.00	12.00
2-4,6	1.70	5.00	12.00
5-L. B. Cole-c	3.50	10.50	24.00
V7#1,3,5, V8#1	1.70	5.00	12.00
2,4,6-L. B. Cole-c. 6-Last Dick Cole	3.50	10.50	24.00
V8#2,3,5-L. B. Cole c/a	4.60	14.00	32.00
4-L. B. Cole-a	2.65	8.00	18.00
37-41: 38,39-L.B. Cole-c. 38-J. Weismuller life story	2.65	8.00	18.00
Accepted Reprint 38-40 (nd); L.B. Cole-c	1.70	5.00	12.00

FOUR STAR BATTLE TALES
Feb-Mar, 1973 - No. 5, Nov-Dec, 1973
National Periodical Publications

FOUR STAR BATTLE TALES (continued)

	Good	Fine	Mint
1-All reprints		.30	.60
2-5: 5-Krigstein-a(r)		.25	.50

NOTE: ***Drucker** a-1,3-5r. **Heath** a-2r. **Kubert** a-4r; c-2.*

FOUR STAR SPECTACULAR
Mar-Apr, 1976 - No. 6, Jan-Feb, 1977
National Periodical Publications

	Good	Fine	Mint
1-Superboy, Wonder Woman reprints begin		.30	.60
2-6: 2-Infinity cover		.25	.50

NOTE: *All contain DC Superhero reprints. No. 1 has 68 pages; No. 2-6, 52 pages. No. 1,4-Hawkman app.; No. 2-Flash app.; No. 3-Green Lantern app; No. 4-Wonder Woman, Superboy app; No. 5-Gr. Arrow, Vigilante app; No. 6-Blackhawk G.A.-r.*

FOUR TEENERS (Formerly Crime Must Pay The Penalty?; Dotty No. 35 on)
April, 1948 (Teen-age comic)
A. A. Wyn

	Good	Fine	Mint
34	1.70	5.00	12.00

FOX AND THE CROW (Stanley & His Monster No. 109 on)
(See Comic Cavalcade & Real Screen Comics)
Dec-Jan, 1951-52 - No. 108, Feb-Mar, 1968
National Periodical Publications

	Good	Fine	Mint
1	41.00	124.00	290.00
2(Scarce)	21.00	63.00	150.00
3-5	13.00	40.00	90.00
6-10	9.00	27.00	63.00
11-20	5.70	17.00	40.00
21-40	3.50	10.50	24.00
41-60	2.00	6.00	14.00
61-80	1.50	4.50	10.00
81-94	1.00	3.00	7.00
95-Stanley & His Monster begins(origin)	1.50	4.50	10.00
96-99,101-108	.85	2.50	6.00
100	1.15	3.50	8.00

NOTE: *Many covers by **Mort Drucker.***

FOX AND THE HOUND, THE (Disney)
Aug, 1981 - No. 3, Oct, 1981
Whitman Publishing Co.

	Good	Fine	Mint
11292 ('81)-Based on animated movie		.30	.60
2,3		.30	.60

FOX GIANTS
1944 - 1950 (132 - 196 pgs.)
Fox Features Syndicate

	Good	Fine	Mint
Album of Crime nn(1949, 132p)	22.00	65.00	154.00
Album of Love nn(1949, 132p)	16.00	48.00	110.00
All Famous Crime Stories nn('49, 132p)	22.00	65.00	154.00
All Good Comics 1(1944, 132p)(R.W. Voigt)-The Bouncer, Purple Tigress, Puppeteer, Green Mask; Infinity-c	16.00	48.00	110.00
All Great nn(1944, 132p)-Capt. Jack Terry, Rick Evans, Jaguar Man	16.00	48.00	110.00
All Great nn(Chicago Nite Life News)(1945, 132p)-Green Mask, Bouncer, Puppeteer, Rick Evans, Rocket Kelly	20.00	60.00	140.00
All-Great Confessions nn(1949, 132p)	16.00	48.00	110.00
All Great Crime Stories nn('49, 132p)	22.00	65.00	154.00
All Great Jungle Adventures nn('49, 132p)	22.00	65.00	154.00
All Real Confession Mag. 3 (3/49, 132p)	16.00	48.00	110.00
All Real Confession Mag. 4 (4/49, 132p)	16.00	48.00	110.00
All Your Comics 1(1944, 132p)-The Puppeteer, Red Robbins, & Merciless the Sorcerer	16.00	48.00	110.00
Almanac Of Crime nn(1948, 148p)	24.00	72.00	168.00
Almanac Of Crime 1(1950, 132p)	24.00	72.00	168.00
Book Of Love nn(1950, 132p)	16.00	48.00	110.00
Burning Romances 1(1949, 132p)	20.00	60.00	140.00
Crimes Incorporated nn(1950, 132p)	22.00	65.00	154.00
Daring Love Stories nn(1950, 132p)	16.00	48.00	110.00
Everybody's Comics 1(1944, 196p)-The Green Mask, The Puppeteer, The Bouncer; (50 cents)	20.00	60.00	140.00
Everybody's Comics 1(1946, 196p)-Green Lama, The Puppeteer	16.00	48.00	110.00
Everybody's Comics 1(1946, 196p)-Same as '45 Ribtickler	13.00	40.00	90.00
Everybody's Comics nn(1947, 132p)-Jo-Jo, Purple Tigress, Cosmo Cat, Bronze Man	16.00	48.00	110.00
Exciting Romance Stories nn('49, 132p	16.00	48.00	110.00
Intimate Confessions nn(1950, 132p)	16.00	48.00	110.00
Journal Of Crime nn(1949, 132p)	22.00	66.00	154.00
Love Problems nn(1949, 132p)	16.00	48.00	110.00
Love Thrills nn(1950, 132p)	16.00	48.00	110.00
March of Crime nn('48, 132p)-female w/rifle-c	22.00	65.00	154.00
March of Crime nn('49, 132p)-cop w/pistol-c	22.00	65.00	154.00
March of Crime nn(1949, 132p)-coffin & man w/machine-gun-c	22.00	65.00	154.00
Revealing Love Stories nn(1950, 132p)	16.00	48.00	110.00
Ribtickler nn(1945, 196p, 50–)-Chicago Nite Life News; Marvel Mutt, Cosmo Cat, Flash Rabbit, The Nebbs app.	16.00	48.00	110.00
Romantic Thrills nn(1950, 132p)	16.00	48.00	110.00
Secret Love nn(1949, 132p)	16.00	48.00	110.00
Secret Love Stories nn(1949, 132p)	16.00	48.00	110.00
Strange Love nn(1950, 132p)-Photo-c	22.00	65.00	154.00
Sweetheart Scandals nn(1950, 132p)	16.00	48.00	110.00
Teen-Age Love nn(1950, 132p)	16.00	48.00	110.00
Throbbing Love nn(1950, 132p)-Photo-c	22.00	65.00	154.00
Truth About Crime nn(1949, 132p)	22.00	65.00	154.00
Variety Comics 1(1946, 132p)-Blue Beetle, Jungle Jo	16.00	48.00	110.00
Variety Comics nn(1950, 132p)	16.00	48.00	110.00
Western Roundup nn(1950, 132p)-Hoot Gibson	16.00	48.00	110.00

Note: Each of the above usually contain four remaindered Fox books minus covers. Since these missing covers often had the first page of the first story, most Giants therefore are incomplete. Approximate values are listed. Books with appearances of Phantom Lady, Rulah, Jo-Jo, etc. could bring more.

FOXHOLE
9-10/54 - No. 4, 3-4/55; No. 5, 7/55 - No. 7, 3/56
Mainline/Charlton Comics No. 5 on

	Good	Fine	Mint
1-Kirby-c	4.35	13.00	30.00
2-Kirby c/a(2)	4.35	13.00	30.00
3,5-Kirby-c only	2.00	6.00	14.00
4,7	.85	2.50	6.00
6-Kirby c/a(2)	3.85	11.50	27.00
Super Reprints No. 10-12,15-18	.30	.80	1.60

NOTE: ***Kirby** a(r)-Super No. 11,12,18. **Powell** a(r)-Super No. 15,16.*

FOXY FAGAN
Dec, 1946 - No. 7, Summer, 1948
Dearfield Publishing Co.

	Good	Fine	Mint
1-Foxy Fagan & Little Buck begin	4.60	14.00	32.00
2	2.15	6.50	15.00
3-7	1.65	5.00	11.50

FOXY GRANDPA
1901 - 1916 (Hardcover; strip reprints)
N. Y. Herald/Frederick A. Stokes Co./M. A. Donahue & Co./Bunny Publ.(L. R. Hammersly Co.)

	Good	Fine	VF-NM
1901-9x15" in color-N. Y. Herald	25.00	75.00	175.00
1902-"Latest Larks of...," 32 pgs. in color, 9½x15½"	25.00	75.00	175.00
1902-"The Many Advs. of...," 9x15", 148pgs. in color (Hammersly)	33.00	100.00	230.00

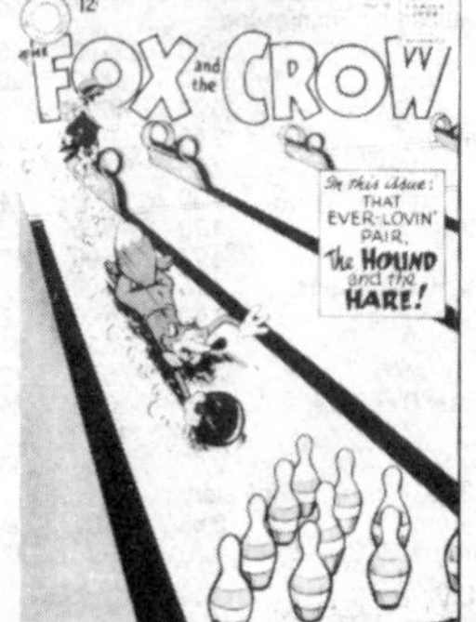

Fox and the Crow #78, © DC

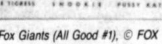

Fox Giants (All Good #1), © FOX

Fox Giants (Teen-Age Love nn), © FOX

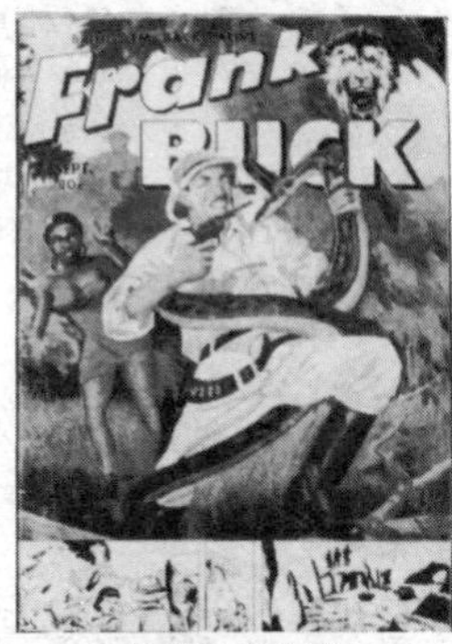

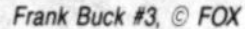

Frank Buck #3, © FOX

Frankenstein #5, © MCG

Frankenstein Comics #20, © PRIZE

FOXY GRANDPA (continued) — Good / Fine / VF-NM

1903-"Latest Advs.," 9x15", 24 pgs. in color, Hammersly Co. — 25.00 75.00 175.00

1903-". . .'s New Advs.," 10x15, 32 pgs. in color, Stokes — 25.00 75.00 175.00

1904-"Up to Date," 10x15", 28 pgs. in color, Stokes — 25.00 75.00 175.00

1905-"& Flip Flaps," 9½x15½", 52 pgs., in color — 25.00 75.00 175.00

1905-"The Latest Advs. of," 9x15", 28 pgs., in color, M.A. Donohue Co.; re-issue of 1902 ish — 15.00 45.00 105.00

1905-"Merry Pranks of," 9½x15½", 52 pgs. in color, Donahue — 15.00 45.00 105.00

1905-"Latest Larks of," 9½x15½", 52 pgs. in color, Donahue; re-issue of 1902 ish — 15.00 45.00 105.00

1906-"Frolics," 10x15", 30 pgs. in color, Stokes — 15.00 45.00 105.00

1907 — 13.00 40.00 90.00

1908?-"Triumphs," 10x15" — 13.00 40.00 90.00

1908?-"& Little Brother," 10x15" — 13.00 40.00 90.00

1911-"Latest Tricks," r-1910,1911 Sundays in color-Stokes Co. — 14.00 42.00 100.00

1914-9½x15½", 24 pgs., 6 color cartoons/page, Bunny Publ. — 10.00 30.00 70.00

1916-"Merry Book," 10x15", 30 pgs. in color, Stokes — 10.00 30.00 70.00

FOXY GRANDPA SPARKLETS SERIES
1908 (6½x7¾"; 24 pgs. in color)
M. A. Donahue & Co.

". . . Rides the Goat," ". . .& His Boys," ". . .Playing Ball," ". . .Fun on the Farm," ". . .Fancy Shooting," ". . .Show the Boys Up Sports," ". . .Plays Santa Claus"
each. . . . — 15.00 45.00 105.00

900-. . .Playing Ball; Bunny illos; 8 pgs., linen like pgs., no date — 8.00 24.00 56.00

FRACTURED FAIRY TALES (TV)
October, 1962 (Jay Ward)
Gold Key — Good / Fine / Mint

1 (10022-210) — 3.50 10.50 24.00

FRAGGLE ROCK
April, 1985 - No. 8, Sept, 1986
Star Comics (Marvel)

1 — .40 .80
2-8 — .35 .70

FRANCIS, BROTHER OF THE UNIVERSE
1980 (75 cents) (52 pgs.) (One Shot)
Marvel Comics Group

Buscema/Marie Severin-a; story of Francis Bernadone celebrating his 800th birthday in 1982 — .30 .60

FRANCIS THE FAMOUS TALKING MULE (All based on movie) (See 4-Color No. 335, 465, 501, 547, 579, 621, 655, 698, 710, 745, 810, 863, 906, 953, 991, 1068, 1090)

FRANK BUCK (Formerly My True Love)
No. 70, May, 1950 - No. 3, Sept, 1950
Fox Features Syndicate

70-Wood a(p)(3) — 8.00 24.00 56.00
71-Wood a? (9 pgs.), 3 — 4.35 13.00 30.00

FRANKENSTEIN (See Movie Classics)
Aug-Oct, 1964; No. 2, Sept, 1966 - No. 4, Mar, 1967
Dell Publishing Co.

1(12-283-410)(1964) — .70 2.00 4.00
2-Intro. & origin super-hero character (9/66) — .35 1.00 2.00
3,4 — .50 1.00

FRANKENSTEIN (The Monster of. . .)
Jan, 1973 - No. 18, Sept, 1975
Marvel Comics Group — Good / Fine / Mint

1-Ploog-a begins — .30 .60
2-18: 8,9-Dracula app. — .25 .50
Power Record giveaway-(12¼x12¼"; 16 pgs.); Adams, Ploog-a — .60 1.20

NOTE: ***Adkins** c-17i. **Buscema** a-7-10p. **Ditko** a-12r. **G. Kane** c-15p. **Orlando** a-8r. **Ploog** a-1-3, 4p, 5p, 6; c-1-6. **Wrightson** c-18i.*

FRANKENSTEIN COMICS (Also See Prize Comics)
Sum, 1945 - V5/5(No.33), Oct-Nov, 1954
Prize Publications (Crestwood/Feature)

1-Frankenstein begins by Dick Briefer (origin); Frank Sinatra parody — 25.00 75.00 175.00
2 — 12.00 36.00 84.00
3-5 — 10.00 30.00 70.00
6-10: 7-S&K a(r)/Headline Comics. 8(7-8/47)-Superman satire — 9.00 27.00 63.00
11-17(1-2/49)-11-Boris Karloff parody c/story. 17-Last humor issue — 6.00 18.00 42.00
18(3/52)-New origin, horror series begins — 9.00 27.00 63.00
19,20(V3No.4, 8-9/52) — 5.50 16.50 38.00
21(V3/5), 22(V3/6) — 5.50 16.50 38.00
23(V4/1)-No.28(V4/6) — 4.60 14.00 32.00
29(V5/1)-No.33(V5/5) — 4.60 14.00 32.00

NOTE: ***Meskin** a-21, 29.*

FRANKENSTEIN, JR. (. . .& the Impossibles) (TV)
January, 1967 (Hanna-Barbera)
Gold Key

1 — 1.35 4.00 8.00

FRANKIE COMICS (. . .& Lana No. 13-15) (Formerly Movie Tunes; becomes Frankie Fuddle No. 16 on)
No. 4, Wint, 1946-47 - No. 15, June, 1949
Marvel Comics (MgPC)

4-Mitzi, Margie, Daisy app. — 4.00 12.00 28.00
5-8 — 2.00 6.00 14.00
9-Transvestism story — 2.50 7.50 17.00
10-15: 13-Anti-Wertham editorial — 1.50 4.50 10.00

FRANKIE DOODLE (See Single Series #7 and Sparkler, both series)

FRANKIE FUDDLE (Formerly Frankie & Lana)
No. 16, Aug, 1949 - No. 17, Nov, 1949
Marvel Comics

16,17 — 1.70 5.00 12.00

FRANK LUTHER'S SILLY PILLY COMICS (See Jingle Dingle. . .)
1950 (10 cents)
Children's Comics

1-Characters from radio, records, & TV — 2.30 7.00 16.00

FRANK MERRIWELL AT YALE (Speed Demons No. 5 on?)
June, 1955 - No. 4, Jan, 1956
Charlton Comics

1 — 1.70 5.00 12.00
2-4 — 1.00 3.00 7.00

FRANTIC (Magazine) (See Zany & Ratfink)
Oct, 1958 - V2No.2, April, 1959 (Satire)
Pierce Publishing Co.

V1No.1,2 — .70 2.00 4.00
V2No.1,2 — .35 1.00 2.00

FRECKLES AND HIS FRIENDS (See Famous Comics Cartoon Book & Honeybee Birdwhistle. . .)

FRECKLES AND HIS FRIENDS
No. 5, 11/47 - No. 12, 8/49; 11/55 - No. 4, 6/56

FRECKLES AND HIS FRIENDS (cont.)
Standard Comics/Argo

	Good	Fine	Mint
5-Reprints	4.00	12.00	28.00
6-12-Reprints; 11-Lingerie panels	2.00	6.00	14.00

NOTE: *Some copies of No. 8 & 9 contain a printing oddity. The negatives were elongated in the engraving process, probably to conform to page dimensions on the filler pages. Those pages only look normal when viewed at a 45 degree angle.*

	Good	Fine	Mint
1(Argo,'55)-Reprints	2.30	7.00	16.00
2-4	1.30	4.00	9.00

FREDDY (Formerly My Little Margie's Boy Friends)
June, 1958 - No. 47, Feb, 1965 (Also see Blue Bird)
Charlton Comics

	Good	Fine	Mint
V2No.12	.85	2.50	6.00
13-15	.50	1.50	3.00
16-47	.35	1.00	2.00
Schiff's Shoes Presents . . . No. 1(1959)-Giveaway	.35	1.00	2.00

FREDDY
May-July, 1963 - No. 3, Oct-Dec, 1964
Dell Publishing Co.

	Good	Fine	Mint
1-3	.55	1.65	4.00

FREE COMICS TO YOU FROM . . . (name of shoe store) (Has clown on cover & another with a rabbit)(like comics from Weather Bird & Edward's Shoes)
Circa 1956, 1960-61
Shoe Store Giveaway

Contains a comic bound with new cover - several combinations possible; Some Harvey titles known. contents determines price.

FREEDOM AGENT (Also see John Steele)
April, 1963
Gold Key

	Good	Fine	Mint
1 (10054-304)	1.00	3.00	7.00

FREEDOM FIGHTERS (See Justice League No. 107,108)
Mar-Apr, 1976 - No. 15, July-Aug, 1978
National Periodical Publications/DC Comics

	Good	Fine	Mint
1-Uncle Sam, The Ray, Black Condor, Doll Man, Human Bomb, & Phantom Lady begin		.35	.70
2-15: 7-1st app. Crusaders. 10-Origin Doll Man. 11-Origin The Ray. 12-Origin Firebrand. 13-Origin Black Condor. 15-Origin Phantom Lady		.25	.50

NOTE: ***Buckler** c-5-11p, 13p, 14p.*

FREEDOM TRAIN
1948 (Giveaway)
Street & Smith Publ.

	Good	Fine	Mint
Powell-c	1.70	5.00	10.00

FRENZY (Magazine) (Satire)
April, 1958 - No. 6, March, 1959
Picture Magazine

	Good	Fine	Mint
1	.70	2.00	4.00
2-6	.35	1.00	2.00

FRIDAY FOSTER
October, 1972
Dell Publishing Co.

	Good	Fine	Mint
1	.85	2.50	5.00

FRIENDLY GHOST, CASPER, THE (See Casper. . .)
8/58 - No. 224, 10/82; No. 225, 10/86 - Present
Harvey Publications

	Good	Fine	Mint
1-Infinity-c	13.00	40.00	90.00
2	6.45	20.00	45.00
3-10: 6-X-Mas-c	4.00	12.00	28.00
11-20: 18-X-Mas-c	2.65	8.00	18.00
21-30	1.20	3.50	8.00
31-50	.70	2.00	5.00
51-100: 54-X-Mas-c	.55	1.60	3.20
101-150		.60	1.20
151-238: 173,179,185-Cub Scout Specials. 239,240-Begin $1.00 issues		.35	.70
American Dental Assoc. giveaway-Small size (1967, 16 pgs.)	.50	1.50	3.00

FRIGHT
June, 1975 (August on inside)
Atlas/Seaboard Periodicals

	Good	Fine	Mint
1-Origin The Son of Dracula; Frank Thorne c/a		.40	.80

FRISKY ANIMALS (Formerly Frisky Fables)
No. 44, Jan, 1951 - No. 58, 1954
Star Publications

	Good	Fine	Mint
44-Super Cat	5.00	15.00	35.00
45-Classic L. B. Cole-c	8.00	24.00	56.00
46-51,53-58-Super Cat	4.35	13.00	30.00
52-L. B. Cole c/a, 3pgs.	5.00	15.00	35.00

NOTE: *All have **L. B. Cole**-c. No. 47-No Super Cat. **Disbrow** a-49,52. **Fago** a-51.*

FRISKY ANIMALS ON PARADE (Formerly Parade; becomes Super-spook)
Sept, 1957 - No. 3, Dec/Jan, 1957-1958
Ajax-Farrell Publ. (Four Star Comic Corp.)

	Good	Fine	Mint
1-L. B. Cole-c	3.75	11.25	26.00
2-No L. B. Cole-c	1.85	5.50	13.00
3-L. B. Cole-c	2.65	8.00	18.00

FRISKY FABLES (Frisky Animals No. 44 on)
Spring, 1945 - No. 44, Oct-Nov, 1949
Premium Group/Novelty Publ.

	Good	Fine	Mint
V1/1-Al Fago c/a	4.60	14.00	32.00
2,3(1945)	2.30	7.00	16.00
4-7(1946)	1.50	4.50	10.00
V2/1-9,11,12(1947)	1.15	3.50	8.00
10-Christmas-c	1.30	4.00	9.00
V3/1-12(1948): 4-Flag-c. 9-Infinity-c	1.00	3.00	7.00
V4/1-7	1.00	3.00	7.00
36-44(V4/8-12, V5/1-4)-L. B. Cole-c; 40-X-mas-c	4.65	14.00	32.00
Accepted Reprint No. 43 (nd); L.B. Cole-c	1.70	5.00	12.00

FRITZI RITZ (See Single Series No. 5,1(reprint), United Comics and Comics on Parade)

FRITZI RITZ
Fall/48 - No. 42, 1/55; No. 43, 1955 - No. 55, 9-11/57; No. 56, 12-2/57-58 - No. 59, 9-11/58
United Features Synd./St. John No. 43-55/Dell No. 56 on

	Good	Fine	Mint
nn(1948)-Special Fall ish.	5.00	15.00	35.00
2	2.30	7.00	16.00
3-5	1.70	5.00	12.00
6-10: 6-Abbie & Slats app. 7-Lingerie panel	1.50	4.50	10.00
11-19,21-28	1.15	3.50	8.00
20-Strange As It Seems; Russell Patterson Cheesecake-a; negligee panel	1.50	4.50	10.00
29-Five pg. Abbie & Slats; 1 pg. Mamie by Russell Patterson	1.15	3.50	8.00
30-59: 36-1 pg. Mamie by Patterson. 43-Peanuts by Schulz	.85	2.50	6.00

NOTE: *Abbie & Slats in No. 7, 8, 11, 18, 20, 27, 29. Li'l Abner in No. 35, 36.*

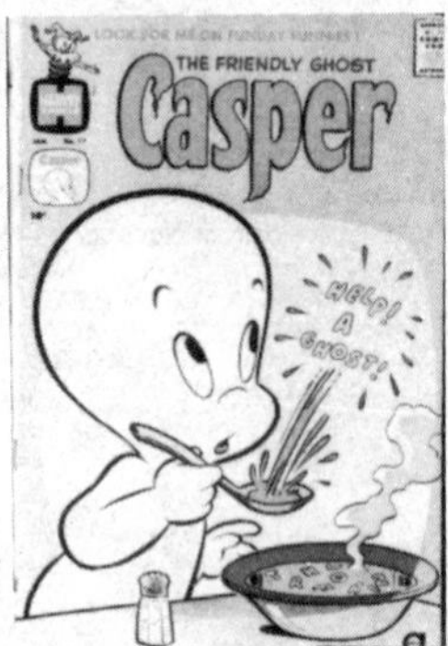

The Friendly Ghost, Casper #17, © Paramount

Frisky Animals #51, © STAR

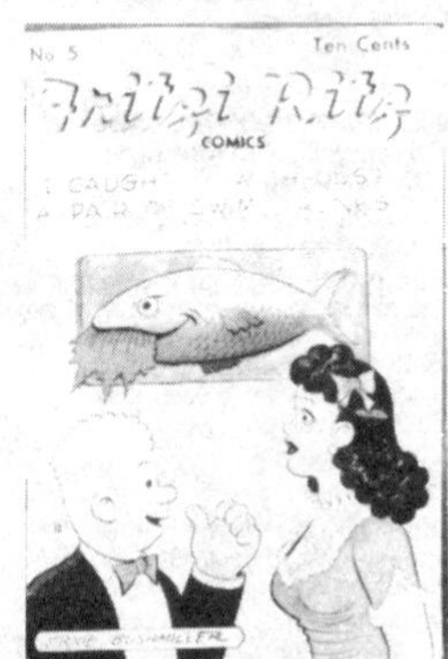

Fritzi Ritz #5, © UFS

The Frogmen #5, © DELL

Frontline Combat #6, © WMG

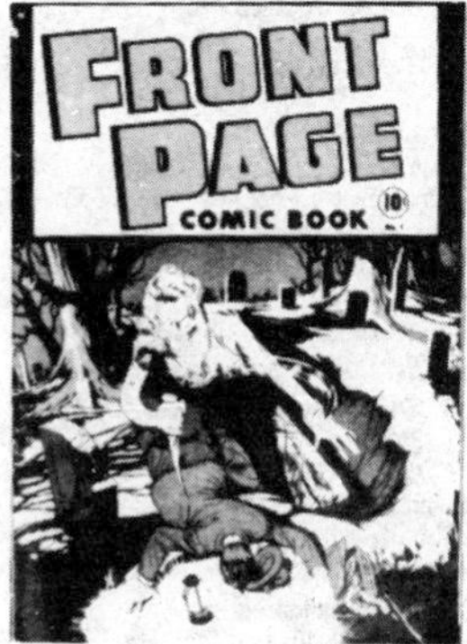

Front Page Comic Book #1, © HARV

FROGMAN COMICS
Jan-Feb, 1952 - No. 11, May, 1953
Hillman Periodicals

	Good	Fine	Mint
1	3.50	10.50	24.00
2	1.70	5.00	12.00
3,4,6-11: 4-Meskin-a	1.30	4.00	9.00
5-Krigstein, Torres-a	3.00	9.00	21.00

FROGMEN, THE
No. 1258, Feb-Apr, 1962 - No. 11, Nov-Jan/1964-65
Dell Publishing Co.

	Good	Fine	Mint
4-Color 1258-Evans-a	2.65	8.00	18.00
2,3-Evans-a; part Frazetta inks in No. 2,3	3.50	10.50	24.00
4,6-11	1.00	3.00	7.00
5-Toth-a	2.00	6.00	14.00

FROM BEYOND THE UNKNOWN
10-11/69 - No.25, 11-12/73 (No.7-11: 64 pgs.; No.12-17: 52 pgs.)
National Periodical Publications

	Good	Fine	Mint
1		.30	.60
2-10: 7-Intro. Col. Glenn Merrit		.25	.50
11-25: Star Rovers reprints begin No. 18,19. Space Museum in No. 23-25		.25	.50

NOTE: ***Adams** c-3, 6, 8, 9. **Anderson** c-2, 4, 5, 10, 11i, 15-17, 22; reprints-3, 4, 6-8, 10, 11, 13-16, 24, 25. **Infantino** reprints-1-5, 7-19, 23-25; c-11p. **Kaluta** c-18,19. **Kubert** c-1,7, 12-14. **Toth** a-2r. **Wood** a-13i. Photo-c 22.*

FROM HERE TO INSANITY (Satire) (Eh No. 1-7)
(See Frantic & Frenzy)
No. 8, Feb, 1955 - V3No.1, 1956
Charlton Comics

	Good	Fine	Mint
8	3.00	9.00	21.00
9	2.00	6.00	14.00
10-Ditko-c/a, 3 pgs.	5.00	15.00	35.00
11,12-All Kirby except 4 pgs.	6.00	18.00	42.00
V3No.1(1956)-Ward-c/a(2)(signed McCartney); 5 pgs. Wolverton; 3 pgs. Ditko; magazine format	13.50	40.50	95.00

FRONTIER DAYS
1956 (Giveaway)
Robin Hood Shoe Store (Brown Shoe)

	Good	Fine	Mint
1	1.35	4.00	8.00

FRONTIER DOCTOR (See 4-Color No. 877)

FRONTIER FIGHTERS
Sept-Oct, 1955 - No. 8, Nov-Dec, 1956
National Periodical Publications

	Good	Fine	Mint
1-Davy Crockett, Buffalo Bill by Kubert, Kit Carson begin (Scarce)	18.00	54.00	125.00
2	11.00	33.00	76.00
3-8	8.50	25.50	60.00

NOTE: *Buffalo Bill by **Kubert** in all.*

FRONTIER ROMANCES
Nov-Dec, 1949 - No. 2, Jan-Feb, 1950
Avon Periodicals/I. W.

	Good	Fine	Mint
1-Used in **SOTI**, pg. 180(General reference) & illo. "Erotic spanking in a western comic book;"	33.00	100.00	230.00
2 (Scarce)	16.00	48.00	110.00
1-I.W.(reprints Avon's No. 1)	2.75	8.00	16.00
I.W. Reprint No. 9	1.35	4.00	8.00

FRONTIER SCOUT: DAN'L BOONE (Formerly Death Valley; The Masked Raider No. 14 on)
No. 10, Jan, 1956 - No. 13, Aug, 1956; No. 14, March, 1965
Charlton Comics

	Good	Fine	Mint
10	2.00	6.00	14.00
11-13(1956)	1.15	3.50	8.00
V2No.14(3/65)	.35	1.00	2.00

FRONTIER TRAIL (The Rider No. 1-5)
No. 6, May, 1958
Ajax/Farrell Publ.

	Good	Fine	Mint
6	1.15	3.50	8.00

FRONTIER WESTERN
Feb, 1956 - No. 10, Aug, 1957
Atlas Comics (PrPI)

	Good	Fine	Mint
1	4.60	14.00	32.00
2,3,6-Williamson-a, 4 pgs. each	4.35	13.00	30.00
4,7,9,10: 10-Check-a	1.65	5.00	11.50
5-Crandall, Baker, Wildey, Davis-a; Williamson text illos	3.35	10.00	23.00
8-Crandall, Morrow, & Wildey-a	1.85	5.50	13.00

NOTE: ***Drucker** a-3,4. **Heath** c-5. **Severin** c-6,8,10. Ringo Kid in No. 4.*

FRONTLINE COMBAT
July-Aug, 1951 - No. 15, Jan, 1954
E. C. Comics

	Good	Fine	Mint
1	34.00	102.00	240.00
2	23.00	70.00	160.00
3	17.00	51.00	120.00
4-Used in **SOTI**, pg. 257; contains "Airburst" by Kurtzman which is his personal all-time favorite story	14.00	42.00	100.00
5	12.00	36.00	84.00
6-10	10.00	30.00	70.00
11-15	8.00	24.00	56.00

NOTE: ***Davis** a-in all; c-11,12. **Evans** a-10-15. **Heath** a-1. **Kubert** a-14. **Kurtzman** a-1-5; c-1-9. **Severin** a-5-7, 9, 13, 15. **Severin/Elder** a-2-11; c-10. **Toth** a-8, 12. **Wood** a-1-4, 6-10, 12-15; c-13-15. Special issues: No. 7 (Iwo Jima), No. 9 (Civil War), No. 12 (Air Force). (Canadian reprints known; see Table of Contents.)*

FRONT PAGE COMIC BOOK
1945
Front Page Comics (Harvey)

	Good	Fine	Mint
1-Kubert-a; intro. & 1st app. Man in Black by Powell; Fuje-c	13.00	40.00	90.00

FROST AND FIRE (See DC Science Fic. Graphic Novel)

FROSTY THE SNOWMAN
No. 359, Nov, 1951 - No. 1272, Dec-Feb?/1961-62
Dell Publishing Co.

	Good	Fine	Mint
4-Color 359	2.30	7.00	16.00
4-Color 435	1.70	5.00	12.00
4-Color 514,601,661	1.50	4.50	10.00
4-Color 748,861,950,1065	1.30	4.00	9.00
4-Color 1153,1272	1.15	3.50	8.00

FRUITMAN SPECIAL
Dec, 1969 (68 pages)
Harvey Publications

	Good	Fine	Mint
1-Funny super hero	1.00	3.00	6.00

F-TROOP (TV)
Aug, 1966 - No. 7, Aug, 1967 (All have photo-c)
Dell Publishing Co.

	Good	Fine	Mint
1	2.00	6.00	14.00
2-7	1.15	3.50	8.00

FUGITIVES FROM JUSTICE
Feb, 1952 - No. 5, Oct, 1952
St. John Publishing Co.

	Good	Fine	Mint
1	5.00	15.00	35.00
2-Matt Baker-a; Vic Flint strip reprints begin, end No. 5	5.00	15.00	35.00
3-Reprints panel from Authentic Police Cases that was used in **SOTI** with changes; Tuska-a	8.00	24.00	56.00
4	2.35	7.00	16.00
5-Bondage-c	3.35	10.00	23.00

FULL COLOR COMICS
1946
Fox Features Syndicate

	Good	Fine	Mint
nn	4.60	14.00	32.00

FULL OF FUN
Aug, 1957 - No. 2, Nov, 1957; 1964
Red Top (Decker Publ.)(Farrell)/I. W. Enterprises

1(1957)-Dave Berg-a	1.60	4.70	11.00
2-Reprints Bingo, the Monkey Doodle Boy	1.00	3.00	7.00
8-I.W. Reprint('64)	.30	.80	1.60

FUN AT CHRISTMAS (See March of Comics No. 138)

FUN CLUB COMICS (See Interstate Theatres . . .)

FUN COMICS (Mighty Bear No. 13 on)
Jan, 1953 - No. 12, Oct, 1953
Star Publications

9(Giant)-L. B. Cole-c	5.50	16.50	38.00
10-12-L. B. Cole-c	3.50	10.50	24.00

FUNDAY FUNNIES (See Famous TV. . ., and Harvey Hits No. 35,40)

FUN-IN (TV)(Hanna-Barbera)
Feb, 1970 - No. 10, Jan, 1972; No. 11, 4/74 - No. 15, 12/74
Gold Key

1-Dastardly & Muttley in Their Flying Machines; Perils of Penelope Pitstop in 1-4; It's the Wolf in all	.85	2.50	5.00
2-4,6-Cattanooga Cats in 2-4	.50	1.50	3.00
5,7-Motormouse & Autocat, Dastardly & Muttley in both; It's the Wolf in No. 7	.40	1.20	2.40
8,10-The Harlem Globetrotters, Dastardly & Muttley in No. 10	.40	1.20	2.40
9-Where's Huddles?, Dastardly & Muttley, Motormouse & Autocat app.	.40	1.20	2.40
11-15: 11-Butch Cassidy. 12,15-Speed Buggy. 13-Hair Bear Bunch. 14-Inch High Private Eye	.25	.75	1.50

FUNKY PHANTOM, THE (TV)
Mar, 1972 - No. 13, Mar, 1975 (Hanna-Barbera)
Gold Key

1	.85	2.50	5.00
2-13	.40	1.20	2.40

FUNLAND
No date (25 cents)
Ziff-Davis (Approved Comics)

Contains games, puzzles, etc.	4.60	14.00	32.00

FUNLAND COMICS
1945
Croyden Publishers

1	3.50	10.50	24.00

FUNNIES, THE (Also see Comic Cuts)
1929 - No. 36, 10/18/30 (10 cents; 5 cents No.22 on) (16 pgs.)
Full tabloid size in color; not reprints; published every Saturday
Dell Publishing Co.

1-My Big Brudder, Johnathan, Jazzbo & Jim, Foxy Grandpa, Sniffy, Jimmy Jams & other strips begin; first four-color comic newsstand publication; also contains magic, puzzles & stories	25.00	75.00	175.00
2-21 (1930, 30 cents)	9.00	27.00	63.00
22(nn-7/12/30-5 cents)	6.50	19.50	45.00
23(nn-7/19/30-5 cents), 24(nn-7/26/30-5 cents), 25(nn-8/2/30), 26(nn-8/9/30), 27(nn-8/16/30), 28(nn-8/23/30), 29(nn-8/30/30), 30(nn-9/6/30), 31(nn-9/13/30), 32(nn-9/20/30), 33(nn-9/27/30), 34(nn-10/4/30), 35(nn-10/11/30), 36(nn, no date-10/18/30) each. . . .	6.50	19.50	45.00

FUNNIES, THE (New Funnies No. 65 on)
Oct, 1936 - No. 64, May, 1942
Dell Publishing Co.

	Good	Fine	Mint
1-Tailspin Tommy, Mutt & Jeff, Alley Oop, Capt. Easy, Don Dixon begin	60.00	180.00	420.00
2-Scribbly by Mayer begins	30.00	90.00	210.00
3	25.00	75.00	175.00
4,5: 4-Christmas-c	22.00	65.00	154.00
6-10	17.00	51.00	120.00
11-20: 16-Christmas-c	14.00	42.00	100.00
21-29	12.00	36.00	84.00
30-John Carter of Mars (origin) begins by Edgar Rice Burroughs	40.00	120.00	280.00
31-44: 33-John Coleman Burroughs art begins on John Carter	22.00	65.00	154.00
45-Origin Phantasmo, the Master of the World & intro. his sidekick Whizzer McGee	18.00	54.00	125.00
46-50: 46-The Black Knight begins, ends No. 62	15.00	45.00	105.00
51-56-Last ERB John Carter of Mars	15.00	45.00	105.00
57-Intro. & origin Captain Midnight	38.00	115.00	265.00
58-60	16.00	48.00	110.00
61-Andy Panda begins by Walter Lantz	17.00	51.00	120.00
62,63-Last Captain Midnight cover	15.00	45.00	105.00
64-Format change; Oswald the Rabbit, Felix the Cat, Li'l Eight Ball app.; origin & 1st app. Woody Woodpecker in Oswald; last Capt. Midnight	30.00	90.00	210.00

NOTE: ***Mayer** c-26. **McWilliams** art in many issues on "Rex King of the Deep."*

FUNNIES ANNUAL, THE
1959 ($1.00)(B&W; tabloid-size, approx. 7x10")
Avon Periodicals

1-(Rare)-Features the best newspaper comic strips of the year: Archie, Snuffy Smith, Beetle Bailey, Henry, Blondie, Steve Canyon, Buz Sawyer, The Little King, Hi & Lois, Popeye, & others. Also has a chronological history of the comics from 2000 B.C. to 1959.	23.00	70.00	160.00

FUNNIES ON PARADE (Premium)
1933 (Probably the 1st comic book) (36 pgs.; slick cover)
No date or publisher listed
Eastern Color Printing Co.

nn-Contains Sunday page reprints of Mutt & Jeff, Joe Palooka, Hairbreadth Harry, Reg'lar Fellers, Skippy, & others (10,000 print run). This book was printed for Proctor & Gamble to be given away & came out before Famous Funnies or Century of Comics.	170.00	515.00	1200.00

FUNNY ANIMALS (See Fawcett's Funny Animals)
Sept, 1984 - No. 2, Nov, 1984
Charlton Comics

1,2-Atomic Mouse-r		.30	.60

FUNNYBONE
1944 (132 pages)
La Salle Publishing Co.

	7.00	21.00	50.00

FUNNY BOOK (. . .Magazine) (Hocus Pocus No. 9)
Dec, 1942 - No. 9, Aug-Sept, 1946
Parents' Magazine Press

1-Funny animal; Alice In Wonderland app.	5.50	16.50	38.00
2	2.65	8.00	18.00
3-9	1.75	5.25	12.00

FUNNY COMICS (7 cents)
1955 (36 pgs.; 5x7"; in color)
Modern Store Publ.

1-Funny animal	.50	1.50	3.50

FUNNY COMIC TUNES (See Funny Tunes)

The Funnies #25, © DELL

Funnies on Parade nn, © EAS

Funnybone nn, © La Salle Publ.

Funny Pages #10, © CEN

Funny Stuff #18, © DC

Funny Tunes #19, © MCG

FUNNY FABLES
Aug, 1957 - V2No. 2, Nov, 1957
Decker Publications (Red Top Comics)

	Good	Fine	Mint
V1No.1	1.30	4.00	9.00
V2No.1,2	.70	2.00	5.00

FUNNY FILMS
Sept-Oct, 1949 - No. 29, May-June, 1954 (No. 1-4, 52 pgs.)
American Comics Group(Michel Publ./Titan Publ.)

	Good	Fine	Mint
1-Puss An' Boots, Blunderbunny begin	5.50	16.50	38.00
2	2.65	8.00	18.00
3-10	1.65	5.00	12.00
11-20	1.30	4.00	9.00
21-29	1.00	3.00	7.00

FUNNY FOLKS (Hollywood. . . on cover only No. 17-26; becomes Hollywood Funny Folks No. 27 on)
April-May, 1946 - No. 26, June-July, 1950
National Periodical Publications

	Good	Fine	Mint
1-1st app. Nutsy Squirrel by Rube Grossman	14.00	42.00	100.00
2	7.00	21.00	50.00
3-5	5.70	17.00	40.00
6-10	3.70	11.00	26.00
11-26	2.65	8.00	18.00

NOTE: ***Sheldon Mayer*** *a-in some issues.*

FUNNY FROLICS
Summer, 1945 - No. 5, Dec, 1946
Timely/Marvel Comics (SPI)

	Good	Fine	Mint
1-Sharpy Fox, Puffy Pig, Krazy Krow	6.00	18.00	42.00
2	3.50	10.50	24.00
3,4	2.65	8.00	18.00
5-Kurtzman-a	3.70	11.00	26.00

FUNNY FUNNIES
April, 1943 (68 pages)
Nedor Publishing Co.

	Good	Fine	Mint
1 (Funny animals)	8.00	24.00	56.00

FUNNYMAN
Dec, 1947; No. 1, Jan, 1948 - No. 6, Aug, 1948
Magazine Enterprises

	Good	Fine	Mint
nn(12/47)-Prepublication B&W undistributed copy by Siegel & Shuster-(5¾x8"), 16 pgs.; Sold in San Francisco in 1976 for $300.00			
1-Siegel & Shuster in all	11.50	34.50	80.00
2	8.50	25.50	60.00
3-6	7.00	21.00	50.00

FUNNY MOVIES (See 3-D Funny Movies)

FUNNY PAGES (Formerly The Comics Magazine)
No. 6, Nov, 1936 - No. 42, Oct, 1940
Comics Magazine Co./Ultem Publ.(Chesler)/Centaur Publications

	Good	Fine	Mint
V1/6 (nn, nd)-The Clock begins (2 pgs.), ends No. 11 (1st app.)	35.00	105.00	245.00
7-11	23.00	70.00	160.00
V2/1 (9/37)(V2/2 on-c; V2/1 in indicia)	18.00	54.00	125.00
V2/2 (10/37)(V2/3 on-c; V2/2 in indicia)	18.00	54.00	125.00
3(11/37)-5	18.00	54.00	125.00
6(1st Centaur, 3/38)	28.00	84.00	195.00
7-9	20.00	60.00	140.00
10(Scarce)-1st app. of The Arrow by Gustavson (Blue costume)	80.00	240.00	560.00
11,12	40.00	120.00	280.00
V3/1-6	40.00	120.00	280.00
7-1st Arrow-c; 9/39	50.00	150.00	350.00
8	40.00	120.00	280.00
9-Tarpe Mills jungle-c	40.00	120.00	280.00
10-2nd Arrow-c	43.00	130.00	300.00
V4/1(1/40, Arrow-c)-(Rare)-The Owl & The Phantom Rider app.; origin Mantoka, Maker of Magic by Jack Cole. Mad Ming begins, ends #42. Tarpe Mills-a	50.00	150.00	350.00
35-Arrow-c	36.00	108.00	250.00
36-38-Mad Ming-c	36.00	108.00	250.00
39-42-Arrow-c. 42-Last Arrow	36.00	108.00	250.00

NOTE: ***Burgos*** *c-V3/10.* ***Jack Cole*** *a-V2/3, 7, 8, 10, 11, V3/2, 6, 9, 10, V4/1, 37.* ***Eisner*** *a-V1/7, 8, 10.* ***Everett*** *a-V2/11 (illos).* ***Gill Fox*** *a-V2/11.* ***Sid Greene*** *a-39.* ***Guardineer*** *a-V2/2, 3, 5.* ***Gustavson*** *a-V2/5, 11, 12, V3/1-10, 35, 38-42; c-V3/7, 35, 39-42.* ***Bob Kane*** *a-V3/1.* ***McWilliams*** *a-V2/12, V3/1, 3-6.* ***Tarpe Mills*** *a-V3/8-10, V4/1; c-V3/9.* ***Ed Moore Jr.*** *a-V2/12.* ***Bob Wood*** *a-V2/2, 3, 8, 11, V3/6, 9, 10; c-V2/6, 7.*

FUNNY PICTURE STORIES (Comic Pages V3/4 on)
Nov, 1936 - V3/3, May, 1939
Comics Magazine Co./Centaur Publications

	Good	Fine	Mint
V1/1-The Clock begins (c-feature)(See Funny Pages for 1st app.)	62.00	185.00	435.00
2	30.00	90.00	210.00
3-9: 4-Eisner-a; Christmas-c	22.00	65.00	154.00
V2/1 (9/37; V1/10 on-c; V2/1 in indicia)-Jack Strand begins	18.00	54.00	125.00
2 (10/37; V1/11 on-c; V2/2 in indicia)	18.00	54.00	125.00
3-5: 4-Xmas-c	15.00	45.00	105.00
6-(1st Centaur, 3/38)	25.00	75.00	175.00
7-11	17.00	51.00	120.00
V3/1-3	14.00	42.00	100.00

NOTE: ***Guardineer*** *a-V1/11.* ***Bob Wood*** *a/c-V1/11.*

FUNNY STUFF (Becomes The Dodo & the Frog No. 80)
Summer, 1944 - No. 79, July-Aug, 1954
All-American/National Periodical Publications No. 7 on

	Good	Fine	Mint
1-The Three Mouseketeers & The "Terrific Whatzit" begin-Sheldon Mayer-a	35.00	105.00	245.00
2-Sheldon Mayer-a	17.00	51.00	120.00
3-5	10.00	30.00	70.00
6-10	7.00	21.00	50.00
11-20: 18-Dodo & the Frog begin?	5.00	15.00	35.00
21,23-30: 24-Infinity-c	3.50	10.50	24.00
22-Superman cameo	12.00	36.00	84.00
31-79: 75-Bo Bunny by Mayer	2.30	7.00	16.00
Wheaties Giveaway(1946, 6½x8¼") (Scarce)	8.00	24.00	56.00

NOTE: ***Mayer*** *a-1-8, 55, ,57, 58, 61, 62, 64, 65, 68, 70, 72, 74-79; c-6.*

FUNNY STUFF STOCKING STUFFER
March, 1985 (52 pgs.)
DC Comics

	Good	Fine	Mint
1-Almost every DC funny animal		.60	1.25

FUNNY 3-D
December, 1953
Harvey Publications

	Good	Fine	Mint
1	7.00	21.00	50.00

FUNNY TUNES (Animated Funny Comic Tunes No. 16-22; Funny Comic Tunes No. 23, on covers only; formerly Human Torch; Oscar No. 24 on)
No. 16, Summer, 1944 - No. 23, Fall, 1946
U.S.A. Comics Magazine Corp. (Timely)

	Good	Fine	Mint
16-Silly, Ziggy, Krazy Krow begin	4.60	14.00	32.00
17-22	2.65	8.00	18.00
23-Kurtzman-a	3.70	11.00	26.00

FUNNY TUNES
July, 1953 - No. 3, Dec-Jan, 1953-54
Avon Periodicals

	Good	Fine	Mint
1-Space Mouse begins	2.65	8.00	18.00

FUNNY TUNES (continued)

	Good	Fine	Mint
2,3	1.60	4.70	11.00

FUNNY WORLD
1947 - 1948
Marbak Press

	Good	Fine	Mint
1-Newspaper strip reprints in all	3.50	10.50	24.00
2,3	2.30	7.00	16.00

FUNTASTIC WORLD OF HANNA-BARBERA, THE (TV)
Dec, 1977 - No. 3, June, 1978 ($1.25) (Oversized)
Marvel Comics Group

	Good	Fine	Mint
1-The Flintstones Christmas Party(12/77); 2-Yogi Bear's Easter Parade(3/78); 3-Laff-a-lympics(6/78) each....	.35	1.00	2.00

FUN TIME
1953 - No. 4, Winter, 1953-54
Ace Periodicals

	Good	Fine	Mint
1,2	1.50	4.50	10.00
3,4 (100 pgs. each)	4.00	12.00	28.00

FUN WITH SANTA CLAUS (See March of Comics No. 11,108,325)

FURTHER ADVENTURES OF INDIANA JONES, THE
Jan, 1983 - No. 34, Mar, 1986
Marvel Comics Group

	Good	Fine	Mint
1-Byrne/Austin-a		.60	1.20
2-Byrne/Austin-c/a		.35	.70
3-34		.35	.70

NOTE: ***Austin*** *a-6i, 9i; c-1i, 2i, 6i, 9i.* ***Chaykin*** *a-6p; c-6p, 8p-10p.* ***Ditko*** *a-21p, 25, 26, 34.* ***Golden*** *c-26.* ***Simonson*** *c-9.*

FURY (Straight Arrow's Horse...) (See A-1 No. 119)

FURY (TV)
No. 781, Mar, 1957 - Nov, 1962 (All photo-c)
Dell Publishing Co./Gold Key

	Good	Fine	Mint
4-Color 781	4.00	12.00	28.00
4-Color 885,975	3.00	9.00	21.00
4-Color 1031,1080,1133,1172,1218,1296, 01292-208(No.1-'62)	3.00	9.00	21.00
10020-211(11/62-G.K.)-Crandall-a	3.00	9.00	21.00

(See March of Comics No. 200)

FURY OF FIRESTORM, THE (Becomes Firestorm The Nuclear Man #65 on; also see Firestorm)
June, 1982 - No. 64, Oct, 1987 (#19-on: 75 cents)
DC Comics

	Good	Fine	Mint
1-Intro The Black Bison; brief origin	.40	1.25	2.50
2	.25	.75	1.50
3-18: 17-1st app. Firehawk		.60	1.20
19-40: 22-Origin. 24-1st app. Blue Devil. 39-Weasel's i.d. revealed.		.50	1.00
41,42-Crisis x-over		.50	1.00
43-49: 48-Intro. Moonbow		.45	.90
50-61: 53-Origin/1st app. Silver Shade. 55,56-Legends x-over		.40	.80
61-Test cover	3.35	10.00	20.00
62-64		.40	.80
Annual 1(11/83), 2(11/84), 3(11/85)		.65	1.30
Annual 4(10/86), 5((10/87)		.65	1.30

NOTE: ***Colan*** *a-19p, Annual 4p.* ***Giffen*** *a-Annual 4p.* ***Tuska*** *a-17p, 18p, 32p, 45p.*

FUTURE COMICS
June, 1940 - No. 4, Sept, 1940
David McKay Publications

	Good	Fine	Mint
1-Origin The Phantom; The Lone Ranger, & Saturn Against the Earth begin	105.00	315.00	735.00
2	50.00	150.00	350.00
3,4	40.00	120.00	280.00

FUTURE WORLD COMICS
Summer, 1946 - No. 2, Fall, 1946
George W. Dougherty

	Good	Fine	Mint
1,2	8.00	24.00	56.00

FUTURE WORLD COMIX (Warren Presents... on cover)
September, 1978
Warren Publications

	Good	Fine	Mint
1		.50	1.00

FUTURIANS, THE
Sept, 1985 - No. 3, 1985 ($1.50, color)
Lodestone Publ.

	Good	Fine	Mint
1	.50	1.50	3.00
2	.35	1.00	2.00
3	.25	.75	1.50

G-8 (See G-Eight)

GABBY (Formerly Ken Shannon)
No. 11, July, 1953; No. 2, Sept, 1953 - No. 9, Sept, 1954
Quality Comics Group

	Good	Fine	Mint
11(No.1)(7/53)	2.30	7.00	16.00
2	1.15	3.50	8.00
3-9	1.00	3.00	7.00

GABBY GOB (See Harvey Hits No. 85,90,94,97,100,103,106,109)

GABBY HAYES WESTERN (Movie star) (See Monte Hale, & Western Hero)
Nov, 1948 - No. 50, Jan, 1953; Dec, 1954 - No. 59, Jan, 1957
Fawcett/Toby Press/Charlton Comics No. 51 on

	Good	Fine	Mint
1-Gabby & his horse Corker begin; Photo front/back-c begin	19.00	57.00	132.00
2	9.50	28.50	66.00
3-5	7.00	21.00	50.00
6-10	5.70	17.00	40.00
11-20: 19-Last photo back-c?	4.60	14.00	32.00
21-49	3.00	9.00	21.00
50-(1/53)-Last Fawcett issue; last photo-c?	3.50	10.50	24.00
51-(12/54)-1st Charlton issue; photo-c	3.50	10.50	24.00
52-59(Charlton '54-57): 53,55-Photo-c	1.85	5.50	13.00
1(Toby)(12/53)-Photo-c	5.00	15.00	35.00
Quaker Oats Giveaway nn(No. 1-5, 1951) (Dell?)	2.50	7.50	17.00

GAGS
July, 1937 - V3No.10, Oct, 1944 (13¾x10¾")
United Features Synd./Triangle Publ. No. 9 on

	Good	Fine	Mint
1(7/37)-52 pgs.; 20 pgs. Grin & Bear It, Fellow Citizen	3.00	9.00	21.00
V1#9 (36 pgs.) (7/42)	2.00	6.00	14.00
V3#10	1.50	4.50	10.00

GALACTIC WAR COMIX (Warren Presents... on cover)
December, 1978
Warren Publications

	Good	Fine	Mint
nn-Wood, Williamson-r		.50	1.00

GALLANT MEN, THE (TV)
October, 1963 (Photo-c)
Gold Key

	Good	Fine	Mint
1(10085-310)-Manning-a	1.15	3.50	8.00

GALLEGHER, BOY REPORTER (TV)
May, 1965 (Disney) (Photo-c)
Gold Key

	Good	Fine	Mint
1(10149-505)	1.15	3.50	8.00

Fury #01292-208, © Independent TV Corp.

Future Comics #3, © DMP

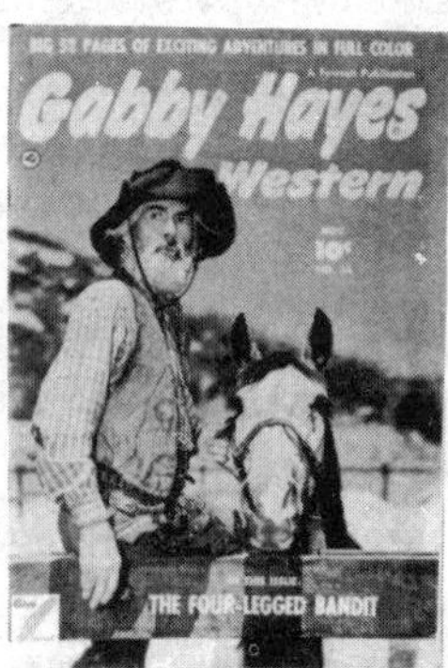

Gabby Hayes Western #24, © FAW

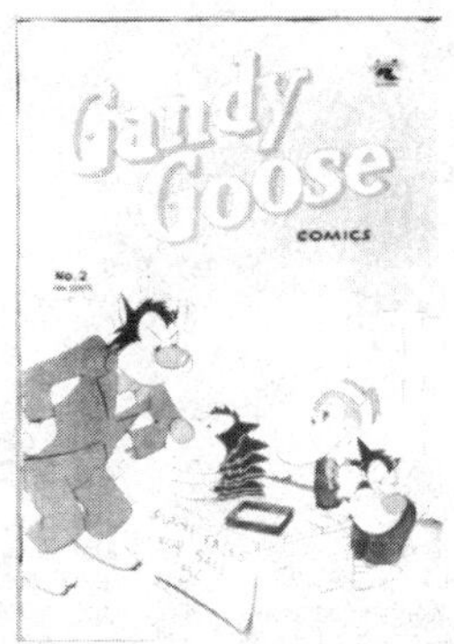

Gandy Goose #2, © STJ

Gang Busters #5, © DC

Gay Comics #35, © MCG

GANDY GOOSE (See Paul Terry's & Terry-Toons Comics)
Mar, 1953 - No. 5, Nov, 1953; No. 5, Fall, 1956 - No. 6, Sum/58
St. John Publ. Co./Pines No. 5,6

	Good	Fine	Mint
1	2.30	7.00	16.00
2	1.15	3.50	8.00
3-5(1953)(St. John)	.85	2.50	6.00
5,6(1956-58)(Pines)	.75	2.25	5.00

GANG BUSTERS
1938 - 1943
David McKay/Dell Publishing Co.

	Good	Fine	Mint
Feature Books 17(McKay)('38)	20.00	60.00	140.00
Large Feat. Comic 10('39)-(Scarce)	25.00	75.00	175.00
Large Feat. Comic 17('41)	16.00	48.00	110.00
4-Color 7(1940)	17.00	51.00	120.00
4-Color 23,24('42-43)	12.00	36.00	84.00

GANG BUSTERS (Radio/TV)
Dec-Jan, 1947-48 - No. 67, Dec-Jan, 1958-59 (No. 1-23, 52 pgs.)
National Periodical Publications

	Good	Fine	Mint
1	23.00	70.00	160.00
2	11.00	32.00	76.00
3-8	6.50	19.50	45.00
9,10-Photo-c	7.00	21.00	50.00
11-13-Photo-c	5.70	17.00	40.00
14,17-Frazetta-a, 8 pgs. each. 14-Photo-c	17.00	51.00	120.00
15,16,18-20	4.00	12.00	28.00
21-30	3.00	9.00	21.00
31-44: 44-Last Pre-code (2-3/55)	2.30	7.00	16.00
45-67	1.50	4.50	10.00

NOTE: ***Barry** a-6, 8, 10. **Drucker** a-51. **Moreira** a-48, 50, 59. **Roussos** a-8.*

GANGSTERS AND GUN MOLLS
Sept, 1951 - No. 4, June, 1952
Avon Periodical/Realistic Comics

	Good	Fine	Mint
1-Wood-a, 1 pg; c-/Avon paperback 292	17.00	51.00	120.00
2-Check-a, 8 pgs.; Kamen-a	12.00	36.00	84.00
3-Marijuana mention story; used in **POP**, pg. 84-85	12.00	36.00	84.00
4	10.00	30.00	70.00

GANGSTERS CAN'T WIN
Feb-Mar, 1948 - No. 9, June-July, 1949
D. S. Publishing Co.

	Good	Fine	Mint
1	8.50	25.50	60.00
2	4.35	13.00	30.00
3	6.00	18.00	42.00
4-Acid in face story	6.00	18.00	42.00
5,6-Ingels-a. 5-McWilliams-a	6.00	18.00	42.00
7-McWilliams-a	3.00	9.00	21.00
8-9	3.00	9.00	21.00

GANG WORLD
No. 5, Nov, 1952 - No. 6, Jan, 1953
Standard Comics

	Good	Fine	Mint
5-Bondage-c	6.50	19.50	45.00
6-Opium story	3.70	11.00	26.00

GARGOYLE
June, 1985 - No. 4, Sept, 1985 (Limited series)
Marvel Comics Group

	Good	Fine	Mint
1- Character from The Defenders; Wrightson-c	.25	.75	1.50
2-4		.50	1.00

GARRISON'S GORILLAS (TV)
Jan, 1968 - No. 4, Oct, 1968; No. 5, Oct, 1969 (Photo-c)
Dell Publishing Co.

	Good	Fine	Mint
1	1.50	4.50	10.00
2-5: 5-Reprints No. 1	1.00	3.00	7.00

GASOLINE ALLEY (Also see Super Comics 117)
1929 (B&W daily strip reprints)(7x8¾"; hardcover)
Reilly & Lee Publishers

	Good	Fine	Mint
By King (96 pgs.)	8.00	24.00	56.00

GASOLINE ALLEY
Oct, 1950 - No. 2, 1950 (Newspaper reprints)
Star Publications

	Good	Fine	Mint
1-Contains 1 pg. intro. history of the strip (The Life of Skeezix); reprints 15 scenes of highlights from 1921-1935, plus an adventure from 1935 and 1936 strips; a 2-pg. filler is included on the life of the creator Frank King, with photo of the cartoonist.	9.00	27.00	62.00
2-(1936-37 reprints)-L. B. Cole-c	9.50	28.50	66.00

(See Super Book No. 21)

GASP!
March, 1967 - No. 4, Aug, 1967
American Comics Group

	Good	Fine	Mint
1-L.S.D. drug mention	1.00	3.00	6.00
2-4	.70	2.00	4.00

GAY COMICS (Honeymoon No. 41)
Mar, 1944 (no month); No. 18, Fall, 1944 - No. 40, Oct, 1949
Timely Comics/USA Comic Mag. Co. No. 18-24

	Good	Fine	Mint
1-Wolverton's Powerhouse Pepper; Tessie the Typist begins (One Shot)	17.00	51.00	120.00
18-Wolverton-a	8.50	25.50	60.00
19-29-Wolverton-a in all. 24,29-Kurtzman-a	6.50	19.50	45.00
30,33,36,37-Kurtzman's "Hey Look"	2.15	6.50	15.00
31-Kurtzman's "Hey Look"(1), Giggles 'N' Grins (1½)	2.15	6.50	15.00
32,35,38-40	1.65	5.00	11.50
34-Three Kurtzman's "Hey Look"	3.00	9.00	21.00

GAY COMICS (Also see Tickle, Smile, & Whee Comics)
1955 (52 pgs.; 5x7¼"; 7 cents)
Modern Store Publ.

	Good	Fine	Mint
1	.50	1.50	3.00

GAY PURR-EE (See Movie Comics)

GEEK, THE (See Brother Power. . .)

G-8 AND HIS BATTLE ACES
October, 1966
Gold Key

	Good	Fine	Mint
1 (10184-610)-Painted-c	1.75	5.25	12.00

GEM COMICS
April, 1945 (52 pgs.) (Bondage-c)
Spotlight Publishers

	Good	Fine	Mint
1-Little Mohee, Steve Strong app.	6.00	18.00	42.00

GENE AUTRY (See March of Comics No. 25,28,39,54,78,90,104,120,135,150, & Western Roundup)

GENE AUTRY COMICS (Movie, Radio star; singing cowboy)
(Dell takes over with No. 11)
1941 (On sale 12/31/41) - No. 10, 1943 (68 pgs.)
Fawcett Publications

	Good	Fine	Mint
1 (Rare)-Gene Autry & his horse Champion begin	100.00	300.00	700.00
2	43.00	130.00	300.00
3-5	33.00	100.00	230.00
6-10	28.00	84.00	195.00

GENE AUTRY COMICS (. . .& Champion No. 102 on)
No. 11, 1943 - No. 121, Jan-Mar, 1959 (TV)-later issues
Dell Publishing Co.

GENE AUTRY COMICS (continued)

	Good	Fine	Mint
11,12(1943-2/44)-Continuation of Fawcett series (60pgs. each); No. 11-photo back-c	30.00	90.00	210.00
4-Color 47(1944, 60 pgs.)	30.00	90.00	210.00
4-Color 57(11/44),66('45)(52 pgs. each)	24.00	72.00	170.00
4-Color 75,83('45, 36 pgs. each)	20.00	60.00	140.00
4-Color 93,100('45-46, 36 pgs. each)	16.00	60.00	140.00
1(5-6/46, 52 pgs.)	30.00	90.00	210.00
2(7-8/46)-Photo-c begin, end No. 111	14.00	42.00	100.00
3-5: 4-Intro Flapjack Hobbs	11.00	32.00	76.00
6-10	8.00	24.00	56.00
11-20: 20-Panhandle Pete begins	5.50	16.50	38.00
21-29(36pgs.)	4.00	12.00	28.00
30-40(52pgs.)	4.00	12.00	28.00
41-56(52pgs.)	3.00	9.00	21.00
57-66(36pgs.): 58-X-mas-c	2.00	6.00	14.00
67-80(52pgs.)	2.35	7.00	16.00
81-90(52pgs.): 82-X-mas-c. 87-Blank inside-c	1.75	5.25	12.00
91-99(36pgs. No. 91-on). 94-X-mas-c	1.50	4.50	10.00
100	2.00	6.00	14.00
101-111-Last Gene Autry photo-c	1.50	4.50	10.00
112-121-All Champion painted-c	1.15	3.50	8.00
...Adventure Comics And Play-Fun Book ('40s)-36 pgs., 8x6½"; games, comics, magic	10.00	30.00	70.00
Pillsbury Premium('47)-36 pgs., 6½x7½"; games, comics, puzzles	10.00	30.00	70.00
Quaker Oats Giveaway(1950)-2½x6¾"; 5 different versions; "Death Card Gang, Phantoms of the Cave, Riddle of Laughing Mtn., Secret of Lost Valley." each....	5.00	15.00	35.00
3-D Giveaway(1953)-Pocket-size; 5 different	5.00	15.00	35.00

NOTE: *Photo back-c, 4-18,20-45,48-65.* ***Manning*** *a-118.* ***Jesse Marsh*** *art: 4-Color No. 66, 75, 93, 100, No. 1-25, 27-37, 39, 40.*

GENE AUTRY'S CHAMPION (TV)
No. 287, 8/50; No. 319, 2/51; No. 3, 8-10/51 - No. 19, 8-10/55
Dell Publishing Co.

	Good	Fine	Mint
4-Color 287('50, 52pgs.)-Photo-c	4.00	12.00	28.00
4-Color 319('51), 3-(Painted-c begin)	3.00	9.00	21.00
4-19: 19-Last painted-c	1.30	4.00	9.00

GENE AUTRY TIM (Formerly Tim) (Becomes Tim in Space)
1950 (Half-size) (Black & White Giveaway)
Tim Stores

	Good	Fine	Mint
Several issues (All Scarce)	5.00	15.00	35.00

GENERAL DOUGLAS MACARTHUR
1951
Fox Features Syndicate

	Good	Fine	Mint
nn	9.00	27.00	63.00

GENERIC COMIC BOOK, THE
April, 1984 (One-shot)
Marvel Comics Group

	Good	Fine	Mint
1		.30	.60

GENTLE BEN (TV)
Feb, 1968 - No. 5, Oct, 1969 (All photo-c)
Dell Publishing Co.

	Good	Fine	Mint
1	1.15	3.50	8.00
2-5: 5-Reprints No. 1	.75	2.25	5.00

GEORGE OF THE JUNGLE (TV)
Feb, 1969 - No. 2, Oct, 1969 (Jay Ward)
Gold Key

	Good	Fine	Mint
1,2	1.70	5.00	12.00

GEORGE PAL'S PUPPETOONS
Dec, 1945 - No. 18, Dec, 1947; No. 19, 1950
Fawcett Publications

	Good	Fine	Mint
1-Captain Marvel on cover	16.00	48.00	110.00
2	8.00	24.00	56.00
3-10	5.70	17.00	40.00
11-19	3.50	10.50	24.00

GEORGIE COMICS (...& Judy Comics No. 20-35?)
Spring, 1945 - No. 39, Oct, 1952
Timely Comics/GPI No. 1-34

	Good	Fine	Mint
1-Dave Berg-a	6.50	19.50	45.00
2	3.50	10.50	24.00
3-5,7,8	2.15	6.50	15.00
6-Georgie visits Timely Comics	2.65	8.00	18.00
9,10-Kurtzman's "Hey Look" (1 & ?); Margie app.	3.35	10.00	23.00
11,12: 11-Margie, Millie app.	1.70	5.00	12.00
13-Kurtzman's "Hey Look," 3 pgs.	2.85	8.50	20.00
14-Wolverton art, 1 pg. & Kurtzman's "Hey Look"	3.00	9.00	21.00
15,16,18-20	1.30	4.00	9.00
17,29-Kurtzman's "Hey Look," 1 pg.	2.15	6.50	15.00
21-24,27,28,30-39: 21-Anti-Wertham editorial	1.00	3.00	7.00
25-Painted cover by classic pin-up artist Peter Driben	2.65	8.00	18.00
26-Logo design swipe from Archie Comics	1.00	3.00	7.00

GERALD McBOING-BOING AND THE NEARSIGHTED MR. MAGOO
(TV)(Mr. Magoo No. 6)
Aug-Oct, 1952 - No. 5, Aug-Oct, 1953
Dell Publishing Co.

	Good	Fine	Mint
1	4.60	14.00	32.00
2-5	3.50	10.50	24.00

GERONIMO
1950 - No. 4, Feb, 1952
Avon Periodicals

	Good	Fine	Mint
1-Indian Fighter; Maneely-a; Texas Rangers r-/Cowpuncher No. 1; Fawcette-c	8.50	25.50	60.00
2-On the Warpath; Kit West app.; Kinstler c/a	5.00	15.00	35.00
3-And His Apache Murderers; Kinstler c/a(2); Kit West, drug story r-Cowpuncher No. 6	5.00	15.00	35.00
4-Savage Raids of; Kinstler c/a(3)	4.00	12.00	28.00

GERONIMO JONES
Sept, 1971 - No. 9, Jan, 1973
Charlton Comics

	Good	Fine	Mint
1		.50	1.00
2-9		.30	.60
Modern Comics Reprint #7('78)		.20	.40

GETALONG GANG, THE
May, 1985 - No. 6, 1986
Star Comics (Marvel)

	Good	Fine	Mint
1-6: Saturday morning TV stars		.35	.70

GET LOST
Feb-Mar, 1954 - No. 3, June-July, 1954 (Satire)
Mikeross Publications

	Good	Fine	Mint
1	5.70	17.00	40.00
2-Has 4 pg. E.C. parody featuring "the Sewer Keeper"	4.00	12.00	28.00
3	3.00	9.00	21.00

GET SMART (TV)
June, 1966 - No. 8, Sept, 1967 (All have photo-c)
Dell Publishing Co.

	Good	Fine	Mint
1	2.65	8.00	18.00
2-Ditko-a	2.65	8.00	18.00

Gene Autry Comics #1 (Dell), © Gene Autry

George Pal's Puppetoons #18, © George Pal

Georgie #2, © MCG

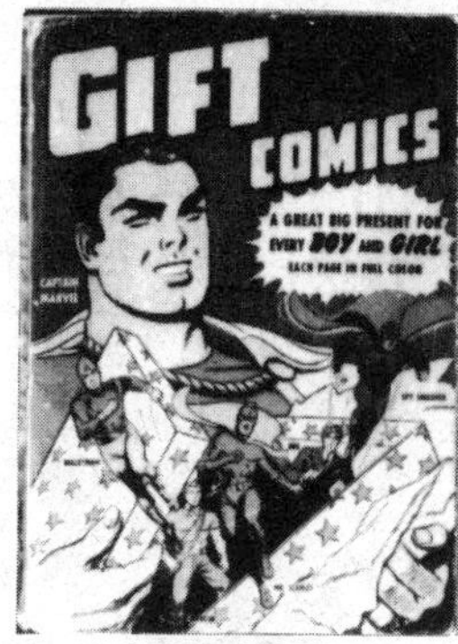

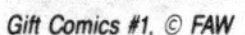
Gift Comics #1, © FAW

G.I. Jane #11, © Merit

G.I. Joe # 25, © Z-D

G.I. COMBAT (continued)

	Good	Fine	Mint
21-31,33,35-43	1.70	5.00	12.00
32-Nuclear attack-c	3.50	10.50	24.00
34-Crandall-a	3.35	10.00	23.00

G. I. COMBAT
No. 44, Jan, 1957 - No. 288, Mar, 1987
National Periodical Publications/DC Comics

	Good	Fine	Mint
44	10.00	30.00	70.00
45	5.15	15.50	36.00
46-50	2.85	8.50	20.00
51-60	1.70	5.00	12.00
61-66,68-80	1.15	3.50	8.00
67-1st Tank Killer	2.65	8.00	18.00
81,82,84-86	.70	2.00	4.00
83-1st Big Al, Little Al, & Charlie Cigar	1.35	4.00	9.00
87-1st Haunted Tank	2.65	8.00	18.00
88-90: Last 10 cent issue	.50	1.50	3.00
91-113,115-120	.35	1.00	2.00
114-Origin Haunted Tank	1.00	3.00	6.00
121-137,139,140		.50	1.00
138-Intro. The Losers (Capt. Storm, Gunner/Sarge, Johnny Cloud) in Haunted Tank	.25	.80	1.60
141-150,152,154		.40	.80
151,153-Medal of Honor series by Maurer		.40	.80
155-200,207,208		.35	.70
201-206,209-245,247-259 ($1.00 size). 232-Origin Kana the Ninja. 244-Death of Slim Stryker; 1st app. The Mercenaries. 257-Intro. Stuart's Raiders		.50	1.00
246-(72 pgs.)30th Anniversary issue		.50	1.00
260-281 ($1.25 size). 264-Intro Sgt. Bullet and the Bravos of Vietnam; origin Kana		.60	1.20
282-288 (75 cents)		.40	.80

NOTE: **Adams** c-168, 201, 202. **Check** a-168, 173. **Drucker** a-48, 61, 63, 66, 71, 72, 76, 134, 140, 141, 144, 147, 148, 153. **Evans** a-135, 138, 158, 164, 166, 202, 204, 205, 215, 256. **Giffen** a-267. **Glanzman** a-most issues. **Kubert/Heath** a-most issues; **Kubert** covers most issues. **Morrow** a-159-161(2 pgs.). **Redondo** a-189, 240i, 243i. **Sekowsky** a-162p. **Severin** a-152. **Simonson** c-169. **Thorne** a-152, 156. **Wildey** a-153. Johnny Cloud app.-No. 112, 115, 120. Mlle. Marie app.-No. 123, 132, 200. Sgt. Rock app.-No. 111-113, 115, 120, 125, 141, 146, 147, 149, 200. USS Stevens by **Glanzman**-No. 145, 150-153, 157.

G. I. COMICS (Also see Jeep & Overseas Comics)
1945 (distributed to U. S. armed forces)
Giveaways

	Good	Fine	Mint
1-49-Contains Prince Valiant by Foster, Blondie, Smilin' Jack, Mickey Finn, Terry & the Pirates, Donald Duck, Alley Oop, Moon Mullins & Capt. Easy strip reprints	4.00	12.00	28.00

GIDGET (TV)
April, 1966 - No. 2, Dec, 1966
Dell Publishing Co.

	Good	Fine	Mint
1,2: 1-Sally Field photo-c	1.70	5.00	12.00

GIFT (See The Crusaders)

GIFT COMICS (50 cents)
1942 - No. 4, 1949 (No.1-3: 324 pgs.; No. 4: 152 pgs.)
Fawcett Publications

	Good	Fine	Mint
1-Captain Marvel, Bulletman, Golden Arrow, Ibis the Invincible, Mr. Scarlet, & Spy Smasher app. Not rebound, remaindered comics, printed at same time as originals	110.00	330.00	770.00
2	80.00	240.00	560.00
3	57.00	170.00	400.00
4-The Marvel Family, Captain Marvel, etc.; each issue can vary in contents	38.00	115.00	265.00

GIFTS FROM SANTA (See March of Comics No. 137)

GIGGLE COMICS (Spencer Spook No. 100) (Also see Ha Ha)
Oct, 1943 - No. 99, Jan-Feb, 1955
Creston No.1-63/American Comics Group No. 64 on

	Good	Fine	Mint
1	11.00	33.00	76.00
2	5.00	15.00	35.00
3-5: Ken Hultgren-a begins?	3.50	10.50	24.00
6-10: 9-1st Superkatt	2.65	8.00	18.00
11-20	1.70	5.00	12.00
21-40	1.30	4.00	9.00
41-54,56-59,61-99: 95-Spencer Spook app.	1.00	3.00	7.00
55,60-Milt Gross-a	1.30	4.00	9.00

G-I IN BATTLE (G-I No. 1 only)
Aug, 1952 - No. 9, July, 1953; Mar, 1957 - No. 6, May, 1958
Ajax-Farrell Publ./Four Star

	Good	Fine	Mint
1	2.35	7.00	16.00
2	1.15	3.50	8.00
3-9	.85	2.50	6.00
Annual 1(1952, 100 pgs.)	11.00	33.00	76.00
1(1957-Ajax)	1.50	4.50	10.00
2-6	.70	2.00	5.00

G. I. JANE
May, 1953 - No. 11, Mar, 1955 (Misdated 3/54)
Stanhall/Merit No. 11

	Good	Fine	Mint
1	3.70	11.00	26.00
2-7(5/54)	1.85	5.50	13.00
8-10(12/54, Stanhall)	1.60	4.70	11.00
11 (3/55, Merit)	1.50	4.50	10.00

G. I. JOE (Also see Advs. of. . ., Showcase #53,54 & The Yardbirds)
No. 10, 1950; No. 11, 4-5/51 - No. 51, 6/57 (52pgs., 10-14,6-17?)
Ziff-Davis Publ. Co.

	Good	Fine	Mint
10(No.1, 1950)-Saunders painted-c begin	3.70	11.00	26.00
11-14(10/51)	2.15	6.50	15.00
V2No.6(12/51)-17-(Last 52pgs.?)	1.85	5.50	13.00
18-(100 pg. Giant-'52)	6.50	19.50	45.00
19-30	1.60	4.70	11.00
31-47,49-51	1.30	4.00	9.00
48-Atom bomb story	1.70	5.00	12.00

NOTE: **Powell** a-V2/7, 8, 11. **Norman Saunders** painted c-10-14, 6-14, 26, 30, 31, 35, 38, 39. Bondage c-29,35,38. **Tuska** a-7.

G. I. JOE (America's Movable Fighting Man)
1967 (36 pages) (5-1/8"x8-3/8")
Custom Comics

	Good	Fine	Mint
Schaffenberger-a		.40	.80

G. I. JOE AND THE TRANSFORMERS
Jan, 1987 - No. 4, Apr, 1987 (mini-series)
Marvel Comics Group

	Good	Fine	Mint
1	.35	1.00	2.00
2-4	.25	.75	1.50

G. I. JOE, A REAL AMERICAN HERO (See Official Handbook. . .)
June, 1982 - Present
Marvel Comics Group

	Good	Fine	Mint
1-Printed on Baxter paper	4.15	12.50	25.00
2-Printed on reg. paper	6.00	17.50	35.00
2 (2nd printing)	.85	2.50	5.00
3-5	2.70	8.00	16.00
3-5 (2nd printing)	.85	2.50	5.00
6,8	3.35	10.00	20.00
6,8 (2nd printing)	.85	2.50	5.00
7,9,10	2.50	7.50	15.00
7,9,10 (2nd printing)	.85	2.50	5.00
11-Intro Airborne	1.70	5.00	10.00
12	2.50	7.50	15.00
13-15	2.15	6.50	13.00

G.I. JOE, A REAL... (continued)

	Good	Fine	Mint
14 (2nd printing)	.70	2.00	4.00
16	2.00	6.00	12.00
17-20	1.30	4.00	8.00
17-19 (2nd printing)	.50	1.50	3.00
21,22	1.70	5.00	10.00
23-25	1.00	3.00	6.00
21,23,25 (2nd printing)	.60	1.75	3.50
26-Origin Snake-Eyes; ends No. 27	1.30	4.00	8.00
27	1.50	4.50	9.00
26,27 (2nd printing)	.40	1.25	2.50
28-30	.85	2.50	5.00
29,30 (2nd printing)	.30	.90	1.80
31-35: 33-New headquarters	.70	2.00	4.00
36-40	.50	1.50	3.00
34,35,36,37 (2nd printing)	.25	.75	1.50
41-49	.40	1.25	2.50
50-Double size; intro Special Missions	.70	2.00	4.00
51-60	.35	1.10	2.20
51 (2nd printing)		.40	.80
61-70		.60	1.20
Special Treasury Edition (1982)-r/#1	1.30	4.00	8.00
...Yearbook 1 ('84)-r/#1	1.15	3.50	7.00
...Yearbook 2 ('85)	.70	2.00	4.00
...Yearbook 3 ('86, 68 pgs.)	.50	1.50	3.00
...Yearbook 4 ('87)	.30	.90	1.80

NOTE: ***Golden** c-23. **Heath** a-24. 2nd printings exist.*

G. I. JOE COMICS MAGAZINE
Dec, 1986 - Present ($1.50, digest-size)
Marvel Comics Group

	Good	Fine	Mint
1-G.I. Joe-r	.35	1.00	2.00
2-8	.25	.75	1.50

G.I. JOE IN 3-D
1987 - Present ($2.50) (with glasses)
Blackthorne Publishing

	Good	Fine	Mint
1,2	.40	1.25	2.50

G. I. JOE ORDER OF BATTLE, THE
Dec, 1986 - No. 4, Mar, 1987 (mini-series)
Marvel Comics Group

	Good	Fine	Mint
1	.70	2.00	4.00
2-4	.35	1.00	2.00

G. I. JOE SPECIAL MISSIONS
Oct, 1986 - Present
Marvel Comics Group

	Good	Fine	Mint
1	.60	1.75	3.50
2	.35	1.00	2.00
3-8	.25	.75	1.50

G. I. JUNIORS (See Harvey Hits No. 86, 91, 95, 98, 101, 104, 107, 110, 112, 114, 116, 118, 120, 122)

GIL THORP
May-July, 1963
Dell Publishing Co.

	Good	Fine	Mint
1-Caniffish-a	1.75	5.25	12.00

GINGER (Li'l Jinx No. 11 on?)
1951 - No. 10, Summer, 1954
Archie Publications

	Good	Fine	Mint
1	5.50	16.50	38.00
2	3.15	9.50	22.00
3-6	2.35	7.00	16.00
7-10-Katy Keene app.	3.70	11.00	26.00

G.I. RAMBOT
April, 1987 - Present?($1.95, color)
Wonder Color Comics/Pied Piper #2

	Good	Fine	Mint
1,2	.25	.75	1.50

GIRL COMICS (Girl Confessions No. 13 on)
Nov, 1949 - No. 12, Jan, 1952 (Photo-c 1-4)
Marvel/Atlas Comics(CnPC)

	Good	Fine	Mint
1	6.00	18.00	42.00
2-Kubert-a	3.15	9.50	22.00
3-Everett-a; Liz Taylor photo-c	4.00	12.00	28.00
4-11	1.70	5.00	12.00
12-Krigstein-a	3.15	9.50	22.00

GIRL CONFESSIONS (Formerly Girl Comics)
No. 13, Mar, 1952 - No. 35, Aug, 1954
Atlas Comics (CnPC/ZPC)

	Good	Fine	Mint
13-Everett-a	3.15	9.50	22.00
14,15,19,20	1.60	4.70	11.00
16-18-Everett-a	2.30	7.00	16.00
21-35	1.30	4.00	9.00

GIRL FROM U.N.C.L.E., THE (TV)
Jan, 1967 - No. 5, Oct, 1967
Gold Key

	Good	Fine	Mint
1-McWilliams-a; photo-c	2.65	8.00	18.00
2-5-Leonard Swift-Courier No. 5	1.70	5.00	12.00

GIRLS' FUN & FASHION MAGAZINE (Formerly Polly Pigtails)
V5No.44, Jan, 1950 - V5No.47, July, 1950
Parents' Magazine Institute

	Good	Fine	Mint
V5#44	1.85	5.50	13.00
45-47	1.00	3.00	7.00

GIRLS IN LOVE
May, 1950 - No. 2, July, 1950
Fawcett Publications

	Good	Fine	Mint
1,2-Photo-c	4.35	13.00	30.00

GIRLS IN LOVE (Formerly G. I. Sweethearts No. 45)
No. 46, Sept, 1955 - No. 57, Dec, 1956
Quality Comics Group

	Good	Fine	Mint
46	2.65	8.00	18.00
47-56: 54-'Commie' story	1.30	4.00	9.00
57-Matt Baker c/a	3.35	10.00	23.00

GIRLS IN WHITE (See Harvey Comics Hits No. 58)

GIRLS' LIFE
Jan, 1954 - No. 6, Nov, 1954
Atlas Comics (BFP)

	Good	Fine	Mint
1-Patsy Walker	3.15	9.50	22.00
2	1.60	4.70	11.00
3-6	1.15	3.50	8.00

GIRLS' LOVE STORIES
Aug-Sept, 1949 - No. 180, Nov-Dec, 1973 (No. 1-13, 52 pgs.)
National Comics(Signal Publ. No.9-65/Arleigh No.83-117)

	Good	Fine	Mint
1-Toth, Kinstler-a, 8 pgs. each; photo-c	16.00	48.00	110.00
2-Kinstler-a?	8.00	24.00	56.00
3-10: 1-9-Photo-c	5.00	15.00	35.00
11-20	3.15	9.50	22.00
21-33: 21-Kinstler-a. 33-Last pre-code (1-2/55)	2.00	6.00	14.00
34-50	1.60	4.70	11.00
51-99	.85	2.50	6.00
100	1.00	3.00	7.00
101-146: 113-117-April O'Day app.	.40	1.25	2.50
147-151-"Confessions" serial		.50	1.00
152-180: 161-170, 52 pgs.		.30	.60

GIRLS' ROMANCES
Feb-Mar, 1950 - No. 160, Oct, 1971 (No. 1-11, 52 pgs.)

G.I. Joe, A Real American Hero #50, © MCG

Ginger #3, © AP

Girls' Love Stories #16, © DC

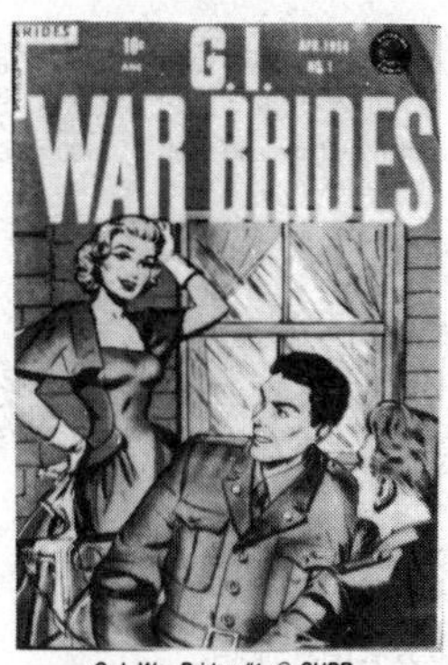

G. I. War Brides #1, © SUPR

Glamorous Romances #87, © ACE

Godzilla #3, © MCG

GIRLS' ROMANCES (continued) — Good / Fine / Mint
National Per. Publ.(Signal Publ. No.7-79/Arleigh No.84)

	Good	Fine	Mint
1-Photo-c	16.00	48.00	110.00
2-Photo-c; Toth-a	8.00	24.00	56.00
3-10: 3-6-Photo-c	5.00	15.00	35.00
11,12,14-20	3.15	9.50	22.00
13-Toth-c	3.50	10.50	24.00
21-31: 31-Last pre-code (2-3/55)	2.00	6.00	14.00
32-50	1.50	4.50	10.00
51-99	.85	2.50	6.00
100	1.00	3.00	7.00
101-108,110-133,135-160	.45	1.35	3.00
109-Beatles c/story	2.00	6.00	14.00
134-Adams-c	.55	1.65	4.00

G. I. SWEETHEARTS (Formerly Diary Loves; Girls In Love #46 on)
No. 32, June, 1953 - No. 45, May, 1955
Quality Comics Group

	Good	Fine	Mint
32	2.30	7.00	16.00
33-45: 43-Last pre-code? (1/55)	1.30	4.00	9.00

G. I. TALES (Sgt. Barney Barker No. 1-3)
No. 4, Feb, 1957 - No. 6, July, 1957
Atlas Comics (MCI)

	Good	Fine	Mint
4-Severin-a(4)	1.70	5.00	12.00
5	.85	2.50	6.00
6-Orlando, Powell, & Woodbridge-a	1.35	4.00	9.00

G. I. WAR BRIDES
April, 1954 - No. 8, June, 1955
Superior Publishers Ltd.

	Good	Fine	Mint
1	2.30	7.00	16.00
2	1.20	3.50	8.00
3-8: 4-Kamenesque-a; lingerie panels	1.00	3.00	7.00

G. I. WAR TALES
Mar-Apr, 1973 - No. 4, Oct-Nov, 1973
National Periodical Publications

	Good	Fine	Mint
1,3-Reprints		.15	.30
2-Adams-a(r), 4-Krigstein-a(r)		.15	.30

NOTE: ***Drucker** a-3r,4r. **Heath** a-4r. **Kubert** a-2,3; c-4r.*

GLADSTONE COMIC ALBUM
1987 - Present (8½x11")($5.95)
Gladstone Publishing

	Good	Fine	Mint
1-U. Scrooge, Barks-r; Beck-c	1.00	3.00	5.95
2-Donald Duck, Barks-r	1.00	3.00	5.95
3-Mickey Mouse-r by Gottfredson	1.00	3.00	5.95
4-Uncle Scrooge-r by Barks	1.00	3.00	5.95

GLAMOROUS ROMANCES (Formerly Dotty)
No. 41, Sept, 1949 - No. 90, Oct, 1956 (Photo-c 68-90)
Ace Magazines (A. A. Wyn)

	Good	Fine	Mint
41-Dotty app.	2.30	7.00	16.00
42-72,74-80: 50-61-Painted-c. 80-Last pre-code (2/55)	1.15	3.50	8.00
73-L.B. Cole-a(r)-/All Love #27	1.65	5.00	11.50
81-90	1.00	3.00	7.00

GLOBAL FORCE
1987 - Present ($1.95, color)
Silverline Comics

	Good	Fine	Mint
1,2	.30	.90	1.80

GNOME MOBILE, THE (See Movie Comics)

GOBLIN, THE
June, 1982 - No. 4, Dec, 1982 (Magazine, $2.25)
Warren Publishing Co.

	Good	Fine	Mint
1-The Gremlin app; Golden-a(p)	.35	1.10	2.25
2-4: 2-1st Hobgoblin	.35	1.10	2.25

GODFATHERS, THE (See The Crusaders)

GOD IS
1973, 1975 (35-49 Cents)
Spire Christian Comics (Fleming H. Revell Co.)

	Good	Fine	Mint
By Al Hartley		.40	.80

GODS FOR HIRE
Dec, 1986 - Present? ($1.50, color)
Hot Comics

	Good	Fine	Mint
1	.25	.75	1.50

GOD'S HEROES IN AMERICA
1956 (nn) (68 pgs.) (25-35 cents)
Catechetical Guild Educational Society

	Good	Fine	Mint
307	1.70	5.00	10.00

GOD'S SMUGGLER (Religious)
1972 (39 & 49 cents)
Spire Christian Comics/Fleming H. Revell Co.

	Good	Fine	Mint
1-Two variations exist		.40	.80

GODZILLA
August, 1977 - No. 24, July, 1979
Marvel Comics Group

	Good	Fine	Mint
1-Mooney-i		.50	1.00
2-24: 3-Champions x-over; 4,5-Sutton-a		.30	.60

GO-GO
June, 1966 - No. 9, Oct, 1967
Charlton Comics

	Good	Fine	Mint
1-Miss Bikini Luv begins; Rolling Stones, Beatles, Elvis, Sonny & Cher, Sinatra, Bob Dylan parody; Herman's Hermits pin-ups	2.00	6.00	14.00
2-Ringo Starr, David McCallum, Beatles photo cover; Beatles story and photos	2.00	6.00	14.00
3-Blooperman begins, ends No. 6	.85	2.50	5.00
4	.85	2.50	5.00
5-Super Hero & TV satire by J. Aparo & Grass Green begin	1.20	3.50	7.00
6-9: 6-8-Aparo-a. 6-Petulia Clark photo-c	.85	2.50	5.00

GO-GO AND ANIMAL (See Tippy's Friends. . .)

GOING STEADY (Formerly Teen-Age Temptations)
No. 10, 1954 - No. 13, June, 1955; No. 14, Oct, 1955
St. John Publishing Co.

	Good	Fine	Mint
10(1954)-Matt Baker c/a	6.50	19.50	45.00
11(2/55, last precode), 12(4/55)-Baker-c	3.15	9.50	22.00
13(6/55)-Baker c/a	4.35	13.00	30.00
14(10/55)-Matt Baker-c/a, 25 pgs.	4.65	14.00	33.00

GOING STEADY (Formerly Personal Love)
V3No.3, Feb., 1960 - V3No.6, Aug, 1960
Prize Publications/Headline

	Good	Fine	Mint
V3#3-6	.50	1.50	3.00

GOING STEADY WITH BETTY (Betty & Her Steady No. 2)
Nov-Dec, 1949
Avon Periodicals

	Good	Fine	Mint
1	6.00	18.00	42.00

GOLDEN ARROW (See Fawcett Miniatures, Mighty Midget & Whiz Comics)

GOLDEN ARROW (. . .Western No. 6)
Wint, 1942-43 - No. 6, Spring, 1947
Fawcett Publications

	Good	Fine	Mint
1-Golden Arrow begins	12.00	36.00	84.00
2	6.00	18.00	42.00

GOLDEN ARROW (continued)

	Good	Fine	Mint
3-5	3.70	11.00	26.00
6-Krigstein-a	4.35	13.00	30.00
Well Known Comics (1944; 12 pgs.; 8½x10½"; paper-c; glued binding)-Bestmaid/Samuel Lowe giveaway; printed in green	6.00	18.00	42.00

GOLDEN COMICS DIGEST
May, 1969 - No. 48, Jan, 1976
Gold Key

NOTE: *Whitman editions exist of many titles and are generally valued less.*

	Good	Fine	Mint
1-Tom & Jerry, Woody Woodpecker, Bugs Bunny	1.15	3.50	8.00
2-Hanna-Barbera TV Fun Favorites	.50	1.50	3.00
3-Tom & Jerry, Woody Woodpecker	.50	1.50	3.00
4-Tarzan; Manning & Marsh-a	1.70	5.00	12.00
5,8-Tom & Jerry, W. Woodpecker, Bugs Bunny	.35	1.00	2.00
6-Bugs Bunny	.35	1.00	2.00
7-Hanna-Barbera TV Fun Favorites	.35	1.00	2.00
9-Tarzan	1.50	4.50	10.00
10-Bugs Bunny	.35	1.00	2.00
11-Hanna-Barbera TV Fun Favorites	.25	.75	1.50
12-Tom & Jerry, Bugs Bunny, W. Woodpecker Journey to the Sun	.25	.75	1.50
13-Tom & Jerry	.25	.75	1.50
14-Bugs Bunny Fun Packed Funnies	.25	.75	1.50
15-Tom & Jerry, W. Woodpecker, Bugs Bunny	.25	.75	1.50
16-Woody Woodpecker Cartoon Special	.25	.75	1.50
17-Bugs Bunny	.25	.75	1.50
18-Tom & Jerry; Barney Bear-r by Barks	.60	1.75	3.50
19-Little Lulu	1.70	5.00	12.00
20-Woody Woodpecker Falltime Funtime	.25	.75	1.50
21-Bugs Bunny Showtime	.25	.75	1.50
22-Tom & Jerry Winter Wingding	.25	.75	1.50
23-Little Lulu & Tubby Fun Fling	1.70	5.00	12.00
24-Woody Woodpecker Fun Festival	.25	.75	1.50
25,28-Tom & Jerry	.25	.75	1.50
26-Bugs Bunny Halloween Hulla-Boo-Loo; Dr. Spektor article, also No. 25	.25	.75	1.50
27-Little Lulu & Tubby in Hawaii	1.50	4.50	10.00
29-Little Lulu & Tubby	1.50	4.50	10.00
30-Bugs Bunny Vacation Funnies	.25	.75	1.50
31-Turok, Son of Stone; reprints 4-Color #596,656	1.15	3.50	8.00
32-Woody Woodpecker Summer Fun	.25	.75	1.50
33-Little Lulu & Tubby Halloween Fun; Dr. Spektor app.	1.70	5.00	12.00
34-Bugs Bunny Winter Funnies	.25	.75	1.50
35-Tom & Jerry Snowtime Funtime	.25	.75	1.50
36-Little Lulu & Her Friends	1.70	5.00	12.00
37-Woody Woodpecker County Fair	.25	.75	1.50
38-The Pink Panther	.25	.75	1.50
39-Bugs Bunny Summer Fun	.25	.75	1.50
40-Little Lulu & Tubby Trick or Treat; all by Stanley	1.70	5.00	12.00
41-Tom & Jerry Winter Carnival		.50	1.00
42-Bugs Bunny		.50	1.00
43-Little Lulu in Paris	1.70	5.00	12.00
44-Woody Woodpecker Family Fun Festival		.50	1.00
45-The Pink Panther		.60	1.20
46-Little Lulu & Tubby	1.50	4.50	10.00
47-Bugs Bunny		.50	1.00
48-The Lone Ranger	.50	1.50	3.00

NOTE: *No. 1-30, 164 pages; No. 31 on, 132 pages.*

GOLDEN LAD
July, 1945 - No. 5, June, 1946
Spark Publications

	Good	Fine	Mint
1-Origin Golden Lad & Swift Arrow	23.00	70.00	160.00
2-Mort Meskin-a	11.50	34.00	80.00
3,4: 3-Mort Meskin-a	11.00	33.00	76.00
5-Origin Golden Girl; Shaman & Flame app.	12.00	36.00	84.00

NOTE: *All **Robinson, Meskin,** and **Roussos** art.*

GOLDEN LEGACY
1966 - 1972 (Black History) (25 cents)
Fitzgerald Publishing Co.

1-Toussaint L'Ouverture (1966), 2-Harriet Tubman (1967), 3-Crispus Attucks & the Minutemen (1967), 4-Benjamin Banneker (1968), 5-Matthew Henson (1969), 6-Alexander Dumas & Family (1969), 7-Frederick Douglass, Part 1 (1969), 8-Frederick Douglass, Part 2 (1970), 9-Robert Smalls (1970), 10-J. Cinque & the Amistad Mutiny (1970), 11-Men in Action: White, Marshall J. Wilkins (1970), 12-Black Cowboys (1972), 13-The Life of Martin Luther King, Jr. (1972), 14-The Life of Alexander Pushkin (1971), 15-Ancient African Kingdoms (1972), 16-Black Inventors (1972)

	Good	Fine	Mint
each....		.50	1.00
1-10,12,13,15,16(1976)-Reprints		.15	.30

GOLDEN LOVE STORIES (Formerly Golden West Love)
No. 4, April, 1950
Kirby Publishing Co.

	Good	Fine	Mint
4-Powell-a; Glenn Ford & Janet Leigh photo-c	6.50	19.50	45.00

GOLDEN PICTURE CLASSIC, A
1956, 1957 (Text stories w/illustrations in color; 100 pgs. each)
(Softcover 49-50 cents; hardcover 69 cents - $1.00)
Western Printing Co. (Simon & Shuster)

CL-401: Treasure Island; CL-402: Tom Sawyer; CL-403: Black Beauty; CL-404: Little Women; CL-405: Heidi; CL-406: Ben Hur; CL-407: Around the World in 80 Days; CL-408: Sherlock Holmes; CL-409: The Three Musketeers; CL-410: The Merry Advs. of Robin Hood; CL-411: Hans Brinker; CL-412: The Count of Monte Cristo

	Good	Fine	Mint
Softcover editions....	1.35	4.00	8.00
Hardcover editions....	2.65	8.00	16.00

NOTE: *Issues CL-401 to CL-412 were issued in 1956 with numbers CL-1-49 to CL-12-49. The 1957 hardcover editions were numbered CL-101 to CL-112.*

GOLDEN PICTURE STORY BOOK
Dec, 1961 (52 pgs.; 50 cents; large size)
Racine Press (Western)

	Good	Fine	Mint
ST-1-Huckleberry Hound (TV)	3.00	9.00	21.00
ST-2-Yogi Bear (TV)	3.00	9.00	21.00
ST-3-Babes in Toyland (Walt Disney's...)-Annette Funicello photo-c	3.00	9.00	21.00
ST-4-(...of Disney Ducks)-Walt Disney's Wonderful World of Ducks (Donald Duck, Uncle Scrooge, Donald's Nephews, Grandma Duck, Ludwig Von Drake, & Gyro Gearloose stories)	4.00	12.00	28.00

GOLDEN WEST LOVE (Golden Love Stories No. 4)
Sept-Oct, 1949 - No. 3, Feb, 1950 (No. 1, 52 pgs.)
Kirby Publishing Co.

	Good	Fine	Mint
1-Powell-a in all; Roussos-a	6.50	19.50	45.00
2,3: 3-Photo-c	5.00	15.00	35.00

GOLDEN WEST RODEO TREASURY (See Dell Giants)

GOLDILOCKS (See March of Comics No. 1)

GOLDILOCKS & THE THREE BEARS
1943 (Giveaway)
K. K. Publications

	Good	Fine	Mint
	6.75	20.00	40.00

GOLD KEY CHAMPION
Mar, 1978 - No. 2, May, 1978 (52 pages) (50 cents)
Gold Key

	Good	Fine	Mint
1-Space Family Robinson; ½-r		.40	.80
2-Mighty Samson; ½-r		.40	.80

Golden Arrow #3, © FAW

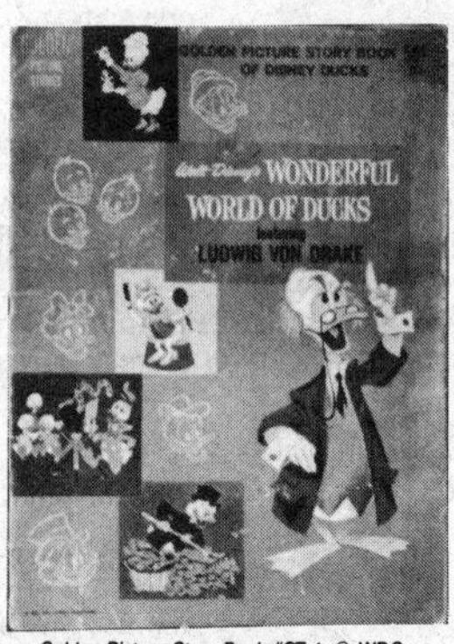

Golden Picture Story Book #ST-4, © WDC

Gold Key Champion #1, © GK

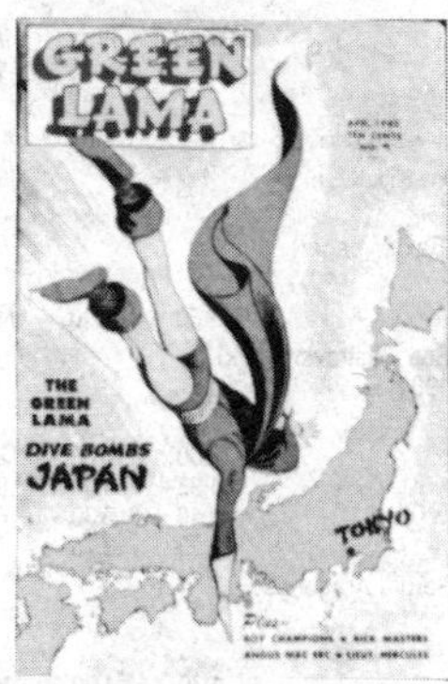

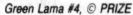

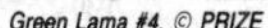
Green Lama #4, © PRIZE

Green Lantern #7 (1st series), © DC

Green Lantern #10 (2nd series), © DC

GREEN LAMA (continued)
Spark Publications/Prize No. 7 on

	Good	Fine	Mint
1-Intro. The Green Lama, Lt. Hercules & The Boy Champions; Mac Raboy-a #1-8	45.00	135.00	315.00
2-Lt. Hercules borrows the Human Torch's powers for one panel	32.00	95.00	225.00
3,6-8: 7-Christmas-c	23.00	70.00	160.00
4-Dick Tracy take-off in Lt. Hercules story by H. L. Gold (sci-fiction writer)	23.00	70.00	160.00
5-Lt. Hercules story; Little Orphan Annie, Smilin' Jack & Snuffy Smith take-off; Mac Raboy-c	23.00	70.00	160.00

NOTE: ***Robinson** a-3-5.*

GREEN LANTERN (1st Series) (See All-American, All Flash Quarterly, All Star Comics, The Big All-American & Comic Cavalcade)
Fall, 1941 - No. 38, May-June, 1949
National Periodical Publications/All-American

	Good	Fine	Mint
1-Origin retold	357.00	1070.00	2500.00
2-1st book-length story	160.00	480.00	1120.00
3	125.00	375.00	875.00
4	85.00	255.00	600.00
5	70.00	210.00	490.00
6-8: 8-Hop Harrigan begins	60.00	180.00	420.00
9,10: 10-Origin Vandal Savage	50.00	150.00	350.00
11-17,19,20: 12-Origin Gambler	42.00	125.00	295.00
18-Christmas-c	46.00	140.00	320.00
21-29: 27-Origin Sky Pirate	37.00	110.00	260.00
30-Origin/1st app. Streak the Wonder Dog by Toth	37.00	110.00	260.00
31-35	32.00	95.00	225.00
36-38: 37-Sargon the Sorcerer app.	37.00	110.00	260.00

NOTE: *Book-length stories No. 2-8. **Toth** a-28, 30, 31, 34-38; c-28, 30, 34, 36-38.*

GREEN LANTERN (2nd Series) (See Adventure, DC Spec., DC Spec. Series, Flash, Showcase & Tales of The. . .Corps; Gr. Lant. Corps #206 on)
7-8/60 - No. 89, 4-5/72; No. 90, 8-9/76 - No. 205, 10/86
National Periodical Publications/DC Comics

	Good	Fine	Mint
1-Origin retold; Gil Kane-a begins	63.00	156.00	438.00
2-1st Pieface	24.00	60.00	170.00
3	14.00	36.00	100.00
4,5: 5-Origin & 1st app. Hector Hammond; 1st 5700 A.D. story	12.00	29.00	82.00
6-10: 6-Intro Tomar-re the alien G.L. 7-Origin Sinestro. 9-1st Jordan Brothers; last 10 cent issue	6.00	16.00	44.00
11-15: 13-Flash x-over. 14-Origin Sonar	4.50	12.00	32.00
16-20: 16-Origin Star Sapphire. 20-Flash x-over	3.15	9.50	22.00
21-30: 21-Origin Dr. Polaris. 23-1st Tattooed Man. 24-Origin Shark. 29-JLA cameo; 1st Blackhand	2.30	7.00	16.00
31-39	1.60	4.75	9.50
40-1st app. Crisis; 1st G.A. Green Lantern in Silver Age; origin The Guardians	13.00	32.00	90.00
41-50: 42-Zatanna x-over. 43-Flash x-over. 45-G.A. Green Lantern x-over	1.00	3.00	6.00
51-75: 52,61-G.A. Green Lantern x-over. 69-Wood inks	.75	2.25	4.50
76-Begin Green Lantern/Green Arrow series by Neal Adams	5.50	16.50	33.00
77	2.15	6.50	13.00
78-80	1.70	5.00	10.00
81,82: 82-One pg. Wrightson inks	1.20	3.50	7.00
83-G.L. reveals i.d. to Carol Ferris	1.20	3.50	7.00
84-Adams/Wrightson-a, 22 pgs.	1.20	3.50	7.00
85,86(52 pgs.)-Drug propaganda books. 86-G.A. Gr. Lant.-r; Toth-a	1.70	5.00	10.00
87,89(52 pgs.): 89-G.A. Green Lantern-r	.90	2.75	5.50
88(52 pgs.,'72)-Unpubbed G.A. Gr. Lantern story; Gr. Lant.-r/Showcase 23. Adams-a(1 pg.)	.35	1.00	2.00
90('76)-99		.50	1.00
100-(Giant)-1st app. new Air Wave	.40	1.10	2.20
101-107,113-119		.40	.80
108-110(44 pgs.)-G.A. Gr. Lant. stories		.40	.80
111-Origin retold; G.A. Gr. Lant. app.		.40	.80
112-G.A. Gr. Lant. origin retold		.40	.80
120-130		.35	.70
131-135,138-140,145-149: 131,132-Tales of the G.L. Corps. 132-Adam Strange begins new series, ends 147. 148-Tales of the G.L. Corps begins, ends #173		.35	.70
136,137-1st app. Citadel	.30	.90	1.80
141-1st app. Omega Men	.85	2.50	5.00
142,143-The Omega Men app.; Perez-c	.50	1.50	3.00
144-Omega Men app. (2 pgs.)		.50	1.00
150-Anniversary ish., 52 pgs.		.50	1.00
151-159,162-170: 159-Origin Evil Star		.40	.80
160,161-Omega Men app.	.25	.75	1.50
171-193,196,197: (75– cover). 174-Book-length stories begin		.40	.80
194,195-Crisis x-over. 195-Guy Gardner becomes Gr. Lantern		.50	1.00
198,200 ($1.25): 198-Crisis x-over		.60	1.25
199,201-224		.40	.80
Annual 1 (See Tales Of The. . .)			

NOTE: ***Adams** a-76, 77p-87p, 89; c-63, 76-89. **Austin** a-93i, 94i, 171i, Annual 3i. **Buckler** c-136p. **Greene** a-39-49i, 58-63i; c-54-58i. **Grell** a-90, 91, 92-100p, 106p, 108-110p; c-90, 93-100, 101p, 102-106, 108-112. **Gil Kane** a-1-49p, 50-57, 58-61p, 68-75p, 85p(r), 87p(r), 88p(r), 156, 177, 184p; c-1-52, 54-61p, 67-75, 123, 154, 156, 165-71, 177, 184. **Newton** a-148p, 149p, 181. **Perez** c-132p, 141-144. **Sekowsky** a-65p, 170p. **Sparling** a-63p. **Starlin** c-129, 133. **Staton** a-117p, 123-127p, 128, 129-31p, 132-39, 140p, 141-46, 147p, 148-50, 151-55p, 207p-213p, 217p, Annual 3; c-107p, 117p, 135(i), 136p, 145p, 146, 147, 148-152p, 155p, 207p-213p, 217p. **Toth** a-86r, 171p. **Tuska** a-166-68p, 170p. **Willingham** a-213p, 219p, Annual 2, 3p; c-218p, 219p.*

GREEN LANTERN CORPS Formerly Green Lantern)
No. 206, Nov, 1986 - Present
DC Comics

	Good	Fine	Mint
206-221		.50	1.00
. .Corps Annual 2 (12/86)-Moore scripts		.65	1.30
. .Corps Annual 3 (8/87)-Moore scripts; Byrne-a		.65	1.30

GREEN LANTERN/GREEN ARROW
Oct, 1983 - No. 7, April, 1984
DC Comics

	Good	Fine	Mint
1-Reprints begin	.45	1.25	2.50
2-6 (52 pgs.)	.45	1.25	2.50
7 (60 pgs.; $2.50)	.45	1.25	2.50

NOTE: ***Adams** a-1-7; c-1-4. **Wrightson** a-4, 5.*

GREEN MASK, THE (The Bouncer No. 11 on? See Mystery Men)
Summer, 1940 - No. 9, 2/42; No. 10, 8/44 - No. 11, 11/44;
V2/1, Spr, 1945 - No. 6, 10-11/46
Fox Features Syndicate

	Good	Fine	Mint
V1/1-Origin The Green Mask & Domino; reprints/Mystery Men No. 1-3,5-7; Lou Fine-c	75.00	225.00	525.00
2-Zanzibar The Magician by Tuska	35.00	105.00	245.00
3-Powell-a; Marijuana story	22.00	65.00	154.00
4-Navy Jones begins, ends No. 6	18.00	54.00	125.00
5	15.00	45.00	105.00
6-The Nightbird begins, ends No. 9; bondage/torture-c	13.00	40.00	90.00
7-9	11.00	32.00	76.00
10,11: 10-Origin One Round Hogan & Rocket Kelly	10.00	30.00	70.00
V2/1	7.00	21.00	50.00
2-6	5.70	17.00	40.00

GREEN PLANET, THE
1962 (One Shot)
Charlton Comics

	Good	Fine	Mint
nn	1.75	5.25	12.00

GREEN TEAM (See First Issue Special)

GREETINGS FROM SANTA (See March of Comics No. 48)

GRENDEL (Also see Primer No. 2 and Mage)
Dec, 1985 - No. 3, 1986
Comico

	Good	Fine	Mint
1	7.00	20.00	40.00
2	5.00	15.00	30.00
3	5.00	15.00	30.00

GRENDEL
Oct, 1986 - Present ($1.50, color)
Comico

	Good	Fine	Mint
1	.85	2.50	5.00
1-2nd printing	.25	.75	1.50
2	.45	1.30	2.60
2-2nd printing	.25	.75	1.50
3-5	.35	1.10	2.20
6-10	.30	.95	1.90
11-15	.25	.80	1.60

GREYFRIARS BOBBY (See 4-Color No. 1189)

GREYLORE
12/85 - No. 6, 9/86 ($1.50-$1.75, full color, high quality paper)
Sirius Comics

	Good	Fine	Mint
1	.25	.75	1.50
2-6		.60	1.20

GRIM GHOST, THE
Jan, 1975 - No. 3, July, 1975
Atlas/Seaboard Publ.

	Good	Fine	Mint
1-Origin		.40	.80
2,3-Heath-c		.30	.60

GRIMJACK
Aug, 1984 - Present
First Comics

	Good	Fine	Mint
1	.40	1.20	2.40
2-5	.35	1.00	2.00
6-10	.25	.80	1.60
11-25: 20-Sutton c/a begins		.70	1.40
26-2nd color Teenage Mutant Ninja Turtles	.75	2.25	4.50
27-38: 30-Dynamo Joe x-over		.65	1.30
39-45	.30	.90	1.80

GRIMM'S GHOST STORIES (See Dan Curtis)
Jan, 1972 - No. 60, June, 1982 (Painted-c No. 1-56)
Gold Key/Whitman No. 55 on

	Good	Fine	Mint
1	.50	1.50	3.00
2-4,6,7,9,10	.25	.75	1.50
5,8-Williamson-a	.40	1.25	2.50
11-16,18-20		.50	1.00
17-Crandall-a	.35	1.00	2.00
21-35: No. 32,34-reprints		.50	1.00
36-55,57-60: 43,44-(52 pgs.)		.40	.80
56-Williamson-a		.50	1.00
Mini-Comic No. 1 (3¼x6½", 1976)		.30	.60

NOTE: *Reprints-No. 32?, 34?, 39, 43, 44, 47?, 53; 56-60(⅓).* ***Bolle*** *a-23-25, 27, 29(2), 33, 35, 43r, 45(2), 48(2), 50, 52.* ***Lopez*** *a-24, 25.* ***McWilliams*** *a-33, 44r, 48, 58.* ***Win Mortimer*** *a-31, 33, 49, 51, 55, 56, 58(2), 59, 60.* ***Roussos*** *a-25, 30.* ***Sparling*** *a-23, 24, 28, 30, 31, 33, 43r, 45, 51(2), 52, 56, 58, 59(2), 60.*

GRIN (The American Funny Book) (Magazine)
Nov, 1972 - No. 3, April, 1973 (52 pgs.) (Satire)
APAG House Pubs

	Good	Fine	Mint
1		.60	1.20
2,3		.40	.80

GRIN & BEAR IT (See Large Feature Comic No. 28)

GRIT GRADY (See Holyoke One-Shot No. 1)

GROO SPECIAL
Oct, 1984 (52 pgs.; $2.00; Baxter paper)
Eclipse Comics

	Good	Fine	Mint
1	2.30	7.00	14.00

GROO THE WANDERER (See Destroyer Duck)
Dec, 1982 - No. 8, March, 1984
Pacific Comics

	Good	Fine	Mint
1-Aragones c/a(p) in all	2.00	6.00	12.00
2	1.35	4.00	8.00
3-7	1.10	3.30	6.60
8	1.25	3.75	7.50

GROO THE WANDERER (Sergio Aragones'. . .)
March, 1985 - Present
Epic Comics (Marvel)

	Good	Fine	Mint
1-Aragones-c/a	1.30	4.00	8.00
2	.85	2.50	5.00
3-5	.60	1.80	3.60
6-10	.40	1.25	2.50
11-20	.35	1.00	2.00
21-26	.25	.75	1.50
27-38 ($1.00)		.60	1.20

GROOVY (Cartoon Comics - not CCA approved)
March, 1968 - No. 3, July, 1968
Marvel Comics Group

	Good	Fine	Mint
1-3	.85	2.50	5.00

GUADALCANAL DIARY (Also see American Library)
1945 (One Shot) (See Thirty Seconds Over Tokyo)
David McKay Publishing Co.

	Good	Fine	Mint
nn-B&W text & pictures; painted-c	11.50	34.00	80.00

GUERRILLA WAR (Formerly Jungle War Stories)
No. 12, July-Sept, 1965 - No. 14, Mar, 1966
Dell Publishing Co.

	Good	Fine	Mint
12-14	.50	1.50	3.00

GUILTY (See Justice Traps the Guilty)

GULF FUNNY WEEKLY (Gulf Comic Weekly No. 1-4)
1933 - No. 422, 5/23/41 (in full color; 4 pgs.; tabloid size to 2/3/39; 2/10/39 on, regular comic book size)(early issues undated)
Gulf Oil Company (Giveaway)

	Good	Fine	Mint
1	10.00	30.00	60.00
2-30	4.00	12.00	24.00
31-100	3.00	9.00	18.00
101-196	2.00	6.00	12.00
197-Wings Winfair begins(1/29/37); by Fred Meagher beginning in 1938	15.00	45.00	90.00
198-300 (last tabloid size)	7.00	20.00	40.00
301-350	3.35	10.00	20.00
351-422	2.35	7.00	14.00

GULLIVER'S TRAVELS (See Dell Jr. Treasury No. 3)
Sept-Nov, 1965 - No. 3, May, 1966
Dell Publishing Co.

	Good	Fine	Mint
1	1.50	4.50	10.00
2,3	.85	2.50	6.00

GUMBY 3-D
Oct, 1986 - Present ($2.50)
Blackthorne Publishing

Grimjack #3, © First Comics

Groo Special #1, © Aragones

Gulliver's Travels #1, © DELL

Guns Against Gangsters #5, © NOVP

Gunsmoke #2 (GK), © CBS

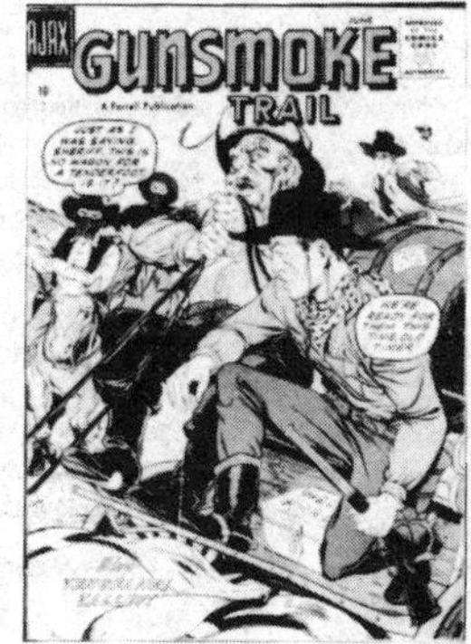

Gunsmoke Trail #1, © Four Star

GUMBY 3-D (continued)

	Good	Fine	Mint
1-6	.40	1.25	2.50
...Summer Fun Special #1 ('87) Comico	.75	2.25	4.50

GUMPS, THE
1918 - No. 8, 1931 (10x10")(52 pgs.; black & white)
Landfield-Kupfer/Cupples & Leon No. 2

	Good	Fine	Mint
Book No.2(1918)-(Rare); 5¼x13⅓"; paper cover; 36 pgs. daily strip reprints by Sidney Smith	14.00	42.00	100.00
nn(1924)-by Sidney Smith	9.00	27.00	63.00
2,3	8.00	24.00	56.00
4-7	7.00	21.00	50.00
8-(10x14"); 36 pgs.; B&W; National Arts Co.	7.00	21.00	50.00

GUMPS, THE (. . . in Radioland)
1937 (95 pgs.) (Mostly text)
Pebco Tooth Paste Premium

	Good	Fine	Mint
	7.00	21.00	50.00

GUMPS, THE (Also see Merry Christmas. . .)
1945 - No. 5, Nov-Dec, 1947
Dell Publ. Co./Bridgeport Herald Corp.

	Good	Fine	Mint
4-Color 73 (Dell)(1945)	6.00	18.00	42.00
1 (3-4/47)	6.00	18.00	42.00
2-5	4.00	12.00	28.00

GUNFIGHTER (Fat & Slat #1-4) (Becomes Haunt of Fear #15 on)
No. 5, Summer, 1948 - No. 14, Mar-Apr, 1950
E. C. Comics

	Good	Fine	Mint
5,6-Moon Girl in each	32.00	95.00	225.00
7-14: 14-Bondage-c	22.00	65.00	154.00

NOTE: *Craig & H. C. Kiefer art in most issues. Feldstein/Craig a-10. Feldstein a-7-11. Harrison/Wood a-13, 14. Ingels a-5-14; c-7-12.*

GUNFIGHTERS, THE
1963 - 1964
Super Comics (Reprints)

	Good	Fine	Mint
10,11(Billy the Kid), 12(Swift Arrow), 15(Straight Arrow-Powell-a), 16,18-All reprints	.50	1.50	3.00

GUNFIGHTERS, THE (Formerly Kid Montana)
No. 51, 10/66 - No. 52, 10/67; No. 53, 6/79 - No. 85, 7/84
Charlton Comics

	Good	Fine	Mint
51,52	.30	.80	1.60
53,54-Williamson a(r)/Wild Bill Hickok		.40	.80
55,57-85		.30	.60
56-Williamson/Severin-c/a; r-Sheriff of Tombstone		.40	.80
85-S&K-r/1955 Bullseye		.40	.80

GUN GLORY (See 4-Color No. 846)

GUNHAWK, THE (Formerly Whip Wilson)(See Wild Western)
No. 12, Nov, 1950 - No. 18, Dec, 1951
Marvel Comics/Atlas (MCI)

	Good	Fine	Mint
12	4.35	13.00	30.00
13-18: 13-Tuska-a	3.50	10.50	24.00

GUNHAWKS (Gunhawk No. 7)
October, 1972 - No. 7, October, 1973
Marvel Comics Group

	Good	Fine	Mint
1-Reno Jones, Kid Cassidy		.40	.80
2-7: 6-Kid Cassidy dies. 7-Reno Jones solo		.25	.50

GUNMASTER (Judo Master No. 89 on; formerly Six-Gun Heroes)
9/64 - No. 4, 1965; No. 84, 7/65 - No. 88, 3-4/66; No. 89, 10/67
Charlton Comics

	Good	Fine	Mint
V1No.1	.50	1.50	3.00
2-4,V5No.84-86: 4-Blank inside-c	.35	1.00	2.00
V5No.87-89	.25	.75	1.50

NOTE: *Vol. 5 was originally cancelled with No. 88 (3-4/66). No. 89 on, became Judo Master, then later in 1967, Charlton issued No. 89 as a Gunmaster one-shot.*

GUNS AGAINST GANGSTERS
Sept-Oct, 1948 - V2No.2, 1949
Curtis Publications/Novelty Press

	Good	Fine	Mint
1-Toni Gayle begins by Schomburg	8.50	25.50	60.00
2	6.00	18.00	42.00
3-6, V2/1,2: 6-Toni Gayle-c	5.50	16.50	38.00

NOTE: *L. B. Cole c-1-6; a-1,2,3(2),4-6.*

GUNSLINGER (See 4-Color No. 1220)

GUNSLINGER (Formerly Tex Dawson. . .)
No. 2, April, 1973 - No. 3, June, 1973
Marvel Comics Group

	Good	Fine	Mint
2,3		.30	.60

GUNSMOKE
Apr-May, 1949 - No. 16, Jan, 1952
Youthful Magazines

	Good	Fine	Mint
1-Gunsmoke & Masked Marvel begin by Ingels; Ingels bondage-c	16.00	48.00	110.00
2-Ingels c/a(2)	8.50	25.50	60.00
3-Ingels bondage-c/a	7.00	21.00	50.00
4-6: Ingels-c	5.00	15.00	35.00
7-10	3.50	10.50	24.00
11-16	2.30	7.00	16.00

GUNSMOKE (TV)
No. 679, 2/56 - No. 27, 6-7/61; 2/69 - No. 6, 2/70
Dell Publishing Co./Gold Key (All have photo-c)

	Good	Fine	Mint
4-Color 679(No. 1)	5.00	15.00	35.00
4-Color 720,769,797,844	3.50	10.50	24.00
6(11-1/57-58), 7	3.50	10.50	24.00
8,9,11,12-Williamson-a in all, 4 pgs. each	4.00	12.00	28.00
10-Williamson/Crandall-a, 4 pgs.	4.00	12.00	28.00
13-27	3.00	9.00	21.00
Gunsmoke Film Story (11/62-G.K. Giant) No. 30008-211	3.50	10.50	24.00
1 (G.K.)	1.70	5.00	12.00
2-6('69-70)	1.00	3.00	6.00

GUNSMOKE TRAIL
June, 1957 - No. 4, Dec, 1957
Ajax-Farrell Publ./Four Star Comic Corp.

	Good	Fine	Mint
1	2.65	8.00	18.00
2-4	1.50	4.50	10.00

GUNSMOKE WESTERN (Formerly Western Tales of Black Rider)
Dec, 1955 - No. 77, July, 1963
Atlas Comics No. 32-35(CPS/NPI); Marvel No. 36 on

	Good	Fine	Mint
32	3.50	10.50	24.00
33,35,36-Williamson-a in each: 5,6 & 4 pgs. plus Drucker No. 33	4.00	12.00	28.00
34-Baker-a, 3pgs.	1.70	5.00	12.00
37-Davis-a(2); Williamson text illo	2.15	6.50	15.00
38,39	1.15	3.50	8.00
40-Williamson/Mayo-a, 4 pgs.	4.00	12.00	28.00
41,42,45-49,51-55,57-60: 49,52-Kid From Texas story. 57-1st Two Gun Kid by Severin. 60-Sam Hawk app. in Kid Colt	1.00	3.00	7.00
43,44-Torres-a	1.50	4.50	10.00
50,61-Crandall-a	1.50	4.50	10.00
56-Matt Baker-a	1.50	4.50	10.00
62-77: 72-Origin Kid Colt	.85	2.50	6.00

NOTE: *Colan a-37. Davis a-37, 52, 54, 55; c-50, 54. Ditko a-56, 66. Jack Keller a-40, 60, 72; c-72. Kirby a-47, 50, 51, 59, 62(3), 63, 65-67, 69, 71, 73, 77; c-56(w/Ditko),57, 58, 60, 61(w/Ayers), 62, 63, 66, 68, 69, 71-77. Severin a-60; c-43. Wildey a-10, 37, 42, 57. Kid Colt in all. Two-Gun Kid in No. 57, 59, 60-63. Wyatt Earp in No. 45, 48, 49, 52, 54, 55, 58.*

GUNS OF FACT & FICTION (See A-1 Comics No. 13)

GUN THAT WON THE WEST, THE
1956 (24 pgs.; regular size) (Giveaway)
Winchester-Western Division & Olin Mathieson Chemical Corp.

	Good	Fine	Mint
nn-Painted-c	2.00	6.00	14.00

GYPSY COLT (See 4-Color No. 568)

GYRO GEARLOOSE (See Walt Disney's C&S #140 & Walt Disney Showcase #18)
No. 1047, Nov-Jan/1959-60 - May-July, 1962 (Disney)
Dell Publishing Co.

	Good	Fine	Mint
4-Color 1047 (No. 1)-Barks c/a	6.00	18.00	42.00
4-Color 1095,1184-All by Carl Barks	5.00	15.00	35.00
4-Color 1267-Barks c/a, 4 pgs.	3.70	11.00	26.00
No. 01-329-207 (5-7/62)-Barks-c only	2.35	7.00	16.00

HAGAR THE HORRIBLE (See Comics Reading Libraries)

HA HA COMICS (Teepee Tim No. 100 on) (Also see Giggle)
Oct, 1943 - No. 99, Jan, 1955
Scope Mag.(Creston Publ.) No. 1-80/American Comics Group

	Good	Fine	Mint
1	11.00	33.00	76.00
2	5.00	15.00	35.00
3-5: Ken Hultgren-a begins?	3.50	10.50	24.00
6-10	2.65	8.00	18.00
11-20: 14-Infinity-c	1.70	5.00	12.00
21-40	1.30	4.00	9.00
41-94,96-99	1.00	3.00	7.00
95-3-D effect-c	4.00	12.00	28.00

HAIR BEAR BUNCH, THE (TV) (See Fun-In No. 13)
Feb, 1972 - No. 9, Feb, 1974 (Hanna-Barbera)
Gold Key

	Good	Fine	Mint
1	.50	1.50	3.00
2-9	.35	1.00	2.00

HALLELUJAH TRAIL, THE (See Movie Classics)

HALL OF FAME FEATURING THE T.H.U.N.D.E.R. AGENTS
May, 1983 - No. 3, Dec, 1983
JC Productions(Archie Comics Group)

	Good	Fine	Mint
1-3: T.H.U.N.D.E.R. Agents-r		.45	.90

HALLOWEEN HORROR
Oct, 1987 (Seduction of the Innocent #7)
Eclipse Comics

	Good	Fine	Mint
1-Pre-code horror-r	.35	1.00	2.00

HANDBOOK OF THE CONAN UNIVERSE, THE
June, 1985 (One Shot)
Marvel Comics Group

	Good	Fine	Mint
1		.65	1.30

HAND OF FATE (Formerly Men Against Crime)
No. 8, Dec, 1951 - No. 26, March, 1955
Ace Magazines

	Good	Fine	Mint
8: Surrealistic text story	8.50	25.50	60.00
9,10	5.00	15.00	35.00
11-18,20,22,23	3.50	10.50	24.00
19-Bondage, hypo needle scenes	4.60	14.00	32.00
21-Necronomicon story; drug belladonna used	5.50	16.50	38.00
24-Electric chair-c	6.00	18.00	42.00
25(11/54), 25(12/54)	4.35	13.00	30.00
26-Nostrand-a	5.00	15.00	35.00

NOTE: ***Cameron** art-No. 9, 10, 18-25; c-13. **Sekowsky** a-8, 9, 13, 14.*

HAND OF FATE
1987 - Present ($1.75, color)
Eclipse Comics

	Good	Fine	Mint
1,2	.30	.90	1.75

HANDS OF THE DRAGON
June, 1975
Seaboard Periodicals (Atlas)

	Good	Fine	Mint
1-Origin; Mooney inks		.50	1.00

HANGMAN COMICS (Special No. 1; Black Hood No. 9 on)
No. 2, Spring, 1942 - No. 8, Fall, 1943 (See Pep Comics)
MLJ Magazines

	Good	Fine	Mint
2-The Hangman, Boy Buddies begin	58.00	175.00	400.00
3-8	30.00	90.00	210.00

NOTE: ***Fuje** a-7(3), 8(3); c-3.*

HANK
1946
Pentagon Publications

	Good	Fine	Mint
nn-Coulton Waugh's newspaper reprint	3.50	10.50	24.00

HANNA-BARBERA (See Golden Comics Digest No. 2,7,11)

HANNA-BARBERA BAND WAGON (TV)
Oct, 1962 - No. 3, April, 1963
Gold Key

	Good	Fine	Mint
1,2-Giants, 84 pgs.	2.50	7.50	20.00
3-Regular size	1.30	4.00	9.00

HANNA-BARBERA HI-ADVENTURE HEROES (See Hi-Adventure. .)

HANNA-BARBERA PARADE (TV)
Sept, 1971 - No. 10, Dec, 1972
Charlton Comics

	Good	Fine	Mint
1	1.20	3.50	7.00
2-6,8-10	.70	2.00	4.00
7-"Summer Picnic"-52 pgs.	.85	2.50	5.00

NOTE: *No. 4 (1/72) went on sale late in 1972 with the January 1973 issues.*

HANNA-BARBERA SPOTLIGHT (See Spotlight)

HANNA-BARBERA SUPER TV HEROES (TV)
April, 1968 - No. 7, Oct, 1969 (Hanna-Barbera)
Gold Key

	Good	Fine	Mint
1-The Birdman, The Herculoids, Moby Dick, Young Samson & Goliath, and The Mighty Mightor begin; Spiegle-a in all	3.00	9.00	21.00
2-The Galaxy Trio only app.; Shazzan begins; no Samson & Goliath	2.00	6.00	14.00
3-7: 3-The Space Ghost app.; also No. 3,6,7, no Herculoids; no Samson & Goliath in No. 4-7	1.70	5.00	12.00

HANNA-BARBERA (TV STARS) (See TV Stars)

HANS AND FRITZ
1929 (28 pgs.; 10x13½"; B&W Sunday strip reprints)
The Saalfield Publishing Co.

	Good	Fine	Mint
193-(Very Rare)-By R. Dirks; contains B&W Sunday strip reprints of Katzenjammer Kids & Hawkshaw the Detective from 1916	25.00	75.00	175.00
. . .The Funny Larks Of 2(1929)	25.00	75.00	175.00

HANS BRINKER (See 4-Color No. 1273)

HANS CHRISTIAN ANDERSEN
1953 (100 pgs. - Special Issue)
Ziff-Davis Publ. Co.

	Good	Fine	Mint
nn-Danny Kaye (movie)-Photo-c	8.00	24.00	56.00

HANSEL & GRETEL (See 4-Color No. 590)

HANSI, THE GIRL WHO LOVED THE SWASTIKA
1973, 1976 (39-49 cents)
Spire Christian Comics (Fleming H. Revell Co.)

	Good	Fine	Mint
		.50	1.00

Ha Ha Comics #70, © ACG

Hand of Fate #9, © ACE

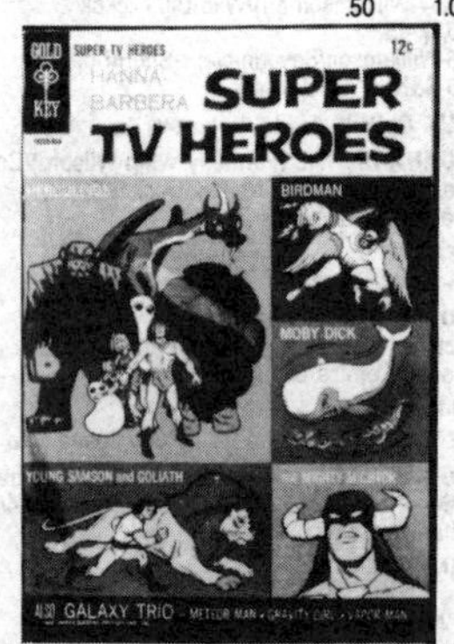

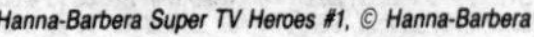
Hanna-Barbera Super TV Heroes #1, © Hanna-Barbera

Hap Hazard Comics #2, © ACE

Happy Comics #19, © STD

Harvey Comics Hits #56, © KING

HAP HAZARD COMICS (Real Love No. 25 on)
1944 - No. 24, Feb, 1949
Ace Magazines (Readers' Research)

	Good	Fine	Mint
1	4.60	14.00	32.00
2	2.30	7.00	16.00
3-10	1.60	4.70	11.00
11-13,15-24	1.15	3.50	8.00
14-Feldstein-c (4/47)	3.50	10.50	24.00

HAP HOPPER (See Comics Revue No. 2)

HAPPIEST MILLIONAIRE, THE (See Movie Comics)

HAPPINESS AND HEALING FOR YOU (Also see Oral Roberts'. . .)
1955 (36 pgs.; slick cover) (Oral Roberts Giveaway)
Commercial Comics

	Good	Fine	Mint
	7.00	20.00	40.00

NOTE: *The success of this book prompted Oral Roberts to go into the publishing business himself to produce his own material.*

HAPPI TIM (See March of Comics No. 182)

HAPPY COMICS (Happy Rabbit No. 41 on)
Aug, 1943 - No. 40, Dec, 1950
Nedor Publ./Standard Comics (Animated Cartoons)

	Good	Fine	Mint
1	8.50	25.50	60.00
2	4.60	14.00	32.00
3-10	3.00	9.00	21.00
11-19	1.70	5.00	12.00
20-31,34-37-Frazetta text illos in all; 2 in No. 34, 3 in No. 27,28,30	3.00	9.00	21.00
32-Frazetta-a, 7 pgs. plus two text illos; Roussos-a	9.00	27.00	63.00
33-Frazetta-a(2), 6 pgs. each (Scarce)	17.00	51.00	120.00
38-40	1.30	4.00	9.00

NOTE: *Al Fago a-27.*

HAPPY DAYS (TV)
March, 1979 - No. 6, Feb, 1980
Gold Key

	Good	Fine	Mint
1	.35	1.00	2.00
2-6		.50	1.00
. . .With the Fonz Kite Fun Book(6¾x5¼",'78)-PG&E	.35	1.00	2.00

HAPPY HOLIDAY (See March of Comics No. 181)

HAPPY HOOLIGAN (See Alphonse. . .)
1903 (18 pgs.) (Sunday strip reprints in color)
Hearst's New York American-Journal

	Good	Fine	Mint
Book 1-by Fred Opper	25.00	75.00	175.00
50 Pg. Edition(1903)-10x15" in color	30.00	90.00	210.00

HAPPY HOOLIGAN (Handy. . .) (See The Travels of. . .)
1908 (32 pgs. in color) (10x15"; cardboard covers)
Frederick A. Stokes Co.

	Good	Fine	Mint
	20.00	60.00	140.00

HAPPY HOOLIGAN (Story of. . .)
1932 (16 pgs.; 9½x12"; softcover)
McLoughlin Bros.

	Good	Fine	Mint
281-Three-color text, pictures on heavy paper	6.00	18.00	42.00

HAPPY HOULIHANS (Saddle Justice No. 3 on)
Fall, 1947 - No. 2, Winter, 1947-48
E. C. Comics

	Good	Fine	Mint
1-Origin Moon Girl	23.00	70.00	160.00
2	11.00	32.00	76.00

HAPPY JACK
August, 1957 - No. 2, Nov, 1957
Red Top (Decker)

	Good	Fine	Mint
V1No.,1,2	1.15	3.50	8.00

HAPPY JACK HOWARD
1957
Red Top (Farrell)/Decker

	Good	Fine	Mint
nn-Reprints Handy Andy story from E. C. Dandy Comics No. 5, renamed "Happy Jack"	1.60	4.70	11.00

HAPPY RABBIT (Formerly Happy Comics)
No. 41, Feb, 1951 - No. 48, April, 1952
Standard Comics (Animated Cartoons)

	Good	Fine	Mint
41	2.30	7.00	16.00
42-48	1.15	3.50	8.00

HARDY BOYS, THE (See 4-Color No. 760,830,887,964-Disney)

HARDY BOYS, THE (TV)
April, 1970 - No. 4, Jan, 1971
Gold Key

	Good	Fine	Mint
1	.85	2.50	5.00
2-4	.40	1.25	2.50

HARLEM GLOBETROTTERS (TV) (See Fun-In No. 8,10)
April, 1972 - No. 12, Jan, 1975 (Hanna-Barbera)
Gold Key

	Good	Fine	Mint
1	.50	1.50	3.00
2-12	.25	.75	1.50

NOTE: *No. 4, 8, and 12 contain 16 extra pages of advertising.*

HAROLD TEEN (See 4-Color No. 2, 209, & Treasure Box of Famous Comics)

HAROLD TEEN (Adv. of. . .)
1929-31 (36-52 pgs.) (Paper covers)
Cupples & Leon Co.

	Good	Fine	Mint
B&W daily strip reprints by Carl Ed	8.00	24.00	56.00

HARVEY
Oct, 1970; No. 2, 12/70; No. 3, 6/72 - No. 6, 12/72
Marvel Comics Group

	Good	Fine	Mint
1	.50	1.50	3.00
2-6	.25	.75	1.50

HARVEY COLLECTORS COMICS (Richie Rich Collectors Comics #10 on, cover title only)
9/75 - No. 15, 1/78; No. 16, 10/79 (52 pgs.)
Harvey Publications

	Good	Fine	Mint
1-Reprints Richie Rich No. 1,2	.70	2.00	4.00
2-10	.40	1.20	2.40
11-16: 16-Sad Sack-r		.50	1.00

NOTE: *All reprints: Casper-No. 2, 7, Richie Rich-No. 1, 3, 5, 6, 8-15, Wendy-No. 4. No. 6 titled 'Richie Rich. . .on inside.*

HARVEY COMICS HITS
No. 51, Oct, 1951 - No. 62, Dec, 1952
Harvey Publications

	Good	Fine	Mint
51-The Phantom	8.50	25.50	60.00
52-Steve Canyon	6.35	19.00	44.00
53-Mandrake the Magician	8.50	25.50	60.00
54-Tim Tyler's Tales of Jungle Terror	6.50	19.50	45.00
55-Mary Worth	3.35	10.00	23.00
56-The Phantom; bondage-c	7.00	21.00	50.00
57-Rip Kirby-"Kidnap Racket;" entire book by Alex Raymond	9.25	28.00	65.00
58-Girls in White	3.00	9.00	21.00
59-Tales of the Invisible Scarlet O'Neil	6.50	20.00	45.00
60-Paramount Animated Comics No.1(2nd app. Baby Huey); 1st Harvey app. Baby Huey	17.00	51.00	120.00
61-Casper the Friendly Ghost; 1st Harvey Casper	16.00	48.00	110.00
62-Paramount Animated Comics	7.00	21.00	50.00

HARVEY COMICS LIBRARY
April, 1952 - No. 2, 1952
Harvey Publications

	Good	Fine	Mint
1-Teen-Age Dope Slaves as exposed by Rex Morgan, M.D.; drug propaganda story; used in **SOTI**, pg. 27	57.00	171.00	400.00
(Prices vary widely on this book)			
2-Sparkle Plenty (Dick Tracy in "Blackmail Terror")	11.50	34.50	80.00

HARVEY COMICS SPOTLIGHT
Sept, 1987 - Present (#1-3, 75 cents, #4-on, $1.00)
Harvey Comics

	Good	Fine	Mint
1-3: 1-Sad Sack, 2-Baby Huey, 3-Little Dot		.40	.75
4-Little Audrey		.50	1.00

HARVEY HITS
Sept, 1957 - No. 122, Nov, 1967
Harvey Publications

	Good	Fine	Mint
1-The Phantom	11.00	33.00	76.00
2-Rags Rabbit(10/57)	1.35	4.00	8.00
3-Richie Rich(11/57)-r/Little Dot; 1st book devoted to Richie Rich; see Little Dot for 1st app.	54.00	160.00	340.00
4-Little Dot's Uncles	8.00	24.00	48.00
5-Stevie Mazie's Boy Friend	1.35	4.00	8.00
6-The Phantom; Kirby-c; 2pg. Powell-a	5.00	15.00	35.00
7-Wendy the Witch	8.00	24.00	48.00
8-Sad Sack's Army Life	2.75	8.00	16.00
9-Richie Rich's Golden Deeds-r (2nd book devoted to Richie Rich)	25.00	75.00	165.00
10-Little Lotta	6.00	18.00	36.00
11-Little Audrey Summer Fun (7/58)	4.35	13.00	26.00
12-The Phantom; Kirby-c; 2pg. Powell-a	4.00	12.00	28.00
13-Little Dot's Uncles (9/58); Richie Rich 1pg.	5.35	16.00	32.00
14-Herman & Katnip (10/58)	1.35	4.00	8.00
15-The Phantom (1958)-1 pg. origin	3.50	10.50	24.00
16-Wendy the Witch (1/59)	4.00	12.00	24.00
17-Sad Sack's Army Life (2/59)	1.35	4.00	8.00
18-Buzzy & the Crow	1.35	4.00	8.00
19-Little Audrey (4/59)	2.75	8.00	16.00
20-Casper & Spooky	4.00	12.00	24.00
21-Wendy the Witch	3.00	9.00	18.00
22-Sad Sack's Army Life	1.00	3.00	6.00
23-Wendy the Witch	3.00	9.00	18.00
24-Little Dot's Uncles (9/59); Richie Rich 1pg.	4.00	12.00	24.00
25-Herman & Katnip (10/59)	1.00	3.00	6.00
26-The Phantom (11/59)	3.50	10.50	24.00
27-Wendy the Good Little Witch	3.00	9.00	18.00
28-Sad Sack's Army Life	.50	1.50	3.00
29-Harvey-Toon (No.1)('60); Casper, Buzzy	2.00	6.00	12.00
30-Wendy the Witch (3/60)	2.75	8.00	16.00
31-Herman & Katnip (4/60)	.70	2.00	4.00
32-Sad Sack's Army Life (5/60)	.50	1.50	3.00
33-Wendy the Witch (6/60)	2.75	8.00	16.00
34-Harvey-Toon (7/60)	1.00	3.00	6.00
35-Funday Funnies (8/60)	.70	2.00	4.00
36-The Phantom (1960)	2.00	6.00	14.00
37-Casper & Nightmare	2.00	6.00	12.00
38-Harvey-Toon	1.35	4.00	8.00
39-Sad Sack's Army Life (12/60)	.50	1.50	3.00
40-Funday Funnies	.50	1.50	3.00
41-Herman & Katnip	.50	1.50	3.00
42-Harvey-Toon (3/61)	.80	2.30	4.60
43-Sad Sack's Army Life (4/61)	.35	1.00	2.00
44-The Phantom	2.00	6.00	14.00
45-Casper & Nightmare	2.00	5.00	10.00
46-Harvey-Toon	.80	2.30	4.60
47-Sad Sack's Army Life (8/61)	.40	1.20	2.40
48-The Phantom (1961)	2.00	6.00	14.00
49-Stumbo the Giant (See Hot Stuff for 1st app.)	5.00	15.00	30.00
50-Harvey-Toon (11/61)	.80	2.30	4.60
51-Sad Sack's Army Life (12/61)	.40	1.20	2.40
52-Casper & Nightmare	1.70	5.00	10.00
53-Harvey-Toons (2/62)	.70	2.00	4.00
54-Stumbo the Giant	2.75	8.00	16.00
55-Sad Sack's Army Life (4/62)	.40	1.20	2.40
56-Casper & Nightmare	1.70	5.00	10.00
57-Stumbo the Giant	2.75	8.00	16.00
58-Sad Sack's Army Life	.40	1.20	2.40
59-Casper & Nightmare (7/62)	1.70	5.00	10.00
60-Stumbo the Giant (9/62)	2.75	8.00	16.00
61-Sad Sack's Army Life	.40	1.20	2.40
62-Casper & Nightmare	1.35	4.00	8.00
63-Stumbo the Giant	2.75	8.00	16.00
64-Sad Sack's Army Life (1/63)	.40	1.20	2.40
65-Casper & Nightmare	1.35	4.00	8.00
66-Stumbo The Giant	2.75	8.00	16.00
67-Sad Sack's Army Life (4/63)	.40	1.20	2.40
68-Casper & Nightmare	1.35	4.00	8.00
69-Stumbo the Giant (6/63)	2.75	8.00	16.00
70-Sad Sack's Army Life (7/63)	.40	1.20	2.40
71-Casper & Nightmare (8/63)	.40	1.20	2.40
72-Stumbo the Giant	2.75	8.00	16.00
73-Little Sad Sack (10/63)	.40	1.20	2.40
74-Sad Sack's Muttsy... (11/63)	.40	1.20	2.40
75-Casper & Nightmare	1.00	3.00	6.00
76-Little Sad Sack	.40	1.20	2.40
77-Sad Sack's Muttsy...	.40	1.20	2.40
78-Stumbo the Giant	2.75	8.00	16.00
79-Little Sad Sack (4/64)	.40	1.20	2.40
80-Sad Sack's Muttsy... (5/64)	.40	1.20	2.40
81-Little Sad Sack	.40	1.20	2.40
82-Sad Sack's Muttsy...	.40	1.20	2.40
83-Little Sad Sack (8/64)	.40	1.20	2.40
84-Sad Sack's Muttsy...	.40	1.20	2.40
85-Gabby Gob (No.1)(10/64)	.40	1.20	2.40
86-G. I. Juniors (No.1)	.40	1.20	2.40
87-Sad Sack's Muttsy...	.40	1.20	2.40
88-Stumbo the Giant (1/65)	2.75	8.00	16.00
89-Sad Sack's Muttsy...	.40	1.20	2.40
90-Gabby Gob	.35	1.00	2.00
91-G. I. Juniors	.35	1.00	2.00
92-Sad Sack's Muttsy... (5/65)	.35	1.00	2.00
93-Sadie Sack (6/65)	.35	1.00	2.00
94-Gabby Gob	.35	1.00	2.00
95-G. I. Juniors	.35	1.00	2.00
96-Sad Sack's Muttsy... (9/65)	.35	1.00	2.00
97-Gabby Gob	.35	1.00	2.00
98-G. I. Juniors (9/65)	.35	1.00	2.00
99-Sad Sack's Muttsy... (12/65)	.35	1.00	2.00
100-Gabby Gob	.35	1.00	2.00
101-G. I. Juniors (2/66)	.35	1.00	2.00
102-Sad Sack's Muttsy... (3/66)	.35	1.00	2.00
103-Gabby Gob	.35	1.00	2.00
104-G. I. Juniors	.35	1.00	2.00
105-Sad Sack's Muttsy...	.35	1.00	2.00
106-Gabby Gob (7/66)	.35	1.00	2.00
107-G. I. Juniors (8/66)	.35	1.00	2.00
108-Sad Sack's Muttsy...	.35	1.00	2.00
109-Gabby Gob	.35	1.00	2.00
110-G. I. Juniors (11/66)	.35	1.00	2.00
111-Sad Sack's Muttsy... (12/66)	.35	1.00	2.00
112-G. I. Juniors	.35	1.00	2.00

Harvey Comics Library #1, © HARV

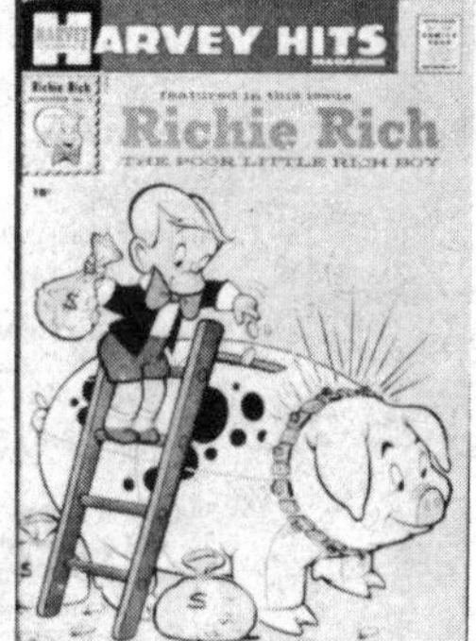

Harvey Hits #3, © HARV

Harvey Hits #15, © KING

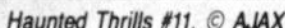
Haunted Thrills #11, © AJAX

Haunt of Fear #18, © WMG

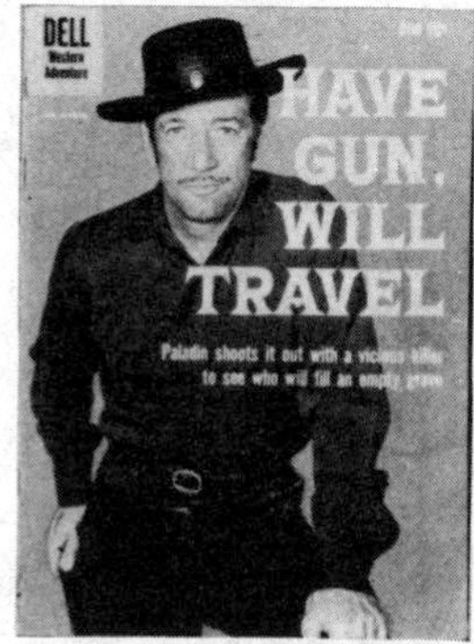

Have Gun Will Travel #4, © DELL

HARVEY HITS (continued)

	Good	Fine	Mint
113-Sad Sack's Muttsy. . .	.35	1.00	2.00
114-G. I. Juniors	.35	1.00	2.00
115-Sad Sack's Muttsy. . .	.35	1.00	2.00
116-G. I. Juniors	.35	1.00	2.00
117-Sad Sack's Muttsy. . .	.35	1.00	2.00
118-G. I. Juniors	.35	1.00	2.00
119-Sad Sack's Muttsy. . . (8/67)	.35	1.00	2.00
120-G. I. Juniors (9/67)	.35	1.00	2.00
121-Sad Sack's Muttsy. . . (10/67)	.35	1.00	2.00
122-G. I. Juniors	.35	1.00	2.00

HARVEY HITS COMICS
Nov, 1986 - Present
Harvey Publications

	Good	Fine	Mint
1-6: Little Lotta, Little Dot, Wendyh & Baby Huey app.		.40	.75

HARVEY POP COMICS (Teen Humor)
Oct, 1968 - No. 2, Nov, 1969
Harvey Publications

	Good	Fine	Mint
1,2-The Cowsills	1.00	3.00	6.00

HARVEY 3-D HITS (See Sad Sack)

HARVEY-TOON (. . . S) (See Harvey Hits No. 29,34,38,42,46,50,53)

HARVEY WISEGUYS
Nov, 1987 - Present (98 pgs., digest-size, $1.25)
Harvey Comics

	Good	Fine	Mint
1-Hot Stuff, Spooky, etc.		.60	1.25

HATARI (See Movie Classics)

HATHAWAYS, THE (See 4-Color No. 1298)

HAUNTED (See This Magazine Is Haunted)

HAUNTED
9/71 - No. 30, 11/76; No. 31, 9/77 - No. 75, 9/84
Charlton Comics

	Good	Fine	Mint
1		.60	1.20
2-5		.50	1.00
6-21		.40	.80
22-75: 64,75-r		.30	.60

NOTE: ***Aparo** c-45. **Ditko** a-1-8, 11-16, 18, 23, 24, 28, 30, 34r, 36r, 39-42r, 47r, 49-51r, 60. c-1-7, 11, 13, 14, 16, 30, 41, 47, 49-51. **Howard** a-18, 22, 32. **Morisi** a-13. **Newton** a-17, 21, 59r; c-21,22(painted). **Staton** a-18, 21, 22, 30, 33; c-18, 33. **Sutton** a-21, 22, 38; c-17, 64r. No. 51 reprints No. 1; No. 49 reprints Tales/Myst. Traveler No. 4.*

HAUNTED LOVE
April, 1973 - No. 11, Sept, 1975
Charlton Comics

	Good	Fine	Mint
1-Tom Sutton-a, 16 pgs.		.50	1.00
2,3,6-11		.30	.60
4,5-Ditko-a		.40	.80
Modern Comics No. 1(1978)		.20	.40

NOTE: ***Howard** a-8i. **Newton** c-8,9. **Staton** a-5.*

HAUNTED THRILLS
June, 1952 - No. 18, Nov-Dec, 1954
Ajax/Farrell Publications

	Good	Fine	Mint
1: r-/Ellery Queen 1	8.50	25.50	60.00
2-L. B. Cole-a r-/Ellery Queen 1	6.50	19.50	45.00
3-5: 3-Drug use story	4.35	13.00	30.00
6-12: 12-Webb-a	3.50	10.50	24.00
13,16,17	2.65	8.00	18.00
14-Jesus Christ apps. in story by Webb	2.65	8.00	18.00
15-Jo-Jo-r	4.00	12.00	28.00
18-Lingerie panels	2.65	8.00	18.00

NOTE: *Kamenish art in most issues.*

HAUNT OF FEAR (Formerly Gunfighter)
No. 15, May-June, 1950 - No. 28, Nov-Dec, 1954
E. C. Comics

	Good	Fine	Mint
15(1950)	100.00	300.00	700.00
16	52.00	156.00	365.00
17-Origin of Crypt of Terror, Vault of Horror, & Haunt of Fear; used in **SOTI**, pg. 43; last pg. Ingels-a used by N.Y. Legis. Comm.	52.00	156.00	365.00
4	40.00	120.00	280.00
5-Injury-to-eye panel, pg. 4	30.00	90.00	210.00
6-10	21.00	62.00	145.00
11-13,15-18	14.00	42.00	100.00
14-Origin Old Witch by Ingels	21.00	62.00	145.00
19-Used in **SOTI**, ill.-"A comic book baseball game" & Senate investigation on juvenile delinq. bondage/decapitation-c	21.00	62.00	150.00
20-Feldstein r-/Vault of Horror No. 12	13.00	40.00	90.00
21,22,25,27	8.50	25.50	60.00
23-Used in **SOTI**, pg. 241	11.00	32.00	75.00
24-Used in Senate Investigative Report, pg. 8	9.35	30.00	65.00
26-Contains anti-censorship editorial, 'Are you a Red Dupe?'	9.35	30.00	65.00
28-Low distribution	9.35	30.00	65.00

(Canadian reprints known; see Table of Contents.)

NOTE: ***Craig** a-15-17, 5, 7, 10, 12, 13; c-15-17, 5-7. **Crandall** a-20, 21, 26, 27. **Davis** a-4-26, 28. **Evans** a-15-19, 22-25, 27. **Feldstein** a-15-17, 20; c-4, 8-10. **Ingels** a-16, 17, 4-28; c-11-28. **Kamen** a-16, 4, 6, 7, 9-11, 13-19, 21-28. **Krigstein** a-28. **Kurtzman** a-15/1, 17/3. **Orlando** a-9, 12. **Wood** a-15, 16, 4-6.*

HAUNT OF HORROR, THE (Magazine)
5/74 - No. 5, 1/75 (75 cents) (B&W)
Cadence Comics Publ. (Marvel)

	Good	Fine	Mint
1-Alcala-a	.85	2.50	5.00
2-Origin & 1st app. Gabriel the Devil Hunter; Satana begins	.70	2.00	4.00
3	.50	1.50	3.00
4-Adams-a	.70	2.00	4.00
5-Evans-a(2)	.50	1.50	3.00
Digest size #1,2 (date?)	.35	1.00	2.00

NOTE: ***Alcala** a-2. **Colan** a-2p. **Heath** r-1. **Krigstein** r-3. **Reese** a-1.*

HAVE GUN, WILL TRAVEL (TV)
No. 931, 8/58 - No. 14, 7-9/62 (All Richard Boone photo-c)
Dell Publishing Co.

	Good	Fine	Mint
4-Color 931(No. 1)	4.35	13.00	30.00
4-Color 983,1044	3.50	10.50	24.00
4 (1-3/60) - 14	3.00	9.00	21.00

HAWAIIAN EYE (TV)
July, 1963 (Troy Donahue, Connie Stevens photo-c)
Gold Key

	Good	Fine	Mint
1 (10073-307)	2.00	6.00	14.00

HAWAIIAN ILLUSTRATED LEGENDS SERIES
1975 (B&W)(Cover printed w/blue, yellow, and green)
Hogarth Press

	Good	Fine	Mint
1-Kalelealuaka, the Mysterious Warrior		.60	1.20
2,3(Exist?)		.40	.80

HAWK, THE (Also see Approved Comics & Tops In Adv.)
Wint/51 - No. 3, 11-12/52; No. 4, 1953 - No. 12, 5/55
Ziff-Davis/St. John Publ. Co. No. 4 on

	Good	Fine	Mint
1-Anderson-a	7.00	21.00	50.00
2-Kubert, Infantino-a; painted-c	4.00	12.00	28.00
3-8,10-11: 8-Reprints #3 with diff.-c. 10-Reprints one story/#2. 11-Buckskin Belle & The Texan app.	3.00	9.00	21.00
9-Baker c/a; Kubert-a(r)/#2	3.50	10.50	24.00

THE HAWK (continued) — Good / Fine / Mint

12-Baker c/a; Buckskin Belle app. 3.50 10.50 24.00
3-D 1(11/53)-Baker-c 16.00 48.00 110.00
NOTE: ***Baker** c-8,9,11. **Tuska** a-9, 12.*

HAWK AND THE DOVE, THE (See Showcase)
Aug-Sept, 1968 - No. 6, June-July, 1969
National Periodical Publications

1-Ditko c/a .50 1.50 3.00
2-6: 5-Teen Titans cameo .35 1.00 2.00
NOTE: ***Ditko** c/a-2. **Gil Kane** a-3p, 4p, 5, 6p; c-3-6.*

HAWKEYE (See Tales Of Suspense #57)
Sept, 1983 - No. 4, Dec, 1983 (Mini-series)
Marvel Comics Group

1-Origin .50 1.00
2-4: 3-Origin Mockingbird .50 1.00

HAWKEYE & THE LAST OF THE MOHICANS (See 4-Color No. 884)

HAWKMAN (See Atom & Hawkman, The Brave & the Bold, DC Comics Presents, Detective, Mystery in Space, Shadow War Of . . ., Showcase, & World's Finest)
Apr-May, 1964 - No. 27, Aug-Sept, 1968
National Periodical Publications

1 6.00 18.00 42.00
2 3.15 9.50 22.00
3-5: 4-Zatanna x-over(origin-1st app.) 1.50 4.50 10.00
6-10: 9-Atom cameo; Hawkman & Atom learn each other's I.D.; 2nd app. Shadow Thief 1.20 3.60 8.50
11-15 .85 2.50 5.00
16-27: Adam Strange x-over No. 18, cameo No. 19. 25-G.A. Hawkman-r .60 1.75 3.50
NOTE: ***Anderson** a-1-21; c-1-21. **Kubert** c-27. **Moldoff** a-25r.*

HAWKMAN
Aug, 1986 - No. 15, Oct, 1987
DC Comics

1 .60 1.20
2-10: 10-Byrne-c .45 .90
11-15 .40 .80
Special #1 .65 1.30

HAWKMOON: THE JEWEL IN THE SKULL
May, 1986 - No. 4, Nov, 1986 (Limited series, Baxter)
First Comics

1-4: Adapts novel by Michael Moorcock .35 1.00 2.00

HAWKMOON: THE MAD GOD'S AMULET
Jan, 1987 - No. 4, July, 1987 (Limited series)
First Comics

1-4: Adapts novel by Michael Moorcock .30 .90 1.80

HAWKMOON: THE SWORD OF DAWN
Sept, 1987 - No. 4, Mar, 1988
First Comics

1-4 .30 .90 1.80

HAWKSHAW THE DETECTIVE (See Advs. of . . ., Hans & Fritz & Okay)
1917 (24 pgs.; B&W; 10½x13½") (Sunday strip reprints)
The Saalfield Publishing Co.

By Gus Mager 7.00 21.00 50.00

HAWTHORN-MELODY FARMS DAIRY COMICS
No date (1950's) (Giveaway)
Everybody's Publishing Co.

Cheerie Chick, Tuffy Turtle, Robin Koo Koo, Donald & Longhorn Legends .70 2.50 5.00

HEADLINE COMICS (. . .Crime No. 32-39)
Feb, 1943 - No. 22, Nov-Dec, 1946; 1947 - No. 77, Oct, 1956
Prize Publications — Good / Fine / Mint

1-Yank & Doodle x-over in Junior Rangers 14.00 42.00 100.00
2 6.00 18.00 42.00
3-Used in **POP**, pg. 84 6.50 19.50 45.00
4-7,9,10: 4,10-Hitler story 4.35 13.00 30.00
8-Classic Hitler-c 6.50 19.50 45.00
11,12 3.00 9.00 21.00
13-15-Blue Streak in all 3.50 10.50 24.00
16-Origin Atomic Man 6.50 19.50 45.00
17,18,20,21: 21-Atomic Man ends 4.00 12.00 28.00
19-S&K-a 9.35 28.00 65.00
22-Kiefer-c 2.00 6.00 14.00
23-(All S&K-a) 9.35 28.00 65.00
24-(All S&K-a); dope-crazy killer story 9.35 28.00 65.00
25-35-S&K c/a. 25-Powell-a 5.50 16.50 38.00
36-S&K-a 3.50 10.50 24.00
37-One pg. S&K, Severin-a 2.35 7.00 16.00
38,40-Meskin-a 1.70 5.00 12.00
39,41-43,45-48,50-55: 51-Kirby-c 1.00 3.00 7.00
44-S&K-c; Severin/Elder, Meskin-a 3.15 9.50 22.00
49-Meskin-a 1.30 4.00 9.00
56,57-S&K-a 2.35 7.00 16.00
58-77: 72-Meskin c/a(i) 1.00 3.00 7.00

HEAP, THE
Sept, 1971 (52 pages)
Skywald Publications

1-Kinstler-a, r-/Strange Worlds No. 8 .50 1.50 3.00

HEART AND SOUL
April-May, 1954 - No. 2, June-July, 1954
Mikeross Publications

1,2 2.30 7.00 16.00

HEART THROBS (Love Stories No. 147 on)
8/49 - No. 8, 10/50; No. 9, 3/52 - No. 146, Oct, 1972
Quality/National No. 47(4-5/57) on (Arleigh No. 48-101)

1-Classic Ward-c, Gustavson-a, 9pgs. 17.00 51.00 120.00
2-Ward c/a, 9 pgs; Gustavson-a 10.00 30.00 70.00
3-Gustavson-a 4.00 12.00 28.00
4,6,8-Ward-a, 8-9 pgs. 6.50 19.50 45.00
5,7 2.15 6.50 15.00
9-Robert Mitchum, Jane Russell photo-c 2.50 7.50 17.50
10,15-Ward-a 4.65 14.00 32.00
11-14,16-20: 12 (7/52) 1.50 4.50 10.00
21-Ward-c 3.65 11.00 25.00
22,23-Ward-a(p) 2.65 8.00 18.00
24-32: 32-Last pre-code (1/55) 1.15 3.50 8.00
33-39,41-46 (12/56; last Quality) 1.00 3.00 7.00
40-Ward-a; r-7 pgs./#21 2.00 6.00 14.00
47-(4-5/57; 1st DC) 3.50 10.50 24.00
48-60 1.15 3.50 8.00
61-70 .70 2.00 5.00
71-100 .50 1.50 3.00
101-The Beatles app. on-c 1.50 4.50 10.00
102-119,121-146: 102-123-(Serial)-Three Girls, Their Lives, Their Loves .25 .75 1.50
120-Adams-c .35 1.00 2.00
NOTE: ***Gustavson** a-8. Photo-c 8, 9, 17.*

HEATHCLIFF
Apr, 1985 - Present
Star Comics (Marvel)

1-15 .35 .70
16-23 ($1.00) .45 .90

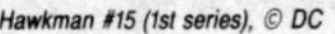
Hawkman #15 (1st series), © DC

Headline Comics #35, © PRIZE

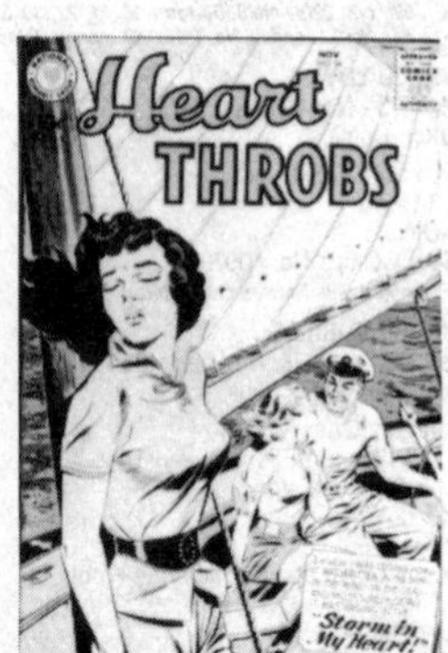

Heart Throbs #56, © DC

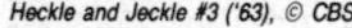
Heckle and Jeckle #3 ('63), © CBS

Hedy Devine Comics #27, © MCG

Hello Pal Comics #3, © HARV

HEATHCLIFF (continued)

	Good	Fine	Mint
Annual 1 ('87)		.60	1.20

HEATHCLIFF'S FUNHOUSE
May, 1987 - Present
Star Comics (Marvel)

	Good	Fine	Mint
1-7		.50	1.00

HECKLE AND JECKLE (See Blue Ribbon, Paul Terry's & Terry-Toons Comics)
10/51 - No. 24, 10/55; No. 25, Fall/56 - No. 34, 6/59
St. John Publ. Co. No. 1-24/Pines No. 25 on

	Good	Fine	Mint
1	13.00	40.00	90.00
2	6.00	18.00	42.00
3-5	4.60	14.00	32.00
6-10	3.50	10.50	24.00
11-20	2.30	7.00	16.00
21-34	1.30	4.00	9.00

HECKLE AND JECKLE (TV) (See New Terrytoons)
11/62 - No. 4, 8/63; 5/66; No. 2, 10/66 - No. 3, 8/67
Gold Key/Dell Publishing Co.

	Good	Fine	Mint
1 (11/62; Gold Key)	1.50	4.50	10.00
2-4	.85	2.50	6.00
1 (5/66; Dell)	1.00	3.00	7.00
2,3	.70	2.00	5.00

(See March of Comics No. 379,472,484)

HECKLE AND JECKLE
1987 - Present ($1.50; color)
Spotlight Comics

	Good	Fine	Mint
1	.25	.75	1.50

HECTOR COMICS
Nov, 1953 - 1954
Key Publications

	Good	Fine	Mint
1	2.00	6.00	14.00
2,3	1.15	3.50	8.00

HECTOR HEATHCOTE (TV)
March, 1964
Gold Key

	Good	Fine	Mint
1 (10111-403)	2.00	6.00	14.00

HEDY DEVINE COMICS (Formerly All Winners No. 21?; Hedy of Hollywood No. 36 on; also see Annie Oakley & Venus)
No. 22, Aug, 1947 - No. 50, Sept, 1952
Marvel Comics (RCM)

	Good	Fine	Mint
22	3.50	10.50	24.00
23,24,27-30: 23-Wolverton-a, 1 pg; Kurtzman's "Hey Look," 2 pgs. 24,27-30-"Hey Look" by Kurtzman, 1-3 pgs.	4.60	14.00	32.00
25-Classic "Hey Look" by Kurtzman-"Optical Illusion"	5.50	16.50	38.00
26-"Giggles & Grins" by Kurtzman	3.50	10.50	24.00
31-34,36-50: 32-Anti-Wertham editorial	1.60	4.70	11.00
35-Four pgs. "Rusty" by Kurtzman	3.50	10.50	24.00

HEDY-MILLIE-TESSIE COMEDY (See Comedy)

HEDY WOLFE
August, 1957
Atlas Publishing Co. (Emgee)

	Good	Fine	Mint
1	2.15	6.50	15.00

HEE HAW (TV)
July, 1970 - No. 7, Aug, 1971
Charlton Press

	Good	Fine	Mint
1-7	.50	1.50	3.00

HEIDI (See Dell Jr. Treasury No. 6)

HELEN OF TROY (See 4-Color No. 684)

HELLBLAZER
Jan, 1988 - Present ($1.25, Adults)
DC Comics

	Good	Fine	Mint
1-4		.60	1.25

HELLO, I'M JOHNNY CASH
1976 (39-49 cents)
Spire Christian Comics (Fleming H. Revell Co.)

	Good	Fine	Mint
nn		.40	.80

HELL ON EARTH (See DC Science Fic. Graphic Novel)

HELLO PAL COMICS (Short Story Comics)
Jan, 1943 - No. 3, May, 1943 (Photo-c)
Harvey Publications

	Good	Fine	Mint
1-Rocketman & Rocketgirl begin; Yankee Doodle Jones app.; Mickey Rooney cover	23.00	70.00	160.00
2-Charlie McCarthy cover	15.00	45.00	105.00
3-Bob Hope cover	16.00	48.00	110.00

HELL-RIDER (Magazine)
Aug, 1971 - No. 2, Oct, 1971 (B&W)
Skywald Publications

	Good	Fine	Mint
1-Origin & 1st app.; Butterfly & Wildbunch begins	.80	2.40	3.60
2	.70	2.00	3.00

NOTE: *#3 advertised in Psycho #5 but did not come out.* **Buckler** *a-1,2.* **Morrow** *c-3.*

HE-MAN (See Masters Of The Universe)

HE-MAN
Fall, 1952
Ziff-Davis Publ. Co. (Approved Comics)

	Good	Fine	Mint
1-Kinstler-c; Powell-a	5.00	15.00	35.00

HE-MAN
May, 1954 - No. 2, July, 1954
Toby Press

	Good	Fine	Mint
1	4.60	14.00	32.00
2	3.00	9.00	21.00

HE-MAN, THE MOVIE
Nov, 1987 ($2.00, 48 pgs.)
Star Comics (Marvel)

	Good	Fine	Mint
1-Adapts movie; Tuska-a(p)	.35	1.00	2.00

HENNESSEY (See 4-Color No. 1200,1280)

HENRY
1935 (52 pages) (Daily B&W strip reprints)
David McKay Publications

	Good	Fine	Mint
1-by Carl Anderson	6.00	18.00	42.00

HENRY
No. 122, Oct, 1946 - No. 65, Apr-June, 1961
Dell Publishing Co.

	Good	Fine	Mint
4-Color 122	5.00	15.00	35.00
4-Color 155 (7/47)	4.00	12.00	28.00
1 (1-3/48)	4.00	12.00	28.00
2	2.00	6.00	14.00
3-10	1.50	4.50	10.00
11-20: 20-Infinity-c	1.15	3.50	8.00
21-30	.85	2.50	6.00
31-40	.55	1.65	4.00
41-65	.40	1.25	3.00

HENRY (See March of Comics No. 43, 58, 84, 101, 112, 129, 147, 162, 178, 189 and Giant Comic Album)

HENRY ALDRICH COMICS (TV)
Aug-Sept, 1950 - No. 22, Sept-Nov, 1954

HENRY ALDRICH COMICS (continued)
Dell Publishing Co.

	Good	Fine	Mint
1-Part series written by John Stanley; Bill Williams-a	3.50	10.50	24.00
2	2.00	6.00	14.00
3-5	1.70	5.00	12.00
6-10	1.50	4.50	10.00
11-22	1.15	3.50	8.00
Giveaway (16p, soft-c, 1951)-Capehart radio	2.00	6.00	12.00

HENRY BREWSTER
Feb, 1966 - V2No.7, Sept, 1967 (All Giants)
Country Wide (M.F. Ent.)

	Good	Fine	Mint
1-6(12/66)-Powell-a in most		.40	.80
V2#7		.30	.60

HERBIE (See Forbidden Worlds)
April-May, 1964 - No. 23, Feb, 1967
American Comics Group

	Good	Fine	Mint
1	6.75	20.00	47.00
2-4	3.35	10.00	23.00
5-Beatles, Dean Martin, F. Sinatra app.	4.00	12.00	28.00
6,7,9,10	2.00	6.00	14.00
8-Origin The Fat Fury	3.00	9.00	21.00
11-22: 14-Nemesis & MagicMan app. 17-R-1st Herbie/F.W. No. 73	1.35	4.00	9.00
23-R-2nd Herbie/F.W. No.94	1.35	4.00	9.00

NOTE: *Most have **Whitney** c/a.*

HERBIE GOES TO MONTE CARLO, HERBIE RIDES AGAIN (See Walt Disney Showcase No. 24, 41)

HERCULES
Oct, 1967 - No. 13, Sept, 1969; Dec, 1968
Charlton Comics

	Good	Fine	Mint
1-Thane of Bagarth series begins; Glanzman-a	.55	1.65	4.00
2-13: 10-Aparo-a	.35	1.00	2.00
8-(Low distribution)(12/68)-35 cents; magazine format; B&W-r	2.35	7.00	16.00
Modern Comics reprint 10('77), 11('78)		.20	.40

HERCULES (See The Mighty...)

HERCULES, PRINCE OF POWER
9/82 - No. 4, 12/82; 3/84 - No. 4, 6/84
Marvel Comics Group

	Good	Fine	Mint
1	.25	.75	1.50
2-4	.25	.75	1.50
V2/1 (Mini-series)	.25	.75	1.50
2-4		.50	1.00

NOTE: ***Layton** a-1, 2, 3p, 4p, V2/1-4; c-1-4, V2/1-4.*

HERCULES UNBOUND
Oct-Nov, 1975 - No. 12, Aug-Sept, 1977
National Periodical Publications

	Good	Fine	Mint
1-Wood inks begin		.40	.80
2-5		.30	.60
6-12: 10-Atomic Knights x-over		.25	.50

NOTE: ***Buckler** c-7p. **Layton** inks-No. 9, 10. **Simonson** a-7-10p, 11, 12; c- 8p, 9-12. **Wood** inks-1-8; c-7i, 8i.*

HERCULES UNCHAINED (See 4-Color No. 1006,1121)

HERE COMES SANTA (See March of Comics No. 30,213,340)

HERE IS SANTA CLAUS
1930s (16 pgs., 8 in color) (stiff paper covers)
Goldsmith Publishing Co. (Kann's in Washington, D.C.)

	Good	Fine	Mint
nn	3.50	10.50	24.00

HERE'S HOW AMERICA'S CARTOONISTS HELP TO SELL U.S. SAVINGS BONDS
1950? (16 pgs.; paper cover)
Harvey Comics giveaway

	Good	Fine	Mint
Contains: Joe Palooka, Donald Duck, Archie, Kerry Drake, Red Ryder,Blondie & Steve Canyon	12.00	35.00	70.00

HERE'S HOWIE COMICS
Jan-Feb, 1952 - No. 18, Nov-Dec, 1954
National Periodical Publications

	Good	Fine	Mint
1	10.00	30.00	70.00
2	4.35	13.00	30.00
3-5	3.70	11.00	26.00
6-10	2.85	8.50	20.00
11-18	2.15	6.50	15.00

HERMAN & KATNIP (See Harvey Hits #14,25,31,41 & Paramount Animated Comics #1)

HERO ALLIANCE, THE
Dec, 1985 - No. 2, Sept, 1986 (No. 2, $1.50)
Sirius Comics

	Good	Fine	Mint
1		.65	1.30
2	.25	.75	1.50
The Special Edition 1 (7/86)-Full color	.25	.75	1.50

HERO ALLIANCE
May, 1987 - Present ($1.95, color)
Wonder Color Comics

	Good	Fine	Mint
1	.30	.95	1.90

HEROES AGAINST HUNGER
1986 (One shot)
DC Comics

	Good	Fine	Mint
1-Superman, Batman app.; Adams-c(p)	.30	.90	1.80

HEROES ALL CATHOLIC ACTION ILLUSTRATED
1943 - V6No.5, March 10, 1948 (paper covers)
Heroes All Co.

	Good	Fine	Mint
V1#1,2-(16 pgs., 8x11")	4.00	12.00	28.00
V2#1(1/44)-3(3/44)-(16 pgs., 8x11")	2.50	7.50	17.50
V3#1(1/45)-10(10/45)-(16 pgs., 8x11")	2.00	6.00	14.00
V4#1-35 (12/20/46)-(16 pgs.)	1.50	4.50	10.00
V5#1(1/10/47)-8(2/28/47)-(16 pgs.)	1.15	3.50	8.00
V5#9(3/7/47)-20(11/25/47)-(32 pgs.)	1.15	3.50	8.00
V6#1(1/10/48)-5(3/10/48)-(32 pgs.)	1.15	3.50	8.00

HEROES FOR HOPE STARRING THE X-MEN
Dec, 1985 ($1.50, One Shot, 52 pgs.)
Marvel Comics Group

	Good	Fine	Mint
1-Proceeds donated to famine relief; scripts by Harlan Ellison, Stephen King; Wrightson, Corben-a	.45	1.30	2.60

HEROES, INC. PRESENTS CANNON
1969 - No. 2, 1976 (Sold at Army PX's)
Wally Wood/CPL/Gang Publ. No. 2

	Good	Fine	Mint
nn-Wood/Ditko-a	1.35	4.00	8.00
2-Wood-c; Ditko, Byrne, Wood-a; 8½x10½"; B&W; $2.00	.70	2.00	4.00

NOTE: *First issue not distributed by publisher; 1,800 copies were stored and 900 copies were stolen from warehouse. Many copies have surfaced in recent years.*

HEROES OF THE WILD FRONTIER (Formerly Baffling Mysteries)
No. 26, 3/55; No. 27, 1/56 - No. 2, 4/56
Ace Periodicals

	Good	Fine	Mint
26(No.1)	2.00	6.00	14.00
27,28,2	1.15	3.50	8.00

HERO FOR HIRE (Power Man No. 17 on)
June, 1972 - No. 16, Dec, 1973
Marvel Comics Group

Henry Aldrich #14, © DELL

Herbie #4, © ACG

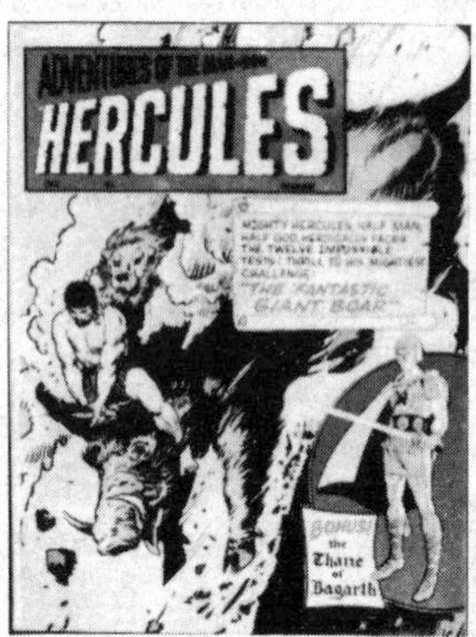

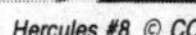
Hercules #8, © CC

Heroic Comics #21, © FF

High School Confidential Diary #1, © CC

Hi-Jinx #6, © ACG

HERO FOR HIRE (continued) — Good / Fine / Mint
- 1-Origin Luke Cage retold; marijuana mention: Tuska-a(p) .50 1.50 3.00
- 2-10: 3-1st app. Mace. 4-1st app. Phil Fox of the Bugle; 2,3-Tuska-a(p) .50 1.00
- 11-16: 14-Origin retold. 15-Everett Subby-r('53). 16-Origin Stilletto; death of Rackham .50 1.00

HEROIC ADVENTURES (See Adventures)

HEROIC COMICS (Reg'lar Fellas #1-15; New Heroic #41 on)
Aug, 1940 - No. 97, June, 1955
Eastern Color Printing Co./Famous Funnies(Funnies, Inc. No. 1)

	Good	Fine	Mint
1-Hydroman(origin) by Bill Everett, The Purple Zombie(origin) & Mann of India by Tarpe Mills begins	40.00	120.00	280.00
2	20.00	60.00	140.00
3,4	17.00	51.00	120.00
5,6	12.00	36.00	84.00
7-Origin Man O'Metal, 1 pg.	15.00	45.00	105.00
8-10: 10-Lingerie panels	8.50	25.50	60.00
11,13: 13-Crandall/Fine-a	7.00	21.00	50.00
12-Music Master(origin) begins by Everett, ends No. 31; last Purple Zombie & Mann of India	9.00	27.00	62.00
14-Hydroman x-over in Rainbow Boy; also in No. 15; origin Rainbow Boy	9.00	27.00	62.00
15-Intro. Downbeat	8.50	25.50	60.00
16-20: 17-Rainbow Boy x-over in Hydroman. 19-Rainbow Boy x-over in Hydroman & vice versa	5.70	17.00	40.00
21-30:25-Rainbow Boy x-over in Hydroman. 28-Last Man O'Metal. 29-Last Hydroman	3.50	10.50	24.00
31,34,38	1.30	4.00	9.00
32,36,37-Toth-a, 3-4 pgs.	2.30	7.00	16.00
33,35-Toth-a, 8 & 9 pgs.	2.65	8.00	18.00
39-42-Toth, Ingels-a	2.65	8.00	18.00
43,46,47,49-Toth-a, 2-4 pgs. 47-Ingels-a	1.70	5.00	12.00
44,45,50-Toth-a, 6-9 pgs.	2.00	6.00	14.00
48,52-54	1.00	3.00	7.00
51-Williamson-a	3.50	10.50	24.00
55-Toth c/a	1.70	5.00	12.00
56-60-Toth-c. 60-Everett-a	1.30	4.00	9.00
61-Everett-a	1.00	3.00	7.00
62,64-Everett-c/a	1.15	3.50	8.00
63-Everett-c	.85	2.50	6.00
65-Williamson/Frazetta-a; Evans-a, 2 pgs.	4.60	14.00	32.00
66,75,94-Frazetta-a, 2 pgs. each	1.70	5.00	12.00
67,73-Frazetta-a, 4 pgs. each	2.65	8.00	18.00
68,74,76-80,84,85,88-93,95-97	.70	2.00	5.00
69,72-Frazetta-a (6 & 8 pgs. each)	4.60	14.00	32.00
70,71,86,87-Frazetta, 3-4 pgs. each; 1 pg. drug mention by Frazetta in #70	2.65	8.00	18.00
81,82-One pg. Frazetta art	1.15	3.50	8.00
83-Frazetta-a, ½ pg.	1.15	3.50	8.00

NOTE: ***Evans** a-64, 65. **Everett** a-(Hydroman-c/a-No. 1-9), 44, 60-64; c-1-9, 62-64. **Sid Greene** a-38-43, 46. **Guardineer** a-42(3), 43, 44, 45(2), 49(3), 50, 60, 61(2), 65, 67(2), 70-72. **Ingels** c-41. **Kiefer** a-46, 48; c-19-22, 24, 44, 46, 48, 51-53, 65, 67-69, 71-74, 76, 77, 79, 80, 82, 85, 88, 89. **Mort Lawrence** a-45. **Tarpe Mills** a-2(2), 3(2), 10. **Ed Moore** a-49, 52-54, 56-63, 65-69, 72-74, 76, 77. **H.G. Peter** a-58-74, 76, 77, 87. **Paul Reinman** a-49. **Rico** a-31. Captain Tootsie by Beck-31, 32. Painted-c #16 on.*

HEX (Replaces Jonah Hex)
Sept, 1985 - No. 18, Feb, 1987
DC Comics

	Good	Fine	Mint
1-Hex in post-atomic war world; origin		.65	1.30
2-18: 6-Origin Stiletta. 13-Intro The Dogs of War (Origin #15)		.40	.80

HEY THERE, IT'S YOGI BEAR (See Movie Comics)

HI-ADVENTURE HEROES (Hanna-Barbera)(TV)
May, 1969 - No. 2, Aug, 1969
Gold Key

	Good	Fine	Mint
1-Three Musketeers, Gulliver, Arabian Knights stories	.55	1.65	4.00
2-Three Musketeers, Micro-Venture, Arabian Knights	.30	.90	2.00

HI AND LOIS (See 4-Color No. 683,774,955)

HI AND LOIS
Nov, 1969 - No. 11, July, 1971
Charlton Comics

	Good	Fine	Mint
1	.50	1.50	3.00
2-11	.35	1.00	2.00

HICKORY
Oct, 1949 - No. 6, Aug, 1950
Quality Comics Group

	Good	Fine	Mint
1-Sahl c/a; Feldstein?-a	5.50	16.50	38.00
2	3.00	9.00	21.00
3-6	2.35	7.00	16.00

HIDDEN CREW, THE (See The United States A. F.)

HIDE-OUT (See 4-Color No. 346)

HIDING PLACE, THE
1973 (35-49 cents)
Spire Christian Comics/Fleming H. Revell Co.

	Good	Fine	Mint
nn		.40	.80

HIGH ADVENTURE
October, 1957
Red Top(Decker) Comics (Farrell)

	Good	Fine	Mint
1-Krigstein-r from Explorer Joe (re-issue on cover)	1.70	5.00	12.00

HIGH ADVENTURE (See 4-Color No. 949,1001)

HIGH CHAPPARAL (TV)
August, 1968 (Photo-c)
Gold Key

	Good	Fine	Mint
1 (10226-808)-Tufts-a	2.30	7.00	16.00

HIGH SCHOOL CONFIDENTIAL DIARY (Confidential Diary #12 on)
June, 1960 - No. 11, March, 1962
Charlton Comics

	Good	Fine	Mint
1	.75	2.25	5.00
2-11	.35	1.00	2.00

HI-HO COMICS
nd (2/46?) - No. 3, 1946
Four Star Publications

	Good	Fine	Mint
1-Funny Animal; L. B. Cole-c	6.00	18.00	42.00
2,3: 2-L. B. Cole-c	3.50	10.50	24.00

HI-JINX
July-Aug, 1947 - 1949
B&I Publ. Co.(American Comics Group)/Creston/LaSalle Publ. Co.

	Good	Fine	Mint
1	4.60	14.00	32.00
2,3	2.30	7.00	16.00
4-7-Milt Gross	3.50	10.50	24.00
132 Pg. issue, nn, nd ('40s)(LaSalle)	6.50	19.50	45.00

HI-LITE COMICS
Fall, 1945
E. R. Ross Publishing Co.

	Good	Fine	Mint
1-Miss Shady	5.00	15.00	35.00

HILLBILLY COMICS
Aug, 1955 - No. 4, July, 1956 (Satire)
Charlton Comics

	Good	Fine	Mint
1	2.65	8.00	18.00

HILLBILLY COMICS (continued)

	Good	Fine	Mint
2-4	1.30	4.00	9.00

HIP-IT-TY HOP (See March of Comics No. 15)

HI-SCHOOL ROMANCE (. . . Romances No. 41 on)
Oct, 1949 - No. 5, June, 1950; No. 6, Dec, 1950 - No. 73, Mar, 1958; No. 74, Sept, 1958 - No. 75, Nov, 1958
Harvey Publications/True Love(Home Comics)

	Good	Fine	Mint
1	3.00	9.00	21.00
2	1.70	5.00	12.00
3-9: 5-Photo-c	1.35	4.00	9.00
10-Rape story	1.70	5.00	12.00
11-20	1.00	3.00	7.00
21-31	.85	2.50	6.00
32-"Unholy passion" story	1.35	4.00	9.00
33-36: 36-Last pre-code (2/55)	.70	2.00	5.00
37-75	.60	1.80	4.00

NOTE: ***Powell** a-1-3, 5, 8, 12-14, 16, 18, 21-23, 25-27, 30-34, 36, 37, 39, 45-48, 50-52, 57, 58, 60, 64, 65, 67, 69.*

HI-SCHOOL ROMANCE DATE BOOK
Nov, 1962 - No. 3, Mar, 1963 (25 cent Giant)
Harvey Publications

	Good	Fine	Mint
1-Powell, Baker-a	2.35	7.00	14.00
2,3	1.00	3.00	6.00

HIS NAME IS SAVAGE (Magazine format)
No. 1, June, 1968 (One Shot)
Adventure House Press

	Good	Fine	Mint
1-Gil Kane-a	1.75	5.25	12.00

HI-SPOT COMICS (Red Ryder No. 1 & No. 3 on)
No. 2, Nov, 1940
Hawley Publications

	Good	Fine	Mint
2-David Innes of Pellucidar; art by J. C. Burroughs; written by Edgar R. Burroughs	50.00	150.00	350.00

HISTORY OF THE DC UNIVERSE
Sept, 1986 - No. 2, Nov, 1986 ($2.95)
DC Comics

	Good	Fine	Mint
1-Perez c/a	.75	2.25	4.50
2	.70	2.00	4.00

HIT COMICS
July, 1940 - No. 65, July, 1950
Quality Comics Group

	Good	Fine	Mint
1-Origin Neon, the Unknown & Hercules; intro. The Red Bee; Bob & Swab, Blaze Barton, the Strange Twins, X-5 Super Agent, Casey Jones & Jack & Jill (ends #7) begin	165.00	495.00	1155.00
2-The Old Witch begins, ends #14	80.00	240.00	560.00
3-Casey Jones ends; transvestism story-'Jack & Jill'	65.00	195.00	455.00
4-Super Agent (ends #17), & Betty Bates (ends #65) begin; X-5 ends	54.00	160.00	380.00
5-Classic cover	80.00	240.00	560.00
6-10: 10-Old Witch by Crandall, 4 pgs.-1st work in comics	45.00	135.00	315.00
11-17: 13-Blaze Barton ends. 17-Last Neon; Crandall Hercules in all	42.00	125.00	295.00
18-Origin Stormy Foster, the Great Defender; The Ghost of Flanders begins; Crandall-c	45.00	135.00	315.00
19,20	42.00	125.00	295.00
21-24: 21-Last Hercules. 24-Last Red Bee & Strange Twins	36.00	108.00	252.00
25-Origin Kid Eternity by Moldoff	45.00	135.00	315.00
26-Blackhawk x-over in Kid Eternity	32.00	95.00	225.00
27-29	20.00	60.00	140.00
30,31-"Bill the Magnificent" by Kurtzman, 11 pgs. in each	17.00	51.00	120.00
32-40: 32-Plastic Man x-over. 34-Last Stormy Foster	9.00	27.00	62.00
41-50	6.00	18.00	42.00
51-60-Last Kid Eternity	5.50	16.50	38.00
61,63-Crandall c/a; Jeb Rivers begins #61	6.00	18.00	42.00
62	4.60	14.00	32.00
64,65-Crandall-a	5.50	16.50	38.00

NOTE: ***Crandall** a-11-17(Hercules), 23, 24(Stormy Foster); c-18-20, 23, 24. **Fine** c-1-14, 16, 17(most). **Ward** c-33. Bondage c-64.*

HI-YO SILVER (See Lone Ranger's Famous Horse. . ., March of Comics No. 215, and The Lone Ranger)

HOCUS POCUS (Formerly Funny Book)
No. 9, Aug-Sept, 1946
Parents' Magazine Press

	Good	Fine	Mint
9	2.00	6.00	14.00

HOGAN'S HEROES (TV) (No. 1-7 have photo-c)
June, 1966 - No. 8, Sept, 1967; No. 9, Oct, 1969
Dell Publishing Co.

	Good	Fine	Mint
1	2.65	8.00	18.00
2,3-Ditko-a(p)	1.70	5.00	12.00
4-9: 9-Reprints #1	1.30	4.00	9.00

HOLIDAY COMICS
1942 (196 pages) (25 cents)
Fawcett Publications

	Good	Fine	Mint
1-Contains three Fawcett comics; Capt. Marvel, Nyoka #1, & Whiz. Not rebound, remaindered comics—printed at the same time as originals	65.00	195.00	455.00

HOLIDAY COMICS
January, 1951 - No. 8, Oct, 1952
Star Publications

	Good	Fine	Mint
1-Funny animal contents (Frisky Fables) in all; L. B. Cole-c	8.50	25.50	60.00
2-Classic L. B. Cole-c	9.00	27.00	62.00
3-8: 5,8-X-Mas-c; all L.B. Cole-c	6.50	19.50	45.00
Accepted Reprint 4 (nd)-L.B. Cole-c	3.00	9.00	21.00

HOLIDAY DIGEST
1988 - Present ($1.25, digest-size)
Harvey Comics

	Good	Fine	Mint
1		.60	1.25

HOLI-DAY SURPRISE (Formerly Summer Fun)
No. 55, Mar, 1967 (25 cents)
Charlton Comics

	Good	Fine	Mint
V2#55-Giant		.40	.80

HOLLYWOOD COMICS
Winter, 1944 (52 pgs.)
New Age Publishers

	Good	Fine	Mint
1-Funny animals	5.00	15.00	35.00

HOLLYWOOD CONFESSIONS
Oct, 1949 - No. 2, Dec, 1949
St. John Publishing Co.

	Good	Fine	Mint
1-Kubert c/a-entire book	11.50	34.00	80.00
2-Kubert c/a(2) (Scarce)	17.00	51.00	120.00

HOLLYWOOD DIARY
Dec, 1949 - No. 5, July-Aug, 1950
Quality Comics Group

	Good	Fine	Mint
1	7.00	21.00	50.00
2-Photo-c	4.60	14.00	32.00
3-5: 3,5-Photo-c	4.00	12.00	28.00

Hi-School Romance Date Book #1, © HARV

Hit Comics #7, © QUA

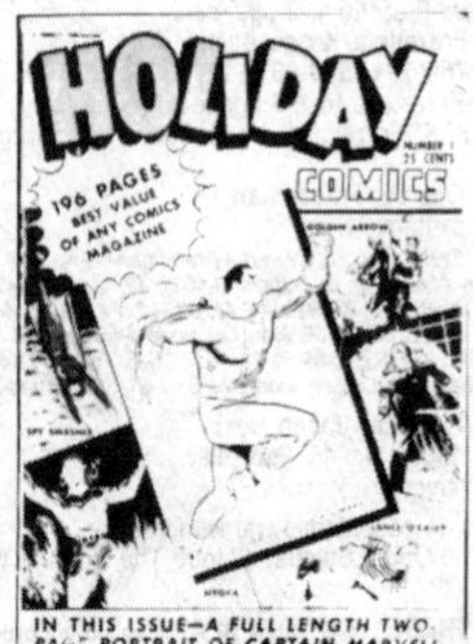

Holiday Comics #1, © FAW

Hollywood Pictorial #3, © STJ

Hollywood Secrets #4, © QUA

Holyoke One-Shot #3, © HOKE

HOLLYWOOD FILM STORIES
April, 1950 - No. 4, Oct, 1950
Feature Publications/Prize

	Good	Fine	Mint
1	7.00	21.00	50.00
2,4	4.60	14.00	32.00
3-A movie magazine; no comics	4.60	14.00	32.00

HOLLYWOOD FUNNY FOLKS (Formerly Funny Folks; Nutsy Squirrel #61 on)
No. 27, Aug-Sept, 1950 - No. 60, July-Aug, 1954
National Periodical Publications

	Good	Fine	Mint
27	3.50	10.50	24.00
28-40	2.00	6.00	14.00
41-60	1.50	4.50	10.00

NOTE: ***Sheldon Mayer** a-27-35, 37-40, 43-46, 48-51, 53, 56, 57, 60.*

HOLLYWOOD LOVE DOCTOR (See Doctor Anthony King . . .)

HOLLYWOOD PICTORIAL (. . . Romances on cover)
No. 3, January, 1950
St. John Publishing Co.

	Good	Fine	Mint
3-Matt Baker-a; photo-c	8.00	24.00	56.00

(Becomes a movie magazine - Hollywood Pictorial West. with No. 4.)

HOLLYWOOD ROMANCES (Formerly Brides In Love)
No. 46, 11/66; No. 47, 10/67; No. 48, 11/68; No. 49, 11/69 - No. 59, 6/71 (Becomes For Lovers Only No. 60-on)
Charlton Comics

	Good	Fine	Mint
V2#46-Rolling Stones c/story	.70	2.00	4.00
V2#47-59: 56-"Born to Heart Break" begins		.30	.60

HOLLYWOOD SECRETS
Nov, 1949 - No. 6, Sept, 1950
Quality Comics Group

	Good	Fine	Mint
1-Ward-c/a, 9pgs.	17.00	51.00	120.00
2-Crandall-a, Ward c/a, 9 pgs.	10.00	30.00	70.00
3-6: All photo-c; 5-Lex Barker (Tarzan)-c	4.35	13.00	30.00
. . . of Romance, I.W. Reprint #9	.85	2.50	5.00

HOLYOKE ONE-SHOT
1944 - 1945 (All reprints)
Holyoke Publishing Co. (Tem Publ.)

	Good	Fine	Mint
1-Grit Grady (on cover only), Miss Victory, Alias X (origin)-All reprints from Captain Fearless	5.00	15.00	35.00
2-Rusty Dugan (Corporal); Capt. Fearless (origin), Mr. Miracle (origin), app.	5.00	15.00	35.00
3-Miss Victory-Crash #4-r; Cat Man (origin), Solar Legion by Kirby app.; Miss Victory on cover only (1945)	11.50	34.00	80.00
4-Mr. Miracle-The Blue Streak app.	4.60	14.00	32.00
5-U.S. Border Patrol Comics (Sgt. Dick Carter of the . . .), Miss Victory (story matches cover #3), Citizen Smith, & Mr. Miracle app.	5.15	15.50	36.00
6-Capt. Fearless, Alias X, Capt. Stone (splash used as cover-#10); Diamond Jim & Rusty Dugan (splash from cover-#2)	4.60	14.00	32.00
7-Z-2, Strong Man, Blue Streak (story matches cover-#8)-Reprints from Crash #2	5.70	17.00	40.00
8-Blue Streak, Strong Man (story matches cover-#7)-Crash reprints-	4.65	14.00	32.00
9-Citizen Smith, The Blue Streak, Solar Legion by Kirby & Strongman, the Perfect Human app.; reprints from Crash #4 & 5; Citizen Smith on cover only-from story in #5(1944-before #3)	7.00	21.00	50.00
10-Captain Stone (Crash reprints); Solar Legion by S&K	7.00	21.00	50.00

HOMER COBB (See Adventures of . . .)

HOMER HOOPER
July, 1953 - No. 4, Dec., 1953
Atlas Comics

	Good	Fine	Mint
1	2.30	7.00	16.00
2-4	1.30	4.00	9.00

HOMER, THE HAPPY GHOST (See Adventures of . . .)
3/55 - No. 22, 11/58; V2No.1, 11/69 - V2No.5, 7/70
Atlas(ACI/PPI/WPI)/Marvel Comics

	Good	Fine	Mint
V1#1	3.00	9.00	21.00
2	1.50	4.50	10.00
3-10	1.15	3.50	8.00
11-22	1.00	3.00	7.00
V2#1 - V2#5 (1969-70)	.50	1.50	3.00

HOME RUN (See A-1 Comics No. 89)

HOME, SWEET HOME
1925 (10¼x10")
M.S. Publishing Co.

	Good	Fine	Mint
nn-By Tuthill	8.00	24.00	56.00

HONEYBEE BIRDWHISTLE AND HER PET PEPI (Introducing)
1969 (24 pgs.; B&W; slick cover)
Newspaper Enterprise Association (Giveaway)

	Good	Fine	Mint
nn-Contains Freckles newspaper strips with a short biography of Henry Fornhals (artist) & Fred Fox (writer) of the strip.	2.75	8.00	16.00

HONEYMOON (Formerly Gay Comics)
No. 41, January, 1950
A Lover's Magazine(USA) (Marvel)

	Good	Fine	Mint
41	2.65	8.00	18.00

HONEYMOONERS, THE
Oct, 1986 ($1.50; in color)
Lodestone Publishing

	Good	Fine	Mint
1-Photo-c	.50	1.50	3.00

HONEYMOONERS, THE
Sept, 1987 - No. 24 ($2.00, color)
Triad Publications

	Good	Fine	Mint
1-3	.35	1.00	2.00
4 ($3.50)	.60	1.75	3.50

HONEYMOON ROMANCE
April, 1950 - No. 2, July, 1950 (25 cents) (digest size)
Artful Publications(Canadian)

	Good	Fine	Mint
1,2-(Rare)	17.00	51.00	120.00

HONEY WEST (TV)
September, 1966 (Photo-c)
Gold Key

	Good	Fine	Mint
1 (10186-609)	4.35	13.00	30.00

HONG KONG PHOOEY (Hanna-Barbera)(TV)
June, 1975 - No. 9, Nov, 1976
Charlton Comics

	Good	Fine	Mint
1-9		.40	.80

HOODED HORSEMAN, THE
No.21, 1-2/52 - No.27, 1-2/53; No.18, 12-1/54-55 - No.27, 6-7/56
American Comics Group (Michel Publ.)

	Good	Fine	Mint
21(1-2/52)-Hooded Horseman, Injun Jones continues	5.00	15.00	35.00
22	3.00	9.00	21.00
23-25,27(1-2/53)	2.30	7.00	16.00
26-Origin/1st app. Cowboy Sahib	3.00	9.00	21.00
18(12-1/54-55)(Formerly Out of the Night)	2.30	7.00	16.00
19-3-D effect-c; last precode, 1-2/55	4.60	14.00	32.00
20-Origin Johnny Injun	2.30	7.00	16.00
21-24,26,27(6-7/56)	2.00	6.00	14.00

THE HOODED HORSEMAN (continued)

	Good	Fine	Mint
25-Cowboy Sahib on cover only; Hooded Horseman i.d. revealed	2.30	7.00	16.00

NOTE: ***Whitney*** *c/a-21('52), 20-22.*

HOODED MENACE, THE (Also see Daring Advs.)
1951 (One Shot)
Realistic/Avon Periodicals

nn-Based on a band of hooded outlaws in the Pacific Northwest, 1900-1906; r-/in Daring Advs. #15	32.00	95.00	225.00

HOODS UP
1953 (16 pgs.; 15 cents) (Eisner c/a in all)
Fram Corp. (Dist. to service station owners)

1-(Very Rare; only 2 known)	33.00	100.00	230.00
2-6-(Very Rare; only 1 known of each)	33.00	100.00	230.00

NOTE: *Convertible Connie gives tips for service stations, selling Fram oil filters.*

HOOT GIBSON WESTERN (Formerly My Love Story; see Fox Giants)
No. 5, May, 1950 - No. 3, Sept, 1950
Fox Features Syndicate

5,6(#1,2)	8.00	24.00	56.00
3-Wood-a	11.50	34.00	80.00

HOPALONG CASSIDY (Also see Bill Boyd Western, Master Comics, Real Western Hero, & Western Hero; Bill Boyd starred as H. Cassidy in the movies; H. Cassidy in movies, radio & TV)
Feb, 1943; No. 2, Summer, 1946 - No. 85, Jan, 1954
Fawcett Publications

1 (1943, 68pgs.)-H. Cassidy & his horse Topper begin (On sale 1/8/43)	85.00	255.00	600.00
2-(Sum, '46)	32.00	95.00	225.00
3,4: 3-(Fall, '46, 52pgs. begin)	16.00	48.00	110.00
5-"Mad Barber" story mentioned in **SOTI**, pgs. 308,309	16.00	48.00	110.00
6-10	12.00	36.00	84.00
11-19: 11,13-19-Photo-c	9.50	28.00	65.00
20-29 (52pgs.)-Painted/photo-c	7.00	21.00	50.00
30,31,33,34,37-39,41 (52pgs.)-Painted-c	5.00	15.00	35.00
32,40 (36pgs.)-Painted-c	4.35	13.00	30.00
35,42,43,45 (52pgs.)-Photo-c	5.00	15.00	35.00
36,44,48 (36pgs.)-Photo-c	4.35	13.00	30.00
46,47,49-51,53,54,56 (52pgs.)-Photo-c	4.60	14.00	32.00
52,55,57-70 (36pgs.)-Photo-c	3.50	10.50	24.00
71-84-Photo-c	2.65	8.00	18.00
85-Last Fawcett issue; photo-c	3.00	9.00	21.00

NOTE: *Line-drawn c-1-10, 12*

Grape Nuts Flakes giveaway(1950,9x6")	7.00	21.00	50.00
...& the Mad Barber(1951 Bond Bread giveaway)-7x5"; used in **SOTI**, pgs. 308,309	17.00	51.00	120.00
...in the Strange Legacy	6.00	18.00	42.00
...Meets the Brend Brothers Bandits	6.00	18.00	42.00
White Tower Giveaway (1946, 16pgs., paper-c)	6.00	18.00	42.00

HOPALONG CASSIDY (TV)
No. 86, Feb, 1954 - No. 135, May-June, 1959 (All-36pgs.)
National Periodical Publications

86-Photo-c continues	9.50	28.00	65.00
87	5.00	15.00	35.00
88-90	3.50	10.50	24.00
91-99 (98 has #93 on-c & is last precode ish, 2/55)	3.00	9.00	21.00
100	4.00	12.00	28.00
101-108-Last photo-c	3.00	9.00	21.00
109-135: 124-Painted-c	3.00	9.00	21.00

NOTE: ***Gil Kane*** *art-1956 up.*

HOPE SHIP
June-Aug, 1963
Dell Publishing Co.

	Good	Fine	Mint
1	1.35	4.00	8.00

HOPPY THE MARVEL BUNNY (See Fawcett's Funny Animals)
Dec, 1945 - No. 15, Sept, 1947
Fawcett Publications

1	9.50	28.00	65.00
2	4.35	13.00	30.00
3-15	3.50	10.50	24.00
...Well Known Comics (1944,8½x10½",paper-c) Bestmaid/Samuel Lowe (Printed in red or blue)	6.75	20.00	40.00

HORACE & DOTTY DRIPPLE (Dotty Dripple No. 1-24)
No. 25, Aug, 1952 - No. 43, Oct, 1955
Harvey Publications

25-43	.70	2.00	5.00

HORIZONTAL LIEUTENANT, THE (See Movie Classics)

HORRIFIC (Terrific No. 14 on)
Sept, 1952 - No. 13, Sept, 1954
Artful/Comic Media/Harwell/Mystery

1	8.00	24.00	56.00
2	4.35	13.00	30.00
3-Bullet in head-c	6.50	19.50	45.00
4,5,7,9,10	3.00	9.00	21.00
6-Jack The Ripper story	3.50	10.50	24.00
8-Origin & 1st app. The Teller(E.C. parody)	4.00	12.00	28.00
11-Swipe/Witches Tales #6,27	2.65	8.00	18.00
12,13	2.65	8.00	18.00

NOTE: ***Don Heck*** *a-8; c-3-13.* ***Hollingsworth*** *a-4.* ***Morisi*** *a-8.* ***Palais*** *a-5, 8, 11.*

HORROR FROM THE TOMB (Mysterious Stories No. 2)
Sept, 1954
Premier Magazine Co.

1-Woodbridge/Torres, Check-a	8.00	24.00	56.00

HORRORS, THE
No. 11, Jan, 1953 - No. 15, Apr, 1954
Star Publications

11-Horrors of War; Disbrow-a(2)	6.00	18.00	42.00
12-Horrors of War; color illo in **POP**	6.00	18.00	42.00
13-Horrors of Mystery; crime stories	5.50	16.50	38.00
14,15-Horrors of the Underworld	5.50	16.50	38.00

NOTE: *All have* ***L. B. Cole*** *covers.* ***Hollingsworth*** *a-13.* ***Palais*** *a-13r.*

HORROR TALES (Magazine)
V1No.7, 6/69 - V6No.6, 12/74; V7No.1, 2/75; V7No.2, 5/76 - V8No.5, 1977; (V1-V6, 52 pgs.; V7, V8No.2, 112 pgs.; V8No.4 on, 68 pgs.) (No V5No.3, V8No.1,3)
Eerie Publications

V1#7-9		.60	1.20
V2#1-6('70), V3#1-6('71)		.40	.80
V4#1-3,5-7('72)		.40	.80
V4#4-LSD story reprint/Weird V3#5	.70	2.00	4.00
V5#1,2,4,5(6/73),5(10/73),6(12/73)		.40	.80
V6#1-6('74),V7#1,2,4('76)		.40	.80
V7#3('76)-Giant issue		.50	1.00
V8#2,4,5('77)		.40	.80

NOTE: *Bondage-c-V6#1,3, V7#2.*

HORSE FEATHERS COMICS
Nov, 1945 - No. 4, 1946
Lev Gleason Publications

1-Wolverton's Scoop Scuttle, 2 pgs.	8.50	25.50	60.00
2	3.00	9.00	21.00
3,4	2.30	7.00	16.00

HORSEMASTERS, THE (See 4-Color No. 1260)

HORSE SOLDIERS, THE (See 4-Color No. 1048)

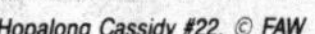
Hopalong Cassidy #22, © FAW

Horrific #1, © Comic Media

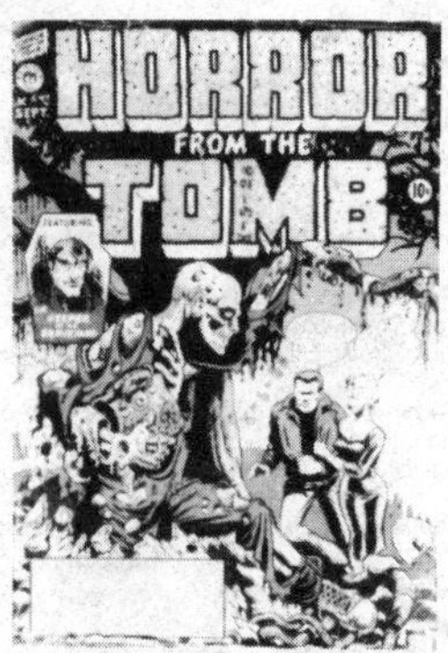

Horror From the Tomb #1, © PG

Howdy Doody #7, © Kagran Corp.

Huckleberry Hound #6 (Dell), © Hanna-Barbera

Hugga Bunch #1, © MCG

HOWARD THE DUCK MAGAZINE (continued)
***Rogers** a-7, 8. **Simonson** a-7.*

HOWARD THE DUCK: THE MOVIE
Dec, 1986 - No. 3, Feb, 1987 (mini-series)
Marvel Comics Group

	Good	Fine	Mint
1-4: Movie adaptation		.40	.80

HOW BOYS AND GIRLS CAN HELP WIN THE WAR
1942 (One Shot) (10 cents)
The Parents' Magazine Institute

	Good	Fine	Mint
1	9.00	27.00	62.00

HOWDY DOODY (TV)(See Poll Parrot)
1/50 - No. 38, 7-9/56; No. 761, 1/57; No. 811, 7/57
Dell Publishing Co.

	Good	Fine	Mint
1-Photo-c; 1st TV comic?	12.00	36.00	84.00
2-Photo-c	5.70	17.00	40.00
3-5: 3,5-Photo-c	4.35	13.00	30.00
6-Used in **SOTI**, pg. 309	4.35	13.00	30.00
7-10	3.00	9.00	21.00
11-20	2.30	7.00	16.00
21-38	1.70	5.00	12.00
4-Color 761,811	3.50	10.50	24.00

HOW IT BEGAN (See Single Series No. 15)

HOW SANTA GOT HIS RED SUIT (See March of Comics No. 2)

HOW STALIN HOPES WE WILL DESTROY AMERICA
1951 (16 pgs.) (Giveaway)
Joe Lowe Co. (Pictorial News)

	Good	Fine	Mint
	47.00	140.00	280.00

(Prices vary widely on this book)

HOW THE WEST WAS WON (See Movie Comics)

HOW TO DRAW FOR THE COMICS
No date (1942?) (64 pgs.; B&W & color) (10 Cents) (No ads)
Street and Smith

nn-Art by Winsor McCay, George Marcoux(Supersnipe artist), Vernon Greene(The Shadow artist), Jack Binder(with biog), Thorton Fisher, Jon Small, & Jack Farr. Has biographies of each artist

	Good	Fine	Mint
	10.00	30.00	70.00

H. R. PUFNSTUF (TV) (See March of Comics 360)
Oct, 1970 - No. 8, July, 1972
Gold Key

	Good	Fine	Mint
1	.60	1.75	3.50
2-8	.30	.90	1.80

HUBERT (See 4-Color No. 251)

HUCK & YOGI JAMBOREE (TV)
March, 1961 (116 pgs.; $1.00) (B&W original material)
(6¼x9"; cardboard cover; high quality paper)
Dell Publishing Co.

	Good	Fine	Mint
	1.70	5.00	12.00

HUCK & YOGI WINTER SPORTS (See 4-Color No. 1310)

HUCK FINN (See New Advs. of. . .)

HUCKLEBERRY FINN (See 4-Color No. 1114)

HUCKLEBERRY HOUND (See Dell Giant No. 31,44, Spotlight No. 1, March of Comics No. 199,214,235, Whitman Comic Books & Golden Picture Story Book)

HUCKLEBERRY HOUND (TV)
No. 990, 5-7/59 - No. 43, 10/70 (Hanna-Barbera)
Dell/Gold Key No. 18 (10/62) on

	Good	Fine	Mint
4-Color 990	2.30	7.00	16.00
4-Color 1050,1054 (12/59)	1.70	5.00	12.00
3(1-2/60) - 7 (9-10/60)	1.70	5.00	12.00
4-Color 1141 (10/60)	1.70	5.00	12.00
8-10	1.30	4.00	9.00
11-17 (6-8/62)	1.00	3.00	7.00
18,19 (84pgs.; 18-20 titled . . .Chuckleberry Tales)	2.25	6.75	18.00
20-30: 20-Titled Chuckleberry Tales	.85	2.50	5.00
31-43: 37-reprints	.70	2.00	4.00
. . .Kite Fun Book('61)-16 pgs.; 5x7¼", soft-c	1.70	5.00	12.00

HUCKLEBERRY HOUND (TV)
Nov, 1970 - No. 8, Jan, 1972 (Hanna-Barbera)
Charlton Comics

	Good	Fine	Mint
1	.35	1.00	2.00
2-8		.50	1.00

HUEY, DEWEY, & LOUIE (See Donald Duck, 1938 for 1st app.)

HUEY, DEWEY, & LOUIE BACK TO SCHOOL (See Dell Giant #22,35,49 & Dell Giants)

HUEY, DEWEY AND LOUIE JUNIOR WOODCHUCKS (Disney)
Aug, 1966 - No. 81, 1984 (See Walt Disney's C&S #125)
Gold Key No. 1-61/Whitman No. 62 on

	Good	Fine	Mint
1	2.65	8.00	18.00
2,3(12/68)	1.70	5.00	12.00
4,5(4/70)-Barks-r	1.70	5.00	12.00
6-17-Written by Barks	1.15	3.50	8.00
18,27-30	.70	2.00	4.00
19-23,25-Written by Barks. 22,23,25-Barks-r	.85	2.50	5.00
24,26-Barks-r	.85	2.50	5.00
31-57,60-81: 41,70,80-Reprints	.25	.75	1.50
58,59-Barks-r	.35	1.00	2.00

NOTE: ***Barks** story reprints-No. 22-26,35,42,45,51.*

HUGGA BUNCH (TV)
Oct, 1986 - Present
Star Comics (Marvel)

	Good	Fine	Mint
1-4		.35	.70
5 ($1.00)		.45	.90

HULK, THE (See The Incredible Hulk)

HULK, THE (Formerly The Rampaging Hulk)
No. 10, 8/78 - No. 27, June, 1981 (Magazine)($1.50)(in color)
Marvel Comics Group

	Good	Fine	Mint
10-12: 11-Moon Knight begins by Colan		.60	1.20
13-27: 13-Color issues begin. 23-Anti-Gay issue		.60	1.20

NOTE: ***Alcala** a(i)-15, 17-20, 22, 24-27. **Buscema** a-23; c-26. **Chaykin** a-21-25. **Colan** a(p)-11, 17, 19, 24-27. **Golden** a-20. **Nebres** a-16. **Simonson** a-27; c-23.*

HUMAN FLY
1963 - 1964 (Reprints)
I.W. Enterprises/Super

	Good	Fine	Mint
I.W. Reprint No. 1-Reprints Blue Beetle No. 44('46)	.70	2.00	4.00
Super Reprint No. 10-Reprints Blue Beetle No. 46('47)	.70	2.00	4.00

HUMAN FLY, THE
Sept, 1977 - No. 19, Mar, 1979
Marvel Comics Group

	Good	Fine	Mint
1-Origin; Spider-Man x-over		.40	.80
2-19: 9-Daredevil x-over; Byrne/Austin-c		.25	.50

NOTE: ***Austin** c-4i. **Elias** a-1, 3p, 4p, 7p, 10-12p, 15p, 18p, 19p. **Layton** c-19.*

HUMAN TORCH, THE (Red Raven #1)(See All-Select, All Winners, Marvel Mystery, USA & Young Men)
No. 2, Fall, 1940 - No. 15, Spring, 1944 (becomes Funny Tunes);
No. 16, Fall, 1944 - No. 35, Mar, 1949 (becomes Love Tales);
No. 36, April, 1954 - No. 38, Aug, 1954
Timely/Marvel Comics (TP 2,3/TCI 4-9/SePI 10/SnPC 11-25/CnPC

HUMAN TORCH, THE (continued)
26-35/Atlas Comics (CPC 36-38))

	Good	Fine	Mint
2(#1)-Intro & Origin Toro; The Falcon, The Fiery Mask, Mantor the Magician, & Microman only app.; Human Torch by Burgos, Sub-Mariner by Everett begin (origin of each in text)	457.00	1370.00	3200.00
(Prices vary widely on this book)			
3(#2)-40pg. H.T. story; H.T. & S.M. battle over who is best artist in text-Everett or Burgos	185.00	555.00	1300.00
4(#3)-Origin The Patriot in text; last Everett Sub-Mariner; Sid Greene-a	140.00	420.00	980.00
5(#4)-The Patriot app; Angel x-over in Sub-Mariner. (Summer, 1941)	100.00	300.00	700.00
5-Human Torch battles Sub-Mariner (Fall,'41)	160.00	480.00	1120.00
6,7,9	65.00	195.00	455.00
8-Human Torch battles Sub-Mariner; Wolverton-a, 1 pg.	100.00	300.00	700.00
10-Human Torch battles Sub-Mariner; Wolverton-a, 1 pg.	80.00	240.00	560.00
11-15	50.00	150.00	350.00
16-20: 20-Last War issue	40.00	120.00	280.00
21-30	32.00	95.00	225.00
31-Namora x-over in Sub-Mariner (also #30); last Toro	25.00	75.00	175.00
32-Sungirl, Namora app.; Sungirl-c	25.00	75.00	175.00
33-Capt. America x-over	25.00	75.00	175.00
34-Sungirl solo	25.00	75.00	175.00
35-Captain America & Sungirl app. (1949)	25.00	75.00	175.00
36-38(1954)-Sub-Mariner in all	20.00	60.00	140.00

NOTE: ***Burgos** c-36. **Everett** a-1-3, 27, 28, 30, 37, 38. **Powell** a-36. **Schomburg** c-5, 7, 12, 14, 15, 16, 19. **Mickey Spillane** text 4-6. Bondage-c No. 2, 12, 19. Since there is a six month delay between No. 15 & 16, it is believed that Funny Tunes No. 16 continued after Human Torch No. 15.*

HUMAN TORCH, THE
Sept, 1974 - No. 8, Nov, 1975
Marvel Comics Group

	Good	Fine	Mint
1		.40	.80
2-8		.25	.50

NOTE: *Golden age Torch-r No. 1-8. **Kirby/Ayers** a-1-5,8r.*

HUMBUG (Satire by Harvey Kurtzman)
8/57 - No. 9, 5/58; No. 10, 6/58; No. 11, 10/58
Humbug Publications

	Good	Fine	Mint
1	6.50	19.50	45.00
2	3.00	9.00	21.00
3-9: 8-Elvis in Jailbreak Rock	2.30	7.00	16.00
10,11-Magazine format	2.30	7.00	16.00
Bound Volume(No.1-6)-Sold by publisher	16.00	48.00	110.00
Bound Volume(No.1-9)	20.00	60.00	140.00

NOTE: ***Davis** a-1-11. **Elder** a-2-4, 6-9, 11. **Heath** a-2, 4-8, 10. **Jaffee** a-2, 4-9. **Kurtzman** a-11. **Wood** a-1.*

HUMDINGER
May-June, 1946 - V2/2, July-Aug, 1947
Novelty Press/Premium Group

	Good	Fine	Mint
1-Jerkwater Line, Mickey Starlight by Don Rico, Dink begin	3.50	10.50	24.00
2	2.00	6.00	14.00
3-6,V2No.1,2	1.30	4.00	9.00

HUMOR (See All Humor Comics)

HUMPHREY COMICS
October, 1948 - No. 22, April, 1952
Harvey Publications

	Good	Fine	Mint
1-Joe Palooka's pal (r); Powell-a	5.70	17.00	40.00
2,3: Powell-a	2.65	8.00	18.00
4-Boy Heroes app.; Powell-a	3.50	10.50	24.00
5-8,10: 7-Little Dot app.	2.00	6.00	14.00
9-Origin Humphrey	2.65	8.00	18.00
11-22	1.60	4.70	11.00

HUNCHBACK OF NOTRE DAME, THE (See 4-Color No. 854)

HUNK
August, 1961 - No. 11, 1963
Charlton Comics

	Good	Fine	Mint
1	.50	1.50	3.00
2-11	.25	.75	1.50

HUNTED (Formerly My Love Memoirs)
No. 13, July, 1950 - No. 2, Sept, 1950
Fox Features Syndicate

	Good	Fine	Mint
13(#1)-Used in **SOTI**, pg. 42 & illo.-"Treating police contemptuously" (lower left); Hollingsworth bondage-c	16.00	48.00	110.00
2	5.50	16.50	38.00

HURRICANE COMICS
1945 (52 pgs.)
Cambridge House

	Good	Fine	Mint
1-(Humor, funny animal)	3.00	9.00	21.00

HYPER MYSTERY COMICS
May, 1940 - No. 2, June, 1940
Hyper Publications

	Good	Fine	Mint
1-Hyper, the Phenomenal begins	40.00	120.00	280.00
2	30.00	90.00	210.00

I AIM AT THE STARS (See 4-Color No. 1148)

I AM COYOTE (See Eclipse Graphic Album Series & Eclipse Mag.)

IBIS, THE INVINCIBLE (See Fawcett Min., Mighty Midget & Whiz)
1943 (Feb) - No. 2, 1943; No. 3, Wint, 1945 - No. 6, Spring, 1948
Fawcett Publications

	Good	Fine	Mint
1-Origin Ibis; Raboy-c; on sale 1/2/43	64.00	190.00	450.00
2-Bondage-c	34.00	100.00	240.00
3-Wolverton-a #3-6 (4 pgs. each)	26.00	80.00	180.00
4-6: 5-Bondage-c. 6-Beck-c	21.00	65.00	150.00

ICEMAN
Dec, 1984 - No. 4, June, 1985 (Limited series)
Marvel Comics Group

	Good	Fine	Mint
1	.35	1.00	2.00
2-4	.25	.75	1.50

IDAHO
June-Aug, 1963 - No. 8, July-Sept, 1965
Dell Publishing Co.

	Good	Fine	Mint
1	1.15	3.50	8.00
2-8	.75	2.25	5.00

IDEAL (. . . a Classical Comic) (2nd Series) (Love Romances No. 6?)
July, 1948 - No. 5, March, 1949 (Feature length stories)
Timely Comics

	Good	Fine	Mint
1-Antony & Cleopatra	12.00	36.00	84.00
2-The Corpses of Dr. Sacotti	10.00	30.00	70.00
3-Joan of Arc; used in **SOTI**, pg. 308-'Boer War'	9.50	28.00	65.00
4-Richard the Lion-hearted; titled ". . .the World's Greatest Comics;" The Witness app.	11.00	33.00	76.00
5-Ideal Love & Romance; photo-c	5.50	16.50	38.00

IDEAL COMICS (1st Series) (Willie No. 5 on)
Fall, 1944 - No. 4, Spring, 1946
Timely Comics (MgPC)

	Good	Fine	Mint
1-Super Rabbit in all	5.70	17.00	40.00
2	4.00	12.00	28.00

The Human Torch #2, © MCG

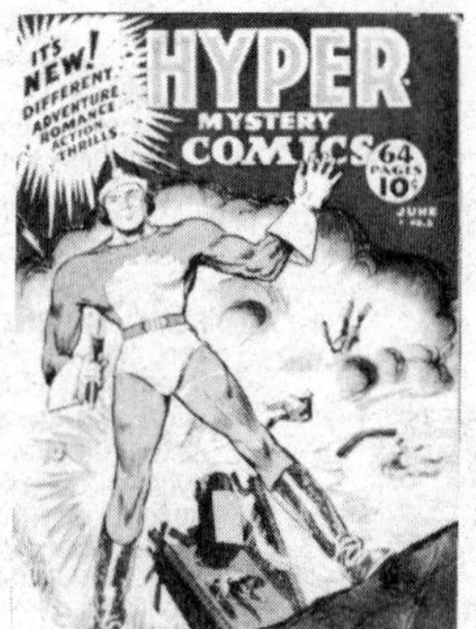

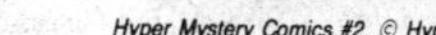
Hyper Mystery Comics #2, © Hyper Publ.

Iceman #1, © MCG

I Love Lucy Comics #3, © Lucille Ball & Desi Arnaz

Impact #3, © WMG

The Incredible Hulk #102, © MCG

IDEAL COMICS (continued)

	Good	Fine	Mint
3,4	3.00	9.00	21.00

IDEAL LOVE & ROMANCE (See Ideal, A Classical Comic)

IDEAL ROMANCE (Formerly Tender Romance)
April, 1954 - No. 8, Feb, 1955 (Diary Confessions No. 9 on)
Key Publications

3	3.00	9.00	21.00
4-8	1.50	4.50	10.00

IDEAL ROMANCES
1950
Stanmor

6	1.70	5.00	12.00

I DREAM OF JEANNIE (TV)
April, 1965 - No. 2, Dec, 1966 (Photo-c)
Dell Publishing Co.

1,2	2.65	8.00	18.00

IF THE DEVIL WOULD TALK
1950; 1958 (32 pgs.; paper cover; in full color)
Roman Catholic Catechetical Guild/Impact Publ.

nn-(Scarce)-About secularism (20-30 copies known to exist); very low distribution	50.00	150.00	350.00
1958 Edition-(Rare)-(Impact Publ.); art & script changed to meet church criticism of earlier edition; only 6 known copies exist	50.00	150.00	350.00
Black & White version of nn edition; small size; only 4 known copies exist	30.00	90.00	200.00

NOTE: *The original edition of this book was printed and killed by the Guild's board of directors. It is believed that a very limited number of copies were distributed. The 1958 version was a complete bomb with very limited, if any, circulation. In 1979, 11 original, 4 1958 reprints, and 4 B&W's surfaced from the Guild's old files in St. Paul, Minnesota.*

ILLUSTRATED GAGS (See Single Series No. 16)

ILLUSTRATED LIBRARY OF. . ., AN (See Classics Illustrated Giants)

ILLUSTRATED STORIES OF THE OPERAS
1943 (16 pgs.; B&W) (25 cents) (cover-B&W & red)
Baily (Bernard) Publ. Co.

nn-(Rare)-Faust (part-r in Cisco Kid #1)	16.00	48.00	110.00
nn-(Rare)-Aida	16.00	48.00	110.00
nn-(Rare)-Carmen; Baily-a	16.00	48.00	110.00
nn-(Rare)-Rigoleito	16.00	48.00	110.00

ILLUSTRATED STORY OF ROBIN HOOD & HIS MERRY MEN, THE (See Robin Hood)

ILLUSTRATED TARZAN BOOK, THE (See Tarzan Book)

I LOVED (Formerly Rulah; Colossal Feature Mag. No. 33 on)
No. 28, July, 1949 - No. 32, Mar, 1950
Fox Features Syndicate

28	4.00	12.00	28.00
29-32	2.65	8.00	18.00

I LOVE LUCY COMICS (TV) (Also see The Lucy Show)
No. 535, Feb, 1954 - No. 35, Apr-June, 1962 (All photo-c)
Dell Publishing Co.

4-Color 535(#1)	8.00	24.00	56.00
4-Color 559 (5/54)(#2)	4.70	17.00	40.00
3 (8-10/54) - 5	5.00	15.00	35.00
6-10	4.35	13.00	30.00
11-20	4.00	12.00	28.00
21-35	3.50	10.50	24.00

I LOVE YOU
June, 1950 (One shot)
Fawcett Publications

1	5.50	16.50	38.00

I LOVE YOU (Formerly In Love)
No. 7, 9/55 - No. 121, 12/76; No. 122, 3/79 - No. 130, 5/80
Charlton Comics

	Good	Fine	Mint
7-Kirby-c, Powell-a	3.70	11.00	26.00
8-10	1.15	3.50	8.00
11-16,18-20	1.00	3.00	7.00
17-68 pg. Giant	1.30	4.00	9.00
21-25,27-50	.55	1.65	4.00
26-Torres-a	1.00	3.00	7.00
51-59	.35	1.00	2.00
60(1/66)-Elvis Presley drawn c/story	5.00	15.00	35.00
61-130		.40	.80

I'M A COP
1954
Magazine Enterprises

1(A-1 111)	4.60	14.00	32.00
2(A-1 126), 3(A-1 128)	2.30	7.00	16.00

NOTE: ***Powell** c/a-1-3.*

I'M DICKENS - HE'S FENSTER (TV)
May-July, 1963 - No. 2, Aug-Oct, 1963 (Photo-c)
Dell Publishing Co.

1,2	1.50	4.50	10.00

I MET A HANDSOME COWBOY (See 4-Color No. 324)

IMMORTAL DOCTOR FATE, THE
Jan, 1985 - No. 3, Mar, 1985 (Mini-series)
DC Comics

1-Simonson c/a		.65	1.30
2,3: 2-Giffen c/a(p)		.65	1.30

IMPACT
Mar-Apr, 1955 - No. 5, Nov-Dec, 1955
E. C. Comics

1	7.00	21.00	50.00
2	5.00	15.00	35.00
3-5: 4-Crandall-a	4.50	13.50	32.00

NOTE: ***Crandall** a-1-4. **Davis** a-2-4; c-1-5. **Evans** a-1, 4, 5. **Ingels** a-in all. **Kamen** a-3. **Krigstein** a-1, 5. **Orlando** a-2, 5.*

INCREDIBLE HULK, THE (See Aurora, Marvel Fanfare, Marvel Treas. Ed. & Rampaging Hulk)
May, 1962 - No. 6, Mar, 1963; No. 102, Apr, 1968 - Present
Marvel Comics Group

1-Origin	94.00	250.00	660.00
2	35.00	90.00	245.00
3-Origin retold	25.00	65.00	175.00
4-6: 4-Brief origin retold. 6-Intro. Teen Brigade	18.00	45.00	128.00
102-(Formerly Tales to Astonish)-Origin retold	2.40	7.00	17.00
103-110: 105-1st Missing Link	.85	2.60	5.20
111-115	.40	1.25	2.50
116-125	.35	1.00	2.00
126-139: 126-1st Barbara Norriss (Valkyrie). 131-1st Jim Wilson, Hulk's new sidekick. 136-1st Xeron, The Star-Slayer	.25	.75	1.50
140-Written by Harlan Ellison; 1st Jarella, Hulk's love	.25	.75	1.50
141-1st app. Doc Samson	.40	1.20	2.40
142-160: 145-52 pgs. 149-1st The Inheritor. 155-1st app. Shaper	.25	.75	1.50
161,163-175,179: 161-The Mimic dies. 163-1st app. The Gremlin. 164-1st app. Capt. Omen & Colonel John D. Armbruster. 166-1st Zzzax. 168-1st The Harpy. 169-1st Bi-Beast. 172-X-Men cameo; origin Juggernaut retold		.50	1.00
162-1st app. The Wendigo	.50	1.50	3.00

INCREDIBLE HULK, THE (continued)

	Good	Fine	Mint
176-178-Warlock app.	.50	1.50	3.00
180-1st app. Wolverine(cameo)	1.70	5.00	10.00
181-Wolverine app.	6.00	18.00	36.00
182-Wolverine cameo; 1st Crackajack Jackson	1.35	4.00	8.00
183-199: 185-Death of Col. Armbruster	.25	.75	1.50
200-Silver Surfer app.	.50	1.50	3.50
201-240: 212-1st The Constrictor		.60	1.20
241-249,251-271: 271-Rocket Raccoon app.		.40	.80
250-Giant size; Silver Surfer app.		.60	1.20
272-Alpha Flight app.	.35	1.00	2.00
273-299,301-313: 279-X-men & Alpha Flight cameos		.40	.80
300-Double size		.50	1.00
314-Byrne-c/a begins, ends #319	.50	1.50	3.00
315-320		.60	1.20
321-339,341,342: 336-X-Factor app.		.40	.80
340-Wolverine app.	.35	1.00	2.00
Giant-Size 1 ('75)	.40	1.10	2.20
Special 1 (10/68)-New material; Steranko-c	1.20	3.50	7.00
Special 2 (10/69)-Origin retold	.70	2.00	4.00
Special 3(1/71)	.50	1.50	3.00
Annual 4 (1/72),5(10/76)		.60	1.20
Annual 6 (11/77)		.50	1.00
Annual 7(8/78)-Byrne/Layton-c/a; Iceman & Angel app.	.50	1.50	3.00
8(11/79), 9(9/80), 10('81)		.50	1.00
Annual 11(10/82)-Miller, Buckler-a(p)		.50	1.00
Annual 12(8/83), 13(11/84)		.50	1.00
Annual 14(12/85), 15(10/86)		.65	1.30
Special 1(. . .Versus Quasimodo,3/83)-Based on Sat. morning cartoon		.25	.50

NOTE: ***Adkins*** *a-111-16i.* ***Austin*** *c-302i.* ***J. Buscema*** *c-202p.* ***Byrne*** *a-314p-319p; c-314-316, 318, 319.* ***Ditko*** *a-2, 6, 249, Annual 2r(3), 3r, 9p; c-2i, 6, 235, 249.* ***Everett*** *c-133i.* ***Golden*** *c-248, 251.* ***Kane*** *c(p)-193, 194, 196, 198.* ***Kirby*** *a-1-5, Special 2, 3p, Annual 5p; c-1-5, Annual 5.* ***Miller*** *c-258p, 261, 264, 268.* ***Mooney*** *a-230p, 287i, 288i.* ***Powell*** *a-Special 3r(2).* ***Severin*** *a(i)-108-110, 131-33, 141-51, 153-55; c(i)-109, 110, 132, 142, 144-55.* ***Simonson*** *c-283.* ***Starlin*** *a-222p; c-217.* ***Staton*** *a(i)-187-89, 191-209.* ***Tuska*** *a-102i, 105i, 106i, 218p.* ***Williamson*** *a-310i; c-310i, 311i.* ***Wrightson*** *c-197.*

INCREDIBLE HULK AND WOLVERINE, THE
Oct, 1986 (One shot)
Marvel Comics Group

	Good	Fine	Mint
1-r-/1st app. Wolverine	.45	1.30	2.60

INCREDIBLE MR. LIMPET, THE (See Movie Classics)

INCREDIBLE SCIENCE FICTION (Formerly Weird Science-Fantasy)
July-Aug, 1955 - No. 33, Jan-Feb, 1956
E. C. Comics

	Good	Fine	Mint
30,33: 33-Story-r/W.F. No. 18	18.00	54.00	125.00
31-Williamson/Krenkel-a, Wood-a(2)	22.00	65.00	154.00
32-Williamson/Krenkel-a	22.00	65.00	154.00

NOTE: ***Davis*** *a-30, 32, 33; c-30-32.* ***Krigstein*** *a-in all.* ***Orlando*** *a-30, 32, 33("Judgement Day" reprint).* ***Wood*** *a-30, 31, 33; c-33.*

INDIANA JONES (See Further Adventures of. . .)

INDIANA JONES AND THE TEMPLE OF DOOM
Sept, 1984 - No. 3, Nov, 1984
Marvel Comics Group

	Good	Fine	Mint
1-3-r/Marvel Super Special; movie adaptation by Guice		.30	.60

INDIAN BRAVES (Baffling Mysteries No. 5 on)
March, 1951 - No. 4, Sept, 1951
Ace Magazines

	Good	Fine	Mint
1	3.00	9.00	21.00
2	1.50	4.50	10.00

	Good	Fine	Mint
3,4	1.15	3.50	8.00
I.W. Reprint No. 1 (no date)	.50	1.50	3.00

INDIAN CHIEF (White Eagle. . .) (Formerly The Chief)
No. 3, July-Sept, 1951 - No. 33, Jan-Mar, 1959
Dell Publishing Co.

	Good	Fine	Mint
3	1.70	5.00	12.00
4-11: 6-White Eagle app.	1.15	3.50	8.00
12-1st White Eagle(10-12/53)-Not same as earlier character	1.70	5.00	12.00
13-29	1.00	3.00	7.00
30-33-Buscema-a	1.15	3.50	8.00

INDIAN CHIEF (See March of Comics No. 94,110,127,140,159,170,187)

INDIAN FIGHTER, THE (See 4-Color No. 687)

INDIAN FIGHTER
May, 1950 - No. 11, Jan, 1952
Youthful Magazines

	Good	Fine	Mint
1	3.00	9.00	21.00
2-Wildey-a/c(bondage)	1.50	4.50	10.00
3-11: 3,4-Wildey-a	1.15	3.50	8.00

INDIAN LEGENDS OF THE NIAGARA (See American Graphics)

INDIANS
Spring, 1950 - No. 17, Spring, 1953
Fiction House Magazines (Wings Publ. Co.)

	Good	Fine	Mint
1-Manzar, White Indian, Long Bow & Orphan of the Storm begin	7.00	21.00	50.00
2-Starlight begins	3.70	11.00	26.00
3-5	3.50	10.50	24.00
6-10	2.30	7.00	16.00
11-17	2.00	6.00	14.00

INDIANS OF THE WILD WEST
Circa 1958? (no date) (Reprints)
I. W. Enterprises

	Good	Fine	Mint
9-Kinstler-c; Whitman-a	.50	1.50	3.00

INDIANS ON THE WARPATH
No date (Late 40s, early 50s) (132 pages)
St. John Publishing Co.

	Good	Fine	Mint
nn-Matt Baker-c; contains St. John comics rebound. Many combinations possible	13.00	40.00	90.00

INDIAN TRIBES (See Famous Indian Tribes)

INDIAN WARRIORS (Formerly White Rider. . .)
No. 7, June, 1951 - No. 11, 1952
Star Publications

	Good	Fine	Mint
7	3.50	10.50	24.00
8-11: 11-White Rider & Superhorse app.; L. B. Cole-c	2.35	7.00	16.00
3-D 1(12/53)-L. B. Cole-c	16.00	48.00	110.00
Accepted Reprint(nn)(inside cover shows White Rider & Superhorse #11)-R-/cover/#7; origin White Rider & . .	1.70	5.00	12.00
Accepted Reprint #8 (nd); L.B. Cole-c	1.70	5.00	12.00

INDOORS-OUTDOORS (See Wisco)

INDOOR SPORTS
nd (64 pgs.; 6x9"; B&W reprints; hardcover)
National Specials Co.

	Good	Fine	Mint
By Tad	3.35	10.00	20.00

INFERIOR FIVE, THE (. . .5 No. 11,12) (See Showcase)
3-4/67 - No. 10, 9-10/68; No. 11, 8-9/72 - No. 12, 10-11/72
National Periodical Publications

	Good	Fine	Mint
1-Sekowsky-a(p)	.50	1.50	3.00
2-Plastic Man app.; Sekowsky-a(p)	.35	1.00	2.00

The Incredible Hulk #181, © MCG

The Incredible Hulk and Wolverine #1, © MCG

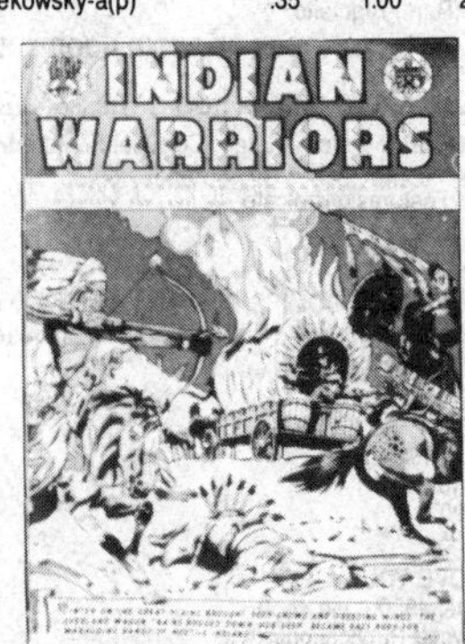

Indian Warriors #7, © STAR

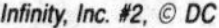
Infinity, Inc. #2, © DC

International Crime Patrol #6, © WMG

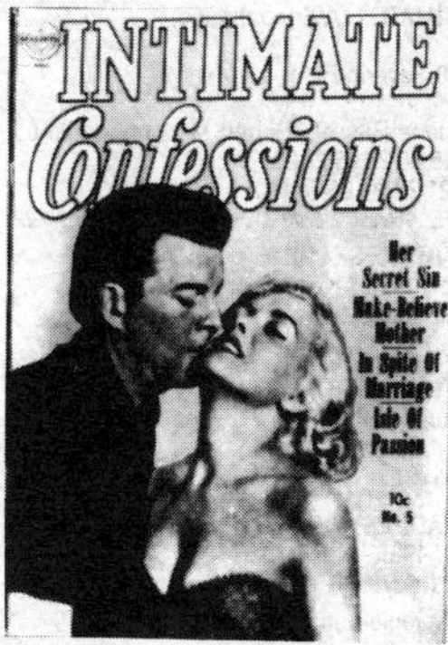

Intimate Confessions #5, © REAL

INFERIOR FIVE, THE (continued) — Good / Fine / Mint
3-10: 10-Superman x-over .25 .75 1.50
11,12-Orlando c/a; both r-/Showcase #62,63 .25 .75 1.50

INFINITY, INC.
March, 1984 - Present ($1.25; Baxter paper; 36 pgs.)
DC Comics
1-Brainwave, Jr., Fury, The Huntress, Jade, Northwind, Nuklon, Obsidian, Power Girl, Silver Scarab & Star Spangled Kid begin .60 1.75 3.50
2-5: 2-Dr. Midnite, G.A. Flash, W. Woman, Dr. Fate, Hourman, Gr. Lantern, Wildcat app. 5-Nudity panels .35 1.10 2.20
6-10 .30 .95 1.90
11-17 .70 1.40
18-22-Crisis x-over. 21-Intro new Hourman & Dr. Midnight .25 .80 1.60
23-30: 26-New Wildcat app. .70 1.40
31-50: 31-Star-Spangled Kid becomes Skyman. 32-Green Fury be-becomes Green Flame. 33-Origin Obsidian .25 .70 1.40
Annual 1 (12/85)-Crisis x-over .35 1.00 2.00
Special 1 ('87, $1.50) .25 .75 1.50
NOTE: ***Kubert*** *r-4.* ***Newton*** *a-12p, 13p(last work 4/85).* ***Tuska*** *a-11p. JSA app. 3-10.*

INFORMER, THE
April, 1954 - No. 5, Dec, 1954
Feature Television Productions
1-Sekowsky-a begins 3.50 10.50 24.00
2 2.30 7.00 16.00
3-5 1.70 5.00 12.00

IN HIS STEPS
1973, 1977 (39, 49 cents)
Spire Christian Comics (Fleming H. Revell Co.)
nn .40 .80

INHUMANOIDS, THE (TV)
Jan, 1987 - Present
Star Comics (Marvel)
1-10: Based on Hasbro toys .50 1.00

INHUMANS, THE (See Amazing Advs.)
Oct, 1975 - No. 12, Aug, 1977
Marvel Comics Group
1 .50 1.00
2-12: 9-Reprints .30 .60
NOTE: ***Buckler*** *c-2p-4p, 5.* ***Gil Kane*** *a-5-7p; c-1p, 7p, 8p.* ***Kirby*** *a-9r.* ***Mooney*** *a-11i.* ***Perez*** *a-1-4p, 8p.*

INKY & DINKY (See Felix's Nephews. . .)

IN LOVE (I Love You No. 7 on)
Aug-Sept, 1954 - No. 6, July, 1955
Mainline/Charlton No. 5 (5/55)-on
1-Simon & Kirby-a 7.00 21.00 50.00
2-S&K-a 3.50 10.50 24.00
3,4-S&K-a 2.65 8.00 18.00
5-S&K-c only 1.65 5.00 11.50
6-No S&K-a 1.15 3.50 8.00

IN LOVE WITH JESUS
1952 (36 pages) (Giveaway)
Catechetical Educational Society
4.00 12.00 28.00

IN SEARCH OF THE CASTAWAYS (See Movie Comics)

INSIDE CRIME (Formerly My Intimate Affair)
No. 3, July, 1950 - No. 2, Sept, 1950
Fox Features Syndicate (Hero Books)
3-Wood-a, 10 pgs.; L. B. Cole-c 10.00 30.00 70.00
2(9/50)-Used in **SOTI**, pg. 182-3; Lingerie panel; r-/Spook #24 — Good / Fine / Mint 9.50 28.00 65.00
nn(no publ. listed, nd) 3.50 10.50 24.00

INSPECTOR, THE (Also see The Pink Panther)
July, 1974 - No. 19, Feb, 1978
Gold Key
1 .60 1.75 3.50
2-5 .30 .90 1.80
6-19: 11-Reprints .50 1.00

INSPECTOR WADE (See Feature Books No. 13, McKay)

INTERNATIONAL COMICS (. . .Crime Patrol No. 6)
Spring, 1947 - No. 5, Nov-Dec, 1947
E. C. Comics
1 30.00 90.00 210.00
2 23.00 70.00 160.00
3-5 20.00 60.00 140.00

INTERNATIONAL CRIME PATROL (Formerly International Comics No. 1-5; becomes Crime Patrol No. 7 on)
Spring, 1948
E. C. Comics
6-Moon Girl app. 30.00 90.00 210.00

INTERSTATE THEATRES' FUN CLUB COMICS
Mid 1940's (10 cents on cover) (B&W cover) (Premium)
Interstate Theatres
Cover features MLJ characters looking at a copy of Top-Notch Comics, but contains an early Detective Comic on inside; many combinations possible
5.35 16.00 24.00

IN THE DAYS OF THE MOB (Magazine)
Fall, 1971 (Black & White)
Hampshire Dist. Ltd. (National)
1-Kirby-a; has John Dillinger wanted poster inside .80 2.40 3.60

IN THE PRESENCE OF MINE ENEMIES
1973 (35-49 cents)
Spire Christian Comics/Fleming H. Revell Co.
.50 1.00

INTIMATE (Teen-Age Love No. 4 on?)
December, 1957 - No. 3, May, 1958
Charlton Comics
1-3 1.00 3.00 7.00

INTIMATE CONFESSIONS (See Fox Giants)

INTIMATE CONFESSIONS
July-Aug, 1951 - No. 7, Aug, 1952; No. 8, Mar, 1953
Realistic Comics
1-Kinstler-c/a; c/Avon paperback 222 50.00 150.00 350.00
2 9.00 27.00 60.00
3-c/Avon paperback 250; Kinstler-c/a 12.00 36.00 80.00
4-c/Avon paperback 304; Kinstler-c 9.00 27.00 60.00
5 9.00 27.00 60.00
6-c/Avon paperback 120 9.00 27.00 60.00
7-Spanking panel 10.00 30.00 70.00
8-c/Avon paperback 375; Kinstler-a 9.00 27.00 60.00

INTIMATE CONFESSIONS
1964
I. W. Enterprises/Super Comics
I.W. Reprint #9,10 .70 2.00 4.00
Super Reprint #12,18 .70 2.00 4.00

INTIMATE LOVE
1950 - No. 28, Aug, 1954
Standard Comics

INTIMATE LOVE (continued)	Good	Fine	Mint
5	2.30	7.00	16.00
6-8-Severin/Elder-a	3.00	9.00	21.00
9	1.15	3.50	8.00
10-Jane Russell, Robert Mitchum photo-c	2.65	8.00	18.00
11-18,20,23,25,27,28	1.00	3.00	7.00
19,21,22,24,26-Toth-a	3.50	10.50	24.00

NOTE: ***Celardo** a-8, 10. **Colletta** a-23. **Moreira** a-13(2). Photo-c-6, 7, 14, 18, 20, 24.*

INTIMATE SECRETS OF ROMANCE
Sept, 1953 - No. 2, April, 1954
Star Publications

	Good	Fine	Mint
1,2-L. B. Cole-c	4.35	13.00	30.00

INTRIGUE
January, 1955
Quality Comics Group

	Good	Fine	Mint
1-Horror; Jack Cole reprt/Web of Evil	7.00	21.00	50.00

INVADERS, THE (TV)
Oct, 1967 - No. 4, Oct, 1968 (All have photo-c)
Gold Key

	Good	Fine	Mint
1-Spiegle-a in all	3.00	9.00	21.00
2-4	2.00	6.00	14.00

INVADERS, THE (Also see Avengers No. 71)
August, 1975 - No. 41, Sept, 1979
Marvel Comics Group

	Good	Fine	Mint
1-Captain America, Sub-Mariner & Human Torch begin	.40	1.20	2.40
2-1st app. Mailbag & Brain-Drain		.60	1.20
3-5: 3-Intro U-Man		.35	.70
6-Liberty Legion app; intro/1st app. Union Jack. Two cover prices, 25 & 30 cents		.35	.70
7-10: 7-Intro Baron Blood; Human Torch origin retold. 9-Origin Baron Blood. 10-G.A. C. Amer.-r		.35	.70
11-Origin Spitfire; intro The Blue Bullet		.25	.50
12-19: 14-1st app. The Crusaders. 16-Re-intro The Destroyer. 17-Intro Warrior Woman. 18-Re-intro The Destroyer w/new origin.		.25	.50
20-Reprints Sub-Mariner story/Motion Picture Funnies Weekly with color added & brief write-up about MPFW		.25	.50
21-r-/Marvel Mystery #10		.25	.50
22-30: 22-New origin Toro. 24-r-/Marvel Mystery #17. 28-Intro new Human Top & Golden Girl. 29-Intro Teutonic Knight		.25	.50
31-40(5/79): 34-Mighty Destroyer joins		.25	.50
41-Double size		.25	.50
Giant Size . . . 1(6/75)-50 cents; origin; GA Sub-Mariner r-/Sub-Mariner 1; intro Master-Man		.50	1.00
Annual 1(9/77)-Schomburg, Rico stories; Schomburg-c; Avengers app; re-intro The Shark & The Hyena		.35	.70

NOTE: ***Buckler** a-5. **Everett** a-21r(1940), 24r, Annual 1r. **Gil Kane** c(p)-13, 17, 18, 20-27. **Kirby** c(p)-3-12, 14-16, 32, 33. **Mooney** a-5, 16, 22.*

INVISIBLE BOY (See Approved Comics)

INVISIBLE MAN, THE (See Superior Stories No. 1)

INVISIBLE SCARLET O'NEIL (Also see Harvey Comics Hits 59)
Dec, 1950 - No. 3, April, 1951
Famous Funnies (Harvey)

	Good	Fine	Mint
1	9.50	28.00	65.00
2,3	6.50	19.50	45.00

IRON CORPORAL, THE (See Army War Heroes)
No. 23, Oct, 1985 - No. 25, Feb, 1986
Charlton Comics

	Good	Fine	Mint
23-25: Glanzman-a(r)		.40	.75

IRON FIST (Also see Marvel Premiere & Powerman & Iron Fist)
Nov, 1975 - No. 15, Sept, 1977
Marvel Comics Group

	Good	Fine	Mint
1-McWilliams-a(i); Iron Man app.	1.85	5.50	11.00
2	1.00	3.00	6.00
3-5	.75	2.25	4.50
6-10: 8-Origin retold	.60	1.80	3.60
11-13: 12-Capt. America app.	.45	1.40	2.80
14-1st app. Saber Tooth	1.15	3.50	7.00
15-New X-Men app., Byrne-a	3.70	11.00	22.00
15 (35 cent edition)	5.00	15.00	30.00

NOTE: ***Adkins** a-8p, 13i; c-8i. **Byrne** a-1-15p; c-8p, 15p. **G. Kane** c-4-6p.*

IRON HORSE (TV)
March, 1967 - No. 2, June, 1967
Dell Publishing Co.

	Good	Fine	Mint
1,2	1.00	3.00	7.00

IRON JAW (Also see The Barbarians)
Jan, 1975 - No. 4, July, 1975
Atlas/Seaboard Publ.

	Good	Fine	Mint
1-Adams-c; Sekowsky-a(p)	.25	.75	1.50
2-Adams-c		.50	1.00
3,4: 4-Origin		.30	.60

IRON MAN (Also see Marvel Double Feat., Marvel Fanfare & Tales of Suspense)
May, 1968 - Present
Marvel Comics Group

	Good	Fine	Mint
1-Origin	9.00	27.00	63.00
2	4.45	13.00	31.00
3-5	2.30	7.00	16.00
6-10	1.50	4.50	10.50
11-15	1.05	3.15	6.30
16-20	.70	2.10	4.20
21-40: 22-Death of Janice Cord. 27-Intro Fire Brand. 33-Intro Spymaster	.55	1.60	3.20
41-46,48-50: 43-Intro The Guardsman. 46-The Guardsman dies. 50-Princess Python app.	.45	1.30	2.60
47-Origin retold; Smith-a(p)	.90	2.75	5.20
51-54	.45	1.30	2.60
55,56-Starlin-a; 55-Starlin-c	.70	2.10	4.20
57-67,69,70: 65-Origin Dr. Spectrum	.35	1.05	2.10
68-Starlin-c; origin retold	.35	1.15	2.30
71-85: 76 r-/#9	.30	.95	1.90
86-1st app. Blizzard	.30	.95	1.90
87-Origin Blizzard	.30	.95	1.90
88-99	.30	.95	1.90
100-Starlin-c	.65	1.90	3.80
101-117: 101-Intro DreadKnight. 109-1st app. new Crimson Dynamo. 110-Origin Jack of Hearts retold	.25	.80	1.60
118-Byrne-a(p)	.70	2.00	4.00
119,120,123-128-Tony Stark recovers from alcohol problem	.45	1.25	2.50
121,122,129-149: 122-Origin		.50	1.00
150-Double size		.60	1.20
151-158,160: 152-New armor		.50	1.00
159-Paul Smith-c/a(p)	.35	1.10	2.20
161-Moon Knight app.		.50	1.00
162-168: 167-Tony Stark alcohol problem starts again		.50	1.00
169-New Iron Man (Jim Rhodes replaces Tony Stark)	.70	2.00	4.00
170	.40	1.25	2.50
171	.25	.75	1.50
172-199: 186-Intro Vibro. 191-Tony Stark new armor		.60	1.20
200-Double size ($1.25)	.35	1.00	2.00

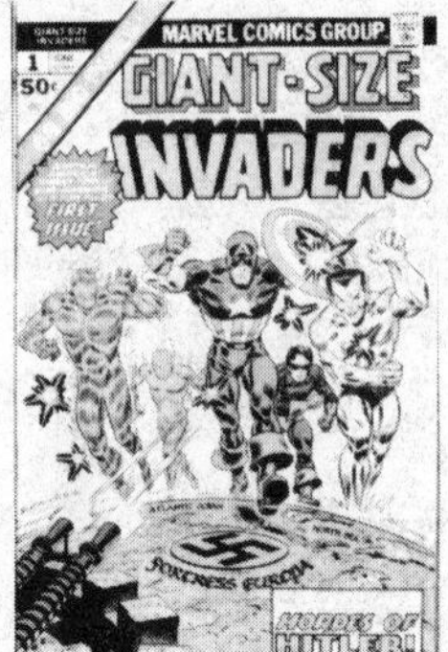

Giant-Size Invaders #1, © MCG

Iron Fist #4, © MCG

Iron Man #17, © MCG

Ironwolf #1, © DC

It Really Happened #8, © STD

It's About Time #1, © GK

IRON MAN (continued)	Good	Fine	Mint
201-224: 213-Intro new Dominic Fortune		.45	.90
225-Double size		.65	1.30
226-230		.40	.80
Giant Size 1('75)-Ditko-a(r)	.35	1.00	2.00
Special 1(8/70)-Everett-c	.70	2.00	4.00
Special 2(11/71)	.35	1.00	2.00
Annual 3(6/76)-Man-Thing app.	.30	.80	1.60
Annual 5(12/82), 6(11/83), 7(10/84)		.65	1.30
Annual 8(10/86)-X-Factor app.		.65	1.30
Annual 9(12/87)		.65	1.30
King Size 4(8/77)-Newton-a(i)	.25	.80	1.60

NOTE: ***Austin** c-105i, 109-11i, 151i. **Byrne** a-118p; c-109p. **Colan** a-Special 1p(3). **Craig** a-1i, 2-4, 5-13i, 14, 15-19i, 24p, 25p, 26-28i; c-2-4. **Ditko** a-160p. **Giffen** a-114p. **G. Kane** c(p)-52-54, 63, 67, 72-75, 77, 78, 88, 98. **Kirby** a-Special 1p; c-80p, 90, 92-95. **Layton** a-116-128i, 130, 131-135i, 137-139, 140-154i, 215i-217i, 218, 219, 220i, 223, Annual 9i; c-116i, 118, 119i, 120, 121, 122i, 123, 124i, 125, 126i, 127-48, 149i, 150i, 151p, 152p, 153, 154i, 155, 156i, 157i, 158, 202, 215i-217i, 218, 219, 220i, 222i, 223, Annual 9i. **Mooney** a-40i, 47i. **Perez** c-103p. **Starlin** a-53p, 55p, 56p; c-55p, 160, 163. **Tuska** a-5-13p, 15-23p, 24i, 32p, 38-46p, 48-54p, 57-61p, 63-69p, 70-72p, 78p, 86-92p, 95-106p, Annual 4p. **Wood** a-Special 1i.*

IRON MAN & SUB-MARINER
April, 1968 (One Shot)
Marvel Comics Group

1-Colan/Craig-a-Iron Man; Colan-c	1.70	5.00	12.00

IRON VIC (See Comics Revue No. 3)
1940; Aug, 1947 - No. 3, 1947
United Features Syndicate/St. John Publ. Co.

Single Series 22	12.00	36.00	84.00
2,3(St. John)	2.00	6.00	14.00

IRONWOLF
1986 ($2.00, one shot)
DC Comics

1	.35	1.00	2.00

ISIS (TV) (Also see Shazam)
Oct-Nov, 1976 - No. 8, Dec-Jan, 1977-78
National Periodical Publications/DC Comics

1-Wood inks		.40	.80
2-8: 5-Isis new look. 7-Origin		.25	.50

ISLAND AT THE TOP OF THE WORLD (See Walt Disney Showcase 27)

ISLAND OF DR. MOREAU, THE (Movie)
October, 1977 (52 pgs.)
Marvel Comics Group

1		.50	1.00

I SPY (TV)
Aug, 1966 - No. 6, Sept, 1968 (Photo-c)
Gold Key

1-Bill Cosby, Robert Culp photo-c	3.50	10.50	24.00
2-6: 3,4-McWilliams-a	2.00	6.00	14.00

IS THIS TOMORROW?
1947 (One Shot) (3 editions) (52 pages)
Catechetical Guild

1-Theme of communists taking over the USA; (no price on cover) Used in **POP**, pg. 102	12.00	36.00	80.00
1-(10 cents on cover)	17.00	51.00	120.00
1-Has blank circle with no price on cover	17.00	51.00	120.00
Black & White advance copy titled "Confidential"-(52 pgs.)-Contains script and art edited out of the color edition, including one page of extreme violence showing mob nailing a Cardinal to a door; (only two known copies)	50.00	150.00	320.00

NOTE: *The original color version first sold for 10 cents. Since sales were good, it was later printed as a giveaway. Approximately four million in total were printed. The two black and white copies listed plus two other versions as well as a full color untrimmed version surfaced in 1979 from the Guild's old files in St. Paul, Minnesota.*

IT! (See Supernatural Thrillers No.1 & Astonishing Tales No.21-24)

IT HAPPENS IN THE BEST FAMILIES
1920 (52 pages) (B&W Sundays)
Powers Photo Engraving Co.

	Good	Fine	Mint
By Briggs	6.00	18.00	42.00
Special Railroad Edition(30 cents)-r-/strips from 1914-1920	5.00	15.00	35.00

IT REALLY HAPPENED
1944 - No. 11, Oct, 1947
William H. Wise No. 1,2/Standard (Visual Editions)

1	5.50	16.50	38.00
2	3.15	9.50	22.00
3-7,9	2.65	8.00	18.00
8-Story of Roy Rogers	5.00	15.00	35.00
10-Honus Wagner story	3.15	9.50	22.00
11-Baker-a	4.35	13.00	30.00

NOTE: ***Guardineer** a-7(2), 8(2), 11. **Schomburg** c-1-7, 9-11.*

IT RHYMES WITH LUST (Also see Bold Stories, Candid Tales)
1950 (Digest size) (128 pages)
St. John Publishing Co.

(Rare)-Matt Baker & Ray Osrin-a	27.00	81.00	190.00

IT'S ABOUT TIME (TV)
January, 1967
Gold Key

1 (10195-701)-Photo-c	2.00	6.00	14.00

IT'S A DUCK'S LIFE
Feb, 1950 - No. 11, Feb, 1952
Marvel Comics/Atlas(MMC)

1-Buck Duck, Super Rabbit begin	4.60	14.00	32.00
2	2.30	7.00	16.00
3-11	1.50	4.50	10.00

IT'S FUN TO STAY ALIVE (Giveaway)
1948 (16 pgs.) (heavy stock paper)
National Automobile Dealers Association

Featuring: Bugs Bunny, The Berrys, Dixie Dugan, Elmer, Tim Tyler, Bruce Gentry, Abbie & Slats, Joe Jinks, The Toodles, & Cokey; all art copyright 1946-48 drawn especially for this book.	10.00	30.00	70.00

IT'S GAMETIME
Sept-Oct, 1955 - No. 4, Mar-Apr, 1956
National Periodical Publications

1-(Scarce)-Infinity-c; Davy Crockett app. in puzzle	20.00	60.00	140.00
2-4(Scarce): 2-Dodo & The Frog	17.00	51.00	120.00

IT'S LOVE, LOVE, LOVE
November, 1957 - No. 2, Jan, 1958 (10 cents)
St. John Publishing Co.

1,2	2.15	6.50	15.00

IVANHOE (See Fawcett Movie Comics No. 20)

IVANHOE
July-Sept, 1963
Dell Publishing Co.

1 (12-373-309)	2.00	6.00	14.00

IWO JIMA (See Spectacular Features Magazine)

JACE PEARSON OF THE TEXAS RANGERS (Tales of the Texas Rangers 4-Color 396; . . .'s Tales of . . . #11-on)(See Western Roundup)
No. 396, 5/52 - No. 1021, 8-10/59 (No #10) (All-Photo-c)
Dell Publishing Co.

JACE PEARSON (continued)

	Good	Fine	Mint
4-Color 396 (#1)	4.35	13.00	30.00
2(5-7/53)	3.00	9.00	21.00
3-9(2-4/55)	3.00	9.00	21.00
4-Color 648(9/55)	3.00	9.00	21.00
11(11-2/55/56) - 14,17-20(6-8/58)	2.65	8.00	18.00
15,16-Toth-a	4.00	12.00	28.00
4-Color 961-Spiegle-a	3.00	9.00	21.00
4-Color 1021	2.65	8.00	18.00

JACK & JILL VISIT TOYTOWN WITH ELMER THE ELF
1949 (16 pgs.) (paper cover)
Butler Brothers (Toytown Stores Giveaway)

	Good	Fine	Mint
	1.70	5.00	10.00

JACK ARMSTRONG
11/47 - No. 9, 9/48; No. 10, 3/49 - No. 13, Sept, 1949
Parents' Institute

	Good	Fine	Mint
1	9.50	28.00	65.00
2	4.60	14.00	32.00
3-5	4.00	12.00	28.00
6-13	2.85	8.50	20.00
12-Premium version(distr. in Chicago only); Free printed on upper right-c; no price (Rare)	10.00	30.00	70.00

JACK HUNTER
July, 1987 - Present ($1.25, color)
Blackthorne Publishing

	Good	Fine	Mint
1-4		.60	1.20

JACKIE GLEASON (Also see The Honeymooners)
1948; Sept, 1955 - No. 5, Dec, 1955
St. John Publishing Co.

	Good	Fine	Mint
1(1948)	27.00	81.00	190.00
2(1948)	16.00	48.00	110.00
1(1955)(TV)-Photo-c	17.00	51.00	120.00
2-5	11.50	34.00	80.00

JACKIE GLEASON AND THE HONEYMOONERS (TV)
June-July, 1956 - No. 12, Apr-May, 1958
National Periodical Publications

	Good	Fine	Mint
1	32.00	95.00	225.00
2	20.00	60.00	140.00
3-11	14.00	42.00	100.00
12 (Scarce)	18.00	54.00	125.00

JACKIE JOKERS (Also see Richie Rich &...)
March, 1973 - No. 4, Sept, 1973
Harvey Publications

	Good	Fine	Mint
1-4; 2-President Nixon app.		.20	.40

JACKIE ROBINSON (Famous Plays of...)
May, 1950 - No. 6, 1952 (Baseball hero)
Fawcett Publications

	Good	Fine	Mint
nn	20.00	60.00	140.00
2	14.00	42.00	100.00
3-6	12.00	36.00	84.00

JACK IN THE BOX (Formerly Yellowjacket No. 1-10)
(Cowboy Western Comics No. 17 on)
Feb, 1946; No. 11, Oct, 1946 - No. 16, Nov-Dec, 1947
Frank Comunale/Charlton Comics No. 11 on

	Good	Fine	Mint
1-Stitches, Marty Mouse & Nutsy McKrow	4.00	12.00	28.00
11-Yellowjacket	4.60	14.00	32.00
12,14-16	1.70	5.00	12.00
13-Wolverton-a	8.50	25.50	60.00

JACK OF HEARTS
Jan, 1984 - No. 4, April, 1984 (Mini-series)
Marvel Comics Group

	Good	Fine	Mint
1-4		.50	1.00

JACKPOT COMICS (Jolly Jingles No. 10 on)
Spring, 1941 - No. 9, Spring, 1943
MLJ Magazines

	Good	Fine	Mint
1-The Black Hood, Mr. Justice, Steel Sterling & Sgt. Boyle begin; Biro-c	86.00	260.00	600.00
2	40.00	120.00	280.00
3	33.00	100.00	230.00
4-Archie begins (on sale 12/41)-(Also see Pep Comics No. 22); Montana-c	100.00	300.00	700.00
5	40.00	120.00	280.00
6-9: 6,7-Bondage-c	34.00	102.00	240.00

JACK Q FROST (See Unearthly Spectaculars)

JACK THE GIANT KILLER (See Movie Classics)

JACK THE GIANT KILLER (New Advs. of...)
Aug-Sept, 1953
Bimfort & Co.

	Good	Fine	Mint
V1#1-H. C. Kiefer-a	7.00	21.00	50.00

JACKY'S DIARY (See 4-Color No. 1091)

JAGUAR, THE (See The Advs. of...)

JAMBOREE
Feb, 1946(no mo. given) - No. 3, April, 1946
Round Publishing Co.

	Good	Fine	Mint
1	3.50	10.50	24.00
2,3	1.70	5.00	12.00

JAMES BOND FOR YOUR EYES ONLY
Oct., 1981 - No. 2, Nov., 1981
Marvel Comics Group

	Good	Fine	Mint
1,2-Movie adaptation r-/Marvel Super Spec.		.30	.60

JANE ARDEN (See Pageant of Comics)
March, 1948 - No. 2, June, 1948
St. John (United Features Syndicate)

	Good	Fine	Mint
1-Newspaper reprints	8.00	24.00	56.00
2	4.60	14.00	32.00

JANN OF THE JUNGLE (Jungle Tales No. 1-7)
No. 8, Nov, 1955 - No. 17, June, 1957
Atlas Comics (CSI)

	Good	Fine	Mint
8(#1)	7.00	21.00	50.00
9,11-15	4.35	13.00	30.00
10-Williamson/Colleta-c	5.50	16.50	38.00
16,17-Williamson/Mayo-a(3), 5 pgs. each	8.50	25.50	60.00

NOTE: ***Everett** c-15-17. **Heck** a-8, 15, 17. **Shores** a-8.*

JASON & THE ARGONAUTS (See Movie Classics)

JAWS 2 (See Marvel Super Special, A)

JCP FEATURES
Feb, 1982-c; Dec, 1981-indicia ($2.00, One-shot, B&W)
J.C. Productions (Archie)

	Good	Fine	Mint
1-T.H.U.N.D.E.R. Agents; Black Hood by Morrow & Adams	.35	1.00	2.00

JEANIE COMICS (Cowgirl Romances No. 28) (Formerly Daring)
No. 13, April, 1947 - No. 27, Oct, 1949
Marvel Comics/Atlas(CPC)

	Good	Fine	Mint
13-Mitzi, Willie begin	5.50	16.50	38.00
14,15	3.50	10.50	24.00
16-Used in **Love and Death** by Legman; Kurtzman's "Hey Look"	5.50	16.50	38.00
17-19,22-Kurtzman's "Hey Look," 1-3 pgs. each	3.50	10.50	24.00

Jace Pearson of the Texas Rangers #5, © DELL

Jackie Gleason #1 ('55), © STJ

Jackie Robinson #4, © FAW

Jeep Comics #3, © R.B. Leffingwell

Jesse James #6, © AVON

Jet Aces #1, © FH

JEANIE COMICS (continued) — Good / Fine / Mint

20,21,23-27 — 2.00 6.00 14.00

JEEP COMICS (Also see G.I. and Overseas Comics)
Winter, 1944 - No. 3, Mar-Apr, 1948
R. B. Leffingwell & Co.

- 1-Capt. Power, Criss Cross & Jeep & Peep (costumed) begin — 7.00 21.00 50.00
- 2,3 — 4.35 13.00 30.00
- 1-29(Giveaway)-Strip reprints in all; Tarzan, Flash Gordon, Blondie, The Nebbs, Little Iodine, Red Ryder, Don Winslow, The Phantom, Johnny Hazard, Katzenjammer Kids; distr. to U.S. Armed Forces in mid 1940's — 3.35 10.00 20.00

NOTE: ***L. B. Cole** c-3.*

JEFF JORDAN, U.S. AGENT
Dec, 1947 - Jan, 1948
D. S. Publishing Co.

- 1 — 4.00 12.00 28.00

JEMM, SON OF SATURN
9/84 - No. 12, 8/85 (12 part maxi-series; mando paper)
DC Comics

- 1-Colan p-all; c-1-5p,7-12p — .50 1.00
- 2-12: 3-Origin — .50 1.00

JERRY DRUMMER (Formerly Soldier & Marine V2No.9)
No. 10, Apr, 1957 - No. 12, Oct, 1957
Charlton Comics

- V2#10, V3#11,12 — 1.15 3.50 8.00

JERRY IGER'S CLASSIC SHEENA (Also see Sheena 3-D Special)
April, 1985 (One-shot)
Blackthorne Publishing

- 1 — .25 .75 1.50

JERRY IGER'S FAMOUS FEATURES
July, 1984 (One-shot)
Pacific Comics

- 1-Unpub. Flamingo & Wonder Boy by Baker — .25 .75 1.50

JERRY LEWIS (See Adventures of. . .)

JESSE JAMES (See 4-Color No. 757 & The Legend of. . .)

JESSE JAMES (See Badmen of the West & Blazing Sixguns)
Aug, 1950 - No. 29, Aug-Sept, 1956
Avon Periodicals

- 1-Kubert Alabam r-/Cowpuncher #1 — 11.00 33.00 76.00
- 2-Kubert-a(3) — 8.50 25.50 60.00
- 3-Kubert Alabam r-/Cowpuncher #2 — 7.00 21.00 50.00
- 4-No Kubert — 2.85 8.50 20.00
- 5,6-Kubert Jesse James-a(3); one pg. Wood-a, #5 — 7.00 21.00 50.00
- 7-Kubert Jesse James-a(2) — 6.00 18.00 42.00
- 8-Kinstler-a(3) — 4.00 12.00 28.00
- 9,10-No Kubert — 2.85 8.50 20.00
- 11-14 (Exist?) — 2.15 6.50 15.00
- 15-Kinstler r-/#3 — 2.15 6.50 15.00
- 16-Kinstler r-/#3 & Sheriff Bob Dixon's Chuck Wagon #1 with name changed to Sheriff Tom Wilson — 2.65 8.00 18.00
- 17-Jesse James r-/#4; Kinstler-c idea from Kubert splash in #6 — 1.70 5.00 12.00
- 18-Kubert Jesse James r-/#5 — 1.70 5.00 12.00
- 19-Kubert Jesse James-r — 1.70 5.00 12.00
- 20-Williamson/Frazetta-a; r-Chief Vic. Apache Massacre; Kubert Jesse James r-/#6 — 8.50 25.50 60.00
- 21-Two Jesse James r-/#4, Kinstler r-/#4 — 1.70 5.00 12.00
- 22,23-No Kubert — 1.60 4.70 11.00
- 24-New McCarty strip by Kinstler plus Kinstler r-/#9 — 1.60 4.70 11.00
- 25-New McCarty Jesse James strip by Kinstler; Kinstler J. James r-/#7,9 — 1.60 4.70 11.00
- 26,27-New McCarty J. James strip plus a Kinstler/McCann Jesse James-r — 1.60 4.70 11.00
- 28-Reprints most of Red Mountain, Featuring Quantrells Raiders — 1.60 4.70 11.00
- 29 — 1.60 4.70 11.00
- Annual(nn; 1952; 25 cents)-". . . Brings Six-Gun Justice to the West"(100 pgs.)-3 earlier issues rebound; Kubert, Kinstler-a(3) — 17.00 51.00 120.00

NOTE: *Mostly reprints No. 10 on.* ***Kinstler** a-3, 4, 7-9, 15r, 16(2), 21-27; c-3, 4, 9, 17, 18, 20-27.*

JESSE JAMES
July, 1953
Realistic Publications

- nn-Reprints Avon's #1, same cover, colors different — 4.35 13.00 30.00

JEST (Kayo No. 12) (Formerly Snap)
1944
Harry 'A' Chesler

- 10-Johnny Rebel & Yankee Boy app. in text — 4.00 12.00 28.00
- 11-Little Nemo in Adventure Land — 4.60 14.00 32.00

JESTER
1945
Harry 'A' Chesler

- 10 — 3.50 10.50 24.00

JESUS
1979 (49 cents)
Spire Christian Comics (Fleming H. Revell Co.)

- nn — .30 .60

JET (See Jet Powers)

JET ACES
1952 - 1953
Fiction House Magazines

- 1 — 4.60 14.00 32.00
- 2 — 3.15 9.50 22.00
- 3,4 — 2.50 7.50 17.00

JET DREAM (. . .& Her Stuntgirl Counterspies)
June, 1968
Gold Key

- 1 — 1.70 5.00 12.00

JET FIGHTERS
No. 5, Nov, 1952 - No. 7, Mar, 1953
Standard Magazines

- 5,7-Toth-a — 5.00 15.00 35.00
- 6-Celardo-a — 1.85 5.50 13.00

JET POWERS (American Air Forces No. 5 on)
1950 - 1951
Magazine Enterprises

- 1(A-1 30)-Powell-a begins — 13.00 40.00 90.00
- 2(A-1 32) — 9.50 28.50 65.00
- 3(A-1 35)-Williamson/Evans-a — 18.00 54.00 125.00
- 4(A-1 38)-Williamson/Wood-a; "The Rain of Sleep" drug story — 18.00 54.00 125.00
- I.W. Reprint 1,2(1963)-r-/No. 1,2 — 1.00 3.00 6.00

JET PUP (See 3-D Features)

JETSONS, THE (TV)(See March of Comics 276,330,348, Spotlight 3)
Jan, 1963 - No. 36, Oct, 1970 (Hanna-Barbera)
Gold Key

JETSONS, THE (continued)

	Good	Fine	Mint
1	4.35	13.00	30.00
2	2.35	7.00	16.00
3-10	1.75	5.25	12.00
11-20	1.50	4.50	10.00
21-36	1.15	3.50	8.00

JETSONS, THE (TV) (Hanna-Barbera)
Nov, 1970 - No. 20, Dec, 1973
Charlton Comics

1	2.00	6.00	14.00
2	1.00	3.00	7.00
3-10	.85	2.50	6.00
11-20	.75	2.25	5.00

JETTA OF THE 21ST CENTURY
No. 5, 1952 - No. 7, Mar, 1953 (Teen-age Archie type)
Standard Comics

5	5.50	16.50	38.00
6,7	2.85	8.50	20.00

JIGGS & MAGGIE (See 4-Color No. 18)

JIGGS & MAGGIE
No. 11, 1949(Aug.) - No. 21, 2/53; No. 22, 4/53 - No. 27, 2-3/54
Standard Comics/Harvey Publications No. 22 on

11	5.70	17.00	40.00
12-15,17-21	3.00	9.00	21.00
16-Wood text illos.	4.00	12.00	28.00
22-25,27: 22-24-Little Dot app.	2.15	6.50	15.00
26-Four pgs. partially in 3-D	9.50	28.00	65.00

NOTE: *Sunday page reprints by* **McManus** *loosely blended into story continuity. Advertised on covers as "All New."*

JIGSAW (Big Hero Adventures)
Sept, 1966 - No. 2, Dec, 1966 (36 pgs.)
Harvey Publications (Funday Funnies)

1-Origin; Crandall-a, 5pgs.	.70	2.00	4.00
2-Man From S.R.A.M.	.35	1.00	2.00

JIGSAW OF DOOM (See Complete Mystery No. 2)

JIM BOWIE (Formerly Danger; Black Jack No. 20 on)
No. 15, 1955? - No. 19, April, 1957
Charlton Comics

15	2.00	6.00	14.00
16-19	1.15	3.50	8.00

JIM BOWIE (See 4-Color No. 893,993, & Western Tales)

JIM DANDY
May, 1956 - No. 3, Sept, 1956 (Charles Biro)
Dandy Magazine (Lev Gleason)

1	2.30	7.00	16.00
2,3	1.15	3.50	8.00

JIM HARDY (Also see Treasury of Comics No. 2&5 & Sparkler)
1939 - 1940; 1947
United Features Syndicate/Spotlight Publ.

Single Series 6	16.00	48.00	110.00
Single Series 27('40)	11.50	34.00	80.00
1('47)-Spotlight Publ.	4.35	13.00	30.00
2	2.30	7.00	16.00

JIM HARDY
1944 (132 pages, 25 cents) (Tip Top, Sparkler-r)
Spotlight/United Features Syndicate

(1944)-Origin Mirror Man; Triple Terror app.	15.00	45.00	105.00

JIMINY CRICKET (See 4-Color No. 701,795,897,989, Mickey Mouse Mag. V5/3 & Walt Disney Showcase #37)

JIMMY (James Swinnerton)
1905 (10x15") (40 pages in color)
N. Y. American & Journal

	Good	Fine	Mint
	15.00	45.00	105.00

JIMMY DURANTE (See A-1 Comics No. 18,20)

JIMMY OLSEN (See Superman's Pal . . .)

JIMMY WAKELY (Cowboy movie star)
Sept-Oct, 1949 - No. 18, July-Aug, 1952 (52pgs., 1-13)
National Periodical Publications

1-Photo-c, 52pgs. begin; Alex Toth-a; Kit Colby Girl Sheriff begins	25.00	75.00	175.00
2-Toth-a	18.00	54.00	125.00
3,6,7-Frazetta-a in all, 3 pgs. each; Toth-a in all. 7-Last photo-c?	20.00	60.00	140.00
4-Frazetta-a, 3pgs.; Kurtzman "Pot-Shot Pete," 1pg; Toth-a	20.00	60.00	140.00
5,8-15,18-Toth-a; 12,14-Kubert-a, 3 & 2 pgs.	13.00	40.00	90.00
16,17	9.50	28.00	65.00

JIM RAY'S AVIATION SKETCH BOOK
Feb, 1946 - No. 2, May-June, 1946
Vital Publishers

1,2-Picture stories about planes and pilots	10.00	30.00	70.00

JIM SOLAR (See Wisco/Klarer)

JINGLE BELLS (See March of Comics No. 65)

JINGLE BELLS CHRISTMAS BOOK
1971 (20 pgs.; B&W inside; slick cover)
Montgomery Ward (Giveaway)

		.40	.80

JINGLE DINGLE CHRISTMAS STOCKING COMICS
V2No.1, 1951 (no date listed) (100 pgs.; giant-size)(25 cents)
Stanhall Publications (Publ.-annually)

V2#1-Foodini & Pinhead, Silly Pilly plus games & puzzles	5.50	16.50	38.00

JINGLE JANGLE COMICS (Also see Puzzle Fun)
Feb, 1942 - No. 42, Dec, 1949
Eastern Color Printing Co.

1-Pie-Face Prince of Old Pretzleburg, & Jingle Jangle Tales by George Carlson, Hortense, & Benny Bear begin	19.00	57.00	132.00
2,3-No Pie-Face Prince	8.50	25.50	60.00
4-Pie-Face Prince cover	8.50	25.50	60.00
5	7.50	22.50	52.50
6-10: 8-No Pie-Face Prince	6.50	19.50	45.00
11-15	4.00	12.00	28.00
16-30: 17,18-No Pie-Face Prince	3.00	9.00	21.00
31-42	2.20	6.50	15.00

NOTE: **George Carlson** *a-(2) in all except No. 2, 3, 8, 17, 18; c-1-6.* **Carlson** *1 pg. puzzles in 9, 10, 12-15, 18, 20.* **Carlson** *illustrated a series of Uncle Wiggily books in 1930's.*

JING PALS
Feb, 1946 - No. 4, Aug?, 1946 (Funny animal)
Victory Publishing Corporation

1-Wishing Willie, Puggy Panda & Johnny Rabbit begin	4.00	12.00	28.00
2-4	2.30	7.00	16.00

JINKS, PIXIE, AND DIXIE (See Whitman Comic. . .)
1965 (Giveaway) (Hanna-Barbera)
Florida Power & Light

	.35	1.00	2.00

JOAN OF ARC (See A-1 Comics No. 21 & Ideal a Classical Comic)

The Jetsons #3 (GK), © Hanna-Barbera

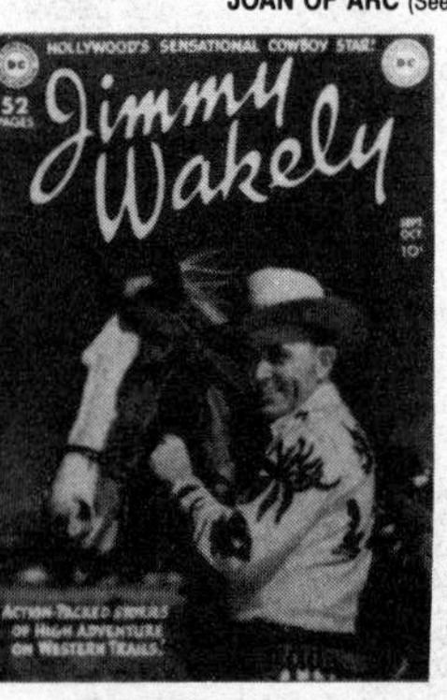

Jimmy Wakely #1, © DC

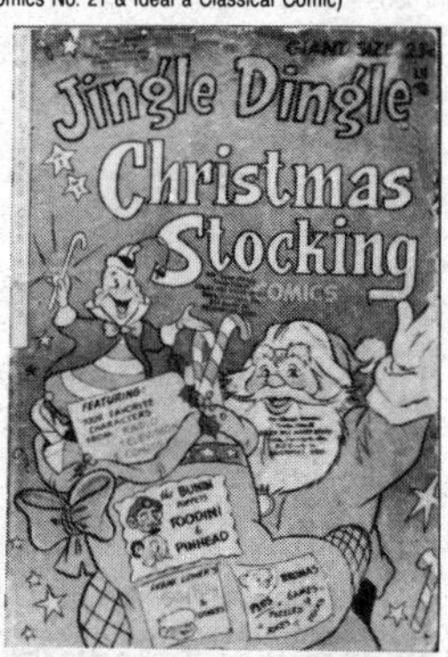

Jingle Dingle Christmas Stocking #1, © Stanhall

Joe Palooka #118 © HARV

John Carter of Mars #2 (GK), © ERB

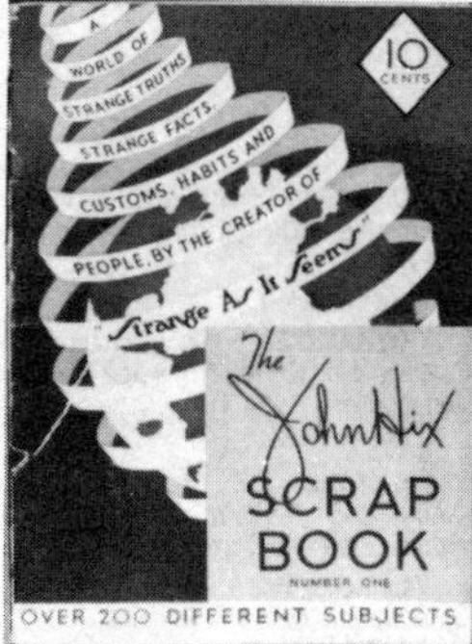

The John Hix Scrap Book #1, © EAS

JOAN OF ARC
No date (28 pages)
Catechetical Guild (Topix) (Giveaway)

	Good	Fine	Mint
	7.00	21.00	50.00

NOTE: *Unpublished version exists which came from the Guild's files.*

JOE COLLEGE
Fall, 1949 - No. 2, Winter, 1950
Hillman Periodicals

	Good	Fine	Mint
1,2-Powell-a; 1-Briefer-a	2.65	8.00	18.00

JOE JINKS (See Single Series No. 12)

JOE LOUIS (Also see True Comics #5)
Sept, 1950 - No. 2, Nov, 1950 (Photo-c)
Fawcett Publications

	Good	Fine	Mint
1	18.00	54.00	125.00
2	14.00	42.00	100.00

JOE PALOOKA
1933 (B&W daily strip reprints) (52 pages)
Cupples & Leon Co.

	Good	Fine	Mint
nn-(Scarce)-by Fisher	40.00	120.00	280.00

JOE PALOOKA (1st Series)(Also see Big Shot)
1942 - 1944
Columbia Comic Corp. (Publication Enterprises)

	Good	Fine	Mint
1-1st to portray American president; gov't permission required	25.00	75.00	175.00
2 (1943)-Hitler-c	13.00	40.00	90.00
3,4	10.00	30.00	70.00

JOE PALOOKA (2nd Series) (Battle Adv. #68-74; . . . Advs. #75,77-81,83-85,87; Champ of the Comics #76,82,86,89-93) (See All-New)
Nov, 1945 - No. 118, Mar, 1961
Harvey Publications

	Good	Fine	Mint
1	19.00	57.00	132.00
2	10.00	30.00	70.00
3,4,6	6.50	19.50	45.00
5-Boy Explorers by S&K (7-8/46)	9.50	28.00	65.00
7-1st Powell Flyin' Fool, ends #25	5.70	17.00	40.00
8-10	5.00	15.00	35.00
11-14,16-20: 19-Freedom Train-c	4.00	12.00	28.00
15-Origin Humphrey; Super heroine Atoma app. by Powell	5.00	15.00	35.00
21-30: 30-Nude female painting	3.00	9.00	21.00
31-61: 35-1st app. Little Max? 44-Joe Palooka marries Ann Howe	2.30	7.00	16.00
62-S&K Boy Explorers-r	3.00	9.00	21.00
63-80: 66,67-'commie' torture story	1.70	5.00	12.00
81-99,101-115	1.50	4.50	10.00
100	1.75	5.25	12.00
116-S&K Boy Explorers (r) (Giant, '60)	2.85	8.50	20.00
117,118-Giants	2.65	8.00	18.00
. . . Body Building Instruction Book (1958 Sports Toy giveaway, 16 pgs, 5¼x7")-Origin	4.60	14.00	32.00
. . . Fights His Way Back (1945 Giveaway, 24 pgs.) Family Comics	13.00	40.00	90.00
. . . in Hi There! (1949 Red Cross giveaway, 12 pgs., 4¾x6")	4.00	12.00	28.00
. . . in It's All in the Family (1945 Red Cross giveaway, 16 pgs., regular size)	6.50	19.50	45.00
. . . Visits the Lost City(1945)(One Shot)(nn)(50 cents)-164 page continuous story strip reprint. Has biography & photo of Ham Fisher; possibly the single longest comic book story published (159 pgs.?)	45.00	135.00	315.00

NOTE: ***Nostrand/Powell** a-73. **Powell** a-7, 8, 10, 12, 17, 19, 26-45, 47-53, 70, 73 at least. Black Cat text stories #8, 12, 13, 19. Bondage c-50.*

JOE YANK
March, 1952 - 1954
Standard Comics (Visual Editions)

	Good	Mint	Mint
5-Celardo, Tuska-a	2.15	6.50	15.00
6-Toth, Severin/Elder-a	4.00	12.00	28.00
7	1.30	4.00	9.00
8-Toth-c	2.65	8.00	18.00
9-16: 12-Andru-a	1.00	3.00	7.00

JOHN BOLTON'S HALLS OF HORROR
June, 1985 - No. 2, June, 1985 ($1.75 cover)
Eclipse Comics

	Good	Fine	Mint
1,2-British-r	.30	.90	1.80

JOHN CARTER OF MARS (See 4-Color No. 375,437,488, The Funnies & Weird Worlds)

JOHN CARTER OF MARS
April, 1964 - No. 3, Oct, 1964
Gold Key

	Good	Fine	Mint
1(10104-404)-Reprints 4-Color 375; Jesse Marsh-a	2.50	7.50	17.50
2(407), 3(410)-Reprints 4-Color 437 & 488; Marsh-a	2.00	6.00	14.00

JOHN CARTER OF MARS
1970 (72 pgs.; paper cover; 10½x16½"; B&W)
House of Greystroke

	Good	Fine	Mint
1941-42 Sunday strip reprints; John Coleman Burroughs-a	2.35	7.00	16.00

JOHN CARTER, WARLORD OF MARS
June, 1977 - No. 28, Oct, 1979
Marvel Comics Group

	Good	Fine	Mint
1-Origin by Gil Kane		.50	1.00
2-10-Last Kane issue		.30	.60
11-17,19-28: 11-Origin Dejah Thoris		.25	.50
18-Miller-a(p)	.35	1.00	2.00
Annual 1(10/77), 2(9/78), 3(10/79)		.40	.80

NOTE: ***Austin** c-24i. **Gil Kane** a-1-10p; c-1p, 2p, 3, 4-9p, 10, 15p, Annual 1p. **Layton** a-17i. **Miller** c-25, 26p. **Nebres** a-2-4i, 8-16i; c(i)-6-9, 11-22, 25, Annual 1. **Perez** c-24p. **Simonson** a-15p. **Sutton** a-7i.*

JOHN F. KENNEDY, CHAMPION OF FREEDOM
1964 (no month) (25 cents)
Worden & Childs

	Good	Fine	Mint
nn-Photo-c	2.65	8.00	18.00

JOHN F. KENNEDY LIFE STORY
Aug-Oct, 1964; Nov, 1965; June, 1966 (12 cents)
Dell Publishing Co.

	Good	Fine	Mint
12-378-410	2.00	6.00	14.00
12-378-511 (reprint)	1.35	4.00	9.00
12-378-606 (reprint)	1.00	3.00	7.00

JOHN FORCE (See Magic Agent)

JOHN HIX SCRAP BOOK, THE
Late 1930's (no date) (68 pgs.; reg. size; 10 cents)
Eastern Color Printing Co. (McNaught Synd.)

	Good	Fine	Mint
1-Strange As It Seems (resembles Single Series books)	8.50	25.50	60.00
2-Strange As It Seems	6.50	19.50	45.00

JOHN LAW DETECTIVE (See Smash Comics #3)
April, 1983 ($1.50; Baxter paper)
Eclipse Comics

	Good	Fine	Mint
1-Three Eisner stories originally drawn in 1948 for the never published John Law No. 1; original cover pencilled in 1948 & inked in 1982 by Eisner	.25	.75	1.50

JOHNNY APPLESEED (See Story Hour Series)

JOHNNY CASH (See Hello, I'm . . .)

JOHNNY DANGER
1950
Toby Press

	Good	Fine	Mint
1	5.50	16.50	38.00

JOHNNY DANGER PRIVATE DETECTIVE
1954 (Reprinted in Danger No. 11 (Super))
Toby Press

1-Opium den story	4.35	13.00	30.00

JOHNNY DYNAMITE (Formerly Dynamite No. 1-9)
No. 10, 6/55 - No. 12, 10/55 (Foreign Intrigues No. 13 on)
Charlton Comics

10-12	2.00	6.00	14.00

JOHNNY HAZARD
No. 5, Aug, 1948 - No. 8, May, 1949
Best Books (Standard Comics)

5-Strip reprints by Frank Robbins	8.00	24.00	56.00
6,8-Strip reprints by Frank Robbins	5.50	16.50	38.00
7-New art, not Robbins	4.00	12.00	28.00
35	4.00	12.00	28.00

JOHNNY JASON (. . .Teen Reporter)
Feb-Apr, 1962 - No. 2, June-Aug, 1962
Dell Publishing Co.

4-Color 1302, 2(01380-208)	1.15	3.50	8.00

JOHNNY JINGLE'S LUCKY DAY
1956 (16 pgs.; 7¼x5-1/8") (Giveaway) (Disney)
American Dairy Association

	2.35	7.00	14.00

JOHNNY LAW, SKY RANGER
Apr, 1955 - No. 3, Aug, 1955; No. 4, Nov, 1955
Good Comics (Lev Gleason)

1-Edmond Good-a	3.15	9.50	22.00
2-4	1.85	5.50	13.00

JOHNNY MACK BROWN (TV western star; see Western Roundup)
No. 269, Mar, 1950 - No. 963, Feb, 1959 (All Photo-c)
Dell Publishing Co.

4-Color 269(3/50, 52pgs.)-J. Mack Brown & his horse Rebel begin; photo front/back-c begin; Marsh-a begins, ends #9	8.00	24.00	56.00
2(10-12/50, 52pgs.)	5.00	15.00	35.00
3(1-3/51, 52pgs.)	3.50	10.50	24.00
4-10 (9-11/52)(36pgs.)	3.00	9.00	21.00
4-Color 455,493,541,584,618	3.00	9.00	21.00
4-Color 645,685,722,776,834,963	3.00	9.00	21.00
4-Color 922-Manning-a	3.50	10.50	24.00

JOHNNY NEMO
Sept, 1985 - No. 3, Feb, 1986 (Mini-series)
Eclipse Comics

1,2 ($1.75 cover)	.30	.90	1.75
3 ($2.00 cover)	.35	1.00	2.00

JOHNNY RINGO (See 4-Color No. 1142)

JOHNNY STARBOARD (See Wisco)

JOHNNY THUNDER
Feb-Mar, 1973 - No. 3, July-Aug, 1973
National Periodical Publications

1-Johnny Thunder & Nighthawk-r begin	.25	.75	1.50
2,3: 2-Trigger Twins app.		.50	1.00

NOTE: *Drucker a-2r, 3r. G. Kane a-2r, 3r. Toth a-1r, 3r; c-1r, 3r. Also see All-American, All-Star Western and Western Comics.*

JOHN PAUL JONES (See Four Color No. 1007)

JOHN STEED & EMMA PEEL (See The Avengers)

JOHN STEELE SECRET AGENT (Also see Freedom Agent)
December, 1964 (Freedom Agent)
Gold Key

1	1.50	4.50	10.00

JOHN WAYNE ADVENTURE COMICS (Movie star; See Big Tex, Oxydol-Dreft & With The Marines. . .#1)
Winter, 1949 - No. 31, May, 1955 (Photo-c, 1-12,17,25-on)
Toby Press

1 (36pgs.)-Photo-c begin	32.00	95.00	225.00
2 (36pgs.)-Williamson/Frazetta-a(2) (one r-/Billy the Kid #1), 6 & 2 pgs; photo back-c	33.00	100.00	230.00
3 (36pgs.)-Williamson/Frazetta-a(2), 16 pgs. total; photo back-c	33.00	100.00	230.00
4 (52pgs.)-Williamson/Frazetta-a(2), 16pgs total	33.00	100.00	230.00
5 (52pgs.)-Kurtzman-a-(Alfred "L" Newman in Potshot Pete)	21.00	64.00	150.00
6 (52pgs.)-Williamson/Frazetta-a, 10pgs; Kurtzman a-'Pot-Shot Pete,' 5pgs.; & "Genius Jones," 1pg.	31.00	93.00	215.00
7 (52pgs.)-Williamson/Frazetta-a, 10pgs.	26.00	78.00	182.00
8 (36pgs.)-Williamson/Frazetta-a(2), 12 & 9 pgs.	31.00	93.00	215.00
9-11: Photo western-c	13.00	40.00	90.00
12-Photo war-c; Kurtzman-a, 2pgs. "Genius"	14.00	42.00	100.00
13-15: 13-Line-drawn-c begin, end #24	12.00	36.00	84.00
16-Williamson/Frazetta r-from Billy the Kid #1	17.00	51.00	120.00
17-Photo-c	13.00	40.00	90.00
18-Williamson/Frazetta-a r-/#4 & 8, 19pgs.	21.00	64.00	150.00
19-24: 23-Evans-a?	11.00	32.00	76.00
25-Photo-c return; end #31; Williamson/Frazetta-a r-/Billy the Kid #3	21.00	64.00	150.00
26-28,30-Photo-c	13.00	40.00	90.00
29-Williamson/Frazetta-a r-/#4	20.00	60.00	140.00
31-Williamson/Frazetta-a r-/#2	20.00	60.00	140.00

NOTE: *Williamsonish art in later issues by Gerald McCann.*

JO-JO COMICS (. . .Congo King #7-29; My Desire #30 on)
(Also see Fantastic Fears and Jungle Jo)
1945 - No. 29, July, 1949 (two No.7's; no No. 13)
Fox Features Syndicate

nn(1945)-Funny animal	4.00	12.00	28.00
2(Sum,'46)-6: Funny animal; 2-Ten pg. Electro story	2.30	7.00	16.00
7(7/47)-Jo-Jo, Congo King begins	22.00	65.00	154.00
7(No.8) (9/47)	17.00	51.00	120.00
8-10(No.9-11): 8-Tanee begins	13.00	40.00	90.00
11,12(No.12,13),14,16	11.50	34.00	80.00
15-Cited by Dr. Wertham in 5/47 Saturday Review of Literature	13.00	40.00	90.00
17-Kamen bondage-c	13.00	40.00	90.00
18-20	11.50	34.00	80.00
21-29	10.00	30.00	70.00

NOTE: *Many bondage-c/a by Baker/Kamen/Feldstein/Good. No. 7's have Princesses Gwenna, Geesa, Yolda, & Safra before settling down on Tanee.*

JO-JOY (Adventures of. . .)
1945 - 1953 (Christmas gift comic)
W. T. Grant Dept. Stores

1945-53 issues	1.50	4.50	10.00

JOKEBOOK COMICS DIGEST ANNUAL (. . .Mag. No. 5 on)
10/77 - No. 13, 10/83 (Digest Size)
Archie Publications

Johnny Mack Brown #6, © DELL

John Wayne Adventure Comics #29, © TOBY

Jo-Jo Comics #10, © FOX

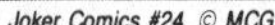
Joker Comics #24, © MCG

Jonah Hex #15, © DC

Jon Sable, Freelance #6, © First

JOKEBOOK COMICS . . . (continued)

	Good	Fine	Mint
1(10/77)-Reprints; Adams-a		.60	1.20
2(4/78)-13		.60	1.20

JOKER, THE (See Batman, Brave & the Bold, and Detective)
May, 1975 - No. 9, Sept-Oct, 1976
National Periodical Publications

	Good	Fine	Mint
1-Two-Face app.		.30	.60
2-4, V2/5-9		.25	.50

JOKER COMICS (Adventures Into Terror No. 43 on)
April, 1942 - No. 42, August, 1950
Timely/Marvel Comics No. 36 on (TCI/CDS)

	Good	Fine	Mint
1-(Rare)-1st app. Powerhouse Pepper by Wolverton; Stuporman app. from Daring	75.00	225.00	525.00
2-Wolverton-a continued; 1st app. Tessie the Typist	31.00	93.00	220.00
3-5-Wolverton-a	22.00	65.00	154.00
6-10-Wolverton-a	15.00	45.00	105.00
11-20-Wolverton-a	12.00	36.00	84.00
21,22,24-27,29,30-Wolverton cont'd. & Kurtzman's "Hey Look" in #24-27	9.50	28.50	65.00
23-1st "Hey Look" by Kurtzman; Wolverton-a	11.00	32.00	76.00
28,32,34,37-41	1.70	5.00	12.00
31-Last Powerhouse Pepper; not in #28	7.00	21.00	50.00
33,35,36-Kurtzman's "Hey Look"	3.00	9.00	21.00
42-Only app. 'Patty Pinup,' a clone of Millie the Model	2.00	6.00	14.00

JOLLY CHRISTMAS, A (See March of Comics No. 269)

JOLLY CHRISTMAS BOOK (See Christmas Journey Through Space)
1951; 1954; 1955 (36 pgs.; 24 pgs.)
Promotional Publ. Co.

	Good	Fine	Mint
1951-(Woolworth giveaway)-slightly oversized; no slick cover; Marv Levy c/a	2.00	6.00	14.00
1954-(Hot Shoppes giveaway)-regular size-reprints 1951 issue; slick cover added; 24 pgs.; no ads	2.00	6.00	14.00
1955-(J. M. McDonald Co. giveaway)-regular size	1.50	4.50	10.00

JOLLY COMICS
1947
Four Star Publishing Co.

	Good	Fine	Mint
1	3.00	9.00	21.00

JOLLY JINGLES (Formerly Jackpot)
No. 10, Sum, 1943 - No. 16, Wint, 1944/45
MLJ Magazines

	Good	Fine	Mint
10-Super Duck begins (origin & 1st app.)	14.00	42.00	100.00
11	6.50	19.50	45.00
12-16: 12: Woody The Woodpecker app.	3.50	10.50	24.00

JONAH HEX (See All-Star Western, Hex and Weird Western Tales)
Mar-Apr, 1977 - No. 92, Aug, 1985
National Periodical Publications/DC Comics

	Good	Fine	Mint
1	.50	1.50	3.00
2-6,8-10: 9-Wrightson-c		.50	1.00
7-Explains Hex's face disfigurement	.25	.75	1.50
11-20: 12-Starlin-c		.40	.80
21-92: 31,32-Origin retold		.25	.50

NOTE: ***Aparo*** *c-76p.* ***Ayers*** *a(p)-35-37, 41,44-53, 56, 58-82.* ***Kubert*** *c-43-46.* ***Morrow*** *c-10.* ***Spiegle****(Tothish) a-34, 38, 40, 49, 52.*

JONAH HEX AND OTHER WESTERN TALES (Blue Ribbon Digest)
Sept-Oct, 1979 - No. 3, Jan-Feb, 1980 (100 pgs.)
DC Comics

	Good	Fine	Mint
1-3: 1-Origin Scalphunter-r; painted-c. 2-Weird Western Tales-r; Adams, Toth, Aragones, Gil Kane-a		.40	.80

JONAH HEX SPECTACULAR (See DC Special Series No. 16)

JONESY (Formerly Crack Western)
No. 85, Aug, 1953; No. 2, Oct, 1953 - No. 8, Oct, 1954
Comic Favorite/Quality Comics Group

	Good	Fine	Mint
85(#1)	2.65	8.00	18.00
2	1.30	4.00	9.00
3-8	.85	2.50	6.00

JON JUAN (Also see Great Lover Romances)
Spring, 1950
Toby Press

	Good	Fine	Mint
1-All Schomburg-a (signed Al Reid on-c); written by Siegel; used in **SOTI**, pg. 38	11.00	32.00	76.00

JONNI THUNDER
Feb, 1985 - No. 4, Aug, 1985 (Mini-series)
DC Comics

	Good	Fine	Mint
1-Origin		.50	1.00
2-4		.45	.90

JONNY QUEST (TV)
December, 1964 (Hanna-Barbera)
Gold Key

	Good	Fine	Mint
1 (10139-412)	4.60	14.00	32.00

JONNY QUEST (TV)
June, 1986 - Present (Hanna-Barbera)
Comico

	Good	Fine	Mint
1	.85	2.50	5.00
2	.60	1.80	3.60
3	.50	1.50	3.00
4-10	.35	1.00	2.00
11-20	.25	.75	1.50

NOTE: ***Pini*** *a-2.* ***Rude*** *a-1.* ***Spiegle*** *a-12.* ***Staton*** *a-11.* ***Stevens*** *c-3, 5.* ***Wildey*** *a-1, c-1, 12.* ***Williamson*** *a-4; c-4i.*

JONNY QUEST CLASSICS (TV)
May, 1987 - Present ($2.00, color) (Hanna-Barbera)
Comico

	Good	Fine	Mint
1-3-Wildey c/a	.35	1.00	2.00

JON SABLE, FREELANCE (Also see Sable)
6/83 - No. 56, 2/88 (#1-17, $1; #18-33, $1.25; #34-on, $1.75)
First Comics

	Good	Fine	Mint
1-Created, story/a&c by Mike Grell	.75	2.25	4.50
2-5: 3-5-Origin, parts 1-3	.45	1.40	2.80
6-10: 6-Origin, part 4	.40	1.25	2.50
11-20: 14-Mando paper begins	.35	1.10	2.20
21-33: 25-30-Shatter app.	.30	.90	1.80
34-56: 34-Deluxe format begins ($1.75)	.30	.95	1.90

NOTE: ***Aragones*** *a-33.* ***Grell*** *a-1-43; c-1-52, 53p, 54.*

JOSEPH & HIS BRETHREN (See The Living Bible)

JOSIE (She's . . . #1-16) (. . . & the Pussycats #45 on) (See Archie Giant Series 528,540,551,562, 571)
2/63 - No. 106, 10/82
Archie Publications/Radio Comics

	Good	Fine	Mint
1	8.00	24.00	56.00
2	3.70	11.00	26.00
3-5	2.65	8.00	18.00
6-10	1.70	5.00	12.00
11-20	1.15	3.50	8.00
21,23-30	.75	2.25	5.00
22-Mighty Man & Mighty (Josie Girl) app.	.75	2.25	5.00
31-54	.45	1.35	3.00
55-74(52pg. ish.)		.50	1.00
75-106		.35	.70

JOURNAL OF CRIME (See Fox Giants)

JOURNEY INTO FEAR
May, 1951 - No. 21, Sept, 1954
Superior-Dynamic Publications

	Good	Fine	Mint
1-Baker-a(2)-r	13.00	40.00	90.00
2	8.00	24.00	56.00
3,4	6.50	19.50	45.00
5-10	5.00	15.00	35.00
11-14,16-21	4.35	13.00	30.00
15-Used in **SOTI**, pg. 389	8.00	24.00	56.00

NOTE: *Kamenish, 'headlight'-a most issues.* ***Robinson*** *a-10.*

JOURNEY INTO MYSTERY (1st Series) (Thor No. 126 on)
6/52 - No. 48, 8/57; No. 49, 11/58 - No. 125, 2/66
Atlas(CPS No.1-48/AMI No.49-68/Marvel No.69(6/61) on)

	Good	Fine	Mint
1	43.00	130.00	300.00
2	23.00	70.00	160.00
3,4	18.00	54.00	125.00
5-11	11.50	34.00	80.00
12-20,22: 22-Davisesque-a; last pre-code issue (2/55)	8.00	24.00	56.00
21-Kubert-a; Tothish-a by Andru	8.50	25.50	60.00
23-32,35-38,40: 24-Torres?-a	4.00	12.00	28.00
33-Williamson-a	7.00	21.00	50.00
34-Krigstein-a	6.00	18.00	42.00
39-Wood-a	6.00	18.00	42.00
41-Crandall-a; Frazettaesque-a by Morrow	3.85	11.50	27.00
42,48-Torres-a	3.85	11.50	27.00
43,44-Williamson/Mayo-a in both	3.85	11.50	27.00
45,47,52,53	2.65	8.00	18.00
46-Torres & Krigstein-a	3.85	11.50	27.00
49-Matt Fox, Check-a	3.50	11.50	24.00
50-Davis-a	2.85	8.50	20.00
51-Kirby/Wood-a	2.85	8.50	20.00
54-Williamson-a	2.85	8.50	20.00
55-61,63-73: 66-Return of Xemnu	2.15	6.50	15.00
62-1st app. Xemnu (Titan) called "The Hulk"	4.00	12.00	28.00
74-82-Fantasy content #74 on. 75-Last 10 cent issue. 80-Anti-communist propaganda story by Ditko	1.70	5.00	12.00
83-R-/from the Golden Record Comic Set	1.50	4.50	10.00
with the record....	4.00	12.00	28.00
83-Origin & 1st app. The Mighty Thor by Kirby (8/62)	68.00	175.00	475.00
84	14.00	36.00	100.00
85-1st app. Loki & Heimdall	11.50	29.00	80.00
86-1st app. Odin	8.50	21.00	60.00
87,88	7.00	18.00	50.00
89-Origin Thor reprint/#83	7.00	18.00	50.00
90-No Kirby-a; Aunt May proto-type	4.60	12.00	32.00
91,92,94-96-Sinnott-a	3.65	9.00	25.00
93,97-Kirby-a; Tales of Asgard series begins #97(Origin which concludes #99)	4.00	10.00	28.00
98-100-Kirby/Heck-a. 98-Origin/1st app. The Human Cobra. 99-1st app. Surtur & Mr. Hyde	3.25	8.00	22.00
101-104,110: 102-Intro Sif	1.85	5.50	11.00
105-109-Ten extra pages Kirby-a. 107-1st app. Grey Gargoyle	1.85	5.50	11.00
111,113,114,116-125: 119-Intro Hogun, Fandrall, Volstagg	1.15	3.50	7.00
112-Thor Vs. Hulk; origin Loki begins; ends #113	1.85	5.50	11.00
115-Detailed origin Loki	1.85	5.50	11.00
Annual 1('65)-1st app. Hercules; Kirby c/a	2.50	7.50	15.00

NOTE: ***Ayers*** *a-14.* ***Bailey*** *a-43.* ***Briefer*** *a-5, 12.* ***Check*** *a-17.* ***Colan*** *a-23, 81.* ***Ditko*** *a-33, 38, 50-96; c-71, 88i.* ***Ditko/Kirby*** *a-50-83.* ***Everett*** *a-20, 48; c-4-7, 9, 37, 39, 40-42, 44, 45, 47.* ***Forte*** *a-19.* ***Heath*** *a-4, 5, 11, 14; c-1, 11, 15, 51.* ***Kirby*** *a(p)-60, 66, 76, 80, 83-89, 93, 97, 98, 100(w/Heck), 101-125; c-50-82(w/Ditko), 83-152p.* ***Leiber/Fox*** *a-93, 98-102.* ***Morrow*** *a-41, 42.* ***Orlando*** *a-30, 45, 57.* ***Mac Pakula****(Tothish) a-9.* ***Powell*** *a-20, 27, 34.* ***Reinman*** *a-87, 92, 96i.* ***Robinson*** *a-9.* ***Robert Sale*** *a-14.* ***Severin*** *a-27.* ***Tuska*** *a-11.* ***Wildey*** *a-16.*

JOURNEY INTO MYSTERY (2nd Series)
Oct, 1972 - No. 19, Oct, 1975
Marvel Comics Group

	Good	Fine	Mint
1-Robert Howard adaptation; Starlin/Ploog-a		.40	.80
2,3,5-Bloch adaptation; 5-Last new story		.30	.60
4-H. P. Lovecraft adaptation		.30	.60
6-19		.30	.60

NOTE: ***Adams*** *a-2i.* ***Ditko*** *a(r)-7, 10, 12, 14, 15, 19; c-10.* ***Everett*** *a-9r, 14r.* ***G. Kane*** *a-1p, 2p; c-1-3p.* ***Kirby*** *a-7r, 13r, 18r, 19r; c-7.* ***Mort Lawrence*** *a-2r.* ***Maneely*** *a-3r.* ***Orlando*** *a-16r.* ***Reese*** *a-1, 2i.* ***Starlin*** *a-3p.* ***Torres*** *a-16r.* ***Wildey*** *a-9r, 14r.*

JOURNEY INTO UNKNOWN WORLDS (Formerly Teen)
No. 36, 9/50 - No. 38, 2/51; No. 4, 4/51 - No. 59, 8/57
Atlas Comics (WFP)

	Good	Fine	Mint
36(#1)-Science fiction/weird	27.00	80.00	190.00
37(#2)-Science fiction; Everett-c/a	21.00	64.00	150.00
38(#3)-Science fiction	17.00	51.00	120.00
4-6,8,10-Science fiction/weird	10.00	30.00	70.00
7-Wolverton-a-"Planet of Terror," 6 pgs; electric chair c-inset/story	20.00	60.00	140.00
9-Giant eyeball story	11.00	32.00	76.00
11,12-Krigstein-a	8.50	25.50	60.00
13,16,17,20	5.00	15.00	35.00
14-Wolverton-a-"One of Our Graveyards Is Missing," 4 pgs; Tuska-a	18.50	55.00	130.00
15-Wolverton-a-"They Crawl By Night," 5 pgs.	18.50	55.00	130.00
18,19-Matt Fox-a	6.00	18.00	42.00
21-26,28-33-Last pre-code (2/55). 21-Decapitation-c. 24-Sci/fic story. 26-Atom bomb panel	2.65	8.00	18.00
27-Sid Check-a	3.00	9.00	21.00
34-Kubert, Torres-a	3.65	11.00	25.00
35-Torres-a	3.00	9.00	21.00
36-42	2.00	6.00	14.00
43-Krigstein-a	3.35	10.00	23.00
44-Davis-a	3.35	10.00	23.00
45,55,59-Williamson-a in all; with Mayo #55,59. Crandall-a, #55,59	5.00	15.00	35.00
46,47,49,52,56-58	1.70	5.00	12.00
48,53-Crandall-a; Check-a, #48	4.45	13.00	30.00
50-Davis, Crandall-a	4.00	12.00	28.00
51-Ditko, Wood-a	3.65	11.00	25.00
54-Torres-a	2.85	8.50	20.00

NOTE: ***Ayers*** *a-24, 43,* ***Berg*** *a-38(No.3), 43.* ***Lou Cameron*** *a-33.* ***Colan*** *a-37(No.2), 6, 17, 20, 39.* ***Ditko*** *a-45, 51.* ***Evans*** *a-20.* ***Everett*** *a-37(No.2), 11, 14, 41, 55, 56; c-11, 13, 14, 17, 22, 47, 48, 50, 53-55, 59.* ***Fox*** *a-21i.* ***Heath*** *a-36(No.1), 4, 6-8, 17, 20, 22, 36i.* ***Mort Lawrence*** *a-38, 39.* ***Maneely*** *a-7, 8, 15, 16, 22, 49; c-25, 52.* ***Morrow*** *a-48.* ***Orlando*** *a-44, 57.* ***Powell*** *a-42, 53, 54.* ***Reinman*** *a-8.* ***Rico*** *a-21.* ***Robert Sale*** *a-24.* ***Sekowsky*** *a-4, 5, 9.* ***Severin*** *a-38, 51; c-38, 48i, 56.* ***Sinnott*** *a-9, 21.* ***Tuska*** *a-38(No.3).* ***Wildey*** *a-25, 44.*

JOURNEY OF DISCOVERY WITH MARK STEEL (See Mark Steel)

JOURNEY TO THE CENTER OF THE EARTH (See 4-Color No. 1060)

JUDE, THE FORGOTTEN SAINT
1954 (16 pgs.; 8x11"; full color; paper cover)
Catechetical Guild Education Society

	Good	Fine	Mint
nn	2.00	6.00	14.00

JUDGE COLT
Oct, 1969 - No. 4, Sept, 1970
Gold Key

	Good	Fine	Mint
1	.85	2.50	6.00
2-4	.70	2.00	4.00

JUDGE DREDD
Nov, 1983 - No. 35, 1986; Oct, 1986 - Present

Journey Into Fear #4, © SUPR

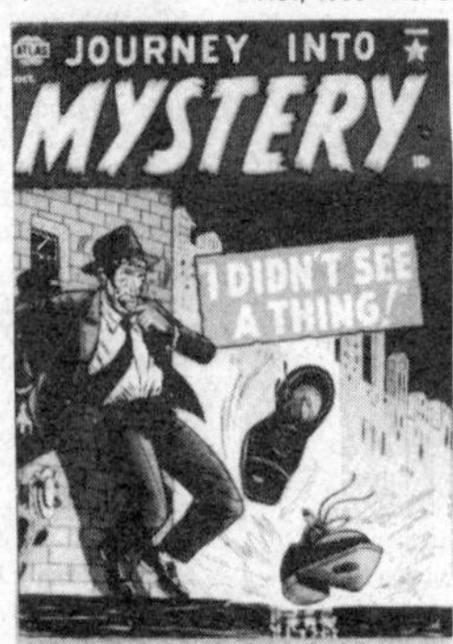

Journey Into Mystery #3 (1st series), © MCG

Journey Into Unknown Worlds #20, © MCG

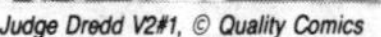
Judge Dredd V2#1, © Quality Comics

Judy Canova #3, © FOX

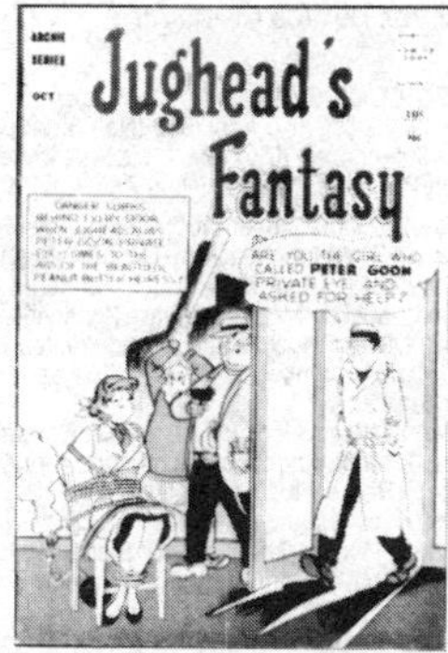

Jughead's Fantasy #2, © AP

JUDGE DREDD (continued)
Eagle Comics/IPC Magazines Ltd./Quality Comics No. 34 on

	Good	Fine	Mint
1-Bolland c/a begins	.70	2.00	4.00
2,3	.40	1.25	2.50
4-10	.35	1.00	2.00
11-20	.30	.90	1.80
21-35	.25	.75	1.50
V2#1-('86)-New look begins	.25	.75	1.50
V2#2-12		.55	1.10
Special 1		.60	1.20

JUDGE DREDD'S CRIME FILE
Aug, 1985 - No. 6, Feb, 1986 (Mini-series)
Eagle Comics

	Good	Fine	Mint
1-6: 1-Byrne-a	.30	.85	1.70

JUDGE DREDD: THE EARLY CASES
Feb, 1986 - No. 6, July, 1986 (Mega-series, Mando paper)
Eagle Comics

	Good	Fine	Mint
1-6: 2000 A.D.-r	.30	.85	1.70

JUDGE DREDD: THE JUDGE CHILD QUEST
Aug, 1984 - No. 5, Oct, 1984 (Limited series, Baxter paper)
Eagle Comics

	Good	Fine	Mint
1-5: 2000 A.D.-r; Bolland c/a	.30	.85	1.70

JUDGE PARKER
Feb, 1956
Argo

	Good	Fine	Mint
1	2.30	7.00	16.00
2	1.30	4.00	9.00

JUDO JOE
Aug, 1953 - No. 3, Dec, 1953
Jay-Jay Corp.

	Good	Fine	Mint
1-Drug ring story	3.50	10.50	24.00
2,3: 3-Hypo needle story	2.00	6.00	14.00

JUDOMASTER (Gun Master No. 84-89) (See Special War Series)
No. 89, May-June, 1966 - No. 98, Dec, 1967 (two No. 89's)
Charlton Comics

	Good	Fine	Mint
89-98: 91-Sarge Steel begins. 93-Intro. Tiger	.50	1.50	3.00
93,94,96,98(Modern Comics reprint, 1977)		.15	.30

NOTE: ***Morisi*** *Thunderbolt No. 90.*

JUDY CANOVA (Formerly My Experience)
May, 1950 - No. 3, Sept, 1950
Fox Features Syndicate

	Good	Fine	Mint
23(#1)-Wood-c,a(p)?	7.00	21.00	50.00
24-Wood-a(p)	7.00	21.00	50.00
3-Wood-c; Wood/Orlando-a	9.50	28.00	65.00

JUDY GARLAND (See Famous Stars)

JUDY JOINS THE WAVES
1951 (For U.S. Navy)
Toby Press

	Good	Fine	Mint
nn	2.30	7.00	16.00

JUGHEAD (Formerly Archie's Pal . . .)
No. 127, Dec, 1965 - No. 352, 1987
Archie Publications

	Good	Fine	Mint
127-130	.85	2.50	5.00
131,133,135-160	.60	1.75	3.50
132-Shield-c; The Fly & Black Hood app.; Shield cameo	.60	1.75	3.50
134-Shield-c	.60	1.75	3.50
161-200	.35	1.00	2.00
201-240		.50	1.00
241-352: 300-Anniversary issue		.30	.60

JUGHEAD
Aug, 1987 - Present
Archie Enterprises

	Good	Fine	Mint
1-4		.40	.75

JUGHEAD AS CAPTAIN HERO
Oct, 1966 - No. 7, Nov, 1967
Archie Publications

	Good	Fine	Mint
1	2.50	7.50	15.00
2	1.35	4.00	8.00
3-7	.85	2.50	5.00

JUGHEAD JONES COMICS DIGEST, THE (. . . Magazine No. 10-on)
June, 1977 - Present (Digest-size)
Archie Publications

	Good	Fine	Mint
1-Adams-a; Capt. Hero-r	.70	2.00	4.00
2(9/77)-Adams-a	.35	1.00	2.00
3-50: 7-Origin Jaguar-r; Adams-a. 13-r-/1957 Jughead's Folly		.50	1.00

JUGHEAD'S EAT-OUT COMIC BOOK MAGAZINE (See Archie Giant Series Mag. No. 170)

JUGHEAD'S FANTASY
Aug, 1960 - No. 3, Dec, 1960
Archie Publications

	Good	Fine	Mint
1	10.00	30.00	70.00
2	7.00	21.00	50.00
3	5.70	17.00	40.00

JUGHEAD'S FOLLY
1957
Archie Publications (Close-Up)

	Good	Fine	Mint
1-Jughead a la Elvis (Rare)	25.00	75.00	175.00

JUGHEAD'S JOKES
Aug, 1967 - No. 78, Sept, 1982
(No. 1-8, 38 on: reg. size; No. 9-23: 68 pgs.; No. 24-37: 52 pgs.)
Archie Publications

	Good	Fine	Mint
1	3.50	10.50	21.00
2	1.70	5.00	10.00
3-5	1.00	3.00	6.00
6-10	.70	2.00	4.00
11-30	.25	.75	1.50
31-50		.45	.90
51-78		.30	.60

JUGHEAD'S SOUL FOOD
1979 (49 cents)
Spire Christian Comics (Fleming H. Revell Co.)

	Good	Fine	Mint
		.30	.60

JUGHEAD WITH ARCHIE DIGEST (. . . Plus Betty & Veronica & Reggie Too No. 1,2; . . . Magazine No. 33 on)
March, 1974 - Present (Digest Size; $1.00-$1.25)
Archie Publications

	Good	Fine	Mint
1	1.15	3.50	7.00
2	.50	1.50	3.00
3-10	.25	.75	1.50
11-20: Capt. Hero r-in #14-16; Pureheart the Powerful #18,21,22; Capt. Pureheart #17,19		.50	1.00
21-85: 29-The Shield-r. 30-The Fly-r		.50	1.00

JUKE BOX COMICS
March, 1948 - No. 6, 1949
Famous Funnies

	Good	Fine	Mint
1-Toth c/a; Hollingsworth-a	18.00	54.00	125.00
2-Transvestism story	8.50	25.50	60.00

JUKE BOX COMICS (continued)

	Good	Fine	Mint
3-6	7.00	21.00	50.00

JUMBO COMICS (Created by S.M. Iger)
Sept, 1938 - No. 167, Apr, 1953 (No.1-3: 68 pgs.; No.4-8: 52 pgs.)
(No. 1-8 oversized-10½x14½''; black & white)
Fiction House Magazines (Real Adv. Publ. Co.)

	Good	Fine	Mint
1-(Rare)-Sheena Queen of the Jungle by Meskin, The Hawk by Eisner, The Hunchback by Dick Briefer(ends #8) begin; 1st comic art by Jack Kirby (Count of Monte Cristo & Wilton of the West); Mickey Mouse appears (1 panel) with brief biography of Walt Disney. **Note:** Sheena was created by Iger for publication in England as a newspaper strip. The early issues of Jumbo contain Sheena strip-r	325.00	975.00	2275.00
2-(Rare)-Origin Sheena. Diary of Dr. Hayward by Kirby (also #3) plus 2 other stories; contains strip from Universal Film featuring Edgar Bergen & Charlie McCarthy	160.00	480.00	1120.00
3-Last Kirby issue	120.00	360.00	840.00
4-(Scarce)-Origin The Hawk by Eisner; Wilton of the West by Fine (ends #14)(1st comic work); Count of Monte Cristo by Fine (ends #15); The Diary of Dr. Hayward by Fine (cont'd. #8,9)	125.00	375.00	875.00
5	80.00	240.00	560.00
6-8-Last B&W issue. #8 was a N. Y. World's Fair Special Edition	65.00	195.00	455.00
9-Stuart Taylor begins by Fine; Fine-c; 1st color issue(8-9/39)-8¼x10¼''(oversized in width only)	68.00	204.00	475.00
10-13: 10-Regular size 68 pg. issues begin; Sheena dons new costume #10	35.00	105.00	245.00
14-Lightning begins (Intro.)	35.00	105.00	245.00
15-20	22.00	65.00	154.00
21-30: 22-1st Tom, Dick & Harry; origin The Hawk retold	20.00	60.00	140.00
31-40: 35 shows V2#11 (correct number does not appear)	18.50	56.00	130.00
41-50	16.50	50.00	115.00
51-60: 52-Last Tom, Dick & Harry	14.00	42.00	100.00
61-70: 68-Sky Girl begins, ends #130; not in #79	11.00	32.00	76.00
71-80	9.50	28.00	65.00
81-93,95-99: 89-ZX5 becomes a private eye	9.50	28.00	65.00
94-Used in **Love and Death** by Legman	10.00	30.00	70.00
100	11.00	32.00	76.00
101-110: 103-Lingerie panel	8.00	24.00	56.00
111-140	6.50	19.50	45.00
141-149-Two Sheena stories. 141-Long Bow, Indian Boy begins, ends #160	8.00	24.00	56.00
150-154,156-158	6.50	19.50	45.00
155-Used in **POP**, pg. 98	7.00	21.00	50.00
159-163: Space Scouts serial in all; 163-Suicide Smith app.	6.50	19.50	45.00
164-The Star Pirate begins, ends #165	6.50	19.50	45.00
165-167: 165,167-Space Rangers app.	6.50	19.50	45.00

NOTE: *Bondage covers, negligee panels, torture, etc. are common in this series. Hawks of the Seas, Inspector Dayton, Spies in Action, Sports Shorts, & Uncle Otto by* ***Eisner****, #1-7. Hawk by* ***Eisner****-#10-15;* ***Eisner*** *c-1, 3-6, 12, 13, 15. 1pg. Patsy pin-ups in 92-97, 99-101. Sheena by* ***Meskin****-#1, 4; by* ***Powell****-#2, 3, 5-28. Sky Girl by* ***Matt Baker****-#69-78, 80-124.* ***Bailey*** *a-3-8.* ***Briefer*** *a-1-8, 10.* ***Fine*** *c-8-11.* ***Kamen*** *a-101, 105, 123, 132; c-105.* ***Bob Kane*** *a-1-8.*

JUMPING JACKS PRESENTS THE WHIZ KIDS
1978 (In 3-D) with glasses (4 pages)
Jumping Jacks Stores giveaway

	Good	Fine	Mint
nn		.40	.80

JUNGLE ACTION
Oct, 1954 - No. 6, Aug, 1955
Atlas Comics (IPC)

	Good	Fine	Mint
1-Leopard Girl begins; Maneely c/a-all	8.00	24.00	56.00
2-(3-D effect cover)	10.00	30.00	70.00
3-6: 3-Last precode (2/55)	5.70	17.00	40.00

JUNGLE ACTION
Oct, 1972 - No. 24, Nov, 1976
Marvel Comics Group

	Good	Fine	Mint
1-Lorna, Jann-r		.40	.80
2-5: 5-Black Panther begins (new-a)		.30	.60
6-18-All new stories. 8-Origin Black Panther		.30	.60
19-23-KKK x-over. 23-r-/No. 22		.30	.60
24-1st Wind Eagle		.30	.60

NOTE: ***Buckler*** *a-6-9pp, 22; c-8p, 12p.* ***Buscema*** *a-5p; c-22.* ***Byrne*** *c-23.* ***Gil Kane*** *c-2, 4, 10p, 11p, 13-17, 19, 24.* ***G. Kane*** *a-8p.* ***Kirby*** *c-18.* ***Russell*** *a-13i.* ***Starlin*** *c-3p.*

JUNGLE ADVENTURES
1963 - 1964 (Reprints)
Super Comics

	Good	Fine	Mint
10,12(Rulah), 15(Kaanga/Jungle #152)	1.35	4.00	9.00
17(Jo-Jo)	1.35	4.00	9.00
18-Reprints/White Princess of the Jungle #1; no Kinstler-a; origin of both White Princess & Cap'n Courage	1.75	5.25	12.00

JUNGLE ADVENTURES
March, 1971 - No. 3, June, 1971
Skywald Comics

	Good	Fine	Mint
1-Zangar origin; reprints of Jo-Jo, Blue Gorilla(origin)/White Princess #3, Kinstler-a/White Princess #2	.50	1.50	3.00
2-Zangar, Sheena/Sheena #17 & Jumbo #162, Jo-Jo, origin Slave Girl Princess-r	.50	1.50	3.00
3-Zangar, Jo-Jo, White Princess-r	.50	1.50	3.00

JUNGLE BOOK, THE (See Movie Comics & Walt Disney Showcase #45)

JUNGLE CAT (See 4-Color No. 1136)

JUNGLE COMICS
Jan, 1940 - No. 163, Summer, 1954
Fiction House Magazines

	Good	Fine	Mint
1-Origin The White Panther, Kaanga, Lord of the Jungle, Tabu, Wizard of the Jungle; Wambi, the Jungle Boy & Camilla begin	105.00	315.00	735.00
2-Fantomah, Mystery Woman of the Jungle begins	50.00	150.00	350.00
3,4	40.00	120.00	280.00
5	33.00	100.00	230.00
6-10	27.00	81.00	190.00
11-20	20.00	60.00	140.00
21-30: 25 shows V2#1 (correct number does not appear). #27-New origin Fantomah, Daughter of the Pharoahs; Camilla dons new costume	17.00	51.00	120.00
31-40	15.00	45.00	105.00
41,43-50	11.50	34.00	80.00
42-Kaanga by Crandall, 12 pgs.	14.00	42.00	100.00
51-60	10.00	30.00	70.00
61-70	8.50	25.50	60.00
71-80: 79-New origin Tabu	8.00	24.00	56.00
81-97,99,101-110	6.50	19.50	45.00
98-Used in **SOTI**, pg. 185 & illo-''In ordinary comic books, there are pictures within pictures for children who know how to look''; used by N.Y. Legis. Comm.	14.00	42.00	100.00
100	8.00	24.00	56.00
111-142,144,146-150: 135-Desert Panther begins in Terry Thunder-(origin), not in #137; ends (dies) #138	6.50	19.50	45.00
143,145-Used in **POP**, pg. 99	7.00	21.00	50.00
151-157,159-163: 152-Tiger Girl begins	6.50	19.50	45.00
158-Sheena app.	8.00	24.00	56.00
I.W. Reprint #1,9: 9-r-/#151	1.00	3.00	6.00

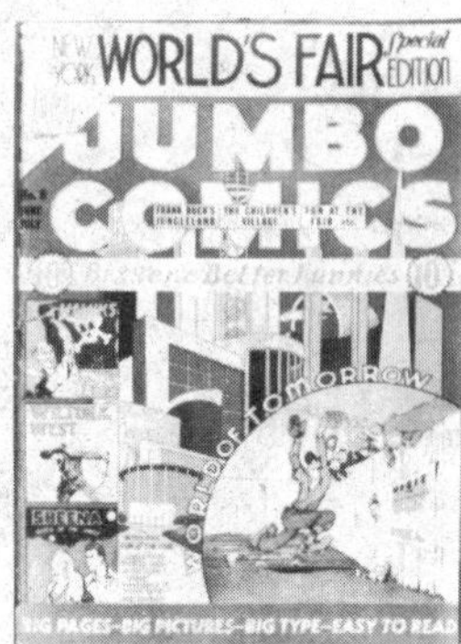

Jumbo Comics #8, © FH

Jumbo Comics #79, © FH

Jungle Comics #41, © FH

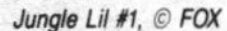
Jungle Lil #1, © FOX

Jungle Thrills 3-D #1, © STAR

Junior Comics #11, © FOX

JUNGLE COMICS (continued)

NOTE: *Bondage covers, negligee panels, torture, etc. are common to this series. Camilla by* ***Fran Hopper****-#73, 78, 80-90; by* ***Baker****-#101, 103, 106, 107, 109, 111-13. Kaanga by* ***John Celardo****-#80-110; by* ***Maurice Whitman****-#124-163. Tabu by* ***Whitman****-No. 93-110.* ***Celardo*** *a-78; c-98, 99, 106, 109, 112.* ***Eisner*** *c-2, 5, 6.* ***Fine*** *c-1.* ***Larsen*** *a-65, 66, 72, 74, 75, 79, 83, 84, 87-90.*

JUNGLE GIRL (See Lorna, . . .)

JUNGLE GIRL (Nyoka, Jungle Girl No. 2 on)
Fall, 1942 (No month listed) (Based on film character)
Fawcett Publications

	Good	Fine	Mint
1-Bondage-c	43.00	130.00	300.00

JUNGLE JIM
Jan, 1949 - No. 20, Apr, 1951
Standard Comics (Best Books)

	Good	Fine	Mint
11	3.50	10.50	24.00
12-20	2.00	6.00	14.00

JUNGLE JIM
No. 490, 8/53 - No. 1020, 8-10/59
Dell Publishing Co.

	Good	Fine	Mint
4-Color 490	2.65	8.00	18.00
4-Color 565(6/54)	2.00	6.00	14.00
3(10-12/54)-5	1.70	5.00	12.00
6-19(1-3/59)	1.50	4.50	10.00
4-Color 1020(#20)	1.70	5.00	12.00

JUNGLE JIM
December, 1967
King Features Syndicate

	Good	Fine	Mint
5-Reprints Dell #5; Wood-c	.85	2.55	6.00

JUNGLE JIM (Continued from Dell)
No. 22, Feb, 1969 - No. 28, Feb, 1970 (No. 21 was an overseas edition only)
Charlton Comics

	Good	Fine	Mint
22-Dan Flagg begins; Ditko/Wood-a	1.50	4.50	10.00
23-28: 23-Last Dan Flagg; Howard-c. 24-Jungle People begin. 27-Ditko/Howard-a. 28-Ditko-a	.85	2.55	6.00

JUNGLE JO
Mar, 1950 - No. 6, Mar, 1951
Fox Feature Syndicate (Hero Books)

	Good	Fine	Mint
nn-Jo-Jo blanked out, leaving Congo King; came out after Jo-Jo #29 (intended as Jo-Jo #30?)	11.00	32.00	76.00
1-Tangi begins; part Wood-a	12.00	36.00	84.00
2	9.50	28.00	65.00
3-6	8.50	25.50	60.00

JUNGLE LIL (Dorothy Lamour No. 2 on) (Also see Feature Stories Magazine)
April, 1950
Fox Feature Syndicate (Hero Books)

	Good	Fine	Mint
1	11.00	32.00	76.00

JUNGLE TALES (Jann of the Jungle No. 8 on)
Sept, 1954 - No. 7, Sept, 1955
Atlas Comics (CSI)

	Good	Fine	Mint
1-Jann of the Jungle	8.00	24.00	56.00
2-7: 3-Last precode (1/55)	5.70	17.00	40.00

NOTE: ***Heck*** *a-6, 7.* ***Maneely*** *a-2; c-1, 3.* ***Shores*** *a-5-7.* ***Tuska*** *a-2.*

JUNGLE TALES OF TARZAN
Dec, 1964 - No. 4, July, 1965
Charlton Comics

	Good	Fine	Mint
1	1.50	4.50	10.00
2-4	1.15	3.50	8.00

NOTE: ***Giordano*** *c-3p.* ***Glanzman*** *a-1-3.* ***Montes/Bache*** *a-4.*

JUNGLE TERROR (See Comics Hits No. 54)

JUNGLE THRILLS (Terrors of the Jungle No. 17)
No. 16, February, 1952
Star Publications

	Good	Fine	Mint
16-Phantom Lady & Rulah story-reprint/All Top No. 15; used in **POP**, pg. 98,99; L. B. Cole-c	15.00	45.00	105.00
3-D 1(12/53)-Jungle Lil & Jungle Jo appear; L. B. Cole-c	20.00	60.00	140.00
7-Titled 'Picture Scope Jungle Adventures;'(1954, 36 pgs, 15 cents)-3-D effect c/stories; story & coloring book; Disbrow-a/script; L.B. Cole-c	11.50	34.00	80.00

JUNGLE TWINS, THE (Tono & Kono)
4/72 - No. 17, 11/75; No. 18, 5/82
Gold Key/Whitman No. 18 on

	Good	Fine	Mint
1	.30	.90	1.80
2-5		.60	1.20
6-18: 18-r		.40	.80

NOTE: *UFO c/story No. 13. Painted-c No. 1-17.* ***Spiegle*** *c-18.*

JUNGLE WAR STORIES (Guerrilla War No. 12 on)
July-Sept, 1962 - No. 11, Apr-June, 1965
Dell Publishing Co.

	Good	Fine	Mint
01-384-209	.55	1.60	4.00
2-11	.50	1.50	3.00

JUNIE PROM
Winter, 1947-48 - No. 7, Aug, 1949
Dearfield Publishing Co.

	Good	Fine	Mint
1-Teen-age	4.00	12.00	28.00
2	2.00	6.00	14.00
3-7	1.50	4.50	10.00

JUNIOR COMICS
No. 9, Sept, 1947 - No. 16, July, 1948
Fox Feature Syndicate

	Good	Fine	Mint
9-Feldstein c/a	32.00	95.00	225.00
10-16-Feldstein c/a	29.00	87.00	200.00

JUNIOR FUNNIES (Formerly Tiny Tot Funnies No. 9)
No. 10, Aug, 1951 - No. 13, Feb, 1952
Harvey Publications (King Features Synd.)

	Good	Fine	Mint
10-Partial reprints in all-Blondie, Popeye, Felix, Katzenjammer Kids	1.50	4.50	10.00
11-13	1.20	3.50	8.00

JUNIOR HOPP COMICS
Feb, 1952 - No. 3, July, 1952
Stanmor Publ.

	Good	Fine	Mint
1	3.50	10.50	24.00
2,3: 3-Dave Berg-a	1.85	5.50	13.00

JUNIOR MEDICS OF AMERICA, THE
1957 (15 cents)
E. R. Squire & Sons

	Good	Fine	Mint
1359	1.30	4.00	9.00

JUNIOR MISS
Winter, 1944; No. 24, April, 1947 - No. 39, Aug, 1950
Timely/Marvel Comics (CnPC)

	Good	Fine	Mint
1-Frank Sinatra & June Allyson life story	6.50	19.50	45.00
24	3.50	10.50	24.00
25-38	1.85	5.50	13.00
39-Kurtzman-a	2.30	7.00	16.00

NOTE: *Painted-c 35-37. 37-all romance. 35,36,38-mostly teen humor.*

JUNIOR PARTNERS (Formerly Oral Roberts' True Stories)
No. 120, Aug, 1959 - V3No.12, Dec, 1961
Oral Roberts Evangelistic Assn.

	Good	Fine	Mint
120(#1)	1.70	5.00	12.00

JUNIOR PARTNERS (continued)	Good	Fine	Mint
2(9/59)	1.15	3.50	8.00
3-12(7/60)	.60	1.80	4.00
V2#1(8/60)-5(12/60)	.50	1.50	3.00
V3#1(1/61)-12	.35	1.00	2.00

JUNIOR TREASURY (See Dell Junior. . .)

JUNIOR WOODCHUCKS (See Huey, Dewey & Louie. . .)

JUSTICE
Nov, 1986 - Present
Marvel Comics Group

Issue	Good	Fine	Mint
1		.50	1.00
2-15		.40	.80

JUSTICE COMICS (Tales of Justice #53 on; formerly Wacky Duck)
No. 7, Fall/47 - No. 9, 6/48; No. 4, 8/48 - No. 52, 3/55
Marvel/Atlas comics (NPP 7-9,4-19/CnPC 20-23/MjMC 24-38/Male 39-52

Issue	Good	Fine	Mint
7('47)	4.35	13.00	30.00
8-Kurtzman-a-"Giggles 'N' Grins," (3)	3.50	10.50	24.00
9('48)	3.00	9.00	21.00
4	2.30	7.00	16.00
5-9: 8-Anti-Wertham editorial	1.70	5.00	12.00
10-15-Photo-c	1.70	5.00	12.00
16-30	1.30	4.00	9.00
31-40,42-47,49-52-Last precode	1.15	3.50	8.00
41-Electrocution-c	3.70	11.00	26.00
48-Pakula & Tuska-a	1.50	4.50	10.00

NOTE: ***Maneely*** *c-44.* ***Pakula*** *a-43, 45.* ***Louis Ravielli*** *a-39.* ***Robinson*** *a-22, 25, 41.* ***Wildey*** *a-52.*

JUSTICE, INC. (The Avenger)
May-June, 1975 - No. 4, Nov-Dec, 1975
National Periodical Publications

Issue	Good	Fine	Mint
1-McWilliams-a; origin		.40	.80
2-4		.25	.50

NOTE: ***Kirby*** *c-2, 3p; a-2-4p.* ***Kubert*** *c-1, 4.*

JUSTICE LEAGUE (. . .International #7 on)
May, 1987 - Present
DC Comics

Issue	Good	Fine	Mint
1	2.00	6.00	12.00
2	1.15	3.50	7.00
3-Regular cover	.70	2.00	4.00
3-Limited cover	5.00	15.00	30.00
4	.60	1.75	3.50
5,6: 5-Origin Gray Man	.35	1.00	2.00
7-Double size ($1.25)	.35	1.10	2.20
8-10	.25	.75	1.50
11-14		.50	1.00
Annual 1 (9/87)	.40	1.25	2.50

JUSTICE LEAGUE OF AMERICA (See Brave & the Bold)
(See Official. . .Index)
10-11/60 - No. 261, 4/87 (52pgs.-91-99,139-157)
National Periodical Publications/DC Comics

Issue	Good	Fine	Mint
1-Origin Despero	82.00	205.00	575.00
2	29.00	73.00	200.00
3-Origin/1st app. Kanjar Ro	21.00	52.00	145.00
4,5: 4-Green Arrow joins JLA. 5-Origin Dr. Destiny	12.00	30.00	85.00
6-8,10: 6-Origin Prof. Amos Fortune. 7-Last 10 cent issue. 10-Origin Felix Faust; 1st app. Time Lord	9.00	23.00	65.00
9-Origin J.L.A.	13.00	32.00	90.00
11-15: 12-Origin & 1st app. Dr. Light. 13-Speedy app. 14-Atom joins JLA	5.45	14.00	38.00
16-20: 17-Adam Strange flashback	3.55	9.00	25.00
21,22: 21-Re-intro. of JSA. 22-JSA x-over	8.00	21.00	58.00
23-28: 24-Adam Strange app. 28-Robin app.	1.70	5.00	12.00
29,30-JSA x-over	1.70	5.00	12.00
31-Hawkman joins JLA, Hawkgirl cameo	1.40	4.25	8.50
32-Intro & Origin Brain Storm	1.40	4.25	8.50
33-36,40	1.25	3.75	7.50
37,38-JSA x-over	1.50	4.50	9.00
39-Giant G-16	2.00	6.00	12.00
41-Intro & Origin The Key	1.25	3.75	7.50
42-45: 42-Metamorpho app. 43-Intro. Royal Flush Gang	.85	2.50	5.00
46,47-JSA x-over	1.25	3.75	7.50
48-Giant G-29	1.30	4.00	8.00
49-57,59,60: 55-Intro. Earth 2 Robin	.85	2.50	5.00
58-Giant G-41	1.15	3.50	7.00
61-66,68-70: 64-Intro/origin Red Tornado. 69-Wonder Woman quits	.70	2.00	4.00
67-Giant G-53	.85	2.50	5.00
71-75,77-80: 71-Manhunter leaves JLA. 74-Black Canary joins. 78-Re-intro Vigilante	.45	1.40	2.80
76-Giant G-65	.70	2.00	4.00
81-84,86-92: 83-Death of Spectre	.45	1.40	2.80
85,93-(Giant G-77,G-89; 68 pgs.)	.70	2.00	4.00
94-Origin Sandman (Adv. #40) & Starman (Adv. #61); Deadman x-over; Adams-a	1.85	5.50	11.00
95-Origin Dr. Fate & Dr. Midnight reprint (More Fun #67, All-American #25)	.50	1.50	3.00
96-Origin Hourman (Adv. #48); Wildcat-r	.50	1.50	3.00
97-Origin JLA retold; Sargon, Starman-r	.60	1.75	3.50
98,99: 98-G.A. Sargon, Starman-r. 99-G.A. Sandman, Starman, Atom-r	.40	1.25	2.50
100	.74	2.25	4.50
101,102: 102-Red Tornado dies	.75	2.25	4.50
103-106: 103-Phantom Stranger joins. 105-Elongated Man joins. 106-New Red Tornado joins	.40	1.25	2.50
107,108-G.A. Uncle Sam, Black Condor, The Ray, Dollman, Phantom Lady, & The Human Bomb x-over	.75	2.25	4.50
109-Hawkman resigns	.35	1.00	2.00
110-116: All 100 pg. issues; 111-Shining Knight, Green Arrow-r. 112-Crimson Avenger, Vigilante, origin Starman-r	.35	1.00	2.00
117-190: 117-Hawkman rejoins. 128-Wonder Woman rejoins. 129-Death of Red Tornado. 135-37-G.A. Bulletman, Bulletgirl, Spy Smasher, Mr. Scarlet, Pinky & Ibis x-over. 137-Superman battles G.A. Capt. Marvel. 144-Origin retold; origin J'onn J'onnz. 145-Red Tornado resurrected. 161-Zatanna joins & new costume. 171-Mr. Terrific murdered. 179-Firestorm joins. 181-Gr. Arrow leaves	.25	.75	1.50
191,194-199		.50	1.00
192-Real origin Red Tornado, ends #193		.50	1.00
193-Free 16pg. insert-All-Star Squadron (1st app.)	.35	1.00	2.00
200-Anniversary ish. (76pgs., $1.50); origin retold; Green Arrow rejoins	.40	1.25	2.50
201-220: 203-Intro/origin new Royal Flush Gang. 208-All-Star Squadron app. 219,220-Origin Black Canary		.65	1.30
221-249 (75 cents): 228-Re-intro Martian Manhunter. 233-New J.L.A. begins. 243-Aquaman leaves. 244,245-Crisis x-over. 253-Origin Despero. 258-Death of Vibe. 260-Death of Steel		.60	1.20
250-Batman rejoins		.60	1.20
251-260		.50	1.00
261-Last issue	.50	1.50	3.00
Annual 1(7/83)	.40	1.25	2.50
Annual 2(10/84)-Intro new J.L.A.	.25	.70	1.40
Annual 3(11/85)-Crisis x-over	.25	.75	1.50

NOTE: ***Adams*** *c-63, 66, 67, 70, 74, 79, 81, 82, 86-89, 91, 92, 94, 96-98, 138, 139.*

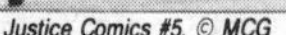
Justice Comics #5, © MCG

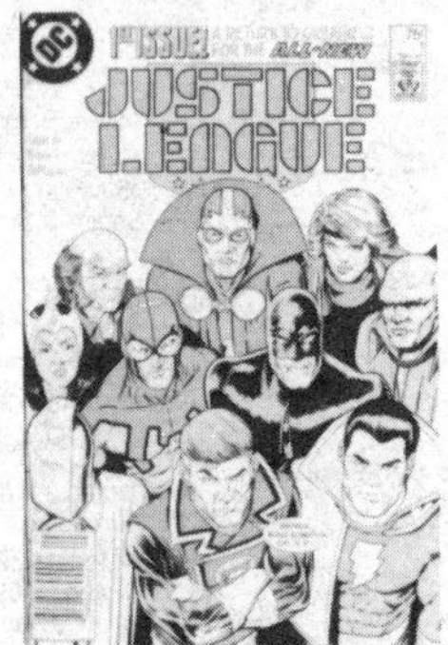

Justice League #1, © DC

Justice League of America #18, © DC

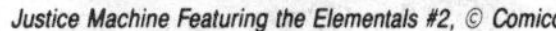

Justice Machine Featuring the Elementals #2, © Comico

Justice Traps the Guilty #22, © PRIZE

Kathy #15, © STD

JUSTICE LEAGUE (continued)
***Aparo** a-200. **Austin** a-200i. **Baily** a-96r. **Burnley** a-94r, 98r, 99r. **Greene** a-46-61i, 64-73i, 110i(r). **Grell** c-117, 122. **Kaluta** c-154p. **Gil Kane** a-200. **Krigstein** a-96(r-Sensation #84.) **Kubert** a-200; c-72, 73. **Nino** a-228i, 230i. **Orlando** c-151i. **Perez** a-184-86p, 192-97p, 200p; c-184p, 186, 192-195, 196p, 197p, 199, 200, 201p, 202, 203-05p, 207-09, 212-15, 217, 219, 220. **Reinman** a-97r. **Roussos** a-62i. **Sekowsky** a-44-63p, 110-12p(r); c-46-48p, 51p. **Smith** c-185i. **Starlin** c-178-80, 183, 185p. **Staton** a-244p; c-157p, 244p. **Toth** a-110r. **Tuska** a-153, 228p, 241-243p. JSA x-over-55, 56, 64, 65, 73, 74, 82, 83, 91, 92, 101, 102, 107, 108, 110, 113, 115, 123, 124, 135-37, 147, 148, 159, 160, 171, 172, 183-85, 195-97, 207, 208, 209, 219, 220, 231, 232.*

JUSTICE MACHINE, THE
June, 1981 - No. 5, Nov, 1983 ($2.00, No. 1-3, Magazine size)
Noble Comics

	Good	Fine	Mint
1-Byrne-c(p)	4.20	12.50	25.00
2-Austin-c(i)	2.00	6.00	12.00
3	1.70	5.00	10.00
4,5	1.00	3.00	6.00
Annual 1 (1/84, 68 pgs.)(published by Texas Comics); 1st app. The Elementals	3.35	10.00	20.00

JUSTICE MACHINE
Jan, 1987 - Present ($1.50, color)
Comico

	Good	Fine	Mint
1	.35	1.00	2.00
2-9	.25	.75	1.50

JUSTICE MACHINE FEATURING THE ELEMENTALS
May, 1986 - No. 4, Aug, 1986 (mini-series)
Comico

	Good	Fine	Mint
1	.50	1.50	3.00
2-4	.35	1.00	2.00

JUSTICE TRAPS THE GUILTY (Fargo Kid V11No.3 on)
Oct-Nov, 1947 - V11No.2(No.92), Apr-May, 1958
Prize/Headline Publications

	Good	Fine	Mint
V2#1-S&K c/a; electrocution-c	11.50	34.00	80.00
2-S&K-c/a	6.00	18.00	42.00
3-5-S&K c/a	5.00	15.00	35.00
6-S&K c/a; Feldstein-a	6.00	18.00	42.00
7,9-S&K c/a	4.00	12.00	28.00
8,10-Krigstein-a; S&K-c. 10-S&K-a	5.00	15.00	35.00
11,19-S&K-c	2.00	6.00	14.00
12,14-17,20-No S&K	1.30	4.00	9.00
13-Used in **SOTI**, pg. 110-111	4.00	12.00	28.00
18-S&K-c, Elder-a	1.85	5.50	13.00
21-S&K c/a	1.85	5.50	13.00
22,23,27-S&K-c	1.70	5.00	11.50
24-26,28-50	1.00	3.00	7.00
51-57,59-70	.85	2.50	6.00
58-Illo. in **SOTI**, "Treating police contemptuously"(top left); text on heroin	9.50	28.00	65.00
71-75,77-92	.85	2.50	6.00
76-Orlando-a	1.00	3.00	7.00

NOTE: ***Bailey** a-12, 13. **Elder** a-8. **Kirby** a-19p. **Meskin** a-22, 27, 63, 64. **Robinson/Meskin** a-5, 19. **Severin** a-8, 11p. Photo-c No. 15, 16.*

JUST KIDS
1932 (16 pages; 9½x12"; paper cover)
McLoughlin Bros.

	Good	Fine	Mint
283-Three-color text, pictures on heavy paper	5.00	15.00	35.00

JUST MARRIED
January, 1958 - No. 114, Dec, 1976
Charlton Comics

	Good	Fine	Mint
1	1.50	4.50	10.00
2	.75	2.25	5.00
3-10	.45	1.35	3.00
11-30	.25	.75	1.50
31-50		.30	.60
51-114		.20	.40

KA'A'NGA COMICS (. . . Jungle King)(See Jungle Comics)
Spring, 1949 - No. 20, Summer, 1954
Fiction House Magazines (Glen-Kel Publ. Co.)

	Good	Fine	Mint
1-Ka'a'nga, Lord of the Jungle begins	20.00	60.00	140.00
2 (Wint., '49-'50)	10.00	30.00	70.00
3,4	8.50	25.50	60.00
5-Camilla app.	6.00	18.00	42.00
6-9: 7-Tuska-a. 9-Tabu, Wizard of the Jungle app.	4.35	13.00	30.00
10-Used in **POP**, pg. 99	4.60	14.00	34.00
11-15	3.50	10.50	24.00
16-Sheena app.	3.70	11.00	26.00
17-20	3.00	9.00	21.00
I.W. Reprint #1 (r-/#18) Kinstler-c	.70	2.00	4.00
I.W. Reprint #8 (reprints #10)	.70	2.00	4.00

KAMANDI, THE LAST BOY ON EARTH (Also see Cancelled Comic Cavalcade and Brave & the Bold No. 120)
Oct-Nov, 1972 - No. 59, Sept-Oct, 1978
National Periodical Publications/DC Comics

	Good	Fine	Mint
1-Origin	.35	1.00	2.00
2-10: 4-Intro. Prince Tuftan of the Tigers		.50	1.00
11-31: 29-Superman x-over. 31-Intro Pyra		.30	.60
32-68 pg. Giant; origin from No. 1		.50	1.00
33-40-Last Kirby issue		.30	.60
41-58: 43-46-Tales of the Great Disaster		.20	.40
59-Starlin c(p)/a(p)		.50	1.00

NOTE: ***Ayers** a(p)-48-59 (most). **Giffen** a-44-47p. **Kirby** a-1-40p; c-1-33. **Kubert** c-34-41. **Nasser** a-45p, 46p. **Starlin** c-57, 59p.*

KARATE KID (See Action, Adventure, Legion of Super-Heroes, & Superboy)
Mar-Apr, 1976 - No. 15, July-Aug, 1978
National Periodical Publications/DC Comics

	Good	Fine	Mint
1-Meets Iris Jacobs; Estrada/Staton-a		.40	.80
2-15: 2-Major Disaster app. 15-Continued into Kamandi #58		.30	.60

NOTE: ***Grell** c-1-4, 5p, 6p, 7, 8. **Staton** a-1-9i. Legion x-over-No. 1, 2, 4, 6, 10, 12, 13. Princess Projectra x-over-#8, 9*

KASCO KOMICS
1945; 1949 (regular size; paper cover)
Kasko Grainfeed (Giveaway)

	Good	Fine	Mint
1(1945)-Similar to Katy Keene; Bill Woggon-a; 28 pgs.; 6-7/8"x9-7/8"	9.35	28.00	65.00
2(1949)	8.00	24.00	55.00

KATHY
September, 1949 - 1953
Standard Comics

	Good	Fine	Mint
1	3.15	9.50	22.00
2-Schomburg-c	1.70	5.00	12.00
3-5	1.30	4.00	9.00
6-16	.85	2.50	6.00

KATHY
Oct, 1959 - No. 27, Feb, 1964
Atlas Comics/Marvel (ZPC)

	Good	Fine	Mint
1	2.15	6.50	15.00
2	1.15	3.50	8.00
3-15	.75	2.25	5.00
16-27	.45	1.25	2.50

KAT KARSON
No date (Reprint)
I. W. Enterprises

KAT KARSON (continued)	Good	Fine	Mint
1-Funny animals	.50	1.50	3.00

KATY AND KEN VISIT SANTA WITH MISTER WISH
1948 (16 pgs.; paper cover)
S. S. Kresge Co. (Giveaway)

	Good	Fine	Mint
	2.35	7.00	14.00

KATY KEENE (Also see Kasco Komics, Laugh, Pep, Suzie, & Wilbur)
1949 - No. 4, 1951; No. 5, 3/52 - No. 62, Oct, 1961
Archie Publ./Close-Up/Radio Comics

	Good	Fine	Mint
1-Bill Woggon-a begins	60.00	180.00	420.00
2	30.00	90.00	210.00
3-5	26.00	78.00	180.00
6-10	21.00	62.00	150.00
11,13-20	18.50	56.00	130.00
12-(Scarce)	20.00	60.00	140.00
21-40	12.00	36.00	84.00
41-62	8.50	25.50	60.00
Annual 1('54)	32.00	95.00	225.00
Annual 2-6('55-59)	16.00	48.00	110.00
3-D 1(1953-Large size)	27.00	81.00	190.00
Charm 1(9/58)	15.00	45.00	105.00
Glamour 1(1957)	15.00	45.00	105.00
Spectacular 1('56)	15.00	45.00	105.00

KATY KEENE COMICS DIGEST MAGAZINE
1987 - Present ($1.25, digest size, annual)
Close-Up, Inc. (Archie Ent.)

	Good	Fine	Mint
1		.70	1.35

KATY KEENE FASHION BOOK MAGAZINE
1955 - No. 13, Sum, '56 - No. 23, Wint, '58-59 (nn 3-10)
Radio Comics/Archie Publications

	Good	Fine	Mint
1	30.00	90.00	210.00
2	17.00	51.00	120.00
11-18: 18-Photo Bill Woggon	13.00	40.00	90.00
19-23	10.00	30.00	70.00

KATY KEENE HOLIDAY FUN (See Archie Giant Series Mag. No. 7,12)

KATY KEENE PINUP PARADE
1955 - No. 15, Summer, 1961 (25 cents)
Radio Comics/Archie Publications

	Good	Fine	Mint
1	30.00	90.00	210.00
2	17.00	51.00	120.00
3-5	14.00	42.00	100.00
6-10,12-14: 8-Mad parody. 10-Photo Bill Woggon	11.50	34.00	80.00
11-Story of how comics get CCA approved, narrated by Katy	14.00	42.00	100.00
15(Rare)-Photo artist & family	30.00	90.00	210.00

KATY KEENE SPECIAL (Katy Keene No. 7 on)
Sept, 1983 - Present
Archie Enterprises

	Good	Fine	Mint
1-Woggon-r; new Woggon-c		.50	1.00
2-25: 3-Woggon-r		.30	.60

KATZENJAMMER KIDS, THE
1903 (50 pgs.; 10x15¼"; in color)
New York American & Journal

(by Rudolph Dirks, strip 1st appeared in 1898)

	Good	Fine	Mint
1903 (Rare)	25.00	75.00	175.00
1905-Tricks of...(10x15)	18.00	54.00	125.00
1906-Stokes-10x16", 32 pgs. in color	18.00	54.00	125.00
1910-The Komical...(10x15)	18.00	54.00	125.00
1921-Embee Dist. Co., 10x16", 20 pgs. in color	15.00	45.00	105.00

KATZENJAMMER KIDS, THE (See Giant Comic Album)
1945-1946; Summer, 1947 - No. 27, Feb-Mar, 1954
David McKay Publ./Standard No.12-21(Spring/'50 - 53)/Harvey No. 22, 4/53 on

	Good	Fine	Mint
Feature Books 30	8.00	24.00	56.00
Feature Books 32,35('45),41,44('46)	6.00	18.00	42.00
Feature Book 37-Has photos & biog. of Harold Knerr	7.00	21.00	50.00
1(1947)	7.00	21.00	50.00
2	3.70	11.00	26.00
3-11	2.85	8.50	20.00
12-14(Standard)	2.00	6.00	14.00
15-21(Standard)	1.50	4.50	10.00
22-25,27(Harvey): 22-24-Henry app.	1.15	3.50	8.00
26-½ in 3-D	11.00	33.00	76.00

KAYO (Formerly Jest?)
March, 1945
Harry 'A' Chesler

	Good	Fine	Mint
12-Green Knight, Capt. Glory, Little Nemo (not by McCay)	4.60	14.00	32.00

KA-ZAR (Also see X-Men #10)
Aug, 1970 - No. 3, Mar, 1971 (Giant-Size, 68 pgs.)
Marvel Comics Group

	Good	Fine	Mint
1-Reprints earlier Ka-Zar stories; Avengers x-over in Hercules; Daredevil, X-Men app; hidden profanity-c	.25	.75	1.50
2,3-Daredevil app., Ka-Zar origin No. 2; Angel in both		.50	1.00

NOTE: *Kirby c/a-all. Colan a-1p(r).*

KA-ZAR (See Savage Tales #6)
Jan, 1974 - No. 20, Feb, 1977 (Regular Size)
Marvel Comics Group

	Good	Fine	Mint
1		.60	1.20
2-10: 4-Brunner-c		.40	.80
11-20		.30	.60

NOTE: ***Alcala** a-6i, 8i. **J. Buscema** a-6-10p; c-1, 5, 7. **Heath** a-12. **Gil Kane** c(p)-3, 5, 8-11, 15, 20. **Kirby** c-12p. **Reinman** a-1p.*

KA-ZAR THE SAVAGE (See Marvel Fanfare)
4/81 - No. 34, 10/84 (Regular size) (Mando paper No. 10 on)
Marvel Comics Group

	Good	Fine	Mint
1	.25	.75	1.50
2-9		.50	1.00
10-First direct sale	.35	1.00	2.00
11-Origin Zabu		.50	1.00
12-Two versions: With & without panel missing (1600 printed with panel)		.50	1.00
13-28,30-34: 21-26-Spider-Man x-over		.40	.80
29-Double size; Ka-Zar & Shanna wed		.40	.80

NOTE: ***B. Anderson** a-1p-15p, 18, 19; c-1-17, 18p, 20(back-c). **Gil Kane** a-11, 12, 14. Photo-c No. 26.*

KEEN DETECTIVE FUNNIES (Formerly Det. Picture Stories?)
No. 8, July, 1938 - No. 24, Sept, 1940
Centaur Publications

	Good	Fine	Mint
V1#8-The Clock continues-r/Funny Pic. Stories 1	55.00	165.00	385.00
9-Tex Martin by Eisner	35.00	105.00	245.00
10,11	28.00	84.00	195.00
V2#1,2-The Eye Sees by Frank Thomas begins; ends #23(Not in V2#3&5). 2-Jack Cole-a	25.00	75.00	175.00
3-TNT Todd begins	25.00	75.00	175.00
4,5: 5-Dean Denton app.	25.00	75.00	175.00
6,9-11: 11-Dean Denton begins	25.00	75.00	175.00
7-The Masked Marvel by Ben Thompson begins	50.00	150.00	350.00

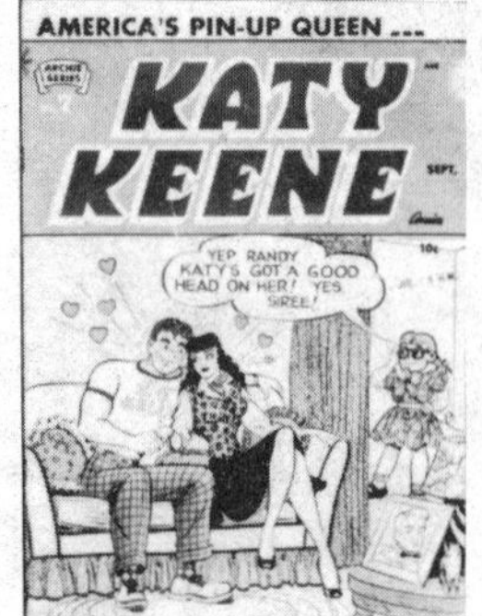

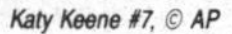
Katy Keene #7, © AP

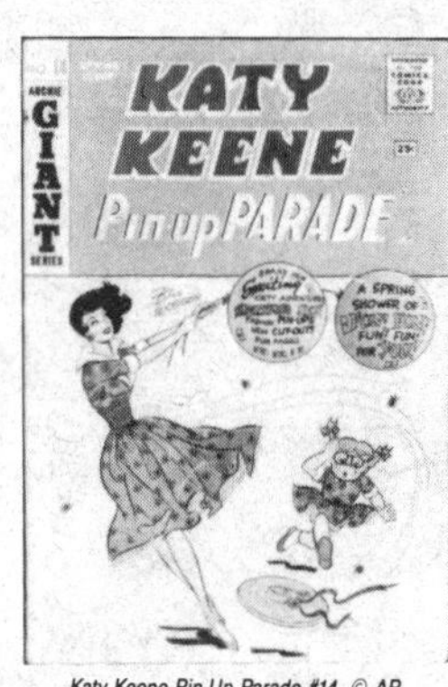

Katy Keene Pin-Up Parade #14, © AP

Keen DETECTIVE FUNNIES
10¢
AUG
The GANG BUSTER

Keen Detective Funnies #9, © CEN

Ken Maynard Western #6, © FAW

Kerry Drake Detective Cases #12, © HARV

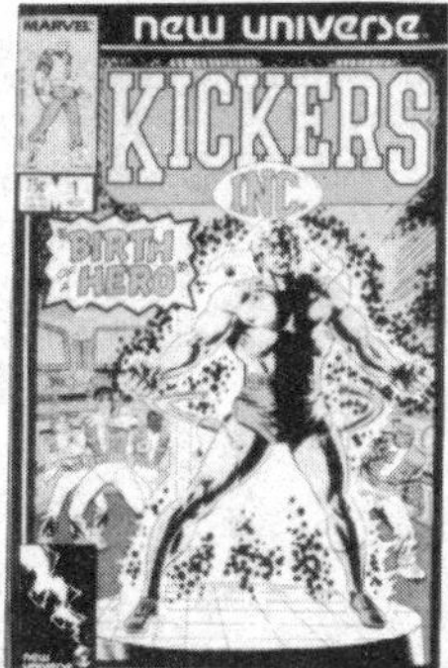

Kickers, Inc. #1, © MCG

KEEN DET. FUNNIES (continued) Good Fine Mint
8-Nudist ranch panel w/four girls 30.00 90.00 210.00
12(12/39)-Origin The Eye Sees by Frank Thomas; death of Masked Marvel's sidekick ZL 35.00 105.00 245.00
V3#1,2 30.00 90.00 210.00
18,19,21,22: 18-Bondage/torture-c 30.00 90.00 210.00
20-Classic Eye Sees-c by Thomas 35.00 105.00 245.00
23-Air Man begins (intro) 35.00 105.00 245.00
24-Air Man-c 35.00 105.00 245.00
NOTE: ***Burgos*** *a-V2#2.* ***Jack Cole*** *a-V2#2.* ***Eisner*** *a-V2#6r.* ***Ken Ernst*** *a-V2#4-7, 9, 10, 19, 21.* ***Everett*** *a-V2#6, 7, 9, 11, 12, 20.* ***Guardineer*** *a-V2#5, 66.* ***Gustavson*** *a-V2#4-6.* ***Simon*** *c-V3#1.*

KEEN KOMICS
V2No.1, May, 1939 - V2No.3, Nov, 1939
Centaur Publications
V2#1(Large size)-Dan Hastings (s/f), The Big Top, Bob Phantom the Magician, The Mad Goddess app. 30.00 90.00 210.00
V2#2(Reg. size)-The Forbidden Idol of Machu Picchu; Cut Carson by Burgos begins 21.00 64.00 150.00
V2#3-Saddle Sniffl by Jack Cole, Circus Pays, Kings Revenge app. 21.00 64.00 150.00
NOTE: ***Binder*** *a-V2/2.* ***Burgos*** *a-V2/2,3.* ***Ken Ernst*** *a-V2/3.* ***Gustavson*** *a-V2/2.* ***Jack Cole*** *a-V2/3.*

KEEN TEENS
1945 - No. 6, Sept, 1947
Life's Romances Publ./Leader/Magazine Enterprises
nn-14 pgs. Claire Voyant (cont'd. in other nn issue) movie photos, Dotty Dripple, Gertie O'Grady & Sissy 8.50 25.50 60.00
nn-16 pgs. Claire Voyant & 16 pgs. movie photos 8.50 25.50 60.00
3-6: 4-Glenn Ford-c. 5-Perry Como-c 2.65 8.00 18.00

KEEPING UP WITH THE JONESES
1920 - No. 2, 1921 (52 pgs.; 9¼x9¼"; B&W daily strip reprints)
Cupples & Leon Co.
1,2-By Pop Momand 7.00 21.00 50.00

KELLYS, THE (Formerly Rusty; Spy Cases No. 26 on)
No. 23, Jan, 1950 - No. 25, June, 1950
Marvel Comics (HPC)
23 4.00 12.00 28.00
24,25: 24-Margie app. 2.30 7.00 16.00

KEN MAYNARD WESTERN (Movie star)(See Wow Comics, '36)
Sept, 1950 - No. 8, Feb, 1952 (All-36pgs; photo front/back-c)
Fawcett Publications
1-K. Maynard & his horse Tarzan begin 20.00 60.00 140.00
2 13.00 40.00 90.00
3-8 11.50 34.50 80.00

KEN SHANNON (Gabby No. 11)
Oct, 1951 - No. 15, 1953 (a private eye)
Quality Comics Group
1-Crandall-a 10.00 30.00 70.00
2-Crandall c/a(2); text on narcotics 8.50 25.50 60.00
3-5-Crandall-a 5.00 15.00 35.00
6 3.50 10.50 24.00
7,9,10-Crandall-a 4.60 14.00 32.00
8-Opium den drug use story 5.00 15.00 35.00
11-15 (Exist?) 2.30 7.00 16.00
NOTE: ***Jack Cole*** *a-1-9. No. 11-15 published after title change to Gabby.*

KEN STUART
Jan, 1949 (Sea Adventures)
Publication Enterprises
1-Frank Borth-c/a 3.00 9.00 21.00

KENT BLAKE OF THE SECRET SERVICE (Spy)
May, 1951 - No. 14, July, 1953
Marvel/Atlas Comics(20CC)
Good Fine Mint
1-Injury to eye, bondage, torture 5.00 15.00 35.00
2-Drug use w/hypo scenes 2.65 8.00 18.00
3-14 1.50 4.50 10.00
NOTE: ***Heath*** *c-5, 7.* ***Infantino*** *c-12.* ***Sinnott*** *a-2(3).*

KERRY DRAKE (Also see Green Hornet)
Jan, 1956 - No. 2, March, 1956
Argo
1,2-Newspaper-r 2.30 7.00 16.00

KERRY DRAKE DETECTIVE CASES (. . . Racket Buster No. 32,33)
(Also see Chamber of Clues)
1944; No. 6, Jan, 1948 - No. 33, Aug, 1952
Life's Romances/Compix/Magazine Ent. No.1-5/Harvey No.6 on
nn(1944)(A-1 Comics)(slightly over-size) 11.50 34.00 80.00
2 7.00 21.00 50.00
3-5(1944) 6.00 18.00 42.00
6,8(1948); 8-Bondage-c 3.50 10.50 24.00
7-Kubert-a; biog of Andriola 4.00 12.00 28.00
9,10-Two-part marijuana story; Kerry smokes marijuana-No. 10 6.75 20.00 47.00
11-15 3.00 9.00 21.00
16-33 2.35 7.00 16.00
. . . in the Case of the Sleeping City-(1951-Publishers Synd.)-16 pg. giveaway for armed forces; paper cover 2.35 7.00 16.00
NOTE: ***Berg*** *a-5.* ***Powell*** *a-10-13, 23.*

KEWPIES
Spring, 1949
Will Eisner Publications
1-Feiffer-a; used in **SOTI** in a non-seductive context, pg. 35 17.00 51.00 120.00

KEY COMICS
Jan, 1944 - No. 5, Aug, 1946
Consolidated Magazines
1-The Key, Will-O-The-Wisp begin 7.00 21.00 50.00
2 4.00 12.00 28.00
3-5 3.00 9.00 21.00

KEY COMICS
1951 - 1956 (32 pages) (Giveaway)
Key Clothing Co./Peterson Clothing
Contains a comic from different publishers bound with new cover. Cover changed each year. Many combinations possible. Distributed in Nebraska, Iowa, & Kansas. Contents would determine price, 40-60 percent of original.

KEY RING COMICS
1941 (16 pgs.; two colors) (sold 5 for 10 cents)
Dell Publishing Co.
1-Sky Hawk 2.00 6.00 12.00
1-Viking Carter 2.00 6.00 12.00
1-Features Sleepy Samson 2.00 6.00 12.00
1-Origin Greg Gilday r-/War Comics No. 2 2.35 7.00 14.00
1-Radior(Super hero) 2.35 7.00 14.00
NOTE: *Each book has two holes in spine to put in binder.*

KICKERS, INC.
Nov, 1986 - No. 12, Oct, 1987
Marvel Comics Group
1 .50 1.00
2-12 .40 .80

KID CARROTS
September, 1953
St. John Publishing Co.
1 1.15 3.50 8.00

KID COLT OUTLAW (Kid Colt #1-4; . . .Outlaw #5-on)(Also see All Western Winners, Best Western,Black Rider, Two-Gun Kid, Two-Gun Western, Western Winners, Wild Western, & Wisco)
8/48 - No. 139, 3/68; No. 140, 11/69 - No. 229, 4/79
Marvel Comics(LCC) 1-16; Atlas(LMC) 17-102; Marvel 103-on

	Good	Fine	Mint
1-Kid Colt & his horse Steel begin; Two-Gun Kid app.	24.00	72.00	170.00
2	11.50	34.00	80.00
3-5: 4-Anti-Wertham editorial; Tex Taylor app. 5-Blaze Carson app.	7.00	21.00	50.00
6-8: 6-Tex Taylor app; 7-Nimo the Lion begins, ends #10	5.00	15.00	35.00
9,10 (52pgs.)	5.70	17.00	40.00
11-Origin	5.70	17.00	40.00
12-20	3.50	10.50	24.00
21-32	2.65	8.00	18.00
33-45: Black Rider in all	2.00	6.00	14.00
46,47,49,50	1.70	5.00	12.00
48-Kubert-a	2.15	6.50	15.00
51-53,55,56	1.50	4.50	10.00
54-Williamson/Maneely-c	2.50	7.50	17.00
57-60,66: 4-pg. Williamson-a in all. 59-Reprint Rawhide Kid #79	3.65	11.00	25.00
61-63,67-78,80-85	1.00	3.00	7.00
64,65-Crandall-a	1.30	4.00	9.00
79-Origin retold	1.30	4.00	9.00
86-Kirby-a(r)	1.00	3.00	7.00
87-Davis-a(r)	1.30	4.00	9.00
88,89-Williamson-a in both (4 pgs.). 89-Redrawn Matt Slade #2	2.15	6.50	15.00
90-99	.45	1.25	3.00
100-Last 10 cent ish.	.55	1.65	4.00
101-120	.25	.75	1.50
121-140: 121-Rawhide Kid x-over. 125-Two-Gun Kid x-over. 130-132 -68pg. issues with one new story each; 130-Origin. 140-Reprints begin		.30	.60
141-160: 156-Giant; reprints		.30	.60
161-229: 170-Origin retold		.25	.50
. . .Album (no date; 1950's; Atlas Comics)-132 pgs.; random binding, cardboard cover, B&W stories; contents can vary	10.00	30.00	70.00
Giant Size 1(1/75), 2(4/75), 3(7/75)		.40	.80

NOTE: ***Ayers*** *a-many.* ***Colan*** *a-52, 53; c(p)-223, 228, 229.* ***Crandall*** *a-140r, 167r.* ***Everett*** *a-137i, 225i(r).* ***Heath*** *c-34, 35, 39, 46, 48, 49, 57.* ***Jack Keller*** *a-25(2), 26-68(3-4), 78, 94p, 98, 99, 108, 110, 132.* ***Kirby*** *a-86r, 93, 96, 119, 176(part); c-87, 92-95, 97, 99-112, 114-117, 121-123, 197r.* ***Maneely*** *a-12, 68, 81; c-41-43, 52, 53, 62, 65, 68, 78, 81.* ***Morrow*** *a-173r.* ***Rico*** *a-13, 18.* ***Severin*** *c-58.* ***Shores*** *a-39, 41-43; c-24.* ***Sutton*** *a-137p, 225p(r).* ***Wildey*** *a-82.* ***Williamson*** *a-147r, 170r, 172r.* ***Woodbridge*** *a-64, 81. Black Rider in #33-45, 74, 86. Iron Mask in #110, 114, 121, 127. Sam Hawk in #84, 101, 111, 121, 146, 174, 181, 188.*

KID COWBOY (Also see Approved Comics #4)
1950 - 1954 (painted covers)
Ziff-Davis Publ./St. John (Approved Comics)

	Good	Fine	Mint
1-Lucy Belle begins	4.00	12.00	28.00
2	2.30	7.00	16.00
3-14: 11-Bondage-c	1.70	5.00	12.00

NOTE: ***Berg*** *a-5.* ***Maneely*** *c-2.*

KIDDIE KAPERS
1945?(nd); Oct, 1957; 1963 - 1964
Decker Publ. (Red Top-Farrell)

	Good	Fine	Mint
1(nd, 1945-46?)-Infinity-c	2.30	7.00	16.00
1(10/57)(Decker)-Little Bit reprints from Kiddie Karnival	.85	2.50	6.00
Super Reprint #7, 10('63), 12, 14('63), 15,17('64), 18('64)	.35	1.00	2.00

KIDDIE KARNIVAL
1952 (100 pgs.) (One Shot)
Ziff-Davis Publ. Co. (Approved Comics)

	Good	Fine	Mint
nn-Rebound Little Bit #1,2	5.00	15.00	35.00

KID ETERNITY (Becomes Buccaneers) (See Hit)
Spring, 1946 - No. 18, Nov, 1949
Quality Comics Group

	Good	Fine	Mint
1	30.00	90.00	210.00
2	14.00	42.00	100.00
3-Mac Raboy-a	15.00	45.00	105.00
4-10	8.50	25.50	60.00
11-18	5.50	16.50	38.00

KID FROM DODGE CITY, THE
July, 1957 - No. 2, Sept, 1957
Atlas Comics (MMC)

	Good	Fine	Mint
1	2.30	7.00	16.00
2-Everett-c	1.15	3.50	8.00

KID FROM TEXAS, THE (A Texas Ranger)
June, 1957 - No. 2, Aug, 1957
Atlas Comics (CSI)

	Good	Fine	Mint
1-Powell-a	2.65	8.00	18.00
2	1.30	4.00	9.00

KID KOKO
1958
I. W. Enterprises

	Good	Fine	Mint
Reprint No. 1,2-(reprints M.E.'s Koko & Kola No. 4, 1947)	.50	1.50	3.00

KID KOMICS (. . .Movie Komics No. 11)
Feb, 1943 - No. 10, Spring, 1946
Timely Comics (USA 1,2/FCI 3-10)

	Good	Fine	Mint
1-Origin Captain Wonder & sidekick Tim Mullrooney, & Subbie; intro the Sea-Going Lad, Pinto Pete, & Trixy Trouble; Knuckles & White-wash Jones only app.; Wolverton art, 7 pgs.	105.00	315.00	735.00
2-The Young Allies, Red Hawk, & Tommy Tyme begin; last Captain Wonder & Subbie	60.00	180.00	420.00
3-The Vision & Daredevils app.	40.00	120.00	280.00
4-The Destroyer begins; Sub-Mariner app.; Red Hawk & Tommy Tyme end	34.00	100.00	240.00
5,6	25.00	75.00	175.00
7-10: The Whizzer app. 7; Destroyer not in #7,8; 10-Last Destroyer, Young Allies & Whizzer	21.00	62.00	146.00

KID MONTANA (Formerly Davy Crockett Frontier Fighter; The Gunfighters No. 51 on)
V2No.9, Nov, 1957 - No. 50, Mar, 1965
Charlton Comics

	Good	Fine	Mint
V2#9	2.00	6.00	14.00
10	1.00	3.00	7.00
11,12,14-20	.70	2.00	5.00
13-Williamson-a	1.70	5.00	12.00
21-35	.45	1.35	3.00
36-50		.40	.80

NOTE: *Title change to Montana Kid on cover only on No. 44; remained Kid Montana on inside.*

KID MOVIE KOMICS (Formerly Kid Komics; Rusty No. 12 on)
No. 11, Summer, 1946
Timely Comics

	Good	Fine	Mint
11-Silly Seal & Ziggy Pig; 2 pgs. Kurtzman "Hey Look" plus 6 pg. story	8.00	24.00	56.00

KIDNAPPED (See 4-Color No. 1101 & Movie Comics)

KIDNAP RACKET (See Comics Hits No. 57)

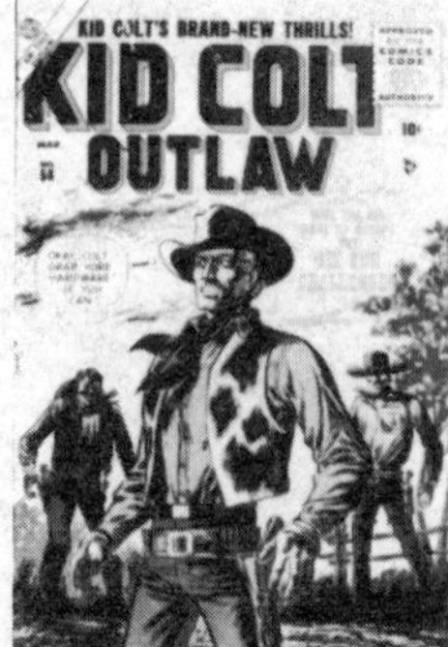

Kid Colt Outlaw #58, © MCG

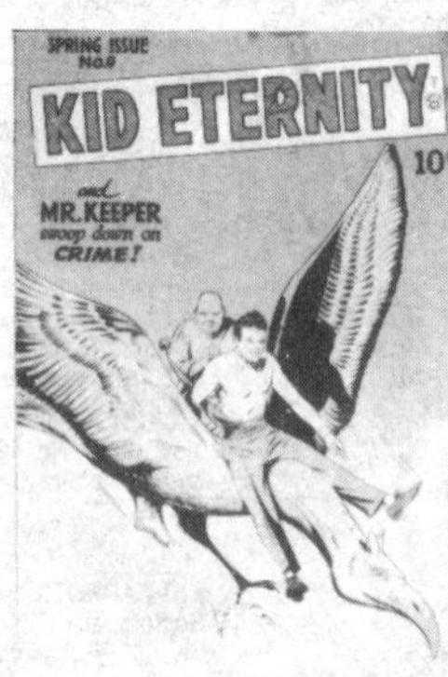

Kid Eternity #9, © QUA

Kid Komics #8, © MCG

The Kilroys #22, © ACG

King Comics #11, © KING

King of the Royal Mounted #18, © Zane Grey

KID SLADE GUNFIGHTER (Formerly Matt Slade. . .)
No. 5, Jan, 1957 - No. 8, July, 1957
Atlas Comics (SPI)

	Good	Fine	Mint
5-Severin-a; Maneely-c	2.65	8.00	18.00
6,8	1.30	4.00	9.00
7-Williamson/Mayo-a, 4 pgs.	3.50	10.50	24.00

KID ZOO COMICS
July, 1948 (52 pgs.)
Street & Smith Publications

	Good	Fine	Mint
1-Funny Animal	3.50	10.50	24.00

KILLER
March, 1985 (One-shot)(Baxter paper)
Eclipse Comics

	Good	Fine	Mint
1	.30	.90	1.80

KILLERS, THE
1947 - 1948 (No month)
Magazine Enterprises

	Good	Fine	Mint
1-Mr. Zin, the Hatchet Killer; mentioned in **SOTI**, pgs. 179,180; Used by N.Y. Legis. Comm. L. B. Cole-c	50.00	150.00	350.00
2-(Scarce)-Hashish smoking story; "Dying, Dying, Dead" drug sty; Whitney, Ingels-a; Whitney hanging-c	50.00	150.00	350.00

KILROYS, THE
June-July, 1947 - No. 54, June-July, 1955
B&I Publ. Co. No. 1-19/American Comics Group

	Good	Fine	Mint
1	6.50	19.50	45.00
2	3.50	10.50	24.00
3-5: 5-Gross-a	2.65	8.00	18.00
6-10: 8-Milt Gross's Moronica	2.00	6.00	14.00
11-20: 14-Gross-a	1.70	5.00	12.00
21-30	1.30	4.00	9.00
31-47,50-54	.85	2.50	6.00
48,49-(3-D effect)	6.50	19.50	45.00

KING CLASSICS
1977 (85 cents each) (36 pages, cardboard covers)
King Features (Printed in Spain for U.S. distr.)

1-Connecticut Yankee, 2-Last of the Mohicans, 3-Moby Dick, 4-Robin Hood, 5-Swiss Family Robinson, 6-Robinson Crusoe, 7-Treasure Island, 8-20,000 Leagues, 9-Christmas Carol, 10-Huck Finn, 11-Around the World in 80 Days, 12-Davy Crockett, 13-Don Quixote, 14-Gold Bug, 15-Ivanhoe, 16-Three Musketeers, 17-Baron Munchausen, 18-Alice in Wonderland, 19-Black Arrow, 20-Five Weeks in a Balloon, 21-Great Expectations, 22-Gulliver's Travels, 23-Prince & Pauper, 24-Lawrence of Arabia

	Good	Fine	Mint
(Originals, 1977-78) each....	1.00	3.00	7.00
Reprints, 1979; HRN-24)	.85	2.50	5.00

NOTE: *The first eight issues were not numbered. Issues No. 25-32 were advertised but not published. The 1977 originals have HRN 32a; the 1978 originals have HRN 32b.*

KING COLT (See 4-Color No. 651)

KING COMICS (Strip reprints)
Apr, 1936 - No. 159, Feb, 1952 (Winter on cover)
David McKay Publications/Standard No. 156-on

	Good	Fine	Mint
1-Flash Gordon by Alex Raymond; Brick Bradford, Mandrake the Magician & Popeye begin	230.00	690.00	1610.00
2	105.00	315.00	735.00
3	75.00	225.00	525.00
4	50.00	150.00	350.00
5	40.00	120.00	280.00
6-10: 9-X-Mas-c	25.00	75.00	175.00
11-20	20.00	60.00	140.00
21-30	17.00	51.00	120.00
31-40: 33-Last Segar Popeye	15.00	45.00	105.00
41-50: 46-Little Lulu, Alvin & Tubby app. as text illos by Marge Buell 50-The Lone Ranger begins	13.00	40.00	90.00
51-60: 52-Barney Baxter begins?	10.00	30.00	70.00
61-The Phantom begins	9.50	28.00	65.00
62-99	8.00	24.00	56.00
100	9.50	28.00	65.00
101-115-Last Raymond issue	6.00	18.00	42.00
116-145: 117-Phantom origin retold	5.00	15.00	35.00
146,147-Prince Valiant in both	3.70	11.00	26.00
148-155-Flash Gordon ends	3.70	11.00	26.00
156-159	2.85	8.50	20.00

NOTE: ***Marge Buell** text illos in No. 24-46 at least.*

KING CONAN (Conan The King No. 20 on)
March, 1980 - No. 19, Nov, 1983 (52 pgs.)
Marvel Comics Group

	Good	Fine	Mint
1	.50	1.50	3.00
2-6: 4-Death of Thoth Amon	.30	.90	1.80
7-1st Paul Smith-a, 2 pgs. (9/81)	.35	1.00	2.00
8-10		.60	1.20
11-19		.50	1.00

NOTE: ***Buscema** a-1p-9p, 17p; c(p)-1-5, 7-9, 14, 17. **Kaluta** c-19. **Nebres** a-17i, 18, 19i. **Severin** c-18. **Simonson** c-6.*

KING KONG (See Movie Comics)

KING LEONARDO & HIS SHORT SUBJECTS (TV)
Nov-Jan, 1961-62 - No. 4, Sept, 1963
Dell Publishing Co./Gold Key

	Good	Fine	Mint
4-Color 1242,1278	3.50	10.50	24.00
01390-207(5-7/62)(Dell)	3.00	9.00	21.00
1 (10/62)	3.00	9.00	21.00
2-4	1.70	5.00	12.00

KING LOUIE & MOWGLI
May, 1968 (Disney)
Gold Key

	Good	Fine	Mint
1 (10223-805)	1.50	4.50	10.00

KING OF DIAMONDS (TV)
July-Sept, 1962
Dell Publishing Co.

	Good	Fine	Mint
01-391-209-Photo-c	1.75	5.25	12.00

KING OF KINGS (See 4-Color No. 1236)

KING OF THE BAD MEN OF DEADWOOD
1950 (See Wild Bill Hickok #16)
Avon Periodicals

	Good	Fine	Mint
nn-Kinstler-c; Kamen/Feldstein-a r-/Cowpuncher 2	9.50	28.00	65.00

KING OF THE ROYAL MOUNTED (See Large Feat. Comic No. 9, Feature Books No. 1 (McKay), & Super Book No. 2,6)

KING OF THE ROYAL MOUNTED (Zane Grey's)
No. 207, Dec, 1948 - No. 935, Sept-Nov, 1958
Dell Publishing Co.

	Good	Fine	Mint
4-Color 207('48)	11.50	34.00	80.00
4-Color 265,283	7.00	21.00	50.00
4-Color 310,340	4.60	14.00	32.00
4-Color 363,384	4.00	12.00	28.00
8(6-8/52)-10	4.00	12.00	28.00
11-20	3.50	10.50	24.00
21-28(3-5/58)	3.00	9.00	21.00
4-Color 935(9-11/58)	3.00	9.00	21.00

NOTE: *4-Color No. 207,265,283,310,340,363,384 are all newspaper reprints with **Jim Gary** art. No. 8 on are all Dell originals. **Painted** c-No. 9-on.*

KING RICHARD & THE CRUSADERS (See 4-Color No. 588)

KING SOLOMON'S MINES
1951 (Movie)
Avon Periodicals

KING SOLOMON'S MINES (continued)	Good	Fine	Mint
nn(#1 on 1st page)	20.00	60.00	140.00

KISS (See Marvel Comics Super Special & Howard the Duck #12, 13)

KIT CARSON (See Frontier Fighters)

KIT CARSON (Formerly All True Detective Cases No. 4; Fighting Davy Crockett No. 9; see Blazing Sixguns)
1950; No. 2, 8/51 - No. 3, 12/51; No. 5, 11-12/54 - No. 8, 9/55
Avon Periodicals

	Good	Fine	Mint
nn(#1) (1950)	6.50	19.50	45.00
2(8/51)	3.70	11.00	26.00
3(12/51)	3.00	9.00	21.00
5-6,8('54-'55)	2.65	8.00	18.00
7-Kinstler-a(2)	3.00	9.00	21.00
I.W. Reprint #10('63)	.85	2.50	5.00

NOTE: ***Kinstler*** *c-1-3,5-8.*

KIT CARSON & THE BLACKFEET WARRIORS
1953
Realistic

	Good	Fine	Mint
nn-Reprint; Kinstler-c	4.60	14.00	32.00

KIT KARTER
May-July, 1962
Dell Publishing Co.

	Good	Fine	Mint
1	1.15	3.50	8.00

KITTY
October, 1948
St. John Publishing Co.

	Good	Fine	Mint
1-Lily Renee-a	2.65	8.00	18.00

KITTY PRYDE AND WOLVERINE
Nov, 1984 - No. 6, April, 1985 (6 issue mini-series)
Marvel Comics Group

	Good	Fine	Mint
1	.45	1.40	2.80
2-6	.40	1.20	2.40

KLARER GIVEAWAYS (See Wisco)

KNIGHTS OF THE ROUND TABLE (See 4-Color No. 540)

KNIGHTS OF THE ROUND TABLE
No. 10, April, 1957
Pines Comics

	Good	Fine	Mint
10	1.30	4.00	9.00

KNIGHTS OF THE ROUND TABLE
Nov-Jan, 1963/64
Dell Publishing Co.

	Good	Fine	Mint
1 (12-397-401)	2.00	6.00	14.00

KNOCK KNOCK (. . .Who's There?)
1936 (52 pages) (8x9", B&W)
Whitman Publ./Gerona Publications

	Good	Fine	Mint
801-Joke book; Bob Dunn-a	5.00	15.00	35.00

KNOCKOUT ADVENTURES
Winter, 1953-54
Fiction House Magazines

	Good	Fine	Mint
1-Reprints/Fight Comics #53	4.00	12.00	28.00

KNOW YOUR MASS
1958 (100 Pg. Giant) (35 cents) (square binding)
Catechetical Guild

	Good	Fine	Mint
303-In color	4.00	12.00	28.00

KOBRA (See DC Special Series No. 1)
Feb-Mar, 1976 - No. 7, Mar-Apr, 1977
National Periodical Publications

	Good	Fine	Mint
1-Art plotted by Kirby		.40	.80
2-7: 3-Giffen-a		.25	.50

NOTE: ***Austin*** *a-3i.* ***Buckler*** *a-5p; c-5p.* ***Kubert*** *c-4.* ***Nasser*** *a-6p, 7.*

KOKEY KOALA
May, 1952
Toby Press

	Good	Fine	Mint
1	1.85	5.50	13.00

KOKO AND KOLA
Fall, 1946 - No. 5, May, 1947; No. 6, 1950
Compix/Magazine Enterprises

	Good	Fine	Mint
1-Funny animal	3.00	9.00	21.00
2	1.50	4.50	10.00
3-5,6(A-1 28)	1.15	3.50	8.00

KO KOMICS
October, 1945
Gerona Publications

	Good	Fine	Mint
1-The Duke of Darkness & The Menace (hero)	6.50	19.50	45.00

KOMIC KARTOONS
Fall, 1945 - No. 2, Winter, 1945
Timely Comics (EPC)

	Good	Fine	Mint
1,2-Andy Wolf, Bertie Mouse	5.00	15.00	35.00

KOMIK PAGES
April, 1945 (All-r)
Harry 'A' Chesler, Jr. (Our Army, Inc.)

	Good	Fine	Mint
10(#1 on inside)-Land O' Nod by Rick Yager (2 pgs.), Animal Crackers, Foxy GrandPa, Tom, Dick & Mary, Cheerio Minstrels, Red Starr plus other 1-2 pg. strips; Cole-a	6.50	19.50	45.00

KONA (. . .Monarch of Monster Isle)
Feb-Apr, 1962 - No. 21, Jan-Mar, 1967
Dell Publishing Co.

	Good	Fine	Mint
4-Color 1256	2.65	8.00	18.00
2-10: 4-Anak begins	1.15	3.50	8.00
11-21	.75	2.25	4.50

NOTE: ***Glanzman*** *a-all issues.*

KONGA (Fantastic Giants No. 24) (See Return of. . .)
1960; No. 2, Aug, 1961 - No. 23, Nov, 1965
Charlton Comics

	Good	Fine	Mint
1(1960)-Based on movie	11.50	34.00	80.00
2	5.70	17.00	40.00
3-5	4.35	13.00	30.00
6-15	3.00	9.00	21.00
16-23	1.70	5.00	12.00

NOTE: ***Ditko*** *a-1, 3-15; c-4, 6-9.* ***Glanzman*** *a-12.* ***Montes & Bache*** *a-16-23.*

KONGA'S REVENGE (Formerly Return of. . .)
No. 2, Summer, 1963 - No. 3, Fall, 1964; Dec, 1968
Charlton Comics

	Good	Fine	Mint
2,3: 2-Ditko c/a	2.00	6.00	14.00
1('68)-Reprints Konga's Revenge No. 3	1.00	3.00	7.00

KONG THE UNTAMED
June-July, 1975 - No. 5, Feb-Mar, 1976
National Periodical Publications

	Good	Fine	Mint
1		.40	.80
2-5		.25	.50

NOTE: ***Alcala*** *a-1-3.* ***Wrightson*** *c-1,2.*

KOOKIE
Feb-Apr, 1962 - No. 2, May-July, 1962
Dell Publishing Co.

	Good	Fine	Mint
1,2-Written by John Stanley; Bill Williams-a	4.00	12.00	28.00

Kit Carson #3, © AVON

Knights of the Round Table #1, © DELL

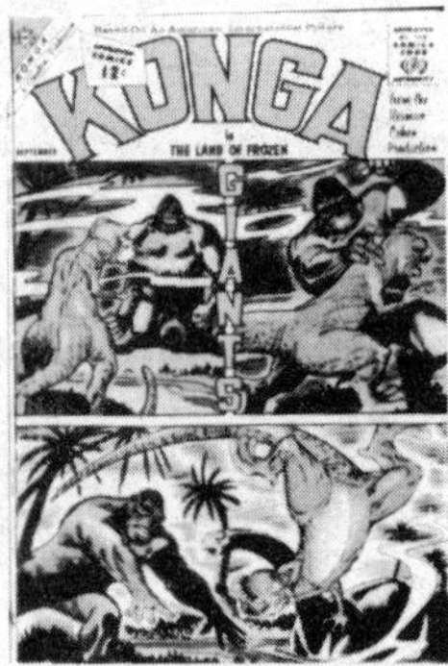

Konga #8, © CC

Korak, Son of Tarzan #10, © ERB

Krazy Komics #5, © MCG

Kull and the Barbarians #1, © MCG

K. O. PUNCH, THE (Also see Lucky Fights It Through)
1948 (Educational giveaway)
E. C. Comics

	Good	Fine	Mint
Feldstein-splash; Kamen-a	117.00	340.00	700.00

KORAK, SON OF TARZAN (Edgar Rice Burroughs)
Jan, 1964 - No. 45, Jan, 1972 (Painted-c No. 1-?)
Gold Key

	Good	Fine	Mint
1-Russ Manning-a	3.00	9.00	21.00
2-11-Russ Manning-a	1.50	4.50	10.00
12-21: 14-Jon of the Kalahari ends. 15-Mabu, Jungle Boy begins; Manning-a #21	.85	2.50	6.00
22-30	.60	1.80	4.00
31-45	.50	1.50	3.00

NOTE: ***Warren Tufts** a-12, 13.*

KORAK, SON OF TARZAN (Tarzan Family No. 60 on)
No. 46, May-June, 1972 - No. 56, Feb-Mar, 1974; No. 57, May-June, 1975 - No. 59, Sept-Oct, 1975 (Edgar Rice Burroughs)
National Periodical Publications

	Good	Fine	Mint
46-(52 pgs.)-Carson of Venus begins (origin); Pellucidar feature		.50	1.00
47-50: 49-Origin Korak retold		.35	.70
51-59: 56-Last Carson of Venus		.25	.50

NOTE: ***Kaluta** a-46-56. All have covers by **Joe Kubert**. **Manning** strip reprints-No. 57-59. **Frank Thorn** a-46-51.*

KOREA MY HOME (Also see Yalta to Korea)
nd (1950s)
Johnstone and Cushing

	Good	Fine	Mint
nn-Anti-communist; Korean War	15.00	45.00	105.00

KORG: 70,000 B. C. (TV)
May, 1975 - No. 9, Nov, 1976 (Hanna-Barbera)
Charlton Publications

	Good	Fine	Mint
1	.25	.75	1.50
2-9		.50	1.00

KORNER KID COMICS
1947
Four Star Publications

	Good	Fine	Mint
1	3.00	9.00	21.00

KRAZY KAT
1946 (Hardcover)
Holt

	Good	Fine	Mint
Reprints daily & Sunday strips by Herriman	26.00	78.00	180.00
with dust jacket (Rare)....	54.00	162.00	380.00

KRAZY KAT (See Ace Comics & March of Comics No. 72,87)

KRAZY KAT COMICS (...& Ignatz the Mouse early issues)
May-June, 1951 - Jan, 1964 (None by Herriman)
Dell Publishing Co./Gold Key

	Good	Fine	Mint
1(1951)	4.00	12.00	28.00
2-5 (#5, 8-10/52)	2.65	8.00	18.00
4-Color 454,504	2.00	6.00	14.00
4-Color 548,619,696 (4/56)	1.70	5.00	12.00
1(10098-401)(1/64-Gold Key)(TV)	1.70	5.00	12.00

KRAZY KOMICS (1st Series) (Cindy No. 27 on)
July, 1942 - No. 26, Spr, 1947 (Also see Ziggy Pig)
Timely Comics (USA No. 1-21/JPC No. 22-26)

	Good	Fine	Mint
1-Ziggy Pig & Silly Seal begins	14.00	42.00	100.00
2	7.00	21.00	50.00
3-10	4.60	14.00	32.00
11,13,14	3.50	10.50	24.00
12-Timely's entire art staff drew themselves into a Creeper story	4.60	14.00	32.00
15-Has "Super Soldier" by Pfc. Stan Lee	3.50	10.50	24.00
16-24,26	2.30	7.00	16.00
25-Kurtzman-a, 6 pgs.	4.00	12.00	28.00

KRAZY KOMICS (2nd Series)
Aug, 1948 - No. 2, Nov, 1948
Timely/Marvel Comics

	Good	Fine	Mint
1-Wolverton (10 pgs.) & Kurtzman (8 pgs.)-a; Eustice Hayseed begins, Li'l Abner swipe	16.00	48.00	110.00
2-Wolverton-a, 10 pgs.; Powerhouse Pepper cameo	9.50	28.00	65.00

KRAZY KROW
Summer, 1945 - No. 3, Wint, 1945/46
Marvel Comics (ZPC)

	Good	Fine	Mint
1	4.60	14.00	32.00
2,3	2.30	7.00	16.00
I.W. Reprint #1('57), 2('58), 7	.30	.80	1.60

KRAZYLIFE
1945 (no month)
Fox Features Syndicate

	Good	Fine	Mint
1-Funny animal	4.60	14.00	32.00

KREE/SKRULL WAR STARRING THE AVENGERS, THE
Sept, 1983 - No. 2, Oct, 1983 ($2.50, 68 pgs.; Baxter paper)
Marvel Comics Group

	Good	Fine	Mint
1,2	.45	1.25	2.50

NOTE: ***Adams** p-1r, 2. **Buscema** a-1r, 2r. **Simonson** c(p)/a(p)-1.*

KRIM-KO COMICS
1936 - 1939 (4 pg. giveaway) (weekly)
Krim-ko Chocolate Drink

	Good	Fine	Mint
Lola, Secret Agent; 184 issues - all original stories each....	1.35	4.00	8.00

KROFFT SUPERSHOW (TV)
April, 1978 - No. 6, Jan, 1979
Gold Key

	Good	Fine	Mint
1		.60	1.20
2-6		.35	.70

KRULL
Nov, 1983 - No. 2, Dec, 1983
Marvel Comics Group

	Good	Fine	Mint
1,2-Film adapt. r/Marvel Super Spec.		.25	.50

KRYPTON CHRONICLES
Sept, 1981 - No. 3, Nov, 1981
DC Comics

	Good	Fine	Mint
1-Buckler-c(p)		.40	.80
2,3		.30	.60

KULL & THE BARBARIANS (Magazine)
May, 1975 - No. 3, Sept, 1975 (B&W) ($1.00)
Marvel Comics Group

	Good	Fine	Mint
1-Andru/Wood-r/Kull #1; 2 pgs. Adams; Gil Kane, Severin-a	.40	1.25	2.50
2-Red Sonja by Chaykin begins; Adams-i; Gil Kane-a	.30	.90	1.80
3-Origin Red Sonja by Chaykin; Adams-a; Solomon Kane app.	.30	.90	1.80

KULL THE CONQUEROR (...the Destroyer #11 on; see Marvel Preview)
June, 1971 - No. 2, Sept, 1971; No. 3, July, 1972 - No. 15, Aug, 1974; No. 16, Aug, 1976 - No. 29, Oct, 1978
Marvel Comics Group

	Good	Fine	Mint
1-Andru/Wood-a; origin Kull	.70	2.00	4.00
2-5	.25	.75	1.50

KULL THE CONQUEROR (continued)

	Good	Fine	Mint
6-10		.60	1.20
11-15-Ploog-a		.40	.80
16-29		.30	.60

NOTE: *No. 1,2,7-9,11 are based on Robert E. Howard stories.* ***Alcala*** *a-17p, 18-20i; c-24.* ***Ditko*** *a-12r, 15r.* ***Gil Kane*** *c-15p, 21.* ***Nebres*** *a-22i-27i; c-25i, 27i.* ***Ploog*** *c-11, 12p, 13.* ***Severin*** *a-2-9i, 10p; c-2-10i, 19.* ***Starlin*** *c-14.*

KULL THE CONQUEROR
Dec, 1982 - No. 2, Mar, 1983 (52 pgs., printed on Baxter paper)
Marvel Comics Group

	Good	Fine	Mint
1-Buscema-a(p)	.45	1.25	2.50
2	.35	1.00	2.00

KULL THE CONQUEROR (No. 9,10 titled 'Kull')
5/83 - No. 10, 6/85 (52 pgs.; $1.25-60 cents; Mando paper)
Marvel Comics Group

	Good	Fine	Mint
V3No.1,2($1.25)		.65	1.30
3,4($1.00)		.50	1.00
5-10(60-65 cents)		.30	.60

KUNG FU (See Deadly Hands of..., & Master of...)

KUNG FU FIGHTER (See Richard Dragon...)

LABOR IS A PARTNER
1949 (32 pgs. in color; paper cover)
Catechetical Guild Educational Society

	Good	Fine	Mint
nn-Anti-communism	30.00	80.00	160.00
Confidential Preview-(B&W, 8½x11", saddle stitched)-only one known copy; text varies from color version, advertises next book on secularism (If the Devil Would Talk)	35.00	100.00	200.00

LABYRINTH
Nov, 1986 - No. 3, Jan, 1987 (mini-series)
Marvel Comics Group

	Good	Fine	Mint
1-3: R-/Marv. Super Spec. #40		.40	.80

LAD: A DOG
1961 - No. 2, July-Sept, 1962
Dell Publishing Co.

	Good	Fine	Mint
4-Color 1303 (movie), 2	2.30	7.00	16.00

LADY AND THE TRAMP (See Dell Giants, 4-Color No. 629,634, & Movie Comics)

LADY AND THE TRAMP IN "BUTTER LATE THAN NEVER"
1955 (16 pgs., 5x7¼", soft-c) (Walt Disney)
American Dairy Association (Premium)

	Good	Fine	Mint
	3.00	9.00	21.00

LADY BOUNTIFUL
1917 (10¼x13½"; 24 pgs.; B&W; cardboard cover)
Saalfield Publ. Co./Press Publ. Co.

	Good	Fine	Mint
by Gene Carr; 2 panels per page	6.00	18.00	42.00

LADY COP (See First Issue Special)

LADY FOR A NIGHT (See Cinema Comics Herald)

LADY LUCK (Formerly Smash No. 1-85)
Dec, 1949 - No. 90, Aug, 1950
Quality Comics Group

	Good	Fine	Mint
86(#1)	30.00	90.00	210.00
87-90	23.00	70.00	160.00

LAFF-A-LYMPICS (TV)(See The Funtastic World of Hanna-Barbera)
Mar, 1978 - No. 13, Mar, 1979
Marvel Comics Group

	Good	Fine	Mint
1		.30	.60
2-13		.25	.50

LAFFY-DAFFY COMICS
Feb, 1945 - No. 2, March, 1945
Rural Home Publ. Co.

	Good	Fine	Mint
1,2	2.30	7.00	16.00

LANA (Little Lana & True Life Tales No. 8 on?)
Aug, 1948 - No. 7, Aug, 1949 (Also see Annie Oakley)
Marvel Comics (MjMC)

	Good	Fine	Mint
1-Rusty, Millie begin	4.00	12.00	28.00
2-Kurtzman's "Hey Look" (1); last Rusty	3.50	10.50	24.00
3-7: 3-Nellie begins	1.70	5.00	12.00

LANCELOT & GUINEVERE (See Movie Classics)

LANCELOT LINK, SECRET CHIMP (TV)
April, 1971 - No. 8, Feb, 1973
Gold Key

	Good	Fine	Mint
1-Photo-c	1.35	4.00	8.00
2-8: 2-Photo-c	.85	2.50	5.00

LANCELOT STRONG (See The Shield)

LANCE O'CASEY (See Mighty Midget & Whiz Comics)
Spring, 1946 - No. 3, Fall, 1946; No. 4, Summer, 1948
Fawcett Publications

	Good	Fine	Mint
1	8.00	24.00	56.00
2	4.60	14.00	32.00
3,4	4.00	12.00	28.00

LANCER (TV)(Western)
Feb, 1969 - No. 3, Sept, 1969 (All photo-c)
Gold Key

	Good	Fine	Mint
1	2.00	6.00	14.00
2,3	1.50	4.50	10.00

LAND OF THE GIANTS (TV)
Nov, 1968 - No. 5, Sept, 1969
Gold Key

	Good	Fine	Mint
1-Photo-c	1.50	4.50	10.00
2-5: 4,5-Photo-c	1.00	3.00	7.00

LAND OF THE LOST COMICS (Radio)
July-Aug, 1946 - No. 9, Spring, 1948
E. C. Comics

	Good	Fine	Mint
1	16.00	48.00	110.00
2	11.00	32.00	76.00
3-9	9.50	28.00	65.00

LAND UNKNOWN, THE (See 4-Color No. 845)

LARAMIE (TV)
Aug, 1960 - July, 1962 (All photo-c)
Dell Publishing Co.

	Good	Fine	Mint
4-Color 1125	4.35	13.00	30.00
4-Color 1223,1284	3.50	10.50	24.00
01-418-207	3.50	10.50	24.00

LAREDO (TV)
June, 1966
Gold Key

	Good	Fine	Mint
1 (10179-606)-Photo-c	2.00	6.00	14.00

LARGE FEATURE COMIC (Formerly called Black & White)
1939 - No. 13, 1943
Dell Publishing Co.

	Good	Fine	Mint
1 **(Series I)**-Dick Tracy Meets the Blank	75.00	225.00	525.00
2-Terry & the Pirates (#1)	37.00	110.00	260.00
3-Heigh-Yo Silver! The Lone Ranger (text & ill.)(76 pgs.). Also exists as a Whitman #710	38.00	115.00	265.00
4-Dick Tracy Gets His Man	43.00	130.00	300.00
5-Tarzan (#1) by Harold Foster (origin); reprints 1st dailies from '29	76.00	228.00	532.00

6-Terry & the Pirates & The Dragon Lady; reprints dailies from

Lady Luck #87, © QUA

Lana #2, © MCG

Land of the Giants #1, © GK

Large Feature Comic #11, © N.Y. News Synd.

Lash LaRue Western #11, © FAW

Lassie #1, © M.G.M.

LARGE FEATURE COMIC (continued)

	Good	Fine	Mint
1936	36.00	108.00	252.00
7-(Scarce)-52 pgs.; The Lone Ranger-Hi-Yo Silver the Lone Ranger to the Rescue. Also exists as a Whitman #715	49.00	145.00	340.00
8-Dick Tracy Racket Buster	37.00	110.00	260.00
9-King of the Royal Mounted	16.00	48.00	110.00
10-(Scarce)-Gang Busters (No. appears on inside front cover); first slick cover	25.00	75.00	175.00
11-Dick Tracy Foils the Mad Doc Hump	37.00	110.00	260.00
12-Smilin' Jack	22.00	65.00	154.00
13-Dick Tracy & Scotty	37.00	110.00	260.00
14-Smilin' Jack	22.00	65.00	154.00
15-Dick Tracy & the Kidnapped Princess	37.00	110.00	260.00
16-Donald Duck-1st app. Daisy Duck on back cover (6/41-Disney)	145.00	435.00	1015.00
(Prices vary widely on this book)			
17-Gang Busters (1941)	16.00	48.00	110.00
18-Phantasmo	14.00	42.00	100.00
19-Dumbo Comic Paint Book (Disney); partial-r 4-Color 17	100.00	300.00	700.00
20-Donald Duck Comic Paint Book (Rarer than #16) (Disney)	205.00	615.00	1435.00
(Prices vary widely on this book)			
21-Private Buck	6.50	19.50	45.00
22-Nuts & Jolts	6.50	19.50	45.00
23-The Nebbs	7.00	21.00	50.00
24-Popeye (Thimble Theatre) ½ by Segar	32.00	95.00	225.00
25-Smilin' Jack	22.00	65.00	154.00
26-Smitty	13.00	40.00	90.00
27-Terry & the Pirates	25.00	75.00	175.00
28-Grin & Bear It	5.70	17.00	40.00
29-Moon Mullins	11.50	34.00	80.00
30-Tillie the Toiler	10.00	30.00	70.00
1 **(Series II)**-Peter Rabbit by Cady	26.00	78.00	182.00
2-Winnie Winkle (#1)	9.00	27.00	62.00
3-Dick Tracy	35.00	105.00	245.00
4-Tiny Tim (#1)	16.00	48.00	110.00
5-Toots & Casper	5.70	17.00	40.00
6-Terry & the Pirates	25.00	75.00	175.00
7-Pluto Saves the Ship (#1)(Disney) written by Carl Barks, Jack Hannah, & Nick George. (Barks' 1st comic book work)	55.00	165.00	385.00
8-Bugs Bunny (#1)('42)	47.00	141.00	330.00
9-Bringing Up Father	7.00	21.00	50.00
10-Popeye (Thimble Theatre)	26.00	78.00	180.00
11-Barney Google & Snuffy Smith	11.00	32.00	75.00
12-Private Buck	5.70	17.00	40.00
13-(nn)-1001 Hours Of Fun; puzzles & games; by A. W. Nugent. This book was bound as #13 with Large Feat. Comics in Publishers files	6.50	19.50	45.00

NOTE: *The Black & White Feature Books are oversized 8½x11-3/8" comics with color covers and black and white interiors. The first nine issues all have rough, heavy stock covers and, except for No. 7, all have 76 pages, including covers. No. 7 and No. 10-on all have 52 pages. Beginning with No. 10 the covers are slick and thin and, because of their size, are difficult to handle without damaging. For this reason, they are seldom found in fine to mint condition. The paper stock, unlike Wow No. 1 and Capt. Marvel No. 1, is itself not unstable . . . just thin.*

LARRY DOBY, BASEBALL HERO
1950 (Cleveland Indians)
Fawcett Publications

	Good	Fine	Mint
nn-Bill Ward-a	22.00	65.00	154.00

LARRY HARMON'S LAUREL AND HARDY (. . . Comics)
July-Aug, 1972 (Regular size)
National Periodical Publications

	Good	Fine	Mint
1	.45	1.25	2.50

LARS OF MARS
Apr-May, 1951 - No. 11, July-Aug, 1951
Ziff-Davis Publishing Co.

	Good	Fine	Mint
10-Origin; Anderson-a(3) in each	24.00	72.00	170.00
11-Painted-c	21.00	64.00	150.00

LARS OF MARS 3-D
Apr, 1987 ($2.50)
Eclipse Comics

	Good	Fine	Mint
1-r/Lars of Mars #10,11 in 3-D + new story	.40	1.25	2.50

LASER ERASER & PRESSBUTTON (See Axel Pressbutton & Miracleman 9)
11/85 - No. 12, 1987 (12 issue series)
Eclipse Comics

	Good	Fine	Mint
1-4		.40	.80
5,6 (.95 cents)		.50	1.00
7-12		.50	1.00
. . . in 3-D 1 (8/86, $2.50)	.40	1.25	2.50
2-D 1 (B&W, limited to 100 copies signed & numbered)	.85	2.50	5.00

LASH LARUE WESTERN (Movie star; king of the bullwhip)
Sum, 1949 - No. 46, Jan, 1954 (36pgs., 1-7,9,13,16-on)
Fawcett Publications

	Good	Fine	Mint
1-Lash & his horse Black Diamond begin; photo front/back-c begin	35.00	105.00	245.00
2(11/49)	22.00	65.00	154.00
3-5	19.50	58.00	135.00
6,7,9: 6-Last photo back-c; intro. Frontier Phantom (Lash's twin brother)	13.00	40.00	90.00
8,10 (52pgs.)	13.50	41.00	95.00
11,12,14,15 (52pgs.)	8.50	25.50	60.00
13,16-20 (36pgs.)	8.00	24.00	56.00
21-30: 21-The Frontier Phantom app.	6.50	19.50	45.00
31-45	5.00	15.00	35.00
46-Last Fawcett issue & photo-c	6.50	19.50	45.00

LASH LARUE WESTERN (Continues from Fawcett)
No. 47, Mar-Apr, 1954 - No. 84, June, 1961
Charlton Comics

	Good	Fine	Mint
47-Photo-c	5.00	15.00	35.00
48	3.50	10.50	24.00
49-60	3.00	9.00	21.00
61-66,69,70: 52-r/#8; 53-r/#22	2.65	8.00	18.00
67,68-(68 pgs.). 68-Check-a	3.00	9.00	21.00
71-83	1.70	5.00	12.00
84-Last issue	2.00	6.00	14.00

LASSIE (TV)(M-G-M's. . . No. 1-36)
Oct-Dec, 1950 - No. 70, July, 1969
Dell Publishing Co./Gold Key No. 59 (10/62) on

	Good	Fine	Mint
1	4.00	12.00	28.00
2	2.30	7.00	16.00
3-10	1.70	5.00	12.00
11-19: 12-Rocky Langford (Lassie's master) marries Gerry Lawrence. 15-1st app. Timbu	1.50	4.50	10.00
20-22-Matt Baker-a	2.00	6.00	14.00
23-40: 33-Robinson-a. 39-1st app. Timmy as Lassie picks up her TV family	.85	2.50	6.00
41-70: 63-Last Timmy. 64-r-/#19. 65-Forest Ranger Corey Stuart begins, ends #69. 70-Forest Rangers Bob Ericson & Scott Turner app. (Lassie's new masters)	.55	1.65	4.00
11193(1978-Golden Press)-224 pgs.; $1.95; Baker-a(r), 92 pgs.	.55	1.65	4.00
The Adventures of. . . (Red Heart Dog Food giveaway, 1949)-16 pgs, soft-c	3.50	10.50	24.00
Kite Fun Book('73)-(16 pgs.; 5x7")	2.00	6.00	14.00

LASSIE (continued)
NOTE: *Photo c-57. (See March of Comics No. 210, 217, 230, 254, 266, 278, 296, 308, 324, 334, 346, 358, 370, 381, 394, 411, 432)*

LAST DAYS OF THE JUSTICE SOCIETY SPECIAL
1986 (One shot, 68 pgs.)
DC Comics

	Good	Fine	Mint
1	.50	1.50	3.00

LAST DAYS OF THE VIKING HEROES
Mar, 1987 - Present ($1.50, color)
Genesis West Comics

	Good	Fine	Mint
1-4	.25	.75	1.50

LAST HUNT, THE (See 4-Color No. 678)

LAST OF THE COMANCHES (See Wild Bill Hickok #28)
1953 (Movie)
Avon Periodicals

	Good	Fine	Mint
nn-Kinstler c/a, 21pgs.; Ravielli-a	8.50	25.50	60.00

LAST OF THE ERIES, THE (See American Graphics)

LAST OF THE FAST GUNS, THE (See 4-Color No. 925)

LAST OF THE MOHICANS (See King Classics)

LAST STARFIGHTER, THE
Oct, 1984 - No. 3, Dec, 1984
Marvel Comics Group

	Good	Fine	Mint
1-3: Movie adaptation-r/Marvel Super Special; Guice-c		.30	.60

LAST TRAIN FROM GUN HILL (See 4-Color No. 1012)

LATEST ADVENTURES OF FOXY GRANDPA (See Foxy. . .)

LATEST COMICS (Super Duper No. 3?)
March, 1945
Spotlight Publ./Palace Promotions (Jubilee)

	Good	Fine	Mint
1-Super Duper	3.50	10.50	24.00
2-Bee-29 (nd)	2.30	7.00	16.00

LAUGH
June, 1987 - Present
Archie Enterprises

	Good	Fine	Mint
1-5		.40	.75

LAUGH COMICS (Formerly Black Hood #1-19) (Laugh #226 on)
No. 20, Fall, 1946 - No. 400, 1987
Archie Publications (Close-Up)

	Good	Fine	Mint
20-Archie begins; Katy Keene & Taffy begin by Woggon	38.00	115.00	265.00
21-23,25	18.00	54.00	125.00
24-"Pipsy" by Kirby, 6 pgs.	18.00	55.00	125.00
26-30	10.00	30.00	70.00
31-40	8.00	24.00	50.00
41-60: 41,54-Debbi by Woggon	4.50	13.50	30.00
61-80: 67-Debbi by Woggon	2.85	8.50	20.00
81-99	2.00	6.00	14.00
100	3.00	9.00	21.00
101-126: 125-Debbi app.	1.35	4.00	9.00
127,130,131,133,135,140-142,144-Jaguar app.	1.35	4.00	9.00
128,129,132,134,138,139-Fly app.	1.35	4.00	9.00
136,143-Flygirl app.	1.35	4.00	9.00
137-Flyman & Flygirl app.	1.35	4.00	9.00
145-160: 157-Josie app.	.75	2.25	4.50
161-165,167-200	.50	1.50	3.00
166-Beatles-c	.85	2.50	5.00
201-240	.25	.75	1.50
241-280		.40	.80
281-400: 381-384-Katy Keene app.; by Woggon-381,382		.30	.60

NOTE: *Josie app.-No. 145, 160, 164. Katy Keene app.-No. 20-125, 129, 130, 133. Many issues contain paper dolls.*

LAUGH COMICS DIGEST (. . .Mag. No. 23 on)
8/74; No. 2, 9/75; No. 3, 3/76 - Present (Digest-size)
Archie Publications (Close-Up No. 1, 3 on)

	Good	Fine	Mint
1-Adams-a	.70	2.00	4.00
2,7,8,19-Adams-a	.35	1.00	2.00
3-6,9,10		.50	1.00
11-18,20-75		.50	1.00

NOTE: ***Katy Keene** in 23, 25, 27, 32-38, 40, 45-48, 50. **The Fly**-r in 19, 20. **The Jaguar**-r in 25, 27. **Mr. Justice**-r in 21. **The Web**-r in 23.*

LAUGH COMIX (Formerly Top Notch Laugh; Suzie No. 49 on)
No. 46, Summer, 1944 - No. 48, Winter, 1944-45
MLJ Magazines

	Good	Fine	Mint
46-Wilbur & Suzie in all	6.50	19.50	45.00
47,48	4.60	14.00	32.00

LAUGH-IN MAGAZINE (Magazine)
Oct, 1968 - No. 12, Oct, 1969 (50 cents) (Satire)
Laufer Publ. Co.

	Good	Fine	Mint
V1#1	.85	2.50	5.00
2-12	.50	1.50	3.00

LAUREL & HARDY (See Larry Harmon's. . . & March of Comics No. 302,314)

LAUREL AND HARDY (. . .Comics)
March, 1949 - No. 28, 1951
St. John Publishing Co.

	Good	Fine	Mint
1	25.00	75.00	175.00
2	12.00	36.00	84.00
3,4	10.00	30.00	70.00
5-10	8.00	24.00	56.00
11-28	6.00	18.00	42.00

LAUREL AND HARDY (TV)
Oct, 1962 - No. 4, Sept-Nov, 1963
Dell Publishing Co.

	Good	Fine	Mint
12-423-210 (8-10/62)	1.75	5.25	12.00
2-4 (Dell)	1.30	4.00	9.00

LAUREL AND HARDY
Jan, 1967 - No. 2, Oct, 1967 (Larry Harmon's)
Gold Key

	Good	Fine	Mint
1,2: 1-Photo back-c	1.15	3.50	8.00

LAW AGAINST CRIME (Law-Crime on cover)
April, 1948 - No. 3, Aug, 1948
Essenkay Publishing Co.

	Good	Fine	Mint
1-(#1-3: ½ funny animal, ½ crime)-L. B. Cole electrocution-c/a	23.00	70.00	160.00
2-L. B. Cole c/a	16.00	48.00	110.00
3-L. B. Cole c/a; used in **SOTI**, pg. 180,181 & illo-"The wish to hurt or kill couples in lovers' lanes;" reprinted in All-Famous Crime #9	24.00	72.00	170.00

LAWBREAKERS (. . .Suspense Stories No. 10 on)
Mar, 1951 - No. 9, Oct-Nov, 1952
Law and Order Magazines (Charlton Comics)

	Good	Fine	Mint
1	6.00	18.00	42.00
2	3.00	9.00	21.00
3,5,6,8,9	2.15	6.50	15.00
4-"White Death" junkie story	4.60	14.00	32.00
7-"The Deadly Dopesters" drug story	3.70	11.00	26.00

LAWBREAKERS ALWAYS LOSE!
Spring, 1948 - No. 10, Oct, 1949
Marvel Comics (CBS)

	Good	Fine	Mint
1-2pg. Kurtzman-a, 'Giggles 'n Grins'	7.00	21.00	50.00
2	3.50	10.50	24.00

Laugh Comics #32, © AP

Laurel and Hardy #3, © DELL

Lawbreakers #1, © CC

Lawman #4, © Warner Bros.

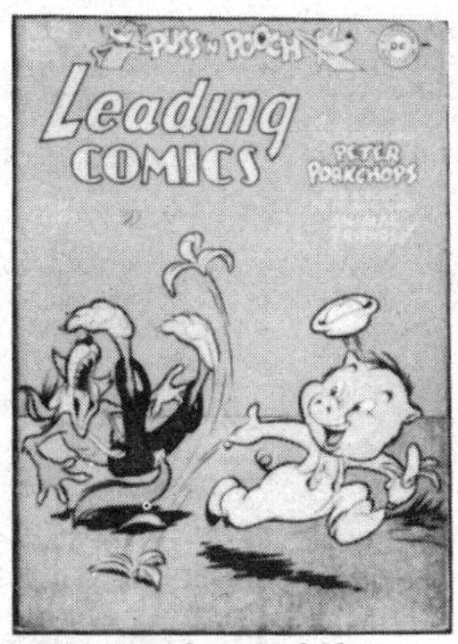

Leading Comics #23, © DC

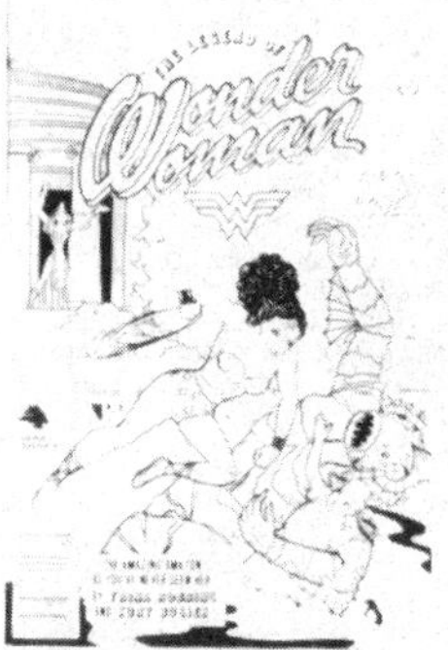

The Legend of Wonder Woman #1, © DC

LAWBREAKERS ALWAYS LOSE (cont'd)	**Good**	**Fine**	**Mint**
3-5: 4-Vampire story	2.65	8.00	18.00
6(2/49)-Has editorial defense against charges of Dr. Wertham	3.70	11.00	26.00
7-Used in **SOTI**, illo-"Comic-book philosophy;"	9.00	27.00	63.00
8-10: 9,10-Photo-c	1.85	5.50	13.00

LAWBREAKERS SUSPENSE STORIES (Formerly Lawbreakers; Strange Suspense Stories No. 16 on)
No. 10, Jan, 1953 - No. 15, Nov, 1953
Capitol Stories/Charlton Comics

10	4.00	12.00	28.00
11 (3/53)-Severed tongues c/story & woman negligee scene	19.50	58.00	135.00
12-14	3.00	9.00	21.00
15-Acid-in-face c/story; hands dissolved in acid story	9.00	27.00	62.00

LAW-CRIME (See Law Against Crime)

LAWMAN (TV)
No. 970, Feb, 1959 - No. 11, Apr-June, 1962 (All photo-c)
Dell Publishing Co.

4-Color 970(#1)	4.60	14.00	32.00
4-Color 1035('60)	3.50	10.50	24.00
3(2-4/60)-Toth-a	4.60	14.00	32.00
4-11	3.00	9.00	21.00

LAWRENCE (See Movie Classics)

LEADING COMICS (. . .Screen Comics No. 42 on)
Winter, 1941-42 - No. 41, Feb-Mar, 1950
National Periodical Publications

1-Origin The Seven Soldiers of Victory; Crimson Avenger, Green Arrow & Speedy, Shining Knight, The Vigilante, Star Spangled Kid & Stripsey begin. The Dummy (Vigilante villain) app.	125.00	375.00	875.00
2-Meskin-a	58.00	160.00	370.00
3	45.00	135.00	315.00
4,5	37.00	110.00	260.00
6-10	32.00	95.00	225.00
11-14(Spring, 1945)	22.00	65.00	154.00
15-Content change to funny animal	7.00	21.00	50.00
16-22,24-30	3.30	10.00	23.00
23-1st app. Peter Porkchops by Otto Feur	8.00	24.00	56.00
31,32,34-41	2.65	8.00	18.00
33-(Scarce)	5.00	15.00	35.00

NOTE: ***Rube Grossman**-a(Peter Porkchops)-most #15-on; c-15-41. **Post** a-23-37, 39, 41.*

LEADING SCREEN COMICS (Formerly Leading Comics)
No. 42, Apr-May, 1950 - No. 77, Aug-Sept, 1955
National Periodical Publications

42	3.70	11.00	26.00
43-77	2.30	7.00	16.00

NOTE: ***Grossman** a-most. **Mayer** a-45-48, 50, 54-57, 60, 62-74, 75(3), 76, 77.*

LEATHERNECK THE MARINE (See Mighty Midget Comics)

LEAVE IT TO BEAVER (TV)
No. 912, June, 1958 - May-July, 1962 (All photo-c)
Dell Publishing Co.

4-Color 912	8.50	25.50	60.00
4-Color 999,1103,1191,1285, 01-428-207	7.00	21.00	50.00

LEAVE IT TO BINKY (Binky No. 72 on) (See Super DC Giant and Showcase) (No. 1-22, 52 pgs.)
2-3/48 - No. 60, 10/58; No. 61, 6-7/68 - No. 71, 2-3/70
National Periodical Publications

	Good	**Fine**	**Mint**
1	11.50	34.00	80.00
2	5.70	17.00	40.00
3-5	4.60	14.00	32.00
6-10	3.70	11.00	26.00
11-20	2.65	8.00	18.00
21-28,30-45: 45-Last pre-code (2/55)	1.60	4.70	11.00
29-Used in **POP**, pg. 78	2.35	7.00	16.00
46-60	1.00	3.00	7.00
61-71	.70	2.00	4.00

NOTE: ***Drucker** a-28. **Mayer** a-1, 2, 15.*

LEE HUNTER, INDIAN FIGHTER (See 4-Color No. 779,904)

LEFT-HANDED GUN, THE (See 4-Color No. 913)

LEGEND OF CUSTER, THE (TV)
January, 1968
Dell Publishing Co.

1	1.15	3.50	8.00

LEGEND OF JESSE JAMES, THE (TV)
February, 1966
Gold Key

10172-602	1.75	5.25	12.00

LEGEND OF LOBO, THE (See Movie Comics)

LEGEND OF WONDER WOMAN, THE
May, 1986 - No. 4, Aug, 1986 (mini-series)
DC Comics

1-4		.60	1.20

LEGEND OF YOUNG DICK TURPIN, THE (TV)
May, 1966 (Disney TV episode)
Gold Key

1 (10176-605)-Photo/painted-c	1.15	3.50	8.00

LEGENDS
Nov, 1986 - No. 6, Apr, 1987 (mini-series)
DC Comics

1-Bryne c/a(p) begins. 1st new Capt. Marvel	.35	1.00	2.00
2	.25	.80	1.60
3-5: 3-Intro new Suicide Squad	.25	.70	1.40
6-New Justice League app.	.45	1.40	2.80

LEGENDS OF DANIEL BOONE, THE
Oct-Nov, 1955 - No. 8, Dec-Jan, 1956-57
National Periodical Publications

1 (Scarce)	16.50	50.00	115.00
2 (Scarce)	11.00	32.00	76.00
3-8 (Scarce)	9.50	28.00	65.00

LEGIONNAIRES THREE
Jan, 1986 - No. 4, May, 1986 (Mini-series)
DC comics

1-4		.40	.80

LEGION OF MONSTERS (Magazine)(Also see Marvel Premiere #28 & Marvel Preview #8)
September, 1975 (black & white)
Marvel Comics Group

1-Origin & 1st app. Legion of Monsters; Adams-c; Morrow-a; origin & only app. The Manphibian	.35	1.00	2.00

LEGION OF SUBSTITUTE HEROES SPECIAL
July, 1985 (One Shot)
DC Comics

1-Giffen c/a(p)	.25	.75	1.50

LEGION OF SUPER-HEROES (See Action, Adventure, All New Collectors Ed., Limited Collectors Ed., Superboy, & Superman)
Feb, 1973 - No. 4, July-Aug, 1973
National Periodical Publications

LEGION OF SUPER HEROES (cont'd) — Good / Mint / Mint

1-Legion & Tommy Tomorrow reprints begin .70 2.00 4.00
2-4: 3-r/Adv. 340, Action 240. 4-r/Adv. 341, Action 233 .35 1.00 2.00

LEGION OF SUPER-HEROES, THE (Formerly Superboy; Tales of The Legion No. 314 on)(See Secrets of . . .)
No. 259, Jan, 1980 - No. 313, July, 1984
DC Comics

259(#1)-Superboy leaves Legion .60 1.75 3.50
260-264,266-270 .35 1.00 2.00
265-Contains 28pg. insert 'Superman & the TR5-80 Computer;' origin Tyroc; Tyroc leaves Legion .35 1.00 2.00
271-284: 272-Blok joins; origin; 20pg. insert-Dial 'H' For Hero. 277-Intro Reflecto. 280-Superboy re-joins legion. 282-Origin Reflecto .25 .75 1.50
285,286-Giffen back up story .50 1.50 3.00
287-Giffen-a on Legion begins .70 2.00 4.00
288-290: 290-Great Darkness saga begins, ends #294 .40 1.25 2.50
291-293 .25 .75 1.50
294-Double size (52 pgs.); Giffen-a(p) .30 .90 1.80
295-299: 297-Origin retold .60 1.20
300-Double size, 64 pgs., Mando paper; c/a by almost everyone at D.C. .40 1.25 2.50
301-305: 304-Karate Kid & Princess Projectra resign .60 1.20
306-313 (75 cent cover price): 306-Brief origin Star Boy .45 .90
Annual 1(1982)-Giffen c/a; 1st app./origin new Invisible Kid who joins Legion .35 1.00 2.00
Annual 2(10/83)-Giffen-c; Karate Kid & Princess Projectra wed .25 .75 1.50
Annual 3('84) .25 .75 1.50

NOTE: ***Aparo*** *c-282, 283.* ***Austin*** *c-268i.* ***Buckler*** *c-273p, 274p, 276p.* ***Colan*** *a-311p.* ***Ditko*** *a(p)-267, 268, 272, 274, 276, 281.* ***Giffen*** *a-285p-313p, Annual No. 1p; c-287p, 288p, 289, 290p, 291p, 292, 293, 294-299p, 300, 301p-313p, Annual 1p, 2p.* ***Perez*** *c-268p, 277-80, 281p.* ***Starlin*** *a-265.* ***Staton*** *a-259p, 260p, 280.* ***Tuska*** *a-308p.*

LEGION OF SUPER-HEROES
Aug, 1984 - Present ($1.25-$1.50, deluxe format)
DC Comics

1 .50 1.50 3.00
2-5: 4-Death of Karate Kid. 5-Death of Nemesis Kid .40 1.25 2.50
6-10 .35 1.00 2.00
11-14: 12-Cosmic Boy, Lightning Lad, & Saturn Girl resign. 14-Intro new members: Tellus, Sensor Girl, Quislet .25 .75 1.50
15-18-Crisis x-over .35 1.00 2.00
19-44: 25-Sensor Girl i.d. revealed as Princess Projectra. 35-Saturn Girl rejoins .25 .75 1.50
45 ($2.95, 68 pgs.) .50 1.50 2.95
Annual 1 (10/85)-Crisis x-over .35 1.10 2.20
Annual 2 (10/86), 3 (10/87) .35 1.00 2.00

NOTE: ***Byrne*** *c-36p.* ***Giffen*** *a(p)-1, 2, Annual 1p, 2; c-1-5p, Annual 1.* ***Orlando*** *a-6p.* ***Steacy*** *c-Annual 3.*

LENNON SISTERS LIFE STORY, THE (See 4-Color No. 951,1014)

LEO THE LION
No date (10 cents)
I. W. Enterprises

1-Reprint .50 1.50 3.00

LEROY
Nov, 1949 - No. 6, Nov, 1950
Standard Comics

1 2.30 7.00 16.00
2-Frazetta text illo. 3.00 9.00 18.00

Good / Fine / Mint

3-6: 3-Lubbers-a 1.30 4.00 9.00

LET'S PRETEND
May-June, 1950 - No. 3, Sept-Oct, 1950
D. S. Publishing Co.

1 5.50 16.50 38.00
2,3 3.00 9.00 21.00

LET'S READ THE NEWSPAPER
1974
Charlton Press

Features Quincy by Ted Sheares .30 .60

LET'S TAKE A TRIP (TV) (CBS TV Presents)
Spring, 1958
Pines

1-Marv Levy c/a 1.15 3.50 8.00

LETTERS TO SANTA (See March of Comics No. 228)

LIBERTY COMICS (Miss Liberty No. 1)
1945 - 1946 (MLJ & other reprints)
Green Publishing Co.

4 7.00 21.00 50.00
5 (5/46)-The Prankster app; Starr-a 5.00 15.00 35.00
10-Hangman & Boy Buddies app.; Suzie & Wilbur begin; reprint of Hangman #8 6.50 19.50 45.00
11(V2/2, 1/46)-Wilbur in women's clothes 9.50 28.00 65.00
12-Black Hood & Suzie app. 5.70 17.00 40.00
14,15-Patty of Airliner; Starr-a in both 3.00 9.00 21.00

LIBERTY GUARDS
No date (1946?)
Chicago Mail Order

nn-Reprints Man of War #1 with cover of Liberty Scouts #1; Gustavson-c 17.00 51.00 120.00

LIBERTY PROJECT, THE
June, 1987 - Present ($1.75)
Eclipse Comics

1 .35 1.00 2.00
2-7 .30 .85 1.70

LIBERTY SCOUTS (See Man of War & Liberty Guards)
June, 1941 - No. 3, Aug, 1941
Centaur Publications

2(#1)-Origin The Fire-Man, Man of War; Vapo-Man & Liberty Scouts begin; Gustavson-c/a 60.00 180.00 420.00
3(#2)-Origin & 1st app. The Sentinel; Gustavson-c/a 45.00 135.00 315.00

LIDSVILLE (TV)
Oct, 1972 - No. 5, Oct, 1973
Gold Key

1 1.15 3.50 7.00
2-5 .70 2.00 4.00

LIEUTENANT, THE (TV)
April-June, 1964
Dell Publishing Co.

1-Photo-c 1.15 3.50 8.00

LT. ROBIN CRUSOE, U.S.N. (See Movie Comics and Walt Disney Showcase 26)

LIFE OF CAPTAIN MARVEL, THE
Aug, 1985 - No. 5, Dec, 1985 ($2.00 cover; Baxter paper)
Marvel Comics Group

1-5: r-/Starlin issues of Capt. Marvel .35 1.00 2.00

Legion of Super-Heroes #1 ('73), © DC

The Legion of Super-Heroes #312, © DC

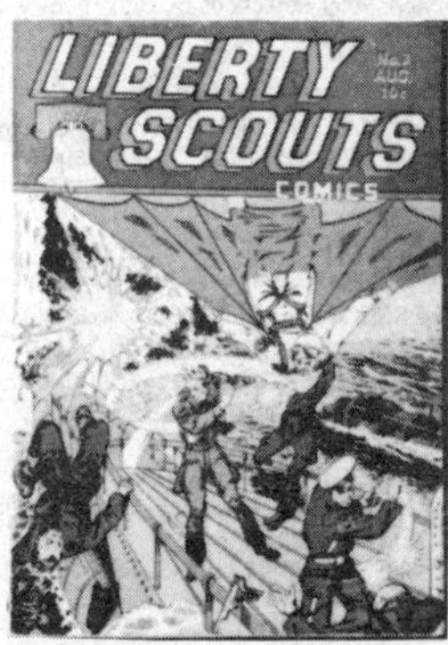

Liberty Scouts #3, © CEN

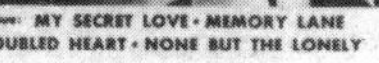

Life Story #1, © FAW

Life With Archie #15, © AP

Lightning Comics #6, © ACE

LIFE OF CHRIST, THE
1949 (100 pages) (35 cents)
Catechetical Guild Educational Society

	Good	Fine	Mint
301-Reprints from Topix(1949)-V5#11,12	4.00	12.00	28.00

LIFE OF CHRIST VISUALIZED
1942 - 1943
Standard Publishers

1-3: All came in cardboard case	2.75	8.00	16.00

LIFE OF CHRIST VISUALIZED
1946? (48 pgs. in color)
The Standard Publ. Co.

	1.00	3.00	6.00

LIFE OF ESTHER VISUALIZED
1947 (48 pgs. in color)
The Standard Publ. Co.

2062	1.00	3.00	6.00

LIFE OF JOSEPH VISUALIZED
1946 (48 pgs. in color)
The Standard Publ. Co.

1054	1.00	3.00	6.00

LIFE OF PAUL (See The Living Bible)

LIFE OF POPE JOHN PAUL II, THE
Jan, 1983
Marvel Comics Group

1	.25	.75	1.50

LIFE OF RILEY, THE (See 4-Color No. 917)

LIFE OF THE BLESSED VIRGIN
1950 (68 pages) (square binding)
Catechetical Guild (Giveaway)

nn-Contains "The Woman of the Promise" & "Mother of Us All" rebound	4.00	12.00	24.00

LIFE'S LIKE THAT
1945 (68 pgs.; B&W; 25 cents)
Croyden Publ. Co.

nn-Newspaper Sunday strip-r by Neher	2.00	6.00	14.00

LIFE'S LITTLE JOKES
No date (1924) (52 pgs.; B&W)
M.S. Publ. Co.

By Rube Goldberg	12.00	36.00	84.00

LIFE STORIES OF AMERICAN PRESIDENTS (See Dell Giants)

LIFE STORY
4/49 - V8/46, 1/53; V8/47, 4/53 (All have photo-c?)
Fawcett Publications

V1#1	4.00	12.00	28.00
2	1.85	5.50	13.00
3-6	1.60	4.70	11.00
V2#7-12	1.50	4.50	10.00
V3#13-Wood-a	6.50	19.50	45.00
V3#14-18, V4#19-21,23,24	1.30	4.00	9.00
V4#22-Drug use story	1.50	4.50	10.00
V5#25-30, V6#31-36	1.15	3.50	8.00
V7#37,40-42, V8#44,45	1.00	3.00	7.00
V7#38, V8#43-Evans-a	1.85	5.50	13.00
V7#39-Drug Smuggling & Junkie sty	1.30	4.00	9.00
V8#46,47 (Scarce)	1.15	3.50	8.00

NOTE: ***Powell*** *a-13,23,24,26,28,30,32,39.*

LIFE WITH ARCHIE
Sept, 1958 - Present
Archie Publications

	Good	Fine	Mint
1	19.00	57.00	132.00
2	10.00	30.00	70.00
3-5	7.00	20.00	50.00
6-10	3.50	10.50	24.00
11-20	1.70	5.00	12.00
21-30	1.25	3.75	8.50
31-41	.85	2.50	6.00
42-45: 42-Pureheart begins	.70	2.00	4.00
46-Origin Pureheart	.85	2.50	5.00
47-50: 50-United Three begin; Superteen, Capt. Hero app.	.50	1.50	3.00
51-59-Pureheart ends	.50	1.50	3.00
60-100: 60-Archie band begins	.35	1.00	2.00
101-150		.50	1.00
151-262		.30	.60

LIFE WITH MILLIE (Formerly A Date With Millie) (Modeling With Millie No. 21 on)
No. 8, Dec, 1960 - No. 20, Dec, 1962
Atlas/Marvel Comics Group

8	1.70	5.00	12.00
9-11	1.20	3.50	7.00
12-20	.85	2.50	5.00

LIFE WITH SNARKY PARKER (TV)
August, 1950
Fox Feature Syndicate

1	7.00	21.00	50.00

LIGHT IN THE FOREST (See 4-Color No. 891)

LIGHTNING COMICS (Formerly Sure-Fire No. 1-3)
No. 4, Dec, 1940 - No. 13(V3No.1), June, 1942
Ace Magazines

4	29.00	87.00	200.00
5,6: 6-Dr. Nemesis begins	20.00	60.00	140.00
V2#1-6: 2-"Flash Lightning" becomes "Lash..."	17.00	51.00	120.00
V3#1-Intro. Lightning Girl & The Sword	17.00	51.00	120.00

NOTE: ***Anderson*** *a-V2No.6. Bondage-c V2No.6.*

LI'L (See Little)

LILY OF THE ALLEY IN THE FUNNIES
No date (1920's?) (10¼x15½"; 28 pgs. in color)
Whitman Publishers

W936 - by T. Burke	6.00	18.00	42.00

LIMITED COLLECTORS' EDITION (See Famous 1st Edition & Rudolph the Red Nosed Reindeer; becomes All-New Collectors' Edition)
(No.21-34,51-59: 84 pgs.; No.35-41: 68 pgs.; No.42-50: 60 pgs.)
C-21, Summer, 1973 - No. C-59, 1978 ($1.00) (10x13½")
National Periodical Publications/DC Comics

nn(C-20)-Rudolph	.70	2.00	4.00
C-21: Shazam (TV); Captain Marvel Jr. reprint by Raboy	.50	1.50	3.00
C-22: Tarzan; complete origin reprinted from #207-210; all Kubert	.50	1.50	3.00
C-23: House of Mystery; Wrightson, Adams, Wood, Toth, Orlando-a	.35	1.00	2.00
C-24: Rudolph The Red-nosed Reindeer	.35	1.00	2.00
C-25: Batman; Adams-c/a	.50	1.50	3.00
C-27: Shazam (TV)	.35	1.00	2.00
C-29: Tarzan; reprints "Return of Tarzan" from #219-223 by Kubert	.50	1.50	3.00
C-31: Superman; origin-r; Adams-a	.50	1.50	3.00
C-32: Ghosts (new-a)	.35	1.00	2.00
C-33: Rudolph The Red-nosed Reindeer(new-a)	.35	1.00	2.00

LIMITED COLL. EDITION (continued) — Good / Fine / Mint

C-34: Xmas with the Super-Heroes; unpublished Angel & Ape story by Oksner & Wood .50 1.50 3.00
C-35: Shazam; cover features TV's Captain Marvel, Jackson Bostwick (TV) .35 1.00 2.00
C-36: The Bible; all new adaptation beginning with Genesis by Kubert, Redondo & Mayer .50 1.50 3.00
C-37: Batman; r-1946 Sundays .35 1.00 2.00
C-38: Superman; 1 pg. Adams .35 1.00 2.00
C-39: Secret Origins/Super Villains; Adams-a(r) .35 1.00 2.00
C-40: Dick Tracy by Gould featuring Flattop; newspaper-r from 12/21/43 - 5/17/44 .50 1.50 3.00
C-41: Super Friends; Toth-c/a .35 1.00 2.00
C-42: Rudolph .35 1.00 2.00
C-43: Christmas with the Super-Heroes; Wrightson, S&K, Adams-a .50 1.50 3.00
C-44: Batman; Adams-r; painted-c .35 1.00 2.00
C-45: Secret Origins/Super Villains; Flash-r/105 .35 1.00 2.00
C-46: Justice League of America; 3 pg. Toth-a .50 1.50 3.00
C-47: Superman Salutes the Bicentennial (Tomahawk interior); 2 pgs. new-a .25 .75 1.50
C-48: The Superman-Flash Race; 6 pgs. Adams-a .35 1.00 2.00
C-49: Superboy & the Legion of Super-Heroes .35 1.00 2.00
C-50: Rudolph The Red-nosed Reindeer .25 .75 1.50
C-51: Batman; Adams-c/a .50 1.50 3.00
C-52: The Best of DC; Adams-c/a; Toth, Kubert-a .35 1.00 2.00
C-57: Welcome Back, Kotter-r(TV)(5/78) .25 .75 1.50
C-59: Batman's Strangest Cases; Adams, Wrightson-r; Adams/Wrightson-c .35 1.00 2.00

NOTE: *All-r with exception of some special features and covers.* ***Aparo*** *a-52r; c-37.* ***Giordano*** *a-39, 45.* ***Grell*** *c-49.* ***Infantino*** *a-25, 39, 44, 45, 52.*

LINDA (Phantom Lady No. 5 on)
Apr-May, 1954 - No. 4, Oct-Nov, 1954
Ajax-Farrell Publ. Co.

	Good	Fine	Mint
1-Kamenish-a	6.50	19.50	45.00
2-Lingerie panel	4.35	13.00	30.00
3,4	4.00	12.00	28.00

LINDA CARTER, STUDENT NURSE
Sept, 1961 - No. 9, Jan, 1963
Atlas Comics (AMI)

	Good	Fine	Mint
1	1.15	3.50	8.00
2-9	.70	2.00	5.00

LINDA LARK
Oct-Dec, 1961 - No. 8, Aug-Oct, 1963
Dell Publishing Co.

	Good	Fine	Mint
1	1.00	3.00	7.00
2-8	.55	1.65	4.00

LINUS, THE LIONHEARTED (TV)
September, 1965
Gold Key

	Good	Fine	Mint
1 (10155-509)	2.00	6.00	14.00

LION, THE (See Movie Comics)

LION OF SPARTA (See Movie Classics)

LIPPY THE LION AND HARDY HAR HAR (TV)
March, 1963 (Hanna-Barbera)
Gold Key

	Good	Fine	Mint
1 (10049-303)	2.00	6.00	14.00

LI'L ABNER (See Comics on Parade, Tip Top, Tip Topper & Sparkler)
1939 - 1940
United Features Syndicate

	Good	Fine	Mint
Single Series 4 ('39)	29.00	87.00	200.00
Single Series 18 ('40) (#18 on inside, #2 on cover)	22.00	65.00	154.00

LI'L ABNER (Al Capp's) (See Oxydol-Dreft)
No. 61, Dec, 1947 - No. 97, Jan, 1955
Harvey Publ. No. 61-69 (2/49)/Toby Press No. 70 on

	Good	Fine	Mint
61(#1)-Wolverton-a	12.00	36.00	84.00
62-65	8.50	25.50	60.00
66,67,69,70	7.00	21.00	50.00
68-Full length Fearless Fosdick story	8.50	25.50	60.00
71-74,76,80	5.70	17.00	40.00
75,77-79,86,91-All with Kurtzman art; 91 reprints #77	6.50	19.50	45.00
81-85,87-90,92-94,96,97: 93-reprints #71	4.60	14.00	32.00
95-Full length Fearless Fosdick story	6.50	19.50	45.00
. . .& the Creatures from Drop-Outer Space-nn (Job Corps giveaway; 36pgs., in color	5.00	15.00	35.00
. . .Joins the Navy (1950) (Toby Press Premium)	5.00	15.00	35.00
. . .by Al Capp Giveaway (Circa 1955, nd)	5.00	15.00	35.00

NOTE: ***Powell*** *a-61, 65.*

LI'L ABNER
1951
Toby Press

	Good	Fine	Mint
1	6.50	19.50	45.00

LI'L ABNER'S DOGPATCH (See Al Capp's. . .)

LITTLE AL OF THE F.B.I.
No. 10, 1950 (no month) - No. 11, Apr-May, 1951
Ziff-Davis Publications (Saunders painted-c)

	Good	Fine	Mint
10(1950)	4.60	14.00	32.00
11(1951)	3.50	10.50	24.00

LITTLE AL OF THE SECRET SERVICE
No. 10, 7-8/51; No, 2, 9-10/51; No. 3, Wint., 1951
Ziff-Davis Publications (Saunders painted-c)

	Good	Fine	Mint
10(#1)-Spanking panel	6.50	19.50	45.00
2,3	3.50	10.50	24.00

LITTLE AMBROSE
September, 1958
Archie Publications

	Good	Fine	Mint
1	7.00	21.00	50.00

LITTLE ANGEL
No. 5, Sept, 1954; No. 6, Sept, 1955 - No. 16, Sept, 1959
Standard (Visual Editions)/Pines

	Good	Fine	Mint
5	2.30	7.00	16.00
6-16	1.15	3.50	8.00

LITTLE ANNIE ROONEY
1935 (48 pgs.; B&W dailies) (25 cents)
David McKay Publications

	Good	Fine	Mint
Book 1-Daily strip-r by Darrell McClure	8.00	24.00	56.00

LITTLE ANNIE ROONEY (See Treasury of Comics)
1938; Aug, 1948 - No. 3, Oct, 1948
David McKay/St. John/Standard

	Good	Fine	Mint
Feature Books 11 (McKay, 1938)	16.00	48.00	110.00
1 (St. John)	5.70	17.00	40.00
2,3	3.00	9.00	21.00

LITTLE ARCHIE (The Adventures of. . . #13-on) (Also see Archie Giant Series #527,534,538,545,549,556,566,570)

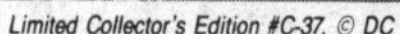
Limited Collector's Edition #C-37, © DC

Linda #1, © AJAX

Little Al of the F.B.I. #11, © Z-D

Little Audrey #12 (St. John), © HARV

Little Beaver #8, © DELL

Little Dot #3, © HARV

LITTLE ARCHIE (continued)
1956 - No. 180, 2/83 (Giants No. 3-84)
Archie Publications

	Good	Fine	Mint
1-(Scarce)	23.00	70.00	160.00
2	11.50	34.00	80.00
3-5	7.00	21.00	50.00
6-10	5.00	15.00	35.00
11-20	3.35	10.00	23.00
21-30	2.00	6.00	14.00
31-40: Little Pureheart begins #40, ends #42,44	1.00	3.00	7.00
41-60: 42-Intro. The Little Archies. 59-Little Sabrina begins	.50	1.50	3.00
61-80	.35	1.00	2.00
81-100		.50	1.00
101-180		.40	.80
...In Animal Land 1('57)	9.20	27.50	64.00
...In Animal Land 17(Winter, 1957-58)-19(Summer,'58)-Formerly Li'l Jinx	4.50	13.50	31.00

LITTLE ARCHIE COMICS DIGEST ANNUAL (...Mag. #5 on)
Oct, 1977 - Present (Digest-size)
Archie Publications

	Good	Fine	Mint
1(10/77)-Reprints	.35	1.00	2.00
2(4/78)-Adams-a		.50	1.00
3(11/78)-The Fly-r by S&K; Adams-a		.50	1.00
4(4/79) - 24('87)		.50	1.00

LITTLE ARCHIE MYSTERY
Aug, 1963 - No. 2, Oct, 1963
Archie Publications

	Good	Fine	Mint
1	7.50	22.50	45.00
2	3.35	10.00	20.00

LITTLE ASPIRIN (See Wisco)
July, 1949 - No. 3, Dec, 1949 (52 pages)
Marvel Comics (CnPC)

	Good	Fine	Mint
1-Kurtzman-a, 4 pgs.	5.70	17.00	40.00
2-Kurtzman-a, 4 pgs.	3.00	9.00	21.00
3-No Kurtzman	1.50	4.50	10.00

LITTLE AUDREY (Also see Playful...)
April, 1948 - No. 24, June, 1952
St. John Publ.

	Good	Fine	Mint
1-1st app. Little Audrey	17.00	51.00	120.00
2	9.00	27.00	62.00
3-5	7.00	21.00	50.00
6-10	4.00	12.00	28.00
11-20	2.00	6.00	14.00
21-24	1.30	4.00	9.00

LITTLE AUDREY (See Harvey Hits #11,19)
No. 25, Aug, 1952 - No. 53, April, 1957
Harvey Publications

	Good	Fine	Mint
25	4.35	13.00	30.00
26-30: 26-28-Casper app.	2.00	6.00	14.00
31-40: 32-35-Casper app.	1.50	4.50	10.00
41-53	1.00	3.00	7.00
...Clubhouse 1 (9/61, Giant)	3.00	9.00	18.00

LITTLE AUDREY (...Yearbook)
1950 (260 pages) (50 cents)
St. John Publishing Co.

	Good	Fine	Mint
Contains 8 complete 1949 comics rebound; Casper, Alice in Wonderland, Little Audrey, Abbott & Costello, Pinocchio, Moon Mullins, Three Stooges (from Jubilee), Little Annie Rooney app. (Rare)	45.00	135.00	315.00

(Also see All Good & Treasury of Comics)

NOTE: *This book contains remaindered St. John comics; many variations possible.*

LITTLE AUDREY & MELVIN (Audrey &... No. 62)
May, 1962 - No. 61, Dec, 1973
Harvey Publications

	Good	Fine	Mint
1	5.35	16.00	32.00
2-5	2.75	8.00	16.00
6-10	1.70	5.00	10.00
11-20	1.00	3.00	6.00
21-40	.70	2.00	4.00
41-61	.50	1.50	3.00

LITTLE AUDREY TV FUNTIME
Sept, 1962 - No. 33, Oct, 1971 (All giants)
Harvey Publications

	Good	Fine	Mint
1-Richie Rich app.	3.35	10.00	20.00
2,3: Richie Rich app.	2.00	6.00	12.00
4,5	1.70	5.00	10.00
6-10	.85	2.50	5.00
11-20	.70	2.00	4.00
21-33	.50	1.50	3.00

LITTLE BAD WOLF (See 4-Color #403,473,564, Walt Disney's C&S #52, Walt Disney Showcase #21 & Wheaties)

LITTLE BEAVER
No. 211, Jan, 1949 - No. 870, Jan, 1958 (All painted-c)
Dell Publishing Co.

	Good	Fine	Mint
4-Color 211('49)-All Harman-a	3.00	9.00	21.00
4-Color 267,294,332(5/51)	2.00	6.00	14.00
3(10-12/51)-8(1-3/53)	1.70	5.00	12.00
4-Color 483(8-10/53),529	1.70	5.00	12.00
4-Color 612,660,695,744,817,870	1.30	4.00	9.00

LITTLE BIT
March, 1949 - No. 2, 1949
Jubilee/St. John Publishing Co.

	Good	Fine	Mint
1,2	1.50	4.50	10.00

LITTLE DOT (See Tastee-Freez Comics, Li'l Max, Humphrey, and Sad Sack)
Sept, 1953 - No. 164, April, 1976
Harvey Publications

	Good	Fine	Mint
1-Intro./1st app. Richie Rich & Little Lotta	45.00	135.00	320.00
2	21.00	64.00	150.00
3	15.00	45.00	105.00
4	11.00	32.50	75.00
5-Origin dots on Little Dot's Dress	12.50	37.50	85.00
6-Richie Rich, Little Lotta, & Little Dot all on cover; 1st Richie Rich cover featured	12.50	37.50	85.00
7-10	5.00	15.00	35.00
11-20	4.00	12.00	28.00
21-40	2.00	6.00	14.00
41-60	1.00	3.00	7.00
61-80	.70	2.00	4.00
81-100	.50	1.50	3.00
101-130	.35	1.00	2.00
131-164		.50	1.00

NOTE: *Richie Rich & Little Lotta in all.*

LITTLE DOT DOTLAND (Dot Dotland No. 62,63)
July, 1962 - No. 61, Dec, 1973
Harvey Publications

	Good	Fine	Mint
1-Richie Rich begins	3.50	10.50	24.00
2,3	1.70	5.00	12.00
4,5	1.50	4.50	10.00
6-10	1.15	3.50	8.00
11-20	.85	2.50	6.00
21-30	.50	1.50	3.00
31-61	.35	1.00	2.00

LITTLE DOT'S UNCLES & AUNTS (See Harvey Hits No. 4,13,24)
Oct, 1961 - No. 52, April, 1974
Harvey Enterprises

	Good	Fine	Mint
1-Richie Rich begins	3.50	10.50	24.00
2,3	1.70	5.00	12.00
4,5	1.50	4.50	10.00
6-10	1.15	3.50	8.00
11-20	.85	2.50	6.00
21-30: 24,25-Giant size	.50	1.50	3.00
31-52	.35	1.00	2.00

LITTLE EVA
May, 1952 - No. 31, Nov, 1956
St. John Publishing Co.

	Good	Fine	Mint
1	5.70	17.00	40.00
2	2.65	8.00	18.00
3-5	2.00	6.00	14.00
6-10	1.30	4.00	9.00
11-31	1.15	3.50	8.00
3-D 1,2(10/53-11/53); 1-Infinity-c	12.00	36.00	84.00
I.W. Reprint #1-3,6-8	.30	.90	1.80
Super Reprint #10,12('63),14,16,18('64)	.30	.90	1.80

LITTLE FIR TREE, THE
1942 (8½x11") (12 pgs. with cover)
W. T. Grant Co. (Christmas giveaway)

8 pg. Kelly-a reprint/Santa Claus Funnies not signed.
(One copy in M sold for $1750.00 in 1986)

LI'L GENIUS (Summer Fun No. 54) (See Blue Bird)
1954 - No. 52, 1/65; No. 53, 10/65; No. 54, 10/85 - No. 55, 1/86
Charlton Comics

	Good	Fine	Mint
1	2.65	8.00	18.00
2	1.30	4.00	9.00
3-15,19,20	1.00	3.00	7.00
16,17-(68 pgs.)	1.15	3.50	8.00
18-(100 pgs., 10/58)	1.85	5.50	13.00
21-35	.75	2.25	5.00
36-53	.50	1.50	3.00
54,55	.25	.75	1.50

LI'L GHOST
Feb, 1958 - No. 3, Mar, 1959
St. John Publishing Co./Fago No. 1 on

	Good	Fine	Mint
1(St. John)	2.30	7.00	16.00
1(Fago)	1.75	5.25	12.00
2,3	1.00	3.00	7.00

LITTLE GIANT COMICS
7/38 - No. 3, 10/38; No. 4, 2/39 (132 pgs.) (6¾x4½")
Centaur Publications

	Good	Fine	Mint
1-B&W with color-c	21.00	64.00	145.00
2,3-B&W with color-c	17.00	51.00	120.00
4 (6-5/8x9-3/8")(68 pgs., B&W inside)	18.00	54.00	125.00

NOTE: ***Gustavson** a-1. **Pinajian** a-4. **Bob Wood** a-1.*

LITTLE GIANT DETECTIVE FUNNIES
Oct, 1938 - No. 4, Jan, 1939 (132 pgs., B&W) (6¾x4½")
Centaur Publications

	Good	Fine	Mint
1-B&W with color-c	21.00	64.00	145.00
2,3	17.00	51.00	120.00
4(1/39)-B&W; color-c; 68 pgs., 6½x9½"; Eisner-r	18.00	54.00	125.00

LITTLE GIANT MOVIE FUNNIES
Aug, 1938 - No. 2, Oct, 1938 (132 pgs., B&W) (6¾x4½")
Centaur Publications

	Good	Fine	Mint
1-Ed Wheelan's "Minute Movies"-r	21.00	64.00	145.00
2-Ed Wheelan's "Minute Movies"-r	16.00	48.00	110.00

LITTLE GROUCHO (. . .Grouchy No. 2) (See Tippy Terry)
Feb-Mar, 1955 - No. 2, June-July, 1955
Reston Publ. Co.

	Good	Fine	Mint
16, 1	2.00	6.00	14.00
2(6-7/55)	1.15	3.50	8.00

LITTLE HIAWATHA (See 4-Color #439,787,901,988 & Walt Disney's C&S #143)

LITTLE IKE
April, 1953 - No. 4, Oct, 1953
St. John Publishing Co.

	Good	Fine	Mint
1	3.00	9.00	21.00
2	1.50	4.50	10.00
3,4	1.15	3.50	8.00

LITTLE IODINE (See Giant Comic Album)
April, 1949 - No. 56, Apr-June, 1962 (52pgs., 1-4)
Dell Publishing Co.

	Good	Fine	Mint
4-Color 224-By Jimmy Hatlo	3.75	11.25	26.00
4-Color 257	2.85	8.50	20.00
1(3-5/50)	2.85	8.50	20.00
2-5	1.75	5.25	12.00
6-10	1.15	3.50	8.00
11-20	1.00	3.00	7.00
21-30	.85	2.50	6.00
31-40	.55	1.65	4.00
41-56	.45	1.35	3.00

LITTLE JACK FROST
1951
Avon Periodicals

	Good	Fine	Mint
1	3.50	10.50	24.00

LI'L JINX (Formerly Ginger?) (Little Archie in Animal Land #17)
(Also see Pep Comics #62)
No. 1(#11), Nov, 1956 - No. 16, Sept, 1957
Archie Publications

	Good	Fine	Mint
11 (#1)	4.60	14.00	32.00
12-16	3.00	9.00	21.00

LI'L JINX (See Archie Giant Series Magazine No. 223)

LI'L JINX CHRISTMAS BAG (See Archie Giant Series Mag. No. 195,206,219)

LI'L JINX GIANT LAUGH-OUT
No. 33, Sept, 1971 - No. 43, Nov, 1973 (52 pgs.)
Archie Publications

	Good	Fine	Mint
33-43	.35	1.00	2.00

(See Archie Giant Series Mag. No. 176,185)

LITTLE JOE (See 4-Color No. 1)

LITTLE JOE
April, 1953
St. John Publishing Co.

	Good	Fine	Mint
1	1.30	4.00	9.00

LITTLE JOHNNY & THE TEDDY BEARS
1907 (10x14") (32 pgs. in color)
Reilly & Britton Co.

	Good	Fine	Mint
By J. R. Bray	15.00	45.00	105.00

LI'L KIDS
8/70 - No. 2, 10/70; No. 3, 11/71 - No. 12, 6/73
Marvel Comics Group

	Good	Fine	Mint
1	.50	1.50	3.00
2-12: 10,11-Calvin app.	.25	.75	1.50

LITTLE KING (See 4-Color No. 494,597,677)

LITTLE KLINKER
Nov, 1960 (20 pgs.) (slick cover)
Little Klinker Ventures (Montgomery Ward Giveaway)

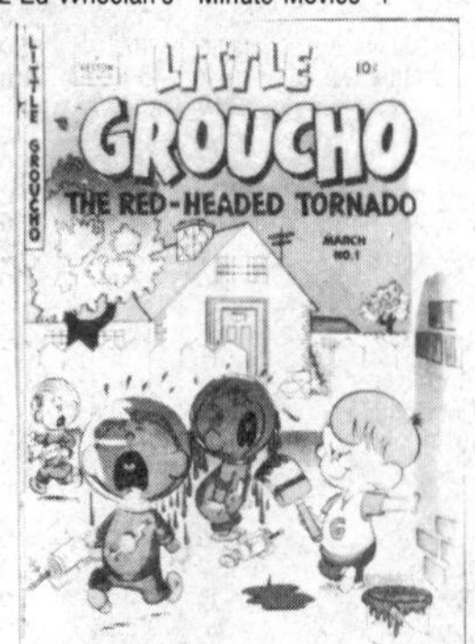

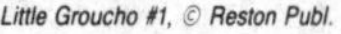
Little Groucho #1, © Reston Publ.

Little Iodine #56, © DELL

Little Joe #1, © STJ

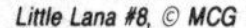
Little Lana #8, © MCG

Little Lotta #30, © HARV

Little Miss Muffet #12, © KING

LITTLE KLINKER (continued)	Good	Fine	Mint
		1.00	2.00

LITTLE LANA (Formerly Lana)
No. 8, Nov, 1949 - No. 9, Mar, 1950
Marvel Comics (MjMC)

	Good	Fine	Mint
8,9	1.60	4.70	11.00

LITTLE LENNY
June, 1949 - No. 3, Nov, 1949
Marvel Comics (CDS)

	Good	Fine	Mint
1	2.65	8.00	18.00
2,3	1.30	4.00	9.00

LITTLE LIZZIE
6/49 - No. 5, 4/50; 9/53 - No. 3, Jan, 1954
Marvel Comics (PrPI)/Atlas (OMC)

	Good	Fine	Mint
1	2.65	8.00	18.00
2-5	1.30	4.00	9.00
1 (1953)	2.00	6.00	14.00
2,3	1.00	3.00	7.00

LITTLE LOTTA (See Harvey Hits No. 10)
11/55 - No. 110, 11/73; No. 111, 9/74 - No. 121, 5/76
Harvey Publications

	Good	Fine	Mint
1-Richie Rich & Little Dot begin	16.00	48.00	110.00
2,3	7.00	21.00	50.00
4,5	4.35	13.00	30.00
6-10	3.00	9.00	21.00
11-20	1.70	5.00	12.00
21-40	1.15	3.50	8.00
41-60	.85	2.50	6.00
61-80	.50	1.50	3.00
81-100	.35	1.00	2.00
101-121	.25	.75	1.50

LITTLE LOTTA FOODLAND
9/63 - No. 14, 10/67; No. 15, 10/68 - No. 29, Oct, 1972
Harvey Publications

	Good	Fine	Mint
1	4.00	12.00	28.00
2,3	2.00	6.00	14.00
4,5	1.70	5.00	12.00
6-10	1.30	4.00	9.00
11-20	.85	2.50	6.00
21-29	.70	2.00	4.00

LITTLE LULU (Formerly Marge's...)
No. 207, Sept., 1972 - No. 268, April, 1984
Gold Key 207-257/Whitman 258 on

	Good	Fine	Mint
207,209,220-Stanley-r	.60	1.75	3.50
208,210-219	.49	1.25	2.50
221-240,242-253	.25	.80	1.60
241,254,255,263,265,268-Stanley-r	.25	.80	1.60
256-262,264,266-267		.50	1.00

LITTLE MARY MIXUP (See Single Series No. 10,26)

LITTLE MAX COMICS (Joe Palooka's Pal; see Joe Palooka)
Oct, 1949 - No. 73, Nov, 1961
Harvey Publications

	Good	Fine	Mint
1-Infinity-c; Little Dot begins	7.00	21.00	50.00
2-Little Dot app.	3.50	10.50	24.00
3-Little Dot app.	2.75	8.00	19.00
4-10: 5-Little Dot app., 1pg.	1.50	4.50	10.00
11-20	1.00	3.00	7.00
21-68,70-72: 23-Little Dot app. 38-r/20	.75	2.25	5.00
69,73-Richie Rich app.	.85	2.50	6.00

LI'L MENACE
Dec, 1958 - No. 3, May, 1959
Fago Magazine Co.

	Good	Fine	Mint
1-Peter Rabbit app.	1.85	5.50	13.00
2-Peter Rabbit (Vincent Fago's)	1.15	3.50	8.00
3	.85	2.50	6.00

LITTLE MISS MUFFET
Dec, 1948 - No. 13, March, 1949
Standard Comics/King Features Synd.

	Good	Fine	Mint
11-Strip reprints; Fanny Cory-a	3.50	10.50	24.00
12,13-Strip reprints; Fanny Cory-a	1.70	5.00	12.00

LITTLE MISS SUNBEAM COMICS
June-July, 1950 - No. 4, Dec-Jan, 1950-51
Magazine Enterprises/Quality Bakers of America

	Good	Fine	Mint
1	4.60	14.00	32.00
2	2.65	8.00	18.00
3,4	2.35	7.00	16.00
...Advs. In Space ('55)	1.50	4.50	10.00
Bread Giveaway 1-4(Quality Bakers, 1949-50)-14 pgs. each	1.50	4.50	10.00
Bread Giveaway (1957,61; 16pgs, reg. size)	1.15	3.50	8.00

LITTLE MONSTERS, THE (See March of Comics No. 423 & Three Stooges No. 17)
Nov, 1964 - No. 44, Feb, 1978
Gold Key

	Good	Fine	Mint
1	1.15	3.50	8.00
2	.70	2.00	4.00
3-10	.50	1.50	3.00
11-20	.35	1.00	2.00
21-44: 20,34-39,43-reprints		.40	.80

LITTLE NEMO (See Cocomalt, Future Comics, Help, Jest, Kayo, Punch, Red Seal, & Superworld; most by Winsor McCay Jr., son of famous artist) (Other McCay books: see Little Sammy Sneeze & Dreams of the Rarebit Fiend)

LITTLE NEMO (...in Slumberland)
1906, 1909 (Sunday strip reprints in color) (cardboard covers)
Doffield & Co.(1906)/Cupples & Leon Co.(1909)

	Good	Fine	Mint
1906-11x16½" in color by Winsor McCay; 30 pgs. (Very Rare)	120.00	320.00	735.00
1909-10x14" in color by Winsor McCay (Very Rare)	100.00	280.00	630.00

LITTLE NEMO (...in Slumberland)
1945 (28 pgs.; 11x7¼"; B&W)
McCay Features/Nostalgia Press('69)

	Good	Fine	Mint
1905 & 1911 reprints by Winsor McCay	2.65	8.00	18.00
1969-70 (exact reprint)	1.50	4.00	8.00

LITTLE NEMO IN SLUMBERLAND 3-D
Jan, 1987 ($2.50)
Blackthorne Publishing

	Good	Fine	Mint
1-Winsor McCay-r in 3-D	.40	1.25	2.50

LITTLE ORPHAN ANNIE (See Annie, Marvel Super Special, Merry Christmas..., & Super Book No. 7, 11, 23)

LITTLE ORPHAN ANNIE (See Treasury Box of...)
1926 - 1934 (Daily strip reprints) (7x8¾") (B&W)
Cupples & Leon Co.

(Hardcover Editions, 100 pages)

	Good	Fine	Mint
1(1926)-Little Orphan Annie	15.00	45.00	105.00
2('27)-In the Circus	11.50	34.00	80.00
3('28)-The Haunted House	11.50	34.00	80.00
4('29)-Bucking the World	11.50	34.00	80.00
5('30)-Never Say Die	11.50	34.00	80.00
6('31)-Shipwrecked	11.50	34.00	80.00
7('32)-A Willing Helper	8.50	25.50	60.00
8('33)-In Cosmic City	8.50	25.50	60.00
9('34)-Uncle Dan	11.50	34.00	80.00

LITTLE ORPHAN ANNIE (continued)
NOTE: *Hardcovers with dust jackets are worth 20-50 percent more; the earlier the book, the higher the percentage. Each book reprints dailies from the previous year.*

LITTLE ORPHAN ANNIE
No. 7, 1937 - No. 3, Sept-Nov, 1948
David McKay Publ./Dell Publishing Co.

	Good	Fine	Mint
Feature Books(McKay) 7-('37) (Very Rare)	70.00	210.00	490.00
4-Color 12(1941)	28.00	84.00	195.00
4-Color 18('43)-Flag-c	21.00	64.00	150.00
4-Color 52('44)	15.00	45.00	105.00
4-Color 76('45)	13.00	40.00	90.00
4-Color 107('46)	11.00	32.00	76.00
4-Color 152('47)	8.00	24.00	56.00
4-Color 206(12/48)	5.50	16.50	38.00
1(3-5/48)	12.00	36.00	84.00
2,3	7.00	21.00	50.00
Junior Commandos Giveaway(same cover as 4-Color No. 18, K.K. Publ.(Big Shoe Store); same back cover as '47 Popped Wheat giveaway; 16 pgs.	14.50	43.50	100.00
Popped Wheat Giveaway('47)-16 pgs. full color; '40 reprints	.85	2.50	6.00
Quaker Sparkies Giveaway(1940)	6.00	18.00	42.00
Quaker Sparkies Giveaway(1941, Full color-20 pgs.); "LOA and the Rescue," "LOA and the Kidnappers," each....	5.50	16.50	38.00
Quaker Sparkies Giveaway(1942, Full color-20 pgs..); "LOA and Mr. Grudge" and "LOA and the Great Am"	4.00	12.00	28.00

LI'L PALS
Sept, 1972 - No. 5, May, 1973
Marvel Comics Group

	Good	Fine	Mint
1-5		.40	.80

LI'L PAN
No. 6, Dec-Jan, 1947 - No. 8, Apr-May, 1947
Fox Features Syndicate

	Good	Fine	Mint
6	2.30	7.00	16.00
7,8	1.60	4.70	11.00

LITTLE PEOPLE (See 4-Color No. 485, 573, 633, 692, 753, 809, 868, 908, 959, 1024, 1062)

LITTLE RASCALS (See 4-Color No. 674, 778, 825, 883, 936, 974, 1030, 1079, 1137, 1174, 1224, 1297)

LI'L RASCAL TWINS (Formerly Nature Boy)
1957 - No. 18, Jan, 1960
Charlton Comics

	Good	Fine	Mint
6-Li'l Genius & Tomboy in all	1.50	4.50	10.00
7-18	.75	2.25	5.00

LITTLE ROQUEFORT
June, 1952 - No. 9, Oct, 1953; No. 10, Summer, 1958
St. John Publishing Co./Pines No. 10

	Good	Fine	Mint
1	2.65	8.00	18.00
2	1.30	4.00	9.00
3-10	1.15	3.50	8.00

LITTLE SAD SACK (See Harvey Hits No. 73,76,79,81,83)
Oct, 1964 - No. 19, Nov, 1967
Harvey Publications

	Good	Fine	Mint
1-Richie Rich app. cover only	1.35	4.00	9.00
2-19	.35	1.00	2.00

LITTLE SAMMY SNEEZE
1905 (28 pgs. in color; 11x16½")
New York Herald Co.

	Good	Fine	Mint
By Winsor McCay (Rare)	150.00	425.00	850.00

NOTE: *Rarely found in fine to mint condition.*

LITTLE SCOUTS
No. 321, Mar, 1951 - No. 587, Oct, 1954
Dell Publishing Co.

	Good	Fine	Mint
4-Color #321 ('51)	1.30	4.00	9.00
2(10-12/51) - 6(10-12/52)	.85	2.50	6.00
4-Color #462,506,550,587	.85	2.50	6.00

LITTLE SHOP OF HORRORS SPECIAL
Feb, 1987 ($2.00, 68 pgs.)
DC Comics

	Good	Fine	Mint
1-Colan-a	.35	1.00	2.00

LITTLE SPUNKY
No date (1963?) (10 cents)
I. W. Enterprises

	Good	Fine	Mint
1-Reprint	.30	.80	1.60

LITTLE STOOGES, THE (The Three Stooges' Sons)
Sept, 1972 - No. 7, Mar, 1974
Gold Key

	Good	Fine	Mint
1-Norman Maurer cover/stories in all	.70	2.00	4.00
2-7	.35	1.00	2.00

LITTLEST OUTLAW (See 4-Color No. 609)

LITTLEST SNOWMAN, THE
No. 755, 12/56; No. 864, 12/57; 12-2/1963-64
Dell Publishing Co.

	Good	Fine	Mint
4-Color #755,864, 1(1964)	2.00	6.00	14.00

LI'L TOMBOY (Formerly Fawcett's Funny Animals)
V14No.92, 10/56; No. 93, 3/57 - No. 107, 2/60
Charlton Comics

	Good	Fine	Mint
V14#92	1.75	5.25	12.00
93-107: 97-Atomic Bunny app.	.85	2.50	6.00

LI'L WILLIE COMICS (Formerly & becomes Willie Comics #22 on)
July, 1949 - No. 21, Sept, 1949
Marvel Comics (MgPC)

	Good	Fine	Mint
20,21: 20-Little Aspirin app.	1.50	4.50	10.00

LIVE IT UP
1973, 1976 (39-49 cents)
Spire Christian Comics (Fleming H. Revell Co.)

	Good	Fine	Mint
nn		.40	.80

LIVING BIBLE, THE
Fall, 1945 - No. 3, Spring, 1946
Living Bible Corp.

	Good	Fine	Mint
1-Life of Paul	7.00	21.00	50.00
2-Joseph & His Brethren	5.00	15.00	35.00
3-Chaplains of War (classic-c)	10.00	30.00	70.00

NOTE: *All have* ***L. B. Cole*** *-c.*

LOBO
Dec, 1965 - No. 2, Oct, 1966
Dell Publishing Co.

	Good	Fine	Mint
1,2	.85	2.50	6.00

LOCKE!
1987 - Present ($1.25, color)
Blackthorne Publishing

	Good	Fine	Mint
1-3		.60	1.25

LOCO (Magazine) (Satire)
Aug, 1958 - V1No.3, Jan, 1959
Satire Publications

	Good	Fine	Mint
V1#1-Chic Stone-a	1.00	3.00	7.00
V1#2,3-Severin-a, 2 pgs. Davis; 3-Heath-a	.70	2.00	4.00

LOGAN'S RUN
Jan, 1977 - No. 7, July, 1977

Little Orphan Annie #3 (Dell), © News Synd.

Little Scouts #2, © DELL

L'il Willie #20, © MCG

The Lone Ranger #118, © Lone Ranger

The Lone Ranger's Companion... #4, © Lone Ranger

Lone Rider #2, © Farrell Publ.

LOGAN'S RUN (continued)
Marvel Comics Group

	Good	Fine	Mint
1		.40	.80
2-7		.25	.50

NOTE: ***Austin*** *a-6i.* ***Gulacy*** *c-6.* ***Kane*** *c-7p.* ***Perez*** *a-1-5p; c-1-5p.* ***Sutton*** *a-6p, 7p.*

LOIS LANE (Also see Superman's Girlfriend . . .)
Aug, 1986 - No. 2, Sept, 1986 (52 pgs.)
DC Comics

1,2-Morrow c/a	.25	.75	1.50

LOLLY AND PEPPER
No. 832, Sept, 1957 - July, 1962
Dell Publishing Co.

4-Color 832	1.70	5.00	12.00
4-Color 940,978,1086,1206	1.30	4.00	9.00
01-459-207	1.30	4.00	9.00

LOMAX (See Police Action)

LONE EAGLE (The Flame No. 5 on)
Apr-May, 1954 - No. 4, Oct-Nov, 1954
Ajax/Farrell Publications

1	3.50	10.50	24.00
2-4	2.00	6.00	14.00

LONELY HEART (Formerly Dear Lonely Hearts; Dear Heart #15 on)
No. 9, March, 1955 - No. 14, Feb, 1956
Ajax/Farrell Publ. (Excellent Publ.)

9-Kamenesque-a; (Last precode)	3.00	9.00	21.00
10-14	1.50	4.50	10.00

LONE RANGER, THE (See Aurora, Dell Giants, Feature Books #21, 24(McKay), Future Comics, Magic Comics & March of Comics #165, 174, 193, 208, 225, 238, 310, 322, 338, 350)

LONE RANGER, THE
No. 3, 1939 - No. 167, Feb, 1947
Dell Publishing Co.

Large Feat. Comic 3('39)-Heigh-Yo Silver; text with ill. by Robert Weisman	38.00	115.00	265.00
Large Feat. Comic 7('39)-Ill. by Henry Valleley; Hi-Yo Silver the Lone Ranger to the Rescue	49.00	145.00	340.00
4-Color 82('45)	24.00	72.00	170.00
4-Color 98('45),118('46)	21.00	64.00	150.00
4-Color 125('46),136('47)	15.00	45.00	105.00
4-Color 151,167('47)	12.00	36.00	84.00

LONE RANGER COMICS, THE (10 cents)
1939(inside) (shows 1938 on-c) (68 pgs. in color; regular size)
Lone Ranger, Inc. (Ice cream mail order)

(Scarce)-not by Valleley	48.00	145.00	335.00

LONE RANGER, THE (Movie, radio & TV; Clayton Moore starred as L. Ranger in the movies; No. 1-37: strip reprints)(See Dell Giants)
Jan-Feb, 1948 - No. 145, May-July, 1962
Dell Publishing Co.

	Good	Fine	Mint
1 (36pgs.)-The L. Ranger, his horse Silver, companion Tonto & his horse Scout begin	40.00	120.00	280.00
2 (52pgs. begin, end #41)	20.00	60.00	140.00
3-5	17.00	51.00	120.00
6,7,9,10	14.00	42.00	100.00
8-Origin retold; indian back-c begin, end #35	17.00	51.00	120.00
11-20: 11-"Young Hawk" Indian boy serial begins, ends #145	9.50	28.00	65.00
21,22,24-31: 51-Reprint. 31-1st Mask logo	7.00	21.00	50.00
23-Origin retold	10.00	30.00	70.00
32-37: 32-Painted-c begin. 36-Animal photo back-c begin, end #49. 37-Last newspaper-r issue; new outfit	5.70	17.00	40.00
38-41 (All 52pgs.)	4.00	12.00	28.00
42-50 (36pgs.)	3.00	9.00	21.00
51-74 (52pgs.): 71-Blank inside-c	3.00	9.00	21.00
75-99: 76-Flag-c. 79-X-mas-c	2.35	7.00	16.00
100	3.50	10.50	24.00
101-111: Last painted-c	2.00	6.00	14.00
112-Clayton Moore photo-c begin, end #145	10.00	30.00	70.00
113-117	5.70	17.00	40.00
118-Origin Lone Ranger, Tonto, & Silver retold; Special anniversary issue	10.00	30.00	70.00
119-145: 139-Last issue by Fran Striker	4.60	14.00	32.00
Cheerios Giveaways (1954, 16 pgs., 2½x7", soft-c) #1-"The Lone Ranger, His Mask & How He Met Tonto." #2-"The Lone Ranger & the Story of Silver" each....	4.60	14.00	32.00
Doll Giveaways (Gabriel Ind.)(1973, 3¼x5")-"The Story of The L.R." & The Carson City Bank Robbery."	.85	2.50	6.00
How the L. R. Captured Silver Book(1936)-Silvercup Bread giveaway	27.00	81.00	190.00
...In Milk for Big Mike(1955, Dairy Association giveaway), soft-c 5x7¼", 16 pgs.	7.00	21.00	50.00
Merita Bread giveaway('54; 16 pgs.; 5x7¼")-"How to Be a L. R. Health & Safety Scout"	7.00	21.00	50.00

NOTE: ***Hank Hartman*** *painted c(signed)-65, 66, 70, 75, 82; unsigned-64?, 67-69?, 71, 72, 73?, 74?, 76-78, 80, 81, 83-91, 92?, 93-111.* ***Ernest Nordli*** *painted c(signed)-42, 50, 52, 53, 56, 59, 60; unsigned-39-41, 44-49, 51, 54, 55, 57, 58, 61-63?*

LONE RANGER, THE
9/64 - No. 16, 12/69; No. 17, 11/72; No. 18, 9/74 - No. 28, 3/77
Gold Key (Reprints No. 13-20)

1-Retells origin	2.15	6.50	15.00
2	1.30	4.00	9.00
3-10: Small Bear-r in No. 6-10	1.00	3.00	7.00
11-17: Small Bear-r in No. 11,12	.85	2.50	6.00
18-28	.55	1.65	4.00
Golden West 1(30029-610)-Giant, 10/66-r/most Golden West #3-including Clayton Moore photo front/back-c	4.35	13.00	30.00

LONE RANGER'S COMPANION TONTO, THE (TV)
No. 312, Jan, 1951 - No. 33, Nov-Jan/58-59 (All painted-c)
Dell Publishing Co.

4-Color 312(1951)	7.00	21.00	50.00
2(8-10/51),3: (#2 titled 'Tonto')	3.50	10.50	24.00
4-10	2.00	6.00	14.00
11-20	1.75	5.25	12.00
21-33	1.30	4.00	9.00

NOTE: ***Ernest Nordli*** *painted c(signed)-2, 7; unsigned-3-6, 8-11, 12?, 13, 14, 18?, 22-24? See Aurora Comic Booklets.*

LONE RANGER'S FAMOUS HORSE HI-YO SILVER, THE (TV)
No. 369, Jan, 1952 - No. 36, Oct-Dec, 1960 (All painted-c)
Dell Publishing Co.

4-Color 369-Silver's origin as told by The L.R.	4.35	13.00	30.00
4-Color 392(4/52)	2.65	8.00	18.00
3(7-9/52)-10(4-6/52)	1.50	4.50	10.00
11-36	1.15	3.50	8.00

LONE RIDER
April, 1951 - No. 26, July, 1955 (36pgs., 3-on)
Superior Comics(Farrell Publications)

1 (52pgs.)-The Lone Rider & his horse Lightnin begin; Kamenish-a begins	6.00	18.00	42.00
2 (52pgs.)-The Golden Arrow begins (origin)	3.50	10.50	24.00
3-6: 6-Last Golden Arrow	2.65	8.00	18.00
7-Swift Arrow begins; origin of his shield	3.00	9.00	21.00
8-Origin Swift Arrow	4.00	12.00	28.00
9,10	2.00	6.00	14.00
11-14	1.60	4.70	11.00

LONE RIDER (continued)

	Good	Fine	Mint
15-Golden Arrow origin-r from #2, changing name to Swift Arrow	2.00	6.00	14.00
16-20,22-26: 23-Apache Kid app.	1.30	4.00	9.00
21-3-D effect-c	4.60	14.00	32.00

LONE WOLF AND CUB
May, 1987 - Present ($1.95, B&W, deluxe size)
First Comics

	Good	Fine	Mint
1	1.70	5.00	10.00
1-2nd print, 3rd print		1.00	2.00
2	.85	2.50	5.00
3	.55	1.60	3.20
4-8: 6-72 pg. origin issue	.40	1.25	2.50

LONG BOW (. . . Indian Boy)
1951 - No. 9, Wint, 1952/53
Fiction House Magazines (Real Adventures Publ.)

	Good	Fine	Mint
1	5.00	15.00	35.00
2	3.00	9.00	21.00
3-9	2.30	7.00	16.00

LONG JOHN SILVER & THE PIRATES (Formerly Terry & the Pirates)
No. 30, Aug, 1956 - No. 32, March, 1957 (TV)
Charlton Comics

	Good	Fine	Mint
30-32: Whitman-c	2.30	7.00	16.00

LONGSHOT
Sept, 1985 - No. 6, Feb, 1986 (Limited-series)
Marvel Comics Group

	Good	Fine	Mint
1-Arthur Adams-c/a in all	1.50	4.50	9.00
2	1.00	3.00	6.00
3-5	.85	2.50	5.00
6-Double size	1.15	3.50	7.00

LOONEY TUNES AND MERRIE MELODIES COMICS ("Looney Tunes" No. 166 (8/55) on)
1941 - No. 246, July-Sept, 1962
Dell Publishing Co.

	Good	Fine	Mint
1-Porky Pig, Bugs Bunny, Elmer Fudd, Mary Jane & Sniffles, Pat, Patsy and Pete begin (1st comic book app.). Bugs Bunny story by Win Smith (early Mickey Mouse artist)	95.00	285.00	665.00
2 (11/41)	48.00	145.00	335.00
3-Kandi the Cave Kid begins by Walt Kelly; also in #4-6,8,11,15	42.00	125.00	295.00
4-Kelly-a	37.00	110.00	260.00
5-Bugs Bunny The Super Rabbit app. (1st funny animal super hero?); Kelly-a	27.00	81.00	190.00
6,8-Kelly-a	20.00	60.00	140.00
7,9,10	15.00	45.00	105.00
11,15-Kelly-a; 15-X-Mas-c	15.00	45.00	105.00
12-14,16-19	12.00	36.00	84.00
20-25: Pat, Patsy & Pete by Kelly in all	12.00	36.00	84.00
26-30	8.50	25.50	60.00
31-40	6.00	18.00	42.00
41-50	4.00	12.00	28.00
51-60	3.00	9.00	21.00
61-80	2.00	6.00	14.00
81-99: 87-X-Mas-c	1.70	5.00	12.00
100	2.00	6.00	14.00
101-120	1.50	4.50	10.00
121-150	1.15	3.50	8.00
151-200	.85	2.50	6.00
201-246	.55	1.65	4.00

LOONEY TUNES (2nd Series)
April, 1975 - No. 47, July, 1984
Gold Key/Whitman

	Good	Fine	Mint
1		.50	1.00
2-47: Reprints-#1-4,16; 38-46(1/3r)		.30	.60

LOONY SPORTS (Magazine)
Spring, 1975 (68 pages)
3-Strikes Publishing Co.

	Good	Fine	Mint
1-Sports satire	.30	.80	1.60

LOOY DOT DOPE (See Single Series No. 13)

LORD JIM (See Movie Comics)

LORDS OF THE ULTRA-REALM
June, 1986 - No. 6, Nov, 1986 (mini-series)
DC Comics

	Good	Fine	Mint
1	.50	1.50	3.00
2-6	.30	.85	1.70
Special 1(12/87, $2.25)	.40	1.15	2.30

LORNA THE JUNGLE GIRL (. . . Jungle Queen No. 1-5)
July, 1953 - No. 26, Aug, 1957
Atlas Comics (NPI 1/OMC 2-11/NPI 12-26)

	Good	Fine	Mint
1-Origin	9.50	28.00	65.00
2-Intro. & 1st app. Greg Knight	5.00	15.00	35.00
3-5	4.35	13.00	30.00
6-11: 11-Last pre-code (1/55)	3.50	10.50	24.00
12-17,19-26	2.65	8.00	18.00
18-Williamson/Colleta-c	4.00	12.00	28.00

NOTE: ***Everett** c-21, 23-26. **Heath** c-6, 7. **Maneely** c-12, 15. **Romita** a-20, 22. **Shores** a-16; c-13, 16. **Tuska** a-6.*

LOSERS SPECIAL(Also see G.I.Combat #138)
Sept, 1985 ($1.25 cover) (One Shot)(See Our Fighting Forces #123)
DC Comics

	Good	Fine	Mint
1-Capt. Storm, Gunner & Sarge; Crisis x-over		.65	1.30

LOST IN SPACE (Space Family Robinson . . ., on Space Station One)(Formerly Space Family Robinson, see Gold Key Champion)
No. 37, 10/73 - No. 54, 11/78; No. 55, 3/81 - No. 59, 5/82
Gold Key

	Good	Fine	Mint
37-48	.35	1.00	2.00
49-59: Reprints-#49,50,55-59		.50	1.00

NOTE: ***Spiegle** a-37-59. All have painted-c.*

LOST PLANET
May, 1987 - No. 6, Mar, 1988 (mini-series, $1.75, color)
Eclipse Comics

	Good	Fine	Mint
1-4	.30	.85	1.70

LOST WORLD, THE (See 4-Color No. 1145)

LOST WORLDS
No. 5, Oct, 1952 - No. 6, Dec, 1952
Standard Comics

	Good	Fine	Mint
5-"Alice in Terrorland" by Toth; J. Katz-a	11.50	34.00	80.00
6-Toth-a	8.00	24.00	56.00

LOTS 'O' FUN COMICS
1940's? (5 cents) (heavy stock; blue covers)
Robert Allen Co.

nn-Contents can vary; Felix, Planet Comics known; contents would determine value. Similar to Up-To-Date Comics. Remainders - re-packaged.

LOU GEHRIG (See The Pride of the Yankees)

LOVE ADVENTURES (Actual Confessions No. 13)
10/49; No. 2, 1/50; No. 3, 2/51 - No. 12, 8/52
Marvel (IPS)/Atlas Comics (MPI)

	Good	Fine	Mint
1	3.00	9.00	21.00
2-Powell-a; Tyrone Power, Gene Tierney photo-c	3.00	9.00	21.00
3-8,10-12: 8-Robinson-a	1.50	4.50	10.00

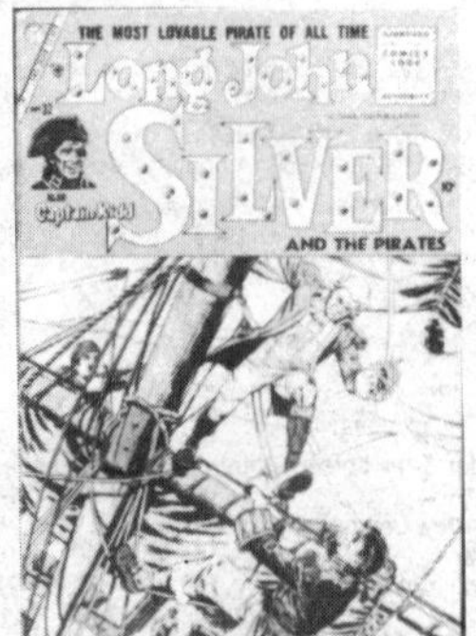

Long John Silver and the Pirates #32, © CC

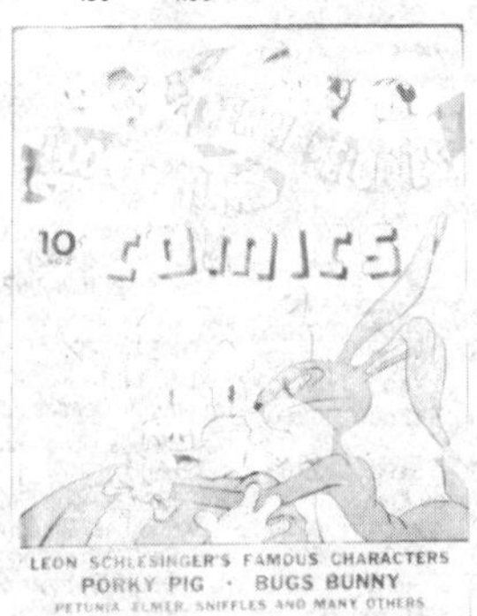

Looney Tunes #2 (1st series), © L. Schlesinger

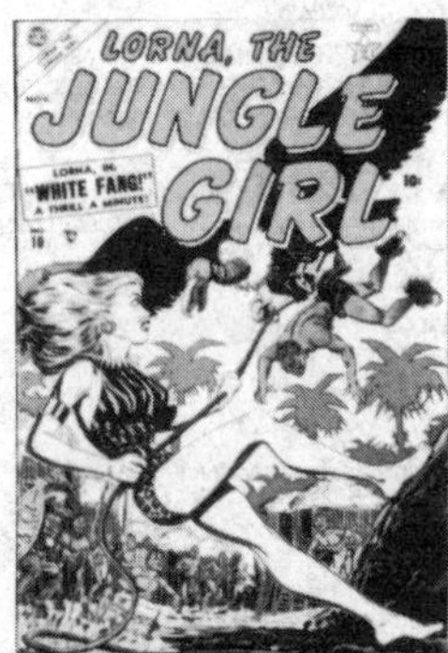

Lorna the Jungle Girl #10, © MCG

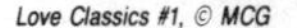
Love Classics #1, © MCG

Love Diary #1, © QUA

Love Journal #14, © Our Publ.

LOVE ADVENTURES (continued)	Good	Fine	Mint
9-Everett-a	2.00	6.00	14.00

LOVE AND MARRIAGE
March, 1952 - No. 16, Sept, 1954
Superior Comics Ltd.

	Good	Fine	Mint
1	4.00	12.00	28.00
2	2.00	6.00	14.00
3-10	1.50	4.50	10.00
11-16	1.15	3.50	8.00
I.W. Reprint #1,2,8,11,14	.30	.80	1.60
Super Reprint #10('63),15,17('64)	.30	.80	1.60

NOTE: *All issues have Kamenish art.*

LOVE AND ROCKETS
July, 1982 - Present (Adults only)
Fantagraphics Books

	Good	Fine	Mint
1-B&W-c ($2.95)(800 printed)	30.00	90.00	180.00
1 (Fall, '82; 2nd printing; color-c)	17.00	50.00	100.00
1-2nd printing	.60	1.75	3.50
2	5.00	15.00	30.00
3-5	3.00	9.00	18.00
6-10	1.50	4.50	9.00
11-15	.70	2.00	4.00
16-24	.40	1.15	2.30

LOVE AND ROMANCE
Sept, 1971 - No. 24, Sept, 1975
Charlton Comics

	Good	Fine	Mint
1		.30	.60
2-24		.15	.30

LOVE AT FIRST SIGHT
Oct, 1949 - No. 42, Aug, 1956 (Photo-c 21-42)
Ace Magazines (RAR Publ. Co./Periodical House)

	Good	Fine	Mint
1-Painted-c	4.00	12.00	28.00
2-Painted-c	2.00	6.00	14.00
3-10: 4-Painted-c	1.50	4.50	10.00
11-20	1.15	3.50	8.00
21-33: 33-Last pre-code	1.00	3.00	7.00
34-42: 36,37-Photo-c	.85	2.50	6.00

LOVE BUG, THE (See Movie Comics)

LOVE CLASSICS
Nov, 1949 - No. 2, Feb, 1950
A Lover's Magazine/Marvel Comics

	Good	Fine	Mint
1,2: 2-Virginia Mayo photo-c; 30 pg. story 'I Was a Small Town Flirt'	4.00	12.00	28.00

LOVE CONFESSIONS
Oct, 1949 - No. 54, Dec, 1956 (Photo-c 6,11-18,21)
Quality Comics Group

	Good	Fine	Mint
1-Ward c/a, 9 pgs; Gustavson-a	14.00	42.00	100.00
2-Gustavson-a	5.00	15.00	35.00
3	3.50	10.50	24.00
4-Crandall-a	4.65	14.00	32.00
5-Ward-a, 7 pgs.	5.50	16.50	38.00
6,7,9	1.70	5.00	12.00
8-Ward-a	4.65	14.00	32.00
10-Ward-a(2)	4.65	14.00	32.00
11-13,15,16,18	1.70	5.00	12.00
14,17,19,22-Ward-a; 17-Faith Domerque photo-c	3.85	11.50	27.00
20-Baker-a, Ward-a(2)	4.65	14.00	32.00
21,23-28,30-38,40,41: Last precode, 2/55	1.15	3.50	8.00
29-Ward-a	3.65	11.00	25.00
39-Matt Baker-a	1.70	5.00	12.00
42-44,46-48,50-54: 47-Ward-c?	1.00	3.00	7.00
45-Ward-a	2.15	6.50	15.00
49-Baker c/a	2.65	8.00	18.00

LOVE DIARY
July, 1949 - No. 48, Oct, 1955 (Photo-c 1-24,27,29)
Our Publishing Co./Toytown/Patches

	Good	Fine	Mint
1-Krigstein-a	6.00	18.00	42.00
2,3-Krigstein & Mort Leav-a in each	4.00	12.00	28.00
4-8	1.70	5.00	12.00
9,10-Everett-a	2.00	6.00	14.00
11-20	1.30	4.00	9.00
21-30,32-48: 47-Last precode (12/54)	1.00	3.00	7.00
31-J. Buscema headlights-c	1.15	3.50	8.00

LOVE DIARY (Diary Loves #2 on)
September, 1949
Quality Comics Group

	Good	Fine	Mint
1-Ward-c, 9 pgs.	11.50	34.50	80.00

LOVE DIARY
July, 1958 - No. 102, Dec, 1976
Charlton Comics

	Good	Fine	Mint
1	2.00	6.00	14.00
2	1.00	3.00	7.00
3-5,7-10	.55	1.65	4.00
6-Torres-a	1.15	3.50	8.00
11-20: 16,20-Leav-a	.35	1.00	2.50
21-40		.50	1.00
41-102: 45-Leav-a		.20	.40

NOTE: *Photo c-10, 20.*

LOVE DOCTOR (See Dr. Anthony King . . .)

LOVE DRAMAS (True Secrets No. 3 on?)
Oct, 1949 - No. 2, Jan, 1950
Marvel Comics (IPS)

	Good	Fine	Mint
1-Jack Kamen-a	5.50	16.50	38.00
2	3.00	9.00	21.00

LOVE EXPERIENCES (Challenge of the Unknown No. 6)
10/49 - No. 5, 1950; No. 6, 4/51 - No. 38, 6/56
Ace Periodicals (A.A. Wyn/Periodical House)

	Good	Fine	Mint
1	3.50	10.50	24.00
2	1.70	5.00	12.00
3-5: 5-Painted-c	1.30	4.00	9.00
6-10	1.00	3.00	7.00
11-30: 30-Last pre-code (2/55)	.85	2.50	6.00
31-38: 38-Indicia date-6/56; c-date-8/56	.75	2.25	5.00

NOTE: ***Anne Brewster** a-15. Photo c-4,15-35,38.*

LOVE JOURNAL
No. 10, Oct, 1951 - No. 25, July, 1954
Our Publishing Co.

	Good	Fine	Mint
10	2.65	8.00	18.00
11-25	1.30	4.00	9.00

LOVELAND
Nov, 1949 - No. 2, Feb, 1950
Mutual Mag./Eye Publ. (Marvel)

	Good	Fine	Mint
1,2-Photo-c	2.65	8.00	18.00

LOVE LESSONS
Oct, 1949 - No. 5, June, 1950
Harvey Comics/Key Publ. No. 5

	Good	Fine	Mint
1-Metallic silver-c printed over the cancelled covers of Love Letters #1; indicia title is 'Love Letters'	3.50	10.50	24.00
2-Powell-a	1.50	4.50	10.00
3-5: 3-Photo-c	1.15	3.50	8.00

LOVE LETTERS (10/49, Harvey; advertised but never published; covers were printed before cancellation and were used as the cover to Love Lessions #1)

LOVE LETTERS (Love Secrets No. 32 on)
11/49 - No. 31, 6/53; No. 32, 2/54 - No. 51, Dec, 1956
Quality Comics Group

	Good	Fine	Mint
1-Ward-c, Gustavson-a	9.00	27.00	62.00
2-Ward-c, Gustavson-a	8.50	25.50	60.00
3-Gustavson-a	5.00	15.00	35.00
4-Ward-a, 9 pgs.	8.50	25.50	60.00
5-8,10	1.70	5.00	12.00
9-One pg. Ward-"Be Popular with the Opposite Sex"; Robert Mitchum photo-c	3.50	10.50	24.00
11-Ward-r/Broadway Romances 2 & retitled	3.50	10.50	24.00
12-15,18-20	1.30	4.00	9.00
16,17-Ward-a; 16-Anthony Quinn photo-c. 17-Jane Russell photo-c	4.60	14.00	32.00
21-29	1.15	3.50	8.00
30,31(6/53)-Ward-a	2.65	8.00	18.00
32(2/54) - 38: Last precode, 2/55	1.00	3.00	7.00
39-48	.70	2.00	5.00
49,50-Baker-a	2.65	8.00	18.00
51-Baker-c	2.15	6.50	15.00

NOTE: *Photo-c on most 3-28.*

LOVE LIFE
1951
P. L. Publishing Co.

	Good	Fine	Mint
1	2.65	8.00	18.00

LOVELORN (Confessions of the Lovelorn No. 52 on)
Aug-Sept, 1949 - No. 51, July, 1954 (No. 1-26, 52 pgs.)
American Comics Group (Michel Publ./Regis Publ.)

	Good	Fine	Mint
1	3.00	9.00	21.00
2	1.50	4.50	10.00
3-10	1.30	4.00	9.00
11-20,22-48: 18-Drucker-a, 2pgs.	.85	2.50	6.00
21-Prostitution story	1.65	5.00	11.50
49-51-Has 3-D effect	5.70	17.00	40.00

LOVE MEMORIES
1949 (no month) - No. 4, July, 1950 (Photo-c all)
Fawcett Publications

	Good	Fine	Mint
1	3.50	10.50	24.00
2-4	1.70	5.00	12.00

LOVE MYSTERY
June, 1950 - No. 3, Oct, 1950
Fawcett Publications

	Good	Fine	Mint
1-Photo-c; George Evans-a	8.00	24.00	56.00
2,3-Evans-a. 3-Powell-a; photo-c	5.50	16.50	38.00

LOVE PROBLEMS (See Fox Giants)

LOVE PROBLEMS AND ADVICE ILLUSTRATED (Becomes Romance Stories of True Love No. 45 on)
June, 1949 - No. 6, Apr, 1950; No. 7, Jan, 1951 - No. 44, Mar, 1957
McCombs/Harvey Publ./Home Comics

	Good	Fine	Mint
V1#1	3.00	9.00	21.00
2	1.50	4.50	10.00
3-10	1.15	3.50	8.00
11-13,15-23,25-31: 31-Last pre-code (1/55)	.70	2.00	5.00
14,24-Rape scene	.85	2.50	6.00
32-37,39-44	.60	1.80	4.00
38-S&K-c	1.35	4.00	9.00

NOTE: ***Powell*** *a-1,2,7-14,17-25,28,29,33,40,41. No. 3 has True Love... on inside.*

LOVE ROMANCES (Formerly Ideal No. 5?)
No. 6, May, 1949 - No. 106, July, 1963
Timely/Marvel/Atlas(TCI No. 7-71/Male No. 72-106)

	Good	Fine	Mint
6-Photo-c	3.00	9.00	21.00
7-Kamen-a	2.00	6.00	14.00
8-Kubert-a; photo-c	3.15	9.50	22.00
9-20: 9-12-Photo-c	1.30	4.00	9.00
21,24-Krigstein-a	2.50	7.50	17.00
22,23,25-35,37,39,40	1.00	3.00	7.00
36,38-Krigstein-a	2.00	6.00	14.00
41-43,46-48,50-52,54-56,58-74	.85	2.50	6.00
44-lingerie panel	.85	2.50	6.00
45,57-Matt Baker-a	1.65	5.00	11.50
49,53-Toth-a, 6 & ? pgs.	2.00	6.00	14.00
75,77,82-Matt Baker-a	1.65	5.00	11.50
76,78-81,84,86-95: Last 10 cent ish.?	.55	1.65	4.00
83-Kirby-c, Severin-a	1.30	4.00	9.00
85,96-Kirby c/a	1.30	4.00	9.00
97,100-104	.35	1.00	2.40
98-Kirby-a(4)	2.35	7.00	16.00
99,105,106-Kirby-a	1.00	3.00	7.00

NOTE: ***Anne Brewster*** *a-67, 72.* ***Colletta*** *a-37, 40, 42, 44, 67(2); c-42, 44, 49, 80.* ***Everett*** *c-70.* ***Kirby*** *c-80, 85, 88.* ***Robinson*** *a-29.*

LOVERS (Formerly Blonde Phantom)
No. 23, May, 1949 - No. 86, Aug?, 1957
Marvel Comics No. 23,24/Atlas No. 25 on (ANC)

	Good	Fine	Mint
23-Photo-c	3.00	9.00	21.00
24-Tothish plus Robinson-a; photo-c	1.60	4.70	11.00
25,30-Kubert-a; 7, 10 pgs.	2.65	8.00	18.00
26-29,31-36,39,40: 26,27-photo-c	1.15	3.50	8.00
37,38-Krigstein-a	2.65	8.00	18.00
41-Everett-a(2)	1.85	5.50	13.00
42,44-65: 65-Last pre-code (1/55)	.85	2.50	6.00
43-1pg. Frazetta ad	1.30	4.00	9.00
66,68-86	.75	2.25	5.00
67-Toth-a	2.30	7.00	16.00

NOTE: ***Anne Brewster*** *a-86.* ***Colletta*** *a-54, 59, 62, 64, 69; c-64.* ***Powell*** *a-27, 30.* ***Robinson*** *a-54, 56.*

LOVERS' LANE
Oct, 1949 - No. 41, June, 1954 (No. 1-18, 52 pgs.)
Lev Gleason Publications

	Good	Fine	Mint
1	3.00	9.00	21.00
2	1.50	4.50	10.00
3-10	1.15	3.50	8.00
11-19	.85	2.50	6.00
20-Frazetta 1 pg. ad	1.30	4.00	9.00
21-38,40,41	.85	2.50	6.00
39-Story narrated by Frank Sinatra	1.85	5.50	13.00

NOTE: ***Briefer*** *a-6, 21.* ***Fuje*** *a-4, 16; c-many.* ***Guardineer*** *a-1.* ***Kinstler*** *c-41.* ***Tuska*** *a-6. Painted-c 1-18. Photo-c 19-21, 22, 26, 28.*

LOVE SCANDALS
Feb, 1950 - No. 5, Oct, 1950 (No. 3-5 - photo covers)
Quality Comics Group

	Good	Fine	Mint
1-Ward c/a, 9 pgs.	11.50	34.00	80.00
2,3: 2-Gustavson-a	3.65	11.00	25.00
4-Ward c/a, 18 pgs; Gil Fox-a	10.00	30.00	70.00
5-C. Cuidera-a; tomboy story 'I Hated Being a Woman'	3.65	11.00	25.00

LOVE SECRETS (Formerly Love Letters No. 31)
No. 32, Aug, 1953 - No. 56, Dec, 1956
Quality Comics Group

	Good	Fine	Mint
32	2.65	8.00	18.00
33,35-39	1.30	4.00	9.00
34-Ward-a	3.75	11.25	26.00
40-Matt Baker-c	2.50	7.50	17.00
41-43: 43-Last precode (3/55)	1.15	3.50	8.00

Love Letters #20, © QUA

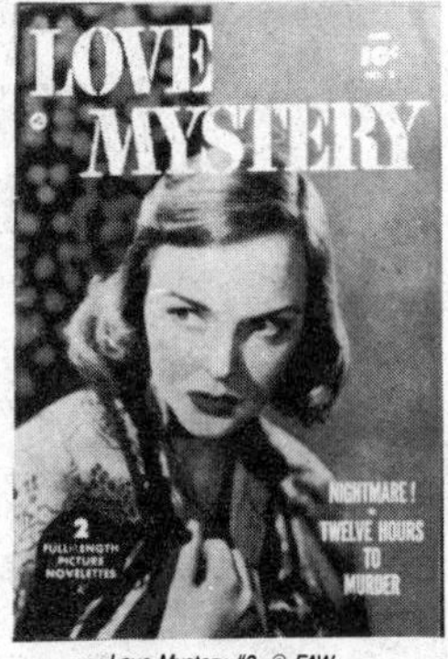

Love Mystery #2, © FAW

Love Romances #8, © MCG

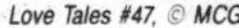
Love Tales #47, © MCG

Lucky Star #5, © Nation Wide

The Lucy Show #2, © Desilu

LOVE SECRETS (continued)	**Good**	**Fine**	**Mint**
44,47-50,53,54	.85	2.50	6.00
45,46-Ward-a. 46-Baker-a	2.85	8.50	20.00
51,52-Ward(r). 52-r/Love Confessions #17	1.65	5.00	11.50
55,56-Baker-a; cover-#56	1.65	5.00	11.50

LOVE SECRETS
Oct, 1949 - No. 2, Jan, 1950 (52 pgs., photo-c)
Marvel Comics(IPC)

1	3.00	9.00	21.00
2	2.65	8.00	18.00

LOVE STORIES
No. 6, 1950 - No. 18, Aug, 1954
Fox Feature Syndicate/Star Publ. No. 13 on

6,8-Wood-a	8.00	24.00	56.00
7,9-12	2.85	8.50	20.00
13-18-L. B. Cole-a	3.35	10.00	23.00

LOVE STORIES (Formerly Heart Throbs)
No. 147, Nov, 1972 - No. 152, Oct-Nov, 1973
National Periodical Publications

147-152		.20	.40

LOVE STORIES OF MARY WORTH (See Harvey Comics Hits No. 55 & Mary Worth)
Sept, 1949 - No. 5, May, 1950
Harvey Publications

1-1940's newspaper reprints-#1-4	3.50	10.50	24.00
2	2.50	7.50	17.00
3-5: 3-Kamen/Baker-a?	2.35	7.00	16.00

LOVE TALES (Formerly The Human Torch No. 35)
No. 36, 5/49 - No. 58, 8/52; No. 59, date? - No. 75, Sept, 1957
Marvel/Atlas Comics (ZPC No. 36-50/MMC No. 67-75)

36-Photo-c	3.00	9.00	21.00
37	1.50	4.50	10.00
38-44,46-50: 40,41-Photo-c	1.00	3.00	7.00
45-Powell-a	1.20	3.50	8.00
51,69-Everett-a	1.65	5.00	11.50
52-Krigstein-a	2.15	6.50	15.00
53-60: 60-Last pre-code (2/55)	.85	2.50	6.00
61-68,70-75	.55	1.65	4.00

LOVE, 10 STORIES
July, 1955
Charlton Comics

6	.85	2.50	6.00

LOVE THRILLS (See Fox Giants)

LOVE TRAILS
Dec, 1949 - No. 2, Mar, 1950 (52 pgs.)
A Lover's Magazine (CDS)(Marvel)

1,2: 1-Photo-c	3.00	9.00	21.00

LOWELL THOMAS' HIGH ADVENTURE (See 4-Color No. 949,1001)

LT. (See Lieutenant)

LUCKY COMICS
Jan, 1944; No. 2, Summer, 1945 - No. 5, Summer, 1946
Consolidated Magazines

1-Lucky Starr, Bobbie	4.00	12.00	28.00
2-5	2.00	6.00	14.00

LUCKY DUCK
No. 5, Jan, 1953 - No. 8, Sept, 1953
Standard Comics (Literary Ent.)

5-Irving Spector-a	2.65	8.00	18.00
6-8-Irving Spector-a	1.70	5.00	12.00

LUCKY FIGHTS IT THROUGH (Also see The K. O. Punch)
1949 (16 pgs. in color; paper cover) (Giveaway)
Educational Comics

	Good	**Fine**	**Mint**
(Very Rare)-1st Kurtzman work for E. C.; V.D. prevention	142.00	425.00	1000.00

(Prices vary widely on this book)

NOTE: *Subtitled "The Story of That Ignorant, Ignorant Cowboy." Prepared for Communications Materials Center, Columbia University.*

LUCKY "7" COMICS
1944 (No date listed)
Howard Publishers Ltd.

1-Congo Raider, Punch Powers; bondage-c	10.00	30.00	70.00

LUCKY STAR (Western)
1950 - No. 7, 1951; No. 8, 1953 - No. 14, 1955 (5x7¼"; full color)
Nation Wide Publ. Co.

1-Jack Davis-a	4.60	14.00	32.00
2,3-(52 pgs.)-Davis-a	3.00	9.00	21.00
4-7-(52 pgs.)-Davis-a	2.65	8.00	18.00
8-14-(36 pgs.)	1.70	5.00	12.00
Given away with Lucky Star Western Wear by the Juvenile Mfg. Co.	1.70	5.00	12.00

LUCY SHOW, THE (TV) (Also see I Love Lucy)
June, 1963 - No. 5, June, 1964 (Photo-c, 1,2)
Gold Key

1	4.00	12.00	28.00
2	2.85	8.50	20.00
3-5: Photo back-c,1,2,4,5	2.30	7.00	16.00

LUCY, THE REAL GONE GAL (Meet Miss Pepper No. 5 on)
June, 1953 - No. 4, Dec, 1953
St. John Publishing Co.

1-Negligee panels	3.50	10.50	24.00
2	1.70	5.00	12.00
3,4: 3-Drucker-a	1.50	4.50	10.00

LUDWIG BEMELMAN'S MADELEINE & GENEVIEVE (See 4-Color #796)

LUDWIG VON DRAKE (TV)(Disney)(See Walt Disney's C&S #256)
Nov-Dec, 1961 - No. 4, June-Aug, 1962
Dell Publishing Co.

1	1.70	5.00	12.00
2-4	1.15	3.50	8.00
...Fish Stampede (1962, Fritos giveaway)-16 pgs., 3¼x7", soft-c; also see D. Duck & M. Mouse	1.70	5.00	12.00

LUGER
Oct, 1986 - No. 3, Feb, 1987 (mini-series, $1.75)
Eclipse Comics

1-3	.30	.90	1.80

LUKE CAGE (See Hero for Hire)

LUKE SHORT'S WESTERN STORIES
No. 580, Aug, 1954 - No. 927, Aug, 1958
Dell Publishing Co.

4-Color 580(8/54)	2.00	6.00	14.00
4-Color 651(9/55)-Kinstler-a	2.65	8.00	18.00
4-Color 739,771,807,875,927	2.00	6.00	14.00
4-Color 848	2.65	8.00	18.00

LUNATICKLE (Magazine) (Satire)
Feb, 1956 - No. 2, Apr, 1956
Whitstone Publ.

1,2-Kubert-a	1.50	4.50	9.00

LYNDON B. JOHNSON
March, 1965
Dell Publishing Co.

LYNDON B. JOHNSON (continued)

	Good	Fine	Mint
12-445-503-Photo-c	1.50	4.50	10.00

MACHINE MAN (Also see 2001. . .)
4/78 - No. 9, 12/78; No. 10, 8/79 - No.19, 2/81
Marvel Comics Group

	Good	Fine	Mint
1		.60	1.20
2-17,19: 19-Intro Jack O'Lantern		.30	.60
18-Wendigo, Alpha Flight-ties into X-Men #140	.85	2.50	5.00

NOTE: ***Austin*** *c-7i, 19i.* ***Buckler*** *c-17p, 18p.* ***Byrne*** *c-14p, 16p.* ***Ditko*** *a-10-19; c-10-13, 14i, 15, 16.* ***Kirby*** *a-1-9p; c-1-5, 7-9p.* ***Layton*** *c-7i.* ***Miller*** *c-19p.* ***Simonson*** *c-6.*

MACHINE MAN
Oct, 1984 - No. 4, Jan, 1985 (Limited-series)
Marvel Comics Group

	Good	Fine	Mint
1-Barry Smith-c/a(i) in all	.25	.75	1.50
2-4		.60	1.20

MACKENZIE'S RAIDERS (See 4-Color No. 1093)

MACO TOYS COMIC
1959 (36 pages; full color) (Giveaway)
Maco Toys/Charlton Comics

	Good	Fine	Mint
1-All military stories featuring Maco Toys	1.00	3.00	6.00

MACROSS (Robotech: The Macross Saga No. 2 on)
Dec, 1984 ($1.50)
Comico

	Good	Fine	Mint
1	3.15	11.00	22.00

MAD
Oct-Nov, 1952 - Present (No. 24 on, magazine format)
(Kurtzman editor No. 1-28, Feldstein No. 29 on)
E. C. Comics

	Good	Fine	Mint
1-Wood, Davis, Elder start as regulars	80.00	240.00	560.00
2-Davis-c	38.00	115.00	265.00
3	23.00	70.00	160.00
4-Reefer mention story "Flob Was a Slob" by Davis	23.00	70.00	160.00
5-Low distribution; Elder-c	48.00	145.00	335.00
6-10	16.00	48.00	110.00
11-Wolverton-a	16.00	48.00	110.00
12-15	14.00	42.00	100.00
16-23(5/55): 21-1st app. Alfred E. Neuman on-c in fake ad. 22-all by Elder. 23-Special cancel announcement	11.00	32.00	76.00
24(7/55)-1st magazine issue (25 cents); Kurtzman logo & border on-c	21.00	64.00	150.00
25-Jaffee starts as regular writer	11.50	34.00	80.00
26	7.50	22.00	52.00
27-Davis-c; Jaffee starts as story artist; new logo	7.50	22.00	52.00
28-Elder-c; Heath back-c; last issue edited by Kurtzman; (three cover variations exist with different wording on contents banner on lower right of cover; value of each the same)	6.50	19.50	45.00
29-Wood-c; Kamen-a; Don Martin starts as regular; Feldstein editing begins	6.50	19.50	45.00
30-1st A. E. Neuman cover by Mingo; Crandall inside-c; last Elder art; Bob Clarke starts as regular	7.50	22.00	52.00
31-Freas starts as regular; last Davis art until #99	5.50	16.50	38.00
32-Orlando, Drucker, Woodbridge start as regulars; Wood back-c	5.00	15.00	35.00
33-Orlando back-c	5.00	15.00	35.00
34-Berg starts as regular	4.35	13.00	30.00
35-Mingo wraparound-c; Crandall-a	4.35	13.00	30.00
36-40	3.15	9.50	22.00
41-50	2.30	7.00	16.00
51-60: 60-Two Clarke-c; Prohias starts as regular	1.30	4.00	9.00
61-70: 64-Rickard starts as regular. 68-Martin-c	1.15	3.50	8.00
71-80: 76-Aragones starts as regular	1.00	3.00	7.00
81-90: 86-1st Fold-in. 89-One strip by Walt Kelly. 90-Frazetta back-c	.85	2.50	6.00
91-100: 91-Jaffee starts as story artist. 99-Davis-a resumes	.70	2.00	4.00
101-120: 101-Infinity-c. 105-Batman TV show take-off. 106-Frazetta back-c	.50	1.50	3.00
121-140: 130-Torres starts as regular. 122-Drucker & Mingo-c. 128-Last Orlando. 135,139-Davis-c	.40	1.25	2.50
141-170: 165-Martin-c. 169-Drucker-c	.25	.75	1.50
171-200: 173,178-Davis-c. 176-Drucker-c. 182-Bob Jones starts as regular. 186-Star Trek take-off. 187-Harry North starts as regular. 196-Star Wars take-off	.25	.75	1.50
201-270: 203-Star Wars take-off. 204-Hulk TV show take-off. 208-Superman movie take-off		.50	1.00

NOTE: ***Jules Feiffer*** *a(r)-42.* ***Freas****-most-c and back covers-40-74.* ***Heath*** *a-14, 27.* ***Kamen*** *a-29.* ***Krigstein*** *a-12, 17, 24, 26.* ***Kurtzman*** *c-1, 3, 4, 6-10, 13, 14, 16, 18.* ***Mingo*** *c-30-37, 75-111.* ***John Severin*** *a-1-6, 9, 10.* ***Wolverton*** *c-11; a-11, 17, 29, 31, 36, 40, 82, 137.* ***Wood*** *a-24-45, 59; c-26, 29.* ***Woodbridge*** *a-43.*

MAD (See . . .Follies, . . .Special, More Trash from. . ., and The Worst from. . .)

MAD ABOUT MILLIE
April, 1969 - No. 17, Dec, 1970
Marvel Comics Group

	Good	Fine	Mint
1-Giant issue	.50	1.50	3.00
2-17: 16,17-r	.35	1.00	2.00
Annual 1(11/71)		.50	1.00

MADAME XANADU
July, 1981 (No ads; $1.00; 32 pgs.)
DC Comics

	Good	Fine	Mint
1-Marshall Rogers-a(25 pgs.); Kaluta-c/a(2 pgs.); pin-up of Madame Xanadu		.50	1.00

MADBALLS
9/86 - No. 3, 11/86; No. 4, 6/87 - Present
Star Comics (Marvel)

	Good	Fine	Mint
1-9: Based on toys		.50	1.00

MAD FOLLIES (Special)
1963 - No. 7, 1969
E. C. Comics

	Good	Fine	Mint
nn(1963)-Paperback book covers	6.50	19.50	45.00
2(1964)-Calendar	4.00	12.00	28.00
3(1965)-Mischief Stickers	3.00	9.00	21.00
4(1966)-Mobile; reprints Frazetta back-c/Mad #90	3.70	11.00	26.00
5(1967)-Stencils	3.00	9.00	21.00
6(1968)-Mischief Stickers	1.85	5.50	13.00
7(1969)-Nasty Cards	1.85	5.50	13.00

NOTE: ***Clarke*** *c-4.* ***Mingo*** *c-1-3.* ***Orlando*** *a-5.*

MAD HATTER, THE (Costume Hero)
Jan-Feb, 1946 - No. 2, Sept-Oct, 1946
O. W. Comics Corp.

	Good	Fine	Mint
1-Freddy the Firefly begins; Giunta-a	17.00	51.00	120.00
2-Has ad for E.C.'s Animal Fables #1	11.50	34.00	80.00

MADHOUSE
3-4/54 - No. 4, 9-10/54; 6/57 - No. 4, Dec?, 1957
Ajax/Farrell Publ. (Excellent Publ./4-Star)

	Good	Fine	Mint
1(1954)	7.00	21.00	50.00
2,3	3.50	10.50	24.00
4-Surrealistic-c	5.70	17.00	40.00

Machine Man #14, © MCG

Mad #2, © WMG

Mad #31, © WMG

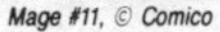
Mage #11, © Comico

Magic Comics #21, © DMP

Magik #1, © MCG

MADHOUSE (continued) — Good / Fine / Mint
1(1957) 3.00 9.00 21.00
2-4 1.70 5.00 12.00

MADHOUSE (Formerly Madhouse Glads; . . . Comics No. 104? on)
No. 95, 9/74 - No. 97, 1/75; No. 98, 8/75 - No. 130, 10/82
Red Circle Productions/Archie Publications

95-Horror stories through #97 .60 1.20
96 .60 1.20
97-Intro. Henry Hobson; Morrow, Thorne-a .40 .80
98-130-Satire/humor stories .30 .60
Annual 8(1970-71)- 12(1974-75)-Formerly Madhouse Ma-ad Annual. 11-Wood-a(r) .40 .80
. . . Comics Digest 1(1975-76)- 8(8/82)(. . . Mag. #5 on) .50 1.00

NOTE: ***B. Jones** a-96. **McWilliams** a-97. **Morrow** a-96; c-95-97. **Wildey** a-95, 96. See Archie Comics Digest #1, 13.*

MADHOUSE GLADS (Formerly . . . Ma-ad; Madhouse #95 on)
No. 73, May, 1970 - No. 94, Aug, 1974 (No. 78-92: 52 pgs.)
Archie Publications

73 .25 .50
74-94 .20 .40

MADHOUSE MA-AD (. . . Jokes #67-70; . . . Freak-Out #71-74)
(Formerly Archie's Madhouse) (Becomes Madhouse Glads #75 on)
No. 67, April, 1969 - No. 72, Jan, 1970
Archie Publications

67-72 .25 .50
. . . Annual 7(1969-70)-Formerly Archie's Madhouse Annual; becomes Madhouse Annual .30 .60

MAD MONSTER PARTY (See Movie Classics)

MAD SPECIAL (. . . Super Special)
Fall, 1970 - Present (84 - 116 pages)
E. C. Publications, Inc.

Fall 1970(#1)-Bonus-Voodoo Doll; contains 17 pgs. new material 3.00 9.00 21.00
Spring 1971(#2)-Wall Nuts; 17 pgs. new material 2.00 6.00 14.00
3-Protest Stickers 2.00 6.00 14.00
4-8: 4-Mini Posters. 5-Mad Flag. 7-Presidential candidate posters, Wild Shocking Message posters. 8-TV Guise 1.50 4.50 10.00
9(1972)-Contains Nostalgic Mad #1 (28pp) 1.30 4.00 9.00
10,11,13: 10-Nonsense Stickers (Don Martin). 11-33⅓ RPM record. 13-Sickie Stickers; 3 pgs. new Wolverton 1.30 4.00 9.00
12-Contains Nostalgic Mad #2 (36 pgs.); Davis, Wolverton-a 1.30 4.00 9.00
14-Vital Message posters & Art Depreciation paintings 1.00 3.00 7.00
15-Contains Nostalgic Mad #3 (28 pgs.) 1.30 4.00 9.00
16,17,19,20: 16-Mad-hesive Stickers. 17-Don Martin posters. 20-Martin Stickers .85 2.50 6.00
18-Contains Nostalgic Mad #4 (36 pgs.) 1.00 3.00 7.00
21,24-Contains Nostalgic Mad #5 (28 pgs.) & #6 (28 pgs.) 1.00 3.00 7.00
22,23,25-27,29,30: 22-Diplomas. 23-Martin Stickers. 25-Martin Posters 26-33⅓ RPM record. 27-Mad Shock-Sticks. 29-Mad Collectable-Correctables Posters. 30-The Movies .55 1.65 4.00
28-Contains Nostalgic Mad #7 (36 pgs.) .75 2.25 5.00
31,33-40 .55 1.65 4.00
32-Contains Nostalgic Mad #8 .85 2.50 6.00

NOTE: *#28-30: no number on cover. **Mingo** c-9, 11, 15, 19, 23.*

MAGE (The Hero Discovered . . .)
1984 (no month) - No. 15, 12/86 ($1.50; 36 pgs; Mando paper)
Comico

Good / Fine / Mint
1-Violence 2.00 6.00 12.00
2 1.50 4.50 9.00
3-5: 3-Intro Edsel .85 2.50 5.00
6-Grendel begins (1st in color) 2.65 8.00 16.00
7-1st new Grendel story 1.15 3.50 7.00
8-14: 13-Grendel dies. 14-Grendel ends .55 1.60 3.20
15-Dbl. size, photo-c .70 2.00 4.00

MAGIC AGENT (See Unknown Worlds)
Jan-Feb, 1962 - No. 3, May-June, 1962
American Comics Group

1-Origin & 1st app. John Force .40 1.20 2.40
2,3 .30 .80 1.60

MAGIC COMICS
Aug, 1939 - No. 123, Nov-Dec, 1949
David McKay Publications

1-Mandrake the Magician, Henry, Popeye (not by Segar), Blondie, Barney Baxter, Secret Agent X-9 (not by Raymond), Bunky by Billy DeBeck & Thornton Burgess text stories illustrated by Harrison Cady begin 72.00 215.00 500.00
2 35.00 105.00 245.00
3 25.00 75.00 175.00
4 20.00 60.00 140.00
5 17.00 51.00 120.00
6-10 14.00 42.00 100.00
11-16,18-20 11.00 32.00 76.00
17-The Lone Ranger begins 12.00 36.00 84.00
21-30 8.50 25.50 60.00
31-40 6.50 19.50 45.00
41-50 5.50 16.50 38.00
51-60 4.35 13.00 30.00
61-70 3.50 10.50 24.00
71-99 2.85 8.50 20.00
100 3.50 10.50 24.00
101-106,109-123 2.15 6.50 15.00
107,108-Flash Gordon app; not by Raymond 3.75 11.25 26.00

MAGICA DE SPELL (See Walt Disney Showcase No. 30)

MAGIC OF CHRISTMAS AT NEWBERRYS, THE
1967 (20 pgs.; slick cover; B&W inside)
E. S. London (Giveaway)
.60 1.20

MAGIC SWORD, THE (See Movie Classics)

MAGIK
Dec, 1983 - No. 4, Mar, 1984 (mini-series)
Marvel Comics Group

1-Illyana & Storm series from X-Men .25 .75 1.50
2-4 .60 1.20

NOTE: ***Buscema** a-1p,2p; c-1p.*

MAGILLA GORILLA (TV) (Hanna-Barbera)
May, 1964 - No. 10, Dec, 1968
Gold Key

1 1.70 5.00 12.00
2-10: 3-Vs. Yogi Bear for President .85 2.50 6.00
Kite Fun Book ('64, 16 pgs., 5x7¼", soft-c) 2.00 6.00 12.00

MAGILLA GORILLA (TV)(See Spotlight #4)
Nov, 1970 - No. 5, July, 1971 (Hanna-Barbera)
Charlton Comics

1-5 .70 2.00 4.00

MAGNUS, ROBOT FIGHTER (. . . 4000 A.D.)(See Doctor Solar)
Feb, 1963 - No. 46, Jan, 1977 (Painted-covers)
Gold Key

MAGNUS, ROBOT FIGHTER (continued)	Good	Fine	Mint
1-Origin Magnus; Aliens series begins	7.00	21.00	50.00
2,3	3.50	10.50	24.00
4-10	2.00	6.00	14.00
11-20	1.50	4.50	10.00
21,22,24-28: 22-Origin-r/#1. 28-Aliens ends	.85	2.50	6.00
23-Exists with two different prices, 12 cents and 15 cents	.85	2.50	6.00
29-46-Reprints	.50	1.50	3.00

NOTE: ***Manning*** *a-1-22, 29-43(r).* ***Spiegle*** *a-23, 44r.*

MAID OF THE MIST (See American Graphics)

MAJOR HOOPLE COMICS
nd (Jan, 1943)
Nedor Publications

	Good	Fine	Mint
1-Mary Worth, Phantom Soldier by Moldoff app.	14.00	42.00	100.00

MAJOR INAPAK THE SPACE ACE
1951 (20 pages) (Giveaway)
Magazine Enterprises (Inapac Foods)

	Good	Fine	Mint
1-Bob Powell-a	.30	.80	1.60

NOTE: *Many warehouse copies surfaced in 1973.*

MAJOR VICTORY COMICS
1944 - No. 3, Summer, 1945
H. Clay Glover/Service Publ./Harry 'A' Chesler

	Good	Fine	Mint
1-Origin Major Victory by C. Sultan (reprint from Dynamic #1); Spider Woman 1st app.	22.00	65.00	154.00
2-Dynamic Boy app.	14.00	42.00	100.00
3-Rocket Boy app.	11.50	34.00	80.00

MALTESE FALCON (See Feature Books No. 48 (McKay))

MALU IN THE LAND OF ADVENTURE
1964 (See White Princess of Jungle #2)
I. W. Enterprises

	Good	Fine	Mint
1-Reprints Avon's Slave Girl Comics #1; Severin-c	4.75	14.00	28.00

MAMMOTH COMICS
1938 (84 pages) (Black & White, 8½x11½")
Whitman Publishing Co.(K. K. Publications)

	Good	Fine	Mint
1-Terry & the Pirates, Dick Tracy, Little Orphan Annie, Wash Tubbs, & other reprints	50.00	150.00	350.00

MAMMY YOKUM & THE GREAT DOGPATCH MYSTERY
1951 (Giveaway)
Toby Press

	Good	Fine	Mint
Li'l Abner	10.00	30.00	70.00

MAN-BAT (Also see Detective No. 400, Brave & the Bold, and Batman Family)
Dec-Jan, 1975-76 - No. 2, Feb-Mar, 1976; Dec, 1984
National Periodical Publications/DC Comics

	Good	Fine	Mint
1-Ditko-a(p); Aparo-c; She-Bat app.		.30	.60
2-Aparo-c		.30	.60
...Vs. Batman 1 (12/84)-Adams-a(r)	.45	1.25	2.50

MAN COMICS
Dec, 1949 - No. 28, Sept, 1953 (52 pgs., No. 1-4)
Marvel/Atlas Comics (NPI)

	Good	Fine	Mint
1-Tuska-a	3.50	10.50	24.00
2-Tuska-a	1.70	5.00	12.00
3-5	1.50	4.50	10.00
6-8	1.30	4.00	9.00
9-13,15: 9-Format changes to war	.85	2.50	6.00
14-Krenkel (3pgs.), Pakula-a	1.70	5.00	12.00
16-21,23-28: 28-Crime ish.	.70	2.00	5.00
22-Krigstein-a, 5 pgs.	2.65	8.00	18.00

NOTE: ***Berg*** *a-14, 15.* ***Colan*** *a-21.* ***Everett*** *a-8, 22; c-22, 25.* ***Heath*** *a-11, 17. Kubertish a-by* ***Bob Brown-3. Maneely*** *c-10, 11.* ***Robinson*** *a-10, 14.*

MANDRAKE THE MAGICIAN (See Defenders Of The Earth, Feature Books #18,19,23,46,52,55, Tiny Tot Funnies & Wow Comics, 1st series)

MANDRAKE THE MAGICIAN (See Harvey Comics Hits No. 53)
No. 752, Nov, 1956; Sept, 1966 - No. 10, Nov, 1967
Dell Publishing Co./King Comics

	Good	Fine	Mint
4-Color 752('56)	3.70	11.00	26.00
1(King)-Begin S.O.S. Phantom series, ends #3	.85	2.50	6.00
2-5: 4-Girl Phantom app. 5-Brick Bradford app., also #6	.70	2.00	5.00
6,7,9: 7-Origin Lothar. 9-Brick Bradford app.	.60	1.80	4.00
8-Jeff Jones-a	1.00	3.00	7.00
10-Rip Kirby app.; Raymond-a (14 pgs.)	1.70	5.00	12.00

MANDRAKE THE MAGICIAN GIANT COMIC ALBUM
1972 (48 pgs.; 11x14"; B&W; cardboard covers)
Modern Promotions

	Good	Fine	Mint
nn-Strip reprints by Lee Falk	1.70	5.00	12.00

MAN FROM ATLANTIS (TV)
Feb, 1978 - No. 7, Aug, 1978
Marvel Comics Group

	Good	Fine	Mint
1-(84 pgs.; $1.00)-Sutton-a(p), Buscema-c; origin		.30	.60
2-7		.25	.50

MAN FROM U.N.C.L.E., THE (TV)
Feb, 1965 - No. 22, April, 1969 (All photo covers)
Gold Key

	Good	Fine	Mint
1	4.60	14.00	32.00
2-Photo back c-2-8	2.65	8.00	18.00
3-10: 7-Jet Dream begins	1.70	5.00	12.00
11-22: 21,22-Reprints	1.50	4.50	10.00

MAN FROM WELLS FARGO (TV)
No. 1287, Feb-Apr, 1962 - May-July, 1962 (Photo-c)
Dell Publishing Co.

	Good	Fine	Mint
4-Color 1287, 01-495-207	3.00	9.00	21.00

MANHUNT! (Becomes Red Fox #15 on)
Oct, 1947 - No. 14, 1953
Magazine Enterprises

	Good	Fine	Mint
1-Red Fox by L. B. Cole, Undercover Girl by Whitney, Space Ace begin; negligee panels	17.00	51.00	120.00
2-Electrocution-c	13.00	40.00	90.00
3-6	11.50	34.00	80.00
7-9: 7-Space Ace ends. 8-Trail Colt begins	9.50	28.00	65.00
10-G. Ingels-a	9.50	28.00	65.00
11(8/48)-Frazetta-a, 7 pgs.; The Duke, Scotland Yard begin	18.00	54.00	125.00
12	6.50	19.50	45.00
13(A-1 63)-Frazetta, r-/Trail Colt #1, 7 pgs.	15.00	45.00	105.00
14(A-1 77)-Classic bondage-c; last L. B. Cole Red Fox; Ingels-a	9.50	28.00	65.00

NOTE: ***Guardineer*** *a-1-5; c-8.* ***Whitney*** *a-2-14; c-1-6,10. Red Fox by* ***L. B. Cole****-#1-14. #15 was advertised but came out as Red Fox #15. Bondage c-6.*

MANHUNTER (See First Issue Special)
May, 1984 (76 pgs; high quality paper)
DC Comics

	Good	Fine	Mint
1-Simonson c/a(r)/Detective	.45	1.25	2.50

MAN IN BLACK (See Thrill-O-Rama) (Also see All New Comics, Front Page, Strange Story & Tally-Ho Comics)
Sept, 1957 - No. 4, Mar, 1958
Harvey Publications

	Good	Fine	Mint
1-Bob Powell c/a	6.00	18.00	42.00
2-4: Powell c/a	5.00	15.00	35.00

Major Victory #2, © CHES

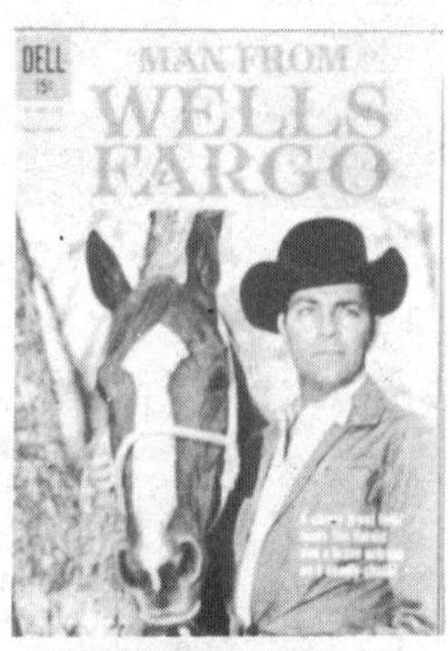

Man From Wells Fargo #01-495-207, © DELL

Man In Black #1, © HARV

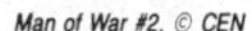
Man of War #2, © CEN

Man-Thing #2, © MCG

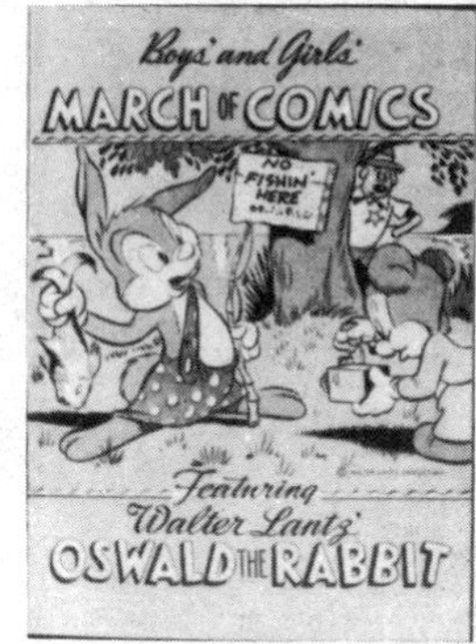

March of Comics #7, © W. Lantz

MAN IN FLIGHT (See 4-Color No. 836)

MAN IN SPACE (See Dell Giant No. 27 & 4-Color No. 716,954)

MAN OF PEACE, POPE PIUS XII
1950 (See Pope Pius XII . . . & Topix V2No.8)
Catechetical Guild

	Good	Fine	Mint
All Powell-a	5.35	16.00	32.00

MAN OF STEEL, THE
1986 (June) - No. 6, 1986 (mini-series)
DC Comics

	Good	Fine	Mint
1-Byrne story, c/art begins; origin	.35	1.00	2.00
1-Alternate-c for newsstand sales	.30	.90	1.80
2-6: 2-Intro. Lois Lane, Jimmy Olsen. 3-Intro/origin Magpie. 4-Intro. new Lex Luthor		.60	1.20
. . .The Complete Saga-Contains #1-6, given away in contest	.35	1.00	2.00
Limited Edition, softcover	6.00	18.00	35.00

MAN OF WAR (See Liberty Scouts & Liberty Guards)
Nov, 1941 - No. 2, Jan, 1942
Centaur Publications

	Good	Fine	Mint
1-The Fire-Man, Man of War, The Sentinel, Liberty Guards, & Vapo-Man begin; Gustavson-c/a; Flag-c	65.00	195.00	455.00
2-The Ferret app.; Gustavson-c/a	52.00	155.00	365.00

MAN OF WAR
Aug, 1987 - Present ($1.75, color)
Eclipse Comics

	Good	Fine	Mint
1,2	.30	.85	1.70

MAN O' MARS
1953; 1964
Fiction House Magazines

	Good	Fine	Mint
1-Space Rangers	12.00	36.00	84.00
I.W. Reprint #1/Man O'Mars #1; Murphy Anderson-a	2.75	8.00	16.00

MANTECH ROBOT WARRIORS
Sept, 1984 - No. 4, April, 1985
Archie Enterprises, Inc.

	Good	Fine	Mint
1-4		.40	.80

MAN-THING (See Fear, Marvel Fanfare, Monsters Unleashed & Savage Tales)
Jan, 1974 - No. 22, Oct, 1975; Nov, 1979 - V2No. 11, July, 1981
Marvel Comics Group

	Good	Fine	Mint
1-Howard the Duck cont./Fear 19.(2nd app.)	.85	2.50	5.00
2-4	.25	.70	1.40
5-11-Ploog-a		.50	1.00
12-22: 19-1st app. Scavenger. 21-Origin Scavenger & Man-Thing. 22-Howard the Duck cameo		.30	.60
V2#1(1979)		.40	.80
2-11: 6-Golden-c		.25	.50
Giant Size 1(8/74)-Ploog c/a		.60	1.20
Giant Size 2,3		.50	1.00
Giant Size 4(5/75)-Howard the Duck by Brunner; Ditko-a(r)	.85	2.50	5.00
Giant Size 5(8/75)-Howard the Duck by Brunner (p)	.85	2.50	5.00

NOTE: ***Alcala*** *a-14, Gnt Size 3.* ***Brunner*** *c-1, Gnt Size 4.* ***J. Buscema*** *a-12p, 13p, 16p, Gnt Size 2p, 5p; c-Gnt Size 2.* ***Ditko*** *a-Gnt Size 1r, 3r, 4r.* ***Gil Kane*** *c-4p, 10p, 12-20p, 21, Gnt-Size 3p, 5p.* ***Kirby*** *a-Gnt Size 1-3r.* ***Mooney*** *a-17, 18, 19p, 20-22, V2No.1-3p.* ***Ploog*** *Man-Thing-5p, 6p, 7, 8, 9-11p, Gnt Size 1p; c-5, 6, 8, 9, 11.* ***Powell*** *a-Gnt Size 2r.* ***Sutton*** *a-13i, Gnt-Size 3r, 5i.*

MAN WITH THE X-RAY EYES, THE (See X, . . . under Movie Comics)

MANY GHOSTS OF DR. GRAVES, THE (Doctor Graves No. 73 on)
5/67 - No. 60, 12/76; No. 61, 9/77 - No. 62, 10/77; No. 63, 2/78 - No. 65, 4/78; No. 66, 6/81 - No. 72, 5/82
Charlton Comics

	Good	Fine	Mint
1	.40	1.20	2.40
2-10		.50	1.00
11-20		.40	.80
21-44,46,48,50-72		.30	.60
45-1st Newton comic book work, 8pgs.	.35	1.00	2.00
47,49-Newton-a		.40	.80
Modern Comics Reprint 12,25 ('78)		.20	.40

NOTE: ***Aparo*** *a-66r, 69r; c-66, 67.* ***Byrne*** *c-54.* ***Ditko*** *a-1, 7, 9, 11-13, 15-18, 20-22, 24, 26, 35, 37, 38, 40-44, 47, 48, 51-54, 58, 60r-65r, 70, 72; c-11-13, 16-18, 22, 24, 26-35, 38, 40, 55, 58, 62-65.* ***Howard*** *c-48.* ***Newton*** *a-45, 47p, 49p; c-49, 52.* ***Sutton*** *c/a-42, 49.*

MANY LOVES OF DOBIE GILLIS (TV)
May-June, 1960 - No. 26, Oct, 1964
National Periodical Publications

	Good	Fine	Mint
1	8.50	25.50	60.00
2-5	4.00	12.00	28.00
6-10	3.50	10.50	24.00
11-26	2.65	8.00	18.00

MARAUDER'S MOON (See 4-Color No. 848)

MARCH OF COMICS (Boys' and Girls' . . . #1-353)
1946 - No. 488, Apr, 1982 (#1-4: No #'s)
(K.K. Giveaway) (Founded by Sig Feuchtwanger)
K. K. Publications/Western Publishing Co.

Early issues were full size, 32 pages, and were printed with and without an extra cover of slick stock, just for the advertiser. The binding was stapled if the slick cover was added; otherwise, the pages were glued together at the spine. Most 1948 - 1951 issues were full size, 24 pages, pulp covers. Starting in 1952 they were half-size and 32 pages with slick covers. 1959 and later issues had only 16 pages plus covers. 1952 -1959 issues read oblong; 1960 and later issues read upright.

	Good	Fine	Mint
1(nn)(1946)-Goldilocks; Kelly back-c; 16pgs., stapled	24.00	72.00	170.00
2(nn)(1946)-How Santa Got His Red Suit; Kelly-a(11 pgs., r-/4-Color 61)('44); 16pgs., stapled	24.00	72.00	170.00
3(nn)(1947)-Our Gang (Walt Kelly)	40.00	110.00	235.00
4(nn)Donald Duck by Carl Barks, "Maharajah Donald," 28 pgs.; Kelly-c?	428.00	1285.00	3000.00
5-Andy Panda	13.00	40.00	90.00
6-Popular Fairy Tales; Kelly-c; Noonan-a(2)	17.00	50.00	120.00
7-Oswald the Rabbit	17.00	50.00	120.00
8-Mickey Mouse, 32 pgs.	50.00	150.00	330.00
9(nn)-The Story of the Gloomy Bunny	8.00	24.00	56.00
10-Out of Santa's Bag	6.75	20.00	47.00
11-Fun With Santa Claus	5.35	16.00	37.00
12-Santa's Toys	5.35	16.00	37.00
13-Santa's Surprise	5.35	16.00	37.00
14-Santa's Candy Kitchen	5.35	16.00	37.00
15-Hip-It-Ty Hop & the Big Bass Viol	5.35	16.00	37.00
16-Woody Woodpecker (1947)	8.50	25.00	60.00
17-Roy Rogers (1948)	20.00	60.00	140.00
18-Popular Fairy Tales	10.00	30.00	70.00
19-Uncle Wiggily	7.50	22.50	52.00
20-Donald Duck by Carl Barks, "Darkest Africa," 22 pgs.; Kelly-c	257.00	770.00	1800.00
21-Tom and Jerry	7.50	22.50	52.00
22-Andy Panda	7.50	22.50	52.00
23-Raggedy Ann; Kerr-a	12.00	35.00	84.00
24-Felix the Cat, 1932 daily strip reprints by Otto Messmer	18.00	54.00	125.00
25-Gene Autry	20.00	60.00	140.00
26-Our Gang; Walt Kelly	20.00	60.00	140.00
27-Mickey Mouse	34.00	100.00	238.00
28-Gene Autry	20.00	60.00	140.00
29-Easter Bonnet Shop	4.00	12.00	28.00
30-Here Comes Santa	3.35	10.00	22.00
31-Santa's Busy Corner	3.35	10.00	22.00
32-No book produced			

MARCH OF COMICS (continued)	Good	Fine	Mint
33-A Christmas Carol	3.35	10.00	22.00
34-Woody Woodpecker	5.85	17.50	40.00
35-Roy Rogers (1948)	19.00	57.00	135.00
36-Felix the Cat(1949)-by Messmer; '34 daily strip-r	15.00	45.00	105.00
37-Popeye	12.50	37.50	87.00
38-Oswald the Rabbit	5.85	17.50	40.00
39-Gene Autry	19.00	57.00	135.00
40-Andy and Woody	5.85	17.50	40.00
41-Donald Duck by Carl Barks, "Race to the South Seas," 22 pgs.; Kelly-c; on Disney's reprint band list	200.00	600.00	1400.00
42-Porky Pig	5.85	17.50	40.00
43-Henry	3.75	11.00	26.00
44-Bugs Bunny	5.85	17.50	40.00
45-Mickey Mouse	27.00	80.00	190.00
46-Tom and Jerry	5.85	17.50	40.00
47-Roy Rogers	17.00	51.00	120.00
48-Greetings from Santa	2.75	8.00	19.00
49-Santa Is Here	2.75	8.00	19.00
50-Santa Claus' Workshop (1949)	2.75	8.00	19.00
51-Felix the Cat (1950) by Messmer	12.50	37.50	87.00
52-Popeye	10.00	30.00	70.00
53-Oswald the Rabbit	5.85	17.50	40.00
54-Gene Autry	16.00	48.00	110.00
55-Andy and Woody	5.00	15.00	35.00
56-Donald Duck-not by Barks; Barks art on back-c	22.00	65.00	140.00
57-Porky Pig	5.00	15.00	35.00
58-Henry	3.00	9.00	21.00
59-Bugs Bunny	5.00	15.00	35.00
60-Mickey Mouse	18.00	55.00	125.00
61-Tom and Jerry	4.35	13.00	30.00
62-Roy Rogers	16.00	48.00	110.00
63-Welcome Santa; ½-size, oblong	2.75	8.00	19.00
64(nn)-Santa's Helpers; ½-size, oblong	2.75	8.00	19.00
65(nn)-Jingle Bells (1950)-½-size, oblong	2.75	8.00	19.00
66-Popeye (1951)	8.35	25.00	58.00
67-Oswald the Rabbit	4.00	12.00	28.00
68-Roy Rogers	14.00	42.00	100.00
69-Donald Duck; Barks-a on back-c	19.00	57.00	125.00
70-Tom and Jerry	4.00	12.00	28.00
71-Porky Pig	4.00	12.00	28.00
72-Krazy Kat	6.00	18.00	42.00
73-Roy Rogers	12.00	36.00	84.00
74-Mickey Mouse (1951)	14.00	42.50	96.00
75-Bugs Bunny	4.00	12.00	28.00
76-Andy and Woody	4.00	12.00	28.00
77-Roy Rogers	13.00	40.00	80.00
78-Gene Autry(1951)-Last regular size issue	13.00	40.00	80.00
79-Andy Panda (1952)-5x7" size	2.75	8.00	19.00
80-Popeye	7.50	22.50	52.00
81-Oswald the Rabbit	3.00	9.00	21.00
82-Tarzan	13.00	40.00	90.00
83-Bugs Bunny	3.00	9.00	21.00
84-Henry	2.35	7.00	16.00
85-Woody Woodpecker	2.35	7.00	16.00
86-Roy Rogers	10.00	30.00	70.00
87-Krazy Kat	4.75	14.00	33.00
88-Tom and Jerry	2.35	7.00	16.00
89-Porky Pig	2.35	7.00	16.00
90-Gene Autry	10.00	30.00	70.00
91-Roy Rogers & Santa	10.00	30.00	70.00
92-Christmas with Santa	2.00	6.00	14.00
93-Woody Woodpecker (1953)	2.35	7.00	16.00
94-Indian Chief	5.50	16.50	40.00
95-Oswald the Rabbit	2.35	7.00	16.00

	Good	Fine	Mint
96-Popeye	7.00	20.00	50.00
97-Bugs Bunny	2.35	7.00	16.00
98-Tarzan-Photo-c	13.00	40.00	90.00
99-Porky Pig	2.35	7.00	16.00
100-Roy Rogers	8.00	24.00	56.00
101-Henry	2.00	6.00	14.00
102-Tom Corbett (TV)	10.00	30.00	70.00
103-Tom and Jerry	2.00	6.00	14.00
104-Gene Autry	8.00	24.00	56.00
105-Roy Rogers	8.00	24.00	56.00
106-Santa's Helpers	2.00	6.00	14.00
107-Santa's Christmas Book - not published			
108-Fun with Santa (1953)	2.00	6.00	14.00
109-Woody Woodpecker (1954)	2.00	6.00	14.00
110-Indian Chief	3.50	10.50	24.00
111-Oswald the Rabbit	2.00	6.00	14.00
112-Henry	1.70	5.00	12.00
113-Porky Pig	2.00	6.00	14.00
114-Tarzan (Russ Manning)	13.00	40.00	90.00
115-Bugs Bunny	2.00	6.00	14.00
116-Roy Rogers	8.00	24.00	56.00
117-Popeye	7.00	20.00	50.00
118-Flash Gordon	10.00	30.00	70.00
119-Tom and Jerry	2.00	6.00	14.00
120-Gene Autry	8.00	24.00	56.00
121-Roy Rogers	8.00	24.00	56.00
122-Santa's Surprise (1954)	1.50	4.50	10.00
123-Santa's Christmas Book	1.50	4.50	10.00
124-Woody Woodpecker (1955)	1.70	5.00	12.00
125-Tarzan-Photo-c	12.00	36.00	84.00
126-Oswald the Rabbit	1.70	5.00	12.00
127-Indian Chief	3.00	9.00	21.00
128-Tom and Jerry	1.70	5.00	12.00
129-Henry	1.50	4.50	10.00
130-Porky Pig	1.70	5.00	12.00
131-Roy Rogers	8.00	24.00	56.00
132-Bugs Bunny	1.70	5.00	12.00
133-Flash Gordon	8.50	25.50	60.00
134-Popeye	4.00	12.00	28.00
135-Gene Autry	7.00	21.00	50.00
136-Roy Rogers	7.00	21.00	50.00
137-Gifts from Santa	1.35	4.00	9.00
138-Fun at Christmas (1955)	1.35	4.00	9.00
139-Woody Woodpecker (1956)	1.70	5.00	12.00
140-Indian Chief	3.00	9.00	21.00
141-Oswald the Rabbit	1.70	5.00	12.00
142-Flash Gordon	8.50	25.50	60.00
143-Porky Pig	1.70	5.00	12.00
144-Tarzan (Russ Manning)	11.00	34.00	76.00
145-Tom and Jerry	1.70	5.00	12.00
146-Roy Rogers-Photo-c	8.00	24.00	56.00
147-Henry	1.35	4.00	9.00
148-Popeye	4.00	12.00	28.00
149-Bugs Bunny	1.70	5.00	12.00
150-Gene Autry	7.00	21.00	50.00
151-Roy Rogers	7.00	21.00	50.00
152-The Night Before Christmas	1.35	4.00	9.00
153-Merry Christmas (1956)	1.35	4.00	9.00
154-Tom and Jerry (1957)	1.70	5.00	12.00
155-Tarzan-Photo-c	11.00	34.00	76.00
156-Oswald the Rabbit	1.70	5.00	12.00
157-Popeye	3.00	9.00	21.00
158-Woody Woodpecker	1.70	5.00	12.00
159-Indian Chief	3.00	9.00	21.00
160-Bugs Bunny	1.70	5.00	12.00
161-Roy Rogers	5.70	17.00	40.00

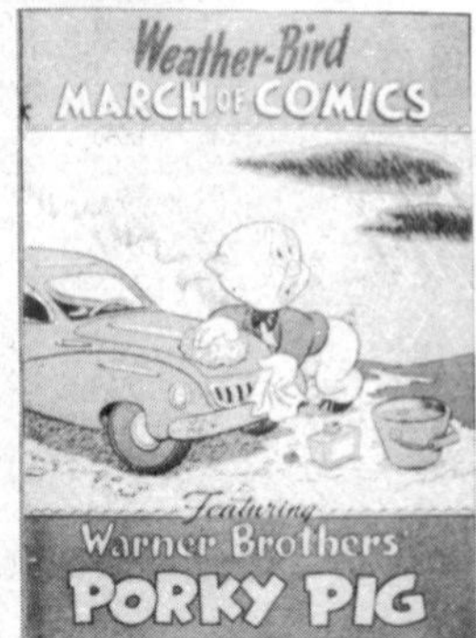

March of Comics #42, © Warner Bros.

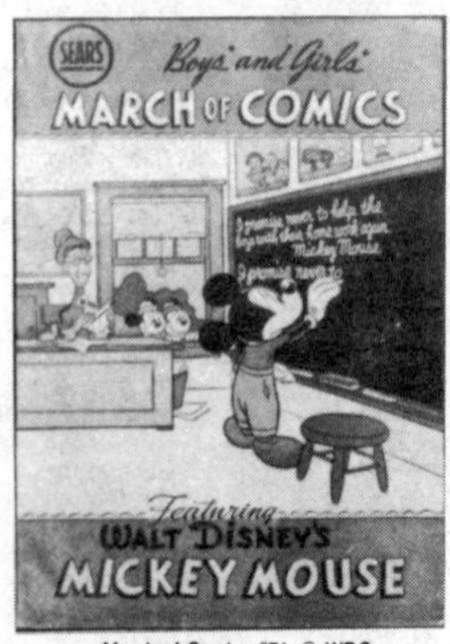

March of Comics #74, © WDC

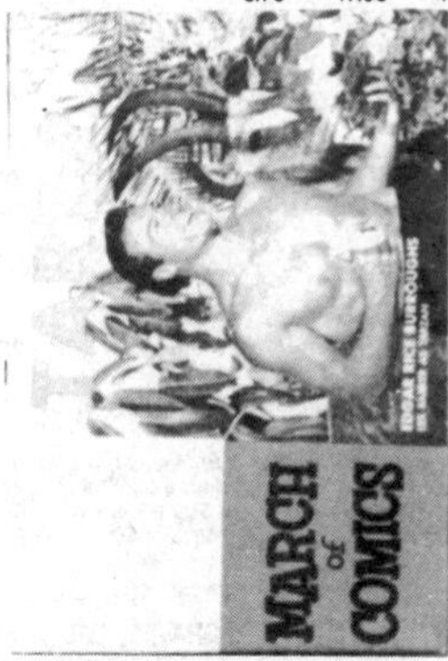

March of Comics #125, © ERB

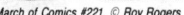

March of Comics #221, © Roy Rogers

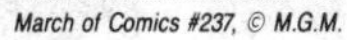

March of Comics #237, © M.G.M.

March of Comics #292, © WEST

MARCH OF COMICS (continued)	Good	Fine	Mint
162-Henry	1.35	4.00	9.00
163-Rin Tin Tin (TV)	3.00	9.00	21.00
164-Porky Pig	1.70	5.00	12.00
165-The Lone Ranger	6.50	19.50	45.00
166-Santa and His Reindeer	1.35	4.00	9.00
167-Roy Rogers and Santa	5.70	17.00	40.00
168-Santa Claus' Workshop (1957)	1.35	4.00	9.00
169-Popeye (1958)	3.00	9.00	21.00
170-Indian Chief	3.00	9.00	21.00
171-Oswald the Rabbit	1.50	4.50	10.00
172-Tarzan	9.50	28.00	65.00
173-Tom and Jerry	1.50	4.50	10.00
174-The Lone Ranger	6.50	19.50	45.00
175-Porky Pig	1.50	4.50	10.00
176-Roy Rogers	5.50	16.50	38.00
177-Woody Woodpecker	1.50	4.50	10.00
178-Henry	1.35	4.00	9.00
179-Bugs Bunny	1.50	4.50	10.00
180-Rin Tin Tin (TV)	3.00	9.00	21.00
181-Happy Holiday	1.20	3.50	8.00
182-Happi Tim	1.50	4.50	10.00
183-Welcome Santa (1958)	1.20	3.50	8.00
184-Woody Woodpecker (1959)	1.50	4.50	10.00
185-Tarzan-Photo-c	9.50	28.00	65.00
186-Oswald the Rabbit	1.50	4.50	10.00
187-Indian Chief	3.00	9.00	21.00
188-Bugs Bunny	1.50	4.50	10.00
189-Henry	1.20	3.50	8.00
190-Tom and Jerry	1.50	4.50	10.00
191-Roy Rogers	5.50	16.50	38.00
192-Porky Pig	1.50	4.50	10.00
193-The Lone Ranger	6.50	19.50	45.00
194-Popeye	3.00	9.00	21.00
195-Rin Tin Tin (TV)	3.00	9.00	21.00
196-Sears Special - not published			
197-Santa Is Coming	1.20	3.50	8.00
198-Santa's Helpers (1959)	1.20	3.50	8.00
199-Huckleberry Hound (TV)(1960)	1.70	5.00	12.00
200-Fury (TV)	3.00	9.00	21.00
201-Bugs Bunny	1.35	4.00	9.00
202-Space Explorer	4.60	14.00	32.00
203-Woody Woodpecker	1.35	4.00	9.00
204-Tarzan	6.50	19.50	45.00
205-Mighty Mouse	2.50	7.50	17.50
206-Roy Rogers-Photo-c	5.50	16.50	38.00
207-Tom and Jerry	1.35	4.00	9.00
208-The Lone Ranger-Clayton Moore photo-c	8.00	24.00	56.00
209-Porky Pig	1.35	4.00	9.00
210-Lassie (TV)	3.00	9.00	21.00
211-Sears Special - not published			
212-Christmas Eve	1.20	3.50	8.00
213-Here Comes Santa (1960)	1.20	3.50	8.00
214-Huckleberry Hound (TV)(1961)	1.70	5.00	12.00
215-Hi Yo Silver	4.00	12.00	28.00
216-Rocky & His Friends (TV)	3.50	10.50	24.00
217-Lassie (TV)	2.35	7.00	16.00
218-Porky Pig	1.35	4.00	9.00
219-Journey to the Sun	3.00	9.00	21.00
220-Bugs Bunny	1.35	4.00	9.00
221-Roy and Dale-Photo-c	5.00	15.00	35.00
222-Woody Woodpecker	1.35	4.00	9.00
223-Tarzan	6.50	19.50	45.00
224-Tom and Jerry	1.35	4.00	9.00
225-The Lone Ranger	5.00	15.00	35.00
226-Christmas Treasury (1961)	1.20	3.50	8.00
227-Sears Special - not published?			

	Good	Fine	Mint
228-Letters to Santa (1961)	1.20	3.50	8.00
229-The Flintstones (TV)(1962)	3.50	10.50	24.00
230-Lassie (TV)	2.35	7.00	16.00
231-Bugs Bunny	1.20	3.50	8.00
232-The Three Stooges	5.00	15.00	35.00
233-Bullwinkle (TV)	4.35	13.00	30.00
234-Smokey the Bear	1.35	4.00	9.00
235-Huckleberry Hound (TV)	1.70	5.00	12.00
236-Roy and Dale	3.65	11.00	25.00
237-Mighty Mouse	2.00	6.00	14.00
238-The Lone Ranger	5.00	15.00	35.00
239-Woody Woodpecker	1.35	4.00	9.00
240-Tarzan	5.70	17.00	40.00
241-Santa Claus Around the World	1.20	3.50	8.00
242-Santa's Toyland (1962)	1.20	3.50	8.00
243-The Flintstones (TV)(1963)	3.00	9.00	21.00
244-Mister Ed (TV)-Photo-c	2.00	6.00	14.00
245-Bugs Bunny	1.35	4.00	9.00
246-Popeye	2.50	7.50	17.50
247-Mighty Mouse	2.00	6.00	14.00
248-The Three Stooges	5.00	15.00	35.00
249-Woody Woodpecker	1.35	4.00	9.00
250-Roy and Dale	3.65	11.00	25.00
251-Little Lulu	13.00	40.00	85.00
252-Tarzan	5.50	16.50	40.00
253-Yogi Bear (TV)	2.00	6.00	14.00
254-Lassie (TV)	2.35	7.00	16.00
255-Santa's Christmas List	1.20	3.50	8.00
256-Christmas Party (1963)	1.20	3.50	8.00
257-Mighty Mouse	2.00	6.00	14.00
258-The Sword in the Stone (Disney)	5.00	15.00	35.00
259-Bugs Bunny	1.35	4.00	9.00
260-Mister Ed (TV)	1.70	5.00	12.00
261-Woody Woodpecker	1.35	4.00	9.00
262-Tarzan	5.50	16.50	40.00
263-Donald Duck-not Barks	6.00	18.00	36.00
264-Popeye	2.50	7.50	17.50
265-Yogi Bear (TV)	1.70	5.00	12.00
266-Lassie (TV)	2.00	6.00	14.00
267-Little Lulu; Irving Tripp-a	10.00	30.00	70.00
268-The Three Stooges	4.35	13.00	30.00
269-A Jolly Christmas	1.20	3.50	8.00
270-Santa's Little Helpers	1.20	3.50	8.00
271-The Flintstones (TV)(1965)	3.00	9.00	21.00
272-Tarzan	5.50	16.50	40.00
273-Bugs Bunny	1.35	4.00	9.00
274-Popeye	2.50	7.50	17.50
275-Little Lulu-Irving Tripp-a	8.35	25.00	55.00
276-The Jetsons (TV)	4.35	13.00	30.00
277-Daffy Duck	1.35	4.00	9.00
278-Lassie (TV)	2.00	6.00	14.00
279-Yogi Bear (TV)	1.70	5.00	12.00
280-The Three Stooges-Photo-c	4.35	13.00	30.00
281-Tom and Jerry	1.00	3.00	7.00
282-Mister Ed (TV)	1.70	5.00	12.00
283-Santa's Visit	1.20	3.50	8.00
284-Christmas Parade (1965)	1.20	3.50	8.00
285-Astro Boy (TV)	17.00	51.00	120.00
286-Tarzan	5.00	15.00	35.00
287-Bugs Bunny	1.00	3.00	7.00
288-Daffy Duck	1.00	3.00	7.00
289-The Flintstones (TV)	2.30	7.00	16.00
290-Mister Ed (TV)-Photo-c	1.30	4.00	9.00
291-Yogi Bear (TV)	1.30	4.00	9.00
292-The Three Stooges-Photo-c	4.35	13.00	30.00
293-Little Lulu; Irving Tripp-a	5.75	17.25	40.00

MARCH OF COMICS (continued)	Good	Fine	Mint
294-Popeye	2.50	7.50	17.50
295-Tom and Jerry	.85	2.50	6.00
296-Lassie (TV)-Photo-c	1.70	5.00	12.00
297-Christmas Bells	1.20	3.50	8.00
298-Santa's Sleigh (1966)	1.20	3.50	8.00
299-The Flintstones (TV)(1967)	2.30	7.00	16.00
300-Tarzan	5.00	15.00	35.00
301-Bugs Bunny	.85	2.50	6.00
302-Laurel and Hardy (TV)-Photo-c	2.65	8.00	18.00
303-Daffy Duck	.70	2.00	5.00
304-The Three Stooges-Photo-c	3.50	10.50	24.00
305-Tom and Jerry	.70	2.00	5.00
306-Daniel Boone (TV)-Photo-c	2.65	8.00	18.00
307-Little Lulu; Irving Tripp-a	5.00	15.00	35.00
308-Lassie (TV)-Photo-c	1.50	4.50	10.00
309-Yogi Bear (TV)	1.00	3.00	7.00
310-The Lone Ranger-Clayton Moore photo-c	5.70	17.00	40.00
311-Santa's Show	1.00	3.00	7.00
312-Christmas Album (1967)	1.00	3.00	7.00
313-Daffy Duck (1968)	.70	2.00	5.00
314-Laurel and Hardy (TV)	2.65	8.00	18.00
315-Bugs Bunny	.85	2.50	6.00
316-The Three Stooges	3.50	10.50	24.00
317-The Flintstones (TV)	1.70	5.00	12.00
318-Tarzan	4.65	13.00	32.00
319-Yogi Bear (TV)	1.00	3.00	7.00
320-Space Family Robinson (TV); Spiegle-a	5.70	17.00	40.00
321-Tom and Jerry	.70	2.00	5.00
322-The Lone Ranger	4.35	13.00	30.00
323-Little Lulu-not Stanley	3.00	9.00	21.00
324-Lassie (TV)-Photo-c	1.50	4.50	10.00
325-Fun with Santa	1.00	3.00	7.00
326-Christmas Story (1968)	1.00	3.00	7.00
327-The Flintstones (TV)(1969)	1.70	5.00	12.00
328-Space Family Robinson (TV); Spiegle-a	5.70	17.00	40.00
329-Bugs Bunny	.85	2.50	6.00
330-The Jetsons (TV)	3.50	10.50	24.00
331-Daffy Duck	.70	2.00	5.00
332-Tarzan	3.65	11.00	25.00
333-Tom and Jerry	.70	2.00	5.00
334-Lassie (TV)	1.15	3.50	8.00
335-Little Lulu	3.00	9.00	21.00
336-The Three Stooges	3.50	10.50	24.00
337-Yogi Bear (TV)	1.00	3.00	7.00
338-The Lone Ranger	4.35	13.00	30.00
339-(Did not come out)			
340-Here Comes Santa (1969)	1.00	3.00	7.00
341-The Flintstones (TV)	1.70	5.00	12.00
342-Tarzan	3.65	11.00	25.00
343-Bugs Bunny	.70	2.00	5.00
344-Yogi Bear (TV)	.85	2.50	6.00
345-Tom and Jerry	.70	2.00	5.00
346-Lassie (TV)	1.15	3.50	8.00
347-Daffy Duck	.70	2.00	5.00
348-The Jetsons (TV)	3.00	9.00	21.00
349-Little Lulu-not Stanley	2.50	7.50	17.50
350-The Lone Ranger	3.65	11.00	25.00
351-Beep-Beep, the Road Runner	1.35	4.00	9.00
352-Space Family Robinson (TV)-Spiegle-a	5.70	17.00	40.00
353-Beep-Beep, the Road Runner (1971)	1.35	4.00	9.00
354-Tarzan (1971)	3.00	9.00	21.00
355-Little Lulu-not Stanley	2.50	7.50	17.50
356-Scooby Doo, Where Are You? (TV)	1.70	5.00	12.00
357-Daffy Duck & Porky Pig	.70	2.00	5.00
358-Lassie (TV)	1.15	3.50	8.00
359-Baby Snoots	1.35	4.00	9.00
360-H. R. Pufnstuf (TV)-Photo-c	1.00	3.00	7.00
361-Tom and Jerry	.70	2.00	5.00
362-Smokey the Bear (TV)	.70	2.00	5.00
363-Bugs Bunny & Yosemite Sam	.70	2.00	5.00
364-The Banana Splits (TV)-Photo-c	.85	2.50	6.00
365-Tom and Jerry (1972)	.70	2.00	5.00
366-Tarzan	3.00	9.00	21.00
367-Bugs Bunny & Porky Pig	.70	2.00	5.00
368-Scooby Doo (TV)(4/72)	1.50	4.50	12.00
369-Little Lulu-not Stanley	2.00	6.00	14.00
370-Lassie (TV)-Photo-c	1.15	3.50	8.00
371-Baby Snoots	1.00	3.00	7.00
372-Smokey the Bear (TV)	.70	2.00	5.00
373-The Three Stooges	3.00	9.00	21.00
374-Wacky Witch	.70	2.00	5.00
375-Beep-Beep & Daffy Duck	.70	2.00	5.00
376-The Pink Panther (1972)	1.35	4.00	9.00
377-Baby Snoots (1973)	1.00	3.00	7.00
378-Turok, Son of Stone	5.75	17.25	40.00
379-Heckle & Jeckle New Terrytoons	.50	1.50	3.00
380-Bugs Bunny & Yosemite Sam	.50	1.50	3.00
381-Lassie (TV)	.85	2.50	6.00
382-Scooby Doo, Where Are You? (TV)	1.50	4.50	10.00
383-Smokey the Bear (TV)	.50	1.50	3.00
384-Pink Panther	1.00	3.00	7.00
385-Little Lulu	2.00	6.00	14.00
386-Wacky Witch	.50	1.50	3.00
387-Beep-Beep & Daffy Duck	.50	1.50	3.00
388-Tom and Jerry (1973)	.50	1.50	3.00
389-Little Lulu-not Stanley	2.00	6.00	14.00
390-Pink Panther	.70	2.00	5.00
391-Scooby Doo (TV)	1.30	4.00	9.00
392-Bugs Bunny & Yosemite Sam	.50	1.50	3.00
393-New Terrytoons (Heckle & Jeckle)	.50	1.50	3.00
394-Lassie (TV)	.70	2.00	5.00
395-Woodsy Owl	.50	1.50	3.00
396-Baby Snoots	.70	2.00	5.00
397-Beep-Beep & Daffy Duck	.50	1.50	3.00
398-Wacky Witch	.50	1.50	3.00
399-Turok, Son of Stone	5.00	15.00	35.00
400-Tom and Jerry	.50	1.50	3.00
401-Baby Snoots (1975) (r-/No. 371)	.70	2.00	5.00
402-Daffy Duck (r-/No. 313)	.50	1.50	3.00
403-Bugs Bunny (r-/No. 343)	.50	1.50	3.00
404-Space Family Robinson (TV)(r-/No. 328)	4.60	14.00	32.00
405-Cracky	.50	1.50	3.00
406-Little Lulu (r-/No. 355)	1.70	5.00	12.00
407-Smokey the Bear (TV)(r-/No. 362)	.50	1.50	3.00
408-Turok, Son of Stone	4.35	13.00	30.00
409-Pink Panther	.50	1.50	3.00
410-Wacky Witch	.35	1.00	2.00
411-Lassie (TV)(r-/No. 324)	.70	2.00	5.00
412-New Terrytoons (1975)	.35	1.00	2.00
413-Daffy Duck (1976)(r-/No. 331)	.35	1.00	2.00
414-Space Family Robinson (r-/No. 328)	3.00	9.00	21.00
415-Bugs Bunny (r-/No. 329)	.35	1.00	2.00
416-Beep-Beep, the Road Runner (r-/No. 353)	.35	1.00	2.00
417-Little Lulu (r-/No. 323)	1.50	4.50	10.00
418-Pink Panther (r-/No. 384)	.35	1.00	2.00
419-Baby Snoots (r-/No. 377)	.50	1.50	3.00
420-Woody Woodpecker	.35	1.00	2.00
421-Tweety & Sylvester	.35	1.00	2.00
422-Wacky Witch (r-/No. 386)	.35	1.00	2.00
423-Little Monsters	.50	1.50	3.00
424-Cracky (12/76)	.35	1.00	2.00
425-Daffy Duck	.35	1.00	2.00

March of Comics #299, © Hanna-Barbera

March of Comics #350, © Lone Ranger

March of Comics #394, © M.G.M.

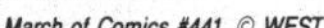

March of Comics #441, © WEST

March of Crime #7 (#1), © FOX

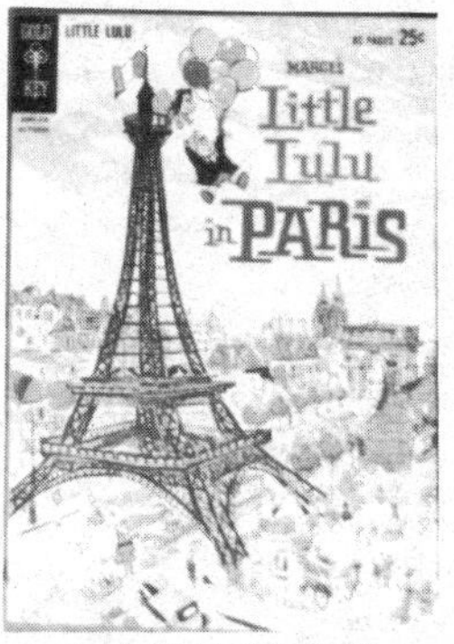

Marge's Little Lulu #165, © WEST

MARCH OF COMICS (continued)	Good	Fine	Mint
426-Underdog (TV)	.85	2.50	6.00
427-Little Lulu (r/No. 335)	1.15	3.50	8.00
428-Bugs Bunny	.35	1.00	2.00
429-The Pink Panther	.35	1.00	2.00
430-Beep-Beep, the Road Runner	.35	1.00	2.00
431-Baby Snoots	.50	1.50	3.00
432-Lassie (TV)	.50	1.50	3.00
433-Tweety & Sylvester	.35	1.00	2.00
434-Wacky Witch	.35	1.00	2.00
435-New Terrytoons	.35	1.00	2.00
436-Wacky Advs. of Cracky	.35	1.00	2.00
437-Daffy Duck	.35	1.00	2.00
438-Underdog (TV)	.85	2.50	6.00
439-Little Lulu (r/No. 349)	1.15	3.50	8.00
440-Bugs Bunny	.35	1.00	2.00
441-The Pink Panther	.35	1.00	2.00
442-Beep-Beep, the Road Runner	.35	1.00	2.00
443-Baby Snoots	.50	1.50	3.00
444-Tom and Jerry	.35	1.00	2.00
445-Tweety and Sylvester	.35	1.00	2.00
446-Wacky Witch	.35	1.00	2.00
447-Mighty Mouse	.50	1.50	3.00
448-Cracky	.35	1.00	2.00
449-Pink Panther	.35	1.00	2.00
450-Baby Snoots	.35	1.00	2.00
451-Tom and Jerry	.35	1.00	2.00
452-Bugs Bunny	.35	1.00	2.00
453-Popeye	.35	1.00	2.00
454-Woody Woodpecker	.35	1.00	2.00
455-Beep-Beep, the Road Runner	.35	1.00	2.00
456-Little Lulu (r/No. 369)	.85	2.50	6.00
457-Tweety & Sylvester	.35	1.00	2.00
458-Wacky Witch	.35	1.00	2.00
459-Mighty Mouse	.50	1.50	3.00
460-Daffy Duck	.35	1.00	2.00
461-The Pink Panther	.35	1.00	2.00
462-Baby Snoots	.35	1.00	2.00
463-Tom and Jerry	.35	1.00	2.00
464-Bugs Bunny	.35	1.00	2.00
465-Popeye	.35	1.00	2.00
466-Woody Woodpecker	.35	1.00	2.00
467-Underdog (TV)	.70	2.00	4.00
468-Little Lulu (r/No. 385)	.70	2.00	4.00
469-Tweety & Sylvester	.35	1.00	2.00
470-Wacky Witch	.35	1.00	2.00
471-Mighty Mouse	.50	1.50	3.00
472-Heckle & Jeckle(12/80)	.35	1.00	2.00
473-Pink Panther(1/81)	.35	1.00	2.00
474-Baby Snoots	.35	1.00	2.00
475-Little Lulu (r/No. 323)	.50	1.50	3.00
476-Bugs Bunny	.35	1.00	2.00
477-Popeye	.35	1.00	2.00
478-Woody Woodpecker	.35	1.00	2.00
479-Underdog (TV)	.70	2.00	4.00
480-Tom and Jerry	.35	1.00	2.00
481-Tweety and Sylvester	.35	1.00	2.00
482-Wacky Witch	.35	1.00	2.00
483-Mighty Mouse	.50	1.50	3.00
484-Heckle & Jeckle	.35	1.00	2.00
485-Baby Snoots	.35	1.00	2.00
486-The Pink Panther	.35	1.00	2.00
487-Bugs Bunny	.35	1.00	2.00
488-Little Lulu (r/No. 335)	.50	1.50	3.00

MARCH OF CRIME (My Love Affair No. 1-6) (See Fox Giants)
No. 7, 7/50 - No. 2, 9/50; No. 3, 9/51
Fox Features Syndicate

	Good	Fine	Mint
7(No.1)(7/50)-Wood-a	11.50	34.00	80.00
2(9/50)-Wood-a (exceptional)	11.00	32.00	76.00
3(9/51)	4.35	13.00	30.00

MARCO POLO
1962 (Movie classic)
Charlton Comics Group

	Good	Fine	Mint
nn (Scarce)-Glanzman-a, 25pgs.	8.00	24.00	56.00

MARGARET O'BRIEN (See The Adventures of . . .)

MARGE'S LITTLE LULU (Little Lulu No. 207 on)
No. 74, 6/45 - No. 164, 7-9/62; No. 165, 10/62 - No. 206, 8/72
Dell Publishing Co./Gold Key 165-206

Marjorie Henderson Buell, born in Philadelphia, Pa., in 1904, created Little Lulu, a cartoon character that appeared weekly in the Saturday Evening Post from Feb. 23, 1935 through Dec. 30, 1944. She was not responsible for any of the comic books. **John Stanley** did pencils only on all Little Lulu Comics through at least No. 175. He did pencils and inks on Four Color 74,97 only. He did storyboards (layouts), pencils, and scripts in all cases and inking only on covers. His word balloons were written in cursive. The Whitman artists in Poughkeepsie, N.Y. blew up the pencilled pages, inked the blowups, and lettered them. The earlier issues had to be approved by Buell prior to publication.

	Good	Fine	Mint
4-Color 74('45)-Intro Lulu, Tubby & Alvin	84.00	250.00	590.00
4-Color 97(2/46)	45.00	135.00	315.00
(Above two books done entirely by John Stanley - cover, pencils, and inks.)			
4-Color 110('46)-1st Alvin Story Telling Time; 1st app. Willy	32.00	95.00	220.00
4-Color 115-1st app. Boys' Clubhouse	32.00	95.00	220.00
4-Color 120, 131: 120-1st app. Eddie	28.00	84.00	195.00
4-Color 139('47),146,158	26.00	78.00	185.00
4-Color 165 (10/47)-Smokes doll hair & has wild hallucinations. 1st Tubby detective story	26.00	78.00	185.00
1(1-2/48)-Lulu's Diary feat. begins	54.00	162.00	380.00
2-1st app. Gloria; 1st Tubby story in a L.L. comic	27.00	81.00	190.00
3-5	24.00	72.00	170.00
6-10: 7-1st app. Annie	17.00	51.00	120.00
11-20	14.00	42.00	100.00
21-30: 26-r/F.C. 110. 30-Xmas-c	11.00	32.00	76.00
31-38,40	9.50	28.50	65.00
39-Intro. Witch Hazel in "That Awful Witch Hazel"	11.00	32.00	76.00
41-60: 45-2nd Witch Hazel app. 49-Gives Stanley & others credit	8.50	25.50	60.00
61-80: 63-1st app. Chubby (Tubby's cousin). 80-Intro. Little Itch (2/55)	5.70	17.00	40.00
81-99	4.00	12.00	28.00
100	4.60	14.00	32.00
101-130	3.50	10.50	24.00
131-164	2.65	8.00	18.00
165-Giant; . . . In Paris ('62)	3.75	11.25	30.00
166-Giant; . . . Christmas Diary ('62-'63)	3.75	11.25	30.00
167-169	2.15	6.50	15.00
170,172,175,176,178-196,198-200-Stanley-r	1.30	4.00	9.00
171,173,174,177,197	.85	2.50	6.00
201,203,206-Last issue to carry Marge's name	.55	1.65	4.00
202,204,205-Stanley-r	1.00	3.00	7.00
. . . & Tubby in Japan (12 cents)(5-7/62) 01476-207	5.00	15.00	35.00
. . . Summer Camp 1(8/67-G.K.-Giant) '57-58-r	4.00	12.00	28.00
. . . Trick 'N' Treat 1(12-)(12/62-Gold Key)	4.35	13.00	30.00

NOTE: *See* ***Dell Giant Comics*** *#23, 29, 36, 42, 50, &* ***Dell Giants*** *for annuals. All Giants not by* ***Stanley*** *from L.L. & Tubby in Alaska (7/59)-on. Christmas c-7, 18, 30, 42, 78, 90, 250.*

MARGE'S LITTLE LULU (See Golden Comics Digest #19, 23, 27, 29, 33, 36, 40, 43, 46 & March of Comics #251, 267, 275, 293, 307, 323, 335, 349, 355, 369, 385, 406,

MARGE'S LITTLE LULU (continued)
417, 427, 439, 456, 468, 475, 488)

MARGE'S TUBBY (Little Lulu)(See Dell Giants)
No. 381, Aug, 1952 - No. 49, Dec-Feb, 1961-62
Dell Publishing Co./Gold Key

	Good	Fine	Mint
4-Color 381-Stanley script; Irving Tripp-a	11.00	33.00	76.00
4-Color 430,444-Stanley-a	6.00	18.00	42.00
4-Color 461 (4/53)-1st Tubby & Men From Mars story; Stanley-a	6.00	18.00	42.00
5 (7-9/53)-Stanley-a	5.00	15.00	35.00
6-10	3.50	10.50	24.00
11-20	2.85	8.50	20.00
21-30	2.35	7.00	16.00
31-49	2.00	6.00	14.00
. . .& the Little Men From Mars No. 30020-410(10/64-G.K.)-25 cents; 68 pgs.	5.00	15.00	40.00

NOTE: ***Lloyd White** did all art except F.C. 430, 444, 461, 5.*

MARGIE (See My Little. . .)

MARGIE (TV)
No. 1307, Mar-May, 1962 - No. 2, July-Sept, 1962 (Photo-c)
Dell Publishing Co.

	Good	Fine	Mint
4-Color 1307, 2	2.00	6.00	14.00

MARGIE COMICS (Formerly Comedy) (Reno Browne No. 50 on)
No. 35, Winter, 1946-47 - No. 49, Dec, 1949
Marvel Comics (ACI)

	Good	Fine	Mint
35	3.35	10.00	23.00
36-38,42,45,47-49	1.65	5.00	11.50
39,41,43(2),44,46-Kurtzman's "Hey Look"	2.50	7.50	17.50
40-Three "Hey Looks," three "Giggles & Grins" by Kurtzman	3.75	11.25	26.00

MARINES (See Tell It to the. . .)

MARINES ATTACK
Aug, 1964 - No. 9, Feb-Mar, 1966
Charlton Comics

	Good	Fine	Mint
1		.40	.80
2-9		.30	.60

MARINES AT WAR (Tales of the Marines No. 4)
No. 5, April, 1957 - No. 7, Aug, 1957
Atlas Comics (OPI)

	Good	Fine	Mint
5-7	.50	1.50	3.50

NOTE: ***Colan** a-5. **Drucker** a-5. **Everett** a-5. **Maneely** a-5. **Orlando** a-7. **Severin** c-5.*

MARINES IN ACTION
June, 1955 - No. 14, Sept, 1957
Atlas News Co.

	Good	Fine	Mint
1-Rock Murdock, Boot Camp Brady begin	1.50	4.50	10.00
2-14	.70	2.00	5.00

NOTE: ***Berg** a-2, 8, 9, 11, 14. **Heath** c-2, 9. **Severin** a-4; c-7-11, 14.*

MARINES IN BATTLE
Aug, 1954 - No. 25, Sept, 1958
Atlas Comics (ACI No. 1-12/WPI No. 13-25)

	Good	Fine	Mint
1-Heath-c; Iron Mike McGraw by Heath; history of U.S. Marine Corps. begins	2.65	8.00	18.00
2	1.30	4.00	9.00
3-6,8-10: 4-Last precode (2/55)	1.15	3.50	8.00
7-Six pg. Kubert/Moskowitz-a	1.70	5.00	12.00
11-16,18-22,24	.70	2.00	5.00
7-Williamson-a, 3 pgs.	3.00	9.00	21.00
23-Crandall-a; Mark Murdock app.	1.70	5.00	12.00
25-Torres-a	1.70	5.00	12.00

NOTE: ***Berg** a-22. **Drucker** a-6. **Everett** a-4, 15; c-21. **Maneely** c-24. **Orlando** a-14. **Pakula** a-6. **Powell** a-16. **Severin** c-12.*

MARINE WAR HEROES (Charlton Premiere No. 19)
Jan, 1964 - No. 18, Mar, 1967
Charlton Comics

	Good	Fine	Mint
1		.40	.80
2-18		.30	.60

NOTE: ***Montes/Bache** a-1,14,18; c-1.*

MARK, THE
Sept, 1987 - Present ($1.75, $1.95, color)
Dark Horse Comics

	Good	Fine	Mint
1	.30	.85	1.70
2,3	.35	1.00	1.95

MARK HAZZARD: MERC
Nov, 1986 - No. 12, Oct, 1987
Marvel Comics Group

	Good	Fine	Mint
1-Morrow-a begins		.60	1.20
2-12		.45	.90
Annual 1(11/87)		.60	1.25

MARK OF ZORRO (See 4-Color No. 228)

MARK STEEL
1967, 1968, 1972 (24 pgs.) (Color)
American Iron & Steel Institute (Giveaway)

	Good	Fine	Mint
1967,1968-"Journey of Discovery with. . ."; Neal Adams art	2.35	7.00	16.00
1972-". . .Fights Pollution;" Adams-a	1.35	4.00	8.00

MARK TRAIL
Oct, 1955 - No. 5, Summer, 1959
Standard Magazines (Hall Syndicate)/Fawcett Publ. No. 5

	Good	Fine	Mint
1-Sunday strip-r	3.70	11.00	26.00
2-5	1.85	5.50	13.00
. . .Adventure Book of Nature 1(Summer, 1958; Pines)-100 pg. Giant; contains 78 Sunday strip-r	4.60	14.00	32.00

MARMADUKE MONK
No date; 1963 (10 cents)
I. W. Enterprises/Super Comics

	Good	Fine	Mint
1-I.W. Reprint, 14-(Super Reprint)('63)		.60	1.20

MARMADUKE MOUSE
Spring, 1946 - No. 65, Dec, 1956
Quality Comics Group (Arnold Publ.)

	Good	Fine	Mint
1	4.60	14.00	32.00
2	2.30	7.00	16.00
3-10	1.70	5.00	12.00
11-30	1.30	4.00	9.00
31-65	1.00	3.00	7.00
Super Reprint #14(1963)		.60	1.20

MARS
Jan, 1984 - No. 12, Jan, 1985 (Mando paper)
First Comics

	Good	Fine	Mint
1-12: 2-The Black Flame begins. 10-Dynamo Joe begins		.50	1.00

MARS
Oct, 1987 - Present ($1.95, color)
Epic Comics (Marvel)

	Good	Fine	Mint
1	.35	1.00	2.00

MARS & BEYOND (See 4-Color No. 866)

MARSHAL LAW
Dec, 1987 - Present
Epic comics (Marvel)

	Good	Fine	Mint
1	.60	1.75	3.50
2,3	.35	1.00	2.00

Marge's Tubby #12, © WEST

Marines in Action #2, © MCG

Mark Trail's Adventure Book of Nature #1, © Pines

M.A.R.S. Patrol Total War #5, © WEST

Marvel Collectors' Item Classics #1, © MCG

Marvel Comics #1, © MCG

M.A.R.S. PATROL TOTAL WAR (Total War No. 1,2)
No. 3, Sept, 1966 - No. 10, Aug, 1969 (All-Painted-c)
Gold Key

	Good	Fine	Mint
3-Wood-a	1.50	4.50	10.00
4-10	.85	2.50	6.00

MARTHA WAYNE (See The Story of. . .)

MARTIN KANE (Formerly My Secret Affair) (Radio-TV)
No. 4, June, 1950 - No. 2, Aug, 1950
Fox Features Syndicate (Hero Books)

4(#1)-Wood-c/a(2); used in **SOTI**, pg. 160; photo back cvr.	14.00	42.00	100.00
2-Orlando-a, 5pgs; Wood-a(2)	8.50	25.50	60.00

MARTY MOUSE
No date (1958?) (10 cents)
I. W. Enterprises

1-Reprint		.60	1.20

MARVEL ADVENTURES (. . .Adventure No. 4 on)
Dec, 1975 - No. 6, Oct, 1976
Marvel Comics Group

1-No. 1-6 r-/Daredevil 22-27		.25	.50
2-6		.20	.40

MARVEL AND DC PRESENT (Featuring the Uncanny X-Men and the New Teen titans)
Nov, 1982 (One Shot, 68pgs, $2.00 cover, printed on Baxter paper)
Marvel Comics Group/DC Comics

1-Simonson/Austin c/a; Perez-a(p)	.75	2.25	4.50

MARVEL BOY (Astonishing #3 on; see Marvel Super Action #4)
Dec, 1950 - No. 2, Feb, 1951
Marvel Comics (MPC)

1-Origin Marvel Boy by Russ Heath	26.00	78.00	182.00
2-Everett-a	22.00	65.00	154.00

MARVEL CHILLERS
Oct, 1975 - No. 7, Oct, 1976
Marvel Comics Group

1-Intro. Modred the Mystic; Kane-c(p)		.30	.60
2-5,7: 3-Tigra, the Were-Woman begins (origin), ends No. 7. 7-Kirby-c, Tuska-p		.25	.50
6-Byrne-a(p); Buckler-c(p)		.50	1.00

MARVEL CLASSICS COMICS SERIES FEATURING. . . (Also see Pendulum Ill. Class.)
1976 - No. 36, Dec, 1978 (52 pgs., no ads)
Marvel Comics Group

1-Dr. Jekyll and Mr. Hyde		.50	1.00
2-27,29-36: 2-Time Machine, 3-Hunchback of Notre Dame, 4-20,000 Leagues Under the Sea, 5-Black Beauty, 6-Gulliver's Travels, 7-Tom Sawyer, 8-Moby Dick, 9-Dracula, 10-Red Badge of Courage, 11-Mysterious Island, 12-The Three Musketeers, 13-Last of the Mohicans, 14-War of the Worlds, 15-Treasure Island, 16-Ivanhoe, 17-The Count of Monte Cristo, 18-The Odyssey, 19-Robinson Crusoe, 20-Frankenstein, 21-Master of the World, 22-Food of the Gods, 23-The Moonstone, 24-She, 25-The Invisible Man, 26-The Illiad, 27-Kidnapped, 29-Prisoner of Zenda, 30-Arabian Nights, 31-First Man in the Moon, 32-White Fang, 33-The Prince and the Pauper, 34-Robin Hood, 35-Alice in Wonderland, 36-A Christmas Carol each. . . .		.30	.60
28-First M. Golden-a; The Pit and the Pendulum	.85	2.50	5.00

NOTE: ***Adkins** c-1i, 4i, 12i. **Alcala** a-34i; c-34. **Bolle** a-35. **Buscema** c-17p, 19p, 26p. **Golden** a-28. **Gil Kane** c-1-16p, 21p, 22p, 24p, 32p. **Nebres** a-5; c-24i. **Nino** a-2, 8, 12. **Redondo** a-1, 9. No. 1-12 were reprinted from Pendulum Ill. Classics.*

MARVEL COLLECTORS ITEM CLASSICS
1965 - No. 22, Aug, 1969 (Marvel's Greatest No. 23 on)
Marvel Comics Group(ATF)

	Good	Fine	Mint
1-Fantastic Four & other-r begin	1.00	3.00	6.00
2 (4/66) - 4	.40	1.25	2.50
5-22		.75	1.50

NOTE: *All reprints; **Ditko, Kirby** art in all.*

MARVEL COMICS (Marvel Mystery No. 2 on)
October, November, 1939
Timely Comics (Funnies, Inc.)

NOTE: The first issue was originally dated October 1939. Most copies have a black circle stamped over the date (on cover and inside) with "November" printed over it. However, some copies do not have the November overprint and could have a higher value. Most No. 1's have printing defects, i.e., tilted pages which caused trimming into the panels usually on right side and bottom. Covers exist with and without gloss finish.

	Good	Fine	VF-NM
1-Origin Sub-Mariner by Bill Everett(1st newsstand app.); 1st 8 pgs. was produced for **Motion Picture Funnies Weekly** #1 which was probably not distributed outside of advance copies; Human Torch by Carl Burgos, Kazar the Great, & Jungle Terror (only app.); intro. The Angel by Gustavson, The Masked Raider (ends #12); cover by sci/fi pulp illustrator Frank R. Paul	4200.00	12,600.00	27,000.00

(Only one known copy exists in Mint condition which traded twice in 1986 for $69,000 & later for $82,000, & once in 1987 for $82,000. Two other copies are known in NM-M condition & their value would vary beyond the VF-NM price)

MARVEL COMICS SUPER SPECIAL (Marvel Super Special #5 on; also see Howard the Duck #12) (Magazine) ($1.50)
September, 1977 - No. 41(?), Nov, 1986 (nn 7)
Marvel Comics Group

	Good	Fine	Mint
1-Kiss, 40 pgs. comics plus photos & features; Simonson-a(p)	3.00	9.00	21.00
2-Conan (3/78)	.50	1.50	3.00
3-Close Encounters of the Third Kind (6/78); Simonson-a	.35	1.00	2.00
4-The Beatles Story (8/78)-Perez/Janson-a	1.00	3.00	6.00
5-Kiss (12/78)	2.65	8.00	18.00
6-Jaws II (12/78)	.25	.75	1.50
8-Battlestar Galactica-tabloid size	.35	1.00	2.00
8-Battlestar Galactica publ. in reg. magazine format; low distribution ($1.50)8½x11"	.85	2.50	5.00
9-Conan	.35	1.00	2.00
10-Star Lord	.35	1.00	2.00
11-13-Weirdworld begins #11; 25 copy special press run of each with gold seal and signed by artists (Proof quality), Spring-June, 1979	10.00	30.00	60.00
11-Weirdworld (regular issue)	.70	2.00	4.00
12-Weirdworld (regular issue)	.40	1.25	2.50
13-Weirdworld (regular issue)	.30	.90	1.80
14-Adapts movie 'Meteor'		.60	1.20
15-Star Trek with photos & pin-ups($1.50)		.60	1.20
15-with $2.00 price(scarce); the price was changed at tail end of a 200,000 press run	.70	2.00	4.00
16-20: 16-'Empire Strikes Back'-Williamson-a, 17-Xanadu, 18-Raiders of the Lost Ark, 19-For Your Eyes Only (James Bond), 20-Dragonslayer each. . . .	.30	.90	1.80
21-40 (Movie adaptations): 21-Conan, 22-Bladerunner; Williamson-a; Steranko-c, 23-Annie, 24-The Dark Crystal, 25-Rock and Rule-w/photos, 26-Octopussy (James Bond), 27-Fire and Ice (Return of the Jedi), 28-Krull, 29-Tarzan of the Apes (Greystoke movie), 30-Indiana Jones and the Temple of Doom, 31-The Last Starfighter, 32-The Muppets Take Manhattan, 33-Buckaroo Bonzai, 34-Sheena, 35-Conan The Destroyer, 36-Dune, 37-2010, 38-Red Sonja-movie adapt., 39-Santa Claus: The Movie, 40-Labyrinth each. . . .	.35	1.00	2.00

MARVEL COMICS SUPER SPEC. (cont.) Good Fine Mint
41-Howard The Duck-movie adapt.(11/86) .45 1.25 2.50

NOTE: ***J. Buscema*** *a-1, 2, 9, 11-13, 18p, 21, 35, 40; c-11(part), 12.* ***Chaykin*** *a-9, 19p; c-18, 19.* ***Colan*** *a(p)-6, 10, 14.* ***Spiegle*** *a-29.*

MARVEL DOUBLE FEATURE
Dec, 1973 - No. 21, Mar, 1977
Marvel Comics Group

1-Captain America & Iron Man-r begin .30 .60
2-21: 17-r/Iron Man & Sub-Mariner No. 1 .25 .50

NOTE: ***Colan*** *a-1-19p(r).* ***Gil Kane*** *a-15p(r).* ***Kirby*** *a-1r, 2-8p(r), 17p(r); c-17-20.*

MARVEL FAMILY (Also see Captain Marvel No. 18)
Dec, 1945 - No. 89, Jan, 1954
Fawcett Publications

1-Origin Captain Marvel, Captain Marvel Jr., Mary Marvel, & Uncle Marvel retold; Black Adam origin & 1st app.
55.00 165.00 385.00
2 30.00 90.00 210.00
3 21.00 64.00 150.00
4,5 16.00 48.00 110.00
6-10: 7-Shazam app. 13.00 40.00 90.00
11-20 9.50 28.50 65.00
21-30 7.00 21.00 50.00
31-40 5.70 17.00 40.00
41-46,48-50 4.60 14.00 32.00
47-Flying Saucer c/stry 5.70 17.00 40.00
51-76,79,80,82-89 4.00 12.00 28.00
77-Communist Threat-c 6.50 19.50 45.00
78,81-Used in **POP**, pgs. 92,93 4.60 14.00 32.00

MARVEL FANFARE
March, 1982 - Present ($1.25-$1.50, slick paper) (Direct Sale only)
Marvel Comics Group

1-Spider-Man/Angel team-up; 1st Paul Smith story
1.35 4.00 8.00
2-Spider-Man, Ka-Zar, The Angel. F.F. origin retold
1.50 4.50 9.00
3-X-Men & Ka-Zar .85 2.50 5.00
4-X-Men & Ka-Zar 1.00 3.00 6.00
5-Dr. Strange, Capt. America .50 1.50 3.00
6-Spider-Man, Scarlet Witch .35 1.10 2.20
7-Incredible Hulk; Daredevil backup .35 1.10 2.20
8-Dr. Strange; Wolf Boy begins .35 1.10 2.20
9-Man-Thing by Morrow .35 1.10 2.20
10-13-Black Widow .35 1.10 2.20
14-The Vision .35 1.00 2.00
15-The Thing by Barry Smith, c/a .35 1.00 2.00
16,17-Skywolf .35 1.00 2.00
18-Capt. America; Miller c/a .25 .80 1.60
19-Cloak and Dagger .25 .80 1.60
20,21-The Thing/Incredible Hulk .25 .80 1.60
22,23-Iron Man vs. Dr. Octopus .25 .80 1.60
24-26-Weirdworld-Ploog/Russell-a .25 .80 1.60
27-37: 27-Daredevil/Spider-Man. 28-Alpha Flight. 29-Hulk. 30-Moon Knight. 31,32-Capt. America. 33-X-Men. 34-37-Warriors Three
.25 .75 1.50

NOTE: ***Art Adams*** *c-13.* ***Austin*** *a-1i, 4i, 33i; c-8i, 33i.* ***Byrne*** *a-1p, 29; c-29.* ***Golden*** *a-1, 2, 4p; c-1, 2.* ***Infantino*** *c/a(p)-8.* ***Gil Kane*** *a-8-11p.* ***Miller*** *c-1(Back-c).* ***Perez*** *a-10, 11p, 12, 13p; c-10p-13p.* ***Rogers*** *a-5p; c-5p.* ***Russell*** *a-5i, 6i, 8-11i; c-5i, 6.* ***Paul Smith*** *a-1p, 32, 4p; c-4p.* ***Williamson*** *a-30.*

MARVEL FEATURE (See Marvel Two-In-One)
Dec, 1971 - No. 12, Nov, 1973 (No. 1,2: 25 cents)
Marvel Comics Group

1-Origin The Defenders; Sub-Mariner, The Hulk & Dr. Strange; G.A. Sub-Mariner-r, Adams-c 1.35 4.00 8.00
2-G.A. 1950s Sub-Mariner-r .70 2.00 4.00
3-Defender series ends .70 2.00 4.00

Good Fine Mint
4-7: 4-Begin Ant-Man series; brief origin .50 1.00
8-Origin Antman & The Wasp .50 1.00
9,10-Last Ant-Man. 9-Iron Man app. .50 1.00
11,12-Thing team-ups. 11-Origin Fantastic-4 retold
.50 1.00

NOTE: ***Bolle*** *a-9i.* ***Everett*** *a-1i, 3i.* ***Kane*** *c-3p, 7p.* ***Russell*** *a-7-10p.* ***Starlin*** *a-8, 11, 12.*

MARVEL FEATURE (Also see Red Sonja)
Nov, 1975 - No. 7, Nov, 1976
Marvel Comics Group

1-Red Sonja begins; Adams r/Savage Sword of Conan #1
.25 .80 1.60
2-7 .50 1.00

NOTE: ***Thorne*** *c/a-2-7.*

MARVEL FUMETTI BOOK
April, 1984 (One shot) ($1.00 cover price)
Marvel Comics Group

1 .40 .80

MARVEL GRAPHIC NOVEL
1982 - Present ($5.95-$6.95)
Marvel Comics Group (Epic Comics)

1 (First Printing)-Death of Captain Marvel 2.50 7.50 15.00
1 (2nd & 3rd Printing) 1.00 3.00 6.00
2-Elric: The Dreaming City .85 2.50 5.00
3-Dreadstar; Starlin-a, 48pgs. 1.00 3.00 6.00
4-The New Mutants-Origin 1.35 4.00 8.00
5-X-Men; book-length story 1.35 4.00 8.00
6-The Star Slammers, 7-Killraven, 8-Super Boxers, 9-The Futurians
10-Heartburst, 11-Void Indigo, 12-The Dazzler, 13-Starstruck, 14-The Swords Of The Swashbucklers, 15-The Raven Banner (Asgard),
16-The Aladdin Effect, 17-Revenge Of The Living Monolith,
18-She Hulk 1.00 3.00 6.00
19-The Witch Queen of Acheron (Conan) 1.20 3.50 7.00
20-Greenberg the Vampire; Wrightson c/a 1.70 5.00 10.00
21-Marada The She-Wolf 1.20 3.50 7.00
22-Amaz. Spider-Man in Hooky by Wrightson 1.70 5.00 10.00
23-Dr. Strange. 24-Love And War by Miller. 26-Silver Surfer. 27-The Death of Groo. 28-Conan The Reaver. 29-The Big Chance (Thing vs. Hulk) 1.00 3.00 6.00
25-Dracula 1.20 3.50 7.00

NOTE: ***Aragones*** *a-27.* ***Byrne*** *c/a-18.* ***Kaluta*** *c/a-13.* ***Miller*** *a-23p.* ***Russell*** *c/a-2.* ***Simonson*** *a-5, 6; c-6.* ***Starlin*** *c/a-1,3.* ***Wrightson*** *c/a(painted)-20; c-29i.*

MARVEL MINI-BOOKS
1966 (50 pgs., B&W; 5/8''x7/8'') (6 different issues)
Marvel Comics Group (Smallest comics ever published)

Captain America, Spider-Man, Sgt. Fury, Hulk, Thor
.35 1.00 2.00
Millie the Model .50 1.00

NOTE: *Each came in six different color covers, usually one color: Pink, yellow, green, etc.*

MARVEL MOVIE PREMIERE (Magazine)
Sept, 1975 (One Shot) (Black & White)
Marvel Comics Group

1-Burroughs "The Land That Time Forgot" adaptation
.35 1.00 2.00

MARVEL MOVIE SHOWCASE
Nov, 1982 - No. 2, Dec, 1982 (68 pgs.)
Marvel Comics Group

1,2-Star Wars movie adaptation r/Star Wars #1-6
.60 1.20

MARVEL MOVIE SPOTLIGHT
Nov, 1982 (68 pgs.)
Marvel Comics Group

Marvel Family #77, © FAW

Marvel Fanfare #9, © MCG

Marvel Movie Showcase #2, © Lucasfilms

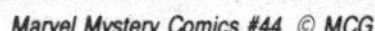
Marvel Mystery Comics #44, © MCG

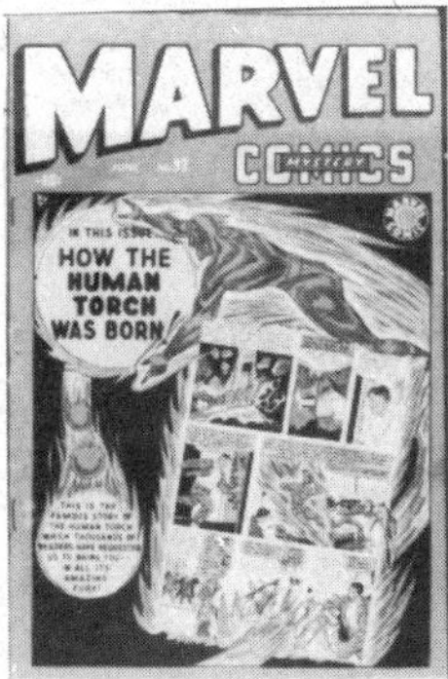

Marvel Mystery Comics #92, © MCG

Marvel Premiere #10, © MCG

Good Fine Mint

1-Edited r/Raiders of the Lost Ark #1-3; Buscema-c/a(p)
.40 .80

MARVEL MYSTERY COMICS (Formerly Marvel Comics) (Marvel Tales No. 93 on)
No. 2, Dec, 1939 - No. 92, June, 1949
Timely /Marvel Comics (TP 2-17/TCI 18-54/MCI 55-92)

2-American Ace begins, ends #3; Human Torch (blue costume) by Burgos, Sub-Mariner by Everett continues; 2pg. origin recap Human Torch 630.00 1890.00 4400.00
3-New logo from Marvel pulp begins 360.00 1080.00 2520.00
4-Intro. Electro, the Marvel of the Age (ends #19), The Ferret, Mystery Detective (ends #9) 290.00 870.00 2030.00
5 (Scarce) 455.00 1365.00 3185.00
6,7 180.00 540.00 1260.00
8-Human Torch & Sub-Mariner battle 235.00 700.00 1645.00
9-(Scarce)-Human Torch & Sub-Mariner battle
288.00 865.00 2015.00
10-Human Torch & Sub-Mariner battle, conclusion; Terry Vance, the Schoolboy Sleuth begins, ends #57 155.00 465.00 1085.00
11 115.00 345.00 800.00
12-Classic Kirby-c 115.00 345.00 800.00
13-Intro. & 1st app. The Vision by S&K; Sub-Mariner dons new costume, ends #15 130.00 390.00 910.00
14-16 80.00 240.00 560.00
17-Human Torch/Sub-Mariner team-up by Everett/Burgos; pin-up on back-c 92.00 275.00 645.00
18 74.00 220.00 520.00
19-Origin Toro in text 78.00 235.00 545.00
20-Origin The Angel in text 74.00 220.00 520.00
21-Intro. & 1st app. The Patriot; not in #46-48; pin-up on back-c
67.00 200.00 470.00
22-25: 23-Last Gustavson Angel; origin The Vision in text. 24-Injury-to-eye story 59.00 178.00 415.00
26-30: 27-Ka-Zar ends; last S&K Vision who battles Satan. 28-Jimmy Jupiter in the Land of Nowhere begins, ends #48; Sub-Mariner vs. The Flying Dutchman 52.00 156.00 365.00
31-Sub-Mariner by Everett ends, begins again #84
51.00 154.00 360.00
32-1st app. The Boboes 51.00 154.00 360.00
33,35-40: 40-Zeppelin-c 51.00 154.00 360.00
34-Everett, Burgos, Martin Goodman, Funnies, Inc. office appear in story & battles Hitler; last Burgos Human Torch
59.00 178.00 415.00
41-43,45-48-Last Vision & Flag-c 46.00 138.00 320.00
44-Classic Super Plane-c 46.00 138.00 320.00
49-Origin Miss America 59.00 178.00 415.00
50-Mary becomes Miss Patriot (origin) 45.00 135.00 315.00
51-60: 53-Bondage-c 41.00 122.00 285.00
61,62,64-Last German War-c 37.00 110.00 260.00
63-Classic Hitler War-c; The Villainess Cat-Woman only app.
37.00 110.00 260.00
65,66-Last Japanese War-c 37.00 110.00 260.00
67-75: 74-Last Patriot. 75-Young Allies begin 35.00 105.00 245.00
76-78: 76-10 Chapter Miss America serial begins, ends #85.
35.00 105.00 245.00
79-New cover format; Super Villains begin on cover; last Angel
31.50 95.00 220.00
80-1st app. Capt. America in Marvel Comics 35.00 105.00 245.00
81-Captain America app. 31.50 95.00 220.00
82-Origin Namora; 1st Sub-Mariner/Namora team-up; Captain America app. 53.00 160.00 370.00
83,85: 83-Last Young Allies. 85-Last Miss America; Blonde Phantom app. 31.50 95.00 220.00
84-Blonde Phantom, Sub-Mariner by Everett begins; Captain America app. 36.00 108.00 250.00

Good Fine Mint

86-Blonde Phantom i.d. revealed; Captain America app.; last Bucky app. 36.00 108.00 250.00
87-1st Capt. America/Golden Girl team-up 40.00 120.00 280.00
88-Golden Girl, Namora, & Sungirl (1st in Marvel Comics) x-over; Captain America, Blonde Phantom, Sun Girl app.; last Toro
36.00 108.00 250.00
89-1st Human Torch/Sun Girl team-up; 1st Captain America solo; Blonde Phantom app. 38.00 115.00 265.00
90-Blonde Phantom un-masked; Captain America app.
34.00 102.00 240.00
91-Capt. America app.; intro Venus; Blonde Phantom & Sub-Mariner end 34.00 102.00 240.00
92-Feature story on the birth of the Human Torch and the death of Professor Horton (his creator); 1st app. The Witness in Marvel Comics; Captain America app. 63.00 190.00 440.00
(Very rare) 132 Pg. issue, B&W, 25 cents (1943-44)-printed in N. Y.; square binding, blank inside covers; has Marvel No. 33-c in color; contains 2 Capt. America & 2 Marvel Mystery Comics-r (Two known copies) 250.00 750.00 1750.00

NOTE: ***Everett*** *c-7-9, 27, 84.* ***Schomburg*** *c-3-11, 13-15, 18, 19, 22-29, 33, 35, 36, 39-48, 50-57, 59, 63-66. Bondage covers-3, 4, 7, 12, 28, 29, 49, 50, 52, 56, 57, 65.*

MARVEL NO-PRIZE BOOK, THE
Jan, 1983 (One Shot, Direct Sale only)
Marvel Comics Group

1-Golden-c .50 1.00

MARVEL PREMIERE
April, 1972 - No. 61, Aug, 1981
Marvel Comics Group

1-Origin Warlock by Gil Kane/Adkins; origin Counter-Earth
1.00 3.00 6.00
2-Warlock ends; Kirby Yellow Claw-r .85 2.50 5.00
3-Dr. Strange series begins, Smith-a(p) 1.25 3.75 7.50
4-Smith/Brunner-a .70 2.00 4.00
5-10: 10-Death of the Ancient One .35 1.00 2.00
11-14: 11-Origin-r by Ditko. 14-Intro. God; last Dr. Strange
.30 .80 1.60
15-Iron Fist begins (origin), ends 25 .85 2.50 5.00
16-20 .35 1.00 2.00
21-24,26-28: 26-Hercules. 27-Satana. 28-Legion of Monsters
.25 .80 1.60
25-Byrne's 1st Iron Fist .85 2.50 5.00
29-56: 35-Origin/1st app. 3-D Man. 47-Origin new Ant-Man
.40 .80
57-Dr. Who (1st U.S. app.) .35 1.00 2.00
58-60-Dr. Who .25 .75 1.50
61-Star Lord .50 1.00

NOTE: ***Austin*** *a-50i, 56i; c-46i, 50i, 56i, 58.* ***Brunner*** *a-4i, 6p, 9-14p; c-9-14.* ***Byrne*** *a-47p, 48p.* ***Giffen*** *a-31p, 44p; c-44.* ***Gil Kane*** *a-1p, 2p, 15p; c-1p, 22-24p, 27p, 36p, 37p.* ***Kirby*** *c-26, 29-31, 35.* ***Layton*** *a-47i, 48i; c-47.* ***McWilliams*** *a-25i.* ***Miller*** *c-49p, 53p, 58p.* ***Nebres*** *a-44i; c-38i.* ***Nino*** *a-38i.* ***Perez*** *c/a-38p, 45p, 46p.* ***Ploog*** *a-38; c-5-7.* ***Russell*** *a-7p.* ***Simonson*** *a-60; c-57.* ***Starlin*** *a-8p; c-8.* ***Sutton*** *a-41, 43, 50p, 61; c-50p, 61. No. 57-60 were published with two different prices on cover.*

MARVEL PRESENTS
October, 1975 - No. 12, Aug, 1977
Marvel Comics Group

1-Bloodstone app. .40 .80
2-Origin Bloodstone; Kirby-c .30 .60
3-Guardians of the Galaxy .50 1.00
4-7,9,11,12-Guardians of the Galaxy .40 .80
8-Reprints Silver Surfer No. 2 .40 .80
10-Starlin-a(p) .40 .80

NOTE: ***Austin*** *a-6i.* ***Kane*** *c-1p.*

MARVEL PREVIEW (Magazine) (Bizarre Advs. No. 25 on)
Feb, 1975 - No. 24, Winter, 1980 (B&W) ($1.00)

MARVEL PREVIEW (continued)
Marvel Comics Group

	Good	Fine	Mint
1-Man Gods From Beyond the Stars; Adams-a(i) & cover; Nino-a	.70	2.00	4.00
2-Origin The Punisher (see Amaz. Spider-Man 129); 1st app. Dominic Fortune; Morrow-c	3.00	9.00	21.00
3-Blade the Vampire Slayer	.30	.90	1.80
4-Star-Lord & Sword in the Star (origins & 1st app.)	1.20	3.50	7.00
5,6-Sherlock Holmes	.50	1.50	3.00
7-9: 7-Satana, Sword in the Star app., 8-Legion of Monsters, 9-Man-God; origin Star Hawk, ends No.20	.35	1.00	2.00
10-Thor the Mighty; Starlin-a	.40	1.25	2.50
11-Star-Lord; Byrne-a	.40	1.25	2.50
12-20: 12-Haunt of Horror, 15-Star-Lord, 16-Detectives, 17-Black Mark by G. Kane, 18-Star-Lord, 19-Kull, 20-Bizarre Advs.		.50	1.00
21,22,24: 21-Moon Knight; Ditko-a, 22-King Arthur. 24-Debut Paradox		.50	1.00
23-Miller-a; Bizarre Advs.	.35	1.00	2.00

NOTE: ***Buscema*** *a-22, 23.* ***Byrne*** *a-11.* ***Colan*** *a-16p, 18p, 23p; c-16p.* ***Giffen*** *a-7.* ***Infantino*** *a-14.* ***Kaluta*** *a-12.* ***Miller*** *a-23.* ***Morrow*** *a-8i; c-2-4.* ***Perez*** *a-20p.* ***Ploog*** *a-8.* ***Starlin*** *c-13, 14.*

MARVEL SAGA, THE
Dec, 1985 - Present
Marvel Comics Group

	Good	Fine	Mint
1	.35	1.00	2.00
2,3	.25	.75	1.50
4-10		.55	1.10
11-25		.50	1.00

MARVEL'S GREATEST COMICS (Marvel Coll. Item Classics #1-22)
No. 23, Oct, 1969 - No. 96, Jan, 1981
Marvel Comics Group

	Good	Fine	Mint
23-34,38-96		.25	.50
35-37-Silver Surfer-r/Fantastic Four #48-50		.40	.80

NOTE: *Dr. Strange, Fantastic-4, Iron Man, Watcher-#23,24. Capt. America, Dr. Strange, Iron Man, Fantastic-4-#25-28. Fantastic Four-#38-60.* ***Buscema*** *a-85-92r; c-87-92r.* ***Ditko*** *a-23-28r.* ***Kirby*** *a(r)-1-82; c-75, 77p, 80p.*

MARVELS OF SCIENCE
March, 1946 - No. 4, June, 1946
Charlton Comics

	Good	Fine	Mint
1-(1st Charlton comic)-A-Bomb sty	6.00	18.00	42.00
2-4	3.00	9.00	21.00

MARVEL SPECIAL EDITION (Also see Special Collectors' Edition)
1975 - 1978 (84 pgs.) (Oversized)
Marvel Comics Group

	Good	Fine	Mint
1-Spider-Man(r); Ditko-a(r)	.25	.75	1.50
1-Star Wars ('77); r-Star Wars #1-3	.25	.75	1.50
2-Star Wars ('78); r-Star Wars #4-6		.50	1.00
3-Star Wars ('78, 116 pgs.); r-Star Wars #1-6		.50	1.00
3-Close Encounters ('78, 56 pgs., movie)		.50	1.00
V2No.2(Spr. '80, $2.00, oversized)-"Star Wars: The Empire Strikes Back;" r-/Marvel Comics S. Special 16		.50	1.00

NOTE: ***Chaykin*** *c/a-1(1977), 2, 3.*

MARVEL SPECTACULAR
Aug, 1973 - No. 19, Nov, 1975
Marvel Comics Group

	Good	Fine	Mint
1-Thor-r begin by Kirby		.30	.60
2-19		.25	.50

MARVEL SPOTLIGHT
11/71 - No. 33, 4/77; 7/79 - V2No. 11, 3/81
Marvel Comics Group

	Good	Fine	Mint
1-Origin Red Wolf; Wood inks, Adams-c	.45	1.30	2.60
2-(Giant, 52pgs.)-Venus-r by Everett; origin Werewolf by Ploog; Adams-c	.30	.90	1.80
3,4-Werewolf ends No. 4		.60	1.20
5-Origin/1st app. Ghost Rider	1.35	4.00	8.00
6-8-Last Ploog issue	.50	1.50	3.00
9-11-Last Ghost Rider	.25	.75	1.50
12-20: 12-The Son of Satan begins (Origin)		.40	.80
21-27: 25-Sinbad. 26-Scarecrow. 27-Sub-Mariner		.30	.60
28,29-Moon Knight	.50	1.50	3.00
30-The Warriors Three, 31-Nick Fury		.30	.60
32-Intro/partial origin Spider-Woman		.50	1.00
33-Deathlok		.40	.80
V2#1-7,9-11: Capt. Marvel #1-4. 5-Dragon Lord. 6,7-StarLord; origin #6. 9-11-Capt. Universe app.		.30	.60
8-Capt. Marvel; Miller a(p)	.35	1.00	2.00

NOTE: ***Austin*** *c-V2/2i, 8.* ***J. Buscema*** *c/a-30p.* ***Ditko*** *a-V2/4, 5, 9-11; c-V2/4, 9-11.* ***Kane*** *c-21p, 32p.* ***Kirby*** *c-29.* ***McWilliams*** *a-20i.* ***Miller*** *a-V2/8p; c-V2/2, 5p, 7p, 8p.* ***Mooney*** *a-8i, 10i, 14-17p, 24p, 27, 32i.* ***Nasser*** *a-33i.* ***Ploog*** *a-2-5, 6-8p; c-3-9.* ***Sutton*** *a-9-11p, V2/6, 7. No. 29-25 cent & 30 cent issues exist.*

MARVEL SUPER ACTION (Magazine)
January, 1976 (One Shot) (76 pgs.; black & white)
Marvel Comics Group

	Good	Fine	Mint
1-Origin & 2nd app. Dominic Fortune; The Punisher app., Weird World & The Huntress; Evans & Ploog-a	.70	2.00	4.00

MARVEL SUPER-ACTION
May, 1977 - No. 37, Nov, 1981
Marvel Comics Group

	Good	Fine	Mint
1-Capt. America-r by Kirby begin		.30	.60
2-5: 4-Marvel Boy-r(origin)/M. Boy #1		.25	.50
6-37: 11-C.A. Origin-r. 14-37-Avengers-r		.25	.50

NOTE: ***Buscema*** *a(r)-14p, 15p; c-18-20, 22, 35r-37.* ***Evans*** *a-1.* ***Everett*** *a-4.* ***Heath*** *a-4.* ***Ploog*** *a-1.* ***Smith*** *a-27r, 28r.* ***Steranko*** *a(r)-12p, 13p; c-12, 13.*

MARVEL SUPER-HERO CONTEST OF CHAMPIONS
June, 1982 - No. 3, Aug, 1982 (Mini-Series)
Marvel Comics Group

	Good	Fine	Mint
1-Features nearly all Marvel characters currently appearing in comics	.85	2.50	5.00
2	.70	2.00	4.00
3	.85	2.50	5.00

MARVEL SUPER HEROES
October, 1966
Marvel Comics Group

	Good	Fine	Mint
1-r-origin Daredevil; Avengers-r; G.A. Sub-Mariner & H. Torch-r/M. Mystery No. 8	.60	1.75	3.50

MARVEL SUPER-HEROES (Fantasy Masterpieces #1-11)
(Also see Giant Size Super Heroes)
No. 12, 12/67 - No. 31, 11/71; No. 32, 9/72 - No. 105, 1/82
Marvel Comics Group

	Good	Fine	Mint
12-Origin & 1st app. Capt. Marvel of the Kree; G.A. H. Torch, Destroyer, Capt. America, Black Knight, Sub-Mariner-r	.60	1.75	3.50
13-G.A. Black Knight, Torch, Vision, Capt. America, Sub-Mariner-r; Capt. Marvel app.	.25	.75	1.50
14-G.A. Sub-Mariner, Torch, Mercury, Black Knight, Capt. America reprints; Spider-Man app.	.25	.75	1.50
15-Black Bolt cameo in Medusa; G.A. Black Knight, Sub-Mariner, Black Marvel, Capt. America-r	.25	.75	1.50
16-Origin & 1st app. Phantom Eagle; G.A. Torch, Capt. America, Black Knight, Patriot, Sub-Mariner-r		.40	.80
17-Origin Black Knight; G.A. Torch, Sub-Mariner, All-Winners Squad reprints		.40	.80
18-Origin Guardians of the Galaxy; G.A. Sub-Mariner, All-Winners Squad-r	.40	1.20	2.40

Marvel Preview #21, © MCG

Marvel Spotlight #4 (1st series), © MCG

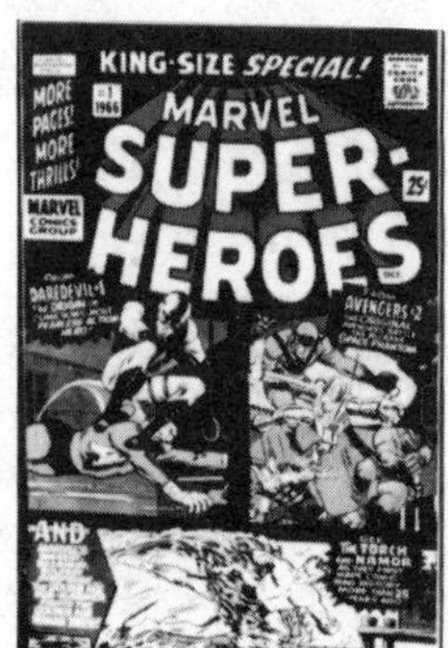

Marvel Super Heroes #1, © MCG

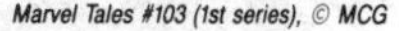
Marvel Tales #103 (1st series), © MCG

Marvel Tales #2 (2nd series), © MCG

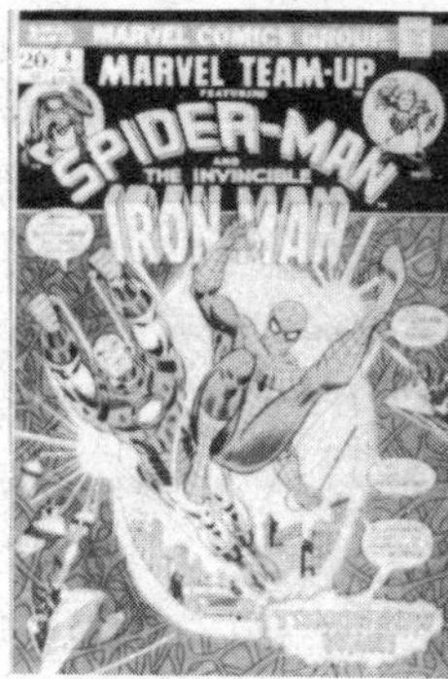

MARVEL COMICS GROUP
MARVEL TEAM-UP
SPIDER-MAN
THE INVINCIBLE
IRON MAN

Marvel Team-Up #9, © MCG

MARVEL SUPER-HEROES (continued)

	Good	Fine	Mint
19-G.A. Torch, Marvel Boy, Black Knight, Sub-Mariner-r; Smith-c(p) Tuska-a(r)		.40	.80
20-Reprints Young Men #24 w/-c		.40	.80
21-105: All-r ish. 31-Last Giant ish.		.25	.50

NOTE: ***Austin*** *a-104.* ***Colan*** *a-12p, 13p, 15p, 18p; c-12, 13, 15, 18.* ***Everett*** *a-14i, 15i(r), 18r, 19r, 33r; c-85(r). New* ***Kirby*** *c-22, 27.* ***Maneely*** *a-15r, 19r.* ***Severin*** *a-83-85i(r), 100-02r; c-100-02r.* ***Starlin*** *c-47.* ***Tuska*** *a-19p.*

MARVEL SUPER-HEROES SECRET WARS (See Secret Wars II)
May, 1984 - No. 12, Apr, 1985 (Limited series)
Marvel Comics Group

	Good	Fine	Mint
1	.60	1.75	3.50
2-4	.35	1.10	2.20
5-7: 6-The Wasp dies. 7-Intro. new Spider-Woman	.35	1.00	2.00
8-Spider-Man's new costume explained	.40	1.25	2.50
9-12	.35	1.00	2.00

MARVEL SUPER SPECIAL (See Marvel Comics Super. . .)

MARVEL TAILS STARRING PETER PORKER THE SPECTACULAR SPIDER-HAM
Nov, 1983 (One Shot)
Marvel Comics Group

	Good	Fine	Mint
1-Peter Porker, the Spectacular Spider-Ham, Captain Americat, Goose Rider, Hulk Bunny app.		.30	.60

MARVEL TALES (Marvel Mystery No. 1-92)
No. 93, Aug, 1949 - No. 159, Aug, 1957
Marvel/Atlas Comics (MCI)

	Good	Fine	Mint
93	27.00	81.00	190.00
94-Everett-a	22.00	65.00	154.00
95,96,99,101,103,105: 96-Bondage-c	11.00	33.00	76.00
97-Sun Girl, 2 pgs; Kirbyish-a; one story used in N.Y. State Legislative document	16.50	50.00	115.00
98-Krigstein-a	12.00	36.00	84.00
100	12.00	36.00	84.00
102-Wolverton-a "The End of the World," 6 pgs.	24.00	74.00	170.00
104-Wolverton-a "Gateway to Horror," 6 pgs; Heath-c	22.00	65.00	154.00
106,107-Krigstein-a. 106-Decapitation story	11.00	32.00	76.00
108-120: 120-Jack Katz-a	5.70	17.00	40.00
121,123-131: 128-Flying Saucer-c. 131-Last precode (2/55)	5.00	15.00	35.00
122-Kubert-a	6.00	18.00	42.00
132,133,135-141,143,145	3.00	9.00	21.00
134-Krigstein, Kubert-a; flying saucer-c	4.60	14.00	32.00
142-Krigstein-a	4.00	12.00	28.00
144-Williamson/Krenkel-a, 3 pgs.	4.60	14.00	32.00
146,148-151,154,155,158	2.00	6.00	14.00
147-Ditko-a	3.50	10.50	24.00
152-Wood, Morrow-a	3.70	11.00	26.00
153-Everett End of World c/story	3.50	10.50	24.00
156-Torres-a	3.00	9.00	21.00
157,159-Krigstein-a	4.00	12.00	28.00

NOTE: ***Andru*** *a-103.* ***Briefer*** *a-118.* ***Check*** *a-147.* ***Colan*** *a-105, 107, 118, 120, 121, 127, 131.* ***Drucker*** *a-127, 135, 141, 146, 150.* ***Everett*** *a-98, 104, 106(2), 108(2), 131, 148, 151, 153, 155; c-109, 111, 114, 117, 127, 143, 147-151, 153, 155, 156.* ***Forte*** *a-125, 130.* ***Heath*** *a-118, 119; c-104-106, 130.* ***Gil Kane*** *a-117.* ***Lawrence*** *a-130.* ***Maneely*** *a-111, 126, 129; c-108, 116, 120, 129, 152.* ***Mooney*** *a-114.* ***Morrow*** *a-150, 152, 156.* ***Orlando*** *a-149, 151, 157.* ***Pakula*** *a-121, 144, 150, 152, 156.* ***Powell*** *a-136, 137, 150, 154.* ***Rico*** *a-97, 99.* ***Romita*** *a-108.* ***Sekowsky*** *a-96-98.* ***Sinnott*** *a-105.* ***Tuska*** *a-114* ***Whitney*** *a-107.* ***Wildey*** *a-126, 138.*

MARVEL TALES (. . .Annual #1,2: . . .Starring Spider-Man #123 on)
1964 - Present (No. 1-32, 72 pgs.)
Marvel Comics Group

	Good	Fine	Mint
1-Origin Spider-Man, Hulk, Ant/Giant Man, Iron Man, Thor, & Sgt. Fury; all-r	7.50	22.50	52.00
2 ('65)-r-X-Men #1(origin), Avengers #1(origin) & origin Dr. Strange/Str. Tales #115	2.65	8.00	18.00
3 (7/66)-Spider-Man-r begin	1.00	3.00	6.00
4,5	.60	1.75	3.50
6-10	.50	1.50	3.00
11-15: 13-Origin Marvel Boy-r/M. Boy #1	.25	.75	1.50
16-30: 30-New Angel story	.25	.75	1.50
31-74,76,80-97		.40	.80
75-Origin Spider-Man-r		.50	1.00
77-79-Drug issues-r/Spider-Man No. 96-98		.50	1.00
98-Death of Gwen Stacy-r/A. Spider-Man #121		.60	1.20
99-Death Green Goblin-r/A. Spider-Man #122		.60	1.20
100-(52 pgs.)-New Hawkeye/Two Gun Kid sty		.40	.80
101-105,107-133-All Spider-Man-r		.35	.70
106-1st Punisher-r/A. Spider-Man #129	.70	2.00	4.00
134-136-Dr. Strange-r begin; SpM stories continue. 134-Dr. Strange r/Strange Tales 110		.35	.70
137-Origin-r Dr. Strange; shows original unprinted-c & origin Spider-Man/Amazing Fantasy 15		.50	1.00
137-Nabisco giveaway		.50	1.00
138-Reprints all Amazing Spider-Man #1		.50	1.00
139-144: r-/Amazing Spider-Man #2-7 with original covers		.40	.80
145-190: Spider-Man-r		.40	.80
191 (68 pgs., $1.50)-r-Spider-Man 96-98		.40	.80
192 (52 pgs., $1.25)-r-Spider-Man 121,122		.40	.80
193-199		.40	.80
200-Double size ($1.25)-Miller c/a(p)		.65	1.30
201-208,210		.40	.80
209-Reprints 1st app The Punisher/Amazing Spider-Man #129	.25	.75	1.50

NOTE: *All are reprints.* ***Austin*** *a-100i.* ***Byrne*** *a-193p-198p, 201p-206p.* ***Ditko*** *a-1-30, 83, 100, 137-55.* ***G. Kane*** *a-71, 81, 98-101p; c-125-127p, 130p, 137-55.* ***Mooney*** *a-63, 95-97i, 103(i).* ***Nasser*** *a-100p.*

MARVEL TEAM-UP (See Marvel Treas. Ed. #18 & Official Marvel Index To. . .)
March, 1972 - No. 150, Feb, 1985
Marvel Comics Group

NOTE: *Spider-Man team-ups in all but Nos. 18,23,26,29,32,35,97,104,105,137.*

	Good	Fine	Mint
1-H-T	3.35	10.00	20.00
2,3-H-T	1.50	4.50	9.00
4-X-Men	1.65	5.00	10.00
5-10: 5-Vision. 6-Thing. 7-Thor. 8-The Cat. 9-Iron Man. 10-H-T	.75	2.25	4.50
11-20: 11-Inhumans. 12-Werewolf. 13-Capt. America. 14-Sub-Mariner 15-Ghost Rider (new.). 16-Capt. Marvel. 17-Mr. Fantastic. 18-H-T/Hulk. 19-Ka-Zar. 20-Black Panther	.50	1.50	3.00
21-30: 21-Dr. Strange. 22-Hawkeye. 23-H-T/Iceman. 24-Brother Voodoo. 25-Daredevil. 26-H-T/Thor. 27-Hulk. 28-Hercules. 29-H-T/Iron Man. 30-Falcon	.35	1.00	2.00
31-40: 31-Iron Fist. 32-H-T/Son of Satan. 33-Nighthawk. 34-Valkyrie. 35-H-T/Dr. Strange. 36-Frankenstein. 37-Man-Wolf. 38-Beast. 39-H-T. 40-Sons of the Tiger/H-T	.25	.75	1.50
41-50: 41-Scarlet Witch. 42-The Vision. 43-Dr. Doom; retells origin. 44-Moondragon. 45-Killraven. 46-Deathlok. 47-Thing. 48-Iron Man. 49,50-Dr. Strange/Iron Man		.60	1.20
51,52,56-58: 51-Dr. Strange/Iron Man. 52-Capt. America. 56-Daredevil. 57-Black Widow. 58-Ghost Rider		.50	1.00
53-Woodgod/Hulk; new X-Men, 1st by Byrne	1.20	3.50	7.00
54-Hulk/Woodgod; Byrne-a(p)	.70	2.00	4.00
55,59,60: 55-Warlock. 59-Yellowjacket/The Wasp. 60-The Wasp-All Byrne-a	.70	2.00	4.00

61-70: 61-H-T. 62-Ms. Marvel. 63-Iron Fist. 64-Daughters of the Dragon. 65-Capt. Britain (1st U.S. app.). 66-Capt. Britain; 1st

MARVEL TEAM-UP (continued) Good Fine Mint

app. Arcade. 67-Tigra. 68-Man-Thing. 69-Havock. 70-Thor-All Bryne-a .45 1.25 2.50

71,72,76: 71-Falcon. 72-Iron Man. 76-Dr. Strange. Byrne-c .50 1.00

73,77,78,80: 73-Daredevil. 77-Ms. Marvel. 78-Wonder Man. 80-Dr. Strange/Clea .40 .80

74-Not Ready for Prime Time Players (Belushi) .40 .80

75,79: 75-Power Man. 79-Mary Jane Watson as Red Sonja. Both Byrne-a(p) .45 1.25 2.50

81-88,90: 81-Satana. 82-Black Widow. 83-Nick Fury. 84-Shang-Chi. 85-Shang-Chi/Black Widow/Nick Fury. 86-Guardians of the Galaxy. 87-Black Panther. 88-The Invisible Girl. 90-Beast .40 .80

89-Nightcrawler .25 .75 1.50

91-99: 91-Ghost Rider. 92-Hawkeye. 93-Werewolf by Night. 94-SpM vs. The Shroud. 95-Nick Fury/Shield; intro. Mockingbird. 96-Howard The Duck. 97-Spider-Woman/Hulk. 98-Black Widow. 99-Machine Man .40 .80

100-Fantastic-4(Double size); origin/1st app. Karma, one of the New Mutants; origin Storm; X-Men x-over; Miller-a/c(p); Byrne-a 1.00 3.00 6.00

101-116: 101-Nighthawk(Ditko-a). 102-Doc Samson. 103-Ant-Man. 104-Hulk/Ka-Zar. 105-Hulk/Powerman/Iron Fist. 106-Capt. America. 107-She-Hulk. 108-Paladin; Dazzler cameo. 109-Paladin/Dazzler. 110-Iron Man. 111-Devil-Slayer. 112-King Kull. 113-Quasar. 114-Falcon. 115-Thor. 116-Valkyrie .40 .80

117-Wolverine .50 1.50 3.00

118-Professor X .25 .75 1.50

119-149: 118-Professor X. 119-Gargoyle. 120-Dominic Fortune. 121-Human Torch. 122-Man-Thing. 123-Daredevil. 124-The Beast. 125-Tigra. 126-Hulk & Powerman/Son of Satan. 127-The Watcher. 128-Capt. America. 129-The Vision. 130-Scarlet Witch. 131-Frogman. 132-Mr. Fantastic. 133-Fantastic-4. 134-Jack of Hearts. 135-Kitty Pryde; X-Men cameo. 136-Wonder Man. 137-Aunt May/Franklin Richards. 138-Sandman. 139-Nick Fury, 140-Black Widow. 141-Daredevil; new SpM/Black Widow app. 142-Captain Marvel. 143-Starfox. 144-Moon Knight. 145-Iron Man. 146-Nomad. 147-Human Torch; SpM old costume. 148-Thor. 149-Cannonball .40 .80

150-X-Men ($1.00); B. Smith-c .50 1.50 3.00

Annual 1(1976)-New X-Men app. 1.30 4.00 8.00

Annual 2(12/79)-SpM/Hulk .25 .75 1.50

Annual 3(11/80)-Hulk/Power Man/Machine Man/Iron Fist; Miller-c(p) .60 1.20

Annual 4(10/81)-SpM/Daredevil/Moon Knight/Power Man/Iron Fist; brief origins of each; Miller-c(p)/a .35 1.00 2.00

Annual 5(1982)-SpM/The Thing/Scarlet Witch/Dr. Strange/Quasar .50 1.00

Annual 6(10/83)-New Mutants, Cloak & Dagger app. .25 .75 1.50

Annual 7(10/84)-Alpha Flight; Byrne-c(i) .50 1.00

NOTE: ***Art Adams*** *c-141p.* ***Austin*** *a-79i; c-76i, 79i, 96i, 101i, 112i, 130i.* ***Bolle*** *a-9i.* ***Byrne*** *a(p)-53-55, 59-70, 75, 79, 100; c-68p, 70p, 72p, 75, 76p, 79p, 129i, 133i.* ***Colan*** *a-87p.* ***Ditko*** *a-101.* ***Kane*** *a(p)-4-6, 13, 14, 16-19, 23; c(p)-4, 13, 14, 17-19, 23, 25, 26, 32-35, 37, 41, 44, 45, 47, 53, 54.* ***Miller*** *c-95p, 99p, 102p, 106.* ***Mooney*** *a-2i, 7i, 8, 10p, 11p, 16i, 24p, 29p, 72, 93i, Annual 5i.* ***Nasser*** *a-89p; c-101p.* ***Simonson*** *c-99i, 148.* ***Paul Smith*** *c-131, 132.* ***Starlin*** *c-27.* ***Sutton*** *a-93p. "H-T" means Human Torch; "SpM" means Spider-Man; "S-M" means Sub-Mariner.*

MARVEL TREASURY EDITION ($1.50-$2.50)
Sept, 1974 - No. 28, 1981 (100 pgs.; oversized, reprints)
Marvel Comics Group

1-Spider-Man .35 1.00 2.00

2-Fantastic Four, Silver Surfer .50 1.00

3-The Mighty Thor .50 1.00

4-Conan; Smith-c/a .25 .75 1.50

5-14,16,17: 5-The Hulk (origin), 6-Doctor Strange, 7-Avengers, 8-Christmas stories; Spider-Man, Hulk, Nick Fury, 9-Giant; Super-hero Team-up, 10-Thor, 11-Fantastic Four, 12-Howard the Duck, 13-Giant Super-hero Holiday Grab-Bag, 14-Spider-Man, 16-Super-hero Team-up; The Defenders (origin) & Valkyrie, 17-The Hulk .50 1.00

15-Conan; Smith, Adams-a .35 1.00 2.00

18-Marvel Team-up; Spider-Man's 1st team-ups with the X-Men .25 .75 1.50

19-28: 19-Conan the Barbarian, 20-Hulk, 21-Fantastic Four, 22-Spider-Man, 23-Conan, 24-Rampaging Hulk, 25-Spider-Man vs. The Hulk, 26-The Hulk; Wolverine app., 27-Spider-Man, 28-Spider-Man/Superman; (origin of each) .50 1.00

NOTE: *Reprints-2,3,5,7-9,13,14,16,17.* ***Adams*** *a-6(i), 15.* ***Brunner*** *a-6, 12; c-6.* ***Buscema*** *a-15, 19, 28; c-28.* ***Colan*** *c-12p.* ***Ditko*** *a-1, 6.* ***Kirby*** *a-2, 10, 11; c-7.* ***Smith*** *c/a-4.*

MARVEL TREASURY OF OZ (See MGM's Marvelous. . .)
1975 (oversized) ($1.50)
Marvel Comics Group

1-The Marvelous Land of Oz; Buscema-a .60 1.20

MARVEL TREASURY SPECIAL (Also see 2001: A Space Odyssey)
1974; 1976 (84 pgs.; oversized) ($1.50)
Marvel Comics Group

Vol. 1-Spider-Man, Torch, Sub-Mariner, Avengers "Giant Superhero Holiday Grab-Bag" .50 1.00

Vol. 1-Capt. America's Bicentennial Battles (6/76)-Kirby-a; Smith inks, 11 pgs. .50 1.00

MARVEL TRIPLE ACTION
2/72 - No. 24, 3/75; No. 25, 8/75 - No. 47, 4/79
Marvel Comics Group

1-Giant (52 pgs.) .40 .80

2-4 .30 .60

5-47: 7-Starlin-c. 45,46-X-Men-r .25 .50

Giant-Size 1(5/75), 2(7/75) .25 .50

NOTE: *Fantastic Four reprints-No. 1-4; Avengers reprints-No. 5 on.* ***Buscema*** *a(r)-35p, 36p, 38p, 39p, 41, 42, 43p, 44p, 46p, 47p.* ***Ditko*** *a-2r; c-47.* ***Kirby*** *a(r)-1-4p.* ***Tuska*** *a(r)-40p, 43i, 46i, 47i.*

MARVEL TWO-IN-ONE (See The Thing)
January, 1974 - No. 100, June, 1983
Marvel Comics Group

1-Thing team-ups begin 1.20 3.50 7.00

2-4: 3-Daredevil app. .60 1.75 3.50

5-Guardians of the Galaxy .70 2.00 4.00

6-10 .50 1.50 3.00

11-20 .35 1.10 2.20

21-40: 29-2nd app. Spider-Woman .25 .70 1.40

41,42,44-49 .50 1.00

43,50,53-55-Byrne-a. 54-Death of Deathlok .45 1.25 2.50

51-Miller-a(p) .50 1.50 3.00

52-Moon Knight app. .35 1.00 2.00

56-82: 60-Intro. Impossible Woman. 61-63-Warlock app. .40 .80

83,84-Alpha Flight app. .50 1.50 3.00

85-99: 93-Jocasta dies. 96-X-Men cameo .30 .60

100-Double size, Byrne scripts .25 .75 1.50

Annual 1(6/76)-Liberty Legion x-over .30 .80 1.60

Annual 2(2/77)-Starlin c/a; Thanos dies 1.25 3.75 7.50

Annual 3(7/78), 4(9/79) .50 1.00

Annual 5(9/80), 6(10/81) .40 .80

Annual 7(10/82)-The Thing/Champion; Sasquatch, Colossus app. .50 1.00

NOTE: ***Austin*** *c-42i, 54i, 56i, 58i, 61i, 63i, 66i.* ***John Buscema*** *a-30p, 45; c-30p.* ***Byrne*** *a-43p, 50p, 53-55p; c-43, 53p, 56p, 98i, 99i.* ***Gil Kane*** *a-1p, 2p; c(p)-1-3, 9, 11, 14, 28.* ***Kirby*** *c-10, 12, 19p, 20, 25, 27.* ***Mooney*** *a-18i, 38i, 90i.* ***Nasser*** *a-70p.* ***Perez*** *a-56-58p, 60p, 64p, 65p; c-32p, 33p, 42p, 50-52p, 54p, 55p, 57p, 58p, 61-66p, 70p.* ***Roussos*** *a-Annual 1i.* ***Simonson*** *c-43i; Annual 6i.* ***Starlin*** *c-6, Annual 1.* ***Tuska*** *a-6p.*

Marvel Team-Up #100, © MCG

MARVEL COMICS GROUP
35¢
starring
AVENGERS
THE AVENGERS VS. THE X-MEN!

Marvel Triple Action #46, © MCG

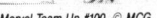

Marvel Two-In-One #100, © MCG

Mary Marvel Comics #12, © FAW

Masked Ranger #1, © PG

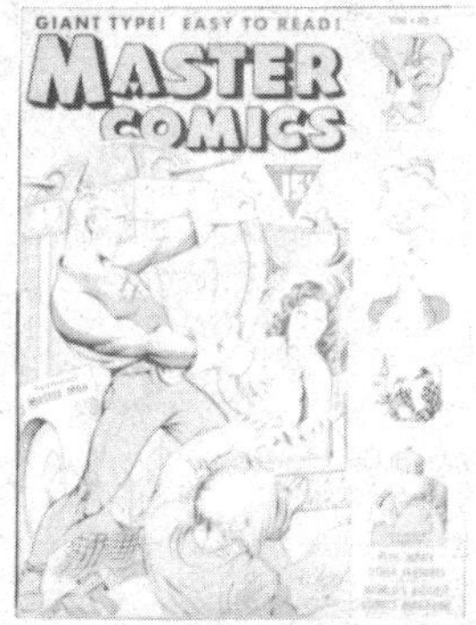

Master Comics #3, © FAW

MARVEL UNIVERSE (See Official Handbook. . .)

MARVIN MOUSE
September, 1957
Atlas Comics (BPC)

	Good	Fine	Mint
1-Everett c/a; Maneely-a	2.30	7.00	16.00

MARY JANE & SNIFFLES (See 4-Color No. 402,474)

MARY MARVEL COMICS (Monte Hale No. 29 on) (Also see Captain Marvel No. 18, Marvel Family, Shazam, & Wow)
Dec, 1945 - No. 28, Sept, 1948
Fawcett Publications

	Good	Fine	Mint
1-Intro/origin Georgia Sivana	50.00	150.00	350.00
2	25.00	75.00	175.00
3	18.00	54.00	125.00
4	14.00	42.00	100.00
5-8: 8-Bulletgirl x-over in Mary Marvel	12.00	36.00	84.00
9,10	9.50	28.00	65.00
11-20	7.00	21.00	50.00
21-28	6.00	18.00	42.00

MARY POPPINS (See Walt Disney Showcase No. 17 & Movie Comics)

MARY'S GREATEST APOSTLE (St. Louis Grignion de Montfort)
No date (16 pages; paper cover)
Catechetical Guild (Topix) (Giveaway)

	Good	Fine	Mint
	2.35	7.00	16.00

MARY WORTH (See Love Stories of. . . & Harvey Comic Hits No. 55)
March, 1956
Argo

	Good	Fine	Mint
1	3.15	9.50	22.00

MASK
Dec, 1985 - No. 4, Mar, 1986 (mini-series)
DC Comics

	Good	Fine	Mint
1-(Sat. morning TV show)	.35	1.00	2.00
2-4	.25	.70	1.40

MASK
Feb, 1987 - No. 9, Oct, 1987
DC Comics

	Good	Fine	Mint
1		.60	1.20
2-9		.45	.90

MASK COMICS
Feb-Mar, 1945 - No. 2, Apr-May, 1945; No. 2, Fall, 1945
Rural Home Publications

	Good	Fine	Mint
1-Classic L. B. Cole Satan-c/a; Palais-a	72.00	215.00	500.00
2-(Scarce)Classic L. B. Cole Satan-c; Black Rider, The Boy Magician, & The Collector app.	36.00	108.00	250.00
2(Fall, 1945)-No publ.-same as regular No. 2; L. B. Cole-c	26.00	78.00	180.00

MASKED BANDIT, THE
1952
Avon Periodicals

	Good	Fine	Mint
nn-Kinstler-a	8.50	25.50	60.00

MASKED MAN, THE
12/84 - No. 10, 4/86 ($1.75-$2.00; 32 pgs.; Baxter paper)
Eclipse Comics

	Good	Fine	Mint
1-Origin retold	.35	1.00	2.00
2-8: 3-Origin Aphid-Man	.30	.90	1.80
9,10 ($2.00; B&W)	.30	.90	1.80

MASKED MARVEL (See Keen Det. Funnies)
Sept, 1940 - No. 3, Dec, 1940
Centaur Publications

	Good	Fine	Mint
1-The Masked Marvel begins	68.00	205.00	475.00
2,3: 2-Gustavson, Tarpe Mills-a	43.00	130.00	300.00

MASKED RAIDER, THE (Billy The Kid #9 on; Frontier Scout, Daniel Boone #10-13; also see Blue Bird)
6/55 - No. 8, 7/57; No. 14, 8/58 - No. 30, 6/61
Charlton Comics

	Good	Fine	Mint
1-Painted-c	3.50	10.50	24.00
2	1.85	5.50	13.00
3-8: 8-Billy The Kid app.	1.50	4.50	10.00
14,16-30: 22-Rocky Lane app.	1.00	3.00	7.00
15-Williamson-a, 7 pgs.	2.35	7.00	16.00

MASKED RANGER
April, 1954 - No. 9, Aug, 1955
Premier Magazines

	Good	Fine	Mint
1-The M. Ranger, his horse Streak, & The Crimson Avenger (origin) begin, end #9; Woodbridge/Frazetta-a; Check-a	12.00	36.00	84.00
2,3	3.50	10.50	24.00
4-8-All Woodbridge-a. 5-Jesse James by Woodbridge. 6-Billy The Kid by Woodbridge. 7-Wild Bill Hickok by Woodbridge. 8-Jim Bowie's Life Story	4.35	13.00	30.00
9-Torres-a; Wyatt Earp by Woodbridge	5.00	15.00	35.00

NOTE: ***Woodbridge** c/a-1,4-9.*

MASK OF DR. FU MANCHU, THE (See Dr. Fu Manchu)
1951
Avon Periodicals

	Good	Fine	Mint
1-Sax Rohmer adapt.; Wood c/a, 26 pgs., Hollingsworth-a	85.00	255.00	595.00

MASQUE OF THE RED DEATH (See Movie Classics)

MASTER COMICS
Mar, 1940 - No. 133, Apr, 1953 (No. 1-6: oversized issues)
(#1-3, 15 cents, 52pgs.; #4-6, 10 cents, 36pgs.)
Fawcett Publications

	Good	Fine	Mint
1-Origin Masterman; The Devil's Dagger, El Carim, Master of Magic, Rick O'Say, Morton Murch, White Rajah, Shipwreck Roberts, Frontier Marshall, Streak Sloan, Mr. Clue begin (all features end #6)	135.00	405.00	950.00
2	65.00	195.00	455.00
3-5	38.00	115.00	265.00
6-Last Masterman	34.00	102.00	240.00

NOTE: *Issues 1-6 are rarely found in near mint to mint condition due to large-size format.*

	Good	Fine	Mint
7-(10/40)-Bulletman, Zorro, the Mystery Man (ends #22), Lee Granger, Jungle King, & Buck Jones begin; only app. The War Bird & Mark Swift & the Time Retarder	85.00	255.00	600.00
8-The Red Gaucho (ends #13), Captain Venture (ends #22) & The Planet Princess begin	40.00	120.00	280.00
9,10: 10-Lee Granger ends	35.00	105.00	245.00
11-Origin Minute-Man	68.00	205.00	475.00
12	46.00	140.00	320.00
13-Origin Bulletgirl	62.00	185.00	435.00
14-16: 14-Companions Three begins, ends #31	38.00	115.00	265.00
17-20: 17-Raboy-a on Bulletman begins. 20-Captain Marvel cameo app. in Bulletman	42.00	125.00	295.00
21-(Scarce)-Captain Marvel x-over in Bulletman; Capt. Nazi origin	171.00	515.00	1200.00
22-Captain Marvel Jr. x-over in Bulletman; Capt. Nazi app; bondage-c	140.00	420.00	980.00
23-Capt. Marvel Jr. begins, vs. Capt. Nazi	110.00	330.00	770.00
24,25,29	40.00	120.00	280.00
26-28,30-Captain Marvel Jr. vs. Capt. Nazi. 30-Flag-c	40.00	120.00	280.00

MASTER COMICS (continued)

	Good	Fine	Mint
31,32: 32-Last El Carim & Buck Jones; Balbo, the Boy Magician intro. in El Carim	28.00	84.00	195.00
33-Balbo, the Boy Magician (ends #47), Hopalong Cassidy (ends #49) begins	28.00	84.00	195.00
34-Capt. Marvel Jr. vs. Capt. Nazi	28.00	84.00	195.00
35	28.00	84.00	195.00
36-40: 40-Flag-c	26.00	78.00	180.00
41-Bulletman, Capt. Marvel Jr. & Bulletgirl x-over in Minute-Man; only app. Crime Crusaders Club (Capt. Marvel Jr., Minute-Man, Bulletman & Bulletgirl)-only team in Fawcett Comics	28.00	84.00	195.00
42-47,49: 47-Hitler becomes Corpl. Hitler Jr. 49-Last Minute-Man	16.00	48.00	110.00
48-Intro. Bulletboy; Capt. Marvel cameo in Minute-Man	16.50	50.00	115.00
50-Radar, Nyoka the Jungle Girl begin; Capt. Marvel x-over in Radar; origin Radar	11.00	32.00	76.00
51-58	7.00	21.00	50.00
59-62: Nyoka serial "Terrible Tiara" in all; 61-Capt. Marvel Jr. 1st meets Uncle Marvel	9.00	27.00	63.00
63-80	5.70	17.00	40.00
81-92,94-99: 88-Hopalong Cassidy begins (ends #94). 95-Tom Mix begins (ends #133)	5.00	15.00	35.00
93-Krigstein-a	5.50	16.50	38.00
100	5.70	17.00	40.00
101-106-Last Bulletman	3.70	11.00	26.00
107-131	3.50	10.50	24.00
132-B&W and color illos in **POP**	4.85	14.50	34.00
133-Bill Battle app.	5.70	17.00	40.00

NOTE: ***Mac Raboy*** *a-15-39, 40 in part, 42, 58; c-21-49, 51, 52, 54, 56, 58, 59.*

MASTER DETECTIVE
1964 (Reprint)
Super Comics

	Good	Fine	Mint
10,17,18: 17-Young King Cole; McWilliams-a	.40	1.20	2.40

MASTER OF KUNG FU (Formerly Special Marvel Edition)
No. 17, April, 1974 - No. 125, June, 1983
Marvel Comics Group

	Good	Fine	Mint
17-Starlin-a; intro Black Jack Tarr	.40	1.20	2.40
18-20: 19-Man-Thing app.	.35	1.00	2.00
21-23,25-30		.60	1.20
24-Starlin, Simonson-a	.25	.75	1.50
31-40: 33-1st Leiko Wu		.40	.80
41-99		.30	.60
100-(Double size)		.60	1.20
101-117,119-124: 104-Cerebus cameo		.30	.60
118,125-(Double size)		.50	1.00
Giant Size 1(9/74)-Russell-a; Yellow Claw-r	.25	.75	1.50
Giant Size 2-r/Yellow Claw #1		.60	1.20
Giant Size 3,4(6/75)-r/Yellow Claw		.60	1.20
Annual 1(4/76)-Iron Fist		.60	1.20

NOTE: ***Austin*** *c-63i, 74i.* ***Buscema*** *c-44p.* ***Gulacy*** *a(p)-18-20, 22, 25, 29-31, 33-35, 38, 39, 40(p&i), 42-50, Giant Size #1, 2; c-51, 55, 64, 67.* ***Gil Kane*** *c(p)-20, 38, 39, 42, 45, 59, 63.* ***Nebres*** *c-73i.* ***Starlin*** *a-17p; c-54.* ***Sutton*** *a-42i.*

MASTER OF THE WORLD (See 4-Color No. 1157)

MASTERS OF TERROR (Magazine)
July, 1975 - No. 2, Sept, 1975 (Black & White) (All Reprints)
Marvel Comics Group

	Good	Fine	Mint
1-Brunner, Smith-a; Morrow-c; Adams-a(i)(r); Starlin-a(p) Gil Kane-a	.30	.90	1.80
2-Reese, Kane, Mayerik-a; Steranko-c		.60	1.20

MASTERS OF THE UNIVERSE
Dec, 1982 - No. 3, Feb, 1983 (mini-series)
DC Comics

	Good	Fine	Mint
1		.60	1.20
2,3: 2-Origin He-Man & Ceril		.50	1.00

NOTE: ***Alcala*** *a-1i, 2i.* ***Tuska*** *a-1-3p; c-1-3p.* #2 has 75 & 95 cent cover price.

MASTERS OF THE UNIVERSE (Comic Album)
1984 (8½x11"; $2.95; 64 pgs.)
Western Publishing Co.

	Good	Fine	Mint
11362-Based on Mattel toy & cartoon	.50	1.50	2.95

MASTERS OF THE UNIVERSE (TV)
May, 1986 - Present
Star Comics (Marvel)

	Good	Fine	Mint
1		.55	1.10
2-7		.40	.80
8-12 ($1.00)		.50	1.00
...The Motion Picture (11/87, $2.00, Star Comics)	.35	1.00	2.00

MASTERWORKS SERIES OF GREAT COMIC BOOK ARTISTS, THE
May, 1983 - No. 3, Dec, 1983 (Baxter paper)
Sea Gate Distributors/DC Comics

	Good	Fine	Mint
1,2-Shining Knight by Frazetta r-/Adventure. 2-Tomahawk by Frazetta-r	.25	.75	1.50
3-Wrightson-c/a(r)	.25	.75	1.50

MATT SLADE GUNFIGHTER (Stories of Romance & Kid Slade Gunfighter No. 5 on?; See Western Gunfighters)
May, 1956 - No. 4, Nov, 1956
Atlas Comics (SPI)

	Good	Fine	Mint
1-Williamson/Torres-a	5.50	16.50	38.00
2-Williamson-a	4.00	12.00	28.00
3,4	2.00	6.00	14.00

MAUD
1906 (32 pgs. in color; 10x15½") (cardboard covers)
Frederick A. Stokes Co.

	Good	Fine	Mint
By Fred Opper	12.00	36.00	84.00

MAVERICK (TV)
No. 892, 4/58 - No. 19, 4-6/62 (All have photo-c)
Dell Publishing Co.

	Good	Fine	Mint
4-Color 892 (#1): James Garner/Jack Kelly photo-c begin	4.60	14.00	32.00
4-Color 930,945,962,980,1005 (6-8/59)	4.00	12.00	28.00
7 (10-12/59) - 14: Last Garner/Kelly-c	3.50	10.50	24.00
15-19: Jack Kelly/Roger Moore photo-c	3.50	10.50	24.00

MAVERICK MARSHAL
Nov, 1958 - No. 7, May, 1960
Charlton Comics

	Good	Fine	Mint
1	1.30	4.00	9.00
2-7	.70	2.00	5.00

MAX BRAND (See Silvertip)

MAYA (See Movie Classics)
March, 1968
Gold Key

	Good	Fine	Mint
1 (10218-803)(TV)	1.15	3.50	8.00

MAZIE (...& Her Friends) (See Tastee-Freez)
1953 - No. 12, 1954; No. 13, 12/54 - No. 22, 9/56; No. 23, 9/57 - No. 28, 8/58
Mazie Comics(Magazine Publ.)/Harvey Publ. No. 13-on

	Good	Fine	Mint
1	1.30	4.00	9.00
2	.70	2.00	5.00
3-10	.60	1.80	4.00
11-28	.25	.75	1.50

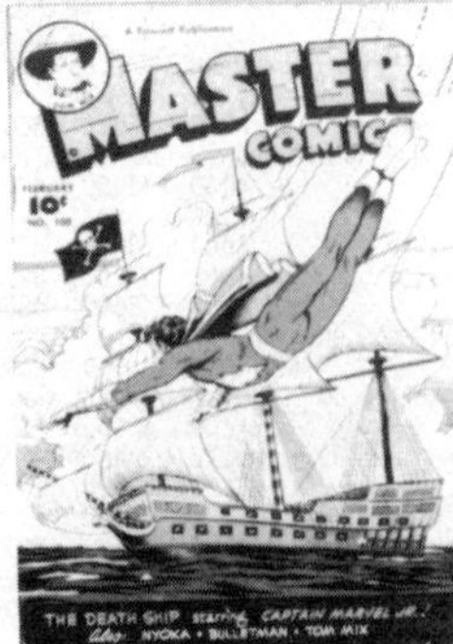

MASTER COMICS
10¢
THE DEATH SHIP starring CAPTAIN MARVEL JR.
Also NYOKA • BULLETMAN • TOM MIX

Master Comics #100, © FAW

Master of Kung-Fu #63, © MCG

Maverick #15, © Warner Bros.

'Mazing Man #1, © DC

MD #1, © WMG

Meet Miss Bliss #1, © MCG

MAZIE
1950 - 1951 (5 cents) (5x7¼"-miniature)(52 pgs.)
Nation Wide Publishers

	Good	Fine	Mint
1-Teen-age	1.15	3.50	8.00
2-7	.60	1.80	4.00

MAZING MAN
Jan, 1986 - No. 12, Dec, 1986
DC Comics

	Good	Fine	Mint
1		.50	1.00
2-11: 7,8-Hembeck-a		.40	.80
12-Dark Knight part-c by Miller		.50	1.00
Special 1('87), 2(4/88) (both $2.00)	.30	.90	1.80

McCRORY'S CHRISTMAS BOOK
1955 (36 pgs.; slick cover)
Western Printing Co. (McCrory Stores Corp. giveaway)

	Good	Fine	Mint
	1.35	4.00	8.00

McCRORY'S TOYLAND BRINGS YOU SANTA'S PRIVATE EYES
1956 (16 pgs.)
Promotional Publ. Co. (Giveaway)

	Good	Fine	Mint
Has 9 pg. story plus 7 pg. toy ads	1.00	3.00	6.00

McCRORY'S WONDERFUL CHRISTMAS
1954 (20 pgs.; slick cover)
Promotional Publ. Co. (Giveaway)

	Good	Fine	Mint
	1.35	4.00	8.00

McHALE'S NAVY (TV) (See Movie Classics)
May-July, 1963 - No. 3, Nov-Jan, 1963-64 (Photo-c)
Dell Publishing Co.

	Good	Fine	Mint
1	1.50	4.50	10.00
2,3	1.00	3.00	7.00

McKEEVER & THE COLONEL (TV)
Feb-Apr, 1963 - No. 3, Aug-Oct, 1963
Dell Publishing Co.

	Good	Fine	Mint
1-Photo-c	2.00	6.00	14.00
2,3	1.50	4.50	10.00

McLINTOCK (See Movie Comics)

MD
Apr-May, 1955 - No. 5, Dec-Jan, 1955-56
E. C. Comics

	Good	Fine	Mint
1-Not approved by code	5.75	17.50	40.00
2-5	4.35	13.00	30.00

NOTE: ***Crandall, Evans, Ingels, Orlando*** *art in all issues;* ***Craig*** *c-1-5.*

MECHA
June, 1987 - Present ($1.75, color)
Dark Horse Comics

	Good	Fine	Mint
1-3	.30	.90	1.80

MECHANICS
Oct, 1985 - No. 3, Dec, 1985 ($2.00 cover; adults only)
Fantagraphics Books

	Good	Fine	Mint
1-Love & Rockets in all	.60	1.75	3.50
2,3	.35	1.00	2.00

MEDAL FOR BOWZER, A
No date (1948-50?)
Will Eisner Giveaway

	Good	Fine	Mint
Eisner-c/script	14.00	42.00	100.00

MEDAL OF HONOR COMICS
Spring, 1946
A. S. Curtis

	Good	Fine	Mint
1	4.35	13.00	30.00

MEET ANGEL (Formerly Angel & the Ape)
No. 7, Nov-Dec, 1969
National Periodical Publications

	Good	Fine	Mint
7-Wood-a(i)	.25	.75	1.50

MEET CORLISS ARCHER (My Life No. 4 on)(Radio/Movie)
March, 1948 - No. 3, July, 1948
Fox Features Syndicate

	Good	Fine	Mint
1-Feldstein c/a	25.00	75.00	175.00
2-Feldstein-c only	18.00	54.00	125.00
3-Part Feldstein-c only	13.00	40.00	90.00

NOTE: *No. 1-3 used in* ***Seduction of the Innocent****, pg. 39.*

MEET HERCULES (See Three Stooges)

MEET HIYA A FRIEND OF SANTA CLAUS
1949 (18 pgs.?) (paper cover)
Julian J. Proskauer (Giveaway)

	Good	Fine	Mint
	3.00	9.00	18.00

MEET MERTON
Dec, 1953 - No. 4, June, 1954
Toby Press

	Good	Fine	Mint
1-Dave Berg-a	2.15	6.50	15.00
2-Dave Berg-a	1.15	3.50	8.00
3,4-Dave Berg-a	.85	2.50	6.00
I.W. Reprint #9		.50	1.00
Super Reprint #11('63), 18		.40	.80

MEET MISS BLISS
May, 1955 - No. 4, Nov., 1955
Atlas Comics (LMC)

	Good	Fine	Mint
1	3.50	10.50	24.00
2-4	1.70	5.00	12.00

MEET MISS PEPPER (Formerly Lucy. . .)
No. 5, April, 1954 - No. 6, June, 1954
St. John Publishing Co.

	Good	Fine	Mint
5-Kubert/Maurer-a	11.00	33.00	76.00
6-Kubert/Maurer-a; Kubert-c	8.50	25.50	60.00

MEET THE NEW POST GAZETTE SUNDAY FUNNIES
3/12/49 (16 pgs.; paper covers) (7¼x10¼")
Commercial Comics (insert in newspaper)
Pittsburgh Post Gazette

Dick Tracy by Gould, Gasoline Alley, Terry & the Pirates, Brenda Starr, Buck Rogers by Yager, The Gumps, Peter Rabbit by Fago, Superman, Funnyman by Siegel & Shuster, The Saint, Archie, & others done especially for this book. A fine copy sold at auction in 1985 for $276.00.

Estimated value. . . . $150—$300

MEGALITH
Mar, 1985 - Present
Continuity Comics

	Good	Fine	Mint
1,2-Neal Adams-a	.35	1.00	2.00

MEGATON
11/83; No. 2, 10/85 - Present (B&W)
Megaton Publ.

	Good	Fine	Mint
1,2 ($2.00)	.35	1.00	2.00
3-8 ($1.50)	.25	.75	1.50
V2#1,2 ($1.50, color)	.25	.75	1.50
Special 1,2 ($2.00, '87)	.35	1.00	2.00

MEGATON MAN
Dec, 1984 - No. 10, 1986 ($2.00; Baxter paper)
Kitchen Sink Enterprises

	Good	Fine	Mint
1-Silver-Age heroes parody	1.25	3.75	7.50
2	.45	1.25	2.50
3-10: 6-Border Worlds begins	.35	1.00	2.00

MEL ALLEN SPORTS COMICS
No. 5, Nov, 1949 - No. 6, Jan, 1950?
Standard Comics

	Good	Fine	Mint
5(#1 on inside)-Tuska-a	5.00	15.00	35.00
6	2.65	8.00	18.00

MELVIN MONSTER
Apr-June, 1965 - No. 10, Oct, 1969
Dell Publishing Co.

	Good	Fine	Mint
1-by John Stanley	6.00	18.00	42.00
2-10-All by Stanley. #10 r-/#1	4.00	12.00	28.00

MELVIN THE MONSTER (Dexter The Demon #7)
July, 1956 - No. 6, July, 1957
Atlas Comics (HPC)

	Good	Fine	Mint
1	2.65	8.00	18.00
2-6: 4-Maneely c/a	1.30	4.00	9.00

MENACE
March, 1953 - No. 11, May, 1954
Atlas Comics (HPC)

	Good	Fine	Mint
1-Everett-a	8.50	25.50	60.00
2-Post-atom bomb disaster by Everett; anti-Communist propaganda/torture scenes	5.00	15.00	35.00
3,4,6-Everett-a	4.35	13.00	30.00
5-Origin & 1st app. The Zombie by Everett (reprinted in Tales of the Zombie #1)(7/53)	7.00	21.00	50.00
7,10,11: 7-Frankenstein story. 10-H-Bomb panels	3.50	10.50	24.00
8-End of world story	3.50	10.50	24.00
9-Everett-a r-in Vampire Tales #1	4.00	12.00	28.00

NOTE: ***Colan** a-6. **Everett** a-1-6, 9; c-1-6. **Heath** a-1-8; c-10. **Katz** a-11. **Maneely** a-3. **Powell** a-11. **Romita** a-3, 6, 11. **Shelly** a-10. **Sinnott** a-2. **Tuska** a-1, 2, 5.*

MEN AGAINST CRIME (Formerly Mr. Risk)
No. 3, Feb, 1951 - No. 7, Oct, 1951 (Hand of Fate No. 8 on)
Ace Magazines

	Good	Fine	Mint
3-Mr. Risk app.	3.50	10.50	24.00
4-7: 4-Colan-a; entire book reprinted as Trapped! #4	1.85	5.50	13.00

MEN, GUNS, & CATTLE (See Classics Special)

MEN IN ACTION (Battle Brady #10 on)
April, 1952 - No. 9, Dec, 1952
Atlas Comics (IPS)

	Good	Fine	Mint
1	3.00	9.00	21.00
2	1.20	3.50	8.00
3-6,8,9: 3-Heath c/a	1.00	3.00	7.00
7-Krigstein-a	2.75	8.00	18.00

MEN IN ACTION
April, 1957 - No. 9, 1958
Ajax/Farrell Publications

	Good	Fine	Mint
1	2.00	6.00	14.00
2	1.00	3.00	7.00
3-9	.85	2.50	6.00

MEN INTO SPACE (See 4-Color No. 1083)

MEN OF BATTLE (See New. . .)

MEN OF COURAGE
1949
Catechetical Guild

	Good	Fine	Mint
Contains bound Topix comics-V7#2,4,6,8,10,16,18,20	3.00	9.00	21.00

MEN OF WAR
August, 1977 - No. 26, March, 1980
DC Comics, Inc.

	Good	Fine	Mint
1-Origin Gravedigger, cont'd. in No. 2		.30	.60
2-26		.25	.50

NOTE: ***Chaykin** a-9, 10, 12-14, 19, 20. **Evans** c-25. **Kubert** c-2-23, 24p, 26.*

MEN'S ADVENTURES (Formerly True Adventures)
No. 4, Aug, 1950 - No. 28, July, 1954
Marvel/Atlas Comics (CCC)

	Good	Fine	Mint
4(#1)	5.00	15.00	35.00
5-Flying Saucer story	2.65	8.00	18.00
6-8: 8-Sci/fic story	2.00	6.00	14.00
9-20: All war format	1.15	3.50	8.00
21,22,24-26: All horror format	1.30	4.00	9.00
23-Crandall-a; Fox-a(i)	3.00	9.00	21.00
27,28-Captain America, Human Torch, & Sub-Mariner app. in each	18.00	54.00	125.00

NOTE: ***Berg** a-16. **Burgos** c-27. **Everett** a-10, 14, 22, 25, 28; c-14, 21-23. **Heath** a-8, 24. **Lawrence** a-23. **Mac Pakula** a-25. **Post** a-23. **Powell** a-27. **Reinman** a-12. **Robinson** c-19. **Romita** a-22. **Sinnott** a-21. Adventure-#4-8; War-#9-20; Horror-#21-26.*

MEN WHO MOVE THE NATION
(Giveaway) (Black & White)

	Good	Fine	Mint
Neal Adams-a	2.65	8.00	16.00

MEPHISTO VERSUS FOUR HEROES
Apr, 1987 - No. 4, July, 1987 ($1.50, mini-series)
Marvel Comics Group

	Good	Fine	Mint
1	.35	1.00	2.00
2-4	.30	.80	1.60

MERC (See Mark Hazzard: Merc)

MERLIN JONES AS THE MONKEY'S UNCLE (See Movie Comics and The Misadventures of . . . under Movie Comics)

MERLINREALM 3-D (Blackthorne 3-D series No. 2)
Oct, 1985 ($2.25)
Blackthorne Publ., Inc.

	Good	Fine	Mint
1-1st printing	.35	1.15	2.30

MERRILL'S MARAUDERS (See Movie Classics)

MERRY CHRISTMAS (See A Christmas Adv., Donald Duck . . ., Dell Giant No. 39, & March of Comics No. 153)

MERRY CHRISTMAS, A
1948 (nn) (Giveaway)
K. K. Publications (Child Life Shoes)

	Good	Fine	Mint
	2.75	8.00	16.00

MERRY CHRISTMAS
1956 (7¼x5¼")
K. K. Publications (Blue Bird Shoes Giveaway)

	Good	Fine	Mint
	1.00	3.00	6.00

MERRY CHRISTMAS FROM MICKEY MOUSE
1939 (16 pgs.) (Color & B&W)
K. K. Publications (Shoe store giveaway)

	Good	Fine	Mint
Donald Duck & Pluto app.; text with art (Rare); c-reprint/Mickey Mouse Mag. V3/3 (12/37)	70.00	200.00	400.00

MERRY CHRISTMAS FROM SEARS TOYLAND
1939 (16 pgs.) (In color)
Sears Roebuck Giveaway

	Good	Fine	Mint
Dick Tracy, Little Orphan Annie, The Gumps, Terry & the Pirates	15.00	45.00	90.00

MERRY COMICS
December, 1945 (No cover price)
Carlton Publishing Co.

	Good	Fine	Mint
nn-Boogeyman app.	3.70	11.00	26.00

Menace #3, © MCG

Men In Action #6, © MCG

Men's Adventures #14, © MCG

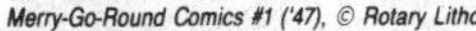
Merry-Go-Round Comics #1 ('47), © Rotary Litho.

Metal Men #6, © DC

Metamorpho #9, © DC

MERRY COMICS
1947
Four Star Publications

	Good	Fine	Mint
1	3.50	10.50	24.00

MERRY-GO-ROUND COMICS
1944 (132 pgs.; 25 cents); 1946; 9-10/47 - No. 2, 1948
LaSalle Publ. Co./Croyden Publ./Rotary Litho.

	Good	Fine	Mint
nn(1944)(LaSalle)	6.50	19.50	45.00
21	1.70	5.00	12.00
1(1946)(Croyden)	3.00	9.00	21.00
V1#1,2(9-10/47, 1948; 52 pgs.)(Rotary Litho. Co. Ltd., Canada); Ken Hultgren-a	2.00	6.00	14.00

MERRY MAILMAN (See Funny Animals)

MERRY MOUSE
June, 1953 - No. 4, Jan-Feb, 1954
Avon Periodicals

	Good	Fine	Mint
1	3.00	9.00	21.00
2-4	1.60	4.70	11.00

METAL MEN (See Brave & the Bold, DC Comics Presents, and Showcase)
4-5/63 - No. 41, 12-1/69-70; No. 42, 2-3/73 - No. 44, 7-8/73; No. 45, 4-5/76 - No. 56, 2-3/78
National Periodical Publications/DC Comics

	Good	Fine	Mint
1	4.30	13.00	30.00
2	1.70	5.00	12.00
3-5	1.30	4.00	9.00
6-10	1.00	3.00	6.00
11-26	.70	2.00	4.00
27-Origin Metal Men	.70	2.00	4.00
28-41(1968-70)	.35	1.00	2.00
42-44(1973)-Reprints	.25	.75	1.50
45('76)-49-Simonson-a in all	.25	.75	1.50
50-56: 50-Part-r. 54,55-Green Lantern x-over	.25	.75	1.50

NOTE: *Aparo c-53-56.* ***Giordano*** *c-45, 46.* ***Kane*** *a-30, 31p; c-31.* ***Simonson*** *a-45-49; c-47-52.* ***Staton*** *a-50-56.*

METAMORPHO (See Action, Brave & the Bold, First Issue Special, & World's Finest)
July-Aug, 1965 - No. 17, Mar-Apr, 1968
National Periodical Publications

	Good	Fine	Mint
1	1.70	5.00	12.00
2-5	.85	2.50	5.00
6-9	.50	1.50	3.00
10-Origin & 1st app. Element Girl (1-2/67)	.50	1.50	3.00
11-17	.35	1.00	2.00

NOTE: ***Ramona Fraden*** *a-1-4.* ***Orlando*** *a-5, 6; c-5-9, 11.* ***Sal Trapani*** *a-7-16.*

METEOR COMICS
November, 1945
L. L. Baird (Croyden)

	Good	Fine	Mint
1-Captain Wizard, Impossible Man, Race Wilkins app.; origin Baldy Bean, Capt. Wizard's sidekick; Bare-breasted mermaids story	11.00	32.00	76.00

MGM'S MARVELOUS WIZARD OF OZ
November, 1975 (84 pgs.; oversize) ($1.50)
Marvel Comics Group/National Periodical Publications

	Good	Fine	Mint
1-Adaptation of MGM's movie (See Marvel Treasury of. . .)	.70	2.00	4.00

M.G.M'S MOUSE MUSKETEERS (Formerly M.G.M.'s The Two Mouseketeers)
No. 670, Jan, 1956 - No. 1290, Mar-May, 1962
Dell Publishing Co.

	Good	Fine	Mint
4-Color 670	1.00	3.00	7.00
4-Color 711,728,764	.85	2.50	6.00
8 (4-6/57) - 21 (3-5/60)	.75	2.25	5.00
4-Color 1135,1175,1290	.85	2.50	6.00

M.G.M.'S SPIKE AND TYKE
No. 499, Sept, 1953 - No. 1266, Dec-Feb, 1961-62
Dell Publishing Co.

	Good	Fine	Mint
4-Color 499	1.30	4.00	9.00
4-Color 577,638	1.00	3.00	7.00
4(12-2/55-56)-10	.85	2.50	6.00
11-24(12-2/60-61)	.75	2.25	5.00
4-Color 1266	.85	2.50	6.00

M.G.M.'S THE TWO MOUSKETEERS (See 4-Color 475,603,642)

MICHAELANGELO, TEENAGE MUTANT NINJA TURTLE
1986 (One shot) ($1.50)
Mirage Studios

	Good	Fine	Mint
1	.90	2.75	5.50

MICKEY AND DONALD
Mar, 1988 - Present
Gladstone Publishing

	Good	Fine	Mint
1-Don Rosa-a; r-/1949 Firestone giv.		.50	.95

MICKEY AND DONALD IN VACATIONLAND (See Dell Giant No. 47)

MICKEY & THE BEANSTALK (See Story Hour Series)

MICKEY & THE SLEUTH (See Walt Disney Showcase No. 38,39,42)

MICKEY FINN
Nov?, 1942 - V3No. 2, May, 1952
Eastern Color 1-4/McNaught Synd. No. 5 on (Columbia)/Headline V3No.2

	Good	Fine	Mint
1	12.00	36.00	84.00
2	6.00	18.00	42.00
3-Charlie Chan app.	4.00	12.00	28.00
4	2.65	8.00	18.00
5-10	1.70	5.00	12.00
11-15(1949): 12-Sparky Watts app.	1.50	4.50	10.00
V3#1,2(1952)	1.15	3.50	8.00

MICKEY MOUSE
1931 - 1934 (52 pgs.; 10x9¾''; cardboard covers)
David McKay Publications

	Good	Fine	Mint
1(1931)	80.00	240.00	430.00
2(1932)	60.00	180.00	315.00
3(1933)-All color Sunday reprints; page #'s 5-17, 32-48 reissued in Whitman #948	120.00	350.00	600.00
4(1934)	50.00	150.00	290.00

NOTE: *Each book reprints strips from previous year - dailies in black and white in #1,2,4; Sundays in color in No. 3. Later reprints exist; i.e., #2 (1934).*

MICKEY MOUSE
1933 (Copyright date, printing date unknown)
(30 pages; 10x8¾''; cardboard covers)
Whitman Publishing Co.

	Good	Fine	Mint
948-(1932 Sunday strips in color)	80.00	240.00	400.00

NOTE: *Some copies were bound with a second front cover upside-down instead of the regular back cover; both covers have the same art, but different right and left margins. The above book is an exact, but abbreviated reissue of David McKay No. 3 but with ½-inch of border trimmed from the top and bottom.*

MICKEY MOUSE (See The Best of Walt Disney Comics, Cheerios giveaways, 40 Big Pages. . ., Gladstone Comic Album, Merry Christmas From. . ., Walt Disney's C&S & Wheaties)

MICKEY MOUSE (. . .Secret Agent No. 107-109; Walt Disney's. . . No. 148-205?) (See Dell Giants for annuals)
No. 16, 1941 - No. 84, 7-9/62; No. 85, 11/62 - No. 218, 7/84; No. 219, 10/86-on
Dell Publ. Co./Gold Key No. 85-204/Whitman No. 205-218/

MICKEY MOUSE (continued)
Gladstone No. 219 on

	Good	Fine	VF-NM
4-Color 16(1941)-1st M.M. comic book-"vs. the Phantom Blot" by Gottfredson	250.00	750.00	1750.00
(Prices vary widely on this book)			

	Good	Fine	Mint
4-Color 27(1943)-"7 Colored Terror"	45.00	135.00	315.00
4-Color 79(1945)-By Carl Barks (1 story)	57.00	171.00	400.00
4-Color 116(1946)	14.00	42.00	100.00
4-Color 141,157(1947)	13.00	40.00	90.00
4-Color 170,181,194('48)	11.50	34.00	80.00
4-Color 214('49),231,248,261	8.50	25.00	60.00
4-Color 268-Reprints/WDC&S #22-24 by Gottfredson ("Surprise Visitor")	8.50	25.00	60.00
4-Color 279,286,296	7.00	21.00	50.00
4-Color 304,313(#1),325(#2),334	5.00	15.00	35.00
4-Color 343,352,362,371,387	4.00	12.00	28.00
4-Color 401,411,427(10-11/52)	3.50	10.50	24.00
4-Color 819-M.M. in Magicland	2.00	6.00	14.00
4-Color 1057,1151,1246(1959-61)-Album	1.70	5.00	12.00
28(12-1/52-53)-32,34	1.70	5.00	12.00
33-(Exists with 2 dates, 10-11/53 & 12-1/54)	1.70	5.00	12.00
35-50	1.15	3.50	8.00
51-73,75-80	.85	2.50	6.00
74-Story swipe-'The Rare Stamp Search'/4-Color 422-'The Gilded Man	1.15	3.50	8.00
81-99: 93,95-titled "Mickey Mouse Club Album"	.85	2.50	6.00
100-105: Reprints 4-Color 427,194,279,170,343,214 in that order	1.00	3.00	7.00
106-120	.75	2.25	5.00
121-130	.70	2.00	4.00
131-146	.50	1.50	3.00
147-Reprints "The Phantom Fires" from WDC&S 200-202	.85	2.50	5.00
148-Reprints "The Mystery of Lonely Valley" from WDC&S 208-210	.85	3.50	5.00
149-158	.35	1.00	2.00
159-Reprints "The Sunken City" from WDC&S 205-207	.70	2.00	4.00
160-170: 162-170-r	.35	1.00	2.00
171-178,180-199		.50	1.00
179-(52 pgs.)		.40	.80
200-r-Four Color 371		.40	.80
201-218		.40	.80
219-1st Gladstone issue; The Seven Ghosts serial-r begins by Gottfredson	.40	1.25	2.50
220-236: 222-Editor-in Grief strip-r		.50	1.00

NOTE: *Reprints No. 195-97, 198(⅔), 199(⅓), 200-208, 211(½), 212, 213, 215(⅓), 216-218.*

	Good	Fine	Mint
Album 01-518-210(Dell), 1(10082-309)(9/63-Gold Key)	.85	2.50	6.00
...& Goofy "Bicep Bungle"(1952, 16 pgs., 3¼x7") Fritos giveaway, soft-c (also see D. Duck & Ludwig Von Drake)	2.35	7.00	14.00
...& Goofy Explore Business(1978)		.40	.80
...& Goofy Explore Energy(1976-1978) 36 pgs.; Exxon giveaway in color; regular size		.40	.80
...& Goofy Explore Energy Conservation(1976-1978)-Exxon		.40	.80
...& Goofy Explore The Universe of Energy(1985) 20pgs.; Exxon giveaway in color; regular size		.40	.80
Club 1(1/64-G.K.)(TV)	1.75	5.25	12.00
Mini Comic 1(1976)(3¼x6½")-Reprints 158			.15
New Mickey Mouse Club Fun Book 11190 (Golden Press, $1.95; 224pgs, 1977)	.40	1.20	2.40
Surprise Party 1(30037-901, G.K.)(1/69)-40th Anniversary (see Walt Disney Showcase #47)	2.35	7.00	16.00
Surprise Party 1(1979)-r-/'69 ish	.35	1.00	2.00

MICKEY MOUSE BOOK
1930 (4 printings, 20pgs., magazine size, paperbound)
Bibo & Lang

nn-Very first Disney book with games, cartoons & songs; only Disney book to offer the origin of Mickey (based on a story originated by 11 yr. old Bobette Bibo). First app. Mickey & Minnie Mouse. Clarabelle Cow & Horace Horsecollar app. on back cover. Walt Disney, so the story goes, named him 'Mickey Mouse' after the green color of Ireland because he ate old green cheese. The book was printed in black & green to reinforce the Irish theme.

NOTE: The first printing has a daily Win Smith M. Mouse strip at bottom of back cover; the reprints are blank in this area. Most copies are missing pages 9 & 10 which contain a puzzle to be cut out. Ub Iwerks-c

	Good	Fine	VF-NM
First Printing (complete)	150.00	400.00	900.00
First Printing (Pgs. 9&10 missing)	43.00	130.00	300.00
2nd-4th Printings (complete)	95.00	285.00	665.00
2nd-4th Printings (pgs. 9&10 missing)	36.00	108.00	250.00

MICKEY MOUSE CLUB MAGAZINE (See Walt Disney...)

MICKEY MOUSE CLUB SPECIAL (See The New Mickey Mouse...)

MICKEY MOUSE COMICS DIGEST
1986 - No. 6, 1987 (96 pgs.)
Gladstone Publishing

	Good	Fine	Mint
1-3 ($1.25)		.60	1.25
4-6 ($1.50)	.25	.75	1.50

MICKEY MOUSE MAGAZINE
V1No.1, Jan, 1933 - V1No.9, Sept, 1933 (5¼x7¼")
No. 1-3 published by Kamen-Blair (Kay Kamen, Inc.)
Walt Disney Productions

(Scarce)-Distributed by leading stores through their local theatres. First few issues had 5 cents listed on cover, later ones had no price.

	Good	Fine	VF-NM
V1#1	120.00	360.00	840.00
2-9	60.00	180.00	400.00

MICKEY MOUSE MAGAZINE
V1No.1, Nov, 1933 - V2No.12, Oct, 1935
Mills giveaways issued by different dairies
Walt Disney Productions

	Good	Fine	Mint
V1#1	25.00	75.00	175.00
2-12	15.00	45.00	105.00
V2#1-12	10.00	30.00	70.00

MICKEY MOUSE MAGAZINE (Becomes Walt Disney's Comics & Stories) (No V3/1, V4/6)
Summer, 1935 (June-Aug, indicia) - V5/12, Sept, 1940
V1/1-5, V3/11,12, V4/1-3 are 44 pgs; V2/3-100 pgs; V5/12-68 pgs; rest are 36 pgs.
K. K. Publications/Western Publishing Co.

	Good	Fine	VF-NM
V1#1 (Large size, 13¼x10¼"; 25 cents)-Contains puzzles, games, cels, stories and comics of Disney characters. Promotional magazine for Disney cartoon movies and paraphernalia	128.00	385.00	900.00

Note: *Some copies were autographed by the editors & given away with all early one year subscriptions.*

	Good	Fine	VF-NM
2 (Size change, 11½x8½"; 10/35; 10 cents)-High quality paper begins; Messmer-a	75.00	225.00	525.00
3,4: 3-Messmer-a	45.00	135.00	315.00
5-1st Donald Duck solo-c; last 44pg. & high quality paper issue	45.00	135.00	315.00

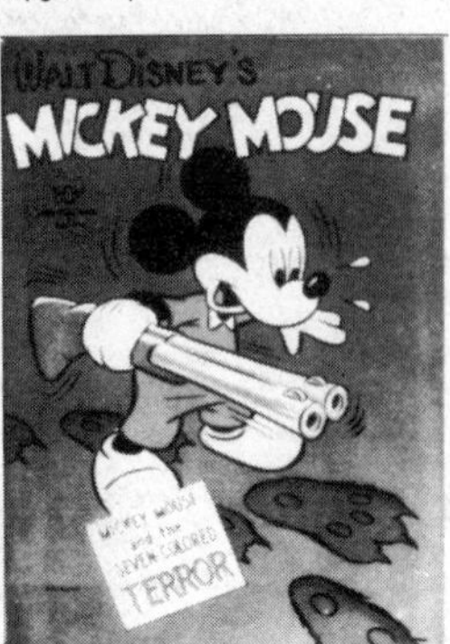

Mickey Mouse Four Color #27, © WDC

Mickey Mouse Club #1, © WDC

Mickey Mouse Magazine #4 (2/34), © WDC

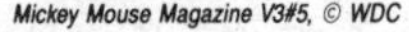
Mickey Mouse Magazine V3#5, © WDC

Mickey Mouse Magazine V5#1, © WDC

Micronauts #2 (1st series), © MCG

MICKEY MOUSE MAGAZINE (continued) Good Fine VF-NM

6-9: 6-36 pg. issues begin; Donald becomes editor. 8-2nd Donald solo-c. 9-1st Mickey/Minnie-c 33.00 100.00 230.00

10-12, V2#1,2: 11-1st Pluto/Mickey-c; Donald fires himself and appoints Mickey as editor 28.00 84.00 195.00

V2#3-Special 100 pg. Christmas issue (25 cents); Messmer-a; Donald becomes editor of Wise Quacks 55.00 165.00 385.00

4-Mickey Mouse Comics & Roy Ranger (adventure strip) begin; both end V2#9; Messmer-a 25.00 75.00 175.00

Good Fine Mint

5-Ted True (adventure strip, ends V2#9) & Silly Symphony Comics (ends V3#3) begin 22.00 65.00 154.00

6-9: 6-1st solo Minnie-c. 6-9-Mickey Mouse Movies cut-out in each 22.00 65.00 154.00

10-1st full color issue; Mickey Mouse (by Gottfredson; ends V3#12) & Silly Symphony (ends V3/3) full color Sunday-r, Peter The Farm Detective (ends V5#8) & Ole Of The North (ends V3#3) begins 28.00 84.00 195.00

11-13: 12-Hiawatha-c & feat. sty 22.00 65.00 154.00

V3#2-Big Bad Wolf Halloween-c 22.00 65.00 154.00

3 (12/37)-1st app. Snow White & The Seven Dwarfs (before release of movie)(possibly 1st in print); Mickey Christmas-c 30.00 90.00 210.00

4 (1/38)-Snow White & The Seven Dwarfs serial begins (on stands before release of movie); Ducky Symphony (ends V3#11) begins 25.00 75.00 175.00

5-1st Snow White & Seven Dwarfs-c (St. Valentine's Day) 25.00 75.00 175.00

6-Snow White serial ends; Lonesome Ghosts app. (2 pp.) 21.00 62.00 145.00

7-Seven Dwarfs Easter-c 20.00 60.00 140.00

8-10: 9-Dopey-c. 10-1st solo Goofy-c 19.00 57.00 132.00

11,12 (44 pgs; 8 more pages color added). 11-Mickey The Sheriff serial (ends V4#3) & Donald Duck strip-r (ends V3#12) begin. Color feature on Snow White's Forest Friends 22.00 65.00 154.00

V4#1 (10/38; 44 pgs.)-Brave Little Tailor-c/feature story, nominated for Academy Award; Bobby & Chip by Otto Messmer (ends V4#2) & The Practical Pig (ends V4#2) begin 22.00 65.00 154.00

2 (44 pgs.)-1st Huey, Dewey & Louie-c 21.00 62.00 145.00

3 (12/38, 44 pgs.)-Ferdinand The Bull-c/feature story, Academy Award winner; Mickey Mouse & The Whalers serial begins, ends V4#12 22.00 65.00 154.00

4-Donald's Lucky Day c/story (film co-written by Carl Barks. Spotty, Mother Pluto strip-r begin, end V4#8 19.00 57.00 132.00

5-St. Valentine's day-c. 1st Pluto solo-c 21.00 62.00 145.00

7 (3/39)-The Ugly Duckling-c/feature story, Academy Award winner; The Hockey Champ feature with gags created by Carl Barks 21.00 62.00 145.00

7 (4/39)-Goofy & Wilbur The Grasshopper classic-c/feature story from 1st Goofy cartoon movie; Donald's Cousin Gus & Beach Picnic features with gags created by Carl Barks; Timid Elmer begins, ends V5#5 21.00 62.00 145.00

8-Big Bad Wolf-c from Practical Pig movie poster; Practical Pig feature story 21.00 62.00 145.00

9-Donald Duck & Mickey Mouse Sunday-r begin; The Pointer feature story, nominated for Academy Award & Sea Scouts (with Barks gags) feature story app. 21.00 62.00 145.00

10-Classic July 4th drum & fife-c; last Donald Sunday-r 25.00 75.00 175.00

11-1st slick-c; last over-sized ish 19.00 57.00 132.00

12 (9/39; format change, 10¼x8¼")-1st full color, cover to cover issue. Donald's Penguin-c/feature story with gags created by Carl Barks 24.00 72.00 165.00

V5#1-Black Pete-c; Officer Duck-c/feature story; Autograph Hound feature story; Robinson Crusoe serial begins

Good Fine Mint

24.00 72.00 165.00

2-Goofy-c; 1st app. Pinocchio (cameo) 24.00 72.00 165.00

3 (12/39)-Pinocchio Christmas-c (Before movie release). Pinocchio serial begins; 1st app. Jiminy Crickett 30.00 90.00 210.00

4,5: 5-Jiminy Crickett-c; Pinocchio serial ends; Donald's Dog Laundry feature story 25.00 75.00 175.00

6-Tugboat Mickey feature story; Rip Van Winkle feature begins, ends V5#8 24.00 72.00 165.00

7-2nd Huey, Dewey & Louie-c 24.00 72.00 165.00

8-Last magazine size issue; 2nd solo Pluto-c; Figaro & Cleo feature story 24.00 72.00 165.00

9 (6/40; change to comic book size)-Jiminy Crickett feature story; Donald-c & Sunday-r begin 35.00 100.00 245.00

10-Special Independence Day issue 35.00 100.00 245.00

11-Hawaiian Holiday & Mickey's Trailor feature stories; last 36 pg. issue 35.00 100.00 245.00

12 (Format change)-The transition issue (68 pgs.) becoming a comic book. With only a title change to follow, becomes Walt Disney's Comics & Stories #1 with the next issue 130.00 390.00 910.00

V4#1 (Giveaway) 18.50 55.00 130.00

NOTE: *Otto **Messmer**-a is in many issues of the first two-three years.*

MICKEY MOUSE MARCH OF COMICS

1947 - 1951 (Giveaway) (See March of Comics No. 447)

K. K. Publications

8(1947)-32 pgs. 50.00 150.00 330.00

27(1948) 34.00 100.00 238.00

45(1949) 27.00 80.00 190.00

60(1950) 18.00 55.00 125.00

74(1951) 14.00 42.50 96.00

MICKEY MOUSE SUMMER FUN (See Dell Giants)

MICKEY MOUSE'S SUMMER VACATION (See Story Hour Series)

MICROBOTS, THE

December, 1971 (One Shot)

Gold Key

1 (10271-112) .85 2.50 5.00

MICRONAUTS

Jan, 1979 - No. 59, Aug, 1984 (Mando paper No. 53 on)

Marvel Comics Group

1-Intro/1st app. Baron Karza .40 1.25 2.50

2-5 .60 1.20

6-10: 7-Man-Thing app. 8-1st app. Capt. Universe. 9-1st app. Cilicia .45 .90

11-20: 13-1st app. Jasmine. 15-Death of Microtron. 15-17-Fantastic-4 app. 17-Death of Jasmine. 20 Ant-Man app. .45 .90

21-30: 21-Microverse series begins. 25-Origin Baron Karza. 25-29-Nick Fury app. 27-Death of Biotron .45 .90

31-34: Dr. Strange app. #34,35 .45 .90

35-Double size; origin Microverse; intro Death Squad .45 .90

36-Giffen-a(p) .45 .90

37-New X-Men app.; Giffen-a(p) .35 1.00 2.00

38-First direct sale .25 .80 1.60

39,40: 40-Fantastic-4 app. .45 .90

41-59: 57-Double size .35 .70

nn-Reprints #1-3; blank UPC; diamond on top .20 .40

Annual 1(12/79)-Ditko c/a .30 .90 1.80

Annual 2(10/80)-Ditko c/a .50 1.00

NOTE: *No. 38-on distributed only through comic shops. **Adams** c-7i. **Chaykin** a-13-18p. **Ditko** a-39p. **Giffen** a-36p, 37p. **Golden** a-1-12p; c-2-6p, 7-23, 24p, 38, 39. **Guice** a-48-58p; c-49-58. **Gil Kane** a-38, 40p-45p; c-40-45. **Layton** c-33-37. **Miller** c-31.*

MICRONAUTS

Oct, 1984 - No. 20, May, 1986

MICRONAUTS (continued)
Marvel Comics Group

	Good	Fine	Mint
V2#1-20		.35	.70

NOTE: ***Golden*** *a-1; c-1, 6.* ***Guice*** *a-4p; c-2p.*

MICRONAUTS SPECIAL EDITION
Dec, 1983 - No. 5, Apr, 1984 ($2.00; mini-series; Baxter paper)
Marvel Comics Group

1: 1-5 r-/original series 1-12	.25	.80	1.60
2-5: Guice-c(p)-all	.25	.70	1.40

MIDGET COMICS (Fighting Indian Stories)
Feb, 1950 - No. 2, Apr, 1950 (5-3/8"x7-3/8")
St. John Publishng Co.

1-Matt Baker-c	4.00	12.00	28.00
2-Tex West, Cowboy Marshal	2.00	6.00	14.00

MIDNIGHT
April, 1957 - No. 6, June, 1958
Ajax/Farrell Publ. (Four Star Comic Corp.)

1-Reprints from Voodoo & Strange Fantasy with some changes	3.50	10.50	24.00
2-5	1.50	4.50	10.00
6-Baker-r/Phantom Lady	3.50	10.50	24.00

MIDNIGHT MYSTERY
Jan-Feb, 1961 - No. 7, Oct, 1961
American Comics Group

1-Sci/Fic story	2.30	7.00	16.00
2-7: 7-Reinman-a	1.15	3.50	8.00

NOTE: ***Reinman*** *a-1, 3.* ***Whitman*** *a-1, 4-6; c-1, 3, 5, 7.*

MIDNIGHT TALES
Dec, 1972 - No. 18, May, 1976
Charlton Press

V1#1		.60	1.20
2-10,15-18		.40	.80
11-14-Newton-a		.40	.80
12,17(Modern Comics reprint, 1977)		.15	.30

NOTE: ***Adkins*** *a-12i, 13i.* ***Ditko*** *a-12.* ***Howard*** *(Wood imitator) a-1-15, 17, 18; c-1-18.* ***Staton*** *a-6, 8, 9, 13.* ***Sutton*** *a-8, 9.*

MIGHTY ATOM, THE (. . .& the Pixies #6)
(Formerly The Pixies No. 1-5)
No. 6, 1949; 11/57 - No. 6, 8-9/58
Magazine Enterprises

6(1949-M.E.)-no month (1st Series)	2.30	7.00	16.00
1-6(2nd Series)-Pixies-r	1.00	3.00	7.00
I.W. Reprint #1(nd)	.30	.90	1.80
Giveaway(1959, '63, Whitman)-Evans-a	1.35	4.00	8.00
Giveaway (1967r, 1968r, 1973r, 1976r)		.50	1.00

MIGHTY BEAR (Formerly Fun Comics, Mighty Ghost #4)
No. 13, Jan, 1954 - No. 14, Mar, 1954; 9/57 - No. 3, 2/58
Star Publ. No. 13,14/Ajax-Farrell (Four Star)

13,14-L. B. Cole-c	3.00	9.00	21.00
1-3('57-'58)Four Star (Ajax)	1.00	3.00	7.00

MIGHTY COMICS (. . . Presents) (Formerly Flyman)
No. 40, Nov, 1966 - No. 50, Oct, 1967
Radio Comics (Archie)

	Good	Fine	Mint
40-Web	1.00	3.00	6.00
41-Shield, Black Hood	.85	2.50	5.00
42-Black Hood	.85	2.50	5.00
43-Shield, Web & Black Hood	.85	2.50	5.00
44-Black Hood, Steel Sterling & The Shield	.85	2.50	5.00
45-Shield & Hangman; origin Web retold	.85	2.50	5.00
46-Steel Sterling, Web & Black Hood	.85	2.50	5.00
47-Black Hood & Mr. Justice	.85	2.50	5.00
48-Shield & Hangman; Wizard x-over in Shield	.85	2.50	5.00
49-Steel Sterling & Fox; Black Hood x-over in Steel Sterling	.85	2.50	5.00
50-Black Hood & Web; Inferno x-over in Web	.85	2.50	5.00

NOTE: ***Paul Reinman*** *a-40-50.*

MIGHTY CRUSADERS, THE (Also see Fly Man, Advs. of the Fly)
Nov, 1965 - No. 7, Oct, 1966
Mighty Comics Group (Radio Comics)

1-Origin The Shield	1.50	4.50	10.00
2-Origin Comet	1.00	3.00	7.00
3-Origin Fly-Man	.85	2.50	5.00
4-Fireball, Inferno, Firefly, Web, Fox, Bob Phantom, Blackjack, Hangman, Zambini, Kardak, Steel Sterling, Mr. Justice, Wizard, Capt. Flag, Jaguar x-over	1.00	3.00	6.00
5-Intro. Ultra-Men (Fox, Web, Capt. Flag) & Terrific Three (Jaguar, Mr. Justice, Steel Sterling)	.85	2.50	5.00
6,7: 7-Steel Sterling feature; origin Fly-Girl	.85	2.50	5.00

NOTE: ***Reinman*** *a-6.*

MIGHTY CRUSADERS, THE (All New Advs. of. . .No. 2)
3/83 - No. 13, 9/85 ($1.00, 36 pgs, Mando paper)
Red Circle Prod./Archie Ent. No. 6 on

1-Origin Black Hood, The Fly, Fly Girl, The Shield, The Wizard, The Jaguar, Pvt. Strong & The Web		.45	.90
2-13: 2-Mister Midnight begins. 4-Darkling replaces Shield. 5-Origin Jaguar, Shield begins. 7-Untold origin Jaguar		.45	.90

NOTE: ***Buckler*** *a-1-3, 4i, 5p, 7p, 8i, 9i; c-1-10p.*

MIGHTY GHOST (Formerly Mighty Bear)
No. 4, June, 1958
Ajax/Farrell Publ.

4	1.00	3.00	7.00

MIGHTY HERCULES, THE (TV)
July, 1963 - No. 2, Nov, 1963
Gold Key

1,2(10072-307,311)	2.65	8.00	18.00

MIGHTY HEROES, THE (TV) (Funny)
Mar, 1967 - No. 4, July, 1967
Dell Publishing Co.

1-1957 Heckle & Jeckle-r	.70	2.00	4.00
2,3	.50	1.50	3.00
4-Two 1958 Mighty Mouse-r	.50	1.50	3.00

MIGHTY MARVEL WESTERN, THE
10/68 - No. 46, 9/76 (No. 1-14: 68 pgs.; No. 15,16: 52 pgs.)
Marvel Comics Group

1-Begin Kid Colt, Rawhide Kid, Two-Gun Kid-r		.40	.80
2-10		.30	.60
11-20		.30	.60
21-30: 24-Kid Colt-r end. 25-Matt Slade-r begin		.30	.60
31,33-36,38-46: 31-Baker-r		.30	.60
32-Origin-r/Ringo Kid #23; Williamson-r/Kid Slade #7		.30	.60
37-Williamson, Kirby-r/Two-Gun Kid 51		.30	.60

NOTE: ***Jack Davis*** *a(r)-21-24.* ***Kirby*** *a(r)-1-3, 6, 9, 12, 14, 16, 26, 29, 32, 36, 41, 43, 44; c-29.* ***Maneely*** *a(r)-22. No Matt Slade-No. 43.*

MIGHTY MIDGET COMICS, THE (Miniature)
No date; circa 1942-1943 (36 pages) (Approx. 5x4")
(Black & White & Red) (Sold 2 for 5 cents)
Samuel E. Lowe & Co.

Bulletman #11(1943)-R-/cover/Bulletman #3	3.00	9.00	21.00
Captain Marvel #11	3.00	9.00	21.00

Captain Marvel #11 (Same as above except for full color ad on

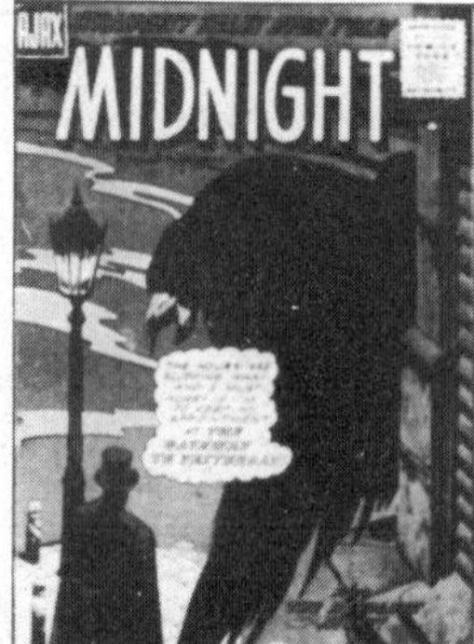

Midnight #2, © AJAX

Mighty Comics #40, © AP

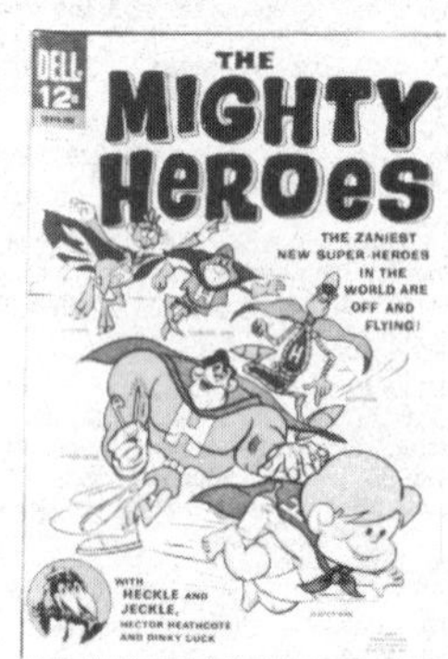

The Mighty Heroes #1, © CBS

Mighty Mouse #22 (52 pg. ed.), © M.G.M.

Mike Barnett, Man Against Crime #6, © FAW

Military Comics #10, © QUA

MIGHTY MIDGET COMICS (continued)	Good	Fine	Mint
back cover; this issue was glued to cover of Captain Marvel #20 and is not found in fine-mint condition)	3.00	9.00	21.00
Captain Marvel Jr. #11	3.00	9.00	21.00
Captain Marvel Jr. #11 (Same as above except for full color ad on back-c; this issue was glued to cover of Captain Marvel #21 and is not found in fine-mint condition)	3.00	9.00	21.00
Golden Arrow #11	2.00	6.00	14.00
Ibis the Invincible #11(1942)-Origin; r-/cover/Ibis #1	3.00	9.00	21.00
Spy Smasher #11(1942)	3.00	9.00	21.00

NOTE: *The above books came in a box called "box full of books" and was distributed with other Samuel Lowe puzzles, paper dolls, coloring books, etc. They are not titled Mighty Midget Comics. All have a war bond seal on back cover which is otherwise blank. These books came in a "Mighty Midget" flat cardboard counter display rack.*

	Good	Fine	Mint
Balbo, the Boy Magician #12	1.50	4.50	10.00
Bulletman #12	3.00	9.00	21.00
Commando Yank #12	2.00	6.00	14.00
Dr. Voltz the Human Generator	1.50	4.50	10.00
Lance O'Casey #12	1.50	4.50	10.00
Leatherneck the Marine	1.50	4.50	10.00
Minute Man #12	3.00	9.00	21.00
Mister Q	1.50	4.50	10.00
Mr. Scarlet & Pinky #12	3.00	9.00	21.00
Pat Wilton & His Flying Fortress	1.50	4.50	10.00
The Phantom Eagle #12	2.00	6.00	14.00
State Trooper Stops Crime	1.50	4.50	10.00
Tornado Tom; r-/from Cyclone #1-3; origin	2.00	6.00	12.00

MIGHTY MOUSE (See Adventures of..., Dell Giant #43, Giant Comics Edition, March of Comics #205, 237, 247, 257, 459, 471, 483, Oxydol-Dreft, Paul Terry's, & Terry-Toons Comics)

MIGHTY MOUSE (1st Series)
Fall, 1946 - No. 4, Summer, 1947
Timely/Marvel Comics (20th Century Fox)

	Good	Fine	Mint
1	40.00	120.00	280.00
2	20.00	60.00	140.00
3,4	15.00	45.00	105.00

MIGHTY MOUSE (2nd Series) (Paul Terry's... No. 62-71)
Aug, 1947 - No. 67, 11/55; No. 68, 3/56 - No. 83, 6/59
St. John Publishing Co./Pines No. 68 (3/56) on

	Good	Fine	Mint
5(#1)	13.00	40.00	90.00
6-10	6.50	19.50	45.00
11-19	4.00	12.00	28.00
20-25-(52 pgs.)	3.50	10.50	24.00
20-25-(36 pg. editions)	3.00	9.00	21.00
26-37	2.30	7.00	16.00
38-45-(100 pgs.)	5.00	15.00	35.00
46-83: 62,64,67-Painted-c. 82-Infinity-c	1.50	4.50	10.00
Album 1(10/52)-100 pgs.	11.00	32.00	76.00
Album 2(11/52-St. John) - 3(12/52) (100 pgs.)	8.50	25.50	60.00
Fun Club Magazine 1(Fall, 1957-Pines) (TV-Tom Terrific)	5.70	17.00	40.00
Fun Club Magazine 2-6(Winter, 1958-Pines)	3.50	10.50	24.00
3-D 1-(1st printing-9/53)(St. John)-stiff covers	18.00	54.00	125.00
3-D 1-(2nd printing-10/53)-slick, glossy covers, slightly smaller	15.00	45.00	105.00
3-D 2(11/53), 3(12/53)-(St. John)	13.00	40.00	90.00

MIGHTY MOUSE (TV)(3rd Series)(Formerly Advs. of Mighty Mouse)
No. 161, Oct, 1964 - No. 172, Oct, 1968
Gold Key/Dell Publishing Co. No. 166-on

	Good	Fine	Mint
161(10/64)-165(9/65)-(Becomes Advs. of... No. 166 on)	1.50	4.50	10.00
166(3/66), 167(6/66)-172	1.15	3.50	8.00

MIGHTY MOUSE
1987 - Present ($1.50, color)
Spotlight Comics

	Good	Fine	Mint
1-3: New stories begin	.25	.75	1.50
...And Friends Holiday Special (11/87, $1.75)	.30	.90	1.75

MIGHTY MOUSE ADVENTURES (Advs. of... No. 2 on)
November, 1951
St. John Publishing Co.

	Good	Fine	Mint
1	14.00	42.00	100.00

MIGHTY MOUSE ADVENTURE STORIES
1953 (384 pgs.) (50 Cents)
St. John Publishing Co.

	Good	Fine	Mint
Rebound issues	25.00	75.00	175.00

MIGHTY SAMSON (Also see Gold Key Champion)
7/64 - No.20, 11/69?; No.21, 8/72; No.22, 12/73 - No.31, 3/76; No. 32, 8/82 (Painted-c No. 1-31)
Gold Key

	Good	Fine	Mint
1-Origin; Thorne-a begins	1.15	3.50	8.00
2-5	.75	2.25	5.00
6-10: 7-Tom Morrow begins, ends No. 20	.50	1.50	3.00
11-20	.35	1.00	2.00
21-32: 21,22,32-r		.50	1.00

MIGHTY THOR (See Thor)

MIKE BARNETT, MAN AGAINST CRIME (TV)
Dec, 1951 - No. 6, 1952
Fawcett Publications

	Good	Fine	Mint
1	4.35	13.00	30.00
2	2.65	8.00	18.00
3,4,6	2.00	6.00	14.00
5-"Market for Morphine" cover/story	3.75	11.25	26.00

MIKE SHAYNE PRIVATE EYE
Nov-Jan, 1962 - No. 3, Sept-Nov, 1962
Dell Publishing Co.

	Good	Fine	Mint
1	1.30	4.00	9.00
2,3	1.00	3.00	7.00

MILITARY COMICS (Becomes Modern #44 on)
Aug, 1941 - No. 43, Oct, 1945
Quality Comics Group

	Good	Fine	Mint
1-Origin Blackhawk by C. Cuidera, Miss America, The Death Patrol by Jack Cole (also #2-7,27-30), & The Blue Tracer by Guardineer; X of the Underground, The Yankee Eagle, Q-Boat & Shot & Shell, Archie Atkins, Loops & Banks by Bud Ernest (Bob Powell) (ends #13) begin	210.00	630.00	1470.00
2-Secret War News begins (by McWilliams #2-16); Cole-a	105.00	335.00	735.00
3-Origin/1st app. Chop Chop	78.00	235.00	545.00
4	70.00	210.00	490.00
5-The Sniper begins; Miss America in costume #4-7	57.00	170.00	400.00
6-9: 8-X of the Underground begins (ends #13). 9-The Phantom Clipper begins (ends #16)	45.00	135.00	315.00
10-Classic Eisner-c	50.00	150.00	350.00
11-Flag-c	37.00	110.00	260.00
12-Blackhawk by Crandall begins, ends #22	50.00	150.00	350.00
13-15: 14-Private Dogtag begins (ends #83)	35.00	105.00	245.00
16-20: 16-Blue Tracer ends. 17-P.T. Boat begins	28.00	84.00	195.00
21-31: 22-Last Crandall Blackhawk. 27-Death Patrol revived	25.00	75.00	175.00
32-43	22.00	65.00	154.00

NOTE: ***Berg** a-6. **J. Cole** a-1-3, 27-32. **Crandall** a-12-22; c-13-22. **Eisner** c-1, 9, 10. **McWilliams** a-2-16. **Powell** a-1-13. **Ward** Blackhawk-30, 31(15 pgs. each); c-29, 30.*

MILITARY WILLY
1907 (14 pgs.; ½ in color (every other page))

MILITARY WILLY (continued)
(regular comic book format)(7x9½")(stapled)
J. I. Austen Co.

	Good	Fine	Mint
By F. R. Morgan	10.00	30.00	70.00

MILLENIUM
Jan, 1988 - No. 8, Feb, 1988 (Weekly mini-series)
DC Comics

	Good	Fine	Mint
1-Staton c/a begins	.35	1.00	2.00
2-4	.25	.75	1.50
5-8		.60	1.20

MILLIE, THE LOVABLE MONSTER
Sept-Nov, 1962 - No. 6, Jan, 1973
Dell Publishing Co.

	Good	Fine	Mint
12-523,211, 2(8-10/63)	1.00	3.00	7.00
3(8-10/64)	.85	2.50	6.00
4(7/72), 5(10/72), 6(1/73)	.70	2.00	4.00

NOTE: ***Woggon** a-3-6; c-3-6. 4 reprints 1; 5 reprints 2; 6 reprints 3.*

MILLIE THE MODEL (See Modeling With . . . , A Date With . . . , and Life With . . .)
1945 - No. 207, December, 1973
Marvel/Atlas/Marvel Comics (SPI/Male/VPI)

	Good	Fine	Mint
1	17.00	51.00	120.00
2 (10/46)-Millie becomes The Blonde Phantom to sell Blonde Phantom perfume; a pre-Blonde Phantom app. (see All-Select #11, Fall, '46)	11.00	32.00	76.00
3-7: 7-Willie smokes extra strong tobacco	5.00	15.00	35.00
8,10-Kurtzman's "Hey Look"	5.00	15.00	35.00
9-Powerhouse Pepper by Wolverton, 4 pgs.	8.50	25.50	60.00
11-Kurtzman-a	4.00	12.00	28.00
12,15,17-20	2.00	6.00	14.00
13,14,16-Kurtzman's "Hey Look"	3.00	9.00	21.00
21-30	1.70	5.00	12.00
31-60	1.00	3.00	7.00
1-99	.70	2.00	4.00
100	.85	2.50	6.00
101-106,108-207: 154-New Millie begins (10/67). 192-(52 pgs.)	.35	1.00	2.00
107-Jack Kirby app. in story	.35	1.00	2.00
Annual 1(1962)	2.65	8.00	18.00
Annual 2-10(1963-11/71)	1.15	3.50	8.00
Queen-Size 11(9/74), 12(1975)	.70	2.00	4.00

MILLION DOLLAR DIGEST
Aug, 1986 - Present ($1.25, digest size)
Harvey Publications

	Good	Fine	Mint
1-7		.60	1.25

MILT GROSS FUNNIES
Aug, 1947 - No. 2, Sept, 1947
Milt Gross, Inc. (ACG?)

	Good	Fine	Mint
1,2	3.70	11.00	26.00

MILTON THE MONSTER & FEARLESS FLY (TV)
May, 1966
Gold Key

	Good	Fine	Mint
1 (10175-605)	2.00	6.00	14.00

MINUTE MAN (See Master & Mighty Midget Comics)
Sum, 1941 - No. 3, Spring, 1942
Fawcett Publications

	Good	Fine	Mint
1	60.00	180.00	420.00
2,3	45.00	135.00	315.00

MINUTE MAN
No date (B&W; 16 pgs.; paper cover blue & red)
Sovereign Service Station giveaway

	Good	Fine	Mint
American history	1.00	3.00	6.00

MINUTE MAN ANSWERS THE CALL, THE
1942 (4 pages)
By M. C. Gaines (War Bonds giveaway)

	Good	Fine	Mint
Sheldon Moldoff-a	5.00	15.00	35.00

MIRACLE COMICS
Feb, 1940 - No. 4, March, 1941
Hillman Periodicals

	Good	Fine	Mint
1-Sky Wizard, Master of Space, Dash Dixon, Man of Might, Dusty Doyle, Pinkie Parker, The Kid Cop, K-7, Secret Agent, The Scorpion, & Blandu, Jungle Queen begin; Masked Angel only app.	45.00	135.00	315.00
2	28.00	84.00	195.00
3,4: 3-Bill Colt, the Ghost Rider begins. 4-The Veiled Prophet & Bullet Bob app.	25.00	75.00	175.00

MIRACLEMAN
Aug, 1985 - Present (Mando paper, 7-10)
Eclipse Comics

	Good	Fine	Mint
1-r-/of British Marvelman series; Alan Moore scripts in all	.35	1.00	2.00
1-Gold edition	4.15	12.50	25.00
1-Silver edition	.85	2.50	5.00
2-15: 9,10-Origin Miracleman. 9-Shows graphic scenes of childbirth		.50	1.00
3-D 1 (12/85)	.40	1.25	2.50
2-D 1 (B&W, 100 copy limited signed & numbered edition)	.85	2.50	5.00

MIRACLE OF THE WHITE STALLIONS, THE (See Movie Comics)

MIRACLE SQUAD, THE
Aug, 1986 - No. 4, 1987 ($2.00, color, mini-series)
Upshot Graphics (Fantagraphics Books)

	Good	Fine	Mint
1-4	.35	1.00	2.00

MISADVENTURES OF MERLIN JONES, THE (See Movie Comics & Merlin Jones as the Monkey's Uncle under Movie Comics)

MISCHIEVOUS MONKS OF CROCODILE ISLE, THE
1908 (8½x11½"; 4 pgs. in color; 12 pgs.)
J. I. Austen Co., Chicago

	Good	Fine	Mint
By F. R. Morgan; reads longwise	6.00	18.00	42.00

MISS AMERICA COMICS (Miss America Mag. No. 2 on)
1944 (One Shot)
Marvel Comics (20CC)

	Good	Fine	Mint
1-2 pgs. pin-ups	48.00	145.00	335.00

MISS AMERICA MAGAZINE (Formerly Miss America) (Miss America #51 on)
V1#2, Nov, 1944 - No. 93, Nov, 1958
Miss America Publ. Corp./Marvel/Atlas (MAP)

	Good	Fine	Mint
V1#2: Photo-c of teenage girl in Miss America costume; Miss America, Patsy Walker (intro.) comic stories plus movie reviews & stories; intro. Buzz Baxter & Hedy Wolfe	43.00	130.00	300.00
3-5-Miss America & Patsy Walker stories	16.00	48.00	110.00
6-Patsy Walker only	4.00	12.00	28.00
V2#1(4/45)-6(9/45)-Patsy Walker continues	2.00	6.00	14.00
V3#1(10/45)-6(4/46)	2.00	6.00	14.00
V4#1(5/46)-3(7/46)	1.60	4.70	11.00
V4#4 (8/46; 68pgs.)	1.60	4.70	11.00
V4#5 (9/46)-Liz Taylor photo-c	3.15	9.50	22.00
V4#6 (10/46; 92pgs.)	1.60	4.70	11.00
V5#1(11/46)-6(4/47), V6#1(5/47)-3(7/47)	1.60	4.70	11.00
V7#1(8/47)-14,16-23(6/49)	1.30	4.00	9.00
V7#15-All comics	1.60	4.70	11.00

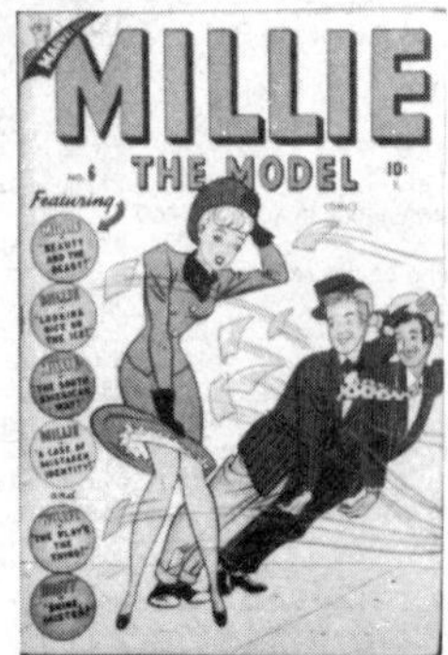

Millie The Model #6, © MCG

Minute Man #2, © FAW

Miss America Comics #1, © MCG

Miss Fury #7, © MCG

Mission Impossible #5, © Paramount Pictures

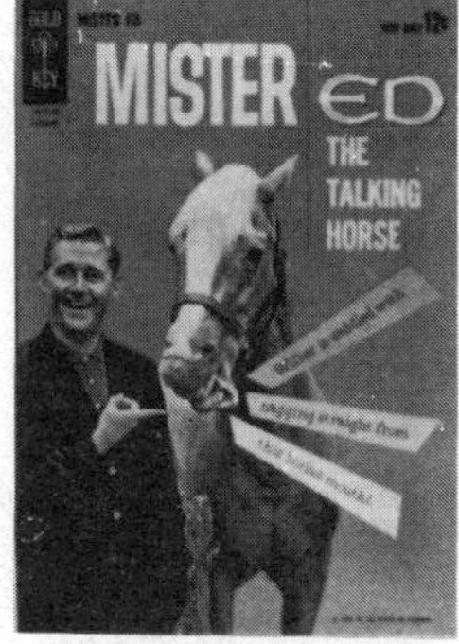

Mister Ed, The Talking Horse #2, © GK

MISS AMERICA MAGAZINE (continued)

	Good	Fine	Mint
V7#24(7/49)-Kamen-a	1.50	4.50	10.00
V7#25(8/49), 27-44(3/52), VII,nn(5/52)	1.30	4.00	9.00
V7#26(9/49)-All comics	1.60	4.70	11.00
V1,nn(7/52)-V1,nn(1/53)(#46-49)	1.30	4.00	9.00
V7#50(Spring '53), V1#51-V7?#54(7/53)	1.15	3.50	8.00
55-93	1.15	3.50	8.00

NOTE: *Photo-c #1, V2#4, V3#5, V4#4,6, V7#15, 24, 26, 34, 37, 38.*

MISS BEVERLY HILLS OF HOLLYWOOD
Mar-Apr, 1949 - No. 9, July-Aug, 1950
National Periodical Publications

1	17.00	51.00	120.00
2-William Holden photo-c	13.00	40.00	90.00
3-5: 3-Photo-c	11.00	32.00	76.00
6,7,9	9.50	28.00	65.00
8-Reagan photo on-c	13.00	40.00	90.00

MISS CAIRO JONES
1945
Croyden Publishers

1-Bob Oksner daily newspaper-r (1st strip story); lingerie panels	11.00	32.00	76.00

MISS FURY COMICS (Newspaper strip reprints)
Winter, 1942-43 - No. 8, Winter, 1946
Timely Comics (NPI 1/CmPI 2/MPC 3-8)

1-Origin Miss Fury by Tarpe' Mills (68 pgs.) in costume w/pin-ups	135.00	405.00	945.00
2-(60 pgs.)-In costume w/pin-ups	60.00	180.00	420.00
3-(60 pgs.)-In costume w/pin-ups	50.00	150.00	350.00
4-(52 pgs.)-Costume, 2 pgs. w/pin-ups	42.00	125.00	295.00
5-(52 pgs.)-In costume w/pin-ups	37.00	110.00	260.00
6-(52 pgs.)-Not in costume in inside stories, w/pin-ups	33.00	100.00	230.00
7,8-(36 pgs.)-In costume 1 pg. each, no pin-ups	33.00	100.00	230.00

MISSION IMPOSSIBLE (TV)
5/67 - No. 4, 10/68; No. 5, 10/69 (No. 1-5 have photo-c)
Dell Publishing Co.

1	3.50	10.50	24.00
2-5	2.65	8.00	18.00

MISS LIBERTY (Becomes Liberty)
1945 (MLJ reprints)
Burten Publishing Co.

1-The Shield & Dusty, The Wizard, & Roy, the Super Boy app.; r-/Shield-Wizard #13	12.00	36.00	84.00

MISS MELODY LANE OF BROADWAY
Feb-Mar, 1950 - No. 3, June-July, 1950
National Periodical Publications

1	17.00	51.00	120.00
2,3	13.00	40.00	90.00

MISS PEACH
Oct-Dec, 1963; 1969
Dell Publishing Co.

1-Jack Mendelsohn-a/script	4.35	13.00	30.00
...Tells You How to Grow(1969; 25 cents)-Mell Lazarus-a; also given away (36 pgs.)	2.65	8.00	18.00

MISS PEPPER (See Meet Miss Pepper)

MISS SUNBEAM (See Little Miss...)

MISS VICTORY (See Holyoke One-Shot No. 3)
1945 (See Veri Best Sure Fire & ...Sure Shot Comics)
Holyoke Publishing Co. (Tem)

	Good	Fine	Mint
1	13.00	40.00	90.00
2	11.00	32.00	76.00

MR. & MRS.
1922 (52 & 28 pgs.) (9x9½", cardboard-c)
Whitman Publishing Co.

By Briggs (B&W, 52pgs.)	6.00	18.00	42.00
28 pgs.-(9x9½")-Sunday strips-r in color	12.00	36.00	84.00

MR. & MRS. BEANS (See Single Series No. 11)

MR. & MRS. J. EVIL SCIENTIST (TV)(See The Flintstones)
Nov, 1963 - No. 4, Sept, 1966 (Hanna-Barbera)
Gold Key

1-From The Flintstones	1.30	4.00	9.00
2-4	.85	2.50	6.00

MR. ANTHONY'S LOVE CLINIC
Nov, 1949 - No. 5, Apr-May, 1950
Hillman Periodicals

1-Photo-c	3.70	11.00	26.00
2	2.00	6.00	14.00
3-5: 5-Photo-c	1.70	5.00	12.00

MR. BUG GOES TO TOWN (See Cinema Comics Herald)

MR. DISTRICT ATTORNEY (Radio/TV)
Jan-Feb, 1948 - No. 67, Jan-Feb, 1959 (52 pgs. 1-23)
National Periodical Publications

1	18.00	54.00	125.00
2	8.50	25.50	60.00
3-5	7.00	21.00	50.00
6-10	5.70	17.00	40.00
11-20	4.60	14.00	32.00
21-43: 43-Last pre-code (1-2/55)	3.50	10.50	24.00
44-67	2.30	7.00	16.00

MR. DISTRICT ATTORNEY (See 4-Color No. 13)

MISTER ED, THE TALKING HORSE (TV)
Mar-May, 1962 - No. 6, Feb, 1964 (All photo-c; photo back-c, 1-6)
Dell Publishing Co./Gold Key

4-Color 1295	2.30	7.00	16.00
1(11/62)-6 (Gold Key)-Photo-c	1.30	4.00	9.00

(See March of Comics No. 244,260,282,290)

MR. MAGOO (TV) (The Nearsighted..., ...& Gerald McBoing Boing 1954 issues; formerly Gerald...)
No. 6, Nov-Jan, 1953-54; 1963 - 1965
Dell Publishing Co.

6	4.00	12.00	28.00
4-Color 561(5/54),602(11/54)	4.00	12.00	28.00
4-Color 1235,1305('61)	3.50	10.50	24.00
3(9-11/63) - 5	3.00	9.00	21.00
4-Color 1235(12-536-505)(3-5/65)-2nd Printing	2.00	6.00	14.00

MISTER MIRACLE (See Brave & the Bold & Canc. Comic Caval.)
3-4/71 - No. 18, 2-3/74; No. 19, 9/77 - No. 25, 8-9/78; 1987
National Periodical Publications/DC Comics (#7,8-52 pgs.)

1	.35	1.00	2.00
2	.25	.75	1.50
3-10: 4-Boy Commando-r begin. 9-Origin Mr. Miracle		.60	1.20
11-17: 15-Intro/1st app. Shilo Norman		.40	.80
18-Barda & Scott Free wed; New Gods app.		.40	.80
19-22-Rogers-a(p)		.40	.80
23-25-Golden-a(p)		.25	.50
Special 1(1987, 52 pgs., $1.25)		.65	1.30

NOTE: ***Austin** a-19i. **Ditko** a-6r. **Golden** c-25p. **Heath** a-24i, 25i; c-25i. **Kirby** a(p)/c-1-18. **Nasser** a-19i. **Rogers** c-19, 20p, 21p, 22-24. **Wolverton** a-6r. 4-8 contain **Simon & Kirby** Boy Commando reprints from Detective 82,76, Boy Commandos 1,3,*

MISTER MIRACLE (continued)
Detective 64 in that order.

MR. MIRACLE (See Holyoke One-Shot No. 4)

MR. MONSTER (See Airboy-Mr. Monster Special & Vanguard Ill. #7)
Jan, 1985 - No. 10, June, 1987 ($1.75; Baxter paper)
Eclipse Comics

	Good	Fine	Mint
1	1.70	5.00	10.00
2-Dave Stevens-c	.70	2.00	4.00
3-9: 3-Alan Moore scripts	.50	1.50	3.00
10-6-D issue	.30	.90	1.80
. . . In 3-D	.35	1.00	2.00

MR. MONSTER'S HIGH-OCTANE HORROR
Aug, 1986 ($1.75)
Eclipse Comics

	Good	Fine	Mint
1-Bissette, Evans, Wolverton-r	.30	.85	1.70
. . . Three Dimensional High-Octane Horror (5/86)-Powell, Kubert Gilbert-a(r)	.40	1.25	2.50
. . . in 2-D: 100 copies signed & numbered (B&W)	1.00	3.00	6.00

MR. MONSTER'S HI-SHOCK SCHLOCK
Mar, 1987 - Present ($1.75, color)
Eclipse Comics

	Good	Fine	Mint
1,2: 40s & 50s horror-r	.30	.90	1.75

MR. MONSTER'S HI-VOLTAGE SUPER SCIENCE
Jan, 1987 - Present
Eclipse Comics

	Good	Fine	Mint
1-Vic Torry & His Flying Saucer-r	.30	.90	1.75

MR. MONSTER'S TRUE CRIME
Sept, 1986 - No. 2, Nov, 1986 ($1.75)
Eclipse Comics

	Good	Fine	Mint
1,2-r-/True Crime	.30	.90	1.80

MR. MONSTER'S WEIRD TALES OF THE FUTURE
July, 1987 - Present ($1.75, color)
Eclipse Comics

	Good	Fine	Mint
1-Wolverton-r	.30	.90	1.80

MR. MUSCLES (Formerly Blue Beetle No. 18-21)
No. 22, Mar, 1956 - No. 23, Aug, 1956
Charlton Comics

	Good	Fine	Mint
22,23	1.70	5.00	12.00

MISTER MYSTERY
Sept, 1951 - No. 19, Oct, 1954
Mr. Publ. (Media Publ.) No. 1-3/SPM Publ./Stanmore (Aragon)

	Good	Fine	Mint
1-Kurtzmanesque horror story	16.00	48.00	110.00
2,3-Kurtzmanesque story	11.00	32.00	76.00
4,6: Bondage-c; 6-Torture	11.00	32.00	76.00
5,8,10	9.50	28.00	65.00
7-"The Brain Bats of Venus" by Wolverton; partially re-used in Weird Tales of the Future #7	37.00	110.00	260.00
9-Nostrand-a	9.50	28.00	65.00
11-Wolverton "Robot Woman" story/Weird Mysteries #2, cut up, rewritten & partially redrawn	18.00	54.00	125.00
12-Classic injury to eye-c	25.00	75.00	175.00
13,14,17,19	6.00	18.00	42.00
15-"Living Dead" junkie story	9.00	27.00	63.00
16-Bondage-c	9.00	27.00	63.00
18-"Robot Woman" by Wolverton reprinted from Weird Mysteries #2; bondage-c	16.00	48.00	110.00

NOTE: ***Andru** c/a-1, 2. **Bailey** c-10-19(most). Bondage c-7.*

MISTER Q (See Mighty Midget Comics)

MR. RISK (Formerly All Romances; Men Against Crime No. 3 on)
No. 7, Oct, 1950 - No. 2, Dec, 1950
Ace Magazines

	Good	Fine	Mint
7,2	2.00	6.00	14.00

MR. SCARLET & PINKY (See Mighty Midget Comics)

MISTER UNIVERSE (Professional wrestler)
July, 1951; No. 2, Oct, 1951 - No. 5, April, 1952
Mr. Publications Media Publ. (Stanmor, Aragon)

	Good	Fine	Mint
1	6.50	19.50	45.00
2-'Jungle That Time Forgot', 24pg. story	4.60	14.00	32.00
3-Marijuana story	4.60	14.00	32.00
4,5-"Goes to War"	2.30	7.00	16.00

MR. X
June, 1984 - Present ($1.50-$1.75; direct sales; Baxter paper; color)
Mr. Publications/Vortex Comics

	Good	Fine	Mint
1	1.15	3.50	7.00
2	.70	2.00	4.00
3-12	.40	1.25	2.50
Graphic Novel ($11.95)	2.00	6.00	12.00

MISTY
Dec, 1985 - No. 6, May, 1986 (mini-series)
Star Comics (Marvel)

	Good	Fine	Mint
1-Millie The Model's niece		.35	.70
2-6		.40	.80

MITZI COMICS (. . . Boy Friend No. 2 on)
Spring, 1948 (One Shot)
Timely Comics

	Good	Fine	Mint
1-Kurtzman's "Hey Look" plus 3 pgs. "Giggles 'n' Grins"	5.00	15.00	35.00

MITZI'S BOY FRIEND (Formerly Mitzi; becomes Mitzi's Romances)
No. 2, June, 1948 - No. 7, April, 1949
Marvel Comics

	Good	Fine	Mint
2	2.30	7.00	16.00
3-7	1.50	4.50	10.00

MITZI'S ROMANCES (Formerly Mitzi's Boy Friend)
No. 8, June, 1949 - No. 10, Dec, 1949
Timely/Marvel Comics

	Good	Fine	Mint
8	2.30	7.00	16.00
9,10: 10-Painted-c	1.50	4.50	10.00

MOBY DICK (See 4-Color #717, Feature Presentations #6, and King Classics)

MOBY DUCK (See W. D. Showcase #2,11, Donald Duck #112)
10/67 - No. 11, 10/70; No. 12, 1/74 - No. 30, 2/78
Gold Key (Disney)

	Good	Fine	Mint
1	.85	2.50	6.00
2-5	.70	2.00	4.00
6-11	.35	1.00	2.00
12-30: 21,30-r		.60	1.20

MODEL FUN (With Bobby Benson)
No. 3, Winter, 1954-55 - No. 5, July, 1955
Harle Publications

	Good	Fine	Mint
3-Bobby Benson	2.30	7.00	16.00
4,5-Bobby Benson	1.50	4.50	10.00

MODELING WITH MILLIE (Formerly Life With Millie)
No. 21, Feb, 1963 - No. 54, June, 1967
Atlas/Marvel Comics Group (Male Publ.)

	Good	Fine	Mint
21	.85	2.50	5.00
22-30	.50	1.50	3.00
31-54	.25	.75	1.50

MODERN COMICS (Formerly Military Comics #1-43)
No. 44, Nov, 1945 - No. 102, Oct, 1950

Mr. Monster #9, © Eclipse Comics

Mister Mystery #13, © Stanmore

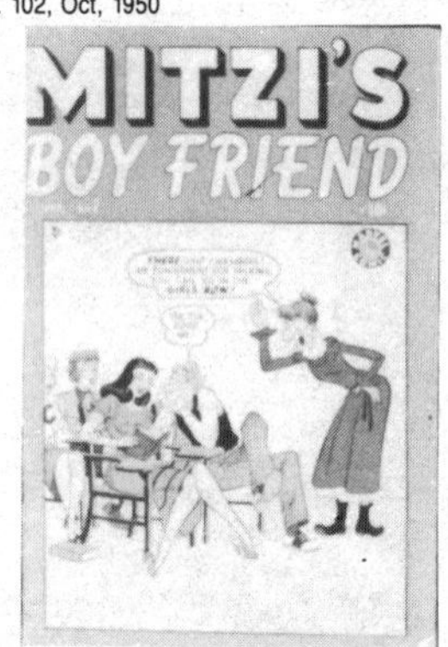

Mitzi's Boy Friend #7, © MCG

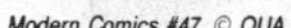
Modern Comics #47, © QUA

Modern Love #5, © WMG

Monster #1, © FH

MODERN COMICS (continued)
Quality Comics Group

	Good	Fine	Mint
44	20.00	60.00	140.00
45-52: 49-1st app. Fear, Lady Adventuress	13.00	40.00	90.00
53-Torchy by Ward begins (9/46)	18.00	54.00	125.00
54-60: 55-J. Cole-a	12.00	36.00	84.00
61-77,79,80: 73-J. Cole-a	11.50	34.00	80.00
78-1st app. Madame Butterfly	12.00	36.00	84.00
81-99,101: 82,83-One pg. J. Cole-a	11.00	32.00	76.00
100	11.50	34.00	80.00
102-(Scarce)-J. Cole-a; some issues have Spirit by Eisner	14.00	42.00	100.00

NOTE: ***Crandall*** *Blackhawk-No. 46-51, 54, 56, 58-60, 64, 67-70, 73, 82, 83.* ***Jack Cole*** *a-73.* ***Gustavson*** *a-47.* ***Ward*** *Blackhawk-No. 52, 53, 55 (15 pgs. each). Torchy in No. 53-102; by* ***Ward*** *only in No. 53-89(9/49); by* ***Gil Fox*** *No. 93, 102.*

MODERN LOVE
June-July, 1949 - No. 8, Aug-Sept, 1950
E. C. Comics

	Good	Fine	Mint
1	40.00	120.00	280.00
2-Craig/Feldstein-c	31.00	92.00	220.00
3-Spanking panels	26.00	78.00	180.00
4-6 (Scarce): 4-Bra/panties panels	37.00	110.00	260.00
7,8	28.00	84.00	195.00

NOTE: ***Feldstein*** *a-in most issues.* ***Ingels*** *a-1, 2, 4-7.* ***Wood*** *a-7. (Canadian reprints known; see Table of Contents.)*

MOD LOVE
1967 (36 pages) (50 cents)
Western Publishing Co.

	Good	Fine	Mint
1	1.50	4.50	10.00

MODNIKS, THE
Aug, 1967 - No. 2, Aug, 1970
Gold Key

	Good	Fine	Mint
10206-708(#1), 2	.75	2.25	5.00

MOD SQUAD (TV)
Jan, 1969 - No. 3, Oct, 1969 - No. 8, April, 1971
Dell Publishing Co.

	Good	Fine	Mint
1	1.50	4.50	10.00
2-8: 8 reprints #2. 3-Photo-c	1.00	3.00	7.00

MOD WHEELS
March, 1971 - No. 19, Jan, 1976
Gold Key

	Good	Fine	Mint
1	1.00	3.00	6.00
2-19: 11,15-Extra 16pgs. ads	.50	1.50	3.00

MOE & SHMOE COMICS
Spring, 1948 - No. 2, Summer, 1948
O. S. Publ. Co.

	Good	Fine	Mint
1	3.00	9.00	21.00
2	2.00	6.00	14.00

MOEBIUS
Oct, 1987 - Present ($9.95, $12.95, graphic novel, adults)
Epic Comics (Marvel)

	Good	Fine	Mint
1,2	1.70	5.00	9.95
3 ($12.95)	2.15	6.50	12.95

MOLLY MANTON'S ROMANCES (My Love No. 3)
Sept, 1949 - No. 2, Dec, 1949 (52 pgs.)
Marvel Comics (SePI)

	Good	Fine	Mint
1-Photo-c	3.70	11.00	26.00
2-Titled 'Romances of . . .'; photo-c	2.65	8.00	18.00

MOLLY O'DAY (Super Sleuth)
February, 1945 (1st Avon comic)
Avon Periodicals

	Good	Fine	Mint
1-Molly O'Day, The Enchanted Dagger by Tuska (r-/Yankee #1), Capt'n Courage, Corporal Grant app.	30.00	90.00	210.00

MONKEES, THE (TV)(Also see Circus Boy, Not Brand Echh #3 & Teen Beam)
March, 1967 - No. 17, Oct, 1969 (No. 1-4,6,7,10 have photo-c)
Dell Publishing Co.

	Good	Fine	Mint
1	3.50	10.50	24.00
2-17: 17 reprints #1	1.70	5.00	12.00

MONKEY & THE BEAR, THE
Sept, 1953 - No. 3, Jan, 1954
Atlas Comics (ZPC)

	Good	Fine	Mint
1-Howie Post-a	1.75	5.25	12.00
2,3	1.00	3.00	7.00

MONKEYSHINES COMICS (Ernie No. 24? on)
Summer, 1944 - No. 26, May, 1949
Ace Periodicals/Publishers Specialists/Current Books/Unity Publ.

	Good	Fine	Mint
1	3.50	10.50	24.00
2	1.70	5.00	12.00
3-10	1.30	4.00	9.00
11-26: 23-Fago c/a	1.15	3.50	8.00

MONKEY SHINES OF MARSELEEN
1909 (11½x17") (28 pages in two colors)
Cupples & Leon Co.

	Good	Fine	Mint
By Norman E. Jennett	9.00	27.00	63.00

MONKEY'S UNCLE, THE (See Merlin Jones As . . . under Movie Comics)

MONROES, THE (TV)
April, 1967
Dell Publishing Co.

	Good	Fine	Mint
1-Photo-c	1.75	5.25	12.00

MONSTER
1953
Fiction House Magazines

	Good	Fine	Mint
1-Dr. Drew by Grandenetti; reprint from Rangers Comics	14.00	42.00	100.00
2	11.50	34.00	80.00

MONSTER CRIME COMICS (Also see Crime Must Stop)
October, 1952 (52 pgs., 15 cents)
Hillman Periodicals

	Good	Fine	Mint
1 (Scarce)	33.00	100.00	230.00

MONSTER HOWLS (Magazine)
December, 1966 (Satire) (35 cents) (68 pgs.)
Humor-Vision

	Good	Fine	Mint
1	.85	2.50	5.00

MONSTER HUNTERS
8/75 - No. 9, 1/77; No. 10, 10/77 - No. 18, 2/79
Charlton Comics

	Good	Fine	Mint
1-Howard-a, Newton-c		.40	.80
2-Ditko-a		.40	.80
3-11		.30	.60
12,13,15-18-All reprints		.25	.50
14-Special all-Ditko issue		.50	1.00
1,2(Modern Comics reprints, 1977)		.15	.30

NOTE: ***Ditko*** *a-6, 8, 10, 13-15r, 18r; c-13-15, 18.* ***Howard*** *r-13.* ***Morisi*** *a-1.* ***Staton*** *a-1,13.* ***Sutton*** *a-2, 4; c-2, 4.*

MONSTER OF FRANKENSTEIN (See Frankenstein)

MONSTERS ON THE PROWL (Chamber of Darkness No. 1-8)
No. 9, 2/71 - No. 27, 11/73; No. 28, 6/74 - No. 30, 10/74
Marvel Comics Group (No. 13,14: 52 pgs.)

MONSTERS ON THE PROWL (continued)

	Good	Fine	Mint
9-Smith inks		.50	1.00
10-30		.30	.60

NOTE: ***Ditko*** *a-9r, 14r, 16r.* ***Kirby*** *r-10-17, 21, 23, 25, 27, 28, 30; c-9, 25.* ***Kirby/Ditko*** *r-14, 17-20, 22, 24, 26, 29.* ***Marie/John Severin*** *a-16(Kull). 9-13, 15-contain one new story. Woodish art by* ***Reese****-11.*

MONSTERS UNLEASHED (Magazine)
July, 1973 - No. 11, April, 1975; Summer, 1975 (B&W)
Marvel Comics Group

	Good	Fine	Mint
1	.35	1.00	2.00
2-The Frankenstein Monster begins		.60	1.20
3-Adams-c; The Man-Thing begins (origin-r)-Adams-a	.25	.75	1.50
4-Intro. Satana, the Devil's daughter; Krigstein-r	.25	.75	1.50
5-7: 7-Williamson-a(r)		.60	1.20
8,10,11: 8-Adams-r. 10-Origin Tigra		.50	1.00
9-Wendigo app.	.40	1.25	2.50
Annual 1(Summer,'75)-Kane-a		.50	1.00

NOTE: ***Boris*** *c-2, 6.* ***Brunner*** *a-2; c-11.* ***J. Buscema*** *a-2p, 4p, 5p.* ***Colan*** *a-1, 4r.* ***Davis*** *a-3r.* ***Everett*** *a-2r.* ***G. Kane*** *a-3.* ***Morrow*** *a-3; c-1.* ***Perez*** *a-8.* ***Reese*** *a-1, 2.* ***Tuska*** *a-3p.* ***Wildey*** *a-1r.*

MONTANA KID, THE (See Kid Montana)

MONTE HALE WESTERN (Movie star; Formerly Mary Marvel #1-28; also see Western Hero, Picture News #8 & X-Mas Comics)
No. 29, Oct, 1948 - No. 88, Jan, 1956
Fawcett Publications/Charlton No. 83 on

	Good	Fine	Mint
29-(#1, 52pgs.)-Photo-c begin, end #82; Monte Hale & his horse Pardner begin	18.00	54.00	125.00
30-(52 pgs.)-Big Bow and Little Arrow begin, end #34; Captain Tootsie by Beck	10.00	30.00	70.00
31-36,38-40-(52 pgs.): 34-Gabby Hayes begins, ends #80. 39-Captain Tootsie by Beck	8.00	24.00	56.00
37,41,45,49-(36 pgs.)	5.50	16.50	38.00
42-44,46-48,50-(52 pgs.): 47-Big Bow & Little Arrow app.	6.00	18.00	42.00
51,52,54-56,58,59-(52 pgs.)	4.35	13.00	30.00
53,57-(36 pgs.): 53-Slim Pickens app.	3.70	11.00	26.00
60-81: 36pgs. #60-on. 80-Gabby Hayes ends	3.70	11.00	26.00
82-Last Fawcett issue (6/53)	4.60	14.00	32.00
83-1st Charlton issue (2/55); B&W photo back-c begin. Gabby Hayes returns, ends #86	4.60	14.00	32.00
84 (4/55)	4.00	12.00	28.00
85-86	3.65	11.00	25.00
87-Wolverton-r, ½pg.	4.00	12.00	28.00
88-Last issue	4.00	12.00	28.00

NOTE: ***Gil Kane*** *a-33?, 34?* ***Rocky Lane*** *½-1 pg. (Carnation ad)-38, 40, 41, 43, 44, 46, 55.*

MONTY HALL OF THE U.S. MARINES (See With the Marines. . .)
Aug, 1951 - No. 11, 1953
Toby Press

	Good	Fine	Mint
1	3.65	11.00	25.00
2	2.85	8.50	20.00
3-5	2.50	7.50	17.00
6-11	1.85	5.50	13.00

NOTE: *3-5 full page pin-ups (Pin-Up Pete) by* ***Jack Sparling*** *in all.*

MOON, A GIRL. . .ROMANCE, A (Becomes Weird Fantasy #13 on; formerly Moon Girl #1-8)
No. 9, Sept-Oct, 1949 - No. 12, Mar-Apr, 1950
E. C. Comics

	Good	Fine	Mint
9-Moon Girl cameo; spanking panels	52.00	156.00	365.00
10,11	40.00	120.00	280.00
12-(Scarce)	55.00	165.00	385.00

NOTE: ***Feldstein, Ingels*** *art in all. Canadian reprints known; see Table of Contents.*

MOON GIRL AND THE PRINCE (#1) (Moon Girl #2-6; Moon Girl Fights Crime #7,8; becomes A Moon, A Girl, Romance #9 on)
Fall, 1947 - No. 8, Summer, 1949
E. C. Comics (Also see Happy Houlihans)

	Good	Fine	Mint
1-Origin Moon Girl	60.00	180.00	420.00
2	35.00	105.00	245.00
3,4: 4-Moon Girl vs. a vampire	30.00	90.00	210.00
5-E.C.'s 1st horror story, "Zombie Terror"	62.00	185.00	435.00
6-8 (Scarce): 7-Origin Star (Moongirl's sidekick)	34.00	102.00	240.00

NOTE: *#2 & #3 are 52 pgs., #4 on, 36 pgs. Canadian reprints known; (see Table of Contents.)*

MOON KNIGHT (Also see Marvel Preview, Marvel Spotlight & Werewolf by Night #32)
November, 1980 - No. 38, July, 1984 (Mando paper No. 33 on)
Marvel Comics Group

	Good	Fine	Mint
1-Origin resumed in #4	.40	1.25	2.50
2-5: 4-Intro Midnight Man	.25	.75	1.50
6-14		.60	1.20
15-First direct sale; Miller c(p)	.50	1.50	3.00
16	.25	.75	1.50
17-24	.25	.70	1.40
25-Double size	.25	.75	1.50
26-34,36-38		.40	.80
35-(52 pgs., $1.00)-X-men app.	.25	.75	1.50

NOTE: ***Austin*** *c-27i, 31i.* ***Kaluta*** *c-36-38.* ***Miller*** *c-9, 12p, 13p, 15p, 27p.*

MOON KNIGHT
June, 1985 - No. 6, Dec, 1985
Marvel Comics Group

	Good	Fine	Mint
1(V2#1)-Double size; new costume		.50	1.00
2-6		.50	1.00

MOON KNIGHT SPECIAL EDITION
Nov, 1983 - No. 3, Jan, 1984 (mini-series) (Baxter paper)
Marvel Comics Group

	Good	Fine	Mint
1-3: 1-Hulk-r	.25	.75	1.50

MOON MULLINS
1927 - 1933 (52 pgs.) (daily B&W strip reprints)
Cupples & Leon Co.

	Good	Fine	Mint
Series 1('27)-By Willard	11.00	32.00	76.00
Series 2('28), Series 3('29), Series 4('30)	8.00	24.00	56.00
Series 5('31), 6('32), 7('33)	6.00	18.00	42.00
Big Book 1('30)-B&W	14.00	42.00	100.00

MOON MULLINS (See Superbook No. 3)
1941 - 1945
Dell Publishing Co.

	Good	Fine	Mint
4-Color 14(1941)	17.00	51.00	120.00
Large Feature Comic 29(1941)	11.50	34.00	80.00
4-Color 31(1943)	10.00	30.00	70.00
4-Color 81(1945)	5.50	16.50	38.00

MOON MULLINS
Dec-Jan, 1947-48 - No. 8, 1949 (52 pgs.)
Michel Publ. (American Comics Group)

	Good	Fine	Mint
1-Alternating Sunday & daily strip-r	7.00	21.00	50.00
2	4.00	12.00	28.00
3-8	3.50	10.50	24.00

NOTE: ***Milt Gross*** *a-2, 4-6, 8.* ***Willard*** *r-all.*

MOON PILOT (See 4-Color No. 1313)

MOONSHADOW
5/85 - No. 12, 2/87 ($1.50-$1.75)(Adults only)
Epic Comics (Marvel)

	Good	Fine	Mint
1-Origin	.45	1.40	2.80

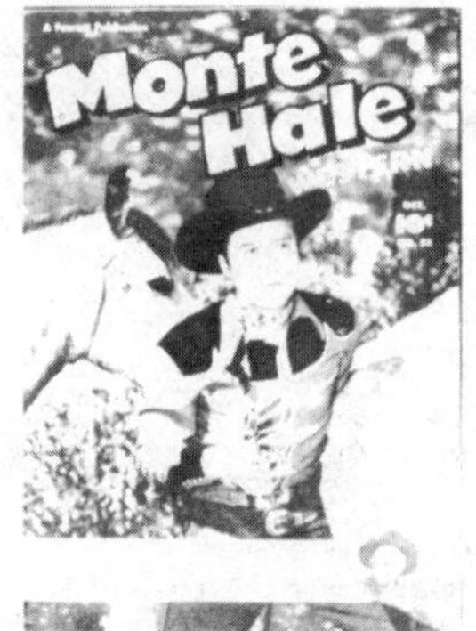

Monte Hale Western #53, © FAW

Monty Hall of the U.S. Marines #1, © TOBY

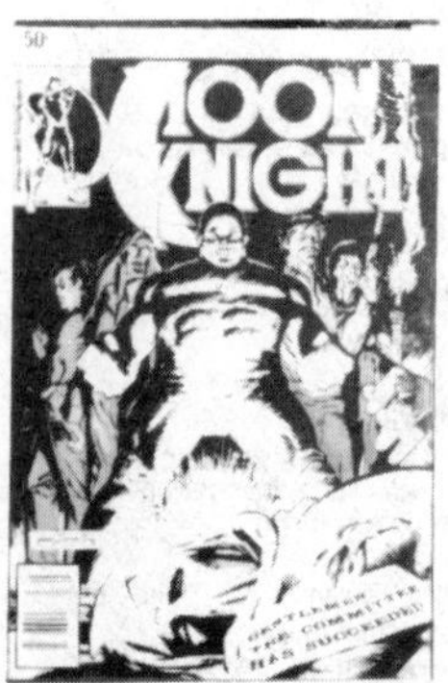

Moon Knight #4 (1st series), © MCG

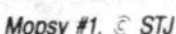
Mopsy #1, © STJ

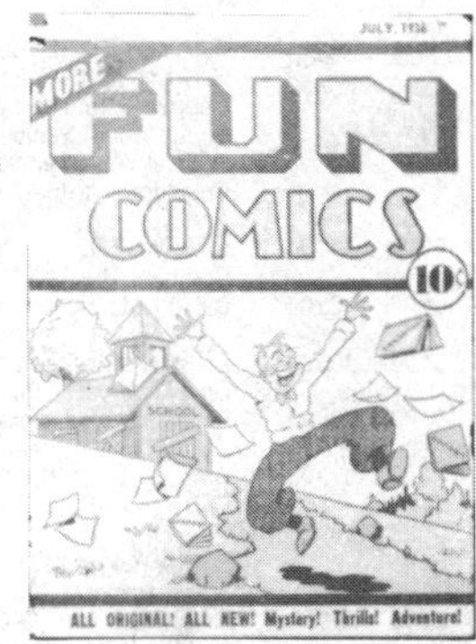

More Fun Comics #11, © DC

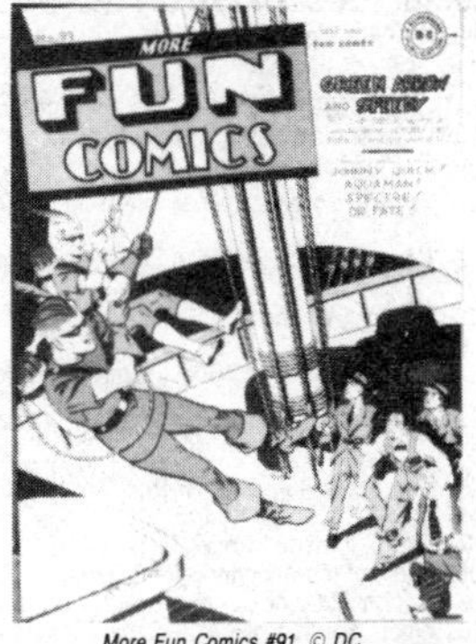

More Fun Comics #91, © DC

MOONSHADOW (continued) — Good / Fine / Mint
2-12: 11-Origin .30 .90 1.80

MOON-SPINNERS, THE (See Movie Comics)

MOPSY (See TV Teens & Pageant of Comics)
Feb, 1948 - No. 19, Sept, 1953
St. John Publ. Co.
1-Part-r; r-/"Some Punkins" by Neher 8.50 25.50 60.00
2 4.60 14.00 32.00
3-10(1953): 8-Lingerie panels 4.00 12.00 28.00
11-19: 19-Lingerie-c 3.50 10.50 24.00
NOTE: *#1, 4-6, 8, 13, 19 have paper dolls.*

MORE FUN COMICS (Formerly New Fun #1-6)
No. 7, Jan, 1936 - No. 127, Nov-Dec, 1947 (No. 7,9-11 paper-c)
National Periodical Publications — Good / Fine / VF-NM
7(1/36)-Oversized, paper-c; 1 pg. Kelly-a 185.00 555.00 1300.00
8(2/36)-Oversized (10x12"), slick-c; 1 pg. Kelly-a 160.00 480.00 1120.00
9(3-4/36)(Very Rare)-Last Henri Duval by Siegel & Shuster 160.00 480.00 1120.00
10,11(7/36): 11-1st 'Calling All Cars' by Siegel & Shuster 105.00 335.00 735.00
12(8/36)-Slick-c begin 90.00 270.00 630.00
V2#1(9/36, #13) 90.00 270.00 630.00
2(10/36, #14)-Dr. Occult in costume (Superman prototype) begins, ends #17; see The Comics Magazine 95.00 285.00 665.00
V2#3(11/36, #15), 16(V2#4), 17(V2#5)-Cover numbering begins #16 60.00 180.00 420.00
18-20(V2#8, 5/37) 42.00 125.00 295.00

Good / Fine / Mint
21(V2#9)-24(V2#12, 9/37) 37.00 110.00 260.00
25(V3#1, 10/37)-27(V3#3, 12/37) 37.00 110.00 260.00
28-30: 30-1st non-funny cover 37.00 110.00 260.00
31-35: 32-Last Dr. Occult 32.00 95.00 225.00
36-40: 36-The Masked Ranger begins, ends #41 30.00 90.00 210.00
41-50 27.00 81.00 190.00
51-1st app. The Spectre (in costume) in one panel ad at end of Buccaneer story 54.00 160.00 380.00
52-Origin The Spectre (out of costume), Part 1 by Bernard Baily; last Wing Brady (Rare) 1220.00 3650.00 8500.00
53-Origin The Spectre (out of costume), Part 2; Capt. Desmo begins (Scarce) 785.00 2355.00 5500.00
(Prices vary widely on above two books)
54-The Spectre in costume; last King Carter 285.00 855.00 2000.00
55-(Scarce)-Dr. Fate begins (Intro & 1st app.); last Bulldog Martin 271.00 810.00 1900.00
56-60: 56-Congo Bill begins 130.00 390.00 910.00
61-66: 63-Last St. Bob Neal. 64-Lance Larkin begins 95.00 285.00 665.00
67-(Scarce)-Origin Dr. Fate; last Congo Bill & Biff Bronson 135.00 405.00 950.00
68-70: 68-Clip Carson begins. 70-Last Lance Larkin 80.00 240.00 560.00
71-(Scarce)-Origin & 1st app. Johnny Quick by Mort Wysinger 130.00 390.00 910.00
72-Dr. Fate's new helmet; last Sgt. Carey, Sgt. O'Malley & Captain Desmo 70.00 210.00 490.00
73-(Rare)-Origin & 1st app. Aquaman; intro. Green Arrow & Speedy 200.00 600.00 1400.00
74-2nd Aquaman 75.00 225.00 525.00
75-80: 76-Last Clip Carson; Johnny Quick by Meskin begins, ends #97. 80-1st small logo 70.00 210.00 490.00
81-88: 87-Last Radio Squad 53.00 160.00 370.00

Good / Fine / Mint
89-Origin Green Arrow & Speedy Team-up 60.00 180.00 420.00
90-99: 93-Dover & Clover begin. 97-Kubert-a. 98-Last Dr. Fate 33.00 100.00 230.00
100 46.00 138.00 320.00
101-Origin & 1st app. Superboy (not by Siegel & Shuster); last Spectre issue 235.00 705.00 1650.00
102-2nd Superboy, 1st Superboy-c 58.00 175.00 405.00
103-3rd Superboy 44.00 130.00 305.00
104-107: 107-Last J. Quick & Superboy; Superboy-c 36.00 108.00 250.00
108-120: 108-Genius Jones begins 5.70 17.00 40.00
121-124,126: 121-123,126-Post-c 4.60 14.00 32.00
125-Superman on cover 25.00 75.00 175.00
127-(Scarce)-Post c/a 13.00 40.00 90.00
NOTE: *Cover features: The Spectre-#52-55, 57-60, 62-67. Dr. Fate-#55, 56, 61, 68-76. The Green Arrow & Speedy-#77-85, 88-97, 99, 101; w/Dover & Clover-#98. Johnny Quick-#86, 87, 100. Superboy-#101-107. Genius Jones-#108-127.* ***Bailey*** *a-45.* ***Al Capp*** *a-45(signed Koppy).* ***Kiefer*** *a-20.* ***Moldoff*** *c-51.*

MORE SEYMOUR (See Seymour My Son)
October, 1963
Archie Publications
1 1.35 4.00 8.00

MORE TRASH FROM MAD (Annual)
1958 - No. 12, 1969
E. C. Comics
nn(1958)-8 pgs. color Mad reprint from #20 8.00 24.00 56.00
2(1959)-Market Product Labels 5.70 17.00 40.00
3(1960)-Text book covers 4.60 14.00 32.00
4(1961)-Sing Along with Mad booklet 4.60 14.00 32.00
5(1962)-Window Stickers; r-/from Mad #39 3.00 9.00 21.00
6(1963)-TV Guise booklet 3.50 10.50 24.00
7(1964)-Alfred E. Neuman commemorative stamps 2.00 6.00 14.00
8(1965)-Life size poster-A. E. Neuman 2.00 6.00 14.00
9,10(1966-67)-Mischief Sticker 1.50 4.50 10.00
11(1968)-Campaign poster & bumper sticker 1.50 4.50 10.00
12(1969)-Pocket medals 1.50 4.50 10.00
NOTE: ***Kelly Freas*** *c-1, 2, 4.* ***Mingo*** *c-3, 5-9, 12.*

MORGAN THE PIRATE (See 4-Color No. 1227)

MORLOCK 2001 (. . .& the Midnight Men No. 3)
Feb, 1975 - No. 3, July, 1975
Atlas/Seaboard Publ.
1-Origin & 1st app. .50 1.00
2 .30 .60
3-Ditko/Wrightson-a; origin The Midnight Man & The Midnight Men .60 1.20

MORTIE (Mazie's Friend)
Dec, 1952 - No. 4, June, 1953?
Magazine Publishers
1 2.30 7.00 16.00
2 1.15 3.50 8.00
3,4 .85 2.50 6.00

MORTY MEEKLE (See 4-Color No. 793)

MOSES & THE TEN COMMANDMENTS (See Dell Giants)

MOTHER GOOSE (See Christmas With Mother Goose & 4-Color #41, 59, 68, 862)

MOTHER OF US ALL
1950? (32 pgs.)
Catechetical Guild Giveaway
2.00 6.00 12.00

MOTHER TERESA OF CALCUTTA
1984

MOTHER TERESA OF CALCUTTA (continued)
Marvel Comics Group

	Good	Fine	Mint
1		.60	1.25

MOTION PICTURE COMICS (See Fawcett Movie Comics)
1950 - No. 114, Jan, 1953 (All-photo-c)
Fawcett Publications

	Good	Fine	Mint
101-"Vanishing Westerner"-Monte Hale (1950)	20.00	60.00	140.00
102-"Code of the Silver Sage"-Rocky Lane (1/51)	18.00	54.00	125.00
103-"Covered Wagon Raid"-Rocky Lane (3/51)	18.00	54.00	125.00
104-"Vigilante Hideout"-Rocky Lane (5/51)-book length Powell-a	18.00	54.00	125.00
105-"Red Badge of Courage"-Audie Murphy; Bob Powell-a (7/51)	24.00	72.00	170.00
106-"The Texas Rangers"-George Montgomery (9/51)	21.00	64.00	150.00
107-"Frisco Tornado"-Rocky Lane (11/51)	17.00	51.00	120.00
108-"Mask of the Avenger"-John Derek	13.00	40.00	90.00
109-"Rough Rider of Durango"-Rocky Lane	17.00	51.00	120.00
110-"When Worlds Collide"-George Evans-a (1951); Williamson & Evans drew themselves in story; (Also see Famous Funnies No. 72-88)	68.00	205.00	475.00
111-"The Vanishing Outpost"-Lash LaRue	20.00	60.00	140.00
112-"Brave Warrior"-Jon Hall & Jay Silverheels	12.00	36.00	84.00
113-"Walk East on Beacon"-George Murphy; Shaffenberger-a	8.50	25.50	60.00
114-"Cripple Creek"-George Montgomery (1/53)	10.00	30.00	70.00

MOTION PICTURE FUNNIES WEEKLY (Amazing Man No. 5 on?)
1939 (36 pgs.)(Giveaway)(Black & White)
No month given; last panel in Sub-Mariner story dated 4/39
(Also see Colossus, Green Giant & Invaders No. 20)
First Funnies, Inc.

	Good	Fine	Mint
1-Origin & 1st printed app. Sub-Mariner by Bill Everett (8 pgs.); Fred Schwab-c; reprinted in Marvel Mystery #1 with color added over the craft tint which was used to shade the black & white version; Spy Ring, American Ace (reprinted in Marvel Mystery No. 3) app. (Rare)-only seven (7) known copies, all with brown pages.	2500.00	5000.00	----
Covers only to #2-4 (set)			600.00

NOTE: The only seven known copies (with an eighth suspected) were discovered in 1974 in the estate of the deceased publisher. Covers only to issues No. 2-4 were also found which evidently were printed in advance along with #1. #1 was to be distributed only through motion picture movie houses. However, it is believed that only advanced copies were sent out and the motion picture houses not going for the idea. Possible distribution at local theaters in Boston suspected. The last panel of Sub-Mariner contains a rectangular box with "Continued Next Week" printed in it. When reprinted in Marvel Mystery, the box was left in with lettering omitted.

MOUNTAIN MEN (See Ben Bowie)

MOUSE MUSKETEERS (See M.G.M.'s. . .)

MOUSE ON THE MOON, THE (See Movie Classics)

MOVIE CLASSICS
Jan, 1953 - Dec, 1969
Dell Publishing Co.

(Before 1962, most movie adapt. were part of the 4-Color Series)

	Good	Fine	Mint
Around the World Under the Sea 12-030-612 (12/66)	1.30	4.00	9.00
Bambi 3(4/56)-Disney; r-/4-Color 186	1.30	4.00	9.00
Battle of the Bulge 12-056-606 (6/66)	1.30	4.00	9.00
Beach Blanket Bingo 12-058-509	4.00	12.00	28.00
Bon Voyage 01-068-212 (12/62)-Disney; photo-c	1.30	4.00	9.00
Castilian, The 12-110-401	1.75	5.25	12.00
Cat, The 12-109-612 (12/66)	1.00	3.00	7.00
Cheyenne Autumn 12-112-506 (4-6/65)	3.35	10.00	23.00
Circus World, Samuel Bronston's 12-115-411; John Wayne app. John Wayne photo-c	4.00	12.00	28.00
Countdown 12-150-710 (10/67); James Caan photo-c	1.30	4.00	9.00
Creature, The 1 (12-142-302) (12-2/62-63)	2.30	7.00	16.00
Creature, The 12-142-410 (10/64)	1.30	4.00	9.00
David Ladd's Life Story 12-173-212 (10-12/62)-Photo-c	5.70	17.00	40.00
Die, Monster, Die 12-175-603 (3/66)-Photo-c	1.75	5.25	12.00
Dirty Dozen 12-180-710 (10/67)	2.00	6.00	14.00
Dr. Who & the Daleks 12-190-612 (12/66)-Photo-c	11.00	33.00	75.00
Dracula 12-231-212 (10-12/62)	1.70	5.00	12.00
El Dorado 12-240-710 (10/67)-John Wayne; photo-c	6.00	18.00	42.00
Ensign Pulver 12-257-410 (8-10/64)	1.30	4.00	9.00
Frankenstein 12-283-305 (3-5/63)	1.75	5.25	12.00
Great Race, The 12-299-603 (3/66)-Natallie Wood, Tony Curtis photo-c	2.00	6.00	14.00
Hallelujah Trail, The 12-307-602 (2/66) (Shows 1/66 inside); Burt Lancaster, Lee Remick photo-c	3.35	10.00	23.00
Hatari 12-340-301 (1/63)-John Wayne	4.00	12.00	28.00
Horizontal Lieutenant, The 01-348-210 (10/62)	1.30	4.00	9.00
Incredible Mr. Limpet, The 12-370-408; Don Knotts photo-c	1.30	4.00	9.00
Jack the Giant Killer 12-374-301 (1/63)	4.00	12.00	28.00
Jason & the Argonauts 12-376-310 (8-10/63)-Photo-c	4.65	14.00	32.00
Lancelot & Guinevere 12-416-310 (10/63)	4.00	12.00	28.00
Lawrence 12-426-308 (8/63)-Story of Lawrence of Arabia; movie ad on back-c; not exactly like movie	3.00	9.00	21.00
Lion of Sparta 12-439-301 (1/63)	1.30	4.00	9.00
Mad Monster Party 12-460-801 (9/67)	4.35	13.00	30.00
Magic Sword, The 01-496-209 (9/62)	3.00	9.00	21.00
Masque of the Red Death 12-490-410 (8-10/64)-Vincent Price photo-c	2.00	6.00	14.00
Maya 12-495-612 (12/66)-Part photo-c	2.00	6.00	14.00
McHale's Navy 12-500-412 (10-12/64)	1.50	4.50	10.00
Merrill's Marauders 12-510-301 (1/63)-Photo-c	1.30	4.00	9.00
Mouse on the Moon, The 12-530-312 (10/12/63)-Photo-c	1.50	4.50	10.00
Mummy, The 12-537-211 (9-11/62) 2 different back-c issues	2.00	6.00	14.00
Music Man, The 12-538-301 (1/63)	1.30	4.00	9.00
Naked Prey, The 12-545-612 (12/66)-Photo-c	3.00	9.00	21.00
Night of the Grizzly, The 12-558-612 (12/66)-Photo-c	2.00	6.00	14.00
None But the Brave 12-565-506 (4-6/65)	2.65	8.00	18.00
Operation Bikini 12-597-310 (10/63)-Photo-c	1.75	5.25	12.00
Operation Crossbow 12-590-512 (10-12/65)	1.75	5.25	12.00
Prince & the Pauper, The 01-654-207 (5-7/62)-Disney	1.75	5.25	12.00
Raven, The 12-680-309 (9/63)-Vincent Price photo-c	2.00	6.00	14.00
Ring of Bright Water 01-701-910 (10/69) (inside shows No. 12-701-909)	2.00	6.00	14.00
Runaway, The 12-707-412 (10-12/64)	1.00	3.00	7.00
Santa Claus Conquers the Martians 12-725-603 (3/60)-Regular issue with number & price; photo-c	5.00	15.00	30.00
Another version given away with a Golden Record, SLP 170, nn, no price (3/66) Complete with record	8.50	25.50	60.00
Six Black Horses 12-750-301 (1/63)-Photo-c	1.75	5.25	12.00

Motion Picture Comics #102, © Republic Pictures

Movie Classics (The Creature), © DELL

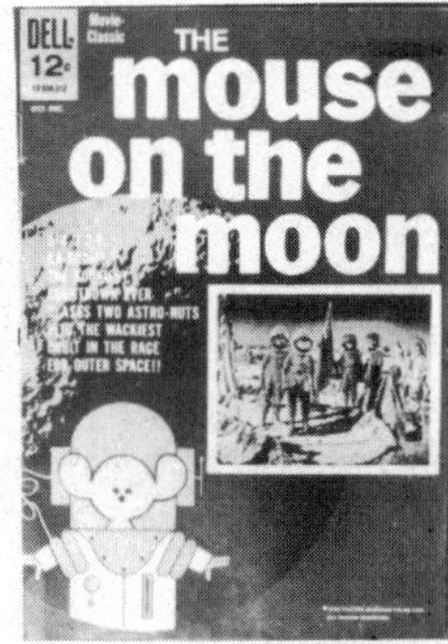

Movie Classics (Mouse on the Moon), © DELL

Movie Classics (Ski Party), © DELL

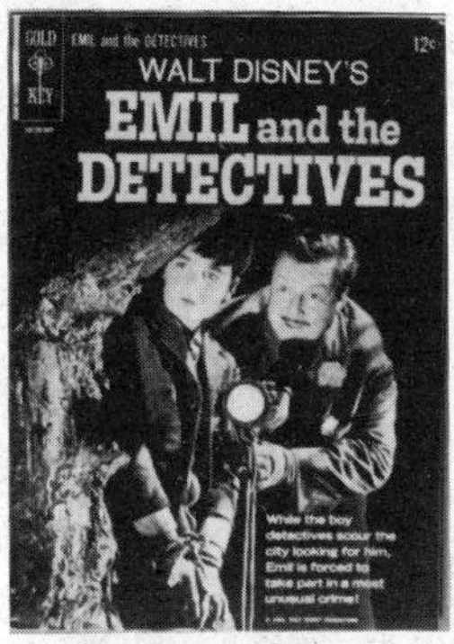

Movie Comics (Emil and the Detectives), © WDC

Movie Comics (Jungle Book #30033-803), © WDC

MOVIE CLASSICS (continued) — Good / Fine / Mint

Ski Party 12-743-511 (9-11/65)-Frankie Avalon photo-c 3.35 10.00 23.00
Smoky 12-746-702 (2/67) 1.15 3.50 8.00
Sons of Katie Elder 12-748-511 (9-11/65); John Wayne app., Photo-c 7.00 21.00 50.00
Tales of Terror 12-793-302 (2/63)-Evans-a 1.15 3.50 8.00
Taras Bulba (1962) (Exist?) 7.00 21.00 50.00
Three Stooges Meet Hercules 01-828-208 (8/62)-Photo-c 3.00 9.00 21.00
Tomb of Ligeia 12-830-506 (4-6/65) 1.30 4.00 9.00
Treasure Island 01-845-211 (7-9/62)-Disney; r-/4-Color 624 1.00 3.00 7.00
Twice Told Tales (Nathaniel Hawthorne) 12-840-401 (11-1/63-64); photo-c 1.75 5.25 12.00
Two on a Guillotine 12-850-506 (4-6/65) 1.30 4.00 9.00
Valley of Gwangi 01-880-912 (12/69) 4.00 12.00 28.00
War Gods of the Deep 12-900-509 (7-9/65) 1.30 4.00 9.00
War Wagon, The 12-533-709 (9/67); John Wayne app. 6.00 18.00 42.00
Who's Minding the Mint? 12-924-708 (8/67)-Photo-c 1.30 4.00 9.00
Wolfman, The 12-922-308 (6-8/63) 1.30 4.00 9.00
Wolfman, The 1(12-922-410)(8-10/64)-2nd printing; 4-/#12-922-308 1.30 4.00 9.00
Zulu 12-950-410 (8-10/64)-Photo-c 4.00 12.00 28.00

MOVIE COMICS (See Fawcett Movie Comics & Cinema Comics Herald)

MOVIE COMICS
April, 1939 - No. 6, Sept, 1939 (Most all photo-c)
National Periodical Publications/Picture Comics

1-"Gunga Din,""Son of Frankenstein,""The Great Man Votes," "Fisherman's Wharf,"&"Scouts to the Rescue part 1; Wheelan "Minute Movies" begin 142.00 425.00 1000.00
2-"Stagecoach,""The Saint Strikes Back,""King of the Turf," "Scouts to the Rescue" part 2, "Arizona Legion" 86.00 260.00 600.00
3-"East Side of Heaven,""Mystery in the White Room,""Four Feathers,""Mexican Rose" with Gene Autry, "Spirit of Culver," "Many Secrets,""The Mikado" 71.00 215.00 500.00
4-"Captain Fury," Gene Autry in "Blue Montana Skies,""Streets of N.Y." with Jackie Cooper, "Oregon Trail" part 1 with Johnny Mack Brown, "Big Town Czar" with Barton MacLane, & "Star Reporter" with Warren Hull 64.00 190.00 450.00
5-"Man in the Iron Mask,""Five Came Back,""Wolf Call,""The Girl & the Gambler,""The House of Fear,""The Family Next Door,""Oregon Trail" part 2 64.00 190.00 450.00
6-"The Phantom Creeps,""Chumps at Oxford,"&"The Oregon Trail" part 3 86.00 260.00 600.00

NOTE: *Above books contain many original movie stills with dialogue from movie scripts.*

MOVIE COMICS
Dec, 1946 - No. 4, 1947
Fiction House Magazines

1-Big Town & Johnny Danger begin; Celardo-a 23.00 70.00 160.00
2-"White Tie & Tails" with William Bendix; Mitzi of the Movies begins by Matt Baker, ends #4 15.00 45.00 105.00
3-Andy Hardy 15.00 45.00 105.00
4-Mitzi In Hollywood by Matt Baker 19.00 57.00 132.00

MOVIE COMICS
Oct, 1962 - March, 1972
Gold Key/Whitman

Alice in Wonderland 10144-503 (3/65)-Disney; partial reprint of 4-Color 331 1.75 5.25 12.00
Aristocats, The 1 (30045-103)(3/71)-Disney; with pull-out poster (25 cents) 3.00 9.00 21.00
Bambi 1 (10087-309)(9/63)-Disney; reprints 4-Color 186 2.00 6.00 14.00
Bambi 2 (10087-607)(7/66)-Disney; reprints 4-Color 186 1.70 5.00 12.00
Beneath the Planet of the Apes 30044-012 (12/70)-with pull-out poster; photo-c 3.00 9.00 21.00
Big Red 10026-211 (11/62)-Disney-Photo-c 1.15 3.50 8.00
Big Red 10026-503 (3/65)-Disney; reprints 10026-211-Photo-c 1.15 3.50 8.00
Blackbeard's Ghost 10222-806 (6/68)-Disney 1.50 4.50 10.00
Buck Rogers Giant Movie Ed. 11296 (Whitman), 02489 (Marvel)-2 formats; 1979; tabloid size; $1.50; adaptation of movie; Bolle, McWilliams-a .30 .80 1.60
Bullwhip Griffin 10181-706 (6/67)-Disney; Manning-a; photo-c 2.35 7.00 16.00
Captain Sindbad 10077-309 (9/63)-Manning-a; photo-c 3.50 10.50 24.00
Chitty Chitty Bang Bang 1 (30038-902)(2/69)-with pull-out poster; Disney; photo-c 3.00 9.00 21.00
Cinderella 10152-508 (8/65)-Disney; reprints 4-Color 786 1.50 4.50 10.00
Darby O'Gill & the Little People 10251-001(1/70)-Disney; reprints 4-Color 1024 (Toth-a)-Photo-c 2.65 8.00 18.00
Dumbo 1 (10090-310)(10/63)-Disney; reprints 4-Color 668 1.50 4.50 10.00
Emil & the Detectives 10120-502 (2/65)-Disney; photo-c 2.35 7.00 16.00
Escapade in Florence 1 (10043-301)(1/63)-Disney; starring Annette 4.00 12.00 28.00
Fall of the Roman Empire 10118-407 (7/64); Sophia Loren photo-c 1.75 5.25 12.00
Fantastic Voyage 10178-702 (2/67)-Wood/Adkins-a; photo-c 2.35 7.00 16.00
55 Days at Peking 10081-309 (9/63)-Photo-c 2.00 6.00 14.00
Fighting Prince of Donegal, The 10193-701 (1/67)-Disney 1.50 4.50 10.00
First Men in the Moon 10132-503 (3/65)-Fred Fredericks-a; photo-c 2.00 6.00 14.00
Gay Purr-ee 30017-301(1/63, 84pgs.) 2.85 8.50 20.00
Gnome Mobile, The 10207-710 (10/67)-Disney 2.00 6.00 14.00
Goodbye, Mr. Chips 10246-006 (6/70)-Peter O'toole photo-c 1.75 5.25 12.00
Happiest Millionaire, The 10221-804 (4/68)-Disney 1.15 3.50 8.00
Hey There, It's Yogi Bear 10122-409 (9/64)-Hanna-Barbera 1.75 5.25 12.00
Horse Without a Head, The 10109-401 (1/64)-Disney 1.50 4.50 10.00
How the West Was Won 10074-307 (7/63)-Tufts-a 3.00 9.00 21.00
In Search of the Castaways 10048-303 (3/63)-Disney; Haley Mills-photo-c 3.50 10.50 24.00
Jungle Book, The 1 (6022-801)(1/68-Whitman)-Disney; large size (10x13½"); 59 cents 1.70 5.00 12.00
Jungle Book, The 1 (30033-803)(3/68, 68 pgs.)-Disney; same contents as Whitman #1 1.30 4.00 9.00
Jungle Book, The 1 (6/78, $1.00 tabloid) .60 1.20
Jungle Book ('84)-r-/Giant .40 .80
Kidnapped 10080-306 (6/63)-Disney; reprints 4-Color 1101; photo-c 1.15 3.50 8.00
King Kong 30036-809(9/68-68 pgs.)-painted-c 2.35 7.00 16.00
King Kong nn-Whitman Treasury($1.00,68pgs.,1968), same cover as Gold Key issue .70 2.00 4.00
King Kong 11299(#1-786, 10x13¼", 68pgs., $1.00, 1978) .50 1.00

MOVIE COMICS (continued) — Good / Fine / Mint

Lady and the Tramp 10042-301 (1/63)-Disney; r-4-Color 629 — 1.50 4.50 10.00

Lady and the Tramp 1 (1967-Giant; 25 cents)-Disney; r-part of Dell #1 — 2.50 7.50 20.00

Lady and the Tramp 2 (10042-203)(3/72)-Disney; r-4-Color 629 — 1.15 3.50 8.00

Legend of Lobo, The 1 (10059-303)(3/63)-Disney; photo-c — 1.15 3.50 8.00

Lt. Robin Crusoe, U.S.N. 10191-610 (10/66)-Disney; Dick Van Dyke photo-c — 1.50 4.50 10.00

Lion, The 10035-301 (1/63)-Photo-c — 1.15 3.50 8.00

Lord Jim 10156-509 (9/65)-Photo-c — 1.75 5.25 12.00

Love Bug, The 10237-906 (6/69)-Disney-Buddy Hackett photo-c — 1.50 4.50 10.00

Mary Poppins 10136-501 (1/65)-Disney; photo-c — 2.65 8.00 18.00

Mary Poppins 30023-501 (1/65-68 pgs.)-Disney; photo-c — 3.00 9.00 24.00

McLintock 10110-403 (3/64); John Wayne app.; photo-c — 6.50 19.50 45.00

Merlin Jones as the Monkey's Uncle 10115-510 (10/65)-Disney; Annette Funicello front/back photo-c — 2.00 6.00 14.00

Miracle of the White Stallions, The 10065-306 (6/63)-Disney — 1.75 5.25 12.00

Misadventures of Merlin Jones, The 10115-405 (5/64)-Disney Annette Funicello photo front/back-c — 2.50 7.50 15.00

Moon-Spinners, The 10124-410 (10/64)-Disney; Haley Mills photo-c — 3.50 10.50 24.00

Mutiny on the Bounty 1 (10040-302)(2/63)-Marlon Brando photo-c — 1.75 5.25 12.00

Nikki, Wild Dog of the North 10141-412 (12/64)-Disney; reprints 4-Color 1226 — 1.15 3.50 8.00

Old Yeller 10168-601 (1/66)-Disney; reprints 4-Color 869; photo-c — 1.15 3.50 8.00

One Hundred & One Dalmations 1 (10247-002) (2/70)-Disney; reprints 4-Color 1183 — 1.50 4.50 10.00

Peter Pan 1 (10086-309)(9/63)-Disney; reprints 4-Color 442 — 2.00 6.00 12.00

Peter Pan 2 (10086-909)(9/69)-Disney; reprints 4-Color 442 — 1.15 3.50 8.00

Peter Pan 1 ('83)-r/4-Color 442 — .40 .80

P.T. 109 10123-409 (9/64)-John F. Kennedy — 2.65 8.00 18.00

Rio Conchos 10143-503(3/65) — 2.35 7.00 16.00

Robin Hood 10163-506 (6/65)-Disney; reprints 4-Color 413 — 1.50 4.50 10.00

Shaggy Dog & the Absent-Minded Professor 30032-708 (8/67-Giant, 68 pgs.)-Disney; reprints 4-Color 985,1199 — 2.50 7.50 20.00

Sleeping Beauty 1 (30042-009)(9/70)-Disney; reprints 4-Color 973; with pull-out poster — 2.65 8.00 18.00

Snow White & the Seven Dwarfs 1 (10091-310)(10/63)-Disney; reprints 4-Color 382 — 1.75 5.25 12.00

Snow White & the Seven Dwarfs 10091-709 (9/67)-Disney; reprints 4-Color 382 — 1.50 4.50 10.00

Snow White & the Seven Dwarfs nn(2/84)-r-/4-Color 382 — .40 .80

Son of Flubber 1 (10057-304)(4/63)-Disney; sequel to "The Absent-Minded Professor" — 1.75 5.25 12.00

Summer Magic 10076-309 (9/63)-Disney; Haley Mills; Manning-a — 4.00 12.00 28.00

Swiss Family Robinson 10236-904 (4/69)-Disney; reprints 4-Color 1156; photo-c — 1.75 5.25 12.00

Sword in the Stone, The 30019-402 (2/64-Giant, 84 pgs.)-Disney — 2.50 7.50 20.00

That Darn Cat 10171-602 (2/66)-Disney; Haley Mills photo-c — 3.50 10.50 24.00

Those Magnificent Men in Their Flying Machines 10162-510 (10/65); photo-c — 1.75 5.25 12.00

Three Stooges in Orbit 30016-211 (11/62-Giant, 32 pgs.)-All photos from movie; stiff-photo-c — 4.60 14.00 32.00

Tiger Walks, A 10117-406 (6/64)-Disney; Torres, Tufts-a; photo-c — 2.35 7.00 16.00

Toby Tyler 10142-502 (2/65)-Disney; reprints 4-Color 1092; photo-c — 1.50 4.50 10.00

Treasure Island 1 (10200-703)(3/67)-Disney; reprints 4-Color 624; photo-c — 1.15 3.50 8.00

20,000 Leagues Under the Sea 1 (10095-312)(12/63)-Disney; reprints 4-Color 614 — 1.15 3.50 8.00

Wonderful Adventures of Pinocchio, The 1 (10089-310)(10/63)-Disney; reprints 4-Color 545 — 1.15 3.50 8.00

Wonderful Adventures of Pinocchio, The 10089-109 (9/71)-Disney; reprints 4-Color 545 — 1.15 3.50 8.00

Wonderful World of the Brothers Grimm 1 (10008-210)(10/62) — 2.65 8.00 18.00

X, the Man with the X-Ray Eyes 10083-309 (9/63)-Ray Milland photo on-c — 3.00 9.00 21.00

Yellow Submarine 35000-902 (2/69-Giant, 68 pgs.)-with pull-out poster; The Beatles cartoon movie — 6.00 18.00 42.00

MOVIE LOVE (See Personal Love)
Feb, 1950 - No. 22, Aug, 1953
Famous Funnies

	Good	Fine	Mint
1	5.00	15.00	35.00
2	2.65	8.00	18.00
3-7,9	2.35	7.00	16.00
8-Williamson/Frazetta-a, 6 pgs.	26.00	78.00	180.00
10-Frazetta-a, 6 pgs.	32.00	95.00	225.00
11,12,14-16	2.15	6.50	15.00
13-Ronald Reagan photo-c with 1 pg. bio.	10.00	30.00	70.00
17-One pg. Frazetta ad	3.15	9.50	22.00
18-22	1.85	5.50	13.00

NOTE: *Each issue has a full-length movie adaptation with photo covers.*

MOVIE THRILLERS
1949 (Movie adaptation; photo-c)
Magazine Enterprises

	Good	Fine	Mint
1-"Rope of Sand" with Burt Lancaster	17.00	51.00	120.00

MOVIE TOWN ANIMAL ANTICS (Formerly Animal Antics; Raccoon Kids #52 on)
No. 24, Jan-Feb, 1950 - No. 51, July-Aug, 1954
National Periodical Publications

	Good	Fine	Mint
24-Raccoon Kids continue	4.00	12.00	28.00
25-51	3.00	9.00	21.00

NOTE: ***Sheldon Mayer** a-28-33, 35, 37-41, 43, 44, 47, 49-51.*

MOVIE TUNES COMICS (Formerly Animated . . . ; Frankie No. 4 on)
No. 3, Fall, 1946
Marvel Comics (MgPC)

	Good	Fine	Mint
3-Super Rabbit, Krazy Krow, Silly Seal & Ziggy Pig	3.70	11.00	26.00

MOWGLI JUNGLE BOOK (See 4-Color No. 487,582,620)

MR. (See Mister)

MS. MARVEL
Jan, 1977 - No. 23, Apr, 1979
Marvel Comics Group

	Good	Fine	Mint
1-Buscema-a		.50	1.00
2-Origin		.30	.60
3-23: 5-Vision app. 20-New costume		.25	.50

NOTE: ***Austin** c-14i, 16i, 17i, 22i. **Buscema** a-1-3p; c(p)-2, 4, 6, 7, 15. **Infantino** a-14p, 19p. **Gil Kane** c-8. **Mooney** a-4-8p, 13p, 15-18p. **Starlin** c-12.*

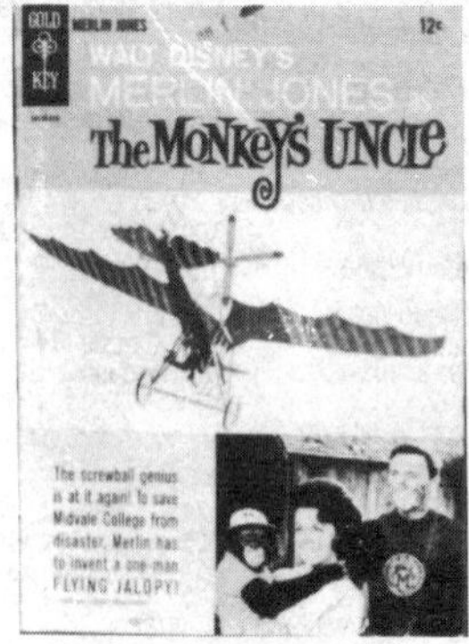

Movie Comics (Merlin Jones as...), © WDC

Movie Love #8, © FF

Movie Thrillers #1, © ME

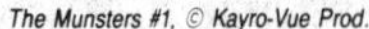

The Munsters #1, © Kayro-Vue Prod.

Murder, Incorporated #1, © FOX

Murderous Gangsters #3, © REAL

MS. MYSTIC (Also see Captain Victory. . .)
10/82 - No. 2, 2/84
Pacific Comics

	Good	Fine	Mint
1-Origin; intro Erth, Ayre, Fyre & Watr; Adams script/a/c	.35	1.00	2.00
2 ($1.50)-Adams c/a & script	.25	.75	1.50

MS. TREE'S THRILLING DETECTIVE ADVENTURES (Ms. Tree #4 on) (Baxter paper #4-9)
2/83 - No. 9, 7/84; No. 10, 8/84 - No. 18, 5/85; No. 19, 6/85 -Present
Eclipse Comics/Aardvark-Vanaheim 10-18/Renegade Press 19 on

	Good	Fine	Mint
1		.50	1.00
2-8: 2-Scythe begins	.25	.75	1.50
9-Last Eclipse & last color issue		.50	1.00
10,11 (Aardvark-Vanaheim) B&W		.50	1.00
12-44 ($1.70; $2.00 #34 on)	.30	.85	1.70
Summer Special 1(8/86)	.35	1.00	2.00
. . .1950s 3-D Crime (7/87, no glasses)-Johnny Dynamite in 3-D	.40	1.25	2.50

NOTE: *Miller pin-up-1-4,6. Johnny Dynamite-r begin #36.*

MS. TREE/MIKE MIST IN 3-D
Aug, 1985 (One Shot)
Renegade Press

	Good	Fine	Mint
1-With glasses	.40	1.25	2.50

MS. VICTORY SPECIAL
Jan, 1985
Americomics

	Good	Fine	Mint
1	.30	.85	1.70

MUGGSY MOUSE
1951 - 1953; 1963
Magazine Enterprises

	Good	Fine	Mint
1(A-1 33)	2.00	6.00	14.00
2(A-1 36)-Racist-c	3.50	10.50	24.00
3(A-1 39), 4(A-1 95), 5(A-1 99)	1.00	3.00	7.00
Super Reprint #14(1963)	.30	.80	1.60
I.W. Reprint #1,2 (nd)	.30	.80	1.60

MUGGY-DOO, BOY CAT
July, 1953 - No. 4, Jan, 1954
Stanhall

	Good	Fine	Mint
1-Irving Spector-a	2.15	6.50	15.00
2-4	1.15	3.50	8.00
Super Reprint #12('63), 16('64)		.50	1.00

MUMMY, THE (See Movie Classics)

MUNDEN'S BAR ANNUAL
April, 1988 (52pgs.; $2.95; color)
First Comics

	Good	Fine	Mint
1-r/from Grimjack; Fish Police story	.50	1.50	3.00

MUNSTERS, THE (TV)
Jan, 1965 - No. 16, Jan, 1968
Gold Key

	Good	Fine	Mint
1 (10134-501)-Photo-c	5.00	15.00	35.00
2	3.00	9.00	21.00
3-5: 4-Photo-c	2.65	8.00	18.00
6-16	2.00	6.00	14.00

MUPPET BABIES, THE (TV)
Aug, 1985 - Present (Children's book)
Star Comics (Marvel)

	Good	Fine	Mint
1-13		.35	.70
14-18 ($1.00)		.45	.90

MUPPETS TAKE MANHATTAN, THE
Nov, 1984 - No. 3, Jan, 1985
Marvel Comics Group

	Good	Fine	Mint
1-3-Movie adapt. r-/Marvel Super Special		.30	.60

MURDER, INCORPORATED (My Private Life No. 16 on)
1/48 - No. 15, 12/49; (2 No.9's); 6/50 - No. 3, 8/51
Fox Feature Syndicate

	Good	Fine	Mint
1 (1st Series)	13.00	40.00	90.00
2-Transvestite, electrocution story	10.00	30.00	70.00
3-7,9(4/49),10(5/49),11-15	5.00	15.00	35.00
8-Used in **SOTI**, pg. 160	9.00	27.00	63.00
9(3/49)-Possible use in **SOTI**, pg. 145; r-Blue Beetle #56('48)	9.00	27.00	63.00
5(6/50)(2nd Series)-Formerly My Desire	4.00	12.00	28.00
2(8/50)-Morisi-a	2.65	8.00	18.00
3(8/51)-Used in **POP**, pg. 81; Rico-a; lingerie-c/panels	5.50	16.50	38.00

MURDEROUS GANGSTERS
July, 1951; No. 2, Dec, 1951 - No. 4, June, 1952
Avon Periodicals/Realistic No. 3 on

	Good	Fine	Mint
1-Pretty Boy Floyd, Leggs Diamond; 1 pg. Wood	17.00	51.00	120.00
2-Baby-Face Nelson; 1 pg. Wood	11.00	32.00	76.00
3	9.50	28.00	65.00
4-"Murder by Needle" drug story; Mort Lawrence-a; Kinstler-c	11.00	32.00	76.00

MURDER TALES (Magazine)
V1No.10, Nov, 1970 - V1No.11, Jan, 1971 (52 pages)
World Famous Publications

	Good	Fine	Mint
V1#10-One pg. Frazetta ad	.50	1.50	3.00
11-Guardineer-r; bondage-c	.25	.75	1.50

MUSHMOUSE AND PUNKIN PUSS (TV)
September, 1965 (Hanna-Barbera)
Gold Key

	Good	Fine	Mint
1 (10153-509)	2.35	7.00	16.00

MUSIC MAN, THE (See Movie Classics)

MUTANTS & MISFITS
1987 - Present ($1.95, color)
Silverline Comics (Solson)

	Good	Fine	Mint
1,2	.35	1.00	2.00

MUTINY (Stormy Tales of Seven Seas)
Oct, 1954 - No. 3, Feb, 1955
Aragon Magazines

	Good	Fine	Mint
1	5.00	15.00	35.00
2,3: 2-Capt. Mutiny. 3-Bondage-c	2.30	7.00	16.00

MUTINY ON THE BOUNTY (See Classics Ill. 100 & Movie Comics)

MUTT & JEFF (. . .Cartoon, The) (See Xmas Comics)
1910 - 1916 (5¾x15½") (Hardcover-B&W)
Ball Publications

	Good	Fine	V. Fine
1(1910)(68 pgs., 50 cents)	25.00	75.00	175.00
2(1911), 3(1912)(68 pgs.)	25.00	75.00	175.00
4(1915)(68 pgs., 50 cents) (Rare)	30.00	90.00	210.00
5(1916)(84 pages, 60 cents) (Rare)	35.00	105.00	245.00

NOTE: *Cover variations exist showing Mutt & Jeff reading various newspapers; i.e., The Oregon Journal, The American, and The Detroit News. Reprinting of each issue began soon after publication. No. 5 may not have been reprinted. Values listed include the reprints.*

MUTT & JEFF
1916 - 1933? (B&W dailies) (9½x9½"; stiff cover; 52 pgs.)
Cupples & Leon Co.

	Good	Fine	V.Fine
6-22-By Bud Fisher	13.00	40.00	90.00

NOTE: *Later issues are somewhat rarer.*

MUTT & JEFF (continued)

	Good	Fine	VF
nn(1920)-(Advs. of . . .) 16x11''; 20 pgs.; reprints 1919 Sunday strips	25.00	75.00	175.00
Big Book nn(1926, 144pgs., hardcovers)	20.00	60.00	140.00
w/dust jacket	30.00	90.00	210.00
Big Book 1(1928)-Thick book (hardcovers)	20.00	60.00	140.00
w/dust jacket	30.00	90.00	210.00
Big Book 2(1929)-Thick book (hardcovers)	20.00	60.00	140.00
w/dust jacket	30.00	90.00	210.00

NOTE: *The Big Books contain three previous issues rebound.*

MUTT & JEFF
1921 (9x15'')
Embee Publ. Co.

	Good	Fine	VF
Sunday strips in color (Rare)	45.00	135.00	315.00

MUTT AND JEFF
Summer, 1939 (nd) - No. 148, Nov, 1965
All American/National 1-103(6/58)/Dell 104(10/58)-115 (10-12/59)/Harvey 116(2/60)-148

	Good	Fine	Mint
1(nn)-Lost Wheels	65.00	195.00	455.00
2(nn)-Charging Bull (Summer 1940, nd)	38.00	115.00	265.00
3(nn)-Bucking Broncos (Summer 1941, nd)	25.00	75.00	175.00
4(Winter,'41), 5(Summer,'42)	18.00	54.00	125.00
6-10	10.00	30.00	70.00
11-20	6.00	18.00	42.00
21-30	5.00	15.00	35.00
31-50	3.00	9.00	21.00
51-75-Last Fisher issue. 53-Last 52pgs.	2.00	6.00	14.00
76-99,101-103	1.50	4.50	10.00
100	1.75	5.25	12.00
104-148: 117,118,120-131-Richie Rich app.	.85	2.50	6.00
. . . Jokes 1-3(8/60-61, Harvey)-84 pgs.; Richie Rich in all; Little Dot in #2,3	1.50	4.50	10.00
. . . New Jokes 1-4(10/63-11/65, Harvey)-68 pgs.; Richie Rich in #1-3; Stumbo in #1	.75	2.25	5.00

NOTE: *Issues 1-74 by* ***Bud Fisher****. 86 on by* ***Al Smith****. Issues from 1963 on have* ***Fisher*** *reprints. Clarification: early issues signed by Fisher are mostly drawn by Smith.*

MY BROTHERS' KEEPER
1973 (36 pages) (35-49 cents)
Spire Christian Comics (Fleming H. Revell Co.)

	Good	Fine	Mint
nn		.50	1.00

MY CONFESSIONS (My Confession #7&8; formerly Western True Crime; A Spectacular Feature Magazine #11)
No. 7, Aug, 1949 - No. 10, Jan-Feb, 1950
Fox Feature Syndicate

	Good	Fine	Mint
7-Wood-a, 10 pgs.	10.00	30.00	70.00
8-Wood-a, 18 pgs.	8.00	24.00	56.00
9,10	3.50	10.50	24.00

MY DATE COMICS
July, 1947 - V1No.4, Jan, 1948 (1st Romance comic)
Hillman Periodicals

	Good	Fine	Mint
1-S&K-c/a	10.00	30.00	70.00
2-4-S&K, Dan Barry-a	6.00	18.00	42.00

MY DESIRE (Formerly Jo-Jo) (Murder, Inc. #5 on)
No. 30, Aug, 1949 - No. 4, April, 1950
Fox Feature Syndicate

	Good	Fine	Mint
30(#1)	4.35	13.00	30.00
31 (#2), 3,4	2.85	8.50	20.00
31 (Canadian edition)	1.50	4.50	10.00
32(12/49)-Wood-a	8.00	24.00	56.00

MY DIARY
Dec, 1949 - No. 2, Mar, 1950
Marvel Comics (A Lovers Mag.)

	Good	Fine	Mint
1,2	3.50	10.50	24.00

MY DOG TIGE (Buster Brown's Dog)
1957 (Giveaway)
Buster Brown Shoes

	Good	Fine	Mint
	1.70	5.00	10.00

MY EXPERIENCE (Formerly All Top; Judy Canova #23 on)
No. 19, Sept, 1949 - No. 22, Mar, 1950
Fox Feature Syndicate

	Good	Fine	Mint
19-Wood-a	10.00	30.00	70.00
20	2.85	8.50	20.00
21-Wood-a(2)	11.00	33.00	76.00
22-Wood-a, 9 pgs.	8.00	24.00	56.00

MY FAVORITE MARTIAN (TV)
1/64; No.2, 7/64 - No. 9, 10/66 (No. 1,3-9 have photo-c)
Gold Key

	Good	Fine	Mint
1-Russ Manning-a	3.50	10.50	24.00
2	2.00	6.00	14.00
3-9	1.70	5.00	12.00

MY FRIEND IRMA (Radio/TV) (Formerly Western Life Romances)
No. 3, June, 1950 - No. 47, Dec, 1954; No. 48, Feb, 1955
Marvel/Atlas Comics (BFP)

	Good	Fine	Mint
3	4.35	13.00	30.00
4-Kurtzman-a, 10 pgs.	6.00	18.00	42.00
5-''Egghead Doodle'' by Kurtzman, 4 pgs.	4.35	13.00	30.00
6,8-10: 9-paper dolls, 1pg; Millie app.	2.00	6.00	14.00
7-One pg. Kurtzman	2.65	8.00	18.00
11-22	1.50	4.50	10.00
23-One pg. Frazetta	1.50	4.50	10.00
24-48	1.00	3.00	7.00

MY GIRL PEARL
4/55 - No. 4, 10/55; No. 5, 7/57 - No. 6, 9/57; No. 7, 8/60 - No. 11, ?/61
Atlas Comics

	Good	Fine	Mint
1	3.00	9.00	21.00
2	1.50	4.50	10.00
3-6	1.00	3.00	7.00
7-11	.55	1.65	4.00

MY GREATEST ADVENTURE (Doom Patrol No. 86 on)
Jan-Feb, 1955 - No. 85, Feb, 1964
National Periodical Publications

	Good	Fine	Mint
1-Before CCA	32.00	95.00	225.00
2	15.00	45.00	105.00
3-5	11.50	34.00	80.00
6-10	6.00	18.00	42.00
11-15,19	3.50	10.50	24.00
16,20,21,28-Kirby-a	3.70	11.00	26.00
17,18-Kirby-a; 18-Kirby-c	4.35	13.00	30.00
22-27,29,30	2.50	7.50	17.00
31-57,59	1.50	4.50	10.00
58,60,61-Toth-a; Last 10 cent ish.	1.70	5.00	12.00
62-76,78,79	.60	1.75	3.50
77-Toth-a	1.00	3.00	7.00
80-(6/63)-Intro/origin Doom Patrol; origin Robotman, Negative Man, & Elasti-Girl	8.50	25.50	60.00
81,85-Toth-a	3.50	10.50	24.00
82-84	1.70	5.00	12.00

NOTE: ***Anderson*** *a-42.* ***Colan*** *a-77.* ***Meskin*** *a-25, 26, 32, 39, 45, 50, 56, 57, 61, 64, 70, 73, 74, 76, 79; c-76.* ***Moreira*** *a-11, 17, 20, 23, 25, 27, 37, 40-43, 46, 48, 55-57, 59, 60, 62-65, 67, 69, 70.* ***Roussos*** *c/a-71-73.*

MY GREATEST THRILLS IN BASEBALL
Date? (16 pg. Giveaway)
Mission of California

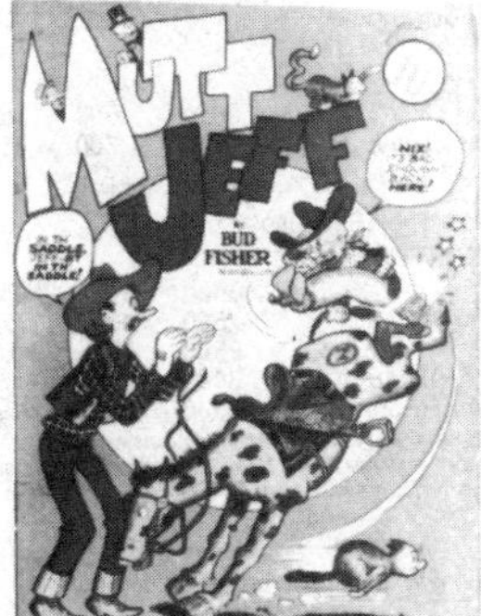

Mutt and Jeff #3, © Ball Syndicate

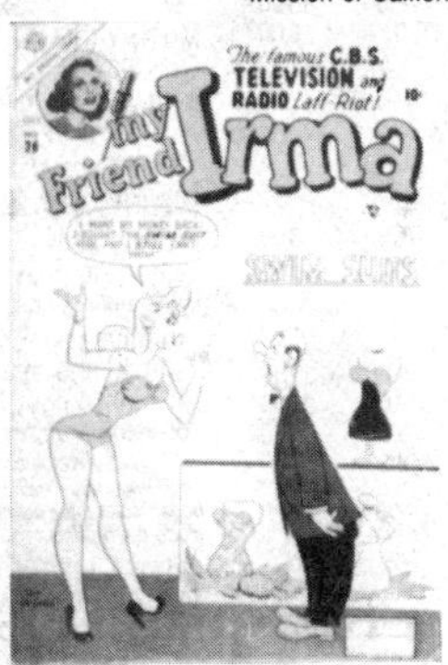

My Friend Irma #36, © MCG

My Greatest Adventure #15, © DC

My Great Love #2, © FOX

My Little Margie #13, © CC

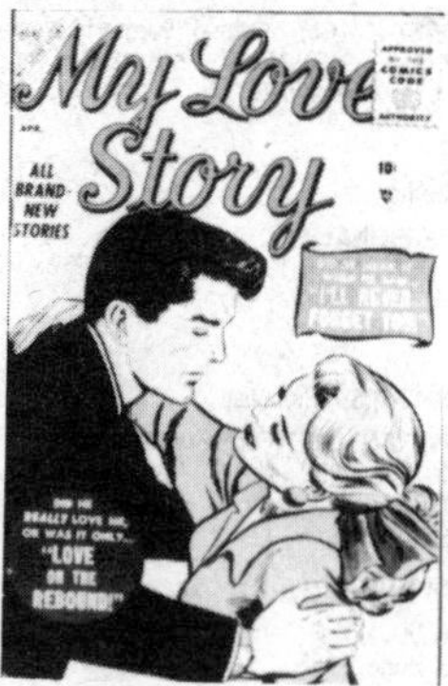

My Love Story #1, © MCG

MY GREATEST THRILLS IN B.B. (cont.)

	Good	Fine	Mint
By Mickey Mantle	20.00	60.00	140.00

MY GREAT LOVE
Oct, 1949 - No. 4, Apr, 1950
Fox Feature Syndicate

	Good	Fine	Mint
1	5.00	15.00	35.00
2-4	2.85	8.50	20.00

MY INTIMATE AFFAIR (Inside Crime No. 3)
Mar, 1950 - No. 2, May, 1950
Fox Feature Syndicate

	Good	Fine	Mint
1	5.00	15.00	35.00
2	2.85	8.50	20.00

MY LIFE (Formerly Meet Corliss Archer)
No. 4, Sept, 1948 - No. 15, July, 1950
Fox Feature Syndicate

	Good	Fine	Mint
4-Used in **SOTI**, pg. 39; Kamen/Feldstein-a	16.00	48.00	110.00
5-Kamen-a	8.00	24.00	56.00
6-Kamen/Feldstein-a	8.00	24.00	56.00
7-Wash cover	4.65	14.00	32.00
8,9,11-15	2.85	8.50	20.00
10-Wood-a	8.00	24.00	56.00

MY LITTLE MARGIE (TV)
July, 1954 - No. 54, Nov, 1964
Charlton Comics

	Good	Fine	Mint
1-Photo-c	6.50	19.50	45.00
2-Photo-c	2.65	8.00	18.00
3-7,10	1.75	5.25	12.00
8,9-Infinity-c	2.00	6.00	14.00
11,14-19	1.15	3.50	8.00
12,13-Photo-c (#13, 8/56)	1.50	4.50	10.00
20-(100 page ish)	2.65	8.00	18.00
21-35-Last 10 cent ish?	.75	2.25	5.00
36-53	.45	1.35	3.00
54-Beatles on cover; lead story spoofs the Beatle haircut craze of the 1960's	4.65	14.00	32.00

NOTE: *Doll cut-outs in 32,33,40,45,50.*

MY LITTLE MARGIE'S BOY FRIENDS (TV)(Freddy V2/12 on)
Aug, 1955 - No. 11, Apr?, 1958
Charlton Comics

	Good	Fine	Mint
1-Has several Archie swipes	3.50	10.50	24.00
2	1.70	5.00	12.00
3-11	1.00	3.00	7.00

MY LITTLE MARGIE'S FASHIONS (TV)
Feb, 1959 - No. 5, Nov, 1959
Charlton Comics

	Good	Fine	Mint
1	2.65	8.00	18.00
2-5	1.30	4.00	9.00

MY LOVE (Formerly Molly Manton's Romances No. 1 & 2)
July, 1949 - No. 4, Apr, 1950 (All photo-c)
Marvel Comics (CLDS)

	Good	Fine	Mint
1-Photo-c	2.65	8.00	18.00
2-4: 2(exist?)	1.30	4.00	9.00

MY LOVE
Sept, 1969 - No. 39, Mar, 1976
Marvel Comics Group

	Good	Fine	Mint
1-9		.30	.60
10-Williamson-r/My Own Romance #71; Kirby-a		.60	1.20
11-20: 14-Morrow-c/a		.20	.40
21,22,24-39: 38,39-Reprints		.20	.40
23-Steranko-r/Our Love Story #5	.35	1.00	2.00
Special(12/71)		.30	.60

MY LOVE AFFAIR (March of Crime No. 7 on)
July, 1949 - No. 6, May, 1950
Fox Feature Syndicate

	Good	Fine	Mint
1	5.50	16.50	38.00
2	3.00	9.00	21.00
3-6-Wood-a	8.00	24.00	56.00

MY LOVE LIFE (Formerly Zegra)
No. 6, June, 1949 - No. 13, Aug, 1950; No. 13, Sept, 1951
Fox Feature Syndicate

	Good	Fine	Mint
6-Kamenish-a	6.50	19.50	45.00
7-13	3.00	9.00	21.00
13 (9/51)	2.30	7.00	16.00

MY LOVE MEMOIRS (Formerly Women Outlaws; Hunted #13 on)
No. 9, Nov, 1949 - No. 12, May, 1950
Fox Feature Syndicate

	Good	Fine	Mint
9,11,12-Wood-a	8.00	24.00	56.00
10	2.85	8.50	20.00

MY LOVE SECRET (Formerly Phantom Lady) (Animal Crackers #31)
No. 24, June, 1949 - No. 30, June, 1950; 1954
Fox Feature Syndicate/M. S. Distr.

	Good	Fine	Mint
24-Kamen/Feldstein-a	7.00	21.00	50.00
25-Possible caricature of Wood on-c?	3.50	10.50	24.00
26,28-Wood-a	8.00	24.00	56.00
27,29,30: 30-photo-c	2.65	8.00	18.00
53-(Reprint, M.S. Distr.) 1954? nd given; formerly Western Thrillers (Crimes by Women #54). Photo-c	1.70	5.00	11.50

MY LOVE STORY (Hoot Gibson Western #5 on)
Sept, 1949 - No. 4, Mar, 1950
Fox Feature Syndicate

	Good	Fine	Mint
1	5.50	16.50	38.00
2	3.00	9.00	21.00
3,4-Wood-a	8.00	24.00	56.00

MY LOVE STORY
April, 1956 - No. 9, Aug, 1957
Atlas Comics (GPS)

	Good	Fine	Mint
1	2.30	7.00	16.00
2	1.15	3.50	8.00
3-Matt Baker-a	2.15	6.50	15.00
4-6,8,9	.85	2.50	6.00
7-Matt Baker, Toth-a	2.15	6.50	15.00

NOTE: ***Colletta*** *a 1(2), 4(2), 5.*

MY ONLY LOVE
July, 1975 - No. 9, Nov, 1976
Charlton Comics

	Good	Fine	Mint
1,2,4-9		.20	.40
3-Toth-a	.35	1.00	2.00

MY OWN ROMANCE (Formerly My Romance; Teen-Age Romance #77 on)
No. 4, Mar, 1949 - No. 76, July, 1960
Marvel/Atlas (MjPC/RCM No. 4-59/ZPC No. 60-76)

	Good	Fine	Mint
4-Photo-c	3.50	10.50	24.00
5-10: 9,10-Photo-c	1.70	5.00	12.00
11-20: 14-Powell-a	1.30	4.00	9.00
21-42: 42-Last pre-code	1.00	3.00	7.00
43-54,56-60	.75	2.25	5.00
55-Toth-a	2.30	7.00	16.00
61-70,72-76	.55	1.65	4.00
71-Williamson-a	3.75	11.25	26.00

NOTE: ***Colletta*** *a-45(2), 48, 50, 55; c-58i, 61.* ***Everett*** *a-25; c-58p.* ***Morisi*** *a-18.* ***Romita*** *a-36.* ***Tuska*** *a-10.*

MY PAST (. . .Confessions) (Formerly Western Thrillers)
No. 7, Aug, 1949 - No. 11, April, 1950 (Crimes Inc. No. 12)
Fox Feature Syndicate

	Good	Fine	Mint
7	4.35	13.00	30.00
8-10	3.00	9.00	21.00
11-Wood-a	8.00	24.00	56.00

MY PERSONAL PROBLEM
Nov, 1955 - No. 4, Nov, 1956; Oct, 1957 - No. 3, May, 1958
Ajax/Farrell/Steinway Comic

	Good	Fine	Mint
1	2.65	8.00	18.00
2-4	1.50	4.50	10.00
1(10/57)-3('58)-Steinway	1.15	3.50	8.00

MY PRIVATE LIFE (Formerly Murder, Inc.)
No. 16, Feb, 1950 - No. 17, April, 1950
Fox Feature Syndicate

	Good	Fine	Mint
16,17	3.50	10.50	24.00

MYRA NORTH (See 4-Color No. 3)

MY REAL LOVE
No. 5, June, 1952
Standard Comics

	Good	Fine	Mint
5-Toth-a, 3 pgs.; Tuska, Cardy, Vern Greene-a; photo-c	4.35	13.00	30.00

MY ROMANCE (My Own Romance #4 on)
Sept, 1948 - No. 3, Jan, 1949
Marvel Comics (RCM)

	Good	Fine	Mint
1	3.50	10.50	24.00
2,3: 2-Anti-Wertham editorial (11/48)	1.70	5.00	12.00

MY ROMANTIC ADVENTURES (Formerly Romantic Adventures)
No. 68, Aug, 1956 - No. 138, Mar, 1964
American Comics Group

	Good	Fine	Mint
68	1.85	5.50	13.00
69-85	1.00	3.00	7.00
86-Three pg. Williamson-a (2/58)	2.85	8.50	20.00
87-100	.50	1.50	3.50
101-138	.35	1.00	2.00

NOTE: ***Whitney*** *art in most.*

MY SECRET (Our Secret No. 4 on)
Aug, 1949 - No. 3, Oct, 1949
Superior Comics, Ltd.

	Good	Fine	Mint
1	3.70	11.00	26.00
2,3	2.65	8.00	18.00

MY SECRET AFFAIR (Martin Kane #4)
Dec, 1949 - No. 3, April, 1950
Hero Book (Fox Feature Syndicate)

	Good	Fine	Mint
1-Harrison/Wood-a, 10 pgs.	9.50	28.50	65.00
2-Wood-a (poor)	5.50	16.50	38.00
3-Wood-a	8.00	24.00	56.00

MY SECRET CONFESSION
September, 1955
Sterling Comics

	Good	Fine	Mint
1-Sekowsky-a	2.00	6.00	14.00

MY SECRET LIFE (Formerly West. Outlaws; Romeo Tubbs #26 on)
No. 22, July, 1949 - No. 27, May, 1950
Fox Feature Syndicate

	Good	Fine	Mint
22	3.70	11.00	26.00
23,26-Wood-a, 6 pgs.	8.00	24.00	56.00
24,25,27	2.30	7.00	16.00

NOTE: *The title was changed to Romeo Tubbs after #25 even though #26 & 27 did come out.*

MY SECRET LIFE (Formerly Young Lovers; Sue & Sally Smith #48 on)
No. 19, Aug, 1957 - No. 47, Sept, 1962
Charlton Comics

	Good	Fine	Mint
19	.80	2.40	5.50
20-35	.45	1.35	2.50
36-47: 44-Last 10 cent ish.		.50	1.00

MY SECRET MARRIAGE
May, 1953 - No. 24, July, 1956
Superior Comics, Ltd.

	Good	Fine	Mint
1	3.50	10.50	24.00
2	1.70	5.00	12.00
3-24	1.30	4.00	9.00
I.W. Reprint #9	.30	.90	1.80

NOTE: *Many issues contain Kamenish art.*

MY SECRET ROMANCE (A Star Presentation #3)
Jan, 1950 - No. 2, March, 1950
Hero Book (Fox Feature Syndicate)

	Good	Fine	Mint
1-Wood-a	9.00	27.00	62.00
2-Wood-a	8.00	24.00	56.00

MY SECRET STORY (Formerly Captain Kidd #25; Sabu #30 on)
No. 26, Oct, 1949 - No. 29, April, 1950
Fox Feature Syndicate

	Good	Fine	Mint
26	4.00	12.00	28.00
27-29	3.00	9.00	21.00

MYSTERIES (. . .Weird & Strange)
May, 1953 - No. 11, Jan, 1955
Superior/Dynamic Publ. (Randall Publ. Ltd.)

	Good	Fine	Mint
1	8.00	24.00	56.00
2-A-Bomb blast story	4.35	13.00	30.00
3-9,11	3.00	9.00	21.00
10-Kamenish c/a r-/Strange Mysteries #2; cover from a panel in S.M. #2	3.70	11.00	26.00

MYSTERIES OF SCOTLAND YARD (See A-1 Comics No. 121)

MYSTERIES OF UNEXPLORED WORLDS (See Blue Bird) (Son of Vulcan V2#49 on)
Aug, 1956 - No. 48, Sept, 1965
Charlton Comics

	Good	Fine	Mint
1	9.00	27.00	63.00
2-No Ditko	2.65	8.00	18.00
3,4,6,8,9-Ditko-a	5.70	17.00	40.00
5-Ditko c/a (all)	6.50	19.50	45.00
7-(68 pg. ish); Ditko-a	7.00	21.00	50.00
10-Ditko-c/a(4)	6.50	19.50	45.00
11-Ditko-c/a(3)-signed J. Kotdi	5.70	17.00	40.00
12,19,21-24,26-Ditko-a	4.00	12.00	28.00
13-18,20	1.30	4.00	9.00
25,27-30	1.00	3.00	7.00
31-45	.45	1.35	3.00
46(5/65)-Son of Vulcan begins (origin)	.70	2.00	4.00
47,48	.50	1.50	3.00

NOTE: ***Ditko*** *c-3-6, 10, 11, 19, 21-24.*

MYSTERIOUS ADVENTURES
March, 1951 - No. 24, Mar, 1955; No. 25, Aug, 1955
Story Comics

	Good	Fine	Mint
1	12.00	36.00	84.00
2	5.70	17.00	40.00
3,4,6,9,10	4.35	13.00	30.00
5-Bondage-c; torture	5.00	15.00	35.00
7-Daggar in eye panel; dismemberment	8.50	25.50	60.00
8-Eyeball story	7.00	21.00	50.00
11(12/52)-Used in **SOTI**, pg. 84.	9.50	28.00	65.00

My Personal Problem #1 (10/57), © Steinway

My Secret Confession #1, © Sterling Comics

Mysteries of Unexplored Worlds #14, © CC

Mysterious Adventures #14, © Story Comics

Mysterious Suspense #1, © CC

Mystery In Space #60, © DC

MYSTERIOUS ADVENTURES (continued) — Good / Fine / Mint

12-Dismemberment, eyes ripped out — 10.00 30.00 70.00
13-Dismemberment — 9.50 28.00 65.00
14,19 — 4.60 14.00 32.00
15-Violence; beheading, acid in face, face carved with knife — 10.00 30.00 70.00
16-Violence, dismemberment, injury to eye — 10.00 30.00 70.00
17-Violence, dismemberment — 10.00 30.00 70.00
18-Used in Sentate Investigative report, pgs. 5,6; E.C. swipe/T.F.T.C. 35 — 10.00 30.00 70.00
20-Violence, head split open, fried body organs-used by Wertham in the Senate hearings — 10.00 30.00 70.00
21-Blood drainage story, hanging panels, intestines pulled out; bondage/beheading-c — 10.00 30.00 70.00
22-'Cinderella' parody — 4.60 14.00 32.00
23-Disbrow-a — 5.70 17.00 40.00
24,25 — 4.35 13.00 30.00

NOTE: *Tothish art by* ***Ross Andru****-#22, 23.* ***Bache*** *a-8.* ***Cameron*** *a-5-7.* ***Harrison*** *a-12.* ***Hollingsworth*** *a-3-8, 12.* ***Schaffenberger*** *a-24, 25.* ***Wildey*** *a-17.*

MYSTERIOUS ISLAND (See 4-Color No. 1213)

MYSTERIOUS ISLE
Nov-Jan, 1963/64 (Jules Verne)
Dell Publishing Co.

1 — 1.00 3.00 7.00

MYSTERIOUS STORIES (Horror From the Tomb #1)
Dec-Jan, 1954-1955 - No. 7, Dec, 1955
Premier Magazines

2-Woodbridge-c — 7.00 21.00 50.00
3-Woodbridge c/a — 5.70 17.00 40.00
4-7: 5-Cinderella parody. 6-Woodbridge-c — 4.60 14.00 32.00

NOTE: ***Hollingsworth*** *a-2,4.*

MYSTERIOUS SUSPENSE
October, 1968
Charlton Comics

1-The Question app. by Ditko-c/a — 1.75 5.25 12.00

MYSTERIOUS TRAVELER (See Tales of the...)

MYSTERIOUS TRAVELER COMICS (Radio)
Nov, 1948 - No. 4, 1949
Trans-World Publications

1-Powell-c/a(2); Poe adaptation, 'Tell Tale Heart' — 17.00 51.00 120.00
2-4 — 11.50 34.50 80.00

MYSTERY COMICS
1944 - No. 4, 1944 (No month given)
William H. Wise & Co.

1-The Magnet, The Silver Knight, Brad Spencer, Wonderman, Dick Devins, King of Futuria, & Zudo the Jungle Boy begin — 28.00 85.00 200.00
2-Bondage-c — 19.00 55.00 130.00
3-Lance Lewis, Space Detective begins — 17.00 51.00 120.00
4(V2No.1 inside) — 17.00 51.00 120.00

NOTE: ***Schomburg*** *c-1-4.*

MYSTERY COMICS DIGEST
March, 1972 - No. 26, Oct, 1975
Gold Key

1-Ripley's; reprint of Ripley's #1 origin Ra-Ka-Tep the Mummy; Wood-a — .85 2.50 5.00
2-Boris Karloff; Wood-a; 1st app. Werewolf Count Wulfstein — .40 1.25 2.50
3-Twilight Zone (TV); Crandall, Toth & George Evans-a; 1st app. Tragg & Simbar the Lion Lord; 2 Crandall/Frazetta-a r-Twilight Zone #1 — .40 1.25 2.50

Good / Fine / Mint

4-Ripley's Believe It or Not; 1st app. Baron Tibor, the Vampire — .35 1.00 2.00
5-Boris Karloff Tales of Mystery; 1st app. Dr. Spektor — .35 1.00 2.00
6-Twilight Zone (TV); 1st app. U.S. Marshal Reid & Sir Duane — .35 1.00 2.00
7-Ripley's Believe It or Not; origin The Lurker in the Swamp; 1st app. Duroc — .60 1.20
8-Boris Karloff Tales of Mystery — .60 1.20
9-Twilight Zone (TV); Williamson, Crandall, McWilliams-a; 2nd Tragg app. — .40 1.25 2.50
10,13-Ripley's Believe It or Not — .50 1.00
11,14-Boris Karloff Tales of Mystery. 14-1st app. Xorkon — .40 .80
12,15-Twilight Zone (TV) — .40 .80
16,19,22,25-Ripley's Believe It or Not — .40 .80
17-Boris Karloff Tales of Mystery; Williamson-r — .25 .75 1.50
18,21,24-Twilight Zone (TV) — .40 .80
20,23,26-Boris Karloff Tales of Mystery — .40 .80

NOTE: *Dr. Spektor app.-#5,10-12,21. Durak app.-#15. Duroc app.-#14 (later called Durak). King George 1st app.-#8.*

MYSTERY IN SPACE
Apr-May, 1951 - No. 110, Sept, 1966; (No. 1-3: 52 pgs.)
No. 111, Sept, 1980 - No. 117, March, 1981
National Periodical Publications

1-Frazetta-a, 8 pgs.; Knights of the Galaxy begins, ends #8 — 110.00 330.00 770.00
2 — 45.00 135.00 315.00
3 — 37.00 110.00 260.00
4,5 — 25.00 75.00 175.00
6-10: 7-Toth-a — 19.00 55.00 130.00
11-15: 13-Toth-a — 13.50 40.00 95.00
16-18,20-25: Interplanetary Insurance feature by Infantino in all. 24-Last precode issue — 12.00 36.00 84.00
19-Virgil Finlay-a — 15.00 45.00 105.00
26-34,36-40: 26-Space Cabbie begins — 8.00 24.00 56.00
35-Kubert-a — 8.50 25.50 60.00
41-52: 47-Space Cabbie feature ends — 4.35 13.00 30.00
53-Adam Strange begins (1st app. in Showcase) — 30.00 90.00 210.00
54 — 13.00 40.00 92.00
55 — 9.50 28.00 66.00
56-60 — 6.50 19.50 46.00
61-71: 61-1st app. Adam Strange foe Ulthoon. 62-1st app. A.S. foe Mortan. 63-Origin Vandor. 66-Star Rovers begin. 68-Dust Devils app. 71-Last 10 cent ish. — 3.70 11.00 26.00
72-80: 75-JLA x-over in Adam Strange — 2.85 8.50 20.00
81-86 — 1.70 5.00 12.00
87-90-Hawkman in all — 1.15 3.50 8.00
91-102: 91-End Infantino art on Adam Strange. 92-Space Ranger begins. 94,98-Adam Strange/Space Ranger team-up. 102-Adam Strange ends — .75 2.25 4.50
103-Origin Ultra, the Multi-Alien; Space Ranger ends — .75 2.25 4.50
104-110(9/66) — .35 1.10 2.20
111(9/80)-117 — .60 1.20

NOTE: ***Anderson*** *a-2, 4, 8-10, 12-17, 19, 45-48, 51, 57, 61-64, 70, 76, 87-98; c-9, 10, 15-25, 87, 89, 105-108, 110.* ***Aparo*** *a-111.* ***Austin*** *a-112i.* ***Craig*** *a-114, 116.* ***Ditko*** *a-111, 114-116.* ***Drucker*** *a-13, 14.* ***Golden*** *a-113p.* ***Sid Greene*** *a-78, 91.* ***Infantino*** *a-1-8, 11, 14-25, 27-46, 48, 49, 51, 53-91, 103, 117; c-60-86, 88, 90, 91, 105, 107.* ***Gil Kane*** *a-18, 100-102; c-52, 101.* ***Kubert*** *a-113; c-111-15.* ***Newton*** *a-117p.* ***Rogers*** *a-111.* ***Sekowsky*** *a-52.* ***Simon & Kirby*** *a-4(2 pgs.).* ***Spiegle*** *a-111, 114.* ***Starlin*** *c-116.* ***Sutton*** *a-112.* ***Tuska*** *a-115p, 117p.*

MYSTERY MEN COMICS
Aug, 1939 - No. 31, Feb, 1942
Fox Features Syndicate

MYSTERY MEN COMICS (continued)

	Good	Fine	Mint
1-Intro. & 1st app. The Blue Beetle, The Green Mask, Rex Dexter of Mars by Briefer, Zanzibar by Tuska, Lt. Drake, D-13-Secret Agent by Powell, Chen Chang, Wing Turner, & Captain Denny Scott	115.00	345.00	800.00
2	55.00	165.00	385.00
3 (10/39)	45.00	135.00	315.00
4-Capt. Savage begins	40.00	120.00	280.00
5	32.00	95.00	225.00
6-8	28.00	84.00	195.00
9-The Moth begins	23.50	70.00	165.00
10-Wing Turner by Kirby	22.00	65.00	155.00
11-Intro. Domino	18.50	55.00	130.00
12,14-18	16.00	48.00	110.00
13-Intro. Lynx & sidekick Blackie	18.50	55.00	130.00
19-Intro. & 1st app. Miss X (ends #21)	18.50	55.00	130.00
20-25,27-31	15.00	45.00	105.00
26-The Wraith begins	15.00	45.00	105.00

NOTE: ***Briefer*** *a-1, 3, 5, 6, 8, 24.* ***Cuidera*** *a-22.* ***Lou Fine*** *c-1-9.* ***Powell*** *a-1-9, 24.* ***Simon*** *c-10-12.* ***Tuska*** *a-1-9, 22, 24. Bondage-c 1, 3, 7, 8, 25, 27-29, 31.*

MYSTERY TALES
March, 1952 - No. 54, Aug, 1957
Atlas Comics (20CC)

	Good	Fine	Mint
1	12.00	36.00	84.00
2-Krigstein-a	6.50	19.50	45.00
3-9: 6-A-Bomb panel	4.00	12.00	28.00
10-Story similar to 'The Assassin' from Shock SuspenStories	4.60	14.00	32.00
11,13-20	2.65	8.00	18.00
12-Matt Fox-a	3.50	10.50	24.00
21-Matt Fox-a; decapitation story	3.50	10.50	24.00
22-Forte/Matt Fox c; a(i)	4.60	14.00	32.00
23-26 (2/55)-Last precode issue	2.30	7.00	16.00
27,29-32,34,35,37,38,41-43,48,49	1.60	4.70	11.00
28-Jack Katz-a	2.65	8.00	18.00
33-Crandall-a	3.65	11.00	25.00
36,39-Krigstein-a	3.65	11.00	25.00
40,45-Ditko-a	3.65	11.00	25.00
44,51-Williamson/Mayo-a	4.65	14.00	32.00
46-Williamson/Krenkel-a	4.65	14.00	32.00
47-Crandall, Ditko, Powell-a	4.00	12.00	28.00
50-Torres, Morrow-a	3.35	10.00	23.00
52,53	1.60	4.70	11.00
54-Crandall, Check-a	3.00	9.00	21.00

NOTE: ***Berg*** *a-17, 51.* ***Colan*** *a-1, 3, 18, 35, 43.* ***Everett*** *a-2, 29, 33, 35, 41, 43; c-8-11, 14, 38, 39, 41, 43, 44, 46, 48-51, 53.* ***Fass*** *a-16.* ***Forte*** *a-21, 22.* ***Matt Fox*** *a-12?, 21, 22; c-22.* ***Heath*** *a-3; c-3, 15, 17, 26.* ***Heck*** *a-25.* ***Kinstler*** *a-15.* ***Mort Lawrence*** *a-26, 32, 34.* ***Maneely*** *a-1, 9, 14, 22; c-12, 23, 24, 27.* ***Mooney*** *a-3, 40.* ***Morisi*** *a-43, 49, 52.* ***Morrow*** *a-50.* ***Pakula*** *a-16.* ***Powell*** *a-21, 29, 37, 38, 47.* ***Robinson*** *a-7p, 42.* ***Roussos*** *a-44.* ***Severin*** *c-52.* ***Tuska*** *a-10, 12, 14.* ***Whitney*** *a-2.*

MYSTERY TALES
1964
Super Comics

	Good	Fine	Mint
Super Reprint #16,17('64)	.50	1.50	3.00
Super Reprint #18-Kubert art/Strange Terrors #4	.50	1.50	3.00

MYSTIC (3rd Series)
March, 1951 - No. 61, Aug, 1957
Marvel/Atlas Comics (CLDS 1/CSI 2-21/OMC 22-35/CSI 35-61)

	Good	Fine	Mint
1-Atom bomb panels	14.00	42.00	100.00
2	7.00	21.00	50.00
3-Eyes torn out	4.60	14.00	32.00
4-"The Devil Birds" by Wolverton, 6 pgs.	19.00	56.00	130.00
5,7-10	4.00	12.00	28.00
6-"The Eye of Doom" by Wolverton, 7 pgs.	19.00	56.00	130.00
11-20: 16-Bondage/torture c/story	3.50	10.50	24.00
21-25,27-30,32-36-Last precode (3/55)	3.00	9.00	21.00
26-Atomic War, severed head stories	3.50	10.50	24.00
31-Sid Check-a	3.00	9.00	21.00
37-51,53-57,61	1.70	5.00	12.00
52-Wood, Crandall-a	4.35	13.00	30.00
58,59-Krigstein-a	3.50	10.50	24.00
60-Williamson/Mayo-a, 4 pgs.	3.85	11.50	27.00

NOTE: ***Andru*** *a-23, 25.* ***Ayers*** *c-8.* ***Check*** *a-60.* ***Colan*** *a-3, 7, 12, 21, 37.* ***Drucker*** *a-46, 52, 56.* ***Everett*** *a-8, 9, 17, 40, 44, 57; c-18, 21, 42, 47, 49, 51-55, 58, 59, 61.* ***Fox*** *a-24i.* ***Heath*** *a-10; c-10, 22, 23, 25, 30.* ***Infantino*** *a-12.* ***Kane*** *a-8, 24p.* ***Jack Katz*** *a-31, 33.* ***Mort Lawrence*** *a-19, 37.* ***Maneely*** *a-22, 24, 58; c-28, 29, 31.* ***Moldoff*** *a-29.* ***Morrow*** *a-51.* ***Orlando*** *a-57, 61.* ***Powell*** *a-52, 55, 56.* ***Robinson*** *a-5.* ***Romita*** *a-11.* ***Sekowsky*** *a-1, 2, 4, 5.* ***Severin*** *c-56.* ***Whitney*** *a-33.* ***Wildey*** *a-28, 30. Canadian reprints known-title 'Startling'.*

MYSTICAL TALES
June, 1956 - No. 8, Aug, 1957
Atlas Comics (CCC 1/EPI 2-8)

	Good	Fine	Mint
1-Everett c/a	8.00	24.00	56.00
2,4: 2-Berg-a	3.70	11.00	26.00
3-Crandall-a	4.60	14.00	32.00
5-Williamson-a, 4 pgs.	5.50	16.50	38.00
6-Torres, Krigstein-a	4.60	14.00	32.00
7-Torres, Orlando, Crandall, Everett-a	4.00	12.00	28.00
8-Krigstein, Check-a	4.60	14.00	32.00

NOTE: ***Everett*** *a-1, 7; c-2-4, 6, 7.* ***Orlando*** *a-1, 2.* ***Powell*** *a-1, 4.*

MYSTIC COMICS (1st Series)
March, 1940 - No. 10, Aug, 1942
Timely Comics (TPI 1-5/TCI 8-10)

	Good	Fine	Mint
1-Origin The Blue Blaze, The Dynamic Man, & Flexo the Rubber Man; Zephyr Jones, 3X's & Deep Sea Demon app.; The Magician begins;c-from Spider pulp V18#1, 6/39	360.00	1080.00	2520.00
2-The Invisible Man & Master Mind Excello begin; Space Rangers, Zara of the Jungle, Taxi Taylor app	145.00	435.00	1015.00
3-Origin Hercules, who last appears in #4	115.00	345.00	805.00
4-Origin The Thin Man & The Black Widow; Merzak the Mystic app.; last Flexo, Dynamic Man, Invisible Man & Blue Blaze. (Some issues have date sticker on cover; others have July w/August overprint in silver color); Roosevelt assassination-c	135.00	405.00	945.00
5-Origin The Black Marvel, The Blazing Skull, The Sub-Earth Man, Super Slave & The Terror; The Moon Man & Black Widow app.	130.00	390.00	910.00
6-Origin The Challenger & The Destroyer	110.00	330.00	770.00
7-The Witness begins (origin); origin Davey & the Demon; last Black Widow; Simon & Kirby-c	90.00	270.00	630.00
8	77.00	230.00	540.00
9-Gary Gaunt app.; last Black Marvel, Mystic & Blazing Skull	77.00	230.00	530.00
10-Father Time, World of Wonder, & Red Skeleton app.; last Challenger & Terror	77.00	230.00	530.00

NOTE: ***Schomburg*** *a-1-4. Bondage c-1,2,9.*

MYSTIC COMICS (2nd Series)
Oct, 1944 - No. 4, Winter, 1944-45
Timely Comics (ANC)

	Good	Fine	Mint
1-The Angel, The Destroyer, The Human Torch, Terry Vance the Schoolboy Sleuth, & Tommy Tyme begin	64.00	192.00	450.00
2-Last Human Torch & Terry Vance; bondage-hypo-c	40.00	120.00	280.00
3-Last Angel (two stories) & Tommy Tyme	37.00	110.00	260.00
4-The Young Allies app.	32.00	95.00	225.00

MY STORY (. . .True Romances in Pictures #5,6) (Formerly Zago)
No. 5, May, 1949 - No. 12, Aug, 1950
Hero Books (Fox Features Syndicate)

	Good	Fine	Mint
5-Kamen/Feldstein-a	7.00	21.00	50.00

Mystery Men Comics #5, © FOX

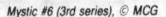

Mystic #6 (3rd series), © MCG

Mystic Comics #2 (1st series), © MCG

Nancy & Sluggo #178, © UFS

Nathaniel Dusk #4, © DC

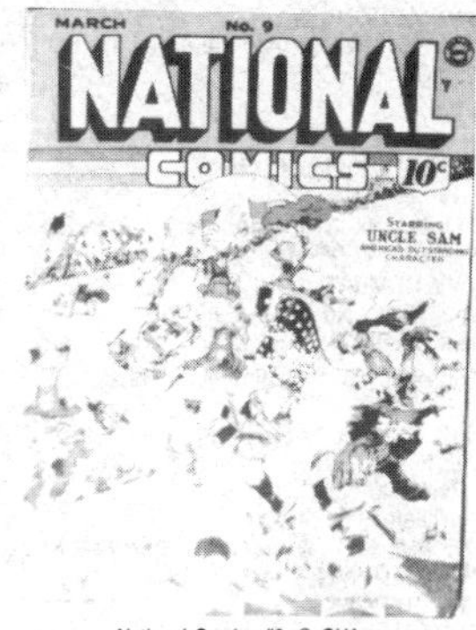

National Comics #9, © QUA

MY STORY (continued)

	Good	Fine	Mint
6-8,11,12	3.00	9.00	21.00
9,10-Wood-a	8.00	24.00	56.00

MY TRUE LOVE (Formerly Western Killers #64; Frank Buck #70 on)
No. 65, July, 1949 - No. 69, March, 1950
Fox Features Syndicate

	Good	Fine	Mint
65	4.35	13.00	30.00
66-69: 69-Morisi-a	3.00	9.00	21.00

NAKED PREY, THE (See Movie Classics)

NAM, THE (See Savage Tales #1, 2nd series)
Dec, 1986 - Present
Marvel Comics Group

	Good	Fine	Mint
1-Golden a(p)/c begins	2.30	7.00	14.00
1 (2nd printing)	.70	2.00	4.00
2	1.40	4.25	8.50
3,4	.70	2.00	4.00
5,6	.55	1.60	3.20
7	.70	2.00	4.00
8-10	.35	1.00	2.00
11-18	.25	.75	1.50

NAMORA
Fall, 1948 - No. 3, Dec, 1948
Marvel Comics (PrPl)

	Good	Fine	Mint
1-Sub-Mariner x-over in Namora; Everett-a	60.00	180.00	420.00
2-The Blonde Phantom & Sub-Mariner story; Everett-a	50.00	150.00	350.00
3-(Scarce)-Sub-Mariner app.; Everett-a	44.00	132.00	310.00

NANCY AND SLUGGO
No. 16, 1949 - No. 23, 1954
United Features Syndicate

	Good	Fine	Mint
16(#1)	3.00	9.00	21.00
17-23	1.85	5.50	13.00

NANCY & SLUGGO (Nancy #146-173; formerly Sparkler Comics)
No. 121, Apr, 1955 - No. 192, Oct, 1963
St. John/Dell No. 146-187/Gold Key No. 188 on

	Good	Fine	Mint
121(4/55)(St. John)	2.65	8.00	18.00
122-145(7/57)(St. John)	1.85	5.50	13.00
146(9/57)-Peanuts begins, ends #192 (Dell)	1.60	4.70	11.00
147-161 (Dell)	1.50	4.50	10.00
162-165,177-180-John Stanley-a	3.00	9.00	21.00
166-176-Oona & Her Haunted House series; Stanley-a	3.50	10.50	24.00
181-187(3-5/62)(Dell)	1.30	4.00	9.00
188(10/62)-192 (G.Key)	1.30	4.00	9.00
4-Color 1034(9-11/59)-Summer Camp	1.70	5.00	12.00

(See Dell Giant #34,45 & Dell Giants)

NANNY AND THE PROFESSOR (TV)
Aug, 1970 - No. 2, Oct, 1970 (Photo-c)
Dell Publishing Co.

	Good	Fine	Mint
1(01-546-008), 2	1.70	5.00	12.00

NAPOLEON (See 4-Color No. 526)

NAPOLEON & SAMANTHA (See Walt Disney Showcase No. 10)

NAPOLEON & UNCLE ELBY (See Clifford McBride's. . .)
Nov?, 1942 (68 pages) (One Shot)
Eastern Color Printing Co.

	Good	Fine	Mint
1	12.00	36.00	84.00
1945-American Book-Strafford Press (128 pgs.) (8x10½''-B&W reprints; hardcover)	6.00	18.00	42.00

NATHANIEL DUSK
Feb, 1984 - No. 4, May, 1984 (mini-series; Baxter paper)
DC Comics (Direct Sale only)

	Good	Fine	Mint
1-Intro/origin		.60	1.20
2-4 ($1.25): Colan c/a		.60	1.20

NATHANIEL DUSK II
Oct, 1985 - No. 4, Jan, 1986 (mini-series; Baxter paper)
DC Comics

	Good	Fine	Mint
1 ($2.00 cover); Colan c/a	.30	.90	1.80
2-4		.55	1.10

NATIONAL COMICS
July, 1940 - No. 75, Nov, 1949
Quality Comics Group

	Good	Fine	Mint
1-Uncle Sam begins; Origin sidekick Buddy by Eisner; origin Wonder Boy & Kid Dixon; Merlin the Magician (ends #45); Cyclone, Kid Patrol, Sally O'Neal Policewoman, Pen Miller (ends #22), Prop Powers (ends #26), & Paul Bunyan (ends #22) begin	160.00	480.00	1120.00
2	75.00	225.00	525.00
3-Last Eisner Uncle Sam	60.00	180.00	420.00
4-Last Cyclone	43.00	130.00	300.00
5-Quick Silver begins (3rd w/lightning speed?); origin Uncle Sam	55.00	165.00	385.00
6-11: 8-Jack & Jill begins (ends #22). 9-Flag-c	40.00	120.00	280.00
12	30.00	90.00	210.00
13-16-Lou Fine-a	37.00	110.00	260.00
17,19-22	27.00	81.00	190.00
18-(12/41)-Shows orientals attacking Pearl Harbor; on stands one month before actual event	33.00	100.00	230.00
23-The Unknown & Destroyer 171 begin	30.00	90.00	210.00
24-26,28,30: 26-Wonder Boy ends	21.00	63.00	145.00
27-G-2 the Unknown begins (ends #46)	21.00	63.00	145.00
29-Origin The Unknown	21.00	63.00	145.00
31-33: 33-Chic Carter begins (ends #47)	18.00	54.00	125.00
34-40: 35-Last Kid Patrol	11.00	32.00	76.00
41-47,49,50: 42-The Barker begins	8.50	25.50	60.00
48-Origin The Whistler	8.50	25.50	60.00
51-Sally O'Neil by Ward, 8 pgs. (12/45)	11.50	34.50	80.00
52-60	6.50	19.50	45.00
61-67: 67-Format change; Quicksilver app.	4.65	14.00	32.00
68-75: The Barker ends	2.85	8.50	20.00

NOTE: ***Cole*** *Quicksilver-13;* *Barker-43; c-46.* ***Crandall*** *Uncle Sam-11-13 (with* ***Fine****), 25, 26; c-24-26, 30-33, 43.* ***Crandall*** *Paul Bunyan-10-13.* ***Fine*** *Uncle Sam-13 (w/****Crandall****), 17, 18; c-1-14, 16, 18, 21.* ***Guardineer*** *Quicksilver-27.* ***Gustavson*** *Quicksilver -14-26.* ***McWilliams*** *a-23-28, 55, 57. Uncle Sam-c #1-41. Bondage c-5.*

NATIONAL CRUMB, THE (Magazine-Size)
August, 1975 (52 pages) (Satire)
Mayfair Publications

	Good	Fine	Mint
1	.70	2.00	4.00

NATIONAL VELVET (TV)
May-July, 1961 - March, 1963 (All photo-c)
Dell Publishing Co./Gold Key

	Good	Fine	Mint
4-Color 1195	2.30	7.00	16.00
4-Color 1312	2.00	6.00	14.00
01-556-207,12-556-210	1.70	5.00	12.00
1(12/62), 2(3/63)-Gold Key	1.70	5.00	12.00

NATURE BOY (Formerly Danny Blaze; Li'l Rascal Twins #6 on)
No. 3, March, 1956 - No. 5, Feb, 1957
Charlton Comics

	Good	Fine	Mint
3-Origin; Blue Beetle story; Buscema-a	10.00	30.00	70.00
4,5	6.50	19.50	45.00

NOTE: ***Buscema*** *a-3, 4p, 5.* ***Powell*** *a-4.*

NATURE OF THINGS (See 4-Color No. 727,842)

NAVY ACTION (Sailor Sweeney #12-14)
Aug, 1954 - No. 11, Apr, 1956; No. 15, 1/57 - No. 18, 8/57
Atlas Comics (CDS)

	Good	Fine	Mint
1-Powell-a	3.00	9.00	21.00
2	1.50	4.50	10.00
3-11: 4-Last precode (2/55)	1.20	3.50	8.00
15-18	.85	2.50	6.00

NOTE: ***Berg** a-9. **Colan** a-8. **Drucker** a-7, 17. **Everett** a-3, 7, 16; c-16, 17. **Maneely** a-8, 18. **Pakula** a-3. **Reinman** a-17.*

NAVY COMBAT
June, 1955 - No. 20, Oct, 1958
Atlas Comics (MPI)

1-Torpedo Taylor begins by D. Heck	3.00	9.00	21.00
2	1.50	4.50	10.00
3-10	1.15	3.50	8.00
11-13,15,16,18-20	1.00	3.00	7.00
14-Torres-a	2.00	6.00	14.00
17-Williamson-a, 4 pgs.	2.75	8.00	18.00

NOTE: ***Berg** a-10,11. **Drucker** a-7, 11. **Everett** a-3, 20; c-8 & 9 w/**Tuska**, 10, 13-16. **Pakula** a-7. **Powell** a-20.*

NAVY HEROES
1945
Almanac Publishing Co.

1-Heavy in propaganda	3.50	10.50	24.00

NAVY: HISTORY & TRADITION
1958 - 1961 (nn) (Giveaway)
Stokes Walesby Co./Dept. of Navy

1772-1778, 1778-1782, 1782-1817, 1817-1865, 1865-1936, 1940-1945	2.00	6.00	14.00
1861: Naval Actions of the Civil War: 1865	2.00	6.00	14.00

NAVY PATROL
May, 1955 - No. 4, Nov, 1955
Key Publications

1	2.00	6.00	14.00
2-4	1.00	3.00	7.00

NAVY TALES
Jan, 1957 - No. 4, July, 1957
Atlas Comics (CDS)

1-Everett-c; Berg, Powell-a	3.00	9.00	21.00
2-Williamson/Mayo-a, 5 pgs; Crandall-a	3.50	10.50	24.00
3,4-Krigstein-a; Severin-c	2.00	6.00	14.00

NAVY TASK FORCE
Feb, 1954 - No. 8, April, 1956
Stanmor Publications/Aragon Mag. No. 4-8

1	2.00	6.00	14.00
2	1.00	3.00	7.00
3-8	.85	2.50	6.00

NAVY WAR HEROES
Jan, 1964 - No. 7, Mar-Apr, 1965
Charlton Comics

1		.40	.80
2-7		.30	.60

NAZA (Stone Age Warrior)
Nov-Jan, 1963/64 - No. 9, March, 1966
Dell Publishing Co.

1 (12-555-401)-Painted-c	.85	2.50	6.00
2-9: 2-4-Painted-c	.55	1.65	4.00

NEBBS, THE
1928 (Daily B&W strip reprints; 52 pages)
Cupples & Leon Co.

By Sol Hess; Carlson-a	5.00	15.00	35.00

NEBBS, THE
1941 - 1945
Dell Publishing Co./Croydon Publishing Co.

	Good	Fine	Mint
Large Feat. Comic 23(1941)	7.00	21.00	50.00
1(1945, 36 pgs.)-Reprints	4.00	12.00	28.00

NEGRO (See All-Negro)

NEGRO HEROES (True, Real Heroes, & Calling All Girls-r)
Spring, 1947 - No. 2, Summer, 1948
Parents' Magazine Institute

1	25.00	75.00	175.00
2	28.00	84.00	195.00

NEGRO ROMANCE (Negro Romances #4?)
June, 1950 - No. 3, Oct, 1950
Fawcett Publications

1-Evans-a	60.00	180.00	420.00
2,3	47.00	140.00	330.00

NEGRO ROMANCES (Formerly Negro Romance?)
No. 4, May, 1955 (Romantic Secrets #5 on?)
Charlton Comics

4-Reprints Fawcett #2	32.00	95.00	225.00

NELLIE THE NURSE
1945 - No. 36, Oct, 1952; 1957
Marvel/Atlas Comics (SPI/LMC)

1	8.50	25.50	60.00
2	4.00	12.00	28.00
3,4	3.50	10.50	24.00
5-Kurtzman's "Hey Look"	4.00	12.00	28.00
6-8,10: 7,8-Georgie app. 10-Millie app.	2.30	7.00	16.00
9-Wolverton-a, 1 pg.	2.65	8.00	18.00
11,14-16,18-Kurtzman's "Hey Look"	3.50	10.50	24.00
12-"Giggles 'n' Grins" by Kurtzman	2.65	8.00	18.00
13,17,19,20: 17-Annie Oakley app.	2.00	6.00	14.00
21-27,29,30	1.70	5.00	12.00
28-Kurtzman's Rusty reprint	2.00	6.00	14.00
31-36	1.30	4.00	9.00
1('57)-Leading Mag. (Atlas)-Everett-a, 20p.	1.15	3.50	8.00

NELLIE THE NURSE (See 4-Color No. 1304)

NEMESIS THE WARLOCK
Sept, 1984 - No. 7, Mar, 1985 (Limited series; 36 pgs.)
Eagle Comics (Baxter paper)

1-2000 A.D. reprints	.25	.75	1.50
2-7	.25	.75	1.50

NEUTRO
January, 1967
Dell Publishing Co.

1-Jack Sparling c/a	.75	2.25	5.00

NEVADA (See Zane Grey's Stories of the West #1)

NEVER AGAIN (War stories; becomes Soldier & Marine V2#9)
Aug, 1955 - No. 2, Oct?, 1955; No. 8, July, 1956 (no No. 3-7)
Charlton Comics

1	3.00	9.00	21.00
2,8	1.60	4.70	11.00

NEW ADVENTURE COMICS (Formerly New Comics; becomes Adventure Comics #32 on)
V1No.12, Jan, 1937 - No. 31, Oct, 1938
National Periodical Publications

	Good	Fine	VF-NM
V1#12-Federal Men by Siegel & Shuster continues; Jor-L mentioned	80.00	240.00	560.00
V2#1(2/37, #13), V2#2 (#14)	60.00	180.00	420.00

Navy Action #1, © MCG

Naza #1, © DELL

Nellie the Nurse #16, © MCG

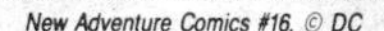
New Adventure Comics #16, © DC

The New DNAgents #1, © Evanier & Meugniot

New Funnies #69, © DELL

NEW ADVENTURE COMICS (continued) — Good / Fine / Mint

15(V2#3)-20(V2#8): 15-1st Adventure logo. 16-1st Shuster-c; 1st non-funny cover. 17-Nadir, Master of Magic begins, ends #30 — 60.00 180.00 420.00
21(V2#9),22(V2#10, 2/37) — 50.00 150.00 350.00
23-31 — 40.00 120.00 280.00

NEW ADVENTURE OF WALT DISNEY'S SNOW WHITE AND THE SEVEN DWARFS, A (See Snow White Bendix Giveaway)

NEW ADVENTURES OF CHARLIE CHAN, THE (TV)
May-June, 1958 - No. 6, Mar-Apr, 1959
National Periodical Publications

1 (Scarce) — 17.00 51.00 120.00
2 (Scarce) — 9.50 28.00 65.00
3-6 (Scarce) — 8.00 24.00 56.00

NOTE: ***Sid Greene** a-1-6i. **Gil Kane** a-1-6p.*

NEW ADVENTURES OF HUCK FINN, THE (TV)
December, 1968 (Hanna-Barbera)
Gold Key

1-"The Curse of Thut" — 1.00 3.00 7.00

NEW ADVENTURES OF PETER PAN (Disney)
1953 (36 pgs.; 5x7¼") (Admiral giveaway)
Western Publishing Co.

4.65 14.00 32.00

NEW ADVENTURES OF PINOCCHIO (TV)
Oct-Dec, 1962 - No. 3, Sept-Nov, 1963
Dell Publishing Co.

12-562-212 — 4.00 12.00 28.00
2,3 — 3.50 10.50 24.00

NEW ADVENTURES OF ROBIN HOOD (See Robin Hood)

NEW ADVENTURES OF SHERLOCK HOLMES (See 4-Color #1169, 1245)

NEW ADVENTURES OF SUPERBOY, THE
Jan, 1980 - No. 54, June, 1984
DC Comics

1 — .60 1.20
2-5 — .50 1.00
6-10 — .40 .80
11-47: 11-Superboy gets new power. 15-Superboy gets new parents. 28-Dial "H" For Hero begins, ends #49. 45-47-1st app. Sunburst — .30 .60
48,49,51-54 (75 cent-c) — .40 .80
50 ($1.25, 52 pgs.) — .60 1.25

NOTE: ***Buckler** a-9p; c-36p. **Giffen** a-50; c-50. 40i. **Gil Kane** c-32p, 33p, 35, 39, 41-49. **Miller** c-51. **Starlin** a-7.*

NEW ADVENTURES OF THE PHANTOM BLOT, THE (See Phantom Blot, The)

NEW AMERICA
Nov., 1987 - No. 4, 1988 (Color, $1.75, Baxter)
Eclipse Comics

1-4: Scout mini-series — .30 .90 1.75

NEW ARCHIES, THE
Oct, 1987 - Present
Archie Comic Publ.

1-3 — .40 .75

NEW BOOK OF COMICS (Also see Big Book Of Fun)
1937; Spring, 1938 (100 pgs. each) (Reprints)
National Periodical Publications

1(Rare)-1st regular size comic annual; 2nd DC annual; contains r-/New Comics #1-4 & More Fun #9; r-Federal Men (8pgs.), Henri Duval (1pg.), & Dr. Occult in costume (1pg.) by Siegel & Shuster; Moldoff, Sheldon Mayer (15pgs.)-a — 242.00 725.00 1700.00

Good / Fine / Mint

2-Contains r-/More Fun #15 & 16; r-/Dr. Occult in costume (a Superman proto-type), & Calling All Cars (4pgs.) by Siegel & Shuster — 150.00 450.00 1050.00

NEW COMICS (New Adventure #12 on)
12/35 - No. 11, 12/36 (No. 1-6, paper cover) (No. 1-5, 84 pgs.)
National Periodical Publications

V1#1-Billy the Kid, Sagebrush 'n' Cactus, Jibby Jones, Needles, The Vikings, Sir Loin of Beef, Now-When I Was a Boy, & other 1-2 pg. strips; 2 pgs. Kelly art(1st)-(Gulliver's Travels); Sheldon Mayer-a(1st) — 300.00 900.00 2100.00
2-Federal Men by Siegel & Shuster begins (Also see The Comics Magazine #2); Sheldon Mayer, Kelly-a. (Rare) — 165.00 495.00 1155.00
3-6: 3,4-Sheldon Mayer-a which continues in The Comics Magazine #1; 5-Kiefer-a — 95.00 285.00 665.00
7-11 — 75.00 225.00 525.00

NOTE: *#1-6 rarely occur in mint condition.*

NEW DEFENDERS (See Defenders)

NEW DNAGENTS, THE (Formerly DNAgents)
Oct, 1985 - No. 17, Mar, 1987 (Mando paper)
Eclipse Comics

V2#1-Origin recap — .50 1.00
2-6 — .40 .80
7-12: (95 cent-c). 9,10-Airboy app. — .50 1.00
13-17 ($1.25-c) — .60 1.20
3-D 1 (1/86) — .35 1.15 2.30
2-D 1 (1/86)-Limited ed. (100 copies) — .85 2.50 5.00

NEW FUN COMICS (More Fun #7 on)
Feb, 1935 - No. 6, Oct, 1935 (10x15", No. 1-4,6-slick covers)
(No. 1-5, 36 pgs; 68 pgs. No. 6-on)
National Periodical Publications — Good / Fine / V. Fine

V1#1 (1st DC comic); 1st app. Oswald The Rabbit — 645.00 1935.00 4200.00
2(3/35)-(Very Rare) — 500.00 1500.00 3250.00
3-5(8/35): 5-Soft-c — 225.00 675.00 1465.00
6(10/35)-1st Dr. Occult by Siegel & Shuster(Leger & Reuths); last "New Fun" title. "New Comics" #1 begins in Dec. which is reason for title change to More Fun; Henri Duval (ends #9) by Siegel & Shuster begins; Paper-c — 275.00 825.00 1790.00

NEW FUNNIES (The Funnies #1-64; Walter Lantz . . . #109 on; #259,260,272,273-New TV. . .; #261-271-TV Funnies)
No. 65, July, 1942 - No. 288, Mar-Apr, 1962
Dell Publishing Co. — Good / Fine / Mint

65(#1)-Andy Panda in a world of real people, Raggedy Ann, Oswald the Rabbit (with Woody Woodpecker x-overs), & Li'l Eight Ball begin — 35.00 105.00 245.00
66-70: 67-Billy & Bonnie Bee by Frank Thomas & Felix The Cat begin. 69-2pg. Kelly-a; The Brownies begin (not by Kelly) — 16.00 48.00 110.00
71-75: 72-Kelly illos. 75-Brownies by Kelly? — 10.00 30.00 70.00
76-Andy Panda (Carl Barks & Pabian-a); Woody Woodpecker x-over in Oswald ends — 57.00 171.00 400.00
77,78: 78-Andy Panda in a world with real people ends — 10.00 30.00 70.00
79-81 — 7.00 21.00 50.00
82-Brownies by Kelly begins; Homer Pigeon begins — 8.50 25.50 60.00
83-85-Brownies by Kelly in ea. 83-X-mas-c. 85-Woody Woodpecker, 1pg. strip begins — 8.50 25.50 60.00
86-90: 90-Woody Woodpecker stories begin — 4.00 12.00 28.00
91-99 — 2.65 8.00 18.00
100 (6/45) — 3.00 9.00 21.00
101-110 — 2.00 6.00 14.00

NEW FUNNIES (continued)	Good	Fine	Mint
111-120: 119-X-mas-c	1.50	4.50	10.00
121-150: 143-X-mas-c	1.15	3.50	8.00
151-200: 155-X-mas-c. 168-X-mas-c, 182-Origin & 1st app. Knothead & Splinter. 191-X-mas-c	.85	2.50	6.00
201-240	.55	1.65	4.00
241-288: 270-Walter Lantz c-app. 281-1st story swipe/WDC&S #100	.45	1.35	3.00

NOTE: *Early issues written by* ***John Stanley.***

NEW GODS, THE (New Gods #12 on)(See Adventure, First Issue Spec. & Super-Team Family)
2-3/71 - No. 11, 10-11/72; No. 12, 7/77 - No. 19, 7-8/78
National Periodical Publications/DC Comics

	Good	Fine	Mint
1-Intro/1st app. Orion	.60	1.75	3.50
2	.40	1.25	2.50
3,4: 4-Origin Manhunter-r	.25	.75	1.50
5-11: 5-Young Gods feature. 7-Origin Orion. 7,8-Young Gods app. 9-1st app. Bug	.25	.75	1.50
12-19		.40	.80

NOTE: *No. 4-9(52 pgs.) contain Manhunter-r by* ***Simon & Kirby*** *from Adventure #73, 74, 75, 76, 77, 78 with covers in that order.* ***Adkins*** *i-12-14, 17-19.* ***Buckler*** *a-15p; c-14p, 15p.* ***Kirby*** *c/a-1-11p.* ***Newton*** *p-12-14, 16-19.* ***Starlin*** *c-17.* ***Staton*** *c-19p.*

NEW GODS, THE
5/84 - No. 6, 11/84 ($2.00; direct sale; Baxter paper)
DC Comics

	Good	Fine	Mint
1-New Kirby-c begin; r-/New Gods 1&2	.35	1.00	2.00
2-6: 6-Original art by Kirby	.35	1.00	2.00

NEW HEROIC (See Heroic)

NEWLYWEDS
1907 - 1917 (cardboard covers)
Saalfield Publ. Co.

	Good	Fine	Mint
. . .& Their Baby' by McManus; Saaalfield, 1907, 13x10," 52pgs. daily strips in full color	24.00	72.00	170.00
. . .& Their Baby's Comic Pictures, The, by McManus, Saalfield, 1917, 14x10," 22pgs, oblong, cardboard-c, reprints 'Newlyweds' (Baby Snookums stips) mainly from 1916; blue cover; says for painting & crayoning, but some pages in color. (Scarce)	18.00	54.00	125.00

NEW MEN OF BATTLE, THE
1949 (nn) (Carboard covers)
Catechetical Guild

	Good	Fine	Mint
nn(V8#1-V8#6)-192pgs.; contains 6 issues of Topix rebound	2.00	6.00	14.00
nn(V8#7-V8#11)-160pgs.; contains 5 issues of Topix	2.00	6.00	14.00

NEW MUTANTS, THE (Also see Marvel Graphic Novel)
March, 1983 - Present
Marvel Comics Group

	Good	Fine	Mint
1	1.25	3.75	7.50
2,3	.60	1.75	3.50
4-10: 10-1st app. Magma	.45	1.40	2.80
11-20: 18-Intro. Warlock	.40	1.15	2.30
21-Double size; new Warlock origin	.45	1.40	2.80
22-30: 23-25-Cloak & Dagger app.	.40	1.15	2.30
31-40		.90	1.80
41-49		.60	1.20
50-58 ($1.25)	.30	.90	1.80
59-Fall of The Mutants begins, ends #61	.35	.90	1.80
60-Double size	.25	.70	1.40
61	.25	.70	1.40
62-65		.45	.90
Annual 1 (1984)	.35	1.10	2.20
Annual 2 (10/86; $1.25)	.25	.80	1.60
Annual 3(9/87, $1.25)	.25	.70	1.40
Special 1-Special Edition ('85; 64 pgs.)-ties in with X-Men Alpha Flight mini-series; A. Adams/Austin-a	.75	2.20	4.40

NOTE: ***Art Adams*** *c-38, 39.* ***Austin*** *c-57i.* ***Sienkiewicz*** *c/a-18-25.* ***Simonson*** *c-11p.* ***B. Smith*** *c-46.* ***W. Smith*** *c-43.*

NEW PEOPLE, THE (TV)
Jan, 1970 - No. 2, May, 1970
Dell Publishing Co.

	Good	Fine	Mint
1,2	1.15	3.50	8.00

NEW ROMANCES
No. 5, May, 1951 - No. 21, Apr?, 1954
Standard Comics

	Good	Fine	Mint
5	3.50	10.50	24.00
6-9: 6-Barbara Bel Geddes, Richard Basehart "Fourteen Hours;"	1.70	5.00	12.00
10,14,16,17-Toth-a	4.00	12.00	28.00
11-Toth-a; Liz Taylor, Montgomery Cliff photo-c	5.00	15.00	35.00
12,13,15,18-21	1.15	3.50	8.00

NOTE: ***Celardo*** *a-9.* ***Moreira*** *a-6.* ***Tuska*** *a-7, 20. Photo c-6-9, 11, 13, 14, 16.*

NEW TALENT SHOWCASE (Talent Showcase No. 16 on)
Jan, 1984 - No. 19, Oct, 1985 (Direct sales only)
DC Comics

	Good	Fine	Mint
1-10: Features new strips & artists		.35	.70
11-19 ($1.25): 18-Williamson c(i)		.35	.70

NEW TEEN TITANS, THE (See DC Comics Presents 26, Marvel and DC Present & Teen Titans; Tales of the Teen Titans #41 on)
November, 1980 - No. 40, March, 1984
DC Comics

	Good	Fine	Mint
1-Robin, Kid Flash, Wonder Girl, The Changeling, Starfire, The Raven, Cyborg begin; partial origin	2.50	7.50	15.00
2	1.35	4.00	8.00
3-Origin Starfire; Intro The Fearsome 5	1.00	3.00	6.00
4-Origin continues; J.L.A. app.	1.00	3.00	6.00
5,6: 6-Raven origin	.70	2.00	4.00
7-10: 7-Cyborg origin. 8-Origin Kid Flash retold. 10-Origin Changeling retold	.70	2.00	4.00
11,12	.50	1.50	3.00
13-15: 13-Return of Madame Rouge & Capt. Zahl; Robotman revived. 14-Return of Mento; origin Doom Patrol. 15-Death of Madame Rouge & Capt. Zahl; intro. new Brotherhood of Evil	.35	1.00	2.00
16-1st app. Capt. Carrot (free 16 pg. preview)	.25	.75	1.50
17-20: 18-Return of Starfire. 19-Hawkman teams-up	.25	.75	1.50
21-23: 21-Intro Night Force in free 16 pg. insert; intro Brother Blood. 23-1st app. Vigilante (not in costume), & Blackfire	.35	1.00	2.00
24-Omega Men app.	.35	1.00	2.00
25-30: 25-Omega Men cameo. 26-1st Terra. 29-The New Brotherhood of Evil & Speedy app. 30-Terra joins the Titans	.35	1.00	2.00
31-40: 38-Origin Wonder Girl. 39-Kid Flash quits		.50	1.00
Annual 1(11/82)-Omega Men app.	.25	.75	1.50
Annual 2(9/83)-1st app. Vigilante in costume		.50	1.00
Annual 3(1984)-Death of Terra		.50	1.00
nn(11/83-Keebler Co. Giveaway)-In cooperation with "The President's Drug Awareness Campaign."		.60	1.20
nn-(re-issue of above on Mando paper for direct sales market); America Soft Drink Ind. version; I.B.M. Corp. version		.50	1.00

NOTE: ***Perez*** *a-1-4p, 6-40p, Annual 1p, 2p; c-1-12, 13-17p, 18-21, 22p, 23p, 24-37,38,39(painted), 40, Annual 1, 2.*

The New Gods #3 (1st series), © DC

The New Mutants #7, © MCG

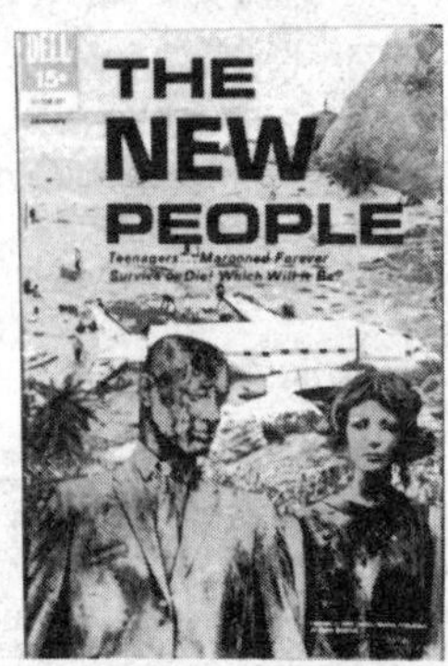

The New People #1, © Thomas/Spelling Prod.

The New Teen Titans Annual #2, © DC

Next Man #3, © Comico

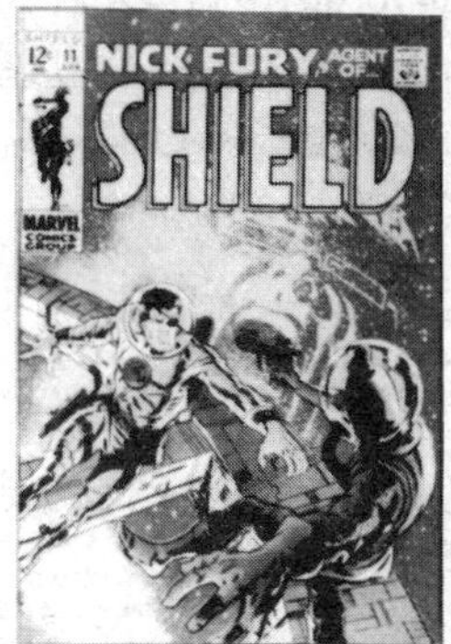

Nick Fury, Agent of Shield #11, © MCG

NEW TEEN TITANS, THE
Aug, 1984 - Present ($1.25,$1.50; deluxe format)
DC Comics

	Good	Fine	Mint
1-New storyline; Perez c/a	1.00	3.00	6.00
2,3	.60	1.75	3.50
4-10: 5-Death of Trigon. 7-9-Origin Lilith. 8-Intro Kole. 10-Kole joins	.35	1.10	2.20
11-42: 13,14-Crisis x-over. 20-Original T. Titans return	.25	.80	1.60
Annual 1 (9/85)-Intro. Vanguard	.35	1.10	2.20
Annual 2 (8/86; $2.50): Byrne c/a; origin Brother Blood; intro new Dr. Light	.50	1.50	3.00
Annual 3 (11/87)-Intro. Danny Chase	.35	1.10	2.30

NOTE: *__Orlando__ c-33p. __Perez__ c/a 1-6; c-20, 22, 23.*

NEW TERRYTOONS (TV)
6-8/60 - No. 8, 3-5/62; 10/62 - No. 54, 1/79
Dell Publishing Co./Gold Key

1('60-Dell)-Deputy Dawg begins	1.50	4.50	10.00
2-8('62)	.85	2.50	6.00
1(30010-210)(10/62-G.Key, 84 pgs.)-Heckle & Jeckle begins	2.50	7.50	20.00
2(30010-301)-84 pgs.	2.00	6.00	16.00
3-10	.75	2.25	5.00
11-20	.50	1.50	3.00
21-30	.25	.75	1.50
31-54		.40	.80

NOTE: *Reprints: #4-12, 38, 40, 47. (See March of Comics #393, 412, 435)*

NEW TESTAMENT STORIES VISUALIZED
1946 - 1947
Standard Publishing Co.

"New Testament Heroes—Acts of Apostles Visualized, Book I"
"New Testament Heroes—Acts of Apostles Visualized, Book II"
"Parables Jesus Told" Set.... 10.00 30.00 60.00

NOTE: *All three are contained in a cardboard case, illustrated on front and info about the set.*

NEW TV FUNNIES (See New Funnies)

NEW WAVE, THE
6/10/86 - No. 14, 4/87 (#1-8, bi-weekly, 20 pgs.; #9-14, monthly)
Eclipse Comics

1-Origin		.30	.60
2-8: 6-Origin Megabyte		.30	.60
9-14 ($1.50)	.25	.75	1.50
...Versus the Volunteers 3-D 1,2(4/87)	.40	1.25	2.50

NEW YORK GIANTS (See Thrilling True Story of the Baseball Giants)

NEW YORK STATE JOINT LEGISLATIVE COMMITTEE TO STUDY THE PUBLICATION OF COMICS, THE
1951, 1955
N.Y. State Legislative Document

This document was referenced by Wertham for **Seduction of the Innocent**. Contains numerous repros from comics showing violence, sadism, torture, and sex.
1955 version (196p, No. 37, 2/23/55)-Sold for $180 in 1986.

NEW YORK WORLD'S FAIR
1939, 1940 (100pgs.; cardboard covers) (DC's 4th & 5th annuals)
National Periodical Publications

1939-Scoop Scanlon, Superman (blonde haired Superman on-c), Sandman, Zatara, Slam Bradley, Ginger Snap by Bob Kane begin	242.00	725.00	1700.00
1940-Batman, Hourman, Johnny Thunderbolt app.	143.00	430.00	1000.00

NOTE: The 1939 edition was published at 25 cents. Since all other comics were 10 cents, it didn't sell. Remaining copies were repriced with 15 cents stickers placed over the 25 cents price. Four variations on the 15 cents stickers known. It was advertised in other DC comics at 25 cents. Everyone who sent a quarter through the mail for it received a free Superman #1 or#2 to make up the dime difference. The 1940 edition was priced at 15 cents.

Not distributed to the stands (?)

NEXT MAN
Feb, 1985 - No. 5, Oct, 1985 ($1.50 cover; Baxter paper)
Comico

	Good	Fine	Mint
1	.50	1.50	3.00
2-5	.30	.90	1.80

NEXUS (Also see First Comics Graphic Novel)
6/81 - No. 6, 3/84; No. 7, 4/85 - Present
(Direct sale only, 36 pgs.; V2/1('83)-printed on Baxter paper
Capital Comics/First Comics No. 7 on

1-B&W version; magazine size	6.00	18.00	36.00
1-B&W 1981 limited edition; 500 copies printed and signed; same as above except this version has a 2-pg. poster & a pencil sketch on paperboard by Rude	8.00	24.00	48.00
2-B&W, magazine size	2.65	8.00	16.00
3-B&W, magazine size; contains 33⅓ rpm record ($2.95 price)	1.10	3.30	6.60
V2#1-Color version	.70	2.00	4.00
2-8: 2-Nexus' origin begins	.50	1.50	3.00
9-43	.30	1.00	2.00

NOTE: *__Bissette__ c-29. __Rude__ c-3(B&W), V2#1-22, 24-27; a-1-3, V2#1-7, 8p-16p, 18p-22p, 24p-27p. __Paul Smith__ c/a-37.*

NICKEL COMICS
1938 (Pocket size - 7½x5½")(132 pgs.)
Dell Publishing Co.

1-"Bobby & Chip" by Otto Messmer, Felix the Cat artist. Contains some English reprints	20.00	50.00	140.00

NICKEL COMICS
May, 1940 - No. 8, Aug, 1940 (36 pgs.; Bi-Weekly; 5 cents)
Fawcett Publications

1-Origin/1st app. Bulletman	80.00	240.00	560.00
2	40.00	120.00	280.00
3	35.00	105.00	245.00
4-The Red Gaucho begins	30.00	90.00	210.00
5-7	25.00	75.00	175.00
8-World's Fair-c; Bulletman moved to Master Comics #7 in Oct.	25.00	75.00	175.00

NOTE: *__Beck__ c-5-8. __Jack Binder__ c-1-4. Bondage c-5.*

NICK FURY, AGENT OF SHIELD (See Shield & Marv. Spotlight #31)
6/68 - No. 15, 11/69; No. 16, 11/70 - No. 18, 3/71
Marvel Comics Group

1	1.50	4.50	9.00
2,3	1.00	3.00	6.00
4-Origin retold	.85	2.50	5.00
5-Classic-c	1.00	3.00	6.00
6,7	.70	2.00	4.00
8-11: 9-Hate Monger begins (ends #11). 11-Smith-c		.50	1.00
12-Smith c/a	.35	1.00	2.00
13-15		.40	.80
16-18-All reprints; 52 pgs.		.30	.60

NOTE: *__Adkins__ a-3i. __Craig__ a-10i. __Sid Greene__ a-12i. __Kirby__ a-16-18r. __Springer__ a-4, 6, 7, 8p, 9, 10p, 11; c-8, 9. __Steranko__ a(p)-1-3, 5; c-1-7.*

NICK FURY, AGENT OF SHIELD
Dec, 1983 - No. 2, Jan, 1984 ($2.00; 52 pgs.; Baxter paper)
Marvel Comics Group

1,2-Nick Fury-r; Steranko-c/a		.60	1.20

NICK HALIDAY
May, 1956
Argo

1-Daily & Sunday strip-r by Petree	3.50	10.50	24.00

NIGHT AND THE ENEMY (Graphic Novel)
1988 (8½x11") (color; 80pgs.; $11.95)

NIGHT AND THE ENEMY (continued)
Comico

	Good	Fine	Mint
1-Harlan Ellison scripts/Ken Steacy-c/a; r/Epic Ill. & new-a	2.00	6.00	11.95

NIGHT BEFORE CHRISTMAS, THE (See March of Comics No. 152)

NIGHTCRAWLER
Nov, 1985 - No. 4, Feb, 1986 (mini-series; from X-Men)
Marvel Comics Group

1-Cockrum c/a	.40	1.25	2.50
2-4	.25	.75	1.50

NIGHT FORCE, THE
Aug, 1982, No. 14, Sept, 1983
DC Comics

1		.40	.80
2-14: 13-Origin The Baron. 14-Nudity panels		.30	.60

NOTE: ***Colan*** *c/a-1-14p.* ***Giordano*** *c-1i, 2i, 4i, 5i, 7i, 12i.*

NIGHTINGALE, THE
1948 (14 pgs., 7¼x10¼", ½B&W) (10 cents)
Henry H. Stansbury Once-A-Time Press, Inc.

(Very Rare)-Low distribution; distributed to Westchester County & Bronx, N.Y. only; used in **Seduction of the Innocent**, pf. 312,313 as the 1st and only "good" comic book ever published. Ill. by Doug kingman; 1,500 words of text, printed on high quality paper & no word balloons. Copyright registered 10/22/48, distributed week of 12/5/48. (By Hans Christian Andersen) Estimated value............................$125

NIGHTMARE
Summer, 1952 - No. 2, Fall, 1952; No. 3,4, 1953 (Painted-c)
Ziff-Davis (Approved Comics)/St. John No. 3,4

1-1pg. Kinstler-a; Tuska-a(2)	13.00	40.00	90.00
2-Kinstler-a-Poe's "Pit & the Pendulum"	10.00	30.00	70.00
3-Kinstler-a	9.00	27.00	63.00
4	7.00	21.00	50.00

NIGHTMARE (Formerly Weird Horrors #1-9) (Amazing Ghost Stories #14 on)
No. 10, Dec, 1953 - No. 13, Aug, 1954
St. John Publishing Co.

10-Reprints Ziff-Davis Weird Thrillers #2 with new Kubert-c plus 2 pgs. Kinstler, & Toth-a	16.50	50.00	115.00
11-Krigstein-a; Poe adapt., "Hop Frog"	11.00	32.00	76.00
12-Kubert bondage-c; adaptation of Poe's 'The Black Cat;' Cannibalism story	9.00	27.00	63.00
13-Reprints Z-D Weird Thrillers 3 with new cover; Powell-a(2), Tuska-a; Baker-c	5.70	17.00	40.00

NOTE: ***Anderson*** *a-10.* ***Colan*** *a-10.*

NIGHTMARE (Magazine)
Dec, 1970 - No. 23, Feb, 1975 (B&W) (68 pages)
Skywald Publishing Corp.

1-Everett-a	1.00	3.00	6.00
2-5: 4-Decapitation story	.70	2.00	4.00
6-Kaluta-a	.70	2.00	4.00
7,9,10	.50	1.50	3.00
8-Features E. C. movie "Tales From the Crypt;" reprints some E.C. comics panels	1.30	4.00	9.00
11-20: 12-Excessive gore, severed heads. 20-Severed head-c	.35	1.00	2.00
21-(1974 Summer Special)-Kaluta-a	.35	1.00	2.00
22-Tomb of Horror issue	.35	1.00	2.00
23-(1975 Winter Special)	.35	1.00	2.00
Annual 1(1972)-B.Jones-a	.50	1.50	3.00
Winter Special 1(1973)	.50	1.50	3.00
Yearbook-nn(1974)	.50	1.50	3.00

NOTE: ***Adkins*** *a-5.* ***Boris*** *c-2, 3, 5 (#4 is not by Boris).* ***Byrne*** *a-20p.* ***Everett*** *a-4, 5.* ***Jones*** *a-6, 21; c-6.* ***Katz*** *a-5.* ***Reese*** *a-4, 5.* ***Wildey*** *a-5, 6, 21, '74 Yearbook.* ***Wrightson*** *a-9.*

NIGHTMARE & CASPER (See Harvey Hits #71) (Casper & Nightmare #6 on)
Aug, 1963 - No. 5, Aug, 1964 (25 cents)
Harvey Publications

	Good	Fine	Mint
1	5.35	16.00	32.00
2-5	2.35	7.00	14.00

NIGHTMARES (See Do You Believe in...)

NIGHTMARES
May, 1985 - No. 2, May, 1985 (Baxter paper)
Eclipse Comics

1,2	.30	.90	1.80

NIGHTMASK
Nov, 1986 - No. 12, Oct, 1987
Marvel Comics Group

1		.45	.90
2-12		.40	.80

NIGHT MUSIC (See Eclipse Graphic Album Series)
Dec, 1984 - No. 6, 1985? ($1.75, Baxter paper)
Eclipse Comics

1-3: 3-Russell's Jungle Book adapt.	.30	.90	1.80
4,5-Pelleas And Melisande (dbl. titled)	.30	.90	1.80
6-Salome' (dbl. titled)	.30	.90	1.80

NIGHT NURSE
Nov, 1972 - No. 4, May, 1973
Marvel Comics Group

1-4		.40	.80

NIGHT OF MYSTERY
1953 (no month) (One Shot)
Avon Periodicals

nn-1pg. Kinstler-a, Hollingsworth-c	12.00	36.00	84.00

NIGHT OF THE GRIZZLY, THE (See Movie Classics)

NIGHT RIDER
Oct, 1974 - No. 6, Aug, 1975
Marvel Comics Group

1-#1-6 reprints Ghost Rider #1-6		.50	1.00
2-6		.30	.60

NIGHTWINGS (See DC Science Fic. Graphic Novel)

NIKKI, WILD DOG OF THE NORTH (See 4-Color No. 1226 & Movie Comics)

1984 (Magazine) (1994 #11 on)
June, 1978 - No. 10, Jan, 1980 ($1.50)
Warren Publishing Co.

1	.50	1.50	3.00
2-10	.30	.90	1.80

NOTE: ***Alacla*** *a-1-3. 5i.* ***Corben*** *a-1-8; c-1,2.* ***Nino*** *a-1-10, 20(2).* ***Thorne*** *a-7-10.* ***Wood*** *a-1, 2, 5i.*

1994 (Formerly 1984) (Magazine)
No. 11, Feb, 1980 - No. 29, Feb, 1983
Warren Publishing Co.

11-29: 27-The Warhawks return	.35	1.00	2.00

NOTE: ***Corben*** *c-26.* ***Nino*** *a-11-21, 25, 26, 28; c-21.* ***Redondo*** *c-20.* ***Thorne*** *a-11-14, 17-21, 25, 26, 28, 29.*

NIPPY'S POP
1917 (Sunday strip reprints-B&W) (10½x13½")
The Saalfield Publishing Co.

32 pages	5.00	15.00	35.00

NOAH'S ARK
1973 (35-49 Cents)
Spire Christian Comics/Fleming H. Revell Co.

By Al Hartley		.40	.80

The Night Force #3, © DC

Nightmare #12, © STJ

Night of Mystery #1, © AVON

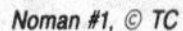
Noman #1, © TC

Not Brand Echh #5, © MCG

Nutty Comics #6, © HARV

NOMAN
Nov, 1966 - No. 2, March, 1967 (68 pgs.)
Tower Comics

	Good	Fine	Mint
1-Wood/Williamson-c; Lightning begins; Dynamo cameo; Kane-a(p)	1.70	5.00	12.00
2-Wood-c only; Dynamo x-over; Whitney-a-#1,2	1.00	3.00	7.00

NONE BUT THE BRAVE (See Movie Classics)

NOODNIK COMICS (See Pinky the Egghead)
1953; No. 2, Feb, 1954 - No. 5, Aug, 1954
Comic Media/Mystery/Biltmore

	Good	Fine	Mint
3-D(1953-Comic Media)(#1)	19.00	57.00	132.00
2-5	2.00	6.00	14.00

NORTH AVENUE IRREGULARS (See Walt Disney Showcase #49)

NORTH TO ALASKA (See 4-Color No. 1155)

NORTHWEST MOUNTIES (Also see Approved Comics)
Oct, 1948 - No. 4, July, 1949
Jubilee Publications/St. John

	Good	Fine	Mint
1-Rose of the Yukon by Matt Baker; Walter Johnson-a; Lubbers-c	16.50	50.00	115.00
2-Baker-a; Lubbers-c. Ventrilo app.	12.00	36.00	84.00
3-Bondage-c, Baker-a; Sky Chief, K-9 app.	13.00	40.00	90.00
4-Baker-c, 2 pgs.; Blue Monk app.	13.00	40.00	90.00

NO SLEEP 'TIL DAWN (See 4-Color No. 831)

NOT BRAND ECHH (Brand Echh #1-4)
Aug, 1967 - No. 13, May, 1969 (No. 9-13: 68 pages)
Marvel Comics Group

	Good	Fine	Mint
1	1.25	3.75	7.50
2-4: 3-Origin Thor, Hulk & Capt. America; Monkees, Alfred E. Neuman cameo. 4-X-Men app.	.75	2.25	4.50
5-Origin & intro. Forbush Man	.65	1.90	3.80
5-8: 5-Origin/intro. Forbush Man. 7-Origin Fantastical-4 & Stupor-man. 8-Beatles cameo; X-Men satire	.65	1.90	3.80
9-13-All Giants. 9-Beatles cameo. 10-All-r; The Old Witch, Crypt Keeper & Vault Keeper cameos. 12,13-Beatles cameo, Avengers satire #12	.45	1.40	2.80

NOTE: *Colan a-4p, 5p, 8p.* ***Everett*** *a-1i.* ***Kirby*** *a(p)-1,3,5-7,10; c-1.* ***Severin*** *a-1; c-3, 7, 8.* ***Sutton*** *a-4, 5i, 7i, 8; c-5. Archie satire-No. 9.*

NO TIME FOR SERGEANTS (TV)
No. 914, July, 1958 - No. 3, Aug-Oct, 1965
Dell Publishing Co.

	Good	Fine	Mint
4-Color 914 (Movie)-Toth-a	5.70	17.00	40.00
1(2-4/65)-3 (TV)	2.00	6.00	14.00

NOVA (The Man Called... No. 22-25)
Sept, 1976 - No. 25, May, 1979
Marvel Comics Group

	Good	Fine	Mint
1-Origin	.40	1.25	2.50
2,3		.60	1.20
4-10		.35	.70
11-20: Nick Fury & Shield app. #15-18		.25	.50
21-25: 21,22-The Comet (MLJ) app.		.25	.50

NOTE: ***Austin*** *c-21i, 23i.* ***John Buscema*** *a(p)-1, 2, 3p, 8p, 21; c-1p, 2, 15.* ***Infantino*** *a(p)-15-20, 22-25; c-17-20, 21p, 23p, 24p.* ***Kirby*** *c-4p, 5, 7.* ***Nebres*** *c-25i.* ***Simonson*** *a-23i.*

NOW AGE ILLUSTRATED (See Pendulum Ill. Classics)

NUKLA
Oct-Dec, 1965 - No. 4, Sept, 1966
Dell Publishing Co.

	Good	Fine	Mint
1-Origin Nukla	1.15	3.50	8.00
2,3	.75	2.25	5.00
4-Ditko-a, c(p)	.85	2.50	6.00

NURSE BETSY CRANE (Formerly Teen Secret Diary)
Aug, 1961 - No. 27, Mar, 1964 (See Soap Opera Romances)
Charlton Comics

	Good	Fine	Mint
V2#12-27		.60	1.20

NURSE HELEN GRANT (See The Romances of...)

NURSE LINDA LARK (See Linda Lark)

NURSERY RHYMES
1950 - No. 10, July-Aug, 1951
Ziff-Davis Publ. Co. (Approved Comics)

	Good	Fine	Mint
2	5.00	15.00	35.00
3-10: 10-Howie Post-a	3.00	9.00	21.00

NURSES, THE (TV)
April, 1963 - No. 3, Oct, 1963 (All photo-c)
Gold Key

	Good	Fine	Mint
1	1.50	4.50	10.00
2,3	.85	2.50	6.00

NUTS! (Satire)
March, 1954 - No. 5, Nov, 1954
Premiere Comics Group

	Good	Fine	Mint
1-Hollingsworth-a	6.00	18.00	42.00
2,4,5: 5-Capt. Marvel parody	4.00	12.00	28.00
3-Drug "reefers" mentioned	5.00	15.00	35.00

NUTS (Magazine) (Satire)
Feb, 1958 - No. 2, April, 1958
Health Knowledge

	Good	Fine	Mint
1	2.65	8.00	18.00
2	1.70	5.00	12.00

NUTS & JOLTS (See Large Feat. Comic No. 22)

NUTSY SQUIRREL (Formerly Hollywood Funny Folks)
(Also see Comic Cavalcade)
No. 61, 9-10/54 - No. 69, 1-2/56; No. 70, 8-9/56 - No. 71, 10-11/56; No. 72, 11/57
National Periodical Publications

	Good	Fine	Mint
61-Mayer-a; Grossman-a in all	2.65	8.00	18.00
62-72: Mayer a-62,65,67-72	1.50	4.50	10.00

NUTTY COMICS
Winter, 1946
Fawcett Publications

	Good	Fine	Mint
1-Capt. Kidd story; 1pg. Wolverton-a	6.00	18.00	42.00

NUTTY COMICS
1945 - No. 8, June-July, 1947
Home Comics (Harvey Publications)

	Good	Fine	Mint
nn-Helpful Hank, Bozo Bear & others	3.00	9.00	21.00
2-4	2.00	6.00	14.00
5-8: 5-Rags Rabbit begins; infinity-c	1.50	4.50	10.00

NUTTY LIFE
No. 2, Summer, 1946
Fox Features Syndicate

	Good	Fine	Mint
2	3.00	9.00	21.00

NYOKA, THE JUNGLE GIRL (Formerly Jungle Girl; see Master & X-Mas Comics)
No. 2, Winter, 1945 - No. 77, June, 1953 (Movie serial)
Fawcett Publications

	Good	Fine	Mint
2	30.00	90.00	210.00
3	17.00	51.00	120.00
4,5	14.00	42.00	100.00
6-10	10.00	30.00	70.00
11,13,14,16-18-Krigstein-a	10.00	30.00	70.00
12,15,19,20	8.00	24.00	56.00

NYOKA, THE JUNGLE GIRL (continued)

	Good	Fine	Mint
21-30	5.00	15.00	35.00
31-40	3.65	11.00	25.00
41-50	2.85	8.50	20.00
51-60	2.15	6.50	15.00
61-77	1.70	5.00	11.50

NOTE: *Photo-c from movies 25-70. Bondage c-4, 5, 7, 8, 14, 24.*

NYOKA, THE JUNGLE GIRL (Formerly Zoo Funnies; Space Adventures #23 on)
No. 14, Nov, 1955 - No. 22, Nov, 1957
Charlton Comics

14	2.65	8.00	18.00
15-22	1.70	5.00	12.00

OAKY DOAKS
July, 1942 (One Shot)
Eastern Color Printing Co.

1	12.00	36.00	84.00

OAKLAND PRESS FUNNYBOOK, THE
9/17/78 - 4/13/80 (16 pgs.) (Weekly)
Full color in comic book form; changes to tabloid size 4/20/80-on
The Oakland Press

Contains Tarzan by Manning, Marmaduke, Bugs Bunny, etc. (low distribution); 9/23/79 - 4/13/80 contain Buck Rogers by Gray Morrow & Jim Lawrence	.30	.80	1.60

OBIE
1953 (6 cents)
Store Comics

1	.70	2.00	4.00

OBNOXIO THE CLOWN
April, 1983 (One Shot) (From Crazy Magazine)
Marvel Comics Group

1-Vs. the X-Men		.30	.60

OCCULT FILES OF DR. SPEKTOR, THE
4/73 - No. 24, 2/77; No. 25, 5/82 (Painted-c No. 1-24)
Gold Key/Whitman No. 25

1-1st app. Lakota; Baron Tibor begins	.70	2.00	4.00
2-5	.35	1.00	2.00
6-10	.25	.75	1.50
11-13: 11-1st app. Spektor as Werewolf		.50	1.00
14-Dr. Solar app.		.50	1.00
15-25: 25-Reprints		.50	1.00
9(Modern Comics reprint, 1977)		.15	.30

NOTE: ***Also see** Dan Curtis, Golden Comics Digest 33, Mystery Comics Digest 5, & Spine Tingling Tales.*

ODELL'S ADVENTURES IN 3-D (See Adventures in. . .)

OFFICIAL CRISIS INDEX, THE
March, 1986
Independent Comics Group (Eclipse)

1	.30	.90	1.80

OFFICIAL CRISIS ON INFINITE EARTHS CROSSOVER INDEX, THE
July, 1986
Independent Comics Group (Eclipse)

1	.50	1.50	3.00

OFFICIAL DOOM PATROL INDEX, THE
Feb, 1986 - No. 2, Mar, 1986 (2 part series)
Independent Comics Group (Eclipse)

1,2	.35	1.00	2.00

OFFICIAL HANDBOOK OF THE MARVEL UNIVERSE, THE
Jan, 1983 - No. 15, May, 1984
Marvel Comics Group

	Good	Fine	Mint
1-Lists Marvel heroes & villains (letter A)	.85	2.50	5.00
2 (B-C)	.70	2.00	4.00
3-5: 3-(C-D). 4-(D-G). 5-(H-J)	.60	1.75	3.50
6-9: 6-(K-L). 7-(M). 8-(N-P). 9-(Q-S)	.45	1.40	2.80
10-12: 10-(S). 11-(S-U). 12-(U-Z)	.40	1.20	2.40
13-15: 13,14-Book of the Dead. 15-Weaponry catalogue	.35	1.00	2.00

NOTE: ***Byrne** c/a(p)-1-14; c-15p. **Grell** a-9. **Layton** a-2, 5, 7. **Miller** a-2, 3. **Nebres** a-3, 4, 8. **Simonson** a-11. **Paul Smith** a-1-3, 6, 7, 9, 10, 12. **Starlin** a-7. **Steranko** a-8p.*

OFFICIAL HANDBOOK OF THE MARVEL UNIVERSE, THE
Dec, 1985 - Present ($1.50 cover; maxi-series)
Marvel Comics Group

1(V2/1)	.70	2.00	4.00
2-5	.50	1.50	3.00
6-10	.40	1.25	2.50
11-20	.35	1.00	2.00
Trade paperback Vol. 1	1.15	3.50	7.00

OFFICIAL HAWKMAN INDEX, THE
Nov, 1986 - No. 2, Dec, 1986 ($2.00)
Independent Comics Group

1,2	.35	1.00	2.00

OFFICIAL JUSTICE LEAGUE OF AMERICA INDEX, THE
April, 1986 - No. 8, Mar, 1987 ($2.00, Baxter)
Independent Comics Group (Eclipse)

1-8	.35	1.10	2.20

OFFICIAL LEGION OF SUPER-HEROES INDEX, THE
Dec, 1986 - Present ($2.00)
Independent Comics Group

1-4	.35	1.00	2.00

OFFICIAL MARVEL INDEX TO MARVEL TEAM-UP
Jan, 1986 - Present
Marvel Comics Group

1-6		.65	1.30

OFFICIAL MARVEL INDEX TO THE AMAZING SPIDER-MAN
Apr, 1985 - No. 9, Dec, 1985
Marvel Comics Group

1	.25	.75	1.50
2-9		.65	1.30

OFFICIAL MARVEL INDEX TO THE AVENGERS
June, 1987 - Present ($2.95)
Marvel Comics Group

1-5	.50	1.50	3.00

OFFICIAL MARVEL INDEX TO THE FANTASTIC FOUR
Dec, 1985 - No. 12, Dec?, 1986
Marvel Comics Group

1-12		.65	1.30

OFFICIAL MARVEL INDEX TO THE X-MEN, THE
Mar, 1987 - Present ($2.95)
Marvel Comics Group

1-5	.50	1.50	3.00

OFFICIAL SOUPY SALES COMIC (See Soupy Sales)

OFFICIAL TEEN TITANS INDEX, THE
Aug, 1985 - No. 5, 1986 ($1.50 cover)
Independent Comics Group (Eclipse)

1-5	.25	.75	1.50

OFFICIAL TRUE CRIME CASES (Formerly Sub-Mariner #23; All-True Crime Cases #26 on)
No. 24, Fall, 1947 - No. 25, Winter, 1947-48

Nyoka, The Jungle Girl #38, © FAW

Official Legion of Super-Heroes Index #1, © ICG

Official Marvel Index to the X-Men #2, © MCG

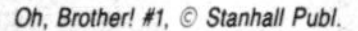
Oh, Brother! #1, © Stanhall Publ.

Oklahoma Kid #1, © AJAX

Omac #5, © DC

OFFICIAL TRUE CRIME CASES (continued)
Marvel Comics (OCI)

	Good	Fine	Mint
24(#1)-Burgos-a	5.00	15.00	35.00
25-Kurtzman's "Hey Look"	4.00	12.00	28.00

OF SUCH IS THE KINGDOM
1955 (36 pgs., 15¢)
George A. Pflaum

nn-R-/1951 Treasure Chest	1.15	3.50	8.00

O.G. WHIZ
2/71 - No. 6, 5/72; No. 7, 5/78 - No. 11, 1/79 (No. 7-52 pgs.)
Gold Key

1,2-John Stanley scripts	4.35	13.00	30.00
3-6(1972)	1.70	5.00	12.00
7-11('78-'79)-Part-r: 9-Tubby app.	.60	1.75	3.50

OH, BROTHER! (Teen Comedy)
Jan, 1953 - No. 5, Oct, 1953
Stanhall Publ.

1	1.85	5.50	13.00
2-5	1.00	3.00	7.00

OH SKIN-NAY!
1913
P.F. Volland & Co.

nn-The Days Of Real Sport by Briggs	8.00	24.00	56.00

OH SUSANNA (See 4-Color No. 1105)

OKAY COMICS
July, 1940
United Features Syndicate

1-Captain & the Kids & Hawkshaw the Detective reprints	15.00	45.00	105.00

OK COMICS
July, 1940 - No. 2, Oct, 1940
United Features Syndicate

1-Little Giant, Phantom Knight, Sunset Smith, & The Teller Twins begin	25.00	75.00	175.00
2 (Rare)-Origin Mister Mist	25.00	75.00	175.00

OKLAHOMA KID
June, 1957 - No. 4, 1958
Ajax/Farrell Publ.

1	2.65	8.00	18.00
2-4	1.30	4.00	9.00

OKLAHOMAN, THE (See 4-Color No. 820)

OLD GLORY COMICS
1944 (Giveaway)
Chesapeake & Ohio Railway

Capt. Fearless reprint	2.35	7.00	16.00

OLD IRONSIDES (See 4-Color No. 874)

OLD YELLER (See 4-Color #869, Movie Comics, and Walt Disney Showcase #25)

OMAC (One Man Army, . . . Corps. No. 4 on)
Sept-Oct, 1974 - No. 8, Nov-Dec, 1975
National Periodical Publications

1-Origin		.40	.80
2-8: 8-2pg. Adams ad		.25	.50

NOTE: *Kirby a-1-8p; c-1-7p. Kubert c-8. See Kamandi No. 59 & Cancelled Comic Cavalcade.*

O'MALLEY AND THE ALLEY CATS
April, 1971 - No. 9, Jan, 1974 (Disney)
Gold Key

1	1.15	3.50	8.00
2-9	.70	2.00	4.00

OMEGA ELITE
1987 - Present ($1.25, color)
Blackthorne Publishing

1-Starlin-c		.60	1.25

OMEGA MEN, THE (See Green Lantern #141)
Dec, 1982 - No. 38, May, 1986 ($1.00-$1.50; Baxter paper)
DC Comics

1	.25	.75	1.50
2-Origin Broot		.45	.90
3-30: 7-Origin The Citadel. 26,27-Alan Moore scripts. 30-Intro new Primus		.45	.90
31-38: 31-Crisis x-over. 34,35-Teen Titans x-over		.45	.90
Annual 1(11/84, 52 pgs.), 2(11/85)	.25	.70	1.40

NOTE: *Giffen c/a-1-6p. Morrow a-24r. Nino a-16, 21; c-16, 21.*

OMEGA THE UNKNOWN
March, 1976 - No. 10, Oct, 1977
Marvel Comics Group

1		.40	.80
2-10: 2-Hulk app. 3-Electro app.		.30	.60

NOTE: *Kane c(p)-3, 5, 8, 9. Mooney a-1-3, 4p, 5, 6p, 7, 8i, 9, 10.*

OMNI MEN
1987 - Present ($1.25, color)
Blackthorne Publishing

1-3		.60	1.25

ONE, THE
July, 1985 - No. 6, Feb, 1986 (mini-series; adults only)
Epic Comics (Marvel)

1-Post nuclear holocaust super-hero	.25	.75	1.50
2-6: 2-Intro. The Other	.25	.75	1.50

ONE HUNDRED AND ONE DALMATIANS (See 4-Color No. 1183, Movie Comics, and Walt Disney Showcase No. 9,51)

100 PAGES OF COMICS
1937 (Stiff covers; square binding)
Dell Publishing Co.

101(Found on back cover)-Alley Oop, Wash Tubbs, Capt. Easy, Og Son of Fire, Apple Mary, Tom Mix, Dan Dunn, Tailspin Tommy, Doctor Doom	45.00	135.00	315.00

100-PAGE SUPER SPECTACULAR (See DC . . .)

$1,000,000 DUCK (See Walt Disney Showcase No. 5)

ONE MILLION YEARS AGO (Tor #2 on)
September, 1953
St. John Publishing Co.

1-Origin; Kubert-a	15.00	45.00	105.00

ONE SHOT (See 4-Color . . .)

1001 HOURS OF FUN (See Large Feature Comic No. 13)

ON STAGE (See 4-Color No. 1336)

ON THE AIR
1947 (Giveaway) (paper cover)
NBC Network Comic

(Rare)	9.50	28.50	65.00

ON THE DOUBLE (See 4-Color No. 1232)

ON THE LINKS
December, 1926 (48 pages) (9x10")
Associated Feature Service

Daily strip-r	6.50	19.50	45.00

ON THE ROAD WITH ANDRAE CROUCH
1973, 1977 (39 cents)
Spire Christian Comics (Fleming H. Revell)

	Good	Fine	Mint
nn		.50	1.00

ON THE SPOT (Pretty Boy Floyd . . .)
Fall, 1948
Fawcett Publications

	Good	Fine	Mint
nn-Bondage-c	11.00	32.00	76.00

OPERATION BIKINI (See Movie Classics)

OPERATION BUCHAREST (See The Crusaders)

OPERATION CROSSBOW (See Movie Classics)

OPERATION PERIL
Oct-Nov, 1950 - No. 16, Apr-May, 1953
American Comics Group (Michel Publ.)

	Good	Fine	Mint
1-Time Travelers, Danny Danger (by Leonard Starr) & Typhoon Tyler (by Ogden Whitney) begin	8.00	24.00	56.00
2	5.00	15.00	35.00
3-5: 3-Horror story	4.35	13.00	30.00
6-12-Last Time Travelers	4.00	12.00	28.00
13-16: All war format	1.35	4.00	9.00

NOTE: ***Starr** a-2. **Whitney** a-1,2,6-10,12; c-1,8,9.*

ORAL ROBERTS' TRUE STORIES (Junior Partners No. 120 on)
1956 (no month) - No. 119, 7/59 (15 cents)(No #102: 25 cents)
TelePix Publ. (Oral Roberts' Evangelistic Assoc./Healing Waters)

	Good	Fine	Mint
V1No.1(1956)-(Not code approved)-"The Miracle Touch"	6.00	18.00	42.00
102-(only issue approved by code)(10/56)	3.00	9.00	21.00
103-119: 115-(114 on inside)	2.00	6.00	14.00

NOTE: *Also see Happiness & Healing For You.*

ORANGE BIRD, THE
No date (1980) (36 pgs.; in color; slick cover)
Walt Disney Educational Media Co.

	Good	Fine	Mint
Included with educational kit on foods		.30	.60

ORIGINAL E-MAN AND MICHAEL MAUSER, THE
Oct, 1985 - No. 7, April, 1986 ($1.75 cover; Baxter paper)
First Comics

	Good	Fine	Mint
1-Has r-/Charlton's E-Man & Vengeance Squad	.35	1.00	2.00
2-6	.30	.90	1.80
7 ($2.00; 44 pgs.)-Staton-a	.35	1.00	2.00

ORIGINAL SHIELD, THE
April, 1984 - No. 4, Oct, 1984
Archie Enterprises, Inc.

	Good	Fine	Mint
1-Origin Shield		.35	.70
2-4		.35	.70

ORIGINAL SWAMP THING SAGA, THE (See DC Spec. Series #2,14,17,20)

OSCAR COMICS (Formerly Funny Tunes; Awful . . . #11 & 12)
No. 24, Spring, 1947 - No. 10, Apr, 1949; No. 13, Oct, 1949
Marvel Comics

	Good	Fine	Mint
24(1947)	3.50	10.50	24.00
25(Sum, '47)-Wolverton-a plus Kurtzman's "Hey Look"	5.70	17.00	40.00
3-9,13: 8-Margie app.	2.30	7.00	16.00
10-Kurtzman's "Hey Look"	3.50	10.50	24.00

OSWALD THE RABBIT (Also see New Fun Comics #1)
No. 21, 1943 - No. 1268, 12-2/61-62 (Walter Lantz)
Dell Publishing Co.

	Good	Fine	Mint
4-Color 21(1943)	18.00	54.00	125.00
4-Color 39(1943)	13.00	40.00	90.00
4-Color 67(1944)	8.50	25.50	60.00
4-Color 102(1946)-Kelly-a, 1 pg.	8.50	25.50	60.00
4-Color 143,183	3.50	10.50	24.00
4-Color 225,273	2.30	7.00	16.00
4-Color 315,388	1.50	4.50	10.00
4-Color 458,507,549,593	1.00	3.00	7.00
4-Color 623,697,792,894,979,1268	.85	2.50	6.00

OSWALD THE RABBIT (See March of Comics #7, 38, 53, 67, 81, 95, 111, 126, 141, 156, 171, 186, The Funnies, New Funnies & Super Book #8, 20)

OUR ARMY AT WAR (Sgt. Rock #302 on)
Aug, 1952 - No. 301, Feb, 1977
National Periodical Publications

	Good	Fine	Mint
1	30.00	90.00	210.00
2	14.00	42.00	100.00
3	13.00	40.00	90.00
4-Krigstein-a	13.00	40.00	90.00
5-7	6.50	19.50	45.00
8-11,14-Krigstein-a	7.00	21.00	50.00
12,15-20	5.00	15.00	35.00
13-Krigstein c/a	7.00	21.00	50.00
21-30	3.50	10.50	24.00
31-40	2.40	7.25	17.00
41-60	2.15	6.50	15.00
61-70	1.50	4.50	10.00
71-80	1.15	3.50	8.00
81-1st Sgt. Rock app. by Andru & Esposito in Easy Co. story	13.00	40.00	90.00
82-Sgt. Rock cameo in Easy Co. story (6 panels)	4.50	13.50	32.00
83-1st Kubert Sgt. Rock	6.50	20.00	45.00
84,86-90	2.85	8.50	20.00
85-1st app. & origin Ice Cream Soldier	3.70	11.00	26.00
91-All Sgt. Rock issue	3.70	11.00	26.00
92-100: 92-1st app. Bulldozer. 95-1st app. Zack	1.00	3.00	7.00
101-120: 101-1st app. Buster. 111-1st app. Wee Willie & Sunny. 113-1st app. Jackie Johnson. 118-Sunny dies. 120-1st app. Wildman	.90	2.75	5.50
121-127,129-150: 126-1st app. Canary. 139-1st app. Little Sure Shot	.75	2.25	4.50
128-Training & origin Sgt. Rock	1.00	3.00	6.00
151-Intro. Enemy Ace by Kubert	1.00	3.00	6.00
152-157,159-163,165-170: 153,155-Enemy Ace stories. 157-Two pg. pin-up. 162,163-Viking Prince x-over in Sgt. Rock	.70	2.00	4.00
158-1st app. & origin Iron Major(1965), formerly Iron Captain	.85	2.50	5.00
164-Giant G-19	.85	2.50	5.00
171-176,178-181	.25	.75	1.50
177-(80 pg. Giant G-32)	.35	1.00	2.00
182,183,186-Adams-a; 186-Origin retold	.70	2.00	4.00
184,185,187-189,191-199: 184-Wee Willie dies. 189-Intro. The Teen-age Underground Fighters of Unit 3		.50	1.00
190-(80 pg. Giant G-44)	.25	.75	1.50
200-12 pg. Rock story told in verse; Evans-a		.50	1.00
201-Krigstein-r/No. 14		.50	1.00
202,206-215		.35	.70
203-(80 pg. Giant G-56)-All-r, no Sgt. Rock		.50	1.00
204,205-All-r, no Sgt. Rock		.35	.70
216-(80 pg. Giant G-68)		.50	1.00
217-228		.35	.70
229-(80 pg. Giant G-80)		.50	1.00
230-239,241		.30	.60
240-Adams-a		.60	1.20
242-(50 cent ish. DC-9)-Kubert-c		.50	1.00
243-248,250-301		.30	.60
249-Wood-a		.50	1.00

Operation Peril #5, © ACG

The Original Shield #1, © AP

Our Army At War #49, © DC

Our Gang Comics #39, © M.G.M.

Outcasts #1, © DC

Outer Space #25, © CC

OUR ARMY AT WAR (continued)

NOTE: ***Alcala*** *a-251.* ***Drucker*** *a-27, 67, 68, 79, 82, 83, 96, 164, 177, 203, 212, 243r, 244, 269r, 275r, 280r.* ***Evans*** *a-165-175, 200, 266, 269, 270, 274, 276, 278, 280.* ***Glanzman*** *a-218, 220, 222, 223, 225, 227, 230-32, 238, 240, 241, 244, 247, 248, 256-59, 261, 265-67, 271, 282, 283, 298.* ***Grell*** *a-287.* ***Heath*** *a-50, & most 176-271.* ***Kubert*** *a-38,59, 67, 68 & most issues from 83-165.* ***Maurer*** *a-233, 237, 239, 240, 280, 284, 288, 290, 291, 295.* ***Severin*** *a-252, 265, 267, 269r, 272.* ***Toth*** *a-235, 241, 254.* ***Wildey*** *a-283-85, 287p.*

OUR FIGHTING FORCES
Oct-Nov, 1954 - No. 181, Sept-Oct, 1978
National Periodical Publications/DC Comics

	Good	Fine	Mint
1-Grandenetti c/a	22.00	65.00	154.00
2	11.00	32.00	76.00
3-Kubert c	9.00	27.00	63.00
4,5	6.50	19.50	45.00
6-9	5.00	15.00	35.00
10-Wood-a	7.00	21.00	50.00
11-20	3.00	9.00	21.00
21-30	2.30	7.00	16.00
31-40	1.70	5.00	12.00
41-44: 41-Unknown Soldier tryout	1.30	4.00	9.00
45-Gunner & Sarge begin (ends #94)	5.00	15.00	33.00
46-50	.75	2.20	4.40
51-90: 64-Last 10 cent issue	.60	1.75	3.50
91-100: 95-Devil-Dog begins, ends 98. 99-Capt. Hunter begins, ends #106	.35	1.10	2.20
101-122: 106-Hunters Hellcats begin. 116-Mlle. Marie app. 121-Intro. Heller		.50	1.00
123-Losers (Capt. Storm, Gunner/Sarge, Johnny Cloud) begin		.40	.80
124-181: 134,146-Toth-a		.30	.60

NOTE: ***Adams*** *c-147.* ***Drucker*** *a-28, 37, 39, 42-44, 49, 53, 133r.* ***Evans*** *a-149, 164-74, 177-81.* ***Glanzman*** *a-125-28, 132, 134, 138-41, 143, 144.* ***Heath*** *a-2, 16, 18, 28, 41, 44, 49, 114, 135r-138r.* ***Kirby*** *a-151-162p; c-152-159.* ***Kubert*** *c/a in many issues.* ***Maurer*** *a-135.* ***Redondo*** *a-166.* ***Severin*** *a-123-30, 131i, 132-50.*

OUR FIGHTING MEN IN ACTION (See Men In Action)

OUR FLAG COMICS
Aug, 1941 - No. 5, April, 1942
Ace Magazines

	Good	Fine	Mint
1-Captain Victory, The Unknown Soldier & The Three Cheers begin	85.00	255.00	600.00
2-Origin The Flag	40.00	120.00	280.00
3-5: 5-Intro & 1st app. Mr. Risk	35.00	105.00	245.00

NOTE: ***Anderson*** *a-1, 4.* ***Mooney*** *a-1, 2.*

OUR GANG COMICS (With Tom & Jerry No. 39-59; becomes Tom & Jerry No. 60 on; based on film characters)
Sept-Oct, 1942 - No. 59, June, 1949
Dell Publishing Co.

	Good	Fine	Mint
1-Our Gang & Barney Bear by Kelly, Tom & Jerry, Pete Smith, Flip & Dip, The Milky Way begin	60.00	180.00	420.00
2	27.00	81.00	190.00
3-5	18.00	54.00	125.00
6-Bumbazine & Albert only app. by Kelly	31.00	92.00	220.00
7-No Kelly story	14.00	42.00	100.00
8-Benny Burro begins by Barks	31.00	92.00	215.00
9-Barks-a(2): Benny Burro & Happy Hound; no Kelly story	25.00	75.00	175.00
10-Benny Burro by Barks	20.00	60.00	140.00
11-1st Barney Bear & Benny Burro by Barks; Happy Hound by Barks	20.00	60.00	140.00
12-20	12.00	36.00	84.00
21-30	9.00	27.00	63.00
31-36-Last Barks issue	6.50	19.50	45.00
37-40	2.65	8.00	18.00
41-50	2.00	6.00	14.00
51-57	1.75	5.25	12.00
58,59-No Kelly art or Our Gang story	1.50	4.50	12.00

NOTE: ***Barks*** *art in part only.* ***Barks*** *did not write Barney Bear stories #30-34. (See March of Comics #3,26). Early issues have photo back-c.*

OUR LADY OF FATIMA
3/11/55 (15 cents) (36 pages)
Catechetical Guild Educational Society

	Good	Fine	Mint
395	3.00	9.00	21.00

OUR LOVE (Romantic Affairs #3)
Sept, 1949 - No. 2, Jan, 1950
Marvel Comics (SPC)

	Good	Fine	Mint
1	3.50	10.50	24.00
2-Photo-c	1.70	5.00	12.00

OUR LOVE STORY
Oct, 1969 - No. 38, Feb, 1976
Marvel Comics Group

	Good	Fine	Mint
1	.55	1.65	4.00
2-4,6-13: 9-J. Buscema-a	.35	1.00	2.00
5-Steranko-a	1.30	4.00	9.00
14-New story by Gary Fredrich & Tarpe' Mills	.55	1.65	4.00
15-38		.40	.80

OUR MISS BROOKS (See 4-Color No. 751)

OUR SECRET (Formerly My Secret)
No. 4, Dec, 1949 - No. 8, Aug, 1950
Superior Comics Ltd.

	Good	Fine	Mint
4-Kamen-a; spanking scene	4.00	12.00	28.00
5,6,8	2.65	8.00	18.00
7-Contains 9 pg. story intended for unpublished Ellery Queen No. 5	3.00	9.00	21.00

OUTBURSTS OF EVERETT TRUE
1921 (32 pages) (B&W)
Saalfield Publ. Co.

	Good	Fine	Mint
1907 (2-panel strips reprint)	7.00	21.00	50.00

OUTCASTS
Oct, 1987 - Present ($1.75, mini-series, color)
DC Comics

	Good	Fine	Mint
1	.35	1.00	2.00
2-4	.30	.90	1.80

OUTER LIMITS, THE (TV)
Jan-Mar, 1964 - No. 18, Oct, 1969
Dell Publishing Co.

	Good	Fine	Mint
1	2.35	7.00	16.00
2	1.30	4.00	9.00
3-10	.85	2.50	6.00
11-18: 17 reprints #1; 18-r-#2	.55	1.65	4.00

OUTER SPACE (Formerly This Mag. Is Haunted, 2nd Series)
May, 1958 - No. 25, Dec, 1959; Nov, 1968
Charlton Comics

	Good	Fine	Mint
17-Williamson/Wood style art; not by them (Sid Check?)	3.50	10.50	24.00
18-20-Ditko-a	5.00	15.00	35.00
21-25: 21-Ditko-c	2.65	8.00	18.00
V2#1(11/68)-Ditko-a, Boyette-c	1.00	3.00	7.00

OUTLAW (See Return of the. . .)

OUTLAW FIGHTERS
Aug, 1954 - No. 5, April, 1955
Atlas Comics (IPC)

	Good	Fine	Mint
1-Tuska-a	3.50	10.50	24.00
2-5: 5-Heath-a, 7pgs.	1.85	5.50	13.00

OUTLAW KID, THE (1st Series; see Wild Western)
Sept, 1954 - No. 19, Sept, 1957
Atlas Comics (CCC No. 1-11/EPI No. 12-29)

	Good	Fine	Mint
1-Origin; The Outlaw Kid & his horse Thunder begin; Black Rider app.	5.70	17.00	40.00
2-Black Rider app.	3.00	9.00	21.00
3-Woodbridge/Williamson-a	2.40	7.25	17.00
4-7,9	1.85	5.50	13.00
8-Williamson/Woodbridge-a, 4 pgs.	3.85	11.50	27.00
10-Williamson-a	3.85	11.50	27.00
11-17,19	1.50	4.50	10.00
18-Williamson-a	3.35	10.00	23.00

NOTE: ***Berg*** *a-7, 13.* ***Maneely*** *c-1, 5-8, 11, 12, 18.* ***Severin*** *c-10.* ***Shores*** *a-1.* ***Wildey*** *a-1(3), 4-8, 10-18; c-4.*

OUTLAW KID, THE (2nd Series)
Aug, 1970 - No. 30, Oct, 1975
Marvel Comics Group

	Good	Fine	Mint
1,2-Reprints; Wildey-a		.40	.80
3,9-Williamson-a(r)		.40	.80
4-8		.30	.60
10-Origin; new material begins, ends #16		.25	.50
11-30: 27-Origin r-/No. 10		.25	.50

NOTE: ***Berg*** *a-7.* ***Gil Kane*** *c-10, 11, 15, 28.* ***Roussos*** *a-10i, 27i(r).* ***Severin*** *c-1.* ***Wildey*** *a-1r, 3r, 6r, 7r, 9, 19, 21, 22, 26.* ***Williamson*** *a-28r.* ***Woodbridge*** *a(p)-9r.*

OUTLAWS
Feb-Mar, 1948 - No. 9, June-July, 1949
D. S. Publishing Co.

	Good	Fine	Mint
1	10.00	30.00	70.00
2-Ingels-a	10.00	30.00	70.00
3,5,6: 3-Not Frazetta	4.00	12.00	28.00
4-Orlando-a	5.50	16.50	38.00
7,8-Ingels-a in each	8.00	24.00	56.00
9-(Scarce)-Frazetta-a, 7 pgs.	27.00	81.00	190.00

NOTE: *No. 3 was printed in Canada with* ***Frazetta*** *art "Prairie Jinx," 7 pgs.* ***McWilliams*** *a-6.*

OUTLAWS, THE (Formerly Western Crime Cases?)
No. 10, May, 1952 - No. 13, Sept, 1953; No. 14, April, 1954
Star Publishing Co.

	Good	Fine	Mint
10-L. B. Cole-c	3.50	10.50	24.00
11-14-L. B. Cole-c. 14-Kamen, Feldstein-a	2.35	7.00	16.00

OUTLAWS OF THE WEST (Formerly Cody of the Pony Express #10)
No. 11, 7/57 - No. 81, 5/70; No. 82, 7/79 - No. 88, 4/80
Charlton Comics

	Good	Fine	Mint
11	2.65	8.00	18.00
12,13,15-17,19,20	1.30	4.00	9.00
14-(68 pgs.)	1.60	4.70	11.00
18-Ditko-a	3.50	10.50	24.00
21-30	.75	2.25	5.00
31-50	.45	1.35	3.00
51-70: 54-Kid Montana app. 64-Captain Doom begins (1st app.)		.40	.80
71-81: 73-Origin & 1st app. The Sharp Shooter, last app. No. 74. 75-Last Capt. Doom. 80,81-Ditko-a		.40	.80
82-88		.30	.60
64,79(Modern Comics-r, 1977, '78)		.15	.30

OUTLAWS OF THE WILD WEST
1952 (132 pages) (25¢)
Avon Periodicals

	Good	Fine	Mint
1-Wood back-c; Kubert-a (3 Jesse James-r)	15.00	45.00	105.00

OUT OF SANTA'S BAG (March of Comics No. 10)

OUT OF THE NIGHT (The Hooded Horseman #18 on)
Feb-Mar, 1952 - No. 17, Oct-Nov, 1954
American Comics Group (Creston/Scope)

	Good	Fine	Mint
1-Williamson/LeDoux-a, 9 pgs	17.00	51.00	120.00
2-Williamson-a, 5 pgs.	13.50	40.00	95.00
3,5-10: 9-Sci/Fic sty	4.35	13.00	30.00
4-Williamson-a, 7 pgs.	13.50	40.00	95.00
11,12,14-16	3.00	9.00	21.00
13-Nostrand-a	4.35	13.00	30.00
17-E.C. Wood swipe; lingerie panels	3.50	10.50	24.00

NOTE: ***Landau*** *a-14, 16, 17.* ***Shelly*** *a-12.*

OUT OF THE PAST A CLUE TO THE FUTURE
1946? (16 pages) (paper cover)
E. C. Comics (Public Affairs Comm.)

	Good	Fine	Mint
Based on public affairs pamphlet-"What Foreign Trade Means to You"	10.00	30.00	70.00

OUT OF THE SHADOWS
No. 5, July, 1952 - No. 14, Aug, 1954
Standard Comics/Visual Editions

	Good	Fine	Mint
5-Toth-p; Moreira, Tuska-a	7.00	21.00	50.00
6-Toth/Celardo-a	6.50	19.50	45.00
7-Jack Katz-a(2)	4.00	12.00	28.00
8,10	3.00	9.00	21.00
9-Crandall-a(2)	5.00	15.00	35.00
11-Toth-a, 2 pgs.	3.50	10.50	24.00
12-Toth/Peppe-a(2)	7.00	21.00	50.00
13-Cannabalism story	4.35	13.00	30.00
14-Toth-a	5.00	15.00	35.00

NOTE: ***Katz*** *a-6(2), 7(2), 11, 12.* ***Sekowsky*** *a-10, 13.*

OUT OF THIS WORLD
June, 1950 (One Shot)
Avon Periodicals

	Good	Fine	Mint
1-Kubert-a(2) (one reprint/Eerie #1-'47) plus Crom the Barbarian by Giunta (origin)	35.00	105.00	245.00

OUT OF THIS WORLD
Aug, 1956 - No. 16, Dec, 1959
Charlton Comics

	Good	Fine	Mint
1	5.00	15.00	35.00
2	2.30	7.00	16.00
3-6-Ditko-a(4) each	8.00	24.00	56.00
7-(68 pgs.; 15 cents)-Ditko-c/a(4)	8.50	25.50	60.00
8-(68 pgs.)-Ditko-a(2)	6.00	18.00	42.00
9-12,16-Ditko-a	5.00	15.00	35.00
13-15	1.50	4.50	10.00

NOTE: ***Ditko*** *c-3-7,11,12,16.* ***Reinman*** *a-10.*

OUT OUR WAY WITH WORRY WART (See 4-Color No. 680)

OUTPOSTS
June, 1987 - Present ($1.25, color)
Blackthorne Publishing

	Good	Fine	Mint
1-4		.60	1.20

OUTSIDERS, THE (Also see Batman & the...)
Nov, 1985 - No. 28, Feb, 1988
DC Comics

	Good	Fine	Mint
1	.30	.90	1.80
2-28: 21-Intro. Strike Force Kobra. 22-E.C. parody; Orlando-a. 25-Atomic Knight app.	.25	.75	1.50
Annual 1 (12/86; $2.50)	.40	1.25	2.50
Special 1 (7/87, $1.50)	.25	.75	1.50

OUTSTANDING AMERICAN WAR HEROES
1944 (16 pgs.) (paper cover)
The Parents' Institute

	Good	Fine	Mint
nn-Reprints from True Comics	2.30	7.00	16.00

The Outlaw Kid #1 (9/54), © MCG

Outlaws #6, © D.S. Publ.

Out of This World #1, © CC

Oxydol-Dreft #4, © Oxydol-Dreft

Panhandle Pete and Jennifer #1, © J.C. Laue Publ.

Panic #3, © WMG

OVERSEAS COMICS (Also see G.I. & Jeep Comics)
1944 (7¼x10¼"; 16 pgs. in color)
Giveaway (Distributed to U.S. armed forces) **Good Fine Mint**
23-65-Bringing Up Father, Popeye, Joe Palooka, Dick Tracy, Superman, Gasoline Alley, Buz Sawyer, Li'l Abner, Blondie, Terry & the Pirates, Out Our Way 3.00 9.00 21.00

OWL, THE
April, 1967; No. 2, April, 1968
Gold Key
1,2-Written by Jerry Siegel .85 2.50 6.00

OXYDOL-DREFT
1950 (Set of 6 pocket-size giveaways; distributed through the mail as a set) (Scarce)
Oxydol-Dreft
1-Li'l Abner, 2-Daisy Mae, 3-Shmoo 7.00 21.00 42.00
4-John Wayne; Williamson/Frazetta-c from John Wayne No. 3 9.00 28.00 56.00
5-Archie 6.00 18.00 36.00
6-Terrytoons Mighty Mouse 4.70 14.00 28.00
NOTE: *Set is worth more with original envelope.*

OZ (See MGM's Marvelous..., Marvel Treasury... & First Comics Graphic Novel)

OZARK IKE
Feb, 1948; Nov, 1948 - No. 24, Dec, 1951; No. 25, Sept, 1952
Dell Publishing Co./Standard Comics
4-Color 180(1948-Dell) 5.75 17.25 40.00
B11, B12, 13-15 4.35 13.00 30.00
16-25 3.50 10.50 24.00

OZ-WONDERLAND WAR
Jan, 1986 - No. 3, March, 1986 (mini-series)
DC Comics
1-3 .35 1.00 2.00

OZZIE & BABS (TV Teens No. 14 on)
1947 - No. 13, Fall, 1949
Fawcett Publications
1 4.00 12.00 28.00
2 2.00 6.00 14.00
3-13 1.50 4.50 10.00

OZZIE & HARRIET (See The Adventures of...)

PACIFIC COMICS GRAPHIC NOVEL
Sept, 1984
Pacific Comics
1-The Seven Samuroid; Brunner-a 1.00 3.00 6.00

PACIFIC PRESENTS
10/82 - No. 2, 4/83; No. 3, 3/84 - No. 4, 6/84
Pacific Comics
1-The Rocketeer by Stevens app. .45 1.30 2.60
2-4: 2-Nudity panels. 3-1st Vanity .25 .75 1.50
NOTE: ***Conrad*** *a-3, 4; c-3.* ***Ditko*** *a-1-3.* ***Stevens*** *c/a-1, 2.*

PADRE OF THE POOR
nd (Giveaway) (16 pgs.; paper cover)
Catechetical Guild
2.35 7.00 14.00

PAGEANT OF COMICS (See Jane Arden & Mopsy)
Sept, 1947 - No. 2, Oct, 1947
Archer St. John
1-Mopsy strip-r 4.60 14.00 32.00
2-Jane Arden strip-r 4.60 14.00 32.00

PANCHO VILLA
1950
Avon Periodicals **Good Fine Mint**
nn-Kinstler-c 12.00 36.00 84.00

PANHANDLE PETE AND JENNIFER (TV)
July, 1951 - No. 3, Nov, 1951
J. Charles Laue Publishing Co.
1 3.00 9.00 21.00
2,3 2.00 6.00 14.00

PANIC (Companion to Mad)
Feb-Mar, 1954 - No. 12, Dec-Jan, 1955-56
E. C. Comics (Tiny Tot Comics)
1-Used in Senate Investigation hearings; Elder draws entire E. C. staff 7.00 21.00 50.00
2 5.50 16.50 38.00
3-Senate Subcommittee parody; Davis draws Gaines, Feldstein & Kelly, 1 pg.; Old King Cole smokes marijuana 3.70 11.00 26.00
4-Infinity-c 3.70 11.00 26.00
5-11 3.50 10.50 24.00
12 (Low distribution; many thousands were destroyed) 4.60 14.00 32.00
NOTE: ***Davis*** *a-1-12; c-12.* ***Elder*** *a-1-12.* ***Feldstein*** *c-1-3,5.* ***Kamen*** *a-1.* ***Orlando*** *a-1-9.* ***Wolverton*** *c-4, panel-3.* ***Wood*** *a-2-9, 11, 12.*

PANIC (Magazine) (Satire)
7/58 - No. 6, 7/59; V2No.10, 12/65 - V2No.12, 1966
Panic Publications
1 2.00 6.00 14.00
2-6 1.15 3.50 8.00
V2No.10-12: Reprints earlier issues .70 2.00 4.00
NOTE: ***Davis*** *a-3(2 pgs.), 4, 5, 10; c-10.* ***Elder*** *a-5.* ***Powell*** *a-V2#10.* ***Torres*** *a-1-5.*

PARADAX (Also see Strange Days)
1986 (One Shot)
Eclipse Comics
1 .35 1.00 2.00

PARADE (See Hanna-Barbera...)

PARADE COMICS (Frisky Animals on Parade No. 2 on)
Sept, 1957
Ajax/Farrell Publ. (World Famous Publ.)
1 1.30 4.00 9.00
NOTE: *Cover title: Frisky Animals on Parade.*

PARADE OF PLEASURE
1954 (192 pgs.) (Hardback book)
Derric Verschoyle Ltd., London, England
By Geoffrey Wagner. Contains section devoted to the censorship of American comic books with illustrations in color and black and white. (Also see **Seduction of the Innocent**). Distributed in USA by Library Publishers, N. Y. 30.00 90.00 210.00
with dust jacket.... 55.00 165.00 385.00

PARAMOUNT ANIMATED COMICS (Also see Harvey Comics Hits #60,62)
Feb, 1953 - No. 22, July, 1956
Harvey Publications
1-Baby Huey, Herman & Katnip, Buzzy the Crow begin 9.00 27.00 62.00
2 6.00 18.00 42.00
3-6 5.00 15.00 35.00
7-Baby Huey becomes permanent cover feature; cover title becomes Baby Huey with #9 9.00 27.00 62.00
8-10: 9-Infinity-c 4.00 12.00 28.00
11-22 2.65 8.50 18.00

PARENT TRAP, THE (See 4-Color No. 1210)

PAROLE BREAKERS
Dec, 1951 - No. 3, July, 1952
Avon Periodicals/Realistic

	Good	Fine	Mint
1(No.2 on inside)-c-/Avon paperback 283	15.00	45.00	105.00
2-Kubert-a; c-/Avon paperback 114	12.00	36.00	84.00
3-Kinstler-c	10.00	30.00	70.00

PARTRIDGE FAMILY, THE (TV)
March, 1971 - No. 21, Dec, 1973
Charlton Comics

	Good	Fine	Mint
1	1.15	3.50	8.00
2-4,6-21	.70	2.00	4.00
5-Partridge Family Summer Special (52 pgs.); The Shadow, Lone Ranger, Charlie McCarthy, Flash Gordon, Hopalong Cassidy, Gene Autry & others app.	1.50	4.50	10.00

PASSION, THE
1955
Catechetical Guild

	Good	Fine	Mint
394	3.35	10.00	20.00

PAT BOONE (TV)(Also see Superman's Girlfriend Lois Lane #9)
Sept-Oct, 1959 - No. 5, May-Jun, 1960
National Periodical Publications

	Good	Fine	Mint
1-Photo-c	13.50	40.00	95.00
2-5: 4-Previews 'Journey To The Center Of The Earth'. 5-Photo-c	10.00	30.00	70.00

PATCHES
Mar-Apr, 1945 - No. 11, Nov, 1947
Rural Home/Patches Publ. (Orbit)

	Good	Fine	Mint
1-L. B. Cole-c	8.50	25.50	60.00
2	4.35	13.00	30.00
3-8,10,11: 5-L.B. Cole-c	3.70	11.00	26.00
9-Leav/Krigstein-a, 16 pgs.	4.35	13.00	30.00

PATHWAYS TO FANTASY
July, 1984
Pacific Comics

	Good	Fine	Mint
1-Barry Smith-c/a; J. Jones-a	.25	.75	1.50

PATORUZU (See Adventures of...)

PATSY & HEDY
Feb, 1952 - No. 110, Feb, 1967
Atlas Comics/Marvel (GPI/Male)

	Good	Fine	Mint
1	5.00	15.00	35.00
2	2.65	8.00	18.00
3-10	2.00	6.00	14.00
11-20	1.30	4.00	9.00
21-40	1.00	3.00	7.00
41-60	.55	1.65	4.00
61-110: 88-Lingerie panel	.30	.80	1.60
Annual 1('63)	1.70	5.00	12.00

PATSY & HER PALS
May, 1953 - No. 29, Aug, 1957
Atlas Comics (PPI)

	Good	Fine	Mint
1	4.35	13.00	30.00
2	2.15	6.50	15.00
3-10	1.70	5.00	12.00
11-29: 24-Everett-c	1.15	3.50	8.00

PATSY WALKER (Also see Girls' Life & Miss America Magazine)
1945 (no month) - No. 124, Dec, 1965
Marvel/Atlas Comics (BPC)

	Good	Fine	Mint
1	15.00	45.00	105.00
2	7.00	21.00	50.00
3-10: 5-Injury-to-eye-c	4.65	14.00	32.00
11,12,15,16,18	2.50	7.50	17.50
13,14,17,19-22-Kurtzman's "Hey Look"	3.75	11.25	26.00
23,24	2.15	6.50	15.00
25-Rusty by Kurtzman; painted-c	3.85	11.50	27.00
26-29,31: 28-31-52 pgs.	1.85	5.50	13.00
30-Egghead Doodle by Kurtzman, 1pg. (52 pgs.)	3.35	10.00	23.00
32-57: Last precode (3/55)	1.15	3.50	8.00
58-80	.80	2.40	5.50
81-99: 92,98-Millie x-over	.45	1.35	3.00
100	.55	1.60	4.00
101-124	.25	.75	1.50
Fashion Parade 1('66)-68 pgs.	1.50	4.50	10.00

NOTE: *Painted c-25-28. 21-Anti-Wertham editorial.* ***Al Jaffee*** *c-57, 58.*

PAT THE BRAT (Adventures of Pipsqueak #34 on)
June, 1953; Summer, 1955 - No. 33, July, 1959
Archie Publications (Radio)

	Good	Fine	Mint
nn(6/53)	5.70	17.00	40.00
1(Summer, 1955)	4.00	12.00	28.00
2-4-(5/56) (#5-14 not published)	2.00	6.00	14.00
15-(7/56)-33	1.15	3.50	8.00

PAT THE BRAT COMICS DIGEST MAGAZINE
October, 1980
Archie Publications

	Good	Fine	Mint
1		.50	1.00

PATTY POWERS (Formerly Della Vision #3)
No. 4, Oct, 1955 - No. 7, Oct, 1956
Atlas Comics

	Good	Fine	Mint
4	2.00	6.00	14.00
5-7	1.15	3.50	8.00

PAT WILTON (See Mighty Midget Comics)

PAUL
1978 (49 cents)
Spire Christian Comics (Fleming H. Revell Co.)

	Good	Fine	Mint
		.40	.80

PAULINE PERIL (See The Close Shaves of...)

PAUL REVERE'S RIDE (See 4-Color #822 & Walt Disney Showcase #34)

PAUL TERRY'S ADVENTURES OF MIGHTY MOUSE (See Adventures of...)

PAUL TERRY'S COMICS (Formerly Terry-Toons Comics; becomes Adventures of Mighty Mouse No. 126 on)
No. 85, Mar, 1951 - No. 125, May, 1955
St. John Publishing Co.

	Good	Fine	Mint
85,86-Same as Terry-Toons #85, & 86 with only a title change	3.50	10.50	24.00
87-99	2.15	6.50	15.00
100	2.65	8.00	18.00
101-104,107-125-Mighty Mouse	1.70	5.00	12.00
105,106-Giant Comics Edition, 100pgs. (9/53, ?)	5.50	16.50	38.00

PAUL TERRY'S HOW TO DRAW FUNNY CARTOONS
1940's (14 pages) (Black & White)
Terrytoons, Inc. (Giveaway)

	Good	Fine	Mint
Heckle & Jeckle, Mighty Mouse, etc.	5.50	16.50	38.00

PAUL TERRY'S MIGHTY MOUSE (See Mighty Mouse)

PAUL TERRY'S MIGHTY MOUSE ADVENTURE STORIES
1953 (384 pgs.) (50 cents) (cardboard covers)
St. John Publishing Co.

	Good	Fine	Mint
nn	30.00	90.00	210.00

Parole Breakers #1, © AVON

Patsy and Hedy #17, © MCG

Patsy Walker #4, © MCG

Peanuts #6, © C. Schulz

Penny #3, © AVON

Pep Comics #2, © AP

PAWNEE BILL
Feb, 1951 - No. 3, July, 1951
Story Comics

	Good	Fine	Mint
1-Bat Masterson, Wyatt Earp app.	4.00	12.00	28.00
2,3: 3-Origin Golden Warrior; Cameron-a	2.00	6.00	14.00

PAY-OFF (This Is the . . ., . . . Crime, . . . Detective Stories)
July-Aug, 1948 - No. 5, Mar-Apr, 1949 (52 pages)
D. S. Publishing Co.

1	4.60	14.00	32.00
2	3.00	9.00	21.00
3-5	2.15	6.50	15.00

PEACEMAKER, THE (Also see Fightin' 5)
Mar, 1967 - No. 5, Nov, 1967
Charlton Comics

1-Fightin' Five begins	.30	.90	1.80
2,3,5		.60	1.20
4-Origin The Peacemaker	.30	.80	1.60
1,2(Modern Comics reprint, 1978)		.15	.30

PEACEMAKER
Jan, 1988 - No. 4, April, 1988 ($1.25, color, mini-series)
DC Comics

1-4		.65	1.30

PEANUTS (Charlie Brown) (See Fritzi Ritz, Nancy & Sluggo, Tip Top, Tip Topper & United Comics)
No. 878, 2/58 - No. 13, 5-7/62; 5/63 - No. 4, 2/64
Dell Publishing Co./Gold Key

4-Color 878(#1)	4.35	13.00	30.00
4-Color 969,1015('59)	3.50	10.50	24.00
4(2-4/60)	2.65	8.00	18.00
5-13	1.70	5.00	12.00
1(G.Key)	2.00	6.00	14.00
2-4	1.50	4.50	10.00
1(1953-54)-Reprints United Features' Strange As It Seems, Willie, Fernand	4.00	12.00	28.00

PEBBLES & BAMM BAMM (TV)
Jan, 1972 - No. 36, Dec, 1976 (Hanna-Barbera)
Charlton Comics

1	1.30	4.00	8.00
2-10	.70	2.00	4.00
11-36	.50	1.50	3.00

PEBBLES FLINTSTONE (TV)
Sept, 1963 (Hanna-Barbera)
Gold Key

1 (10088-309)	2.00	6.00	14.00

PECKS BAD BOY
1906 - 1908 (Strip reprints) (11¼x15¾")
Thompson of Chicago (by Walt McDougal)

. . .& Cousin Cynthia(1907)-In color	15.00	45.00	105.00
. . .& His Chums(1908)-Hardcover; in full color; 16 pgs.	15.00	45.00	105.00
Advs. of . . . And His Country Cousins (1906)-In color, 18 pgs., oblong	15.00	45.00	105.00
Advs. of . . . in Pictures(1908)-In color; Stanton & Van V. Liet Co.	15.00	45.00	105.00

PEDRO (Also see Romeo Tubbs)
No. 18, June, 1950 - No. 2, Aug, 1950?
Fox Features Syndicate

18(#1)-Wood c/a(p)	10.00	30.00	70.00
2-Wood-a?	8.50	25.50	60.00

PEE-WEE PIXIES (See The Pixies)

PELLEAS AND MELISANDE (See Night Music No. 4,5)

PENALTY (See Crime Must Pay the. . .)

PENDULUM ILLUSTRATED BIOGRAPHIES
1979 (B&W)
Pendulum Press

19-355x-George Washington/Thomas Jefferson, 19-3495-Charles Lindbergh/Amelia Earhart, 19-3509-Harry Houdini/Walt Disney, 19-3517-Davy Crockett/Daniel Boone-Redondo-a, 19-3525-Elvis Presley/Beatles, 19-3533-Benjamin Franklin/Martin Luther King Jr, 19-3541-Abraham Lincoln/Franklin D. Roosevelt, 19-3568-Marie Curie/Albert Einstein-Redondo-a, 19-3576-Thomas Edison/Alexander Graham Bell-Redondo-a, 19-3584-Vince Lombardi/Pele, 19-3592-Babe Ruth/Jackie Robinson, 19-3606-Jim Thorpe/Althea Gibson

Softback	1.50
Hardback	4.50

NOTE: *Above books still available from publisher.*

PENDULUM ILLUSTRATED CLASSICS (Now Age Illustrated)
1973 - 1978 (62pp, B&W, 5-3/8x8") (Also see Marvel Classics)
Pendulum Press

64-100x(1973)-Dracula-Redondo art, 64-131x-The Invisible Man-Nino art, 64-0968-Dr Jekyll and Mr Hyde-Redondo art, 64-1005-Black Beauty, 64-1010-Call of the Wild, 64-1020-Frankenstein, 64-1025-Hucklebury Finn, 64-1030-Moby Dick-Nino-a, 64-1040-Red Badge of Courage, 64-1045-The Time Machine-Nino-a, 64-1050-Tom Sawyer, 64-1055-Twenty Thousand Leagues Under the Sea, 64-1069-Treasure Island, 64-1328(1974)-Kidnapped, 64-1336-Three Musketeers-Nino art, 64-1344-A Tale of Two Cities, 64-1352-Journey to the Center of the Earth, 64-1360-The War of the Worlds-Nino-a, 64-1379-The Greatest Advs of Sherlock Holmes-Redondo art, 64-1387-Mysterious Island, 64-1395-Hunchback of Notre Dame, 64-1409-Helen Keller-story of my life, 64-1417-Scarlet Letter, 64-1425-Gulliver's Travels, 64-2618(1977)-Around the World in Eighty Days, 64-2626-Captains Courageous, 64-2634-Connecticut Yankee, 64-2642-The Hound of the Baskervilles, 64-2650-The House of Seven Gables, 64-2669-Jane Eyre, 64-2677-The Last of the Mohicans, 64-2685-The Best of O'Henry, 64-2693-The Best of Poe-Redondo-a, 64-2707-Two Years Before the Mast, 64-2715-White Fang, 64-2723-Wuthering Heights, 64-3126(1978)-Ben Hur-Redondo art, 64-3134-A Christmas Carol, 64-3142-The Food of the Gods, 64-3150-Ivanhoe, 64-3169-The Man in the Iron Mask, 64-3177-The Prince and the Pauper, 64-3185-The Prisoner of Zenda, 64-3193-The Return of the Native, 64-3207-Robinson Crusoe, 64-3215-The Scarlet Pimpernal, 64-3223-The Sea Wolf, 64-3231-The Swiss Family Robinson, 64-3851-Billy Budd, 64-386x-Crime and Punishment, 64-3878-Don Quixote, 64-3886-Great Expectations, 64-3894-Heidi, 64-3908-The Iliad, 64-3916-Lord Jim, 64-3924-The Mutiny on Board H.M.S. Bounty, 64-3932-The Odyssey, 64-3940-Oliver Twist, 64-3959-Pride and Prejudice, 64-3967-The Turn of the Screw

Softback	1.45
Hardback	4.50

NOTE: *All of the above books can be ordered from the publisher; some were reprinted as Marvel Classic Comics No. 1-12.*

PENDULUM ILLUSTRATED ORIGINALS
1979 (in color)
Pendulum Press

	Good	Fine	Mint
94-4254-Solarman: The Beginning	.30	.80	1.60

PENNY
1947 - No. 6, 9-10/49 (Newspaper reprints)
Avon Comics

1-Photo & biography of creator	4.60	14.00	32.00
2-5	2.30	7.00	16.00
6-Perry Como photo-c	2.65	8.00	18.00

PEP COMICS (See Archie Giant Series Mag. #576)
Jan, 1940 - Present
MLJ Magazines/Archie Publications No. 56 (3/46) on

1-Intro. The Shield by Irving Novick (1st patriotic hero); origin The Comet by Jack Cole, The Queen of Diamonds & Kayo Ward; The Rocket, The Press Guardian (The Falcon #1 only), Sergeant Boyle, Fu Chang, & Bentley of Scotland Yard	150.00	450.00	1050.00
2-Origin The Rocket	65.00	195.00	455.00
3	50.00	150.00	350.00
4-Wizard cameo	43.00	130.00	300.00
5-Wizard cameo in Shield story	43.00	130.00	300.00

PEP COMICS (continued)

	Good	Fine	Mint
6-10: 6-Transvestite story in Sgt. Boyle. 8-Last Cole Comet, no Cole art in #6,7	33.00	100.00	230.00
11-Dusty, Shield's sidekick begins; last Press Guardian, Fu Chang	32.00	95.00	225.00
12-Origin Fireball; last Rocket & Queen of Diamonds	43.00	130.00	300.00
13-15	30.00	90.00	210.00
16-Origin Madam Satan; blood drainage-c	43.00	130.00	300.00
17-Origin The Hangman; death of The Comet	90.00	270.00	630.00
18-20-Last Fireball	28.00	84.00	195.00
21-Last Madam Satan	28.00	84.00	195.00
22-Intro. & 1st app. Archie, Betty, & Jughead(12/41); (also see Jack-pot)	200.00	600.00	1400.00
(Prices vary widely on this book.)			
23	55.00	165.00	385.00
24,25	48.00	145.00	335.00
26-1st app. Veronica Lodge	54.00	162.00	380.00
27-30: 30-Capt. Commando begins	38.00	115.00	265.00
31-35: 34-Bondage/Hypo-c	27.00	81.00	190.00
36-1st Archie-c	45.00	135.00	315.00
37-40	22.00	65.00	154.00
41-50: 41-Archie-c begin. 47-Last Hangman issue. 48-Black Hood begins (5/44); ends #51,59,60	16.00	48.00	110.00
51-60: 52-Suzie begins. 56-Last Capt. Commando. 59-Black Hood not in costume; spanking & lingerie panels; Archie dresses as his aunt; Suzie ends. 60-Katy Keene begins, ends #154	11.50	34.00	80.00
61-65-Last Shield. 62-1st app. Li'l Jinx	8.50	25.50	60.00
66-80: 66-G-Man Club becomes Archie Club (2/48)	6.50	19.50	45.00
81-99	4.35	13.00	30.00
100	5.00	15.00	35.00
101-130	2.00	6.00	14.00
131-149	1.00	3.00	7.00
150,152,157,159-Jaguar stories in all	.65	2.00	4.50
151,154,160-The Fly stories in all	.65	2.00	4.50
153,155,156,158-Flygirl stories in all	.65	2.00	4.50
161-167,169-200	.35	1.00	2.50
168-Jaguar app.	.55	1.65	4.00
201-260		.50	1.00
261-411: 383-Marvelous Maureen begins (Sci/fi). 393-Thunderbunny begins		.35	.70

NOTE: ***Biro*** *a-2, 4, 5.* ***Jack Cole*** *a-1-5, 8.* ***Fuje*** *a-39, 47.* ***Meskin*** *a-2, 4, 5, 11(2).* ***Schomburg*** *c-38.* ***Bob Wood*** *a-2, 4-6, 11. Katy Keene by* ***Bill Woggon*** *in many later issues. Bondage c-7, 12, 15, 18, 21, 31, 32.*

PEPE (See 4-Color No. 1194)

PERCY & FERDIE
1921 (52 pages) (B&W dailies, 10x10", cardboard-c)
Cupples & Leon Co.

	Good	Fine	Mint
By H. A. MacGill	6.00	18.00	42.00

PERFECT CRIME, THE
Oct, 1949 - No. 33, Feb?, 1953 (No. 5-12, 52 pgs.)
Cross Publications

	Good	Fine	Mint
1-Powell-a(2)	5.70	17.00	40.00
2	4.00	12.00	28.00
3-7,9,10: 7-Steve Duncan begins, ends #30	3.50	10.50	24.00
8-Heroin drug story	5.50	16.50	38.00
11-Used in **SOTI**, pg. 159; bondage-c	6.00	18.00	42.00
12-14	2.15	6.50	15.00
15-"The Most Terrible Menace"-2 pg. drug editorial	3.85	11.50	27.00
16,17,19-25,27-29,31-33	1.70	5.00	12.00
18-Drug cover, heroin drug propaganda story, plus 2 pg. drug editorial	8.00	24.00	56.00
26-Drug-c with hypodermic; drug propaganda story	8.50	25.50	60.00
30-Strangulation cover	6.00	18.00	42.00

NOTE: ***Powell*** *a-No. 1,2,4.* ***Wildey*** *a-1,5.*

PERFECT LOVE
No. 10, 8-9/51 (cover date; 5-6/51 indicia date); No. 2, 10-11/51 -No. 10, 12/53
Ziff-Davis(Approved Comics)/St. John No. 9 on

	Good	Fine	Mint
10(#1)(8-9/51)	5.00	15.00	35.00
2(10-11/51)	3.00	9.00	21.00
3,6,7: 3-Painted-c.	2.30	7.00	16.00
4,8 (Fall, '52)-Kinstler-a; last Z-D issue	2.65	8.00	18.00
5-Woodbridge-a?	2.30	7.00	16.00
9,10 (10/53, 12/53, St. John): 10-Photo-c	2.30	7.00	16.00

PERRI (See 4-Color No. 847)

PERRY MASON (See Feature Books No. 49,50 (McKay))

PERRY MASON MYSTERY MAGAZINE (TV)
June-Aug, 1964 - No. 2, Oct-Dec, 1964
Dell Publishing Co.

	Good	Fine	Mint
1,2	1.30	4.00	9.00

PERSONAL LOVE (Also see Movie Love)
Jan, 1950 - No. 33, June, 1955
Famous Funnies

	Good	Fine	Mint
1	5.70	17.00	40.00
2	3.50	10.50	24.00
3-7,10	3.00	9.00	21.00
8,9-Kinstler-a	3.50	10.50	24.00
11-Toth-a	5.50	16.50	38.00
12,16,17-One pg. Frazetta	3.50	10.50	24.00
13-15,18-23	2.30	7.00	16.00
24,25,27,28-Frazetta-a in all-8,7,8&6 pgs.	26.00	78.00	180.00
26,29-31,33: 31-Last pre-code (2/55)	1.70	5.00	12.00
32-Classic Frazetta-a, 8 pgs.	45.00	135.00	315.00

NOTE: *All have photo-c.* ***Everett*** *a-5, 9, 10, 24.*

PERSONAL LOVE (Going Steady V3#3 on)
V1No.1, Sept, 1957 - V3No.2, Nov-Dec, 1959
Prize Publ. (Headline)

	Good	Fine	Mint
V1#1	2.00	6.00	14.00
2	1.15	3.50	8.00
3-6(7-8/58)	.85	2.50	6.00
V2#1(9-10/58)-V2#6(7-8/59)	.75	2.25	5.00
V3#1-Wood/Orlando-a	1.50	4.50	10.00
2	.55	1.65	4.00

NOTE: *Photo covers on most issues.*

PETER COTTONTAIL
Jan, 1954; Feb, 1954 - No. 2, Mar, 1954
Key Publications

	Good	Fine	Mint
1(1/54)-Not 3-D	3.50	10.50	24.00
1(2/54)-(3-D); written by Bruce Hamilton	13.50	40.00	95.00
2-Reprints 3-D #1 but not in 3-D	2.30	7.00	16.00

PETER GUNN (See 4-Color No. 1087)

PETER PAN (See New Adventures of. . ., 4-Color #442,446,926, Movie Classics & Comics & Walt Disney Showcase #36)

PETER PANDA
Aug-Sept, 1953 - No. 31, Aug-Sept, 1958
National Periodical Publications

	Good	Fine	Mint
1-Grossman-c/a in all	11.50	34.00	80.00
2	5.70	17.00	40.00
3-10	4.60	14.00	32.00

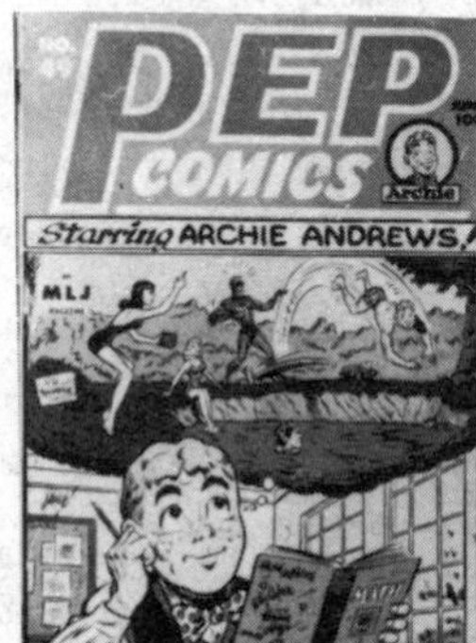

Pep Comics #49, © AP

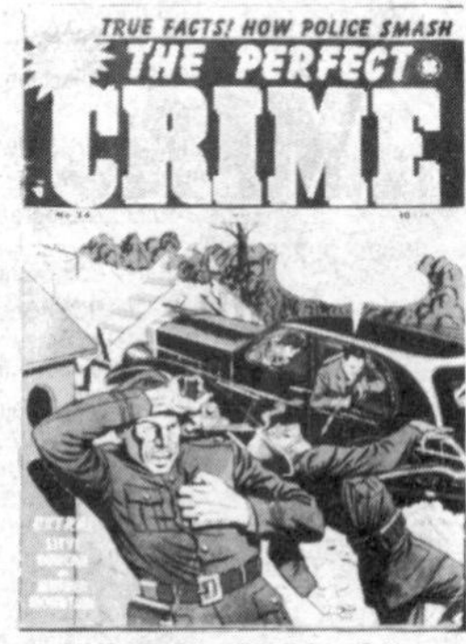

The Perfect Crime #24, © Cross Publ.

Perfect Love #5, © STJ

Peter Paul's 4 In 1 Jumbo Comic...#1, © Capitol Stories

Peter Rabbit #8, © AVON

Peter Wheat #1, © Baker's Assoc.

PETER PANDA (continued) — Good / Fine / Mint
11-31 2.15 6.50 15.00

PETER PAN TREASURE CHEST (See Dell Giants)

PETER PARKER (See The Spectacular Spider-Man)

PETER PAT (See Single Series No. 8)

PETER PAUL'S 4 IN 1 JUMBO COMIC BOOK
No date (1953)
Capitol Stories
1-Contains 4 comics bound; Space Adventures, Space Western, Crime & Justice, Racket Squad in Action 15.00 45.00 105.00

PETER PENNY AND HIS MAGIC DOLLAR
1947 (16 pgs.; paper cover; regular size)
American Bankers Association, N. Y. (Giveaway)
nn-(Scarce)-Used in **SOTI**, pg. 310, 311 7.00 21.00 50.00
Another version (7¼x11")-redrawn, 16 pgs., paper-c 5.00 15.00 35.00

PETER PIG
No. 5, May, 1953 - No. 6, Aug, 1953
Standard Comics
5,6 1.30 4.00 9.00

PETER PORKCHOPS (See Leading Comics #23)
Nov-Dec, 1949 - No. 61, Sept-Nov, 1959; No. 62, Oct-Dec, 1960
National Periodical Publications
1 13.00 40.00 90.00
2 6.50 19.50 45.00
3-10 4.60 14.00 32.00
11-30 3.00 9.00 21.00
31-62 1.70 5.00 12.00
NOTE: *Otto Feur a-all. **Sheldon Mayer** a-30-38, 40-44, 46-52, 61.*

PETER PORKER, THE SPECTACULAR SPIDER-HAM
May, 1985 - No. 15, Sept, 1987
Star Comics (Marvel)
1 .25 .75 1.50
2-6 .50 1.00
7-15: 13-Halloween ish. .35 .70

PETER POTAMUS (TV)
January, 1965 (Hanna-Barbera)
Gold Key
1 2.00 6.00 14.00

PETER RABBIT (See Large Feature Comic No. 1)

PETER RABBIT
1922 - 1923 (9¼x6¼") (paper cover)
John H. Eggers Co. The House of Little Books Publishers
B1-B4-(Rare)-(Set of 4 books which came in a cardboard box)-Each book reprints ½ of a Sunday page per page and contains 8 B&W and 2 color pages; by Harrison Cady
each.... 18.00 54.00 125.00

PETER RABBIT (Adventures of...)
1947 - No. 34, Aug-Sept, 1956
Avon Periodicals
1(1947)-Reprints 1943-44 Sunday strips; contains a biography & drawing of Cady 23.00 70.00 160.00
2 18.00 54.00 125.00
3-6(1949)-Last Cady issue 16.50 50.00 115.00
7-10(1950-8/51) 3.00 9.00 21.00
11(11/51)-34('56)-Avon's character 1.85 5.50 13.00
...Easter Parade (132 pgs.; 1952) 9.50 28.50 65.00
...Jumbo Book(1954-Giant Size, 25 cents)-6 pgs.; Jesse James by Kinstler 14.00 42.00 100.00

PETER RABBIT
1958
Fago Magazine Co. — Good / Fine / Mint
1 2.35 7.00 16.00

PETER, THE LITTLE PEST (No. 4 titled Petey)
Nov, 1969 - No. 4, May, 1970
Marvel Comics Group
1 .50 1.50 3.00
2-4-Reprints Dexter the Demon & Melvin the Monster .35 1.00 2.00

PETER WHEAT (The Adventures of...)
1948 - 1956? (16 pgs. in color) (paper covers)
Bakers Associates Giveaway
nn(No.1)-States on last page, end of 1st Adventure of...; Kelly-a 22.00 65.00 140.00
nn(4 issues)-Kelly-a 17.00 50.00 100.00
6-10-All Kelly-a 12.00 36.00 72.00
11-20-All Kelly-a 10.00 30.00 60.00
21-35-All Kelly-a 8.00 24.00 48.00
36-66 5.00 15.00 30.00
...Artist's Workbook ('54, digest size) 4.50 13.50 27.00
...Four-In-One Fun Pack (Vol. 2, '54), oblong, comics w/puzzles 5.00 15.00 30.00
...Fun Book ('52, 32pgs., paper-c, B&W & color, 8¼"x10¾"), contains cut-outs, puzzles, games, magic & pages to color 7.00 21.00 50.00
NOTE: ***Al Hubbard** art No. 36 on; written by Del Connell.*

PETER WHEAT NEWS
1948 - No. 30, 1950 (4 pgs. in color)
Bakers Associates
Vol. 1-All have 2 pgs. Peter Wheat by Kelly 20.00 60.00 140.00
2-10 13.00 40.00 80.00
11-20 6.75 20.00 40.00
21-30 4.00 12.00 24.00
NOTE: *Early issues have no date & Kelly art.*

PETE'S DRAGON (See Walt Disney Showcase #43)

PETE THE PANIC
November, 1955? (mid 1950s)
Stanmor Publications
nn 1.15 3.50 8.0(

PETEY (See Peter, the Little Pest)

PETTICOAT JUNCTION (TV)
Oct-Dec, 1964 - No. 5, Oct-Dec, 1965 (Photo-c)
Dell Publishing Co.
1 3.50 10.50 24.C
2-5 1.70 5.00 12.C

PETUNIA (See 4-Color No. 463)

PHANTASMO (See Large Feat. Comic No. 18)

PHANTOM, THE
1939 - 1949
David McKay Publishing Co.
Feature Books 20 37.00 110.00 260
Feature Books 22 32.00 95.00 225
Feature Books 39 22.00 65.00 154
Feature Books 53,56,57 17.00 51.00 12C

PHANTOM, THE (See Ace Comics, Eat Right to Work..., Future Comics, Har Comics Hits No.51,56 & Harvey Hits No. 1, 6, 12, 15, 26, 36, 44, 48)

PHANTOM, THE (nn 29-Published overseas only) (Also see Comi(Reading Library)
Nov, 1962 - No. 17, July, 1966; No. 18, Sept, 1966 - No. 28, Dec,

THE PHANTOM (continued)
1967; No. 30, Feb, 1969 - No. 74, Jan, 1977
Gold Key (No.1-17)/King (No.18-28)/Charlton (No.30 on)

	Good	Fine	Mint
1-Manning-a	3.50	10.50	24.00
2-King, Queen & Jack begins, ends #11	1.50	4.50	10.00
3-10	1.00	3.00	7.00
11-17: 12-Track Hunter begins	.70	2.00	5.00
18-Flash Gordon begins; Wood-a	1.00	3.00	7.00
19,20-Flash Gordon ends	.70	2.00	5.00
21-24,26,27: 21-Mandrake begins. 20,24-Girl Phantom app. 26-Brick Bradford app.	.55	1.65	4.00
25-Jeff Jones-a; 1 pg. Williamson ad	.85	2.50	6.00
28(nn)-Brick Bradford app.	.70	2.00	5.00
30-40: 36,39-Ditko-a	.55	1.65	4.00
41-66: 46-Intro. The Piranha. 62-Bolle-c	.50	1.50	3.00
67-71,73-Newton c/a; 67-Origin retold	.50	1.50	3.00
72	.35	1.00	2.00
74-Newton Flag-c; Newton-a	.50	1.50	3.00

NOTE: ***Aparo** a-36-38; c-35-38, 60, 61. Painted-c No. 1-17.*

PHANTOM BLOT, THE (#1 titled New Adventures of. . .)
Oct, 1964 - No. 7, Nov, 1966 (Disney)
Gold Key

	Good	Fine	Mint
1	2.00	6.00	14.00
2-1st Super Goof	1.50	4.50	10.00
3-7	1.15	3.50	8.00

PHANTOM EAGLE (See Mighty Midget Comics & Marvel Super Heroes No. 16)

PHANTOM LADY (1st Series) (My Love Secret #24 on) (Also see All Top, Daring Adventures, Jungle Thrills, and Wonder Boy)
Aug, 1947 - No. 23 April, 1949
Fox Features Syndicate

	Good	Fine	Mint
13(#1)-Phantom Lady by Matt Baker begins; The Blue Beetle app.	110.00	330.00	770.00
14(#2)	68.00	205.00	475.00
15-P.L. injected with experimental drug	58.00	175.00	405.00
16-Negligee-c, panels	58.00	175.00	405.00
17-Classic bondage cover; used in **SOTI**, illo-"Sexual stimulation by combining 'headlights' with the sadist's dream of tying up a woman"	145.00	435.00	1015.00
18,19	52.00	155.00	365.00
20-23: 23-Bondage-c	44.00	132.00	310.00

NOTE: ***Matt Baker** a-in all; c-13, 15-21. **Kamen** a-22, 23.*

PHANTOM LADY (2nd Series) (See Terrific Comics) (Formerly Linda)
Dec-Jan, 1955 - No. 4, June, 1955
Ajax/Farrell Publ.

	Good	Fine	Mint
V1#5(#1)-by Matt Baker	25.00	75.00	175.00
V1#2-Last pre-code	20.00	60.00	140.00
3,4-Red Rocket	17.00	51.00	120.00

PHANTOM PLANET, THE (See 4-Color No. 1234)

PHANTOM STRANGER, THE (1st Series)
Aug-Sept, 1952 - No. 6, June-July, 1953
National Periodical Publications

	Good	Fine	Mint
1 (Scarce)	47.00	140.00	330.00
2 (Scarce)	35.00	105.00	245.00
3-6 (Scarce)	30.00	90.00	210.00

PHANTOM STRANGER, THE (2nd Series) (See Showcase)
May-June, 1969 - No. 41, Feb-Mar, 1976
National Periodical Publications

	Good	Fine	Mint
1	.85	2.50	5.00
2,3,5-10	.35	1.00	2.00
4-Adams-a	.85	2.50	5.00
11-22: 22-Dark Circle begins		.50	1.00
23-Spawn of Frankenstein begins by Kaluta; series ends #30	.25	.75	1.50
24,25		.50	1.00
26-31: 31-The Black Orchid begins		.30	.60
32,35,36-Black Orchid by Redondo		.30	.60
33,34,37,38-41: 33, 39-41-Deadman app.		.30	.60

NOTE: ***Adams** a-4; c-3-19. **Aparo** a-7-26; c-20-24, 33-41. **B. Bailey** a-27-30. **Dezuniga** a-14-16, 19-22, 31, 34. **Grell** a-33. **Kaluta** a-23-25; c-26. **Meskin** r-15, 16, 18. **Sparling** a-20. **Starr** a-17r. **Toth** a-15r. Black Orchid by **Carrilo**-38-41. Dr. 13 solo in-13, 18, 20. Frankenstein by **Kaluta**-23-25; by **Baily**-27-30. No Black Orchid-33, 34, 37.*

PHANTOM STRANGER
Oct, 1987 - No. 4, Jan, 1988 (mini-series, 75 cents, color)
DC Comics

	Good	Fine	Mint
1	.25	.75	1.50
2-4		.50	1.00

PHANTOM WITCH DOCTOR
1952 (Also see Eerie No. 8)
Avon Periodicals

	Good	Fine	Mint
1-Kinstler-c, 7 pgs.	20.00	60.00	140.00

PHANTOM ZONE, THE
January, 1982 - No. 4, April, 1982
DC Comics

	Good	Fine	Mint
1-Superman app. in all		.40	.80
2-4: Batman, Gr. Lantern app.		.30	.60

NOTE: ***Colan** a-1-4p; c-1-4p. **Giordano** c-1-4i.*

PHIL RIZZUTO (Baseball Hero)
1951 (New York Yankees)
Fawcett Publications

	Good	Fine	Mint
nn	18.00	54.00	125.00

PHOENIX
Jan, 1975 - No. 4, Oct, 1975
Atlas/Seaboard Publ.

	Good	Fine	Mint
1-Origin		.30	.60
2,3: 3-Origin & only app. The Dark Avenger		.25	.50
4-New origin/costume The Protector (formerly Phoenix)		.25	.50

NOTE: ***Infantino** appears in No. 1,2. **Austin** a-3i. **Thorne** c-3.*

PHOENIX-THE UNTOLD STORY
April, 1984 (One shot; $2.00)
Marvel Comics Group

	Good	Fine	Mint
1-Byrne/Austin-r/X-Men 137 with original unpubbed ending	.70	2.00	4.00

PICNIC PARTY (See Dell Giants)

PICTORIAL CONFESSIONS (Pictorial Romances #4 on)
Sept, 1949 - No. 3, Dec, 1949
St. John Publishing Co.

	Good	Fine	Mint
1-Baker-c/a(3)	12.00	36.00	84.00
2-Baker-a; photo-c	6.00	18.00	42.00
3-Kubert, Baker-a; part Kubert-c	8.50	25.50	60.00

PICTORIAL LOVE STORIES (Formerly Tim McCoy)
No. 22, Oct, 1949 - No. 26, July, 1950
Charlton Comics

	Good	Fine	Mint
22-26-"Me-Dan Cupid" in all	5.00	15.00	35.00

PICTORIAL LOVE STORIES
October, 1952
St. John Publishing Co.

	Good	Fine	Mint
1-Baker c/a	10.00	30.00	70.00

PICTORIAL ROMANCES (Formerly Pictorial Confessions)
No. 4, Jan, 1950; No. 5, Jan, 1951 - No. 24, Mar, 1954
St. John Publishing Co.

The Phantom #22, © KING

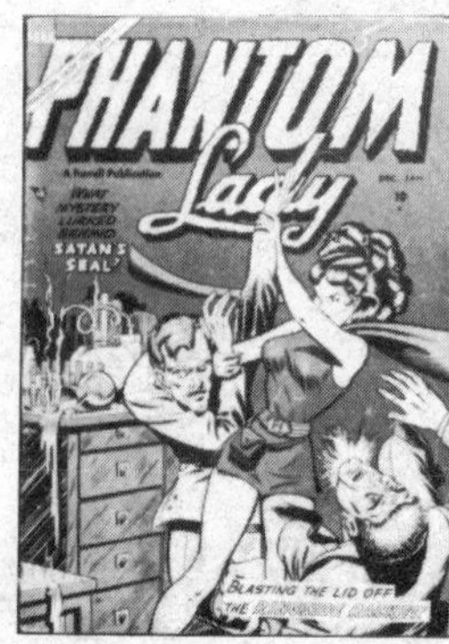

Phantom Lady #5, © AJAX

The Phantom Stranger #1 (3rd series), © DC

Pictorial Romances #7, © STJ

Picture Parade #2, © GIL

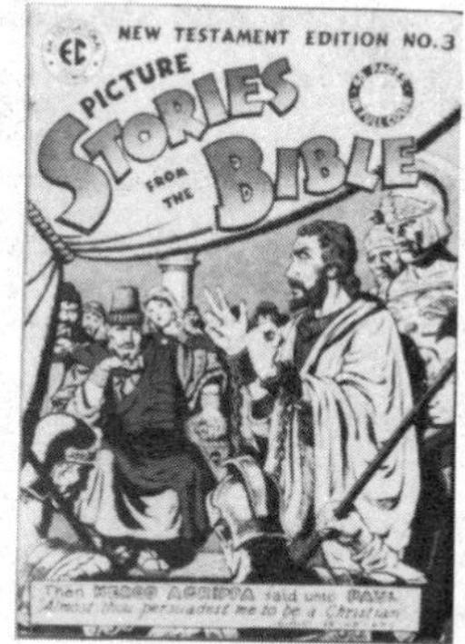

Picture Stories From the Bible (New Test. #3), © WMG

PICTORIAL ROMANCES (continued) — Good / Fine / Mint

4-All Baker 9.50 28.50 65.00
5,10-All Matt Baker issues 7.00 21.00 50.00
6-9,12,13,15,16-Baker-c, 2-3 stories 5.00 15.00 35.00
11-Baker c/a(3); Kubert-a 6.00 18.00 42.00
14,21-24-Baker-c/a each 3.70 11.00 26.00
17-20(7/53)-100 pgs. each; Baker-c/a 10.00 30.00 70.00

NOTE: ***Matt Baker*** *art in most issues.* ***Estrada*** *a-19(2).*

PICTURE NEWS
Jan, 1946 - No. 10, Jan-Feb, 1947
Lafayette Street Corp.

1-Milt Gross begins, ends No. 6; 4 pg. Kirby-a; A-Bomb-c/story 9.50 28.00 65.00
2-Atomic explosion panels; Frank Sinatra, Perry Como stories 4.35 13.00 30.00
3-Atomic explosion panels; Frank Sinatra, June Allyson stories 3.50 10.50 24.00
4-Atomic explosion panels; "Caesar and Cleopatra" movie adaptation; Jackie Robinson story 4.00 12.00 28.00
5-7: 5-Hank Greenberg story. 6-Joe Louis c/story 2.65 8.00 18.00
8-Monte Hale story(9-10/46; 1st?) 4.00 12.00 28.00
9-A-Bomb story; "Crooked Mile" movie adaptation; Joe DiMaggio story 4.00 12.00 28.00
10-A-Bomb story; Krigstein, Gross-a 4.35 13.00 30.00

PICTURE PARADE (Picture Progress #5 on)
Sept, 1953 - V1/4, Dec, 1953 (28 pages)
Gilberton Company (Also see A Christmas Adventure)

V1#1-Andy's Atomic Adventures-A-bomb blast-c; (Teachers version distr. to schools exists 5.00 15.00 35.00
2-Around the World with the United Nations 4.00 12.00 28.00
3-Adventures of the Lost One(The Amer. Indian), 4-A Christmas Adventure (r-under same title in '69) 4.00 12.00 28.00

PICTURE PROGRESS (Formerly Picture Parade)
V1No.5, Jan, 1954 - V3No.2, Oct, 1955 (28-36 pgs.)
Gilberton Corp.

V1#5-News in Review 1953, 6-The Birth of America, 7-The Four Seasons, 8-Paul Revere's Ride, 9-The Hawaiian Islands(5/54),
V2#1-The Story of Flight(9/54), 2-Vote for Crazy River(The Meaning of Elections), 3-Louis Pasteur, 4-The Star Spangled Banner, 5-News in Review 1954, 6-Alaska: The Great Land, 7-Life in the Circus, 8-The Time of the Cave Man, 9-Summer Fun(5/55) each.... 2.00 6.00 14.00
V3#1-The Man Who Discovered America, 2-The Lewis & Clark Expedition each.... 2.00 6.00 14.00

PICTURE SCOPE JUNGLE ADVENTURES (See Jungle Thrills)

PICTURE STORIES FROM AMERICAN HISTORY
1945 - 1947 (68 - 52 pages)
National/All-American/E. C. Comics

1 6.00 18.00 42.00
2-4 4.00 12.00 28.00

PICTURE STORIES FROM SCIENCE
Spring, 1947 - No. 2, Fall, 1947
E.C. Comics

1,2 7.00 21.00 50.00

PICTURE STORIES FROM THE BIBLE
Fall, 1942-3 & 1944-46
National/All-American/E.C. Comics

1-4('42-Fall,'43)-Old Testament (DC) 7.00 21.00 50.00
Complete Old Testament Edition, 232pgs.(1943-DC); contains #1-4 10.00 30.00 70.00

Good / Fine / Mint

Complete Old Testament Edition (1945-publ. by Bible Pictures Ltd.)-232 pgs., hardbound, in color with dust jacket 10.00 30.00 70.00

NOTE: *Both Old and New Testaments published in England by Bible Pictures Ltd. in hardback, 1943, in color, 376 pages, and were also published by Scarf Press in 1979 (Old Test., $9.95) and in 1980 (New Test., $7.95)*

1-3(New Test.; 1944-46, DC)-52pgs. ea. 6.00 18.00 42.00
The Complete Life of Christ Edition (1945)-96pgs.; contains #1&2 of the New Testament Edition 8.00 24.00 56.00
1,2(Old Testament-r in comic book form)(E.C., 1946; 52pgs.) 6.00 18.00 42.00
1-3(New Testament-r in comic book form)(E.C., 1946; 52pgs.) 6.00 18.00 42.00
Complete New Testament Edition (1946-E.C.)-144 pgs.; contains #1-3 8.50 25.50 60.00

PICTURE STORIES FROM WORLD HISTORY
Spring, 1947 - No. 2, Summer, 1947 (52,48 pgs.)
E.C. Comics

1,2 6.00 18.00 42.00

PINHEAD & FOODINI (TV)(Also see Foodini)
July, 1951 - No. 4, Jan, 1952
Fawcett Publications

1-Photo-c 6.00 18.00 42.00
2-Photo-c 4.35 13.00 30.00
3,4: 3-Photo-c 2.65 8.00 18.00

PINK LAFFIN
1922 (9x12")(strip-r)
Whitman Publishing Co.

...the Lighter Side of Life,...He Tells 'Em,...and His Family, ...Knockouts; Ray Gleason-a (All rare) each... 7.00 21.00 50.00

PINK PANTHER, THE (TV)
April, 1971 - No. 87, 1984
Gold Key

1-The Inspector begins 1.20 3.50 8.00
2-10 .70 2.00 4.00
11-30: Warren Tufts-a #16-on .40 1.20 2.50
31-60 .25 .75 1.50
61-87 .50 1.00
Kite Fun Book(1972)-16pgs. .70 2.00 4.00
Mini-comic No. 1(1976)(3¼x6½") .50 1.00

NOTE: *Pink Panther began as a movie cartoon. (See Golden Comics Digest #38, 45 and March of Comics #376, 384, 390, 409, 418, 429, 441, 449, 461, 473, 486; No. 37, 72, 80-85 contain reprints.*

PINKY LEE (See Adventures of...)

PINKY THE EGGHEAD
1963 (Reprints from Noodnik)
I.W./Super Comics

I.W. Reprint #1,2(nd) .60 1.20
Super Reprint #14 .60 1.20

PINOCCHIO (See 4-Color #92,252,545,1203, Movie Comics under Wonderful Advs. of..., Mickey Mouse Mag. V5#3, Wonderful Advs. of...,World's Greatest Stories #2 & New Advs. of...)

PINOCCHIO
1940 (10 pages; linen-like paper)
Montgomery Ward Co. (Giveaway)

12.00 36.00 84.00

PINOCCHIO AND THE EMPEROR OF THE NIGHT
1988 (52 pgs., $1.25)
Marvel Comics

1-Adapts film .60 1.25

PINOCCHIO LEARNS ABOUT KITES (Also see Donald Duck & Brer Rabbit (Disney)
1954 (8 pages) (Premium)
Pacific Gas & Electric Co./Florida Power & Light

	Good	Fine	Mint
	20.00	60.00	130.00

PIN-UP PETE (Also see Monty Hall . . . & Great Lover Romances)
1952
Toby Press

	Good	Fine	Mint
1-Jack Sparling pin-ups	8.50	25.50	60.00

PIONEER MARSHAL (See Fawcett Movie Comics)

PIONEER PICTURE STORIES
Dec, 1941 - No. 9, Dec, 1943
Street & Smith Publications

	Good	Fine	Mint
1	8.50	25.50	60.00
2	5.00	15.00	35.00
3-9	4.00	12.00	28.00

PIONEER WEST ROMANCES (Firehair #1,2,7-11)
No. 3, Summer, 1949 - No. 6, Winter, 1949-50
Fiction House Magazines

	Good	Fine	Mint
2-Firehair continues	7.00	21.00	50.00
4-6	5.70	17.00	40.00

PIPSQUEAK (See The Adventures of . . .)

PIRACY
Oct-Nov, 1954 - No. 7, Oct-Nov, 1955
E. C. Comics

	Good	Fine	Mint
1-Williamson/Torres-a	12.00	36.00	85.00
2-Williamson/Torres-a	9.00	27.00	62.00
3-7	7.00	21.00	50.00

NOTE: ***Crandall** a-in all; c-2-4. **Davis** a-1, 2, 6. **Evans** a-3-7; c-7. **Ingels** a-3-7. **Krigstein** a-3-5, 7; c-5, 6. **Wood** a-1, 2; c-1.*

PIRANA (See Thrill-O-Rama No. 2,3)

PIRATE CORPS, THE
1987 - Present ($1.95, color #3 on)
Eternity Comics

	Good	Fine	Mint
1-4	.35	1.00	1.95

PIRATE OF THE GULF, THE (See Superior Stories No. 2)

PIRATES COMICS
Feb-Mar, 1950 - No. 4, Aug-Sept, 1950 (All 52 pgs.)
Hillman Periodicals

	Good	Fine	Mint
1	5.70	17.00	40.00
2-Berg-a	3.00	9.00	21.00
3,4-Berg-a	2.65	8.00	18.00

P.I.'S: MICHAEL MAUSER AND MS. TREE, THE
Jan, 1985 - No. 3, May, 1985 (mini-series)
First Comics

	Good	Fine	Mint
1-3: Staton c/a(p)		.65	1.30

PITT, THE
1988 (one shot, $3.25)
Marvel Comics

	Good	Fine	Mint
1-Ties into Starbrand, D.P. 7	.55	1.60	3.25

PIUS XII MAN OF PEACE
No date (12 pgs.; 5½x8½") (B&W)
Catechetical Guild Giveaway

	Good	Fine	Mint
	4.00	12.00	28.00

PIXIE & DIXIE & MR. JINKS (TV)(See Whitman Comic Books)
July-Sept, 1960 - Feb, 1963 (Hanna-Barbera)
Dell Publishing Co./Gold Key

	Good	Fine	Mint
4-Color 1112	2.00	6.00	14.00
4-Color 1196,1264	1.70	5.00	12.00
01-631-207 (Dell)	1.50	4.50	10.00
1(2/63-G.K.)	1.50	4.50	10.00

PIXIE PUZZLE ROCKET TO ADVENTURELAND
November, 1952
Avon Periodicals

	Good	Fine	Mint
1	5.00	15.00	35.00

PIXIES, THE (Advs. of . . .) (Mighty Atom #6 on)
Winter, 1946 - No. 4, Fall?, 1947; No. 5, 1948
Magazine Enterprises

	Good	Fine	Mint
1-Mighty Atom	3.00	9.00	21.00
2-5-Mighty Atom	1.60	4.70	11.00
I.W. Reprint #1(1958), 8-(Pee-Wee Pixies), 10-I.W. on cover, Super on inside	.40	1.20	2.40

PLANET COMICS
Jan, 1940 - No. 73, Winter, 1953
Fiction House Magazines

	Good	Fine	Mint
1-Origin Auro, Lord of Jupiter; Flint Baker & The Red Comet begin; Eisner/Fine-c	300.00	900.00	2100.00
2-(Scarce)	150.00	450.00	1050.00
3-Eisner-c	122.00	365.00	854.00
4-Gale Allen and the Girl Squadron begins	105.00	315.00	735.00
5,6-(Scarce)	95.00	285.00	665.00
7-11	80.00	240.00	560.00
12-The Star Pirate begins	80.00	240.00	560.00
13-15: 13-Reff Ryan begins. 15-Mars, God of War begins	60.00	180.00	420.00
16-20,22	55.00	165.00	385.00
21-The Lost World & Hunt Bowman begin	60.00	180.00	420.00
23-26: 26-The Space Rangers begin	55.00	165.00	385.00
27-30	45.00	135.00	315.00
31-35: 33-Origin Star Pirates Wonder Boots, reprinted in #52. 35-Mysta of the Moon begins	38.00	115.00	265.00
36-45: 41-New origin of "Auro, Lord of Jupiter." 42-Last Gale Allen. 43-Futura begins	33.00	100.00	230.00
46-52,54-60	24.00	72.00	170.00
53-Used in **SOTI**, pg. 32; bondage-c	26.00	78.00	180.00
61-64	17.00	51.00	120.00
65-68,70: 65-70-All partial-r of earlier issues	16.00	48.00	110.00
69-Used in **POP**, pgs. 101,102	17.00	51.00	120.00
71-73-No series stories	13.50	40.00	95.00
I.W. Reprint #1(nd)-r-/#70; c-from Attack on Planet Mars	2.65	8.00	18.00
I.W. Reprint #8 (r-/#72), 9-r-/#73	2.65	8.00	18.00

NOTE: *#33-38, 40-51-Star Pirate by **Anderson**. **Evans** a-50-64 (Lost World). **Fine** c-2, 5. **Ingels** a-24-31, 56-61 (Auro, Lord of Jupiter). Mysta of the Moon by **Maurice Whitman**-51, 52; by **Matt Baker**-53-59. Star Pirate by **Tuska**-30; by **M. Whitman**-54-56. **Starr** a-59.*

PLANET OF THE APES (Magazine) (Also see Advs. on the . . .)
Aug, 1974 - No. 29, Feb, 1977 (B&W) (Based on movies)
Marvel Comics Group

	Good	Fine	Mint
1-Ploog-a	.40	1.25	2.50
2-Ploog-a	.35	1.00	2.00
3-10	.25	.70	1.40
11-20		.50	1.00
21-29		.40	.80

NOTE: ***Alcala** a-7-11, 17-22, 24. **Ploog** a-1-8, 11, 13, 14, 19. **Sutton** a-11, 12, 15, 17, 19, 20, 23, 24, 29.*

PLANET OF VAMPIRES
Feb, 1975 - No. 3, July, 1975
Seaboard Publications (Atlas)

	Good	Fine	Mint
1-Adams-c(i); 1st Broderick c/a(p)		.40	.80
2-Adams-c, 3-Heath-c/a		.30	.60

Pixie & Dixie & Mr. Jinks #1, © Hanna-Barbera

The Pixies #4, © ME

Planet Comics #26, © FH

Plastic Man #46, © QUA

Pogo Possum #8, © Walt Kelly

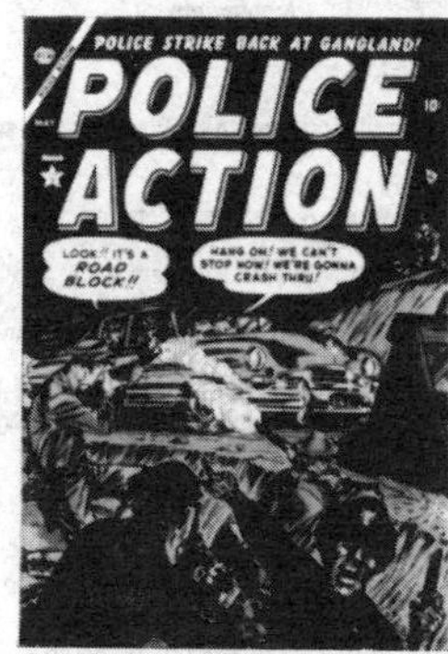

Police Action #3, © MCG

PLANET TERRY
April, 1985 - No. 12, 1986 (children's comic)
Star Comics (Marvel)

	Good	Fine	Mint
1-12		.35	.70

PLASTIC MAN (Also see Police & Smash #17)
Sum, 1943 - No. 64, Nov, 1956
Vital Publ. No. 1,2/Quality Comics No. 3 on

	Good	Fine	Mint
nn(#1)-'In The Game of Death;' Jack Cole-a begins; ends-#64?	105.00	335.00	735.00
2(nn, 2/44)-'The Gay Nineties Nightmare'	68.00	205.00	475.00
3 (Spr, '46)	44.00	132.00	310.00
4 (Sum, '46)	38.00	115.00	265.00
5 (Aut, '46)	33.00	100.00	230.00
6-10: 8-Extreme violence	23.00	70.00	160.00
11-20	21.00	62.00	145.00
21-30: 26-Last non-r issue?	16.00	48.00	110.00
31-39	12.00	36.00	84.00
40-Used in **POP**, pg. 91	13.00	40.00	90.00
41-64: 53-Last precode issue	9.50	28.50	65.00
Super Reprint 11('63, r-/#16), 16 (r-#21, Cole-a), 18('64-Spirit app. by Eisner/Police 95)	2.00	6.00	14.00

NOTE: ***Cole** r-44,49,56,58,59 at least.*

PLASTIC MAN (See Brave & the Bold and DC Special #15)
11-12/66 - No. 10, 5-6/68; No. 11, 2-3/76 - No. 20, 10-11/77
National Periodical Publications/DC Comics

	Good	Fine	Mint
1	.70	2.00	4.00
2-5: 4-Infantino-c	.35	1.00	2.00
6-10('68)		.60	1.20
11('76)-20: 17-Origin retold		.40	.80

NOTE: ***Gil Kane** c/a-1. **Mortimer** a-4. **Sparling** a-10.*

PLAYFUL LITTLE AUDREY (Also see Little Audrey #25)
6/57 - No. 110, 11/73; No. 111, 8/74 - No. 121, 4/76
Harvey Publications

	Good	Fine	Mint
1	11.50	34.50	80.00
2	5.70	17.00	40.00
3-5	5.00	15.00	35.00
6-10	3.35	10.00	23.00
11-20	1.70	5.00	12.00
21-40	1.35	4.00	9.00
41-60	.85	2.50	5.00
61-80	.50	1.50	3.00
81-99	.40	1.25	2.50
100	.70	2.00	4.00
101-121	.35	1.00	2.00

PLOP!
Sept-Oct, 1973 - No. 24, Nov-Dec, 1976
National Periodical Publications

	Good	Fine	Mint
1,5-Wrightson-a		.40	.80
2-4,6-10		.30	.60
11-24: 21-24-Giant size, 52 pgs.		.25	.50

NOTE: ***Alcala** a-1-3. **Anderson** a-5. **Aragones** a-1-22, 24. **Ditko** a-16p. **Evans** a-1. **Orlando** a-21, 22; c-21. **Sekowsky** a-5, 6p. **Toth** a-11. **Wolverton** a-4, 22, 23(1 pg.); c-1-12, 14, 17, 18. **Wood** a-14, 16i, 18-24; c-13, 15, 16, 19.*

PLUTO (See Cheerios Premiums, Four Color #537, Mickey Mouse Mag. Walt Disney Showcase #4,7,13,20,23,33 & Wheaties)
No. 7, 1942; No. 429, 10/52 - No. 1248, 11-1/61-62 (Walt Disney)
Dell Publishing Co.

	Good	Fine	Mint
Large Feature Comic 7(1942)	55.00	165.00	385.00
4-Color 429,509	2.00	6.00	14.00
4-Color 595,654	1.70	5.00	12.00
4-Color 736,853,941,1039,1143,1248	1.30	4.00	9.00

POCAHONTAS
1941 - No. 2, 1942
Pocahontas Fuel Company

	Good	Fine	Mint
nn(No.1), 2	4.35	13.00	30.00

POCKET COMICS
Aug, 1941 - No. 4, Jan, 1942 (Pocket size; 100 pgs.)
Harvey Publications

	Good	Fine	Mint
1-Origin The Black Cat, Cadet Blakey the Spirit of '76, The Red Blazer, The Phantom, Sphinx, & The Zebra; Phantom Ranger, British Agent #99, Spin Hawkins, Satan, Lord of Evil begin	36.00	108.00	252.00
2	23.00	70.00	160.00
3,4	18.00	54.00	125.00

POGO PARADE (See Dell Giants)

POGO POSSUM (Also see Animal Comics & Special Delivery)
April, 1946 - No. 16, April-June, 1954
Dell Publishing Co.

	Good	Fine	Mint
4-Color 105(1946)-Kelly-a	54.00	160.00	380.00
4-Color 148-Kelly-a	45.00	135.00	315.00
1-(10-12/49)-Kelly art in all	40.00	120.00	280.00
2	20.00	60.00	140.00
3-5	15.00	45.00	105.00
6-10: 10-Infinity-c	12.00	36.00	84.00
11-16: 11-X-mas-c	10.00	30.00	70.00

NOTE: *#1-4,9-13: 52 pgs.; #5-8,14-16: 36 pgs.*

POLICE ACTION
Jan, 1954 - No. 7, Nov, 1954
Atlas News Co.

	Good	Fine	Mint
1	4.00	12.00	28.00
2	2.00	6.00	14.00
3-7: 7-Powell-a	1.70	5.00	12.00

NOTE: ***Ayers** a-4. **Maneely** a-3. **Reinman** a-6.*

POLICE ACTION
Feb, 1975 - No. 3, June, 1975
Atlas/Seaboard Publ.

	Good	Fine	Mint
1-Lomax, N.Y.P.D., Luke Malone begin; McWilliams-a; bondage-c		.40	.80
2,3: 2-Origin Luke Malone, Manhunter		.30	.60

NOTE: ***Ploog** art in all. **Sekowsky/McWilliams** a-1-3. **Thorne** c-3.*

POLICE AGAINST CRIME
April, 1954 - No. 9, Aug, 1955
Premiere Magazines

	Good	Fine	Mint
1-Disbrow-a; extreme violence - man's face slashed with knife; Hollingsworth-a	5.00	15.00	35.00
2-Hollingsworth-a	2.85	8.50	20.00
3-9	1.85	5.50	13.00

POLICE BADGE #479 (Spy Thrillers #1-4)
No. 5, Sept, 1955
Atlas Comics (PrPI)

	Good	Fine	Mint
5-Maneely-c	1.75	5.25	12.00

POLICE CASE BOOK (See Giant Comics Editions)

POLICE CASES (See Authentic. . . & Record Book of. . .)

POLICE COMICS
Aug, 1941 - No. 127, Oct, 1953
Quality Comics Group (Comic Magazines)

	Good	Fine	Mint
1-Origin Plastic Man by Jack Cole, The Human Bomb by Gustavson, & No. 711; intro. Chic Carter by Eisner, The Firebrand by R. Crandall, The Mouthpiece, Phantom Lady, & The Sword	240.00	720.00	1680.00
2-Plastic Man smuggles opium	123.00	370.00	860.00
3	100.00	300.00	700.00
4	86.00	260.00	600.00
5-Plastic Man forced to smoke marijuana	86.00	260.00	600.00

POLICE COMICS (continued)

	Good	Fine	Mint
6,7	78.00	235.00	545.00
8-Origin Manhunter	90.00	270.00	630.00
9,10	73.00	220.00	510.00
11-The Spirit strip-r begin by Eisner(Origin-strip #1)	120.00	360.00	840.00
12-Intro. Ebony	78.00	235.00	545.00
13-Intro. Woozy Winks; last Firebrand	78.00	235.00	545.00
14-19: 15-Last No. 711; Destiny begins	50.00	150.00	350.00
20-The Raven x-over in Phantom Lady; features Jack Cole himself	50.00	150.00	350.00
21,22-Raven & Spider Widow x-over in Phantom Lady #21, cameo in Phantom Lady #22	35.00	105.00	245.00
23-30: 23-Last Phantom Lady. 24-Chic Carter becomes The Sword, only issue. 24-26-Flatfoot Burns by Kurtzman in all	32.00	95.00	225.00
31-41-Last Spirit-r by Eisner	23.00	70.00	160.00
42,43-Spirit-r by Eisner/Fine	20.00	60.00	140.00
44-Fine Spirit-r begin, end #88,90,92	16.00	48.00	110.00
45-50-(#50 on-c, #49 on inside)(1/46)	16.00	48.00	110.00
51-60: 58-Last Human Bomb	12.00	36.00	84.00
61,62,64-88	11.00	32.00	76.00
63-(Some issues have #65 printed on cover, but #63 on inside) Kurtzman-a, 6pgs.	11.00	32.00	76.00
89,91,93-No Spirit	10.00	30.00	70.00
90,92-Spirit by Fine	11.00	32.00	76.00
94-99,101,102: Spirit by Eisner in all; 101-Last Manhunter. 102-Last Spirit & Plastic Man by Jack Cole	14.00	42.00	100.00
100	16.00	48.00	110.00
103-Content change to crime - Ken Shannon	7.00	21.00	50.00
104-111,114-127-Crandall-a most issues	5.00	15.00	35.00
112-Crandall-a	5.00	15.00	35.00
113-Crandall-c/a(2), 9 pgs. each	5.50	16.50	38.00

NOTE: *Most Spirit stories signed by **Eisner** are not by him; all are reprints. **Cole** c-20, 24-26, 28, 29, 31, 36-38, 40, 46, 68, 69, 73. **Crandall** Firebrand-1-8. Spirit by **Eisner** 1-41, 94-102; by **Eisner/Fine**-42, 43; by **Fine**-44-88, 90, 92. 103, 109, Bondage c-103, 109, 125.*

POLICE LINE-UP
Aug, 1951 - No. 4, July, 1952
Realistic Comics/Avon Periodicals

	Good	Fine	Mint
1-Wood-a, 1 pg. plus part-c; spanking panel-r/Saint #5	13.50	40.00	95.00
2-Classic story "The Religious Murder Cult," drugs, perversion r-/Saint #5; c-/Avon paperback 329	12.00	36.00	84.00
3-Kubert-a(r)/part-c, Kinstler-a	8.00	24.00	56.00
4-Kinstler-a	8.00	24.00	56.00

POLICE THRILLS
1954
Ajax/Farrell Publications

	Good	Fine	Mint
1	2.65	8.00	18.00

POLICE TRAP (Public Defender In Action #7 on)
8-9/54 - No. 4, 2-3/55; No. 5, 7/55 - No. 6, 9/55
Mainline No. 1-4/Charlton No. 5,6

	Good	Fine	Mint
1-S&K covers-all issues	5.00	15.00	35.00
2-4	2.65	8.00	18.00
5,6-S&K-c/a	4.60	14.00	32.00

POLICE TRAP
No. 11, 1963; No. 16-18, 1964
Super Comics

	Good	Fine	Mint
Reprint #11,16-18	.50	1.50	3.00

POLL PARROT
Poll Parrot Shoe Store/International Shoe
1950 - 1951; 1959 - 1962
K. K. Publications (Giveaway)

	Good	Fine	Mint
1 ('50)-Howdy Doody; small size	2.00	6.00	14.00
2-4('50)-Howdy Doody	1.15	3.50	8.00
2('59)-16('61): 2-The Secret of Crumbley Castle. 5-Bandit Busters. 7-The Make-Believe Mummy. 8-Mixed Up Mission('60). 10-The Frightful Flight. 11-Showdown at Sunup. 13-...and the Runaway Genie. 14-Bully for You. 16-...& the Rajah's Ruby('62)	.50	1.50	3.00

POLLY & HER PALS (See Comic Monthly No. 1)

POLLYANNA (See 4-Color No. 1129)

POLLY PIGTAILS (Girls' Fun & Fashion Mag. #44 on)
Jan, 1946 - V4No.43, Oct-Nov, 1949
Parents' Magazine Institute/Polly Pigtails

	Good	Fine	Mint
1-Infinity-c	4.60	14.00	32.00
2	2.15	6.50	15.00
3-5	1.75	5.25	12.00
6-10	1.35	4.00	9.00
11-30	1.15	3.50	8.00
31-43	1.00	3.00	7.00

PONY EXPRESS (See Four Color No. 942)

PONYTAIL
7-9/62 - No. 12, 10-12/65; No. 13, 11/69 - No. 20, 1/71
Dell Publishing Co./Charlton No. 13 on

	Good	Fine	Mint
12-641-209(#1)	.75	2.25	5.00
2-12	.50	1.50	3.00
13-20	.35	1.00	2.00

POP COMICS (7 cents)
1955 (36 pgs.; 5x7"; in color)
Modern Store Publ.

	Good	Fine	Mint
1-Funny animal	.50	1.50	3.00

POPEYE (See Comic Album #7,11,15, Comics Reading Libraries, Eat Right to Work..., Giant Comic Album, March of Comics #37, 52, 66, 80, 96, 117, 134, 148, 157, 169, 194, 246, 264, 274, 294, 453, 465, 477 & Wow Comics, 1st series)

POPEYE (See Thimble Theatre)
1935 (25 cents; 52 pgs.; B&W) (By Segar)
David McKay Publications

	Good	Fine	Mint
1-Daily strip serial reprints-"The Gold Mine Thieves"	42.00	125.00	295.00
2-Daily strip-r	34.00	105.00	240.00

NOTE: *Popeye first entered Thimble Theatre in 1929.*

POPEYE
1937 - 1939 (All by Segar)
David McKay Publications

	Good	Fine	Mint
Feature Books nn (100 pgs.) (Very Rare)	385.00	1155.00	2700.00
Feature Books 2 (52 pgs.)	47.00	140.00	330.00
Feature Books 3 (100 pgs.)-r-/nn issue with a new-c	40.00	120.00	280.00
Feature Books 5,10 (76 pgs.)	32.00	95.00	225.00
Feature Books 14 (76 pgs.) (Scarce)	46.00	138.00	320.00

POPEYE (Strip reprints through 4-Color #70)
1941 - 1947; No. 1, 2-4/48 - No. 65, 7-9/62; No. 66, 10/62 - No. 80, 5/66; No. 81, 8/66 - No. 92, 12/67; No. 94, 2/69 - No. 138, 1/77; No. 139, 5/78 - No. 171, 7/84 (no No.93,160,161)
Dell No. 1-65/Gold Key No. 66-80/King No. 81-92/Charlton No. 94-138/Gold Key No. 139-155/Whitman No. 156 on

	Good	Fine	Mint
Large Feat. Comic 24('41)-½ by Segar	32.00	95.00	225.00
4-Color 25('41)-by Segar	35.00	105.00	245.00
Large Feature Comic 10('43)	26.00	78.00	180.00
4-Color 17('43)-by Segar	28.00	84.00	195.00
4-Color 26('43)-by Segar	26.00	78.00	180.00
4-Color 43('44)	17.00	51.00	120.00
4-Color 70('45)-Title: ...& Wimpy	14.00	42.00	100.00

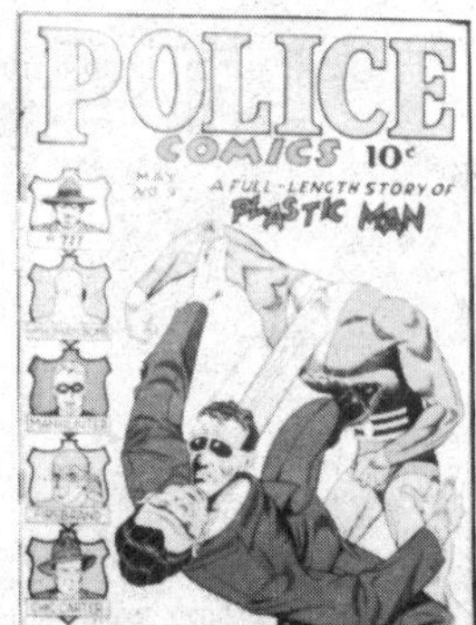

Police Comics #9, © QUA

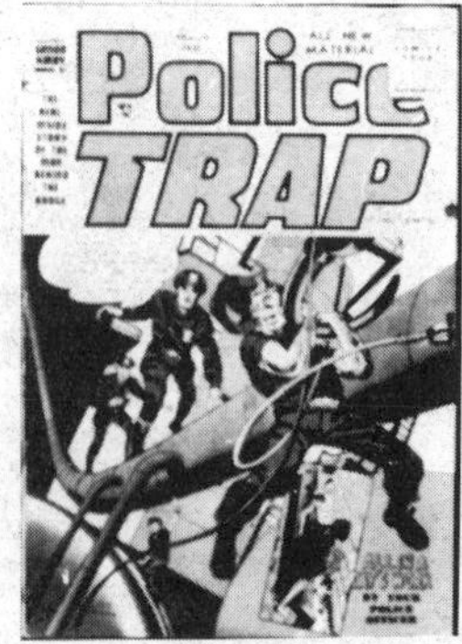

Police Trap #4, © CC

Polly Pigtails #30, © PMI

Popeye #41, © KING

Popular Comics #60, © DELL

Popular Teen-Agers #21, © STAR

POPEYE (continued)

	Good	Fine	Mint
4-Color 113('46-original strips begin),127,145('47),168	8.00	24.00	56.00
1(2-4/48)(Dell)	19.00	58.00	135.00
2	10.00	30.00	70.00
3-10	8.50	25.50	60.00
11-20	5.70	17.00	40.00
21-40	4.35	13.00	30.00
41-45,47-50	3.00	9.00	21.00
46-Origin Swee' Pee	4.35	13.00	30.00
51-60	2.00	6.00	14.00
61-65 (Last Dell ish.)	1.70	5.00	12.00
66,67-both 84 pgs. (G. Key)	3.00	9.00	24.00
68-80	1.70	5.00	12.00
81-92,94-100	.85	2.50	6.00
101-130	.70	2.00	5.00
131-143,145-159,162-171	.55	1.65	4.00
144-50th Anniversary issue	.55	1.65	4.00

NOTE: *Reprints-#145, 147, 149, 151, 153, 155, 157, 163-68(1/3), 170.*

	Good	Fine	Mint
Bold Detergent giveaway (Same as regular issue #94)	.35	1.00	2.00
. . .Kite Fun Book ('77, 5x7¼", 16p., soft-c)	1.00	3.00	6.00

POPEYE
1972 - 1974 (36 pgs. in color)
Charlton (King Features) (Giveaway)

	Good	Fine	Mint
E-1 to E-15 (Educational comics)	.25	.75	1.50
nn-Popeye Gettin' Better Grades-4 pgs. used as intro. to above giveaways (in color)	.25	.75	1.50

POPEYE CARTOON BOOK
1934 (40 pgs. plus cover)(8½x13")(cardboard covers)
The Saalfield Publ. Co.

2095-(Rare)-1933 strip reprints in color by Segar; each page con tains a vertical half of a Sunday strip, so the continuity reads row by row completely across each double page spread. If each page is read by itself, the continuity makes no sense. Each double page spread reprints one complete Sunday page (from 1933).

	Good	Fine	Mint
2095	77.00	230.00	540.00
12 Page Version	42.00	125.00	295.00

POPEYE SPECIAL
Summer, 1987 ($1.75, color)
Ocean Comics

	Good	Fine	Mint
1-Origin	.50	1.50	3.00

POPPLES (TV, Movie)
Dec, 1986 - Present
Star Comics (Marvel)

	Good	Fine	Mint
1-3-Based on toys		.35	.70
4,5 ($1.00)		.45	.90

POPPO OF THE POPCORN THEATRE
10/29/55 - 1956 (published weekly)
Fuller Publishing Co. (Publishers Weekly)

	Good	Fine	Mint
1	2.00	6.00	14.00
2-13	1.00	3.00	7.00

NOTE: *By* ***Charles Biro***. *10 cent-c price, given away by supermarkets such as IGA.*

POP-POP COMICS
No date (Circa 1945) (52 pgs.)
R. B. Leffingwell Co.

	Good	Fine	Mint
1-Funny animal	3.70	11.00	26.00

POPSICLE PETE FUN BOOK
1947, 1948
Joe Lowe Corp.

	Good	Fine	Mint
nn-36 pgs. in color; Sammy 'n' Claras, The King Who Couldn't Sleep & Popsicle Pete stories, games, cut-outs	4.60	14.00	32.00
Adventure Book ('48)	3.70	11.00	26.00

POPULAR COMICS
Feb, 1936 - No. 145, July-Sept, 1948
Dell Publishing Co.

	Good	Fine	Mint
1-Dick Tracy, Little Orphan Annie, Terry & the Pirates, Gasoline Alley, Moon Mullins, The Gumps begin (all strip-r)	103.00	310.00	720.00
2	50.00	150.00	350.00
3	40.00	120.00	280.00
4,5	30.00	90.00	210.00
6-10: 8-Scribbly app.	25.00	75.00	175.00
11-20	20.00	60.00	140.00
21-27-Last Terry & the Pirates, Little Orphan Annie, & Dick Tracy	16.00	48.00	110.00
28-37: 35-Christmas-c	13.50	40.00	95.00
38-43-Tarzan in text only	15.00	45.00	105.00
44,45	10.00	30.00	70.00
46-Origin Martan, the Marvel Man	14.00	42.00	100.00
47-50	10.00	30.00	70.00
51-Origin The Voice (The Invisible Detective) strip begins	11.00	32.00	76.00
52-59: 55-End of World sty	9.00	27.00	62.00
60-Origin Professor Supermind and Son	10.00	30.00	70.00
61-71: 63-Smilin' Jack begins	8.50	25.50	60.00
72-The Owl & Terry & the Pirates begin; Smokey Stover reprints begin	11.50	34.00	80.00
73-75	9.00	27.00	62.00
76-78-Capt. Midnight in all	11.00	32.00	76.00
79-85-Last Owl	8.00	24.00	56.00
86-99: 98-Felix the Cat, Smokey Stover-r begin	6.50	19.50	45.00
100	8.00	24.00	56.00
101-130: 115-Last Dick Tracy-r	4.35	13.00	30.00
131-145	3.70	11.00	26.00

POPULAR FAIRY TALES (See March of Comics No. 6,18)

POPULAR ROMANCE
No. 5, Dec, 1949 - No. 29, 1954
Better-Standard Publications

	Good	Fine	Mint
5	3.50	10.50	24.00
6-9	2.15	6.50	15.00
10-Wood-a, 2 pgs.	3.65	11.00	25.00
11,12,14-21,28,29	1.70	5.00	12.00
13-Severin/Elder-a, 3 pgs.	2.00	6.00	14.00
22-27-Toth-a	4.60	14.00	32.00

NOTE: *All have photo-c.* ***Tuska*** *art in most issues.*

POPULAR TEEN-AGERS (Secrets of Love) (Formerly School Day Romances)
Sept, 1950 - No. 23, Nov, 1954
Star Publications

	Good	Fine	Mint
5-Toni Gay, Honey Bunn, etc.; L. B. Cole-c	10.00	30.00	70.00
6-8-Toni Gay, Honey Bunn, etc.; all have L. B. Cole-c; 6-Negligee panels	9.00	27.00	62.00
9-(. . .Romances; change to romance format)	3.50	10.50	24.00
10-(. . .Secrets of Love)	3.50	10.50	24.00
11,16,18,19,22,23	2.85	8.50	20.00
12,13,17,20,21-Disbrow-a	3.50	10.50	24.00
14-Harrison/Wood-a; 2 spanking scenes	11.50	34.50	80.00
15-Wood?, Disbrow-a	8.00	24.00	55.00
Accepted Reprint 5,6 (nd); L.B. Cole-c	2.00	6.00	14.00

NOTE: *All have* ***L. B. Cole*** *covers.*

PORE LI'L MOSE
1902 (30 pgs.; 10½x15"; in full color)

PORE LI'L MOSE (continued)
New York Herald Publ. by Grand Union Tea
Cupples & Leon Co.

	Good	Fine	Mint
By R. F. Outcault; 1 pg. strips about early Negroes	30.00	90.00	210.00

PORKY PIG (. . .& Bugs Bunny #40-69)
No. 16, 1942 - No. 109, July, 1984
Dell Publishing Co./Gold Key No. 1-93/Whitman No. 94 on

	Good	Fine	Mint
4-Color 16(1942)	32.00	95.00	225.00
4-Color 48(1944)-Carl Barks-a	62.00	185.00	435.00
4-Color 78(1945)	11.50	34.00	80.00
4-Color 112(7/46)	7.00	21.00	50.00
4-Color 156,182,191('49)	5.00	15.00	35.00
4-Color 226,241('49),260,271,277,284,295	3.50	10.50	24.00
4-Color 303,311,322,330	2.30	7.00	16.00
4-Color 342,351,360,370,385,399,410,426	1.70	5.00	12.00
25 (11-12/52)-30	1.15	3.50	8.00
31-50	.55	1.65	4.00
51-81(3-4/62)	.45	1.35	3.00
1(1/65-G.K.)(2nd Series)	.75	2.25	5.00
2,4,5-Reprints 4-Color 226,284 & 271 in that order	.45	1.35	3.00
3,6-10	.35	1.00	2.00
11-50		.50	1.00
51-109		.30	.60
Kite Fun Book (1960, 16pgs., 5x7¼", soft-c)	2.00	6.00	12.00

NOTE: *Reprints-#1-8, 9-35(⅔); 36-46,58,67,69-74,76,78,102-109(⅓-½).*

PORKY PIG (See March of Comics #42, 57, 71, 89, 99, 113, 130, 143, 164, 175, 192, 209, 218, 367, and Super Book #6, 18, 30)

PORKY'S BOOK OF TRICKS
1942 (48 pages) (8½x5½")
K. K. Publications (Giveaway)

	Good	Fine	Mint
7 pg. comic story, text stories, plus games & puzzles	25.00	75.00	175.00

POST GAZETTE (See Meet the New. . .)

POWDER RIVER RUSTLERS (See Fawcett Movie Comics)

POWER COMICS
1944 - 1945
Holyoke Publ. Co./Narrative Publ.

	Good	Fine	Mint
1-L. B. Cole-c	15.00	45.00	105.00
2-4: 2-Dr. Mephisto begins. 3,4-L. B. Cole-c; Miss Espionage app. each	13.00	40.00	90.00

POWER FACTOR
1987 - Present ($1.95, color)
Wonder Color Comics

	Good	Fine	Mint
1	.35	1.00	2.00

POWERHOUSE PEPPER COMICS (See Gay & Joker Comics)
No. 1, 1943; No. 2, May, 1948 - No. 5, Nov, 1948
Marvel Comics (20CC)

	Good	Fine	Mint
1-(60 pgs.)-Wolverton-a	55.00	165.00	385.00
2-Wolverton-a	33.00	100.00	230.00
3,4-Both by Wolverton	32.00	95.00	225.00
5-(Scarce)-Wolverton-a	38.00	115.00	265.00

POWER LORDS
Dec, 1983 - No. 3, Feb, 1984 (Mando paper)
DC Comics

	Good	Fine	Mint
1-3-Based on Revell toys		.40	.80

POWER MAN (Formerly Hero for Hire; . . .& Iron Fist #68 on)
No. 17, Feb, 1974 - No. 125, Sept, 1986
Marvel Comics Group

	Good	Fine	Mint
17-20: 17-Iron Man app.	.40	1.20	2.40
21-31: 31-Part Adams-i		.60	1.20
32-47: 36-Reprint. 45-Starlin-c		.50	1.00
48-Byrne-a; Powerman/Iron Fist 1st meet	.50	1.50	3.00
49,50-Byrne-a(p); 50-Iron Fist joins Cage	.50	1.50	3.00
51-56,58-60: 58-Intro El Aguila		.40	.80
57-New X-Men app.	.85	2.50	5.00
61-74: 68-Miller c/a		.30	.60
75-Double size; Larkin painted-c	.25	.75	1.50
76-99,101-124: 87-Moon Knight app. 90-Unus app. 109-The Reaper app.		.30	.60
100-Double size; painted-c; origin K'un L'un		.50	1.00
125-Double size		.60	1.20
Giant-Size 1('75)	.30	.80	1.60
Annual 1(11/76)		.50	1.00

NOTE: ***Austin** c-102i. **Byrne** a-48-50; c-102, 104, 106, 107. **Kane** c(p)-24, 25, 28, 48. **Miller** c-66, 67, 70-74, 80i. **Mooney** a-53i, 55i. **Nebres** a-76p. **Nino** a-42i, 43i. **Perez** a-27. **Tuska** a-17p, 20p, 24p.*

POWERMOWERMAN AND POWER MOWER SAFETY
1966 (16 pgs.) (Giveaway)
Frank Burgmeier Co. (Outdoor Power Equipment Inst.)

	Good	Fine	Mint
nn-Vaughn Bode'-a	22.00	65.00	130.00

POWER PACK
Aug, 1984 - Present
Marvel Comics Group

	Good	Fine	Mint
1-($1.00)	.55	1.65	3.30
2-5	.40	1.20	2.40
6-8-Cloak & Dagger app.	.35	1.00	2.00
9-18		.65	1.30
19-Dbl. size; Cloak & Dagger, Wolverine app.	.35	1.10	2.20
20-24		.50	1.00
25-Double size	.25	.80	1.60
26-Direct sale; Cloak & Dagger app.		.50	1.00
27-Mutant massacre	.55	1.65	3.30
28-36		.50	1.00

POW MAGAZINE (Bob Sproul's) (Satire Magazine)
Aug, 1966 - No. 3, Feb, 1967 (30 cents)
Humor-Vision

	Good	Fine	Mint
1-3: 2-Jones-a. 3-Wrightson-a	.85	2.50	6.00

PREHISTORIC WORLD (See Classics Special)

PREMIERE (See Charlton Premiere)

PRESTO KID, THE (See Red Mask)

PRETTY BOY FLOYD (See On the Spot)

PREZ (See Cancelled Comic Cavalcade & Supergirl #10)
Aug-Sept, 1973 - No. 4, Feb-Mar, 1974
National Periodical Publications

	Good	Fine	Mint
1-Origin		.30	.60
2-4		.25	.50

PRICE, THE (See Eclipse Graphic Album Series)

PRIDE AND THE PASSION, THE (See 4-Color No. 824)

PRIDE OF THE YANKEES, THE
1949 (The Life of Lou Gehrig)
Magazine Enterprises

	Good	Fine	Mint
nn-Ogden Whitney-a	22.00	65.00	154.00

PRIMAL MAN (See The Crusaders)

PRIMER (Comico. . .)
1982 - No. 6, 1985 (B&W)
Comico

	Good	Fine	Mint
1 (52 pgs.)	1.00	3.00	6.00
2-1st app. Grendel by Wagner	7.50	22.50	45.00
3-5	.70	2.00	4.00

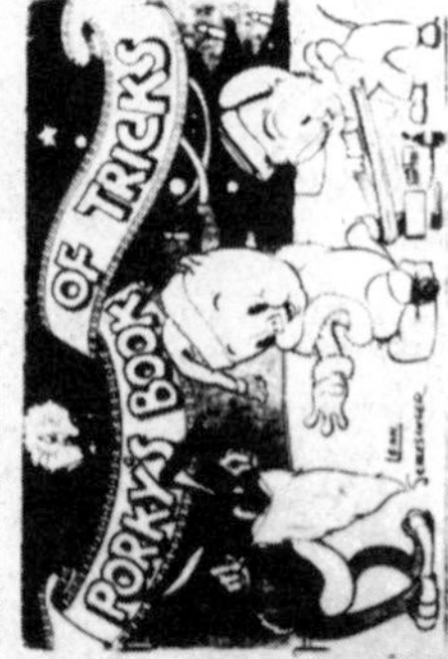

Porky's Book of Tricks nn, © Warner Bros.

Power Comics #2, © HOKE

Power Man #17, © MCG

Prison Break! #1, © REAL

Prize Comics #5, © PRIZE

Prize Mystery #1, © Key Publ.

	Good	Fine	Mint
PRIMER (continued)			
6-Intro Evangeline	1.85	5.50	11.00

PRIMUS (TV)
Feb, 1972 - No. 7, Oct, 1972
Charlton Comics

1-5,7-Staton-a in all	.35	1.00	2.00
6-Drug propaganda story	.35	1.00	2.00

PRINCE & THE PAUPER, THE (See Movie Classics)

PRINCE NAMOR, THE SUB-MARINER
Sept, 1984 - No. 4, Dec, 1984 (mini-series)
Marvel Comics Group

1		.60	1.20
2-4		.45	.90

PRINCE NIGHTMARE
1987 - Present ($2.95, color, 68 pgs.)
Aaaargh! Associated Artists

Book 1	.50	1.50	3.00

PRINCE VALIANT (See Comics Reading Libraries, Feature Books No. 26, McKay, and 4-Color No. 567, 650, 699, 719, 788, 849, 900)

PRISCILLA'S POP (See 4-Color No. 569,630,704,799)

PRISON BARS (See Behind . . .)

PRISON BREAK!
1951 (Sept) - No. 5, Sept, 1952
Avon Periodicals/Realistic No. 4 on

1-Wood-c & 1 pg.; has r-/Saint #7 retitled Michael Strong Private Eye	17.00	51.00	120.00
2-Wood-c/Kubert-a plus 2 pgs. Wood-a	12.00	36.00	84.00
3-Orlando, Check-a; c-/Avon paperback 179	10.00	30.00	70.00
4,5: Kinstler-c. 5-Infantino-a	9.00	27.00	62.00

PRISON RIOT
1952
Avon Periodicals

1-Marijuana Murders-1 pg. text; Kinstler-c	13.00	40.00	90.00

PRISON TO PRAISE
1974 (35 cents)
Logos International

True Story of Merlin R. Carothers		.30	.60

PRIVATE BUCK (See Large Feature Comic No. 12 & 21)

PRIVATEERS
Aug, 1987 - Present ($1.50, color)
Vanguard Graphics

1-3	.25	.75	1.50

PRIVATE EYE (Rocky Jordan . . . #6-8)
Jan, 1951 - No. 8, March, 1952
Atlas Comics (MCI)

1	4.35	13.00	30.00
2,3-Tuska c/a(3)	2.65	8.00	18.00
4-8	2.30	7.00	16.00

NOTE: ***Henkel** a-6(3), 7; c-7. **Sinnott** a-6.*

PRIVATE EYE (See Mike Shayne . . .)

PRIVATE SECRETARY
Dec-Feb, 1962-63 - No. 2, Mar-May, 1963
Dell Publishing Co.

1,2	1.00	3.00	7.00

PRIVATE STRONG (See The Double Life of . . .)

PRIZE COMICS (. . . Western #69 on) (Also see Treasure Comics)
March, 1940 - No. 68, Feb-Mar, 1948
Prize Publications

	Good	Fine	Mint
1-Origin Power Nelson, The Futureman & Jupiter, Master Magician; Ted O'Neil, Secret Agent M-11, Jaxon of the Jungle, Bucky Brady & Storm Curtis begin	64.00	192.00	450.00
2-The Black Owl begins	32.00	95.00	225.00
3,4	24.00	72.00	170.00
5,6: Dr. Dekkar, Master of Monsters app. in each	22.00	65.00	154.00
7-Black Owl by S&K; origin/1st app. Dr. Frost & Frankenstein; The Green Lama, Capt. Gallant, The Great Voodini & Twist Turner begin; Kirby-c	50.00	150.00	350.00
8,9-Black Owl & Ted O'Neil by S&K	25.00	75.00	175.00
10-12,14-20: 11-Origin Bulldog Denny. 16-Spike Mason begins	22.00	65.00	154.00
13-Origin Yank & Doodle	27.00	81.00	190.00
21-24	12.00	36.00	84.00
25-30	9.50	28.50	65.00
31-33	7.00	21.00	50.00
34-Origin Airmale, & Yank & Doodle; The Black Owl joins army, Yank & Doodle's father assumes Black Owl's role	8.00	24.00	56.00
35-40: 35-Flying Fist & Bingo begin. 37-Intro. Stampy, Airmale's sidekick	6.00	18.00	42.00
41-50: 45-Yank & Doodle learn Black Owl's I.D. (their father). 48-Prince Ra begins	4.60	14.00	32.00
51-62,64-68: 53-Transvestism sty. 55-No Frankenstein. 64-Black Owl retires	4.00	12.00	28.00
63-Simon & Kirby c/a	6.00	18.00	42.00

NOTE: ***Briefer** a 7-on. **J. Binder** a-16.*

PRIZE COMICS WESTERN (Prize #1-68)
No. 69(V7No.2), Apr-May, 1948 - No. 119, Nov-Dec, 1956
Prize Publications (Feature) (No. 69-84, 52 pgs.)

69(V7#2)	5.60	16.50	38.00
70-75	4.00	12.00	28.00
76-Randolph Scott photo-c; "Canadian Pacific" movie adapt.	5.50	16.50	38.00
77-Photo-c; Severin, Mart Bailey-a; 'Streets of Laredo' movie adapt.	4.60	14.00	32.00
78-Photo-c; Kurtzman-a, 10 pgs.; Severin, Mart Bailey-a; 'Bullet Code,' & 'Roughshod' movie adapt.	7.00	21.00	50.00
79-Photo-c; Kurtzman-a, 8 pgs.; Severin & Elder, Severin, Mart Bailey-a; 'Stage To Chino' movie adapt.	7.00	21.00	50.00
80,81-Photo-c; Severin/Elder-a(2)	4.60	14.00	32.00
82-Photo-c; 1st app. The Preacher by Mart Bailey; Severin/Elder-a(3)	4.60	14.00	32.00
83,84	3.70	11.00	26.00
85-American Eagle by John Severin begins (1-2/50)	9.50	28.00	65.00
86,92,95,101-105	4.00	12.00	28.00
87-91,93,94,96-99,110,111-Severin/Elder a(2-3) each	4.60	14.00	32.00
100	6.00	18.00	42.00
106-108,112	3.50	10.50	24.00
109-Severin/Williamson-a	5.50	16.50	38.00
113-Williamson/Severin-a(2)	6.00	18.00	42.00
114-119: Drifter series in all; by Mort Meskin 114-118	2.65	8.00	18.00

NOTE: ***Fass** a-81. **Severin & Elder** c-88, 92, 94-96, 98. **Severin** a-72, 75, 77-79, 83-86, 96, 97, 100-105; c-most 85-109. **Simon & Kirby** c-75, 83.*

PRIZE MYSTERY
May, 1955 - No. 3, Sept, 1955
Key Publications

1	2.65	8.00	18.00
2,3	1.60	4.70	11.00

PROFESSIONAL FOOTBALL (See Charlton Sport Library)

PROFESSOR COFFIN
No. 19, Oct, 1985 - No. 21, Feb, 1986
Charlton Comics

	Good	Fine	Mint
19-21: Wayne Howard-a(r)		.40	.80

PROJECT: HERO
Aug, 1987 ($1.50, color)
Vanguard Graphics (Canadian)

	Good	Fine	Mint
1	.25	.75	1.50

PROWLER
July, 1987 - Present ($1.75, color)
Eclipse Comics

	Good	Fine	Mint
1,2	.30	.85	1.70

PSI FORCE
Nov, 1986 - Present
Marvel Comics Group

	Good	Fine	Mint
1		.60	1.20
2-18		.50	1.00
Annual 1 (10/87)		.60	1.25

PSYCHO (Magazine)
Jan, 1971 - No. 24, Mar, 1975 (68 pgs.; B&W) (no No.22?)
Skywald Publishing Corp.

	Good	Fine	Mint
1-All reprints	.70	2.00	4.00
2-Origin & 1st app. The Heap, & Frankenstein series by Adkins	.35	1.00	2.00
3-10	.30	.80	1.60
11-21,23: 13-Cannabalism. 18-Injury to eye-c. 20-Severed Head-c		.50	1.00
24-1975 Winter Special		.60	1.20
Annual 1('72)	.30	.80	1.60
Fall Special('74)		.60	1.20
Yearbook(1974-nn)		.60	1.20

NOTE: ***Boris*** *c-3, 5.* ***Buckler*** *a-4 ,5.* ***Everett*** *a-3-6.* ***J. Jones*** *a-6, 7, 9; c-12.* ***Kaluta*** *a-13.* ***Katz/Buckler*** *a-3.* ***Morrow*** *a-1.* ***Reese*** *a-5.* ***Sutton*** *a-3.* ***Wildey*** *a-5.*

PSYCHOANALYSIS
Mar-Apr, 1955 - No. 4, Sept-Oct, 1955
E. C. Comics

	Good	Fine	Mint
1-All Kamen; not approved by code	6.00	18.00	42.00
2-4-Kamen-a in all	4.60	14.00	32.00

PSYCHOBLAST
Nov,1987 - Present ($1.75, color)
First Comics

	Good	Fine	Mint
1-6	.30	.90	1.80

P.T. 109 (See Movie Comics)

PUBLIC DEFENDER IN ACTION (Formerly Police Trap)
No. 7, Mar, 1956 - No. 12, Oct, 1957
Charlton Comics

	Good	Fine	Mint
7	2.65	8.00	18.00
8-12	1.50	4.50	10.00

PUBLIC ENEMIES
1948 - No. 9, June-July, 1949
D. S. Publishing Co.

	Good	Fine	Mint
1	5.00	15.00	35.00
2-Used in **SOTI**, pg. 95	7.00	21.00	50.00
3-5	3.00	9.00	21.00
6,8,9	2.65	8.00	18.00
7-McWilliams-a; injury to eye panel	4.60	14.00	32.00

PUDGY PIG
Sept, 1958 - No. 2, Nov, 1958
Charlton Comics

	Good	Fine	Mint
1,2	.75	2.25	5.00

PUNCH & JUDY COMICS
1944 - V3No.9, Dec, 1951
Hillman Periodicals

	Good	Fine	Mint
V1#1-(60 pgs.)	5.00	15.00	35.00
2	2.65	8.00	18.00
3-12(7/46)	1.70	5.00	12.00
V2#1,3-9	1.30	4.00	9.00
V2#2,10-12, V3#1-Kirby-a(2) each	6.50	19.50	45.00
V3#2-Kirby-a	5.50	16.50	38.00
3-9	1.15	3.50	8.00

PUNCH COMICS
Dec, 1941 - No. 26, Dec, 1947
Harry 'A' Chesler

	Good	Fine	Mint
1-Mr. E, The Sky Chief, Hale the Magician, Kitty Kelly begin	35.00	105.00	245.00
2-Captain Glory app.	18.00	54.00	125.00
3	15.00	45.00	105.00
4	13.00	40.00	90.00
5	11.00	32.00	76.00
6-8	9.50	28.50	65.00
9-Rocketman & Rocket Girl & The Master Key begin	11.00	32.00	76.00
10-Sky Chief app.; J. Cole-a; Master Key r-/Scoop 3	9.50	28.50	65.00
11-Origin Master Key-r/Scoop 1; Sky Chief, Little Nemo app.; Jack Cole-a; Fineish art by Sultan	10.00	30.00	70.00
12-Rocket Boy & Capt. Glory app; Skull-c	8.50	25.50	60.00
13-17,19: 13-Cover has list of 4 Chesler artists' names on tombstone	8.00	24.00	56.00
18-Bondage-c; hypodermic panels	10.00	30.00	70.00
20-Unique cover with bare-breasted women	16.00	48.00	110.00
21-Hypo needle story	8.50	25.50	60.00
22-26: 22,23-Little Nemo-not by McCay	7.00	21.00	50.00

PUNCHY AND THE BLACK CROW
No. 10, Oct, 1985 - No. 12, Feb, 1986
Charlton Comics

	Good	Fine	Mint
10-12: Al Fago funny animal-r		.40	.80

PUNISHER (Also see Amaz. Spider-Man, Captain America #241, Daredevil #182-184, Marvel Preview #2, Marvel Super Action & Spect. Spider-Man #81-83)
Jan, 1986 - No. 5, May, 1986 (mini-series)
Marvel Comics Group

	Good	Fine	Mint
1-Double size	2.00	6.00	12.00
2	1.15	3.50	7.00
3	.75	2.25	4.50
4,5	.60	1.80	3.60

PUNISHER
July, 1987 - Present
Marvel Comics Group

	Good	Fine	Mint
V2#1	.75	2.25	4.50
2	.40	1.20	2.40
3-5	.30	.90	1.80
6-10		.60	1.20

PUPPET COMICS
Spring, 1946 - No. 2, Summer, 1946
George W. Dougherty Co.

	Good	Fine	Mint
1,2-Funny animal	3.00	9.00	21.00

PUPPETOONS (See George Pal's . . .)

PURE OIL COMICS (Also see Salerno Carnival of Comics, 24 Pages of Comics, & Vicks Comics)
Late 1930's (24 pgs.; regular size) (paper cover)
Pure Oil Giveaway

Psychoblast #1, © First Comics

Punch and Judy Comics V2#1, © HILL

Punch Comics #11, © CHES

The Purple Claw #3, © TOBY

Queen of the West, Dale Evans #3, © Roy Rogers

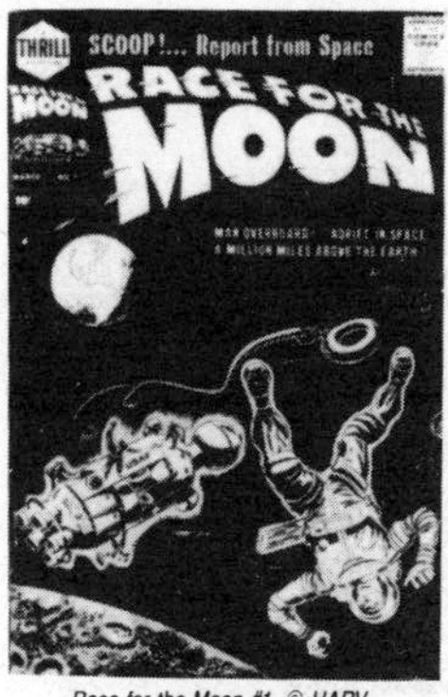

Race for the Moon #1, © HARV

PURE OIL COMICS (continued) — Good / Fine / Mint

nn-Contains 1-2 pg. strips; i.e., Hairbreadth Harry, Skyroads, Buck Rogers by Calkins & Yager, Olly of the Movies, Napoleon, S'Matter Pop, etc. — 25.00 / 75.00 / 175.00
Also a 16 pg. 1938 giveaway with Buck Rogers — 20.00 / 60.00 / 140.00

PURPLE CLAW, THE (Also see Tales of Horror)
Jan, 1953 - No. 3, May, 1953
Minoan Publishing Co./Toby Press

1-Origin — 8.50 / 25.50 / 60.00
2,3: 1-3 r-in Tales of Horror #9-11 — 5.00 / 15.00 / 35.00
I.W. Reprint #8-Reprints #1 — .80 / 2.40 / 4.80

PUSSYCAT (Magazine)
Oct, 1968 (B&W reprints from Men's magazines)
Marvel Comics Group

1-(Scarce)-Ward, Everett, Wood-a; Everett-c — 12.00 / 36.00 / 84.00

PUZZLE FUN COMICS (Also see Jingle Jangle)
Spring, 1946 - No. 2, Summer, 1946 (52 pgs.)
George W. Dougherty Co.

1(1946)-Gustavson-a — 7.00 / 21.00 / 50.00
2 — 5.50 / 16.50 / 38.00

*NOTE: #1,2('46) each contain a **George Carlson** cover plus a 6 pg. story "Alec in Fumbleland;" also many puzzles in each.*

QUAKER OATS (Also see Cap'n Crunch)
1965 (Giveaway) (2½x5½") (16 pages)
Quaker Oats Co.

"Plenty of Glutton," "Lava Come-Back," "Kite Tale," "A Witch in Time" — .50 / 1.00

QUEEN OF THE WEST, DALE EVANS (TV)(See Western Roundup)
No. 479, 7/53 - No. 22, 1-3/59 (All photo-c; photo back c-4-8, 15)
Dell Publishing Co.

4-Color 479('53) — 5.50 / 16.50 / 38.00
4-Color 528('54) — 4.00 / 12.00 / 28.00
3(4-6/54)-Toth-a — 5.00 / 15.00 / 35.00
4-Toth, Manning-a — 5.00 / 15.00 / 35.00
5-10-Manning-a. 5-Marsh-a? — 3.50 / 10.50 / 24.00
11,19,21-No Manning 21-Tufts-a — 2.65 / 8.00 / 18.00
12-18,20,22-Manning-a — 3.00 / 9.00 / 21.00

QUENTIN DURWARD (See 4-Color No. 672)

QUESTAR ILLUSTRATED SCIENCE FICTION CLASSICS
1977 (224 pgs.) ($1.95)
Golden Press

11197-Stories by Asimov, Sturgeon, Silverberg & Niven; Star stream-r — .50 / 1.50 / 3.00

QUESTION, THE (See Mysterious Suspense)

QUESTION, THE
Feb, 1987 - Present (Mature readers)
DC Comics

1-Sienkiewicz painted-c begin — .40 / 1.25 / 2.50
2-15: 8-Intro. The Mikado — .25 / .75 / 1.50

QUESTPROBE
8/84; (One-shot) 9/85 - No. 4, 12/85 (limited series)
Marvel Comics Group

1 (8/84) — .40 / .80
1-4 — .40 / .80

QUICK-DRAW McGRAW (TV) (Hanna-Barbera)
No. 1040, 12-2/59-60 - No. 11, 7-9/62; No. 12, 11/62; No. 13, 2/63; No. 14, 4/63; No. 15, 6/69 (See Whitman Comic Books)
Dell Publishing Co./Gold Key No. 12 on

4-Color 1040 — 2.30 / 7.00 / 16.00
2(4-6/60)-6 — 1.30 / 4.00 / 9.00
7-11 — .85 / 2.50 / 6.00
12,13-Title change to . . . Fun-Type Roundup (84 pgs.) — 2.50 / 7.50 / 20.00
14,15 — .85 / 2.50 / 6.00

(See Whitman Comic Books)

QUICK-DRAW McGRAW (TV)(See Spotlight #2)
Nov, 1970 - No. 8, Jan, 1972 (Hanna-Barbera)
Charlton Comics

1 — .85 / 2.50 / 5.00
2-8 — .50 / 1.50 / 3.00

QUICK-TRIGGER WESTERN (. . . Action #12; formerly Cowboy Action)
No. 12, May, 1956 - No. 19, Sept, 1957
Atlas Comics (ACI No. 12/WPI No. 13-19)

12-Baker-a — 3.50 / 10.50 / 24.00
13-Williamson-a, 5 pgs. — 4.00 / 12.00 / 28.00
14-Everett, Crandall, Torres-a; Heath-c — 3.50 / 10.50 / 24.00
15-Torres, Crandall-a — 2.65 / 8.00 / 18.00
16-Orlando, Kirby-a — 2.30 / 7.00 / 16.00
17-Crandall-a — 2.00 / 6.00 / 14.00
18-Baker-a — 2.00 / 6.00 / 14.00
19 — 1.30 / 4.00 / 9.00

*NOTE: **Morrow** a-18. **Powell** a-14. **Severin** c-13,16,17,19.*

QUINCY (See Comics Reading Libraries)

RACCOON KIDS, THE (Formerly Movietown Animal Antics)
No. 52, Sept-Oct, 1954 - No. 64, Nov, 1957
National Periodical Publications (Arleigh No. 63,64)

52-Doodles Duck by Mayer — 3.50 / 10.50 / 24.00
53-64: 53-62-Doodles Duck by Mayer — 2.00 / 6.00 / 14.00

RACE FOR THE MOON
March, 1958 - No. 3, Nov, 1958
Harvey Publications

1-Powell-a(5); ½-pg. S&K-a; c-redrawn from Galaxy Science Fiction pulp (5/53) — 5.00 / 15.00 / 35.00
2-Kirby/Williamson c(r)/a(3) — 13.50 / 40.50 / 95.00
3-Kirby/Williamson c/a(4) — 14.50 / 43.50 / 100.00

RACKET SQUAD IN ACTION
May-June, 1952 - No. 29, March, 1958
Capitol Stories/Charlton Comics

1 — 6.50 / 19.50 / 45.00
2-4 — 2.65 / 8.00 / 18.00
5-Dr. Neff, Ghost Breaker app; headlights-c — 3.50 / 10.50 / 24.00
6-Dr. Neff, Ghost Breaker app. — 2.65 / 8.00 / 18.00
7-10: 10-Explosion-c — 2.30 / 7.00 / 16.00
11-Ditko c/a — 7.00 / 21.00 / 50.00
12-Ditko explosion-c (classic); Shuster-a(2) — 16.00 / 48.00 / 110.00
13-Shuster c/a; acid in woman's face — 2.30 / 7.00 / 16.00
14-"Shakedown"-marijuana story — 5.00 / 15.00 / 35.00
15-28 — 1.85 / 5.50 / 13.00
29-(68 pgs.)(15 cents) — 2.15 / 6.50 / 15.00

RADIANT LOVE (Formerly Daring Love #1)
No. 2, Dec, 1953 - No. 6, Aug, 1954
Gilmor Magazines

2 — 2.65 / 8.00 / 18.00
3-6 — 1.70 / 5.00 / 12.00

RAGAMUFFINS
Jan, 1985 (One Shot)
Eclipse Comics

1-Eclipse Magazine-r, w/color — .30 / .90 / 1.80

RAGGEDY ANN AND ANDY (See Dell Giants, March of Comics #23 & New Funnies)
No. 5, 1942 - No. 533, 2/54; 10-12/64 - No. 4, 3/66
Dell Publishing Co.

	Good	Fine	Mint
4-Color 5(1942)	27.00	81.00	190.00
4-Color 23(1943)	20.00	60.00	140.00
4-Color 45(1943)	15.00	45.00	105.00
4-Color 72(1945)	13.00	40.00	90.00
1(6/46)-Billy & Bonnie Bee by Frank Thomas	14.00	42.00	100.00
2,3: 3-Egbert Elephant by Dan Noonan begins	7.00	21.00	50.00
4-Kelly-a, 16 pgs.	8.00	24.00	56.00
5-10: 7-Little Black Sambo, Black Mumbo & Black Jumbo only app; Christmas-c	6.00	18.00	42.00
11-20	4.65	14.00	32.00
21-Alice In Wonderland cover/story	4.65	14.00	32.00
22-27,29-39(8/49), 4-Color 262(1/50)	3.50	10.50	24.00
28-Kelly-c	4.00	12.00	28.00
4-Color 306,354,380,452,533	3.00	9.00	21.00
1(10-12/64-Dell)	1.15	3.50	8.00
2,3(10-12/65), 4(3/66)	.75	2.25	5.00

NOTE: ***Kelly** art ("Animal Mother Goose")-No. 1-34, 36, 37; c-28. Peterkin Pottle by **John Stanley** in 32-38.*

RAGGEDY ANN AND ANDY
Dec, 1971 - No. 6, Sept, 1973
Gold Key

1	.70	2.00	4.00
2-6	.35	1.00	2.00

RAGGEDY ANN & THE CAMEL WITH THE WRINKLED KNEES (See Dell Jr. Treasury No. 8)

RAGMAN (See Batman Family #20 & Cancelled Comic Cavalcade)
Aug-Sept, 1976 - No. 5, June-July, 1977
National Periodical Publications

1-Origin		.40	.80
2-Origin concludes; Kubert-c		.30	.60
3-5: 4-Drug use story		.25	.50

NOTE: ***Kubert** a-4 ,5; c-1-5. **Redondo** studios a-1-4.*

RAGS RABBIT (See Harvey Hits #2 & Tastee Freez)
No. 11, June, 1951 - No. 18, March, 1954
Harvey Publications

11(See Nutty Comics #5 for 1st app.)	1.00	3.00	7.00
12-18	.85	2.50	6.00

RAIDERS OF THE LOST ARK
Sept, 1981 - No. 3, Nov, 1981 (Movie adaptation)
Marvel Comics Group

1		.40	.80
2,3: 3-Final chapter of movie adapt.		.30	.60

NOTE: ***Buscema** a(p)-1-3; c(p)-1. **Simonson** a-2i, 3i.*

RAINBOW BRITE AND THE STAR STEALER
1985
DC Comics

nn-Movie adapt.		.40	.80

RALPH KINER, HOME RUN KING
1950 (Pittsburgh Pirates)
Fawcett Publications

nn	18.00	54.00	125.00

RAMAR OF THE JUNGLE (TV)
1954 (no month); No. 2, 9/55 - No. 5, 9/56
Toby Press No. 1/Charlton No. 2 on

1-Jon Hall photo-c	5.50	16.50	38.00
2-5	4.00	12.00	28.00

RAMPAGING HULK, THE (Magazine) (The Hulk #10 on; see Marvel Treas. Ed.)
Jan, 1977 - No. 9, June, 1978
Marvel Comics Group

	Good	Fine	Mint
1-Bloodstone featured	.50	1.50	3.00
2-Old X-Men app; origin old & new X-Men in text	.35	1.00	2.00
3-9		.50	1.00

NOTE: ***Alcala** a-1-3i, 5i, 8i. **Buscema** a-1. **Giffen** a-4. **Nino** a-4i. **Simonson** a-1-3p. **Starlin** a-4(w/Nino), 7; c-4, 5, 7.*

RANGE BUSTERS
Sept, 1950 - No. 8, 1951
Fox Features Syndicate

1	5.70	17.00	40.00
2	3.00	9.00	21.00
3-8	2.65	8.00	18.00

RANGE BUSTERS (Formerly Cowboy Love?; Wyatt Earp, Frontier Marshall #11 on)
No. 8, May, 1955 - No. 10, Sept, 1955
Charlton Comics

8	2.65	8.00	18.00
9,10	1.30	4.00	9.00

RANGELAND LOVE
Dec, 1949 - No. 2, Mar, 1950
Atlas Comics (CDS)

1,2	4.00	12.00	28.00

RANGER, THE (See 4-Color No. 255)

RANGE RIDER (See Flying A's. . .)

RANGE RIDER, THE (See 4-Color No. 404)

RANGE ROMANCES
Dec, 1949 - No. 5, Aug, 1950
Comic Magazines (Quality Comics)

1-Gustavson-c/a	11.50	34.00	80.00
2-Crandall-c/a; "spanking" scene	16.00	48.00	110.00
3-Crandall, Gustavson-a; photo-c	9.00	27.00	62.00
4-Crandall-a; photo-c	7.00	21.00	50.00
5-Gustavson-a; Crandall-a(p)	8.00	24.00	56.00

RANGERS COMICS (. . .of Freedom #1-7)
Oct, 1941 - No. 69, Winter, 1952-53
Fiction House Magazines (Flying stories)

1-Intro. Ranger Girl & The Rangers of Freedom; ends #7, cover app. only-#5	65.00	195.00	455.00
2	30.00	90.00	210.00
3	25.00	75.00	175.00
4,5	22.00	65.00	154.00
6-10: 8-U.S. Rangers begin	19.00	57.00	132.00
11,12-Commando Rangers app.	17.00	51.00	120.00
13-Commando Ranger begins-not same as Comm. Rangers	17.00	51.00	120.00
14-20	12.00	36.00	84.00
21-Intro/origin Firehair (begins)	15.00	45.00	105.00
22-30: 23-Kazanda begins, ends #28. 28-Origin Tiger Man. 30-Crusoe Island begins, ends #40	11.00	32.00	76.00
31-40: 33-Hypodermic panels	10.00	30.00	70.00
41-46	8.00	24.00	56.00
47-56-"Eisnerish" Dr. Drew by Grandenetti	9.00	27.00	62.00
57-60-Straight Dr. Drew by Grandenetti	6.50	19.50	45.00
61,62,64-66: 64-Suicide Smith begins	5.50	16.50	38.00
63-Used in **POP**, pgs. 85, 99	5.70	17.00	40.00
67-69: 67-Space Rangers begin, end #69	5.50	16.50	38.00

NOTE: *Bondage, discipline covers, lingerie panels are common. **Baker** a-36-38. **John Celardo** a-36-39. **Lee Elias** a-21-28. **Evans** a-19, 38-45, 47, 52. **Ingels** a-13-16. **Larsen***

Raggedy Ann and Andy #5, © DELL

Ramar of the Jungle #3, © CC

Rangers Comics #7, © FH

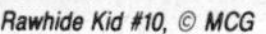

Rawhide Kid #10, © MCG

Real Clue Crime Stories V2#5, © HILL

Real Fact Comics #20, © DC

RANGERS COMICS (continued)
*a-34. **Bob Lubbers** a-30-38, 40, 42, 44. **Moreira** a-44, 45. **Tuska** a-16, 17, 19, 22.*

RANGO (TV)
August, 1967
Dell Publishing Co.

	Good	Fine	Mint
1-Photo-c	1.75	5.25	12.00

RAPHAEL (See Teenage Mutant Ninja Turtles)
1985 (One Shot)
Mirage Studios

1	.90	2.75	5.50
1-2nd printing; new-c & 8pgs.-a		.75	1.50

RATFINK (See Frantic & Zany)
October, 1964
Canrom, Inc.

1-Woodbridge-a	2.35	7.00	14.00

RAT PATROL, THE (TV)
March, 1967 - No. 5, Nov, 1967; No. 6, Oct, 1969
Dell Publishing Co.

1-Christopher George photo-c	3.00	9.00	21.00
2	2.00	6.00	14.00
3-6: 3-6-Photo-c	1.50	4.50	10.00

RAVEN, THE (See Movie Classics)

RAVENS AND RAINBOWS
Dec, 1983 (Baxter paper)
Pacific Comics

1-Jeff Jones-c/a(r); nudity scenes	.25	.75	1.50

RAWHIDE (TV)
Sept-Nov, 1959 - June-Aug, 1962; July, 1963 - No. 2, Jan, 1964
Dell Publishing Co./Gold Key

4-Color 1028	8.50	25.50	60.00
4-Color 1097,1160,1202,1261,1269	6.00	18.00	42.00
01-684-208(8/62-Dell)	5.70	17.00	40.00
1(10071-307, G.K.), 2	5.00	15.00	35.00

NOTE: *All have Clint Eastwood photo-c. **Tufts** a-1028.*

RAWHIDE KID
3/55 - No. 16, 9/57; No. 17, 8/60 - No. 151, 5/79
Atlas/Marvel Comics (CnPC No. 1-16/AMI No. 17-30)

1-Rawhide Kid, his horse Apache & sidekick Randy begin; Wyatt Earp app.	12.00	36.00	84.00
2	5.70	17.00	40.00
3-5	3.50	10.50	24.00
6,8-10	2.65	8.00	18.00
7-Williamson-a, 4 pgs.	3.50	10.50	24.00
11-15	1.70	5.00	12.00
16-Torres-a	2.15	6.50	15.00
17-Origin by J. Kirby	3.00	9.00	21.00
18-22,24-30	1.15	3.50	8.00
23-Origin by J. Kirby	2.65	8.00	18.00
31,32,36-44: 40-Two-Gun Kid x-over. 42-1st Larry Lieber issue	.85	2.50	6.00
33-35-Davis-a. 35-Intro & death of The Raven	1.30	4.00	9.00
45-Origin retold	1.50	4.50	10.00
46-Toth-a	1.50	4.50	10.00
47-70: 50-Kid Colt x-over. 64-Kid Colt story. 66-Two-Gun Kid story. 67-Kid Colt story	.70	2.00	4.00
71-85: 79-Williamson-a(r)	.35	1.00	2.00
86-Origin-r; Williamson-a r-/Ringo Kid No. 13, 4 pgs.	.40	1.25	2.50
87-99,101-115: Last new story	.25	.75	1.50
100-Origin retold & expanded	.30	.90	1.80
116-151	.25	.75	1.50
Special 1(9/71)-Reprints	.25	.75	1.50

NOTE: ***Ayers** a-16. **Colan** c-145p, 148p. **Davis** a-125r. **Everett** a-54i, 65, 66, 88, 96i, 148i(r). **Gulacy** c-147. **Heath** c-4. **G. Kane** c-101, 144. **Keller** a-5. **Kirby** a-17-32, 34, 42, 43, 84, 86, 92, 109r, 112r, 137r, Spec. 1; c-17-35, 40, 41, 43-47, 137. **Maneely** c-1, 2. **McWilliams** a-41. **Severin** a-16; c-8. **Torres** a-99r. **Williamson** a-95r, 111r.*

RAWHIDE KID
Aug, 1985 - No. 4, Nov, 1985 (mini-series)
Marvel Comics Group

	Good	Fine	Mint
1	.25	.70	1.40
2-4		.50	1.00

REAL ADVENTURE COMICS (Action Adventure #2 on)
April, 1955
Gillmor Magazines

1	1.50	4.50	10.00

REAL CLUE CRIME STORIES (Formerly Clue)
June, 1947 - V8No.3, May, 1953
Hillman Periodicals

V2#4(#1)-S&K c/a(3); Dan Barry-a	10.00	30.00	70.00
5-7-S&K c/a(3-4); 7-Iron Lady app.	8.50	25.50	60.00
8-12	1.85	5.50	13.00
V3#1-8,10-12, V4#1-8,11,12	1.60	4.70	11.00
9-Used in **SOTI**, pg. 102	4.60	14.00	32.00
V4#9,10-Krigstein-a	3.00	9.00	21.00
V5#1-5,7,8,10,12	1.15	3.50	8.00
6,9,11-Krigstein-a	2.35	7.00	16.00
V6#1-5,8,9,11	1.00	3.00	7.00
6,7,10,12-Krigstein-a. 10-Bondage-c	2.00	6.00	14.00
V7#1-3,5,7-11, V8#1-3	1.00	3.00	7.00
4,12-Krigstein-a	2.00	6.00	14.00
6-1 pg. Frazetta ad	1.15	3.50	8.00

NOTE: ***Barry** a-9, 10. **Briefer** a-V6#6. **Fuje** a- V2#11. **Infantino** a-V2#8. **Lawrence** a-V5#7. **Powell** a-V4#11, 12. V5#4,7 are 68 pgs.*

REAL EXPERIENCES (Formerly Tiny Tessie)
No. 25, January, 1950
Atlas Comics (20CC)

25	1.60	4.70	11.00

REAL FACT COMICS
Mar-Apr, 1946 - No. 21, July-Aug, 1949
National Periodical Publications

1-S&K-a; Harry Houdini sty; Just Imagine begins (not by Finlay)	17.00	51.00	120.00
2-S&K-a; Rin-Tin-Tin sty	10.00	30.00	70.00
3-H.G. Wells, Lon Chaney sty	5.00	15.00	35.00
4-Virgil Finlay-a on 'Just Imagine' begins, ends #12 (2 pgs. ea.); Jimmy Stewart sty	10.00	30.00	70.00
5-Batman/Robin-c; 5pg. story about creation of Batman & Robin	28.00	84.00	195.00
6-Origin & 1st app. Tommy Tomorrow by Finlay; Flag-c; 1st writing by Harlan Ellison (letter column, non-professional)	35.00	105.00	245.00
7-(No. 6 on inside)-Roussos-a	4.35	13.00	30.00
8-2nd app. Tommy Tomorrow by Finlay	20.00	60.00	140.00
9-S&K-a; Glenn Miller sty	7.00	21.00	50.00
10-Vigilante by Meskin	7.00	21.00	50.00
11,12: 11-Kinstler-a	4.35	13.00	30.00
13-Tommy Tomorrow cover/story	17.00	51.00	120.00
14,17,18	4.00	12.00	28.00
15-Nuclear Explosion part-c	4.35	13.00	30.00
16-Tommy Tomorrow app.; 1st Planeteers?	17.00	51.00	120.00
19-Sir Arthur Conan Doyle sty	4.00	12.00	28.00
20-Kubert-a, 4 pgs.	8.00	24.00	56.00
21-Kubert-a, 2 pgs.	4.00	12.00	28.00

NOTE: ***Roussos** a-1-4.*

REAL FUN OF DRIVING!!, THE
1965, 1967 (Regular size)

THE REAL FUN OF DRIVING (continued)
Chrysler Corp.

	Good	Fine	Mint
Shaffenberger-a, 12pgs.	.85	2.50	5.00

REAL FUNNIES
Jan, 1943 - No. 3, June, 1943
Nedor Publishing Co.

	Good	Fine	Mint
1-Funny animal, humor; Black Terrier app. (clone of The Black Terror)	9.00	27.00	62.00
2,3	4.35	13.00	30.00

REAL HEROES COMICS
Sept, 1941 - No. 16, Oct, 1946
Parents' Magazine Institute

	Good	Fine	Mint
1-Roosevelt c/story	9.00	27.00	62.00
2	3.50	10.50	24.00
3-5,7-10	2.65	8.00	18.00
6-Lou Gehrig c/sty	3.00	9.00	21.00
11-16: 13-Kiefer-a	1.85	5.50	13.00

REAL HIT
1944 (Savings Bond premium)
Fox Features Publications

	Good	Fine	Mint
1-Blue Beetle-r	8.00	24.00	56.00

NOTE: *Two versions exist, with and without covers. The coverless version has the title, No. 1 and price printed at top of splash page.*

REALISTIC ROMANCES
July-Aug, 1951 - No. 17, Aug-Sept, 1954 (no No. 9-14)
Realistic Comics/Avon Periodicals

	Good	Fine	Mint
1-Kinstler-a; c-/Avon paperback 211	8.50	25.50	60.00
2	4.00	12.00	28.00
3,4	3.35	10.00	23.00
5,8-Kinstler-a	3.65	11.00	25.00
6-c-Diversey Prize Novels 6; Kinstler-a	4.00	12.00	28.00
7-Evans-a?; c-/Avon paperback 360	4.00	12.00	28.00
15,17	2.65	8.00	18.00
16-Kinstler marijuana story-r/Romantic Love #6	5.00	15.00	35.00
I.W. Reprint #1,8,9	.45	.90	1.80

NOTE: ***Astarita** a-2-4,7,8.*

REAL LIFE COMICS
Sept, 1941 - No. 59, Sept, 1952
Nedor/Better/Standard Publ./Pictorial Magazine No. 13

	Good	Fine	Mint
1-Uncle Sam c/story	11.00	32.00	76.00
2	5.00	15.00	35.00
3-Hitler cover	7.00	21.00	50.00
4,5: 4-Story of American flag "Old Glory"	3.50	10.50	24.00
6-10	2.65	8.00	18.00
11-20: 17-Albert Einstein sty.	2.15	6.50	15.00
21-23,25,26,28-30	1.65	5.00	11.50
24-Story of Baseball	2.30	7.00	16.00
27-Schomburg A-Bomb-c; sty. of A-Bomb	3.50	10.50	24.00
31-33,35,36,42-44,48,49	1.30	4.00	9.00
34,37-41,45-47: 34-Jimmy Stewart sty. 37-Sty. of motion pictures; Bing Crosby sty. 38-Jane Froman sty. 39-"1,000,000 A.D." sty. 40-Bob Feller sty. 41-Jimmie Foxx sty.; "Home Run" Baker sty. 45-Sty. of Olympic games; Burl Ives sty. 46-Douglas Fairbanks Jr. & Sr. sty. 47-George Gershwin sty.	1.50	4.50	10.00
50-Frazetta-a, 5 pgs.	11.50	34.00	80.00
51-Jules Verne "Journey to the Moon" by Evans	5.00	15.00	35.00
52-Frazetta-a, 4 pgs.; Severin/Elder-a(2); Evans-a	12.00	36.00	84.00
53-57-Severin/Elder-a	3.00	9.00	21.00
58-Severin/Elder-a(2)	3.50	10.50	24.00
59-1pg. Frazetta; Severin/Elder-a	3.50	10.50	24.00

NOTE: *Some issues had two titles. **Guardineer** a-40(2), 44. **Schomburg** c-1, 2, 4, 5, 7, 11, 13-21, 23, 24, 26, 28, 30-32, 34-40, 42, 44-47.*

REAL LIFE SECRETS (Real Secrets #3 on)
Sept, 1949 - No. 2, Nov?, 1949
Ace Periodicals

	Good	Fine	Mint
1-Painted-c	3.00	9.00	21.00
2	1.50	4.50	10.00

REAL LIFE STORY OF FESS PARKER (Magazine)
1955
Dell Publishing Co.

	Good	Fine	Mint
1	5.00	15.00	35.00

REAL LIFE TALES OF SUSPENSE (See Suspense)

REAL LOVE (Formerly Hap Hazard)
No. 25, April, 1949 - No. 76, Nov, 1956
Ace Periodicals (A. A. Wyn)

	Good	Fine	Mint
25	3.50	10.50	24.00
26	1.70	5.00	12.00
27-L. B. Cole-a	3.00	9.00	21.00
28-35	1.15	3.50	8.00
36-66: 66-Last pre-code (2/55)	1.00	3.00	7.00
67-76	.75	2.25	5.00

NOTE: *Photo-c No. 50-76. Painted-c No. 46.*

REAL McCOYS, THE (TV)
No. 1071, 1-3/60 - 5-7/1962 (Photo-c)
Dell Publishing Co.

	Good	Fine	Mint
4-Color 1071-Toth-a	5.00	15.00	35.00
4-Color 1134-Toth-a	5.00	15.00	35.00
4-Color 1193,1265	4.35	13.00	30.00
01-689-207 (5-7/62)	3.50	10.50	24.00

REAL SCREEN COMICS (#1 titled Real Screen Funnies; TV Screen Cartoons #129-138)
Spring, 1945 - No. 128, May-June, 1959
National Periodical Publications

	Good	Fine	Mint
1-The Fox & the Crow, Flippity & Flop begin	48.00	145.00	335.00
2	24.00	72.00	170.00
3-5	13.00	40.00	90.00
6-10	9.50	28.50	65.00
11-20: 13-Crow x-over in Flippity & Flop	7.00	21.00	50.00
21-30	5.00	15.00	35.00
31-50	3.70	11.00	26.00
51-99	2.65	8.00	18.00
100	3.50	10.50	24.00
101-128	2.00	6.00	14.00

REAL SECRETS (Formerly Real Life Secrets)
No. 3, Jan, 1950 - No. 5, May, 1950
Ace Periodicals

	Good	Fine	Mint
3-Photo-c	3.00	9.00	21.00
4,5	1.60	4.70	11.00

REAL SPORTS COMICS (All Sports Comics #2 on)
Oct-Nov, 1948
Hillman Periodicals

	Good	Fine	Mint
1-12 pg. Powell-a	11.00	32.00	76.00

REAL WAR STORIES
July, 1987 - Present (52 pgs., $2.00, color)
Eclipse Comics

	Good	Fine	Mint
1-Bolland, Bissette, Totleben-a	.35	1.00	2.00

REAL WESTERN HERO (Formerly Wow #1-69; becomes Western Hero #76 on)
No. 70, Sept, 1948 - No. 75, Feb, 1949 (All 52 pgs.)
Fawcett Publications

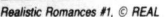

Realistic Romances #1, © REAL

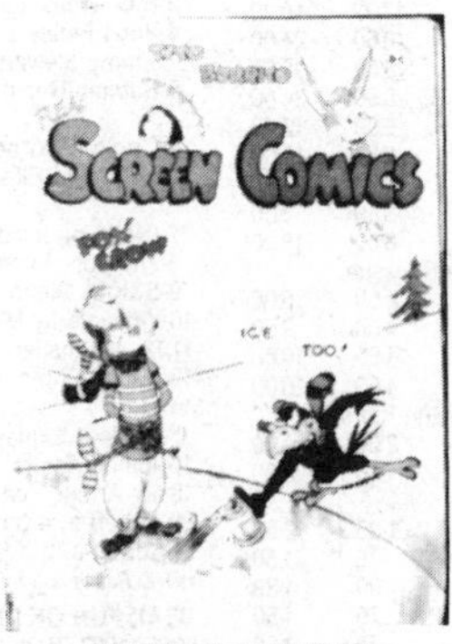

Real Screen Comics #5, © DC

Real Sports Comics #1, © HILL

Real Western Hero #74, © FAW

Red Band Comics #3, © Enwil Assoc.

Red Dragon Comics #1 ('47), © S & S

REAL WESTERN HERO (continued) — Good / Fine / Mint

70(#1)-Tom Mix, Monte Hale, Hopalong Cassidy, Young Falcon begin — 14.00 42.00 100.00
71-Gabby Hayes begins; Captain Tootsie by Beck — 10.00 30.00 70.00
72-75: 72-Captain Tootsie by Beck. 75-Big Bow and Little Arrow app. — 8.00 24.00 56.00

NOTE: *Painted/photo c-70-73; painted c-74,75.*

REAL WEST ROMANCES
4-5/49 - V1#6, 3/50; V2/1, Apr-May, 1950 (All 52 pgs. & photo-c)
Crestwood Publishing Co./Prize Publ.

V1#1-S&K-a(p) — 7.00 21.00 50.00
2-Spanking panel — 7.00 21.00 50.00
3-Kirby-a(p) only — 3.00 9.00 21.00
4-S&K-a; Whip Wilson, Reno Browne photo-c — 4.60 14.00 32.00
5-Audie Murphy, Gale Storm photo-c; S&K-a — 3.70 11.00 26.00
6-S&K-a — 3.70 11.00 26.00
V2#1-Kirby-a(p) — 3.00 9.00 21.00

NOTE: ***Meskin** a-V1#5. **Severin & Elder** a-V1#3-6, V2#1. **Leonard Starr** a-1-3. Photo-c V1#2-5, V2#1.*

REAP THE WILD WIND (See Cinema Comics Herald)

REBEL, THE (See 4-Color No. 1076,1138,1207,1262)

RECORD BOOK OF FAMOUS POLICE CASES
1949 (132 pages) (25 cents)
St. John Publishing Co.

nn-Kubert-a(3) r-/Son of Sinbad; Baker-c — 17.00 51.00 120.00

RED ARROW
May-June, 1951 - No. 3, Oct, 1951
P. L. Publishing Co.

1 — 3.00 9.00 21.00
2,3 — 1.70 5.00 12.00

RED BALL COMIC BOOK
1947 (Red Ball Shoes giveaway)
Parents' Magazine Institute

Reprints from True Comics — 1.50 4.50 10.00

RED BAND COMICS
Feb, 1945 - No. 4, May, 1945
Enwil Associates

1 — 8.50 25.50 60.00
2-Origin Boogeyman & Santanas — 7.00 21.00 50.00
3,4-Captain Wizard app. in both; identical contents in each — 6.00 18.00 42.00

RED CIRCLE COMICS
Jan, 1945 - No. 4, April, 1945
Rural Home Publications (Enwil)

1-The Prankster & Red Riot begin — 8.50 25.50 60.00
2-Starr-a; The Judge (costumed hero) app. — 6.50 19.50 45.00
3,4-Starr-a. 3-The Prankster not in costume; Starr-c — 4.35 13.00 30.00
4-(dated 4/45)-Leftover covers to #4 were later restapled over early 1950s coverless comics. Variations in the coverless comics used are endless; Woman Outlaws, Dorothy Lamour, Crime Does Not Not Pay, Sabu, Diary Loves, Love Confessions & Young Love V3/3 known — 4.00 12.00 28.00

RED CIRCLE SORCERY (Chilling Advs. in Sorcery #1-5)
No. 6, Apr, 1974 - No. 11, Feb, 1975
Red Circle Productions (Archie)

6-11 — .40 .80

NOTE: ***Chaykin** a-6, 10. **B. Jones** a-7(w/Wrightson, Kaluta, J. Jones). **McWilliams** a-10. **Morrow** a-6, 8, 11i; c-6-11. **Thorne** a-8, 10. **Toth** a-8, 9. **Wood** a-10.*

RED DRAGON COMICS (1st Series) (Trail Blazers #1-4)
No. 5, Jan, 1943 - No. 9, Jan, 1944
Street & Smith Publications — Good / Fine / Mint

5-Origin Red Rover, the Crimson Crimebuster; Rex King, Man of Adventure, Captain Jack Commando, & The Minute Man begin; text origin Red Dragon — 27.00 81.00 190.00
6-Origin The Black Crusader & Red Dragon (3/43) — 20.00 60.00 140.00
7 — 16.00 48.00 110.00
8-The Red Knight app. — 16.00 48.00 110.00
9-Origin Chuck Magnon, Immortal Man — 16.00 48.00 110.00

RED DRAGON COMICS (2nd Series)
Nov, 1947 - No. 6, Jan, 1949; No. 7, July, 1949
Street & Smith Publications

1-Red Dragon begins; Elliman, Nigel app.; Ed Cartier-c/a — 25.00 75.00 175.00
2-Cartier-c — 20.00 60.00 140.00
3-1st app. Dr. Neff by Powell; Elliman, Nigel app. — 16.00 48.00 110.00
4-Cartier c/a — 17.00 51.00 120.00
5-7 — 12.00 36.00 84.00

NOTE: ***Maneely** a-5,7. **Powell** a-2-7; c-3,5,7.*

REDDY GOOSE
No. 2, Jan, 1959 - No. 16, July, 1962 (Giveaway)
International Shoe Co. (Western Printing)

nn,2-16 — .50 1.50 3.00

REDDY KILOWATT (5 cents) (Also see Story of Edison)
1946 - No. 2, 1947; 1956 - 1960 (no month) (16 pgs.; paper cover)
Educational Comics (E. C.)

nn-Reddy Made Magic — 12.00 35.00 70.00
nn-Reddy Made Magic (1958) — 5.35 16.00 32.00
2-Edison, the Man Who Changed the World (¾" smaller than #1) — 12.00 35.00 70.00
...Comic Book 2 (1954)-"Light's Diamond Jubilee" — 6.75 20.00 40.00
...Comic Book 2 (1958)-"Wizard of Light," 16 pgs. — 5.35 16.00 32.00
...Comic Book 3 (1956)-"The Space Kite," 8 pgs.; Orlando story; regular size — 5.35 16.00 32.00
...Comic Book 3 (1960)-"The Space Kite," 8 pgs.; Orlando story; regular size — 4.75 14.00 28.00

NOTE: *Several copies surfaced in 1979.*

REDDY MADE MAGIC
1956, 1958 (16 pages) (paper cover)
Educational Comics (E. C.)

1-Reddy Kilowatt-r (splash panel changed) — 8.00 24.00 48.00
1 (1958 edition) — 5.00 15.00 30.00

RED EAGLE (See Feature Books No. 16, McKay)

REDEYE (See Comics Reading Libraries)

RED FOX (Manhunt #1-14)
1954
Magazine Enterprises

15(A-1 108)-Undercover Girl app.; L.B. Cole c/a (Red Fox); r-from Manhunt; Powell-a — 7.00 21.00 50.00

RED GOOSE COMIC SELECTIONS (See Comic Selections)

RED HAWK (See A-1 Comics No. 90)

RED ICEBERG, THE
1960 (10 cents) (16 pgs.) (Communist propaganda)
Impact Publ. (Catechetical Guild)

(Rare)-'We The People'-back-c — 37.00 110.00 240.00
2nd version-'Impact Press'-back-c — 43.00 130.00 280.00

THE RED ICEBERG (continued)

NOTE: *This book was the Guild's last anti-communist propaganda book and had very limited circulation. 3 - 4 copies surfaced in 1979 from the defunct publisher's files. Other copies do turn up.*

RED MASK (Formerly Tim Holt)
No. 42, 6-7/1954 - No. 53, 5/56; No. 54, 9/57
Magazine Enterprises No. 42-53/Sussex No. 54

	Good	Fine	Mint
42-Ghost Rider by Ayers continues, ends #50; Black Phantom continues; 3-D effect c/stories begin	11.00	32.00	76.00
43-3-D effect-c/stories	9.00	27.00	62.00
44-50-3-D effect stories only. 50-Last Ghost Rider	8.00	24.00	56.00
51-The Presto Kid begins by Ayers (1st app.); Presto Kid-c begins, ends #54; last 3-D effect story	8.00	24.00	56.00
52-Origin The Presto Kid	8.00	24.00	56.00
53,54-Last Black Phantom	5.00	15.00	35.00
I.W. Reprint #1 (r-/#52), 2,3 (r-/#51), 8 (nd; Kinstler-c)	.80	2.40	4.80

NOTE: ***Ayers*** *art on Ghost Rider & Presto Kid.* ***Bolle*** *art in all (Red Mask).* ***Guardineer*** *a-52.* ***Black Phantom*** *in #42-44, 47-50, 53, 54.*

RED MOUNTAIN FEATURING QUANTRELL'S RAIDERS
1952 (Movie) (Also see Jesse James #28)
Avon Periodicals

	Good	Fine	Mint
Alan Ladd; Kinstler c/a	14.00	42.00	100.00

"RED" RABBIT COMICS
Jan, 1947 - No. 22, Aug-Sept, 1951
Dearfield Comic/J. Charles Laue Publ. Co.

	Good	Fine	Mint
1	4.00	12.00	28.00
2	2.00	6.00	14.00
3-10	1.70	5.00	12.00
11-22	1.50	4.50	9.00

RED RAVEN COMICS (Human Torch #2 on)
August, 1940 (Also see Sub-Mariner #26, 2nd series)
Timely Comics

	Good	Fine	Mint
1-Origin Red Raven; Comet Pierce & Mercury by Kirby, The Human Top & The Eternal Brain; intro. Magar, the Mystic & only app.; Kirby-c	415.00	1245.00	2900.00

(Prices vary widely on this book)

RED RYDER COMICS (Hi Spot #2)(Movies, radio)
(Also see Crackajack Funnies)
9/40; No. 3, 8/41 - No. 5, 12/41; No. 6, 4/42 - No. 151, 4-6/57
Hawley Publ. No. 1-5/Dell Publishing Co.(K.K.) No. 6 on

	Good	Fine	Mint
1-Red Ryder, his horse Thunder, Little Beaver & his horse Papoose strip reprints begin by Fred Harman; 1st meeting of Red & Little Beaver; Harman line-drawn-c #1-85	75.00	225.00	525.00
3-(Scarce)-Alley Oop, King of the Royal Mtd., Capt. Easy, Freckles & His Friends, Dan Dunn strip-r begin	45.00	135.00	315.00
4,5	25.00	75.00	175.00
6-1st Dell issue	25.00	75.00	175.00
7-10	19.00	57.00	132.00
11-20	13.00	40.00	90.00
21-32-Last Alley Oop, Dan Dunn, Capt. Easy, Freckles	8.50	25.50	60.00
33-40 (52 pgs.)	5.50	16.50	38.00
41 (52 pgs.)-Rocky Lane photo back-c; photo back-c begin, end #57	6.00	18.00	42.00
42-46 (52 pgs.). 46-Last Red Ryder strip-r	5.00	15.00	35.00
47-53 (52 pgs.). 47-New stories on Red Ryder begin	4.00	12.00	28.00
54-57 (36 pgs.)	3.50	10.50	24.00
58-73 (36 pgs.). 73-Last King of the Royal Mtd. strip-r by Jim Gary	3.00	9.00	21.00
74-85,93 (52 pgs.)-Harman line-drawn-c	3.50	10.50	24.00
86-92 (52 pgs.)-Harman painted-c	3.50	10.50	24.00
94-96 (36 pgs.)-Harman painted-c	2.15	6.50	15.00
97,98,107,108 (36 pgs.)-Harman line-drawn-c	2.15	6.50	15.00
99,101-106 (36 pgs.)-Jim Bannon Photo-c	2.15	6.50	15.00
100 (36 pgs.)-Bannon photo-c	2.65	8.00	18.00
109-118 (52 pgs.)-Harman line-drawn-c	1.85	5.50	13.00
119-129 (52 pgs.). 119-Painted-c begin, not by Harman, end #151	1.60	4.70	11.00
130-144 (36 pgs., #130-on)	1.50	4.50	10.00
145-148: 145-Title change to Red Ryder Ranch Magazine with photos	1.30	4.00	9.00
149-151: 149-Title changed to Red Ryder Ranch Comics	1.30	4.00	9.00
4-Color 916 (7/58)	1.60	4.70	11.00
Buster Brown Shoes Giveaway (1941, 32pgs., color, soft-c)	17.00	52.00	120.00
Red Ryder Super Book Of Comics 10 (1944; paper-c; 32 pgs.; blank back-c)-Magic Morro app.	17.00	52.00	120.00
Red Ryder Victory Patrol-nn(1944, 32 pgs.)-r-/#43,44; comic has a paper-c & is stapled inside a triple cardboard fold-out-c; contains membership card, decoder, map of R.R. home range, etc. Herky app. (Langendorf Bread giveaway; sub-titled 'Super Book of Comics')	30.00	90.00	210.00
Wells Lamont Corp. giveaway (1950)-16 pgs. in color; regular size; paper-c; 1941-r	17.00	52.00	120.00

NOTE: ***Fred Harman*** *a-1-99; c-1-98, 107-118. Don Red Barry, Allan Rocky Lane, Wild Bill Elliott & Jim Bannon starred as Red Ryder in the movies. Robert Blake starred as Little Beaver.*

RED RYDER PAINT BOOK
1941 (148 pages) (8½x11½")
Whitman Publishing Co.

	Good	Fine	Mint
Reprints 1940 daily strips	13.00	40.00	90.00

RED SEAL COMICS
10/45 - No. 18, 10/46; No. 19, 6/47 - No. 22, 12/47
Harry 'A' Chesler/Superior Publ. No. 19 on

	Good	Fine	Mint
14-The Black Dwarf begins; Little Nemo app; bondage/hypo-c; Tuska-a	16.00	48.00	110.00
15-Torture story	13.00	40.00	90.00
16-Used in **SOTI**, pg. 181, illo-"Outside the forbidden pages of de Sade, you find draining a girl's blood only in children's comics;" drug club story r-later in Crime Reporter #1; Veiled Avenger & Barry Kuda app; Tuska-a	19.00	57.00	132.00
17-Lady Satan, Yankee Girl & Sky Chief app; Tuska-a	11.00	32.00	76.00
18,20-Lady Satan & Sky Chief app.	11.00	32.00	76.00
19-No Black Dwarf-on cover only; Zor, El Tigre app.	9.00	27.00	62.00
21-Lady Satan & Black Dwarf app.	9.00	27.00	62.00
22-Zor, Rocketman app.	9.00	27.00	62.00

REDSKIN (Famous Western Badmen #13 on)
Sept, 1950 - No. 12, Oct, 1952
Youthful Magazines

	Good	Fine	Mint
1	3.50	10.50	24.00
2	2.00	6.00	14.00
3-12: 6,12-Bondage-c	1.70	5.00	12.00

RED SONJA (Also see Conan #23 & Marvel Feature)
1/77 - No. 15, 5/79; V1/1, 2/83 - V2/2, 3/83;
V3/1, 8/83 - V3/4, 2/84; V3/5, 1/85 - V3/13, 1986
Marvel Comics Group

	Good	Fine	Mint
1	.35	1.10	2.20
2-5	.30	.80	1.60
6-10		.40	.80
11-15, V1#1,V2#2		30	.60
V3#1,2 ($1.00)		.50	1.00

Red Mask #51, © ME

Red Ryder Comics #5, © DELL

Red Seal Comics #20, © SUPR

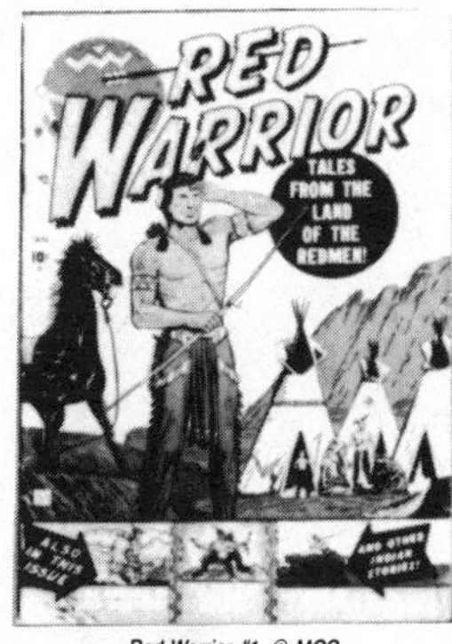

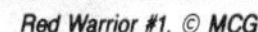
Red Warrior #1, © MCG

Reese's Pieces #1, © Eclipse Comics

Return of the Outlaw #4, © TOBY

RED SONJA (continued)

	Good	Fine	Mint
V3#3-13 (65-75 cents)		.35	.70

NOTE: ***Brunner** c-12-14. **J. Buscema** a(p)-12, 13, 15; c-V1No.1. **Nebres** a-V3/3i. **N. Redondo** a-8i, V3/2i, 3i. **Simonson** a-V3No.1. **Thorne** a-1-11; c-1-11.*

RED SONJA: THE MOVIE
Nov, 1985 - No. 2, Dec, 1985 (limited-series)
Marvel Comics Group

	Good	Fine	Mint
1,2-Movie adapt-r		.40	.80

RED TORNADO
July, 1985 - No. 4, Oct, 1985 (mini-series)
DC Comics

	Good	Fine	Mint
1-4		.40	.80

RED WARRIOR
Jan, 1951 - No. 6, Dec, 1951
Marvel/Atlas Comics (TCI)

	Good	Fine	Mint
1-Tuska-a	4.00	12.00	28.00
2	2.30	7.00	16.00
3-6: 4-Origin White Wing, his horse	2.00	6.00	14.00

RED WOLF
May, 1972 - No. 9, Sept, 1973
Marvel Comics Group

	Good	Fine	Mint
1-Kane/Severin-c		.30	.60
2-9: 9-Origin sidekick, Lobo (wolf)		.25	.50

NOTE: ***G. Kane** c-1p, 2.*

REESE'S PIECES
Oct, 1985 - No. 2, Oct, 1985
Eclipse Comics

	Good	Fine	Mint
1,2-B&W-r in color	.30	.90	1.80

REFORM SCHOOL GIRL!
1951
Realistic Comics

	Good	Fine	Mint
nn-Used in **SOTI**, pg. 358, & cover ill. with caption "Comic books are supposed to be like fairy tales"	107.00	321.00	750.00

(Prices vary widely on this book)

NOTE: *The cover and title originated from a digest-sized book published by Diversey Publishing Co. of Chicago in 1948. The original book "House of Fury," Doubleday, came out in 1941. The girl's real name which appears on the cover of the digest and comic is Marty Collins, Canadian model and ice skating star who posed for this special color photograph for the Diversey novel.*

REGGIE (Formerly Archie's Rival. . .; Reggie & Me #19 on)
No. 15, Sept, 1963 - No. 18, Nov, 1965
Archie Publications

	Good	Fine	Mint
15(9/63), 16(10/64)	3.35	10.00	20.00
17(8/65), 18(11/65)	3.35	10.00	20.00

NOTE: *Cover title No. 15,16 is Archie's Rival. . . .*

REGGIE AND ME (Formerly Reggie)
No. 19, 8/66 - No. 126, 9/80 (No. 50-68: 52 pgs.)
Archie Publications

	Good	Fine	Mint
19-Evilheart app.	1.70	5.00	10.00
20-23-Evilheart app.; with Pureheart #22	.85	2.50	5.00
24-40	.35	1.00	2.00
41-60		.40	.80
61-126		.25	.50

REGGIE'S JOKES (See Reggie's Wise Guy Jokes)

REGGIE'S WISE GUY JOKES
Aug, 1968 - No. 60, Jan, 1982 (No. 5 on are Giants)
Archie Publications

	Good	Fine	Mint
1	1.70	5.00	10.00
2-4	.75	2.25	4.50
5-10	.25	.75	1.50
11-28		.40	.80

	Good	Fine	Mint
29-60		.25	.50

REGISTERED NURSE
Summer, 1963
Charlton Comics

	Good	Fine	Mint
1-Reprints Nurse Betsy Crane & Cynthia Doyle	.35	1.00	2.00

REG'LAR FELLERS (See Treasure Box of. . .)
1921 - 1929
Cupples & Leon Co./MS Publishng Co.

	Good	Fine	Mint
1(1921)-52 pgs. B&W dailies (Cupples & Leon, 10x10")	8.00	24.00	56.00
1925, 48 pgs. B&W dailies (MS Publ.)	8.00	24.00	56.00
Softcover (1929, nn, 36 pgs.)	8.00	24.00	56.00
Hardcover (1929)-B&W reprints, 96 pgs.	8.50	25.50	60.00

REG'LAR FELLERS
No. 5, Nov, 1947 - No. 6, Mar, 1948
Visual Editions (Standard)

	Good	Fine	Mint
5,6	3.00	9.00	21.00

REG'LAR FELLERS HEROIC (See Heroic)

RELUCTANT DRAGON, THE (See 4-Color No. 13)

REMEMBER PEARL HARBOR
1942 (68 pages)
Street & Smith Publications

	Good	Fine	Mint
nn	17.00	51.00	120.00

RENO BROWNE, HOLLYWOOD'S GREATEST COWGIRL (Formerly Margie; Apache Kid #53 on)
No. 50, April, 1950 - No. 52, Sept, 1950
Marvel Comics (MPC)

	Good	Fine	Mint
50	8.00	24.00	56.00
51,52	6.50	19.50	45.00

REPTILICUS (Reptisaurus #3 on)
Aug, 1961 - No. 2, Oct, 1961
Charlton Comics

	Good	Fine	Mint
1 (Movie)	4.00	12.00	28.00
2	2.65	8.00	18.00

REPTISAURUS (Reptilicus #1,2)
Jan, 1962 - No. 8, Dec, 1962; Summer, 1963
Charlton Comics

	Good	Fine	Mint
V2#3-8: 8-Montes/Bache c/a	1.50	4.50	10.00
Special Edition 1 (1963)	1.50	4.50	10.00

RESCUERS, THE (See Walt Disney Showcase No. 40)

RESTLESS GUN (See 4-Color No. 934,986,1045,1089,1146)

RETURN FROM WITCH MOUNTAIN (See Wald Disney Showcase #44)

RETURN OF GORGO, THE (Formerly Gorgo's Revenge)
No. 2, Summer, 1963 - No. 3, Fall, 1964
Charlton Comics

	Good	Fine	Mint
2,3-Ditko-a, c-#3	2.65	8.00	18.00

RETURN OF KONGA, THE (Konga's Revenge #2 on)
1962
Charlton Comics

	Good	Fine	Mint
nn	2.30	7.00	16.00

RETURN OF THE OUTLAW
Feb, 1953 - No. 11, 1955
Toby Press (Minoan)

	Good	Fine	Mint
1-Billy the Kid	3.00	9.00	21.00
2	1.50	4.50	10.00
3-11	1.15	3.50	8.00

REVEALING LOVE STORIES (See Fox Giants)

REVEALING ROMANCES
Sept, 1949 - No. 6, Aug, 1950
Ace Magazines

	Good	Fine	Mint
1	3.00	9.00	21.00
2	1.50	4.50	10.00
3-6	1.15	3.50	8.00

REVENGERS, THE (Featuring Armor And Silverstreak)
Sept, 1985 ($2.00); 1987
Continuity Comics

1-Origin; Adams c/a	.35	1.00	2.00
1-Newsstand, 1987, $2.00	.35	1.00	2.00

REVENGERS STARRING MEGALITH
Sept, 1985
Continuity Comics

1-Adams c/a, scripts	.35	1.00	2.00

REX ALLEN COMICS (Movie star)(Also see 4-Color #877 & Western Roundup)
No. 316, Feb, 1951 - No. 31, Dec-Feb, 1958-59 (All-photo-c)
Dell Publishing Co.

4-Color 316(#1)(52 pgs.)-Rex Allen & his horse Koko begin; Marsh-a	8.50	25.50	60.00
2 (9-11/51, 36 pgs.)	5.00	15.00	35.00
3-10	4.35	13.00	30.00
11-20	3.50	10.50	24.00
21-23,25-31	3.00	9.00	21.00
24-Toth-a	4.00	12.00	28.00

NOTE: ***Manning*** *a-20,27-30. Photo back-c 316,2-12,20,21.*

REX DEXTER OF MARS (See Mystery Men Comics)
Fall, 1940
Fox Features Syndicate

1-Rex Dexter, Patty O'Day, & Zanzibar (Tuska-a) app.; Briefer-c/a	62.00	185.00	435.00

REX HART (Formerly Blaze Carson; Whip Wilson #9 on)
No. 6, Aug, 1949 - No. 8, Feb, 1950 (All photo-c)
Timely/Marvel Comics (USA)

6-Rex Hart & his horse Warrior begin; Black Rider app; Captain Tootsie by Beck	6.00	18.00	42.00
7,8: 18pg. Thriller in each. 8-Blaze the Wonder Collie app. in text	5.00	15.00	35.00

REX MORGAN, M.D. (Also see Harvey Comics Library)
Dec, 1955 - No. 3, 1956
Argo Publ.

1-Reprints Rex Morgan daily newspaper strips & daily panel-r of "These Women" by D'Alessio & "Timeout" by Jeff Keate	4.35	13.00	30.00
2,3	2.65	8.00	18.00

REX THE WONDER DOG (See The Adventures of. . .)

RHUBARB, THE MILLIONAIRE CAT (See 4-Color No. 423,466,563)

RIBTICKLER (Also see Fox Giants)
1945 - No. 9, Aug, 1947; 1957 - 1959
Fox Features Synd./Green Publ. (1957)/Norlen (1959)

1	3.00	9.00	21.00
2	1.50	4.50	10.00
3-9: 7-Cosmo Cat app.	1.15	3.50	8.00
3,7,8 (Green Publ.-1957)	.75	2.25	5.00
3,7,8 (Norlen Mag.-1959)	.75	2.25	5.00

RICHARD DRAGON, KUNG-FU FIGHTER (See Brave & the Bold)
Apr-May, 1975 - No. 18, Nov-Dec, 1977
National Periodical Publications/DC Comics

	Good	Fine	Mint
1,2: 2-Starlin-a(p). 3-Kirby-c; a(p).		.45	.90
3-18: 4-8-Wood inks		.30	.60

RICHARD THE LION-HEARTED (See Ideal a Classic. . .)

RICHIE RICH (See Harvey Collectors Comics, Harvey Hits, Little Dot, Little Lotta, Little Sad Sack, Mutt & Jeff, Super Richie, and 3-D Dolly)

RICHIE RICH (. . .the Poor Little Rich Boy) (See Harvey Hits #3,9)
11/60 - No. 218, 10/82; No. 219, 10/86 - Present
Harvey Publications

1-(See Little Dot for 1st app.)	90.00	250.00	440.00
2	40.00	100.00	180.00
3-5	20.00	60.00	120.00
6-10: 8-Christmas-c	12.50	37.50	75.00
11-20	5.35	16.00	32.00
21-40	3.00	9.00	18.00
41-60	2.00	6.00	12.00
61-80: 65-1st app. Dollar the Dog	1.20	3.50	7.00
81-100	.70	2.00	4.00
101-120	.50	1.50	3.00
121-140	.40	1.25	2.50
141-160: 145-Infinity-c	.35	1.00	2.00
161-180	.25	.75	1.50
181-200		.50	1.00
201-234		.40	.75

RICHIE RICH AND. . .
Oct, 1987 - Present
Harvey Comics

1,2 (75 cents)		.40	.75
3,4 ($1.00)		.50	1.00

RICHIE RICH AND BILLY BELLHOPS
October, 1977 (One Shot) (52pgs.)
Harvey Publications

1	.50	1.50	3.00

RICHIE RICH AND CADBURY
10/77; No. 2, 9/78 - No. 23, 7/82 (No. 1-10, 52pgs.)
Harvey Publications

1	.70	2.00	4.00
2-5	.35	1.00	2.00
6-10		.50	1.00
11-23		.40	.80

RICHIE RICH AND CASPER
Aug, 1974 - No. 45, Sept, 1982
Harvey Publications

1	1.15	3.50	7.00
2-5	.50	1.50	3.00
6-10: 10-X-Mas-c	.35	1.00	2.00
11-20		.50	1.00
21-40		.40	.80
41-45		.30	.60

RICHIE RICH AND DOLLAR THE DOG
9/77 - No. 24, 8/82 (No. 1-10, 52pgs.)
Harvey Publications

1	.70	2.00	4.00
2-5	.35	1.00	2.00
6-24		.50	1.00

RICHIE RICH AND DOT
October, 1974 (One Shot)
Harvey Publications

1	1.00	3.00	6.00

RICHIE RICH AND GLORIA
Sept, 1977 - No. 25, Sept, 1982 (No. 1-11, 52pgs.)

Rex Allen Comics #12, © DELL

Ribtickler #1, © FOX

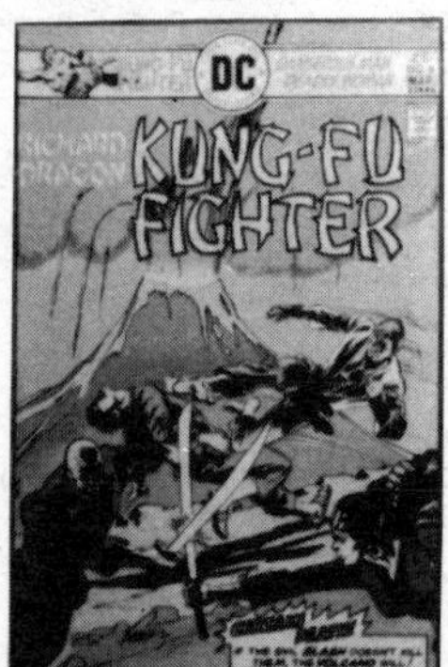

Richard Dragon, Kung-Fu Fighter #6, © DC

Richie Rich #2, © HARV

Richie Rich Millions #22, © HARV

Richie Rich Success Stories #17, © HARV

RICHIE RICH AND GLORIA (continued)
Harvey Publications

	Good	Fine	Mint
1	.70	2.00	4.00
2-5	.35	1.00	2.00
6-25		.40	.80

RICHIE RICH AND HIS GIRLFRIENDS
April, 1979 - No. 16, Dec, 1982
Harvey Publications

	Good	Fine	Mint
1	.50	1.50	3.00
2-10	.35	1.00	2.00
11-16		.40	.80

RICHIE RICH AND HIS MEAN COUSIN REGGIE
April, 1979 - No. 4, Apr?, 1980 (50 cents) (No. 1,2-52pgs.)
Harvey Publications

	Good	Fine	Mint
1	.35	1.00	2.00
2-4	.25	.75	1.50

RICHIE RICH AND JACKIE JOKERS
Nov, 1973 - No. 48, Dec, 1982
Harvey Publications

	Good	Fine	Mint
1	1.70	5.00	10.00
2-5	.85	2.50	5.00
6-10	.50	1.50	3.00
11-20	.35	1.00	2.00
21-40		.50	1.00
41-48		.40	.80

RICHIE RICH AND TIMMY TIME
Sept, 1977 (50 Cents) (One Shot) (52 pages)
Harvey Publications

	Good	Fine	Mint
1	.50	1.50	3.00

RICHIE RICH BANK BOOKS
Oct, 1972 - No. 59, Sept, 1982
Harvey Publications

	Good	Fine	Mint
1	2.00	6.00	12.00
2-5	1.00	3.00	6.00
6-10	.70	2.00	4.00
11-20	.50	1.50	3.00
21-30	.35	1.00	2.00
31-40		.50	1.00
41-59		.40	.80

RICHIE RICH BEST OF THE YEARS
Oct, 1977 - No. 6, June, 1980 (Digest) (128 pages)
Harvey Publications

	Good	Fine	Mint
1(10/77)-Reprints, #2(10/78)-Reprints, #3(6/79-75 cents)	.35	1.00	2.00
4-6(11/79-6/80-95 cents)		.50	1.00

RICHIE RICH BILLIONS
10/74 - No. 48, 10/82 (No. 1-33, 52pgs.)
Harvey Publications

	Good	Fine	Mint
1	1.70	5.00	10.00
2-5	.85	2.50	5.00
6-10	.70	2.00	4.00
11-20	.35	1.00	2.00
21-30		.50	1.00
31-48		.40	.80

RICHIE RICH CASH
Sept, 1974 - No. 47, Aug, 1982
Harvey Publications

	Good	Fine	Mint
1	1.70	5.00	10.00
2-5	.85	2.50	5.00
6-10	.50	1.50	3.00
11-20	.35	1.00	2.00
21-30		.50	1.00
31-47		.40	.80

RICHIE RICH, CASPER & WENDY NATIONAL LEAGUE
June, 1976 (52 pages)
Harvey Publications

	Good	Fine	Mint
1	.70	2.00	3.00

RICHIE RICH COLLECTORS COMICS (See Harvey Coll. Comics)

RICHIE RICH DIAMONDS
8/72 - No. 59, 8/82 (No. 1-12,23-45, 52pgs.)
Harvey Publications

	Good	Fine	Mint
1	2.65	8.00	16.00
2-5	1.00	3.00	6.00
6-10	.70	2.00	4.00
11-20	.50	1.50	3.00
21-30	.35	1.00	2.00
31-40: 39-Origin Little Dot		.50	1.00
41-50		.40	.80
51-59		.30	.60

RICHIE RICH DIGEST
Oct, 1986 - Present ($1.25, digest-size)
Harvey Publications

	Good	Fine	Mint
1-12		.60	1.25

RICHIE RICH DIGEST STORIES (. . . Magazine No. ?-on)
10/77 - No. 17, 10/82 (Digest) (132 pages) (75-95 cents)
Harvey Publications

	Good	Fine	Mint
1-Reprints	.30	.80	1.60
2-17: 4-Infinity-c		.40	.80

RICHIE RICH DIGEST WINNERS
12/77 - No. 16, 9/82 (Digest) (132 pages) (75-95 Cents)
Harvey Publications

	Good	Fine	Mint
1	.30	.80	1.60
2-16		.40	.80

RICHIE RICH DOLLARS & CENTS
8/63 - No. 109, 8/82 (No. 1-61,72-94, 52pgs.)
Harvey Publications

	Good	Fine	Mint
1	8.00	24.00	56.00
2	4.00	12.00	24.00
3-5	2.35	7.00	14.00
6-10	1.70	5.00	10.00
11-20: #11-68 pgs.	1.35	4.00	8.00
21-30	.85	2.50	5.00
31-50	.50	1.50	3.00
51-70	.35	1.00	2.00
71-90 (Early issues are reprints)		.50	1.00
91-99,101-109		.40	.80
100-Anniversary issue		.40	.80

RICHIE RICH FORTUNES
Sept, 1971 - No. 63, July, 1982 (No. 1-17, 52pgs.)
Harvey Publications

	Good	Fine	Mint
1	2.35	7.00	16.00
2-5	1.15	3.50	7.00
6-10	.85	2.50	5.00
11-20	.70	2.00	4.00
21-30	.35	1.00	2.00
31-40		.50	1.00
41-63		.40	.80

RICHIE RICH GEMS
Sept, 1974 - No. 43, Sept, 1982
Harvey Publications

	Good	Fine	Mint
1	1.70	5.00	10.00

RICHIE RICH GEMS (continued)

	Good	Fine	Mint
2-5	.85	2.50	5.00
6-10	.50	1.50	3.00
11-20	.35	1.00	2.00
21-30		.50	1.00
31-43		.40	.80

RICHIE RICH GOLD AND SILVER
Sept, 1975 - No. 42, Oct, 1982 (No. 1-27, 52pgs.)
Harvey Publications

	Good	Fine	Mint
1	1.35	4.00	8.00
2-5	.70	2.00	4.00
6-10	.35	1.00	2.00
11-20		.50	1.00
21-42		.40	.80

RICHIE RICH HOLIDAY DIGEST MAGAZINE
January, 1980 - No. 3, Jan, 1982
Harvey Publications

	Good	Fine	Mint
1-3: All X-Mas-c		.50	1.00

RICHIE RICH INVENTIONS
Oct, 1977 - No. 26, Oct, 1982 (No. 1-11, 52pgs.)
Harvey Publications

	Good	Fine	Mint
1	.70	2.00	4.00
2-5	.35	1.00	2.00
6-10		.50	1.00
11-26		.40	.80

RICHIE RICH JACKPOTS
Oct, 1972 - No. 58, Aug, 1982 (No. 41-43, 52pgs.)
Harvey Publications

	Good	Fine	Mint
1	2.00	6.00	12.00
2-5	1.00	3.00	6.00
6-10	.70	2.00	4.00
11-20	.35	1.00	2.00
21-30	.25	.75	1.50
31-50		.50	1.00
51-58		.40	.80

RICHIE RICH MILLION DOLLAR DIGEST (. . . Magazine No. ?-on)
October, 1980 - No. 10, Oct, 1982
Harvey Publications

	Good	Fine	Mint
1-10		.50	1.00

RICHIE RICH MILLION $ DIGEST
1986 - Present ($1.25, digest-size)
Harvey Publications

	Good	Fine	Mint
1-8		.60	1.25

RICHIE RICH MILLIONS
9/61; No. 2, 9/62 - No. 113, 10/82 (No. 1-66,52-68pgs.; 85-97, 52pgs.)
Harvey Publications

	Good	Fine	Mint
1	10.00	30.00	70.00
2	5.00	15.00	35.00
3-10	3.35	10.00	23.00
11-20	1.70	5.00	12.00
21-30	1.00	3.00	6.00
31-40	.80	2.30	4.60
41-50	.50	1.50	3.00
51-70	.35	1.00	2.00
71-90	.30	.80	1.60
91-100 (Early issues are reprints)		.50	1.00
101-113		.40	.80

RICHIE RICH MONEY WORLD
Sept, 1972 - No. 59, Sept, 1982
Harvey Publications

	Good	Fine	Mint
1	2.35	7.00	14.00
2-5	1.00	3.00	6.00
6-10: 9,10-R. Rich mistakenly named Little Lotta on covers	.50	1.50	3.00
11-20	.35	1.10	2.20
21-30	.25	.75	1.50
31-50		.50	1.00
51-59		.40	.80

RICHIE RICH PROFITS
Oct, 1974 - No. 47, Sept, 1982
Harvey Publications

	Good	Fine	Mint
1	2.00	6.00	12.00
2-5	1.00	3.00	6.00
6-10	.50	1.50	3.00
11-20	.35	1.00	2.00
21-30		.50	1.00
31-47		.40	.80

RICHIE RICH RELICS
1988 - Present
Harvey Comics

	Good	Fine	Mint
1		.40	.75

RICHIE RICH RICHES
7/72 - No. 59, 8/82 (No. 1-13, 41-45, 52pgs.)
Harvey Publications

	Good	Fine	Mint
1	2.00	6.00	12.00
2-5	1.00	3.00	6.00
6-10	.50	1.50	3.00
11-20	.35	1.00	2.00
21-40		.50	1.00
41-59		.40	.80

RICHIE RICH SUCCESS STORIES
11/64 - No. 105, 9/82 (No. 1-16,18-56, 67-90, 52pgs; 17-68pgs..)
Harvey Publications

	Good	Fine	Mint
1	8.00	24.00	56.00
2-5	3.00	9.00	21.00
6-10	2.00	6.00	12.00
11-30: 27-1st Penny Van Dough (8/69)	1.00	3.00	6.00
31-50	.50	1.50	3.00
51-70	.35	1.00	2.00
71-90 (Early issues are reprints)		.50	1.00
91-105		.40	.80

RICHIE RICH TREASURE CHEST DIGEST (. . . Mag. #3)
4/82 - No. 3, 8/82 (95 Cents, Digest Magazine)
Harvey Publications

	Good	Fine	Mint
1-3		.50	1.00

RICHIE RICH VACATIONS DIGEST
11/77; No. 2, 10/78 - No. 7, 10/81; No. 8, 8/82 (Digest, 132 pgs.)
Harvey Publications

	Good	Fine	Mint
1-Reprints	.30	.80	1.60
2-8		.50	1.00

RICHIE RICH VAULTS OF MYSTERY
Nov, 1974 - No. 47, Sept, 1982
Harvey Publications

	Good	Fine	Mint
1	1.50	4.50	9.00
2-10	.70	2.00	4.00
11-20	.35	1.00	2.00
21-30	.25	.75	1.50
31-47		.40	.80

RICHIE RICH ZILLIONZ
10/76 - No. 33, 9/82 (No. 1-4, 68pgs.; No. 5-18, 52pgs.)
Harvey Publications

	Good	Fine	Mint
1	1.35	4.00	8.00
2-5	.70	2.00	4.00
6-10	.35	1.00	2.00
11-20		.50	1.00
21-33		.40	.80

RICKY
September, 1953
Standard Comics (Visual Editions)

	Good	Fine	Mint
5	1.15	3.50	8.00

RICKY NELSON (TV)(See Sweethearts V2#42)
No. 956, 12/58 - No. 1192, 6/61 (All photo-c)
Dell Publishing Co.

	Good	Fine	Mint
4-Color 956,998	8.50	25.50	60.00
4-Color 1115,1192-Manning-a	8.50	25.50	60.00

RIDER, THE (Frontier Trail #6)
March, 1957 - No. 5, 1958
Ajax/Farrell Publ. (Four Star Comic Corp.)

	Good	Fine	Mint
1-Swift Arrow, Lone Rider begin	2.65	8.00	18.00
2-5	1.30	4.00	9.00

RIFLEMAN, THE (TV)
No. 1009, 7-9/59 - No. 12, 7-9/62; No. 13, 11/62 - No. 20, 10/64
Dell Publ. Co./Gold Key No. 13 on

	Good	Fine	Mint
4-Color 1009	6.00	18.00	42.00
2 (1-3/60)	4.60	14.00	32.00
3-Toth-a, 4 pgs.	5.70	17.00	40.00
4,5,7-10	3.50	10.50	24.00
6-Toth-a, 4pgs.	4.00	12.00	28.00
11-20	3.00	9.00	21.00

NOTE: ***Warren Tufts*** *a-2-9. All have photo-c. Photo back-c, No. 13-15.*

RIMA, THE JUNGLE GIRL
Apr-May, 1974 - No. 7, Apr-May, 1975
National Periodical Publications

	Good	Fine	Mint
1-Origin, part 1		.60	1.20
2-4-Origin, part 2,3,&4		.40	.80
5-7: 7-Origin & only app. Space Marshal		.30	.60

NOTE: ***Kubert*** *c-1-7.* ***Nino*** *a-1-5.* ***Redondo*** *a-1-6.*

RING OF BRIGHT WATER (See Movie Classics)

RINGO KID, THE (2nd Series)
1/70 - No. 23, 11/73; No. 24, 11/75 - No. 30, 11/76
Marvel Comics Group

	Good	Fine	Mint
1(1970)-Williamson-a r-from #10, 1956		.40	.80

Ringo Kid Western #7, © MCG

Rin Tin Tin #12, © Screen Gems

Ripley's Believe It Or Not! #53, © GK

THE RINGO KID (continued)

	Good	Fine	Mint
2-30: 20-Williamson-r/#1		.25	.50

NOTE: ***Wildey*** *a-13r.*

RINGO KID WESTERN, THE (1st Series)(See Wild Western)
Aug, 1954 - No. 21, Sept, 1957
Atlas Comics (HPC)/Marvel Comics

	Good	Fine	Mint
1-Origin; The Ringo Kid & his horse Arab begin	5.70	17.00	40.00
2-Black Rider app.	3.00	9.00	21.00
3-5	2.00	6.00	14.00
6-8-Severin-a(3) each	3.00	9.00	21.00
9,11,14-21	1.30	4.00	9.00
10,13-Williamson-a, 4 pgs.	3.35	10.00	23.00
12-Orlando-a, 4 pgs.	1.70	5.00	12.00

NOTE: ***Berg*** *a-8.* ***Maneely*** *a-1, 4, 5, 15, 18, 20, 21; c-1, 6, 13, 15, 16, 18, 20.* ***J. Severin*** *c-10, 11.* ***Sinnott*** *a-1.* ***Wildey*** *a-16-18.*

RIN TIN TIN (See March of Comics No. 163,180,195)

RIN TIN TIN (TV) (. . & Rusty #21 on; see Western Roundup)
Nov, 1952 - No. 38, May-July, 1961; 1963 (All Photo-c)
Dell Publishing Co./Gold Key

	Good	Fine	Mint
4-Color 434 (#1)	4.00	12.00	28.00
4-Color 476,523	3.00	9.00	21.00
4(3-5/54)-10	2.65	8.00	18.00
11-20	2.00	6.00	14.00
21-38	1.70	5.00	12.00
1(11/63-G.K.) . . . & Rusty	1.70	5.00	12.00

RIO
June, 1987 (64 pgs., $8.95, color)
Comico

	Good	Fine	Mint
1-Wildey-c/a	1.50	4.50	8.95

RIO BRAVO (See 4-Color No. 1018)

RIO CONCHOS (See Movie Comics)

RIOT (Satire)
Apr, 1954 - No. 3, Aug, 1954; No. 4, Feb, 1956 - No. 6, June, 1956
Atlas Comics (ACI No. 1-5/WPI No. 6)

	Good	Fine	Mint
1-Russ Heath-a	5.00	15.00	35.00
2-Li'l Abner satire by Post	3.50	10.50	24.00
3-Last precode (8/54)	3.00	9.00	21.00
4-Infinity-c; Marilyn Monroe '7 Year Itch' movie satire; Mad Rip-off ads	4.35	13.00	30.00
5-Marilyn Monroe, John Wayne parody	5.00	15.00	35.00
6-Lorna of the Jungle satire by Everett; Dennis the Menace satire cover/story	3.00	9.00	21.00

NOTE: ***Berg*** *a-3.* ***Everett*** *a-1, 4, 6.* ***Maneely*** *a-1, 2, 4-6; c-6.* ***Reinman*** *a-2.* ***Severin*** *a-1, 4-6.*

RIPCORD (See 4-Color No. 1294)

RIP HUNTER TIME MASTER (See Showcase)
Mar-Apr, 1961 - No. 29, Nov-Dec, 1965
National Periodical Publications

	Good	Fine	Mint
1	7.00	21.00	50.00
2	4.35	13.00	30.00
3-5: 5-Last 10 cent issue	2.30	7.00	16.00
6,7-Toth-a in each	2.65	8.00	18.00
8-15	1.50	4.50	10.00
16-29: 29-G. Kane-c	.85	2.50	6.00

RIP KIRBY (See Feat. Books No. 51,54, Harvey Comics Hits No.57, & Street Comix)

RIPLEY'S BELIEVE IT OR NOT!
Sept, 1953 - No. 4, March, 1954
Harvey Publications

	Good	Fine	Mint
1-Powell-a	5.70	17.00	40.00
2-4	3.00	9.00	21.00
J. C. Penney giveaway (1948)	3.50	10.50	24.00

RIPLEY'S BELIEVE IT OR NOT! (Formerly . . .True War Stories)
No. 4, April, 1967 - No. 94, Feb, 1980
Gold Key

	Good	Fine	Mint
4-McWilliams-a	1.15	3.50	8.00
5-Subtitled "True War Stories;" Evans-a	.75	2.25	5.00
6-9: 6-McWilliams-a. 8-Orlando-a	.75	2.25	5.00
10-Evans-a(2)	.75	2.25	5.00
11-14,16-20	.55	1.65	4.00
15-Evans-a	.55	1.65	4.00
21-30	.50	1.50	3.00
31-38,40-60	.35	1.00	2.00
39-Crandall-a	.40	1.25	2.50
61-94: 74,77-83 (52 pgs.)	.25	.75	1.50
Story Digest Mag. 1(6/70)-4¾x6½"	.50	1.50	3.00

NOTE: ***Evanish*** *art by* ***Luiz Dominguez*** *#22-25, 27, 30, 31, 40.* ***McWilliams*** *a-65, 70, 89.* ***Sparling*** *c-68. Reprints-#74,77-84,87 (part); 91,93 (all).* ***Williamson, Wood****-a-80r/#1.*

RIPLEY'S BELIEVE IT OR NOT! (See Ace Comics, All-American Comics, Mystery Comics Digest No. 1, 4, 7, 10, 13, 16, 19, 22, 25)

RIPLEY'S BELIEVE IT OR NOT TRUE GHOST STORIES (Becomes . . .True War Stories) (See Dan Curtis)
June, 1965 - No. 2, Oct, 1966
Gold Key

	Good	Fine	Mint
1-Williamson, Wood & Evans-a; photo-c	2.00	6.00	14.00
2-Orlando, McWilliams-a	1.15	3.50	8.00
Mini-Comic 1(1976-3¼x6½")		.30	.60
11186(1977)-Golden Press; 224 pgs. ($1.95)-Reprints	.50	1.50	3.00
11401(3/79)-Golden Press; 96 pgs. ($1.00)-Reprints		.60	1.20

RIPLEY'S BELIEVE IT OR NOT TRUE WAR STORIES (Formerly . . .True Ghost Stories; becomes Ripley's Believe It or Not #4 on)
Nov, 1966
Gold Key

	Good	Fine	Mint
1(#3)-Williamson-a	1.50	4.50	10.00

RIPLEY'S BELIEVE IT OR NOT! TRUE WEIRD
June, 1966 - No. 2, Aug, 1966 (B&W Magazine)
Ripley Enterprises

	Good	Fine	Mint
1,2-Comic stories & text	.40	1.20	2.40

RIVETS (See 4-Color No. 518)

RIVETS (A dog)
Jan, 1956 - No. 3, May, 1956
Argo Publ.

	Good	Fine	Mint
1-Reprints Sunday & daily newspaper strips	2.30	7.00	16.00
2,3	1.30	4.00	9.00

ROAD RUNNER, THE (See Beep Beep. . .)

ROBERT E. HOWARD'S CONAN THE BARBARIAN
1983 (No month) ($2.50, printed on Baxter paper)
Marvel Comics Group

	Good	Fine	Mint
1-r-/Savage Tales No. 2,3 by Smith; c-r/Conan No. 21 by Smith	.45	1.25	2.50

ROBIN (See Aurora)

ROBIN HOOD (See 4-Color No. 413,669, King Classics, Movie Comics, & The Advs. of. . .)

ROBIN HOOD (. . .& His Merry Men, The Illustrated Story of. . .) (See Classic Comics No. 7)

ROBIN HOOD (New Adventures of. . .)
1952 (36 pages) (5x7¼")
Walt Disney Productions (Flour giveaways)
"New Adventures of Robin Hood," "Ghosts of Waylea Castle," &

	Good	Fine	Mint
ROBIN HOOD (continued)			
"The Miller's Ransom" each....	1.70	5.00	12.00

ROBIN HOOD (Adventures of... #7, 8)
No. 52, Nov, 1955 - No. 6, June, 1957
Magazine Enterprises (Sussex Publ. Co.)

52-Origin Robin Hood & Sir Gallant of the Round Table	3.50	10.50	24.00
53, 3-6	2.30	7.00	16.00
I.W. Reprint #1,2 (r-#4), 9 (r-#52)(1963)	.40	1.20	2.40
Super Reprint #10 (r-#53?), 11,15 (r-#5), 17('64)	.40	1.20	2.40

NOTE: ***Bolle*** *a-in all.* ***Powell*** *a-6.*

ROBIN HOOD (Not Disney)
May-July, 1963 (One shot)
Dell Publishing Co.

1	1.00	3.00	7.00

ROBIN HOOD ($1.50)
1973 (Disney) (8½x11"; cardboard covers) (52 pages)
Western Publishing Co.

96151-"Robin Hood," based on movie, 96152-"The Mystery of Sherwood Forest," 96153-"In King Richard's Service," 96154-"The Wizard's Ring" each....	.70	2.00	4.00

ROBIN HOOD AND HIS MERRY MEN (Formerly Danger & Adv.)
No. 28, April, 1956 - No. 38, Aug, 1958
Charlton Comics

28	2.00	6.00	14.00
29-37	1.15	3.50	8.00
38-Ditko-a, 5 pgs.	3.50	10.50	24.00

ROBIN HOOD'S FRONTIER DAYS (...Western Tales)
No date (Circa 1955) 20 pages, slick-c (Seven issues?)
Shoe Store Giveaway (Robin Hood Stores)

nn	2.00	6.00	14.00
nn-Issues with Crandall-a	3.00	9.00	21.00

ROBIN HOOD TALES (National Periodical #7 on)
Feb, 1956 - No. 6, Nov-Dec, 1956
Quality Comics Group (Comic Magazines)

1	3.50	10.50	24.00
2-5-Matt Baker-a	4.00	12.00	28.00
6	1.85	5.50	13.00
Frontier Days giveaway (1956)	1.50	4.50	10.00

ROBIN HOOD TALES (Continued from Quality)
No. 7, Jan-Feb, 1957 - No. 14, Mar-Apr, 1958
National Periodical Publications

7	7.00	21.00	50.00
8-14	6.00	18.00	42.00

ROBINSON CRUSOE (Also see King Classics)
Nov-Jan, 1963-64
Dell Publishing Co.

1	1.00	3.00	7.00

ROBO-HUNTER
April, 1984 - No. 6, 1984
Eagle Comics

1-6-2000 A.D.-r		.50	1.00

ROBOTECH DEFENDERS
Mar, 1985 - No. 2, Apr, 1985 (mini-series)
DC Comics

1,2	.40	1.20	2.40

ROBOTECH IN 3-D
Aug, 1987 ($2.50)
Comico

	Good	Fine	Mint
1-Adapts TV show; Steacy-c	.40	1.25	2.50

ROBOTECH MASTERS (TV)
July, 1985 - Present
Comico

1	.50	1.50	3.00
2,3	.35	1.00	2.00
4-20	.25	.75	1.50

ROBOTECH THE GRAPHIC NOVEL
Aug, 1986 ($5.95, 8½x11", 52 pgs.)
Comico

1-Origin SDF-1; intro T.R. Edwards	1.00	3.00	5.95
1-2nd printing	1.00	3.00	5.95

ROBOTECH: THE MACROSS SAGA (Formerly Macross)(TV)
No. 2, Feb, 1985 - Present
Comico

2	1.30	4.00	8.00
3-5	.50	1.50	3.00
6,7	.40	1.25	2.50
8-24	.25	.75	1.50

ROBOTECH: THE NEW GENERATION (TV)
July, 1985 - Present
Comico

1	.50	1.50	3.00
2-4	.35	1.00	2.00
5-20	.25	.75	1.50

ROBOTIX
Feb, 1986 (One Shot)
Marvel Comics Group

1-Based on toy		.50	1.00

ROBOTMEN OF THE LOST PLANET (Also see Space Thrillers)
1952
Avon Periodicals

1-3pg. Kinstler-a	56.00	170.00	390.00

ROB ROY (See 4-Color No. 544)

ROCK AND ROLLO (Formerly T.V. Teens)
V2No.14, Oct, 1957 - No. 19, Sept, 1958
Charlton Comics

14-19	.85	2.50	6.00

ROCKET COMICS
Mar, 1940 - No. 3, May, 1940
Hillman Periodicals

1-Rocket Riley, Red Roberts the Electro Man(Origin), The Phantom Ranger, The Steel Shark, The Defender, Buzzard Barnes, Lefty Larson, & Man With a Thousand Faces begin	58.00	175.00	405.00
2,3	35.00	105.00	245.00

ROCKETEER, THE (See Eclipse Graphic Album Series, Pacific Presents & Starslayer #2)

ROCKETEER SPECIAL EDITION, THE
Nov, 1984 ($1.50; Baxter paper)
Eclipse Comics

1-Dave Stevens-c/a	.50	1.50	3.00

ROCKET KELLY
1944; Fall, 1945 - No. 5, 10-11/46
Fox Features Syndicate

nn (1944)	7.00	21.00	50.00
1	7.00	21.00	50.00
2-The Puppeteer app. (costumed hero)	5.00	15.00	35.00

Robin Hood Tales #6, QUA

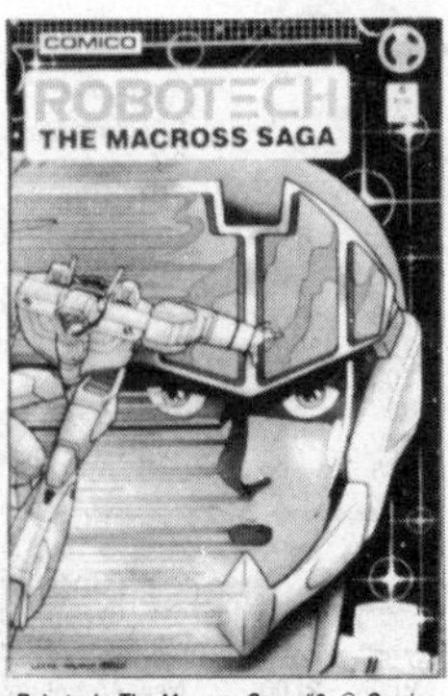

Robotech: The Macross Saga #6, © Comico

The Rocketeer Special Edition #1, © Eclipse

Rocketman #1, © AJAX

Rocky and His Fiendish Friends #2, © Jay Ward

Rogue Trooper #1, © Quality Comics

	Good	Fine	Mint
ROCKET KELLY (continued)			
3-5: 5-(#5 on cover, #4 inside)	4.35	13.00	30.00

ROCKETMAN (See Hello Pal & Scoop Comics)
June, 1952
Ajax/Farrell Publications

1-Rocketman & Cosmo 11.50 34.00 80.00

ROCKET RACCOON
May, 1985 - No. 4, Aug, 1985 (mini-series)
Marvel Comics Group

1 .25 .75 1.50
2-4 .50 1.00

ROCKETS AND RANGE RIDERS
May, 1957 (16 pages, soft-c) (Giveaway)
Richfield Oil Corp.

Toth-a 10.50 30.00 70.00

ROCKET SHIP X
September, 1951; 1952
Fox Features Syndicate

1 32.00 95.00 225.00
1952 (nn, nd, no publ.)-Edited '51-c 22.00 65.00 154.00

ROCKET TO ADVENTURE LAND (See Pixie Puzzle. . .)

ROCKET TO THE MOON
1951
Avon Periodicals

nn-Orlando c/a; adapts Otis Aldebert Kline's "Maza of the Moon" 55.00 165.00 385.00

ROCK HAPPENING (Harvey Pop Comics:)
Sept, 1969 - No. 2, Nov, 1969
Harvey Publications

1,2 1.00 3.00 7.00

ROCKY AND HIS FIENDISH FRIENDS (TV)
Oct, 1962 - No. 5, Sept, 1963 (Jay Ward)
Gold Key

1 (84 pgs.) 5.00 15.00 40.00
2,3 (84 pgs.) 4.00 12.00 32.00
4,5 (Regular size) 3.00 9.00 21.00
Kite Fun Book ('63, 16p, soft-c, 5x7¼") 4.35 13.00 30.00
Kite Fun Book ('70, 16p, soft-c, 5x7¼") 3.00 9.00 21.00

ROCKY AND HIS FRIENDS (See 4-Color No. 1128, 1152, 1166, 1208, 1275, 1311 and March of Comics No. 216)

ROCKY JONES SPACE RANGER (See Space Adventures No. 15-18)

ROCKY JORDAN PRIVATE EYE (See Private Eye)

ROCKY LANE WESTERN (Rocky Allan Lane starred in Republic movies (for a short time as Red Ryder) & TV)(See Black Jack)
May, 1949 - No. 87, Nov, 1959
Fawcett Publications/Charlton No. 56 on

1 (36 pgs.)-Rocky, his stallion Black Jack, & Slim Pickens begin; photo-c begin, end No. 57; photo back-c 25.00 75.00 175.00
2 (36 pgs.)-Last photo back-c 12.00 36.00 84.00
3-5 (52 pgs.). 4-Captain Tootsie by Beck 10.00 30.00 70.00
6,10 (36 pgs.) 8.00 24.00 56.00
7-9 (52 pgs.) 8.50 25.50 60.00
11-13,15-17 (52 pgs.): 15-Black Jack's Hitching Post begins, ends #25 6.50 19.50 45.00
14,18 (36 pgs.) 5.70 17.00 40.00
19-21,23,24 (52 pgs.): 20-Last Slim Pickens. 21-Dee Dickens begins, ends #55,57,65-68 5.70 17.50 40.00
22,25-28,30 (36 pgs. begin) 5.50 16.50 38.00
29-Classic complete novel "The Land of Missing Men,"-hidden land of ancient temple ruins (r-in #65) 6.50 19.50 45.00

	Good	Fine	Mint
31-40	5.00	15.00	35.00
41-54	4.35	13.00	30.00
55-Last Fawcett issue (1/54)	5.00	15.00	35.00
56-1st Charlton issue (2/54)-Photo-c	5.00	15.00	35.00
57,60-Photo-c	3.50	10.50	24.00
58,59,61-64: 59-61-Young Falcon app. 64-Slim Pickens app.	3.00	9.00	21.00
65-R-/#29, "The Land of Missing Men"	3.50	10.50	24.00
66-68: Reprints #30,31,32	2.30	7.00	16.00
69-78,80-86	2.30	7.00	16.00
79-Giant Edition, 68 pgs.	3.50	10.50	24.00
87-Last issue	3.00	9.00	21.00

NOTE: ***Complete novels** in #10, 14, 18, 22, 25, 30-32, 36, 38, 39, 49. **Captain Tootsie** in #4, 12, 20. **Big Bow and Little Arrow** in #11, 28, 63. **Black Jack's Hitching Post** in #15-25, 64, 73.*

ROD CAMERON WESTERN (Movie star)
Feb, 1950 - No. 20, April, 1953
Fawcett Publications

1-Rod Cameron, his horse War Paint, & Sam The Sheriff begin; photo front/back-c begin 21.00 62.00 150.00
2 11.50 34.00 80.00
3-Novel length story "The Mystery of the Seven Cities of Cibola" 9.50 28.00 65.00
4-10: 9-Last photo back-c 8.00 24.00 56.00
11-19 6.50 19.50 45.00
20-Last issue & photo-c 7.00 21.00 50.00

NOTE: ***Novel length stories** in No. 1-8,12-14.*

RODEO RYAN (See A-1 Comics No. 8)

ROGER BEAN, R. G. (Regular Guy)
1915 - 1917 (34 pgs.; B&W; 4¾x16"; cardboard covers)
(No. 1 & 4 bound on side, No. 3 bound at top)
The Indiana News Co.

1-By Chic Jackson (48 pgs.) 6.00 18.00 42.00
2-4 4.35 13.00 30.00

ROGER DODGER (Also in Exciting #57 on)
No. 5, Aug, 1952
Standard Comics

5 1.15 3.50 8.00

ROG 2000
June, 1982 ($2.95)
Pacific Comics

nn-Byrne c/a-r .70 2.00 4.00

ROG 2000
1987 - No. 2 ($2.00, mini-series, color)
Fantagraphics Books

1,2-Byrne-r .35 1.00 2.00

ROGUE TROOPER
Oct, 1986 - Present (color)
Quality Comics

1-5 .35 .70
6-Double size ($1.50) .25 .70 1.40
7-12 .45 .90

ROLY POLY COMIC BOOK
1945 - 1946 (MLJ reprints)
Green Publishing Co.

1-Red Rube & Steel Sterling begin 9.50 28.50 65.00
6-The Blue Circle & The Steel Fist app. 5.00 15.00 35.00
10-Origin Red Rube retold; Steel Sterling story (Zip #41) 5.50 16.50 38.00
11,12,14: 11,14-The Black Hood app. 5.50 16.50 38.00
15-The Blue Circle & The Steel Fist app.; cover exact swipe from

ROLY POLY COMIC BOOK (continued)

	Good	Fine	Mint
Fox Blue Beetle #1	13.50	41.00	95.00

ROM
December, 1979 - Present
Marvel Comics Group

	Good	Fine	Mint
1-Based on a Parker Bros. toy-origin	.60	1.75	3.50
2	.35	1.10	2.20
3-5: 3-Miller-c	.30	.90	1.80
6-10	.25	.70	1.40
11-16: 13-Saga of the Space Knights begins		.55	1.10
17,18-X-Men app.	.45	1.40	2.80
19-24,26-30: 19-X-Men cameo		.45	.90
25-Double size		.60	1.20
31,33-49		.35	.70
32-X-Men cameo		.40	.80
50-Double size		.50	1.00
51-56		.35	.70
57-Alpha Flight app.	.25	.75	1.50
58-75: 65-X-Men & Beta Ray Bill app.		.40	.80
Annual 1(11/82)		.60	1.20
Annual 2(11/83), 3(1984)		.50	1.00
Annual 4(1985)		.60	1.20

NOTE: ***Austin*** *c-3i, 18i, 61i.* ***Byrne*** *a-74i; c-56, 57, 74.* ***Ditko*** *a-59-64p.* ***Golden*** *c-7-12, 19.* ***Guice*** *a-61i; c-55, 58, 60p.* ***Layton*** *a-59i; c-15, 59i.* ***Miller*** *c-3p, 17p, 18p.* ***Russell*** *a(i)-64, 65, 67, 69; c-64, 65i, 66.* ***P. Smith*** *c-59p.* ***Starlin*** *c-67.*

ROMANCE (See True Stories of . . .)

ROMANCE AND CONFESSION STORIES (See Giant Comics Ed.)
No date (1949) (100pgs.)
St. John Publishing Co.

	Good	Fine	Mint
1-Baker c/a; remaindered St. John love comics	20.00	60.00	140.00

ROMANCE DIARY
December, 1949 - No. 2, March, 1950
Marvel Comics (CDS)(CLDS)

	Good	Fine	Mint
1,2	3.50	10.50	24.00

ROMANCE OF FLYING, THE (See Feature Books No. 33)

ROMANCES OF MOLLY MANTON (See Molly Manton)

ROMANCES OF NURSE HELEN GRANT, THE
August, 1957
Atlas Comics (VPI)

	Good	Fine	Mint
1	1.30	4.00	9.00

ROMANCES OF THE WEST
Nov, 1949 - No. 2, Mar, 1950
Marvel Comics (SPC)

	Good	Fine	Mint
1-Movie photo of Calamity Jane/Sam Bass	5.70	17.00	40.00
2	3.70	11.00	26.00

ROMANCE STORIES OF TRUE LOVE (Formerly Love Problems & Advice)
No. 45, 5/57 - No. 50, 3/58; No. 51, 9/58 - No. 52, 11/58
Harvey Publications

	Good	Fine	Mint
45-51	1.00	3.00	7.00
52-Matt Baker-a	2.35	7.00	16.00

NOTE: ***Powell*** *a-45,46,48-50.*

ROMANCE TALES
No. 7, Oct, 1949 - No. 9, March, 1950 (No. 7,8-photo-c)
Marvel Comics (CDS)

	Good	Fine	Mint
7	2.65	8.00	18.00
8,9: 8-Everett-a	1.70	5.00	12.00

ROMANCE TRAIL
July-Aug, 1949 - No. 6, May-June, 1950
National Periodical Publications

	Good	Fine	Mint
1-Kinstler, Toth-a; Photo-c	13.50	40.00	95.00
2-Kinstler-a; photo-c	7.00	21.00	50.00
3-Photo-c; Kinstler, Toth-a	7.00	21.00	50.00
4-Photo-c; Toth-a	6.50	19.50	45.00
5,6: 5-Photo-c	5.50	16.50	38.00

ROMAN HOLIDAYS, THE (TV)
Feb, 1973 - No. 4, Nov, 1973 (Hanna-Barbera)
Gold Key

	Good	Fine	Mint
1	1.35	4.00	8.00
2-4	1.00	3.00	6.00

ROMANTIC ADVENTURES (My . . . #49-67, covers only)
Mar-Apr, 1949 - No. 67, July, 1956 (My . . . No. 68 on)
American Comics Group (B&I Publ. Co.)

	Good	Fine	Mint
1	3.50	10.50	24.00
2	1.70	5.00	12.00
3-10	1.15	3.50	8.00
11-20 (4/52)	.85	2.50	6.00
21-46,48-52: 52-Last Pre-code (2/55)	.65	2.00	4.50
47-3-D effect	.85	2.50	6.00
53-67	.50	1.50	3.50

NOTE: *No. 1-22, 52 pgs.* ***Shelly*** *a-40.* ***Whitney*** *art in many issues.*

ROMANTIC AFFAIRS (Formerly Our Love?)
No. 3, March, 1950
Marvel Comics (Select Publications)

	Good	Fine	Mint
3-Photo-c	1.70	5.00	12.00

ROMANTIC CONFESSIONS
Oct, 1949 - V3No.1, April-May, 1953
Hillman Periodicals

	Good	Fine	Mint
V1#1-McWilliams-a	4.00	12.00	28.00
2-Briefer-a; negligee panels	2.15	6.50	15.00
3-12	1.50	4.50	10.00
V2#1,2,4-8,10-12	1.15	3.50	8.00
3-Krigstein-a	2.65	8.00	18.00
9-One pg. Frazetta ad	1.50	4.50	10.00
V3#1	1.00	3.00	7.00

NOTE: ***McWilliams*** *a-V2#2.*

ROMANTIC HEARTS
Mar, 1951 - No. 9, Aug, 1952; July, 1953 - No. 12, July, 1955
Story Comics/Master/Merit Pubs.

	Good	Fine	Mint
1(3/51) (1st Series)	3.50	10.50	24.00
2	1.70	5.00	12.00
3-9	1.50	4.50	10.00
1(7/53) (2nd Series)	2.00	6.00	14.00
2	1.30	4.00	9.00
3-12	1.00	3.00	7.00

ROMANTIC LOVE
No. 4, June, 1950
Quality Comics Group

	Good	Fine	Mint
4 (6/50)(Exist?)	1.70	5.00	12.00
I.W. Reprint #2,3,8		.60	1.20

ROMANTIC LOVE
Sept-Oct, 1949 - No. 23, Sept-Oct, 1954 (no No. 14-19)
Avon Periodicals/Realistic

	Good	Fine	Mint
1-c-/Avon paperback 252	10.00	30.00	70.00
2	5.00	15.00	35.00
3-c-/paperback Novel Library 12	5.00	15.00	35.00
4-c-/paperback Diversey Prize Novel 5	5.00	15.00	35.00
5-c-/paperback Novel Library 34	5.00	15.00	35.00
6-"Thrill Crazy"-marijuana story; c-/Avon paperback 207; Kinstler-a	7.00	21.00	50.00
7,8: 8-Astarita-a(2)	4.35	13.00	30.00

Rom #65, © MCG

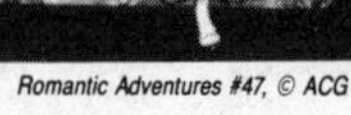

Romantic Adventures #47, © ACG

Romantic Hearts #1 (7/53), © Merit Pubs.

Ronin #5, © DC

Rootie Kazootie #4, © DELL

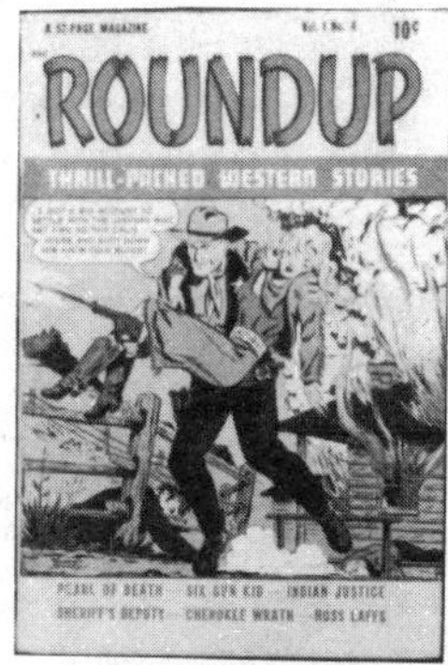

Roundup #4, © D. S. Publishing

ROMANTIC LOVE (continued)	**Good**	**Fine**	**Mint**
9-c-/paperback/Novel Library 41; Kinstler-a	5.00	15.00	35.00
10-c-/Avon paperback 212	5.00	15.00	35.00
11-c-/paperback Novel Library 17; Kinstler-a	5.00	15.00	35.00
12-c-/paperback Novel Library 13	5.00	15.00	35.00
13,21,22	4.35	13.00	30.00
20-Kinstler-c/a	4.35	13.00	30.00
23-Kinstler-c	3.65	11.00	25.00
nn(1-3/53)(Realistic-r)	2.85	8.50	20.00

NOTE: ***Astarita*** *a-7,10,11,21.*

ROMANTIC MARRIAGE (Cinderella Love #25 on)
No. 1-3 (1950, no month); No. 4, 5-6/51 - No. 17, 9/52; No. 18, 9/53 - No. 24, Sept, 1954
Ziff-Davis/St. John No. 18 on

	Good	Fine	Mint
1-Photo-c	5.50	16.50	38.00
2	3.00	9.00	21.00
3-9: 3,8,9-Painted-c; 5,7-Photo-c	2.30	7.00	16.00
10-Unusual format; front-c is a painted-c; back-c is a photo-c complete with logo, price, etc.	3.50	10.50	24.00
11-17 (9/52; last Z-D ish.): 13-Photo-c	2.00	6.00	14.00
18-22,24	2.00	6.00	14.00
23-Baker-c	2.30	7.00	16.00

ROMANTIC PICTURE NOVELETTES
1946
Magazine Enterprises

	Good	Fine	Mint
1-Mary Worth-r	7.00	21.00	50.00

ROMANTIC SECRETS (Becomes Time For Love)
Sept, 1949 - No. 39, 4/53; No. 5, 10/55 - No. 52, 11/64
Fawcett/Charlton Comics No. 5 (10/55) on

	Good	Fine	Mint
1	3.50	10.50	24.00
2,3	1.65	5.00	12.00
4,9-Evans-a	2.65	8.00	18.00
5-8,10	1.50	4.50	10.00
11-23	1.15	3.50	8.00
24-Evans-a	2.30	7.00	16.00
25-39	.85	2.50	6.00
5 (Charlton)(10/55, formerly Negro Romances #4?)	1.85	5.50	13.00
6-10	1.00	3.00	7.00
11-20	.45	1.35	3.00
21-35: Last 10 cent ish?	.35	1.00	2.50
36-52('64)		.40	.80

NOTE: ***Bailey*** *a-20.* ***Powell*** *a(1st series)-5,7,10,12,16,17,20,26,29,33,34,36,37. Photo c(1st series)-1-5, 25, 27, 33.* ***Sekowsky*** *a-26.*

ROMANTIC STORY
11/49 - No. 22, Sum, 1953; No. 23, 5/54 - No. 130, 11/73
Fawcett/Charlton Comics No. 23 on

	Good	Fine	Mint
1	4.35	13.00	30.00
2	2.15	6.50	15.00
3-5	1.65	5.00	12.00
6-14	1.50	4.50	10.00
15-Evans-a	2.30	7.00	16.00
16-22(Sum, '53; last Fawcett ish.). 21-Toth-a?	1.15	3.50	8.00
23-39,41-50: 29-Wood swipes	1.15	3.50	8.00
40-(100 pgs.)	3.15	9.50	22.00
51-56,58-80	.45	1.35	3.00
57-Hypo needle story	.70	2.00	4.00
81-130		.40	.80

NOTE: ***Powell*** *a-7,8,16,20,30. Photo c-8,10,11,13,19,24.*

ROMANTIC THRILLS (See Fox Giants)

ROMANTIC WESTERN
Winter, 1949 - No. 3, June, 1950 (Photo-c all)
Fawcett Publications

	Good	**Fine**	**Mint**
1	5.50	16.50	38.00
2-Williamson, McWilliams-a	8.00	24.00	56.00
3	3.50	10.50	23.00

ROMEO TUBBS (Formerly My Secret Life)
No. 26, 5/50 - No. 28, 7/50; No. 1, 1950; No. 27, 12/52
Fox Feature Syndicate/Green Publ. Co. No. 27

	Good	Fine	Mint
26	4.60	14.00	32.00
27-Contains Pedro on inside; Wood-a	6.50	19.50	45.00
28, 1	3.50	10.50	24.00

RONALD McDONALD (TV)
Sept, 1970 - No. 4, March, 1971
Charlton Press (King Features Synd.)

	Good	Fine	Mint
1		.50	1.00
2-4		.25	.50

RONIN
July, 1983 - No. 6, Apr, 1984 (mini-series) (52 pgs., $2.50)
DC Comics

	Good	Fine	Mint
1-Miller script, c/a in all	.70	2.10	4.20
2	.60	1.80	3.60
3-5	.55	1.60	3.20
6	.70	2.10	4.20
Trade paperback	2.50	7.50	15.00

ROOK
November, 1979 - No. 14, April, 1982
Warren Publications

	Good	Fine	Mint
1-Nino-a		.40	.80
2-14: 3,4-Toth-a		.30	.60

ROOKIE COP (Formerly Crime and Justice?)
Nov, 1955 - No. 33, Aug, 1957
Charlton Comics

	Good	Fine	Mint
27	2.30	7.00	16.00
28-33	1.30	4.00	9.00

ROOM 222 (TV)
Jan, 1970; No. 2, May, 1970 - No. 4, Jan, 1971
Dell Publishing Co.

	Good	Fine	Mint
1,2,4: 2,4-Photo-c. 4 r-/#1	1.75	5.25	12.00
3-Marijuana story	1.50	4.50	10.00

ROOTIE KAZOOTIE (TV)(See 3-D-ell)
No. 415, Aug, 1952 - No. 6, Oct-Dec, 1954
Dell Publishing Co.

	Good	Fine	Mint
4-Color 415	3.00	9.00	21.00
4-Color 459,502	2.65	8.00	18.00
4(4-6/54)-6	2.00	6.00	14.00

ROOTS OF THE SWAMPTHING
July, 1986 - No. 5, Nov, 1986 ($2.00, Baxter)
DC Comics

	Good	Fine	Mint
1-5: All Wrightson-r	.35	1.00	2.00

ROUND THE WORLD GIFT
No date (mid 1940's) (4 pages)
National War Fund (Giveaway)

	Good	Fine	Mint
	10.00	30.00	70.00

ROUNDUP (Western Crime)
July-Aug, 1948 - No. 5, Mar-Apr, 1949 (52 pgs.)
D. S. Publishing Co.

	Good	Fine	Mint
1-1pg. Frazetta on 'Mystery of the Hunting Lodge'?; Ingels-a?	5.70	17.00	40.00
2-Marijuana drug mention story	4.60	14.00	32.00
3-5	3.00	9.00	21.00

ROYAL ROY
May, 1985 - No. 6, 1986 (Children's book)
Star Comics (Marvel)

	Good	Fine	Mint
1-6		.35	.70

ROY CAMPANELLA, BASEBALL HERO
1950
Fawcett Publications

nn	18.00	54.00	125.00

ROY ROGERS (See March of Comics No. 17, 35, 47, 62, 68, 73, 77, 86, 91, 100, 105, 116, 121, 131, 136, 146, 151, 161, 167, 176, 191, 206, 221, 236, 250)

ROY ROGERS AND TRIGGER
April, 1967
Gold Key

1-Photo-c; reprints	2.00	6.00	14.00

ROY ROGERS COMICS (See Western Roundup)
No. 38, 4/44 - No. 177, 12/47 (52 pgs.-No. 38-166)
Dell Publishing Co.

4-Color 38 (1944)-49pg. story; photo front/back-c on all 4-Color ish.	42.00	125.00	295.00
4-Color 63 (1945)-Color photos inside-c	28.00	84.00	195.00
4-Color 86,95 (1945)	21.00	62.00	148.00
4-Color 109 (1946)	17.00	51.00	120.00
4-Color 117,124,137,144	12.00	36.00	84.00
4-Color 153,160,166: 166-48pg. story	9.00	27.00	62.00
4-Color 177 (36 pgs.)-32pg. story	9.00	27.00	62.00

ROY ROGERS COMICS (. . .& Trigger #92(8/55)-on)(Roy starred in Republic movies, radio & TV) (Singing cowboy) (Also see Dale Evans, Queen of the West. . ., It Really Happened #8 & Roy Roger's Trigger)
Jan, 1948 - No. 145, Sept-Oct, 1961 (36pgs. No. 1-19)
Dell Publishing Co.

1-Roy, his horse Trigger, & Chuck Wagon Charley's Tales begin; photo-c begin, end #145	32.00	95.00	225.00
2	16.00	48.00	110.00
3-5	13.00	40.00	90.00
6-10	10.00	30.00	70.00
11-19: 19-. . .Charley's Tales ends	7.00	21.00	50.00
20 (52 pgs.)-Trigger feature begins, ends #46	7.00	21.00	50.00
21-30 (52 pgs.)	6.00	18.00	42.00
31-46 (52 pgs.): 37-X-mas-c	5.00	15.00	35.00
47-56 (36 pgs.): 47-Chuck Wagon Charley's Tales returns, ends #133 49-X-mas-c. 55-Last photo back-c	4.00	12.00	28.00
57 (52 pgs.)-Heroin drug propaganda story	4.60	14.00	32.00
58-70 (52 pgs.): 61-X-mas-c	3.50	10.50	24.00
71-80 (52 pgs.): 73-X-mas-c	2.65	8.00	18.00
81-91 (36 pgs. #81-on): 85-X-mas-c	2.35	7.00	16.00
92-Title changed to Roy Rogers and Trigger (8/55)	2.35	7.00	16.00
93-99,101-110,112-118	2.35	7.00	16.00
100-Trigger feature returns, ends #133?	4.00	12.00	28.00
111,119-124-Toth-a	4.35	13.00	30.00
125-131	3.00	9.00	21.00
132-144-Manning-a. 144-Dale Evans feat.	3.50	10.50	24.00
145-Last issue	4.00	12.00	28.00
. . .& the Man From Dodge City (Dodge giveaway, 16 pgs., 1954)-Frontier, Inc. (5x7¼")	9.00	27.00	62.00
Official R.R. Riders Club Comics (1952; 16 pgs., reg. size, paper-c)	10.00	30.00	70.00

NOTE: ***Buscema** a-2 each-74-108. **Manning** a-123, 124, 132-144. **Marsh** a-110. Photo back-c No. 1-9, 11-35, 38-55.*

ROY ROGERS' TRIGGER (TV)
No. 329, May, 1951 - No. 17, June-Aug, 1955
Dell Publishing Co.

	Good	Fine	Mint
4-Color 329-Painted-c	5.00	15.00	35.00
2 (9-11/51)-Photo-c	3.50	10.50	24.00
3-5: Painted-c #3-on	1.70	5.00	12.00
6-17	1.15	3.50	8.00

RUDOLPH, THE RED NOSED REINDEER (See Limited Collectors Edition #20,24,33,42,50)

RUDOLPH, THE RED NOSED REINDEER
1939 (2,400,000 copies printed); Dec, 1951
Montgomery Ward (Giveaway)

Paper cover - 1st app. in print; written by Robert May; ill. by Denver Gillen	8.35	25.00	50.00
Hardcover version	10.00	30.00	70.00
1951 version (Has 1939 date)-36 pgs., illos in three colors; red-c	3.00	9.00	21.00

RUDOLPH, THE RED-NOSED REINDEER
1950 - No. 13?, Winter, 1962-63
(Issues are not numbered) (15 different issues known)
National Periodical Publications

1950 issue; Grossman-c/a begins	4.00	12.00	28.00
1951-54 issues (4 total)	3.00	9.00	21.00
1955-62 issues (8 total)	1.60	4.70	11.00

NOTE: *The 1962-63 issue is 84 pages. 13 total issues published.*

RUFF & REDDY (TV)
No. 937, 9/58 - No. 12, 1-3/62 (Hanna-Barbera)
Dell Publishing Co./Gold Key

4-Color 937(1st Hanna-Barbera book)	2.30	7.00	16.00
4-Color 981,1038	1.70	5.00	12.00
4(1-3/60)-12	1.15	3.50	8.00

RUGGED ACTION (Strange Stories of Suspense #5 on)
Dec, 1954 - No. 4, June, 1955
Atlas Comics (CSI)

1	3.00	9.00	21.00
2-4: 2-Last precode (2/55)	1.50	4.50	10.00

RULAH JUNGLE GODDESS (Formerly Zoot; I Loved #28 on) (Also see Terrors of the Jungle)
No. 17, Aug, 1948 - No. 27, June, 1949
Fox Features Syndicate

17	25.00	75.00	175.00
18-Classic girl-fight interior splash	22.00	65.00	154.00
19,20	20.00	60.00	140.00
21-Used in **SOTI**, pg. 388,389	22.00	65.00	154.00
22-Used in **SOTI**, pg. 22,23	20.00	60.00	140.00
23-27	15.00	45.00	105.00

NOTE: ***Kamen** c-17-19,21,22.*

RUNAWAY, THE (See Movie Classics)

RUN BABY RUN
1974 (39 cents)
Logos International

By Tony Tallarico from Nicky Cruz's book		.30	.60

RUN, BUDDY, RUN (TV)
June, 1967 (Photo-c)
Gold Key

1 (10204-706)	1.30	4.00	9.00

RUST
July, 1987 - Present ($1.50 color)
Now Comics

1-3	.25	.70	1.40
4-6-($1.75)	.25	.75	1.70

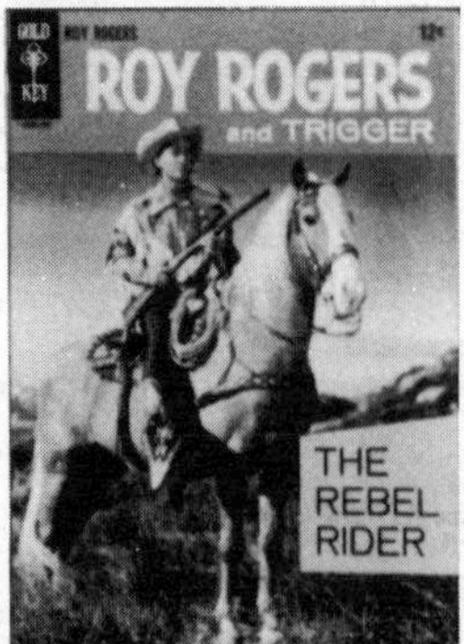

Roy Rogers and Trigger #1, © Roy Rogers

Ruff and Reddy #9, © Hanna-Barbera

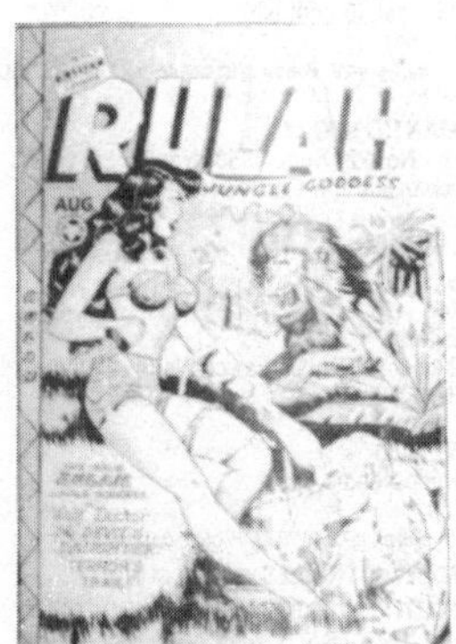

Rulah Jungle Goddess #17, © FOX

Sabre #1, © Eclipse Comics

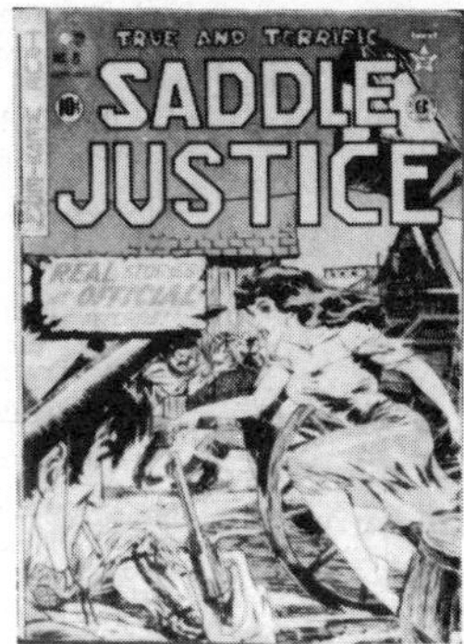

Saddle Justice #8, © WMG

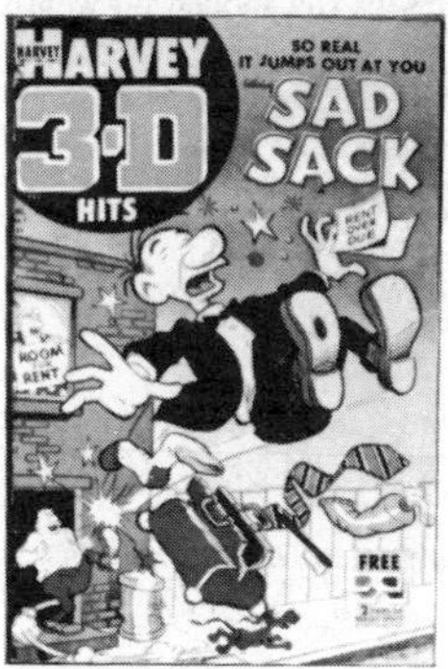

Sad Sack 3-D #1, © HARV

RUSTY, BOY DETECTIVE
Mar-April, 1955 - No. 5, Nov, 1955
Good Comics/Lev Gleason

	Good	Fine	Mint
1-Bob Wood, Carl Hubbell-a begins	2.65	8.00	18.00
2-5	1.50	4.50	10.00

RUSTY COMICS (Formerly Kid Movie Comics; Rusty and Her Family #21, 22; The Kelleys #23 on)
No. 12, Apr, 1947 - No. 22, Sept, 1949
Marvel Comics (HPC)

	Good	Fine	Mint
12-Mitzi app.	5.50	16.50	38.00
13	2.65	8.00	18.00
14-Wolverton's Powerhouse Pepper (4 pgs.) plus Kurtzman's "Hey Look"	5.70	17.00	40.00
15-17-Kurtzman's "Hey Look"	4.60	14.00	32.00
18,19	2.00	6.00	14.00
20-Kurtzman, 5 pgs.	4.65	14.00	32.00
21,22-Kurtzman, 17 & 22 pgs.	8.00	24.00	56.00

RUSTY DUGAN (See Holyoke One-Shot No. 2)

RUSTY RILEY (See 4-Color No. 418,451,486,554)

SAARI (The Jungle Goddess)
November, 1951
P. L. Publishing Co.

	Good	Fine	Mint
1	16.00	48.00	110.00

SABLE (Formerly Jon Sable, Freelance)
Mar, 1988 - Present ($1.75, color)
First Comics

	Good	Fine	Mint
1,2	.30	.90	1.75

SABOTAGE (See The Crusaders)

SABRE (See Eclipse Graphic Album Series)
10/78; 1/79; 8/82 - No. 14, 8/85; (Baxter paper No. 4 on)
Eclipse Comics

	Good	Fine	Mint
1-($1.00)-Sabre & Morrigan Tales begin	.25	.75	1.50
2,3-($1.00)		.50	1.00
4-10: ($1.50); 4-6-Origin Incredible Seven		.50	1.00
11,12		.50	1.00
13,14 ($2.00 cover)		.50	1.00

NOTE: ***Colan*** *c-11p.* ***Gulacy*** *c/a-1, 2.*

SABRINA'S CHRISTMAS MAGIC (See Archie Giant Series Mag. No. 196, 207, 220, 231, 243, 455, 467, 479, 491, 503, 515)

SABRINA, THE TEEN-AGE WITCH (TV) (See Archie's TV Laugh-Out, Archie Madhouse & Archie Giant Series #544)
April, 1971 - No. 77, Jan, 1983 (Giants No. 1-17)
Archie Publications

	Good	Fine	Mint
1	2.00	6.00	14.00
2	1.00	3.00	7.00
3-5: 3,4-Archie's Group x-over	.50	1.50	3.00
6-10	.25	.75	1.50
11-20		.40	.80
21-77		.25	.50

SABU, "ELEPHANT BOY" (Movie; formerly My Secret Story)
No. 30, June, 1950 - No. 2, Aug, 1950
Fox Features Syndicate

	Good	Fine	Mint
30(#1)-Wood-a; photo-c	9.00	27.00	62.00
2-Photo-c; Kamen-a	6.00	18.00	42.00

SACRAMENTS, THE
October, 1955 (25 cents)
Catechetical Guild Educational Society

	Good	Fine	Mint
304	2.00	6.00	12.00

SACRED AND THE PROFANE, THE (See Eclipse Graphic Album Series)

SAD CASE OF WAITING ROOM WILLIE, THE
1950? (nd) (14 pgs. in color; paper covers; regular size)
American Visuals Corp. (For Baltimore Medical Society)

	Good	Fine	Mint
By Will Eisner (Rare)	27.00	81.00	190.00

SADDLE JUSTICE (Happy Houlihans #1,2; becomes Saddle Romances #9 on)
No. 3, Spring, 1948 - No. 8, Sept-Oct, 1949
E. C. Comics

	Good	Fine	Mint
3-The first E. C. by Bill Gaines to break away from M. C. Gaines' old Educational Comics format. Craig, Feldstein, H. C. Kiefer, & Stan Asch-a. Mentioned in **Love and Death**	30.00	90.00	210.00
4-1st Graham Ingels E. C.-a	30.00	90.00	210.00
5-8-Ingels-a in all	26.00	78.00	180.00

NOTE: ***Craig*** *and* ***Feldstein*** *art in most issues. Canadian reprints known; see Table of Contents.*

SADDLE ROMANCES (Saddle Justice #3-8; continued as Weird Science #12 on)
No. 9, Nov-Dec, 1949 - No. 11, Mar-Apr, 1950
E. C. Comics

	Good	Fine	Mint
9-Ingels-a	30.00	90.00	210.00
10-Wood's 1st work at E. C.; Ingels-a	32.00	95.00	225.00
11-Ingels-a	30.00	90.00	210.00

NOTE: *Canadian reprints known; see Table of Contents.*

SADIE SACK (See Harvey Hits No. 93)

SAD SACK AND THE SARGE
Sept, 1957 - No. 155, June, 1982
Harvey Publications

	Good	Fine	Mint
1	5.00	15.00	35.00
2	2.00	6.00	14.00
3-10	1.70	5.00	12.00
11-20	1.00	3.00	6.00
21-50	.40	1.20	2.40
51-100		.50	1.00
101-155		.25	.50

SAD SACK COMICS (See Harvey Collector's Comics 16, Little Sad Sack, Tastee Freez Comics 4 & True Comics #55)
Sept, 1949 - No. 287, Oct, 1982
Harvey Publications

	Good	Fine	Mint
1-Infinity-c; Little Dot begins (1st app.); civilian issues begin, end No. 21	18.00	54.00	125.00
2-Flying Fool by Powell	8.50	25.50	60.00
3	5.50	16.50	38.00
4-10	3.50	10.50	24.00
11-21	2.35	7.00	16.00
22-("Back In The Army Again" on covers #22-36). "The Specialist" story about Sad Sack's return to Army	1.35	4.00	8.00
23-50	.85	2.50	5.00
51-100	.40	1.20	2.40
101-150		.50	1.00
151-222		.25	.50
223-228 (25 cent Giants, 52 pgs.)		.40	.80
229-287: 286,287 had limited distribution		.25	.50
3-D 1 (1/54-titled "Harvey 3-D Hits")	10.00	30.00	70.00
Armed Forces Complimentary copies, HD #1-40 ('57-'62)	.40	1.20	2.40

NOTE: *The* ***Sad Sack Comics*** *comic book was a spin-off from a Sunday Newspaper strip launched through John Wheeler's Bell Syndicate. The previous Sunday page and the first 21 comics depicted the Sad Sack in civvies. Unpopularity caused the Sunday page to be discontinued in the early '50s. Meanwhile Sad Sack returned to the Army, by popular demand, in issue No. 22, remaining there ever since. Incidentally, relatively few of the first 21 issues were ever collected and remain scarce due to this.*

SAD SACK FUN AROUND THE WORLD
1974 (no month)
Harvey Publications

	Good	Fine	Mint
1-About Great Britain		.40	.80

SAD SACK GOES HOME
1951 (16 pgs. in color)
Harvey Publications

	Good	Fine	Mint
nn-by George Baker	3.50	10.50	24.00

SAD SACK LAUGH SPECIAL
Winter, 1958-59 - No. 93, Feb, 1977
Harvey Publications

	Good	Fine	Mint
1	2.65	8.00	18.00
2-10	1.35	4.00	8.00
11-30	.70	2.00	4.00
31-50	.40	1.20	2.40
51-93		.50	1.00

SAD SACK NAVY, GOBS 'N' GALS
Aug, 1972 - No. 8, Oct, 1973
Harvey Publications

	Good	Fine	Mint
1		.50	1.00
2-8		.30	.60

SAD SACK'S ARMY LIFE (See Harvey Hits No. 8, 17, 22, 28, 32, 39, 43, 47, 51, 55, 58, 61, 64, 67, 70)

SAD SACK'S ARMY LIFE (. . .Parade #1-57, . . .Today #58 on)
Oct, 1963 - No. 60, Nov, 1975; No. 61, May, 1976
Harvey Publications

	Good	Fine	Mint
1	2.00	6.00	14.00
2-10	1.00	3.00	6.00
11-20	.40	1.20	2.40
21-40		.50	1.00
41-61		.30	.60

SAD SACK'S FUNNY FRIENDS (See Harvey Hits #75)
Dec, 1955 - No. 75, Oct, 1969
Harvey Publications

	Good	Fine	Mint
1	3.50	10.50	24.00
2-10	1.70	5.00	10.00
11-20	.85	2.50	5.00
21-30	.40	1.20	2.40
31-50		.50	1.00
51-75		.30	.60

SAD SACK'S MUTTSY (See Harvey Hits No. 74, 77, 80, 82, 84, 87, 89, 92, 96, 99, 102, 105, 108, 111, 113, 115, 117, 119, 121)

SAD SACK USA (. . .Vacation #8)
Nov, 1972 - No. 7, Nov, 1973; No. 8, Oct, 1974
Harvey Publications

	Good	Fine	Mint
1		.50	1.00
2-8		.25	.50

SAD SACK WITH SARGE & SADIE
Sept, 1972 - No. 8, Nov, 1973
Harvey Publications

	Good	Fine	Mint
1		.50	1.00
2-8		.25	.50

SAD SAD SACK WORLD
Oct, 1964 - No. 46, Dec, 1973
Harvey Publications

	Good	Fine	Mint
1	.85	2.50	5.00
2-10	.40	1.20	2.40
11-46		.50	1.00

SAGA OF BIG RED, THE
Sept, 1976 ($1.25) (In color)
Omaha World-Herald

	Good	Fine	Mint
nn-by Win Mumma; story of the Nebraska Cornhuskers (sports)	.30	.80	1.60

SAGA OF CRYSTAR, CRYSTAL WARRIOR, THE
May, 1983 - No. 11, Feb, 1985
Marvel Comics Group

	Good	Fine	Mint
1-($2.00; Baxter paper)	.35	1.00	2.00
2-5		.30	.60
6-Golden-c	.25	.75	1.50
7-11: Golden c-7-9,11; 10,11($1.00); 11-Alpha Flight app.		.30	.60

SAGA OF RA'S AL GHUL, THE
Jan, 1988 - No. 4, Apr, 1988 (mini-series, $2.50, color)
DC Comics

	Good	Fine	Mint
1-4	.40	1.25	2.50

SAGA OF SWAMP THING, THE (Swamp Thing #39-41,46 on)
May, 1982 - Present (Later issues for mature readers)
DC Comics

	Good	Fine	Mint
1-Origin retold; Phantom Stranger series begins; ends No. 13; movie adapt.		.50	1.00
2-15: 2-Photo-c		.35	.70
16-19: Bissette-a	.35	1.00	2.00
20-1st Alan Moore issue	2.65	8.00	16.00
21-New origin	3.15	9.50	19.00
22-25	1.25	3.75	7.50
26-30	.85	2.60	5.20
31-35	.40	1.25	2.50
36-40	.35	1.00	2.00
41-45	.25	.75	1.50
46-52: 46-Crisis x-over		.60	1.20
53-Double size ($1.25)	.25	.75	1.50
54-60		.45	.90
61-66: Direct only. 64-Last Moore ish.		.50	1.00
Annual 1(11/82)-Movie Adaptation		.50	1.00
Annual 2(1/85)	.35	1.00	2.00
Annual 3(10/87, $2.00)	.35	1.00	2.00
Saga of the Swamp Thing ($10.95, '87)-reprints #20-26	1.85	5.50	10.95

NOTE: ***Bissette*** *a(p)-16-19, 21-27, 29, 30, 34-36, 39-42, 44, 46, 50, 64p; c-17i, 24p-32p, 35p-37p, 40p, 44p, 46p-50p, 51-56, 57i, 58, 61, 62, 63p.* ***Spiegle*** *a-1-3, 6.* ***Totleben*** *a(i)-10, 16-27, 29, 31, 34-40, 42, 44, 46, 48, 50, 53, 55i; c-25-32i, 33, 35-40i, 42i, 44i, 46-50i, 53, 55i, 59p, 64, 65.* ***Wrightson*** *a-18i(r), 33r; c-57p.*

SAILOR SWEENEY (Navy Action #1-11, 15 on)
No. 12, July, 1956 - No. 14, Nov, 1956
Atlas Comics (CDS)

	Good	Fine	Mint
12-14: 12-Shores-a. 13-Severin-c	1.70	5.00	12.00

SAINT, THE(Also see Movie Comics(DC) #2 & Silver Streak #18)
Aug, 1947 - No. 12, Mar, 1952
Avon Periodicals

	Good	Fine	Mint
1-Kamen bondage c/a	28.00	84.00	195.00
2	15.00	45.00	105.00
3,4: 4-Lingerie panels	12.00	36.00	84.00
5-Spanking panel	18.00	54.00	125.00
6-Miss Fury app., 14 pgs.	20.00	60.00	140.00
7-c-/Avon paperback 118	11.00	32.00	76.00
8,9(12/50): Saint strip-r in #8-12; 9-Kinstler-c	9.00	27.00	62.00
10-Wood-a, 1 pg; c-/Avon paperback 289	9.00	27.00	62.00
11	6.50	19.50	45.00
12-c-/Avon paperback 123	8.50	25.50	60.00

NOTE: *Lucky Dale, Girl Detective in #1,2,4,6.* ***Hollingsworth*** *a-4, 6.*

SALERNO CARNIVAL OF COMICS (Also see Pure Oil Comics, 24 Pages of Comics, & Vicks Comics)
Late 1930s (16 pgs.) (paper cover) (Giveaway)

Sad Sack's Funny Friends #4, © HARV

The Saga of Swamp Thing #19, © DC

The Saint #1, © AVON

Samson #1, © FOX

Samurai #5, © Aircel Publ.

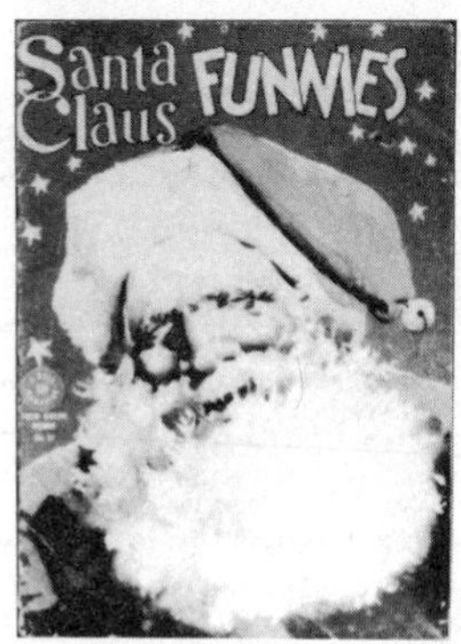
Santa Claus Funnies #91, © DELL

SALERNO CARNIVAL OF COMICS (continued)
Salerno Cookie Co.

	Good	Fine	Mint
nn-Color reprints of Calkins' Buck Rogers & Skyroads, plus other strips from Famous Funnies	25.00	75.00	175.00

SALIMBA (3-D)
1986 - No. 2, Sept, 1986
Blackthorne Publ.

1,2-Jungle girl stories	.35	1.10	2.25

SALOME' (See Night Music No. 6)

SAM HILL PRIVATE EYE
1950 - No. 7, 1951
Close-Up

1-Negligee panel	4.35	13.00	30.00
2	2.65	8.00	18.00
3-7	2.00	6.00	14.00

SAM SLADE ROBOHUNTER
Oct, 1986 - Present
Quality Comics

1-5		.35	.70
6-12 ($1.25)-Origin Ro-Busters		.55	1.10

SAMSON (1st Series) (Capt. Aero #7 on)
Fall, 1940 - No. 6, Sept, 1941 (See Fantastic Comics)
Fox Features Syndicate

1-Powell-a, signed 'Rensie;' Wing Turner by Tuska app.	50.00	150.00	350.00
2-Dr. Fung by Powell	24.00	72.00	170.00
3-Navy Jones app.; Simon-c	19.00	57.00	132.00
4-Yarko the Great, Master Magician by Eisner begins; Fine-c?	16.00	48.00	110.00
5,6: 6-Origin The Topper	16.00	48.00	110.00

SAMSON (2nd Series) (See Spectacular Features Magazine)
No. 12, April, 1955 - No. 14, Aug, 1955
Ajax/Farrell Publications (Four Star)

12-Wonder Boy	7.00	21.00	50.00
13,14: 13-Wonder Boy, Rocket Man	5.00	15.00	35.00

SAMSON (See Mighty Samson)

SAMSON & DELILAH (See A Spectacular Feature Magazine)

SAMUEL BRONSTON'S CIRCUS WORLD (See Circus World under Movie Comics)

SAMURAI
1985 - Present ($1.70, B&W)
Aircel Publ.

1	3.15	9.50	22.00
1 (2nd printing)	.50	1.50	3.00
1 (3rd printing)	.30	.85	1.70
2	1.00	3.00	6.00
2 (2nd printing)	.30	.85	1.70
3-5	.50	1.50	3.00
6-17	.35	1.00	2.00

SANDMAN, THE
Winter, 1974; No. 2, Apr-May, 1975 - No. 6, Dec-Jan, 1975-76
National Periodical Publications

1-Kirby-a		.30	.60
2-6: 6-Kirby/Wood c/a		.25	.50

NOTE: *Kirby a-1p, 4-6p; c-1-5.*

SANDS OF THE SOUTH PACIFIC
January, 1953
Toby Press

1	8.50	25.50	60.00

SANTA AND HIS REINDEER (See March of Comics No. 166)

SANTA AND POLLYANNA PLAY THE GLAD GAME
Aug, 1960 (16 pages) (Disney giveaway)
Sales Promotion

	Good	Fine	Mint
	1.00	3.00	6.00

SANTA AND THE ANGEL (See 4-Color No. 259 & Dell Jr. Treasury No. 7)

SANTA & THE BUCCANEERS
1959
Promotional Publ. Co. (Giveaway)

Reprints 1952 Santa & the Pirates	.50	1.50	3.00

SANTA & THE CHRISTMAS CHICKADEE
1974 (20 pgs.)
Murphy's (Giveaway)

		.50	1.00

SANTA & THE PIRATES
1952
Promotional Publ. Co. (Giveaway)

Marv Levy c/a	.85	2.50	5.00

SANTA AT THE ZOO (See 4-Color No. 259)

SANTA CLAUS
Apr, 1986 - No. 3, June, 1986 (mini-series)
Star Comics (Marvel)

1-3: r-/Marvel Super Sp. 39		.40	.80

SANTA CLAUS AROUND THE WORLD (See March of Comics No. 241)

SANTA CLAUS CONQUERS THE MARTIANS (See Movie Classics)

SANTA CLAUS FUNNIES
No date (1940s) (Color & B&W; 8x10''; 12pgs., heavy paper)
W. T. Grant Co. (Giveaway)

March Of Comics-r?	6.75	20.00	40.00

SANTA CLAUS FUNNIES (Also see Dell Giants)
Dec?, 1942 - No. 1274, Dec, 1961
Dell Publishing Co.

nn(#1)(1942)-Kelly-a	27.00	81.00	190.00
2(12/43)-Kelly-a	19.00	57.00	132.00
4-Color 61(1944)-Kelly-a	19.00	57.00	132.00
4-Color 91(1945)-Kelly-a	14.00	42.00	100.00
4-Color 128('46),175('47)-Kelly-a	12.00	36.00	84.00
4-Color 205,254-Kelly-a	11.00	32.00	76.00
4-Color 302,361	2.30	7.00	16.00
4-Color 525,607,666,756,867	1.70	5.00	12.00
4-Color 958,1063,1154,1274	1.50	4.50	10.00

NOTE: *Most issues contain only one **Kelly** story.*

SANTA CLAUS PARADE
1951; 1952; 1955 (25 cents)
Ziff-Davis (Approved Comics)/St. John Publishing Co.

nn(1951-Ziff-Davis)-116 pgs. (Xmas Special)	5.50	16.50	38.00
2(12/52-Ziff-Davis)-100 pgs.; Dave Berg-a	4.35	13.00	30.00
V1#3(1/55-St. John)-100 pgs.	3.70	11.00	26.00

SANTA CLAUS' WORKSHOP (See March of Comics No. 50,168)

SANTA IS COMING (See March of Comics No. 197)

SANTA IS HERE (See March of Comics No. 49)

SANTA ON THE JOLLY ROGER
1965
Promotional Publ. Co. (Giveaway)

Marv Levy c/a	.50	1.50	3.00

SANTA! SANTA!
1974 (20 pgs.)
R. Jackson (Montgomery Ward giveaway)

SANTA! SANTA! (continued) — Good / Fine / Mint
.50 1.00

SANTA'S BUSY CORNER (See March of Comics No. 31)

SANTA'S CANDY KITCHEN (See March of Comics No. 14)

SANTA'S CHRISTMAS BOOK (See March of Comics No. 123)

SANTA'S CHRISTMAS COMICS
December, 1952 (100 pages)
Standard Comics (Best Books)

nn-Supermouse, Dizzy Duck, Happy Rabbit, etc. 4.35 13.00 30.00

SANTA'S CHRISTMAS COMIC VARIETY SHOW
1943 (24 pages)
Sears Roebuck & Co.

Contains puzzles & new comics of Dick Tracy, Little Orphan Annie, Moon Mullins, Terry & the Pirates, etc. 7.50 22.50 52.00

SANTA'S CHRISTMAS LIST (See March of Comics No. 255)

SANTA'S CHRISTMAS TIME STORIES
nd (late 1940s) (16 pgs.; paper cover)
Premium Sales, Inc. (Giveaway)

2.00 6.00 12.00

SANTA'S CIRCUS
1964 (half-size)
Promotional Publ. Co. (Giveaway)

Marv Levy c/a .50 1.50 3.00

SANTA'S FUN BOOK
1951, 1952 (regular size, 16 pages, paper-c)
Promotional Publ. Co. (Murphy's giveaway)

1.70 5.00 10.00

SANTA'S GIFT BOOK
No date (16 pgs.)
No Publisher

Puzzles, games only 1.00 3.00 6.00

SANTA'S HELPERS (See March of Comics No. 64,106,198)

SANTA'S LITTLE HELPERS (See March of Comics No. 270)

SANTA'S NEW STORY BOOK
1949 (16 pgs.; paper cover)
Wallace Hamilton Campbell (Giveaway)

3.00 9.00 18.00

SANTA'S REAL STORY BOOK
1948, 1952 (16 pgs.)
Wallace Hamilton Campbell/W. W. Orris (Giveaway)

2.35 7.00 14.00

SANTA'S RIDE
1959
W. T. Grant Co. (Giveaway)

1.35 4.00 8.00

SANTA'S RODEO
1964 (half-size)
Promotional Publ. Co. (Giveaway)

Marv Levy-a .70 2.00 4.00

SANTA'S SECRETS
1951, 1952? (16 pgs.; paper cover)
Sam B. Anson Christmas giveaway

2.00 6.00 12.00

SANTA'S SHOW (See March of Comics No. 311)

SANTA'S SLEIGH (See March of Comics No. 298)

SANTA'S STORIES
1953 (regular size; paper cover)
K. K. Publications (Klines Dept. Store) — Good / Fine / Mint

Kelly-a 12.00 36.00 84.00

SANTA'S SURPRISE (See March of Comics No. 13)

SANTA'S SURPRISE
1947 (36 pgs.; slick cover)
K. K. Publications (Giveaway)

2.75 8.00 16.00

SANTA'S TINKER TOTS
1958
Charlton Comics

1-Based on "The Tinker Tots Keep Christmas" 1.15 3.50 7.00

SANTA'S TOYLAND (See March of Comics No. 242)

SANTA'S TOYS (See March of Comics No. 12)

SANTA'S TOYTOWN FUN BOOK
1952, 1953?
Promotional Publ. Co. (Giveaway)

Marv Levy-c 1.00 3.00 6.00

SANTA'S VISIT (See March of Comics No. 283)

SANTIAGO (See 4-Color No. 723)

SARGE SNORKEL (Beetle Bailey)
Oct, 1973 - No. 17, Dec, 1976
Charlton Comics

1 .50 1.00
2-17 .30 .60

SARGE STEEL (Becomes Secret Agent #9 on)
Dec, 1964 - No. 8, Mar-Apr, 1966
Charlton Comics

1-Origin .35 1.00 2.00
2-8: 6-Judo Master app. .25 .75 1.50

SAVAGE COMBAT TALES
Feb, 1975 - No. 3, July, 1975
Atlas/Seaboard Publ.

1-3: 1-Sgt. Stryker's Death Squad begins (origin). 2-Only app. Warhawk .30 .60

NOTE: ***McWilliams*** *a-1-3; c-1.* ***Sparling*** *a-1, 3.* ***Toth*** *a-2.*

SAVAGE RAIDS OF GERONIMO (See Geronimo No. 4)

SAVAGE RANGE (See 4-Color No. 807)

SAVAGE SHE-HULK, THE
Feb, 1980 - No. 25, Feb, 1982
Marvel Comics Group

1-Origin & 1st app. .50 1.00
2-25: 25-52 pgs. .30 .60

NOTE: ***Austin*** *a-25i; c-23i-25i.* ***J. Buscema*** *a-1p; c-1, 2p.* ***Golden*** *c-8-11.*

SAVAGE SWORD OF CONAN, THE (Magazine)
Aug, 1974 - Present (B&W)(Mature readers)
Marvel Comics Group

1-Smith-r; Buscema/Adams/Krenkel-a; origin Blackmark by Gil Kane(part 1) & Red Sonja (3rd app.) 2.50 7.50 15.00
2-Adams-c; Chaykin/Adams-a 1.25 3.75 7.50
3-Severin/Smith-a; Adams-a 1.00 3.00 6.00
4-Adams/Kane-a(r) .85 2.50 5.00
5-10 .70 2.00 4.00
11-20 .60 1.75 3.50
21-30 .50 1.50 3.00
31-50 .35 1.00 2.00
51-146: 70-Article on movie. 83-Red Sonja-r by Adams from #1

Santa's Surprise, © WEST

The Savage She-Hulk #24, © MCG

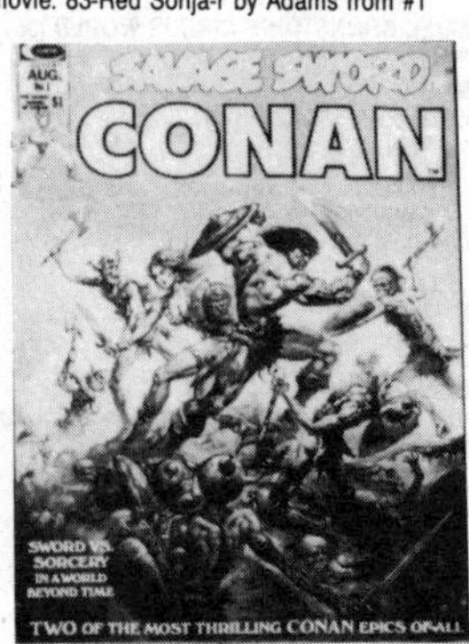

The Savage Sword of Conan #1, © MCG

Savage Tales #4 (1st series), © MCG

The Scarecrow of Romney Marsh #1, © WDC

Science Comics #1 (2nd series), © Humor Publ.

SAVAGE SWORD OF CONAN (continued) — Good / Fine / Mint

	Good	Fine	Mint
	.25	.75	1.50
Annual 1('75)-B&W, Smith-r (Conan #10,13)	.50	1.50	3.00

NOTE: ***Adams** a-14p, 60, 83p(r). **Alcala** a-2 ,4, 7, 12, 15-20, 23, 24, 28, 59, 67, 69, 75, 76i, 80i, 82i, 83i, 89. **Austin** a-78i. **Boris** c-1, 4, 5, 7, 9, 10, 12, 15. **Brunner** a-30; c-8, 30. **Buscema** a-1-5, 7, 10-12, 15-24, 26-28, 31, 32, 36-43, 45, 47-58p, 60-67p, 70, 71-74p, 76-81p, 87-96p, 98, 99p-101p; c-40. **Corbin** a-4, 16, 29. **Finlay** a-16. **Golden** a-98, 101. **Kaluta** a-11, 18; c-3, 91, 93. **Gil Kane** a-2, 3, 8, 13r, 29, 47, 64, 65, 67, 85p, 86p. **Krenkel** a-9, 11, 14, 16, 24. **Morrow** a-7. **Nebres** a-93i, 101i, 107, 114. **Newton** a-6. **Nino** a/c-6. **Redondo** c-48, 50, 52, 56, 57, 85i, 90, 96i. **Simonson** a-7, 8, 12, 15-17. **Smith** a-7, 16, 24, 82r. **Starlin** c-26. No. 8 & 10 contain a Robert E. Howard Conan adaptation.*

SAVAGE TALES (Magazine) (B&W)
May, 1971; No. 2, 10/73; No. 3, 2/74 - No. 12, Summer, 1975
Marvel Comics Group

	Good	Fine	Mint
1-Origin & 1st app. The Man-Thing by Morrow; Conan the Barbarian by Barry Smith, Femizons by Romita begin; Ka-Zar app.	7.00	20.00	40.00
2-Smith, Brunner, Morrow, Williamson, Wrightson-a (reprint/Creatures on the Loose #10); King Kull app.	2.50	7.50	15.00
3-Smith, Brunner, Steranko, Williamson-a	1.70	5.00	10.00
4,5-Adams-c; last Conan (Smith-r/#4) plus Kane/Adams-a. 5-Brak the Barbarian begins, ends #8	1.00	3.00	6.00
6-Ka-Zar begins; Williamson-r; Adams-c	.50	1.50	3.00
7-Buscema/Adams-a	.50	1.50	3.00
8-Shanna, the She-Devil begins, ends #10; Williamson-r	.50	1.50	3.00
9,11	.40	1.20	2.40
10-Adams-a(i)	.50	1.50	3.00
Annual 1(Summer'75)(#12 on inside)-Ka-Zar origin by G. Kane; B&W; Smith-r/Astonishing Tales	.40	1.20	2.40

NOTE: ***Boris** c-7,10. **Buscema** a-5r, 6p, 8p; c-2. **Fabian** c-8. **Heath** a-10p, 11p. **Kaluta** c-9. **Maneely** a-2r. **Starlin** a-5. Robert E. Howard adaptations-1-4.*

SAVAGE TALES (Magazine size)
Nov, 1985 - No. 9?, Mar, 1987 (B&W) ($1.50) (Mature readers)
Marvel Comics Group

	Good	Fine	Mint
1-1st app. The Nam; Golden-a	1.50	4.50	10.00
2-9: Golden-a	.25	.75	1.50

SCAMP (Walt Disney)(See Walt Disney's C&S #204)
No. 703, 5/56 - No. 1204, 8-10/61; 11/67 - No. 45, 1/79
Dell Publishing Co./Gold Key

	Good	Fine	Mint
4-Color 703(No. 1)	1.70	5.00	12.00
4-Color 777,806('57),833	1.15	3.50	8.00
5(3-5/58)-10(6-8/59)	.85	2.50	6.00
11-16(12-2/60-61)	.70	2.00	5.00
4-Color 1204(1961)	.85	2.50	6.00
1(12/67-G.K.)-Reprints begin	.55	1.65	4.00
2(3/69)-10	.35	1.00	2.00
11-20	.25	.75	1.50
21-45		.40	.80

NOTE: *New stories-No. 20(in part), 22-25, 27, 29-31, 34, 36-40, 42-45. New covers-No. 11, 12, 14, 15, 17-25, 27, 29-31, 34, 36-38.*

SCAR FACE (See The Crusaders)

SCARECROW OF ROMNEY MARSH, THE (See W.D. Showcase #53)
April, 1964 - No. 3, Oct, 1965 (Disney TV Show)
Gold Key

	Good	Fine	Mint
10112-404 (#1)	2.65	8.00	18.00
2,3	1.70	5.00	12.00

SCARLET O'NEIL (See Harvey Comics Hits No. 59)

SCARY TALES
8/75 - No. 9, 1/77; No. 10, 9/77 - No. 20, 6/79; No. 21, 8/80 - No. 46, 10/84
Charlton Comics

	Good	Fine	Mint
1-Origin & 1st app. Countess Von Bludd, not in No. 2		.40	.80
2-11		.30	.60
12-36,39,46-All reprints		.30	.60
37,38,40-45-New-a. 38-Mr. Jigsaw app.		.30	.60
1(Modern Comics reprint, 1977)		.15	.30

NOTE: ***Adkins** a-31i; c-31i. **Ditko** a-3, 5, 7, 8(2), 11, 12, 14-16r, 18(3)r, 19r, 21r, 30r, 32, 39r; c-5, 11, 14, 18, 30, 32. **Newton** a-31p; c-31p. **Powell** a-18r. **Staton** a-1(2 pgs.), 4, 20r; c-1, 20. **Sutton** a-9; c-4, 9.*

SCHOOL DAY ROMANCES (. . .of Teen-Agers #4) (Popular Teen-Agers #5 on)
Nov-Dec, 1949 - No. 4, May-June, 1950
Star Publications

	Good	Fine	Mint
1-Tony Gayle (later Gay), Gingersnapp	7.00	21.00	50.00
2,3	4.00	12.00	28.00
4-Ronald Reagan photo-c	11.00	32.00	76.00

NOTE: *All have **L. B. Cole** covers.*

SCHWINN BICYCLE BOOK (. . . Bike Thrills, 1959)
1949; 1952; 1959 (10 cents)
Schwinn Bicycle Co.

	Good	Fine	Mint
1949	2.30	7.00	16.00
1952-Believe It or Not type facts; comic format; 36 pgs.	1.35	4.00	8.00
1959	1.00	3.00	6.00

SCIENCE COMICS (1st Series)
Feb, 1940 - No. 8, Sept, 1940
Fox Features Syndicate

	Good	Fine	Mint
1-Origin Dynamo (called Electro in #1), The Eagle, & Navy Jones; Marga, The Panther Woman, Cosmic Carson & Perisphere Payne, Dr. Doom begin; bondage/hypo-c	100.00	300.00	700.00
2	55.00	165.00	385.00
3,4: 4-Kirby-a	44.00	132.00	310.00
5-8	30.00	90.00	210.00

NOTE: *Cosmic Carson by **Tuska**-No. 1-3; by **Kirby**-No. 4. **Lou Fine** c-1-3 only.*

SCIENCE COMICS (2nd Series)
January, 1946 - No. 5, 1946
Humor Publications (Ace Magazines?)

	Good	Fine	Mint
1-Palais c/a in No. 1-3; A-Bomb-c	3.50	10.50	24.00
2	2.00	6.00	14.00
3-Feldstein-a, 6 pgs.	5.00	15.00	35.00
4,5	1.85	5.50	13.00

SCIENCE COMICS
May, 1947 (8 pgs. in color)
Ziff-Davis Publ. Co.

	Good	Fine	Mint
nn-Could be ordered by mail for 10 cents; like the nn Amazing Advs. (1950)-used to test the market	20.00	60.00	140.00

SCIENCE COMICS
March, 1951
Export Publication Ent., Toronto, Canada
Distr. in U.S. by Kable News Co.

	Good	Fine	Mint
1-Science Adventure stories plus some true science features	1.85	5.50	13.00

SCIENCE FICTION SPACE ADVENTURES (See Space Adventures)

SCOOBY DOO (. . .Where are you? No. 1-16,26; . . .Mystery Comics No. 17-25,27 on) (TV)
March, 1970 - No. 30, Feb, 1975
Gold Key

	Good	Fine	Mint
1	2.65	8.00	18.00
2-5	1.30	4.00	9.00
6-10	.85	2.50	6.00
11-20: 11-Tufts-a	.70	2.00	4.00

SCOOBY DOO (continued)

	Good	Fine	Mint
21-30	.40	1.25	2.50

(See March of Comics No. 356,368,382,391)

SCOOBY DOO (TV)
April, 1975 - No. 11, Dec, 1976 (Hanna Barbera)
Charlton Comics

	Good	Fine	Mint
1	1.00	3.00	7.00
2-5	.60	1.75	3.50
6-11	.40	1.25	2.50

SCOOBY-DOO (TV)
Oct, 1977 - No. 9, Feb, 1979
Marvel Comics Group

	Good	Fine	Mint
1-Dyno-Mutt begins	.40	1.25	2.50
2-9		.50	1.00

SCOOP COMICS
November, 1941 - No. 8, 1946
Harry 'A' Chesler (Holyoke)

	Good	Fine	Mint
1-Intro. Rocketman & Rocketgirl; origin The Master Key; Dan Hastings begins; Charles Sultan c/a	28.00	84.00	195.00
2-Rocket Boy app; Injury to eye story (Same as Spotlight #3)	17.00	51.00	120.00
3-Injury to eye story-r from #2	13.00	40.00	90.00
4-8	10.00	30.00	70.00

SCOOTER (See Swing with . . .)

SCOOTER
April, 1946
Rucker Publ. Ltd. (Canadian)

	Good	Fine	Mint
1	2.00	6.00	14.00

SCORPION
Feb, 1975 - No. 3, July, 1975
Atlas/Seaboard Publ.

	Good	Fine	Mint
1-Intro.; bondage-c by Chaykin		.40	.80
2-Wrightson, Kaluta, Simonson-a(i)		.30	.60
3-Mooney-a(i)		.25	.50

NOTE: ***Chaykin** a-1,2.*

SCORPIO ROSE
Jan, 1983; No. 2, Oct, 1983 (Baxter paper)
Eclipse Comics

	Good	Fine	Mint
1-Dr. Orient back-up story begins	.25	.75	1.50
2-Origin	.25	.75	1.50

NOTE: ***Rogers** c/a 1,2.*

SCOTLAND YARD (Inspector Farnsworth of . . .) (Texas Rangers in Action #5 on?)
June, 1955 - No. 4, March, 1956
Charlton Comics Group

	Good	Fine	Mint
1-Tothish-a	4.35	13.00	30.00
2-4: 2-Tothish-a	2.65	8.00	18.00

SCOUT (See New America & Swords of Texas)
12/85 - No. 24, 10/87 ($1.75 - $1.25)
Eclipse Comics

	Good	Fine	Mint
1	.85	2.50	5.00
2-8,11,12: 11-Monday: The Eliminator begins	.35	1.00	2.00
9,10: 9-Airboy app. 10-Bissette-a	.25	.75	1.50
13-15,17,18,20-24 ($1.75)	.35	1.00	2.00
16-Scout 3-D Special ($2.50)	.50	1.50	3.00
16-Scout 2-D	.50	1.50	3.00
19-Contains Flexidisk ($2.50)	.50	1.50	3.00
. . . Handbook 1 (1987, $1.75)	.30	.90	1.75

SCREAM (. . . Comics) (Andy Comics #20 on)
Fall, 1944 - No. 19, April, 1948
Humor Publications/Current Books(Ace Magazines)

	Good	Fine	Mint
1	4.60	14.00	32.00
2	2.30	7.00	16.00
3-15: 11-Racist humor (Indians)	1.70	5.00	12.00
16-Intro. Lily-Belle	1.70	5.00	12.00
17,19	1.50	4.50	10.00
18-Transvestism, hypo needle story	3.50	10.50	24.00

SCREAM (Magazine)
Aug, 1973 - No. 11, Feb, 1975 (68 pgs.) (B&W)
Skywald Publishing Corp.

	Good	Fine	Mint
1	.50	1.50	3.00
2-5: 2-Origin Lady Satan. 3 (12/73)-#3 found on pg. 22	.30	.80	1.60
6-11: 6-Origin The Victims. 9-Severed head-c		.50	1.00

SCRIBBLY (See All-American, Buzzy, The Funnies & Popular Comics)
8-9/48 - No. 13, 8-9/50; No. 14, 10-11/51 - No. 15, 12-1/51-52
National Periodical Publications

	Good	Fine	Mint
1-Sheldon Mayer-a in all; 52pgs. begin	40.00	120.00	280.00
2	22.00	65.00	154.00
3-5	20.00	60.00	140.00
6-10	13.00	40.00	90.00
11-15: 13-Last 52 pgs.	10.00	30.00	70.00

SEA DEVILS (See DC Special #10,19, DC Super-Stars #14,17, Limited Collectors Ed. #39,45, & Showcase)
Sept-Oct, 1961 - No. 35, May-June, 1967
National Periodical Publications

	Good	Fine	Mint
1	6.50	19.50	45.00
2-Last 10 cent issue	3.60	11.00	25.00
3-5	1.70	5.00	12.00
6-10	1.15	3.50	8.00
11,12,14-20	.85	2.50	5.00
13-Kubert, Colan-a	1.00	3.00	6.00
21,23-35	.70	2.00	4.00
22-Intro. International Sea Devils; origin & 1st app. Capt. X & Man Fish	.70	2.00	4.00

NOTE: ***Heath** a-1-10; c-1-10,14-16.*

SEADRAGON (Also see The Epsilon Wave)
May, 1986 - No. 8, 1987? ($1.75, color)
Elite Comics

	Good	Fine	Mint
1-3	.30	.90	1.80
1 (2nd printing)	.30	.85	1.70
4-8	.30	.85	1.70

SEA HOUND, THE (Capt. Silver's Log of . . .)
1945 (no month) - No. 4, Jan-Feb, 1946
Avon Periodicals

	Good	Fine	Mint
nn	4.60	14.00	32.00
2-4	3.00	9.00	21.00

SEA HOUND, THE (Radio)
No. 3, July, 1949 - No. 4, Sept, 1949
Capt. Silver Syndicate

	Good	Fine	Mint
3,4	2.65	8.00	18.00

SEA HUNT (TV)
No. 928, 8/58; No. 994, 10-12/59; No. 4, 1-3/60 - No. 13, 4-6/62
Dell Publishing Co. (All have Lloyd Bridges photo-c)

	Good	Fine	Mint
4-Color 928	4.35	13.00	30.00
4-Color 994, 4-13: Manning-a #4-6,8-11,13	3.50	10.50	24.00
4-Color 1041-Toth-a	5.00	15.00	35.00

SEARCH FOR LOVE
Feb-Mar, 1950 - No. 2, Apr-May, 1950 (52 pgs.)
American Comics Group

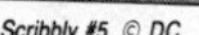
Scribbly #5, © DC

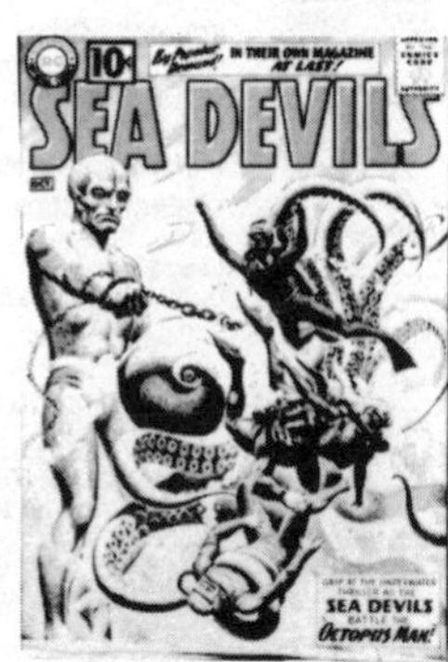

Sea Devils #1, © DC

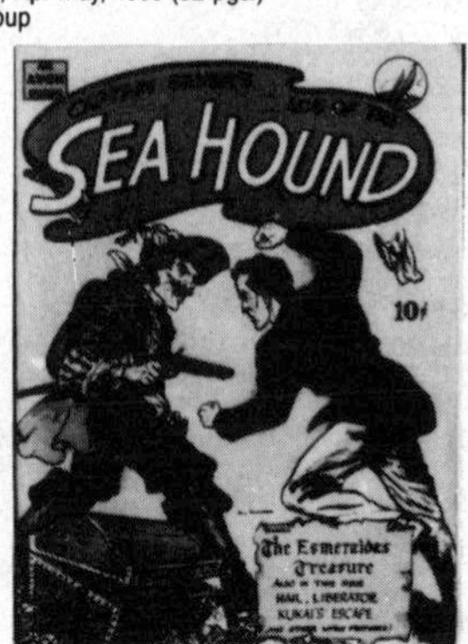

The Sea Hound #1, © AVON

Secret Agent X-9 Book 1, © DMP

Secret Love #1 (12/55), © AJAX

Secret Mysteries #17, © Merit Publ.

SEARCH FOR LOVE (continued)

	Good	Fine	Mint
1	3.50	10.50	24.00
2	1.85	5.50	13.00

SEARCHERS (See 4-Color No. 709)

SEARS (See Merry Christmas From . . .)

SEASON'S GREETINGS
1935 (6¼x5¼") (32 pgs. in color)
Hallmark (King Features)

Cover features Mickey Mouse, Popeye, Jiggs & Skippy. "The Night Before Christmas" told one panel per page, each panel by a famous artist featuring their character. Art by Alex Raymond, Gottfredson, Swinnerton, Segar, Chic Young, Milt Gross, Sullivan (Messmer), Herriman, McManus, Percy Crosby & others (22 artists in all)
Estimated value. . . . $200.00 — $400.00

SECRET AGENT (Formerly Sarge Steel)
Oct, 1966 - V2No.10, Oct, 1967
Charlton Comics

	Good	Fine	Mint
V2#9-Sarge Steel part-r begins	.30	.80	1.60
10-Tiffany Sinn, CIA app. (from Career Girl Romances #39); Aparo-a		.40	.80

SECRET AGENT (TV)
Nov, 1966 - No. 2, Jan, 1968
Gold Key

	Good	Fine	Mint
1,2-Photo-c	1.70	5.00	12.00

SECRET AGENT X-9
1934 (Book 1: 84 pgs.; Book 2: 124 pgs.) (8x7½")
David McKay Publications

	Good	Fine	Mint
Book 1-Contains reprints of the first 13 weeks of the strip by Alex Raymond; complete except for 2 dailies	34.00	100.00	240.00
Book 2-Contains reprints immediately following contents of Book 1, for 20 weeks by Alex Raymond; complete except for two dailies. Note: Raymond mis-dated the last five strips from 6/34, and while the dating sequence is confusing, the continuity is correct.	27.00	81.00	190.00

SECRET AGENT X-9 (See Feature Books No. 8, McKay)

SECRET AGENT Z-2 (See Holyoke One-Shot No. 7)

SECRET DIARY OF EERIE ADVENTURES
1953 (One Shot) (Giant-100 pgs.)
Avon Periodicals

	Good	Fine	Mint
(Rare) Kubert-a; Hollingsworth-c; Check back-c	82.00	246.00	575.00

SECRET HEARTS
9-10/49 - No. 6, 7-8/50; No. 7, 12-1/51-52 - No. 153, 7/71
(No. 1-6, photo-c; all 52 pgs.)
National Periodical Publications (Beverly)(Arleigh No. 50-113)

	Good	Fine	Mint
1	12.00	36.00	84.00
2-Toth-a	6.00	18.00	42.00
3,6 (1950)	4.60	14.00	32.00
4,5-Toth-a	5.70	17.00	40.00
7(12-1/51-52) (Rare)	5.50	16.50	38.00
8-10 (1952)	3.00	9.00	21.00
11-20	2.40	7.25	17.00
21-26: 26-Last pre-code (2-3/55)	2.00	6.00	14.00
27-40	1.70	5.00	12.00
41-50	1.00	3.00	7.00
51-60	.55	1.65	4.00
61-75: Last 10 cent ish?	.35	1.00	2.00
76-109		.60	1.20
110-"Reach for Happiness" serial begins, ends #138		.50	1.00
111-119,121-133,135-138		.40	.80
120,134-Adams-c	.30	.80	1.60
139,140		.25	.50
141,142-"20 Miles to Heartbreak," Chapter 2 & 3 (See Young Love for Chapter 1 & 4); Toth, Colletta-a		.40	.80
143-148,150-153: 144-Morrow-a		.25	.50
149-Toth-a		.50	1.00

SECRET ISLAND OF OZ, THE (See First Comics Graphic Novel)

SECRET LOVE (See Fox Giants)

SECRET LOVE
12/55 - No. 3, 8/56; 4/57 - No. 5, 2/58; No. 6, 6/58
Ajax-Farrell/Four Star Comic Corp. No. 2 on

	Good	Fine	Mint
1(12/55-Ajax)	2.30	7.00	16.00
2,3	1.30	4.00	9.00
1(4/57-Ajax)	1.85	5.50	13.00
2-6: 5-Bakerish-a	1.15	3.50	8.00

SECRET LOVE (See Sinister House of . . .)

SECRET LOVES
Nov, 1949 - No. 6, Sept, 1950
Comic Magazines/Quality Comics Group

	Good	Fine	Mint
1-Ward-c	9.00	27.00	62.00
2-Ward-c	8.50	25.50	60.00
3-Crandall-a	5.50	16.50	38.00
4,6	2.85	8.50	20.00
5-Suggestive art-"Boom Town Babe"	4.35	13.00	30.00

SECRET LOVE STORIES (See Fox Giants)

SECRET MISSIONS
February, 1950
St. John Publishing Co.

	Good	Fine	Mint
1-Kubert-c	7.00	21.00	50.00

SECRET MYSTERIES (Formerly Crime Mysteries & Crime Smashers)
No. 16, Nov, 1954 - No. 19, July, 1955
Ribage/Merit Publications No. 17 on

	Good	Fine	Mint
16-Horror, Palais-a	4.35	13.00	30.00
17-19-Horror; #17-mis-dated 3/54?	3.00	9.00	21.00

SECRET ORIGINS (See 80 Page Giant #8)
Aug-Oct, 1961 (Annual) (Reprints)
National Periodical Publications

	Good	Fine	Mint
1('61)-Origin Adam Strange (Showcase #17), Green Lantern (G.L. #1), Challs (partial/Showcase #6, 6 pgs. Kirby-a). J'onn J'onzz (Det. #225), New Flash (Showcase #4). Green Arrow (1pg. text). Superman-Batman team (W. Finest #94). Wonder Woman (W. Woman #105)	10.00	30.00	70.00

SECRET ORIGINS
Feb-Mar, 1973 - No. 6, Jan-Feb, 1974; No. 7, Oct-Nov, 1974
National Periodical Publications (All reprints)

	Good	Fine	Mint
1-Origin Superman, Batman, The Ghost, The Flash (Showcase #4); Infantino & Kubert-a	.25	.75	1.50
2-Origin new Green Lantern, the new Atom, & Supergirl; Kane-a		.50	1.00
3-Origin Wonder Woman, Wildcat		.50	1.00
4-Origin Vigilante by Meskin, Kid Eternity		.50	1.00
5-Origin The Spectre; Colan-c(p)		.45	.90
6-Origin Blackhawk & Legion of Super Heroes		.45	.90
7-Origin Robin, Aquaman		.45	.90

SECRET ORIGINS
April, 1986 - Present (All origins)(52 pgs. #6 on)
DC Comics

	Good	Fine	Mint
1-Origin Superman	.50	1.50	3.00
2-5: 2-Blue Beetle. 3-Capt. Marvel. 4-Firestorm, 5-Crimson Avenger, Shadow Lass, Dollman	.30	.90	1.80

SECRET ORIGINS (continued)

	Good	Fine	Mint
6-10: 6-G.A. Batman. 7-Green Lantern, G.A. Sandman, 8-Doll Man, 9-G.A. Flash, Skyman, 10-Phantom Stranger.	.25	.75	1.50
11-20: 11-G.A. Hawkman, Power Girl, 12-Challs of Unknown, G.A. Fury, 13-Nightwing, Johnny Thunder, 14-Suicide Squad, 15-Spectre, Deadman, 16-G.A. Hourman, Warlord, 17-Adam Strange, Dr. Occult, 18-G.A. Gr. Lantern, The Creeper, 19-Uncle Sam, The Guardian, 20-Batgirl, G.A. Dr. Mid-Nite		.65	1.30
21-25: 21-Jonah Hex, Black Candor. 22-Manhunters. 23-Floronic Man/Guardians of the Universe. 24-Blue Devil/Dr. Fate. 25-L.S.H./Atom		.65	1.30
Annual 1 (8/87)-Doom Patrol by Byrne c/a	.35	1.00	2.00

NOTE: ***Boland** c-7. **Giffen** a-18p. **Gil Kane** a-2; c-2p. **Morrow** a-21. **Orlando** a-10. **Tuska** a-9p.*

SECRET ORIGINS OF SUPER-HEROES (See DC Special Series #10,19)

SECRET ROMANCE
10/68 - No. 41, 11/76; No. 42, 3/79 - No. 48, 2/80
Charlton Comics

	Good	Fine	Mint
1		.40	.80
2-48: 9-Reese-a		.20	.40

NOTE: *Beyond the Stars app.-No. 9,11,12,14.*

SECRET ROMANCES
April 1951 - No. 27, July, 1955
Superior Publications Ltd.

	Good	Fine	Mint
1	4.60	14.00	32.00
2	2.65	8.00	18.00
3-10	2.35	7.00	16.00
11-13,15-18,20-27	1.65	5.00	11.50
14,19-Lingerie panels	2.65	8.00	18.00

SECRET SERVICE (See Kent Blake of the...)

SECRET SIX
Apr-May, 1968 - No. 7, Apr-May, 1969
National Periodical Publications

	Good	Fine	Mint
1-Origin	.35	1.00	2.00
2-7		.50	1.00

SECRET SOCIETY OF SUPER-VILLAINS
May-June, 1976 - No. 15, June-July, 1978
National Periodical Publications/DC Comics

	Good	Fine	Mint
1-Origin; JLA cameo		.65	1.30
2-5: 2-Re-intro/origin Capt. Comet; Gr. Lantern x-over		.30	.60
6-15: 9,10-Creeper x-over. 15-G.A. Atom, Dr. Midnite, & JSA app.		.25	.50

NOTE: ***Jones** a-'77 Special. **Orlando** a-11i.*

SECRET SOCIETY OF SUPER-VILLAINS SPECIAL (See DC Special Series #6)

SECRETS OF HAUNTED HOUSE
4-5/75 - No. 5, 12-1/75-76; No. 6, 6-7/77 - No. 14, 10-11/78; No. 15, 8/79 - No. 46, 3/82
National Periodical Publications/DC Comics

	Good	Fine	Mint
1		.50	1.00
2-46: 31-Mr. E series begins, ends #41		.25	.50

NOTE: ***Buckler** c-32-40p. **Ditko** a-9, 12, 41, 45. **Golden** a-10. **Howard** a-13i. **Kaluta** c-8, 10, 11, 14, 16, 29. **Kubert** c-41, 42. **Sheldon Mayer** a-43p. **McWilliams** a-35. **Newton** a-30p. **Nino** a-1, 13, 19. **Orlando** c-13, 30, 43, 45i. **Redondo** a-4, 29. **Rogers** c-26. **Spiegle** a-31-41. **Wrightson** c-5, 44.*

SECRETS OF HAUNTED HOUSE SPECIAL (See DC Spec. Ser. No. 12)

SECRETS OF LIFE (See 4-Color No. 749)

SECRETS OF LOVE (See Popular Teen-Agers...)

SECRETS OF LOVE AND MARRIAGE
Aug, 1956 - V2No.25, June, 1961
Charlton Comics

	Good	Fine	Mint
V2#1	1.30	4.00	9.00
V2#2-6	.55	1.65	4.00
V2#7-9(All 68 pgs.)	.45	1.35	3.00
10-25	.35	1.00	2.00

SECRETS OF MAGIC (See Wisco)

SECRETS OF SINISTER HOUSE (S.H. of Secret Love #1-4)
No. 5, June-July, 1972 - No. 18, June-July, 1974
National Periodical Publications

	Good	Fine	Mint
5-9: 7-Redondo-a		.30	.60
10-Adams-a(i)	.50	1.50	3.00
11-18: 17-Toth-r?		.25	.50

NOTE: ***Alcala** a-6, 13, 14. **Kaluta** c-6, 7, 11. **Nino** a-8, 11-13. c-6. Ambrose Bierce adaptation-#14.*

SECRETS OF THE LEGION OF SUPER-HEROES
Jan, 1981 - No. 3, March, 1981 (mini-series)
DC Comics

	Good	Fine	Mint
1-Origin of the Legion		.50	1.00
2-Retells origins of Brainiac 5, Shrinking Violet, Sun-Boy, Bouncing Boy, Ultra-Boy, Matter-Eater Lad, Mon-El, Karate Kid, & Dream Girl		.40	.80
3		.40	.80

SECRETS OF TRUE LOVE
February, 1958
St. John Publishing Co.

	Good	Fine	Mint
1	1.50	4.50	10.00

SECRETS OF YOUNG BRIDES
No. 5, 9/57 - No. 44, 10/64; 7/75 - No. 9, 11/76
Charlton Comics

	Good	Fine	Mint
5	1.30	4.00	9.00
6-10: 8-Negligee panel	.55	1.65	4.00
11-20	.45	1.35	3.00
21-30: Last 10 cent ish?	.35	1.00	2.00
31-44		.50	1.00
1-9		.25	.50

SECRET SQUIRREL (TV)
October, 1966 (Hanna-Barbera)
Gold Key

	Good	Fine	Mint
1	2.00	6.00	14.00
Kite Fun Book (1966, 16p, 5x7¼", soft-c)	2.30	7.00	16.00

SECRET STORY ROMANCES (Becomes True Tales of Love?)
Nov, 1953 - No. 21, Mar, 1956
Atlas Comics (TCI)

	Good	Fine	Mint
1-Everett-a	3.00	9.00	21.00
2	1.50	4.50	10.00
3-11: 11-Last pre-code (2/55)	1.15	3.50	8.00
12-21	1.00	3.00	7.00

NOTE: ***Colletta** a-10,14,15,17,21; c-10,14,17.*

SECRET VOICE, THE (See Great American Comics)

SECRET WARS II (Also see Marvel Super Heroes...)
July, 1985 - No. 9, Mar, 1986 (maxi-series)
Marvel Comics Group

	Good	Fine	Mint
1-Byrne/Austin-c	.35	1.00	2.00
2-9: 9-Double sized (75 cents)	.25	.75	1.50

SECTAURS
June, 1985 - No. 8?, 1986
Marvel Comics Group

	Good	Fine	Mint
1-Based on Coleco Toys		.50	1.00
2-10		.45	.90

Secret Romance #1, © CC

Secret Six #1, © DC

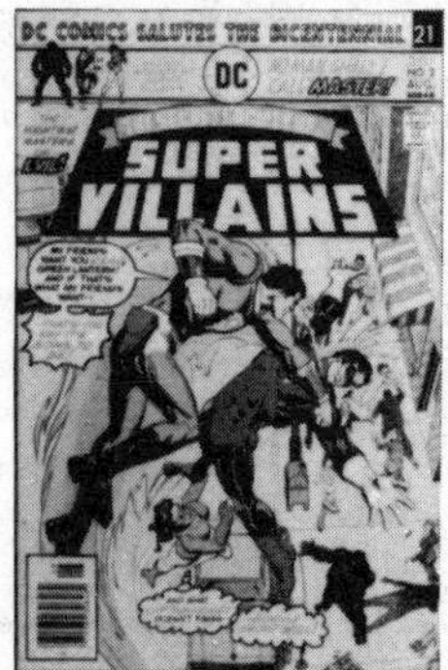

Secret Society of Super-Villains #2, © DC

Sensation Comics #56, © DC

Sensation Mystery #110, © DC

Sergeant Bilko #9, © DC

SEDUCTION OF THE INNOCENT (Also see N. Y. State Joint Legis. Committee to Study. . .)
1953, 1954 (399 pages) (Hardback)
Rinehart & Co., Inc., N. Y. (Also printed in Canada by Clarke, Irwin & Co. Ltd., Toronto)

Written by Dr. Fredric Wertham — **Good / Fine / Mint**

(1st Version)-with bibliographical note intact (several copies got out before the comic publishers forced the removal of this page) 70.00 150.00
with dust jacket. . . . 120.00 280.00
(2nd Version)- 42.00 90.00
with dust jacket. . . . 65.00 140.00
(3rd Version)-Published in England by Kennikat Press, 1954, 399pp. has bibliographical page 30.00 60.00
1972 r-/of 3rd version; 400pgs w/bibliography page; Kennikat Press 10.00 20.00

NOTE: *Material from this book appeared in the November, 1953(Vol.70, pp50-53,214) issue of the* ***Ladies' Home Journal*** *under the title "What Parents Don't Know About Comic Books." With the release of this book, Dr. Wertham reveals seven years of research attempting to link juvenile delinquency to comic books. Many illustrations showing excessive violence, sex, sadism, and torture are shown. This book was used at the Kefauver Senate hearings which led to the Comics Code Authority. Because of the influence this book had on the comic industry and the collector's interest in it, we feel this listing is justified. Also see* ***Parade of Pleasure.***

SEDUCTION OF THE INNOCENT!
Nov, 1985 - No. 3, 1986 ($1.75 cover)
Eclipse Comics

1-3 .30 .90 1.80
. . .3-D 1(10/85; $2.25 cover)-Contains unpub. Advs. Into Darkness #15 (pre-code) (36 pgs.) .40 1.15 2.30
2-D 1 (100 copy limited signed & numbered edition)(B&W) .85 2.50 5.00
. . .3-D 2 (4/86)-Baker, Toth-a .40 1.25 2.50
2-D 2 (100 copy limited signed & numbered edition)(B&W) .85 2.50 5.00

SELECT DETECTIVE
Aug-Sept, 1948 - No. 3, Dec-Jan, 1948-49
D. S. Publishing Co.

1-Matt Baker-a 6.50 19.50 45.00
2-Baker, McWilliams-a 4.60 14.00 32.00
3 4.00 12.00 28.00

SENSATIONAL POLICE CASES (Becomes Captain Steve Savage, 2nd series)
1952; 1954
Avon Periodicals

nn-100 pg. issue (1952, 25 cents)-Kubert & Kinstler-a 17.00 51.00 120.00
1 (1954) 5.70 17.00 40.00
2,3: 2-Kirbyish-a 4.35 13.00 30.00
4-Reprint/Saint #5 4.35 13.00 30.00

SENSATIONAL POLICE CASES
No date (1963?)
I. W. Enterprises

Reprint #5-Reprints Prison Break #5(1952-Avon); Infantino-a .80 2.40 4.80

SENSATION COMICS (. . .Mystery #110 on)
Jan, 1942 - No. 109, May-June, 1952
National Periodical Publ./All-American

1-Origin Mr. Terrific, Wildcat, The Gay Ghost, & Little Boy Blue; Wonder Woman(cont'd from All Star #8), The Black Pirate begin; intro. Justice & Fair Play Club 265.00 800.00 1850.00
1-Reprint, Oversize 13½"x10." **WARNING:** This comic is an exact duplicate reprint of the original except for its size. DC published it in 1974 with a second cover titling it as a Famous First Edition. There have been many reported cases of the outer cover being removed and the interior sold as the original edition. The reprint with the new outer cover removed is practically worthless.

Good / Fine / Mint

2 125.00 375.00 875.00
3-W. Woman gets secretary's job 73.00 220.00 510.00
4-1st app. Stretch Skinner in Wildcat 65.00 195.00 455.00
5-Intro. Justin, Black Pirate's son 48.00 145.00 335.00
6-Origin/1st app. Wonder Woman's magic lasso 40.00 120.00 280.00
7-10 38.00 115.00 265.00
11-20: 13-Hitler, Tojo, Mussolini-c 32.00 95.00 225.00
21-30 22.00 65.00 154.00
31-33 18.00 54.00 125.00
34-Sargon, the Sorcerer begins, ends 36; begins again 52 18.00 54.00 125.00
35-40: 38-X-Mas-c 15.00 45.00 105.00
41-50: 43-The Whip app. 13.00 40.00 90.00
51-60: 51-Last Black Pirate. 56,57-Sargon by Kubert 12.00 36.00 84.00
61-80: 63-Last Mr. Terrific. 65,66-Wildcat by Kubert. 68-Origin Huntress. 73-Bondage-c 11.00 32.00 76.00
81-Used in SOTI, pg. 33,34; Krigstein-a 14.00 42.00 100.00
82-90: 83-Last Sargon. 86-The Atom app. 90-Last Wildcat 9.50 28.50 65.00
91-Streak begins by Alex Toth 9.50 28.50 65.00
92,93: 92-Toth-a, 2 pgs. 8.50 25.50 60.00
94-1st all girl issue 11.00 32.00 76.00
95-99,101-106: Wonder Woman ends. 99-1st app. Astra, Girl of the Future, ends 106. 105-Last 52 pgs. 11.00 32.00 76.00
100 13.00 40.00 90.00
107-(Scarce)-1st mystery issue; Toth-a 17.00 51.00 115.00
108-(Scarce)-J. Peril by Toth(p) 12.00 36.00 84.00
109-(Scarce)-J. Peril by Toth(p) 17.00 51.00 115.00

NOTE: ***Krigstein*** *a-(Wildcat)-81, 83, 84.* ***Moldoff*** *Black Pirate-1-25; Black Pirate not in 34-36, 43-48. Wonder Woman by* ***H. G. Peter,*** *all issues except #8, 17-19, 21.*

SENSATION MYSTERY (Sensation #1-109)
No. 110, July-Aug, 1952 - No. 116, July-Aug, 1953
National Periodical Publications

110-Johnny Peril 10.00 30.00 70.00
111-116-Johnny Peril in all 9.50 28.50 65.00

NOTE: ***Colan*** *a-114p.* ***Giunta*** *a-112.* ***G. Kane*** *c-112, 113, 115.*

SENTINELS OF JUSTICE, THE (See Captain Paragon & . . .)

SERGEANT BARNEY BARKER (G. I. Tales #4 on)
Aug, 1956 - No. 3, Dec, 1956
Atlas Comics (MCI)

1-Severin-a(4) 5.00 15.00 35.00
2,3-Severin-a(4) 3.00 9.00 21.00

SERGEANT BILKO (Phil Silvers) (TV)
May-June, 1957 - No. 18, Mar-Apr, 1960
National Periodical Publications

1 13.00 40.00 90.00
2 9.00 27.00 62.00
3-5 8.00 24.00 56.00
6-18: 11,15-Photo-c 5.70 17.00 40.00

SGT. BILKO'S PVT. DOBERMAN (TV)
June-July, 1958 - No. 11, Feb-Mar, 1960
National Periodical Publications

1 10.00 30.00 70.00
2 7.00 21.00 50.00
3-5 5.00 15.00 35.00
6-11: 9-Photo-c 4.00 12.00 28.00

SGT. DICK CARTER OF THE U.S. BORDER PATROL (See Holyoke One-Shot)

SGT. FURY (& His Howling Commandos)(See Spec. Marv. Ed.)
May, 1963 - No. 167, Dec, 1981
Marvel Comics Group

	Good	Fine	Mint
1-1st app. Sgt. Fury; Kirby/Ayers c/a	16.00	40.00	110.00
2-Kirby-a	5.00	13.00	36.00
3-5: 3-Reed Richards x-over. 4-Death of Junior Juniper. 5-1st Baron Strucker app.; Kirby-a	1.50	3.50	10.00
6-10: 8-Baron Zemo, 1st Percival Pinkerton app. 10-1st app. Capt. Savage (the Skipper)	.85	2.50	5.00
11,12,14-20: 14-1st Blitz Squad. 18-Death of Pamela Hawley	.70	2.00	4.00
13-Captain America app.; Kirby-a	1.00	3.00	6.00
21-30: 25-Red Skull app. 27-1st Eric Koenig app., origin Fury's eye patch	.40	1.25	2.50
31-40: 34-Origin Howling Commandos. 35-Eric Koeing joins Howlers	.40	1.25	2.50
41-60: 43-Bob Hope, Glen Miller app. 44-Flashback-Howlers 1st mission. 51-Roosevelt, Churchill, Stalin app.	.40	1.25	2.50
61-100: 64-Capt. Savage & Raiders x-over. 76-Fury's Father app. in WWI story. 98-Deadly Dozen x-over. 100-Captain America, Fantastic Four cameos; Stan Lee, Martin Goodman & others app.	.25	.75	1.50
101-Origin retold	.25	.75	1.50
102-166: 113,121-166-r	.25	.75	1.50
167-Reprints #1	.25	.75	1.50
Annual 1('65)	1.00	3.00	6.00
Special 2-7('66-11/71)	.25	.75	1.50

NOTE: ***Ditko*** *a-15i.* ***Gil Kane*** *c-37, 96.* ***Kirby*** *a-1-8, 13p, 167p. Special 5; c-1-20, 25, 167p.* ***Severin*** *a-44-46, 48, 162, 164; inks-49-79; c-44, 46, 110, 149i, 155i, 162-166.* ***Sutton*** *a-57p. Reprints in #80, 82, 85, 87, 89, 91, 93, 95, 99, 101, 103, 105, 107, 109, 111, 145.*

SGT. FURY AND HIS HOWLING DEFENDERS (See The Defenders)

SERGEANT PRESTON OF THE YUKON (TV)
No. 344, Aug, 1951 - No. 29, Nov-Jan, 1958-59
Dell Publishing Co.

	Good	Fine	Mint
4-Color 344(#1)-Sergeant Preston & his dog Yukon King begin; painted-c begin, end #18	4.00	12.00	28.00
4-Color 373,397,419('52)	3.00	9.00	21.00
5(11-1/52-53)-10(2-4/54)	2.65	8.00	18.00
11,12,14-17	2.00	6.00	14.00
13-Origin S. Preston	2.65	8.00	18.00
18-Origin Yukon King; last painted-c	2.65	8.00	18.00
19-29: All photo-c	2.65	8.00	18.00

SERGEANT PRESTON OF THE YUKON
1956 (4 comic booklets) (Soft-c, 16p, 7x2½" & 5x2½")
Giveaways with Quaker Cereals

	Good	Fine	Mint
"How He Found Yukon King, The Case That Made Him A Sergeant, How Yukon King Saved Him From The Wolves, How He Became A Mountie" each...	4.00	12.00	28.00

SGT. ROCK (Formerly Our Army at War)
No. 302, March, 1977 - Present
National Periodical Publications/DC Comics

	Good	Fine	Mint
302-422: 318-Reprints		.50	1.00
Annual 2(9/82), 3(8/83), 4(8/84)		.50	1.00

NOTE: ***Estrada*** *a-322, 327, 331, 336, 337, 341, 342i.* ***Glanzman*** *a-384.* ***Kubert*** *a-302, 303, 305r, 306, 328, 356, 368, 373; c-317, 318r, 319-323, 325-333-on, Annual 2, 3.* ***Spiegle*** *a-382, Annual 2, 3.* ***Thorne*** *a-384.* ***Toth*** *a-385r.*

SGT. ROCK SPECIAL (See DC Special Series No. 3)

SGT. ROCK SPECTACULAR (See DC Special Series No. 13)

SGT. ROCK'S PRIZE BATTLE TALES (See DC Spec. Series #18)
Winter, 1964 (One Shot) (Giant - 80 pgs.)
National Periodical Publications

	Good	Fine	Mint
1-Kubert, Heath-r; new Kubert-c	1.00	3.00	6.00

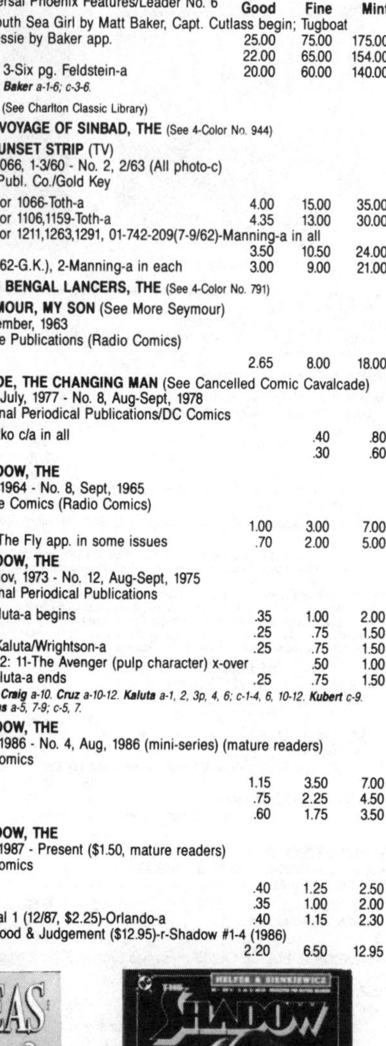

SERGIO ARAGONES' GROO THE WANDERER (See Groo...)

SEVEN DEAD MEN (See Complete Mystery No. 1)

SEVEN DWARFS (See 4-Color No. 227,382)

SEVEN SEAS COMICS
Apr, 1946 - No. 6, 1947 (no month)
Universal Phoenix Features/Leader No. 6

	Good	Fine	Mint
1-South Sea Girl by Matt Baker, Capt. Cutlass begin; Tugboat Tessie by Baker app.	25.00	75.00	175.00
2	22.00	65.00	154.00
3-6: 3-Six pg. Feldstein-a	20.00	60.00	140.00

NOTE: ***Baker*** *a-1-6; c-3-6.*

1776 (See Charlton Classic Library)

7TH VOYAGE OF SINBAD, THE (See 4-Color No. 944)

77 SUNSET STRIP (TV)
No. 1066, 1-3/60 - No. 2, 2/63 (All photo-c)
Dell Publ. Co./Gold Key

	Good	Fine	Mint
4-Color 1066-Toth-a	4.00	15.00	35.00
4-Color 1106,1159-Toth-a	4.35	13.00	30.00
4-Color 1211,1263,1291, 01-742-209(7-9/62)-Manning-a in all	3.50	10.50	24.00
1(11/62-G.K.), 2-Manning-a in each	3.00	9.00	21.00

77TH BENGAL LANCERS, THE (See 4-Color No. 791)

SEYMOUR, MY SON (See More Seymour)
September, 1963
Archie Publications (Radio Comics)

	Good	Fine	Mint
1	2.65	8.00	18.00

SHADE, THE CHANGING MAN (See Cancelled Comic Cavalcade)
June-July, 1977 - No. 8, Aug-Sept, 1978
National Periodical Publications/DC Comics

	Good	Fine	Mint
1-Ditko c/a in all		.40	.80
2-8		.30	.60

SHADOW, THE
Aug, 1964 - No. 8, Sept, 1965
Archie Comics (Radio Comics)

	Good	Fine	Mint
1	1.00	3.00	7.00
2-8-The Fly app. in some issues	.70	2.00	5.00

SHADOW, THE
Oct-Nov, 1973 - No. 12, Aug-Sept, 1975
National Periodical Publications

	Good	Fine	Mint
1-Kaluta-a begins	.35	1.00	2.00
2	.25	.75	1.50
3,4-Kaluta/Wrightson-a	.25	.75	1.50
5,7-12: 11-The Avenger (pulp character) x-over		.50	1.00
6-Kaluta-a ends	.25	.75	1.50

NOTE: ***Craig*** *a-10.* ***Cruz*** *a-10-12.* ***Kaluta*** *a-1, 2, 3p, 4, 6; c-1-4, 6, 10-12.* ***Kubert*** *c-9.* ***Robbins*** *a-5, 7-9; c-5, 7.*

SHADOW, THE
May, 1986 - No. 4, Aug, 1986 (mini-series) (mature readers)
DC Comics

	Good	Fine	Mint
1	1.15	3.50	7.00
2,3	.75	2.25	4.50
4	.60	1.75	3.50

SHADOW, THE
Aug, 1987 - Present ($1.50, mature readers)
DC Comics

	Good	Fine	Mint
1	.40	1.25	2.50
2-10	.35	1.00	2.00
Annual 1 (12/87, $2.25)-Orlando-a	.40	1.15	2.30
...Blood & Judgement ($12.95)-r-Shadow #1-4 (1986)	2.20	6.50	12.95

Sgt. Fury Annual #1, © MCG

Seven Seas Comics #5, © Univ. Phoenix Feat.

The Shadow #1 ('87), © DC

Shadow Comics V7#11, © S & S

Sharp Comics #2, © H. C. Blackerby

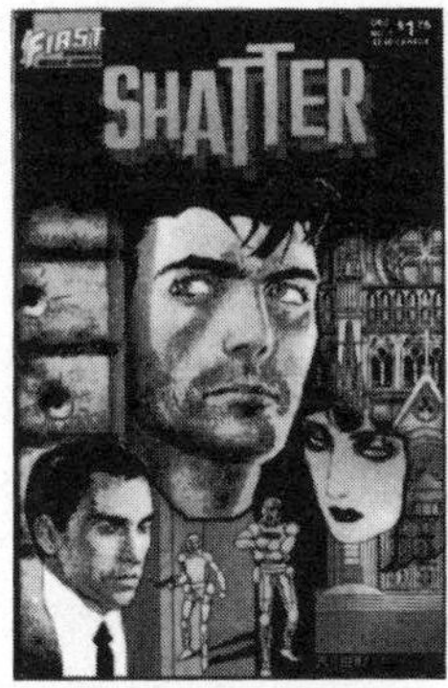

Shatter #1 (12/85), © First Comics

SHADOW COMICS (Pulp, radio)
March, 1940 - V9No.5, Aug, 1949
Street & Smith Publications

	Good	Fine	Mint

NOTE: *The Shadow first appeared in Fame & Fortune Magazine, 1929, began on radio the same year, and was featured in pulps beginning in 1931.*

V1#1-Shadow, Doc Savage, Bill Barnes, Nick Carter, Frank Merriwell, Iron Munro, the Astonishing Man begin 107.00 320.00 750.00
2-The Avenger begins, ends #6; Capt. Fury only app. 46.00 138.00 320.00
3(nn-5/40)-Norgil the Magician app. (also #9) 36.00 108.00 250.00
4,5: 4-The Three Musketeers begins, ends #8. 5-Doc Savage ends 30.00 90.00 210.00
6,8,9 22.00 65.00 154.00
7-Origin & 1st app. Hooded Wasp & Wasplet; series ends V3#8 25.00 75.00 175.00
10-Origin The Iron Ghost, ends #11; The Dead End Kids begins, ends #14 22.00 65.00 154.00
11-Origin The Hooded Wasp & Wasplet retold 22.00 65.00 154.00
12-Dead End Kids app. 19.00 57.00 132.00
V2#1,2(11/41): 2-Dead End Kid story 17.00 51.00 120.00
3-Origin & 1st app. Supersnipe; series begins 22.00 65.00 154.00
4,5: 4-Little Nemo story 13.00 40.00 90.00
6-9: 6-Blackstone the Magician app. 12.00 36.00 84.00
10-Supersnipe app. 12.00 36.00 84.00
11,12 12.00 36.00 84.00
V3#1-12: 10-Doc Savage begins, not in V5#5, V6#10-12, V8#4 10.00 30.00 70.00
V4#1-12 9.50 28.50 65.00
V5#1-12 7.50 22.50 52.00
V6#1-11: 9-Intro. Shadow, Jr. 6.50 19.50 45.00
12-Powell-c/a; atom bomb panels 11.50 34.00 80.00
V7#1,2,5,7-9,12: 2,5-Shadow, Jr. app.; Powell-a 11.50 34.00 80.00
3,6,11-Powell c/a 13.00 40.00 90.00
4-Powell c/a; Atom bomb panels 14.00 42.00 100.00
10(1/48)-Flying Saucer issue; Powell c/a (2nd of this theme; see The Spirit 9/28/47) 16.00 48.00 110.00
V8#1-12-Powell-a 12.00 36.00 84.00
V9#1,5-Powell-a 11.50 34.00 80.00
2-4-Powell c/a 12.00 36.00 84.00

NOTE: ***Powell** art in most issues beginning V6#12.*

SHADOW OF THE BATMAN
Dec, 1985 - No. 5, Apr, 1986 ($1.75 cover; mini-series)
DC Comics

1 .35 1.00 2.00
2-5: Detective-r .30 .90 1.80

NOTE: ***Austin** a-2-4i. **Rogers** c/a 1-5.*

SHADOW PLAY
June, 1982
Whitman Publications

1 .30 .60

SHADOWS FROM BEYOND (Formerly Unusual Tales)
October, 1966
Charlton Comics

V2#50-Ditko-c .35 1.00 2.00

SHADOW WAR OF HAWKMAN
May, 1985 - No. 4, Aug, 1985 (mini-series)
DC Comics

1-Alcala inks .50 1.00
2-4 .50 1.00

SHAGGY DOG & THE ABSENT-MINDED PROFESSOR (See 4-Color #985, Movie Comics & Walt Disney Showcase #46)

SHANNA, THE SHE-DEVIL (See Savage Tales #8)
Dec, 1972 - No. 5, Aug, 1973
Marvel Comics Group

	Good	Fine	Mint

1-Steranko-c; Tuska-a .40 .80
2-5: 2-Steranko-c .30 .60

SHARK FIGHTERS, THE (See 4-Color No. 762)

SHARP COMICS (Slightly large size)
Winter, 1945-46 - V1No.2, Spring, 1946 (52 pgs.)
H. C. Blackerby

V1#1-Origin Dick Royce Planetarian 11.00 32.00 76.00
2-Origin The Pioneer; Michael Morgan, Dick Royce, Sir Gallagher, Planetarian, Steve Hagen, Weeny and Pop app. 8.00 24.00 56.00

SHARPY FOX
1958; 1963
I. W. Enterprises/Super Comics

1,2-I.W. Reprint (1958) .30 .80 1.60
14-Super Reprint (1963) .30 .80 1.60

SHATTER
June, 1985 (One Shot; Baxter paper)
First Comics

1-1st computer-generated artwork in a comic book .70 2.00 4.00
1-2nd printing .35 1.00 2.00

NOTE: *1st printings have the number "1" included in the row of numbers at the bottom of the indicia.*

SHATTER
Dec, 1985 - Present ($1.75 cover; deluxe paper)
First Comics

1-Continues computer-generated art and lettering .40 1.25 2.50
2-14 .30 .90 1.80

SHAZAM (See Giant Comics to Color & Limited Collector's Edition)

SHAZAM! (TV)(See World's Finest)
Feb, 1973 - No. 35, May-June, 1978
National Periodical Publications/DC Comics

1-1st revival of original Captain Marvel(origin retold), by Beck; Captain Marvel Jr. & Mary Marvel x-over .60 1.20
2-7,9,10: 2-Infinity-c; re-intro Mr. Mind & Tawney. 4-Origin retold. 10-Last Beck ish. .50 1.00
8-100 pgs.; reprints Capt. Marvel Jr. by Raboy; origin/C.M. #80; origin Mary Marvel/C.M. #18 .60 1.20
11-Shaffenberger-a begins .50 1.00
12-17-All 100 pgs.; 15-Lex Luthor x-over .60 1.20
18-35: 25-1st app. Isis. 34-Origin Capt. Nazi & Capt. Marvel Jr. retold .50 1.00

NOTE: *Reprints in #1-8,10,12-17,21-24. **Beck** a-1-10, 12-17r, 21-24r; c-1, 3-9. **Nasser** c-35p. **Newton** a-35p. **Rayboy** a-5r, 8r, 17r. **Shaffenberger** a-11, 14-20, 25, 26, 27p, 28, 29-31p, 33i, 35i; c-20, 22, 23, 25, 26i, 27i, 28-33.*

SHAZAM: THE NEW BEGINNING
Apr, 1987 - No. 4, July, 1987 (mini-series)
DC Comics

1-New origin Capt. Marvel .25 .75 1.50
2-4 .60 1.20

SHEA THEATRE COMICS
No date (1940's) (32 pgs.)
Shea Theatre

Contains Rocket Comics; MLJ cover in mono color 10.00 20.00 30.00

SHEENA, QUEEN OF THE JUNGLE (See Jumbo Comics, Jerry Iger's Classic . . ., & 3-D . . .)
Spring, 1942 - No. 18, Winter, 1952-53
Fiction House Magazines

	Good	Fine	Mint
1-Sheena begins	90.00	270.00	630.00
2 (Winter, 1942/43)	45.00	135.00	315.00
3 (Spring, 1943)	33.00	100.00	230.00
4, 5 (Fall, 1948 - Sum., '49)	19.00	57.00	132.00
6,7 (Spring, '50 - '50, 52 pgs.)	17.00	51.00	120.00
8-10('50, 36 pgs.)	16.00	48.00	110.00
11-17	13.00	40.00	90.00
18-Used in **POP**, pg. 98	13.50	40.00	95.00
I.W. Reprint #9-Reprints #17	2.50	7.50	15.00

SHEENA, QUEEN OF THE JUNGLE
Dec, 1984 - No. 2, Feb, 1985 (Limited series)
Marvel Comics Group

	Good	Fine	Mint
1,2-r-/Marvel Super Special; movie adaption		.40	.80

SHEENA 3-D (. . .SPECIAL, Blackthorne)
Jan, 1985; May, 1985 ($2.00)
Eclipse Comics/Blackthorne Publishing

	Good	Fine	Mint
1	.45	1.25	2.50
1-r-/1953 3-D Sheena	.35	1.00	2.00

SHE-HULK (See The Savage She-Hulk)

SHERIFF BOB DIXON'S CHUCK WAGON (TV)
November, 1950 (See Wild Bill Hickok #22)
Avon Periodicals

	Good	Fine	Mint
1-Kinstler c/a(3)	6.50	19.50	45.00

SHERIFF OF COCHISE, THE
1957 (16 pages) (TV Show)
Mobil Giveaway

	Good	Fine	Mint
Shaffenberger-a	1.00	3.00	7.00

SHERIFF OF TOMBSTONE
Nov, 1958 - No. 17, Sept, 1961
Charlton Comics

	Good	Fine	Mint
V1#1-Williamson/Severin-c	3.00	9.00	21.00
2	1.50	4.50	10.00
3-17	.95	2.85	6.50

SHERLOCK HOLMES (See 4-Color #1169,1245, Marvel Prev. & Spect. Stories)

SHERLOCK HOLMES (All New Baffling Advs. of)
(Young Eagle No. 3 on?)
Oct, 1955 - No. 2, Mar, 1956
Charlton Comics

	Good	Fine	Mint
1-Dr. Neff, Ghost Breaker app.	18.00	54.00	125.00
2	16.00	48.00	110.00

SHERLOCK HOLMES (Also see The Joker)
Sept-Oct, 1975
National Periodical Publications

	Good	Fine	Mint
1-Cruz-a; Simonson-c		.50	1.00

SHERRY THE SHOWGIRL (Showgirls No. 4)
7/56 - No. 3, 12/56; No. 5, 4/57 - No. 7, 8/57
Atlas Comics

	Good	Fine	Mint
1	3.00	9.00	21.00
2	1.70	5.00	12.00
3,5-7	1.30	4.00	9.00

SHIELD (Nick Fury & His Agents of . . .) (See Nick Fury)
Feb, 1973 - No. 5, Oct, 1973
Marvel Comics Group

	Good	Fine	Mint
1-Steranko-c		.50	1.00
2-Steranko-c		.30	.60
3-5: 1-5 all contain-r from Strange Tales #146-155.			
3-5-Cover-r		.30	.60

NOTE: *Buscema a-3p(r). Kirby layouts 1-5. Steranko a-4r.*

SHIELD, THE (Becomes Shield-Steel Sterling #3; #1 titled 'Lancelot Strong;' also see Advs. of the Fly, Double Life of Private Strong, Fly Man, Mighty Comics, & The Mighty Crusaders)
June, 1983 - No. 2, Aug, 1983
Archie Enterprises, Inc.

	Good	Fine	Mint
1,2: Steel Sterling app.		.45	.90

SHIELD-STEEL STERLING (Formerly The Shield)
No. 3, Dec, 1983 (Becomes Steel Sterling No. 4)
Archie Enterprises, Inc.

	Good	Fine	Mint
3-Nino-a		.45	.90

SHIELD WIZARD COMICS (Also see Pep & Top-Notch Comics)
Summer, 1940 - No. 13, Spring, 1944
MLJ Magazines

	Good	Fine	Mint
1-(V1#5 on inside)-Origin The Shield by Irving Novick & The Wizard by Ed Ashe, Jr; Flag-c	100.00	300.00	700.00
2-Origin The Shield retold; intro. Wizard's sidekick, Roy	48.00	145.00	335.00
3,4	32.00	95.00	225.00
5-Dusty, the Boy Detective begins	27.00	81.00	190.00
6-8: 6-Roy the Super Boy begins	24.00	72.00	170.00
9,10	21.00	64.00	150.00
11-13: 13-Bondage-c	19.00	57.00	132.00

SHIP AHOY
November, 1944 (52 pgs.)
Spotlight Publishers

	Good	Fine	Mint
1-L. B. Cole-c	5.00	15.00	35.00

SHMOO (See Al Capp's . . . & Washable Jones & . . .)

SHOCK (Magazine)
(Reprints from horror comics) (Black & White)
May, 1969 - V3No.4, Sept, 1971
Stanley Publications

	Good	Fine	Mint
V1#1-Cover-r/Weird Tales of the Future #7 by Bernard Baily	.70	2.00	4.00
2-Wolverton-r/Weird Mysteries 5; r-Weird Mysteries 7 used in **SOTI**; cover r-/Weird Chills #1	.70	2.00	4.00
3,5,6	.30	.90	1.80
4-Harrison/Williamson-r/Forbidden Worlds #6	.60	1.75	3.50
V2#2, V1#8, V2#4-6, V3#1-4	.30	.90	1.80

NOTE: *Disbrow r-V2#4; bondage c-V1#4, V2#6, V3#1.*

SHOCK DETECTIVE CASES (Formerly Crime Fighting Detective)
(Becomes Spook Detective Cases No. 22)
No. 20, Sept, 1952 - No. 21, Nov, 1952
Star Publications

	Good	Fine	Mint
20,21-L.B. Cole-c	4.00	12.00	28.00

NOTE: *Palais a-20. No. 21-Fox-r.*

SHOCK ILLUSTRATED (Magazine format)
Sept-Oct, 1955 - No. 3, Spring, 1956
E. C. Comics

	Good	Fine	Mint
1-All by Kamen; drugs, prostitution, wife swapping	3.50	10.50	24.00
2-Williamson-a redrawn from Crime SuspenStories #13 plus Ingels, Crandall, & Evans	4.00	12.00	28.00
3-Only 100 known copies bound & given away at E.C. office; Crandall, Evans-a	100.00	300.00	700.00

(Prices vary widely on this book)

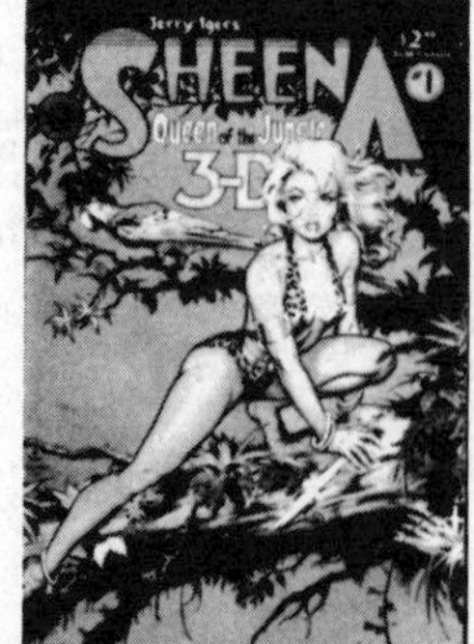

Sheena 3-D Special #1 (Blackthorne), © Caplin-Iger Co.

Shield Wizard Comics #6, © AP

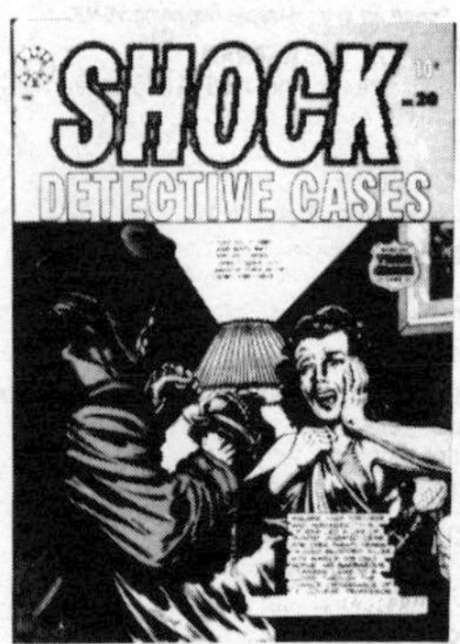

Shock Detective Cases #20, © STAR

Shock Suspenstories #13, © WMG

Showcase #17, © DC

Showcase #37, © DC

SHOCKING MYSTERY CASES (Formerly Thrilling Crime Cases)
No. 50, Sept, 1952 - No. 60, Oct, 1954
Star Publications

	Good	Fine	Mint
50-Disbrow "Frankenstein" story	10.00	30.00	70.00
51-Disbrow-a	4.75	14.00	33.00
52-55,57-60	4.00	12.00	28.00
56-Drug use story	4.75	14.00	33.00

NOTE: *L. B. Cole covers on all; a-60(2 pgs.). **Hollingsworth** a-52. **Morisi** a-55.*

SHOCKING TALES DIGEST MAGAZINE
Oct, 1981 (95 cents)
Harvey Publications

	Good	Fine	Mint
1-1957-58-r; Powell, Kirby, Nostrand-a		.50	1.00

SHOCK SUSPENSTORIES
Feb-Mar, 1952 - No. 18, Dec-Jan, 1954-55
E. C. Comics

	Good	Fine	Mint
1-Classic Feldstein electrocution-c. Bradbury adaptation	43.00	130.00	300.00
2	26.00	78.00	180.00
3	17.00	51.00	120.00
4-Used in **SOTI**, pg. 387,388	19.00	58.00	130.00
5	17.00	51.00	115.00
6,7: 6-Classic bondage-c. 7-Classic face melting-c	20.00	60.00	140.00
8-Williamson-a	18.00	55.00	120.00
9-11: 10-Junkie story	13.00	40.00	90.00
12-"The Monkey"-classic junkie cover/story; drug propaganda ish.	18.00	54.00	125.00
13-Frazetta's only solo story for E.C., 7 pgs.	23.00	70.00	160.00
14-Used in Senate Investigation hearings	10.00	30.00	70.00
15-Used in 1954 Reader's Digest article, "For the Kiddies to Read"	10.00	30.00	70.00
16-"Red Dupe" editorial; rape story	10.00	30.00	70.00
17,18	10.00	30.00	70.00

NOTE: ***Craig** a-11; c-11. **Crandall** a-9-13, 15-18. **Davis** a-1-5. **Evans** a-7, 8, 14-18; c-16-18. **Feldstein** c-1, 7-9, 12. **Ingels** a-1, 2, 6. **Kamen** a-in all. **Krigstein** a-14, 18. **Orlando** a-1, 3-7, 9, 10, 12, 16, 17. **Wood** a-2-15; c-2-6, 14.*

SHOGUN WARRIORS
Feb, 1979 - No. 20, Sept, 1980
Marvel Comics Group

	Good	Fine	Mint
1-Raydeen, Combatra, & Dangard Ace begin		.40	.80
2-20		.25	.50

SHOOK UP (Magazine) (Satire)
November, 1958
Dodsworth Publ. Co.

	Good	Fine	Mint
V1#1	1.00	3.00	6.00

SHORT RIBS (See 4-Color No. 1333)

SHORT STORY COMICS (See Hello Pal, . . .)

SHORTY SHINER
June, 1956 - No. 3, Oct, 1956
Dandy Magazine (Charles Biro)

	Good	Fine	Mint
1	1.85	5.50	13.00
2,3	1.15	3.50	8.00

SHOTGUN SLADE (See 4-Color No. 1111)

SHOWCASE (See Cancelled Comic Cavalcade & New Talent . . .)
3-4/56 - No. 93, 9/70; No. 94, 8-9/77 - No. 104, 9/78
National Periodical Publications/DC Comics

	Good	Fine	Mint
1-Fire Fighters	64.00	193.00	450.00
2-King of the Wild; Kubert-a	24.00	70.00	165.00
3-The Frogmen	20.00	60.00	140.00
4-Origin The Flash (Silver Age) & The Turtle; Kubert-a	207.00	620.00	1450.00
5-Manhunters	18.00	54.00	125.00
6-Origin Challengers by Kirby, partly r-/in Secret Origins #1 & Challengers of the Unknown #64,65	50.00	150.00	350.00
7-Challengers by Kirby r-in/Challengers of the Unknown #75	28.00	86.00	200.00
8-The Flash; intro/origin Capt. Cold	73.00	218.00	510.00
9,10-Lois Lane	27.00	81.00	190.00
11,12-Challengers by Kirby	24.00	70.00	167.00
13-The Flash; origin Mr. Element	54.00	162.00	380.00
14-The Flash; origin Dr. Alchemy, former Mr. Element	54.00	162.00	380.00
15,16-Space Ranger	13.50	40.50	95.00
17-Adam Strange-Origin & 1st app.	34.00	103.00	240.00
18,19-Adam Strange	21.00	64.00	150.00
20-1st app/origin Rip Hunter; Moriera-a	6.80	21.00	48.00
21-Rip Hunter; Sekowsky c/a	6.80	21.00	48.00
22-Origin & 1st app. Silver Age Green Lantern by Gil Kane	71.00	212.00	495.00
23,24-Green Lantern. 23-Nuclear explosion-c	28.00	84.00	195.00
25,26-Rip Hunter by Kubert	4.00	12.00	28.00
27-29-Sea Devils by Heath, c/a	3.50	10.50	24.00
30-Origin Aquaman	5.15	15.50	36.00
31-33-Aquaman	2.30	7.00	16.00
34-Origin & 1st app. Silver Age Atom by Kane & Anderson	7.00	21.00	50.00
35-The Atom by Gil Kane; last 10 cent ish.	4.00	12.00	28.00
36-The Atom by Gil Kane	4.00	12.00	28.00
37-1st app. Metal Men	4.35	13.00	30.00
38-40-Metal Men	2.00	6.00	14.00
41,42-Tommy Tomorrow	1.15	3.50	8.00
43-Dr. No (James Bond); Nodel-a; originally done for Classics Ill. Series (appeared as British Classics Ill. No. 158A)	16.00	48.00	115.00
44-Tommy Tomorrow	1.00	3.00	6.00
45-Sgt. Rock; origin retold; Heath-c	1.35	4.00	9.00
46,47-Tommy Tomorrow	.85	2.50	5.00
48,49-Cave Carson	.85	2.50	5.00
50,51-I Spy (Danger Trail-r by Infantino), King Farady story (not reprint-#50)	.85	2.50	5.00
52-Cave Carson	.85	2.50	5.00
53,54-G.I. Joe; Heath-a	.85	2.50	5.00
55,56-Dr. Fate & Hourman	.85	2.50	5.00
57,58-Enemy Ace by Kubert	.85	2.50	5.00
59-Teen Titans	3.00	9.00	18.00
60-The Spectre by Anderson	.85	2.50	5.00
61,64-The Spectre by Anderson	.70	2.00	4.00
62-Origin/1st app. Inferior Five	.25	.75	1.50
63,65-Inferior Five	.25	.75	1.50
66,67-B'wana Beast		.50	1.00
68,69,71-Maniaks		.40	.80
70-Binky		.40	.80
72-Top Gun (Johnny Thunder-r)-Toth-a		.60	1.20
73-Creeper; Ditko c/a	.85	2.50	5.00
74-Anthro; Post c/a	.30	.80	1.60
75-Hawk & the Dove; Ditko c/a	.60	1.80	3.60
76-Bat Lash	.40	1.20	2.40
77-Angel & Ape		.60	1.20
78-Jonny Double		.60	1.20
79-Dolphin; Aqualad origin-r	.30	.90	1.80
80-Phantom Stranger-r; Adams-c	.50	1.50	3.00
81-Windy & Willy	.30	.90	1.80
82-Nightmaster by Grandenetti & Giordano; Kubert-c	.30	.90	1.80
83,84-Nightmaster by Wrightson/Jones/Kaluta in each; Kubert-c. 84-Origin retold	1.35	4.00	8.00
85-87-Firehair; Kubert-a	.50	1.50	3.00
88-90-Jason's Quest: 90-Manhunter 2070 app.		.50	1.00

SHOWCASE (continued) — Good / Fine / Mint
91-93-Manhunter 2070; origin-92 — .50 — 1.00
94-Intro/origin new Doom Patrol & Robotman — .80 — 1.60
95,96-The Doom Patrol. 95-Origin Celsius — .50 — 1.00
97-99-Power Girl; origin-97,98; JSA cameos — .40 — .80
100-(52 pgs.)-Features most Showcase characters — .50 — 1.00
101-103-Hawkman; Adam Strange x-over — .40 — .80
104-(52 pgs.)-O.S.S. Spies at War — .40 — .80
NOTE: ***Anderson** a-22-24i, 34-36i, 55, 56, 60, 61, 64, 101-03i; c-50i, 51i, 55, 56, 60, 61, 64. **Aparo** c-94-96. **Estrada** a-104. **Infantino** a/c-4, 8, 13, 14; c-50p, 51p. **Gil Kane** a-22-24p, 34-36p; c-17-19, 22-24, 31, 34-36. **Kirby** c-6, 7, 11, 12. **Kubert** a-2, 4i, 25, 26, 45, 53, 54, 72; c-25, 26, 53, 54, 57, 58, 82-87, 101-04. **Orlando** a-62p, 63p, 97i; c-62, 63, 97i. **Sekowsky** a-65p. **Sparling** a-78. **Staton** a-94, 95-99p, 100; c-97-100p.*

SHOWGIRLS (Formerly Sherry the Showgirl #3)
No. 4, 1-2/57?; June, 1957 - No. 2, Aug, 1957
Atlas Comics (MPC No. 2)
4 — 1.60 — 4.70 — 11.00
1-Millie, Sherry, Chili, Pearl & Hazel begin — 3.50 — 10.50 — 24.00
2 — 1.85 — 5.50 — 13.00

SHROUD OF MYSTERY
June, 1982
Whitman Publications
1 — .30 — .60

SICK (Magazine) (Satire)
Aug, 1960 - No. 140?, 1980?
Feature Publ./Headline Publ./Crestwood Publ. Co./Hewfred Publ./
Pyramid Comm./Charlton Publ. No. 109 (4/76) on
V1#1-Torres-a — 5.00 — 15.00 — 35.00
2-5-Torres-a in all — 2.65 — 8.00 — 18.00
6 — 1.50 — 4.50 — 10.00
V2#1-8(#7-14) — 1.15 — 3.50 — 8.00
V3#1-8(#15-22) — .85 — 2.50 — 6.00
V4#1-5(#23-27) — .85 — 2.50 — 5.00
28-40 — .60 — 1.75 — 3.50
41-140: 45 has #44 on-c & #45 on inside — .40 — 1.25 — 2.50
Annual 1969, 1970, 1971 — .85 — 2.50 — 5.00
Annual 2-4('80) — .60 — 1.75 — 3.50
Special 2 ('78) — .35 — 1.00 — 2.00
NOTE: ***Davis** c/a in most issues of #16-27, 30-32, 34, 35. **Simon** a-1-3. **Torres** a-V2#7, V4#2, V6#1-3. Civil War Blackouts-23, 24.*

SIDESHOW
1949 (One Shot)
Avon Periodicals
1-(Rare)-Similar to Bachelor's Diary — 16.00 — 48.00 — 110.00

SIEGEL AND SHUSTER: DATELINE 1930s
11/84 - No. 2, 9/85 (Baxter paper No. 1; $1.50)
Eclipse Comics
1-Unpubbed samples of strips from 1935; includes 'Interplanetary Police;' Shuster-c — .25 — .75 — 1.50
2 (B&W)-Unpubbed strips — .25 — .75 — 1.50

SILK HAT HARRY'S DIVORCE SUIT
1912 (5¾x15½") (B&W)
M. A. Donoghue & Co.
Newspaper reprints by Tad (Thomas Dorgan) — 7.00 — 21.00 — 50.00

SILLY PILLY (See Frank Luther's. . .)

SILLY SYMPHONIES (See Dell Giants)

SILLY TUNES
Fall, 1945 - No. 7, June, 1947
Timely Comics
1-Silly Seal, Ziggy Pig begin — 5.00 — 15.00 — 35.00
2 — 2.65 — 8.00 — 18.00
3-7 — 2.00 — 6.00 — 14.00

SILVER (See Lone Ranger's Famous Horse. . .)

SILVERBLADE
Sept, 1987 - Present
DC Comics
Good / Fine / Mint
1 — .25 — .75 — 1.50
2-5 — .25 — .70 — 1.40

SILVERHAWKS
Aug, 1987 - Present ($1.00)
Star Comics (Marvel)
1-3 — .50 — 1.00

SILVERHEELS
Dec, 1983 - No. 3, May, 1984
Pacific Comics
1-3 — .35 — 1.00 — 2.00

SILVER KID WESTERN
Oct, 1954 - No. 5, 1955
Key/Stanmor Publications
1 — 3.00 — 9.00 — 21.00
2 — 1.50 — 4.50 — 10.00
3-5 — 1.15 — 3.50 — 8.00
I.W. Reprint #1,2 — .50 — 1.50 — 3.00

SILVER STAR
Feb, 1983 - No. 6, Jan, 1984
Pacific Comics
1-Kirby/Royer-a — .50 — 1.00
2-6 — .50 — 1.00
NOTE: ***Kirby** a-1-5p; c-1-5p.*

SILVER STREAK COMICS (Crime Does Not Pay #22 on)
Dec, 1939 - May, 1942; 1946 (Silver logo-#1-5)
Your Guide Publs. No. 1-7/New Friday Publs. No. 8-17/Comic House Publ./Newsbook Publ.
1-Intro. The Claw by Cole (r-/in Daredevil #21), Red Reeves, Boy Magician, & Captain Fearless; The Wasp, Mister Midnight begin; Spirit Man app. Silver metallic-c begin, end #5 (Scarce) — 290.00 — 870.00 — 2030.00
2-The Claw by Cole; Simon c/a — 125.00 — 345.00 — 875.00
3-1st app. & origin Silver Streak (2nd with lightning speed); Dickie Dean the Boy Inventor, Lance Hale, Ace Powers, Bill Wayne, & The Planet Patrol begin — 110.00 — 330.00 — 770.00
4-Sky Wolf begins; Silver Streak by Jack Cole (new costume); intro. Jackie, Lance Hale's sidekick — 60.00 — 180.00 — 420.00
5-Jack Cole c/a(2) — 68.00 — 205.00 — 475.00
6-(Scarce)-Origin & 1st app. Daredevil (blue & yellow costume) by Jack Binder; The Claw returns; classic Cole Claw-c — 250.00 — 750.00 — 1750.00
(Prices vary widely on this book)
7-Claw vs. Daredevil (new costume-blue & red) by Jack Cole & 3 other Cole stories (38 pgs.) — 155.00 — 465.00 — 1085.00
8-Claw vs. Daredevil by Cole; last Cole Silver Streak — 93.00 — 280.00 — 650.00
9-Claw vs. Daredevil by Cole — 68.00 — 205.00 — 475.00
10-Origin Captain Battle; Claw vs. Daredevil by Cole — 64.00 — 192.00 — 450.00
11-Intro. Mercury by Bob Wood, Silver Streak's sidekick; conclusion Claw vs. Daredevil by Rico; in 'Presto Martin,' 2nd pg., news paper says 'Roussos does it again.' — 44.00 — 132.00 — 310.00
12-14: 13-Origin Thun-Dohr — 35.00 — 105.00 — 245.00
15-17-Last Daredevil issue — 31.00 — 92.00 — 215.00
18-The Saint begins; by Leslie Charteris (See Movie Comics 2, DC) — 26.00 — 78.00 — 185.00
19-21(1942): 20,21 have Wolverton's Scoop Scuttle — 16.50 — 50.00 — 115.00

Siegel and Shuster: Dateline 1930s #1, © Siegel & Shuster

Silverblade #1, © DC

Silver Streak Comics #3, © LEV

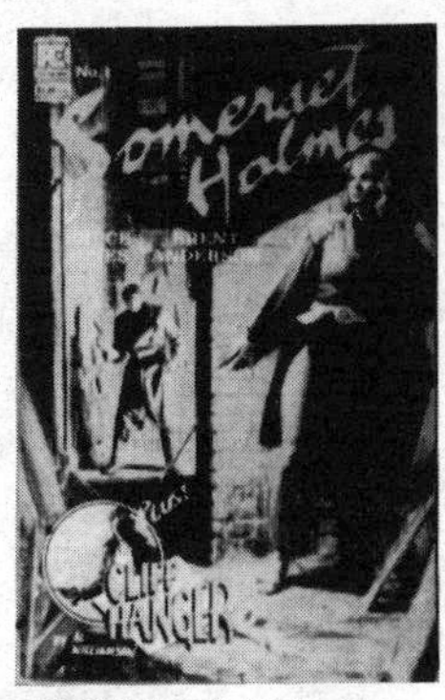

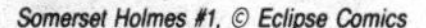
Somerset Holmes #1, © Eclipse Comics

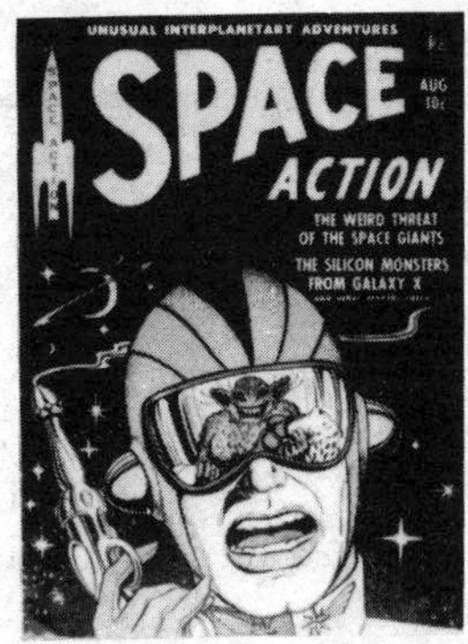

Space Action #2, © ACE

Space Adventures #16, © CC

SOJOURN (continued) — Good / Fine / Mint
2 .30 .80 1.60

SOLDIER & MARINE COMICS (Fightin' Army #16 on)
No. 11, 12/54 - No. 15, 8/55; V2No.9, 12/56
Charlton Comics (Toby Press of Conn. V1No.11)

V1#11 (12/54) 1.00 3.00 7.00
V1#12(2/55)-15 .50 1.50 3.50
V2#9(Formerly Never Again; Jerry Drummer V2#10 on) .50 1.50 3.50

NOTE: ***Bob Powell** a-11.*

SOLDIER COMICS
Jan, 1952 - No. 11, Sept, 1953
Fawcett Publications

1 3.00 9.00 21.00
2 1.50 4.50 10.00
3-5 1.35 4.00 9.00
6,7,9-11 .85 2.50 6.00
8-Illo. in **POP** 2.00 6.00 14.00

SOLDIERS OF FORTUNE
Feb-Mar, 1951 - No. 13, Feb-Mar, 1953
American Comics Group (Creston Publ. Corp.)

1-Capt. Crossbones by Shelly, Ace Carter, Lance Larson begin 5.50 17.00 40.00
2 4.00 12.00 28.00
3-10: 6-Bondage-c 3.00 9.00 21.00
11-13 (War format) 1.00 3.00 7.00

NOTE: ***Shelly** a-1-3, 5. **Whitney** a-6, 8-11, 13; c-1-3, 5, 6. Most issues are 52 pages.*

SOLDIERS OF FREEDOM
1987 - Present ($1.75, color)
Americomics

1,2 .30 .90 1.80

SOLO AVENGERS
Dec, 1987 - Present
Marvel Comics

1-5 .40 .75

SOLOMON AND SHEBA (See 4-Color No. 1070)

SOLOMON KANE
Sept, 1985 - No. 6, Mar, 1986 (mini-series)
Marvel Comics Group

1 .50 1.00
2-6: 3,4-Williamson-a .45 .90

SOMERSET HOLMES (See Eclipse Graphic Album Series)
9/83 - No. 4, 4/84; No. 5, 11/84 - No. 6, 12/84 ($1.50; Baxter)
Pacific Comics/Eclipse Comics No. 5, 6

1-B. Anderson c/a; Cliff Hanger by Williamson begins, ends #6 .40 1.25 2.50
2-6 .35 1.00 2.00

SONG OF PAIN AND SORROW
1986 (Proceeds donated to famine relief)
DC Comics

1-Top artist line-up .40 .80

SONG OF THE SOUTH (See 4-Color No. 693 & Brer Rabbit)

SONIC DISRUPTORS
Dec, 1987 - No. 12, 1988 ($1.75, limited series)
DC Comics

1-5 .30 .90 1.75

SON OF AMBUSH BUG (Also see Ambush Bug)
July, 1986 - No. 6, Dec, 1986
DC Comics

Good / Fine / Mint
1-Giffen c/a(p) in all .50 1.00
2-6 .40 .80

SON OF BLACK BEAUTY (See 4-Color No. 510,566)

SON OF FLUBBER (See Movie Comics)

SON OF SATAN (Also see Marvel Spotlight)
Dec, 1975 - No. 8, Feb, 1977
Marvel Comics Group

1-Mooney-a .40 .80
2-Origin The Possessor .25 .50
3-8: 4,5-Russell-a(p). 8-Heath-a .20 .40

SON OF SINBAD (Also see Daring Adventures, Abbott & Costello)
February, 1950
St. John Publishing Co.

1-Kubert c/a 26.00 78.00 180.00

SON OF TOMAHAWK (See Tomahawk)

SON OF VULCAN (Mysteries of Unexplored Worlds #1-48; Thunderbolt, V3#51 on)
Nov, 1965 - V2No.50, Jan, 1966
Charlton Comics

49,50 .30 .90 1.80

SONS OF KATIE ELDER (See Movie Classics)

SORCERY (See Chilling Adventures in . . . & Red Circle . . .)

SORORITY SECRETS
July, 1954
Toby Press

1 2.30 7.00 16.00

SOUPY SALES COMIC BOOK (TV)(The Official . . .)
1965
Archie Publications

1 4.60 14.00 32.00

SPACE ACE
1952
Magazine Enterprises

5(A-1 61)-Guardineer-a 13.00 40.00 90.00

SPACE ACTION
June, 1952 - No. 3, Oct, 1952
Ace Magazines (Junior Books)

1 21.00 62.00 145.00
2,3 17.00 51.00 120.00

SPACE ADVENTURES (War At Sea #22 on)
7/52 - No. 21, 5/56; No. 23, 5/58 - No. 59, 11/64; V3/60, 10/67; V1/2, 7/68 - V1No.8, 7/69; No. 9, 5/78 - No. 13, 3/79
Capitol Stories/Charlton Comics

1 11.00 32.00 76.00
2 5.50 16.50 38.00
3-5 4.60 14.00 32.00
6,8,9 4.00 12.00 28.00
7-Transvestism story 6.00 18.00 42.00
10-Ditko c/a 16.50 50.00 115.00
11-Ditko c/a(2) 16.50 50.00 115.00
12-Ditko-c (Classic) 19.00 57.00 132.00
13-(Fox-r, 10-11/54); Blue Beetle story 5.00 15.00 35.00
14-Blue Beetle story (Fox-r, 12-1/54-55) 4.00 12.00 28.00
15,17-19: 15-18-Rocky Jones app.(TV) 3.50 10.50 24.00
16-Krigstein 9.00 27.00 62.00
20-Reprints Fawcett's "Destination Moon" 10.00 30.00 70.00
21-(8/56) (no #22) 5.00 15.00 35.00
23-(5/58; formerly Nyoka, The Jungle Girl)-Reprints Fawcett's "Destination Moon" 8.50 25.50 60.00

SPACE ADVENTURES (continued)

	Good	Fine	Mint
24,25,31,32-Ditko-a	5.50	16.50	38.00
26,27-Ditko-a(4) each	7.00	21.00	50.00
28-30	1.70	5.00	12.00
33-1st app./origin Captin Atom by Ditko (3/60)	12.00	36.00	84.00
34-40,42-All Captain Atom by Ditko	5.50	16.50	38.00
41,43,46-59	.50	1.50	3.00
44,45-Mercury Man in each	.50	1.50	3.00
V3#60(10/67)-Origin Paul Mann & The Saucers From the Future		.40	.80
2-8('68-'69)-All Ditko-a; Aparo-a #2		.30	.60
9-13('78-'79)-Capt. Atom-r/Space Advs. by Ditko; 9-Origin-r		.30	.60

NOTE: ***Aparo** a-V3#60. **Ditko** c-12, 31-42. **Shuster** a-11.*

SPACE BUSTERS
Spring/52 - No. 3, Fall/52 (Painted covers by Norman Saunders)
Ziff-Davis Publ. Co.

	Good	Fine	Mint
1-Krigstein-a	28.00	84.00	195.00
2,3: 2-Two pgs. Kinstler-a; bondage-c	22.00	65.00	154.00

NOTE: ***Anderson** a-2.*

SPACE CADET (See Tom Corbett, . . .)

SPACE COMICS
No. 4, Mar-Apr, 1954 - No. 5, May-June, 1954
Avon Periodicals

	Good	Fine	Mint
4,5-Space Mouse, Peter Rabbit, Super Pup, & Merry Mouse app.	2.30	7.00	16.00
I.W. Reprint #8 (nd)-Space Mouse-r	.50	1.50	2.25

SPACE DETECTIVE
July, 1951 - No. 4, July, 1952
Avon Periodicals

	Good	Fine	Mint
1-Red Hathway, Space Det. begins, ends #4; Wood c/a(3)-23 pgs.; "Opium Smugglers of Venus" drug story; Lucky Dale-r/Saint #4	62.00	185.00	435.00
2-Tales from the Shadow Squad story; Wood/Orlando-c; Wood inside layouts	30.00	90.00	210.00
3-Kinstler-c	19.00	57.00	132.00
4-Kinstler-a	19.00	57.00	132.00
I.W. Reprint #1(Reprints #2), 8(Reprints cover #1 & part Famous Funnies #191)	1.35	4.00	8.00
I.W. Reprint #9	1.35	4.00	8.00

SPACE EXPLORER (See March of Comics No. 202)

SPACE FAMILY ROBINSON (TV)(. . . Lost in Space #15 on)(Lost in Space #37 on)
Dec, 1962 - No. 36, Oct, 1969 (All painted covers)
Gold Key

	Good	Fine	Mint
1-(low distr.); Spiegle-a in all	6.50	19.50	45.00
2(3/63)-Became Lost in Space	3.50	10.50	24.00
3-10: 6-Captain Venture begins	1.60	4.70	11.00
11-20	1.00	3.00	7.00
21-36	.55	1.65	4.00

SPACE FAMILY ROBINSON (See March of Comics No. 320,328,352,404,414)

SPACE GHOST (TV)
March, 1967 (Hanna-Barbera) (TV debut was 9/66)
Gold Key

	Good	Fine	Mint
1 (10199-703)-Spiegle-a	5.70	17.00	40.00

SPACE GHOST (TV) (Graphic Novel)
1988 (One Shot) (52pgs.; deluxe format; $3.50)
Comico

	Good	Fine	Mint
1-(Hanna-Barbera)	.60	1.75	3.50

SPACE KAT-ETS (in 3-D)
Dec, 1953 (25 cents)
Power Publishing Co.

	Good	Fine	Mint
1	17.00	51.00	120.00

SPACEMAN (Speed Carter. . .)
Sept, 1953 - No. 6, July, 1954
Atlas Comics (CnPC)

	Good	Fine	Mint
1	13.00	40.00	90.00
2	9.00	27.00	62.00
3-6	7.00	21.00	50.00

NOTE: ***Everett** c-1, 3. **Maneely** a-1-8?; c-6. **Tuska** a-5(3).*

SPACE MAN
No. 1253, 1-3/62 - No. 8, 3-5/64; No. 9, 7/72 - No. 10, 10/72
Dell Publishing Co.

	Good	Fine	Mint
4-Color 1253 (1-3/62)	2.65	8.00	18.00
2,3	1.30	4.00	9.00
4-8	.85	2.50	6.00
9-Reprints #1253	.40	1.25	2.80
10-Reprints #2	.35	1.00	2.00

SPACE MOUSE (Also see Space Comics)
April, 1953 - No. 5, Apr-May, 1954
Avon Periodicals

	Good	Fine	Mint
1	3.70	11.00	26.00
2	2.15	6.50	15.00
3-5	1.50	4.50	10.00

SPACE MOUSE (Walter Lantz. . .#1; see Comic Album #17)
No. 1132, 8-10/60 - No. 5, 11/63 (Walter Lantz)
Dell Publishing Co./Gold Key

	Good	Fine	Mint
4-Color 1132,1244	1.15	3.50	8.00
1(11/62)(G.K.)	1.15	3.50	8.00
2-5	.85	2.50	6.00

SPACE MYSTERIES
1964 (Reprints)
I.W. Enterprises

	Good	Fine	Mint
1-r-/Journey Into Unknown Worlds #4 w/new-c	.50	1.50	3.00
8,9	.50	1.50	3.00

SPACE: 1999 (TV)
Nov, 1975 - No. 7, Nov, 1976
Charlton Comics

	Good	Fine	Mint
1-Staton-c/a; origin Moonbase Alpha		.60	1.20
2-Staton-a		.50	1.00
3-6: All byrne-a; c-5	.50	1.50	3.00
7		.50	1.00

SPACE: 1999 (TV)(Magazine)
Nov, 1975 - No. 8, Nov, 1976 (B&W)
Charlton Comics

	Good	Fine	Mint
1-Origin Moonbase Alpha; Morrow c/a	.50	1.50	3.00
2,3-Morrow c/a	.30	.90	1.80
4-8 (#7 shows #6 on inside)	.30	.80	1.60

SPACE PATROL (TV)
Summer/52 - No. 2, Oct-Nov/52 (Painted-c by Norman Saunders)
Ziff-Davis Publishing Co. (Approved Comics)

	Good	Fine	Mint
1-Krigstein-a	33.00	100.00	230.00
2-Krigstein-a	28.00	84.00	195.00
. . .'s Special Mission (8 pgs., B&W, Giveaway)	50.00	150.00	300.00

SPACE PIRATES (See Archie Giant Series No. 533)

SPACE SQUADRON (Space Worlds No. 6)
June, 1951 - No. 5, Feb, 1952
Marvel/Atlas Comics (ACI)

	Good	Fine	Mint
1	16.50	50.00	115.00

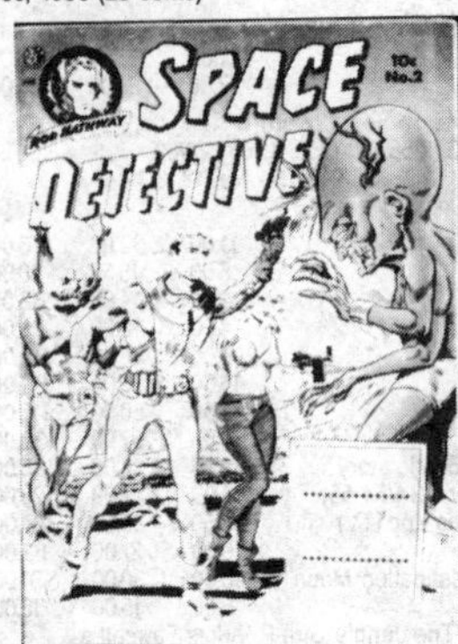

Space Detective #2, © AVON

Spaceman #6, © MCG

Space Mysteries #1, © I.W. Enterprises

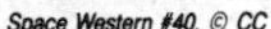
Space Western #40, © CC

Sparkie, Radio Pixie #2, © Z-D

Sparkler Comics #5, © UFS

SPACE SQUADRON (continued) — Good / Fine / Mint
2 — 12.00 36.00 84.00
3-5 — 10.00 30.00 70.00

SPACE THRILLERS
1954 (Giant) (25 cents)
Avon Periodicals
nn-(Scarce)-Robotmen of the Lost Planet; contains 3 rebound comics of The Saint & Strange Worlds. Contents could vary — 68.00 205.00 475.00

SPACE TRIP TO THE MOON (See Space Adventures No. 23)

SPACE WAR (Fightin' Five No. 28 on)
Oct, 1959 - No. 27, Mar, 1964; No. 28, Mar, 1978 - No. 34, 3/79
Charlton Comics
V1#1 — 4.00 12.00 28.00
2,3 — 1.85 5.50 13.00
4,5,8,10-Ditko c/a — 6.00 18.00 42.00
6-Ditko-a — 4.60 14.00 32.00
7,9,11-15: Last 10 cent ish? — 1.15 3.50 8.00
16-27 — .85 2.50 6.00
28,29,33,34-Ditko c/a(r) — 2.00 6.00 14.00
30-Ditko c/a(r); Staton, Sutton/Wood-a — 2.30 7.00 16.00
31-Ditko c/a; atom-blast-c — 2.30 7.00 16.00
32-r-/Charlton Premiere V2#2 — .30 .90 1.80
NOTE: *Sutton a-30, 33.*

SPACE WESTERN (Formerly Cowboy Western Comics; becomes Cowboy Western Comics #46 on)
No. 40, Oct, 1952 - No. 45, Aug, 1953
Charlton Comics (Capitol Stories)
40 — 22.00 65.00 154.00
41,43-45 — 16.00 48.00 110.00
42-Atom bomb explosion-c — 18.00 54.00 125.00

SPACE WORLDS (Space Squadron #1-5)
No. 6, April, 1952
Atlas Comics (Male)
6 — 8.00 24.00 56.00

SPANKY & ALFALFA & THE LITTLE RASCALS (See The Little Rascals)

SPANNER'S GALAXY
Dec, 1984 - No. 6, May, 1985 (mini-series)
DC Comics
1-Mandrake c/a begins — .50 1.00
2-6: 2-Intro sidekick Gadg — .40 .80

SPARKIE, RADIO PIXIE (Big John & Sparkie #4)
Winter, 1951 - No. 3, 1952
Ziff-Davis Publ. Co.
1 — 5.70 17.00 40.00
2,3 — 4.60 14.00 32.00

SPARKLE COMICS
Oct-Nov, 1948 - No. 33, Dec-Jan, 1953-54
United Features Syndicate
1-Li'l Abner, Nancy, Captain & the Kids — 5.50 16.50 38.00
2 — 2.65 8.00 18.00
3-10 — 2.15 6.50 15.00
11-20 — 1.50 4.50 10.00
21-33 — 1.15 3.50 8.00

SPARKLE PLENTY (See 4-Color No. 215 & Harvey Com. Libr. No. 2)

SPARKLER COMICS (1st Series)
July, 1940 - No. 2, 1940
United Feature Comic Group
1-Jim Hardy — 15.00 45.00 105.00
2-Frankie Doodle — 11.00 32.00 76.00

SPARKLER COMICS (2nd Series)(Nancy & Sluggo #121 on)
July, 1941 - No. 120, Jan, 1955
United Features Syndicate — Good / Fine / Mint
1-Origin Sparkman; Tarzan (by Hogarth in all issues), Captain & the Kids, Ella Cinders, Danny Dingle, Dynamite Dunn, Nancy, Abbie & Slats, Frankie Doodle, Broncho Bill begin — 55.00 165.00 385.00
2 — 25.00 75.00 175.00
3,4 — 22.00 65.00 154.00
5-10: 9-Sparkman's new costume — 17.00 51.00 120.00
11-13,15-20: 12-Sparkman new costume-color change. 19-1st Race Riley — 15.00 45.00 105.00
14-Hogarth Tarzan-c — 18.00 54.00 125.00
21-24,26,27,29,30: 22-Race Riley & the Commandos strips begin, ends #44 — 11.00 32.00 76.00
25,28,31,34,37,39-Tarzan-c by Hogarth — 15.00 45.00 105.00
32,33,35,36,38,40 — 7.00 21.00 50.00
41,43,45,46,48,49 — 5.00 15.00 35.00
42,44,47,50-Tarzan-c — 9.00 27.00 62.00
51,52,54-70: 57-Li'l Abner begins (not in #58); Fearless Fosdick app.-#58 — 3.70 11.00 26.00
53-Tarzan-c — 7.00 21.00 50.00
71-80 — 3.00 9.00 21.00
81,82,84-90: 85-Li'l Abner ends. 86-Lingerie panels — 2.30 7.00 16.00
83-Tarzan-c — 4.00 12.00 28.00
91-96,98-99 — 2.00 6.00 14.00
97-Origin Casey Ruggles by Warren Tufts — 4.00 12.00 28.00
100 — 2.65 8.00 18.00
101-107,109-112,114-120 — 1.50 4.50 10.00
108,113-Toth-a — 4.00 12.00 28.00

SPARKLING LOVE
June, 1950; 1953
Avon Periodicals/Realistic (1953)
1(Avon)-Kubert-a — 11.50 34.00 80.00
nn(1953)-Reprint; Kubert-a — 5.00 15.00 35.00

SPARKLING STARS
June, 1944 - No. 33, March, 1948
Holyoke Publishing Co.
1-Hell's Angels, FBI, Boxie Weaver & Ali Baba begin — 5.50 16.50 38.00
2 — 3.50 10.50 24.00
3-Actual FBI case photos & war photos — 2.30 7.00 16.00
4-10: 7-X-mas-c — 1.85 5.50 13.00
11-19: 13-Origin/1st app. Jungo The Man-Beast — 1.60 4.70 11.00
20,30-Fangs the Wolf Boy app. — 1.85 5.50 13.00
21-29,32,33: 29-Bondage-c — 1.60 4.70 11.00
31-Spanking panel; Sid Greene-a — 1.85 5.50 13.00

SPARK MAN
1945 (One Shot) (36 pages)
Frances M. McQueeny
1-Origin Spark Man; female torture story; cover redrawn from Sparkler No. 1 — 11.00 32.00 76.00

SPARKY WATTS
Nov?, 1942 - No. 10, 1949
Columbia Comic Corp.
1(1942)-Skyman & The Face app. — 11.50 34.00 80.00
2(1943) — 5.50 16.50 38.00
3(1944) — 5.00 15.00 35.00
4(1944)-Origin — 4.35 13.00 30.00
5(1947)-Skyman app. — 3.50 10.50 24.00
6('47),7,8('48),9,10('49) — 2.30 7.00 16.00

SPARTACUS (See 4-Color No. 1139)

SPECIAL AGENT (Steve Saunders. . .)
Dec, 1947 - No. 8, Sept, 1949
Parents' Magazine Institute (Commended Comics No. 2)

	Good	Fine	Mint
1	3.70	11.00	26.00
2	1.85	5.50	13.00
3-8	1.30	4.00	9.00

SPECIAL COLLECTORS' EDITION
Dec, 1975 (No month given) (10¼x13½")
Marvel Comics Group

	Good	Fine	Mint
1-Kung Fu, Iron Fist & Sons of the Tiger	.30	.90	1.80

SPECIAL COMICS (Hangman #2 on)
Winter, 1941-42
MLJ Magazines

	Good	Fine	Mint
1-Origin The Boy Buddies (Shield & Wizard x-over); death of The Comet; origin The Hangman retold	82.00	245.00	575.00

SPECIAL DELIVERY
1951 (32 pgs.; B&W)
Post Hall Synd. (Giveaway)

Origin of Pogo, Swamp, etc.; 2 pg. biog. on Walt Kelly
(One copy sold in 1980 for $150.00)

SPECIAL EDITION (See Gorgo, Reptisaurus)

SPECIAL EDITION (U. S. Navy Giveaways)
1944 - 1945 (Regular comic format with wording simplified, 52pgs.)
National Periodical Publications

	Good	Fine	Mint
1-Action (1944)-reprints Action 80	65.00	195.00	455.00
2-Action (1944)-reprints Action 81	65.00	195.00	455.00
3-Superman (1944)-reprints Superman 33	65.00	195.00	455.00
4-Detective (1944)-reprints Det. 97	65.00	195.00	455.00
5-Superman (1945)-reprints Superman 34	70.00	210.00	490.00
6-Action (1945)-reprints Action 84	70.00	210.00	490.00

SPECIAL EDITION COMICS
1940 (Aug.) (One Shot, 68pgs.)
Fawcett Publications

	Good	Fine	Mint
1-1st book devoted entirely to Captain Marvel; C.C. Beck c/a; only app. of C. Marvel with belt buckle; C. Marvel appears with button-down flap, 1st story (came out before Captain Marvel #1)	215.00	645.00	1720.00

NOTE: *Prices vary widely on this book. Since this book is all Captain Marvel stories, it is actually a pre-Captain Marvel No. 1. There is speculation that this book almost became* ***Captain Marvel*** *No. 1. After* ***Special Edition*** *was published, there was an editor change at Fawcett. The new editor commissioned Kirby to do a nn* ***Captain Marvel*** *book early in 1941. This book was followed by a 2nd book several months later. This 2nd book was advertised as a No. 3 (making Special Edition the No. 1, & the nn issue the No. 2). However, the 2nd book did come out as a No. 2.*

SPECIAL EDITION X-MEN
Feb, 1983 (One Shot) (Baxter paper, $2.00)
Marvel Comics Group

	Good	Fine	Mint
1-r-/Giant-Size X-Men plus one new story	.85	2.50	5.00

SPECIAL MARVEL EDITION (Master of Kung Fu #17 on)
Jan, 1971 - No. 16, Feb, 1974
Marvel Comics Group

	Good	Fine	Mint
1-Thor begins (r)		.35	.70
2-4-Last Thor (r); all Giants		.30	.60
5-14: Sgt. Fury-r; 11 r-/Sgt. Fury #13 (Captain America)		.30	.60
15-Master of Kung Fu begins; Starlin-a; origin & 1st app. Nayland Smith & Dr. Petric		.60	1.20
16-1st app. Midnight; Starlin-a		.60	1.20

SPECIAL MISSIONS (See G.I. Joe. . .)

SPECIAL WAR SERIES (Attack V4#3 on?)
Aug, 1965 - No. 4, Nov, 1965
Charlton Comics

	Good	Fine	Mint
V4No.1-D-Day (See D-Day listing)		.50	1.00
2-Attack!		.40	.80
3-War & Attack		.40	.80
4-Judomaster	.85	2.50	5.00

SPECTACULAR ADVENTURES (See Adventures)

SPECTACULAR FEATURE MAGAZINE, A (Formerly My Confessions)
(Spectacular Features Magazine #12)
No. 11, April, 1950
Fox Feature Syndicate

	Good	Fine	Mint
11-Samson & Delilah	11.00	32.00	76.00

SPECTACULAR FEATURES MAGAZINE (Formerly A Spectacular Feature Magazine)
No. 12, June, 1950 - No. 3, Aug, 1950
Fox Feature Syndicate

	Good	Fine	Mint
12-Iwo Jima; photo flag-c	11.00	32.00	76.00
3-Drugs/prostitution story	8.50	25.50	60.00

SPECTACULAR SPIDER-MAN, THE (See Marvel Treasury Edition and Marvel Special Edition)

SPECTACULAR SPIDER-MAN, THE (Magazine)
July, 1968 - No. 2, Nov, 1968 (35 cents)
Marvel Comics Group

	Good	Fine	Mint
1-(Black & White)	1.20	3.50	7.00
2-(Color)-Green Goblin app.	1.00	3.00	6.00

SPECTACULAR SPIDER-MAN, THE (Peter Parker. . #54 on)
Dec, 1976 - Present
Marvel Comics Group

	Good	Fine	Mint
1	1.30	4.00	8.00
2-5	.70	2.00	4.00
6-10	.60	1.75	3.50
11-20	.45	1.35	2.70
21,24-26	.35	1.15	2.30
22,23-Moon Knight app.	.45	1.40	2.80
27-Miller's 1st Daredevil	1.60	4.75	9.50
28-Miller Daredevil (p)	1.20	3.70	7.40
29-57,59: 33-Origin Iguana	.35	1.00	2.00
58-Byrne a(p)	.45	1.40	2.80
60-Double size; origin retold with new facts revealed	.35	1.05	2.10
61-63,65-68,71-74	.25	.75	1.50
64-1st Cloak & Dagger app.	1.40	4.20	8.40
69,70-Cloak & Dagger app.	.70	2.10	4.20
75-Double size	.30	.90	1.80
76-80	.25	.75	1.50
81,82-Punisher app.	.85	2.50	5.00
83-Origin Punisher retold	1.00	3.00	6.00
84-93,97-99: 98-Intro The Spot	.25	.70	1.40
94-96-Cloak & Dagger app.	.25	.70	1.40
100-Double size	.25	.70	1.40
101-130: 107-Death of Jean DeWolf. 111-Secret Wars II tie-in. 128-Black Cat new costume		.50	1.00
131-Six part Kraven tie-in	.50	1.50	3.00
132-138		.40	.80
Annual 1 (12/79)	.25	.75	1.50
Annual 2 (8/80)-1st app. & origin Rapier	.25	.75	1.50
Annual 3 (11/81)-Last Manwolf	.25	.75	1.50
Annual 4 (11/84), 5 (10/85)	.25	.75	1.50
Annual 6 ('85), 7 (11/87)	.25	.75	1.50

NOTE: ***Austin*** *c-21i.* ***Byrne*** *c(p)-17, 43, 58, 101, 102.* ***Giffen*** *a-120p.* ***Miller*** *c-46p, 48p, 50, 51p, 52p, 54p, 55, 56p, 57, 60.* ***Mooney*** *a-7i, 11i, 21p, 23p, 25p, 26p, 29-34p, 36p, 37p, 39i, 41, 42i, 49p, 50i, 51i, 53p, 54-57i, 59-66i, 68i, 71i, 73-79i, 81-83i, 85i, 87-99i,*

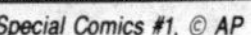
Special Comics #1, © AP

Special Edition X-Men #1, © MCG

The Spectacular Spider-Man #3, © MCG

The Spectre #1 (4/87), © DC

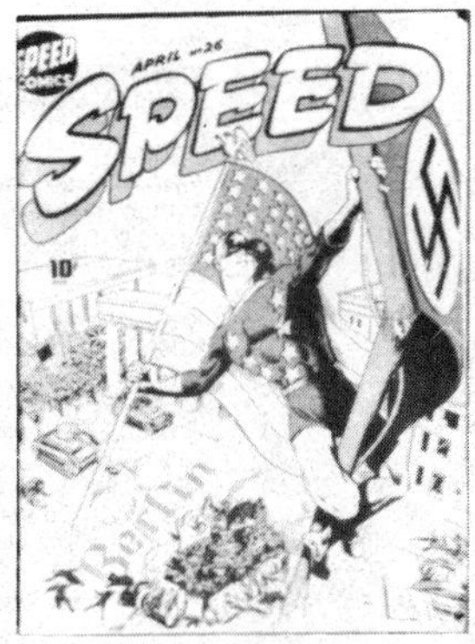

Speed Comics #26, © HARV

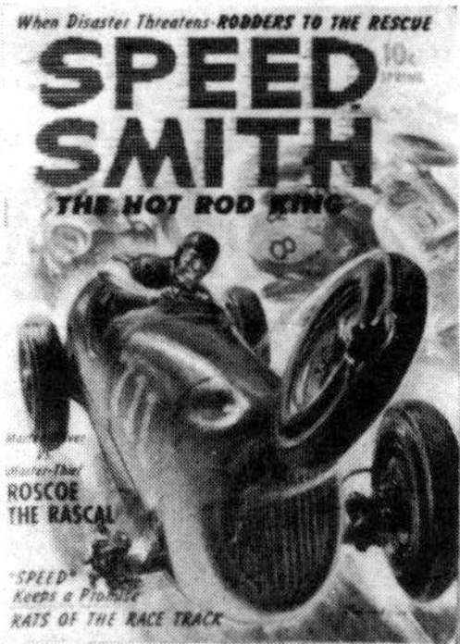

Speed Smith the Hot Rod King #1, © Z-D

SPECTACULAR SPIDER-MAN (continued)
102i, 125p, Annual 1i, 2p. ***Nasser*** *c-37p.* ***Perez*** *c-10.* ***Simonson*** *c-54i.*

SPECTACULAR STORIES MAGAZINE (Formerly A Star Presentation)
No. 4, July, 1950 - No. 3, Sept, 1950
Fox Feature Sydicate (Hero Books)

	Good	Fine	Mint
4-Sherlock Holmes	16.50	50.00	115.00
3-The St. Valentine's Day Massacre	10.00	30.00	70.00

SPECTRE, THE (See Adventure, Showcase, & More Fun)
Nov-Dec, 1967 - No. 10, May-June, 1969
National Periodical Publications

1-Anderson c/a	1.50	4.50	9.00
2-5-Adams c/a; 3-Wildcat x-over	1.00	3.00	6.00
6-8,10: 7-Hourman app.	.50	1.50	3.00
9-Wrightson-a	.70	2.00	4.00

NOTE: ***Anderson*** *inks-No. 6-8.*

SPECTRE, THE
April, 1987 - Present ($1.00, deluxe format)
DC Comics

1-Colan-a(p) begins; Kaluta-c	.35	1.00	2.00
2-13: 3-Kaluta-c	.25	.75	1.50

SPEED BUGGY (TV)(Also see Fun-In #12,15)
July, 1975 - No. 9, Nov, 1976 (Hanna-Barbera)
Charlton Comics

1-9		.25	.50

SPEED CARTER SPACEMAN (See Spaceman)

SPEED COMICS (New Speed)
Oct, 1939 - No. 44, 1-2/47 (No.14-16: pocket size, 100 pgs.)
Brookwood Publ./Speed Publ./Harvey Publications No. 12 on

1-Origin Shock Gibson; Ted Parrish, the Man with 1000 Faces begins; Powell-a	65.00	195.00	455.00
2-Powell-a	32.00	95.00	225.00
3	20.00	60.00	140.00
4-Powell-a	17.00	51.00	120.00
5	16.00	48.00	110.00
6-12 (3/41): 7-Mars Mason begins, ends #11. 12-The Wasp begins; Major Colt app. (Capt. Colt #12)	13.00	40.00	90.00
13-Intro. Captain Freedom & Young Defenders; Girl Commandos, Pat Parker, War Nurse begins; Major Colt app.	20.00	60.00	140.00
14-16 (100 pg. pocket size, 1941): 15-Pat Parker dons costume, last in costume #23; no Girl Commandos	15.00	45.00	105.00
17-Black Cat begins (origin), r-/Pocket #1; not in #40,41	25.00	75.00	175.00
18-20	13.50	40.00	95.00
21,22,25-30: 26-Flag-c	11.50	34.00	80.00
23-Origin Girl Commandos	17.00	51.00	120.00
24-Pat Parker team-up with Girl Commandos	11.50	34.00	80.00
31-44: 35-Bondage-c. 38-Flag-c	9.00	27.00	62.00

NOTE: ***Briefer*** *a-7.* ***Kubert*** *a-7-11(Mars Mason), 37, 38, 42-44.* ***Powell*** *a-1, 2, 4-7, 28, 31, 44.* ***Schomburg*** *c-31, 32, 34-36.* ***Tuska*** *a-3, 6, 7. Bondage c-18.*

SPEED DEMONS (Formerly Frank Merriwell at Yale?; Submarine Attack #11 on)
No. 5, Feb, 1957 - No. 10, 1958
Charlton Comics

5-10	.35	1.00	2.00

SPEED RACER
July, 1987 - Present (No. 1-3: $1.50, 4 on: $1.75; color)
Now Comics

1	.50	1.50	3.00
1-2nd printing	.25	.75	1.50
2-6	.30	.90	1.80

SPEED SMITH THE HOT ROD KING
Spring, 1952
Ziff-Davis Publishing Co.

	Good	Fine	Mint
1-Saunders painted-c	4.70	17.00	40.00

SPEEDY GONZALES (See 4-Color No. 1084)

SPEEDY RABBIT
nd (1953); 1963
Realistic/I. W. Enterprises/Super Comics

nn (1953)	.70	2.00	5.00
I.W. Reprint #1 (2 versions w/diff. c/stories exist)	.30	.80	1.60
Super Reprint #14(1963)	.30	.80	1.60

SPELLBINDERS
Dec, 1986 - Present (52 pgs.)
Quality Comics

1-10: Nemesis The Warlock, Amadeus Wolf		.65	1.30

SPELLBOUND (See The Crusaders)

SPELLBOUND (Tales to Hold You . . . #1, Stories . . .)
3/52 - No. 23, 6/54; No. 24, 10/55 - No. 34, 6/57
Atlas Comics (ACI 1-15/Male 16-23/BPC 24-34)

1	12.00	36.00	84.00
2-Edgar A. Poe app.	6.50	19.50	45.00
3-5: 3-Cannibalism story	5.00	15.00	35.00
6-Krigstein-a	5.00	15.00	35.00
7-10	3.50	10.50	24.00
11-16,18-20	3.00	9.00	21.00
17-Krigstein-a	4.35	13.00	30.00
21-23-Last precode (6/54)	2.65	8.00	18.00
24,26-28,30,31,34	1.70	5.00	12.00
25-Orlando-a	1.85	5.50	13.00
29-Ditko-a	2.65	8.00	18.00
32,33-Torres-a	3.85	11.50	27.00

NOTE: ***Colan*** *a-17.* ***Everett*** *a-2, 5, 7, 10, 16, 28, 31; c-2, 8, 9, 14, 17-19, 28, 30.* ***Forte/Fox*** *a-16.* ***Heath*** *a-2, 4, 8, 9, 12, 14, 16; c-3, 4, 12, 16, 20, 21.* ***Infantino*** *a-15.* ***Maneely*** *a-7, 14, 27; c-24, 31.* ***Mooney*** *a-5, 13, 18.* ***Mac Pakula*** *a-22, 32.* ***Post*** *a-8.* ***Powell*** *a-19, 20, 32.* ***Robinson*** *a-1.* ***Romita*** *a-24, 26, 27.* ***Severin*** *c-29.* ***Sinnott*** *a-8, 16.*

SPELLBOUND
Jan, 1988 - No. 6, Apr, 1988 ($1.50, bi-weekly)
Marvel Comics

1-5	.25	.75	1.50
6 (52 pgs., $2.25)	.35	1.10	2.25

SPENCER SPOOK (Formerly Giggle; see Advs. of. . .)
No. 100, Mar-Apr, 1955 - No. 101, May-June, 1955
American Comics Group

100,101	1.15	3.50	8.00

SPIDER-MAN (See Amazing. . ., Marvel Tales, Marvel Team-Up, Spectacular. . ., Spidey Super Stories & Web Of. . .)

SPIDER-MAN AND DAREDEVIL
March, 1984 (One-Shot; $2.00; deluxe paper)
Marvel Comics Group

1-r-/Spectacular Spider-Man Nos. 26-28 by Frank Miller	.35	1.00	2.00

SPIDER-MAN AND HIS AMAZING FRIENDS
Dec, 1981 (One shot)
Marvel Comics Group

1-Adapted from TV cartoon show; Green Goblin app.; Spiegle-a(p)	.25	.75	1.50

SPIDER-MAN COMICS MAGAZINE
Jan, 1987 - Present ($1.50, Digest-size)
Marvel Comics Group

SPIDER-MAN COMICS MAG. (continued)

	Good	Fine	Mint
1-10-Reprints	.25	.75	1.50

SPIDER-MAN GRAPHIC NOVEL
Summer, 1987 ($5.95)
Marvel Comics

	Good	Fine	Mint
1-Kingpin app.	1.00	3.00	5.95

SPIDER-MAN VS. WOLVERINE
Feb, 1987 (One-shot, 68 pgs.)
Marvel Comics Group

	Good	Fine	Mint
1-Williamson-i; intro Charlemagne	.70	2.00	4.00

SPIDER-WOMAN (Also see Marvel Spotlight #32)
April, 1978 - No. 50, June, 1983 (See Marvel Two-In-One)
Marvel Comics Group

	Good	Fine	Mint
1-New origin & mask added		.50	1.00
2-20: 20-Spider-Man app.		.35	.70
21-36,39-49: 37-Photo-c; 47-New look		.25	.50
37,38-New X-Men x-over; 37-1st Siryn; origin retold	.35	1.10	2.20
50-Double size; photo-c; Death of S-W		.50	1.00

NOTE: *Austin a-37i.* ***Byrne*** *c-26p.* ***Layton*** *c-19.* ***Miller*** *c-32p.*

SPIDEY SUPER STORIES (Spider-Man)
Oct, 1974 - No. 57, Mar, 1982 (35 cents) (no ads)
Marvel/Children's TV Workshop

	Good	Fine	Mint
1-(Stories simplified)		.30	.60
2-57		.25	.50

SPIKE AND TYKE (See M.G.M.'s. . .)

SPIN & MARTY (TV) (Walt Disney's)(See W. Disney Showcase #32)
No. 714, June, 1956 - No. 1082, Mar-May, 1960 (All photo-c)
Dell Publishing Co. (Mickey Mouse Club)

	Good	Fine	Mint
4-Color 714	3.50	10.50	24.00
4-Color 767,808	3.00	9.00	21.00
4-Color 826-Annette Funicello photo-c	6.00	18.00	42.00
5(3-5/58) - 9(6-8/59)	2.65	8.00	18.00
4-Color 1026,1082	2.65	8.00	18.00

SPINE-TINGLING TALES (Doctor Spektor Presents. . .)
May, 1975 - No. 4, Jan, 1976
Gold Key

	Good	Fine	Mint
1-1st Tragg r-/Mystery Comics Digest #3		.40	.80
2-Origin Ra-Ka-Tep r-/Mystery Comics Digest #1; Dr. Spektor #12		.40	.80
3-All Durak issue; (r)		.40	.80
4-Baron Tibor's 1st app. r-/Mystery Comics Digest #4		.40	.80

SPIRAL PATH, THE
July, 1986 - No. 2, 1986 ($1.75, Baxter, color)
Eclipse Comics

	Good	Fine	Mint
1,2	.30	.90	1.80

SPIRAL ZONE
Oct, 1987 - Present ($1.00)
DC Comics

	Good	Fine	Mint
1,2-Based on Tonka toys		.50	1.00

SPIRIT, THE (Weekly Comic Book)
6/2/40 - 10/5/52 (16 pgs.; 8 pgs.) (no cover) (in color)
(Distributed through various newspapers and other sources)
Will Eisner

NOTE: ***Eisner*** *script, pencils/inks for the most part from 6/2/40-4/26/42; a few stories assisted by Jack Cole, Fine, Powell and Kotsky.*

	Good	Fine	Mint
6/2/40(#1)-Origin; reprinted in Police #11; Lady Luck (Brenda Banks) by Chuck Mazoujian & Mr. Mystic by S. R. (Bob) Powell begin	75.00	220.00	485.00
6/9/40(#2)	30.00	90.00	200.00
6/16/40(#3)-Black Queen app. in Spirit	20.00	60.00	125.00
6/23/40(#4)-Mr. Mystic receives magical necklace	17.00	50.00	105.00
6/30/40(#5)	17.00	50.00	105.00
7/7/40(#6)-Black Queen app. in Spirit	17.00	50.00	105.00
7/14/40(#7)-8/4/40(#10)	12.50	37.50	75.00
8/11/40-9/22/40	12.00	35.00	70.00
9/29/40-Ellen drops engagement with Homer Creep	10.00	30.00	60.00
10/6/40-11/3/40	10.00	30.00	60.00
11/10/40-The Black Queen app.	10.00	30.00	60.00
11/17/40, 11/24/40	10.00	30.00	60.00
12/1/40-Ellen spanking by Spirit on cover & inside; Eisner-1st 3 pgs., J. Cole rest	15.00	45.00	90.00
12/8/40-3/9/41	7.75	23.00	46.00
3/16/41-Intro. & 1st app. Silk Satin	13.00	40.00	80.00
3/23/41-6/1/41: 5/11/41-Last Lady Luck by Mazoujian; 5/18/41-Lady Luck by Nick Viscardi begins, ends 2/22/42	7.75	23.00	46.00
6/8/41-2nd app. Satin; Spirit learns Satin is also a British agent	12.00	35.00	70.00
6/15/41-1st app. Twilight	9.20	27.50	55.00
6/22/41-Hitler app. in Spirit	7.00	21.00	42.00
6/29/41-1/25/42,2/8/42	7.00	21.00	42.00
2/1/42-1st app. Duchess	9.20	27.50	55.00
2/15/42-4/26/42-Lady Luck by Klaus Nordling begins 3/1/42	7.00	21.00	42.00
5/3/42-8/16/42-Eisner/Fine/Quality staff assists on Spirit	4.00	12.00	24.00
8/23/42-Satin cover splash; Spirit by Eisner/Fine although signed by Fine	10.00	30.00	60.00
8/30/42,9/27/42-10/11/42,10/25/42-11/8/42-Eisner/Fine/Quality staff assists on Spirit	4.00	12.00	24.00
9/6/42-9/20/42,10/18/42-Fine/Belfi art on Spirit; scripts by Manly Wade Wellman	2.75	8.00	16.00
11/15/42-12/6/42,12/20/42,12/27/42,1/17/43-4/18/43,5/9/43-8/8/43-Wellman/Woolfolk scripts, Fine pencils, Quality staff inks	2.75	8.00	16.00
12/13/42,1/3/43,1/10/43,4/25/43,5/2/43-Eisner scripts/layouts; Fine pencils, Quality staff inks	3.35	10.00	20.00
8/15/43-Eisner script/layout; pencils/inks by Quality staff; Jack Cole-a	2.00	6.00	12.00
8/22/43-12/12/43-Wellman/Woolfolk scripts, Fine pencils, Quality staff inks; Mr. Mystic by Guardineer-10/10/43-10/24/43	2.00	6.00	12.00
12/19/43-8/13/44-Wellman/Woolfolk/Jack Cole scripts; Cole, Fine & Robin King-a; Last Mr. Mystic-5/14/44	1.70	5.00	10.00
8/22/44-12/16/45-Wellman/Woolfolk scripts; Fine art with unknown staff assists	1.70	5.00	10.00

NOTE: *Scripts/layouts by Eisner, or Eisner/Nordling, Eisner/Mercer or Spranger/Eisner; inks by Eisner or Eisner/Spranger in issues 12/23/45-2/2/47.*

	Good	Fine	Mint
12/23/45-1/6/46	5.35	16.00	32.00
1/13/46-Origin Spirit retold	8.50	25.00	50.00
1/20/46-1st postwar Satin app.	7.50	22.50	45.00
1/27/46-3/10/46: 3/3/46-Last Lady Luck by Nordling	5.35	16.00	32.00
3/17/46-Intro. & 1st app. Nylon	7.50	22.50	45.00
3/24/46,3/31/46,4/14/46	5.35	16.00	32.00
4/7/46-2nd app. Nylon	7.00	20.00	40.00
4/21/46-Intro. & 1st app. Mr. Carrion & His Buzzard Pet Julia	9.20	27.50	55.00
4/28/46-5/12/46,5/26/46-6/30/46: Lady Luck by Fred Schwab in issues 5/5/46-11/3/46	5.35	16.00	32.00
5/19/46-2nd app. Mr. Carrion	6.75	20.00	40.00

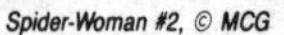
Spider-Woman #2, © MCG

Spin & Marty #8, © WDC

The Spirit, 11/2/41, © Will Eisner

The Spirit, 10/27/46, © Will Eisner

The Spirit, 10/29/50, © Will Eisner

The Spirit #8 (Quality), © Will Eisner

THE SPIRIT (continued)	**Good**	**Fine**	**Mint**
7/7/46-Intro. & 1st app. Dulcet Tone & Skinny	8.35	25.00	50.00
7/14/46-9/29/46	5.35	16.00	32.00
10/6/46-Intro. & 1st app. P'Gell	10.00	30.00	60.00
10/13/46-11/3/46,11/16/46-11/24/46	5.35	16.00	32.00
11/10/46-2nd app. P'Gell	7.00	21.00	42.00
12/1/46-3rd app. P'Gell	6.00	18.00	36.00
12/8/46-2/2/47	5.00	15.00	30.00

NOTE: *Scripts, pencils/inks by Eisner except where noted in issues 2/9/47-12/19/48.*

	Good	Fine	Mint
2/9/47-7/6/47: 6/8/47-Eisner self satire	5.00	15.00	30.00
7/13/47-"Hansel & Gretel" fairy tales	7.50	22.50	45.00
7/20/47-Li'L Abner, Daddy Warbucks, Dick Tracy, Fearless Fosdick parody; A-Bomb blast-c	7.50	22.50	45.00
7/27/47-9/14/47	5.00	15.00	30.00
9/21/47-Pearl Harbor flashback	5.00	15.00	30.00
9/28/47-1st mention of Flying Saucers in comics-3 months after 1st sighting in Idaho on 6/25/47	11.00	32.00	64.00
10/5/47-"Cinderella" fairy tales	7.50	22.50	45.00
10/12/47-11/30/47	5.00	15.00	30.00
12/7/47-Intro. & 1st app. Powder Pouf	8.50	25.50	50.00
12/14/47-12/28/47	5.00	15.00	30.00
1/4/48-2nd app. Powder Pouf	6.75	20.00	40.00
1/11/48-1st app. Sparrow Fallon; Powder Pouf app.	6.75	20.00	40.00
1/18/48-He-Man ad cover; satire issue	6.75	20.00	40.00
1/25/48-Intro. & 1st app. Castanet	7.50	22.50	45.00
2/1/48-2nd app. Castanet	5.35	16.00	32.00
2/8/48-3/7/48	5.00	15.00	30.00
3/14/48-Only app. Kretchma	5.35	16.00	32.00
3/21/48,3/28/48,4/11/48-4/25/48	5.00	15.00	30.00
4/4/48-Only app. Wild Rice	5.35	16.00	32.00
5/2/48-2nd app. Sparrow	5.00	15.00	30.00
5/9/48-6/27/48,7/11/48,7/18/48	5.00	15.00	30.00
7/4/48-Spirit by Andre Le Blanc	2.75	8.00	16.00
7/25/48-Ambrose Bierce's "The Thing" adaptation classic by Eisner/Grandenetti	11.00	32.00	64.00
8/1/48-8/15/48,8/29/48-9/12/48	5.00	15.00	30.00
8/22/48-Poe's "Fall of the House of Usher" classic by Eisner/Grandenetti	11.00	32.00	64.00
9/19/48-Only app. Lorelei	6.00	18.00	36.00
9/26/48-10/31/48	5.00	15.00	30.00
11/7/48-Only app. Plaster of Paris	6.75	20.00	40.00
11/14/48-12/19/48	5.00	15.00	30.00

NOTE: *Scripts by Eisner or Feiffer or Eisner/Feiffer or Nordling. Art by Eisner with backgrounds by Eisner, Grandenetti, Le Blanc, Stallman, Nordling, Dixon and/or others in issues 12/26/48-4/1/51 except where noted.*

	Good	Fine	Mint
12/26/48-Reprints some covers of 1948 with flashbacks	5.00	15.00	30.00
1/2/49-1/16/49	5.00	15.00	30.00
1/23/49,1/30/49-1st & 2nd app. Thorne	6.75	20.00	40.00
2/6/49-8/14/49	5.00	15.00	30.00
8/21/49,8/28/49-1st & 2nd app. Monica Veto	6.75	20.00	40.00
9/4/49,9/11/49	5.00	15.00	30.00
9/18/49-Love comic cover; has gag love comic ads on inside	7.35	22.00	44.00
9/25/49-Only app. Ice	6.35	19.00	38.00
10/2/49,10/9/49-Autumn News appears & dies in 10/9 ish.	6.35	19.00	38.00
10/16/49-11/27/49,12/18/49,12/25/49	5.00	15.00	30.00
12/4/49,12/11/49-1st & 2nd app. Flaxen	6.00	18.00	36.00
1/1/50-Flashbacks to all of the Spirit girls-Thorne, Ellen, Satin, & Monica	9.00	27.00	54.00
1/8/50-Intro. & 1st app. Sand Saref	12.00	36.00	72.00
1/15/50-2nd app. Saref	9.20	27.50	55.00
1/22/50-2/5/50	5.00	15.00	30.00
2/12/50-Roller Derby ish.	5.75	17.00	34.00
2/19/50-Half Dead Mr. Lox - Classic horror	6.35	19.00	38.00
2/26/50-4/23/50,5/14/50,5/28/50,7/23/50-9/3/50	5.00	15.00	30.00
4/30/50-Script/art by Le Blanc with Eisner framing	1.70	5.00	10.00
5/7/50,6/4/50-7/16/50-Abe Kanegson-a	1.70	5.00	10.00
5/21/50-Script by Feiffer/Eisner, art by Blaisdell, Eisner framing	1.70	5.00	10.00
9/10/50-P'Gell returns	6.75	20.00	40.00
9/17/50-1/7/51	5.00	15.00	30.00
1/14/51-Life Magazine cover; brief biography of Comm. Dolan, Sand Saref, Silk Satin, P'Gell, Sammy & Willum, Darling O'Shea, & Mr. Carrion & His Pet Buzzard Julia, with pin-ups by Eisner	6.35	19.00	38.00
1/21/51,2/4/51-4/1/51	5.00	15.00	30.00
1/28/51-"The Meanest Man in the World" classic by Eisner	6.35	19.00	38.00
4/8/51-7/29/51,8/12/51-Last Eisner issue	5.00	15.00	30.00
8/5/51,8/19/51-7/20/52-Not Eisner	1.70	5.00	10.00
7/27/52-(Rare)-Denny Colt in Outer Space by Wally Wood; 7 pg. S/F story of E.C. vintage	50.00	150.00	300.00
8/3/52-(Rare)-"Mission. . .The Moon" by Wood	50.00	150.00	300.00
8/10/52-(Rare)-"A DP On The Moon" by Wood	50.00	150.00	300.00
8/17/52-(Rare)-"Heart" by Wood/Eisner	42.00	125.00	250.00
8/24/52-(Rare)-"Rescue" by Wood	50.00	150.00	300.00
8/31/52-(Rare)-"The Last Man" by Wood	50.00	150.00	300.00
9/7/52-(Rare)-"The Man in The Moon" by Wood	50.00	150.00	300.00
9/14/52-(Rare)-Eisner/Wenzel-a	10.00	30.00	60.00
9/21/52-(Rare)-"Denny Colt, Alias The Spirit/Space Report" by Eisner/Wenzel	20.00	60.00	125.00
9/28/52-(Rare)-"Return From The Moon" by Wood	50.00	150.00	300.00
10/5/52-(Rare)-"The Last Story" by Eisner	20.00	60.00	125.00

Large Tabloid pages from 1946 on (Eisner) - Price 30 percent over listed prices.

NOTE: *Spirit sections came out in both large and small format. Some newspapers went to the 8-pg. format months before others. Some printed the pages so they cannot be folded into a small comic book section; these are worth less. (Also see Three Comics & Spiritman).*

SPIRIT, THE (Section)
January 9, 1966
N. Y. Sunday Herald Tribune

	Good	Fine	Mint
New 5-pg. Spirit story by Eisner; 2 pg. article on super-heroes; 2 pgs. color strips (BC, Miss Peach, Peanuts, Wizard of Id)	13.00	40.00	80.00

SPIRIT, THE (1st Series)
1944 - No. 22, Aug, 1950
Quality Comics Group (Vital)

	Good	Fine	Mint
nn(#1)-"Wanted Dead or Alive"	38.00	115.00	265.00
nn(#2)-"Crime Doesn't Pay"	24.00	72.00	170.00
nn(#3)-"Murder Runs Wild"	18.00	54.00	125.00
4,5	13.50	40.00	95.00
6-10	12.00	36.00	84.00
11	11.00	32.00	76.00
12-17-Eisner-c	19.00	57.00	132.00
18-21-Strip-r by Eisner; Eisner-c	27.00	81.00	190.00
22-Used by N.Y. Legis. Comm; Classic Eisner-c	42.00	125.00	295.00
Super Reprint #11-r-/Quality Spirit #19 by Eisner	1.35	4.00	8.00
Super Reprint #12-r-/Quality Spirit #17 by Fine	1.00	3.00	6.00

SPIRIT, THE (2nd Series)
Spring, 1952 - 1954
Fiction House Magazines

	Good	Fine	Mint
1-Not Eisner	17.00	51.00	120.00
2-Eisner c/a(2)	20.00	60.00	140.00
3-Eisner/Grandenetti-c	13.00	40.00	90.00
4-Eisner/Grandenetti-c; Eisner-a	16.00	48.00	110.00
5-Eisner c/a(4)	20.00	60.00	140.00

SPIRIT, THE
Oct, 1966 - No. 2, Mar, 1967 (Giant Size, 68 pgs.)
Harvey Publications

	Good	Fine	Mint
1-Eisner-r plus 9 new pgs.(Origin Denny Colt, Take 3, plus 2 filler pages)	4.00	12.00	24.00
2-Eisner-r plus 9 new pgs.(Origin of the Octopus)	4.00	12.00	24.00

SPIRIT, THE (Underground)
Jan, 1973 - No. 2, Sept, 1973 (Black & White)
Kitchen Sink Enterprises (Krupp Comics)

	Good	Fine	Mint
1-New Eisner-c, 4 pgs. new Eisner-a plus-r (titled Crime Convention)	1.00	3.00	6.00
2-New Eisner-c, 4 pgs. new Eisner-a plus-r(titled Meets P'Gell)	1.35	4.00	8.00

SPIRIT, THE (Magazine)
4/74 - No. 16, 10/76; No. 17, Winter, 1977 - No. 41, 6/83
Warren Publ. Co./Krupp Comic Works No. 17 on

	Good	Fine	Mint
1-Eisner-r begin	.80	2.40	4.80
2-5	.50	1.50	3.00
6-9,11-16: 7-All Ebony ish. 8-Female Foes ish. 12-X-Mas ish.	.40	1.20	2.40
10-Origin	.50	1.40	2.80
17,18(8/78)		.60	1.20
19-21-New Eisner-a plus Wood #20,21		.60	1.20
22,23-Wood-r		.60	1.20
24-35: 28-r-last story (10/5/52)		.60	1.20
36-Begin Spirit Section-r; r-1st story (6/2/40) in color; new Eisner c/a (18 pgs.)($2.95)	.50	1.50	3.00
37-r-2nd story in color plus 18 pgs. new Eisner-a	.50	1.50	3.00
38-41: r-3rd-6th story in color	.50	1.50	3.00
Special 1('75)-All Eisner-a	.30	.90	1.80

NOTE: *Covers pencilled/inked by* ***Eisner*** *only No. 1-9,12-16; painted by Eisner & Ken Kelly No. 10 & 11; painted by Eisner No. 17-up; one color story reprinted in No. 1-10.* ***Austin*** *a-30i.* ***Byrne*** *a-30p.* ***Miller*** *a-30p.*

SPIRIT, THE
Oct, 1983 - Present (Baxter paper) ($2.00)
Kitchen Sink Enterprises

	Good	Fine	Mint
1-Origin; r/12/23/45 Spirit Section	.55	1.60	3.20
2-r/sections 1/20/46-2/10/46	.55	1.60	3.20
3-r/sections 2/17/46-3/10/46	.55	1.60	3.20
4-r/sections 3/17/46-4/7/46	.55	1.60	3.20
5-11 ($2.95 cover)	.50	1.50	3.00
12-38 ($1.95 cover, B&W)	.35	1.00	2.00
. . . In 3-D (11/85)-Eisner-r; new Eisner-c	.35	1.00	2.00

SPIRITMAN (Also see Three Comics)
No date (1944) (10 cents)
(Triangle Sales Co. ad on back cover)
No publisher listed

	Good	Fine	Mint
1-Three 16pg. Spirit sections bound together, (1944, 48 pgs., 10 cents)	12.00	35.00	84.00
2-Two Spirit sections (3/26/44, 4/2/44) bound together; by Lou Fine	9.20	27.50	64.00

SPIRIT WORLD (Magazine)
Fall, 1971 (Black & White)
National Periodical Publications

	Good	Fine	Mint
1-Kirby-a/Adams-c	.70	2.00	4.00

SPITFIRE
1944 (Aug) - 1945 (Female undercover agent)
Malverne Herald (Elliot)(J. R. Mahon)

	Good	Fine	Mint
132,133: Both have Classics Gift Box ads on b/c with checklist to #20	6.50	19.50	45.00

SPITFIRE AND THE TROUBLESHOOTERS
Oct, 1986 - No. 9, June, 1987 (Codename: Spitfire #10 on)
Marvel Comics Group

	Good	Fine	Mint
1		.50	1.00
2-9		.40	.80

SPITFIRE COMICS (Also see Double Up)
Aug, 1941 - No. 2, Oct, 1941 (Pocket size; 100 pgs.)
Harvey Publications

	Good	Fine	Mint
1-Origin The Clown, The Fly-Man, The Spitfire & The Magician From Bagdad	22.00	65.00	154.00
2	18.00	54.00	125.00

SPOOF!
Oct, 1970 - No. 2, Nov, 1972 - No. 5, May, 1973
Marvel Comics Group

	Good	Fine	Mint
1-Infinity-c		.30	.60
2-5		.25	.50

SPOOK (Formerly Shock Detective Cases)
No. 22, Jan, 1953 - No. 30, Oct, 1954
Star Publications

	Good	Fine	Mint
22-Sgt. Spook-r; acid in face story	7.00	21.00	50.00
23,25,27: 27-two Sgt. Spook-r	5.00	15.00	35.00
24-Used in **SOTI**, pg. 182,183-r/Inside Crime 2; Transvestism story	8.50	25.50	60.00
26-Disbrow-a	5.75	17.00	40.00
28,29-Rulah app.; Jo-Jo in #29	5.75	17.00	40.00
30-Disbrow c/a(2); only Star-c	5.75	17.00	40.00

NOTE: ***L. B. Cole*** *covers-all issues; a-28(1pg.).* ***Disbrow*** *a-26(2), 28, 29(2), 30(2); No. 30 r-/Blue Bolt Weird Tales No. 114.*

SPOOK COMICS
1946
Baily Publications/Star

	Good	Fine	Mint
1-Mr. Lucifer app.	8.00	24.00	56.00

SPOOKY (The Tuff Little Ghost)
11/55 - 139, 11/73; No. 140, 7/74 - No. 155, 3/77; No. 156, 12/77 - No. 158, 4/78; No. 159, 9/78; No. 160, 10/79; No. 161, 9/80
Harvey Publications

	Good	Fine	Mint
1-Nightmare begins (See Casper 19)	12.00	36.00	84.00
2	6.00	18.00	42.00
3-10(1956-57)	3.00	9.00	21.00
11-20(1957-58)	1.50	4.50	10.00
21-40(1958-59)	.70	2.00	5.00
41-60	.50	1.50	3.00
61-80	.35	1.10	2.20
81-100	.30	.90	1.80
101-120	.25	.70	1.40
121-140		.60	1.20
141-161		.40	.80

SPOOKY HAUNTED HOUSE
Oct, 1972 - No. 15, Feb, 1975
Harvey Publications

	Good	Fine	Mint
1	1.00	3.00	6.00
2-5	.50	1.50	3.00
6-10	.30	.80	1.60
11-15		.60	1.20

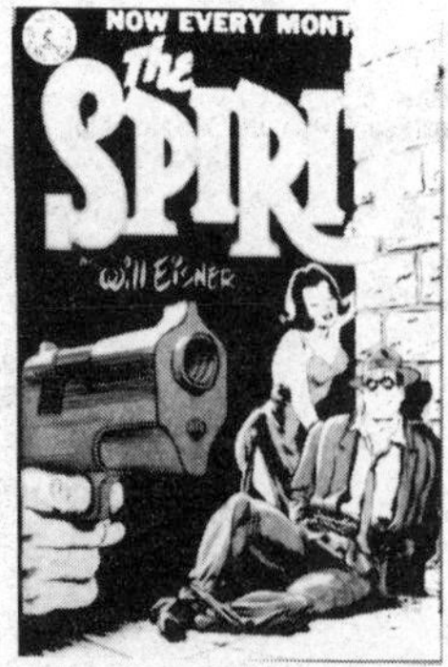

The Spirit #12 (Kitchen Sink), © Will Eisner

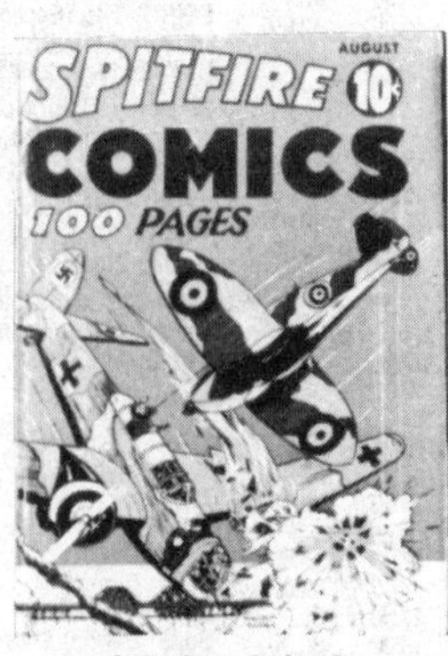

Spitfire Comics #1, © HARV

Spook #27, © STAR

Sport Stars #1, © MCG

Spy and Counterspy #1, © ACG

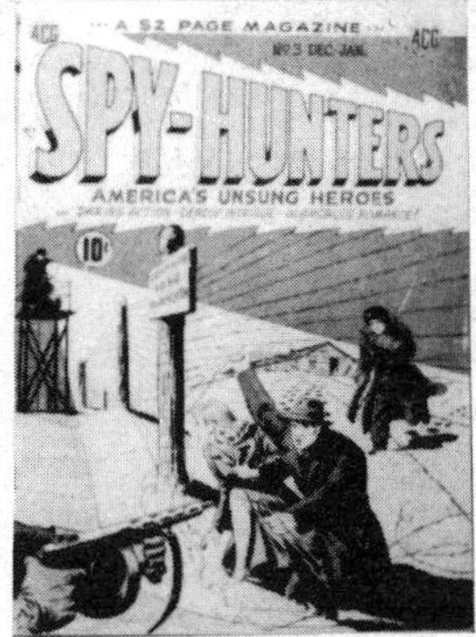

Spy-Hunters #3, © ACG

SPOOKY MYSTERIES
No date (1946) (10 cents)
Your Guide Publ. Co.

	Good	Fine	Mint
1-Mr. Spooky, Super Snooper, Pinky, Girl Detective app.	3.70	11.00	26.00

SPOOKY SPOOKTOWN
6/62 - No. 52, 12/73; No. 53, 10/74 - No. 66, Dec, 1976
Harvey Publications

	Good	Fine	Mint
1-Casper, Spooky	5.85	17.50	35.00
2	3.00	9.00	18.00
3-5	2.75	8.00	16.00
6-10	1.35	4.00	8.00
11-20	1.00	3.00	6.00
21-40	.50	1.50	3.00
41-66	.30	.80	1.60

SPORT COMICS (True Sport Picture Stories #4 on?)
Oct, 1940(No mo.) - No. 4, Nov, 1941
Street & Smith Publications

	Good	Fine	Mint
1-Life story of Lou Gehrig	13.00	40.00	90.00
2	7.00	21.00	50.00
3,4	6.00	18.00	42.00

SPORT LIBRARY (See Charlton Sport . . .)

SPORTS ACTION (Formerly Sport Stars)
No. 2, Feb, 1950 - No. 14, Sept, 1952
Marvel/Atlas Comics (ACI No. 2,3/SAI No. 4-14)

	Good	Fine	Mint
2-Powell painted-c	5.00	15.00	35.00
3-Everett-a	4.00	12.00	28.00
4-11,14: Weiss-a. 9,10-Maneely-c	3.50	10.50	24.00
12-Everett-c	4.00	12.00	28.00
13-Krigstein-a	4.35	13.00	30.00

NOTE: *Title may have changed after No. 3, to Crime Must Lose No. 4 on, due to publisher change.*

SPORT STARS
2-3/46 - No. 4, 8-9/46 (½ comic, ½ photo magazine)
Parents' Magazine Institute (Sport Stars)

	Good	Fine	Mint
1-"How Tarzan Got That Way" story of Johnny Weissmuller	9.50	28.50	65.00
2-Baseball greats	6.50	19.50	45.00
3,4	4.60	14.00	32.00

SPORT STARS (Sports Action #2 on)
Nov, 1949
Marvel Comics (ACI)

	Good	Fine	Mint
1-Knute Rockne; painted-c	9.50	28.50	65.00

SPORT THRILLS (Formerly Dick Cole)
No. 11, Nov, 1950 - No. 15, Nov, 1951
Star Publications

	Good	Fine	Mint
11-Dick Cole app.	4.35	13.00	30.00
12-L. B. Cole c/a	3.50	10.50	24.00
13-15-All L. B. Cole-c; 13-Dick Cole app.	3.50	10.50	24.00
Accepted Reprint #11 (#15 on-c, nd); L.B. Cole-c	1.70	5.00	12.00
Accepted Reprint #12 (nd); L.B. Cole-c	1.70	5.00	12.00

SPOTLIGHT (TV)
Sept, 1978 - No. 4, Mar, 1979 (Hanna-Barbera)
Marvel Comics Group

	Good	Fine	Mint
1-Huckleberry Hound, 2-Quick Draw McGraw, 3-The Jetsons, 4-Magilla Gorilla		.25	.50

SPOTLIGHT COMICS
Nov, 1944 - No. 3, 1945
Harry 'A' Chesler (Our Army, Inc.)

	Good	Fine	Mint
1-The Black Dwarf, The Veiled Avenger, & Barry Kuda begin; Tuska-c	18.00	54.00	125.00
2	15.00	45.00	105.00
3-Injury to eye story(Same as Scoop #3)	16.00	48.00	110.00

SPOTTY THE PUP
No. 2, Oct-Nov?, 1953 - No. 3, Dec-Jan, 1953-54
Avon Periodicals/Realistic Comics

	Good	Fine	Mint
2,3	1.50	4.50	10.00
nn (1953, Realistic-r)	.85	2.50	6.00

SPUNKY (. . .Junior Cowboy)(. . .Comics #2 on)
April, 1949 - No. 7, Nov, 1951
Standard Comics

	Good	Fine	Mint
1,2-Text illos by Frazetta	3.50	10.50	24.00
3-7	1.30	4.00	9.00

SPUNKY THE SMILING SPOOK
Aug, 1957 - No. 4, May, 1958
Ajax/Farrell (World Famous Comics/Four Star Comic Corp.)

	Good	Fine	Mint
1-Reprints from Frisky Fables	1.85	5.50	13.00
2-4	1.00	3.00	7.00

SPY AND COUNTERSPY (Spy Hunters #3 on)
Aug-Sept, 1949 - No. 2, Oct-Nov, 1949
American Comics Group

	Good	Fine	Mint
1-Origin, 1st app. Jonathan Kent, Counterspy	4.60	14.00	32.00
2	3.00	9.00	21.00

SPY CASES (Formerly The Kellys)
No. 26, Sept, 1950 - No. 19, Oct, 1953
Marvel/Atlas Comics (Hercules Publ.)

	Good	Fine	Mint
26	4.00	12.00	28.00
27,28(2/51): 27-Everett-a; bondage-c	3.00	9.00	21.00
4(4/51)-6,7,9,10: 7-Tuska-a	1.70	5.00	12.00
8-A-Bomb-c/story	2.30	7.00	16.00
11-19: 13-War format	1.50	4.50	10.00

SPY FIGHTERS
March, 1951 - No. 15, July, 1953
Marvel/Atlas Comics (CSI)

	Good	Fine	Mint
1	4.60	14.00	32.00
2-Tuska-a	2.00	6.00	14.00
3-13	1.60	4.70	11.00
14,15-Pakula-a(3), Ed Win-a	1.85	5.50	13.00

SPY-HUNTERS (Formerly Spy & Counterspy)
No. 3, Dec-Jan, 1949-50 - No. 24, June-July, 1953
American Comics Group

	Good	Fine	Mint
3-Jonathan Kent begins, ends No. 10	4.60	14.00	32.00
4-10: 4,8-Starr-a	3.00	9.00	21.00
11-15,17-22,24	1.70	5.00	12.00
16-Williamson-a (9 pgs.)	5.50	16.50	38.00
23-Graphic torture, injury to eye panel	6.00	18.00	42.00

NOTE: ***Whitney** a-many issues; c-8, 10, 11, 16.*

SPYMAN (Top Secret Adventures on cover)
Sept, 1966 - No. 3, Feb, 1967
Harvey Publications

	Good	Fine	Mint
1-Steranko-a(p)-1st pro work; 1pg. Adams ad; Tuska c/a, Crandall-a(i)	.50	1.50	3.00
2,3: Simon-c. 2-Steranko-a(p)	.35	1.00	2.00

SPY SMASHER (See Mighty Midget, Whiz & X-Mas Comics)
Fall, 1941 - No. 11, Feb, 1943
Fawcett Publications

	Good	Fine	Mint
1-Spy Smasher begins; silver metallic-c	95.00	285.00	665.00
2-Raboy-c	47.00	141.00	330.00
3,4: 3-Bondage-c	40.00	120.00	280.00
5-7: Raboy-a; 6-Raboy c/a	35.00	105.00	245.00

SPY SMASHER (continued) — Good / Fine / Mint

8-11: 10-Hitler-c 30.00 90.00 210.00

Well Known Comics (1944, 12 pgs., 8½x10½", paper-c, glued binding, printed in green; Bestmaid/Samuel Lowe giveaway
15.00 45.00 90.00

SPY THRILLERS (Police Badge No. 479 #5)
Nov, 1954 - No. 4, May, 1955
Atlas Comics (PrPI)

	Good	Fine	Mint
1	3.50	10.50	24.00
2-Last precode (1/55)	1.70	5.00	12.00
3,4	1.30	4.00	9.00

SQUADRON SUPREME
Sept, 1985 - No. 12, Aug, 1986 (maxi-series)
Marvel Comics Group

	Good	Fine	Mint
1	.30	.90	1.80
2-11		.50	1.00
12-Double size ($1.25)	.25	.75	1.50

SQUEEKS
Oct, 1953 - No. 5, June, 1954
Lev Gleason Publications

	Good	Fine	Mint
1-Biro-c	2.65	8.00	18.00
2-Biro-c	1.30	4.00	9.00
3-5: 3-Biro-c	1.00	3.00	7.00

STAINLESS STEEL RAT
Oct, 1985 - No. 6, Mar, 1986 (limited-series)
Eagle Comics

	Good	Fine	Mint
1 (52 pgs.; $2.25 cover)	.35	1.10	2.20
2-6 (36 pgs.)	.25	.75	1.50

STALKER
June-July, 1975 - No. 4, Dec-Jan, 1975-76
National Periodical Publications

	Good	Fine	Mint
1-Origin & 1st app; Ditko/Wood c/a		.40	.80
2-4-Ditko/Wood c/a		.30	.60

STAMP COMICS (Stamps... on-c; Thrilling Advs. In...#8)
Oct, 1951 - No. 7, Oct, 1952 (No. 1: 15 cents)
Youthful Magazines/Stamp Comics, Inc.

	Good	Fine	Mint
1('Stamps' on indicia No. 1)	9.00	27.00	62.00
2	5.00	15.00	35.00
3-6: 3,4-Kiefer, Wildey-a	4.35	13.00	30.00
7-Roy Krenkel, 4 pgs.	8.00	24.00	56.00

NOTE: *Promotes stamp collecting; gives stories behind various commemorative stamps. No. 2, 10 cents printed over 15 cents c-price.* ***Kiefer*** *a-1-7.* ***Kirkel*** *a-1-6.* ***Napoli*** *a-2-7.* ***Palais*** *a-2-4, 7.*

STANLEY & HIS MONSTER (Formerly The Fox & the Crow)
No. 109, Apr-May, 1968 - No. 112, Oct-Nov, 1968
National Periodical Publications

	Good	Fine	Mint
109-112	.70	2.00	5.00

STAR BLAZERS
Apr, 1987 - No. 4, July, 1987 (mini-series, color, $1.75)
Comico

	Good	Fine	Mint
1-4	.30	.95	1.90

STAR BRAND
Oct, 1986 - Present
Marvel Comics Group

	Good	Fine	Mint
1	.35	1.00	2.00
2		.50	1.00
3-14: 3-Williamson-i		.40	.80
Annual 1 (10/87)		.65	1.30

STAR COMICS
Feb, 1937 - V2No.7 (No. 23), Aug, 1939 (#1-6: large size)
Ultem Publ. (Harry 'A' Chesler)/Centaur Publications

	Good	Fine	Mint
V1#1-Dan Hastings (s/f) begins	54.00	162.00	375.00
2	26.00	78.00	180.00
3-6 (#6, 9/37): 5-Little Nemo	23.00	70.00	160.00
7-9: 8-Severed head centerspread; Impy & Little Nemo by Windsor McKay Jr, Popeye app. by Bob Wood; Mickey Mouse-c app.	22.00	65.00	154.00
10 (1st Centaur; 3/38)-Impy by Winsor McCay Jr; Don Marlow by Guardineer begins	32.00	95.00	225.00
11-1st Jack Cole comic-a, 1 pg. (4/38)	20.00	60.00	140.00
12-15: 12-Riders of the Golden West begins; Little Nemo app. 15-Speed Silvers by Gustavson & The Last Pirate by Burgos begins	20.00	60.00	140.00
16 (12/38)-The Phantom Rider begins, ends V2#6	20.00	60.00	140.00
V2#1(#17, 2/39)	20.00	60.00	140.00
2-7(#18-23): 2-Diana Deane by Tarpe Mills app. 3-Drama of Hollywood by Mills begins. 7-Jungle Queen app.	18.00	54.00	125.00

NOTE: ***Biro*** *c-9, 10.* ***Burgos*** *a-15, 16, V2#1-7.* ***Ken Ernst*** *a-10, 12, 14.* ***Gill Fox*** *c-V2#2.* ***Guardineer*** *a-6, 8-14.* ***Gustavson*** *a-13-16, V2#1-7.* ***Tarpe Mills*** *a-15, V2#1-7.* ***Bob Wood*** *a-10, 12, 13; c-8.*

STAR COMICS MAGAZINE
Dec, 1986 - Present ($1.50, Digest-size)
Star Comics (Marvel)

	Good	Fine	Mint
1-10: Heathcliff, Muppet Babies, Ewoks, Carebears, Top Dog app.	.25	.75	1.50

STAR FEATURE COMICS
1963
I. W. Enterprises

	Good	Fine	Mint
Reprint #9-Stunt-Man Stetson app.	.50	1.50	3.00

STARFIRE
Aug-Sept, 1976 - No. 8, Oct-Nov, 1977
National Periodical Publications/DC Comics

	Good	Fine	Mint
1-Origin & 1st app; (CCA stamp fell off cover art; so it **was** approved by code)		.50	1.00
2-8		.30	.60

STAR HUNTERS (See DC Super Stars #16)
Oct-Nov, 1977 - No. 7, Oct-Nov, 1978
National Periodical Publications/DC Comics

	Good	Fine	Mint
1-Newton-a(p)		.30	.60
2-6		.25	.50
7-Giant		.30	.60

NOTE: ***Buckler*** *a-4p-7p; c-1p-7p.* ***Layton*** *a-1i-5i; c-1i-6i.* ***Nasser*** *a-3p.* ***Sutton*** *a-6i.*

STARK TERROR (Magazine)
Dec, 1970 - No. 5, Aug, 1971 (52 pages) (B&W)
Stanley Publications

	Good	Fine	Mint
1-Bondage, torture-c	.50	1.50	3.00
2-4 (Gillmor/Aragon-r)	.30	.80	1.60
5 (ACG-r)		.60	1.20

STARLET O'HARA IN HOLLYWOOD
Dec, 1948 - No. 4, Sept, 1949
Standard Comics

	Good	Fine	Mint
1-Owen Fitzgerald-a in all	6.50	19.50	45.00
2	4.35	13.00	30.00
3,4	3.70	11.00	26.00

STAR-LORD THE SPECIAL EDITION (Also see Marvel Comics Super Special #10, Marvel Premiere & Preview & Marvel Spotlight V2#6,7)
Feb, 1982 (One Shot) (Direct sale, 1st Baxter paper comic)
Marvel Comics Group

	Good	Fine	Mint
1-Byrne/Austin-a; Austin-c, Golden-a(p)	.50	1.50	3.00

STARMAN (See Adventure, First Issue Special, Justice League & Showcase)

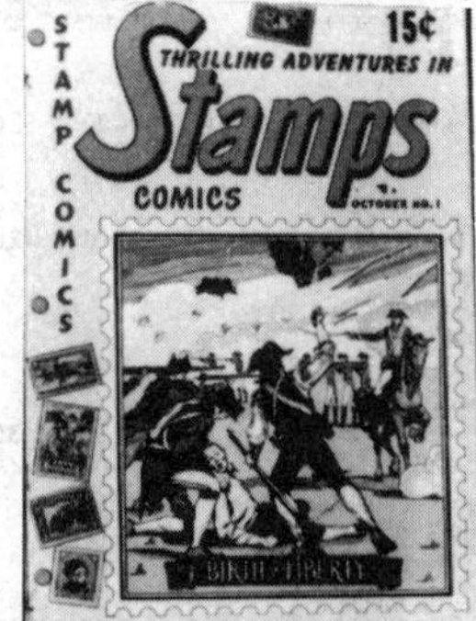

Stamp Comics #1, © YM

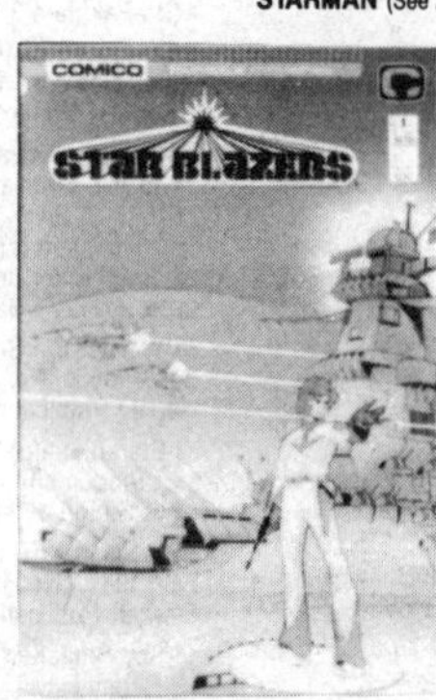

Star Blazers #1, © Comico

Star Comics #16, © CEN

Stars and Stripes Comics #5, © CEN

Starslayer #5, © First Comics

Star Spangled Comics #88, © DC

STARMASTERS
Mar, 1984
Americomics

	Good	Fine	Mint
1-The Women of W.O.S.P. & Breed begin	.25	.75	1.50

STAR PRESENTATION, A (Formerly My Secret Romance #1,2; Spectacular Stories #4) (Also see This Is Suspense)
No. 3, May, 1950
Fox Features Syndicate (Hero Books)

3-Dr. Jekyll & Mr. Hyde by Wood & Harrison (reprinted in Startling Terror Tales #10); 'The Repulsing Dwarf' by Wood; Wood-c	43.00	130.00	300.00

STAR QUEST COMIX (Warren Presents... on cover)
October, 1978
Warren Publications

1		.50	1.00

STAR RAIDERS (See DC Graphic Novel No. 1)

STAR RANGER (Cowboy Comics #13 on)
Feb, 1937 - No. 12, May, 1938 (Large size: No. 1-6)
Ultem Publ./Centaur Publications

1-(1st Western comic)-Ace & Deuce, Air Plunder	54.00	162.00	375.00
2	26.00	78.00	180.00
3-6	23.00	70.00	160.00
7-9: 8-Christmas-c	22.00	65.00	154.00
V2#10 (1st Centaur; 3/38)	32.00	95.00	225.00
11,12	20.00	60.00	140.00

NOTE: ***J. Cole** a-10, 12; c-12. **Ken Ernst** a-11. **Gill Fox** a-8(illo), 9, 10. **Guardineer** a-3, 6, 7, 8(illos), 9, 10, 12. **Gustavson** a-8-10, 12. **Bob Wood** a-8-10.*

STAR RANGER FUNNIES (Formerly Cowboy Comics?)
V1No.15, Oct, 1938 - V2No.5, Oct, 1939
Centaur Publications

V1#15-Eisner, Gustavson-a	33.00	100.00	230.00
V2#1 (1/39)	23.00	70.00	160.00
2-5: 2-Night Hawk by Gustavson. 4-Kit Carson app.	20.00	60.00	140.00

NOTE: ***Jack Cole** a-V2#1,3; c-V2#1. **Guardineer** a-V2#3. **Gustavson** a-V2#2. **Pinajian** c/a-V2#5.*

STAR REACH CLASSICS
Mar, 1984 - No. 6, Aug, 1984 ($1.50; color; Baxter paper)
Eclipse Comics

1-Adams-r/Star Reach #1	.25	.75	1.50
2-6	.25	.75	1.50

NOTE: ***Brunner** c/a-4r. **Nino** a-3r. **Russell** c/a-3r.*

STARR FLAGG, UNDERCOVER GIRL (See Undercover...)

STARRIORS
Aug, 1984 - No. 4, Feb, 1985 (limited-series)
Marvel Comics Group

1-Based on Tomy Toy robots		.50	1.00
2-4		.45	.90

STARS AND STRIPES COMICS
May, 1941 - No. 6, Dec, 1941
Centaur Publications

2(#1)-The Shark, The Iron Skull, Aman, The Amazing Man, Mighty Man, Minimidget begin; The Voice & Dash Dartwell, the Human Meteor, Reef Kinkaid app.; Gustavson Flag-c	82.00	245.00	575.00
3-Origin Dr. Synthe; The Black Panther app.	57.00	170.00	400.00
4-Origin/1st app. The Stars and Stripes; injury to eye-c	48.00	145.00	335.00
5(#5 on cover & inside)	32.00	95.00	225.00

	Good	Fine	Mint
5(#6)-(#5 on cover, #6 on inside)	32.00	95.00	225.00

NOTE: ***Gustavson** c/a-3.*

STARSLAYER
9/81 - No. 6, 4/83; No. 7, 8/83 - No. 34, 11/85
Pacific Comics/First Comics No. 7 on

1-Origin; excessive blood & gore	.50	1.50	3.00
2-Intro & origin the Rocketeer by Dave Stevens	.85	2.50	5.00
3-Rocketeer continues	.70	2.20	4.40
4	.35	1.00	2.00
5-Preview of Groo the Wanderer by Aragones	1.00	3.00	6.00
6,7: 7-Grell-a ends	.35	1.00	2.00
5-2nd app. Groo the Wanderer by Aragones	.70	2.00	4.00
	.25	.75	1.50
8-21: 10-Intro Grimjack (ends #17). 19-Starslayer meets Grimjack; book length story. 20-The Black Flame begins, ends #33		.50	1.00
22-34 ($1.25)		.65	1.30

NOTE: ***Grell** a-1-7; c-1-8. **Sutton** a-17p, 20-22p.*

STAR SPANGLED COMICS (...War Stories #131 on)
Oct, 1941 - No. 130, July, 1952
National Periodical Publications

1-Origin Tarantula; Captain X of the R.A.F., Star Spangled Kid(See Action #40) & Armstrong of the Army begin	107.00	320.00	750.00
2	50.00	150.00	350.00
3-5	34.00	102.00	240.00
6-Last Armstrong/Army	23.00	70.00	160.00
7-Origin/1st app. The Guardian by S&K, & Robotman by Paul Cassidy; The Newsboy Legion & TNT begin; last Captain X	135.00	405.00	945.00
8-Origin TNT & Dan the Dyna-Mite	68.00	205.00	475.00
9,10	60.00	180.00	420.00
11-17	48.00	145.00	335.00
18-Origin Star Spangled Kid	60.00	180.00	420.00
19-Last Tarantula	48.00	145.00	335.00
20-Liberty Belle begins	48.00	145.00	335.00
21-29-Last S&K issue; 23-Last TNT. 25-Robotman by Jimmy Thompson begins	35.00	105.00	245.00
30-40	17.00	51.00	120.00
41-50	13.50	40.00	95.00
51-64: Last Newsboy Legion & The Guardian; 53 by S&K	13.00	40.00	90.00
65-Robin begins with cover app.	15.00	45.00	105.00
66-68,70-80	10.00	30.00	70.00
69-Origin Tomahawk	13.50	40.00	95.00
81-Origin Merry, Girl of 1000 Gimmicks	10.00	30.00	70.00
82,83,85,86: 83-Capt. Compass begins, ends #130	10.00	30.00	70.00
84,87 (Rare)	11.00	32.00	76.00
88-94: Batman-c/stories in all. 88-Last Star Spangled Kid. 91-Federal Men begin, end #93. 94-Manhunters Around the World begin, end #121	11.00	32.00	76.00
95-99	8.50	25.50	60.00
100	11.00	32.00	76.00
101-112,114,115,117-121: 114-Retells Robin's origin. 120-Last 52 pgs.	6.50	19.50	45.00
113-Frazetta-a, 10 pgs.	22.00	65.00	154.00
116-Flag-c	8.00	24.00	56.00
122-Ghost Breaker begins (origin), ends #130	6.50	19.50	45.00
123-129	6.00	18.00	42.00
130	7.00	21.00	50.00

NOTE: *Most all issues after No. 29 signed by **Simon & Kirby** are **not** by them. **Batman** c/stories-88-94.*

STAR SPANGLED WAR STORIES (Star Spangled Comics #1-130; The Unknown Soldier #205 on) (See Showcase)

No. 131, 8/52 - No. 133, 10/52; No. 3, 11/52 - No. 204, 2-3/77
National Periodical Publications

	Good	Fine	Mint
131(#1)	20.00	60.00	140.00
132	13.00	40.00	90.00
133-Used in **POP**, Pg. 94	13.00	40.00	90.00
3-5: 4-Devil Dog Dugan app.	9.50	28.50	65.00
6-Evans-a	7.00	21.00	50.00
7-10	5.50	16.50	38.00
11-20	4.35	13.00	30.00
21-30	3.50	10.50	24.00
31-33,35-40	2.65	8.00	18.00
34-Krigstein-a	4.35	13.00	30.00
41-50	2.15	6.50	15.00
51-83: 67-Easy Co. story w/o Sgt. Rock	1.85	5.50	13.00
84-Origin Mlle. Marie	4.00	12.00	28.00
85-89-Mlle. Marie in all	2.30	7.00	16.00
90-1st Dinosaur issue	7.00	21.00	50.00
91-100	1.70	5.00	12.00
101-120	1.00	3.00	7.00
121-133,135-137-Last dinosaur story; Heath Birdman-#129,131	.70	2.00	4.00
134,144-Adams-a plus Kubert #144	.85	2.50	5.00
138-Enemy Ace begins by Joe Kubert	.70	2.00	4.00
139-143,145-148,152,153,155	.45	1.25	2.50
149,150-Viking Prince by Kubert	.50	1.50	3.00
151-1st Unknown Soldier	.35	1.00	2.00
154-Origin Unknown Soldier	.35	1.00	2.00
156-1st Battle Album		.50	1.00
157-161-Last Enemy Ace		.50	1.00
162-204: 181-183-Enemy Ace vs. Balloon Buster serial app.		.40	.80

NOTE: ***Drucker** a-59, 61, 64, 66, 67, 73-84. **Estrada** a-149. **John Giunta** a-72. **Glanzman** a-167, 171, 172, 174. **Heath** c-67. **Kaluta** a-197i; c-167. **Kubert** a-6-162(most later issues), 200. **Maurer** a-160. **Severin** a-65. **Simonson** a-170, 172, 174, 180. **Sutton** a-168. **Thorne** a-183. **Toth** a-164. **Wildey** a-161. Suicide Squad in 110, 116-18, 120, 121, 127.*

STARSTREAM (Adventures in Science Fiction)

1976 (68 pgs.; cardboard covers) (79 cents)
Whitman/Western Publishing Co.

	Good	Fine	Mint
1-Bolle-a	.30	.80	1.60
2-4-McWilliams & Bolle-a		.60	1.20

STARSTRUCK

Mar, 1985 - No. 6, Feb, 1986 ($1.50; adults only)
Epic Comics (Marvel)

	Good	Fine	Mint
1-Nudity & strong language	.30	.85	1.70
2-6	.25	.70	1.40

NOTE: ***Kaluta** a-1-6; c-1-6.*

STAR STUDDED

1945 (25 cents; 132 pgs.); 1945 (196 pgs.)
Cambridge House/Superior Publishers

	Good	Fine	Mint
1-Captain Combat by Giunta, Ghost Woman, Commandette, & Red Rogue app.	11.00	32.00	76.00
nn-The Cadet, Edison Bell, Hoot Gibson, Jungle Lil (196 pgs.); copies vary - Blue Beetle in some	8.50	25.50	60.00

STAR TEAM

1977 (20 pgs.) (6½x5")
Marvel Comics Group (Ideal Toy Giveaway)

	Good	Fine	Mint
nn		.15	.30

STARTLING COMICS

June, 1940 - No. 53, May, 1948
Better Publications (Nedor)

	Good	Fine	Mint
1-Origin Captain Future, Mystico (By Eisner/Fine), the Wonder Man; The Masked Rider begins; drug use story	58.00	175.00	405.00
2	25.00	75.00	175.00
3	19.00	57.00	132.00
4	13.50	40.00	95.00
5-9	11.00	32.00	76.00
10-Origin & 1st app. The Fighting Yank	46.00	138.00	320.00
11-15: 12-Hitler, Hirohito, Mussolini-c	12.00	36.00	84.00
16-Origin The Four Comrades; not in #32,35	16.00	48.00	110.00
17-Last Masked Rider & Mystico	10.00	30.00	70.00
18-Origin Pyroman	24.00	72.00	170.00
19	11.00	32.00	76.00
20-The Oracle begins; not in #26,28,33,34	11.00	32.00	76.00
21-Origin The Ape, Oracle's enemy	9.50	28.50	65.00
22-33	9.50	28.50	65.00
34-Origin The Scarab & only app.	10.00	30.00	70.00
35-Hypodermic syringe attacks Fighting Yank in drug story	10.00	30.00	70.00
36-43: 36-Last Four Comrades. 40-Last Capt. Future & Oracle. 41-Front Page Peggy begins. 43-Last Pyroman	9.50	28.50	65.00
44-Lance Lewis, Space Detective begins; Ingels-c	15.00	45.00	105.00
45-Tygra begins (origin)	13.00	40.00	90.00
46-Ingels c/a	13.00	40.00	90.00
47-53: 49-Last Fighting Yank. 50,51-Sea-Eagle app.	11.00	32.00	76.00

NOTE: ***Ingels** c-44, 46(Wash). **Schomburg (Xela)** c-21-43; 47-53 (airbrush). **Tuska** c-45? Bondage c-16, 21, 46-49.*

STARTLING TERROR TALES

5/52 - No. 14, 2/53; No. 4, 4/53 - No. 11, 1954
Star Publications

	Good	Fine	Mint
10-(1st Series)-Wood/Harrison-a (r-A Star Presentation #3) Disbrow/Cole-c	18.00	54.00	125.00
11-L. B. Cole Spider-c; r-Fox's "A Feat. Presentation #5"	9.00	27.00	62.00
12,14	3.65	11.00	25.00
13-Jo-Jo-r; Disbrow-a	4.00	12.00	28.00
4-7,9,11('53-54) (2nd Series)	3.00	9.00	21.00
8-Spanking scene; Palais-a(r)	5.00	15.00	35.00
10-Disbrow-a	4.00	12.00	28.00

NOTE: ***L. B. Cole** covers-all issues. **Palais** a-V2#11r.*

STAR TREK (TV) (See Dan Curtis)

7/67; No. 2, 6/68; No. 3, 12/68; No. 4, 6/69 - No. 61, 3/79
Gold Key

	Good	Fine	Mint
1	6.50	19.50	45.00
2-5	3.50	10.50	24.00
6-10: 1-9-Photo-c	2.00	6.00	14.00
11-20	1.30	4.00	9.00
21-30	.85	2.50	6.00
31-40	.55	1.65	4.00
41-61: 52-Drug propaganda story	.35	1.00	2.00
...the Enterprise Logs nn(8/76)-Golden Press, 224 pgs. ($1.95)-Reprints No. 1-8 plus 7 pgs. by McWilliams (#11185)	1.00	3.00	6.00
...the Enterprise Logs Vol.2('76)-Reprints #9-17 (#11187)	.85	2.50	5.00
...the Enterprise Logs Vol.3('77)-Reprints #18-26 (#11188); McWilliams-a (4 pgs.)	.70	2.00	4.00
Star Trek Vol.4(Winter'77)-Reprints #27,28,30-36,38 (#11189) plus 3 pgs. new art	.70	2.00	4.00

NOTE: ***McWilliams** a-38, 40-44, 46-61. #29 reprints #1; #35 reprints #4; #37 reprints #5; #45 reprints #7. The tabloids all have photo covers and blank inside covers. Painted covers #10-44, 46-59.*

Startling Comics #53, © BP

Startling Terror Tales #6, © STAR

Star Trek #5 (G.K.), © Paramount

Star Trek Annual #2 (DC), © Paramount

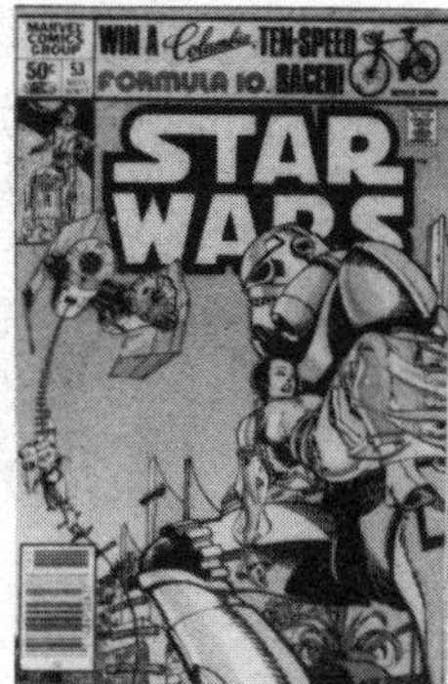

Star Wars #53, © Lucasfilms

Steel Sterling #6, © AP

STAR TREK
April, 1980 - No. 18, Feb, 1982
Marvel Comics Group

	Good	Fine	Mint
1-r/Marvel Super Special; movie adapt.	.25	.75	1.50
2-18		.50	1.00

NOTE: ***Austin*** *c-18i.* ***Buscema*** *a-13.* ***Gil Kane*** *a-15.* ***Miller*** *c-5.* ***Nasser*** *c/a-7.* ***Simonson*** *c-17.*

STAR TREK
Feb, 1984 - Present (Mando paper)
DC Comics

	Good	Fine	Mint
1-Sutton-a(p)	.75	2.25	4.50
2-5	.60	1.75	3.50
6-10 (75 cent cover)	.35	1.10	2.20
11-20	.30	.85	1.70
21-32		.60	1.20
33 ($1.25)	.30	.85	1.70
34-50		.50	1.00
Annual 1 (10/85)	.35	1.00	2.00
Annual 2 (9/86)	.30	.90	1.80

NOTE: ***Morrow*** *a-28, 35, 36.* ***Orlando*** *c-8i.* ***Perez*** *c-1-3.* ***Spiegle*** *a-19.* ***Starlin*** *c-24, 25.* ***Sutton*** *a-1-6p, 8-18p, 20-27p, 29p, 31-34p, 39-45p; c-4-6p, 8-22p.*

STAR TREK MOVIE SPECIAL
June, 1984 - No. 2, 1987 (68pgs; $1.50)
DC Comics

	Good	Fine	Mint
1-Adapts Star Trek III; Sutton-a(p)	.25	.75	1.50
2-Adapts Star Trek IV; Sutton-a	.35	1.00	2.00

STAR TREK: THE NEXT GENERATION (TV)
Feb, 1988 - Present
DC Comics

	Good	Fine	Mint
1-3: Based on TV show	.25	.75	1.50

STAR WARS (Movie) (See Contemporary Motivators, The Droids, The Ewoks, Marvel Movie Showcase & Marvel Special Edition)
July, 1977 - No. 107, Sept, 1986
Marvel Comics Group

	Good	Fine	Mint
1-(Regular 30 cent edition)-Price in square w/UPC code	1.35	4.00	8.00
1-(35 cent cover; limited distribution - 1500 copies?)- Price in square w/UPC code	23.00	70.00	160.00
2-4	.70	2.00	4.00
5-10	.50	1.50	3.00
11-20	.35	1.00	2.00
21-37	.25	.75	1.50
38-Golden c/a	.35	1.00	2.00
39-The Empire Strikes Back r-begin, ends #44; Williamson c/a	.35	1.00	2.00
40-44-Williamson c/a	.35	1.00	2.00
45-49,51-99: 81-Painted-c		.40	.80
50-(75 cents, 52pgs.) Williamson-a		.50	1.00
100-Double size		.65	1.30
101-107		.35	.70
1-9-Reprints; has "reprint" in upper lefthand corner of cover or on inside or price and number inside a diamond with no date or UPC on cover; 30 cents and 35 cents issues published		.25	.50
Annual 1 (12/79)	.35	1.00	2.00
Annual 2 (11/82), 3(12/83)		.60	1.20

NOTE: ***Austin*** *c-11-15i, 21i, 38; c-12-15i, 21i.* ***Byrne*** *c-13p.* ***Chaykin*** *a-1-10p; c-1.* ***Leialoha*** *inks-2-5.* ***Miller*** *c-47p.* ***Nebres*** *c/a-Annual 2i.* ***Simonson*** *a-16p, 49p, 51-63p, 65p, 66p; c-16, 49-51, 52p, 53-62, Annual 1.* ***Williamson*** *a-39-44p, 50p; c-39, 40, 41-44p, 98.*

STAR WARS: RETURN OF THE JEDI
Oct, 1983 - No. 4, Jan, 1984 (Mini-series)
Marvel Comics Group

	Good	Fine	Mint
1-4-Williamson-a(p) in all		.30	.60
Oversized issue ('83; 10¾x8¼"; 68 pgs.; cardboard-c)-Reprints above 4 issues	.50	1.50	2.95

STATIC (Also see Ditko's World)
No. 11, Oct, 1985 - No. 12, Dec, 1985
Charlton Comics

	Good	Fine	Mint
11,12: Ditko c/a		.40	.80

STEEL CLAW, THE
Dec, 1986 - No. 4, Mar, 1987 (mini-series)
Quality Comics

	Good	Fine	Mint
1-3		.45	.90
4 ($1.50)		.60	1.20

STEELGRIP STARKEY
July, 1986 - No. 6, June, 1987 (mini-series)($1.50, Baxter)
Epic Comics (Marvel)

	Good	Fine	Mint
1-6	.25	.75	1.50

STEEL STERLING (Formerly Shield-Steel Sterling)
No. 4, Jan, 1984 - No. 7, July, 1984
Archie Enterprises, Inc.

	Good	Fine	Mint
4-7: 6-McWilliams-a		.40	.80

STEEL, THE INDESTRUCTIBLE MAN
March, 1978 - No. 5, Oct-Nov, 1978
DC Comics, Inc.

	Good	Fine	Mint
1		.30	.60
2-5: 5-Giant		.25	.50

STEVE CANYON (See 4-Color No. 519, 578, 641, 737, 804, 939, 1033, and Harvey Comics Hits No. 52)

STEVE CANYON
1959 (96 pgs.; no text; 6¾x9"; hardcover)(B&W inside)
Grosset & Dunlap

	Good	Fine	Mint
100100-Reprints 2 stories from strip (1953, 1957)	3.00	9.00	21.00
100100 (softcover edition)	2.50	7.50	17.00

STEVE CANYON COMICS
Feb, 1948 - No. 6, Dec, 1948 (Strip reprints) No. 4,5-52pgs.
Harvey Publications

	Good	Fine	Mint
1-Origin; has biog of Milton Caniff; Powell-a, 2pgs.; Caniff-a	13.50	40.50	95.00
2-Caniff, Powell-a	10.00	30.00	70.00
3-6: Caniff, Powell-a in all	8.50	25.50	60.00
Dept. Store giveaway #3(6/48, 36pp)	8.50	25.50	60.00
. . .'s Secret Mission (1951, 16 pgs., Armed Forces giveaway) -Caniff-a	8.00	24.00	56.00
Strictly for the Smart Birds-16 pgs., 1951; Information Comics Div. (Harvey) Premium	8.00	24.00	56.00

STEVE CANYON IN 3-D
June, 1986 (One shot, $2.25)
Kitchen Sink Press

	Good	Fine	Mint
1	.35	1.15	2.30

STEVE DONOVAN, WESTERN MARSHAL (TV)
No. 675, Feb, 1956 - No. 880, Feb, 1958 (All photo-c)
Dell Publishing Co.

	Good	Fine	Mint
4-Color 675-Kinstler-a	3.50	10.50	24.00
4-Color 768-Kinstler-a	3.00	9.00	21.00
4-Color 880	2.00	6.00	14.00

STEVE ROPER
April, 1948 - No. 5, Dec, 1948
Famous Funnies

	Good	Fine	Mint
1-Contains 1944 daily newspaper-r	4.00	12.00	28.00
2	2.00	6.00	14.00

STEVE ROPER (continued) | Good | Fine | Mint
3-5 1.70 5.00 12.00

STEVE SAUNDERS SPECIAL AGENT (See Special Agent)

STEVE SAVAGE (See Captain . . .)

STEVE ZODIAC & THE FIRE BALL XL-5 (TV)
January, 1964
Gold Key
1 (10108-401) 3.70 11.00 26.00

STEVIE
Nov, 1952 - No. 6, April, 1954
Mazie (Magazine Publ.)
1 1.15 3.50 8.00
2-6 .85 2.50 6.00

STEVIE MAZIE'S BOY FRIEND (See Harvey Hits No. 5)

STEWART THE RAT (See Eclipse Graphic Album Series)

STONEY BURKE (TV)
June-Aug, 1963 - No. 2, Sept-Nov, 1963
Dell Publishing Co.
1,2 1.15 3.50 8.00

STONY CRAIG
1946 (No #)
Pentagon Publishing Co.
Reprints Bell Syndicate's "Sgt. Stony Craig" newspaper strips
3.00 9.00 21.00

STORIES BY FAMOUS AUTHORS ILLUSTRATED (Fast Fiction #1-5)
Fall, 1950 - No. 13, May, 1951
Seaboard Publ./Famous Authors Ill.
1-Scarlet Pimpernel-Baroness Orczy 13.00 40.00 90.00
2-Capt. Blood-Rafael Sabatini 12.00 36.00 84.00
3-She, by Haggard 16.00 48.00 110.00
4-The 39 Steps-John Buchan 8.00 24.00 56.00
5-Beau Geste-P. C. Wren 8.00 24.00 56.00
NOTE: *The above five issues are exact reprints of Fast Fiction #1-5 except for the title change and new Kiefer covers on #1 and 2. The above 5 issues were released before Famous Authors #6.*
6-Macbeth, by Shakespeare; Kiefer art (8/50); used in **SOTI**, pg. 22,143. Kiefer-c 11.50 34.00 80.00
7-The Window; Kiefer-c/a 8.00 24.00 56.00
8-Hamlet, by Shakespeare; Kiefer-c/a 11.50 34.00 80.00
9-Nicholas Nickleby, by Dickens; G. Schrotter-a
8.00 24.00 56.00
10-Romeo & Juliet, by Shakespeare; Kiefer-c/a
8.00 24.00 56.00
11-Ben-Hur; Schrotter-a 10.00 30.00 70.00
12-La Svengali; Schrotter-a 10.00 30.00 70.00
13-Scaramouche; Kiefer-c/a 10.00 30.00 70.00

STORIES OF CHRISTMAS
1942 (32 pages; paper cover) (Giveaway)
K. K. Publications
Adaptation of "A Christmas Carol;" Kelly story-"The Fir Tree" Infinity-c 40.00 100.00 200.00

STORIES OF ROMANCE (Formerly Matt Slade Gunfighter?)
No. 5, Mar, 1956 - No. 13, Aug, 1957
Atlas Comics (LMC)
5-Baker-a? 2.15 6.50 15.00
6-13 1.15 3.50 8.00
NOTE: ***Ann Brewster** a-13. **Colletta** a-9(2); c-5.*

STORMY (See 4-Color No. 537)

STORY HOUR SERIES (Disney)
1948, 1949; 1951-1953 (36 pgs.) (4½x6¼")
Given away with subscription to Walt Disney's Comics & Stories
Whitman Publishing Co. | Good | Fine | Mint
nn(1948)-Mickey Mouse and Boy Thursday 5.00 15.00 35.00
nn(1948)-Mickey Mouse Miracle Maker 5.00 15.00 35.00
nn(1948)-Minnie Mouse and Antique Chair 5.00 15.00 35.00
nn(1949)-The Three Orphan Kittens(B&W & color)
2.35 7.00 16.00
nn(1949)-Danny-The Little Black Lamb 2.35 7.00 16.00
800-Donald Duck in "Bringing Up the Boys"
1948 Paper Cover 8.00 24.00 56.00
1953 4.00 12.00 28.00
801-Mickey Mouse's Summer Vacation
1948 Paper Cover 4.00 12.00 28.00
1951, 1952 edition 2.00 6.00 14.00
802-Bugs Bunny's Adventures
1948 Paper Cover 3.00 9.00 21.00
803-Bongo
1948 Paper Cover 3.35 8.00 18.00
804-Mickey and the Beanstalk
1948 Paper Cover 3.35 10.00 23.00
808-15(1949)-Johnny Appleseed 2.75 8.00 18.00
1948 Hard Cover Edition of each. . . . $2.00 - $3.00 more

STORY OF EDISON, THE
1956 (16 pgs.) (Reddy Killowatt)
Educational Comics
Reprint of Reddy Killowatt #2(1947) 4.75 14.00 30.00

STORY OF HARRY S. TRUMAN, THE
1948 (16 pgs.) (in color, regular size)(Soft-c)
Democratic National Committee (Giveaway)
Gives biography on career of Truman; used in **SOTI**, pg. 311
15.00 45.00 105.00

STORY OF JESUS (See Classics Special)

STORY OF MANKIND, THE (See 4-Color No. 851)

STORY OF MARTHA WAYNE, THE
April, 1956
Argo Publ.
1-Newspaper-r 1.60 4.70 11.00

STORY OF RUTH, THE (See 4-Color No. 1144)

STORY OF THE COMMANDOS, THE (Combined Operations)
1943 (68 pgs.; B&W) (15 cents)
Long Island Independent (Distr. by Gilberton)
nn-All text (no comics); photos & illustrations; ads for Classic Comics on back cover (Rare) 11.50 34.00 80.00

STORY OF THE GLOOMY BUNNY, THE (See March of Comics No. 9)

STRAIGHT ARROW (Radio)(See Best of the West, Great Western)
Feb-Mar, 1950 - No. 55, Mar, 1956 (all 36 pgs.)
Magazine Enterprises
1-Straight Arrow (alias Steve Adams) & his palomino Fury begin; 1st mention of Sundown Valley & the Secret Cave; Whitney-a
17.00 51.00 120.00
2-Red Hawk begins by Powell (Origin), ends #55
8.50 25.50 60.00
3-Frazetta-c 16.00 48.00 120.00
4,5: 4-Secret Cave-c 5.00 15.00 35.00
6-10 4.35 13.00 30.00
11-Classic story "The Valley of Time," with an ancient civilization made of gold 4.35 13.00 30.00
12-19 3.00 9.00 21.00
20-Origin S. Arrow's Shield 4.35 13.00 30.00
21-Origin Fury 5.00 15.00 35.00
22-Frazetta-c 13.00 40.00 90.00

Stories By Famous Authors Illustrated #8, © Seaboard

Stories of Romance #9, © MCG

Straight Arrow #20, © ME

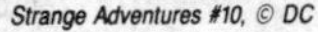
Strange Adventures #10, © DC

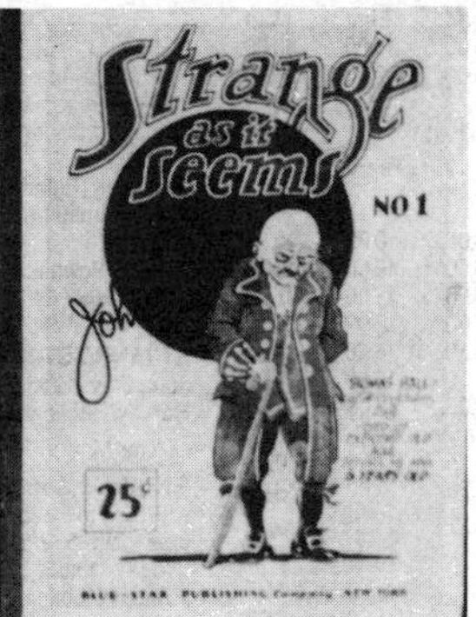

Strange As It Seems #1, © UFS

Strange Fantasy #5, © AJAX

STRAIGHT ARROW (continued) — Good / Fine / Mint

23,25-30: 25-Secret Cave-c. 28-Red Hawk meets The Vikings
2.65 8.00 18.00
24-Classic story "The Dragons of Doom!" with prehistoric pteradactyls 4.00 12.00 28.00
31-38 2.15 6.50 15.00
39-Classic story "The Canyon Beast," with a dinosaur egg hatching a Tyranosaurus Rex 3.00 9.00 21.00
40-Classic story "Secret of The Spanish Specters," with Conquistadors lost treasure 3.00 9.00 21.00
41,42,44-54: 45-Secret Cave-c 1.85 5.50 13.00
43-Intro & 1st app. Blaze, S. Arrow's Warrior dog
2.15 6.50 15.00
55-Last issue 2.65 8.00 18.00

NOTE: ***Fred Meagher** a 1-55; c-1,2,4-21,23-55. **Powell** a 2-55. Many issues advertise the radio premiums associated with Straight Arrow.*

STRAIGHT ARROW'S FURY (See A-1 Comics No. 119)

STRANGE
March, 1957 - No. 6, May, 1958
Ajax-Farrell Publ. (Four Star Comic Corp.)

1 4.00 12.00 28.00
2 2.00 6.00 14.00
3-6 1.70 5.00 12.00

STRANGE ADVENTURES
Aug-Sept, 1950 - No. 244, Oct-Nov, 1973 (No. 1-12: 52 pgs.)
National Periodical Publications

1-Adaptation of "Destination Moon;" Kris KL-99 & Darwin Jones begin; photo-c 85.00 255.00 595.00
2 42.00 125.00 295.00
3,4 26.00 78.00 180.00
5-8,10: 7-Origin Kris KL-99 24.00 72.00 170.00
9-Intro. & origin Captain Comet (6/51) 65.00 195.00 455.00
11,14,15 17.00 51.00 120.00
12,13,17-Toth-a 19.00 57.00 132.00
16,18-20 12.00 36.00 84.00
21-30 11.00 32.00 76.00
31,34-38 9.00 27.00 62.00
32,33-Krigstein-a 10.00 30.00 70.00
39-Ill. in SOTI-"Treating police contemptuously" (top right)
17.00 51.00 120.00
40-49-Last Capt. Comet; not in 45,47,48 8.00 24.00 56.00
50-53-Last pre-code issue 5.70 17.00 40.00
54-70 3.50 10.50 24.00
71-99 2.65 8.00 18.00
100 3.50 10.50 24.00
101-110: 104-Space Museum begins by Sekowsky
1.70 5.00 12.00
111-116,118-120: 114-Star Hawkins begins, ends #185; Heath-a in Wood E.C. style 1.50 4.50 10.00
117-Origin Atomic Knights 7.00 21.00 50.00
121-134: 124-Origin Faceless Creature. 134-Last 10 cent issue
1.00 3.00 7.00
135-145 .85 2.50 5.00
146-160: 159-Star Rovers app. 160-Last Atomic Knights
.50 1.50 3.00
161-179: 161-Last Space Museum. 163-Star Rovers app. 170-Infinity-c. 177-Origin Immortal Man .35 1.00 2.00
180-Origin Animal Man .35 1.00 2.00
181-186,188-204: 201-Last Animal Man .50 1.00
187-Origin The Enchantress .50 1.00
205-Intro & origin Deadman by Infantino 2.50 7.50 15.00
206-Adams-a begins 1.35 4.00 8.00
207-210 1.15 3.50 7.00
211-216-Last Deadman 1.00 3.00 6.00
217-Adam Strange & Atomic Knights-r begin .25 .50

Good / Fine / Mint

218-225: 222-New Adam Strange story .25 .50
226-236(68-52 pgs.): 231-Last Atomic Knights-r .25 .50
237-244 .25 .50

NOTE: ***Adams** a-206-216; c-207-216, 228, 235. **Anderson** a-8-52, 94, 96, 97, 99, 115, 117, 119-163, 217r, 218r, 222-25r, 222, 226, 242i(r); c/r-157i, 190i, 217-224, 228-31, 233, 235-39, 241-43. **Ditko** a-188, 189. **Drucker** a-42, 43, 45. **Finlay** a-2, 3, 6, 7, 210r, 229r. **Infantino** a-10-101, 106-151, 154, 157-163, 180, 190, 223-25p(r), 242p(r); c/r-190p, 197, 199-211, 218-221, 223-244. **Kaluta** c-238, 240. **Gil Kane** a-8-116, 124, 125, 130, 138, 146-157, 173-186, 204r, 222r, 227-231r; c-154p, 157p. **Kubert** a-55(2 pgs.), 226; c-219, 220, 225-227, 232, 234. **Moriera** c-71. **Morrow** c-230. **Powell** a-4. **Mike Sekowsky** a-71p, 97-162p, 217p(r), 218p(r); c-206, 217-219r. **Simon & Kirby** a-2r (2 pg.) **Sparling** a-201. **Toth** a-8, 12, 13, 17-19. **Wood** a-154i. **Chris KL99** in 1-3, 5, 7, 9, 11, 15. **Capt. Comet** covers-9-14, 17-19, 24, 26, 27, 32-44.*

STRANGE AS IT SEEMS (See Famous Funnies-A Carnival of Comics, Feature Funnies #1, The John Hix Scrap Book & Peanuts)

STRANGE AS IT SEEMS
1932 (64 pgs.; B&W; square binding)
Blue-Star Publishing Co.

1-Newspaper-r 11.50 34.00 80.00
NOTE: *Published with and without No. 1 and price on cover.*
Ex-Lax giveaway(1936,24pgs,5x7",B&W)-McNaught Synd.
2.00 6.00 14.00

STRANGE AS IT SEEMS
1939
United Features Syndicate

Single Series 9, 1,2 11.50 34.00 80.00

STRANGE CONFESSIONS
Jan-Mar, 1952 - No. 4, Fall, 1952
Ziff-Davis Publ. Co. (Approved)

1(Scarce)-Photo-c; Kinstler-a 18.00 54.00 125.00
2(Scarce) 11.50 34.00 80.00
3(Scarce)-#3 on-c, #2 on inside 11.00 32.00 76.00
4(Scarce)-Reformatory girl story 11.00 32.00 76.00

STRANGE DAYS
Oct, 1984 - No. 3, Apr, 1985 ($1.75; Baxter paper)
Eclipse Comics

1-3-Freakwave & Johnny Nemo & Paradax from Vanguard Ill.; nudity, violence, strong language .25 .75 1.50

STRANGE FANTASY
Aug, 1952 - No. 14, Oct-Nov, 1954
Harvey Publ./Ajax-Farrell No. 2 on

2(8/52)-Jungle Princess story; no Black Cat; Kamenish-a; r-/Ellery Queen #1 6.50 19.50 45.00
2(10/52)-No Black Cat or Rulah; Bakerish, Kamenish-a; hypo/meat-hook-c 6.00 18.00 42.00
3-Rulah story, called Pulah 6.00 18.00 42.00
4-Rocket Man app. 4.60 14.00 32.00
5,6,8,10,12,14 3.50 10.50 24.00
7-Madam Satan/Slave story 4.00 12.00 28.00
9(w/Black Cat), 9(w/Boy's Ranch; S&K-a) 6.00 18.00 42.00
9-Regular issue 3.70 11.00 26.00
11-Jungle story 4.00 12.00 28.00
13-Bondage-c; Rulah (Kolah) story 6.00 18.00 42.00

STRANGE GALAXY (Magazine)
V1No.8, Feb, 1971 - No. 11, Aug, 1971 (B&W)
Eerie Publications

V1#8-Cover-r/from Fantastic V19#3 (2/70) (a pulp)
.50 1.50 3.00
9-11 .35 1.00 2.00

STRANGE JOURNEY
Sept, 1957 - No. 4, June, 1958 (Farrell reprints)
America's Best (Steinway Publ.) (Ajax/Farrell)

STRANGE JOURNEY (continued)

	Good	Fine	Mint
1	5.00	15.00	35.00
2-4	3.00	9.00	21.00

STRANGE LOVE (See Fox Giants)

STRANGE MYSTERIES
Sept, 1951 - No. 21, Jan, 1955
Superior/Dynamic Publications

	Good	Fine	Mint
1-Kamenish-a begins	13.00	40.00	90.00
2	6.50	19.50	45.00
3-5	5.00	15.00	35.00
6-8	4.00	12.00	28.00
9-Bondage 3-D effect-c	5.50	16.50	38.00
10-Used in **SOTI**, pg. 181	5.50	16.50	38.00
11-18	3.00	9.00	21.00
19-r-/Journey Into Fear #1; cover is a splash from one story; Baker-a(2)(r)	5.75	17.25	40.00
20,21-Reprints; 20-r-/#1 with new-c	2.65	8.00	18.00

STRANGE MYSTERIES
1963 - 1964
I. W. Enterprises/Super Comics

	Good	Fine	Mint
I.W. Reprint #9; Rulah-r	.60	1.80	3.60
Super Reprint #10-12,15-17('63-'64): #12-reprints Tales of Horror #5 (3/53) less-c. #15,16-reprints The Dead Who Walk	.60	1.80	3.60
Super Reprint #18-R-/Witchcraft #1; Kubert-a	.60	1.80	3.60

STRANGE PLANETS
1958; 1963-64
I. W. Enterprises/Super Comics

	Good	Fine	Mint
I.W. Reprint #1(nd)-E. C. Incred. S/F #30 plus-c/Strange Worlds #3	5.00	15.00	35.00
I.W. Reprint #8	1.35	4.00	9.00
I.W. Reprint #9-Orlando/Wood-a (Strange Worlds #4); c-from Flying Saucers #1	6.00	18.00	42.00
Super Reprint #10-22 pg. Wood-a from Space Detective #1; c-/ Attack on Planet Mars	6.00	18.00	42.00
Super Reprint #11-25 pg. Wood-a from An Earthman on Venus	9.20	27.50	64.00
Super Reprint #12-Orlando-a from Rocket to the Moon	5.85	17.50	40.00
Super Reprint #15-Reprints Atlas stories; Heath, Colan-a	1.35	4.00	9.00
Super Reprint #16-Avon's Strange Worlds #6; Kinstler, Check-a	2.00	6.00	14.00
Super Reprint #17	1.35	4.00	9.00
Super Reprint #18-Reprints Daring Adventures; Space Busters, Explorer Joe, The Son of Robin Hood; Krigstein-a	2.00	6.00	14.00

STRANGE SPORTS STORIES (See Brave & the Bold, DC Special, and DC Super Stars #10)
Sept-Oct, 1973 - No. 6, July-Aug, 1974
National Periodical Publications

	Good	Fine	Mint
1		.30	.60
2-6: 3-Swan/Anderson-a		.25	.50

STRANGE STORIES FROM ANOTHER WORLD
No. 2, Aug, 1952 - No. 5, Feb, 1953 (Unknown World #1)
Fawcett Publications

	Good	Fine	Mint
2-Saunders painted-c	11.00	32.00	76.00
3-5-Saunders painted-c	7.00	21.00	50.00

STRANGE STORIES OF SUSPENSE (Rugged Action #1-4)
No. 5, Oct, 1955 - No. 16, Aug, 1957
Atlas Comics (CSI)

	Good	Fine	Mint
5(#1)	6.00	18.00	42.00
6,9	3.50	10.50	24.00
7-E. C. swipe cover/Vault of Horror #32	4.00	12.00	28.00
8-Williamson/Mayo-a; Pakula-a	5.00	15.00	35.00
10-Crandall, Torres, Meskin-a	5.00	15.00	35.00
11,13	2.00	6.00	14.00
12-Torres, Pakula-a	2.65	8.00	18.00
14-Williamson-a	3.65	11.00	25.00
15-Krigstein-a	2.85	8.50	20.00
16-Fox, Powell-a	3.50	10.50	24.00

NOTE: ***Everett** a-6, 7, 13; c-9, 11-14. **Heath** a-5. **Maneely** c-5. **Morrow** a-13. **Powell** a-8. **Severin** c-7. **Wildey** a-14.*

STRANGE STORY (Also see Front Page)
June-July, 1946 (52 pages)
Harvey Publications

	Good	Fine	Mint
1-The Man in Black Called Fate by Powell	8.00	24.00	56.00

STRANGE SUSPENSE STORIES (Lawbreakers Suspense Stories #10-15; This Is Suspense #23-26; Captain Atom V1#78 on)
6/52 - No. 5, 2/53; No. 16, 1/54 - No. 22, 11/54; No. 27, 10/55 - No. 77, 10/65; V3No. 1, 10/67 - V1No.9, 9/69
Fawcett Publications/Charlton Comics No. 16 on

	Good	Fine	Mint
1-(Fawcett)-Powell, Sekowsky-a	14.00	42.00	100.00
2-George Evans horror story	8.50	25.50	60.00
3-5 (2/53)-George Evans horror stories	7.00	21.00	50.00
16(1-2/54)	5.00	15.00	35.00
17,21	4.00	12.00	28.00
18-E.C. swipe/HOF 7; Ditko c/a(2)	10.00	30.00	70.00
19-Ditko electric chair-c; Ditko-a	11.50	34.00	80.00
20-Ditko c/a(2)	10.00	30.00	70.00
22(11/54)-Ditko-c, Shuster-a; last pre-code issue; becomes This Is Suspense	7.00	21.00	50.00
27(10/55)-(Formerly This Is Suspense #26?)	1.75	5.25	12.00
28-30,38	1.50	4.50	10.00
31-33,35,37,40,51-Ditko c/a(2-3)	4.60	14.00	32.00
34-Story of ruthless business man-Wm. B. Gaines; Ditko-c/a	6.50	19.50	45.00
36-(68 pgs.); Ditko-a	6.00	18.00	42.00
39,41,52,53-Ditko-a	4.00	12.00	28.00
42-44,46,49,54-60	1.15	3.50	8.00
45,47,48,50-Ditko c/a	3.50	10.50	24.00
61-74	.50	1.50	3.00
75(6/65)-Origin Captain Atom by Ditko-r/Space Advs.	5.50	16.50	38.00
76,77-Ditko Captain Atom-r/Space Advs.	2.00	6.00	14.00
V3#1(10/67)-4		.40	.80
V1#2-9: 2-Ditko-a, atom bomb-c		.30	.60

NOTE: ***Alascia** a-19. **Aparo** a-V3/1. **Bailey** a-1-3; c-5. **Evans** c-4. **Powell** a-4. **Shuster** a-19, 21.*

STRANGE TALES (Dr. Strange #169 on)
6/51 - No. 168, 5/68; No. 169, 9/73 - No. 188, 11/76
Atlas (CCPC No. 1-67/ZPC No. 68-79/VPI No. 80-85)/Marvel No. 86(7/61) on

	Good	Fine	Mint
1	60.00	180.00	420.00
2	28.00	84.00	195.00
3,5: 3-Atom bomb panels	20.00	60.00	140.00
4-"The Evil Eye," cosmic eyeball sty	22.00	65.00	154.00
6-9	15.00	45.00	105.00
10-Krigstein-a	16.00	48.00	110.00
11-14,16-20	6.00	18.00	42.00
15-Krigstein-a	7.00	21.00	50.00
21,23-27,29-32,34-Last precode ish(2/55): 27-Atom bomb panels	5.00	15.00	35.00
22-Krigstein, Forte/Fox-a	5.50	16.50	38.00
28-Jack Katz story used in Senate Investigation report, pgs. 7 & 169	5.50	16.50	38.00

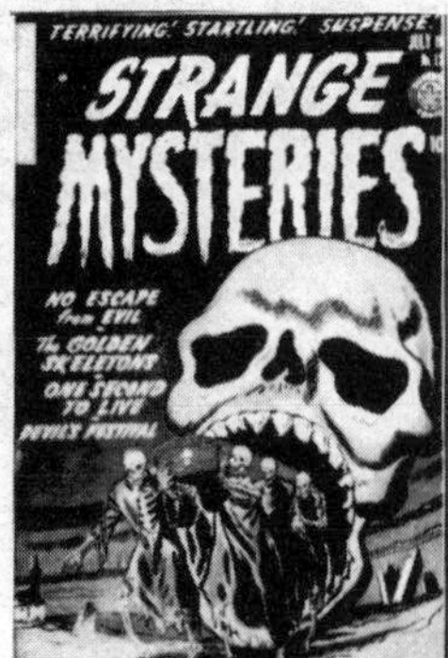

Strange Mysteries #12, © SUPR

Strange Stories From Another World #3, © FAW

Strange Suspense Stories #1, © CC

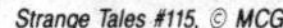
Strange Tales #115, © MCG

Strange Terrors #4, © STJ

Strange World of Your Dreams #4, © PRIZE

STRANGE TALES (continued)	**Good**	**Fine**	**Mint**
33-Davis-a	5.50	16.50	38.00
35-41,43,44	3.00	9.00	21.00
42,45,59,61-Krigstein-a; #61 (2/58)	4.00	12.00	28.00
46-52,54,55,57,60: 60 (8/57)	2.30	7.00	16.00
53-Torres, Crandall-a	4.00	12.00	28.00
56-Crandall-a	3.70	11.00	26.00
58,64-Williamson-a in each, with Mayo-#58	4.00	12.00	28.00
62-Torres-a	2.65	8.00	18.00
63,65	2.30	7.00	16.00
66-Crandall-a	2.65	8.00	18.00
67-80-Ditko/Kirby-a. 79-Dr. Strange proto-type app.	2.30	7.00	16.00
81-92-Last 10 cent ish. Ditko/Kirby-a	2.00	6.00	14.00
93-100-Kirby-a	1.60	4.70	11.00
101-Human Torch begins by Kirby (10/62)	18.00	46.00	130.00
102	8.50	21.00	60.00
103-105	7.00	17.00	48.00
106,108,109	4.85	12.00	34.00
107-Human Torch/Sub-Mariner battle	5.40	13.50	38.00
110-Intro Dr. Strange, Ancient One & Wong by Ditko	14.00	36.00	100.00
111-2nd Dr. Strange	3.50	9.00	25.00
112,113	2.30	6.00	16.00
114-Acrobat disguised as Captain America, 1st app. since the G.A.; intro. & 1st app. Victoria Bentley	3.15	8.00	22.00
115-Origin Dr. Strange; Sandman (villain) app.	7.00	17.00	48.00
116-120: 116-Thing/Torch battle	1.15	2.85	8.00
121-125: 123-Thor app.	.70	2.00	4.00
126-129,131-133: Thing/Torch team-up in all; 126-Intro Clea	.70	2.00	4.00
130-The Beatles cameo	1.00	3.00	6.00
134-Last Human Torch; Wood-a(i)	.70	2.00	4.00
135-Origin Nick Fury, Agent of Shield by Kirby	1.00	3.00	6.00
136-147,149: 146-Last Ditko Dr. Strange who is in consecutive stories since No. 113	.35	1.00	2.00
148-Origin Ancient One	.45	1.25	2.50
150(11/66)-J. Buscema 1st work at Marvel	.30	1.00	2.00
151-1st Marvel work by Steranko (w/Kirby)	.50	1.50	3.00
152,153-Kirby/Steranko-a	.35	1.00	2.00
154-158-Steranko-a/script	.35	1.00	2.00
159-Origin Nick Fury; Intro Val; Captain America app; Steranko-a	.45	1.25	2.50
160-162-Steranko-a/scripts; Cap. America app.	.35	1.00	2.00
163-166,168-Steranko-a(p)	.35	1.00	2.00
167-Steranko pen/script; classic flag-c	.50	1.50	3.00
169,170-Brother Voodoo origin in each; series ends #173		.30	.60
171-177: 174-Origin Golem. 177-Brunner-c		.30	.60
178-Warlock by Starlin with covers; origin Warlock & Him	1.00	3.00	6.00
179-181-Warlock by Starlin with covers. 179-Intro/1st app. Pip the Troll. 180-Intro Gamora	.60	1.75	3.50
182-188		.25	.50
Annual 1(1962)-Reprints from Str. Tales #73,76,78, Tales of Suspense #7,9, Tales to Astonish #1,6,7, & Journey Into Mystery #53,55,59	8.50	21.00	60.00
Annual 2(1963)-r-/from Str. Tales #67, Str. Worlds (Atlas) #1-3, World of Fantasy #16, Human Torch vs. Spider-Man by Kirby/-Ditko; Kirby-c	6.50	16.00	45.00

NOTE: ***Briefer*** *a-17.* ***Burgos*** *a-123p.* ***J. Buscema*** *a-174p.* ***Colan*** *a-11, 20, 53, 169-73p, 188p.* ***Davis*** *c-71.* ***Ditko*** *a-46, 50, 67-122, 123-25p, 126-146, 175r, 182-88r; c-33, 51, 93, 115, 121, 146.* ***Everett*** *a-4, 21, 40-42, 73, 147-52, 164i; c-10, 11, 13, 24, 45, 49-54, 56, 58, 60, 61, 63, 148, 150, 152, 158i.* ***Forte*** *a-27, 43, 50, 53, 60.* ***Heath*** *c-20.* ***Kamen*** *a-45.* ***G. Kane*** *c-170-72-, 173, 182p.* ***Kirby*** *Human Torch-101-105, 108, 109, 114, 120; Nick Fury-135p, 141-43p; (Layouts)-135-153; other* ***Kirby*** *a-73, 79p, 84p, 97-99p; c-68-70, 72-92, 94, 95, 101-114, 116-123, 125-130, 132-135, 136p, 138-145, 147, 149, 151p.* ***Lawrence*** *a-29.* ***Leiber/Fox*** *a-110, 111, 113.* ***Maneely*** *a-3, 42.* ***Moldoff*** *a-20.* ***Mooney*** *a-174i.* ***Morisi*** *a-53.* ***Orlando*** *a-41, 44, 46, 49, 52.* ***Powell*** *a-42, 44, 49, 54, 130-34p; c-131p.* ***Reinman*** *a-50, 74, 88, 91, 95, 104, 106, 112i, 124-127i.* ***Robinson*** *a-17.* ***Sekowski*** *a-3, 11.* ***Starlin*** *a-178, 179, 180p, 181p; c-178-80, 181p.* ***Steranko*** *a-151-61, 162-68p; c-151i, 153, 155, 157, 159, 161, 163, 165, 167.* ***Tuska*** *a-14, 166p.* ***Wildey*** *a-42.* ***Woodbridge*** *a-59. Fantastic Four cameo-101-134. Jack Katz app.-26.*

STRANGE TALES
Apr, 1987 - Present
Marvel Comics Group

	Good	**Fine**	**Mint**
V2#1		.50	1.00
2-14		.40	.80

STRANGE TALES OF THE UNUSUAL
Dec, 1955 - No. 11, Aug, 1957
Atlas Comics (ACI No. 1-4/WPI No. 5-11)

	Good	Fine	Mint
1-Powell-a	7.00	21.00	50.00
2	3.50	10.50	24.00
3-Williamson-a, 4 pgs.	4.65	14.00	32.00
4,6,8,11	1.70	5.00	12.00
5-Crandall, Ditko-a	4.00	12.00	28.00
7-Kirby, Orlando-a	3.00	9.00	21.00
9-Krigstein-a	3.00	9.00	21.00
10-Torres, Morrow-a	2.65	8.00	18.00

NOTE: ***Baily*** *a-6.* ***Everett*** *a-2, 6; c-6, 9, 11.* ***Heck*** *a-1.* ***Maneely*** *c-1.* ***Orlando*** *a-7.* ***Romita*** *a-1.*

STRANGE TERRORS
June, 1952 - No. 7, Mar, 1953
St. John Publishing Co.

	Good	Fine	Mint
1-Bondage-c; Zombies spelled Zoombies on-c; Finesque-a	10.00	30.00	70.00
2	4.60	14.00	32.00
3-Kubert-a; painted-c	9.00	27.00	62.00
4-Kubert-a(r-/in Mystery Tales No. 18); Ekgren-c; Fineesque-a; Jerry Iger caricature	16.50	50.00	115.00
5-Kubert-a; painted-c	9.00	27.00	62.00
6-Giant, 100 pgs.(1/53); bondage-c	12.00	36.00	84.00
7-Giant, 100 pgs.; Kubert c/a	16.50	50.00	115.00

NOTE: ***Cameron*** *a-6, 7.* ***Morisi*** *a-6.*

STRANGE WORLD OF YOUR DREAMS
Aug, 1952 - No. 4, Jan-Feb, 1953
Prize Publications

	Good	Fine	Mint
1-Simon & Kirby-a	17.00	51.00	120.00
2,3-Simon & Kirby-a. 2-Meskin-a	13.00	40.00	90.00
4-S&K-c; Meskin-a	11.50	34.00	80.00

STRANGE WORLDS (#18 continued from Avon's Eerie #1-17)
Nov, 1950 - No. 22, Sept-Oct, 1955 (no No. 11-17)
Avon Periodicals

	Good	Fine	Mint
1-Kenton of the Star Patrol by Kubert (r-/Eerie #1-'47); Crom the Barbarian by John Giunta	38.00	115.00	265.00
2-Wood-a; Crom the Barbarian by Giunta; Dara of the Vikings app.; used in **SOTI**, pg. 112; injury to eye panel	33.00	100.00	230.00
3-Wood/Orlando-a(Kenton), Wood/Williamson/Frazetta/Krenkel/Orlando-a (7 pgs.); Malu Slave Girl Princess app.; Kinstler-c	77.00	230.00	540.00
4-Wood c/a (Kenton); Orlando-a; origin The Enchanted Daggar; Sultan-a	32.00	95.00	225.00
5-Orlando/Wood-a (Kenton); Wood-c	27.00	81.00	190.00
6-Kinstler-a(2); Orlando/Wood-c, Check-a	17.00	51.00	120.00
7-Kinstler, Fawcette & Becker/Alascia-a	13.00	40.00	90.00
8-Kubert, Kinstler, Hollingsworth & Lazarus-a; Lazarus-c	14.00	42.00	100.00
9-Kinstler, Fawcette, Alascia-a	13.00	40.00	90.00
10	12.00	36.00	84.00
18-Reprints "Attack on Planet Mars" by Kubert	13.50	40.00	95.00
19-Reprints Avon's Robotmen of the Lost Planet			

STRANGE WORLDS (continued)

	Good	Fine	Mint
	13.50	40.00	95.00
20-War stories; Wood-c(r)/U.S. Paratroops #1	3.65	11.00	25.00
21,22-War stories	3.35	10.00	23.00
I.W. Reprint #5-Kinstler-a(r)/Avon's #9	1.35	4.00	8.00

STRANGE WORLDS
Dec, 1958 - No. 5, Aug, 1959
Marvel Comics (MPI No. 1,2/Male No. 3,5)

	Good	Fine	Mint
1-Kirby & Ditko-a; flying saucer ish.	13.00	40.00	90.00
2-Ditko c/a	7.00	21.00	50.00
3-Kirby-a(2)	6.50	19.50	45.00
4-Williamson-a	9.50	28.50	65.00
5-Ditko-a	6.50	19.50	45.00

NOTE: ***Buscema*** *a-3.* ***Ditko*** *a-1-5; c-2.* ***Kirby*** *a-1, 3; c-1, 3-5.*

STRAWBERRY SHORTCAKE
June, 1985 - No. 7, 1986 (Children's comic)
Star Comics (Marvel)

	Good	Fine	Mint
1-7: Howie Post-a		.35	.70

STREET COMIX (50 cents)
1973 (36 pgs.; B&W) (20,000 print run)
Street Enterprises/King Features

	Good	Fine	Mint
1-Rip Kirby		.40	.80
2-Flash Gordon		.60	1.20

STREETFIGHTER
8/86 - No. 4, Spr, 1987 ($1.75, color, mini-series)
Ocean Comics

	Good	Fine	Mint
1-4: 2-Origin begins	.25	.85	1.70

STRICTLY PRIVATE
Nov?, 1942
Eastern Color Printing Co.

	Good	Fine	Mint
1,2	9.00	27.00	62.00

STRIKE!
Aug, 1987 - Present ($1.75, color)
Eclipse Comics

	Good	Fine	Mint
1	.35	1.00	2.00
2-5	.30	.90	1.75

STRIKEFORCE: MORITURI
Dec, 1986 - Present
Marvel Comics Group

	Good	Fine	Mint
1	.40	1.25	2.50
2-5	.30	.90	1.80
6-12,14		.60	1.20
13-Double size	.25	.75	1.50
15-18 ($1.00)		.50	1.00

STRONG MAN (Also see Complimentary Comics)
Mar-Apr, 1955 - No. 4, Sept-Oct, 1955
Magazine Enterprises

	Good	Fine	Mint
1(A-1 130)-Powell-a	8.00	24.00	56.00
2(A-1 132), 3(A-1 134), 4(A-1 139)-Powell-a	5.70	17.00	40.00

STRONTIUM DOG
Dec, 1985 - No. 4, Mar, 1986 (mutie series. $1.25 cover)
Eagle Comics

	Good	Fine	Mint
1-4		.65	1.30
Special 1 ('86)-Moore scripts	.25	.75	1.50

STRONTIUM DOG
July, 1987 - Present ($1.25, color)
Quality Comics

	Good	Fine	Mint
1-5		.60	1.25
Special 1	.25	.75	1.50

STUMBO THE GIANT (See Harvey Hits No. 49,54,57,60,63,66,69,72,78,88)

STUMBO TINYTOWN
Oct, 1963 - No. 13, Nov, 1966
Harvey Publications

	Good	Fine	Mint
1	8.50	25.50	60.00
2	4.30	13.00	30.00
3-5	3.00	9.00	21.00
6-13	2.00	6.00	14.00

STUNTMAN COMICS
Apr-May, 1946 - No. 2, June-July, 1946; No. 3, Oct-Nov, 1946
Harvey Publications

	Good	Fine	Mint
1-Origin Stuntman by S&K reprinted in Black Cat #9	47.00	141.00	330.00
2-S&K-a	31.00	92.00	215.00

3-Small size (5½x8½''; B&W; 32 pgs.); distributed to mail subscribers only; S&K-a; Kid Adonis by S&K reprinted in Green Hornet #37. Estimated value. . . $250.00-$400.00

(Also see All-New #15, Boy Explorers #2, Flash Gordon #5 & Thrills of Tomorrow)

SUBMARINE ATTACK (Formerly Speed Demons)
No. 11, May, 1958 - No. 54, Feb-Mar, 1966
Charlton Comics

	Good	Fine	Mint
11	.70	2.00	4.00
12-20	.35	1.00	2.00
21-54		.60	1.20

NOTE: ***Glanzman*** *c/a-25.* ***Montes/Bache*** *a-38, 40, 41.*

SUB-MARINER (See All-Select, All-Winners, Blonde Phantom, Daring, Human Torch, Marvel Mystery, Motion Picture Funnies Weekly, Namora, Prince Namor, The. . ., USA & Young Men)

SUB-MARINER, THE (2nd Series)(Sub-Mariner #31 on)(Also see Marvel Spotlight #27 & Tales To Astonish, 2nd series)
May, 1968 - No. 72, Sept, 1974 (No. 43: 52 pgs.)
Marvel Comics Group

	Good	Fine	Mint
1-Origin Sub-Mariner	1.70	5.00	10.00
2-Triton app.	.55	1.65	3.30
3-10: 5-1st Tiger Shark	.35	1.10	2.20
11-13,15-20: 19-1st Sting Ray		.65	1.30
14-Sub-Mariner vs. G.A. Human Torch; death of Toro	.35	1.00	2.00
21-33,36,37,39,40: 37-Death of Lady Dorma		.40	.80
34-Silver Surfer, Hulk app.		.50	1.00
35-Ties into 1st Defenders story; Avengers, Silver Surfer, Hulk app.		.50	1.00
38-Origin		.60	1.20
41-49: 44,45-Sub-Mariner vs. H. Torch		.40	.80
50-60: 50-1st app. Nita, Namor's niece. 57-Venus app.		.30	.60
61-Last artwork by Everett; 1st 4 pgs. completed by Mortimer; pgs. 5-20 by Mooney		.25	.50
62-72: 62-1st Tales of Atlantis, ends No. 66		.25	.50
Special 1(1/71)		.50	1.00
Special 2(1/72)-Everett-a		.40	.80

NOTE: ***Bolle*** *a-67i.* ***Buscema*** *a(p)-1-8, 20, 24.* ***Colan*** *a-10p, 11p, 40p, 43p, 46-49p, Spec. 1p, 2; c(p)-10, 11, 40.* ***Craig*** *a-17, 19-23i.* ***Everett*** *a-45r, 50-55, 57, 58, 59-61(plot), 63(plot); c-47, 48i, 55, 57-59i, 61, Spec. 2.* ***G. Kane*** *c(p)-42-52, 58, 66, 70, 71.* ***Mooney*** *a-24i, 25i, 32-35i, 39i, 42i, 44i, 45i, 60i, 61i, 65p, 66p, 68i.* ***Severin*** *c/a-38i.* ***Starlin*** *c-59p.* ***Tuska*** *a-41p, 42p, 69-71p.* ***Wrightson*** *a-36i.*

SUB-MARINER COMICS (1st Series) (The Sub-Mariner #1,2 33-42) (Official True Crime Cases #24 on; Amazing Mysteries #32 on; Best Love #33 on)
Spring, 1941 - No. 23, Sum, '47; No. 24, Wint, '47 - No. 31, 4/49; No. 32, 7/49; No. 33, 4/54 - No. 42, 10/55
Timely/Marvel Comics (TCI 1-7/SePI 8/MPI 9-32/Atlas Comics (CCC 33-42))

	Good	Fine	Mint
1-The Sub-Mariner by Everett & The Angel begin	357.00	1070.00	2500.00

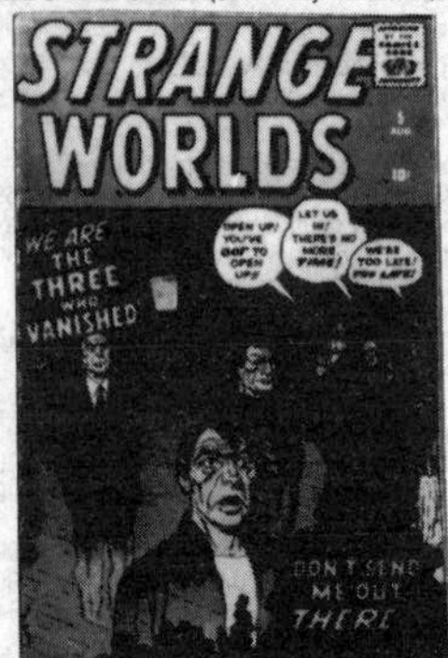

Strange Worlds #5, © MCG

Street Fighter #1, © Ocean Comics

The Sub-Mariner #1, © MCG

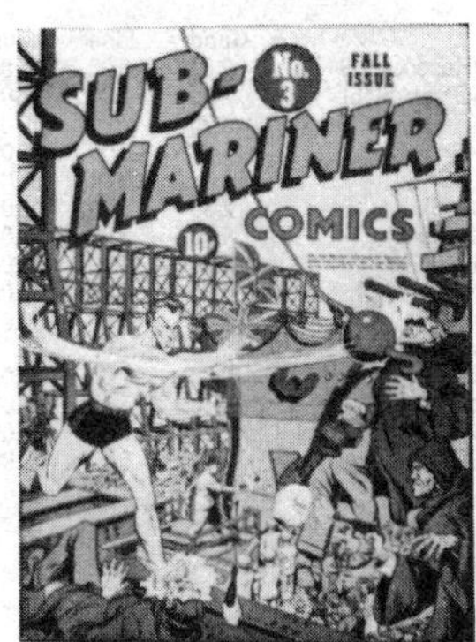

Sub-Mariner Comics #3, © MCG

Suicide Squad #3, © DC

Sunny, America's Sweetheart #11, © FOX

SUB-MARINER COMICS (continued)

	Good	Fine	Mint
2-Everett-a	180.00	540.00	1260.00
3-Churchill assassination-c; 40 pg. S-M story	125.00	375.00	875.00
4-Everett-a, 40 pgs.; 1 pg. Wolverton-a	110.00	330.00	770.00
5	80.00	240.00	560.00
6-10: 9-Wolverton-a, 3 pgs.; flag-c	60.00	180.00	420.00
11-15	42.00	125.00	295.00
16-20	37.00	110.00	260.00
21-Last Angel; Everett-a	28.00	86.00	200.00
22-Young Allies app.	29.00	86.00	200.00
23-The Human Torch, Namora x-over	29.00	86.00	200.00
24-Namora x-over	29.00	86.00	200.00
25-The Blonde Phantom begins, ends No. 31; Kurtzman-a; Namora x-over	35.00	105.00	245.00
26,27	32.00	95.00	225.00
28-Namora cover; Everett-a	32.00	95.00	225.00
29-31 (4/49): 29-The Human Torch app. 31-Capt. America app.	32.00	95.00	225.00
32 (7/49, Scarce)-Origin Sub-Mariner	50.00	150.00	350.00
33 (4/54)-Origin Sub-Mariner; The Human Torch app.; Namora x-over in Sub-Mariner, #33-42	29.00	86.00	200.00
34,35-Human Torch in each	20.00	60.00	140.00
36,37,39-41: 36,39-41-Namora app.	20.00	60.00	140.00
38-Origin Sub-Mariner's wings; Namora app.	26.00	78.00	182.00
42-Last issue	23.00	70.00	160.00

NOTE: *Angel by* ***Gustavson-#1. Everett*** *a-1-4, 22, 24, 26-42; c-2, 32, 33, 40.* ***Maneely*** *c-37, 39, 41.* ***Schomburg*** *c-1-4, 6, 8-14, 16-18, 20. Bondage c-13, 22, 24, 25, 34.*

SUE & SALLY SMITH (Formerly My Secret Life)
No. 48, 11/62 - No. 54, 11/63 (Flying Nurses)
Charlton Comics

	Good	Fine	Mint
V2#48-54		.20	.40

SUGAR & SPIKE (Also see The Best of DC)
Apr-May, 1956 - No. 98, Oct-Nov, 1971
National Periodical Publications

	Good	Fine	Mint
1 (Scarce)	50.00	150.00	350.00
2	25.00	75.00	175.00
3-5	22.00	65.00	154.00
6-10	15.00	45.00	105.00
11-20	11.50	34.00	80.00
21-29,31-40	5.70	17.00	40.00
30-Scribbly x-over	7.00	21.00	50.00
41-60	2.65	8.00	18.00
61-80: 72-Origin & 1st app. Bernie the Brain	1.70	5.00	12.00
81-98: 85-68 pgs.; r-#72. #96-68 pgs. #97,98-52 pgs.	1.35	4.00	9.00

NOTE: ***All written and drawn by Sheldon Mayer.***

SUGAR BEAR
No date (16 pages) (2½x4½")
Post Cereal Giveaway

	Good	Fine	Mint
"The Almost Take Over of the Post Office," "The Race Across the Atlantic," "The Zoo Goes Wild" each...		.40	.80

SUGAR BOWL COMICS
May, 1948 - 1949
Famous Funnies

	Good	Fine	Mint
1-Toth-c/a	6.50	19.50	45.00
2,4,5	2.15	6.50	15.00
3-Toth-a	4.35	13.00	30.00

SUGARFOOT (See 4-Color No. 907,992,1059,1098,1147,1209)

SUICIDE SQUAD
May, 1987 - Present
DC Comics

	Good	Fine	Mint
1	.25	.75	1.50
2-12		.40	.80

SUMMER FUN (See Dell Giants)

SUMMER FUN (Formerly Li'l Genius; Holiday Surprise No. 55)
No. 54, Oct, 1966 (Giant)
Charlton Comics

	Good	Fine	Mint
54		.40	.80

SUMMER LOVE (Formerly Brides in Love?)
V2/46, 10/65; V2/47, 10/66; V2/48, 11/68
Charlton Comics

	Good	Fine	Mint
V2#46-Beatle c/sty	2.00	6.00	14.00
47-Beatle story	2.00	6.00	14.00
48	.35	1.00	2.00

SUMMER MAGIC (See Movie Comics)

SUNDANCE (See 4-Color No. 1126)

SUNDANCE KID
June, 1971 - No. 3, Sept, 1971 (52 pages)
Skywald Publications

	Good	Fine	Mint
1-Durango Kid; 2 Kirby Bullseye-r		.60	1.20
2-Swift Arrow, Durango Kid, Bullseye by S&K; Meskin plus 1 pg. origin		.40	.80
3-Durango Kid, Billy the Kid, Red Hawk-r		.30	.60

SUNDAY FUNNIES
1950
Harvey Publications

	Good	Fine	Mint
1	1.50	4.50	10.50

SUN DEVILS
July, 1984 - No. 12, June, 1985 (12-issue series; $1.25)
DC Comics

	Good	Fine	Mint
1-12: 6-Death of Sun Devil		.60	1.20

SUN FUN KOMIKS
1939 (15 cents; black, white & red)
Sun Publications

	Good	Fine	Mint
1-Satire on comics	12.00	36.00	84.00

SUN GIRL
Aug, 1948 - No. 3, Dec, 1948
Marvel Comics (CCC)

	Good	Fine	Mint
1-Sun Girl begins; Miss America app.	50.00	150.00	350.00
2,3: 2-The Blonde Phantom begins	37.00	110.00	260.00

SUNNY, AMERICA'S SWEETHEART
No. 11, Dec, 1947 - No. 14, June, 1948
Fox Features Syndicate

	Good	Fine	Mint
11-Feldstein c/a	25.00	75.00	175.00
12-14-Feldstein c/a; 14-Lingerie panels	22.00	65.00	154.00
I.W. Reprint #8-Feldstein-a; r-Fox issue	4.00	12.00	28.00

SUN-RUNNERS (Also see Tales of the...)
2/84 - No. 3, 5/84; No. 4, 11/84 - No. 7, '86 (Baxter paper)
Pacific Comics/Eclipse Comics No. 4 on

	Good	Fine	Mint
1-7: P. Smith-a	.25	.80	1.60
Christmas Special 1	.30	.95	1.90

SUNSET CARSON (Also see Cowboy Western)
Feb, 1951 - No. 4, 1951
Charlton Comics

	Good	Fine	Mint
1-Photo-c	32.00	95.00	225.00
2	20.00	60.00	140.00
3,4	17.00	51.00	120.00

SUPER ANIMALS PRESENTS PIDGY & THE MAGIC GLASSES
Dec, 1953
Star Publications

SUPER ANIMALS PRESENTS (continued)

	Good	Fine	Mint
3-D 1-L. B. Cole-c	20.00	60.00	140.00

SUPER BOOK OF COMICS
nd (1943?) (32 pgs., soft-c) (Pan-Am & Kelloggs giveaways)
Western Publishing Co.

	Good	Fine	Mint
1-Dick Tracy (Rare)	26.00	78.00	180.00
2-Smitty	5.00	15.00	35.00
3-Moon Mullins?	4.00	12.00	28.00
4-Smitty	4.00	12.00	28.00
5-Terry & the Pirates	9.00	27.00	62.00
6-Don Winslow, McWilliams-a	5.00	15.00	35.00
7-Little Orphan Annie?	5.00	15.00	35.00
8-Dick Tracy?	10.00	30.00	70.00
9-Terry & the Pirates	8.00	24.00	56.00

SUPER-BOOK OF COMICS
(Omar Bread & Hancock Oil Co. giveaways)
1944 - No. 30, 1947 (Omar); 1947 - 1948 (Hancock) (16 pgs.)
Western Publishing Co.

Note: The Hancock issues are all exact reprints of the earlier Omar issues. The issue numbers were removed in some of the reprints.

	Good	Fine	Mint
1-Dick Tracy (Omar, 1944)	14.00	42.00	100.00
1-Dick Tracy (Hancock, 1947)	10.00	30.00	70.00
2-Bugs Bunny (Omar, 1944)	3.50	10.50	24.00
2-Bugs Bunny (Hancock, 1947)	2.65	8.00	18.00
3-Terry & the Pirates (Omar, 1944)	8.00	24.00	56.00
3-Terry & the Pirates (Hancock, 1947)	6.00	18.00	42.00
4-Andy Panda (Omar, 1944)	3.50	10.50	24.00
4-Andy Panda (Hancock, 1947)	2.65	8.00	18.00
5-Smokey Stover (Omar, 1945)	2.65	8.00	18.00
5-Smokey Stover (Hancock, 1947)	1.70	5.00	12.00
6-Porky Pig (Omar, 1945)	3.50	10.50	24.00
6-Porky Pig (Hancock, 1947)	2.65	8.00	18.00
7-Smilin' Jack (Omar, 1945)	3.50	10.50	24.00
7-Smilin' Jack (Hancock, 1947)	2.65	8.00	18.00
8-Oswald the Rabbit (Omar, 1945)	2.65	8.00	18.00
8-Oswald the Rabbit (Hancock, 1947)	1.70	5.00	12.00
9-Alley Oop (Omar, 1945)	8.00	24.00	56.00
9-Alley Oop (Hancock, 1947)	6.00	18.00	42.00
10-Elmer Fudd (Omar, 1945)	2.65	8.00	18.00
10-Elmer Fudd (Hancock, 1947)	1.70	5.00	12.00
11-Little Orphan Annie (Omar, 1945)	4.35	13.00	30.00
11-Little Orphan Annie (Hancock, 1947)	3.00	9.00	21.00
12-Woody Woodpecker (Omar, 1945)	2.65	8.00	18.00
12-Woody Woodpecker (Hancock, 1947)	1.70	5.00	12.00
13-Dick Tracy (Omar, 1945)	9.00	27.00	62.00
13-Dick Tracy (Hancock, 1947)	7.00	21.00	50.00
14-Bugs Bunny (Omar, 1945)	2.65	8.00	18.00
14-Bugs Bunny (Hancock, 1947)	1.70	5.00	12.00
15-Andy Panda (Omar, 1945)	2.30	7.00	16.00
15-Andy Panda (Hancock, 1947)	1.70	5.00	12.00
16-Terry & the Pirates (Omar, 1945)	7.00	21.00	50.00
16-Terry & the Pirates (Hancock, 1947)	5.00	15.00	35.00
17-Smokey Stover (Omar, 1946)	2.65	8.00	18.00
17-Smokey Stover (Hancock, 1948?)	1.70	5.00	12.00
18-Porky Pig (Omar, 1946)	2.30	7.00	16.00
18-Porky Pig (Hancock, 1948?)	1.70	5.00	12.00
19-Smilin' Jack (Omar, 1946)	2.65	8.00	18.00
nn-Smilin' Jack (Hancock, 1948)	1.70	5.00	12.00
20-Oswald the Rabbit (Omar, 1946)	2.30	7.00	16.00
nn-Oswald the Rabbit (Hancock, 1948)	1.70	5.00	12.00
21-Gasoline Alley (Omar, 1946)	4.00	12.00	28.00
nn-Gasoline Alley (Hancock, 1948)	3.00	9.00	21.00
22-Elmer Fudd (Omar, 1946)	2.30	7.00	16.00
nn-Elmer Fudd (Hancock, 1948)	1.70	5.00	12.00
23-Little Orphan Annie (Omar, 1946)	3.50	10.50	24.00
nn-Little Orphan Annie (Hancock, 1948)	2.65	8.00	18.00
24-Woody Woodpecker (Omar, 1946)	2.30	7.00	16.00
nn-Woody Woodpecker (Hancock, 1948)	1.70	5.00	12.00
25-Dick Tracy (Omar, 1946)	7.00	21.00	50.00
nn-Dick Tracy (Hancock, 1948)	5.00	15.00	35.00
26-Bugs Bunny (Omar, 1946))	2.30	7.00	16.00
nn-Bugs Bunny (Hancock, 1948)	1.70	5.00	12.00
27-Andy Panda (Omar, 1946)	2.30	7.00	16.00
27-Andy Panda (Hancock, 1948)	1.70	5.00	12.00
28-Terry & the Pirates (Omar, 1946)	7.00	21.00	50.00
28-Terry & the Pirates (Hancock, 1948)	5.00	15.00	35.00
29-Smokey Stover (Omar, 1947)	2.30	7.00	16.00
29-Smokey Stover (Hancock, 1948)	1.70	5.00	12.00
30-Porky Pig (Omar, 1947)	2.30	7.00	16.00
30-Porky Pig (Hancock, 1948)	1.70	5.00	12.00

SUPERBOY (See Adventure, Aurora, DC Comics Presents, DC Super Stars, 80 page Giant No. 10, More Fun, and The New Advs. of. . .)

SUPERBOY (. . .& the Legion of Super Heroes with #231)
(Becomes The Legion of Super Heroes No. 259 on)
Mar-Apr, 1949 - No. 258, Dec, 1979 (No. 1-16, 52 pgs.)
National Periodical Publications/DC Comics

	Good	Fine	Mint
1	220.00	660.00	1540.00
2-Used in **SOTI**, pg. 35-36,226	84.00	252.00	590.00
3	60.00	180.00	420.00
4,5: 5-Pre-Supergirl tryout	50.00	150.00	350.00
6-10: 8-1st Superbaby. 10-1st Lana Lang	36.00	108.00	250.00
11-15	30.00	90.00	210.00
16-20	21.00	62.00	145.00
21-26,28-30	15.00	45.00	105.00
27-Low distribution	16.00	48.00	110.00
31-38: 38-Last pre-code ish.	11.00	32.00	76.00
39-50 (7/56)	8.00	24.00	56.00
51-60: 55-Spanking-c	5.50	16.50	38.00
61-67	4.35	13.00	30.00
68-Origin & 1st app. original Bizarro (10-11/58)	7.00	21.00	50.00
69-77,79: 75-Spanking-c. 76-1st Supermonkey. 77-Pre-Pete Ross tryout	3.15	9.50	22.00
78-Origin Mr. Mxyzptlk & Superboy's costume	4.80	14.50	34.00
80-1st meeting Superboy/Supergirl (4/60)	3.15	9.50	22.00
81,84,85,87,88	2.65	8.00	18.00
82-1st Bizarro Krypto	2.65	8.00	18.00
83-Origin & 1st app. Kryptonite Kid	2.65	8.00	18.00
86(1/61)-4th Legion app; Intro Pete Ross	7.00	21.00	50.00
89(6/61)-Mon-el 1st app.	5.75	17.25	40.00
90-92: 90-Pete Ross learns Superboy's I.D. 92-Last 10 cent issue	2.15	6.50	15.00
93(12/61)-10th Legion app; Chameleon Boy app.	3.00	9.00	21.00
94-97,99	1.50	4.50	10.00
98(7/62)-19th Legion app; Origin & intro. Ultra Boy; Pete Ross joins Legion	2.50	7.50	17.00
100-Ultra Boy app; 1st app. Phantom Zone villains, Dr. Xadu & Erndine. 2 pg. map of Krypton; origin Superboy retold; r-cover of Superman 1; Pete Ross joins Legion	5.15	15.00	36.00
101-120: 104-Origin Phantom Zone. 115-Atomic bomb-c. 117-Legion app.	1.00	3.00	6.00
121-128: 124(10/65)-1st app. Insect Queen (Lana Lang). 125-Legion cameo. 126-Origin Krypto the Super Dog retold with new facts	.50	1.50	3.00
129,138 (80-pg. Giant G-22,35)	.60	1.75	3.50
130-137,139,140: 131-Legion cameo (statues). 132-1st app. Supremo	.40	1.25	2.50
141-146,148-155,157-164,166-173,175,176: 145-Superboy's parents regain their youth. 172,173,176-Legion app.; 172-Origin Yango (Super Ape)	.35	1.00	2.00

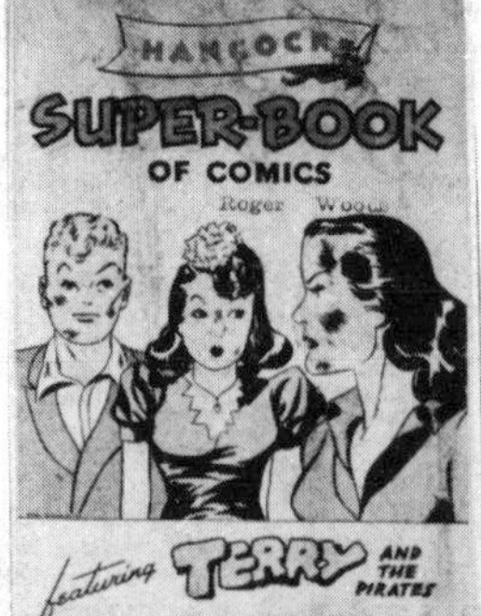

Super Book of Comics #28, © News Synd.

Superboy #9, © DC

Superboy #120, © DC

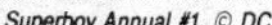
Superboy Annual #1, © DC

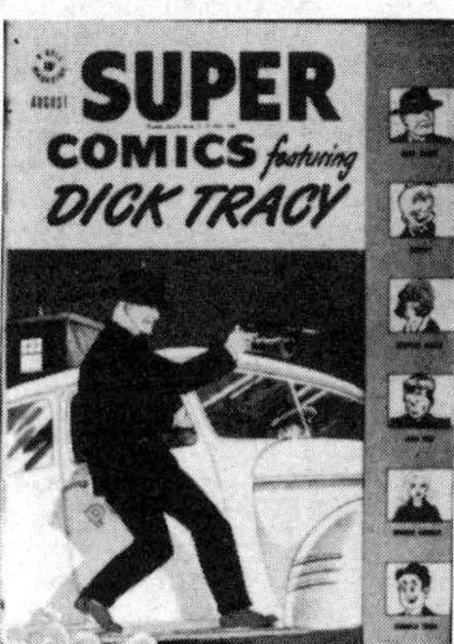

Super Comics #111, © DELL

Super DC Giant #S-16, © DC

SUPERBOY (continued)

	Good	Fine	Mint
147(6/68)-Giant G-47; origin Saturn Girl, Lightning Lad, & Cosmic Boy	.85	2.50	5.00
156,165,174 (Giants G-59,71,83)	.50	1.50	3.00
177-184,186,187 (All 52 pgs.): 184-Origin Dial H for Hero-r		.50	1.00
185-100 pg. Super Spec. No. 12; Legion app.-c, story; Teen Titans, Kid Eternity, Star Spangled Kid-r	.25	.75	1.50
188-190: 188-Origin Karkan		.50	1.00
191-Origin Sunboy retold; Legion app.		.50	1.00
192-196: 193-Chameleon Boy & Shrinking Violet get new costumes. 195-1st app. Erg/Wildfire; Phantom Girl gets new costume. 196-Last Superboy solo story		.50	1.00
197-Legion begins; Lightning Lad's new costume	.75	2.25	4.50
198,199: 198-Element Lad & Princess Projectra get new costumes	.35	1.00	2.00
200-Bouncing Boy & Duo Damsel marry; Jonn' Jonzz' cameo	.75	2.25	4.50
201,204,206,207,209: 201-Re-intro Erg as Wildfire. 204-Supergirl resigns from Legion. 206-Ferro Lad & Invisible Kid app. 209-Karate Kid new costume	.35	1.00	2.00
202,205-(100 pgs.): 202-Light Lass gets new costume	.45	1.25	2.50
203-Invisible Kid dies	.50	1.50	3.00
208-(68 pgs.)	.45	1.25	2.50
210-Origin Karate Kid	.45	1.25	2.50
211-215,217-220: 212-Matter-Eater Lad resigns	.30	.90	1.80
216-1st app. Tyroc who joins Legion in #218	.30	.90	1.80
221-249: 226-Intro. Dawnstar. 228-Death of Chemical King. 240-origin Dawnstar		.60	1.20
250-258: 253-Intro Blok		.50	1.00
Annual 1(Sum/64)-Origin Krypto-r	2.15	6.50	15.00

NOTE: ***Adams*** *c-143, 145, 146, 148-155, 157-161, 163, 164, 166-168, 172, 173, 175, 176, 178.* ***Ditko*** *a-257p.* ***Grell*** *a-202i, 203-219, 220-24p, 235p; c-207-232, 235, 236p, 237, 239p, 240p, 243p, 246, 258.* ***Nasser*** *a(p)-222, 225, 226, 230, 231, 233, 236.* ***Simonson*** *a-237p.* ***Starlin*** *a(p)-239, 250, 251; c-238.* ***Staton*** *a-227p, 243-249p, 252-258p; c-247-51p.* ***Tuska*** *a-172, 173, 176, 235p.* ***Wood*** *inks-152-155, 157-161. Legion app.-172, 173, 176, 177, 183, 184, 188, 190, 191, 193, 195.*

SUPERBOY SPECTACULAR
1980 (Giant)
DC comics

	Good	Fine	Mint
1-Comic shop distr. only; mostly-r		.50	1.00

SUPER BRAT
January, 1954 - No. 4, July, 1954
Toby Press

	Good	Fine	Mint
1 (1954)	1.60	4.70	11.00
2-4: 4-Li'l Teevy by Mel Lazarus	.75	2.25	5.00
I.W. Reprint #1,2,3,7,8('58)		.40	.80
I.W. (Super) Reprint #10('63)		.40	.80

SUPERCAR (TV)
Nov, 1962 - No. 4, Aug, 1963 (All painted covers)
Gold Key

	Good	Fine	Mint
1	3.50	10.50	24.00
2-4	2.00	6.00	14.00

SUPER CAT (Also see Frisky Animals)
Sept, 1957 - No. 4, May, 1958
Ajax/Farrell Publ. (Four Star Comic Corp.)

	Good	Fine	Mint
1('57-Ajax)	1.50	4.50	10.00
2-4	.85	2.50	6.00

SUPER CIRCUS (TV)
January, 1951 - No. 5, 1951 (Mary Hartline)
Cross Publishing Co.

	Good	Fine	Mint
1-Cast photos on-c	2.65	8.00	18.00
2	2.00	6.00	14.00
3-5	1.50	4.50	10.00

SUPER CIRCUS (TV)
No. 542, March, 1954 - No. 694, Mar, 1956 (Feat. Mary Hartline)
Dell Publishing Co.

	Good	Fine	Mint
4-Color 542,592,694	2.30	7.00	16.00

SUPER COMICS
May, 1938 - No. 121, Feb-Mar, 1949
Dell Publishing Co.

	Good	Fine	Mint
1-Terry & The Pirates, The Gumps, Dick Tracy, Little Orphan Annie, Gasoline Alley, Little Joe, Smilin' Jack, Smokey Stover, Smitty, Tiny Tim, Moon Mullins, Harold Teen, Winnie Winkle begin	70.00	210.00	490.00
2	34.00	102.00	280.00
3	27.00	81.00	190.00
4,5	22.00	65.00	154.00
6-10	18.00	54.00	125.00
11-20	16.00	48.00	110.00
21-29: 21-Origin Magic Morro (2/40)	13.00	40.00	90.00
30-"Sea Hawk" movie adaptation-c/story with Errol Flynn	13.00	40.00	90.00
31-40	10.00	30.00	70.00
41-50: 43-Terry & The Pirates ends	8.50	25.50	60.00
51-60	6.00	18.00	42.00
61-70: 67-X-mas-c	5.00	15.00	35.00
71-80	4.35	13.00	30.00
81-99	3.70	11.00	26.00
100	5.00	15.00	35.00
101-115-Last Dick Tracy (moves to own title)	3.50	10.50	24.00
116,118-All Smokey Stover	2.85	8.50	20.00
117-All Gasoline Alley	2.85	8.50	20.00
119-121: 119-121-Terry & The Pirates app.	2.85	8.50	20.00

SUPER COPS, THE
July, 1974 (One Shot)
Red Circle Productions (Archie)

	Good	Fine	Mint
1-Morrow-c/a		.30	.60

SUPER CRACKED (See Cracked)

SUPER DC GIANT (25 cents) (No #1-12)
No. 13, 9-10/70 - No. 26, 7-8/71; No. 27, Summer, 1976
National Periodical Publications

	Good	Fine	Mint
S-13-Binky		.40	.80
S-14-Top Guns of the West; Kubert-c; Trigger Twins, Johnny Thunder, Wyoming Kid-r		.30	.60
S-15-Western Comics; Kubert-c; Pow Wow Smith, Vigilante, Buffalo Bill-r		.30	.60
S-16-Best of the Brave & the Bold; Kubert-a		.40	.80
S-17-Love 1970		.40	.80
S-18-Three Mouseketeers; Dizzy Dog, Doodles Duck, Bo Bunny-r; Sheldon Mayer-a		.40	.80
S-19-Jerry Lewis; no Adams-a		.40	.80
S-20-House of Mystery; Adams-c; Kirby-a(3)(r)		.40	.80
S-21-Love 1971		.30	.60
S-22-Top Guns of the West		.30	.60
S-23-The Unexpected		.30	.60
S-24-Supergirl		.40	.80
S-25-Challengers of the Unknown; all Kirby/Wood-r		.40	.80
S-26-Aquaman (1971)		.40	.80
27-Strange Flying Saucers Adventures (Fall, '76)		.30	.60

NOTE: ***Sid Greene*** *a-27p(r).* ***Heath*** *a-27r.* ***G. Kane*** *a-14r, 15r, 27p(r).*

SUPER-DOOPER COMICS
1946 (10 cents)(32 pages)(paper cover)
Able Manufacturing Co.

SUPER-DOOPER COMICS (continued)

	Good	Fine	Mint
1-The Clock, Gangbuster app.	5.00	15.00	35.00
2	2.15	6.50	15.00
3,4,6	1.75	5.25	12.00
5,7-Capt. Freedom & Shock Gibson	3.00	9.00	21.00
8-Shock Gibson, Sam Hill	3.00	9.00	21.00

SUPER DUCK COMICS (The Cockeyed Wonder) (See Jolly Jingles)
Fall, 1944 - No. 94, Dec, 1960
MLJ Mag. No. 1-4(9/45)/Close-Up No. 5 on (Archie)

	Good	Fine	Mint
1-Origin	16.00	48.00	110.00
2	7.00	21.00	50.00
3-5: 3-1st Mr. Monster	5.70	17.00	40.00
6-10	4.00	12.00	28.00
11-20	2.30	7.00	16.00
21,23-40	1.70	5.00	12.00
22-Used in **SOTI**, pg. 35,307,308	3.50	10.50	24.00
41-60	1.15	3.50	8.00
61-94	1.00	3.00	7.00

SUPER DUPER
1941
Harvey Publications

	Good	Fine	Mint
5-Captain Freedom & Shock Gibson app.	10.00	30.00	70.00
8,11	5.00	15.00	35.00

SUPER DUPER COMICS (Formerly Latest Comics?)
May-June, 1947
F. E. Howard Publ.

	Good	Fine	Mint
3-Mr. Monster app.	3.00	9.00	21.00

SUPER FRIENDS (TV) (Also see Best of DC & Limited Coll. Ed.)
Nov, 1976 - No. 47, Aug, 1981
National Periodical Publications/DC Comics

	Good	Fine	Mint
1-Superman, Batman, Wonder Woman, Aquaman, Atom, Robin, Wendy, Marvin & Wonder Dog begin		.30	.60
2-10: 7-1st app. Wonder Twins, & The Seraph. 8-1st app. Jack O'Lantern		.25	.50
11-47: 13-1st app. Dr. Mist. 14-Origin Wonder Twins. 25-1st app. Green Fury. 31-Black Orchid app. 47-Origin Green Fury		.25	.50

NOTE: ***Estrada** a-1p, 2p. **Orlando** a-1p. **Staton** a-43, 45.*

SUPER FRIENDS SPECIAL, THE
1981 (Giveaway) (no code or price) (no ads)
DC Comics

	Good	Fine	Mint
1		.30	.60

SUPER FUN
January, 1956 (By A.W. Nugent)
Gillmor Magazines

	Good	Fine	Mint
1-Comics, puzzles, cut-outs	1.15	3.50	8.00

SUPER FUNNIES (. . .Western Funnies #3,4)
Dec, 1953 - No. 4, June, 1954
Superior Comics Publishers Ltd. (Canada)

	Good	Fine	Mint
1-(3-D)-Dopey Duck; make your own 3-D glasses cut-out inside front-c; did not come w/glasses	22.00	65.00	154.00
2-Horror & crime satire	2.00	6.00	14.00
3-Geronimo, Billy The Kid app.	1.50	4.50	10.00
4-(Western-Phantom Ranger)	1.50	4.50	10.00

SUPERGEAR COMICS
1976 (4 pages in color) (slick paper)
Jacobs Corp. (Giveaway)

	Good	Fine	Mint
(Rare)-Superman, Lois Lane; Steve Lombard app.	1.00	3.00	6.00

NOTE: *500 copies printed, over half destroyed?*

SUPERGIRL (See Action, Adv., Brave & the Bold, Daring New Advs. of. . ., Super DC Giant, Superman Family, & Super-Team Family)
11/72 - No. 9, 12-1/73-74; No. 10, 9-10/74
National Periodical Publications

	Good	Fine	Mint
1-Zatanna begins; ends No. 5		.50	1.00
2-5: 5-Zatanna origin-r		.40	.80
6-10: 8-JLA x-over		.30	.60

NOTE: *Zatanna in No. 1-5,7(Guest); Prez-No. 10.*

SUPERGIRL (Formerly Daring New Advs. of. . .)
No. 14, Dec, 1983 - No. 23, Sept, 1984
DC Comics

	Good	Fine	Mint
14,15,17-23: 20-New Teen Titans app.		.40	.80
16-Ambush Bug app.		.60	1.20
Movie Special (1985)-Adapts movie		.60	1.20
Giveaway ('84, Baxter, nn)(American Honda/U.S. Dept. Transportation)-Torres-a		.60	1.20

SUPER GOOF (Walt Disney)
Oct, 1965 - No. 74, 1982
Gold Key No. 1-57/Whitman No. 58 on

	Good	Fine	Mint
1	1.15	3.50	8.00
2-10	.55	1.65	4.00
11-20	.45	1.35	3.00
21-30	.35	1.00	2.00
31-50		.50	1.00
51-74		.30	.60

NOTE: *Reprints in No. 16,24,28,29,37,38,43,45,46,54(½),56-58,65(½),72(r-No.2).*

SUPER GREEN BERET (Tod Holton . . .)
April, 1967 - No. 2, June, 1967 (68 pages)
Lightning Comics (Milson Publ. Co.)

	Good	Fine	Mint
1,2	.70	2.00	4.00

SUPER HEROES (See Marvel . . . & Giant-Size. . .)

SUPER HEROES
Jan, 1967 - No. 4, June, 1967
Dell Publishing Co.

	Good	Fine	Mint
1-Origin & 1st app. Fab 4	1.15	3.50	8.00
2-4	.85	2.50	6.00

SUPER-HEROES BATTLE SUPER-GORILLAS (See DC Special #16)
Winter, 1976-77 (One Shot)
National Periodical Publications

	Good	Fine	Mint
1-Superman, Batman, Flash stories; Infantino-a(p); all-r		.30	.60

SUPER HEROES PUZZLES AND GAMES
1979 (32 pgs.) (regular size)
General Mills Giveaway (Marvel Comics Group)

	Good	Fine	Mint
Four 2-pg. origin stories of Spider-Man, Captain America, The Hulk, Spider-Woman	.50	1.50	3.00

SUPERHEROES VERSUS SUPERVILLAINS
July, 1966 (no month given)
Archie Publications

	Good	Fine	Mint
1-Flyman, Black Hood, The Web, Shield-r; Reinman-a	1.30	4.00	9.00

SUPERICHIE (Formerly Super Richie)
No. 5, Oct, 1976 - No. 18, Jan, 1979
Harvey Publications

	Good	Fine	Mint
5-18		.25	.50

SUPERIOR STORIES
May-June, 1955 - No. 4, Nov-Dec, 1955
Nesbit Publishing Co.

	Good	Fine	Mint
1-Invisible Man app.	5.50	16.50	38.00
2-The Pirate of the Gulf by J.H. Ingrahams	3.00	9.00	21.00

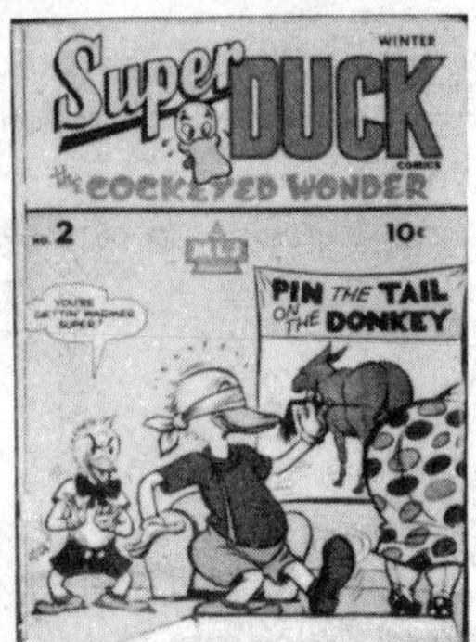

Super Duck Comics #2, © AP

Super Funnies #2, © SUPR

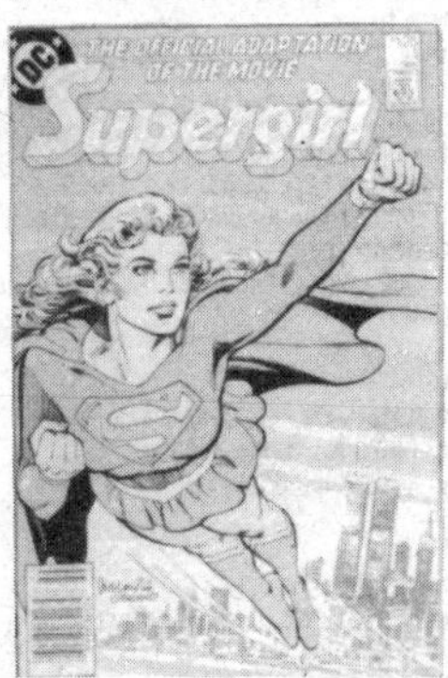

Supergirl Movie Special #1, © DC

Super Magician Comics #3, © S & S

Superman #3, © DC

Superman #100, © DC

SUPERIOR STORIES (continued) — Good / Fine / Mint
3-Wreck of the Grosvenor 3.00 9.00 21.00
4-O'Henry's "The Texas Rangers" 3.70 11.00 26.00
NOTE: ***Morisi** c/a in all.*

SUPER MAGIC (Super Magician #2 on)
May, 1941
Street & Smith Publications
V1#1-Blackstone the Magician app.; origin & 1st app. Rex King (Black Fury); not Eisner-c 30.00 90.00 210.00

SUPER MAGICIAN COMICS (Super Magic No. 1)
No. 2, Sept, 1941 - V5No.8, Feb-Mar, 1947
Street & Smith Publications
V1#2-Rex King, Man of Adventure app. 11.00 32.00 76.00
3-Tao-Anwar, Boy Magician begins 7.00 21.00 50.00
4-Origin Transo 6.00 18.00 42.00
5-12: 8-Abbott & Costello sty. 11-Supersnipe app. 6.00 18.00 42.00
V2#1-The Shadow app. 5.00 15.00 35.00
2-12: 5-Origin Tigerman. 8-Red Dragon begins 3.70 11.00 26.00
V3#1-12: 5-Origin Mr. Twilight 3.70 11.00 26.00
V4#1-12: 11-Nigel Elliman begins 3.50 10.50 24.00
V5#1-6 3.50 10.50 24.00
7,8-Red Dragon by Cartier 10.00 30.00 70.00

SUPERMAN (See Action Comics, Advs. of..., All-New Coll. Ed., All-Star Comics, Best of DC, Brave & the Bold, DC Comics Presents, Limited Coll. Ed., Man of Steel, Special Edition, Taylor's Christmas Tabloid, Three-Dimension Advs., World's Finest Comics & World of Krypton)

SUPERMAN (Adventures Of...#424 on)
Summer, 1939 - No. 423, Sept, 1986
National Periodical Publications/DC Comics
1(r.n)-1st four Action stories reprinted; origin Superman by Siegel & Shuster; has a new 2 pg. origin plus 4 pgs. omitted in Action story 3200.00 9500.00 20,800.00
(No known copy exists beyond Vf-NM condition)
1-Reprint, Oversize 13½"x10." **WARNING:** This comic is an exact duplicate reprint of the original except for its size. DC published it in 1978 with a second cover titling it as a Famous First Edition. There have been many reported cases of the outer cover being removed and the interior sold as the original edition. The reprint with the new outer cover removed is practically worthless.
2-All daily strip-r 450.00 1350.00 3150.00
3-2nd story-r from Action #5; 3rd story-r from Action #6 320.00 960.00 2240.00
4-1st mention of Daily Planet 225.00 675.00 1575.00
5 185.00 555.00 1300.00
6,7: 7-1st Perry White? 140.00 420.00 980.00
8-10: 10-1st bald Luthor 112.00 335.00 785.00
11-13,15: 13-Jimmy Olsen app. 80.00 240.00 560.00
14-Patriotic Shield-c 95.00 285.00 665.00
16-20: 17-Hitler, Hirohito-c 70.00 210.00 490.00
21-23,25 55.00 165.00 385.00
24-Flag-c 65.00 195.00 455.00
26-29: 28-Lois Lane Girl Reporter series begins, ends #40,42 50.00 150.00 350.00
28-Overseas edition for Armed Forces; same as reg. #28 50.00 150.00 350.00
30-Origin & 1st app. Mr. Mxyztplk (pronounced "Mix-it-plk"); name later became Mxyzptlk ("Mix-yez-pit-l-ick"); the character was inspired by a combination of the name of Al Capp's Joe Blyfstyk (the little man with the black cloud over his head) & the devilish antics of Bugs Bunny 87.00 260.00 610.00
31,32,34-40 38.00 115.00 265.00
33-(3-4/45)-3rd app. Mxyztplk 43.00 130.00 300.00
41-50: 45-Lois Lane as Superwoman (see Action 60 for 1st app.) 30.00 90.00 210.00

Good / Fine / Mint
51,52 25.00 75.00 175.00
53-Origin Superman retold 55.00 165.00 385.00
54,56-60 25.00 75.00 175.00
55-Used in **SOTI**, pg. 33 27.00 81.00 190.00
61-Origin Superman retold; origin Green Kryptonite (1st Kryptonite story) 44.00 132.00 310.00
62-65,67-70: 62-Orson Welles app. 65-1st Krypton Foes: Mala, K120, & U-Ban 25.00 75.00 175.00
66-2nd Superbaby story 26.00 78.00 180.00
71-75: 75-Some have #74 on-c 24.00 72.00 168.00
72-Giveaway(9-10/51)-(Rare)-Price blackened out; came with banner wrapped around book 30.00 90.00 210.00
76-Batman x-over; Superman & Batman learn each other's I.D. 55.00 165.00 385.00
77-80: 78-Last 52 pgs. 21.00 62.00 148.00
81-Used in **POP**, pg. 88 21.00 62.00 148.00
82-90 19.00 57.00 132.00
91-95: 95-Last precode ish. 18.00 54.00 125.00
96-99 13.00 40.00 90.00
100 (11/55) 38.00 115.00 268.00
101-110 11.00 32.00 75.00
111-120 8.50 25.50 60.00
121-130: 123-Pre-Supergirl tryout. 127-Origin/1st app. Titano. 128-Red Kryptonite used (4/59). 129-Intro/origin Lori Lemaris, The Mermaid 6.70 20.00 47.00
131-139: 139-Lori Lemaris app. 5.00 15.00 35.00
140-1st Blue Kryptonite & Bizarro Supergirl; origin Bizarro Jr. #1 4.60 14.00 32.00
141-145,148: 142-2nd Batman x-over 2.85 8.50 20.00
146-Superman's life story 4.35 13.00 30.00
147(8/61)-7th Legion app; 1st app. Legion of Super-Villains; intro. Adult Legion 5.50 16.50 38.00
149(11/61)-9th Legion app.-cameo; last 10 cent issue 5.50 16.50 38.00
150,151,153-154,158-160: 158-1st app. Flamebird & Nightwing & Nor-Kan of Kandor 2.15 6.50 15.00
152(4/62)-15th Legion app. 2.15 6.50 15.00
155(8/62)-20th Legion app; Lightning Man & Cosmic Man, & Adult Legion app. 2.15 6.50 15.00
156,162-Legion app. 2.15 6.50 15.00
157-Gold Kryptonite used (see Adv. 299); Mon-el app.; Lightning Lad cameo (11/62) 2.15 6.50 15.00
161-1st told death of Ma and Pa Kent 2.15 6.50 15.00
163-166,168-180: 169-Last Sally Selwyn. 172,173-Legion cameo 1.15 3.50 8.00
167-New origin Brainiac & Brainiac 5; intro Tixarla (Later Luthor's wife) 1.50 4.50 10.00
181,182,184-186,188-192,194-196,198-200: 181-1st 2965 story/series 189-Origin/destruction of Krypton II. 199-1st Superman/Flash race 1.00 3.00 6.00
183,187,193,197 (Gnts G-18,G-23,G-31,G-36) 1.25 3.75 7.50
201,203-206,208-211,213-216,218-221,223-226,228-231,234-238: 213-Brainiac-5 app. .70 2.00 4.00
202,207,212,217,222,227,239 (Giants G-42,G-48,G-54,G-60,G-66, G-72,G-84). 207-Legion app. .85 2.50 5.00
232(Giant, G-78)-All Krypton issue .85 2.50 5.00
233-1st app. Morgan Edge, Clark Kent switch from newspaper reporter to TV newscaster .70 2.00 4.00
240-Kaluta-a .40 1.25 2.50
241-244 (52 pgs.). 243-G.A.-r/No. 38 .35 1.00 2.00
245-DC 100 pg. Super Spec. #7; Air Wave, Kid Eternity, Hawkman, Atom-r .45 1.40 2.80
246-248,250,251,253 (All 52 pgs.): 246-G.A.-r/#40. 248-World of Krypton story. 251-G.A.-r/#45. 253-Finlay-a, 2pgs., G.A.-r/#13 .50 1.00
249,254-Adams-a. 249-(52 pgs.); origin & 1st app. Terra-Man

SUPERMAN (continued) — Good / Fine / Mint

by Adams (inks) .85 2.50 5.00
252-DC 100 pg. Super Spec. #13; Ray, Black Condor, Starman, Dr. Fate, Hawkman, Spectre app.; Adams-c .70 2.00 4.00
255-263: 263-Photo-c .50 1.00
264-1st app. Steve Lombard .25 .75 1.50
265-271,273-277,279-283,285-299: 292-Origin Lex Luthor retold .50 1.00
272,278,284-All 100 pgs. G.A.-r in all .25 .75 1.50
300-Retells origin .50 1.50 3.00
301-330: 301,320-Solomon Grundy app. 323-Intro. Atomic Skull. 327-329-(44 pgs.). 330-More facts revealed about I. D. .50 1.00
331-389: 338-The bottled city of Kandor enlarged. 372-Superman 2021 app. 376-Free 16 pg. preview of Daring, New Advs. of Supergirl .50 1.00
390-399 (75 cent cover) .50 1.00
400 (10/84, $1.50, 68 pgs.)-Many top artists featured .35 1.00 2.00
401-422: 415-Crisis x-over .45 .90
423 .50 1.50 3.00
Annual 1(10/60)-Reprints 1st Supergirl/Action #252; r-/Lois Lane #1 14.00 42.00 100.00
Annual 2(1960)-Brainiac, Titano, Metallo, Bizarro origin-r 10.00 30.00 70.00
Annual 3(1961) 7.00 21.00 48.00
Annual 4(1961)-11th Legion app; 1st Legion origins-text & pictures 5.50 16.50 38.00
Annual 5(Sum, '62)-All Krypton issue 3.50 10.50 24.00
Annual 6(Wint, '62-'63)-Legion-r/Adv. #247 2.65 8.00 18.00
Annual 7(Sum/'63)-Origin-r/Superman-Batman team/Adv. 275; r-1955 Superman dailies 2.15 6.50 15.00
Annual 8(Wint, '63-'64) 1.70 5.00 12.00
Annual 9(9/83)-Toth/Austin-a .25 .75 1.50
Annual 10(11/84; $1.25) .25 .75 1.50
Annual 11(9/85)-Moore scripts .25 .75 1.50
Annual 12 (8/86) .25 .75 1.50
Special 1(3/83)-G. Kane c/a; r-that appeared in Germany .25 .75 1.50
Special 2(3/84, 48pgs.) .25 .75 1.50
Special 3(4/85; $1.25) .25 .75 1.50
The Amazing World of Superman "Official Metropolis Edition" ($2.00; 1973, 14x10½")-Origin retold 1.35 4.00 8.00
Kelloggs Giveaway-(⅔ normal size, 1954)-r-two stories/Superman #55 30.00 90.00 200.00
. . .Movie Special-(9/83)-Adaptation of Superman III .50 1.00
Pizza Hut Premium(12/77)-Exact-r of #97,113 .25 .75 1.50
Radio Shack Giveaway-36pgs. (7/80) 'The Computers That Saved Metropolis;' Starlin/Giordano-a; advertising insert in Action 509, New Advs. of Superboy 7, Legion of Super-Heroes 265, & House of Mystery 282. (All comics were 64 pgs.) Cover of inserts printed on newsprint. Giveaway contains 4 extra pgs. of Radio Shack advertising that inserts do not. .25 .75 1.50
Radio Shack Giveaway-(7/81) 'Victory by Computer' .25 .75 1.50
Radio Shack Giveaway-(7/82) 'Computer Masters of Metropolis' .50 1.00
11195(2/79,224pp,$1.95)-Golden Press .40 1.20 2.40

NOTE: ***Adams*** *a-249i, 254p; c-204-208, 210, 212-215, 219, 231, 233-237, 240-243, 249-252, 254, 263, 307, 308, 313, 314, 317.* ***Adkins*** *a-323i.* ***Austin*** *c-368i.* ***Wayne Boring*** *art-late 1940's to early 1960's.* ***Buckler*** *a-352p, 363p, 364p, 369p; c-324-327p, 356p, 363p, 368p, 369p, 373p, 376p, 378p.* ***Burnley*** *a-252r.* ***Fine*** *a-252r.* ***Gil Kane*** *a-272r, 367, 372, 375; c-374p, 375p, 377, 381, 382, 384-90, 392, Annual 9.* ***Kubert*** *c-216.* ***Morrow*** *a-238.* ***Perez*** *c-364p.* ***Starlin*** *c-355.* ***Staton*** *a-354i, 355i.* ***Williamson*** *a-408-410i, 412i, 416i; c-408i, 409i.* ***Wrightson*** *a-416.*

SUPERMAN
Jan, 1987 - Present
DC Comics — Good / Fine / Mint

1-Byrne c/a; intro Metallo .40 1.25 2.50
2-16 .50 1.00
Annual 1 (8/87)-No Byrne-a .65 1.30

SUPERMAN & THE GREAT CLEVELAND FIRE (Giveaway)
1948 (4 pages, no cover)(Hospital Fund)
National Periodical Publications

in full color 43.00 130.00 300.00

SUPERMAN FAMILY, THE (Formerly Superman's Pal Jimmy Olsen)
No. 164, Apr-May, 1974 - No. 222, Sept, 1982
National Periodical Publications/DC Comics

164-Jimmy Olsen, Supergirl, Lois Lane begin .60 1.20
165-176 (100-68 pgs.) .45 .90
177-181 (52 pgs.) .40 .80
182-$1.00 ish. begin; Marshal Rogers-a; Krypto begins, ends #192 .25 .75 1.50
183-193,195-222: 183-Nightwing-Flamebird begins, ends #194. 189-Brainiac 5, Mon-el app. 191-Superboy begins, ends #198. 200-Book length story .40 .80
194-Rogers-a .25 .75 1.50

NOTE: ***Adams*** *c-182-185.* ***Anderson*** *a-186i.* ***Buckler*** *c-190p, 191p, 209p, 210p, 215p, 217p, 220p.* ***Jones*** *a-191-193.* ***Gil Kane*** *c-221p, 222p.* ***Mortimer*** *a-191-93p, 199p, 201-22p.* ***Orlando*** *a-186i, 187i.* ***Rogers*** *a-182, 194.* ***Staton*** *a-191-194, 196p.* ***Tuska*** *a-203p, 207-209p.*

SUPERMAN (Miniature)
1942; 1955 - 1956 (3 issues; no #'s; 32 pgs.)
The pages are numbered in the 1st issue: 1-32; 2nd: 1A-32A, and 3rd: 1B-32B
National Periodical Publications

No date-Py-Co-Pay Tooth Powder giveaway (8 pgs.; circa 1942) 45.00 135.00 315.00
1-The Superman Time Capsule (Kellogg's Sugar Smacks)(1955) 20.00 60.00 140.00
1A-Duel in Space 16.00 48.00 110.00
1B-The Super Show of Metropolis (also #1-32, no B) 16.00 48.00 110.00

NOTE: *Numbering variations exist. Each title could have any combination-No. 1, 1A, or 1B.*

SUPERMAN IV MOVIE SPECIAL
Oct, 1987 (one shot, $2.00, color)
DC Comics

1 .35 1.00 2.00

SUPERMAN RECORD COMIC
1966 (Golden Records)
National Periodical Publications

(with record)-Record reads origin of Superman from comic; came with iron-on patch, decoder, membership card & button; comic r-/Superman 125, 146 4.00 12.00 28.00
comic only 1.50 4.50 12.00

SUPERMAN'S BUDDY (Costume Comic)
1954 (4 pgs.) (One Shot) (Came in box w/costume; slick-paper/c)
National Periodical Publications

1-(Rare)-w/box & costume 60.00 180.00 420.00
Comic only 32.00 95.00 225.00

SUPERMAN'S CHRISTMAS ADVENTURE
1940, 1944 (16 pgs.) (Giveaway)
Distr. by Nehi drinks, Bailey Store, Ivey-Keith Co., Kennedy's Boys Shop, Macy's Store
National Periodical Publications

1(1940)-by Burnley 72.00 215.00 505.00

Superman #252, © DC

Superman #300, © DC

Superman Miniature #1, © DC

Superman's Girlfriend Lois Lane #2, © DC

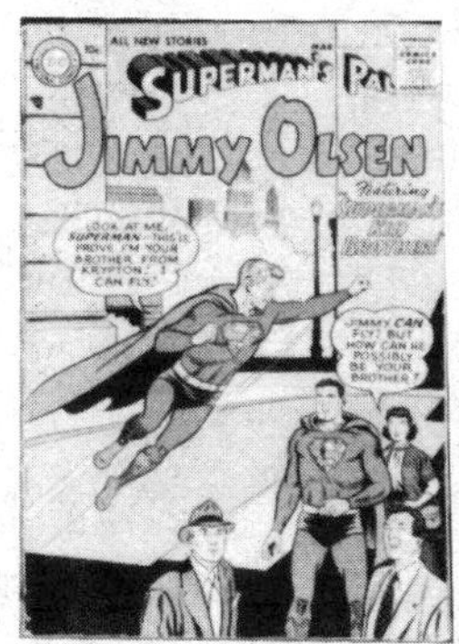

Superman's Pal Jimmy Olsen #19, © DC

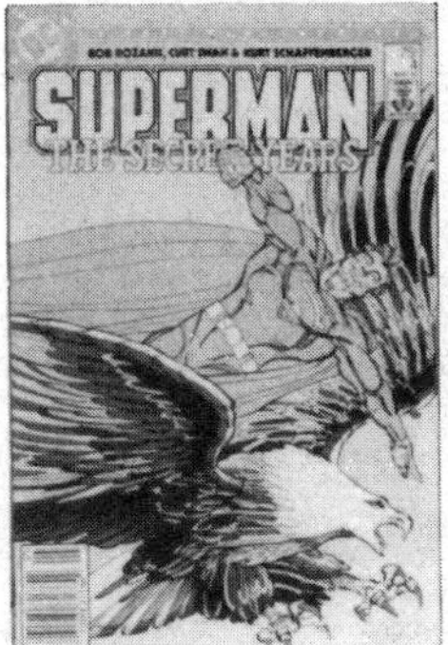

Superman: The Secret Years #4, © DC

SUPERMAN'S CHRISTMAS ADV. (cont.)	**Good**	**Fine**	**Mint**
nn(1944)	56.00	168.00	390.00

SUPERMAN SCRAPBOOK (Has blank pages; contains no comics)

SUPERMAN'S GIRLFRIEND LOIS LANE (See 80 Pg. Giants No. 3,14, Showcase, & Superman Family)

SUPERMAN'S GIRLFRIEND LOIS LANE (Also see Lois Lane)
3-4/58 - No. 136, 1-2/74; No. 137, 9-10/74
National Periodical Publications

	Good	Fine	Mint
1	43.00	128.00	300.00
2	19.00	58.00	136.00
3	14.00	42.00	100.00
4,5	11.50	34.00	80.00
6-10: 9-Pat Boone app.	7.00	21.00	50.00
11-20: 14-Supergirl x-over	3.60	11.00	25.00
21-29: 23-1st app. Lena Thorul, Lex Luthor's sister. 29-Aquaman, Batman, Green Arrow cameo; last 10 cent issue	1.70	5.00	12.00
30-32,34-49: 47-Legion app.	1.00	3.00	6.00
33(5/62)-Mon-el app.	1.50	4.50	9.00
50-Triplicate Girl, Phantom Girl & Shrinking Violet app.	.70	2.00	4.00
51-55,57-67,69,70	.25	.75	1.50
56-Saturn Girl app.	.35	1.00	2.00
68-(Giant G-26)	.35	1.00	2.00
71-76,78: 74-1st Bizarro Flash		.50	1.00
77-(Giant G-39)		.60	1.20
79-Adams-c begin, end No. 95,108		.50	1.00
80-85,87-94: 89-Batman x-over; all Adams-c		.40	.80
86-(Giant G-51)-Adams-c		.60	1.20
95-(Giant G-63)-Wonder Woman x-over; Adams-c		.60	1.20
96-103,106,107,109-111		.25	.50
104-(Giant G-75)		.50	1.00
105-Origin & 1st app. The Rose & the Thorn		.25	.50
108-Adams-c		.25	.50
112,114-123 (52 pgs.): 111-Morrow-a. 122-G.A.-r/Superman #30. 123-G.A. Batman-r		.25	.50
113-(Giant G-87)		.40	.80
124-137: 130-Last Rose & the Thorn. 132-New Zatanna story. 136-Wonder Woman x-over		.25	.50
Annual 1(Sum,'62)	2.15	6.50	15.00
Annual 2(Sum,'63)	1.15	3.50	8.00

NOTE: ***Buckler** a-117-121p. **Curt Swan** a-1-50(most).*

SUPERMAN'S PAL JIMMY OLSEN (Superman Family #164 on)
(See 80 Page Giants)
Sept-Oct, 1954 - No. 163, Feb-Mar, 1974
National Periodical Publications

	Good	Fine	Mint
1	71.00	215.00	500.00
2	30.00	90.00	210.00
3-Last pre-code ish.	20.00	60.00	140.00
4,5	14.00	42.00	100.00
6-10	10.00	30.00	70.00
11-20	6.50	19.50	45.00
21-30: 29-1st app. Krypto in J.O.	3.15	9.50	22.00
31-40: 31-Origin Elastic Lad. 33-One pg. biography of Jack Larson (TV Jimmy Olsen). 36-Intro Lucy Lane	1.85	5.50	13.00
41-47,49,50: 41-1st J.O. Robot	1.15	3.50	8.00
48-Intro/origin Superman Emergency Squad	1.30	4.00	9.00
51-56: 56-Last 10 cent issue	.75	2.25	5.00
57-61,64-69: 57-Olsen marries Supergirl	.55	1.60	3.20
62(7/62)-18th Legion app.; Mon-el, Elastic Lad app.	1.35	4.00	8.00
63(9/62)-Legion of Super-Villains app.	.60	1.80	3.60
70-Element Lad app.	.55	1.60	3.20
71,74,75,78,80-84,86,89,90: 86-J.O. Robot becomes Congorilla	.35	1.00	2.00
72(10/63)-Legion app; Elastic Lad (Olsen) joins	.50	1.50	3.00
73-Ultra Boy app.	.40	1.25	2.50
76,85-Legion app.	.50	1.50	3.00
77-Olsen with Colossal Boy's powers & costume; origin Titano retold	.40	1.25	2.50
79(9/64)-Titled The Red-headed Beatle of 1000 B.C.	.40	1.25	2.50
87-Legion of Super-Villains app.	.50	1.50	3.00
88-Star Boy app.	.35	1.00	2.00
91-94,96-98,101-103,105,107-110		.50	1.00
95,104 (Giants G-25,G-38). 95-Transvestite story		.60	1.20
99-Legion app; Olsen with powers/costumes of Lightning Lad, Sun Boy, & Star Boy	.30	1.00	2.00
100-Legion cameo app.	.30	1.00	2.00
106-Legion app.		.60	1.20
111,112,114-121,123-130,132		.25	.50
113,122,131 (Giants G-50,G-62,G-74)		.50	1.00
133-Newsboy Legion by Kirby begins	.30	1.00	2.00
134-139: 135-G.A. Guardian app. 136-Origin new Guardian		.50	1.00
140-(Giant G-86)		.50	1.00
141-Newsboy Legion reprints by S&K begin (52 pg. issues begin)		.40	.80
142-148-Newsboy Legion-r		.40	.80
149,150-G.A. Plastic Man reprint in both; last 52 pg. ish. 150-Newsboy Legion app.		.25	.50
151-163		.25	.50

NOTE: *Issues No. 141-148 contain **Simon & Kirby** Newsboy Legion reprints from Star Spangled No. 7, 8, 9, 10, 11, 12, 13, 14 in that order. **Adams** c-109-112, 115, 117, 118, 120, 121, 132, 134-136, 147, 148. **Kirby** a-133-139p, 141-148p; c-133, 139, 145p. **Kirby/Adams** c-137, 138, 141-144, 146.*

SUPERMAN SPECTACULAR (Also see DC Special Series #5)
1982 (Magazine size)(Square binding)
DC Comics

	Good	Fine	Mint
1	.35	1.00	2.00

SUPERMAN: THE SECRET YEARS
Feb, 1985 - No. 4, May, 1985 (mini-series)
DC Comics

	Good	Fine	Mint
1-Miller-c on all	.25	.75	1.50
2-4		.50	1.00

SUPERMAN 3-D (See Three-Dimension Adventures)

SUPERMAN-TIM (Becomes Tim)
1942 - May, 1950 (½-size) (B&W Giveaway)
Superman-Tim Stores/National Periodical Publications

	Good	Fine	Mint
8/42, 2/43, 3/43, 6/43, 8/43, 9/43, 3/44, 11/49 issues-Two pg. Superman illos	8.00	24.00	56.00
10/43, 12/43, 2/44, 4/44-1/45, 3/45, 4/45, 4/46 issues-No Superman	5.50	16.50	40.00
2/45, 6/46, 8/46, 11/46, 3/47, 5/47-8/47, 10/47 issues-Superman story	13.00	40.00	90.00
2/48, 6/48, 8/48-11/48, 2/49-4/49, 12/49-5/50 issues-No Superman	4.65	14.00	32.00

SUPERMAN VS. THE AMAZING SPIDER-MAN
(Also see Marvel Treasury Edition No. 28)
April, 1976 (100 pgs.) ($2.00) (Over-sized)
National Periodical Publications/Marvel Comics Group

	Good	Fine	Mint
1	.50	1.50	3.00
1-2nd printing; 5000 numbered copies signed by Stan Lee & Carmine Infantino on front cover & sold through mail	.85	2.50	5.00

SUPERMAN WORKBOOK
1945 (One Shot) (68 pgs; reprints) (B&W)
National Periodical Publ./Juvenile Group Foundation

SUPERMAN WORKBOOK (continued)	Good	Fine	Mint
c-r/Superman #14	60.00	180.00	420.00

SUPERMOUSE (. . .the Big Cheese; see Coo Coo Comics)
12/48 - No. 34, 9/55; No. 35, 4/56 - No. 45, Fall, 1958
Standard Comics/Pines No. 35 on (Literary Ent.)

	Good	Fine	Mint
1-Frazetta text illos (3)	13.00	40.00	90.00
2-Frazetta text illos	7.00	21.00	50.00
3,5,6-Text illos by Frazetta in all	5.50	16.50	38.00
4-Two pg. text illos by Frazetta	5.70	17.00	40.00
7-10	1.85	5.50	13.00
11-20: 13-Racist humor (Indians)	1.30	4.00	9.00
21-45	.85	2.50	6.00
1-Summer Holiday issue (Summer,'56-Pines)-100 pgs.	3.00	9.00	21.00
2-Giant Summer issue (Summer,'58-Pines)-100 pgs.	2.65	8.00	18.00

SUPER-MYSTERY COMICS
July, 1940 - V8#6, July, 1949
Ace Magazines (Periodical House)

	Good	Fine	Mint
V1#1-Magno, the Magnetic Man & Vulcan begin	60.00	180.00	420.00
2	28.00	84.00	195.00
3-The Black Spider begins	22.00	65.00	154.00
4-Origin Davy	20.00	60.00	140.00
5-Intro. The Clown	20.00	60.00	140.00
6(2/41)	17.00	51.00	120.00
V2#1(4/41)-Origin Buckskin	17.00	51.00	120.00
2-6(2/42): 3-The Clown app.	15.00	45.00	105.00
V3#1(4/42),2: 1-Vulcan & Black Ace begin	13.00	40.00	90.00
3-Intro. The Lancer; Dr. Nemesis & The Sword begin; Kurtzman c/a(2) (Mr. Risk & Paul Revere Jr.)	19.00	57.00	132.00
4-Kurtzman-a	15.00	45.00	105.00
5-Kurtzman-a(2); L.B. Cole-a; Mr. Risk app.	16.00	48.00	110.00
6(10/43)-Mr. Risk app.; Kurtzman's Paul Revere Jr.; L.B. Cole-a	16.00	48.00	110.00
V4#1(1/44)-L.B. Cole-a	11.00	32.00	76.00
2-6(4/45): 2,5,6-Mr. Risk app.	9.50	28.50	65.00
V5#1(7/45)-6	8.00	24.00	56.00
V6#1-6: 3-Torture story. 4-Last Magno. Mr. Risk app. in #2,4-6	6.50	19.50	45.00
V7#1-6, V8#1-4,6	6.50	19.50	45.00
V8#5-Meskin, Tuska, Sid Greene-a	8.00	24.00	56.00

NOTE: ***Sid Greene*** *a-V7#4.* ***Mooney*** *c-V2#5, 6.* ***Palais*** *c/a-V5#3,4. Bondage c-V2#5, 6, V3#2, 5.*

SUPERNATURAL THRILLERS
12/72 - No. 6, 11/73; No. 7, 7/74 - No. 15, 10/75
Marvel Comics Group

	Good	Fine	Mint
1-It!-Sturgeon adaptation, 2-The Invisible Man, 3-The Valley of the Worm		.40	.80
4-Dr. Jekyll & Mr. Hyde, 5-The Living Mummy, 6-The Headless Horseman		.25	.50
7-15: 7-The Living Mummy begins		.25	.50

NOTE: ***Brunner*** *c-11.* ***Buckler*** *a-5p.* ***Ditko*** *a-8r, 9r.* ***G. Kane*** *a-3p; c-3, 9p, 15p.* ***Mayerik*** *a-2p, 7, 8, 9p, 10p, 11.* ***McWilliams*** *a-14i.* ***Mortimer*** *a-4.* ***Steranko*** *c-1, 2.* ***Sutton*** *a-15.* ***Tuska*** *a-6p. Robert E. Howard story-No. 3.*

SUPER POWERS
7/84 - No. 5, 11/84; 9/85 - No. 6, 2/86; 9/86 - No. 4, 12/86
DC Comics

	Good	Fine	Mint
1-Kirby-c		.60	1.20
2-5		.45	.90
1-('85)Kirby c/a in all; 1st app Samurai from Super Friends TV show; Capt. Marvel, Dr. Fate join		.50	1.00
2-6		.45	.90
1-4 ('86)		.40	.80

SUPER PUP
No. 4, Mar-Apr, 1954 - No. 5, 1954
Avon Periodicals

	Good	Fine	Mint
4,5	1.30	4.00	9.00

SUPER RABBIT (See All Surprise, Animated Movie Tunes, Comedy Comics, Comic Capers, Ideal Comics, It's A Duck's Life, Movie Tunes & Wisco)
Fall, 1943 - No. 14, Nov, 1948
Timely Comics (CmPl)

	Good	Fine	Mint
1	24.00	72.00	170.00
2	12.00	36.00	84.00
3-5	7.00	21.00	50.00
6-Origin	5.70	17.00	40.00
7-10; 9-Infinity-c	4.35	13.00	30.00
11-Kurtzman's "Hey Look"	5.50	16.50	38.00
12-14	3.50	10.50	24.00
I.W. Reprint #1,2('58),7,10('63)	.70	2.00	4.00

SUPER RICHIE (Superichie #5 on)
Sept, 1975 - No. 4, Mar, 1976 (52 pages)
Harvey Publications

	Good	Fine	Mint
1	.35	1.00	2.00
2-4		.50	1.00

SUPERSNIPE COMICS (Army & Navy #1-5)
Oct, 1942 - V5No.1, Aug-Sept, 1949 (Also see Shadow Comics V2/3)
Street & Smith Publications

	Good	Fine	Mint
V1#6-Rex King Man of Adventure(costumed hero) by Jack Binder begins; Supersnipe by George Marcoux continues from Army & Navy #5; Bill Ward-a	25.00	75.00	175.00
7-12: 9-Doc Savage x-over in Supersnipe. 11-Little Nemo app.	16.00	48.00	110.00
V2#1-12: 1-Huck Finn by Clare Dwiggins begins, ends V3#5	11.50	34.00	80.00
V3#1-12: 8-Bobby Crusoe by Dwiggins begins, ends V3#12	8.50	25.50	60.00
V4#1-12, V5#1	6.00	18.00	42.00

NOTE: *Doc Savage in some issues.*

SUPERSPOOK (Formerly Frisky Animals on Parade)
No. 4, June, 1958
Ajax/Farrell Publications

	Good	Fine	Mint
4	1.30	4.00	9.00

SUPER SPY (See Wham)
Oct, 1940 - No. 2, Nov, 1940 (Reprints)
Centaur Publications

	Good	Fine	Mint
1-Origin The Sparkler	55.00	165.00	385.00
2-The Inner Circle, Dean Denton, Tim Blain, The Drew Ghost, The Night Hawk by Gustavson, & S.S. Swanson by Glanz app.	40.00	120.00	280.00

SUPER STAR HOLIDAY SPECIAL (See DC Special Series No. 21)

SUPER-TEAM FAMILY
10-11/75 - No. 15, 3-4/78 (No.1-4: 68 pgs.; No.5 on: 52 pgs.)
National Periodical Publications/DC Comics

	Good	Fine	Mint
1-Reprints; Adams, Kane/Wood		.40	.80
2-7: 4-7-Reprints		.25	.50
8-15-New stys; Chall. of the Unknown in 8-10		.25	.50

NOTE: ***Adams*** *a-1r-3r.* ***Brunner*** *c-3.* ***Buckler*** *c-8p.* ***Estrada*** *a-2.* ***Tuska*** *a-7r.* ***Wood*** *a-1i(r), 3.*

SUPER TV HEROES (See Hanna-Barbera . . .)

SUPER-VILLAIN CLASSICS
May, 1983 (One Shot)

Super-Mystery Comics V3#5, © ACE

Super Rabbit #1, © MCG

Supersnipe Comics V1#6, © S & S

Sure-Fire Comics #1, © ACE

Suspense #1, © MCG

Suzie Comics #56, © AP

SUPER-VILLAIN CLASSICS (continued)
Marvel Comics Group

	Good	Fine	Mint
1-"Galactus the Origin"		.50	1.00

SUPER-VILLAIN TEAM-UP
8/75 - No. 14, 10/77; No. 15, 11/78; No. 16, 5/79; No. 17, 6/80
Marvel Comics Group

	Good	Fine	Mint
1-Sub-Mariner app.		.60	1.20
2-17: 5-1st Shroud. 7-Origin The Shroud		.30	.60
Giant-Size 1(3/75, 68 pgs.)-Craig inks-r		.50	1.00
Giant-Size 2(6/75, 68 pgs.)-Dr. Doom, Sub-Mariner app.		.40	.80

NOTE: ***Buckler** c-4p, 5p, 7p. **Buscema** c-1. **Byrne/Austin** c-14. **Ditko** a-Gnt-Size 2r. **Evans** a-1p, 3p. **Everett** a-1p. **Giffen** a-8p, 13p; c-13p. **Kane** c-2p, 9p. **Mooney** a-4i. **Sekowsky** a-Gnt-size 2p. **Starlin** c-6. **Tuska** a-1p, 15p(r). **Wood** a-15p(r).*

SUPER WESTERN COMICS (Also see Buffalo Bill)
Aug, 1950 - No. 4, Mar, 1951
Youthful Magazines

	Good	Fine	Mint
1-Buffalo Bill begins; Powell-a	3.50	10.50	24.00
2-4	1.85	5.50	13.00

SUPER WESTERN FUNNIES (See Super Funnies)

SUPERWORLD COMICS
April, 1940 - No. 3, Aug, 1940
Hugo Gernsback (Komos Publ.)

	Good	Fine	Mint
1-Origin Hip Knox, Super Hypnotist; Mitey Powers & Buzz Allen, the Invisible Avenger, Little Nemo begin; cover by Frank R. Paul	85.00	255.00	600.00
2-Marvo 1,2 Go+, the Super Boy of the Year 2680	50.00	150.00	350.00
3	45.00	135.00	315.00

SURE-FIRE COMICS (Lightning Comics #4 on)
June, 1940 - No. 4, Oct, 1940 (Two No. 3's)
Ace Magazines

	Good	Fine	Mint
V1#1-Origin Flash Lightning; X-The Phantom Fed, Ace McCoy, Buck Steele, Marvo the Magician, The Raven, Whiz Wilson (Time Traveler) begin	50.00	150.00	350.00
2	30.00	90.00	210.00
3(9/40)	24.00	72.00	170.00
3(#4)(10/40)-nn on-c, #3 on inside	24.00	72.00	170.00

SURF 'N' WHEELS
Nov, 1969 - No. 6, Sept, 1970
Charlton Comics

	Good	Fine	Mint
1		.40	.80
2-6		.25	.50

SURGE
July, 1984 - No. 4, Jan, 1985 (mini-series) ($1.50; Baxter paper)
Eclipse Comics

	Good	Fine	Mint
1-4-Ties into DNAgents series	.30	.90	1.80

SURPRISE ADVENTURES (Formerly Tormented)
Mar, 1955 - No. 5, July, 1955
Sterling Comic Group

	Good	Fine	Mint
3-5: 3,5-Sekowsky-a	1.30	4.00	9.00

SUSIE Q. SMITH (See Four Color 323,377,453,553)

SUSPENSE (Radio/TV; Real Life Tales of... #1-4) (Amazing Detective Cases #3 on?...change to horror)
Dec, 1949 - No. 29, Apr, 1953 (No. 1-8,17-23: 52 pgs.)
Marvel/Atlas Comics (CnPC No. 1-10/BFP No. 11-29)

	Good	Fine	Mint
1-Powell-a; Peter Lorre, Sidney Greenstreet photo-c from Hammett's 'The Maltese Falcon'	13.00	40.00	90.00
2-Crime stories; photo-c	6.50	19.50	45.00
3-Change to horror	6.50	19.50	45.00
4,7-10	4.35	13.00	30.00
5-Krigstein, Tuska, Everett-a	5.00	15.00	35.00
6-Tuska, Everett, Morisi-a	4.35	13.00	30.00
11-17,19,20: 14-Hypo-c; A-Bomb panels	3.70	11.00	26.00
18,22-Krigstein-a	4.35	13.00	30.00
21,23,26-29	3.00	9.00	21.00
24-Tuska-a	3.50	10.50	24.00
25-Electric chair c/a	6.00	18.00	42.00

NOTE: ***Briefer** a-5, 7, 27. **Colan** a-8(2), 9. **Everett** a-5, 6(2), 19, 23, 28; c-21-23, 26. **Fuje** a-29. **Heath** a-5, 6, 8, 10, 12, 14; c-14, 19, 24. **Maneely** a-29; c-10. **Morisi** a-6. **Palais** a-10. **Rico** a-7-9. **Robinson** a-29. **Romita** a-25. **Sekowsky** a-11, 13, 14. **Sinnott** a-23, 25. **Tuska** a-5, 6, 12; c-12. **Whitney** a-15, 16, 22.*

SUSPENSE COMICS
Dec, 1943 - No. 12, Dec?, 1946
Continental Magazines

	Good	Fine	Mint
1-The Grey Mask begins; bondage/torture-c; L. B. Cole-a, 7pgs.	30.00	90.00	210.00
2-Intro. The Mask; Rico, Giunta, L. B. Cole-a, 7pgs.	19.00	57.00	132.00
3-L.B. Cole-a; Schomburg-c	19.00	57.00	132.00
4-6: 5-Schomburg-c	17.00	51.00	120.00
7,9,10	16.00	48.00	110.00
8-Classic L. B. Cole spider-c	38.00	115.00	265.00
11-Classic Devil-c	25.00	75.00	175.00
12-r-No.7-c	16.00	48.00	110.00

NOTE: ***L. B. Cole** c-6-12. **Larsen** a-11. **Palais** a-10,11.*

SUSPENSE DETECTIVE
June, 1952 - No. 5, Mar, 1953
Fawcett Publications

	Good	Fine	Mint
1-Evans-a, 11 pgs; Baily c/a	8.50	25.50	60.00
2-Evans-a, 10 pgs.	5.00	15.00	35.00
3,5	4.00	12.00	28.00
4-Bondage-c	5.00	15.00	35.00

NOTE: ***Baily** a-4, 5. **Sekowsky** a-2, 4, 5; c-5.*

SUSPENSE STORIES (See Strange Suspense Stories)

SUZIE COMICS (Formerly Laugh Comix; see Top-Notch #28)
No. 49, Spring, 1945 - No. 100, Aug, 1954
Close-Up No. 49,50/MLJ Mag./Archie No. 51 on

	Good	Fine	Mint
49-Ginger begins	11.00	32.00	76.00
50-55: 54-Transvestism story	8.00	24.00	56.00
56-Katy Keene begins by Woggon	7.00	21.00	50.00
57-65	4.60	14.00	32.00
66-80	4.00	12.00	28.00
81-87,89-99	3.50	10.50	24.00
88-Used in **POP**, pg. 76,77; Bill Woggon draws himself in story	4.60	14.00	32.00
100-Last Katy Keene	4.00	12.00	28.00

NOTE: ***Katy Keene** in 53-82,85-100.*

SWAMP FOX, THE (See 4-Color #1179 & Walt Disney Presents #2)

SWAMP FOX, THE
1960 (14 pgs, small size) (Canada Dry Premiums)
Walt Disney Productions

	Good	Fine	Mint
Titles: (A)-Tory Masquerade, (B)-Rindau Rampage, (C)-Turnabout Tactics; each came in paper sleeve, books 1,2 & 3;			
Set with sleeves	3.50	10.50	24.00
Comic only	1.00	3.00	6.00

SWAMP THING (See Brave & Bold, DC Comics Presents 8, DC Spec. Series 2, 14, 17, 20, House of Sec. 92, Roots of the..., & The Saga of...)
Oct-Nov, 1972 - No. 24, Aug-Sept, 1976
National Periodical Publications/DC Comics

	Good	Fine	Mint
1-c/a by Wrightson begin	1.00	3.00	6.00
2	.50	1.50	3.00

SWAMP THING (continued)	Good	Fine	Mint
3-Intro. Patchworkman	.40	1.25	2.50
4-10: 7-Batman app. 10-Last Wrightson issue	.35	1.00	2.00
11-23-Redondo-a; 23-Swamp Thing reverts back to Dr. Holland		.50	1.00
24		.50	1.00

NOTE: *J. Jones a-9i. Kaluta a-9i. Redondo c-12-19, 21.*

SWAT MALONE
Sept, 1955
Swat Malone Enterprises

V1#1-Hy Fleishman-a	3.50	10.50	24.00

SWEENEY (Buz Sawyer's Pal, Roscoe. . .)
1949
Standard Comics

4,5-Crane-a #5	3.00	9.00	21.00

SWEE'PEA (See 4-Color No. 219)

SWEETHEART DIARY (Cynthia Doyle No. 66-on)
Wint, 1949 - No. 14, 1/53; No. 33, 4/56 - No. 65, 8/62
(No. 1-14, photo-c)
Fawcett Publications/Charlton Comics No. 33 on

1	5.50	16.50	38.00
2	3.00	9.00	21.00
3,4-Wood-a	8.00	24.00	56.00
5-10: 8-Bailey-a	2.35	7.00	16.00
11-14-Last Fawcett issue	1.30	4.00	9.00
33 (4/56; 1st Charlton ish.)(Formerly Sweetheart Love Story?)	1.15	3.50	8.00
34-40	.85	2.50	6.00
41-60	.35	1.00	2.00
61-65		.40	.80

SWEETHEART LOVE STORY (Formerly Cowboy Love #28-31? Sweetheart Diary No. 33-on?)
No. 32, Oct, 1955
Charlton Comics

32	.55	1.65	4.00

SWEETHEARTS (Formerly Captain Midnight)
No. 68, 10/48 - No. 121, 5/53; No. 122, 3/54 - No. 137, 12/73
Fawcett Publications/Charlton No. 122 on

68-Robert Mitchum photo-c	4.60	14.00	32.00
69-80: 72-Baker-a?	2.00	6.00	14.00
81-84,86-93,95-99	1.50	4.50	10.00
85,94,103,105,110,117-George Evans-a	2.35	7.00	16.00
100	1.85	5.50	13.00
101-Powell-a	1.65	5.00	11.50
102,104,106-109,112-116,118,121	1.15	3.50	8.00
111-1 pg. Ronald Reagan biog	3.00	9.00	21.00
119-Marilyn Monroe photo-c; also appears in story; part Wood-a	8.00	24.00	56.00
120-Atom Bomb story	3.00	9.00	21.00
122-(1st Charlton?)-Marijuana story	2.15	6.50	15.00
123-125 (Exist?)	1.00	3.00	7.00
V2/26 (?/54)-28: Last Pre-code ish	.85	2.50	6.00
29-39,41,43-45,47-50	.60	1.80	4.00
40-Photo-c; Tommy Sands story	1.00	3.00	7.00
42-Ricky Nelson photo-c/sty	1.30	4.00	9.00
46-Jimmy Rodgers photo-c/sty	1.00	3.00	7.00
51-60	.55	1.65	4.00
61-80	.30	1.00	2.00
81-100		.50	1.00
101-137		.25	.50

NOTE: *Photo c-68-121.*

SWEETHEART SCANDALS (See Fox Giants)

SWEETIE PIE (See 4-Color No. 1185,1241)

SWEETIE PIE
Dec, 1955 - No. 15, Fall, 1957
Ajax-Farrell/Pines (Literary Ent.)

	Good	Fine	Mint
1-By Napine Seltzer	2.35	7.00	16.00
2 (5/56; last Ajax?)	1.15	3.50	8.00
3-15 (#3-10, exist?)	.85	2.50	6.00

SWEET LOVE
Sept, 1949 - No. 5, May, 1950
Home Comics (Harvey)

1-Photo-c	2.00	6.00	14.00
2	1.50	4.50	10.00
3,4: 3-Powell-a	1.35	4.00	9.00
5-Kamen, Powell-a; photo-c	2.75	8.00	18.00

SWEET ROMANCE
October, 1968
Charlton Comics

1		.40	.80

SWEET SIXTEEN
Aug-Sept, 1946 - No. 13, Jan, 1948
Parents' Magazine Institute

1-Van Johnson's life story; Dorothy Dare, Queen of Hollywood Stunt Artists begins (in all issues)	4.35	13.00	30.00
2-Jane Powell, Roddy McDowall "Holiday in Mexico" photo-c	3.00	9.00	21.00
3-6,8-11: 6-Dick Haymes story	2.35	7.00	16.00
7-Ronald Reagan's life story	10.00	30.00	70.00
12-Bob Cummings, Vic Damone story	3.50	10.50	24.00
13-Robert Mitchum's life story	4.00	12.00	28.00

SWIFT ARROW (Also see Lone Rider)
2-4/54 - No. 5, 10-11/54; 4/57 - No. 3, 9/57
Ajax/Farrell Publications

1(1954) (1st Series)	4.00	12.00	28.00
2	1.85	5.50	13.00
3-5: 5-Lone Rider sty	1.70	5.00	12.00
1 (2nd Series) (Swift Arrow's Gunfighters #4)	1.70	5.00	12.00
2,3: 2-Lone Rider begins	1.50	4.50	10.00

SWIFT ARROW'S GUNFIGHTERS (Formerly Swift Arrow)
No. 4, Nov, 1957
Ajax/Farrell Publ. (Four Star Comic Corp.)

4	1.50	4.50	10.00

SWING WITH SCOOTER
6-7/66 - No. 35, 8-9/71; No. 36, 10-11/72
National Periodical Publications

1	.75	2.25	5.00
2-10	.50	1.50	3.00
11-32,35,36	.25	.75	1.50
33-Interview with David Cassidy	.25	.75	1.50
34-Interview with Ron Ely (Doc Savage)	.25	.75	1.50

NOTE: *Orlando a-1-11; c-1-11, 13. No. 20, 33, 34: 68 pgs.; No. 35: 52 pgs.*

SWISS FAMILY ROBINSON (See 4-Color #1156, King Classics, & Movie Comics)

SWORD & THE DRAGON, THE (See 4-Color #1118)

SWORD & THE ROSE, THE (See 4-Color #505,682)

SWORD IN THE STONE, THE (See March of Comics #258 & Movie Comics)

SWORD OF LANCELOT (See Movie Comics)

SWORD OF SORCERY
Feb-Mar, 1973 - No. 5, Nov-Dec, 1973
National Periodical Publications

1-Leiber Fafhrd & The Grey Mouser; Adams/Bunkers inks; also #2;

Swamp Thing #12, © DC

Sweetheart Diary #1, © CC

Sweet Love #5, © HARV

BY GIL KANE AND JAN STRNAD
SWORD OF THE ATOM

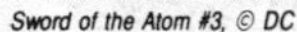
Sword of the Atom #3, © DC

Tales Calculated To Drive You Bats #2, © AP

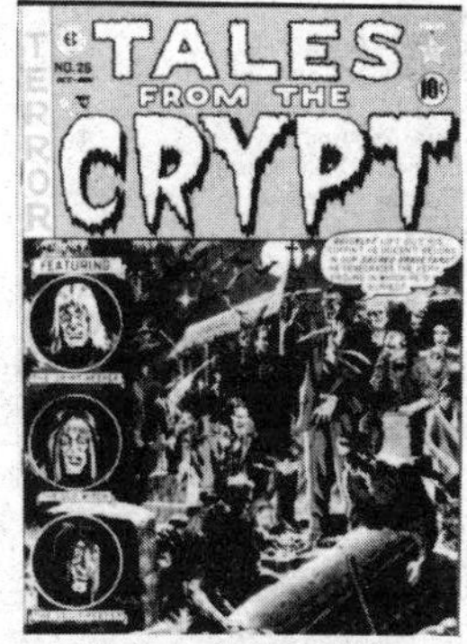

Tales From the Crypt #26, © WMG

SWORD OF SORCERY (continued)

	Good	Fine	Mint
Kaluta-c	.25	.75	1.50
2-Wrightson-c(i); Adams-a(i)	.25	.75	1.50
3-5: 5-Starlin-a; Conan cameo		.60	1.20

NOTE: ***Chaykin*** *a-1p, 2-4; c-2p, 3-5.* ***Kaluta*** *a-3i.* ***Simonson*** *a-1i, 3p, 4, 5p; c-5.* ***Starlin*** *a-5p.*

SWORD OF THE ATOM
Sept, 1983 - No. 4, Dec, 1983 (Mini-series)
DC Comics

	Good	Fine	Mint
1-Kane c/a begins		.50	1.00
2-4		.40	.80
Special 1(7/84), 2(7/85): Kane c/a each		.65	1.30

SWORDS OF TEXAS
10/87 - No. 4, 1988 ($1.75, color)
Eclipse Comics

	Good	Fine	Mint
1-4: Scout app.	.30	.90	1.75

SWORDS OF THE SWASHBUCKLERS (See Marvel Graphic Novel)
5/85 - No. 12, 6/87 ($1.50; Mature readers)
Epic Comics (Marvel)

	Good	Fine	Mint
1-Butch Guice-c/a cont'd from Marvel Graphic Novel	.35	1.00	2.00
2-12	.25	.80	1.60

SYPHONS
July, 1986 - No. 7, 1987 ($1.50, $1.75, color)
Now Comics

	Good	Fine	Mint
1-7	.25	.75	1.50

TAFFY
Mar-Apr, 1945 - No. 12, 1948
Rural Home/Orbit Publ.

	Good	Fine	Mint
1-L.B. Cole-c; origin of Wonderworm plus 7 chapter WWII funny animal adv.	5.00	15.00	35.00
2-L.B. Cole-c	3.50	10.50	24.00
3,4,6-12: 6-Perry Como c/story. 7-Duke Ellington, 2pgs.	2.65	8.00	18.00
5-L.B. Cole-c; Van Johnson story	3.50	10.50	24.00

TAILSPIN
November, 1944
Spotlight Publishers

	Good	Fine	Mint
nn-Firebird app.; L.B. Cole-c	5.00	15.00	35.00

TAILSPIN TOMMY STORY & PICTURE BOOK
1931? (nd) (Color stip reprints; 10½x10")
McLoughlin Bros.

	Good	Fine	Mint
266-by Forrest	12.00	36.00	84.00

TAILSPIN TOMMY
1932 (100 pages)(hardcover)
Cupples & Leon Co.

	Good	Fine	Mint
(Rare)-B&W strip reprints from 1930 by Hal Forrest & Glenn Claffin	15.00	45.00	105.00

TAILSPIN TOMMY
1940; 1946
United Features Syndicate/Service Publ. Co.

	Good	Fine	Mint
Single Series 23('40)	13.00	40.00	90.00
Best Seller (nd, '46)-Service Publ. Co.	7.00	21.00	50.00

TALENT SHOWCASE (See New Talent Showcase)

TALES CALCULATED TO DRIVE YOU BATS
Nov, 1961 - No. 7, Nov, 1962; 1966
Archie Publications

	Good	Fine	Mint
1	3.00	9.00	18.00
2	1.50	4.50	9.00
3-6	1.20	3.50	7.00
7-Story line change	.70	2.00	4.00
1('66)-25 cents	.80	2.40	4.80

TALES FROM THE CRYPT (Formerly The Crypt Of Terror)
No. 20, Oct-Nov, 1950 - No. 46, Feb-Mar, 1955
E.C. Comics

	Good	Fine	Mint
20	42.00	125.00	295.00
21-Kurtzman-r/Haunt of Fear #15/1	35.00	105.00	245.00
22-Moon Girl costume at costume party, one panel	28.00	84.00	195.00
23-25	21.00	62.00	146.00
26-30	16.50	50.00	115.00
31-Williamson-a(1st at E.C.); B&W and color illos. in **POP**; Kamen draws himself, Gaines & Feldstein; Ingels, Craig & Davis draw themselves in his story	21.00	62.00	146.00
32,35-39	13.00	40.00	90.00
33-Origin The Crypt Keeper	21.00	62.00	146.00
34-Used in **POP**, pg. 83; lingerie panels	13.00	40.00	90.00
40-Used in Senate hearings & in Hartford Cournat anti-comics editorials-1954	13.00	40.00	90.00
41-45: 45-2pgs. showing E.C. staff	11.50	34.00	80.00
46-Low distribution; pre-advertised cover for unpublished 4th horror title 'Crypt of Terror' used on this book	13.00	40.00	90.00

NOTE: ***Craig*** *a-20, 22-24; c-20.* ***Crandall*** *a-38, 44.* ***Davis*** *a-24-46; c-29-46.* ***Elder*** *a-37, 38.* ***Evans*** *a-32-34, 36, 40, 41, 43, 46.* ***Feldstein*** *a-20-23; c-21-25, 28.* ***Ingels*** *a-in all.* ***Kamen*** *a-20, 22, 25, 27-31, 33-36, 39, 41-45.* ***Krigstein*** *a-40, 42, 45.* ***Kurtzman*** *a-21.* ***Orlando*** *a-27-30, 35, 37, 39, 41-45.* ***Wood*** *a-21, 24, 25; c-26, 27. Canadian reprints known; see Table of Contents.*

TALES FROM THE CRYPT (Magazine)
No. 10, July, 1968 (35 cents)(B&W)
Eerie Publications

	Good	Fine	Mint
10-Contains Farrell reprints from 1950s	.50	1.50	3.00

TALES FROM THE GREAT BOOK
Feb, 1955 - No. 4, Jan, 1956
Famous Funnies

	Good	Fine	Mint
1	3.00	9.00	21.00
2-4-Lehti-a in all	1.50	4.50	10.00

TALES FROM THE TOMB
Oct, 1962 - No. 2, Dec, 1962
Dell Publishing Co.

	Good	Fine	Mint
1(02-810-210)(Giant)-All stories written by John Stanley	1.35	5.25	12.00
2	1.35	4.00	9.00

TALES FROM THE TOMB (Magazine)
V1#6, July, 1969 - V6#6, Dec, 1974 (52 pgs.)
Eerie Publications

	Good	Fine	Mint
V1#6-8	.70	2.00	4.00
V2#1-3,5,6: 6-Rulah-r	.40	1.25	2.50
4-LSD story-r/Weird V3#5	.85	2.50	5.00
V3#1-Rulah-r	.70	2.00	4.00
2-6('70),V4#1-6('72),V5#1-6('73),V6#1-6('74)	.40	1.25	2.50

TALES OF ASGARD
Oct, 1968 (68 pages); Feb, 1984 ($1.25, 52 pgs.)
Marvel Comics Group

	Good	Fine	Mint
1-Thor r-/from Journey into Mystery #97-106; new Kirby-c	.25	.75	1.50
V2#1 (2/84)-Thor-r; Simonson-c		.40	.80

TALES OF DEMON DICK & BUNKER BILL
1934 (78 pgs; 5x10½"; B&W)(hardcover)
Whitman Publishing Co.

	Good	Fine	Mint
793-by Dick Spencer	7.00	21.00	50.00

TALES OF EVIL
Feb, 1975 - No. 3, July, 1975
Atlas/Seaboard Publ.

	Good	Fine	Mint
1		.30	.60
2-Intro. The Bog Beast		.25	.50
3-OriginThe Man-Monster		.25	.50

NOTE: ***Lieber*** *c-1.* ***Sekowsky*** *a-1.* ***Sutton*** *a-2.* ***Thorne*** *c-2.*

TALES OF GHOST CASTLE
May-June, 1975 - No. 3, Sept-Oct, 1975
National Periodical Publications

	Good	Fine	Mint
1-3: 1,3-Redondo-a. 2-Nino-a		.25	.50

TALES OF G.I. JOE
Jan, 1988 - Present (color)
Marvel Comics

	Good	Fine	Mint
1 ($2.25)	.40	1.15	2.30
2-4 ($1.50)	.25	.75	1.50

TALES OF HORROR
June, 1952 - No. 13, Oct, 1954
Toby Press/Minoan Publ. Corp.

	Good	Fine	Mint
1	7.00	21.00	50.00
2-Torture scenes	5.00	15.00	35.00
3-8,13	3.50	10.50	24.00
9-11-Reprints Purple Claw #1-3	4.35	13.00	30.00
12-Myron Fass c/a; torture scenes	4.00	12.00	28.00

NOTE: ***Andru*** *a-5.* ***Bailey*** *a-5.* ***Myron Fass*** *a-2,s 3, 12; c-1-3, 12.* ***Hollingsworth*** *a-2.* ***Sparling*** *a-6, 9; c-9.*

TALES OF JUSTICE
No. 53, May, 1955 - No. 67, Aug, 1957
Atlas Comics(MjMC No. 53-66/Male No. 67)

	Good	Fine	Mint
53	3.50	10.50	24.00
54-57	2.15	6.50	15.00
58,59-Krigstein-a	3.00	9.00	21.00
60-63,65	1.30	4.00	9.00
64,67-Crandall-a	2.15	6.50	15.00
66-Torres, Orlando-a	2.15	6.50	15.00

NOTE: ***Everett*** *a-53, 60.* ***Orlando*** *a-65, 66.* ***Powell*** *a-54.* ***Severin*** *c-58, 65.*

TALES OF SUSPENSE (Captain America #100 on)
Jan, 1959 - No. 99, March, 1968
Atlas (WPI No. 1,2/Male No. 3-12/VPI No. 13-18)/Marvel No. 19 on

	Good	Fine	Mint
1-Williamson-a, 5 pgs.	33.00	100.00	230.00
2,3	13.00	40.00	90.00
4-Williamson-a, 4 pgs; Kirby/Everett c/a	14.00	42.00	100.00
5-10	7.50	22.50	52.00
11,13-20: 14-Intro. Colossus. 16-Intro Metallo (Pre-Iron Man prototype)	5.70	17.00	40.00
12-Crandall-a	6.00	18.00	42.00
21-25: 25-Last 10 cent ish.	3.15	9.50	22.00
26-38: 32-Sazzik The Sorcerer app. (Dr. Strange proto-type)	2.65	8.00	18.00
39-Origin & 1st app. Iron Man; 1st Iron Man story-Kirby layouts	60.00	150.00	420.00
40-Iron Man in new armor	21.00	54.00	150.00
41	11.50	29.00	80.00
42-45: 45-Intro. & 1st app. Happy & Pepper	4.30	11.00	30.00
46,47	2.30	5.70	16.00
48-New Iron Man armor	2.85	7.15	20.00
49-51: 50-1st app. Mandarin	1.45	3.60	10.00
52-1st app. The Black Widow	1.70	4.30	12.00
53-Origin The Watcher (5/64); Black Widow app.	1.45	3.60	10.00
54-56	1.00	3.00	6.00
57-1st app./Origin Hawkeye (9/64)	2.00	6.00	14.00
58-Captain America begins (10/64)	.70	2.00	4.00
59-Iron Man plus Captain America features begin; intro Jarvis, Avenger's butler	.70	2.00	4.00
60,61,64	.40	1.25	2.50
62-Origin Mandarin (2/65)	.50	1.50	3.00
63-Origin Captain America (3/65)	.70	2.00	4.00
65-1st Silver-Age Red Skull (6/65)	.40	1.25	2.50
66-Origin Red Skull	.40	1.25	2.50
67-94,96-99: 69-1st app. Titanium Man. 75-Intro/1st spp. Agent 13 later named Sharon Carter. 76-Intro Batroc & Sharon Carter, Agent 13 of Shield. 79-Intro Cosmic Cube. 94-Intro Modok	.40	1.25	2.50
95-Capt. America's i.d. revealed	.40	1.25	2.50

NOTE: ***Colan*** *a-39, 73-99p; c(p)-73, 75, 77, 79, 81, 83, 85-87, 89, 91, 93, 95, 97, 99.* ***Craig*** *a-99i.* ***Crandall*** *a-12.* ***Davis*** *a-38.* ***Ditko/Kirby*** *art in most issues No. 1-15, 17-49.* ***Everett*** *a-8.* ***Forte*** *a-5, 9.* ***Gil Kane*** *a-88p, 89-91; c-88, 89-91p.* ***Kirby*** *a(p)-40, 41, 43, 59-75, 77-86, 92-99; layouts-69-75, 77; c(p)-29-56, 58-72, 74, 76, 78, 80, 82, 84, 86, 92, 94, 96, 98.* ***Leiber/Fox*** *a-42, 43, 45, 51.* ***Reinman*** *a-26, 44i, 49i, 52i, 53i.* ***Tuska*** *a-58, 70-74.* ***Wood*** *c/a-71i.*

TALES OF SWORD & SORCERY (See Dagar)

TALES OF TERROR
1952 (no month)
Toby Press Publications

	Good	Fine	Mint
1-Fawcette-c; Ravielli-a	4.00	12.00	28.00

NOTE: *This title was cancelled due to similarity to the E.C. title.*

TALES OF TERROR (See Movie Classics)

TALES OF TERROR (Magazine)
Summer, 1964
Eerie Publications

	Good	Fine	Mint
1	1.00	3.00	7.00

TALES OF TERROR
July, 1985 - Present ($2.00; Baxter paper; mature readers)
Eclipse Comics

	Good	Fine	Mint
1	.40	1.25	2.50
2-13: 3-Morrow-a. 7-Bissette, Bolton-a	.35	1.00	2.00

TALES OF TERROR ANNUAL
1951 - 1953 (25 cents)
E.C. Comics

	Good	Fine	Mint
nn(1951)(Scarce)-Infinity-c	200.00	600.00	1400.00
2(1952)	100.00	300.00	700.00
3(1953)	70.00	210.00	490.00

No. 1 contains three horror and one science fiction comic which came out in 1950. No. 2 contains a horror, crime and science fiction book which generally had cover dates in 1951, and No. 3 had horror, crime, and shock books that generally appeared in 1952. All E.C. annuals contain four complete books that did not sell on the stands which were rebound in the annual format, minus the covers, and sold from the E.C. office and on the stands in key cities. The contents of each annual may vary in the same year.

TALES OF TERROR ILLUSTRATED (See Terror Ill.)

TALES OF TEXAS JOHN SLAUGHTER (See 4-Color No. 997)

TALES OF THE GREEN BERET
Jan, 1967 - No. 5, Oct, 1969
Dell Publishing Co.

	Good	Fine	Mint
1	1.00	3.00	7.00
2-5: 5 reprints #1	.75	2.25	5.00

NOTE: ***Glanzman*** *a 1-4.*

TALES OF THE GREEN LANTERN CORPS
May, 1981 - No. 3, July, 1981
DC Comics

	Good	Fine	Mint
1-Origin of G.L. & the Guardians; Staton-a(p)		.45	.90
2,3-Staton-a(p)		.30	.60
Annual 1 (1/85)-G. Kane c/a		.65	1.30

TALES OF THE INVISIBLE SCARLET O'NEIL (See Harv. Comics Hits #59)

Tales of Suspense #11, © MCG

Tales of Terror #1, © Eclipse Comics

Tales of the Green Lantern Corps #3, © DC

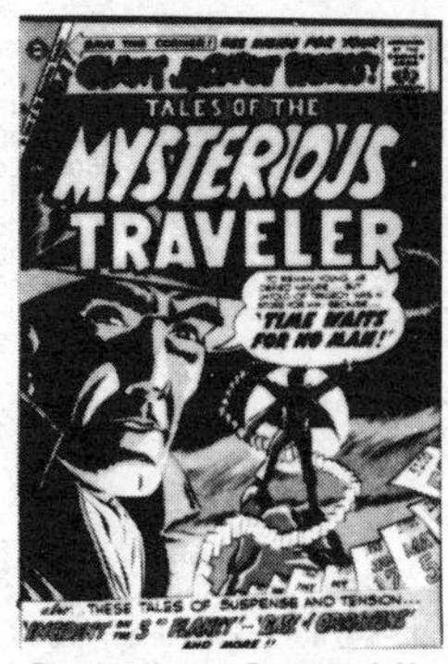

Tales of the Mysterious Traveler #13, © CC

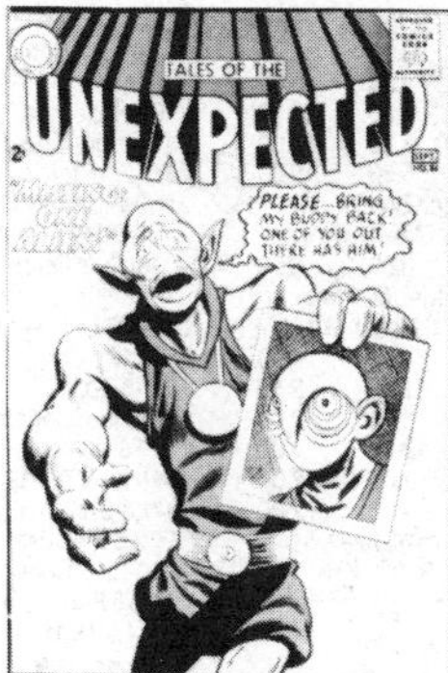

Tales of the Unexpected #84, © DC

Tales To Astonish #1, © MCG

TALES OF THE KILLERS (Magazine)
V1No.10, Dec, 1970 - V1No.11, Feb, 1971 (52pgs.)(B&W)
World Famous Periodicals

	Good	Fine	Mint
V1#10-One pg. Frazetta	.85	2.50	6.00
11	.70	2.00	4.00

TALES OF THE LEGION (Formerly The Legion of Super-Heroes)
No. 314, Aug, 1984 - Present
DC Comics

	Good	Fine	Mint
314-320: 314-Origin The White Witch		.40	.80
321-354: r-/Legion S.H. (Baxter series)		.45	.90
Annual 4 ('86), 5 (10/87)		.60	1.20

TALES OF THE MARINES (Devil-Dog Dugan #3)
Feb, 1957 (Marines At War #5 on)
Atlas Comics (OPI)

	Good	Fine	Mint
4-Powell-a	1.20	3.50	8.00

TALES OF THE MYSTERIOUS TRAVELER (See Mysterious. . .)
8/56 - No. 13, 6/59; V2/14, 10/85 - No. 15, 12/85
Charlton Comics

	Good	Fine	Mint
1-No Ditko-a	12.00	36.00	84.00
2-Ditko-a(1)	10.00	30.00	70.00
3-Ditko c/a(1)	8.50	25.50	60.00
4-6-Ditko c/a(3-4)	12.00	36.00	84.00
7-9-Ditko-a(1-2)	8.00	24.00	56.00
10,11-Ditko-c/a(3-4)	10.00	30.00	70.00
12,13	3.50	10.50	24.00
14,15 (1985)-Ditko c/a		.40	.80

TALES OF THE NEW TEEN TITANS
June, 1982 - No. 4, Sept, 1982 (mini-series)
DC Comics

	Good	Fine	Mint
1-Origin Cyborg-book length story	.30	.90	1.80
2-Origin Raven-book length story	.25	.75	1.50
3-Origin Changeling	.25	.75	1.50
4-Origin Starfire	.25	.75	1.50

NOTE: ***Perez** a-1-4p; c-1-4.*

TALES OF THE PONY EXPRESS (See 4-Color No. 829, 942)

TALES OF THE SUN RUNNERS
July, 1986 - Present ($1.50, color)
Sirius Comics/Amazing Comics No. 3 on

	Good	Fine	Mint
V2#1	.25	.75	1.50
V2#2,3 ($1.95)	.35	1.00	2.00
Christmas Special 1(12/86)	.25	.75	1.50

TALES OF THE TEENAGE MUTANT NINJA TURTLES
May, 1987 - Present (B&W, $1.50)
Mirage Studios

	Good	Fine	Mint
1-3	.25	.75	1.50

TALES OF THE TEEN TITANS (Formerly The New. . .)
No. 41, April, 1984 - Present
DC Comics

	Good	Fine	Mint
41-49,51-59: 44-1st app/origin Terminator; Jericho & Nightwing join. 46-Aqualad & Aquagirl join. 53-Intro Azreal. 56-Intro Jinx. 57-Neutron app. 59-r/DC Comics Presents 26		.45	.90
50-Double size		.60	1.20
60-88: r/New Teen Titans Baxter series. 69-Origin Kole		.40	.80
Annual 3('84; $1.25)-Death of Terra		.60	1.20
Annual 4(11/86)-r, 5('87)		.60	1.20

TALES OF THE TEXAS RANGERS (See Jace Pearson. . .)

TALES OF THE UNEXPECTED (The Unexpected #105 on)(See Super DC Giant)
Feb-Mar, 1956 - No. 104, Dec-Jan, 1967-68
National Periodical Publications

	Good	Fine	Mint
1	26.00	80.00	185.00
2	11.50	34.00	80.00
3-5	7.00	21.00	50.00
6-10	4.85	14.50	34.00
11,12,14	2.65	8.00	18.00
13,15-18,21-23: Kirby-a. 16-Character named 'Thor' with a magic hammer - not like later thor	3.60	11.00	25.00
19,20,24-39: 24-Cameron-c/a	1.70	5.00	12.00
40-Space Ranger begins, ends #82	9.30	28.00	65.00
41-50	1.30	4.00	9.00
51-67: 67-Last 10 cent ish.	.85	2.50	6.00
68-100: 91-1st Automan (also in #94,97)	.40	1.25	2.50
101-104		.60	1.20

NOTE: ***Adams** c-104. **Anderson** a-50. **Brown** a-50-82(Space Ranger). **Heath** a-31, 49. **Bob Kane** a-48. **Kirby** a-12, 24; c-22. **Meskin** a-15, 18, 26, 27, 35, 66. **Moreira** a-16, 39, 38, 44, 62; c-38.*

TALES OF THE WEST (See 3-D. . .)

TALES OF THE WIZARD OF OZ (See 4-Color No. 1308)

TALES OF THE ZOMBIE (Magazine)
Aug, 1973 - No. 10, Mar, 1975 (75 cents)(B&W)
Marvel Comics Group

	Good	Fine	Mint
V1#1-Reprint/Menace #5; origin	1.00	3.00	6.00
2,3: 2-Everett biography & memorial	.70	2.00	4.00
V2#1(#4)-Photos,text of Bond movie 'Live & Let Die'	.70	2.00	4.00
5-10: 8-Kaluta-a	.70	2.00	4.00
Annual 1(Summer,'75)(#11)-B&W; Everett, Buscema-a	.70	2.00	4.00

NOTE: ***Alcala** a-7-9. **Boris** c-1-4. **Colan** a-2r, 6. **Heath** a-5r. **Reese** a-2. **Tuska** a-2r.*

TALES OF THUNDER
March, 1985
Deluxe Comics

	Good	Fine	Mint
1-Dynamo, Iron Maiden & Menthor app.; Giffen-a	.35	1.00	2.00

TALES OF VOODOO (Magazine)
V1No.11, Nov, 1968 - V7No.6, Nov, 1974
Eerie Publications

	Good	Fine	Mint
V1#11	.85	2.50	6.00
V2#1(3/69)-V2#4(9/69)	.50	1.50	3.00
V3#1-6('70): 4-'Claws of the Cat' redrawn from Climax #1	.50	1.50	3.00
V4#1-6('71), V5#1-6('72), V6#1-6('73), V7#1-6('74)	.50	1.50	3.00
Annual 1	.70	2.00	4.00

NOTE: *Bondage-c-V1No.10, V2No.4, V3No.4.*

TALES OF WELLS FARGO (See 4-Color No. 876, 968, 1023,1075, 1113, 1167, 1215, & Western Roundup)

TALES TO ASTONISH
Jan, 1959 - No. 101, March, 1968
Atlas (MAP No. 1/ZPC No. 2-14/VPI No. 15-21/Marvel No. 22 on

	Good	Fine	Mint
1-Jack Davis-a	34.00	102.00	240.00
2-Ditko-c	16.00	48.00	110.00
3	12.00	36.00	84.00
4	8.00	24.00	56.00
5-Williamson-a, 4 pgs.	10.00	30.00	70.00
6-10	6.00	18.00	42.00
11-20	4.00	12.00	28.00
21-26	2.65	8.00	18.00
27-1st Antman app. (1/62); last 10 cent ish.	78.00	200.00	550.00
28-34	2.00	6.00	14.00
35-2nd Antman, 1st in costume; begin series	29.00	71.00	200.00
36	11.50	29.00	80.00

TALES TO ASTONISH (continued) — Good / Fine / Mint

	Good	Fine	Mint
37-40	5.15	13.00	36.00
41-43	2.15	5.35	15.00
44-Origin & 1st app. The Wasp	2.60	6.50	18.00
45-48: 46-1st Crimson Dynamo	1.70	4.30	12.00
49-Antman becomes Giant Man	2.60	6.50	18.00
50-60: 50-Origin/1st app. Human Top. 52-Origin/1st app. Black Knight. 59-Giant Man vs. Hulk feat. story. 60-Giant Man/Hulk dbl. feat. begins	1.00	3.00	6.00
61-70: 62-1st app./origin The Leader; new Wasp costume. 65-New Giant Man costume. 68-New Human Top costume. 69-Last Giant Man. 70-Sub-Mariner begins	.70	2.00	4.00
71-80	.40	1.25	2.50
81-91: 90-1st app. The Abomination	.35	1.00	2.00
92,93-Silver Surfer app.	.70	2.00	4.00
94-99	.35	1.00	2.00
100,101: 100-Hulk battles Sub-Mariner	.30	1.00	2.00

NOTE: ***Berg** a-1. **Burgos** a-62-64p. **Buscema** a-85-87p. **Colan** a(p)-70-76, 78-82, 84, 85, 101; c(p)-71-76, 78, 80, 82, 84, 86, 88, 90. **Ditko** a-most issues-1-48, 50i, 60-67. **Everett** a-78, 79i, 80-84, 85-90i, 94i, 95, 96; c(i)-79-81, 83, 86, 88. **Forte** a-6. **Kane** a-76, 88-91; c-89, 91. **Kirby** a(p)-1-34(most), 35-40, 44, 49-51, 68-70, 82, 83; layouts-71-84; c(p)-1, 5, 27, 35-48, 50-70, 72, 73, 75, 77, 78, 79, 81, 85, 90. **Leiber/Fox** a-47, 48, 50, 51. **Powell** a-65-69p, 73, 74. **Reinman** a-6, 36, 45, 46, 54i, 56-60i.*

TALES TO ASTONISH (2nd Series)
Dec, 1979 - No. 14, Jan, 1981
Marvel Comics Group

	Good	Fine	Mint
V1#1-Buscema-r from Sub-Mariner #1		.30	.60
2-14: Reprints Sub-Mariner 2-14		.25	.50

TALES TO HOLD YOU SPELLBOUND (See Spellbound)

TALKING KOMICS
1957 (20 pages) (Slick covers)
Belda Record & Publ. Co.

Each comic contained a record that followed the story - much like the Golden Record sets. Known titles: Chirpy Cricket, Lonesome Octopus, Sleepy Santa, Grumpy Shark, Flying Turtle, Happy Grasshopper with records 80 2.40 4.80

TALLY-HO COMICS
December, 1944
Swappers Quarterly (Baily Publ. Co.)

	Good	Fine	Mint
nn-Frazett's 1st work as Giunta's assistant; Man in Black story; violence	18.00	54.00	126.00

TALOS OF THE WILDERNESS SEA
Aug, 1987 (One Shot, $2.00, color)
DC Comics

	Good	Fine	Mint
1	.35	1.00	2.00

TAMMY, TELL ME TRUE (See 4-Color No. 1233)

TARANTULA (See Weird Suspense)

TARAS BULBA (See Movie Classics)

TARGET COMICS (. . .Western Romances #106 on)
Feb, 1940 - V10/3(#105), Aug, Sept, 1949
Funnies, Inc./Novelty Publications/Star Publications

	Good	Fine	Mint
V1#1-Origin & 1st app. Manowar, The White Streak by Burgos, & Bulls-Eye Bill by Everett; City Editor (ends #5), High Grass Twins by Jack Cole(ends #4), T-Men by Joe Simon(ends #9), Rip Rory (ends #4), Fantastic Feature Films by Tarpe Mills (ends #39, & Calling 2-R(ends #14) begin; Marijuana use story	145.00	435.00	1015.00
2	70.00	210.00	490.00
3,4	50.00	150.00	350.00
5-Origin The White Streak in text; Space Hawk by Wolverton begins (See Circus)	115.00	345.00	805.00
6-The Chameleon by Everett begins; White Streak origin cont'd. in text	65.00	195.00	455.00
7-Wolverton-c (Scarce)	154.00	460.00	1075.00
8,9,12	48.00	145.00	335.00
10-Intro. & 1st app. The Target; Kirby-c	65.00	195.00	455.00
11-Origin The Target & The Targeteers	58.00	175.00	405.00
V2#1,2: 1-Target by Bob wood	35.00	105.00	245.00
3-5: 4-The Cadet begins	23.00	70.00	160.00
6-9:Red Seal with White Streak in 6-10	23.00	70.00	160.00
10-Classic-c	26.00	78.00	180.00
11,12	23.00	70.00	160.00
V3#1-10-Last Wolverton issue	23.00	70.00	160.00
11,12	3.50	10.50	24.00
V4#1-5,7-12	2.00	6.00	14.00
6-Targetoons by Wolverton, 1 pg.	2.15	6.50	15.00
V5#1-8	1.70	5.00	12.00
V6#1-10, V7#1-12	1.30	4.00	9.00
V8#1,3-5,8,9,11,12	1.30	4.00	9.00
2,6,7-Krigstein-a	1.70	5.00	12.00
10-L.B. Cole-c	4.60	14.00	32.00
V9/1,3,6,8,10,12, V10/2-L.B. Cole-c	4.60	14.00	32.00
V9/2,4,5,7,9,11, 10/1,3	1.30	4.00	9.00

NOTE: ***Jack Cole** a-1-8. **Everett** c-1-9. **Tarpe Mills** a-1-4, 6, 8, 11, V3#1. **Rico** a-V7#4, 10, V8#5, 6, V9#3. **Simon** a-1, 2.*

TARGET: THE CORRUPTORS (TV)
No. 1306, Mar-May, 1962 - No. 3, Oct-Dec, 1962 (Photo-c)
Dell Publishing Co.

	Good	Fine	Mint
4-Color 1306, #2,3	2.30	7.00	16.00

TARGET WESTERN ROMANCES (Formerly Target)
No. 106, Oct-Nov, 1949 - No. 107, Dec-Jan, 1949-50
Star Publications

	Good	Fine	Mint
106-Silhouette nudity panel; L.B. Cole-c	8.50	25.50	60.00
107-L.B. Cole-c; lingerie panels	5.70	17.00	40.00

TARGITT
March, 1975 - No. 3, July, 1975
Atlas/Seaboard Publ.

	Good	Fine	Mint
1-Origin; Nostrand-a in all		.30	.60
2,3: 2-1st in costume		.25	.50

TARZAN (See Aurora, Comics on Parade, Crackajack, DC 100-Page Super Spec., Famous Feat. Stories 1, Golden Comics Digest #4,9, Jeep Comics 1-29, Jungle Tales of . . ., Limited Coll. Edition, Popular, Sparkler, Sport Stars 1, Tip Top & Top Comics)

TARZAN
No. 5, 1939 - No. 161, Aug, 1947
Dell Publishing Co./United Features Syndicate

	Good	Fine	Mint
Large Feat. Comic 5('39)-(Scarce)-by Hal Foster; r-1st dailies from 1929	76.00	228.00	532.00
Single Series 20(:40)-by Hal Foster	68.00	205.00	475.00
4-Color 134(2/47)-Marsh-a	32.00	95.00	225.00
4-Color 161(8/47)-Marsh-a	28.00	84.00	195.00

TARZAN (. . .of the Apes #138 on)
1-2/48 - No. 131, 7-8/62; No. 132, 11/62 - No. 206, 2/72
Dell Publishing Co./Gold Key No. 132 on

	Good	Fine	Mint
1-Jesse Marsh-a begins	55.00	165.00	385.00
2	32.00	95.00	225.00
3-5	23.00	70.00	160.00
6-10: 6-1st Tantor the Elephant. 7-1st Valley of the Monsters	19.00	57.00	132.00
11-15: 11-Two Against the Jungle begins, ends #24. 13-Lex Barker photo-c begin	16.00	48.00	110.00
16-20	12.00	36.00	84.00
21-24,26-30	9.00	27.00	62.00
25-1st "Brothers of the Spear" episode; series ends #156,160,161, 196-206	11.00	32.00	76.00
31-40	5.00	15.00	35.00

Tales To Astonish #59, © MCG

Target Comics V2#1, © STAR

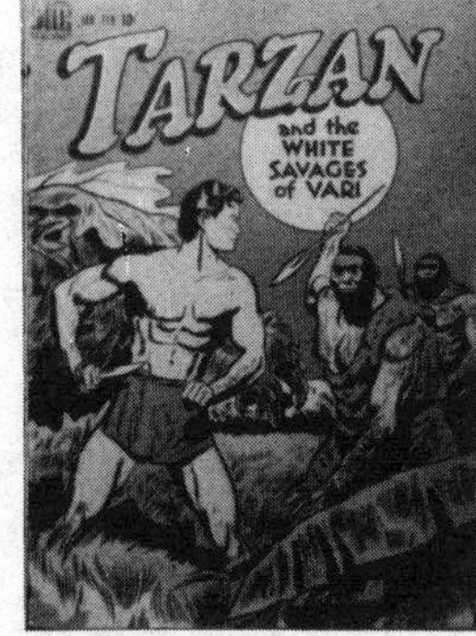

Tarzan #1 (Dell), © ERB

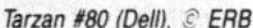
Tarzan #80 (Dell), © ERB

Tarzan #2 (Marvel), © ERB

Tastee-Freez Comics #3, © Paramount

TARZAN (continued)

	Good	Fine	Mint
41-54: Last Barker photo-c	3.70	11.00	26.00
55-60: 56-Eight pg. Boy story	3.15	9.50	22.00
61,62,64-70	2.35	7.00	16.00
63-Two Tarzan stories, 1 by Manning	2.65	8.00	18.00
71-79	2.00	6.00	14.00
80-99: 80-Gordon Scott photo-c begin	2.30	7.00	16.00
100	2.65	8.00	18.00
101-109	1.70	5.00	12.00
110 (Scarce)-Last photo-c	2.00	6.00	14.00
111-120	1.30	4.00	9.00
121-131: Last Dell issue	1.00	3.00	7.00
132-154: Gold Key issues	.85	2.50	6.00
155-Origin Tarzan	1.00	3.00	7.00
156-161: 157-Banlu, Dog of the Arande begins, ends #159, 195. 169-Leopard Girl app.	.70	2.00	5.00
162,165,168,171-Ron Ely photo-c	.85	2.50	6.00
163,164,166-167,169-170: 169-Leopard Girl app.	.55	1.65	4.00
172-199,201-206: 178-Tarzan origin r-/#155; Leopard Girl app, also in #179, 190-193	.50	1.50	3.00
200 (Scarce)	.75	2.25	5.00
Story Digest 1(6/70)-G.K.	.75	2.25	5.00

NOTE: *No. 162, 165, 168, 171 are TV issues. No. 1-153 all have* ***Marsh*** *art on Tarzan. No. 154-161, 163, 164, 166, 167, 172-177 all have* ***Manning*** *art on Tarzan. No. 178, 202 have* ***Manning*** *Tarzan reprints. No "Brothers of the Spear" in No. 1-24, 157-159, 162-195. No. 39-126, 128-156 all have* ***Russ Manning*** *art on "Brothers of the Spear." No. 196-201, 203-205 all have* ***Manning*** *B.O.T.S. reprints; No. 25-38, 127 all have* ***Jesse Marsh*** *art on B.O.T.S. No. 206 has a* ***Marsh*** *B.O.T.S. reprint.* ***Doug Wildey*** *art-No. 179-187. Many issues have front and back photo covers.*

TARZAN (Continuation of Gold Key series)
No. 207, April, 1972 - No. 258, Feb, 1977
Naional Periodical Publications

	Good	Fine	Mint
207-Origin Tarzan by Joe Kubert, part 1; John Carter begins (origin); 52 pg. issues thru #209	.40	1.20	2.40
208-210: Origin, parts 2-4. 209-Last John Carter. 210-Kubert-a		.60	1.20
211-Hogarth, Kubert-a		.50	1.00
212-214: Adaptations from "Jungle Tales of Tarzan." 213-Beyond the Farthest Star begins, ends #218		.45	.90
215-218,224,225-All by Kubert. 215-part Foster-r		.45	.90
219-223: Adapts "The Return of Tarzan" by Kubert		.45	.90
226-229: 226-Manning-a		.30	.60
230-100 pgs.; Kubert, Kaluta-a(p); Korak begins, ends #234; Carson of Venus app.		.50	1.00
231-234: Adapts "Tarzan and the Lion Man;" all 100 pgs.; Rex, the Wonder Dog r-#232, 233		.45	.90
235-Last Kubert issue; 100 pgs.		.45	.90
236-258: 238-68 pgs. 240-243 adapts "Tarzan & the Castaways." 250-256 adapts "Tarzan the Untamed." 252,253-r/#213		.25	.50
Comic Digest 1(Fall,'72)(DC)-50 cents; 160 pgs.; digest size; Kubert-c, Manning-a	.35	1.00	2.00

NOTE: ***Anderson*** *a-207, 209, 217, 218.* ***Chaykin*** *a-216.* ***Finlay*** *a(r)-212.* ***Foster*** *strip-r No. 208, 209, 211, 221.* ***Heath*** *a-230i.* ***G. Kane*** *a-232p, 233p.* ***Kubert*** *a-207-25, 227-35, 257r, 258r; c-207-249, 253.* ***Lopez*** *a-250-550p; c-250p, 251, 252, 254.* ***Manning*** *strip-r 230-235, 238.* ***Morrow*** *a-208.* ***Nino*** *a-231-234.* ***Sparling*** *a-230.* ***Starr*** *a-233r.*

TARZAN
June, 1977 - No. 29, Oct, 1979
Marvel Comics Group

	Good	Fine	Mint
1		.35	.70
2-29: 2-Origin by J. Buscema		.25	.50
Annual 1 (10/77)		.35	.70
Annual 2 (11/78), Annual 3 (10/79)		.25	.50

NOTE: ***Adams*** *c-11i, 12i.* ***Alcala*** *a-9i, 10i; c-8i, 9i.* ***Buckler*** *c-25-27p, Annual 3p.* ***John Buscema*** *a-1-3, 4-18p; c-1-7, 8p, 9p, 10, 11p, 12p, 13, 14p-19p, 21p, 22, 23p, 24p, 28p.* ***Buscema*** *c/a-Annual 1.* ***Mooney*** *a-22i.* ***Nebres*** *a-22i.* ***Russell*** *a-29i.*

TARZAN BOOK (The Illustrated . . .)
1929 (80 pages)(7x9")
Grosset & Dunlap

	Good	Fine	Mint
1(Rare)-Contains 1st B&W Tarzan newspaper comics from 1929. Cloth reinforced spine & dust jacket (50 cents)			
with dust jacket . . .	48.00	145.00	335.00
without dust jacket . . .	20.00	60.00	140.00
2nd Printing(1934)-76 pgs.; 25 cents; 4 Foster pages dropped; paper spine, circle in lower right cover with 25 cents price. The 25 cents is barely visible on some copies.	14.00	42.00	100.00
1967-House of Greystoke reprint-7x10", using the complete 300 illustrations/text from the 1929 edition minus the original indicia, foreword, etc. Initial version bound in gold paper & sold for $5. Officially titled **Burroughs Biblophile #2**. A very few additional copies were bound in heavier blue paper.			
Gold binding . . .	2.65	8.00	18.00
Blue binding . . .	3.50	10.50	24.00

TARZAN FAMILY, THE (Formerly Korak)
No. 60, Nov-Dec, 1975 - No. 66, Nov-Dec, 1976
(No. 60-62: 68 pgs.; No. 63 on: 52 pgs.)
National Periodical Publications

	Good	Fine	Mint
60-Korak begins; Kaluta-r		.30	.60
61-66		.25	.50

NOTE: *Carson of Venus-r 60-65. New John Carter-62-64, 65r, 66r. New Korak-60-66. Pellucidar feature-66.* ***Foster*** *Sunday r-60('32)-63.* ***Kaluta*** *Carson of Venus-60-65.* ***Kubert*** *c-60-64.* ***Manning*** *strip-r 60-62, 64.* ***Morrow*** *a-66r.*

TARZAN KING OF THE JUNGLE (See Dell Giant #37,51)

TARZAN, LORD OF THE JUNGLE
Sept, 1965 (Giant)(soft paper cover)(25 cents)
Gold Key

	Good	Fine	Mint
1-Marsh-r	2.65	8.00	18.00

TARZAN MARCH OF COMICS (See March of Comics No. 82, 98, 114, 125, 144, 155, 172, 185, 204, 223, 240, 252, 262, 272, 286, 300, 332, 342, 354, 366)

TARZAN OF THE APES
July, 1984 - No. 2, Aug, 1984
Marvel Comics Group

	Good	Fine	Mint
1,2-Origin-/Marvel Super Spec.		.30	.60

TARZAN OF THE APES TO COLOR
1933 (24 pages)(10¾x15¼")(Coloring book)
Saalfield Publishing Co.

	Good	Fine	Mint
988-(Very Rare)-Contains 1929 daily-r with some new art by Hal Foster. Two panels blown up large on each page; 25 percent in color; believed to be the only time these panels ever appeared in color.	72.00	215.00	505.00

TARZAN'S JUNGLE ANNUAL (See Dell Giants)

TARZAN'S JUNGLE WORLD (See Dell Giant #25)

TASMANIAN DEVIL & HIS TASTY FRIENDS
November, 1962
Gold Key

	Good	Fine	Mint
1-Bugs Bunny & Elmer Fudd x-over	4.00	12.00	28.00

TASTEE-FREEZ COMICS
1957 (36 pages)(10 cents)(6 different issues)
Harvey Comics

	Good	Fine	Mint
1-Little Dot, 3-Casper	3.35	10.00	23.00
2-Rags Rabbit, 5-Mazie	2.00	6.00	14.00
4-Sad Sack	2.00	6.00	14.00
6-Dick Tracy	4.00	12.00	28.00

TAYLOR'S CHRISTMAS TABLOID
Mid 1930s, Cleveland, Ohio
Dept. Store Giveaway (Tabloid size; in color)

TAYLOR'S CHRISTMAS TABLOID (cont.)

	Good	Fine	Mint
nn-(Very Rare)-Among the earliest pro work of Siegel & Shuster; one full color page called "The Battle in the Stratosphere," with a pre-Superman look; Shuster art thoughout. (Only 1 known copy) Estimated value. . .			$800.00

TEAM AMERICA (See Capt. America 269)
June, 1982 - No. 12, May, 1983
Marvel Comics Group

	Good	Fine	Mint
1-Origin; Ideal Toy motorcycle characters		.40	.80
2-12: 11-Ghost Rider app. 12-Double size		.30	.60

TEDDY ROOSEVELT & HIS ROUGH RIDERS
1950
Avon Periodicals

	Good	Fine	Mint
1-Kinstler-c; Palais-a; Flag-c	10.00	30.00	70.00

TEDDY ROOSEVELT ROUGH RIDER (See Classics Special)

TEE AND VEE CROSLEY IN TELEVISION LAND COMICS
(Also see Crosley's House of Fun)
1951 (52 pgs.; 8x11"; paper cover; in color)
Crosley Division, Avco Mfg. Corp. (Giveaway)

	Good	Fine	Mint
Many stories, puzzles, cut-outs, games, etc.	2.65	8.00	18.00

TEENA
1948 - No. 22, Oct, 1950
Magazine Enterprises/Standard Comics

	Good	Fine	Mint
A-1 #11	2.30	7.00	16.00
A-1 #12, 15	1.70	5.00	12.00
20-22 (Standard)	1.15	3.50	8.00

TEEN-AGE BRIDES (True Bride's Experiences #8)
Aug, 1953 - No. 7, Aug, 1954
Harvey/Home Comics

	Good	Fine	Mint
1-Powell-a	2.00	6.00	14.00
2-Powell-a	1.50	4.50	10.00
3-7: 3,6-Powell-a	1.35	4.00	9.00

TEEN-AGE CONFESSIONS (See Teen Confessions)

TEEN-AGE CONFIDENTIAL CONFESSIONS
July, 1960 - No. 22, 1964
Charlton Comics

	Good	Fine	Mint
1	.55	1.65	4.00
2-10	.35	1.00	2.00
11-22		.50	1.00

TEEN-AGE DIARY SECRETS (Formerly Blue Ribbon Comics; becomes Diary Secrets #10 on)
Sept, 1949 - No. 9, Aug, 1950
St. John Publishing Co.

	Good	Fine	Mint
nn(9/49)-oversized issue; Baker-a	9.50	28.50	65.00
6-8-Photo-c; Baker-a(2-3) in each	6.50	19.50	45.00
9-Pocket size	8.00	24.00	56.00

TEEN-AGE DOPE SLAVES (See Harvey Comics Library No. 1)

TEENAGE HOTRODDERS (Top Eliminator #25 on)
April, 1963 - No. 24, July, 1967
Charlton Comics

	Good	Fine	Mint
1	.70	2.00	4.00
2-24	.35	1.00	2.00

TEEN-AGE LOVE (See Fox Giants)

TEEN-AGE LOVE (Formerly Intimate?)
V2No.4, July, 1958 - No. 96, Dec, 1973
Charlton Comics

	Good	Fine	Mint
V2#4	1.00	3.00	7.00
5-9	.60	1.75	3.50
10(9/59)-35		1.00	2.00
36-96: 61&62-Jonnie Love begins (origin)		.20	.40

TEENAGE MUTANT NINJA TURTLES (Also see Anything Goes, Donatello, First Comics Graphic Novel, Grimjack #26, Michaelangelo, Tales Of The. . . & Raphael)
1984 - Present (B&W)
Mirage Studios

	Good	Fine	Mint
1-1st printing	26.00	78.50	157.00
1-2nd printing	5.30	16.00	32.00
1-3rd printing	1.30	3.90	7.80
1-4th,5th printing; new-c	.70	2.10	4.20
2-1st printing	6.15	18.50	37.00
2-2nd printing	1.40	4.20	8.40
2-3rd printing; new Corbin-c & story	.55	1.60	3.20
3	2.65	8.00	16.00
3-2nd printing	.50	1.50	3.00
4	1.60	4.75	9.50
4-2nd printing (5/87)	.35	1.05	2.10
5	1.15	3.40	6.80
5-2nd printing	.35	1.00	2.00
6	.85	2.50	5.00
6-2nd printing	.35	1.00	2.00
7-4pg. Corbin color insert; 1st color TMNT	.70	2.00	4.00
8-13: 8-Rion 2990 begins	.50	1.50	3.00
Book 1,2($1.50, B&W): 2-Corben-c	.25	.75	1.50

TEEN-AGE ROMANCE (Formerly My Own Romance)
No. 77, Sept, 1960 - No. 86, March, 1962
Marvel Comics (ZPC)

	Good	Fine	Mint
77-86	.60	1.80	3.60

TEEN-AGE ROMANCES
Jan, 1949 - No. 45, Dec, 1955
St. John Publ. co. (Approved Comics)

	Good	Fine	Mint
1-Baker c/a(1)	13.00	40.00	90.00
2-Baker c/a	8.00	24.00	56.00
3-Baker c/a(3); spanking panel	8.50	25.50	60.00
4,5,7,8-Photo-c; Baker-a(2-3) each	5.70	17.00	40.00
6-Slightly large size; photo-c; part magazine; Baker-a (10/49)	5.70	17.00	40.00
9-Baker c/a; Kubert-a	8.50	25.50	60.00
10-12,20-Baker c/a(2-3) each	5.70	17.00	40.00
13-19,21,22-Complete issues by Baker	9.00	27.00	62.00
23-25-Baker c/a(2-3) each	4.85	14.50	34.00
26,27,22,24,36-42-Last Precode, 3/55; Baker-a. 38-Suggestive-c	3.50	10.50	24.00
28-30-No Baker-a	1.70	5.00	12.00
31-Baker-c	2.15	6.50	15.00
32-Baker c/a, 1pg.	2.15	6.50	15.00
35-Baker c/a, 16pgs.	3.65	11.00	25.00
43-45-Baker-a	2.50	7.50	17.00

TEEN-AGE TALK
1964
I.W. Enterprises

	Good	Fine	Mint
Reprint #1-Monkees photo-c	1.00	3.00	6.00
Reprint #5,8,9	.30	.80	1.60

TEEN-AGE TEMPTATIONS (Going Steady #10 on)(See True Love Pic)
Oct, 1952 - No. 9, Aug, 1954
St. John Publishing co.

	Good	Fine	Mint
1-Baker c/a; has story "Reform School Girl" by Estrada	15.00	45.00	105.00
2-Baker-c	5.00	15.00	35.00
3-7,9-Baker c/a	8.50	25.50	60.00
8-Teenagers smoke reefers; Baker c/a	9.00	27.00	62.00

NOTE: ***Estrada** a-1, 4, 5.*

Teena #22, © STD

Teen-Age Confidential Confessions #1, © CC

Teen-Age Temptations #1, © STJ

Teen Beam #2, © DC

Teen Titans #21, © DC

Tell It to the Marines #14, © TOBY

TEEN BEAM (Teen Beat #1)
No. 2, Jan-Feb, 1968 (Monkees photo-c)
National Periodical Publications

	Good	Fine	Mint
2-Orlando, Drucker-a(r)	.75	2.25	5.00

TEEN BEAT (Teen Beam #2)
Nov-Dec, 1967
National Periodical Publications

1-Photos & text only; Monkees photo-c	1.15	3.50	8.00

TEEN COMICS (Formerly All Teen; Journey into Unknown Worlds #36 on)
No. 21, April, 1947 - No. 35, May, 1950
Marvel comics (WFP)

21-Kurtzman's "Hey Look"; Patsy Walker, Cindy, Georgie, Margie app.	3.70	11.00	26.00
22,23,25,27,29,31-35	2.00	6.00	14.00
24,26,28,30-Kurtzman's "Hey Look"	3.00	9.00	21.00

TEEN CONFESSIONS
Aug, 1959 - No. 97, Nov, 1976
Charlton Comics

1	3.00	9.00	21.00
2	1.30	4.00	9.00
3-10	.95	2.80	6.50
11-30	.40	1.20	2.80
31-Beatles-c	1.80	5.50	12.00
32-36,38-97: 89,90-Newton-c		.50	1.00
37 (1/66)-Beatles Fan Club story; Beatles-c	1.80	5.50	12.00

TEENIE WEENIES, THE
1950 - 1951 (Newspaper reprints)
Ziff-Davis Publishing Co.

10,11	4.60	14.00	32.00

TEEN-IN (Tippy Teen)
Summer, 1968 - No. 4, Fall, 1969
Tower Comics

nn(Summer,'68), nn(Spring,'69),3,4	.70	2.00	4.00

TEEN LIFE (Formerly Young Life)
No. 3, Winter, 1945 - No. 5, Fall, 1945
New Age/Quality Comics Group

3-June Allyson photo-c	3.00	9.00	21.00
4-Duke Ellington story	2.15	6.50	15.00
5-Van Johnson, Woody Herman & Jackie Robinson articles	3.00	9.00	21.00

TEEN ROMANCES
1964
Super Comics

10,11,15-17-Reprints		.30	.60

TEEN SECRET DIARY (Nurse Betsy Crane #12 on)
Oct, 1959 - No. 11, June, 1961; No. 1, 1972
Charlton Comics

1	1.30	4.00	9.00
2	.55	1.65	4.00
3-11	.35	1.00	2.50
1(1972)		.30	.60

TEEN TALK (See Teen)

TEEN TITANS (See Brave & the Bold, DC Super-Stars #1, Marvel & DC Present, New Teen Titans, Official...Index and Showcase)
1-2/66 - No. 43, 1-2/73; No. 44, 11/76 - No. 53, 2/78
National Periodical Publications/DC Comics

	Good	Fine	Mint
1-Titans join peace corps; Batman, Flash, Aquaman, Wonder Woman cameos	7.00	21.00	50.00
2	2.85	8.50	20.00
3-5: 4-Speedy app.	1.50	4.50	10.00
6-10: 6-Doom Patrol app.	1.00	3.00	7.00
11-18: 11-Speedy app.	.85	2.50	5.00
19-Wood-i; Speedy begins as regular	.85	2.50	5.00
20-22: All Adams-a. 21-Hawk & Dove app. 22-Origin Wonder Girl	1.10	3.25	6.50
23-Wonder Girl dons new costume	.70	2.00	4.00
24	.70	2.00	4.00
25-Flash, Aquaman, Batman, Green Arrow, Green Lantern, Superman, & Hawk & Dove guests	.70	2.00	4.00
26-30: 29-Hawk & Dove & Ocean Master app. 30-Aquagirl app.	.70	2.00	4.00
31-43: 31-Hawk & Dove app. 36,37-Superboy-r. 38-Green Arrow/ Speedy-r; Aquaman/Aqualad story. 39-Hawk & Dove-r. (36-39, 52 pgs.)	.50	1.50	3.00
44-47,49-52: 44-Mal becomes the Guardian. 46-Joker's Daughter begins. 50-Intro. Teen Titans West; 1st revival original Bat-Girl	.35	1.00	2.00
48-Intro Bumblebee; Joker's daughter becomes Harlequin	.35	1.00	2.00
53-Origin retold	.35	1.00	2.00

NOTE: *Aparo a-36.* ***Buckler*** *c-46-53.* ***Kane*** *a(p)-19,22-24, 39r.* ***Tuska*** *a(p)-31,36,38,39.*

TEEN TITANS SPOTLIGHT
Aug, 1986 - Present
DC Comics

1		.60	1.20
2,3		.45	.90
4-10: 7-Guice's 1st work at DC		.40	.80
11-21		.35	.70

TEEPEE TIM (Formerly Ha Ha Comics)
No. 100, Feb-Mar, 1955 - No. 102, June-July, 1955
American Comics Group

100-102	.55	1.65	4.00

TEGRA JUNGLE EMPRESS (Zegra #2 on)
August, 1948
Fox Features Syndicate

1-Blue Beetle, Rocket Kelly app.; used in **SOTI**, pg. 31	18.00	54.00	125.00

TELEVISION (See TV)

TELEVISION COMICS
No. 5, Feb, 1950 - No. 8, Nov, 1950
Standard Comics (Animated Cartoons)

5-1st app. Willy Nilly	2.00	6.00	14.00
6-8: 6 has No. 2 on inside	1.15	3.50	8.00

TELEVISION PUPPET SHOW
1950 - No. 2, Nov, 1950
Avon Periodicals

1,2	4.35	13.00	30.00

TELEVISION TEENS MOPSY (See TV Teens)

TELL IT TO THE MARINES
Mar, 1952 - No. 15, July, 1955
Toby Press Publications

1-Lover O'Leary and His Liberty Belles (with Pin-ups), ends #6	5.00	15.00	35.00
2-Madame Cobra app. c/story	3.50	10.50	24.00
3,5	2.65	8.00	18.00
4-Transvestism story	4.35	13.00	30.00
6-15: 7-9,14-Photo-c	1.50	4.50	10.00
I.W. Reprint #1,9	.30	.90	1.80
Super Reprint #16('64)	.30	.90	1.80

TEN COMMANDMENTS (See Moses & the...and Classics Special)

TENDER LOVE STORIES
Feb, 1971 - No. 4, July, 1971 (All 52pgs.)(25 cents)
Skywald Publ. Corp.

	Good	Fine	Mint
1-4	.30	.80	1.60

TENDER ROMANCE (Ideal Romance #3 on)
Dec., 1953 - No. 2, Feb, 1954
Key Publications (Gilmour Magazines)

	Good	Fine	Mint
1-Headlight & lingerie panels	5.50	16.50	38.00
2	2.65	8.00	18.00

TENNESSEE JED (Radio)
nd (1945) (16 pgs.; paper cover; regular size; giveaway)
Fox Syndicate? (Wm. C. Popper & Co.)

	Good	Fine	Mint
nn	7.00	21.00	50.00

TENNIS (For Speed, Stamina, Strength, Skill)
1956 (16 pgs.; soft cover; 10 cents)
Tennis Educational Foundation

	Good	Fine	Mint
Book 1-Endorsed by Gene Tunney, Ralph Kiner, etc. showing how tennis has helped them	1.50	4.50	10.00

TENSE SUSPENSE
Dec, 1958 - No. 2, Feb, 1959
Fago Publications

	Good	Fine	Mint
1,2	1.30	4.00	9.00

TEN STORY LOVE (Formerly a pulp magazine with same title)
V29/3, 6-7/51 - V36/5(#209), 9/56 (#3-6, 52 pgs.)
Ace Periodicals

	Good	Fine	Mint
V29#3(#177)-Part comic, part text	3.00	9.00	21.00
4-6(1/52)	1.50	4.50	10.00
V30#1(3/52)-6(1/53)	1.15	3.50	8.00
V31#1(2/53),V32#2(4/53)-6(12/53)	.85	2.50	6.00
V33#1(1/54)-3(5#54, #195), V34#4(7/54, #196)-6(10/54, #198)	.80	2.40	5.50
V35#1(12/54, #199)-3(4/55, #201)-Last precode	.75	2.25	5.00
V35#4-6(9/55, #201-204), V36#1(11/55, #205)-3, 5(9/56, #209)	.55	1.65	4.00
V36#4-L.B. Cole-a	1.15	3.50	8.00

TEN WHO DARED (See 4-Color No. 1178)

TERRAFORMERS
April, 1987 - Present ($1.95, color)
Wonder Color Comics/Pied Piper No. 3 on

	Good	Fine	Mint
1,2	.35	1.00	2.00

TERRANAUTS
Aug, 1986 - Present ($1.75, color)
Fantasy General Comics

	Good	Fine	Mint
1,2	.30	.85	1.70

TERRIFIC COMICS
Jan, 1944 - No. 6, Nov, 1944
Continental Magazines

	Good	Fine	Mint
1-Kid Terrific; opium story	25.00	75.00	175.00
2-The Boomerang by L.B. Cole & Ed Wheelan's "Comics" McCormick, called the world's No. 1 comic book fan begins; Schomburg-c	21.00	62.00	148.00
3,4: 3-Diana becomes Boomerang's costumed aide	19.00	57.00	132.00
5-The Reckoner begins; Boomerang & Diana by L.B. Cole; Schomburg bondage-c	21.00	62.00	148.00
6-L.B. Cole c/a	22.90	65.00	154.00

NOTE: *L.B. Cole a-1, 2(2), 3-6. **Fuje** a-5, 6. **Rico** a-2.*

TERRIFIC COMICS (Formerly Horrific, Wonder Boy #17 on)
No. 14, Dec, 1954 - No. 16, Mar, 1955
Mystery Publ.(Comic Media)/(Ajax/Farrell)

	Good	Fine	Mint
14-Art swipe/Advs. into Unknown 37; injury-to-eye-c; page-2, panel 5 swiped from Phantom Stranger #4; surrealistic Palais-a; Human Cross story	5.00	15.00	30.00
15,16-No Phantom Lady. 16-Wonder Boy app. (precode)	4.00	12.00	28.00

TERRIFYING TALES
No. 11, Jan, 1953 - No. 15, Apr, 1954
Star Publications

	Good	Fine	Mint
11-Used in **POP**, pgs. 99,100; all Jo-Jo-r	14.00	42.00	100.00
12-All Jo-Jo-r; L.B. Cole splash	11.00	32.00	76.00
13-All Rulah-r; classic devil-c	16.00	48.00	110.00
14-All Rulah reprints	11.00	32.00	76.00
15-Rulah, Zago-r; used in **SOTI**-r/Rulah #22	11.00	32.00	76.00

NOTE: *All issues have **L.B. Cole** covers; bondage covers-No. 12-14.*

TERROR ILLUSTRATED (Adult Tales of . . .)
Nov-Dec, 1955 - No. 2, Spring, 1956 (Magazine)
E.C. Comics

	Good	Fine	Mint
1	5.70	17.00	40.00
2	5.00	15.00	35.00

TERRORS OF THE JUNGLE (Formerly Jungle Thrills)
No. 17, May, 1952 - No. 10, Sept, 1954
Star Publications

	Good	Fine	Mint
17-Reprints Rulah #21, used in **SOTI**; L.B. Cole bondage-c	13.00	40.00	90.00
18-Jo-Jo-r	8.50	25.50	60.00
19,20(1952)-Jo-Jo-r; Disbrow-a	8.00	24.00	56.00
21-Jungle Jo, Tangi-r; used in **POP**, pg. 100 & color illos.	10.00	30.00	70.00
4,6,7-Disbrow-a	8.00	24.00	56.00
5,8,10: All Disbrow-a. 5-Jo-Jo-r. 8-Rulah, Jo-Jo-r. 10-Rulah-r	8.00	24.00	56.00
9-Jo-Jo-r; Disbrow-a; Tangi by Orlando	8.00	24.00	56.00

NOTE: ***L.B. Cole** c-all; bondage c-17, 19, 21, 5, 7.*

TERROR TALES (See Beware Terror Tales)

TERROR TALES (Magazine)
V1#7, 1969 - V6#6, 12/74; V7#1, 4/76 - V10, 1979?
(V1-V6, 52 pgs.; V7 on, 68 pgs.)
Eerie Publications

	Good	Fine	Mint
V1#7	.70	2.00	5.00
V1#8-11('69): 9-Bondage-c	.50	1.50	3.00
V2#1-6('70), V3#1-6('71), V4#1-6('72), V5#1-6('73), V6#1-6('74)	.50	1.50	3.00
V7#1,4(no V7#2), V8#1-3('77), V9, V10	.50	1.50	3.00
V7#3-LSD story-r/Weird V3#5	.50	1.50	3.00

TERRY AND THE PIRATES (See Merry Christmas . . ., Superbook No. 3,5,9,16,28, & Super Comics)

TERRY AND THE PIRATES
1939 - 1953 (By Milton Caniff)
Dell Publishing Co.

	Good	Fine	Mint
Large Feat. Comic 2('39)	37.00	110.00	260.00
Large Feat. Comic 6('39)-1936 dailies	36.00	108.00	252.00
4-Color 9(1940)	37.00	110.00	260.00
Large Feature Comic 27('41), 6('42)	25.00	75.00	175.00
4-Color 44('43)	22.00	65.00	154.00
4-Color 101('45)	14.00	42.00	100.00
Buster Brown Shoes giveaway(1938)-32 pgs.; in color	20.00	60.00	140.00
Canada Dry Premiums-Books No. 1-3(1953-Harvey)-2x5"; 36 pgs.	5.00	15.00	35.00
Family Album(1942)	8.50	25.50	60.00
Gambles Giveaway ('38)-16 pgs.	4.35	13.00	26.00
Gillmore Giveaway('38)-24 pgs.	5.00	15.00	30.00

Tense Suspense #1, © Fago Publ.

Terrifying Tales #11, © STAR

Terrors of the Jungle #10, © STAR

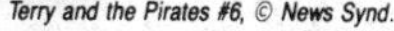
Terry and the Pirates #6, © News Synd.

Tessie the Typist #14, © MCG

Texas Kid #9, © MCG

TERRY AND THE PIRATES (continued) — Good / Fine / Mint
Popped Wheat Giveaway('38)-Reprints in full color; Caniff-a
.85 2.50 5.00
Shoe Store giveaway('38, 16pp, soft-c)(2-diff.) 3.00 9.00 18.00
Sparked Wheat Giveaway('42)-16 pgs. in full color
4.60 14.00 32.00

TERRY AND THE PIRATES
1941 (16 pgs.; regular size)
Libby's Radio Premium

"Adventure of the Ruby of Genghis Khan" - Each pg. is a puzzle that must be completed to read the story 8.50 25.50 60.00

TERRY AND THE PIRATES (Formerly Boy Explorers; Long John Silver & the Pirates #30 on) (Daily strip-r) (Two #26's)
No. 3, 4/47 - No. 26, 4/51; No. 26, 6/55 - No. 28, 10/55
Harvey Publications/Charlton No. 26-28

	Good	Fine	Mint
3(#1)-Boy Explorers by S&K; Terry & the Pirates begin by Caniff	20.00	60.00	140.00
4-S&K Boy Explorers	13.00	40.00	90.00
5-10	7.00	21.00	50.00
11-Man in Black app. by Powell	7.00	21.00	50.00
12-20: 16-Girl threatened with red hot poker	5.35	16.00	37.00
21-26(4/51)-Last Caniff issue	4.75	14.00	33.00
26-28('55)(Formerly This Is Suspense)-Not by Caniff	3.50	10.50	24.00

NOTE: ***Powell** a (Tommy Tween)-5-10,12,14; 15-17(½-2 pgs.).*

TERRY BEARS COMICS (TerryToons, The... #4)
June, 1952 - No. 3, Oct, 1952
St. John Publishing Co.

	Good	Fine	Mint
1-3	1.60	4.70	11.00

TERRY-TOONS COMICS (1st Series) (Becomes Paul Terry's Comics #85 on; later issues titled "Paul Terry's...) (See Giant Comics Ed.)
Oct, 1942 - No. 86, Feb?, 1951 (Two #60s)
Timely/Marvel No. 1-60 (8/47)(Becomes Best Western No. 58 on?, Marvel)/St. John No. 60 (9/47) on

	Good	Fine	Mint
1 (Scarce)	40.00	120.00	280.00
2	20.00	60.00	140.00
3-5	12.00	36.00	84.00
6-10	8.50	25.50	60.00
11-20	5.50	16.50	38.00
21-37	3.70	11.00	26.00
38-Mighty Mouse begins (1st app.)(11/45)	32.00	95.00	225.00
39	11.00	32.00	76.00
40-49: 43-Infinity-c	4.35	13.00	30.00
50-1st app. Heckle & Jeckle	10.00	30.00	70.00
51-60(8/47): 55-Infinity-c. 60(9/47)-Atomic explosion panel	3.50	10.50	24.00
61-84	2.15	6.50	15.00
85,86-Same book as Paul Terry's Comics #85,86 with only a title change	2.15	6.50	15.00

TERRY-TOONS COMICS (2nd Series)
June, 1952 - No. 9, Nov, 1953
St. John Publishing Co./Pines

	Good	Fine	Mint
1	3.70	11.00	26.00
2	2.30	7.00	16.00
3-9	1.70	5.00	12.00
Giant Summer Fun Book 101,102(Summer,'57-Summer,'58)(TV, Tom Terrific app.)	2.00	6.00	14.00

TERRYTOONS, THE TERRY BEARS (Formerly Terry Bears)
No. 4, Summer, 1958
Pines Comics

	Good	Fine	Mint
4	1.15	3.50	8.00

TESSIE THE TYPIST (Tiny Tessie #24; see Gay & Joker Comics)
Summer, 1944 - No. 23, Aug, 1949
Timely/Marvel Comics (20CC)

	Good	Fine	Mint
1-Doc Rockblock & others by Wolverton	19.00	57.00	132.00
2-Wolverton's Powerhouse Pepper	11.00	32.00	76.00
3-No Wolverton	3.50	10.50	24.00
4,5,7,8-Wolverton-a	6.50	20.00	45.00
6-Kurtzman's "Hey Look," 2 pgs. Wolverton	7.00	21.00	50.00
9-Wolverton's Powerhouse Pepper (8 pgs.) & Kurtzman's "Hey Look" (1)	8.00	24.00	56.00
10-4 pgs. Wolverton's Powerhouse Pepper	6.50	20.00	45.00
11-8 pgs. Wolverton's Powerhouse Pepper	8.00	24.00	56.00
12-4 pgs. Wolverton's Powerhouse Pepper & 1 pg. Kurtzman's "Hey Look"	6.50	20.00	45.00
13-4 pgs. Wolverton's Powerhouse Pepper	6.00	18.00	42.00
14-1 pg. Wolverton's Dr. Whackyhack, 1½ pgs. Kurtzman's "Hey Look"	4.35	13.00	30.00
15-3 pgs. Kurtzman's "Hey Look" & 3 pgs. Giggles 'n' Grins	4.35	13.00	30.00
16-18-Kurtzman's "Hey Look" (?, 2 & 1)	3.35	10.00	23.00
19-Eight pg. Annie Oakley	2.15	6.50	15.00
20-23: 20-Anti-Wertham editorial (2/49)	1.70	5.00	11.50

NOTE: *Lana app.-21. Millie The Model app.-13,15,17,21. Rusty app.-10,11,13,15,17.*

TEXAN, THE (Fightin' Marines #15 on; Fightin' Texan #16 on)
Aug, 1948 - No. 15, Oct, 1951
St. John Publishing Co.

	Good	Fine	Mint
1-Buckskin Belle	5.70	17.00	40.00
2	3.00	9.00	21.00
3,5,10: 10-Over-sized issue	2.35	7.00	16.00
4,7,15-Baker c/a	5.00	15.00	35.00
6,9-Baker-c	3.00	9.00	21.00
8,11,13,14-Baker c/a(2-3) each	5.00	15.00	35.00
12-All Matt Baker; Peyote story	6.00	18.00	42.00

NOTE: ***Matt Baker** c-6-15. **Larsen** a-6, 8. **Tuska** a-1, 2, 8.*

TEXAN, THE (See 4-Color No. 1027,1096)

TEXAS JOHN SLAUGHTER (See 4-Color #997,1181 & W. Disney Presents #2)

TEXAS KID (See Two-Gun Western, Wild Western)
Jan, 1951 - No. 10, July, 1952
Marvel/Atlas Comics (LMC)

	Good	Fine	Mint
1-Origin; Texas Kid (alias Lance Temple) & his horse Thunder begin; Tuska-a	5.00	15.00	35.00
2	2.30	7.00	16.00
3-10	2.00	6.00	14.00

NOTE: ***Maneely** a-1-4 c-3, 5-10.*

TEXAS RANGERS, THE (See Superior Stories No. 4 and Jace Pearson of...)

TEXAS RANGERS IN ACTION (Formerly Captain Gallant or Scotland Yard?) (See Blue Bird Comics)
No. 5, July, 1956 - No. 79, Aug, 1970
Charlton Comics

	Good	Fine	Mint
5	2.00	6.00	14.00
6-10	1.00	3.00	7.00
11-Williamson-a(5,5,&8 pgs.); Torres-a	4.35	13.00	30.00
12,14-20	.55	1.65	4.00
13-Williamson-a, 5 pgs; Torres-a	3.35	10.00	23.00
21-30: 30-Last 10 cent ish?	.45	1.35	3.00
31-59	.25	.80	1.60
60-Rileys Rangers begin		.40	.80
61-70: 65-1st app. The Man Called Loco, origin-#67		.30	.60
71-79		.25	.50
76(Modern Comics-r, 1977)		.15	.30

TEXAS SLIM (See A-1 Comics No. 2-8,10)

TEX DAWSON, GUN-SLINGER (Gunslinger #2 on)
January, 1973
Marvel Comics Group

	Good	Fine	Mint
1-Steranko-c; Williamson-a(r); Tex Dawson-r		.30	.60

TEX FARNUM (See Wisco)

TEX FARRELL
Mar-Apr, 1948
D. S. Publishing Co.

	Good	Fine	Mint
1-Tex Farrell & his horse Lightning begin; Shelly-c	4.60	14.00	32.00

TEX GRANGER (Formerly Calling All Boys)
No. 18, June, 1948 - No. 24, Sept, 1949
Parents' Magazine Institute/Commended

	Good	Fine	Mint
18-Tex Granger & his horse Bullet begin	3.50	10.50	24.00
19	2.30	7.00	16.00
20-24	1.70	5.00	12.00

TEX MORGAN (See Blaze Carson, Wild Western)
Aug, 1948 - No. 9, Feb, 1950
Marvel Comics (CCC)

	Good	Fine	Mint
1-Tex Morgan, his horse Lightning & sidekick Lobo begin	8.00	24.00	56.00
2	5.70	17.00	40.00
3-6: 4-Arizona Annie app.	4.00	12.00	28.00
7-9: All photo-c. 7-Captain Tootsie by Beck. 8-18pg. story "The Terror of Rimrock Valley;" Diablo app.	5.70	17.00	40.00

NOTE: *Tex Taylor app.-6,7,9.*

TEX RITTER WESTERN (Movie star; singing cowboy; see Six-Gun Heroes, Western Hero)
Oct, 1950 - No. 46, May, 1959 (Photo-c, 1-21)
Fawcett No. 1-20 (1/54)/Charlton No. 21 on

	Good	Fine	Mint
1-Tex Ritter, his stallion White Flash & dog Fury begin; photo front/back-c begin	22.00	65.00	154.00
2	13.00	40.00	90.00
3-5: 5-Last photo back-c	11.00	32.00	76.00
6-10	9.00	27.00	62.00
11-19	5.70	17.00	40.00
20-Last Fawcett issue (1/54)	6.50	19.50	45.00
21-1st Charlton issue; photo-c (3/54)	6.50	19.50	45.00
22	3.50	10.50	24.00
23-30: 23-25-Young Falcon app.	2.65	8.00	18.00
31-38,40-45	2.15	6.50	15.00
39-Williamson-c/a (1/58)	4.35	13.00	30.00
46-Last issue	2.65	8.00	18.00

NOTE: *B&W photo back-c No. 23-32.*

TEX TAYLOR (See Blaze Carson, Kid Colt, Tex Morgan, Wild West, Wild Western, & Wisco)
Sept, 1948 - No. 9, March, 1950
Marvel Comics (HPC)

	Good	Fine	Mint
1-Tex Taylor & his horse Fury begin	8.00	24.00	56.00
2	5.70	17.00	40.00
3	4.00	12.00	28.00
4-6: All photo-c. 4-Anti-Wertham editorial. 5,6-Blaze Carson app.	4.35	13.00	30.00
7-Photo-c; 18pg. Movie-Length Thriller "Trapped in Time's Lost Land!" with sabre toothed tigers, dinosaurs; Diablo app.	5.70	17.00	40.00
8-Photo-c; 18pg. Movie-Length Thriller "The Mystery of Devil-Tree Plateau!" with dwarf horses, dwarf people & a lost miniature Inca type village; Diablo app.	5.70	17.00	40.00
9-Photo-c; 18pg. Movie-Length Thriller "Guns Along the Border!" Captain Tootsie by Schreiber; Nimo The Mountain Lion app.	5.70	17.00	40.00

THANE OF BAGARTH
No. 24, Oct, 1985 - No. 25, Dec, 1985
Charlton Comics

	Good	Fine	Mint
24,25		.40	.80

THAT'S MY POP! GOES NUTS FOR FAIR
1939 (76 pages) (B&W)
Bystander Press

	Good	Fine	Mint
nn-by Milt Gross	6.50	19.50	45.00

THAT DARN CAT (See Movie Comics & Walt Disney Showcase No.19)

THAT THE WORLD MAY BELIEVE
No date (16 pgs.) (Graymoor Friars distr.)
Catechetical Guild Giveaway

	Good	Fine	Mint
	1.70	5.00	10.00

THAT WILKIN BOY (Meet Bingo. . .)
Jan, 1969 - No. 52, Oct, 1982
Archie Publications

	Good	Fine	Mint
1	1.35	4.00	8.00
2-10	.70	2.00	4.00
11-26 (last Giant issue)	.35	1.00	2.00
27-52		.50	1.00

T.H.E. CAT (TV)
Mar, 1967 - No. 4, Oct, 1967 (All have photo-c)
Dell Publishing Co.

	Good	Fine	Mint
1	1.50	4.50	10.00
2-4	1.00	3.00	7.00

THERE'S A NEW WORLD COMING
1973 (35-49 Cents)
Spire Christian Comics/Fleming H. Revell Co.

	Good	Fine	Mint
		.50	1.00

THEY ALL KISSED THE BRIDE (See Cinema Comics Herald)

THEY RING THE BELL
1946
Fox Feature Syndicate

	Good	Fine	Mint
1	5.70	17.00	40.00

THIEF OF BAGHDAD (See 4-Color No. 1229)

THIMBLE THEATRE STARRING POPEYE
1931, 1932 (52 pgs.; 25 cents; B&W)
Sonnet Publishing Co.

	Good	Fine	Mint
1-Daily strip serial reprints in both by Segar	45.00	135.00	315.00
2	40.00	120.00	280.00

NOTE: *Probably the first Popeye reprint book. Popeye first entered Thimble Theatre in 1929.*

THIMK (Magazine) (Satire)
May, 1958 - No. 6, May, 1959
Counterpart

	Good	Fine	Mint
1	2.00	6.00	14.00
2-6	1.15	3.50	8.00

THING!, THE (Blue Beetle #18 on)
Feb, 1952 - No. 17, Nov, 1954
Song Hits No. 1,2/Capitol Stories/Charlton

	Good	Fine	Mint
1	17.00	51.00	120.00
2,3	13.00	40.00	90.00
4-6,8,10	11.00	32.00	76.00
7-Injury to eye-c & inside panel. E.C. swipes from VOH #28	20.00	60.00	140.00
9-Used in **SOTI**, pg. 388 & illo-"Stomping on the face is a form of brutality which modern children learn early"	23.00	70.00	160.00

11-Necronomicon story; Hansel & Gretel parody; Injury-to-eye panel;

Tex Morgan #8, © MCG

Tex Ritter Western #7, © CC

The Thing! #3, © CC

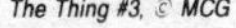
The Thing #3, © MCG

This Magazine Is Haunted #7, © CC

Thor #270, © MCG

THE THING! (continued)	Good	Fine	Mint
Check-a	17.00	51.00	120.00
12-"Cinderella" parody; Ditko-c/a; lingerie panels	29.00	87.00	200.00
13,15-Ditko c/a(3 & 5); 13-Ditko E.C. swipe/HOF #15/1-"House of Horror"	29.00	87.00	200.00
14-Extreme violence/torture; Rumpelstiltskin story; Ditko c/a(4)	29.00	87.00	200.00
16-Injury to eye panel	14.50	43.50	100.00
17-Ditko-c; classic parody-"Through the Looking Glass;" Powell-a(r)	23.00	70.00	160.00

NOTE: *Excessive violence, severed heads, injury to eye are common No. 5 on.*

THING, THE (Also see Marvel Fanfare & Marvel Two-In-One)
July, 1983 - No. 36, June, 1986
Marvel Comics Group

	Good	Fine	Mint
1-Byrne scripts 1-13,18 on; life story of Ben Grimm		.60	1.20
2-10		.45	.90
11-36		.40	.80

NOTE: ***Byrne** a-2i, 7; c-1, 7.*

THIRTEEN (. . .Going on 18)
11-1/61-62 - No. 25, 12/67; No. 26, 7/69 - No. 29, 1/71
Dell Publishing Co.

	Good	Fine	Mint
1	3.50	10.50	24.00
2-10	2.65	8.00	18.00
11-29: 26-29-r	2.00	6.00	14.00

NOTE: ***John Stanley** script-No. 3-29; art?*

THIRTY SECONDS OVER TOKYO (Also see Guadacanal Diary)
1943 (Movie) (Also see American Library)
David McKay Co.

	Good	Fine	Mint
nn(B&W, text & pictures)	14.00	42.00	100.00

THIS IS SUSPENSE! (Formerly Strange Suspense Stories; Strange Suspense Stories #27 on)
No. 23, Feb, 1955 - No. 26, Aug, 1955
Charlton Comics

	Good	Fine	Mint
23-Wood-a(r)/A Star Presentation #3-"Dr. Jekyll & Mr. Hyde"	9.50	28.50	65.00
24-Evans-a	3.50	10.50	24.00
25,26	1.85	5.50	13.00

THIS IS THE PAYOFF (See Pay-Off)

THIS IS WAR
No. 5, July, 1952 - No. 9, May, 1953
Standard Comics

	Good	Fine	Mint
5-Toth-a	5.00	15.00	35.00
6,9-Toth-a	4.00	12.00	28.00
7,8	1.20	3.50	8.00

THIS IS YOUR LIFE, DONALD DUCK (See 4-Color No. 1109)

THIS MAGAZINE IS CRAZY (Crazy V3#3 on)
V3#2, July, 1957 (68 pgs.) (25 cents) (Satire)
Charlton Publ. (Humor Magazines)

	Good	Fine	Mint
V3#2	1.00	3.00	6.00

THIS MAGAZINE IS HAUNTED (Danger and Adventure #22 on)
Oct, 1951 - No. 14, 12/53; No. 15, 2/54 - V3/21, Nov, 1954
Fawcett Publications/Charlton No. 15(2/54) on

	Good	Fine	Mint
1-Evans-a(i?)	13.00	40.00	90.00
2,5-Evans-a	9.50	28.50	65.00
3,4	5.00	15.00	35.00
6-9,11,12,14	4.00	12.00	28.00
10-Severed head-c	6.00	18.00	42.00
13-Severed head story	5.50	16.50	38.00
15,20	3.50	10.50	24.00
16,19-Ditko-c. 19-Injury-to-eye panel; story r-/#1	8.50	25.50	60.00
17-Ditko-c/a(3); blood drainage story	13.00	40.00	90.00
18-Ditko-c/a; E.C. swipe/Haunt of Fear 5; injury-to-eye panel	11.00	32.00	76.00
21-Ditko-c, Evans-a	8.50	25.50	60.00

NOTE: ***Bailey** a-1, 3, 4, 21r/No.1. **Powell** a-3-5, 11, 12, 17. **Shuster** a-18-20.*

THIS MAGAZINE IS HAUNTED (2nd Series) (Formerly Zaza the Mystic; Outer Space #17 on)
V2No.12, July, 1957 - V2No.16, April, 1958
Charlton Comics

	Good	Fine	Mint
V2#12-14-Ditko c/a in all	9.50	28.50	65.00
15-No Ditko-c/a	1.30	4.00	9.00
16-Ditko-a	6.00	18.00	42.00

THIS MAGAZINE IS WILD (See Wild)

THIS WAS YOUR LIFE (Religious)
1964 (3½x5½") (40 pgs.) (Black, white & red)
Jack T. Chick Publ.

	Good	Fine	Mint
		.40	.80
Another version (5x2¾", 26pgs.)		.60	1.20

THOR (Formerly Journey Into Mystery)(Also see Marvel Preview, Marvel Spec., Marvel Treas. Ed., Spec. Marv. Ed. & Tales of Asgard)
March, 1966 - Present
Marvel Comics Group

	Good	Fine	Mint
126	.85	2.50	5.00
127-133,135-140	.50	1.50	3.00
134-Intro High Evolutionary	.85	2.50	5.00
141-145,150: 146-Inhumans begin, end #151	.35	1.00	2.00
146,147-Origin The Inhumans	.40	1.20	2.40
148,149-Origin Black Bolt in each; 149-Origin Medusa, Crystal, Maximus, Gorgon, Kornak	.35	1.00	2.00
151-157,159,160	.35	1.00	2.00
158-Origin-r/No. 83; origin Dr. Blake, concludes #159	.50	1.50	3.00
161,163,164,167,170-179-Last Kirby issue	.35	1.00	2.00
162,168,169-Origin Galactus	.35	1.10	2.20
165,166-Warlock(Him) app.	.50	1.50	3.00
180,181-Adams-a	.70	2.00	4.00
182-192,194-199	.25	.75	1.50
193-(52 pgs.); Silver Surfer x-over	.85	2.50	5.00
200	.45	1.25	2.50
201-226: 225-Intro. Firelord		.50	1.00
227-299: 294-Origin Asgard & Odin		.40	.80
300-End of Asgard; origin of Odin & The Destroyer	.25	.75	1.50
301-336		.40	.80
337-Simonson-a; Beta Ray Bill becomes new Thor	1.00	3.00	6.00
338	.40	1.25	2.50
339,340: 340-Donald Blake returns as Thor	.25	.75	1.50
341-350		.50	1.00
351-373,375-381: 373-X-Factor tie-in		.50	1.00
374-Mutant massacre; X-Factor app.	.50	1.50	3.00
382-Anniversary issue ($1.25)	.25	.70	1.40
383,385-390		.40	.80
384-Intro. new Thor	.35	1.00	2.00
Giant-Size 1('75)		.50	1.00
Special 2(9/66)-See Journey Into Myst. for 1st annual	.35	1.00	2.00
Special 3,4('67-12/71)	.35	1.00	2.00
Annual 5(11/76)		.50	1.00
Annual 6(10/77), 7(9/78), 8(11/79)		.40	.80
Annual 9(11/81), 10(11/82), 11(11/83)		.40	.80

THOR (continued) — Good / Fine / Mint

Annual 12(11/84) .40 .80
Annual 13(12/85) .65 1.30

NOTE: ***Adams*** *c-179-181.* ***Austin*** *a-342i, 346i; c-312i.* ***Buscema*** *a(p)-178, 182-213, 215-226, 231-238, 241-253, 254r, 256-259, 272-278, 283-285, 370, Annual 6, 8; c(p)-175, 182-196, 198-200, 202-204, 206, 211, 212, 215, 219, 221, 226, 256, 259, 261, 262, 272-278, 283, 289, 370, Annual 6.* ***Everett*** *a(i)-143, 170-175; c(i)-171, 172, 174, 176, 241.* ***Gil Kane*** *a-318p; c(p)-201, 205, 207-10, 216, 220, 222, 223, 231, 233-40, 242, 243, 318.* ***Kirby*** *a(p)-126-177, 179, 194, 254r; c(p)-126-169, 171-174, 176, 177, 178, 249-253, 255, 257, 258, Annual 5, Special 1-4.* ***Mooney*** *a(i)-201, 204, 214-16, 218, 322i, 324i, 325i, 327i.* ***Simonson*** *a-260-71p, 337-54, 357-367, 380, Annual 7p; c-260, 263-71, 337-55, 357-369, 371, 373-382, Annual 7.* ***Starlin*** *c-213.*

THOSE MAGNIFICENT MEN IN THEIR FLYING MACHINES (See Movie Comics)

THREE CABALLEROS (See 4-Color No. 71)

THREE CHIPMUNKS, THE (See 4-Color No. 1042)

THREE COMICS (Also see Spiritman)
1944 (10 cents, 48pgs.) (2 different covers exist)
The Penny King Co.

1,3,4-Lady Luck, Mr. Mystic, The Spirit app. (3 Spirit sections bound together)-Lou Fine-a 13.00 40.00 90.00

NOTE: *No. 1 contains Spirit Sections 4/9/44 - 4/23/44, and No. 4 is also from 4/44.*

3-D (NOTE: The prices of all the 3-D comics listed include glasses. Deduct 40-50 percent if glasses are missing, and reduce slightly if glasses are loose.)

3-D ACTION
Jan, 1954 (Oversized) (15 cents)
Atlas Comics (ACI)

1-Battle Brady 19.00 57.00 132.00

3-D ADVENTURE COMICS
Aug, 1986 (One shot)
Stats, Etc.

1-Promo material .25 .75 1.50

3-D ALIEN TERROR
June, 1986
Eclipse Comics

1-Morrow-a; Old Witch, Crypt-Keeper, Vault Keeper cameo .45 1.25 2.50
...in 2-D: 100 copies signed & numbered (B&W) .85 2.50 5.00

3-D ANIMAL FUN (See Animal Fun)

3-D BATMAN
1953, Reprinted in 1966
National Periodical Publications

1953-Reprints Batman #42 & 48; Tommy Tomorrow app. 47.00 141.00 330.00
1966-Tommy Tomorrow app. 11.50 34.00 80.00

3-D CIRCUS
1953 (25 cents)
Fiction House Magazines

1 19.00 57.00 132.00

3-D COMICS (See Tor, 3-D, and Mighty Mouse)

3-D DOLLY
December, 1953
Harvey Publications

1-Richie Rich story redrawn from his 1st app. in Little Dot #1 11.50 34.50 80.00

3-D-ELL
1953 (3-D comics) (25 cents)
Dell Publishing Co.

1,2-Rootie Kazootie 18.00 54.00 125.00
3-Flukey Luke 17.00 51.00 120.00

3-D FEATURES PRESENT JET PUP
Oct-Dec, 1953
Dimensions Public — Good / Fine / Mint

1-Irving Spector-a(2) 19.00 57.00 132.00

3-D FUNNY MOVIES
1953 (25 cents)
Comic Media

1 18.00 54.00 125.00

3-D HEROES (Blackthorne 3-D series #3)
Feb, 1986 ($2.25)
Blackthorne Publishing, Inc.

1 1.25 2.50

THREE-DIMENSION ADVENTURES (Superman)
1953 (Large size)
National Periodical Publications

Origin Superman (new art) 55.00 165.00 385.00

THREE DIMENSIONAL ALIEN WORLDS (See Alien Worlds)
July, 1984 (One-Shot)
Pacific Comics

1-Bolton/Stevens, Art Adams-a .85 2.50 5.00

THREE DIMENSIONAL DNAGENTS (See New DNAgents)

THREE DIMENSIONAL E. C. CLASSICS (Three Dimensional Tales From the Crypt No. 2)
Spring, 1954 (Prices include glasses)
E. C. Comics

1-Reprints: Wood (Mad #3), Krigstein (W.S. #7), Evans (F.C. #13), & Ingels (CSS #5); Kurtzman-c 33.00 100.00 230.00

NOTE: *Stories redrawn to 3-D format. Original stories not necessarily by artists listed. CSS: Crime SuspenStories; F.C.: Frontline Combat; W.S.: Weird Science.*

THREE DIMENSIONAL TALES FROM THE CRYPT (Formerly Three Dimensional E. C. Classics)
Spring, 1954 (Prices include glasses)
E. C. Comics

2-Davis (TFTC #25), Elder (VOH #14), Craig (TFTC #24), & Orlando (TFTC #22) stories; Feldstein-c 35.00 105.00 245.00

NOTE: *Stories redrawn to 3-D format. Original stories not necessarily by artists listed. TFTC: Tales From the Crypt; VOH: Vault of Horror.*

3-D LOVE
December, 1953 (25 cents)
Steriographic Publ. (Mikeross Publ.)

1 19.00 57.00 132.00

3-D NOODNICK (See Noodnick)

3-D ROMANCE
January, 1954 (25 cents)
Steriographic Publ. (Mikeross Publ.)

1 19.00 57.00 132.00

3-D SHEENA, JUNGLE QUEEN
1953
Fiction House Magazines

1 32.00 95.00 225.00

3-D TALES OF THE WEST
Jan, 1954 (Oversized) (15 cents)
Atlas Comics (CPS)

1 (3-D) 19.00 57.00 132.00

3-D THREE STOOGES (Also see Three Stooges)
Sept, 1986 - Present ($2.50)
Eclipse Comics

1-3 .60 1.80 3.60
1,2 (2-D) .85 2.50 5.00

3-D Alien Terror #1, © Eclipse Comics

3-D Circus #1, © FH

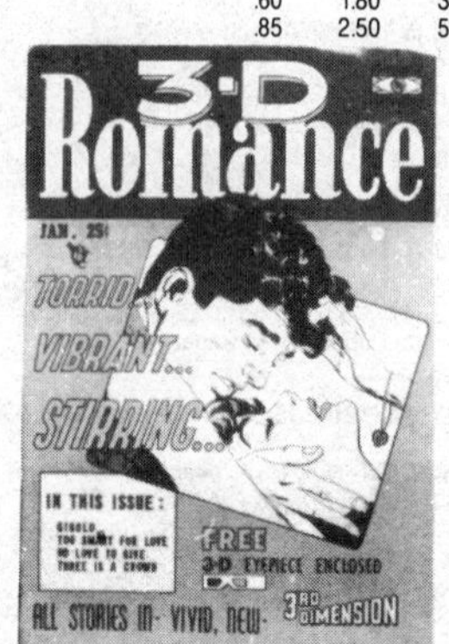

3-D Romance #1, © Steriographic Publ.

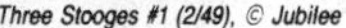
Three Stooges #1 (2/49), © Jubilee

Thriller #4, © DC

Thrilling Comics #14, © STD

3-D WHACK (See Whack)

3-D ZONE
Feb, 1987 - Present ($2.50)
The 3-D Zone(Renegade Press)

	Good	Fine	Mint
1-6: 1-r-/A Star Presentation, 2-Wolverton-r, 3-Picture Scope Jungle Advs., 4-Electric Fear, 5-Krazy Kat-r, 6-Ratfink,	.40	1.25	2.50
7-10: 7-Hollywood 3-D; Jayne Mansfield photo-c, 8-High Seas 3-D, 9-Redmask-r, 10-Jet 3-D; Powell & Williamson-r	.40	1.25	2.50

3 FUNMAKERS, THE
1908 (64 pgs.) (10x15")
Stokes and Company

Maude, Katzenjammer Kids, Happy Hooligan (1904-06 Sunday strip reprints in color)	24.00	72.00	170.00

3 LITTLE PIGS (See 4-Color No. 218)

3 LITTLE PIGS, THE (See Walt Disney Showcase #15,21)
May, 1964 - No. 2, Sept, 1968 (Walt Disney)
Gold Key

1-Reprints 4-Color 218	1.00	3.00	7.00
2	.75	2.25	5.00

THREE MOUSEKETEERS, THE (1st Series)
3-4/56 - No. 24, 9-10/59; No. 25, 8-9/60 - No. 26, 10-12/60
National Periodical Publications

1	6.00	18.00	42.00
2	3.50	10.50	24.00
3-10	2.65	8.00	18.00
11-26	1.70	5.00	12.00

NOTE: ***Rube Grossman** a-1-26. **Sheldon Mayer** a-1-8; c-1,3,4,6,7.*

THREE MOUSEKETEERS, THE (2nd Series) (See Super DC Giant)
May-June, 1970 - No. 7, May-June, 1971
National Periodical Publications

1-Mayer-a	.25	.75	1.50
2-7-Mayer-a (68 pgs. #5-7)		.30	.60

THREE NURSES (Formerly Confidential Diary; Career Girl Romances #24 on)
V3#18, May, 1963 - V3#23, Mar, 1964
Charlton Comics

V3#18-23		.50	1.00

THREE RASCALS
1958; 1963
I. W. Enterprises

I.W. Reprint #1 (Says Super Comics on inside)-(M.E.'s Clubhouse Rascals), #2('58)	.30	.80	1.60
10('63)-Reprints #1	.30	.80	1.60

THREE RING COMICS
March, 1945
Spotlight Publishers

1	2.65	8.00	18.00

THREE ROCKETEERS (See Blast-Off)

THREE STOOGES (See Comic Album No. 18, The Little Stooges, March of Comics No. 232, 248, 268, 280, 292, 304, 316, 336, 373, Movie Classics & Comics, & 3-D Three Stooges)

THREE STOOGES
Feb, 1949 - No. 2, May, 1949; Sept, 1953 - No. 7, Oct, 1954
Jubilee No. 1,2/St. John No. 1 (9/53) on

	Good	Fine	Mint
1-(Scarce, 1949)-Kubert-a; infinity-c	40.00	120.00	280.00
2-(Scarce)-Kubert, Maurer-a	32.00	95.00	225.00
1(9/53)-Hollywood Stunt Girl by Kubert, 7 pgs.	28.00	84.00	195.00
2(3-D, 10/53)-Stunt Girl story by Kubert	20.00	60.00	140.00
3(3-D, 11/53)	17.00	51.00	120.00
4(3/54)-7(10/54)	10.00	30.00	70.00

NOTE: *All issues have **Kubert-Maurer** art.*

THREE STOOGES
No. 1043, Oct-Dec, 1959 - No. 55, June, 1972
Dell Publishing Co./Gold Key No. 10 (10/62) on

4-Color 1043 (#1)	5.00	15.00	35.00
4-Color 1078,1127,1170,1187	3.50	10.50	24.00
6(9-11/61) - 10: 6-Professor Putter begins; ends #16	2.65	8.00	18.00
11-14,16-20: 17-The Little Monsters begin (5/64)(1st app.?)	3.00	9.00	21.00
15-Go Around the World in a Daze (movie scenes)	3.50	10.50	24.00
21,23-30	1.70	5.00	12.00
22-Movie scenes/'The Outlaws Is Coming'	3.50	10.50	24.00
31-55	1.50	4.50	10.00

NOTE: *All Four Colors, 6-50,52-55 have photo-c.*

3 WORLDS OF GULLIVER (See 4-Color No. 1158)

THRILL COMICS (See Flash Comics, Fawcett)

THRILLER
Nov, 1983 - No. 12, Nov, 1984 ($1.25; Baxter paper)
DC Comics

1-Intro Seven Seconds		.50	1.00
2-10: 2-Origin. 5,6-Elvis satire		.50	1.00
11,12 ($2.00; 52 pgs.)		.50	1.00

THRILLING ADVENTURES IN STAMPS COMICS
Jan, 1953 (25 cents) (100 pages) (Formerly Stamp Comics)
Stamp Comics, Inc. (Very Rare)

V1#8-Harrison, Wildey, Kiefer, Napoli-a	12.00	36.00	84.00

THRILLING ADVENTURE STORIES
Feb, 1975 - No. 2, July-Aug, 1975 (B&W) (68 pgs.)
Atlas/Seaboard Publ.

1-Tigerman, Kromag the Killer begin; Heath, Thorne-a	.40	1.20	2.40
2-Toth, Severin, Simonson-a; Adams-c	.40	1.20	2.40

THRILLING COMICS
Feb, 1940 - No. 80, April, 1951
Better Publ./Nedor/Standard Comics

1-Origin Doc Strange (37 pgs.); Nickie Norton of the Secret Service begins	53.00	160.00	370.00
2-The Rio Kid, The Woman in Red, Pinocchio begins	24.00	72.00	168.00
3-The Ghost & Lone Eagle begin	22.00	65.00	154.00
4-10	14.00	42.00	100.00
11-18,20	11.00	32.00	76.00
19-Origin The American Crusader, ends #39,41	16.00	48.00	110.00
21-30: 24-Intro. Mike, Doc Strange's sidekick. 29-Last Rio Kid	9.50	28.50	65.00
31-40: 36-Commando Cubs begin	7.00	21.00	50.00
41-52: 41-Hitler bondage-c. 52-The Ghost ends	5.70	17.00	40.00
53-The Phantom Detective begins; The Cavalier app.; no Commando Cubs	5.70	17.00	40.00
54-The Cavalier app.; no Commando Cubs	5.70	17.00	40.00
55-Lone Eagle ends	5.70	17.00	40.00
56-Princess Pantha begins	11.50	34.00	80.00
57-60	11.00	32.00	76.00
61-65: 61-Ingels-a; The Lone Eagle app. 65-Last Phantom Detective & Commando Cubs	11.50	34.00	80.00

THRILLING COMICS (continued)

	Good	Fine	Mint
66-Frazetta text illo	10.00	30.00	70.00
67,70-73: Frazetta-a(5-7 pgs.) in each. 72-Sea Eagle app.	17.00	51.00	120.00
68,69-Frazetta-a(2), 8 & 6 pgs.; 9 & 7 pgs.	18.00	54.00	125.00
74-Last Princess Pantha; Tara app.	5.50	16.50	38.00
75-78: 75-Western format begins	3.00	9.00	21.00
79-Krigstein-a	4.60	14.00	32.00
80-Severin & Elder, Celardo, Moreira-a	4.60	14.00	32.00

NOTE: *Bondage c-5, 9, 13, 20, 22, 27-30, 38, 41, 52, 54.* ***Kinstler*** *a-45, 48.* ***Leo Morey*** *a-7.* ***Schomburg (Xela)*** *c-No. 36-71; airbrush 62-71. Woman in Red not in No. 19, 23, 31-33, 39-45. No. 72 exists as a Canadian reprint with no Frazetta story.*

THRILLING CRIME CASES (Shocking Mystery Cases #50 on)
No. 41, June-July, 1950 - No. 49, 1952
Star Publications

	Good	Fine	Mint
41	4.75	14.25	33.00
42-44-Chameleon story-Fox-r	4.35	13.00	30.00
45-48: 47-Used in **POP**, pg. 84	4.00	12.00	28.00
49-Classic L. B. Cole-c	11.00	32.00	76.00

NOTE: *All have* ***L. B. Cole-c****; a-43p, 45p, 46p, 49(2pgs.).* ***Disbrow*** *a-48.* ***Hollingsworth*** *a-48.*

THRILLING ROMANCES
No. 5, Dec, 1949 - No. 26, June, 1954
Standard Comics

	Good	Fine	Mint
5	3.50	10.50	24.00
6,8	1.70	5.00	12.00
7-Severin/Elder-a, 7 pgs.	3.00	9.00	21.00
9,10-Severin/Elder-a	2.35	7.00	16.00
11,14-21,26	1.15	3.50	8.00
12-Wood-a, 2 pgs.; photo-c	4.35	13.00	30.00
13-Severin-a	2.00	6.00	14.00
22-25-Toth-a	3.70	11.00	26.00

NOTE: *All photo-c.* ***Celardo*** *a-9,16.* ***Colletta*** *a-23, 24(2).* ***Tuska*** *a-9.*

THRILLING TRUE STORY OF THE BASEBALL GIANTS
1952 (2nd issue titled . . . Baseball Yankees)
Fawcett Publications

	Good	Fine	Mint
Each. . . . (photo-c)	20.00	60.00	140.00

THRILLOGY
Jan, 1984 (One-shot)
Pacific Comics

	Good	Fine	Mint
1-Conrad c/a		.50	1.00

THRILL-O-RAMA
Oct, 1965 - No. 3, Dec, 1966
Harvey Publications (Fun Films)

	Good	Fine	Mint
1-Fate (Man in Black) by Powell app.; Doug Wildey-a; Simon-c	.85	2.50	6.00
2-Pirana begins; Williamson 2 pgs.; Fate (Man in Black) app.; Tuska/Simon-c	.85	2.50	6.00
3-Fate (Man in Black) app.; Sparling-c	.50	1.50	3.00

THRILLS OF TOMORROW (Formerly Tomb of Terror)
No. 17, Oct, 1954 - No. 20, April, 1955
Harvey Publications

	Good	Fine	Mint
17-Powell-a (horror); r/Witches Tales #7.	2.35	7.00	16.00
18-Powell-a (horror); r/Tomb of Terror #1	2.00	6.00	14.00
19,20-Stuntman by S&K (r/from Stuntman 1 & 2); 19 has origin & is last pre-code (2/55)	13.50	40.50	95.00

NOTE: ***Palais*** *a-17.*

THROBBING LOVE (See Fox Giants)

THROUGH GATES OF SPLENDOR
1973, 1974 (36 pages) (39-49 cents)
Spire Christian Comics (Fleming H. Revell Co.)

	Good	Fine	Mint
nn		.40	.80

THUMPER (See 4-Color No. 19 & 243)

THUN'DA
1952 - 1953
Magazine Enterprises

	Good	Fine	Mint
1(A-1 47)-Origin; Frazetta c/a; only comic done entirely by Frazetta; Cave Girl app.	100.00	300.00	700.00
2(A-1 56)	12.00	36.00	84.00
3(A-1 73), 4(A-1 78)	9.00	27.00	62.00
5(A-1 83), 6(A-1 86)	8.00	24.00	56.00

NOTE: ***Powell*** *c/a-2-6.*

THUN'DA TALES
1987 (one shot, color, $2.00)
Fantagraphics Books

	Good	Fine	Mint
1	.35	1.00	2.00

THUNDER AGENTS
11/65 - No. 17, 12/67; No. 18, 9/68, No. 19, 11/68, No. 20, 11/69 (No. 1-16: 68 pgs.; No. 17 on: 52 pgs.)
Tower Comics

	Good	Fine	Mint
1-Origin & 1st app. Dynamo, Noman, Menthor, & The Thunder Squad; 1st app. The Iron Maiden	4.35	13.00	30.00
2-Death of Egghead	2.00	6.00	14.00
3-5: 4-Guy Gilbert becomes Lightning who joins Thunder Squad; Iron Maiden app.	1.50	4.50	10.00
6-10: 7-Death of Menthor. 8-Origin & 1st app. The Raven	1.00	3.00	6.00
11-15: 13-Undersea Agent app.; no Raven sty	.85	2.50	5.00
16-19	.60	1.75	3.50
20-All reprints	.40	1.25	2.50

NOTE: ***Crandall*** *a-1, 4p, 5p, 18, 20r; c-18.* ***Ditko*** *a-6, 7p, 12p, 13, 14p, 16, 18.* ***Kane*** *a-1, 5p, 6p, 14, 16p; c-14, 15.* ***Tuska*** *a-1p, 7, 8, 10, 13-17, 19.* ***Whitney*** *a-9p, 10, 13, 15, 17, 18; c-17.* ***Wood*** *a-1-11,(w/Ditko-12,18), (inks-No. 9, 13, 14, 16, 17), 19i, 20r; c-1-8, 9i, 10-13(No. 10* ***w/Williamson****(p)), 16.*

T.H.U.N.D.E.R. AGENTS (See Wally Wood's. . ., Hall of Fame Featuring the. . . & JCP Features)
May, 1983 - No. 2, Jan, 1984
JC Comics (Archie Publications)

	Good	Fine	Mint
1,2-New material	.35	1.00	2.00

THUNDER BIRDS (See Cinema Comics Herald)

THUNDERBOLT (See The Atomic. . .)

THUNDERBOLT (Peter Cannon. . .) (Formerly Son of Vulcan #50)
Jan, 1966; No. 51, Mar-Apr, 1966 - No. 60, Nov, 1967
Charlton Comics

	Good	Fine	Mint
1-Origin	.50	1.50	3.00
51	.30	.80	1.60
52-58: 54-Sentinels begin. 58-Last Thunderbolt & Sentinels		.60	1.20
59,60: 60-Prankster app.		.50	1.00
Modern Comics-r. 57,58('77)		.15	.30

NOTE: ***Aparo*** *a-60.* ***Morisi*** *a-1, 51-56, 58; c-1, 51-56, 58, 59.*

THUNDERBUNNY (Also see Charlton Bullseye & Pep #393)
Jan, 1984 (Direct sale only)
Red Circle Comics

	Good	Fine	Mint
1-Origin		.60	1.20

THUNDERCATS (TV)
Dec, 1985 - Present
Star Comics (Marvel)

	Good	Fine	Mint
1-Mooney c/a begins	.85	2.50	5.00
2-(65 & 75 cent cover exist)	.45	1.25	2.50
3-22: 12-Begin $1.00-c		.50	1.00

THUNDER MOUNTAIN (See 4-Color No. 246)

Thrilling Crime Cases #44, © STAR

Thunder Agents #6, © TC

Thunderbolt #56, © CC

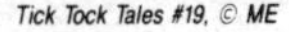
Tick Tock Tales #19, © ME

The Time Tunnel #1, © GK

Tim Holt #22, © ME

TICKLE COMICS (Also see Gay, Smile, & Whee Comics)
1955 (52 pages) (5x7¼") (7 cents)
Modern Store Publ.

	Good	Fine	Mint
1	.40	1.20	2.40

TICK TOCK TALES
Jan, 1946 - No.34, 1951
Magazine Enterprises

	Good	Fine	Mint
1	4.00	12.00	28.00
2	2.00	6.00	14.00
3-10	1.60	4.70	11.00
11-34: 19-Flag-c	1.00	3.00	7.00

TIGER (Also see Comics Reading Libraries)
March, 1970 - No. 6, Jan, 1971 (15 cents)
Charlton Press (King Features)

	Good	Fine	Mint
1	.30	.80	1.60
2-6		.50	1.00

TIGER BOY (See Unearthly Spectaculars)

TIGER GIRL
September, 1968
Gold Key

	Good	Fine	Mint
1 (10227-809)	1.75	5.25	12.00

NOTE: ***Sparling*** *c/a; written by Jerry Siegel.*

TIGERMAN (Also see Thrilling Adv. Stories)
April, 1975 - No. 3, Sept, 1975
Seaboard Periodicals (Atlas)

	Good	Fine	Mint
1		.40	.80
2,3-Ditko-p in each		.30	.60

TIGER WALKS, A (See Movie Comics)

TILLIE THE TOILER
1925 - 1933 (52 pgs.) (B&W daily strip reprints)
Cupples & Leon Co.

	Good	Fine	Mint
nn (No. 1)	8.00	24.00	56.00
2-8	5.50	16.50	40.00

NOTE: *First strip app. was January, 1921.*

TILLIE THE TOILER (See Comic Monthly)
No. 15, 1941 - No. 237, July, 1949
Dell Publishing Co.

	Good	Fine	Mint
4-Color 15(1941)	17.00	51.00	120.00
Large Feature Comic 30(1941)	10.00	30.00	70.00
4-Color 8(1942)	10.00	30.00	70.00
4-Color 22(1943)	8.00	24.00	56.00
4-Color 55(1944)	6.00	18.00	42.00
4-Color 89(1945)	5.50	16.50	38.00
4-Color 106('45),132('46)	4.60	14.00	32.00
4-Color 150,176,184	3.50	10.50	24.00
4-Color 195,213,237	3.00	9.00	21.00

TILLY AND TED-TINKERTOTLAND
1945 (Giveaway) (20 pgs.)
W. T. Grant Co.

	Good	Fine	Mint
nn-Christmas comic	1.70	5.00	12.00

TIM (Formerly Superman-Tim; becomes Gene Autry-Tim)
June, 1950 (Half-size, B&W)
Tim Stores

	Good	Fine	Mint
4 issues	2.50	7.50	15.00

TIME BANDITS
Feb, 1982 (One shot)
Marvel Comics Group

	Good	Fine	Mint
1-Movie adaptation		.50	1.00

TIME BEAVERS (See First Comics Graphic Novel)

TIME FOR LOVE (Formerly Romantic Secrets)
V2#53, Oct, 1966 - No. 47, May, 1976
Charlton Comics

	Good	Fine	Mint
V2#53(10/66), 1(10/67), 2(12/67)		.40	.80
3-47		.15	.30

TIMELESS TOPIX (See Topix)

TIME MACHINE, THE (See 4-Color No. 1085)

TIMESPIRITS
Jan, 1985 - No. 8, Mar, 1986 ($1.50, Baxter paper; adults only)
Epic Comics (Marvel)

	Good	Fine	Mint
1	.30	.90	1.80
2-8: 4-Williamson-a	.25	.75	1.50

TIME TO RUN
1973 (39, 49 cents)
Spire Christian Comics (Fleming H. Revell Co.)

	Good	Fine	Mint
nn-by Al Hartley (from Billy Graham movie)		.40	.80

TIME TUNNEL, THE (TV)
Feb, 1967 - No. 2, July, 1967
Gold Key

	Good	Fine	Mint
1,2-Photo back-c	1.75	5.25	12.00

TIME TWISTERS
Sept, 1987 - Present ($1.25, color)
Quality Comics

	Good	Fine	Mint
1-3: Alan Moore scripts		.60	1.25

TIME 2: THE EPIPHANY (See First Comics Graphic Novel)

TIME WARP
Oct-Nov, 1979 - No. 5, July, 1980 ($1.00)
DC Comics, Inc.

	Good	Fine	Mint
1		.40	.80
2-5		.30	.60

NOTE: ***Aparo*** *a-1.* ***Buckler*** *a-1p.* ***Chaykin*** *a-2.* ***Ditko*** *a-1-4.* ***Kaluta*** *c-1-5.* ***G. Kane*** *a-2.* ***Nasser*** *a-4.* ***Newton*** *a-1-5p.* ***Orlando*** *a-2.* ***Sutton*** *a-1-3.*

TIME WARRIORS THE BEGINNING
1986 (Aug) - Present (color)
Fantasy General Comics

	Good	Fine	Mint
1-Alpha Track/Skellon Empire	.25	.75	1.50
2		.40	.75

TIM HOLT (Movie star) (Becomes Red Mask #42 on; also see Crack Western #72, & Great Western)
1948 - No. 41, April-May, 1954 (All 36 pgs.)
Magazine Enterprises

	Good	Fine	Mint
1(A-1 14)-Photo-c begin, end No. 18, 29; Tim Holt, His horse Lightning & sidekick Chito begin	28.00	84.00	195.00
2(A-1 17)(9-10/48)	17.00	51.00	120.00
3(A-1 19)-Photo back-c	12.00	36.00	84.00
4(1-2/49),5: 5-Photo back-c	10.00	30.00	70.00
6-1st app. The Calico Kid (alias Rex Fury), his horse Ebony & Sidekick Sing-Song (begin series); photo back-c	11.00	32.00	76.00
7-10: 7-Calico Kid by Ayers. 8-Calico Kid by Guardineer (r-/in Great Western 10). 9-Map of Tim's Home Range	8.00	24.00	56.00
11-The Calico Kid becomes The Ghost Rider (Origin & 1st app.) by Dick Ayers (r-/in Great Western 8); his horse Spectre & sidekick Sing-Song begin series	22.00	65.00	154.00
12-16,18-Last photo-c	5.70	17.00	40.00
17-Frazetta Ghost Rider-c	23.00	70.00	160.00
19,22,24: 19-Last Tim Holt-c; Bolle line-drawn-c begin	4.35	13.00	30.00
20-Tim Holt becomes Redmask (Origin); begin series; Redmask-c #20-on	8.50	25.50	60.00
21-Frazetta Ghost Rider/Redmask-c	20.00	60.00	140.00

TIM HOLT (continued)

	Good	Fine	Mint
23-Frazetta Redmask-c	17.00	51.00	120.00
25-1st app. Black Phantom	8.50	25.50	60.00
26-30: 28-Wild Bill Hickok, Bat Masterson team up with Redmask. 29-B&W photo-c	4.35	13.00	30.00
31-33-Ghost Rider ends	3.50	10.50	24.00
34-Tales of the Ghost Rider begins (horror)-Classic "The Flower Women" & "Hard Boiled Harry!"	4.35	13.00	30.00
35-Last Tales of the Ghost Rider	3.50	10.50	24.00
36-The Ghost Rider returns, ends No. 41; liquid hallucinogenic drug story	4.60	14.00	32.00
37-Ghost Rider classic "To Touch Is to Die!," about Inca treasure	4.60	14.00	32.00
38-The Black Phantom begins; classic Ghost Rider "The Phantom Guns of Feather Gap!"	4.60	14.00	32.00
39-41: All 3-D effect c/stories	11.00	32.00	76.00

NOTE: ***Dick Ayers*** *a-7, 9-41.* ***Bolle*** *a-1-41; c-19,20,22,24-28,30-41.*

TIM IN SPACE (Formerly Gene Autry Tim; becomes Tim Tomorrow)
1950 (½-size giveaway) (B&W)
Tim Stores

	Good	Fine	Mint
	1.70	5.00	10.00

TIM McCOY (Formerly Zoo Funnies; Pictorial Love Stories #22 on)
No. 16, Oct, 1948 - No. 21, Aug-Sept, 1949
Charlton Comics

	Good	Fine	Mint
16	12.00	36.00	84.00
17-21	10.00	30.00	70.00

TIM McCOY, POLICE CAR 17
1934 (32 pgs.) (11x14¾") (B&W) (Like Feature Books)
Whitman Publishing Co.

	Good	Fine	Mint
674-1933 movie ill.	9.50	28.50	65.00

TIMMY (See 4-Color No. 715,823,923,1022)

TIMMY THE TIMID GHOST (Formerly Win-A-Prize?; see Blue Bird)
No. 3, 2/56 - No. 44, 10/64; No. 45, 9/66; 10/67 - No. 23, 7/71; V4/24, 9/85 - No. 26, 1/86
Charlton Comics

	Good	Fine	Mint
3(1956) (1st Series)	2.00	6.00	14.00
4,5	1.00	3.00	7.00
6-10	.50	1.50	3.50
11,12(4/58,10/58)(100pgs.)	.90	2.70	6.50
13-20	.45	1.35	3.00
21-45('66)		.50	1.00
1(10/67)		.30	.60
2-23		.25	.50
24-26 (1985): Fago-r		.40	.80
Shoe Store Giveaway		.40	.80

TIM TOMORROW (Formerly Tim In Space)
8/51, 9/51, 10/51, Christmas, 1951 (5x7¾")
Tim Stores

	Good	Fine	Mint
Prof. Fumble & Captain Kit Comet in all	1.35	4.00	8.00

TIM TYLER (See Harvey Comics Hits No. 54)

TIM TYLER (Also see Comics Reading Libraries)
1942
Better Publications

	Good	Fine	Mint
1	5.00	15.00	35.00

TIM TYLER COWBOY
No. 11, Nov, 1948 - No. 18, 1950
Standard Comics

	Good	Fine	Mint
11	3.70	11.00	26.00
12-18	2.30	7.00	16.00

TINKER BELL (See 4-Color No. 896,982, & Walt Disney Showcase No. 37)

TINY FOLKS FUNNIES (See 4-Color No. 60)

TINY TESSIE (Tessie No. 1-23; Real Experiences #25)
No. 24, Oct, 1949
Marvel Comics (20CC)

	Good	Fine	Mint
24	1.50	4.50	10.00

TINY TIM
No. 4, 1941 - No. 235, July, 1949
Dell Publishing Co.

	Good	Fine	Mint
Large Feature Comic 4('41)	16.00	48.00	110.00
4-Color 20(1941)	17.00	51.00	120.00
4-Color 42(1943)	9.50	28.50	65.00
4-Color 235	3.00	9.00	21.00

TINY TOT COMICS
Mar, 1946 - No. 10, Nov-Dec, 1947 (For younger readers)
E. C. Comics

	Good	Fine	Mint
1(nn)	12.00	36.00	84.00
2 (5/46)	9.50	28.50	65.00
3-10: 10-Christmas-c	8.00	24.00	56.00

TINY TOT FUNNIES (Formerly Family Funnies)
June, 1951 (Becomes Junior Funnies)
Harvey Publ. (King Features Synd.)

	Good	Fine	Mint
9-Flash Gordon, Mandrake	2.50	7.50	17.00

TINY TOTS COMICS
1943 (Not reprints)
Dell Publishing Co.

	Good	Fine	Mint
1-Kelly-a(2)	30.00	90.00	210.00

TIPPY & CAP STUBBS (See 4-Color No. 210,242)

TIPPY'S FRIENDS GO-GO & ANIMAL
July, 1966 - No. 15, Oct, 1969 (25 cents)
Tower Comics

	Good	Fine	Mint
1	.75	2.25	5.00
2-7,9-15: 12-15 titled "Tippy's Friend Go-Go"	.50	1.50	3.50
8-Beatles on front/back-c	2.00	6.00	14.00

TIPPY TEEN (See Vicki)
Nov, 1965 - No. 27, Feb, 1970 (25 cents)
Tower Comics

	Good	Fine	Mint
1	.70	2.00	4.00
2-27: 5-1pg. Beatle pin-up	.35	1.00	2.00
Special Collectors' Eds. (1969-nn; 25 cents)	.35	1.00	2.00

TIPPY TERRY
1963
Super/I. W. Enterprises

	Good	Fine	Mint
Super Reprint #14('63)-Little Grouchy reprints		.60	1.20
I.W. Reprint #1 (nd)		.60	1.20

TIP TOP COMICS
4/36 - No. 210, 1957; No. 211, 11-1/57-58 - No. 225, 5-7/61
United Features No. 1-187/St. John No. 188-210/Dell Publishing Co. No. 211 on

	Good	Fine	Mint
1-Tarzan by Hal Foster, Li'l Abner begin; strip-r	115.00	345.00	805.00
2	54.00	162.00	380.00
3	40.00	120.00	280.00
4	33.00	100.00	230.00
5-10: 7-Photo & biography of Edgar Rice Burroughs. 8-Christmas-c	27.00	80.00	190.00
11-20: 20-Christmas-c	20.00	60.00	140.00
21-40: 36-Kurtzman panel (1st published comic work)	17.00	51.00	120.00
41-Has 1st Tarzan Sunday	17.00	51.00	120.00
42-50: 43-Mort Walker panel	15.00	45.00	105.00
51-53	12.00	36.00	84.00

54-Origin Mirror Man & Triple Terror, also featured on cover

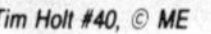
Tim Holt #40, © ME

Tiny Tot Comics #5, © WMG

Tip Top Comics #9, © UFS

T-Man #32, © QUA

Tomahawk #8, © DC

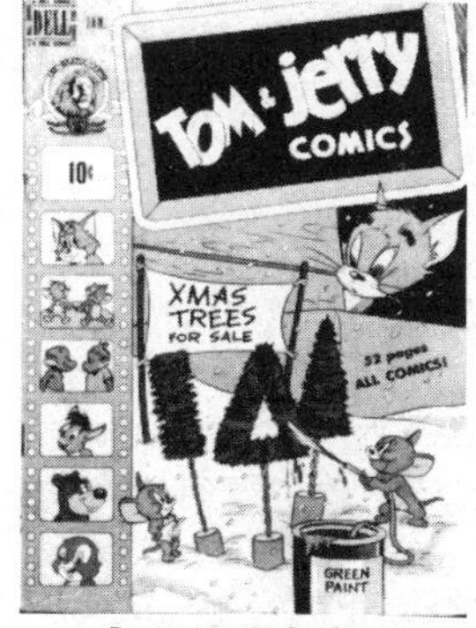

Tom and Jerry #66, © M.G.M.

TIP TOP COMICS (continued)

	Good	Fine	Mint
	17.00	51.00	120.00
55,56,58,60: Last Tarzan by Foster	11.00	32.00	76.00
57,59,61,62-Tarzan by Hogarth	15.00	45.00	105.00
63-80: 65,67-70,72-74,77,78-No Tarzan	8.00	24.00	56.00
81-90	7.00	21.00	50.00
91-99	5.00	15.00	35.00
100	5.70	17.00	40.00
101-140: 110-Gordo story. 111-Li'l Abner app. 118, 132-no Tarzan	3.50	10.50	24.00
141-170: 145,151-Gordo story. 157-Last Li'l Abner; lingerie panels	2.35	7.00	16.00
171-188-Tarzan reprints by B. Lubbers in all. #177?-Peanuts by Schulz begins; no Peanuts in #178,179,181-183	2.65	8.00	18.00
189-225	1.50	4.50	10.00
Bound Volumes (Very Rare) sold at 1939 World's Fair; bound by publ. in pictorial comic boards. (Also see Comics on Parade)			
Bound issues 1-12	150.00	450.00	1050.00
Bound issues 13-24	90.00	270.00	630.00
Bound issues 25-36	70.00	210.00	490.00

NOTE: *Tarzan covers-No. 3, 9, 11, 13, 16, 18, 21, 24, 27, 30, 32-34, 36, 37, 39, 41, 43, 45, 47, 50, 52 (all worth 10-20 percent more). Tarzan by* ***Foster****-No. 1-40, 44-50; by* ***Rex Maxon****-No. 41-43; by* ***Byrne Hogarth****-No. 57, 59, 62.*

TIP TOPPER COMICS
1949 - 1954
United Features Syndicate

	Good	Fine	Mint
1-Li'l Abner, Abbie & Slats	3.50	10.50	24.00
2	2.00	6.00	14.00
3-5	1.70	5.00	12.00
6-25: 17-22,24,26-Peanuts app. (2 pgs.)	1.50	4.50	10.00
26-28-Twin Earths	3.50	10.50	24.00

NOTE: *Many lingerie panels in Fritzi Ritz stories.*

T-MAN
Sept, 1951 - No. 38, Dec, 1956
Quality Comics Group

	Good	Fine	Mint
1-Jack Cole-a	9.50	28.50	65.00
2-Crandall-c	5.35	16.00	37.00
3,6-8: Crandall-c	.35	13.00	30.00
4,5-Crandall c/a each; 5-Drug test	4.85	14.50	34.00
9-Crandall-c	3.50	10.50	24.00
10,12	2.50	7.50	17.50
11-Used in **POP**, pg. 95 & color illo.	5.70	17.00	40.00
13-19,21-24,26	2.15	6.50	15.00
20-Nuclear explosion-c	5.00	15.00	35.00
25-All Crandall-a	4.00	12.00	28.00
27-38	1.70	5.00	12.00

NOTE: *Anti-communist stories are common. Bondage c-15.*

TNT COMICS
Feb, 1946 (36 pgs.)
Charles Publishing Co.

	Good	Fine	Mint
1-Yellowjacket app.	6.50	19.50	45.00

TOBY TYLER (See Movie Comics & 4-Color No. 1092)

TODAY'S BRIDES
Nov, 1955 - No. 4, Nov, 1956
Ajax/Farrell Publishing Co.

	Good	Fine	Mint
1	3.00	9.00	21.00
2-4	1.50	4.50	10.00

TODAY'S ROMANCE
No. 5, March, 1952 - No. 8, Sept, 1952
Standard Comics

	Good	Fine	Mint
5	2.65	8.00	18.00
6-Toth-a	3.50	10.50	24.00

	Good	Fine	Mint
7,8	1.30	4.00	9.00

TOKA (Jungle King)
Aug-Oct, 1964 - No. 10, Jan, 1967
Dell Publishing Co.

	Good	Fine	Mint
1	.50	1.50	3.00
2	.35	1.00	2.00
3-10	.25	.70	1.40

TOMAHAWK (Son of . . . #131-140 on-c; see Star Spangled Comics)
Sept-Oct, 1950 - No. 140, May-June, 1972
National Periodical Publications

	Good	Fine	Mint
1	35.00	105.00	245.00
2-Frazetta/Williamson-a, 4 pgs.	21.00	64.00	150.00
3-5	11.00	32.00	76.00
6-10: 7-Last 52 pgs.	8.00	24.00	56.00
11-20	5.00	15.00	35.00
21-27,30	3.50	10.50	24.00
28-1st app. Lord Shilling (arch-foe)	4.35	13.00	30.00
29-Frazetta-r/Jimmy Wakely #3, 3 pgs.	12.00	36.00	84.00
31-40	2.65	8.00	18.00
41-50	2.00	6.00	14.00
51-56,58-60	1.50	4.50	10.00
57-Frazetta-r/Jimmy Wakely #6, 3 pgs.	6.50	19.50	45.00
61-77: 77-Last 10 cent ish.	.85	2.50	6.00
78-85: 81-1st app. Miss Liberty. 83-Origin Tomahawk's Rangers	.35	1.00	2.00
86-100: 96-Origin/1st app. The Hood, alias Lady Shilling		.50	1.00
101-130,132-138,140: 107-Origin/1st app. Thunder-Man		.30	.60
131-Frazetta-r/Jimmy Wakely #7, 3 pgs.; origin Firehair retold	.35	1.00	2.00
139-Frazetta-r/Star Spangled #113		.50	1.00

NOTE: ***Adams*** *c-116-119, 121, 123-130. Firehair by* ***Kubert****-131-134, 136.* ***Maurer*** *a-138.* ***Severin*** *a-135.*

TOM AND JERRY (See Comic Album No. 4, 8, 12, Dell Giant No. 21, Dell Giants, Golden Comics Digest No. 1, 5, 8, 13, 15, 18, 22, 25, 28, 35, & March of Comics No. 21, 46, 61, 70, 88, 103, 119, 128, 145, 154, 173, 190, 207, 224, 281, 295, 305, 321, 333, 345, 361, 365, 388, 400, 444, 451, 463, 480)

TOM AND JERRY (. . Comics, early issues) (M.G.M.)
(Formerly Our Gang No. 1-59) (See Dell Giants for annuals)
No. 193, 6/48; No. 60, 7/49 - No. 212, 7-9/62; No. 213, 11/62 - No. 291, 2/75; No. 292, 3/77 - No. 342, 5/82 - No. 344, 1982?
Dell Publishing Co./Gold Key No. 213-327/Whitman No. 328 on

	Good	Fine	Mint
4-Color 193 (#1)	6.50	19.50	45.00
60	3.70	11.00	26.00
61	3.00	9.00	21.00
62-70: 66-X-mas-c	2.35	7.00	16.00
71-80	1.75	5.25	12.00
81-99: 90-X-mas-c	1.50	4.50	10.00
100	1.75	5.25	12.00
101-120	1.15	3.50	8.00
121-140: 126-X-mas-c	.85	2.50	6.00
141-160	.75	2.25	5.00
161-200	.55	1.65	4.00
201-212(7-9/62)(Last Dell ish.)	.45	1.35	3.00
213,214-(84 pgs.)-titled ". . . Funhouse"	1.50	4.50	12.00
215-240: 215-titled ". . . Funhouse"	.45	1.35	3.00
241-270	.35	1.00	2.00
271-300: 286 "Tom & Jerry"	.25	.75	1.50
301-344		.40	.80
Mouse From T.R.A.P. 1(7/66)-Giant, G. K.	1.50	4.50	12.00
Summer Fun 1(7/67, 68pgs.)(Gold Key)-R-/Barks' Droopy/Summer Fun No. 1	1.50	4.50	12.00
. . . Kite Fun Book (1958, 5x7¼", 16pgs.)	1.50	4.50	12.00

TOM AND JERRY (continued)

NOTE: *No. 60-87, 98-121, 268, 277, 289, 302 are 52 pages. Reprints-No. 225, 241, 245, 247, 252, 254, 266, 268, 270, 292-327, 329-342, 344.*

TOMB OF DARKNESS (Formerly Beware)
No. 9, July, 1974 - No. 23, Nov, 1976
Marvel Comics Group

	Good	Fine	Mint
9-19: 17-Woodbridge-r/Astonishing #62		.25	.50
20-Everett Venus r-/Venus #19		.25	.50
21-23: 23-Everett-a(r)		.25	.50

NOTE: ***Ditko** a-15r, 19r.*

TOMB OF DRACULA (See Giant-Size Dracula & Dracula Lives)
April, 1972 - No. 70, Aug, 1979
Marvel Comics Group

	Good	Fine	Mint
1-Colan-p in all	.85	2.50	5.00
2-9: 3-Intro. Dr. Rachel Van Helsing & Inspector Chelm. 6-Adams-c	.30	.90	1.80
10-1st app. Blade the Vampire Slayer	.35	1.00	2.00
11,12,14-20: 12-Brunner-c(p)		.60	1.20
13-Origin Blade the Vampire Slayer	.25	.70	1.40
21-40		.45	.90
41-70: 43-Wrightson-c. 70-Double size		.35	.70

NOTE: ***Colan** a-1-70p; c(p)-8, 38-42, 44-56, 58-70.*

TOMB OF DRACULA (Magazine)
Nov, 1979 - No. 6, Sept, 1980 (B&W)
Marvel Comics Group

	Good	Fine	Mint
1		.60	1.20
2,4-6: 2-Ditko-a (36 pgs.)	.35	1.00	2.00
3-Miller-a	.35	1.00	2.00

NOTE: ***Buscema** a-4p, 5p. **Chaykin** c-5, 6. **Colan** a(p)-1, 3-6. **Miller** a-3.*

TOMB OF LIGEIA (See Movie Classics)

TOMB OF TERROR (Thrills of Tomorrow #17 on)
June, 1952 - No. 16, July, 1954
Harvey Publications

	Good	Fine	Mint
1	6.50	19.50	45.00
2	4.35	13.00	30.00
3-Bondage-c; atomic disaster story	5.00	15.00	35.00
4-7: 4-Heart ripped out	4.35	13.00	30.00
8-12-Nostrand-a	4.35	13.00	30.00
13-Special S/F ish	6.00	18.00	42.00
14-Check-a; special S/F ish	6.00	18.00	42.00
15-S/F ish.; c-shows head exploding; Nostrand-a(r)	8.00	24.00	55.00
16-Special S/F ish; Nostrand-a	6.00	18.00	42.00

NOTE: ***Kremer** a-1, 7; c-1. **Palais** a-2, 3, 5-7. **Powell** a-1, 3, 5, 9-16. **Sparling** a-12, 13, 15.*

TOMBSTONE TERRITORY (See 4-Color No. 1123)

TOM CAT (Formerly Bo, Atom The Cat #9 on)
No. 4, Apr, 1956 - No. 8, July, 1957
Charlton Comics

	Good	Fine	Mint
4	1.30	4.00	9.00
5-8	.75	2.25	5.00

TOM CORBETT, SPACE CADET (TV)
No. 378, 1-2/52 - No. 11, 9-11/54 (All painted covers)
Dell Publishing Co.

	Good	Fine	Mint
4-Color 378-McWilliams-a	5.00	15.00	35.00
4-Color 400,421-McWilliams-a	4.00	12.00	28.00
4(11-1/53) - 11	2.65	8.00	18.00

TOM CORBETT SPACE CADET (See March of Comics No. 102)

TOM CORBETT SPACE CADET (TV)
May-June, 1955 - V2No.3, Sept-Oct, 1955
Prize Publications

	Good	Fine	Mint
V2#1	7.00	21.00	50.00
2,3	6.00	18.00	42.00

TOM LANDRY AND THE DALLAS COWBOYS
1973 (35-49 cents)
Spire Christian Comics/Fleming H. Revell Co.

	Good	Fine	Mint
nn	.25	.75	1.50

TOM MIX (. . .Commandos Comics #10-12)
Sept, 1940 - No. 12, Nov, 1942 (36 pages); 1983 (One-shot)
Given away for two Ralston box-tops; in cereal box, 1983
Ralston-Purina Co.

	Good	Fine	Mint
1-Origin (life) Tom Mix; Fred Meagher-a	60.00	180.00	420.00
2	35.00	105.00	245.00
3-9	30.00	90.00	210.00
10-12: 10-Origin Tom Mix Commando Unit; Speed O'Dare begins. 12-Sci/fi-c	22.00	65.00	154.00
1983-'Taking of Grizzly Grebb,' Toth-a; 16 pg. miniature	1.00	3.00	6.00

TOM MIX WESTERN (Movie, radio star) (Also see The Comics, Crackajack Funnies, Master Comics, 100 Pages Of Comics, Real Western Hero, Six Gun Heroes, Western Hero & X-Mas Comics)
Jan, 1948 - No. 61, May, 1953 (52pgs., 1-17)
Fawcett Publications

	Good	Fine	Mint
1 (Photo-c, 52 pgs.)-Tom Mix & his horse Tony begin; Tumbleweed Jr begins, ends #52,54,55	35.00	105.00	245.00
2 (Photo-c)	20.00	60.00	140.00
3-5 (Painted/photo-c): 5-Billy the Kid & Oscar app.	16.00	48.00	110.00
6,7 (Painted/photo-c)	13.00	40.00	90.00
8-Kinstler tempera-c	13.00	40.00	90.00
9,10 (Painted/photo-c)-Used in **SOTI**, pgs. 323-325	13.00	40.00	90.00
11-Kinstler oil-c	11.00	32.00	76.00
12 (Painted/photo-c)	10.00	30.00	70.00
13-17 (Painted-c, 52 pgs.)	10.00	30.00	70.00
18,22 (Painted-c, 36 pgs.)	8.00	24.00	56.00
19 (Photo-c, 52 pgs.)	10.00	30.00	70.00
20,21,23 (Painted-c, 52 pgs.)	8.00	24.00	56.00
24,25,27-29 (52 pgs.): 24-Photo-c begin, end #61. 29-Slim Pickens app.	8.00	24.00	56.00
26,30 (36 pgs.)	7.00	21.00	50.00
31-33,35-37,39,40,42 (52 pgs.): 39-Red Eagle app.	6.00	18.00	42.00
34,38 (36 pgs. begin)	5.00	15.00	35.00
41,43-60	3.50	10.50	24.00
61-Last issue	4.60	14.00	32.00

NOTE: *Photo-c from 1930s Tom Mix movies (he died in 1940). Many issues contain ads for Tom Mix, Rocky Lane, Space Patrol and other premiums. **Captain Tootsie** by C.C. Beck in No. 6-11, 20.*

TOMMY OF THE BIG TOP
No. 10, Sept, 1948 - No. 12, Mar, 1949
King Features Syndicate/Standard Comics

	Good	Fine	Mint
10	2.65	8.00	18.00
11,12	1.50	4.50	10.00

TOM SAWYER (See Famous Stories & Advs. of. . .)

TOM SAWYER & HUCK FINN
1925 (52 pgs.) (10¾x10") (stiff covers)
Stoll & Edwards Co.

	Good	Fine	Mint
By Dwiggins; reprints 1923, 1924 Sunday strips in color	8.00	24.00	56.00

TOM SAWYER COMICS
1951? (paper cover)
Giveaway

Tomb of Dracula #1, © MCG

Tom Corbett, Space Cadet #8, © DELL

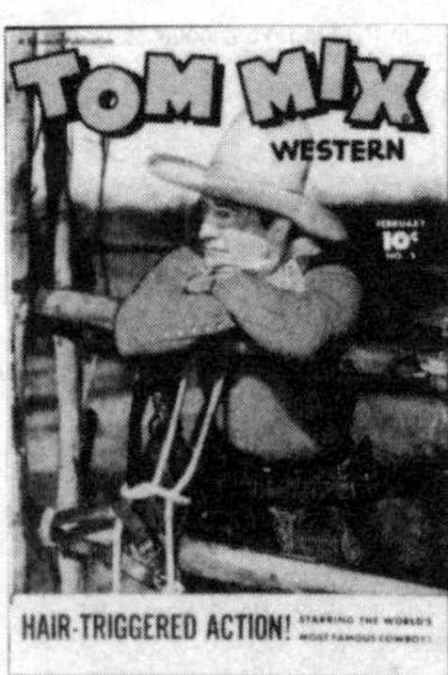

Tom Mix Western #2, © FAW

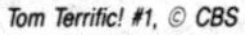
Tom Terrific! #1, © CBS

Tony Trent #3, © Z-D

Top Cat #3 (Dell), © Hanna-Barbera

TOM SAWYER COMICS (continued)

	Good	Fine	Mint
Contains a coverless Hopalong Cassidy from 1951; other combinations possible.	1.00	3.00	6.00

TOM SKINNER-UP FROM HARLEM (See Up From Harlem)

TOM TERRIFIC! (TV)(See Mighty Mouse Fun Club Mag. #1)
Summer, 1957 - No. 6, Fall, 1958 (Paul Terry)
Pines Comics

	Good	Fine	Mint
1	7.00	21.00	50.00
2-6	4.60	14.00	32.00

TOM THUMB (See 4-Color No. 972)

TOM-TOM, THE JUNGLE BOY
1947; Nov, 1957 - No. 3, Mar, 1958
Magazine Enterprises

	Good	Fine	Mint
1-Funny animal	3.00	9.00	21.00
2,3(1947)	1.85	5.50	13.00
1(1957)(& Itchi the Monk), 2,3('58)	.85	2.50	6.00
I.W. Reprint No. 1,2,8,10		.40	.80

TONKA (See 4-Color No. 966)

TONTO (See The Lone Ranger's Companion. . .)

TONY TRENT (The Face #1,2)
1948 - 1949
Big Shot/Columbia Comics Group

	Good	Fine	Mint
3,4: 3-The Face app.	4.60	14.00	32.00

TOODLE TWINS, THE
1-2/51 - No. 10, 7-8/51; 1956 (Newspaper reprints)
Ziff-Davis (Approved Comics)/Argo

	Good	Fine	Mint
1	3.00	9.00	21.00
2	2.00	6.00	14.00
3-9	1.70	5.00	12.00
10-Painted-c, some newspaper-r	1.70	5.00	12.00
1(Argo, 3/56)	1.50	4.50	10.00

TOONERVILLE TROLLEY
1921 (Daily strip reprints) (B&W) (52 pgs.)
Cupples & Leon Co.

	Good	Fine	Mint
1-By Fontaine Fox	12.00	36.00	84.00

TOOTS & CASPER (See Large Feature Comic No. 5)

TOP ADVENTURE COMICS
1964 (Reprints)
I. W. Enterprises

	Good	Fine	Mint
1-Reprints/Explorer Joe #2; Krigstein-a	.70	2.00	4.00
2-Black Dwarf	.80	2.40	4.80

TOP CAT (TV) (Hanna-Barbera)
12-2/61-62 - No. 3, 6-8/62; No. 4, 10/62 - No. 31, 9/70
Dell Publishing Co./Gold Key No. 4 on

	Good	Fine	Mint
1	2.00	6.00	14.00
2-5	1.30	4.00	9.00
6-10	.85	2.50	6.00
11-20	.55	1.65	4.00
21-31: 21,24,25,29-Reprints	.50	1.50	3.00
Kite Fun Book (1963, 16pgs., 5x7¼'', soft-c)	1.15	3.50	8.00

TOP CAT (TV) (Hanna-Barbera)
Nov, 1970 - No. 20, Nov, 1973
Charlton Comics

	Good	Fine	Mint
1	.85	2.50	5.00
2-10	.50	1.50	3.00
11-20	.25	.75	1.50

NOTE: *No. 8 (1/72) went on sale late in 1972 between No. 14 and No. 15 with the January 1973 issues.*

TOP COMICS
July, 1967 (All rebound issues)
K. K. Publications/Gold Key

	Good	Fine	Mint
nn-The Gnome-Mobile (Disney-movie)	.50	1.50	3.00
1-Beagle Boys (#7), Bugs Bunny, Chip 'n' Dale, Daffy Duck (#50), Flintstones, Flipper, Huckleberry Hound, Huey, Dewey & Louie, Junior Woodchucks, The Jetsons, Lassie, The Little Monsters (#71), Moby Duck, Porky Pig (has Gold Key label - says Top Comics on inside), Scamp, Super Goof, Tarzan of the Apes (#169) Three Stooges (#35), Tom & Jerry, Top Cat (#21), Tweety & Sylvester (#7), Walt Disney C&S (#322), Woody Woodpecker, Yogi Bear, Zorro known; each character given own book	.30	.90	1.80
1-Uncle Scrooge (#70)	1.00	3.00	6.00
1-Donald Duck (not Barks), Mickey Mouse	.70	2.00	4.00
2-Bugs Bunny, Daffy Duck, Donald Duck (not Barks), Mickey Mouse (#114), Porky Pig, Super Goof, Three Stooges, Tom & Jerry, Tweety & Sylvester, Uncle Scrooge (#71)-Barks-c, Walt Disney's C&S (r-/#325), Woody Woodpecker, Yogi Bear (#30), Zorro (r-#8; Toth-a)	.30	.90	1.80
2-Snow White & 7 Dwarfs(6/67)(1944-r)	.80	2.40	4.80
3-Donald Duck	.50	1.50	3.00
3-Uncle Scrooge (#72)	1.00	3.00	6.00
3-The Flintstones, Mickey Mouse (r-/#115), Tom & Jerry, Woody Woodpecker, Yogi Bear		.50	1.00
4-The Flintstones, Mickey Mouse, Woody Woodpecker		.50	1.00

NOTE: *Each book in this series is identical to its counterpart except for cover, and came out at same time. The number in parentheses is the original issue it contains.*

TOP DETECTIVE COMICS
1964 (Reprints)
I. W. Enterprises

	Good	Fine	Mint
9-Young King Cole & Dr. Drew (not Grandenetti)	.40	1.20	2.40

TOP DOG
Apr, 1985 - No. 14, June, 1987 (Children's book)
Star Comics (Marvel)

	Good	Fine	Mint
1-13		.35	.70
14		.50	1.00

TOP ELIMINATOR (Formerly Teenage Hotrodders; Drag 'n' Wheels #30 on)
No. 25, Sept, 1967 - No. 29, July, 1968
Charlton Comics

	Good	Fine	Mint
25-29		.40	.80

TOP FLIGHT COMICS
1947; July, 1949
Four Star Publications/St. John Publishing Co.

	Good	Fine	Mint
1	3.00	9.00	21.00
1(7/49)-Hector the Inspector	2.00	6.00	14.00

TOP GUN (See 4-Color No. 927)

TOP GUNS (See Super DC Giant & Showcase No. 72)

TOPIX (. . .Comics) (Timeless Topix-early issues) (Also see Men of Courage & Treasure Chest)(V1-V5/1,V7/1-20-paper-c)
11/42 - V10No.15, 1/28/52 (Weekly - later issues)
Catechetical Guild Educational Society

	Good	Fine	Mint
V1#1(8pgs.,8x11'')	6.00	18.00	36.00
2,3(8pgs.,8x11'')	3.35	10.00	20.00
4-8(16pgs.,8x11'')	2.50	7.50	15.00
V2#1-10(16pgs.,8x11''): V2#8-Pope Pius XII	2.50	7.50	15.00
V3#1-10(16pgs.,8x11'')	2.00	6.00	12.00
V4#1-10	2.00	6.00	12.00

V5#1(10/46,52pgs.)-9,12-15(12/47)-#13 shows V5#4

TOPIX (continued)

	Good	Fine	Mint
	1.00	3.00	6.00
10,11-Life of Christ eds.	2.35	7.00	14.00
V6#1-14	.70	2.00	4.00
V7#1(9/1/48)-20(6/15/49), 32pgs.	.70	2.00	4.00
V8#1(9/19/49)-3,5-11,13-30(5/15/50)	.70	2.00	4.00
4-Dagwood Splits the Atom(10/10/49)-Magazine format	1.35	4.00	8.00
12-Ingels-a	2.75	8.00	16.00
V9#1(9/25/50)-11,13-30(5/14/51)	.50	1.50	3.00
12-Special 36pg. Xmas ish., text illos format	.85	2.50	5.00
V10#1(10/1/51)-15	.50	1.50	3.00

NOTE: ***Hollingsworth*** *a-V10#14.*

TOP JUNGLE COMICS
1964 (Reprint)
I. W. Enterprises

	Good	Fine	Mint
1(nd)-Reprints White Princess of the Jungle #3, minus cover	.80	2.40	4.80

TOP LOVE STORIES
No. 8, 11-12/49 - No. 3, 5/51 - No. 19, 3/54
Star Publications

	Good	Fine	Mint
8	3.85	11.50	27.00
9, 3-5,7-9	3.00	9.00	21.00
6-Wood-a	6.35	19.00	44.00
10-16,18,19-Disbrow-a	3.35	10.00	23.00
17-Wood art (Fox-r)	5.00	15.00	35.00

NOTE: *All have* ***L. B. Cole*** *covers.*

TOP-NOTCH COMICS (. . . Laugh #28-45; Laugh #46 on)
Dec, 1939 - No. 45, June, 1944
MLJ Magazines

	Good	Fine	Mint
1-Origin The Wizard; Kardak the Mystic Magician, Swift of the Secret Service (ends No. 3), Air Patrol, The Westpointer, Manhunters (by J. Cole), Mystic (ends #2) & Scott Rand (ends #3) begin	80.00	240.00	560.00
2-Dick Storm (ends #8), Stacy Knight M.D. (ends #4) begin; Jack Cole-a	40.00	120.00	280.00
3-Bob Phantom, Scott Rand on Mars begin; J. Cole-a	33.00	100.00	230.00
4-Origin/1st app. Streak Chandler on Mars; Moore of the Mounted only app.; J. Cole-a	28.00	84.00	195.00
5-Flag-c; origin/1st app. Galahad; Shanghai Sheridan begins (ends #8); Shield cameo	22.00	65.00	154.00
6-The Shield app.	20.00	60.00	140.00
7-The Shield x-over in Wizard; The Wizard dons new costume	30.00	90.00	210.00
8-Origin The Firefly & Roy, the Super Boy	35.00	105.00	245.00
9-Origin & 1st app. The Black Hood; Fran Frazier begins	80.00	240.00	560.00
10	35.00	105.00	245.00
11-20	22.00	65.00	154.00
21-30: 23,24-No Wizard, Roy app. in each. 25-Last Bob Phantom, Roy app. 26-Roy app. 27-Last Firefly. 28-Suzie begins. 29-Last Kardak	19.00	57.00	132.00
31-44: 33-Dotty & Ditto by Woggon begins. 44-Black Hood series ends	10.00	30.00	70.00
45-Last issue	6.00	18.00	42.00

NOTE: ***J. Binder*** *a-1-3.* ***Meskin*** *a-2,3, 15.* ***Woggon*** *a-33-40, 42. Bondage c-17, 19.*

TOPPER & NEIL (See 4-Color No. 859)

TOPPS COMICS
1947
Four Star Publications

	Good	Fine	Mint
1-L. B. Cole-c	4.00	12.00	28.00

TOPS
July, 1949 - No. 2, Sept, 1949 (68 pgs, 25 cents)(10¼x13¼")
(Large size-magazine format; for the adult reader)
Tops Magazine, Inc. (Lev Gleason)

	Good	Fine	Mint
1 (Rare)-Story by Dashiell Hammett; Crandall/Lubbers, Tuska, Dan Barry, Fuje-a; Biro painted-c	55.00	165.00	385.00
2 (Rare)-Crandall/Lubbers, Biro, Kida, Fuje, Guardineer-a	47.00	140.00	330.00

TOPS COMICS (See Tops in Humor)
1944 (Small size, 32 pgs.) (7¼x5")
Consolidated Book (Lev Gleason)

	Good	Fine	Mint
2001-The Jack of Spades	8.50	25.50	60.00
2002-Rip Raider	4.00	12.00	28.00
2003-Red Birch (gag cartoons)	1.00	3.00	7.00

TOPS COMICS
1944 (132 pages) (10 cents)
Consolidated Book Publishers

	Good	Fine	Mint
nn(Color-c, inside in red shade & some in full color)-Ace Kelly by Rick Yager, Black Orchid, Don on the Farm, Dinky Dinkerton (Rare)	13.00	40.00	90.00

NOTE: *This book is printed in such a way that when the staple is removed, the strips on the left side of the book correspond with the same strips on the right side. Therefore, if strips are removed from the book, each strip can be folded into a complete comic section of its own.*

TOP SECRET
January, 1952
Hillman Publ.

	Good	Fine	Mint
1	6.50	19.50	45.00

TOP SECRET ADVENTURES (See Spyman)

TOP SECRETS (. . .of the F.B.I.)
Nov, 1947 - No. 10, July-Aug, 1949
Street & Smith Publications

	Good	Fine	Mint
1-Powell c/a	10.00	30.00	70.00
2-Powell-c/a	6.50	19.50	45.00
3-6,8-10-Powell-a	5.70	17.00	40.00
7-Used in **SOTI**, pg. 90 & illo.-"How to hurt people;" used by N.Y. Legis. Comm.; Powell c/a	11.00	32.00	76.00

NOTE: ***Powell*** *c-1-3,5-10.*

TOPS IN ADVENTURE
Fall, 1952 (132 pages)
Ziff-Davis Publishing Co.

	Good	Fine	Mint
1-Crusader from Mars & The Hawk; Powell-a	20.00	60.00	140.00

TOPS IN HUMOR (See Tops Comics?)
1944 (Small size) (7¼x5")
Consolidated Book Publ. (Lev Gleason)

	Good	Fine	Mint
2001(#1)-Origin The Jack of Spades, Ace Kelly by Rick Yager, Black Orchid (female crime fighter) app.	9.50	28.50	65.00
2	4.60	14.00	32.00

TOP SPOT COMICS
1945
Top Spot Publ. Co.

	Good	Fine	Mint
1-The Menace, Duke of Darkness app.	7.00	21.00	50.00

TOPSY-TURVY
April, 1945
R. B. Leffingwell Publ.

	Good	Fine	Mint
1	2.30	7.00	16.00

TOR (Formerly One Million Years Ago)
No. 2, Oct, 1953 - No. 3, May, 1954 - No. 5, Oct, 1954
St. John Publishing Co.

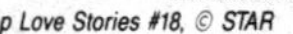
Top Love Stories #18, © STAR

Top-Notch Comics #23, © AP

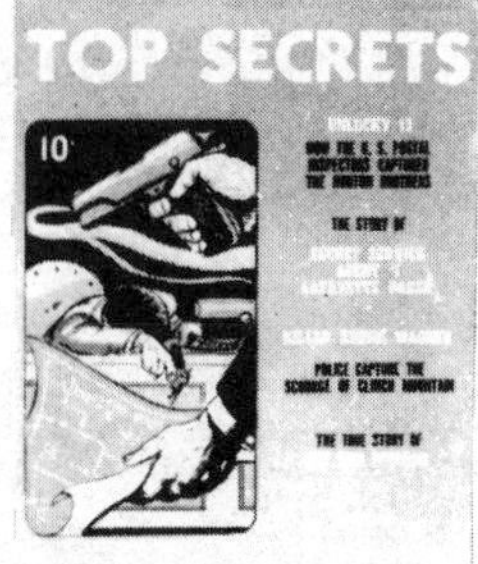

Top Secrets #2, © S & S

Tor 3-D #1, © Eclipse Comics

The Tormented #2, © Sterling Comics

The Transformers #2, © MCG

TOR (continued) — Good / Fine / Mint

3-D 2(10/53)-Kubert-a 10.00 30.00 70.00
3-D 2(10/53)-Oversized, otherwise same contents 9.00 27.00 62.00
3-D 2(11/53)-Kubert-a 9.00 27.00 62.00
3-5-Kubert-a; 3-Danny Dreams by Toth 10.00 30.00 70.00

NOTE: *The two October 3-D's have same contents and **Powell** art; the Nov. issue is titled 3-D Comics.*

TOR (See Sojourn)
May-June, 1975 - No. 6, Mar-Apr, 1976
National Periodical Publications

1-New origin by Kubert .30 .60
2-6: 2-Origin-r/St. John #1 .25 .50

NOTE: ***Kubert** a-1; 2-6r; c-1-6. **Toth** a(p)-3r.*

TOR 3-D
July, 1986 - No. 2, Aug, 1986
Eclipse Comics

1-r-/One Million Years Ago .40 1.25 2.50
2-D 1-Limited signed & numbered edition .85 2.50 5.00
2-r-/Tor 3-D No. 2 .40 1.25 2.50
2-D 2-Limited signed & numbered edition .85 2.50 5.00

TORCHY (. . . Blonde Bombshell) (See Dollman, Military, & Modern)
Nov, 1949 - No. 6, Sept, 1950
Quality Comics Group

1-Bill Ward-c, Gil Fox-a 75.00 225.00 525.00
2,3-Fox c/a 32.00 95.00 225.00
4-Fox c/a(3), Ward-a, 9pgs. 42.00 125.00 295.00
5,6-Ward c/a, 9 pgs; Fox-a(3) each 52.00 155.00 365.00
Super Reprint #16('64)-R-/#4 with new-c 6.00 18.00 36.00

TORMENTED, THE (Surprise Adventure #3)
July, 1954 - No. 2, Sept, 1954
Sterling Comics

1,2 4.35 13.00 30.00

TORNADO TOM (See Mighty Midget Comics)

TOTAL WAR (M.A.R.S. Patrol #3 on)
July, 1965 - No. 2, Oct, 1965 (Painted covers)
Gold Key

1,2-Wood-a 1.70 5.00 12.00

TOUGH KID SQUAD COMICS
March, 1942
Timely Comics (TCI)

1-(Scarce)-Origin The Human Top & The Tough Kid Squad; The Flying Flame app. 250.00 750.00 1750.00

TOWER OF SHADOWS (Creatures on the Loose #10 on)
Sept, 1969 - No. 9, Jan, 1971
Marvel Comics Group

1-Steranko, Craig-a .50 1.00
2-Neal Adams-a .40 .80
3-Smith, Tuska-a .40 .80
4-Kirby/Everett-c .25 .50
5,7-Smith(p), Wood-a (Wood draws himself-1st pg., 1st panel-#5) .25 .75 1.50
6,8: Wood-a; 8-Wrightson-c .40 .80
9-Wrightson-c; Roy Thomas app. .25 .50
Special 1(12/71)-Adams-a .25 .50

NOTE: ***J. Buscema** a-1p, 2p. **Colan** a-3p, 6p. **J. Craig** a-1. **Ditko** a-6, 8, 9r, Special 1. **Everett** a-9(i)r; c-5i. **Kirby** a-9(p)r. **Severin** c-5p, 6. **Steranko** a-1. **Wood** a-5-8. Issues 1-9 contain new stories with some pre-Marvel age reprints in 6-9. H. P. Lovecraft adaptation-9.*

TOWN & COUNTRY
May, 1940
Publisher?

Good / Fine / Mint

Origin The Falcon 20.00 60.00 140.00

TOWN THAT FORGOT SANTA, THE
1961 (24 pages) (Giveaway)
W. T. Grant Co.

nn 1.35 4.00 9.00

TOYLAND COMICS
Jan, 1947 - No. 4, July?, 1947
Fiction House Magazines

1 7.00 21.00 50.00
2-4: 3-Tuska-a 4.35 13.00 30.00
148 pg. issue 10.00 30.00 70.00

NOTE: *All above contain strips by **Al Walker**.*

TOY TOWN COMICS
1945 - No. 7, May, 1947
Toytown/Orbit Publ./B. Antin/Swapper Quarterly

1-Mertie Mouse; L. B. Cole-c/a 7.00 21.00 50.00
2-L. B. Cole-a 3.70 11.00 26.00
3-7-L. B. Cole-a 3.00 9.00 21.00

TRAGG AND THE SKY GODS (See Mystery Comics Digest #3,9 & Spine Tingling Tales) (Painted-c #3-8)
June, 1975 - No. 8, Feb, 1977; No. 9, May, 1982
Gold Key/Whitman No. 9

1-Origin .60 1.20
2-9: 4-Sabre-Fang app. 8-Ostellon app.; 9-r #1 .40 .80

NOTE: ***Santos** a-1,2,9r; c-3-7. **Spiegel** a-3-8.*

TRAIL BLAZERS (Red Dragon #5 on)
1941 - 1942
Street & Smith Publications

1-True stories of American heroes 11.00 32.00 76.00
2 7.00 21.00 50.00
3,4 6.50 19.50 45.00

TRAIL COLT
1949
Magazine Enterprises

nn(A-1 24)-7 pg. Frazetta-a r-in Manhunt #13; Undercover Girl app.; The Red Fox by L. B. Cole; Ingels-c; (Scarce) 24.00 72.00 168.00
2(A-1 26)-Undercover Girl; Ingels-c; L. B. Cole-a, 6pgs. 17.00 51.00 120.00

TRANSFORMERS, THE (TV)
Sept, 1984 - Present (75 cents, $1.00)
Marvel Comics Group

1-Based on Hasbro toy 1.00 3.00 6.00
2,3 .50 1.50 3.00
4-10 .35 1.10 2.20
11-15 .65 1.30
16-27: 21-Intro The Aerialbots .40 .80
28-40 ($1.00) .45 .90

NOTE: *Second and third printings of all issues exist.*

TRANSFORMERS COMICS MAGAZINE, THE
Oct, 1986 - Present ($1.50, Digest-size)
Marvel Comics Group

1-10 .25 .75 1.50

TRANSFORMERS: HEADMASTERS
July, 1987 - No. 4, 1987 (mini-series)
Marvel Comics Group

1 .35 1.00 2.00
2-4 .25 .75 1.50

TRANSFORMERS IN 3-D
1987 - Present ($2.50)
Blackthorne Publishing

	Good	Fine	Mint
1,2	.40	1.25	2.50

TRANSFORMERS, THE MOVIE
Dec, 1986 - No. 3, Feb, 1987 (mini-series)
Marvel Comics Group

	Good	Fine	Mint
1-Adapts animated movie	.25	.75	1.50
2,3		.50	1.00

TRANSFORMERS UNIVERSE, THE
Dec, 1986 - No. 4, March, 1987 ($1.25, mini-series)
Marvel Comics Group

	Good	Fine	Mint
1-A guide to all characters	.35	1.00	2.00
2-4		.65	1.30

TRAPPED
1951 (Giveaway) (16 pages) (soft cover)
Harvey Publications (Columbia University Press)

	Good	Fine	Mint
Drug education comic (30,000 printed?) distributed to schools. Mentioned in **SOTI**, pgs. 256,350	2.00	6.00	12.00

NOTE: *Many copies surfaced in 1979 causing a setback in price; beware of trimmed edges, because many copies have a brittle edge.*

TRAPPED!
Oct, 1954 - No. 5, June?, 1955
Periodical House Magazines (Ace)

	Good	Fine	Mint
1 (All-r)	3.50	10.50	24.00
2-5: 4-r-entire Men Against Crime 4	1.85	5.50	13.00

NOTE: ***Colan** a-1, 4. **Sekowsky** a-1.*

TRAVELS OF HAPPY HOOLIGAN, THE
1906 (10¼"x15¾", 32 pgs., cardboard covers)
Frederick A. Stokes Co.

	Good	Fine	Mint
1905-r	18.00	54.00	125.00

TRAVELS OF JAIMIE McPHEETERS,THE (TV)
December, 1963
Gold Key

	Good	Fine	Mint
1-Kurt Russell	1.50	4.50	10.00

TREASURE BOX OF FAMOUS COMICS
Mid 1930's (36 pgs.) (6-7/8"x8½") (paper covers)
Cupples & Leon Co.

	Good	Fine	Mint
Box plus 5 titles: Reg'lar Fellers(1928), Little Orphan Annie(1926), Smitty(1928), Harold Teen(1931), How D. Tracy & D. Tracy Jr. Caught The Racketeers (1933) (These are abbreviated versions of hardcover editions) (Set)....	70.00	200.00	425.00

NOTE: *Dates shown are copyright dates; all books actually came out in 1934 or later.*

TREASURE CHEST (Catholic Guild; also see Topix)
3/12/46 - V27#8, July, 1972 (Educational comics)
George A. Pflaum (not publ. during summer)

	Good	Fine	Mint
V1#1	7.00	21.00	50.00
2-6 (5/21/46): 5-Dr. Styx app. by Baily	3.00	9.00	21.00
V2#1 (9/3/46) - 6	1.50	4.50	10.00
V3#1-5,7-20 (1st slick cover)	1.50	4.50	10.00
V3#6-Jules Verne's "Voyage to the Moon"	3.35	10.00	22.00
V4#1-20 (9/9/48-5/31/49)	1.35	4.00	8.00
V5#1-20 (9/6/49-5/31/50)	1.00	3.00	6.00
V6#1-20 (9/14/50-5/31/51)	1.00	3.00	6.00
V7#1-20 (9/13/51-6/5/52)	.70	2.00	4.00
V8#1-20 (9/11/52-6/4/53)	.70	2.00	4.00
V9#1-20 ('53-'54)	.50	1.50	3.00
V10#1-20 ('54-'55)	.50	1.50	3.00
V11('55-'56), V12('56-'57)	.50	1.50	3.00
V13#1,3-5,7,9,10,12-V17#1 ('57-'63)	.35	1.00	2.00
V13#2,6,8,11-Ingels-a	2.00	6.00	14.00
V17#2-'This Godless Communism' series begins (Not in V17#3,7,11) Cover shows hammer & sickle over Statue of Liberty; 8pg. Crandall-a of family life under communism	8.00	24.00	56.00
V17#3-7,9,11,13-15,17,19	.30	.80	1.60
V17#8-Shows red octopus encompassing Earth, firing squad; 8pg. Crandall-a	6.00	18.00	42.00
V17#10-'This Godless Communism'-how Stalin came to power, part I; Crandall-a	6.00	18.00	42.00
V17#12-Stalin in WWII, forced labor, death by exhaustion; Crandall-a	6.00	18.00	42.00
V17#16-Kruschev takes over; de-Stalinization	6.00	18.00	42.00
V17#18-Kruschev's control; murder of revolters, brainwash, space race by Crandall	6.00	18.00	42.00
V17#20-End of series; Kruschev-people are puppets, firing squads hammer & sickle over Statue of Liberty, snake around communist manifesto by Crandall	6.00	18.00	42.00
V18,V19#5,11-20,V20('64-'65)		.40	.80
V18#5-'What About Red China?'-describes how communists took over China	2.75	8.00	16.00
V19#1-4,6-10-'Red Victim' anti-communist series in all	2.75	8.00	16.00
V21-V25('65-'70)-(two V24#5's 11/7/68 & 11/21/68) (no V24#6)		.30	.60
V26, V27#1-8 (V26,27-68 pgs.)		.30	.60
Summer Edition V1#1-6('66), V2#1-6('67)		.20	.40

NOTE: ***Anderson** a-V18/13. **Borth** a-V7/10-19 (serial), V8/8-17 (serial), V9/1-10 (serial), V13/2, 6, 11, V15/2, V18/1, V19/4, 11, 19, V20/10, 15, 16, 18, V21/5, V22/7, 9, 14, V24/7, Summer Ed. V1/3, 5. **Crandall** a-V7/20, V16/7, 9, 12, 14, 17, 20; V17/1, 2, 4, 5, 14, 16-18, 20; V18/1, 7, 9, 10, 15, 17, 19; V19/4, 11, 13, 16, 19; V20/1, 2, 6, 9, 10, 12, 14-16, 18, 20; V21/1-3, 5, 8, 9, 11, 13, 16, 17; V22/3, 7, 9-11, 14, 16, 20; V23/3, 6, 9, 13, 16; V24/7, 8, 10; V25/16; V27/1, 3-5r, 6r, 8(2 pg.), Summer Ed. V1/3, 5; c-V16/7, V18/10, V19/4, V21/5, 9, V22/7, 11, V23/9, 16 at least. **Powell** a-V10/11. V19/11, 15, V10/13, V13/6, 8 all have wraparound covers. All the above Crandall issues should be priced by condition from $4-8.00 unless already priced.*

TREASURE CHEST OF THE WORLD'S BEST COMICS
1945 (500 pgs.) (hardcover)
Superior, Toronto, Canada

	Good	Fine	Mint
Contains Blue Beetle, Captain Combat, John Wayne, Dynamic Man, Nemo, Li'l Abner; contents can vary - represents random binding of extra books; Capt. America on-c	32.00	95.00	225.00

TREASURE COMICS
No date (1943) (324 pgs.; cardboard covers) (50 cents)
Prize Publications? (no publisher listed)

	Good	Fine	Mint
nn-(Rare)-Contains Prize Comics #7-11 from 1942 (blank inside-c)	130.00	390.00	910.00

TREASURE COMICS
June-July, 1945 - No. 12, Fall, 1947
Prize Publications (American Boys' Comics)

	Good	Fine	Mint
1-Paul Bunyan & Marco Polo begin; Highwayman & Carrot Topp only app.; Kiefer-a	8.50	25.50	60.00
2-Arabian Knight, Gorilla King, Dr. Styx begin	4.35	13.00	30.00
3,4,9,12	3.00	9.00	21.00
5-Marco Polo-c; Kirby a(p); Krigstein-a	6.00	18.00	42.00
6,11-Krigstein-a; c-#11	5.50	16.50	38.00
7,8-Frazetta, 5 pgs. each	20.00	60.00	140.00
10-Jr. Rangers by Kirby; Kirby-c	7.00	21.00	50.00

TREASURE ISLAND (See 4-Color No. 624, King Classics, & Movie Classics & Comics)

TREASURY OF COMICS
1947; No. 2, July, 1947 - No. 4, Sept, 1947; No. 5, Jan, 1948
St. John Publishing Co.

	Good	Fine	Mint
nn(#1)-Abbie 'n' Slats (nn on-c, #1 on inside)	7.00	21.00	50.00

Trapped! #3, © ACE

Treasure Chest V10#13, © G.A. Pflaum

Treasure Comics #3, © PRIZE

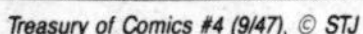
Treasury of Comics #4 (9/47), © STJ

True Comics #78, © PMI

True Complete Mystery #5, © MCG

TREASURY OF COMICS (continued)

	Good	Fine	Mint
2-Jim Hardy	5.00	15.00	35.00
3-Bill Bumlin	4.00	12.00	28.00
4-Abbie 'n' Slats	5.00	15.00	35.00
5-Jim Hardy Comics #1	5.00	15.00	35.00

TREASURY OF COMICS
Mar, 1948 - No. 5, 1948; 1948-1950-(Over 500 pgs., $1.00)
St. John Publishing Co.

1	10.00	30.00	70.00
2(#2 on-c, #1 on inside)	6.00	18.00	42.00
3-5	5.00	15.00	35.00
1-(1948, 500 pgs., hard-c)-Abbie & Slats, Abbott & Costello, Casper, Little Annie Rooney, Little Audrey, Jim Hardy, Ella Cinders (16 books bound together) (Rare)	90.00	270.00	630.00
1(1949, 500pgs.)-Same format as above	90.00	270.00	630.00
1(1950, 500pgs.)-Same format as above; different-c; (Also see Little Audrey Yearbook) (Rare)	90.00	270.00	630.00

TREASURY OF DOGS, A (See Dell Giants)

TREASURY OF HORSES, A (See Dell Giants)

TRIALS OF LULU AND LEANDER, THE
1906 (32 pgs. in color) (10x16")
William A. Stokes Co.

By F. M. Howarth	12.00	36.00	84.00

TRIGGER (See Roy Rogers . . .)

TRIGGER TWINS
Mar-Apr, 1973 (One Shot)
National Periodical Publications

1-Trigger Twins & Pow Wow Smith-r; Infantino-a(p)		.40	.80

TRIPLE GIANT COMICS (See Archie All-Star Spec. under Archie Comics)

TRIPLE THREAT
Winter, 1945
Special Action/Holyoke/Gerona Publ.

1-Duke of Darkness, King O'Leary	5.00	15.00	35.00

TRIP WITH SANTA ON CHRISTMAS EVE, A
No date (early 50's) (16 pgs.; full color; paper cover)
Rockford Dry Goods Co. (Giveaway)

	2.00	6.00	12.00

TROUBLE SHOOTERS, THE (See 4-Color No. 1108)

TRUE ADVENTURES (Formerly True Western)(Men's Advs. #4 on)
No. 3, May, 1950
Marvel Comics (CCC)

3-Powell, Sekowsky-a	4.60	14.00	32.00

TRUE ANIMAL PICTURE STORIES
Winter, 1947 - No. 2, Spr-Summer, 1947
True Comics Press

1,2	2.65	8.00	18.00

TRUE AVIATION PICTURE STORIES (Aviation Adventures & Model Building #16)
1942 - No. 15, Sept-Oct, 1946
Parents' Magazine Institute

1-(#1 & 2 titled . . . Aviation Comics Digest)(not digest size)	6.00	18.00	42.00
2	3.50	10.50	24.00
3-14	2.65	8.00	18.00
15-(titled "True Aviation Advs. & Model Building")	2.65	8.00	18.00

TRUE BRIDE'S EXPERIENCES (Formerly Teen-Age Brides)
(True Bride-To-Be Romances No. 17 on)
No. 8, Oct, 1954 - No. 16, Feb, 1956
True Love (Harvey Publications)

	Good	Fine	Mint
8	1.70	5.00	12.00
9,10: 10-Last pre-code (2/55)	1.35	4.00	9.00
11-15	1.00	3.00	7.00
16-Spanking issue	5.00	15.00	35.00

NOTE: ***Powell*** *a-8-10, 12, 13.*

TRUE BRIDE-TO-BE ROMANCES (Formerly True Bride's Exp.)
No. 17, Apr, 1956 - No. 30, Nov, 1958
Home Comics/True Love (Harvey)

17-S&K-c, Powell-a	2.00	6.00	14.00
18-20,22,25-28,30	1.00	3.00	7.00
21,23,24-Powell-a	1.20	3.50	8.00
29-Powell, 1 pg. Baker-a	1.35	4.00	9.00

TRUE COMICS (Also see Outstanding American War Heroes)
April, 1941 - No. 84, Aug, 1950
True Comics/Parents' Magazine Press

1-Marathon run story	11.50	34.00	80.00
2-Everett-a	6.50	19.50	45.00
3-5: 3-Baseball Hall of Fame sty. 4-Sty. of American flag "Old Glory." 5-Life story of Joe Louis	5.50	16.50	38.00
6-Baseball World Series sty.	4.35	13.00	30.00
7-10	3.70	11.00	26.00
11-20: 13-Harry Houdini sty. 14-Charlie McCarthy sty. 15-Flag-c; Bob Feller sty. 17-Brooklyn Dodgers sty. 18-Story of America begins, ends #26	3.00	9.00	21.00
21-30	2.65	8.00	18.00
31-Red Grange story	2.30	7.00	16.00
32-45	1.70	5.00	12.00
46-George Gershwin sty.	1.70	5.00	12.00
47-Atomic bomb issue	3.50	10.50	24.00
48-67: 55(12/46)-1st app. Sad Sack by Baker, ½ pg. 58-Jim Jeffries (boxer) sty.; Harry Houdini sty. 59-Bob Hope sty. 66-Will Rogers story	1.30	4.00	9.00
68-1st oversized ish?; Steve Saunders, Special Agent begins	2.00	6.00	14.00
69-72,74-79: 69-Jack Benny sty.	1.15	3.50	8.00
73-Walt Disney's life story	2.00	6.00	14.00
80-84 (Scarce)-All distr. to subscribers through mail only; paper-c	18.00	54.00	125.00

(Prices vary widely on these books)

NOTE: ***Bob Kane*** *a-7.* ***Palais*** *a-80.* ***Powell*** *c/a-80. No. 80-84 have soft covers and combined with Tex Granger, Jack Armstrong, and Calling All Kids. No. 68-78 featured true FBI adventures.*

TRUE COMICS AND ADVENTURE STORIES
1965 (Giant) (25 cents)
Parents' Magazine Institute

1,2-Fighting Hero of Viet Nam; LBJ on-c	.50	1.50	3.00

TRUE COMPLETE MYSTERY (Formerly Complete Mystery)
No. 5, April, 1949 - No. 8, Oct, 1949
Marvel Comics (PrPl)

5	5.70	17.00	40.00
6-8: 6,8-Photo-c	4.60	14.00	32.00

TRUE CONFESSIONS
1949
Fawcett Publications

1	5.00	15.00	35.00

TRUE CONFIDENCES
1949 (Fall) - No. 4, June, 1950 (All photo-c)
Fawcett Publications

1-Has ad for Fawcett Love Adventures #1, but publ. as Love Memoirs #1 as Marvel publ. the title first	5.00	15.00	35.00
2-4: 4-Powell-a	2.30	7.00	16.00

TRUE CRIME CASES
1944; V1No.6, June-July 1949 - V2No.1, Aug-Oct, 1949
St. John Publishing Co.

	Good	Fine	Mint
1944-(100 pgs.)	17.00	51.00	120.00
V1#6, V2#1	3.50	10.50	24.00

TRUE CRIME COMICS (Also see Complete Book of. . .)
No. 2, May, 1947; No. 3, Jul-Aug, 1948 - No. 6, June-Jul, 1949; V2No.1, Aug-Sept, 1949
Magazine Village

	Good	Fine	Mint
2-Jack Cole c/a; used in **SOTI**, pg. 81,82 plus illo.-"A sample of the injury-to-eye motif" & illo.-"Dragging living people to death;" used in **POP**, pg. 105; "Murder, Morphine and Me" classic drug propaganda story used by N.Y. Legis. Comm.	87.00	261.00	610.00
3-Classic Cole c/a; drug sty with hypo, opium den & withdrawing addict	56.00	168.00	390.00
4-Jack Cole-c/a; c-taken from a story panel in #3; r-(2) **SOTI** & **POP** stories/#2	50.00	150.00	350.00
5-Jack Cole-c; Marijuana racket story	25.00	75.00	175.00
6	10.00	30.00	70.00
V2#1-Used in **SOTI**, pgs. 81,82 & illo.-"Dragging living people to death;" Toth, Wood (3 pgs.), Roussos-a; Cole-r from #2	36.00	108.00	252.00

NOTE: *V2#1 was reprinted in Canada as V2#9 (12/49); same cover & contents minus Wood-a.*

TRUE GHOST STORIES (See Ripley's. . .)

TRUE LIFE ROMANCES (. . .Romance on cover)
Dec, 1955 - No. 3, Aug, 1956
Ajax/Farrell Publications

	Good	Fine	Mint
1	3.50	10.50	24.00
2	1.70	5.00	12.00
3-Disbrow-a	2.65	8.00	18.00

TRUE LIFE SECRETS
Mar-April, 1951 - No. 28, Sept, 1955; No. 29, Jan, 1956
Romantic Love Stories/Charlton

	Good	Fine	Mint
1	4.35	13.00	30.00
2	2.65	8.00	18.00
3-12,15-19	2.00	6.00	14.00
13-Headlight-a	5.35	16.00	37.00
14-Drug mention story(marijuana)	3.15	9.50	22.00
20-22,24-29	1.50	4.50	10.00
23-Suggestive-c	2.65	8.00	18.00

TRUE LIFE TALES (Formerly Lana?)
No. 8, Oct, 1949 - No. 2, Jan, 1950
Marvel Comics (CCC)

	Good	Fine	Mint
8(10/49), 2(1/50)-Photo-c	2.65	8.00	18.00

TRUE LOVE
Jan, 1986 - No. 2, Jan, 1986 ($2.00, Baxter paper)
Eclipse Comics

	Good	Fine	Mint
1,2-Love stories-r from pre-code Standard Comics; Toth-a	.35	1.00	2.00

TRUE LOVE CONFESSIONS
May, 1954 - No. 11, Jan, 1956
Premier Magazines

	Good	Fine	Mint
1-Marijuana story	4.00	12.00	28.00
2	1.70	5.00	12.00
3-11	1.30	4.00	9.00

TRUE LOVE PICTORIAL
1952 - No. 11, Aug, 1954
St. John Publishing Co.

	Good	Fine	Mint
1	5.50	16.50	38.00
2	2.65	8.00	18.00
3-5(All 100 pgs.): 5-Formerly Teen-Age Temptations (4/53); Kubert-a-#3,5; Baker-a-#3-5	15.00	45.00	105.00
6,7-Baker c/a	5.70	17.00	40.00
8,10,11-Baker c/a	5.00	15.00	35.00
9-Baker-c	3.70	11.00	26.00

TRUE MOVIE AND TELEVISION (Part magazine)
No. 1, Aug, 1950 - No. 3, Nov, 1950 (52 pgs.) (10 cents)
Toby Press

	Good	Fine	Mint
1-Liz Taylor photo-c; Gene Autry, Shirley Temple, Li'l Abner app.	18.00	54.00	125.00
2-Frazetta John Wayne illo	11.50	34.00	80.00
3-June Allyson-c; Montgomery Cliff, Esther Williams, Andrews Sisters app; Li'l Abner feat.	11.50	34.00	80.00

NOTE: ***16 pages in color, rest movie material in black & white.***

TRUE SECRETS (Formerly Love Dramas?)
No. 3, Mar, 1950; No. 4, Feb, 1951 - No. 40, Sept, 1956
Marvel (IPS)/Atlas Comics (MPI)

	Good	Fine	Mint
3 (52 pgs.)	3.50	10.50	24.00
4,5,7-10	1.70	5.00	12.00
6,22-Everett-a	2.30	7.00	16.00
11-20	1.30	4.00	9.00
21,23-28: 28-Last pre-code (2/55)	1.00	3.00	7.00
29-40	.85	2.50	6.00

NOTE: ***Colletta** a-34, 36; c-24.*

TRUE SPORT PICTURE STORIES (Formerly Sport Comics)
Feb, 1942? - V5/2, July-Aug, 1949
Street & Smith Publications

	Good	Fine	Mint
V1#5	8.50	25.50	60.00
6-12 (1942-43)	5.00	15.00	35.00
V2#1-12 (1944-45)	4.00	12.00	28.00
V3#1-12 (1946-47)	3.00	9.00	21.00
V4#1-12 (1948-49), V5/1,2	2.30	7.00	16.00

NOTE: ***Powell** a-V3#10, V4#1-4, 6-8, 10-12; V5#1, 2; c-V4#5, 6, 9, 10.*

TRUE STORIES OF ROMANCE
Jan, 1950 - No. 3, May, 1950 (All photo-c)
Fawcett Publications

	Good	Fine	Mint
1	4.35	13.00	30.00
2,3	2.65	8.00	18.00

TRUE STORY OF JESSE JAMES, THE (See 4-Color No. 757)

TRUE SWEETHEART SECRETS
May, 1950 - No. 11, Jan, 1953 (All photo-c?)
Fawcett Publications

	Good	Fine	Mint
1-Photo-c; Debbie Reynolds?	4.35	13.00	30.00
2-Wood-a, 11 pgs.	8.00	24.00	56.00
3-11: 4,5-Powell-a	2.35	7.00	16.00

TRUE TALES OF LOVE (Formerly Secret Story Romances)
No. 22, April, 1956 - No. 31, Sept, 1957
Atlas Comics (TCI)

	Good	Fine	Mint
22	1.60	4.70	11.00
23-31-Colletta-a in most	.85	2.50	6.00

TRUE TALES OF ROMANCE
No. 4, June, 1950
Fawcett Publications

	Good	Fine	Mint
4	2.65	8.00	18.00

TRUE 3-D
Dec, 1953 - No. 2, Feb, 1954
Harvey Publications

	Good	Fine	Mint
1-Nostrand, Powell-a	5.70	17.00	40.00

True Crime Comics #5, © Magazine Village

True Life Romances #1, © AJAX

True Sport Picture Stories V2#4, © S & S

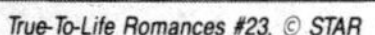
True-To-Life Romances #23, © STAR

Tuff Ghosts Starring Spooky #20, © HARV

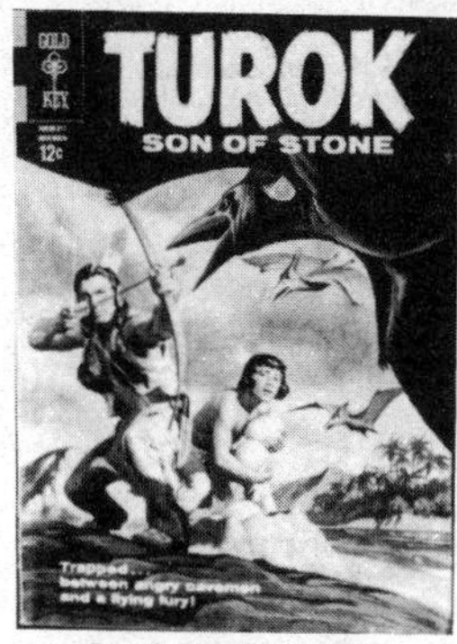

Turok, Son of Stone #36, © GK

TRUE 3-D (continued)

	Good	Fine	Mint
2-Powell-a	10.00	30.00	70.00

NOTE: *Many copies of No. 1 surfaced in 1984.*

TRUE-TO-LIFE ROMANCES
No. 9, 1-2/50; No. 3, 4/50 - No. 23, 10/54
Star Publications

	Good	Fine	Mint
9(1950)	5.00	15.00	35.00
3-10	4.35	13.00	30.00
11,22,23	4.00	12.00	28.00
12-14,17-21-Disbrow-a	6.00	16.00	37.00
15,16-Wood & Disbrow-a in each	8.35	25.00	58.00

NOTE: ***Kamen** a-13. **Kamen/Feldstein** a-14. All have **L.B. Cole** covers.*

TRUE WAR EXPERIENCES
Aug, 1952 - No. 4, Dec, 1952
Harvey Publications

	Good	Fine	Mint
1	2.35	7.00	16.00
2-4	1.35	4.00	9.00

TRUE WAR ROMANCES
Sept, 1952 - No. 21, June, 1955
Quality Comics Group

	Good	Fine	Mint
1-Photo-c	4.60	14.00	32.00
2	2.30	7.00	16.00
3-10: 9-Whitney-a	1.85	5.50	13.00
11-21: 14-Whitney-a	1.50	4.50	10.00

TRUE WAR STORIES (See Ripley's...)

TRUE WESTERN (True Adventures #3)
Dec, 1949 - No. 2, March, 1950
Marvel Comics (MMC)

	Good	Fine	Mint
1-Photo-c	4.60	14.00	32.00
2: Alan Ladd photo-c	5.00	15.00	35.00

TRUE WEST ROMANCE
1952
Quality Comics Group

	Good	Fine	Mint
21 (Exist?)	2.65	8.00	18.00

TRUMP (Magazine format)
Jan, 1957 - No. 2, Mar, 1957
HMH Publishing Co.

	Good	Fine	Mint
1-Harvey Kurtzman satire	8.50	25.50	60.00
2-Harvey Kurtzman satire	6.50	19.50	45.00

NOTE: ***Davis, Elder, Heath, Jaffee** art-#1,2; **Wood**-#1. #2-article by Mel Brooks.*

TRUMPETS WEST (See 4-Color No. 875)

TRUTH ABOUT CRIME (See Fox Giants)

TRUTH ABOUT MOTHER GOOSE (See 4-Color No. 862)

TRUTH BEHIND THE TRIAL OF CARDINAL MINDSZENTY, THE (See Cardinal...)

TRUTHFUL LOVE (Formerly Youthful Love)
No. 2, July, 1950
Youthful Magazines

	Good	Fine	Mint
2-Ingrid Bergman's true life story	2.30	7.00	16.00

TRY-OUT WINNER BOOK
Mar, 1988
Marvel Comics

	Good	Fine	Mint
1-Spider-Man vs. Doc. Octopus		.60	1.25

TUBBY (See Marge's...)

TUFF GHOSTS STARRING SPOOKY
7/62 - No. 39, 11/70; No. 40, 9/71 - No. 43, 10/72
Harvey Publications

	Good	Fine	Mint
1	4.00	12.00	24.00
2-5	2.00	6.00	12.00
6-10	1.35	4.00	8.00
11-20	.70	2.00	4.00
21-30	.50	1.50	3.00
31-43		.50	1.00

TUFFY
1949 - 1950
Standard Comics

	Good	Fine	Mint
1-All by Sid Hoff	2.65	8.00	18.00
2	1.30	4.00	9.00
3-10	1.15	3.50	8.00

TUFFY TURTLE
No date
I. W. Enterprises

	Good	Fine	Mint
1-Reprint	.30	.80	1.60

TUROK, SON OF STONE (See Golden Comics Digest #31, March of Comics #378,399,408, and Dan Curtis)
No. 596, 12/54 - No. 29, 6-8/62; No. 30, 12/62 - No. 125, 1/80; No. 126, 3/81 - No. 130, 4/82
Dell Publ. Co. No. 1-29/Gold Key No. 30-125/Whitman No. 126 on

	Good	Fine	Mint
4-Color 596 (12/54)(#1)	19.00	57.00	132.00
4-Color 656 (10/55)	13.00	40.00	90.00
3(3-5/56)-5	10.00	30.00	70.00
6-10	6.50	19.50	45.00
11-20	3.50	10.50	24.00
21-30: 30-back-c pinups begin	1.70	5.00	12.00
31-50: 31-Drug use story	.85	2.50	6.00
51-60	.70	2.00	4.00
61-83: 63-Only line drawn-c	.35	1.00	2.00
84-Origin & 1st app. Hutec	.35	1.00	2.00
85-130: 114-(52 pgs.)		.50	1.00
Giant 1(30031-611) (11/66)	3.50	10.50	28.00

NOTE: ***Alberto Gioletti** painted-c No. 30-129. **Sparling** a-126-30. Reprints-#36, 54, 57, 75, 112, 118, 125, 127-130(⅓).*

TURTLE SOUP
Sept., 1987 (One shot, B&W, $2.00, 76 pgs.)
Mirage Studios

	Good	Fine	Mint
1-Feat. Teenage Mutant Ninja Turtles	.25	.75	1.50

TV CASPER & COMPANY
Aug, 1963 - No. 46, April, 1974 (25 cent Giants)
Harvey Publications

	Good	Fine	Mint
1	4.00	12.00	24.00
2-5	2.00	6.00	12.00
6-10	1.35	4.00	8.00
11-20	.70	2.00	4.00
21-30	.50	1.50	3.00
31-46		.50	1.00

TV FUNDAY FUNNIES (See Famous TV...)

TV FUNNIES (See New Funnies)

TV FUNTIME (See Little Audrey)

TV LAUGHOUT (See Archie's...)

TV SCREEN CARTOONS (Formerly Real Screen)
No. 129, July-Aug, 1959 - No. 138, Jan-Feb, 1961
National Periodical Publications

	Good	Fine	Mint
129-138 (Scarce)	1.60	4.70	11.00

TV STARS (TV)(Hanna-Barbera)
Aug, 1978 - No. 4, Feb, 1979
Marvel Comics Group

	Good	Fine	Mint
1-Sparling-a		.50	1.00
2,4		.40	.80

TV STARS (continued)

	Good	Fine	Mint
3-Toth-c/a	.50	1.50	3.00

TV TEENS (Formerly Ozzie & Babs; Rock and Rollo #14 on)
Feb, 1954 - V2No.13, July, 1956
Charlton Comics

	Good	Fine	Mint
V1#14-Ozzie & Babs	3.00	9.00	21.00
15	1.70	5.00	12.00
V2#3(6/54) - 7-Don Winslow	2.00	6.00	14.00
8(7/55)-13-Mopsy	1.70	5.00	12.00

TWEETY AND SYLVESTER (1st Series)
No. 406, June, 1952 - No. 37, June-Aug, 1962
Dell Publishing Co.

	Good	Fine	Mint
4-Color 406	1.30	4.00	9.00
4-Color 489,524	1.00	3.00	7.00
4 (3-5/54) - 20	.85	2.50	6.00
21-37	.55	1.65	4.00

(See March of Comics No. 421,433,445,457,469,481)

TWEETY AND SYLVESTER (2nd Series)
Nov, 1963; No. 2, Nov, 1965 - No. 121, July, 1984
Gold Key No. 1-102/Whitman No. 103 on

	Good	Fine	Mint
1	.85	2.50	6.00
2-10	.45	1.35	3.00
11-30	.25	.75	1.50
31-70		.50	1.00
71-121: 99,119-r(1/3)		.30	.60
Kite Fun Book (1965, 16pgs., 5x7¼", soft-c)	.50	1.50	3.00
Mini Comic No. 1(1976)-3¼x6½"		.30	.60

12 O'CLOCK HIGH (TV)
Jan-Mar, 1965 - No. 2, Apr-June, 1965 (Photo-c)
Dell Publishing Co.

	Good	Fine	Mint
1,2	2.30	7.00	16.00

24 PAGES OF COMICS (No title) (Also see Pure Oil Comics, Salerno Carnival of Comics, & Vicks Comics)
Late 1930s
Giveaway by various outlets including Sears

	Good	Fine	Mint
Contains strip reprints-Buck Rogers, Napoleon, Sky Roads, War on Crime	20.00	60.00	140.00

20,000 LEAGUES UNDER THE SEA (See 4-Color No. 614, King Classics, and Movie Comics)

TWICE TOLD TALES (See Movie Classics)

TWILIGHT AVENGER, THE
July, 1986 - No. 4, Jan, 1987 ($1.75, color, mini-series)
Elite Comics

	Good	Fine	Mint
1-4	.35	1.00	2.00

TWILIGHT ZONE, THE (TV) (See Dan Curtis)
No. 1173, 3-5/61 - No. 91, 4/79; No. 92, 5/82
Dell Publishing Co./Gold Key/Whitman No. 92

	Good	Fine	Mint
4-Color 1173-Crandall/Evans-c/a	4.60	14.00	32.00
4-Color 1288-Crandall/Evans c/a	3.70	11.00	26.00
01-860-207 (5-7/62-Dell)	3.00	9.00	21.00
12-860-210 on-c; 01-860-210 on inside(8-10/62-Dell)-Evans c/a; Crandall/Frazetta-a(2)	3.00	9.00	21.00
1(11/62-Gold Key)-Crandall,Evans-a	3.00	9.00	21.00
2,5-8,10,11	1.15	3.50	8.00
3,4,9-Toth-a, 11,10 & 15 pgs.	1.75	5.25	12.00
12-Williamson-a	1.65	5.00	10.00
13,15-Crandall-a	1.65	5.00	10.00
14-Williamson/Orlando/Crandall/Torres-a	2.00	6.00	12.00
16-20	.85	2.50	6.00
21-Crandall-a(r)	.70	2.00	4.00
22-24	.50	1.50	3.00
25-Evans/Crandall-a(r)	.50	1.50	3.00
26-Crandall, Evans-a(r)	.50	1.50	3.00
27-Evans-a(2)(r)	.50	1.50	3.00
28-32: 32-Evans-a(r)	.35	1.00	2.00
33-42,44-50,52-70	.25	.75	1.50
43-Crandall-a	.30	.90	1.80
51-Williamson-a	.30	.90	1.80
71-92: 71-Reprint. 83,84-(52 pgs.)		.50	1.00
Mini Comic #1(1976-3¼x6½")		.30	.60

NOTE: ***Bolle*** *a-13(w/**McWilliams**), 50, 57, 59.* ***McWilliams*** *a-59.* ***Orlando*** *a-19, 20, 22, 23.* ***Sekowsky*** *a-3. (See Mystery Comics Digest 3, 6, 9, 12, 15, 18, 21, 24). Reprints-26(1/3), 71, 73, 79, 83, 84, 86, 92. Painted-c 1-91.*

TWINKLE COMICS
May, 1945
Spotlight Publishers

	Good	Fine	Mint
1	5.00	15.00	35.00

TWIST, THE
July-September, 1962
Dell Publishing Co.

	Good	Fine	Mint
01-864-209-painted-c	3.00	9.00	21.00

TWISTED TALES
11/82 - No. 8, 5/84; No. 9, 11/84; No. 10, 12/84 (Baxter paper)
Pacific Comics/Independent Comics Group No. 9, 10/Blackthorne

	Good	Fine	Mint
1-Nudity/Violence in all	.50	1.50	3.00
2-10	.25	.75	1.50
3-D 1-r/earlier issues in 3-D	.45	1.25	2.50

NOTE: ***Alcala*** *a-1.* ***John Bolton*** *painted c-4, 6, 7; a-7.* ***Conrad*** *a-1.* ***Corben*** *a-1, 3, 5; c-1, 3, 5.* ***Guice*** *a-8.* ***Morrow*** *a-10.* ***Ploog*** *a-2.* ***Wildey*** *a-3.* ***Wrightson*** *a(Painted)-10; c-2.*

TWISTED TALES
1988 ($3.95, bi-annual, 52 pgs.)
Eclipse Comics

	Good	Fine	Mint
1	.70	2.00	3.95

TWISTED TALES OF BRUCE JONES, THE
Feb, 1986 - No. 4, Mar, 1986 ($1.75, Baxter)
Eclipse Comics

	Good	Fine	Mint
1-4	.30	.90	1.80

TWO BIT THE WACKY WOODPECKER (See Wacky. . .)
1951 - No. 3, May, 1953
Toby Press

	Good	Fine	Mint
1	2.15	6.50	15.00
2,3	1.15	3.50	8.00

TWO FACES OF COMMUNISM (Also see Double Talk)
1961 (36 pgs.; paper cover) (Giveaway)
Christian Anti-Communism Crusade, Houston, Texas

	Good	Fine	Mint
	10.00	30.00	70.00

TWO-FISTED TALES (Formerly Haunt of Fear #15-17)
No. 18, Nov-Dec, 1950 - No. 41, Feb-Mar, 1955
E. C. Comics

	Good	Fine	Mint
18(#1)-Kurtzman-c	61.00	182.00	430.00
19-Kurtzman-c	45.00	135.00	315.00
20-Kurtzman-c	27.00	81.00	190.00
21,22-Kurtzman-c	21.00	62.00	145.00
23-25-Kurtzman-c	15.00	45.00	105.00
26-35: 33-"Atom Bomb" by Wood	12.00	36.00	80.00
36-41	7.35	22.00	50.00
Two-Fisted Annual, 1952	61.00	182.00	430.00
Two-Fisted Annual, 1953	45.00	135.00	315.00

NOTE: ***Berg*** *a-29.* ***Craig*** *a-18, 19, 32.* ***Crandall*** *a-35, 36.* ***Davis*** *a-20-36, 40; c-30, 34, 35, 41, Annual 2.* ***Evans*** *a-34, 40, 41; c-40.* ***Feldstein*** *a-18.* ***Krigstein*** *a-41.* ***Kubert*** *a-32, 33.* ***Kurtzman*** *a-18-25; c-18-29, 31, Annual 1.* ***Severin*** *a-26, 28, 29, 31, 34-41*

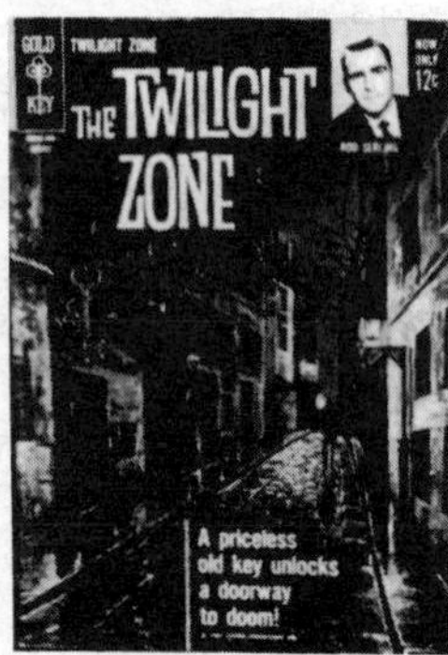

The Twilight Zone #4, © GK

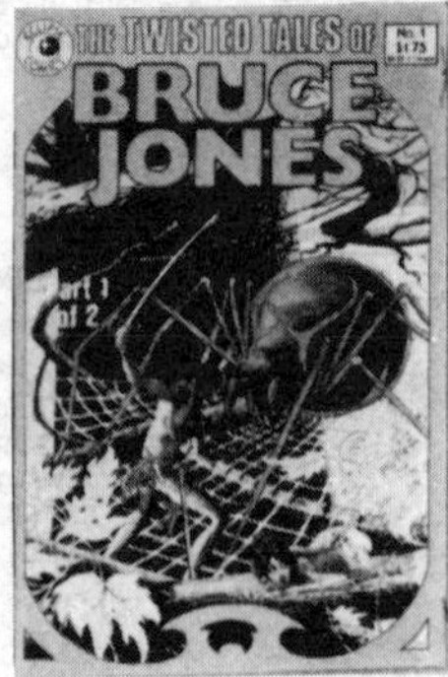

The Twisted Tales of Bruce Jones #1, © Eclipse

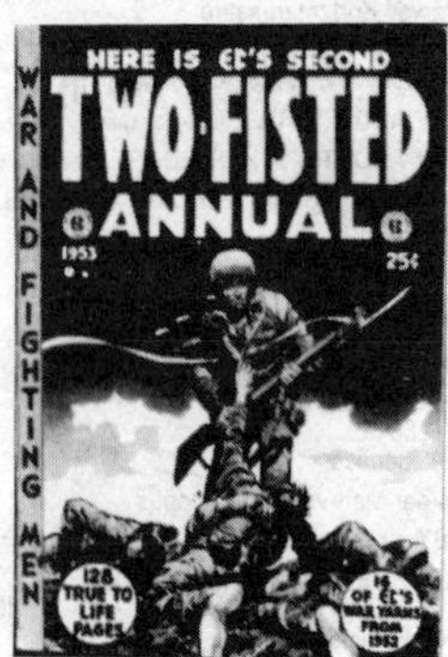

Two-Fisted Tales Annual #2, © WMG

Two Gun Western #11 (1st series), © MCG

2000 A.D. Presents #5, © Quality Comics

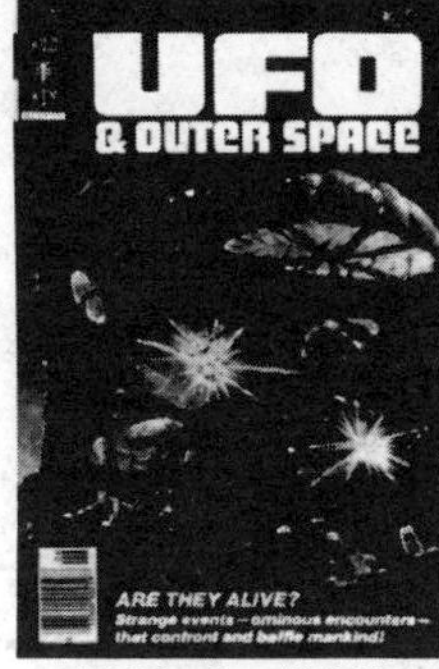

UFO & Outer Space #14, © GK

TWO-FISTED TALES (continued)

*(No.37-39 are **all-Severin** issues); c-36-39. **Severin/Elder** a-19-29, 31, 33, 36. **Wood** a-18-28, 30-35, 41; c-32, 33. Special issues: #26 (ChanJin Reservoir), 31 (Civil War), 35 (Civil War). Canadian reprints known; see Table of Contents.*

TWO-GUN KID (Also see All Western Winners, Best Western, Black Rider, Blaze Carson, Kid Colt, Western Winners, Wild West, & Wild Western)
3/48(No mo.) - No. 10, 11/49; No. 11, 12/53 - No. 59, 4/61; No. 60, 11/62 - No. 92, 3/68; No. 93, 7/70 - No. 136, 4/77
Marvel/Atlas (MCI No. 1-10/HPC No. 11-59/Marvel No. 60 on)

	Good	Fine	Mint
1-Two-Gun Kid & his horse Cyclone begin; The Sheriff begins	24.00	72.00	170.00
2	11.00	32.00	76.00
3,4: 3-Annie Oakley app.	8.00	24.00	56.00
5-Pre-Black Rider app. (Wint. 48/49); Spanking panel. Anti-Wertham editorial (1st?)	10.00	30.00	70.00
6-10 (11/49)	4.70	17.00	40.00
11 (12/53)-Black Rider app.	4.35	13.00	30.00
12-Black Rider app.	4.35	13.00	30.00
13-20	3.70	11.00	26.00
21-24,26-29	3.00	9.00	21.00
25,30-Williamson-a in both, 5 & 4 pgs.	4.00	12.00	28.00
31-33,35,37-40	2.00	6.00	14.00
34-Crandall-a	2.65	8.00	18.00
36,41,42,48-Origin in all	2.30	7.00	16.00
43,44,47	1.30	4.00	9.00
45,46-Davis-a	2.15	6.50	15.00
49,50,52,55,57-Severin-a(3) in each	1.30	4.00	9.00
51-Williamson-a, 5pgs.	2.75	8.25	19.00
53,54,56	.70	2.00	4.00
58,60-New origin. 58-Last 10 cent ish.	.70	2.00	4.00
59,61-80: 64-Intro. Boom-Boom	.25	.75	1.50
81-92: 92-Last new story		.30	.60
93-100,102-136		.25	.50
101-Origin retold/#58		.30	.60

NOTE: ***Ayers** a-26, 27. **Davis** c-45-47. **Everett** a-82, 91. **Fuje** a-13. **Heath** c-13, 21, 23. **Keller** a-16, 19, 28. **Kirby** a-54, 55, 57-62, 75-77, 90, 95, 101, 119, 120, 129; c-10, 52, 54-65, 67-72, 74-76, 116. **Maneely** a-20; c-16, 19, 20, 25-28, 49. **Powell** a-38, 102, 104. **Severin** a-29, 51. **Whitney** a-87, 89-91, 98-113, 124, 129; c-87, 89, 91, 113. **Wildey** a-21. **Williamson** a-110r. Kid Colt in No. 13, 14, 16-19, 21.*

TWO GUN WESTERN (1st Series) (Formerly Casey Crime Photographer)
No. 5, Nov, 1950 - No. 14, June, 1952
Marvel/Atlas Comics (MPC)

	Good	Fine	Mint
5-The Apache Kid (Intro & origin) & his horse Nightwind begin by Buscema	6.00	18.00	42.00
6-10: 8-Kid Colt, The Texas Kid & his horse Thunder begin?	3.50	10.50	24.00
11-14: 13-Black Rider app.	2.65	8.00	18.00

NOTE: ***Maneely** a-9; c-11-13. **Wildey** a-8.*

2-GUN WESTERN (2nd Series) (Formerly Billy Buckskin; Two-Gun Western #5 on)
No. 4, May, 1956
Atlas Comics (MgPC)

	Good	Fine	Mint
4-Apache Kid; Ditko-a	5.00	15.00	35.00

TWO-GUN WESTERN (Formerly 2-Gun Western)
No. 5, July, 1956 - No. 12, Sept, 1957
Atlas Comics (MgPC)

	Good	Fine	Mint
5-Apache Kid, Kid Colt Outlaw, Doc Holiday begin	3.00	9.00	21.00
6,7,10,12	1.70	5.00	12.00
8-Crandall-a	3.00	9.00	21.00
9,11-Williamson-a in both, 5 pgs. each	3.65	11.00	25.00

NOTE: ***Morrow** a-9,10. **Powell** a-7, 11. **Severin** c-10.*

TWO MOUSEKETEERS, THE (See 4-Color No. 475,603,642 under M.G.M.'s . . . ; becomes M.G.M.'s Mouse Musketeers)

TWO ON A GUILLOTINE (See Movie Classics)

2000 A.D. MONTHLY
4/85 - No. 6, 9/85; 4/86 - Present (Mando paper)
Eagle Comics/Quality Comics No. 5 on

	Good	Fine	Mint
1-5: #1-4-r/British series featuring Judge Dredd; Alan Moore scripts begin		.50	1.00
6 ($1.25)		.60	1.25
1-18-New look		.60	1.25

2001: A SPACE ODYSSEY (Marvel Treasury Special)
Oct, 1976 (One Shot) (Over-sized)
Marvel Comics Group

	Good	Fine	Mint
1-Kirby, Giacoia-a	.35	1.00	2.00

2001, A SPACE ODYSSEY
Dec, 1976 - No. 10, Sept, 1977 (Regular size)
Marvel Comics Group

	Good	Fine	Mint
1-Kirby c/a in all		.30	.60
2-10: 8-Origin/1st app. Machine Man (called Mr. Machine)		.25	.50
Howard Johnson giveaway(1968, 8pp); 6pg. movie adaptation, 2pg. games, puzzles		.25	.50

2010
Apr, 1985 - No. 2, May, 1985
Marvel Comics Group

	Good	Fine	Mint
1,2-r/Marvel Super Special		.40	.80

UFO & ALIEN COMIX
Jan, 1978 (One Shot)
Warren Publishing Co.

	Good	Fine	Mint
Toth, Severin-a(r)	.30	.80	1.60

UFO & OUTER SPACE (Formerly UFO Flying Saucers)
No. 14, June, 1978 - No. 25, Feb, 1980 (all painted covers)
Gold Key

	Good	Fine	Mint
14-Reprints UFO Flying Saucers #3	.35	1.00	2.00
15,16-Reprints		.60	1.20
17-20-New material	.25	.75	1.50
21-25: 23-McWilliams-a. 24-3 pg.-r. 25-r-UFO Flying Saucers #2 w/cover		.50	1.00

UFO ENCOUNTERS
May, 1978 (228 pages) ($1.95)
Western Publishing Co.

	Good	Fine	Mint
11192-Reprints UFO Flying Saucers	.70	2.00	4.00
11404-Vol.1 (128 pgs.)-See UFO Mysteries for Vol.2	.35	1.00	2.00

UFO FLYING SAUCERS (UFO & Outer Space #14 on)
Oct, 1968 - No. 13, Jan, 1977 (No. 2 on, 36 pgs.)
Gold Key

	Good	Fine	Mint
1(30035-810) (68 pgs.)	1.15	3.50	8.00
2(11/70), 3(11/72), 4(11/74)	1.00	3.00	6.00
5(2/75)-13: Bolle-a No. 4 on	.70	2.00	4.00

UFO MYSTERIES
1978 (96 pages) ($1.00) (Reprints)
Western Publishing Co.

	Good	Fine	Mint
11400(96 pgs., $1.00)	.25	.75	1.50
11404(Vol.2)-Cont'd from UFO Encounters, pgs. 129-224	.25	.75	1.50

UNBIRTHDAY PARTY WITH ALICE IN WONDERLAND (See 4-Color #341)

UNCANNY TALES
June, 1952 - No. 56, Sept, 1957

UNCANNY TALES (continued)
Atlas Comics (PrPI/PPI)

	Good	Fine	Mint
1-Heath-a	14.00	42.00	100.00
2	6.50	19.50	45.00
3-5	5.70	17.00	40.00
6-Wolvertonish-a by Matt Fox	6.50	19.50	45.00
7,8,10: 8-Tothish-a	5.50	16.50	38.00
9-Crandall-a	6.00	18.00	42.00
11-20: 17-Atom bomb panels; anti-communist story. 19-Krenkel-a	4.00	12.00	28.00
21-27: 25-Nostrand-a?	3.50	10.50	24.00
28-Last precode ish (1/55); Kubert-a; #1-28 contain 2-3 sci/fic stories each	4.60	14.00	32.00
29-41,43-49,52	1.60	4.70	11.00
42,54,56-Krigstein-a	2.85	8.50	20.00
50,53,55-Torres-a	2.85	8.50	20.00
51,57-Williamson-a (#57, exist?)	3.85	11.50	27.00

NOTE: ***Bailey*** *a-51.* ***Briefer*** *a-19, 20.* ***Colan*** *a-11, 16, 17.* ***Drucker*** *a-37, 42, 45.* ***Everett*** *a-2, 12, 32, 36, 39, 47, 48; c-7, 11, 17, 39, 41, 50, 52, 53.* ***Forte*** *a-27.* ***Heath*** *a-13, 14; c-10.* ***Keller*** *a-3.* ***Lawrence*** *a-14, 17, 19, 23, 27, 28, 35.* ***Maneely*** *a-4, 8, 10, 16, 29, 35; c-33, 38.* ***Moldoff*** *a-23.* ***Morrow*** *a-46, 51.* ***Orlando*** *a-49, 50, 53.* ***Powell*** *a-12, 18, 38, 43, 50, 53, 56.* ***Robinson*** *a-3, 13.* ***Roussos*** *a-8.* ***Sekowsky*** *a-25.* ***Tothish****-a by* ***Andru****-27.* ***Wildey*** *a-48.*

UNCANNY TALES
Dec, 1973 - No. 12, Oct, 1975
Marvel Comics Group

	Good	Fine	Mint
1-Crandall-a(r-'50s #9)		.30	.60
2-12		.25	.50

NOTE: ***Ditko*** *reprints-No. 4, 6-8, 10-12.*

UNCANNY X-MEN, THE (See X-Men)

UNCANNY X-MEN AND THE NEW TEEN TITANS (See Marvel and DC Present)

UNCANNY X-MEN AT THE STATE FAIR OF TEXAS, THE
1983 (36 pgs.)(One-Shot)
Marvel Comics Group

	Good	Fine	Mint
nn	1.00	3.00	6.00

UNCLE CHARLIE'S FABLES
Jan, 1952 - No. 5, Sept, 1952
Lev Gleason Publications

	Good	Fine	Mint
1-Norman Maurer-a; has Biro's picture	3.70	11.00	26.00
2-Fuje-a; Biro photo; painted-c	2.65	8.00	18.00
3-5	2.00	6.00	14.00

UNCLE DONALD & HIS NEPHEWS DUDE RANCH (See Dell Giant #52)

UNCLE DONALD & HIS NEPHEWS FAMILY FUN (See Dell Giant #38)

UNCLE JOE'S FUNNIES
1938
Centaur Publications

	Good	Fine	Mint
1-Games/puzzles, some interior art; Bill Everett-c	19.00	57.00	132.00

UNCLE MILTY (TV)
Dec, 1950 - No. 4, July, 1951
Victoria Publications/True Cross

	Good	Fine	Mint
1-Milton Berle	14.00	42.00	100.00
2	7.00	21.00	50.00
3,4	6.00	18.00	42.00

UNCLE REMUS & HIS TALES OF BRER RABBIT (See 4-Color No. 129, 208, 693)

UNCLE SAM QUARTERLY (Blackhawk #9 on)
Autumn, 1941 - No. 8, Fall, 1943 (Also see National Comics)
Quality Comics Group

	Good	Fine	Mint
1-Origin Uncle Sam; Fine/Eisner-c, chapter headings, 2 pgs. by Eisner. (2 versions: dark cover, no price; light cover with price); Jack Cole-a	95.00	285.00	665.00
2-Cameos by The Ray, Black Condor, Quicksilver, The Red Bee, Alias the Spider, Hercules & Neon the Unknown; Eisner, Fine c/a	46.00	138.00	320.00
3-Tuska-a	32.00	95.00	225.00
4	27.00	81.00	190.00
5-8	22.00	65.00	154.00

NOTE: ***Kotzky*** *or* ***Tuska*** *a-4-8.*

UNCLE SAM'S CHRISTMAS STORY
1958
Promotional Publ. Co. (Giveaway)

	Good	Fine	Mint
Reprints 1956 Christmas USA	1.00	3.00	7.00

UNCLE SCROOGE (Disney)(See Dell Giants 33,55 & WDC&S #98)
No. 386, 3/52 - No. 39, 8-10/62; No. 40, 12/62 - No. 209, 1984; No. 210, 10/86 - Present
Dell No. 1-39/Gold Key No. 40-173/Whitman No. 174-209/Gladstone No. 210-on

	Good	Fine	Mint
4-Color 386(#1)-in "Only a Poor Old Man" by Carl Barks; r-in Uncle Scrooge & Donald Duck #1('65) & The Best of Walt Disney Comics('74)	56.00	168.00	390.00
4-Color 456(#2)-in "Back to the Klondike" by Carl Barks; r-in Best of U.S. & D.D. #1('66)	26.00	78.00	180.00
4-Color 495(No.3)-r-in #105	23.00	70.00	160.00
4(12-2/53-54)	18.00	54.00	125.00
5-r-in W.D. Digest #1	14.00	42.00	100.00
6-r-in U.S. #106,165 & Best of U.S. & D.D. #1('66)	13.00	40.00	90.00
7-r-in Best of D.D. & U.S. #2('67)	10.00	30.00	70.00
8-10: 8-r-in #111. 9-r-in #104. 10-r-in #67	8.00	24.00	56.00
11-20	6.50	19.50	45.00
21-30	5.50	16.50	38.00
31-40	4.60	14.00	32.00
41-50	3.50	10.50	24.00
51-60	3.00	9.00	21.00
61-66,68-70: 70-Last Barks issue with original story	2.30	7.00	16.00
67,72,73-Barks-r	1.50	4.50	10.00
71-Written by Barks only	1.70	5.00	12.00
74-One pg. Barks-r	1.15	3.50	7.00
75-81,83-Not by Barks	1.15	3.50	7.00
82,84-Barks-r begin	1.15	3.50	7.00
85-100	1.00	3.00	6.00
101-110	.85	2.50	5.00
111-120	.70	2.00	4.00
121-141,143-152,154-157	.60	1.75	3.50
142-Reprints 4-Color 456 with-c	.70	2.00	4.00
153,158,162-164,166,168-170,178,180: No barks		.40	.80
159-160,165,167,172-176-Barks-a		.60	1.20
161(r-#14), 171(r-#11), 177(r-#16), 179(r-#9), 183(r-#6)-Barks-r		.60	1.20
181(r-4-Color 495), 195(r-4-Color 386)	.25	.70	1.40
182,186,191-194,197-202,204-206: No Barks		.40	.80
184,185,187,188-Barks-a		.50	1.00
189(r-#5), 190(r-#4), 196(r-#16), 203(r-#12), 207(r-#93,92), 208(r-U.S. #18), 209(r-U.S. #21)-Barks-r		.60	1.20
210-1st Gladstone issue	.50	1.50	3.00
211-218		.60	1.20
219-Son Of The Sun by Rosa	1.35	4.00	8.00
220-226: 210(r-WDC&S 134, 1st Beagle Boys)		.50	1.00
Uncle Scrooge & Money(G.K.)-Barks-r/from WDC&S #130 (3/67)	4.00	12.00	24.00
Mini Comic #1(1976)(3¼x6½")-R-/U.S. #115; Barks-c			.20

NOTE: ***Barks*** *c-4-Color 386, 456, 495, #4-37, 39, 40, 43-71.*

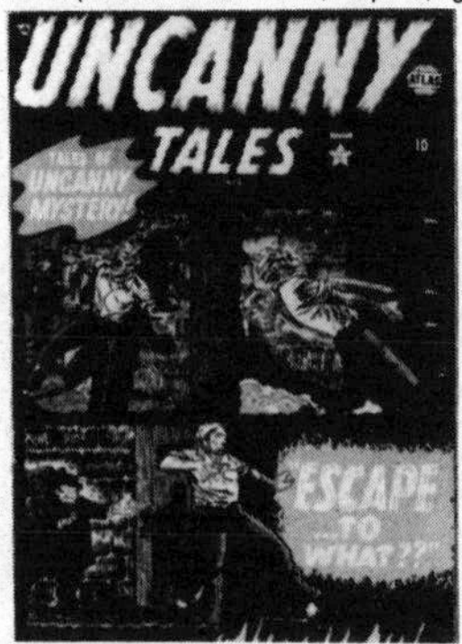

Uncanny Tales #3, © MCG

Uncle Sam Quarterly #2, © QUA

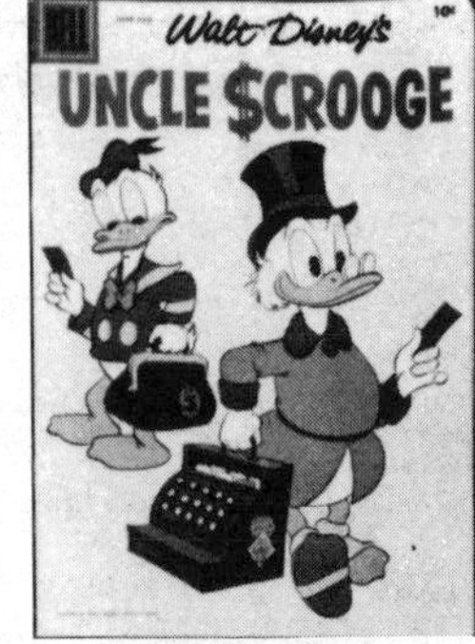

Uncle Scrooge #22, © WDC

Uncle Scrooge and Donald Duck #1, © WDC

Underworld Crime #7, © FAW

United Comics #8, © UFS

UNCLE SCROOGE ADVENTURES
Nov, 1987 - Present
Gladstone Publishing

	Good	Fine	Mint
1-5: Barks-r		.50	.95

UNCLE SCROOGE & DONALD DUCK
June, 1965 (25 cents) (Paper cover)
Gold Key

	Good	Fine	Mint
1-Reprint of 4-Color 386(#1) & lead story from 4-Color 29	8.35	25.00	50.00

UNCLE SCROOGE COMICS DIGEST
1986 - No. 6, 1987 ($1.25, Digest-size)
Gladstone Publishing

	Good	Fine	Mint
1-6		.60	1.25

UNCLE SCROOGE GOES TO DISNEYLAND (See Dell Giants)
Aug, 1985 ($2.50)
Gladstone Publishing Ltd.

	Good	Fine	Mint
1-r/Dell Giant w/new-c by Mel Crawford, based on old cover	.40	1.25	2.50
Comics Digest 1 ($1.50, digest size)	.25	.75	1.50

UNCLE WIGGILY (See 4-Color No. 179, 221, 276, 320, 349, 391, 428, 503, 543, & March of Comics No. 19)

UNDERCOVER GIRL (Starr Flagg)
1952 - 1954
Magazine Enterprises

	Good	Fine	Mint
5(#1)(A-1 62)	15.00	45.00	105.00
6(A-1 98), 7(A-1 118)-All have Starr Flagg	13.00	40.00	90.00

NOTE: ***Powell** c-6,7. **Whitney** a-5-7.*

UNDERDOG (TV) (See March of Comics 426,438,467,479)
July, 1970 - No. 10, Jan, 1972; Mar, 1975 - No. 23, Feb, 1979
Charlton Comics/Gold Key

	Good	Fine	Mint
1	1.50	4.50	10.00
2-10	.70	2.00	4.00
1 (G.K.)	1.00	3.00	6.00
2-10	.50	1.50	3.00
11-23: 13-1st app. Shack of Solitude	.25	.75	1.50
Kite Fun Book('74)-5x7"; 16 pgs.	.50	1.50	3.00

UNDERDOG
1987 - Present ($1.50, color)
Spotlight Comics

	Good	Fine	Mint
1-3	.25	.75	1.50

UNDERSEA AGENT
Jan, 1966 - No. 6, Mar, 1967 (68 pages)
Tower Comics

	Good	Fine	Mint
1-Davy Jones, Undersea Agent begins	.70	2.00	4.00
2-6: 2-Jones gains magnetic powers. 5-Origin & 1st app. of Merman. 6-Kane?/Wood-c(r)	.50	1.50	3.00

NOTE: ***Gil Kane** a-3-6; c-4, 5. **Moldoff** a-2i.*

UNDERSEA FIGHTING COMMANDOS
May, 1952 - No. 5, Jan, 1953; 1964
Avon Periodicals

	Good	Fine	Mint
1	4.00	12.00	28.00
2	2.50	7.50	17.50
3-5	2.15	6.50	15.00
I.W. Reprint #1,2('64)	.85	2.00	4.00

UNDERWATER CITY, THE (See 4-Color No. 1328)

UNDERWORLD (True Crime Stories)
Feb-Mar, 1948 - No. 9, June-July, 1949 (52 pgs.)
D. S. Publishing Co.

	Good	Fine	Mint
1-Moldoff-c; excessive violence	12.00	36.00	84.00
2-Moldoff-c; Ma Barker story used in **SOTI**, pg. 95; female electrocution panel; lingerie art	13.00	40.00	90.00
3-McWilliams c/a; extreme violence, mutilation	10.00	30.00	70.00
4-Used in **Love and Death** by Legman; Ingels-a	7.00	21.00	50.00
5-Ingels-a	5.00	15.00	35.00
6-9: 8-Ravielli-a	4.00	12.00	28.00

UNDERWORLD
Dec, 1987 - No. 4, Mar, 1988 (mini-series, $1.00)
DC Comics

	Good	Fine	Mint
1-4		.50	1.00

UNDERWORLD CRIME
June, 1952 - No. 9, Oct, 1953
Fawcett Publications

	Good	Fine	Mint
1	8.00	24.00	56.00
2	4.00	12.00	28.00
3-6,8,9 (8,9-exist?)	3.50	10.50	24.00
7-Bondage/torture-c	9.00	27.00	62.00

UNDERWORLD STORY, THE
1950 (Movie)
Avon Periodicals

	Good	Fine	Mint
nn-(Scarce)	12.00	36.00	84.00

UNEARTHLY SPECTACULARS
Oct, 1965 - No. 3, Mar, 1967
Harvey Publications

	Good	Fine	Mint
1-Tiger Boy; Simon-c	.50	1.50	3.00
2-Jack Q. Frost app.; Wood, Williamson, Kane art; r-1 story/ Thrill-O-Rama No. 2	1.70	5.00	10.00
3-Jack Q. Frost app.; Williamson/Crandall-a; r-from Alarming Advs. No. 1, 1962	1.70	5.00	10.00

NOTE: ***Crandall** a-3r. **G. Kane** a-2. **Orlando** a-3. **Simon, Sparling, Wood** c-2. **Simon/Kirby** a-3r. **Torres** a-1. **Wildey** a-1(3). **Williamson** a-2, 3r. **Wood** a-2(2).*

UNEXPECTED, THE (Formerly Tales of the. . .)
No. 105, Feb-Mar, 1968 - No. 222, May, 1982
National Periodical Publications/DC Comics

	Good	Fine	Mint
105-115,117,118,120,122-127		.40	.80
116,119,121,128-Wrightson-a		.50	1.00
129-156: 132-136-(52 pgs.)		.30	.60
157-162-(All 100 pgs.)		.30	.60
163-188		.25	.50
189,190,192-195 ($1.00 size)		.40	.80
191-Rogers-a(p) ($1.00 size)		.50	1.00
196-218,220,221: 205-213-Johnny Peril app. 210-Time Warp app.		.25	.50
219,222-Giffen-a		.30	.60

NOTE: ***Adams** c-110, 112-118, 121, 124. **J. Craig** a-195. **Ditko** a-189, 221p, 222p; c-222. **Drucker** a-107. **Kaluta** c-203, 212. **Kirby** a-127, 162. **Kubert** c-204, 214-16, 219-21. **Mayer** a-217p, 220, 221p. **Moldoff** a-136r. **Moreira** a-133. **Mortimer** a-212p. **Newton** a-204p. **Orlando** a-202; c-191. **Perez** a-217p. **Redondo** a-155, 195. **Reese** a-145. **Sparling** a-107, 205-09p, 212p. **Spiegle** a-217. **Starlin** c-198. **Toth** a-126r, 127r. **Tuska** a-132, 136, 139, 152, 180, 200p. **Wildey** a-193. **Wood** a-122i, 133i, 137i, 138i. **Wrightson** a-161r(2 pgs.). Johnny Peril in #106-117.*

UNEXPECTED ANNUAL, THE (See DC Spec. Series No. 4)

UNIDENTIFIED FLYING ODDBALL (See Walt Disney Showcase #52)

UNITED COMICS
Aug, 1940 - No. 26, Jan-Feb, 1953
United Features Syndicate

	Good	Fine	Mint
1-Fritzi Ritz & Phil Fumble	10.00	30.00	70.00
2-Fritzi Ritz, Abbie & Slats	5.00	15.00	35.00
3-9-Fritzi Ritz, Abbie & Slats	3.50	10.50	24.00
10-26: 25-Peanuts app.	1.85	5.50	13.00

NOTE: *Abbie & Slats reprinted from Tip Top.*

UNITED NATIONS, THE (See Classics Illustrated Special Ed.)

UNITED STATES AIR FORCE PRESENTS: THE HIDDEN CREW
1964 (36 pages) (full color)
U.S. Air Force

	Good	Fine	Mint
Shaffenberger-a	.50	1.50	3.00

UNITED STATES FIGHTING AIR FORCE
Sept, 1952 - No. 29, Oct, 1956
Superior Comics Ltd.

1	3.50	10.50	24.00
2	1.70	5.00	12.00
3-10	1.00	3.00	7.00
11-29	.85	2.50	6.00
I.W. Reprint #1,9(nd)	.40	1.10	2.20

UNITED STATES MARINES
1943 - No. 4, 1944; No. 5, 1952 - 1953
William H. Wise/Life's Romances Publ. Co./Magazine Enterprises No. 5-8/Toby Press

nn-Mart Bailey-a	4.00	12.00	28.00
2-Bailey-a	3.00	9.00	21.00
3,4	2.65	8.00	18.00
5(A-1 55), 6(A-1 60), 7(A-1 68), 8(A-1 72)	2.35	7.00	16.00
7-11 (Toby)	1.00	3.00	7.00

NOTE: ***Powell** a-5-7.*

UNIVERSAL PRESENTS DRACULA (See Dell Giants)

UNKEPT PROMISE
1949 (24 pages)
Legion of Truth (Giveaway)

Anti-alcohol	6.00	18.00	42.00

UNKNOWN MAN, THE
1951 (Movie)
Avon Periodicals

nn-Kinstler-c	12.00	36.00	84.00

UNKNOWN SOLDIER (Formerly Star-Spangled War Stories) (See Brave & the Bold #146)
No. 205, Apr-May, 1977 - No. 268, Oct, 1982
National Periodical Publications/DC Comics

205-268: 251-Enemy Ace begins. 268-Death of Unknown Soldier. 248,249-Origin		.30	.60

NOTE: ***Evans** a-265-67; c-235. **Kubert** c-Most. **Miller** a-219p. **Severin** a-251-53, 260, 261, 265-67. **Simonson** a-254-256. **Spiegle** a-258, 259, 262-64.*

UNKNOWN WORLD (Strange Stories From Another World #2 on)
June, 1952
Fawcett Publications

1-Norman Saunders painted-c	10.00	30.00	70.00

UNKNOWN WORLDS (See Journey Into. . .)

UNKNOWN WORLDS
Aug, 1960 - No. 57, Aug, 1967
American Comics Group/Best Synd. Features

1	3.70	11.00	26.00
2-5	1.70	5.00	12.00
6-15: 15-Last 10 cent ish?	1.15	3.50	8.00
16-19	.85	2.50	6.00
20-Herbie cameo	1.00	3.00	7.00
21-35	.50	1.50	3.00
36-"The People vs. Hendricks" by Craig; most popular ACG story ever	.80	2.30	4.60
37-46	.30	.90	1.80
47-Williamson-a r-from Adventures Into the Unknown #96, 3 pgs.; Craig-a	.80	2.30	4.60
48-57	.60	1.20	

NOTE: ***Ditko** a-49, 50p, 54. **Forte** a-3, 6, 11. **Landau** a-56(2). **Reinman** a-3, 9, 36. **John Force, Magic Agent** app.-No. 35, 36, 48, 50, 52, 54, 56.*

UNKNOWN WORLDS OF FRANK BRUNNER
Aug, 1985 - No. 2, Aug, 1985 ($1.75 cover)
Eclipse Comics

	Good	Fine	Mint
1,2-B&W-r in color	.30	.90	1.80

UNKNOWN WORLDS OF SCIENCE FICTION
12/74 - No. 6, 11/75; 12/76 (B&W Magazine) ($1.00)
Marvel Comics Group

1-Williamson/Wood/Torres/Frazetta r-/Witzend No. 1, Adams r-/Phase 1; Brunner & Kaluta-r	.50	1.50	3.00
2	.40	1.20	2.40
3-6	.40	1.20	2.40
Special 1(12/76)-100 pgs.; Newton-c; Nino-a	.40	1.20	2.40

NOTE: ***Brunner** a-2; c-4, 6. **Chaykin** a-5. **Colan** a(p)-1, 3, 5. **Corben** a-4. **Kaluta** a-2; c-2. **Morrow** a-3, 5. **Nino** a-3, 6. **Perez** a-2, 3.*

UNSANE
June, 1954
Star Publications

15-Disbrow-a(2); L. B. Cole-c	10.00	30.00	70.00

UNSEEN, THE
1952 - No. 15, July, 1954
Visual Editions/Standard Comics

5-Toth-a	7.00	21.00	50.00
6,7,9,10-Jack Katz-a	5.00	15.00	35.00
8,11,13,14	3.70	11.00	26.00
12,15-Toth-a; Tuska-a, #12	6.00	18.00	42.00

NOTE: ***Fawcette** a-13, 14. **Sekowsky** a-7, 8(2), 10, 13.*

UNTAMED LOVE
Jan, 1950 - No. 5, Sept, 1950
Quality Comics Group (Comic Magazines)

1-Ward-c, Gustavson-a	11.00	32.00	76.00
2,4: 2-Photo-c	6.00	18.00	42.00
3,5-Gustavson-a	6.50	19.50	45.00

UNTOLD LEGEND OF THE BATMAN, THE
7/80 - No. 3, 9/80 (mini-series)
DC Comics

1-Origin		.45	.90
2,3		.30	.60

NOTE: ***Aparo** a-1i, 2, 3. **Byrne** a-1p.*

UNTOUCHABLES, THE (TV)
No. 1237, 10-12/61 - No. 4, 8-10/62 (Robert Stack photo-c)
Dell Publishing Co.

4-Color 1237,1286	3.50	10.50	24.00
01-879-207, 12-879-210(01879-210 on inside)	3.00	9.00	21.00
Topps Bubblegum premiums-2½x4½", 8 pgs. (3 different issues) "The Organization, Jamaica Ginger, The Otto Frick Story (drug), 3000 Suspects, The Antidote, Mexican Stakeout, Little Egypt, Purple Gang, Bugs Moran Story, & Lily Dallas Story"	1.70	5.00	12.00

UNUSUAL TALES (Blue Beetle & Shadow From Beyond #50 on)
Nov, 1955 - No. 49, Mar-Apr, 1965
Charlton Comics

1	5.50	16.50	38.00
2	2.30	7.00	16.00
3-5	1.85	5.50	13.00
6-8-Ditko c/a	6.00	18.00	42.00
9-Ditko c/a, 20 pgs.	7.00	21.00	50.00
10-Ditko c/a(4)	8.00	24.00	56.00
11-(68 pgs.); Ditko-a(4)	8.00	24.00	56.00
12,14-Ditko-a	4.35	13.00	30.00
13,16-20	1.15	3.50	8.00

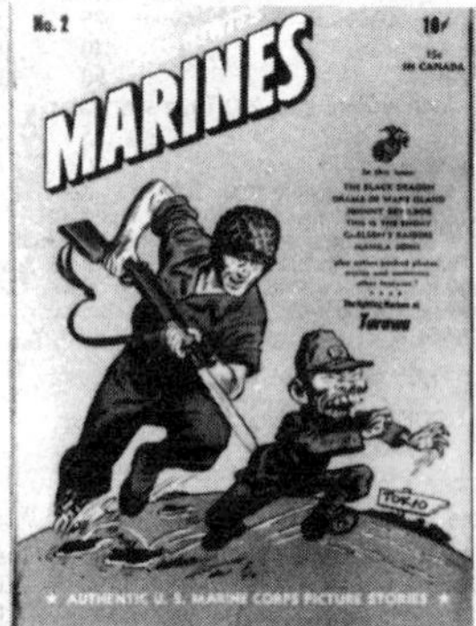

United States Marines #2, © Life's Romances

Unknown Worlds #14, © ACG

Unusual Tales #1, © CC

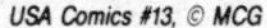
USA Comics #13, © MCG

U.S. Air Force Comics #1, © CC

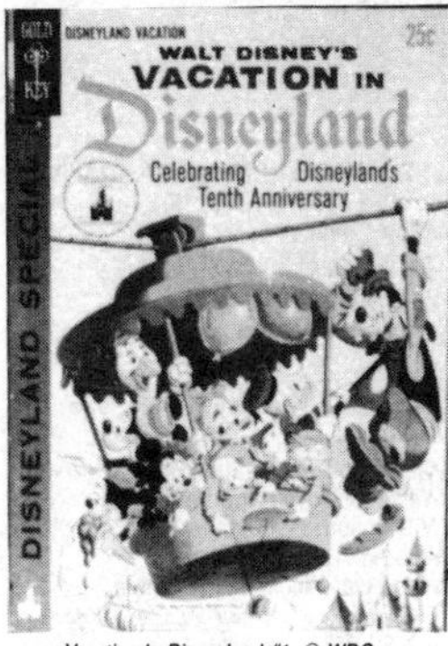

Vacation In Disneyland #1, © WDC

UNUSUAL TALES (continued)

	Good	Fine	Mint
15-Ditko c/a	4.60	14.00	32.00
21,24,28	.75	2.25	5.00
22,25-27,29-Ditko-a	2.30	7.00	16.00
23-Ditko-c	1.15	3.50	8.00
30-49	.50	1.50	3.00

NOTE: ***Colan** a-11. **Ditko** c-22,23,25-27, 31(part).*

UP FROM HARLEM (Tom Skinner. . .)
1973 (35-49 Cents)
Spire Christian Comics (Fleming H. Revell Co.)

	Good	Fine	Mint
		.50	1.00

UP-TO-DATE COMICS
No date (1938) (36 pgs.; B&W cover) (10 cents)
King Features Syndicate

	Good	Fine	Mint
nn-Popeye & Henry cover; The Phantom, Jungle Jim & Flash Gordon by Raymond, The Katzenjammer Kids, Curley Harper & others	16.00	48.00	110.00

(Variations to above contents exist.)

UP YOUR NOSE AND OUT YOUR EAR (Magazine)
April, 1972 - No. 2, June, 1972 (52 pgs.) (Satire)
Klevart Enterprises

	Good	Fine	Mint
V1#1,2	.30	.90	1.80

USA COMICS (Gay Comics #18 on?)
Aug, 1941 - No. 17, Fall, 1945
Timely Comics (USA)

	Good	Fine	Mint
1-Origin Major Liberty (called Mr. Liberty #1), Rockman by Wolverton, & The Whizzer by Avison; The Defender with sidekick Rusty & Jack Frost begin; The Young Avenger only app.; S&K-c plus 1 pg.	285.00	860.00	2000.00
2-Origin Captain Terror & The Vagabond; last Wolverton Rockman	145.00	435.00	1015.00
3-No Whizzer	112.00	335.00	785.00
4-Last Rockman, Major Liberty, Defender, Jack Frost, & Capt. Terror; Corporal Dix app.	94.00	280.00	660.00
5-Origin American Avenger & Roko the Amazing; The Blue Blade, The Black Widow & Victory Boys, Gypo the Gypsy Giant & Hills of Horror only app.; Sergeant Dix begins; no Whizzer	80.00	240.00	560.00
6-Captain America, The Destroyer, Jap Buster Johnson, Jeep Jones begin; Terror Squad only app.	85.00	255.00	595.00
7-Captain Daring, Disk-Eyes the Detective by Wolverton app.; origin & only app. Marvel Boy; Secret Stamp begins; no Whizzer, Sergeant Dix	73.00	220.00	510.00
8-10: 9-Last Secret Stamp. 10-The Thunderbird only app.	53.00	160.00	370.00
11,12: 11-No Jeep Jones	43.00	130.00	300.00
13-17: 13-No Whizzer; Jeep Jones ends. 15-No Destroyer; Jap Buster Johnson ends	32.00	95.00	225.00

U.S. AGENT (See Jeff Jordan. . .)

U.S. AIR FORCE COMICS (Army Attack #38 on)
Oct, 1958 - No. 37, Mar-Apr, 1965
Charlton Comics

	Good	Fine	Mint
1	1.00	3.00	7.00
2	.50	1.50	3.50
3-10	.35	1.00	2.00
11-20		.50	1.00
21-37		.30	.60

NOTE: ***Glanzman** c/a-9, 10, 12. **Montes/Bache** a-33.*

USA IS READY
1941 (68 pgs.) (One Shot)
Dell Publishing Co.

	Good	Fine	Mint
1-War propaganda	16.00	45.00	110.00

U.S. BORDER PATROL COMICS (Sgt. Dick Carter of the. . .) (See Holyoke One Shot)

U.S. FIGHTING MEN
1963 - 1964 (Reprints)
Super Comics

	Good	Fine	Mint
10-Avon's With the U.S. Paratroops	.50	1.50	3.00
11,12,15-18	.30	.80	1.60

U.S. JONES (Also see Wonderworld Comics #28)
Nov, 1941 - No. 2, Jan, 1942
Fox Features Syndicate

	Good	Fine	Mint
1-U.S. Jones & The Topper begin	45.00	135.00	315.00
2	30.00	90.00	210.00

U.S. MARINES
Fall, 1964 (One shot)
Charlton Comics

	Good	Fine	Mint
1	.30	.80	1.60

U.S. MARINES IN ACTION!
Aug, 1952 - No. 3, Dec?, 1952
Avon Periodicals

	Good	Fine	Mint
1-Louis Ravielli c/a	3.35	10.00	23.00
2,3: 3-Kinstler-c	1.65	5.00	11.50

U.S. 1
May, 1983 - No. 12, Oct, 1984
Marvel Comics Group

	Good	Fine	Mint
1		.30	.60
2-12		.25	.50

NOTE: *a-12p. **Golden** c-5-7,9,10,12.*

U.S. PARATROOPS (See With the. . .)

U.S. PARATROOPS
1964?
I. W. Enterprises

	Good	Fine	Mint
1-Wood-c r-/With the. . . #1	.50	1.50	3.00
8-Kinstler-c	.50	1.50	3.00

U.S. TANK COMMANDOS
June, 1952 - No. 4, March, 1953
Avon Periodicals

	Good	Fine	Mint
1-Kinstler-c	3.75	11.25	26.00
2-4: 2-Kinstler-c	2.15	6.50	15.00
I.W. Reprint #1,8	.40	1.10	2.20

NOTE: ***Kinstler** a-3, 4, I.W. #1; c-1-4, I.W. #1, 8.*

"V"
Feb, 1985 - No. 18, July, 1986
DC Comics

	Good	Fine	Mint
1-Based on TV movie & series	.25	.75	1.50
2-18		.45	.90

VACATION COMICS (See A-1 Comics #16)

VACATION DIGEST
Sept, 1987 - Present ($1.25, digest size)
Harvey Comics

	Good	Fine	Mint
1		.60	1.25

VACATION IN DISNEYLAND (Also see Dell Giants)
Aug-Oct, 1959 - May, 1965 (Walt Disney)
Dell Publishing Co./Gold Key (1965)

	Good	Fine	Mint
4-Color 1025-Barks-a	6.00	18.00	42.00
1(30024-508)(G.K.)-Reprints Dell Giant #30 & cover to #1('58)	1.50	4.50	12.00

VACATION PARADE (See Dell Giants)

VALKYRIE (Also see Airboy)
May, 1987 - No. 3, July, 1987 ($1.75, mini-series)

VALKYRIE (continued)
Eclipse Comics

	Good	Fine	Mint
1	.50	1.50	3.00
2	.40	1.25	2.50
3	.35	1.00	2.00

VALLEY OF THE DINOSAURS (TV) (Hanna-Barbera)
April, 1975 - No. 11, Dec, 1976
Charlton Comics

	Good	Fine	Mint
1-Howard inks		.40	.80
2-11: 2-Howard inks		.30	.60

VALLEY OF GWANGI (See Movie Classics)

VALOR
Mar-Apr, 1955 - No. 5, Nov-Dec, 1955
E. C. Comics

	Good	Fine	Mint
1-Williamson/Torres-a; Wood c/a	15.00	45.00	105.00
2-Williamson c/a; Wood-a	13.00	40.00	90.00
3-Williamson, Crandall-a	9.25	28.00	65.00
4-Wood-c	9.25	28.00	65.00
5-Wood c/a; Williamson/Evans-a	8.00	24.00	55.00

NOTE: ***Crandall*** *a-3, 4.* ***Ingels*** *a-1, 2, 4, 5.* ***Krigstein*** *a-1-5.* ***Orlando*** *a-3, 4; c-3.* ***Wood*** *a-1, 2, 5; c-1, 4, 5.*

VALOR THUNDERSTAR AND HIS FIREFLIES
Dec, 1986 - No. 3, 1987 (mini-series, $1.50, color)
Now Comics

	Good	Fine	Mint
1	.25	.75	1.50

VAMPIRELLA (Magazine)(See Warren Presents)
Sept, 1969 - No. 112, Feb, 1983
Warren Publishing Co.

	Good	Fine	Mint
1-Intro. Vampirella	8.50	25.50	60.00
2-Amazonia series begins, ends #12	2.65	8.00	18.00
3 (Low distribution)	10.00	30.00	70.00
4-7	2.00	6.00	14.00
8-Vampi begins by Tom Sutton as serious strip (early issues-gag line)	1.35	4.00	9.00
9-Smith-a	2.00	6.00	14.00
10-No Vampi story	1.35	4.00	9.00
11-15: 11-Origin, 1st app. Pendragon. 12-Vampi by Gonzales begins	1.20	3.50	8.00
16-18,20-25: 17-Tomb of the Gods begins, ends #22	.85	2.50	6.00
19 (1973 Annual)	1.20	3.50	8.00
26,28-36,38-40: 30-Intro. Pantha. 31-Origin Luana, the Beast Girl. 33-Pantha ends	.70	2.00	5.00
27 (1974 Annual)	1.00	3.00	7.00
37 (1975 Annual)	.85	2.50	6.00
41-45	.40	1.25	2.50
46-Origin	.50	1.50	3.00
47-50: 50-Spirit cameo	.30	.90	1.80
51-99: 93-Cassandra St. Knight begins, ends #103; new Pantha series begins, ends 108	.25	.75	1.50
100 (96pg. r-special)-Origin retold	.30	.90	1.80
101-112: 108-Torpedo series by Toth begins	.25	.75	1.50
Annual 1('72)-New origin Vampirella by Gonzales; reprints by Adams(#1), Wood(#9)	8.50	25.00	50.00
Special 1 ('77; large-square bound)	.85	2.50	5.00

NOTE: ***Adams*** *a-1, 10p, 19p.* ***Alcala*** *a-90, 93i.* ***Bode'/Todd*** *c-3.* ***Bode'/Jones*** *c-4.* ***Boris*** *c-9.* ***Brunner*** *a-10.* ***Corben*** *a-30, 31, 33, 54.* ***Crandall*** *a-1, 19.* ***Frazetta*** *c-1, 5, 7, 11, 31.* ***Jones*** *a-5, 9, 12, 27, 32, 33, 34, 50i.* ***Nino*** *a-59i, 61i, 67, 76, 85, 90.* ***Ploog*** *a-14.* ***Smith*** *a-9.* ***Sutton*** *a-11.* ***Toth*** *a-90i, 108, 110.* ***Wood*** *a-9, 10, 12, 19, 27; c-9.* ***Wrightson*** *a-33, 63. All reprint issues-37, 74, 83, 87, 91, 105, 107, 109, 111. Annuals from 1973 on are included in regular numbering. Later annuals are same format as regular issues.*

VAMPIRE TALES (Magazine)
Aug, 1973 - No. 11, June, 1975 (B&W) (75 cents)
Marvel Comics Group

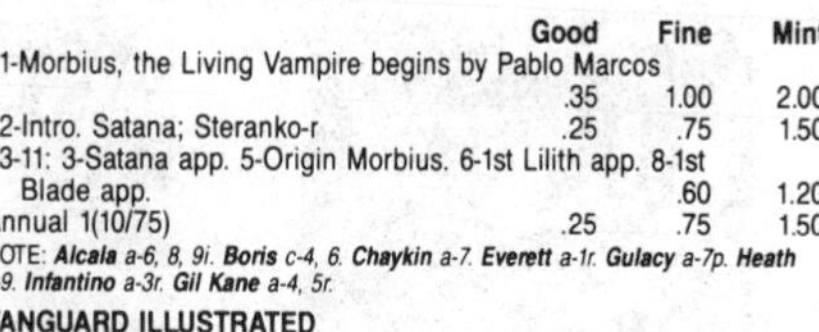

	Good	Fine	Mint
1-Morbius, the Living Vampire begins by Pablo Marcos	.35	1.00	2.00
2-Intro. Satana; Steranko-r	.25	.75	1.50
3-11: 3-Satana app. 5-Origin Morbius. 6-1st Lilith app. 8-1st Blade app.		.60	1.20
Annual 1(10/75)	.25	.75	1.50

NOTE: ***Alcala*** *a-6, 8, 9i.* ***Boris*** *c-4, 6.* ***Chaykin*** *a-7.* ***Everett*** *a-1r.* ***Gulacy*** *a-7p.* ***Heath*** *a-9.* ***Infantino*** *a-3r.* ***Gil Kane*** *a-4, 5r.*

VANGUARD ILLUSTRATED
Nov, 1983 - No. 7, July, 1984
Pacific Comics

	Good	Fine	Mint
1-Nudity scenes		.50	1.00
2-4 (Baxter paper)	.25	.75	1.50
5,6,8-11	.25	.75	1.50
7-1st app. Mr. Monster	1.00	3.00	6.00

NOTE: ***Evans*** *a-7.* ***Kaluta*** *c-5, 7p.* ***Perez*** *a-6; c-6.* ***Rude*** *a-3-5; c-4.*

VANITY (See Pacific Presents)
Jun, 1984 - No. 2, Aug, 1984 ($1.50)
Pacific Comics

	Good	Fine	Mint
1,2-Origin	.25	.75	1.50

VARIETY COMICS
1944 - 1945; 1946
Rural Home Publications/Croyden Publ. Co.

	Good	Fine	Mint
1-Origin Captain Valiant	6.00	18.00	42.00
2-Captain Valiant	3.70	11.00	26.00
3(1946-Croyden)-Captain Valiant	3.00	9.00	21.00
4,5	2.30	7.00	16.00

VARIETY COMICS (See Fox Giants)

VARSITY
1945
Parents' Magazine Institute

	Good	Fine	Mint
1	2.00	6.00	14.00

VAUDEVILLE AND OTHER THINGS
1900 (10½x13") (in color) (18+ pgs.)
Isaac H. Blandiard Co.

	Good	Fine	Mint
By Bunny	17.00	51.00	120.00

VAULT OF EVIL
Feb, 1973 - No. 23, Nov, 1975
Marvel Comics Group

	Good	Fine	Mint
1 (Reprints begin)		.35	.70
2-23: 3,4-Brunner-c		.25	.50

NOTE: ***Ditko*** *a-14r, 15r, 20-22r.* ***Drucker*** *a-10r(Mystic #52), 13r(Uncanny Tales #42).* ***Everett*** *a-11r(Menace #2), 13r(Menace #4); c-10.* ***Krigstein*** *a-20r(Uncanny Tales #54).*

VAULT OF HORROR (War Against Crime #1-11)
No. 12, Apr-May, 1950 - No. 40, Dec-Jan, 1954-55
E. C. Comics

	Good	Fine	Mint
12	107.00	320.00	750.00
13-Morphine story	50.00	150.00	350.00
14	43.00	130.00	300.00
15	36.00	108.00	250.00
16	28.00	84.00	195.00
17-19	21.00	62.00	146.00
20-22,24,25	16.00	48.00	110.00
23-Used in **POP**, pg. 84	16.50	50.00	115.00
26-B&W & color illos in **POP**	16.50	50.00	115.00
27-35	12.00	36.00	84.00
36-"Pipe Dream"-classic opium addict story by Krigstein; 'Twin Bill' cited in articles by T.E. Murphy & Wertham	12.00	36.00	84.00
37-Williamson-a	12.00	36.00	84.00
38-39: 39-Bondage-c	10.00	30.00	70.00

Valkyrie #1, © Eclipse Comics

Vampirella #9, © WP

Vault of Horror #36, © WMG

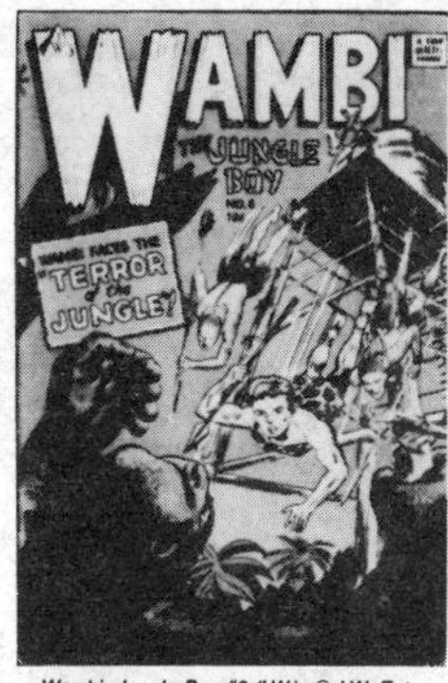

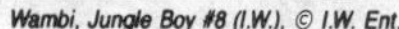
Wambi, Jungle Boy #8 (I.W.), © I.W. Ent.

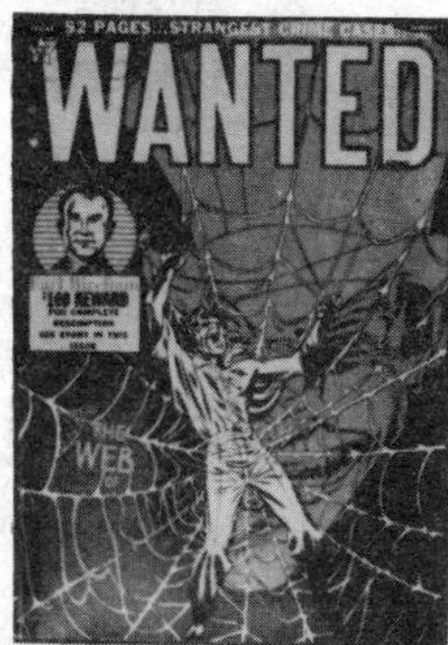

Wanted Comics #33, © Orbit Publ.

War Action #13, © MCG

WALT DISNEY SHOWCASE (continued)

	Good	Fine	Mint
41-Herbie Goes to Monte Carlo (Movie); sequel to "Herbie Rides Again"-Photo-c	.25	.75	1.50
42-Mickey & the Sleuth	.25	.75	1.50
43-Pete's Dragon (Movie)-Photo-c	.35	1.00	2.00
44-Return From Witch Mountain (new) & In Search of the Castaways -r(Movies)-Photo-c; 68 pg. giants begin	.50	1.50	3.00
45-The Jungle Book (Movie); r-#30033-803	.50	1.50	3.00
46-The Cat From Outer Space (Movie)(new), & The Shaggy Dog (Movie)-r/F.C. 985-Photo-c	.50	1.50	3.00
47-Mickey Mouse Surprise Party-r	.50	1.50	3.00
48-The Wonderful Advs. of Pinocchio-r/F.C. 1203; last 68 pg. issue	.50	1.50	3.00
49-North Avenue Irregulars (Movie); Zorro-r/Zorro 11; 52 pgs. begin; photo-c	.25	.75	1.50
50-Bedknobs & Broomsticks-r/#6; Mooncussers-r/World of Adv. #1-Photo-c	.25	.75	1.50
51-101 Dalmatians-r	.25	.75	1.50
52-Unidentified Flying Oddball (Movie); r-/Picnic Party 8-Photo-c	.25	.75	1.50
53-The Scarecrow-r (TV)	.25	.75	1.50
54-The Black Hole (Movie)-Photo-c	.25	.75	1.50

WALT DISNEY'S MAGAZINE (TV)(Formerly Walt Disney's Mickey Mouse Club Magazine) (50 cents) (Bi-monthly)
V2No.4, June, 1957 - V4No.6, Oct, 1959
Western Publishing Co.

	Good	Fine	Mint
V2#4-Stories & articles on the Mouseketeers, Zorro, & Goofy and other Disney characters & people	3.50	10.50	24.00
V2#5, V2#6(10/57)	3.50	10.50	24.00
V3#1(12/57), V3#3-6(10/58)	1.70	5.00	12.00
V3#2-Annette photo-c	4.00	12.00	28.00
V4#1(12/58) - V4#2-4,6(10/59)	1.70	5.00	12.00
V4#5-Annette photo-c	3.00	9.00	21.00

NOTE: *V2#4-V3#6 were 11½x8½", 48 pgs.; V4#1 on were 10x8", 52 pgs. (Peak circulation of 400,000).*

WALT DISNEY'S MERRY CHRISTMAS (See Dell Giant No. 39)

WALT DISNEY'S MICKEY MOUSE CLUB MAGAZINE (TV)(Becomes Walt Disney's Magazine) (Quarterly)
Winter, 1956 - V2#3, April, 1957 (11½x8½") (48 pgs.)
Western Publishing Co.

	Good	Fine	Mint
V1#1	8.50	25.50	60.00
2-4	4.35	13.00	30.00
V2#1-3	3.50	10.50	24.00
Annual(1956)-Two different issues; ($1.50-Whitman); 120 pgs., cardboard covers, 11¾x8¾"; reprints	8.50	25.50	60.00
Annual(1957)-Same as above	5.70	17.00	40.00

WALT DISNEY'S WHEATIES PREMIUMS (See Wheaties)

WALTER LANTZ ANDY PANDA (Also see Andy Panda)
Aug, 1973 - No. 23, Jan, 1978 (Walter Lantz)
Gold Key

	Good	Fine	Mint
1-Reprints	.35	1.00	2.00
2-10-All reprints		.40	.80
11-23: 15,17-19,22-Reprints		.15	.30

WALT KELLY'S CHRISTMAS CLASSICS
1988 ($1.75, color, Baxter)
Eclipse Comics

	Good	Fine	Mint
1-Kelly-r/Peter Wheat & Santa Claus Funnies	.30	.90	1.75

WALT SCOTT'S CHRISTMAS STORIES (See 4-Color No. 959,1062)

WAMBI, JUNGLE BOY (See Jungle Comics)
Spring, 1942 - No. 3, Spring, 1943; No. 4, Fall, 1948 - No. 18, Winter, 1952-53
Fiction House Magazines

	Good	Fine	Mint
1-Wambi, the Jungle Boy begins	25.00	75.00	175.00
2 (1942)	13.00	40.00	90.00
3 (1943)-Kiefer c/a	10.00	30.00	70.00
4 (1948)-Origin in text	5.70	17.00	40.00
5 (Fall, '49, 36pgs.)-Kiefer c/a	5.00	15.00	35.00
6-10: 7-52 pgs.	4.35	13.00	30.00
11-18	3.50	10.50	24.00
I.W. Reprint #8('64)-R-/#12 with new-c	1.00	3.00	6.00

WANTED COMICS
No. 9, Sept-Oct, 1947 - No. 53, April, 1953
Toytown Publications/Patches/Orbit Publ.

	Good	Fine	Mint
9	5.00	15.00	35.00
10,11: 10-Giunta-a; radio's Mr. D. A. app.	3.00	9.00	21.00
12-Used in **SOTI**, pg. 277	6.00	18.00	42.00
13-Heroin drug propaganda story	4.65	14.00	32.00
14-Marijuana drug mention story, 2 pgs.	2.65	8.00	18.00
15-17,19,20	2.00	6.00	14.00
18-Marijuana story, 'Satan's Cigarettes'; r-in #45 & retitled	10.00	30.00	70.00
21-Krigstein-a	2.65	8.00	18.00
22-Extreme violence	3.00	9.00	21.00
23,25-34,36-38,40-44,46-48,53	1.15	3.50	8.00
24-Krigstein-a; 'The Dope King,' marijuana mention story	4.65	14.00	32.00
35-Used in **SOTI**, pg. 160	4.65	14.00	32.00
39-Drug propaganda story "The Horror Weed"	5.50	16.50	38.00
45-Marijuana story from No. 18	5.50	16.50	38.00
49-Has unstable pink-c that fades easily; rare in mint condition	1.85	5.00	11.50
50-surrealist-c; horror stys	5.00	15.00	35.00
51-"Holiday of Horror"-junkie story; drug-c	5.00	15.00	35.00
52-Classic "Cult of Killers" opium use story	5.00	15.00	35.00

NOTE: ***Lawrence** and **Leav** c/a most issues.*

WANTED: DEAD OR ALIVE (See 4-Color No. 1102,1164)

WANTED, THE WORLD'S MOST DANGEROUS VILLAINS
July-Aug, 1972 - No. 9, Aug-Sept, 1973 (All reprints)
National Periodical Publications (See DC Special)

	Good	Fine	Mint
1-Batman, Green Lantern, & Green Arrow		.60	1.20
2-Batman & The Flash		.40	.80
3-Dr. Fate, Hawkman, & Vigilante		.40	.80
4-Green Lantern & Kid Eternity		.40	.80
5-Dollman/Green Lantern		.30	.60
6-Starman/Wildcat/Sargon		.30	.60
7-Johnny Quick/Hawkman/Hourman		.30	.60
8-Dr. Fate/Flash		.30	.60
9-S&K Sandman/Superman		.30	.60

NOTE: ***Kubert** a-3i, 6, 7.*

WAR
7/75 - No. 9, 11/76; No. 10, 9/78 - No. 49?, 1984
Charlton Comics

	Good	Fine	Mint
1		.15	.30
2-49: 47-r		.15	.30
7,9(Modern Comics-r, 1977)		.15	.30

WAR ACTION
April, 1952 - No. 14, June, 1953
Atlas Comics (CPS)

	Good	Fine	Mint
1	3.50	10.50	24.00
2	1.60	4.70	11.00
3-6,8-10,14	1.35	4.00	9.00
7-Pakula-a	1.35	4.00	9.00
11-13-Krigstein-a	2.75	8.00	18.00

NOTE: ***Heath** a-1; c-7, 14. **Keller** a-6. **Maneely** a-1.*

WAR ADVENTURES
Jan, 1952 - No. 13, Feb, 1953
Atlas Comics (HPC)

	Good	Fine	Mint
1-Tuska-a	2.85	8.50	20.00
2	1.50	4.50	10.00
3-7,9-13	1.35	4.00	9.00
8-Krigstein-a	2.75	8.00	18.00

NOTE: ***Heath** a-5; c-4, 5, 13. **Pakula** a-3. **Robinson** a-3; c-10.*

WAR ADVENTURES ON THE BATTLEFIELD (See Battlefield)

WAR AGAINST CRIME! (Vault of Horror #12 on)
Spring, 1948 - No. 11, Feb-Mar, 1950
E. C. Comics

	Good	Fine	Mint
1	37.00	110.00	260.00
2,3	21.00	62.00	146.00
4-9: 9-Morphine drug use story	20.00	60.00	140.00
10-1st Vault Keeper app.	53.00	160.00	370.00
11-2nd Vault Keeper app.	46.00	138.00	320.00

NOTE: *All have **Craig** covers. **Feldstein** a-4, 7-9. **Ingels** a-1, 2, 8.*

WAR AND ATTACK (Also see Special War Series #3)
Fall, 1964 - V2No.63, Dec, 1967
Charlton Comics

	Good	Fine	Mint
1-Wood-a	.85	2.50	5.00
V2#54(6/66)-#63 (Formerly Fightin' Air Force)		.40	.80

NOTE: ***Montes/Bache** a-55, 56, 60, 63.*

WAR AT SEA (Formerly Space Adventures)
No. 22, Nov, 1957 - No. 42, June, 1961
Charlton Comics

	Good	Fine	Mint
22	1.00	3.00	7.00
23-30	.50	1.50	3.50
31-42	.35	1.00	2.00

WAR BATTLES
Feb, 1952 - No. 9, Dec, 1953
Harvey Publications

	Good	Fine	Mint
1	2.75	8.00	18.00
2	1.50	4.50	10.00
3-5,7-9	1.35	4.00	9.00
6-Nostrand-a	2.35	7.00	16.00

NOTE: ***Powell** a-1-3, 7.*

WAR BIRDS
1952
Fiction House Magazines

	Good	Fine	Mint
1	5.00	15.00	35.00
2	2.65	8.00	18.00
3-7 (4-7 exist?)	2.50	7.50	17.50

WAR COMBAT (Combat Casey #6 on)
March, 1952 - No. 5, Nov, 1952
Atlas Comics (LBI 1/SAI 2-5)

	Good	Fine	Mint
1	2.65	8.00	18.00
2	1.30	4.00	9.00
3-5	1.00	3.00	7.00

NOTE: ***Berg** a-2, 4, 5. **Henkel** a-5. **Maneely** a-1, 4.*

WAR COMICS (See Key Ring Comics)
May, 1940 (No mo. given) - No. 8, Feb-Apr, 1943
Dell Publishing Co.

	Good	Fine	Mint
1-Sikandur the Robot Master, Sky Hawk, Scoop Mason, War Correspondent begin	20.00	60.00	140.00
2-Origin Greg Gilday	10.00	30.00	70.00
3-Joan becomes Greg Gilday's aide	7.00	21.00	50.00
4-Origin Night Devils	8.50	25.50	60.00
5-8	5.00	15.00	35.00

WAR COMICS
Dec, 1950 - No. 49, Sept, 1957
Marvel/Atlas (USA No. 1-41/JPI No. 42-49)

	Good	Fine	Mint
1	4.60	14.00	30.00
2	2.30	7.00	16.00
3-10	1.70	5.00	12.00
11-20	1.00	3.00	7.00
21,23-32: Last precode (2/55). 26-Valley Forge story	.85	2.50	6.00
22-Krigstein-a	2.75	8.00	18.00
33-37,39-42,44,45,47,48	.70	2.00	5.00
38-Kubert/Moskowitz-a	2.00	6.00	14.00
43,49-Torres-a. 43-Davis E.C. swipe	2.00	6.00	14.00
46-Crandall-a	2.00	6.00	14.00

NOTE: ***Colan** a-4, 48, 49. **Drucker** a-37, 43, 48. **Everett** a-17. **Heath** a-7-9, 19. **G. Kane** a-19. **Orlando** a-42, 48. **Pakula** a-26. **Reinman** a-26. **Robinson** a-15. **Severin** a-26; c-48.*

WAR DOGS OF THE U.S. ARMY
1952
Avon Periodicals

	Good	Fine	Mint
1-Kinstler c/a	6.35	19.00	44.00

WARFRONT
9/51 - No. 35, 11/58; No. 36, 10/65; No. 37, 9/66 - No. 38, 12/66; No. 39, 2/67
Harvey Publications

	Good	Fine	Mint
1	3.00	9.00	21.00
2	1.50	4.50	10.00
3-10	1.35	4.00	9.00
11,12,14,16-20	.85	2.50	6.00
13,15,22-Nostrand-a	2.75	8.00	18.00
21,23-27,29,31-33,35	.70	2.00	5.00
28,30,34-Kirby-c	1.35	4.00	9.00
36-Dynamite Joe begins, ends #39; Williamson-a	1.35	4.00	9.00
37-Wood-a, 17pgs.	1.35	4.00	9.00
38,39-Wood-a, 2-3 pgs.; Lone Tiger app.	.85	2.50	6.00

NOTE: ***Powell** a-1-6, 9-11, 14, 17, 20, 23, 25-28, 30, 31, 34, 36. **Powell/Nostrand** a-12, 13, 15. **Simon** c-36?, 38.*

WAR FURY
Sept, 1952 - No. 4, March, 1953
Comic Media/Harwell (Allen Hardy Associates)

	Good	Fine	Mint
1-Heck c/a in all	2.65	8.00	18.00
2-4: 4-Morisi-a	1.35	4.00	9.00

WAR GODS OF THE DEEP (See Movie Classics)

WAR HEROES (See Marine War Heroes)

WAR HEROES
July-Sept, 1942 (no month); No. 2, Oct-Dec, 1942 - No. 10, Oct-Dec, 1944; No. 11, Mar, 1945
Dell Publishing Co.

	Good	Fine	Mint
1	7.00	21.00	50.00
2	3.50	10.50	24.00
3,5: 3-Pro-Russian back-c	3.00	9.00	21.00
4-Disney's Gremlins app.	7.00	21.00	50.00
6-11: 6-Tothish-a by Discount	2.65	8.00	18.00

NOTE: *No. 1 was to be released in July, but was delayed. **Cameron** a-6.*

WAR HEROES
May, 1952 - No. 8, April, 1953
Ace Magazines

	Good	Fine	Mint
1	2.65	8.00	18.00
2	1.35	4.00	9.00
3-8	1.20	3.50	8.00

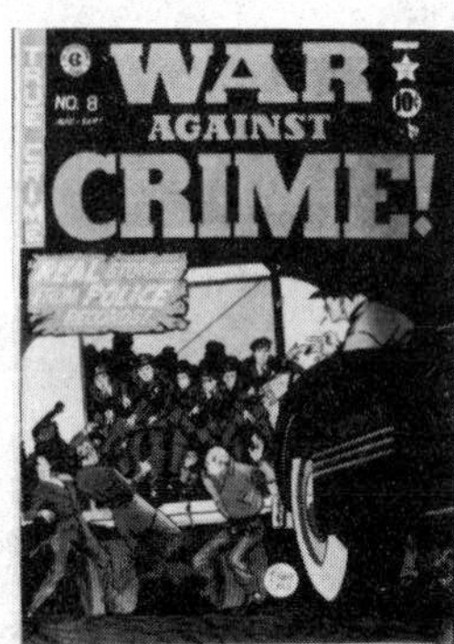

War Against Crime! #8, © WMG

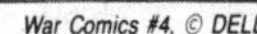
War Comics #4, © DELL

War Heroes #6, © DELL

Warlock #3, © MCG

Warlord #40, © DC

War Stories #7, © DELL

WAR HEROES
Feb, 1963 - No. 27, Nov, 1967
Charlton Comics

	Good	Fine	Mint
1	.50	1.50	3.00
2-10	.30	.80	1.60
11-27: 27-1st Devils Brigade by Glanzman		.30	.60

NOTE: ***Montes/Bache** a-3-7, 21, 25, 27; c-3-7.*

WAR IS HELL
Jan, 1973 - No. 15, Oct, 1975
Marvel Comics Group

	Good	Fine	Mint
1-Williamson-a(r), 3pgs.		.40	.80
2-9-All reprints		.30	.60
10-15		.15	.30

NOTE: ***Bolle** a-3r. **Powell, Woodbridge** a-1. Sgt. Fury reprints-7, 8.*

WARLOCK (The Power of . . .) (See Str. Tales & Marvel Premiere)
Aug, 1972 - No. 8, Oct, 1973; No. 9, Oct, 1975 - No. 15, Nov, 1976
Marvel Comics Group

	Good	Fine	Mint
1-Origin by Kane	.85	2.50	5.00
2,3	.40	1.20	2.40
4-8: 4-Death of Eddie Roberts	.35	1.00	2.00
9-15-Starlin-c/a in all. 10-Origin Thanos & Gamora. 14-Origin Star Thief	.35	1.00	2.00

NOTE: ***Buscema** a-2p; c-8p. **G. Kane** a-1p, 3-5p; c-1p, 2, 3, 4p, 5p, 7p. **Starlin** a-9-14p, 15; c-12p, 13-15. **Sutton** a-1-8i.*

WARLOCK
12/82 - No. 6, 5/83 ($2.00) (slick paper) (Direct Sales only)
Marvel Comics Group

	Good	Fine	Mint
1-Starlin Warlock r-/Str. Tales #178-180; Starlin-c	.35	1.00	2.00
2(1/83)-Starlin Warlock r-/Str. Tales #180,181 & Warlock #9; Starlin-c	.35	1.00	2.00
3-Starlin-a(r)/Warlock #10-12	.35	1.00	2.00
4-Starlin-a(r)/Warlock #12-15	.35	1.00	2.00
5-Starlin-a(r)/Warlock #15	.35	1.00	2.00
6	.35	1.00	2.00
Special Edition #1(12/83)	.35	1.00	2.00

NOTE: ***Byrne** a-5r. **Starlin** a-3-6r; c-1-4.*

WARLORD (See First Issue Special)
Jan-Feb, 1976; No.2, Mar-Apr, 1976; No.3, Oct-Nov, 1976 -Present
National Periodical Publications/DC Comics

	Good	Fine	Mint
1-Story cont'd. from 1st Issue Special #8	2.50	7.50	15.00
2-Intro. Machiste	1.25	3.75	7.50
3-5	.90	2.75	5.50
6-10: 6-Intro Mariah. 7-Origin Machiste. 9-Dons new costume	.85	2.50	5.00
11-20: 11-Origin-r. 12-Intro Aton. 15-Tara returns; Warlord has son	.60	1.80	3.60
21-30: 27-New facts about origin. 28-1st app. Wizard World	.45	1.25	2.50
31-36,39,40: 32-Intro Shakira. 39-Omac ends. 40-Warlord gets new costume	.35	1.00	2.00
37,38-Origin Omac by Starlin. 38-Intro Jennifer Morgan, Warlord's daughter	.35	1.00	2.00
41-47,49-52: 42-47-Omac back-up series. 49-Claw The Unconquered app. 50-Death of Aton. 51-r-/No.1.	.25	.75	1.50
48-(52pgs.)-1st app. Arak; contains free 16pg. Arak Son of Thunder; Claw The Unconquered app.	.35	1.00	2.00
53-80: 55-Arion Lord of Atlantis begins, ends No. 62. 63-The Barren Earth begins; contains free 16pg. Masters of the Universe		.50	1.00
81-99,101-128: 91-Origin w/new facts		.40	.80
100-Double size ($1.25)		.65	1.30
Remco Toy Giveaway (2¾x4")		.50	1.00
Annual 1(11/82)-Grell c, a(p)		.60	1.20
Annual 2(10/83)		.50	1.00
Annual 3(9/84), 4(8/85), 5(9/86), 6(10/87)		.65	1.30

NOTE: ***Grell** a-1-15, 16-50p, 51r, 52p, 59p, Annual 1p; c-1-70, 100-104, 112, 116, 117, Annual 1, 5. **Wayne Howard** a-64i. **Starlin** a-37-39p.*

WARLORDS (See DC Graphic Novel No. 2)

WARP
March, 1983 - No. 19, Feb, 1985 ($1.00-$1,25, Mando paper)
First Comics

	Good	Fine	Mint
1-Sargon-Mistress of War app.	.30	.90	1.80
2-5: 2-Faceless Ones begins		.65	1.30
6-10: 10-New Warp advs., & Outrider begin		.50	1.00
11-19		.45	.90
Special 1(7/83, 36 pgs.)-Origin Chaos-Prince of Madness; origin of Warp Universe begins, ends #3		.50	1.00
Special 2(1/84)-Lord Cumulus vs. Sargon Mistress of War ($1.00)		.50	1.00
Special 3(6/84)-Chaos-Prince of Madness		.50	1.00

NOTE: ***Brunner** a-1-9p; c-1-9. **Chaykin** a(p)-Special 1; c-Special 1. **Ditko** a-2-4. **Staton** a-1i. No. 1-9 are adapted from the Warp plays.*

WARPATH
Nov, 1954 - No. 3, April, 1955
Key Publications/Stanmor

	Good	Fine	Mint
1	3.00	9.00	21.00
2,3	1.70	5.00	12.00

WARP GRAPHICS ANNUAL
Dec, 1985 ($2.50 cover)
WaRP Graphics

	Good	Fine	Mint
1-Elfquest, Blood of the Innocent, Thunderbunny & Myth-adventures app.	.40	1.25	2.50

WARREN PRESENTS
Jan, 1979 - No. 14, Nov, 1981
Warren Publications

	Good	Fine	Mint
1-14-Eerie, Creepy, & Vampirella-r		.50	1.00

WAR REPORT
Sept, 1952 - No. 5, May, 1953
Ajax/Farrell Publications (Excellent Publ.)

	Good	Fine	Mint
1	2.65	8.00	18.00
2	1.35	4.00	9.00
3,5	1.20	3.50	8.00
4-Used in **POP**, pg. 94	2.00	6.00	14.00

WARRIOR COMICS
1945 (1930s DC reprints)
H.C. Blackerby

	Good	Fine	Mint
1-Wing Brady, The Iron Man, Mark Markon	4.60	14.00	32.00

WAR ROMANCES (See True. . .)

WAR SHIPS
1942 (36 pgs.)(Similar to Large Feature Comics)
Dell Publishing Co.

	Good	Fine	Mint
Cover by McWilliams; contains photos & drawings of U.S. war ships	6.00	18.00	42.00

WAR STORIES
1942 - No. 8, Feb-Apr, 1943
Dell Publishing Co.

	Good	Fine	Mint
1	7.00	21.00	50.00
2	4.35	13.00	30.00
3,4,6-8: 6-8-Night Devils	4.00	12.00	38.00
5-Origin The Whistler	5.50	16.50	38.00

WAR STORIES (Korea)
Sept, 1952 - No. 5, May, 1953
Ajax/Farrell Publications (Excellent Publ.)

WAR STORIES (continued)

	Good	Fine	Mint
1	2.65	8.00	18.00
2	1.35	4.00	9.00
3-5	1.20	3.50	8.00

WAR STORIES (See Star Spangled . . .)

WART AND THE WIZARD
Feb, 1964 (Walt Disney)
Gold Key

	Good	Fine	Mint
1 (10102-402)	1.75	5.25	12.00

WARTIME ROMANCES
July, 1951 - No. 18, Nov, 1953
St. John Publishing co.

	Good	Fine	Mint
1-All Baker-a	10.00	30.00	70.00
2-All Baker-a	6.00	18.00	42.00
3,4-All Baker-a	5.75	17.25	40.00
5-8-Baker c/a(2-3) each	5.15	15.50	36.00
9-12,16,18-Baker c/a each	3.75	11.25	26.00
13-15,17-Baker-c only	2.75	8.25	19.00

WAR VICTORY ADVENTURES (#1 titled War Victory Comics)
Summer, 1942 - No. 3, Winter, 1943-44 (5 cents)
U.S. Treasury Dept./War Victory/Harvey Publ.

	Good	Fine	Mint
1-(Promotion of Savings Bonds)-Featuring America's greatest comic art by top syndicated cartoonists; Blondie, Joe Palooka, Green Hornet, Dick Tracy, Superman, Gumps, etc.; (36 pgs.)	18.00	54.00	125.00
2-Powell-a	8.50	25.50	60.00
3-Capt. Red Cross (cover & text only); Powell-a	6.50	19.50	45.00

WAR WAGON, THE (See Movie Classics)

WAR WINGS
October, 1968
Charlton Comics

	Good	Fine	Mint
1		.50	1.00

WASHABLE JONES & SHMOO
June, 1953
Harvey Publications

	Good	Fine	Mint
1	10.00	30.00	70.00

WASH TUBBS (See The Comics & 4-Color #11,28,53)

WASTELAND
Dec, 1987 - Present ($1.75, color, adults)
DC Comics

	Good	Fine	Mint
1-3	.30	.90	1.80

WATCHMEN
Sept, 1986 - No. 12, Oct, 1987 (12 issue maxi-series)
DC Comics

	Good	Fine	Mint
1-Alan Moore scripts in all	1.00	3.00	6.00
2,3	.70	2.00	4.00
4-12	.50	1.50	3.00
Trade paperback ('87, $14.95)	2.50	7.50	15.00

WATCH OUT FOR BIG TALK
1950
Giveaway

	Good	Fine	Mint
Dan Barry-a (about crooked politicians)	2.35	7.00	14.00

WATER BIRDS AND THE OLYMPIC ELK (See 4-Color No. 700)

WAYFARERS, THE
Oct, 1986 ($1.80, color)
Eternity Comics

	Good	Fine	Mint
1-Super-hero team	.30	.90	1.80

WEATHER-BIRD (See Comics From . . . & Free Comics to You . . .)
1958 - No. 16, July, 1962 (Giveaway)
International Shoe Co./Western Printing Co.

	Good	Fine	Mint
1	.70	2.00	4.00
2-16	.45	1.25	2.50

NOTE: *The numbers are located in the lower bottom panel, pg. 1. All feature a character called Weather-Bird.*

WEATHER BIRD COMICS (See Comics From Weather Bird)
1957 (Giveaway)
Weather Bird Shoes

nn-Contains a comic bound with new cover. Several combinations possible; contents determines price (40 - 60 percent of contents).

WEB OF EVIL
Nov, 1952 - No. 21, Dec, 1954
Comic Magazines/Quality Comics Group

	Good	Fine	Mint
1-Used in **SOTI**, pg. 388. Jack Cole-a; morphine use story	14.00	42.00	100.00
2,3-Jack Cole-a	7.00	21.00	50.00
4,6,7-Jack Cole c/a	8.50	25.50	60.00
5-Electrocution-c; Jack Cole-c/a	10.00	30.00	70.00
8-11-Jack Cole-a	4.60	14.00	32.00
12,13,15,16,19-21	3.50	10.50	24.00
14-Part Crandall-c; Old Witch swipe	4.00	12.00	28.00
17-Opium drug propaganda story	4.00	12.00	28.00
18-Acid-in-face story	4.99	12.00	28.00

NOTE: ***Jack Cole** a(2 each)-2, 6, 8, 9. **Ravielli** a-13.*

WEB OF HORROR (Magazine)
Dec, 1969 - No. 3, Apr, 1970
Major Magazines

	Good	Fine	Mint
1-Jones-c; Wrightson-a	3.00	9.00	18.00
2-Jones-c; Wrightson-a(2), Kaluta-a	2.00	6.00	12.00
3-Wrightson-c; Brunner, Kaluta, Bruce Jones, Wrightson-a	2.00	6.00	12.00

WEB OF MYSTERY
Feb, 1951 - No. 29, Sept, 1955
Ace Magazines (A. A. Wyn)

	Good	Fine	Mint
1	9.50	28.50	65.00
2-Bakerish-a	5.70	17.00	40.00
3-10	4.60	14.00	32.00
11-18,20-26: 20-r/The Beyond #1	3.70	11.00	26.00
19-r-Chall. of Unknown #6 used in N.Y. Legislative Committee	4.35	13.00	30.00
27-Bakerish-a(r-/The Beyond #2); last pre-code issue	3.50	10.50	24.00
28,29: 28-All-r	2.65	8.00	18.00

NOTE: *This series was to appear as "Creepy Stories," but title was changed before publication. **Cameron** a-6, 8, 12, 13, 17, 18-20, 22, 24, 25, 27; c-8, 13, 17. **Colan** a-4. **Palais** a-28r. **Sekowsky** a-1-3, 7, 8, 11, 14, 21, 29. **Tothish** a-by Bill Discount #16. #29-all-r, 19-28-partial-r.*

WEB OF SPIDER-MAN, THE
Apr, 1985 - Present
Marvel Comics Group

	Good	Fine	Mint
1	1.25	3.75	7.50
2,3	.80	2.40	4.80
4-8	.55	1.60	3.20
9-13	.45	1.40	2.80
14-20: 19-Intro Humbug & Solo	.35	1.00	2.00
21-28,30	.25	.80	1.60
29-Wolverine app.	.50	1.50	3.00
31-Six part Kraven storyline	.70	2.00	4.00
32-Kraven storyline cont.	.45	1.40	2.80
33,34		.60	1.20
35-38		.50	1.00
Annual 1 (9/85)	.35	1.10	2.20

War Victory Adventures #3, © HARV

Web of Evil #16, © QUA

The Web of Spider-Man #3, © MCG

Weird Chills #1, © Key Publ.

Weird Comics #9, © FOX

Weird Fantasy #18, © WMG

THE WEB OF SPIDER-MAN (continued)

	Good	Fine	Mint
Annual 2 (9/86)-New Mutants; Art Adams-a	.70	2.00	4.00
Annual 3 (10/87)	.25	.75	1.50

WEDDING BELLS
Feb, 1954 - No. 19, 1956
Quality Comics Group

	Good	Fine	Mint
1-Whitney-a	5.50	16.50	38.00
2	2.65	8.00	18.00
3-9	1.70	5.00	12.00
10-Ward-a, 9 pgs.	6.85	20.50	48.00
11-14,17	1.30	4.00	9.00
15-Baker-c	2.00	6.00	14.00
16-Baker-c/a	3.15	9.50	22.00
18,19-Baker-a each	2.65	8.00	18.00

WEEKENDER, THE
1945 - 1946 (52 pages)
Rucker Publ. Co.

	Good	Fine	Mint
V1#4(1945)	8.00	24.00	56.00
V2#1-36 pgs. comics, 16 in newspaper format with photos; partial Dynamic Comics reprints; 4 pgs. of cels from the Disney film Pinocchio; Little Nemo story by Winsor McCay, Jr.; Jack Cole-a	11.50	34.00	80.00

WEEKLY COMIC MAGAZINE
May 12, 1940 (16 pgs.) (Full Color)
Fox Publications

(1st Version)-8 pg. Blue Beetle story, 7 pg. Patty O'Day story; two copies known to exist. Estimated value.... $500.00
(2nd Version)-7 two-pg. adventures of Blue Beetle, Patty O'Day, Yarko, Dr. Fung, Green Mask, Spark Stevens, & Rex Dexter; one copy known to exist Estimated value.... $400.00

Discovered with business papers, letters and exploitation material promoting **Weekly Comic Magazine** for use by newspapers in the same manner of **The Spirit** weeklies. Interesting note: these are dated three weeks before the first **Spirit** comic. Letters indicate that samples may have been sent to a few newspapers. These sections were actually 15½x22" pages which will fold down to an approximate 8x10" comic booklet. Other various comic sections were found with the above, but were more like the Sunday comic sections in format.

WEIRD (Magazine)
1/66 - V8#6, 12/74; V9#1, 1/75 - V10#3, 1977
(V1-V8, 52 pgs.; V9 on, 68 pgs.)
Eerie Publications

	Good	Fine	Mint
V1#10(#1)-Intro. Morris the Caretaker of Weird (ends V2#10); Burgos-a	.70	2.00	4.00
11,12	.35	1.00	2.00
V2#1-4(10/67), V3#1(1/68), V2#6(4/68)-V2#7,9,10(12/68), V3#1(2/69)-V3#4	.35	1.00	2.00
V2#8-Reprints Ditko's 1st story/Fantastic Fears #5	.50	1.50	3.00
5(12/69)-Rulah reprint; "Rulah" changed to "Pulah;" LSD story-reprinted in Horror Tales V4#4, Tales From the Tomb V2#4, & Terror Tales V7#3	.35	1.00	2.00
V4#1-6('70), V5#1-6('71), V6#1-7('72), V7#1-6('73), V8#1-6('74), V9#1-4(1/75-'76)(no V9#1), V10#1-3('77)	.35	1.00	2.00

WEIRD ADVENTURES
May-June, 1951 - No. 3, Sept-Oct, 1951
P. L. Publishing Co. (Canada)

	Good	Fine	Mint
1-"The She-Wolf Killer" by Matt Baker, 6 pgs.	11.50	34.00	80.00
2-Bondage/hypodermic panel; opium den text story	7.00	21.00	50.00
3-Male bondage/torture-c; severed head story	6.50	19.50	45.00

WEIRD ADVENTURES
No. 10, July-Aug, 1951
Ziff-Davis Publishing Co.

	Good	Fine	Mint
10-Painted-c	7.00	21.00	50.00

WEIRD CHILLS
July, 1954 - No. 3, Nov, 1954
Key Publications

	Good	Fine	Mint
1-Wolverton-a r-/Weird Mysteries No. 4; blood transfusion-c	17.00	51.00	120.00
2-Injury to eye-c	19.00	57.00	132.00
3-Bondage E.C. swipe-c	8.00	24.00	56.00

NOTE: ***Baily*** *c-1.*

WEIRD COMICS
April, 1940 - No. 20, Jan, 1942
Fox Features Syndicate

	Good	Fine	Mint
1-The Birdman, Thor, God of Thunder (ends #5), The Sorceress of Zoom, Blast Bennett, Typhon, Voodoo Man, & Dr. Mortal begin; Fine bondage-c	90.00	270.00	630.00
2-Lou Fine-c	45.00	135.00	315.00
3,4: 3-Simon-c. 4-Torture-c	30.00	90.00	210.00
5-Intro. Dart & sidekick Ace (ends #20); bondage/hypo-c	33.00	100.00	230.00
6,7-Dynamite Thor app. in each	30.00	90.00	210.00
8-Dynamo, the Eagle & sidekick Buddy & Marga, the Panther Woman begin	30.00	90.00	210.00
9	23.00	70.00	160.00
10-Navy Jones app.	23.00	70.00	160.00
11-16: 16-Flag-c	20.00	60.00	140.00
17-Origin The Black Rider	20.00	60.00	140.00
18-20: 20-Origin The Rapier; Swoop Curtis app; Churchill, Hitler-c	20.00	60.00	140.00

WEIRD FANTASY (Formerly A Moon, A Girl, Romance; becomes Weird Science-Fantasy #23 on)
No. 13, May-June, 1950 - No. 22, Nov-Dec, 1953
E. C. Comics

	Good	Fine	Mint
13(#1) (1950)	80.00	240.00	560.00
14-Necronomicon story; atomic explosion-c	45.00	130.00	300.00
15,16: 16-Used in **SOTI**, pg. 144	35.00	105.00	245.00
17 (1951)	28.00	85.00	195.00
6-10	21.50	65.00	150.00
11-13 (1952)	16.00	48.00	110.00
14-Frazetta/Williamson(1st team-up at E.C.)/Krenkel-a, 7 pgs.; Orlando draws E.C. staff	30.00	90.00	210.00
15-Williamson/Evans-a(3), 4,3,&7 pgs.	18.00	54.00	125.00
16-19-Williamson/Krenkel-a in all. 18-Williamson/Feldstein-c	16.00	48.00	110.00
20-Frazetta/Williamson-a, 7 pgs.	18.00	54.00	125.00
21-Frazetta/Williamson-c & Williamson/Krenkel-a	30.00	90.00	210.00
22-Bradbury adaptation	12.50	37.50	85.00

NOTE: ***Crandall*** *a-22.* ***Elder*** *a-17.* ***Feldstein*** *a-13(No.1)-8; c-13(No.1)-18 (No.18 w/****Williamson****), 20.* ***Kamen*** *a-13(No.1)-16, 18-22.* ***Krigstein*** *a-22.* ***Kurtzman*** *a-13(No.1)-17(No.5), 6.* ***Orlando*** *a-9-22 (2 stories in No. 16); c-19, 22.* ***Severin/Elder*** *a-18-21.* ***Wood*** *a-13(No.1)-14, 17(2 stories ea. in No. 10-13). Canadian reprints exist; see Table of Contents.*

WEIRD HORRORS (Nightmare #10 on)
June, 1952 - No. 9, Oct, 1953
St. John Publishing Co.

	Good	Fine	Mint
1-Tuska-a	11.50	34.00	80.00
2	6.00	18.00	42.00
3-Finesque-a; hashish story	7.00	21.00	50.00
4,5-Finesque-a	5.70	17.00	40.00
6-Ekgren-c	12.00	36.00	84.00
7-Ekgren-c; Kubert, Cameron-a	13.00	40.00	90.00
8,9-Kubert c/a. 8-Bondage-c	9.50	28.50	65.00

NOTE: ***Cameron*** *a-7, 9.* ***Finesque*** *a-1, 2, 4.* ***Morisi*** *a-3.*

WEIRD MYSTERIES
Oct, 1952 - No. 14, Jan, 1955
Gillmore Publications

	Good	Fine	Mint
1-Partial Wolverton-c swiped from splash page "Flight to the Future" in Weird Tales of the Future #2; "Eternity" has an Ingels swipe	16.00	48.00	110.00
2-"Robot Woman" by Wolverton; Bernard Baily-c-reprinted in Mister Mystery #18; acid in face panel	36.00	108.00	250.00
3,6: 3-Decapitation-c	10.00	30.00	70.00
4-"The Man Who Never Smiled" (3 pgs.) by Wolverton; B. Baily skull-c	27.00	81.00	190.00
5-Wolverton story "Swamp Monster," 6 pgs.; decapitation-c	30.00	90.00	210.00
7-Used in **SOTI**, illo-"Indeed" & illo-"Sex and blood"	20.00	60.00	140.00
8-Wolverton-c panel reprint/No. 5; used in a 1954 Readers Digest anti-comics article by T. E. Murphy entitled "For the Kiddies to Read"	9.50	28.50	65.00
9-Excessive violence, gore & torture	8.00	24.00	56.00
10-Silhouetted nudity panel	7.00	21.00	50.00
11-14 (#13,14-Exist?)	5.70	17.00	40.00

NOTE: ***Baily*** *c-2-8, 10-12.*

WEIRD MYSTERIES (Magazine)
Mar-Apr, 1959 (68 pages) (35 cents) (B&W)
Pastime Publications

	Good	Fine	Mint
1-Torres-a; E. C. swipe from TFTC No. 46 by Tuska-"The Ragman"	2.00	6.00	14.00

WEIRD MYSTERY TALES (See DC 100 Page Super Spectacular)

WEIRD MYSTERY TALES (See Cancelled Comic Cavalcade)
Jul-Aug, 1972 - No. 24, Nov, 1975
National Periodical Publications

	Good	Fine	Mint
1-Kirby-a		.50	1.00
2-24		.20	.40

NOTE: ***Alcala*** *a-5, 10, 13, 14.* ***Aparo*** *c-4.* ***Bolle*** *a-8.* ***Howard*** *a-4.* ***Kaluta*** *a-24; c-1.* ***G. Kane*** *a-10.* ***Kirby*** *a-1, 2p, 3p.* ***Nino*** *a-5, 6, 9, 13, 16, 21.* ***Redondo*** *a-9.* ***Starlin*** *a-2-4.* ***Wood*** *a-23.* ***Wrightson*** *c-21.*

WEIRD SCIENCE (Formerly Saddle Romances) (Becomes Weird Science-Fantasy #23 on)
No. 12, May-June, 1950 - No. 22, Nov-Dec, 1953
E. C. Comics

	Good	Fine	Mint
12(#1) (1950)	82.00	245.00	575.00
13	45.00	135.00	315.00
14,15 (1950)	41.00	123.00	285.00
5-10	25.00	75.00	175.00
11-14 (1952)	16.00	48.00	110.00
15-18-Williamson/Krenkel-a in each; 15-Williamson-a. 17-Used in **POP**, pgs. 81,82	19.00	57.00	130.00
19,20-Williamson/Frazetta-a, 7 pgs each. 19-Used in **SOTI**, illo-"A young girl on her wedding night stabs her sleeping husband to death with a hatpin . . ."	25.00	75.00	175.00
21-Williamson/Frazetta-a, 6 pgs.; Wood draws E.C. staff; Gaines & Feldstein app. in story	25.00	75.00	175.00
22-Williamson/Frazetta/Krenkel-a, 8 pgs.; Wood draws himself in his story - last pg. & panel	25.00	75.00	175.00

NOTE: ***Elder*** *a-14, 19.* ***Evans*** *a-22.* ***Feldstein*** *a-12(No.1)-8; c-12(No.1)-8, 11.* ***Ingels*** *a-15.* ***Kamen*** *a-12(No.1)-13, 15-18, 20, 21.* ***Kurtzman*** *a-12(No.1)-7.* ***Orlando*** *a-10-22.* ***Wood*** *a-12(No.1), 13(No.2), 5-22 (No. 9, 10, 12, 13 all have 2* ***Wood*** *stories); c-9, 10, 12-22. Canadian reprints exist; see Table of Contents.*

WEIRD SCIENCE-FANTASY (Formerly Weird Science & Weird Fantasy) (Becomes Incredible Science Fiction #30)
No. 23 Mar, 1954 - No. 29, May-June, 1955
E. C. Comics

	Good	Fine	Mint
23-Williamson & Wood-a	18.00	55.00	125.00
24-Williamson & Wood-a; Harlan Ellison's 1st professional story, 'Upheaval!,' later adapted into a short story as 'Mealtime,' and then into a TV episode of Voyage to the Bottom of the Sea as 'The Price of Doom'	18.00	55.00	125.00
25-Williamson-c; Williamson/Torres/Krenkel-a plus Wood-a	22.00	65.00	154.00
26-Flying Saucer Report; Wood, Crandall, Orlando-a	17.00	51.00	120.00
27	18.00	55.00	125.00
28-Williamson/Krenkel/Torres-a; Wood-a	22.00	65.00	154.00
29-Frazetta-c; Williamson/Krenkel & Wood-a	42.00	125.00	295.00

NOTE: ***Crandall*** *a-26, 27, 29.* ***Evans*** *a-26.* ***Feldstein*** *c-24, 26, 28.* ***Kamen*** *a-27, 28.* ***Krigstein*** *a-23-25.* ***Orlando*** *a-in all.* ***Wood*** *a-in all; c-23, 27.*

WEIRD SCIENCE-FANTASY ANNUAL
1952, 1953 (Sold thru the E. C. office & on the stands in some major cities)
E. C. Comics

	Good	Fine	Mint
1952	104.00	312.00	725.00
1953	66.00	200.00	460.00

NOTE: *The 1952 annual contains books cover-dated in 1951 & 1952, and the 1953 annual from 1952 & 1953. Contents of each annual may vary in same year.*

WEIRD SUSPENSE
Feb, 1975 - No. 3, July, 1975
Atlas/Seaboard Publ.

	Good	Fine	Mint
1-Tarantula begins		.30	.60
2,3: 3-Buckler-c		.25	.50

WEIRD SUSPENSE STORIES (Canadian reprint of Crime SuspenStories No. 1-3; see Table of Contents)

WEIRD TALES OF THE FUTURE
March, 1952 - No. 8, July, 1953
S.P.M. Publ. No. 1-4/Aragon Publ. No. 5-8

	Good	Fine	Mint
1-Andru-a(2)	24.00	72.00	170.00
2,3-Wolverton-c/a(3) each. 2-"Jumpin Jupiter" satire by Wolverton begins, ends #5	48.00	145.00	335.00
4-"Jumpin Jupiter" satire by Wolverton; partial Wolverton-c	22.00	65.00	154.00
5-Wolverton-c/a(2)	48.00	145.00	335.00
6-Bernard Baily-c	11.00	32.00	76.00
7-"The Mind Movers" from the art to Wolverton's "Brain Bats of Venus" from Mr. Mystery #7 which was cut apart, pasted up, partially redrawn, and rewritten by Harry Kantor, the editor; Bernard Baily-c	23.00	70.00	160.00
8-Reprints Weird Mysteries #1(10/52) minus cover; gory cover showing heart ripped out	9.50	28.50	65.00

WEIRD TALES OF THE MACABRE (Magazine)
Jan, 1975 - No. 2, Mar, 1975 (B&W) (75 cents)
Atlas/Seaboard Publ.

	Good	Fine	Mint
1-Jones-c	.35	1.00	2.00
2-Boris Vallejo-c, Severin-a	.30	.80	1.60

WEIRD TERROR (Also see Horrific)
Sept, 1952 - No. 13, Sept, 1954
Allen Hardy Associates (Comic Media)

	Good	Fine	Mint
1-"Portrait of Death," adapted from Lovecraft's "Pickman's Model;" lingerie panels, Hitler story	8.50	25.50	60.00
2	4.60	14.00	32.00
3,5,7,9,10	4.00	12.00	28.00
4,6-Dismemberment, decapitation	7.00	21.00	50.00
8-Decapitation story; Ambrose Bierce adapt.	6.50	19.50	45.00
11-End of the world story with atomic blast panels; Tothish-a by Bill Discount	6.50	19.50	45.00
12-Discount-a	4.00	12.00	28.00
13-Severed head panels	4.35	13.00	30.00

NOTE: ***Don Heck*** *a/c-most issues.* ***Landau*** *a-6.* ***Morisi*** *a-2-5, 7, 12.* ***Palais*** *a-1, 5, 8(2), 12.* ***Powell*** *a-10.* ***Ravielli*** *a-11, 20.*

Weird Mysteries #6, Gillmore Publ.

Weird Science #15 (#4), © WMG

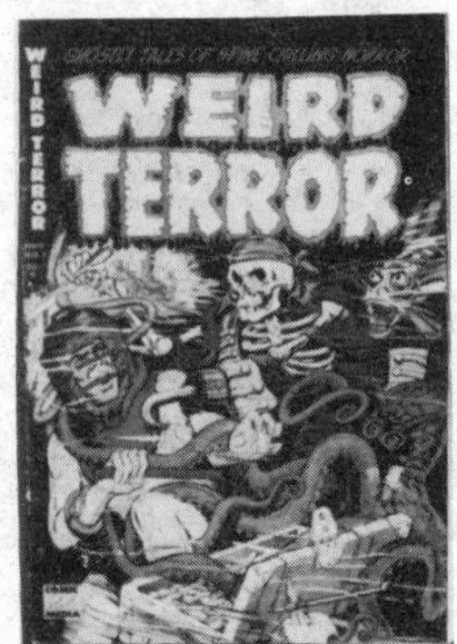

Weird Terror #2, © Comic Media

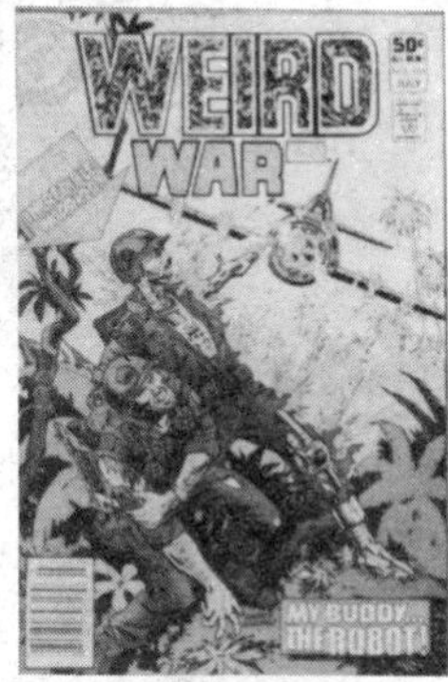

Weird War Tales #101, © DC

Wendy Parker Comics #1, © MCG

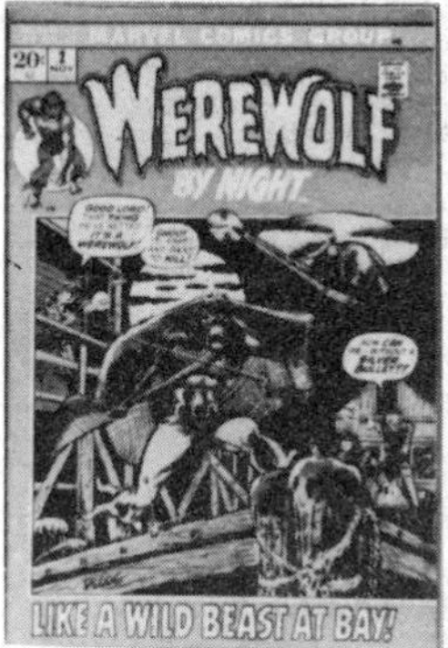

Werewolf By Night #2, © MCG

WEIRD THRILLERS
Sept-Oct, 1951 - No. 5, Oct-Nov, 1952
Ziff-Davis Publ. Co. (Approved Comics)

	Good	Fine	Mint
1-Ron Hatton photo-c	13.00	40.00	90.00
2-Toth, Anderson, Colan-a	11.00	32.00	76.00
3-Two Powell, Tuska-a	8.00	24.00	56.00
4-Kubert, Tuska-a	10.00	30.00	70.00
5-Powell-a	8.00	24.00	56.00

NOTE: ***Anderson** a-2. **Roussos** a-4. No. 2, 3 reprinted in Nightmare No. 10 & 13; No. 4,5 r-/in Amazing Ghost Stories No. 16 & No. 15.*

WEIRD WAR TALES
Sept-Oct, 1971 - No. 124, June, 1983
National Periodical Publications/DC Comics

	Good	Fine	Mint
1	.25	.75	1.50
2-7,9,10: 5,6,10-Toth-a. 7-Krigstein-a		.30	.60
8-Adams c/a(i)	.30	.90	1.80
11-50: 36-Crandall, Kubert r-/No.2		.25	.50
51-63,65-67,69-124: 69-Sci-Fic ish. 93-Origin Creature Commandos. 101-Origin G.I. Robot		.20	.40
64,68-Miller-a		.40	.80

NOTE: ***Austin** a-51i, 52i. **Bailey** a-21, 33. **Crandall** a-2r, 36r. **Ditko** a-46p, 49p, 95, 99, 104-106. **Drucker** a-2, 3. **Evans** a-17, 22, 35, 46, 74, 82; c-73, 74, 82, 83, 85. **Giffen** a-124p. **Grell** a-67. **Heath** a-3, 59. **Howard** a-53i. **Kaluta** c-12. **Gil Kane** c-115, 116, 118. **Kubert** a-1-4, 7, 36, 68, 69; c-51, 60, 62-69, 72, 75-81, 84, 86-88, 90-96, 100, 103, 104, 106, 107, 123, 124. **Lopez** a-108. **Maurer** a-5. **Meskin** a-4r. **Morrow** c-54. **Newton** a-82p, 122p. **Nino** a-9. **Redondo** a-10, 13, 30, 38, 42, 52. **Rogers** a-51p, 52p. **Sekowsky** a-75p. **Simonson** a-10, 72. **Sparling** a-86p. **Spiegle** a-96, 97, 107, 109-112. **Starlin** c-89. **Staton** a-106p; c-108p. **Sutton** a-66, 87, 91, 92, 103. **Tuska** a-103p, 122p.*

WEIRD WESTERN TALES (Formerly All-Star Western)
No. 12, June-July, 1972 - No. 70, Aug, 1980 (No. 12: 52 pgs.)
National Periodical Publications/DC Comics

	Good	Fine	Mint
12-Bat Lash, Pow Wow Smith reprints; El Diablo by Adams/Wrightson	.25	.75	1.50
13,15-Adams-a; c-#15	.25	.75	1.50
14-Toth-a		.40	.80
16-28,30-70: 39-Origin/1st app. Scalphunter		.20	.40
29-Origin Jonah Hex		.40	.80

NOTE: ***Ditko** a-99. **Evans** inks-39-48; c-39i, 40, 47. **G. Kane** a-15. **Kubert** c-12, 33. **Starlin** c-44, 45. **Wildey** a-26.*

WEIRD WONDER TALES
Dec, 1973 - No. 22, May, 1977
Marvel Comics Group

	Good	Fine	Mint
1-Wolverton-a r-from Mystic #6		.40	.80
2-22: 16-18-Venus r-by Everett/Venus #19,18 & 17. 19-22-Dr. Druid (Droom)-r		.25	.50

NOTE: *All Reprints: **Check** a-1. **Colan** a-17r. **Ditko** a-4, 5, 10-13, 19-21. **Drucker** a-12, 20. **Everett** a-3(Spellbound #16), 6(Astonishing #10), 9(Adv. Into Mystery #5). **Kirby** a-6, 11, 13, 16-22; c-17, 19, 20. **Krigstein** a-19. **Kubert** a-22. **Maneely** a-8. **Mooney** a-7p. **Powell** a-7. **Torres** a-7. **Wildey** a-2.*

WEIRD WORLDS (See Adventures Into. . .)

WEIRD WORLDS (Magazine)
V1#10(12/70), V2#1(2/71) - No. 4, Aug, 1971 (52 pgs.)
Eerie Publications

	Good	Fine	Mint
V1#10	.50	1.50	3.00
V2#1-4	.35	1.00	2.00

WEIRD WORLDS
Aug-Sept, 1972 - No. 9, Jan-Feb, 1974; No. 10, Oct-Nov, 1974
National Periodical Publications

	Good	Fine	Mint
1-Edgar Rice Burrough's John Carter of Mars & David Innes begin; Kubert-c		.50	1.00
2-7: 7-Last John Carter		.40	.80
8-10: 8-Iron Wolf begins by Chaykin		.30	.60

NOTE: ***Adams** a-2i, 3i. John Carter by **Anderson**-No. 1-3. **Chaykin** c-7, 8. **Kaluta** a-4; c-5, 6, 10. **Orlando** a-4i; c-2-4. **Wrightson** a-2i.*

WELCOME BACK, KOTTER (TV) (See Limited Collectors Ed. #57)
Nov, 1976 - No. 10, Mar-Apr, 1978
National Periodical Publications/DC Comics

	Good	Fine	Mint
1-Sparling a(p)		.40	.80
2-10: 3-Estrada-a		.30	.60

WELCOME SANTA (See March of Comics No. 63,183)

WELLS FARGO (See Tales of. . .)

WENDY PARKER COMICS
July, 1953 - No. 8, July, 1954
Atlas Comics (OMC)

	Good	Fine	Mint
1	3.00	9.00	21.00
2	1.50	4.50	10.00
3-8	1.15	3.50	8.00

WENDY, THE GOOD LITTLE WITCH
8/60 - No. 82, 11/73; No. 83, 8/74 - No. 93, 4/76
Harvey Publications

	Good	Fine	Mint
1	8.35	25.00	50.00
2	4.00	12.00	24.00
3-5	3.35	10.00	20.00
6-10	2.50	7.50	15.00
11-20	1.70	5.00	10.00
21-30	.85	2.50	5.00
31-50	.50	1.50	3.00
51-70	.40	1.20	2.40
71-93	.25	.75	1.50

NOTE: *(See Casper the Friendly Ghost & Harvey Hits No. 7,16,21,23,27,30,33)*

WENDY WITCH WORLD
10/61; No. 2, 9/62 - No. 52, 12/73; No. 53, 9/74
Harvey Publications

	Good	Fine	Mint
1	5.35	16.00	32.00
2-5	2.75	8.00	16.00
6-10	1.70	5.00	10.00
11-20: 14-Giant	6.00		
21-30	.50	1.50	3.00
31-40	.35	1.00	2.00
41-53		.60	1.20

WEREWOLF (Super Hero)
Dec, 1966 - No. 3, April, 1967
Dell Publishing Co.

	Good	Fine	Mint
1	.35	1.00	2.00
2,3		.50	1.00

WEREWOLF BY NIGHT (See Marvel Spotlight)
Sept, 1972 - No. 43, Mar, 1977
Marvel Comics Group

	Good	Fine	Mint
1-Ploog-a-cont'd./Marvel Spotlight #4	.35	1.00	2.00
2-7-Ploog-a(p) in all		.40	.80
8-10		.30	.60
11-31: 15-New origin Werewolf		.25	.50
32-Origin & 1st app. Moon Knight	1.70	5.00	10.00
33-Moon Knight app.	1.00	3.00	6.00
34-36,38-43: 35-Starlin/Wrightson-c		.25	.50
37-Moon Knight app; part Wrightson-c	.50	1.50	3.00
Giant Size 2(10/74, 68 pgs.)(Formerly G-S Creatures)-Frankenstein app; Ditko-a(r).		.30	.60
Giant Size 3-5(7/75, 68 pgs.); 4-Morbius the Living Vampire app.		.30	.60

NOTE: ***Bolle** a-6i. **Ditko** a-Gnt. Size 2r. **G. Kane** a-11p, 12p; c-21, 22, 24-30, 34p, Gnt. Size 3-5. **Mooney** a-7i. **Ploog** 1-4p, 5, 6p, 7p, 13-16p; c-5-8, 13-16. **Reinman** a-8i. **Sutton** a(i)-9, 11, 16, 35.*

WEREWOLVES & VAMPIRES (Magazine)
1962 (One Shot)
Charlton Comics

WEREWOLVES & VAMPIRES (continued)

	Good	Fine	Mint
1	3.00	9.00	21.00

WEST COAST AVENGERS, THE
Sept, 1984 - No. 4, Dec, 1984 (mini-series; Mando paper)
Marvel Comics Group

	Good	Fine	Mint
1-Hawkeye, Iron Man, Mockingbird, Tigra	.90	2.75	5.50
2-4	.60	1.75	3.50

WEST COAST AVENGERS
Oct, 1985 - Present (regular series)
Marvel Comics Group

	Good	Fine	Mint
1 (V2/1)	.75	2.25	4.50
2,3	.55	1.60	3.20
4-6	.45	1.30	2.60
7-10	.35	1.10	2.20
11-20	.30	.90	1.80
21-30		.60	1.20
31,32		.50	1.00
Annual 1 (10/86)	.35	1.00	2.00
Annual 2 (9/87)	.25	.75	1.50

WESTERN ACTION
1964
I. W. Enterprises

	Good	Fine	Mint
7-Reprint	.30	.90	1.80

WESTERN ACTION
February, 1975
Atlas/Seaboard Publ.

	Good	Fine	Mint
1-Kid Cody by Wildey & The Comanche Kid stories; intro. The Renegade		.30	.60

WESTERN ACTION THRILLERS
April, 1937 (100 pages)(Square binding)
Dell Publishers

	Good	Fine	Mint
1-Buffalo Bill, The Texas Kid, Laramie Joe, Two-Gun Thompson, & Wild West Bill app.	30.00	90.00	210.00

WESTERN ADVENTURES COMICS (Western Love Trails #7 on)
Oct, 1948 - No. 6, Aug, 1949
Ace Magazines

	Good	Fine	Mint
nn(#1)-Sheriff Sal, The Cross-Draw Kid, Sam Bass begin	9.50	28.50	65.00
nn(#2)(12/48)	5.00	15.00	35.00
nn(#3)(2/49)-Used in **SOTI**, pgs. 30,31	5.70	17.00	40.00
4-6	4.00	12.00	28.00

WESTERN BANDITS
1952
Avon Periodicals

	Good	Fine	Mint
1-Butch Cassidy, The Daltons by Larsen; Kinstler-a; c-part r-/paperback Avon Western Novel 1	8.00	24.00	56.00

WESTERN BANDIT TRAILS (See Approved Comics)
Jan, 1949 - No. 3, July, 1949
St. John Publishing Co.

	Good	Fine	Mint
1-Tuska-a; Baker-c; Blue Monk, Ventrilo app.	8.00	24.00	56.00
2-Baker-c	5.70	17.00	40.00
3-Baker c/a, Tuska-a	6.50	19.50	45.00

WESTERN COMICS (See Super DC Giant)
Jan-Feb, 1948 - No. 85, Jan-Feb, 1961 (52pgs., 1-18?)
National Periodical Publications

	Good	Fine	Mint
1-The Wyoming Kid & his horse Racer, The Vigilante (Meskin-a), The Cowboy Marshal, & Rodeo Rick begin	22.00	65.00	154.00
2	12.00	36.00	84.00
3,4-Last Vigilante	10.00	30.00	70.00
5-Nighthawk & his horse Nightwind begin (not in #6); Captain Tootsie by Beck	8.50	25.50	60.00
6,7,9,10	7.00	21.00	50.00
8-Origin Wyoming Kid; 2pg. pin-ups of rodeo queens	8.50	25.50	60.00
11-20	4.60	14.00	32.00
21-40: 27-Last 52 pgs.	3.70	11.00	26.00
41-60: 43-Pow Wow Smith begins, ends #85	3.00	9.00	21.00
61-85-Last Wyoming Kid. 77-Origin Matt Savage Trail Boss. 82-1st app. Fleetfoot, Pow Wow's girlfriend	1.70	5.00	12.00

NOTE: ***Gil Kane, Infantino*** *art in most.* ***Meskin*** *a-1-4.* ***Moreira*** *a-35, 37, 39.* ***Post*** *a-3-5.*

WESTERN CRIME BUSTERS
Sept, 1950 - No. 10, Mar-Apr, 1952
Trojan Magazines

	Good	Fine	Mint
1-Six-Gun Smith, Wilma West, K-Bar-Kate, & Fighting Bob Dale begin	10.00	30.00	70.00
2	6.00	18.00	42.00
3-5	5.50	16.50	38.00
6-Wood-a	15.00	45.00	105.00
7-Six-Gun Smith by Wood	15.00	45.00	105.00
8	5.00	15.00	35.00
9-Tex Gordon & Wilma West by Wood; Lariat Lucy app.	16.00	48.00	110.00
10-Wood-a	13.00	40.00	90.00

WESTERN CRIME CASES (The Outlaws #10 on?)
No. 9, Dec, 1951
Star Publications

	Good	Fine	Mint
9-White Rider & Super Horse; L. B. Cole-c	2.65	8.00	18.00

WESTERN DESPERADO COMICS (Formerly Slam Bang)
1940 (Oct.?)
Fawcett Publications

	Good	Fine	Mint
8-(Rare)	25.00	75.00	175.00

WESTERNER, THE (Wild Bill Pecos)
No. 14, June, 1948 - No. 41, Dec, 1951
"Wanted" Comic Group/Toytown/Patches

	Good	Fine	Mint
14	3.70	11.00	26.00
15-17,19-21: 19-Meskin-a	1.85	5.50	13.00
18,22-25-Krigstein-a	3.50	10.50	24.00
26(4/50)-Origin & 1st app. Calamity Kate, series ends #32; Krigstein-a	4.35	13.00	30.00
27-Krigstein-a(2)	4.65	14.00	32.00
28-41: 33-Quest app. 37-Lobo, the Wolf Boy begins	1.60	4.70	11.00

WESTERNER, THE
1964
Super Comics

	Good	Fine	Mint
Super Reprint #15,16(Crack West. #65), 17	.25	.75	1.50

WESTERN FIGHTERS
Apr-May, 1948 - V4No.7, Mar-Apr, 1953
Hillman Periodicals/Star Publ.

	Good	Fine	Mint
V1#1-Simon & Kirby-c	10.00	30.00	70.00
2-Kirby-a(p)?	3.50	10.50	24.00
3-Fuje-c	3.00	9.00	21.00
4-Krigstein, Ingels-a	4.00	12.00	28.00
5,6,8,9,12	2.30	7.00	16.00
7,10-Krigstein-a	4.00	12.00	28.00
11-Williamson/Frazetta-a	14.00	42.00	100.00
V2#1-Krigstein-a	4.00	12.00	28.00
2-12: 4-Berg-a	1.30	4.00	9.00
V3#1-11	1.15	3.50	8.00
12-Krigstein-a	3.50	10.50	24.00
V4#1,4-7	1.15	3.50	8.00
2,3-Krigstein-a	3.00	9.00	21.00

Western Comics #10, © DC

Western Crime Busters #9, © TM

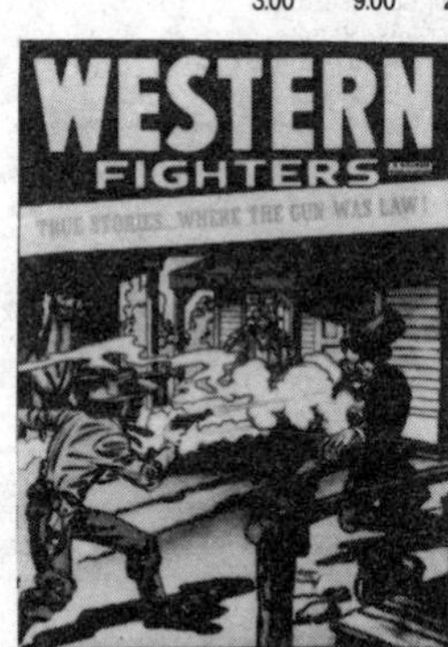

Western Fighters #1, © HILL

Western Frontier #1, © P.L.Publ.

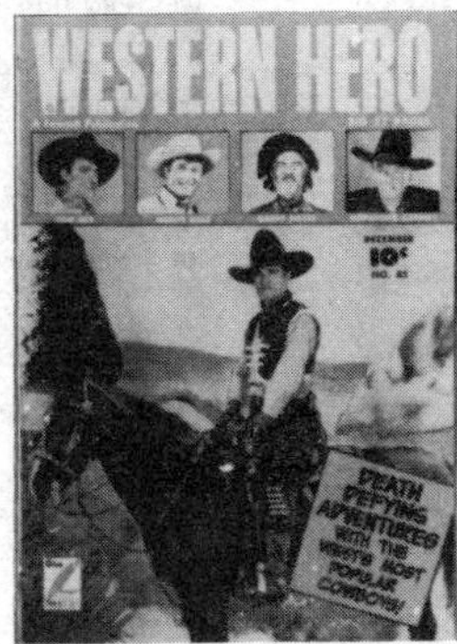

Western Hero #85, © FAW

Western Killers #60, © FOX

WESTERN FIGHTERS (continued) — Good / Fine / Mint

3-D 1(12/53, Star Publ.)-L. B. Cole-c 14.00 42.00 100.00

NOTE: ***Kinstlerish*** *a-V2#6, 8, 9, 12; V3#2, 5-7, 11, 12; V4#1(plus cover).* ***McWilliams*** *a-11.* ***Powell*** *a-V2#2.* ***Rowich*** *c-6.*

WESTERN FRONTIER
Apr-May, 1951 - No. 7, 1952
P. L. Publishers

1 3.50 10.50 24.00
2 1.85 5.50 13.00
3-7 1.30 4.00 9.00

WESTERN GUNFIGHTERS (1st Series) (Apache Kid #11-19)
No. 20, June, 1956 - No. 27, Aug, 1957
Atlas Comics (CPS)

20 3.00 9.00 21.00
21,25-27 1.70 5.00 12.00
22-Wood & Powell-a 6.75 20.25 47.00
23-Williamson-a 4.65 14.00 32.00
24-Toth-a 3.50 10.50 24.00

WESTERN GUNFIGHTERS (2nd Series)
Aug, 1970 - No. 33, Nov, 1975 (No. 1-6: 68 pgs.; No. 7: 52 pgs.)
Marvel Comics Group

1-Ghost Rider, Fort Rango, Renegades & Gunhawk app. .40 .80
2-33: 2-Origin Nightwind (Apache Kid's horse). 7-Origin Ghost Rider retold. 10-Origin Black Rider. 12-Origin Matt Slade .25 .50

NOTE: ***Baker*** *a-2r.* ***Everett*** *a-6i.* ***G. Kane*** *c-29, 31.* ***Kirby*** *a-1p(r), 10, 11.* ***Kubert*** *a-2r.* ***Maneely*** *a-2, 10r.* ***Morrow*** *a-29r.* ***Severin*** *c-10.* ***Smith*** *a-4.* ***Steranko*** *c-14.* ***Sutton*** *a-1, 2i, 3, 4.* ***Torres*** *a-26('57).* ***Wildey*** *a-8r, 9r.* ***Williamson*** *a-2r, 18r.* ***Woodbridge*** *a-27('57). Renegades in #4, 5; Ghost Rider-#1-7.*

WESTERN HEARTS
Dec, 1949 - No. 10, Mar, 1952
Standard Comics

1-Severin-a, Whip Wilson photo-c 6.00 18.00 42.00
2-Williamson/Frazetta-a, 2 pgs; photo-c 11.00 32.00 76.00
3 2.00 6.00 14.00
4-7,10-Severin & Elder, Al Carreno-a. 5,6-Photo-c 2.30 7.00 16.00
8-Randolph Scott/Janis Carter photo-c/'Santa Fe;' Severin & Elder-a 3.00 9.00 21.00
9-Whip Wilson photo-c; Severin & Elder-a 3.00 9.00 21.00

WESTERN HERO (Wow #1-69; Real Western Hero #70-75)
No. 76, Mar, 1949 - No. 112, Mar, 1952
Fawcett Publications

76(#1, 52 pgs.)-Tom Mix, Hopalong Cassidy, Monte Hale, Gabby Hayes, Young Falcon (ends #78,80), & Big Bow and Little Arrow (ends #102,105) begin; painted-c begin 11.00 32.00 76.00
77 (52 pgs.) 7.00 21.00 50.00
78,80-82 (52 pgs.): 81-Capt. Tootsie by Beck 7.00 21.00 50.00
79,83 (36 pgs.): 83-Last painted-c 5.70 17.00 40.00
84-86,88-90 (52 pgs.): 84-Photo-c begin, end #112. 86-Last Hopalong Cassidy 6.00 18.00 42.00
87,91,95,99 (36 pgs.): 87-Bill Boyd begins, ends #95 5.00 15.00 35.00
92-94,96-98,101 (52 pgs.): 96-Tex Ritter begins. 101-Red Eagle app. 5.70 17.00 40.00
100 (52 pgs.) 6.00 18.00 42.00
102-111 (36pgs. begin) 5.00 15.00 35.00
112-Last issue 5.70 17.00 40.00

NOTE: *½-1 pg. Rocky Lane (Carnation) in 80-83,86,88,97.*

WESTERN KID (1st Series)
Dec, 1954 - No. 17, Aug, 1957
Atlas Comics (CPC)

Good / Fine / Mint

1-Origin; The Western Kid, his horse Whirlwind & dog Lightning begin 5.00 15.00 35.00
2 2.30 7.00 16.00
3-8 1.85 5.50 13.00
9,10-Williamson-a in both, 4 pgs. each 3.85 11.50 27.00
11-17 1.30 4.00 9.00

NOTE: ***Maneely*** *c-2-7, 14.* ***Romita*** *a-1(2), 2(3)-7(3), 12, 14, 17; c-1, 12.* ***Severin*** *c-17.*

WESTERN KID, THE (2nd Series)
Dec, 1971 - No. 5, Aug, 1972
Marvel Comics Group

1-Reprints .25 .50
2,4,5: 2-Severin-c. 4-Everett-r .20 .40
3-Williamson-r .25 .50

WESTERN KILLERS
1948 - No. 64, May, 1949; No. 6, July, 1949
Fox Features Syndicate

nn(nd, F&J Trading Co.)-Range Busters 4.60 14.00 32.00
60-Extreme violence; lingerie panel 6.50 19.50 45.00
61-64, 6: 61-J. Cole-a 3.70 11.00 26.00

WESTERN LIFE ROMANCES (My Friend Irma #3?)
Dec, 1949 - No. 2, Mar, 1950
Marvel Comics (IPP)

1-Photo-c 3.70 11.00 26.00
2-Spanking scene 5.70 17.00 40.00

WESTERN LOVE
July-Aug, 1949 - No. 5, Mar-Apr, 1950 (All photo-c)
Prize Publications

1-S&K-a; Randolph Scott "Canadian Pacific" photo-c (see Prize #76) 6.50 19.50 45.00
2,5-S&K-a 4.60 14.00 32.00
3,4 3.70 11.00 26.00

NOTE: ***Meskin & Severin/Elder*** *a-2-5.*

WESTERN LOVE TRAILS (Formerly Western Adventures)
No. 7, Nov, 1949 - No. 9, Mar, 1950
Ace Magazines (A. A. Wyn)

7 4.00 12.00 28.00
8,9 2.65 8.00 18.00

WESTERN MARSHAL (See Steve Donovan . . . & Ernest Haycox's 4-Color 534, 591, 613, 640 [based on Haycox's "Trailtown"])

WESTERN OUTLAWS (My Secret Life #22 on)
No. 17, Sept, 1948 - No. 21, May, 1949
Fox Features Syndicate

17-Kamen-a; Iger shop-a in all; 1 pg. 'Death and the Devil Pills' r-in Ghostly Weird 122 8.00 24.00 56.00
18-21 3.70 11.00 26.00

WESTERN OUTLAWS
Feb, 1954 - No. 21, Aug, 1957
Atlas Comics (ACI No. 1-14/WPI No. 15-21)

1-Heath, Powell-a 5.00 15.00 35.00
2 2.30 7.00 16.00
3-10: 9,10-Everett-a 1.85 5.50 13.00
11,14-Williamson-a in both, 6 pgs. each 3.85 11.50 27.00
12,18,20,21 1.30 4.00 9.00
13-Baker-a 2.15 6.50 15.00
15-Torres-a 2.35 7.00 16.00
16-Williamson text illo 1.65 5.00 11.50
17-Crandall-a, Williamson text illo 2.65 8.00 18.00
19-Crandall-a 2.00 6.00 14.00

NOTE: ***Bolle*** *a-21.* ***Colan*** *a-17.* ***Heath*** *c-4, 16.* ***Maneely*** *a-16, 17; c-9, 12.* ***Morisi*** *a-18.* ***Powell*** *a-3, 15, 16.* ***Romita*** *a-7.* ***Severin*** *a-16; c-17.*

WESTERN OUTLAWS & SHERIFFS (Formerly Best Western)
No. 60, Dec, 1949 - No. 73, June, 1952
Marvel/Atlas Comics (IPC)

	Good	Fine	Mint
60 (52 pgs.)	4.60	14.00	32.00
61-65: 61-Photo-c	3.00	9.00	21.00
66,68-73	2.30	7.00	16.00
67-Cannibalism story	3.00	9.00	21.00

NOTE: ***Maneely** c-69,70,73. **Robinson** a-68. **Tuska** a-69.*

WESTERN PICTURE STORIES (1st Western Comic)
Feb, 1937 - No. 4, June, 1937
Comics Magazine Company

	Good	Fine	Mint
1-Will Eisner-a	60.00	180.00	420.00
2-Will Eisner-a	35.00	105.00	245.00
3,4: 3-Eisner-a	30.00	90.00	210.00

WESTERN PICTURE STORIES (See Giant Comics Editions No. 6,11)

WESTERN ROMANCES (See Target. . .)

WESTERN ROUGH RIDERS
Nov, 1954 - No. 4, May, 1955
Gillmor Magazines No. 1,4 (Stanmor Publications)

	Good	Fine	Mint
1	2.35	7.00	16.00
2-4	1.15	3.50	8.00

WESTERN ROUNDUP (See Dell Giants)

WESTERN TALES (Formerly Witches. . .)
No. 31, Oct, 1955 - No. 33, July-Sept, 1956
Harvey Publications

	Good	Fine	Mint
31,32-All S&K-a; Davy Crockett app. in ea.	5.00	15.00	35.00
33-S&K-a; Jim Bowie app.	5.00	15.00	35.00

NOTE: *No. 32 & 33 Boy's Ranch-r.*

WESTERN TALES OF BLACK RIDER (Formerly Black Rider; Gunsmoke Western #32 on)
No. 28, May, 1955 - No. 31, Nov, 1955
Atlas Comics (CPS)

	Good	Fine	Mint
28 (#1)	4.00	12.00	28.00
29-31	3.00	9.00	21.00

NOTE: ***Lawrence** a-30. **Maneely** c-29. **Severin** a-28. **Shores** c-31.*

WESTERN TEAM-UP
November, 1973
Marvel Comics Group

	Good	Fine	Mint
1-Origin & 1st app. The Dakota Kid; Rawhide Kid-r; Gunsmoke Kid-r by Jack Davis		.25	.50

WESTERN THRILLERS (My Past Confessions #7 on)
Aug, 1948 - No. 6, June, 1949
Fox Features Syndicate

	Good	Fine	Mint
1-"Velvet Rose"-Kamenish-a; "Two-Gun Sal," "Striker Sisters" (all women outlaws issue)	14.00	42.00	100.00
2	5.00	15.00	35.00
3,6: 3-Tuska-a, Heath-c	4.00	12.00	28.00
4,5-Bakerish-a; Butch Cassidy app. #5	5.70	17.00	40.00
52-(Reprint, M.S. Dist.)-1954? No date given (Becomes My Love Secret #53)	1.60	4.70	11.00

WESTERN THRILLERS (Cowboy Action #5 on)
Nov, 1954 - No. 4, Feb, 1955
Atlas Comics (ACI)

	Good	Fine	Mint
1-Severin-c	4.00	12.00	28.00
2-4	2.00	6.00	14.00

WESTERN TRAILS
May, 1957 - No. 2, July, 1957
Atlas Comics (SAI)

	Good	Fine	Mint
1	2.65	8.00	18.00
2-Severin-c	1.70	5.00	12.00

WESTERN TRUE CRIME (Becomes My Confessions)
No. 15, Aug, 1948 - No. 6, June, 1949
Fox Features Syndicate

	Good	Fine	Mint
15-Kamenish-a	8.50	25.50	60.00
16-Kamenish-a	4.35	13.00	30.00
3,5,6	2.65	8.00	18.00
4-Johnny Craig-a	7.00	21.00	50.00

WESTERN WINNERS (Formerly All-West. Winners; Black Rider #8)
No. 5, June, 1949 - No. 7, Dec, 1949
Marvel Comics (CDS)

	Good	Fine	Mint
5-Two-Gun Kid, Kid Colt, Black Rider	9.50	28.50	65.00
6-Two-Gun Kid, Black Rider, Heath Kid Colt story; Captain Tootsie By Beck	7.00	21.00	50.00
7-Randolph Scott Photo-c w/true stories about the West	7.00	21.00	50.00

WEST OF THE PECOS (See 4-Color No. 222)

WESTWARD HO, THE WAGONS (See 4-Color No. 738)

WHACK (Satire)
Oct, 1953 - No. 3, May, 1954
St. John Publishing Co.

	Good	Fine	Mint
1-(3-D)-Kubert-a	14.00	42.00	100.00
2,3-Kubert-a in each	5.50	16.50	38.00

WHACKY (See Wacky)

WHAM COMICS (See Super Spy)
Nov, 1940 - No. 2, Dec, 1940
Centaur Publications

	Good	Fine	Mint
1-The Sparkler, The Phantom Rider, Craig Carter and the Magic Ring Detector, Copper Slug, Speed Silvers by Gustavson, Speed Centaur & Jon Linton (s/f) begin	55.00	165.00	385.00
2-Origin Blue Fire & Solarman; The Buzzard app.	40.00	120.00	280.00

WHAM-O GIANT COMICS (98 cents)
1967 (Newspaper size) (One Shot) (Full Color)
Wham-O Mfg. Co.

	Good	Fine	Mint
1-Radian & Goody Bumpkin by Wally Wood; 1 pg. Stanley-a; Lou Fine, Tufts-a; wraparound-c	1.50	4.50	10.00

WHAT DO YOU KNOW ABOUT THIS COMICS SEAL OF APPROVAL?
nd (1955) (4pgs.; color; slick paper-c)
No publisher listed (DC Comics Giveaway)

	Good	Fine	Mint
(Rare)	40.00	120.00	280.00

WHAT IF. . .?
Feb, 1977 - No. 47, Oct, 1985 (All 52 pgs.)
Marvel Comics Group

	Good	Fine	Mint
1-Brief origin Spider-Man, Fantastic-4	1.00	3.00	6.00
2-Origin The Hulk retold	.70	2.00	4.00
3-5	.60	1.80	3.60
6-10: 9-Origins Venus, Marvel Boy, Human Robot, 3-D Man	.45	1.25	2.50
11,12	.35	1.10	2.20
13-Conan app.	.70	2.00	4.00
14-26: 22-Origin Dr. Doom retold	.30	.90	1.80
27-X-Men app.; Miller-c	.90	2.75	5.50
28-Daredevil by Miller	1.10	3.30	6.60
29,30: 29-Golden-c	.25	.75	1.50
31-X-Men app.; death of Hulk, Wolverine & Magneto	.35	1.10	2.20
32,36-Byrne-a	.25	.75	1.50
33,34: 34-Marvel crew each draw themselves	.25	.75	1.50
35-What if Elektra had lived?; Miller/Austin-a	.25	.75	1.50
37-47: 37-Old X-Men app.	.25	.75	1.50

Western Outlaws and Sheriffs #62, © MCG

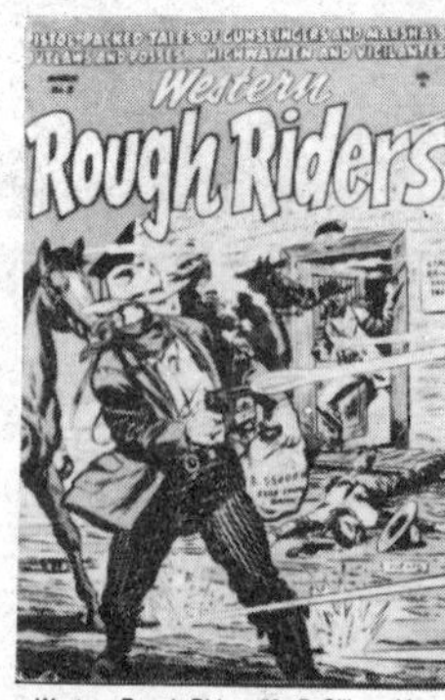

Western Rough Riders #3, © Gillmor Mag.

What If. . .? #31, © MCG

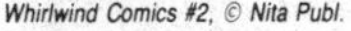
Whirlwind Comics #2, © Nita Publ.

Whisper V2#1, © First Comics

White Indian #11, © ME

WHAT IF. . .? (continued)

NOTE: ***Austin** a-27p, 32i, 34, 35i; c-35i, 36i. **J. Buscema** a-13p, 15p; c-10, 13p, 23p. **Byrne** a-32i, 36; c-36p. **Colan** a-21p; c-17p, 18p, 21p. . **Ditko** a-35. **Golden** c-40, 42. **Guice** a-40p. **Gil Kane** a-3p, 24p; c-2-4p, 7p, 8p. **Kirby** a-11p; c-9p, 11p. **Layton** a-32i, 33i; c-30, 32p, 33i, 34. **Miller** a-28p, 32i, 35p; c-27, 28p. **Mooney** a-8i, 30i. **Perez** a-15p. **Simonson** a-15p, 32i. **Starlin** a-32i. **Stevens** a-16i. **Sutton** a-2i, 18p, 28. **Tuska** a-5p.*

WHAT'S BEHIND THESE HEADLINES
1948 (16 pgs.)
William C. Popper Co.

	Good	Fine	Mint
Comic insert-"The Plot to Steal the World"	1.35	4.00	8.00

WHEATIES (Premiums) (32 titles)
1950 & 1951 (32 pages) (pocket size)
Walt Disney Productions

(Set A-1 to A-8, 1950)

A-1 Mickey Mouse & the Disappearing Island, A-2 Grandma Duck, Homespun Detective, A-3 Donald Duck & the Haunted Jewels, A-4 Donald Duck & the Giant Ape, A-5 Mickey Mouse, Roving Reporter, A-6 Li'l Bad Wolf, Forest Ranger, A-7 Goofy, Tightrope Acrobat, A-8 Pluto & the Bogus Money each. . . . 2.00 6.00 12.00

(Set B-1 to B-8, 1950)

B-1 Mickey Mouse & the Pharoah's Curse, B-2 Pluto, Canine Cowpoke, B-3 Donald Duck & the Buccaneers, B-4 Mickey Mouse & the Mystery Sea Monster, B-5 Li'l Bad Wolf in the Hollow Tree Hideout, B-6 Donald Duck, Trail Blazer, B-7 Goofy & the Gangsters, B-8 Donald Duck, Klondike Kid each. . . . 1.70 5.00 10.00

(Set C-1 to C-8, 1951)

C-1 Donald Duck & the Inca Idol, C-2 Mickey Mouse & the Magic Mountain, C-3 Li'l Bad Wolf, Fire Fighter, C-4 Gus & Jaq Save the Ship, C-5 Donald Duck in the Lost Lakes, C-6 Mickey Mouse & the Stagecoach Bandits, C-7 Goofy, Big Game Hunter, C-8 Donald Duck Deep-Sea Diver each. . . . 1.70 5.00 10.00

(Set D-1 to D-8, 1951)

D-1 Donald Duck in Indian Country, D-2 Mickey Mouse and the Abandoned Mine, D-3 Pluto & the Mysterious Package, D-4 Bre'r Rabbit's Sunken Treasure, D-5 Donald Duck, Mighty Mystic, D-6 Mickey Mouse & the Medicine Man, D-7 Li'l Bad Wolf and the Secret of the Woods, D-8 Minnie Mouse, Girl Explorer
each. . . . 1.70 5.00 10.00

NOTE: *Some copies lack the Wheaties ad.*

WHEE COMICS (Also see Tickle, Gay, & Smile Comics)
1955 (52 pgs.) (5x7¼") (7 cents)
Modern Store Publications

1-Funny animal .40 1.20 2.40

WHEELIE AND THE CHOPPER BUNCH (TV)
July, 1975 - No. 7, July, 1976 (Hanna-Barbera)
Charlton Comics

1,2-Bryne-a (1st work) .85 2.50 5.00
3-7-Staton-a .40 1.25 2.50

WHEN KNIGHTHOOD WAS IN FLOWER (See 4-Color No. 505, 682)

WHEN SCHOOL IS OUT (See Wisco)

WHERE CREATURES ROAM
July, 1970 - No. 8, Sept, 1971
Marvel Comics Group

1-Kirby/Ayers-r .25 .50
2-8-Kirby-r .20 .40

NOTE: ***Ditko** r-1, 2, 4, 7.*

WHERE MONSTERS DWELL
Jan, 1970 - No. 38, Oct, 1975
Marvel Comics Group

1-Kirby/Ditko-a(r) .40 .80
2-10: 4-Crandall-a(r) .30 .60

	Good	Fine	Mint
11,13-37		.20	.40
12-Giant issue		.30	.60
38-Williamson-r/World of Suspense #3		.30	.60

NOTE: ***Ditko** a(r)-4, 8, 10, 17, 19, 23, 24, 37. **Reinman** a-4r. **Severin** c-15.*

WHERE'S HUDDLES? (TV) (See Fun-In #9)
Jan, 1971 - No. 3, Dec, 1971 (Hanna-Barbera)
Gold Key

1 .85 2.50 5.00
2,3: 3 r-most #1 .50 1.50 3.00

WHIP WILSON (Movie star) (Formerly Rex Hart; Gunhawk #12 on; see Western Hearts)
No. 9, April, 1950 - No. 11, Sept, 1950 (52pgs., 9,10; 36pgs., 11)
Marvel Comics

9-Photo-c; Whip Wilson & his horse Bullet begin; origin Bullet; issue #23 listed on splash page; cover changed to #9
12.00 36.00 84.00
10,11-Photo-c 10.00 30.00 70.00
I.W. Reprint #1('64)-Kinstler-c; r-Marvel #11 .85 2.50 6.00

WHIRLWIND COMICS
June, 1940 - No. 3, Sept, 1940
Nita Publication

1-Cyclone begins (origin) 34.00 102.00 240.00
2,3 22.00 65.00 154.00

WHIRLYBIRDS (See 4-Color No. 1124,1216)

WHISPER (Female Ninja)
Dec, 1983 - No. 2, 1984 ($1.50; Baxter paper)
Capital Comics/First Comics

1-Origin; Golden-c 1.25 3.75 7.50
2 .60 1.80 3.60

WHISPER
June, 1986 - Present
First Comics

V2#1-9 .65 1.30
10-12 ($1.75) .30 .90 1.80
Special 1 (11/85, First Comics) .40 1.25 2.50

WHITE CHIEF OF THE PAWNEE INDIANS
1951
Avon Periodicals

nn-Kit West app.; Kinstler-c 6.00 18.00 42.00

WHITE EAGLE INDIAN CHIEF (See Indian Chief)

WHITE INDIAN
July, 1953 - 1954
Magazine Enterprises

11(A-1 94), 12(A-1 101), 13(A-1 104)-Frazetta-r(Dan Brand) in all from Durango Kid 18.00 54.00 126.00
14(A-1 117), 15(A-1 135)-Check-a; Torres-a-#15
6.50 19.50 45.00

NOTE: *#11 reprints from Durango Kid #1-4; #12 from #5, 9, 10, 11; #13 from #7, 12, 13, 16.*

WHITE PRINCESS OF THE JUNGLE (Also see Top Jungle & Jungle Adventures)
July, 1951 - No. 5, Nov, 1952
Avon Periodicals

1-Origin of White Princess & Capt'n Courage (r); Kinstler-c
21.00 62.00 146.00
2-Reprints origin of Malu, Slave Girl Princess from Avon's Slave Girl Comics #1 w/Malu changed to Zora; Kinstler c/a(2)
15.00 45.00 105.00
3-Origin Blue Gorilla; Kinstler c/a 12.00 36.00 84.00
4-Jack Barnum, White Hunter app.; r-/Sheena #9

WHITE PRINCESS OF THE JUNGLE (cont.)

	Good	Fine	Mint
	10.00	30.00	70.00
5-Blue Gorilla by Kinstler	10.00	30.00	70.00

WHITE RIDER AND SUPER HORSE (Indian Warriors #7 on)
Dec, 1950 - No. 6, Mar, 1951 (Also see Western Crime Cases)
Novelty-Star Publications/Accepted Publ.

1	4.35	13.00	30.00
2,3	2.75	8.00	18.00
4-6-Adapt. "The Last of the Mohicans"	3.00	9.00	21.00
Accepted Reprint #5,6 (nd); L.B. Cole-c	1.70	5.00	12.00

NOTE: *All have* **L. B. Cole** *covers.*

WHITE WILDERNESS (See 4-Color No. 943)

WHITMAN COMIC BOOKS
1962 (136 pgs.; 7¾x5¾"; hardcover) (B&W)
Whitman Publishing Co.

1-Yogi Bear, 2-Huckleberry Hound, 3-Mr. Jinks and Pixie & Dixie, 4-The Flintstones, 5-Augie Doggie & Loopy de Loop, 6-Snooper & Blabber Fearless Detectives/Quick Draw McGraw of the Wild West, 7-Bugs Bunny-(r)-/from #47,51,53,54 & 55 each....	.50	1.50	3.00
8-Donald Duck-reprints most of WDC&S No. 209-213. Includes 5 Barks stories, 1 complete Mickey Mouse serial & 1 Mickey Mouse serial missing the 1st episode	7.75	22.00	44.00

NOTE: *Hanna-Barbera No. 1-6(TV), original stories. Dell reprints-No. 7, 8.*

WHIZ COMICS (Formerly Flash & Thrill Comics #1)
No. 2, Feb, 1940 - No. 155, June, 1953
Fawcett Publications

1-(nn on cover, #2 inside)-Origin & 1st newsstand app. Captain Marvel (formerly Captain Thunder) by C. C. Beck (created by Bill Parker), Spy Smasher, Golden Arrow, Ibis the Invincible, Dan Dare, Scoop Smith, Sivana, & Lance O'Casey begin

Good	Fine	VF-NM
2500.00	7500.00	16,250.00

(Only one known copy exists in Mint condition which has not sold)

1-Reprint, oversize 13½"x10". **WARNING:** This comic is an exact duplicate reprint of the original except for its size. DC published it in 1974 with a second cover titling it as a Famous First Edition. There have been many reported cases of the outer cover being removed and the interior sold as the original edition. The reprint with the new outer cover removed is practically worthless.

	Good	Fine	Mint
2-(nn on cover, #3 inside); cover to Flash #1 redrawn, pg. 12, panel 4; Spy Smasher reveals I.D. to Eve	315.00	945.00	2200.00
3-(#3 on cover, #4 inside)-1st app. Beautia	190.00	570.00	1325.00
4-(#4 on cover, #5 inside)	161.00	483.00	1125.00
5-Captain Marvel wears button-down flap on splash page only	120.00	360.00	840.00
6-10: 7-Dr. Voodoo begins (by Raboy-#9-22)	86.00	258.00	600.00
11-14	55.00	165.00	385.00
15-Origin Sivana; Dr. Voodoo by Raboy	73.00	220.00	510.00
16-18-Spy Smasher battles Captain Marvel	73.00	220.00	510.00
19,20	37.00	110.00	260.00
21-Origin & 1st app. Lt. Marvels	42.00	125.00	295.00
22-24: 23-Only Dr. Voodoo by Tuska	32.00	95.00	225.00
25-Origin/1st app. Captain Marvel Jr., x-over in Capt. Marvel; Capt. Nazi app; origin Old Shazam in text	95.00	285.00	665.00
26-30	24.00	72.00	168.00
31,32: 32-1st app. The Trolls	18.50	56.00	130.00
33-Spy Smasher, Captain Marvel x-over on cover and inside	24.00	72.00	168.00
34,36-40-The Trolls in #37	17.00	51.00	120.00
35-Captain Marvel & Spy Smasher-c	19.00	57.00	132.00
41-50: 43-Spy Smasher, Ibis, Golden Arrow x-over in Capt. Marvel. 44-Flag-c. 47-Origin recap (1pg.)	11.00	33.00	76.00
51-60: 52-Capt. Marvel x-over in Ibis. 57-Spy Smasher, Golden Arrow, Ibis cameo	8.00	24.00	56.00
61-70	6.50	19.50	45.00
71,77-80	5.00	15.00	35.00
72-76-Two Captain Marvel stories in each; 76-Spy Smasher becomes Crime Smasher	5.75	17.25	40.00
81-99: 86-Captain Marvel battles Sivana Family. 91-Infinity-c	5.00	15.00	35.00
100	6.50	19.50	45.00
101,103-105	4.00	12.00	28.00
102-Commando Yank app.	4.00	12.00	28.00
106-Bulletman app.	4.00	12.00	28.00
107-141,143-152: 112,139-Infinity-c	3.65	11.00	25.00
142-Used in **POP**, pg. 89	4.35	13.00	30.00
153-155-(Scarce)	8.50	25.50	60.00
Wheaties Giveaway(1946, Miniature)-6½x8¼", 32 pgs.; all copies were taped at each corner to a box of Wheaties and are never found in fine or mint condition; "Capt. Marvel & the Water Thieves," Golden Arrow, Ibis stories	13.00	40.00	80.00

NOTE: **Krigstein** *Golden Arrow-No. 75, 78, 91, 95, 96, 98-100.* **Wolverton** *½ pg. "Culture Corner"-No. 65-68, 70-85, 87-96, 98-100, 102-109, 112-121, 123, 125, 126, 128-131, 133, 134, 136, 142, 143, 146.*

WHODUNIT
Aug-Sept, 1948 - No. 3, Dec-Jan, 1948-49
D.S. Publishing co.

1-Baker-a, 7pgs.	5.50	16.50	38.00
2-Morphine story	3.50	10.50	24.00
3	2.65	8.00	18.00

WHODUNNIT?
June, 1986 - Present
Eclipse Comics

1-3	.35	1.00	2.00

WHO IS NEXT?
January, 1953
Standard Comics

5-Toth, Sekowsky, Andru-a	7.00	21.00	50.00

WHO'S MINDING THE MINT? (See Movie Classics)

WHO'S WHO IN STAR TREK
March, 1987 - No. 2, April, 1987
DC Comics

1,2-Chaykin-c	.25	.75	1.50

WHO'S WHO: THE DEFINITIVE DIRECTORY OF THE DC UNIV.
3/85 - No. 26, 4/87 (26 issue maxi-series, no ads)
DC Comics

1-DC heroes from A-Z	.25	.75	1.50
2-5	.25	.70	1.40
6-10		.60	1.20
11-26		.50	1.00

NOTE: **Kane** *a-1, 3.* **Kirby** *a-3.* **Perez** *c-1, 2, 3-5p, 13, 14p, 15, 16p, 17, 18p.*

WHO'S WHO UPDATE '87
Aug, 1987 - No. 5, Dec, 1987 ($1.25, color)
DC Comics

1	.25	.75	1.50
2-5		.65	1.30

WILBUR COMICS (Also see Zip Comics)
Sum', 1944 - No. 87, 11/59; No. 88, 9/63; No. 89, 10/64; No. 90, 10/65 (No. 1-46: 52 pgs.)
MLJ Magazines/Archie Publ. No. 8, Spr.'46 on

1	22.00	65.00	154.00
2(Fall,'44)	11.00	32.00	76.00
3,4(Wint,'44-'45; Spr,'45)	9.00	27.00	62.00

5-1st app. Katy Keene-begin series; Wilbur story same as Archie story in Archie #1 except that Wilbur replaces Archie

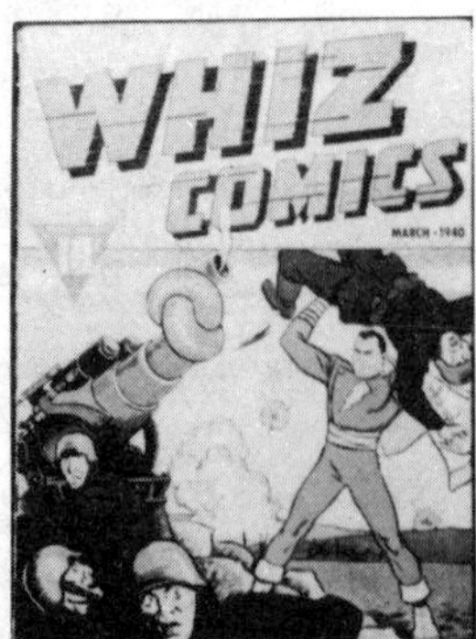

Whiz Comics #2, © FAW

Whiz Comics #25, © FAW

Whiz Comics #129, © FAW

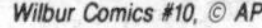
Wilbur Comics #10, © AP

Wild Bill Elliott #17, © DELL

Wild Dog #1, © DC

WILBUR COMICS (continued)

	Good	Fine	Mint
	37.00	110.00	260.00
6-10(Fall,'46): 7-Transvestism issue	9.00	27.00	62.00
11-20	5.00	15.00	35.00
21-30(1949)	4.00	12.00	28.00
31-50	2.00	6.00	14.00
51-69: 59-Last 10 cent ish?	1.15	3.50	8.00
70-90	.85	2.50	5.00

NOTE: *Katy Keene in No. 5-56, 58-69.*

WILD
Feb, 1954 - No. 5, Aug, 1954
Atlas Comics (IPC)

	Good	Fine	Mint
1	5.00	15.00	35.00
2	3.00	9.00	21.00
3-5	2.65	8.00	18.00

NOTE: ***Berg** a-5; c-4. **Colan** a-4. **Everett** a-1-3. **Heath** a-2, 3. **Maneely** a-1-3, 5; c-1, 5. **Post** a-2.*

WILD (This Magazine Is. . .) (Magazine)
Jan, 1968 - No. 3, 1968 (52 pgs.) (Satire)
Dell Publishing Co.

	Good	Fine	Mint
1-3	.85	2.50	5.00

WILD ANIMALS
Dec, 1982 (One-Shot)
Pacific Comics

	Good	Fine	Mint
1-Funny animal; Sergio Aragones-a		.50	1.00

WILD BILL ELLIOTT (Also see Western Roundup)
No. 278, 5/50 - No. 643, 7/55 (No #11,12) (All photo-c)
Dell Publishing Co.

	Good	Fine	Mint
4-Color 278(#1, 52pgs.)-Titled "Bill Elliott;" Bill & his horse Stormy begin; photo front/back-c begin	7.00	21.00	50.00
2 (11/50), 3 (52 pgs.)	4.00	12.00	28.00
4-10(10-12/52)	3.50	10.50	24.00
4-Color 472(6/53),520(12/53)-Last photo back-c	3.50	10.50	24.00
13(4-6/54) - 17(4-6/55)	3.00	9.00	21.00
4-Color 643	3.00	9.00	21.00

WILD BILL HICKOK (Also see Blazing Sixguns)
Sept-Oct, 1949 - No. 28, May-June, 1956
Avon Periodicals

	Good	Fine	Mint
1-Ingels-c	11.50	34.00	80.00
2-Painted-c	5.70	17.00	40.00
3,5-Painted-c	3.00	9.00	21.00
4-Painted-c by Howard Winfield	3.00	9.00	21.00
6-10,12: 8-10-Painted-c; 9-Ingels-a?	3.00	9.00	21.00
11,14-Kinstler c/a	3.65	11.00	25.00
13,15,17,18,20,23	2.15	6.50	15.00
16-Kamen-a; r-3 stories/King of the Badmen of Deadwood	3.00	9.00	21.00
19-Meskin-a	2.15	6.50	15.00
21-Reprints 2 stories/Chief Crazy Horse	2.15	6.50	15.00
22-Kinstler-a; r-/Sheriff Bob Dixon's. . .	2.15	6.50	15.00
24-27-Kinstler-c/a(r)	2.85	8.50	20.00
28-Kinstler-c/a (new); r-/Last of the Comanches	2.85	8.50	20.00
I.W. Reprint #1-Kinstler-c	.50	1.50	3.00
Super Reprint #10-12	.50	1.50	3.00

NOTE: *No. 23, 25 contain numerous editing deletions in both art and script due to code. **Kinstler** c-6, 7, 11-14, 17, 18, 20-22, 24-28. **Howard Larsen** a-1, 2(3), 4(4), 5(3), 7(3), 9(3), 11(4), 12(4), 17, 18, 21(2), 22, 24(3), 26. **Meskin** a-7. **Reinman** a-17.*

WILD BILL HICKOK & JINGLES (TV)(Formerly Cowboy Western)
March, 1958 - 1960 (Also see Blue Bird)
Charlton Comics

	Good	Fine	Mint
68,69-Williamson-a	3.50	10.50	24.00
70-Two pgs. Williamson-a	1.85	5.50	13.00
71-76 (#75,76, exist?)	1.00	3.00	7.00

WILD BILL PECOS (See The Westerner)

WILD BOY OF THE CONGO (Also see Approved Comics)
No. 10, Feb-Mar, 1951 - No. 15, June, 1955
Ziff-Davis No. 10-12,4,5/St. John No. 6 on

	Good	Fine	Mint
10(2-3/51)-Origin; bondage-c by Saunders; used in **SOTI**, pg. 189	6.50	19.50	45.00
11(4-5/51),12(8-9/51)-Norman Saunders-c	3.70	11.00	26.00
4(10-11/51)-Saunders bondage-c	3.70	11.00	26.00
5(Winter,'51)-Saunders-c	3.00	9.00	21.00
6,8,9(10/53),10	2.65	8.00	18.00
7(8-9/52)-Baker-c; Kinstler-a	3.50	10.50	24.00
11-13-Baker-c(St. John)	3.50	10.50	24.00
14(4/55)-Baker-c; r-#12('51)	3.50	10.50	24.00
15(6/55)	2.00	6.00	14.00

WILD DOG
Sept, 1987 - No. 4, Dec, 1987 (4 part mini-series)
DC Comics

	Good	Fine	Mint
1-4		.40	.80

WILD FRONTIER (Cheyenne Kid #8 on)
Oct, 1955 - No. 7, April, 1957
Charlton Comics

	Good	Fine	Mint
1-Davy Crockett	2.30	7.00	16.00
2-6-Davy Crockett in all	1.15	3.50	8.00
7-Origin Cheyenne Kid	1.15	3.50	8.00

WILD KINGDOM (TV)
1965 (Giveaway) (regular size) (16 pgs., slick-c)
Western Printing Co.

	Good	Fine	Mint
Mutual of Omaha's. . .	.85	2.50	6.00

WILD WEST (Wild Western #3 on)
Spring, 1948 - No. 2, July, 1948
Marvel Comics (WFP)

	Good	Fine	Mint
1-Two-Gun Kid, Arizona Annie, & Tex Taylor begin	7.00	21.00	50.00
2-Captain Tootsie by Beck	4.70	17.00	40.00

WILD WEST (Black Fury #1-57)
No. 58, November, 1966
Charlton Comics

	Good	Fine	Mint
V2#58		.50	1.00

WILD WESTERN (Wild West #1,2)
No. 3, 9/48 - No. 57, 9/57 (52pgs, 3-11; 36pgs, 12-on)
Marvel/Atlas Comics (WFP)

	Good	Fine	Mint
3(#1)-Two-Gun Kid, Tex Morgan, Tex Taylor, Kid Colt, & Arizona Annie begin	7.00	21.00	50.00
4-Last Arizona Annie; Captain Tootsie by Beck	5.70	17.00	40.00
5-2nd app. Black Rider (1/49); Blaze Carson, Captain Tootsie by Beck app.	6.50	19.50	45.00
6-8: 6-Blaze Carson app; Anti-Wertham editorial	4.35	13.00	30.00
9-Photo-c; Black Rider begins, ends #19	4.60	14.00	32.00
10-Charles Starrett photo-c	5.70	17.00	40.00
11-(Last 52 pg. issue)	3.50	10.50	24.00
12-14,16-19: All Black Rider-c/stories. 12-14-The Prairie Kid & his horse Fury app.	3.00	9.00	21.00
15-Red Larabee, Gunhawk (Origin), his horse Blaze, & Apache Kid begin, end #22; Black Rider c/story	4.00	12.00	28.00
20-29: 20-Kid Colt-c begin	2.65	8.00	18.00
30-Katz-a	3.00	9.00	21.00
31-37,39,40	1.70	5.00	12.00
38-War issue; Kubert-a	1.70	5.00	12.00

WILD WESTERN (continued)

	Good	Fine	Mint
41-47,49-51,53,57	1.15	3.50	8.00
48-Williamson/Torres-a, 4 pgs; Drucker-a	3.85	11.50	27.00
52-Crandall-a	2.65	8.00	18.00
54,55-Williamson-a in both, 5 & 4 pgs., #54 with Mayo plus 2 text illos.	3.35	10.00	23.00
56-Baker-a?	2.00	6.00	14.00

NOTE: ***Annie Oakley*** *in #46, 47.* ***Arizona Kid*** *in #21, 23.* ***Arrowhead*** *in #34-39.* ***Black Rider*** *in #5, 9-19, 33-44.* ***Fighting Texan*** *in #17.* ***Kid Colt*** *in #4-6, 9-11, 20-47, 52, 54-56.* ***Outlaw Kid*** *in #43.* ***Red Hawkins*** *in #13, 14.* ***Ringo Kid*** *in #26, 41, 43, 44, 46, 47, 52-56.* ***Tex Morgan*** *in #3, 4, 6, 9, 11.* ***Tex Taylor*** *in #3-6, 9, 11.* ***Texas Kid*** *in #23-25.* ***Two-Gun Kid*** *in #3-6, 9, 11, 12, 33-39, 41.* ***Wyatt Earp*** *in #47.* ***Ayers*** *a-41.* ***Berg*** *a-26; c-24.* ***Colan*** *a-49.* ***Forte*** *a-28, 30.* ***Heath*** *a-8; c-34, 44.* ***Keller*** *a-24, 26, 29-40, 44-46, 52.* ***Maneely*** *a-10, 15, 16, 28, 35, 40, 41, 43-45; c-18-22, 33, 35, 36, 39, 45.* ***Morisi*** *a-23, 52.* ***Pakula*** *a-52.* ***Powell*** *a-51.* ***Severin*** *a-46, 47.* ***Shores*** *a-30, 35, 36.* ***Sinnott*** *a-34-39.* ***Wildey*** *a-43. Bondage c-19.*

WILD WESTERN ACTION (Also see The Bravados)
March, 1971 - No. 3, June, 1971 (52 pgs.)
Skywald Publishing Corp. (Reprints)

	Good	Fine	Mint
1-Durango Kid, Straight Arrow; with all references to "Straight" in the story relettered to "Swift;" Bravados begin		.50	1.00
2-Billy Nevada, Durango Kid		.30	.60
3-Red Mask, Durango Kid		.30	.60

WILD WESTERN ROUNDUP
Oct, 1957; 1964
Red Top/Decker Publications/I. W. Enterprises

	Good	Fine	Mint
1(1957)-Kid Cowboy-r	.85	2.50	6.00
I.W. Reprint #1('60-61)	.25	.75	1.50

WILD WEST RODEO
1953 (15 cents)
Star Publications

	Good	Fine	Mint
1-A comic book coloring book with regular full color cover & B&W inside	2.15	6.50	15.00

WILD WILD WEST, THE (TV)
June, 1966 - No. 7, Oct, 1969
Gold Key

	Good	Fine	Mint
1,2-McWilliams-a	2.65	8.00	18.00
3-7	1.70	5.00	12.00

WILKIN BOY (See That. . .)

WILLIE COMICS (Formerly Ideal #1-4; Crime Cases #24 on; Li'l Willie #20 & 21) (See Wisco)
No. 5, Fall, 1946 - No. 19, 4/49; No. 22, 1/50 - No. 23, 5/50 (No No. 20 & 21)
Marvel Comics (MgPC)

	Good	Fine	Mint
5(#1)-Nellie The Nurse, Margie begin	3.50	10.50	24.00
6,8,9	1.85	5.50	13.00
7(1),10,11-Kurtzman's "Hey Look"	3.00	9.00	21.00
12,14-18,22,23	1.50	4.50	10.00
13,19-Kurtzman's "Hey Look"	2.35	7.00	16.00

NOTE: *Cindy app.-17. Jeanie app.-17. Little Lizzie app.-22.*

WILLIE MAYS (See The Amazing. . .)

WILLIE THE PENGUIN
April, 1951 - No. 6, April, 1952
Standard Comics

	Good	Fine	Mint
1	1.15	3.50	8.00
2-6	.55	1.65	4.00

WILLIE THE WISE-GUY
Sept, 1957
Atlas Comics (NPP)

	Good	Fine	Mint
1: Kida, Maneely-a	1.00	3.00	7.00

WILLIE WESTINGHOUSE EDISON SMITH THE BOY INVENTOR
1906 (36 pgs. in color) (10x16")
William A. Stokes Co.

	Good	Fine	Mint
By Frank Crane	15.00	45.00	105.00

WILL ROGERS WESTERN (See Blazing & True Comics #66)
No. 5, June, 1950 - No. 2, Aug, 1950
Fox Features Syndicate

	Good	Fine	Mint
5,2: Photo-c	7.00	21.00	50.00

WILL-YUM (See 4-Color No. 676,765,902)

WIN A PRIZE COMICS (Timmy The Timid Ghost #3 on?)
Feb, 1955 - No. 2, Apr, 1955
Charlton Comics

	Good	Fine	Mint
V1#1-S&K-a; Poe adapt; E.C. War swipe	17.00	51.00	120.00
2-S&K-a	12.00	36.00	84.00

WIND RAGE
1987 - Present ($1.25, color)
Blackthorne Publishing

	Good	Fine	Mint
1		.60	1.25

WINDY & WILLY
May-June, 1969 - No. 4, Nov-Dec, 1969
National Periodical Publications

	Good	Fine	Mint
1-4: r-/Dobie Gillis with some art changes		.50	1.00

WINGS COMICS
Sept, 1940 - No. 124, 1954
Fiction House Magazines

	Good	Fine	Mint
1-Skull Squad, Clipper Kirk, Suicide Smith, Jane Martin, War Nurse, Phantom Falcons, Greasemonkey Griffin, Parachute Patrol & Powder Burns begin	57.00	170.00	400.00
2	28.00	84.00	195.00
3-5	22.00	65.00	154.00
6-10	18.00	54.00	125.00
11-15	15.00	45.00	105.00
16-Origin Captain Wings	16.00	48.00	110.00
17-20	12.00	36.00	84.00
21-30	11.00	32.00	76.00
31-40	10.00	30.00	70.00
41-50	8.00	24.00	56.00
51-60: 60-Last Skull Squad	7.00	21.00	50.00
61-67: 66-Ghost Patrol begins (becomes Ghost Squadron #71)	7.00	21.00	50.00
68,69: 68-Clipper Kirk becomes The Phantom Falcon-origin, Part 1; Part 2-#69	7.00	21.00	50.00
70-72: 70-1st app. The Phantom Falcon in costume, origin-Part 3; Capt. Wings battles Col. Kamikaze in all	5.50	16.50	38.00
73-99	5.50	16.50	38.00
100	6.50	19.50	45.00
101-114,116-124: 111-Last Jane Martin. 112-Flying Saucer c/story	4.00	12.00	28.00
115-Used in **POP**, pg. 89	4.60	14.00	32.00

NOTE: *Bondage covers are common. Captain Wings battles Sky Hag-#75, 76; . . . Mr. Atlantis-#85-92; . . . Mr. Pupin(Red Agent)-#98-103. Capt. Wings by* ***Elias****-#52-64; by* ***Lubbers****-#29-32,70-103; by* ***Renee****-#33-46.* ***Evans*** *a-85-103, 108(Jane Martin).* ***Larsen*** *a-52, 59, 64, 73-77. Jane Martin by* ***Fran Hopper****-#68-84; Suicide Smith by* ***John Celardo****-#76-103; by* ***Hollingsworth****-#105-109; Ghost Patrol by* ***Maurice Whitman****-#83-103; Skull Squad by* ***M. Baker****-#52-60; Clipper Kirk by* ***Baker****-#60, 61; Ghost Squadron by* ***Whitman****-#72-77, 104-110.* ***Tuska*** *a-5.*

WINGS OF THE EAGLES, THE (See 4-Color No. 790)

WINKY DINK (Adventures of. . .)
No. 75, March, 1957 (One Shot)
Pines Comics

	Good	Fine	Mint
75-Marv Levy c/a	1.30	4.00	9.00

WINKY DINK (See 4-Color No. 663)

Willie Comics #23, © MCG

Will Rogers Western #2, © FOX

Wings Comics #101, © FH

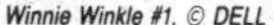
Winnie Winkle #1, © DELL

Witchcraft #5, © AVON

Witches Tales #15, © HARV

WINNIE-THE-POOH
January, 1977 - No. 33, 1984 (Walt Disney)
(Winnie-The-Pooh began as Edward Bear in 1926 by Milne)
Gold Key No. 1-17/Whitman No. 18 on

	Good	Fine	Mint
1-New art	.25	.75	1.50
2-4,6-11		.40	.80
5,12-33-New material		.35	.70

WINNIE WINKLE
1930 - 1933 (52 pgs.) (B&W daily strip reprints)
Cupples & Leon Co.

1	7.00	21.00	50.00
2-4	5.00	15.00	35.00

WINNIE WINKLE
1941 - No. 7, Sept-Nov, 1949
Dell Publishing Co.

Large Feature Comic 2('41)	9.00	27.00	62.00
4-Color 94('45)	7.00	21.00	50.00
4-Color 174	4.00	12.00	28.00
1(3-5/48)-Contains daily & Sunday newspaper-r from 1939-1941	3.50	10.50	24.00
2 (6-8/48)	2.00	6.00	14.00
3-7	1.50	4.50	10.00

WINTERWORLD
Sept, 1987 - Present (mini-series, $1.75, color)
Eclipse Comics

1-3	.30	.90	1.80

WISCO/KLARER COMIC BOOK (Miniature)
1948 - 1964 (24 pgs.) (3½x6¾")
Given away by Wisco "99" Service Stations, Carnation Malted Milk, Klarer Health Wieners, Fleers Dubble Bubble Gum, Rodeo All-Meat Wieners, Perfect Potato Chips, & others; see ad in Tom Mix #21
Vital Publications/Fawcett Publications

Blackstone & the Gold Medal Mystery(1948)	2.35	7.00	14.00
Blackstone "Solves the Sealed Vault Mystery"(1950)	2.35	7.00	14.00
Blaze Carson in "The Sheriff Shoots It Out"(1950)	2.35	7.00	14.00
Captain Marvel & Billy's Big Game (r-/Capt. Marvel Adv. #76)	24.00	70.00	145.00
(Prices vary widely on this book)			
China Boy in "A Trip to the Zoo" #10	.85	2.50	5.00
Indoors-Outdoors Game Book	.85	2.50	5.00
Jim Solar Space Sheriff in "Battle for Mars," "Between Two Worlds," "Conquers Outer Space," "The Creatures on the Comet," "Defeats the Moon Missile Men," "Encounter Creatures on Comet," "Meet the Jupiter Jumpers," "Meets the Man From Mars," "On Traffic Duty," "Outlaws of the Spaceways," "Pirates of the Planet X," "Protects Space Lanes," "Raiders From the Sun," "Ring Around Saturn," "Robots of Rhea," "The Sky Ruby," "Spacetts of the Sky," "Spidermen of Venus," "Trouble on Mercury"	2.35	7.00	14.00
Johnny Starboard & the Underseas Pirates('48)	.70	2.00	4.00
Kid Colt in "He Lived by His Guns"('50)	2.65	8.00	16.00
Little Aspirin as "Crook Catcher" #2('50)	.60	1.80	3.60
Little Aspirin in "Naughty But Nice" #6(1950)	.60	1.80	3.60
Return of the Black Phantom	2.00	6.00	12.00
Secrets of Magic	1.00	3.00	6.00
Slim Morgan "Brings Justice to Mesa City" #3	1.00	3.00	6.00
Super Rabbit(1950)-Cuts Red Tape, Stops Crime Wave!	1.20	3.50	7.00
Tex Farnum, Frontiersman(1948)	1.50	4.50	9.00
Tex Taylor in "Draw or Die, Cowpoke!"('50)	2.35	7.00	14.00
Tex Taylor in "An Exciting Adventure at the Gold Mine"('50)			

	Good	Fine	Mint
	2.35	7.00	14.00
Wacky Quacky in "All-Aboard"	.50	1.50	3.00
When School Is Out	.50	1.50	3.00
Willie in a "Comic-Comic Book Fall" #1	.50	1.50	3.00
Wonder Duck "An Adventure at the Rodeo of the Fearless Quacker!" (1950)	.50	1.50	3.00
Rare uncut version of three; includes Capt. Marvel, Tex Farnum, Black Phantom Estimated value....			$250.00

WISE GUYS
1987 - Present
Harvey Comics

1		.40	.75

WISE LITTLE HEN, THE
1934 (48 pgs.); 1935; 1937 (Story book)
David McKay Publ./Whitman

2nd book app. Donald Duck; Donald app. on cover with Wise Little Hen & Practical Pig; painted cover; same artist as the B&W's from Silly Symphony Cartoon, The Wise Little Hen (1934)(McKay)	25.00	75.00	175.00
1935 Edition with dust jacket; 44 pgs. with color, 8¾x9¾" (Whitman)	20.00	60.00	140.00
888(1937)-9½x13", 12 pgs. (Whitman) Donald Duck app.	14.00	42.00	100.00

WITCHCRAFT (See Strange Mysteries, Super Reprint #18)
Mar-Apr, 1952 - No. 6, Mar, 1953
Avon Periodicals

1-Kubert-a; 1pg. check	22.00	65.00	154.00
2-Kubert & Check-a	13.00	40.00	90.00
3,6: 3-Kinstler, Lawrence-a	9.50	28.50	65.00
4-People cooked alive c/s	10.00	30.00	70.00
5-Kelly Freas-c	14.00	42.00	100.00

NOTE: ***Hollingsworth** a-4-6; c-4, 6.*

WITCHES TALES (Witches Western Tales #29,30)
Jan, 1951 - No. 28, Dec, 1954 (date misprinted as 4/55)
Witches Tales/Harvey Publications

1-1pg. Powell-a	11.50	34.50	80.00
2-Eye injury panel	4.00	12.00	28.00
3-7,9,10	3.35	10.00	23.00
8-Eye injury panels	3.85	11.50	27.00
11-13,15,16: 12-Acid in face story	3.00	9.00	21.00
14,17-Powell/Nostrand-a. 17-Atomic disaster story	5.00	15.00	35.00
18-Nostrand-a; E.C. swipe/Shock S.S.	5.00	15.00	35.00
19-Nostrand-a; E.C. swipe/"Glutton"	5.00	15.00	35.00
20-24-Nostrand-a. 21-E.C. swipe; rape story. 23-Wood E.C. swipes/Two-Fisted Tales #34.	5.00	15.00	35.00
25-Nostrand-a; E.C. swipe/Mad Barber	5.00	15.00	35.00
26-28: 27-r-/#6 with diff.-c. 28-r-/#8 with diff.-c	2.50	7.50	17.00

NOTE: ***Check** a-24. **Kremer** a-18; c-25. **Nostrand** a-17-25; 14, 17(w/**Powell**). **Palais** a-1, 2, 4(2), 5(2), 7-9, 12, 14, 15, 17. **Powell** a-3-7, 10, 11, 19-27. Bondage-c 1, 3, 5, 6, 8, 9.*

WITCHES TALES (Magazine)
V1No.7, July, 1969 - V7No.1, Feb, 1975 (52 pgs.) (B&W)
Eerie Publications

V1#7(7/69) - 9(11/69)	.50	1.50	3.00
V2#1-6('70), V3#1-6('71)	.35	1.00	2.00
V4#1-6('72), V5#1-6('73), V6#1-6('74), V7#1	.35	1.00	2.00

NOTE: *Ajax/Farrell reprints in early issues.*

WITCHES' WESTERN TALES (Formerly Witches Tales) (Western Tales #31 on)
No. 29, Feb, 1955 - No. 30, April, 1955
Harvey Publications

29,30-S&K-r/from Boys' Ranch including-c	6.00	18.00	42.00

WITCHING HOUR, THE
Feb-Mar, 1969 - No. 85, Oct, 1978
National Periodical Publications/DC Comics

	Good	Fine	Mint
1-Toth plus Adams, 3 pgs.	.45	1.30	2.60
2,6		.30	.60
3,5-Wrightson-a; Toth-a(p)	.25	.75	1.50
4,7,9-12: Toth-a in all		.50	1.00
8-Adams-a	.35	1.00	2.00
13-Adams c/a, 2pgs.	.25	.75	1.50
14-Williamson/Garzon, Jones-a; Adams-c	.25	.75	1.50
15-85: 38-(100 pgs.)		.25	.50

NOTE: *Combined with The Unexpected with No. 189.* ***Adams*** *c-7-11, 13, 14.* ***Alcala*** *a-24, 27, 33, 41, 43.* ***Anderson*** *a-9, 38.* ***Cardy*** *c-4, 5.* ***Kaluta*** *a-7.* ***Kane*** *a-12p.* ***Morrow*** *a-10, 13, 15, 16.* ***Nino*** *a-31, 40, 45, 47.* ***Redondo*** *a-20, 23, 24, 34, 65.* ***Reese*** *a-23.* ***Toth*** *a-38r.* ***Tuska*** *a-12.* ***Wood*** *a-12i, 15.*

WITH THE MARINES ON THE BATTLEFRONTS OF THE WORLD
1953 (no month) - No. 2, March, 1954 (photo covers)
Toby Press

	Good	Fine	Mint
1-John Wayne story	10.00	30.00	70.00
2-Monty Hall in #1,2	2.00	6.00	14.00

WITH THE U.S. PARATROOPS BEHIND ENEMY LINES (Also see U.S. Paratroops. . ; #2-4 titled U.S. Paratroops. .)
1951 - No. 6, Dec, 1952
Avon Periodicals

	Good	Fine	Mint
1-Wood-c & inside-c	8.00	24.00	56.00
2	4.35	13.00	30.00
3-6	3.65	11.00	25.00

NOTE: ***Kinstler*** *a-2, 5, 6; c-2, 4, 5.*

WITNESS, THE (Also see Amazing Mysteries, Captain America 71, Ideal 4, Marvel Mystery 92 & Mystic #7)
Sept, 1948
Marvel Comics (MjMe)

	Good	Fine	Mint
1(Scarce)-No Everett-c	35.00	105.00	245.00

WITTY COMICS
1945
Irwin H. Rubin Publ./Chicago Nite Life News No. 2

	Good	Fine	Mint
1-The Pioneer, Junior Patrol	4.00	12.00	28.00
2-The Pioneer, Junior Patrol	2.30	7.00	16.00
3-7-Skyhawk	1.85	5.50	13.00

WIZARD OF OZ (See Classics Ill. Jr. 535, Dell Jr. Treasury No. 5, First Comics Graphic Novel, 4-Color No. 1308, Marvelous. . . , & Marvel Treasury of Oz)

WOLF GAL (See Al Capp's. . .)

WOLFMAN, THE (See Book & Record Set & Movie Classics)

WOLFPACK
Feb, 1988 ($7.95)
Marvel Comics

	Good	Fine	Mint
1-1st app./origin	1.35	4.00	7.95

WOLVERINE (See Kitty Pryde &. . . , Incred. Hulk &. . . , Spider-Man vs. . . , & X-Men)
Sept, 1982 - No. 4, Dec, 1982 (mini-series)
Marvel Comics Group

	Good	Fine	Mint
1-Frank Miller-c/a(p)	1.15	3.50	7.00
2,3-Miller-c/a(p)	1.50	3.00	6.00
4-Miller-c/a(p)	1.10	3.25	6.50

WOMAN OF THE PROMISE, THE
1950 (General Distr.) (32 pgs.) (paper cover)
Catechetical Guild

	Good	Fine	Mint
	5.00	15.00	30.00

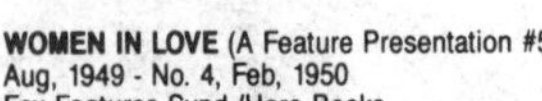

WOMEN IN LOVE (A Feature Presentation #5)
Aug, 1949 - No. 4, Feb, 1950
Fox Features Synd./Hero Books

	Good	Fine	Mint
1	11.00	32.00	76.00
2-Kamen/Feldstein-c	8.50	25.50	60.00
3	5.70	17.00	40.00
4-Wood-a	8.00	24.00	56.00

WOMEN IN LOVE
Winter, 1952 (100 pgs.)
Ziff-Davis Publishing Co.

	Good	Fine	Mint
nn-Kinstler-a (Scarce)	20.00	60.00	140.00

WOMEN OUTLAWS (My Love Memories #9 on)
July, 1948 - No. 8, Sept, 1949 (Also see Red Circle)
Fox Features Syndicate

	Good	Fine	Mint
1-Used in SOTI, illo-"Giving children an image of American womanhood"; negligee panels	25.00	75.00	175.00
2-Spanking panel	20.00	60.00	140.00
3-Kamen-a	16.00	48.00	110.00
4-8	12.00	36.00	84.00
nn(nd)-Contains Cody of the Pony Express	10.00	30.00	70.00

WOMEN TO LOVE
No date (1953)
Realistic

	Good	Fine	Mint
nn-(Scarce)-Reprint/Complete Romance No. 1; c-/Avon paperback 165	20.00	60.00	140.00

WONDER BOY (Formerly Terrific Comics) (See Bomber Comics)
No. 17, May, 1955 - No. 18, July, 1955
Ajax/Farrell Publ.

	Good	Fine	Mint
17-Phantom Lady app. Bakerish a/c	9.50	28.50	65.00
18-Phantom Lady app.	8.50	25.50	60.00

NOTE: *Phantom Lady not by Matt Baker.*

WONDER COMICS (Wonderworld #3 on)
May, 1939 - No. 2, June, 1939
Fox Features Syndicate

	Good	Fine	Mint
1-(Scarce)-Wonder Man only app. by Will Eisner; Dr. Fung (by Powell), K-51 begins; Bob Kane-a; Eisner-c	280.00	840.00	1960.00
2-(Scarce)-Yarko the Great, Master Magician by Eisner begins; 'Spark' Stevens by Bob Kane, Patty O'Day, Tex Mason app. Lou Fine's 1st-c; a(2pgs.)	155.00	465.00	1085.00

WONDER COMICS
May, 1944 - No. 20, Oct, 1948
Great/Nedor/Better Publications

	Good	Fine	Mint
1-The Grim Reaper & Spectro, the Mind Reader begin; Hitler/Hirohito bondage-c	28.00	84.00	195.00
2-Origin The Grim Reaper; Super Sleuths begin, end #8,17	17.00	51.00	120.00
3-5	14.00	42.00	100.00
6-10: 6-Flag-c. 8-Last Spectro. 9-Wonderman begins	12.00	36.00	84.00
11-14-Dick Devens, King of Futuria begins #11, ends #14	14.00	42.00	100.00
15-Tara begins (origin), ends #20	15.00	45.00	105.00
16,18: 16-Spectro app.; last Grim Reaper. 18-The Silver Knight begins	13.50	40.00	95.00
17-Wonderman with Frazetta panels; Jill Trent with all Frazetta inks	17.00	51.00	120.00
19-Frazetta panels	15.00	45.00	105.00
20-Most of Silver Knight by Frazetta	19.00	57.00	132.00

NOTE: ***Ingels*** *c-11, 12.* ***Schomburg (Xela)*** *c-1-10; (airbrush)-13-20. Bondage-c 12, 13, 15.*

WONDER DUCK (See Wisco)
Sept, 1949 - No. 3, Mar, 1950
Marvel Comics (CDS)

Wolverine #2, © MCG

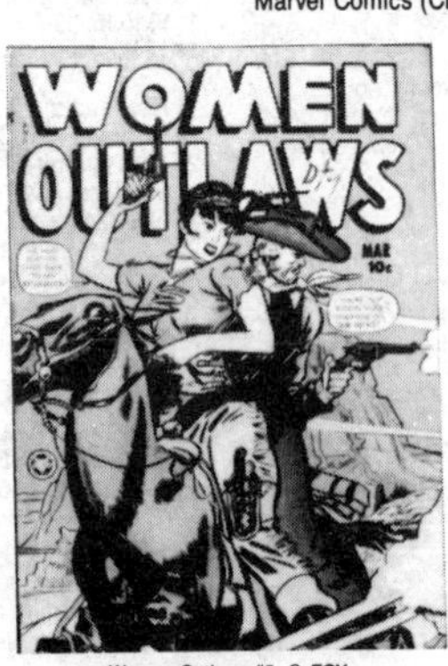

Women Outlaws #5, © FOX

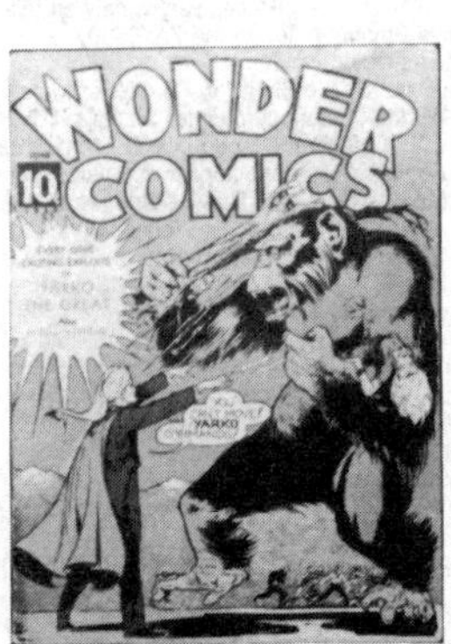

Wonder Comics #2, © FOX

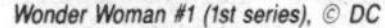
Wonder Woman #1 (1st series), © DC

Wonder Woman #159, © DC

Wonderworld Comics #8, © FOX

WONDER DUCK (continued)

	Good	Fine	Mint
1	3.50	10.50	24.00
2,3	2.30	7.00	16.00

WONDERFUL ADVENTURES OF PINOCCHIO, THE (See Movie Comics & Walt Disney Showcase #48)
April, 1982 (Walt Disney)
Whitman Publishing Co.

	Good	Fine	Mint
3-(Cont. of Movie Comics?); r-/FC #92		.30	.60

WONDERFUL WORLD OF DUCKS (See Golden Picture Story Book)
1975
Colgate Palmolive Co.

	Good	Fine	Mint
1-Mostly-r		.30	.60

WONDERFUL WORLD OF THE BROTHERS GRIMM (See Movie Comics)

WONDERLAND COMICS
Summer, 1945 - No. 9, Feb-Mar, 1947
Feature Publications/Prize

	Good	Fine	Mint
1	3.00	9.00	21.00
2	1.50	4.50	10.00
3-9	1.15	3.50	8.00

WONDER MAN
Mar, 1986 (One-Shot, 52 pgs.)
Marvel Comics Group

	Good	Fine	Mint
1	.25	.75	1.50

WONDERS OF ALADDIN, THE (See 4-Color No. 1255)

WONDER WOMAN (See Adventure, All-Star Comics, Brave & the Bold, DC Comics Presents, Legend of . . ., Sensation Comics, and World's Finest)

WONDER WOMAN
Summer, 1942 - No. 329, Feb, 1986
National Periodical Publications/All-American Publ./DC Comics

	Good	Fine	Mint
1-Origin Wonder Woman retold (see All-Star #8); r-/Famous 1st Editions; H. G. Peter-a begins	275.00	825.00	1925.00
2-Origin & 1st app. Mars; Duke of Deception app.	93.00	280.00	650.00
3	68.00	205.00	475.00
4,5: 5-1st Dr. Psycho app.	50.00	150.00	350.00
6-10: 6-1st Cheetah app.	38.00	115.00	265.00
11-20	28.00	84.00	195.00
21-30	22.00	65.00	154.00
31-40	16.00	48.00	110.00
41-44,46-48	13.00	40.00	90.00
45-Origin retold	22.00	65.00	154.00
49-Used in **SOTI**, pgs. 234,236. Last 52 pg. ish	13.00	40.00	90.00
50-(44 pgs.)-Used in **POP**, pg. 97	10.00	30.00	70.00
51-60	9.50	28.50	65.00
61-72: 62-Origin of W.W. i.d. 64-Story about 3-D movies. 70-1st Angle Man app. 72-Last pre-code	8.00	24.00	56.00
73-90: 80-Origin The Invisible Plane	6.00	18.00	42.00
91-94,96-99: 97-Last H. G. Peter-a. 99-Origin W.W. i.d. with new facts	4.00	12.00	28.00
95-A-Bomb-c	4.65	14.00	32.00
100	5.00	15.00	35.00
101-104,106-110: 107-1st advs. of Wonder Girl; 1st Merboy; tells how W.W. won her costume	3.15	9.50	22.00
105-(Scarce)-Wonder Woman's secret origin; 1st app. Wonder Girl	6.50	19.50	45.00
111-120	1.85	5.50	13.00
121-126: 122-1st app. Wonder Tot. 124-1st app. Won. Wom. Family. 126-Last 10 cent ish.	1.10	3.30	7.50
127-130: 128-Origin The Invisible Plane retold	1.00	3.00	7.00
131-150	.85	2.50	5.00
151-158,160-170	.70	2.00	4.00
159-Origin retold	.85	2.50	5.00
171-178	.50	1.50	3.00
179-195: 179-Wears no costume to issue #203. 180-Death of Steve Trevor. 195-Wood inks?	.45	1.25	2.50
196 (52 pgs.)-Origin r-/All-Star 8	.50	1.50	3.00
197,198 (52 pgs.)-r	.50	1.50	3.00
199,200-Jones-c; 52 pgs.	.85	2.50	5.00
201-210: 204-Return to old costume; death of I Ching. 202-Fafhrd & The Grey Mouser debut		.40	.80
211-217: 211,214(100 pgs.), 217 (68 pgs.)		.35	.70
218-230: 220-Adams assist. 223-Steve Trevor revived as Steve Howard & learns W.W.'s I.D. 228-Both W. Women team up & new World War II stories begin, end #243		.35	.70
231-240: 237-Origin retold		.25	.50
241-260: 241-Intro Bouncer. 248-Steve Trevor Howard dies. 250-Intro/origin Orana, the new W. Woman. 251-Orana dies		.25	.50
261-286: 269-Last Wood a(i) for DC? (7/80). 271-Huntress & 3rd Life of Steve Trevor begin		.30	.60
287-New Teen Titans x-over	.25	.75	1.50
288-299: 288-New costume, logo. 291-93-Three part epic with Super-Heroines		.30	.60
300-Double-sized, 76 pg. anniversary issue; Giffen-a; New Teen Titans, JLA app.	.25	.75	1.50
301-309: 308-Huntress begins		.30	.60
310-328 (75 cent cover)		.40	.80
329-Double size		.65	1.30
Pizza Hut Giveaways (12/77)-Reprints #60,62		.40	.80

NOTE: ***Colan** a-288-305p; c-288-90p. **Giffen** a-300p. **Grell** c-217. **Kaluta** c-297. **Gil Kane** c-294p, 303-05, 307, 312, 314. **Miller** c-298p. **Morrow** c-233. **Nasser** a-232p; c-231p, 232p. **Perez** c-283p, 284p. **Spiegle** a-312. **Staton** a-241p, 271-287p, 289p, 290p, 294-99p; c-241p, 245p, 246p.*

WONDER WOMAN
Feb, 1987 - Present
DC Comics

	Good	Fine	Mint
1-New origin; Perez c/a begins	.50	1.50	3.00
2-5	.25	.75	1.50
6-15		.65	1.30

WONDER WOMAN SPECTACULAR (See DC Special Series No. 9)

WONDER WORKER OF PERU
No date (16 pgs.) (B&W) (5x7")
Catechetical Guild (Giveaway)

	Good	Fine	Mint
	1.70	5.00	10.00

WONDERWORLD COMICS (Formerly Wonder Comics)
No. 3, July, 1939 - No. 33, Jan, 1942
Fox Features Syndicate

	Good	Fine	Mint
3-Intro The Flame by Fine; Dr. Fung (Powell-a), K-51 (Powell-a?), & Yarko the Great, Master Magician (Eisner-a) continues; Eisner/Fine-c	68.00	205.00	475.00
4	48.00	145.00	335.00
5-10	45.00	135.00	315.00
11-Origin The Flame	50.00	150.00	350.00
12-20: 12-Dr. Fung ends	26.00	78.00	182.00
21-Origin The Black Lion & Cub	24.00	72.00	168.00
22-27	19.00	57.00	132.00
28-1st app/origin U.S. Jones; Lu-Nar, the Moon Man begins	22.00	65.00	154.00
29,31-33: 32-Hitler-c	13.50	40.00	95.00
30-Origin Flame Girl	25.00	75.00	175.00

NOTE: *Yarko by **Eisner**-No. 3-11. **Eisner** text illos-3. **Lou Fine** c/a-3-11; c-12, 13, 15; text illos-4. **Powell** a-3-12. **Tuska** a-5-9. Bondage-c 14, 15, 28, 31, 32.*

WOODSY OWL (See March of Comics #395)
Nov, 1973 - No. 10, Feb, 1976

WOODSY OWL (continued)
Gold Key

	Good	Fine	Mint
1	.25	.75	1.50
2-10		.50	1.00

WOODY WOODPECKER (Walter Lantz . . . #73 on?)(See Dell Giants for annuals, The Funnies, New Funnies & Jolly Jingles)
No. 169, 10/47 - No. 72, 5-7/62; No. 73, 10/62 - No. 201, 4/84 (nn 192)
Dell Publishing Co./Gold Key No. 73-187/Whitman No. 188 on

	Good	Fine	Mint
4-Color 169-Drug turns Woody into a Mr. Hyde	5.70	17.00	40.00
4-Color 188	4.35	13.00	30.00
4-Color 202,232,249,264,288	2.65	8.00	18.00
4-Color 305,336,350	1.70	5.00	12.00
4-Color 364,374,390,405,416,431('52)	1.50	4.50	10.00
16 (12-1/52-53) - 30('55)	1.15	3.50	8.00
31-50	.75	2.25	5.00
51-72 (Last Dell)	.55	1.65	4.00
73-75 (Giants, 84 pgs., Gold Key)	1.50	4.50	12.00
76-80	.50	1.50	3.00
81-100	.35	1.00	2.00
101-120		.60	1.20
121-191,193-201		.40	.80
Christmas Parade 1(11/68-Giant)(G.K.)	1.50	4.50	10.00
Clover Stamp-Newspaper Boy Contest('56)-9 pg. story-(Giveaway)	.85	2.50	6.00
In Chevrolet Wonderland(1954-Giveaway)(Western Publ.)-20 pgs., full story line; Chilly Willy app.	2.65	8.00	18.00
Kite Fun Book (1956, 5x7¼", 16p, soft-c)	4.00	12.00	28.00
Meets Scotty McTape(1953-Scotch Tape giveaway)-16 pgs., full size	2.00	6.00	14.00
Summer Fun 1(6/66-G.K.)(84 pgs.)	2.00	6.00	16.00

NOTE: *15 cents editions exist. Reprints-No. 92, 102, 103, 105, 106, 124, 125, 152, 153, 157, 162, 165, 194(⅓)-200(⅓).*

WOODY WOODPECKER (See Comic Album #5,9,13, Dell Giant #24, 40, 54, Dell Giants, The Funnies, Golden Comics Digest #1, 3, 5, 8, 15, 16, 20, 24, 32, 37, 44, March of Comics #16, 34, 85, 93, 109, 124, 139, 158, 177, 184, 203, 222, 239, 249, 261, 420, 454, 466, 478, New Funnies & Super Book #12, 24)

WOOLWORTH'S CHRISTMAS STORY BOOK
1952 - 1954 (16 pgs., paper-c) (See Jolly Christmas Book)
Promotional Publ. Co.(Western Printing Co.)

	Good	Fine	Mint
nn	2.00	6.00	14.00

NOTE: *1952 issue-**Marv Levy** c/a.*

WOOLWORTH'S HAPPY TIME CHRISTMAS BOOK
1952 (Christmas giveaway, 36 pgs.)
F. W. Woolworth Co.(Whitman Publ. Co.)

	Good	Fine	Mint
nn	2.00	6.00	14.00

WORLD AROUND US, THE (Ill. Story of . . .)
Sept, 1958 - No. 36, Oct, 1961 (25 cents)
Gilberton Publishers (Classics Illustrated)

	Good	Fine	Mint
1-Dogs	1.50	4.50	10.00
2-Indians-Crandall-a	1.00	3.00	7.00
3-Horses; L. B. Cole-c	1.35	4.00	9.00
4-Railroads	.85	2.50	6.00
5-Space; Ingels-a	2.85	8.50	20.00
6-The F.B.I.; Disbrow, Evans, Ingels-a	2.00	6.00	14.00
7-Pirates; Disbrow, Ingels-a	2.65	8.00	18.00
8-Flight; Evans, Ingels, Crandall-a	2.00	6.00	14.00
9-Army; Disbrow, Ingels, Orlando-a	2.35	7.00	16.00
10-Navy; Disbrow, Kinstler-a	1.35	4.00	9.00
11-Marine Corps.	1.00	3.00	7.00
12-Coast Guard	1.00	3.00	7.00
13-Air Force; L.B. Cole-c	1.35	4.00	9.00
14-French Revolution; Crandall, Evans-a	3.00	9.00	21.00
15-Prehistoric Animals; Al Williamson-a, 6 & 10 pgs. plus Morrow-a	3.50	10.50	24.00
16-Crusades	2.00	6.00	14.00
17-Festivals-Evans, Crandall-a	2.30	7.00	16.00
18-Great Scientists; Crandall, Evans, Torres, Williamson, Morrow-a	2.65	8.00	18.00
19-Jungle; Crandall, Williamson, Morrow-a	3.70	11.00	26.00
20-Communications; Crandall, Evans-a	3.50	10.50	24.00
21-Presidents	2.00	6.00	14.00
22-Boating; Morrow-a	1.50	4.50	10.00
23-Great Explorers; Crandall, Evans-a	1.50	4.50	10.00
24-Ghosts; Morrow, Evans-a	1.70	5.00	12.00
25-Magic; Evans, Morrow-a	2.35	7.00	16.00
26-The Civil War	2.65	8.00	18.00
27-Mountains (High Advs.); Crandall/Evans, Morrow, Torres-a	2.00	6.00	14.00
28-Whaling; Crandall, Evans, Morrow-a; L.B. Cole-c	1.75	5.25	12.00
29-Vikings; Crandall, Evans, Torres, Morrow-a	2.30	7.00	16.00
30-Undersea Adventure; Crandall/Evans, Kirby-a	3.50	10.50	24.00
31-Hunting; Crandall/Evans, Ingels, Kinstler, Kirby-a	2.65	8.00	18.00
32-For Gold & Glory; Morrow, Kirby, Crandall, Evans-a	2.30	7.00	16.00
33-Famous Teens; Torres, Crandall, Evans-a	2.00	6.00	14.00
34-Fishing; Crandall/Evans, Ingels-a	1.70	5.00	12.00
35-Spies; Kirby, Evans, Morrow-a	1.75	5.25	12.00
36-Fight for Life (Medicine); Kirby-a	1.75	5.25	12.00

(See Classics Ill. Special Edition)

WORLD FAMOUS HEROES MAGAZINE
Oct, 1941 - No. 4, Apr, 1942 (a comic book)
Comic Corp. of America (Centaur)

	Good	Fine	Mint
1-Gustavson-c; Lubbers, Glanzman-a; Davy Crockett story; Flag-c	30.00	90.00	210.00
2-Lou Gehrig life story; Lubbers-a	16.00	48.00	110.00
3,4-Lubbers-a	15.00	45.00	105.00

WORLD FAMOUS STORIES
1945
Croyden Publishers

	Good	Fine	Mint
1-Ali Baba, Hansel & Gretel, Rip Van Winkle, Mid-Summer Night's Dream	4.60	14.00	32.00

WORLD IS HIS PARISH, THE
1953 (15 cents)
George A. Pflaum

	Good	Fine	Mint
The story of Pope Pius XII	3.50	10.50	22.00

WORLD OF ADVENTURE (Walt Disney's . . .)(TV)
April, 1963 - No. 3, Oct, 1963
Gold Key

	Good	Fine	Mint
1-3-Disney TV characters; Savage Sam, Johnny Shiloh, Capt. Nemo, The Mooncussers	.75	2.25	5.00

WORLD OF ARCHIE, THE (See Archie Giant Series Mag. No. 148, 151, 156, 160, 165, 171, 177, 182, 188, 193, 200, 208, 213, 225, 232, 237, 244, 249, 456, 461, 468, 473, 480, 485, 492, 497, 504, 509, 516, 521, 532, 543, 554, 565, 574)

WORLD OF FANTASY
May, 1956 - No. 19, Aug, 1959
Atlas Comics (CPC No. 1-15/ZPC No. 16-19)

	Good	Fine	Mint
1	7.00	21.00	50.00
2-Williamson-a, 4 pgs.	6.00	18.00	42.00
3-Sid Check, Roussos-a	3.00	9.00	21.00
4-7	2.35	7.00	16.00
8-Matt Fox, Orlando, Berg-a	3.50	10.50	24.00
9-Krigstein-a	3.00	9.00	21.00
10,13-15	1.85	5.50	13.00

Woody Woodpecker Summer Fun #1, © W. Lantz

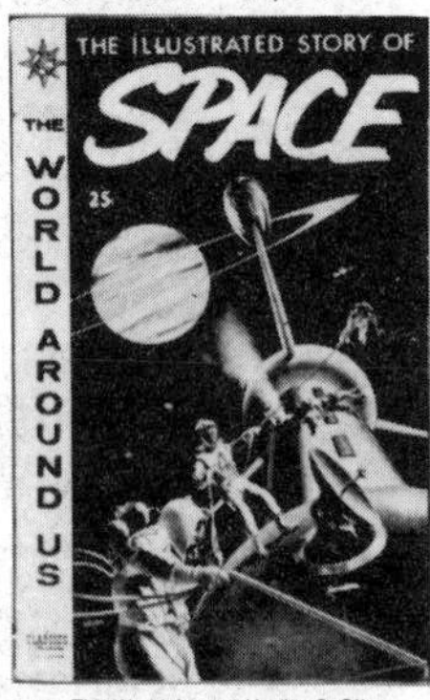

The World Around Us #5, © GIL

World of Fantasy #17, © MCG

World of Suspense #6, © MCG

World's Finest Comics #7, © DC

World's Finest Comics #164, © DC

WORLD OF FANTASY (continued)

	Good	Fine	Mint
11-Torres-a	3.00	9.00	21.00
12-Everett-c	1.85	5.50	13.00
16-Williamson-a, 4 pgs.; Ditko, Kirby-a	4.75	14.25	33.00
17-19-Ditko, Kirby-a	4.00	12.00	28.00

NOTE: ***Berg*** *a-5, 6, 8.* ***Check*** *a-3.* ***Ditko*** *a-17, 19.* ***Everett*** *c-4, 5-7, 9, 13.* ***Kirby*** *c-15, 17-19.* ***Krigstein*** *a-9.* ***Maneely*** *c-14.* ***Morrow*** *a-7, 8, 14.* ***Orlando*** *a-8, 13, 14.* ***Powell*** *a-4, 6.*

WORLD OF GIANT COMICS, THE (See Archie All-Star Specials under Archie Comics)

WORLD OF JUGHEAD, THE (See Archie Giant Series Mag. No. 9, 14, 19, 24, 30, 136, 143, 149, 152, 157, 161, 166, 172, 178, 183, 189, 194, 202, 209, 215, 227, 233, 239, 245, 251, 457, 463, 469, 475, 481, 487, 493, 499, 505, 511, 517, 523, 531, 542, 553, 564, 576)

WORLD OF KRYPTON, THE (World of . . . #3)
7/79 - No. 3, 9/79; 12/87 - No. 4, 3/88 (Both mini-series)
DC Comics, Inc.

	Good	Fine	Mint
1 ('79)-Jor-El marries Lara		.40	.80
2,3: 3-Baby Superman sent to Earth; Krypton explodes; Mon-el app.		.30	.60
1-4 (2nd series)-Byrne scripts		.40	.80

WORLD OF MYSTERY
June, 1956 - No. 7, July, 1957
Atlas Comics (GPI)

	Good	Fine	Mint
1-Torres, Orlando-a	6.00	18.00	42.00
2-Woodish-a	2.00	6.00	14.00
3-Torres, Davis, Ditko-a	4.35	13.00	30.00
4-Davis, Pakula, Powell-a; Ditko-c	4.35	13.00	30.00
5,7: 5-Orlando-a	2.00	6.00	14.00
6-Williamson/Mayo-a, 4 pgs.; Ditko-a; Crandall text illo	4.60	14.00	32.00

NOTE: ***Colan*** *a-7.* ***Everett*** *c-1-3.* ***Romita*** *a-2.* ***Severin*** *c/a-7.*

WORLD OF SMALLVILLE
Apr, 1988 - Present
DC Comics

	Good	Fine	Mint
1-Byrne c/scripts		.40	.80

WORLD OF SUSPENSE
April, 1956 - No. 8, July, 1957
Atlas News Co.

	Good	Fine	Mint
1-Orlando-a	6.00	18.00	42.00
2-Ditko-a	3.00	9.00	21.00
3,7-Williamson-a in both, 4 pgs. each; #7-with Mayo	4.35	13.00	30.00
4-6,8	2.00	6.00	14.00

NOTE: ***Berg*** *a-6.* ***Ditko*** *a-2.* ***Everett*** *a-1, 5; c-6.* ***Heck*** *a-5.* ***Orlando*** *a-5.* ***Powell*** *a-6.* ***Roussos*** *a-6.*

WORLD OF WHEELS (Formerly Dragstrip Hotrodders)
Oct, 1967 - No. 32, June, 1970
Charlton Comics

	Good	Fine	Mint
17-32-Features Ken King		.15	.30
Modern Comics Reprint 23('78)		.15	.30

WORLD OF WOOD
1986 - No. 4 (mini-series, $1.75, color)
Eclipse Comics

	Good	Fine	Mint
1-4	.30	.90	1.80

WORLD'S BEST COMICS (. . . Finest #2 on)
Spring, 1941 (Cardboard-c)(DC's 6th annual format comic)
National Periodical Publications

	Good	Fine	Mint
1-The Batman, Superman, Crimson Avenger, Johnny Thunder, The King, Young Dr. Davis, Zatara, Lando, Man of Magic, & Red, White & Blue begin (inside-c blank)	280.00	840.00	1960.00

WORLDS BEYOND (Worlds of Fear #2 on)
Nov, 1951
Fawcett Publications

	Good	Fine	Mint
1-Powell, Bailey-a	8.00	24.00	56.00

WORLD'S FAIR COMICS (See N. Y. . . .)

WORLD'S FINEST COMICS (World's Best #1)
No. 2, Sum, 1941 - No. 323, Jan, 1986 (early issues-100 pgs.)
National Periodical Publ./DC Comics (No.1-17 cardboard covers)

	Good	Fine	Mint
2	130.00	390.00	910.00
3-The Sandman begins; last Johnny Thunder; origin & 1st app. The Scarecrow	115.00	345.00	805.00
4-Hop Harrigan app.; last Young Dr. Davis	80.00	240.00	560.00
5-Intro. TNT & Dan the Dyna-Mite; last King & Crimson Avenger	80.00	240.00	560.00
6-Star Spangled Kid begins; Aquaman app.; S&K Sandman with Sandy in new costume begins, ends #7	65.00	195.00	455.00
7-Green Arrow begins; last Lando, King, & Red, White & Blue; S&K art	65.00	195.00	455.00
8-Boy Commandos begin	57.00	170.00	400.00
9-Batman cameo in Star Spangled Kid; S&K-a; last 100pg. ish.	52.00	155.00	365.00
10-S&K-a	52.00	155.00	365.00
11-17-Last cardboard cover issue	45.00	135.00	315.00
18-20: 18-Paper covers begin; last Star Spangled Kid	42.00	125.00	295.00
21-30: 30-Johnny Peril app.	30.00	90.00	210.00
31-40: 33-35-Tomahawk app.	26.00	78.00	180.00
41-50: 41-Boy Commandos end. 42-Wyoming Kid begins, ends #63. 43-Full Steam Foley begins, ends #48. 48-Last square binding. 49-Tom Sparks, Boy Inventor begins	20.00	60.00	140.00
51-60: 51-Zatara ends. 59-Manhunters Around the World begins, ends #62	20.00	60.00	140.00
61-64: 63-Capt. Compass app.	17.00	51.00	120.00
65-Origin Superman; Tomahawk begins, ends #101	21.00	64.00	150.00
66-70-(15 cent issues)(Scarce)-Last 68pg. issue	20.00	60.00	140.00
71-(10 cent issue)(Scarce)-Superman & Batman begin as team	27.00	81.00	190.00
72,73-(10 cent issues)(Scarce)	20.00	60.00	140.00
74-80: 74-Last pre-code ish.	10.00	30.00	70.00
81-90: 88-1st Joker/Luthor team-up. 90-Batwoman's 1st app. in World's Finest	6.50	19.50	45.00
91-93,95-99: 96-99-Kirby Green Arrow	4.35	13.00	30.00
94-Origin Superman/Batman team retold	8.50	25.50	60.00
100	8.50	25.50	60.00
101-121: 102-Tommy Tomorrow begins, ends. #124. 113-Intro. Miss Arrowette in Green Arrow; 1st Batmite/ Mxyzptlk team-up. 121-Last 10 cent issue	2.85	8.50	20.00
122-141: 125-Aquaman begins, ends #139. 140-Last Green Arrow	1.50	4.50	10.00
142-Origin The Composite Superman(Villain); Legion app.	1.50	4.50	10.00
143-150: 143-1st Mailbag	1.00	3.00	7.00
151-160: 156-1st Bizarro Batman	.85	2.50	5.00
161,170 (80-Pg. Giant G-28,G-40)	.70	2.00	4.00
162-169,171-174: 168,172-Adult Legion app.	.50	1.50	3.00
175,176-Adams-a; both r-Jonn' Jonzz' origin/Det. 225,226	.70	2.00	4.00
177,178,180-187,189-196,198-204: 182-Silent Knight-r/Brave & Bold #6. 186-Johnny Quick-r. 187-Green Arrow origin-r/Adv. #256. 190-93-Robin-r. 198,199-3rd Superman/Flash race	.25	.70	1.40
179,188,197 (80-Pg. Giant G-52,G-64,G-76)	.35	1.00	2.00
205-6 pgs. Shining Knight by Frazetta/Adv. #153; 52 pgs.; Teen Titans x-over	.35	1.10	2.20

WORLD'S FINEST COMICS (continued) **Good** **Fine** **Mint**

206 (80-Pg. Giant G-88) .25 .75 1.50
207-212 (52 pgs.) .40 .80
213-222: 215-Intro. Batman Jr. & Superman Jr. 217-Metamorpho begins, ends #220; Batman/Superman team-up begins .30 .60
223,226-Adams-a(r); 100 pgs.; 223-Deadman origin; 226-S&K, Toth-r; Manhunter part origin-r/Det. 225,226 .25 .75 1.50
224,225,227,228-(100 pgs.) .50 1.00
229-243: 229-r-/origin Superman-Batman team .25 .50
244-248: 244-Green Arrow, Black Canary, Wonder Woman, Vigilante begin; $1.00 size begins. 246-Death of Stuff in Vigilante; origin Vigilante retold. 248-Last Vigilante .40 .80
249-The Creeper begins by Ditko, ends #255 .50 1.00
250-The Creeper origin retold by Ditko .40 .80
251-262: 253-Captain Marvel begins. 255-Last Creeper. 256-Hawkman begins. 257-Black Lightning begins .40 .80
263-282 ($1.00): 268-Capt. Marvel Jr origin retold. 274-Zatanna begins. 279,280-Capt. Marvel Jr. & Kid Eternity learn they are brothers. 271-Origin Superman/Batman team retold .40 .80
283-297 (36 pgs.). 284-Legion app. .30 .60
298,299 (75 cent issues begin) .40 .80
300-(52pgs., $1.25)-New Teen Titans app. by Perez .60 1.20
301-323: 304-Origin Null and Void .40 .80
Giveaway (c. 1944-45, 8 pgs., in color, paper-c)-Johnny Everyman-r/W. Finest 10.00 30.00 70.00

NOTE: ***Adams*** *a-230r; c-174-176, 178-180, 182, 183, 185, 186, 199-205, 208-211, 244-246, 258.* ***Austin*** *a-244-246i.* ***Burnley*** *a-8, 10; c-7-9, 12.* ***Colan*** *a-274p.* ***Ditko*** *a-249-255.* ***Giffen*** *c-284p.* ***G. Kane*** *a-38, 174r, 282, 283; c-281, 282, 289.* ***Kirby*** *a-187.* ***Kubert*** *Zatara-40-44.* ***Miller*** *c-285p.* ***Morrow*** *a-245-248.* ***Nasser*** *a(p)-244-246, 259, 260.* ***Newton*** *a-253-281p.* ***Orlando*** *a-224r.* ***Perez*** *a-300i; c-271, 276, 277p, 278p.* ***Robinson*** *a-2, 9, 13-15; c-2-4, 6.* ***Rogers*** *a-259p.* ***Roussos*** *a-212r.* ***Simonson*** *c-291.* ***Spiegle*** *a-275-78, 284.* ***Staton*** *a-262p, 273p.* ***Toth*** *a-228r.* ***Tuska*** *a-230r, 250p, 252p, 254p, 257p, 283p, 284p, 308p.*

(Also see 80 Pg. Giant No. 15.)

WORLD'S FINEST COMICS DIGEST (See DC Special Series 23)

WORLD'S GREATEST ATHLETE (See Walt Disney Showcase No. 14)

WORLD'S GREATEST SONGS
Sept, 1954
Atlas Comics (Male)

1-(Scarce) Heath & Harry Anderson-a 11.00 34.00 80.00

WORLD'S GREATEST STORIES
Jan, 1949 - No. 2, May, 1949
Jubilee Publications

1-Alice in Wonderland 8.00 24.00 56.00
2-Pinocchio 6.50 19.50 45.00

WORLD'S GREATEST SUPER HEROES
1977 (3¾x3¾") (24 pgs. in color) (Giveaway)
DC Comics (Nutra Comics) (Child Vitamins, Inc.)

Batman & Robin app.; health tips .25 .75 1.50

WORLDS OF FEAR (Worlds Beyond #1)
V1No.2, Jan, 1952 - V2No.10, June, 1953
Fawcett Publications

V1#2 7.00 21.00 50.00
3-Evans-a 6.50 19.50 45.00
4-6(9/52) 5.70 17.00 40.00
V2#7-9 4.00 12.00 28.00
10-Saunders Painted-c; man with no eyes surrounded by eyeballs-c 10.00 30.00 70.00

NOTE: ***Powell*** *a-2, 4, 5.* ***Sekowsky*** *a-4, 5.*

WORLDS UNKNOWN
May, 1973 - No. 8, Aug, 1974
Marvel Comics Group

Good **Fine** **Mint**

1-R-/from Astonishing #54; Torres, Reese-a .30 .60
2-8 .20 .40

NOTE: ***Adkins/Mooney*** *a-5.* ***Buscema*** *a/c-4p.* ***W. Howard*** *c/a-3i.* ***Kane*** *a(p)-1,2; c(p)-5, 6, 8.* ***Sutton*** *a-2.* ***Tuska*** *a(p)-7, 8; c-7p. No. 7, 8 has Golden Voyage of Sinbad movie adaptation.*

WORLD WAR STORIES
Apr-June, 1965 - No. 3, Dec, 1965
Dell Publishing Co.

1 1.00 3.00 7.00
2,3: 1-3-Glanzman-a .70 2.00 4.00

WORLD WAR II (See Classics Special Ed.)

WORLD WAR III
Mar, 1953 - No. 2, May, 1953
Ace Periodicals

1-(Scarce)-Atomic bomb-c 35.00 105.00 245.00
2-Used in **POP**, pg. 78 and B&W & color illos. 26.00 78.00 182.00

WORST FROM MAD, THE (Annual)
1958 - No. 12, 1969 (Each annual cover is reprinted from the cover of the Mad issues being reprinted)
E. C. Comics

nn(1958)-Bonus; record labels & travel stickers; 1st Mad annual; r-/Mad #29-34 10.00 30.00 70.00
2(1959)-Bonus is small 33⅓ rpm record entitled "Meet the Staff of Mad;" r-/Mad #35-40 14.00 42.00 100.00
3(1960)-20"x30" campaign poster "Alfred E. Neuman for President;" r-/Mad #41-46 7.00 21.00 50.00
4(1961)-Sunday comics section; r-/Mad #47-54 7.00 21.00 50.00
5(1962)-Has 33⅓ record; r-/Mad #55-62 11.50 34.00 80.00
6(1963)-Has 33⅓ record; r-/Mad #63-70 12.00 36.00 84.00
7(1964)-Mad protest signs; r-/Mad #71-76 4.35 13.00 30.00
8(1965)-Build a Mad Zeppelin 5.70 17.00 40.00
9(1966)-33⅓ rpm record 9.50 28.50 65.00
10(1967)-Mad bumper sticker 3.00 9.00 21.00
11(1968)-Mad cover window stickers 3.00 9.00 21.00
12(1969)-Mad picture postcards; Orlando-a 3.00 9.00 21.00

NOTE: *Covers:* ***Bob Clarke****-No. 8.* ***Mingo****-No. 7, 9-12.*

WOTALIFE COMICS
No. 3, Aug-Sept, 1946 - No. 12, July, 1947; 1959
Fox Features Syndicate/Norlen Mag.

3-Cosmo Cat 2.65 8.00 18.00
4-12-Cosmo Cat 1.50 4.50 10.00
1('59-Norlen)-Atomic Rabbit, Atomic Mouse 1.15 3.50 8.00

WOTALIFE COMICS
1957 - No. 5, 1957
Green Publications

1 1.15 3.50 8.00
2-5 .70 2.00 5.00

WOW COMICS
July, 1936 - No. 4, Nov, 1936 (52 pgs., magazine size)
Henle Publishing Co.

1-Fu Manchu; Eisner-a 95.00 285.00 665.00
2-Ken Maynard, Fu Manchu, Popeye by Segar; Eisner-a 65.00 195.00 455.00
3-Eisner-c/a(3); Popeye by Segar, Fu Manchu, Hiram Hick by Bob Kane, Space Limited app. 65.00 195.00 455.00
4-Flash Gordon by Raymond, Mandrake, Popeye by Segar, Tillie The Toiler, Fu Manchu, Hiram Hick by Bob Kane; Eisner-a(3), Briefer-c 90.00 270.00 630.00

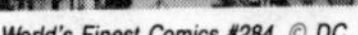
World's Finest Comics #284, © DC

World War III #1, © ACE

Wow Comics #3, © Henle Publ.

Wow Comics #15, © FAW

Xmas Comics #2, © FAW

X-Men #1, © MCG

WOW COMICS (Real Western Hero #70 on)(See X-Mas Comics)
Wint, 1940-41; No. 2, Summer, 1941 - No. 69, Fall, 1948
Fawcett Publications

	Good	Fine	Mint
nn(#1)-Origin Mr. Scarlet by S&K; Atom Blake, Boy Wizard, Jim Dolan, & Rick O'Shay begin; Diamond Jack, The White Rajah, & Shipwreck Roberts, only app.; the cover was printed on unstable paper stock and is rarely found in fine or mint condition; blank inside-c; bondage-c by Beck (Rare)	625.00	1875.00	5000.00
(Prices vary widely on this book)			
2-The Hunchback begins	57.00	170.00	400.00
3	35.00	105.00	245.00
4-Origin Pinky	43.00	130.00	300.00
5	30.00	90.00	210.00
6-Origin The Phantom Eagle; Commando Yank begins	23.00	70.00	160.00
7,8,10	23.00	70.00	160.00
9-Capt. Marvel, Capt. Marvel Jr., Shazam app.; Scarlet & Pinky x-over; Mary Marvel begins (cameo)	30.00	90.00	210.00
11-17,19,20: 15-Flag-c	14.00	42.00	100.00
18-1st app. Uncle Marvel (10/43); infinity-c	16.00	48.00	110.00
21-30: 28-Pinky x-over in Mary Marvel	8.50	25.50	60.00
31-40	5.70	17.00	40.00
41-50	4.35	13.00	30.00
51-58: Last Mary Marvel	3.65	11.00	25.00
59-69: 59-Ozzie begins. 65-69-Tom Mix app.	3.00	9.00	21.00

WRECK OF GROSVENOR (See Superior Stories No. 3)

WRINGLE WRANGLE (See 4-Color No. 821)

WULF THE BARBARIAN
Feb, 1975 - No. 4, Sept, 1975
Atlas/Seaboard Publ.

	Good	Fine	Mint
1-Origin		.40	.80
2-Intro. Berithe the Swordswoman; Adams, Wood, Reese-a		.30	.60
3,4		.25	.50

WYATT EARP (Hugh O'Brian Famous Marshal)
No. 860, 11/57 - No. 13, 12-2/1960-61 (Photo-c)
Dell Publishing Co.

	Good	Fine	Mint
4-Color 860 (#1)-Manning-a	5.00	15.00	35.00
4-Color 890,921(6/58)-All Manning-a	3.50	10.50	24.00
4 (9-11/58) - 12-Manning-a	3.00	9.00	21.00
13-Toth-a	4.00	12.00	28.00

WYATT EARP
11/55 - No. 29, 6/60; No. 30, 10/72 - No. 34, 6/73
Atlas Comics/Marvel No. 23 on (IPC)

	Good	Fine	Mint
1	5.00	15.00	35.00
2-Williamson-a, 4 pgs.	4.35	13.00	30.00
3-6,8-11	1.70	5.00	12.00
7,12-Williamson-a, 4pgs. ea.; #12 with Mayo	3.50	10.50	24.00
13-19	1.50	4.50	10.00
20-Torres-a	1.85	5.50	13.00
21-Davis-c	1.50	4.50	10.00
22-24,26-29: 22-Ringo Kid app. 23-Kid From Texas app. 29-Last 10 cent issue	.75	2.25	5.00
25-Davis-a	1.30	4.00	9.00
30-Williamson-r ('72)		.40	.80
31,33,34-Reprints		.25	.50
32-Torres-a(r)		.30	.60

NOTE: ***Everett** c-6. **Kirby** c-25, 29. **Maneely** c-12, 17, 20. **Maurer** a-4. **Severin** a-10; c-10, 14. **Wildey** a-5, 17, 24, 28.*

WYATT EARP FRONTIER MARSHAL (Formerly Range Busters)
No. 12, Jan, 1956 - No. 72, Dec, 1967 (Also see Blue Bird)
Charlton Comics

	Good	Fine	Mint
12	1.85	5.50	13.00
13-19	1.00	3.00	7.00
20-Williamson-a(4), 8,5,5,& 7 pgs.; 68 pgs.	5.50	16.50	38.00
21-30	.55	1.65	4.00
31-72: 31-Crandall-r		.50	1.00

X-FACTOR
Feb, 1986 - Present
Marvel Comics Group

	Good	Fine	Mint
1-Double size; Layton/Guice-a	1.15	3.50	7.00
2,3	.70	2.00	4.00
4,5	.60	1.75	3.50
6-10	.45	1.40	2.80
11-20	.35	1.00	2.00
21-23	.25	.70	1.40
24-26: Fall Of The Mutants	.35	1.00	2.00
27,28		.50	1.00
Annual 1 (10/86), 2 (10/87)	.35	1.00	2.00

XMAS COMICS
12?/1941 - No. 2, 12?/1942 (324 pgs.) (50 cents)
No. 3, 12?/1943 - No. 7, 12?/1947 (132 pgs.)
Fawcett Publications

	Good	Fine	Mint
1-Contains Whiz #21, Capt. Marvel #3, Bulletman #2, Wow #3, & Master #18; Raboy back-c. Not rebound, remaindered comics printed at same time as originals	122.00	365.00	854.00
2-Capt. Marvel, Bulletman, Spy Smasher	62.00	185.00	435.00
3-7-Funny animals	14.00	42.00	100.00

XMAS COMICS
No. 4, Dec, 1949 - No. 7, Dec, 1952 (196 pgs.)
Fawcett Publications

	Good	Fine	Mint
4-Contains Whiz, Master, Tom Mix, Captain Marvel, Nyoka, Capt. Video, Bob Colt, Monte Hale, Hot Rod Comics, & Battle Stories. Not rebound, remaindered comics—printed at the same time as originals	24.00	72.00	170.00
5-7-Same as above	21.00	62.00	148.00

XMAS FUNNIES
No date (paper cover) (36 pgs.?)
Kinney Shoes (Giveaway)

	Good	Fine	Mint
Contains 1933 color strip-r; Mutt & Jeff, etc.	10.00	30.00	70.00

X-MEN, THE (See Amazing Adventures, Classic X-Men, Heroes For Hope. . ., Kitty Pryde &. . ., Marvel & DC Present, Marvel Fanfare, Marvel Graphic Novel, Marvel Team-up, Marvel Triple Action, Nightcrawler, Official Marvel Index To. . ., Special Edition. . . & The Uncanny. . .)

X-MEN, THE (The Uncanny. . .#142)
Sept, 1963 - Present
Marvel Comics Group

	Good	Fine	Mint
1-Origin X-Men; 1st app. Magneto	86.00	255.00	600.00
2-1st app. The Vanisher	39.00	118.00	275.00
3-1st app. The Blob	18.00	54.00	128.00
4-1st Quick Silver & Scarlet Witch & Brotherhood of the Evil Mutants	15.00	45.00	105.00
5	12.00	36.50	85.00
6-10: 8-1st Unus the Untouchable. 9-Avengers app. 10-1st Silver-Age app. Ka-Zar	8.50	25.50	60.00
11-15: 11-1st app. The Stranger. 12-Origin Prof. X. 14-1st app. Sentinels. 15-Origin Beast	4.70	14.00	33.00
16-20: 19-1st app. The Mimic	3.60	11.00	25.00
21-27,29,30	2.85	8.50	20.00
28-1st app. The Banshee	3.15	9.50	22.00
31-37	1.85	5.50	13.00
38-Origin The X-Men feat. begins, ends #57	2.00	6.00	14.00
39,40: 39-New costumes	1.70	5.00	12.00
41-49: 42-Death of Prof. X (Changeling disguised as). 44-Red Raven			

THE X-MEN (continued)	Good	Fine	Mint
app. (G.A.). 49-Steranko-c; 1st Polaris	1.50	4.50	10.00
50,51-Steranko c/a	2.00	6.00	14.00
52	1.15	3.50	8.00
53-Smith c/a; 1st Smith comic book work	2.30	7.00	16.00
54,55-Smith-c	2.00	6.00	14.00
56-63,65-Adams-a. 56-Intro Havoc without costume. 65-Return of Prof. X. 58-1st app. Havoil	2.85	8.50	20.00
64-1st Sunfire app.	2.00	6.00	14.00
66	1.40	4.25	8.50
67-80: 67-All-r. 67-70,72-(52 pgs.)	1.25	3.75	7.50
81-93-r-#39-45 with-c	1.25	3.75	7.50
94(8/75)-New X-Men begin; Colossus, Nightcrawler, Thunderbird, Storm, Wolverine, & Banshee join; Angel, Marvel Girl, & Iceman resign	15.00	45.00	105.00
95-Death Thunderbird	7.70	23.00	46.00
96-99	5.35	16.00	32.00
98-99 (35 cent cover)	6.00	18.00	36.00
100-Old vs. New X-Men; part origin Phoenix	6.00	18.00	36.00
101-Phoenix origin concludes	5.35	16.00	32.00
102-107: 102-Origin Storm. 104-Intro. Star Jammers. 106-Old vs. New X-Men	3.00	9.00	18.00
108-1st Byrne X-Men	5.35	16.00	32.00
109-1st Vindicator	4.70	14.00	28.00
110,111: 110-Phoenix joins	3.00	9.00	18.00
112-119: 117-Origin Prof. X	2.65	8.00	16.00
120-1st app. Alpha Flight (cameo), story line begins	4.70	14.00	28.00
121-1st Alpha Flight (full story)	5.00	15.00	30.00
122-128: 124-Colossus becomes Proletarian	1.85	5.50	11.00
129-Intro Kitty Pryde	1.85	5.50	11.00
130-1st app. The Dazzler by Byrne	2.35	7.00	14.00
131-135: 131-Dazzler app. 134-Phoenix becomes Dark Phoenix	1.70	5.00	10.00
136,138: 138-Dazzler app.	1.40	4.25	8.50
137-Giant; death of Phoenix	1.85	5.50	11.00
139-Alpha Flight app.; Kitty Pryde joins	2.15	6.50	13.00
140-Alpha Flight app.	2.85	8.50	17.00
141-Intro Future X-Men & The New Brotherhood of Evil Mutants; death of Frank Richards	1.25	3.75	7.50
142,143: 142-Deaths of Wolverine, Storm & Colossus. 143-Last Byrne issue	1.00	3.00	6.00
144-150: 145-Old X-Men app. 148-Spider-Woman, Dazzler app. 150-Double size	.75	2.30	4.60
151-164: 161-Origin Magneto. 162-Wolverine app. 163-Origin Binary. 164-1st app. Binary as Carol Danvers	.60	1.75	3.50
165-Paul Smith-a begins	.75	2.30	4.60
166-Double size; Paul Smith-a	.60	1.75	3.50
167-170: 167-New Mutants x-over. 168-1st app. Madelyne Pryor.	.45	1.40	2.80
171-1st app. Rogue	.75	2.30	4.60
172-174: 174-Phoenix cameo	.40	1.20	2.40
175-Double size; anniversary issue; Phoenix returns? Paul Smith c/a	.45	1.35	2.70
176-185: 181-Sunfire app.	.40	1.20	2.40
186-Double-size; Barry Smith/Austin-a	.45	1.35	2.70
187-192,194-199	.30	.90	1.80
193-Double size	.45	1.35	2.70
200-Double size	.40	1.20	2.40
201-209	.25	.75	1.50
210-213-Mutant Massacre	.40	1.25	2.50
214-224		.60	1.20
225-227: Fall Of The Mutants	.35	1.00	2.00
228-230		.50	1.00
Annual 3(2/80)	1.10	3.25	6.50
Annual 4(11/80)	.90	2.75	5.50
Annual 5(10/81)	.70	2.00	4.00
Annual 6(11/82)	.45	1.40	2.80
Annual 7(1/84), 8(12/84)	.40	1.25	2.50
Annual 9(1985)-New Mutants; Art Adams-a	.85	2.75	5.50
Annual 10(1/87)-Art Adams-a	.85	2.75	5.50
Annual 11(11/87)	.25	.80	1.60
Giant-Size 1(Summer,'75, 50 cents)-1st app. new X-Men; Intro Nightcrawler, Storm, Colossus & Thunderbird; Wolverine app.	13.50	34.00	95.00
Giant-Size 2(11/75)-51 pgs. Adams-a(r)	2.65	8.00	18.00
Special 1(12/70)-Kirby-c/a; origin The Stranger	2.65	8.00	18.00
Special 2(11/71)	2.65	8.00	18.00

NOTE: ***Art Adams*** *a-Annual 9, 10p.* ***Adams*** *c-56-63.* ***Adkins*** *c-34.* ***Austin*** *a-108i, 109i, 111-17i, 119-43i, 196i, 204i, Annual 3i, 7i, 9i; c-109-111i, 114-22i, 123, 124-41i, 142, 143, Annual 3i.* ***Buscema*** *c-42, 43p, 45p.* ***Byrne*** *a-108p, 109p, 111-43p; c-113-16p, 127p, 129p, 131-41p.* ***Ditko*** *a-90r.* ***Everett*** *c-73.* ***Golen*** *a-Annual 7p.* ***G. Kane*** *c(p)-33, 74-76, 79, 80, 94, 95.* ***Kirby*** *a(p)-1-17 (#12-17, 24, 27-29, 32, 67r-layouts); c(p)-1-22, 25, 26, 30, 31, 35.* ***Layton*** *a-105i; c-112i, 113i.* ***Miller*** *c-Annual 3.* ***Perez*** *c/a-Annual 3p; c-112p, 128p, Annual 3p.* ***Roussos*** *a-84i.* ***Simonson*** *a-171p; c-171.* ***B. Smith*** *a-198, 205, 214; c-186, 198.* ***Paul Smith*** *a-165-70p, 172-75p; c-165-70, 172-75.* ***Sparling*** *a-78p.* ***Steranko*** *a-50p, 51p; c-49-51.* ***Sutton*** *a-106i.* ***Toth*** *a-12p, 67p(r).* ***Tuska*** *a-40-42i, 44-46p, 88i(r); c-39-41, 77p, 78p.* ***Williamson*** *a-202i, 203i, 211i; c-202i, 203i, 206i.* ***Wood*** *c-14i. 25 cent & 30 cent issues of No. 98 & 99 exist.*

X-MEN AND ALPHA FLIGHT
Jan, 1986 - No. 2, Jan, 1986 ($1.50 cover; mini-series)
Marvel Comics Group

	Good	Fine	Mint
1,2: 1-Intro The Berserkers; Paul Smith-a	.50	1.50	3.00

X-MEN AND THE MICRONAUTS, THE
Jan, 1984 - No. 4, April, 1984 (mini-series)
Marvel Comics Group

	Good	Fine	Mint
1-Guice-c/a(p) in all	.30	.90	1.80
2-4		.60	1.20

X-MEN CLASSICS
Dec, 1983 - No. 3, Feb, 1984 ($2.00; Baxter paper)
Marvel Comics Group

	Good	Fine	Mint
1-3: Adams-r/X-Men	.50	1.50	3.00

X-MEN VS. THE AVENGERS
Apr, 1987 - No. 4, July, 1987 (4 issue mini-series)(Baxter paper)
Marvel Comics Group

	Good	Fine	Mint
1	.60	1.75	3.50
2-4	.40	1.25	2.50

X, THE MAN WITH THE X-RAY EYES (See Movie Comics)

X-VENTURE
July, 1947 - No. 2, Nov, 1947 (Super heroes)
Victory Magazines Corp.

	Good	Fine	Mint
1-Atom Wizard, Mystery Shadow, Lester Trumble	22.00	65.00	154.00
2	13.50	40.00	95.00

XYR
Nov, 1987 (52pgs., $3.95, color)
Eclipse Comics

	Good	Fine	Mint
1-Multiple ending comic	.70	2.00	3.95

YAK YAK (See 4-Color No. 1186,1348)

YAKKY DOODLE & CHOPPER (TV)
Dec, 1962 (Hanna-Barbera)
Gold Key

	Good	Fine	Mint
1	2.00	6.00	14.00

YALTA TO KOREA
1952 (8 pgs.) (Giveaway) (paper cover)
M. Phillip Corp. (Republican National Committee)

	Good	Fine	Mint
Anti-communist propaganda book	15.00	45.00	90.00

X-Men #121, © MCG

X-Men #168, © MCG

Giant-Size X-Men #1, © MCG

Yogi Bear #6 (Dell), © Hanna-Barbera

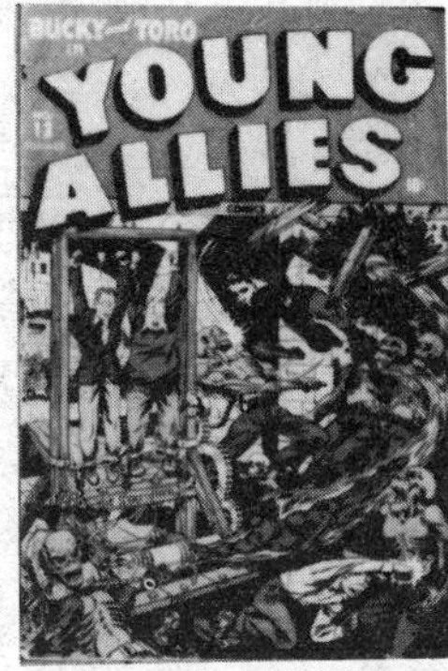

Young Allies Comics #13, © MCG

The Young All-Stars #2, © DC

YANG (See House of Yang)
11/73 - No. 13, 5/76; V14/14, 9/85 - No. 17, 1/86
Charlton Comics

	Good	Fine	Mint
1-Origin		.50	1.00
2-5		.30	.60
6-13(1976)		.20	.40
14-17(1986)		.40	.80
3,10,11(Modern Comics-r, 1977)		.15	.30

YANKEE COMICS
Sept, 1941 - No. 4, Mar, 1942
Harry 'A' Chesler

	Good	Fine	Mint
1-Origin The Echo, The Enchanted Dagger, Yankee Doodle Jones, The Firebrand, & The Scarlet Sentry; Black Satan app.	35.00	105.00	245.00
2-Origin Johnny Rebel; Major Victory app.; Barry Kuda begins	21.00	62.00	148.00
3,4	17.00	51.00	120.00
4 (nd, '40s; 7¼x5", 68pgs, distr. to the service)-Foxy Grandpa, Tom, Dick & Harry, Impy, Ace & Deuce, Dot & Dash, Ima Slooth by Jack Cole (Remington Morse publ.)	1.70	5.00	12.00

YANKS IN BATTLE
Sept, 1956 - No. 4, Dec, 1956
Quality Comics Group

	Good	Fine	Mint
1	2.50	7.50	17.00
2-4	1.20	3.50	8.00

YANKS IN BATTLE
1963
I. W. Enterprises

	Good	Fine	Mint
Reprint #3	.25	.75	1.50

YARDBIRDS, THE (G. I. Joe's Sidekicks)
Summer, 1952
Ziff-Davis Publishing Co.

	Good	Fine	Mint
1-By Bob Oskner	3.50	10.50	24.00

YARNS OF YELLOWSTONE
1972 (36 pages) (50 cents)
World Color Press

	Good	Fine	Mint
Ill. by Bill Chapman	.50	1.50	3.00

YELLOW CLAW
Oct, 1956 - No. 4, April, 1957
Atlas Comics (MjMC)

	Good	Fine	Mint
1-Origin by Joe Maneely	19.00	57.00	132.00
2-Kirby-a	16.00	48.00	110.00
3,4-Kirby-a; 4-Kirby/Severin-a	14.00	42.00	100.00

NOTE: ***Everett** c-3. **Maneely** c-1. **Reinman** a-2i, 3. **Severin** c-2, 4.*

YELLOWJACKET COMICS (Jack in the Box #11 on)
Sept, 1944 - No. 10, June, 1946
E. Levy/Frank Comunale

	Good	Fine	Mint
1-Origin Yellowjacket; Diana, the Huntress begins	13.00	40.00	90.00
2	8.00	24.00	56.00
3,5	7.00	21.00	50.00
4-Poe's 'Fall Of The House Of Usher' adaptation	8.00	24.00	56.00
6-10: 7,8-Has stories narrated by old witch in 'Tales of Terror'	6.50	19.50	45.00

YELLOWSTONE KELLY (See 4-Color No. 1056)

YELLOW SUBMARINE (See Movie Comics)

YOGI BEAR (TV) (Hanna-Barbera)
No. 1067, 12-2/59-60 - No. 9, 7-9/62; No. 10, 10/62 - No. 42, 10/70
Dell Publishing Co./Gold Key No. 10 on

	Good	Fine	Mint
4-Color 1067	2.65	8.00	18.00
4-Color 1104,1162 (5-7/61)	1.70	5.00	12.00
4(8-9/61) - 6(12-1/61-62)	1.50	4.50	10.00
4-Color 1271(11/61), 1349(1/62)	1.50	4.50	10.00
7(2-3/62) - 9(7-9/62)-Last Dell	1.15	3.50	8.00
10(10/62-G.K.), 11(1/63)-titled "Y.B. Jellystone Jollies"-80 pgs.	1.75	5.25	14.00
12(4/63), 14-20	1.00	3.00	6.00
13(7/63)-Surprise Party, 68 pgs.	1.75	5.25	14.00
21-30	.55	1.65	4.00
31-42	.45	1.25	3.00
...Kite Fun Book('62, 16 pgs., soft-c)	1.00	3.00	6.00

YOGI BEAR (See Dell Giant #41, March of Comics #253, 265, 279, 291, 309, 319, 337, 344, Whitman Comic Books & Movie Comics under "Hey There It's...")

YOGI BEAR (TV)
Nov, 1970 - No. 35, Jan, 1976 (Hanna-Barbera)
Charlton Comics

	Good	Fine	Mint
1	.70	2.00	4.00
2-6,8-35: 28-31-partial-r	.35	1.00	2.00
7-Summer Fun (Giant); 52 pgs.	.35	1.00	2.00

YOGI BEAR (TV)(See The Flintstones, 3rd series)
Nov, 1977 - No. 9, Mar, 1979
Marvel Comics Group

	Good	Fine	Mint
1-Flintstones begin		.40	.80
2-9		.20	.40

YOGI BEAR'S EASTER PARADE (See The Funtastic World of Hanna-Barbera #2)

YOGI BERRA (Baseball hero)
1951 (Yankee catcher)
Fawcett Publications

	Good	Fine	Mint
nn	20.00	60.00	140.00

YOSEMITE SAM (...& Bugs Bunny)
Dec, 1970 - No. 81, Feb, 1984
Gold Key/Whitman

	Good	Fine	Mint
1	.70	2.00	4.00
2-10	.40	1.25	2.50
11-30		.60	1.20
31-81: 81-r(⅓)		.30	.60

(See March of Comics No. 363,380,392)

YOUNG ALLIES COMICS (All-Winners #21)
Summer, 1941 - No. 20, Oct, 1946
Timely Comics (USA 1-7/NPI 8,9/YAI 10-20)

	Good	Fine	Mint
1-Origin The Young Allies; 1st meeting of Capt. America & Human Torch; Red Skull app.; S&K c/splash	205.00	615.00	1435.00
2-Captain America & Human Torch app.; Simon & Kirby-c	90.00	270.00	630.00
3-Fathertime, Captain America & Human Torch app.	73.00	220.00	510.00
4-The Vagabond & Red Skull, Capt. America, Human Torch app.	57.00	170.00	400.00
5-Captain America & Human Torch app.	42.00	125.00	295.00
6-10: 10-Origin Tommy Tyme & Clock of Ages; ends #19	32.00	95.00	225.00
11-20: 12-Classic decapitation story	25.00	75.00	175.00

YOUNG ALL-STARS
June, 1987 - Present ($1.00, deluxe format, color)
DC Comics

	Good	Fine	Mint
1	.70	2.00	4.00
2,3	.50	1.50	3.00
4-7: 7 ($1.25)	.25	.75	1.50
8-10		.60	1.20

YOUNG BRIDES
Sept-Oct, 1952 - No. 29, Jul-Aug, 1956 (Photo-c #1-3)
Feature/Prize Publications

	Good	Fine	Mint
V1#1-Simon & Kirby-a	5.70	17.00	40.00
2-S&K-a	3.00	9.00	21.00
3-6-S&K-a	2.65	8.00	18.00
V2#1,3-7,10-12 (#7-18)-S&K-a	2.15	6.50	15.00
2,8,9-No S&K-a	1.00	3.00	7.00
V3#1-3(#19-21)-Last precode (3-4/55)	.85	2.50	6.00
4,6(#22,24), V4#1,3(#25,27)	.75	2.25	5.00
V3#5(#23)-Meskin-c	1.15	3.50	8.00
V4#2(#26-All S&K ish	2.00	6.00	14.00
V4#4(#28)-S&K-a, V4#5(#29)	1.15	3.50	8.00

YOUNG DR. MASTERS (See Advs. of Young Dr. Masters)

YOUNG DOCTORS, THE
January, 1963 - No. 6, Nov, 1963
Charlton Comics

	Good	Fine	Mint
V1#1-6		.40	.80

YOUNG EAGLE
12/50 - No. 10, 6/52; No. 3, 7/56 - No. 5, 4/57 (Photo-c, 1-10)
Fawcett Publications/Charlton

	Good	Fine	Mint
1	5.70	17.00	40.00
2	3.50	10.50	24.00
3-9	2.65	8.00	18.00
10-Origin Thunder, Young Eagle's Horse	2.35	7.00	16.00
3-5(Charlton)-Formerly Sherlock Holmes?	1.00	3.00	7.00

YOUNG HEARTS
Nov, 1949 - No. 2, Feb, 1950
Marvel Comics (SPC)

	Good	Fine	Mint
1-Photo-c	3.00	9.00	21.00
2	1.60	4.70	11.00

YOUNG HEARTS IN LOVE
1964
Super Comics

	Good	Fine	Mint
17,18-17-r/Young Love V5#6, 4-5/62	.25	.75	1.50

YOUNG HEROES (Formerly Forbidden Worlds #34)
No. 35, Feb-Mar, 1955 - No. 37, June-July, 1955
American Comics Group (Titan)

	Good	Fine	Mint
35-37-Frontier Scout	1.30	4.00	9.00

YOUNG KING COLE (Becomes Criminals on the Run)
Fall, 1945 - V3/12, July, 1948
Premium Group/Novelty Press

	Good	Fine	Mint
V1#1-Toni Gayle begins	6.00	18.00	42.00
2	4.00	12.00	28.00
3-6	3.50	10.50	24.00
V2#1-7(7/47)	2.65	8.00	18.00
V3#1,3-6,12	2.00	6.00	14.00
2-L.B. Cole-a	2.65	8.00	18.00
7-L.B. Cole-c/a	4.00	12.00	28.00
8-11-L.B. Cole-c	3.35	10.00	23.00

YOUNG LAWYERS, THE (TV)
Jan, 1971 - No. 2, April, 1971
Dell Publishing co.

	Good	Fine	Mint
1,2	1.15	3.50	8.00

YOUNG LIFE (Teen Life #3 on)
Spring, 1945 - No. 2, Summer, 1945
New Age Publ./Quality Comics Group

	Good	Fine	Mint
1-Skip Homeier, Louis Prima stories	3.50	10.50	24.00
2-Frank Sinatra c/story	2.65	8.00	18.00

YOUNG LOVE
2-3/49 - No. 73, 12-1/56-57; V3#5, 2-3/60 - V7#1, 6-7/63
Prize(Feature)Publ.(Crestwood)

	Good	Fine	Mint
V1#1-S&K c/a(2)	10.00	30.00	70.00
2-Photo-c begin; S&K-a	4.35	13.00	30.00
3-S&K-a	3.00	9.00	21.00
4-5-Minor S&K-a	2.15	6.50	15.00
V2#1(#7)-S&K-a	3.00	9.00	21.00
2-5(#8-11)-Minor S&K-a	1.70	5.00	12.00
6,8(#12,14)-S&K-c only	2.15	6.50	15.00
7,9-12(#13,15-18)-S&K c/a	3.00	9.00	21.00
V3#1-4(#19-22)-S&K c/a	2.15	6.50	15.00
5-7,9-12(#23-25,27-30)-Photo-c resume; S&K-a	1.70	5.00	12.00
8(#26)-No S&K	1.30	4.00	9.00
V4#1,6(#31,36)-S&K-a	1.70	5.00	12.00
2-5,7-12(#32-35,37-42)-Minor S&K-a	1.50	4.50	10.00
V5#1-12(#43-54), V6#1-9(#55-63)-Last precode; S&K-a-some	1.15	3.50	8.00
V6#10-12(#64-66)	1.00	3.00	7.00
V7#1-7(#67-73)	.55	1.65	4.00
V3#5(2-3/60),6(4-5/60)(Formerly All For Love)	.45	1.35	3.00
V4#1(6-7/60)-6(4-5/61)	.45	1.35	3.00
V5#1(6-7/61)-6(4-5/62)	.45	1.35	3.00
V6#1(6-7/62)-6(4-5/63), V7#1	.35	1.00	2.00

NOTE: ***Severin/Elder*** *a-V1#3.* ***S&K*** *art not in #53, 57, 58, 61, 63-65.* ***Meskin*** *a-27. Photo c-V3#5-V5#11.*

YOUNG LOVE
#39, 9-10/63 - #120, Wint./75-76; #121, 10/76 - #126, 7/77
National Periodical Publ.(Arleigh Publ. Corp #49-60)/DC Comics

	Good	Fine	Mint
39-50	.50	1.50	3.00
51-70: 64-Simon & Kirby-a	.25	.75	1.50
71,72,74-77,80		.40	.80
73,78,79-Toth-a		.60	1.20
81-126: 107-114 (100 pgs.). 122-Toth-a		.30	.60

YOUNG LOVER ROMANCES (Formerly & becomes Great Lover. . ?)
No. 4, June, 1952 - No. 5, Aug, 1952
Toby Press

	Good	Fine	Mint
4,5-Photo-c	1.30	4.00	9.00

YOUNG LOVERS (My Secret Life #19 on)
No. 16, 7/56 - No. 18, 5/57 (Formerly Brenda Starr?)
Charlton Comics

	Good	Fine	Mint
16,17('56)	1.30	4.00	9.00
18-Elvis Presley picture-c, text story (biography)	23.00	70.00	160.00

YOUNG MARRIAGE
June, 1950
Fawcett Publications

	Good	Fine	Mint
1-Powell-a; photo-c	4.00	12.00	28.00

YOUNG MEN (Formerly Cowboy Romances)(. . .on the Battlefield #12-20(4/53);. . .In Action #21)
No. 4, 6/50 - No. 11, 10/51; NO.12, 12/51 - No. 28, 6/54
Marvel/Atlas Comics (IPC)

	Good	Fine	Mint
4	3.50	10.50	24.00
5-11	1.85	5.50	13.00
12-23	1.60	4.70	11.00
24-Origin Captain America, Human Torch, & Sub-Mariner which are revived thru #28. Red Skull app.	27.00	80.00	190.00
25-28	20.00	60.00	140.00

NOTE: ***Berg*** *a-7, 17, 20; c-17.* ***Colan*** *a-15. Sub-Mariner by* ***Everett-#24-28. Everett*** *a-18-20.* ***Heath*** *a-14.* ***Maneely*** *c-15.*

YOUNG REBELS, THE (TV)
January, 1971
Dell Publishing Co.

	Good	Fine	Mint
1-Photo-c	1.00	3.00	6.00

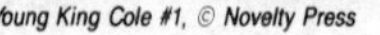
Young King Cole #1, © Novelty Press

Young Love #27, © PRIZE

Young Men #24, © MCG

Young Romance Comics #45, © PRIZE

Zane Grey's Stories of the West #39, © DELL

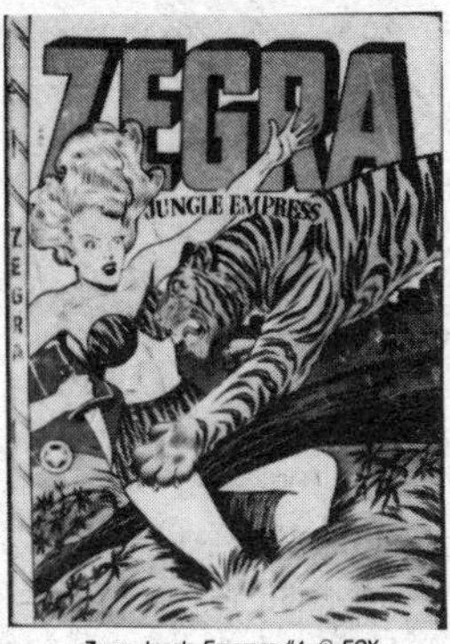

Zegra Jungle Empress #4, © FOX

YOUNG ROMANCE COMICS (The 1st romance comic)
Sept-Oct, 1947 - V16#4, June-July, 1963
Prize/Headline (Feature Publ.)

	Good	Fine	Mint
V1#1-S&K c/a(2)	11.50	34.00	80.00
2-S&K c/a(2-3)	6.50	19.50	45.00
3-6-S&K c/a(2-3) each	5.00	15.00	35.00
V2#1-6(#7-12)-S&K c/a(2-3) each	4.35	13.00	30.00
V3#1-3(#13-15)-Last line drawn-c; S&K c/a	2.15	6.50	15.00
4-12(#16-24)-Photo-c; S&K-a	2.15	6.50	15.00
V4#1-11(#25-35)-S&K-a	1.70	5.00	12.00
12(#36)-S&K, Toth-a	4.00	12.00	28.00
V5#1-12(#37-48), V6#4-12(#52-60)-S&K-a	1.70	5.00	12.00
V6#1-3(#49-51)-No S&K-a	1.50	4.50	10.00
V7#1-11(#61-71)-S&K-a in most	1.70	5.00	12.00
V7#12(#72), V8#1-3(#73-75)-Last precode (12-1/54-55)-No S&K-a	1.00	3.00	7.00
V8#4(#76, 4-5/55), 5(#77)-No S&K	.85	2.50	6.00
V8#6-8(#78-80, 12-1/55-56)-S&K-a	1.30	4.00	9.00
V9#3,5,6(#81, 2-3/56, 83,84)-S&K-a	1.15	3.50	8.00
4, V10#1(#82,85)-All S&K-a	1.50	4.50	10.00
V10#2-6(#86-90, 10-11/57)-S&K-a	1.15	3.50	8.00
V11#1,2,5,6(#91,92,95,96)-S&K-a	1.15	3.50	8.00
3,4(#93,94), V12#2,4,5(#98,100,101)-No S&K	.85	2.50	6.00
V12#1,3,6(#97,99,102)-S&K-a	1.15	3.50	8.00
V13#1(#103)-S&K, Powell-a	1.30	4.00	9.00
2-6(#104-108)	.45	1.35	3.00
V14#1-6, V15#1-6, V16#1-4(#109-124)	.35	1.00	2.00

NOTE: ***Meskin** a-16, 24(2), 47. **Robinson/Meskin** a-6. **Leonard Starr** a-11. Photo c-16-65.*

YOUNG ROMANCE COMICS
No. 125, Aug-Sept, 1963 - No. 208, Nov-Dec, 1975
National Periodical Publ.(Arleigh Publ. Corp. No. 127)

	Good	Fine	Mint
125-153,155-162	.40	1.20	2.40
154-Adams-c	.50	1.50	3.00
163,164-Toth-a		.50	1.00
165-196: 170-Michell from Young Love ends; Lily Martin, the Swinger begins		.40	.80
197 (100 pgs.)-208		.25	.50

YOUR DREAMS (See Strange World of . . .)

YOUR TRIP TO NEWSPAPERLAND
June, 1955 (12 pgs.; 14x11½")
Philadelphia Evening Bulletin (Printed by Harvey Press)

	Good	Fine	Mint
Joe Palooka takes kids on tour through newspaper	2.65	8.00	18.00

YOUR UNITED STATES
1946
Lloyd Jacquet Studios

	Good	Fine	Mint
Used in **SOTI**, pg. 309,310; Sid Greene-a	10.00	30.00	70.00

YOUTHFUL HEARTS (Daring Confessions #4 on)
May, 1952 - No. 3, 1952
Youthful Magazines

	Good	Fine	Mint
1-"Monkey on Her Back" swipes E.C. drug story from Shock SuspenStories #12	10.00	30.00	70.00
2,3	4.60	14.00	32.00

NOTE: ***Doug Wildey** art in all.*

YOUTHFUL LOVE (Truthful Love #2)
May, 1950
Youthful Magazines

	Good	Fine	Mint
1	3.00	9.00	21.00

YOUTHFUL ROMANCES (Daring Love #15 & 17)
8-9/49 - No. 14, 10/52; #16, 3/53; #18, 7/53 - No. 8, 5/54
Pix-Parade #-14/Ribage

	Good	Fine	Mint
1-(1st ser.)-Titled Youthful Love-Romances	7.00	21.00	50.00
2	4.00	12.00	28.00
3-5	3.50	10.50	24.00
6,7,9-14(10/52, Pix-Parade; becomes Daring Love #15)	2.30	7.00	16.00
8-Wood-c	8.50	25.50	60.00
16(3/53, Ribage; Formerly Daring Love #15; becomes Daring Love #17)	2.35	7.00	16.00
18(7/53, Ribage; formerly Daring Love #17)	2.35	7.00	16.00
5(9/53, Ribage)	1.85	5.50	13.00
6,7(#7, 2/54)	1.50	4.50	10.00
8(5/54)	1.50	4.50	10.00

ZAGO, JUNGLE PRINCE (My Story #5 on)
Sept, 1948 - No. 4, March, 1949
Fox Features Syndicate

	Good	Fine	Mint
1-Blue Beetle app.-partial r-/Atomic #4 (Toni Luck)	14.00	42.00	100.00
2,3-Kamen-a	11.00	32.00	76.00
4-Baker-c	10.00	30.00	70.00

ZANE GREY'S STORIES OF THE WEST
No. 197, 9/48 - 11/64 (All painted-c)
Dell Publishing Co./Gold Key 11/64

	Good	Fine	Mint
4-Color 197(9/48)	5.00	15.00	35.00
4-Color 222,230,236('49)	4.00	12.00	28.00
4-Color 246,255,270,301,314,333,346	3.00	9.00	21.00
4-Color 357,372,395,412,433,449,467,484	2.30	7.00	16.00
4-Color 511-Kinstler-a	2.65	8.00	18.00
4-Color 532,555,583,604,616,632(5/55)	2.30	7.00	16.00
27(9-11/55) - 39(9-11/58)	2.00	6.00	14.00
4-Color 996(5-7/59)	2.00	6.00	14.00
10131-411-(11/64-G.K.)-Nevada; r-4-Color #996	1.15	3.50	8.00

ZANY (Magazine)(Satire)(See Ratfink & Frantic)
Sept, 1958 - No. 4, May, 1959
Candor Publ. Co.

	Good	Fine	Mint
1-Bill Everett-c	2.65	8.00	18.00
2-4	1.50	4.50	10.00

ZATANNA SPECIAL
1987 (One shot, $2.00)
DC Comics

	Good	Fine	Mint
1	.35	1.00	2.00

ZAZA, THE MYSTIC (Formerly Charlie Chan; This Magazine is Haunted V2#12 on)
April, 1956 - No. 11, Sept, 1956
Charlton Comics

	Good	Fine	Mint
10,11	2.65	8.00	18.00

ZEGRA JUNGLE EMPRESS (Formerly Tegra)(My Love Life #6 on)
No. 2, Oct, 1948 - No. 5, April, 1949
Fox Features Syndicate

	Good	Fine	Mint
2	17.00	51.00	120.00
3-5	12.00	36.00	84.00

ZERO PATROL, THE
Nov, 1984 - Present ($2.00, color)
Continuity Comics

	Good	Fine	Mint
1-5: Adams c/a	.35	1.00	2.00

ZIGGY PIG-SILLY SEAL COMICS (See Animated Movie-Tunes, Krazy Komics & Silly Tunes)
Fall, 1944 - No. 6, Fall, 1946
Timely Comics (CmPL)

	Good	Fine	Mint
1-Vs. the Japs	6.50	19.50	45.00
2	3.00	9.00	21.00

ZIGGY PIG-SILLY SEAL COMICS (cont.)

	Good	Fine	Mint
3-5	2.65	8.00	18.00
6-Infinity-c	5.00	15.00	35.00
I.W. Reprint #1('58)-r/Krazy Komics	.50	1.50	3.00
I.W. Reprint #2,7,8	.25	.75	1.50

ZIP COMICS
Feb, 1940 - No. 47, Summer, 1944
MLJ Magazines

	Good	Fine	Mint
1-Origin Kalathar the Giant Man, The Scarlet Avenger, & Steel Sterling; Mr. Satan, Nevada Jones & Zambini, the Miracle Man, War Eagle, Captain Valor begins	86.00	260.00	600.00
2	42.00	125.00	295.00
3	33.00	100.00	230.00
4,5	28.00	84.00	195.00
6-9: 9-Last Kalthar & Mr. Satan	24.00	72.00	170.00
10-Inferno, the Flame Breather begins, ends #13	22.00	65.00	154.00
11,12: 11-Inferno without costume	20.00	60.00	140.00
13-17,19: 17-Last Scarlet Avenger	20.00	60.00	140.00
18-Wilbur begins (1st app.)	22.00	65.00	154.00
20-Origin Black Jack (1st app.)	30.00	90.00	210.00
21-26: 25-Last Nevada Jones. 26-Black Witch begins; last Captain Valor	19.00	57.00	132.00
27-Intro. Web	28.00	84.00	195.00
28-Origin Web	28.00	84.00	195.00
29,30	16.00	48.00	110.00
31-38: 34-1st Applejack app. 35-Last Zambini, Black Jack. 38-Last Web issue	12.00	36.00	84.00
39-Origin Red Rube (8/43)	12.00	36.00	84.00
40-47: 45-Wilbur ends	8.00	24.00	56.00

NOTE: ***Biro*** *a-5, 9, 17; c-5, 9.* ***Meskin*** *a-1-3, 5-7, 9, 10, 12, 13, 15, 16 at least. Bondage c-8, 9, 33, 34.*

ZIP-JET (Hero)
Feb, 1953 - No. 2, Apr-May, 1953
St. John Publishing Co.

	Good	Fine	Mint
1,2-Rocketman-r/Punch Comics; #1-c from splash in Punch #10	13.00	40.00	90.00

ZIPPY THE CHIMP (CBS TV Presents. . .)
No. 50, March, 1957 - No. 51, Aug, 1957
Pines (Literary Ent.)

	Good	Fine	Mint
50,51	1.15	3.50	8.00

ZODY, THE MOD ROB
July, 1970
Gold Key

	Good	Fine	Mint
1	.70	2.00	4.00

ZOO ANIMALS
No. 8, 1954 (36 pages; 15 cents)
Star Publications

	Good	Fine	Mint
8-(B&W for coloring)	1.30	4.00	9.00

ZOO FUNNIES (Tim McCoy #16 on)
Nov, 1945 - No. 15, 1947
Charlton Comics/Children Comics Publ.

	Good	Fine	Mint
101(#1)(1945)	4.00	12.00	28.00
2(9/45)	2.00	6.00	14.00
3-5	1.70	5.00	12.00
6-15: 8-Diana the Huntress app.	1.30	4.00	9.00

ZOO FUNNIES (Becomes Nyoka, The Jungle Girl #14 on?)
July, 1953 - No. 13, Sept, 1955; Dec, 1984
Capitol Stories/Charlton Comics

	Good	Fine	Mint
1-1st app.? Timothy The Ghost; Fago-c/a	3.00	9.00	21.00
2	1.50	4.50	10.00
3-7	1.15	3.50	8.00
8-13-Nyoka app.	3.00	9.00	21.00
1('84)		.40	.80

ZOONIVERSE
8/86 - No. 6, 6/87 ($1.25, color, mini-series; Mando paper)
Eclipse Comics

	Good	Fine	Mint
1-4		.65	1.30
5,6 ($1.70)	.25	.75	1.50

ZOO PARADE (See 4-Color No. 662)

ZOOM COMICS
December, 1945 (One Shot)
Carlton Publishing Co.

	Good	Fine	Mint
nn-Dr. Mercy, Satannas, from Red Band Comics; Capt. Milksop origin retold	13.00	40.00	90.00

ZOOT (Rulah #17 on)
nd (1946) - No. 16, July, 1948 (Two #13s & 14s)
Fox Features Syndicate

	Good	Fine	Mint
nn-Funny animal only	7.00	21.00	50.00
2-The Jaguar app.	6.00	18.00	42.00
3(Fall,'46) - 6-Funny animals & teen-age	3.50	10.50	24.00
7-Rulah, Jungle Goddess begins (6/47); origin & 1st app.	27.00	81.00	190.00
8-10	20.00	60.00	140.00
11-Kamen bondage-c	22.00	65.00	154.00
12-Injury-to-eye panels	13.00	40.00	90.00
13(2/48), 14(3/48)	13.00	40.00	90.00
13(4/48), 14(5/48)	13.00	40.00	90.00
15,16	13.00	40.00	90.00

ZORRO (Walt Disney with #882)(TV)(See Eclipse Graphic Album)
May, 1949 - No. 15, Sept-Nov, 1961 (Photo-c 882 on)
Dell Publishing Co.

	Good	Fine	Mint
4-Color 228	14.00	42.00	100.00
4-Color 425,497	6.50	19.50	45.00
4-Color 538-Kinstler-a	7.00	21.00	50.00
4-Color574,617,732	6.50	19.50	45.00
4-Color 882-Photo-c begin; Toth-a	5.00	15.00	35.00
4-Color 920,933,960,976-Toth-a in all	5.00	15.00	35.00
4-Color 1003('59)	4.00	12.00	28.00
4-Color 1037-Annette Funicello photo-c	6.50	19.50	45.00
8(12-2/59-60)	3.00	9.00	21.00
9,12-Toth-a	3.50	10.50	24.00
10,11,13-15-Last photo-c	2.30	7.00	16.00

NOTE: ***Warren Tufts*** *a-4-Color 1037, 8, 9, 13.*

ZORRO (Walt Disney)(TV)
Jan, 1966 - No. 9, March, 1968 (All photo-c)
Gold Key

	Good	Fine	Mint
1-Toth-a	2.35	7.00	16.00
2,4,5,7-9-Toth-a	1.75	5.25	12.00
3,6-Tufts-a	1.50	4.50	10.00

NOTE: *#1-9 are reprinted from Dell issues.* ***Tufts*** *a-3,4. #3-r/#12-c & #8 inside; #4-r/#9-c & insides; #6-r/#11(all); #7a-r/#14-c.*

ZOT!
4/84 - No. 10, 7/85; No. 11, 1/87 - Present ($1.50, Baxter paper)
Eclipse Comics

	Good	Fine	Mint
1	.45	1.30	2.60
2,3	.35	1.00	2.00
4-15: 4-Origin. 11 (New series begins)	.25	.75	1.50

Z-2 COMICS (Secret Agent. . .)(See Holyoke One-Shot No. 7)

ZULU (See Movie Classics)

Zip-Jet #1, © STJ

Zorro #7 (GK), © WDC

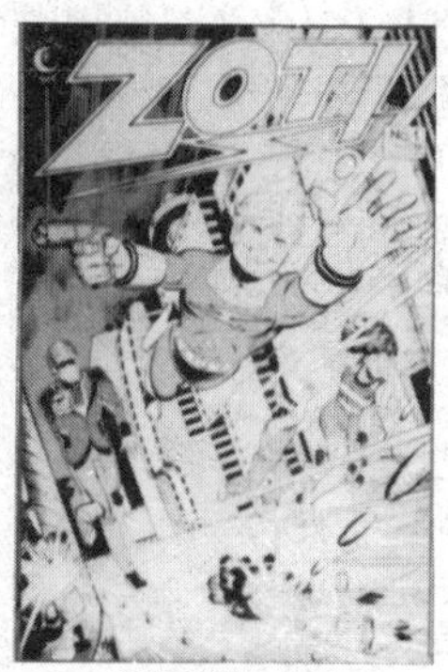

Zot! #1, © Eclipse Comics

DOUG SULIPA'S

comic world

175 Ashford Drive, Winnipeg, Manitoba Canada R2N 1K7
Ph: (204) 256-5713 (Moving our store; write for new address)

Over 1 MILLION comics in stock. Send 50¢ for my huge catalogue with the low, low prices and see why I have over 10,000 people on my mailing list. Marvel, D.C., Harvey, Dell, Mads, Classics Illustrated, Gold Key, Archie, Disneys, Charlton, Playboys, Pacific, esoteric comics, Warren magazines, Big Little Books, comic digests, Arkham House, hardcovers, Trek items, R.E.H. National Lampoons, etc., etc. We also buy and trade. Also specializing in rare paperbacks (SF, Mystery, Harlequin, TV, etc.)—Inquire.

FANTASY EXPRESS

NEW COMIC SUBSCRIPTIONS

20% OFF EVERYTHING TO ANYONE! 30% off if over $100.00 a month.

The most efficient, fast and progressive service with the best selection!!

ONE PICTURE IS WORTH 400,000 WORDS

FANTAZIA

Just let your imagination run wild . . . then TRIPLE IT!!!

2 So. Central Ave., Hartsdale, NY 10530

(914) 946-3306 Daniel $ Dupcak (914) 946-1236

EVER WONDER WHAT OVER $20,000,000 WORTH OF GOLD & SILVER AGE COMICS, SPORT/NON-SPORT CARDS & MEMORABILIA, & RECORDS WOULD LOOK LIKE ALL UNDER ONE ROOF? Where else in the world can you see Action 1-10's Superman 1-10's, Complete DC, Timely & Marvel Key, Origin, & First Appearance issues in your choice of grade as easily as most dealers can offer you X-Men 170 up? Who else can offer you a complete run of Captain America, Human Torch, Fantastic Four, Miller Daredevils or a plain old X-Men/Micronauts Mini Series with equal facility **at a moments notice?** Who indeed! . . . FANTAZIA . . . The only collector's shop in the universe that deserves the title ''Endless Convention.'' Stop by when in New York, it's worth the trip from anywhere in the country; we guarantee you won't be disappointed. Call for easy access directions from all N.Y. airports & railway systems as well as simple road directions.

If you're selling a collection, sell to us; the company that most dealers earn 90% of their yearly income from. Your books will probably wind up in our hands anyway; why **shouldn't** you be the one to benefit from increased dividends on your collection; eliminate the ''middle-man'' dealer! If you have one of our priority wants, and you're thinking of consignment to one of those services who can't afford to buy your book(s) outright and cons you into believing consignment is the ''best way to go,'' stop & think! We'll take items we want for a full 10% **above** the full projected precentage ''cut of sale price estimate'' you might or might not get 5 years down the road from ''efficient consignment'' services. And of course if you have a Superman 1, Action 1, Detective 1, 27, 29, 33, Marvel 1, All American 16, Flash 1, New Comics 1, New Fun 1-6, More Fun 52, All Star 3 or simply a nice small quality collection give us a call **LAST.** Once you get your **top** offer that's the time to call Fantazia and separate the men from the sheep! We'll go head to herd against any self-appointed ''low-ball grading'' (only when buying **your** books), ''sorry we have too many of these and can only pay 10% of guide this month,'' ''this isn't Mint,'' top prices paid dealers in the world; without the aces and wool up our sleeves. RHETORIC? HARDLY! Rhetoric doesn't sell 17 Superman 1's in a year, produce millions of dollars worth of books at the drop of a hat and manage maintaining a CBG Customer Service Award over thousands of mutual satisfaction transactions. Hard work and truly unlimited cash does; **our own!** Not our stock broker, banker, backers, partners, or loan sharks. That's what gives us the competitive edge on outbiding **anyone** on your collection. We've no one to answer to but ourselves and whether you buy or sell at Fantazia the benifits are yours. We work closer in profit margin than **any** other dealer(s) in the world. We have no ''extra mouths to feed'' when a purchase or sales is made. It's single arithmetic . . . Fantazia . . . you just can't do any better!

EXPENSIVE ITEMS ARE NOT LEFT OVERNIGHT IN STORE

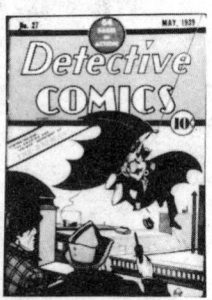

YOU'RE GONNA LOVE...

25 YEARS OF
X-TRAORDINARY
HISTORY
CONTINUES...
X-MEN™
X-FACTOR™
EXCALIBUR™
NEW MUTANTS™
WOLVERINE™
1963-1988
COMICS IN A CLASS
BY THEMSELVES.
FROM MARVEL®.

X-MEN
"IF ICEMAN SHOULD FAIL!"
THE X-MEN
THE SURPRISE OF THE YEAR!
IN THIS JAM-PACKED ISSUE, YOU WILL MEET... THE X-MEN'S NEW LEADER!
"THE RETURN OF THE BLOB!"
THE X-MEN
"WHERE WALKS THE JUGGERNAUT!"
X-MEN
SPECIAL GUEST STAR ISSUE
X-MEN
MORE DANGEROUS THAN EVER
STRIKE AGAIN!

Hit Comics #2, 1940. © QUA

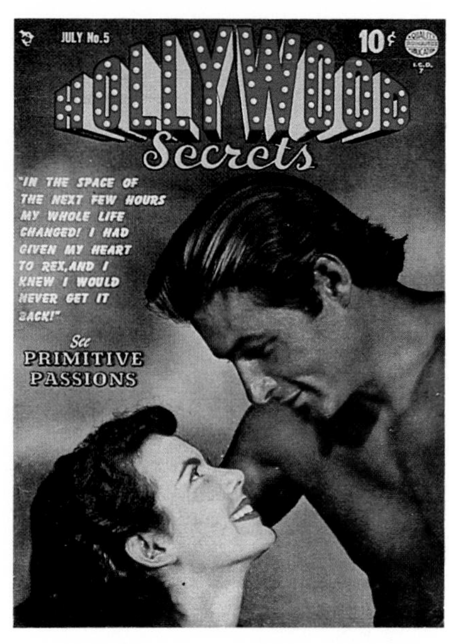

Hollywood Secrets #5, 1950. © QUA

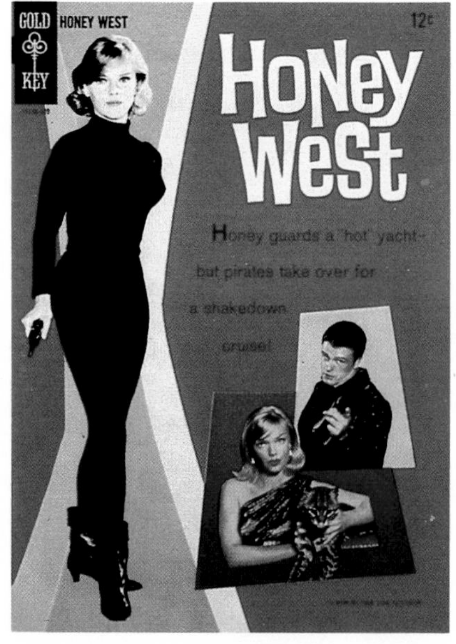

Honey West #1, 1966. © Four Star TV

The Human Torch #23, 1946. © MCG

Jackie Robinson #1, 1949. © FAW

The Jetsons #1, 1962. © Hanna-Barbera

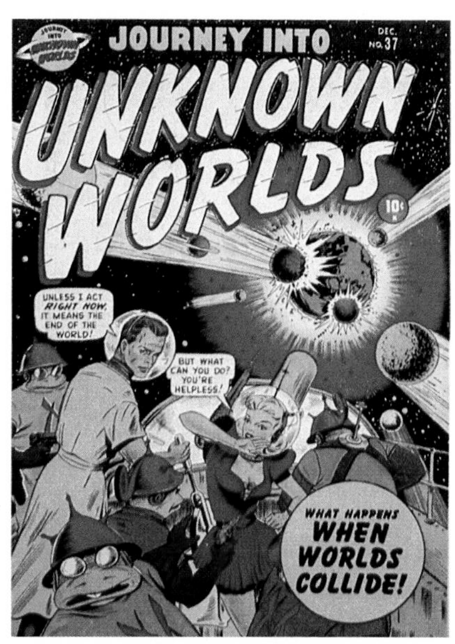

Journey Into Unknown Worlds #37(#2), 1950. © MCG

Jumbo Comics #133, 1950. © FH

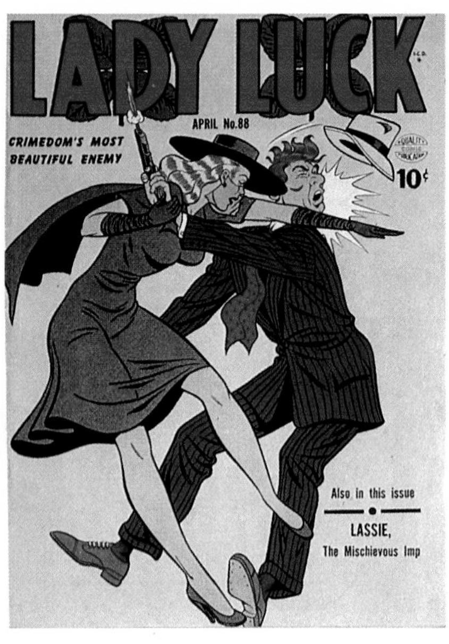

Lady Luck #88, 1950. © QUA

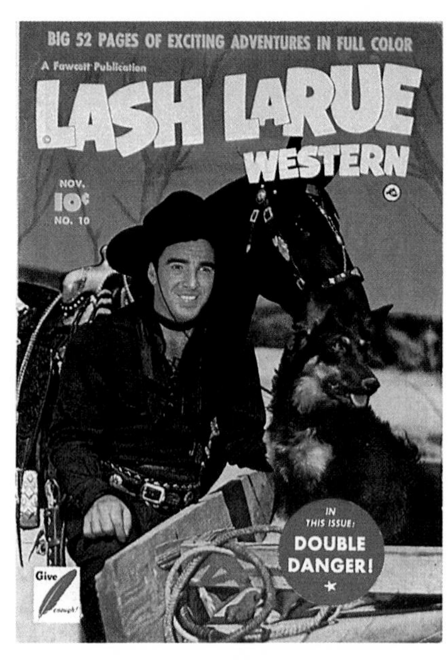

Lash LaRue Western #10, 1950. © FAW

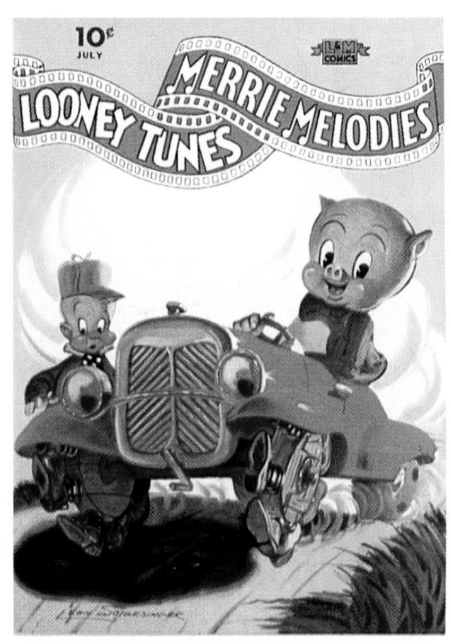

Looney Tunes #9, 1942. © Leon Schlesinger

The Marvel Family #60, 1951. © FAW

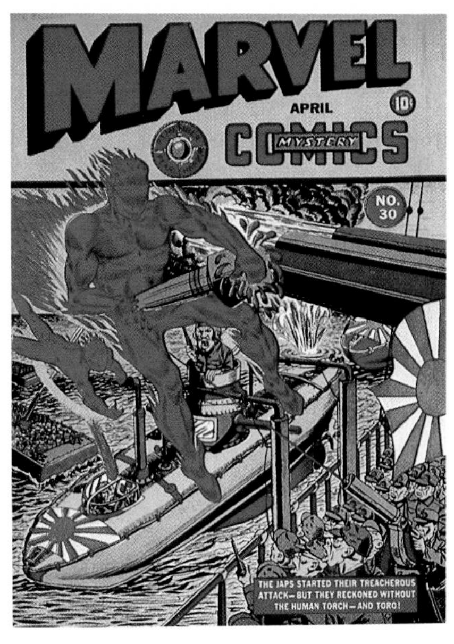

Marvel Mystery Comics #30, 1942. Remember Pearl Harbor issue. © MCG

Mighty Mouse (Dell Giant #43), 1961. © CBS

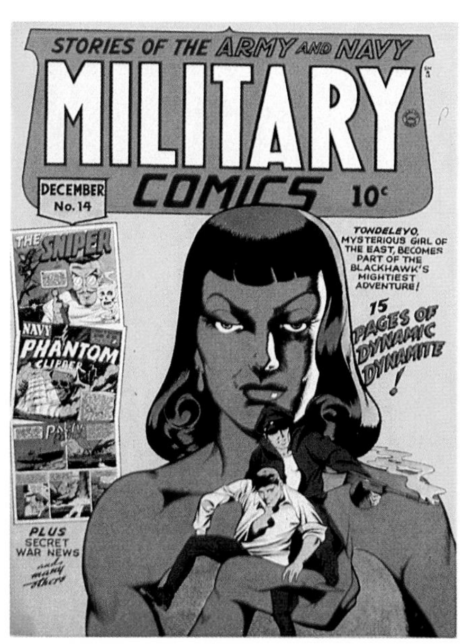

Military Comics #14, 1942. © QUA

Monte Hale Western #36, 1949. © FAW

More Fun Comics #87, 1943. © DC

Motion Picture Comics #102, 1951. © FAW

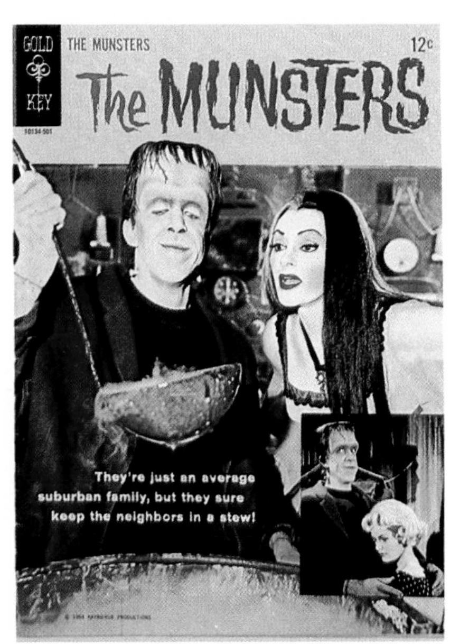

The Munsters #1, 1964. © Kayro-Vue Prod.

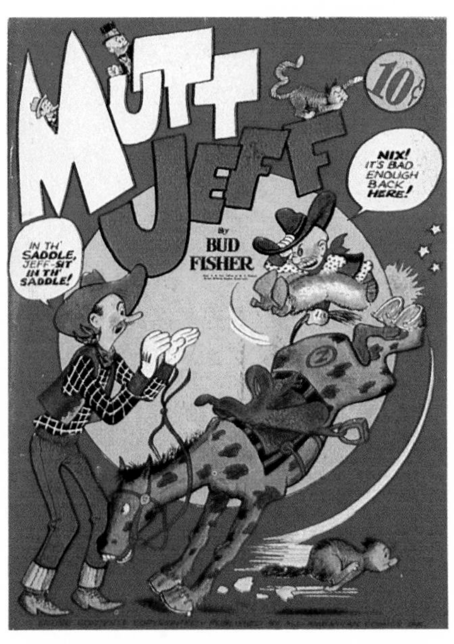

Mutt and Jeff #3, 1941. © Ball Synd.

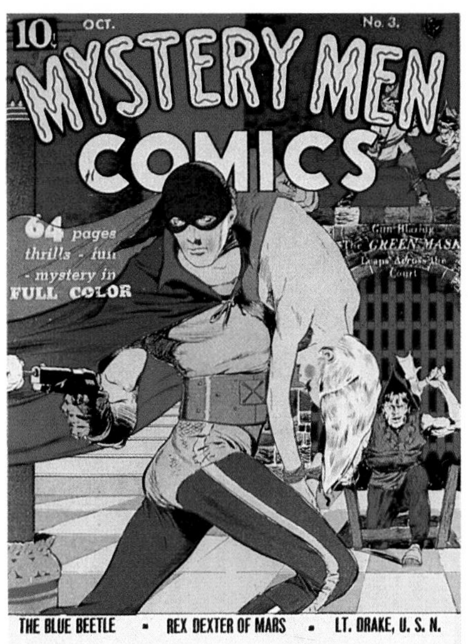

Mystery Men Comics #3, 1939. Lou Fine cover art. © FOX

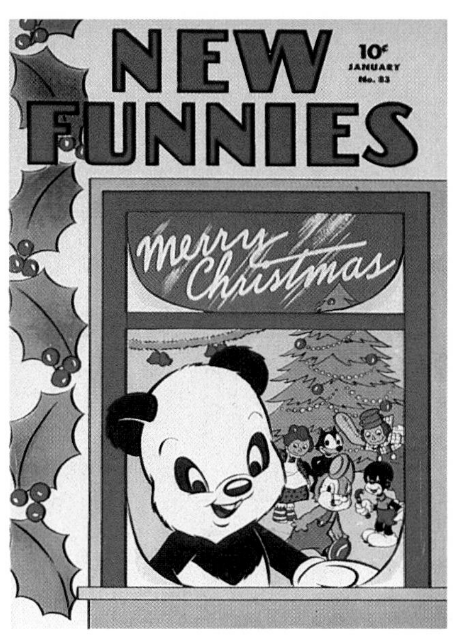

New Funnies #83, 1944. © Walter Lantz

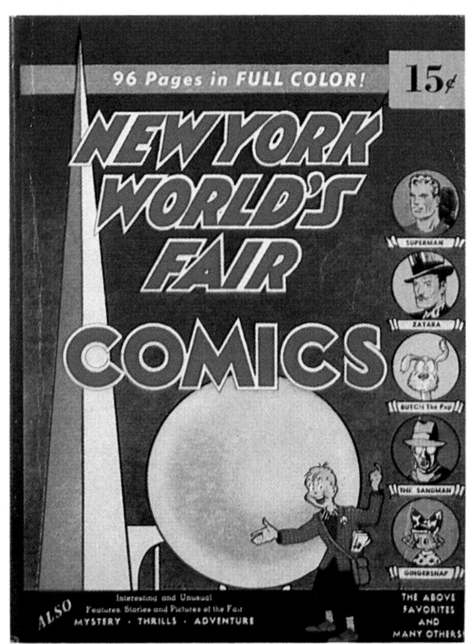

New York Worlds Fair 1939, 1939. © DC

Pep Comics #2, 1940. © AP

Peter Pan Treasure Chest 1953. © WDC

Phantom Lady #15, 1947. © FOX

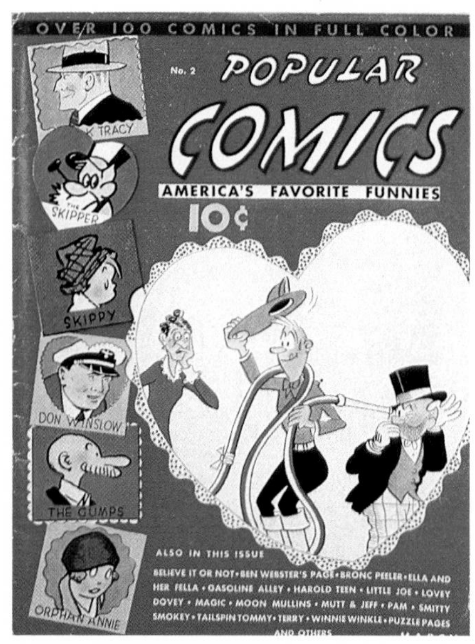

Popular Comics #2, 1936. © DELL

Peter Pan Treasure Chest 1953. © WDC

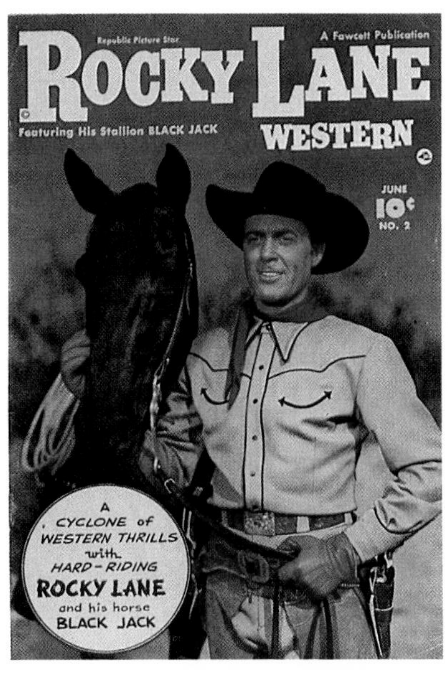

Rocky Lane Western #2, 1949. © FAW

Sensation Comics #38, 1945. © DC

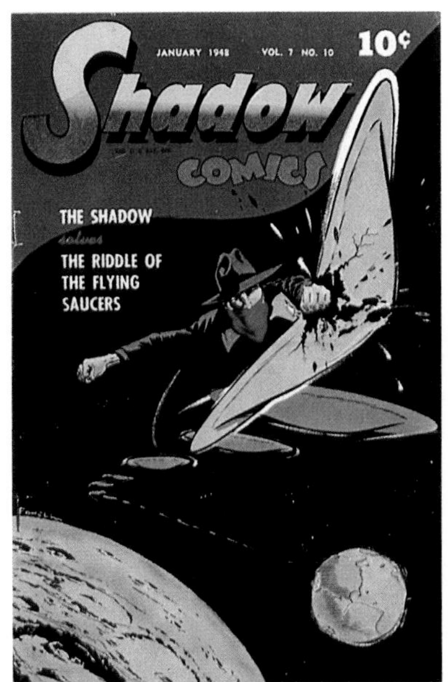

Shadow Comics V7#10, 1948. Bob Powell cover art. 2nd mention of flying saucers in comics. © S&S

Stars and Stripes #3, 7/41. © CEN

Sub-Mariner Comics #6, 1941. © MCG

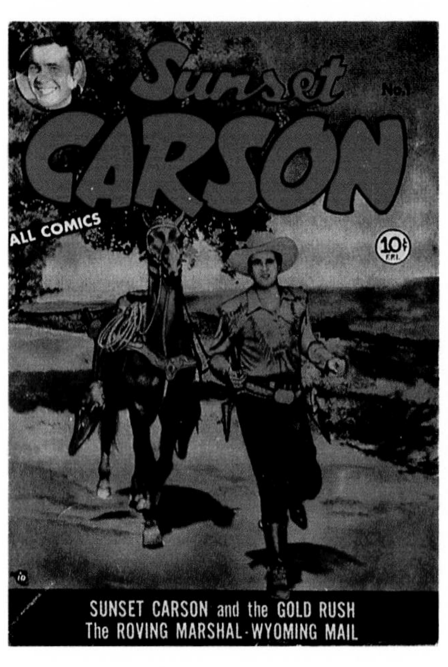

Sunset Carson #1, 1951. © CC

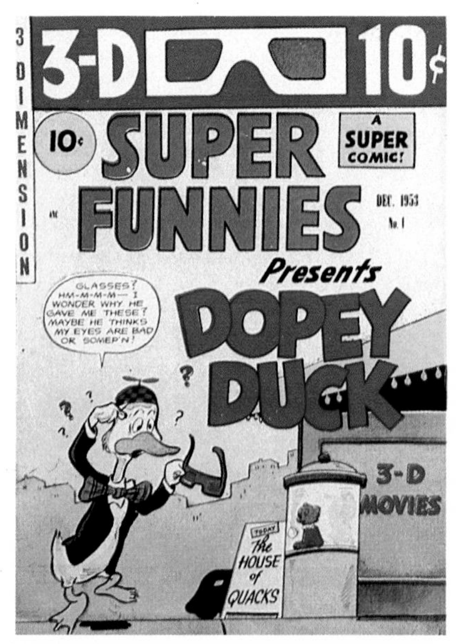

Super Funnies #1, 1953. © SUPR

Superman #5, 1940. © DC

WE'VE ALWAYS BEEN AMONG THE BEST.

NOW WE'RE AMONG THE BIGGEST ...

Funny Business, the Comic Book Emporium, is proud to announce our relocation to a new store, 5 times LARGER than our former store. Browse to your heart's content. Over half a million books in stock: Marvels, DCs, Independents, Classics ... tee shirts, buttons, records, portfolios, mylars, boxes, plastic bags ... you name it. The new address is 656 Amsterdam Ave., NYC, NY 10025; the phone number stays the same: 212-799-9477.

A visit to the new store will provide you with a once-in-a-lifetime experience. Visit our private Art Gallery. Original unpublished art by the finest comic artists in the World. See a Frank Miller *Dark Knight* done in 1984 before he did the book. See the works of Neal Adams, George Perez, Gil Kane, John Buscema, Walt Simonson, Mike Kaluta, Klaus Jansen, Paul Smith, Jose Garcia Lopez, Bill Sienkiewicz, Al Milgrom, Jackson (Butch) Guice, Bill Willingham and Rich Rankin, Howard Chaykin, John Romita, Keith Giffen, Dave Cockrum, Jim Aparo, Bob Hall, and—would you believe—Len Wein and Bill Mantlo, including a collection of *Batmans* (my favorite), like you never saw. (Is it really true that The Joker looks like me? Charles Vess apparently thinks so.) The gallery's not for sale, but you'll love looking at it.

Did you ask about mail-order? Our new spacious area provides for this often-asked-for service. So, send your want list. Also, send for a copy of our very special books-for-a-buck-or-less-much-less list. 1,000's of Marvels and DCs and specials.

AND FINALLY ... WE'RE BUYING. We're buying everything, but in particular we're BUYING GOLDEN AGE.

WE'RE expanding our Golden Age Department, and we are actively purchasing everything from *Superman* #1 to *Dotty Dripple*. Store stock, accumulations, collections, we want 'em all. Immediate payment, no delay. Call or write now.

FUNNY BUSINESS

656 Amsterdam Ave. (Corner of 92nd Street)
New York, NY 10025
212-799-9477

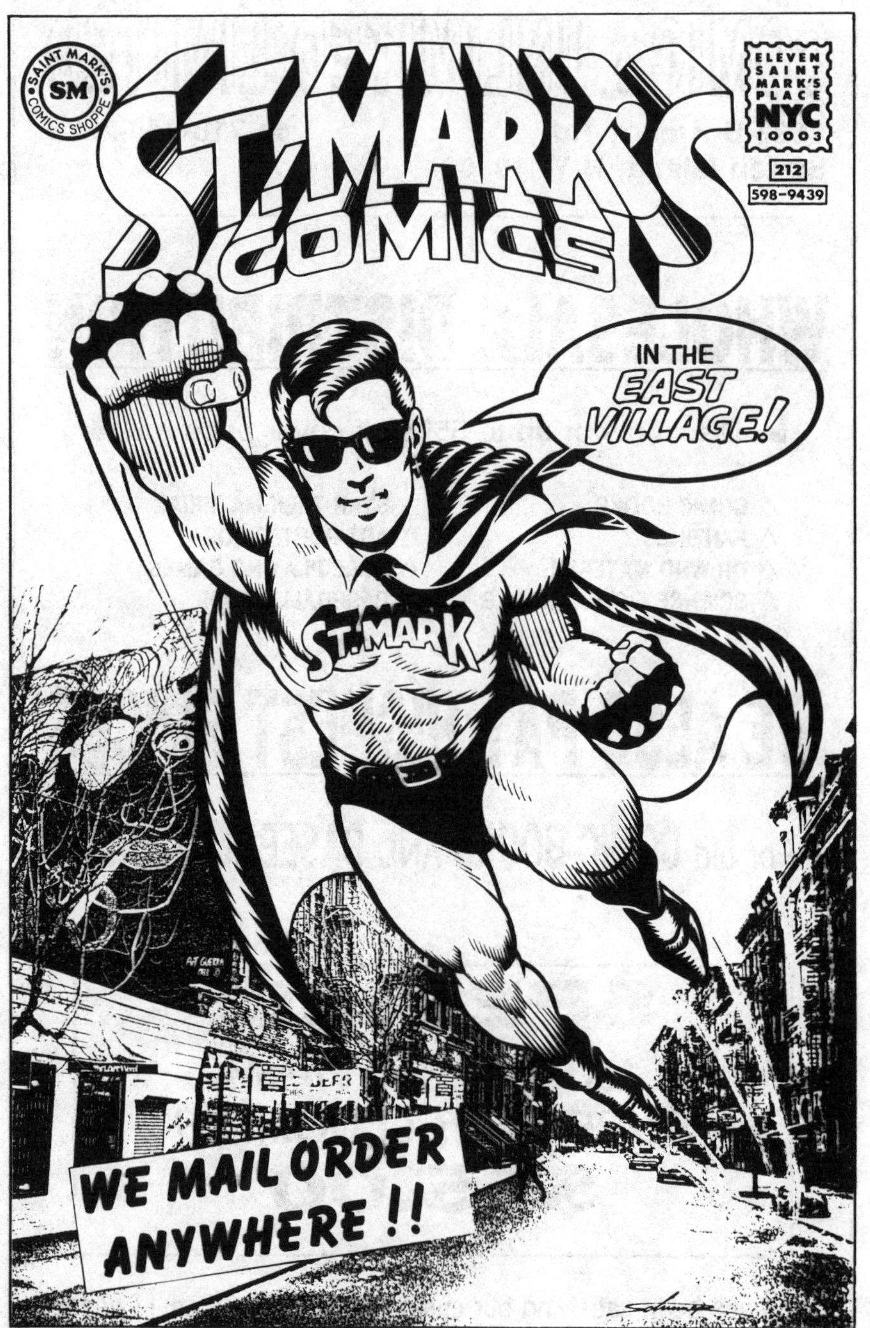

SAINT MARK'S
SM
COMICS SHOPPE
ST. MARK'S
COMICS
ELEVEN SAINT MARK'S PLACE NYC 10003
212
598-9439
IN THE EAST VILLAGE!
ST. MARK
WE MAIL ORDER ANYWHERE !!

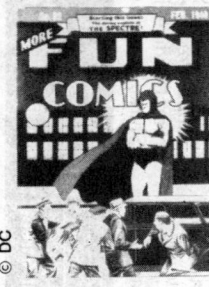

ROBERT D. CRESTOHL (Price Guide Advisor)
& GERRY ROSS (The Comic Master)

P.O. Box 4953, St. Laurent,
(Montreal), Quebec, Canada H4L-4Z6
(514) 630-4518 or (514) 620-4421

WE BUY EARLY MARVELS (1961-1965) AT 70%-100% OF GUIDE!!

We specialize in buying and selling early MARVELS in all conditions ranging from FAIR to MINT. Below, you will find what are currently regarded as the highest BUYING PRICES in the industry. Grading must conform with Overstreet standards, as outlined in the guide. Note that by sending your comics you agree to abide by our grading standards. Pack securely, address on three sides and insure. We reserve the right to adjust prices without notice, however the majority of these prices will be constant over the next year. Offer expires April 30, 1989. Not responsible for typographical errors. We have over 20 years of experience buying and selling comics and you can expect reliable, courteous treatment. Packages will bring instant payment in **U.S. FUNDS**. Feel free to call beforehand if you wish. We also purchase Golden Age D.C. and pay similarly high. If looking to buy Marvels, read our selling prices elsewhere in this book. We also buy store sellouts and large collections. Please pack all material securely.

	FAIR	FAIR/ GOOD	GOOD	GOOD/ VG	VERY GOOD	VG/ FINE	FINE	VERY FINE	NEAR MINT	MINT
AMAZING FANTASY 15	$50.00	$75.00	$100.00	$150.00	$200.00	$300.00	$400.00	$550.00	$700.00	$1080.00
AMAZING SPIDERMAN 1	40.00	60.00	80.00	110.00	160.00	210.00	290.00	380.00	500.00	720.00
2	18.00	27.00	36.00	43.00	50.00	75.00	100.00	140.00	180.00	270.00
3	11.00	16.00	22.00	26.00	30.00	45.00	60.00	90.00	120.00	160.00
4	8.00	12.00	16.00	19.00	22.50	31.00	45.00	60.00	80.00	135.00
5, 6	7.00	10.50	14.00	15.50	17.50	26.00	35.00	47.00	60.00	105.00
7-10	5.00	7.50	10.00	11.00	12.50	18.50	25.00	35.00	45.00	78.00
11-15	3.00	4.50	6.00	7.00	8.00	12.00	16.00	23.00	30.00	51.00
16-20	2.00	3.00	4.00	4.50	5.00	7.50	10.00	14.00	18.00	30.00
21-30; 100	1.00	1.50	2.00	2.25	2.50	3.75	5.00	6.00	7.00	19.00
AVENGERS 1	20.00	30.00	40.00	50.00	60.00	90.00	120.00	200.00	300.00	375.00
2, 4	7.50	10.50	15.00	18.00	20.00	30.00	40.00	60.00	100.00	130.00
3	5.00	7.50	10.00	12.50	15.00	22.00	30.00	40.00	60.00	78.00
5-10	2.50	3.75	5.00	5.50	6.00	9.00	12.00	20.00	30.00	36.00
DAREDEVIL 1	15.00	22.50	30.00	35.00	40.00	60.00	80.00	100.00	120.00	210.00
2	6.00	9.00	12.00	13.75	15.00	22.50	30.00	45.00	60.00	90.00
4, 5	2.00	3.00	4.00	4.50	5.00	7.50	10.00	14.00	18.00	25.00
FANTASTIC FOUR 1	50.00	75.00	100.00	150.00	200.00	300.00	400.00	550.00	700.00	1080.00
2	25.00	37.50	50.00	67.00	75.00	110.00	150.00	210.00	280.00	400.00
3	20.00	30.00	40.00	50.00	60.00	90.00	120.00	170.00	220.00	320.00
4	17.50	25.00	35.00	40.00	45.00	67.50	90.00	120.00	160.00	250.00
5	12.50	17.50	25.00	30.00	35.00	53.00	70.00	95.00	120.00	195.00
6-10	7.00	10.00	14.00	17.00	20.00	30.00	40.00	55.00	70.00	120.00
11, 12	5.00	7.50	10.00	12.50	15.00	22.50	30.00	40.00	50.00	90.00
13-15	4.00	6.00	8.00	10.00	12.50	18.75	25.00	32.00	40.00	60.00
16-20	2.50	3.75	5.00	6.50	7.50	8.50	15.00	20.00	25.00	39.00
21-30, 48	1.75	2.25	3.50	3.75	4.00	6.00	8.00	11.00	14.00	20.00
31-40	0.75	1.25	1.50	1.85	2.25	3.50	4.50	5.75	7.00	12.00
INCREDIBLE HULK 1	35.00	50.00	70.00	85.00	100.00	150.00	200.00	275.00	350.00	500.00
2	12.50	17.50	25.00	30.00	35.00	52.50	70.00	95.00	120.00	180.00
3	9.00	13.50	18.00	22.00	25.00	37.50	50.00	70.00	90.00	130.00
4, 5, 6	6.00	9.00	12.00	15.00	17.50	25.00	35.00	47.00	60.00	196.00
IRONMAN 1	–	–	6.00	7.50	9.00	13.50	18.00	23.00	27.00	45.00
TALES OF SUSPENSE 39	17.50	22.50	35.00	42.50	50.00	75.00	100.00	140.00	180.00	285.00
40	7.00	10.50	14.00	15.00	17.50	25.00	35.00	50.00	65.00	95.00
41	3.50	5.25	7.00	8.50	10.00	15.00	20.00	27.00	35.00	50.00
42-45	1.50	2.25	3.00	3.50	4.00	6.00	8.00	10.00	12.00	18.00
TALES TO ASTONISH 27	22.50	32.50	45.00	52.00	60.00	90.00	120.00	170.00	220.00	375.00
THOR 83	20.00	30.00	40.00	55.00	70.00	105.00	140.00	195.00	250.00	360.00
84	6.00	9.00	12.00	16.00	20.00	30.00	40.00	50.00	60.00	75.00
85	5.00	8.00	11.00	13.00	15.00	22.50	30.00	40.00	50.00	60.00
86	4.00	6.00	8.00	9.50	11.00	16.00	23.00	28.00	32.00	45.00
87-89	3.00	4.00	5.00	8.00	11.00	16.00	23.00	28.00	32.00	37.50
X-MEN 1	25.00	47.00	70.00	85.00	100.00	150.00	200.00	275.00	350.00	450.00
2	12.50	18.75	25.00	30.00	37.50	55.00	75.00	100.00	120.00	220.00
3, 4	5.00	7.50	10.00	12.50	15.00	22.50	30.00	40.00	50.00	96.00
5	3.50	5.25	7.00	8.50	11.00	16.00	22.00	28.75	35.00	63.00
6-10	2.00	3.00	4.00	5.00	6.00	9.00	12.00	17.00	22.00	45.00
11-20	–	1.50	3.00	4.75	6.00	8.50	11.00	13.00	17.00	19.00
21-44	–	–	1.95	2.50	3.80	5.25	7.00	8.50	10.00	14.00
56-63, 65	–	–	1.80	2.00	3.25	4.75	6.50	7.75	9.00	13.00
94	–	–	8.75	13.50	17.50	23.00	35.00	42.50	50.00	75.00
95	–	–	4.50	7.50	9.00	13.50	18.00	23.00	28.00	36.00
96-98, 100, 101, 108, 109, 120, 121	–	–	3.00	4.50	6.00	9.00	12.00	15.00	18.00	22.00
102-107, 110, 111	–	–	1.80	2.50	3.50	5.50	6.75	8.00	10.00	13.00
112-119	–	–	–	1.50	3.00	4.50	6.00	7.50	9.00	12.00
122-130, 137, 139, 140	–	–	–	1.00	2.25	2.75	4.15	5.00	7.00	8.00
131-136, 138	–	–	–	–	1.75	3.00	3.50	4.75	6.00	7.00
Giant Size 1	–	–	7.00	10.50	14.00	21.00	28.00	35.00	45.00	60.00

We pay similarly high prices for later issues of the same titles (50%-75% of guide).

COMICS UNLIMITED LTD.

6833 AMBOY RD.
STATEN ISLAND, N.Y. 10309
718-948-2223

WHOLESALE DISTRIBUTORS

of the complete line

of  role

TSR, Inc.

TSR, Inc.

Playing systems and aids. Featuring Dungeons and Dragons, Marvel Super Heroe game, Indiana Jones game and other exciting role playing systems.

ATTENTION RETAILERS

You can greatly increase your profits by carrying the hot selling line of Marvel Super Heroe games and modules.

For more information
Call or write for details.

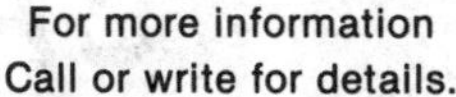

TROPIC
COMICS
313 S. STATE ROAD 7
PLANTATION FL 33317
(305) 587-8878
742 N.E. 167th ST
N MIAMI BEACH FL 33162
(305) 940-8700
HOTFOOT
(WILLIAM "BIG" VOGAL)
SAYS:
COMIX
TROPIC COMICS BURNS ALL COMPETITION IN
SOUTH FLORIDA! THE HOTTEST PRICES ON
OUR HUGE INVENTORY OF MARVELS, DC'S,
ALTERNATES AND GOLDEN AGE. ALL NEW
COMICS ROASTED TO A 20% DISCOUNT!
HORGUS HORGUS HORGUS!!
(ADVISORS TO OVERSTREET'S)

JIM HARMON'S GOLDEN AGE **VIDEO**

Action gems from the producer-writer-costar of nationally sponsored 1983 TOM MIX radio dramas, author of best-selling books.

SUPERMAN FLEISHER CARTOONS -- complete sets of 17 -- full color -- 1940's all-time peak super-hero animation. We discovered lost prints. All other offers are poorer copies of our high grade tape. DOUBLE SPECIAL: 1 FOR YOU + 1 FOR A GIFT -- BOTH FOR $45, OR A SINGLE SET FOR $34.

SPECIAL -- Serials on two quality tapes -- $29.00 each:
The Green Hornet. 13 episodes, 1940 serial. Comics and radio masked hero, origin.
Gordon of Ghost City. Buck Jones' first Western serial. 12 chapters. Fine image.
Phantom Empire. Gene Autry. Cowboys, robots, ray guns. 12 terrific installments.

OTHER $29.00 SPECIALS: *Gang Busters, Dick Tracy, Flash Gordon Conquers the Universe.*

STATE VHS OR BETA.
Postage $2.00 (U.S.)
Free complete video catalog (public domain)
Free old radio mystery audio cat. available.

JIM HARMON
634 So. Orchard Dr., Burbank, CA 91506
(Phone 818-843-5472).

THE COMPLEAT PAPERBACKER

15711 E. AMAR RD, LA PUENTE, CA 91744 **phone (818)330-0400**

• *WHEN IN SOUTHERN CALIF. VISIT THE* **NO. 1** *STORE IN THE* **SAN GABRIEL VALLEY** *FOR A* **COMPLETE** *LINE OF* **COMICS, SCIENCE-FICTION** *AND* **OCCULT** *BOOKS.*

• *SITUATED AT* **15711 E. AMAR RD., LA PUENTE** *BETWEEN THE* **POMONA** *AND* **SAN BERNARDINO FREEWAYS**, *WE ARE ONE TRAFFIC LIGHT EAST OF* **HACIENDA**

OPEN 7 DAYS A WEEK, FROM 10:A.M. TO 8:P.M. WEEKDAYS, AND ON SAT. & SUN. FROM 10:A.M. TO 5:P.M. PHONE (818) 330-0400

WE ALSO HAVE THOUSANDS OF PAPERBACKS IN ALL CATEGORIES:-NOVELS, GOTHICS, MYSTERIES, WESTERNS, & LIGHT ROMANCES TOGETHER WITH NON-FICTION.

WHAT?

-STILL CAN'T SPELL "COMPLETE" EITHER!

* HARDBACK TURTLE

REMEMBER- LOOK FOR THE STORE WITH THE MISSPELLED SIGN!

Collecting Supplies

COMIC STORAGE BAGS

- Hi clarity
- 2″ flaps
- 3 mil
- Pre-counted in 100's

NAME	SIZE	QUANTITY	PRICE
Current	6⅞″x10½″	1,000–1,900	$2.00/100
Regular	7⅛″x10½″	1,000–1,900	$2.00/100
Golden Age	7¾″x10½″	500–1,900	$3.00/100
Magazine	8¾″x11″	500–1,900	$3.00/100

DISCOUNT QUANTITIES

Current and Regular

No. of Cases	No. of Bags	Weight	Unit Price	Price
1 Case	2,000	24 lbs.	$18.50/1000	$ 37.00
5 Cases	10,000	120 lbs.	$17.00/1000	$170.00
13 Cases	26,000	312 lbs.	$16.50/1000	$429.00
25 Cases	50,000	600 lbs	$15.50/1000	$775.00

Golden Age

No. of Cases	No. of Bags	Weight	Unit Price	Price
1 Case	2,000	40 lbs.	$23.00/1000	$ 46.00

Magazine

No. of Cases	No. of Bags	Weight	Unit Price	Price
1 Case	2,000	31 lbs.	$27.00/1000	$ 54.00

The Strongest Storage Boxes In Fandom!

Our boxes have become the industry standard. 275 lb. double-walled thickness (twice that on the handles) makes our product strong enough to stand on. Easy fold construction requires no tape or staples.

Bin Boxes

2 lbs.

- Perfect for shelves
- 11″x8″x14″ long

4-29 boxes $2.50 each
30-90 boxes $1.50 each
120 or more $1.25 each

Comic Boxes

3 lbs.

- Holds over 300 comics
- 11″x8″x26½″ long

Magazine Boxes

2 lbs.

- Holds 100 Mags
- 9″x12″x16″ long

Prices below for both COMIC and MAGAZINE boxes

2-5 boxes . . . . $3.50 each
6-19 boxes . . . . $2.50 each
20-39 boxes . . . . $2.00 each
40-74 boxes . . . . $1.75 each
75-499 boxes . . . . $1.60 each
500-up boxes . . . . $1.40 each

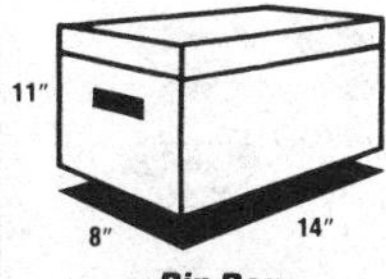

Bin Box

Comic Box

Magazine Box

Advanced Collecting Supplies

Acid-Free Backing Board

White on both sides; lab tested to be Acid-Free.
All sizes available at $12 per 100 (5 lbs.).

Regular: 6[13]/16″ x 10½″
1000 (45 lbs.) $39.00
5000 or more $35.00/1000

Golden Age: 7[9]/16″ x 10½″

Magazine: 8⅝″ x 11″
1000 (45 lbs) $50.00

5-Mil Mylar®

Typical Mylar® bags are 4-mil thick. Now FFD has 20% more protection at less cost than ever! Compare with other (bigger) ads in this edition. (50-5 lbs.)

Regular: 7¼″ x 10½″
20-49 bags/70¢ each
50-250 bags/40¢ each
300-900 bags/37¢ each
1000-up bags/35¢ each

Gold 7¾″ x 10½″
Old Gold 8¼″ x 10½″
20-49/75¢ each. . . . 50-250/45¢ each
300-950/42¢ each. 1000-up/37¢ each

Mylar is a registered trademark of DuPont Co.

2 Flap Lok-Top™ Mylars®

Add 15¢ to prices at left.

SHIPPING: We charge exact costs. Extra money refunded. UPS COD's cost an extra $2.20 per package.

Total Weight	If your zip code starts with: 1,2,4 or 6	0,3,5,7 8 or 9
1-5 lbs.	$ 2.50	$ 3.25
6-12 lbs.	$ 3.75	$ 6.00
13-20	$ 5.50	$ 9.50
21-28 lbs.	$ 7.00	$13.00
29-36	$ 9.00	$16.00
37-50	$12.00	$22.00

Over 50 lbs.—Add weights together i.e. 60 lbs. to 46408 would be $10.00 & $3.75.

Friendly Frank's DISTRIBUTION, INC.

3990 Broadway, Gary, IN 46408-2705 • (219) 884-5052, 884-5053
727 Factory Road, Addison, IL 60101 • (312) 543-6262

AURORA

Captain
Action

ALL NEW COMICS!

The Comic Shop Subscription Service Entering its 5th year! Still offering you the best in service! When you join our subscription service you get;

- *Fast reliable service.*
- *Free subscriptions to Marvel Age, DC Releases & The Comic Shop News, plus newsletters from all the major publishers!*
- *Access to our huge selection of back issues.*
- *25% off all new comics.*
- *We also stock toys, games, baseball cards, comic bags & supplies.*
- *And there's more!*

For complete information, simply write to:

"The Comic Shop"
P.O. Box 18178
Portland, OR 97218

...and we'll send you everything you need to get started!

OUR 16th YEAR SERVING THE NEW YORK TRI-STATE AREA
TOMORROW'S TREASURES
WANTED:
COMIC COLLECTIONS LARGE & SMALL 1933-1969
WE TRAVEL ANYWHERE
$$$ READY CASH $$$
SPECIALIZING IN:
MARVELS • DC'S • SILVER AGE •
EC'S • DISNEYS
SEND YOUR INQUIRIES TO:
RICHARD MUCHIN
P.O. BOX 925
COMMACK, NY 11725
PHONE:
(516) 543-7574
MAIL ORDER SERVICE GUARANTEED
SEND WANT LISTS
BATMAN
CRIME
Steve Lowenthal

SUPERMAN

The Man of Steel

by John Byrne and Dick Giordano

The Man of Steel was recently changed to be made more "vulnerable and human," in short more acceptable to an eighties audience. The first comic book in the new series sold almost one million copies in its first month—more than any other comic book in twenty years.

Now, here's a full-color collection of the first six books in the new series, produced in the "Graphic Novel" format, just in time for Superman's 50th anniversary.

$12.95 345-35093-6

Available at your bookstore or use this coupon.

BALLANTINE MAIL SALES
Dept. TA, 201 E. 50th St., New York, N.Y. 10022

Please send me the BALLANTINE or DEL REY BOOKS I have checked above. I am enclosing $ . . . . (add $1.00 per copy to cover postage and handling). Send check or money order—no cash or C.O.D.'s please. Prices and numbers are subject to change without notice. Valid in U.S. only. All orders are subject to availability of books.

Name ______________________

Address ______________________

City ______________ State ________ Zip Code ________

Allow at least 4 weeks for delivery.

30 HC-4

The HOUSE OF COLLECTIBLES Series

☐ Please send me the following price guides—
☐ I would like the most current edition of the books listed below.

THE OFFICIAL PRICE GUIDES TO:

☐	199-3	**American Silver & Silver Plate** 5th Ed.	$11.95
☐	513-1	**Antique Clocks** 3rd Ed.	10.95
☐	283-3	**Antique & Modern Dolls** 3rd Ed.	10.95
☐	287-6	**Antique & Modern Firearms** 6th Ed.	11.95
☐	738-X	**Antiques & Collectibles** 8th Ed.	10.95
☐	289-2	**Antique Jewelry** 5th Ed.	11.95
☐	539-5	**Beer Cans & Collectibles** 4th Ed.	7.95
☐	521-2	**Bottles Old & New** 10th Ed.	10.95
☐	532-8	**Carnival Glass** 2nd Ed.	10.95
☐	295-7	**Collectible Cameras** 2nd Ed.	10.95
☐	548-4	**Collectibles of the '50s & '60s** 1st Ed.	9.95
☐	740-1	**Collectible Toys** 4th Ed.	10.95
☐	531-X	**Collector Cars** 7th Ed.	12.95
☐	538-7	**Collector Handguns** 4th Ed.	14.95
☐	748-7	**Collector Knives** 9th Ed.	12.95
☐	361-9	**Collector Plates** 5th Ed.	11.95
☐	296-5	**Collector Prints** 7th Ed.	12.95
☐	001-6	**Depression Glass** 2nd Ed.	9.95
☐	589-1	**Fine Art** 1st Ed.	19.95
☐	311-2	**Glassware** 3rd Ed.	10.95
☐	243-4	**Hummel Figurines & Plates** 6th Ed.	10.95
☐	523-9	**Kitchen Collectibles** 2nd Ed.	10.95
☐	291-4	**Military Collectibles** 5th Ed.	11.95
☐	525-5	**Music Collectibles** 6th Ed.	11.95
☐	313-9	**Old Books & Autographs** 7th Ed.	11.95
☐	298-1	**Oriental Collectibles** 3rd Ed.	11.95
☐	746-0	**Overstreet Comic Book** 17th Ed.	11.95
☐	522-0	**Paperbacks & Magazines** 1st Ed.	10.95
☐	297-3	**Paper Collectibles** 5th Ed.	10.95
☐	744-4	**Political Memorabilia** 1st Ed.	10.95
☐	529-8	**Pottery & Porcelain** 6th Ed.	11.95
☐	524-7	**Radio, TV & Movie Memorabilia** 3rd Ed.	11.95
☐	288-4	**Records** 7th Ed.	10.95
☐	247-7	**Royal Doulton** 5th Ed.	11.95
☐	280-9	**Science Fiction & Fantasy Collectibles** 2nd Ed.	10.95
☐	747-9	**Sewing Collectibles** 1st Ed.	8.95
☐	358-9	**Star Trek/Star Wars Collectibles** 2nd Ed.	8.95
☐	086-5	**Watches** 8th Ed.	12.95
☐	248-5	**Wicker** 3rd Ed.	10.95

THE OFFICIAL:

☐	445-3	**Collector's Journal** 1st Ed.	4.95
☐	549-2	**Directory to U.S. Flea Markets** 1st Ed.	4.95
☐	365-1	**Encyclopedia of Antiques** 1st Ed.	9.95
☐	369-4	**Guide to Buying and Selling Antiques** 1st Ed.	9.95
☐	414-3	**Identification Guide to Early American Furniture** 1st Ed.	9.95
☐	413-5	**Identification Guide to Glassware** 1st Ed.	9.95
☐	448-8	**Identification Guide to Gunmarks** 2nd Ed.	9.95
☐	412-7	**Identification Guide to Pottery & Porcelain** 1st Ed.	$9.95
☐	415-1	**Identification Guide to Victorian Furniture** 1st Ed.	9.95

THE OFFICIAL (SMALL SIZE) PRICE GUIDES TO:

☐	309-0	**Antiques & Flea Markets** 4th Ed.	4.95
☐	269-8	**Antique Jewelry** 3rd Ed.	4.95
☐	085-7	**Baseball Cards** 8th Ed.	4.95
☐	647-2	**Bottles** 3rd Ed.	4.95
☐	544-1	**Cars & Trucks** 3rd Ed.	5.95
☐	519-0	**Collectible Americana** 2nd Ed.	4.95
☐	294-9	**Collectible Records** 3rd Ed.	4.95
☐	306-6	**Dolls** 4th Ed.	4.95
☐	359-7	**Football Cards** 7th Ed.	4.95
☐	540-9	**Glassware** 3rd Ed.	4.95
☐	526-3	**Hummels** 4th Ed.	4.95
☐	279-5	**Military Collectibles** 3rd Ed.	4.95
☐	745-2	**Overstreet Comic Book Companion** 1st Ed.	4.95
☐	278-7	**Pocket Knives** 3rd Ed.	4.95
☐	527-1	**Scouting Collectibles** 4th Ed.	4.95
☐	494-1	**Star Trek/Star Wars Collectibles** 3rd Ed.	3.95
☐	307-4	**Toys** 4th Ed.	4.95

THE OFFICIAL BLACKBOOK PRICE GUIDES OF:

☐	743-6	**U.S. Coins** 26th Ed.	3.95
☐	742-8	**U.S. Paper Money** 20th Ed.	3.95
☐	741-X	**U.S. Postage Stamps** 10th Ed.	3.95

THE OFFICIAL INVESTORS GUIDE TO BUYING & SELLING:

☐	534-4	**Gold, Silver & Diamonds** 2nd Ed.	12.95
☐	535-2	**Gold Coins** 2nd Ed.	12.95
☐	536-0	**Silver Coins** 2nd Ed.	12.95
☐	537-9	**Silver Dollars** 2nd Ed.	12.95

THE OFFICIAL NUMISMATIC GUIDE SERIES:

☐	254-X	**The Official Guide to Detecting Counterfeit Money** 2nd Ed.	7.95
☐	257-4	**The Official Guide to Mint Errors** 4th Ed.	7.95

SPECIAL INTEREST SERIES:

☐	506-9	**From Hearth to Cookstove** 3rd Ed.	17.95
☐	530-1	**Lucky Number Lottery Guide** 1st Ed.	4.95
☐	504-2	**On Method Acting** 8th Printing	6.95

	TOTAL	

SEE REVERSE SIDE FOR ORDERING INSTRUCTIONS

LAWN COMICS

Y BECOMING AMERICA'S #1 MAIL
DISCOUNT SUBSCRIPTION SERVICE

HE ARE 3 REASONS WHY:

1. **SERVICE**

- NO MINIMUMS ON ANY PURCHASE.
- GOT A QUESTION ? CALL OUR TOLL FREE NUMBER 1-800-342-3992
- WE HAVE A 100% FILL RATE ON ALL ORDERS THAT WE RECIEVE BY OUR DEADLINE DATE.
- YOU CHOOSE THE SHIPPING FREQUENCY: WEEKY, BI-WEEKLY, OR MONTHLY. ONLY $1.75 PER SHIPMENT.
- ALL NEW COMIC ORDERS CAN BE PLACED UP TO THE SAME WEEK THEY COME OUT.

2. **SELECTION**

- WE CARRY EVERY COMIC PRINTED.
- WE ALSO CARRY JUST ABOUT EVERY SIGNED AND NUMERED HARD COVER, SOFT COVER, GRAPHIC NOVEL, PRINT, PORTFOLIO, AND COMIC RELATED ITEM.

3. **PRICE**

- ALL NEW COMICS ARE DISCOUNTED AT LEAST 40%.
- ALL OTHER COMIC RELATED ITEMS ARE SOLD AT A SUBSTANTIAL DISCOUNT.

OAKLAWN COMICS 4929 W. 95th St.
Oaklawn, Ill. 60453 / Phone: (312) 445-7873

THE DISCOUNT EXPERTS

STARBASE 21
2130 S. Sheridan Tulsa, OK 74114
Comics & Science Fiction
★ All New Marvel, D.C., & Independent Comics
★ Old Comics/Over 100,000 Back Issues
★ New & Used Science Fiction Paperbacks
★ Movie Posters
★ Japanese Animation Books & Models
★ Star Trek & Star Wars Collectibles
★ Doctor Who Paperbacks & Collectibles
(918) 838-3388
MON.-SAT 11-7 SUN. 12-6
Copyright 1988 Marvel Comics A New World Company. All rights reserved

1,000,000 COMIX INC.

THE LEADING INTERNATIONAL FRANCHISOR OF COMIC BOOK STORES OFFERS YOU A UNIQUE OPPORTUNITY.

Comic collecting is the fastest growing recession resistant hobby today. We offer a unique, highly successful, proven formula. An initial 15-40K investment puts successful candidates into a high grossing, upscale "turnkey" store, stocked in depth, that provides immediate upper level income and **SOLID** long term growth. **YOUR GROWTH!**

Equipped with a huge 10,000 back issue opening stock (provided with store opening – no extra cost) including many high priced books, and with continual training, support, and nationwide advertising in the *comic books themselves* franchisees revel in success. W. Strike (Toronto, Mississauga franchise) "Our store in one month alone topped $20,000 in sales". E. Roussell (Moncton, N.B. franchise) "Our store is the nicest looking in all of New Brunswick. The interior design was especially well done. I also have high praise for the inventory control system".

Join the team that has changed comic book retailing. Master franchises are still available for many areas, on a limited basis. If you like comics, kids, and upper level income you owe it to yourself to become your own boss. *Be in business for yourself, but not by yourself.*

$25.00 APPLICATION FEE. You'll receive a video cassette demonstrating our store concept. Include your name, address and a financial curriculum vitae along with your $25.00.

Send to:
1,000,000 COMIX INC.
Comic Master Division
c/o The President
Franchise Department
P.O. Box 4953
St. Laurent (Montreal) Quebec
Canada H4L-4Z6
Franchise Hotline!
(514) 630-4518

Already existing franchises

Montreal
7019 Côte St-Luc Rd.
(514) 486-1175
5010 Samson Blvd. (Chomedey)
(514) 688-5626
Toronto
Mississauga: Birnhamthorpe Rd.
South Common Mall
(416) 828-8208
Burlington: 2400 Guelph Line
(416) 332-5600
Moncton, N.B.
345 Mountain Rd.
(506) 855-0056

Soon opening in...
Oakland, CA
New York
Boston
72 other master franchise areas available

Affiliates
Comix Plus
1475 MacDonald St.
St-Laurent, Que.
Canada
(514) 334-0732

Already own a store? Become a 1,000,000 Comix affiliate. Get **great** back issue discounts on all store packages, catalogs, and more!

WE BUY BIG! WE PAY $35,000 FOR A NEAR MINT ACTION COMICS #1

We're also interested in purchasing large accumulations (1,000-1,000,000) of older comics. We buy anything, pay promptly, and take all you've got. We also want small accumulations of key, higher grade golden age books such as, BATMAN, SUPERMAN, ACTION, ADVENTURE, DETECTIVE, and other D.C. comics. We're also looking for Timelys, Quality, Dell 4-colors, Classics, Pre-Code Horror, E.C., Pulps, 1950's Atlas and Westerns.

CUSTOMIZED START-UP PACKAGES FOR RETAILERS, COLLECTORS, INVESTORS.

These packages are available to retailers as well as collectors. We are able to offer the lowest priced, best quality store or start-up packages in existence! Our warehouse has bulked up even more with an estimated purchase of 1.2 million comics from Glenwood Distribution Inc. (we bought out the majority of their comic stock). Although all store packages are available, it is advised that you phone first, as to assess postage costs to your area. **Coming to Montreal? We'll be glad to help you personally select your stock (by appointment only). Our complete GIANT CATALOG of Golden Age, Silver Age and Marvel comics is available for $1.00 (free with any purchase).**

OUR MOST POPULAR PACKAGES

Package A: 10 key Marvel titles (ASM, Cap. America, Spiderman, Daredevil, Conan, Hulk, Thor, Fantastic Four, Avengers, Peter Parker, Iron Man). Each title includes 30% minimum, (i.e. 25-40 early 12¢ issues or more) of earlier sought after issues per title. 850 comics (or 80-90/title, avg. 85) **Most fine or better**, max. 4 per number, except early issues (VG or better). These packages always includes high-priced books such as Conans between 1-10; Spidermans between 10-20, Daredevils between 3-20, etc. These titles are the most consistent movers in the majority of comic book stores. Suggestions appreciated. Early issues vary with our stock but you can be assured that there will be a healthy chunk of early Marvels in every package. Cost $1,475.00 U.S. *plus postage*. Take half of this package for $845.00 plus postage. Note, many of these Marvels will retail for between $4.00-$10.00; and Marvels are steadily increasing in value all the time, just take a look at this year's Spiderman prices between #20-100. This package boasts many happy customers "I want to thank you and your staff personally for the great job you did in helping us out and setting up our store" *Michael Halbleib, Marvel-us Comics, Great Falls, Montana.*

Package B: Includes Package A plus 50 X-Men between #94-150. Also includes 300 other Marvels (Marvel Team up, 2 in 1, Presents, and others) avg., near fine or better. Sum: 13 titles avg., 80 comics per title and 50 X-Men between #94-150. Total 1,090 key comic books for $1,995.00 U.S. *plus postage.* Note, X-Men are a consistent seller and these are the most in demand numbers.

Package C: X-Men #1-200 plus all annuals (avg., fine or better) $3,000.00 *plus postage*. (Guide value equals $4,116.10 in mint). **OR**, X-Men #1-200 (#1-10 avg., VG; #20-93 avg., fine or better; #94 up avg., very fine or better) $1,995.00 U.S. *plus postage* **OR** #1-20 avg., G/VG; #21-93 avg., VG or better; #94-200 avg., near fine or better $1,450.00 U.S. *plus postage*. This is a truly great investment lot.

Mini X-Men package: #13-200 avg., N/F or better $2,400.00 U.S. *plus postage*. **OR** #13-100 avg., VG or better, #101-120 avg., F– or better, #121 up avg., F or better; $1,390.00 U.S. *plus postage.*

Package D: X-Men #94-150 avg., very fine or better $850.00; Avg., fine or better $650.00; Avg., VG or better $430.00 *plus postage*.

Package E: Convention Special 2,000 Marvel, D.C. and independents. (Max 5 of a number. Most fine or better. Nobody can beat the price of $675.00 *plus postage*).

Package F: Start-up Special 100 Marvel comics, max 5 of a number, many 5-10 years old, most VF or better $25.00 *plus postage.*

Package G: Archie Avalanche. Great store stock. Most $0.65 cover and up; multiples; 300 Archies $49.00 *plus postage* (order in multiples of 300. Call for larger order discounts).

Package H: Cheapie Special. 900 comics; anything and everything. Many with cover prices of $2.00 or more. Multiples. Cost $150.00 *plus postage.*

Package I: Magazine Massacre. 100 mags (many sci-fi, comics, war, etc.) 100 mags at $25.00; some multiples, *plus postage.*

Package J: Amazing, Amazing Spiderman Lot. Instant Spidy collection #1-250 plus annuals avg., F+ or better $3,800.00. ($4,317.00 at mint guide. **OR** #1-20 avg., fine, #21-100 avg., F/VF; #100-250 avg. VF or better (90%) plus annuals avg., fine or better – $2,500.00 **OR** #1-20 avg., G/VG, #21-100 avg., VG/F; #100 up avg., fine or better – $1,999.00 **OR** #1-250 avg., G/VG or better – $1,300.00 (restorers delight!).

Package J1: Mini Spidey Set A) #7-250 plus annuals, most fine or better, a steal at $1,999.00 *plus postage. B)* #7-250 (#7-30 avg., VG/VG+; #31-100 avg., VG; #101 up avg., NF or better) take it for $1,500.00 **OR** #7-250 (#7-30 avg., G/VG; #31-70 avg., VG–; #71-150 avg., VG/VG+; #150 up avg., VG/F or better) $1,300.00 *plus postage.*

Package K: Fantabulous Fantastic Four Lot. #1-300 plus annuals avg., F/VF or better – $4,900.00 ($5,919.00 by guide in mint) **OR** #1-300 plus annuals (#1-20 avg., near fine; #21-100 avg., F/VF or better; #100 up avg., VF or better – $3,500.00 **OR** #1-20 avg., G/VG; #21-100 avg., VG; #100 up avg., fine or better $2,500.00) **OR** #1-150 avg., good or better; #151 up avg., VG or better, most fine. $1,850.00 *plus postage.*

Package K1: Mini FF A) #14-250 plus annuals. (#14-250 avg., NF or better) $2,320.00 *plus postage.* **OR** B) #14-250 (#14-30 avg., VG/F or better, #30-250 avg., NF or better) $1,885.00 *plus postage.* **OR** C) #14-250 (#14-40 avg., G/VG, #41-70 avg., VG–, #71-100 avg., VG, #101-250 avg., VG/F or better) $999.00 *plus postage.*

Package L: Instant Conan #1-200 all high grade (near VF or better) $600.00 *plus postage.*

Package M: Super Special Groo #1 (Pacific scarce) $9.00 (guide equals $11.00) 5 or more $7.50 each.

Package N: Peter Hsu's Scarcest Work – Quadrant. Scarce print runs makes this a truly good investment. #1 (scarce) $100.00 (low quantities) #2 $40.00 (3 or more at $29.00 each) #3 $20.00 (3 or more $16.00 each) #4 (rare) $15.00 (3 or more $10.00 each)

Package O: (Cheap) Quality Special. 100 issues composed of 25 issues each of the following titles between #100-250. Amazing Spiderman, Daredevil, Fantastic Four, Conan; avg., VG/F or better. Cost (believe it or not!) $100.00 *plus postage.*

Package P: Small Quality Special. 50 Marvel comics, mainly 15¢ cover price and higher, all super heros most fine or better $22.00 *plus postage.*

Package Q: Quick Steal! 50 different 12¢ cover priced Marvel comics VG or better, super special; (most super hero) $45.00 *plus postage.*

Package R: Ridiculous and Racy! 50 different comics with a $1.25 or greater cover price for only $15.00 *plus postage.*

Package S: 80% Off Cover Price Special! Includes mainly independents. Lots of good sellable, collectable material (ex. Johnny Quest, Elflord, Samurai, Jon Sable, American Flagg, Lone Wolf) all at 80% off cover, our choice, multiples, order in $50.00 increments. i.e. $50.00 gives you $250.00 (by cover price) of material $100.00 order gives you $500.00 (by cover price) of great merchandise. Make your customers happy.

Package T: The Titanic Complete Marvel collection of key books – Amazing Spiderman, Fantastic Four, Daredevil, Conan, X-Men, and Avengers. #1-250 (except Conan #1-200) avg., N/fine or better, includes all annuals. Guides at around $20,000.00. Your cost $14,000.00 *plus postage.* **OR** same package, avg., VG $8,700.00 **OR** same package, avg., G/VG $5,825.00. The Mini-Mother; Amazing Spiderman #10-200, Fantastic Four #10-200, Daredevil #3-200, Conan #1-200, X-Men #10-200, and Avengers #8-200; A) avg. fine or better $7,120.00 B) avg., VG or better $4,999.00 C) avg., G/VG $3,425.00 *plus postage.*

CLASSIFIED ADVERTISING